UNESCO

STATISTICAL YEARBOOK   ANNUAIRE STATISTIQUE   ANUARIO ESTADÍSTICO

1996

STATISTICAL YEARBOOK ANNUAIRE STATISTIQUE ANUARIO ESTADÍSTICO

UNESCO

1996

Reference Tables
Education
Educational expenditure
Science and technology
Libraries
Book production
Newspapers and other periodicals
Cultural paper
Film and cinema
Radio and television broadcasting
International trade in printed matter

Tableaux de référence
Education
Dépenses de l'éducation
Science et technologie
Bibliothèques
Edition de livres
Journaux et autres périodiques
Papier culturel
Films et cinéma
Radiodiffusion sonore et télévision
Commerce international en matière d'imprimés

Cuadros de referencia
Educación
Gastos de la educación
Ciencia y tecnología
Bibliotecas
Edición de libros
Periódicos y revistas
Papel cultural
Películas y cine
Radiodifusión sonora y televisión
Comercio internacional de impresos

UNESCO Publishing & Bernan Press

Published jointly in 1997 by the
United Nations Educational, Scientific
and Cultural Organization
7, place Fontenoy,
75352 Paris 07 SP, France

and

Bernan Press
4611-F Assembly Drive
Lanham, MD 20706-4391
U.S.A.
(800) 274-4447
Internet: query@bernan.com

Photocomposition by
Automated Graphic Systems
4590 Graphics Drive
White Plains, Maryland 20695
U.S.A.

Publié conjointement en 1997 par
l'Organisation des Nations Unies pour
l'Education, la Science et la Culture
7, place Fontenoy,
75352 Paris 07 SP, France

et

Bernan Press
4611-F Assembly Drive
Lanham, MD 20706-4391
U.S.A.
(800) 274-4447
Internet: query@bernan.com

Photocomposition par
Automated Graphic Systems
4590 Graphics Drive
White Plains, Maryland 20695
U.S.A.

Publicado conjuntamente en 1997
por la Organización de las
Naciones Unidas para la
Educación, la Ciencia y la Cultura
7, place Fontenoy,
75352 Paris 07 S, Francia

y

Bernan Press
4611-F Assembly Drive
Lanham, MD 20706-4391
U.S.A.
(800) 274-4447
Internet: query@bernan.com

Fotocomposición de
Automated Graphic Systems
4590 Graphics Drive
Whitc Plains, Maryland 20695
U.S.A.

98 97   4 3 2 1

ISBN (UNESCO) 92-3-003344-8
ISBN (Bernan Press) 0-89059-064-8

Table of contents

▶ New table introduced in this issue

Table des matières

► Nouveau tableau introduit dans la présente édition

Indice

Introduction

This issue of the *UNESCO Statistical Yearbook* has been prepared by the Division of Statistics with the co-operation of the National Commissions for UNESCO, national statistical services and other national agencies.

In accordance with article VIII of the Constitution of UNESCO, each Member State is requested to report periodically to the Organization on its laws, regulations and statistics relating to its educational, scientific and cultural life and activities. Data are gathered mainly from official replies from some 200 countries and territories to UNESCO questionnaires and special surveys but also from official reports and publications, supplemented by information available to the Secretariat from other national and international sources, in particular from the Statistical Division and the Population Division of the United Nations. Where available data differ from the recommendations adopted or other concepts and definitions employed by UNESCO, the statistical practice of the country is respected and explained in a footnote where possible.

The explanatory texts to the tables, presented in English, French and Spanish, are included with the texts at the beginning of each chapter, except for Chapter 3, where these texts can be found at the end of each individual table. As an aid to Arabic- and Russian-speaking readers of the *Yearbook,* the introductory texts to each chapter have been translated into these two languages and can be found in Appendices F and G of the *Yearbook.*

The reader's attention is drawn to the fact that certain tables which have appeared in preceding editions of the *Yearbook* have not been retained in this edition. A list of these tables is shown in Appendix E which gives the last edition in which they appeared.

All questions and comments, as well as any suggestions for further improvements in subsequent editions of the *Yearbook,* will be gratefully received by the Division of Statistics, UNESCO, 75352 Paris 07 SP, France.

Explanatory note

The data presented in this publication relate in general to territorial units within their present "de facto" boundaries. A complete list of countries and territories follows this note. Changes in country names during recent years are reflected in this list and used in the tables of the *Yearbook.*

It should be noted that:

—Data presented for *Jordan,* except for Table 1.1, refer to the *East Bank* only.

—Statistics concerning *Palestine* are limited to the *Gaza Strip* and *West Bank,* and are to be found following the Asian countries in each of the relevant tables.

—Data for *Germany* prior to 1990 are shown separately for the *Federal Republic of Germany* and the former *German Democratic Republic.*

—The same holds for *Yemen* where data prior to 1990 are shown under *Former Democratic Yemen* and former *Yemen Arab Republic.*

—In 1991, the *Union of Soviet Socialist Republics* formally dissolved into fifteen individual countries (Armenia, Azerbaijan, Belarus, Estonia, Georgia, Kazakstan, Kyrgyzstan, Latvia, Lithuania, Republic of Moldova, Russian Federation, Tajikistan, Turkmenistan, Ukraine and Uzbekistan). Whenever possible, data are shown for the individual countries.

—Data for the former *Yugoslavia* and the former *Czechoslovakia* refer in general to years prior to the changes in these countries. When available, data are shown for the separate republics.

—Until 1991, data for *Ethiopia* include *Eritrea;* however when data for the latter are available for years prior to 1991, they are shown separately from Ethiopia.

—Revised data may be presented in this edition of the *Yearbook* and thus differ from those published for the same year in earlier editions.

Owing to the rounding off of figures, the totals and sub-totals shown in the tables do not always correspond exactly to the sums of their component items.

Explanatory notes concerning selected figures are indicated by the symbol ‡ shown against the name of the relevant continents, regions, countries or territories. The texts of these notes will be found at the end of each table; each note is composed of the name of the continent, region, country or territory (in English), followed by the required explanation, for which the English text is preceded by the symbol E‑‑> , the French text by FR‑>, and the Spanish text by ESP>. For a certain number of tables there is also a general note which precedes the notes for individual countries.

The following symbols are used in the *Yearbook*:

-	Magnitude nil
0 or 0.0	Magnitude less than half of unit employed
. . .	Data not available
.	Category not applicable
*	Provisional or estimated data
./.	Data included elsewhere under another category
→	The figure to the immediate left includes the data for the column(s) in which this symbol appears
←	The figure to the immediate right includes the data for the column(s) in which this symbol appears

A break in the continuity of a time series is indicated by a vertical or horizontal line.

Introduction

Cette édition de l'*Annuaire statistique the l'UNESCO* a été établie par la Division des statistiques, avec la coopération des commissions nationales pour l'UNESCO, des services nationaux de statistique et d'autres agences nationales.

En vertu de l'Article VIII de l'Acte constitutif de l'UNESCO, chaque État membre est tenu d'adresser à l'Organisation un rapport périodique sur les lois, règlements et statistiques relatifs à ses institutions et à son activité dans les domaines de l'éducation, de la science et de la culture. Les données concernant quelques 200 pays et territoires sont recueillies par le Secrétariat, principalement au moyen de questionnaires et d'enquêtes spéciales, mais aussi dans les publications et rapports officiels, le tout étant complété par des renseignements provenant d'autres sources nationales et internationales, en particulier de la Division de Statistique et de la Division de la Population des Nations Unies. Lorsque les données disponibles ne sont pas conformes aux recommandations adoptées ou aux autres concepts et définitions utilisés par l'UNESCO, on a suivi la pratique adoptée par les pays, en l'expliquant, si possible, par une note.

Dans cette édition, les textes d'explications aux tableaux rédigés en anglais, français et espagnol, sont présentés avec les textes d'introduction au début de chaque chapitre, à l'exception du Chapitre 3 où ils sont placés à la fin de chaque tableau. Afin de faciliter l'utilisation de l'*Annuaire* aux lecteurs arabophones et russophones, les textes d'introduction aux chapitres ont été traduits dans ces deux langues. On trouvera ces textes dans les Annexes F et G de l'*Annuaire*.

L'attention du lecteur est attirée sur le fait que certains tableaux qui figuraient dans les éditions précédentes de l'*Annuaire* ne sont pas présentés dans ce volume. On trouvera dans l'Annexe E une liste des tableaux supprimés avec l'indication de la dernière édition dans laquelle ils figuraient.

Prière d'adresser toutes questions ou observations concernant le présent *Annuaire,* ainsi que toutes suggestions, en vue d'améliorer les éditions ultérieures, à la Division des statistiques de l'UNESCO, 75352 Paris 07 SP, France.

Notice explicative

Les données présentées dans cette publication se rapportent, en général, aux territoires tels qu'ils sont délimités par les frontières de fait. Une liste complète des pays et territoires figure à la suite de cette note. Les changements de nom de pays survenus récemment dans certains pays sont reflétés dans cette liste et dans les tableaux de cet *Annuaire*.

Il convient de préciser que:

—Les données relatives à la *Jordanie* se réfèrent, à l'exception du Tableau 1.1, à la rive orientale seulement.

—Les statistiques relatives à la *Palestine* concernent la *Bande de Gaza* et la *Cisjordanie* et se trouvent à la suite des pays asiatiques dans chacun des tableaux où ces données apparaissent.

—Les données antérieures à octobre 1990 concernant l'*Allemagne* sont présentées sous des rubriques séparées pour la *République fédérale d'Allemagne* et l'ancienne *République démocratique allemande*.

—L'en va de même pour le *Yémen* pour lequel les données antérieures à 1990 sont présentées sous les rubriques l'ex *Yémen démocratique* et l'ancienne *République arabe du Yemen*.

—En 1991, l'*Union des républiques socialistes soviétiques* s'est séparée en 15 pays distincts (Arménie, Azerbaïdjan, Bélarus, Estonie, Géorgie, Kazakstan, Kirghizistan, Lettonie, Lituanie, République de Moldova, Fédération de Russie, Tadjikistan, Turkménistan, Ukraine, Ouzbékistan). Les données sont présentées pour ces pays pris séparément quand cela est possible.

—Les données relatives à l'ancienne *Yougoslavie* et à l'ancienne *Tchécoslovaquie* se réfèrent en général aux années antérieures aux changements survenus dans ces pays. Les données des différentes républiques sont présentées si elles sont disponibles.

—Jusqu'en 1991, les données présentées sous la rubrique *Éthiopie* incluent celles de l'*Érythrée;* cependant si des données pour les années antérieures à 1991 sont disponibles pour l'Erythrée, elles sont présentées séparément de l'Éthiopie.

—Les données révisées peuvent être présentées dans cette édition de l'*Annuaire* et elles seront donc différentes des données correspondant à la même année qui figuraient dans les éditions précédentes.

Les chiffres et pourcentages ayant été arrondis, les totaux et les sous-totaux figurant dans les tableaux ne correspondent pas toujours exactement à la somme des éléments qui les composent.

Les notes explicatives concernant certains chiffres sont signalées par le symbole ‡ qui suivent immédiatement le nom des continents, des régions, des pays ou territoires auxquels ils s'appliquent. On trouvera les textes de ces notes à la fin de chaque tableau; chaque note est composée du nom du continent, de la région, du pays ou du territoire (en anglais), suivi de l'explication nécessaire. Le texte anglais est précédé du symbole E—>, le texte français de FR—>, et le texte espagnol de ESP>. Il y a aussi, pour un certain nombre de tableaux, une note générale précédant les notes spécifiques aux pays.

Les symboles utilisés dans l'*Annuaire* sont les suivants:

-	Chiffre nul
0 or 0.0	Chiffre inférieur à la moitié de l'unité employée
...	Données non disponibles
.	Catégorie sans objet
*	Chiffre provisoire ou estimé
./.	Données comprises dans une autre rubrique
→	Le chiffre immédiatement à gauche comprend les données de la (des) colonne(s) où figure ce symbole
←	Le chiffre immédiatement à droite comprend les données de la (des) colonne(s) où figure ce symbole

Une discontinuité dans l'homogénéité des séries est indiquée par un trait vertical ou horizontal.

Introducción

La presente edición del *Anuario estadístico de la UNESCO* ha sido preparada por la División de Estadística, con la cooperación de las comisiones nacionales para la UNESCO, de los servicios nacionales de estadística y otras agencias nacionales.

En virtud del Artículo VIII de la Constitución de la UNESCO cada Estado miembro debe someter a la Organización un informe periódico sobre las leyes, reglamentos y estadísticas relativos a sus instituciones y actividades educativas, científicas y culturales. Estos datos los reúne la Secretaría principalmente por medio de cuestionarios y de encuestas especiales provenientes de unos 200 países y territorios, pero también utilizando las publicaciones e informes oficiales, completándose el todo mediante información procedente de otras fuentes nacionales e internacionales, en particular de la División de Estadística y de la División de Población de las Naciones Unidas. Cuando los datos disponibles difieren de las recomendaciones aprobadas o de los demás conceptos y definiciones utilizados por la UNESCO, se ha adoptado el procedimiento utilizado por el país y explicado, cuando ello es posible, en una nota.

Los textos explicativos a lospresentados en inglés, francfés y español figuran al comienzo de cada capítulo, salvo en el Capítulo 3 donde aparecen al final de cada cuadro. A fin de facilitar el uso del *Anuario* a los lectores de lengua árabe y rusa, los textos de introducción de los capítulos han sido traducidos a estos dos idiomas et figuran en los Apéndices F y G del *Anuario.*

Se desea llamar la atención al lector de que algunos cuadros que han aparecido en ediciones anteriores del *Anuario* no han sido incluídos en la presente edición. Se incluye una lista de dichos cuadros en el Apéndice E, donde se indica la última edición en que éstos fueron publicados.

Se ruega dirigir toda cuestión u observación relativa al presente del mismo *Anuario,* así como todas las sugerencias destinadas a mejorar las ediciones ulteriores, se dirijan a la División de Estadística de la UNESCO, 75352 Paris 07 SP, Francia.

Nota explicativa

En general, los datos que figuran en la presente publicación se refieren a los territorios delimitados por sus fronteras de facto. A continuación de esta nota, se presenta una lista completa de países y territorios. Los cambios ocurridos en estos últimos años con respecto a la nomenclatura de algunos países se han reflejado en esta lista y en los cuadros del *Anuario.*

Se debe señalar que:

—Los datos relativos a *Jordania,* salvo el Cuadro 1.1, se refieren a la orilla oriental solamente.

—Las estadísticas relativas a *Palestina* se refieren al *Estrecho de Gaza* y a *Cisjordania* y figuran inmediatamente después de los países de Asia en los cuadros correspondientes.

—Los datos relativos a *Alemania,* anteriores a 1990, figuran bajo la *República Federal de Alemania* y la ex *República Democrática Alemana,* respectivamente.

—Asimismo para Yemen, cuando los datos son anteriores a 1990, se han presentado bajo ex *Yemen Democrático* y ex *República árabe Yemen.*

—En 1991, la *Unión de Repúblicas Socialistas Soviéticas* se separaron en 15 países diferentes (Armenia, Azerbaiyán, Belarús, Estonia, Georgia, Kazajstán, Kirguistán, Latvia, Lituania, República de Moldova, Federación Rusa, Tajikistán, Turkmenistán, Ucrania, Uzbekistán). En la medida de lo posible, se han presentado los datos por país.

—Los datos relativos a la ex *Yugoslavia* y a la ex *Checoslovaquia* se refieren en general a los años anteriores a los cambios ocurridos en estos países. Los datos relativos a las diferentes repúblicas han sido presentados también, en la medida que estén disponibles.

—Hasta el año 1991, los datos presentados bajo *Etiopía* incluyen a *Eritrea;* sin embargo, si para Eritrea se dispone de datos anteriores a 1991, éstos no se incluyen en los de Etiopía.

—Esta edición del *Anuario* puede contener datos revisados y diferir de aquellos publicados en ediciones anteriores para el mismo año.

Como las cifras y porcentajes se han redondeado, los totales y subtotales que figuran en los cuadros no siempre corresponden exactamente a la suma de los elementos que los componen.

Las notas explicativas relativas a ciertas cifras se señalan por medio del símbolo ‡ que figura inmediatamente después del nombre de los continentes, regiones, países o territorios a que se refieren. El texto aparece al final de cada cuadro; cada nota se compone del nombre del continente, región, país o territorio (en inglés), seguido de la debida explicación. Los textos en inglés, francés y español están precedidos respectivamente de los símbolos E-->, FR->, ESP>. En un determinado número de cuadros figura igualmente una nota general, que precede a las notas correspondientes a los países.

Los símbolos utilizados en el *Anuario* son los siguentes:

-	Cifra nula
0 or 0.0	Cifra inferior a la mitad de la unidad empleada
...	Datos no disponibles
.	Categoría sin objeto
*	Cifra provisional o estimada
./.	Datos comprendidos en otra rúbrica
→	La cifra situada inmediatamente a la izquierda comprende los datos relativos a la(s) columna(s) donde figura ese símbolo
←	La cifra situada inmediatamente a la derecha comprende los datos relativos a la(s) columna(s) donde figura ese símbolo

Una interrupción en la homogeneidad de las series se indica mediante un trazo vertical u horizontal.

List of countries and territories
Liste des pays et territoires
Lista de países y territorios

List of countries and territories

Liste des pays et territoires

Lista de países y territorios

In the tables of this publication, the names of countries and territories are shown in English only. The names in French and Spanish are given in the following pages where they are grouped by continent and arranged in alphabetical order. The number preceding each one refers to the corresponding name in English.

Apart from the continental groupings, eight other groupings are used in certain tables of the **Yearbook.** The countries which compose these groupings can be found at the end of this list, in alphabetical order. There are no international standards on the use of the terms *developed* and *developing* countries, areas or regions. These designations are intended for statistical convenience and do not express a judgement about the stage reached by a particular country or area in the development process.

As in the previous edition of this **Yearbook,** *South Africa* is included in the grouping *Developing Countries* and the states of the former *U.S.S.R.* are included under either *Europe* or *Asia*, and retained under the heading *Developed Countries*. It should also be noted that countries may be included in more than one of the six groupings shown for *Developing Countries*.

Dans les tableaux de cette publication, les noms des pays et des territoires sont donnés en anglais seulement. Les noms en français et en espagnol apparaissent dans la liste ci-après, où les pays ont été classés par continent et dans l'ordre alphabétique de chaque langue. Ils sont précédés d'un numéro qui les renvoie à leur équivalent en anglais.

Outre le groupement par continents, huit autres groupements sont utilisés dans certains tableaux de cet **Annuaire.** Les pays qui composent ces groupes se trouvent à la fin de cette liste, par ordre alphabétique. L'utilisation des expressions pays, zones ou régions *développés* ou *en développement* n'est pas normalisée à l'échelle internationale. Ces appellations sont employées pour des raisons de commodité statistique et n'expriment pas un jugement sur le stade de développement atteint par tel ou tel pays ou zone.

Comme dans l'édition précédente de cet **Annuaire,** *l'Afrique du Sud* est incluse dans la rubrique *Pays en développement.* Les états de l'ancienne *U.R.S.S.* sont présentés en *Europe* ou en *Asie*, et dans le groupement des *Pays développés.* Il est à retenir que quelques pays peuvent appartenir à plus d'un des six groupes présentés sous l'intitulé *Pays en développement.*

En los cuadros de esta publicación, los nombres de los países y territorios se indican en inglés solamente. Los nombres en español y en francés se presentan en la lista que figura a continuación, en la que los países se han clasificado por continente de acuerdo con el orden alfabético de cada lengua. Al lado de los nombres de los países figura un número que corresponde al equivalente del orden alfabético inglés.

*Además de la clasificación por continente, se han presentado también ocho grupos adicionales en algunos de los cuadros de este **Anuario.** Los países que componen estos grupos figuran al final de esta lista, por orden alfabético.- No existe una normalización internacional del empleo de las expresiones países, zonas o regiones desarrolladas o en desarrollo. Estas expresiones se utilizan por conveniencia estadística y no deben interpretarse en el sentido de que expresen un juicio sobre el nivel de desarrollo alcanzado por un país o una zona.*

*Como en la edición precedente del **Anuario,** Africa del Sur se incluye en la clasificación de los Países en desarrollo. Los estados de la ex U.R.S.S. se presentan en Europa o Asia aunque forman parte todavía de los Países desarrollados. Cabe recordar que ciertos países pueden pertenecer a uno o más de los seis grupos que constituyen los Países en desarrollo.*

List of countries and territories
Liste des pays et territoires
Lista de países y territorios

Africa

101 Algeria
102 Angola
103 Benin
104 Botswana
105 Burkina Faso
106 Burundi
107 Cameroon
108 Cape Verde
109 Central African Republic
110 Chad
111 Comoros
112 Congo
113 Côte d'Ivoire
114 Djibouti
115 Egypt
116 Equatorial Guinea
117 Eritrea
118 Ethiopia
119 Gabon
120 Gambia
121 Ghana
122 Guinea
123 Guinea-Bissau
124 Kenya
125 Lesotho
126 Liberia
127 Libyan Arab Jamahiriya
128 Madagascar
129 Malawi
130 Mali
131 Mauritania
132 Mauritius
133 Morocco
134 Mozambique
135 Namibia
136 Niger
137 Nigeria
138 Reunion
139 Rwanda
140 St. Helena
141 Sao Tome and Principe
142 Senegal
143 Seychelles
144 Sierra Leone
145 Somalia
146 South Africa
147 Sudan
148 Swaziland
149 Togo
150 Tunisia
151 Uganda
152 United Republic of Tanzania
153 Western Sahara
154 Zaïre
155 Zambia
156 Zimbabwe

North America

201 Anguilla
202 Antigua and Barbuda
203 Aruba
204 Bahamas

Afrique

146 Afrique du Sud
101 Algérie
102 Angola
103 Bénin
104 Botswana
105 Burkina Faso
106 Burundi
107 Cameroun
108 Cap-Vert
111 Comores
112 Congo
113 Côte d'Ivoire
114 Djibouti
115 Égypte
117 Érythrée
118 Éthiopie
119 Gabon
120 Gambie
121 Ghana
122 Guinée
123 Guinée-Bissau
116 Guinée équatoriale
127 Jamahiriya arabe libyenne
124 Kenya
125 Lesotho
126 Libéria
128 Madagascar
129 Malawi
130 Mali
133 Maroc
132 Maurice
131 Mauritanie
134 Mozambique
135 Namibie
136 Niger
137 Nigéria
151 Ouganda
109 République centrafricaine
152 République—Unie de Tanzanie
138 Réunion
139 Rwanda
153 Sahara occidental
140 Sainte Hélène
141 Sao Tomé-et-Principe
142 Sénégal
143 Seychelles
144 Sierra Leone
145 Somalie
147 Soudan
148 Swaziland
110 Tchad
149 Togo
150 Tunisie
154 Zaïre
155 Zambie
156 Zimbabwe

Amérique du Nord

201 Anguilla
202 Antigua-et-Barbuda
226 Antilles néerlandaises
203 Aruba

Africa

102 Angola
101 Argelia
103 Benín
104 Botswana
105 Burkina Faso
106 Burundi
108 Cabo Verde
107 Camerún
111 Comoras
112 Congo
113 Côte d'Ivoire
110 Chad
114 Djibouti
115 Egipto
117 Eritrea
118 Etiopía
119 Gabón
120 Gambia
121 Ghana
122 Guinea
123 Guinea-Bissau
116 Guinea Ecuatorial
127 Jamahiriya Árabe Libia
124 Kenya
125 Lesotho
126 Liberia
128 Madagascar
129 Malawi
130 Malí
133 Marruecos
132 Mauricio
131 Mauritania
134 Mozambique
135 Namibia
136 Níger
137 Nigeria
138 Reunión
109 República Centroafricana
152 Rep. Unida de Tanzania
139 Rwanda
153 Sahara Occidental
140 Santa Elena
141 Santo Tomé y Príncipe
142 Senegal
143 Seychelles
144 Sierra Leona
145 Somalia
146 Sudáfrica
147 Sudán
148 Swazilandia
149 Togo
150 Túnez
151 Uganda
154 Zaïre
155 Zambia
156 Zimbabwe

América del Norte

201 Anguilla
202 Antigua y Barbuda
226 Antillas Neerlandesas
203 Aruba

List of countries and territories
Liste des pays et territoires
Lista de países y territorios

205 Barbados	204 Bahamas	204 Bahamas
206 Belize	205 Barbade	205 Barbados
207 Bermuda	206 Belize	206 Belice
208 British Virgin Islands	207 Bermudes	207 Bermudas
209 Canada	209 Canada	209 Canadá
210 Cayman Islands	211 Costa Rica	211 Costa Rica
211 Costa Rica	212 Cuba	212 Cuba
212 Cuba	213 Dominique	213 Dominica
213 Dominica	215 El Salvador	215 El Salvador
214 Dominican Republic	236 États-Unis	236 Estados Unidos
215 El Salvador	217 Grenade	217 Granada
216 Greenland	216 Groënland	216 Groenlandia
217 Grenada	218 Guadeloupe	218 Guadalupe
218 Guadeloupe	219 Guatemala	219 Guatemala
219 Guatemala	220 Haïti	220 Haití
220 Haïti	221 Honduras	221 Honduras
221 Honduras	210 Îles Caïmanes	210 Islas Caimán
222 Jamaica	234 Îles Turques et Caïques	234 Islas Turcas y Caicos
223 Martinique	237 Îles Vierges américaines	237 Islas Vírgenes Americanas
224 Mexico	208 Îles Vierges britanniques	208 Islas Vírgenes Británicas
225 Montserrat	222 Jamaïque	222 Jamaica
226 Netherlands Antilles	223 Martinique	223 Martinica
227 Nicaragua	224 Mexique	224 México
228 Panama	225 Montserrat	225 Montserrat
229 Puerto Rico	227 Nicaragua	227 Nicaragua
230 St. Kitts and Nevis	228 Panama	228 Panamá
231 St. Lucia	229 Porto Rico	229 Puerto Rico
232 St. Pierre and Miquelon	214 République dominicaine	214 República Dominicana
233 St. Vincent and the Grenadines	230 Saint-Kitts-et-Nevis	230 Saint Kitts y Nevis
234 Trinidad and Tobago	232 Saint-Pierre-et-Miquelon	232 San Pedro y Miquelón
235 Turks and Caicos Islands	233 Saint-Vincent-et-Grenadines	233 San Vicente y las Granadinas
236 United States	231 Sainte-Lucie	231 Santa Lucía
237 United States Virgin Islands	234 Trinité-et-Tobago	234 Trinidad y Tobago

South America	**Amérique du Sud**	**América del Sur**
301 Argentina	301 Argentine	301 Argentina
302 Bolivia	302 Bolivie	302 Bolivia
303 Brazil	303 Brésil	303 Brasil
304 Chile	304 Chili	305 Colombia
305 Colombia	305 Colombie	304 Chile
306 Ecuador	306 Équateur	306 Ecuador
307 Falkland Islands (Malvinas)	309 Guyana	309 Guyana
308 French Guiana	308 Guyane française	308 Guyana francesa
309 Guyana	307 Îles Falkland (Malvinas)	307 Islas Falkland (Malvinas)
310 Paraguay	310 Paraguay	310 Paraguay
311 Peru	311 Pérou	311 Perú
312 Suriname	312 Suriname	312 Suriname
313 Uruguay	313 Uruguay	313 Uruguay
314 Venezuela	314 Venezuela	314 Venezuela

Asia	**Asie**	**Asia**
401 Afghanistan	401 Afghanistan	401 Afghanistán
402 Armenia	438 Arabie saoudite	438 Arabia Saudí
403 Azerbaijan	402 Arménie	402 Armenia
404 Bahrain	403 Azerbaïdjan	403 Azerbaiyán
405 Bangladesh	404 Bahreïn	404 Bahrein
406 Bhutan	405 Bangladesh	405 Bangladesh
407 Brunei Darussalam	406 Bhoutan	406 Bhután
408 Cambodia	407 Brunéi Darussalam	407 Brunei Darussalam
409 China	408 Cambodge	408 Camboya
410 Cyprus	409 Chine	409 China
411 East Timor	410 Chypre	410 Chipre

List of countries and territories
Liste des pays et territoires
Lista de países y territorios

412 Georgia
413 Hong Kong
414 India
415 Indonesia
416 Iran, Islamic Republic of
417 Iraq
418 Israel
419 Japan
420 Jordan
421 Kazakstan
422 Korea, Democratic People's
   Republic of
423 Korea, Republic of
424 Kuwait
425 Kyrgyzstan
426 Lao People's Democratic
   Republic
427 Lebanon
428 Macau
429 Malaysia
430 Maldives
431 Mongolia
432 Myanmar
433 Nepal
434 Oman
435 Pakistan
436 Philippines
437 Qatar
438 Saudi Arabia
439 Singapore
440 Sri Lanka
441 Syrian Arab Republic
442 Tajikistan
443 Thailand
444 Turkey
445 Turkmenistan
446 United Arab Emirates
447 Uzbekistan
448 Viet Nam
449 Yemen
450 Former Democratic Yemen
451 Former Yemen Arab Rep.

452 *Palestine*
453 Gaza Strip
454 West Bank

Europe

501 Albania
502 Andorra
503 Austria
504 Belarus
505 Belgium
506 Bosnia and Herzegovina
507 Bulgaria
508 Croatia
509 Former Czechoslovakia
510 Czech Republic
511 Denmark
512 Estonia
513 Faeroë Islands
514 Finland
515 France
516 Germany

446 Émirats arabes unis
412 Géorgie
413 Hong-Kong
414 Inde
415 Indonésie
416 Iran, République islamique d'
417 Irak
418 Israël
419 Japon
420 Jordanie
421 Kazakstan
424 Koweït
425 Kirghizistan
427 Liban
428 Macao
429 Malaisie
430 Maldives
431 Mongolie
432 Myanmar
433 Népal
434 Oman
447 Ouzbékistan
435 Pakistan
436 Philippines
437 Qatar
441 République arabe syrienne
423 République de Corée
426 République démocratique
   populaire lao
422 République populaire
   démocratique de Corée
439 Singapour
440 Sri Lanka
442 Tadjikistan
443 Thaïlande
411 Timor oriental
444 Turquie
445 Turkménistan
448 Viet Nam
449 Yémen
450 AncienYémen démocratique
451 Ancienne Rép. arabe yémen

452 *Palestine*
453 Bande de Gaza
454 Cisjordanie

Europe

501 Albanie
516 Allemagne
517 Ancienne R. dém. allemande
518 Rép. fédérale d'Allemagne
502 Andorre
503 Autriche
504 Bélarus
505 Belgique
506 Bosnie-Herzégovine
507 Bulgarie
508 Croatie
511 Danemark
542 Espagne
512 Estonie
538 Fédération de Russie
514 Finlande

446 Emiratos Árabes Unidos
436 Filipinas
412 Georgia
413 Hong-Kong
414 India
415 Indonesia
417 Irak
416 Irán, República Islámica del
418 Israel
419 Japón
420 Jordania
421 Kazajstán
425 Kirguistán
424 Kuwait
427 Líbano
428 Macao
429 Malasia
430 Maldivas
431 Mongolia
432 Myanmar
433 Nepal
434 Omán
435 Pakistán
437 Qatar
441 República Árabe Siria
423 República de Corea
426 República Democrática
   Popular Lao
422 República Popular
   democrática de Corea
439 Singapur
439 Sri Lanka
443 Tailandia
442 Tayikistán
411 Timor Oriental
445 Turkmenistán
444 Turquía
447 Uzbekistán
448 Viet Nam
449 Yemen
450 ex República Árabe Yemen
451 ex Yemen Democrático

452 *Palestina*
454 Cisjordania
453 Estrecho de Gaza

Europa

501 Albania
516 Alemania
517 ex Rep. Democrática Alemana
518 Rep. Federal de Alemania
502 Andorra
503 Austria
504 Belarrús
505 Bélgica
506 Bosnia y Herzegovina
507 Bulgaria
509 ex Checoslovaquia
510 República Checa
508 Croacia
511 Dinamarca
540 Eslovaquia
541 Eslovenia

List of countries and territories
Liste des pays et territoires
Lista de países y territorios

517 Former German Democratic Rep.	515 France	542 España
518 Federal Republic of Germany	519 Gibraltar	512 Estonia
519 Gibraltar	520 Grèce	538 Federación de Rusia
520 Greece	522 Hongrie	514 Finlandia
521 Holy See	513 Îles Féroé	515 Francia
522 Hungary	524 Irlande	519 Gibraltar
523 Iceland	523 Islande	520 Grecia
524 Ireland	525 Italie	522 Hungría
525 Italy	545 L'ex-Rép. yougoslave	524 Irlanda
526 Latvia	de Macédoine	523 Islandia
527 Liechtenstein	526 Lettonie	513 Islas Feroé
528 Lithuania	527 Liechtenstein	525 Italia
529 Luxembourg	528 Lituanie	545 La ex República Yugoslava
530 Malta	529 Luxembourg	de Macedonia
531 Moldova	530 Malte	526 Letonia
532 Monaco	531 Moldova	527 Liechtenstein
533 Netherlands	532 Monaco	528 Lituania
534 Norway	534 Norvège	529 Luxemburgo
535 Poland	533 Pays-Bas	530 Malta
536 Portugal	535 Pologne	531 Moldova
537 Romania	536 Portugal	532 Mónaco
538 Russian Federation	537 Roumanie	534 Noruega
539 San Marino	547 Royaume-Uni	533 Países Bajos
540 Slovakia	539 Saint-Marin	535 Polonia
541 Slovenia	521 Saint-Siège	536 Portugal
542 Spain	540 Slovaquie	547 Reino Unido
543 Sweden	541 Slovénie	537 Rumania
544 Switzerland	543 Suède	539 San Marino
545 The former Yugoslav Rep.	544 Suisse	521 Santa Sede
of Macedonia	509 Ancienne Tchécoslovaquie	543 Suecia
546 Ukraine	510 République tchèque	544 Suiza
547 United Kingdom	546 Ukraine	546 Ucrania
548 Former Yugoslavia	548 Ancienne Yougoslavie	548 ex Yugoslavia
549 Federal Rep. of Yugoslavia	549 Rép. fédérative de Yougoslavie	549 Rep. Federativa de Yugoslavia

Oceania	**Océanie**	**Oceanía**
601 American Samoa	602 Australie	602 Australia
602 Australia	604 Fidji	604 Fiji
603 Cook Islands	606 Guam	606 Guam
604 Fiji	603 Îles Cook	603 Islas Cook
605 French Polynesia	608 Îles Marshall	608 Islas Marshall
606 Guam	613 Îles du Pacifique (Palau)	614 Islas del Pacífico (Palau)
607 Kiribati	616 Îles Salomon	617 Islas Salomón
608 Marshall Islands	607 Kiribati	607 Kiribati
609 Nauru	609 Nauru	609 Nauru
610 New Caledonia	612 Nioué	612 Niue
611 New Zealand	610 Nouvelle-Calédonie	611 Nueva Caledonia
612 Niue	611 Nouvelle-Zélande	612 Nueva Zelandia
613 Pacific Islands (Palau)	614 Papouasie-Nouvelle-Guinée	615 Papua Nueva Guinea
614 Papua New Guinea	605 Polynésie française	605 Polinesia Francesa
615 Samoa	615 Samoa	616 Samoa
616 Solomon Islands	616 Samoa américaines	601 Samoa Americanas
617 Tokelau	617 Tokelaou	618 Tokelau
618 Tonga	618 Tonga	619 Tonga
619 Tuvalu	619 Tuvalu	619 Tuvalu
620 Vanuatu, Republic of	620 Vanuatu, République de	620 Vanuatu, República de

Former U.S.S.R.	**Ancienne U.R.S.S.**	**ex U.R.S.S.**
701 Former U.S.S.R.	701 Ancienne U.R.S.S.	701 ex U.R.S.S.

List of countries and territories
Liste des pays et territoires
Lista de países y territorios

Continents, Major Areas and Groups of Countries
Continents, grandes régions et groupes de pays
Continentes, grandes regiones y grupos de países

Developing Countries / Pays en développement / Países en desarrollo

All countries, excluding the Developed Countries listed below.
Tous les pays, à l'exclusion des Pays développés énumérés ci-dessous.
Todos los países, excepto los Países desarrollados indicados abajo.

Sub-Saharan Africa / Afrique subsaharienne / Africa subsahariana
Angola, Benin, Botswana, Burkina Faso, Burundi, Cameroon, Cape Verde, Central African Republic, Chad, Comoros, Congo, Côte d'Ivoire, Djibouti, Equatorial Guinea, Eritrea, Ethiopia, Gabon, Gambia, Ghana, Guinea, Guinea-Bissau, Kenya, Lesotho, Liberia, Madagascar, Malawi, Mali, Mauritania, Mauritius, Mozambique, Namibia, Niger, Nigeria, Reunion, Rwanda, St. Helena, Sao Tome and Principe, Senegal, Seychelles, Sierra Leone, Somalia, South Africa, Sudan, Swaziland, Togo, Uganda, United Republic of Tanzania, Western Sahara, Zaïre, Zambia, Zimbabwe.

Arab States / États arabes / Estados árabes
Algeria, Bahrain, Djibouti, Egypt, Iraq, Jordan, Kuwait, Lebanon, Libyan Arab Jamahiriya, Mauritania, Morocco, Oman, Palestine: Gaza Strip and West Bank, Qatar, Saudi Arabia, Somalia, Sudan, Syrian Arab Republic, Tunisia, United Arab Emirates, Yemen.

Latin America and the Caribbean / Amérique latine et les Caraïbes / América latina y el Caribe
Anguilla, Antigua and Barbuda, Argentina, Aruba, Bahamas, Barbados, Belize, Bolivia, Brazil, British Virgin Islands, Cayman Islands, Chile, Colombia, Costa Rica, Cuba, Dominica, Dominican Republic, Ecuador, El Salvador, Falkland Islands (Malvinas), French Guiana, Grenada, Guadeloupe, Guatemala, Guyana, Haïti, Honduras, Jamaica, Martinique, Mexico, Montserrat, Netherlands Antilles, Nicaragua, Panama, Paraguay, Peru, Puerto Rico, St. Kitts and Nevis, St. Lucia, St. Vincent and the Grenadines, Suriname, Trinidad and Tobago, Turks and Caicos Islands, U.S. Virgin Islands, Uruguay, Venezuela,

Eastern Asia and Oceania / Asie de l'est et Océanie / Asia del Este y Oceanía
American Samoa, Brunei Darussalam, Cambodia, China, Cook Islands, East Timor, Fiji, French Polynesia, Guam, Hong Kong, Indonesia, Kiribati, Democratic People's Republic of Korea, Republic of Korea, Lao People's Democratic Republic, Macau, Malaysia, Marshall Islands, Mongolia, Myanmar, Nauru, New Caledonia, Niue, Pacific Islands (Palau), Papua New Guinea, Philippines, Samoa, Singapore, Solomon Islands, Thailand, Tokelau, Tonga, Tuvalu, Vanuatu, Viet Nam.

Southern Asia / Asie du Sud / Asia del Sur
Afghanistan, Bangladesh, Bhutan, India, Islamic Republic of Iran, Maldives, Nepal, Pakistan, Sri Lanka.

Least Developed Countries / Pays les moins avancés / Países menos adelantados
Afghanistan, Bangladesh, Benin, Bhutan, Burkina Faso, Burundi, Cambodia, Cape Verde, Central African Republic, Chad, Comoros, Djibouti, Equatorial Guinea, Eritrea, Ethiopia, Gambia, Guinea, Guinea-Bissau, Haïti, Kiribati, Lao People's Democratic Republic, Lesotho, Liberia, Madagascar, Malawi, Maldives, Mali, Mauritania, Mozambique, Myanmar, Nepal, Niger, Rwanda, Samoa, Sao Tome and Principe, Sierra Leone, Solomon Islands, Somalia, Sudan, Togo, Tuvalu, Uganda, United Republic of Tanzania, Vanuatu, Yemen, Zaïre, Zambia.

Developed Countries / Pays développés / Países desarrollados

Albania, Andorra, Armenia, Australia, Austria, Azerbaijan, Belarus, Belgium, Bulgaria, Canada, Czech Republic, Denmark, Estonia, Faeroe Islands, Finland, France, Georgia, Germany, Gibraltar, Greece, Holy See, Hungary, Iceland, Ireland, Israel, Italy, Japan, Kazakstan, Kyrgyzstan, Latvia, Liechtenstein, Lithuania, Luxembourg, Moldova, Monaco, Netherlands, New Zealand, Norway, Poland, Portugal, Romania, Russian Federation, San Marino, Slovakia, Spain, Sweden, Switzerland, Tajikistan, Turkmenistan, Ukraine, United Kingdom, United States, Uzbekistan.

Table on selected indicators

Tableau d'indicateurs selectionnés

Cuadro de indicadores seleccionados

This table presents in a kind of overview a number of indicators in UNESCO'S fields of competence. The exact definitions and interpretation of these indicators are given in footnotes to the table.

Ce tableau présente une synthèse de différents indicateurs relatifs aux domaines de compétence de l'UNESCO. Les définitions exactes et l'interprétation des ces indicateurs sont présentées à la fin du tableau.

Este cuadro presenta una sintesis de diferentes indicadores relativos a las esferas de competencia de la UNESCO. Las definiciones exactas y la interpretación de estos indicadores están presentadas en las notas de este cuadro.

Table on selected indicators

Tableau d'indicateurs selectionnés

Cuadro de indicadores seleccionados

Country Pays País	Adult illiteracy rates estimates for 1995 Taux d'analphabétisme des adultes estimations pour 1995 Tasas de analfabetismo de adultos estimaciones para 1995			Circulation of daily newspapers per 1,000 inhabitants Diffusion de journaux quotidiens pour 1 000 habitants Difusión de periódicos diarios por 1 000 habitantes	Number of television receivers per 1,000 inhabitants Nombre de récepteurs de télévision pour 1 000 habitants Número de receptores de televisión por 1 000 habitantes	Gross enrolment ratios at first and second level Taux bruts d'inscription dans les premier et deuxième degrés Tasas de escolarización brutas en los primer y segundo grados 1994		
	MF	M	F	1994	1994	MF	M	F
	(1)	(2)	(3)	(4)	(5)	(6)	(7)	(8)
Africa								
Algeria	38.4	26.1	51.0	46	79	84	89	79
Angola	...	...	...	11	6.6	45	...	...
Benin	63.0	51.3	74.2	2	5.5	40	54	26
Botswana	30.2	19.5	40.1	24	17	93	91	96
Burkina Faso	80.8	70.5	90.8	0.3	5.5	25	31	19
Burundi	64.7	50.7	77.5	3	1.5	40	44	35
Cameroon	36.6	25.0	47.9	4	24	58	63	53
Cape Verde	28.4	18.6	36.2	-	3.4	83	85A	81
Central African Republic	40.0	31.5	47.6	1	4.9	...	...	...
Chad	51.9	37.9	65.3	0.4	1.4	33	46	20
Comoros	42.7	35.8	49.6	-	0.4	49	53	44
Congo	25.1	16.9	32.8	8	7.0	...	...	...
Côte d'Ivoire	59.9	50.1	70.0	7	60	48	58	39
Djibouti	53.8	39.7	67.3	-	44	26	30	22
Egypt	48.6	36.4	61.2	64	109	86	93	79
Equatorial Guinea	21.5	10.4	31.9	3	9.6	...	...	...
Eritrea	...	...	...	...	0.3	32	37	28
Ethiopia	64.5	54.5	74.7	2	4.3	20	24	16
Gabon	36.8	26.3	46.7	16	38	...	...	...
Gambia	61.4	47.2	75.1	2	2.8	44	53	35
Ghana	35.5	24.1	46.5	18	89	58	65	50
Guinea	64.1	50.1	78.1	-	7.7	30	41	19
Guinea-Bissau	45.1	32.0	57.5	6	...	...	...	...
Kenya	21.9	13.7	30.0	13	11	72	73	71
Lesotho	28.7	18.9	37.7	7	10	72	67	78
Liberia	61.7	46.1	77.6	14	19	...	...	...
Libyan Arab Jamahiriya	23.8	12.1	37.0	13	100	104	...	...
Madagascar	...	...	...	4	20	42	43	42
Malawi	43.6	28.1	58.2	2	...	87	92	83
Mali	69.0	60.6	76.9	4	1.3	20	26	15

School life expectancy: number of years / Espérance de vie scolaire: nombre d'années / Esperanza de vida escolar: número de años 1993	Net enrolment ratio at the first level / Taux nets d'inscription dans le premier degré / Tasas netas de escolarización en el primer grado 1994			Percentage of 1992 cohort reaching grade 5 / Pourcentage de la cohorte 1992 atteign. la 5e année d'études / Porcentaje de la cohorte de 1992 que llega al quinto año	Number of 3rd lev. students per 100,000 inhabitants / No. d'élèves du 3e degré par 100 000 habitants / Número de estudiantes del 3er grado por 100 000 habitantes 1994	Public expenditure on education as % of GNP / Dépenses publiques aff. a l'éducation en % du PNB / Gastos públicos dest. a la educación en % del PNB 1994	Country / Pays / País
MF	MF	M	F	MF	MF		
(9)	(10)	(11)	(12)	(13)	(14)	(15)	
							Africa
10.3	95	99	91	92	1 160	...	Algeria
...	...	...	...	34	71	...	Angola
...	53	71	35	55	208	...	Benin
10.8	96	93	99	84	362	8.5	Botswana
2.9	32	39	25	61	90	3.6	Burkina Faso
4.5	51	56	47	74	73	3.8	Burundi
...	...	...	...		288		Cameroon
8.8	100	100	100		.	4.4	Cape Verde
...	...	...	...	...	150	...	Central African Republic
...	...	...	...	46	70	2.2	Chad
...	51	55	46	78	47	3.7	Comoros
...	...	...	...	...	582	8.3	Congo
...	...	...	...	73	204	6.7	Côte d'Ivoire
...	32	36	28	94	11	3.8	Djibouti
9.8	89	95	82	98	1 542	5.0	Egypt
...	...	...	...	...	164	1.8	Equatorial Guinea
3.3	27	28	25	79	91	...	Eritrea
...	21	24	17	58	68	...	Ethiopia
...	...	...	...	...	373	...	Gabon
5.0	55	64	46	87	147	2.7	Gambia
...	...	...	...	80	126	...	Ghana
...	40	...	...	80	93	2.2	Guinea
...	...	...	...	...	...	...	Guinea-Bissau
...	...	...	...	77*	142	6.8	Kenya
8.3	65	60	71	60	206	4.8	Lesotho
...	...	...	...	...	...	...	Liberia
...	97	98	96	...	1 548	...	Libyan Arab Jamahiriya
...	...	...	...	28	318	...	Madagascar
7.0	92	91	93	37	69	...	Malawi
...	23	28	18	85	73	2.1	Mali

Country Pays País	Adult illiteracy rates estimates for 1995 Taux d'analphabétisme des adultes estimations pour 1995 Tasas de analfabetismo de adultos estimaciones para 1995			Circulation of daily newspapers per 1,000 inhabitants Diffusion de journaux quotidiens pour 1 000 habitants Difusión de periódicos diarios por 1 000 habitantes	Number of television receivers per 1,000 inhabitants Nombre de récepteurs de télévision pour 1 000 habitants Número de receptores de televisión por 1 000 habitantes	Gross enrolment ratios at first and second level Taux bruts d'inscription dans les premier et deuxième degrés Tasas de escolarización brutas en los primer y segundo grados 1994		
	MF	M	F	1994	1994	MF	M	F
	(1)	(2)	(3)	(4)	(5)	(6)	(7)	(8)
Mauritania	62.3	50.4	73.7	0.5	25	44	50	38
Mauritius	17.1	12.9	21.2	68	222	80	79	80
Morocco	56.3	43.4	69.0	13	79	59	68	50
Mozambique	59.9	42.3	76.7	5	3.5	32	37	27
Namibia	...	...	...	102	23	109	106	112
Niger	86.4	79.1	93.4	1	4.9	18	23	13
Nigeria	42.9	32.7	52.7	18	38	63	70	56
Rwanda	39.5	30.2	48.4	0.1	...	50	51	49
Sao Tome and Principe	...	...	...	-	162	...	...	...
Senegal	66.9	57.0	76.8	6	37	38	44	31
Seychelles	...	...	...	44	88	...	...	...
Sierra Leone	68.6	54.6	81.8	2	11	36	43	29
Somalia	...	...	...	1	13	...	...	...
South Africa	18.2	18.1	18.3	33	101	103	102	105
Sudan	53.9	42.3	65.4	23	80	38	43	34
Swaziland	23.3	22.0	24.4	14	20	94	97	92
Togo	48.3	33.0	63.0	2	7.5	64	80	48
Tunisia	33.3	21.4	45.4	46	81	86	89	82
Uganda	38.2	26.3	49.8	2	11	44	...	...
United Republic of Tanzania	32.2	20.6	43.2	8	2.1	44	45	43
Zaire	22.7	13.4	32.3	3	1.5	49	58	39
Zambia	21.8	14.4	28.7	8	27	62	66	58
Zimbabwe	14.9	9.6	20.1	18	27	86	90	81
America, North								
Antigua and Barbuda	...	...	...	-	370	...	...	...
Aruba	...	...	...	757	277	...	...	...
Bahamas	1.8	1.5	2.0	129	226	98	97	99
Barbados	2.6	2.0	3.2	159	279	...	...	...
Belize	...	...	...	-	167	92	92	91
British Virgin Islands	...	...	...	-	213	...	...	...
Canada	...	...	...	189	685	105	105	104
Costa Rica	5.2	5.3	5.0	99	142	81	81	82
Cuba	4.3	3.8	4.7	120	171	90	88	92
Dominica	...	...	...	-	75	...	...	...
Dominican Republic	17.9	18.0	17.8	34	90	84	81	86
El Salvador	28.5	26.5	30.2	50	443	66	66	67
Grenada	...	...	...	-	337	...	...	...
Guatemala	44.4	37.5	51.4	23	53	57	60	53
Haiti	55.0	52.0	57.8	6	4.8	40	41	39
Honduras	27.3	27.4	27.3	44	78	79	...	...
Jamaica	15.0	19.2	10.9	66	142	86	83	88
Mexico	10.4	8.2	12.6	113	163	86	86	85
Netherlands Antilles	...	...	...	269	334	...	...	...
Nicaragua	34.3	35.4	33.4	30	67	79	76	81
Panama	9.2	8.6	9.8	62	170	85	85	85
Saint Kitts and Nevis	...	...	...	-	213	...	...	...
St. Lucia	...	...	...	-	189	...	...	...
St. Vincent and the Grenadines	...	...	...	-	147	...	...	...
Trinidad and Tobago	2.1	1.2	3.0	135	317	87	86	88
United States	...	...	...	228	817	102	103	102
America, South								
Argentina	3.8	3.8	3.8	138	219	93	...	...
Bolivia	16.9	9.5	24.0	69	113	77	81	73
Brazil	16.7	16.7	16.8	45	209	96	...	...
Chile	4.8	4.6	5.0	100	211	89	89	89
Colombia	8.7	8.8	8.6	64	118	89	85	92
Ecuador	9.9	8.0	11.8	72	88	90	91	90
Guyana	1.9	1.4	2.5	97	39	...	...	...
Paraguay	7.9	6.5	9.4	42	83	78	79	78
Peru	11.3	5.5	17.0	86	99	95	...	...
Suriname	7.0	4.9	9.0	103	141	...	...	...

School life expectancy: number of years / Espérance de vie scolaire: nombre d'années / Esperanza de vida escolar: número de años 1993	Net enrolment ratio at the first level / Taux nets d'inscription dans le premier degré / Tasas netas de escolarización en el primer grado 1994			Percentage of 1992 cohort reaching grade 5 / Pourcentage de la cohorte 1992 atteign. la 5e année d'études / Porcentaje de la cohorte de 1992 que llega al quinto año	Number of 3rd lev. students per 100,000 inhabitants / No. d'élèves du 3e degré par 100 000 habitants / Número de estudiantes del 3er grado por 100 000 habitantes 1994	Public expenditure on education as % of GNP / Dépenses publiques aff. a l'éducation en % du PNB / Gastos públicos dest. a la educación en % del PNB 1994	Country / Pays / País
MF	MF	M	F	MF	MF		
(9)	(10)	(11)	(12)	(13)	(14)	(15)	
...	...	...	...	72	393	4.0	Mauritania
...	94	94	94	100	431	...	Mauritius
7.4	69	79	59	80	1 040	5.4	Morocco
3.4	41	46	35	35	35	...	Mozambique
13.2	91	...	...	82	665	8.7	Namibia
...	...	...	...	82	56	...	Niger
...	...	...	...	92*	360	...	Nigeria
5.7	71	71	71	60	50	...	Rwanda
...	...	...	...	...	.	...	Sao Tome and Principe
...	...	...	...	...	298	4.4	Senegal
...	...	...	...	99	.	7.4	Seychelles
...	...	...	...	...	129	...	Sierra Leone
...	...	...	...	...	...	...	Somalia
13.2	96	95	96	76	1 394	7.1	South Africa
...	...	...	...	94	266	...	Sudan
11.2	95	95	96	78	544	6.8	Swaziland
...	69	80	58	...	235	6.1	Togo
10.3	99	100	96	92	1 121	6.3	Tunisia
...	...	...	...	55*	121	1.9	Uganda
...	50	50	51	83	21	...	United Republic of Tanzania
5.5	54	60	47	64	176	...	Zaire
...	69	70	68	...	183	...	Zambia
...	...	...	...	76	588	8.3	Zimbabwe
							America, North
...	...	...	...	...	.	...	Antigua and Barbuda
...	...	...	...	...	.	...	Aruba
12.4	94	93	96	...	...	3.9	Bahamas
...	78	78	78	...	2 493	7.5	Barbados
10.6	97	97	96	68	.	5.7	Belize
...	...	...	...	...	.	...	British Virgin Islands
17.6	97	97	96	97*	6 980	7.6	Canada
10.1	90	...	...	88	2 767	4.7	Costa Rica
11.5	100	99	100	95	1 620	...	Cuba
...	...	...	...	93*	...	...	Dominica
10.3	81	79	83	58*	...	1.9	Dominican Republic
...	70	70	71	58	1 508	1.6	El Salvador
...	...	...	...	...	.	5.3	Grenada
...	...	...	...	...	...	1.6	Guatemala
...	26	25	26	...	...	...	Haiti
8.2	90	89	91	...	865	4.0	Honduras
11.0	100	100	100	96	668	4.7	Jamaica
...	99	...	...	84	1 509	5.8	Mexico
...	...	...	...	...	.	...	Netherlands Antilles
8.6	79	78	81	49	903	...	Nicaragua
...	91	91	92	...	2 736	5.2	Panama
...	...	...	...	...	...	3.3	Saint Kitts and Nevis
...	...	...	...	95	...	5.2	St. Lucia
...	...	...	...	...	...	...	St. Vincent and the Grenadines
10.6	...	...	...	95	673	4.5	Trinidad and Tobago
15.9	100	99	100	...	5 546	5.5	United States
							America, South
13.2	...	...	...	...	3 206	3.8	Argentina
...	91	95	87	60	2 214	5.4	Bolivia
10.9	91	...	...	70	1 080	...	Brazil
11.7	86	86	85	95*	2 369	2.9	Chile
10.6	85	...	...	59	1 703	3.7	Colombia
...	...	...	...	...	2 012	3.0	Ecuador
...	...	...	...	...	1 012	...	Guyana
8.9	90	89	90	71	907	2.9	Paraguay
12.0	88	...	...	...	3 240	...	Peru
...	...	...	...	...	1 079	3.6	Suriname

Country Pays País	Adult illiteracy rates estimates for 1995 Taux d'analphabétisme des adultes estimations pour 1995 Tasas de analfabetismo de adultos estimaciones para 1995			Circulation of daily newspapers per 1,000 inhabitants Diffusion de journaux quotidiens pour 1 000 habitants Difusión de periódicos diarios por 1 000 habitantes	Number of television receivers per 1,000 inhabitants Nombre de récepteurs de télévision pour 1 000 habitants Número de receptores de televisión por 1 000 habitantes	Gross enrolment ratios at first and second level Taux bruts d'inscription dans les premier et deuxième degrés Tasas de escolarización brutas en los primer y segundo grados 1994		
	MF	M	F	1994	1994	MF	M	F
	(1)	(2)	(3)	(4)	(5)	(6)	(7)	(8)
Uruguay	2.7	3.1	2.3	237	232	95	92	98
Venezuela	8.9	8.2	9.7	215	164	86	84	88
Asia								
Afghanistan	68.5	52.8	85.0	11	9.8	34	47	20
Armenia	...	...	...	23	225	87	82	91
Azerbaijan	...	...	...	28	...	97	98	95
Bahrain	14.8	10.9	20.6	128	430	105	104	107
Bangladesh	61.9	50.6	73.9	6	5.8	46	51	40
Bhutan	57.8	43.8	71.9	-	...	...	...	...
Brunei Darussalam	11.8	7.4	16.6	71	241	89	89	89
Cambodia	...	...	...	-	8.0	75	84	65
China	18.5	10.1	27.3	23	189	88	92	84
Cyprus	...	...	...	110	320	99	98	99
Georgia	...	...	...	...	459	80	82	78
Hong Kong	7.8	4.0	11.8	719	291	91	...	...
India	48.0	34.5	62.3	...	40	72	83	62
Indonesia	16.2	10.4	22.0	20	62	80	83	77
Iran, Islamic Republic of	27.9	21.6	34.2	18	62	84	89	78
Iraq	42.0	29.3	55.0	27	75	69	77	61
Israel	...	...	...	281	275	92	91	93
Japan	...	...	...	576	681	100	100	101
Jordan	13.4	6.6	20.6	48	76	...	...	...
Kazakstan	...	...	...	...	250	89	88	89
Korea, Dem. People's Rep. of	...	...	...	213	43	...	...	...
Korea, Republic of	2.0	0.7	3.3	404	323	97	97	97
Kuwait	21.4	17.8	25.1	401	380	66	66	66
Kyrgyzstan	...	...	...	11	...	95	93	96
Lao People's Democratic Rep.	43.4	30.6	55.6	3	8.4	67	78	56
Lebanon	7.6	5.3	9.7	172	360	94	92	95
Malaysia	16.5	10.9	21.9	142	157	78	76	79
Maldives	6.8	6.7	7.0	12	25	90	91	89
Mongolia	...	...	...	88	42	68	60	75
Myanmar	16.9	11.3	22.3	23	5.0	65	...	...
Nepal	72.5	59.1	86.0	8	4.7	74	91	57
Oman	...	...	...	30	662	74	77	72
Pakistan	62.2	50.0	75.6	21	19	42	56	28
Philippines	5.4	5.0	5.7	65	48	99	...	...
Qatar	20.6	20.8	20.1	148	398	87	88	86
Saudi Arabia	37.2	28.5	49.8	54	255	66	69	62
Singapore	8.9	4.1	13.7	364	390	86	...	...
Sri Lanka	9.8	6.6	12.8	25	50	87	85	89
Syrian Arab Republic	29.2	14.3	44.2	18	62	77	82	72
Tajikistan	...	...	...	13	...	83	86	80
Thailand	6.2	4.0	8.4	48	117	68	...	...
Turkey	17.7	8.3	27.6	44	181	80	88	71
Turkmenistan	...	...	...	-	180	...	...	...
United Arab Emirates	20.8	21.1	20.2	161	107	103	102	104
Uzbekistan	...	...	...	7	190	87	90	83
Viet Nam	6.3	3.5	8.8	8	43	73	...	...
Yemen	...	...	...	17	28	70	100	39
Europe								
Albania	...	...	...	54	91	79	78	79
Andorra	...	...	...	63	367	...	...	...
Austria	...	...	...	472	480	105	107	104
Belarus	...	...	...	187	226	95	94	96
Belgium	...	...	...	321	453	101	101	102
Bosnia and Herzegovina	...	...	...	131	...	...	...	...
Bulgaria	...	...	...	209	363	80	81	80
Croatia	...	...	...	575	253	84	83	84
Czech Republic	...	...	...	219	478	94	93	96
Denmark	...	...	...	365	539	107	106	109

School life expectancy: number of years / Espérance de vie scolaire: nombre d'années / Esperanza de vida escolar: número de años 1993	Net enrolment ratio at the first level / Taux nets d'inscription dans le premier degré / Tasas netas de escolarización en el primer grado 1994			Percentage of 1992 cohort reaching grade 5 / Pourcentage de la cohorte 1992 atteign. la 5e année d'études / Porcentaje de la cohorte de 1992 que llega al quinto año	Number of 3rd lev. students per 100,000 inhabitants / No. d'élèves du 3e degré par 100 000 habitants / Número de estudiantes del 3er grado por 100 000 habitantes 1994	Public expenditure on education as % of GNP / Dépenses publiques aff. a l'éducation en % du PNB / Gastos públicos dest. a la educación en % del PNB 1994	Country / Pays / País
MF	MF	M	F	MF	MF		
(9)	(10)	(11)	(12)	(13)	(14)	(15)	
...	94	94	94	94	2 179	2.5	Uruguay
10.5	88	87	90	78	2 757	5.1	Venezuela
							Asia
...	...	...	...	...	162	...	Afghanistan
...	...	...	...	...	3 711	...	Armenia
...	...	...	...	93	1 753	5.5	Azerbaijan
13.0	100	100	100	99	1 436	...	Bahrain
...	70	74	66	...	405	2.3	Bangladesh
...	...	...	...	82	...	2.7	Bhutan
11.6	90	90	89	100	516	...	Brunei Darussalam
...	...	...	...	50	126	...	Cambodia
...	96	97	95	88	377	2.6	China
10.3	96	96	96	100	1 069	4.3	Cyprus
...	82	82	81	...	3 083	1.9	Georgia
...	...	...	...	...	1 677	...	Hong Kong
...	...	...	...	62*	582	3.8	India
9.6	97	100	95	92	951	2.2	Indonesia
...	...	...	...	90	1 148	5.9	Iran, Islamic Republic of
8.3	79	83	74	...	1 240	...	Iraq
...	...	...	...	100*	2 979	6.0	Israel
13.5	100	100	100	100	2 340	4.7	Japan
...	89	89	89	98	2 225	...	Jordan
...	...	...	...	...	2 915	5.4	Kazakstan
...	...	...	...	...	...	...	Korea, Dem.People's Rep. of
13.9	96	95	97	100	4 756	4.5	Korea, Republic of
8.1	64	64	64	99	1 589	5.6	Kuwait
...	...	...	...	...	1 837	6.8	Kyrgyzstan
6.9	68	75	61	53	134	2.3	Lao People's Democratic Rep.
...	...	...	...	...	3 275	2.0	Lebanon
...	...	...	...	98	884	5.3	Malaysia
...	...	...	...	93*	.	8.1	Maldives
7.1	78	76	81	...	1 377	5.2	Mongolia
...	...	...	...	...	528	...	Myanmar
...	...	...	...	52	490	2.9	Nepal
0.5	72	74	71	96	400	4.5	Oman
...	...	...	...	...	294	2.7	Pakistan
10.8	97	...	...	...	2 716	2.9	Philippines
11.0	81	81	80	98	1 389	3.5	Qatar
8.5	63	66	59	94	1 175	6.3	Saudi Arabia
...	100	100	100	100	2 642	3.3	Singapore
...	...	...	...	92	552	3.2	Sri Lanka
9.3	93	98	89	92	1 700	4.2	Syrian Arab Republic
...	...	...	...	...	2 298	9.5	Tajikistan
...	...	...	...	88	2 166	3.8	Thailand
9.3	90	92	87	89	1 918	3.3	Turkey
...	...	...	...	...	2 078	7.9	Turkmenistan
11.4	100	100	99	99	601	2.0	United Arab Emirates
...	...	...	...	100	3 054	11.0	Uzbekistan
...	...	...	...	...	316	...	Viet Nam
...	...	...	...	...	447	...	Yemen
							Europe
...	...	...	...	92*	891	3.0	Albania
...	...	...	...	...	.	...	Andorra
14.7	90	89	91	97*	2 893	5.5	Austria
...	87	88	85	99	2 941	6.1	Belarus
14.4	96	95	97	...	2 776	5.6	Belgium
...	...	...	...	...	...	...	Bosnia and Herzegovina
11.5	83	84	82	93	2 324	4.5	Bulgaria
11.6	82	83	82	98	1 826	...	Croatia
...	...	...	...	98	1 484	5.9	Czech Republic
15.2	99	99	99	100	3 284	8.5	Denmark

Country Pays País	Adult illiteracy rates estimates for 1995 Taux d'analphabétisme des adultes estimations pour 1995 Tasas de analfabetismo de adultos estimaciones para 1995			Circulation of daily newspapers per 1,000 inhabitants Diffusion de journaux quotidiens pour 1 000 habitants Difusión de periódicos diarios por 1 000 habitantes	Number of television receivers per 1,000 inhabitants Nombre de récepteurs de télévision pour 1 000 habitants Número de receptores de televisión por 1 000 habitantes	Gross enrolment ratios at first and second level Taux bruts d'inscription dans les premier et deuxième degrés Tasas de escolarización brutas en los primer y segundo grados 1994		
	MF	M	F	1994	1994	MF	M	F
	(1)	(2)	(3)	(4)	(5)	(6)	(7)	(8)
Estonia	...	...	...	242	367	90	88	92
Finland	...	...	...	473	511	110	105	115
France	...	...	...	237	591	106	105	106
Germany	...	...	...	317	560	100	100	99
Greece	...	...	...	156	206	96	97	95
Hungary	...	...	...	228	429	91	90	91
Iceland	...	...	...	515	320	102	103	101
Ireland	...	...	...	170	302	108	107	109
Italy	...	...	...	105	437	87	87	87
Latvia	...	...	...	228	465	85	84	86
Lithuania	...	...	...	136	386	87	86	88
Luxembourg	...	...	...	384	374	...	...	...
Malta	...	...	...	176	747	97	101	94
Moldova	...	...	...	24	271	80	79	81
Monaco	...	...	...	250	741	...	...	...
Netherlands	...	...	...	334	494	110	112	108
Norway	...	...	...	607	428	108	109	107
Poland	...	...	...	141	308	98	98	97
Portugal	...	...	...	41	321	99	...	...
Romania	...	...	...	297	201	83	83	83
Russian Federation	...	...	...	267	377	94	91	96
San Marino	...	...	...	-	352	...	...	...
Slovakia	...	...	...	256	474	93	92	95
Slovenia	...	...	...	185	320	93	92	94
Spain	...	...	...	104	402	110	106	114
Sweden	...	...	...	483	475	100	100	100
Switzerland	...	...	...	409	416	95	96	95
The Former Yugoslav Rep. of Macedonia				21	166	77	77	77
Ukraine	...	...	...	118	340	90	88	92
United Kingdom	...	...	...	351	439	103	103	104
Federal Rep. of Yugoslavia	...	...	...	90	179	64	63	66
Oceania								
Australia	...	...	...	258	489	96	95	96
Cook Islands	...	...	...	105	179	...	...	...
Fiji	8.4	6.2	10.7	45	17	97	97	97
Kiribati	...	...	...	-	...	...	...	...
New Zealand	...	...	...	297	510	107	107	108
Niue				-	...	...	...	...
Papua New Guinea	27.8	19.0	37.3	15	2.9	50	55	46
Samoa	...	...	...	-	39	...	...	...
Solomon Islands	...	...	...	-	6.0	64	69	58
Tonga	...	...	...	73	16	...	...	...
Tuvalu	...	...	...	-	...	...	...	...
Vanuatu, Republic of	...	...	...	-	13	66	67	65

School life expectancy: number of years / Espérance de vie scolaire: nombre d'années / Esperanza de vida escolar: número de años 1993	Net enrolment ratio at the first level / Taux nets d'inscription dans le premier degré / Tasas netas de escolarización en el primer grado 1994			Percentage of 1992 cohort reaching grade 5 / Pourcentage de la cohorte 1992 atteign. la 5e année d'études / Porcentaje de la cohorte de 1992 que llega al quinto año	Number of 3rd lev. students per 100,000 inhabitants / No. d'élèves du 3e degré par 100 000 habitants / Número de estudiantes del 3er grado por 100 000 habitantes 1994	Public expenditure on education as % of GNP / Dépenses publiques aff. a l'éducation en % du PNB / Gastos públicos dest. a la educación en % del PNB 1994	Country / Pays / País
MF	MF	M	F	MF	MF	MF	
(9)	(10)	(11)	(12)	(13)	(14)	(15)	
11.5	81	82	80	100	1 595	5.8	Estonia
...	...	...	...	100	3 902	8.4	Finland
15.1	99	99	99	...	3 623	5.8	France
14.7	97	97	98	100	2 319	4.8	Germany
14.0	91	91	91	100	3 026	3.0	Greece
12.3	93	92	94	98	1 312	6.7	Hungary
...	...	...	...	...	2 300	5.4	Iceland
13.6	91	90	91	100	3 338	6.4	Ireland
...	...	...	...	100	2 944	5.2	Italy
11.0	81	83	79	95	1 452	6.5	Latvia
...	...	...	...	94	1 898	4.5	Lithuania
...	...	...	...	...	...	...	Luxembourg
13.2	99	100	98	100	1 433	5.1	Malta
...	...	...	...	...	2 291	5.5	Moldova
...	...	...	...	...	...	...	Monaco
15.5	93	92	95	...	3 352	5.5	Netherlands
15.7	99	99	99	100	4 111	9.2	Norway
12.5	97	97	97	100	1 952	5.5	Poland
...	100	100	100	...	2 808	5.4	Portugal
10.6	87	87	86	93	1 086	3.2	Romania
...	96	96	96	97	3 104	4.4	Russian Federation
...	...	...	...	100	.	...	San Marino
...	...	...	...	97	1 369	4.9	Slovakia
...	96	96	97	100	2 077	6.2	Slovenia
14.7	100	99	100	96*	3 719	4.7	Spain
13.9	99	100	99	98	2 697	8.4	Sweden
14.0	100	100	100	100	2 107	5.6	Switzerland
10.1	84	85	84	95	1 290	5.6	The Former Yugoslav Rep. of Macedonia
...	...	...	...	97	3 152	8.2	Ukraine
14.9	100	100	100	...	2 788	5.4	United Kingdom
...	...	...	...	...	1 370	...	Federal Rep. of Yugoslavia
							Oceania
13.6	98	98	99	99*	3 267	6.0	Australia
...	...	...	...	...	...	...	Cook Islands
...	99	99	100	87*	1 076	5.4	Fiji
...	...	...	...	90	.	7.4	Kiribati
16.8	99	100	99	94	4 675	7.3	New Zealand
...	...	...	...	...	...	...	Niue
...	...	...	...	71	...	...	Papua New Guinea
...	...	...	...	...	.	...	Samoa
...	...	...	...	81	...	4.2	Solomon Islands
...	...	...	...	92	...	4.8	Tonga
...	...	...	...	...	...	...	Tuvalu
...	...	...	...	...	.	4.8	Vanuatu, Republic of

General note / Note générale / Nota general:

E––> **Adult illiteracy rates**: Number of adult illiterates (15 years and over) expressed as percentages of the population in the corresponding age-group.

Daily newspapers: Estimated circulation of daily newspapers, expressed in number of copies per 1,000 inhabitants.

Television receivers: Number of television receivers per 1,000 inhabitants. The indicators are based on estimates of the number of receivers in use.

Gross enrolment ratio: Total enrolment in primary and secondary education, regardless of age, expressed as a percentage of the population age-group corresponding to the national regulations for these two levels of education.

School life expectancy: The number of years a child is expected to remain at school or university, including years spent on repetition. It is the sum of the age-specific enrolment ratios for first, second and third level education.

Net enrolment ratio (at the first level): The net enrolment ratio is calculated by using the part of enrolment which corresponds to the age group of first level of education, taking into account the duration of schooling at this level in the different national systems.

Percentage of a cohort reaching Grade 5: Percentage of children starting primary school who eventually attain Grade 5 (Grade 4 if the duration of primary education is four years). The estimate is based on the Reconstructed Cohort Method, which uses data on enrolment and repeaters for two consecutive years.

The symbol * is shown when data on repeaters are missing for the years shown and the Apparent Cohort Method was used for estimating survival. When repetition rates are relatively high and vary between grades this method may overestimate or underestimate the level of survival.

Number of students per 100,000 inhabitants: Total number of students (both national and foreign) enrolled in higher education institutions per 100,000 population.

Public education expenditure as percentage of GNP: Public expenditure on education at all levels of administration expressed as a percentage of the Gross National Product (GNP).

FR–> **Taux d'analphabétisme**: Analphabètes adultes (15 ans et plus) exprimés en pourcentage de la population du groupe d'âge correspondant.

Journaux quotidiens: Circulation estimée de quotidiens, exprimée en nombre d'exemplaires pour 1 000 habitants.

Récepteurs de télévision: Nombre de récepteurs de télévision pour 1 000 habitants. Les indicateurs sont basés sur le nombre estimé de récepteurs en service.

Taux brut de scolarisation: Population inscrite dans l'enseignement du premier et du second degré, quel que soit l'âge des enfants, exprimée en pourcentage de la population scolarisable dans ces deux degrés selon la réglementation nationale.

Espérance de vie scolaire: Le nombre d'années qu'un enfant ou un jeune est probablement appelé à passer à l'école ou à l'université, années de redoublement comprises, calculé par addition des taux de scolarisation par âge simple dans l'enseignement des premier, second et troisième degrés.

Taux d'inscription net (premier degré): Le calcul du taux d'inscription net est basé sur la partie des effectifs dont l'âge correspond au premier degré de scolarité, en tenant compte de la durée de ce degré dans les différents systèmes nationaux.

Pourcentage d'une cohorte atteignant la cinquième année d'études: Pourcentage des enfants entrés à l'école primaire une année scolaire donnée qui atteignent la cinquième année d'études (quatrième année si la durée de l'éducation primaire est de quatre ans). Cette estimation est obtenue par application de la méthode de la cohorte reconstituée, qui se fonde sur les chiffres des inscrits et des redoublants de deux années scolaires consécutives.

Le symbole * indique que, faute de donnée sur les redoublants, on a estimé la survie scolaire par la méthode des cohortes apparentes. Lorsque les taux de redoublement sont assez importants et varient selon la classe, cette méthode peut conduire à surestimer ou à sous-estimer les abandons.

Nombre d'étudiants pour 100 000 habitants: Nombre total d'étudiants (nationaux et étrangers) inscrits dans des institutions d'enseignement supérieur pour 100 000 habitants.

Financement public de l'éducation en pourcentage du PNB: Financement public sur l'éducation à tous les niveaux de l'administration exprimé en pourcentage du Produit National Brut (PNB).

ESP> **Tasa de analfabetismo**: Número de adultos analfabetos (de 15 años o más), expresado como porcentaje de la población en los respectivos grupos de edad.

Diarios: Estimación de la tirada de diarios, expresada en número de ejemplares por cada 1 000 habitantes.

Receptores de televisión: Número de receptores de televisión por cada 1 000 habitantes. Los indicadores se basan en estimaciones del número de receptores en uso.

Tasa bruta de matrícula: Relación entre la matrícula total de los grados de enseñanza primaria y secundaria, sin distinción de edad, y la población que, según los reglamentos nacionales, debería estar matriculada en esos dos grados.

Número esperado de años de educación formal: Esta cifra de *esperanza de escolaridad* es el número de años que se espera va a pasar un alumno en la escuela o la universidad, incluídos los años de repetición. Es la suma de la tasa de matrícula por edades simples del primero, segundo y tercer grado de enseñanza.

Tasa neta de matrícula (primer grado): El cálculo de la tasa neta de matrícula se basa en la parte de los alumnos matriculados en el primer grado de enseñanza cuya edad corresponde a ese grado, teniendo en cuenta su duración en los diferentes sistemas nacionales.

Porcentaje de la cohorte que llega al quinto año de estudio: Porcentaje de alumnos que ingresan en el primer grado de enseñanza un año escolar dado y que llegan al quinto año de estudio (cuarto año de estudio si la duración de la enseñanza primaria es de cuatro años). Esta estimación se obtiene mediante la aplicación del método de la cohorte reconstituida, el cual se basa en el número de alumnos matriculados y los repitentes de dos años escolares consecutivos.

El símbolo * denota que no hay datos sobre repetidores y que para calcular el número de alumnos que continuaron el ciclo se utilizó el método de la cohorte aparente. Cuando la tasa de repetición es relativamente alta y varia de un grado a otro, este método puede sobrevalorar o subestimar el abandono escolar.

Número de alumnos por cada 100 000 habitantes: Número total de estudiantes (nacionales y extranjeros) matriculados en instituciones de enseñanza superior por 100 000 habitantes.

Gastos públicos de educación como porcentaje del PNB: Gastos públicos de educación en todos los niveles de administración expresados como porcentaje del Producto Nacional Bruto (PNB).

Reference tables 1
Tableaux de référence
Cuadros de referencia

1 Reference tables

Tableaux de référence

Cuadros de referencia

The first chapter of the *Yearbook* consists of three tables: one on population, one on illiteracy and one on educational attainment of the population. They provide basic reference data for all the other tables concerned with education, science, culture and the mass media.

The size and density of a country's population directly affect the development of its educational institutions and facilities.

Data on illiteracy and on educational attainment provide an educational profile of the adult population which can serve as a complement to statistics on school and university enrollments.

Table 1.1

Table 1.1 contains data on total population, area and density for certain country groupings and individual countries. The figures presented in this table correspond to the medium variant of the 1994 revision of the population estimates and projections prepared by the United Nations Population Division.

Area figures, include inland waters. Population density figures (inhabitants per square kilometre) are not given for areas of less than 1,000 square kilometres. Readers interested in more detailed information on area, population and age structure are referred to the various editions of the *Demographic Yearbook* and the *Statistical Yearbook* of the United Nations.

Table 1.2

Table 1.2 presents data relating to the adult illiterate population and percentage illiterate, from the latest census or survey held since 1979. These figures were provided by the United Nations Statistical Division or were derived from national publications. The table also shows the latest estimates of adult illiteracy for 1995 as assessed by the UNESCO Division of Statistics in 1994. Readers interested in obtaining comparable statistics for earlier years as well as estimated time-series for selected developing countries may refer to the UNESCO publication : *Compendium of statistics on illiteracy - Edition 1995*.

Table 1.3

Table 1.3 shows the percentage distribution of the adult population according to the highest level of education attained. The data are collected during national population censuses or sample surveys, and were provided by the United Nations Statistical Division or derived from national publications.

Readers interested in data for earlier presented here years are referred to the publication *Statistics of Educational Attainment and Illiteracy, 1970-1980*, CSR-E-44 (UNESCO, 1983).

The six levels of educational attainment are conceptually based on a selection of the categories of the International Standard Classification of Education (ISCED) and may be defined as follows:

No schooling. This term applies to those who have completed less than one year of schooling.

First level not completed. This category includes all those who completed at least one year of education at the first level but who did not complete the final grade at this level. The duration of education at the first level may vary depending on the country: the relevant information is indicated in Table 3.1.

First level completed. Those who completed the final grade of education at the first level (ISCED category *1*) but did not go on to second level studies are included in this group.

S-1: *Entered second level, first stage*. This group comprises those whose level of educational attainment was limited to the lower stage of education at the second level, as defined in Table 3.1 and corresponding to ISCED category *2*.

S-2: *Entered second level, second stage*. This group corresponds to ISCED category *3* and consists of those who moved to the higher stage of second level education from the lower stage, but did not proceed to studies at the third level.

Post-secondary. Anyone who undertook third level studies (ISCED categories *5, 6* or *7*), whether or not they completed the full course, would be counted in this group.

The proportion of the 15-24 age group with some third level education is frequently smaller than that of the 25-34 age group, since a sizeable proportion of the 15-24 age group is too young to have reached third level education. For this reason the total adult age range is taken as 25+ (and not 15+) for the purposes of this table.

Le premier chapitre de l'*Annuaire statistique* se compose de trois tableaux dont un sur la population, un sur l'analphabétisme et un autre sur le niveau d'instruction de la population. Ces tableaux fournissent des données de référence pour tous les autres tableaux sur l'enseignement, la science, la culture et les moyens d'information.

La taille et la densité de la population d'un pays influent sur le développement de ses établissements scolaires et de ses moyens d'enseignement.

Les données concernant l'analphabétisme et le niveau d'instruction présentent un profil éducatif de la population adulte et peuvent servir de complément aux statistiques sur les effectifs scolaires et universitaires.

Tableau 1.1

Le tableau 1.1 contient des données sur la population totale, la superficie et la densité pour l'ensemble du monde, certains groupements de pays et par pays. Les chiffres présentés dans ce tableau correspondent à la variante moyenne des estimations et projections de population élaborée en 1994 par la Division de la Population des Nations Unies.

Les chiffres relatifs à la superficie comprennent les eaux intérieures. La densité de la population (nombre d'habitants au kilomètre carré) n'est pas indiquée lorsque la superficie est inférieure à 1 000 km². Les lecteurs désireux d'avoir des renseignements plus détaillés sur la superficie, la population et la structure par âge sont priés de se reporter aux diverses éditions de l'*Annuaire statistique* et de l'*Annuaire démographique* de l'Organisation des Nations Unies.

Tableau 1.2

Le tableau 1.2 présente des données sur la population adulte analphabète et le pourcentage d'analphabètes, tirées du dernier recensement ou enquête faits depuis 1979. Ces chiffres ont été fournis par la Division de Statistique des Nations Unies ou extraits de publications nationales. Le tableau présente également, pour

1   **Reference tables**
Tableaux de référence
Cuadros de referencia

1995, les estimations sur l'analphabétisme des adultes élaborées en 1994 par la Division des Statistiques de l'UNESCO. Les lecteurs désireux d'obtenir des statistiques comparables pour les années antérieures et les séries chronologiques estimées pour une selection de pays en voie de développement peuvent consulter la publication de l'Unesco : *Compendium des statistiques relatives à l'analphabétisation - Edition 1995.*

Tableau 1.3

Le tableau 1.3 présente la répartition en pourcentage de la population adulte d'après le plus haut niveau d'instruction atteint. Les données sont tirées des recensements nationaux de population et des enquêtes par sondage, dont les résultats nous ont été communiqués par la Division de Statistique des Nations Unies, ou tirées des publications nationales.

Les lecteurs intéressés par des données comparables pour les années antérieures sont priés de consulter la publication *Statistiques sur le niveau d'instruction et l'analphabétisme, 1970-1980,* CSR-E-44, (UNESCO, 1983).

Les six niveaux d'instruction présentés sont conçus à partir d'une sélection de catégories de la Classification Internationale Type de l'Education (CITE), et peuvent être définis comme suit:

Sans scolarité. Il s'agit des personnes qui ont fait moins d'une année de scolarité.

Premier degré non complété. Cette catégorie comprend toutes les personnes qui ont fait au moins une année d'enseignement du premier degré mais qui n'ont pas terminé la dernière année de ce degré. La durée de l'enseignement du premier degré est différente selon les pays: voir à cet égard les informations indiquées dans le tableau 3.1.

Premier degré complété. Comprend les personnes qui ont terminé la dernière année d'étude l'enseignement du premier degré (catégorie *1* de la CITE), mais qui n'ont pas accédé aux études du second degré.

S-1: Accédé au second degré, premier cycle. Ce groupe, qui correspond à la catégorie *2* de la CITE, comprend toutes les personnes dont les études n'ont pas été au-delà du premier cycle de l'enseignement du second degré, tel qu'il est défini dans le tableau 3.1 .

S-2: Accédé au second degré, deuxième cycle. Ce groupe, qui correspond à la catégorie *3* de la CITE, comprend les personnes qui sont passées du premier au deuxième cycle de l'enseignement du second degré, mais qui n'ont pas fait d'études du troisième degré.

Post-secondaire. Toutes les personnes qui ont entrepris des études du troisième degré, (catégories *5, 6* ou *7* de la CITE) qu'elles les aient ou non terminées, sont comptées dans ce groupe.

En ce qui concerne l'enseignement du troisième degré, la proportion du groupe d'âge 15-24 ans est souvent inférieure à celle du groupe d'âge 25-34 ans, par le fait qu'une proportion notable du groupe d'âge 15-24 ans est encore trop jeune pour accéder à l'enseignement du troisième degré. Pour cette raison, on a choisi comme total de la population adulte dans ce tableau le groupe d'âge 25 ans et plus (et non 15 ans et plus).

El primer capítulo del *Anuario Estadístico* se compone de tres cuadros, uno sobre la población, uno sobre el analfabetismo y uno sobre el nivel de instrucción de la población. Estos cuadros presentan datos de referencia para todos los otros cuadros relativos a la educación, la ciencia, la cultura y a los medios de comunicación.

El número y la densidad de la población de un país influyen sobre el desarrollo de sus instituciones de enseñanza y de sus facilidades educativas.

Los datos relativos al analfabetismo y al nivel de instrucción presentan un perfil educativo de la población adulta que sería complementario de las estadísticas sobre la matrícula escolar y universitaria.

Cuadro 1.1

El cuadro 1.1 contiene datos sobre la población total, la superficie y la densidad demográfica de ciertos grupos de países y por país. Las cifras presentadas en este cuadro corresponden a la variante media de la revisión de las estimaciones y proyecciones de población, preparadas en 1994 por la División de Población de las Naciones Unidas.

Las cifras relativas a la superficie comprenden las aguas continentales. No se indica la densidad demográfica (número de habitantes por kilómetro cuadrado) cuando la superficie es inferior a 1 000 km². Los lectores que deseen datos más detallados sobre la superficie, la población y la estructura por edades pueden consultar las diversas ediciones del *Statistical Yearbook - Annuaire Statistique* y *Demographic Yearbook - Annuaire Démographique* de las Naciones Unidas.

Cuadro 1.2

El cuadro 1.2 presenta datos sobre la población adulta analfabeta y el porcentaje de analfabetos obtenidos del último censo o encuesta realizados desde 1979. Estas cifras han sido proporcionadas por la División de Estadística de las Naciones Unidas o extraídas de publicaciones nacionales. El cuadro presenta también las últimas estimaciones de la población de adultos analfabetos para 1995, elaboradas en 1994 por la División de Estadística de la UNESCO. Se remite al lector interesado en obtener estadísticas comparables para años anteriores así como series cronológicas para algunos países en desarrollo seleccionados a la publicación de la UNESCO: *Compendio de estadísticas relativas al analfabetismo - Edición 1995.*

Cuadro 1.3

El cuadro 1.3 presenta la distribución porcentual de la población adulta según el nivel de instrucción más alto alcanzado. Los datos fueron reunidos durante censos nacionales y encuestas por muestreo, cuyos resultados nos fueron comunicados por la División de Estadística de las Naciones Unidas o extraídos de publicaciones nacionales. Se remite al lector interesado en obtener datos para años anteriores a la publicación *Estadísticas sobre el nivel de instrucción y el analfabetismo, 1970-1980,* CSR-E-44 (UNESCO, 1983).

Los seis niveles de instrucción presentados aquí se basan en una selección de las categorías de la Clasificación Internacional Normalizada de la Educación (CINE) y pueden definirse como sigue:

Sin escolaridad: Se trata de las personas que no llegaron a completar un año de estudios.

Primer grado sin completar. Esta categoría comprende todas las personas que terminaron como mínimo un año de enseñanza de primer grado, pero que no finalizaron el último año de estudios de este nivel. La duración de la enseñanza de primer grado puede variar según los países: este tipo de información figura en el cuadro 3.1.

Primer grado completo. Comprende las personas que terminaron el último año de enseñanza de primer grado (categoría *1* de la CINE), pero que no accedieron a la enseñanza de segundo grado.

S-1: Accedieron al segundo grado, primer ciclo. Este grupo comprende todas las personas cuyos estudios no excedieron el primer ciclo de la enseñanza de segundo grado, tal y como se define en el cuadro 3.1 y corresponde a la categoría *2* de la CINE.

S-2: Accedieron al segundo grado, segundo ciclo. Este grupo corresponde a la categoría *3* de la CINE y comprende las personas que pasaron del primero al segundo ciclo de la enseñanza de segundo grado, pero que no hicieron estudios de tercer grado.

Post-secundario. Todas las personas que empezaron estudios de tercer grado, (categorías *5, 6* o *7* de la CINE y comprende las personas terminado, figuran en este grupo.

En lo que concierne a la enseñanza de tercer grado, la proporción del grupo de edad de 15 a 24 años es a menudo inferior a la del grupo de 25 a 34 años de edad, ya que una proporción notable de aquél es todavía demasiado joven para poder ingresar en ese grado de enseñanza. Por este motivo, se ha escogido como total de la población adulta en el cuadro el grupo de edad de 25 años y más (y no el de 15 años y más).

Population, area and density, 1980-1994 **1.1**
Population, superficie et densité, 1980-1994
Población, superficie y densidad, 1980-1994

1.1 Population, area and density, 1980, 1985, 1990, 1993 and 1994

Population, superficie et densité, 1980, 1985, 1990, 1993 et 1994

Población, superficie y densidad, 1980, 1985, 1990, 1993 y 1994

Continents, major areas, and countries Continents, grandes régions et pays Continentes, grandes regiones y países	Estimates of midyear population (thousands) Estimations de la population au milieu de l'année (milliers) Estimaciones de la población a mediado de año (millares)					Area (km²) Superficie (km²) Superficie (km²)	Inhabitants per km² Nombre d'habitants par km² Habitantes por km²
	1980	1985	1990	1993	1994		1994
	(1)	(2)	(3)	(4)	(5)	(6)	(7)
World Total	4 444 361	4 846 339	5 284 843	5 543 608	5 629 635	135 574 876	42
Africa	475 666	548 805	632 672	688 786	708 288	30 250 107	23
America	610 901	662 939	717 557	751 932	763 443	42 056 113	18
Asia	2 642 110	2 903 766	3 186 447	3 349 520	3 403 427	31 744 471	107
Europe	692 997	706 374	721 739	725 679	726 355	22 987 895	32
Oceania	22 687	24 455	26 428	27 691	28 122	8 536 290	3
Developing Countries	3 326 852	3 693 380	4 093 959	4 334 138	4 414 637	80 945 721	55
Sub-Saharan Africa	384 238	444 120	514 236	561 921	578 609	24 231 217	24
Arab States	168 158	196 192	225 751	243 492	249 574	13 680 306	18
Latin America and the Caribbean	358 440	398 416	439 719	465 065	473 544	20 546 088	23
Eastern Asia and Oceania	1 426 567	1 543 989	1 675 583	1 744 833	1 766 804	16 416 656	108
Southern Asia	948 781	1 067 315	1 192 918	1 272 006	1 298 984	6 766 666	192
Least Developed Countries	390 880	441 601	501 517	545 522	561 318	19 276 229	29
Developed Countries	1 117 509	1 152 959	1 190 884	1 209 470	1 214 998	54 629 155	22
Africa							
Algeria	18 740	21 887	24 935	26 722	27 325	2 381 741	11
Angola	6 994	7 976	9 194	10 276	10 674	1 246 700	9
Benin	3 459	3 989	4 633	5 087	5 246	112 622	47
Botswana	906	1 077	1 276	1 401	1 443	581 730	2
Burkina Faso	6 957	7 879	8 987	9 772	10 046	274 000	37
Burundi	4 130	4 750	5 503	6 027	6 209	27 834	223
Cameroon	8 655	9 972	11 526	12 522	12 871	475 442	27
Cape Verde	289	310	341	370	381	4 033	94
Central African Republic	2 313	2 595	2 927	3 156	3 235	622 984	5
Chad	4 477	5 018	5 553	6 010	6 183	1 284 000	5
Comoros	383	455	543	607	630	2 235	282
Congo	1 669	1 923	2 232	2 443	2 516	342 000	7
Côte d'Ivoire	8 194	9 934	11 974	13 316	13 780	322 463	43
Djibouti	281	391	517	557	567	23 200	24
Egypt	43 749	49 749	56 312	60 319	61 636	1 001 449	62
Equatorial Guinea	217	312	352	379	389	28 051	14
Eritrea	2 382	2 698	3 082	3 345	3 437	...	...
Ethiopia	36 368	41 137	47 423	51 859	53 435	...	...
Gabon	806	985	1 146	1 248	1 283	267 668	5
Gambia	641	745	924	1 042	1 081	11 295	96
Ghana	10 735	12 839	15 020	16 446	16 944	238 533	71
Guinea	4 461	4 987	5 755	6 306	6 501	245 857	26
Guinea-Bissau	795	873	964	1 028	1 050	36 125	29
Kenya	16 632	19 880	23 613	26 391	27 343	580 367	47
Lesotho	1 339	1 563	1 792	1 943	1 996	30 355	66

1.1 Population, area and density, 1980-1994
Population, superficie et densité, 1980-1994
Población, superficie y densidad, 1980-1994

Continents, major areas, and countries Continents, grandes régions et pays Continentes, grandes regiones y países	Estimates of midyear population (thousands) Estimations de la population au milieu de l'année (milliers) Estimaciones de la población a mediado de año (millares)					Area (km²) Superficie (km²) Superficie (km²)	Inhabitants per km² Nombre d'habitants par km² Habitantes por km² 1994
	1980	1985	1990	1993	1994		
	(1)	(2)	(3)	(4)	(5)	(6)	(7)
Liberia	1 876	2 199	2 575	2 845	2 941	111 369	26
Libyan Arab Jamahiriya	3 043	3 786	4 545	5 048	5 225	1 759 540	3
Madagascar	9 063	10 632	12 571	13 854	14 303	587 041	24
Malawi	6 183	7 247	9 367	10 520	10 843	118 484	92
Mali	6 863	7 915	9 212	10 135	10 462	1 240 192	8
Mauritania	1 551	1 766	2 003	2 162	2 217	1 025 520	2
Mauritius	966	1 016	1 057	1 091	1 104	2 040	541
Morocco	19 382	21 816	24 334	25 945	26 488	446 550	59
Mozambique	12 095	13 541	14 187	15 102	15 527	801 590	19
Namibia	1 030	1 178	1 349	1 461	1 500	824 292	2
Niger	5 586	6 608	7 731	8 550	8 846	1 267 000	7
Nigeria	72 024	83 068	96 154	105 264	108 467	923 768	117
Reunion	506	550	604	634	644	2 510	257
Rwanda	5 163	6 056	6 986	7 554	7 750	26 338	294
St. Helena	5	6	6	6	6	122	...
Sao Tome and Principe	94	106	119	127	130	964	...
Senegal	5 538	6 375	7 327	7 902	8 102	196 722	41
Seychelles	63	65	70	72	72	455	...
Sierra Leone	3 236	3 582	3 999	4 297	4 402	71 740	61
Somalia	6 713	7 875	8 677	8 955	9 077	637 657	14
South Africa	29 170	33 043	37 066	39 659	40 555	1 221 037	33
Sudan	18 681	21 462	24 585	26 641	27 361	2 505 813	11
Swaziland	560	649	744	809	832	17 364	48
Togo	2 615	3 028	3 531	3 885	4 011	56 785	71
Tunisia	6 384	7 262	8 080	8 570	8 733	163 610	53
Uganda	13 120	15 111	17 949	19 940	20 621	241 038	86
United Republic of Tanzania	18 581	21 798	25 600	28 019	28 846	883 749	33
Western Sahara	130	185	230	261	272	266 000	1
Zaire	27 009	31 701	37 436	41 231	42 552	2 344 858	18
Zambia	5 738	6 862	8 150	8 936	9 196	752 618	12
Zimbabwe	7 126	8 393	9 904	10 739	11 002	390 757	28
America, North							
Anguilla	7	7	7	8	8	96	...
Antigua and Barbuda	61	62	64	65	66	442	...
Aruba	60	63	67	69	69	193	...
Bahamas	210	234	256	268	272	13 878	20
Barbados	249	253	257	260	261	430	...
Belize	146	166	189	204	210	22 696	9
Bermuda	54	56	61	62	63	53	...
British Virgin Islands	12	14	16	18	19	153	...
Canada	24 594	25 942	27 791	28 817	29 141	9 970 610	3
Cayman Islands	17	21	26	29	30	264	...
Costa Rica	2 285	2 642	3 035	3 270	3 347	51 100	65
Cuba	9 710	10 102	10 598	10 875	10 960	110 861	99
Dominica	74	72	71	71	71	751	...
Dominican Republic	5 697	6 376	7 110	7 543	7 684	48 734	158
El Salvador	4 525	4 739	5 172	5 517	5 641	21 041	268
Greenland	50	53	56	57	58	2 175 600	
Grenada	89	90	91	92	92	344	...
Guadeloupe	327	355	391	413	421	1 705	247
Guatemala	6 917	7 963	9 197	10 029	10 322	108 889	95
Haiti	5 353	5 865	6 486	6 893	7 035	27 750	254
Honduras	3 569	4 186	4 879	5 335	5 493	112 088	49
Jamaica	2 133	2 311	2 366	2 411	2 429	10 990	221
Martinique	326	341	360	372	375	1 102	340
Mexico	67 056	75 526	84 511	90 027	91 858	1 958 201	47
Montserrat	12	11	11	11	11	102	...
Netherlands Antilles	174	182	190	195	197	800	...
Nicaragua	2 802	3 229	3 676	4 114	4 275	130 000	33
Panama	1 950	2 167	2 398	2 538	2 585	75 517	34
Puerto Rico	3 206	3 366	3 531	3 618	3 646	8 897	410
Saint Kitts and Nevis	44	43	42	42	41	261	...
St. Lucia	115	124	133	138	140	622	...
St. Pierre and Miquelon	6	6	6	6	6	242	...
St. Vincent and the Grenadines	98	102	107	110	111	388	...
Trinidad and Tobago	1 082	1 161	1 237	1 279	1 292	5 130	252
Turks and Caicos Islands	7	9	12	13	14	430	...

Population, area and density, 1980-1994   1.1
Population, superficie et densité, 1980-1994
Población, superficie y densidad, 1980-1994

Continents, major areas, and countries Continents, grandes régions et pays Continentes, grandes regiones y países	Estimates of midyear population (thousands) Estimations de la population au milieu de l'année (milliers) Estimaciones de la población a mediado de año (millares)					Area (km²) Superficie (km²) Superficie (km²)	Inhabitants per km² Nombre d'habitants par km² Habitantes por km² 1994
	1980	1985	1990	1993	1994		
	(1)	(2)	(3)	(4)	(5)	(6)	(7)
United States	227 757	238 466	249 924	257 925	260 631	9 363 520	28
U.S. Virgin Islands	97	99	102	104	104	347	...
America, South							
Argentina	28 114	30 325	32 547	33 780	34 182	2 780 400	12
Bolivia	5 355	5 895	6 573	7 063	7 237	1 098 581	7
Brazil	121 286	135 042	148 477	156 486	159 143	8 511 965	19
Chile	11 143	12 076	13 154	13 823	14 044	756 626	19
Colombia	26 525	29 481	32 300	33 986	34 545	1 138 914	30
Ecuador	7 961	9 099	10 264	10 981	11 221	283 561	40
Falkland Islands (Malvinas)	2	2	2	2	2	12 173	
French Guiana	68	91	117	134	140	90 000	2
Guyana	759	790	796	816	825	214 969	4
Paraguay	3 136	3 693	4 317	4 701	4 830	406 752	12
Peru	17 321	19 518	21 588	22 886	23 331	1 285 216	18
Suriname	355	377	400	414	419	163 265	3
Uruguay	2 914	3 008	3 094	3 149	3 168	177 414	18
Venezuela	15 091	17 138	19 502	20 913	21 378	912 050	23
Asia							
Afghanistan	16 063	14 519	15 045	17 691	18 879	652 090	29
Armenia	3 072	3 232	3 352	3 495	3 548	29 800	119
Azerbaijan	6 157	6 659	7 117	7 384	7 472	86 600	86
Bahrain	347	414	490	535	549	678	...
Bangladesh	88 221	98 556	108 118	115 203	117 787	143 998	818
Bhutan	1 237	1 376	1 544	1 596	1 614	47 000	34
Brunei Darussalam	193	226	257	274	280	5 765	49
Cambodia	6 498	7 562	8 841	9 683	9 968	181 035	55
China	998 877	1 070 175	1 155 305	1 196 360	1 208 841	9 596 961	126
Cyprus	629	665	702	726	734	9 251	79
East Timor	581	659	740	785	800	14 874	54
Georgia	5 048	5 252	5 418	5 446	5 450	69 700	78
Hong Kong‡	5 039	5 456	5 705	5 809	5 838	1 075	5 431
India	688 856	768 185	850 638	901 459	918 570	3 287 590	279
Indonesia	150 958	167 332	182 812	191 671	194 615	1 904 569	102
Iran, Islamic Republic of	39 254	48 916	58 946	64 169	65 758	1 633 188	40
Iraq	13 007	15 317	18 078	19 454	19 925	438 317	45
Israel	3 879	4 233	4 660	5 254	5 458	21 056	259
Japan	116 807	120 837	123 537	124 536	124 815	377 801	330
Jordan	2 923	3 833	4 259	4 936	5 198	97 740	53
Kazakstan	14 908	15 780	16 670	16 952	17 027	2 717 300	6
Korea, Democratic People's Republic of	18 260	19 888	21 774	23 048	23 483	120 538	195
Korea, Republic of	38 124	40 806	42 869	44 131	44 563	99 263	449
Kuwait	1 375	1 720	2 143	1 775	1 633	17 818	92
Kyrgyzstan	3 617	3 990	4 362	4 590	4 667	198 500	24
Lao People's Democratic Rep.	3 205	3 594	4 202	4 605	4 742	236 800	20
Lebanon	2 669	2 668	2 555	2 807	2 915	10 400	280
Macau	242	284	342	384	398	18	...
Malaysia	13 763	15 677	17 892	19 247	19 695	329 758	60
Maldives	158	184	216	238	246	298	...
Mongolia	1 663	1 909	2 178	2 318	2 363	1 566 500	2
Myanmar	33 821	37 544	41 813	44 596	45 555	676 578	67
Nepal	14 874	16 975	19 253	20 812	21 360	140 797	152
Oman	1 101	1 397	1 751	1 992	2 077	212 457	10
Pakistan	85 299	102 490	121 933	132 941	136 645	796 095	172
Philippines	48 317	54 668	60 779	64 800	66 188	300 000	221
Qatar	229	358	485	529	540	11 000	49
Saudi Arabia	9 604	12 649	16 048	17 119	17 451	2 149 690	8
Singapore	2 415	2 558	2 705	2 793	2 821	618	...
Sri Lanka	14 819	16 114	17 225	17 897	18 125	65 610	276
Syrian Arab Republic	8 704	10 348	12 348	13 696	14 171	185 180	77
Tajikistan	3 955	4 558	5 287	5 767	5 933	143 100	41
Thailand	46 718	51 129	55 583	57 585	58 183	513 115	113
Turkey	44 438	50 345	56 098	59 597	60 771	774 815	78
Turkmenistan	2 864	3 225	3 657	3 921	4 010	488 100	8
United Arab Emirates	1 015	1 379	1 671	1 816	1 861	83 600	22
Uzbekistan	15 936	18 112	20 420	21 860	22 349	447 400	50
Viet Nam	53 711	59 898	66 689	71 324	72 931	331 689	220
Yemen	8 219	9 598	11 311	13 196	13 873	527 968	26

1.1   Population, area and density, 1980-1994
       Population, superficie et densité, 1980-1994
       Población, superficie y densidad, 1980-1994

Continents, major areas, and countries Continents, grandes régions et pays Continentes, grandes regiones y países	Estimates of midyear population (thousands) Estimations de la population au milieu de l'année (milliers) Estimaciones de la población a mediado de año (millares)					Area (km²) Superficie (km²) Superficie (km²)	Inhabitants per km² Nombre d'habitants par km² Habitantes por km²
	1980	1985	1990	1993	1994		1994
	(1)	(2)	(3)	(4)	(5)	(6)	(7)
Palestine							
Gaza Strip	441	517	624	718	752	378	...
West Bank	...	...	...	...	...	...	...
Europe							
Albania	2 671	2 962	3 290	3 389	3 414	28 748	119
Andorra	34	44	52	61	64	453	...
Austria	7 549	7 558	7 705	7 863	7 918	83 853	94
Belarus	9 627	9 958	10 212	10 188	10 163	207 600	49
Belgium	9 852	9 857	9 951	10 046	10 080	30 519	330
Bosnia and Herzegovina	3 914	4 122	4 308	3 707	3 527	51 129	69
Bulgaria‡	8 862	8 960	8 991	8 870	8 818	110 912	80
Channel Islands	129	135	142	146	147	195	...
Croatia	4 377	4 471	4 517	4 511	4 504	56 538	80
Czech Republic	10 283	10 305	10 306	10 296	10 295	78 864	131
Denmark	5 123	5 114	5 140	5 165	5 173	43 077	120
Estonia	1 480	1 536	1 575	1 553	1 541	45 100	34
Faeroe Islands	43	46	47	47	47	1 399	34
Finland	4 780	4 902	4 986	5 058	5 084	338 145	15
France	53 880	55 170	56 718	57 508	57 747	551 500	105
Germany	78 304	77 668	79 365	80 857	81 278	356 733	228
Gibraltar	29	28	28	28	28	6	...
Greece	9 643	9 934	10 238	10 377	10 416	131 990	79
Holy See‡	1	1	1	1	1	...	...
Hungary	10 708	10 579	10 365	10 210	10 161	93 032	109
Iceland	228	241	255	263	266	103 000	3
Ireland	3 401	3 552	3 503	3 524	3 539	70 284	50
Isle of Man	64	64	69	72	73	572	...
Italy	56 434	56 771	57 024	57 127	57 157	301 268	190
Latvia	2 534	2 613	2 671	2 611	2 583	64 600	40
Liechtenstein	25	27	29	30	31	160	...
Lithuania	3 433	3 587	3 711	3 712	3 706	65 200	57
Luxembourg	364	367	381	395	401	2 586	155
Malta	324	344	354	361	364	316	...
Moldova	4 011	4 214	4 362	4 408	4 420	33 700	131
Monaco	27	28	30	31	32	1	...
Netherlands	14 144	14 492	14 952	15 285	15 397	40 844	377
Norway	4 086	4 153	4 242	4 299	4 318	323 877	13
Poland	35 574	37 203	38 119	38 303	38 341	323 250	119
Portugal	9 766	9 904	9 868	9 838	9 830	92 389	106
Romania	22 201	22 725	23 207	23 023	22 922	238 391	96
Russian Federation	138 483	143 033	147 913	147 760	147 370	17 075 400	9
San Marino	21	22	23	24	25	61	...
Slovakia	4 976	5 140	5 256	5 314	5 333	49 012	109
Slovenia	1 832	1 881	1 918	1 937	1 942	20 256	96
Spain	37 542	38 474	39 272	39 514	39 568	505 992	78
Sweden	8 311	8 350	8 559	8 694	8 738	449 964	19
Switzerland	6 319	6 536	6 834	7 056	7 131	41 293	173
The Former Yugoslav Republic of Macedonia	1 795	1 923	2 046	2 119	2 142	25 713	83
Ukraine	49 961	50 914	51 637	51 551	51 465	603 700	85
United Kingdom	56 330	56 618	57 411	57 924	58 092	244 100	238
Federal Republic of Yugoslavia	9 522	9 848	10 156	10 623	10 763	102 173	105
Oceania							
American Samoa	32	39	47	51	53	199	...
Australia	14 569	15 641	16 888	17 617	17 853	7 713 364	2
Cook Islands	18	17	18	19	19	236	...
Fiji	634	699	726	758	771	18 274	42
French Polynesia	151	174	197	211	215	4 000	54
Guam	107	120	134	144	147	549	...
Kiribati	61	67	72	76	78	726	...
Marshall Islands	35	40	46	49	51	181	...
Micronesia	83	95	108	117	121	702	...
Nauru	7	8	10	11	11	21	...

Population, area and density, 1980-1994 1.1
Population, superficie et densité, 1980-1994
Población, superficie y densidad, 1980-1994

Continents, major areas, and countries / Continents, grandes régions et pays / Continents, grandes regiones y países	Estimates of midyear population (thousands) / Estimations de la population au milieu de l'année (milliers) / Estimaciones de la población a mediado de año (millares)					Area (km²) / Superficie (km²) / Superficie (km²)	Inhabitants per km² / Nombre d'habitants par km² / Habitantes por km²
	1980	1985	1990	1993	1994		1994
	(1)	(2)	(3)	(4)	(5)	(6)	(7)
New Caledonia	143	155	168	175	178	18 575	10
New Zealand	3 113	3 247	3 361	3 485	3 531	270 534	13
Niue	3	3	2	2	2	260	...
Northern Mariana Islands	17	19	43	45	46	464	...
Pacific Islands (Palau)	12	14	15	16	17	459	...
Papua New Guinea	3 086	3 442	3 839	4 110	4 205	462 840	9
Pitcairn	0	0	0	0	0	5	...
Samoa	159	160	163	167	169	2 831	60
Solomon Islands	227	270	320	354	366	28 896	13
Tokelau	2	2	2	2	2	12	...
Tonga	92	91	96	97	98	747	...
Tuvalu	8	8	9	10	10	26	...
Vanuatu, Republic of	117	132	150	161	165	12 189	14
Wallis and Fortuna Islands	11	12	14	14	14	200	...

General note / Note générale / Nota general:

E--> Area shown includes land area and inland waters, but excludes uninhabited polar regions and some uninhabited islands. Population density is not shown for territories less than 1,000 km² in area.

FR-> La superficie indiquée est celle des terres et des eaux intérieures, non compris les zones polaires ni quelques îles inhabitées. La densité n'est pas indiquée lorsque la superficie est inférieure à 1 000 km².

ESP> La superficie incluye las tierras y las aguas continentales, y excluye las regiones polares y algunas islas inhabitadas. No se indica la densidad demográfica en el caso de territorios de menos de 1 000 km² de superficie.

ASIA:

Hong Kong:

E--> Land area only. The total including ocean area within administrative boundaries is 2,916 km².

FR-> Superficie terrestre seulement. La superficie totale, en comprenant la zone maritime se trouvant à l'intérieur des limites administratives, est de 2 916 km².

ESP> Superficie terrestre solamente. La superficie total, que abarca la zona marítima que se encuentra dentro de los límites administrativos, es de 2 916 km².

EUROPE:

Bulgaria:

E--> Excluding surface area of frontier rivers.

FR-> Non compris la surface des cours d'eau frontaliers.

ESP> No se incluye la superficie de los ríos fronterizos.

Holy See:

E--> Data refer to the State of the Vatican City, of which the area is 0.44 km².

FR-> Les données se réfèrent à l'Etat de la Cité du Vatican, dont la superficie est de 0,44 km².

ESP> Los datos se refieren al Estado de la Ciudad del Vaticano, cuya superficie es de 0,44 km².

1.2   Illiterate population 15 years and over and percentage of illiterates, by age group

Population analphabète de 15 ans et plus et pourcentage d'analphabètes, par groupe d'âge

Población analfabeta de 15 años y más y porcentaje de analfabetos, por grupo de edad

Country and year of census or survey Pays et année du recensement ou de l'enquête País y año del censo o de la encuesta			Age Âge Edad	Illiterate population Population analphabète Población analfabeta			Percentage of illiterates Pourcentage d'analphabètes Porcentaje de analfabetos		
				Total	Male Masculine Masculina	Female Féminine Femenina	Total	Male Masculin Masculino	Female Féminin Femenino
				(1)	(2)	(3)	(4)	(5)	(6)
Africa									
Algeria	1987	Total population	15 +	6 373 688	2 320 756	4 052 932	50.4	36.6	64.2
			10-14	389 023	78 799	310 224	13.6	5.4	22.4
			15-19	516 984	134 540	382 444	20.9	10.8	31.2
			20-24	683 474	190 255	493 219	31.0	17.1	45.1
			25-34	1 376 076	456 524	919 552	45.4	29.4	62.3
			35-44	1 105 553	401 337	704 216	62.8	45.7	80.0
			45-54	1 095 957	438 841	657 116	80.7	67.2	93.1
			55-64	804 780	340 991	463 789	86.0	75.2	96.1
			65 +	790 864	358 268	432 596	88.5	81.1	95.8
		Dense population	15 +	4 000 189	1 368 739	2 631 450	42.9	29.5	56.2
			10-14	127 623	22 613	105 010	6.3	2.2	10.6
			15-19	217 437	47 763	169 674	12.0	5.3	18.7
			20-24	355 623	85 268	270 355	21.8	10.5	33.1
			25-34	811 766	235 195	576 571	36.1	20.4	52.5
			35-44	730 663	243 111	487 552	55.9	37.4	74.2
			45-54	761 343	289 662	471 681	76.6	60.9	91.0
			55-64	559 961	226 856	333 105	83.1	70.2	95.1
			65 +	563 396	240 884	322 512	86.7	77.6	95.1
		Scattered pop.	15 +	2 373 499	952 017	1 421 482	71.2	55.8	87.2
			10-14	261 400	56 186	206 214	32.3	13.4	53.0
			15-19	299 547	86 777	212 770	45.3	25.2	66.9
			20-24	327 851	104 987	222 864	57.5	35.7	80.8
			25-34	564 310	221 329	342 981	72.5	55.3	90.7
			35-44	374 890	158 226	216 664	82.7	69.4	96.1
			45-54	334 614	149 179	185 435	91.8	84.3	98.8
			55-64	244 819	114 135	130 684	93.2	87.6	98.8
			65 +	227 468	117 384	110 084	93.4	89.6	97.8
	1995	Estimates	15 +	6 582 000	2 249 000	4 333 000	38.4	26.1	51.0
Angola	1985	National estimates	15 +	...	...	...	59.0	51.0	...
Benin	1992	Total population	15 +	1 822 441	688 888	1 133 553	72.5	59.9	83.2
			10-14	337 024	153 090	183 934	59.7	50.8	70.0
			15-19	254 259	97 839	156 420	58.6	45.7	71.1
			20-24	231 942	70 398	161 544	61.5	43.4	75.1
			25-29	254 256	79 444	174 812	68.1	50.8	80.6
			30 +	1 081 984	441 207	640 777	81.5	71.4	90.2
	1995	Estimates	15 +	1 792 000	713 000	1 079 000	63.0	51.3	74.2

Country and year of census or survey Pays et année du recensement ou de l'enquête País y año del censo o de la encuesta			Age Âge Edad	Illiterate population Population analphabète Población analfabeta			Percentage of illiterates Pourcentage d'analphabètes Porcentaje de analfabetos		
				Total	Male Masculine Masculina	Female Féminine Femenina	Total	Male Masculin Masculino	Female Féminin Femenino
				(1)	(2)	(3)	(4)	(5)	(6)
Botswana‡	1991	Total population	15+	340 523	164 045	176 478	45.2	46.8	43.8
			10-14	120 798	63 323	57 475	65.8	70.4	61.4
			15-19	27 858	17 744	10 114	18.3	24.3	12.7
			20-24	25 746	15 078	10 668	22.0	27.8	17.0
			25-29	32 716	16 763	15 953	32.8	36.9	29.3
			30-34	34 672	16 115	18 557	43.0	44.0	42.2
			35-39	33 623	15 061	18 562	50.8	49.4	51.9
			40-44	28 770	13 196	15 574	59.7	56.9	62.3
			45-49	27 700	12 239	15 461	70.9	66.0	75.4
			50-54	26 790	12 290	14 500	79.5	75.9	82.8
			55-59	23 187	10 342	12 845	83.6	81.1	85.6
			60-64	19 338	8 810	10 528	85.0	84.0	85.8
			65+	60 123	26 407	33 716	91.9	90.4	93.0
	1995	Estimates	15+	256 000	79 000	177 000	30.2	19.5	40.1
Burkina Faso	1995	Estimates	15+	4 597 000	1 972 000	2 625 000	80.8	70.5	90.8
Burundi	1990	Total population	15+	1 757 984	691 703	1 066 281	62.2	51.5	72.0
			10-14	238 178	108 182	129 996	38.3	35.0	41.6
			15-19	207 270	91 587	115 683	42.0	37.6	46.2
			20-24	220 644	88 518	132 126	50.8	43.3	57.5
			25-29	237 782	92 152	145 630	58.0	47.2	67.9
			30-34	228 525	86 605	141 920	62.9	49.3	75.8
			35-39	176 130	68 124	108 006	66.0	51.9	79.7
			40-44	126 384	44 876	81 508	68.9	52.2	83.6
			45-49	100 725	35 462	65 263	71.6	54.5	86.4
			50-54	105 531	36 106	69 425	78.0	61.0	91.2
			55-59	77 564	29 982	47 582	81.0	66.7	93.6
			60-64	83 295	31 470	51 825	88.5	78.0	96.4
			65+	194 134	86 821	107 313	93.1	88.2	97.5
Cameroon	1995	Estimates	15+	2 712 000	908 000	1 805 000	36.6	25.0	47.9
Cape Verde	1990	Total population	15+	69 930	21 363	48 567	37.1	25.2	46.7
			10-14	2 630	1 405	1 225	6.2	6.6	5.8
			15-19	3 002	1 403	1 599	8.8	8.1	9.4
			20-24	4 899	1 926	2 973	15.1	12.2	17.9
			25-29	5 971	1 850	4 121	22.7	14.8	29.7
			30-34	7 277	1 924	5 353	38.1	23.2	49.5
			35-39	6 139	1 338	4 801	47.0	26.0	60.6
			40-44	3 435	783	2 652	50.0	29.0	63.5
			45-49	4 304	1 071	3 233	60.4	40.4	72.3
			50-54	7 073	1 949	5 124	64.2	49.3	72.5
			55-59	7 000	2 238	4 762	72.2	55.7	83.8
			60-64	6 300	2 197	4 103	71.6	55.6	84.6
			65+	14 530	4 684	9 846	73.2	56.1	85.6
	1995	Estimates	15+	65 000	19 000	46 000	28.4	18.6	36.2
Chad	1995	Estimates	15+	1 868 000	666 000	1 202 000	51.9	37.9	65.3
Comoros	1980	Total population	15+	88 780	36 429	52 351	52.1	44.0	60.0
			10-14	4 741	2 194	2 547	24.4	21.2	28.1
			15-19	10 079	3 835	6 244	33.4	26.2	40.0
			20-24	10 792	4 037	6 755	44.4	36.5	51.1
			25-34	20 405	7 826	12 579	52.5	43.9	59.7
			35-44	17 428	7 265	10 163	57.8	48.7	66.6
			45-54	12 007	5 346	6 661	60.5	52.0	70.0
			55-64	8 281	3 715	4 566	63.1	54.0	73.1
			65+	9 788	4 405	5 383	70.4	61.6	79.6
	1995	Estimates	15+	143 000	60 000	83 000	42.7	35.8	49.6
Congo	1984	Total population	15+	422 770	142 744	280 026	40.4	28.7	51.0
			10-14	11 748	3 988	7 760	4.8	3.3	6.3
			15-19	19 173	5 626	13 547	9.1	5.5	12.5
			20-24	28 754	8 505	20 249	16.7	10.1	22.9
			25-29	35 646	10 504	25 142	26.1	15.9	35.6
			30-34	34 970	9 835	25 135	34.5	20.4	47.2
			35-39	40 992	11 200	29 792	48.8	27.9	67.9
			40-44	40 837	12 588	28 249	59.9	37.6	81.4
			45-49	47 091	15 553	31 538	68.8	47.9	87.7
			50-54	44 401	16 004	28 397	78.3	62.6	91.3
			55-59	40 348	15 523	24 825	84.5	73.4	93.4
			60-64	34 978	13 598	21 380	89.1	81.4	94.9
			65+	55 580	23 808	31 772	90.8	86.3	94.4
	1995	Estimates	15+	353 000	114 000	239 000	25.1	16.9	32.8

Country and year of census or survey Pays et année du recensement ou de l'enquête País y año del censo o de la encuesta			Age Âge Edad	Illiterate population Population analphabète Población analfabeta			Percentage of illiterates Pourcentage d'analphabètes Porcentaje de analfabetos		
				Total	Male Masculine Masculina	Female Féminine Femenina	Total	Male Masculin Masculino	Female Féminin Femenino
				(1)	(2)	(3)	(4)	(5)	(6)
Côte d'Ivoire	1988	Total population	15+	3 787 385	1 636 497	2 150 888	65.9	55.6	76.6
			10-14	407 837	153 316	254 521	33.5	24.3	43.4
			15-19	466 476	164 029	302 447	45.5	33.6	56.3
			20-24	586 693	231 606	355 087	57.5	46.4	68.2
			25-29	558 366	227 902	330 464	61.6	50.1	73.2
			30-34	436 857	186 046	250 811	63.4	51.0	77.5
			35-39	375 726	163 653	212 073	70.1	56.5	86.0
			40-44	314 677	142 316	172 361	80.0	68.5	92.9
			45-49	288 883	137 871	151 012	84.8	75.6	95.4
			50-54	228 212	113 061	115 151	87.3	79.6	96.5
			55-59	187 710	96 180	91 530	89.8	83.5	97.5
			60-64	131 615	67 962	63 653	91.3	85.9	97.9
			65+	212 170	105 871	106 299	93.8	89.6	98.4
	1995	Estimates	15+	4 339 000	1 859 000	2 480 000	59.9	50.1	70.0
Djibouti	1995	Estimates	15+	181 000	66 000	115 000	53.8	39.7	67.3
Egypt‡	1986	Total population	15+	15 954 760	6 207 399	9 747 361	55.8	42.7	69.4
			10-14	1 109 244	363 013	746 231	19.9	12.4	28.3
			15-19	1 739 105	701 526	1 037 579	34.5	26.1	43.9
			20-24	1 803 031	707 610	1 095 421	42.6	32.0	54.3
			25-29	1 957 351	689 852	1 267 499	53.1	38.8	66.6
			30-34	1 679 997	610 825	1 069 172	55.4	40.5	70.1
			35-44	3 147 225	1 187 132	1 960 093	62.5	46.8	78.5
			45-54	2 533 617	957 797	1 575 820	70.4	54.4	85.8
			55-64	1 784 578	751 534	1 033 044	75.1	61.5	89.7
			65+	1 309 856	601 123	708 733	82.3	71.7	94.0
		Urban population	15+	5 286 517	2 026 804	3 259 713	40.1	30.0	50.8
			10-14	207 025	84 409	122 616	9.0	7.2	11.0
			15-19	427 605	204 885	222 720	19.7	18.0	21.6
			20-24	502 144	210 461	291 683	26.0	20.9	31.7
			25-29	595 263	211 470	383 793	35.9	26.1	45.3
			30-34	575 904	205 632	370 272	39.0	27.7	50.4
			35-44	1 107 293	395 034	712 259	45.6	31.8	60.2
			45-54	906 517	313 170	593 347	53.6	36.8	70.6
			55-64	670 289	257 595	412 694	60.7	45.0	77.4
			65+	501 502	228 557	272 945	68.8	57.2	82.9
		Rural population	15+	10 645 299	4 252 729	6 392 570	68.7	54.2	83.5
			10-14	871 717	269 011	602 706	26.7	15.6	39.1
			15-19	1 222 898	501 178	721 720	43.6	32.3	57.5
			20-24	1 149 710	466 239	683 471	54.4	40.7	70.6
			25-29	1 285 502	469 577	815 925	67.3	50.3	83.6
			30-34	1 060 186	402 265	657 921	70.8	53.8	87.7
			35-44	2 078 319	803 300	1 275 019	77.7	61.8	92.8
			45-54	1 706 106	669 492	1 036 614	83.9	70.5	95.6
			55-64	1 205 276	501 631	703 645	86.5	75.3	96.9
			65+	937 302	439 047	498 255	87.7	80.0	95.8
	1995	Estimates	15+	18 954 000	7 205 000	11 749 000	48.6	36.4	61.2
Equatorial Guinea	1983	Total population	15+	58 847	16 288	42 559	38.0	22.6	51.5
			10-14	14 472	6 760	7 712	45.8	42.6	49.1
			15-19	4 829	1 385	3 444	17.1	10.2	23.4
			20-24	3 583	746	2 837	17.2	8.0	24.5
			25-34	6 157	961	5 196	19.9	6.9	30.6
			35-44	11 533	1 790	9 743	43.2	15.0	66.0
			45-54	12 473	3 372	9 101	56.7	30.9	82.1
			55-64	9 181	3 167	6 014	70.8	51.4	88.4
			65+	11 091	4 867	6 224	85.6	76.7	94.3
		Urban population	15+	8 596	2 252	6 344	18.9	10.0	27.6
			10-14	2 966	1 327	1 639	31.1	28.5	33.5
			15-19	837	305	532	9.2	6.8	11.6
			20-24	658	159	499	8.7	4.7	11.9
			25-34	1 177	226	951	10.1	4.1	15.6
			35-44	1 714	328	1 386	21.8	7.7	37.5
			45-54	1 549	388	1 161	32.3	14.5	55.0
			55-64	1 211	360	851	51.1	31.5	69.4
			65+	1 450	486	964	72.9	57.9	83.8
		Rural population	15+	50 251	14 036	36 215	45.9	28.2	60.7
			10-14	11 506	5 433	6 073	52.2	48.4	56.2
			15-19	3 992	1 080	2 912	20.8	11.9	28.7
			20-24	2 925	587	2 338	22.0	10.0	31.5
			25-34	4 980	735	4 245	25.8	8.7	39.0
			35-44	9 819	1 462	8 357	52.1	19.1	74.8
			45-54	10 924	2 984	7 940	63.5	36.3	88.5
			55-64	7 970	2 807	5 163	75.2	55.9	92.6
			65+	9 641	4 381	5 260	88.0	79.5	96.5
	1995	Estimates	15+	48 000	11 000	37 000	21.5	10.4	31.9

Country and year of census or survey Pays et année du recensement ou de l'enquête País y año del censo o de la encuesta			Age Âge Edad	Illiterate population Population analphabète Población analfabeta			Percentage of illiterates Pourcentage d'analphabètes Porcentage de analfabetos		
				Total	Male Masculine Masculina	Female Féminine Femenina	Total	Male Masculin Masculino	Female Féminin Femenino
				(1)	(2)	(3)	(4)	(5)	(6)
Ethiopia	1984	Total population	15+	13 533 624	5 840 560	7 693 064	75.7	67.3	83.6
			10-14	2 489 248	1 250 225	1 239 023	61.5	58.1	65.2
			15-19	1 519 278	665 903	853 375	54.8	47.4	62.3
			20-24	1 407 046	551 054	855 992	66.3	55.3	76.0
			25-34	3 012 701	1 091 943	1 920 758	73.2	60.9	82.7
			35-44	2 724 943	1 175 524	1 549 419	79.2	69.9	88.2
			45-54	1 956 840	897 205	1 059 635	86.0	78.3	93.8
			55+	2 912 816	1 458 931	1 453 885	92.2	87.8	97.0
		Urban population	15+	873 380	248 975	624 405	33.2	21.2	42.9
			10-14	94 513	39 077	55 436	13.3	11.5	15.1
			15-19	55 787	16 551	39 236	10.5	7.1	13.1
			20-24	52 880	14 415	38 465	16.6	10.4	21.3
			25-34	145 855	32 196	113 659	24.5	12.8	33.1
			35-44	167 735	47 453	120 282	34.8	20.4	48.2
			45-54	150 671	45 266	105 405	51.4	31.8	69.9
			55+	300 452	93 094	207 358	74.1	53.5	89.6
		Rural population	15+	12 660 244	5 591 585	7 068 659	83.0	74.4	91.2
			10-14	2 394 735	1 211 148	1 183 587	71.6	66.9	77.2
			15-19	1 463 491	649 352	814 139	65.3	55.5	76.0
			20-24	1 354 166	536 639	817 527	75.1	62.5	86.5
			25-34	2 866 846	1 059 747	1 807 099	81.4	68.7	91.3
			35-44	2 557 208	1 128 071	1 429 137	86.4	77.8	94.8
			45-54	1 806 169	851 939	954 230	91.1	85.0	97.5
			55+	2 612 364	1 365 837	1 246 527	94.9	91.8	98.4
	1995	Estimates	15+	19 052 000	8 099 000	10 953 000	64.5	54.5	74.7
Gabon	1995	Estimates	15+	295 000	103 000	192 000	36.8	26.3	46.7
Gambia	1995	Estimates	15+	403 000	152 000	251 000	61.4	47.2	75.1
Ghana	1990	National estimates	15+	4 839 557	1 843 221	2 996 236	59.0	45.7	71.9
	1995	Estimates	15+	3 387 000	1 134 000	2 253 000	35.5	24.1	46.5
Guinea	1995	Estimates	15+	2 272 000	886 000	1 386 000	64.1	50.1	78.1
Guinea-Bissau	1979	Total population	7+	436 821	...	...	90.4	...	...
			15+	342 393	130 922	211 471	80.0	66.7	91.4
			10-14	37 342	14 717	22 625	46.0	33.1	61.4
			15-19	40 904	11 824	29 080	56.8	34.7	76.6
			20-24	42 807	11 729	31 078	71.8	48.2	88.2
			25-34	87 539	27 744	59 795	81.8	63.8	94.1
			35-44	64 244	25 068	39 176	87.9	77.5	96.2
			45-54	44 366	20 080	24 286	91.6	86.0	96.8
			55-64	29 199	15 564	13 635	92.0	87.8	97.2
			65+	33 334	18 913	14 421	93.0	89.8	97.7
	1995	Estimates	15+	283 000	98 000	185 000	45.1	32.0	57.5
Kenya	1989	Total population	15+	3 179 856	1 025 621	2 154 235	29.1	19.2	38.5
			10-14	395 209	195 579	199 630	13.5	13.3	13.7
			15-19	223 957	88 993	134 964	9.5	7.7	11.4
			20-24	241 366	74 507	166 779	13.0	8.6	16.8
			25-29	310 076	84 862	225 214	19.4	11.1	27.0
			30-34	312 936	86 860	226 076	27.5	15.2	39.9
			35-39	300 082	83 129	216 953	33.3	18.4	48.2
			40-44	292 629	78 722	213 907	40.8	21.8	59.9
			45-49	278 175	80 585	197 590	49.5	29.2	68.9
			50-54	260 211	82 214	177 997	55.8	35.5	75.8
			55-59	216 481	74 415	142 066	61.4	42.3	80.4
			60+	743 943	291 254	452 689	74.6	60.0	88.4
	1995	Estimates	15+	3 237 000	1 005 000	2 232 000	21.9	13.7	30.0
Lesotho	1995	Estimates	15+	339 000	108 000	231 000	28.7	18.9	37.7
Liberia	1984	Total population	15+	811 187	329 695	481 492	67.9	55.1	80.7
			10-14	175 222	90 108	85 114	72.3	69.6	75.4
			15-19	117 723	43 690	74 033	51.0	38.9	62.5
			20-24	104 482	31 697	72 785	54.0	35.0	70.6
			25-29	103 856	34 115	69 741	61.8	42.2	80.0
			30-34	82 926	29 012	53 914	67.7	48.4	86.1
			35-39	80 537	30 343	50 194	75.2	59.0	90.2
			40-44	63 179	27 815	35 364	79.1	66.6	92.7
			45-49	56 044	26 245	29 799	81.9	71.7	93.7
			50-54	47 885	23 039	24 846	86.3	78.7	94.9
			55-59	33 716	17 342	16 374	87.3	80.8	95.3
			60-64	39 630	20 942	18 688	91.3	87.3	96.2
			65-69	28 043	14 961	13 082	92.3	88.7	96.7
			70-74	17 694	10 216	7 478	92.2	89.9	95.4
			75+	35 472	20 278	15 194	94.5	92.8	97.0
	1995	Estimates	15+	1 013 000	381 000	632 000	61.7	46.1	77.6

Country and year of census or survey Pays et année du recensement ou de l'enquête País y año del censo o de la encuesta			Age Âge Edad	Illiterate population Population analphabète Población analfabeta			Percentage of illiterates Pourcentage d'analphabètes Porcentaje de analfabetos		
				Total	Male Masculine Masculina	Female Féminine Femenina	Total	Male Masculin Masculino	Female Féminin Femenino
				(1)	(2)	(3)	(4)	(5)	(6)
Libyan Arab Jamahiriya	1984	Total population	15+	646 181	192 106	454 075	39.9	23.1	57.7
			15-19	27 889	3 103	24 786	7.5	1.6	13.7
			20-24	41 568	4 098	37 470	15.0	2.9	27.7
			25-29	50 942	5 337	45 605	27.8	5.6	51.9
			30-34	58 615	8 678	49 937	42.4	12.5	72.8
			35-39	62 518	13 611	48 907	53.4	23.0	84.3
			40-44	65 172	19 137	46 035	62.0	34.9	91.7
			45-49	63 125	21 579	41 546	68.1	44.1	95.0
			50-54	63 373	23 380	39 993	75.0	53.9	97.2
			55-59	58 272	23 883	34 389	78.8	61.5	98.0
			60-64	49 324	20 266	29 058	82.5	66.8	98.7
			65+	105 383	49 034	56 349	90.5	82.4	99.1
	1995	Estimates	15+	702 000	189 000	513 000	23.8	12.1	37.0
Madagascar	1995	Estimates	15+	4 324 000	1 570 000	2 754 000	54.3	40.2	68.0
Malawi	1987	Total population	15+	2 214 440	706 326	1 508 114	51.5	34.7	66.5
			10-14	497 653	245 719	251 934	51.0	49.7	52.2
			15-19	309 470	115 022	194 448	40.2	31.2	48.3
			20-24	281 329	82 712	198 617	41.9	27.5	53.7
			25-29	266 203	77 774	188 429	45.1	27.6	61.0
			30-34	217 825	63 653	154 172	49.8	30.6	67.3
			35-39	222 788	67 343	155 445	52.5	33.2	70.1
			40-44	161 097	48 544	112 553	54.9	34.2	74.3
			45-49	159 889	51 055	108 834	59.6	38.7	79.9
			50-54	127 918	38 991	88 927	64.5	42.5	83.5
			55-59	115 471	38 229	77 242	65.7	44.6	85.8
			60-64	101 204	31 917	69 287	72.3	51.2	89.3
			65+	251 246	91 086	160 160	75.2	57.1	91.9
	1995	Estimates	15+	2 588 000	804 000	1 784 000	43.6	28.1	58.2
Mali	1988	Total population	6+	...	...	...	81.2	73.6	88.6
		Urban population	6+	...	...	...	56.0	45.2	66.4
		Rural population	6+	...	...	...	88.5	81.7	95.0
	1995	Estimates	15+	3 917 000	1 668 000	2 249 000	69.0	60.6	76.9
Mauritania	1988	Total population	15+	667 342	268 955	398 387	64.9	53.9	75.4
			10-14	101 654	47 163	54 491	46.5	41.2	52.3
			15-19	94 202	38 198	56 004	49.7	41.2	57.9
			20-24	91 249	34 017	57 232	56.5	45.4	66.1
			25-29	92 443	34 839	57 604	71.1	51.9	91.6
			30-34	77 662	30 912	46 750	66.3	54.8	77.0
			35-39	62 559	26 209	36 350	69.8	58.9	80.5
			40-44	53 104	21 691	31 413	71.9	62.3	80.4
			45-49	40 921	17 418	23 503	73.5	63.1	83.6
			50-54	45 676	19 314	26 362	73.8	64.3	82.6
			55-59	22 897	10 731	12 166	72.2	63.7	81.8
			60-64	30 066	13 182	16 884	73.7	65.3	81.9
			65+	56 563	22 444	34 119	74.6	65.6	82.1
	1995	Estimates	15+	806 000	319 000	487 000	62.3	50.4	73.7
Mauritius	1990	Total population	15+	149 383	54 748	94 635	20.1	14.8	25.3
			12-14	5 452	3 105	2 347	8.4	9.4	7.3
			15-19	8 244	4 567	3 677	8.5	9.3	7.7
			20-24	9 347	4 885	4 462	9.1	9.3	8.9
			25-34	22 417	9 906	12 511	11.3	9.8	12.8
			35-44	26 980	8 844	18 136	19.0	12.4	25.8
			45-54	27 771	9 061	18 710	33.6	22.4	44.2
			55-64	26 890	9 331	17 559	42.7	30.6	53.9
			65+	27 734	8 154	19 580	48.9	34.1	59.8
	1995	Estimates	15+	138 000	52 000	86 000	17.1	12.9	21.2
Morocco	1982	Total population	15+	8 119 233	3 187 079	4 932 154	69.7	56.3	82.5
			10-14	1 095 260	390 245	705 015	42.5	29.5	56.1
			15-19	1 163 698	416 782	746 916	52.5	38.4	65.9
			20-24	1 150 351	425 418	724 933	59.8	46.0	72.6
			25-34	1 661 629	597 359	1 064 270	63.1	46.5	78.8
			35-44	1 346 745	489 349	857 396	78.6	62.6	92.1
			45-54	1 224 627	506 891	717 736	86.3	74.2	97.6
			55-64	837 385	387 104	450 281	89.4	80.6	98.6
			65+	734 798	364 176	370 622	92.3	86.4	98.9

Country and year of census or survey Pays et année du recensement ou de l'enquête País y año del censo o de la encuesta			Age Âge Edad	Illiterate population Population analphabète Población analfabeta			Percentage of illiterates Pourcentage d'analphabètes Porcentage de analfabetos		
				Total	Male Masculine Masculina	Female Féminine Femenina	Total	Male Masculin Masculino	Female Féminin Femenino
				(1)	(2)	(3)	(4)	(5)	(6)
Morocco (cont)		Urban population	15+	2 674 434	911 061	1 763 373	50.2	34.9	64.8
			10-14	163 692	46 819	116 873	15.1	8.6	21.4
			15-19	260 504	70 159	190 345	25.1	13.9	35.6
			20-24	336 431	98 471	237 960	35.7	21.8	48.7
			25-34	535 504	161 951	373 553	41.6	25.0	58.4
			35-44	491 392	151 020	340 372	63.9	42.0	83.2
			45-54	482 910	181 555	301 355	77.6	59.6	94.8
			55-64	325 711	142 499	183 212	83.1	70.3	96.9
			65+	241 982	105 406	136 576	87.6	77.5	97.4
		Rural population	15+	5 444 799	2 276 018	3 168 781	86.2	74.5	97.2
			10-14	931 568	343 426	588 142	62.5	44.0	82.8
			15-19	903 194	346 623	556 571	76.5	59.6	93.1
			20-24	813 920	326 947	486 973	82.9	69.1	95.7
			25-34	1 126 125	435 408	690 717	83.6	68.4	97.1
			35-44	855 353	338 329	517 024	90.6	80.1	99.1
			45-54	741 717	325 336	416 381	93.1	85.8	99.7
			55-64	511 674	244 605	267 069	93.9	88.2	99.8
			65+	492 816	258 770	234 046	94.8	90.6	99.9
	1995	Estimates	15+	9 730 000	3 714 000	6 016 000	56.3	43.4	69.0
Mozambique	1980	Total population	15+	4 522 941	1 634 940	2 888 001	72.7	55.8	87.7
			10-14	859 844	410 939	448 905	58.5	52.3	65.6
			15-19	545 791	185 087	360 704	49.2	32.5	66.7
			20-24	588 471	161 025	427 446	64.9	40.9	83.2
			25-39	1 521 011	489 790	1 031 221	74.4	53.7	91.0
			40-59	1 303 253	548 381	754 872	84.1	72.0	95.9
			60+	564 415	250 657	313 758	92.3	85.6	98.5
		Urban population	15+	342 420	103 490	238 930	39.4	22.0	60.2
			10-14	49 101	21 726	27 375	27.6	23.6	31.9
			15-19	38 486	13 288	25 198	20.7	12.4	31.9
			20-24	51 634	12 812	38 822	31.5	14.7	50.6
			25-39	126 245	33 350	92 895	41.3	20.3	65.7
			40-59	90 939	31 905	59 034	54.8	35.0	79.1
			60+	35 116	12 135	22 981	75.2	56.7	90.7
		Rural population	15+	4 180 521	1 531 450	2 649 071	78.1	62.3	91.5
			10-14	810 743	389 213	421 530	62.7	56.1	70.5
			15-19	507 305	171 799	335 506	54.9	37.2	72.7
			20-24	536 837	148 213	388 624	72.2	48.4	89.0
			25-39	1 394 766	456 440	938 326	80.2	61.1	94.6
			40-59	1 212 314	516 476	695 838	87.7	77.0	97.7
			60+	529 299	238 522	290 777	93.8	87.9	99.2
	1995	Estimates	15+	5 298 000	1 828 000	3 470 000	59.9	42.3	76.7
Namibia‡	1991	Total population	15+	198 460	87 209	111 251	24.2	22.2	26.0
			10-14	33 940	19 512	14 428	19.2	22.2	16.2
			15-19	18 156	11 306	6 850	11.0	13.9	8.1
			20-24	17 057	9 398	7 659	13.0	14.8	11.4
			25-29	17 364	8 560	8 804	15.8	16.3	15.2
			30-34	17 560	7 647	9 913	20.4	18.9	21.7
			35-39	15 196	6 414	8 782	22.8	20.0	25.5
			40-44	16 610	6 816	9 794	30.3	25.5	34.9
			45-49	14 622	6 012	8 610	33.4	28.0	38.6
			50-54	14 616	5 979	8 637	38.2	32.0	44.2
			55-59	11 201	4 604	6 597	40.2	33.2	47.1
			60-64	14 124	5 071	9 053	49.2	39.6	56.9
			65+	41 954	15 402	26 552	61.4	51.8	68.8
		Urban population	15+	31 493	15 727	15 766	10.3	9.9	10.6
			10-14	3 350	1 677	1 673	7.0	7.2	6.7
			15-19	2 315	1 335	980	4.4	5.5	3.5
			20-24	3 010	1 750	1 260	5.6	6.5	4.6
			25-29	3 571	1 927	1 644	6.9	7.3	6.5
			30-34	3 602	1 699	1 903	8.9	8.1	9.8
			35-39	3 090	1 520	1 570	10.2	9.2	11.5
			40-44	3 101	1 544	1 557	14.0	12.2	16.3
			45-49	2 526	1 281	1 245	15.7	13.7	18.4
			50-54	2 322	1 189	1 133	17.9	15.8	20.9
			55-59	1 886	903	983	21.4	17.5	26.9
			60-64	1 664	710	954	27.3	22.7	32.1
			65+	4 406	1 869	2 537	36.6	34.7	38.1

Country and year of census or survey Pays et année du recensement ou de l'enquête País y año del censo o de la encuesta			Age Âge Edad	Illiterate population Population analphabète Población analfabeta			Percentage of illiterates Pourcentage d'analphabètes Porcentage de analfabetos		
				Total	Male Masculine Masculina	Female Féminine Femenina	Total	Male Masculin Masculino	Female Féminin Femenino
				(1)	(2)	(3)	(4)	(5)	(6)
Namibia‡ (cont)									
		Rural population	15+	166 967	71 482	95 485	32.5	30.5	34.2
			10-14	30 590	17 835	12 755	23.8	27.6	19.9
			15-19	15 841	9 971	5 870	14.0	17.5	10.5
			20-24	14 047	7 648	6 399	18.3	20.9	16.0
			25-29	13 793	6 633	7 160	23.5	25.6	21.9
			30-34	13 958	5 948	8 010	30.4	30.4	30.5
			35-39	12 106	4 894	7 212	33.3	31.6	34.6
			40-44	13 509	5 272	8 237	41.4	37.4	44.5
			45-49	12 096	4 731	7 365	43.7	39.1	47.4
			50-54	12 294	4 790	7 504	48.6	43.0	53.1
			55-59	9 315	3 701	5 614	48.8	42.4	54.2
			60-64	12 460	4 361	8 099	55.1	45.0	62.6
			65+	37 548	13 533	24 015	66.7	55.5	75.2
Niger	1988	Total population	15+	3 268 685	1 467 030	1 801 655	89.1	83.1	94.6
			10-14	574 155	292 063	282 092	81.0	77.2	85.4
			15-19	520 646	212 115	308 531	80.8	72.1	88.1
			20-24	504 491	197 145	307 346	85.9	77.9	92.1
			25-29	498 677	197 471	301 206	89.3	82.0	94.8
			30-34	383 979	168 305	215 674	90.5	84.1	96.2
			35-39	305 420	148 617	156 803	91.9	86.7	97.5
			40-44	271 694	130 892	140 802	93.5	88.6	98.7
			45-49	178 906	97 216	81 690	92.9	88.4	98.9
			50-54	179 389	91 291	88 098	94.2	89.7	99.3
			55-59	102 156	58 821	43 335	93.2	89.1	99.3
			60-64	119 982	60 901	59 081	94.8	90.8	99.4
			65+	203 345	104 256	99 089	95.3	91.6	99.5
	1995	Estimates	15+	4 081 000	1 825 000	2 256 000	86.4	79.1	93.4
Nigeria	1995	Estimates	15+	26 075 000	9 731 000	16 344 000	42.9	32.7	52.7
Reunion	1982	Total population	15+	73 220	38 861	34 359	21.4	23.5	19.5
			10-14	2 204	1 393	811	3.4	4.3	2.5
			15-19	2 310	1 673	637	3.3	4.7	1.8
			20-24	2 876	2 025	851	5.9	8.5	3.4
			25-34	7 755	4 980	2 775	10.6	14.1	7.4
			35-44	13 137	7 493	5 644	24.5	28.1	20.9
			45-54	18 181	9 654	8 527	44.0	47.7	40.4
			55-64	14 364	7 140	7 224	49.4	52.0	47.0
			65+	14 597	5 896	8 701	57.6	59.6	56.3
Rwanda	1991	Total population	15+	1 545 540	...	...	42.0	...	...
			10-14	262 065	...	...	28.4	...	...
			15-19	170 170	...	...	23.9	...	...
			20-24	154 365	...	...	26.4	...	...
			25-29	186 680	...	...	35.3	...	...
			30-34	194 460	...	...	40.4	...	...
			35-39	161 100	...	...	45.0	...	...
			40-44	125 195	...	...	51.1	...	...
			45-49	103 470	...	...	58.9	...	...
			50-54	114 540	...	...	66.1	...	...
			55-59	96 330	...	...	71.8	...	...
			60-64	102 505	...	...	81.2	...	...
			65-69	71 100	...	...	84.6	...	...
			70-74	65 625	...	...	89.5	...	...
	1995	Estimates	15+	1 695 000	635 000	1 060 000	39.5	30.2	48.4
St. Helena	1987	Total population	20+	104	65	39	2.7	3.3	2.1
			12-19	16	9	7	1.5	1.6	1.3
			20-29	14	9	5	1.3	1.7	0.9
			30-39	24	17	7	2.6	3.3	1.7
			40-49	10	9	1	1.5	2.2	0.4
			50-59	21	14	7	4.7	6.3	3.2
			60+	35	16	19	5.2	5.5	5.0
Sao Tome and Principe	1981	Total population	15+	22 080	6 755	15 325	42.6	26.8	57.6
			10-14	1 641	751	890	13.9	12.4	15.4
			15-19	1 464	440	1 024	14.0	8.4	19.5
			20-24	1 780	402	1 378	22.3	10.2	34.2
			25-34	3 435	806	2 629	35.9	17.6	52.6
			35-44	3 948	1 227	2 721	54.3	34.3	73.5
			45-54	4 468	1 603	2 865	64.9	46.7	82.9
			55-64	3 447	1 206	2 241	69.8	50.3	88.3
			65+	3 538	1 071	2 467	75.5	53.1	92.4

Country and year of census or survey Pays et année du recensement ou de l'enquête País y año del censo o de la encuesta			Age Âge Edad	Illiterate population Population analphabète Población analfabeta			Percentage of illiterates Pourcentage d'analphabètes Porcentage de analfabetos		
				Total	Male Masculine Masculina	Female Féminine Femenina	Total	Male Masculin Masculino	Female Féminin Femenino
				(1)	(2)	(3)	(4)	(5)	(6)
Senegal	1988	Total population	15+	2 652 915	1 090 771	1 562 144	73.1	63.1	82.1
			10-14	411 714	167 572	244 142	50.3	41.0	59.5
			15-19	425 479	161 399	264 081	59.9	48.4	70.1
			20-24	363 560	140 696	222 864	64.9	54.1	74.3
			25-29	377 551	144 472	233 079	71.0	60.3	79.7
			30-34	261 882	105 529	156 353	69.1	58.3	78.9
			35-39	260 924	103 656	157 268	76.8	65.3	86.9
			40-44	177 884	73 919	103 965	81.3	70.2	91.5
			45-49	189 637	81 763	107 874	86.5	77.0	95.4
			50-54	142 119	64 837	77 282	86.5	77.6	95.8
			55-59	142 090	64 182	77 908	88.8	80.7	96.9
			60+	311 790	150 319	161 471	89.9	83.3	97.1
	1995	Estimates	15+	3 084 000	1 305 000	1 779 000	66.9	57.0	76.8
Seychelles	1987	Total population	15+	7 106	3 789	3 317	15.6	16.9	14.4
			10-14	29	22	7	0.6	1.0	0.3
			15-19	83	52	31	1.1	1.4	0.8
			20-24	257	175	82	3.6	5.1	2.2
			25-29	372	233	139	6.0	7.3	4.5
			30-34	468	281	187	10.3	11.5	8.8
			35-39	476	298	178	14.3	16.2	11.9
			40-44	505	303	202	19.2	21.5	16.5
			45-49	601	352	249	23.7	29.1	18.7
			50-54	728	375	353	29.0	30.9	27.2
			55-59	692	384	308	30.7	34.8	26.7
			60-64	656	332	324	33.4	36.9	30.5
			65+	2 268	1 004	1 264	46.4	50.0	43.9
Sierra Leone	1995	Estimates	15+	1 727 000	668 000	1 059 000	68.6	54.6	81.8
South Africa‡	1980	Total population	15+	3 711 776	1 796 523	1 915 253	23.8	22.5	25.2
			10-14	1 559 863	806 401	753 462	33.4	34.5	32.3
			15-24	761 861	388 658	373 203	14.8	14.7	15.0
			25-34	770 669	398 115	372 554	20.5	19.9	21.2
			35-44	689 843	343 332	346 511	26.1	24.9	27.6
			45-54	588 120	282 738	305 382	32.3	30.4	34.3
			55-64	458 308	202 333	255 975	37.6	34.3	40.7
			65+	442 975	181 347	261 628	43.0	41.0	44.6
	1995	Estimates	15+	4 731 000	2 319 000	2 412 000	18.2	18.1	18.3
Sudan‡	1993	Total population	15+	5 387 588	1 880 349	3 507 239	49.4	35.6	62.5
			15-19	635 232	228 586	406 646	30.1	21.8	38.4
			20-24	552 108	172 165	379 943	33.7	22.6	43.1
			25-29	660 984	185 138	475 846	43.5	28.5	54.9
			30-34	506 853	158 204	348 649	46.1	29.2	62.6
			35-39	622 736	195 518	427 218	56.1	37.2	72.5
			40-44	472 169	164 062	308 107	62.6	44.2	80.3
			45-49	450 014	156 224	293 790	66.4	47.1	84.8
			50-54	395 835	150 692	245 143	71.5	53.5	90.2
			55-59	233 773	95 108	138 665	70.9	53.5	91.2
			60-64	273 505	115 742	157 763	76.2	60.5	94.2
			65-69	171 026	78 373	92 653	75.2	60.5	94.8
			70-74	178 441	77 672	100 769	81.3	67.5	96.5
			65+	584 379	258 910	325 469	79.8	65.8	96.1
		Urban population	15+	1 288 548	458 888	829 660	32.7	22.3	44.0
			15-19	111 190	41 150	70 040	14.9	10.8	19.2
			20-24	121 262	44 487	76 775	17.9	12.7	23.5
			25-29	157 222	50 935	106 287	26.6	17.7	35.1
			30-34	123 607	44 931	78 676	28.5	18.5	41.2
			35-39	158 718	54 022	104 696	39.1	25.5	54.1
			40-44	116 010	42 132	73 878	45.1	30.3	62.6
			45-49	119 950	40 440	79 510	50.8	32.6	71.0
			50-54	102 285	35 540	66 745	57.4	37.4	80.2
			55-59	64 291	23 082	41 209	58.1	38.0	82.6
			60-64	70 338	26 544	43 794	65.3	45.4	88.9
			65-69	45 276	17 662	27 614	66.4	47.0	90.4
			70-74	43 891	16 664	27 227	74.2	55.4	93.6
			65+	143 675	55 625	88 050	72.2	53.3	93.0
		Rural population	15+	4 099 040	1 421 461	2 677 579	59.0	44.1	71.8
			15-19	524 042	187 436	336 606	38.5	28.0	48.5
			20.24	430 846	127 678	303 168	44.5	30.8	54.7
			25-29	503 762	134 203	369 559	54.4	37.1	65.5
			30-34	383 246	113 273	269 973	57.6	37.8	73.7
			35-39	464 018	141 496	322 522	65.5	45.2	81.5
			40-44	356 159	121 930	234 229	71.7	52.6	88.3
			45-49	330 064	115 784	214 280	74.7	55.8	91.4
			50-54	293 550	115 152	178 398	78.2	61.8	94.5
			55-59	169 482	72 026	97 456	77.3	61.5	95.4
			60-64	203 167	89 198	113 969	80.9	67.1	96.5
			65-69	125 750	60 711	65 039	79.0	66.0	96.8
			70-74	134 550	61 008	73 542	83.9	71.7	97.6
			65+	440 704	203 285	237 419	82.6	70.2	97.4

Country and year of census or survey / Pays et année du recensement ou de l'enquête / País y año del censo o de la encuesta			Age Âge Edad	Illiterate population Population analphabète Población analfabeta			Percentage of illiterates Pourcentage d'analphabètes Porcentaje de analfabetos		
				Total	Male Masculine Masculina	Female Féminine Femenina	Total	Male Masculin Masculino	Female Féminin Femenino
				(1)	(2)	(3)	(4)	(5)	(6)
Swaziland	1986	Total population	15+	116 464	48 722	67 742	32.7	30.1	34.8
			10-14	16 296	8 894	7 402	17.5	19.3	15.8
			15-19	10 481	5 577	4 904	13.9	15.3	12.5
			20-24	11 291	4 701	6 590	19.3	19.3	19.4
			25-34	22 184	8 516	13 668	26.8	24.1	28.9
			35-44	21 156	8 220	12 936	38.0	32.5	42.6
			45-54	19 909	9 011	10 898	51.1	46.0	56.4
			55-64	13 233	5 881	7 352	62.3	57.3	67.0
			65+	18 210	6 816	11 394	78.7	71.7	83.6
	1995	Estimates	15+	114 000	50 000	64 000	23.3	22.0	24.4
Togo	1981	Total population	15+	927 712	328 497	599 215	68.6	53.3	81.5
			12-14	50 403	18 605	31 798	28.0	18.8	39.2
			15-19	104 790	30 963	73 827	39.1	22.7	56.3
			20-29	113 598	28 145	85 453	56.5	33.6	72.7
			30-39	138 591	38 674	99 917	68.8	48.1	82.7
			40-49	203 651	66 589	137 062	76.9	59.9	89.2
			50-59	146 581	59 880	86 701	83.8	72.4	93.9
			60-69	86 016	38 790	47 226	87.7	79.7	95.5
			70+	134 485	65 456	69 029	93.3	88.8	98.0
		Urban population	15+	160 398	44 658	115 740	43.1	24.8	60.1
			12-14	7 522	1 433	6 089	15.1	6.0	23.8
			15-19	18 224	3 860	14 364	21.7	9.2	34.4
			20-29	23 331	4 941	18 390	32.3	14.2	49.1
			30-39	26 331	6 264	20 067	42.4	21.7	60.3
			40-49	36 420	10 032	26 388	51.2	29.5	71.1
			50-59	24 331	8 221	16 110	60.6	40.8	80.6
			60-69	13 454	4 822	8 632	66.6	48.7	83.8
			70+	18 307	6 518	11 789	80.7	65.2	92.9
		Rural population	15+	767 314	283 839	483 475	78.3	65.0	89.0
			12-14	42 881	17 172	25 709	33.0	23.0	46.3
			15-19	86 566	27 103	59 463	47.0	28.7	66.4
			20-29	90 267	23 204	67 063	70.0	47.4	83.8
			30-39	112 260	32 410	79 850	80.7	62.9	91.1
			40-49	167 231	56 557	110 674	86.4	73.4	95.0
			50-59	122 250	51 659	70 591	90.7	82.7	97.5
			60-69	72 562	33 968	38 594	93.1	87.6	98.6
			70+	116 178	58 938	57 240	95.7	92.6	99.1
	1995	Estimates	15+	1 085 000	363 000	722 000	48.3	33.0	63.0
Tunisia	1989	Total population	15+	2 095 943	762 085	1 333 858	42.7	30.8	54.8
			10-14	79 907	17 317	62 590	8.3	3.5	13.3
			15-19	113 638	22 245	91 393	13.7	5.3	22.3
			20-24	165 701	37 514	128 187	21.5	9.6	33.8
			25-29	150 890	35 583	115 307	23.4	11.1	35.5
			30-34	157 361	37 875	119 486	29.5	14.2	44.9
			35-39	176 251	47 331	128 920	42.2	23.6	59.4
			40-44	172 330	56 596	115 734	56.4	38.2	73.6
			45-49	196 966	75 151	121 815	71.9	56.2	86.9
			50-54	230 177	97 598	132 579	79.7	66.6	93.2
			55-59	214 289	97 363	116 926	83.7	72.7	95.8
			60-64	172 364	79 906	92 458	85.9	76.4	96.3
			65+	345 976	174 923	171 053	89.6	84.0	96.2
		Urban population	15+	965 831	337 571	628 260	31.9	21.9	42.4
			10-14	14 207	5 038	9 169	2.7	1.9	3.5
			15-19	23 740	5 862	17 878	4.9	2.4	7.6
			20-24	45 576	9 601	35 975	9.6	4.0	15.5
			25-29	52 390	11 426	40 964	12.4	5.4	19.5
			30-34	61 286	13 408	47 878	17.6	7.6	28.0
			35-39	74 583	17 418	57 165	27.8	13.1	42.2
			40-44	83 805	22 904	60 901	42.2	23.3	60.7
			45-49	101 368	33 415	67 953	60.3	40.5	79.4
			50-54	123 645	47 674	75 971	71.1	53.8	89.2
			55-59	115 635	47 425	68 210	76.9	61.2	93.6
			60-64	94 288	40 708	53 580	80.1	66.7	94.5
			65+	189 515	87 730	101 785	85.8	70.8	105.1
		Rural population	15+	1 130 112	424 514	705 598	60.0	44.9	75.1
			10-14	65 700	12 279	53 421	15.1	5.5	25.0
			15-19	89 898	16 383	73 515	25.7	9.3	42.4
			20-24	120 125	27 913	92 212	40.5	18.7	62.6
			25-29	98 500	24 157	74 343	44.2	22.3	65.0
			30-34	96 075	24 467	71 608	52.0	27.4	75.2
			35-39	101 668	29 913	71 755	67.9	43.8	88.0
			40-44	88 525	33 692	54 833	82.8	67.4	96.4
			45-49	95 598	41 736	53 862	90.3	81.2	98.8
			50-54	106 532	49 924	56 608	92.7	86.3	99.1
			55-59	98 654	49 938	48 716	93.3	88.4	98.9
			60-64	78 076	39 198	38 878	94.2	90.0	99.0
			65+	156 461	87 193	69 268	94.7	92.5	97.6
	1995	Estimates	15+	1 930 000	621 000	1 309 000	33.3	21.4	45.4

Country and year of census or survey Pays et année du recensement ou de l'enquête País y año del censo o de la encuesta			Age Âge Edad	Illiterate population Population analphabète Población analfabeta			Percentage of illiterates Pourcentage d'analphabètes Porcentage de analfabetos		
				Total	Male Masculine Masculina	Female Féminine Femenina	Total	Male Masculin Masculino	Female Féminin Femenino
				(1)	(2)	(3)	(4)	(5)	(6)
Uganda	1991	Total population	15+	3 855 388	1 348 282	2 507 106	43.9	31.8	55.2
			10-14	1 209 685	613 453	596 232	54.5	54.3	54.7
			15-19	527 581	205 380	322 201	29.3	23.7	34.4
			20-24	477 479	153 570	323 909	31.3	21.6	39.7
			25-29	479 369	151 277	328 092	37.4	24.8	48.7
			30-34	383 724	121 935	261 789	40.6	26.2	54.5
			35-39	312 027	96 820	215 207	45.1	28.5	61.0
			40-44	278 520	82 796	195 724	51.5	31.7	69.8
			45-49	264 340	84 274	180 066	57.7	37.5	77.3
			50-54	274 061	92 091	181 970	64.0	44.3	82.5
			55-59	181 564	70 111	111 453	67.9	50.8	86.2
			60-64	215 610	82 761	132 849	76.0	61.6	88.9
			65+	461 113	207 267	253 846	82.9	73.3	92.8
		Urban population	15+	187 604	63 442	124 162	17.2	11.8	22.5
			10-14	63 449	27 675	35 774	28.6	28.2	28.9
			15-19	27 129	9 726	17 403	11.9	10.3	13.1
			20-24	28 241	10 259	17 982	11.5	8.8	13.9
			25-29	27 455	9 299	18 156	13.3	8.8	18.0
			30-34	20 346	6 791	13 555	14.8	9.1	21.6
			35-39	15 181	4 900	10 281	17.6	10.2	26.8
			40-44	13 117	3 910	9 207	23.5	12.4	37.9
			45-49	11 373	3 617	7 756	29.2	16.4	46.0
			50-54	12 048	3 797	8 251	37.8	22.5	55.2
			55-59	6 859	2 571	4 288	42.3	28.7	59.1
			60-64	8 567	2 716	5 851	53.6	37.7	66.7
			65+	17 288	5 856	11 432	64.9	50.4	76.2
		Rural population	15+	3 667 784	1 284 840	2 382 944	47.7	34.7	59.7
			10-14	1 146 236	585 778	560 458	57.4	56.8	58.0
			15-19	500 452	195 654	304 798	31.8	25.4	37.9
			20-24	449 238	143 311	305 927	35.1	24.1	44.6
			25-29	451 914	141 978	309 936	42.0	28.1	54.2
			30-34	363 378	115 144	248 234	44.9	29.4	59.5
			35-39	296 846	91 920	204 926	49.0	31.5	65.1
			40-44	265 403	78 886	186 517	54.7	34.4	72.9
			45-49	252 967	80 657	172 310	60.4	39.8	79.7
			50-54	262 013	88 294	173 719	66.1	46.3	84.5
			55-59	174 705	67 540	107 165	69.6	52.3	87.9
			60-64	207 043	80 045	126 998	77.3	63.0	90.3
			65+	443 825	201 411	242 414	83.8	74.3	93.8
	1995	Estimates	15+	4 171 000	1 409 000	2 762 000	38.2	26.3	49.8
United Republic of Tanzania	1995	Estimates	15+	5 171 000	1 618 000	3 553 000	32.2	20.6	43.2
Zaire	1995	Estimates	15+	5 184 000	1 491 000	3 783 000	22.7	13.4	32.3
Zambia‡	1980	Total population	15+	1 308 098	476 250	831 848	46.5	35.3	56.8
			10-14	563 415	284 892	278 523	73.3	74.2	72.5
			15-19	151 951	66 271	85 680	25.6	23.3	27.8
			20-24	113 546	33 015	80 531	24.0	15.5	30.9
			25-44	511 787	140 044	371 743	47.4	28.1	64.1
			45+	530 814	236 920	293 894	79.3	67.2	92.7
	1995	Estimates	15+	1 082 000	346 000	736 000	21.8	14.4	28.7
Zimbabwe	1992	Total population	15-19	52 449	23 448	29 001	4.2	3.8	4.6
			20-24	50 251	14 002	36 249	5.1	3.0	6.9
			25-34	199 899	46 922	152 977	15.2	7.6	21.8
			35-44	199 967	59 652	140 315	23.5	14.8	31.2
			45-54	203 355	68 621	134 734	35.7	24.6	46.3
			55-64	174 514	72 894	101 620	48.3	38.3	59.4
	1995	Estimates	15+	940 000	298 000	642 000	14.9	9.6	20.1
America, North									
Bahamas	1995	Estimates	15+	3 000	1 000	2 000	1.8	1.5	2.0
Barbados	1995	Estimates	15+	5 000	2 000	3 000	2.6	2.0	3.2
Belize	1991	Total population	14+	31 879	16 040	15 839	29.7	29.7	29.7
			14-19	5 110	2 595	2 515	20.7	21.2	20.2
			20-34	10 805	5 418	5 387	25.2	25.4	25.1
			35-49	6 430	3 270	3 160	31.5	31.1	31.9
			50-64	5 287	2 704	2 583	45.1	44.1	46.2
			65+	4 247	2 053	2 194	55.2	55.2	55.3

Country and year of census or survey Pays et année du recensement ou de l'enquête País y año del censo o de la encuesta			Age Âge Edad	Illiterate population Population analphabète Población analfabeta			Percentage of illiterates Pourcentage d'analphabètes Porcentage de analfabetos		
				Total	Male Masculine Masculina	Female Féminine Femenina	Total	Male Masculin Masculino	Female Féminin Femenino
				(1)	(2)	(3)	(4)	(5)	(6)
British Virgin Islands‡	1991	Total population	15+	207	135	72	1.8	2.2	1.3
			15-19	11	9	2	0.9	1.5	0.3
			20-24	11	9	2	0.7	1.2	0.3
			25-34	28	18	10	0.8	1.0	0.6
			35-44	27	14	13	1.1	1.1	1.1
			45-54	28	18	10	2.1	2.6	1.7
			55-64	31	16	15	4.3	4.2	4.4
			65+	71	51	20	7.9	10.5	4.8
Canada	1986	Total population	15+	659 745	...	...	3.4	...	...
Costa Rica	1984	Total population	15+	112 946	55 431	57 515	7.4	7.3	7.4
			10-14	12 377	7 479	4 898	4.6	5.4	3.7
			15-19	7 809	4 626	3 183	2.8	3.3	2.3
			20-24	7 596	4 098	3 498	2.9	3.2	2.6
			25-34	15 123	7 622	7 501	4.0	4.1	3.9
			35-44	19 114	9 114	10 000	8.2	7.9	8.5
			45-54	22 713	10 777	11 936	14.2	13.6	14.7
			55-64	17 367	8 193	9 174	15.7	15.0	16.4
			65+	23 224	11 001	12 223	21.5	21.1	21.9
	1995	Estimates	15+	115 000	59 000	56 000	5.2	5.3	5.0
Cuba‡	1981	Total population	15-49	105 901	...	...	2.2	...	...
			10-14	9 473	...	...	0.8	...	...
			15-19	3 589	...	...	0.3	...	...
			20-24	4 820	...	...	0.6	...	...
			25-34	19 199	...	...	1.4	...	...
			35-44	47 859	...	...	4.2	...	...
			45-49	30 434	...	...	7.1	...	...
	1995	Estimates	15+	364 000	163 000	201 000	4.3	3.8	4.7
Dominican Republic	1981	Total population	15+	1 031 629	518 236	513 809	26.0	26.0	26.0
			10-14	141 434	80 665	60 769	19.4	22.0	16.8
			15-19	110 895	60 289	50 606	16.0	18.0	14.0
			20-24	104 382	53 541	50 841	19.0	20.0	18.0
			25-34	167 188	81 104	86 084	21.7	21.2	22.3
			35-44	135 539	63 042	72 497	27.0	25.0	29.0
			45-54	139 060	64 123	74 937	37.5	33.3	42.0
			55-64	109 144	54 447	54 697	50.0	46.4	54.0
			65+	123 987	61 025	62 962	60.6	58.3	63.1
	1995	Estimates	15+	907 000	465 000	443 000	17.9	18.0	17.8
El Salvador	1980	Total population	15+	818 100	...	...	32.7	...	...
			10-14	126 900	...	...	20.1	...	...
			15-19	83 900	...	...	16.6	...	...
			20-24	69 100	...	...	19.8	...	...
			25-34	129 300	...	...	26.2	...	...
			35-44	144 000	...	...	35.6	...	...
			45-54	149 900	...	...	47.9	...	...
			55-64	118 100	...	...	52.8	...	...
			65+	124 800	...	...	58.7	...	...
		Total population	10+	946 000	403 300	542 700	30.2	26.9	33.2
		Urban population	10+	217 200	64 900	152 300	15.5	10.3	19.6
		Rural population	10+	728 800	338 400	390 400	42.2	39.0	45.5
	1995	Estimates	15+	975 000	432 000	543 000	28.5	26.5	30.2
Guadeloupe	1982	Total population	15+	22 359	11 231	11 128	10.0	10.4	9.6
			10-14	716	432	284	1.7	2.1	1.4
			15-19	490	302	188	1.2	1.4	0.9
			20-24	609	408	201	2.0	2.5	1.4
			25-34	1 582	960	622	3.6	4.6	2.7
			35-44	2 122	1 242	880	6.4	7.8	5.1
			45-54	4 117	2 295	1 822	15.2	17.9	12.7
			55-64	4 403	2 325	2 078	19.6	21.7	17.7
			65+	9 036	3 699	5 337	35.9	34.4	37.1
Guatemala	1985	National estimates	15+	2 519 543	1 070 325	1 449 218	45.0	37.4	52.9
	1995	Estimates	15+	2 627 000	1 111 000	1 516 000	44.4	37.5	51.4

Country and year of census or survey Pays et année du recensement ou de l'enquête País y año del censo o de la encuesta			Age Âge Edad	Illiterate population Population analphabète Población analfabeta			Percentage of illiterates Pourcentage d'analphabètes Porcentaje de analfabetos		
				Total	Male Masculine Masculina	Female Féminine Femenina	Total	Male Masculin Masculino	Female Féminin Femenino
				(1)	(2)	(3)	(4)	(5)	(6)
Haiti	1982	Total population	15+	2 004 791	926 751	1 078 040	65.2	62.7	67.5
			10-14	298 692	160 908	137 784	51.6	55.6	47.6
			15-19	229 764	116 949	112 815	44.9	46.5	43.5
			20-24	243 385	109 656	133 729	53.2	51.4	54.8
			25-34	437 083	188 767	248 316	64.4	60.9	67.4
			35-44	368 294	164 944	203 350	73.6	69.4	77.4
			45-54	293 847	143 543	150 304	75.8	71.9	80.0
			55-64	187 646	91 275	96 371	78.7	75.7	81.9
			65+	244 772	111 617	133 155	82.0	79.1	84.7
	1995	Estimates	15+	2 360 000	1 075 000	1 285 000	55.0	52.0	57.8
Honduras	1985	National estimates	15+	...	...	...	40.5	39.3	41.6
	1995	Estimates	15+	869 000	435 000	434 000	27.3	27.4	27.3
Jamaica	1987	Total population	15+	278 578	173 683	104 895	18.2	23.1	13.5
			15-19	33 492	25 421	8 071	11.8	17.9	5.7
			20-24	28 819	20 186	8 633	11.4	16.1	6.8
			25-29	19 463	13 505	5 958	9.5	13.3	5.7
			30-34	22 872	16 307	6 565	15.4	22.5	8.7
			35-39	17 243	11 154	6 089	15.8	20.9	10.9
			40-44	18 694	10 664	8 030	20.4	23.5	17.4
			45-49	21 918	12 074	9 844	27.4	30.4	24.5
			50-54	26 406	13 616	12 790	36.4	37.7	35.1
			55-59	17 404	10 255	7 149	27.1	32.9	21.6
			60-64	18 895	11 275	7 620	34.6	42.7	27.0
			65+	53 372	29 226	24 146	31.2	36.7	26.4
	1995	Estimates	15+	254 000	161 000	93 000	15.0	19.2	10.9
Martinique	1982	Total population	15+	16 814	8 824	7 990	7.2	8.0	6.6
			10-14	548	313	235	1.4	1.5	1.2
			15-19	393	269	124	0.9	1.2	0.6
			20-24	477	307	170	1.4	1.7	1.1
			25-34	864	544	320	2.1	2.8	1.4
			35-44	1 099	658	441	3.4	4.4	2.5
			45-54	2 703	1 652	1 051	9.0	11.8	6.6
			55-64	3 281	1 871	1 410	13.7	16.7	11.0
			65+	7 997	3 523	4 474	29.2	30.7	28.1
Mexico	1990	Total population	15+	6 161 662	2 305 113	3 856 549	12.4	9.6	15.0
			15-19	381 014	177 910	203 104	3.9	3.7	4.1
			20-24	419 172	164 540	254 632	5.4	4.4	6.2
			25-34	921 198	331 936	589 262	7.8	5.9	9.6
			35-44	1 086 992	380 694	706 298	13.5	9.7	17.0
			45-54	1 123 190	408 552	714 638	20.9	15.6	26.0
			55-64	970 212	358 393	611 819	27.7	21.2	33.7
			65+	1 259 884	483 088	776 796	37.3	30.6	43.2
	1995	Estimates	15+	6 245 000	2 416 000	3 829 000	10.4	8.2	12.6
Netherlands Antilles	1981	Total population	15+	10 236	4 497	5 739	6.2	5.8	6.6
			15-24	1 135	707	428	2.3	2.8	1.7
			25-44	1 970	861	1 109	2.9	2.8	3.1
			45+	7 131	2 929	4 202	14.6	13.2	15.7
Nicaragua	1995	Estimates	15+	822 000	398 000	424 000	34.3	35.4	33.4
Panama	1990	Total population	15+	168 644	80 700	87 944	11.2	10.6	11.7
			10-14	20 540	11 400	9 140	8.0	8.7	7.3
			15-19	12 122	5 774	6 348	4.9	4.6	5.1
			20-24	11 230	5 206	6 024	4.9	4.6	5.3
			25-34	21 500	9 130	12 370	5.9	5.0	6.8
			35-44	28 542	13 339	15 203	11.2	10.4	12.0
			45-54	30 958	15 279	15 679	17.7	17.1	18.3
			55-59	14 215	7 067	7 148	22.8	22.1	23.6
			60+	50 077	24 905	25 172	28.4	28.1	28.8
	1995	Estimates	15+	161 000	76 000	85 000	9.2	8.6	9.8
Puerto Rico‡	1980	Total population	15+	277 461	123 215	154 246	12.2	11.4	12.9
			15-19	19 946	10 856	9 090	5.9	6.4	5.4
			20-24	16 607	8 804	7 803	6.1	6.8	5.5
			25-29	15 213	7 977	7 236	6.4	7.2	5.8
			30-34	16 498	8 483	8 015	7.2	7.9	6.6
			35-44	31 778	14 854	16 924	8.8	8.8	8.9
			45-54	29 275	12 069	17 206	10.7	9.4	11.9
			55-64	34 869	13 752	21 117	15.4	12.6	17.9
			65+	113 275	46 420	66 855	32.8	28.5	36.6

Country and year of census or survey / Pays et année du recensement ou de l'enquête / País y año del censo o de la encuesta			Age / Âge / Edad	Illiterate population / Population analphabète / Población analfabeta			Percentage of illiterates / Pourcentage d'analphabètes / Porcentage de analfabetos		
				Total	Male Masculine Masculina	Female Féminine Femenina	Total	Male Masculin Masculino	Female Féminin Femenino
				(1)	(2)	(3)	(4)	(5)	(6)
Saint Kitts and Nevis	1980	Total population	15+	674	337	337	2.7	2.9	2.5
			15-19	42	27	15	1.3	1.6	0.9
			20-24	38	16	22	0.8	0.7	0.9
			25-29	35	17	18	1.2	1.2	1.3
			30-34	14	7	7	0.8	0.9	0.8
			35-39	26	12	14	2.1	2.1	2.0
			40-44	31	16	15	2.6	3.1	2.3
			45-49	30	15	15	2.3	2.6	2.1
			50-54	39	22	17	2.8	3.7	2.1
			55-59	41	27	14	3.0	4.4	1.9
			60-64	84	45	39	5.1	5.9	4.4
			65+	294	133	161	7.1	8.0	6.6
St. Pierre and Miquelon	1982	Total population	15+	32	16	16	0.7	0.7	0.7
			10-14	2		2	0.3	0.0	0.6
			15-19	3	3		0.5	0.9	0.0
			20-24	3		3	0.6	0.0	1.2
			25-29	3	2	1	0.6	0.8	0.4
			30-34	4	3	1	0.8	1.1	0.4
			35-44	3	2	1	0.4	0.5	0.3
			45-54	6	2	4	1.0	0.7	1.4
			55-64	2		2	0.4	0.0	0.8
			65+	8	4	4	1.5	2.1	1.2
Trinidad and Tobago	1990	Total population	15+	25 910	9 159	16 751	3.1	2.0	4.4
			10-14	820	460	360	0.7	0.8	0.6
			15-19	707	379	328	0.7	0.7	0.7
			20-24	836	439	397	0.7	0.7	0.7
			25-29	1 042	545	497	0.9	0.9	0.9
			30-34	944	484	460	0.9	0.9	1.0
			35-39	883	438	445	1.0	0.9	1.1
			40-44	1 064	485	579	1.5	1.2	1.8
			45-49	1 401	517	884	2.4	1.5	3.6
			50-54	1 943	589	1 354	3.8	2.0	6.3
			55-59	2 417	653	1 764	6.1	2.8	10.9
			60-64	3 100	870	2 230	9.7	4.7	16.5
			65+	11 573	3 760	7 813	17.2	11.0	23.7
	1995	Estimates	15+	18 000	5 000	13 000	2.1	1.2	3.0
United States	1979	Total population	14+	...	...	...	0.5	...	...
			14-24	...	...	...	0.2	...	...
			25-44	...	...	...	0.3	...	...
			45-64	...	...	...	0.7	...	...
			65+	...	...	...	1.4	...	...
America, South									
Argentina	1991	Total population	15+	895 483	416 466	479 017	4.0	3.8	4.1
			10-14	60 507	35 270	25 237	1.8	2.1	1.5
			15-19	44 080	25 977	18 103	1.6	1.8	1.3
			20-24	45 674	24 844	20 830	1.9	2.0	1.7
			25-29	52 210	28 178	24 032	2.3	2.5	2.1
			30-34	61 481	33 239	28 242	2.8	3.0	2.5
			35-39	71 338	36 634	34 704	3.4	3.5	3.2
			40-44	79 489	40 854	38 635	4.1	4.2	3.9
			45-49	75 295	37 607	37 688	4.5	4.5	4.4
			50-54	72 695	33 936	38 759	4.9	4.7	5.1
			55-59	70 298	31 656	38 642	5.2	4.9	5.5
			60-64	75 716	32 005	43 711	5.8	5.3	6.2
			65+	247 207	91 536	155 671	8.6	7.6	9.3
	1995	Estimates	15+	935 000	450 000	485 000	3.8	3.8	3.8
Bolivia	1992	Total population	15+	744 846	213 713	531 133	19.9	11.8	27.5
			10-14	34 068	13 552	20 516	4.2	3.3	5.1
			15-19	35 401	11 209	24 192	5.3	3.4	7.2
			20-24	38 173	10 549	27 624	7.0	4.0	9.7
			25-29	44 381	10 898	33 483	9.5	4.8	13.8
			30-34	54 664	12 952	41 712	13.1	6.3	19.5
			35-39	66 956	15 368	51 588	18.4	8.8	27.1
			40-44	72 919	18 559	54 360	24.6	12.7	36.2
			45-49	76 953	20 287	56 666	31.1	16.8	44.7
			50-54	67 880	19 180	48 700	36.9	21.5	51.3
			55-69	58 221	16 508	41 713	42.1	25.1	57.5
			60-64	68 510	21 780	46 730	47.9	31.7	62.8
			65+	160 788	56 423	104 365	59.0	45.2	70.6

Country and year of census or survey Pays et année du recensement ou de l'enquête País y año del censo o de la encuesta	Age Âge Edad	Illiterate population Population analphabète Población analfabeta			Percentage of illiterates Pourcentage d'analphabètes Porcentage de analfabetos		
		Total	Male Masculine Masculina	Female Féminine Femenina	Total	Male Masculin Masculino	Female Féminin Femenino
		(1)	(2)	(3)	(4)	(5)	(6)
Bolivia (cont)							
Urban population	15+	197 902	39 532	158 370	8.9	3.7	13.5
	10-14	7 594	3 231	4 363	1.6	1.4	1.9
	15-19	8 937	2 529	6 408	2.1	1.2	2.9
	20-24	9 538	2 337	7 201	2.7	1.4	3.8
	25-29	10 595	2 086	8 509	3.6	1.5	5.4
	30-34	14 100	2 514	11 586	5.3	2.0	8.3
	35-39	17 689	2 929	14 760	7.9	2.8	12.5
	40-44	18 789	3 216	15 573	10.9	3.8	17.7
	45-49	20 346	3 459	16 887	15.1	5.4	24.1
	50-54	18 059	3 272	14 787	18.5	7.1	28.6
	55-59	17 150	3 150	14 000	23.9	9.5	36.2
	60-64	19 070	3 807	15 263	27.0	11.6	40.2
	65+	43 629	10 233	33 396	35.3	19.0	48.0
Rural population	15+	546 944	174 181	372 763	36.1	23.0	49.4
	10-14	26 474	10 321	16 153	7.6	5.7	9.8
	15-19	26 464	8 680	17 784	11.0	6.9	15.6
	20-24	28 635	8 212	20 423	14.8	8.4	21.2
	25-29	33 786	8 812	24 974	19.5	10.2	28.9
	30-34	40 564	10 438	30 126	26.5	13.4	40.0
	35-39	49 267	12 439	36 828	34.9	18.1	50.9
	40-44	54 130	15 343	38 787	43.7	24.9	62.4
	45-49	56 607	16 828	39 779	50.1	29.8	70.3
	50-54	49 821	15 908	33 913	57.7	37.0	78.2
	55-59	41 071	13 358	27 713	61.7	40.9	81.8
	60-64	49 440	17 973	31 467	68.4	50.2	86.4
	65+	117 159	46 190	70 969	78.5	65.1	90.7
1995 Estimates	15+	745 000	204 000	541 000	16.9	9.5	24.0
Brazil 1991 Total population	15+	19 294 646	9 300 503	9 994 143	20.1	19.9	20.3
	10-14	3 041 486	1 807 152	1 234 334	17.8	21.0	14.6
	15-19	1 820 461	1 132 987	687 474	12.1	15.2	9.1
	20-24	1 660 354	940 038	720 316	12.2	14.0	10.5
	25-29	1 612 671	867 223	745 448	12.7	14.0	11.5
	30-34	1 552 998	786 344	766 654	14.0	14.5	13.5
	35-39	1 610 122	761 174	848 948	17.0	16.5	17.4
	40-44	1 717 029	800 911	916 118	21.9	20.7	23.0
	45-49	1 611 631	734 519	877 112	26.3	24.5	28.0
	50-54	1 644 332	687 940	956 392	31.8	27.2	36.2
	55-59	1 415 065	598 661	816 404	33.3	29.7	36.7
	60-64	1 360 925	579 511	781 414	37.4	33.8	40.7
	65+	3 289 058	1 411 195	1 877 863	46.4	43.9	48.5
1995 Estimates	15+	18 330 000	9 067 000	9 263 000	16.7	16.7	16.8
Chile 1992 Total population	15+	537 744	247 531	290 213	5.7	5.4	6.0
	10-14	37 462	22 659	14 803	3.0	3.6	2.4
	15-19	16 482	10 135	6 347	1.4	1.6	1.1
	20-24	21 642	12 276	9 366	1.8	2.0	1.5
	25-29	28 031	15 402	12 629	2.3	2.6	2.0
	30-34	29 884	15 518	14 366	2.6	2.8	2.5
	35-39	31 499	14 600	16 899	3.4	3.2	3.5
	40-44	38 634	17 377	21 257	5.0	4.7	5.4
	45-49	45 538	20 444	25 094	7.0	6.5	7.5
	50-54	53 120	23 918	29 202	9.7	9.1	10.3
	55-59	50 219	22 716	27 503	11.4	10.9	11.9
	60-64	56 812	25 368	31 444	13.3	12.8	13.6
	65+	165 883	69 777	96 106	18.9	18.7	19.1
1995 Estimates	15+	485 000	225 000	260 000	4.8	4.6	5.0
Colombia‡ 1985 Total population	12+	2 271 338	1 076 907	1 194 431	11.9	11.6	12.2
	5-6	1 182 439	611 606	570 833	81.4	82.5	80.1
	7-11	791 490	431 722	359 768	25.2	27.1	23.3
	12-17	254 236	148 704	105 532	6.7	7.9	5.6
	18-24	256 635	136 712	119 923	6.3	7.1	5.5
	25-34	342 979	167 892	175 087	8.2	8.4	8.0
	35-44	371 761	170 290	201 471	13.3	12.3	14.3
	45-59	537 254	239 846	297 408	20.8	18.8	22.8
	60+	508 473	213 463	295 010	31.7	27.4	35.8
1995 Estimates	15+	2 047 000	1 010 000	1 037 000	8.7	8.8	8.6

Country and year of census or survey Pays et année du recensement ou de l'enquête País y año del censo o de la encuesta			Age Âge Edad	Illiterate population Population analphabète Población analfabeta			Percentage of illiterates Pourcentage d'analphabètes Porcentaje de analfabetos		
				Total	Male Masculine Masculina	Female Féminine Femenina	Total	Male Masculin Masculino	Female Féminin Femenino
				(1)	(2)	(3)	(4)	(5)	(6)
Ecuador	1990	Total population	15+	691 422	274 731	416 691	11.7	9.5	13.8
			10-14	39 671	20 335	19 366	3.2	3.3	3.2
			15-19	33 695	15 456	18 239	3.2	3.0	3.4
			20-24	40 718	17 141	23 577	4.4	3.9	5.0
			25-29	46 508	17 834	28 674	5.9	4.7	7.0
			30-34	52 860	20 117	32 743	7.9	6.2	9.6
			35-39	60 509	22 779	37 730	10.7	8.3	13.1
			40-44	63 753	24 659	39 094	14.4	11.2	17.7
			45-49	63 969	24 703	39 266	18.2	14.1	22.3
			50-54	65 591	26 079	39 512	22.2	17.8	26.7
			55-59	55 955	22 458	33 497	24.8	20.0	29.6
			60-64	60 809	24 638	36 171	29.9	24.5	35.2
			65+	147 055	58 867	88 188	35.2	29.3	40.6
	1995	Estimates	15+	719 000	289 000	430 000	9.9	8.0	11.8
French Guiana	1982	Total population	15+	8 372	4 321	4 051	17.0	16.4	17.7
			10-14	457	228	229	5.8	5.7	5.8
			15-19	454	200	254	6.4	5.7	7.2
			20-24	792	342	450	10.9	7.9	15.1
			25-34	2 242	1 159	1 083	16.6	16.2	17.2
			35-44	1 719	896	823	19.7	18.8	20.9
			45-54	1 203	685	518	22.2	23.0	21.3
			55-64	907	515	392	25.0	27.0	22.7
			65+	1 055	524	531	28.9	30.8	27.4
Guyana	1995	Estimates	15+	11 000	4 000	7 000	1.9	1.4	2.5
Paraguay	1992	Total population	15+	235 323	96 330	138 993	9.7	8.0	11.4
			10-14	41 813	22 949	18 864	8.0	8.7	7.4
			15-19	16 729	8 077	8 652	4.3	4.1	4.4
			20-24	15 692	7 105	8 587	4.5	4.1	4.9
			25-34	33 470	14 895	18 575	5.6	5.0	6.2
			35-44	37 594	16 028	21 566	8.7	7.3	10.2
			45-54	38 382	15 757	22 625	13.5	11.0	16.1
			55-64	37 631	15 000	22 631	20.2	16.3	24.0
			65+	55 825	19 468	36 357	29.4	22.4	35.3
	1995	Estimates	15+	235 000	97 000	138 000	7.9	6.5	9.4
Peru	1993	Total population	15+	1 784 281	487 113	1 297 168	12.8	7.1	18.3
			10-14	115 929	50 268	65 661	4.4	3.7	5.0
			15-19	91 690	31 393	60 297	3.9	2.6	5.1
			20-29	237 631	69 594	168 037	6.1	3.6	8.3
			30-39	255 411	61 398	194 013	9.0	4.4	13.3
			40-64	810 371	208 188	602 183	21.7	11.2	32.1
			65+	389 178	116 540	272 638	37.9	23.9	50.6
	1995	Estimates	15+	1 736 000	421 000	1 315 000	11.3	5.5	17.0
Suriname	1985	National estimates	15+	...	...	...	10.0	10.0	10.0
	1995	Estimates	15+	20 000	7 000	13 000	7.0	4.9	9.0
Uruguay	1985	Total population	15+	108 400	57 300	51 100	5.0	5.6	4.5
			10-14	4 500	2 900	1 600	1.8	2.2	1.3
			15-19	3 200	1 900	1 300	1.4	1.7	1.1
			20-24	3 900	2 300	1 600	1.7	2.0	1.4
			25-34	9 100	5 500	3 600	2.2	2.7	1.7
			35-44	10 700	6 600	4 100	3.1	3.9	2.3
			45-54	15 400	9 100	6 300	4.7	5.8	3.8
			55-64	20 600	11 200	9 400	6.9	7.9	6.0
			65+	45 500	20 700	24 800	13.9	15.2	13.1
		Urban population	15+	79 800	37 600	42 200	4.3	4.4	4.2
			10-14	3 500	2 200	1 300	1.6	2.0	1.2
			15-19	2 600	1 400	1 200	1.3	1.5	1.2
			20-24	2 900	1 600	1 300	1.5	1.7	1.3
			25-34	6 600	3 700	2 900	1.9	2.2	1.6
			35-44	6 900	3 800	3 100	2.3	2.7	2.0
			45-54	9 900	5 000	4 900	3.6	3.9	3.3
			55-64	14 200	6 800	7 400	5.5	5.9	5.2
			65+	36 700	15 300	21 400	12.5	13.1	12.2
		Rural population	15+	28 600	19 700	8 900	9.6	11.1	7.4
			10-14	1 000	700	300	2.8	3.7	1.9
			15-19	600	500	100	1.8	2.5	0.7
			20-24	1 000	700	300	3.1	3.6	2.3
			25-34	2 500	1 800	700	4.3	5.5	2.8
			35-44	3 800	2 800	1 000	7.5	9.3	4.9
			45-54	5 500	4 100	1 400	11.6	14.1	7.7
			55-64	6 400	4 400	2 000	15.8	17.4	13.2
			65+	8 800	5 400	3 400	26.1	27.8	23.8
	1995	Estimates	15+	65 000	36 000	29 000	2.7	3.1	2.3

Country and year of census or survey Pays et année du recensement ou de l'enquête País y año del censo o de la encuesta			Age Âge Edad	Illiterate population Population analphabète Población analfabeta			Percentage of illiterates Pourcentage d'analphabètes Porcentage de analfabetos		
				Total	Male Masculine Masculina	Female Féminine Femenina	Total	Male Masculin Masculino	Female Féminin Femenino
				(1)	(2)	(3)	(4)	(5)	(6)
Venezuela	1990	Total population	15+	1 130 567	509 864	620 703	10.0	9.1	10.8
			10-14	100 080	61 398	38 682	4.7	5.6	3.7
			15-19	81 640	51 311	30 329	4.2	5.3	3.2
			20-24	81 055	46 542	34 513	4.7	5.4	4.0
			25-34	161 211	83 842	77 369	5.5	5.8	5.2
			35-44	165 234	72 923	92 311	8.1	7.2	8.8
			45-54	184 992	75 371	109 621	15.6	12.8	18.2
			55+	456 435	179 875	276 560	29.7	24.8	34.1
		Urban population	15+	689 885	276 284	413 601	7.1	5.9	8.2
			10-14	52 847	31 795	21 052	3.0	3.6	2.4
			15-19	42 208	25 125	17 083	2.6	3.2	2.1
			20-24	45 062	24 349	20 713	3.0	3.4	2.7
			25-34	88 933	42 879	46 054	3.5	3.5	3.5
			35-44	95 053	37 942	57 111	5.3	4.4	6.2
			45-54	111 633	39 658	71 975	11.1	8.1	13.8
			55+	306 996	106 331	200 665	24.2	18.4	29.0
		Rural population	15+	440 682	233 580	207 102	26.7	25.7	28.0
			10-14	47 233	29 603	17 630	12.4	14.8	9.8
			15-19	39 432	26 186	13 246	12.8	15.3	9.7
			20-24	35 993	22 193	13 800	14.6	16.4	12.5
			25-34	72 278	40 963	31 315	18.8	19.4	18.1
			35-44	70 181	34 981	35 200	26.9	24.5	29.8
			45-54	73 359	35 713	37 646	40.6	35.7	46.8
			55+	149 439	73 544	75 895	55.8	49.5	63.6
	1995	Estimates	15+	1 244 000	571 000	673 000	8.9	8.2	9.7
Asia									
Afghanistan	1995	Estimates	15+	8 169 000	3 229 000	4 940 000	68.5	52.8	85.0
Armenia	1989	Total population	15+	...	...	...	1.2	0.6	1.9
			9-49	...	...	...	0.1	0.1	0.2
		Urban population	15+	...	...	...	0.9	0.5	1.3
			9-49	...	...	...	0.1	0.1	0.1
		Rural population	15+	...	...	...	2.0	0.9	3.1
			9-49	...	...	...	0.2	0.1	0.3
	1995	Estimates	15+	9 000	3 000	6 000	0.4	0.3	0.5
Azerbaijan	1989	Total population	15+	...	...	...	2.7	1.1	4.1
			9-49	...	...	...	0.1	0.1	0.1
		Urban population	15+	...	...	...	1.8	0.7	2.9
			9-49	...	...	...	0.1	0.1	0.1
		Rural population	15+	...	...	...	3.8	1.5	5.7
			9-49	...	...	...	0.1	0.1	0.2
	1995	Estimates	15+	18 000	6 000	12 000	0.4	0.3	0.5
Bahrain	1991	Total population	15+	55 300	24 196	31 104	15.9	11.4	23.0
			10-14	218	99	119	0.5	0.4	0.5
			15-19	343	149	194	0.9	0.8	1.1
			20-24	2 174	1 042	1 132	4.8	4.2	5.4
			25-29	4 877	2 573	2 304	7.9	6.9	9.4
			30-34	6 534	3 434	3 100	10.1	8.1	13.9
			35-39	5 995	2 789	3 206	12.2	8.3	20.6
			40-44	4 731	1 868	2 863	15.9	9.1	31.3
			45-49	4 758	1 480	3 278	27.3	13.3	51.8
			50-54	5 853	2 005	3 848	43.7	25.6	68.9
			55-59	5 523	2 186	3 337	56.5	39.7	78.1
			60-64	5 409	2 349	3 060	69.9	56.4	85.5
			65+	9 103	4 321	4 782	79.8	70.7	90.4
	1995	Estimates	15+	56 000	25 000	31 000	14.8	10.9	20.6
Bangladesh	1981	Total population	15+	32 923 083	14 501 583	18 421 500	70.8	60.3	82.0
			10-14	8 715 441	4 545 096	4 170 345	74.8	73.0	76.9
			15-19	5 232 801	2 375 362	2 857 439	64.2	57.2	71.1
			20-24	4 371 789	1 727 112	2 644 677	64.5	53.2	74.8
			25-34	7 796 087	3 245 033	4 551 054	68.5	56.6	80.5
			35-44	6 020 420	2 670 465	3 349 955	74.0	62.4	86.9
			45-54	4 276 890	1 958 337	2 318 553	77.0	65.2	90.9
			55-64	2 832 959	1 331 169	1 501 790	79.4	67.6	93.9
			65+	2 392 137	1 194 105	1 198 032	81.0	70.0	95.9
		Urban population	15+	3 992 749	1 901 951	2 090 798	51.8	42.0	65.9
			10-14	1 082 320	560 084	522 236	60.3	59.1	61.6
			15-19	636 915	313 349	323 566	46.7	42.1	52.1
			20-24	581 301	262 010	319 291	44.6	35.4	56.7
			25-34	982 615	462 664	519 951	47.8	37.4	63.6
			35-44	712 389	353 247	359 142	54.6	43.6	72.8
			45-54	499 055	233 916	265 139	60.7	47.5	80.5
			55-64	310 324	147 324	163 000	65.5	52.0	85.6
			65+	270 150	129 441	140 709	70.7	57.4	89.9

Country and year of census or survey Pays et année du recensement ou de l'enquête País y año del censo o de la encuesta			Age Âge Edad	Illiterate population Population analphabète Población analfabeta			Percentage of illiterates Pourcentage d'analphabètes Porcentage de analfabetos		
				Total	Male Masculine Masculina	Female Féminine Femenina	Total	Male Masculin Masculino	Female Féminin Femenino
				(1)	(2)	(3)	(4)	(5)	(6)
Bangladesh (cont)									
		Rural population	15+	28 930 334	12 599 632	16 330 702	74.5	64.5	84.7
			10-14	7 633 121	3 985 012	3 648 109	77.5	75.5	79.7
			15-19	4 595 886	2 062 013	2 533 873	67.8	60.9	74.6
			20-24	3 790 488	1 465 102	2 325 386	69.2	58.5	78.2
			25-34	6 813 472	2 782 369	4 031 103	73.0	61.9	83.4
			35-44	5 308 031	2 317 218	2 990 813	77.7	66.8	89.0
			45-54	3 777 472	1 724 421	2 053 414	80.0	68.7	92.5
			55-64	2 522 635	1 183 845	1 338 790	81.5	70.2	95.0
			65+	2 121 987	1 064 664	1 057 323	82.5	72.0	96.7
	1995	Estimates	15+	45 082 000	19 057 000	26 025 000	61.9	50.6	73.9
Bhutan	1995	Estimates	15+	558 000	211 000	347 000	57.8	43.8	71.9
Brunei Darussalam	1991	Total population	15+	20 809	6 887	13 922	12.2	7.5	17.5
			10-14	496	248	248	1.9	1.8	2.0
			15-19	271	131	140	1.2	1.1	1.3
			20-24	661	345	316	2.5	2.6	2.5
			25-29	967	454	513	3.5	3.1	4.0
			30-34	1 252	567	685	4.6	3.9	5.6
			35-39	1 504	499	1 005	6.9	4.1	10.5
			40-44	1 883	447	1 436	12.9	5.4	23.0
			45-49	2 076	488	1 588	24.1	10.0	42.8
			50-54	2 490	578	1 912	36.9	16.0	60.7
			55-59	2 654	694	1 960	52.0	27.6	75.6
			60-64	2 039	705	1 334	56.8	36.6	80.3
			65+	5 012	1 979	3 033	71.7	54.9	89.4
	1995	Estimates	15+	22 000	7 000	15 000	11.8	7.4	16.6
Cambodia‡	1993	Total population	15+	...	...	...	34.7	20.3	46.6
		Phnom Penh	15+	...	...	...	18.0	8.1	36.7
		Other urban	15+	...	...	...	27.3	15.6	36.8
		Rural population	15+	...	...	...	36.5	21.4	49.0
China	1990	Total population	15+	181 609 097	54 359 731	127 249 366	22.2	13.0	31.9
			15-19	6 341 459	1 832 392	4 509 067	5.3	3.0	7.7
			20-24	7 721 519	1 973 154	5 748 365	6.1	3.1	9.3
			25-29	7 284 756	1 495 755	5 789 001	7.0	2.8	11.4
			30-34	10 192 152	2 310 739	7 881 413	12.2	5.3	19.6
			35-39	15 006 097	3 699 505	11 306 592	17.4	8.3	27.1
			40-44	12 712 522	3 405 767	9 306 755	20.0	10.2	30.6
			45-49	13 625 645	3 818 925	9 806 720	27.8	14.8	42.2
			50-54	18 258 819	5 659 339	12 599 480	40.0	23.5	58.6
			55-59	22 153 712	7 239 725	14 913 987	53.1	33.1	75.1
			60+	68 312 416	22 924 430	45 387 986	70.4	49.7	89.3
		Urban population	15+	27 526 502	7 288 509	20 237 993	12.0	6.1	18.4
			15-19	363 509	137 663	225 846	1.3	0.9	1.6
			20-24	532 958	184 363	348 595	1.6	1.0	2.2
			25-29	622 831	167 991	454 840	1.9	1.0	3.0
			30-34	1 102 529	271 117	831 412	4.0	1.9	6.4
			35-39	1 672 684	403 105	1 269 579	6.6	3.0	10.4
			40-44	1 444 036	375 402	1 068 634	7.9	3.9	12.6
			45-49	1 734 921	430 425	1 304 496	12.3	5.8	19.6
			50-54	2 881 078	713 027	2 168 051	21.0	9.9	33.2
			55-59	4 001 241	1 010 703	2 990 538	33.3	15.7	53.6
			60+	13 170 715	3 594 713	9 576 002	54.6	30.5	77.5
		Rural population	15+	154 082 595	47 071 222	107 011 373	26.2	15.7	37.1
			15-19	5 977 950	1 694 729	4 283 221	6.5	3.6	9.6
			20-24	7 188 561	1 788 791	5 399 770	7.8	3.8	11.9
			25-29	6 661 925	1 327 764	5 334 161	9.3	3.6	15.1
			30-34	9 089 623	2 039 622	7 050 001	16.1	7.0	26.0
			35-39	13 333 413	3 296 400	10 037 013	21.9	10.5	33.9
			40-44	11 268 486	3 030 365	8 238 121	24.8	12.8	37.6
			45-49	11 890 724	3 388 500	8 502 224	34.0	18.4	51.3
			50-54	15 377 741	4 946 312	10 431 429	48.2	29.3	69.6
			55-59	18 152 471	6 229 022	11 923 449	61.1	40.5	83.4
			60+	55 141 701	19 329 717	35 811 984	75.7	56.2	93.1
	1995	Estimates	15+	166 173 000	46 651 000	119 522 000	18.5	10.1	27.3
Cyprus	1992	Total population	15+	25 216	4 774	20 442	5.6	2.2	8.9
			15-19	134	66	68	0.3	0.3	0.3
			20-24	189	116	73	0.4	0.5	0.3
			25-34	423	203	220	0.4	0.4	0.5
			35-44	761	342	419	0.9	0.8	1.0
			45-54	1 920	490	1 430	2.9	1.5	4.2
			55-64	4 797	768	4 029	9.6	3.3	15.1
			65+	16 922	2 789	14 203	25.3	9.1	38.9

Country and year of census or survey / Pays et année du recensement ou de l'enquête / País y año del censo o de la encuesta			Age / Âge / Edad	Illiterate population / Population analphabète / Población analfabeta			Percentage of illiterates / Pourcentage d'analphabètes / Porcentage de analfabetos		
				Total	Male Masculine Masculina	Female Féminine Femenina	Total	Male Masculin Masculino	Female Féminin Femenino
				(1)	(2)	(3)	(4)	(5)	(6)
Georgia	1989	Total population	15+	...	...	...	1.0	0.5	1.5
			9-49	...	...	...	0.2	0.1	0.2
		Urban population	15+	...	...	...	0.7	0.3	1.0
			9-49	...	...	...	0.1	0.1	0.1
		Rural population	15+	...	...	...	1.5	0.7	2.2
			9-49	...	...	...	0.2	0.2	0.2
	1995	Estimates	15+	19 000	6 000	13 000	0.5	0.3	0.6
Hong Kong	1995	Estimates	15+	371 000	96 000	275 000	7.8	4.0	11.8
India‡	1981	Total population	15+	238 097 747	93 899 834	144 197 913	59.2	45.2	74.3
			10-14	37 290 123	14 957 724	22 332 399	43.5	33.1	55.2
			15-19	28 582 428	11 480 784	17 101 644	44.6	33.9	56.7
			20-24	27 497 781	9 690 257	17 807 524	48.0	33.5	62.8
			25-34	51 160 336	18 596 823	32 563 513	54.9	39.3	71.0
			35-59	96 946 774	39 730 709	57 216 065	67.2	52.5	83.5
			60+	33 910 428	14 401 261	19 509 167	78.5	65.4	92.2
		Urban population	15+	34 856 080	12 791 547	22 064 533	34.9	23.6	48.1
			10-14	4 243 434	1 792 114	2 451 320	21.9	17.6	26.6
			15-19	3 878 586	1 599 064	2 279 522	23.1	17.9	29.2
			20-24	4 084 855	1 481 444	2 603 411	25.3	17.1	34.8
			25-34	7 568 361	2 641 951	4 926 410	30.5	19.8	43.0
			35-59	14 333 957	5 368 847	8 965 110	42.4	28.5	60.1
			60+	4 990 321	1 700 241	3 290 080	59.1	40.0	78.4
		Rural population	15+	203 241 667	81 108 287	122 133 380	67.3	52.7	82.4
			10-14	33 046 689	13 165 610	19 881 079	49.8	37.6	63.6
			15-19	24 703 842	9 881 720	14 822 122	52.3	39.6	66.3
			20-24	23 412 926	8 208 813	15 204 113	56.9	40.5	72.8
			25-34	43 591 975	15 954 872	27 637 103	63.8	46.9	80.4
			35-59	82 612 817	34 361 862	48 250 955	74.8	60.7	90.0
			60+	28 920 107	12 701 020	16 219 087	83.3	71.5	95.6
	1991	Total population	7+	328 879 000	128 362 000	200 517 000	47.8	35.9	60.7
		Urban population	7+	49 039 000	18 263 000	30 776 000	26.7	18.9	35.9
		Rural population	7+	279 840 000	110 099 000	169 741 000	55.3	42.1	69.4
	1995	Estimates	15+	290 705 000	108 017 000	182 688 000	48.0	34.5	62.3
Indonesia	1990	Total population	15+	20 899 440	6 553 716	14 345 714	18.4	11.7	24.7
			10-14	517 571	266 382	250 739	2.4	2.4	2.4
			15-19	495 618	205 074	290 544	2.6	2.1	3.1
			20-24	838 804	250 957	587 847	5.2	3.3	6.9
			25-34	3 146 738	964 669	2 182 069	11.0	6.9	14.8
			35-44	3 503 544	1 102 704	2 400 840	18.2	11.3	25.3
			45-49	2 129 954	593 810	1 536 144	27.9	15.9	39.5
			50+	10 784 782	3 436 502	7 348 280	46.6	30.9	61.1
	1995	Estimates	15+	21 507 000	6 783 000	14 724 000	16.2	10.4	22.0
Iran, Islamic Republic of‡	1991	Total population	15+	10 652 344	4 113 811	6 538 533	34.3	25.6	43.6
			10-14	451 464	135 118	316 346	6.0	3.5	8.7
			15-19	611 508	190 620	420 888	10.3	6.2	14.8
			20-24	796 723	229 641	567 082	16.1	9.1	23.4
			25-29	910 848	268 564	642 284	22.7	13.3	32.2
			30-34	1 069 799	346 956	722 843	30.5	19.5	41.9
			35-39	1 073 482	357 623	715 859	37.4	24.5	51.0
			40-44	935 172	321 438	613 734	45.9	31.3	60.8
			45-49	839 402	306 559	532 843	53.2	38.4	68.3
			50-54	992 882	413 137	579 745	63.2	50.3	77.4
			55-59	1 003 807	468 183	535 624	69.6	59.0	82.4
			60-64	977 313	479 101	498 212	75.0	66.2	85.9
			65+	1 441 408	731 989	709 419	76.3	68.7	86.0
		Urban population	15+	4 331 207	1 607 450	2 723 757	23.6	16.9	30.9
			10-14	92 247	35 031	57 216	2.2	1.7	2.9
			15-19	144 862	51 009	93 853	4.6	3.1	6.1
			20-24	254 642	73 363	181 279	8.8	5.1	12.5
			25-29	339 377	97 175	242 202	13.3	7.5	19.0
			30-34	417 232	128 820	288 412	18.4	11.1	26.2
			35-39	440 356	140 941	299 415	23.9	14.5	34.1
			40-44	385 450	125 967	259 483	30.4	18.9	43.2
			45-49	363 360	123 639	239 721	37.9	24.6	52.7
			50-54	436 357	168 658	267 699	48.8	35.2	64.6
			55-59	448 771	193 862	254 909	56.8	44.4	72.0
			60-64	425 459	191 088	234 371	62.9	51.5	76.9
			65+	675 341	312 928	362 413	66.1	55.5	79.0

Country and year of census or survey / Pays et année du recensement ou de l'enquête / País y año del censo o de la encuesta			Age / Âge / Edad	Illiterate population / Population analphabète / Población analfabeta			Percentage of illiterates / Pourcentage d'analphabètes / Porcentaje de analfabetos		
				Total	Male Masculine Masculina	Female Féminine Femenina	Total	Male Masculin Masculino	Female Féminin Femenino
				(1)	(2)	(3)	(4)	(5)	(6)
Iran, Islamic Republic of‡ (cont)		Rural population	15+	6 185 869	2 446 186	3 739 683	49.3	37.9	61.4
			10-14	338 640	92 805	245 835	10.0	5.3	15.1
			15-19	445 274	131 547	313 727	16.4	9.3	24.1
			20-24	525 208	150 042	375 166	26.1	14.2	39.0
			25-29	557 618	166 457	391 161	39.1	23.3	55.0
			30-34	637 810	212 118	425 692	52.1	34.9	69.1
			35-39	619 930	210 930	409 000	61.6	43.4	78.7
			40-44	538 674	190 594	348 080	71.2	53.9	86.4
			45-49	468 019	179 280	288 739	76.5	61.6	90.1
			50-54	547 042	239 605	307 437	82.0	71.0	93.3
			55-59	546 815	269 641	277 174	84.9	76.6	94.9
			60-64	542 907	282 541	260 366	87.9	81.7	95.9
			65+	756 572	413 431	343 141	88.2	83.4	94.9
	1994	National estimates	15+	9 788 927	3 950 690	5 838 237	27.7	21.6	34.2
Iraq	1987	Total population	10+	3 102 331	1 139 894	1 962 437	29.2	21.6	36.7
		Urban population	10+	1 834 039	669 288	1 164 751	24.3	17.7	30.9
		Rural population	10+	1 268 292	470 606	797 686	41.2	31.4	50.5
Israel	1992	Total population	15+	183 200	50 500	132 700	5.1	2.9	7.3
			15-17	1 500	600	900	0.5	0.4	0.6
			18-24	6 600	2 100	4 500	1.1	0.7	1.5
			25-34	10 900	3 600	7 300	1.5	1.0	2.0
			35-44	16 700	5 100	11 600	2.4	1.5	3.4
			45-54	26 000	6 400	19 600	6.0	3.0	8.9
			55-64	48 100	11 800	36 300	13.8	7.2	19.5
			65+	73 400	20 900	52 500	15.3	10.0	19.6
	1995	Estimates	15+	176 000	46 000	130 000	4.4	2.3	6.4
Jordan	1991	Total population	15+	373 610	105 950	267 660	16.8	9.2	24.9
			10+14	5 230	2 080	3 150	0.9	0.7	1.1
			15-19	10 960	4 290	6 670	2.1	1.6	2.7
			20-24	14 240	5 080	9 160	3.2	2.2	4.4
			25-29	16 260	4 990	11 270	5.5	3.2	8.0
			30-34	19 050	3 950	15 100	9.9	4.1	15.8
			35-39	25 640	4 240	21 400	17.0	5.9	27.2
			40-44	35 450	4 820	30 630	25.6	7.4	41.9
			45-49	45 380	7 900	37 480	34.4	11.7	58.2
			50-54	49 310	10 860	38 450	45.7	19.5	73.8
			55-59	45 060	13 760	31 300	52.9	29.6	80.9
			60-64	39 800	14 600	25 200	57.7	37.6	83.4
			65+	72 460	31 460	41 000	70.8	55.2	90.5
	1995	Estimates	15+	414 000	105 000	309 000	13.4	6.6	20.6
Kazakstan	1989	Total population	15+	276 835	49 301	227 534	2.5	0.9	3.9
			10-14	4 234	2 474	1 760	0.3	0.3	0.2
			15-19	4 236	2 451	1 785	0.3	0.3	0.3
			20-24	3 418	1 860	1 558	0.3	0.3	0.2
			25-29	3 370	1 819	1 551	0.2	0.2	0.2
			30-34	2 543	1 280	1 263	0.2	0.2	0.2
			35-39	2 041	952	1 089	0.2	0.2	0.2
			40-44	1 654	648	1 006	0.2	0.2	0.2
			45-49	3 613	1 111	2 502	0.5	0.3	0.6
			50-54	12 992	3 065	9 927	1.6	0.8	2.3
			55-59	17 756	4 274	13 482	3.0	1.6	4.3
			60-64	19 822	3 912	15 910	3.3	1.7	4.5
			65+	205 390	27 929	177 461	22.5	10.2	27.7
	1995	Estimates	15+	46 000	15 000	31 000	0.4	0.3	0.5
Korea, Republic of	1985	National estimates	15+	...	...	...	3.0	...	...
	1995	Estimates	15+	697 000	124 000	573 000	2.0	0.7	3.3
Kuwait	1985	Total population	15+	273 513	141 082	132 431	25.5	21.8	31.2
			10-14	6 877	2 184	4 693	4.0	2.5	5.5
			15-19	11 244	2 981	8 263	7.7	4.1	11.4
			20-24	25 583	10 943	14 640	17.2	14.2	20.5
			25-29	40 122	22 762	17 360	21.4	19.8	24.0
			30-34	40 639	23 641	16 998	23.4	21.3	27.1
			35-39	36 196	19 680	16 516	26.3	22.2	33.6
			40-44	31 211	16 247	14 964	31.8	25.1	45.0
			45-49	27 621	14 749	12 872	38.1	30.1	54.8
			50-54	21 257	11 406	9 851	46.0	36.4	66.3
			55-59	13 825	7 125	6 700	50.6	39.1	73.7
			60-64	9 449	4 404	5 045	62.3	48.7	82.3
			65+	16 366	7 144	9 222	78.5	67.1	90.3

Country and year of census or survey / Pays et année du recensement ou de l'enquête / País y año del censo o de la encuesta			Age / Âge / Edad	Illiterate population / Population analphabète / Población analfabeta			Percentage of illiterates / Pourcentage d'analphabètes / Porcentaje de analfabetos		
				Total	Male Masculine Masculina	Female Féminine Femenina	Total	Male Masculin Masculino	Female Féminin Femenino
				(1)	(2)	(3)	(4)	(5)	(6)
Kuwait (cont)		Kuwaiti population	15+	54 411	16 702	37 709	21.8	13.2	30.6
			10-14	1 439	461	978	2.3	1.4	3.1
			15-19	2 016	354	1 662	3.8	1.3	6.3
			20-24	2 235	257	1 978	5.0	1.2	9.0
			25-29	3 153	256	2 897	8.9	1.5	15.7
			30-34	4 147	310	3 837	15.4	2.5	26.7
			35-39	5 197	530	4 667	25.2	5.8	41.0
			40-44	6 686	1 316	5 370	38.3	15.4	60.4
			45-49	7 310	2 410	4 900	46.7	27.6	70.8
			50-54	6 531	2 627	3 904	56.9	40.5	78.3
			55-59	5 208	2 407	2 801	61.2	47.0	82.9
			60-64	4 070	1 953	2 117	68.9	56.3	86.9
			65+	7 858	4 282	3 576	78.2	69.3	92.2
		Non Kuwaiti pop.	15+	219 102	124 380	94 722	26.6	23.9	31.4
			10-14	5 438	1 723	3 715	5.0	3.1	7.0
			15-19	9 228	2 627	6 601	10.1	5.8	14.3
			20-24	23 348	10 686	12 662	22.4	19.6	25.6
			25-29	36 969	22 506	14 463	24.3	22.9	26.9
			30-34	36 492	23 331	13 161	24.9	23.7	27.2
			35-39	30 999	19 150	11 849	26.5	24.2	31.4
			40-44	24 525	14 931	9 594	30.4	26.5	39.4
			45-49	20 311	12 339	7 972	35.8	30.7	48.1
			50-54	14 726	8 779	5 947	42.4	35.3	60.3
			55-59	8 617	4 718	3 899	45.8	36.0	68.3
			60-64	5 379	2 451	2 928	58.0	44.0	79.2
			65+	8 508	2 862	5 646	78.8	64.0	89.2
	1995	Estimates	15+	200 000	83 000	117 000	21.4	17.8	25.1
Kyrgyzstan	1989	Total population	15+	...	...	...	3.0	1.4	4.5
			9-49	...	...	...	0.3	0.3	0.3
		Urban population	15+	...	...	...	1.9	0.8	3.0
			9-49	...	...	...	0.2	0.2	0.2
		Rural population	15+	...	...	...	3.8	1.9	5.7
			9-49	...	...	...	0.3	0.3	0.4
	1995	Estimates	15+	11 000	4 000	7 000	0.4	0.3	0.5
Lao People's Democratic Republic	1985	National estimates	15-45	...	...	...	16.1	8.0	24.2
	1995	Estimates	15+	1 170 000	402 000	768 000	43.4	30.6	55.6
Lebanon	1995	Estimates	15+	151 000	50 000	101 000	7.6	5.3	9.7
Malaysia	1980	Total population	15+	2 399 790	791 000	1 608 790	30.4	20.4	40.3
			10-14	236 460	113 100	123 360	14.5	14.0	15.0
			15-19	156 100	62 300	93 800	10.6	9.0	12.0
			20-29	351 100	116 300	234 800	15.7	11.0	20.0
			30-39	415 900	123 100	292 800	27.0	16.0	38.0
			40-49	503 070	150 300	352 770	46.6	28.0	65.0
			50-59	426 820	135 900	290 920	58.8	38.0	79.0
			60+	546 800	203 100	343 700	74.0	56.0	91.0
	1995	Estimates	15+	2 056 000	682 000	1 374 000	16.5	10.9	21.9
Maldives	1985	Total population	15+	7 598	4 059	3 539	7.7	7.8	7.6
			10-14	1 574	970	604	7.1	8.3	5.7
			15-19	830	517	313	4.0	5.0	3.0
			20-24	860	444	416	4.9	5.1	4.7
			25-29	724	370	354	5.8	5.8	5.7
			30-34	462	222	240	5.6	5.1	6.1
			35-44	1 113	550	563	8.4	7.9	9.0
			45-54	1 780	951	829	12.9	12.5	13.4
			55-64	1 152	620	532	14.3	13.0	16.0
			65+	677	385	292	15.1	13.6	17.6
	1995	Estimates	15+	10 000	5 000	5 000	6.8	6.7	7.0
Mongolia	1988	National estimates	15+	...	...	...	1.3	...	...
Myanmar	1983	Total population	15+	4 492 769	1 460 457	3 032 312	21.4	14.2	28.3
			10-14	622 824	270 742	352 082	14.5	12.4	16.8
			15-19	564 799	216 760	348 039	15.1	11.7	18.4
			20-24	495 692	178 241	317 451	15.1	11.1	18.9
			25-34	857 082	298 750	558 332	17.4	12.3	22.5
			35-44	719 075	223 998	495 077	22.8	14.4	31.0
			45-54	776 231	229 636	546 595	28.6	17.3	39.5
			55-64	580 851	174 523	406 328	31.8	19.6	43.4
			65+	499 039	138 549	360 490	37.2	22.3	50.1
	1995	Estimates	15+	4 913 000	1 617 000	3 296 000	16.9	11.3	22.3

Country and year of census or survey / Pays et année du recensement ou de l'enquête / País y año del censo o de la encuesta			Age / Âge / Edad	Illiterate population / Population analphabète / Población analfabeta			Percentage of illiterates / Pourcentage d'analphabètes / Porcentaje de analfabetos		
				Total	Male Masculine Masculina	Female Féminine Femenina	Total	Male Masculin Masculino	Female Féminin Femenino
				(1)	(2)	(3)	(4)	(5)	(6)
Nepal	1981	Total population	15+	6 998 148	3 053 083	3 945 065	79.4	68.3	90.8
			10-14	1 045 467	452 238	593 229	61.2	49.2	75.3
			15-19	882 010	360 317	521 693	66.4	51.8	82.5
			20-24	981 835	371 373	610 462	73.5	58.3	87.4
			25-34	1 681 560	682 519	999 041	78.7	65.7	90.9
			35-44	1 379 493	621 745	757 748	83.8	74.1	93.8
			45-54	1 005 383	490 314	515 069	86.6	79.1	95.2
			55-64	629 830	309 991	319 839	88.3	81.6	95.9
			65+	438 037	216 824	221 213	89.5	83.6	96.1
		Urban population	15+	306 572	126 552	180 020	52.6	40.3	67.0
			10-14	35 773	15 716	20 057	32.4	26.1	39.9
			15-19	34 976	14 269	20 707	35.9	27.0	46.5
			20-24	42 064	15 484	26 580	42.5	30.1	56.0
			25-34	72 160	27 146	45 014	49.4	35.3	65.1
			35-44	61 588	25 571	36 017	59.5	45.3	76.5
			45-54	44 973	20 047	24 926	66.1	52.6	83.2
			55-64	28 494	13 429	15 065	72.4	60.5	87.8
			65+	22 317	10 606	11 711	76.3	65.7	89.3
		Rural population	15+	6 691 576	2 926 531	3 765 045	81.3	70.4	92.4
			10-14	1 009 664	436 522	573 172	63.2	50.8	77.7
			15-19	847 034	346 048	500 986	68.8	53.8	85.2
			20-24	939 771	355 889	583 882	76.0	60.8	89.7
			25-34	1 609 400	655 373	954 027	80.8	68.2	92.7
			35-44	1 317 905	596 174	721 731	85.4	76.2	94.9
			45-54	960 410	470 267	490 143	87.9	80.9	95.9
			55-64	601 336	296 562	304 774	89.2	82.9	96.3
			65+	415 720	206 218	209 502	90.3	84.8	96.5
	1995	Estimates	15+	9 149 000	3 762 000	5 387 000	72.5	59.1	86.0
Pakistan‡	1981	Total population	15+	34 713 824	16 051 771	18 662 053	74.3	64.6	85.2
			10-14	8 266 534	4 209 928	4 056 606	74.6	69.5	80.7
			15-19	5 093 452	2 423 476	2 669 976	64.1	56.0	73.8
			20-24	4 367 781	1 841 836	2 525 945	66.6	54.9	78.9
			25-34	7 416 063	3 265 279	4 150 784	71.7	60.3	84.4
			35-44	6 375 225	2 720 792	3 654 433	77.2	65.4	89.1
			45-54	5 019 416	2 404 992	2 614 424	81.3	72.3	91.7
			55-64	1 360 802	644 678	716 124	82.9	73.3	94.0
			65+	5 081 085	2 750 718	2 330 367	87.3	81.6	95.3
		Urban population	15+	7 144 396	3 213 688	3 930 708	52.6	43.1	64.1
			10-14	1 692 077	858 530	833 547	54.2	51.9	56.8
			15-19	1 040 029	500 513	539 516	40.9	36.7	45.9
			20-24	895 634	401 912	493 722	42.5	34.7	52.0
			25-34	1 524 788	646 685	878 103	49.0	38.0	62.3
			35-44	1 365 046	552 382	812 664	56.7	43.4	71.7
			45-54	1 060 829	490 636	570 193	63.2	51.7	78.3
			55-64	272 936	122 987	149 949	64.3	50.8	82.2
			65+	985 134	498 573	486 561	74.5	64.5	88.5
		Rural population	15+	27 569 428	12 838 083	14 731 345	83.2	73.9	93.4
			10-14	6 574 457	3 351 398	3 223 059	82.6	76.1	90.5
			15-19	4 053 423	1 922 963	2 130 460	75.0	64.9	87.2
			20-24	3 472 147	1 439 924	2 032 223	78.0	65.5	90.2
			25-34	5 891 275	2 618 594	3 272 681	81.5	70.4	93.3
			35-44	5 010 179	2 168 410	2 841 769	85.6	75.2	95.8
			45-54	3 958 587	1 914 356	2 044 231	88.0	80.6	96.3
			55-64	1 087 866	521 691	566 175	89.4	81.9	97.8
			65+	4 095 951	2 252 145	1 843 806	91.1	86.6	97.3
	1995	Estimates	15+	48 693 000	20 433 000	28 260 000	62.2	50.0	75.6
Philippines	1990	Total population	15+	2 349 731	1 095 697	1 254 034	6.4	6.0	6.8
			10-14	496 389	288 285	208 104	6.6	7.6	5.7
			15-19	240 911	134 871	106 040	3.6	4.1	3.2
			20-24	183 714	95 490	88 224	3.2	3.3	3.0
			25-29	189 347	92 779	96 568	3.8	3.8	3.9
			30-34	161 886	80 248	81 638	3.9	3.8	3.9
			35-39	171 934	81 821	90 113	4.9	4.6	5.2
			40-44	158 189	75 078	83 111	5.7	5.4	6.1
			45-49	184 300	86 852	97 448	8.3	7.8	8.8
			50-54	179 018	82 527	96 491	9.4	8.7	10.0
			55-59	182 769	79 483	103 286	12.7	11.3	14.1
			60-64	182 975	78 364	104 611	16.2	14.3	18.0
			65+	514 688	208 184	306 504	25.0	21.9	27.6

Country and year of census or survey Pays et année du recensement ou de l'enquête País y año del censo o de la encuesta			Age Âge Edad	Illiterate population Population analphabète Población analfabeta			Percentage of illiterates Pourcentage d'analphabètes Porcentage de analfabetos		
				Total	Male Masculine Masculina	Female Féminine Femenina	Total	Male Masculin Masculino	Female Féminin Femenino
				(1)	(2)	(3)	(4)	(5)	(6)
Philippines (cont)		Urban population	15+	500 063	211 986	288 077	2.7	2.4	3.0
			10-14	111 527	63 487	48 040	3.3	3.7	2.8
			15-19	54 153	28 195	25 958	1.7	1.8	1.5
			20-24	37 386	19 086	18 300	1.2	1.3	1.2
			25-29	35 354	16 932	18 422	1.4	1.3	1.4
			30-34	30 368	14 393	15 975	1.4	1.3	1.4
			35-39	30 937	14 052	16 885	1.7	1.5	1.8
			40-44	29 680	13 152	16 528	2.1	1.8	2.3
			45-49	34 035	14 737	19 298	3.1	2.7	3.5
			50-54	35 356	14 729	20 627	3.8	3.3	4.4
			55-59	37 988	14 734	23 254	5.5	4.5	6.5
			60-64	41 159	15 461	25 698	7.7	6.1	9.1
			65+	133 647	46 515	87 132	14.0	11.2	16.2
		Rural population	15+	1 849 668	883 711	965 957	10.3	9.6	11.0
			10-14	384 862	224 798	160 064	9.5	10.8	8.1
			15-19	186 758	106 676	80 082	5.5	6.0	4.9
			20-24	146 328	76 404	69 924	5.3	5.4	5.3
			25-29	153 993	75 847	78 146	6.6	6.4	6.8
			30-34	131 518	65 855	65 663	6.7	6.5	6.8
			35-39	140 997	67 769	73 228	8.5	8.0	9.0
			40-44	128 509	61 926	66 583	9.8	9.3	10.3
			45-49	150 265	72 115	78 150	13.2	12.5	13.8
			50-54	143 662	67 798	75 864	14.6	13.7	15.5
			55-59	144 781	64 749	80 032	19.2	17.2	21.2
			60-64	141 816	62 903	78 913	23.9	21.3	26.3
			65+	381 041	161 669	219 372	34.4	30.3	38.3
	1995	Estimates	15+	2 234 000	1 047 000	1 187 000	5.4	5.0	5.7
Qatar	1986	Total population	15+	64 891	45 253	19 638	24.3	23.2	27.5
			10-14	771	295	476	2.9	2.1	3.7
			15-19	1 258	630	628	5.6	5.1	6.1
			20-24	4 484	3 314	1 170	13.8	15.0	11.2
			25-34	20 896	15 969	4 927	19.5	19.3	19.9
			35-44	18 744	12 945	5 799	28.8	26.2	37.0
			45-54	11 549	7 740	3 809	43.4	37.9	61.6
			55-64	5 027	3 142	1 885	59.6	52.2	78.0
			65+	2 933	1 513	1 420	71.9	62.1	86.4
	1995	Estimates	15+	82 000	60 000	22 000	20.6	20.8	20.1
Saudi Arabia	1982	Total population	15+	...	...	...	48.9	28.9	69.2
	1995	Estimates	15+	3 871 000	1 740 000	2 131 000	37.2	28.5	49.8
Singapore	1990	Total population	15+	226 677	51 307	175 370	10.9	4.9	17.0
			10-14	1 028	551	477	0.5	0.5	0.5
			15-19	1 458	841	617	0.7	0.7	0.6
			20-24	3 230	1 825	1 405	1.4	1.5	1.2
			25-29	5 322	2 577	2 745	1.9	1.8	2.0
			30-34	8 197	3 380	4 817	2.8	2.3	3.4
			35-39	10 522	3 151	7 371	4.2	2.4	5.9
			40-44	14 589	3 459	11 130	7.2	3.3	11.1
			45-49	18 035	3 426	14 609	14.1	5.3	23.1
			50-54	23 949	4 428	19 521	20.4	7.5	33.4
			55-59	30 881	6 245	24 636	30.9	12.6	49.2
			60-64	30 106	6 168	23 938	36.4	15.1	57.2
			65+	80 388	15 807	64 581	49.0	21.4	71.5
	1995	Estimates	15+	196 000	46 000	150 000	8.9	4.1	13.7
Sri Lanka	1981	Total population	15+	1 271 984	424 424	847 560	13.2	8.7	18.0
			10-14	171 994	86 378	85 616	10.2	10.0	10.4
			15-19	153 889	74 994	78 895	9.6	9.2	10.0
			20-24	126 423	53 177	73 246	8.3	6.9	9.6
			25-34	199 104	69 163	129 941	8.3	5.7	10.9
			35-44	201 214	56 206	145 008	13.1	7.2	19.2
			45-54	222 710	60 603	162 107	19.4	10.2	29.2
			55-64	175 347	50 048	125 299	23.0	12.3	35.1
			65+	193 297	60 233	133 064	30.1	17.8	44.0
		Urban population	15+	143 572	51 543	92 029	6.6	4.4	8.9
			10-14	22 997	11 278	11 719	6.6	6.3	6.9
			15-19	18 778	9 220	9 558	5.2	4.8	5.6
			20-24	14 380	6 419	7 961	4.0	3.3	4.8
			25-34	21 074	8 246	12 828	3.8	2.8	4.9
			35-44	20 948	6 847	14 101	6.0	3.7	8.7
			45-54	23 728	7 305	16 423	9.3	5.4	13.7
			55-64	20 163	6 128	14 035	11.8	6.8	17.4
			65+	24 501	7 378	17 123	17.6	10.7	24.3

Country and year of census or survey Pays et année du recensement ou de l'enquête País y año del censo o de la encuesta			Age Âge Edad	Illiterate population Population analphabète Población analfabeta			Percentage of illiterates Pourcentage d'analphabètes Porcentage de analfabetos		
				Total	Male Masculine Masculina	Female Féminine Femenina	Total	Male Masculin Masculino	Female Féminin Femenino
				(1)	(2)	(3)	(4)	(5)	(6)
Sri Lanka (cont)		Rural population	15+	1 128 412	372 881	755 531	15.2	10.0	20.5
			10-14	148 997	75 100	73 897	11.1	11.0	11.3
			15-19	135 111	65 774	69 337	10.9	10.6	11.2
			20-24	112 043	46 758	65 285	9.6	8.1	11.0
			25-34	178 030	60 917	117 113	9.7	6.7	12.6
			35-44	180 266	49 359	130 907	15.2	8.3	22.1
			45-54	198 982	53 298	145 684	22.3	11.7	33.5
			55-64	155 184	43 920	111 264	26.2	13.9	40.3
			65+	168 796	52 855	115 941	33.6	19.6	50.0
	1995	Estimates	15+	1 242 000	413 000	829 000	9.8	6.6	12.8
Syrian Arab Republic‡	1981	Total population	15+	1 982 265	601 390	1 380 875	44.4	26.4	63.0
			10-14	179 000	37 437	141 563	15.3	6.2	25.0
			15-19	213 639	48 663	164 976	21.8	9.6	34.8
			20-24	224 621	48 771	175 850	31.0	13.3	49.1
			25-34	396 959	95 037	301 922	40.9	19.4	62.8
			35-44	338 377	93 641	244 736	52.4	29.3	74.9
			45-54	352 011	122 940	229 071	64.3	43.9	85.7
			55-64	229 011	90 157	138 854	70.5	52.9	90.0
			65+	227 647	102 181	125 466	82.1	70.9	94.2
	1995	Estimates	15+	2 259 000	556 000	1 703 000	29.2	14.3	44.2
Tajikistan	1989	Total population	15+	66 973	17 189	49 784	2.3	1.2	3.4
			10-14	1 389	666	723	0.2	0.2	0.2
			15-19	1 614	731	883	0.3	0.3	0.3
			20-24	1 319	562	557	0.3	0.2	0.3
			25-34	2 445	911	1 534	0.3	0.2	0.4
			35-44	1 592	420	1 172	0.4	0.2	0.6
			45-54	6 702	1 407	5 295	2.1	0.9	3.4
			55-64	15 076	3 761	11 315	5.8	3.0	8.2
			65+	38 225	9 397	28 828	19.9	12.7	24.5
		Urban population	15+	21 332	4 424	16 908	2.0	0.9	3.1
			10-14	331	176	155	0.2	0.2	0.2
			15-19	325	154	171	0.2	0.2	0.2
			20-24	302	127	175	0.2	0.2	0.2
			25-29	396	154	242	0.3	0.2	0.3
			30-34	259	75	184	0.2	0.1	0.3
			35-39	215	56	159	0.2	0.1	0.3
			40-44	202	39	163	0.3	0.1	0.5
			45-49	493	89	404	0.8	0.3	1.3
			50-54	1 687	337	1 350	2.5	1.0	3.8
			55-59	2 349	518	1 831	4.3	2.1	6.2
			60-64	2 110	492	1 618	4.3	2.5	5.6
			65+	12 994	2 383	10 611	17.1	9.6	20.7
		Rural population	15+	45 641	12 765	32 876	2.5	1.4	3.5
			10-14	1 058	490	568	0.3	0.2	0.3
			15-19	1 289	577	712	0.4	0.3	0.4
			20-24	1 017	435	582	0.3	0.3	0.4
			25-29	1 077	456	621	0.4	0.3	0.4
			30-34	713	226	487	0.4	0.2	0.5
			35-39	624	192	432	0.5	0.3	0.6
			40-44	551	133	418	0.7	0.3	1.1
			45-49	1 023	230	793	1.2	0.5	2.0
			50-54	3 499	751	2 748	3.6	1.5	5.8
			55-59	5 317	1 284	4 033	6.1	3.0	9.1
			60-64	5 300	1 467	3 833	7.5	4.1	11.0
			65+	25 231	7 014	18 217	21.8	14.2	27.4
	1995	Estimates	15+	11 000	4 000	7 000	0.3	0.2	0.4
Thailand	1990	Total population	15+	2 572 127	833 682	1 738 445	6.7	4.4	8.8
			10-14	76 116	38 337	37 779	1.3	1.3	1.3
			15-19	82 471	36 059	46 412	1.4	1.3	1.6
			20-24	115 102	44 906	70 196	2.1	1.6	2.5
			25-29	135 216	50 564	84 652	2.6	2.0	3.2
			30-34	148 767	53 907	94 860	3.2	2.4	4.0
			35-39	151 299	52 502	98 797	3.9	2.8	5.0
			40-44	153 038	50 939	102 099	5.1	3.4	6.7
			45-49	171 862	55 536	116 326	6.8	4.5	9.0
			50-54	228 886	73 219	155 667	10.0	6.6	13.2
			55-59	224 893	73 654	151 239	11.8	8.0	15.4
			60-64	249 712	77 140	172 572	16.9	10.8	22.7
			65+	910 881	265 256	645 625	35.8	23.2	46.1

Country and year of census or survey Pays et année du recensement ou de l'enquête País y año del censo o de la encuesta			Age Âge Edad	Illiterate population Population analphabète Población analfabeta			Percentage of illiterates Pourcentage d'analphabètes Porcentage de analfabetos		
				Total	Male Masculine Masculina	Female Féminine Femenina	Total	Male Masculin Masculino	Female Féminin Femenino
				(1)	(2)	(3)	(4)	(5)	(6)
Thailand (cont)		Urban population	15+	258 292	72 530	185 762	3.3	1.9	4.5
			10-14	5 206	2 559	2 647	0.6	0.6	0.6
			15-19	6 859	2 943	3 916	0.6	0.6	0.7
			20-24	9 040	3 492	5 548	0.7	0.6	0.9
			25-29	11 909	4 100	7 809	1.0	0.7	1.3
			30-34	12 796	4 157	8 639	1.2	0.8	1.6
			35-39	12 830	3 713	9 117	1.6	0.9	2.2
			40-44	13 494	3 780	9 714	2.2	1.3	3.1
			45-49	14 740	3 748	10 992	3.2	1.7	4.6
			50-54	24 420	6 280	18 140	6.0	3.2	8.6
			55-59	24 027	6 753	17 274	7.8	4.6	10.7
			60-64	26 418	7 959	18 459	10.9	7.0	14.2
			65+	101 759	25 605	76 154	24.8	14.6	32.3
		Rural population	15+	2 313 835	761 152	1 552 683	7.5	5.0	9.9
			10-14	70 910	35 778	35 132	1.4	1.4	1.4
			15-19	75 612	33 116	42 496	1.7	1.4	1.9
			20-24	106 062	41 414	64 648	2.5	1.9	3.0
			25-29	123 307	46 464	76 843	3.1	2.4	3.8
			30-34	135 971	49 750	86 221	3.8	2.8	4.7
			35-39	138 469	48 789	89 680	4.6	3.2	5.8
			40-44	139 544	47 159	92 385	5.8	4.0	7.6
			45-49	157 122	51 788	105 334	7.6	5.1	10.0
			50-54	204 466	66 939	137 527	10.9	7.3	14.3
			55-59	200 866	66 901	133 965	12.6	8.7	16.3
			60-64	223 294	69 181	154 113	18.1	11.5	24.5
			65+	809 122	239 651	569 471	37.9	24.7	48.9
	1995	Estimates	15+	2 613 000	829 000	1 784 000	6.2	4.0	8.4
Turkey	1990	Total population	15+	7 615 973	1 870 245	5 745 728	20.8	10.1	31.5
			10-14	453 146	160 146	293 000	6.6	4.5	8.8
			15-19	411 135	105 147	305 988	6.6	3.3	10.0
			20-24	432 188	91 877	340 311	8.5	3.6	13.5
			25-29	473 752	82 110	391 642	9.8	3.4	16.5
			30-34	496 471	81 820	414 651	12.1	3.9	20.8
			35-39	568 710	90 883	477 827	16.3	5.1	28.0
			40-44	609 981	104 987	504 994	21.9	7.4	36.9
			45-49	628 208	136 388	491 820	28.5	12.3	45.1
			50-54	754 764	181 642	573 122	37.4	18.5	55.2
			55-59	861 644	259 661	601 983	44.4	26.1	63.6
			60-64	842 071	246 035	596 036	52.1	32.0	70.4
			65+	1 537 049	489 695	1 047 354	63.6	44.9	79.0
		Urban population	15+	3 315 800	745 363	2 570 437	14.9	6.5	23.9
			10-14	160 470	60 167	100 303	4.0	2.9	5.4
			15-19	160 901	47 233	113 668	4.4	2.4	6.7
			20-24	195 051	52 819	142 232	5.9	3.0	9.3
			25-29	221 208	39 577	181 631	7.1	2.5	12.0
			30-34	236 856	39 638	197 218	8.8	2.8	15.3
			35-39	276 671	41 954	234 717	12.2	3.5	21.5
			40-44	283 767	45 034	238 733	16.2	4.9	28.6
			45-49	281 933	55 342	226 591	21.6	8.2	36.2
			50-54	323 554	70 693	252 861	29.1	12.8	45.1
			55-59	356 946	95 562	261 384	35.4	18.5	53.1
			60-64	344 919	87 847	257 072	41.9	22.6	59.1
			65+	633 994	169 664	464 330	53.1	32.7	68.8
		Rural population	15+	4 300 173	1 124 882	3 175 291	29.8	16.2	42.3
			10-14	292 676	99 979	192 697	10.0	6.8	13.2
			15-19	250 234	57 914	192 320	9.9	4.9	14.3
			20-24	237 137	39 058	198 079	13.1	4.8	20.0
			25-29	252 544	42 533	210 011	14.8	5.0	24.3
			30-34	259 615	42 182	217 433	18.4	6.0	30.9
			35-39	292 039	48 929	243 110	24.0	8.1	39.6
			40-44	326 214	59 953	266 261	31.6	12.0	49.8
			45-49	346 275	81 046	265 229	38.6	18.7	57.1
			50-54	431 210	110 949	320 261	47.5	25.8	67.0
			55-59	504 698	164 099	340 599	54.2	34.4	74.9
			60-64	497 152	158 188	338 964	62.8	41.6	82.4
			65+	903 055	320 031	583 024	73.8	55.9	89.6
	1995	Estimates	15+	7 232 000	1 737 000	5 495 000	17.7	8.3	27.6
Turkmenistan	1989	Total population	15+	...	...	...	2.3	1.2	3.4
			9-49	...	...	...	0.3	0.2	0.3
		Urban population	15+	...	...	...	1.8	0.8	2.8
			9-49	...	...	...	0.2	0.2	0.3
		Rural population	15+	...	...	...	2.8	1.5	3.9
			9-49	...	...	...	0.3	0.2	0.4
	1995	Estimates	15+	8 000	3 000	5 000	0.3	0.2	0.4

Country and year of census or survey Pays et année du recensement ou de l'enquête País y año del censo o de la encuesta			Age Âge Edad	Illiterate population Population analphabète Población analfabeta			Percentage of illiterates Pourcentage d'analphabètes Porcentage de analfabetos		
				Total	Male Masculine Masculina	Female Féminine Femenina	Total	Male Masculin Masculino	Female Féminin Femenino
				(1)	(2)	(3)	(4)	(5)	(6)
United Arab Emirates	1985	Total population	15+	269 983	185 397	84 586	28.8	27.7	31.3
			10-14	3 663	1 483	2 180	3.8	2.9	4.7
			15-19	6 778	2 920	3 858	9.2	7.5	11.2
			20-24	27 646	18 829	8 817	22.5	24.9	18.6
			25-29	53 966	40 347	13 619	26.6	27.9	23.4
			30-34	46 387	34 979	11 408	25.0	24.8	25.5
			35-39	39 994	28 647	11 347	27.9	25.6	36.1
			40-44	27 980	19 773	8 207	33.5	29.8	48.1
			45-49	22 130	14 819	7 311	40.3	34.5	61.6
			50-54	15 174	9 453	5 721	51.0	43.1	73.2
			55-59	8 888	5 038	3 850	57.3	47.7	77.7
			60-64	6 882	3 485	3 397	71.5	62.9	83.2
			65+	14 158	7 107	7 051	82.6	77.0	89.2
	1995	Estimates	15+	272 000	192 000	80 000	20.8	21.1	20.2
Uzbekistan	1989	Total population	15+	...	...	...	2.8	1.5	4.0
			9-49	...	...	...	0.3	0.3	0.4
		Urban population	15+	...	...	...	2.4	1.2	3.5
			9-49	...	...	...	0.3	0.3	0.3
		Rural population	15+	...	...	...	3.2	1.8	4.5
			9-49	...	...	...	0.3	0.3	0.4
	1995	Estimates	15+	45 000	16 000	29 000	0.3	0.2	0.4
Viet Nam	1989	Total population	15+	4 871 866	1 287 769	3 584 097	12.4	7.0	17.2
			10-14	522 432	252 566	269 866	6.9	6.5	7.4
			15-19	453 740	220 420	233 320	6.7	6.5	6.8
			20-24	349 425	149 744	199 681	5.8	5.2	6.4
			25-29	307 867	114 976	192 891	5.4	4.3	6.5
			30-34	262 588	87 778	174 810	5.5	3.9	7.1
			35-44	420 866	110 428	310 438	7.6	4.3	10.5
			45-54	559 936	104 954	454 982	14.3	6.0	21.1
			55-59	431 010	82 321	348 689	21.9	8.9	33.4
			60+	2 086 434	417 148	1 669 286	45.0	21.6	61.8
	1995	Estimates	15+	2 916 000	785 000	2 131 000	6.3	3.5	8.8
Europe									
Belarus	1989	Total population	15+	165 406	21 917	143 489	2.1	0.6	3.4
			10-14	1 731	1 005	726	0.2	0.3	0.2
			15-19	1 766	1 030	736	0.2	0.3	0.2
			20-24	1 536	862	674	0.2	0.2	0.2
			25-29	1 446	758	688	0.2	0.2	0.2
			30-34	1 308	709	599	0.2	0.2	0.1
			35-39	1 014	501	513	0.1	0.1	0.1
			40-44	831	408	423	0.2	0.2	0.2
			45-49	1 176	515	661	0.2	0.2	0.2
			50-54	3 849	1 202	2 647	0.6	0.4	0.7
			55-59	7 126	1 677	5 449	1.2	0.6	1.6
			60-64	9 230	1 704	7 526	1.6	0.7	2.1
			65+	136 124	12 551	123 573	12.8	3.9	16.7
		Urban population	15+	44 702	4 618	40 084	0.9	0.2	1.5
			10-14	741	423	318	0.1	0.2	0.1
			15-19	674	387	287	0.1	0.2	0.1
			20-24	431	242	189	0.1	0.1	0.1
			25-29	394	194	200	0.1	0.1	0.1
			30-34	296	154	142	0.0	0.0	0.0
			35-39	203	99	104	0.0	0.0	0.0
			40-44	175	74	101	0.0	0.0	0.0
			45-49	236	80	156	0.1	0.0	0.1
			50-54	794	234	560	0.2	0.1	0.3
			55-59	1 466	345	1 121	0.5	0.3	0.7
			60-64	1 867	311	1 556	0.7	0.3	0.9
			65+	38 166	2 498	35 668	8.7	1.8	11.7
		Rural population	15+	120 704	17 299	103 405	4.3	1.4	6.7
			10-14	990	582	408	0.4	0.5	0.4
			15-19	1 092	643	449	0.6	0.6	0.5
			20-24	1 105	620	485	0.6	0.6	0.6
			25-29	1 052	564	488	0.5	0.5	0.5
			30-34	1 012	555	457	0.5	0.5	0.5
			35-39	811	402	409	0.5	0.4	0.5
			40-44	656	334	322	0.5	0.5	0.5
			45-49	940	435	505	0.5	0.5	0.5
			50-54	3 055	968	2 087	1.1	0.8	1.4
			55-59	5 660	1 332	4 328	1.8	1.0	2.5
			60-64	7 363	1 393	5 970	2.5	1.2	3.3
			65+	97 958	10 053	87 905	15.8	5.5	20.1
	1995	Estimates	15+	38 000	10 000	28 000	0.5	0.3	0.6

Country and year of census or survey Pays et année du recensement ou de l'enquête País y año del censo o de la encuesta			Age Âge Edad	Illiterate population Population analphabète Población analfabeta			Percentage of illiterates Pourcentage d'analphabètes Porcentaje de analfabetos		
				Total	Male Masculine Masculina	Female Féminine Femenina	Total	Male Masculin Masculino	Female Féminin Femenino
				(1)	(2)	(3)	(4)	(5)	(6)
Bulgaria	1992	Total population	15+	147 389	44 123	103 266	2.1	1.3	2.9
			10-14	5 566	2 765	2 801	0.9	0.9	1.0
			15-19	5 305	2 445	2 860	0.8	0.8	0.9
			20-24	4 502	2 016	2 486	0.8	0.7	0.9
			25-29	3 885	1 746	2 139	0.7	0.6	0.8
			30-34	4 139	1 809	2 330	0.7	0.6	0.8
			35-39	3 897	1 613	2 284	0.7	0.5	0.8
			40-44	4 895	1 782	3 113	0.8	0.6	1.0
			45-49	6 446	2 114	4 332	1.1	0.8	1.5
			50-54	8 809	2 592	6 217	1.8	1.1	2.5
			55-59	14 654	4 129	10 525	2.7	1.6	3.8
			60-64	17 705	5 355	12 350	3.4	2.1	4.5
			65+	73 152	18 522	54 630	6.0	3.5	8.0
	1995	Estimates	15+	125 000	39 000	86 000	1.7	1.1	2.3
Croatia	1991	Total population	15+	126 624	22 915	103 709	3.3	1.2	5.1
			14-10	814	428	386	0.2	0.3	0.2
			15-19	1 099	518	581	0.3	0.3	0.4
			20-24	1 255	582	673	0.4	0.4	0.4
			25-34	3 253	1 436	1 817	0.5	0.4	0.5
			35-44	4 211	1 593	2 618	0.6	0.4	0.7
			45-54	10 067	2 106	7 961	1.8	0.8	2.8
			55-64	29 097	4 700	24 397	4.9	1.7	7.8
			65+	77 642	11 980	65 662	12.4	5.2	16.6
		Urban population	15+	30 414	4 548	25 866	1.5	0.5	2.3
			14-10	352	173	179	0.2	0.2	0.2
			15-19	414	175	239	0.2	0.2	0.3
			20-24	433	176	257	0.3	0.2	0.3
			25-34	1 018	377	641	0.3	0.2	0.3
			35-44	1 203	409	794	0.3	0.2	0.4
			45-54	2 389	460	1 929	0.7	0.3	1.2
			55-64	6 462	845	5 617	2.2	0.6	3.6
			65+	18 495	2 106	16 389	6.3	1.9	9.0
		Rural population	15+	96 210	18 367	77 843	5.4	2.1	8.5
			14-10	462	255	207	0.3	0.4	0.3
			15-19	685	343	342	0.5	0.5	0.5
			20-24	822	406	416	0.6	0.5	0.6
			25-34	2 235	1 059	1 176	0.7	0.6	0.8
			35-44	3 008	1 184	1 824	1.0	0.7	1.4
			45-54	7 678	1 646	6 032	3.1	1.3	5.0
			55-64	22 635	3 855	18 780	7.6	2.8	11.8
			65+	59 147	9 874	49 273	17.6	8.0	23.2
	1995	Estimates	15+	87 000	32 000	55 000	2.4	1.8	2.9
Estonia	1989	Total population	15+	3 329	687	2 642	0.3	0.1	0.4
			10-14	164	97	67	0.1	0.2	0.1
			15-19	152	107	45	0.1	0.2	0.1
			20-24	133	79	54	0.1	0.1	0.1
			25-34	141	78	63	0.1	0.1	0.1
			35-44	113	55	58	0.1	0.1	0.1
			45-54	150	80	70	0.1	0.1	0.1
			55-64	375	146	229	0.2	0.2	0.2
			65+	2 265	142	2 123	1.3	0.3	1.7
	1995	Estimates	15+	3 000	1 000	1 000	0.2	0.2	0.2
Greece	1991	Total population	15+	389 067	90 049	299 018	4.8	2.3	7.0
			10-14	2 872	718	2 154	0.4	0.2	0.6
			15-19	3 950	2 513	1 437	0.5	0.7	0.4
			20-24	3 878	2 298	1 580	0.6	0.7	0.5
			25-29	4 237	1 867	2 370	0.7	0.6	0.7
			30-34	5 888	3 231	2 657	0.9	1.0	0.8
			35-39	5 673	2 442	3 231	0.9	0.8	0.9
			40-44	7 037	2 657	4 380	1.0	0.8	1.3
			45-49	8 617	2 801	5 816	1.4	0.9	1.9
			50-54	21 184	4 524	16 660	3.2	1.4	4.8
			55-59	43 158	12 136	31 022	6.4	3.6	9.1
			60-64	39 926	8 976	30 950	6.0	2.8	8.9
			65+	245 519	46 604	198 915	16.3	6.9	24.1
		Urban population	15+	160 639	37 197	123 442	3.1	1.5	4.5
			10-14	1 652	431	1 221	0.3	0.2	0.5
			15-19	2 513	1 652	861	0.5	0.7	0.3
			20-24	2 442	1 508	934	0.5	0.7	0.4
			25-29	2 944	1 364	1 580	0.7	0.6	0.7
			30-34	3 806	2 082	1 724	0.8	0.9	0.7
			35-39	3 016	1 221	1 795	0.7	0.6	0.8
			40-44	4 021	1 293	2 728	0.9	0.6	1.1
			45-49	3 591	1 436	2 155	0.9	0.7	1.1
			50-54	8 617	1 580	7 037	2.1	0.8	3.2
			55-59	19 245	5 242	14 003	4.7	2.5	7.0
			60-64	17 450	3 734	13 716	4.5	2.0	6.7
			65+	92 994	16 085	76 909	11.5	4.5	16.9

Country and year of census or survey Pays et année du recensement ou de l'enquête País y año del censo o de la encuesta			Age Âge Edad	Illiterate population Population analphabète Población analfabeta			Percentage of illiterates Pourcentage d'analphabètes Porcentaje de analfabetos		
				Total	Male Masculine Masculina	Female Féminine Femenina	Total	Male Masculin Masculino	Female Féminin Femenino
				(1)	(2)	(3)	(4)	(5)	(6)
Greece (cont)		Rural population	15+	181 537	41 363	140 174	8.9	4.1	13.6
			10-14	862	287	575	0.5	0.3	0.7
			15-19	1 077	574	503	0.6	0.7	0.6
			20-24	1 293	718	575	1.1	1.1	1.1
			25-29	1 149	503	646	1.0	0.8	1.3
			30-34	1 652	862	790	1.4	1.5	1.4
			35-39	1 795	790	1 005	1.4	1.3	1.5
			40-44	2 011	934	1 077	1.4	1.3	1.5
			45-49	3 447	1 005	2 442	2.6	1.5	3.8
			50-54	9 551	2 298	7 253	5.6	2.8	8.2
			55-59	17 953	4 955	12 998	9.1	5.3	12.6
			60-64	17 378	3 950	13 428	8.5	3.9	13.1
			65+	124 231	24 774	99 457	23.0	9.9	34.4
		Semi-urban pop.	15+	46 891	11 489	35 402	5.4	2.7	8.0
			10-14	358	-	358	0.4	-	0.8
			15-19	360	287	73	0.4	0.7	0.2
			20-24	143	72	71	0.3	0.3	0.2
			25-29	144	-	144	0.2	-	0.5
			30-34	430	287	143	0.6	0.9	0.4
			35-39	862	431	431	1.2	1.2	1.2
			40-44	1 005	430	575	1.3	1.1	1.5
			45-49	1 579	360	1 219	2.3	1.0	3.6
			50-54	3 016	646	2 370	4.0	1.7	6.3
			55-59	5 960	1 939	4 021	8.0	5.0	11.2
			60-64	5 098	1 292	3 806	6.9	3.6	10.0
			65+	28 294	5 745	22 549	18.5	7.9	28.3
	1995	Estimates	15+	283 000	73 000	210 000	3.3	1.7	4.7
Hungary	1980	Total population	15+	95 542	27 756	67 786	1.1	0.7	1.5
			15-19	4 510	2 204	2 306	0.7	0.7	0.7
			20-24	4 699	2 133	2 566	0.6	0.5	0.6
			25-34	9 162	3 603	5 559	0.6	0.4	0.7
			35-44	12 387	4 206	8 181	0.9	0.6	1.2
			45-54	14 163	4 446	9 717	1.0	0.7	1.4
			55-64	9 976	2 791	7 185	0.9	0.6	1.2
			65+	40 645	8 373	32 272	2.8	1.4	3.7
	1995	Estimates	15+	69 000	26 000	43 000	0.8	0.7	1.0
Italy	1981	Total population	15+	1 572 556	539 781	1 032 775	3.5	2.5	4.5
			11-14	11 073	6 206	4 867	0.3	0.3	0.3
			15-19	14 797	6 715	8 082	0.3	0.3	0.4
			20-24	16 702	6 845	9 857	0.4	0.3	0.5
			25-44	151 731	55 259	96 472	1.0	0.7	1.3
			45-54	284 741	103 065	181 676	4.0	3.0	5.0
			55+	297 696	105 308	192 388	5.1	3.9	6.2
			65+	806 889	262 589	544 300	10.8	8.6	12.3
	1995	Estimates	15+	932 000	337 000	595 000	1.9	1.4	2.4
Latvia	1989	Total population	15+	11 476	2 327	9 149	0.5	0.2	0.8
			10-14	544	336	208	0.3	0.4	0.2
			15-19	445	272	173	0.2	0.3	0.2
			20-24	352	204	148	0.2	0.2	0.2
			25-34	552	296	256	0.1	0.1	0.1
			35-44	428	212	216	0.1	0.1	0.1
			45-54	600	278	322	0.2	0.2	0.2
			55-64	888	275	613	0.3	0.2	0.3
			65+	8 211	790	7 421	2.6	0.8	3.4
		Urban population	15+	6 358	971	5 387	0.4	0.1	0.7
			10-14	157	97	60	0.1	0.2	0.1
			15-19	179	116	63	0.1	0.2	0.1
			20-24	144	86	58	0.1	0.1	0.1
			25-34	208	116	92	0.1	0.1	0.1
			35-44	164	72	92	0.1	0.1	0.1
			45-54	236	97	139	0.1	0.1	0.1
			55-64	407	101	306	0.2	0.1	0.2
			65+	5 020	383	4 637	2.5	0.6	3.3
		Rural population	15+	5 118	1 356	3 762	0.9	0.5	1.2
			10-14	387	239	148	0.7	0.9	0.6
			15-19	266	156	110	0.5	0.6	0.5
			20-24	208	118	90	0.4	0.5	0.4
			25-34	344	180	164	0.3	0.3	0.3
			35-44	264	140	124	0.3	0.3	0.3
			45-54	364	181	183	0.4	0.4	0.4
			55-64	481	174	307	0.5	0.5	0.6
			65+	3 191	407	2 784	2.9	1.2	3.7
	1995	Estimates	15+	5 000	2 000	3 000	0.3	0.2	0.3
Liechtenstein	1981	Total population	10+	68	33	35	*0.3	*0.3	*0.3

Country and year of census or survey Pays et année du recensement ou de l'enquête País y año del censo o de la encuesta			Age Âge Edad	Illiterate population Population analphabète Población analfabeta			Percentage of illiterates Pourcentage d'analphabètes Porcentage de analfabetos		
				Total	Male Masculine Masculina	Female Féminine Femenina	Total	Male Masculin Masculino	Female Féminin Femenino
				(1)	(2)	(3)	(4)	(5)	(6)
Lithuania	1989	Total population	15+	44 308	10 436	33 872	1.6	0.8	2.2
			9-14	1 221	705	516	0.4	0.4	0.3
			15-19	1 021	590	431	0.4	0.4	0.3
			20-24	807	447	360	0.3	0.3	0.3
			25-34	1 296	724	572	0.2	0.2	0.2
			35-44	871	424	447	0.2	0.2	0.2
			45-54	2 045	856	1 189	0.5	0.4	0.5
			55-65	4 712	1 547	3 165	1.2	0.9	1.4
			65+	33 556	5 848	27 708	8.6	4.3	10.8
	1995	Estimates	15+	16 000	5 000	11 000	0.5	0.4	0.7
Malta	1985	Total population	20+	33 740	16 802	16 938	14.3	14.8	13.9
			10-19	534	391	143	1.1	1.5	0.6
			20-24	838	626	212	3.1	4.5	1.6
			25-34	3 682	2 474	1 208	6.6	8.8	4.4
			35-44	4 548	2 779	1 769	8.9	11.0	6.8
			45-54	5 478	2 642	2 836	15.0	15.5	14.6
			55-64	7 469	3 244	4 225	23.9	22.4	25.3
			65+	11 725	5 037	6 688	35.0	34.7	35.3
	1995	Estimates	15+	25 000	13 000	12 000	8.7	9.4	8.1
Moldova	1989	Total population	15+	113 193	20 078	93 115	3.6	1.4	5.6
			10-14	950	510	440	0.3	0.3	0.2
			15-19	882	452	430	0.3	0.3	0.3
			20-24	810	422	388	0.3	0.3	0.3
			25-29	910	455	455	0.2	0.3	0.3
			30-34	852	410	442	0.2	0.2	0.2
			35-39	735	347	388	0.2	0.2	0.2
			40-44	466	189	277	0.2	0.2	0.3
			45-49	721	233	488	0.3	0.2	0.4
			50-54	3 373	688	2 685	1.4	0.6	2.1
			55-59	7 622	1 127	6 495	3.6	1.2	5.6
			60-64	16 439	2 469	13 970	8.5	3.1	12.2
			65+	80 383	13 286	67 097	22.8	10.2	30.2
		Urban population	15+	...	...	...	1.8	0.6	2.8
		Rural population	15+	...	...	...	5.3	2.1	8.0
	1995	Estimates	15+	34 000	25 000	9 000	1.1	1.6	0.5
Portugal	1981	Total population	15+	1 506 206	524 461	981 745	20.6	15.2	25.4
			10-14	14 268	8 243	6 025	1.7	1.9	1.4
			15-19	16 704	9 895	6 809	1.9	2.3	1.6
			20-24	16 812	9 245	7 567	2.2	2.4	2.0
			25-34	39 323	17 479	21 844	3.0	2.7	3.3
			35-44	144 913	48 854	96 059	12.7	9.0	16.1
			45-54	318 764	111 132	207 632	27.5	20.3	34.0
			55-64	366 996	128 626	238 370	38.1	28.7	46.2
			65+	602 694	199 230	403 464	53.6	43.6	60.3
	1995	Estimates	15+	827 000	283 000	544 000	10.4	7.5	13.0
Romania	1992	Total population	15+	577 376	125 372	452 004	3.3	1.5	5.0
			10-14	13 893	6 952	6 941	1.2	1.2	1.2
			15-19	19 721	9 483	10 238	1.0	1.0	1.1
			20-24	15 509	7 001	8 508	0.8	0.7	0.8
			25-29	10 908	4 642	6 266	0.9	0.7	1.0
			30-34	13 390	5 466	7 924	0.9	0.7	1.0
			35-39	13 649	5 474	8 175	0.8	0.6	1.0
			40-44	13 199	4 735	8 464	0.9	0.6	1.1
			45-49	14 529	4 647	9 882	1.2	0.8	1.7
			50-54	35 738	8 887	26 851	2.7	1.4	3.9
			55-59	67 398	12 572	54 826	4.9	1.9	7.7
			60-64	68 194	12 285	55 909	5.5	2.1	8.6
			65+	305 141	50 180	254 961	12.2	4.8	17.4
	1995	Estimates	15+	387 000	97 000	290 000	2.1	1.1	3.1
Russian Federation	1989	Total population	15+	2 274 572	279 490	1 995 082	2.0	0.5	3.2
			10-14	34 485	20 137	14 348	0.3	0.4	0.3
			15-19	30 216	17 241	12 975	0.3	0.3	0.3
			20-24	25 079	13 886	11 193	0.3	0.3	0.2
			25-29	28 666	15 443	13 223	0.2	0.2	0.2
			30-34	23 841	12 653	11 188	0.2	0.2	0.2
			35-39	20 204	10 122	10 082	0.2	0.2	0.2
			40-44	13 585	6 112	7 473	0.2	0.2	0.2
			45-49	21 788	8 599	13 189	0.3	0.2	0.3
			50-54	62 280	19 172	43 108	0.6	0.4	0.8
			55-59	100 179	27 863	72 316	1.2	0.7	1.5
			60-64	108 270	22 965	85 305	1.3	0.7	1.7
			65+	1 840 464	125 434	1 715 030	13.0	3.4	16.4
	1995	Estimates	15+	543 000	146 000	397 000	0.5	0.3	0.6

Country and year of census or survey Pays et année du recensement ou de l'enquête País y año del censo o de la encuesta			Age Âge Edad	Illiterate population Population analphabète Población analfabeta			Percentage of illiterates Pourcentage d'analphabètes Porcentaje de analfabetos		
				Total	Male Masculine Masculina	Female Féminine Femenina	Total	Male Masculin Masculino	Female Féminin Femenino
				(1)	(2)	(3)	(4)	(5)	(6)
Slovenia	1991	Total population	15+	7 422	2 963	4 459	0.5	0.4	0.5
			15-19	302	162	140	0.2	0.2	0.2
			20-24	397	222	175	0.3	0.3	0.2
			25-29	415	187	228	0.3	0.2	0.3
			30-34	427	202	225	0.3	0.3	0.3
			35-39	465	210	255	0.3	0.3	0.3
			40-44	513	237	276	0.4	0.3	0.4
			45-49	431	195	236	0.4	0.3	0.4
			50-54	623	254	369	0.5	0.4	0.6
			55-59	797	313	484	0.7	0.6	0.8
			60-64	706	290	416	0.7	0.6	0.7
			65-69	550	187	363	0.7	0.6	0.7
			70-74	330	108	222	0.8	0.7	0.8
			75+	1 466	396	1 070	1.6	1.4	1.8
		Urban population	15+	2 123	695	1 428	0.3	0.2	0.3
			10-14	46	28	18	0.1	0.1	0.0
			15-19	116	56	60	0.2	0.2	0.2
			20-24	155	80	75	0.2	0.2	0.2
			25-29	148	62	86	0.2	0.2	0.2
			30-34	156	60	96	0.2	0.2	0.2
			35-39	147	67	80	0.2	0.2	0.2
			40-44	138	49	89	0.2	0.1	0.2
			45-49	127	40	87	0.2	0.1	0.3
			50-54	171	47	124	0.3	0.2	0.4
			55-59	207	57	150	0.4	0.2	0.5
			60-64	179	56	123	0.4	0.3	0.4
			65-69	132	29	103	0.3	0.2	0.4
			70-74	95	14	81	0.5	0.2	0.6
			75+	352	78	274	0.9	0.7	1.1
		Rural population	15+	5 299	2 268	3 031	0.7	0.6	0.8
			10-14	61	34	27	0.1	0.1	0.1
			15-19	186	106	80	0.3	0.3	0.2
			20-24	242	142	100	0.3	0.4	0.3
			25-29	267	125	142	0.4	0.3	0.4
			30-34	271	142	129	0.4	0.4	0.4
			35-39	318	143	175	0.4	0.4	0.5
			40-44	375	188	187	0.6	0.5	0.6
			45-49	304	155	149	0.6	0.5	0.6
			50-54	452	207	245	0.8	0.7	0.9
			55-59	590	256	334	1.0	1.0	1.1
			60-64	527	234	293	1.0	1.0	1.0
			65-69	418	158	260	1.0	1.0	1.0
			70-74	235	94	141	1.0	1.2	0.9
			75+	1 114	318	796	2.1	1.9	2.3
Spain	1991	Total population	15+	1 081 742	293 343	788 399	3.5	1.9	4.9
			10-14	9 475	5 078	4 397	0.3	0.3	0.3
			15-19	13 052	6 988	6 064	0.4	0.4	0.4
			20-24	15 551	8 082	7 469	0.5	0.5	0.5
			25-29	17 494	8 692	8 802	0.6	0.6	0.6
			30-34	20 598	9 298	11 300	0.7	0.7	0.8
			35-44	57 441	21 746	36 595	1.2	0.9	1.5
			45-54	129 891	36 778	93 113	3.1	1.8	4.4
			55-64	260 642	77 723	182 919	6.0	3.7	8.1
			65+	567 073	124 036	443 037	10.6	5.6	14.1
	1995	Estimates	15+	957 000	291 000	666 000	2.9	1.8	3.9
Ukraine	1989	Total population	15+	...	...	...	1.6	0.5	2.6
			9-49	...	...	...	0.1	0.2	0.1
		Urban population	15+	...	...	...	1.1	0.3	1.8
			9-49	...	...	...	0.1	0.1	0.1
		Rural population	15+	...	...	...	2.7	0.9	4.2
			9-49	...	...	...	0.3	0.3	0.2
	1995	Estimates	15+	484 000	334 000	150 000	1.2	1.8	0.7
Former Yugoslavia	1981	Total population	15+	1 764 042	370 558	1 393 484	10.4	4.5	16.1
			10-14	16 860	6 515	10 345	0.9	0.7	1.2
			15-19	22 836	7 443	15 393	1.2	0.8	1.7
			20-24	28 758	8 367	20 391	1.5	0.9	2.2
			25-34	72 165	16 864	55 301	2.0	0.9	3.2
			35-44	156 651	24 179	132 472	5.7	1.8	9.6
			45-54	389 603	60 674	328 929	13.1	4.1	21.7
			55-64	356 605	58 091	298 514	20.1	7.5	29.8
			65+	737 424	194 940	542 484	34.6	21.5	44.2

Country and year of census or survey Pays et année du recensement ou de l'enquête País y año del censo o de la encuesta			Age Âge Edad	Illiterate population Population analphabète Población analfabeta			Percentage of illiterates Pourcentage d'analphabètes Porcentage de analfabetos		
				Total	Male Masculine Masculina	Female Féminine Femenina	Total	Male Masculin Masculino	Female Féminin Femenino
				(1)	(2)	(3)	(4)	(5)	(6)
Former Yugoslavia (cont)		Urban population	15+	377 921	68 227	309 694	4.8	1.8	7.5
			10-14	6 678	2 597	4 081	0.9	0.7	1.1
			15-19	7 922	2 534	5 388	1.0	0.7	1.4
			20-24	9 205	2 638	6 567	1.1	0.6	1.5
			25-34	18 882	4 700	14 182	1.0	0.5	1.5
			35-44	32 434	4 882	27 552	2.2	0.7	3.8
			45-54	78 992	10 533	68 459	5.7	1.5	9.7
			55-64	73 527	10 381	63 146	9.6	3.1	14.8
			65+	156 959	32 559	124 400	19.4	9.9	25.8
		Rural population	15+	1 386 121	302 331	1 083 790	15.4	6.8	23.9
			10-14	10 182	3 918	6 264	1.0	0.7	1.3
			15-19	14 914	4 909	10 005	1.4	0.9	1.9
			20-24	19 553	5 729	13 824	2.0	1.1	3.0
			25-34	53 283	12 164	41 119	3.2	1.4	5.3
			35-44	124 217	19 297	104 920	9.3	2.8	15.9
			45-54	310 611	50 141	260 470	19.6	6.5	32.2
			55-64	283 078	47 710	235 368	28.1	11.0	41.1
			65+	580 465	162 381	418 084	44.0	28.2	56.2
Federal Republic of Yugoslavia	1991	Total population	15+	463 291	79 258	384 033	6.7	2.4	10.8
			10-14	4 315	2 178	2 137	0.7	0.7	0.7
			15-19	5 792	2 412	3 380	1.0	0.8	1.2
			20-24	6 117	2 287	3 830	1.1	0.8	1.3
			25-29	6 041	2 080	3 961	1.0	0.7	1.4
			30-34	7 210	2 412	4 798	1.1	0.8	1.5
			35-39	8 169	2 628	5 541	1.1	0.7	1.6
			40-44	8 948	2 496	6 452	1.4	0.8	2.0
			45-49	11 284	2 549	8 735	2.5	1.1	3.8
			50-54	25 062	3 983	21 079	4.5	1.5	7.3
			55-59	60 313	8 102	52 211	10.1	2.8	16.9
			60-64	78 225	9 381	68 844	14.0	3.6	23.0
			65+	246 130	40 928	205 202	25.5	10.1	36.5
		Urban population	15+	117 552	19 630	97 922	3.2	1.1	5.1
			10-14	2 316	1 111	1 205	0.7	0.6	0.7
			15-19	2 913	1 102	1 811	0.9	0.7	1.1
			20-24	3 027	1 013	2 014	1.0	0.7	1.3
			25-29	2 805	843	1 962	0.9	0.5	1.2
			30-34	3 090	875	2 215	0.9	0.5	1.2
			35-39	3 156	924	2 232	0.8	0.5	1.0
			40-44	2 998	794	2 204	0.8	0.4	1.1
			45-49	3 483	713	2 770	1.3	0.6	2.1
			50-54	6 805	1 144	5 661	2.2	0.8	3.6
			55-59	14 126	1 878	12 248	4.7	1.3	7.9
			60-64	18 265	2 214	16 051	7.0	1.9	11.5
			65+	56 884	8 130	48 754	13.9	4.9	20.0
		Rural population	15+	345 739	59 628	286 111	10.8	3.7	17.7
			10-14	1 999	1 067	932	0.8	0.8	0.8
			15-19	2 879	1 310	1 569	1.1	0.9	1.2
			20-24	3 090	1 274	1 816	1.2	0.9	1.4
			25-29	3 236	1 237	1 999	1.3	0.9	1.7
			30-34	4 120	1 537	2 583	1.6	1.1	2.1
			35-39	5 013	1 704	3 309	1.7	1.1	2.5
			40-44	5 950	1 702	4 248	2.3	1.2	3.4
			45-49	7 801	1 836	5 965	4.0	1.9	6.1
			50-54	18 257	2 839	15 418	7.2	2.3	11.8
			55-59	46 187	6 224	39 963	15.6	4.4	25.9
			60-64	59 960	7 167	52 793	19.9	5.1	33.0
			65+	189 246	32 798	156 448	34.1	13.8	49.2
	1995	Estimates	15+	178 000	60 000	118 000	2.1	1.4	2.7
Oceania									
American Samoa‡	1980	Total population	15+	507	240	267	2.7	2.5	2.8
			15-19	88	41	47	2.3	2.2	2.4
			20-24	74	28	46	2.4	2.0	2.8
			25-34	92	51	41	2.1	2.3	1.8
			35-44	56	31	25	1.8	1.8	1.8
			45-54	71	36	35	3.1	3.1	3.2
			55-64	57	26	31	4.0	3.6	4.5
			65+	69	27	42	7.3	5.8	8.8

Country and year of census or survey Pays et année du recensement ou de l'enquête País y año del censo o de la encuesta		Age Âge Edad	Illiterate population Population analphabète Población analfabeta			Percentage of illiterates Pourcentage d'analphabètes Porcentage de analfabetos		
			Total	Male Masculine Masculina	Female Féminine Femenina	Total	Male Masculin Masculino	Female Féminin Femenino
			(1)	(2)	(3)	(4)	(5)	(6)
Fiji‡	1986 Total population	15+	56 203	21 633	34 570	12.8	9.8	15.8
		10-14	2 787	1 570	1 217	3.5	3.9	3.1
		15-19	1 557	824	733	2.1	2.2	2.0
		20-24	2 114	959	1 155	2.9	2.6	3.1
		25-29	3 285	1 346	1 939	5.2	4.2	6.2
		30-34	4 347	1 637	2 710	8.6	6.5	10.7
		35-39	5 172	1 832	3 340	12.4	8.7	16.1
		40-44	5 633	1 921	3 712	16.2	10.9	21.6
		45-49	6 106	2 118	3 988	21.2	14.7	27.8
		50-54	6 083	2 161	3 922	26.8	18.8	35.1
		55-59	5 841	2 240	3 601	34.2	25.6	43.3
		60-64	4 811	1 903	2 908	39.9	30.7	49.8
		65+	11 254	4 692	6 562	53.6	44.9	62.3
	1995 Estimates	15+	43 000	16 000	27 000	8.4	6.2	10.7
Guam	1990 Total population	15+	1 004	511	493	1.0	1.0	1.0
		10-14	378	188	190	3.2	3.1	3.3
		15-19	10	5	5	0.1	0.1	0.1
		20-24	23	12	11	0.2	0.1	0.2
		25-34	75	47	28	0.3	0.3	0.2
		35-44	99	74	25	0.5	0.7	0.3
		45-54	102	73	29	1.0	1.3	0.6
		55-64	100	48	52	1.3	1.2	1.5
		65+	217	64	153	4.1	2.5	5.7
New Caledonia	1989 Total population	15+	7 654	3 367	4 287	6.9	6.0	7.9
		10-14	462	243	219	2.6	2.7	2.5
		15-19	198	106	92	1.1	1.1	1.0
		20-24	216	122	94	1.5	1.6	1.3
		25-29	281	123	158	2.1	1.8	2.3
		30-34	249	125	124	2.1	2.1	2.1
		35-44	981	446	535	4.8	4.1	5.6
		45-54	1 623	656	967	11.1	8.5	13.9
		55-64	1 812	750	1 062	19.6	15.7	23.8
		65+	2 294	1 039	1 255	31.0	30.2	31.7
Pacific Islands‡	1980 Total population	15+	5 798	2 454	3 344	8.1	6.7	9.5
		10-14	1 782	963	819	10.1	10.5	9.7
		15-19	871	458	413	6.2	6.5	6.0
		20-24	594	284	310	5.1	5.0	5.2
		25-34	961	403	558	5.4	4.4	6.5
		35-44	689	229	460	7.1	4.5	9.9
		45-54	812	308	504	10.4	7.5	13.5
		55-64	831	350	481	13.7	11.3	16.3
		65+	1 040	422	618	22.2	18.6	25.4
Papua New Guinea	1995 Estimates	15+	724 000	257 000	467 000	27.8	19.0	37.3
Vanuatu, Republic of	1979 Total population	15+	28 647	13 823	14 824	47.1	42.7	52.2
		10-24	5 004	2 538	2 466	34.7	33.1	36.4
		15-19	3 125	1 431	1 694	25.7	22.6	29.0
		20-24	3 157	1 364	1 793	31.1	26.2	36.3
		25-34	6 243	2 700	3 543	42.3	35.9	49.0
		35-44	6 018	2 793	3 225	59.0	50.8	68.6
		45-54	4 327	2 264	2 063	69.3	63.8	76.5
		55-64	3 059	1 679	1 380	75.8	71.6	81.8
		65+	2 718	1 592	1 126	83.9	81.8	87.0
Former U.S.S.R.								
Former U.S.S.R.	1989 Total population	15+	4 282 023	644 964	3 637 059	2.0	0.7	3.2
	Urban population	15+	1 912 673	245 609	1 667 064	1.4	0.4	2.1
	Rural population	15+	2 369 350	399 355	1 969 995	3.4	1.2	5.3

AFRICA:
Botswana:
E--> In 1991, illiterates are defined as *persons with less than five years of schooling*.
FR-> En 1991, les analphabètes sont définis comme *toute personne ayant suivi moins de cinq années d'études*.
ESP> En 1991, los analfabetos son definidos como *las personas que tienen menos de cinco años de estudios*.
Egypt:
E--> In 1986, data refer to Egyptian nationals only and excluding unemployed population.
FR-> En 1986, les données se réfèrent aux nationaux égyptiens seulement et non comprises la population sans emploi.
ESP> Para 1986, los datos se refieren a los ciudadanos egipcios solamente y no incluyen a la población sin empleo.
Namibia:
E--> Excluding unemployed population.
FR-> Non compris la population sans emploi.
ESP> No se incluye la población sin empleo.
South Africa:
E--> In 1980, not including Botphuthatswana, Transkei and Veda.
FR-> En 1980, non compris le Botphuthatswana, le Transkei et le Veda.
ESP> En 1980, excluídos el Botphuthatswana, el Transkei y el Veda.
Sudan:
E--> In 1993, data refer to Nothern States only and do not include homeless and / or nomade populations.
F--> En 1993, les données se réfèrent aux états du nord seulement et ne comprennent pas les populations sans domicile et / ou nomades.
ESP> Para 1993, los datos se refieren a los estados del norte del país solamente y no incluyen a la población sin domicilio ni a la población nómada.
Zambia:
E--> In 1980, illiterates are defined *as persons with less than five years of schooling*.
FR-> En 1980, les analphabètes sont définis comme *toute personne ayant suivi moins de cinq années d'études*.
ESP> En 1980, los analfabetos son definidos como *tienen menos de cinco años de estudios*.
AMERICA, NORTH:
British Virgin Islands:
E--> In 1991, illiterates are defined as *persons with less than five years of schooling*.
FR-> En 1991, les analphabètes sont définis comme *toute personne ayant suivi moins de cinq années d'études*.
ESP> En 1991, los analfabetos son definidos como *tienen menos de cinco años de estudios*.
Cuba:
E--> In 1981, data do not include functionally and physically handicapped.
FR-> En 1981, les données ne comprennent pas les handicapés physiques et fonctionnels.
ESP> En 1981, los datos excluyen los incapacitados funcionales y físicos.
Puerto Rico:
E--> *De jure* population, including armed forces stationed in the area.
FR-> Population de droit, y compris les militaires en garnison sur le territoire.
ESP> Población *de jure*, incluidos los militares destacados en la zona.

AMERICA, SOUTH:
Colombia:
E--> In 1985, including persons of unknown literacy situation.
FR-> En 1985, y compris les personnes dont le niveau d'alphabétisation est inconnu.
ESP> En 1985, incluídas las personas cuyo nivel de alfabetización es desconocido.
ASIA:
Cambodia:
E--> Based on a sample survey.
FR-> D'après une enquête par sondage.
ESP> Según una encuesta por muestreo.
India:
E--> In 1981, including data for Jammu and Kashmir, the final status of which has not yet been determined.
FR-> En 1981, y compris les données pour Jammu et Cachemire dont le statut final n'a pas encore été déterminé.
ESP> En 1981, incluídos los datos para Jammu y Cachemira, cuyo estatuto definitivo no ha sido determinado todavía.
Iran, Islamic Republic of:
E--> In 1991, the total is not the sum of urban and rural areas as these two areas do not include nomades and unsettled population.
FR-> En 1991, le total n'est pas la somme des zones urbaine et rurale car ces deux zones n'incluent pas les nomades et les populations non sedentarisées.
ESP> En 1991, el total no representa la suma de las zonas urbanas y rurales, pues no incluyen a las poblaciones nómadas y no sedentarias.
Pakistan:
E--> In 1981, not including Jammu, Kashmir, the final status of which has not yet been determined, and Junagardh, Manavadar, Gilgit and Baltistan and federally administrated tribal areas.
FR-> En 1981, non compris le Jammu, le Cachemire, dont le statut final n'a pas encore été déterminé, ainsi que le Junagardh, le Manavadar, le Gilgit, le Baltistan et les zones tribales administrées fédérativement.
ESP> En 1981, excluído Jammu y Cachemira, cuyo estatuto definitivo no ha sido determinado todavía, así como Junagardh, Manavadar, Gilgit, Baltistan y las zonas tribales bajo administración federal.
Syrian Arab Republic:
E--> In 1981, national population only.
FR-> En 1981, population nationale seulement.
ESP> En 1981, población nacional solamente.
OCEANIA:
American Samoa:
E--> *De jure* population including armed forces stationed in the area.
FR-> Population de droit y compris les militaires en garnison sur le territoire.
ESP> Población *de jure* incluídos los militares destacados en la zona.
Fiji:
E--> In 1986, illerates are defined as *persons with less than five years of schooling*.
FR-> En 1986, les analphabètes sont définis comme *toute personne ayant suivi moins de cinq années d'études*.
ESP> En 1986, los analfabetos son definidos como *tienen menos de cinco años de estudios*.
Pacific Islands:
E--> *De jure* population including armed forces stationed in the area.
FR-> Population de droit y compris les militaires en garnison sur le territoire.
ESP> Población *de jure* incluídos los militares destacados en la zona.

1.3   Educational attainment
Niveau d'instruction
Nivel de instrucción

1.3 Percentage distribution of population 25 years and over, by educational attainment

Répartition en pourcentage de la population de 25 ans et plus selon le niveau d'instruction

Distribución porcentual de la población de 25 años y más según el nivel de instrucción

S-1 = First stage	S-1 = Premier cycle	S-1 = Primer ciclo
S-2 = Second stage	S-2 = Deuxième cycle	S-2 = Segundo ciclo

					Highest level attained / Niveau d'instruction atteint — Nivel de instrucción alcanzado					
						First level		Entered second level		Post-secondary
Country	Year	Sex	Age group	Total population	No schooling	Premier degré / Primer grado		Accédé au second degré		Post-secondaire
Pays	Année	Sexe	Groupe d'âge	Population totale	Sans scolarité	Incompleted / Non complété	Completed / Complété	Accedieron al segundo grado		Post-secundaria
País	Año	Sexo	Grupo de edad	Población total	Sin escolaridad	Incompleto	Completo	S-1	S-2	
				(1)	(2)	(3)	(4)	(5)	(6)	(7)
Africa										
Benin	1979	MF	25+	1 191 179	89.2	8.3	——>	1.4	0.8	0.3
		F	25+	651 159	94.3	4.4	——>	0.9	0.4	0.1
	1992	MF	25+	1 700 914	78.5	10.8	——>	8.2	——>	1.3
Botswana	1981	MF	25+	310 303	54.7	31.1	9.4	3.1	1.3	0.5
		F	25+	172 274	51.4	36.3	8.7	2.5	0.8	0.2
Burundi	1990	MF	25+	1 897 323	75.4	19.9	——>	2.5	——>	0.6
		F	25+	1 001 183	85.5	11.3	——>	1.6	——>	0.2
Central African Republic	1988	MF	25+	920 929	70.7	19.5	——>	7.3	——>	2.0
		F	25+	481 154	82.6	12.9	——>	3.2	——>	0.8
Congo	1984	MF	25+	646 626	58.8	13.0	8.5	11.0	5.9	3.0
		F	25+	345 173	72.0	10.0	5.6	8.2	3.0	1.1
Côte d'Ivoire‡	1988	MF	25+	739 179	...	...	48.2	43.1	——>	8.7
		F	25+	217 251	...	...	58.2	36.4	——>	5.4
Egypt‡										
Total population	1986	MF	25+	19 441 903	64.1	16.5	——>	14.8	——>	4.6
		F	25+	9 721 464	78.6	10.3	——>	9.3	——>	1.8
Urban population		MF	25+	9 089 987	47.8	21.6	——>	22.4	——>	8.2
		F	25+	4 427 377	61.8	17.5	——>	17.1	——>	3.6
Rural population		MF	25+	10 351 916	78.4	12.0	——>	8.1	——>	1.5
		F	25+	5 294 087	92.6	4.3	——>	2.8	——>	0.2
Guinea-Bissau	1979	MF	7+	483 336	91.1	8.0	——>	0.6	0.2	0.1
Kenya‡	1979	MF	25+	4 818 310	58.6	32.2	——>	7.9	1.3	——>
		F	25+	2 442 417	73.0	23.0	——>	3.4	0.6	——>
Libyan Arab Jamahiriya‡	1984	MF	25+	966 774	59.7	15.4	8.5	5.2	8.5	2.7
		F	25+	493 212	79.4	6.4	3.0	1.6	4.3	5.2
Malawi	1987	MF	25+	2 859 826	55.0	31.8	8.0	2.7	2.1	0.4
		F	25+	1 495 441	71.5	22.7	3.7	1.2	0.8	0.2
Mauritania	1988	MF	25+	679 667	60.8	34.1	——>	3.8	——>	1.3
		F	25+	352 864	68.3	29.7	——>	1.7	——>	0.3

Educational attainment 1.3
Niveau d'instruction
Nivel de instrucción

						Highest level attained / Niveau d'instruction atteint Nivel de instrucción alcanzado				
Country	Year	Sex	Age group	Total population	No schooling	First level Premier degré Primer grado		Entered second level Accédé au second degré Accedieron al segundo grado		Post-secondary Post-secondaire
Pays	Année	Sexe	Groupe d'âge	Population totale	Sans scolarité	Incompleted Non complété Incompleto	Completed Complété Completo			Post-secundaria
País	Año	Sexo	Grupo de edad	Población total	Sin escolaridad			S-1	S-2	
				(1)	(2)	(3)	(4)	(5)	(6)	(7)
Mauritius	1983	MF	25+	440 134	23.9	52.0	——>	20.6	——>	3.6
		F	25+	230 126	32.4	48.1	——>	17.5	——>	1.9
	1990	MF	25+	540 244	18.3	42.6	6.1	7.2	23.9	1.9
		F	25+	274 291	25.8	42.1	6.1	5.9	19.2	0.9
Mozambique‡	1980	MF	25+	4 242 819	81.0	18.1	——>	0.8	——>	0.1
		F	25+	2 257 630	94.0	5.7	——>	0.3	——>	0.0
Namibia‡ Total population	1991	MF	25+	340 552	...	49.1	——>	43.8	——>	4.0
		F	25+	172 581	...	50.0	——>	43.7	——>	3.7
Urban population		MF	25+	165 393	...	33.2	——>	56.3	——>	5.8
		F	25+	76 869	...	30.8	——>	59.4	——>	5.7
Rural population		MF	25+	175 159	...	64.2	——>	32.0	——>	2.2
		F	25+	95 712	...	65.4	——>	31.2	——>	2.1
Sao Tome and Principe‡	1981	MF	25+	33 308	56.6	18.0	19.3	4.6	1.3	0.3
		F	25+	17 330	74.6	11.8	9.7	3.0	0.7	0.1
Seychelles	1987	MF	25+	30 912	12.1	44.9	——>	35.7	——>	4.6
Sierra Leone	1985	MF	5+	1 315 897	64.5	18.7	1.8	9.7	3.8	1.5
South Africa‡	1980	MF	25+	10 460 159	32.0	28.0	11.8	16.8	10.0	1.3
	1985	MF	25+	10 388 428	24.8	41.6	4.8	20.6	5.9	2.3
		F	25+	5 288 066	26.9	40.7	4.6	20.0	6.2	1.5
Sudan‡ Total population	1983	MF	25+	6 492 263	76.7	18.6	——>	1.9	2.0	0.8
		F	25+	3 351 247	88.8	9.1	——>	0.9	0.9	0.3
Urban population		MF	25+	1 499 492	54.3	31.6	——>	5.4	6.1	2.7
		F	25+	695 700	71.3	21.0	——>	3.3	3.3	1.1
Rural population		MF	25+	4 992 771	83.4	14.7	——>	0.9	0.8	0.2
		F	25+	2 655 547	93.4	5.9	——>	0.3	0.2	0.1
Swaziland	1986	MF	25+	221 672	42.0	24.0	10.5	13.2	6.3	3.3
		F	25+	100 013	38.0	22.9	10.8	14.8	8.4	4.2
Togo	1981	MF	25+	1 084 488	76.5	13.5	——>	8.7	——>	1.3
		F	25+	604 296	87.3	7.9	——>	4.2	——>	0.5
Tunisia	1980	MF	25+	2 379 900	72.1	17.2	——>	4.1	4.8	1.8
		F	25+	1 205 800	85.0	9.5	——>	2.3	2.5	0.7
Total population	1984	MF	25+	2 714 100	66.3	18.9	——>	12.0	——>	2.8
		F	25+	1 347 700	79.0	12.7	——>	6.9	——>	1.3
Urban population		MF	25+	1 504 300	53.4	23.7	——>	18.2	——>	4.7
		F	25+	746 600	67.9	18.2	——>	11.6	——>	2.3
Rural population		MF	25+	1 209 800	82.3	12.8	——>	4.4	——>	0.6
		F	25+	601 100	92.7	5.9	——>	1.2	——>	0.2
Uganda	1991	MF	25+	5 455 582	46.1	41.4	——>	8.9	1.3	0.5
		F	25+	2 791 949	60.8	32.4	——>	5.6	0.5	0.2
Zambia‡ Total population	1980	MF	25+	1 880 124	49.8	37.0	——>	12.8	——>	0.4
		F	25+	961 086	64.2	29.6	——>	6.0	——>	0.2
Urban population		MF	25+	744 957	34.5	40.8	——>	23.8	——>	0.9
		F	25+	314 509	45.1	40.5	——>	14.0	——>	0.4
Rural population		MF	25+	1 135 167	59.9	34.4	——>	5.6	——>	0.1
		F	25+	646 577	73.6	24.3	——>	2.1	——>	0.0
Total population	1993	MF	14+	...	18.6	54.8	——>	12.9	12.2	1.5
		F	14+	...	18.3	57.6	——>	13.4	9.8	1.0
Urban population		MF	14+	...	8.9	46.5	——>	19.1	22.4	3.1
Rural population		MF	14+	...	26.7	59.6	——>	8.2	4.9	0.5
Zimbabwe	1992	MF	25+	3 445 195	22.3	53.2	——>	19.4	——>	4.9
		F	25+	1 801 364	29.2	54.2	——>	13.1	——>	3.4

1.3　Educational attainment
Niveau d'instruction
Nivel de instrucción

Country Pays País	Year Année Año	Sex Sexe Sexo	Age group Groupe d'âge Grupo de edad	Total population Population totale Población total	No schooling Sans scolarité Sin escolaridad	First level / Premier degré / Primer grado — Incompleted / Non complété / Incompleto	First level — Completed / Complété / Completo	Entered second level / Accédé au second degré / Accedieron al segundo grado — S-1	Entered second level — S-2	Post-secondary Post-secondaire Post-secundaria
				(1)	(2)	(3)	(4)	(5)	(6)	(7)
America, North										
Aruba	1991	MF	25+	41 180	14.9	37.3	——>	37.7	——>	7.0
		F	25+	18 751	14.9	36.9	——>	39.7	——>	5.5
Bahamas	1990	MF	25+	104 472	3.5	25.4	——>	57.7	——>	13.5
		F	25+	54 844	3.2	25.6	——>	57.9	——>	13.4
Barbados	1980	MF	25+	116 874	0.8	63.5	——>	32.3	——>	3.3
		F	25+	68 807	0.9	65.2	——>	32.0	——>	1.9
Belize	1980	MF	25+	45 596	10.7	75.3	——>	11.7	——>	2.3
		F	25+	22 632	10.5	76.6	——>	11.7	——>	1.2
	1991	MF	25+	66 520	13.0	64.3	——>	14.9	——>	6.6
		F	25+	32 586	12.8	65.4	——>	15.1	——>	5.8
Bermuda	1991	MF	25+	38 873	0.5	18.2	——>	63.0	——>	18.4
		F	25+	20 373	0.4	17.1	——>	65.0	——>	17.5
British Virgin Islands	1980	MF	25+	5 136	2.4	65.8	——>	23.3	——>	8.5
		F	25+	2 437	2.4	64.7	——>	25.4	——>	7.4
	1991	MF	25+	8 986	0.7	43.2	——>	34.8	6.4	13.6
		F	25+	4 297	0.6	39.4	——>	37.6	6.8	14.1
Canada 　Total population	1981	MF	25+	13 971 280	2.0	14.2	9.5	36.8	——>	37.4
		F	25+	7 161 655	2.2	14.2	9.4	39.6	——>	34.7
Urban population		MF	25+	10 743 370	1.9	13.1	8.5	39.4	——>	37.1
		F	25+	5 597 975	2.2	13.6	8.7	39.1	——>	36.3
Rural population		MF	25+	3 227 895	2.3	18.1	12.7	37.6	——>	29.3
		F	25+	1 563 690	2.0	16.2	11.9	41.0	——>	28.8
Total population	1991	MF	25+	17 471 920	1.0	4.0	11.7	34.3	27.7	21.4
		F	25+	8 996 970	1.1	4.0	11.6	35.7	28.0	19.6
Urban population		MF	25+	13 514 580	1.0	3.8	10.3	32.9	28.2	23.7
		F	25+	7 056 000	1.2	4.0	10.8	34.3	28.5	21.2
Rural population		MF	25+	3 957 340	0.9	4.5	16.1	39.1	25.8	13.6
		F	25+	1 940 970	0.8	3.7	14.7	40.6	26.2	13.9
Cuba 　Total population	1981	MF	25-49	3 013 315	3.7	22.6	27.6	40.2	——>	5.9
		F	25-49	1 511 380	4.1	27.0	28.4	35.9	——>	4.5
Urban population		MF	25-49	2 165 853	2.0	16.8	26.0	47.4	——>	7.8
Rural population		MF	25-49	847 462	8.1	37.5	31.6	21.9	——>	1.0
Dominica	1981	MF	25+	27 508	6.6	80.5	——>	11.1	——>	1.7
		F	25+	14 581	6.8	81.6	——>	10.6	——>	1.0
El Salvador‡ 　Total population	1980	MF	10+	3 132 400	30.2	60.7	——>	6.9	——>	2.3
		F	10+	1 635 100	33.1	58.3	——>	6.6	——>	1.9
Urban population		MF	10+	1 405 000	15.5	66.2	——>	13.5	——>	4.8
		F	10+	776 200	19.6	64.0	——>	12.5	——>	3.9
Rural population		MF	10+	1 727 400	42.2	56.2	——>	1.4	——>	0.2
		F	10+	858 900	45.4	53.1	——>	1.3	——>	0.2
Grenada	1981	MF	25+	33 401	2.2	87.8	——>	8.5	——>	1.5
		F	25+	18 362	2.3	88.3	——>	8.5	——>	0.8
Guadeloupe	1982	MF	25+	150 253	10.7	54.6	——>	29.5	——>	5.2
		F	25+	79 984	10.3	53.6	——>	31.8	——>	4.2
Guatemala	1981	MF	25+	2 060 399	55.0	27.3	8.6	2.9	4.0	2.2
		F	25+	1 052 347	61.6	22.1	7.9	2.6	4.6	1.2
Haiti	1982	MF	25+	2 103 124	77.0	15.2	——>	7.2	——>	0.7
		F	25+	1 093 992	81.3	12.3	——>	5.9	——>	0.4
Total population	1986	MF	25+	2 229 501	59.5	30.5	——>	9.3	——>	0.7
Urban population		MF	25+	551 865	31.6	37.1	——>	28.9	——>	2.4
Rural population		MF	25+	1 677 636	68.6	28.4	——>	2.8	——>	0.2

Educational attainment 1.3
Niveau d'instruction
Nivel de instrucción

Country / Pays / País	Year / Année / Año	Sex / Sexe / Sexo	Age group / Groupe d'âge / Grupo de edad	Total population / Population totale / Población total	Highest level attained / Niveau d'instruction atteint / Nivel de instrucción alcanzado					
					No schooling / Sans scolarité / Sin escolaridad	First level / Premier degré / Primer grado		Entered second level / Accédé au second degré / Accedieron al segundo grado		Post-secondary / Post-secondaire / Post-secundaria
						Incompleted / Non complété / Incompleto	Completed / Complété / Completo	S-1	S-2	
				(1)	(2)	(3)	(4)	(5)	(6)	(7)
Honduras‡										
Total population	1983	MF	25 +	...	33.5	51.3	——>	4.3	7.6	3.3
		F	25 +	...	34.1	51.1	——>	4.4	8.3	2.2
Urban population		MF	25 +	...	17.3	51.8	——>	8.2	15.4	7.4
		F	25 +	...	19.4	51.8	——>	8.4	15.8	4.6
Rural population		MF	25 +	...	46.1	51.0	——>	1.2	1.6	0.1
		F	25 +	...	46.9	50.3	——>	1.0	1.7	0.1
Jamaica	1982	MF	25 +	703 714	3.2	79.8	——>	15.0	——>	2.0
		F	25 +	365 612	3.0	79.4	——>	15.8	——>	1.8
Martinique	1982	MF	25 +	157 574	8.1	55.5	——>	30.9	——>	5.6
		F	25 +	85 288	6.7	55.4	——>	33.2	——>	4.7
Mexico	1980	MF	25 +	24 309 593	34.2	31.4	17.2	11.8	——>	5.3
		F	25 +	12 455 708	37.1	30.7	18.0	11.5	——>	2.7
	1990	MF	25 +	31 188 180	18.8	28.6	19.9	12.7	10.7	9.2
		F	25 +	16 206 466	21.4	29.0	19.9	12.1	11.1	6.5
Montserrat	1980	MF	25 +	5 544	1.7	84.6	——>	7.9	——>	5.8
		F	25 +	3 023	1.7	84.4	——>	9.9	——>	4.0
Netherlands Antilles	1981	MF	25 +	115 087	61.3	——>	——>	32.2	——>	6.4
		F	25 +	62 076	67.3	——>	——>	27.8	——>	4.9
Panama‡										
Total population	1980	MF	25 +	725 878	18.3	27.1	23.2	11.7	11.5	8.3
		F	25 +	358 714	19.1	26.3	23.1	11.6	12.2	7.8
Urban population		MF	25 +	391 047	7.0	17.9	25.1	17.7	18.2	14.1
		F	25 +	205 098	7.5	18.8	25.5	17.0	18.7	12.5
Rural population		MF	25 +	334 831	31.5	37.7	20.9	4.7	3.6	1.5
		F	25 +	153 616	34.4	36.3	19.8	4.5	3.6	1.4
Total population	1990	MF	25 +	1 035 339	11.7	20.2	21.8	12.6	16.4	13.2
		F	25 +	513 435	12.4	19.2	20.3	12.1	17.1	13.5
Puerto Rico‡	1980	MF	25 +	1 577 686	8.0	17.8	11.4	16.4	27.9	18.4
		F	25 +	839 399	9.1	17.8	11.9	15.7	27.2	18.3
Saint Kitts and Nevis	1980	MF	25 +	16 771	1.1	29.0	——>	66.6	——>	2.3
		F	25 +	9 267	1.0	29.8	——>	67.0	——>	1.4
St. Lucia	1980	MF	25 +	39 599	17.5	74.5	——>	6.8	——>	1.3
		F	25 +	21 756	16.8	75.6	——>	6.8	——>	0.7
St. Vincent and the Grenadines	1980	MF	25 +	32 444	2.4	88.0	——>	8.2	——>	1.4
		F	25 +	17 893	2.5	88.6	——>	8.0	——>	0.9
Trinidad and Tobago	1980	MF	25 +	408 215	1.3	29.4	42.6	19.7	4.0	2.9
		F	25 +	201 148	1.3	29.9	42.4	20.4	4.1	1.9
Turks and Caicos Islands	1980	MF	25 +	2 859	0.9	74.6	——>	16.9	——>	7.7
		F	25 +	1 545	1.0	77.5	——>	16.4	——>	5.1
United States‡	1980	MF	25 +	132 835 687	1.0	6.3	——>	15.5	45.2	31.9
		F	25 +	70 419 233	1.0	6.0	——>	15.8	49.1	28.1
	1994	MF	25 +	164 511 000	0.6	8.2	——>	44.6	——>	46.5
		F	25 +	85 972 000	0.6	8.1	——>	46.8	——>	44.6
U.S. Virgin Islands‡	1980	MF	25 +	44 986	1.5	26.3	7.8	14.4	25.7	24.4
		F	25 +	24 145	1.5	26.1	7.9	14.3	26.6	23.5
America, South										
Argentina	1980	MF	25 +	14 913 575	7.1	33.4	33.0	20.4	——>	6.1
		F	25 +	7 711 356	6.7	32.1	35.2	20.1	——>	5.8
	1991	MF	25 +	17 340 713	5.7	22.3	34.6	25.3	——>	12.0
		F	25 +	9 074 589	6.2	22.8	34.7	24.5	——>	11.8

1.3 Educational attainment
Niveau d'instruction
Nivel de instrucción

Country / Pays / País	Year / Année / Año	Sex / Sexe / Sexo	Age group / Groupe d'âge / Grupo de edad	Total population / Population totale / Población total	No schooling / Sans scolarité / Sin escolaridad	First level / Premier degré / Primer grado — Incompleted / Non complété / Incompleto	First level — Completed / Complété / Completo	Entered second level / Accédé au second degré / Accedieron al segundo grado — S-1	Entered second level — S-2	Post-secondary / Post-secondaire / Post-secundaria
				(1)	(2)	(3)	(4)	(5)	(6)	(7)
Bolivia‡										
Total population	1992	MF	25+	2 533 393	23.5	20.4	6.6	15.2	15.7	9.9
		F	25+	1 314 371	31.9	19.5	5.9	12.5	13.2	7.9
Urban population		MF	25+	1 454 355	13.1	15.6	7.0	16.1	23.7	15.7
		F	25+	769 608	18.4	17.5	7.1	15.2	20.8	12.6
Rural population		MF	25+	1 079 038	37.5	26.9	6.1	14.0	4.9	2.0
		F	25+	544 763	50.9	22.3	4.1	8.7	2.5	1.2
Brazil‡										
Total population	1980	MF	25+	48 310 722	32.9	50.4	4.9	6.9	——>	5.0
		F	25+	24 576 023	35.2	48.8	4.6	7.2	——>	4.1
Urban population		MF	25+	34 355 258	22.8	54.7	6.5	9.2	——>	6.8
		F	25+	17 928 564	25.9	53.1	6.0	9.4	——>	5.6
Rural population		MF	25+	13 955 463	57.7	40.0	0.9	1.0	——>	0.4
		F	25+	6 647 459	60.5	37.3	0.9	1.1	——>	0.3
Total population	1989	MF	10+	110 157 487	18.7	57.0	6.9	11.9	5.5	——>
		F	10+	56 707 493	18.7	56.3	6.9	12.7	5.4	——>
Urban population		MF	10+	83 338 354	13.3	56.6	8.2	14.7	7.2	——>
		F	10+	43 726 380	14.1	55.5	8.1	15.4	6.8	——>
Rural population		MF	10+	26 819 133	35.4	58.1	2.8	3.2	0.5	——>
		F	10+	12 981 113	34.1	59.0	2.9	3.5	0.5	——>
Chile	1982	MF	25+	5 204 698	9.4	56.6	——>	26.9	——>	7.2
		F	25+	2 724 739	10.0	56.9	——>	27.1	——>	5.9
	1992	MF	25+	...	5.8	48.0	——>	33.9	——>	12.3
		F	25+	...	6.3	48.6	——>	33.5	——>	11.6
Ecuador	1982	MF	25+	2 887 330	25.4	17.0	34.1	8.1	7.9	7.6
		F	25+	1 457 435	29.6	16.8	31.1	8.3	8.7	5.6
	1990	MF	25+	3 953 452	1.7	43.7	——>	22.6	——>	12.7
		F	25+	2 014 479	1.8	42.6	——>	22.2	——>	11.1
French Guiana	1982	MF	25+	34 145	20.8	40.5	——>	32.4	——>	6.4
Guyana	1980	MF	25+	270 849	8.1	72.9	——>	17.3	——>	1.8
		F	25+	138 083	10.6	73.0	——>	15.5	——>	0.9
Paraguay	1982	MF	25+	1 139 583	14.1	51.1	15.5	9.0	7-0	3.4
		F	25+	573 256	17.9	49.5	15.3	7.7	7.0	2.5
	1992	MF	15+	2 427 485	7.0	38.4	22.8	12.8	12.2	6.6
		F	15+	1 219 289	8.6	38.1	23.0	11.4	11.8	6.6
Peru	1981	MF	25+	6 526 328	20.1	27.3	17.2	10.7	10.7	10.1
		F	25+	3 308 370	28.8	24.4	15.5	8.6	9.7	7.7
	1993	MF	20+	9 916 161	0.4	30.0	7.6	11.8	22.9	27.3
		F	20+	4 721 582	0.5	31.2	8.2	11.2	21.4	27.5
Uruguay	1985	MF	25+	1 701 705	4.7	58.0	——>	29.2	——>	8.1
		F	25+	903 318	3.6	57.5	——>	30.0	——>	8.9
Venezuela‡	1981	MF	25+	5 542 852	23.5	47.2	——>	22.3	——>	7.0
		F	25+	2 802 602	26.4	46.2	——>	21.9	——>	5.5
Total population	1990	MF	25+	7 680 427	21.2	55.0	——>	12.0	——>	11.8
		F	25+	3 930 584	22.9	53.8	——>	12.1	——>	11.3
Urban population		MF	25+	6 591 116	17.2	55.9	——>	13.4	——>	13.5
		F	25+	3 442 360	19.3	54.7	——>	13.3	——>	12.6
Rural population		MF	25+	1 089 311	45.2	49.8	——>	3.5	——>	1.6
		F	25+	488 224	48.1	46.8	——>	3.6	——>	1.5

Educational attainment 1.3
Niveau d'instruction
Nivel de instrucción

Country / Pays / País	Year / Année / Año	Sex / Sexe / Sexo	Age group / Groupe d'âge / Grupo de edad	Total population / Population totale / Población total (1)	No schooling / Sans scolarité / Sin escolaridad (2)	First level / Premier degré / Primer grado		Entered second level / Accédé au second degré / Accedieron al segundo grado		Post-secondary / Post-secondaire / Post-secundaria (7)
						Incompleted / Non complété / Incompleto (3)	Completed / Complété / Completo (4)	S-1 (5)	S-2 (6)	
Asia										
Afghanistan										
Total population	1979	MF	25+	4 891 473	89.0	6.5	0.3	1.1	——>	3.0
		F	25+	2 405 187	97.6	1.4	0.1	0.3	——>	0.6
Urban population		MF	25+	717 983	72.1	12.0	1.1	3.5	——>	11.4
		F	25+	335 968	88.2	5.7	0.8	1.6	——>	3.7
Rural population		MF	25+	4 173 490	92.0	5.5	0.2	0.7	——>	1.6
		F	25+	2 069 219	99.2	0.7	0.0	0.0	——>	0.0
Bahrain	1991	MF	25+	263 720	38.4	26.2	——>	25.1	——>	10.3
		F	25+	96 080	46.0	18.3	——>	25.3	——>	10.4
Bangladesh										
Total population	1981	MF	25+	31 593 122	70.4	16.7	——>	7.4	4.2	1.3
		F	25+	14 904 705	84.0	11.5	——>	3.3	0.8	0.3
Urban population		MF	25+	5 036 383	52.0	18.4	——>	13.6	10.7	5.3
		F	25+	1 987 459	69.3	15.4	——>	9.5	4.1	1.7
Rural population		MF	25+	26 556 739	73.9	16.3	——>	6.2	3.0	0.5
		F	25+	12 917 246	86.3	10.9	——>	2.4	0.3	0.0
Brunei Darussalam	1981	MF	25+	75 283	32.1	28.3	——>	30.1	——>	9.4
		F	25+	33 701	45.8	21.7	——>	25.6	——>	6.9
Cambodia										
Total population	1993	MF	5+	8 664 920	30.5	47.0	——>	16.2	4.1	1.0
		F	5+	4 571 987	37.8	46.1	——>	12.1	2.7	0.5
Phnom Penh		MF	5+	647 546	16.8	40.2	——>	25.0	10.9	6.4
		F	5+	331 136	22.1	42.4	——>	23.7	7.5	3.4
Other urban pop.		MF	5+	713 628	25.9	43.0	——>	21.3	7.4	1.1
		F	5+	376 883	31.3	42.9	——>	18.7	5.5	0.6
Rural population		MF	5+	7 303 746	32.2	48.0	——>	15.0	3.2	0.5
		F	5+	3 863 968	39.7	46.7	——>	10.4	2.0	0.2
China‡	1982	MF	25+	466 915 380	44.5	——>	32.7	16.1	5.6	1.0
		F	25+	227 191 450	62.3	——>	23.6	9.9	3.7	0.5
	1990	MF	25+	571 589 800	29.3	34.3	——>	34.4	——>	2.0
Cyprus	1980	MF	20+	...	8.0	55.0	——>	29.0	——>	8.0
		F	20+	...	14.0	55.0	——>	25.0	——>	6.0
	1992	MF	25+	363 573	5.1	13.0	30.6	34.2	——>	17.0
		F	25+	186 432	8.2	16.2	30.1	31.0	——>	14.4
Hong Kong‡	1981	MF	25+	2 601 296	22.5	16.7	23.1	13.2	17.3	7.1
		F	25+	1 239 697	35.9	15.3	19.5	9.9	14.4	5.0
	1991	MF	25+	3 530 524	15.7	30.3	——>	17.8	25.5	10.6
		F	25+	1 747 296	22.8	29.3	——>	14.6	25.0	8.3
India	1981	MF	25+	280 599 720	72.5	11.3	——>	13.7	——>	2.5
		F	25+	135 517 843	85.2	7.2	——>	6.6	——>	1.1
Indonesia										
Total population	1980	MF	25+	58 441 240	41.1	31.6	16.8	4.7	4.9	0.8
		F	25+	29 764 530	53.9	26.6	12.9	3.3	3.0	0.4
Urban population		MF	25+	12 518 959	21.9	26.0	23.1	12.1	14.1	2.9
		F	25+	6 288 212	34.8	24.2	20.3	9.8	9.5	1.4
Rural population		MF	25+	45 922 281	45.9	33.6	15.1	2.7	2.5	0.2
		F	25+	23 476 318	59.0	27.3	10.8	1.5	1.3	0.1
Total population	1990	MF	25+	78 497 680	54.5	26.4	——>	16.8	——>	2.3
		F	25+	39 961 034	62.8	23.3	——>	12.4	——>	1.4

1.3 Educational attainment
Niveau d'instruction
Nivel de instrucción

Country / Pays / País	Year / Année / Año	Sex / Sexe / Sexo	Age group / Groupe d'âge / Grupo de edad	Total population / Population totale / Población total	Highest level attained / Niveau d'instruction atteint / Nivel de instrucción alcanzado					
					No schooling / Sans scolarité / Sin escolaridad	First level / Premier degré / Primer grado		Entered second level / Accédé au second degré / Accedieron al segundo grado		Post-secondary / Post-secondaire / Post-secundaria
						Incompleted / Non complété / Incompleto	Completed / Complété / Completo	S-1	S-2	
				(1)	(2)	(3)	(4)	(5)	(6)	(7)
Iran, Islamic Republic of										
Total population	1987	MF	10+	10 628 447	52.8	21.6	——>	11.6	——>	4.1
		F	10+	5 349 328	60.2	18.9	——>	8.8	——>	2.9
Rural population		MF	10+	3 079 311	64.6	19.1	——>	5.6	——>	1.0
		F	10+	1 579 988	73.0	15.6	——>	2.1	——>	0.3
Urban population		MF	10+	7 549 136	48.0	22.6	——>	14.0	——>	5.4
		F	10+	3 769 340	54.8	20.3	——>	11.7	——>	4.0
Israel	1983	MF	25+	2 043 720	10.5	42.4	——>	35.9	——>	11.2
		F	25+	1 059 465	14.2	41.5	——>	35.3	——>	9.0
Japan‡										
Total population	1980	MF	25+	73 368 684	0.4	——>	45.6	——>	39.7	14.3
		F	25+	38 110 839	0.6	——>	47.6	——>	42.1	9.5
Urban population		MF	25+	55 235 050	0.3	——>	40.6	——>	42.5	16.5
		F	25+	28 596 309	0.4	——>	42.8	——>	45.8	11.0
Rural population		MF	25+	18 133 634	0.7	——>	60.6	——>	31.0	7.6
		F	25+	9 514 530	0.9	——>	62.9	——>	30.9	5.1
Total population	1990	MF	25+	81 991 363	0.3	33.6	——>	43.7	——>	20.7
		F	25+	42 625 628	0.3	35.7	——>	45.9	——>	16.4
Kazakstan	1989	MF	25+	8 414 539	7.7	29.2	——>	50.7	——>	12.4
		F	25+	4 528 351	11.0	29.2	——>	48.1	——>	11.7
Korea, Republic of	1980	MF	25+	16 457 362	19.7	34.5	——>	18.2	18.7	8.9
		F	25+	8 503 065	26.9	39.4	——>	16.7	12.9	4.0
	1990	MF	25+	23 408 288	11.0	0.8	20.9	18.9	35.0	13.4
		F	25+	11 983 259	16.3	1.0	25.2	20.3	30.0	7.2
Kuwait										
Total population	1980	MF	25+	568 086	58.0	7.6	——>	9.6	14.8	10.1
		F	25+	205 573	62.7	6.4	——>	8.7	14.7	7.4
Kuwaiti population		MF	25+	176 011	69.5	7.8	——>	9.5	9.0	4.2
		F	25+	89 718	80.0	4.5	——>	6.1	6.6	2.8
Non-Kuwaiti pop.		MF	25+	392 075	52.8	7.5	——>	9.6	17.4	12.7
		F	25+	115 855	49.3	7.9	——>	10.7	21.0	11.0
Total population	1988	MF	10+	1 409 065	17.6	18.4	——>	22.7	14.6	11.1
		F	10+	615 017	21.4	18.0	——>	20.7	14.2	10.2
Kuwaiti population		MF	10+	384 951	15.2	21.0	——>	29.8	13.1	12.3
		F	10+	193 473	22.0	19.9	——>	26.2	11.7	12.0
Non-Kuwaiti pop.		MF	10+	1 024 114	18.5	17.5	——>	20.0	15.1	10.7
		F	10+	421 544	21.2	17.2	——>	18.1	15.3	9.3
Macau	1991	MF	25+	212 363	13.1	16.0	19.9	25.2	19.9	5.9
		F	25+	108 515	18.8	16.7	20.2	22.3	17.3	4.7
Malaysia										
Total population	1980	MF	25+	5 146 888	36.6	21.1	21.1	18.1	1.3	1.9
		F	25+	2 587 961	49.0	18.8	16.9	13.5	0.8	1.0
Myanmar	1983	MF	25+	13 948 584	55.8	27.7	——>	14.5	——>	2.0
		F	25+	7 122 177	60.4	28.9	——>	9.2	——>	1.5
Nepal‡										
Total population	1981	MF	25+	6 146 768	90.3	4.8	——>	3.7	——>	1.1
Urban population		MF	25+	2 878 386	95.7	2.9	——>	1.1	——>	0.3
Rural population		MF	25+	855 819	43.8	31.3	——>	20.8	——>	4.1
Total population	1991	MF	6+	15 145 071	69.6	16.2	——>	8.9	2.0	1.5
Pakistan‡										
Total population	1981	MF	25+	30 707 279	78.9	8.7	——>	10.5	——>	1.9
		F	25+	14 400 805	90.4	4.7	——>	4.2	——>	0.7

Educational attainment 1.3
Niveau d'instruction
Nivel de instrucción

Country / Pays / País	Year / Année / Año	Sex / Sexe / Sexo	Age group / Groupe d'âge / Grupo de edad	Total population / Population totale / Población total (1)	No schooling / Sans scolarité / Sin escolaridad (2)	First level / Premier degré / Primer grado — Incompleted / Non complété / Incompleto (3)	First level — Completed / Complété / Completo (4)	Entered second level / Accédé au second degré / Accedieron al segundo grado — S-1 (5)	S-2 (6)	Post-secondary / Post-secondaire / Post-secundaria (7)
Pakistan‡ (cont)										
Urban population		MF	25+	8 709 327	59.5	12.9	——>	22.1	——>	5.4
		F	25+	3 901 096	73.9	10.8	——>	12.8	——>	2.6
Rural population		MF	25+	21 997 952	86.8	6.9	——>	5.9	——>	0.5
		F	25+	10 499 709	96.5	2.4	——>	1.0	——>	0.1
Total population	1990	MF	25+	...	73.8	9.7	——>	5.8	8.2	2.5
		F	25+	...	87.9	5.3	——>	2.2	3.8	0.9
Urban population		MF	25+	...	59.2	11.8	——>	8.8	14.5	5.7
		F	25+	...	74.9	8.4	——>	4.9	9.2	2.6
Rural population		MF	25+	...	80.4	8.7	——>	4.4	5.4	1.1
		F	25+	...	94.1	3.7	——>	1.0	1.2	0.0
Philippines	1980	MF	25+	17 865 290	11.7	31.3	22.8	18.9	——>	15.2
		F	25+	8 980 215	13.3	31.4	23.7	16.6	——>	15.1
	1990	MF	25+	24 156 427	6.7	46.9	——>	27.2	——>	18.7
		F	25+	12 167 641	7.5	47.8	——>	25.3	——>	18.9
Qatar‡	1981	MF	10+	188 940	48.9	15.0	——>	11.7	12.8	11.6
		F	10+	61 732	49.1	15.9	——>	11.7	13.6	9.7
	1986	MF	25+	211 485	53.5	9.8	——>	10.1	13.3	13.3
		F	25+	50 673	56.0	6.7	——>	7.5	14.6	15.3
Singapore‡	1980	MF	25+	1 176 282	43.7	38.3	——>	9.6	5.0	3.4
		F	25+	583 726	54.3	31.2	——>	8.7	3.8	2.0
	1990	MF	25+	1 596 600	64.0	——>	——>	23.2	8.1	4.7
		F	25+	807 800	65.9	——>	——>	23.9	6.8	3.5
Sri Lanka										
Total population	1981	MF	25+	6 490 502	15.9	48.9	——>	34.1	——>	1.1
		F	25+	3 163 187	22.7	45.3	——>	31.3	——>	0.8
Urban population		MF	25+	1 471 818	8.8	39.5	——>	49.2	——>	2.4
		F	25+	694 072	12.3	40.5	——>	45.4	——>	1.7
Rural population		MF	25+	5 018 684	18.0	51.6	——>	29.7	——>	0.7
		F	25+	2 469 115	25.6	46.6	——>	27.3	——>	0.5
Tajikistan	1989	MF	25+	1 916 494	9.8	13.0	——>	65.5	——>	11.7
		F	25+	984 302	13.5	15.3	——>	63.1	——>	8.1
Thailand	1980	MF	25+	17 491 470	20.5	67.3	2.4	4.5	2.3	2.9
		F	25+	9 000 023	26.3	65.4	1.6	2.6	1.7	2.4
	1990	MF	6+	49 076 100	10.7	69.6	——>	13.7	——>	5.1
		F	6+	24 835 200	12.8	70.0	——>	11.4	——>	5.1
Turkey‡	1985	MF	25+	21 366 259	40.0	44.5	——>	4.6	——>	10.8
		F	25+	10 708 464	54.4	36.1	——>	2.8	——>	6.7
Total population	1993	MF	25+	...	30.6	6.6	40.6	21.9	——>	——>
		F	25+	...	43.2	8.1	34.7	13.7	——>	——>
Urban population		MF	6+	...	16.8	14.3	33.5	35.2	——>	——>
		F	6+	...	23.7	14.5	34.1	27.5	——>	——>
Rural population		MF	6+	...	28.2	17.8	40.3	13.4	——>	——>
		F	6+	...	37.1	17.2	38.5	6.9	——>	——>
Viet Nam	1979	MF	25+	19 402 270	28.4	——>	42.8	——>	27.7	1.2
		F	25+	10 564 766	31.7	——>	43.8	——>	18.5	0.6
	1989	MF	25+	26 466 214	16.6	69.8	——>	10.6	——>	2.6
		F	25+	14 315 859	23.4	66.2	——>	8.4	——>	1.7
Europe										
Austria	1981	MF	25+	4 558 681	.	49.3	——>	——>	47.5	3.3
		F	25+	2 508 936	.	61.9	——>	——>	36.6	1.6
Belarus										
Total population	1979	MF	10+	...	40.6	——>	——>	41.5	10.2	7.7
		F	10+	...	45.1	——>	——>	36.8	11.1	7.0
Urban population		MF	10+	...	24.0	——>	——>	49.9	14.2	12.0
		F	10+	...	26.4	——>	——>	46.9	15.6	11.1

1.3 Educational attainment
Niveau d'instruction
Nivel de instrucción

Country / Pays / País	Year / Année / Año	Sex / Sexe / Sexo	Age group / Groupe d'âge / Grupo de edad	Total population / Population totale / Población total	No schooling / Sans scolarité / Sin escolaridad	First level / Premier degré / Primer grado		Entered second level / Accédé au second degré / Accedieron al segundo grado		Post-secondary / Post-secondaire / Post-secundaria
						Incompleted / Non complété / Incompleto	Completed / Complété / Completo	S-1	S-2	
				(1)	(2)	(3)	(4)	(5)	(6)	(7)
Belarus (cont)										
Rural population		MF	10+	...	60.2	——>	——>	31.7	5.5	2.6
		F	10+	...	66.6	——>	——>	25.1	5.8	2.5
Bulgaria‡										
Total population	1992	MF	25+	5 649 672	4.7	12.5	31.9	35.7	——>	15.0
		F	25+	2 931 909	6.2	14.8	29.8	33.9	——>	15.2
Urban population		MF	25+	3 666 533	2.4	6.0	25.7	44.5	——>	21.2
		F	25+	1 909 391	3.1	7.3	24.5	43.5	——>	21.5
Rural population		MF	25+	1 983 139	9.0	24.7	43.5	19.3	——>	3.5
		F	25+	1 022 518	11.9	28.8	39.8	16.1	——>	3.4
Croatia‡	1981	MF	15+	3 637 769	14.2	51.2	——>	31.0	——>	3.6
		F	15+	1 904 061	18.7	55.3	——>	23.5	——>	2.5
Total population	1991	MF	25+	2 969 584	10.2	43.6	——>	39.5	——>	6.4
		F	25+	1 587 468	14.4	48.8	——>	31.6	——>	4.9
Urban population		MF	15+	2 083 869	4.5	34.9	——>	50.4	——>	8.8
		F	15+	1 102 581	6.5	40.9	——>	44.2	——>	7.0
Rural population		MF	15+	1 774 217	13.3	56.0	——>	27.8	——>	1.2
		F	15+	911 371	18.6	58.4	——>	20.5	——>	0.9
Former Czechoslovakia	1980	MF	25+	9 274 694	0.4	47.6	——>	45.9	——>	6.0
		F	25+	4 899 960	0.5	58.3	——>	37.2	——>	4.0
Czech Republic	1991	MF	25+	6 580 525	0.3	31.4	——>	58.6	——>	8.5
		F	25+	3 485 093	0.4	40.8	——>	51.7	——>	6.0
Denmark‡	1991	MF	25+	2 742 734	-	38.7	——>	3.4	38.2	19.6
		F	25+	1 363 396	-	44.3	——>	3.6	32.6	19.5
Estonia										
Total population	1989	MF	25+	1 001 198	2.2	39.0	——>	45.1	——>	13.7
		F	25+	559 294	2.9	38.5	——>	45.3	——>	13.2
Urban population		MF	25+	720 479	1.9	32.4	——>	49.6	——>	16.1
		F	25+	406 333	2.7	32.2	——>	49.8	——>	15.4
Rural population		MF	25+	280 719	2.9	56.1	——>	33.6	——>	7.4
		F	25+	152 961	3.6	55.5	——>	33.6	——>	7.3
Finland	1980	MF	20+	3 442 000	*1.2	50.0	——>	7.7	29.2	11.9
		F	20+	1 815 000	*1.0	51.2	——>	8.9	28.5	10.4
	1990	MF	25+	3 387 384	...	49.4	——>	35.3	——>	15.4
		F	25+	1 784 166	...	51.4	——>	35.3	——>	13.3
France	1990	MF	25+	37 354 255	...	51.1	——>	36.9	——>	11.4
		F	25+	19 647 744	...	55.1	——>	34.2	——>	10.3
Greece	1981	MF	25+	5 966 511	11.5	16.9	44.3	6.1	13.6	7.6
		F	25+	3 113 632	17.7	18.4	41.7	4.2	13.1	4.9
Total population	1991	MF	25+	6 738 566	5.7	12.7	44.2	6.7	22.0	8.7
Urban population		MF	25+	4 269 892	3.6	8.7	37.9	7.8	29.6	12.4
Rural population		MF	25+	1 741 823	10.3	21.5	56.7	3.9	6.2	1.3
Semi urban pop.		MF	25+	726 851	6.4	15.6	51.1	7.2	14.5	5.2
Hungary‡	1980	MF	25+	6 903 881	1.3	8.0	3.2	57.0	23.6	7.0
		F	25+	3 670 474	1.7	8.7	3.4	61.5	19.6	5.0
	1990	MF	25+	6 798 765	1.3	24.3	33.6	——>	30.7	10.1
		F	25+	3 644 553	1.6	28.8	34.9	——>	26.0	8.7
Ireland	1981	MF	25+	1 793 855	52.3	——>	——>	39.8	——>	7.9
		F	25+	909 047	50.2	——>	——>	43.2	——>	6.5
Total population	1991	MF	25+	1 983 547	0.0	0.0	38.5	43.7	——>	14.6
		F	25+	1 020 854	0.0	0.0	36.8	45.4	——>	14.2
Urban population		MF	25+	1 120 973	0.0	0.0	33.3	45.4	——>	17.5
		F	25+	598 607	0.0	0.0	34.2	46.0	——>	15.8
Rural population		MF	25+	862 574	0.0	0.0	45.3	41.5	——>	10.7
		F	25+	422 247	0.0	0.0	40.5	44.7	——>	11.9

Educational attainment 1.3
Niveau d'instruction
Nivel de instrucción

Country / Pays / País	Year / Année / Año	Sex / Sexe / Sexo	Age group / Groupe d'âge / Grupo de edad	Total population / Population totale / Población total	No schooling / Sans scolarité / Sin escolaridad	First level / Premier degré / Primer grado		Entered second level / Accédé au second degré / Accedieron al segundo grado		Post-secondary / Post-secondaire / Post-secundaria
						Incompleted / Non complété / Incompleto	Completed / Completé / Completo	S-1	S-2	
				(1)	(2)	(3)	(4)	(5)	(6)	(7)
Italy‡	1981	MF	25+	35 596 616	19.3	47.4	——>	18.0	11.2	4.1
		F	25+	18 790 372	23.2	48.8	——>	15.3	9.8	2.9
Latvia	1989	MF	25+	1 725 639	0.6	18.5	21.2	46.3	——>	13.4
		F	25+	968 037	0.9	21.4	19.3	45.3	——>	13.0
Lithuania	1989	MF	25+	2 282 191	9.1	21.3	——>	57.0	——>	12.6
		F	25+	1 255 511	11.7	22.8	——>	53.1	——>	12.3
Luxembourg	1991	MF	25+	262 628	...	39.7	——>	40.3	——>	10.8
		F	25+	136 326	...	44.4	——>	37.2	——>	7.9
Moldova	1989	MF	25+	2 499 613	12.7	17.1	——>	58.9	——>	11.3
		F	25+	1 363 236	16.8	17.7	——>	55.0	——>	10.6
Norway‡	1980	MF	25+	2 574 641	1.8	0.0	——>	60.0	26.2	11.9
		F	25+	1 324 409	1.6	0.0	——>	65.7	23.8	8.8
Total population	1990	MF	25+	2 803 030	0.1	0.1	——>	32.9	46.4	17.9
		F	25+	1 442 854	0.1	0.1	——>	36.4	45.1	15.9
Urban population		MF	25+	2 024 051	0.1	0.1	——>	29.1	46.5	21.1
		F	25+	1 060 370	0.1	0.1	——>	33.5	45.3	18.3
Rural population		MF	25+	762 807	0.0	0.0	——>	42.9	46.2	9.4
		F	25+	375 419	0.0	0.0	——>	44.6	44.6	9.3
Poland										
Total population	1988	MF	25+	22 986 018	1.5	5.6	37.2	47.8	——>	7.9
		F	25+	12 120 238	2.0	6.8	40.6	43.5	——>	7.0
Urban population		MF	25+	14 284 765	0.9	2.4	29.3	56.2	——>	11.3
		F	25+	7 673 764	1.2	3.1	33.7	52.3	——>	9.8
Rural population		MF	25+	8 701 253	2.5	10.9	50.2	34.1	——>	2.2
		F	25+	4 446 474	3.4	13.3	52.6	28.5	——>	2.1
Portugal	1981	MF	25+	5 696 282	27.5	58.5	——>	10.6	——>	3.5
		F	25+	3 057 786	33.4	55.1	——>	9.3	——>	2.2
	1991	MF	25+	6 280 792	16.1	61.5	——>	14.8	——>	7.7
		F	25+	3 348 946	20.1	59.7	——>	12.9	——>	7.2
Romania										
Total population	1992	MF	25+	13 602 159	5.4	24.4	——>	63.2	——>	6.9
		F	25+	7 072 132	8.1	28.1	——>	58.4	——>	5.4
Urban population		MF	25+	7 143 727	1.8	12.9	——>	73.4	——>	12.0
		F	25+	3 719 797	2.6	16.2	——>	71.7	——>	9.5
Rural population		MF	25+	6 458 432	9.5	37.2	——>	52.0	——>	1.4
		F	25+	3 352 335	14.1	41.2	——>	43.7	——>	1.0
Russian Federation	1989	MF	25+	86 016 990	...	36.9	——>	49.0	——>	14.1
		F	25+	46 006 781	...	37.5	——>	48.7	——>	13.8
Slovakia	1991	MF	25+	3 144 143	0.7	37.9	——>	50.9	——>	9.5
		F	25+	1 657 128	0.9	46.5	——>	44.1	——>	7.5
Slovenia	1991	MF	25+	1 272 409	0.7	45.1	——>	42.4	——>	10.4
		F	25+	673 756	0.9	53.5	——>	35.0	——>	9.2
Spain‡										
Total population	1981	MF	25+	21 758 498	35.1	11.8	32.7	7.6	5.7	7.1
		F	25+	11 411 664	38.9	11.8	32.5	7.2	4.1	5.5
Urban population		MF	25+	17 054 758	33.7	11.1	31.4	8.9	6.7	8.2
		F	25+	9 023 931	37.6	11.2	31.7	8.5	4.8	6.2
Rural population		MF	25+	4 703 741	40.6	14.3	37.3	2.7	2.0	3.1
		F	25+	2 387 733	44.1	14.0	35.7	2.4	1.4	2.5
Total population	1991	MF	25+	24 667 414	30.4	34.9	——>	25.5	——>	8.4
		F	25+	12 906 677	33.7	35.2	——>	22.9	——>	7.2
Sweden	1986	MF	16-74	6 114 449	...	28.1	——>	15.6	37.0	13.8
		F	16-74	3 057 014	...	28.8	——>	16.4	36.3	13.6
	1990	MF	16-74	6 212 805	...	23.2	——>	15.4	39.9	15.8
		F	16-74	3 099 034	...	23.7	——>	16.1	39.5	15.8
	1995	MF	16-74	6 329 913	...	18.2	——>	14.7	44.1	21.0
		F	16-74	3 153 976	...	18.1	——>	14.5	44.0	21.5

1.3 Educational attainment
Niveau d'instruction
Nivel de instrucción

Country / Pays / País	Year / Année / Año	Sex / Sexe / Sexo	Age group / Groupe d'âge / Grupo de edad	Total population / Population totale / Población total	No schooling / Sans scolarité / Sin escolaridad	First level – Incompleted / Non complété / Incompleto	First level – Completed / Complété / Completo	Entered second level S-1	S-2	Post-secondary / Post-secondaire / Post-secundaria
				(1)	(2)	(3)	(4)	(5)	(6)	(7)
Switzerland	1980	MF	25+	3 232 206	...	75.6	——>	8.9	——>	11.5
		F	25+	1 626 305	...	78.4	——>	11.7	——>	5.6
Former Yugoslavia	1981	MF	25+	13 083 762	15.8	53.9	——>	23.4	——>	6.8
		F	25+	6 786 385	23.3	56.1	——>	15.8	——>	4.8
Oceania										
American Samoa‡	1980	MF	25+	12 184	2.5	24.3	9.0	22.1	25.5	16.6
		F	25+	5 966	2.6	27.4	9.4	23.2	24.6	12.8
	1990	MF	25+	19 570	1.9	16.8	——>	58.7	——>	22.6
		F	25+	9 578	2.0	17.5	——>	60.5	——>	20.0
Fiji	1986	MF	25+	287 175	10.9	35.9	23.9	24.9	——>	4.5
		F	25+	147 154	14.8	35.0	24.9	21.9	——>	3.4
Guam‡	1980	MF	25+	46 906	1.5	16.5	3.3	44.4	——>	34.4
		F	25+	22 366	2.1	19.4	3.5	44.2	——>	30.8
	1990	MF	25+	66 700	...	13.9	——>	46.2	——>	39.9
		F	25+	30 956	...	16.1	——>	46.2	——>	37.8
New Caledonia	1989	MF	25+	69 922	6.5	51.2	——>	34.8	——>	7.5
		F	25+	33 800	7.8	51.9	——>	34.3	——>	6.0
New Zealand Total population	1981	MF	25+	1 720 383	1.2	41.5	——>	——>	26.6	30.6
		F	25+	884 310	1.2	42.3	——>	——>	28.9	27.6
Urban population		MF	25+	1 450 758	1.2	41.3	——>	——>	26.0	31.5
		F	25+	757 791	1.3	42.8	——>	——>	28.3	27.6
Rural population		MF	25+	269 625	1.0	42.8	——>	——>	30.1	26.1
		F	25+	126 519	0.9	39.1	——>	——>	32.3	27.7
Total population	1991	MF	25+	1 992 354	0.0	36.8	——>	16.3	7.8	39.1
		F	25+	1 029 375	0.0	39.5	——>	19.6	8.0	32.9
Pacific Islands‡	1980	MF	25+	46 177	17.8	36.8	10.9	10.1	13.5	10.9
		F	25+	22 398	21.7	41.8	11.7	8.3	10.2	6.3
Papua New Guinea	1980	MF	25+	1 135 783	82.6	8.2	5.0	3.9	0.3	——>
		F	25+	551 886	87.3	7.2	3.6	1.8	0.0	——>
Samoa	1981	MF	25+	48 872	3.0	53.7	2.4	12.9	25.4	2.7
		F	25+	24 633	3.0	53.6	1.8	13.2	25.4	2.8
Tonga	1986	MF	25+	33 911	9.6	34.6	——>	51.1	——>	2.8
		F	25+	17 737	10.2	36.2	——>	49.7	——>	2.0
Vanuatu, Rep. of Total population	1979	MF	25+	38 488	37.2	34.3	6.5	14.7	7.3	——>
		F	25+	17 612	43.5	33.7	5.8	11.8	5.2	——>
Former U.S.S.R.										
Former U.S.S.R. Total population	1979	MF	10+	...	36.2	——>	——>	44.8	10.7	8.3
		F	10+	...	40.3	——>	——>	40.6	11.5	7.6
Urban population		MF	10+	...	27.6	——>	——>	47.6	13.3	11.4
		F	10+	...	30.7	——>	——>	44.3	14.5	10.5
Rural population		MF	10+	...	50.8	——>	——>	39.9	6.3	3.0
		F	10+	...	56.4	——>	——>	34.4	6.6	2.6
Total population	1989	MF	25+	170 405 095	7.9	——>	14.9	63.3	——>	13.9
		F	25+	94 283 525	11.3	——>	16.1	59.8	——>	12.7
Urban population		MF	25+	114 957 247	5.3	——>	11.0	65.9	——>	17.8
		F	25+	63 675 776	7.8	——>	12.1	63.7	——>	16.4
Rural population		MF	25+	55 447 848	13.2	——>	22.9	57.8	——>	6.0
		F	25+	30 607 749	18.7	——>	24.6	51.7	——>	5.0

Educational attainment 1.3
Niveau d'instruction
Nivel de instrucción

General note / Note générale / Nota general:

E--> Unless otherwise indicated, persons whose level of education has not been stated are included in the total population. Their percentage distribution, although not shown in the table, can be derived by subtracting the sum of the other percentage distributions from 100.

FR--> Sauf mention spéciale, les personnes dont le niveau d'instruction n'est pas connu a été inclus dans le total de la population. Bien que le pourcentage relatif à cette catégorie ne soit pas présentée dans le tableau, il peut être obtenu en soustrayant de 100 la somme des pourcentages présentés.

ESP> De no ser indicado, las personas sobre las cuales se desconoce el nivel de instrucción se han incluído en el total de la población. Aunque el cuadro no presenta una distribución porcentual de esta categoría, se podrá obtener ésta sustrayendo de 100 la suma de los porcentajes presentados.

AFRICA:

Côte d'Ivoire:

E--> Excluding less then first level and never attended school.

FR--> Non compris les personnes n'ayant jamais fréquenté une institution scolaire et celles qui ont un niveau inférieur au premier degré.

ESP> No se incluye a aquellas personas que no se han inscrito nunca en un establecimiento de enseñanza ni aquéllas con un nivel inferior al primer grado de enseñanza.

Egypt:

E--> Egyptian population only. Second level also includes third level education not leading to a university degree.

FR--> Population égyptienne seulement. Le second niveau inclut aussi l'enseignement du troisième degré ne conduisant pas à un grade universitaire.

ESP> Poblacion egipcia solamente. El segundo nivel incluye también la enseñanza de tercer grado que no conduce a un título universitario.

Kenya:

E--> Persons who did not state their level of education have been included in the category *no schooling*.

FR--> Les personnes dont le niveau d'instruction est inconnu sont inclues dans la catégorie *sans scolarité*.

ESP> Las personas cuyo nivel de instrucción se desconoce figuran en la categoría *sin escolaridad*.

Libyan Arab Jamahiriya:

E--> Persons who can read and write have been counted with *incomplete first level*.

FR--> Les personnes sachant lire et écrire ont été inclues dans la catégorie *premier degré incomplet*.

ESP> Las personas que saben leer y escribir han sido incluídas en la categoría *primer grado incompleto*.

Mozambique:

E--> Illiteracy data have been used for the category *no schooling*.

FR--> Les données relatives à l'analphabétisme ont été utilisées pour la catégorie *sans scolarité*.

ESP> Se han utilizado los datos relativos al analfabetismo en la categoría *sin escolaridad*.

Namibia:

E--> Excluding population attending and never attended school.

FR--> Non compris les personnes encore inscrites dans une institution scolaire et celles n'ayant jamais fréquenté une institution scolaire.

ESP> No se incluye a aquellas personas que están escolarizadas ni aquéllas que nunca estuvieron inscritas en un establecimiento de enseñanza.

Sao Tome and Principe:

E--> Illiteracy data have been used for the category *no schooling*.

FR--> Les données relatives à l'analphabétisme ont été utilisées pour la catégorie *sans scolarité*.

ESP> Se han utilizado los datos relativos al analfabetismo en la categoría *sin escolaridad*.

South Africa:

E--> Not including Botphuthatswana, Transkei and Veda.

FR--> Non compris le Botphuthatswana,le Transkei et Veda.

ESP> Excluídos Botphuthaswana, Transkei y Veda.

Sudan:

E--> Persons who can read and write have been counted with *incomplete first level*. Persons who did not state their level of education have been included in the in the category *no schooling*.

FR--> Les personnes sachant lire et écrire on été incluses dans la catégorie *premier degré incomplet*. Les personnes dont le niveau d'instruction est inconnu sont incluses dans la catégorie *sans scolarité*.

ESP> Las personas que saben leer y escribir han sido incluídas en la categoría *primer grado incompleto*. Las personas cuyo nivel de instrucción se desconoce figuran en la categoría *sin escolaridad*.

Zambia:

E--> For 1993, based on a sample survey referring to 35,502 persons.

FR--> En 1993, d'après une enquête par sondage portant sur 35 502 personnes.

ESP> En 1993, según una encuesta por muestreo relativa a 35 502 personas.

AMERICA, NORTH:

El Salvador:

E--> Illiteracy data have been used for the category *no schooling*.

FR--> Les données relatives à l'analphabétisme ont été utilisées pour la catégorie *sans scolarité*.

ESP> Se han utilizado los datos relativos al analfabetismo en la categoría *sin escolaridad*.

Honduras:

E--> Based on a sample survey referring to 51,372 persons.

FR--> D'après une enquête par sondage portant sur 51 372 personnes.

ESP> Según una encuesta por muestreo relativa a 51 372 personas.

Panama:

E--> In 1990, excluding transients and residents of former Canal Zone.

FR--> En 1990, non compris les personnes de passage et les résidents de l'ancienne Zone du Canal.

ESP> En 1990, no se incluyen las personas de pasaje y los residentes de la antigua zona del Canal.

Puerto Rico:

E--> *De jure* population, but including armed forces stationed in the area, based on a 20 % sample of census returns.

FR--> Population de droit, mais y compris les militaires en garnison sur le territoire, d'après un échantillon portant sur 20 % des bulletins de recensement.

ESP> Población *de jure*, pero incluídos los militares destacados en la zona, según una muestra basada en el 20 % de los boletines de censo.

United States:

E--> In 1994, the category *no schooling* refer to those who have less than first grade of first level.

FR--> En 1994, la catégorie *sans scolarité* se réfère aux personnes dont le niveau d'instruction est inférieur à la première année d'étude de l'enseignement primaire.

ESP> En 1994, la categoría *sin escolaridad* se refiere a las personas cuyo nivel de instrucción es inferíor al primer año de estudios de la enseñanza primaria.

U.S. Virgin Islands:

E--> *De jure* population, but including armed forces stationed in the area.

FR--> Population de droit, mais y compris les militaires en garnison sur le territoire.

ESP> Población *de jure*, pero incluídos los militares destacados en la zona.

AMERICA, SOUTH:

Bolivia:

E--> For 1992, first stage of second level of education refers to *Intermedio* level of education. Second stage of second level refers to *Medio* level, *Tecnica* and *Normal* education.

FR--> En 1992, le premier cycle du second degré se réfère au niveau *Intermedio*. Le deuxième cycle du second degré se réfère au niveau *Medio*, et aux enseignements *Tecnica*, et *Normal*.

ESP> En 1992, el primer ciclo de la enseñanza de segundo grado se refiere al nivel de instrucción *Intermedio*. El segundo ciclo se refiere a los niveles de instrucción *Medio*, y a la enseñanza *Técnica* y *Normal*.

Brazil:

E--> For 1989, not including rural population of the region north of Brazil.

FR--> En 1989, non compris la population rurale du Nord du Brésil.

ESP> En 1989, excluída la población rural del norte de Brasil.

Venezuela:

E--> For 1990, persons who did not state their level of education have been included in the category *no schooling*.

FR--> En1990, les personnes dont le niveau d'instruction est inconnu sont incluses dans la catégorie *sans scolarité*.

ESP> En 1990, las personas cuyo nivel de instrucción se desconoce figuran en la categoría *sin escolaridad*.

ASIA:

China:

E--> In 1982, based on a 10% sample of census returns.

FR--> Pour 1982, d'après un échantillon portant sur 10% des bulletins de recensement.

ESP> Para 1982, según una muestra basada en el 10% de los boletines de censo.

1.3 Educational attainment
Niveau d'instruction
Nivel de instrucción

Hong Kong:
E--> In 1981, the category *first level completed* comprises the last two grades of education at first level.
FR-> En 1981, la catégorie *premier degré complète* comprend les deux dernières années d'études de l'enseignement du premier degré.
ESP> En 1981, la categoría *primer grado completo* comprende los dos últimos años de estudios de la enseñanza de primer grado.

Japan:
E--> For 1990, the distribution by level of education do not take into account those still attending school.
FR-> En 1990, la distribution par niveau d'éducation ne prend pas en compte les personnes encore inscrites dans une institution scolaire.
ESP> En 1990, no se incluyen las personas que están todavía inscritas en una institución escolar.

Nepal:
E--> The category of *no schooling* comprises illiterates.
FR-> La catégorie *sans scolarité* comprend les analphabètes.
ESP> La categoría *sin escolaridad* comprende los analfabetos.

Pakistan:
E--> The category of *no schooling* comprises illiterates. For 1990, household survey results based on a sample of 6,393 households.
FR-> La catégorie *sans scolarité* comprend les analphabètes. En 1990, d'après une enquête des ménages portant sur 6 393 ménages.
ESP> La categoría *sin escolaridad* comprende los analfabetos. En 1990, según una encuesta de hogares relativa a 6 393 viviendas.

Qatar:
E--> For 1981, illiteracy data have been used for the category no schooling.
FR-> En 1981, les données relatives à l'analphabétisme ont été utilisées pour la catégorie *sans scolarité*.
ESP> En 1981, se han utilizado los datos relativos al analfabetismo en la categoría *sin escolaridad*.

Singapore:
E--> For 1990, not including persons still enrolled in schools.
FR-> En 1990, non compris les personnes encore inscrites dans les institutions scolaires.
ESP> En 1990, excluídas las personas que están todavía inscritas en las instituciónes escolares.

Turkey:
E--> Based on a sample survey referring to 8,619 households (5,563 urban, 3,056 rural).
FR-> D'après une enquête, par sondage portant sur 8 619 ménages (5 563 urbains, 3 056 ruraux).
ESP> Según una encuesta por muestreo relativa a 8 619 hogares (5 563 urbanos, 3 056 rurales).

EUROPE:
Bulgaria:
E--> The category *first not completed* comprises 4 first grades of primary education (from I to IV). The category *first completed* comprises the last 4 grades of primary education (from V to VIII).
FR-> La catégorie *premier degré non complet* comprend les 4 premières années d'études de l'enseignement primaire (de I à IV). La catégorie *premier degré complet* comprend les 4 dernières années d'études de l'enseignement primaire (de V à VIII).
ESP> La categoría *primer grado incompleto* comprende los 4 primeros años de estudios de la enseñanza primaria (de I a IV). La categoría *primer grado completo* comprende los 4 últimos años de estudios de la enseñanza de primaria (de V a VIII).

Croatia:
E--> Not including expatriate workers.
FR-> Non compris les travailleurs expatriés.
ESP> Excluídos los trabajadores expatriados.

Denmark:
E--> Not including persons whose educational level is unknown.
FR-> Non compris les personnes pour lesquelles leurs niveaux d'instruction sont inconnus.
ESP> Excluídas las personas cuyo nivel de instrucción se desconoce.

Hungary:
E--> In 1990, not including persons still enrolled in schools.
FR-> En 1990, non compris les personnes encore inscrites dans les institutions scolaires.
ESP> En 1990, excluídas las personas que están todavía inscritas en las instituciones escolares.

Italy:
E--> Illiteracy data have been used for the category *no schooling*.
FR-> Les données relatives à l'analphabétisme ont été utilisées pour la catégorie *sans scolarité*.
ESP> Se han utilizado los datos relativos al analfabetismo en la categoría *sin escolaridad*.

Norway:
E--> In 1980, persons who did not state their level of education have been included in the category *no schooling*.
FR-> En 1980, les personnes dont le niveau d'instruction est inconnu sont incluses dans la catégorie *sans scolarité*.
ESP> En 1980, las personas cuyo nivel de instrucción se desconoce figuran en la categoría *sin escolaridad*.

Spain:
E--> In 1981, illiteracy data have been used for the category *no schooling*.
FR-> En 1981, les données relatives à l'analphabétisme ont été utilisées pour la catégorie *sans scolarité*.
ESP> En 1981, se han utilizado los datos relativos al analfabetismo en la categoría *sin escolaridad*.

OCEANIA:
American Samoa:
E--> *De jure* population, including armed forces stationed in the area.
FR-> Population de droit, y compris les militaires en garnison sur le territoire.
ESP> Población *de jure*, incluídos los militares destacados en la zona.

Guam:
E--> *De jure* population, including armed forces stationed in the area.
FR-> Population de droit, y compris les militaires en garnison sur le territoire.
ESP> Población *de jure*, incluídos los militares destacados en la zona.

Pacific Islands:
E--> *De jure* population, including armed forces stationed in the area.
FR-> Population de droit, y compris les militaires en garnison sur le territoire.
ESP> Población *de jure*, incluídos los militares destacados en la zona.

Education

Education

Educación

The following three chapters of the *Yearbook* assemble most of the basic statistical information collected and compiled by UNESCO regarding population, adult illiteracy and public and private education at all levels. The thirty tables provide world-wide statistical data on such subjects as: the number of schools; teachers and pupils by level and type of education; students and graduates in higher education by field of study and level of programme; foreign students in higher education by country of origin and by host country; and public expenditure on education by purpose and by level of education. As far as possible, data refer to the school years beginning in 1980, 1985 and 1990 as well as the three most recent years.

For the purpose of these tables, the definitions and classifications set out in the Revised Recommendation concerning the International Standardization of Educational Statistics, adopted by the General Conference of UNESCO at its twentieth session (Paris, 1978), and those presented in the International Standard Classification of Education (ISCED) have been applied as far as possible. In accordance therewith education is classified by level as follows:

Education preceding the first level (ISCED level 0), which provides education for children who are not old enough to enter school at the first level (e.g. at nursery school, kindergarten, infant school).

Education at the first level (ISCED level 1), of which the main function is to provide the basic elements of education (e.g. at elementary school, primary school).

Education at the second level (ISCED levels 2 and 3), provided at middle school, secondary school, high school, teacher-training school at this level and schools of a vocational or technical nature. This level of education is based upon at least four years' previous instruction at first level and provides general and/or specialized instruction.

Education at the third level (ISCED levels 5, 6 and 7), provided at universities, teachers' colleges, higher professional schools, which requires, as a minimum condition of admission, the successful completion of education at the second level, or evidence of the attainment of an equivalent level of knowledge.

Special education, covering all types of education given to children who suffer from physical, mental, visual, social, hearing or speech handicaps, or from reading and writing difficulties.

The following definitions are reproduced from the Recommendation:

A pupil (student) is a person enrolled in a school for systematic instruction at any level of education.

A teacher is a person directly engaged in instructing a group of pupils (students). Heads of educational institutions, supervisory and other personnel should be counted as teachers only when they have regular teaching functions.

A school (educational institution) is a group of pupils (students) of one or more grades organized to receive instruction of a given type and level under one teacher, or under more than one teacher under the direct supervision of the head of the establishment.

(a) *A public school* is a school operated by a public authority (national, federal, state or provincial, or local), whatever the origin of its financial resources.

(b) *A private school* is a school not operated by a public authority, whether or not it receives financial support from such authorities. Private schools may be defined as aided or non-aided, respectively, according as they derive or do not derive financial support from public authorities.

The enrolment data throughout these tables refer, in general, to the beginning of the school or academic year. In this connection, it should be pointed out that enrolment data may vary substantially according to the date at which the count is taken, i.e. at the beginning, in the middle, at the end of the school year, an average count, etc.

The years stated indicate the school or academic year. Appendix B gives information on the dates of commencement and end of the school and fiscal years in each country and territory.

Les trois chapitres de l'*Annuaire* qui suivent contiennent la plupart des données statistiques de base recueillies et élaborées par l'UNESCO relatives a la population, à l'analphabétisme des adultes et des enseignements publics et privés de tous les degrés. Les quelque trente tableaux qui suivent présentent pour l'ensemble du monde, des données statistiques sur: le nombre d'écoles, le nombre de maîtres et d'élèves par degré et type d'enseignement; le nombre d'étudiants et de diplômés de l'enseignement supérieur, par domaine d'études et par niveau de programmes; le nombre d'étudiants étrangers, par pays d'origine et par pays d'accueil; enfin, les dépenses publiques afférentes à l'enseignement, selon leur destination et par degré d'enseignement. Dans la mesure du possible, les chiffres présentés se rapportent aux années scolaires commençant en 1980, 1985, 1990 et aux trois années les plus récentes.

Les définitions et classifications qui figurent dans la Recommandation révisée concernant la normalisation internationale des statistiques de l'éducation, adoptée par la Conférence générale de l'UNESCO à sa vingtième session (Paris, 1978), ainsi que celles qui apparaissent dans la Classification Internationale Type de l'Education (CITE), ont été utilisées, autant que possible, dans ces tableaux. Aux termes de ces définitions, l'enseignement est classé par degré, de la façon suivante:

Enseignement précédant le premier degré (Niveau 0 de la CITE), dispensé, par exemple, dans les écoles maternelles ou les jardins d'enfants, qui assure léducation des enfants trop jeunes pour être admis à l'enseignement du premier degré.

Enseignement du premier degré (Niveau 1 de la CITE), dispensé, par exemple, dans les écoles élémentaires ou les écoles primaires, qui a pour fonction principale de fournir les premiers éléments de l'instruction.

Enseignement du second degré (Niveaux 2 et 3 de la CITE), dispensé, par exemple dans les écoles moyennes, les lycées, les collèges, les gymnases, les athénées, les écoles complémentaires, ainsi que dans les écoles de ce degré destinées à la formation des maîtres et dans les écoles à caractère technique ou professionnel. Ce niveau d'enseignement implique quatre années au moins d'études préalables dans le premier degré et donne une formation générale ou spécialisée (ou les deux).

Enseignement du troisième degré (Niveaux 5, 6 et 7 de la CITE), dispensé, par exemple, dans les universités, les diverses grandes écoles et instituts supérieurs, y compris les écoles normales supérieures, qui exige comme condition minimale d'admission d'avoir suivi avec succès un enseignement complet du second degré ou de faire preuve de connaissances équivalentes.

Education spéciale, englobant tous les types d'enseignement destinés aux enfants déficients physiques, mentaux, visuels, auditifs, souffrant de difficultés de la parole ou de troubles de lecture et d'écriture et aux inadaptés sociaux.

Les définitions ci-après sont tirées de la Recommandation:

Elève (étudiant): personne inscrite dans un établissement d'enseignement pour recevoir un enseignement systématique de n'importe quel degré.

Maître: personne assurant directement l'instruction d'un groupe d'élèves (étudiants); les chefs d'établissements, ainsi que les membres du personnel d'inspection, de surveillance et autres, ne devraient être rangés parmi les maîtres que s'ils exercent régulièrement des fonctions d'enseignement.

Etablissement d'enseignement (école, institut, etc.): institution groupant des élèves (étudiants) d'une ou plusieurs années en vue de leur faire donner un enseignement d'un certain type et d'un certain degré par un ou plusieurs maîtres relevant directement d'un chef d'établissement.

(a) *Etablissement d'enseignement public*: établissement dont le fonctionnement est assuré par les pouvoirs publics (nationaux, fédéraux, d'état ou provinciaux, ou locaux) quelle que soit l'origine de ses ressources financières.

(b) *Etablissement d'enseignement privé*: établissement dont le fonctionnement n'est pas assuré par les pouvoirs publics qu'il reçoive ou non une aide financière de ceux-ci. Les établissements d'enseignement privé peuvent être classés en établissements subventionnés et établissements non subventionnés, selon qu'ils reçoivent ou non une aide financière des pouvoirs publics.

Dans tous les tableaux, les données concernant les effectifs se rapportent d'ordinaire au début de l'année scolaire ou universitaire. A ce propos, il y a lieu de rappeler que les effectifs peuvent varier sensiblement, selon qu'il s'agisse de chiffres relevés au début, au milieu ou à la fin de l'année scolaire ou encore de moyennes, etc.

Les années indiquées sont les années scolaires ou universitaires. L'annexe B fournit des renseignements sur le commencement et la fin des années scolaires et budgétaires dans chaque pays et territoire.

Los tres capítulos siguientes del *Anuario* contienen la mayor parte de los datos estadísticos básicos solicitados por la UNESCO en relación con la población, el analfabetismo de adultos, los establecimientos docentes, públicos y privados, de todos los grados (niveles) de la enseñanza. En los treinta cuadros que figuran a continuación se presentan datos estadísticos mundiales sobre el número de establecimientos docentes; el número de maestros y profesores y de alumnos por grado (nivel) y tipo de enseñanza; el número de estudiantes y diplomados de la enseñanza de tercer grado (superior), por sexo, sector de estudios y por nivel de los programas; el número de estudiantes extranjeros, por país de origen y por país huésped; por último, los gastos públicos de educación desglosados según su destino y por grado de enseñanza. En la medida de lo posible los datos se refieren a los años escolares que empezaron en 1980, en 1985 y a los cuatro años más recientes.

En esos cuadros se ha utilizado en lo posible las definiciones y clasificaciones que figuran en la Recomendación revisada sobre la normalización internacional de las estadísticas relativas a la educación aprobada por la Conferencia General de la UNESCO en su 20a reunión (París, 1978) y las deficiones que se encuentran en la Clasificación Internacional Normalizada de la Educación (CINE). Con arreglo a esas definiciones, la enseñanza queda clasificada por grados como sigue:

Enseñanza anterior al primer grado (Nivel 0 de la CINE), por ejemplo, la que se da en guarderías infantiles, escuelas de párvulos o jardines de infancia : para los niños que no están aún en edad de ser admitidos en la enseñanza de primer grado.

Enseñanza de primer grado (Nivel 1 de la CINE), por ejemplo, la que se da en escuelas elementales o en escuelas primarias, cuya función principal consiste en proporcionar los primeros elementos de la instrucción.

Enseñanza de segundo grado (Niveles 2 y 3 de la CINE), por ejemplo, la que se da en escuelas de enseñanza media, secundarias, institutos, liceos, colegios, escuelas técnicas, escuelas normales de este grado, que implica cuatro años como mínimo de estudios previos en el primer grado y que da una formación general o especializada, o de ambas clases.

Enseñanza de tercer grado (Niveles 5, 6 y 7 de la CINE), por ejemplo, la que se da en las universidades, las escuelas técnicas superiores, las grandes escuelas especiales y las escuelas normales superiores, para la admisión a la cual se exige como condición mínima haber completado con éxito la enseñanza de segundo grado o demostrar la posesión de conocimientos equivalentes.

Educación especial: comprende toda la enseñanza general o profesional destinada a los deficientes físicos o mentales, visuales, auditivos, que sufren de dificultades de la palabra o de trastornos para la lectura y a los inadaptados sociales.

Las siguientes definiciones están tomadas de la recomendación:

Alumno (estudiante): la persona matriculada en un establecimiento docente para recibir una enseñanza sistemática de cualquier grado.

Maestro o profesor: la persona que se ocupa directamente de la instrucción de un grupo de alumnos (estudiantes). No debería incluirse entre los maestros o profesores a los directores de los establecimientos docentes, ni al personal de inspección, vigilancia, etc, más que cuando ejerzan regularmente funciones de enseñanza.

Establecimiento docente (escuela, instituto, etc.): grupo de alumnos (estudiantes) de uno o de varios años de estudios organizados para recibir una enseñanza de determinado tipo y determinado grado dada por uno o varios profesores, bajo la autoridad de un director de establecimiento.

(a) *Establecimiento docente público*: establecimiento cuyo funcionamiento depende del poder público (nacional, federal, provincial o local), cualquiera que sea el origen de sus recursos económicos.

(b) *Establecimiento docente privado*: establecimiento cuyo funcionamiento no depende del poder público, tanto si recibe una ayuda económica de éste como en caso contrario. Los establecimientos docentes privados pueden clasificarse en establecimientos subvencionados y establecimientos no subvencionados, según reciban o no una ayuda económica de los poderes públicos.

En todos los cuadros, los datos relativos a la matrícula se refieren habitualmente al principio del año escolar o universitario. Procede recordar a este respecto que la matrícula puede variar sensiblemente según se trate de cifras calculadas al principio, a mediados o al final del año escolar, de promedios, etc.

Los años indicados son los años escolares o universitarios. En el apéndice B se presentan datos sobre el comienzo y el final de los años escolares y de los ejercicios económicos en cada país y territorio.

2 Summary tables for all levels of education, by continents, major areas and groups of countries

Tableaux récapitulatifs pour tous les degrés d'enseignement, par continents, grandes régions et groupes de pays

Cuadros recapitulativos para todos los grados de enseñanza, por continentes, grandes regiones y grupos de países

This chapter, comprising 11 tables, provides a summary presentation of data on population as well as statistics for all levels of education. Together these tables convey a general picture of the quantitative development since 1980 and also of the present situation of adult illiteracy, education and expenditure on education in the whole world and in each major area and group of countries.

Table 2.1

Table 2.1 presents estimates and projections of the total population and the population below age 25, for the world, by continents, major areas and groups of countries, for the years 1970, 1980, 1990, 1995 and 2000 and 2010. Separate estimates are given for age-groups 0-4, 5-9, 10-14, 15-19 and 20-24 years, covering the ages of most relevance for education. The figures presented in this table correspond to the medium variant of the 1994 revision of the population estimates and projections prepared by the United Nations Population Division.

Table 2.2

This table presents data for 1980, 1985, 1990 and 1995 relating to the estimated adult illiterate population and percentage of illiterates by continent, major areas and groups of countries, as assessed by the Unesco Division of Statistics in 1994.

Table 2.3

The data in this table are based mainly on the enrolment and teaching staff figures shown for each individual country and territory in Table 3.3.

Tables 2.4 - 2.8

These tables present regional trends of enrolment and teaching staff by level of education. The definitions for each level are given in the introductory text to the *Education* section. Data in these tables are based mainly on the enrolment and the teaching staff figures shown for each individual country and territory in Tables 3.4, 3.7 and 3.10 of the *Yearbook*. However in case of changes in the national education systems, data have been standardised to reflect the latest education structure for each country. It should be noted that the breakdown and percentage distribution by level of education are influenced by the length of schooling at each level, which in turn depends on the criteria applied in the national definitions of levels (see Table 3.1). Since these criteria, particularly as concerns primary and secondary education, vary from country to country, caution should be exercised in making comparisons between areas.

Table 2.9

This table shows the distribution of enrolment and teaching staff at the second level by type of education. The data are based mainly on the enrolment and teaching staff figures shown for each individual country and territory in Table 3.7. Care should be exercised when making comparisons between areas and also in interpreting changes observed within a given area during the period under review because of the differences in the curricula and classifications used by countries and territories to define the role and function of teacher training and technical and vocational education at the second level.

Table 2.10

This table presents adjusted gross enrolment ratios by level of education and by sex. Data are based on the enrolment estimates presented in Table 2.4, and the medium variant of the population estimates and projections prepared by the United Nations Population Division, 1994 revision. A gross enrolment ratio for a given level of education is derived by dividing the total enrolment for this level of education, regardless of age, by the population of the age group which according to national regulations, should be enrolled at this level. The term *adjusted* indicates that the population groups used in deriving these ratios for a particular region have been obtained by taking into account the structure of education of each country in the region. However, for third level education, a standard duration of 5 years following the end of second level general education was used for all countries. All ratios are expressed as percentages and may be greater than 100 because of late entry, repetition, etc.

Table 2.11

The purpose of this table is to show the general trends in public expenditure on education, expressed in United States dollars at current market prices.

For most countries statistics for Gross National Product (GNP) and exchange rates have been obtained from the World Bank and the International Monetary Fund respectively.

The data shown in this table should be considered as approximate indications of the public resources allocated to education. The comparative analysis of data expressed in U.S. dollars should be treated with great caution, due to the fact that the official exchange rates used for the conversions produce unrealistic U.S. dollar values for a number of countries. Moreover, it should be noted that these values are expressed at current prices and are therefore affected by inflation.

Ce chapitre, qui comprend 11 tableaux, présente des données récapitulatives sur la population ainsi que des statistiques pour tous les degrés d'enseignement. Ces tableaux donnent également une idée générale de l'évolution quantitative à partir de 1980, ainsi que la situation actuelle de l'analphabétisme des adultes, l'enseignement et des dépenses afférentes à l'enseignement dans le monde et dans chaque grande région et groupe de pays.

Tableau 2.1
Dans le tableau 2.1 figurent les estimations et les projections pour les années 1970, 1980, 1990, 1995, 2000 et 2010 de la population totale et de la population de moins de 25 ans pour le monde entier, par continents, par grandes régions et par groupes de pays. Des estimations sont données séparément pour les groupes d'âge 0-4, 10-14, 15-19 et 20-24 ans, qui sont ceux qui présentent le plus d'intérêt du point de vue de l'éducation. Les données présentées dans ce tableau correspondent à la variante moyenne des estimations et projections de la population effectuées par la Division de la Population de l'Organisation des Nations Unies en 1994.

Tableau 2.2
Ce tableau présente les estimations du nombre d'analphabètes adultes pour les années 1980, 1985, 1990 et 1995, ainsi que les pourcentages d'analphabètes par continent, grandes régions et groupes de pays , élaborés en 1994 par la Division des Statistiques de l'Unesco.

Tableau 2.3
Les données présentées dans ce tableau sont basées, pour la plupart, sur les effectifs scolaires et le personnel enseignant indiqués pour chaque pays et territoire dans le tableau 3.3.

Tableaux 2.4 - 2.8
Ces tableaux montrent l'évolution par régions des effectifs scolaires et du personnel enseignant pour les différents degrés d'enseignement. Pour la définition de chaque degré d'enseignement se reporter au texte introductif de la partie *Education*. Les données sont basées, pour la plupart, sur les effectifs scolaires et le personnel enseignant indiqués pour chaque pays et territoire dans les tableaux 3.4, 3.7 et 3.10 de l'*Annuaire*. Toutefois, en cas de changement dans les systèmes nationaux d'enseignement les données ont été normalisées afin de refléter les dernières structures nationales d'enseignement. Il y a lieu de noter que la répartition, en chiffres absolus ou en pourcentages, entre les différents degrés d'enseignement dépend du nombre d'années d'études correspondant à chaque degré et, par la suite, des critères appliqués dans chaque pays pour définir les degrés d'enseignement (voir tableau 3.1). Comme ces critères varient d'un pays à un autre, notamment en ce qui concerne le premier et le second degré, il convient de faire preuve de prudence lorsqu'on veut procéder à des comparaisons entre les régions.

Tableau 2.9
Ce tableau présente la répartition des effectifs d'étudiants et d'enseignants par type d'enseignement du second degré. Les données sont basées, pour la plupart, sur les effectifs d'étudiants et le personnel enseignant indiqués pour chaque pays et territoire dans le tableau 3.7. Il convient de faire preuve de prudence lorsqu'on veut procéder à des comparaisons entre les régions ou interpréter les modifications constatées dans une région donnée pendant la période considérée, compte tenu des différences existant dans les programmes d'études et les classifications utilisées par les pays et territoires pour définir le rôle et la fonction de l'enseignement normal et de l'enseignement technique et professionnel.

Tableau 2.10
Ce tableau présente les taux d'inscription scolaire bruts ajustés par degré d'enseignement et par sexe. Les données présentées dans ce tableau correspondent aux estimations des effectifs d'élèves présentées dans le tableau 2.4 et à la variante moyenne des estimations et projections de la population effectuées par la Division de la Population des Nations Unies en 1994.

Un taux d'inscription scolaire brut pour un niveau d'éducation donné est obtenu en divisant le total des effectifs scolaires de ce niveau d'éducation, sans tenir compte de l'âge, par la population du groupe d'âge, qui, suivant les systèmes nationaux, devrait être scolarisée à ce niveau. Le terme *ajusté* indique que les groupes de population utilisés pour le calcul de ces taux pour une région donnée ont été obtenus en tenant compte des systèmes d'éducation pour chaque pays de la région. Cependant, pour l'enseignement du troisième degré, une durée normalisée de 5 ans, à partir de la fin de l'enseignement général du second degré, a été utilisée pour tous les pays. Tous les taux sont exprimés en pourcentages et peuvent être supérieurs à 100, en raison des admissions tardives, redoublements, etc.

Tableau 2.11
Ce tableau a pour objet de montrer l'évolution des dépenses publiques d'enseignement exprimées en dollars des Etats-Unis aux prix courants du marché.

Pour la majeure partie des pays, les données sur le produit national brut (PNB) et les taux de change sont fournis respectivement par la Banque Mondiale et le Fonds Monétaire International.

Toutes les données doivent être considérées comme des indications générales et approximatives de l'ordre de grandeur des ressources publiques consacrées à l'enseignement. L'analyse comparative des données exprimées en dollars des Etats-Unis, doit être faite avec beaucoup de prudence, car les taux de change officiels utilisés pour les conversions fournissent des valeurs en dollars irréalistes pour un certain nombre de pays. Il faut aussi signaler que ces valeurs sont exprimées en prix courants et sont donc affectées par l'inflation.

Este capítulo, que comprende 11 cuadros, presenta datos recapitulativos sobre población así como estadísticas para todos los grados de enseñanza. Estos cuadros dan igualmente una idea general del desarrollo cuantitativo a partir de 1980, así como de la situación actual del analfabetismo de adultos, de la enseñanza y de los gastos destinados a la educación en el mundo y en cada de las grandes regiones y grupos de países.

Cuadro 2.1
En el cuadro 2.1 figuran las estimaciones y las proyecciones para los años 1970, 1980, 1990, 1995, 2000 y 2010 de la población total y de la población de menos de 25 años, para el mundo, por continentes, por grandes regiones y grupos de países. Se presentan por separado estimaciones relativas a los grupos de 0-4, 5-9, 10-14, 15-19, y 20-24 años de edad, que presentan un mayor interés del punto de vista de la educación. Los datos presentados en este cuadro corresponden a la variante media de las estimaciones y proyecciones de la población, evaluadas por la División de la Población de las Naciones Unidas en 1994.

Cuadro 2.2
Este cuadro presenta las estimaciones del número de analfabetos adultos para 1980, 1985, 1990 y 1995 y los porcentajes de analfabetos por continente, grandes regiones y grupos de países, preparados en 1994 por la División de Estadística de la Unesco.

Cuadro 2.3
Los datos de este cuadro se basan principalmente en las cifras de la matrícula escolar y del personal docente que figuran en el cuadro 3.3 para cada país y territorio.

Cuadros 2.4 - 2.8
Estos cuadros presentan la evolución por regiones de la matrícula escolar y del personel docente para cada grado de enseñanza. Para la definición de los distintos grados de enseñanza refiérase a la introducción del capítulo *Educación*. Los datos presentados en estos cuadros se basan en principalmente en matrícula escolar y de personal docente para cada país o territorio en los cuadros 3.4, 3.7 y 3.10 del *Anuario* . Sin embargo, se han normalizado los datos; en el caso de cambios en los sistemas nacionales de educacúon para que reflejen las nuevas estructuras de los sistemas educativos de cada país. Cabe señalar que la distribución en valores absolutos y

en porcentajes, entre los distintos grados de enseñanza depende del número de años de estudios correspondientes a cada grado, que a su vez depende de los criterios aplicados en cada país para definir los grados de enseñanza (véase el cuadro 3.1). Como estos criterios varían de un país a otro en particular respecto del primero y del segundo grado, las comparaciones entre las regiones deben ser efectuadas con prudencia.

Cuadro 2.9
Este cuadro presenta la distribución de la matrícula escolar y del personal docente por tipo de enseñanza de segundo grado. Los datos se basan principalmente en las cifras de la matrícula escolar y del personal docente que figuran en el cuadro 3.7 para cada país y territorio. Las comparaciones entre las regiones o la interpretación de los cambios observados dentro de una misma región durante el período considerado deben efectuarse con prudencia, debido a las diferencias existentes en los programas de estudio y las clasificaciones utilizadas por los países y territorios para definir el papel y las funciones de la enseñanza normal y de la enseñanza técnica y profesional.

Cuadro 2.10
Este cuadro presenta las tasas de escolarización brutas ajustadas por nivel de educación y por sexo. Los datos se refieren a las estimaciones de las matrículas escolares presentadas en el cuadro 2.4 y a la variante media de las estimaciones y proyecciones de la población evaluadas por la División de la Población de las Naciones Unidas en 1994.

Una tasa bruta para un nivel de educación dado se obtiene dividiendo el total de la matrícula del nivel de educación en cuestión, independientemente de la edad, por la población del grupo de edad que, de acuerdo con las normas nacionales, debe de estar inscrita en ese nivel. El término *ajustado* indica que los grupos de población utilizados en el cálculo de estas tasas para una región dada fueron obtenidos tomando en cuenta los sistemas de educación de cada país de la región. Sin embargo, para la educación de tercer grado, una duración fija de 5 años al final de la educación secundaria general fué utilizada para todos los países. Todas las tasas están expresadas en porcentajes y pueden ser superiores al 100% debidoa inscripciones retrasadas, repetición, etc.

Cuadro 2.11

El objeto de este cuadro es presentar la evolución de los gastos públicos de educación, expresados en precios corrientes del mercado y en dólares de los Estados Unidos.

Para la mayoría de los países, los datos relativos al producto nacional bruto (PNB) y los tipos de cambio han sido proporcionados por el Banco Mundial y el Fondo Monetario Internacional respectivamente.

Los datos presentados en este cuadro han de considerarse como una indicación general y aproximada del orden de magnitud de los recursos públicos dedicados a la educación. El análisis comparativo de los datos expresados en dólares de los Estados Unidos debe ser llevado a cabo con prudencia ya que las tasas de cambio oficiales utilizadas en las conversiones proporcionan valores en dólares irrealistas para un cierto número de países. Hay que señalar también que estos valores están expresados en precios corrientes y por ende afectados por la inflación.

2.1 Estimated total population and population 0-24 years old, by continents, major areas and groups of countries, 1970-2010

Estimation de la population totale et de la population de 0 à 24 ans, par continents, grandes régions et groupes de pays, 1970-2010

Estimación de la población total y de la población de 0 a 24 años, por continentes, grandes regiones y grupos de países, 1970-2010

A = all ages   A = tous les âges   A = todas las edades

Continents, major areas and groups of countries / Continents, grandes régions et groupes de pays / Continentes, grandes regiones y grupos de países	Age group / Groupe d'âge / Grupo de edad	Estimated population (thousands) / Estimation de la population (en milliers) / Población estimada (en miles)						Annual average increase / Accroissement moyen annuel / Crecimiento medio annual		
		1970	1980	1990	1995	2000	2010	1970-1990 (%)	1990-2000 (%)	2000-2010 (%)
		(1)	(2)	(3)	(4)	(5)	(6)	(7)	(8)	(9)
World total	A	3 697 141	4 444 361	5 284 843	5 716 426	6 158 051	7 032 294	1.8	1.5	1.3
	0-4	521 972	539 287	625 067	634 693	655 441	677 588	0.9	0.5	0.3
	5-9	460 340	525 716	563 357	609 847	620 992	652 478	1.0	1.0	0.5
	10-14	404 048	499 887	517 738	558 400	605 297	639 560	1.2	1.6	0.6
	15-19	365 373	450 274	517 894	514 306	554 937	613 828	1.8	0.7	1.0
	20-24	300 039	393 351	492 157	513 748	510 122	598 053	2.5	0.4	1.6
	0-24	2 051 764	2 408 509	2 716 204	2 830 983	2 946 781	3 181 500	1.4	0.8	0.8
Africa	A	364 206	475 666	632 672	728 074	831 596	1 069 378	2.8	2.8	2.5
	0-4	65 076	85 640	111 372	125 406	136 928	161 598	2.7	2.1	1.7
	5-9	53 116	68 707	92 196	105 290	119 273	143 637	2.8	2.6	1.9
	10-14	44 626	57 833	77 453	90 015	103 088	129 030	2.8	2.9	2.3
	15-19	37 229	49 843	65 121	76 131	88 616	115 645	2.8	3.1	2.7
	20-24	30 596	42 054	55 173	63 783	74 647	100 047	3.0	3.1	3.0
	0-24	230 642	304 076	401 315	460 625	522 552	649 956	2.8	2.7	2.2
America	A	509 694	610 901	717 557	774 846	830 155	935 414	1.7	1.5	1.2
	0-4	63 948	68 950	75 922	79 217	79 101	79 271	0.9	0.4	0.0
	5-9	62 775	65 222	72 438	75 426	78 733	78 490	0.7	0.8	0.0
	10-14	57 702	63 428	68 418	72 459	75 412	78 691	0.9	1.0	0.4
	15-19	50 857	63 132	65 581	68 371	72 365	78 666	1.3	1.0	0.8
	20-24	43 098	57 243	63 180	65 381	68 145	75 156	1.9	0.8	1.0
	0-24	278 379	317 974	345 538	360 853	373 755	390 274	1.1	0.8	0.4
Asia	A	2 147 491	2 642 110	3 186 447	3 457 957	3 735 846	4 263 948	2.0	1.6	1.3
	0-4	338 097	332 617	386 932	385 953	395 619	393 322	0.7	0.2	-0.1
	5-9	285 673	338 440	346 742	378 155	378 815	387 293	1.0	0.9	0.2
	10-14	242 756	323 672	319 584	343 680	375 713	387 978	1.4	1.6	0.3
	15-19	221 241	279 088	333 332	317 083	341 571	375 233	2.1	0.2	0.9
	20-24	175 517	235 640	318 267	330 138	314 488	371 709	3.0	-0.1	1.7
	0-24	1 263 281	1 509 452	1 704 853	1 755 003	1 806 201	1 915 529	1.5	0.6	0.6
Europe	A	656 441	692 997	721 739	726 999	729 803	728 741	0.5	0.1	0.0
	0-4	52 707	49 921	48 410	41 531	41 111	40 581	-0.4	-1.6	-0.1
	5-9	56 673	51 082	49 658	48 505	41 546	40 284	-0.7	-1.8	-0.3
	10-14	56 986	52 715	50 058	49 878	48 572	41 102	-0.6	-0.3	-1.7
	15-19	54 262	56 108	51 495	50 466	49 990	41 592	-0.3	-0.3	-1.8
	20-24	49 180	56 427	53 311	52 058	50 566	48 574	0.4	-0.5	-0.4
	0-24	269 807	266 253	252 932	242 437	231 785	212 131	-0.3	-0.9	-0.9
Oceania	A	19 310	22 687	26 428	28 549	30 652	34 814	1.6	1.5	1.3
	0-4	2 139	2 155	2 429	2 593	2 687	2 825	0.6	1.0	0.5
	5-9	2 109	2 262	2 321	2 472	2 630	2 780	0.5	1.3	0.6
	10-14	1 977	2 241	2 225	2 364	2 510	2 762	0.6	1.2	1.0
	15-19	1 779	2 112	2 365	2 253	2 390	2 695	1.4	0.1	1.2
	20-24	1 649	1 982	2 225	2 385	2 274	2 563	1.5	0.2	1.2
	0-24	9 652	10 752	11 565	12 066	12 490	13 624	0.9	0.8	0.9

Continents, major areas and groups of countries — Continents, grandes régions et groupes de pays — Continentes, grandes regiones y grupos de países	Age group — Groupe d'âge — Grupo de edad	Estimated population (thousands) — Estimation de la population (en milliers) — Población estimada (en miles)						Annual average increase — Accroissement moyen annuel — Crecimiento medio annual		
		1970	1980	1990	1995	2000	2010	1970-1990 (%)	1990-2000 (%)	2000-2010 (%)
		(1)	(2)	(3)	(4)	(5)	(6)	(7)	(8)	(9)
Developing countries	A	2 666 053	3 326 852	4 093 959	4 496 091	4 913 559	5 748 205	2.2	1.8	1.6
	0-4	435 034	455 333	539 979	555 176	576 710	598 964	1.1	0.7	0.4
	5-9	366 530	439 391	478 091	524 422	541 280	574 456	1.3	1.2	0.6
	10-14	310 224	411 603	432 924	472 552	519 543	560 206	1.7	1.8	0.8
	15-19	276 543	355 867	430 079	428 714	468 711	533 361	2.2	0.9	1.3
	20-24	218 345	299 423	402 817	424 958	424 112	511 540	3.1	0.5	1.9
	0-24	1 606 672	1 961 612	2 283 883	2 405 814	2 530 346	2 778 519	1.8	1.0	0.9
Sub-Saharan Africa	A	292 751	384 238	514 236	595 874	685 573	896 271	2.9	2.9	2.7
	0-4	52 971	70 779	94 147	108 262	119 386	144 230	2.9	2.4	1.9
	5-9	42 611	56 291	76 150	88 341	102 355	126 098	2.9	3.0	2.1
	10-14	35 442	46 653	63 282	74 056	86 236	111 718	2.9	3.1	2.6
	15-19	29 695	40 129	52 990	62 029	72 751	98 867	2.9	3.2	3.1
	20-24	24 970	33 373	44 264	51 728	60 662	83 362	2.9	3.2	3.2
	0-24	185 688	247 224	330 831	384 416	441 388	564 275	2.9	2.9	2.5
Arab States	A	125 952	168 158	225 751	255 067	288 989	362 037	3.0	2.5	2.3
	0-4	22 088	28 898	35 861	38 071	41 048	45 736	2.5	1.4	1.1
	5-9	18 571	23 791	31 617	34 814	37 337	43 076	2.7	1.7	1.4
	10-14	15 758	20 686	27 483	31 152	34 541	40 112	2.8	2.3	1.5
	15-19	13 008	17 667	23 232	27 157	30 932	36 845	2.9	2.9	1.8
	20-24	10 234	15 239	20 342	22 898	26 921	34 058	3.5	2.8	2.4
	0-24	79 659	106 281	138 535	154 092	170 778	199 827	2.8	2.1	1.6
Latin America and the Caribbean	A	283 214	358 440	439 719	482 005	523 875	603 843	2.2	1.8	1.4
	0-4	44 915	50 690	55 065	56 673	57 180	56 897	1.0	0.4	0.0
	5-9	40 554	46 789	52 388	54 219	55 880	56 485	1.3	0.6	0.1
	10-14	34 549	43 208	49 295	52 003	53 846	56 118	1.8	0.9	0.4
	15-19	29 448	39 535	45 846	48 827	51 536	55 102	2.2	1.2	0.7
	20-24	24 039	33 204	41 854	45 182	48 174	52 805	2.8	1.4	0.9
	0-24	173 505	213 425	244 447	256 904	266 616	277 406	1.7	0.9	0.4
Eastern Asia and Oceania	A	1 172 154	1 426 567	1 675 583	1 788 429	1 899 641	2 092 691	1.8	1.3	1.0
	0-4	188 567	160 456	182 929	171 335	172 511	164 978	-0.2	-0.6	-0.4
	5-9	158 305	182 139	161 681	180 733	169 626	163 745	0.1	0.5	-0.4
	10-14	131 208	183 822	156 378	160 738	179 882	170 502	0.9	1.4	-0.5
	15-19	125 763	155 167	180 397	155 376	159 848	168 202	1.8	-1.2	0.5
	20-24	94 354	128 055	181 422	178 807	154 085	177 944	3.3	-1.6	1.5
	0-24	698 196	809 639	862 806	846 988	835 952	845 370	1.1	-0.3	0.1
Southern Asia	A	754 496	948 781	1 192 918	1 326 258	1 466 065	1 746 631	2.3	2.1	1.8
	0-4	122 599	141 455	168 919	178 444	184 915	187 682	1.6	0.9	0.1
	5-9	102 504	126 350	153 011	162 884	173 405	184 230	2.0	1.3	0.6
	10-14	89 265	113 010	133 111	151 164	161 477	179 706	2.0	2.0	1.1
	15-19	74 740	99 148	123 353	131 819	150 117	171 494	2.5	2.0	1.3
	20-24	61 758	85 802	110 517	121 979	130 675	159 677	3.0	1.7	2.0
	0-24	450 865	565 764	688 912	746 289	800 588	882 789	2.1	1.5	1.0
Least developed countries	A	303 801	390 880	501 517	577 230	662 033	846 268	2.5	2.8	2.5
	0-4	54 579	69 924	86 996	99 465	109 356	125 753	2.4	2.3	1.4
	5-9	43 267	57 537	72 748	81 796	94 411	113 358	2.6	2.6	1.8
	10-14	36 511	48 637	61 662	70 901	80 135	102 732	2.7	2.7	2.5
	15-19	29 977	40 570	53 536	60 610	69 974	91 519	2.9	2.7	2.7
	20-24	25 756	33 733	45 255	52 689	59 847	77 715	2.9	2.8	2.6
	0-24	190 090	250 400	320 197	365 460	413 722	511 077	2.6	2.6	2.1
Developed countries	A	1 030 762	1 117 509	1 190 884	1 219 880	1 244 007	1 283 543	0.7	0.4	0.3
	0-4	86 906	83 924	85 060	79 496	78 707	78 602	-0.1	-0.8	0.0
	5-9	93 789	86 295	85 236	85 395	79 689	77 997	-0.5	-0.7	-0.2
	10-14	93 798	88 255	84 787	85 815	85 723	79 324	-0.5	0.1	-0.8
	15-19	88 799	94 385	87 784	85 561	86 190	80 437	-0.1	-0.2	-0.7
	20-24	81 669	93 896	89 306	88 754	85 975	86 475	0.4	-0.4	0.1
	0-24	444 961	446 754	432 172	425 020	416 284	402 835	-0.1	-0.4	-0.3

General note / Note générale / Nota general:

E--> For composition of major areas and groups of countries, see the *List of countries and territories*, page xii. Data may not add up to totals and subtotals because of rounding and also because population data by age are not available for countries with a population of less than 150,000.

FR-> Pour la composition des grandes régions et des groupes de pays, voir la *Liste de pays et territoires*, page xii. Les totaux et sous totaux peuvent ne pas être la somme des différents éléments à cause des arrondis et du fait que, pour les pays dont la population est inférieur à 150 000 habitants, la répartition par âge n'est pas disponible.

ESP> Puede verse la composición de las grandes regiones y grupos de países en la *Lista de países y territorios*, página xii. Los totales y subtotales no siempre corresponden a la suma de sus partes, pues son el resultado de cifras redondeadas y de que no se dispone para algunos países cuya población es inferior a 150 000 habitantes, de la distribución por edad.

2.2 Estimated illiterate population 15 years and over and percentage of illiterates

Estimation de la population analphabète de 15 ans et plus et pourcentage d'analphabètes

Estimación de la población analfabeta de 15 años y más y porcentaje de analfabetos

Continents, major areas and groups of countries / Continents, grandes régions et groupes de pays / Continentes, grandes regiones y grupos de países	Year / Année / Año	Illiterate population / Population analphabète / Población analfabeta			Percentage of illiterates / Pourcentage d'analphabètes / Porcentaje de analfabetos		
		Total	Male Masculine Masculina	Female Féminine Femenina	Total	Male Masculin Masculino	Female Féminin Femenino
	(1)	(2)	(3)	(4)	(5)	(6)	
World total	1980	877	326	551	30.5	22.8	38.1
	1985	886	326	560	27.5	20.3	34.6
	1990	885	324	561	24.7	18.1	31.3
	1995	885	320	565	22.6	16.4	28.8
Africa	1980	159	62	96	60.2	48.0	71.9
	1985	167	65	102	54.8	43.1	66.2
	1990	173	66	107	49.2	38.1	60.1
	1995	179	67	111	43.8	33.5	54.0
America	1980	48	21	27	11.6	10.2	12.9
	1985	47	21	27	10.4	9.3	11.5
	1990	45	20	25	9.1	8.2	9.9
	1995	45	20	25	8.3	7.6	8.9
Asia	1980	647	237	410	39.3	28.2	50.7
	1985	654	235	418	34.6	24.5	45.1
	1990	653	233	419	30.6	21.4	40.1
	1995	651	228	422	27.7	19.1	36.6
Europe	1980	22	6	17	4.1	2.2	5.8
	1985	17	5	12	3.0	1.8	4.1
	1990	12	4	8	2.1	1.4	2.7
	1995	9	3	6	1.5	1.2	1.8
Oceania	1980	1.3	0.5	0.8	7.9	6.0	9.8
	1985	1.2	0.5	0.8	6.8	5.1	8.5
	1990	1.2	0.4	0.7	5.9	4.5	7.4
	1995	1.1	0.4	0.7	5.2	3.9	6.5
Developing countries	1980	848	318	531	42.0	31.1	53.2
	1985	863	319	544	37.1	27.0	47.5
	1990	868	318	550	32.8	23.7	42.2
	1995	872	315	557	29.6	21.1	38.3
Sub-Saharan Africa	1980	126	50	76	59.8	48.2	70.8
	1985	132	51	81	54.4	43.3	65.1
	1990	137	53	84	48.7	38.2	58.9
	1995	141	53	87	43.2	33.4	52.7
Arab States	1980	56	21	34	59.2	45.0	73.8
	1985	60	23	37	53.6	40.1	67.8
	1990	63	24	39	48.3	35.5	61.9
	1995	65	24	41	43.4	31.6	55.8
Latin America and the Caribbean	1980	44	19	25	20.3	17.9	22.5
	1985	44	19	25	17.6	15.7	19.5
	1990	43	19	24	15.1	13.6	16.5
	1995	43	19	23	13.4	12.3	14.5
Eastern Asia and Oceania	1980	276	90	186	30.7	19.6	42.0
	1985	259	81	178	24.8	15.3	34.7
	1990	231	70	161	19.7	11.8	27.8
	1995	210	60	149	16.4	9.4	23.7
Southern Asia	1980	346	139	207	60.9	47.2	75.5
	1985	370	146	224	57.1	43.7	71.5
	1990	394	153	241	53.4	40.2	67.4
	1995	416	159	256	49.8	37.1	63.4
Least developed countries	1980	136	55	81	63.5	51.7	75.1
	1985	145	58	87	59.5	48.1	70.8
	1990	154	61	93	55.2	44.1	66.3
	1995	166	65	101	51.2	40.5	61.9
Developed countries	1980	29	8	21	3.4	2.0	4.6
	1985	23	7	16	2.5	1.6	3.3
	1990	17	6	11	1.8	1.3	2.3
	1995	13	5	8	1.3	1.1	1.6

General note / Note générale / Nota general:

E--> For composition of major areas and groups of countries, see the *List of countries and territories*, page xii.

FR-> Pour la composition des grandes régions et des groupes de pays, voir la *Liste de pays et territoires*, page xii.

ESP> Puede verse la composición de las grandes regiones y grupos de países en la *Lista de países y territorios*, página xii.

Education preceding the first level
Enseignement précédant le premier degré
Enseñanza anterior al primer grado
2.3

2.3 Teaching staff and enrolment for education preceding the first level

Personnel enseignant et effectifs scolaires pour l'enseignement précédant le premier degré

Personal docente y matrícula escolar para la enseñanza anterior al primer grado

% 1980-85, 1985-90 and 1990-94 = average annual increase in teaching staff and enrolment from 1980 to 1985, from 1985 to 1990 and from 1990 to 1994, as percentage.

% 1980-85, 1985-90, et 1990-94 = accroissement moyen annuel du personnel enseignant et des effectifs scolaires de 1980 à 1985, de 1985 à 1990 et de 1990 à 1994, en pourcentage.

% 1980-85, 1985-90 y 1990-94 = crecimiento medio anual del personal docente y de la matrícula escolar de 1980 a 1985, de 1985 a 1990 y de 1990 a 1994, en porcentaje.

Continents, major areas and groups of countries / Continents, grandes régions et groupes de pays / Continentes, grandes regiones y grupos de países	Year / Année / Año	Teaching staff Personnel enseignant Personal docente			Enrolment Effectifs scolaires Matrícula escolar			
		Total (000)	Female Femmes Femenino (000)	% F	Total (000)	Female Filles Femenina (000)	% F	Private Privé Privada %
World total	1980	3 026	2 854	94	58 152	27 956	48	21
	1985	3 914	3 702	95	72 252	34 666	48	21
	1990	4 704	4 454	95	85 996	41 354	48	21
	1993	4 778	4 500	94	91 690	43 785	48	21
	1994	4 892	4 609	94	93 857	44 874	48	21
	% 1980-85	5.3	5.3		4.4	4.4		
	% 1985-90	3.7	3.8		3.5	3.6		
	% 1990-94	1.0	0.9		2.2	2.1		
Africa	1980	72	38	53	2 240	893	40	58
	1985	94	56	60	2 746	1 171	43	64
	1990	125	83	66	3 446	1 508	44	62
	1993	144	106	74	4 036	1 780	44	58
	1994	150	112	75	4 136	1 831	44	58
	% 1980-85	5.5	8.1		4.2	5.6		
	% 1985-90	5.9	8.2		4.6	5.2		
	% 1990-94	4.7	7.8		4.7	5.0		
America	1980	406	390	96	10 300	4 998	49	32
	1985	643	617	96	16 136	7 909	49	28
	1990	822	794	97	19 914	9 653	48	28
	1993	900	856	95	21 195	10 303	49	27
	1994	990	943	95	22 853	11 123	49	27
	% 1980-85	9.6	9.6		9.4	9.6		
	% 1985-90	5.0	5.2		4.3	4.1		
	% 1990-94	4.8	4.4		3.5	3.6		
Asia	1980	957	843	88	22 663	10 797	48	19
	1985	1 287	1 188	92	29 230	13 838	47	20
	1990	1 709	1 580	92	38 050	18 264	48	19
	1993	1 867	1 715	92	44 108	20 950	47	17
	1994	1 878	1 724	92	44 500	21 159	48	17
	% 1980-85	6.1	7.1		5.2	5.1		
	% 1985-90	5.8	5.9		5.4	5.7		
	% 1990-94	2.4	2.2		4.0	3.7		
Europe	1980	1 581	1 572	99	22 670	11 130	49	15
	1985	1 879	1 830	97	23 846	11 605	49	13
	1990	2 033	1 983	98	24 224	11 752	49	13
	1993	1 850	1 806	98	21 963	10 564	48	18
	1994	1 856	1 813	98	21 978	10 571	48	18
	% 1980-85	3.5	3.1		1.0	0.8		
	% 1985-90	1.6	1.6		0.3	0.3		
	% 1990-94	-2.3	-2.2		-2.4	-2.6		

2.3 Education preceding the first level
Enseignement précédant le premier degré
Enseñanza anterior al primer grado

Continents, major areas and groups of countries / Continents, grandes régions et groupes de pays / Continentes, grandes regiones y grupos de países	Year / Année / Año	Teaching staff / Personnel enseignant / Personal docente			Enrolment / Effectifs scolaires / Matrícula escolar			
		Total (000)	Female Femmes Femenino (000)	% F	Total (000)	Female Filles Femenina (000)	% F	Private Privé Privada %
Oceania	1980	10	10	100	279	136	49	19
	1985	11	11	100	293	142	48	21
	1990	15	15	100	363	177	49	21
	1993	17	17	100	387	189	49	20
	1994	18	17	94	390	190	49	20
	% 1980-85	1.9	1.9		1.0	0.9		
	% 1985-90	6.4	6.4		4.4	4.5		
	% 1990-94	4.7	3.2		1.8	1.8		
Developing countries	1980	895	757	85	25 094	11 825	47	21
	1985	1 380	1 244	90	36 878	17 394	47	23
	1990	1 927	1 753	91	48 815	23 319	48	22
	1993	2 180	1 976	91	57 178	27 229	48	20
	1994	2 292	2 084	91	59 496	28 391	48	20
	% 1980-85	9.0	10.4		8.0	8.0		
	% 1985-90	6.9	7.1		5.8	6.0		
	% 1990-94	4.4	4.4		5.1	5.0		
Sub-Saharan Africa	1980	38	33	87	1 543	694	45	39
	1985	54	47	87	1 841	867	47	49
	1990	74	64	86	2 366	1 129	48	48
	1993	93	81	87	2 888	1 372	48	47
	1994	98	87	89	2 959	1 406	48	46
	% 1980-85	7.3	7.3		3.6	4.6		
	% 1985-90	6.5	6.4		5.1	5.4		
	% 1990-94	7.3	8.0		5.8	5.6		
Arab States	1980	53	23	43	1 189	430	36	84
	1985	68	34	50	1 605	607	38	81
	1990	89	53	60	1 921	743	39	77
	1993	104	70	67	2 318	969	42	72
	1994	105	71	68	2 367	995	42	72
	% 1980-85	5.1	8.1		6.2	7.1		
	% 1985-90	5.5	9.3		3.7	4.1		
	% 1990-94	4.2	7.6		5.4	7.6		
Latin America and the Caribbean	1980	177	174	98	4 738	2 355	50	30
	1985	366	355	97	9 406	4 590	49	25
	1990	519	507	98	12 139	5 911	49	24
	1993	595	578	97	13 505	6 679	49	24
	1994	683	664	97	15 157	7 496	49	24
	% 1980-85	15.6	15.3		14.7	14.3		
	% 1985-90	7.2	7.4		5.2	5.2		
	% 1990-94	7.1	7.0		5.7	6.1		
Eastern Asia and Oceania	1980	538	461	86	15 159	7 261	48	11
	1985	746	718	96	19 664	9 418	48	12
	1990	1 049	1 010	96	26 658	12 958	49	11
	1993	1 188	1 126	95	32 789	15 721	48	9
	1994	1 204	1 141	95	33 276	15 975	48	9
	% 1980-85	6.8	9.3		5.3	5.3		
	% 1985-90	7.1	7.1		6.3	6.6		
	% 1990-94	3.5	3.1		5.7	5.4		
Southern Asia	1980	61	38	62	2 284	999	44	22
	1985	107	50	47	4 065	1 740	43	44
	1990	147	68	46	5 415	2 389	44	47
	1993	153	70	46	5 566	2 429	44	46
	1994	153	70	46	5 614	2 453	44	45
	% 1980-85	11.9	5.6		12.2	11.7		
	% 1985-90	6.6	6.3		5.9	6.5		
	% 1990-94	1.0	0.7		0.9	0.7		
Least developed countries	1980	23	11	48	911	440	48	71
	1985	65	24	37	2 347	1 046	45	86
	1990	99	35	35	3 331	1 484	45	87
	1993	104	39	38	3 614	1 653	46	84
	1994	105	39	37	3 634	1 663	46	84
	% 1980-85	23.1	16.9		20.8	18.9		
	% 1985-90	8.8	7.8		7.3	7.2		
	% 1990-94	1.5	2.7		2.2	2.9		

Education preceding the first level **2.3**
Enseignement précédant le premier degré
Enseñanza anterior al primer grado

Continents, major areas and groups of countries	Year	Teaching staff / Personnel enseignant / Personal docente			Enrolment / Effectifs scolaires / Matrícula escolar			
Continents, grandes régions et groupes de pays	Année		Female Femmes			Female Filles		Private Privé
Continentes, grandes regiones y grupos de países	Año	Total (000)	Femenino (000)	% F	Total (000)	Femenina (000)	% F	Privada %
Developed countries	1980	2 131	2 097	98	33 058	16 131	49	21
	1985	2 534	2 458	97	35 374	17 272	49	20
	1990	2 777	2 701	97	37 181	18 035	49	21
	1993	2 598	2 524	97	34 512	16 556	48	23
	1994	2 600	2 525	97	34 361	16 483	48	23
	% 1980-85	3.5	3.2		1.4	1.4		
	% 1985-90	1.8	1.9		1.0	0.9		
	% 1990-94	-1.6	-1.7		-2.0	-2.2		

General note / Note générale / Nota general:

E--> For composition of major areas and groups of countries, see the *List of countries and territories*, page xii. Data do not include the Democratic People's Republic of Korea.

FR-> Pour la composition des grandes régions et des groupes de pays, voir la *Liste de pays et territoires*, page xii. Les données n'incluent pas la République populaire démocratique de Corée.

ESP> Puede verse la composición de las grandes regiones y grupos de países en la *Lista de países y territorios*, página xii. Los datos no incluyen la República Popular Democrática de Corea.

2.4 Enrolment by level of education
Effectifs scolaires par degré d'enseignement
Matrícula escolar por grado de enseñanza

2.4 Total and female enrolment by level of education

Effectifs scolaires, total et féminin, par degré d'enseignement

Matrícula escolar, total y femenina, por grado de enseñanza

(See introductory text concerning Tables 2.4 - 2.8)

(Voir le texte d'introduction relatif aux tableaux 2.4 - 2.8)

(Véase el texto de introducción relativo a los cuadros 2.4 - 2.8)

% 1980-85, 1985-90 and 1990-94 = average annual increase in enrolment from 1980 to 1985, 1985 to 1990 and from 1990 to 1994, as percentage.

% 1980-85, 1985-90 et 1990-94 = accroissement moyen annuel des effectifs scolaires de 1980 à 1985, de 1985 à 1990 et de 1990 à 1994, en porcentaje.

% 1980-85, 1985-90 y 1990-94 = crecimiento medio anual de la matrícula escolar de 1980 a 1985, de 1985 a 1990 y de 1990 a 1994, en porcentaje.

Continents, major areas and groups of countries / Continents, grandes régions et groupes de pays / Continentes, grandes regiones y grupos de países	Year / Année / Año	Total enrolment (thousands) Effectifs scolaires total (milliers) Matrícula escolar total (miles)				Female enrolment (thousands) Effectifs scolaires féminins (milliers) Matrícula escolar femenina (miles)			
		Total	1st level 1er degré 1er grado	2nd level 2nd degré 2do grado	3rd level 3ème degré 3er grado	Total	1st level 1er degré 1er grado	2nd level 2nd degré 2do grado	3rd level 3ème degré 3er grado
		(1)	(2)	(3)	(4)	(5)	(6)	(7)	(8)
World total	1980	856 890	541 484	264 371	51 035	379 529	242 578	114 234	22 717
	1985	918 111	567 238	290 680	60 194	409 707	256 496	126 374	26 836
	1990	979 667	596 697	314 150	68 820	443 885	273 240	139 256	31 389
	1993	1 043 315	626 422	341 345	75 547	476 837	288 472	153 287	35 078
	1994	1 067 192	638 908	351 098	77 185	488 273	294 128	158 255	35 891
	% 1980-85	1.4	0.9	1.9	3.4	1.5	1.1	2.0	3.4
	% 1985-90	1.3	1.0	1.6	2.7	1.6	1.3	2.0	3.2
	% 1990-94	2.2	1.7	2.8	2.9	2.4	1.9	3.2	3.4
Africa	1980	78 023	62 606	13 874	1 543	33 006	27 185	5 403	417
	1985	94 086	72 385	19 509	2 192	40 593	32 071	7 880	641
	1990	107 894	80 639	24 307	2 949	47 628	36 221	10 443	963
	1993	120 300	88 821	27 987	3 492	53 679	40 143	12 331	1 205
	1994	125 572	92 473	29 466	3 632	56 179	41 881	13 023	1 275
	% 1980-85	3.8	2.9	7.1	7.3	4.2	3.4	7.8	9.0
	% 1985-90	2.8	2.2	4.5	6.1	3.2	2.5	5.8	8.5
	% 1990-94	3.9	3.5	4.9	5.3	4.2	3.7	5.7	7.3
America	1980	147 253	87 921	40 885	18 446	72 196	42 882	20 241	9 073
	1985	156 332	92 705	43 376	20 251	76 772	44 975	21 629	10 168
	1990	166 968	100 329	43 655	22 984	82 646	48 687	21 991	11 968
	1993	175 769	105 121	46 552	24 095	87 195	50 994	23 355	12 847
	1994	179 099	106 900	47 963	24 236	88 892	51 843	24 081	12 968
	% 1980-85	1.2	1.1	1.2	1.9	1.2	1.0	1.3	2.3
	% 1985-90	1.3	1.6	0.1	2.6	1.5	1.6	0.3	3.3
	% 1990-94	1.8	1.6	2.4	1.3	1.8	1.6	2.3	2.0
Asia	1980	494 850	335 949	144 613	14 288	207 211	145 740	56 587	4 884
	1985	531 605	348 848	162 664	20 093	225 293	153 514	64 765	7 013
	1990	567 817	364 116	180 249	23 451	245 925	163 169	74 118	8 637
	1993	609 095	382 302	199 642	27 151	267 455	172 915	84 120	10 420
	1994	622 850	389 032	205 694	28 125	273 966	175 869	87 315	10 782
	% 1980-85	1.4	0.8	2.4	7.1	1.7	1.0	2.7	7.5
	% 1985-90	1.3	0.9	2.1	3.1	1.8	1.2	2.7	4.3
	% 1990-94	2.3	1.7	3.4	4.6	2.7	1.9	4.2	5.7
Europe	1980	131 949	52 255	63 352	16 342	64 813	25 458	31 196	8 160
	1985	131 174	50 719	63 284	17 172	64 681	24 701	31 194	8 786
	1990	131 776	48 889	64 079	18 808	65 143	23 860	31 788	9 495
	1993	132 564	47 312	65 221	20 031	65 773	23 047	32 531	10 195
	1994	134 008	47 583	66 003	20 422	66 459	23 137	32 868	10 454
	% 1980-85	-0.1	-0.6	-0.0	1.0	-0.0	-0.6	-0.0	1.5
	% 1985-90	0.1	-0.7	0.2	1.8	0.1	-0.7	0.4	1.6
	% 1990-94	0.4	-0.7	0.7	2.1	0.5	-0.8	0.8	2.4
Oceania	1980	4 815	2 752	1 647	416	2 303	1 313	807	183
	1985	4 913	2 581	1 846	486	2 369	1 235	906	228
	1990	5 211	2 724	1 859	628	2 543	1 302	916	325
	1993	5 586	2 865	1 942	779	2 735	1 372	951	411
	1994	5 662	2 920	1 972	770	2 777	1 398	969	410
	% 1980-85	0.4	-1.3	2.3	3.2	0.6	-1.2	2.3	4.5
	% 1985-90	1.2	1.1	0.1	5.3	1.4	1.1	0.2	7.3
	% 1990-94	2.1	1.8	1.5	5.2	2.2	1.8	1.4	6.0

Enrolment by level of education 2.4
Effectifs scolaires par degré d'enseignement
Matrícula escolar por grado de enseñanza

Continents, major areas and groups of countries / Continents, grandes régions et groupes de pays / Continentes, grandes regiones y grupos de países	Year / Année / Año	Total enrolment (thousands) Effectifs scolaires total (milliers) Matrícula escolar total (miles)				Female enrolment (thousands) Effectifs scolaires féminins (milliers) Matrícula escolar femenina (miles)			
		Total	1st level 1er degré 1er grado	2nd level 2nd degré 2do grado	3rd level 3ème degré 3er grado	Total	1st level 1er degré 1er grado	2nd level 2nd degré 2do grado	3rd level 3ème degré 3er grado
		(1)	(2)	(3)	(4)	(5)	(6)	(7)	(8)
Developing countries	1980	626 057	449 360	159 764	16 932	266 365	197 667	62 788	5 910
	1985	686 695	477 170	184 806	24 720	295 830	212 608	74 357	8 864
	1990	745 382	507 251	208 777	29 354	327 979	229 663	87 165	11 151
	1993	805 383	537 427	234 288	33 667	358 767	245 089	100 342	13 336
	1994	827 238	549 376	243 013	34 849	369 253	250 528	104 881	13 845
	% 1980-85	1.9	1.2	3.0	7.9	2.1	1.5	3.4	8.4
	% 1985-90	1.7	1.2	2.5	3.5	2.1	1.6	3.2	4.7
	% 1990-94	2.6	2.0	3.9	4.4	3.0	2.2	4.7	5.6
Sub-Saharan Africa	1980	60 009	50 554	8 891	563	25 658	22 294	3 239	125
	1985	71 052	57 838	12 308	906	31 049	25 841	4 985	224
	1990	80 449	64 402	14 660	1 387	35 770	29 056	6 276	438
	1993	89 776	70 848	17 137	1 791	40 166	32 075	7 508	583
	1994	94 023	73 999	18 117	1 907	42 077	33 523	7 916	638
	% 1980-85	3.4	2.7	6.7	10.0	3.9	3.0	9.0	12.4
	% 1985-90	2.5	2.2	3.6	8.9	2.9	2.4	4.7	14.4
	% 1990-94	4.0	3.5	5.4	8.3	4.1	3.6	6.0	9.9
Arab States	1980	30 993	21 310	8 196	1 487	12 546	8 743	3 341	462
	1985	39 762	26 152	11 589	2 021	16 361	11 069	4 598	695
	1990	47 809	30 353	14 936	2 520	20 456	13 245	6 299	912
	1993	52 334	32 785	16 713	2 835	22 875	14 537	7 239	1 098
	1994	54 485	34 480	17 117	2 888	23 958	15 236	7 598	1 124
	% 1980-85	5.1	4.2	7.2	6.3	5.5	4.8	6.6	8.5
	% 1985-90	3.8	3.0	5.2	4.5	4.6	3.7	6.5	5.6
	% 1990-94	3.3	3.2	3.5	3.5	4.0	3.6	4.8	5.4
Latin America and The Caribbean	1980	87 211	65 310	16 972	4 930	42 454	31 855	8 460	2 139
	1985	97 081	70 231	20 486	6 364	47 318	34 036	10 435	2 847
	1990	104 962	75 518	22 087	7 357	51 535	36 681	11 396	3 458
	1993	110 291	79 018	23 495	7 778	54 369	38 305	12 154	3 909
	1994	113 251	80 485	24 856	7 910	55 885	39 000	12 858	4 027
	% 1980-85	2.2	1.5	3.8	5.2	2.2	1.3	4.3	5.9
	% 1985-90	1.6	1.5	1.5	2.9	1.7	1.5	1.8	4.0
	% 1990-94	1.9	1.6	3.0	1.8	2.0	1.5	3.1	3.9
Eastern Asia and Oceania	1980	295 151	210 876	79 012	5 263	130 082	95 701	32 484	1 898
	1985	291 489	203 117	79 236	9 136	129 855	93 159	33 481	3 215
	1990	286 135	194 829	80 662	10 644	130 896	91 567	35 426	3 903
	1993	296 546	197 753	86 274	12 519	137 672	93 693	39 115	4 864
	1994	301 022	198 994	88 942	13 086	139 841	94 355	40 424	5 063
	% 1980-85	-0.2	-0.7	0.1	11.7	-0.0	-0.5	0.6	11.1
	% 1985-90	-0.4	-0.8	0.4	3.1	0.2	-0.3	1.1	4.0
	% 1990-94	1.3	0.5	2.5	5.3	1.7	0.8	3.4	6.7
Southern Asia	1980	142 308	95 838	42 407	4 063	50 979	36 447	13 491	1 041
	1985	175 593	113 608	56 450	5 535	65 925	45 408	18 928	1 588
	1990	213 477	136 041	70 995	6 440	83 673	56 117	25 512	2 045
	1993	243 528	151 601	84 539	7 388	97 908	63 823	31 758	2 327
	1994	251 398	156 127	87 607	7 665	101 632	65 814	33 408	2 411
	% 1980-85	4.3	3.5	5.9	6.4	5.3	4.5	7.0	8.8
	% 1985-90	4.0	3.7	4.7	3.1	4.9	4.3	6.2	5.2
	% 1990-94	4.2	3.5	5.4	4.4	5.0	4.1	7.0	4.2
Least developed countries	1980	48 420	39 831	7 927	662	18 633	16 082	2 380	171
	1985	56 011	44 839	10 144	1 029	22 378	18 687	3 421	270
	1990	65 829	52 756	11 899	1 175	27 567	22 923	4 335	309
	1993	73 923	58 816	13 576	1 532	30 929	25 603	4 918	408
	1994	77 936	62 239	14 089	1 607	32 529	26 936	5 174	419
	% 1980-85	3.0	2.4	5.1	9.2	3.7	3.0	7.5	9.6
	% 1985-90	3.3	3.3	3.2	2.7	4.3	4.2	4.8	2.7
	% 1990-94	4.3	4.2	4.3	8.1	4.2	4.1	4.5	7.9
Developed countries	1980	230 833	92 124	104 607	34 103	113 164	44 911	51 446	16 807
	1985	231 416	90 068	105 874	35 474	113 877	43 888	52 017	17 972
	1990	234 285	89 446	105 373	39 466	115 906	43 577	52 091	20 238
	1993	237 932	88 995	107 057	41 880	118 070	43 383	52 945	21 742
	1994	239 954	89 532	108 085	42 336	119 020	43 600	53 374	22 046
	% 1980-85	0.1	-0.5	0.2	0.8	0.1	-0.5	0.2	1.3
	% 1985-90	0.2	-0.1	-0.1	2.2	0.4	-0.1	0.0	2.4
	% 1990-94	0.6	0.0	0.6	1.8	0.7	0.0	0.6	2.2

2.4 Enrolment by level of education
Effectifs scolaires par degré d'enseignement
Matrícula escolar por grado de enseñanza

General note / Note générale / Nota general:

E--> For composition of major areas and groups of countries, see the *List of countries and territories*, page xii. Data do not include the Democratic People's Republic of Korea. Figures also do not include education and special education provided outside regular schools. Second level education includes general, teacher training and vocational education. Third level education includes universities and other institutions of higher education. The data shown in this table are standardised and based on the present national system of education of each country.

FR-> Pour la composition des grandes régions et des groupes de pays, voir la *Liste des pays et territoires*, page xii. Les données ne comprennent pas la République populaire démocratique de Corée. Les chiffres ne comprennent pas non plus l'éducation des adultes, ni l'enseignement spécial dispensé en dehors des établissements scolaires ordinaires. L'enseignement du second degré comprend les enseignements général, normal et technique.

L'enseignement du troisième degré comprend les universités et autres établissements d'enseignement supérieur. Les données dans ce tableau ont été compilées à partir des données par pays, classées selon le système national d'enseignement actuellement en vigueur.

ESP> Puede verse la composición de las grandes regiones y grupos de países en la *Lista de países y territorios*, página xii. Los datos no incluyen la República Popular Democrática de Corea. Las cifras no comprenden además la educación de adultos y, en lo que toca a la enseñanza especial, solo comprenden la impartida en establecimientos de enseñanza ordinaria. La enseñanza de segundo grado incluye las enseñanza general, normal y técnica. La enseñanza de tercer grado incluye las universidades y otros establecimientos de enseñanza superior. Los datos presentados en este cuadro están basados en los datos por país, clasificados según el sistema nacional de educación actualmente vigente .

Enrolment: distribution by level and percentage female   2.5
Effectifs scolaires: répartition par degré et pourcentage de filles
Matrícula escolar: distribución por grado y porcentaje de alumnas

2.5 Distribution of enrolment by level of education and percentage female enrolment at each level

Répartition des effectifs scolaires par degré d'enseignement et pourcentage de filles dans chaque degré

Distribución de la matrícula escolar por grado de enseñanza y porcentaje de mujeres en cado grado

(See introductory text concerning Tables 2.4 - 2.8)   (Voir le texte d'introduction relatif aux tableaux 2.4 - 2.8)   (Véase el texto de introducción relativo a los cuadros 2.4 - 2.8)

Continents, major areas and groups of countries / Continents, grandes régions et groupes de pays / Continentes, grandes regiones y grupos de países	Year / Année / Año	Percentage distribution of enrolment / Distribution en pourcentage de l'effectif scolaire / Distribución en porcentaje de la matrícula escolar				Percentage female enrolment by level / Pourcentage de l'effectif scolaire féminin par degré / Porcentaje de la matrícula escolar femenina por grado		
		Total	1st level / 1er degré / 1er grado	2nd level / 2nd degré / 2do grado	3rd level / 3ème degré / 3er grado	1st level / 1er degré / 1er grado	2nd level / 2nd degré / 2do grado	3rd level / 3ème degré / 3er grado
World total	1980	100.0	63.2	30.9	6.0	45	43	45
	1985	100.0	61.8	31.7	6.6	45	43	45
	1990	100.0	60.9	32.1	7.0	46	44	46
	1993	100.0	60.0	32.7	7.2	46	45	46
	1994	100.0	59.8	33.0	7.2	46	45	47
Africa	1980	100.0	80.2	17.8	2.0	43	39	27
	1985	100.0	76.9	20.7	2.3	44	40	29
	1990	100.0	74.7	22.5	2.7	45	43	33
	1993	100.0	73.8	23.3	2.9	45	44	35
	1994	100.0	73.6	23.5	2.9	45	44	35
America	1980	100.0	59.7	27.8	12.5	49	50	49
	1985	100.0	59.3	27.7	13.0	49	50	50
	1990	100.0	60.1	26.1	13.8	49	50	52
	1993	100.0	59.8	26.5	13.7	49	50	53
	1994	100.0	59.7	26.8	13.5	48	50	54
Asia	1980	100.0	67.9	29.2	2.9	43	39	34
	1985	100.0	65.6	30.6	3.8	44	40	35
	1990	100.0	64.1	31.7	4.1	45	41	37
	1993	100.0	62.8	32.8	4.5	45	42	38
	1994	100.0	62.5	33.0	4.5	45	42	38
Europe	1980	100.0	39.6	48.0	12.4	49	49	50
	1985	100.0	38.7	48.2	13.1	49	49	51
	1990	100.0	37.1	48.6	14.3	49	50	50
	1993	100.0	35.7	49.2	15.1	49	50	51
	1994	100.0	35.5	49.3	15.2	49	50	51
Oceania	1980	100.0	57.2	34.2	8.6	48	49	44
	1985	100.0	52.5	37.6	9.9	48	49	47
	1990	100.0	52.3	35.7	12.1	48	49	52
	1993	100.0	51.3	34.8	13.9	48	49	53
	1994	100.0	51.6	34.8	13.6	48	49	53
Developing countries	1980	100.0	71.8	25.5	2.7	44	39	35
	1985	100.0	69.5	26.9	3.6	45	40	36
	1990	100.0	68.1	28.0	3.9	45	42	38
	1993	100.0	66.7	29.1	4.2	46	43	40
	1994	100.0	66.4	29.4	4.2	46	43	40
Sub-Saharan Africa	1980	100.0	84.2	14.8	0.9	44	36	22
	1985	100.0	81.4	17.3	1.3	45	41	25
	1990	100.0	80.1	18.2	1.7	45	43	32
	1993	100.0	78.9	19.1	2.0	45	44	33
	1994	100.0	78.7	19.3	2.0	45	44	33

2.5 Enrolment: distribution by level and percentage female
Effectifs scolaires: répartition par degré et pourcentage de filles
Matrícula escolar: distribución por grado y porcentaje de alumnas

Continents, major areas and groups of countries / Continents, grandes régions et groupes de pays / Continentes, grandes regiones y grupos de países	Year / Année / Año	Percentage distribution of enrolment / Distribution en pourcentage de l'effectif scolaire / Distribución en porcentaje de la matrícula escolar				Percentage female enrolment by level / Pourcentage de l'effectif scolaire féminin par degré / Porcentaje de la matrícula escolar femenina por grado		
		Total	1st level / 1er degré / 1er grado	2nd level / 2nd degré / 2do grado	3rd level / 3ème degré / 3er grado	1st level / 1er degré / 1er grado	2nd level / 2nd degré / 2do grado	3rd level / 3ème degré / 3er grado
Arab States	1980	100.0	68.8	26.4	4.8	41	41	31
	1985	100.0	65.8	29.1	5.1	42	40	34
	1990	100.0	63.5	31.2	5.3	44	42	36
	1993	100.0	62.6	31.9	5.4	44	43	39
	1994	100.0	63.3	32.4	5.3	44	44	39
Latin America and the Caribbean	1980	100.0	74.9	19.5	5.7	49	50	43
	1985	100.0	72.3	21.1	6.6	48	51	45
	1990	100.0	71.9	21.0	7.0	49	52	47
	1993	100.0	71.6	21.3	7.1	48	52	50
	1994	100.0	71.1	21.9	7.0	48	52	51
Eastern Asia and Oceania	1980	100.0	71.4	26.8	1.8	45	41	36
	1985	100.0	69.7	27.2	3.1	46	42	35
	1990	100.0	68.1	28.2	3.7	47	44	37
	1993	100.0	66.7	29.1	4.2	47	45	39
	1994	100.0	66.1	29.5	4.3	47	45	39
Southern Asia	1980	100.0	67.3	29.8	2.9	38	32	26
	1985	100.0	64.7	32.1	3.2	40	34	29
	1990	100.0	63.7	33.3	3.0	41	36	32
	1993	100.0	62.3	34.7	3.0	42	38	31
	1994	100.0	62.1	34.8	3.0	42	38	31
Least developed countries	1980	100.0	82.3	16.4	1.4	40	30	26
	1985	100.0	80.1	18.1	1.8	42	34	26
	1990	100.0	80.1	18.1	1.8	43	36	26
	1993	100.0	79.6	18.4	2.1	44	36	27
	1994	100.0	79.9	18.1	2.1	43	37	26
Developed countries	1980	100.0	39.9	45.3	14.8	49	49	49
	1985	100.0	38.9	45.8	15.3	49	49	51
	1990	100.0	38.2	45.0	16.8	49	49	51
	1993	100.0	37.4	45.0	17.6	49	49	52
	1994	100.0	37.3	45.0	17.6	49	49	52

General note / Note générale / Nota general:

E--> For composition of major areas and groups of countries, see the *List of countries and territories*, page xii. Data do not include the Democratic People's Republic of Korea. Figures also do not include adult education and special education provided outside regular schools. Second level education includes general, teacher training and vocational education. Third level education includes universities and other institutions of higher education. The data shown in this table are standardised and based on the present national system of education of each country.

FR-> Pour la composition des grandes régions et des groupes de pays, voir la *Liste des pays et territoires*, page xii. Les données ne comprennent pas la République populaire démocratique de Corée. Les chiffres ne comprennent pas non plus l'éducation des adultes, ni l'enseignement spécial dispensé en dehors des établissements scolaires ordinaires. L'enseignement du second degré comprend les enseignements général, normal et technique.

L'enseignement du troisième degré comprend les universités et autres établissements d'enseignement supérieur. Les données dans ce tableau ont été compilées à partir des données par pays, classées selon le système national d'enseignement actuellement en vigueur.

ESP> Puede verse la composición de las grandes regiones y grupos de países en la *Lista de países y territorios*, página xii. Los datos no incluyen la República Popular Democrática de Corea Las cifras no comprenden además la educación de adultos y, en lo que toca a la enseñanza especial, solo comprenden la impartida en establecimientos de enseñanza ordinaria. La enseñanza de segundo grado incluye las enseñanza general, normal y técnica. La enseñanza de tercer grado incluye las universidades y otros establecimientos de enseñanza superior. Los datos presentados en este cuadro están basados en los datos por país, clasificados según el sistema nacional de educación actualmente vigente.

Teaching staff by level of education 2.6
Personnel enseignant par degré d'enseignement
Personal docente por grado de enseñanza

2.6 Total and female teaching staff by level of education

Personnel enseignant, total et féminin, par degré d'enseignement

Personal docente, total y femenino, por grado de enseñanza

(See introductory text concerning Tables 2.4 - 2.8)

% 1980-85, 1985-90 and 1990-94 = average annual increase in enrollment from 1980 to 1985, 1985 to 1990 and from 1990 to 1994, as percentage.

(Voir le texte d'introduction relatif aux tableaux 2.4 - 2.8)

% 1980-85, 1985-90 et 1990-94 = ccroissement moyen annuel des effectifs scolaires de 1980 à 1985, de 1985 à 1990 et de 1990 à 1994, en pourcentage.

(Véase el texto de introducción relativo a los cuadros 2.4 - 2.8)

% 1980-85, 1985-90 y 1990-94 = acrecimiento medio anual de la matrícula escolar de 1980 a 1985, de 1985 a 1990 y de 1990 a 1994, en porcentaje.

Continents, major areas and groups of countries — Continents, grandes régions et groupes de pays — Continentes, grandes regiones y grupos de países	Year — Année — Año	Total teaching staff (thousands) — Personnel enseignant total (milliers) — Personal docente total (miles)			Female teaching staff (thousands) — Personnel enseignant féminin (milliers) — Personal docente femenino (miles)	
		Total	1st level — 1er degré — 1er grado	2nd level — 2nd degré — 2do grado	3rd level — 3ème degré — 3er grado	1st level — 1er degré — 1er grado	2nd level — 2nd degré — 2do grado
World total	1980	38 129	19 032	15 338	3 759	10 032	6 226
	1985	41 929	20 855	16 751	4 323	11 343	7 211
	1990	46 905	22 725	19 206	4 974	12 790	8 642
	1993	49 613	23 920	20 336	5 356	13 732	9 415
	1994	50 494	24 324	20 681	5 488	13 945	9 640
	% 1980-85	1.9	1.8	1.8	2.8	2.5	3.0
	% 1985-90	2.3	1.7	2.8	2.8	2.4	3.7
	% 1990-94	1.9	1.7	1.9	2.5	2.2	2.8
Africa	1980	2 340	1 686	561	94	603	190
	1985	3 047	2 038	879	131	802	293
	1990	3 788	2 390	1 240	157	995	433
	1993	4 196	2 681	1 332	183	1 197	471
	1994	4 360	2 789	1 378	194	1 252	492
	% 1980-85	5.4	3.9	9.4	6.9	5.9	9.0
	% 1985-90	4.4	3.2	7.1	3.7	4.4	8.1
	% 1990-94	3.6	3.9	2.7	5.4	5.9	3.2
America	1980	7 746	3 840	2 762	1 144	3 006	1 278
	1985	8 200	4 162	2 780	1 258	3 274	1 413
	1990	9 168	4 691	2 970	1 507	3 711	1 522
	1993	9 690	5 035	3 083	1 573	3 969	1 550
	1994	9 839	5 123	3 128	1 588	4 037	1 565
	% 1980-85	1.1	1.6	0.1	1.9	1.7	2.0
	% 1985-90	2.3	2.4	1.3	3.7	2.5	1.5
	% 1990-94	1.8	2.2	1.3	1.3	2.1	0.7
Asia	1980	19 547	10 849	7 491	1 207	4 372	2 295
	1985	21 629	11 825	8 264	1 540	5 023	2 814
	1990	24 216	12 731	9 726	1 759	5 734	3 645
	1993	25 563	13 216	10 354	1 993	6 110	4 086
	1994	25 947	13 381	10 517	2 049	6 165	4 207
	% 1980-85	2.0	1.7	2.0	5.0	2.8	4.2
	% 1985-90	2.3	1.5	3.3	2.7	2.7	5.3
	% 1990-94	1.7	1.3	2.0	3.9	1.8	3.6
Europe	1980	8 224	2 530	4 411	1 283	1 971	2 411
	1985	8 749	2 695	4 692	1 362	2 156	2 627
	1990	9 404	2 768	5 125	1 511	2 254	2 969
	1993	9 817	2 839	5 413	1 565	2 356	3 232
	1994	10 000	2 881	5 504	1 616	2 390	3 297
	% 1980-85	1.2	1.3	1.2	1.2	1.8	1.7
	% 1985-90	1.5	0.5	1.8	2.1	0.9	2.5
	% 1990-94	1.5	1.0	1.8	1.7	1.5	2.7

2.6   Teaching staff by level of education
Personnel enseignant par degré d'enseignement
Personal docente por grado de enseñanza

Continents, major areas and groups of countries Continents, grandes ré-gions et groupes de pays Continentes, grandes regiones y grupos de países	Year Année Año	Total teaching staff (thousands) Personnel enseignant total (milliers) Personal docente total (miles)				Female teaching staff (thousands) Personnel enseignant féminin (milliers) Personal docente femenino (miles)	
		Total	1st level 1er degré 1er grado	2nd level 2nd degré 2do grado	3rd level 3ème degré 3er grado	1st level 1er degré 1er grado	2nd level 2nd degré 2do grado
Oceania	1980	272	129	112	31	81	51
	1985	305	135	137	33	88	65
	1990	331	144	146	41	96	73
	1993	346	149	154	43	100	77
	1994	348	151	155	42	101	78
	% 1980-85	2.3	0.9	4.1	1.3	1.7	5.0
	% 1985-90	1.6	1.3	1.3	4.4	1.8	2.3
	% 1990-94	1.3	1.2	1.5	0.6	1.3	1.7
Developing countries	1980	23 690	14 198	8 148	1 344	6 309	2 581
	1985	27 013	15 848	9 372	1 793	7 421	3 279
	1990	30 747	17 482	11 163	2 102	8 602	4 222
	1993	32 567	18 402	11 789	2 375	9 273	4 611
	1994	33 223	18 753	12 022	2 448	9 441	4 753
	% 1980-85	2.7	2.2	2.8	5.9	3.3	4.9
	% 1985-90	2.6	2.0	3.6	3.2	3.0	5.2
	% 1990-94	2.0	1.8	1.9	3.9	2.4	3.0
Sub-Saharan Africa	1980	1 687	1 310	334	43	454	119
	1985	2 084	1 510	510	64	574	170
	1990	2 478	1 719	681	78	671	223
	1993	2 746	1 929	718	100	816	233
	1994	2 859	2 010	740	109	856	243
	% 1980-85	4.3	2.9	8.8	8.3	4.8	7.4
	% 1985-90	3.5	2.6	6.0	4.0	3.2	5.6
	% 1990-94	3.6	4.0	2.1	8.7	6.3	2.2
Arab States	1980	1 208	722	403	83	300	129
	1985	1 713	987	615	111	471	215
	1990	2 254	1 252	870	132	643	340
	1993	2 549	1 412	989	149	746	395
	1994	2 657	1 482	1 023	152	774	416
	% 1980-85	7.2	6.5	8.8	6.0	9.4	10.8
	% 1985-90	5.6	4.9	7.2	3.5	6.4	9.6
	% 1990-94	4.2	4.3	4.1	3.6	4.7	5.2
Latin America and the Caribbean	1980	3 731	2 260	1 083	388	1 725	511
	1985	4 446	2 601	1 338	506	2 001	641
	1990	5 136	3 005	1 520	611	2 318	740
	1993	5 459	3 216	1 581	662	2 466	739
	1994	5 594	3 295	1 623	676	2 527	754
	% 1980-85	3.6	2.9	4.3	5.5	3.0	4.6
	% 1985-90	2.9	2.9	2.6	3.8	3.0	2.9
	% 1990-94	2.2	2.3	1.7	2.6	2.2	0.5
Eastern Asia and Oceania	1980	12 093	7 467	4 150	476	3 064	1 185
	1985	12 922	7 883	4 334	704	3 480	1 425
	1990	14 282	8 281	5 201	800	3 933	1 900
	1993	14 627	8 319	5 391	917	4 107	2 084
	1994	14 750	8 341	5 464	945	4 127	2 121
	% 1980-85	1.3	1.1	0.9	8.1	2.6	3.8
	% 1985-90	2.0	1.0	3.7	2.6	2.5	5.9
	% 1990-94	0.8	0.2	1.2	4.3	1.2	2.8
Southern Asia	1980	4 472	2 214	1 948	310	651	535
	1985	5 333	2 648	2 323	362	786	716
	1990	6 044	3 001	2 621	421	925	891
	1993	6 584	3 294	2 808	482	1 025	1 016
	1994	6 749	3 393	2 856	500	1 043	1 070
	% 1980-85	3.6	3.6	3.6	3.1	3.8	6.0
	% 1985-90	2.5	2.5	2.4	3.1	3.3	4.5
	% 1990-94	2.8	3.1	2.2	4.4	3.0	4.7
Least developed countries	1980	1 232	879	316	38	243	73
	1985	1 524	1 071	404	49	317	101
	1990	1 822	1 252	509	62	423	121
	1993	1 985	1 343	564	78	471	134
	1994	2 056	1 392	582	83	467	139
	% 1980-85	4.3	4.0	5.0	5.2	5.5	6.7
	% 1985-90	3.6	3.2	4.7	4.8	5.9	3.7
	% 1990-94	3.1	2.7	3.4	7.6	2.5	3.5

Teaching staff by level of education **2.6**
Personnel enseignant par degré d'enseignement
Personal docente por grado de enseñanza

Continents, major areas and groups of countries Continents, grandes ré-gions et groupes de pays Continentes, grandes re-giones y grupos de países	Year Année Año	Total teaching staff (thousands) Personnel enseignant total (milliers) Personal docente total (miles)				Female teaching staff (thousands) Personnel enseignant féminin (milliers) Personal docente femenino (miles)	
		Total	1st level 1er degré 1er grado	2nd level 2nd degré 2do grado	3rd level 3ème degré 3er grado	1st level 1er degré 1er grado	2nd level 2nd degré 2do grado
Developed countries	1980	14 439	4 834	7 190	2 415	3 723	3 645
	1985	14 916	5 007	7 379	2 530	3 922	3 932
	1990	16 158	5 243	8 043	2 872	4 188	4 420
	1993	17 046	5 518	8 547	2 981	4 459	4 804
	1994	17 271	5 571	8 659	3 040	4 504	4 887
	% 1980-85	0.7	0.7	0.5	0.9	1.0	1.5
	% 1985-90	1.6	0.9	1.7	2.6	1.3	2.4
	% 1990-94	1.7	1.5	1.9	1.4	1.8	2.5

General note / Note générale / Nota general:

E--> For composition of major areas and groups of countries, see the *List of countries and territories*, page XII. Data do not include the Democratic People's Republic of Korea. Figures also do not include adult education and special education provided outside regular schools. Second level education includes general, teacher training and vocational education. Third level education includes universities and other institutions of higher education. The data shown in this table are standardised and based on the present national system of education of each country.

FR-> Pour la composition des grandes régions et des groupes de pays, voir la *Liste des pays et territoires*, page XII. Les données ne comprennent pas la République populaire démocratique de Corée. Les chiffres ne comprennent pas non plus l'éducation des adultes, ni l'enseignement spécial dispensé en dehors des établissements scolaires ordinaires. L'enseignement du second degré comprend les enseignements général, normal et technique. L'enseignement du troisième degré comprend les universités et autres établissements d'enseignement supérieur. Les données dans ce tableau ont été compilées à partir des données par pays, classées selon le système national d'enseignement actuellement en vigueur.

ESP> Puede verse la composición de las grandes regiones y grupos de países en la *Lista de países y territorios*, página XII. Los datos no incluyen la República Popular Democrática de Corea. Las cifras no comprenden además la educación de adultos y, en lo que toca a la enseñanza especial, solo comprenden la impartida en establecimientos de enseñanza ordinaria. La enseñanza de segundo grado incluye las enseñanza general, normal y técnica. La enseñanza de tercer grado incluye las universidades y otros establecimientos de enseñanza superior. Los datos presentados en este cuadro están basados en los datos por país, clasificados según el sistema nacional de educación actualmente vigente.

2.7 Teaching staff: distribution by level and percentage female
Personnel enseignant: répartition par degré et pourcentage de femmes
Personal docente: distribución por grado y porcentaje de mujeres

2.7 Teaching staff: distribution by level of education and percentage female at first and second level

Personnel enseignant: répartition par degré d'enseignement et pourcentage de femmes aux premier et second degrés

Personal docente: distribución por grado de enseñanza y porcentaje de mujeres en el primer y segundo grados

(See introductory text concerning Tables 2.4 - 2.8)   (Voir le texte d'introduction relatif aux tableaux 2.4 - 2.8)   (Véase el texto de introducción relativo a los cuadros 2.4 - 2.8)

Continents, major areas and groups of countries / Continents, grandes régions et groupes de pays / Continentes, grandes regiones y grupos de países	Year / Année / Año	Percentage distribution of teaching staff / Distribution en pourcentage du personnel enseignant / Distribución en porcentaje del personal docente				Percentage female teaching staff by level / Pourcentage du personnel enseignant féminin par degré / Porcentaje del personal docente femenino por grado	
		Total	1st level / 1er degré / 1er grado	2nd level / 2nd degré / 2do grado	3rd level / 3ème degré / 3er grado	1st level / 1er degré / 1er grado	2nd level / 2nd degré / 2do grado
World total	1980	100.0	49.9	40.2	9.9	53	41
	1985	100.0	49.7	40.0	10.3	54	43
	1990	100.0	48.4	40.9	10.6	56	45
	1993	100.0	48.2	41.0	10.8	57	46
	1994	100.0	48.2	41.0	10.9	57	47
Africa	1980	100.0	72.1	24.0	4.0	36	34
	1985	100.0	66.9	28.8	4.3	39	33
	1990	100.0	63.1	32.7	4.1	42	35
	1993	100.0	63.9	31.7	4.4	45	35
	1994	100.0	64.0	31.6	4.4	45	36
America	1980	100.0	49.6	35.7	14.8	78	46
	1985	100.0	50.8	33.9	15.3	79	51
	1990	100.0	51.2	32.4	16.4	79	51
	1993	100.0	52.0	31.8	16.2	79	50
	1994	100.0	52.1	31.8	16.1	79	50
Asia	1980	100.0	55.5	38.3	6.2	40	31
	1985	100.0	54.7	38.2	7.1	42	34
	1990	100.0	52.6	40.2	7.3	45	37
	1993	100.0	51.7	40.5	7.8	46	39
	1994	100.0	51.6	40.5	7.9	46	40
Europe	1980	100.0	30.8	53.6	15.6	78	55
	1985	100.0	30.8	53.6	15.6	80	56
	1990	100.0	29.4	54.5	16.1	81	58
	1993	100.0	28.9	55.1	15.9	83	60
	1994	100.0	28.8	55.0	16.2	83	60
Oceania	1980	100.0	47.4	41.2	11.4	63	46
	1985	100.0	44.3	44.9	10.8	65	47
	1990	100.0	43.5	44.1	12.4	67	50
	1993	100.0	43.1	44.5	12.4	67	50
	1994	100.0	43.4	44.5	12.1	67	50

Teaching staff: distribution by level and percentage female **2.7**
Personnel enseignant: répartition par degré et pourcentage de femmes
Personal docente: distribución por grado y porcentaje de mujeres

Continents, major areas and groups of countries Continents, grandes régions et groupes de pays Continentes, grandes regiones y grupos de países	Year Année Año	Percentage distribution of teaching staff Distribution en pourcentage du personnel enseignant Distribución en porcentaje del personal docente				Percentage female teaching staff by level Pourcentage du personnel enseignant féminin par degré Porcentage del personal docente femenino por grado	
		Total	1st level 1er degré 1er grado	2nd level 2nd degré 2do grado	3rd level 3ème degré 3er grado	1st level 1er degré 1er grado	2nd level 2nd degré 2do grado
Developing countries	1980	100.0	59.9	34.4	5.7	44	32
	1985	100.0	58.7	34.7	6.6	47	35
	1990	100.0	56.9	36.3	6.8	49	38
	1993	100.0	56.5	36.2	7.3	50	39
	1994	100.0	56.4	36.2	7.4	50	40
Sub-Saharan Africa	1980	100.0	77.7	19.8	2.5	35	36
	1985	100.0	72.5	24.5	3.1	38	33
	1990	100.0	69.4	27.5	3.1	39	33
	1993	100.0	70.2	26.1	3.6	42	32
	1994	100.0	70.3	25.9	3.8	43	33
Arab States	1980	100.0	59.8	33.4	6.9	42	32
	1985	100.0	57.6	35.9	6.5	48	35
	1990	100.0	55.5	38.6	5.9	51	39
	1993	100.0	55.4	38.8	5.8	53	40
	1994	100.0	55.8	38.5	5.7	52	41
Latin America and the Caribbean	1980	100.0	60.6	29.0	10.4	76	47
	1985	100.0	58.5	30.1	11.4	77	48
	1990	100.0	58.5	29.6	11.9	77	49
	1993	100.0	58.9	29.0	12.1	77	47
	1994	100.0	58.9	29.0	12.1	77	46
Eastern Asia and Oceania	1980	100.0	61.7	34.3	3.9	41	29
	1985	100.0	61.0	33.5	5.4	44	33
	1990	100.0	58.0	36.4	5.6	47	37
	1993	100.0	56.9	36.9	6.3	49	39
	1994	100.0	56.5	37.0	6.4	49	39
Southern Asia	1980	100.0	49.5	43.6	6.9	29	27
	1985	100.0	49.7	43.6	6.8	30	31
	1990	100.0	49.7	43.4	7.0	31	34
	1993	100.0	50.0	42.6	7.3	31	36
	1994	100.0	50.3	42.3	7.4	31	37
Least developed countries	1980	100.0	71.3	25.6	3.1	28	23
	1985	100.0	70.3	26.5	3.2	30	25
	1990	100.0	68.7	27.9	3.4	34	24
	1993	100.0	67.7	28.4	3.9	35	24
	1994	100.0	67.7	28.3	4.0	34	24
Developed countries	1980	100.0	33.5	49.8	16.7	77	51
	1985	100.0	33.6	49.5	17.0	78	53
	1990	100.0	32.4	49.8	17.8	80	55
	1993	100.0	32.4	50.1	17.5	81	56
	1994	100.0	32.3	50.1	17.6	81	56

General note / Note générale / Nota general:

E--> For composition of major areas and groups of countries, see the *List of countries and territories*, page xii. Data do not include the Democratic People's Republic of Korea. Figures also do not include adult education and special education provided outside regular schools. Second level education includes general, teacher training and vocational education. Third level education includes universities and other institutions of higher education. The data shown in this table are standardised and based on the present national system of education of each country.

FR-> Pour la composition des grandes régions et des groupes de pays, voir la *Liste des pays et territoires*, page xii. Les données ne comprennent pas la République populaire démocratique de Corée. Les chiffres ne comprennent pas non plus l'éducation des adultes, ni l'enseignement spécial dispensé en dehors des établissements scolaires ordinaires. L'enseignement du second degré comprend les enseignements général, normal et technique.

L'enseignement du troisième degré comprend les universités et autres établissements d'enseignement supérieur. Les données dans ce tableau ont été compilées à partir des données par pays, classées selon le système national d'enseignement actuellement en vigueur.

ESP> Puede verse la composición de las grandes regiones y grupos de países en la *Lista de países y territorios*, página xii. Los datos no incluyen la República Popular Democrática de Corea. Las cifras no comprenden además la educación de adultos y, en lo que toca a la enseñanza especial, solo comprenden la impartida en establecimientos de enseñanza ordinaria. La enseñanza de segundo grado incluye las enseñanza general, normal y técnica. La enseñanza de tercer grado incluye las universidades y otros establecimientos de enseñanza superior. Los datos presentados en este cuadro están basados en los datos por país, clasificados según el sistema nacional de educación actualmente vigente.

2.8 Enrolment: index numbers
Effectifs scolaires: indices
Matrícula escolar: índices

2.8 Index numbers: total and female enrolment by level of education (1980 = 100)

Indices: total des effectifs scolaires et effectifs féminins par degré d'enseignement (1980 = 100)

Indices: total de la matrícula escolar y matrícula escolar femenina por grado de enseñanza (1980 = 100)

(See introductory text concerning Tables 2.4 - 2.8)   (Voir le texte d'introduction relatif aux tableaux 2.4 - 2.8)   (Véase el texto de introducción relativo a los cuadros 2.4 - 2.8)

Continents, major areas and groups of countries / Continents, grandes régions et groupes de pays / Continentes, grandes regiones y grupos de países	Year / Année / Año	Total enrolment — Total des effectifs scolaires — Total de la matrícula escolar				Female enrolment — Effectifs féminins — Matrícula femenina			
		Total	1st level / 1er degré / 1er grado	2nd level / 2nd degré / 2do grado	3rd level / 3ème degré / 3er grado	Total	1st level / 1er degré / 1er grado	2nd level / 2nd degré / 2do grado	3rd level / 3ème degré / 3er grado
World total	1980	100	100	100	100	100	100	100	100
	1985	107	104	109	117	107	105	110	118
	1990	114	110	118	134	116	112	121	138
	1993	121	115	129	148	125	118	134	154
	1994	124	117	132	151	128	120	138	157
Africa	1980	100	100	100	100	100	100	100	100
	1985	120	115	140	142	122	117	145	153
	1990	138	128	175	191	144	133	193	230
	1993	154	141	201	226	162	147	228	288
	1994	160	147	212	235	170	154	241	305
America	1980	100	100	100	100	100	100	100	100
	1985	106	105	106	109	106	104	106	112
	1990	113	114	106	124	114	113	108	131
	1993	119	119	113	130	120	118	115	141
	1994	121	121	117	131	123	120	118	142
Asia	1980	100	100	100	100	100	100	100	100
	1985	107	103	112	140	108	105	114	143
	1990	114	108	124	164	118	111	130	176
	1993	123	113	138	190	129	118	148	213
	1994	125	115	142	196	132	120	154	220
Europe	1980	100	100	100	100	100	100	100	100
	1985	99	97	99	105	99	97	99	107
	1990	99	93	101	115	100	93	101	116
	1993	100	90	102	122	101	90	104	124
	1994	101	91	104	124	102	90	105	128
Oceania	1980	100	100	100	100	100	100	100	100
	1985	102	93	112	116	102	94	112	124
	1990	108	98	112	150	110	99	113	177
	1993	116	104	117	187	118	104	117	224
	1994	117	106	119	185	120	106	120	224
Developing countries	1980	100	100	100	100	100	100	100	100
	1985	109	106	115	145	111	107	118	149
	1990	119	112	130	173	123	116	138	188
	1993	128	119	146	198	134	123	159	225
	1994	132	122	152	205	138	126	167	234

Enrolment: index numbers 2.8
Effectifs scolaires: indices
Matrícula escolar: índices

Continents, major areas and groups of countries / Continents, grandes régions et groupes de pays / Continentes, grandes regiones y grupos de países	Year / Année / Año	Total enrolment / Total des effectifs scolaires / Total de la matrícula escolar				Female enrolment / Effectifs féminins / Matrícula femenina			
		Total	1st level / 1er degré / 1er grado	2nd level / 2nd degré / 2do grado	3rd level / 3ème degré / 3er grado	Total	1st level / 1er degré / 1er grado	2nd level / 2nd degré / 2do grado	3rd level / 3ème degré / 3er grado
Sub-Saharan Africa	1980	100	100	100	100	100	100	100	100
	1985	118	114	138	161	121	116	154	179
	1990	134	127	165	246	139	130	194	350
	1993	150	140	193	318	157	144	232	466
	1994	157	146	204	339	164	150	244	510
Arab States	1980	100	100	100	100	100	100	100	100
	1985	128	122	141	135	130	126	137	150
	1990	154	142	182	169	163	151	188	197
	1993	168	153	203	190	182	166	216	237
	1994	175	161	208	194	190	174	227	243
Latin America and the Caribbean	1980	100	100	100	100	100	100	100	100
	1985	111	107	120	129	111	106	123	133
	1990	120	115	130	149	121	115	134	161
	1993	126	120	138	157	128	120	143	182
	1994	129	123	146	160	131	122	151	188
Eastern Asia and Oceania	1980	100	100	100	100	100	100	100	100
	1985	98	96	100	173	99	97	103	169
	1990	96	92	102	202	100	95	109	205
	1993	100	93	109	237	105	97	120	256
	1994	101	94	112	248	107	98	124	266
Southern Asia	1980	100	100	100	100	100	100	100	100
	1985	123	118	133	136	129	124	140	152
	1990	150	141	167	158	164	153	189	196
	1993	171	158	199	181	192	175	235	223
	1994	176	162	206	188	199	180	247	231
Least developed countries	1980	100	100	100	100	100	100	100	100
	1985	115	112	127	155	120	116	143	157
	1990	135	132	150	177	147	142	182	180
	1993	152	147	171	231	165	159	206	238
	1994	160	156	177	242	174	167	217	245
Developed countries	1980	100	100	100	100	100	100	100	100
	1985	100	97	101	104	100	97	101	106
	1990	101	97	100	115	102	97	101	120
	1993	103	96	102	122	104	96	102	129
	1994	103	97	103	124	105	97	103	131

General note / Note générale / Nota general:

E--> For composition of major areas and groups of countries, see the *List of countries and territories*, page xii. Data do not include the Democratic People's Republic of Korea. Figures also do not include adult education and special education provided outside regular schools. Second level education includes general, teacher training and vocational education. Third level education includes universities and other institutions of higher education. The data shown in this table are standardised and based on the present national system of education of each country.

FR-> Pour la composition des grandes régions et des groupes de pays, voir la *Liste des pays et territoires*, page xii. Les données ne comprennent pas la République populaire démocratique de Corée. Les chiffres ne comprennent pas non plus l'éducation des adultes, ni l'enseignement spécial dispensé en dehors des établissements scolaires ordinaires. L'enseignement du second degré comprend les enseignements général, normal et technique.

L'enseignement du troisième degré comprend les universités et autres établissements d'enseignement supérieur. Les données dans ce tableau ont été compilées à partir des données par pays, classées selon le système national d'enseignement actuellement en vigueur.

ESP> Puede verse la composición de las grandes regiones y grupos de países en la *Lista de países y territorios*, página xii. Los datos no incluyen la República Popular Democrática de Corea. Las cifras no comprenden además la educación de adultos y, en lo que toca a la enseñanza especial, solo comprenden la impartida en establecimientos de enseñanza ordinaria. La enseñanza de segundo grado incluye las enseñanza general, normal y técnica. La enseñanza de tercer grado incluye las universidades y otros establecimientos de enseñanza superior. Los datos presentados en este cuadro están basados en los datos por país, clasificados según el sistema nacional de educación actualmente vigente.

2.9 Enrolment and teachers at the second level: % distribution
Effectifs et personnel enseignant du second degré: répartition en %
Matrícula escolar y personal docente de segundo grado: distribución en %

2.9 Education at the second level: distribution of enrolment and teaching staff by type of education

Enseignement du second degré: répartition des effectifs scolaires et du personnel enseignant par type d'enseignement

Enseñanza de segundo grado: distribución de la matrícula escolar y del personal docente por tipo de enseñanza

Continents, major areas and groups of countries	Year	Enrolment / Effectifs scolaires / Matrícula escolar				Teaching staff / Personnel enseignant / Personal docente			
Continents, grandes régions et groupes de pays	Année	Total	General education / Enseignement général / Enseñanza general	Teacher training / Enseignement normal / Enseñanza normal	Vocational / Enseignement technique / Enseñanza técnica	Total	General education / Enseignement général / Enseñanza general	Teacher training / Enseignement normal / Enseñanza normal	Vocational / Enseignement technique / Enseñanza técnica
Continentes, grandes regiones y grupos de países	Año	(%)	(%)	(%)	(%)	(%)	(%)	(%)	(%)
World total	1980	100.0	88.7	1.1	10.2	100.0	87.0	1.4	11.5
	1985	100.0	87.4	1.1	11.5	100.0	84.8	1.6	13.6
	1990	100.0	87.6	0.9	11.5	100.0	84.7	1.4	14.0
	1993	100.0	87.9	0.9	11.2	100.0	85.0	1.2	13.8
	1994	100.0	87.7	0.9	11.4	100.0	84.9	1.2	13.9
Africa	1980	100.0	86.1	4.6	9.3	100.0	80.6	5.8	13.6
	1985	100.0	86.7	4.0	9.3	100.0	83.4	4.8	11.8
	1990	100.0	88.4	2.4	9.1	100.0	83.9	3.4	12.6
	1993	100.0	86.9	2.3	10.8	100.0	83.3	3.1	13.6
	1994	100.0	86.1	2.5	11.4	100.0	82.3	3.3	14.4
America	1980	100.0	88.2	1.8	10.0	100.0	87.7	2.1	10.3
	1985	100.0	87.0	1.7	11.2	100.0	84.7	2.7	12.6
	1990	100.0	85.9	1.7	12.4	100.0	84.0	2.4	13.7
	1993	100.0	85.8	1.8	12.4	100.0	84.3	2.1	13.6
	1994	100.0	85.4	1.9	12.7	100.0	84.4	2.2	13.4
Asia	1980	100.0	94.7	0.6	4.7	100.0	93.2	0.9	5.9
	1985	100.0	93.2	0.6	6.2	100.0	90.8	0.9	8.3
	1990	100.0	92.7	0.5	6.8	100.0	89.8	0.8	9.4
	1993	100.0	92.6	0.4	7.0	100.0	89.9	0.7	9.4
	1994	100.0	92.3	0.5	7.2	100.0	89.8	0.7	9.5
Europe	1980	100.0	75.7	0.9	23.4	100.0	76.8	1.4	21.8
	1985	100.0	72.9	0.9	26.2	100.0	74.2	1.4	24.4
	1990	100.0	73.8	1.0	25.2	100.0	75.1	1.4	23.5
	1993	100.0	75.5	0.9	23.6	100.0	76.0	1.2	22.7
	1994	100.0	75.3	0.9	23.8	100.0	76.1	1.2	22.7
Oceania	1980	100.0	98.5	0.2	1.3	100.0	98.2	0.0	1.8
	1985	100.0	98.4	0.2	1.5	100.0	98.5	0.0	1.5
	1990	100.0	98.0	0.2	1.9	100.0	97.9	0.0	2.1
	1993	100.0	95.7	0.2	4.2	100.0	96.1	0.0	3.2
	1994	100.0	94.9	0.2	5.0	100.0	95.5	0.0	4.5

Enrolment and teachers at the second level: % distribution 2.9
Effectifs et personnel enseignant du second degré: répartition en %
Matrícula escolar y personal docente de segundo grado: distribución en %

Continents, major areas and groups of countries / Continents, grandes régions et groupes de pays / Continentes, grandes regiones y grupos de países	Year / Année / Año	Enrolment Effectifs scolaires Matrícula escolar				Teaching staff Personnel enseignant Personal docente			
		Total (%)	General education Enseignement général Enseñanza general (%)	Teacher training Enseignement normal Enseñanza normal (%)	Vocational Enseignement technique Enseñanza técnica (%)	Total (%)	General education Enseignement général Enseñanza general (%)	Teacher training Enseignement normal Enseñanza normal (%)	Vocational Enseignement technique Enseñanza técnica (%)
Developing countries	1980	100.0	91.9	1.4	6.7	100.0	89.4	1.9	8.6
	1985	100.0	90.5	1.4	8.1	100.0	87.0	2.1	10.9
	1990	100.0	90.1	1.1	8.8	100.0	86.2	1.7	12.1
	1993	100.0	89.9	1.0	9.1	100.0	86.1	1.5	12.4
	1994	100.0	89.6	1.1	9.4	100.0	85.9	1.6	12.5
Sub-Saharan Africa	1980	100.0	87.4	6.1	6.5	100.0	81.6	7.7	10.7
	1985	100.0	88.7	5.4	5.8	100.0	85.5	6.5	7.8
	1990	100.0	90.7	3.4	5.8	100.0	86.5	4.7	8.7
	1993	100.0	90.6	3.6	5.7	100.0	86.2	5.3	8.5
	1994	100.0	90.5	3.8	5.6	100.0	85.9	5.7	8.5
Arab States	1980	100.0	87.5	1.8	10.7	100.0	83.8	2.8	13.4
	1985	100.0	86.5	1.5	12.0	100.0	83.7	2.2	14.1
	1990	100.0	87.4	1.1	11.6	100.0	83.4	1.6	15.0
	1993	100.0	85.0	0.6	14.4	100.0	83.2	0.9	15.8
	1994	100.0	83.4	0.7	16.0	100.0	82.0	0.9	17.2
Latin America and the Caribbean	1980	100.0	71.6	4.3	24.2	100.0	68.6	5.3	26.2
	1985	100.0	72.6	3.7	23.7	100.0	68.3	5.6	26.1
	1990	100.0	72.1	3.3	24.6	100.0	68.7	4.6	26.7
	1993	100.0	71.9	3.6	24.5	100.0	69.3	4.2	26.5
	1994	100.0	71.8	3.6	24.6	100.0	69.9	4.3	25.8
Eastern Asia and Oceania	1980	100.0	94.9	1.0	4.1	100.0	93.2	1.4	5.3
	1985	100.0	91.5	1.1	7.3	100.0	88.9	1.6	9.6
	1990	100.0	89.8	0.9	9.3	100.0	87.1	1.3	11.6
	1993	100.0	88.9	0.9	10.3	100.0	86.9	1.1	11.9
	1994	100.0	88.4	0.9	10.7	100.0	86.7	1.1	12.2
Southern Asia	1980	100.0	98.2	0.1	1.7	100.0	97.2	0.2	2.6
	1985	100.0	98.2	0.1	1.8	100.0	97.0	0.1	2.9
	1990	100.0	98.2	0.1	1.7	100.0	97.0	0.2	2.8
	1993	100.0	98.3	0.1	1.6	100.0	96.9	0.2	3.0
	1994	100.0	98.3	0.1	1.6	100.0	96.9	0.1	2.9
Least developed countries	1980	100.0	92.4	3.3	4.3	100.0	89.6	5.0	5.3
	1985	100.0	91.4	3.5	5.0	100.0	87.7	5.4	6.7
	1990	100.0	91.4	3.4	5.2	100.0	87.6	4.7	7.7
	1993	100.0	91.1	3.7	5.2	100.0	87.4	5.0	7.4
	1994	100.0	90.8	4.0	5.2	100.0	86.9	5.5	7.6
Developed countries	1980	100.0	83.7	0.6	15.7	100.0	84.3	0.8	14.8
	1985	100.0	82.1	0.5	17.3	100.0	82.0	0.9	17.1
	1990	100.0	82.6	0.6	16.8	100.0	82.6	0.9	16.5
	1993	100.0	83.6	0.5	15.8	100.0	83.4	0.8	15.8
	1994	100.0	83.5	0.5	16.0	100.0	83.4	0.8	15.8

General note / Note générale / Nota general:

E--> For composition of major areas and groups of countries, see the *List of countries and territories*, page xii. Data do not include the Democratic People's Republic of Korea.

FR-> Pour la composition des grandes régions et des groupes de pays, voir la *Liste de pays et territoires*, page xii. Les données n'incluent pas la République populaire démocratique de Corée.

ESP> Puede verse la composición de las grandes regiones y grupos de países en la *Lista de países y territorios*, página xii. Los datos no incluyen la República Popular Democrática de Corea.

2.10   Gross enrolment ratios
Taux d'inscription bruts
Tasas de escolarización brutas

2.10   Estimated gross enrolment ratios by level of education

Estimation des taux d'inscription bruts
par degré d'enseignement

Estimación de las tasas de escolarización brutas
por grado de enseñanza

Continents, major areas and groups of countries / Continents, grandes régions et groupes de pays / Continentes, grandes regiones y grupos de países	Year / Année / Año	Level of education / Degré d'enseignement / Grado de enseñanza											
		First level Premier degré Primer grado			Second level Second degré Segundo grado			Third level Troisième degré Tercer grado			All levels Tous les degrés Todos los grados		
		MF	M	F	MF	M	F	MF	M	F	MF	M	F
		(1)	(2)	(3)	(4)	(5)	(6)	(7)	(8)	(9)	(10)	(11)	(12)
World total	1980	96.1	103.6	88.2	46.3	51.3	41.1	12.2	13.2	11.1	55.2	60.0	50.1
	1985	99.5	106.5	92.2	47.8	52.6	42.7	12.8	13.8	11.7	55.6	60.1	50.9
	1990	99.6	105.6	93.4	51.2	55.5	46.6	13.7	14.5	12.8	57.1	60.9	53.0
	1993	99.4	104.7	93.8	54.4	58.5	50.2	14.9	15.6	14.2	59.2	62.7	55.5
	1994	99.5	104.9	94.0	55.4	59.4	51.2	15.3	15.9	14.6	59.9	63.4	56.2
Africa	1980	79.5	89.6	69.3	21.9	26.7	17.1	3.5	5.1	1.9	41.9	48.2	35.5
	1985	79.0	87.5	70.5	27.1	32.1	22.1	4.3	6.1	2.5	43.9	49.7	38.1
	1990	75.8	82.9	68.6	29.1	33.0	25.1	5.1	6.9	3.4	43.6	48.4	38.7
	1993	76.8	83.6	69.9	30.5	33.8	27.0	5.5	7.2	3.8	44.4	48.9	39.9
	1994	77.8	84.6	70.9	31.1	34.5	27.7	5.6	7.2	3.9	45.0	49.5	40.5
America	1980	103.6	104.6	102.5	64.1	63.8	64.4	30.7	30.9	30.4	70.5	71.0	70.0
	1985	104.6	106.2	102.9	68.3	67.4	69.2	32.1	31.7	32.6	72.6	73.0	72.3
	1990	106.4	107.9	104.8	66.3	64.8	67.9	36.0	34.2	37.9	74.6	74.3	74.9
	1993	108.0	109.6	106.4	68.8	67.4	70.1	36.9	34.1	39.8	76.3	75.8	76.8
	1994	108.8	110.5	107.2	70.2	68.8	71.6	36.8	33.8	39.8	77.0	76.5	77.6
Asia	1980	96.4	105.9	86.3	39.5	46.6	32.0	5.6	7.1	3.9	51.0	57.5	44.1
	1985	102.7	111.4	93.3	40.9	47.7	33.6	6.7	8.4	4.8	51.1	57.1	44.8
	1990	104.5	112.0	96.6	46.0	52.4	39.1	7.2	8.8	5.4	53.2	58.4	47.6
	1993	104.1	110.5	97.3	50.5	56.7	43.9	8.4	10.0	6.7	56.1	61.0	50.9
	1994	103.7	110.1	97.0	51.7	57.7	45.3	8.8	10.5	6.9	56.9	61.8	51.7
Europe	1980	107.4	107.6	107.1	84.4	83.8	85.0	29.3	28.7	29.8	73.5	73.2	73.8
	1985	107.4	107.7	107.1	87.6	86.9	88.4	31.7	30.4	33.1	75.6	75.0	76.2
	1990	103.8	103.8	103.7	91.8	90.5	93.1	35.7	34.6	36.8	77.7	76.9	78.5
	1993	100.3	100.5	100.1	94.0	92.2	95.9	38.6	37.1	40.1	78.7	77.6	79.9
	1994	101.4	101.7	101.0	95.2	93.5	97.0	39.5	37.8	41.4	79.8	78.7	81.0
Oceania	1980	104.4	106.1	102.3	63.4	62.5	64.3	20.9	22.8	18.9	66.6	67.5	65.7
	1985	100.3	101.8	98.8	67.3	66.8	67.9	22.9	23.5	22.2	66.1	66.5	65.6
	1990	103.1	104.9	101.2	68.0	67.2	69.0	28.2	26.6	30.0	68.6	68.4	68.8
	1993	104.1	106.1	102.2	71.9	71.3	72.4	34.3	31.6	37.1	72.3	72.0	72.7
	1994	104.5	106.5	102.5	73.0	72.3	73.6	33.8	30.9	36.9	72.9	72.5	73.3

Gross enrolment ratios 2.10
Taux d'inscription bruts
Tasas de escolarización brutas

Continents, major areas and groups of countries / Continents, grandes régions et groupes de pays / Continentes, grandes regiones y grupos de países	Year / Année / Año	Level of education / Degré d'enseignement / Grado de enseñanza											
		First level Premier degré Primer grado			Second level Second degré Segundo grado			Third level Troisième degré Tercer grado			All levels Tous les degrés Todos los grados		
		MF	M	F	MF	M	F	MF	M	F	MF	M	F
		(1)	(2)	(3)	(4)	(5)	(6)	(7)	(8)	(9)	(10)	(11)	(12)
Developing countries	1980	94.7	103.5	85.4	35.5	42.0	28.7	5.2	6.6	3.7	50.2	56.2	43.8
	1985	98.7	106.9	90.2	37.6	43.7	31.1	6.5	8.1	4.8	50.7	56.3	44.8
	1990	99.1	106.0	91.8	41.8	47.4	35.8	7.1	8.6	5.5	52.2	57.1	47.2
	1993	99.1	105.2	92.6	45.6	50.8	40.1	8.1	9.5	6.6	54.6	59.1	49.9
	1994	99.1	105.3	92.7	46.7	51.8	41.4	8.3	9.8	6.8	55.4	59.9	50.8
Sub-Saharan Africa	1980	77.4	86.6	68.2	17.5	22.3	12.7	1.6	2.5	.7	39.7	45.5	33.8
	1985	76.0	83.8	68.1	21.2	25.2	17.2	2.2	3.4	1.1	40.7	45.7	35.6
	1990	72.5	79.3	65.7	21.6	24.7	18.5	3.0	4.1	1.9	39.6	43.9	35.3
	1993	72.9	79.5	66.3	23.0	25.7	20.2	3.5	4.7	2.3	40.3	44.4	36.1
	1994	73.9	80.5	67.2	23.5	26.4	20.6	3.6	4.8	2.4	40.9	45.1	36.7
Arab States	1980	79.5	91.7	66.7	36.6	42.4	30.5	9.2	12.5	5.9	47.5	55.3	39.3
	1985	83.3	94.2	72.0	45.6	53.7	37.0	10.7	13.7	7.6	52.6	60.5	44.3
	1990	84.1	93.0	74.9	50.6	57.3	43.7	11.8	14.7	8.8	55.1	61.6	48.2
	1993	85.2	93.1	77.0	51.7	57.4	45.7	12.3	14.7	9.8	55.7	61.4	49.8
	1994	85.7	93.9	77.1	53.0	57.7	48.1	12.2	14.5	9.7	56.6	62.1	50.8
Latin America and the Caribbean	1980	104.8	106.1	103.4	45.4	45.0	45.7	13.7	15.5	12.0	64.3	65.4	63.2
	1985	105.8	107.9	103.6	51.1	49.6	52.7	15.7	17.3	14.1	66.1	67.1	65.0
	1990	106.8	108.6	105.0	51.7	49.6	53.9	17.0	17.9	16.1	67.0	67.6	66.4
	1993	108.6	110.5	106.5	53.2	50.7	55.6	17.1	16.9	17.3	67.9	68.2	67.7
	1994	109.7	111.7	107.6	55.6	53.1	58.2	17.2	16.7	17.6	69.0	69.1	68.8
Eastern Asia and Oceania	1980	109.2	116.1	101.8	43.0	49.3	36.3	3.7	4.7	2.8	57.0	62.1	51.6
	1985	116.5	123.0	109.7	40.5	45.6	35.1	5.3	6.7	3.8	53.8	58.1	49.2
	1990	118.2	121.9	114.4	46.1	50.4	41.5	5.8	7.1	4.4	54.7	57.7	51.4
	1993	113.1	115.2	110.9	52.0	55.4	48.4	7.3	8.6	5.8	57.8	60.2	55.2
	1994	111.2	113.0	109.3	53.8	57.2	50.2	7.8	9.3	6.2	58.8	61.2	56.3
Southern Asia	1980	77.1	92.0	61.1	28.3	37.1	18.7	4.4	6.3	2.4	38.9	48.0	29.1
	1985	85.3	98.4	71.2	33.8	43.1	23.6	5.3	7.3	3.2	43.4	52.1	34.0
	1990	90.7	103.0	77.4	39.4	48.5	29.6	5.5	7.3	3.7	47.8	56.0	39.0
	1993	96.2	107.9	83.8	44.1	53.0	34.4	6.1	7.9	4.0	51.7	59.5	43.2
	1994	97.8	109.6	85.3	44.6	53.2	35.4	6.2	8.1	4.1	52.4	60.2	44.0
Least developed countries	1980	63.9	75.7	52.0	14.3	19.8	8.7	1.8	2.7	1.0	31.5	38.5	24.5
	1985	64.5	74.0	54.7	16.0	21.0	10.9	2.5	3.6	1.3	32.1	38.1	26.0
	1990	66.6	74.3	58.8	16.8	21.0	12.4	2.4	3.6	1.3	33.2	38.1	28.2
	1993	69.0	77.0	60.8	17.7	22.1	13.0	2.9	4.3	1.6	34.5	39.6	29.3
	1994	71.2	79.9	62.4	17.8	22.2	13.3	3.0	4.4	1.6	35.4	40.7	30.0
Developed countries	1980	103.7	103.9	103.4	86.5	86.1	87.0	36.1	35.9	36.2	75.9	75.8	75.9
	1985	104.1	104.4	103.9	90.8	90.4	91.2	38.7	37.5	39.9	78.5	78.1	78.9
	1990	103.0	103.2	102.7	92.4	91.4	93.4	44.2	42.2	46.3	80.7	79.8	81.7
	1993	101.6	101.8	101.4	94.4	93.4	95.5	47.4	44.6	50.3	82.2	81.0	83.4
	1994	102.1	102.4	101.8	95.3	94.4	96.3	48.0	45.1	51.1	83.0	81.8	84.2

General note / Note générale / Nota general:

E--> For composition of major areas and groups of countries, see the *List of countries and territories*, page xii. Data do not include the Democratic People's Republic of Korea. Figures also do not include data relating to adult education and to special education provided outside regular schools. Second level education includes general, teacher training and vocational education. Third level education includes universities and other institutions of higher education. The data shown in this table are standardised and based on the present national system of education of each country.

FR--> Pour la composition des grandes régions et des groupes de pays, voir la *Liste des pays et territoires*, page xii. Les données ne comprennent pas la République populaire démocratique de Corée. Les chiffres ne comprennent pas non plus l'éducation des adultes, ni l'enseignement spécial dispensé en dehors des établissements scolaires ordinaires. L'enseignement du second degré comprend les enseignements général, normal et technique.

L'enseignement du troisième degré comprend les universités et autres établissements d'enseignement supérieur. Les données dans ce tableau ont été compilées à partir des données par pays, classées selon le système national d'enseignement actuellement en vigueur.

ESP> Puede verse la composición de las grandes regiones y grupos de países en la *Lista de países y territorios*, página xii. Excluídas la República Popular Democrática de Corea Las cifras no comprenden además la educación de adultos y, en lo que toca a la enseñanza especial, solo comprenden la impartida en establecimientos de enseñanza ordinaria. La enseñanza de segundo grado incluye las enseñanza general, normal y técnica. La enseñanza de tercer grado incluye las universidades y otros establecimientos de enseñanza superior. Los datos presentados en este cuadro están basados en los datos por país, clasificados según el sistema nacional de educación actualmente vigente.

2.11 Public expenditure on education
Dépenses publiques afférentes à l'enseignement
Gastos públicos destinados a la educación

2.11 Public expenditure on education, in United States dollars

Dépenses publiques afférentes à l'enseignement, en dollars des Etats-Unis

Gastos públicos destinados a la educación, en dólares de los Estados Unidos

Continents, major areas and groups of countries Continents, grandes régions et groupes de pays Continentes, grandes regiones y grupos de países	Public expenditure on education (in billions of dollars) Dépenses publiques afférentes à l'enseignement (en milliards de dollars) Gastos públicos destinados a la educación (en billones de dólares)				Public expenditure on education as % of GNP Dépenses publiques afférentes à l'enseignement en % du PNB Gastos públicos destinados a la educación en % del PNB				Public expenditure on education per inhabitant ($) Dépenses publiques afférentes à l'enseignement, par habitant ($) Gastos públicos destinados a la educación por habitante ($)			
	1980	1985	1990	1994	1980	1985	1990	1994	1980	1985	1990	1994
World total	526.1	565.3	1 014.8	1 275.7	4.9	4.9	4.9	5.2	129	126	208	244
Africa	22.9	22.0	26.1	26.3	5.3	5.7	5.8	6.1	48	40	41	37
America	188.6	249.5	375.6	477.5	4.9	4.9	5.2	5.4	309	377	524	626
Asia	103.5	117.4	227.0	315.7	4.4	4.3	4.2	4.4	41	43	75	98
Europe	200.6	165.8	367.5	432.7	5.1	5.1	5.1	5.4	418	340	741	863
Oceania	10.4	10.6	18.6	23.5	5.6	5.6	5.6	6.1	467	439	715	850
Developing countries	101.6	100.2	161.7	191.9	3.8	4.0	4.0	4.2	31	28	41	45
Sub-Saharan Africa	15.8	11.3	15.2	16.3	5.1	4.8	5.3	5.9	41	26	30	28
Arab States	18.0	23.6	24.8	27.5	4.1	5.8	5.3	5.5	109	122	112	112
Latin America and the Caribbean	33.5	27.9	45.3	72.1	3.8	3.9	4.0	4.5	94	70	103	152
Eastern Asia and Oceania	16.0	20.1	31.8	52.0	2.8	3.2	3.0	3.3	12	14	20	31
Southern Asia	12.8	14.7	35.8	16.9	4.1	3.3	3.9	3.8	13	14	30	13
Least developed countries	3.1	2.7	4.2	4.3	2.7	2.8	2.9	2.8	8	6	9	8
Developed countries	424.5	465.1	853.1	1 083.7	5.3	5.1	5.2	5.4	500	533	949	1179

General note / Note générale / Nota general:

E––> For composition of major areas and groups of countries, see the *List of countries and territories*, page xii. Certain data in this table differ from those for the same year presented in earlier editions of the *Yearbook*. These differences should be taken to reflect revisions made as a result of the receipt of additional information and of revisions made by World Bank and the International Monetary Fund (IMF) on the GNP and exchange rate series respectively. It should also be noted that any significant decreases in the estimated amounts on public expenditure on education (see Southern Asia) are due to exchange rate fluctuations in certain countries.

Data for countries of the *Former U.S.S.R.* are not included in either the world total or regional totals due to the lack of information necessary for the calculation of valid estimates for these countries.

FR–> Pour la composition des grandes régions et groupes de pays, voir la *Liste des pays et territoires*, page xii. Certaines des données présentées dans ce tableau diffèrent de celles correspondant à la même année et figurant dans les éditions précédentes. Ces différences sont dues aux révisions effectuées à la suite de nouveaux renseignements reçus ainsi qu'aux révisions des séries du PNB et du taux de change effectuées respectivement par la Banque Mondiale et le Fonds Monétaire International (FMI). Il

faut aussi noter que les diminutions significatives dans les montants estimés des dépenses publiques afférentes à l'enseignement (voir Asie du Sud) sont dues aux fluctuations du taux de change dans certains pays.

Les données concernant les pays de *l'ancienne U.R.S.S.* ne sont incluses ni dans le total mondial ni dans les totaux régionaux à cause du manque d'information nécessaire pour le calcul d'estimations fiables pour ces pays.

ESP> Puede verse la composición de las grandes regiones y grupos de paises en la *Lista de países y territorios*, página xii. Ciertos datos presentados en este cuadro difieren de los correspondientes al mismo año que figuran en las ediciones anteriores del *Anuario*. Debe considerarse que se trata de cifras revisadas de acuerdo con las nuevas informaciones recibidas así como las revisiones de las series del PNB y los tipos de cambio proporcionadas por el Banco Mundial y el Fondo Monetario Internacional (FMI), respectivamente. Se debe observar que la disminución importante de los gastos públicos estimados destinados a la educación (véase Asia del Sur) se deben a las fluctuaciones de los tipos de cambio en algunos paises.

No se han incluído los datos relativos a los países de la *ex URSS* ni en el total mundial ni en los totales regionales, por falta de información necesaria para la preparación de estimaciones fiables para esos paises.

3   Education

Education

Educación

This chapter provides statistics on education preceding the first level, as well as on that at the first, second, and third levels of education. Data are also provided on educational systems and on enrolment ratios for the different levels. Data on the number of students and teachers are provided for all levels of education; data on number of institutions are provided for education preceding the first level and for education at the first level; data on enrolment and graduates at the third level are presented with different disaggregations.

The tables in this chapter can be subdivided into three groups.

The first group, which includes Tables 3.1 and 3.2, provides information by country on the entrance ages and duration of compulsory education for first and second level general education and enrolment ratios by level of education.

The second group consists of six tables, 3.3 to 3.8 concerned with education preceding the first level, and first and second level

education. In consulting these tables, reference should be made to the information on duration of schooling, etc., contained in Tables 3.1, 3.1a and 3.1b. In general, the data shown in all tables are for the school years beginnig in 1980, 1985, 1990 and the three latest years for which data are available.

The third group consists of six tables, 3.9 to 3.14, on the development of third level education.

According to the definition adopted by UNESCO, education at the third level requires, as a minimum condition of entry, the successful completion of education at the second level or proof of equivalent knowledge or experience. Third level education can be given in different types of institutions, such as universities, teacher-training institutes, technical institutes, etc.

Definitions of fields of study according to ISCED
(International Standard Classification of Education)

ISCED Codes

Levels	Fields of Study		
5, 6, 7	14	EDUCATION SCIENCE AND TEACHER TRAINING	General teacher training, teacher training programmes with specialization in vocational subjects, education science.
5, 6, 7	22, 26	HUMANITIES, RELIGION AND THEOLOGY	Languages and literature, linguistics, comparative literature, programmes for interpreters and translators, history, archaeology, philosophy. Religion and theology.
5, 6, 7	18	FINE AND APPLIED ARTS	Art studies, drawing and painting, sculpturing, handicrafts, music, drama, photography and cinematography, interior design, history and philosophy of art.
5, 6, 7	38	LAW	Law, programmes for 'notaires', local magistrates, jurisprudence.
5, 6, 7	30	SOCIAL AND BEHAVIOURAL SCIENCE	Social and behavioural science, economics, demography, political science, sociology, anthropology, psychology, geography, studies of regional cultures.
5, 6, 7	34	COMMERCIAL AND BUSINESS ADMINISTRATION	Business administration and commercial programmes, accountancy, secretarial programmes, business machine operation and electronic data processing, financial management, public administration, institutional administration.
5, 6, 7	84	MASS COMMUNICATION AND DOCUMENTATION	Journalism, programmes in radio and television broadcasting, public relations, communications arts, library science, programmes for technicians in museums and similar repositories, documentation techniques.
5, 6, 7	66	HOME ECONOMICS (domestic science)	Household arts, consumer food research and nutrition.
5	78	SERVICE TRADES	Cooking (restaurant and hotel-type), retailing, tourist trades, other service trades programmes.
5, 6, 7	42	NATURAL SCIENCE	Biological science, chemistry, geological science, physics, astronomy, meteorology, oceanography.
5, 6, 7	46	MATHEMATICS AND COMPUTER SCIENCE	General programmes in mathematics, statistics, actuarial science, computer science.
5, 6, 7	50	MEDICAL SCIENCE AND HEALTH-RELATED	Medecine, surgery and medical specialities, hygiene and public health, physiotherapy and occupational therapy; nursing, midwifery, medical X-ray techniques and other programmes in medical diagnostic and treatment techniques; medical technology, dentistry, stomatology and odontology, dental techniques, pharmacy, optometry.
5, 6, 7	54	ENGINEERING	Chemical engineering and materials techniques, civil engineering, electrical and electronics engineering, surveying, industrial engineering, metallurgical engineering, mining engineering, mechanical engineering, agricultural and forestry engineering techniques, fishery engineering techniques.
5, 6, 7	58	ARCHITECTURE AND TOWN PLANNING	Architecture, town planning, landscape architecture.
5	52	TRADE, CRAFT AND INDUSTRIAL PROGRAMMES	Food processing, electrical and electronics trades, metal trades, mechanical trades, air-conditioning trades; textile techniques, graphic arts, laboratory technicians, optical lens making.
5	70	TRANSPORT AND COMMUNICATIONS	Air crew and ships' officer programmes, railway operating trades, road motor vehicle operation programmes, postal service programmes.
5, 6, 7	62	AGRICULTURE, FORESTRY AND FISHERY	General programmes in agriculture, animal husbandry, horticulture, crop husbandry, agricultural economics, food sciences and technology, soil and water sciences, veterinary medicine, forestry, forest products technology, fishery science and technology.
5	01		General programmes.
5, 6, 7	89	OTHER PROGRAMMES	Criminology, civil security and military programme, social welfare, vocational counselling, physical education, environmental studies, nautical science. Other programmes.

Ce chapitre présente des statistiques relatives à l'enseignement précédant le premier degré, ainsi qu'aux enseignements du premier, du second et du troisième degré. Des données sont présentées sur les systèmes nationaux d'enseignement et les taux d'inscription scolaire ainsi que sur le personnel enseignant et les effectifs scolaires pour tous les niveaux d'enseignement; le nombre d'écoles est également indiqué pour les enseignements précédant le premier degré et du premier degré; les chiffres sur les effectifs et les diplômés du troisième degré sont présentés selon différentes répartitions. Les tableaux de ce chapitre peuvent être subdivisés en trois catégories:

La première catégorie, qui inclut les tableaux 3.1 et 3.2, procure des informations par pays sur l'âge d'admission et les durées de l'enseignement obligatoire dans les enseignements du premier degré et du second degré général, ainsi que les taux d'inscription par degré d'enseignement.

Une deuxième catégorie comprend six tableaux, 3.3 à 3.8, qui se réfèrent à l'enseignement précédant le premier degré et aux enseignements du premier et du second degré. Ces tableaux doivent être consultés en se référant aux renseignements sur la durée de la scolarité, contenus dans les tableaux 3.1, 3.1a et 3.1b. En général, les données présentées dans ces tableaux correspondent aux années scolaires commençant en 1980, 1985, 1990 et aux trois dernières années pour lesquelles les données sont disponibles.

La troisième section comprend six tableaux statistiques sur l'enseignement du troisième degré (tableaux 3.9 à 3.14).

L'enseignement du troisième degré, d'après la définition adoptée par l'UNESCO, est celui qui exige comme condition minimale d'admission d'avoir suivi avec succès un enseignement complet du second degré ou de faire preuve de connaissances ou expériences équivalentes. Il peut être dispensé dans différents types d'établissements tels que les universités, les écoles normales supérieures, les écoles techniques supérieures, etc.

Définitions des domaines d'études d'après la CITE
(Classification internationale type de l'éducation

Codes CITE

Niveaux   Domaines d'études

Niveaux		Domaines d'études	
5, 6, 7,	14	SCIENCES DE L'ÉDUCATION ET FORMATION D'ENSEIGNANTS	Formation de personnel enseignant, préparation générale à l'enseignement, préparation à l'enseignement avec spécialisation dans des disciplines à caractère professionnel, sciences de l'éducation.
5, 6, 7,	22, 26	LETTRES, RELIGION ET THÉOLOGIE	Langues et littératures, linguistique, littérature comparée, formation d'interprètes et de traducteurs, histoire, archéologie, philosophie. Religion et théologie.
5, 6, 7,	18	BEAUX-ARTS ET ARTS APPLIQUÉS	Études artistiques, dessin et peinture, sculpture, arts artisanaux, musique, arts du spectacle, photographie et cinématographie, décoration, histoire et philosophie de l'art.
5, 6, 7,	38	DROIT	Droit, notariat, formation de magistrats locaux, jurisprudence.
5, 6, 7,	30	SCIENCES SOCIALES ET SCIENCES DU COMPORTEMENT	Sciences sociales et sciences du comportement, sciences économiques, science politique, démographie, sociologie, anthropologie, psychologie, géographie, études des cultures régionales.
5, 6, 7,	34	FORMATION AU COMMERCE ET À L'ADMINISTRATION DES ENTREPRISES	Administration des entreprises et enseignement commercial, comptabilité, secrétariat, mécanographie et traitement électronique de l'information, gestion financière, administration publique, administration d'établissements et de collectivités.
5, 6, 7,	84	INFORMATION ET DOCUMENTATION	Journalisme, formations pour la radio et la télévision, relations avec le public, techniques de l'information, bibliothéconomie, formation des techniciens pour les musées et établissements analogues, techniques de la documentation.
5, 6, 7,	66	ENSEIGNEMENT MÉNAGER	Arts ménagers, alimentation familiale, diététique et nutrition.
5	78	FORMATION POUR LE SECTEUR TERTIAIRE	Hôtellerie et restauration, commerce de détail, services de tourisme, autres formations pour le secteur tertiaire.
5, 6, 7,	42	SCIENCES EXACTES ET NATURELLES	Sciences biologiques, chimie, sciences géologiques, physique, astronomie, météorologie, océanographie.
5, 6, 7,	46	MATHÉMATIQUES ET INFORMATIQUE	Mathématiques générales, statistique, science actuarielle, informatique.
5, 6, 7,	50	SCIENCES MÉDICALES, SANTÉ ET HYGIÈNE	Médecine, chirurgie et spécialisations médicales, hygiène et santé publique, physiothérapie et ergothérapie ; formation d'infirmiers, de sages-femmes, de radiologues et autres formations aux techniques du diagnostic et du traitement des maladies, technologie médicale, art dentaire, stomatologie et odontologie, technologie dentaire, pharmacie, optométrie.
5, 6, 7,	54	SCIENCES DE L'INGÉNIEUR	Génie chimique et technologie des matériaux, génie civil, électrotechnique et électronique, topographie, organisation industrielle, métallurgie, techniques minières, mécanique, technologie agricole et forestière, techniques de la pêche.
5, 6, 7,	58	ARCHITECTURE ET URBANISME	Architecture, urbanisme, formation d'architectes paysagistes.
5	52	MÉTIERS DE LA PRODUCTION INDUSTRIELLE	Traitement des denrées alimentaires ; formation en électricité, en électronique, au travail des métaux, à la mécanique, aux techniques du conditionnement d'air ; technologie des textiles, arts graphiques, techniciens de laboratoire, fabrication de verres optiques.
5	70	TRANSPORTS ET TÉLÉCOMMUNICATIONS	Formation de personnel des transports aériens, maritimes, ferroviaires, routiers et des services postaux.
5, 6, 7,	62	AGRICULTURE, SYLVICULTURE ET HALIEUTIQUE	Enseignement agricole, zootechnie, horticulture, culture de plein champ, économie agricole, science et technologie de l'alimentation, pédologie et hydrologie, médecine vétérinaire, sylviculture, technologie des produits forestiers, halieutique (science et technologie de la pêche).
5	01		Programmes d'enseignement général.
5, 6, 7,	89	AUTRES PROGRAMMES	Criminologie, formation militaire et pour la sécurité civile, formation de personnel des services sociaux, formation des conseillers d'orientation professionnelle, éducation physique, programmes relatifs à l'environnement, sciences nautiques. Autres programmes.

Este capítulo facilita datos estadísticos sobre la enseñanza anterior al primer grado, así como sobre las enseñanzas de primero, segundo y tercer grado. También se presentan datos relativos a los sistemas de enseñanza, a las tasas de escolarización, al personal docente y a los alumnos para todos los grados de enseñanza. Se indican asimismo el número de escuelas en las enseñanzas anterior al primer grado y de primer grado; las cifras relativas a la matrícula escolar y los diplomados de la enseñanzas de tercer grado se presentan bajo distintas formas.Los cuadros incluídos en este capítulo pueden subdividerse en tres secciones;

La primera sección, que comprende los cuadros 3.1 y 3.2, facilita la información, por países, sobre la edad de admisión, la duración de la enseñanza obligatoria en las enseñanzas de primero y de segundo grado (general), y las tasas de escolarización para los diferentes grados de enseñanza.

La segunda sección comprende seis cuadros, 3.3 a 3.8, que se refieren a la enseñanza anterior al primer grado y a las enseñanzas de primero y de segundo grado. Al consultar los cuadros de esta sección, hay que referirse a las informaciones sobre la duración de la escolaridad, etc. que figuran en los cuadros 3.1, 3.1a y 3.1b. En general, los datos presentados en estos cuadros corresponden a los años escolares que empezaron en 1980, 1985, 1990 y los tres últimos años para los que se dispone de datos.

La tercera sección comprende seis cuadros estadísticos sobre la enseñanza de tercer grado (cuadros 3.9 a 3.14).

Según la definición adoptada por la UNESCO, la enseñanza de tercer grado es aquélla en la que se exige, como condición mínima de admisión, haber terminado con éxito la enseñanza de segundo grado o demostrar la posesión de conocimientos equivalentes. Puede dispensarse en distintos tipos de establecimientos docentes tales como las universidades, las escuelas normales superiores, las escuelas técnicas superiores, etc.

Definiciones de los sectores de estudio según la CINE
(Clasificación Internacional Normalizada de la Educación)

Cifra de la CINE

Grados   Sectores de estudios

5, 6, 7,	14	CIENCIAS DE LA EDUCACIÓN Y FORMACIÓN DE PERSONAL DOCENTE	Programas generales de formación de personal docente, formación de personal docente con especialización en materias profesionales o técnicas, ciencias de la educación.
5, 6, 7,	22, 26	HUMANIDADES, RELIGIÓN Y TEOLOGÍA	Lenguas y literatura, lingüística, literatura comparada, formación de traductores e intérpretes, historia, arqueología, filosofía. Religión y teología.
5, 6, 7,	18	BELLAS ARTES Y ARTES APLICADAS	Estudios artísticos, dibujo y pintura, escultura, artesanía, música, arte dramático, fotografía y cinematografía, decoración, historia y filosofía del arte.
5, 6, 7,	38	DERECHO	Derecho, formación de notarios, formación de magistrados locales, jurisprudencia.
5, 6, 7,	30	CIENCIAS SOCIALES Y DEL COMPORTAMIENTO	Ciencias sociales y del comportamiento, economía, ciencias políticas, demografía, sociología, antropología, psicología, geografía, estudio de las culturas regionales.
5, 6, 7,	34	ENSEÑANZA COMERCIAL Y DE ADMINISTRACIÓN DE EMPRESAS	Administración de empresas y enseñanza comercial, contabilidad, programas de secretaría, manejo de máquinas de oficina y tratamiento electrónico de datos, gestión financiera, administración pública, administración de instituciones.
5, 6, 7,	84	DOCUMENTACIÓN Y COMUNICACIÓN SOCIAL	Periodismo, formación de personal de radio y televisión, relaciones públicas, comunicación, bibliotecología, formación de personal técnico de museos y establecimientos análogos, técnicas de la documentación.
5, 6, 7,	66	ECONOMÍA DOMÉSTICA (enseñanza del hogar)	Artes del hogar, nutrición e investigación sobre el consumo de alimentos y la alimentación familiar.
5	78	FORMACIÓN PARA EL SECTOR DE LOS SERVICIOS	Arte culinario (hotelería y restaurantes), venta al detalle, turismo, otros programas relativos al sector de los servicios.
5, 6, 7,	42	CIENCIAS NATURALES	Ciencias biológicas, química, ciencias geológicas, física, astronomía, meteorología, oceanografía.
5, 6, 7,	46	MATEMÁTICAS E INFORMÁTICA	Programas generales de matemáticas, estadística, ciencia actuarial, informática.
5, 6, 7,	50	CIENCIAS MÉDICAS, SANIDAD E HIGIENE	Medicina, cirugía y especialidades médicas, higiene y sanidad pública, fisioterapia y ergoterapia; formación de enfermeros y de comadronas, tecnología médica de los rayos X y otras tecnologías del diagnóstico y tratamiento médicos, tecnología médica; odontología y estomatología, tecnología dentaria, farmacia, optometría.
5, 6, 7,	54	INGENIERÍA Y TECNOLOGÍA	Ingeniería química y tecnología de materiales, ingeniería civil, ingeniería eléctrica y electrónica, topografía, organización industrial, ingeniería metalúrgica, ingeniería de minas, ingeniería mecánica, ingeniería agronómica, ingeniería forestal (de montes).
5, 6, 7,	58	ARQUITECTURA Y URBANISMO	Arquitectura, urbanismo, arquitectura paisajística.
5	52	ARTES Y OFICIOS INDUSTRIALES	Tratamiento y elaboración de alimentos; oficios de la electricidad, de la electrónica, del metal, oficios relativos a la mecánica, al acondicionamiento de aire; técnicas textiles, artes gráficas, técnicas de laboratorio, fabricación de cristales y lentes ópticos.
5	70	TRANSPORTES Y COMUNICACIONES	Formación de personal para los transportes aéreos, marítimos, por ferrocarril y por carretera; programas relativos a los servicios postales.
5, 6, 7,	62	ENSEÑANZA AGRONÓMICA, DASONÓMICA Y PESQUERA	Agronomía, zootecnia, horticultura, agricultura, economía agraria, tecnología y ciencias de la alimentación, hidrología y edafología, veterinaria, dasonomía, tecnología de los productos forestales, ciencia y tecnología pesquera (haliéutica).
5	01		Enseñanza general.
5, 6, 7,	89	OTROS PROGRAMAS	Criminología, enseñanza militar y programas relativos a la seguridad civil, asistencia social, orientación profesional, educación física, estudios mesológicos, ciencia náutica. Otros programas.

National education systems 3.1
Systèmes nationaux d'enseignement
Sistemas nacionales de enseñanza

3.1 National education systems

Systèmes nationaux d'enseignement

Sistemas nacionales de enseñanza

P—P = First level S—S = Second level S1-S1 = Second level, first stage S2-S2 = Second level, second stage	P—P = Premier degré S—S = Second degré S1-S1 = Second degré, premier cycle S2-S2 = Second degré, deuxième cycle	P—P = Primer grado S—S = Segundo grado S1-S1 = Segundo grado, primer ciclo S2-S2 = Segundo grado, segundo ciclo
For countries marked with the symbol #, the educational system allows for other alternatives (see Table 3.1A)	Pour les pays signalés par le symbole #, le système d'enseignement permet d'autres structures (voir le Tableau 3.1A)	En los países marcados con el símbolo #, el sistema de la enseñanza permite otras estructuras (véase el Cuadro 3.1A)
Please refer to the explanatory text at the end of the table.	Prière de se référer au texte explicatif à la fin du tableau	Referirse al texto explicativo al final del cuadro

Country Pays País	Compulsory education Scolarité obligatoire Escolaridad obligatoria		Entrance age to education preceding the first level Âge d'admission dans l'enseignement précédant le premier degré Edad de admisión en la enseñanza anterior al primer grado	Entrance age and duration of first and second level (general) education Âge d'admission et durée des enseignements du premier et du second degré (général) Edad de admisión y duración de las enseñanzas de primer y de segundo grado (general) Age / Âge / Edad																	
	Age limits Limites d'âge Limites de edad	Duration (years) Durée (années) Duración (años)		4	5	6	7	8	9	10	11	12	13	14	15	16	17	18	19	20
Africa																				
Algeria	6-15	9	4		P—P—P—P—P—P S1—S1—S1 S2—S2—S2															
Angola	7-15	8	5		P—P—P—P S1—S1—S1—S1 S2—S2—S2															
Benin	6-11	6	3		P—P—P—P—P—P S1—S1—S1—S1 S2—S2—S2															
Botswana	-	-	-		P—P—P—P—P—P—P S1—S1 S2—S2—S2															
Burkina Faso	7-14	6	3		P—P—P—P—P—P S1—S1—S1—S1 S2—S2—S2															
Burundi	7-13	6	3		P—P—P—P—P—P S1—S1—S1—S1 S2—S2—S2															
Cameroon																					
Eastern	6-12	6	4		P—P—P—P—P—P S1—S1—S1—S1 S2—S2—S2															
Western	-	-	3		P—P—P—P—P—P—P S1—S1—S1—S1—S1 S2—S2															
Cape Verde	7-13	6	4		P—P—P—P—P—P S1—S1—S1 S2—S2—S2															
Central African Republic	6-14	6	4		P—P—P—P—P—P S1—S1—S1—S1 S2—S2—S2															
Chad	6-14	8	4		P—P—P—P—P—P S1—S1—S1—S1 S2—S2—S2															
Comoros	7-16	9	4		P—P—P—P—P—P S1—S1—S1—S1 S2—S2—S2															
Congo	6-16	10	3		P—P—P—P—P—P S1—S1—S1—S1 S2—S2—S2															
Côte d'Ivoire #	7-13	6	4		P—P—P—P—P—P S1—S1—S1—S1 S2—S2—S2															
Djibouti	6-12	6	4		P—P—P—P—P—P S1—S1—S1—S1 S2—S2—S2															
Egypt	6-11	5	4		P—P—P—P—P S1—S1—S1 S2—S2—S2															

3.1 National education systems
Systèmes nationaux d'enseignement
Sistemas nacionales de enseñanza

Country / Pays / País	Compulsory education / Scolarité obligatoire / Escolaridad obligatoria — Age limits / Limites d'âge / Limites de edad	Duration (years) / Durée (années) / Duración (años)	Entrance age to education preceding the first level / Âge d'admission dans l'enseignement précédant le premier degré / Edad de admisión en la enseñanza anterior al primer grado	Entrance age and duration of first and second level (general) education — Age / Âge / Edad (4–20)
Equatorial Guinea	6-11	5	2	P—P—P—P—P S1—S1—S1—S1 S2—S2—S2
Eritrea	7-13	7	5	P—P—P—P—P S1—S1 S2—S2—S2—S2
Ethiopia	7-13	6	4	P—P—P—P—P—P S1—S1 S2—S2—S2—S2
Gabon	6-16	10	3	P—P—P—P—P—P S1—S1—S1—S1 S2—S2—S2
Gambia	-	-	...	P—P—P—P—P—P S1—S1—S1—S1—S1 S2—S2
Ghana #	6-14	9	4	P—P—P—P—P—P S1—S1—S1 S2—S2—S2—S2
Guinea	7-13	6	-	P—P—P—P—P—P S1—S1—S1—S1 S2—S2—S2
Guinea-Bissau	7-13	6	3	P—P—P—P—P—P S1—S1—S1 S2—S2
Kenya	6-14	8	3	P—P—P—P—P—P—P—P S—S—S—S
Lesotho	6-13	7	-	P—P—P—P—P—P—P S1—S1—S1 S2—S2
Liberia	7-16	9	4	P—P—P—P—P—P S1—S1—S1 S2—S2—S2
Libyan Arab Jamahiriya	6-15	9	4	P—P—P—P—P—P—P—P—P S—S—S
Madagascar	6-13	5	3	P—P—P—P—P S1—S1—S1—S1 S2—S2—S2
Malawi	6-14	8	-	P—P—P—P—P—P—P—P S1—S1 S2—S2
Mali #	7-16	9	3	P—P—P—P—P—P S1—S1—S1 S2—S2—S2
Mauritania	-	-	3	P—P—P—P—P—P S1—S1—S1 S2—S2—S2
Mauritius	5-12	7	3	P—P—P—P—P—P S1—S1—S1 S2—S2—S2—S2
Morocco	7-13	6	5	P—P—P—P—P—P S1—S1—S1 S2—S2—S2—S2
Mozambique #	7-13	7	-	P—P—P—P—P S1—S1 S2—S2—S2—S2—S2
Namibia #	6-16	10	6	P—P—P—P—P—P—P S—S—S—S—S
Niger	7-15	8	5	P—P—P—P—P—P S1—S1—S1—S1 S2—S2—S2
Nigeria	6-12	6	3	P—P—P—P—P—P S1—S1—S1 S2—S2—S2
Reunion	6-16	10	2	P—P—P—P—P S1—S1—S1—S1 S2—S2—S2
Rwanda	7-13	7	3	P—P—P—P—P—P—P S—S—S—S—S—S
St. Helena	5-15	10	3	P—P—P—P—P—P S1—S1—S1—S1 S2—S2
Sao Tome and Principe	7-14	4	3	P—P—P—P S1—S1—S1—S1 S2—S2—S2
Senegal #	7-13	6	3	P—P—P—P—P—P S1—S1—S1—S1 S2—S2—S2
Seychelles	6-15	9	4	P—P—P—P—P—P S—S—S—S—S
Sierra Leone	-	-	3	P—P—P—P—P—P—P S1—S1—S1—S1 S2—S2
Somalia	6-14	8	5	P—P—P—P—P—P—P—P S—S—S—S
South Africa	7-16	10	5	P—P—P—P—P—P—P S1—S1—S1 S2—S2
Sudan	7-12	6	5	P—P—P—P—P—P S1—S1—S1 S2—S2—S2
Swaziland	6-13	7	3	P—P—P—P—P—P—P S1—S1—S1 S2—S2
Togo	6-12	6	3	P—P—P—P—P—P S1—S1—S1—S1 S2—S2—S2
Tunisia	6-16	9	3	P—P—P—P—P—P S1—S1—S1 S2—S2—S2—S2
Uganda	-	-	...	P—P—P—P—P—P—P S1—S1—S1—S1 S2—S2
United Republic of Tanzania	7-13	7	3	P—P—P—P—P—P—P S1—S1—S1—S1 S2—S2
Western Sahara	6-16	8	4	P—P—P—P—P S1—S1—S1 S2—S2—S2
Zaire	6-12	6	3	P—P—P—P—P—P S1—S1 S2—S2—S2—S2

National education systems 3.1
Systèmes nationaux d'enseignement
Sistemas nacionales de enseñanza

Country / Pays / País	Compulsory education — Age limits / Limites d'âge / Limites de edad	Compulsory education — Duration (years) / Durée (années) / Duración (años)	Entrance age to education preceding the first level / Âge d'admission dans l'enseignement précédant le premier degré / Edad de admisión en la enseñanza anterior al primer grado	Entrance age and duration of first and second level (general) education — Age / Âge / Edad (4–20)
Zambia	7-14	7	3	P—P—P—P—P—P—P S1—S1 S2—S2—S2
Zimbabwe	7-15	8	5	P—P—P—P—P—P—P S—S—S—S—S—S
America, North				
Anguilla	5-16	12	3	P—P—P—P—P—P S—S—S—S—S—S
Antigua and Barbuda #	5-16	11	-	P—P—P—P—P—P—P S1—S1—S1 S2—S2
Bahamas	5-14	10	3	P—P—P—P—P—P S1—S1—S1 S2—S2—S2
Barbados	5-16	12	3	P—P—P—P—P—P—P S—S—S—S—S—S
Belize	5-14	10	3	P—P—P—P—P—P—P—P S—S—S
Bermuda	5-16	11,12	4	P—P—P—P—P—P—P S—S—S—S
British Virgin Islands #	5-11	7	3	P—P—P—P—P—P S1—S1—S1 S2—S2
Canada #	6-16	10	4	P—P—P—P—P—P S1—S1—S1 S2—S2—S2
Cayman Islands	5-15	10	-	P—P—P—P—P—P—P S—S—S—S—S—S
Costa Rica #	6-15	9	5 1/2	P—P—P—P—P—P S1—S1—S1 S2—S2
Cuba	6-11	6	5	P—P—P—P—P—P S1—S1—S1 S2—S2—S2
Dominica	5-15	10	3	P—P—P—P—P—P—P S—S—S—S—S
Dominican Republic	6-14	9	3	P—P—P—P—P—P—P—P S—S—S—S
El Salvador	7-15	9	4	P—P—P—P—P—P—P—P—P S—S—S
Grenada #	5-16	11	3	P—P—P—P—P—P—P S—S—S—S—S
Guadeloupe	6-16	10	2	P—P—P—P—P S1—S1—S1—S1 S2—S2—S2
Guatemala	7-14	6	5	P—P—P—P—P—P S1—S1—S1 S2—S2—S2
Haiti #	6-12	6	3	P—P—P—P—P—P S1—S1—S1 S2—S2—S2
Honduras	7-13	6	4	P—P—P—P—P—P S1—S1—S1 S2—S2
Jamaica	6-12	6	3	P—P—P—P—P—P S1—S1—S1 S2—S2—S2—S2
Martinique	6-16	10	2	P—P—P—P—P S1—S1—S1 S2—S2—S2
Mexico	6-14	6	4	P—P—P—P—P—P S1—S1—S1 S2—S2—S2
Montserrat	5-16	11	3	P—P—P—P—P—P—P S1—S1—S1—S1—S1
Netherlands Antilles	-	-	4	P—P—P—P—P—P S—S—S—S—S
Nicaragua	7-12	6	3	P—P—P—P—P—P S1—S1—S1 S2—S2
Panama	6-15	6	5	P—P—P—P—P—P S1—S1—S1 S2—S2—S2
Puerto Rico	8-14	7	...	P—P—P—P—P—P—P—P S—S—S—S
St. Kitts and Nevis #	5-17	12	3	P—P—P—P—P—P S1—S1—S1—S1 S2—S2
St. Lucia	5-15	10	-	P—P—P—P—P—P S1—S1—S1 S2—S2
St. Pierre and Miquelon	6-16	10	2	P—P—P—P—P S1—S1—S1—S1 S2—S2—S2
St. Vincent and the Grenadines	...	...	3	P—P—P—P—P—P—P S1—S1—S1—S1—S1 S2—S2
Trinidad and Tobago	6-12	7	3	P—P—P—P—P—P—P S1—S1—S1 S2—S2
Turcs and Caicos Islands	7-14	7	4 1/2	P—P—P—P—P—P S—S—S—S—S

3.1 National education systems
Sysièmes nationaux d'enseignement
Sistemas nacionales de enseñanza

Country / Pays / País	Compulsory education / Scolarité obligatoire / Escolaridad obligatoria		Entrance age to education preceding the first level / Âge d'admission dans l'enseignement précédant le premier degré / Edad de admisión en la enseñanza anterior al primer grado	Entrance age and duration of first and second level (general) education / Âge d'admission et durée des enseignements du premier et du second degré (général) / Edad de admisión y duración de las enseñanzas de primer y de segundo grado (general) — Age / Âge / Edad
	Age limits / Limites d'âge / Limites de edad	Duration (years) / Durée (années) / Duración (años)		
United States #	7-16	10	3	P—P—P—P—P—P S1—S1—S1 S2—S2—S2
U.S. Virgin Islands	5-16	10	4	P—P—P—P—P—P S1—S1—S1 S2—S2—S2
America, South				
Argentina #	6-14	7	3	P—P—P—P—P—P—P S1—S1—S1 S2—S2
Bolivia	6-13	8	4	P—P—P—P—P—P—P—P S—S—S—S
Brazil	7-14	8	4	P—P—P—P—P—P—P—P S—S—S
Chile	6-13	8	5	P—P—P—P—P—P—P—P S1—S1 S2—S2
Colombia	6-12	5	3	P—P—P—P—P S1—S1—S1—S1 S2—S2
Ecuador	6-14	6	4	P—P—P—P—P—P S1—S1—S1 S2—S2—S2
Falkland Islands (Malvinas)	5-15	10	-	P—P—P—P—P—P S—S—S—S—S
French Guiana	6-16	10	2	P—P—P—P—P S1—S1—S1—S1 S2—S2—S2
Guyana	6-14	10	4	P—P—P—P—P—P S1—S1—S1—S1—S1 S2—S2
Paraguay	6-12	6	6	P—P—P—P—P—P S1—S1—S1 S2—S2—S2
Peru	6-16	11	3	P—P—P—P—P—P S1—S1 S2—S2—S2
Suriname	6-16	11	4	P—P—P—P—P—P S1—S1—S1—S1 S2—S2—S2
Uruguay	6-14	6	3	P—P—P—P—P—P S1—S1—S1 S2—S2—S2
Venezuela	5-15	10	3	P—P—P—P—P—P—P—P—P S—S
Asia				
Afghanistan	7-13	6	3	P—P—P—P—P—P S—S—S—S—S—S
Armenia	6-17	9	3	P—P—P S1—S1—S1—S1—S1 S2—S2
Azerbaijan	6-17	11	3	P—P—P S1—S1—S1—S1—S1 S2—S2
Bahrain #	6-17	12	3	P—P—P—P—P—P S1—S1—S1 S2—S2—S2
Bangladesh	6-10	5	5	P—P—P—P—P S1—S1—S1—S1—S1 S2—S2
Bhutan	-	-	5	P—P—P—P—P—P—P S1—S1 S2—S2
Brunei Darussalam #	5-16	12	5	P—P—P—P—P—P S1—S1—S1—S1—S1 S2—S2
Cambodia	6-12	6	5	P—P—P—P—P S1—S1—S1 S2—S2—S2
China #	7-16	9	3	P—P—P—P—P S1—S1—S1 S2—S2
Cyprus‡#	6-15	9	3	P—P—P—P—P—P S1—S1—S1 S2—S2—S2
East Timor	...	...	...	P—P—P—P S1—S1—S1—S1—S1 S2—S2
Georgia	6-14	9	3	P—P—P—P S1—S1—S1—S1—S1 S2—S2
Hong Kong #	6-15	9	3	P—P—P—P—P—P S1—S1—S1—S1—S1 S2—S2
India‡	6-14	8	3	P—P—P—P—P S1—S1—S1 S2—S2—S2—S2
Indonesia	7-13	6	5	P—P—P—P—P—P S1—S1—S1 S2—S2—S2
Iran, Islamic Rep. of	6-10	5	5	P—P—P—P—P S1—S1—S1 S2—S2—S2—S2
Iraq	6-12	6	4	P—P—P—P—P—P S1—S1—S1 S2—S2—S2
Israel #	5-15	11	2	P—P—P—P—P—P—P—P S—S—S—S
Japan #	6-15	9	3	P—P—P—P—P—P S1—S1—S1 S2—S2—S2
Jordan	6-15	10	4	P—P—P—P—P—P—P—P—P—P S—S

National education systems **3.1**
Systèmes nationaux d'enseignement
Sistemas nacionales de enseñanza

Country / Pays / País	Compulsory education / Scolarité obligatoire / Escolaridad obligatoria — Age limits / Limites d'âge / Limites de edad	Duration (years) / Durée (années) / Duración (años)	Entrance age to education preceding the first level / Âge d'admission dans l'enseignement précédant le premier degré / Edad de admisión en la enseñanza anterior al primer grado	Entrance age and duration of first and second level (general) education — Age / Âge / Edad (4–20)
Kazakstan	6-18	11	...	P— P— P— P S1—S1—S1—S1—S1 S2—S2
Korea, Democratic Peoples Rep. of	5-15	10	4	P— P— P— P S— S— S— S— S— S
Korea, Republic of	6-15	9	4	P— P— P— P— P— P S1—S1—S1 S2—S2—S2
Kuwait	6-14	8	4	P— P— P— P S1—S1—S1—S1 S2—S2—S2—S2
Kyrgyzstan	7-16	10	3	P— P— P S1—S1—S1—S1—S1 S2—S2
Lao People's Democratic Republic	6-15	5	3	P— P— P— P— P S1—S1—S1 S2—S2—S2
Lebanon	-	-	3	P— P— P— P— P S1—S1—S1—S1 S2—S2—S2
Macau	6-12	5	3	P— P— P— P— P— P S— S— S— S— S— S
Malaysia #	6-16	11	5	P— P— P— P— P— P S1—S1—S1 S2—S2—S2—S2
Maldives	-	-	4	P— P— P— P— P S1—S1—S1—S1—S1 S2—S2
Mongolia	8-16	8	3	P— P— P S1—S1—S1—S1—S1 S2—S2
Myanmar	5-10	5	4	P— P— P— P— P S1—S1—S1—S1 S2—S2
Nepal	6-11	5	3	P— P— P— P— P S1—S1—S1 S2—S2
Oman	-	-	4	P— P— P— P— P— P S1—S1—S1 S2—S2—S2
Pakistan	-	-	3	P— P— P— P— P S1—S1—S1 S2—S2—S2—S2
Philippines	7-13	6	5	P— P— P— P— P— P S— S— S— S
Qatar	-	-	4	P— P— P— P— P— P S1—S1—S1 S2—S2—S2
Saudi Arabia	-	-	4	P— P— P— P— P— P S1—S1—S1 S2—S2—S2
Singapore #	-	-	4	P— P— P— P— P— P S1—S1—S1—S1 S2—S2—S2
Sri Lanka	5-15	11	4	P— P— P— P— P S1—S1—S1—S1—S1 S2—S2
Syrian Arab Republic	6-11	6	3	P— P— P— P— P— P S1—S1—S1 S2—S2—S2
Tajikistan	7-17	9	3	P— P— P— P S1—S1—S1—S1—S1 S2—S2
Thailand	6-11	6	3	P— P— P— P— P— P S1—S1—S1 S2—S2—S2
Turkey	6-14	5	4	P— P— P— P— P S1—S1—S1 S2—S2—S2
Turkmenistan	...	...	...	P— P— P— P S— S— S— S— S— S
United Arab Emirates	6-12	6	4	P— P— P— P— P— P S1—S1—S1 S2—S2—S2
Uzbekistan	...	...	3	P— P— P— P S1—S1—S1—S1—S1 S2—S2
Viet Nam	6-11	5	3	P— P— P— P— P S1—S1—S1—S1 S2—S2
Yemen	6-15	9	3	P— P— P— P— P— P— P— P— P S— S— S
Former Democratic Yemen	7-14	8	3	P— P— P— P— P— P— P— P S— S— S— S
Former Yemen Arab Republic	6-12	6	3	P— P— P— P— P— P S1—S1—S1 S2—S2—S2
Palestine	6-15	10	4	P— P— P— P— P— P S1—S1—S1—S1 S2—S2
Gaza Strip	6-14	9	4	P— P— P— P— P— P S1—S1—S1 S2—S2—S2
West Bank	6-15	10	4	P— P— P— P— P— P S1—S1—S1—S1 S2—S2
Europe				
Albania	6-14	8	3	P— P— P— P— P— P— P— P S— S— S— S

3.1 National education systems
Systèmes nationaux d'enseignement
Sistemas nacionales de enseñanza

Country / Pays / País	Compulsory education — Age limits / Limites d'âge / Limites de edad	Compulsory education — Duration (years) / Durée (années) / Duración (años)	Entrance age to education preceding the first level / Âge d'admission dans l'enseignement précédant le premier degré / Edad de admisión en la enseñanza anterior al primer grado	Entrance age and duration of first and second level (general) education (Age 4–20)
Andorra #				
French Schools	6-16	10	3	P—P—P—P—P S1—S1—S1—S1 S2—S2—S2
Spanish Schools	6-15	10	2	P—P—P—P—P S1—S1—S1 S2—S2—S2—S2
Austria #	6-15	9	3	P—P—P—P S1—S1—S1—S1 S2—S2—S2—S2
Belarus #	6-15	9	3	P—P—P—P S1—S1—S1—S1—S1 S2—S2
Belgium	6-18	12	2 1/2	P—P—P—P—P—P S1—S1—S1 S2—S2—S2
Bulgaria	7-16	8	3	P—P—P—P—P—P—P—P S—S—S—S
Croatia	7-15	8	3	P—P—P—P—P—P—P—P S—S—S—S
Former Czechoslovakia	6-16	10	3	P—P—P—P—P—P—P—P S—S—S—S
Czech Republic	6-15	9	3	P—P—P—P S1—S1—S1—S1 S2—S2—S2—S2
Denmark	7-15	9	6	P—P—P—P—P—P S1—S1—S1 S2—S2—S2
Estonia	7-17	9	3	P—P—P—P—P—P S1—S1—S1 S2—S2—S2
Finland	7-15	9	3	P—P—P—P—P—P S1—S1—S1 S2—S2—S2
France	6-16	10	2	P—P—P—P—P S1—S1—S1—S1 S2—S2—S2
Germany‡	6-18	12	3	P—P—P—P S1—S1—S1—S1—S1 S2—S2—S2
Former German Democratic Republic	6-16	10	3	P—P—P—P S—S—S—S—S—S
Federal Republic of Germany‡	6-18	12	3	P—P—P—P S1—S1—S1—S1—S1 S2—S2—S2
Gibraltar	4-15	12	3	P—P—P—P—P—P—P—P S1—S1—S1—S1 S2—S2
Greece #	6-15	9	4	P—P—P—P—P—P S1—S1—S1 S2—S2—S2
Hungary	6-16	10	3	P—P—P—P—P—P—P—P S—S—S—S
Iceland	7-15	8	5	P—P—P—P—P—P S1—S1—S1 S2—S2—S2—S2
Ireland #	6-15	9	4	P—P—P—P—P—P S1—S1—S1 S2—S2
Italy	6-13	8	3	P—P—P—P—P S1—S1—S1 S2—S2—S2—S2—S2
Latvia	7-15	9	3	P—P—P—P S1—S1—S1—S1 S2—S2—S2
Liechtenstein #	6-14	8	4	P—P—P—P S1—S1—S1 S2—S2—S2
Lithuania	7-16	9	3	P—P—P—P S1—S1—S1—S1 S2—S2—S2
Luxembourg	6-15	9	4	P—P—P—P—P—P S1—S1—S1 S2—S2—S2—S2
Malta #	5-16	10	3	P—P—P—P—P—P S1—S1—S1—S1 S2—S2
Moldova	7-16	11	3	P—P—P—P S1—S1—S1—S1 S2—S2—S2
Monaco	6-16	10	3	P—P—P—P—P S1—S1—S1—S1 S2—S2—S2
Netherlands #	5-16	11	4	P—P—P—P—P—P S1—S1—S1 S2—S2—S2
Norway	7-15	9	4	P—P—P—P—P—P S1—S1—S1 S2—S2
Poland	7-14	8	3	P—P—P—P—P—P—P—P S—S—S—S
Portugal	6-15	9	3	P—P—P—P—P—P S1—S1—S1 S2—S2—S2
Romania	7-14	8	3	P—P—P—P S1—S1—S1—S1 S2—S2—S2—S2
Russian Federation #	7-17	9	3	P—P—P S1—S1—S1—S1—S1 S2—S2
San Marino	6-13	8	3	P—P—P—P—P S1—S1—S1 S2—S2—S2—S2—S2
Slovakia	6-15	9	3	P—P—P—P S1—S1—S1—S1 S2—S2—S2—S2
Slovenia	7-15	8	3	P—P—P—P S1—S1—S1—S1 S2—S2—S2—S2

National education systems
Systèmes nationaux d'enseignement
Sistemas nacionales de enseñanza

3.1

Country / Pays / País	Compulsory education / Scolarité obligatoire / Escolaridad obligatoria — Age limits / Limites d'âge / Limites de edad	Compulsory education — Duration (years) / Durée (années) / Duración (años)	Entrance age to education preceding the first level / Âge d'admission dans l'enseignement précédant le premier degré / Edad de admisión en la enseñanza anterior al primer grado	Entrance age and duration of first and second level (general) education — Age / Âge / Edad (4–20)
Spain	6-15	10	2	P—P—P—P—P S1—S1—S1 S2—S2—S2—S2
Sweden #	7-15	9	3	P—P—P—P—P—P S1—S1—S1 S2—S2—S2
Switzerland #	7-15	8,9	5	P—P—P—P—P—P S1—S1—S1 S2—S2—S2—S2
The Former Yugoslav Rep. of Macedonia	7-15	8	3	P—P—P—P—P—P—P—P S—S—S—S
Ukraine #	7-15	8	3	P—P—P—P S1—S1—S1—S1—S1 S2—S2
United Kingdom	5-16	11	3	P—P—P—P—P S1—S1—S1 S2—S2—S2—S2
Former Yugoslavia	7-15	8	3	P—P—P—P S1—S1—S1—S1 S2—S2—S2—S2
Federal Republic of Yugoslavia	7-15	8	3	P—P—P—P S1—S1—S1—S1 S2—S2—S2—S2
Oceania				
American Samoa	6-18	12	3	P—P—P—P—P—P—P—P S1—S1 S2—S2
Australia #	6-16	10,11	5	P—P—P—P—P—P S1—S1—S1 S2—S2—S2
Cook Islands	5-15	10	4	P—P—P—P—P—P S1—S1—S1 S2—S2—S2
Fiji #	-	-	3	P—P—P—P—P—P S—S—S—S—S—S
French Polynesia	5-16	12	2	P—P—P—P—P S1—S1—S1—S1 S2—S2—S2
Guam	5-16	11	5	P—P—P—P—P—P S1—S1—S1 S2—S2—S2
Kiribati #	6-14	9	4	P—P—P—P—P—P—P S—S—S—S—S
Nauru	6-16	10	4	P—P—P—P—P—P S—S—S—S—S
New Caledonia	6-16	10	3	P—P—P—P—P S1—S1—S1—S1 S2—S2—S2
New Zealand #	6-16	11	2	P—P—P—P—P—P S1—S1—S1—S1 S2—S2—S2
Niue	5-14	10	4	P—P—P—P—P—P S—S—S—S—S
Pacific Islands	6-14	8	4	P—P—P—P—P—P—P—P S1—S1 S2—S2
Papua New Guinea	-	-	5	P—P—P—P—P—P S1—S1—S1—S1 S2—S2
Samoa	-	-	3	P—P—P—P—P—P—P S1—S1—S1—S1 S2—S2
Solomon Islands #	-	-	3	P—P—P—P—P—P S1—S1—S1 S2—S2
Tokelau Islands	5-16	12	3	P—P—P—P—P—P—P—P—P S—S
Tonga #	6-14	8	3	P—P—P—P—P—P S—S—S—S—S—S—S
Tuvalu #	7-15	9	3	P—P—P—P—P—P—P S—S—S—S—S—S
Vanuatu, Republic of	6-12	6	3	P—P—P—P—P—P S1—S1—S1—S1 S2—S2—S2

This table provides a summary presentation of selected elements of the education systems. The information given here facilitates the correct interpretation of the figures shown in the other tables on education.

The first two columns provide data on compulsory education regulations. The first column shows lower and upper age limits. Thus 6-14, for example, means that children are subject to compulsory education laws, unless exempted, from their sixth to their fourteenth birthday. The second column shows the number of years of compulsory school attendance. For example, regulations may stipulate that the duration of compulsory education shall be six grades between the ages of 6 and 14. This means that a child ceases to be subject to the regulations either on his fourteenth birthday or on completion of six years of schooling (though he might then be only 12 or 13 years old).

However, in many countries and territories where the urgent problem is to provide a sufficient number of schools for all children, the existence of compulsory education laws may be only of academic interest since almost all such regulations exempt a child from attending if there is no suitable school within reasonable distance of his or her home.

The third column gives the age at which children are accepted for education preceding the first level, which for most countries is still provided on a limited basis, often restricted to urban areas and even there it is frequently only a small proportion of children within the ages shown in this table who actually receive pre-school education.

The diagrams for all countries and territories which follow these three columns provide a pictorial representation of the duration and age of admission into first level and second level general education according to the education system presently in force. Information

3.1 National education systems
Systèmes nationaux d'enseignement
Sistemas nacionales de enseñanza

on teacher training and technical and vocational education is not presented. The symbol *P* shows the duration of first level education, the symbol *S1* that of the first stage of second level general education and the symbol *S2* the duration of the second stage of second level general education. It should be noted that some countries and territories make no distinction between the two stages of second level general education. In these cases the duration is shown simply by the symbol *S*. For a certain number of countries

the entrance age and duration of education at these two levels vary according to the area or type of schools. The most common system is shown in the diagram.

Table 3.1A indicates the other existing possibilities and Table 3.1B shows any changes in the education system which have occurred since 1980. This table should be consulted when referring to the enrolment data given in Tables 3.3 to 3.8.

Ce tableau présente des données sommaires sélectionnées sur les systèmes d'enseignement. L'information ainsi présentée doit aider à interpréter correctement les chiffres qui figurent dans les autres tableaux consacrés à l'éducation.

Les deux premières colonnes présentent les données relatives à l'obligation scolaire. Dans la première colonne sont précisées les limites d'âge minimum et maximum. C'est ainsi que les deux chiffres 6-14 signifient que les lois instituant la scolarité obligatoire s'appliquent, sauf exception, aux enfants de 6 à 14 ans. La deuxième colonne indique le nombre d'années pendant lesquelles les enfants sont tenus de fréquenter l'école. Les règlements peuvent stipuler, par exemple, que l'enseignement obligatoire est de six années d'études (entre l'âge de 6 et 14 ans). En d'autres termes, l'enfant cesse d'être soumis à l'obligation scolaire soit lorsqu'il a atteint l'âge de 14 ans, soit lorsqu'il a terminé sa sixième année d'études (même s'il n'a alors que 12 ou 13 ans).

Néanmoins, dans beaucoup de pays et territoires, le problème le plus urgent consiste à disposer d'un nombre suffisant d'écoles pour tous les enfants, l'existence d'une loi sur la scolarité obligatoire n'ayant qu'un intérêt théorique, puisque la plupart de ces règlementations dispensent un enfant de fréquentation scolaire s'il n'existe pas une école à une distance raisonnable de son domicile.

La troisième colonne indique l'âge d'admission des enfants dans l'enseignement précédant le premier degré, qui dans la plupart des pays, n'est encore dispensé que d'une façon limitée et généralement dans les zones urbaines, où une faible proportion

seulement des enfants compris dans l'âge indiqué peuvent en bénéficier.

Le diagramme qui suit les trois colonnes donne pour tous les pays et territoires une représentation graphique de la durée et de l'âge d'admission dans l'enseignement du premier degré et l'enseignement général du second degré, en accord avec les systèmes d'enseignement actuellement en vigueur. Les renseignements concernant l'enseignement normal et l'enseignement technique et professionnel du second degré ne sont pas présentés. Le symbole *P* montre la durée de l'enseignement du premier degré, le symbole *S1* celle du premier cycle de l'enseignement général du second degré et le symbole *S2* la durée du deuxième cycle de l'enseignement général du second degré. Il faut noter que quelques pays et territoires ne font pas de distinction entre les deux cycles de l'enseignement général du second degré. Dans ces cas, la durée de l'enseignement est montrée par le symbole *S*. Pour un certain nombre de pays, l'âge d'admission et la durée de l'enseignement dans ces deux degrés peuvent varier selon la zone ou le type d'école. Pour ces pays, le système le plus courant a été porté sur le diagramme.

Le tableau 3.1A indique les autres possibilités existantes et le tableau 3.1B précise les changements qui se sont produits dans le système d'enseignement d'un certain nombre de pays depuis 1980. Ce tableau doit être consulté lorsque l'on se réfère aux effectifs scolaires qui figurent dans les tableaux 3.3 à 3.8.

Este cuadro presenta un resumen de datos seleccionados sobre los sistemas de enseñanza. La información así procurada debe facilitar una interpretación correcta de las cifras que figuran en los otros cuadros relativos a la educación.

Las dos primeras columnas presentan datos relativos a la escolaridad obligatoria. En la primera se precisan los límites de edad mínima y máxima. Por ejemplo, las cifras 6-14 significan que la ley que instituye la escolaridad obligatoria se aplica sin excepción a los niños de 6 a 14 años de edad. En la segunda columna puede verse el número de años durante los cuales los niños han de asistir a la escuela. Se puede estipular, por ejemplo, que la duración de la enseñanza obligatoria es de 6 años de estudios entre los 6 y los 14 años de edad. En otras palabras, el niño deja de estar sometido a la obligación escolar o bien al cumplir los 14 años o bien cuando termina su sexto año de estudios (aunque sólo tenga entonces 12 o 13 años).

Ahora bien, en muchos países y territorios el problema más urgente consiste en disponer de un número suficiente de escuelas para todos los niños; la existencia de una ley sobre la escolaridad obligatoria no tiene sino un interés teórico, dado que la mayoría de esas disposiciones eximen a los niños de la asistencia escolar si no existe una escuela a distancia razonable de su domicilio.

La tercera columna indica la edad de admisión de los niños en la enseñanza anterior al primer grado. En muchos países, la enseñanza anterior al primer grado sigue dispensándose todavía

de un modo limitado generalmente a las zonas urbanas, donde sólo puede beneficiarse de ella una pequeña proporción de los niños de la edad indicada.

El diagrama que sigue las tres columnas muestra para todos los países y territorios una representación gráfica sobre la duración y la edad de admisión en la enseñanza de primer grado y en la enseñanza general de segundo grado, de acuerdo con los sistemas de educación actualmente en vigor. No se presentan aquí las informaciones relativas a la enseñanza normal y a la enseñanza técnica y profesional. El símbolo *P* indica la duración del primer grado de enseñanza, el símbolo *S1* la duración del primer ciclo de la enseñanza general de segundo grado y el símbolo *S2* la duración del segundo ciclo de la enseñanza general de segundo grado. Cabe observar que para algunos países y territorios no existe ninguna distinción entre los dos ciclos de enseñanza general de segundo grado. En tales casos, el símbolo *S* indica la duración de este grado de enseñanza. Además, para un cierto número de países, la edad de admisión y la duración de la enseñanza en estos dos grados pueden variar según la zona o el tipo de escuela. El diagrama muestra el sistema más común.

El cuadro 3.1A indica las otras posibilidades existentes y el cuadro 3.1B precisa los cambios que se han producido en el sistema de enseñanza de un cierto número de países desde 1980. Consúltese este cuadro cuando precise información sobre la matrícula escolar que figura en los cuadros 3.3 a 3.8.

ASIA:
Cyprus:
 E––> Greek education only.
 FR–> Enseignement grec seulement.
 ESP> Enseñanza griega solamente.
India:
 E––> This information pertains to the majority of states.
 FR–> Ces informations concernent la majorité des états.
 ESP> Esta información se refiere a la mayoría de los estados.
EUROPE:
Germany:
 E––> In the individual *Lander* there may be variations from the structure indicated.

 FR–> Dans les différents *Lander* il peut y avoir des variations par rapport à la structure indiquée.
 ESP> En los differentes *Lander* pueden encontrarse variaciones con respecto a la estructura indicada.
Federal Republic of Germany:
 E––> In the individual *Lander* there may be variations from the structure indicated.
 FR–> Dans les différents *Lander* il peut y avoir des variations par rapport à la structure indiquée.
 ESP> En los differentes *Lander* pueden encontrarse variaciones con respecto a la estructura indicada.

National education systems **3.1**
Systèmes nationaux d'enseignement
Sistemas nacionales de enseñanza

3.1A National education systems: other structures

Systèmes nationaux d'enseignement: autres structures en vigueur

Sistemas nacionales de enseñanza: otras estructuras en vigor

Country / Pays / País	Entrance age to first level / Âge d'admission dans le premier degré / Edad de admisión en el primer grado	Duration (years) Durée (années) Duración (años) 1st level / 1er degré / 1er grado	2nd level (general) / 2nd degré (général) / 2do grado (general)
Africa			
Côte d'Ivoire	6		
Ghana			3+3
Mali	7		2+4
Mozambique			2+4
Namibia			6
Senegal	6		
America, North		7	
Antigua and Barbuda		7	
British Virgin Islands		8	
Canada		8	3+4,5
Costa Rica			3+3
Grenada		8	
Haiti		7	3+4
St. Kitts and Nevis			5+2
United States		8	4
America, South			
Argentina			3+3 3+4
Asia			
Azerbaijan		4	
Bahrain			4+4
Brunei Darussalam		7	
China	6	6	3+3
Cyprus		7	3+4
Hong Kong			3+2
Israel			5

Country / Pays / País	Entrance age to first level / Âge d'admission dans le premier degré / Edad de admisión en el primer grado	Duration (years) Durée (années) Duración (años) 1st level / 1er degré / 1er grado	2nd level (general) / 2nd degré (général) / 2do grado (general)
Japan			3+4
Kyrgyzstan			4
Malaysia			3+3
Singapore		8	4+3
Europe			
Andorra			
Spanish Schools			4+4
Austria			4+5
Belarus	7		
Greece			3+4
Ireland			4+2
Liechtenstein			5+3
Malta	6		
Moldova	6		
Netherlands			4+2
Russian Federation	6	4	
Sweden			3+2
Switzerland	6	4,5	4+4 3+5 5+2
Ukraine	6	3	
Oceania			
Australia	5	7	
Fiji		8	4
Kiribati		9	7
Papua New Guinea		8	
Solomon Islands	7,8,9		3+3
Tonga			6
Tuvalu		10	

3.1 National education systems
Systèmes nationaux d'enseignement
Sistemas nacionales de enseñanza

3.1B Structural changes in education systems since 1980/81

Changements de structure dans les systèmes d'enseignement depuis 1980/81

Cambios de estructura en los sistemas de enseñanza desde 1980/81

Country / Pays / País	Year of change / Année du changement / Año del cambio	First level of education Enseignement du premier degré Ensenanza de primer grado Duration (years) / Durée (années) / Duración (años)		General education at the second level Enseignement général du second degré Enseñanza general de segundo grado Duration (years) / Durée (années) / Duración (años)	
		from / de	to / à/a	from / de	to / à/a
Africa					
Algeria	1988/89			4+3	3+3
Angola	1985/86			4+2	4+3
Cape Verde	1990/91			3+2	3+3
Egypt	1989/90	6	5		
Eritrea	1991/92	6	5		
Guinea	1985/86			3+3	4+3
Kenya	1985	7	8	6	5
	1990			5	4
Libyan Arab Jamahiriya	1985/86	6	9	3+3	3
Morocco	1990/91	5	6	4+3	3+3
Mozambique	1984			2+3	2+5
	1987	4	5		
Nigeria	1988			5	3+3
Rwanda	1991/92	8	7		
Seychelles	1984/85			4	2
America, North					
Dominican Republic	1986/87	6	8	6	4
Asia					
Afghanistan	1990	8	6	4	6
Bhutan	1986	6	7	3+2	2+2
Cambodia	1986/87	4	5		
Jordan	1989/90	6	10	3+3	2
Nepal	1981	3	5	4+3	2+3
Singapore	1981			4+2	4+3
Sri Lanka	1987	6	5	5+2	6+2
Europe					
Belarus	1986	5	6		
	1990	6	4	5	7
Bulgaria	1987			3	4
Former Czechoslovakia	1984	9	8		
Romania	1988	8	4	4	8
Ukraine	1986	5	6		
	1992	6	4	3+2	5+2
Oceania					
Niue	1988	7	8	5	4
	1991	8	6	4	6

Enrolment ratios 3.2
Taux d'inscription
Tasas de escolarización

3.2 Enrolment ratios by level of education

Taux d'inscription par degré d'enseignement

Tasas de escolarización por grado de enseñanza

As the school year, in a number of countries, does not coincide with the academic year, the year shown in this table is the one in which the school or academic year starts.

Please refer to the explanatory text at the end of the table.

Dans certains pays l'année scolaire et l'année universitaire ne coincidant pas, l'année figurant dans ce tableau se réfère au début de l'année scolaire ou académique.

Prière de se référer au texte explicatif à la fin du tableau.

Como en algunos países, el año escolar y el año universitario no coinciden, el año presentado en este cuadro corresponde al comienzo del año escolar o universitario.

Referirse al texto explicativo al final del cuadro.

Country	Year	Sex	Enrolment ratios / Taux d'inscription / Tasas de escolarización						
			Pre-primary	First level		Second level		1st + 2nd levels	3rd level
Pays	Année	Sexe	Pré-primaire	Premier degré		Second degré		1er + 2nd degré	3ème degré
País	Año	Sexo	Preprimaria	Primer grado		Segundo grado		1er + 2do grado	3er grado
			Gross Brut Bruta	Gross Brut Bruta	Net Net Neta	Gross Brut Bruta	Net Net Neta	Gross Brut Bruta	Gross Brut Bruta
Africa									
Algeria	1980				(6-11)		(12-18)	(6-18)	(19-23)
		MF	-	94	81	33	31	65	5.9
		M	-	108	91	40	37	75	8.5
		F	-	81	71	26	24	54	3.1
	1990				(6-11)		(12-17)	(6-17)	(18-22)
		MF	-	100	93	61	54	82	11.4
		M	-	108	99	67	60	89	...
		F	-	92	87	54	48	74	...
	1992		(4-5)		(6-11)		(12-17)	(6-17)	(18-22)
		MF	1	103	94	61	55	83	11.4
		M	1	111	99	66	59	90	14.3
		F	1	96	89	55	50	77	8.4
	1993								
		MF	2	104	95	62	55	84	...
		M	2	111	99	66	59	90	...
		F	2	97	90	57	51	78	...
	1994								
		MF	2	105	95	62	55	84	...
		M	2	111	99	66	59	89	...
		F	2	98	91	58	52	79	...
Angola‡	1980		(4-6)		(7-10)		(11-16)	(7-16)	(17-21)
		MF	60	175	...	20	...	88	0.4
		M	71	...	...	...	...	...	...
		F	48	...	...	...	...	...	...
	1985		(5)		(6-9)		(10-16)	(6-16)	(17-21)
		MF	90	107	...	14	...	53	0.7
		M	99	118	...	...	...	...	...
		F	80	96	...	...	...	...	...
	1989								
		MF	65	99	...	12	...	48	0.8
		M	70	103	...	...	...	...	1.3
		F	60	95	...	...	...	...	0.3

3.2 Enrolment ratios
Taux d'inscription
Tasas de escolarización

			Enrolment ratios / Taux d'inscription / Tasas de escolarización						
Country	Year	Sex	Pre-primary	First level		Second level		1st + 2nd levels	3rd level
Pays	Année	Sexe	Pré-primaire	Premier degré		Second degré		1er + 2nd degré	3ème degré
País	Año	Sexo	Preprimaria	Primer grado		Segundo grado		1er + 2do grado	3er grado
			Gross Brut Bruta	Gross Brut Bruta	Net Net Neta	Gross Brut Bruta	Net Net Neta	Gross Brut Bruta	Gross Brut Bruta
Angola‡ (cont)									
	1990								
		MF	53	91	...	12	...	45	0.8
		M	71	95	...	...	...	...	...
		F	36	87	...	...	...	...	...
	1991								
		MF	68	88	...	14	...	45	0.7
Benin	1980		(3-4)		(5-10)		(11-17)	(5-17)	(18-22)
		MF	2	64	...	16	...	41	1.5
		M	...	87	...	24	...	57	...
		F	...	41	...	9	...	25	...
	1985		(3-5)		(6-11)		(12-18)	(6-18)	(19-23)
		MF	3	68	53	18	...	44	2.6
		M	3	90	71	25	...	59	4.4
		F	2	45	35	10	...	28	0.8
	1990								
		MF	3	63	...	11	...	38	2.7
		M	3	84	...	16	...	52	4.7
		F	3	41	...	7	...	25	0.7
	1991								
		MF	3	66	53	12	...	40	2.5
		M	3	88	71	17	...	54	4.3
		F	2	44	35	7	...	26	0.8
	1992								
		MF	...	71	...	...	...	...	2.3
		M	...	...	...	...	...	...	3.9
		F	...	...	...	...	...	...	0.8
	1993								
		MF	...	72	...	...	...	...	2.4
		M	...	...	...	...	...	...	4.0
		F	...	...	...	...	...	...	0.8
Botswana	1980				(6-12)		(13-17)	(6-17)	(18-22)
		MF	-	91	75	19	14	64	1.2
		M	-	83	69	17	12	58	1.6
		F	-	100	82	20	17	70	0.8
	1985				(7-13)		(14-18)	(7-18)	(19-23)
		MF	-	105	89	29	22	77	1.8
		M	-	99	84	27	20	73	2.0
		F	-	110	94	31	25	81	1.6
	1990								
		MF	-	114	94	42	33	88	3.1
		M	-	110	90	40	30	84	3.2
		F	-	119	98	45	36	91	2.9
	1992								
		MF	-	116	97	52	42	92	3.4
		M	-	113	93	49	38	89	3.3
		F	-	120	100	55	45	95	3.6
	1993								
		MF	-	115	96	57	45	93	3.7
		M	-	113	93	53	42	91	3.5
		F	-	118	99	60	49	96	4.0
	1994								
		MF	-	115	...	56	...	92	4.9
		M	-	114	...	54	...	91	...
		F	-	115	...	58	...	93	...
Burkina Faso‡	1980		(4-6)		(7-12)		(13-19)	(7-19)	(20-24)
		MF	0.1	18	15	3	...	11	0.3
		M	0.1	23	19	4	...	14	0.4
		F	0.1	14	11	2	...	8	0.1
	1985								
		MF	0.2	29	25	5	4	17	0.6
		M	...	37	31	6	5	22	0.9
		F	...	21	18	3	2	12	0.3
	1990								
		MF	1	37	29	8	...	22	0.7
		M	1	45	36	10	...	28	1.1
		F	1	28	23	5	...	17	0.3

Enrolment ratios **3.2**
Taux d'inscription
Tasas de escolarización

			Enrolment ratios / Taux d'inscription / Tasas de escolarización						
Country Pays País	Year Année Año	Sex Sexe Sexo	Pre-primary Pré-primaire Preprimaria	First level Premier degré Primer grado		Second level Second degré Segundo grado		1st + 2nd levels 1er + 2nd degré 1er + 2do grado	3rd level 3ème degré 3er grado
			Gross Brut Bruta	Gross Brut Bruta	Net Net Neta	Gross Brut Bruta	Net Net Neta	Gross Brut Bruta	Gross Brut Bruta
Burkina Faso‡ (cont)	1991								
		MF	...	37	30	8	7	23	0.9
		M	...	46	37	10	9	29	1.4
		F	...	29	23	5	5	17	0.4
	1992								
		MF	...	38	31	8	7	24	1.1
		M	...	47	38	11	10	30	1.6
		F	...	30	24	6	5	18	0.5
	1993								
		MF	...	39	32	9	7	25	1.0
		M	...	48	39	12	10	31	1.6
		F	...	31	25	6	5	19	0.5
Burundi‡	1980		(4-6)		(7-12)		(13-19)	(7-19)	(20-24)
		MF	0.3	26	20	3	...	15	0.5
		M	0.3	32	23	4	...	18	0.7
		F	0.3	21	16	2	...	11	0.2
	1985								
		MF	0.4	52	41	4	3	28	0.6
		M	0.4	61	47	5	3	33	0.9
		F	0.4	44	35	2	2	23	0.3
	1990								
		MF	0.5	72	...	6	...	41	0.7
		M	0.5	79	...	7	...	45	1.1
		F	0.5	66	...	4	...	36	0.4
	1991								
		MF	...	70	...	6	...	39	0.8
		M	...	77	...	7	...	44	1.1
		F	...	63	...	4	...	35	0.4
	1992								
		MF	...	69	51	7	5	40	0.8
		M	...	76	56	8	6	44	1.2
		F	...	62	47	5	4	35	0.4
Cameroon	1980		(4-5)		(6-11)		(12-18)	(6-18)	(19-23)
		MF	7	98	...	18	15	60	1.6
		M	7	107	...	24	19	67	...
		F	7	89	...	13	11	53	...
	1985								
		MF	11	102	...	23	...	64	2.2
		M	12	111	...	28	...	71	...
		F	11	93	...	17	...	57	...
	1990								
		MF	13	101	...	28	...	66	3.2
		M	13	109	...	32	...	72	...
		F	13	93	...	23	...	59	...
	1991								
		MF	13	96	...	28	...	63	...
		M	12	100	...	33	...	68	...
		F	13	92	...	24	...	59	...
	1993								
		MF	12	91	...	27	...	60	...
		M	12	95	...	33	...	65	...
		F	12	86	...	22	...	55	...
	1994								
		MF	11	89	...	27	...	58	...
		M	11	93	...	32	...	63	...
		F	11	84	...	22	...	53	...
Cape Verde‡	1980		(5-6)		(7-12)		(13-17)	(7-17)	(18-22)
		MF	...	114	90	8	...	66	-
		M	...	119	93	9	...	69	-
		F	...	110	88	7	...	63	-
	1985								
		MF	...	117	96	13	...	71	-
		M	...	120	98	15	...	73	-
		F	...	114	95	12	...	68	-

3.2 Enrolment ratios
Taux d'inscription
Tasas de escolarización

Country / Pays / País	Year / Année / Año	Sex / Sexe / Sexo	Pre-primary / Pré-primaire / Preprimaria Gross Brut Bruta	First level / Premier degré / Primer grado Gross Brut Bruta	First level Net Net Neta	Second level / Second degré / Segundo grado Gross Brut Bruta	Second level Net Net Neta	1st + 2nd levels / 1er + 2nd degré / 1er + 2do grado Gross Brut Bruta	3rd level / 3ème degré / 3er grado Gross Brut Bruta
Cape Verde‡ (cont)	1989								
		MF	...	122	100	20	...	80	-
		M	...	125	100	21	...	82	-
		F	...	119	99	20	...	78	-
	1990		(5-6)		(7-12)		(13-18)	(7-18)	(19-23)
		MF	...	123	...	25	...	...	
	1993								
		MF	...	131	100	27	22	83	-
		M	...	132	100	28	22	85	-
		F	...	130	100	26	22	81	-
Central African Republic	1980		(4-5)		(6-11)		(12-18)	(6-18)	(19-23)
		MF	7	71	56	14	...	43	0.9
		M	8	92	73	21	...	57	1.6
		F	7	51	41	7	...	29	0.1
	1985								
		MF	8	75	61	16	...	47	1.2
		M	9	93	74	24	...	61	2.2
		F	8	58	48	8	...	34	0.2
	1989								
		MF	7	71	58	12	...	42	1.4
		M	9	88	71	17	...	54	2.5
		F	5	55	46	6	...	31	0.5
	1991								
		MF	...	...	...	...	...	...	1.7
		M	...	...	...	...	...	...	2.9
		F	...	...	...	...	...	...	0.6
Chad	1985		(4-5)		(6-11)		(12-18)	(6-18)	(19-23)
		MF	...	43	...	...	...	...	...
		M	...	63	...	...	...	...	...
		F	...	24	...	...	...	...	...
	1990								
		MF	...	59	...	8	...	34	...
		M	...	82	...	13	...	48	...
		F	...	37	...	3	...	20	...
	1992								
		MF	...	59	...	9	...	35	0.8
		M	...	80	...	...	...	...	1.5
		F	...	38	...	...	...	...	0.1
	1993								
		MF	...	56	...	8	...	33	0.8
		M	...	76	...	13	...	46	1.5
		F	...	36	...	3	...	20	0.1
	1994								
		MF	...	55	...	...	...	...	...
		M	...	75	...	...	...	...	...
		F	...	36	...	...	...	...	...
Comoros‡	1980		(4-5)		(6-11)		(12-18)	(6-18)	(19-23)
		MF	68	88	...	23	...	57	-
		M	69	100	...	30	...	67	-
		F	67	75	...	15	...	47	-
	1985								
		MF	...	82	62	28	...	56	-
		M	...	92	...	34	...	64	-
		F	...	72	...	23	...	48	-
	1990								
		MF	...	76	...	...	...	...	0.5
		M	...	86	...	...	...	...	0.9
		F	...	65	...	...	...	...	0.2
	1991		(4-6)		(7-12)		(13-19)	(7-19)	(20-24)
		MF	...	79	...	18	...	50	...
		M	...	85	...	22	...	55	...
		F	...	73	...	15	...	45	...

Enrolment ratios   3.2
Taux d'inscription
Tasas de escolarización

Country / Pays / País	Year / Année / Año	Sex / Sexe / Sexo	Enrolment ratios / Taux d'inscription / Tasas de escolarización						
			Pre-primary / Pré-primaire / Preprimaria	First level / Premier degré / Primer grado		Second level / Second degré / Segundo grado		1st + 2nd levels / 1er + 2nd degré / 1er + 2do grado	3rd level / 3ème degré / 3er grado
			Gross Brut Bruta	Gross Brut Bruta	Net Net Neta	Gross Brut Bruta	Net Net Neta	Gross Brut Bruta	Gross Brut Bruta
Chad (cont)									
	1992	MF	...	74	...	17	...	47	...
		M	...	78	...	19	...	50	...
		F	...	70	...	14	...	44	...
	1993	MF	...	75	51	19	...	49	...
		M	...	81	55	21	...	53	...
		F	...	69	46	17	...	44	...
Congo‡			(3-5)	(6-11)		(12-18)		(6-18)	(19-23)
Côte d'Ivoire‡	1980		(5-6)	(7-12)		(13-19)		(7-19)	(20-24)
		MF	1	79	...	19	...	51	2.9
		M	1	95	...	27	...	63	4.7
		F	1	63	...	12	...	39	1.0
	1985	MF	1	75	...	20	...	50	2.7
		M	1	88	...	28	...	60	4.3
		F	1	62	...	12	...	39	1.1
	1990	MF	1	71	54	23	...	48	3.1
		M	1	83	...	31	...	59	5.1
		F	1	59	...	15	...	38	1.0
	1991	MF	1	69	52	24	...	48	...
		M	1	81	...	32	...	58	...
		F	1	58	...	16	...	38	...
	1993	MF	2	69	...	25	...	48	...
		M	3	80	...	33	...	58	...
		F	2	58	...	17	...	39	...
	1994	MF	3	68	...	...	...	...	...
		M	3	78	...	...	...	...	...
		F	3	59	...	...	...	...	...
Djibouti	1980		(4-5)	(6-11)		(12-18)		(6-18)	(19-23)
		MF	...	37	...	12	...	25	-
	1985	MF	1	40	31	12	11	26	-
		M	1	47	37	14	13	31	-
		F	1	33	26	9	8	21	-
	1990	MF	1	38	32	12	...	25	-
		M	1	45	...	14	...	30	-
		F	1	32	...	9	...	21	-
	1992	MF	1	35	29	11	...	23	0.1
		M	0.5	39	33	13	...	26	0.1
		F	1	30	26	10	...	20	0.1
	1993	MF	1	36	30	12	...	24	...
		M	1	41	34	14	...	28	...
		F	1	31	26	10	...	21	...
	1994	MF	1	38	32	13	...	26	...
		M	1	43	36	15	...	30	...
		F	1	33	28	10	...	22	...
Egypt	1980		(4-5)	(6-11)		(12-17)		(6-17)	(18-22)
		MF	3	73	...	50	...	62	16.1
		M	3	84	...	61	...	73	21.4
		F	3	61	...	39	...	50	10.6
	1985	MF	5	85	...	61	...	74	18.2
		M	5	94	...	72	...	84	23.6
		F	5	76	...	50	...	64	12.4

3.2 Enrolment ratios
Taux d'inscription
Tasas de escolarización

Country	Year	Sex	Enrolment ratios / Taux d'inscription / Tasas de escolarización						
			Pre-primary	First level		Second level		1st + 2nd levels	3rd level
Pays	Année	Sexe	Pré-primaire	Premier degré		Second degré		1er + 2nd degré	3ème degré
País	Año	Sexo	Preprimaria	Primer grado		Segundo grado		1er + 2do grado	3er grado
			Gross Brut Bruta	Gross Brut Bruta	Net Net Neta	Gross Brut Bruta	Net Net Neta	Gross Brut Bruta	Gross Brut Bruta
Egypt (cont)									
	1990		(4-5)		(6-10)		(11-16)	(6-16)	(17-21)
		MF	6	94	...	76	...	85	17.5
		M	6	102	...	84	...	93	22.5
		F	6	86	...	68	...	77	12.1
	1992								
		MF	7	95	...	75	...	85	17.1
		M	7	102	...	82	...	92	22.1
		F	7	87	...	67	...	77	11.8
	1993								
		MF	7	97	89	76	65	86	16.9
		M	8	105	95	81	70	93	21.8
		F	7	89	82	69	60	79	11.6
	1994								
		MF	8	98	...	77	...	87	...
		M	8	105	...	82	...	93	...
		F	8	91	...	71	...	81	...
Equatorial Guinea‡			(3-5)		(6-10)		(11-17)	(6-17)	(18-22)
Eritrea‡	1988		(5-6)		(7-12)		(13-18)	(7-18)	(19-23)
		MF	...	28	...	16	...	23	...
		M	...	30	...	16	...	24	...
		F	...	27	...	15	...	21	...
	1990								
		MF	3	23	...	15	...	19	...
		M	3	23	...	15	...	20	...
		F	3	22	...	14	...	19	...
	1992		(5-6)		(7-11)		(12-17)	(7-17)	(18-22)
		MF	4	43	...	14	...	28	...
		M	3	47	...	15	...	31	...
		F	4	38	...	13	...	26	...
	1993								
		MF	4	47	26	15	11	31	...
		M	4	52	27	17	12	35	...
		F	4	41	24	13	10	27	...
	1994								
		MF	4	49	27	16	12	32	1.0
		M	4	54	28	19	13	37	1.7
		F	4	43	25	13	11	28	0.3
Ethiopia	1980		(4-6)		(7-12)		(13-18)	(7-18)	(19-23)
		MF	...	34	...	8	...	22	0.4
		M	...	44	...	11	...	29	...
		F	...	23	...	6	...	16	...
	1985								
		MF	2	35	...	12	...	25	0.7
		M	...	42	...	14	...	29	1.1
		F	...	28	...	9	...	20	0.3
	1990								
		MF	2	31	...	13	...	23	0.8
		M	2	36	...	15	...	27	1.2
		F	2	25	...	12	...	19	0.3
	1991								
		MF	1	25	...	12	...	19	0.7
		M	1	29	...	13	...	21	1.1
		F	1	22	...	11	...	17	0.3
	1992								
		MF	1	23	...	11	...	18	...
		M	1	27	...	12	...	20	...
		F	1	19	...	11	...	15	...
	1993								
		MF	1	27	21	11	...	20	...
		M	1	33	24	11	...	24	...
		F	1	21	17	10	...	16	...
Gabon‡			(3-5)		(6-11)		(12-18)	(6-18)	(19-23)

Enrolment ratios 3.2
Taux d'inscription
Tasas de escolarización

Country / Pays / País	Year / Année / Año	Sex / Sexe / Sexo	Pre-primary / Pré-primaire / Preprimaria — Gross Brut Bruta	First level / Premier degré / Primer grado — Gross Brut Bruta	First level — Net Net Neta	Second level / Second degré / Segundo grado — Gross Brut Bruta	Second level — Net Net Neta	1st + 2nd levels / 1er + 2nd degré / 1er + 2do grado — Gross Brut Bruta	3rd level / 3ème degré / 3er grado — Gross Brut Bruta
Gambia‡	1980		(6-7)		(8-13)		(14-20)	(8-20)	(21-25)
		MF	...	51	48	11	...	32	...
		M	...	67	63	16	...	42	...
		F	...	35	33	7	...	21	...
	1985								
		MF	...	68	62	16	13	43	...
		M	...	84	77	23	19	55	...
		F	...	52	48	10	8	32	...
	1990		(5-6)		(7-12)		(13-19)	(7-19)	(20-24)
		MF	...	65	...	16	...	41	...
		M	...	77	...	21	...	50	...
		F	...	52	...	10	...	32	...
	1991								
		MF	24	65	51	16	16	41	...
		M	...	78	60	22	21	50	...
		F	...	53	42	11	11	32	...
	1992								
		MF	...	67	55	19	18	44	1.6
		M	...	79	64	25	24	53	2.1
		F	...	56	46	13	12	35	1.2
Ghana	1980		(4-5)		(6-11)		(12-18)	(6-18)	(19-23)
		MF	23	80	...	41	...	61	1.6
		M	24	89	...	51	...	70	2.5
		F	21	71	...	31	...	52	0.6
	1985								
		MF	25	76	...	40	...	58	1.4
		M	...	...	...	...	...	...	2.3
		F	...	...	...	...	...	...	0.6
	1990								
		MF	...	77	...	37	...	58	1.4
		M	...	84	...	45	...	65	2.2
		F	...	69	...	29	...	50	0.6
	1991								
		MF	...	76	...	37	...	58	...
		M	...	83	...	45	...	65	...
		F	...	70	...	29	...	50	...
Guinea	1980				(7-12)		(13-18)	(7-18)	(19-23)
		MF	-	36	...	17	...	28	4.5
		M	-	48	...	24	...	37	7.3
		F	-	25	...	10	...	18	1.8
	1985				(7-12)		(13-19)	(7-19)	(20-24)
		MF	-	34	27	13	9	24	2.1
		M	-	47	36	18	13	33	3.5
		F	-	22	18	7	5	15	0.6
	1990								
		MF	-	37	...	10	...	24	1.1
		M	-	50	...	15	...	33	2.0
		F	-	24	...	5	...	15	0.1
	1991								
		MF	-	37	...	11	...	25	...
		M	-	50	...	16	...	34	...
		F	-	24	...	5	...	15	...
	1992								
		MF	-	42	...	12	...	28	...
		M	-	57	...	17	...	38	...
		F	-	27	...	6	...	17	...
	1993								
		MF	-	46	40	12	...	30	...
		M	-	61	...	18	...	41	...
		F	-	30	...	6	...	19	...
Guinea-Bissau	1980		(4-6)		(7-12)		(13-17)	(7-17)	(18-22)
		MF	2	68	47	6	3	42	...
		M	2	94	63	10	4	59	...
		F	2	43	31	2	1	26	...

3.2 Enrolment ratios
Taux d'inscription
Tasas de escolarización

Country Pays País	Year Année Año	Sex Sexe Sexo	Enrolment ratios / Taux d'inscription / Tasas de escolarización						
			Pre-primary Pré-primaire Preprimaria	First level Premier degré Primer grado		Second level Second degré Segundo grado		1st + 2nd levels 1er + 2nd degré 1er + 2do grado	3rd level 3ème degré 3er grado
			Gross Brut Bruta	Gross Brut Bruta	Net Net Neta	Gross Brut Bruta	Net Net Neta	Gross Brut Bruta	Gross Brut Bruta
Guinea-Bissau (cont)	1986								
		MF	2	61	46	7	...	39	...
		M	...	80	60	11	...	51	...
		F	...	43	33	4	...	27	...
	1987								
		MF	2	59	45	6	...	37	...
		M	2	77	58	9	...	49	...
		F	1	41	32	3	...	25	...
	1988								
		MF	2	60	...	7	...	38	0.5
		M	2	77	...	9	...	49	0.9
		F	1	42	...	4	...	27	0.1
Kenya	1980		(3-5)	(6-12)			(13-18)	(6-18)	(19-23)
		MF	...	115	91	20	...	78	0.9
		M	...	120	92	23	...	82	1.4
		F	...	110	89	16	...	73	0.3
	1985		(3-5)	(6-13)			(14-18)	(6-18)	(19-23)
		MF	26	99	...	21	...	75	1.2
		M	26	102	...	26	...	78	1.8
		F	26	96	...	16	...	71	0.7
	1990								
		MF	34	95	...	...	...	...	1.6
		M	32	97	...	...	...	...	2.3
		F	36	93	...	...	...	...	0.9
	1991		(3-5)	(6-13)			(14-17)	(6-17)	(18-22)
		MF	35	93	...	28	...	75	...
		M	...	95	...	31	...	77	...
		F	...	92	...	24	...	73	...
	1992								
		MF	35	92	...	27	...	73	...
		M	35	93	...	30	...	75	...
		F	35	91	...	24	...	72	...
	1993								
		MF	34	91	...	25	...	72	...
		M	34	92	...	28	...	73	...
		F	33	91	...	23	...	71	...
Lesotho	1980			(6-12)			(13-17)	(6-17)	(18-22)
		MF	-	102	66	18	13	71	1.5
		M	-	85	54	14	9	59	...
		F	-	120	78	21	17	83	...
	1985								
		MF	-	110	71	23	13	78	1.7
		M	-	97	61	18	8	68	1.3
		F	-	124	81	27	18	89	2.1
	1990								
		MF	-	105	68	25	...	76	1.7
		M	-	94	61	20	...	67	1.8
		F	-	115	76	30	...	84	1.7
	1992								
		MF	-	102	68	26	16	74	2.2
		M	-	94	61	21	11	67	2.0
		F	-	111	75	31	22	81	2.4
	1993								
		MF	-	98	65	26	17	71	2.3
		M	-	90	59	22	12	65	2.0
		F	-	105	71	31	22	77	2.5
	1994								
		MF	-	99	65	28	...	72	...
		M	-	93	60	23	...	67	...
		F	-	104	71	34	...	78	...
Libyan Arab Jamahiriya	1980		(4-5)		(6-11)		(12-17)	(6-17)	(18-22)
		MF	4	125	100	76	62	104	7.8
		M	5	129	100	88	71	112	11.2
		F	4	120	100	63	53	96	4.1

Enrolment ratios 3.2
Taux d'inscription
Tasas de escolarización

Country Pays País	Year Année Año	Sex Sexe Sexo	Enrolment ratios / Taux d'inscription / Tasas de escolarización							
			Pre- primary Pré- primaire Preprimaria	First level Premier degré Primer grado			Second level Second degré Segundo grado		1st + 2nd levels 1er + 2nd degré 1er + 2do grado	3rd level 3ème degré 3er grado
			Gross Brut Bruta	Gross Brut Bruta	Net Net Neta		Gross Brut Bruta	Net Net Neta	Gross Brut Bruta	Gross Brut Bruta
Libyan Arab Jamahiriya (cont))	1985		(4-5)		(6-14)			(15-17)	(6-17)	(18-22)
		MF	6	109	...		59	...	98	9.2
		M	6	113	...		61	...	102	...
		F	6	104	...		57	...	94	...
	1990									
		MF	...	106	...		86	...	102	...
		M	...	110	...		85	...	104	...
		F	...	103	...		87	...	99	...
	1991									
		MF	...	108	...		95	...	105	16.4
		M	...	111	...		95	...	107	17.5
		F	...	105	...		95	...	103	15.3
	1992									
		MF	...	106	97		97	...	104	...
		M	...	107	98		...	...	...	...
		F	...	104	96		...	...	...	...
	1993									
		MF	...	110	...		...	...	...	...
		M	...	110	...		...	...	...	...
		F	...	110	...		...	...	...	...
Madagascar‡	1980		(3-5)		(6-10)			(11-17)	(6-17)	(18-22)
		MF	...	136	...		...	...	...	2.6
		M	...	139	...		...	...	...	...
		F	...	133	...		...	...	...	...
	1984									
		MF	...	112	...		30	...	68	3.8
		M	...	116	...		33	...	72	4.8
		F	...	108	...		27	...	65	2.9
	1990									
		MF	...	87	...		17	...	50	3.1
		M	...	88	...		17	...	51	3.4
		F	...	85	...		17	...	49	2.8
	1991									
		MF	...	79	...		15	...	45	...
		M	...	83	...		15	...	47	...
		F	...	76	...		15	...	44	...
	1992									
		MF	...	76	...		15	...	44	3.5
		M	...	77	...		15	...	45	3.9
		F	...	74	...		15	...	43	3.0
	1993									
		MF	...	73	...		14	...	42	...
		M	...	75	...		14	...	43	...
		F	...	72	...		14	...	42	...
Malawi	1980				(6-13)			(14-17)	(6-17)	(18-22)
		MF	-	60	43		3	...	44	0.6
		M	-	72	48		5	...	53	0.9
		F	-	48	38		2	...	35	0.4
	1985									
		MF	-	60	43		4	...	44	0.6
		M	-	68	46		6	...	51	0.9
		F	-	52	41		3	...	37	0.3
	1990									
		MF	-	68	50		4	2	50	0.7
		M	-	74	52		5	2	55	0.9
		F	-	62	48		3	2	45	...
	1992									
		MF	-	80	52		4	2	59	0.8
		M	-	84	50		6	2	62	1.1
		F	-	77	54		3	2	56	0.5
	1993									
		MF	-	82	63		5	2	60	0.8
		M	-	84	61		6	2	62	1.1
		F	-	80	65		4	2	58	0.5

3.2 Enrolment ratios
Taux d'inscription
Tasas de escolarización

Country Pays País	Year Année Año	Sex Sexe Sexo	Enrolment ratios / Taux d'inscription / Tasas de escolarización						
			Pre-primary Pré-primaire Preprimaria	First level Premier degré Primer grado		Second level Second degré Segundo grado		1st + 2nd levels 1er + 2nd degré 1er + 2do grado	3rd level 3ème degré 3er grado
			Gross Brut Bruta	Gross Brut Bruta	Net Net Neta	Gross Brut Bruta	Net Net Neta	Gross Brut Bruta	Gross Brut Bruta
Malawi (cont)	1994								
		MF	-	120	92	5	2	87	...
		M	-	126	91	6	2	92	...
		F	-	114	93	4	2	83	...
Mali	1980		(5-6)		(7-12)		(13-18)	(7-18)	(19-23)
		MF	...	26	20	8		18	0.8
		M	...	33	...	12	...	24	1.4
		F	...	18	...	5	...	12	0.2
	1985								
		MF	...	23	...	6	...	15	0.9
		M	...	29	...	9	...	20	1.6
		F	...	17	...	4	...	11	0.2
	1990								
		MF	...	23	18	6	5	15	0.8
		M	...	29	23	9	6	20	1.4
		F	...	17	13	4	3	11	0.2
	1992								
		MF	...	27	21	...	...	...	...
		M	...	34	26	...	...	...	...
		F	...	21	16	...	...	...	...
	1993								
		MF	2	30	23	8	...	20	...
		M	3	37	28	11	...	26	...
		F	2	23	18	6	...	15	...
	1994								
		MF	3	32	...	...	...	...	...
		M	3	39	...	...	...	...	...
		F	2	25	...	...	...	...	...
Mauritania	1980				(6-11)		(12-17)	(6-17)	(18-22)
		MF	...	37	...	11	...	25	...
		M	...	47	...	17	...	34	...
		F	...	26	...	4	...	16	...
	1985								
		MF	...	48	...	15	...	33	2.8
		M	...	58	...	22	...	42	...
		F	...	39	...	8	...	25	...
	1990								
		MF	...	48	...	14	...	33	...
		M	...	56	...	19	...	39	...
		F	...	41	...	9	...	27	...
	1992								
		MF	...	61	...	15	...	40	3.7
		M	...	68	...	19	...	46	6.3
		F	...	55	...	10	...	34	1.1
	1993								
		MF	...	69	...	15	...	44	4.1
		M	...	76	...	19	...	50	6.8
		F	...	62	...	11	...	38	1.4
	1994								
		MF	...	74	...	...	...	...	...
		M	...	81	...	...	...	...	...
		F	...	66	...	...	...	...	...
Mauritius	1980		(3-4)		(5-10)		(11-17)	(5-17)	(18-22)
		MF	27	93	79	50		70	1.0
		M	27	94	80	51	...	71	1.4
		F	26	91	79	49		69	0.6
	1985								
		MF	...	110	100	49	...	77	1.1
		M	...	110	100	51	...	78	1.3
		F	...	109	100	46		76	0.8
	1990								
		MF	...	109	95	53	...	79	3.5
		M	...	109	95	53	...	79	4.4
		F	...	109	95	53	...	79	2.6

Enrolment ratios 3.2
Taux d'inscription
Tasas de escolarización

Country / Pays / País	Year / Année / Año	Sex / Sexe / Sexo	Enrolment ratios / Taux d'inscription / Tasas de escolarización						
			Pre-primary / Pré-primaire / Preprimaria	First level / Premier degré / Primer grado		Second level / Second degré / Segundo grado		1st + 2nd levels / 1er + 2nd degré / 1er + 2do grado	3rd level / 3ème degré / 3er grado
			Gross Brut Bruta	Gross Brut Bruta	Net Net Neta	Gross Brut Bruta	Net Net Neta	Gross Brut Bruta	Gross Brut Bruta
Mauritius (cont)	1991								
		MF	...	109	91	55	...	79	4.1
		M	...	109	91	54	...	79	4.7
		F	...	109	92	56	...	80	3.5
	1992								
		MF	...	107	...	57	...	79	4.3
		M	...	107	...	56	...	79	...
		F	...	107	...	57	...	80	...
	1993								
		MF	...	106	94	59	...	80	4.8
		M	...	107	94	58	...	79	...
		F	...	106	94	60	...	80	...
Morocco	1980		(5-6)		(7-11)		(12-18)	(7-18)	(19-23)
		MF	50	83	62	26	20	52	5.9
		M	74	102	75	32	25	65	9.0
		F	25	63	47	20	16	39	2.7
	1985								
		MF	57	77	61	35	26	54	8.6
		M	79	93	73	42	31	65	11.8
		F	35	60	48	28	22	43	5.5
	1990		(5-6)		(7-12)		(13-18)	(7-18)	(19-23)
		MF	65	67	58	35	28	52	10.1
		M	89	79	68	41	31	61	12.5
		F	40	54	48	29	24	42	7.6
	1992								
		MF	62	73	63	36	29	55	10.3
		M	85	85	73	42	33	64	12.5
		F	37	60	53	30	24	46	8.1
	1993								
		MF	61	77	66	37	...	57	10.3
		M	85	89	76	43	...	66	12.2
		F	37	64	56	31	...	48	8.3
	1994								
		MF	61	80	69	38	30	59	10.0
		M	84	92	79	43	34	68	11.6
		F	38	68	59	32	26	50	8.4
Mozambique	1980		(4-5)		(6-9)		(10-16)	(6-16)	(17-21)
		MF	...	99	36	5	...	43	0.1
		M	...	114	39	8	...	51	0.1
		F	...	84	33	3	...	35	0.1
	1985		(6)		(7-10)		(11-17)	(7-17)	(18-22)
		MF	...	86	51	7	...	40	0.1
		M	...	98	55	10	...	46	0.2
		F	...	75	46	5	...	33	0.1
	1990		(-)		(7-11)		(12-18)	(7-18)	(19-23)
		MF	-	66	46	8	...	35	...
		M	-	75	...	10	...	41	...
		F	-	57	...	6	...	30	...
	1993								
		MF	-	60	41	7	7	32	0.4
		M	-	69	46	9	8	37	0.6
		F	-	51	35	6	5	27	0.2
	1994								
		MF	-	62	...	7	...	33	...
		M	-	72	...	9	...	39	...
		F	-	52	...	6	...	27	...
	1995								
		MF	-	65	...	8	...	35	...
		M	-	75	...	10	...	41	...
		F	-	54	...	6	...	29	...
Namibia	1986		(6)		(7-13)		(14-18)	(7-18)	(19-23)
		MF	13	135	...	39	...	99	...

3.2 Enrolment ratios
Taux d'inscription
Tasas de escolarización

Country / Pays / País	Year / Année / Año	Sex / Sexe / Sexo	Pre-primary / Pré-primaire / Preprimaria — Gross Brut Bruta	First level / Premier degré / Primer grado — Gross Brut Bruta	— Net Net Neta	Second level / Second degré / Segundo grado — Gross Brut Bruta	— Net Net Neta	1st + 2nd levels / 1er + 2nd degré / 1er + 2do grado — Gross Brut Bruta	3rd level / 3ème degré / 3er grado — Gross Brut Bruta
Namibia (cont)	1990	MF	15	129	...	43	...	97	...
		M	14	123	...	38	...	91	...
		F	15	135	...	49	...	103	...
	1992	MF	13	136	89	55	30	106	...
		M	13	134	86	49	26	102	...
		F	13	138	93	61	35	110	...
	1993	MF	12	134	...	59	...	106	7.3
		M	11	133	...	53	...	103	5.6
		F	12	136	...	65	...	109	9.0
	1994	MF	11	137	91	63	35	109	8.2
		M	10	136	...	57	...	106	6.4
		F	11	138	...	69	...	112	10.1
Niger	1980		(5-6)		(7-12)		(13-19)	(7-19)	(20-24)
		MF	1	25	21	5	4	15	0.3
		M	1	33	...	7	5	20	0.5
		F	1	18	...	3	2	11	0.1
	1985	MF	1	26	25	5	...	16	...
		M	1	33	32	8	...	21	...
		F	1	18	17	3	...	11	...
	1990	MF	2	29	25	7	6	18	...
		M	2	37	32	9	8	24	...
		F	2	21	18	4	3	13	...
	1992	MF	2	28	...	6	...	18	...
		M	2	36	...	9	...	23	...
		F	2	21	...	4	...	13	...
	1993	MF	...	28	...	7	...	18	...
		M	...	35	...	...	...	...	...
		F	...	21	...	...	...	...	...
	1994	MF	...	30	...	7	...	19	...
		M	...	...	...	9	...	...	...
		F	...	...	...	5	...	...	...
Nigeria	1980		(3-5)		(6-11)		(12-18)	(6-18)	(19-23)
		MF	...	105	...	16	...	61	2.2
		M	...	118	...	22	...	71	...
		F	...	92	...	11	...	52	...
	1985		(3-5)		(6-11)		(12-16)	(6-16)	(17-21)
		MF	...	96	...	33	...	70	3.3
		M	...	107	...	38	...	79	4.9
		F	...	85	...	27	...	61	1.8
	1990		(3-5)		(6-11)		(12-17)	(6-17)	(18-22)
		MF	...	85	...	23	...	57	...
		M	...	97	...	26	...	65	...
		F	...	74	...	19	...	50	...
	1992	MF	...	87	...	26	...	60	...
		M	...	97	...	29	...	67	...
		F	...	77	...	24	...	53	...
	1993	MF	...	90	...	29	...	63	...
		M	...	101	...	31	...	70	...
		F	...	79	...	26	...	55	...
	1994	MF	...	89	...	30	...	63	...
		M	...	100	...	33	...	70	...
		F	...	79	...	28	...	56	...
Reunion‡			(2-5)		(6-10)		(11-17)	(6-17)	(18-22)

Enrolment ratios 3.2
Taux d'inscription
Tasas de escolarización

Country / Pays / País	Year / Année / Año	Sex / Sexe / Sexo	Pre-primary / Pré-primaire / Preprimaria Gross Brut Bruta	First level / Premier degré / Primer grado Gross Brut Bruta	First level Net Net Neta	Second level / Second degré / Segundo grado Gross Brut Bruta	Second level Net Net Neta	1st + 2nd levels / 1er + 2nd degré / 1er + 2do grado Gross Brut Bruta	3rd level / 3ème degré / 3er grado Gross Brut Bruta
Rwanda	1980		(4-6)		(7-14)		(15-20)	(7-20)	(21-25)
		MF	...	63	59	3	...	42	0.3
		M	...	66	62	4	...	44	0.6
		F	...	60	57	3	...	40	0.1
	1985								
		MF	...	63	60	6	...	42	0.4
		M	...	65	61	7	...	44	0.7
		F	...	61	58	5	...	41	0.1
	1990								
		MF	...	70	66	8	7	47	...
		M	...	70	66	9	8	48	...
		F	...	69	66	7	6	47	...
	1991		(4-6)		(7-13)		(14-19)	(7-19)	(20-24)
		MF	...	77	71	10	8	50	...
		M	...	78	71	11	9	51	...
		F	...	76	71	9	7	49	...
Senegal	1980		(3-5)		(6-11)		(12-18)	(6-18)	(19-23)
		MF	2	46	37	11	...	29	2.7
		M	1	55	44	15	...	36	4.4
		F	2	37	30	7	...	23	1.0
	1985		(4-6)		(7-12)		(13-19)	(7-19)	(20-24)
		MF	2	56	48	14	...	36	2.4
		M	2	67	57	18	...	44	3.8
		F	2	46	39	9	...	28	1.0
	1990								
		MF	2	59	...	16	...	38	3.0
		M	...	68	...	21	...	45	...
		F	...	50	...	11	...	31	...
	1991								
		MF	2	59	48	17	...	39	3.3
		M	2	67	55	22	...	45	5.0
		F	2	50	42	12	...	32	1.6
	1992								
		MF	2	58	...	16	...	38	3.4
		M	...	67	...	21	...	44	...
		F	...	50	...	11	...	31	...
	1993								
		MF	2	60	50	...	...	...	...
		M	2	68	...	...	...	...	...
		F	2	51	...	...	...	...	...
Sierra Leone	1980		(3-4)		(5-11)		(12-18)	(5-18)	(19-23)
		MF	...	52	...	14	...	35	0.8
		M	...	61	...	20	...	43	...
		F	...	43	...	8	...	28	...
	1985								
		MF	...	63	...	18	...	43	1.8
		M	...	...	...	...	...	...	3.0
		F	...	...	...	...	...	...	0.6
	1989								
		MF	...	56	...	17	...	38	1.4
		M	...	66	...	23	...	47	2.4
		F	...	45	...	12	...	30	0.5
	1990								
		MF	...	51	...	17	...	36	1.3
		M	...	60	...	22	...	43	...
		F	...	42	...	12	...	29	...
Somalia‡	1980		(4-5)		(6-13)		(14-17)	(6-17)	(18-22)
		MF	0.5	19	14	8	4	16	...
		M	0.5	24	18	11	6	21	...
		F	0.5	14	10	4	2	11	...
	1985								
		MF	0.3	11	8	7	3	10	2.1
		M	0.3	15	11	9	4	13	3.4
		F	0.3	8	6	5	2	7	0.8
South Africa	1980		(5-5)		(6-12)		(13-17)	(6-17)	(18-22)
		MF	...	85	...	...	...	...	...

3.2 Enrolment ratios
Taux d'inscription
Tasas de escolarización

			Enrolment ratios / Taux d'inscription / Tasas de escolarización						
			Pre-primary	First level		Second level		1st + 2nd levels	3rd level
Country	Year	Sex	Pré-primaire	Premier degré		Second degré		1er + 2nd degré	3ème degré
Pays	Année	Sexe							
País	Año	Sexo	Preprimaria	Primer grado		Segundo grado		1er + 2do grado	3er grado
			Gross Brut Bruta	Gross Brut Bruta	Net Net Neta	Gross Brut Bruta	Net Net Neta	Gross Brut Bruta	Gross Brut Bruta
South Africa (cont)	1986								
		MF	10	103	...	55	...	86	...
		M	10	103	...	52	...	84	...
		F	10	103	...	59	...	86	...
	1990								
		MF	17	109	89	68	...	93	12.8
		M	16	109	87	63	...	91	14.2
		F	17	109	90	73	...	95	11.4
	1991								
		MF	17	111	92	71	46	96	13.2
		M	17	112	90	66	43	94	14.4
		F	18	111	93	77	49	98	12.1
	1993								
		MF	25	115	...	77	...	101	14.7
		M	24	116	...	71	...	98	15.9
		F	25	115	...	84	...	103	13.5
	1994								
		MF	28	117	96	82	52	103	15.9
		M	...	119	95	76	47	102	16.6
		F	...	115	96	88	57	105	15.2
Sudan	1980		(5-6)		(7-12)		(13-18)	(7-18)	(19-23)
		MF	13	50	...	16	...	35	1.7
		M	...	59	...	20	...	41	2.5
		F	...	41	...	12	...	28	0.9
	1985								
		MF	17	50	...	20	...	37	2.0
		M	...	59	...	23	...	43	2.4
		F	...	41	...	17	...	31	1.4
	1990								
		MF	19	50	...	23	...	38	3.0
		M	24	57	...	25	...	43	3.2
		F	13	43	...	20	...	33	2.8
	1991								
		MF	23	52	...	21	...	38	...
		M	24	59	...	24	...	43	...
		F	22	45	...	19	...	34	...
	1993								
		MF	...	55	...	...	...	...	...
		M	...	61	...	...	...	...	...
		F	...	48	...	...	...	...	...
Swaziland	1980		(3-5)		(6-12)		(13-17)	(6-17)	(18-22)
		MF	...	103	80	38	...	79	3.6
		M	...	104	...	39	...	80	4.4
		F	...	102	...	37	...	78	2.8
	1985								
		MF	...	102	79	39	...	79	4.4
		M	...	104	78	40	...	81	...
		F	...	100	80	38	...	77	...
	1990								
		MF	17	111	88	44	...	85	4.1
		M	12	114	87	45	...	87	4.8
		F	22	108	88	44	...	84	3.5
	1992								
		MF	...	117	93	53	...	92	3.9
		M	...	120	93	54	...	94	4.2
		F	...	114	93	52	...	90	3.7
	1993								
		MF	26	120	93	51	...	93	5.1
		M	...	123	93	51	...	95	6.1
		F	...	116	93	50	...	90	4.1
	1994								
		MF	...	122	95	52	37	94	...
		M	...	125	95	53	34	97	...
		F	...	119	96	51	40	92	...

Enrolment ratios **3.2**
Taux d'inscription
Tasas de escolarización

Country / Pays / País	Year / Année / Año	Sex / Sexe / Sexo	Pre-primary / Pré-primaire / Preprimaria Gross Brut Bruta	First level / Premier degré / Primer grado Gross Brut Bruta	First level Net Net Neta	Second level / Second degré / Segundo grado Gross Brut Bruta	Second level Net Net Neta	1st + 2nd levels / 1er + 2nd degré / 1er + 2do grado Gross Brut Bruta	3rd level / 3ème degré / 3er grado Gross Brut Bruta
Togo‡	1980		(3-5)		(6-11)		(12-18)	(6-18)	(19-23)
		MF	3	118	...	33	...	77	2.1
		M	3	146	...	51	...	100	3.5
		F	3	91	...	16	...	55	0.6
	1985	MF	3	93	...	21	...	58	1.9
		M	3	114	...	32	...	75	3.4
		F	3	71	...	10	...	42	0.5
	1990	MF	3	110	75	23	18	68	...
		M	3	132	87	35	26	86	...
		F	3	87	62	12	10	51	...
	1991	MF	...	107	...	23	...	67	2.5
		M	...	128	...	35	...	84	4.5
		F	...	86	...	12	...	50	0.6
	1993	MF	3	102	69	23	...	64	2.7
		M	3	122	80	34	...	80	4.7
		F	3	81	58	12	...	48	0.6
	1994	MF	...	...	...	...	...	...	3.1
		M	...	...	...	...	...	...	5.4
		F	...	...	...	...	...	...	0.8
Tunisia‡	1980		(3-5)		(6-11)		(12-18)	(6-18)	(19-23)
		MF	...	103	83	27	23	64	4.9
		M	...	118	93	34	28	75	6.7
		F	...	88	72	20	18	53	3.0
	1985	MF	...	116	94	39	...	77	5.6
		M	...	126	100	46	...	85	7.0
		F	...	106	87	32	...	68	4.1
	1990	MF	9	116	96	45	...	80	8.4
		M	...	123	100	50	...	86	10.0
		F	...	109	92	40	...	74	6.8
	1992	MF	...	116	98	49	...	82	10.5
		M	...	122	100	53	...	87	12.2
		F	...	111	94	45	...	77	8.8
	1993	MF	...	118	98	52	...	84	11.4
		M	...	123	100	55	...	88	12.9
		F	...	113	95	49	...	80	9.8
	1994	MF	...	118	99	56	...	86	12.0
		M	...	123	100	58	...	89	13.4
		F	...	113	96	53	...	82	10.6
Uganda‡	1980				(6-12)		(13-18)	(6-18)	(19-23)
		MF	...	50	...	5	...	32	0.5
		M	...	56	...	7	...	37	0.8
		F	...	43	...	3	...	27	0.2
	1985	MF	...	70	...	10	...	46	0.8
		M	...	...	...	...	...	...	1.2
		F	...	...	...	...	...	...	0.3
	1990	MF	...	70	...	12	...	47	1.1
		M	...	78	...	16	...	53	1.6
		F	...	62	...	9	...	41	0.6
	1991	MF	...	70	...	11	...	47	1.3
		M	...	77	...	...	...	...	1.8
		F	...	64	...	...	...	...	0.7

3.2 Enrolment ratios
Taux d'inscription
Tasas de escolarización

Country / Pays / País	Year / Année / Año	Sex / Sexe / Sexo	Enrolment ratios / Taux d'inscription / Tasas de escolarización						
			Pre-primary / Pré-primaire / Preprimaria	First level / Premier degré / Primer grado		Second level / Second degré / Segundo grado		1st + 2nd levels / 1er + 2nd degré / 1er + 2do grado	3rd level / 3ème degré / 3er grado
			Gross Brut Bruta	Gross Brut Bruta	Net Net Neta	Gross Brut Bruta	Net Net Neta	Gross Brut Bruta	Gross Brut Bruta
Uganda‡ (cont)	1992								
		MF	...	...	...	11	...	...	1.2
		M	...	...	...	14	...	...	1.8
		F	...	...	...	8	...	...	0.7
	1993								
		MF	...	67	...	11	...	44	1.3
		M	...	74	...	...	...	...	1.9
		F	...	59	...	...	...	...	0.8
United Republic of Tanzania	1980		(4-6)		(7-13)		(14-19)	(7-19)	(20-24)
		MF	...	93	68	3	...	57	...
		M	...	99	...	4	...	62	...
		F	...	86	...	2	...	53	...
	1985								
		MF	...	75	56	3	...	46	0.3
		M	...	76	55	4	...	47	0.4
		F	...	74	56	2	...	45	0.1
	1990								
		MF	...	70	52	5	...	43	...
		M	...	70	51	6	...	44	...
		F	...	69	52	4	...	42	...
	1991								
		MF	...	70	51	5	...	44	...
		M	...	71	51	6	...	45	...
		F	...	70	51	4	...	43	...
	1992								
		MF	...	70	...	5	...	43	...
		M	...	71	...	6	...	45	...
		F	...	69	...	5	...	42	...
	1993								
		MF	...	70	50	5	...	44	...
		M	...	71	50	6	...	45	...
		F	...	69	51	5	...	43	...
Zaire‡	1980		(3-5)		(6-11)		(12-17)	(6-17)	(18-22)
		MF	...	92	...	24	...	62	1.2
		M	...	108	...	35	...	76	...
		F	...	77	...	13	...	49	...
	1985								
		MF	...	86	...	23	...	58	1.4
		M	...	105	...	32	...	73	...
		F	...	68	...	13	...	44	...
	1990								
		MF	...	70	54	...	...	...	1.9
		M	...	80	61	...	...	...	...
		F	...	60	47	...	...	...	...
	1991								
		MF	...	68	53	21	15	48	...
		M	...	78	59	28	19	56	...
		F	...	59	47	14	11	39	...
	1992								
		MF	1	70	52	23	16	49	...
		M	1	78	58	31	21	58	...
		F	1	61	47	14	12	40	...
	1993								
		MF	...	68	54	24	17	49	...
		M	...	78	60	33	23	58	...
		F	...	58	47	15	11	39	...
Zambia‡	1980		(3-6)		(7-13)		(14-18)	(7-18)	(19-23)
		MF	...	90	77	16	...	64	1.5
		M	...	97	81	22	...	71	...
		F	...	83	73	11	...	57	...
	1985								
		MF	...	100	...	18	...	70	1.9
		M	...	106	...	23	...	76	3.2
		F	...	94	...	13	...	64	0.6

Enrolment ratios 3.2
Taux d'inscription
Tasas de escolarización

Country / Pays / País	Year / Année / Año	Sex / Sexe / Sexo	Pre-primary Préprimaire Preprimaria Gross Brut Bruta	First level Premier degré Primer grado Gross Brut Bruta	First level Net Net Neta	Second level Second degré Segundo grado Gross Brut Bruta	Second level Net Net Neta	1st + 2nd levels 1er + 2nd degré 1er + 2do grado Gross Brut Bruta	3rd level 3ème degré 3er grado Gross Brut Bruta
Zambia‡ (cont)	1990	MF	...	92	...	...	...	...	2.0
		M	...	...	...	...	...	...	2.9
		F	...	...	...	...	...	...	1.1
	1994	MF	...	82	69	25	...	62	...
		M	...	85	70	31	...	66	...
		F	...	79	68	19	...	58	...
Zimbabwe	1980		(5-6)		(7-13)		(14-19)	(7-19)	(20-24)
		MF	...	85	...	8	...	54	1.3
	1985	MF	...	136	...	41	...	96	3.9
		M	...	140	...	50	...	103	...
		F	...	131	...	33	...	90	...
	1990	MF	...	116	...	49	...	88	5.2
		M	...	117	...	53	...	90	...
		F	...	115	...	46	...	86	...
	1991	MF	...	122	...	52	...	92	4.5
		M	...	124	...	58	...	97	6.6
		F	...	119	...	45	...	88	2.4
	1992	MF	...	119	...	47	...	89	6.1
		M	...	120	...	53	...	92	8.9
		F	...	117	...	41	...	86	3.3
	1993		(5)		(6-12)		(13-18)	(6-18)	(19-23)
		MF	...	115	...	44	...	86	...
		M	...	119	...	49	...	90	...
		F	...	111	...	39	...	81	...
America, North									
Bahamas	1980		(3-4)		(5-10)		(11-16)	(5-16)	(17-21)
		MF	...	99	99	88	88	94	16.7
	1985	MF	...	99	99	86	82	92	17.5
		M	...	100	100	81	78	90	...
		F	...	98	98	91	87	94	...
	1990	MF	...	101	...	...	...	...	...
	1991	MF	7	101	95	94	87	98	...
		M	7	101	94	94	87	97	...
		F	7	102	96	94	88	98	...
	1992	MF	7	101	94	95	89	98	...
		M	7	100	93	95	88	97	...
		F	7	103	96	95	89	99	...
	1993	MF	7	97	95	91	87	94	...
		M	7	...	...	...	...	...	...
		F	7	...	...	...	...	...	...
Barbados	1980		(3-4)		(5-11)		(12-17)	(5-17)	(18-22)
		MF	41	85	84	88	74	87	14.8
		M	40	85	83	88	73	86	13.9
		F	42	86	85	88	75	87	15.7
	1989	MF	...	95	82	85	75	90	17.0
		M	...	95	82	90	78	92	13.6
		F	...	95	82	80	72	88	20.6
	1990	MF	...	...	...	...	...	...	27.1

3.2   Enrolment ratios
      Taux d'inscription
      Tasas de escolarización

Country / Pays / País	Year / Année / Año	Sex / Sexe / Sexo	Pre-primary / Pré-primaire / Preprimaria — Gross Brut Bruta	First level / Premier degré / Primer grado — Gross Brut Bruta	First level — Net Net Neta	Second level / Second degré / Segundo grado — Gross Brut Bruta	Second level — Net Net Neta	1st + 2nd levels / 1er + 2nd degré / 1er + 2do grado — Gross Brut Bruta	3rd level / 3ème degré / 3er grado — Gross Brut Bruta
Barbados (cont)	1991								
		MF	...	90	78	...	...	...	28.5
		M	...	90	78	...	...	...	25.1
		F	...	91	78	...	...	...	31.9
	1992								
		MF	...	...	...	...	...	...	26.2
	1994								
		MF	...	...	...	...	...	...	28.1
		M	...	...	...	...	...	...	22.2
		F	...	...	...	...	...	...	34.2
Belize	1980		(3-5)		(6-13)		(14-17)	(6-17)	(18-22)
		MF	14	107	...	38	...	86	-
	1985		(3-4)		(5-12)		(13-16)	(5-16)	(17-21)
		MF	...	103	87	42	...	85	-
		M	...	106	89	39	...	86	-
		F	...	100	85	46	...	84	-
	1990								
		MF	23	112	...	41	29	90	-
		M	21	114	...	38	27	91	-
		F	25	109	...	44	31	89	-
	1991								
		MF	28	111	94	45	35	91	-
		M	27	113	95	41	30	91	-
		F	28	109	93	50	39	90	-
	1992								
		MF	28	109	96	47	36	90	-
		M	27	111	97	46	35	91	-
		F	28	107	95	48	37	88	-
	1994								
		MF	28	111	97	49	36	92	-
		M	27	113	97	46	33	92	-
		F	29	109	96	52	39	91	-
Canada	1980		(4-5)		(6-11)		(12-17)	(6-17)	(18-22)
		MF	55	99	...	88	...	93	57.1
		M	55	99	...	87	...	92	56.1
		F	55	99	...	89	...	93	58.0
	1985								
		MF	57	103	95	99	88	101	69.6
		M	57	104	95	99	88	102	62.0
		F	58	102	95	99	89	100	77.7
	1990								
		MF	60	103	97	101	89	102	94.7
		M	61	104	97	101	88	102	85.3
		F	60	102	97	101	89	101	104.3
	1991								
		MF	62	103	97	102	90	103	97.8
		M	62	104	98	102	90	103	88.0
		F	62	102	97	102	90	102	107.8
	1992								
		MF	61	103	96	105	90	104	102.9
		M	61	104	96	105	90	104	94.2
		F	61	102	96	105	90	103	111.8
	1993								
		MF	62	103	97	106	91	105	102.9
		M	62	104	97	106	91	105	95.8
		F	62	102	96	106	92	104	110.2
Costa Rica	1980		(5)		(6-11)		(12-16)	(6-16)	(17-21)
		MF	39	105	89	48	39	78	21.0
		M	39	106	89	44	36	77	...
		F	39	104	90	51	43	80	...
	1985								
		MF	52	97	84	40	34	73	22.0
		M	51	98	83	38	32	72	...
		F	53	96	84	42	36	73	...

Enrolment ratios 3.2
Taux d'inscription
Tasas de escolarización

Country / Pays / País	Year / Année / Año	Sex / Sexe / Sexo	Pre-primary / Pré-primaire / Preprimaria — Gross Brut Bruta	First level / Premier degré / Primer grado — Gross Brut Bruta	First level — Net Net Neta	Second level / Second degré / Segundo grado — Gross Brut Bruta	Second level — Net Net Neta	1st + 2nd levels / 1er + 2nd degré / 1er + 2do grado — Gross Brut Bruta	3rd level / 3ème degré / 3er grado — Gross Brut Bruta
Costa Rica (cont)	1990		61	101	87	42	36	76	26.3
		M	61	102	86	41	35	76	...
		F	61	100	87	43	37	76	...
	1991	MF	67	103	87	43	37	78	30.3
		M	67	103	87	42	35	78	...
		F	67	102	88	45	38	78	...
	1993	MF	66	105	91	47	41	81	...
		M	66	106	...	45	...	80	...
		F	66	105	...	49	...	81	...
	1994	MF	67	106	90	49	43	81	...
		M	67	107	...	47	...	81	...
		F	67	105	...	51	...	82	...
Cuba	1980		(5)		(6-11)		(12-17)	(6-17)	(18-22)
		MF	59	106	95	81	...	93	17.3
		M	59	109	95	79	...	94	17.8
		F	59	103	95	83	...	93	16.7
	1985	MF	79	101	91	82	67	91	20.1
		M	87	105	91	80	63	90	18.3
		F	71	98	91	85	71	91	22.1
	1990	MF	103	99	93	89	69	93	20.9
		M	113	100	93	83	64	91	17.4
		F	93	97	93	95	74	96	24.5
	1992	MF	94	102	97	82	...	92	18.1
		M	104	103	97	77	...	89	14.9
		F	83	102	98	87	...	94	21.3
	1993	MF	94	104	100	77	58	90	16.6
		M	107	104	99	73	55	88	14.1
		F	81	104	100	81	62	92	19.3
	1994	MF	90	104	100	75	...	90	13.9
		M	...	104	99	70	...	88	...
		F	...	103	100	79	...	92	...
Dominican Republic	1980		(3-6)		(7-12)		(13-18)	(7-18)	(19-23)
		MF	4	118	...	42	...	81	...
	1985	MF	10	126	70	51	...	89	18.0
		M	...	123	70	44	...	85	...
		F	...	129	69	57	...	94	...
	1989		(3-6)		(7-14)		(15-18)	(7-18)	(19-23)
		MF	15	96	...	...	...	...	...
		M	15	96	...	...	...	...	...
		F	15	97	...	...	...	...	...
	1993	MF	20	97	81	37	24	78	...
		M	19	95	79	30	20	75	...
		F	20	99	83	43	29	81	...
	1994		(3-5)		(6-13)		(14-17)	(6-17)	(18-22)
		MF	...	103	81	41	22	84	...
		M	...	103	79	34	18	81	...
		F	...	104	83	47	26	86	...
El Salvador‡	1980		(4-6)		(7-15)		(16-18)	(7-18)	(19-23)
		MF	11	75	...	24	...	64	13.0
		M	11	75	...	26	...	65	15.0
		F	12	75	...	23	...	64	11.0
	1984	MF	13	74	65	26	15	64	15.3
		M	13	73	64	25	13	63	17.7
		F	14	75	66	28	17	65	13.0

3.2 Enrolment ratios
Taux d'inscription
Tasas de escolarización

			Enrolment ratios / Taux d'inscription / Tasas de escolarización						
Country Pays País	Year Année Año	Sex Sexe Sexo	Pre- primary Pré- primaire Preprimaria	First level Premier degré Primer grado		Second level Second degré Segundo grado		1st + 2nd levels 1er + 2nd degré 1er + 2do grado	3rd level 3ème degré 3er grado
			Gross Brut Bruta	Gross Brut Bruta	Net Net Neta	Gross Brut Bruta	Net Net Neta	Gross Brut Bruta	Gross Brut Bruta
El Salvador‡ (cont)	1989								
		MF	...	79	71	26	15	67	16.4
		M	...	78	70	26	14	67	19.1
		F	...	79	72	26	16	68	13.9
	1991								
		MF	19	76	...	25	...	65	15.2
		M	18	76	...	22	...	64	17.5
		F	20	77	...	27	...	66	13.1
	1992								
		MF	22	78	70	26	...	66	...
		M	21	78	70	25	...	66	...
		F	22	79	71	28	...	67	...
	1993								
		MF	25	79	...	29	...	67	15.4
		M	24	79	...	27	...	67	15.7
		F	26	80	...	30	...	68	15.1
Guadeloupe‡			(2-5)	(6-10)		(11-17)		(6-17)	(18-22)
Guatemala	1980		(5-6)	(7-12)		(13-18)		(7-18)	(19-23)
		MF	21	71	58	18	13	47	8.1
		M	22	77	...	20	...	51	...
		F	19	65	...	17	...	43	...
	1985								
		MF	26	76	...	19	...	51	8.1
		M	27	83	...	...	...	...	...
		F	25	70	...	...	...	...	...
	1991								
		MF	25	79	...	23	...	54	...
		M	25	84	...	...	...	...	...
		F	24	73	...	...	...	...	...
	1992								
		MF	...	83	...	...	...	...	...
	1993								
		MF	31	84	...	24	...	57	...
		M	32	89	...	25	...	60	...
		F	31	78	...	23	...	53	...
Haiti‡	1980		(4-5)	(6-11)		(12-17)		(6-17)	(18-22)
		MF	...	76	38	14	...	47	0.9
		M	...	82	38	14	...	51	1.3
		F	...	70	37	13	...	44	0.5
	1985		(3-5)	(6-11)		(12-17)		(6-17)	(18-22)
		MF	...	97	55	18	...	60	1.1
		M	...	103	57	19	...	63	1.6
		F	...	91	54	17	...	56	0.6
	1990								
		MF	41	56	26	22	...	40	...
		M	42	58	25	22	...	41	...
		F	40	54	26	21	...	39	...
Honduras	1980		(5-6)	(7-12)		(13-17)		(7-17)	(18-22)
		MF	14	98	78	30	...	70	7.5
		M	16	98	78	29	...	70	9.2
		F	12	99	78	31	...	71	5.7
	1985								
		MF	18	108	...	37	...	79	8.8
		M	...	108	...	...	...	...	10.9
		F	...	109	...	...	...	...	6.7
	1991								
		MF	19	108	89	33	21	77	8.6
		M	19	105	...	29	...	74	9.9
		F	20	110	...	37	...	80	7.3
	1992								
		MF	...	...	...	...	...	...	8.6
		M	...	...	...	...	...	...	9.6
		F	...	...	...	...	...	...	7.6

Enrolment ratios 3.2
Taux d'inscription
Tasas de escolarización

Country / Pays / País	Year / Année / Año	Sex / Sexe / Sexo	Pre-primary / Pré-primaire / Preprimaria — Gross Brut Bruta	First level / Premier degré / Primer grado — Gross Brut Bruta	First level — Net Net Neta	Second level / Second degré / Segundo grado — Gross Brut Bruta	Second level — Net Net Neta	1st + 2nd levels / 1er + 2nd degré / 1er + 2do grado — Gross Brut Bruta	3rd level / 3ème degré / 3er grado — Gross Brut Bruta
Honduras (cont)	1993								
		MF	20	112	90	32	...	79	8.7
		M	20	111	89	...	...	...	10.0
		F	20	112	91	...	...	...	7.4
	1994								
		MF	...	...	...	...	...	...	9.3
		M	...	...	...	...	...	...	10.7
		F	...	...	...	...	...	...	7.7
Jamaica‡	1980		(3-5)		(6-11)		(12-18)	(6-18)	(19-23)
		MF	70	103	96	67	64	84	6.7
		M	67	103	95	63	61	82	...
		F	73	104	97	71	88	87	...
	1985								
		MF	76	100	94	59	57	78	4.4
		M	...	99	92	56	54	76	5.0
		F	...	101	95	62	60	80	3.8
	1990								
		MF	84	108	100	64	62	84	6.0
		M	83	107	100	60	59	81	6.8
		F	85	109	100	68	66	87	5.3
	1992								
		MF	82	109	100	66	64	86	5.9
		M	85	109	100	62	61	83	6.6
		F	78	108	100	70	68	88	5.2
Martinique‡			(2-5)		(6-10)		(11-17)	(6-17)	(18-22)
Mexico	1980		(4-5)		(6-11)		(12-17)	(6-17)	(18-22)
		MF	25	122	...	48	...	89	14.2
		M	25	122	...	51	...	90	18.9
		F	25	121	...	46	...	87	9.4
	1985								
		MF	59	123	100	56	46	91	15.4
		M	58	124	...	57	...	92	19.4
		F	59	122	...	55	...	89	11.3
	1990								
		MF	62	115	100	55	46	85	14.1
		M	61	117	...	55	...	86	16.2
		F	63	114	...	55	...	85	12.0
	1992								
		MF	63	113	100	56	...	85	13.4
		M	62	114	...	56	...	86	14.6
		F	64	111	...	56	...	84	12.2
	1993								
		MF	65	112	99	58	...	86	13.8
		M	64	114	...	57	...	86	14.7
		F	66	110	...	58	...	85	12.8
	1994								
		MF	67	111	...	60	...	87	...
Netherlands Antilles‡			(4-5)		(6-11)		(12-16)	(6-16)	(17-21)
Nicaragua	1980		(3-6)		(7-12)		(13-17)	(7-17)	(18-22)
		MF	8	98	73	42	23	75	13.0
		M	8	95	72	39	21	72	...
		F	8	101	74	45	25	78	...
	1985								
		MF	14	100	76	34	19	74	9.7
		M	14	95	73	23	15	67	9.2
		F	15	106	78	45	24	81	10.0
	1990								
		MF	12	98	76	40	...	75	9.3
		M	12	95	74	35	...	72	10.7
		F	13	101	77	44	...	78	8.3
	1992								
		MF	12	102	80	42	...	78	9.7
		M	12	100	79	40	...	76	10.9
		F	13	104	82	44	...	80	8.8

Country / Pays / País	Year / Année / Año	Sex / Sexe / Sexo	Pre-primary / Pré-primaire / Preprimaria — Gross / Brut / Bruta	First level / Premier degré / Primer grado — Gross / Brut / Bruta	First level — Net / Net / Neta	Second level / Second degré / Segundo grado — Gross / Brut / Bruta	Second level — Net / Net / Neta	1st + 2nd levels / 1er + 2nd degré / 1er + 2do grado — Gross / Brut / Bruta	3rd level / 3ème degré / 3er grado — Gross / Brut / Bruta
Nicaragua (cont)	1993								
		MF	15	103	80	41	26	78	...
		M	14	101	79	39	25	76	...
		F	15	105	81	44	28	80	...
	1994								
		MF	17	104	79	43	...	79	...
		M	17	102	78	40	...	76	...
		F	18	105	81	47	...	81	...
Panama	1980		(5-5)	106	(6-11)	61	(12-17)	(6-17)	(18-22)
		MF	33	106	89	61	46	85	20.9
		M	33	108	88	58	43	85	18.7
		F	34	105	89	65	49	86	23.1
	1985								
		MF	51	106	90	60	48	84	24.6
		M	50	109	90	57	45	84	20.6
		F	52	104	90	63	51	84	28.6
	1990								
		MF	53	106	91	63	51	85	21.5
		M	53	108	91	60	48	85	...
		F	53	104	92	65	53	85	...
	1992								
		MF	56	105	...	64	...	85	25.3
	1993								
		MF	60	105	...	65	...	86	27.3
	1994								
		MF	60	106	...	66	...	87	27.5
Trinidad and Tobago	1980		(3-4)		(5-11)	70	(12-16)	(5-16)	(17-21)
		MF	8	99	90	70		87	4.4
		M	...	98	89	...	...	...	5.0
		F	...	100	91	...	...	...	3.8
	1985								
		MF	8	96	92	81	...	90	5.4
		M	...	96	91	...	...	...	6.6
		F	...	97	93	...	...	...	4.1
	1990								
		MF	8	95	89	81	...	90	6.3
		M	8	95	89	80	...	89	7.1
		F	8	95	89	83	...	90	5.5
	1991								
		MF	...	95	89	79	...	89	6.6
		M	...	95	89	78	...	89	7.8
		F	...	95	89	80	...	89	5.4
	1992								
		MF	9	95	88	78	65	88	7.2
		M	9	95	88	77	64	88	8.4
		F	9	95	88	80	67	89	6.0
	1993								
		MF	...	94	...	76	...	87	7.6
		M	...	94	...	74	...	86	8.9
		F	...	94	...	78	...	88	6.2
United States‡	1980		(3-5)	100	(6-11)	91	(12-17)	(6-17)	(18-22)
		MF	53	100	96	91	...	95	55.6
		M	54	101	96	90	...	95	53.3
		F	51	100	97	92	...	96	58.0
	1985								
		MF	61	101	94	98	91	99	60.7
		M	60	101	94	97	91	99	57.0
		F	62	101	94	98	92	99	64.6
	1990								
		MF	65	105	99	92	85	99	74.1
		M	66	106	99	92	84	99	65.9
		F	64	104	99	93	86	99	82.7
	1991								
		MF	...	...	...	...	...	...	78.6

Enrolment ratios 3.2
Taux d'inscription
Tasas de escolarización

Country / Pays / País	Year / Année / Año	Sex / Sexe / Sexo	Pre-primary / Pré-primaire / Preprimaria — Gross Brut Bruta	First level / Premier degré / Primer grado — Gross Brut Bruta	First level — Net Net Neta	Second level / Second degré / Segundo grado — Gross Brut Bruta	Second level — Net Net Neta	1st + 2nd levels / 1er + 2nd degré / 1er + 2do grado — Gross Brut Bruta	3rd level / 3ème degré / 3er grado — Gross Brut Bruta
United States‡ (cont)	1992	MF	...	105	98	98	89	101	80.1
		M	...	106	98	98	89	102	70.4
		F	...	104	98	98	90	101	90.2
	1993	MF	62	107	100	97	90	102	79.7
		M	64	107	99	98	89	103	70.0
		F	60	106	100	97	90	102	89.9
America, South									
Argentina‡	1980		(4-5)		(6-12)		(13-17)	(6-17)	(18-22)
		MF	40	106	...	56	...	87	21.8
		M	...	106	...	...	...	...	21.8
		F	...	106	...	...	...	...	21.9
	1985	MF	50	105	...	70	...	92	35.7
		M	49	105	...	66	...	90	33.6
		F	51	105	...	74	...	94	37.8
	1990	MF	...	106	...	68	...	91	...
	1991	MF	47	108	95	72	59	94	40.7
		M	...	108	95	70	55	93	...
		F	...	107	95	75	62	94	...
	1993	MF	47	107	...	62	...	89	39.1
	1994	MF	51	111	...	67	...	93	35.8
		M	...	...	...	...	...	...	32.0
		F	...	...	...	...	...	...	39.7
Bolivia	1980		(4-5)		(6-13)		(14-17)	(6-17)	(18-22)
		MF	27	87	79	37	16	72	16.4
		M	28	92	84	42	18	78	...
		F	27	81	74	32	14	66	...
	1986	MF	38	95	86	39	27	78	22.5
		M	38	100	90	42	29	83	...
		F	38	89	82	36	25	73	...
	1990	MF	32	95	91	37	29	77	22.2
		M	32	99	95	40	32	81	...
		F	32	90	87	34	27	73	...
Brazil	1980		(4-6)		(7-14)		(15-17)	(7-17)	(18-22)
		MF	14	99	81	34	14	81	11.1
		M	14	101	...	31	13	82	11.3
		F	14	97	...	36	16	80	10.9
	1985	MF	37	101	82	36	15	84	...
	1990	MF	48	109	89	39	16	91	11.3
		M	...	...	...	...	...	...	11.3
		F	...	...	...	...	...	...	11.4
	1992	MF	53	111	90	43	19	94	11.5
		M	...	...	...	...	...	...	9.9
		F	...	...	...	...	...	...	13.0
	1993	MF	55	112	90	44	19	94	11.5
		M	...	...	...	...	...	...	9.2
		F	...	...	...	...	...	...	13.7
	1994	MF	55	114	91	46	20	96	11.4
		M	...	...	...	...	...	...	8.5
		F	...	...	...	...	...	...	14.4

3.2 Enrolment ratios
Taux d'inscription
Tasas de escolarización

Country Pays País	Year Année Año	Sex Sexe Sexo	Enrolment ratios / Taux d'inscription / Tasas de escolarización						
			Pre-primary Pré-primaire Preprimaria	First level Premier degré Primer grado		Second level Second degré Segundo grado		1st + 2nd levels 1er + 2nd degré 1er + 2do grado	3rd level 3ème degré 3er grado
			Gross Brut Bruta	Gross Brut Bruta	Net Net Neta	Gross Brut Bruta	Net Net Neta	Gross Brut Bruta	Gross Brut Bruta
Chile	1980		(5-5)		(6-13)		(14-17)	(6-17)	(18-22)
		MF	71	109	...	52	...	90	12.3
		M	70	110	...	49	...	89	13.8
		F	71	108	...	56	...	90	10.7
	1985								
		MF	82	105	...	67	...	92	15.5
		M	82	106	...	64	...	92	17.4
		F	82	103	...	69	...	92	13.5
	1991								
		MF	74	100	89	72	55	91	23.2
		M	74	101	90	69	53	91	...
		F	75	99	88	74	56	91	...
	1992								
		MF	86	99	86	69	52	89	25.8
		M	85	99	87	67	50	89	...
		F	86	98	84	72	55	90	...
	1993								
		MF	...	98	87	67	53	88	26.7
		M	...	99	88	65	51	88	...
		F	...	98	87	70	55	89	...
	1994								
		MF	90	99	86	68	54	89	...
		M	89	100	86	66	52	89	...
		F	90	98	85	70	55	89	...
Colombia‡	1980		(3-5)		(6-10)		(11-16)	(6-16)	(17-21)
		MF	9	124	...	41	...	78	9.1
		M	...	123	...	40	...	77	10.1
		F	...	126	...	41	...	79	8.2
	1985								
		MF	12	113	72	48	...	79	11.3
		M	12	111	...	48	...	78	11.6
		F	12	114	...	49	...	80	11.0
	1990								
		MF	...	110	...	...	...	...	...
	1992								
		MF	20	117	83	61	44	87	15.5
		M	20	116	...	56	...	84	15.0
		F	21	117	...	67	...	90	15.9
	1993								
		MF	22	119	85	62	41	89	...
		M	22	118	...	57	...	85	...
		F	22	120	...	68	...	92	...
	1994								
		MF	28	121	87	64	46	90	17.5
		M	...	...	...	...	...	...	17.1
		F	...	...	...	...	...	...	17.9
Ecuador	1980		(4-5)		(6-11)		(12-17)	(6-17)	(18-22)
		MF	11	117	...	53	...	88	34.9
		M	10	119	...	53	...	89	43.2
		F	11	116	...	53	...	87	26.3
	1985								
		MF	18	119	...	58	...	91	...
		M	17	120	...	57	...	91	...
		F	18	118	...	59	...	91	...
	1990								
		MF	21	116	...	55	...	88	20.0
	1991								
		MF	22	126	...	56	...	93	...
	1992								
		MF	23	123	...	55	...	90	...
		M	23	124	...	54	...	91	...
		F	24	122	...	56	...	90	...

Enrolment ratios **3.2**
Taux d'inscription
Tasas de escolarización

Country Pays País	Year Année Año	Sex Sexe Sexo	Pre-primary Pré-primaire Preprimaria Gross Brut Bruta	First level Premier degré Primer grado Gross Brut Bruta	Net Net Neta	Second level Second degré Segundo grado Gross Brut Bruta	Net Net Neta	1st + 2nd levels 1er + 2nd degré 1er + 2do grado Gross Brut Bruta	3rd level 3ème degré 3er grado Gross Brut Bruta
Guyana‡	1980		(4-5)		(6-11)		(12-18)	(6-18)	(19-23)
		MF	67	101	...	57	...	78	3.0
		M	67	103	...	56	...	78	3.5
		F	67	100	...	58	...	78	2.6
	1985								
		MF	72	103	...	54	...	76	2.5
		M	71	104	...	53	...	75	2.6
		F	73	101	...	56	...	76	2.4
	1988								
		MF	71	112	...	57	...	82	5.1
		M	71	113	...	56	...	82	5.7
		F	71	111	...	59	...	82	4.4
	1992								
		MF	79	...	...	...	...	...	9.3
		M	79	...	...	...	...	...	9.7
		F	79	...	...	...	...	...	8.9
Paraguay	1980		(6)		(7-12)		(13-18)	(7-18)	(19-23)
		MF	12	104	87	26	...	67	8.3
		M	...	107	88	...	...	...	...
		F	...	100	86	...	...	...	...
	1985								
		MF	19	104	88	30	...	69	8.7
		M	19	106	89	30	...	70	...
		F	20	101	88	30	...	68	
	1990								
		MF	28	108	95	30	25	72	8.1
		M	28	110	96	30	25	73	8.6
		F	29	106	95	31	26	72	7.6
	1992								
		MF	32	109	97	34	29	76	...
		M	31	111	98	34	28	76	...
		F	33	108	96	35	29	75	...
	1993								
		MF	41	112	96	37	32	79	9.9
		M	40	114	97	36	31	79	9.4
		F	42	110	96	38	33	78	10.5
	1994		(5)		(6-11)		(12-17)	(6-17)	(18-22)
		MF	37	109	90	39	34	78	...
		M	36	111	89	38	33	79	...
		F	37	108	90	40	35	78	...
Peru	1980		(3-5)		(6-11)		(12-16)	(6-16)	(17-21)
		MF	15	114	86	59	...	91	17.3
		M	14	117	...	63	...	94	22.1
		F	15	111	...	54	...	87	12.4
	1985								
		MF	21	121	96	63	49	96	22.4
		M	20	123	...	66	...	99	...
		F	21	118	...	60	...	93	...
	1990								
		MF	30	118	...	67	...	96	30.4
	1992								
		MF	32	117	...	65	...	94	31.3
	1993								
		MF	34	119	88	65	46	95	...
	1994								
		MF	36	123	...	74	...	101	30.9
Suriname‡			(4-5)		(6-11)		(12-18)	(6-18)	(19-23)
Uruguay	1980		(2-5)		(6-11)		(12-17)	(6-17)	(18-22)
		MF	19	107	...	62	...	85	16.7
		M	...	107	...	61	...	85	15.5
		F	...	107	...	62	...	85	17.9

3.2 Enrolment ratios
Taux d'inscription
Tasas de escolarización

			Enrolment ratios / Taux d'inscription / Tasas de escolarización						
Country / Pays / País	Year / Année / Año	Sex / Sexe / Sexo	Pre-primary / Pré-primaire / Preprimaria	First level / Premier degré / Primer grado		Second level / Second degré / Segundo grado		1st + 2nd levels / 1er + 2nd degré / 1er + 2do grado	3rd level / 3ème degré / 3er grado
			Gross Brut Bruta	Gross Brut Bruta	Net Net Neta	Gross Brut Bruta	Net Net Neta	Gross Brut Bruta	Gross Brut Bruta
Uruguay (cont)									
	1985	MF	25	107	88	72	...	90	...
		M	25	107	...	...	...	...	...
		F	25	106	...	...	...	...	...
	1990	MF	32	108	...	81	...	95	30.1
		M	...	109	...	...	...	...	...
		F	...	108	...	...	...	...	...
	1992	MF	34	108	93	83	...	95	27.3
		M	33	108	92	...	...	...	...
		F	34	107	93	...	...	...	...
	1993	MF	33	109	94	81	...	95	...
		M	32	109	94	...	...	...	...
		F	33	108	95	...	...	...	...
	1994	MF	33	109	94	81	...	95	...
		M	34	110	94	74	...	92	...
		F	33	109	94	88	...	98	...
Venezuela	1980		(4-6)		(7-15)		(16-18)	(7-18)	(19-23)
		MF	34	93	82	21	14	76	20.6
		M	...	...	...	18	...	...	...
		F	...	...	...	25	...	...	...
	1985	MF	39	97	84	24	16	80	25.3
		M	39	95	...	21	14	78	29.3
		F	40	98	...	27	18	82	21.1
	1990		(3-5)		(6-14)		(15-16)	(6-16)	(17-21)
		MF	41	96	88	35	19	86	29.0
		M	40	94	87	29	15	84	...
		F	41	97	89	40	22	88	...
	1991	MF	43	97	89	35	19	87	28.5
		M	42	96	88	29	15	85	...
		F	43	98	90	40	23	89	...
	1992	MF	43	96	88	35	20	86	...
		M	42	95	87	29	16	84	...
		F	43	97	90	41	24	88	...
	1993	MF	43	94	...	35	...	85	...
		M	42	93	...	29	...	83	...
		F	43	96	...	41	...	87	...
Asia									
Afghanistan‡	1980		(3-6)		(7-14)		(15-18)	(7-18)	(19-23)
		MF	...	34	29	10	...	27	...
		M	...	54	46	16	...	43	...
		F	...	12	11	4	...	10	...
	1985	MF	1	20	17	8	...	16	...
		M	1	27	23	11	...	22	...
		F	1	13	11	5	...	11	...
	1990		(3-6)		(7-12)		(13-18)	(7-18)	(19-23)
		MF	1	27	...	9	...	18	1.7
		M	1	35	...	8	...	22	2.3
		F	1	19	...	9	...	14	1.1
	1993	MF	...	31	29	15	...	24	...
		M	...	46	42	22	...	34	...
		F	...	16	14	8	...	12	...
	1994	MF	...	44	...	22	...	34	...
		M	...	59	...	34	...	47	...
		F	...	29	...	9	...	20	...

Enrolment ratios 3.2
Taux d'inscription
Tasas de escolarización

Country / Pays / País	Year / Année / Año	Sex / Sexe / Sexo	Pre-primary / Pré-primaire / Preprimaria Gross Brut Bruta	First level / Premier degré / Primer grado Gross Brut Bruta	First level Net Net Neta	Second level / Second degré / Segundo grado Gross Brut Bruta	Second level Net Net Neta	1st + 2nd levels / 1er + 2nd degré / 1er + 2do grado Gross Brut Bruta	3rd level / 3ème degré / 3er grado Gross Brut Bruta
Afghanistan‡ (cont)	1995								
		MF	...	48	...	22	...	36	...
		M	...	63	...	32	...	49	...
		F	...	32	...	11	...	22	...
Armenia	1980		(3-6)		(7-9)		(10-16)	(7-16)	(17-21)
		MF	54	...		...		...	30.0
	1985	MF	56	...	...	...	...	...	33.4
	1990	MF	39	...	...	...	...	...	44.2
	1991	MF	39	...	...	...	...	...	48.9
	1992	MF	36	...		...		...	...
	1993	MF	32	90	...	85	...	87	...
		M	...	87	...	80	...	82	...
		F	...	93	...	90	...	91	...
Azerbaijan	1980		(3-6)		(7-9)		(10-16)	(7-16)	(17-21)
		MF	20	115	...	93	...	99	24.0
	1985	MF	21	119	...	95	...	102	24.5
	1990	MF	20	114	...	89	...	97	24.4
		M	...	115	...	89	...	97	...
		F	...	114	...	90	...	98	...
	1991	MF	19	114	...	89	...	98	25.3
		M	21	114	...	89	...	97	...
		F	17	114	...	90	...	98	...
	1992	MF	18	114	...	89	...	97	21.9
		M	20	115	...	89	...	98	25.6
		F	16	114	...	89	...	97	17.9
	1993	MF	18	117	...	86	...	97	19.8
		M	19	120	...	87	...	98	21.9
		F	17	115	...	85	...	95	17.5
Bahrain	1980		(3-5)		(6-11)		(12-17)	(6-17)	(18-22)
		MF	15	104	80	64	55	85	5.0
		M	15	111	84	70	58	92	5.3
		F	14	97	76	58	51	78	4.8
	1985	MF	27	112	96	97	77	106	12.8
		M	27	109	94	98	76	104	9.7
		F	27	116	98	97	77	107	16.4
	1990	MF	27	110	99	100	85	105	17.7
		M	27	110	99	98	84	105	15.0
		F	27	110	99	101	86	106	20.8
	1992	MF	33	110	100	99	85	105	20.1
		M	33	109	99	97	84	103	16.6
		F	32	111	100	101	87	106	23.9
	1993	MF	33	111	100	99	85	105	20.2
		M	34	109	100	98	84	104	16.6
		F	33	112	100	101	87	107	24.0
	1994	MF	34	111	100	99	85	105	...
		M	35	110	100	97	84	104	...
		F	33	113	100	100	87	107	...

3.2 Enrolment ratios
Taux d'inscription
Tasas de escolarización

Country / Pays / País	Year / Année / Año	Sex / Sexe / Sexo	Enrolment ratios / Taux d'inscription / Tasas de escolarización						
			Pre-primary / Pré-primaire / Preprimaria	First level / Premier degré / Primer grado		Second level / Second degré / Segundo grado		1st + 2nd levels / 1er + 2nd degré / 1er + 2do grado	3rd level / 3ème degré / 3er grado
			Gross Brut Bruta	Gross Brut Bruta	Net Net Neta	Gross Brut Bruta	Net Net Neta	Gross Brut Bruta	Gross Brut Bruta
Bangladesh‡	1980		(4)		(5-9)		(10-16)	(5-16)	(17-21)
		MF	...	61	...	18	...	38	2.8
		M	...	75	...	26	...	49	4.6
		F	...	46	...	9	...	26	0.8
	1985		(5)		(6-10)		(11-17)	(6-17)	(18-22)
		MF	...	64	57	18	18	39	4.8
		M	...	72	65	26	...	47	7.5
		F	...	54	49	11	...	30	1.9
	1990								
		MF	74	79	70	19	18	46	3.9
		M	79	84	74	25	23	51	6.4
		F	68	73	66	13	13	40	1.3
Bhutan‡					(6-12)		(13-16)	(6-16)	(17-21)
Brunei Darussalam	1980		(3-5)		(6-11)		(12-18)	(6-18)	(19-23)
		MF	42	109	82	61	51	84	0.6
		M	42	111	83	59	48	84	0.6
		F	42	106	82	63	54	84	0.7
	1985								
		MF	43	106	...	65	...	86	...
	1991								
		MF	48	104	84	68	63	86	...
		M	49	107	85	65	60	86	...
		F	46	101	83	70	66	86	...
	1992								
		MF	50	105	86	69	60	87	6.0
		M	52	108	87	65	56	86	5.1
		F	49	102	86	73	64	87	6.9
	1993								
		MF	59	107	89	71	61	89	...
		M	60	111	90	67	58	89	...
		F	59	104	89	74	63	89	...
	1994								
		MF	54	109	90	70	61	89	...
		M	55	113	90	67	58	89	...
		F	54	106	89	73	65	89	...
Cambodia	1990		(3-5)		(6-10)		(11-16)	(6-16)	(17-21)
		MF	5	113	...	27	...	73	1.2
		M	6	...	...	...	...	...	...
		F	5	...	...	...	...	...	...
	1993								
		MF	5	117	...	26	...	75	1.5
		M	5	128	...	33	...	84	2.4
		F	5	107	...	19	...	66	0.5
	1994								
		MF	5	118	...	25	...	75	1.4
		M	5	130	...	31	...	84	2.4
		F	5	106	...	18	...	65	0.5
China	1980		(3-6)		(7-11)		(12-16)	(7-16)	(17-21)
		MF	13	113	...	46	...	80	1.7
		M	...	121	...	54	...	88	2.3
		F	...	104	...	37	...	71	1.0
	1985								
		MF	20	123	...	39	...	77	2.8
		M	20	132	...	45	...	85	3.9
		F	19	114	...	33	...	70	1.7
	1990								
		MF	23	127	99	48	...	85	2.9
		M	23	132	100	53	...	90	4.0
		F	23	121	96	41	...	79	1.8
	1991								
		MF	25	124	98	51	...	86	3.2
		M	25	128	99	56	...	91	4.4
		F	24	120	96	45	...	81	1.9

Enrolment ratios 3.2
Taux d'inscription
Tasas de escolarización

Country Pays País	Year Année Año	Sex Sexe Sexo	Enrolment ratios / Taux d'inscription / Tasas de escolarización						
			Pre-primary Pré-primaire Preprimaria	First level Premier degré Primer grado		Second level Second degré Segundo grado		1st + 2nd levels 1er + 2nd degré 1er + 2do grado	3rd level 3ème degré 3er grado
			Gross Brut Bruta	Gross Brut Bruta	Net Net Neta	Gross Brut Bruta	Net Net Neta	Gross Brut Bruta	Gross Brut Bruta
China (cont)	1992								
		MF	26	120	96	54	...	87	3.5
		M	27	124	98	59	...	92	4.8
		F	26	117	95	48	...	83	2.1
	1993								
		MF	27	118	96	55	...	88	3.8
		M	27	120	97	60	...	92	5.3
		F	27	116	95	51	...	84	2.3
Cyprus‡	1980		(2-5)		(6-11)		(12-17)	(6-17)	(20-24)
		MF	...	104	100	95	87	99	4.0
		M	...	104	100	95	86	99	5.0
		F	...	104	100	95	88	99	3.0
	1985								
		MF	...	103	98	94	85	98	7.0
		M	...	103	99	93	84	98	7.0
		F	...	102	98	95	86	98	7.0
	1990								
		MF	57	103	100	90	86	97	15.0
		M	57	103	99	89	85	97	14.0
		F	56	103	100	91	88	98	16.0
	1991								
		MF	59	102	98	94	90	98	14.0
		M	59	101	97	93	89	98	14.0
		F	60	102	98	96	92	99	14.0
	1992								
		MF	...	101	98	93	89	97	14.0
		M	...	101	98	92	88	97	14.0
		F	...	101	98	94	90	98	14.0
	1993								
		MF	63	101	97	95	91	98	15.0
		M	63	101	97	94	90	98	14.0
		F	63	101	97	96	92	99	16.0
	1994								
		MF	59	100	96	97	92	99	17.0
		M	60	100	96	96	90	98	15.0
		F	58	100	96	98	93	99	19.0
Georgia	1980		(3-5)		(6-9)		(10-16)	(6-16)	(17-21)
		MF	...	...	...	...	...	...	29.7
	1985								
		MF							33.0
	1990								
		MF	...	...	...	...	...	...	36.6
	1994								
		MF	...	82	82	79	...	80	41.5
		M	...	82	82	82	...	82	35.5
		F	...	81	81	76	...	78	48.0
Hong Kong‡	1980		(3-5)		(6-11)		(12-18)	(6-18)	(19-23)
		MF	81	107	95	64	61	81	10.3
		M	81	107	95	63	59	81	13.8
		F	81	106	96	65	62	82	6.6
	1985								
		MF	92	105	...	71	...	86	13.3
		M	91	106	...	69	...	85	16.9
		F	92	105	...	73	...	87	9.4
	1990								
		MF	80	102	...	80	...	90	19.6
		M	79	102	...	...	...	...	22.8
		F	81	103	...	...	...	...	16.3
	1992								
		MF	82	100	...	82	...	90	20.7
		M	82	99	...	...	...	...	23.3
		F	83	100	...	...	...	...	17.9

3.2   Enrolment ratios
Taux d'inscription
Tasas de escolarización

Country Pays País	Year Année Año	Sex Sexe Sexo	Pre-primary Pré-primaire Preprimaria Gross Brut Bruta	First level Premier degré Primer grado Gross Brut Bruta	First level Net Net Neta	Second level Second degré Segundo grado Gross Brut Bruta	Second level Net Net Neta	1st + 2nd levels 1er + 2nd degré 1er + 2do grado Gross Brut Bruta	3rd level 3ème degré 3er grado Gross Brut Bruta
Hong Kong‡ (cont)	1993								
		MF	85	98	...	84	...	90	22.7
		M	84	98	...	...	...	...	25.0
		F	85	99	...	...	...	...	20.1
	1994								
		MF	85	99	...	85	...	91	...
		M	84	97	...	...	...	...	...
		F	86	100	...	...	...	...	...
India	1980		(4)		(5-9)		(10-16)	(5-16)	(17-21)
		MF	5	83	...	30	...	54	5.2
		M	5	98	...	39	...	65	7.4
		F	5	67	...	20	...	41	2.9
	1985		(4-5)		(6-10)		(11-17)	(6-17)	(18-22)
		MF	3	96	...	37	...	63	6.0
		M	3	110	...	48	...	75	8.1
		F	3	80	...	26	...	50	3.8
	1990								
		MF	3	98	...	44	...	68	6.0
		M	4	111	...	54	...	79	7.7
		F	3	84	...	32	...	56	4.2
	1991								
		MF	3	99	...	44	...	69	...
		M	3	111	...	55	...	80	...
		F	3	85	...	33	...	57	...
	1992								
		MF	3	101	...	48	...	72	...
		M	4	112	...	58	...	82	...
		F	3	89	...	37	...	60	...
	1993								
		MF	...	102	...	49	...	72	...
		M	...	113	...	59	...	83	...
		F	...	91	...	38	...	62	...
Indonesia‡	1980		(5-6)		(7-12)		(13-18)	(7-18)	(19-23)
		MF	12	107	88	29	...	72	...
		M	...	115	93	35	...	79	...
		F	...	100	83	23	...	65	...
	1985								
		MF	15	117	98	41	...	81	...
		M	...	120	100	...	...	...	...
		F	...	114	95	...	...	...	...
	1990								
		MF	18	115	97	44	38	80	8.5
		M	...	117	100	48	40	83	...
		F	...	114	95	40	35	77	...
	1991								
		MF	18	114	97	43	38	79	9.4
		M	...	115	100	48	42	82	...
		F	...	113	95	39	34	77	...
	1992								
		MF	18	114	97	43	37	79	9.3
		M	...	116	99	48	41	83	11.1
		F	...	112	95	39	34	76	7.4
	1993								
		MF	18	115	97	45	...	80	...
		M	...	117	100	49	...	83	...
		F	...	113	95	41	...	77	...
Iran, Islamic Republic of	1980		(5)		(6-10)		(11-17)	(6-17)	(18-22)
		MF	14	87	...	42	...	63	0.0
	1985								
		MF	7	96	79	44	...	68	4.1
		M	7	106	85	52	...	77	5.7
		F	6	85	72	35	...	59	2.4

Enrolment ratios 3.2
Taux d'inscription
Tasas de escolarización

Country / Pays / País	Year / Année / Año	Sex / Sexe / Sexo	Pre-primary / Pré-primaire / Preprimaria — Gross Brut Bruta	First level / Premier degré / Primer grado — Gross Brut Bruta	First level — Net Net Neta	Second level / Second degré / Segundo grado — Gross Brut Bruta	Second level — Net Net Neta	1st + 2nd levels / 1er + 2nd degré / 1er + 2do grado — Gross Brut Bruta	3rd level / 3ème degré / 3er grado — Gross Brut Bruta
Iran, Islamic Republic of (cont)	1990								
		MF	12	110	...	54	...	80	9.1
		M	13	118	...	62	...	88	12.3
		F	12	102	...	45	...	73	5.7
	1992								
		MF	9	109	...	62	...	84	11.6
		M	9	114	...	70	...	91	15.7
		F	8	104	...	53	...	77	7.2
	1993								
		MF	7	105	...	66	...	84	12.3
		M	7	109	...	74	...	90	16.7
		F	6	101	...	58	...	78	7.7
	1994								
		MF	7	101	...	69	...	84	12.7
		M	7	104	...	76	...	89	17.0
		F	7	97	...	62	...	78	8.2
Iraq‡	1980		(4-5)		(6-11)		(12-17)	(6-17)	(18-22)
		MF	9	113	99	57	47	89	8.7
		M	9	119	100	76	62	100	11.6
		F	9	107	94	38	31	77	5.6
	1985								
		MF	8	108	93	54	...	83	11.5
		M	9	116	99	68	...	94	14.4
		F	8	99	87	39	...	71	8.6
	1990								
		MF	8	111	...	47	...	82	12.6
		M	8	120	...	57	...	91	15.3
		F	7	102	...	36	...	72	9.8
	1992								
		MF	8	91	79	44	37	69	...
		M	8	98	83	53	44	77	...
		F	7	83	74	34	30	61	...
	1994								
		MF	7	...	...	...	...	...	...
		M	7	...	...	...	...	...	...
		F	7	...	...	...	...	...	...
Israel	1980		(2-5)		(6-13)		(14-17)	(6-17)	(18-22)
		MF	71	95		73	...	88	29.4
		M	73	...	...	...	...	...	28.0
		F	69	...	...	...	...	...	31.0
	1985								
		MF	77	97	...	80	...	92	33.1
		M	...	95	...	76	...	90	33.9
		F	...	98	...	85	...	94	32.2
	1990								
		MF	83	95	...	85	...	92	33.0
		M	...	93	...	82	...	90	33.0
		F	...	96	...	89	...	94	33.1
	1991								
		MF	83	96	...	88	...	93	34.1
		M	...	95	...	84	...	92	...
		F	...	96	...	91	...	94	...
	1992								
		MF	81	95	...	87	...	93	35.3
		M	...	95	...	84	...	91	35.3
		F	...	96	...	91	...	94	35.4
	1993								
		MF	80	95	...	86	...	92	34.2
		M	...	95	...	83	...	91	...
		F	...	95	...	89	...	93	...
Japan‡	1980		(3-5)		(6-11)		(12-17)	(6-17)	(18-22)
		MF	41	101	100	93	93	97	30.5
		M	41	101	100	92	92	97	40.4
		F	41	101	100	94	94	98	20.3

3.2 Enrolment ratios
Taux d'inscription
Tasas de escolarización

Country / Pays / País	Year / Année / Año	Sex / Sexe / Sexo	Pre-primary / Pré-primaire / Preprimaria — Gross / Brut / Bruta	First level / Premier degré / Primer grado — Gross / Brut / Bruta	First level — Net / Net / Neta	Second level / Second degré / Segundo grado — Gross / Brut / Bruta	Second level — Net / Net / Neta	1st + 2nd levels / 1er + 2nd degré / 1er + 2do grado — Gross / Brut / Bruta	3rd level / 3ème degré / 3er grado — Gross / Brut / Bruta
Japan‡ (cont)	1985								
		MF	46	102	100	95	95	98	27.8
		M	45	102	100	94	...	98	35.5
		F	46	102	100	96	...	99	19.8
	1990								
		MF	48	100	100	97	97	98	29.1
		M	48	100	100	96	...	98	35.1
		F	49	100	100	98	...	99	22.9
	1992								
		MF	49	101	100	95	...	98	...
		M	48	101	100	94	...	97	...
		F	49	101	100	97	...	99	...
	1993								
		MF	49	102	100	98	...	100	...
		M	49	102	100	98	...	100	...
		F	50	102	100	99	...	101	...
	1994								
		MF	49	102	100	...	...	...	...
		M	48	102	100	...	...	...	...
		F	49	102	100	...	...	...	...
Jordan	1980		(4-5)		(6-11)		(12-17)	(6-17)	(20-24)
		MF	12	104	93	75	68	91	26.6
		M	14	105	94	79	70	93	28.9
		F	11	102	91	73	60	90	24.2
	1989		(4-5)		(6-15)		(16-17)	(6-17)	(20-24)
		MF	21	97	91	63	42	92	24.5
		M	22	96	90	63	41	91	22.6
		F	19	96	92	62	43	93	26.7
	1992								
		MF	25	94	89	...	...	...	...
		M	27	94	89	...	...	...	...
		F	24	95	89	...	...	...	...
Kazakstan‡	1980		(3-6)		(7-10)		(11-17)	(7-17)	(18-22)
		MF	...	85	...	93	...	90	34.1
	1985								
		MF	...	88	...	103	...	97	36.8
	1990								
		MF	...	88	...	98	...	94	40.2
	1992								
		MF	...	88	...	93	...	91	38.8
	1993								
		MF	...	86	...	91	...	89	35.3
		M	...	86	...	89	...	88	31.1
		F	...	86	...	92	...	89	39.8
	1994								
		MF	...	87	...	...	...	...	33.6
		M	...	...	...	...	...	...	29.6
		F	...	...	...	...	...	...	37.8
Korea, Republic of	1980		(5)		(6-11)		(12-17)	(6-17)	(18-22)
		MF	8	110	100	78	70	94	14.7
		M	8	109	100	82	73	95	21.3
		F	7	111	100	74	67	92	7.5
	1985								
		MF	42	97	94	92	84	94	34.0
		M	43	96	94	93	85	94	45.8
		F	41	98	95	91	84	94	21.2
	1990								
		MF	55	105	100	90	86	97	38.6
		M	56	105	100	91	87	98	51.3
		F	55	105	100	88	85	96	25.1
	1993								
		MF	71	101	99	93	87	97	48.2
		M	71	100	98	93	88	97	60.4
		F	71	102	100	92	87	97	35.2

Enrolment ratios 3.2
Taux d'inscription
Tasas de escolarización

Country	Year	Sex	Enrolment ratios / Taux d'inscription / Tasas de escolarización						
			Pre-primary	First level		Second level		1st + 2nd levels	3rd level
Pays	Année	Sexe	Pré-primaire	Premier degré		Second degré		1er + 2nd degré	3ème degré
País	Año	Sexo	Preprimaria	Primer grado		Segundo grado		1er + 2do grado	3er grado
			Gross Brut Bruta	Gross Brut Bruta	Net Net Neta	Gross Brut Bruta	Net Net Neta	Gross Brut Bruta	Gross Brut Bruta
Korea, Republic of (cont)									
	1994								
		MF	80	98	96	96	92	97	50.8
		M	80	97	95	97	92	97	63.6
		F	80	99	97	96	92	97	37.3
	1995								
		MF	84	95	93	99	95	98	54.8
		M	84	95	93	100	95	97	67.9
		F	84	96	94	99	95	98	40.9
Kuwait‡	1980		(4-5)		(6-9)		(10-17)	(6-17)	(18-22)
		MF	37	102	85	80	...	89	11.3
		M	38	105	89	84	...	92	8.6
		F	36	100	80	76	...	85	14.8
	1985								
		MF	46	103	87	91	...	96	16.6
		M	47	104	88	95	...	99	15.3
		F	45	102	85	87	...	92	17.9
	1990								
		MF	33	60	...	43	...	50	15.0
		M	33	62	...	43	...	50	13.1
		F	33	59	...	43	...	49	16.8
	1992								
		MF	44	60	...	55	...	57	18.7
		M	44	60	...	55	...	57	16.8
		F	44	60	...	55	...	57	20.6
	1993								
		MF	45	65	55	60	56	62	...
		M	46	65	55	60	56	62	...
		F	44	65	54	60	55	62	...
	1994								
		MF	51	69	64	65	...	66	24.2
		M	51	69	64	65	...	66	21.5
		F	50	69	64	64	...	66	26.9
Kyrgyzstan‡	1980		(3-6)		(7-9)		(10-16)	(7-16)	(17-21)
		MF	...	116	...	110	...	112	26.7
		M	...	118	...	112	...	114	...
		F	...	115	...	108	...	110	...
	1985								
		MF	30	123	...	110	...	114	28.1
		M	30	123	...	111	...	115	...
		F	31	123	...	108	...	113	...
	1990								
		MF	34	112	...	101	...	104	25.8
		M	33	112	...	100	...	104	...
		F	34	112	...	102	...	105	...
	1992								
		MF	23	110	...	94	...	100	23.9
		M	23	110	...	93	...	98	...
		F	24	111	...	96	...	101	...
	1993								
		MF	14	111	...	89	...	96	20.1
		M	14	110	...	86	...	94	19.2
		F	14	112	...	91	...	98	21.0
	1994								
		MF	9	111	...	86	...	95	...
		M	...	110	...	84	...	93	...
		F	...	111	...	89	...	96	...
Lao People's Democratic Republic	1980		(3-5)		(6-10)		(11-16)	(6-16)	(17-21)
		MF	2	113	...	21	...	66	0.4
		M	2	123	...	25	...	73	0.6
		F	2	104	...	16	...	59	0.3
	1985								
		MF	6	111	...	23	...	67	1.6
		M	7	121	...	27	...	74	2.0
		F	6	100	...	19	...	59	1.1

3.2 Enrolment ratios
Taux d'inscription
Tasas de escolarización

			Enrolment ratios / Taux d'inscription / Tasas de escolarización						
			Pre-primary	First level		Second level		1st + 2nd levels	3rd level
Country	Year	Sex	Pré-primaire	Premier degré		Second degré		1er + 2nd degré	3ème degré
Pays	Année	Sexe						1er + 2do	3er
País	Año	Sexo	Preprimaria	Primer grado		Segundo grado		grado	grado
			Gross Brut Bruta	Gross Brut Bruta	Net Net Neta	Gross Brut Bruta	Net Net Neta	Gross Brut Bruta	Gross Brut Bruta
Lao People's Democratic Rep. (cont)	1989								
		MF	7	103	68	25	...	64	1.2
		M	7	117	...	31	...	74	1.7
		F	7	88	...	20	...	54	0.8
	1991								
		MF	6	98	59	22	15	60	...
		M	6	112	66	27	17	70	...
		F	6	84	53	17	13	51	...
	1992								
		MF	6	104	64	24	15	64	1.4
		M	6	119	71	30	18	75	2.0
		F	7	89	57	18	13	54	0.8
	1993								
		MF	7	107	68	25	18	67	1.5
		M	6	123	75	31	21	78	2.2
		F	7	92	61	19	15	56	0.8
Lebanon	1980		(3-5)	(6-10)		(11-17)		(6-17)	(18-22)
		MF	59	111	...	59	...	82	30.1
		M	...	...	...	...	...	...	40.5
		F	...	...	...	...	...	...	20.6
	1985								
		MF	...	...	...	...	...	...	27.8
	1988								
		MF	71	118	...	66	...	87	...
		M	72	121	...	65	...	88	...
		F	69	115	...	68	...	87	...
	1991								
		MF	68	118	...	74	...	93	28.9
		M	69	120	...	71	...	92	29.6
		F	68	116	...	76	...	93	28.2
	1993								
		MF	73	115	...	76	...	93	...
		M	74	117	...	73	...	92	...
		F	71	114	...	78	...	93	...
	1994								
		MF	74	112	...	79	...	94	...
		M	75	114	...	75	...	92	...
		F	73	110	...	83	...	95	...
Malaysia	1980		(4-5)	(6-11)		(12-18)		(6-18)	(19-23)
		MF	23	93	...	48	...	70	4.1
		M	...	93	...	50	...	71	5.2
		F	...	92	...	46	...	68	3.1
	1985								
		MF	37	101	...	53	...	75	5.9
		M	...	101	...	53	...	76	6.6
		F	...	100	...	53	...	75	5.2
	1990								
		MF	31	93	...	58	...	76	7.2
		M	31	93	...	56	...	75	7.4
		F	32	93	...	60	...	77	6.8
	1992								
		MF	36	93	...	60	...	77	9.2
		M	35	93	...	58	...	76	...
		F	36	94	...	62	...	79	...
	1993								
		MF	35	93	...	61	...	78	9.6
		M	34	93	...	58	...	76	...
		F	35	93	...	64	...	79	...
	1994								
		MF	...	93	...	61	...	78	...
		M	...	93	...	...	...	...	...
		F	...	94	...	...	...	...	...
Maldives	1980		(4-5)	(6-10)		(11-17)		(6-17)	(18-22)
		MF	...	145	...	4	...	70	-

Enrolment ratios **3.2**
Taux d'inscription
Tasas de escolarización

Country / Pays / País	Year / Année / Año	Sex / Sexe / Sexo	Pre-primary / Pré-primaire / Preprimaria — Gross / Brut / Bruta	First level / Premier degré / Primer grado — Gross / Brut / Bruta	First level — Net / Net / Neta	Second level / Second degré / Segundo grado — Gross / Brut / Bruta	Second level — Net / Net / Neta	1st + 2nd levels / 1er + 2nd degré / 1er + 2do grado — Gross / Brut / Bruta	3rd level / 3ème degré / 3er grado — Gross / Brut / Bruta
Maldives (cont)	1992								
		MF	21	130	...	44	...	85	-
		M	22	132	...	44	...	86	-
		F	20	128	...	44	...	85	-
	1993								
		MF	59	134	...	49	...	90	-
		M	59	136	...	49	...	91	-
		F	59	133	...	49	...	89	-
Mongolia	1980		(4-7)		(8-10)		(11-17)	(8-17)	(18-22)
		MF	25	107	...	91	...	96	...
		M	...	107	...	85	...	92	...
		F	...	107	...	97	...	100	...
	1985								
		MF	28	101	...	92	...	95	21.6
	1990								
		MF	39	97	...	86	...	90	14.4
		M	...	95	...	...	...	...	...
		F	...	100	...	...	...	...	...
	1991								
		MF	38	88	...	77	...	81	12.7
	1994								
		MF	...	84	78	60	56	68	13.6
		M	...	82	76	50	47	60	8.2
		F	...	87	81	70	66	75	19.2
Myanmar‡	1980		(4)		(5-9)		(10-15)	(5-15)	(16-20)
		MF	...	91	...	22	...	56	4.7
		M	...	93	...	...	...	...	...
		F	...	89	...	...	...	...	...
	1985								
		MF	...	98	...	23	...	58	4.5
		M	...	101	...	24	...	60	4.2
		F	...	96	...	22	...	56	4.8
	1990								
		MF	...	105	...	23	...	62	4.3
		M	...	107	...	23	...	63	3.8
		F	...	104	...	23	...	61	4.9
	1992								
		MF	...	110	...	25	...	66	5.3
		M	...	112	...	...	...	...	4.4
		F	...	108	...	...	...	...	6.2
	1993								
		MF	...	106	...	26	...	65	5.1
	1994								
		MF	...	100	...	30	...	65	...
Nepal	1980		(3-5)		(6- 8)		(9-15)	(6-15)	(16-20)
		MF	...	84	...	21	...	43	2.7
		M	...	117	...	33	...	62	4.2
		F	...	49	...	9	...	23	1.1
	1985		(3-5)		(6-10)		(11-15)	(6-15)	(16-20)
		MF	...	75	...	25	...	52	4.3
		M	...	101	...	37	...	72	...
		F	...	47	...	12	...	31	...
	1990								
		MF	...	103	...	31	...	70	4.9
		M	...	128	...	43	...	89	7.5
		F	...	77	...	18	...	50	2.3
	1991								
		MF	...	105	...	33	...	72	5.6
		M	...	127	...	45	...	89	8.5
		F	...	81	...	20	...	53	2.7
	1992								
		MF	...	109	...	35	...	74	5.1
		M	...	130	...	46	...	91	...
		F	...	87	...	23	...	57	...

3.2 Enrolment ratios
Taux d'inscription
Tasas de escolarización

Country / Pays / País	Year / Année / Año	Sex / Sexe / Sexo	Pre-primary / Pré-primaire / Preprimaria — Gross Brut Bruta	First level / Premier degré / Primer grado — Gross Brut Bruta	First level — Net Net Neta	Second level / Second degré / Segundo grado — Gross Brut Bruta	Second level — Net Net Neta	1st + 2nd levels / 1er + 2nd degré / 1er + 2do grado — Gross Brut Bruta	3rd level / 3ème degré / 3er grado — Gross Brut Bruta
Nepal (cont)	1993								
		MF	...	109	...	36	...	75	4.8
		M	...	129	...	...	...	...	...
		F	...	88	...	...	...	...	...
Oman‡	1980		(4-5)		(6-11)		(12-17)	(6-17)	(18-22)
		MF	1	52	44	12	11	35	0.0
		M	1	69	56	19	16	47	0.0
		F	0.5	36	32	6	5	23	-
	1985								
		MF	2	75	65	28	...	55	0.9
		M	2	83	69	38	...	65	1.0
		F	2	66	62	18	...	46	0.7
	1990								
		MF	3	85	70	45	...	68	4.2
		M	3	89	72	50	...	73	4.6
		F	3	81	67	40	...	63	3.8
	1992								
		MF	3	86	73	55	...	73	4.9
		M	4	90	74	59	...	77	5.0
		F	3	83	71	52	...	69	4.9
	1993								
		MF	3	85	73	61	52	74	...
		M	4	87	74	64	55	77	...
		F	3	82	72	57	50	71	...
	1994								
		MF	4	83	72	64	...	74	...
		M	4	85	74	67	...	77	...
		F	3	80	71	61	...	72	...
Pakistan‡	1980		(3-4)		(5-9)		(10-16)	(5-16)	(17-21)
		MF	...	39	...	14	...	25	...
		M	...	51	...	20	...	34	...
		F	...	27	...	8	...	16	...
	1985								
		MF	...	44	...	17	...	29	2.5
		M	...	56	...	24	...	38	3.5
		F	...	30	...	10	...	19	1.4
	1990								
		MF	...	56	...	23	...	39	2.9
		M	...	76	...	30	...	52	3.7
		F	...	36	...	15	...	25	2.0
	1991								
		MF	...	60	...	25	...	42	...
		M	...	81	...	33	...	56	...
		F	...	39	...	17	...	28	...
	1992								
		MF	...	64	...	...	...	...	...
		M	...	87	...	...	...	...	...
		F	...	41	...	...	...	...	...
	1993								
		MF	...	69	...	...	...	...	...
		M	...	94	...	...	...	...	...
		F	...	42	...	...	...	...	...
Philippines	1980		(5-6)		(7-12)		(13-16)	(7-16)	(17-21)
		MF	4	112	94	64	45	94	24.4
		M		114	95	60	42	94	22.5
		F	...	110	92	69	48	94	26.2
	1985								
		MF	6	107	96	64	50	91	24.9
		M	6	108	97	64	49	91	...
		F	7	107	96	65	50	91	...
	1990								
		MF	12	113	...	73	...	98	27.4
		M	...	...	...	...	...	...	23.0
		F	...	...	...	...	...	...	31.9

Enrolment ratios 3.2
Taux d'inscription
Tasas de escolarización

Country / Pays / País	Year / Année / Año	Sex / Sexe / Sexo	Pre-primary / Pré-primaire / Preprimaria — Gross / Brut / Bruta	First level / Premier degré / Primer grado — Gross / Brut / Bruta	First level — Net / Net / Neta	Second level / Second degré / Segundo grado — Gross / Brut / Bruta	Second level — Net / Net / Neta	1st + 2nd levels / 1er + 2nd degré / 1er + 2do grado — Gross / Brut / Bruta	3rd level / 3ème degré / 3er grado — Gross / Brut / Bruta
Philippines (cont)	1992								
		MF	...	112	99	77	59	99	26.5
		M	...	...	...	...	...	...	22.1
		F	...	...	...	...	...	...	30.9
	1993								
		MF	12	111	97	79	60	99	26.8
		M	...	110	...	...	...	...	21.7
		F	...	111	...	...	...	...	32.0
	1994								
		MF	...	111	...	80	...	99	...
Qatar	1980		(4-5)		(6-11)		(12-17)	(6-17)	(18-22)
		MF	25	105	85	66	51	87	10.4
		M	26	108	88	64	50	87	6.3
		F	23	103	83	68	52	87	17.1
	1985								
		MF	33	109	91	82	66	97	20.7
		M	34	110	88	78	63	97	12.7
		F	31	107	94	86	69	98	33.8
	1990								
		MF	28	97	87	81	67	90	27.0
		M	29	101	88	77	64	91	14.7
		F	27	94	85	84	70	90	42.9
	1992								
		MF	28	89	79	84	70	87	28.6
		M	31	91	80	82	68	87	15.1
		F	26	86	78	86	72	86	44.5
	1993								
		MF	31	90	81	83	69	87	27.3
		M	33	92	81	82	68	88	15.0
		F	30	87	80	84	71	86	41.6
	1994								
		MF	30	87	...	82	...	84	27.5
		M	32	89	...	82	...	86	14.8
		F	29	84	...	82	...	83	42.1
Saudi Arabia	1980		(4-5)		(6-11)		(12-17)	(6-17)	(18-22)
		MF	5	61	49	29	21	47	7.1
		M	5	74	60	36	26	57	9.0
		F	4	49	37	23	16	37	4.6
	1985								
		MF	6	65	51	40	27	54	10.6
		M	7	73	60	48	32	62	11.8
		F	6	57	42	31	22	46	9.2
	1990								
		MF	7	73	59	44	31	60	11.6
		M	8	78	65	49	34	65	12.2
		F	7	68	53	39	28	55	10.9
	1991								
		MF	8	73	59	45	32	61	11.9
		M	7	77	64	50	30	65	13.5
		F	8	69	54	41	34	57	10.1
	1992								
		MF	8	75	61	49	34	63	13.7
		M	9	78	65	54	38	67	14.1
		F	8	73	57	43	30	59	13.2
	1993								
		MF	8	77	63	52	37	66	13.9
		M	7	79	66	57	41	69	14.9
		F	9	75	59	47	33	62	12.8
Singapore‡	1980		(4-5)		(6-11)		(12-17)	(6-17)	(18-22)
		MF	13	108	99	58	...	81	7.8
		M	13	109	100	56	...	81	9.1
		F	13	106	99	59	...	81	6.3
	1985		(4-5)		(6-11)		(12-18)	(6-18)	(19-23)
		MF	21	115	...	62	...	85	14.4
		M	21	117	...	61	...	85	17.6
		F	20	113	...	64	...	85	11.0

3.2 Enrolment ratios
Taux d'inscription
Tasas de escolarización

| Country

Pays

País | Year

Année

Año | Sex

Sexe

Sexo | Enrolment ratios / Taux d'inscription / Tasas de escolarización |||||||
| | | | Pre-primary

Pré-primaire

Preprimaria | First level

Premier degré

Primer grado || Second level

Second degré

Segundo grado || 1st + 2nd levels

1er + 2nd degré

1er + 2do grado | 3rd level

3ème degré

3er grado |
			Gross Brut Bruta	Gross Brut Bruta	Net Net Neta	Gross Brut Bruta	Net Net Neta	Gross Brut Bruta	Gross Brut Bruta
Singapore‡ (cont)	1990								
		MF	21	107	...	69	...	86	24.5
		M	22	...	...	...	...	...	28.2
		F	21	...	...	...	...	...	20.7
	1991								
		MF	...	107	...	68	...	86	27.2
		M	...	...	...	...	...	...	30.7
		F	...	...	...	...	...	...	23.4
	1993								
		MF		...	...	...	...	...	33.6
		M		...	...	...	...	...	37.2
		F		...	...	...	...	...	29.8
	1994								
		MF		...	...	...	...	...	35.2
		M		...	...	...	...	...	38.2
		F		...	...	...	...	...	31.8
Sri Lanka‡	1980		(4)		(5-10)		(11-17)	(5-17)	(18-22)
		MF	...	103	...	55	...	77	2.7
		M	...	105	...	52	...	77	3.1
		F	...	100	...	57	...	77	2.4
	1985								
		MF	...	103	...	63	...	82	3.7
		M	...	104	...	60	...	81	4.4
		F	...	101	...	66	...	83	3.0
	1990		(4)		(5-9)		(10-17)	(5-17)	(18-22)
		MF	...	105	...	74	...	87	5.2
		M	...	106	...	71	...	85	6.2
		F	...	104	...	77	...	88	4.1
	1992								
		MF	...	105	...	74	...	86	5.4
		M	...	106	...	71	...	85	6.4
		F	...	104	...	78	...	88	4.4
	1993								
		MF	...	106	...	74	...	86	...
		M	...	106	...	71	...	85	...
		F	...	105	...	78	...	88	...
	1994								
		MF	...	105	...	75	...	87	6.1
		M	...	106	...	71	...	85	7.1
		F	...	104	...	79	...	89	5.0
Syrian Arab Republic	1980		(3-5)		(6-11)		(12-17)	(6-17)	(18-22)
		MF	4	100	89	46	39	75	16.9
		M	4	111	99	57	48	86	23.4
		F	3	88	80	35	30	64	10.1
	1985								
		MF	6	110	98	58	51	87	17.1
		M	6	117	100	69	59	95	21.6
		F	5	103	92	48	43	78	12.4
	1990								
		MF	6	109	99	52	46	84	18.3
		M	7	115	100	60	53	91	21.9
		F	6	103	93	44	39	77	14.6
	1992								
		MF	6	107	96	48	44	81	17.6
		M	7	112	100	54	49	87	20.2
		F	6	101	92	43	39	75	14.8
	1993								
		MF	6	105	95	47	42	79	...
		M	7	111	100	52	47	85	...
		F	6	99	91	42	38	74	...
	1994								
		MF	6	103	93	45	40	77	...
		M	7	108	98	50	44	82	...
		F	6	97	89	41	37	72	...
Tajikistan‡	1980		(3-6)		(7-10)		(11-17)	(7-17)	(18-22)
		MF	13	...	...	...	...	...	23.6

Enrolment ratios **3.2**
Taux d'inscription
Tasas de escolarización

Country / Pays / País	Year / Année / Año	Sex / Sexe / Sexo	Pre-primary / Pré-primaire / Preprimaria — Gross Brut Bruta	First level / Premier degré / Primer grado — Gross Brut Bruta	First level — Net Net Neta	Second level / Second degré / Segundo grado — Gross Brut Bruta	Second level — Net Net Neta	1st + 2nd levels / 1er + 2nd degré / 1er + 2do grado — Gross Brut Bruta	3rd level / 3ème degré / 3er grado — Gross Brut Bruta
Tajikistan‡ (cont)	1985	MF	...	...	...	...	...	...	20.1
	1990	MF	16	91	...	...	...	...	22.3
		M	...	92	...	...	...	...	...
		F	...	90	...	...	...	...	...
	1992	MF	11	85	...	91	...	89	24.8
		M	...	87	...	94	...	91	...
		F	...	84	...	88	...	86	...
	1993	MF	11	89	...	79	...	83	...
		M	...	91	...	83	...	86	...
		F	...	88	...	75	...	80	...
	1994	MF	10	89	...	...	...	...	...
		M	...	91	...	...	...	...	...
		F	...	88	...	...	...	...	...
Thailand‡	1980		(4-6)		(7-12)		(13-18)	(7-18)	(19-23)
		MF	10	99	...	29	...	66	14.7
		M	10	100	...	30	...	67	...
		F	10	97	...	28	...	65	...
	1985	MF	18	96	...	30	...	63	19.0
	1990		(3-5)		(6-11)		(12-17)	(6-17)	(18-22)
		MF	44	99	...	30	...	64	15.7
		M	43	100	...	31	...	64	...
		F	44	99	...	29	...	63	...
	1992	MF	50	98	...	37	...	67	18.7
		M	49	98	...	38	...	67	17.5
		F	50	97	...	37	...	66	20.0
	1993	MF	45	88	...	44	...	66	...
	1994	MF	51	87	...	49	...	68	20.6
Turkey	1980		(4-5)		(6-10)		(11-16)	(6-16)	(17-21)
		MF	0.4	96	...	35	...	64	5.4
		M	1	102	...	44	...	72	7.7
		F	0.3	90	...	24	...	56	2.9
	1985	MF	5	113	98	42	36	74	8.9
		M	5	117	...	52	...	81	11.6
		F	5	110	...	30	...	67	6.0
	1990	MF	4	110	100	54	48	81	12.9
		M	5	115	...	66	...	89	16.5
		F	4	106	...	42	...	72	9.0
	1991	MF	5	108	98	57	50	81	13.9
		M	5	113	...	69	...	90	17.7
		F	5	103	...	44	...	73	9.8
	1992	MF	5	103	93	61	54	81	15.7
		M	5	107	...	74	...	89	19.9
		F	5	98	...	48	...	72	11.2
	1993	MF	5	97	90	64	56	80	19.6
		M	5	101	92	76	67	88	23.9
		F	5	94	87	50	46	71	15.1
Turkmenistan	1980		(3-6)		(7-10)		(11-17)	(7-17)	(18-22)
		MF	...	...	...	...	...	...	22.5
	1985	MF	...	...	...	...	...	...	22.4

3.2   Enrolment ratios
Taux d'inscription
Tasas de escolarización

Country Pays País	Year Année Año	Sex Sexe Sexo	Enrolment ratios / Taux d'inscription / Tasas de escolarización						
			Pre-primary Pré-primaire Preprimaria	First level Premier degré Primer grado		Second level Second degré Segundo grado		1st + 2nd levels 1er + 2nd degré 1er + 2do grado	3rd level 3ème degré 3er grado
			Gross Brut Bruta	Gross Brut Bruta	Net Net Neta	Gross Brut Bruta	Net Net Neta	Gross Brut Bruta	Gross Brut Bruta
Turkmenistan (cont)	1990								
		MF	...	...	...	...	...	...	21.8
United Arab Emirates	1980		(4-5)		(6-11)		(12-17)	(6-17)	(18-22)
		MF	37	89	74	52	...	75	3.1
		M	40	90	72	55	...	76	2.4
		F	35	88	75	49	...	73	4.6
	1985								
		MF	63	110	86	61	...	89	7.6
		M	65	110	86	61	...	90	5.4
		F	61	109	86	62	...	89	10.6
	1990								
		MF	59	119	100	77	68	101	10.9
		M	60	120	100	72	64	99	5.7
		F	58	119	100	82	73	104	17.6
	1992								
		MF	61	110	100	83	74	99	10.5
		M	62	111	100	78	70	97	5.6
		F	60	109	99	89	79	101	16.5
	1993								
		MF	64	110	100	89	79	101	...
		M	66	112	100	84	75	100	...
		F	62	108	99	94	84	102	...
	1994								
		MF	64	110	100	92	83	103	...
		M	65	112	100	88	79	102	...
		F	62	108	99	97	87	104	...
Uzbekistan‡	1980		(3-5)		(6-9)		(10-16)	(6-16)	(17-21)
		MF	66	82	...	106	...	96	28.5
		M	...	83	...	117	...	104	...
		F	...	80	...	94	...	88	...
	1985								
		MF	71	87	...	107	...	99	30.1
		M	...	88	...	117	...	106	...
		F	...	85	...	97	...	92	...
	1990								
		MF	73	82	...	100	...	93	30.6
		M	...	83	...	104	...	95	...
		F	...	81	...	95	...	90	...
	1992								
		MF	63	76	...	95	...	87	31.8
		M	64	76	...	100	...	90	...
		F	62	76	...	90	...	84	...
	1993								
		MF	60	77	...	93	...	86	...
		M	61	77	...	98	...	90	...
		F	59	77	...	88	...	83	...
	1994								
		MF	54	77	...	93	...	87	...
		M	55	78	...	99	...	90	...
		F	53	76	...	87	...	83	...
Viet Nam	1980		(3-5)		(6-10)		(11-17)	(6-17)	(18-22)
		MF	35	109	95	42	...	71	2.1
		M	33	111		44	...	73	3.4
		F	37	106	...	40	...	68	0.9
	1985								
		MF	33	103	...	43	...	69	2.4
		M	31	106	...	44	...	71	...
		F	35	100	...	41	...	67	...
	1990								
		MF	28	103	...	33	...	64	2.8
	1992								
		MF	28	108	...	32	...	66	...
	1993								
		MF	30	111	...	35	...	68	3.2

Enrolment ratios **3.2**
Taux d'inscription
Tasas de escolarización

Country / Pays / País	Year / Année / Año	Sex / Sexe / Sexo	Pre-primary / Pré-primaire / Preprimaria Gross Brut Bruta	First level / Premier degré / Primer grado Gross Brut Bruta	First level Net Net Neta	Second level / Second degré / Segundo grado Gross Brut Bruta	Second level Net Net Neta	1st + 2nd levels / 1er + 2nd degré / 1er + 2do grado Gross Brut Bruta	3rd level / 3ème degré / 3er grado Gross Brut Bruta
Viet Nam (cont)	1994								
		MF	...	114	...	41	...	73	...
Yemen	1990		(3-5)		(6-14)		(15-17)	(6-17)	(18-22)
		MF	1	...	...	...	...	...	...
		M	1	...	...	...	...	...	...
		F	1	...	...	...	...	...	...
	1991								
		MF	1	...	...	...	...	...	4.4
		M	1	...	...	...	...	...	7.0
		F	1	...	...	...	...	...	1.5
	1993								
		MF	1	83	...	23	...	70	...
		M	1	118	...	37	...	100	...
		F	1	47	...	9	...	39	...
Europe									
Albania	1980		(3-5)		(6-13)		(14-17)	(6-17)	(18-22)
		MF	46	113	...	67	...	98	7.6
		M	...	116	...	70	...	100	7.5
		F	...	111	...	63	...	95	7.8
	1985								
		MF	52	103	...	72	...	93	10.5
		M	...	104	...	75	...	95	10.3
		F	...	102	...	68	...	91	10.7
	1990								
		MF	59	100	...	78	...	93	10.0
		M	...	100	...	84	...	95	10.0
		F	...	100	...	72	...	91	10.0
	1992								
		MF	...	...	...	...	...	...	10.4
		M	...	...	...	...	...	...	10.2
		F	...	...	...	...	...	...	10.5
	1993								
		MF	35	96	...	40	...	78	9.5
		M	...	95	...	38	...	77	8.7
		F	...	97	...	41	...	79	10.4
	1994								
		MF	35	98	...	36	...	79	...
		M	...	98	...	36	...	78	...
		F	...	99	...	37	...	79	...
Austria	1980		(3-5)		(6-9)		(10-17)	(6-17)	(18-22)
		MF	63	99	99	93	...	94	21.9
		M	63	99	99	98	...	98	25.2
		F	63	98	98	87	...	90	18.5
	1985								
		MF	71	100	...	99	...	99	26.4
		M	72	101	...	103	...	102	28.4
		F	71	99	...	94	...	95	24.3
	1990								
		MF	70	102	...	104	...	103	35.2
		M	70	102	...	107	...	105	37.5
		F	70	102	...	100	...	101	32.8
	1991								
		MF	70	103	...	106	...	105	38.3
		M	71	103	...	109	...	107	40.3
		F	70	103	...	102	...	103	36.1
	1992								
		MF	72	104	100	107	91	106	40.6
		M	72	104	100	110	92	108	42.3
		F	72	104	100	104	91	104	38.7
	1993								
		MF	75	103	100	107	91	105	43.2
		M	75	103	100	109	91	107	44.6
		F	75	103	100	104	91	104	41.8

3.2 Enrolment ratios
Taux d'inscription
Tasas de escolarización

			Enrolment ratios / Taux d'inscription / Tasas de escolarización						
Country	Year	Sex	Pre-primary	First level		Second level		1st + 2nd levels	3rd level
Pays	Année	Sexe	Pré-primaire	Premier degré		Second degré		1er + 2nd degré	3ème degré
País	Año	Sexo	Preprimaria	Primer grado		Segundo grado		1er + 2do grado	3er grado
			Gross Brut Bruta	Gross Brut Bruta	Net Net Neta	Gross Brut Bruta	Net Net Neta	Gross Brut Bruta	Gross Brut Bruta
Belarus	1980		(3-6)		(7-11)		(12-16)	(7-16)	(17-21)
		MF	58	104	...	98	...	101	39.0
	1985								
		MF	67	109	...	99	...	104	44.9
	1990		(3-5)		(6-9)		(10-16)	(6-16)	(17-21)
		MF	84	95	...	93	...	94	45.9
		M	...	...	...	...	...	...	44.6
		F	...	...	...	...	...	...	47.1
	1992								
		MF	79	96	...	91	...	93	44.5
		M	...	96	...	88	...	91	43.1
		F	...	96	...	95	...	95	45.9
	1993								
		MF	79	96	...	92	...	94	42.4
		M	...	96	...	89	...	92	40.9
		F	...	95	...	96	...	96	43.8
	1994								
		MF	82	97	97	94	...	95	...
		M	88	98	98	92	...	94	...
		F	76	95	95	97	...	96	...
Belgium	1980		(3-5)		(6-11)		(12-17)	(6-17)	(18-22)
		MF	103	104	97	91	...	97	26.0
		M	103	104	97	90	...	97	28.9
		F	104	103	98	92	...	98	23.0
	1985								
		MF	110	99	94	102	89	100	32.2
		M	111	99	94	101	87	100	34.3
		F	110	99	95	102	90	101	30.0
	1990								
		MF	105	100	97	103	88	102	40.2
		M	105	100	96	103	86	101	40.7
		F	105	101	98	103	89	102	39.6
	1991								
		MF	111	99	96	103	88	101	...
		M	111	99	95	103	87	101	...
		F	111	100	97	104	90	102	...
Bulgaria	1980		(4-6)		(7-14)		(15-17)	(7-17)	(18-22)
		MF	104	98	96	84	73	94	16.2
		M	105	98	96	85	73	95	13.8
		F	104	98	96	84	72	94	18.7
	1985								
		MF	93	102	...	102	...	102	18.9
		M	94	103	...	101	...	102	16.8
		F	92	102	...	102	...	102	21.2
	1990								
		MF	89	95	84	73	61	87	30.2
		M	88	96	84	71	60	87	28.7
		F	89	94	83	75	63	87	31.7
	1992								
		MF	79	89	80	70	61	82	30.4
		M	80	90	80	68	59	83	25.5
		F	79	88	79	72	62	82	35.5
	1993		(3-6)		(7-14)		(15-18)	(7-18)	(19-23)
		MF	56	86	82	68	57	79	32.2
		M	56	87	83	66	57	80	25.9
		F	56	84	81	70	58	79	38.7
	1994								
		MF	57	86	83	70	58	80	34.3
		M	57	88	84	68	57	81	26.5
		F	56	84	82	72	58	80	42.5
Croatia	1980		(3-6)		(7-14)		(15-18)	(7-18)	(19-23)
		MF	...	...	...	...	...	...	19.0

Enrolment ratios **3.2**
Taux d'inscription
Tasas de escolarización

Country / Pays / País	Year / Année / Año	Sex / Sexe / Sexo	Pre-primary / Pré-primaire / Preprimaria — Gross Brut Bruta	First level / Premier degré / Primer grado — Gross Brut Bruta	First level — Net Net Neta	Second level / Second degré / Segundo grado — Gross Brut Bruta	Second level — Net Net Neta	1st + 2nd levels / 1er + 2nd degré / 1er + 2do grado — Gross Brut Bruta	3rd level / 3ème degré / 3er grado — Gross Brut Bruta
Croatia (cont)	1985								
		MF	...	105	...	...	...	...	17.7
		M	...	105	...	...	...	...	...
		F	...	106	...	...	...	...	...
	1990								
		MF	...	85	79	77	66	82	23.9
		M	...	85	79	73	63	81	...
		F	...	84	79	80	69	83	...
	1992								
		MF	23	86	...	77	...	83	25.7
		M	24	86	...	73	...	82	26.2
		F	23	85	...	81	...	84	25.2
	1993								
		MF	26	87	...	83	...	86	27.2
		M	27	87	...	80	...	85	27.9
		F	25	87	...	86	...	87	26.5
	1994								
		MF	29	86	82	78	66	84	27.1
		M	30	87	83	75	63	83	27.0
		F	29	86	82	81	68	84	27.2
Czech Republic	1980		(3-5)		(6-9)		(10-17)	(6-17)	(18-22)
		MF	...	...	...	...	...	...	17.5
	1985								
		MF	...	99	...	...	...	...	16.2
	1990								
		MF	95	96	...	...	...	...	16.0
	1992								
		MF	88	99	...	88	...	91	14.6
		M	...	99	...	86	...	90	15.9
		F	...	99	...	90	...	93	13.2
	1993								
		MF	88	99	...	86	...	90	18.3
		M	...	99	...	85	...	89	18.9
		F	...	100	...	88	...	91	17.8
	1994								
		MF	88	100	...	92	...	94	19.2
		M	...	100	...	90	...	93	19.9
		F	...	100	...	94	...	96	18.4
Denmark	1980		(6)		(7-12)		(13-18)	(7-18)	(19-23)
		MF	88	96	96	105	88	100	28.3
		M	88	96	96	105	87	101	28.3
		F	88	95	95	104	89	100	28.3
	1985								
		MF	94	99	99	105	83	102	29.1
		M	94	99	99	106	83	102	28.8
		F	94	98	98	105	84	102	29.5
	1990								
		MF	99	98	98	109	87	104	36.5
		M	99	98	98	108	86	104	34.1
		F	99	98	98	110	88	105	39.0
	1991								
		MF	101	97	97	110	87	104	38.7
		M	101	96	96	109	86	103	35.8
		F	101	97	97	111	88	105	41.7
	1992								
		MF	98	97	97	114	87	106	40.9
		M	98	97	97	112	86	105	38.0
		F	98	98	97	115	88	107	44.0
	1993								
		MF	100	99	99	115	...	107	44.8
		M	100	99	99	113	...	106	42.7
		F	99	99	99	117	...	109	47.1

3.2 Enrolment ratios
Taux d'inscription
Tasas de escolarización

Country / Pays / País	Year / Année / Año	Sex / Sexe / Sexo	Enrolment ratios / Taux d'inscription / Tasas de escolarización						
			Pre-primary / Pré-primaire / Preprimaria	First level / Premier degré / Primer grado		Second level / Second degré / Segundo grado		1st + 2nd levels / 1er + 2nd degré / 1er + 2do grado	3rd level / 3ème degré / 3er grado
			Gross Brut Bruta	Gross Brut Bruta	Net Net Neta	Gross Brut Bruta	Net Net Neta	Gross Brut Bruta	Gross Brut Bruta
Estonia‡	1980		(3-5)		(6-11)		(12-16)	(6-16)	(17-21)
		MF	...	98	...		...	...	24.4
		M	...	98	...	...	...	...	21.7
		F	...	98	...	...	...	...	27.4
	1985								
		MF	...	97	...	116	...	105	23.9
		M	...	96	...	110	...	102	19.4
		F	...	98	...	122	...	108	28.6
	1990		(3-6)		(7-11)		(12-17)	(7-17)	(18-22)
		MF	74	105	94	95	...	100	26.0
		M	75	107	94	88	...	97	25.2
		F	73	103	93	101	...	102	27.0
	1992								
		MF	60	101	91	92	82	96	24.6
		M	60	102	91	90	81	95	23.7
		F	60	100	95	94	84	97	25.5
	1993								
		MF	62	99	89	91	80	95	23.4
		M	61	99	88	83	76	91	21.9
		F	62	99	90	97	83	98	25.0
	1994								
		MF	69	101	90	91	...	96	24.0
		M	69	103	90	92	...	97	22.2
		F	69	100	90	90	...	95	25.8
Finland	1980		(3-6)		(7-12)		(13-18)	(7-18)	(19-23)
		MF	27	96	...	100	...	98	32.2
		M	...	97	...	94	...	95	32.5
		F	...	96	...	105	...	101	31.8
	1985								
		MF	28	102	...	106	...	104	34.1
		M	...	103	...	98	...	100	34.2
		F	...	102	...	114	...	108	34.0
	1990								
		MF	34	99	...	116	93	107	48.9
		M	...	99	...	106	92	103	46.0
		F	...	99	...	127	94	112	52.0
	1991								
		MF	35	99	...	121	...	110	52.7
		M	...	99	...	109	...	104	48.9
		F	...	99	...	133	...	115	56.6
	1992								
		MF	36	100	...	123	...	111	58.7
		M	36	100	...	112	...	106	54.1
		F	35	99	...	135	...	117	63.5
	1993								
		MF	37	100	...	119	...	110	63.2
		M	37	100	...	110	...	105	58.2
		F	37	100	...	130	...	115	68.5
France	1980		(2-5)		(6-10)		(11-17)	(6-17)	(18-22)
		MF	76	111	100	85	79	95	25.3
		M	77	112	...	77	...	92	...
		F	76	110	...	92	...	99	...
	1985								
		MF	89	109	97	90	82	97	29.8
		M	89	110	97	86	78	95	29.2
		F	88	107	97	94	85	99	30.3
	1990								
		MF	83	108	100	99	...	103	39.6
		M	83	109	100	96	...	101	36.6
		F	83	108	100	101	...	104	42.8
	1992								
		MF	83	106	99	102	86	103	46.1
		M	83	107	99	100	85	103	41.4
		F	83	105	99	104	89	104	51.0

Enrolment ratios **3.2**
Taux d'inscription
Tasas de escolarización

Country	Year	Sex	Enrolment ratios / Taux d'inscription / Tasas de escolarización						
			Pre-primary	First level		Second level		1st + 2nd levels	3rd level
Pays	Année	Sexe	Pré-primaire	Premier degré		Second degré		1er + 2nd degré	3ème degré
País	Año	Sexo	Preprimaria	Primer grado		Segundo grado		1er + 2do grado	3er grado
			Gross Brut Bruta	Gross Brut Bruta	Net Net Neta	Gross Brut Bruta	Net Net Neta	Gross Brut Bruta	Gross Brut Bruta
France (cont)	1993								
		MF	84	106	99	106	90	106	49.7
		M	85	107	99	104	88	105	44.2
		F	84	105	99	107	92	106	55.4
	1994								
		MF	84	105	...	...	...	...	...
Germany	1990		(3-5)		(6-9)		(10-18)	(6-18)	(19-23)
		MF	...	101	...	98	...	99	33.9
	1991								
		MF	94	99	...	100	...	100	35.0
		M	...	98	...	101	...	100	40.0
		F	...	100	...	99	...	99	29.8
	1992								
		MF	101	98	98	101	85	100	32.9
		M	101	97	97	102	85	100	38.5
		F	101	98	98	100	86	99	27.0
	1993								
		MF	101	97	97	101	86	100	35.6
		M	101	97	97	101	85	100	41.1
		F	101	98	98	100	86	99	29.7
Greece	1980		(4-5)		(6-11)		(12-17)	(6-17)	(18-22)
		MF	54	103	96	81	...	92	17.1
		M	53	103	96	85	...	94	19.6
		F	54	103	97	77	...	89	14.5
	1985								
		MF	57	104	99	90	81	97	24.2
		M	56	104	99	92	81	98	23.6
		F	57	104	99	89	81	97	24.8
	1990								
		MF	55	98	94	99	88	98	25.5
		M	55	97	93	100	87	98	24.6
		F	56	98	94	98	89	98	26.6
	1991								
		MF	57	96	93	101	88	99	25.9
		M	56	96	92	101	87	99	24.9
		F	58	97	93	100	89	98	26.9
	1992								
		MF	60	95	91	97	86	96	39.9
		M	58	94	91	97	84	96	39.1
		F	61	95	91	98	88	97	40.7
	1993								
		MF	61	95	91	98	86	96	42.5
		M	61	95	91	99	86	97	43.9
		F	62	95	91	96	86	95	40.9
Hungary	1980		(3-5)		(6-13)		(14-17)	(6-17)	(18-22)
		MF	96	96	95	70	...	88	14.1
		M	97	96	94	72	...	89	13.9
		F	95	97	95	67	...	88	14.4
	1985								
		MF	91	99	97	72	70	91	15.4
		M	91	99	97	72	69	91	13.9
		F	91	99	98	72	70	91	16.9
	1990								
		MF	113	95	91	79	75	89	14.0
		M	115	95	91	78	73	89	13.6
		F	111	95	92	79	76	89	14.4
	1992								
		MF	116	94	...	...	...	...	15.1
		M	...	...	...	...	...	...	14.6
		F	...	...	...	...	...	...	15.7
	1993								
		MF	114	95	92	81	75	90	16.9
		M	115	95	91	79	72	89	15.6
		F	112	95	92	82	77	90	18.2

3.2 Enrolment ratios
Taux d'inscription
Tasas de escolarización

Country	Year	Sex	Enrolment ratios / Taux d'inscription / Tasas de escolarización						
			Pre-primary	First level		Second level		1st + 2nd levels	3rd level
Pays	Année	Sexe	Pré-primaire	Premier degré		Second degré		1er + 2nd degré	3ème degré
País	Año	Sexo	Preprimaria	Primer grado		Segundo grado		1er + 2do grado	3er grado
			Gross Brut Bruta	Gross Brut Bruta	Net Net Neta	Gross Brut Bruta	Net Net Neta	Gross Brut Bruta	Gross Brut Bruta
Hungary (cont)									
	1994	MF	111	97	93	81	73	91	...
		M	112	97	92	79	71	90	...
		F	109	97	94	83	76	91	...
Iceland	1980		(5-6)		(7-12)		(13-19)	(7-19)	(20-24)
		MF	48	99	...	86		92	16.9
		M	...	...	...	...	...	...	13.1
		F	...	...	...	...	...	...	21.0
	1985	MF	55	99	...	91	...	94	21.1
		M	54	99	...	95	...	96	18.4
		F	56	99	...	87	...	92	23.8
	1990	MF	49	103	...	100	...	101	24.8
		M	48	104	...	103	...	103	20.8
		F	49	102	...	97	...	99	28.9
	1991	MF	46	102	...	102	...	102	29.6
		M	45	104	...	105	...	105	24.1
		F	48	101	...	99	...	100	35.4
	1992	MF	46	100	...	103	...	102	27.0
		M	46	102	...	105	...	104	22.3
		F	46	98	...	101	...	100	32.0
	1993	MF	48	98	...	105	...	102	28.8
		M	49	100	...	105	...	103	25.0
		F	47	96	...	105	...	101	32.6
Ireland	1980		(4-5)		(6-11)		(12-16)	(6-16)	(17-21)
		MF	97	100	100	90	78	95	18.1
		M	98	100	100	85	75	93	21.1
		F	96	100	100	95	80	98	15.0
	1985	MF	106	100	100	98	81	99	22.3
		M	107	100	100	93	79	97	24.8
		F	105	100	100	103	84	101	19.8
	1990	MF	102	103	100	101	80	102	29.3
		M	102	103	100	96	78	100	30.8
		F	101	103	100	105	82	104	27.7
	1991	MF	104	103	100	102	81	103	32.5
		M	104	103	100	98	79	101	33.4
		F	104	103	100	107	83	105	31.4
	1992	MF	106	103	100	105	82	104	34.2
		M	106	103	100	101	80	102	34.5
		F	106	103	100	110	84	106	33.9
	1993	MF	106	104	100	113	84	108	36.4
		M	107	104	100	110	82	107	36.7
		F	106	104	100	115	86	109	36.1
Italy	1980		(3-5)		(6-10)		(11-18)	(6-18)	(19-23)
		MF	78	100	...	72	...	82	27.0
		M	78	100	...	73	...	83	30.6
		F	79	100	...	70	...	81	23.3
	1985	MF	85	96	...	73	...	81	25.5
		M	85	97	...	74	...	82	27.0
		F	85	96	...	73	...	81	23.8
	1990	MF	92	97	...	79	...	85	30.8
		M	92	97	...	79	...	85	31.8
		F	93	97	...	79	...	85	29.8

Enrolment ratios **3.2**
Taux d'inscription
Tasas de escolarización

Country Pays País	Year Année Año	Sex Sexe Sexo	Enrolment ratios / Taux d'inscription / Tasas de escolarización						
			Pre- primary Pré- primaire Preprimaria	First level Premier degré Primer grado		Second level Second degré Segundo grado		1st + 2nd levels 1er + 2nd degré 1er + 2do grado	3rd level 3ème degré 3er grado
			Gross Brut Bruta	Gross Brut Bruta	Net Net Neta	Gross Brut Bruta	Net Net Neta	Gross Brut Bruta	Gross Brut Bruta
Italy (cont)	1991								
		MF	93	99	...	80	...	86	32.9
		M	93	99	...	80	...	86	32.6
		F	94	99	...	80	...	86	33.2
	1992								
		MF	95	100	...	81	...	87	35.2
		M	94	98	...	81	...	87	34.1
		F	95	101	...	81	...	88	36.3
	1993								
		MF	95	98	...	81	...	87	37.3
		M	95	98	...	81	...	87	35.9
		F	96	99	...	82	...	87	38.8
Latvia	1980		(3-6)		(7-10)		(11-18)	(7-18)	(19-23)
		MF	58	77	...	100	...	92	23.5
		M	57	78	...	...	...	...	19.7
		F	58	77	...	...	...	...	27.6
	1985								
		MF	66	80	...	102	...	95	22.5
		M	...	79	...	...	...	...	17.9
		F	...	80	...	...	...	...	27.3
	1990								
		MF	55	95	...	93	...	94	25.2
		M	55	95	...	93	...	94	21.9
		F	56	94	...	93	...	94	28.7
	1992								
		MF	36	87	83	87	...	87	23.0
		M	36	88	84	87	...	87	21.0
		F	36	87	83	88	...	88	25.2
	1993								
		MF	34	83	...	87	77	85	21.4
		M	34	83	...	84	...	84	18.3
		F	34	82	...	90	...	87	24.7
	1994								
		MF	39	83	81	86	78	85	21.8
		M	40	85	83	84	...	84	18.9
		F	38	81	79	89	...	86	24.7
Lithuania	1980		(3-6)		(7-10)		(11-18)	(7-18)	(19-23)
		MF	51	79	...	113	...	102	34.6
		M	...	79	...	...	...	...	28.2
		F	...	78	...	...	...	...	41.3
	1985								
		MF	64	80	...	104	...	96	32.3
		M	...	80	...	...	...	...	23.3
		F	...	80	...	...	...	...	41.4
	1990								
		MF	58	89	...	91	...	90	34.0
		M	...	91	...	...	...	...	...
		F	...	88	...	...	...	...	...
	1992								
		MF	40	91	...	83	...	86	28.5
		M	...	93	...	82	...	86	24.1
		F	...	90	...	83	...	85	33.2
	1993								
		MF	34	92	...	81	...	85	26.5
		M	34	95	...	...	...	...	21.6
		F	35	90	...	...	...	...	31.6
	1994								
		MF	33	96	...	82	81	87	26.7
		M	...	97	...	80	80	86	21.8
		F	...	95	...	84	83	88	31.7
Luxembourg‡	1980		(4-5)		(6-11)		(12-18)	(6-18)	(19-23)
		MF	93	87	77	71	...	78	2.6
		M	93	86	76	79	...	82	3.3
		F	93	88	78	62	...	73	1.8

3.2 Enrolment ratios
Taux d'inscription
Tasas de escolarización

Country / Pays / País	Year / Année / Año	Sex / Sexe / Sexo	Enrolment ratios / Taux d'inscription / Tasas de escolarización						
			Pre-primary / Pré-primaire / Preprimaria	First level / Premier degré / Primer grado		Second level / Second degré / Segundo grado		1st + 2nd levels / 1er + 2nd degré / 1er + 2do grado	3rd level / 3ème degré / 3er grado
			Gross Brut Bruta	Gross Brut Bruta	Net Net Neta	Gross Brut Bruta	Net Net Neta	Gross Brut Bruta	Gross Brut Bruta
Luxembourg‡ (cont)	1985								
		MF	95	89	81	75	66	81	2.6
		M	...	88	80	76	66	81	3.4
		F	...	89	82	74	67	80	1.8
	1990								
		MF	93	91	...	74	...	82	...
		M	...	88	...	...	...	...	...
		F	...	94	...	...	...	...	...
	1991								
		MF	95	...	...	78	...	...	...
		M	...	...	...	76	...	...	...
		F	...	...	...	79	...	...	...
	1992								
		MF	...	...	...	78	...	...	...
		M	...	...	...	78	...	...	...
		F	...	...	...	78	...	...	...
	1993								
		MF	103	...	...	...	...	...	...
Malta	1980		(4)		(5-10)		(11-17)	(5-17)	(18-22)
		MF	145	113	98	75	71	93	3.2
		M	150	114	99	80	73	96	4.7
		F	140	112	98	70	69	90	1.6
	1985								
		MF	139	107	97	78	74	92	5.8
		M	141	109	97	79	73	94	7.6
		F	136	104	96	77	75	90	3.9
	1990		(3-4)		(5-10)		(11-17)	(5-17)	(18-22)
		MF	105	110	99	85	80	96	13.0
		M	108	112	100	88	81	99	14.1
		F	101	107	98	82	80	94	11.7
	1991								
		MF	110	107	99	88	82	97	14.8
		M	109	109	100	91	83	99	15.3
		F	111	105	98	84	82	94	14.2
	1992								
		MF	113	108	100	88	83	97	18.6
		M	113	109	100	91	83	99	18.9
		F	114	106	99	84	82	94	18.4
	1993								
		MF	115	108	99	88	83	97	20.0
		M	115	110	100	93	85	101	19.8
		F	115	107	98	83	80	94	20.2
Moldova	1980		(3-6)		(7-10)		(11-18)	(7-18)	(19-23)
		MF	58	83	...	78	...	80	29.7
		M	60	83	...	78	...	80	...
		F	57	82	...	78	...	80	...
	1985								
		MF	66	84	...	86	...	85	32.8
		M	68	85	...	83	...	84	...
		F	65	84	...	89	...	87	...
	1990								
		MF	73	93	...	80	...	85	35.5
		M	74	93	...	77	...	83	...
		F	71	93	...	83	...	87	...
	1992								
		MF	61	92	...	75	...	81	...
		M	62	92	...	71	...	78	...
		F	60	91	...	78	...	83	...
	1993								
		MF	57	90	...	74	...	80	31.6
		M	58	90	...	70	...	78	...
		F	56	90	...	77	...	82	...
	1994								
		MF	49	94	...	72	...	80	30.4
		M	51	95	...	71	...	79	28.2
		F	48	94	...	74	...	81	32.6

Enrolment ratios 3.2
Taux d'inscription
Tasas de escolarización

Country / Pays / País	Year / Année / Año	Sex / Sexe / Sexo	Pre-primary / Pré-primaire / Preprimaria — Gross Brut Bruta	First level / Premier degré / Primer grado — Gross Brut Bruta	First level — Net Net Neta	Second level / Second degré / Segundo grado — Gross Brut Bruta	Second level — Net Net Neta	1st + 2nd levels / 1er + 2nd degré / 1er + 2do grado — Gross Brut Bruta	3rd level / 3ème degré / 3er grado — Gross Brut Bruta
Netherlands	1980		(4-5)		(6-11)		(12-17)	(6-17)	(18-22)
		MF	107	100	93	93	81	96	29.3
		M	108	99	91	95	80	97	34.7
		F	106	101	94	90	82	95	23.8
	1985								
		MF	106	99	92	117	89	109	31.8
		M	105	98	91	120	87	110	36.8
		F	107	100	94	114	90	108	26.6
	1990								
		MF	99	102	95	120	84	111	39.8
		M	99	101	93	124	83	113	43.4
		F	100	104	97	115	85	110	36.1
	1991								
		MF	99	98	95	121	84	110	42.2
		M	98	97	93	125	83	111	45.2
		F	101	99	96	116	86	108	39.1
	1992								
		MF	98	97	94	123	86	110	44.8
		M	98	96	92	126	84	111	47.5
		F	98	99	96	120	87	110	42.1
	1993								
		MF	97	97	93	123	...	110	47.1
		M	96	96	92	129	...	112	49.7
		F	97	98	95	118	...	108	44.4
Norway	1980		(4-6)		(7-12)		(13-18)	(7-18)	(19-23)
		MF	44	100	98	94	84	97	25.5
		M	...	100	98	92	82	96	26.0
		F	...	100	99	96	86	98	25.0
	1985								
		MF	66	97	96	97	86	97	29.6
		M	...	97	96	95	84	96	27.8
		F	...	97	96	100	88	98	31.6
	1990								
		MF	88	100	100	103	88	102	42.3
		M	...	100	100	101	87	101	38.8
		F	...	100	100	105	88	103	46.0
	1991								
		MF	96	100	100	105	89	103	46.1
		M	...	100	100	105	88	103	42.0
		F	...	101	100	106	89	103	50.3
	1992								
		MF	106	100	99	113	90	106	50.3
		M	...	100	99	114	90	107	45.8
		F	...	100	99	111	90	106	55.1
	1993								
		MF	113	99	99	116	92	108	54.4
		M	...	99	99	118	92	109	49.2
		F	...	99	99	114	92	107	59.9
Poland	1980		(3-6)		(7-14)		(15-18)	(7-18)	(19-23)
		MF	55	100	98	77	70	92	18.1
		M	...	100	98	75	68	91	15.6
		F	...	99	98	80	74	92	20.7
	1985								
		MF	51	101	99	78	73	94	17.1
		M	...	102	100	76	70	94	14.8
		F	...	100	99	81	76	94	19.5
	1990								
		MF	47	98	97	81	76	93	21.7
		M	...	99	97	80	73	93	18.7
		F	...	98	97	83	79	93	25.0
	1992								
		MF	41	98	96	83	77	93	23.4
		M	...	99	96	81	74	93	20.0
		F	...	97	96	85	81	94	27.1

3.2 Enrolment ratios
Taux d'inscription
Tasas de escolarización

Country Pays País	Year Année Año	Sex Sexe Sexo	Enrolment ratios / Taux d'inscription / Tasas de escolarización						
			Pre-primary Pré-primaire Preprimaria	First level Premier degré Primer grado		Second level Second degré Segundo grado		1st + 2nd levels 1er + 2nd degré 1er + 2do grado	3rd level 3ème degré 3er grado
			Gross Brut Bruta	Gross Brut Bruta	Net Net Neta	Gross Brut Bruta	Net Net Neta	Gross Brut Bruta	Gross Brut Bruta
Poland (cont)	1993								
		MF	42	98	96	84	78	93	27.5
		M	...	98	96	82	74	93	23.3
		F	...	97	96	87	82	94	31.9
	1994								
		MF	45	99	97	96	83	98	...
		M	...	100	97	95	80	98	...
		F	...	98	97	96	86	97	...
Portugal	1980		(3-5)	(6-11)		(12-17)		(6-17)	(18-22)
		MF	20	123	98	37	...	79	10.7
		M	20	124	97	34	...	78	10.7
		F	20	123	100	40	...	80	10.7
	1985								
		MF	30	129	100	57	...	92	12.3
		M	30	132	100	53	...	92	11.3
		F	30	125	100	62	...	93	13.3
	1990								
		MF	49	118	97	68	...	92	22.6
		M	49	120	97	63	...	90	19.7
		F	49	115	98	74	...	93	25.6
	1991								
		MF	...	120	100	79	...	98	23.4
		M	...	122	100	...	...	...	18.1
		F	...	118	100	...	...	...	28.8
	1992								
		MF	...	...	...	...	...	...	30.6
		M	...	...	...	...	...	...	30.3
		F	...	...	...	...	...	...	30.9
	1993								
		MF	53	117	...	84	...	99	34.5
Romania	1980		(3-5)	(6-13)		(14-17)		(6-17)	(18-22)
		MF	83	102	...	71	...	93	12.1
		M	83	102	...	73	...	94	13.6
		F	84	101	...	69	...	92	10.5
	1985								
		MF	75	98	...	84	...	93	10.0
		M	74	98	...	87	...	94	10.7
		F	76	98	...	81	...	92	9.1
	1990		(3-5)	(6-9)		(10-17)		(6-17)	(18-22)
		MF	76	91	...	92	...	92	...
		M	75	91	...	92	...	92	...
		F	78	91	...	92	...	91	...
	1992								
		MF	76	86	86	82	72	84	11.8
		M	74	87	87	83	71	84	12.4
		F	78	86	86	82	73	83	11.3
	1993		(3-6)	(7-10)		(11-18)		(7-18)	(19-23)
		MF	53	87	87	79	73	82	12.9
		M	52	87	87	78	72	81	13.5
		F	54	86	86	80	74	82	12.3
	1994								
		MF	53	94	94	78	72	83	...
		M	52	94	94	77	71	83	...
		F	54	93	93	78	73	83	...
Russian Federation	1980		(3-6)	(7-9)		(10-16)		(7-16)	(17-21)
		MF	67	102	...	96	...	98	46.1
		M	...	102	...	95	...	97	39.5
		F	...	102	...	97	...	99	53.1
	1985								
		MF	73	104	...	97	...	99	54.3
		M	...	104	...	96	...	98	45.9
		F	...	104	...	98	...	100	62.9
	1990								
		MF	74	109	...	94	...	99	52.2
		M	...	109	...	91	...	97	46.1
		F	...	109	...	96	...	100	58.6

Enrolment ratios 3.2
Taux d'inscription
Tasas de escolarización

Country Pays País	Year Année Año	Sex Sexe Sexo	Enrolment ratios / Taux d'inscription / Tasas de escolarización						
			Pre-primary Pré-primaire Preprimaria	First level Premier degré Primer grado			Second level Second degré Segundo grado		1st + 2nd levels 1er + 2nd degré 1er + 2do grado	3rd level 3ème degré 3er grado
			Gross Brut Bruta	Gross Brut Bruta	Net Net Neta	Gross Brut Bruta	Net Net Neta	Gross Brut Bruta	Gross Brut Bruta
Russian Federation (cont)	1992								
		MF	65	109	...	89	...	95	47.0
		M	...	109	...	86	...	93	41.2
		F	...	109	...	93	...	98	53.0
	1993								
		MF	63	107	96	88	...	94	45.3
		M	66	107	96	84	...	91	40.5
		F	60	107	96	91	...	96	50.2
	1994								
		MF	...	109	94	...	...	...	43.3
		M	...	109	94	...	...	...	37.7
		F	...	108	94	...	...	...	49.0
Slovakia	1980		(3-5)	(6-9)		(10-17)		(6-17)	(18-22)
		MF	81	...	...	...	...	...	...
	1985	MF	87	...	...	...	...	...	...
	1990	MF	86	...	...	...	...	...	...
	1992								
		MF	78	101	...	88	...	92	16.1
		M	...	101	...	86	...	91	16.4
		F	...	101	...	90	...	93	15.8
	1993								
		MF	77	101	...	89	...	93	17.1
		M	...	101	...	87	...	91	17.2
		F	...	101	...	90	...	94	17.0
	1994								
		MF	74	101	...	90	...	93	18.7
		M	...	101	...	88	...	92	18.7
		F	...	101	...	93	...	95	18.7
Slovenia	1991		(3-6)	(7-10)		(11-18)		(7-18)	(19-23)
		MF	...	...	...	...	...	...	27.0
		M	...	...	...	...	...	...	25.0
		F	...	...	...	...	...	...	29.1
	1992								
		MF	57	96	...	89	...	91	27.6
		M	58	96	...	88	...	90	24.6
		F	56	96	...	91	...	92	30.7
	1993								
		MF	61	97	...	89	...	91	28.1
		M	62	97	...	88	...	90	24.4
		F	60	97	...	90	...	92	32.0
	1994								
		MF	63	100	96	90	...	93	30.1
		M	65	100	96	89	...	92	25.6
		F	61	100	97	91	...	94	34.8
Spain	1980		(2-5)	(6-10)		(11-17)		(6-17)	(18-22)
		MF	44	109	100	87	74	96	23.2
		M	43	110	100	85	74	95	25.7
		F	46	109	100	89	74	97	20.5
	1985								
		MF	51	110	100	98	...	103	28.5
		M	51	111	100	95	...	101	28.5
		F	52	109	100	102	...	105	28.6
	1990								
		MF	58	107	100	105	...	106	36.7
		M	56	107	100	101	...	103	35.1
		F	59	108	100	109	...	109	38.5
	1991								
		MF	61	105	100	108	87	107	39.1
		M	61	105	99	103	86	104	37.1
		F	62	105	100	112	89	110	41.1

3.2 Enrolment ratios
Taux d'inscription
Tasas de escolarización

			Enrolment ratios / Taux d'inscription / Tasas de escolarización						
Country Pays País	Year Année Año	Sex Sexe Sexo	Pre- primary Pré- primaire Preprimaria	First level Premier degré Primer grado		Second level Second degré Segundo grado		1st + 2nd levels 1er + 2nd degré 1er + 2do grado	3rd level 3ème degré 3er grado
			Gross Brut Bruta	Gross Brut Bruta	Net Net Neta	Gross Brut Bruta	Net Net Neta	Gross Brut Bruta	Gross Brut Bruta
Spain (cont)	1992								
		MF	65	105	100	110	90	108	41.1
		M	64	105	99	105	88	105	38.7
		F	66	105	100	115	92	112	43.7
	1993								
		MF	67	104	...	113	...	110	44.1
		M	67	104	...	107	...	106	42.1
		F	68	105	...	120	...	114	46.2
Sweden	1980		(4-6)		(7-12)		(13-18)	(7-18)	(19-23)
		MF	71	97	...	88	...	92	30.8
		M	...	96	...	83	...	90	...
		F	...	97	...	93	...	95	...
	1985		(3-6)		(7-12)		(13-18)	(7-18)	(19-23)
		MF	62	98	...	91	...	94	30.0
		M	...	...	...	...	...	...	28.1
		F	...	...	...	...	...	...	32.1
	1990								
		MF	65	100	100	90	85	95	32.0
		M	...	100	100	88	85	94	28.9
		F	...	100	100	92	86	96	35.3
	1991								
		MF	67	100	100	92	86	96	34.6
		M	...	100	100	90	86	95	31.1
		F	...	101	100	94	87	97	38.3
	1992								
		MF	67	101	100	96	90	99	38.3
		M	...	101	100	96	90	98	34.6
		F	...	101	100	97	91	99	42.1
	1993								
		MF	65	100	99	99	93	100	40.1
		M	64	100	100	99	93	100	35.6
		F	67	100	99	100	94	100	44.9
Switzerland‡	1980		(4-6)		(7-12)		(13-19)	(7-19)	(20-24)
		MF	53	...	...	...	...	90	18.3
		M	53	...	...	...	...	92	25.6
		F	53	...	...	...	...	87	11.1
	1985								
		MF	57	95	95	88	78	91	21.0
		M	57	94	94	92	82	93	28.1
		F	56	95	95	83	74	88	13.7
	1990								
		MF	60	102	100	90	79	95	25.7
		M	60	101	100	83	81	96	32.5
		F	60	103	100	87	76	94	18.4
	1991								
		MF	59	103	100	91	79	96	27.4
		M	59	102	100	93	81	97	34.4
		F	59	104	100	88	77	95	19.9
	1992								
		MF	59	102	100	91	79	96	28.9
		M	60	101	100	94	82	97	36.0
		F	59	103	100	89	77	95	21.4
	1993								
		MF	91	101	...	91	...	95	30.6
		M	92	100	...	93	...	96	37.7
		F	90	102	...	89	...	95	23.0
The Former Yugoslav Rep. of Macedonia	1980		(3-6)		(7-14)		(15-18)	(7-18)	(19-23)
		MF	...	100	...	61	...	87	27.5
	1985								
		MF	...	101	...	56	...	86	22.6
	1990								
		MF	...	93	93	53	...	80	15.5
		M	...	93	93	...	...	...	14.7
		F	...	92	92	...	...	...	16.5

Enrolment ratios 3.2
Taux d'inscription
Tasas de escolarización

Country / Pays / País	Year / Année / Año	Sex / Sexe / Sexo	Enrolment ratios / Taux d'inscription / Tasas de escolarización						
			Pre-primary Pré-primaire Preprimaria	First level Premier degré Primer grado		Second level Second degré Segundo grado		1st + 2nd levels 1er + 2nd degré 1er + 2do grado	3rd level 3ème degré 3er grado
			Gross Brut Bruta	Gross Brut Bruta	Net Net Neta	Gross Brut Bruta	Net Net Neta	Gross Brut Bruta	Gross Brut Bruta
The Former Yugoslav Rep. of Macedonia (cont)	1992								
		MF	21	89	...	54	...	78	15.5
		M	21	89	...	53	...	78	14.6
		F	21	88	...	55	...	78	16.5
	1993								
		MF	21	87	...	54	...	77	16.1
		M	22	88	...	53	...	77	14.8
		F	21	87	...	55	...	77	17.6
	1994								
		MF	23	87	87	55	49	77	17.1
		M	23	88	88	55	49	77	15.3
		F	23	87	87	56	50	77	19.1
Ukraine	1980		(3-6)	(7-11)		(12-16)		(7-16)	(17-21)
		MF	60	102	...	94	...	98	41.6
		M	...	103	...	...	...	...	...
		F	...	102	...	...	...	...	...
	1985								
		MF	65	103	...	96	...	100	46.9
		M	68	...	...	...	...	...	...
		F	62	...	...	...	...	...	...
	1990		(3- 5)	(6-11)		(12-16)		(6-16)	(17-21)
		MF	85	89	...	93	...	91	46.5
		M	89	89	...	...	...	...	44.8
		F	82	89	...	...	...	...	48.2
	1991								
		MF	84	90	...	91	...	90	45.9
		M	86	90	...	...	...	...	44.9
		F	81	89	...	...	...	...	46.9
	1992		(3-6)	(7-10)		(11-17)		(7-17)	(18-22)
		MF	56	88	...	91	...	90	...
		M	59	89	...	88	...	88	...
		F	53	87	...	95	...	92	...
	1993								
		MF	54	87	...	92	...	90	...
		M	57	87	...	88	...	88	...
		F	51	87	...	95	...	92	...
United Kingdom‡	1980		(3-4)	(5-10)		(11-17)		(5-17)	(18-22)
		MF	42	103	100	83	79	92	19.1
		M	42	103	100	82	78	91	23.7
		F	42	103	100	85	81	93	14.3
	1985								
		MF	49	104	100	84	80	92	21.7
		M	50	104	100	82	78	91	23.1
		F	48	105	100	86	82	93	20.1
	1990								
		MF	51	104	100	86	80	95	29.1
		M	51	104	100	85	79	94	29.5
		F	51	105	100	88	81	96	28.8
	1991								
		MF	52	103	100	90	82	96	33.0
		M	52	103	100	88	81	95	33.1
		F	52	104	100	92	84	97	32.9
	1992								
		MF	27	112	100	92	85	102	37.4
		M	27	112	100	91	83	101	36.9
		F	27	113	100	94	86	103	37.9
	1993								
		MF	27	114	100	94	...	103	40.6
		M	27	114	100	93	...	103	39.4
		F	27	114	100	95	...	104	41.9
Federal Republic of Yugoslavia‡	1990		(3-6)	(7-10)		(11-18)		(7-18)	(19-23)
		MF	...	72	69	63	62	66	...
		M	...	71	69	62	61	66	...
		F	...	73	70	64	63	67	...

3.2 Enrolment ratios
Taux d'inscription
Tasas de escolarización

Country Pays País	Year Année Año	Sex Sexe Sexo	Enrolment ratios / Taux d'inscription / Tasas de escolarización						
			Pre-primary Pré-primaire Preprimaria	First level Premier degré Primer grado		Second level Second degré Segundo grado		1st + 2nd levels 1er + 2nd degré 1er + 2do grado	3rd level 3ème degré 3er grado
			Gross Brut Bruta	Gross Brut Bruta	Net Net Neta	Gross Brut Bruta	Net Net Neta	Gross Brut Bruta	Gross Brut Bruta
Federal Republic of Yugoslavia‡ (cont)									
	1991								
		MF	41	72	...	65	...	67	18.0
		M	41	72	...	64	...	66	16.7
		F	41	73	...	65	...	68	19.3
	1992								
		MF	25	72	...	65	...	67	18.9
		M	25	72	...	64	...	66	17.3
		F	25	73	...	65	...	68	20.7
	1993								
		MF	23	70	...	62	...	64	18.3
		M	23	68	...	61	...	63	16.3
		F	23	71	...	63	...	66	20.4
Oceania									
Australia	1980		(5)		(6-11)		(12-17)	(6-17)	(18-22)
		MF	68	112	100	71	70	92	25.4
		M	68	113	100	70	69	91	27.2
		F	67	111	100	72	71	92	23.5
	1985								
		MF	71	107	98	80	78	93	27.7
		M	72	107	98	79	77	93	28.3
		F	71	106	98	81	79	93	27.0
	1990								
		MF	71	108	99	82	79	94	35.5
		M	71	108	99	80	77	94	32.8
		F	71	107	99	83	80	95	38.2
	1992								
		MF	71	108	99	84	80	96	40.7
		M	71	108	99	83	79	96	37.2
		F	70	108	99	86	82	97	44.4
	1993								
		MF	71	108	98	84	81	96	41.9
		M	71	108	98	83	79	95	38.2
		F	71	107	99	86	82	96	45.7
	1994								
		MF	72	107	...	84	...	96	40.9
		M	72	107	...	83	...	95	37.0
		F	72	106	...	86	...	96	44.8
Fiji	1980		(3-5)		(6-11)		(12-17)	(6-17)	(18-22)
		MF	9	119	92	55	...	88	2.5
		M	9	119	92	53	...	88	...
		F	9	119	92	57	...	89	...
	1985								
		MF	7	122	97	51	...	90	3.2
		M	...	122	97	51	...	90	3.9
		F	...	122	97	51	...	89	2.4
	1990								
		MF	13	125	...	...	...	...	...
		M	13	...	...	...	...	...	...
		F	14	...	...	...	...	...	...
	1991								
		MF	14	126	100	61	...	96	11.9
		M	...	126	100	62	...	96	...
		F	...	126	100	60	...	95	...
	1992								
		MF	15	128	99	64	...	97	...
		M	15	128	99	64	...	97	...
		F	16	127	100	65	...	97	...
French Polynesia‡	1987		(3-5)		(6-10)		(11-17)	(6-17)	(18-22)
		MF	102	129	...	62	...	90	...
		M	103	134	...	...	...	...	...
		F	102	123	...	...	...	...	...
	1990								
		MF	108	129	...	70	61	95	...
		M	108	131	...	64	...	93	...
		F	108	126	...	75	...	97	...

Enrolment ratios 3.2
Taux d'inscription
Tasas de escolarización

Country / Pays / País	Year / Année / Año	Sex / Sexe / Sexo	Pre-primary / Pré-primaire / Preprimaria	First level / Premier degré / Primer grado		Second level / Second degré / Segundo grado		1st + 2nd levels / 1er + 2nd degré / 1er + 2do grado	3rd level / 3ème degré / 3er grado
			Gross Brut Bruta	Gross Brut Bruta	Net Net Neta	Gross Brut Bruta	Net Net Neta	Gross Brut Bruta	Gross Brut Bruta
French Polynesia‡ (cont)	1992								
		MF	106	125	100	77	...	98	1.1
		M	107	127	100	68	...	94	1.1
		F	104	123	100	87	...	103	1.1
	1994								
		MF	101	120	100	...	...	...	...
		M	102	122	100	...	...	...	...
		F	99	118	100	...	...	...	...
New Caledonia	1985		(3-5)		(6-10)		(11-17)	(6-17)	(18-22)
		MF	82	122	89	74	...	94	5.1
		M	82	126	89	69	...	93	5.8
		F	82	118	88	78	...	95	4.5
	1990								
		MF	99	128	97	79	69	99	...
		M	98	129	96	76	65	98	...
		F	99	126	97	83	73	100	...
	1991								
		MF	...	125	98	85	72	101	...
		M	...	125	98	82	69	100	...
		F	...	124	99	88	75	102	...
	1992								
		MF	...	123	...	...	...	...	...
	1994								
		MF	113	123	...	...	...	...	...
New Zealand	1980		(3-4)		(5-10)		(11-17)	(5-17)	(18-22)
		MF	73	111	100	83	81	96	27.0
		M	73	111	100	82	81	95	31.4
		F	74	111	100	84	82	96	22.5
	1985								
		MF	91	107	100	85	84	94	33.1
		M	91	108	100	84	83	94	35.3
		F	92	106	100	87	85	95	30.8
	1990		(2-4)		(5-10)		(11-17)	(5-17)	(18-22)
		MF	74	106	100	89	85	96	39.7
		M	74	106	100	88	84	96	37.8
		F	74	105	100	90	86	96	41.7
	1992								
		MF	81	102	99	95	88	98	51.9
		M	82	103	99	95	87	98	47.3
		F	80	101	98	95	89	98	56.6
	1993								
		MF	77	102	...	104	...	103	57.5
		M	77	102	...	103	...	103	51.9
		F	77	101	...	104	...	103	63.3
	1994								
		MF	75	102	99	112	95	107	59.8
		M	75	103	100	111	93	107	52.5
		F	74	101	99	114	96	108	67.3
Papua New-Guinea‡	1980		(5-6)		(7-12)		(13-18)	(7-18)	(19-23)
		MF	...	59	...	12	...	38	1.8
		M	...	66	...	15	...	43	2.7
		F	...	51	...	8	...	32	0.9
	1985								
		MF	...	...	...	...	...	...	1.6
		M	...	...	...	...	...	...	2.2
		F	...	...	...	...	...	...	0.8
	1990								
		MF	...	72	...	12	...	44	...
		M	...	78	...	15	...	48	...
		F	...	66	...	10	...	39	...
	1993								
		MF	...	78	...	14	...	48	...
		M	...	84	...	17	...	52	...
		F	...	71	...	12	...	44	...

3.2 Enrolment ratios
Taux d'inscription
Tasas de escolarización

Country / Pays / País	Year / Année / Año	Sex / Sexe / Sexo	Enrolment ratios / Taux d'inscription / Tasas de escolarización						
			Pre-primary / Pré-primaire / Preprimaria	First level / Premier degré / Primer grado		Second level / Second degré / Segundo grado		1st + 2nd levels / 1er + 2nd degré / 1er + 2do grado	3rd level / 3ème degré / 3er grado
			Gross Brut Bruta	Gross Brut Bruta	Net Net Neta	Gross Brut Bruta	Net Net Neta	Gross Brut Bruta	Gross Brut Bruta
Papua New Guinea‡ (cont)	1994								
		MF	1	81	...	15	...	50	...
		M	1	88	...	18	...	55	...
		F	1	74	...	12	...	46	...
	1995								
		MF	1	82	...	14	...	50	3.2
		M	1	88	...	17	...	55	4.2
		F	1	75	...	11	...	46	2.1
Solomon Islands	1980			(7-12)		(13-17)		(7-17)	(18-22)
		MF	...	76	...	16	...	52	...
		M	...	85	...	22	...	59	...
		F	...	65	...	9	...	43	...
	1985			(6-11)		(12-16)		(6-16)	(17-21)
		MF	...	79	...	19	...	55	...
	1990								
		MF	...	84	...	14	...	55	...
		M	...	90	...	17	...	60	...
		F	...	78	...	11	...	50	...
	1992								
		MF	...	90	...	16	...	59	...
		M	...	97	...	19	...	65	...
		F	...	82	...	12	...	53	...
	1993								
		MF	...	94	...	17	...	62	...
		M	...	102	...	21	...	68	...
		F	...	87	...	13	...	56	...
	1994								
		MF	...	97	...	17	...	64	...
		M	...	104	...	21	...	69	...
		F	...	90	...	14	...	58	...
Vanuatu, Republic of	1985			(6-11)		(12-18)		(6-18)	(19-23)
		MF	...	100	...	...	...	...	...
	1988								
		MF	...	102	...	...	...	...	-
	1989								
		MF	...	109	74	16	15	65	-
		M	...	112	76	18	16	69	-
		F	...	106	72	14	13	62	-
	1990								
		MF	...	106	...	...	...	...	-
		M	...	109	...	...	...	...	-
		F	...	103	...	...	...	...	-
	1991								
		MF	...	105	...	18	17	65	-
		M	...	108	...	21	19	68	-
		F	...	102	...	16	15	61	-
	1992								
		MF	...	106	...	20	...	66	-
		M	...	105	...	23	...	67	-
		F	...	107	...	18	...	65	-

This table presents enrolment ratios for countries and territories whose population exceeds 150,000. For countries with a population of less than 150,000, data by single years of age are not available. Demographic data are based on estimates and projections of the United Nations Population Division, as assessed in 1994; the enrolment data used to calculate the gross enrolment ratios appear in Tables 3.3, 3.4, 3.7 and 3.10 of this *Yearbook*. Where enrolment data by age for the primary and secondary levels are also available, a net enrolment ratio has been calculated.

All ratios are expressed as percentages. The gross enrolment ratio is the total enrolment, regardless of age, divided by the population of the official age group which corresponds to a specific level of education. The net enrolment ratio is calculated by using only that part of the enrolment which corresponds to the age group of the level considered.

The gross enrolment ratio for pre-primary education is the total enrolment in education preceding the first level, regardless of age, expressed as a percentage of the population age-group corresponding to the national regulations for this level of education. As regulations for this level are extremely flexible, caution should be exercised in making inter-country comparisons.

The ratios for first and second level education have been calculated taking into account the different national systems of education and the duration of schooling at the first and second levels (general). At the third level the ratios are expressed as a percentage of the population in the five-year age-group following on from the offficial secondary school leaving age.

Enrolment ratios
Taux d'inscription
Tasas de escolarización

3.2

The age groups used to calculate enrolment ratios for the primary and secondary levels shown in the table, have been determined according to the following rules:

1. For countries which have a single school system at each level, the age group is defined in conformity with the normal entrance age and normal duration of general schooling at the first and second levels as given in Table 3.1.

2. In the case of countries with several systems of different duration, the system followed by the majority of the pupils has been used.

3. The durations used are those which were operative in the year considered.

The age group for the combined ratio for the first and second levels is defined by taking the whole range covering the two age groups defined for the first and second levels.

Enrolment ratios for the second level are based on the total enrolment including general education, teacher-training and technical and vocational education. Table 3.7 should be consulted for more details on enrolment data. It should be emphasized that the gross enrolment ratios at the pre-primary and the first and second levels include all pupils whatever their ages, whereas the population is limited to the range of official school ages defined according to the above-mentioned rules. Therefore, for countries with almost universal education among the school-age population at the first level, the gross enrolment ratio will exceed 100 if the actual age distribution of pupils extends beyond the official school ages.

Furthermore, in certain countries where first level education covers 100% of the population, their net enrolment ratio at this level can be less than 100 if some children of primary school age have not yet left their pre-primary schools.

Ce tableau présente des taux d'inscription pour les pays et territoires dont la population est supérieure à 150 000 habitants. Pour les pays dont la population est inférieure à 150 000 habitants, les données par année d'âge simple ne sont pas disponibles. Les données démographiques sont basées sur les estimations et projections de la population effectuées par la Division de la Population des Nations Unies en 1994; les effectifs qui ont servi pour calculer les taux d'inscription bruts sont ceux qui figurent dans les tableaux 3.3, 3.4, 3.7 et 3.10 de cet *Annuaire*. Lorsqu'on disposait des effectifs par âge des enseignements du premier et du second degré, on a calculé également un taux d'inscription net.

Tous les taux d'inscription sont exprimés en pourcentages. Pour un degré d'enseignement donné, le taux d'inscription brut est le rapport entre le total des effectifs scolaires, quel que soit l'âge des élèves, et la population du groupe d'âge officiel correspondant à ce degré. Le taux d'inscription net est calculé en ne prenant en compte que la partie des effectifs dont les âges correspondent au degré d'enseignement.

Le taux d'inscription brut dans l'enseignement préprimaire est le rapport entre le total des effectifs à ce degré d'enseignement, tous âges confondus, et la population d'âge correspondant à la durée de l'enseignement préprimaire, d'après la réglementation en vigueur dans chaque pays. La réglementation pour ce degré d'enseignement pouvant être très souple, il convient d'être prudent dans la comparaison des taux entre pays.

Les taux pour les premier et second degrés ont été calculés en tenant compte de la diversité des systèmes nationaux d'enseignement et de la durée des études du premier et du second degré (général). Pour l'enseignement du troisième degré les taux sont exprimés en pourcentage de la population du groupe d'âge quinquennal qui suit l'âge théorique de sortie l'enseignement du second degré.

Les groupes d'âge utilisés pour calculer les taux d'inscription relatifs aux enseignements du premier et du second degré qui figurent dans le tableau ont été déterminés en accord avec les normes suivantes:

1. Pour les pays qui ont un type d'enseignement unique à tous les degrés, le groupe d'âge est déterminé conformément à l'âge normal d'admission et à la durée normale des études générales primaires et secondaires qui figurent dans le tableau 3.1.

2. Dans le cas des pays qui ont plusieurs types d'enseignement de durée différente, on a choisi le système qui s'applique à la majorité des élèves.

3. Les durées d'enseignement sont celles qui étaient en vigueur pour chaque année considérée.

Le groupe d'âge considéré pour le calcul du taux concernant la totalité du premier et du second degré est déterminé par les limites extrêmes de l'ensemble des deux groupes d'âge définis pour le premier et le second degré.

Les taux d'inscription pour le second degré sont calculés à partir des effectifs globaux des trois types d'enseignement du second degré (général, normal, technique et professionnel). On trouvera des renseignements plus détaillés sur ces effectifs dans le tableau 3.7. Il convient de noter que les taux d'inscription bruts dans le préprimaire et dans le premier et le second degré comprennent les élèves de tous les âges alors que la population considérée est limitée aux groupes d'âges officiels déterminés selon les règles susmentionnées. Par conséquent, dans les pays où, pour le premier degré, la population d'âge scolaire est presque entièrement scolarisée, le taux d'inscription brut dépassera 100 si la répartition effective des élèves par âge déborde les limites d'âge officielles.

De même, dans certains pays où l'enseignement du premier degré scolarise 100% de la population, le taux net d'inscription pour ce niveau peut être inférieur à 100 si une partie des enfants ayant déjà atteint l'âge officiel d'entrée à l'école primaire n'a, en fait, pas encore quitté l'enseignement préprimaire.

Este cuadro presenta las tasas de escolarización para los países y territorios cuya población sobrepasa los 150 000 habitantes. Para los países cuya población es inferior a 150 000 habitantes, no se dispone de datos por años de edad simple. Los datos demográficos se refieren a las estimaciones y proyecciones de población preparadas por la División de la Población de la Organización de las Naciones Unidas en 1994; la matrícula que sirvió para el cálculo de las tasas de escolarización brutas es la que figura en los cuadros 3.3, 3.4, 3.7 y 3.10 del presente *Anuario*. Cuando se disponía de la matrícula por edad de las enseñanzas de primer y segundo grado, se calculó también la tasa de escolarización neta.

Todas las tasas de escolarización se expresan en porcentaje. La tasa de escolarización bruta es la relación entre, el total de la matrícula escolar, independiente de la edad de los alumnos, y la población del grupo de edad oficial correspondiente a ese grado. La tasa de escolarización neta se calcula tomando en consideración solamente aquella parte de la matrícula cuya edad corresponde al grado de enseñanza dado considerado.

La tasa de escolarización bruta de la enseñanza preprimaria es la relación entre el total de la matrícula escolar, de todas las edades, en este grado de enseñanza y la población del grupo de edad correspondiente a la duración de la enseñanza preprimaria, conforme a la reglamentación vigente en cada país. Sin embargo, como las reglamentaciones que rigen este nivel de enseñanza son flexibles, cabe proceder con prudencia al efectuar comparaciones entre los países.

Las tasas para el primer y el segundo grado se han calculado teniendo en cuenta la diversidad de los sistemas de enseñanza y de la duración de los estudios de primer y de segundo grado (general). Para la enseñanza de tercer grado, las tasas se expresan en porcentaje de la población del grupo de edad quinquenal subsiguiente a la edad teórica del fin de los estudios de la enseñanza de segundo grado.

Los grupos de edad utilizados para calcular las tasas de escolarización relativas a las enseñanzas de primer y de segundo grado que figuran en el cuadro han sido determinados como sigue:

1. Para los países que tienen un solo sistema de enseñanza para cada grado, el grupo de edad ha sido determinado de acuerdo con la edad normal de admisión y la duración normal de los estudios generales de primaria y secundaria, tal como figura en el cuadro 3.1.

2. En el caso de países con varios sistemas de enseñanza de diferente duración, se ha escogido el sistema que se aplica a la mayoría de los alumnos.

3. La duración de escolaridad considerada es la que estaba en vigor en los años correspondientes.

El grupo de edad considerado para el cálculo de la tasa combinada relativa al total de las enseñanzas de primer y de segundo grado queda determinado por los límites extremos del conjunto de los dos grupos de edad, definidos para ambos grados.

Las tasas de escolarización para el segundo grado incluyen la matrícula global de los tres tipos de enseñanza (general, normal y técnica y profesional). Para más detalles sobre la matrícula, consúltese el cuadro 3.7. Conviene señalar que las tasas de escolarización brutas para la enseñanza anterior al primer grado y de primer y segundo grado comprenden alumnos de todas las edades, mientras que la población considerada se limita a los grupos de edad oficiales, determinados según las normas antes mencionadas. Por consiguiente, en los países donde, para el primer grado, la población de edad escolar está casi completamente escolarizada, la tasa de escolarización bruta sobrepasará 100 si la distribución de los alumnos por edad desborda los límites de edad oficiales.

3.2   Enrolment ratios
Taux d'inscription
Tasas de escolarización

Además, en algunos países donde la enseñanza de primer grado cubre el 100% de la población, la tasa neta de escolarización en este grado puede ser inferior a 100 si una parte de los alumnos

en edad oficial de admisión en primaria no ha terminado la enseñanza preprimaria.

General note / Note générale / Nota general:

E--> Due to inconsistencies in the enrolment and/or population data enrolment ratios are not shown for certain countries.

FR-> Pour certains pays les taux d'inscriptions ne sont pas présentés à cause d'inconsistances dans les données sur les effectifs scolaires ou dans celles sur la population.

ESP> Para algunos no se presentan las tasas de escolarización debido a inconsistencias en los datos sobre los efectivos y/o en los datos sobre la población.

AFRICA:

Angola:

E--> For pre-primary education, data refer to initiation classes where pupils learn Portuguese.

FR-> Pour l'enseignement préprimaire, les données se réfèrent aux classes d'initiation où les élèves apprennent le portugais.

ESP> Para la enseñanza preprimaria, los datos se refieren a las clases de iniciación donde los alumnos aprenden el portugués.

Burkina Faso:

E--> For 1990/91, data on pre-primary education refer to 1989/90.

FR-> Pour 1990/91, les données relatives à l'enseignement préprimaire se réfèrent à 1989/90.

ESP> Para 1990/91, los datos relativos a la enseñanza preprimaria se refieren a 1989/90.

Burundi:

E--> For 1990/91, data on pre-primary education refer to 1988/89.

FR-> Pour 1990/91, les données relatives à l'enseignement préprimaire se réfèrent à 1988/89.

ESP> Para 1990/91, los datos relativos a la enseñanza preprimaria se refieren a 1988/89.

Cape Verde:

E--> For 1990/91, data on second level refer to 1991/92.

FR-> Pour 1990/91, les données relatives au second degré se réfèrent à 1991/92.

ESP> Para 1990/91, los datos relativos al segundo grado se refieren a 1991/92.

Comoros:

E--> For 1990/91, data on third level refer to 1989/90.

FR-> Pour 1990/91, les données relatives au troisième degré se réfèrenT à 1989/90.

ESP> Para 1990/91, los datos relativos al tercer grado se refieren a 1989/90.

Congo:

E--> See general note.

FR-> Voir la note générale.

ESP> Véase la nota general.

Côte d'Ivoire:

E--> For 1990/91, data on third level refer to 1988/89.

FR-> Pour 1990/91, les données relatives au troisième degré se réfèrent à 1988/89.

ESP> Para 1990/91, los datos relativos al tercer grado se refieren a 1988/89.

Equatorial Guinea:

E--> See general note.

FR-> Voir la note générale.

ESP> Véase la nota general.

Eritrea:

E--> For 1990/91, data on pre-primary education refer to 1991/92.

FR-> Pour 1990/91, les données relatives au troisième degré se réfèrent à 1991/92.

ESP> Para 1990/91, los datos relativos al tercer grado se refieren a 1991/92.

Gabon:

E--> See general note.

FR-> Voir la note générale.

ESP> Véase la nota general.

Gambia:

E--> For 1992/93, data on third level refer to 1994/95.

FR-> Pour 1992/93, les données relatives au troisième degré se réfèrent à 1994/95.

ESP> Para 1992/93, los datos relativos al tercer grado se refieren a 1994/95.

Madagascar:

E--> For 1984/85, data on third level refer to 1985/86.

FR-> Pour 1984/85, les données relatives au troisième degré se réfèrent à 1985/86.

ESP> Para 1984/85, los datos relativos al tercer grado se refieren a 1985/86.

Reunion:

E--> See general note.

FR-> Voir la note générale.

ESP> Véase la nota general.

Somalia:

E--> For 1985/86, data on third level refer to 1986/87.

FR-> Pour 1985/86, les données relatives au troisième degré se réfèrent à 1986/87.

ESP> Para 1985/86, los datos relativos al tercer grado se refieren a 1986/87.

Togo:

E--> For 1991/92, data on third level refer to 1992/93.

FR-> Pour 1991/92, les données relatives au troisième degré se réfèrent à 1992/93.

ESP> Para 1991/92, los datos relativos al tercer grado se refieren a 1992/93.

Tunisia:

E--> For 1990/91, data on pre-primary education refer to 1991/92.

FR-> Pour 1990/91, les données relatives à l'enseignement préprimaire se réfèrent à 1991/92.

ESP> Para 1990/91, los datos relativos a la enseñanza preprimaria se refieren a 1990/91.

Uganda:

E--> Government maintained and aided schools only.

FR-> Ecoles publiques et subventionnées seulement.

ESP> Escuelas públicas y subvencionadas solamente.

Zaire:

E--> For 1990/91, data on third level refer to 1988/89.

FR-> Pour 1990/91, les données relatives au troisième degré se réfèrent à 1988/89.

ESP> Para 1990/91, los datos relativos al tercer grado se refieren a 1988/89.

Zambia:

E--> For 1990, data on third level refer to 1989.

FR-> Pour 1990, les données relatives au troisième degré se réfèrent à 1989.

ESP> Para 1990, los datos relativos al tercer grado se refieren a 1989.

AMERICA, NORTH:

El Salvador:

E--> For 1991, data on third level refer to 1990.

FR-> Pour 1991, les données relatives au troisième degré se réfèrent à 1990.

ESP> Para 1991, los datos relativos al tercer grado se refieren a 1990.

Guadeloupe:

E--> See general note.

FR-> Voir la note générale.

ESP> Véase la nota general.

Haiti:

E--> For 1990/91, infant classes are included with pre-primary education.

FR-> Pour 1990/91, les classes enfantines sont incluses dans l'enseignement préprimaire.

ESP> Para 1990/91, las clases *enfantines* están incluídas en la enseñanza preprimaria.

Jamaica:

E--> For 1992/93 data on third level refer to 1991/92.

FR-> Pour 1992/93, les données relatives au troisième degré se réfèrent à 1991/92.

ESP> Para 1992/93, los datos relativos al tercer grado se refieren a 1991/92.

Martinique:

E--> See general note.

FR-> Voir la note générale.

ESP> Véase la nota general.

Netherlands Antilles:

E--> See general note.

FR-> Voir la note générale.

ESP> Véase la nota general.

United States:

E--> Enrolment ratios for first level refer to grades 1 to 6; those for second level to grades 7 to 12.

FR-> Les taux d'inscription pour le premier degré se réfèrent aux classes allant de la première à la sixième année d'études; ceux pour le second degré aux classes allant de la septième à la douzième année.

ESP> Las tasas de escolarización para la enseñanza de primer grado se refieren a los años de estudio de 1 a 6; las tasas

Enrolment ratios 3.2
Taux d'inscription
Tasas de escolarización

para la enseñanza de segundo grado se refieren a los años de estudio de 7 a 12.

AMERICA, SOUTH:

Argentina:

E--> For 1993, data on third level refer to 1992.

FR-> Pour 1993, les données relatives au troisième degré se réfèrent à 1992.

ESP> Para 1993, los datos relativos al tercer grado se refieren a 1992.

Colombia:

E--> For 1992, data on third level refer to 1991.

FR-> Pour 1992, les données relatives au troisième degré se réfèrent à 1991.

ESP> Para 1992, los datos relativos al tercer grado se refieren a 1991.

Guyana:

E--> For 1988/89 and 1992/93 data on third level refer to 1989/90 and 1993/94 respectively.

FR-> Pour 1988/89 et 1992/93, les données relatives au troisième degré se réfèrent à 1989/90 et 1993/94 respectivement.

ESP> Para 1988/89 y 1992/93, los datos relativos al tercer grado se refieren a 1989/90 y 1993/94 respectivamente.

Suriname:

E--> See general note.

FR-> Voir la note générale.

ESP> Véase la nota general.

ASIA:

Afghanistan:

E--> For 1990, data on pre-primary education refer to 1988.

FR-> Pour 1990, les données relatives à l'enseignement préprimaire se réfèrent à 1988.

ESP> Para 1990, los datos relativos a la enseñanza preprimaria se refieren a 1988.

Bangladesh:

E--> For 1990, data on pre-primary education refer to 1988.

FR-> Pour 1990, les données relatives à l'enseignement préprimaire se réfèrent à 1988.

ESP> Para 1990, los datos relativos a la enseñanza preprimaria se refieren a 1988.

Bhutan:

E--> See general note.

FR-> Voir la note générale.

ESP> Véase la nota general.

Cyprus:

E--> Not including Turkish enrolment and population.

FR-> Non compris les effectifs et la population turques.

ESP> No incluídas la matrícula y la población turcas.

Hong Kong:

E--> For 1985/86 and 1990/91, data on third level refer to 1984/85 and 1991/92 respectively.

FR-> Pour 1985/86 et 1990/91, les données relatives au troisième degré se réfèrent à 1984/85 et 1991/92 respectivement.

ESP> Para 1985/86 y 1990/91, los datos relativos al tercer grado se refieren a 1984/85 y 1991/92 respectivamente.

Indonesia:

E--> For 1990/91, data on third level refer to 1989/90.

FR-> Pour 1990/91, les données relatives au troisième degré se réfèrent à 1989/90.

ESP> Para 1990/91, los datos relativos al tercer grado se refieren a 1989/90.

Iraq:

E--> For 1990/91, data on third level refer to 1988/89.

FR-> Pour 1990/91, les données relatives au troisième degré se réfèrent à 1988/89.

ESP> Para 1990/91, los datos relativos al tercer grado se refieren a 1988/89.

Japan:

E--> For 1990/91, data on third level refer to 1989/90.

FR-> Pour 1990/91, les données relatives au troisième degré se réfèrent à 1989/90.

ESP> Para 1990/91, los datos relativos al tercer grado se refieren a 1989/90.

Kazakstan:

E--> For 1992/93, data on third level refer to 1991/92.

FR-> Pour 1992/93, les données relatives au troisième degré se réfèrent à 1991/92.

ESP> Para 1992/93, los datos relativos al tercer grado se refieren a 1991/92.

Kuwait:

E--> For 1990/91, data on third level refer to 1989/90.

FR-> Pour 1990/91, les données relatives au troisième degré se réfèrent à 1989/90.

ESP> Para 1990/91, los datos relativos al tercer grado se refieren a 1989/90.

Kyrgyzstan:

E--> For 1992/93, data on third level refer to 1991/92.

FR-> Pour 1992/93, les données relatives au troisième degré se réfèrent à 1991/92.

ESP> Para 1992/93, los datos relativos al tercer grado se refieren a 1991/92.

Myanmar:

E--> For 1990/91, data on third level refer to 1991/92.

FR-> Pour 1990/91, les données relatives au troisième degré se réfèrent à 1991/92.

ESP> Para 1990/91, los datos relativos al tercer grado se refieren a 1991/92.

Oman:

E--> For 1992/93, data on third level refer to 1991/92.

FR-> Pour 1992/93, les données relatives au troisième degré se réfèrent à 1991/92.

ESP> Para 1992/93, los datos relativos al tercer grado se refieren a 1991/92.

Pakistan:

E--> For 1990/91, data on third level refer to 1989/90.

FR-> Pour 1990/91, les données relatives au troisième degré se réfèrent à 1989/90.

ESP> Para 1990/91, los datos relativos al tercer grado se refieren a 1989/90.

Singapore:

E--> For 1990, data on pre-primary education refer to 1989.

FR-> Pour 1990, les données relatives au préprimaire se réfèrent à 1989.

ESP> Para 1990, los datos relativos a la enseñanza preprimaria se refieren a 1989.

Sri Lanka:

E--> For 1992, data on third level refer to 1991.

FR-> Pour 1992, les données relatives au troisième degré se réfèrent à 1991.

ESP> Para 1992, los datos relativos al tercer grado se refieren a 1991.

Tajikistan:

E--> For 1992/93, data on third level refer to 1991/92.

FR-> Pour 1992/93, les données relatives au troisième degré se réfèrent à 1991/92.

ESP> Para 1992/93, los datos relativos al tercer grado se refieren a 1991/92.

Thailand:

E--> For 1990/91, data on third level refer to 1989/90.

FR-> Pour 1990/91, les données relatives au troisième degré se réfèrent à 1989/90.

ESP> Para 1990/91, los datos relativos al tercer grado se refieren a 1989/90.

Uzbekistan:

E--> For 1992/93, data on third level refer to 1991/92.

FR-> Pour 1992/93, les données relatives au troisième degré se réfèrent à 1991/92.

ESP> Para 1992/93, los datos relativos al tercer grado se refieren a 1991/92.

EUROPE:

Estonia:

E--> Due to the change in 1989 of the official entry age in first level education from 6 to 7, the enrolment ratios from 1990/91 to 1994/95 had to be calculated on the basis of the age-group 7-11 although this level comprises six grades. The age group 7-12 will be used only from 1996/97 onwards.

FR--> En raison de changement intervenu en 1989 dans l'âge d'entrée dans l'enseignement du premier degré qui est passé de 6 à 7 ans, les taux d'inscription de 1990/91 à 1994/95 ont été calculés sur le groupe d'âges 7-11 ans bien que ce degré d'enseignement comporte six années d'études. Le groupe d'âges 7-12 ans ne sera utilisé qu'à partir de l'année scolaire 1996/97.

ESP> Debido a un cambio en 1989 de la edad oficial de entrada en la enseñanza de primer grado, que pasó de 6 años a 7 años de edad, las tasas de escolarización de 1990/91 a 1994/95 debieren calcularse sobre la base del grupo de edad de 7-11 años, aunque este nivel comprende seis años de estudios. Se utilizará el grupo de edad de 7-12 años a partir del año escolar 1996/97.

Luxembourg:

E--> Some students from Luxembourg pursue their studies in neighbouring countries.

FR-> Une partie des étudiants luxembourgeois poursuivent leurs études dans les pays voisins.

ESP> Una parte de los estudiantes de Luxemburgo cursan sus estudios en los países vecinos.

Switzerland:

E--> In order to show representative enrolment ratios and as the institutional system of education differs from canton to canton, the first six years of enrolment have been taken for the first level, and the following seven years for the second level, throughout the country.

FR-> Pour montrer des taux significatifs et puisque le système institutionel de l'éducation varie d'un canton à l'autre, le taux de

3.2 Enrolment ratios
Taux d'inscription
Tasas de escolarización

scolarisation pour le premier degré a été calculé sur la base des premières six années d'enseignement et le second degré sur la base des sept années suivantes, pour l'ensemble du pays.

ESP> Para mostrar tasas representativas y dado que el sistema institutional de la educación varía de un cantón al otro, las tasas de escolarización para el primer grado se refieren a los seis primeros años de escolaridad y las del segundo grado se refieren a los siete años siguientes, para todo el país.

United Kingdom:

E--> From 1992/93, education provided in infant classes in primary schools, previously considered as pre-primary education, is included with education at the first level.

FR-> A partir de 1992/93, l'enseignement dispensé dans les classes enfantines des écoles primaires, considéré auparavant comme de l'enseignement préprimaire, est inclus dans l'enseignement du premier degré.

ESP> A partir de 1992/93, la enseñanza impartida en las clases de párvulos de las escuelas primarias, considerada antes como educación preprimaria, se incluye en la educación de primer grado.

Federal Republic of Yugoslavia:

E--> For 1993/94, data on third level refer to 1994/95.

FR-> Pour 1993/94, les données relatives au troisième degré se réfèrent à 1994/95.

ESP> Pour 1993/94, los datos relativos al tercer grado se refieren a 1994/95.

OCEANIA:

French Polynesia:

E--> For 1992/93, data on third level refer to 1991/92.

FR-> Pour 1992/93, les données relatives au troisième degré se réfèrent à 1991/92.

ESP> Para 1992/93, los datos relativos al tercer grado se refieren a 1991/92.

Papua New-Guinea:

E--> Education at the second level does not include colleges of distance education.

FR-> L'enseignement du second degré n'inclut pas les établissements d'enseignement à distance.

ESP> La enseñanza de segundo grado no incluye los establecimientos de enseñanza a distancia.

Education preceding the first level 3.3
Enseignement précédant le premier degré
Enseñanza anterior al primer grado

3.3 Education preceding the first level: schools, teachers and pupils

Enseignement précédant le premier degré: écoles, personnel enseignant et élèves

Enseñanza anterior al primer grado: escuelas, personal docente, y alumnos

Please refer to the explanatory text at the end of the table.

Prière de se référer au texte explicatif à la fin du tableau.

Referirse al texto explicativo al final del cuadro.

Country Pays País	Year Année Año	Schools Écoles Escuelas	Teaching staff Personnel enseignant Personal docente			Pupils enrolled Élèves inscrits Alumnos matriculados			
			Total	Female Féminin Femenino	% F	Total	Female Féminin Femenino	% F	% Private Privé Privada
		(1)	(2)	(3)	(4)	(5)	(6)	(7)	(8)
Africa									
Algeria	1992/93	...	1 042	836	80	21 120	10 399	49	-
	1993/94	...	1 229	1 142	93	27 409	13 032	48	-
	1994/95	...	1 280	1 085	85	27 657	13 309	48	-
Angola‡	1980/81	...	...	...	...	390 512	157 803	40	-
	1985/86	...	...	...	...	230 154	103 139	45	-
	1990/91	...	...	...	...	164 146	55 817	34	-
	1991/92	...	...	...	...	214 867	...	...	...
Benin	1980/81	92	174	...	...	3 779	...	...	...
	1985/86	241	526	289	55	11 302	5 090	45	-
	1990/91	306	598	328	55	13 623	6 177	45	8
	1991/92	309	612	335	55	13 827	6 299	46	8
Burkina Faso‡	1980/81	...	...	...	...	732	319	44	90
	1985/86	...	...	...	...	1 075	...	...	...
	1989/90	95	259	253	98	7 655	3 911	51	44
Burundi‡	1980/81	...	15	15	100	1 004	498	50	...
	1985/86	...	32	30	94	1 774	883	50	26
	1988/89	...	49	40	82	2 381	1 161	49	28
Cameroon	1980/81	436	1 512	1 494	99	40 574	19 920	49	49
	1985/86	536	2 454	2 444	100	73 486	35 758	49	43
	1990/91	807	3 567	3 562	100	93 771	46 818	50	36
	1991/92	935	3 490	3 477	100	94 068	46 985	50	37
	1993/94	1 018	3 755	*3 750	*100	91 179	45 170	50	41
	1994/95	1 061	3 778	3 733	99	91 242	45 206	50	41
Cape Verde	1981/82	...	...	...	...	1 823	...	...	...
	1986/87	58	136	136	100	4 523	...	...	...
Central African Republic	1986/87	164	360	360	100	11 450	4 503	39	...
	1987/88	173	572	...	...	11 677	...	...	...
Comoros	1980/81	...	600	200	33	17 778	8 598	48	-
Congo	1980/81	36	334	334	100	3 498	1 736	50	-
	1985/86	51	537	537	100	5 595	2 756	49	-
	1990/91	56	645	645	100	5 810	2 897	50	-
	1991/92	63	685	685	100	6 836	3 511	51	9
	1993/94	53	619	619	100	4 415	2 301	52	8
Cote d'Ivoire	1980/81	...	179	179	100	6 291	2 953	47	76
	1985/86	...	...	...	...	8 570	4 104	48	63
	1990/91	...	...	...	...	11 624	5 624	48	67
	1991/92	...	...	...	...	11 217	5 422	48	67
	1993/94	...	...	...	...	22 458	10 981	49	...
	1994/95	...	...	...	...	25 638	12 323	48	...
Djibouti	1985/86	1	...	...	...	234	116	50	100
	1990/91	1	...	...	...	220	130	59	100
	1992/93	1	...	...	...	218	142	65	100
	1993/94	2	...	...	...	236	150	64	100
	1994/95	2	6	6	100	259	148	57	100

3.3 Education preceding the first level
Enseignement précédant le premier degré
Enseñanza anterior al primer grado

Country Pays País	Year Année Año	Schools Écoles Escuelas	Teaching staff Personnel enseignant Personal docente			Pupils enrolled Élèves inscrits Alumnos matriculados			
			Total	Female Féminin Femenino	% F	Total	Female Féminin Femenino	% F	% Private Privé Privada
		(1)	(2)	(3)	(4)	(5)	(6)	(7)	(8)
Egypt	1980/81	433	...	...	...	74 921	36 809	49	94
	1985/86	602	...	...	...	128 272	62 368	49	93
	1990/91	1 075	8 015	7 649	95	198 742	96 749	49	87
	1992/93	1 335	9 184	8 818	96	235 733	113 995	48	83
	1993/94	1 569	9 692	9 344	96	246 100	118 432	48	77
	1994/95	1 790	9 216	8 976	97	257 815	124 092	48	72
Equatorial Guinea									
	1992/93	72	142	...	...	4 048	...	...	...
	1993/94	85	171	171	100	3 788	1 864	49	...
Eritrea	1991/92	65	201	201	100	6 461	3 319	51	98
	1992/93	72	227	227	100	7 031	3 605	51	97
	1993/94	77	244	243	100	7 748	3 839	50	95
	1994/95	80	256	255	100	8 032	3 930	49	96
Ethiopia	1985/86	708	1 532	...	...	69 736	...	...	100
	1990/91	786	2 091	1 956	94	73 668	36 919	50	100
	1991/92	632	1 531	1 474	96	58 444	29 099	50	100
	1992/93	550	1 486	1 443	97	57 006	28 537	50	100
	1993/94	652	1 638	1 597	97	66 086	33 158	50	100
Gabon	1991/92	9	37	36	97	950	485	51	52
Gambia	1991/92	...	408	...	...	13 118	...	...	...
Ghana‡	1980/81	1 160	...	...	...	158 395	72 682	46	11
	1985/86	2 399	10 218	9 921	97	171 182	...	...	...
	1988/89	3 932	14 665	13 737	94	285 865	141 806	50	18
	1989/90	4 735	15 152	...	...	323 406	156 104	48	...
Guinea	1993/94	113	302	242	80	10 260	4 593	45	95
Guinea-Bissau‡	1980/81	6	46	45	98	459	225	49	-
	1986/87	17	61	53	87	1 246	...	...	-
	1988/89	5	43	37	86	754	370	49	-
Kenya	1985	11 780	15 676	15 676	100	582 505	290 211	50	...
	1990	17 000	22 000	21 800	99	850 000	450 000	53	...
	1991	17 650	24 809	...	...	908 966	...	...	...
	1992	...	25 681	25 000	97	931 826	*465 000	*50	...
	1993	18 487	26 625	...	...	924 094	452 070	49	...
Liberia	1980	60	...	...	...	80 215	33 745	42	42
	1984	...	...	...	...	70 507	...	...	43
Libyan Arab Jamahiriya	1980/81	45	515	515	100	9 008	4 146	46	-
	1985/86	78	1 051	1 051	100	15 028	7 243	48	-
Mali	1993/94	151	503	...	...	15 908	7 610	48	...
	1994/95	...	531	475	89	17 165	8 211	48	...
Mauritania	1992/93	36	108	108	100	800	...	...	56
Mauritius	1980	349	453	451	100	11 704	5 712	49	100
Morocco‡	1980/81	27 245	29 611	1 532	5	579 547	143 127	25	100
	1985/86	30 180	33 919	3 491	10	723 770	216 025	30	100
	1990/91	33 345	39 805	8 080	20	812 487	248 574	31	100
	1992/93	31 928	36 464	8 125	22	779 043	229 694	29	100
	1993/94	31 898	36 203	9 623	27	783 456	232 334	30	100
	1994/95	32 021	36 553	10 692	29	796 669	241 277	30	100
Mozambique‡	1985	...	...	...	...	62 940	29 647	47	-
	1987	-	-	-	-	-	-	-	-
Namibia	1986	...	...	...	...	4 568	...	...	...
	1990	...	...	...	...	5 649	2 991	53	...
	1992	97	217	216	100	5 482	2 714	50	14
	1993	...	...	...	...	4 900	2 476	51	...
	1994	...	...	...	...	4 579	2 306	50	...
Niger	1980/81	21	85	85	100	2 561	1 268	50	54
	1985/86	24	115	115	100	3 980	1 967	49	44
	1990/91	81	317	317	100	11 696	5 593	48	22
	1991/92	87	317	317	100	13 182	6 363	48	21
	1992/93	88	367	367	100	12 600	6 366	51	22
Reunion	1980/81	...	...	...	...	33 816	...	...	8
	1985/86	142	1 212	1 181	97	37 694	18 651	49	8
	1990/91	...	...	...	...	41 294	...	...	...
	1992/93	...	...	...	...	42 730	...	...	8
	1993/94	172	...	...	...	43 737	...	...	8
	1994/95	...	...	...	...	44 312	...	...	7

Education preceding the first level 3.3
Enseignement précédant le premier degré
Enseñanza anterior al primer grado

Country Pays País	Year Année Año	Schools Écoles Escuelas	Teaching staff Personnel enseignant Personal docente			Pupils enrolled Élèves inscrits Alumnos matriculados			
			Total	Female Féminin Femenino	% F	Total	Female Féminin Femenino	% F	% Private Privé Privada
		(1)	(2)	(3)	(4)	(5)	(6)	(7)	(8)
Rwanda	1986/87	102	154	122	79	*8 000	*3 500	*44	*100
	1987/88	150	...	...	...	*8 000	...	...	...
St. Helena	1980/81	3	9	9	100	60	36	60	-
	1985/86	3	6	6	100	88	60	68	-
Sao Tome and Principe	1980/81	...	...	...	...	2 430	...	...	...
	1986/87	...	...	...	...	3 240	1 621	50	...
	1989/90	13	116	108	93	3 446	1 744	51	...
Senegal	1980/81	98	...	...	...	8 445	4 315	51	80
	1985/86	124	547	...	...	12 764	6 509	51	57
	1990/91	161	666	501	75	17 042	...	...	58
	1991/92	173	714	528	74	17 432	8 614	49	59
	1992/93	...	...	...	...	17 592	...	...	...
	1993/94	196	751	580	77	17 305	8 526	49	60
Seychelles	1980	34	91	91	100	2 568	...	...	-
	1985	38	109	109	100	3 180	...	...	-
	1990	34	*173	*173	*100	3 412	*1 705	*50	...
	1992	35	176	176	100	3 199	1 602	50	2
	1993	34	159	159	100	3 125	1 528	49	1
	1994	35	175	175	100	3 167	1 537	49	2
Somalia	1980/81	17	143	134	94	2 089	1 087	52	-
	1985/86	16	133	125	94	1 558	882	57	-
South Africa‡	1986	...	...	...	...	69 790	34 189	49	...
	1990	...	...	...	...	125 393	62 488	50	...
	1992	...	...	...	...	178 125	90 235	51	...
	1993	...	...	...	...	193 176	96 126	50	...
	1994	...	...	...	...	286 663	...	...	8
Sudan‡	1980/81	3 135	3 183	...	...	148 879	...	...	69
	1985/86	4 003	5 569	2 278	41	235 943	...	...	69
	1990/91	5 914	8 055	3 770	47	283 126	100 279	35	...
	1991/92	6 525	8 478	3 939	46	350 306	164 699	47	...
Swaziland	1990	384	623	...	...	12 000	7 757	65	...
	1993	446	816	...	...	19 182	...	...	...
Togo	1980/81	148	237	237	100	8 424	4 121	49	54
	1985/86	212	364	364	100	9 740	4 733	49	48
	1990/91	252	383	383	100	10 949	5 409	49	51
	1993/94	241	395	395	100	10 526	5 235	50	45
Tunisia	1987/88	520	1 376	1 376	100	39 819	...	...	...
	1989/90	649	1 726	1 716	99	43 765	...	...	63
	1991/92	845	2 192	...	...	58 488	...	...	...
Zaire	1992/93	429	768	404	53	33 235	17 279	52	86
America, North									
Bahamas‡	1991/92	5	19	19	100	248	124	50	...
	1992/93	14	47	47	100	788	390	49	69
	1993/94	7	21	21	100	325	200	62	...
Barbados	1980/81	132	...	...	...	3 936	1 962	50	*20
Belize	1980/81	55	130	...	...	2 000	...	...	...
	1990/91	73	143	...	...	2 695	1 428	53	...
	1991/92	81	170	169	99	3 250	1 647	51	...
	1992/93	83	176	175	99	3 377	1 661	49	...
	1994/95	90	190	189	99	3 533	1 804	51	...
Bermuda‡	1980/81	31	...	...	...	1 067	545	51	60
	1984/85	32	37	37	100	1 287	637	49	66
British Virgin Islands	1980/81	8	15	12	80	299	134	45	100
	1990/91	...	...	...	...	228	...	...	100
	1991/92	...	...	...	...	320	160	50	100
	1994/95	5	52	52	100	482	...	...	100
Canada	1980/81	...	...	...	...	397 266	193 807	49	3
	1985/86	...	12 625	...	...	422 085	205 391	49	3
	1990/91	...	15 471	10 796	70	472 802	230 057	49	4
	1991/92	...	15 857	10 947	69	486 609	237 183	49	4
	1992/93	...	15 839	10 994	69	482 377	234 624	49	4
	1993/94	...	15 968	11 053	69	490 845	238 754	49	4

3.3 Education preceding the first level
Enseignement précédant le premier degré
Enseñanza anterior al primer grado

Country Pays País	Year Année Año	Schools Écoles Escuelas	Teaching staff Personnel enseignant Personal docente			Pupils enrolled Élèves inscrits Alumnos matriculados			
			Total	Female Féminin Femenino	% F	Total	Female Féminin Femenino	% F	% Private Privé Privada
		(1)	(2)	(3)	(4)	(5)	(6)	(7)	(8)
Costa Rica	1980	370	673	...	...	21 857	10 792	49	13
	1985	536	1 302	...	...	36 356	18 020	50	11
	1990	791	1 989	...	...	46 638	22 912	49	11
	1992	879	2 090	...	...	52 644	25 884	49	10
	1993	913	2 284	...	...	53 774	26 327	49	10
	1994	964	2 435	...	...	55 125	27 035	49	11
Cuba	1980/81	...	5 047	4 998	99	123 741	60 386	49	-
	1985/86	...	4 635	4 635	100	108 881	47 347	43	-
	1990/91	...	6 980	6 980	100	166 337	72 977	44	-
	1992/93	...	6 968	6 968	100	161 699	69 827	43	-
	1993/94	...	6 933	6 933	100	165 278	68 968	42	-
	1994/95	...	6 512	6 512	100	160 283	...	...	-
Dominica	1985/86	54	86	86	100	2 500	...	...	72
	1990/91	65	100	100	100	2 246	1 152	51	100
	1991/92	70	108	107	99	2 000	1 047	52	100
	1992/93	72	131	130	99	3 000	...	...	100
Dominican Rep.	1980/81	286	...	...	...	27 278	...	...	87
	1985/86	...	...	...	...	67 615	...	...	79
	1993/94	...	...	...	...	148 435	75 380	51	55
El Salvador‡	1980	459	1 036	1 036	100	48 684	25 350	52	20
	1991	1 271	975	970	99	83 865	42 868	51	37
	1992	1 596	1 038	1 027	99	97 700	49 623	51	33
	1993	2 312	2 522	...	...	113 440	57 815	51	30
Grenada	1980/81	67	115	113	98	2 500	...	...	...
	1986/87	68	146	145	99	3 283	1 646	50	...
	1987/88	70	150	149	99	3 584	1 816	51	...
Guadeloupe	1980/81	...	...	...	...	16 875	...	...	11
	1985/86	96	615	...	...	18 866	9 300	49	10
	1990/91	119	709	...	...	19 983	9 801	49	9
	1992/93	121	639	636	100	21 201	10 388	49	9
	1993/94	121	760	...	...	22 089	10 883	49	10
	1994/95	...	...	...	...	22 678	...	...	10
Guatemala‡	1980	564	1 700	...	...	48 869	24 464	50	38
	1985	2 864	4 407	...	...	133 726	63 522	48	25
	1991	...	...	...	...	145 719	70 496	48	31
	1993	4 553	7 708	...	...	193 061	92 745	48	32
Haiti‡	1987/88	...	...	...	...	228 877	109 874	48	86
	1990/91	...	...	...	...	230 391	110 600	48	86
Honduras	1980	441	833	...	...	33 034	13 874	42	16
	1985	...	...	...	...	48 610	...	...	...
	1991	973	1 870	1 870	100	60 137	30 413	51	18
	1993	1 210	2 220	2 220	100	64 876	31 964	49	21
Jamaica‡	1980/81	...	...	...	...	119 508	61 592	52	85
	1985/86	1 581	...	...	...	125 046	...	...	84
	1990/91	1 681	4 158	...	...	133 687	67 154	50	84
	1992/93	...	...	...	...	114 427	53 567	47	...
Martinique	1980/81	...	...	...	...	17 678	...	...	4
	1986/87	75	598	586	98	18 422	8 893	48	4
	1990/91	...	...	...	...	20 122	...	...	4
	1992/93	86	...	...	...	21 285	10 509	49	5
	1993/94	84	696	655	94	21 342	10 524	49	4
	1994/95	...	...	...	...	21 475	...	...	4
Mexico	1980/81	13 021	32 368	32 368	100	1 071 619	531 704	50	11
	1985/86	35 649	80 529	80 529	100	2 381 412	1 188 108	50	6
	1990/91	46 736	104 972	104 972	100	2 734 054	1 362 041	50	9
	1992/93	51 554	114 335	114 335	100	2 858 890	1 419 258	50	9
	1993/94	55 083	121 589	*121 589	*100	2 980 024	1 480 944	50	8
	1994/95	58 868	129 576	*129 576	*100	3 092 834	...	...	8
Montserrat‡	1981/82	9	20	19	95	278	124	45	...
	1993/94	12	31	31	100	407	199	49	12
Netherlands Antilles	1991/92	74	314	...	...	7 462	...	...	74
Nicaragua	1980	463	924	915	99	30 524	15 649	51	43
	1985	686	1 983	1 906	96	62 784	32 509	52	26
	1990	978	1 893	1 868	99	63 201	32 514	51	24
	1992	1 152	2 102	...	...	66 727	34 282	51	28
	1993	1 403	2 508	2 472	99	79 543	40 391	51	36
	1994	2 100	3 409	3 314	97	97 163	49 119	51	27

Education preceding the first level 3.3
Enseignement précédant le premier degré
Enseñanza anterior al primer grado

Country / Pays / País	Year / Année / Año	Schools / Écoles / Escuelas	Teaching staff / Personnel enseignant / Personal docente			Pupils enrolled / Élèves inscrits / Alumnos matriculados			
			Total	Female Féminin Femenino	% F	Total	Female Féminin Femenino	% F	% Private Privé Privada
		(1)	(2)	(3)	(4)	(5)	(6)	(7)	(8)
Panama	1980	365	645	644	100	18 136	9 063	50	34
	1985	637	1 121	1 109	99	27 501	13 736	50	27
	1990	793	1 413	...	...	30 719	15 033	49	27
	1992	835	1 452	...	...	33 248	...	...	30
	1993	887	1 544	...	...	35 582	...	...	28
	1994	902	1 644	...	...	35 863	...	...	31
Saint Kitts and Nevis	1985/86	36	46	45	98	1 501	740	49	75
	1991/92	56	89	89	100	1 693	...	...	71
	1992/93	...	116	116	100	1 706	839	49	74
	1993/94	47	99	...	...	1 708	...	...	73
St. Lucia	1985/86	105	202	...	...	3 711	...	...	95
	1990/91	...	340	...	...	5 366	...	...	100
	1991/92	125	318	...	...	5 300	...	...	100
	1992/93	150	310	310	100	4 566	...	...	100
St. Pierre and Miquelon	1980/81	4	18	18	100	356	169	47	78
	1985/86	4	18	18	100	361	186	52	76
	1990/91	...	...	...	...	343	...	...	...
	1992/93	...	...	...	...	307	...	...	...
	1994/95	...	...	...	...	298	...	...	...
St. Vincent and the Grenadines	1981/82	30	...	...	...	967	468	48	100
	1986/87	66	171	170	99	2 150	1 089	51	100
	1990/91	77	180	180	100	2 492	1 296	52	100
	1993/94	97	175	174	99	2 500	...	...	100
Trinidad and Tobago‡	1980/81	39	117	117	100	1 739	...	...	...
	1985/86	49	147	147	100	2 035	...	...	...
	1989/90	158	366	352	96	5 049	3 100	61	...
	1990/91	43	121	121	100	1 429	733	51	...
	1992/93	50	126	126	100	1 418	691	49	...
United States	1980/81	...	...	...	...	5 163 000	2 449 000	47	36
	1985/86	...	...	...	...	6 306 000	3 113 000	49	35
	1990/91	...	...	...	...	7 300 000	3 511 000	48	38
	1993/94	...	...	...	...	7 198 000	3 384 000	47	34
U.S. Virgin Isl.‡	1980/81	...	71	...	...	2 561	...	...	31
	1985/86	58	71	...	...	2 656	...	...	29
	1990/91	66	129	...	...	2 595	...	...	41
	1992/93	62	121	...	...	2 606	...	...	36
America, South									
Argentina	1980	6 622	...	36 117	...	480 216	...	...	32
	1985	8 015	36 287	36 117	100	693 259	348 639	50	31
	1991	9 693	48 821	...	...	914 686	...	...	...
	1003	...	...	...	...	933 345	...	...	31
	1994	...	62 521	59 006	94	1 014 027	...	...	31
Bolivia	1980	...	...	...	...	90 031	44 503	49	...
	1986	2 038	2 386	...	...	133 677	65 713	49	11
	1990	...	2 895	2 767	96	121 132	59 669	49	10
Brazil	1980	15 320	58 788	57 458	98	1 335 317	660 412	49	46
	1987	90 673	199 986	...	...	4 735 873	...	...	30
	1989	95 754	211 356	...	...	4 839 083	...	...	27
	1991	109 786	256 208	...	...	5 283 894	...	...	25
	1992	126 428	258 157	...	...	5 574 514	...	...	23
	1993	135 012	272 619	...	...	5 780 566	...	...	22
Chile	1980	...	...	...	...	174 909	...	...	20
	1985	...	...	...	...	202 252	99 714	49	44
	1990	4 180	...	...	...	220 396	108 786	49	48
	1991	4 302	8 542	8 363	98	205 283	101 532	49	49
	1992	...	...	...	...	241 759	119 010	49	47
	1994	4 389	9 415	9 140	97	263 337	129 654	49	48
Colombia	1980	3 281	6 742	...	...	174 369	...	...	64
	1985	5 127	10 891	...	...	285 286	142 380	50	61
	1989	6 920	13 794	...	...	328 425	163 910	50	53
	1992	9 737	19 763	19 022	96	468 379	237 468	51	58
	1993	9 886	20 770	...	...	506 080	249 194	49	57
	1994	12 914	28 946	...	...	627 782	...	...	55
Ecuador	1980/81	736	1 858	1 768	95	50 819	25 760	51	42
	1985/86	...	3 846	3 652	95	93 665	47 249	50	...
	1990/91	...	6 301	...	...	115 024	...	...	...
	1991/92	...	5 799	...	...	123 074	...	...	...
	1992/93	...	5 895	5 552	94	130 378	66 036	51	40

3.3 Education preceding the first level
Enseignement précédant le premier degré
Enseñanza anterior al primer grado

Country / Pays / País	Year / Année / Año	Schools / Écoles / Escuelas	Teaching staff / Personnel enseignant / Personal docente			Pupils enrolled / Élèves inscrits / Alumnos matriculados			
			Total	Female Féminin Femenino	% F	Total	Female Féminin Femenino	% F	% Private Privé Privada
		(1)	(2)	(3)	(4)	(5)	(6)	(7)	(8)
French Guiana	1980/81	...	...	...	...	3 879	...	...	12
	1990/91	...	...	...	...	7 231	...	...	10
	1992/93	...	...	...	...	7 786	...	...	10
	1993/94	42	...	...	...	8 113	4 001	49	9
	1994/95	...	...	...	...	8 583	...	...	9
Guyana	1980/81	374	2 018	1 975	98	27 955	14 020	50	-
	1985/86	...	1 399	1 387	99	25 685	12 984	51	-
	1992/93	372	1 495	1 491	100	29 678	14 632	49	-
Paraguay	1980	...	...	...	...	10 928	...	...	...
	1985	70	...	...	...	19 052	9 530	50	54
	1990	...	...	...	...	34 157	17 076	50	55
	1992	76	2 255	...	...	41 627	*20 873	*50	50
	1993	...	2 997	2 687	90	55 318	27 738	50	47
	1994	...	2 447	...	...	51 671	25 615	50	38
Peru	1980	3 271	6 778	6 689	99	228 168	114 940	50	27
	1985	5 268	11 206	11 059	99	342 779	172 141	50	23
	1990	...	22 271	...	...	504 175	...	...	18
	1992	10 644	21 726	...	...	536 607	...	...	20
	1993	...	20 572	...	...	560 573	...	...	20
	1994	13 148	27 219	...	...	597 382	...	...	22
Suriname	1980/81	...	693	693	100	17 314	8 467	49	...
	1985/86	...	676	675	100	17 226	8 441	49	...
	1990/91	...	675	675	100	16 968	8 281	49	...
	1991/92	...	675	675	100	17 827	8 787	49	...
	1992/93	...	672	672	100	18 720	9 079	48	...
	1993/94	...	...	...	...	20 979	10 360	49	...
Uruguay‡	1980	...	1 001	...	...	42 444	...	...	25
	1985	968	2 012	...	...	55 092	27 457	50	26
	1991	1 508	...	...	...	66 841	32 994	49	29
	1992	1 567	2 400	...	...	68 048	33 792	50	29
	1993	...	1 662	...	...	67 209	33 331	50	31
	1994	1 668	2 596	...	...	68 999	33 392	48	30
Venezuela	1980/81	...	16 487	...	...	421 183	...	...	17
	1985/86	1 407	22 102	21 747	98	561 846	278 497	50	15
	1990/91	...	26 074	25 739	99	634 812	314 457	50	15
	1991/92	...	27 792	27 424	99	674 644	333 898	49	16
	1992/93	...	29 009	28 594	99	683 495	338 149	49	17
	1993/94	...	29 942	29 436	98	695 320	343 937	49	...
Asia									
Afghanistan	1980	36	369	369	100	4 470	2 010	45	-
	1985	...	873	873	100	17 000	7 545	44	-
	1988	263	...	...	...	19 660	9 601	49	-
Armenia	1980/81	...	11 593	...	...	134 839	...	...	...
	1985/86	...	13 234	...	...	149 768	...	...	...
	1990/91	...	11 954	...	...	113 303	...	...	...
	1991/92	...	12 121	...	...	114 964	...	...	...
	1992/93	...	12 398	...	...	105 325	...	...	...
	1993/94	...	11 966	...	...	93 052	...	...	...
Azerbaijan	1980/81	...	13 628	13 628	100	109 721	...	...	...
	1985/86	...	15 331	15 331	100	125 636	...	...	...
	1990/91	...	18 516	18 516	100	132 338	...	...	...
	1991/92	...	19 193	19 193	100	128 785	56 665	44	...
	1992/93	2 120	19 251	19 251	100	123 094	54 161	44	...
	1993/94	2 115	20 140	20 140	100	124 371	55 469	45	...
Bahrain	1980/81	...	...	...	...	3 730	1 768	47	100
	1985/86	56	255	255	100	7 608	3 599	47	100
	1990/91	...	344	344	100	9 056	4 412	49	100
	1992/93	75	420	419	100	11 492	5 519	48	100
	1993/94	79	464	464	100	12 008	5 752	48	100
	1994/95	90	514	513	100	12 807	5 990	47	100
Bangladesh	1988	51 495	63 054	11 625	18	2 317 181	1 033 417	45	100
Brunei Darussalam	1980	143	324	248	77	6 760	3 251	48	51
	1985	141	366	...	...	8 055	...	...	...
	1991	161	451	404	90	9 278	4 410	48	57
	1992	159	471	424	90	9 869	4 673	47	57
	1993	165	538	495	92	11 729	5 648	48	65
	1994	165	506	468	92	10 717	5 172	48	64
Cambodia	1980/81	149	630	...	...	15 077	...	...	...
	1985/86	689	2 398	...	...	56 165	...	...	...
	1990/91	397	2 959	2 428	82	49 277	23 138	47	...
	1993/94	203	2 058	2 058	100	53 080	26 848	51	...
	1994/95	219	1 954	1 954	100	49 542	24 810	50	...

Education preceding the first level 3.3
Enseignement précédant le premier degré
Enseñanza anterior al primer grado

Country / Pays / País	Year / Année / Año	Schools / Écoles / Escuelas	Teaching staff / Personnel enseignant / Personal docente			Pupils enrolled / Élèves inscrits / Alumnos matriculados			
			Total	Female / Féminin / Femenino	% F	Total	Female / Féminin / Femenino	% F	% Private / Privé / Privada
		(1)	(2)	(3)	(4)	(5)	(6)	(7)	(8)
China	1980/81	170 419	410 700	335 100	82	11 507 700	...	...	-
	1985/86	172 262	549 900	527 200	96	14 796 900	6 971 700	47	-
	1990/91	172 322	749 600	721 700	96	19 722 300	9 369 200	48	-
	1991/92	164 465	768 900	726 200	94	22 092 900	10 383 600	47	-
	1992/93	172 506	815 000	770 200	95	24 282 100	11 408 700	47	-
	1993/94	165 197	836 000	786 800	94	25 525 400	11 975 900	47	-
Cyprus‡	1980/81	259	418	416	100	10 397	5 007	48	49
	1985/86	423	676	672	99	16 810	7 985	48	58
	1990/91	572	1 030	1 022	99	23 694	11 363	48	68
	1992/93	608	1 242	1 226	99	24 977	11 959	48	68
	1993/94	630	1 269	1 255	99	25 236	12 062	48	66
	1994/95	642	1 308	1 295	99	25 819	12 271	48	66
Hong Kong	1980/81	761	5 177	5 064	98	197 410	94 788	48	100
	1985/86	828	6 959	6 850	98	229 089	110 974	48	100
	1990/91	810	7 595	...	...	196 466	*95 480	*49	100
	1992/93	777	7 993	...	...	189 730	*92 020	*49	100
	1993/94	761	8 222	...	...	187 549	*90 774	*48	100
	1994/95	739	8 107	8 066	99	180 109	87 276	*48	100
India	1980/81	10 802				918 238	416 848	45	...
	1985/86	11 187	...	...	...	1 235 750	560 150	45	...
	1990/91	15 427	...	...	...	1 510 090	687 278	46	...
	1991/92	13 515	...	...	...	1 435 724	639 116	45	...
	1992/93	13 662	...	...	...	1 463 486	652 090	45	...
Indonesia	1980/81	19 868	37 100	...	...	1 005 226	...	...	99
	1985/86	26 419	58 341	...	...	1 258 468	...	...	100
	1990/91	39 121		...	...	1 604 254	...	...	100
	1991/92	40 284	70 509	...	...	1 554 755	...	...	100
	1992/93	43 155	86 738	...	...	1 567 236	...	...	100
	1993/94	40 007	95 585	...	...	1 596 283	...	...	100
Iran, Islamic Republic of	1980/81	2 791	9 356	...	...	172 000	...	...	-
	1985/86	1 732	5 795	5 791	100	106 986	50 376	47	-
	1990/91	3 586	8 520	8 504	100	227 492	108 151	48	-
	1992/93	3 003	6 885	6 860	100	168 864	81 307	48	-
	1993/94	2 483	6 469	6 446	100	132 653	63 534	48	-
	1994/95	2 715	6 151	6 131	100	141 728	67 782	48	-
Iraq	1980/81	387	3 235	3 235	100	76 507	36 671	48	-
	1985/86	584	4 657	4 657	100	81 431	38 604	47	-
	1990/91	646	4 908	4 908	100	86 508	41 225	48	-
	1992/93	578	4 778	4 778	100	90 836	43 656	48	-
	1994/95	576	4 972	4 972	100	93 028	45 220	49	-
Israel	1980/81	...	...	...	...	269 506	127 832	47	17
	1985/86	...	...	...	...	292 000	...	...	...
	1990/91	...	...	...	...	329 050	...	...	...
	1991/92	...	...	...	...	336 500	...	...	...
	1992/93	...	...	...	...	338 180	...	...	...
	1993/94	...	...	...	...	344 900	...	...	...
Japan	1980/81	14 893	110 037	97 083	88	2 407 093	1 177 453	49	73
	1985/86	15 220	107 606	94 762	88	2 067 951	1 012 435	49	75
	1990/91	15 076	109 753	97 419	89	2 007 964	987 014	49	78
	1992/93	15 006	102 279	95 974	94	1 948 868	958 956	49	80
	1993/94	14 958	102 828	96 584	94	1 909 136	939 051	49	80
	1994/95	14 901	103 014	96 801	94	1 852 183	912 089	49	80
Jordan	1980/81	207	737	731	99	19 598	8 372	43	99
	1985/86	358	1 336	1 332	100	27 954	12 554	45	98
	1990/91	546	1 933	1 932	100	44 856	20 406	45	99
	1991/92	575	2 115	2 113	- 100	49 422	22 530	46	98
	1992/93	600	2 016	2 002	99	52 284	23 848	46	96
	1993/94	666	2 422	2 417	100	55 996	25 606	46	99
Korea, Democratic People's Rep.	1987/88	16 964	35 000	35 000	100	728 000	350 000	48	-
Korea, Rep. of	1980/81	901	3 339	2 846	85	66 433	30 041	45	97
	1985/86	6 242	9 281	8 342	90	314 692	148 371	47	54
	1990/91	8 354	18 511	17 309	94	414 532	196 842	47	69
	1992/93	8 498	21 133	20 047	95	450 882	214 341	48	74
	1993/94	8 515	22 212	21 075	95	469 380	222 077	47	76
	1994/95	8 910	24 288	23 037	95	510 100	240 150	47	78
Kuwait	1980/81	109	1 696	1 696	100	29 965	14 262	48	41
	1985/86	161	2 539	2 539	100	42 830	20 665	48	37
	1990/91	...	2 343	2 343	100	37 771	18 688	49	9
	1992/93	169	2 634	2 632	100	47 677	23 505	49	17
	1993/94	177	2 747	2 747	100	46 482	22 648	49	21
	1994/95	193	2 927	2 925	100	49 016	23 920	49	22

3.3 Education preceding the first level
Enseignement précédant le premier degré
Enseñanza anterior al primer grado

Country / Pays / País	Year / Année / Año	Schools / Écoles / Escuelas	Teaching staff / Personnel enseignant / Personal docente			Pupils enrolled / Élèves inscrits / Alumnos matriculados			
			Total	Female Féminin Femenino	% F	Total	Female Féminin Femenino	% F	% Private Privé Privada
		(1)	(2)	(3)	(4)	(5)	(6)	(7)	(8)
Kyrgyzstan	1985/86	...	...	...	...	122 900	61 500	50	...
	1990/91	...	...	...	...	158 500	79 300	50	...
	1992/93	...	...	...	...	113 500	56 800	50	...
	1993/94	...	...	...	...	68 700	34 400	50	...
	1994/95	639	...	...	...	45 680	...	...	...
Lao People's Democratic Rep.	1980/81	153	252	252	100	5 296	2 719	51	-
	1985/86	500	1 327	1 327	100	21 625	9 534	44	-
	1989/90	638	1 519	1 519	100	28 167	14 008	50	-
	1991/92	608	1 618	1 618	100	25 675	13 627	53	-
	1992/93	659	1 755	1 750	100	27 389	14 498	53	8
	1993/94	750	1 883	1 883	100	29 703	15 353	52	11
Lebanon	1980/81	...	6 604	...	...	123 530	...	...	81
	1986/87	1 776	5 257	...	...	129 590	...	...	79
	1991/92	1 757	...	...	...	131 074	63 707	49	83
	1993/94	...	...	...	...	148 400	71 644	48	85
	1994/95	1 819	...	...	...	157 083	75 790	48	85
Macau	1990/91	...	...	...	...	20 814	10 090	48	...
	1991/92	...	...	...	...	21 573	10 419	48	...
	1992/93	...	...	...	...	21 600	10 352	48	...
Malaysia	1980	3 087	...	...	...	170 955	...	...	...
	1985	5 757	9 056	8 889	98	293 801	...	...	45
	1989/90	6 046	10 773	...	...	328 813	161 704	49	...
	1990/91	6 502	10 918	...	...	372 767	183 332	49	...
	1991/92	6 352	11 341	10 882	96	383 715	188 216	49	43
	1992/93	6 824	16 453	15 514	94	370 337	181 654	49	42
Maldives‡	1981	1	...	...	...	1 651	...	...	...
	1986	...	...	...	...	2 327	...	...	...
	1992	8	...	...	...	3 298	1 582	48	97
	1993	...	...	...	...	9 592	4 695	49	93
Mongolia	1980/81	617	1 813	1 813	100	49 800	...	...	-
	1985/86	680	2 205	...	...	62 470	...	...	-
	1990/91	909	3 747	...	...	97 212	...	...	-
	1991/92	883	4 088	...	...	95 715	...	...	-
Oman	1980/81	3	11	10	91	396	175	44	100
	1985/86	7	71	71	100	1 665	732	44	100
	1990/91	8	181	181	100	3 682	1 697	46	100
	1992/93	...	223	223	100	4 435	1 982	45	100
	1993/94	5	238	238	100	4 728	2 077	44	100
	1994/95	6	280	280	100	5 235	2 302	44	100
Philippines	1980/81	...	...	...	...	*123 571	...	...	...
	1985/86	2 334	4 636	...	...	189 654	98 020	52	61
	1990/91	4 201	9 644	...	...	397 364	...	...	58
	1993/94	5 035	...	...	...	416 894	...	...	53
Qatar	1980/81	19	...	...	...	2 587	1 203	47	100
	1985/86	36	247	247	100	4 859	2 244	46	100
	1990/91	53	287	285	99	5 230	2 492	48	100
	1992/93	57	348	341	98	5 905	2 651	45	100
	1993/94	59	294	294	100	6 756	3 165	47	100
	1994/95	64	302	302	100	6 786	3 192	47	100
Saudi Arabia	1980/81	195	1 127	1 098	97	28 045	12 375	44	87
	1985/86	492	3 001	2 941	98	51 604	23 654	46	78
	1990/91	646	4 839	4 839	100	67 069	30 378	45	79
	1991/92	725	5 182	5 182	100	73 523	36 512	50	78
	1992/93	806	5 098	5 098	100	81 464	37 102	46	78
	1993/94	752	6 704	6 234	93	84 992	46 105	54	78
Singapore	1980	122	...	...	...	11 142	5 240	47	63
	1985	108	684	684	100	15 658	7 344	47	69
	1989	104	776	776	100	17 858	8 429	47	72
Syrian Arab Rep.	1980/81	351	1 082	1 052	97	33 611	14 985	45	100
	1985/86	610	2 028	2 018	100	61 988	28 056	45	62
	1990/91	...	3 122	3 066	98	83 552	38 379	46	61
	1992/93	1 052	3 922	3 739	95	90 439	41 538	46	92
	1993/94	1 046	4 020	3 908	97	90 530	41 656	46	86
	1994/95	1 037	4 054	3 885	96	90 681	41 675	46	90
Tajikistan	1980/81	...	7 391	...	...	61 558	...	...	...
	1990/91	...	10 827	...	...	105 527	...	...	...
	1992/93	...	9 988	...	...	81 839	...	...	...
	1993/94	...	9 345	...	...	80 848	...	...	...
	1994/95	...	8 879	...	...	76 087	...	...	...

Education preceding the first level
Enseignement précédant le premier degré
Enseñanza anterior al primer grado

3.3

Country Pays País	Year Année Año	Schools Écoles Escuelas	Teaching staff Personnel enseignant Personal docente			Pupils enrolled Élèves inscrits Alumnos matriculados			
			Total	Female Féminin Femenino	% F	Total	Female Féminin Femenino	% F	% Private Privé Privada
		(1)	(2)	(3)	(4)	(5)	(6)	(7)	(8)
Thailand	1980/81	...	...	...	...	367 313	178 662	49	55
	1985/86	12 996	33 119	...	...	672 080	...	...	41
	1990/91	...	64 628	...	...	1 463 660	721 530	49	...
	1992/93	29 529	83 072	...	...	1 678 350	826 779	49	24
	1993/94	30 538	82 451	...	...	1 530 382	...	...	28
	1994/95	31 647	...	...	...	1 748 272	...	...	...
Turkey‡	1980/81	117	262	255	97	4 691	2 090	45	80
	1985/86	3 551	5 903	5 868	99	117 819	56 712	48	4
	1990/91	3 819	7 119	7 090	100	119 819	56 622	47	6
	1991/92	4 454	7 976	7 942	100	132 724	62 541	47	5
	1992/93	4 683	8 593	8 372	97	136 117	64 506	47	4
	1993/94	4 908	8 908	8 874	100	143 349	67 226	47	5
United Arab Emirates‡	1980/81	20	359	359	100	17 263	7 930	46	69
	1985/86	32	590	590	100	35 360	16 668	47	62
	1990/91	48	2 269	2 244	99	47 049	22 453	48	64
	1991/92	48	2 374	2 344	99	49 064	23 479	48	66
	1992/93	55	2 575	2 554	99	51 885	24 727	48	66
	1993/94	65	2 760	2 737	99	55 566	26 393	47	67
Uzbekistan	1980/81	...	50 500	...	...	915 200	...	...	...
	1985/86	...	68 200	...	...	1 095 600	...	...	...
	1990/91	...	89 800	...	...	1 349 400	...	...	...
	1992/93	...	101 700	...	...	1 211 500	590 300	49	...
	1993/94	...	100 200	...	...	1 166 300	562 500	48	...
	1994/95	...	96 100	...	...	1 071 400	515 500	48	...
Viet Nam	1980/81	6 121	57 605	57 605	100	1 595 724	823 806	52	-
	1985/86	6 446	65 718	65 718	100	1 701 681	885 567	52	-
	1990/91	...	65 400	...	...	1 534 900	...	...	...
	1991/92	...	69 800	...	...	1 496 100	...	...	...
	1992/93	6 806	69 619	...	...	1 538 882	...	...	...
	1993/94	6 870	65 691	...	...	1 652 947	...	...	...
Yemen	1990/91	51	665	...	...	10 067	4 748	47	...
	1991/92	61	645	...	...	10 283	4 836	47	...
	1993/94	62	680	...	...	11 999	5 698	47	...
Former Democratic Yemen	1980/81	26	311	307	99	5 541	2 562	46	-
	1985/86	29	387	...	...	11 578	5 605	48	-
Palestine	1994/95	436	1 211	1 210	100	36 829	17 706	48	100
Gaza Strip	1985/86	54	...	...	...	6 597	...	...	100
	1990/91	83	...	...	...	8 336	...	...	100
	1991/92	83	...	...	...	9 395	...	...	100
	1992/93	102	...	...	...	11 151	...	...	100
	1993/94	89	...	...	...	10 299	...	...	100
West Bank	1985/86	145	...	...	...	13 448			100
	1990/91	297	1 262	1 255	99	21 822	10 904	50	100
	1991/92	305	...	...	...	23 176	11 183	48	100
	1992/93	337	...	...	...	27 492	...	...	100
	1993/94	377	...	...	...	32 044	15 623	49	100
Europe									
Albania	1980/81	2 667	4 162	4 162	100	92 490	...	...	-
	1985/86	3 064	4 850	4 850	100	110 603	...	...	-
	1990/91	3 426	5 664	5 664	100	130 007	...	...	-
	1993/94	2 656	4 578	4 578	100	80 395	...	...	-
	1994/95	2 668	4 428	4 428	100	80 348	...	...	-
Austria	1980/81	3 423	7 069	7 030	99	165 611	81 262	49	28
	1985/86	3 667	8 159	8 113	99	181 582	88 540	49	27
	1990/91	3 915	9 329	9 295	100	194 829	94 633	49	26
	1991/92	3 983	9 634	9 615	100	197 186	95 703	49	26
	1992/93	4 084	9 981	9 961	100	202 294	97 962	48	26
	1993/94	4 212	11 536	11 317	98	209 743	101 570	48	26
Belarus	1980/81	3 488	36 400	...	...	345 300	...	...	-
	1985/86	4 476	52 000	...	...	407 100	...	...	-
	1990/91	5 215	62 300	...	...	419 600	...	...	-
	1992/93	4 938	56 100	...	...	380 200	...	...	-
	1993/94	4 811	54 800	...	...	367 600	...	...	-
	1994/95	4 674	55 300	...	...	368 700	166 000	45	-
Belgium	1980/81	4 325	17 116	17 075	100	383 955	188 248	49	58
	1985/86	4 087	19 793	19 691	99	391 848	191 208	49	58
	1990/91	4 058	...	...	...	374 343	182 180	49	57
	1991/92	3 992	...	...	...	398 005	193 641	49	57

Education preceding the first level
Enseignement précédant le premier degré
Enseñanza anterior al primer grado

Country Pays País	Year Année Año	Schools Écoles Escuelas	Teaching staff Personnel enseignant Personal docente			Pupils enrolled Élèves inscrits Alumnos matriculados			
			Total	Female Féminin Femenino	% F	Total	Female Féminin Femenino	% F	% Private Privé Privada
		(1)	(2)	(3)	(4)	(5)	(6)	(7)	(8)
Bulgaria	1980/81	6 185	28 996	28 996	100	420 804	204 002	48	-
	1985/86	5 054	28 864	28 864	100	360 395	174 649	48	-
	1990/91	4 590	28 776	28 776	100	303 779	148 397	49	-
	1992/93	4 429	27 400	27 400	100	263 004	127 750	49	0
	1993/94	3 856	25 623	25 516	100	247 472	119 892	48	0
	1994/95	3 659	24 091	24 018	100	246 608	119 550	48	0
Croatia	1990/91	930	5 619	...	...	...	...	...	...
	1992/93	814	4 820	...	...	54 715	26 072	48	0
	1993/94	846	5 081	...	...	59 767	28 499	48	2
	1994/95	871	5 320	5 308	100	65 395	31 098	48	2
Former Czechoslovakia	1980/81	11 119	47 290	47 290	100	694 720		...	-
	1985/86	11 477	51 104	51 104	100	681 515		...	-
Czech Republic	1990/91	...	32 112	...	...	352 139		...	-
	1992/93	6 817	29 937	29 937	100	325 591		...	0
	1993/94	6 601	27 394	27 394	100	331 509		...	1
	1994/95	6 526	27 695	27 695	100	338 119		...	2
Denmark‡	1980/81	...	...	...	...	62 936	30 864	49	8
	1985/86	...	3 592	2 037	57	56 735	27 743	49	8
	1990/91	...	3 663	...	...	51 583	25 208	49	9
	1991/92	...	3 830	...	...	53 138	26 054	49	9
	1992/93	...	4 023	...	...	53 102	25 845	49	10
	1993/94	...		...	...	56 251	27 254	48	10
Estonia	1988/89	...	10 040	...	...	66 875		...	-
	1990/91	...	10 917	...	...	70 807	34 401	49	-
	1992/93	...	8 698	8 685	100	56 831	27 720	49	-
	1993/94	...	8 163	8 144	100	57 212	28 060	49	-
	1994/95	...	8 093	8 078	100	61 940	30 117	49	0
Finland	1980/81	...	...	...	...	64 000	...	...	...
	1985/86	...	...	...	...	76 097	...	...	...
	1990/91	...	...	...	...	86 400	...	...	3
	1991/92	...	...	...	...	88 492	...	...	3
	1992/93	...	...	...	...	89 670	43 676	49	2
	1993/94	...	...	...	...	92 229	45 192	49	6
France‡	1980/81	16 080	66 948	...	...	2 383 465	1 163 500	49	13
	1985/86	17 776	71 705	69 093	96	2 563 464	1 247 108	49	13
	1990/91	18 850	...	...	...	2 555 684	1 246 014	49	12
	1992/93	19 041	...	...	...	2 549 638	1 246 554	49	12
	1993/94	19 028	106 700	83 200	78	2 566 197	1 244 451	48	12
	1994/95	...	...	...	...	2 530 800	...	...	...
Germany	1991/92	...	...	...	...	2 516 250	...	...	...
	1992/93	43 552	137 330	132 787	97	2 712 643	1 322 087	49	53
	1993/94	43 660	137 557	133 010	97	2 716 409	1 320 122	49	53
Former German Democratic Rep.	1980/81	12 145	56 448	56 448	100	663 491	...	...	-
	1985/86	13 148	69 612	69 612	100	788 232	...	...	-
	1989/90	13 452	73 383	73 383	100	747 140	...	...	-
Federal Republic of Germany	1980/81	26 793	...	...	...	*1 535 959	*751 010	*49	...
	1985/86	*26 874	...	...	...	*1 582 051	*755 064	*48	...
	1990/91	28 848	*85 201	*72 665	*85	1 755 944	851 196	48	*67
Gibraltar‡	1980/81	1	2	2	100	28	11	39	...
	1984/85	2	5	5	100	150	53	35	...
Greece	1980/81	4 576	6 514	6 514	100	145 924	71 173	49	9
	1985/86	5 203	7 617	7 617	100	160 079	78 152	49	4
	1990/91	5 518	8 400	8 384	100	136 536	66 497	49	5
	1991/92	5 529	8 377	8 357	100	135 014	66 147	49	5
	1992/93	5 544	8 179	8 103	99	134 991	66 692	49	4
	1993/94	5 588	8 400	8 376	100	132 818	65 167	49	4
Hungary	1980/81	4 690	29 437	29 437	100	478 100	230 493	48	-
	1985/86	4 823	33 548	33 548	100	424 678	206 606	49	-
	1990/91	4 718	33 635	33 534	100	391 129	187 805	48	0
	1992/93	4 730	33 140	...	...	394 420	...	...	...
	1993/94	4 712	32 957	32 957	100	397 153	191 484	48	2
	1994/95	4 719	37 470	...	...	396 184	190 357	48	1
Iceland	1980/81	...	...	...	...	4 041	...	...	...
	1985/86	...	...	...	...	4 528	2 222	49	...
	1990/91	...	...	...	...	4 174	2 043	49	...
	1991/92	...	...	...	...	3 988	2 024	51	...
	1992/93	...	...	...	...	3 985	1 951	49	...
	1993/94	...	...	...	...	4 117	1 982	48	...

Education preceding the first level
Enseignement précédant le premier degré
Enseñanza anterior al primer grado

3.3

Country Pays País	Year Année Año	Schools Écoles Escuelas	Teaching staff Personnel enseignant Personal docente			Pupils enrolled Élèves inscrits Alumnos matriculados			
			Total	Female Féminin Femenino	% F	Total	Female Féminin Femenino	% F	% Private Privé Privada
		(1)	(2)	(3)	(4)	(5)	(6)	(7)	(8)
Ireland	1980/81	...	4 782	3 523	74	137 533	66 568	48	100
	1985/86	...	5 164	3 921	76	147 908	71 501	48	100
	1990/91	...	4 541	3 481	77	127 512	61 517	48	100
	1991/92	...	4 613	3 548	77	126 168	61 228	49	100
	1992/93	...	4 598	3 549	77	122 991	59 740	49	100
	1993/94	...	4 730	3 657	77	118 205	57 284	48	100
Italy	1980/81	30 295	108 261	...	...	1 870 477	917 854	49	38
	1985/86	28 943	108 184	...	...	1 660 986	805 727	49	32
	1990/91	27 716	108 339	107 353	99	1 552 694	759 111	49	29
	1991/92	27 463	103 540	102 920	99	1 552 255	758 946	49	29
	1992/93	27 274	104 715	104 086	99	1 569 811	767 638	49	29
	1993/94	26 895	120 387	119 530	99	1 577 842	771 565	49	29
Latvia	1980/81	...	...	...	...	84 165	41 300	49	-
	1985/86	...	...	...	...	95 684	...	...	-
	1990/91	...	12 336	...	...	90 832	44 608	49	-
	1992/93	750	8 435	...	...	58 088	28 347	49	-
	1993/94	647	7 383	...	...	53 352	25 966	49	-
	1994/95	608	8 716	...	...	58 947	28 053	48	0
Lithuania	1980/81	...	14 335	...	...	110 778	...	...	-
	1985/86	...	18 902	...	...	136 210	...	...	-
	1990/91	...	22 026	...	...	134 765	...	...	-
	1992/93	...	14 472	...	...	92 027	...	...	-
	1993/94	811	11 676	11 621	100	78 596	39 123	50	-
	1994/95	748	11 511	11 465	100	74 936	...	...	0
Luxembourg	1980/81	...	415	411	99	7 621	3 703	49	1
	1985/86	...	440	...	...	7 779	...	...	...
	1990/91	...	...	...	...	8 354	...	...	...
	1991/92	...	467	...	...	8 689	...	...	...
	1993/94	...	491	...	...	9 408	...	...	1
Malta	1980/81	42	428	372	87	7 691	3 630	47	51
	1985/86	43	324	324	100	7 899	3 818	48	56
	1990/91	58	688	688	100	11 313	5 364	47	38
	1991/92	49	692	692	100	11 770	5 791	49	36
	1992/93	47	697	697	100	12 025	5 921	49	37
	1993/94	52	739	739	100	12 226	6 000	49	36
Moldova	1980/81	...	18 051	18 051	100	175 660	84 317	48	...
	1985/86	...	22 620	22 620	100	209 349	100 488	48	...
	1990/91	...	28 067	28 067	100	248 384	119 224	48	...
	1992/93	...	25 728	25 728	100	207 288	99 498	48	...
	1993/94	...	23 587	23 587	100	190 235	91 313	48	...
	1994/95	...	21 680	21 680	100	162 062	76 169	47	...
Monaco	1980/81	5	...	...	...	330	151	46	...
	1990/91	9	47	30	64	903	429	48	33
	1991/92	9	52	39	75	962	448	47	32
	1993/94	9	44	...	...	1 055	523	50	30
	1994/95	9	46	...	...	1 034	493	48	28
Netherlands‡	1980/81	8 727	22 361	22 361	100	409 576	198 795	49	70
	1985/86	8 401	21 426	21 426	100	359 130	176 497	49	68
	1990/91	8 450	21 019	21 019	100	360 880	177 951	49	69
	1991/92	8 435	22 200	22 200	100	367 602	182 586	50	68
	1992/93	8 331	22 700	22 700	100	368 473	180 491	49	68
	1993/94	8 139	23 000	23 000	100	369 764	181 593	49	68
Norway	1980/81	2 554	16 866	...	...	78 189	...	...	41
	1985/86	3 281	...	...	...	98 454	...	...	37
	1990/91	4 649	35 891	34 152	95	139 350	...	...	36
	1991/92	5 214	34 534	33 165	96	155 153	...	...	38
	1992/93	5 836	37 549	35 951	96	174 096	...	...	37
	1993/94	6 444	43 862	41 483	95	190 064	...	...	37
Poland	1980/81	31 014	57 730	57 137	99	1 349 528	...	...	0
	1985/86	26 344	78 092	76 798	98	1 360 044	...	...	0
	1990/91	25 732	89 864	...	...	1 226 101	...	...	0
	1992/93	21 043	75 350	...	...	1 011 369	...	...	1
	1993/94	21 055	74 593	...	...	979 112	...	...	2
	1994/95	21 017	75 215	...	...	997 824	...	...	2
Portugal	1980/81	1 916	5 047	4 974	99	100 178	48 389	48	31
	1985/86	2 547	6 408	6 323	99	128 089	62 226	49	58
	1990/91	4 879	9 700	9 495	98	181 450	87 943	48	64
	1993/94	5 406	9 064	...	...	181 000	...	...	58
Romania	1980/81	13 467	38 512	38 512	100	935 711	461 084	49	-
	1985/86	12 811	33 522	33 522	100	864 332	426 792	49	-
	1990/91	12 529	37 007	37 007	100	752 141	375 347	50	-
	1992/93	12 603	36 447	36 447	100	752 063	376 242	50	0
	1993/94	12 715	37 303	37 126	100	712 136	354 861	50	0
	1994/95	12 665	37 603	37 288	99	715 514	356 475	50	0

3.3 Education preceding the first level
Enseignement précédant le premier degré
Enseñanza anterior al primer grado

Country Pays País	Year Année Año	Schools Écoles Escuelas	Teaching staff Personnel enseignant Personal docente			Pupils enrolled Élèves inscrits Alumnos matriculados			
			Total	Female Féminin Femenino	% F	Total	Female Féminin Femenino	% F	% Private Privé Privada
		(1)	(2)	(3)	(4)	(5)	(6)	(7)	(8)
Russian Federation	1980/81	...	532 000	...	...	5 703 000	...	...	-
	1985/86	...	677 000	...	...	6 488 000	...	...	-
	1990/91	...	770 000	...	...	7 042 000	...	...	-
	1991/92	...	768 000	...	...	6 882 000	3 217 000	47	-
	1992/93	...	687 000	...	...	6 058 000	...	...	0
	1993/94	78 333	646 000	...	...	5 696 000	2 657 000	47	*7
San Marino	1980/81	17	91	91	100	877	430	49	-
	1985/86	16	109	109	100	814	388	48	-
	1990/91	15	108	108	100	759	373	49	-
	1991/92	15	103	103	100	750	346	46	-
	1992/93	15	103	103	100	785	363	46	-
	1993/94	15	102	102	100	811	377	46	-
Slovakia	1980/81	3 723	16 180	...	...	231 155	...	...	-
	1985/86	3 976	18 249	...	...	249 448	...	...	-
	1990/91	4 025	18 620	...	...	216 336	...	...	-
	1992/93	3 642	17 218	...	...	188 502	...	...	-
	1993/94	3 482	15 834	...	...	183 872	...	...	0
	1994/95	3 343	14 639	...	...	174 436	...	...	0
Slovenia	1992/93	774	4 809	4 719	98	53 543	25 666	48	-
	1993/94	773	4 803	4 780	100	55 460	26 599	48	-
	1994/95	776	4 944	4 902	99	55 233	26 263	48	0
Spain	1980/81	...	35 588	34 386	97	1 182 425	593 030	50	45
	1985/86	...	39 573	36 723	93	1 127 348	555 852	49	38
	1990/91	15 260	40 051	38 172	95	994 322	491 140	49	39
	1991/92	15 404	43 922	42 020	96	1 025 797	500 946	49	38
	1992/93	17 816	48 767	46 708	96	1 052 488	513 474	49	36
	1993/94	17 866	48 489	46 442	96	1 077 797	525 821	49	35
Sweden	1980/81	8 504	...	...	...	226 571	...	...	...
	1985/86	...	...	...	...	224 161	...	...	...
	1990/91	...	...	...	...	262 320	...	...	...
	1991/92	...	...	...	...	283 506	...	...	...
	1992/93	...	...	...	...	292 541	...	...	...
	1993/94	8 982	74 167	72 190	97	295 529	147 763	50	8
Switzerland	1980/81	...	...	...	...	120 315	58 402	49	7
	1985/86	...	...	...	...	123 128	59 848	49	3
	1990/91	...	...	...	...	139 798	68 225	49	5
	1991/92	...	...	...	...	141 360	68 832	49	5
	1992/93	3 600	...	...	...	144 469	70 258	49	6
	1993/94	...	...	...	...	149 250	72 461	49	6
The Former Yugoslav Rep. of Macedonia	1992/93	49	2 967	2 865	97	30 946	14 956	48	-
	1993/94	49	2 938	2 913	99	30 432	14 645	48	-
	1994/95	...	3 027	3 000	99	31 980	15 527	49	-
Ukraine	1980/81	21 200	194 700	...	...	1 779 300	...	...	-
	1985/86	22 600	236 000	...	...	1 902 600	894 200	47	-
	1990/91	23 600	212 600	...	...	1 939 600	911 600	47	-
	1991/92	23 500	212 200	...	...	1 875 000	892 600	48	-
	1992/93	23 700	201 400	...	...	1 663 200	775 100	47	-
	1993/94	23 100	191 500	...	...	1 566 600	728 500	47	-
United Kingdom‡	1980/81	1 251	...	...	...	326 400	158 900	49	8
	1985/86	1 262	...	...	...	665 000	315 000	47	5
	1990/91	1 364	30 900	29 500	95	792 700	388 100	49	6
	1991/92	1 380	32 100	30 600	95	810 600	396 500	49	6
	1992/93	1 406	12 100	12 100	100	426 900	209 700	49	...
	1993/94	...	12 280	12 280	100	430 927	210 144	49	...
Former Yugoslavia	1980/81	3 177	29 436	27 632	94	290 870	139 284	48	-
	1985/86	3 852	37 686	35 588	94	374 740	180 440	48	-
	1990/91	4 139	46 273	43 743	95	423 899	204 513	48	-
Federal Republic of Yugoslavia	1991/92	2 658	29 879	28 232	94	261 988	126 145	48	-
	1992/93	1 682	16 306	15 367	94	159 719	77 015	48	-
	1993/94	1 638	15 622	14 633	94	146 212	70 659	48	-
Oceania									
American Samoa	1980/81	111	...	...	...	1 922	891	46	7
	1985/86	97	98	98	100	2 001	941	47	10
	1989/90	95	103	102	99	2 874	1 454	51	17
	1991/92	92	123	122	99	2 694	...	...	11
Australia‡	1980	...	...	...	...	165 742	80 485	49	22
	1985	...	...	...	...	161 974	78 433	48	26
	1990	...	...	...	...	180 470	88 117	49	26
	1992	...	...	...	...	181 358	88 356	49	26
	1993	...	...	...	...	182 269	88 878	49	...
	1994	...	...	...	...	186 163	90 742	49	...

Education preceding the first level 3.3
Enseignement précédant le premier degré
Enseñanza anterior al primer grado

Country / Pays / País	Year / Année / Año	Schools / Écoles / Escuelas	Teaching staff / Personnel enseignant / Personal docente			Pupils enrolled / Élèves inscrits / Alumnos matriculados			
			Total	Female Féminin Femenino	% F	Total	Female Féminin Femenino	% F	% Private Privé Privada
		(1)	(2)	(3)	(4)	(5)	(6)	(7)	(8)
Cook Islands	1985	...	...	...	...	412	...	...	...
	1988	24	23	22	96	360	...	...	...
Fiji	1980	163	196	196	100	4 493	2 201	49	100
	1985	244	308	306	99	4 206	...	...	100
	1990	299	375	...	...	7 506	3 760	50	100
	1991	327	...	...	...	7 839	...	...	100
	1992	334	422	...	...	8 209	4 114	50	100
French Polynesia‡	1984/85	67	462	462	100	11 937	5 854	49	19
	1990/91	75	626	521	98	15 860	7 765	49	17
	1992/93	77	669	660	99	16 472	7 905	48	16
	1994/95	71	...	...	...	16 545	7 936	48	16
Nauru	1985	4	20	20	100	383	187	49	-
New Caledonia	1980	...	...	...	...	10 313	5 121	50	25
	1985	52	355	...	...	8 647	4 280	49	33
	1990	73	428	...	...	10 745	5 261	49	31
	1991	80	461	...	...	11 431	5 531	48	31
	1994	...	...	...	...	12 776	...	...	...
New Zealand‡	1980	1 208	...	...	...	56 858	27 653	49	0
	1985	1 388	1 459	1 444	99	60 666	29 590	49	0
	1990	2 890	...	...	...	118 367	57 765	49	0
	1992	3 336	5 567	5 448	98	135 732	65 778	48	0
	1993	3 000	...	...	...	132 932	64 856	49	...
	1994	3 720	7 174	6 793	95	131 311	64 006	49	...
Papua New Guinea‡	1987	...	...	...	...	1 196	519	43	100
	1990	...	...	...	...	934	434	46	100
	1991	...	...	...	...	698	328	47	100
	1992	...	...	...	...	856	411	48	100
	1994	9	20	15	75	1 524	703	46	60
Solomon Islands‡	1990	...	...	...	...	10 122	4 711	47	...
	1992	...	...	...	...	12 705	5 900	46	9
	1993	...	...	...	...	12 839	6 059	47	9
	1994	...	...	...	...	12 627	5 950	47	...
Tokelau	1981	3	3	3	100	56	27	48	-
	1991	3	5	5	100	133	64	48	-
Vanuatu, Republic of	1980	34	49	49	100	1 187	557	47	66
	1992	252	...	...	...	5 178	*2 500	*48	100

The data refer to education preceding the first level, e.g. kindergarten, nursery schools as well as infant classes attached to schools at higher levels. Day nurseries, child care and play centres, etc. are excluded. Unless otherwise stated, data cover both public and private establishments. Figures on teaching staff refer, in general, to both full-time and part-time teachers. The enrolment in private institutions (aided and unaided) as a percentage of the total number of children enrolled in education preceding the first level is also shown. In some cases, the data given should be considered as a approximate indication of the importance of education preceding the first level since complete data are not available. Table 3.1 should be consulted for complementary information.

Les données se rapportent à l'enseignement qui précède le premier degré (jardins d'enfants, écoles maternelles et classes enfantines ouvertes dans des écoles de niveau plus élevé). Les centres de puériculture, garderies, crèches, etc. sont exclus. Sauf indication contraire, les données se rapportent à la fois aux établissements publics et aux établissements privés. Les chiffres relatifs au personnel enseignant englobent, en général, le personnel à plein temps et le personnel à temps partiel. Le pourcentage des effectifs inscrits dans les établissements privés (subventionnés et non subventionnés) par rapport au total des effectifs del'enseignement précédant le premier degré a été indiqué. Il convient cependant de considérer les données de ce tableau comme une indication approximative de l'importance de l'enseignement précédant le premier degré, car on ne dispose pas de données complètes dans tous les cas. Pour des renseignements complémentaires, veuillez consulter le tableau 3.1.

Los datos se refieren a la enseñanza anterior al primer grado (jardines de la infancia, escuelas maternales y clases de párvulos adscritas a establecimientos docentes de grado superior). En la medida de lo posible, se han excluído las guarderías, centros de juego, etc. Cuando no se indica otra cosa, los datos comprenden a la vez los establecimientos públicos y los privados. Las cifras relativas al personal docente abarcan, en general, el personal que trabaja en régimen de jornada completa y el de jornada parcial. Se indica el porcentage a la matrícula correspondiente a los establecimientos privados (subvencionados y no subvencionados) con respecto a la matrícula total de la enseñanza anterior al primer grado. Procede, sin embargo, considerar los datos de este cuadro como una indicación aproximada de la importancia de la enseñanza anterior al primer grado, ya que no se dispone de datos completos en todos los casos. Para toda información complementaria, debe consultarse el cuadro 3.1.

3.3 Education preceding the first level
Enseignement précédant le premier degré
Enseñanza anterior al primer grado

AFRICA:
Angola:
E--> Data refer to initiation classes where pupils learn Portuguese.
FR-> Les données se réfèrent aux classes d'initiation où les élèves apprennent le portugais.
ESP> Los datos se refieren a las clases de iniciación donde los alumnos aprenden el portugués.
Burkina Faso:
E--> For 1989/90, data on teaching staff refer to public education only.
FR-> En 1989/90, les données sur le personnel enseignant se réfèrent à l'enseignement public seulement.
ESP> Para 1989/90 los datos sobre el personal docente se refieren a la enseñanza pública solamente.
Burundi:
E--> Data for 1980/81 refer to public education only.
FR-> En 1980/81, les données se réfèrent à l'enseignement public seulement.
ESP> Para 1980/81, los datos se refieren a la enseñanza pública solamente.
Equatorial Guinea:
E--> Data refer to public education only.
FR-> Les données se réfèrent à l'enseignement public seulement.
ESP> Los datos se refieren a la enseñanza pública solamente.
Ghana:
E--> Data for 1985/86 refer to public education only.
FR-> En 1985/86, les données se réfèrent à l'enseignement public seulement.
ESP> Para 1985/86, los datos se refieren a la enseñanza pública solamente.
Guinea-Bissau:
E--> Except for 1986/87, data refer to *Sector autonomo Bissau* only.
FR-> A l'exception de 1986/87, les données se réfèrent au *Sector autonomo Bissau* seulement.
ESP> Excepto para 1986/87, los datos se refieren al *Sector autonomo Bissau* solamente.
Morocco:
E--> For 1980/81, data on teaching staff refer to Koranic schools only.
FR-> En 1980/81, les données sur le personnel enseignant se réfèrent aux écoles coraniques seulement.
ESP> Para 1980/81, los datos sobre el personal docente se refieren a las escuelas coránicas solamente.
Mozambique:
E--> Data refer to initiation classes where pupils learn Portuguese.
FR-> Les données se réfèrent aux classes d'initiation où les élèves apprennent le portugais.
ESP> Los datos se refieren a las clases de iniciación donde los alumnos aprenden el portugués.
South Africa:
E--> Until 1993, data do not include the former Independent States (Transkei, Bophuthatswana, Venda and Ciskei).
FR-> Jusqu'en 1993, les données n'incluent pas les anciens Etats indépendants (Transkei, Bophuthatswana, Venda et Ciskei).
ESP> Hasta 1993, los datos no incluyen los antiguos estados independientes (Transkei, Bophuthatswana, Venda y Ciskei).
Sudan:
E--> Data include Koranic schools *Khalwas* which accept pupils of all ages (161,882 pupils in 1985/86).
FR-> Les données incluent les écoles coraniques *Khalwas* qui acceptent les élèves de tous âges (161 882 élèves en 1985/86).
ESP> Los datos incluyen las escuelas coránicas *Khalwas* que admiten a los alumnos de todas las edades (161 882 alumnos en 1985/86).
AMERICA, NORTH:
Bahamas:
E--> Data for 1991/92 and 1993/94 refer to public education only.
FR-> Les données de 1991/92 et 1993/94 se réfèrent à l'enseignement public seulement.
ESP> Los datos de 1991/92 y 1993/94 se refieren a la enseñanza pública solamente.
Bermuda:
E--> Data on teaching staff refer to public education only.
FR-> Les données relatives au personnel enseignant se réfèrent à l'enseignement public seulement.
ESP> Los datos sobre el personal docente se refieren a la enseñanza pública solamente.
El Salvador:
E--> Data on teaching staff for 1991 and 1992 refer to public education only.
FR-> Les données relatives au personnel enseignant pour 1991 et 1992 se réfèrent à l'enseignement public seulement.

ESP> Los datos relativos al personal docente para 1991 y 1992 se refieren a la enseñanza pública solamente.
Guatemala:
E--> For 1980, data do not include classes where pupils learn Spanish (la castellanización).
FR-> Pour 1980, les données n'incluent pas les classes où les élèves apprennent l'espagnol (la castellanización).
ESP> Para 1980, los datos no incluyen las clases donde los alumnos aprenden el español (la castellanización).
Haiti:
E--> Data refer to infant classes.
FR-> Les données se réfèrent aux classes enfantines.
ESP> Los datos se refieren a las clases infantiles.
Jamaica:
E--> Data for 1992/93 refer to public and aided schools only.
FR-> Les données de 1992/93 se réfèrent aux écoles publiques et subventionnées seulement.
ESP> Los datos de 1992/93 se refieren a las escuelas públicas y subvencionadas solamente.
Montserrat:
E--> Data for 1981/82 refer to public education only.
FR-> Les données de 1981/82 se réfèrent à l'enseignement public seulement.
ESP> Los datos de 1981/82 se refieren a la enseñanza pública solamente.
Trinidad and Tobago:
E--> With the exception of 1989/90, data refer to public education only.
FR-> A l'exception de 1989/90, les données se réfèrent à l'enseignement public seulement.
ESP> Excepto para 1989/90, los datos se refieren a la enseñanza pública solamente.
U.S. Virgin Islands:
E--> For 1985/86, data on teaching staff refer to public education only.
FR-> En 1985/86, les données relatives au personnel enseignant se réfèrent à l'enseignement public seulement.
ESP> Para 1985/86, los datos relativos al personal docente se refieren a la enseñanza pública solamente.
AMERICA, SOUTH:
Uruguay:
E--> For 1980 and 1993, data on teaching staff refer to public education only.
FR-> Pour 1980 et 1993 les données relatives au personnel enseignant se réfèrent à l'enseignement public seulement.
ESP> Para 1980 y 1993 los datos sobre el personal docente se refieren a la enseñanza pública solamente.
ASIA:
Cyprus:
E--> Not including Turkish schools.
FR-> Non compris les écoles turques.
ESP> Excluyendo las escuelas turcas.
Maldives:
E--> The increase in enrolment from 1992 to 1993 is due to the fact that pre-schools, which were exclusively found in the capital, have now expanded into the atolls.
FR-> De 1992 à 1993 l'augmentation des effectifs est due au fait que les écoles préprimaires qui n'existaient que dans la capitale, se sont maintenant développées dans les atolls.
ESP> De 1992 a 1993 el aumento de la matrícula se debe a que las escuelas preprimarias, existentes solamente en la capital, se han extendido también a los atolones.
Turkey:
E--> For 1980/81, data refer to kindergarten only.
FR-> Pour 1980/81, les données se réfèrent aux jardins d'enfants seulement.
ESP> Para 1980/81, los datos se refieren a los jardines infantiles solamente.
United Arab Emirates:
E--> Data on schools and those on teaching staff for 1980/81 and 1985/86 refer to public education only.
FR-> Les données sur les écoles et celles sur le personnel enseignant en 1980/81 et 1985/86 se réfèrent à l'enseignement public seulement.
ESP> Los datos sobre las escuelas y sobre el personal docente para 1980/81 y 1985/86 se refieren a la enseñanza pública solamente.
EUROPE:
Denmark:
E--> From 1990/91, data on teaching staff are expressed in full-time equivalent.
FR-> A partir de 1990/91, les données relatives au personnel enseignant sont exprimées en équivalents plein-temps.
ESP> A partir de 1990/91, los datos sobre el personal docente están expresados en equivalentes de jornada completa.

Education preceding the first level
Enseignement précédant le premier degré
Enseñanza anterior al primer grado

3.3

France:
E--> In 1980/81 and 1985/86 data on teaching staff refer to public education only.

FR-> En 1980/81 et 1985/86, les données relatives au personnel enseignant se réfèrent à l'enseignement public seulement.

ESP> En 1980/81 y 1985/86 los datos sobre el personal docente se refieren a la enseñanza pública solamente.

Gibraltar:
E--> Data refer to public education only.

FR-> Les données se réfèrent à l'enseignement public seulement.

ESP> Los datos se refieren a la enseñanza pública solamente.

Netherlands:
E--> The number of schools refers to the total number of pre-primary schools and primary schools.

FR-> Le nombre d'écoles se réfère au total des écoles préprimaires et primaires.

ESP> El número de escuelas se refiere al total de las escuelas preprimarias y primarias.

United Kingdom:
E--> Data for 1980/81 refer to full-time pupils only. From 1992/93, the data only refer to nursery schools and nursery classes within primary schools; education provided in infant classes in primary schools is now included with education at the first level.

FR-> Les données pour 1980/81 se réfèrent aux élèves à plein temps seulement. Depuis 1992/93, les données ne se réfèrent qu'aux écoles maternelles et aux classes maternelles dans les écoles primaires; l'enseignement dispensé dans les classes enfantines des écoles primaires est à présent compris dans l'enseignement du premier degré.

ESP> Los datos para 1980/81 se refieren a los alumnos de jornada completa solamente. A partir de 1992/93, los datos sólo se refieren a las guarderías y a las secciones de guadería adscritas a escuelas primarias; la enseñanza impartida en las clases de párvulos de las escuelas primarias está ahora comprendida en la enseñanza de primer grado.

OCEANIA:
Australia:
E--> Data refer only to pre-primary classes in primary schools (pre-year 1).

FR-> Les données se réfèrent seulement aux classes du préprimaire rattachées aux écoles primaires (*pre-year 1*).

ESP> Los datos se refieren solamente a las clases de preprimaria adscritas a las escuelas primarias (*pre-year 1*).

French Polynesia:
E--> For 1990/91, data on female teachers and the percentage female refer to public education only.

FR-> Pour 1990/91, les données relatives au personnel enseignant féminin et au pourcentage se réfèrent à l'enseignement public seulement.

ESP> Para 1990/91, los datos sobre el personal docente femenino y el porcentaje se refieren a la enseñanza.

New Zealand:
E--> Data for 1980 and 1985 do not include licensed childcare centres.

FR-> Les données pour 1980 et 1985 ne comprennent pas les *licensed childcare centres*.

ESP> Los datos para 1980 y 1985 no comprenden los *licensed childcare centres*.

Papua New Guinea:
E--> For 1994, data on teaching staff refer to public education only.

FR-> Pour 1994, les données relatives au personnel enseignant se réfèrent à l'enseignement public seulement.

ESP> Para 1994, los datos relativos el personal docente se refieren a la enseñanza pública solamente.

Solomon Islands:
E--> Data refer to preparatory classes.

FR-> Les données se réfèrent aux classes préparatoires.

ESP> Los datos se refieren a las clases preparatorias.

3.4 First level: schools, teachers and pupils
Premier degré: écoles, enseignants et élèves
Primer grado: escuelas, personal docente y alumnos

3.4 Education at the first level: schools, teachers and pupils

Enseignement du premier degré: écoles, personnel enseignant et élèves

Enseñanza de primer grado: escuelas, personal docente y alumnos

Please refer to the explanatory text at the end of the table

Prière de se référer au texte explicatif à la fin du tableau

Referirse al texto explicativo al final del cuadro

Country / Pays / País	Year / Année / Año	Schools / Écoles / Escuelas	Teaching staff / Personnel enseignant / Personal docente			Pupils enrolled / Élèves inscrits / Alumnos matriculados			Pupil/teacher ratio / Nombre d'élèves par maître / Número de alumnos por maestro
			Total	Female / Féminin / Femenino	% F	Total	Female / Féminin / Femenino	% F	
		(1)	(2)	(3)	(4)	(5)	(6)	(7)	(8)
Africa									
Algeria	1980/81	9 263	88 481	32 506	37	3 118 827	1 307 550	42	35
	1985/86	11 360	125 034	49 807	40	3 481 288	1 516 157	44	28
	1990/91	13 135	151 262	59 074	39	4 189 152	1 877 990	45	28
	1992/93	13 970	161 802	65 512	40	4 436 363	2 011 685	45	27
	1993/94	14 734	164 982	70 492	43	4 515 274	2 061 359	46	27
	1994/95	14 836	166 771	71 817	43	4 548 827	2 086 456	46	27
Angola	1980/81	6 090	...	...	...	1 300 673	...	...	...
	1985/86	...	31 161	...	...	974 498	440 764	45	31
	1990/91	...	31 062	...	...	990 155	*475 500	*48	32
	1991/92	...	...	...	...	989 443	...	...	...
Benin	1980/81	2 275	7 994	1 848	23	379 926	121 745	32	48
	1985/86	2 715	13 452	3 284	24	444 163	148 882	34	33
	1990/91	2 864	13 556	...	...	490 129	163 048	33	36
	1991/92	2 904	13 422	...	...	534 810	179 612	34	40
	1992/93	...	13 184	...	...	599 830	...	...	45
	1993/94	...	12 890	...	...	628 689	...	...	49
Botswana	1980	415	5 316	3 827	72	171 914	93 793	55	32
	1985	528	6 980	5 435	78	223 608	117 185	52	32
	1990	602	8 956	7 150	80	283 516	146 299	52	32
	1992	643	10 463	8 057	77	301 482	154 068	51	29
	1993	657	11 190	8 582	77	305 479	154 728	51	27
	1994	669	11 726	...	...	310 050	...	...	26
Burkina Faso	1980/81	936	3 700	747	20	201 595	74 367	37	54
	1985/86	1 758	...	...	...	351 807	129 838	37	...
	1990/91	2 486	8 903	2 405	27	504 414	193 652	38	57
	1991/92	2 590	9 165	...	...	530 013	205 296	39	58
	1992/93	2 741	9 412	2 298	24	562 644	218 396	39	60
	1993/94	2 971	10 300	2 408	23	600 032	233 806	39	58
Burundi	1981/82	792	5 252	2 487	47	206 408	79 400	38	39
	1985/86	1 023	6 866	3 260	47	385 936	161 473	42	56
	1990/91	1 342	9 465	4 376	46	633 203	288 896	46	67
	1991/92	1 373	9 582	4 498	47	631 039	283 768	45	66
	1992/93	1 418	10 400	4 865	47	651 086	292 906	45	63
Cameroon	1980/81	4 971	26 763	5 248	20	1 379 205	626 966	45	52
	1985/86	5 856	33 598	8 993	27	1 705 319	777 820	46	51
	1990/91	6 709	38 430	11 534	30	1 964 146	904 179	46	51
	1991/92	6 890	40 012	12 647	32	1 915 148	913 132	48	48
	1993/94	...	...	...	...	1 892 778	891 530	47	...
	1994/95	6 801	40 970	12 973	32	1 896 722	893 617	47	46

First level: schools, teachers and pupils   3.4
Premier degré: écoles, enseignants et élèves
Primer grado: escuelas, personal docente y alumnos

Country / Pays / País	Year / Année / Año	Schools / Écoles / Escuelas	Teaching staff / Personnel enseignant / Personal docente			Pupils enrolled / Élèves inscrits / Alumnos matriculados			Pupil/teacher ratio / Nombre d'élèves par maître / Número de alumnos por maestro
			Total	Female / Féminin / Femenino	% F	Total	Female / Féminin / Femenino	% F	
		(1)	(2)	(3)	(4)	(5)	(6)	(7)	(8)
Cape Verde‡	1980/81	...	1 436	...	...	57 587	27 985	49	...
	1985/86	436	1 493	...	...	57 909	28 625	49	...
	1989/90	*367	2 028	1 221	60	67 761	33 238	49	33
	1990/91	370	...	...	...	69 832	...	...	...
	1993/94	...	2 657	1 560	59	78 173	38 336	49	29
Central African Republic	1980/81	825	4 130	1 016	25	246 174	90 468	37	60
	1985/86	961	4 718	1 178	25	309 656	120 968	39	66
	1989/90	986	3 581	942	26	323 661	125 578	39	90
Chad	1985/86	1 243	4 779	168	4	337 616	95 323	28	71
	1990/91	2 073	7 980	470	6	525 165	162 857	31	66
	1992/93	2 739	9 126	...	...	553 105	177 592	32	61
	1993/94	...	8 905	632	7	542 405	175 318	32	61
	1994/95	...	8 826	690	8	547 695	177 897	32	62
Comoros‡	1980/81	236	1 292	95	7	59 709	24 777	41	46
	1985/86	253	1 901	393	21	66 084	28 241	43	35
	1990/91	257	1 995	...	...	72 824	30 300	42	37
	1991/92	255	1 894	...	...	75 577	34 252	45	40
	1992/93	268	1 771	...	...	73 827	34 050	46	41
	1993/94	275	1 737	...	...	77 837	34 745	45	43
Congo	1980/81	1 335	7 186	1 794	25	390 676	188 431	48	54
	1985/86	1 558	7 745	2 307	30	475 805	231 062	49	61
	1990/91	1 655	7 578	2 457	32	503 918	234 479	47	66
	1991/92	1 620	7 789	2 579	33	492 286	236 763	48	63
	1993/94	1 623	6 891	2 341	34	505 925	242 762	48	73
Côte d'Ivoire‡	1980/81	4 807	26 460	4 070	15	1 024 585	409 859	40	39
	1985/86	5 796	33 500	6 289	19	1 214 511	502 672	41	36
	1990/91	6 765	39 002	7 340	19	1 414 865	586 272	41	36
	1991/92	6 844	39 057	7 387	19	1 447 785	603 492	42	37
	1993/94	7 249	39 691	7 976	20	1 553 540	650 608	42	40
	1994/95	...	...	...	...	1 612 417	693 184	43	...
Djibouti	1980/81	45	419	...	...	16 841	...	...	40
	1985/86	58	514	...	...	25 212	10 423	41	49
	1990/91	69	742	...	...	31 706	13 149	41	43
	1993/94	74	787	294	37	33 005	14 264	43	42
	1994/95	81	932	309	33	35 024	15 153	43	38
	1995/96	...	...	...	...	36 710	15 692	43	...
Egypt‡	1980/81	12 120	...	...	...	4 662 816	1 875 949	40	...
	1985/86	14 057	194 929	93 253	48	6 214 250	2 684 574	43	31
	1990/91	16 481	279 315	144 200	52	6 964 306	3 088 768	44	27
	1992/93	15 647	288 891	154 745	54	6 791 128	3 069 511	45	24
	1993/94	17 799	288 939	155 075	54	7 732 308	3 463 823	45	24
	1994/95	16 088	291 400	156 101	54	7 313 038	3 344 785	46	24
Equatorial Guinea‡	1980/81	...	647	...	...	44 499	...	...	69
	1992/93	749	1 352	371	27	72 725	35 229	48	54
	1993/94	781	1 381	367	27	75 751	37 127	49	55
Eritrea‡	1988/89	246	3 163	1 420	45	128 504	60 593	47	41
	1990/91	214	2 895	1 311	45	109 087	53 020	49	38
	1992/93	447	4 954	1 841	37	184 492	82 356	45	37
	1993/94	491	5 272	1 865	35	207 099	91 988	44	39
	1994/95	507	5 583	1 974	35	224 287	99 743	44	40
Ethiopia	1980/81	5 822	33 322	7 296	22	2 130 716	744 068	35	64
	1985/86	7 900	50 922	13 056	26	2 448 778	957 535	39	48
	1990/91	8 256	68 370	16 341	24	2 466 464	980 634	40	36
	1991/92	8 434	68 399	17 078	25	2 063 636	863 242	42	30
	1992/93	8 120	69 743	17 820	26	1 855 894	757 054	41	27
	1993/94	8 674	75 736	20 162	27	2 283 638	873 077	38	30
Gabon	1980/81	864	3 441	939	27	155 081	76 209	49	45
	1985/86	946	4 008	1 409	35	183 607	90 480	49	46
	1988/89	1 000	4 289	1 564	36	207 023	102 842	50	48
	1991/92	1 024	4 782	...	...	210 000	104 181	50	44
Gambia‡	1980/81	148	1 808	610	34	43 432	15 147	35	24
	1985/86	189	2 979	1 078	36	69 017	26 694	39	23
	1990/91	230	2 757	*850	*31	86 307	*35 000	*41	31
	1991/92	231	2 876	880	31	90 645	36 870	41	32
	1992/93	245	3 193	995	31	97 262	40 314	41	30
Ghana‡	1980/81	7 848	47 921	20 123	42	1 377 734	611 328	44	29
	1985/86	9 004	64 795	26 085	40	1 505 819	...	...	23
	1990/91	11 165	66 946	23 936	36	1 945 422	879 430	45	29
	1991/92	...	*72 925	*25 635	*35	2 011 602	918 411	46	*28

First level: schools, teachers and pupils
Premier degré: écoles, enseignants et élèves
Primer grado: escuelas, personal docente y alumnos

Country / Pays / País	Year / Année / Año	Schools / Écoles / Escuelas	Teaching staff / Personnel enseignant / Personal docente			Pupils enrolled / Élèves inscrits / Alumnos matriculados			Pupil/teacher ratio / Nombre d'élèves par maître / Número de alumnos por maestro
			Total	Female Féminin Femenino	% F	Total	Female Féminin Femenino	% F	
		(1)	(2)	(3)	(4)	(5)	(6)	(7)	(8)
Guinea	1980/81	2 555	7 165	985	14	257 547	85 842	33	36
	1985/86	2 285	7 605	1 437	19	276 438	87 544	32	36
	1990/91	2 476	8 699	1 957	22	346 807	109 351	32	40
	1991/92	2 586	7 374	1 554	21	359 406	113 250	32	49
	1992/93	2 685	8 577	2 004	23	421 869	133 777	32	49
	1993/94	2 849	9 718	2 184	22	471 792	154 138	33	49
Guinea-Bissau	1980/81	...	3 257	782	24	74 539	23 549	32	23
	1986/87	795	3 121	713	23	77 004	27 171	35	25
	1987/88	632	3 065	661	22	75 892	26 708	35	25
	1988/89	...	...	...	...	79 035	28 291	36	...
Kenya‡	1980	10 268	102 489	...	...	3 926 629	1 864 014	47	38
	1985	12 936	138 374	47 487	34	4 702 414	2 267 511	48	34
	1990	15 196	172 117	64 508	37	5 392 319	2 625 943	49	31
	1991	15 196	173 090	65 482	38	5 455 996	2 659 024	49	32
	1992	15 465	176 359	78 106	44	5 554 977	2 714 485	49	31
	1993	15 804	*179 200	*79 370	*44	*5 643 000	*2 772 900	*49	*31
Lesotho	1980	1 074	5 097	3 818	75	244 838	143 472	59	48
	1985	1 141	5 663	4 343	77	314 003	174 701	56	55
	1990	1 190	6 448	5 154	80	351 632	192 433	55	55
	1992	1 201	7 051	5 592	79	362 657	196 158	54	51
	1993	1 209	7 292	5 817	80	354 275	189 571	54	49
	1994	1 234	7 433	5 892	79	366 935	194 218	53	49
Liberia‡	1980	...	...	...	...	147 216	52 129	35	...
	1986	...	...	...	...	80 048	...	...	...
Libyan Arab Jamahiriya‡	1980/81	2 607	36 591	17 160	47	662 843	314 570	47	18
	1985/86	4 164	63 122	35 187	56	1 011 952	475 591	47	16
	1990/91	...	85 537	...	...	1 175 229	558 477	48	14
	1991/92	...	99 623	66 829	67	1 238 986	593 594	48	12
	1992/93	...	103 791	...	...	1 254 242	604 948	48	12
	1993/94	...	...	...	...	1 357 040	666 920	49	...
Madagascar	1980/81	13 594	39 474	...	...	1 723 779	844 822	49	44
	1984/85	13 973	42 462	...	...	1 625 216	783 716	48	38
	1990/91	13 791	38 933	...	...	1 570 721	773 797	49	40
	1991/92	13 686	39 637	...	...	1 496 845	713 328	48	38
	1992/93	13 508	38 743	...	...	1 490 317	726 412	49	38
	1993/94	13 624	37 676	21 029	56	1 504 668	737 641	49	40
Malawi‡	1980/81	2 340	12 540	...	...	809 862	333 495	41	65
	1985/86	2 520	15 440	5 124	33	942 539	408 727	43	61
	1990/91	2 906	22 942	7 176	31	1 400 682	633 127	45	61
	1992/93	3 118	26 333	9 064	34	1 795 451	847 974	47	68
	1993/94	3 319	27 948	9 620	34	1 895 423	912 126	48	68
	1994/95	3 425	45 775	17 489	38	2 860 819	1 345 317	47	62
Mali	1980/81	1 160	6 862	1 368	20	291 159	105 115	36	42
	1985/86	1 259	8 593	1 850	22	292 395	108 875	37	34
	1990/91	1 461	8 156	1 846	23	340 573	124 407	37	42
	1992/93	1 589	8 688	1 898	22	438 302	165 693	38	50
	1993/94	1 728	8 363	1 962	23	497 869	192 207	39	60
	1994/95	1 732	8 274	1 905	23	542 891	212 833	39	66
Mauritania	1980/81	599	2 183	198	9	90 530	32 057	35	41
	1985/86	875	2 785	411	15	140 871	56 362	40	51
	1990/91	1 261	3 741	667	18	167 229	70 588	42	45
	1992/93	1 451	4 276	765	18	219 258	97 277	44	51
	1993/94	1 635	4 686	853	18	248 048	111 058	45	53
	1994/95	...	5 181	1 046	20	268 216	120 504	45	52
Mauritius	1980	267	6 379	...	...	128 758	63 033	49	20
	1985	280	6 450	2 763	43	140 714	69 528	49	22
	1990	289	6 507	...	...	137 491	67 936	49	21
	1991	290	6 369	2 842	45	135 233	66 720	49	21
	1992	283	6 272	2 888	46	129 738	64 066	49	21
	1993	281	5 931	2 779	47	125 543	62 000	49	21
Morocco‡	1980/81	2 332	56 908	16 990	30	2 172 289	804 056	37	37
	1985/86	3 570	81 867	27 334	33	2 279 887	871 164	38	28
	1990/91	...	91 680	34 128	37	2 483 691	989 391	40	27
	1992/93	4 420	98 734	37 891	38	2 727 833	1 105 995	41	28
	1993/94	4 741	102 452	39 186	38	2 873 883	1 180 935	41	28
	1994/95	5 144	106 393	40 293	38	3 006 631	1 249 589	42	28
Mozambique‡	1980	5 730	17 030	3 714	22	1 387 192	590 101	43	81
	1985	3 679	20 286	4 390	22	1 248 074	546 101	44	*63
	1990	3 441	23 107	...	...	1 260 218	542 908	43	55
	1993	3 466	22 396	5 127	23	1 227 341	521 422	42	55
	1994	3 669	...	...	...	1 301 833	547 066	42	...
	1995	4 149	24 575	5 591	23	1 415 428	592 133	42	58

First level: schools, teachers and pupils 3.4
Premier degré: écoles, enseignants et élèves
Primer grado: escuelas, personal docente y alumnos

Country / Pays / País	Year / Année / Año	Schools / Écoles / Escuelas	Teaching staff / Personnel enseignant / Personal docente			Pupils enrolled / Élèves inscrits / Alumnos matriculados			Pupil/ teacher ratio / Nombre d'élèves par maître / Número de alumnos por maestro
			Total	Female / Féminin / Femenino	% F	Total	Female / Féminin / Femenino	% F	
		(1)	(2)	(3)	(4)	(5)	(6)	(7)	(8)
Namibia	1986	...	...	...	...	294 985	...	...	...
	1990	...	...	...	...	314 105	163 336	52	...
	1992	1 213	10 912	7 087	65	349 167	176 160	50	32
	1993	...	...	...	...	352 900	177 089	50	...
	1994	...	...	...	...	367 669	183 706	50	...
Niger	1980/81	1 686	5 518	1 673	30	228 855	80 784	35	41
	1985/86	1 850	7 383	2 421	33	275 902	99 241	36	37
	1990/91	2 307	8 835	2 880	33	368 732	133 252	36	42
	1992/93	2 422	10 027	3 457	34	386 056	142 257	37	39
	1993/94	2 656	12 216	...	...	394 063	147 498	37	32
	1994/95	...	...	...	...	440 460	...	...	...
Nigeria‡	1979/80	35 723	343 551	...	...	12 117 483	5 295 363	44	35
	1984/85	35 281	308 072	125 628	41	13 025 267	5 768 791	44	42
	1990	35 443	331 915	142 416	43	13 607 249	5 877 572	43	41
	1992	36 610	384 212	172 562	45	14 805 937	6 532 113	44	39
	1993	38 254	428 097	191 831	45	15 870 280	6 939 680	44	37
	1994	38 649	435 210	201 905	46	16 190 947	7 134 580	44	37
Reunion	1980/81	...	...	...	...	79 143	...	...	...
	1985/86	349	3 811	2 537	67	73 985	35 516	48	19
	1990/91	...	...	...	...	71 966	...	...	...
	1992/93	...	...	...	...	71 303	...	...	...
	1993/94	343	...	...	...	70 735	34 797	49	...
	1994/95	...	...	...	...	73 250	...	...	...
Rwanda‡	1980/81	1 567	11 912	4 577	38	704 924	337 625	48	59
	1985/86	1 594	14 896	6 628	44	836 877	409 081	49	56
	1990/91	1 671	19 183	8 884	46	1 100 437	547 869	50	57
	1991/92	1 710	18 937	8 986	47	1 104 902	548 171	50	58
St. Helena	1980/81	8	39	37	95	717	369	51	18
	1985/86	8	32	31	97	582	318	55	18
Sao Tome and Principe‡	1980/81	...	588	...	...	16 376	...	...	32
	1986/87	63	574	339	59	17 010	8 175	48	35
	1989/90	64	559	289	52	19 822	9 394	47	35
Senegal	1980/81	1 672	9 175	2 202	24	419 748	166 913	40	46
	1985/86	2 322	12 559	3 347	27	583 890	235 319	40	46
	1990/91	2 458	13 394	...	...	708 448	297 375	42	53
	1991/92	2 434	12 307	3 317	27	725 496	307 353	42	59
	1992/93	2 454	12 711	...	...	738 556	314 020	43	58
	1993/94	2 559	14 436	3 559	25	773 386	329 081	43	54
Seychelles‡	1980	27	658	529	80	14 468	7 356	51	22
	1985	25	652	555	85	14 368	7 073	49	22
	1991	...	...	...	...	10 134	4 968	49	...
	1992	...	...	...	...	9 931	4 836	49	...
	1993	26	548	483	88	9 873	4 797	49	18
	1994	26	588	509	87	9 911	4 876	49	17
Sierra Leone‡	1980/81	1 199	9 528	...	...	315 145	131 661	42	33
	1985/86	1 807	10 837	...	...	421 689	...	...	39
	1989/90	1 806	11 280	...	...	391 152	160 098	41	35
	1990/91	1 795	10 850	...	...	367 426	151 560	41	34
Somalia	1980/81	1 408	8 122	2 365	29	271 704	98 053	36	33
	1985/86	1 224	10 338	4 664	45	196 496	66 753	34	19
South Africa‡	1980	...	*160 286	...	...	*4 352 916	...	...	*27
	1986	...	...	...	...	4 737 367	2 340 178	49	...
	1990	...	...	...	...	6 951 777	3 448 868	50	...
	1991	15 858	270 365	158 118	58	7 210 021	3 573 615	50	27
	1993	...	...	...	...	5 758 389	2 850 973	50	...
	1994	20 428	213 890	124 929	58	7 971 770	3 906 652	49	37
Sudan	1980/81	6 027	43 451	13 497	31	1 464 227	591 173	40	34
	1985/86	6 775	50 089	22 038	44	1 738 341	702 987	40	35
	1990/91	7 939	60 047	30 651	51	2 042 743	872 174	43	34
	1991/92	8 016	64 227	33 263	52	2 168 180	932 517	43	34
	1993/94	9 681	66 268	38 303	58	2 377 437	1 040 244	44	36
Swaziland	1980	450	3 278	2 590	79	112 019	55 937	50	34
	1985	466	4 107	3 278	80	139 345	69 042	50	34
	1990	497	5 083	4 025	79	166 454	82 665	50	33
	1992	515	5 504	4 271	78	180 285	89 111	49	33
	1993	520	5 696	4 387	77	186 271	91 630	49	33
	1994	521	5 887	4 547	77	192 599	94 792	49	33

3.4

First level: schools, teachers and pupils
Premier degré: écoles, enseignants et élèves
Primer grado: escuelas, personal docente y alumnos

Country / Pays / País	Year / Année / Año	Schools / Écoles / Escuelas	Teaching staff / Personnel enseignant / Personal docente			Pupils enrolled / Élèves inscrits / Alumnos matriculados			Pupil/ teacher ratio / Nombre d'élèves par maître / Número de alumnos por maestro
			Total	Female Féminin Femenino	% F	Total	Female Féminin Femenino	% F	
		(1)	(2)	(3)	(4)	(5)	(6)	(7)	(8)
Togo	1980/81	2 205	9 193	1 972	21	506 356	194 064	38	55
	1985/86	2 336	10 049	2 008	20	462 858	177 373	38	46
	1990/91	2 494	11 105	2 085	19	646 962	255 642	40	58
	1991/92	...	...	...	...	652 548	260 853	40	...
	1993/94	2 594	12 487	2 007	16	663 126	265 252	40	53
Tunisia	1980/81	2 661	27 375	8 003	29	1 054 027	438 252	42	39
	1985/86	3 373	40 887	15 641	38	1 291 490	574 817	45	32
	1990/91	3 866	50 609	22 659	45	1 405 665	643 910	46	28
	1992/93	4 080	55 013	26 005	47	1 440 960	668 436	46	26
	1993/94	4 201	56 154	26 867	48	1 476 329	688 292	47	26
	1994/95	4 321	58 738	28 300	48	1 481 759	694 360	47	25
Uganda‡	1980	4 276	38 422	*11 410	*30	1 292 377	*558 300	*43	34
	1985	7 025	61 424	...	...	2 117 000	...	...	34
	1990	8 080	84 149	25 117	30	*2 470 000	*1 096 000	*44	*29
	1991	8 046	78 259	...	...	2 576 537	1 175 151	46	33
	1993	8 431	79 024	24 773	31	2 456 352	1 087 690	44	31
United Rep. of Tanzania‡	1980	9 794	81 153	29 927	37	3 367 644	1 585 140	47	...
	1985	10 173	92 586	...	...	3 169 759	1 580 130	50	34
	1990	10 417	96 850	39 966	41	3 379 000	1 673 765	50	35
	1991	10 451	98 174	39 758	40	3 512 347	1 734 011	49	36
	1992	10 960	101 306	42 007	41	3 603 488	1 769 580	49	36
	1993	10 892	101 816	43 132	42	3 736 734	1 837 429	49	37
Zaire	1980/81	10 536	...	...	...	*4 195 699	*1 745 385	*42	...
	1985/86	10 068	...	...	...	*4 650 756	*1 827 111	*39	...
	1990/91	11 955	*114 000	...	...	4 562 430	1 944 978	43	*40
	1991/92	11 948	114 967	22 601	20	4 622 758	1 987 645	43	40
	1992/93	12 658	117 267	22 827	19	4 870 933	2 122 843	44	42
	1993/94	12 987	112 041	26 934	24	4 939 297	2 103 195	43	44
Zambia	1980	2 819	21 455	8 584	40	1 041 938	487 435	47	49
	1985	3 128	27 302	11 818	43	1 348 318	635 530	47	49
	1990	3 587	33 200	...	...	1 461 206	...	...	44
	1994	3 715	36 697	16 234	44	1 507 660	720 122	48	41
Zimbabwe	1980	3 157	28 118	...	...	1 235 036	...	...	44
	1985	4 216	56 067	24 347	43	2 214 963	1 073 658	48	40
	1990	4 534	59 154	23 213	39	2 116 414	1 052 869	50	36
	1991	4 549	58 436	23 597	40	2 289 309	1 124 109	49	39
	1992	4 567	60 834	24 874	41	2 301 642	1 141 553	50	38
	1993	4 578	52 415	21 934	42	2 376 048	1 147 392	48	45
America, North									
Antigua and Barbuda	1991/92	...	...	...	...	9 298	4 568	49	...
Bahamas‡	1980/81	...	1 261	...	...	32 854	...	...	20
	1985/86	88	1 767	...	...	32 848	16 215	49	...
	1990/91	...	...	...	...	32 873	...	...	...
	1991/92	...	...	...	...	33 374	*16 480	*49	...
	1992/93	...	...	...	...	33 917	*16 850	*50	...
	1993/94	115	1 581	1 446	91	33 343	...	...	21
Barbados‡	1980/81	134	*1 172	...	...	31 147	15 497	50	24
	1984/85	125	1 441	...	...	30 161	14 605	48	21
	1989/90	...	1 602	1 227	77	28 516	13 984	49	18
	1991/92	106	1 553	1 120	72	26 662	13 164	49	17
Belize‡	1980/81	197	1 421	...	...	34 615	...	...	24
	1985/86	...	1 555	1 121	72	39 212	18 917	48	25
	1990/91	236	...	...	...	46 023	*22 270	*48	...
	1991/92	237	1 776	1 261	71	46 874	22 697	48	26
	1992/93	270	1 818	1 292	71	48 397	23 418	48	27
	1994/95	276	1 976	1 390	70	51 155	24 735	48	26
Bermuda	1980/81	22	312	...	...	5 934	2 885	49	19
	1984/85	22	309	278	80	5 398	2 692	50	17
British Virgin Islands	1980/81	18	109	92	84	1 974	982	50	18
	1984/85	19	...	...	...	2 069	987	48	...
	1990/91	...	126	...	...	2 340	1 102	47	19
	1991/92	19	151	...	...	2 443	1 153	47	16
	1993/94	20	166	147	89	2 502	1 204	48	15
	1994/95	...	169	143	85	2 625	1 266	48	16
Canada‡	1980/81	...	...	...	...	2 184 919	1 064 543	49	...
	1985/86	...	135 010	...	...	2 254 887	1 086 611	48	17
	1990/91	12 346	154 698	106 289	69	2 375 704	1 147 503	48	15
	1991/92	12 456	156 432	107 586	69	2 394 115	1 156 674	48	15
	1992/93	12 376	157 308	108 135	69	2 397 281	1 159 430	48	15
	1993/94	12 344	158 059	108 678	69	2 404 122	1 162 855	48	15

First level: schools, teachers and pupils
Premier degré: écoles, enseignants et élèves
Primer grado: escuelas, personal docente y alumnos

3.4

Country Pays País	Year Année Año	Schools Écoles Escuelas	Teaching staff Personnel enseignant Personal docente			Pupils enrolled Élèves inscrits Alumnos matriculados			Pupil/ teacher ratio Nombre d'élèves par maître Número de alumnos por maestro
			Total	Female Féminin Femenino	% F	Total	Female Féminin Femenino	% F	
		(1)	(2)	(3)	(4)	(5)	(6)	(7)	(8)
Costa Rica	1980	2 936	12 596	...	...	348 674	169 403	49	28
	1985	3 091	11 526	...	...	362 877	175 721	48	31
	1991	3 317	14 078	11 225	80	453 297	220 386	49	32
	1992	3 359	14 584	...	...	471 049	228 900	49	32
	1993	3 442	14 949	...	...	484 958	235 688	49	32
	1994	3 472	15 806	...	...	495 879	240 941	49	31
Cuba	1980/81	12 196	84 041	63 339	75	1 468 538	698 138	48	17
	1985/86	10 187	77 111	59 359	77	1 077 213	509 055	47	14
	1990/91	9 375	70 962	55 987	79	887 737	426 609	48	13
	1992/93	9 368	76 161	...	...	942 431	457 961	49	12
	1993/94	9 440	76 193	59 646	78	983 459	478 746	49	13
	1994/95	9 425	74 225	60 288	81	1 007 769	490 621	49	14
Dominica‡	1980/81	...	...	*541	...	14 815	7 472	50	...
	1985/86	66	808	*541	*67	12 340	5 940	48	*25
	1990/91	65	439	354	81	12 836	6 301	49	29
	1992/93	64	608	440	72	12 795	6 325	49	*29
	1993/94	64	674	412	61	12 822	6 354	50	*29
	1994/95	64	641	469	73	12 627	6 266	50	*29
Dominican Rep.‡	1980/81	4 606	...	...	...	1 105 730	...	...	...
	1985/86	*6 299	*27 952	...	...	1 219 681	614 514	50	*44
	1989/90	4 854	21 850	...	...	1 032 055	510 331	49	...
	1993/94	...	39 464	28 019	71	1 336 211	671 522	50	34
	1994/95	4 001	42 135	29 802	71	1 462 722	727 498	50	35
El Salvador‡	1980	3 196	17 364	11 315	65	834 101	412 743	49	48
	1984	2 631	21 145	14 018	66	883 329	438 883	50	42
	1989	4 160	25 318	17 008	67	1 016 181	503 658	50	40
	1991	3 516	22 622	15 418	68	1 000 671	496 199	50	38
	1992	3 806	23 339	16 127	69	1 028 877	510 001	50	38
	1993	3 961	26 259	18 585	71	1 042 256	515 378	49	34
Grenada	1980/81	57	776	506	65	18 076	8 647	48	23
	1986/87	63	821	574	70	17 963	*8 582	*48	22
	1990/91	...	...	...	...	19 811	*8 933	*45	...
	1991/92	...	...	...	...	21 365	*9 415	*44	...
	1992/93	...	963	...	...	22 345	*10 895	*49	23
Guadeloupe	1980/81	...	...	...	...	53 581	...	...	...
	1985/86	230	1 927	...	...	42 734	...	...	22
	1990/91	222	2 064	...	...	38 531	18 902	49	19
	1992/93	219	1 920	1 232	64	37 765	18 512	49	20
	1993/94	...	...	...	...	37 330	18 209	49	...
	1994/95	...	...	...	...	38 332	...	...	...
Guatemala	1980	6 959	23 770	...	...	803 404	362 083	45	34
	1985	8 016	27 809	...	...	1 016 474	458 469	45	37
	1991	9 362	36 757	...	...	1 249 413	571 218	46	34
	1992	...	...	...	...	1 340 657	...	...	...
	1993	10 770	44 220	...	...	1 393 921	637 548	46	32
	1994	...	...	...	...	1 449 981	...	...	...
Haiti‡	1980/81	3 271	14 581	7 124	49	642 391	294 712	46	44
	1985/86	3 734	23 200	...	...	872 500	407 002	47	38
	1990/91	7 306	26 208	11 681	45	555 433	267 120	48	29
Honduras	1980	5 524	16 385	12 187	74	601 337	298 163	50	37
	1985	...	...	...	...	765 809	380 074	50	...
	1991	7 593	23 872	17 646	74	908 446	456 751	50	38
	1993	8 127	26 561	19 475	73	990 352	490 580	50	37
Jamaica‡	1980/81	894	8 676	7 506	87	359 488	178 053	50	37
	1985/86	...	9 648	8 474	88	340 059	...	...	35
	1990/91	...	8 830	...	...	323 378	160 805	50	37
	1992/93	...	8 315	7 705	93	333 104	*163 200	*49	37
Martinique	1980/81	...	...	...	...	47 382	...	...	...
	1986/87	218	...	...	...	33 492	15 986	48	...
	1990/91	...	...	...	...	32 744	...	...	...
	1992/93	197	...	...	...	32 585	15 955	49	...
	1993/94	190	2 483	1 745	70	33 121	16 231	49	13
	1994/95	...	...	...	...	33 917	...	...	...
Mexico	1980/81	76 179	375 220	...	...	14 666 257	7 151 826	49	39
	1985/86	76 690	449 760	...	...	15 124 160	7 361 273	49	34
	1990/91	82 280	471 625	...	...	14 401 588	6 989 433	49	31
	1992/93	85 249	486 686	...	...	14 425 669	6 996 240	48	30
	1993/94	87 271	496 472	...	...	14 469 450	6 997 719	48	29
	1994/95	91 857	507 669	...	...	14 574 202	...	...	29

3.4 First level: schools, teachers and pupils
Premier degré: écoles, enseignants et élèves
Primer grado: escuelas, personal docente y alumnos

Country / Pays / País	Year / Année / Año	Schools / Écoles / Escuelas	Teaching staff Personnel enseignant Personal docente			Pupils enrolled Élèves inscrits Alumnos matriculados			Pupil/ teacher ratio Nombre d'élèves par maître Número de alumnos por maestro
			Total	Female Féminin Femenino	% F	Total	Female Féminin Femenino	% F	
		(1)	(2)	(3)	(4)	(5)	(6)	(7)	(8)
Montserrat	1980/81	16	...	...	...	1 846	892	48	...
	1985/86	...	...	...	...	1 351	658	49	...
	1990/91	...	...	...	...	1 593	...	...	...
	1991/92	11	*82	...	...	1 570	744	47	*19
	1992/93	...	...	...	...	1 566	...	...	...
	1993/94	11	85	64	75	1 525	704	46	18
Netherlands Antilles	1980/81	...	...	...	...	32 856	16 243	49	...
	1991/92	86	1 077	...	...	22 410	...	...	21
Nicaragua	1980	4 421	13 318	10 391	78	472 167	239 968	51	35
	1985	4 008	16 872	12 595	75	561 551	291 646	52	33
	1990	4 030	19 022	16 531	87	632 882	322 837	51	33
	1992	4 571	18 901	...	...	703 854	355 199	50	37
	1993	4 945	19 913	16 768	84	737 476	370 659	50	37
	1994	4 993	20 626	17 255	84	765 972	382 818	50	37
Panama	1980	2 306	12 361	9 909	80	337 522	162 510	48	27
	1985	2 476	13 359	10 486	78	340 135	162 542	48	25
	1990	2 659	15 249	...	...	351 021	168 235	48	23
	1992	2 712	...	...	...	353 154	...	...	...
	1993	2 732	...	...	...	357 402	...	...	...
	1994	2 791	...	...	...	364 934	...	...	...
Saint Kitts and Nevis	1980/81	...	...	...	...	7 149	3 488	49	...
	1985/86	32	353	...	...	7 810	...	...	22
	1989/90	33	346	...	...	7 665	3 690	48	22
	1991/92	32	350	278	79	7 236	3 509	48	21
	1992/93	...	...	...	...	7 068	3 442	49	...
St. Lucia‡	1980/81	77	957	768	80	29 605	15 079	51	31
	1985/86	83	1 084	862	80	32 817	16 012	49	30
	1990/91	87	1 127	931	83	33 006	*16 061	*49	27
	1991/92	88	1 181	967	82	32 622	*15 795	*48	27
	1992/93	88	1 204	998	83	32 545	15 765	48	27
St. Pierre and Miquelon	1980/81	5	36	26	72	747	364	49	21
	1985/86	5	38	28	74	558	265	47	15
	1990/91	...	...	...	...	556	...	...	...
	1992/93	...	...	...	...	529	...	...	...
	1994/95	...	...	...	...	492	...	...	...
St. Vincent and the Grenadines	1980/81	...	...	...	...	24 158	...	...	...
	1985/86	61	1 263	801	63	24 561	11 918	49	19
	1990/91	64	1 119	746	67	22 030	10 845	49	20
	1993/94	65	*1 080	*725	*67	21 386	10 374	49	*20
Trinidad and Tobago‡	1980/81	464	7 002	4 623	66	167 039	83 524	50	24
	1985/86	468	7 627	5 357	70	168 308	83 708	50	22
	1990/91	476	7 473	5 257	70	193 992	95 612	49	26
	1991/92	475	7 512	5 374	72	196 333	96 854	49	26
	1992/93	...	7 647	5 483	72	197 030	97 180	49	26
	1993/94	476	7 210	5 307	74	195 013	96 281	49	27
Turks and Caicos Islands‡	1980/81	17	80	74	93	1 483	712	48	19
	1984/85	17	68	67	99	1 429	697	49	21
	1993/94	10	86	78	91	1 211	604	50	14
United States	1980/81	...	...	...	...	20 420 000	9 959 000	49	...
	1985/86	76 000	1 425 000	...	...	20 214 000	9 850 000	49	14
	1990/91	...	...	...	...	22 429 000	10 856 000	48	...
	1992/93	...	...	...	...	22 976 240	11 115 649	48	...
	1993/94	72 000	1 660 000	1 394 000	84	23 694 000	11 523 000	49	14
U.S. Virgin Islands‡	1980/81	...	...	...	...	12 641	...	...	...
	1985/86	57	711	...	...	14 948	...	...	14
	1990/91	57	777	671	86	14 319	...	...	14
	1992/93	62	790	...	...	14 544	6 778	47	14
America, South									
Argentina	1980	...	...	...	...	3 917 449	1 927 389	49	...
	1985	20 700	229 715	212 033	92	4 589 291	2 268 227	49	20
	1990	...	...	...	...	4 965 395	...	...	...
	1991	24 511	306 372	...	...	5 041 090	2 475 067	49	16
	1993	...	...	...	...	4 990 486	...	...	...
	1994	25 448	286 885	249 042	87	5 126 307	...	...	18
Bolivia	1980	...	48 894	23 293	48	978 250	456 411	47	20
	1986	12 451	47 363	...	...	1 204 534	565 319	47	25
	1990	...	51 763	29 663	57	1 278 775	604 245	47	25

First level: schools, teachers and pupils **3.4**
Premier degré: écoles, enseignants et élèves
Primer grado: escuelas, personal docente y alumnos

Country / Pays / País	Year / Année / Año	Schools / Écoles / Escuelas	Teaching staff Personnel enseignant Personal docente			Pupils enrolled Élèves inscrits Alumnos matriculados			Pupil/ teacher ratio Nombre d'élèves par maître Número de alumnos por maestro
			Total	Female Féminin Femenino	% F	Total	Female Féminin Femenino	% F	
		(1)	(2)	(3)	(4)	(5)	(6)	(7)	(8)
Brazil	1980	201 926	884 257	748 927	85	22 598 254	10 993 176	49	26
	1985	187 274	1 040 566	...	...	24 769 736	...	...	24
	1990	208 934	1 260 501	...	...	28 943 619	...	...	23
	1992	199 447	1 329 352	...	...	30 106 084	...	...	23
	1993	195 840	1 344 045	...	...	30 548 879	...	...	23
	1994	194 487	1 377 665	...	...	31 220 110	...	...	23
Chile	1980	...	...	...	...	2 185 459	1 069 048	49	...
	1985	8 586	...	...	...	2 062 344	1 003 671	49	...
	1991	8 626	81 742	59 840	73	2 033 982	989 415	49	25
	1992	8 338	...	...	...	2 034 839	994 152	49	...
	1993	...	78 813	56 999	72	2 066 046	1 009 396	49	26
	1994	8 323	78 813	56 999	72	2 119 737	1 032 038	49	27
Colombia	1980	33 557	136 381	107 744	79	4 168 200	2 083 500	50	31
	1985	34 004	132 940	105 014	79	4 039 533	2 019 305	50	30
	1990	40 340	141 936	...	...	4 246 658	...	...	30
	1992	44 139	162 445	129 566	80	4 525 959	2 226 319	49	28
	1993	44 693	166 123	...	...	4 599 132	2 281 437	50	28
	1994	46 458	179 776	...	...	4 648 335	...	...	26
Ecuador	1980/81	11 451	42 415	27 696	65	1 534 258	746 014	49	36
	1985/86	...	53 683	35 036	65	1 738 549	850 354	49	32
	1990/91	...	61 039	...	...	1 846 338	...	...	30
	1991/92	...	63 845	...	...	2 019 850	...	...	32
	1992/93	...	63 347	41 173	65	1 986 753	971 411	49	31
French Guiana	1980/81	...	...	...	...	9 276	...	...	...
	1990/91	...	...	...	...	14 256	...	...	...
	1992/93	...	...	...	...	15 996	...	...	...
	1993/94	78	...	...	...	15 839	7 651	48	...
	1994/95	...	...	...	...	16 449	...	...	...
Guyana‡	1980/81	425	3 909	2 721	70	130 832	64 242	49	33
	1985/86	...	3 879	2 663	69	113 857	56 072	49	*36
	1988/89	414	*4 010	*2 855	*71	118 015	*58 080	*49	*36
Paraguay	1980	...	18 948	...	...	518 968	246 876	48	27
	1985	3 923	22 764	...	...	570 775	272 656	48	25
	1990	4 602	27 831	...	...	687 331	331 801	48	25
	1992	4 807	32 732	18 034	55	749 336	361 929	48	23
	1993	5 172	33 061	...	...	798 981	386 548	48	24
	1994	5 318	34 580	...	...	835 089	403 900	48	24
Peru	1980	20 776	84 360	50 676	60	3 161 375	1 514 621	48	37
	1985	24 327	106 600	64 036	60	3 711 592	1 787 244	48	35
	1990	...	132 556	...	...	3 855 282	...	...	29
	1992	28 712	135 502	...	...	3 853 098	...	...	28
	1993	...	133 080	...	...	3 914 291	...	...	29
	1994	31 315	145 795	...	...	4 031 359	...	...	28
Suriname	1981/82	...	2 793	2 201	79	75 630	36 182	48	27
	1985/86	...	3 010	2 498	83	69 963	33 658	48	23
	1990/91	...	2 686	2 258	84	60 085	29 489	49	22
	1991/92	...	2 982	2 580	87	73 407	35 762	49	25
	1992/93	...	3 695	3 223	87	79 162	37 878	48	21
	1993/94	...	...	...	...	87 882	43 359	49	...
Uruguay	1980	2 294	14 768	...	...	331 247	161 293	49	22
	1985	2 360	14 193	...	...	356 002	173 382	49	25
	1990	2 393	15 827	...	...	346 416	168 783	49	22
	1992	2 419	16 376	...	...	338 020	164 322	49	21
	1993	...	...	...	...	338 204	164 433	49	...
	1994	2 423	15 793	...	...	337 889	164 167	49	21
Venezuela‡	1980/81	...	92 551	...	...	3 158 466	...	...	*26
	1985/86	13 184	108 125	90 249	83	3 539 890	1 767 085	50	*25
	1990/91	15 445	177 049	131 855	74	4 052 947	2 018 163	50	23
	1991/92	15 800	183 298	136 274	74	4 190 047	2 081 105	50	23
	1992/93	15 984	184 321	137 111	74	4 222 035	2 095 340	50	23
	1993/94	...	185 748	138 450	75	4 217 283	2 094 806	50	23
Asia									
Afghanistan‡	1980	3 824	35 364	7 413	21	1 115 993	198 580	18	32
	1985	792	15 581	8 223	53	580 499	179 027	31	37
	1990	586	15 106	8 874	59	622 513	211 667	34	41
	1993	1 753	16 160	6 662	41	786 532	192 920	25	49
	1994	...	20 055	7 557	38	1 161 444	367 866	32	58
	1995	...	...	...	...	1 312 197	420 270	32	...
Armenia	1993/94	...	...	...	...	193 915	97 623	50	...

3.4 First level: schools, teachers and pupils
Premier degré: écoles, enseignants et élèves
Primer grado: escuelas, personal docente y alumnos

Country Pays País	Year Année Año	Schools Écoles Escuelas	Teaching staff Personnel enseignant Personal docente			Pupils enrolled Élèves inscrits Alumnos matriculados			Pupil/ teacher ratio Nombre d'élèves par maître Número de alumnos por maestro
			Total	Female Féminin Femenino	% F	Total	Female Féminin Femenino	% F	
		(1)	(2)	(3)	(4)	(5)	(6)	(7)	(8)
Azerbaijan	1980/81	...	...	...	...	473 298	...	...	...
	1985/86	...	...	...	...	487 748	...	...	...
	1990/91	...	...	...	...	527 370	255 820	49	...
	1991/92	...	...	...	...	539 234	262 633	49	...
	1992/93	4 368	...	...	...	553 862	267 946	48	...
	1993/94	4 406	...	...	...	580 266	275 589	47	...
Bahrain‡	1980/81	...	2 577	1 242	48	48 451	22 439	46	...
	1985/86	...	2 856	1 359	48	57 330	28 181	49	...
	1990/91	112	3 092	1 489	48	66 597	32 466	49	...
	1992/93	114	3 312	2 000	60	68 898	33 716	49	...
	1993/94	118	3 386	2 100	62	70 513	34 612	49	...
	1994/95	124	3 536	2 309	65	72 329	35 446	49	...
Bangladesh	1980	43 936	153 859	12 128	8	8 240 169	3 044 989	37	54
	1985	44 180	189 900	15 192	8	8 920 293	3 568 116	40	47
	1990	45 917	189 508	36 727	19	11 939 949	5 346 707	45	63
Bhutan‡	1980	...	...	...	...	29 899	...	...	...
	1985	145	...	...	...	45 395	15 579	34	...
	1988	150	1 513	...	...	55 340	20 597	37	37
	1993	235	1 859	...	...	56 773	24 207	43	31
	1994	...	...	...	...	60 089	25 924	43	...
Brunei Darussalam	1980	137	1 671	760	45	30 513	14 547	48	18
	1985	140	2 165	...	...	34 815	...	...	16
	1991	149	2 543	1 444	57	38 933	18 368	47	15
	1992	151	2 561	1 477	58	39 782	18 820	47	16
	1993	158	2 646	1 570	59	41 134	19 537	47	16
	1994	158	2 772	1 666	60	42 270	19 991	47	15
Cambodia‡	1980/81	...	30 316	...	...	1 328 053	...	...	44
	1985/86	4 294	35 080	8 704	25	1 315 531	596 487	45	38
	1990/91	4 617	40 820	12 532	31	1 329 573	...	...	33
	1993/94	...	37 616	13 561	36	1 621 685	727 060	45	43
	1994/95	...	37 827	14 071	37	1 703 316	756 135	44	45
China	1980/81	917 316	5 499 400	2 039 100	37	146 270 000	65 174 000	45	27
	1985/86	832 309	5 376 800	2 127 900	40	133 701 800	59 862 200	45	25
	1990/91	766 072	5 581 810	2 408 800	43	122 413 800	56 555 200	46	22
	1991/92	729 158	5 532 300	2 422 700	44	121 641 500	56 546 400	46	22
	1992/93	712 973	5 526 500	2 458 500	44	122 012 800	56 856 000	47	22
	1993/94	696 681	5 551 600	2 506 900	45	124 212 400	58 159 000	47	22
Cyprus‡	1980/81	443	2 193	993	45	48 701	23 789	49	22
	1985/86	380	2 239	1 106	49	50 990	24 646	48	23
	1990/91	383	3 069	1 840	60	62 962	30 379	48	21
	1992/93	391	3 410	2 158	63	64 313	31 008	48	19
	1993/94	381	3 456	2 229	64	64 907	31 370	48	19
	1994/95	383	3 528	2 303	65	64 884	31 368	48	18
Georgia	1994/95	3 170	18 022	16 513	92	291 175	141 206	48	16
Hong Kong‡	1980/81	803	17 937	13 015	73	540 260	258 685	48	30
	1985/86	1 017	19 404	14 385	74	534 903	254 966	48	28
	1990/91	972	19 518	...	...	524 919	*253 540	*48	27
	1992/93	946	18 790	...	...	501 625	*242 280	*48	27
	1993/94	920	19 122	...	...	485 061	*234 280	*48	25
	1994/95	884	18 740	*14 110	*75	476 847	*232 220	*49	*25
India‡	1980/81	485 538	...	...	...	73 873 184	28 537 132	39	...
	1985/86	528 079	1 509 910	414 373	27	87 440 514	35 193 740	40	*46
	1990/91	558 392	1 636 898	470 414	29	99 118 320	41 023 604	41	*47
	1991/92	565 786	1 693 014	498 934	29	101 577 089	42 359 096	42	*47
	1992/93	572 541	1 681 970	492 966	29	105 370 216	44 915 896	43	*48
	1993/94	572 923	1 703 164	506 913	30	108 200 539	46 396 230	43	*48
Indonesia	1980/81	128 875	787 400	...	...	25 537 053	11 786 487	46	32
	1985/86	168 555	1 181 807	...	...	29 897 115	14 320 934	48	25
	1990/91	169 133	1 281 407	647 583	51	29 753 576	14 479 304	49	23
	1991/92	170 780	1 261 089	636 590	50	29 577 704	14 461 795	49	23
	1992/93	171 455	1 276 217	656 338	51	29 598 790	14 354 056	48	23
	1993/94	173 921	1 296 103	674 701	52	29 876 196	14 464 611	48	23
Iran, Islamic Republic of‡	1980/81	39 213	...	...	...	4 799 000	...	...	...
	1985/86	50 432	309 736	160 231	52	6 788 323	2 960 218	44	22
	1990/91	59 280	298 759	158 109	53	9 369 646	4 328 327	46	31
	1992/93	61 323	311 839	172 679	55	9 937 369	4 666 836	47	32
	1993/94	61 683	311 531	172 564	55	9 862 817	4 652 405	47	32
	1994/95	61 889	305 380	167 611	55	9 745 600	4 594 053	47	*32

Country / Pays / País	Year / Année / Año	Schools / Écoles / Escuelas	Teaching staff / Personnel enseignant / Personal docente			Pupils enrolled / Élèves inscrits / Alumnos matriculados			Pupil/ teacher ratio / Nombre d'élèves par maître / Número de alumnos por maestro
			Total	Female / Féminin / Femenino	% F	Total	Female / Féminin / Femenino	% F	
		(1)	(2)	(3)	(4)	(5)	(6)	(7)	(8)
Iraq	1980/81	11 284	94 000	45 516	48	2 615 910	1 212 828	46	28
	1985/86	8 127	118 442	79 063	67	2 816 326	1 260 383	45	24
	1990/91	8 917	134 081	94 029	70	3 328 212	1 479 897	44	25
	1992/93	8 003	131 271	89 684	68	2 857 467	1 277 057	45	22
Israel‡	1980/81	1 576	41 468	...	...	621 912	...	...	*14
	1985/86	1 621	41 943	...	...	699 476	345 943	49	*14
	1990/91	1 514	40 571	33 346	82	724 502	357 997	49	*15
	1991/92	1 525	43 248	35 824	83	748 069	365 124	49	*15
	1992/93	1 533	47 299	39 631	84	763 511	372 667	49	*14
	1993/94	...	48 010	40 255	84	780 575	380 433	49	*14
Japan	1980/81	24 945	470 991	266 971	57	11 826 573	5 764 765	49	25
	1985/86	25 040	464 173	260 169	56	11 095 372	5 412 882	49	24
	1990/91	24 827	452 849	264 513	58	9 373 295	4 575 098	49	21
	1992/93	24 730	...	...	...	8 947 226	4 369 221	49	...
	1993/94	24 676	461 729	278 060	60	8 798 082	4 293 958	49	19
	1994/95	24 635	...	...	...	8 582 871	4 191 649	49	...
Jordan‡	1980/81	1 115	14 303	8 416	59	454 391	216 578	48	32
	1985/86	1 239	16 979	11 193	66	530 906	253 437	48	31
	1990/91	2 457	36 930	22 792	62	926 445	448 098	48	25
	1991/92	2 424	40 694	24 197	59	981 255	480 723	49	24
	1992/93	2 441	45 871	27 962	61	1 014 295	497 866	49	22
	1993/94	2 479	48 150	29 128	60	1 036 079	508 601	49	22
Kazakstan	1980/81	...	...	...	...	1 064 000	...	...	...
	1985/86	...	44 700	42 800	96	1 147 700	...	...	26
	1990/91	...	56 300	54 200	96	1 197 300	...	...	21
	1992/93	...	64 100	62 300	97	1 240 400	...	...	19
	1993/94	...	66 700	64 800	97	1 227 130	604 552	49	18
	1994/95	...	...	...	...	1 252 000	...	...	...
Korea, Democr. People's Rep.	1987/88	4 813	59 000	53 000	90	1 543 000	750 000	49	26
Korea, Rep.	1980/81	6 487	119 064	43 792	37	5 658 002	2 745 382	49	48
	1985/86	6 519	126 785	54 600	43	4 856 752	2 357 028	49	38
	1990/91	6 335	136 800	68 604	50	4 868 520	2 362 050	49	36
	1993/94	6 057	139 381	74 943	54	4 336 252	2 091 636	48	31
	1994/95	5 900	139 096	75 848	55	4 099 395	1 971 311	48	29
	1995/96	5 772	138 282	76 882	56	3 905 163	1 869 239	48	28
Kuwait	1980/81	238	8 035	4 466	56	148 983	71 249	48	19
	1985/86	270	9 623	6 586	68	172 975	84 175	49	18
	1990/91	...	7 034	4 321	61	124 996	59 920	48	18
	1991/92	218	6 967	4 401	63	114 641	56 085	49	16
	1992/93	230	7 526	5 187	69	122 930	60 687	49	16
	1993/94	239	8 278	5 849	71	129 956	64 123	49	16
	1994/95	...	8 815	6 247	71	133 264	65 944	49	15
Kyrgyzstan	1980/81	...	11 000	9 700	88	306 000	149 900	49	28
	1985/86	...	17 900	14 600	82	342 600	169 400	49	19
	1990/91	...	22 100	17 800	81	354 700	176 100	50	16
	1992/93	...	22 800	18 800	82	368 500	183 500	50	16
	1993/94	...	23 000	18 400	80	380 100	189 700	50	17
	1994/95	1 864	23 259	18 964	82	386 829	192 207	50	17
Lao People's Democr. Rep.	1980/81	6 339	16 109	4 849	30	479 291	217 297	45	30
	1985/86	8 011	21 033	6 744	32	523 347	234 790	45	25
	1989/90	6 435	19 970	7 335	37	563 734	245 005	43	28
	1991/92	7 140	21 036	8 589	41	580 792	253 261	44	28
	1992/93	7 643	21 652	8 988	42	637 359	277 274	44	29
	1993/94	8 361	22 649	9 466	42	681 044	295 846	43	30
Lebanon	1980/81	...	22 646	...	...	405 402	...	...	18
	1986/87	...	...	...	...	399 029	...	...	...
	1988/89	...	...	...	...	346 534	167 801	48	...
	1991/92	2 100	...	...	...	345 662	167 607	48	...
	1993/94	...	...	...	...	360 858	175 395	49	...
	1994/95	...	...	...	...	365 174	176 829	48	...
Macau	1990/91	...	...	...	...	34 972	16 694	48	...
	1991/92	...	...	...	...	37 872	18 229	48	...
	1992/93	...	...	...	...	40 665	19 556	48	...
Malaysia	1980	6 414	73 664	32 537	44	2 008 973	975 419	49	27
	1985	6 685	91 424	45 753	50	2 199 096	1 068 148	49	24
	1989/90	6 884	120 505	68 490	57	2 455 522	1 194 161	49	20
	1991/92	6 946	130 482	75 928	58	2 652 397	1 290 631	49	20
	1992/93	6 968	134 579	79 280	59	2 718 906	1 323 714	49	20
	1993/94	6 965	140 342	83 274	59	2 802 677	1 366 984	49	20

First level: schools, teachers and pupils
Premier degré: écoles, enseignants et élèves
Primer grado: escuelas, personal docente y alumnos

Country Pays País	Year Année Año	Schools Écoles Escuelas	Teaching staff Personnel enseignant Personal docente			Pupils enrolled Élèves inscrits Alumnos matriculados			Pupil/ teacher ratio Nombre d'élèves par maître Número de alumnos por maestro
			Total	Female Féminin Femenino	% F	Total	Female Féminin Femenino	% F	
		(1)	(2)	(3)	(4)	(5)	(6)	(7)	(8)
Maldives	1980	...	...	...	...	30 621	...	...	...
	1986	...	...	...	...	39 775	...	...	...
	1992	134	...	...	...	45 333	22 188	49	...
	1993	...	...	...	...	48 321	23 586	49	...
Mongolia	1980/81	...	...	...	...	145 200	71 200	49	...
	1985/86	590	5 064	...	...	153 100	...	...	30
	1990/91	638	5 917	3 460	58	166 200	83 200	50	28
	1991/92	643	6 230	...	...	154 600	...	...	25
	1994/95	638	6 704	...	...	158 990	80 400	51	24
Myanmar	1980/81	21 999	80 343	...	...	4 148 342	1 994 086	48	52
	1985/86	31 499	92 180	55 661	60	4 710 616	2 266 693	48	51
	1990/91	33 305	147 578	95 214	65	5 384 539	2 612 608	49	36
	1992/93	35 657	154 759	102 854	66	5 919 339	2 864 030	48	38
	1993/94	35 727	156 629	...	...	5 896 026	...	...	38
	1994/95	35 744	...	...	...	5 711 202	...	...	...
Nepal‡	1980	10 130	27 805	2 681	10	1 067 912	299 512	28	38
	1985	11 946	51 266	...	...	1 812 098	541 649	30	35
	1990	17 842	71 213	...	...	2 788 644	1 003 810	36	39
	1991	18 694	74 495	10 206	14	2 884 275	1 073 319	37	39
	1992	19 498	77 948	11 685	15	3 034 710	1 161 806	38	39
	1993	20 217	79 590	12 771	16	3 091 684	1 195 930	39	39
Oman	1980/81	178	3 959	1 362	34	91 895	31 455	34	23
	1985/86	349	6 681	2 923	44	177 541	78 360	44	27
	1990/91	431	9 551	4 486	47	262 989	123 604	47	28
	1992/93	416	10 839	5 216	48	289 911	137 568	47	27
	1993/94	415	11 158	5 507	49	297 209	142 125	48	27
	1994/95	425	11 586	5 759	50	301 999	145 072	48	26
Pakistan‡	1980/81	59 165	150 004	48 652	32	5 473 578	1 782 378	33	36
	1985/86	77 207	180 622	57 237	32	7 094 059	2 365 408	33	39
	1990/91	...	271 100	71 900	27	11 451 000	3 689 000	32	42
	1991/92	...	283 100	...	...	12 721 000	4 036 000	32	45
	1992/93	...	...	...	...	14 120 000	4 425 000	31	...
	1993/94	...	...	...	...	15 532 000	4 771 000	31	...
Philippines‡	1980/81	30 595	264 241	211 271	80	8 033 642	3 905 036	49	30
	1985/86	33 104	289 251	...	...	8 925 959	4 367 764	49	31
	1990/91	34 081	317 023	...	...	10 427 077	...	...	33
	1992/93	34 570	294 485	...	...	10 679 748	...	...	34
	1993/94	35 087	320 634	...	...	10 731 453	5 316 112	50	33
	1994/95	35 671	324 418	...	...	10 903 529	...	...	34
Qatar	1980/81	101	2 029	1 159	57	30 078	14 472	48	15
	1985/86	113	3 154	2 070	66	40 636	19 359	48	13
	1990/91	153	4 286	3 103	72	48 650	23 144	48	11
	1992/93	160	4 917	3 567	73	49 059	23 548	48	10
	1993/94	158	5 656	4 327	77	52 016	24 871	48	9
	1994/95	169	5 853	4 595	79	52 130	25 088	48	9
Saudi Arabia	1980/81	5 719	50 511	19 645	39	926 531	360 030	39	18
	1985/86	7 813	83 420	35 393	42	1 344 076	584 190	43	16
	1990/91	9 097	119 881	56 990	48	1 876 916	857 208	46	16
	1991/92	9 490	124 698	58 730	47	1 922 254	893 276	46	15
	1992/93	10 228	141 930	67 627	48	2 025 948	951 065	47	14
	1993/94	11 244	153 556	74 917	49	2 110 893	996 536	47	14
Singapore	1980	335	9 463	6 289	66	291 649	139 276	48	31
	1985	236	10 363	7 192	69	278 060	130 977	47	27
	1990	...	10 006	...	...	257 932	...	...	26
	1991	...	...	...	...	260 286	...	...	...
Sri Lanka‡	1980	8 772	...	...	...	2 081 391	999 173	48	...
	1985	9 349	...	...	...	2 242 645	1 082 127	48	...
	1990	9 574	*72 488	...	...	2 112 023	1 018 321	48	*29
	1992	...	69 965	56 245	80	2 059 203	992 377	48	29
	1993	9 664	70 008	56 195	80	2 012 702	971 905	48	29
	1994	9 648	70 108	57 695	82	1 960 495	945 919	48	28
Syrian Arab Republic	1980/81	7 846	55 346	29 616	54	1 555 921	667 780	43	28
	1985/86	9 039	78 388	47 750	61	2 029 752	930 821	46	26
	1990/91	9 683	97 811	62 730	64	2 452 086	1 140 131	46	25
	1992/93	10 079	106 164	68 073	64	2 573 181	1 200 147	47	24
	1993/94	10 219	110 580	70 537	64	2 624 594	1 224 642	47	24
	1994/95	10 420	113 384	72 584	64	2 651 247	1 237 336	47	23
Tajikistan	1990/91	...	23 807	11 581	49	507 354	247 959	49	21
	1992/93	...	24 977	12 017	48	519 701	251 842	48	21
	1993/94	625	25 664	12 946	50	570 916	277 049	49	22
	1994/95	...	25 968	13 355	51	593 596	288 530	49	23

First level: schools, teachers and pupils 3.4
Premier degré: écoles, enseignants et élèves
Primer grado: escuelas, personal docente y alumnos

Country / Pays / País	Year / Année / Año	Schools / Écoles / Escuelas	Teaching staff Personnel enseignant Personal docente			Pupils enrolled Élèves inscrits Alumnos matriculados			Pupil/ teacher ratio Nombre d'élèves par maître Número de alumnos por maestro
			Total	Female Féminin Femenino	% F	Total	Female Féminin Femenino	% F	
		(1)	(2)	(3)	(4)	(5)	(6)	(7)	(8)
Thailand	1980/81	...	...	...	...	7 392 563	3 562 975	48	...
	1985/86	33 964	*369 822	...	...	7 150 489	...	...	*19
	1990/91	...	314 684	...	...	6 956 717	3 378 159	49	22
	1992/93	34 123	341 122	...	...	6 758 091	3 278 151	49	20
	1993/94	*32 883	*312 962	...	...	*6 098 103	...	...	*19
	1994/95	*32 927	...	...	...	*5 986 446	...	...	...
Turkey	1980/81	45 549	212 456	86 205	41	5 656 494	2 568 623	45	27
	1985/86	47 631	212 717	88 855	42	6 635 858	3 131 419	47	31
	1990/91	51 055	225 852	97 803	43	6 861 711	3 229 812	47	30
	1991/92	50 669	234 961	99 474	42	6 878 923	3 238 599	47	29
	1992/93	49 974	235 721	100 822	43	6 707 725	3 163 808	47	28
	1993/94	49 599	237 943	102 391	43	6 526 296	3 092 337	47	27
United Arab Emirates‡	1980/81	200	5 424	2 949	54	88 617	42 343	48	14
	1985/86	...	6 123	3 310	54	152 125	73 308	48	18
	1990/91	...	12 526	8 049	64	228 980	110 274	48	18
	1992/93	...	13 940	9 450	68	238 469	114 895	48	17
	1993/94	...	14 754	10 133	69	251 182	120 491	48	17
	1994/95	...	15 449	10 670	69	262 628	125 695	48	17
Uzbekistan	1980/81	...	57 700	44 900	78	1 391 000	676 000	49	24
	1985/86	...	66 900	52 100	78	1 612 000	783 100	49	24
	1990/91	...	73 800	58 100	79	1 777 900	872 300	49	24
	1992/93	...	87 700	69 800	80	1 769 300	875 300	49	20
	1993/94	...	91 500	73 600	80	1 852 841	908 832	49	20
	1994/95	...	92 400	76 200	82	1 905 693	925 205	49	21
Viet Nam	1980/81	...	204 104	133 652	65	7 887 439	3 732 913	47	39
	1985/86	12 511	235 791	165 825	70	8 125 836	3 864 348	48	34
	1990/91	...	252 413	...	...	8 862 292	...	...	35
	1992/93	...	264 808	...	...	9 476 441	...	...	36
	1993/94	10 137	275 640	...	...	9 725 095	...	...	35
	1994/95	...	288 200	...	...	10 047 500	...	...	35
Yemen	1993/94	11 013	...	...	...	2 678 863	743 851	28	...
Former Democr. Yemen‡	1980/81	897	10 072	3 439	34	267 456	73 696	28	...
	1985/86	966	...	...	...	334 309	99 011	30	...
	1990/91	1 065	13 240	5 046	38	379 908	143 055	38	29
Former Yemen Arab Rep.‡	1980/81	3 094	9 826	1 046	11	435 913	56 990	13	37
	1985/86	6 252	18 279	1 725	9	981 127	194 049	20	54
	1990/91	...	35 350	4 400	12	1 291 372	306 547	24	37
Palestine	1994/95	...	...	...	...	404 259	196 602	49	...
Gaza Strip	1985/86	...	...	...	...	105 348	...	...	...
	1000/01	...	...	...	...	121 750	...	...	...
	1991/92	170	3 138	...	...	127 257	...	...	41
	1992/93	...	...	...	...	134 937	...	...	...
	1993/94	...	...	...	...	141 902	68 113	48	...
West Bank	1985/86	...	...	...	...	173 081	...	...	...
	1990/91	410	...	...	...	198 740	95 927	48	...
	1991/92	...	...	...	...	209 702	101 492	48	...
	1992/93	...	...	...	...	217 497	...	...	...
	1993/94	...	...	...	...	225 595	109 368	48	...
Europe									
Albania	1980/81	1 559	25 980	13 060	50	552 651	260 895	47	21
	1985/86	1 641	27 167	14 075	52	543 775	258 600	48	20
	1990/91	1 726	28 798	15 826	55	551 294	265 552	48	19
	1993/94	1 777	32 098	19 367	60	535 713	260 396	49	17
	1994/95	1 782	30 893	18 492	60	550 737	265 582	48	18
Austria	1980/81	3 450	27 525	20 776	75	400 397	195 074	49	15
	1985/86	3 760	32 806	25 899	79	343 823	166 176	48	10
	1990/91	3 721	34 232	27 975	82	370 210	180 416	49	11
	1991/92	3 716	34 902	28 767	82	378 676	184 195	49	11
	1992/93	3 715	33 507	27 661	83	382 663	186 133	49	11
	1993/94	3 723	32 059	26 838	84	381 628	185 464	49	12
Belarus‡	1980/81	6 600	90 800	...	...	750 300	...	...	*17
	1985/86	5 900	95 600	...	...	796 600	...	...	*17
	1990/91	5 200	110 600	...	...	614 800	...	...	*17
	1992/93	5 000	117 500	...	...	635 100	311 100	49	*16
	1993/94	4 900	122 700	...	...	634 600	309 500	49	*16
	1994/95	5 000	125 300	...	...	636 300	306 000	48	*16

3.4 First level: schools, teachers and pupils
Premier degré: écoles, enseignants et élèves
Primer grado: escuelas, personal docente y alumnos

Country / Pays / País	Year / Année / Año	Schools / Écoles / Escuelas	Teaching staff / Personnel enseignant / Personal docente			Pupils enrolled / Élèves inscrits / Alumnos matriculados			Pupil/teacher ratio / Nombre d'élèves par maître / Número de alumnos por maestro
			Total	Female / Féminin / Femenino	% F	Total	Female / Féminin / Femenino	% F	
		(1)	(2)	(3)	(4)	(5)	(6)	(7)	(8)
Belgium‡	1980/81	4 968	46 430	27 278	59	842 117	409 890	49	18
	1985/86	4 386	44 190	27 621	63	730 288	357 486	49	17
	1990/91	4 226	72 845	56 636	78	719 372	353 668	49	15
	1991/92	4 158	72 589	56 811	78	711 521	349 289	49	15
Bulgaria	1980/81	3 247	51 581	36 953	72	994 018	482 258	49	19
	1985/86	2 973	61 153	46 012	75	1 080 979	523 816	48	18
	1990/91	2 856	62 501	48 331	77	960 681	461 907	48	15
	1992/93	2 812	61 148	47 818	78	877 189	420 098	48	14
	1993/94	2 770	58 480	46 402	79	839 419	400 646	48	14
	1994/95	2 758	58 201	46 659	80	825 984	394 076	48	14
Croatia	1985/86	2 724	27 165	19 921	73	520 576	253 823	49	19
	1990/91	2 026	23 262	17 511	75	431 586	209 524	49	19
	1992/93	1 891	23 077	17 269	75	436 755	212 035	49	19
	1993/94	1 930	24 067	18 101	75	441 837	214 856	49	18
	1994/95	1 980	24 879	18 796	76	434 418	210 829	49	17
Former Czechoslovakia‡	1980/81	6 753	90 380	71 460	79	1 904 476	937 307	49	21
	1985/86	6 332	96 414	79 114	82	2 074 403	1 018 944	49	22
	1990/91	6 319	100 354	82 308	82	1 924 001	947 032	49	19
Czech Republic	1985/86	...	25 156	...	...	694 659	...	...	28
	1990/91	...	23 368	...	...	546 036	...	...	23
	1992/93	...	24 187	...	...	528 750	259 080	49	22
	1993/94	...	25 138	23 488	93	521 285	255 652	49	21
	1994/95	1 710	25 686	24 057	94	522 741	255 640	49	20
Denmark	1980/81	2 346	...	...	...	434 635	211 959	49	...
	1985/86	2 556	34 744	19 677	57	402 707	196 825	49	12
	1990/91	...	...	...	...	340 267	166 582	49	...
	1991/92	...	...	...	...	327 024	160 126	49	...
	1992/93	...	32 900	19 100	58	323 651	158 950	49	10
	1993/94	...	32 900	19 100	58	326 619	160 043	49	10
Estonia	1980/81	...	...	...	...	125 850	62 060	49	...
	1985/86	...	...	...	...	132 233	65 250	49	...
	1990/91	...	...	...	...	123 675	60 411	49	...
	1992/93	...	...	...	...	119 409	58 356	49	...
	1993/94	...	6 580	6 300	96	118 136	57 733	49	18
	1994/95	...	...	...	...	121 404	58 717	48	...
Finland	1980/81	4 245	25 949	...	...	373 347	181 879	49	14
	1985/86	...	...	...	...	379 339	185 229	49	...
	1990/91	...	...	...	...	390 587	190 330	49	...
	1991/92	...	...	...	...	392 695	191 603	49	...
	1992/93	...	...	...	...	392 754	191 628	49	...
	1993/94	3 968	...	...	...	390 892	190 727	49	...
France‡	1980/81	51 448	192 438	130 307	68	4 610 361	2 235 963	48	*21
	1985/86	47 923	266 523	189 400	71	4 115 846	1 986 129	48	*17
	1990/91	44 311	340 015	259 753	76	4 149 143	2 010 219	48	*18
	1992/93	42 235	342 905	264 470	77	4 060 408	1 967 332	48	*18
	1993/94	41 656	218 100	169 800	78	4 060 607	1 965 709	48	19
	1994/95	...	...	...	...	4 011 046	...	...	...
Germany	1990/91	...	...	...	...	3 431 385	...	...	...
	1991/92	...	...	...	...	3 438 052	1 684 548	49	...
	1992/93	18 871	215 414	180 814	84	3 469 959	1 700 816	49	16
	1993/94	18 867	225 068	191 367	85	3 524 219	1 727 572	49	16
Former German Democr. Rep.	1980/81	5 624	53 396	46 146	86	852 109	409 397	48	16
	1985/86	5 649	58 406	51 660	88	859 830	415 098	48	15
Federal Rep. of Germany	1980/81	18 411	...	...	...	2 783 867	1 359 791	49	...
	1985/86	19 594	*133 471	*105 292	*79	2 271 546	1 110 936	49	*17
Gibraltar	1980/81	13	157	131	83	2 750	1 374	50	18
	1984/85	13	183	141	77	2 830	1 362	48	15
Greece	1980/81	9 461	37 315	17 845	48	900 641	435 000	48	24
	1985/86	8 675	37 994	18 594	49	887 735	429 906	48	23
	1990/91	7 653	43 599	22 762	52	813 353	394 228	48	19
	1991/92	7 526	42 991	22 515	52	784 707	380 614	49	18
	1992/93	7 257	42 045	22 864	54	749 312	363 214	48	18
	1993/94	7 193	43 789	24 267	55	723 701	350 276	48	17

First level: schools, teachers and pupils **3.4**
Premier degré: écoles, enseignants et élèves
Primer grado: escuelas, personal docente y alumnos

Country Pays País	Year Année Año	Schools Écoles Escuelas	Teaching staff Personnel enseignant Personal docente			Pupils enrolled Élèves inscrits Alumnos matriculados			Pupil/ teacher ratio Nombre d'élèves par maître Número de alumnos por maestro
			Total	Female Féminin Femenino	% F	Total	Female Féminin Femenino	% F	
		(1)	(2)	(3)	(4)	(5)	(6)	(7)	(8)
Hungary	1980/81	3 633	75 422	60 673	80	1 162 203	565 243	49	15
	1985/86	3 546	88 066	72 390	82	1 297 818	632 567	49	15
	1990/91	3 548	90 511	75 596	84	1 130 656	551 952	49	12
	1992/93	3 717	88 917	74 338	84	1 044 164	...	...	12
	1993/94	3 771	89 655	74 827	83	1 009 416	493 521	49	11
	1994/95	3 814	89 939	75 282	84	985 291	481 881	49	11
Iceland	1980/81	...	...	...	...	24 736	...	...	...
	1985/86	...	...	...	...	24 603	11 994	49	...
	1990/91	...	...	...	...	25 878	12 626	49	...
	1991/92	...	...	...	...	25 809	12 600	49	...
	1992/93	...	...	...	...	25 234	12 383	49	...
	1993/94	...	...	...	...	24 711	12 129	49	...
Ireland‡	1980/81	3 385	14 636	10 795	74	419 998	205 447	49	29
	1985/86	3 334	15 674	11 907	76	420 236	205 236	49	27
	1990/91	3 320	15 614	11 965	77	416 747	203 506	49	27
	1991/92	3 308	15 775	12 124	77	408 567	198 995	49	26
	1992/93	3 288	15 804	12 171	77	398 736	194 220	49	25
	1993/94	3 276	16 578	12 821	77	391 998	190 467	49	24
Italy	1980/81	30 305	273 744	238 299	87	4 422 888	2 150 146	49	16
	1985/86	27 748	273 800	244 631	89	3 703 108	1 800 587	49	14
	1990/91	24 268	265 553	240 466	91	3 055 883	1 485 252	49	12
	1991/92	22 911	255 429	231 697	91	3 004 264	1 460 072	49	12
	1992/93	22 710	251 621	228 233	91	2 959 564	1 459 066	49	12
	1993/94	21 378	272 667	250 854	92	2 863 003	1 397 145	49	11
Latvia	1980/81	...	...	...	...	107 558	52 660	49	...
	1985/86	...	...	...	...	113 167	55 610	49	...
	1990/91	...	...	...	...	143 338	70 264	49	...
	1992/93	921	...	...	...	137 095	67 327	49	...
	1993/94	1 010	9 329	8 586	92	132 059	64 541	49	14
	1994/95	1 038	10 056	9 228	92	132 465	63 912	48	13
Lithuania	1980/81	...	6 800	6 571	97	172 064	84 426	49	25
	1985/86	...	6 800	6 571	97	172 349	85 075	49	25
	1990/91	...	10 912	10 590	97	197 952	95 947	48	18
	1992/93	...	11 987	11 764	98	207 522	100 569	48	17
	1993/94	...	12 362	12 058	98	212 261	100 965	48	17
	1994/95	...	12 904	12 673	98	221 569	107 096	48	17
Luxembourg	1980/81	...	1 765	882	50	24 628	11 954	49	14
	1985/86	...	1 745	855	49	22 003	10 721	49	13
	1990/91	326	1 764	896	51	23 465	11 902	51	13
Malta	1980/81	102	1 557	993	64	33 063	15 944	48	21
	1985/86	107	1 665	1 123	67	36 240	17 108	47	22
	1990/91	115	1 780	1 411	79	36 899	17 708	48	21
	1991/92	...	1 666	1 345	81	35 626	17 143	48	21
	1992/93	...	1 722	1 408	82	35 488	17 137	48	21
	1993/94	...	1 748	1 447	83	35 366	17 068	48	20
Moldova	1980/81	...	8 003	7 645	96	230 624	113 149	49	29
	1985/86	...	9 500	9 078	96	248 005	121 039	49	26
	1990/91	...	13 024	12 684	97	301 653	148 608	49	23
	1992/93	...	13 295	12 829	96	307 604	150 890	49	23
	1993/94	...	13 230	12 764	96	307 447	151 174	49	23
	1994/95	...	13 344	...	...	322 612	158 080	49	24
Monaco‡	1980/81	3	...	...	...	1 017	471	46	...
	1990/91	7	...	...	...	1 773	897	51	...
	1991/92	7	...	...	...	1 761	869	49	...
	1993/94	7	...	...	...	1 815	889	49	...
	1994/95	7	106	...	...	1 838	866	47	17
Netherlands‡	1980/81	8 727	57 536	26 421	46	1 333 342	658 509	49	23
	1985/86	8 401	66 388	34 889	53	1 109 590	547 513	49	17
	1990/91	8 450	63 022	33 391	53	1 082 022	537 223	50	17
	1991/92	8 435	63 100	33 700	53	1 040 158	514 149	49	16
	1992/93	8 331	64 700	35 400	55	1 046 192	519 688	50	16
	1993/94	8 139	65 747	36 634	56	1 056 769	524 123	50	16
Norway‡	1980/81	3 518	47 739	26 709	56	390 186	190 252	49	*17
	1985/86	3 524	48 763	28 185	58	335 373	163 832	49	*16
	1990/91	3 406	50 614	31 814	63	309 432	150 737	49	*15
	1991/92	3 389	51 814	32 659	63	308 516	150 418	49	*15
	1992/93	3 352	...	...	...	307 461	150 144	49	...
	1993/94	...	...	...	...	309 889	151 179	49	...

3.4 First level: schools, teachers and pupils
Premier degré: écoles, enseignants et élèves
Primer grado: escuelas, personal docente y alumnos

Country / Pays / País	Year / Année / Año	Schools / Écoles / Escuelas	Teaching staff / Personnel enseignant / Personal docente			Pupils enrolled / Élèves inscrits / Alumnos matriculados			Pupil/teacher ratio / Nombre d'élèves par maître / Número de alumnos por maestro
			Total	Female Féminin Femenino	% F	Total	Female Féminin Femenino	% F	
		(1)	(2)	(3)	(4)	(5)	(6)	(7)	(8)
Poland	1980/81	12 593	195 608	...	...	4 167 313	2 025 824	49	21
	1985/86	16 254	267 620	...	...	4 801 307	2 325 579	48	18
	1990/91	17 788	317 474	...	...	5 189 118	2 524 274	49	16
	1992/93	17 268	308 873	...	...	5 231 769	2 540 932	49	17
	1993/94	17 032	311 054	...	...	5 194 245	2 524 238	49	17
	1994/95	20 214	325 812	...	...	5 204 801	2 520 928	48	16
Portugal	1980/81	12 460	68 746	...	...	1 240 307	594 090	48	18
	1985/86	12 741	73 343	*60 800	*83	1 235 312	588 646	48	17
	1990/91	11 532	72 140	58 781	81	1 019 794	485 324	48	14
	1991/92	12 472	71 105	...	...	1 004 848	480 385	48	14
	1993/94	12 069	73 221	...	...	910 650	...	...	12
Romania‡	1980/81	14 381	156 817	109 017	70	3 236 808	1 578 403	49	21
	1985/86	14 076	147 147	103 470	70	3 030 666	1 476 503	49	21
	1990/91	6 070	57 140	47 989	84	1 253 480	613 352	49	22
	1992/93	6 145	57 014	47 358	83	1 201 229	584 917	49	21
	1993/94	6 160	58 195	48 642	84	1 237 655	602 685	49	21
	1994/95	6 162	61 960	52 004	84	1 335 973	650 697	49	22
Russian Federation	1980/81	...	215 000	210 000	98	6 009 000	2 956 000	49	28
	1985/86	...	248 000	244 000	98	6 579 000	3 244 000	49	27
	1990/91	...	340 000	336 000	99	7 596 000	3 737 000	49	22
	1992/93	...	385 000	377 000	98	7 797 000	3 836 000	49	20
	1993/94	66 235	395 000	387 000	98	7 738 000	3 799 000	49	20
	1994/95	...	...	...	...	7 849 000	3 832 000	49	...
San Marino	1980/81	14	145	128	88	1 509	733	49	10
	1985/86	13	158	138	87	1 411	691	49	9
	1990/91	14	208	186	89	1 212	564	47	6
	1991/92	14	218	187	86	1 200	579	48	6
	1992/93	14	221	195	88	1 190	574	48	5
	1993/94	14	219	192	88	1 166	566	49	5
Slovakia	1992/93	2 472	15 859	14 556	92	350 604	171 163	49	22
	1993/94	2 483	15 433	14 097	91	345 594	168 918	49	22
	1994/95	2 481	15 394	14 083	91	338 291	165 422	49	22
Slovenia	1992/93	821	5 935	5 487	92	104 441	50 983	49	18
	1993/94	821	6 513	6 044	93	102 120	50 051	49	16
	1994/95	881	6 780	6 259	92	102 184	49 988	49	15
Spain	1980/81	...	127 679	86 135	67	3 609 623	1 753 535	49	28
	1985/86	18 851	137 807	94 585	69	3 483 948	1 681 536	48	25
	1990/91	18 672	128 034	93 098	73	2 820 497	1 366 826	48	22
	1991/92	18 561	125 828	94 364	75	2 662 490	1 286 059	48	21
	1992/93	17 460	122 050	90 800	74	2 554 083	1 233 431	48	21
	1993/94	16 540	121 353	90 282	74	2 447 859	1 181 724	48	20
Sweden‡	1980/81	4 928	...	...	...	666 679	325 121	49	...
	1985/86	...	...	...	...	612 704	...	...	...
	1990/91	...	92 843	63 963	69	578 359	282 011	49	...
	1991/92	...	92 924	64 301	69	584 203	284 840	49	...
	1992/93	4 221	60 022	47 099	78	594 891	289 681	49	10
	1993/94	4 253	57 331	45 332	79	600 392	292 237	49	10
Switzerland	1980/81	...	...	...	...	450 942	220 942	49	...
	1985/86	...	...	...	...	376 512	184 492	49	...
	1990/91	...	...	...	...	404 154	198 385	49	...
	1991/92	...	...	...	...	414 129	203 380	49	...
	1992/93	...	...	...	...	420 089	206 558	49	...
	1993/94	...	...	...	...	423 399	208 378	49	...
The Former Yugoslav Rep. of Macedonia	1980/81	1 210	12 100	...	...	272 344	...	...	23
	1985/86	1 134	12 929	...	...	273 219	...	...	21
	1990/91	1 067	12 976	...	...	266 813	128 597	48	21
	1992/93	1 049	12 958	6 692	52	261 540	126 097	48	20
	1993/94	1 050	13 102	6 828	52	260 659	125 737	48	20
	1994/95	1 042	13 154	6 913	53	261 105	126 183	48	20
Ukraine‡	1980/81	21 000	79 500	77 500	97	3 591 800	1 758 400	49	*26
	1985/86	20 500	88 200	86 200	98	3 738 900	...	...	*23
	1990/91	20 900	119 600	117 200	98	3 990 500	1 959 500	49	*22
	1991/92	21 000	125 300	122 400	98	4 033 000	1 971 600	49	*21
	1992/93	21 100	130 600	127 900	98	2 682 600	1 304 900	49	21
	1993/94	21 720	133 600	130 600	98	2 658 800	1 300 000	49	20
United Kingdom‡	1980/81	26 504	260 283	203 643	78	4 910 724	2 393 020	49	...
	1985/86	24 756	244 000	194 000	80	4 296 000	2 096 000	49	...
	1990/91	24 135	229 100	178 800	78	4 532 500	2 221 200	49	20
	1991/92	23 958	230 200	180 000	78	4 559 500	2 229 900	49	20
	1992/93	23 829	256 500	199 200	78	5 023 200	2 457 900	49	20
	1993/94	...	271 194	209 806	77	5 143 227	2 509 915	49	19

First level: schools, teachers and pupils
Premier degré: écoles, enseignants et élèves
Primer grado: escuelas, personal docente y alumnos

3.4

Country / Pays / País	Year / Année / Año	Schools / Écoles / Escuelas	Teaching staff / Personnel enseignant / Personal docente				Pupils enrolled / Élèves inscrits / Alumnos matriculados				Pupil/teacher ratio / Nombre d'élèves par maître / Número de alumnos por maestro
				Total	Female Féminin Femenino	% F		Total	Female Féminin Femenino	% F	
		(1)	(2)	(3)	(4)		(5)	(6)	(7)		(8)
Former Yugosalavia	1980/81	12 671	59 391	41 449	70		1 431 582	692 074	48		24
	1985/86	12 148	61 288	43 405	71		1 448 562	701 576	48		24
	1990/91	11 753	61 473	44 254	72		1 392 789	674 308	48		23
Federal Republic of Yugoslavia	1990/91	...	...	...	...		466 692	227 175	49		...
	1991/92	4 424	21 399	15 905	74		470 669	229 078	49		22
	1992/93	4 433	21 368	16 002	75		473 902	230 426	49		22
	1993/94	4 421	...	...	...		460 203	225 896	49		...
Oceania											
American Samoa	1985/86	31	454	284	63		7 704	3 614	47		17
	1989/90	26	461	296	64		8 574	4 039	47		19
	1991/92	30	524	341	65		7 884	3 769	48		15
Australia‡	1980	...	91 280	64 311	70		1 718 352	835 617	49		20
	1985	...	97 070	69 510	72		1 542 101	748 952	49		17
	1990	7 927	95 916	70 497	73		1 583 024	769 337	49		...
	1992	7 923	97 955	72 652	74		1 623 012	789 407	49		...
	1993	7 880	98 526	73 351	74		1 633 797	794 807	49		...
	1994	7 725	98 867	73 850	75		1 639 577	797 944	49		...
Cook Islands	1985	28	162	...	...		2 713	...	...		17
	1988	28	137	95	69		2 376	...	...		17
Fiji	1980	652	4 097	2 349	57		116 139	56 646	49		28
	1985	668	4 396	2 540	58		127 286	61 921	49		29
	1990	681	4 272	...	...		143 552	...	...		34
	1991	692	4 664	2 639	57		144 924	70 508	49		31
	1992	693	4 644	2 606	56		145 630	70 713	49		31
French Polynesia	1987/88	176	1 967	...	...		27 259	12 695	47		14
	1990/91	180	1 976	...	...		28 270	13 489	48		14
	1991/92	...	...	...	...		28 195	...	...		...
	1992/93	176	...	...	...		29 132	13 996	48		...
	1994/95	...	1 974	1 331	67		30 037	14 375	48		15
Guam‡	1980/81	...	674	...	...		18 093	...	...		20
	1985/86	...	711	...	...		16 783	...	...		20
	1988/89	...	701	...	...		15 516	...	...		20
Kiribati	1980	100	435	210	48		13 235	6 457	49		30
	1985	112	460	236	51		13 440	6 625	49		29
	1990	104	514	295	57		14 709	7 298	50		29
	1991	102	533	310	58		15 570	7 680	49		29
	1992	95	545	319	59		16 020	7 904	49		29
	1993	92	537	317	59		16 316	8 067	49		30
Nauru	1985	7	71	43	61		1 451	679	47		20
New Caledonia	1981	...	...	...	...		26 779	12 976	48		...
	1985	211	1 131	...	...		22 517	10 838	48		20
	1990	205	1 147	...	...		22 958	11 098	48		20
	1991	200	1 096	...	...		22 325	10 780	48		20
	1992	...	...	...	...		21 865	...	...		...
	1994	...	...	...	...		22 308	...	...		...
New Zealand	1980	2 345	...	...	...		381 262	185 824	49		...
	1985	...	...	...	...		329 337	160 197	49		...
	1990	2 301	17 729	13 943	79		318 568	154 149	48		18
	1992	2 262	19 583	15 687	80		317 286	153 804	48		16
	1993	...	...	...	...		322 984	156 820	49		...
	1994	2 324	19 443	15 742	81		331 666	161 221	49		17
Niue‡	1980	...	45	...	...		666	...	...		15
	1985	...	29	...	...		503	...	...		17
	1991	...	19	...	...		371	...	...		20
Pacific Islands	1980/81	249	...	...	...		30 159	...	...		...
Papua New Guinea‡	1980	*2 130	*9 549	*2 559	*27		299 823	*123 805	*41		*31
	1987	2 584	12 294	4 021	33		384 367	169 904	44		31
	1990	2 606	13 105	4 227	32		415 195	184 128	44		32
	1993	2 638	13 976	4 860	35		467 938	210 732	45		33
	1994	2 781	15 320	5 557	36		512 129	230 114	45		33
	1995	2 790	13 652	4 980	36		525 995	238 109	45		39
Samoa‡	1980	152	1 438	1 026	71		33 012	15 694	48		29
	1986	...	1 511	1 115	74		31 412	15 218	48		27
	1989	...	...	...	...		37 833	18 097	48		...

3.4 First level: schools, teachers and pupils
Premier degré: écoles, enseignants et élèves
Primer grado: escuelas, personal docente y alumnos

Country Pays País	Year Année Año	Schools Écoles Escuelas	Teaching staff Personnel enseignant Personal docente			Pupils enrolled Élèves inscrits Alumnos matriculados			Pupil/ teacher ratio Nombre d'élèves par maître Número de alumnos por maestro
			Total	Female Féminin Femenino	% F	Total	Female Féminin Femenino	% F	
		(1)	(2)	(3)	(4)	(5)	(6)	(7)	(8)
Solomon Islands	1980	370	1 148	303	26	28 870	11 980	41	25
	1985	423	1 496	...	...	38 716	...	...	26
	1990	518	2 457	...	...	47 598	21 107	44	19
	1992	521	2 490	...	...	53 320	23 581	44	21
	1993	...	2 357	...	...	57 264	25 403	44	24
	1994	...	2 514	...	...	60 493	27 089	45	24
Tokelau	1981	...	21	16	76	434	213	49	21
	1991	...	...	...	...	361	181	50	...
Tonga	1980	110	781	...	...	19 012	...	...	24
	1985	112	744	460	62	17 019	8 162	48	23
	1990	115	689	475	69	16 522	7 915	48	24
	1991	115	714	481	67	16 728	7 985	48	23
	1992	115	784	503	64	16 658	7 960	48	21
	1993	115	754	495	66	16 792	7 994	48	22
Tuvalu‡	1980	...	...	...	...	1 327	...	...	...
	1986	9	58	43	74	1 280	622	49	22
	1990	...	72	52	72	1 485	708	48	21
	1993	...	...	...	...	1 752	838	48	...
	1994	11	...	...	...	1 906	932	49	...
Vanuatu, Rep. of‡	1980	278	986	...	...	23 264	10 593	46	24
	1985	245	...	...	...	22 897	...	...	...
	1990	261	...	...	...	24 471	11 518	47	...
	1991	267	869	350	40	24 952	11 651	47	29
	1992	272	852	...	...	26 267	12 288	47	31

In general, data in this table cover both public and private schools at the first level of education, including primary classes attached to secondary schools. From the school year beginning in 1994, special education should be included. Adult education, is not included however. In consulting this table, reference should be made to the information given on the duration of schooling in Tables 3.1, 3.1a and 3.1b. Figures on teaching staff refer, in principle, to both full- and part-time teachers. Data comparability may thus be affected, particularly as regards the pupil/teacher ratios presented in column 8, as the proportion of part-time teachers varies greatly from one country to another. Instructional personnel without teaching functions (e.g. certain principals, librarians, guidance personnel, etc.) are in general excluded.

En général, les données de ce tableau se rapportent aux établissements d'enseignement du premier degré, publics et privés, y compris les classes primaires rattachées aux établissements du second degré. A partir de l'année scolaire commençant en 1994, l'enseignement spécial devrait être pris en compte. L'enseignement destiné aux adultes n'est pas inclus. Il convient, en consultant ce tableau, de se reporter aux renseignements donnés sur la durée de la scolarité aux tableaux 3.1, 3.1a et 3.1b. Les chiffres relatifs au personnel enseignant représentent, en général, le nombre total de maîtres à plein temps et à temps partiel. Ceci peut affecter la comparabilité des données, surtout en ce qui concerne le nombre d'élèves par maître, présenté à la colonne 8, car la proportion des enseignants à temps partiel peut varier considérablement d'un pays à l'autre. Le personnel qui n'est pas chargé d'enseignement (certains chefs d'établissements, bibliothécaires, conseillers d'orientation professionnelle, etc.) a été en général exclu.

En general, los datos de este cuadro se refieren a los establecimientos de enseñanza de primer grado, públicos y privados, incluídos los adscritos a establecimientos de segundo grado. Desde del año escolar empezaró on 1994, las escuelas especiales deberian ser incluídas. Las escuelas y clases destinadas a los adultos estan excluídas. Al consultar este cuadro, habrá que tener presentes los datos sobre la duración de la escolaridad que figuran en los cuadros 3.1, 3.1a y 3.1b. Las cifras relativas al personal docente representan, en general, el número total de maestros de jornada completa y de jornada parcial. Esto puede afectar la comparabilidad de los datos, sobre todo en lo que concierne al número de alumnos por maestro, tal como se presenta en la columna 8, ya que la proporción de maestros de jornada parcial puede variar considerablemente de un país a otro. En la medida de lo posible, se ha excluído al personal que no se dedica a la enseñanza (por ejemplo, ciertos directores, los bibliotecarios, los consejeros de orientación profesional, etc.).

AFRICA:
Cape Verde:
E--> For 1980/81 and 1985/86 data on teachers refer to *ensino básico elementar* (grades 1-4) only.
FR-> Pour 1980/81 et 1985/86 les données sur le personnel enseignant se réfèrent à l'*ensino básico elementar* (années d'études 1 à 4) seulement.
ESP> Para 1980/81 y 1985/86 los datos sobre el personal docente se refieren al *ensino básico elementar* (años de estudio 1 a 4) solamente.
Comoros:
E--> From 1991/92 data on teaching staff and the pupil/teacher ratio refer to public education only.

FR-> A partir de 1991/92, les données relatives au personnel enseignant et au nombre d'élèves par maître se réfèrent à l'enseignement public seulement.
ESP> A partir de 1991/92, los datos relativos al personal docente y al número de alumnos por maestro se refieren a la enseñanza pública solamente.
Côte d'Ivoire:
E--> From 1985/86, data on teaching staff include education preceding the first level.
FR-> A partir de 1985/86, les données relatives au personnel enseignant incluent l'enseignement précédant le premier degré.
ESP> A partir de 1985/86, los datos relativos al personal docente incluyen la enseñanza anterior al primer grado.

First level: schools, teachers and pupils
Premier degré: écoles, enseignants et élèves
Primer grado: escuelas, personal docente y alumnos

3.4

Egypt:
E--> See Table 3.1b. Data on teaching staff and the pupil/teacher ratio and all data for 1992/93 and 1994/95, do not include Al Azhar.

FR-> Voir le tableau 3.1b. Les données relatives au personnel enseignant et au nombre d'élèves par maître ainsi que toutes les données pour 1992/93 et 1994/95, ne comprennent pas Al Azhar.

ESP> Véase el cuadro 3.1b. Los datos relativos al personal docente y al número de alumnos por maestro y todos los datos para 1992/93 y 1994/95, no incluyen Al Azhar.

Equatorial Guinea:
E--> For 1992/93 data refer to public education only.

FR-> Pour 1992/93, les données se réfèrent à l'enseignement public seulement.

ESP> Para 1992/93, los datos se refieren a la enseñanza pública solamente.

Eritrea:
E--> See Table 3.1b.

FR-> Voir le tableau 3.1b.

ESP> Véase el cuadro 3.1b.

Gambia:
E--> For 1980/81 and 1985/86, data do not include *Action aid* schools.

FR-> Pour 1980/81 et 1985/86, les données n'incluent pas les écoles de *Action aid.*

ESP> Para 1980/81 y 1985/86, los datos no incluyen las escuelas de *Action aid.*

Ghana:
E--> For 1980/81 and 1985/86, data refer to public education only.

FR-> Pour 1980/81 et 1985/86, les données se réfèrent à l'enseignement public seulement.

ESP> Para 1980/81 y 1985/86, los datos se refieren a la enseñanza pública solamente.

Kenya:
E--> See Table 3.1b.

FR-> Voir le tableau 3.1b.

ESP> Véase el cuadro 3.1b.

Liberia:
E--> For 1986, data refer to public education only.

FR-> En 1986, les données se réfèrent à l'enseignement public seulement.

ESP> En 1986, los datos se refieren a la enseñanza pública solamente.

Libyan Arab Jamahiriya:
E--> See Table 3.1b.

FR-> Voir le tableau 3.1b.

ESP> Véase el cuadro 3.1b.

Malawi:
E--> In 1994/95, education at the first level became exempt of school fees.

FR-> En 1994/95, les frais de scolarité sont supprimés pour l'enseignement primaire.

ESP> En 1994/95, los gastos de enseñanza al primer grado han sido suprimidos.

Morocco:
E--> See Table 3.1b. For 1980/81, data on teaching staff and the pupil/teacher ratio refer to public education only.

FR-> Voir le tableau 3.1b. Pour 1980/81 les données sur le personnel enseignant et le nombre d'élèves par maître se réfèrent à l'enseignement public seulement.

ESP> Véase el cuadro 3.1b. Para 1980/81, los datos sobre el personal docente y el número de alumnos por maestro se refieren a la enseñanza pública solamente.

Mozambique:
E--> See Table 3.1b. All data for 1980 and those on teachers and the pupil/teacher ratio for 1985 include initiation classes (education preceding the first level).

FR-> Voir le tableau 3.1b. Toutes les données pour 1980 et celles relatives au personnel enseignant et au nombre d'élèves par maître pour 1985 incluent les classes d'initiation (enseignement précédant le premier degré).

ESP> Véase el cuadro 3.1b. Todos los datos para 1980 y los datos sobre el personal docente y el número de alumnos por maestro para 1985 incluyen las clases de iniciación (enseñanza anterior al primer grado).

Nigeria:
E--> Revised data. From 1990, the school year corresponds to the calendar year.

FR-> Données révisées. A partir de 1990, l'année scolaire correspond à l'année de calendrier.

ESP> Datos revisados. A partir de 1990, el año escolar corresponde al año calendario.

Rwanda:
E--> See Table 3.1b.

FR-> Voir le tableau 3.1b.

ESP> Véase el cuadro 3.1b.

Sao Tome and Principe:
E--> Except for 1989/90, data on teaching staff and the pupil/teacher ratio include education preceding the first level.

FR-> A l'exception de 1989/90, les données relatives au personnel enseignant et au nombre d'élèves par maître incluent l'enseignement précédant le premier degré.

ESP> Excepto para 1989/90, los datos relativos al personal docente y al número de alumnos por maestro incluyen la enseñanza anterior al primer grado.

Seychelles:
E--> See Table 3.1b.

FR-> Voir le tableau 3.1b.

ESP> Véase el cuadro 3.1b.

Sierra Leone:
E--> From 1989/90 data on enrolment refer to approximately 95% of the total number of schools.

FR-> A partir de 1989/90, les données relatives aux élèves se réfèrent à environ 95% du nombre total des écoles.

ESP> A partir de 1989/90 los datos sobre los alumnos se refieren a cerca del 95% del total de las escuelas.

South Africa:
E--> For 1986 and 1993, data do not include the former Independant States (Transkei, Bophuthatswana, Venda and Ciskei).

FR-> Pour 1986 et 1993, les données n'incluent pas les anciens Etats indépendants (Transkei, Bophuthatswana, Venda et Ciskei).

ESP> Para 1986 y 1993, los datos no incluyen los antiguos Estados independientes (Transkei, Bophuthatswana, Venda y Ciskei).

Uganda:
E--> Data refer to government-maintained and aided schools only.

FR-> Les données se réfèrent aux écoles publiques et subventionnées seulement.

ESP> Los datos se refieren a las escuelas públicas y subvencionadas solamente.

United Republic of Tanzania:
E--> Data refer to Tanzania mainland only.

FR-> Les données se réfèrent à la Tanzanie continentale seulement.

ESP> Los datos se refieren a Tanzania continental solamente.

AMERICA, NORTH:
Bahamas:
E--> For 1980/81 data on teaching staff and the pupil/teacher ratio refer to public education only. For 1985/86 data on teaching staff include a part of education at the second level.

FR-> Pour 1980/81, les données relatives au personnel enseignant et au nombre d'élèves par maître se réfèrent à l'enseignement public seulement. En 1985/86, les données sur le personnel enseignant incluent une partie de l'enseignement du second degré.

ESP> Para 1980/81, los datos sobre el personal docente y el número de alumnos por maestro se refieren a la enseñanza pública solamente. Para 1985/86, los datos sobre el personal docente incluyen una parte de la enseñanza de segundo grado.

Barbados:
E--> For 1980/81 data on teaching staff and the pupil/teacher ratio refer to public education only.

FR-> En 1980/81, les données relatives au personnel enseignant et au nombre d'élèves par maître se réfèrent à l'enseignement public seulement.

ESP> En 1980/81, los datos relativos al personal docente y al número de alumnos por maestro se refieren a la enseñanza pública solamente.

Belize:
E--> With the exception of 1992/93 and 1994/95, data refer to government-maintained and aided schools only.

FR-> A l'exception de 1992/93 et 1994/95, les données se réfèrent aux écoles publiques et subventionnées seulement.

ESP> Excepto para 1992/93 y 1994/95, los datos se refieren a las escuelas públicas y subvencionadas solamente.

Canada:
E--> Data on schools have been revised, and include pre-primary and primary schools.

FR-> Les données concernant les écoles ont été révisées et comprennent les écoles préprimaires et primaires.

ESP> Los datos han sido revisados y incluyen las escuelas preprimarias y primarias.

Dominica:
E--> With the exception of 1990/91, data on teaching staff include general education at the second level.

FR-> A l'exception de 1990/91, les données relatives au personnel enseignant incluent l'enseignement général du second degré.

ESP> Excepto para 1990/91, los datos relativos al personal docente incluyen la enseñanza general de segundo grado.

3.4 First level: schools, teachers and pupils
Premier degré: écoles, enseignants et élèves
Primer grado: escuelas, personal docente y alumnos

Dominican Republic:
E--> See Table 3.1b. For 1989/90, data include intermediate education (grades 7 and 8 of *tradicional* education), and refer to public education only.
FR-> Voir le tableau 3.1b. Pour 1989/90 les données incluent l'enseignement intermédiaire (septième et huitième années d'études de l'enseignement *tradicional*), et se réfèrent à l'enseignement public seulement.
ESP> Véase el cuadro 3.1b. Para 1989/90, los datos incluyen la enseñanza intermedia (séptimo y octavo años de estudio de la enseñanza tradicional), y se refieren a la enseñanza pública solamente.

El Salvador:
E--> From 1991, data on teaching staff and the pupil/teacher ratio refer to public education only.
FR-> A partir de 1991, les données relatives au personnel enseignant et au nombre d'élèves par maître se réfèrent à l'enseignement public seulement.
ESP> A partir de 1991, los datos sobre el personal docente y el nùmero de alumnos por maestro se refieren a la enseñanza pública solamente.

Haiti:
E--> Data on teaching staff and the pupil/teacher ratio for 1990/91, and all data for 1980/81 and 1985/86 include infant classes.
FR-> Les données relatives au personnel enseignant et au nombre d'élèves par maître en 1990/91, et toutes les données en 1980/81 et 1985/86 incluent les classes enfantines.
ESP> Los datos sobre el personal docente y el número de alumnos por maestro para 1990/91, y todos los datos para 1980/81 y 1985/86 incluyen las clases infantiles.

Jamaica:
E--> Data on teaching staff and the pupil/teacher ratio for 1980/81 and 1992/93, and all data for 1990/91 refer to public education only.
FR-> Les données relatives au personnel enseignant et au nombre d'élèves par maître en 1980/81 et 1992/93, et toutes les données en 1990/91 se réfèrent à l'enseignement public seulement.
ESP> Los datos sobre el personal docente y el número de alumnos por maestro para 1980/81 y 1992/93, y todos los datos para 1990/91 se refieren a la enseñanza pública solamente.

St. Lucia:
E--> Data on teaching staff and the pupil/teacher ratio for 1985/86, 1990/91 and 1991/92, refer to public education only.
FR-> Les données sur le personnel enseignant et le nombre d'élèves par maître pour 1985/86, 1990/91 et 1991/92, se réfèrent à l'enseignement public seulement.
ESP> Los datos sobre el personal docente y el número de alumnos por maestro para 1985/86, 1990/91 y 1991/92, se refieren a la enseñanza pública solamente.

St. Vincent and the Grenadines:
E--> For 1980/81 and 1985/86, data include secondary classes attached to primary schools.
FR-> Pour 1980/81 et 1985/86, les données incluent les classes secondaires rattachées aux écoles primaires.
ESP> Para 1980/81 y 1985/86, los datos incluyen las clases secundarias adscritas a las escuelas primarias.

Trinidad and Tobago:
E--> Data refer to government-maintained and aided schools only.
FR-> Les données se réfèrent aux écoles publiques et subventionnées seulement.
ESP> Los datos se refieren a las escuelas públicas y subvencionadas solamente.

Turks and Caicos Islands:
E--> Data refer to public education only.
FR-> Les données se réfèrent à l'enseignement public seulement.
ESP> Los datos se refieren a la enseñanza pública solamente.

U.S. Virgin Islands:
E--> Revised data. From 1985/86 data on teaching staff and the pupil/teacher ratio refer to public education only.
FR-> Données révisées. A partir de 1985/86, les données relatives au personnel enseignant et au nombre d'élèves par maître, se réfèrent à l'enseignement public seulement.
ESP> Datos revisados. A partir de 1985/86 los datos relativos al personal docente y el número de alumnos por maestro se refieren a la enseñanza pública solamente.

AMERICA, SOUTH:
Guyana:
E--> From 1985/86, data on teaching staff include secondary classes attached to primary schools.
FR-> A partir de 1985/86, les données relatives au personnel enseignant incluent les classes secondaires rattachées aux écoles primaires.
ESP> A partir de 1985/86, los datos sobre el personal docente incluyen las clases secundarias adscritas a las escuelas primarias.

Venezuela:
E--> Data refer to grades 1 to 9 (basic education). For 1980/81 and 1985/86 data on teaching staff and the pupil/teacher ratio refer to grades 1 to 6 only.
FR-> Les données se réfèrent aux années d'études 1 à 9 (enseignement de base). En 1980/81 et 1985/86 les données sur le personnel enseignant et le nombre d'élèves par maître se réfèrent aux années d'études 1 à 6 seulement.
ESP> Los datos se refieren a los años de estudio 1 a 9 (educación básica). En 1980/81 y 1985/86 los datos sobre el personal docente y el número de alumnos por maestro se refieren a los años de estudio 1 a 6 solamente.

ASIA:
Afghanistan:
E--> See Table 3.1b.
FR-> Voir le tableau 3.1b.
ESP> Véase el cuadro 3.1b.

Bahrain:
E--> Data on schools and teaching staff include part of intermediate education and refer to public education only.
FR-> Les données relatives aux écoles et au personnel enseignant comprennent une partie de l'enseignement intermédiaire et se réfèrent à l'enseignement public seulement.
ESP> Los datos sobre las escuelas y el personal docente comprenden una parte de la enseñanza intermedia y se refieren a la enseñanza pública solamente.

Bhutan:
E--> See Table 3.1b.
FR-> Voir le tableau 3.1b.
ESP> Véase el cuadro 3.1b.

Cambodia:
E--> See Table 3.1b.
FR-> Voir le tableau 3.1b.
ESP> Véase el cuadro 3.1b.

Cyprus:
E--> Not including Turkish schools.
FR-> Non compris les écoles turques.
ESP> Excluídas las escuelas turcas.

Hong Kong:
E--> Since 1990/91, data on teaching staff do not include teachers in international and English Foundation schools (12,482 students in 1994/95).
FR-> A partir de 1990/91, les données sur le personnel enseignant n'incluent pas les enseignants des écoles internationales et de la *English Foundation* (12 482 étudiants en 1994/95).
ESP> A partir de 1990/91, los datos relativos al personal docente no incluyen los docentes de las escuelas internacionales y de la *English Foundation* (12 482 estudiantes en 1994/95).

India:
E--> Data on teaching staff do not include primary classes attached to secondary schools.
FR-> Les données relatives au personnel enseignant ne comprennent pas les classes primaires rattachées aux écoles secondaires.
ESP> Los datos relativos al personal docente no incluyen las clases primarias adscritas a las escuelas secundarias.

Iran, Islamic Republic of:
E--> For 1994/95, data on teaching staff refer to public education only.
FR-> Pour 1994/95, les données relatives au personnel enseignant se réfèrent à l'enseignement public seulement.
ESP> Para 1994/95, los datos relativos al personal docente se refieren a la enseñanza pública solamente.

Israel:
E--> Data on teaching staff do not include intermediate classes.
FR-> Les données relatives au personnel enseignant n'incluent pas les classes intermédiaires.
ESP> Los datos relativos al personal docente no incluyen las clases intermedias.

Jordan:
E--> See Table 3.1b.
FR-> Voir le tableau 3.1b.
ESP> Véase el cuadro 3.1b.

Nepal:
E--> See Table 3.1b.
FR-> Voir le tableau 3.1b.
ESP> Véase el cuadro 3.1b.

Pakistan:
E--> Data include education preceding the first level.
FR-> Les données incluent l'enseignement précédant le premier degré.
ESP> Los datos incluyen la enseñanza anterior al primer grado.

First level: schools, teachers and pupils
Premier degré: écoles, enseignants et élèves
Primer grado: escuelas, personal docente y alumnos **3.4**

Philippines:

E--> Data on teaching staff and the pupil/teacher ratio for 1992/93 and all data for 1980/81 refer to public education only.

FR-> Les données relatives au personnel enseignant et au nombre d'élèves par maître en 1992/93 et toutes les données en 1980/81 se réfèrent à l'enseignement public seulement.

ESP> Los datos sobre el personal docente y el número de alumnos por maestro para 1992/93 y todos los datos para 1980/81 se refieren a la enseñanza pública solamente.

Sri Lanka:

E--> See Table 3.1b.

FR-> Voir le tableau 3.1b.

ESP> Véase el cuadro 3.1b.

United Arab Emirates:

E--> For 1980/81 and 1985/86, data on teaching staff and the pupil/teacher ratio refer to public education only.

FR-> Pour 1980/81 et 1985/86, les chiffres sur le personnel enseignant et le nombre d'élèves par maître se réfèrent à l'enseignement public seulement.

ESP> En 1980/81 y 1985/86, las cifras sobre el personal docente y el número de alumnos por maestro se refieren a la enseñanza pública solamente.

Yemen:

Former Democratic Yemen:

E--> Data on teachers for 1980/81 and all data for 1990/91 do not include schools for nomads.

FR-> Les données relatives au personnel enseignant en 1980/81 et toutes les données en 1990/91 n'incluent pas les écoles de nomades.

ESP> Los datos sobre el personal docente para 1980/81 y todos los datos de 1990/91 no incluyen las escuelas para nómadas.

Former Yemen Arab Republic:

E--> For 1980/81, data on teaching staff and the pupil/teacher ratio refer to public education only.

FR-> Pour 1980/81, les données sur le personnel enseignant et le nombre d'élèves par maître se réfèrent à l'enseignement public seulement.

ESP> Para 1980/81, los datos sobre el personal docente y el número de alumnos por maestro se refieren a la enseñanza pública solamente.

EUROPE:

Belarus:

E--> See Table 3.1b. Data on schools and teaching staff include general education at the second level.

FR-> Voir le tableau 3.1b. Les données relatives aux écoles et au personnel enseignant incluent l'enseignement général du second degré.

ESP> Véase el cuadro 3.1b. Los datos relativos a las escuelas y al personal docente incluyen la enseñanza general de segundo grado.

Belgium:

E--> From 1990/91, data on teaching staff and the pupil/teacher ratio include education preceding the first level.

FR-> A partir de 1990/91, les données relatives au personnel enseignant et au nombre d'élèves par maître incluent l'enseignement précédant le premier degré.

ESP> A partir de 1990/91, los datos relativos al personal docente y al número de alumnos por maestro incluyen la enseñanza anterior al primer grado.

Former Czechoslovakia:

E--> See Table 3.1b.

FR-> Voir le tableau 3.1b.

ESP> Véase el cuadro 3.1b.

France:

E--> In 1980/81, data on teaching staff refer to public education only; in 1985/86, they include private pre-primary teachers and in 1990/91 and 1992/93 they include all pre-primary teachers.

FR-> En 1980/81, les données relatives au personnel enseignant se réfèrent à l'enseignement public seulement, en 1985/86, elles incluent le personnel enseignant de l'enseignement privé du préprimaire et en 1990/91 et 1992/93 elles incluent tout le personnel enseignant du préprimaire.

ESP> En 1980/81, los datos sobre el personal docente se refieren à la enseñanza pública solamente; en 1985/86, ellos incluyen el personal docente de la enseñanza privada preprimaria y en 1990/91 y 1992/93 ellos incluyen todo el personal docente de la enseñanza preprimaria.

Ireland:

E--> The number of schools includes education preceding the first level.

FR-> Le nombre d'écoles comprend l'enseignement précédant le premier degré.

ESP> El número de escuelas incluye la enseñanza anterior al primer grado.

Monaco:

E--> Data for 1980/81 refer to public education only.

FR-> Les données pour 1980/81 se réfèrent à l'enseignement public seulement.

ESP> Los datos para 1980/81 se refieren a la enseñanza pública solamente.

Netherlands:

E--> The number of schools refers to the total number of pre-primary and primary schools.

FR-> Le nombre d'écoles se réfère au total des écoles préprimaires et primaires.

ESP> El número de escuelas se refiere al total de las escuelas preprimarias y primarias.

Norway:

E--> Data on schools and teaching staff include the first stage of general education at the second level.

FR-> Les données relatives aux écoles et au personnel enseignant incluent le premier cycle de l'enseignement général du second degré.

ESP> Los datos relativos a las escuelas y al personal docente incluyen el primer ciclo de la enseñanza general de segundo grado.

Romania:

E--> See Table 3.1b.

FR-> Voir le tableau 3.1b.

ESP> Véase el cuadro 3.1b.

Sweden:

E--> In 1990/91 and 1991/92 data on teaching staff include the first stage of general education at the second level.

FR-> En 1990/91 et 1991/92 les données relatives au personnel enseignant incluent le premier cycle de l'enseignement général du second degré.

ESP> En 1990/91 y 1991/92 los datos relativos al personal docente incluyen el primer ciclo de la enseñanza general de segundo grado.

Ukraine:

E--> See Table 3.1b. Data on schools include general education at the second level. All data on teachers refer to grades 1 to 4, whereas enrolment data refer to these grades only since 1992/93.

FR-> Voir le tableau 3.1b. Les données relatives aux écoles incluent l'enseignement général du second degré. Toutes les données relatives au personnel enseignant se réfèrent à 4 années d'études alors que les effectifs ne se réfèrent à ces années d'études qu'à partir de 1992/93.

ESP> Véase el cuadro 3.1b. Los datos relativos a las escuelas incluyen la enseñanza general de segundo grado. Todos los datos relativos al personal docente se refieren a 4 años de estudios, aunque los efectivos solo se refieren a estos años de estudios a partir de 1992/93.

United Kingdom:

E--> Data on schools refer to public education only. For 1980/81 and 1985/86, data on teaching staff include education preceding the first level. From 1992/93, education provided in infant classes in primary schools, previously considered as pre-primary education, is included with education at the first level.

FR-> Les données relatives aux écoles se réfèrent à l'enseignement public seulement. Pour 1980/81 et 1985/86, les données relatives au personnel enseignant incluent l'enseignement précédant le premier degré. A partir de 1992/93 l'enseignement dispensé dans les classes enfantines des écoles primaires, considéré auparavant comme de l'enseignement préprimaire, est inclus dans l'enseignement du premier degré.

ESP> Los datos relativos a las escuelas se refieren a la enseñanza pública solamente. Para 1980/81 y 1985/86, los datos relativos al personal docente incluyen la enseñanza anterior al primer grado. A partir de 1992/93 la enseñanza impartida en las clases de párvulos de las escuelas primarias, considerada antes como educación preprimaria se incluye en la educación de primer grado.

OCEANIA:

Australia:

E--> Data on teaching staff and the pupil/teacher ratio include pre-primary classes and from 1990, data on teaching staff are expressed in full-time equivalent.

FR-> Les données sur le personnel enseignant et le nombre d'élèves par maître comprennent les classes préprimaires et, à partir de 1990, les données relatives au personnel enseignant sont exprimées en équivalents plein-temps.

ESP> Los datos sobre el personal docente y el número de alumnos por maestro comprenden las clases de preprimaria y, a partir de 1990, los datos relativos al personal docente están expresados en equivalentes de jornada completa.

Guam:

E--> Data on teaching staff and the pupil/teacher ratio refer to public education only.

FR-> Les données sur le personnel enseignant et le nombre d'élèves par maître se réfèrent à l'enseignement public seulement.

ESP> Los datos sobre el personal docente y el número de alumnos por maestro se refieren a la enseñanza pública solamente.

3.4 First level: schools, teachers and pupils
Premier degré: écoles, enseignants et élèves
Primer grado: escuelas, personal docente y alumnos

Niue:

E--> See Table 3.1b.

FR-> Voir le tableau 3.1b.

ESP> Véase el cuadro 3.1b.

Papua New Guinea:

E--> Data for 1993 refer to public education only and from 1994 include grades 7 and 8 which are *Top up schools*.

FR-> Les données pour 1993 se réfèrent à l'enseignement public seulement et à partir de 1994 incluent les septième et huitième années d'études qui correspondent aux *Top up schools*.

ESP> Los datos para 1993 se refieren a la enseñanza pública y a partir de 1994 incluyen los años de estudio séptimo y octavo que corresponden a los *Top up schools*.

Samoa:

E--> Data on teaching staff and the pupil/teacher ratio include Forms I and II (education at the second level).

FR-> Les données sur le personnel enseignant et le nombre d'élèves par maître incluent les *Forms* I et II (enseignement du second degré).

ESP> Los datos sobre el personal docente y el número de alumnos por maestro incluyen las *Forms* I y II (enseñanza de segundo grado).

Tuvalu:

E--> From 1980 to 1990, data include 3 years of education provided in community training centres. For 1990 data refer to public education only.

FR-> De 1980 à 1990, les données incluent 3 années d'enseignement dispensé dans les *community training centres*. En 1990 les données se réfèrent à l'enseignement public seulement.

ESP> De 1980 a 1990, los datos incluyen 3 años de enseñanza dispensada en los *community training centres*. Para 1990 los datos se refieren a la enseñanza pública solamente.

Vanuatu, Republic of:

E--> From 1990, data do not include independent private schools.

FR-> A partir de 1990, les donnnées n'incluent pas les écoles privées indépendantes.

ESP> A partir de 1990, los datos no incluyen las escuelas privadas independientes.

First level: enrolment by grade 3.5
Premier degré: effectifs par année d'études
Primer grado: matrícula escolar por año de estudios

3.5 Education at the first level: distribution of enrolment by grade

Enseignement du premier degré: répartition des effectifs par année d'études

Enseñanza de primer grado: distribución de la matrícula escolar por año de estudios

Please refer to the explanatory text at the end of the table

Prière de se référer au texte explicatif à la fin du tableau

Referirse al texto explicativo al final del cuadro

Country Pays País	Year Année Año	Sex Sexe Sexo	Grades / Années d'études / Año de estudios									
			I	II	III	IV	V	VI	VII	VIII	IX	X
Africa												
Algeria‡	1985/86	MF	19	18	17	16	15	15	0			
		F	20	18	18	16	15	14	0			
	1990/91	MF	19	18	17	16	16	14				
		F	20	18	17	16	15	14				
	1993/94	MF	18	17	18	17	15	15				
		F	18	18	18	17	15	14				
	1994/95	MF	17	17	17	17	16	15				
		F	18	17	17	17	16	15				
Angola	1985/86	MF	38	31	20	11						
		F	40	31	19	10						
	1990/91	MF	35	29	22	14						
		F	*36	*29	*22	*13						
Benin	1985/86	MF	25	19	17	14	12	13				
		F	25	19	17	14	12	12				
	1990/91	MF	32	21	17	12	10	8				
		F	31	22	17	12	10	8				
	1991/92	MF	29	22	18	12	10	9				
		F	30	21	19	12	10	8				
Botswana	1985	MF	17	15	14	15	13	12	14			
		F	16	15	13	14	13	13	15			
	1990	MF	17	15	15	15	12	12	13			
		F	16	15	15	15	13	13	14			
	1993	MF	16	15	15	16	14	13	12			
		F	15	15	15	15	14	14	13			
	1994	MF	16	14	15	16	14	13	13			
Burkina Faso	1985/86	MF	23	22	17	14	11	13				
		F	23	22	17	14	11	12				
	1990/91	MF	21	19	17	14	13	15				
		F	21	20	18	14	13	15				
	1992/93	MF	21	19	17	15	10	18				
		F	21	19	18	15	11	17				
	1993/94	MF	20	21	17	15	10	17				
		F	20	21	17	15	11	16				
Burundi	1985/86	MF	25	20	18	16	11	11				
		F	26	20	18	15	10	10				
	1990/91	MF	22	17	16	16	15	14				
		F	22	17	16	16	15	14				
	1991/92	MF	20	18	15	15	16	16				
		F	20	18	15	15	16	15				
	1992/93	MF	21	17	15	14	16	17				
		F	21	17	15	14	16	16				

First level: enrolment by grade
Premier degré: effectifs par année d'études
Primer grado: matrícula escolar por año de estudios

Country Pays País	Year Année Año	Sex Sexe Sexo	Grades / Années d'études / Año de estudios									
			I	II	III	IV	V	VI	VII	VIII	IX	X
Cameroon	1985/86	MF	25	17	18	14	13	12	2			
		F	25	17	18	14	13	12	2			
	1990/91	MF	23	16	18	14	14	12	2			
		F	23	16	18	14	14	12	2			
Cape Verde	1985/86	MF	26	22	19	17	10	7				
		F	25	22	19	17	10	7				
	1989/90	MF	23	23	18	16	11	9				
		F	23	22	19	16	11	9				
	1993/94	MF	23	19	18	16	13	11				
		F	22	19	18	16	13	11				
Central African Republic	1985/86	MF	23	19	20	14	12	12				
		F	24	19	20	15	11	10				
	1989/90	MF	25	19	20	14	11	11				
		F	27	20	20	14	10	9				
Chad	1985/86	MF	43	21	15	9	6	6				
		F	49	21	14	8	5	4				
	1990/91	MF	31	20	18	12	9	9				
		F	37	22	18	10	7	5				
	1991/92	MF	32	20	18	12	9	9				
		F	36	22	18	11	7	6				
	1993/94	MF	30	21	17	13	9	9				
		F	34	23	17	12	7	6				
Comoros	1985/86	MF	22	18	16	15	14	16				
		F	23	17	16	15	13	15				
	1991/92	MF	25	18	16	14	12	16				
		F	26	17	16	14	12	16				
	1992/93	MF	23	19	17	14	12	15				
		F	24	18	16	14	12	15				
	1993/94	MF	23	19	18	14	12	14				
		F	22	19	17	14	13	15				
Congo	1985/86	MF	21	16	21	17	14	11				
		F	21	16	21	17	14	11				
	1990/91	MF	20	18	21	16	14	11				
		F	20	16	21	17	14	12				
	1991/92	MF	21	16	21	16	14	12				
		F	21	16	21	16	14	12				
	1993/94	MF	21	17	22	16	14	11				
		F	21	17	21	16	14	11				
Côte d'Ivoire	1985/86	MF	20	16	16	14	14	20				
		F	22	17	17	14	14	17				
	1990/91	MF	20	18	17	14	13	17				
		F	21	19	18	14	13	15				
	1991/92	MF	20	17	17	14	14	17				
		F	21	18	18	15	14	15				
	1993/94	MF	22	18	16	14	13	17				
		F	23	18	17	14	13	15				
Djibouti	1985/86	MF	18	18	16	16	16	17				
		F	18	17	16	17	15	17				
	1993/94	MF	19	17	16	15	14	20				
		F	19	18	16	15	13	19				
	1994/95	MF	19	17	16	15	13	19				
		F	20	17	16	15	13	19				
Egypt	1985/86	MF	19	19	17	16	15	14				
		F	20	19	17	16	14	14				
	1990/91	MF	21	21	19	20	20					
		F	21	19	20	20	20					
	1992/93	MF	21	21	20	20	19					
		F	21	21	20	20	18					
	1993/94	MF	21	21	20	20	18					
		F	22	21	20	19	18					

First level: enrolment by grade 3.5
Premier degré: effectifs par année d'études
Primer grado: matrícula escolar por año de estudios

Country / Pays / País	Year / Année / Año	Sex / Sexe / Sexo	I	II	III	IV	V	VI	VII	VIII	IX	X
Eritrea	1988/89	MF	25	18	16	15	13	14				
	1990/91	MF	22	18	16	15	14	15				
	1993/94	MF	31	26	21	13	10					
		F	32	25	20	13	10					
	1994/95	MF	28	22	21	18	11					
		F	29	22	20	18	11					
Ethiopia	1985/86	MF	34	17	14	13	12	11				
		F	34	17	14	12	11	11				
	1990/91	MF	28	18	16	15	12	11				
		F	28	18	16	14	12	12				
	1992/93	MF	34	18	14	13	11	11				
		F	33	17	14	13	12	11				
	1993/94	MF	40	17	13	11	9	9				
		F	37	17	13	12	10	11				
Gabon	1985/86	MF	32	18	16	12	10	11				
		F	32	18	17	12	11	11				
	1991/92	MF	30	20	18	12	10	11				
		F	30	18	18	12	10	11				
Gambia	1985/86	MF	19	17	16	15	15	18				
		F	21	19	16	15	14	15				
	1991/92	MF	24	20	14	13	13	16				
		F	25	21	15	13	13	14				
	1992/93	MF	25	18	18	13	12	14				
		F	25	19	18	13	12	12				
Ghana	1986/87	MF	22	18	17	15	14	14				
	1990/91	MF	22	19	17	16	14	13				
		F	22	19	17	15	14	12				
	1991/92	MF	21	18	17	16	14	13				
		F	22	19	17	16	14	13				
Guinea	1985/86	MF	21	29	15	12	11	12				
		F	23	27	15	12	11	12				
	1990/91	MF	26	20	19	15	11	10				
		F	28	21	19	14	10	9				
	1992/93	MF	28	18	18	13	12	10				
		F	30	20	17	13	11	9				
	1993/94	MF	26	22	16	14	11	10				
		F	29	23	17	13	10	9				
Guinea-Bissau	1986/87	MF	35	24	16	13	7	4				
		F	37	25	16	11	7	4				
	1988/89	MF	34	25	17	13	7	4				
		F	35	25	17	12	7	4				
Kenya	1985	MF	18	15	14	13	12	11	10	8		
		F	18	15	14	14	12	11	9	7		
	1990	MF	17	15	14	13	11	11	11	7		
		F	17	15	14	13	12	11	12	7		
	1992	MF	17	15	14	13	12	11	11	8		
		F	17	15	13	14	12	11	11	7		
	1993	MF	*17	*15	*14	*14	*12	*11	*11	*7		
		F	*17	*14	*14	*14	*12	*11	*11	*7		
Lesotho	1985	MF	26	19	16	13	10	8	8			
		F	24	18	16	13	11	10	9			
	1990	MF	22	18	16	14	12	9	8			
		F	19	17	16	14	13	11	10			
	1993	MF	20	17	16	14	12	10	9			
		F	18	16	16	15	13	12	11			
	1994	MF	20	17	16	15	12	11	9			
		F	19	16	15	15	13	12	10			

First level: enrolment by grade
Premier degré: effectifs par année d'études
Primer grado: matrícula escolar por año de estudios

Country Pays País	Year Année Año	Sex Sexe Sexo	Grades / Années d'études / Año de estudios									
			I	II	III	IV	V	VI	VII	VIII	IX	X
Libyan Arab Jamahiriya	1985/86	MF	13	13	13	14	11	10	10	8	7	
		F	14	13	13	14	11	10	10	8	7	
Madagascar	1987/88	MF	37	22	18	12	11					
		F	35	22	19	13	12					
	1990/91	MF	38	22	18	12	10					
		F	38	22	18	12	11					
	1992/93	MF	37	22	18	12	10					
		F	37	22	18	12	11					
	1993/94	MF	37	23	18	12	10					
		F	36	22	18	12	11					
Malawi	1985/86	MF	27	18	14	10	8	8	6	10		
		F	29	19	14	10	8	8	6	7		
	1990/91	MF	27	19	15	10	9	7	5	8		
		F	29	19	15	10	9	7	5	6		
	1993/94	MF	33	20	14	10	8	6	5	4		
		F	35	21	14	10	7	5	4	3		
	1994/95	MF	35	18	14	10	8	6	5	5		
		F	37	18	14	10	7	5	4	4		
Mali	1985/86	MF	25	20	19	14	12	10				
		F	25	20	19	14	12	9				
	1990/91	MF	25	21	20	14	11	9				
		F	25	21	20	14	11	8				
	1992/93	MF	28	21	19	14	11	8				
		F	30	21	18	14	11	7				
	1993/94	MF	25	22	19	14	11	8				
		F	27	23	19	13	11	8				
Mauritania	1985/86	MF	20	17	17	15	14	16				
		F	21	19	17	15	13	15				
	1990/91	MF	23	18	17	14	12	16				
		F	24	19	17	13	12	15				
	1992/93	MF	29	20	15	12	11	12				
		F	30	21	15	12	10	12				
	1993/94	MF	27	23	17	12	10	12				
		F	28	23	17	12	10	11				
Mauritius	1985	MF	18	10	16	15	20	21				
		F	18	11	16	15	20	20				
	1990	MF	14	15	15	17	17	22				
		F	14	14	16	17	17	22				
	1992	MF	14	14	15	15	16	25				
		F	14	14	15	15	16	25				
	1993	MF	15	15	15	15	16	24				
		F	16	14	15	15	16	24				
Morocco	1985/86	MF	24	17	20	19	20					
		F	25	17	19	19	20					
	1990/91	MF	22	19	17	16	14	12				
		F	23	19	17	16	14	12				
	1993/94	MF	23	20	17	15	14	12				
		F	24	20	17	15	13	11				
	1994/95	MF	22	20	18	15	13	12				
		F	23	20	18	15	13	11				
Mozambique	1985	MF	39	27	21	12						
		F	42	27	21	10						
	1990	MF	33	26	17	14	10					
		F	35	25	17	13	9					
	1992	MF	31	25	20	14	10					
		F	32	25	20	14	10					
	1993	MF	33	24	19	14	10					
		F	35	24	19	13	10					

First level: enrolment by grade 3.5
Premier degré: effectifs par année d'études
Primer grado: matrícula escolar por año de estudios

Country Pays País	Year Année Año	Sex Sexe Sexo	Grades / Années d'études / Año de estudios									
			I	II	III	IV	V	VI	VII	VIII	IX	X
Namibia	1986	MF	23	17	15	15	12	9	9			
	1990	MF	24	16	14	14	12	11	9			
		F	23	15	14	14	13	12	10			
	1994	MF	21	18	16	15	12	9	9			
		F	21	17	16	15	12	10	10			
Niger	1985/86	MF	19	18	15	14	15	19				
		F	19	18	15	15	15	18				
	1990/91	MF	18	18	19	16	14	16				
		F	18	19	19	15	14	15				
	1991/92	MF	18	18	17	16	14	17				
		F	18	18	17	16	14	16				
	1992/93	MF	19	18	17	15	14	18				
		F	19	18	17	15	15	17				
Nigeria	1985/86	MF	21	18	17	16	15	13				
		F	21	18	17	16	15	13				
	1990	MF	23	19	17	16	14	12				
		F	23	19	17	16	14	12				
	1992	MF	21	18	17	16	15	13				
		F	21	18	17	15	15	13				
	1993	MF	21	18	17	16	15	13				
		F	21	18	17	16	15	13				
Reunion	1985/86	MF	21	19	19	20	21					
		F	21	19	19	20	21					
	1986/87	MF	21	19	19	20	21					
		F	21	20	19	20	21					
	1993/94	MF	20	21	20	20	19					
		F	20	21	20	20	20					
Rwanda	1985/86	MF	24	17	14	12	10	9	8	6		
		F	24	17	14	13	11	9	7	6		
	1990/91	MF	23	18	15	13	11	8	6	5		
		F	23	18	15	13	11	8	6	5		
	1991/92	MF	25	18	15	13	11	9	7			
		F	25	18	16	14	11	9	7			
St. Helena	1985/86	MF	17	16	17	16	16	18				
		F	17	14	19	16	17	17				
Sao Tome and Principe	1986/87	MF	33	26	22	19						
		F	32	26	22	20						
	1989/90	MF	31	27	23	18						
		F	31	27	23	19						
Senegal	1985/86	MF	18	19	18	16	14	16				
		F	19	19	18	16	14	15				
	1991/92	MF	19	18	17	15	15	17				
		F	20	19	17	15	14	15				
	1993/94	MF	20	18	17	16	14	15				
		F	21	19	17	15	14	14				
Seychelles	1985	MF	12	11	10	12	12	11	11	11	10	
		F	12	11	11	12	12	11	11	11	10	
	1991	MF	18	17	16	16	16	17				
		F	18	17	15	17	16	17				
	1993	MF	16	17	18	17	16	16				
		F	17	17	18	17	15	16				
	1994	MF	17	16	17	18	17	16				
		F	17	16	16	18	17	15				
Somalia	1985/86	MF	17	14	13	12	12	11	10	12		
		F	18	14	13	11	11	10	10	13		
South Africa	1990	MF	21	16	15	13	13	11	10			
		F	20	16	15	13	13	12	11			
	1991	MF	21	16	15	13	13	11	10			
		F	20	15	15	14	13	12	11			
	1994	MF	20	16	15	14	13	12	11			

First level: enrolment by grade
Premier degré: effectifs par année d'études
Primer grado: matrícula escolar por año de estudios

Country Pays País	Year Année Año	Sex Sexe Sexo	Grades / Années d'études / Año de estudios									
			I	II	III	IV	V	VI	VII	VIII	IX	X
Sudan	1985/86	MF	21	19	17	16	14	13				
		F	21	19	17	16	14	13				
	1990/91	MF	20	19	17	16	14	13				
		F	20	19	17	16	14	14				
	1991/92	MF	21	19	18	16	15	11				
		F	21	19	18	16	15	11				
Swaziland	1985	MF	19	17	16	14	13	11	10			
		F	19	16	16	14	13	12	10			
	1990	MF	21	18	16	13	12	10	9			
		F	20	17	16	13	12	11	10			
	1993	MF	20	18	16	14	13	11	9			
		F	19	17	16	14	13	11	10			
	1994	MF	19	17	16	14	13	11	9			
		F	18	17	16	15	13	12	10			
Togo	1985/86	MF	29	19	18	13	12	10				
		F	30	20	18	12	11	8				
	1990/91	MF	27	20	18	13	12	10				
		F	29	22	19	12	11	8				
	1991/92	MF	26	20	18	13	13	10				
		F	28	21	19	12	11	8				
	1993/94	MF	30	19	17	12	12	9				
		F	32	20	18	12	10	7				
Tunisia‡	1985/86	MF	19	18	17	16	15	14	1	0		
		F	20	18	17	16	14	13	1	0		
	1990/91	MF	17	19	17	15	15	17				
		F	18	19	17	15	14	16				
	1993/94	MF	17	17	18	17	16	15				
		F	17	17	18	16	16	15				
	1994/95	MF	16	17	17	17	16	16				
		F	17	17	17	17	16	16				
Uganda‡	1986	MF	24	18	17	14	11	9	7			
		F	25	19	17	14	11	8	6			
	1990	MF	25	18	17	13	11	9	7			
		F	26	19	17	13	11	9	6			
	1991	MF	24	18	17	14	11	9	7			
	1993	MF	24	17	17	14	12	9	7			
		F	25	18	17	14	11	9	6			
United Republic of Tanzania‡	1985	MF	17	15	15	14	13	13	13			
		F	17	15	15	14	13	13	13			
	1990	MF	18	16	15	16	12	13	9			
		F	18	16	15	16	12	13	9			
	1992	MF	19	16	15	16	13	12	10			
		F	18	16	15	16	13	12	10			
	1993	MF	18	16	15	15	13	12	11			
		F	18	16	15	16	13	12	11			
Zaire	1985/86	MF	27	20	18	14	11	10				
		F	30	21	18	13	10	8				
	1990/91	MF	25	19	18	15	13	11				
		F	26	20	18	14	12	9				
	1992/93	MF	23	19	18	15	13	12				
		F	24	19	18	15	13	11				
	1993/94	MF	24	19	18	15	13	11				
		F	25	19	18	15	13	10				
Zambia	1985	MF	17	16	15	14	13	12	13			
		F	18	16	15	14	13	12	12			
	1988	MF	16	15	15	15	13	12	13			
		F	17	16	15	15	13	12	12			
	1994	MF	16	16	15	15	13	13	12			
		F	17	16	16	15	13	12	11			

First level: enrolment by grade 3.5
Premier degré: effectifs par année d'études
Primer grado: matrícula escolar por año de estudios

Country Pays País	Year Année Año	Sex Sexe Sexo	Grades / Années d'études / Año de estudios									
			I	II	III	IV	V	VI	VII	VIII	IX	X
Zimbabwe	1985	MF	16	15	15	16	16	14	10			
		F	16	15	15	16	16	13	9			
	1990	MF	18	16	15	14	13	13	12			
		F	18	17	15	14	13	12	12			
	1991	MF	18	16	15	14	13	12	12			
		F	18	16	15	14	13	12	12			
	1992	MF	18	16	15	14	13	12	11			
		F	18	16	15	14	13	13	11			
America, North												
Antigua and Barbuda	1991/92	MF	19	14	14	14	13	12	12			
		F	20	14	14	14	13	12	12			
Bahamas	1985/86	MF	19	16	16	17	16	16				
		F	19	16	16	16	17	16				
	1990/91	MF	18	20	16	16	15	15				
	1992/93	MF	18	17	16	17	16	16				
	1993/94	MF	19	17	17	16	16	15				
Barbados	1988/89	MF	15	17	14	14	13	14	14			
		F	15	16	14	14	14	14	14			
	1989/90	MF	15	15	15	14	14	13	14			
		F	15	15	15	14	14	13	14			
	1991/92	MF	14	15	15	15	14	13	13			
		F	14	16	14	15	14	14	13			
Belize	1985/86	MF	19	13	13	12	11	11	10	10		
		F	18	13	14	12	11	11	10	10		
	1990/91	MF	19	14	14	12	12	11	10	9		
		F	*19	*14	*14	*12	*11	*11	*10	*9		
	1992/93	MF	19	14	13	12	12	11	10	9		
		F	19	13	13	13	11	11	10	9		
	1994/95	MF	19	14	13	12	12	11	10	9		
		F	19	14	13	12	12	11	10	9		
British Virgin Islands	1984/85	MF	16	14	14	15	14	13	13	0		
		F	15	13	14	14	14	15	14	0		
	1991/92	MF	15	15	13	13	14	15	14	0		
		F	16	15	12	13	14	15	15	0		
	1993/94	MF	16	13	13	13	14	14	16	0		
		F	17	13	13	14	13	14	16	0		
Canada	1985/86	MF	18	17	17	16	16	16				
		F	17	17	17	16	17	16				
	1990/91	MF	18	17	17	16	16	16				
		F	17	17	17	17	16	16				
	1992/93	MF	17	17	17	17	16	16				
		F	17	17	17	17	17	16				
	1993/94	MF	17	17	17	17	17	16				
		F	17	17	17	17	17	17				
Costa Rica	1985	MF	22	19	17	15	14	12				
		F	22	19	17	15	14	12				
	1990	MF	22	19	17	16	14	12				
		F	21	19	18	16	15	12				
	1993	MF	22	19	17	15	14	13				
		F	21	19	17	15	14	13				
	1994	MF	21	19	18	16	14	12				
		F	20	19	18	16	14	13				

3.5 First level: enrolment by grade
Premier degré: effectifs par année d'études
Primer grado: matrícula escolar por año de estudios

Country Pays País	Year Année Año	Sex Sexe Sexo	I	II	III	IV	V	VI	VII	VIII	IX	X
									Grades / Années d'études / Año de estudios			
Cuba	1985/86	MF F	13 13	15 15	16 16	18 18	19 19	19 19				
	1990/91	MF F	18 18	19 19	17 17	15 15	15 15	15 15				
	1993/94	MF F	18 18	18 17	18 18	16 16	16 16	15 15				
	1994/95	MF F	18 18	19 18	15 15	18 18	15 15	15 15				
Dominica	1985/86	MF F	16 15	14 14	13 13	13 12	13 13	14 13	18 20			
	1990/91	MF F	14 14	15 14	15 16	14 14	14 14	12 12	15 16			
	1993/94	MF F	14 14	14 13	13 12	14 14	14 14	15 15	17 17			
	1994/95	MF F	15 14	13 13	14 13	13 13	13 13	14 13	18 21			
Dominican Republic	1985/86	MF F	31 29	18 18	16 16	14 14	12 12	10 10				
	1989/90	MF F	28 27	16 16	14 14	12 12	10 11	9 10	6 6	5 4		
	1993/94	MF F	25 24	16 15	14 13	12 12	10 11	9 10	8 8	7 7		
	1994/95	MF F	25 23	15 15	14 14	13 13	10 10	9 9	8 8	7 8		
El Salvador	1987	MF F	24 23	17 16	14 14	12 12	10 10	8 8	6 7	5 6	4 5	
	1991	MF F	22 21	15 15	13 13	12 12	10 10	9 9	7 8	6 7	5 6	
	1992	MF F	22 21	15 15	13 13	11 12	10 10	9 9	8 8	6 7	5 6	
	1993	MF F	21 20	15 15	13 13	12 12	10 10	9 9	8 8	7 7	6 6	
Grenada	1992/93	MF F	15 14	15 15	15 15	13 13	13 13	16 17	12 12			
Guadeloupe	1985/86	MF	19	18	20	22	22					
	1990/91	MF F	21 20	20 20	20 21	20 20	19 19					
	1992/93	MF F	20 20	21 21	19 19	20 20	20 20					
	1993/94	MF F	21 21	20 20	20 20	19 19	20 20					
Guatemala	1985	MF F	33 34	21 21	16 16	12 12	9 9	8 8				
	1991	MF F	33 33	21 21	16 16	13 12	10 10	8 8				
	1993	MF F	32 33	20 20	16 16	13 12	10 10	8 8				
Haiti‡	1985/86	MF F	38 38	19 19	16 16	12 12	9 9	6 6				
	1990/91	MF F	26 26	21 21	18 18	15 15	12 12	9 9				
Honduras	1985	MF F	32 31	21 20	16 17	13 13	10 10	8 9				
	1991	MF F	29 31	20 20	17 17	14 13	11 11	9 9				
	1993	MF F	27 26	20 20	17 17	14 14	12 12	10 10				

First level: enrolment by grade   **3.5**
Premier degré: effectifs par année d'études
Primer grado: matrícula escolar por año de estudios

Country / Pays / País	Year / Année / Año	Sex / Sexe / Sexo	Grades / Années d'études / Año de estudios									
			I	II	III	IV	V	VI	VII	VIII	IX	X
Jamaica	1985/86	MF	17	17	17	17	16	16				
	1990/91	MF	17	17	17	17	16	16				
		F	17	17	17	17	16	17				
	1992/93	MF	17	17	17	17	16	16				
		F	16	17	17	17	16	17				
Martinique	1986/87	MF	21	19	19	20	22					
		F	20	19	19	20	22					
	1991/92	MF	21	20	20	19	20					
		F	21	21	20	19	19					
	1992/93	MF	21	21	20	20	19					
		F	21	21	20	20	19					
	1993/94	MF	22	20	20	19	19					
		F	21	20	20	20	19					
Mexico	1985/86	MF	21	18	17	16	15	13				
		F	21	18	17	16	15	13				
	1990/91	MF	21	18	17	16	15	13				
		F	21	18	17	16	15	13				
	1992/93	MF	21	18	17	16	15	13				
		F	20	18	17	16	15	14				
	1993/94	MF	19	19	17	16	15	14				
		F	19	18	17	16	15	14				
Montserrat‡	1993/94	MF	13	14	14	15	18	15	10			
		F	11	16	11	15	19	18	11			
Nicaragua	1985	MF	32	20	19	13	11	6				
		F	30	19	19	13	11	6				
	1990	MF	36	21	15	12	9	7				
		F	34	20	16	13	9	8				
	1993	MF	31	21	16	13	10	9				
		F	29	21	16	14	11	9				
	1994	MF	29	20	17	14	10	9				
		F	28	20	17	14	11	10				
Panama	1985	MF	21	18	17	16	14	13				
		F	21	18	17	16	15	14				
	1990	MF	19	19	18	16	15	14				
		F	19	19	18	16	15	14				
Saint Kitts and Nevis‡	1985/86	MF	14	14	12	15	14	12	20			
		F	15	14	11	14	14	14	18			
	1991/92	MF	14	14	14	14	14	14	15			
		F	14	14	15	15	14	15	14			
St. Lucia‡	1985/86	MF	11	11	12	12	11	11	13	7	11	
		F	11	11	12	12	11	11	13	7	11	
	1990/91	MF	13	12	12	12	11	11	11	8	10	
		F	13	12	13	12	11	11	11	8	10	
	1991/92	MF	12	13	12	12	12	11	11	7	10	
		F	12	13	12	13	12	11	11	6	9	
	1992/93	MF	12	12	12	12	13	12	12	8	7	
		F	12	12	13	12	13	12	12	7	6	
St. Pierre and Miquelon	1985/86	MF	18	21	20	20	20					
		F	17	18	21	22	22					
St. Vincent and the Grenadines	1986/87	MF	16	15	14	14	14	13	14			
		F	15	15	14	14	14	13	15			
	1993/94	MF	28	——>	15	15	15	14	13			
		F	27	——>	14	14	15	15	15			
Trinidad and Tobago‡	1985/86	MF	14	14	14	13	13	11	17	3	1	
		F	14	14	14	13	13	12	17	3	1	
	1990/91	MF	14	14	14	14	13	13	16	2	0	
		F	14	14	14	13	13	13	16	2	0	
	1991/92	MF	13	14	15	14	13	13	16	2	0	
		F	13	14	15	13	13	13	16	2	0	
	1992/93	MF	13	13	14	14	14	13	16	2	0	
		F	13	13	14	14	13	13	17	2	0	

First level: enrolment by grade
Premier degré: effectifs par année d'études
Primer grado: matrícula escolar por año de estudios

Country Pays País	Year Année Año	Sex Sexe Sexo	Grades / Années d'études / Año de estudios									
			I	II	III	IV	V	VI	VII	VIII	IX	X
Turks and Caicos Islands	1993/94	MF	15	20	15	17	17	16	-			
		F	16	19	16	17	16	16	-			
United States	1985/86	MF	18	17	16	16	16	17				
		F	18	17	17	16	16	17				
	1990/91	MF	18	17	17	16	16	16				
		F	18	17	16	17	16	16				
	1993/94	MF	18	17	17	16	16	16				
		F	18	17	16	16	16	16				
U. S. Virgin Islands‡	1985/86	MF	18	17	17	17	16	15				
	1990/91	MF	17	17	18	17	16	15				
		F	17	17	18	17	17	15				
	1992/93	MF	18	17	16	17	16	16				
America, South												
Argentina	1987	MF	19	17	15	14	13	12	10			
	1991	MF	16	15	15	14	14	13	14			
		F	15	15	15	14	14	14	14			
Bolivia	1984	MF	23	17	15	12	11	9	7	6		
		F	24	18	15	12	10	8	6	6		
	1990	MF	20	17	15	13	11	9	8	6		
		F	21	17	15	13	11	9	7	6		
Brazil	1985	MF	27	18	14	11	11	8	6	5		
	1990	MF	28	18	14	11	11	8	6	5		
	1992	MF	21	16	15	13	13	10	7	6		
	1993	MF	21	16	14	12	14	10	7	6		
Chile	1985	MF	14	12	12	13	14	13	12	11		
		F	14	11	11	13	14	13	12	11		
	1990	MF	14	14	14	13	13	12	10	10		
		F	14	14	14	13	13	12	10	10		
	1993	MF	14	12	13	13	13	13	12	10		
		F	14	12	12	13	13	13	12	11		
	1994	MF	15	14	12	12	13	12	12	11		
		F	14	14	12	12	12	12	12	11		
Colombia	1985	MF	31	22	18	16	13					
		F	30	21	19	17	14					
	1990	MF	30	22	18	16	14					
	1993	MF	30	19	19	17	15					
		F	29	19	19	18	16					
	1994	MF	28	20	19	17	15					
Ecuador	1984/85	MF	24	18	17	15	14	12				
	1992/93	MF	26	17	16	15	14	13				
		F	26	17	16	15	14	13				
French Guiana	1993/94	MF	24	22	20	19	16					
		F	23	21	20	19	17					
Guyana	1986/87	MF	17	17	17	17	16	16				
		F	17	17	17	17	16	17				
	1988/89	MF	*16	*17	*18	*17	*16	*16				
		F	*16	*17	*17	*17	*17	*16				
Paraguay	1985	MF	24	20	18	15	12	10				
		F	24	20	18	15	12	10				
	1990	MF	24	21	18	15	12	10				
		F	24	21	18	15	12	10				
	1993	MF	24	19	18	15	13	11				
		F	24	19	18	15	13	11				
	1994	MF	24	20	17	15	13	11				
		F	23	20	17	15	13	11				

First level: enrolment by grade 3.5
Premier degré: effectifs par année d'études
Primer grado: matrícula escolar por año de estudios

Country Pays País	Year Année Año	Sex Sexe Sexo	Grades / Années d'études / Año de estudios									
			I	II	III	IV	V	VI	VII	VIII	IX	X
Peru	1985	MF	26	19	16	15	13	12				
		F	26	19	16	14	13	11				
	1988	MF	24	19	17	15	14	12				
	1993	MF	25	19	17	15	13	11				
Suriname	1984/85	MF	19	17	17	17	16	14				
		F	18	17	17	17	17	15				
	1988/89	MF	21	17	17	17	15	14				
		F	20	16	16	17	16	16				
Uruguay	1985	MF	19	18	17	17	15	14				
		F	19	18	17	17	15	14				
	1990	MF	18	17	17	16	16	16				
		F	18	17	16	16	17	16				
	1993	MF	19	17	17	16	16	15				
		F	19	17	17	16	16	15				
	1994	MF	19	18	17	16	15	15				
		F	19	17	17	16	16	15				
Venezuela	1985/86	MF	17	15	14	12	11	9	9	7	6	
		F	16	14	13	12	11	10	9	8	6	
	1990/91	MF	17	15	13	12	11	10	10	6	5	
		F	16	14	13	12	11	10	10	7	6	
	1991/92	MF	17	15	14	12	11	10	10	6	5	
		F	16	14	13	12	11	10	10	7	6	
	1992/93	MF	16	14	14	13	11	10	10	7	5	
		F	15	14	13	12	11	10	11	7	6	
Asia												
Afghanistan	1985	MF	19	17	13	12	11	10	9	8		
		F	20	18	13	12	11	9	8	8		
	1989	MF	19	18	16	12	11	10	8	7		
		F	19	18	16	12	12	9	7	6		
	1993	MF	18	17	17	16	16	16				
		F	18	17	17	16	16	16				
Armenia	1993/94	MF	33	34	33							
		F	33	33	33							
Azerbaijan	1992/93	MF	31	28	28	13						
		F	31	28	28	13						
	1993/94	MF	33	27	27	13						
		F	33	28	27	13						
Bahrain	1985/86	MF	19	18	18	17	15	13				
		F	19	18	18	17	15	13				
	1990/91	MF	18	18	17	17	16	14				
		F	19	18	17	16	16	14				
	1993/94	MF	18	18	17	17	16	14				
		F	18	18	17	17	16	14				
	1994/95	MF	18	18	17	17	16	14				
		F	18	17	17	16	16	14				
Bangladesh	1985	MF	45	20	15	12	8					
		F	47	20	14	11	8					
	1990	MF	30	22	20	16	13					
		F	30	23	20	15	13					
Bhutan‡	1985	MF	45	18	13	10	8	6				
		F	47	18	12	9	7	6				
	1988	MF	26	24	17	12	9	7	5			
		F	27	25	17	12	9	6	5			
	1993	MF	23	21	17	13	10	9	7			
		F	23	21	17	13	10	9	7			
	1994	MF	19	20	18	15	12	9	7			
		F	20	21	18	14	12	8	7			

3.5 First level: enrolment by grade
Premier degré: effectifs par année d'études
Primer grado: matrícula escolar por año de estudios

Country / Pays / País	Year / Année / Año	Sex / Sexe / Sexo	I	II	III	IV	V	VI	VII	VIII	IX	X
Brunei Darussalam	1986	MF	18	17	16	16	14	12	8			
		F	18	16	16	15	14	12	8			
	1991	MF	18	16	17	16	16	17				
		F	18	16	17	16	16	17				
	1993	MF	18	17	16	16	16	16				
		F	17	17	16	16	16	16				
	1994	MF	18	17	17	16	16	16				
		F	18	17	17	16	16	16				
Cambodia	1985/86	MF	46	18	17	19						
	1988/89	MF	39	22	16	12	11					
	1993/94	MF	38	23	17	12	10					
		F	39	22	17	12	10					
	1994/95	MF	35	24	16	13	12					
		F	36	25	17	12	11					
China	1985/86	MF	22	19	19	19	17	4				
		F	22	20	19	18	16	4				
	1990/91	MF	20	19	18	17	16	9				
		F	20	19	18	17	16	9				
	1992/93	MF	20	18	18	18	16	9				
		F	21	18	18	18	16	9				
	1993/94	MF	21	19	17	17	17	9				
		F	21	19	17	17	16	9				
Cyprus‡	1985/86	MF	20	18	17	17	15	13	0			
		F	20	18	17	17	15	13	0			
	1990/91	MF	17	17	17	16	16	16	0			
		F	17	17	17	16	16	16	0			
	1993/94	MF	17	16	16	17	17	17	0			
		F	17	16	16	16	17	17	0			
	1994/95	MF	17	17	16	16	17	17	0			
		F	17	17	17	16	17	17	0			
Georgia	1994/95	MF	24	25	25	25						
		F	24	25	25	25						
Hong Kong	1985/86	MF	16	16	17	17	17	17				
	1990/91	MF	15	17	17	17	17	17				
	1993/94	MF	15	15	17	17	18	18				
	1994/95	MF	16	15	16	17	17	18				
India	1985/86	MF	30	21	19	16	14					
		F	30	22	19	16	13					
	1992/93	MF	27	22	20	17	15					
		F	28	22	19	16	14					
	1993/94	MF	27	22	19	17	15					
		F	28	22	19	17	14					
Indonesia	1985/86	MF	19	19	18	16	15	13				
		F	19	19	18	16	15	13				
	1990/91	MF	19	18	18	16	15	13				
		F	19	18	18	17	15	13				
	1992/93	MF	19	18	17	16	15	14				
		F	19	18	18	17	15	13				
	1993/94	MF	19	18	17	16	15	14				
		F	19	18	18	16	15	14				
Iran, Islamic Republic of	1985/86	MF	27	21	19	18	16					
		F	28	21	19	17	15					
	1990/91	MF	24	21	19	19	17					
		F	25	21	19	18	17					
	1993/94	MF	21	20	20	20	19					
		F	21	20	20	20	18					
	1994/95	MF	20	20	20	21	20					
		F	20	20	20	21	20					

3-124

First level: enrolment by grade 3.5
Premier degré: effectifs par année d'études
Primer grado: matrícula escolar por año de estudios

Country / Pays / País	Year / Année / Año	Sex / Sexe / Sexo	Grades / Années d'études / Año de estudios									
			I	II	III	IV	V	VI	VII	VIII	IX	X
Iraq	1985/86	MF	20	18	16	15	16	14				
		F	21	19	17	15	16	13				
	1988/89	MF	20	18	17	16	17	12				
		F	21	18	17	16	16	11				
	1992/93	MF	20	18	17	17	17	12				
		F	20	18	17	17	16	11				
Israel	1985/86	MF	13	13	13	13	13	12	12	11		
		F	13	13	13	13	13	12	12	11		
	1990/91	MF	13	13	12	13	12	12	12	12		
		F	13	13	12	13	12	12	12	12		
	1992/93	MF	13	13	13	13	12	12	12	12		
		F	13	13	13	13	12	12	12	12		
	1993/94	MF	13	13	13	13	12	12	12	12		
		F	13	13	13	13	12	12	12	12		
Japan	1985/86	MF	15	16	16	17	18	19				
		F	15	16	16	17	18	19				
	1990/91	MF	16	16	16	16	17	18				
		F	16	16	16	16	17	18				
	1991/92	MF	16	16	17	17	17	18				
		F	16	16	17	16	17	18				
	1993/94	MF	16	16	17	17	17	17				
		F	16	16	17	17	17	17				
Jordan	1985/86	MF	19	17	16	17	16	15				
		F	19	17	16	17	16	15				
	1990/91	MF	12	11	11	11	11	10	10	9	8	7
		F	12	11	11	11	11	10	10	9	8	7
	1992/93	MF	11	11	11	11	11	11	10	9	8	7
		F	11	11	11	11	11	10	10	9	8	7
	1993/94	MF	11	11	11	11	11	11	10	9	8	7
		F	11	11	11	11	11	11	10	9	9	7
Kazakstan	1993/94	MF	30	29	29	13						
		F	30	29	29	13						
Korea, Democratic People's Rep. of	1987/88	MF	26	24	25	24						
		F	26	25	25	24						
Korea, Republic of	1985/86	MF	16	16	15	17	18	19				
		F	16	16	15	17	18	19				
	1990/91	MF	15	17	18	17	17	16				
		F	15	17	18	17	17	16				
	1993/94	MF	14	15	15	17	19	20				
		F	14	15	15	17	19	20				
	1994/95	MF	15	15	16	16	18	20				
		F	15	15	16	16	18	20				
Kuwait	1985/86	MF	26	26	25	23						
		F	26	26	25	23						
	1991/92	MF	23	28	25	24						
		F	24	28	25	23						
	1993/94	MF	27	26	22	25						
		F	27	26	22	25						
	1994/95	MF	28	25	26	21						
		F	27	26	26	22						
Kyrgyzstan	1994/95	MF	32	31	30	7						
		F	32	31	30	7						
Lao People's Democratic Rep.	1985/86	MF	45	22	15	10	8					
		F	46	21	15	11	8					
	1991/92	MF	42	22	15	11	10					
		F	42	22	15	12	9					
	1992/93	MF	41	22	16	12	10					
		F	42	22	16	11	9					
	1993/94	MF	40	22	16	12	10					
		F	40	22	16	12	10					

First level: enrolment by grade
Premier degré: effectifs par année d'études
Primer grado: matrícula escolar por año de estudios

Country Pays País	Year Année Año	Sex Sexe Sexo	Grades / Années d'études / Año de estudios									
			I	II	III	IV	V	VI	VII	VIII	IX	X
Macau	1989/90	MF	20	18	16	16	16	14				
		F	20	17	16	16	16	14				
	1991/92	MF	20	19	17	16	15	13				
		F	21	18	17	15	15	14				
	1992/93	MF	19	19	17	16	15	13				
		F	20	19	17	16	15	14				
Malaysia	1985	MF	17	17	17	17	16	15				
		F	18	17	17	17	16	15				
	1989/90	MF	18	18	17	16	16	15				
		F	18	18	17	16	16	15				
	1990/91	MF	18	17	17	17	16	15				
		F	18	17	17	17	16	15				
	1992/93	MF	19	18	17	16	16	15				
		F	19	18	17	16	16	15				
Maldives	1992	MF	24	21	20	19	16					
		F	24	21	20	19	17					
	1993	MF	21	21	21	18	18					
		F	21	21	21	18	19					
Mongolia	1986/87	MF	35	32	32							
	1994/95	MF	41	32	28							
		F	40	32	28							
Myanmar	1994/95	MF	30	21	19	16	13					
Nepal	1984	MF	42	19	15	13	10					
		F	44	19	15	12	10					
	1988	MF	43	18	15	13	11					
		F	46	18	14	12	10					
	1991	MF	43	19	15	12	10					
		F	45	19	15	12	9					
	1992	MF	42	19	15	14	11					
		F	43	19	15	13	10					
Oman	1985/86	MF	23	21	18	16	12	10				
		F	25	23	19	15	10	8				
	1990/91	MF	19	18	17	17	15	14				
		F	20	18	17	17	15	13				
	1993/94	MF	18	18	18	17	15	14				
		F	19	19	18	17	15	13				
	1994/95	MF	17	18	18	18	16	14				
		F	17	18	18	17	16	14				
Pakistan‡	1986/87	MF	33	21	18	15	13					
		F	37	20	17	14	11					
	1989/90	MF	32	21	18	15	14					
		F	35	20	17	14	13					
Philippines	1985/86	MF	22	19	17	15	14	13				
		F	22	18	17	16	14	14				
	1989/90	MF	22	19	17	16	14	13				
		F	21	18	17	16	14	13				
	1992/93	MF	21	18	17	16	14	14				
	1993/94	MF	21	18	17	16	15	14				
Qatar‡	1985/86	MF	18	18	17	17	16	15				
		F	19	18	17	16	16	14				
	1990/91	MF	14	18	18	17	17	16				
		F	14	18	18	17	17	15				
	1993/94	MF	17	17	17	14	18	17				
		F	17	18	17	14	17	16				
	1994/95	MF	18	17	17	17	15	16				
		F	18	17	18	17	15	16				

First level: enrolment by grade **3.5**
Premier degré: effectifs par année d'études
Primer grado: matrícula escolar por año de estudios

Country / Pays / País	Year / Année / Año	Sex / Sexe / Sexo	Grades / Années d'études / Año de estudios									
			I	II	III	IV	V	VI	VII	VIII	IX	X
Saudi Arabia	1985/86	MF	22	19	17	16	14	11				
		F	23	20	17	16	13	11				
	1990/91	MF	20	18	17	17	15	13				
		F	20	18	17	17	15	12				
	1992/93	MF	20	18	17	17	16	13				
		F	21	18	17	16	15	13				
	1993/94	MF	19	18	18	17	15	13				
		F	20	18	18	16	15	13				
Singapore	1985	MF	14	14	16	15	16	17	5	4		
		F	15	14	16	15	16	18	4	4		
	1989	MF	16	16	16	16	15	15	3	3		
		F	16	16	16	16	16	15	3	3		
Sri Lanka	1985	MF	18	18	17	17	15	14				
		F	18	18	17	16	15	14				
	1990	MF	20	20	21	20	19					
		F	20	20	20	20	19					
	1993	MF	19	20	21	21	20					
		F	19	20	21	21	20					
	1994	MF	19	20	20	21	21					
		F	19	20	20	21	21					
Syrian Arab Republic	1985/86	MF	21	19	18	15	14	14				
		F	21	19	18	15	14	13				
	1990/91	MF	20	18	17	16	16	14				
		F	20	18	17	16	16	14				
	1993/94	MF	19	18	17	16	15	14				
		F	19	18	17	16	15	14				
	1994/95	MF	19	18	17	16	15	14				
		F	19	18	17	16	16	14				
Thailand	1985/86	MF	19	17	16	16	16	16				
	1990/91	MF	18	17	17	17	16	16				
		F	17	17	17	17	16	16				
	1992/93	MF	18	16	16	17	17	16				
Turkey	1985/86	MF	22	20	23	18	18					
		F	22	20	23	18	18					
	1990/91	MF	21	20	20	20	18					
		F	21	20	20	20	18					
	1992/93	MF	21	20	20	20	19					
		F	21	20	20	20	19					
	1993/94	MF	21	20	20	20	20					
		F	21	20	20	20	19					
United Arab Emirates	1985/86	MF	22	20	17	15	14	12				
		F	22	20	17	15	14	12				
	1990/91	MF	19	18	17	17	15	13				
		F	19	19	17	16	15	13				
	1993/94	MF	19	18	17	16	16	14				
		F	19	18	17	16	16	14				
	1994/95	MF	19	18	17	17	16	14				
		F	19	18	17	16	15	14				
Uzbekistan	1993/94	MF	34	32	25	10						
		F	34	32	25	10						
	1994/95	MF	33	33	31	3						
		F	33	33	31	3						
Viet Nam	1985/86	MF	29	22	19	17	14					
		F	28	22	19	16	14					
	1987/88	MF	27	22	19	17	15					
Yemen‡ Former Democratic Yemen	1985/86	MF	19	18	15	13	11	9	8	7		
		F	22	22	15	12	10	7	7	6		
	1988/89	MF	18	17	15	13	12	10	8	7		
		F	20	19	16	13	12	8	6	5		

First level: enrolment by grade
Premier degré: effectifs par année d'études
Primer grado: matrícula escolar por año de estudios

Country Pays País	Year Année Año	Sex Sexe Sexo	Grades / Années d'études / Año de estudios									
			I	II	III	IV	V	VI	VII	VIII	IX	X
Former Yemen Arab Republic‡	1985/86	MF F	27 32	22 26	17 16	13 12	11 8	10 6				
	1987/88	MF F	23 27	20 23	19 19	16 14	12 9	11 7				
Palestine	1994/95	MF F	20 20	17 17	17 17	16 16	15 15	14 14				
Gaza Strip	1985/86	MF	19	17	16	17	16	15				
	1990/91	MF	17	18	18	16	16	15				
	1993/94	MF F	20 20	18 18	17 17	15 15	16 16	14 14				
West Bank	1985/86	MF	18	16	16	18	17	16				
	1990/91	MF F	18 19	17 17	17 17	16 16	16 16	15 15				
	1993/94	MF F	18 18	17 18	18 18	17 17	16 16	15 15				
Europe												
Albania	1985/86	MF F	12 12	13 13	13 13	13 13	13 13	12 12	12 12	12 12		
	1990/91	MF F	13 13	13 13	13 13	13 13	12 12	12 12	12 12	12 12		
	1993/94	MF F	15 15	14 13	12 13	13 13	13 13	12 12	11 11	10 10		
	1994/95	MF F	15 15	14 14	13 13	12 12	13 13	12 12	11 12	10 10		
Austria	1985/86	MF F	25 25	25 25	25 25	25 25						
	1990/91	MF F	25 25	25 25	25 25	25 25						
	1992/93	MF F	25 25	25 25	25 25	25 25						
	1993/94	MF F	26 25	25 25	25 25	25 25						
Belarus	1985/86	MF	28	18	18	18	18					
	1990/91	MF	27	26	23	24						
	1993/94	MF F	25 25	25 25	25 25	25 25						
	1994/95	MF F	26 25	25 25	25 25	25 25						
Belgium	1985/86	MF F	18 18	17 17	17 17	16 16	16 16	16 16				
	1990/91	MF F	17 17	16 16	17 17	17 17	17 17	16 16				
	1991/92	MF F	17 17	16 16	16 16	17 17	17 17	16 17				
Bulgaria	1985/86	MF F	13 13	13 13	13 13	13 13	14 14	12 12	11 11	11 10		
	1990/91	MF F	12 12	11 11	12 12	13 12	14 14	13 13	14 14	12 12		
	1993/94	MF F	14 14	12 13	12 12	13 13	12 12	13 13	13 13	12 11		
	1994/95	MF F	14 14	13 13	12 13	12 12	13 13	12 12	13 13	11 10		
Croatia	1992/93	MF F	12 12	12 12	12 12	12 12	13 13	13 13	13 13	13 13		
	1993/94	MF F	12 12	12 12	12 12	12 12	12 12	13 13	13 13	13 13		
	1994/95	MF F	12 12	12 12	12 12	12 12	13 13	12 12	13 13	13 13		

First level: enrolment by grade **3.5**
Premier degré: effectifs par année d'études
Primer grado: matrícula escolar por año de estudios

Country Pays País	Year Année Año	Sex Sexe Sexo	Grades / Années d'études / Año de estudios									
			I	II	III	IV	V	VI	VII	VIII	IX	X
Czech Republic	1990/91	MF	25	25	25	25						
	1993/94	MF	25	25	25	25						
		F	25	25	25	25						
	1994/95	MF	25	25	25	25						
		F	25	25	25	25						
Denmark	1985/86	MF	15	16	16	18	17	18				
		F	15	15	16	18	17	18				
	1990/91	MF	15	16	16	17	18	18				
		F	15	16	16	17	18	18				
	1992/93	MF	17	16	16	17	17	17				
		F	17	16	16	17	17	17				
	1993/94	MF	17	17	16	16	17	17				
		F	17	17	16	16	17	17				
Estonia	1992/93	MF	17	17	17	15	17	18				
		F	17	17	17	15	17	17				
	1993/94	MF	18	17	17	17	15	17				
		F	18	17	17	17	15	17				
	1994/95	MF	18	17	17	17	17	15				
		F	18	17	17	17	17	15				
Finland	1985/86	MF	17	17	17	17	16	15				
		F	17	17	17	17	16	15				
	1990/91	MF	17	17	16	16	17	16				
		F	17	17	16	16	17	16				
	1992/93	MF	16	17	17	17	16	16				
		F	16	17	17	17	16	16				
	1993/94	MF	16	16	17	17	17	17				
		F	16	16	17	17	17	17				
France	1985/86	MF	21	20	19	19	20					
		F	21	20	20	20	20					
	1990/91	MF	20	19	20	20	20					
		F	20	19	20	20	20					
	1992/93	MF	21	20	19	19	20					
		F	20	20	19	19	20					
	1993/94	MF	21	21	20	19	20					
		F	21	21	20	19	20					
Germany	1992/93	MF	26	25	24	25						
		F	26	25	24	25						
	1993/94	MF	26	25	24	24						
		F	26	25	25	24						
Former German Democratic Rep.	1985/86	MF	27	27	24	22						
		F	27	27	24	22						
	1989/90	MF	25	25	25	25						
		F	25	25	25	25						
Federal Republic of Germany	1985/86	MF	25	25	25	25						
		F	25	25	25	25						
	1990/91	MF	25	25	25	25						
		F	25	25	25	25						
Greece	1985/86	MF	17	16	16	17	16	18				
		F	17	16	16	17	17	17				
	1990/91	MF	15	16	17	17	18	18				
		F	15	16	17	17	18	18				
	1991/92	MF	15	16	16	17	17	19				
		F	15	16	16	17	17	18				
Hungary	1985/86	MF	13	13	13	14	14	12	11	10		
		F	12	13	13	14	14	12	11	10		
	1990/91	MF	11	11	11	11	13	14	14	14		
		F	11	11	11	12	13	14	14	14		
	1993/94	MF	12	12	12	12	12	13	13	14		
		F	12	12	12	12	12	13	13	14		
	1994/95	MF	13	12	12	12	12	13	13	13		
		F	13	12	13	12	12	13	13	13		

First level: enrolment by grade
Premier degré: effectifs par année d'études
Primer grado: matrícula escolar por año de estudios

Country Pays País	Year Année Año	Sex Sexe Sexo	Grades / Années d'études / Año de estudios									
			I	II	III	IV	V	VI	VII	VIII	IX	X
Ireland	1985/86	MF	17	17	16	16	16	17				
		F	17	17	16	16	16	17				
	1990/91	MF	15	16	17	17	17	17				
		F	15	16	17	17	17	17				
	1992/93	MF	15	16	16	17	18	18				
		F	15	16	16	17	18	18				
	1993/94	MF	16	16	16	17	18	18				
		F	16	16	16	17	18	18				
Italy	1985/86	MF	17	19	20	21	22					
		F	17	19	20	21	22					
	1990/91	MF	18	20	20	20	21					
		F	18	20	20	20	21					
	1991/92	MF	19	20	20	21	21					
		F	18	20	20	21	21					
	1993/94	MF	19	19	20	21	21					
		F	19	19	20	21	21					
Latvia	1992/93	MF	23	27	29	21						
		F	23	28	29	21						
	1993/94	MF	28	23	27	22						
		F	28	23	27	22						
	1994/95	MF	30	27	22	22						
		F	30	27	22	22						
Lithuania	1992/93	MF	27	25	24	23						
		F	27	25	24	23						
	1993/94	MF	27	25	24	23						
		F	27	26	24	23						
	1994/95	MF	26	25	25	24						
		F	26	25	25	24						
Luxembourg	1985/86	MF	18	18	18	16	16	14				
		F	18	18	17	16	16	15				
	1987/88	MF	19	17	17	17	16	14				
		F	18	17	17	17	16	14				
Malta	1985/86	MF	16	16	16	16	16	18	2			
		F	16	17	17	16	16	17	1			
	1990/91	MF	16	16	16	16	16	16	3			
		F	15	16	17	17	16	16	3			
	1992/93	MF	16	16	16	17	17	18				
		F	16	15	16	16	17	18				
	1993/94	MF	17	16	16	17	16	18				
		F	17	16	16	17	16	18				
Moldova	1991/92	MF	28	28	27	17						
		F	28	28	27	17						
	1993/94	MF	27	25	26	21						
		F	27	25	26	22						
	1994/95	MF	26	25	24	25						
		F	26	25	24	25						
Monaco	1990/91	MF	21	21	20	20	18					
		F	20	20	20	21	19					
	1993/94	MF	20	20	20	20	20					
		F	17	22	20	21	21					
	1994/95	MF	20	20	20	20	20					
		F	19	17	22	20	22					
Norway	1985/86	MF	16	15	16	17	18	18				
		F	15	15	16	17	18	18				
	1990/91	MF	16	17	17	17	17	17				
		F	16	17	17	17	17	17				
	1992/93	MF	17	16	16	17	17	17				
		F	17	17	16	17	17	17				
	1993/94	MF	17	17	16	16	17	17				
		F	17	17	17	16	17	17				

First level: enrolment by grade **3.5**
Premier degré: effectifs par année d'études
Primer grado: matrícula escolar por año de estudios

Country Pays País	Year Année Año	Sex Sexe Sexo	Grades / Années d'études / Año de estudios									
			I	II	III	IV	V	VI	VII	VIII	IX	X
Poland	1985/86	MF	14	13	13	13	13	12	11	10		
	1990/91	MF	13	13	12	13	13	12	12	12		
		F	13	13	12	13	12	12	12	12		
	1993/94	MF	12	12	13	13	13	12	13	12		
		F	12	12	13	13	13	12	12	12		
	1994/95	MF	11	12	12	13	13	13	12	13		
		F	11	12	13	13	13	13	12	13		
Portugal	1985/86	MF	35	——>	34	——>	16	15				
		F	34	——>	34	——>	16	15				
	1990/91	MF	33	——>	33	——>	18	17				
		F	32	——>	33	——>	18	17				
	1991/92	MF	33	——>	33	——>	18	17				
		F	32	——>	33	——>	18	17				
	1993/94	MF	13	16	17	18	17	19				
Romania	1990/91	MF	22	24	26	28						
		F	22	24	26	28						
	1993/94	MF	29	26	25	20						
		F	29	26	25	20						
	1994/95	MF	28	26	23	23						
		F	28	26	23	23						
Russian Federation	1993/94	MF	32	29	30	9						
		F	32	29	30	9						
	1994/95	MF	32	30	29	9						
		F	32	30	29	9						
San Marino	1985/86	MF	18	20	20	21	21					
		F	19	20	20	20	20					
	1990/91	MF	19	21	20	19	21					
		F	20	21	20	18	21					
	1992/93	MF	18	20	20	21	21					
		F	20	20	20	20	21					
	1993/94	MF	19	18	20	21	22					
		F	18	20	20	20	22					
Slovakia	1992/93	MF	25	25	25	25						
		F	25	25	25	25						
	1993/94	MF	25	25	25	25						
		F	25	25	25	25						
	1994/95	MF	25	24	25	26						
		F	25	25	25	26						
Slovenia	1992/93	MF	24	25	25	26						
		F	24	25	25	26						
	1993/94	MF	24	25	25	26						
		F	24	25	25	26						
	1994/95	MF	25	24	25	26						
		F	25	24	25	26						
Spain	1985/86	MF	18	20	20	20	22					
		F	18	20	20	20	22					
	1990/91	MF	18	19	19	20	23					
		F	18	19	19	20	23					
	1991/92	MF	18	19	19	20	23					
		F	18	19	19	20	23					
	1992/93	MF	18	19	20	20	23					
		F	18	19	20	20	23					
Sweden	1986/87	MF	16	16	16	16	17	18				
		F	16	16	16	16	17	18				
	1990/91	MF	16	17	17	17	17	16				
		F	16	16	17	17	17	16				
	1992/93	MF	18	17	16	16	16	17				
		F	18	17	16	16	16	17				
	1993/94	MF	18	17	17	16	16	16				
		F	18	17	17	16	16	16				

3.5 First level: enrolment by grade
Premier degré: effectifs par année d'études
Primer grado: matrícula escolar por año de estudios

Country / Pays / País	Year / Année / Año	Sex / Sexe / Sexo	Grades / Années d'études / Año de estudios									
			I	II	III	IV	V	VI	VII	VIII	IX	X
Switzerland	1985/86	MF	18	19	19	19	14	11				
		F	18	19	19	19	14	11				
	1990/91	MF	19	20	19	19	13	10				
		F	19	20	19	18	13	10				
	1992/93	MF	18	19	19	19	14	10				
		F	19	19	19	19	14	10				
	1993/94	MF	18	19	19	19	15	11				
		F	18	19	19	19	15	10				
The Former Yugoslav Rep. of Macedonia	1992/93	MF	13	13	13	13	13	12	12	11		
		F	13	13	13	13	13	12	12	11		
	1993/94	MF	13	13	13	13	13	12	12	11		
		F	13	13	13	13	13	12	12	11		
	1994/95	MF	13	13	13	12	13	12	12	12		
		F	13	13	13	13	13	12	12	12		
Ukraine	1985/86	MF	23	19	19	19	19					
	1992/93	MF	28	27	28	16						
		F	28	27	28	16						
	1993/94	MF	29	27	28	16						
		F	29	28	28	16						
Former Yugoslavia	1985/86	MF	25	25	25	25						
		F	25	25	25	25						
Federal Republic of Yugoslavia	1990/91	MF	26	25	25	25						
		F	26	25	25	25						
	1993/94	MF	24	25	26	26						
		F	24	25	25	25						
Oceania												
American Samoa	1985/86	MF	14	13	13	13	13	12	11	10		
		F	14	13	13	13	13	13	11	10		
	1989/90	MF	14	13	13	12	12	12	12	12		
		F	14	13	14	13	13	12	12	11		
	1991/92	MF	15	14	13	13	12	12	11	11		
		F	15	14	12	14	12	11	12	11		
Australia	1985	MF	15	15	15	16	16	17	6			
		F	15	15	15	16	16	17	6			
	1990	MF	16	16	16	16	15	15	5			
		F	16	16	16	16	15	15	5			
	1993	MF	16	16	16	16	16	15	6			
		F	16	16	16	16	16	15	6			
	1994	MF	16	16	16	16	16	16	6			
		F	16	16	16	16	16	16	6			
Cook Islands	1985	MF	16	16	17	17	17	17				
	1988	MF	18	16	15	17	16	18				
Fiji	1985	MF	17	15	14	14	13	12	8	7		
		F	17	15	14	14	13	12	8	7		
	1991	MF	15	14	14	14	14	13	8	7		
		F	15	14	14	14	14	13	9	7		
	1992	MF	15	14	14	14	14	13	9	8		
		F	15	14	14	14	14	13	9	8		
French Polynesia‡	1987/88	MF	22	20	19	19	17	4				
		F	21	21	18	19	17	4				
	1990/91	MF	22	20	19	19	17	3				
		F	22	20	19	19	17	2				
	1992/93	MF	21	21	20	19	18	1				
		F	21	21	20	19	18	1				
	1994/95	MF	22	20	19	19	19	1				
		F	21	20	19	20	19	1				

First level: enrolment by grade 3.5
Premier degré: effectifs par année d'études
Primer grado: matrícula escolar por año de estudios

Country Pays País	Year Année Año	Sex Sexe Sexo	Grades / Années d'études / Año de estudios										
			I	II	III	IV	V	VI	VII	VIII	IX	X
Kiribati	1985	MF	14	11	11	12	10	11	13	8	9	
		F	14	11	12	12	10	11	12	9	10	
	1990	MF	15	*14	13	12	12	12	11	7	6	
		F	14	*14	13	11	12	12	11	7	6	
	1992	MF	15	13	13	13	12	11	12	6	6	
		F	15	13	13	13	12	10	11	6	6	
	1993	MF	14	14	12	12	12	11	11	8	5	
		F	14	14	12	12	13	11	11	7	5	
Nauru	1985	MF	17	16	18	16	15	15	4			
		F	18	16	18	18	14	13	3			
New Caledonia‡	1985	MF	19	18	17	19	19	8	—>	—>		
		F	20	18	17	19	20	6	—>	—>		
	1990	MF	21	20	19	19	18	4	—>	—>		
		F	20	19	19	19	19	4	—>	—>		
	1991	MF	21	20	20	20	19	1	—>	—>		
		F	21	20	19	19	20	1	—>	—>		
New Zealand	1985	MF	16	19	15	16	16	17				
		F	16	19	15	16	16	17				
	1990	MF	17	20	15	16	16	16				
		F	17	20	15	16	16	16				
	1993	MF	18	20	16	16	16	15				
		F	18	20	16	16	16	15				
	1994	MF	17	20	16	16	16	15				
		F	17	20	16	16	16	15				
Niue	1984	MF	16	15	13	13	14	13	17			
		F	13	13	18	13	17	14	13			
	1988	MF	11	17	12	15	11	11	11	12		
		F	15	20	15	12	11	9	10	9		
	1991	MF	16	16	16	18	19	15				
Papua New Guinea‡	1987	MF	22	19	18	15	14	12				
		F	22	19	18	15	14	11				
	1990	MF	24	20	17	15	13	12				
		F	24	20	17	15	13	11				
	1993	MF	*24	*20	*17	*15	*13	*11				
		F	*24	*20	*17	*15	*13	*11				
	1994	MF	23	20	17	15	13	11	1	0		
		F	23	20	17	15	13	11	1	0		
Samoa	1986	MF	14	15	15	14	14	14	14			
		F	14	16	15	13	14	14	14			
Solomon Islands	1984	MF	23	20	17	15	14	10				
	1990	MF	19	17	17	16	15	15				
		F	20	18	17	16	15	15				
	1993	MF	22	19	17	14	14	14				
		F	23	19	17	14	14	13				
	1994	MF	21	19	17	15	13	14				
		F	22	20	17	15	13	13				
Tokelau	1991	MF	12	12	12	12	11	11	9	11	10	
		F	14	12	9	9	12	11	11	12	10	
Tonga	1985	MF	17	19	15	14	14	21				
		F	16	20	16	14	13	20				
	1990	MF	17	12	18	16	16	22				
		F	17	11	19	16	16	21				
	1992	MF	17	16	15	12	18	22				
		F	17	16	16	13	18	20				
	1993	MF	16	16	15	15	13	25				
		F	16	16	15	16	12	26				

3.5 First level: enrolment by grade
Premier degré: effectifs par année d'études
Primer grado: matrícula escolar por año de estudios

Country / Pays / País	Year / Année / Año	Sex / Sexe / Sexo	Grades / Années d'études / Año de estudios									
			I	II	III	IV	V	VI	VII	VIII	IX	X
Tuvalu	1984	MF	11	11	11	11	12	11	8	7	7	11
		F	10	14	11	11	13	13	7	5	6	9
	1990	MF	11	13	13	15	12	9	9	6	5	7
		F	10	15	14	15	13	10	7	4	4	7
	1993	MF	15	15	11	13	11	15	10	10		
		F	14	15	10	13	11	15	11	11		
	1994	MF	13	14	13	11	13	11	14	11		
		F	12	14	13	10	13	11	15	12		
Vanuatu, Rep. of	1989	MF	*17	*18	*17	*16	*15	*17				
		F	*17	*18	*17	*15	*15	*17				
	1991	MF	18	17	16	16	16	17				
		F	18	17	16	16	17	16				
	1992	MF	20	17	16	15	15	17				
		F	21	17	16	15	15	17				

This table presents for total (MF) and female (F) enrolment at the first level a percentage distribution by grade. In general, these percentages are given for the school years beginning in 1985, 1990 and the two latest years for which data are available.

Ce tableau présente la répartition en pourcentage par année d'études de l'ensemble des effectifs (MF) et des effectifs féminins (F) de l'enseignement du premier degré. En général, ces pourcentages sont présentés pour les années scolaires commençant en 1985, 1990 et les deux dernières années pour lesquelles les données sont disponibles.

Este cuadro presenta la distribución porcentual por año de estudios del total de la matrícula escolar (MF) y de la matrícula femenina (F) de la enseñanza de primer grado. En general, los porcentajes se refieren a los años escolares que empezaron en 1985, 1990 y a los dos últimos años para los que se dispone de datos.

AFRICA:
Algeria:
E--> Grade VII refers to terminal classes.
FR-> La septième année d'études se réfère aux classes de fin d'études.
ESP> El séptimo año de estudio se refiere a las clases de fin d'études.
Tunisia:
E--> Grades VII and VIII refer to terminal classes.
FR-> Les septième et huitième années d'études se réfèrent aux classes de fin d'études.
ESP> Los años de estudio séptimo y octavo se refieren a las clases de fin d'études.
Uganda:
E--> Data refer to government-maintained and aided schools only.
FR-> Les données se réfèrent aux écoles publiques et subventionnées seulement.
ESP> Los datos se refieren a las escuelas públicas y subvencionadas solamente.
United Republic of Tanzania:
E--> Tanzania mainland only.
FR-> Tanzanie continentale seulement.
ESP> Tanzania continental solamente.
AMERICA, NORTH:
Dominican Republic:
E--> For 1985/86 and 1989/90 data refer to public education only.
FR-> Pour 1985/86 et 1989/90 les données se réfèrent à l'enseignement public seulement.
ESP> Para 1985/86 y 1989/90, los datos se refieren a la enseñanza pública solamente.
Haiti:
E--> For 1985/86, grade 1 includes infant classes.
FR-> Pour 1985/86, la première année d'études inclut les classes enfantines.
ESP> En 1985/86, el primer año de estudio incluye las clases infantiles.

Montserrat:
E--> Data refer to public education only.
FR-> Les données se réfèrent à l'enseignement public seulement.
ESP> Los datos se refieren a la enseñanza pública solamente.
St. Kitts and Nevis:
E--> For 1985/86, data refer to public education only.
FR-> Pour 1985/86, les données se réfèrent à l'enseignement public seulement.
ESP> Para 1985/86, los datos se refieren a la enseñanza pública solamente.
St. Lucia:
E--> Grades VIII and IX refer to terminal classes.
FR-> Les huitième et neuvième années d'études se réfèrent aux classes de fin d'études.
ESP> Los años de estudio octavo y noveno se refieren a las clases de fin d'études.
Trinidad and Tobago:
E--> Grades VIII and IX refer to post-primary classes.
FR-> Les huitième et neuvième années d'études se réfèrent aux classes post-primaires.
ESP> Los años de estudio octavo y noveno se refieren a las clases postprimarias.
U.S. Virgin Islands:
E--> Revised data.
FR-> Données révisées.
ESP> Datos revisados.
ASIA:
Bhutan:
E--> Grade I refers to pre-primary classes
FR-> La première année d'études se réfère aux classes préprimaires.
ESP> El primer año de estudio se refiere a las clases preprimarias.
Cyprus:
E--> Not including Turkish schools. Grade VII exists in private schools only.
FR-> Non compris les écoles turques. La septième année d'études n'existe que dans les écoles privées.

First level: enrolment by grade **3.5**
Premier degré: effectifs par année d'études
Primer grado: matrícula escolar por año de estudios

ESP> Excluyendo las escuelas turcas. El séptimo año de estudio sólo existe en las escuelas privadas.

Pakistan:

E--> Grade 1 includes pre-primary classes (Kachi).

FR-> La première année d'études inclut les classes préprimaires (Kachi).

ESP> El primer año de estudio incluye las clases preprimarias (Kachi).

Qatar:

E--> Data refer to public education only.

FR-> Les données se réfèrent à l'enseignement public seulement.

ESP> Los datos se refieren a la enseñanza pública solamente.

Yemen:

Former Yemen Arab Republic:

E--> Data refer to public education only.

FR-> Les données se réfèrent à l'enseignement public seulement.

ESP> Los datos se refieren a la enseñanza pública solamente.

OCEANIA:

French Polynesia:

E--> Grade VI refers to terminal classes.

FR-> La sixième année d'études se réfère aux classes de fin d'études,

ESP> El sexto año de estudio se refiere a las clases de *fin d'études*.

New Caledonia:

E--> Grades VI, VII and VIII refer to terminal classes.

FR-> Les sixième, septième et huitième années d'études se réfèrent aux classes de fin d'études.

ESP> Los años de estudio sexto, séptimo y octavo se refieren a las clases de *fin d'études*.

Papua New Guinea:

E--> Since 1994, some non-community schools offer grades VII and VIII.

FR-> A partir de 1994, certaines écoles non communautaire disposent de septième et huitième années d'études.

ESP> A partir de 1994, algunas escuelas no-comunitarias offercen los años de estudio séptimo y octavo.

3.6 First level: repeaters by grade
Premier degré: redoublants par année d'études
Primer grado: repetidores por año de estudios

3.6 Education at the first level: percentage of repeaters by grade

Enseignement du premier degré: pourcentage de redoublants par année d'études

Enseñanza de primer grado: porcentaje de repetidores por año de estudios

Please refer to the explanatory text at the end of the table

Prière de se référer au texte explicatif à la fin du tableau

Referirse al texto explicativo al final del cuadro.

In countries shown with this symbol, a policy of automatic promotion is practised in first level education.

Pour les pays dont le nom est accompagné de ce symbole, une politique de promotion automatique est appliquée pour l'enseignement du premier degré.

En los países que figuran con este símbolo, se aplica una política de promoción automática en la enseñanza de primer grado.

Country / Pays / País	Year / Année / Año	Sex / Sexe / Sexo	Total / Total / Total	Percentage repeaters by grade / Pourcentage de redoublants par année d'études / Porcentaje de repetidores por año de estudios								
				Total	I	II	III	IV	V	VI	VII	VIII	IX
Africa												
Algeria‡	1985/86	MF	261 995	8	6	6	6	6	6	16	26		
		F	90 711	6	5	5	5	5	5	11	22		
	1990/91	MF	385 634	9	8	8	10	9	9	11			
		F	128 773	7	7	7	7	7	6	7			
	1993/94	MF	409 655	9	9	9	9	8	8	12			
		F	137 793	7	8	7	7	6	5	8			
	1994/95	MF	404 201	9	9	8	9	8	8	11			
		F	134 491	6	8	6	7	6	5	7			
Angola	1990/91	MF	331 183	33	36	35	31	28					
Benin	1985/86	MF	119 270	27	21	23	27	26	30	42			
		F	41 475	28	22	23	28	27	32	44			
	1990/91	MF	105 297	21	21	17	22	17	25	34			
		F	36 057	22	22	18	23	18	27	33			
	1991/92	MF	123 654	23	25	17	21	18	28	39			
		F	42 853	24	25	18	22	19	30	38			
Botswana	1985	MF	12 713	6	1	1	1	12	1	1	23		
		F	6 638	6	1	1	1	11	1	1	24		
	1990	MF	13 822	5	1	1	1	12	1	1	18		
		F	6 833	5	1	1	1	9	1	1	19		
	1992	MF	10 005	3	1	1	1	11	1	1	8		
		F	4 619	3	1	1	1	8	1	1	9		
	1993	MF	7 984	3	1	1	1	9	1	1	5		
		F	3 452	2	1	0	1	7	1	1	5		
Burkina Faso	1986/87	MF	60 549	16	12	10	13	12	14	39			
		F	22 946	16	12	11	13	13	16	39			
	1990/91	MF	89 527	18	12	12	15	14	15	41			
		F	34 872	18	13	12	15	15	17	41			
	1992/93	MF	93 606	17	12	11	14	12	16	36			
		F	36 939	17	13	11	15	12	17	36			
	1993/94	MF	95 974	16	12	10	14	12	16	34			
		F	38 145	16	13	10	14	12	17	34			

First level: repeaters by grade
Premier degré: redoublants par année d'études
Primer grado: repetidores por año de estudios
3.6

Country Pays País	Year Année Año	Sex Sexe Sexo	Total Total Total	Percentage repeaters by grade Pourcentage de redoublants par année d'études Porcentaje de repetidores por año de estudios								
				Total	I	II	III	IV	V	VI	VII	VIII	IX
Burundi	1985/86	MF	68 476	18	14	15	16	15	27	30			
		F	28 540	18	14	14	15	16	28	32			
	1990/91	MF	137 802	22	18	18	18	19	27	33			
		F	60 949	21	18	17	18	18	26	31			
	1991/92	MF	145 226	23	21	18	18	21	28	32			
		F	63 851	23	22	17	17	20	27	32			
	1992/93	MF	154 244	24	20	21	19	23	28	31			
		F	68 124	23	20	20	18	22	28	31			
Cameroon	1985/86	MF	499 474	29	36	25	31	24	26	33	9		
		F	221 516	28	34	24	30	23	26	32	9		
	1990/91	MF	573 163	29	34	25	32	25	28	31	7		
		F	252 562	28	33	23	31	23	28	28	6		
Cape Verde	1985/86	MF	16 033	28	36	30	23	22	19	27			
		F	7 461	26	36	29	22	22	10	25			
	1989/90	MF	12 724	19	27	20	13	11	17	22			
		F	5 800	17	25	18	12	10	16	23			
	1993/94	MF	13 229	17	22	18	14	10	16	19			
		F	5 985	16	20	16	12	9	17	20			
Central African Republic	1985/86	MF	91 165	29	31	28	31	26	25	35			
		F	34 737	29	29	27	31	27	26	33			
	1989/90	MF	101 030	31	29	28	32	31	32	40			
		F	40 224	32	30	28	33	33	33	41			
Chad	1987/88	MF	135 635	32	40	29	30	23	22	37			
		F	41 537	35	41	30	32	27	26	36			
	1990/91	MF	*169 600	*32	37	30	32	25	26	38			
		F	*54 800	*34	37	31	34	29	29	36			
	1993/94	MF	*156 000	*29	31	26	27	24	25	39			
		F	*50 700	*29	32	27	28	24	25	37			
Comoros	1985/86	MF	21 552	33	33	29	32	31	31	41			
		F	9 360	33	34	29	32	31	30	43			
	1991/92	MF	29 564	39	34	34	37	36	38	59			
		F	13 351	39	34	34	37	36	38	59			
	1992/93	MF	30 216	41	38	35	38	38	39	61			
	1993/94	MF	27 885	36	35	33	32	32	34	50			
Congo	1985/86	MF	142 051	30	33	20	37	32	28	24			
		F	67 156	29	32	19	36	31	28	23			
	1990/91	MF	183 475	36	36	20	45	39	39	39			
		F	86 860	37	35	22	45	39	40	42			
	1991/92	MF	161 423	33	31	21	44	34	32	30			
		F	75 123	32	30	20	43	33	31	29			
	1993/94	MF	180 397	36	35	22	45	37	37	34			
		F	84 196	35	33	23	44	36	37	35			
Côte d'Ivoire	1985/86	MF	344 236	28	20	20	24	23	28	51			
		F	140 639	28	21	20	25	24	29	49			
	1990/91	MF	343 503	24	22	19	21	17	23	42			
		F	141 123	24	23	19	22	18	24	40			
	1991/92	MF	391 490	27	25	21	23	20	25	46			
		F	165 395	27	26	22	25	21	27	44			
	1993/94	MF	394 756	25	22	19	23	20	25	43			
		F	162 219	25	23	20	23	21	26	40			
Djibouti	1985/86	MF	3 145	12	9	8	9	9	7	32			
	1990/91	MF	4 259	13	8	8	8	8	8	37			
	1993/94	MF	4 445	13	8	8	9	8	8	35			
	1994/95	MF	4 360	12	8	8	7	7	7	33			
Egypt	1985/86	MF	93 214	2	-	0	-	6	-	4			
		F	35 816	1	-	0	-	5	-	4			
	1990/91	MF	551 800	8	-	7	6	9	18				

3.6 First level: repeaters by grade
Premier degré: redoublants par année d'études
Primer grado: repetidores por año de estudios

Country Pays País	Year Année Año	Sex Sexe Sexo	Total Total Total	Percentage repeaters by grade Pourcentage de redoublants par année d'études Porcentaje de repetidores por año de estudios									
				Total	I	II	III	IV	V	VI	VII	VIII	IX
Egypt (cont.)	1992/93	MF	550 600	7	0	7	6	11	14				
		F	211 900	6	0	6	5	10	12				
	1993/94	MF	400 000	5	0	5	5	8	8				
		F	151 000	4	0	4	4	7	7				
Eritrea	1993/94	MF	41 536	20	29	17	11	19	20				
		F	20 956	23	31	19	13	22	25				
	1994/95	MF	42 426	19	30	18	13	14	12				
		F	21 249	21	31	20	16	18	15				
Ethiopia	1986/87	MF	261 253	10	14	8	6	6	5	9			
		F	118 387	11	16	9	7	7	6	13			
	1988/89	MF	260 286	9	15	7	5	5	3	11			
		F	119 709	11	16	8	5	6	4	15			
	1993/94	MF	196 855	9	11	7	6	8	6	10			
		F	90 615	10	13	9	7	9	7	13			
Gabon	1986/87	MF	68 545	36	47	33	33	23	23	38			
		F	33 399	35	46	32	33	23	23	38			
	1988/89	MF	69 875	34	43	30	33	22	22	40			
		F	34 206	33	43	30	32	22	22	38			
	1991/92	MF	70 140	33	43	30	32	22	22	40			
		F	35 014	34	43	30	33	22	22	38			
Gambia	1985/86	MF	11 976	17	18	11	11	11	13	37			
		F	4 186	16	17	11	11	10	12	34			
	1988/89	MF	13 116	18	14	11	11	13	17	37			
		F	4 626	16	15	11	11	12	16	35			
	1991/92	MF	14 499	16	17	9	10	11	15	34			
		F	5 550	15	17	9	10	10	16	30			
	1992/93	MF	13 932	14	17	11	8	10	13	28			
		F	5 445	14	17	11	8	9	13	24			
Ghana	1990/91	MF	56 322	3	6	3	2	2	2	2			
		F	25 964	3	6	3	2	2	2	1			
	1991/92	MF	61 846	3	5	3	3	2	2	2			
		F	28 267	3	5	3	3	2	2	2			
Guinea	1985/86	MF	74 965	27	34	16	27	25	27	44			
		F	26 982	31	35	19	31	32	32	46			
	1990/91	MF	68 821	20	18	20	21	18	19	27			
		F	25 114	23	20	24	24	21	21	30			
	1992/93	MF	87 012	21	19	19	21	20	19	31			
		F	31 306	23	21	22	25	23	23	33			
	1993/94	MF	103 099	22	23	16	23	20	22	31			
		F	37 548	24	24	19	26	24	26	34			
Guinea-Bissau	1986/87	MF	31 530	41	40	44	41	43	33	35			
		F	11 431	42	41	46	42	43	33	39			
	1987/88	MF	31 832	42	44	42	40	40	39	42			
		F	11 381	43	44	43	41	40	41	46			
Lesotho	1985	MF	70 979	23	31	25	21	17	15	13	20		
		F	36 820	21	30	23	19	16	15	14	21		
	1990	MF	76 371	22	31	25	23	19	15	12	13		
		F	37 023	19	29	22	21	16	14	11	14		
	1993	MF	69 301	20	27	23	21	19	15	11	11		
		F	32 511	17	25	19	19	17	13	10	12		
	1994	MF	67 691	18	23	24	21	18	15	11	8		
		F	31 066	16	21	20	18	16	13	10	8		
Madagascar	1987/88	MF	494 492	33	39	31	31	25	33				
		F	225 530	31	36	28	29	24	33				
	1990/91	MF	560 712	36	44	32	31	26	33				
		F	263 576	34	41	30	30	25	34				
	1992/93	MF	488 658	33	39	31	30	24	31				
		F	229 996	32	37	29	29	24	31				
	1993/94	MF	487 162	32	34	30	33	27	36				
		F	229 948	31	33	28	31	27	37				

First level: repeaters by grade 3.6
Premier degré: redoublants par année d'études
Primer grado: repetidores por año de estudios

Country / Pays / País	Year / Année / Año	Sex / Sexe / Sexo	Total / Total / Total	Percentage repeaters by grade / Pourcentage de redoublants par année d'études / Porcentaje de repetidores por año de estudios									
				Total	I	II	III	IV	V	VI	VII	VIII	IX
Malawi	1985/86	MF	167 598	18	19	17	15	12	5	13	14	41	
		F	71 141	17	19	17	16	12	5	14	16	41	
	1990/91	MF	266 197	19	21	18	16	13	14	14	15	40	
		F	119 855	19	21	18	17	14	15	15	17	37	
	1993/94	MF	313 650	17	19	19	17	11	12	10	9	24	
		F	148 687	16	19	18	16	10	12	10	9	20	
	1994/95	MF	513 282	18	18	18	18	18	18	18	18	18	
		F	248 960	19	19	19	19	19	19	19	19	19	
Mali	1985/86	MF	86 433	30	28	28	31	28	31	34			
	1990/91	MF	93 592	27	27	26	31	26	29	26			
		F	34 903	28	26	27	31	27	31	28			
	1992/93	MF	116 590	27	22	24	32	29	30	28			
		F	43 310	26	21	23	32	30	31	28			
	1993/94	MF	126 296	25	25	19	29	27	30	28			
		F	48 077	25	24	18	28	28	31	29			
Mauritania	1985/86	MF	25 824	18	11	17	17	15	18	35			
		F	11 466	20	13	18	19	16	22	36			
	1990/91	MF	30 023	18	12	15	16	15	19	34			
		F	13 393	19	13	16	17	17	20	36			
	1992/93	MF	35 119	16	12	13	15	14	16	33			
		F	16 236	17	12	14	15	16	17	36			
	1993/94	MF	40 803	16	12	13	15	15	18	36			
		F	18 992	17	13	14	15	16	19	38			
Mauritius	1985	MF	8 356	6	-	-	-	-	-	29			
		F	3 917	6	-	-	-	-	-	27			
	1990	MF	6 302	5	-	-	-	-	-	21			
		F	3 080	5	-	-	-	-	-	21			
	1992	MF	10 410	8	-	-	-	-	-	32			
		F	5 010	8	-	-	-	-	-	31			
	1993	MF	9 569	8	-	-	-	-	-	31			
		F	4 689	8	-	-	-	-	-	31			
Morocco	1985/86	MF	451 780	20	13	20	20	17	30				
		F	157 543	18	13	18	18	14	28				
	1990/91	MF	275 042	11	14	13	14	12	9	0			
		F	96 353	10	13	11	12	10	7	0			
	1992/93	MF	338 732	12	13	13	13	12	11	11			
		F	115 985	10	13	11	11	10	8	8			
	1994/95	MF	353 210	12	15	12	12	11	9	10			
		F	124 860	10	14	11	10	8	7	8			
Mozambique	1985	MF	293 905	24	24	24	22	23					
		F	133 348	24	24	25	23	25					
	1990	MF	328 357	26	29	28	27	20	18				
		F	148 234	27	30	29	29	21	18				
	1992	MF	303 747	25	28	27	25	20	20				
		F	134 650	26	29	27	27	21	21				
	1993	MF	316 075	26	27	28	27	22	20				
		F	137 806	26	27	28	28	23	21				
Namibia	1992	MF	85 963	25	34	25	22	24	22	17	16		
		F	40 874	23	32	23	20	23	21	17	17		
	1994	MF	83 830	23	33	24	19	21	20	15	19		
		F	*39 150	*21	31	22	17	20	19	14	20		
Niger	1985/86	MF	41 385	15	2	15	15	15	18	26			
		F	14 886	15	2	15	15	15	18	26			
	1990/91	MF	50 908	14	3	9	11	12	14	37			
		F	18 859	14	3	10	12	12	15	36			
	1991/92	MF	57 002	15	3	10	13	14	16	37			
		F	21 348	16	3	11	14	14	17	38			
	1992/93	MF	67 810	18	6	11	13	13	15	48			
		F	23 126	16	6	10	12	11	14	45			

3.6 First level: repeaters by grade
Premier degré: redoublants par année d'études
Primer grado: repetidores por año de estudios

Country / Pays / País	Year / Année / Año	Sex / Sexe / Sexo	Total / Total / Total	Percentage repeaters by grade / Pourcentage de redoublants par année d'études / Porcentaje de repetidores por año de estudios									
				Total	I	II	III	IV	V	VI	VII	VIII	IX
Reunion	1985/86	MF	12 134	16	18	14	15	16	18				
Rwanda	1985/86	MF	101 184	12	18	13	12	11	9	8	8	7	
		F	47 820	12	18	12	11	10	8	8	7	7	
	1990/91	MF	136 186	12	16	14	13	10	9	9	8	11	
		F	65 812	12	16	13	12	10	9	9	8	12	
	1991/92	MF	156 105	14	18	15	13	12	13	11	11		
		F	74 635	14	17	14	13	12	12	11	11		
Sao Tome and Principe	1986/87	MF	8 078	47	53	45	43	47					
	1989/90	MF	5 842	29	33	29	28	26					
Senegal	1985/86	MF	95 234	16	13	12	12	12	16	34			
		F	38 942	17	14	12	13	13	17	34			
	1989/90	MF	110 485	16	10	11	11	12	17	34			
		F	45 978	16	10	11	12	13	18	34			
	1991/92	MF	116 730	16	11	11	12	13	17	33			
		F	49 286	16	12	11	13	13	17	33			
	1993/94	MF	116 164	15	11	11	12	12	16	30			
		F	50 085	15	11	12	13	13	16	30			
Seychelles #			-	-	-	-	-	-	-	-			
South Africa	1991	MF	889 693	12	15	13	13	11	13	10	9		
		F	382 950	11	13	11	11	9	11	9	9		
Sudan #			-	-	-	-	-	-	-	-			
Swaziland	1985	MF	19 477	14	15	14	15	13	14	13	13		
		F	8 370	12	13	11	12	12	12	12	12		
	1990	MF	24 783	15	18	17	16	13	12	11	11		
		F	10 561	13	16	14	13	11	11	11	10		
	1993	MF	29 397	16	20	16	18	14	13	13	12		
		F	12 374	14	18	13	15	12	12	12	11		
	1994	MF	28 491	15	16	15	17	15	14	12	11		
		F	12 036	13	13	12	14	13	13	12	11		
Togo	1985/86	MF	161 202	35	37	33	37	29	33	39			
		F	63 755	36	37	34	39	31	34	39			
	1990/91	MF	231 466	36	40	33	37	28	35	41			
		F	93 736	37	39	34	39	30	37	41			
	1991/92	MF	241 592	37	41	36	37	28	38	40			
		F	98 313	38	41	36	39	29	38	40			
	1993/94	MF	304 742	46	47	45	48	41	47	48			
		F	122 630	46	46	46	49	41	48	47			
Tunisia	1985/86	MF	262 974	20	19	18	18	19	24	29	-	-	
		F	109 031	19	19	16	16	17	22	28	-	-	
	1990/91	MF	277 752	20	9	15	19	16	24	37			
		F	117 411	18	9	13	17	14	21	37			
	1993/94	MF	263 052	18	14	16	18	16	18	26			
		F	111 010	16	13	14	16	14	15	25			
	1994/95	MF	241 783	16	14	14	17	14	16	22			
		F	101 819	15	13	13	14	12	14	22			
Uganda‡	1986	MF	310 196	14	16	15	14	13	13	14	10		
		F	138 545	14	15	14	13	13	13	15	10		
United Republic of Tanzania‡	1985	MF	30 731	1	3	2	1	0	0	0	0		
	1991	MF	130 790	4	4	3	2	14	0	0	0		
		F	67 080	4	4	3	2	14	0	0	0		
	1992	MF	124 296	3	4	3	2	13	0	0	0		
		F	63 255	4	4	3	2	14	0	0	0		
	1993	MF	115 189	3	4	2	2	11	0	0	0		
		F	58 692	3	4	2	2	12	0	0	0		

First level: repeaters by grade 3.6
Premier degré: redoublants par année d'études
Primer grado: repetidores por año de estudios

Country Pays País	Year Année Año	Sex Sexe Sexo	Total Total Total	Percentage repeaters by grade Pourcentage de redoublants par année d'études Porcentaje de repetidores por año de estudios									
				Total	I	II	III	IV	V	VI	VII	VIII	IX
Zaire	1987/88	MF	904 837	21	23	20	23	21	20	15			
		F	388 622	21	22	20	23	22	21	16			
	1990/91	MF	804 538	18	26	18	19	14	12	7			
		F	350 047	18	26	18	19	14	12	7			
	1993/94	MF	1 035 303	21	22	23	23	20	19	15			
		F	438 792	21	22	21	23	21	19	15			
Zambia	1986	MF	29 811	2	1	0	1	1	1	2	10		
		F	12 315	2	1	0	1	1	1	2	9		
Zimbabwe #			-	-	-	-	-	-	-	-			
America, North													
Antigua and Barbuda	1991/92	MF	269	3	7	3	2	1	0	0	6		
		F	116	3	5	3	2	1	0	-	6		
Bahamas #			-	-	-	-	-	-	-	-			
Belize	1991/92	MF	3 304	7	8	7	6	7	5	7	7	10	
		F	1 407	6	7	6	5	5	5	6	6	9	
	1994/95	MF	5 382	11	14	9	10	10	8	10	10	12	
		F	2 240	9	12	7	8	8	6	8	9	13	
British Virgin Islands	1984/85	MF	199	10	12	8	7	5	10	10	15	43	
		F	81	8	11	8	4	4	7	9	14	-	
	1993/94	MF	165	7	8	2	2	6	5	7	14	-	
		F	58	5	6	1	1	3	1	6	12	-	
Costa Rica	1985	MF	38 355	11	17	13	11	9	6	2			
		F	16 230	9	15	12	9	8	5	1			
	1990	MF	49 139	11	19	13	11	10	8	1			
	1993	MF	39 310	8	17	8	6	6	5	1			
		F	16 333	7	15	7	5	5	4	1			
	1994	MF	43 263	9	18	10	7	7	5	1			
		F	18 134	8	16	9	6	6	4	1			
Cuba	1985/86	MF	34 573	3	0	12	2	3	2	1			
	1990/91	MF	23 386	3	0	8	0	4	2	1			
	1993/94	MF	29 066	3	0	9	0	5	3	1			
	1994/95	MF	27 883	3	0	8	0	4	3	1			
Dominica	1987/88	MF	662	5	5	2	2	3	2	4	16		
		F	282	5	4	2	2	1	0	3	15		
Dominican Republic	1985/86	MF	156 161	17	28	16	13	11	10	9			
	1987/88	MF	176 562	17	25	17	14	13	12	12	14	12	
El Salvador	1984	MF	74 114	8	18	9	6	5	4	3	2	1	1
		F	35 581	8	18	8	6	5	4	3	2	1	1
	1989	MF	80 319	8	19	9	7	5	3	2	2	1	1
		F	37 359	7	18	8	6	5	3	2	1	1	1
	1992	MF	69 417	7	16	8	6	4	3	2	2	1	0
		F	31 561	6	15	7	5	4	3	2	2	1	0
	1993	MF	79 015	8	20	9	6	5	3	3	2	1	0
		F	35 077	7	19	8	6	4	3	2	2	1	0
Guadeloupe	1990/91	MF	2 982	8	13	8	7	6	5				
Guatemala	1985	MF	133 088	13	25	11	8	6	4	1			
	1993	MF	225 940	16	...	...	...	...	...	...			
		F	99 504	16	...	...	...	...	...	...			
Haiti‡	1985/86	MF	82 503	9	8	10	11	11	11	5			
		F	38 595	9	8	10	11	12	11	5			
	1990/91	MF	70 498	13	11	13	15	15	14	7			
		F	33 762	13	11	13	15	15	14	7			
Honduras	1984	MF	113 932	15	26	15	11	8	6	2			
		F	53 199	15	26	14	11	8	5	2			

3.6 First level: repeaters by grade
Premier degré: redoublants par année d'études
Primer grado: repetidores por año de estudios

Country / Pays / País	Year / Année / Año	Sex / Sexe / Sexo	Total / Total / Total	Percentage repeaters by grade / Pourcentage de redoublants par année d'études / Porcentaje de repetidores por año de estudios									
				Total	I	II	III	IV	V	VI	VII	VIII	IX
Honduras (cont.)	1991	MF	109 745	12	22	13	10	7	4	1			
		F	59 484	13	22	14	11	7	5	1			
	1993	MF	116 159	12	23	12	9	6	4	1			
		F	52 018	11	22	11	8	6	3	1			
Jamaica	1985/86	MF	11 800	3	7	2	2	1	2	7			
	1990/91	MF	13 670	4	7	3	2	1	2	10			
		F	6 225	4	5	2	1	1	2	11			
	1992/93	MF	11 565	3	6	2	1	1	2	9			
		F	5 250	3	5	2	1	1	1	10			
Martinique	1991/92	MF	1 761	5	8	6	3	4	5				
Mexico	1985/86	MF	1 496 746	10	19	12	9	7	5	1			
	1990/91	MF	1 352 359	9	18	11	9	7	5	1			
	1992/93	MF	1 254 229	9	17	11	8	7	5	1			
	1993/94	MF	1 046 363	7	13	9	8	6	4	1			
		F	419 453	6	11	8	6	5	3	0			
Montserrat #			-	-	-	-	-	-	-			
Nicaragua	1985	MF	86 482	15	26	19	10	7	4	3			
		F	42 573	15	25	19	10	7	4	3			
	1990	MF	104 852	17	28	11	12	9	9	6			
	1993	MF	125 313	17	30	15	12	10	7	7			
		F	58 069	16	29	14	11	9	7	6			
	1994	MF	115 041	15	27	15	11	9	7	5			
		F	52 084	14	25	13	10	8	6	4			
Panama	1985	MF	44 724	13	21	18	13	10	8	3			
		F	17 533	11	19	15	11	8	6	2			
	1989	MF	34 957	10	17	13	10	7	5	2			
		F	13 996	8	15	11	8	5	4	1			
Saint Kitts and Nevis #			-	-	-	-	-	-	-	-		
St. Lucia #			-	-	-	-	-	-	-	-		
St. Pierre and Miquelon	1985/86	MF	18	3	7	5	-	-	4				
Trinidad and Tobago‡	1987/88	MF	6 467	4	4	——>	1	1	1	1	13	18	30
		F	3 100	3	4	——>	1	1	0	1	13	16	30
	1990/91	MF	6 602	3	3	2	1	1	1	1	12	14	21
		F	3 191	3	3	1	1	1	1	1	13	13	19
	1991/92	MF	6 324	3	3	2	1	1	1	1	11	14	20
		F	3 112	3	3	1	1	0	0	1	13	13	16
	1992/93	MF	7 061	4	4	1	1	1	1	1	13	10	19
		F	3 564	4	3	1	1	0	1	1	14	11	19
Turks and Caicos Islands #			-	-	-	-	-	-	-	-		
U.S. Virgin Islands	1985/86	MF	1 436	10	12	10	9	9	9	9			
	1992/93	MF	6 778	47	45	44	49	48	46	48			
America, South													
Bolivia	1990	MF	39 521	3	3	3	3	3	3	4	4	4	
		F	19 536	3	3	3	3	3	3	4	4	4	
Brazil	1985	MF	4 891 126	20	24	19	16	13	23	20	19	15	
	1987	MF	4 997 435	19	23	21	17	14	23	19	16	11	
	1992	MF	5 244 249	17	24	20	15	11	20	16	13	9	
	1993	MF	5 386 788	18	23	20	15	12	21	17	14	9	
Colombia	1985	MF	684 832	17	25	18	14	11	7				
		F	338 253	17	24	18	15	11	7				
	1991	MF	490 842	11	18	11	9	9	5				
		F	228 644	11	17	10	9	8	5				

First level: repeaters by grade 3.6
Premier degré: redoublants par année d'études
Primer grado: repetidores por año de estudios

Country Pays País	Year Année Año	Sex Sexe Sexo	Total Total Total	Percentage repeaters by grade Pourcentage de redoublants par année d'études Porcentaje de repetidores por año de estudios									
				Total	I	II	III	IV	V	VI	VII	VIII	IX
Colombia (cont.)	1992	MF	558 051	12	20	14	10	7	5				
	1993	MF	336 103	7	11	8	6	5	3				
		F	156 537	7	11	7	6	5	3				
Ecuador	1986/87	MF	120 484	7	10	9	6	6	4	4			
		F	56 011	6	9	8	6	5	3	5			
French Guiana	1993/94	MF	2 276	14	1	2	10	23	45				
		F	1 024	13	1	2	9	21	41				
Paraguay	1985	MF	60 496	11	15	14	12	8	5	2			
		F	25 380	9	13	12	10	7	4	2			
	1990	MF	58 799	9	12	11	9	7	4	1			
		F	24 212	7	11	10	7	5	3	1			
	1993	MF	65 997	8	12	12	9	7	4	1			
		F	27 131	7	10	10	8	5	3	1			
	1994	MF	67 755	8	12	10	9	7	4	1			
		F	27 973	7	11	8	8	5	3	1			
Peru	1985	MF	524 270	14	21	13	12	13	11	8			
Suriname	1984/85	MF	15 500	22	25	21	22	21	21	19			
		F	6 726	20	21	17	18	19	21	21			
	1988/89	MF	15 064	23	27	19	20	24	23	24			
		F	6 495	20	22	15	16	21	20	26			
Uruguay	1985	MF	40 391	11	21	12	10	9	8	4			
		F	16 089	9	19	10	8	7	6	3			
	1990	MF	31 738	9	18	11	8	7	6	3			
		F	12 682	8	16	9	6	6	5	2			
	1993	MF	33 265	10	19	11	8	8	6	3			
		F	13 326	8	17	10	7	6	5	2			
	1994	MF	33 425	10	19	11	8	8	6	3			
		F	13 392	8	17	10	7	6	5	3			
Venezuela	1985/86	MF	359 938	10	14	10	10	9	7	3	12	13	13
	1990/91	MF	448 204	11	17	12	11	9	6	3	16	11	10
		F	186 168	9	15	9	8	7	5	2	15	11	10
	1991/92	MF	469 650	11	18	12	10	9	7	3	16	12	10
		F	193 387	9	15	10	8	7	5	2	14	11	10
	1992/93	MF	478 835	11	18	13	11	10	7	3	15	11	10
		F	194 095	9	15	10	9	7	5	2	13	10	9
Asia													
Afghanistan	1985	MF	33 625	6	5	5	5	5	5	6	8	10	
		F	10 273	6	5	5	5	5	5	6	8	10	
	1993	MF	70 786	9	9	9	9	9	9	9			
		F	17 696	9	9	9	9	9	9	9			
Armenia	1993/94	MF	330	0	0	0	0						
Azerbaijan	1992/93	MF	1 018	0	0	0	0	0					
		F	493	0	0	0	0	0					
	1993/94	MF	1 619	0	0	0	0	0					
		F	769	0	0	0	0	0					
Bahrain	1985/86	MF	4 900	9	8	8	9	10	10	6			
		F	2 452	9	9	9	9	10	9	5			
	1990/91	MF	3 397	5	6	6	5	5	5	4			
		F	1 606	5	6	6	5	5	5	3			
	1993/94	MF	3 580	5	6	6	5	5	5	4			
		F	1 720	5	7	6	5	4	4	3			
	1994/95	MF	3 785	5	6	5	5	5	5	4			
		F	1 641	5	7	5	5	4	4	2			
Bangladesh	1989	MF	770 376	7	7	6	7	8	7				
Bhutan‡	1988	MF	9 280	17	23	20	12	11	11	9	19		
	1993	MF	10 588	19	21	19	17	16	19	15	22		
		F	4 310	18	21	19	15	15	17	15	23		

First level: repeaters by grade
Premier degré: redoublants par année d'études
Primer grado: repetidores por año de estudios

Country Pays País	Year Année Año	Sex Sexe Sexo	Total Total Total	Percentage repeaters by grade Pourcentage de redoublants par année d'études Porcentaje de repetidores por año de estudios									
				Total	I	II	III	IV	V	VI	VII	VIII	IX
Bhutan (cont.)	1994	MF	11 431	19	24	20	18	15	19	19	14		
		F	4 758	18	23	19	17	14	17	20	16		
Brunei Darussalam	1986	MF	3 166	9	7	7	9	10	5	11	14		
		F	1 131	6	6	5	6	8	4	7	11		
	1991	MF	3 791	10	6	6	10	10	7	18			
	1993	MF	4 181	10	7	7	8	14	11	16			
	1994	MF	3 748	9	6	6	7	10	9	15			
Cambodia	1993/94	MF	435 585	27	35	27	21	17	15				
	1994/95	MF	518 269	30	42	26	22	18	30				
		F	225 563	30	41	25	21	17	30				
China	1988/89	MF	9 387 000	7	16	8	7	6	3	0			
	1990/91	MF	7 522 000	6	13	6	6	5	2	0			
	1992/93	MF	5 588 000	5	10	5	4	3	2	0			
	1993/94	MF	4 645 000	4	8	4	3	3	2	0			
Cyprus‡	1985/86	MF	201	0	1	0	-	0	0	0	-		
		F	87	0	1	0	-	0	-	0	-		
	1990/91	MF	238	0	2	0	0	0	0	0	-		
		F	89	0	1	0	0	0	0	0	-		
	1993/94	MF	211	0	2	0	0	0	0	0	2		
		F	81	0	1	0	-	0	0	0	-		
	1994/95	MF	195	0	2	0	0	0	-	0	-		
		F	71	0	1	0	0	-	-	0	-		
Georgia	1994/95	MF	798	0	0	0	0	0					
Hong Kong	1985/86	MF	8 782	2	2	2	2	3	2	0			
	1990/91	MF	6 908	1	2	1	2	2	1	0			
	1993/94	MF	5 890	1	1	1	2	2	1	0			
	1994/95	MF	4 961	1	1	1	1	2	1	0			
India	1986/87	MF	3 419 043	4	4	3	4	5	4				
		F	1 386 186	4	4	3	4	5	4				
	1987/88	MF	3 682 988	4	4	3	4	5	5				
		F	1 461 275	4	4	3	4	5	5				
Indonesia	1985/86	MF	3 254 352	11	18	13	11	9	8	2			
	1990/91	MF	2 877 568	10	17	12	10	8	6	1			
	1992/93	MF	2 659 501	9	16	11	10	8	6	1			
	1993/94	MF	2 515 951	8	15	10	9	7	5	1			
Iran, Islamic Republic of	1985/86	MF	691 394	10	14	9	6	9	10				
	1990/91	MF	877 020	9	12	8	5	9	12				
		F	337 492	8	11	6	4	8	10				
	1993/94	MF	708 504	7	10	7	4	6	8				
		F	266 386	6	9	6	3	5	6				
	1994/95	MF	702 474	7	10	7	4	6	8				
		F	255 275	6	9	6	3	4	6				
Iraq	1985/86	MF	584 550	21	15	15	15	20	34	29			
		F	238 721	19	14	14	14	18	32	25			
	1988/89	MF	585 171	19	16	16	15	17	30	23			
		F	218 136	16	14	14	12	14	27	18			
	1992/93	MF	470 687	16	15	15	14	15	28	10			
		F	172 110	13	13	13	11	12	23	8			
Japan #			-	-	-	-	-	-	-	-			
Jordan‡	1986/87	MF	33 582	6	2	2	3	9	12	9			
		F	16 072	6	2	2	3	10	12	8			
	1990/91	MF	50 404	5	2	2	2	7	9	6	9	7	5 8
		F	22 659	5	2	2	2	7	8	5	8	6	4 7

First level: repeaters by grade 3.6
Premier degré: redoublants par année d'études
Primer grado: repetidores por año de estudios

Country / Pays / País	Year / Année / Año	Sex / Sexe / Sexo	Total / Total / Total	Percentage repeaters by grade / Pourcentage de redoublants par année d'études / Porcentaje de repetidores por año de estudios									
				Total	I	II	III	IV	V	VI	VII	VIII	IX
Jordan (cont.)	1992/93	MF	44 551	4	1	1	2	6	8	6	7	5	4 3
		F	20 319	4	1	1	1	6	7	5	6	5	4 3
	1993/94	MF	16 959	2	1	0	1	2	3	3	3	2	2 0
		F	8 368	2	1	0	1	1	3	3	3	2	2 0
Kazakstan	1993/94	MF	11 711	1	1	1	1	1					
		F	5 759	1	1	1	1	1					
Korea, Republic #		-	-	-	-	-	-	-	-	-			
Kuwait	1985/86	MF	8 998	5	6	5	6	4					
		F	4 344	5	6	6	5	3					
	1991/92	MF	3 214	3	5	3	2	1					
		F	1 734	3	5	3	2	1					
	1993/94	MF	5 394	4	5	3	5	3					
		F	2 618	4	5	3	5	3					
	1994/95	MF	5 056	4	5	4	3	3					
		F	2 454	4	5	4	3	3					
Kyrgyzstan	1994/95	MF	2 349	1	1	1	0	1					
Lao People's Democratic Rep.	1987/88	MF	152 240	27	35	26	22	17	15				
	1991/92	MF	178 181	31	43	28	20	16	19				
		F	74 199	29	42	26	19	14	16				
	1992/93	MF	175 112	27	39	24	17	13	18				
		F	72 046	26	38	23	15	12	15				
	1993/94	MF	178 524	26	40	23	15	11	14				
		F	73 197	25	39	22	13	9	12				
Macau	1989/90	MF	2 363	7	5	6	8	8	10	6			
		F	940	6	4	5	7	7	8	6			
	1991/92	MF	2 649	7	5	5	6	9	12	7			
		F	1 076	6	3	4	4	8	11	6			
	1992/93	MF	2 687	7	5	5	7	8	10	6			
		F	1 592	8	6	6	9	11	11	7			
Malaysia #			-	-	-	-	-	-	-	-			
Mongolia	1994/95	MF	1 632	1	1	1	1						
		F	697	1	1	1	0						
Nepal	1988	MF	446 576	21	31	17	11	12	12				
	1991	MF	789 115	27	43	19	14	15	12				
	1992	MF	807 056	27	42	19	15	13	11				
		F	280 175	24	38	18	12	12	10				
Oman	1985/86	MF	20 809	12	11	10	9	17	14	11			
		F	7 435	9	10	10	7	11	11	7			
	1991/92	MF	25 500	9	10	9	8	10	7	11			
		F	11 000	8	9	10	8	8	7	8			
	1993/94	MF	25 302	9	9	9	8	10	8	8			
		F	10 247	7	9	8	7	8	7	5			
	1994/95	MF	23 793	8	9	9	8	10	6	5			
		F	10 003	7	9	9	7	7	4	4			
Philippines	1985/86	MF	161 618	2	3	2	2	1	1	1			
		F	78 634	2	3	2	2	1	1	1			
	1989/90	MF	206 178	2	4	2	2	1	1	1			
Qatar‡	1985/86	MF	3 406	11	9	8	8	13	16	10			
		F	1 229	8	8	7	7	10	11	5			
	1990/91	MF	2 736	7	7	6	5	6	12	8			
		F	925	5	7	5	4	3	7	5			
	1993/94	MF	1 733	5	4	4	5	4	10	3			
		F	591	3	3	3	3	3	6	2			
	1994/95	MF	1 706	5	3	4	5	3	11	5			
		F	559	3	2	3	3	2	8	2			
Saudi Arabia	1985/86	MF	166 623	12	14	12	12	14	13	7			
		F	51 372	9	12	8	8	10	9	4			

3.6 First level: repeaters by grade
Premier degré: redoublants par année d'études
Primer grado: repetidores por año de estudios

Country / Pays / País	Year / Année / Año	Sex / Sexe / Sexo	Total / Total / Total	Percentage repeaters by grade / Pourcentage de redoublants par année d'études / Porcentaje de repetidores por año de estudios									
				Total	I	II	III	IV	V	VI	VII	VIII	IX
Saudi Arabia (cont.)	1990/91	MF	171 893	9	12	7	7	11	11	5			
		F	59 159	7	10	5	5	8	8	3			
	1992/93	MF	222 130	11	11	7	10	15	15	7			
		F	77 067	8	10	4	6	11	12	5			
	1993/94	MF	186 641	9	10	5	9	12	11	5			
		F	63 837	6	9	3	5	9	8	3			
Sri Lanka	1985	MF	184 115	8	7	8	9	10	9	7			
		F	95 476	9	7	9	10	11	9	7			
	1990	MF	169 870	8	6	9	9	8	7				
		F	69 725	7	6	8	8	7	6				
	1991	MF	162 915	8	5	8	9	9	7				
		F	64 151	6	5	7	7	7	6				
	1992	MF	145 305	7	5	8	8	8	6				
		F	57 238	6	5	6	7	6	5				
Syrian Arab Rep.	1985/86	MF	151 878	7	11	9	7	5	5	6			
		F	62 057	7	11	8	6	5	4	4			
	1990/91	MF	172 607	7	12	8	7	5	4	5			
		F	71 474	6	11	8	6	5	3	3			
	1993/94	MF	184 584	7	12	9	6	5	4	4			
		F	73 560	6	11	8	5	4	3	3			
	1994/95	MF	200 554	8	13	9	7	5	4	6			
		F	78 781	6	12	8	5	4	4	4			
Turkey	1985/86	MF	553 649	8	16	9	8	5	2				
		F	256 208	8	16	9	8	5	2				
	1990/91	MF	463 907	7	13	6	7	4	2				
		F	223 928	7	13	7	7	4	3				
	1992/93	MF	383 961	6	12	5	5	4	2				
		F	188 289	6	11	5	6	4	3				
	1993/94	MF	334 698	5	10	5	5	3	2				
		F	165 369	5	10	5	5	4	3				
United Arab Emirates‡	1985/86	MF	8 638	8	7	7	6	11	9	9			
		F	3 823	7	7	7	5	8	8	7			
	1990/91	MF	9 974	7	7	6	5	8	7	5			
		F	4 522	6	7	7	5	6	6	4			
	1993/94	MF	9 263	6	7	6	4	8	7	4			
		F	3 701	5	7	6	4	5	5	3			
	1994/95	MF	10 103	7	7	7	4	8	9	5			
		F	4 135	5	7	7	4	5	6	5			
Uzbekistan	1993/94	MF	3 983	0	0	0	0	0					
	1994/95	MF	3 217	0	0	0	0	0					
Palestine	1994/95	MF	20 635	5	4	4	5	6	7	6			
		F	9 568	5	4	4	5	5	7	5			
West Bank	1990/91	MF	6 290	3	-	1	1	6	6	5			
		F	3 645	4	-	2	1	7	7	6			
Europe													
Belarus	1985/86	MF	3 600	0	1	0	0	0	0				
	1990/91	MF	7 100	1	2	1	1	1					
	1993/94	MF	7 500	1	2	1	1	1					
		F	3 700	1	2	1	1	1					
	1994/95	MF	7 600	1	2	1	1	1					
		F	3 700	1	2	1	1	1					
Belgium	1985/86	MF	120 541	17	10	13	16	18	22	21			
		F	53 532	15	9	12	14	17	20	19			
	1990/91	MF	113 985	16	11	14	16	17	19	18			
		F	50 492	14	9	13	15	16	17	16			

First level: repeaters by grade 3.6
Premier degré: redoublants par année d'études
Primer grado: repetidores por año de estudios

Country / Pays / País	Year / Année / Año	Sex / Sexe / Sexo	Total / Total / Total	Percentage repeaters by grade / Pourcentage de redoublants par année d'études / Porcentaje de repetidores por año de estudios									
				Total	I	II	III	IV	V	VI	VII	VIII	IX
Bulgaria	1985/86	MF	19 485	2	3	1	1	3	2	2	2	1	
		F	4 686	1	1	1	1	1	1	1	1	1	
	1990/91	MF	42 742	4	5	4	4	6	5	5	4	3	
		F	12 421	3	3	3	3	3	3	3	3	3	
	1993/94	MF	40 631	5	4	4	4	6	6	6	5	3	
		F	13 604	3	4	3	3	5	4	3	3	2	
	1994/95	MF	33 245	4	3	4	4	5	5	5	4	3	
		F	11 448	3	3	3	3	3	3	3	2	2	
Croatia	1993/94	MF	5 428	1	1	1	0	0	3	2	2	1	
	1994/95	MF	5 296	1	1	1	0	0	2	2	3	1	
		F	1 437	1	1	0	0	0	1	1	1	0	
Czech Republic	1993/94	MF	5 662	1	1	1	1	1					
		F	2 204	1	1	1	1	1					
	1994/95	MF	5 609	1	1	1	1	1					
		F	2 203	1	1	1	1	1					
Denmark #			-	-	-	-	-	-	-	-			
Estonia	1992/93	MF	3 445	3	2	2	3	3	3	5			
		F	882	2	2	1	2	2	1	2			
	1993/94	MF	3 165	3	2	2	2	3	3	5			
		F	810	1	1	1	1	2	1	2			
	1994/95	MF	3 962	3	2	2	3	3	3	6			
		F	1 017	2	2	1	2	2	1	3			
Finland	1986/87	MF	1 436	0	1	1	0	0	0	0			
		F	427	0	1	0	0	0	0	0			
	1990/91	MF	1 429	0	1	1	0	0	0	0			
		F	433	0	1	0	0	0	0	0			
	1992/93	MF	1 396	0	1	1	0	0	0	0			
		F	386	0	0	0	0	0	0	0			
	1993/94	MF	1 366	0	1	1	0	0	0	0			
		F	408	0	1	0	0	0	0	0			
France	1985/86	MF	321 699	8	10	7	6	7	9				
	1990/91	MF	206 567	5	8	6	4	4	4				
	1991/92	MF	168 968	4	6	5	4	3	3				
Germany	1992/93	MF	65 664	2	2	2	2	2					
		F	27 000	2	2	2	1	1					
	1993/94	MF	67 284	2	2	2	2	2					
		F	27 816	2	2	2	1	1					
Federal Republic of Germany	1985/86	MF	34 545	2	1	2	1	1					
		F	14 547	1	1	2	1	1					
	1990/91	MF	54 176	2	2	3	2	2					
		F	22 768	2	2	2	2	1					
Greece	1985/86	MF	1 452	0	0	0	0	0	0	0			
		F	597	0	0	0	0	0	0	0			
	1991/92	MF	830	0	0	0	0	0	0	0			
		F	389	0	0	0	0	0	0	0			
Hungary	1985/86	MF	38 643	3	5	3	2	3	4	3	2	0	
		F	13 410	2	4	3	2	2	2	2	1	0	
	1990/91	MF	33 675	3	5	3	3	3	4	4	3	0	
	1993/94	MF	24 796	2	5	2	2	2	3	3	3	0	
	1994/95	MF	23 573	2	4	2	2	2	3	3	2	0	
Ireland	1991/92	MF	8 036	2	2	2	2	2	2	3			
		F	3 709	2	2	2	2	2	2	2			
	1992/93	MF	7 660	2	2	2	2	2	2	3			
		F	3 348	2	1	2	2	2	2	2			
	1993/94	MF	7 350	2	2	2	1	1	2	3			
		F	3 266	2	1	2	2	1	2	3			

3.6 First level: repeaters by grade
Premier degré: redoublants par année d'études
Primer grado: repetidores por año de estudios

Country / Pays / País	Year / Année / Año	Sex / Sexe / Sexo	Total / Total / Total	Percentage repeaters by grade — Pourcentage de redoublants par année d'études — Porcentaje de repetidores por año de estudios									
				Total	I	II	III	IV	V	VI	VII	VIII	IX
Italy	1985/86	MF	37 790	1	1	1	1	1	1				
		F	13 769	1	1	1	1	1	1				
	1990/91	MF	23 976	1	1	1	1	1	1				
		F	8 696	1	1	1	0	0	1				
	1991/92	MF	20 666	1	1	1	1	0	1				
		F	7 602	1	1	1	0	0	1				
	1993/94	MF	17 241	1	1	1	1	0	1				
		F	6 392	0	1	1	0	0	0				
Latvia	1994/95	MF	4 252	3	4	2	3	3					
Lithuania	1993/94	MF	5 353	3	4	2	2	2					
	1994/95	MF	4 370	2	3	2	2	2					
		F	1 320	1	2	1	1	1					
Malta	1985/86	MF	1 054	3	1	1	2	1	2	10	1		
		F	394	2	1	1	2	1	1	8	2		
	1990/91	MF	471	1	1	1	1	1	1	3	0		
		F	200	1	1	1	1	0	1	3	-		
	1992/93	MF	555	2	1	1	1	1	1	4			
		F	222	1	1	1	1	1	1	4			
	1993/94	MF	649	2	1	1	1	1	1	6			
		F	282	2	1	1	1	1	1	5			
Moldova	1994/95	MF	4 515	1	3	1	1	1					
		F	2 212	1	3	1	1	1					
Monaco	1990/91	MF	106	6	5	5	6	6	8				
		F	50	6	5	4	6	4	8				
	1991/92	MF	105	6	5	5	6	6	8				
		F	51	6	5	4	6	5	9				
Norway #			-	-	-	-	-	-	-	-			
Poland	1985/86	MF	138 585	3	3	2	2	4	4	4	3	1	
	1990/91	MF	101 281	2	2	1	1	2	3	3	2	0	
	1993/94	MF	67 169	1	2	1	1	1	2	2	2	0	
	1994/95	MF	68 026	1	2	1	1	1	2	2	2	1	
Portugal	1984/85	MF	222 665	17	23	——>	13	——>	17	14			
		F	92 887	15	20	——>	12	——>	14	12			
	1990/91	MF	145 908	14	19	——>	11	——>	14	11			
		F	58 578	12	17	——>	10	——>	11	9			
Romania	1989/90	MF	24 321	2	4	1	1	1					
		F	9 482	1	3	1	1	1					
	1992/93	MF	50 897	4	6	3	4	4					
		F	19 631	3	5	3	3	3					
	1994/95	MF	36 931	3	5	2	2	2					
Russian Federation	1993/94	MF	153 000	2	3	2	2	2					
		F	75 000	2	2	2	2	2					
	1994/95	MF	147 000	2	2	2	2	2					
		F	73 000	2	2	2	2	2					
San Marino	1985/86	MF	4	0	-	1	-	-	0				
	1990/91	MF	3	0	0	1	-	-	-				
	1992/93	MF	4	0	1	0	0	-	-				
		F	-	-	-	-	-	-	-				
	1993/94	MF	5	0	1	1	0	-	-				
		F	-	-	-	-	-	-	-				
Slovakia	1993/94	MF	7 215	2	4	2	1	1					
		F	3 144	2	3	2	1	1					
	1994/95	MF	7 232	2	4	2	1	1					
		F	3 050	2	4	2	1	1					
Slovenia	1992/93	MF	1 065	1	1	1	1	1					
	1993/94	MF	1 004	1	1	1	1	1					

First level: repeaters by grade 3.6
Premier degré: redoublants par année d'études
Primer grado: repetidores por año de estudios

Country / Pays / País	Year / Année / Año	Sex / Sexe / Sexo	Total / Total / Total	Percentage repeaters by grade / Pourcentage de redoublants par année d'études / Porcentaje de repetidores por año de estudios									
				Total	I	II	III	IV	V	VI	VII	VIII	IX
Slovenia (cont.)	1994/95	MF	1 181	1	2	1	1	1					
Spain	1985/86	MF	170 855	5	2	6	3	3	9				
		F	68 957	4	2	5	3	3	7				
	1989/90	MF	112 598	4	1	6	1	1	8				
		F	46 733	3	1	5	1	1	7				
Sweden #			-	-	-	-	-	-	-	-			
Switzerland	1985/86	MF	7 563	2	2	2	2	2	2	2			
		F	3 193	2	1	2	2	2	2	2			
	1990/91	MF	6 749	2	2	2	2	2	2	1			
		F	2 867	1	1	2	2	1	1	1			
	1992/93	MF	7 159	2	2	2	2	2	1	1			
		F	3 060	1	1	2	2	1	1	1			
	1993/94	MF	7 272	2	2	2	2	2	2	1			
		F	3 073	1	1	2	2	1	1	1			
The Former Yugoslav Rep. of Macedonia	1992/93	MF	5 249	2	2	1	1	1	4	3	3	1	
	1993/94	MF	4 168	2	2	1	1	1	3	2	2	1	
	1994/95	MF	3 735	1	2	1	1	0	3	2	2	1	
		F	1 337	1	2	1	0	0	2	1	1	1	
Ukraine	1990/91	MF	38 000	1	2	1	1	0	1	1			
	1992/93	MF	27 800	1	2	1	1	1					
		F	13 500	1	2	1	1	1					
	1993/94	MF	24 600	1	2	1	1	1					
		F	12 000	1	2	1	1	1					
United Kingdom #			-	-	-	-	-	-	-	-			
Former Yugoslavia	1985/86	MF	25 301	2	3	2	1	1					
Federal Republic of Yugoslavia	1990/91	MF	7 052	2	3	1	1	1					
	1993/94	MF	5 705	1	2	1	1	1					
Oceania													
Fiji	1985	MF	3 777	3	4	2	3	2	3	3	4	2	
		F	1 436	2	3	2	2	1	3	2	3	2	
Kiribati	1985	MF	374	3	5	2	1	1	1	1	3	2	10
		F	187	3	5	2	1	1	1	1	3	1	9
	1990	MF	85	1	1	*1	1	-	0	0	1	0	0
		F	43	1	1	*1	1	-	-	0	2	0	0
	1991	MF	89	1	1	1	1	0	0	-	0	0	1
		F	43	1	1	1	1	1	0	-	0	1	1
	1993	MF	72	0	2	0	0	0	1	0	0	0	-
		F	26	0	1	0	0	-	-	-	0	0	-
New Caledonia‡	1985	MF	3 848	17	20	15	14	19	22	6	——>	——>	
		F	1 632	15	17	13	12	17	19	6	——>	——>	
	1990	MF	3 090	13	19	13	11	13	14	-			
		F	1 327	12	17	11	9	12	13	-			
New Zealand	1985	MF	10 331	3	-	17	-	-	-	-			
		F	4 587	3	-	15	-	-	-	-			
	1990	MF	9 777	3	-	15	-	-	-	-			
		F	4 430	3	-	15	-	-	-	-			
	1991	MF	10 672	3	-	17	-	-	-	-			
		F	4 882	3	-	16	-	-	-	-			
	1992	MF	12 020	4	-	19	-	-	-	-			
		F	5 421	4	-	17	-	-	-	-			
Papua New Guinea #			-	-	-	-	-	-	-	-	-	-	
Solomon Islands	1986	MF	2 884	7	8	6	6	5	7	12			
		F	1 178	7	9	5	5	5	7	12			

3.6　First level: repeaters by grade
Premier degré: redoublants par année d'études
Primer grado: repetidores por año de estudios

Country Pays País	Year Année Año	Sex Sexe Sexo	Total Total Total	Percentage repeaters by grade Pourcentage de redoublants par année d'études Porcentaje de repetidores por año de estudios									
				Total	I	II	III	IV	V	VI	VII	VIII	IX
Solomon Islands (cont.)	1990	MF	4 962	10	7	7	7	7	9	29			
	1993	MF	3 407	6	2	3	3	4	6	22			
	1994	MF	5 239	9	6	5	5	5	9	24			
Tonga	1985	MF	1 282	8	-	-	-	-	-	36			
		F	570	7	-	-	-	-	-	35			
	1990	MF	680	4	1	1	0	1	1	16			
		F	329	4	1	0	0	1	1	18			
	1991	MF	1 494	9	-	-	-	0	4	37			
		F	795	10	-	-	-	0	4	40			
	1993	MF	1 333	8	0	-	-	-	-	32			
		F	602	8	0	-	-	-	-	29			
Tuvalu #		-	-	-	-	-	-	-	-	-	-	-
Vanuatu, Rep. of	1992	MF	3 320	13	10	11	10	10	12	23			
		F	1 406	11	9	9	8	8	12	22			

This table presents the number of repeaters at the first level, and their percentage of total enrolment and of enrolment in each grade. In the cases where the number of repeaters in private institutions was not available, estimates have been made in order to maintain a consistent series on repetition as well as to facilitate the comparison of these data with those for enrolment by grade presented in Table 3.5.
The data shown refer in general to the school years beginning in 1985, 1990 and the two latest years for which they are available.

Ce tableau présente les redoublants du premier degré ainsi que leur pourcentage dans le total des effectifs et des effectifs de chaque année d'études. Lorsque les chiffres sur le nombre de redoublants dans les écoles privées n'étaient pas disponibles, les estimations ont été faites afin d'assurer une série cohérente sur les redoublants et de faciliter la comparabilité de ces données avec celles des effectifs par année d'études présentées dans le tableau 3.5.
Les données se réfèrent, en général aux années scolaires commençant en 1985, 1990 et aux deux dernières pour lesquelles les données sont disponibles.

Este cuadro presenta a los repetidores de la enseñanza del primer grado como así también porcentaje con respecto la matrícula total y a la matrícula en cada año de estudios. Cuando no se disponia del número de repetidores en las escuelas privadas, estimaciones han sido effectuadas para obtener una serie coherente sobre los repetidores y facilitar la comparabilidad de estos datos con los de la matrícula por año de estudios presentados en el cuadro 3.5.
Los datos se refieren, en general a 1985, 1990 y los dos últimos años para los que se dispone de datos.

AFRICA:
Algeria:
　E--> Grade VII refers to terminal classes.
　FR-> La septième année d'études se réfère aux classes de fin d'études
　ESP> El séptimo año de estudio se refiere a las clases de *fin d'études.*
Uganda:
　E--> Data refer to government maintained and aided schools only.
　FR-> Les données se réfèrent aux écoles publiques et subventionnées seulement.
　ESP> Los datos se refieren a las escuelas públicas y subvencionadas solamente.
United Republic of Tanzania:
　E--> Tanzania mainland only.
　FR-> Tanzanie continentale seulement.
　ESP> Tanzania continental solamente.
AMERICA, NORTH:
Dominican Republic:
　E--> Data refer to public education only.
　FR-> Les données se réfèrent à l'enseignement public seulement.
　ESP> Los datos se refieren a la enseñanza pública solamente.
Haiti:
　E--> For 1985, grade 1 includes infant classes.
　FR-> En 1985, la première année d'études inclut les classes enfantines.
　ESP> En 1985, el primer año de estudio incluye las clases infantiles.

Trinidad and Tobago:
　E--> Grades VIII and IX refer to post-primary classes.
　FR-> Les huitième et neuvième années d'études se réfèrent aux classes post-primaires.
　ESP> Los años de estudio octavo y noveno se refieren a las clases postprimarias.
ASIA:
Bhutan:
　E--> Grade I refers to pre-primary classes.
　FR-> La première année d'études se réfère aux classes préprimaires.
　ESP> El primer año de estudio se refiere a las clases preprimarias.
Cyprus:
　E--> Not including Turkish schools. Grade VII exists in private schools only.
　FR-> Non compris les écoles turques. La septième année d'études n'existe que dans les écoles privées.
　ESP> Excluyendo las escuelas turcas. El séptimo año de estudio sólo existe en las escuelas privadas.
Jordan:
　E--> The two figures shown under grade IX refer to grades IX and X respectively.
　FR-> Les deux chiffres présentés sous la neuvième année d'études se réfèrent respectivement aux neuvième et dixième années d'études.
　ESP> Las dos cifras presentadas bajo el noveno año de estudios se refieren respectivamente a los años de estudio noveno y décimo.
Qatar:
　E--> Data refer to public education only.

First level: repeaters by grade **3.6**
Premier degré: redoublants par année d'études
Primer grado: repetidores por año de estudios

FR-> Les données se réfèrent à l'enseignement public seulement.

ESP> Los datos se refieren a la enseñanza pública solamente.

United Arab Emirates:

E--> Data refer to public education only.

FR-> Les données se réfèrent à l'enseignement public seulement.

ESP> Los datos se refieren a la enseñanza pública solamente.

OCEANIA:

New Caledonia:

E--> For 1985, grades VI, VII and VIII refer to terminal classes.

FR-> Pour 1985, les sixième, septième et huitième années d'études se réfèrent aux classes de fin d'études.

ESP> Para 1985, los años de estudio sexto, séptimo y octavo se refieren a las clases de *fin d'études*.

3.7 Second level: teachers and pupils
Second degré: personnel enseignant et élèves
Segundo grado: personal docente y alumnos

3.7 Education at the second level (general, teacher-training and vocational): teachers and pupils

Enseignement du second degré (général, normal et technique): personnel enseignant et élèves

Enseñanza de segundo grado (general, normal y técnica): personal docente y alumnos

Total second level	= Total du second degré	= Total del segundo grado
General education	= Enseignement général	= Enseñanza general
Teacher training	= Enseignement normal	= Enseñanza normal
Vocational education	= Enseignement technique	= Enseñanza técnica

Country / Pays / País	Type of education / Type d'enseignement / Tipo de enseñanza	Year / Année / Año	Teaching staff Personnel enseignant Personal docente			Pupils enrolled Élèves inscrits Alumnos matriculados		
			Total	Female Féminin Femenino	% F	Total	Female Féminin Femenino	% F
			(1)	(2)	(3)	(4)	(5)	(6)
Africa								
Algeria‡	Total second level	1980/81	41 137	...	...	1 028 294	396 245	39
		1985/86	82 218	29 883	36	1 823 392	757 511	42
		1990/91	127 024	49 600	39	2 175 580	943 357	43
		1992/93	135 730	56 891	42	2 305 198	1 027 489	45
		1993/94	143 887	61 892	43	2 412 079	1 093 221	45
		1994/95	146 792	63 284	43	2 472 569	1 136 941	46
	General	1980/81	...	...	...	1 000 486	388 268	39
		1985/86	80 055	29 580	37	1 756 506	737 439	42
		1990/91	120 706	48 564	40	2 022 220	895 633	44
		1992/93	130 413	55 970	43	2 176 076	991 205	46
		1993/94	137 701	60 711	44	2 290 904	1 051 818	46
		1994/95	140 213	61 953	44	2 336 114	1 089 997	47
	Teacher-training	1980/81	1 124	...	...	13 315	4 911	37
		1985/86	-	-	-	-	-	-
		1990/91	-	-	-	-	-	-
		1992/93	-	-	-	-	-	-
		1993/94	-	-	-	-	-	-
		1994/95	-	-	-	-	-	-
	Vocational	1980/81	...	...	...	14 493	3 066	21
		1985/86	2 163	303	14	66 886	20 072	30
		1990/91	6 318	1 036	16	153 360	47 724	31
		1992/93	5 317	921	17	129 122	36 284	28
		1993/94	6 186	1 181	19	121 175	41 403	34
		1994/95	6 579	1 331	20	136 455	46 944	34
Angola	Total second level	1980/81	...	...	...	190 702	...	...
		1985/86	...	...	...	178 910	...	...
		1990/91	...	...	...	186 499	...	...
		1991/92	...	...	...	218 987	...	...
	General	1980/81	...	...	...	185 904	...	...
		1985/86	...	...	...	170 165	...	...
		1990/91	...	...	...	166 812	...	...
		1991/92	...	...	...	196 099	...	...
	Teacher-training	1980/81	...	...	...	2 086	...	...
		1985/86	...	...	...	4 070	...	...
		1990/91	...	...	...	8 753	3 657	42
		1991/92	...	...	...	10 772	...	...

Second level: teachers and pupils 3.7
Second degré: personnel enseignant et élèves
Segundo grado: personal docente y alumnos

Country Pays País	Type of education Type d'enseignement Tipo de enseñanza	Year Année Año	Teaching staff Personnel enseignant Personal docente			Pupils enrolled Élèves inscrits Alumnos matriculados		
			Total	Female Féminin Femenino	% F	Total	Female Féminin Femenino	% F
			(1)	(2)	(3)	(4)	(5)	(6)
Angola (cont)	Vocational	1980/81	...	...	...	2 712	...	...
		1985/86	...	...	...	4 675	...	...
		1990/91	...	...	...	10 934	...	...
		1991/92	...	...	...	12 116	...	...
Benin‡	Total second level	1980/81	...	...	...	89 969	...	...
		1985/86	...	...	...	107 172	30 590	29
		1990/91	...	...	...	...	...	...
		1991/92	...	...	...	...	...	...
	General	1980/81	1 854	...	...	83 207	21 765	26
		1985/86	2 722	...	...	99 345	27 824	28
		1990/91	2 493	...	...	72 256	19 686	27
		1991/92	2 178	...	...	76 672	21 363	28
	Teacher-training	1980/81	...	...	...	788	...	...
		1985/86	57	...	...	1 332	394	30
	Vocational	1980/81	...	...	...	5 974	...	...
		1985/86	...	...	...	6 495	2 372	37
Botswana	Total second level	1980	1 137	417	37	20 969	11 434	55
		1985	1 675	662	40	36 144	19 163	53
		1990	3 716	1 482	40	61 767	32 444	53
		1992	4 467	1 791	40	81 316	43 182	53
		1993	5 269	2 202	42	91 623	48 285	53
		1994	5 678	...	...	93 057	47 706	51
	General	1980	851	300	35	18 325	10 283	56
		1985	1 283	545	42	32 172	17 175	53
		1990	3 067	1 263	41	56 892	30 330	53
		1992	3 835	1 577	41	75 873	40 727	54
		1993	4 391	1 876	43	85 687	45 807	53
		1994	4 712	...	...	86 684	45 695	53
	Teacher-training	1980	59	15	25	844	700	83
		1985	73	27	37	1 188	996	84
		1990	121	68	56	1 361	1 158	85
		1992	114	62	54	1 272	1 087	85
		1993	135	90	67	1 261	1 066	85
		1994	141	...	...	1 085	*816	*75
	Vocational	1980	227	102	45	1 800	451	25
		1985	319	90	28	2 784	992	36
		1990	528	151	29	3 514	956	27
		1992	518	152	29	4 171	1 368	33
		1993	743	236	32	4 675	1 412	30
		1994	825	...	...	5 288	*1 195	*23
Burkina Faso	Total second level	1980/81	...	...	...	27 539	9 224	33
		1985/86	...	...	...	53 565	17 991	34
		1990/91	...	...	...	98 929	*34 003	*34
		1991/92	...	...	...	105 542	*36 342	*34
		1992/93	...	...	...	115 753	*40 457	*35
		1993/94	...	...	...	...	...	...
	General	1980/81	903	...	...	23 420	7 632	33
		1985/86	...	...	...	48 938	15 667	32
		1990/91	3 132	...	...	91 727	30 486	33
		1991/92	3 162	...	...	97 170	32 602	34
		1992/93	...	...	...	107 024	36 306	34
		1993/94	3 346	604	18	116 033	39 551	34
	Teacher-training	1980/81	...	...	...	248	57	23
		1985/86	...	...	...	351	117	33
		1990/91	...	...	...	350	*130	*37
		1991/92	...	...	...	*350	*130	*37
		1992/93	...	...	...	*350	*130	*37
	Vocational	1980/81	194	...	...	3 871	1 535	40
		1985/86	...	...	...	4 276	2 207	52
		1990/91	474	...	...	6 852	3 387	49
		1991/92	...	...	...	8 022	3 610	45
		1992/93	493	...	...	8 379	4 021	48
		1993/94	639	137	21	8 808	4 335	49
Burundi	Total second level	1980/81	...	382	...	19 013	*6 079	*32
		1985/86	1 849	382	21	25 939	8 791	34
		1990/91	2 026	429	21	44 207	16 280	37
		1991/92	2 211	459	21	48 398	18 306	38
		1992/93	2 562	519	20	55 713	21 600	39
	General	1980/81	...	...	...	8 899	2 265	25
		1985/86	785	181	23	13 037	3 918	30
		1990/91	...	...	...	36 773	13 687	37
		1991/92	...	...	...	40 334	15 215	38
		1992/93	...	...	...	46 381	17 675	38

3.7 Second level: teachers and pupils
Second degré: personnel enseignant et élèves
Segundo grado: personal docente y alumnos

Country Pays País	Type of education Type d'enseignement Tipo de enseñanza	Year Année Año	Teaching staff Personnel enseignant Personal docente			Pupils enrolled Élèves inscrits Alumnos matriculados		
			Total	Female Féminin Femenino	% F	Total	Female Féminin Femenino	% F
			(1)	(2)	(3)	(4)	(5)	(6)
Burundi (cont)	Teacher-training	1980/81	412	84	20	6 849	3 213	47
		1985/86	498	138	28	8 032	3 830	48
		1990/91	...	...	...	1 532	708	46
		1991/92	...	...	...	1 890	914	48
		1992/93	...	...	...	2 470	1 233	50
	Vocational	1980/81	*239	*25	*10	3 265	601	18
		1985/86	566	63	11	4 870	1 043	21
		1990/91	493	67	14	5 902	1 885	32
		1991/92	510	91	18	6 174	2 177	35
		1992/93	502	70	14	6 862	2 692	39
Cameroon	Total second level	1980/81	8 926	...	...	234 090	82 720	35
		1985/86	11 096	2 496	22	343 720	132 272	38
		1990/91	19 820	...	...	500 272	207 486	41
		1991/92	...	...	...	...	...	...
		1993/94	...	...	...	550 480	...	...
		1994/95	...	...	...	...	...	...
	General	1980/81	5 944	1 044	18	169 298	57 438	34
		1985/86	7 510	1 571	21	256 453	96 027	37
		1990/91	13 893	...	...	409 729	169 841	41
		1991/92	14 765	2 936	20	443 244	182 694	41
		1993/94	...	...	...	458 141	185 057	40
		1994/95	14 917	3 742	25	459 068	185 248	40
	Teacher-training	1980/81	218	47	22	2 118	768	36
		1985/86	502	115	23	4 058	1 692	42
		1990/91	232	69	30	515	283	55
		1993/94	123	...	...	435	...	...
	Vocational	1980/81	2 764	...	...	62 674	24 514	39
		1985/86	3 084	810	26	83 209	34 553	42
		1990/91	5 695	...	...	90 028	37 362	42
		1991/92	5 658	1 414	25	91 207	39 721	44
		1993/94	...	...	...	91 904	37 587	41
		1994/95	5 885	1 655	28	91 779	37 674	41
Cape Verde‡	Total second level	1980/81	184	...	...	3 341	...	...
		1985/86	...	...	...	...	...	...
		1989/90	...	...	...	7 866	3 963	50
		1991/92	...	...	...	...	...	...
		1993/94	...	...	...	14 097	6 880	49
	General	1980/81	121	...	...	2 733	1 167	43
		1985/86	146	108	74	4 941	2 211	45
		1989/90	238	107	45	7 114	3 664	52
		1991/92	...	...	...	10 309	...	...
		1993/94	438	158	36	11 808	5 987	51
	Teacher-training	1980/81	23	...	...	104	...	...
		1993/94	...	...	...	889	293	33
	Vocational	1980/81	40	...	...	504	198	39
		1985/86	...	...	...	361	172	48
		1991/92	...	...	...	1 149	...	...
		1993/94	94	40	43	1 400	600	43
Central African Republic	Total second level	1980/81	724	114	16	45 211	11 936	26
		1985/86	922	...	...	59 273	15 985	27
		1989/90	1 317	...	...	49 147	14 125	29
	General	1980/81	510	62	12	41 811	10 396	25
		1985/86	769	80	10	56 941	14 936	26
		1989/90	1 216	...	...	45 633	12 657	28
	Teacher-training	1980/81	88	21	24	677	195	29
		1985/86	28	9	32	107	9	8
		1989/90	-	-	-	-	-	-
	Vocational	1980/81	126	31	25	2 723	1 345	49
		1985/86	125	...	...	2 225	1 040	47
		1989/90	101	...	...	3 514	1 468	42
Chad	Total second level	1986/87	...	...	...	44 379	6 991	16
		1990/91	...	...	...	...	...	...
		1991/92	...	...	...	...	...	...
		1993/94	...	...	...	73 666	13 317	18
	General	1986/87	1 077	...	...	40 260	6 046	15
		1990/91	1 359	72	5	59 565	9 382	16
		1991/92	2 062	...	...	72 641	...	...
		1993/94	1 893	*85	*4	69 784	12 187	17
	Teacher-training	1986/87	...	...	...	1 030	162	16
		1993/94	...	...	...	635	153	24

Second level: teachers and pupils
Second degré: personnel enseignant et élèves
Segundo grado: personal docente y alumnos

3.7

Country Pays País	Type of education Type d'enseignement Tipo de enseñanza	Year Année Año	Teaching staff Personnel enseignant Personal docente			Pupils enrolled Élèves inscrits Alumnos matriculados		
			Total	Female Féminin Femenino	% F	Total	Female Féminin Femenino	% F
			(1)	(2)	(3)	(4)	(5)	(6)
Chad (cont)	Vocational	1986/87	...	...	...	3 089	783	25
		1990/91	...	...	...	3 093	967	31
		1991/92	...	...	...	3 310	983	30
		1993/94	...	...	...	3 247	977	30
Comoros	Total second level	1980/81	449	91	20	13 798	4 665	34
		1985/86	...	...	...	21 056	8 169	39
		1989/90	...	...	...	...	...	...
		1991/92	...	...	...	15 878	...	...
		1992/93	...	...	...	...	...	...
		1993/94	...	...	...	17 637	...	...
	General	1980/81	432	88	20	13 528	4 597	34
		1985/86	...	...	...	20 541	8 032	39
		1989/90	557	...	...	14 472	6 008	42
		1991/92	613	...	...	15 647	6 129	39
		1992/93	...	...	...	15 068	6 285	42
		1993/94	...	...	...	17 474	7 643	44
	Teacher-training	1980/81	8	2	25	119	29	24
		1985/86	11	...	...	94	13	14
		1991/92	11	1	9	129	...	...
		1992/93	...	...	...	82	...	...
		1993/94	...	...	...	37	...	...
	Vocational	1980/81	9	1	11	151	39	26
		1985/86	...	...	...	421	124	29
		1991/92	...	...	...	102	...	...
		1993/94	...	...	...	126	35	28
Congo	Total second level	1980/81	*5 117	...	...	187 585	77 222	41
		1985/86	6 322	...	...	222 633	96 908	44
		1990/91	6 851	...	...	182 967	...	...
		1991/92	7 230	...	...	191 459	82 382	43
		1993/94	7 861	...	...	212 850	...	...
	General	1980/81	3 649	...	...	168 718	67 583	40
		1985/86	4 773	...	...	197 491	83 868	42
		1990/91	4 924	...	...	170 409	71 199	42
		1991/92	5 689	...	...	178 753	76 482	43
		1993/94	6 048	...	...	192 229	79 463	41
	Teacher-training	1980/81	229	...	...	1 934	488	25
		1985/86	191	29	15	1 800	662	37
		1990/91	169	...	...	280	...	...
		1991/92	149	27	18	221	76	34
		1993/94	143	18	13	769	475	62
	Vocational	1980/81	*1 239	...	...	16 933	9 151	54
		1985/86	1 358	...	...	23 342	12 378	53
		1990/91	1 758	353	20	12 278	5 715	47
		1991/92	1 392	327	23	12 485	5 824	47
		1993/94	1 670	...	...	19 852	...	...
Côte d'Ivoire‡	Total second level	1980/81	...	...	...	221 940	66 624	30
		1985/86	...	...	...	...	...	...
		1990/91	...	...	...	...	...	...
		1991/92	...	...	...	...	...	...
		1992/93	...	...	...	...	...	...
		1993/94	...	...	...	...	...	...
	General	1980/81	5 192	...	...	198 190	55 826	28
		1985/86	7 188	...	...	260 330	76 364	29
		1990/91	10 788	...	...	361 032	114 832	32
		1991/92	9 324	...	...	396 606	128 778	32
		1992/93	...	...	...	414 504	...	...
		1993/94	9 644	...	...	445 505	150 554	34
	Teacher-training	1980/81	...	...	...	2 454	423	17
		1990/91	...	...	...	2 729	...	...
		1991/92	527	...	...	3 094	...	...
		1993/94	...	...	...	8 882	2 581	29
	Vocational	1980/81	...	...	...	21 296	10 375	49
		1985/86	...	...	...	22 861	8 500	37
Djibouti‡	Total second level	1980/81	278	...	...	5 133	...	...
		1985/86	306	...	...	7 041	2 718	39
		1990/91	...	...	...	9 513	...	...
		1992/93	347	...	...	9 740	4 184	43
		1993/94	367	...	...	10 384	4 380	42
		1994/95	385	...	...	11 384	4 608	40

3.7   Second level: teachers and pupils
Second degré: personnel enseignant et élèves
Segundo grado: personal docente y alumnos

Country Pays País	Type of education Type d'enseignement Tipo de enseñanza	Year Année Año	Teaching staff Personnel enseignant Personal docente			Pupils enrolled Élèves inscrits Alumnos matriculados		
			Total	Female Féminin Femenino	% F	Total	Female Féminin Femenino	% F
			(1)	(2)	(3)	(4)	(5)	(6)
Djibouti‡ (cont)	General	1980/81	179	...	...	3 812	...	...
		1985/86	221	...	...	5 057	1 688	33
		1990/91	305	...	...	7 742	2 709	35
		1992/93	...	...	...	8 083	3 128	39
		1993/94	...	...	...	8 755	3 381	39
		1994/95	...	...	...	9 577	3 598	38
	Teacher-training	1980/81	11	...	...	42	17	40
		1985/86	13	...	...	107	19	18
		1990/91	13	...	...	108	33	31
		1992/93	...	...	...	112	38	34
		1993/94	...	...	...	108	37	34
		1994/95	...	...	...	110	28	25
	Vocational	1980/81	88	...	...	1 279	...	...
		1985/86	72	...	...	1 877	1 011	54
		1990/91	...	...	...	1 663	...	...
		1992/93	...	...	...	1 545	1 018	66
		1993/94	...	...	...	1 521	962	63
		1994/95	...	...	...	1 697	982	58
Egypt‡	Total second level	1980/81	121 999	37 851	31	2 929 168	1 081 504	37
		1985/86	187 580	66 577	35	3 826 601	1 514 049	40
		1990/91	286 797	...	...	5 507 257	2 381 289	43
		1992/93	296 668	118 399	40	5 515 092	2 468 324	45
		1993/94	309 131	123 371	40	6 133 308	2 726 594	44
		1994/95	333 706	133 914	40	6 138 263	2 797 984	46
	General	1980/81	83 364	28 858	35	2 238 882	813 072	36
		1985/86	128 616	49 082	38	2 864 615	1 112 459	39
		1990/91	203 073	...	...	4 434 748	1 916 367	43
		1992/93	204 371	86 380	42	4 058 834	1 814 311	45
		1993/94	209 519	87 652	42	4 433 060	1 953 569	44
		1994/95	219 132	91 582	42	4 153 435	1 900 104	46
	Teacher-training	1980/81	4 148	1 766	43	56 377	25 458	45
		1985/86	6 727	3 020	45	84 587	50 474	60
		1990/91	6 072	...	...	46 350	28 262	61
		1992/93	650	305	47	2 664	954	36
		1993/94	...	...	...	109	24	22
		1994/95	-	-	-	-	-	-
	Vocational	1980/81	34 487	7 227	21	633 909	242 974	38
		1985/86	52 237	14 475	28	877 399	351 116	40
		1990/91	77 652	...	...	1 026 159	436 660	43
		1992/93	91 647	31 714	35	1 453 594	653 059	45
		1993/94	...	...	...	1 700 139	773 001	45
		1994/95	114 574	42 332	37	1 984 828	897 880	45
Equatorial Guinea‡	Total second level	1992/93	566	62	11	17 535	5 367	31
		1993/94	588	67	11	16 616	5 741	35
	General	1992/93	461	57	12	15 180	4 684	31
		1993/94	466	58	12	14 511	5 119	35
	Teacher-training	1992/93	8	1	13	269	53	20
		1993/94	44	5	11	609	150	25
	Vocational	1992/93	97	4	4	2 086	630	30
		1993/94	78	4	5	1 496	472	32
Eritrea	Total second level	1988/89	...	...	...	...	...	...
		1990/91	...	...	...	...	...	...
		1992/93	1 856	242	13	60 955	27 922	46
		1993/94	2 095	248	12	66 524	28 090	42
		1994/95	2 162	251	12	72 969	30 538	42
	General	1988/89	1 762	229	13	59 843	28 658	48
		1990/91	1 609	198	12	59 696	29 042	49
		1992/93	1 759	236	13	59 958	27 765	46
		1993/94	1 993	244	12	65 537	27 976	43
		1994/95	2 029	245	12	71 723	30 316	42
	Teacher-training	1992/93	22	2	9	460	99	22
		1993/94	39	4	10	398	54	14
		1994/95	44	3	7	427	133	31
	Vocational	1988/89	47	...	...	404	61	15
		1990/91	43	...	...	333	40	12
		1992/93	75	4	5	537	58	11
		1993/94	63	-	-	589	60	10
		1994/95	89	3	3	819	89	11

Second level: teachers and pupils 3.7
Second degré: personnel enseignant et élèves
Segundo grado: personal docente y alumnos

Country Pays País	Type of education Type d'enseignement Tipo de enseñanza	Year Année Año	Teaching staff Personnel enseignant Personal docente			Pupils enrolled Élèves inscrits Alumnos matriculados		
			Total	Female Féminin Femenino	% F	Total	Female Féminin Femenino	% F
			(1)	(2)	(3)	(4)	(5)	(6)
Ethiopia	Total second level	1980/81	...	...	...	666 169	...	...
		1985/86	15 861	...	...	...	...	...
		1990/91	23 319	2 296	10	866 016	371 841	43
		1991/92	23 705	2 429	10	782 412	353 992	45
		1992/93	22 600	2 159	10	720 825	334 085	46
		1993/94	...	...	...	...	...	...
	General	1980/81	9 962	1 003	10	426 277	151 542	36
		1985/86	15 218	1 700	11	655 517	255 719	39
		1990/91	22 721	2 254	10	858 846	370 262	43
		1991/92	23 110	2 387	10	775 211	352 063	45
		1992/93	21 970	2 136	10	712 489	331 798	47
		1993/94	21 598	2 130	10	714 622	327 277	46
	Teacher-training	1980/81	240	26	11	4 610	1 307	28
		1985/86	253	27	11	5 683	850	15
		1990/91	293	42	14	3 823	998	26
		1991/92	293	42	14	4 527	1 395	31
		1992/93	320	23	7	5 747	1 818	32
		1993/94	365	24	7	5 782	1 865	32
	Vocational	1985/86	390	...	...	4 969	...	...
		1990/91	305	-	-	3 347	581	17
		1991/92	302	-	-	2 674	534	20
		1992/93	310	-	-	2 589	469	18
Gabon‡	Total second level	1980/81	1 587	387	24	29 406	11 776	40
		1985/86	2 074	460	22	44 124	18 668	42
		1988/89	2 091	...	...	47 828	22 349	47
		1991/92	...	...	...	51 348	27 814	54
	General	1980/81	1 034	285	28	19 998	8 402	42
		1985/86	1 391	342	25	28 887	12 650	44
		1988/89	1 593	...	...	36 783	*17 052	*46
		1991/92	1 356	360	27	42 871	...	...
	Teacher-training	1980/81	181	40	22	3 878	1 810	47
		1985/86	236	53	22	6 581	3 350	51
		1988/89	37	...	...	1 062	506	48
		1991/92	-	-	-	-	-	-
	Vocational	1980/81	372	62	17	5 530	1 564	28
		1985/86	447	65	15	8 656	2 668	31
		1988/89	461	...	...	9 983	4 791	48
		1991/92	476	...	...	8 477	...	...
Gambia	Total second level	1980/81	620	158	25	9 657	2 853	30
		1985/86	695	...	...	15 918	4 746	30
		1990/91	...	...	...	20 400	6 743	33
		1991/92	...	...	...	21 786	7 523	35
		1992/93	1 054	198	19	25 929	9 013	35
	General	1980/81	536	144	27	9 081	2 740	30
	Teacher-training	1980/81	30	3	10	262	53	20
		1985/86	...	...	...	367	127	35
		1990/91	-	-	-	-	-	-
		1991/92	-	-	-	-	-	-
	Vocational	1980/81	54	11	20	314	60	19
Ghana‡	Total second level	1980/81	31 636	6 656	21	693 159	263 097	38
		1985/86	37 290	9 615	26	749 980	...	...
		1989/90	45 597	9 850	22	829 518	323 931	39
		1990/91	...	...	...	...	...	...
		1991/92	...	...	...	...	...	...
	General	1980/81	29 642	6 226	21	654 436	251 664	38
		1985/86	35 085	9 287	26	718 444	...	...
		1989/90	43 349	9 495	22	793 018	313 646	40
		1990/91	39 903	9 760	24	768 603	297 914	39
		1991/92	...	...	...	841 722	328 718	39
	Teacher-training	1980/81	881	194	22	11 600	4 698	41
		1985/86	1 011	219	22	15 169	...	...
		1989/90	1 001	216	22	15 723	7 156	46
	Vocational	1980/81	1 113	236	21	27 123	6 735	25
		1985/86	1 194	109	9	16 367	...	...
		1991/92	...	...	...	22 578	6 914	31
Guinea‡	Total second level	1980/81	...	...	...	98 305	27 599	28
		1985/86	4 642	323	7	92 754	24 493	26
		1990/91	5 976	725	12	85 942	20 929	24
		1991/92	...	...	...	...	...	...
		1992/93	4 719	614	13	106 811	26 443	25
		1993/94	...	...	...	116 377	28 720	25

Second level: teachers and pupils
Second degré: personnel enseignant et élèves
Segundo grado: personal docente y alumnos

Country Pays País	Type of education Type d'enseignement Tipo de enseñanza	Year Année Año	Teaching staff Personnel enseignant Personal docente			Pupils enrolled Élèves inscrits Alumnos matriculados		
			Total	Female Féminin Femenino	% F	Total	Female Féminin Femenino	% F
			(1)	(2)	(3)	(4)	(5)	(6)
Guinea‡ (cont)	General	1980/81	3 520	...	...	89 900	24 942	28
		1985/86	3 764	264	7	86 474	22 194	26
		1990/91	4 846	622	13	75 674	17 739	23
		1991/92	4 572	644	14	87 975	20 905	24
		1992/93	3 417	522	15	97 533	23 703	24
		1993/94	3 629	510	14	108 459	26 444	24
	Teacher-training	1985/86	101	6	6	912	382	42
		1990/91	128	14	11	2 066	985	48
		1992/93	188	...	...	1 568	763	49
		1993/94	194	13	7	1 329	615	46
	Vocational	1985/86	777	53	7	5 368	1 917	36
		1990/91	1 002	89	9	8 202	2 205	27
		1992/93	1 114	...	...	7 710	1 977	26
		1993/94	...	...	...	6 589	1 661	25
Guinea-Bissau	Total second level	1980/81	462	99	21	4 757	939	20
		1986/87	764	100	13	6 450	1 621	25
		1988/89	...	...	...	6 330	2 012	32
	General	1980/81	387	78	20	4 068	876	22
		1986/87	617	69	11	5 665	1 549	27
		1988/89	...	...	...	5 505	1 917	35
	Teacher-training	1980/81	46	20	43	412	25	6
		1986/87	76	24	32	434	49	11
		1988/89	33	18	55	176	39	22
	Vocational	1980/81	29	1	3	277	38	14
		1986/87	71	7	10	351	23	7
		1988/89	74	-	-	649	56	9
Kenya‡	Total second level	1980	17 081	...	...	428 023	174 281	41
		1985	23 055	8 364	36	457 767	173 417	38
		1989	...	...	...	...	...	...
		1991	...	...	...	...	...	...
		1992	...	...	...	...	...	...
		1993	...	...	...	...	...	...
	General	1980	15 916	...	...	407 322	169 401	42
		1985	21 712	8 027	37	437 207	167 174	38
		1989	28 056	8 756	31	640 735	257 600	40
		1991	35 097	11 458	33	614 161	268 373	44
		1992	36 560	12 356	34	629 062	275 690	44
		1993	*37 670	*13 400	*36	*616 200	*273 900	*44
	Teacher-training	1980	732	...	...	12 126	4 880	40
		1985	808	242	30	12 720	5 162	41
		1989	...	...	...	15 456	6 550	42
		1991	...	...	...	17 504	7 696	44
		1992	...	...	...	18 992	8 823	46
	Vocational	1980	433	...	...	8 575		
		1985	535	95	18	7 840	1 081	14
Lesotho‡	Total second level	1980	1 299	...	...	25 292	15 239	60
		1985	1 897	...	...	37 343	22 274	60
		1990	...	...	...	...	...	...
		1992	...	...	...	53 485	31 519	59
		1993	...	...	...	...	...	...
		1994	...	...	...	...	...	...
	General	1980	1 122	534	48	23 355	13 922	60
		1985	1 676	872	52	35 423	21 051	59
		1990	2 213	1 181	53	46 303	27 673	60
		1992	2 443	1 211	50	51 895	30 789	59
		1993	2 526	1 255	50	55 312	32 747	59
		1994	2 597	1 332	51	61 615	36 595	59
	Teacher-training	1980	55	...	...	701	624	89
		1985	93	...	...	657	572	87
		1992	-	-	-	-	-	-
		1993	-	-	-	-	-	-
		1994	-	-	-	-	-	-
	Vocational	1980	122	57	47	1 236	693	56
		1985	128	61	48	1 263	651	52
		1992	...	...	...	1 590	730	46
Liberia	Total second level	1980	...	...	...	54 623	15 343	28
		1984	...	...	...	...	...	...
	General	1980	1 129	258	23	51 666	14 632	28
		1984	...	...	...	43 273		...
	Teacher-training	1980	...	...	...	635	84	13

Second level: teachers and pupils
Second degré: personnel enseignant et élèves
Segundo grado: personal docente y alumnos

3.7

Country Pays País	Type of education Type d'enseignement Tipo de enseñanza	Year Année Año	Teaching staff Personnel enseignant Personal docente			Pupils enrolled Élèves inscrits Alumnos matriculados		
			Total	Female Féminin Femenino	% F	Total	Female Féminin Femenino	% F
			(1)	(2)	(3)	(4)	(5)	(6)
Liberia (cont)	Vocational	1980	...	...	...	2 322	627	27
Libyan Arab Jamahiriya‡	Total second level	1980/81	24 323	5 750	24	296 197	118 953	40
		1985/86	10 765	2 064	19	143 113	67 644	47
		1990/91	...	...	...	257 120	...	...
		1991/92	...	...	...	294 283	...	...
		1992/93	...	...	...	310 556	...	...
		1993/94	...	...	...	...	...	...
	General	1980/81	20 327	4 942	24	253 201	98 134	39
		1985/86	5 977	1 262	21	81 864	38 863	47
		1990/91	9 219	...	...	148 406	78 268	53
		1991/92	14 941	5 920	40	181 368	95 809	53
		1992/93	...	...	...	189 202	...	...
	Teacher-training	1980/81	2 488	631	25	26 988	16 838	62
		1985/86	2 639	555	21	34 746	23 093	66
		1990/91	3 306	...	...	43 142	30 193	70
		1991/92	3 688	...	...	34 289	25 690	75
		1992/93	2 760	...	...	26 393	21 462	81
		1993/94	...	...	...	29 125	23 595	81
	Vocational	1980/81	1 508	177	12	16 008	3 981	25
		1985/86	2 149	247	11	26 503	5 688	21
		1990/91	...	...	...	65 572	...	...
		1991/92	...	...	...	78 626	...	...
		1992/93	...	...	...	94 961	...	...
		1993/94	...	...	...	118 564	...	...
Madagascar‡	Total second level	1979/80	...	...	...	233 578	...	...
		1984/85	...	...	...	...	...	...
		1990/91	...	...	...	...	...	...
		1991/92	...	...	...	...	...	...
		1992/93	...	...	...	...	...	...
		1993/94	...	...	...	...	...	...
	General	1979/80	...	...	...	222 416	...	...
		1984/85	10 383	...	...	288 543	122 529	42
		1990/91	14 856	...	...	322 772	160 333	50
		1991/92	...	...	...	293 721	145 883	50
		1992/93	14 770	...	...	304 796	150 891	50
		1993/94	15 118	...	...	298 241	149 900	50
	Teacher-training	1979/80	66	...	...	1 192	...	...
		1993/94	58	18	31	341	142	42
	Vocational	1979/80	1 209	...	...	9 970	...	...
		1990/91	1 448	...	...	17 033	6 923	41
		1991/92	...	...	...	7 254	2 324	32
		1992/93	1 091	...	...	8 053	2 705	34
Malawi	Total second level	1980/81	878	...	...	18 653	5 248	28
		1985/86	1 192	...	...	25 737	8 136	32
		1990/91	...	...	...	32 275	10 986	34
		1992/93	...	...	...	37 413	12 833	34
		1993/94	...	...	...	47 451	18 219	38
		1994/95	...	...	...	49 412	18 963	38
	General	1980/81	834	...	...	18 006	5 248	29
		1985/86	1 141	...	...	25 177	8 136	32
		1990/91	...	...	...	31 495	10 923	35
		1992/93	...	...	...	36 550	12 768	35
		1993/94	...	...	...	46 444	18 179	39
		1994/95	...	...	...	48 332	18 918	39
	Teacher-training		-	-	-	-	-	-
	Vocational	1980/81	44	-	-	647	-	-
		1985/86	51	-	-	560	-	-
		1990/91	...	...	...	780	63	8
		1992/93	...	...	...	863	65	8
		1993/94	...	...	...	1 007	40	4
		1994/95	...	...	...	1 080	45	4
Mali	Total second level	1979/80	...	...	...	78 707	...	...
		1986/87	...	...	...	63 768	19 036	30
		1990/91	5 748	802	14	78 523	25 369	32
		1991/92	...	...	...	...	...	...
		1993/94	...	...	...	111 568	38 131	34
	General	1979/80	...	...	...	60 065	17 711	29
		1986/87	5 233	828	16	54 964	16 427	30
		1990/91	4 804	702	15	67 111	22 410	33
		1991/92	4 854	803	17	78 920	26 447	34
		1993/94	...	...	...	99 379	34 026	34

3.7 Second level: teachers and pupils
Second degré: personnel enseignant et élèves
Segundo grado: personal docente y alumnos

Country / Pays / País	Type of education / Type d'enseignement / Tipo de enseñanza	Year / Année / Año	Teaching staff / Personnel enseignant / Personal docente			Pupils enrolled / Élèves inscrits / Alumnos matriculados		
			Total	Female Féminin Femenino	% F	Total	Female Féminin Femenino	% F
			(1)	(2)	(3)	(4)	(5)	(6)
Mali (cont)	Teacher-training	1979/80	...	...	...	2 711	508	19
		1986/87	346	32	9	1 692	280	17
		1990/91	182	12	7	894	173	19
		1993/94	75	6	8	313	56	18
	Vocational	1979/80	...	...	...	5 482	1 895	35
		1986/87	...	...	...	7 112	2 329	33
		1990/91	762	88	12	10 518	2 786	26
		1991/92	...	...	...	8 715	2 917	33
		1993/94	...	...	...	11 876	4 049	34
Mauritania‡	Total second level	1980/81	...	...	...	22 102	4 528	20
		1985/86	...	...	...	35 955	...	...
		1990/91	...	...	...	37 653	11 957	32
		1991/92	2 184	...	...	39 821	*13 344	*34
		1992/93	2 236	...	...	43 034	14 334	33
		1993/94	1 938	212	11	45 810	16 204	35
	General	1980/81	646	54	8	20 248	4 291	21
		1985/86	1 378	...	...	33 148	9 398	28
		1990/91	2 091	224	11	36 177	*11 773	*33
		1991/92	2 015	198	10	38 039	*13 006	*34
		1992/93	2 071	202	10	41 071	13 909	34
		1993/94	1 776	204	11	43 861	15 667	36
	Teacher-training	1980/81	51	6	12	850	164	19
		1985/86	66	...	...	953	266	28
		1990/91	47	...	...	676	174	26
		1991/92	51	...	...	752	193	26
		1992/93	49	...	...	791	231	29
		1993/94	57	4	7	820	276	34
	Vocational	1980/81	...	...	...	1 004	73	7
		1985/86	...	...	...	1 854	...	...
		1990/91	115	...	...	800	10	1
		1991/92	118	16	14	1 030	145	14
		1992/93	116	...	...	1 172	194	17
		1993/94	105	4	4	1 129	261	23
Mauritius	Total second level	1980	...	...	...	81 926	39 602	48
		1985	...	...	...	72 551	34 232	47
		1990	...	...	...	79 229	39 357	50
		1991	...	...	...	...	...	...
		1992	...	...	...	86 024	...	...
		1993	...	...	...	...	...	...
	General	1980	3 101	1 220	39	81 656	39 542	48
		1985	3 603	1 466	41	71 686	33 904	47
		1990	3 728	...	...	78 110	39 002	50
		1991	3 949	1 635	41	81 090	41 312	51
		1992	4 050	1 719	42	83 591	42 345	51
		1993	4 160	2 385	57	87 661	44 636	51
	Teacher-training		-	-	-	-	-	-
	Vocational	1980	...	...	...	270	60	22
		1985	...	...	...	865	328	38
		1990	...	...	...	1 119	355	32
		1992	...	...	...	2 433	...	...
Morocco‡	Total second level	1980/81	36 526	...	...	797 110	300 665	38
		1985/86	64 079	17 646	28	1 201 858	474 706	39
		1990/91	76 964	23 240	30	1 123 531	458 808	41
		1992/93	78 580	24 720	31	1 207 734	495 322	41
		1993/94	79 064	25 088	32	1 264 886	522 121	41
		1994/95	80 867	25 757	32	1 298 897	540 952	42
	General	1980/81	...	...	...	787 004	298 344	38
		1985/86	62 904	17 277	27	1 174 599	460 913	39
		1990/91	75 708	22 982	30	1 106 673	452 491	41
		1992/93	77 297	24 420	32	1 191 716	489 180	41
		1993/94	77 753	24 759	32	1 248 324	515 597	41
		1994/95	79 474	25 391	32	1 280 135	533 356	42
	Teacher-training		-	-	-	-	-	-
	Vocational	1980/81	...	...	...	10 106	2 321	23
		1985/86	1 175	369	31	27 259	13 793	51
		1990/91	1 256	258	21	16 858	6 317	37
		1992/93	1 283	300	23	16 018	6 142	38
		1993/94	1 311	329	25	16 562	6 524	39
		1994/95	1 393	366	26	18 762	7 596	40

Second level: teachers and pupils **3.7**
Second degré: personnel enseignant et élèves
Segundo grado: personal docente y alumnos

Country Pays País	Type of education Type d'enseignement Tipo de enseñanza	Year Année Año	Teaching staff Personnel enseignant Personal docente			Pupils enrolled Élèves inscrits Alumnos matriculados		
			Total	Female Féminin Femenino	% F	Total	Female Féminin Femenino	% F
			(1)	(2)	(3)	(4)	(5)	(6)
Mozambique‡	Total second level	1981	3 388	752	22	107 849	30 606	28
		1985	4 688	1 001	21	151 888	47 398	31
		1990	4 657	...	...	160 177	58 452	36
		1993	4 809	954	20	163 747	63 882	39
		1994	...	...	...	171 102	66 151	39
		1995	...	...	...	...	...	...
	General	1981	2 211	576	26	89 835	27 693	31
		1985	3 377	799	24	135 068	44 452	33
		1990	3 437	611	18	145 341	54 975	38
		1993	3 924	773	20	147 201	59 013	40
		1994	...	...	...	150 229	59 554	40
		1995	...	...	...	165 868	66 549	40
	Teacher-training	1981	270	44	16	4 236	602	14
		1985	350	40	11	5 177	842	16
		1990	324	35	11	4 904	1 365	28
		1993	231	24	10	4 902	1 917	39
		1994	...	...	...	5 021	2 086	42
	Vocational	1981	907	132	15	13 778	2 311	17
		1985	961	162	17	11 643	2 104	18
		1990	896	...	...	9 932	2 112	21
		1993	654	157	24	11 644	2 952	25
		1994	...	...	...	15 852	4 511	28
Namibia	Total second level	1986	...	...	...	49 571	...	...
		1990	...	...	...	62 399	34 732	56
		1992	3 999	1 840	46	84 581	46 631	55
		1993	...	...	...	92 725	50 844	55
		1994	...	...	...	101 974	55 591	55
	General	1986	...	...	...	49 417	...	...
		1990	...	...	...	61 801	34 599	56
		1992	3 943	1 829	46	83 862	46 476	55
		1993	...	...	...	92 136	50 718	55
		1994	...	...	...	101 838	55 538	55
	Teacher-training		-	-	-	-	-	-
	Vocational	1986	...	...	...	154	...	...
		1990	...	...	...	598	133	22
		1992	56	11	20	719	155	22
		1993	...	...	...	589	126	21
		1994	...	...	...	136	53	39
Niger	Total second level	1980/81	1 284	267	21	38 861	11 334	29
		1985/86	...	...	...	...	...	...
		1990/91	2 775	490	18	76 758	22 619	29
		1992/93	2 394	420	18	80 009	26 003	33
		1993/94	...	...	...	...	...	...
		1994/95	...	...	...	...	...	...
	General	1980/81	1 164	255	22	36 510	10 765	29
		1985/86	1 963	327	17	51 448	14 398	28
		1990/91	2 534	455	18	74 337	21 884	29
		1992/93	2 219	402	18	77 899	25 514	33
		1993/94	...	...	...	88 810	...	...
		1994/95	...	...	...	89 773	29 474	33
	Teacher-training	1980/81	80	6	8	1 830	525	29
		1990/91	122	19	16	1 578	661	42
		1992/93	76	6	8	1 322	389	29
	Vocational	1980/81	40	6	15	521	44	8
		1985/86	...	...	...	615	72	12
		1990/91	119	16	13	843	74	9
		1992/93	99	12	12	788	100	13
Nigeria‡	Total second level	1979/80	41 581	12 242	29	1 864 713	623 257	33
		1984/85	98 487	...	...	3 561 207	...	...
		1990	142 007	46 402	33	2 908 466	1 243 669	43
		1992	141 491	44 936	32	3 600 620	1 621 575	45
		1993	151 722	52 363	35	4 032 083	1 850 049	46
		1994	152 596	54 949	36	4 451 329	2 031 547	46
	General	1979/80	26 261	3 492	13	1 553 345	543 564	35
	Teacher-training	1979/80	7 940	6 302	79	249 512	71 312	29
	Vocational	1979/80	7 380	2 448	33	61 856	8 381	14
Reunion	Total second level	1980/81	...	...	...	62 613	...	...
		1985/86	3 994	...	...	69 863	38 042	54
		1993/94	5 699	...	...	88 605	44 885	51
		1994/95	...	...	...	90 033	45 365	50

Second level: teachers and pupils
Second degré: personnel enseignant et élèves
Segundo grado: personal docente y alumnos

Country / Pays / País	Type of education / Type d'enseignement / Tipo de enseñanza	Year / Année / Año	Teaching staff Personnel enseignant Personal docente			Pupils enrolled Élèves inscrits Alumnos matriculados		
			Total	Female Féminin Femenino	% F	Total	Female Féminin Femenino	% F
			(1)	(2)	(3)	(4)	(5)	(6)
Reunion (cont)	General	1985/86	2 978	...	...	46 550	27 090	58
		1993/94	4 591	2 002	44	74 827	38 692	52
		1994/95	...	...	...	74 978	38 748	52
	Teacher-training		-	-	-	-	-	-
	Vocational	1985/86	1 016	...	...	23 313	10 952	47
		1993/94	1 108	...	...	13 778	6 193	45
		1994/95	...	...	...	15 055	6 617	44
Rwanda‡	Total second level	1980/81	1 454	234	16	20 672	9 602	46
		1985/86	3 120	288	9	46 998	19 550	42
		1990/91	2 802	565	20	70 400	30 523	43
		1991/92	3 413	731	21	94 586	41 704	44
	General	1980/81	...	...	...	5 022	1 388	28
		1985/86	...	...	...	7 252	1 500	21
		1990/91	...	...	...	16 173	5 784	36
		1991/92	...	...	...	23 039	8 734	38
	Teacher-training	1980/81	...	...	...	3 580	1 606	45
		1985/86	...	...	...	6 101	2 757	45
		1990/91	...	...	...	14 378	7 279	51
		1991/92	...	...	...	20 171	10 331	51
	Vocational	1980/81	...	...	...	12 070	6 608	55
		1985/86	...	...	...	33 645	15 293	45
		1990/91	...	...	...	39 849	17 460	44
		1991/92	...	...	...	51 376	22 639	44
St. Helena	Total second level	1980/81	47	35	74	638	304	48
		1985/86	54	37	69	513	252	49
	General	1980/81	40	32	80	601	295	49
		1985/86	44	34	77	470	245	52
	Teacher-training	1980/81	4	3	75	5	5	100
		1985/86	6	3	50	11	7	64
	Vocational	1980/81	3	-	-	32	4	13
		1985/86	4	-	-	32	-	-
Sao Tome and Principe	Total second level	1980/81	...	...	...	3 815	...	...
		1986/87	...	...	...	5 255	...	...
		1987/88	...	...	...	6 452	3 055	47
		1989/90	...	...	...	...	...	...
	General	1980/81	...	...	...	3 685	...	...
		1986/87	...	...	...	5 031	2 354	47
		1987/88	331	103	31	6 171	2 922	47
		1989/90	318	77	24	7 446	3 454	46
	Teacher-training	1980/81	-	-	-	-	-	-
		1986/87	...	...	...	116	92	79
		1987/88	...	...	...	188	114	61
	Vocational	1980/81	...	...	...	130	...	...
		1986/87	...	...	...	108	...	...
		1987/88	...	...	...	93	19	20
		1989/90	18	-	-	101	33	33
Senegal‡	Total second level	1980/81	4 302	...	...	95 604	31 307	33
		1985/86	...	...	...	130 338	42 937	33
		1990/91	...	...	...	...	...	...
		1991/92	...	...	...	191 431	66 154	35
		1992/93	...	...	...	...	...	...
	General	1980/81	...	...	...	83 431	28 133	34
		1985/86	3 481	597	17	121 104	40 450	33
		1990/91	5 242	...	...	173 383	59 898	35
		1991/92	5 374	748	14	183 071	63 442	35
		1992/93	...	...	...	182 140	64 252	35
	Teacher-training	1980/81	...	...	...	2 241	724	32
		1985/86	93	6	6	464	80	17
		1991/92	...	...	...	789	173	22
	Vocational	1980/81	...	...	...	9 932	2 450	25
		1985/86	...	...	...	8 770	2 407	27
		1990/91	...	...	...	6 435	2 082	32
		1991/92	...	...	...	7 571	2 539	34
		1992/93	...	...	...	7 301	2 535	35

Second level: teachers and pupils 3.7
Second degré: personnel enseignant et élèves
Segundo grado: personal docente y alumnos

Country / Pays / País	Type of education / Type d'enseignement / Tipo de enseñanza	Year / Année / Año	Teaching staff / Personnel enseignant / Personal docente			Pupils enrolled / Élèves inscrits / Alumnos matriculados		
			Total	Female / Féminin / Femenino	% F	Total	Female / Féminin / Femenino	% F
			(1)	(2)	(3)	(4)	(5)	(6)
Seychelles‡	Total second level	1980	127	47	37	924	*438	*47
		1985	364	107	29	3 975	1 997	50
		1990	328	...	...	4 396	...	...
		1992	...	...	...	9 182	4 530	49
		1993	735	382	52	9 111	4 530	50
		1994	757	380	50	9 280	4 621	50
	General	1980	67	30	45	478	226	47
		1985	193	54	28	2 435	1 233	51
		1990	157	...	...	3 034	...	...
		1992	...	...	...	7 726	3 818	49
		1993	576	318	55	7 683	3 834	50
		1994	579	311	54	7 877	3 962	50
	Teacher-training	1980	-	-	-	-	-	-
		1985	22	14	64	170	148	87
		1990	...	...	...	294	...	...
		1992	33	17	52	323	217	67
		1993	27	19	70	290	222	77
		1994	46	34	74	347	235	68
	Vocational	1980	60	17	28	446	212	48
		1985	149	39	26	1 370	616	45
		1990	...	...	...	1 068	...	...
		1992	125	38	30	1 133	495	44
		1993	132	45	34	1 138	474	42
		1994	132	35	27	1 056	424	40
Sierra Leone	Total second level	1980/81	...	...	...	68 199	...	...
		1985/86	3 006	...	...	94 717	...	...
		1989/90	5 451	985	18	101 726	35 317	35
		1990/91	5 969	1 049	18	102 474	37 660	37
	General	1980/81	2 985	...	...	64 808	19 374	30
		1985/86	2 865	...	...	93 509	...	...
		1989/90	5 049	873	17	96 709	33 137	34
		1990/91	5 544	942	17	97 049	34 859	36
	Teacher-training	1980/81	...	...	...	1 500	523	35
		1985/86	-	-	-	-	-	-
		1989/90	-	-	-	-	-	-
		1990/91	-	-	-	-	-	-
	Vocational	1980/81	...	...	...	1 891	...	...
		1985/86	141	...	...	1 208	...	...
		1989/90	402	112	28	5 017	2 180	43
		1990/91	425	107	25	5 425	2 801	52
Somalia	Total second level	1980/81	2 089	153	7	43 841	11 689	27
		1985/86	2 786	320	11	45 686	16 036	35
	General	1980/81	1 345	138	10	33 132	9 294	28
		1985/86	2 149	234	11	39 753	14 675	37
	Teacher-training	1980/81	119	14	12	3 005	853	28
		1985/86	-	-	-	-	-	-
	Vocational	1980/81	625	1	0	7 704	1 542	20
		1985/86	637	86	14	5 933	1 361	23
South Africa‡	Total second level	1986	...	...	...	2 743 184	1 475 412	54
		1990	...	...	...	2 939 270	1 589 180	54
		1991	113 215	71 452	63			
		1993	...	...	...	3 571 395	1 911 420	54
		1994	128 784	81 911	64			
	General	1986	...	...	...	1 594 147	826 670	52
		1990	...	...	...	2 702 103	1 459 573	54
		1991	110 214	70 604	64	2 902 851	1 575 320	54
		1993	...	...	...	2 658 726	1 417 134	53
		1994	...	...	...	3 523 594	1 891 974	54
	Teacher-training		-	-	-	-	-	-
	Vocational	1990	...	...	...	41 081	15 839	39
		1991	3 001	848	28	36 419	13 860	38
		1994	...	...	...	47 801	19 446	41
Sudan	Total second level	1980/81	18 831	...	...	384 194	141 736	37
		1985/86	23 035	7 501	33	556 587	235 400	42
		1990/91	33 628	*11 828	*35	731 624	318 128	43
		1991/92	30 642	9 999	33	718 298	317 277	44
	General	1980/81	17 452	4 487	26	362 992	136 016	37
		1985/86	21 342	7 140	33	525 533	226 445	43
		1990/91	31 535	11 366	36	695 964	308 573	44
		1991/92	29 208	9 755	33	683 982	309 333	45

3.7 Second level: teachers and pupils
Second degré: personnel enseignant et élèves
Segundo grado: personal docente y alumnos

Country Pays País	Type of education Type d'enseignement Tipo de enseñanza	Year Année Año	Teaching staff Personnel enseignant Personal docente			Pupils enrolled Élèves inscrits Alumnos matriculados		
			Total	Female Féminin Femenino	% F	Total	Female Féminin Femenino	% F
			(1)	(2)	(3)	(4)	(5)	(6)
Sudan (cont)	Teacher-training	1980/81	695	180	26	5 657	2 429	43
		1985/86	479	168	35	5 444	2 851	52
		1990/91	683	265	39	5 328	2 876	54
		1991/92	640	128	20	5 328	2 876	54
	Vocational	1980/81	684	...	...	15 545	3 291	21
		1985/86	1 214	193	16	25 610	6 104	24
		1990/91	1 410	*197	*14	30 332	6 679	22
		1991/92	794	116	15	28 988	5 068	17
Swaziland	Total second level	1980	...	...	...	23 665	...	...
		1985	...	...	...	31 109	...	...
		1990	...	...	...	...	...	...
		1992	...	...	...	...	...	...
		1993	...	...	...	...	...	...
		1994	...	...	...	...	...	...
	General	1980	1 292	624	48	23 198	11 370	49
		1985	1 561	725	46	29 914	14 717	49
		1990	2 213	...	...	41 128	20 551	50
		1992	2 703	...	...	51 514	25 896	50
		1993	2 824	...	...	50 304	25 231	50
		1994	2 872	1 245	43	52 571	26 464	50
	Teacher-training	1980	...	...	...	283	218	77
		1985	...	...	...	800	...	...
		1993	-	-	-	-	-	-
		1994	-	-	-	-	-	-
	Vocational	1980	...	...	...	184	...	...
		1985	...	...	...	395	58	15
Togo	Total second level	1980/81	...	...	...	...	...	...
		1985/86	4 351	559	13	97 120	23 025	24
		1990/91	4 492	529	12	125 545	31 766	25
		1991/92	...	...	...	...	...	...
		1993/94	...	...	...	...	...	...
	General	1980/81	3 166	427	13	125 122	30 066	24
		1985/86	4 072	519	13	91 609	21 570	24
		1990/91	4 231	489	12	117 153	29 605	25
		1991/92	3 922	427	11	120 289	29 785	25
		1993/94	2 918	314	11	126 335	32 433	26
	Teacher-training		-	-	-	-	-	-
	Vocational	1985/86	279	40	14	5 511	1 455	26
		1990/91	261	40	15	8 392	2 161	26
Tunisia	Total second level	1980/81	14 328	4 091	29	293 351	107 074	37
		1985/86	25 245	7 918	31	457 630	183 580	40
		1990/91	33 058	10 512	32	564 540	243 427	43
		1992/93	36 535	11 913	33	639 403	287 456	45
		1993/94	38 891	12 980	33	688 004	314 377	46
		1994/95	41 328	14 195	34	749 175	347 051	46
	General	1980/81	...	...	...	209 060	80 493	39
		1985/86	...	...	...	366 995	149 825	41
		1990/91	...	...	...	526 245	228 766	43
		1992/93	...	...	...	627 255	282 820	45
		1993/94	...	...	...	671 975	308 473	46
		1994/95	...	...	...	733 002	341 038	47
	Teacher-training	1980/81	148	36	24	4 101	2 557	62
		1985/86	232	64	28	3 935	2 758	70
		1990/91	191	48	25	1 497	949	63
		1992/93	-	-	-	-	-	-
		1993/94	-	-	-	-	-	-
		1994/95	-	-	-	-	-	-
	Vocational	1980/81	...	...	...	80 190	24 024	30
		1985/86	...	...	...	86 700	30 997	36
		1990/91	...	...	...	36 798	13 712	37
		1992/93	...	...	...	12 148	4 636	38
		1993/94	...	...	...	16 029	5 904	37
		1994/95	...	...	...	16 173	6 013	37
Uganda‡	Total second level	1980	3 833	...	...	86 560	...	...
		1985	8 252	...	...	179 185	...	...
		1990	16 881	...	...	267 520	97 268	36
		1991	15 638	...	...	254 051	...	...
		1992	16 628	...	...	256 669	94 898	37
		1993	16 163	...	...	261 415	...	...

Second level: teachers and pupils 3.7
Second degré: personnel enseignant et élèves
Segundo grado: personal docente y alumnos

Country Pays País	Type of education Type d'enseignement Tipo de enseñanza	Year Année Año	Teaching staff Personnel enseignant Personal docente			Pupils enrolled Élèves inscrits Alumnos matriculados		
			Total	Female Féminin Femenino	% F	Total	Female Féminin Femenino	% F
			(1)	(2)	(3)	(4)	(5)	(6)
Uganda‡ (cont)	General	1980	3 202	...	...	73 092	*21 123	*29
		1985	6 903	...	...	159 702	...	...
		1990	15 128	2 450	16	244 765	90 988	37
		1991	13 491	...	...	228 857	...	...
		1992	14 710	...	...	226 805	86 080	38
		1993	14 620	...	...	231 430	...	...
	Teacher-training	1980	388	...	...	10 027	...	...
		1985	906	...	...	12 551	...	...
		1990	1 022	...	...	14 206	5 833	41
		1991	1 439	...	...	14 305	...	...
		1992	1 149	...	...	16 261	6 992	43
		1993	827	...	...	17 194	7 309	43
	Vocational	1980	243	...	...	3 441	294	9
		1985	443	...	...	6 932	...	...
		1990	731	22	3	8 549	447	5
		1991	708	...	...	10 889	834	8
		1992	769	...	...	13 603	1 826	13
		1993	716	...	...	12 791	...	...
United Republic of Tanzania‡	Total second level	1980	3 837	...	...	78 715	...	...
		1985	5 267	...	...	92 945	...	...
		1990	7 944	1 931	24	167 150	70 337	42
		1991	9 904	2 256	23	183 109	79 430	43
		1992	10 251	2 308	23	189 827	83 258	44
		1993	10 735	2 190	20	196 723	86 392	44
	General	1980	3 158	...	...	67 292	22 388	33
		1985	4 329	1 081	25	83 098	30 558	37
		1990	6 930	1 729	25	150 300	63 148	42
		1991	8 649	2 032	23	166 812	72 136	43
		1992	8 926	2 070	23	175 776	76 291	43
		1993	9 568	1 927	20	180 899	78 305	43
	Teacher-training	1980	679	...	...	11 423	...	...
		1985	938	...	...	9 847	...	...
		1990	1 014	202	20	16 850	7 189	43
		1991	1 255	224	18	16 297	7 294	45
		1992	1 325	238	18	14 051	6 967	50
		1993	1 167	263	23	15 824	8 087	51
	Vocational		-	-	-	-	-	-
Zaire	Total second level	1980/81	...	...	...	861 774	235 610	27
		1985/86	...	...	...	959 934	284 686	30
		1991/92	54 394	7 744	14	1 097 095	356 150	32
		1992/93	59 879	8 996	15	1 218 760	389 110	32
		1993/94	59 325	5 989	10	1 341 446	413 113	31
	General	1991/92	...	...	...	522 690	159 517	31
		1992/93	...	...	...	585 005	175 100	30
		1993/94	...	...	...	640 298	190 942	30
	Teacher-training	1991/92	...	...	...	279 721	91 966	33
		1992/93	...	...	...	304 690	97 277	32
		1993/94	...	...	...	360 249	111 589	31
	Vocational	1991/92	...	...	...	294 684	104 667	36
		1992/93	...	...	...	329 065	116 733	35
		1993/94	...	...	...	340 899	110 582	32
Zambia‡	Total second level	1980	4 882	...	...	102 019	35 718	35
		1985	...	...	...	140 743	...	...
		1988	6 703	1 417	21	170 299	63 219	37
		1990	...	...	...	...	...	...
		1994	...	...	...	...	...	...
	General	1980	4 334	...	...	95 771	33 309	35
		1985	5 758	1 419	25	131 502	48 366	37
		1988	5 786	1 300	22	161 349	60 145	37
		1994	...	...	...	199 081	76 325	38
	Teacher-training	1980	313	60	19	3 742	1 750	47
		1985	...	...	...	4 549	...	...
		1988	471	71	15	4 769	2 139	45
		1990	...	...	...	4 669	...	...
	Vocational	1980	235	7	3	2 506	659	26
		1985	...	...	...	4 692	...	...
		1988	446	46	10	4 181	935	22
		1990	...	...	...	3 313	...	...

3.7 Second level: teachers and pupils
Second degré: personnel enseignant et élèves
Segundo grado: personal docente y alumnos

Country / Pays / País	Type of education / Type d'enseignement / Tipo de enseñanza	Year / Année / Año	Teaching staff / Personnel enseignant / Personal docente			Pupils enrolled / Élèves inscrits / Alumnos matriculados		
			Total	Female Féminin Femenino	% F	Total	Female Féminin Femenino	% F
			(1)	(2)	(3)	(4)	(5)	(6)
Zimbabwe	Total second level	1980	3 782	...	...	74 746	...	...
		1985	...			482 000	...	...
		1990	*24 547	*7 106	*29	661 066	308 677	47
		1991	25 225	8 010	32	710 619	312 665	44
		1992	23 233	7 706	33	657 344	289 274	44
		1993	21 403	6 767	32	639 559	283 971	44
	General	1980	3 736	...	...	74 012	...	...
		1985	17 315	5 139	30	481 708	194 784	40
		1990	*24 547	*7 106	*29	661 066	308 677	47
		1991	25 225	8 010	32	710 619	312 665	44
		1992	23 233	7 706	33	657 344	289 274	44
		1993	21 403	6 767	32	639 559	283 971	44
	Teacher-training		-	-	-	-	-	-
	Vocational	1980	46	...	...	734	734	100
		1985	...	...	...	292	...	...
		1990			-			-
		1991	-		-	-		-
		1992	-	-	-	-	-	-
		1993	-	-	-	-	-	-
America, North								
Antigua and Barbuda	Total second level	1991/92	*400	*348	*87	5 845	2 937	50
	General	1991/92	*400	*348	*87	5 845	2 937	50
	Teacher-training		-	-	-		-	-
	Vocational		-	-	-		-	-
Bahamas‡	Total second level	1980/81	1 018	...	...	28 136	...	...
		1985/86	1 472	...	...	27 604	14 448	52
		1991/92	...	...	...	29 559	14 678	50
		1992/93	...	...	...	29 863	14 792	50
		1993/94	1 775	1 232	69	28 532	...	...
	General	1980/81	1 018	...	...	28 136	...	...
		1985/86	1 472	...	...	27 604	14 448	52
		1991/92	...	...	...	29 559	14 678	50
		1992/93	...	...	...	29 863	14 792	50
		1993/94	1 775	1 232	69	28 532	...	...
	Teacher-training		-	-	-	-	-	-
	Vocational		-	-	-	-	-	-
Barbados‡	Total second level	1980/81	1 231	...	...	28 818	14 363	50
		1988/89	1 481	797	54	25 422	13 009	51
		1989/90	1 224	677	55	24 004	11 255	47
	General	1980/81	1 231	...	...	28 818	14 363	50
		1988/89	1 481	797	54	25 422	13 009	51
		1989/90	1 224	677	55	24 004	11 255	47
	Teacher-training			-	-		-	-
	Vocational			-	-		-	-
Belize	Total second level	1980/81	...	...	...	...	...	...
		1985/86	534	229	43	7 048	3 811	54
		1990/91	564	233	41	7 904	4 176	53
		1991/92	622	287	46	8 901	4 896	55
		1992/93	643	299	47	9 457	4 812	51
		1994/95	740	346	47	10 147	5 307	52
	General	1980/81	338	159	47	5 435	*2 989	*55
		1985/86	515	222	43	6 752	3 642	54
		1990/91	...	...	...	7 799	4 172	53
	Teacher-training	1980/81	-	-		-	-	
		1985/86	13	6	46	195	156	80
		1990/91	-	-	-	-	-	-
		1991/92	-	-	-	-	-	-
		1992/93	-	-	-	-	-	-
		1994/95	-	-	-	-	-	-
	Vocational	1985/86	6	1	17	101	13	13
		1990/91	...	...	...	105	4	4
Bermuda	Total second level	1980/81	...	...	...	...	...	...
		1984/85	...	...	...	...	...	...
	General	1980/81	367	151	41	4 347	2 165	50
		1984/85	418	218	52	4 741	2 391	50

Second level: teachers and pupils 3.7
Second degré: personnel enseignant et élèves
Segundo grado: personal docente y alumnos

Country Pays País	Type of education Type d'enseignement Tipo de enseñanza	Year Année Año	Teaching staff Personnel enseignant Personal docente			Pupils enrolled Élèves inscrits Alumnos matriculados		
			Total	Female Féminin Femenino	% F	Total	Female Féminin Femenino	% F
			(1)	(2)	(3)	(4)	(5)	(6)
Bermuda (cont)	Teacher-training		-		-	-		-
British Virgin Islands	Total second level	1980/81	55	33	60	791	448	57
		1990/91	...	...	...	1 124	596	53
		1991/92	98	...	...	1 134	625	55
		1993/94	115	75	65	1 309	668	51
	General	1980/81	...	...	...	510	279	55
		1990/91	...	...	...	1 124	596	53
		1991/92	98	...	...	1 134	625	55
		1993/94	115	75	65	1 309	668	51
	Teacher-training		-		-	-		-
	Vocational	1980/81	...	...	...	281	169	60
		1990/91	-	-	-	-	-	-
		1991/92	-	-	-	-	-	-
		1993/94	-	-	-	-	-	-
Canada	Total second level	1980/81	...	...	...	2 323 228	1 146 714	49
		1985/86	151 390	...	...	2 250 941	1 097 002	49
		1990/91	164 125	87 875	54	2 292 497	1 118 112	49
		1991/92	166 406	89 315	54	2 337 513	1 137 699	49
		1992/93	167 118	89 588	54	2 414 285	1 176 738	49
		1993/94	168 027	90 130	54	2 472 328	1 206 423	49
	General	1980/81	...	...	...	2 323 228	1 146 714	49
		1985/86	151 390	...	...	2 250 941	1 097 002	49
		1990/91	164 125	87 875	54	2 292 497	1 118 112	49
		1991/92	166 406	89 315	54	2 337 513	1 137 699	49
		1992/93	167 118	89 588	54	2 414 285	1 176 738	49
		1993/94	168 027	90 130	54	2 472 328	1 206 423	49
	Teacher-training		-		-	-		-
	Vocational		-		-	-		-
Costa Rica	Total second level	1980	7 157	...	...	135 830	72 014	53
		1985	6 613	...	...	112 531	58 116	52
		1990	6 889	...	...	130 553	65 508	50
		1992	7 641	...	...	151 513	76 359	50
		1993	8 263	...	...	160 291	81 469	51
		1994	8 845	...	...	169 777	86 315	51
	General	1980	4 903	...	...	105 220	56 586	54
		1985	...	...	...	87 038	45 403	52
		1990	4 671	...	...	101 451	51 518	51
		1992	5 281	...	...	117 975	60 193	51
		1993	5 892	...	...	124 660	64 009	51
		1994	6 316	...	...	132 914	68 460	52
	Teacher-training		-		-	-		-
	Vocational	1980	2 254	...	...	30 610	15 428	50
		1985	...	...	...	25 493	12 713	50
		1990	2 218	...	...	29 102	13 990	48
		1992	2 360	...	...	33 538	16 166	48
		1993	2 371	...	...	35 631	17 460	49
		1994	2 529	...	...	36 863	17 855	48
Cuba	Total second level	1980/81	88 017	40 145	46	1 146 414	577 396	50
		1985/86	100 673	48 444	48	1 156 555	585 507	51
		1990/91	100 118	51 112	51	1 002 338	524 488	52
		1992/93	92 813	45 679	49	819 712	427 038	52
		1993/94	85 094	43 302	51	725 800	374 630	52
		1994/95	68 960	35 244	51	674 152	349 664	52
	General	1980/81	63 685	31 976	50	837 261	423 084	51
		1985/86	65 929	35 179	53	807 597	417 490	52
		1990/91	63 855	35 524	56	672 166	357 930	53
		1992/93	57 455	33 939	59	520 290	281 975	54
		1993/94	53 423	32 290	60	459 140	248 238	54
		1994/95	43 633	26 485	61	445 178	239 037	54
	Teacher-training	1980/81	6 730	3 842	57	80 666	49 862	62
		1985/86	7 283	4 305	59	41 829	29 415	70
		1990/91	6 998	3 943	56	29 559	24 691	84
		1992/93	3 650	2 099	58	14 590	10 576	72
		1993/94	1 675	954	57	7 305	5 871	80
		1994/95	627	265	42	3 779	2 994	79
	Vocational	1980/81	17 602	4 327	25	228 487	104 450	46
		1985/86	27 461	8 960	33	307 129	138 602	45
		1990/91	29 265	11 645	40	300 613	141 867	47
		1992/93	31 708	9 641	30	284 832	134 487	47
		1993/94	29 996	10 058	34	259 355	120 521	46
		1994/95	24 700	8 494	34	225 195	107 633	48

3.7 Second level: teachers and pupils
Second degré: personnel enseignant et élèves
Segundo grado: personal docente y alumnos

Country / Pays / País	Type of education / Type d'enseignement / Tipo de enseñanza	Year / Année / Año	Teaching staff — Total (1)	Female Féminin Femenino (2)	%F (3)	Pupils enrolled — Total (4)	Female Féminin Femenino (5)	%F (6)
Dominica‡	Total second level	1980/81	...	...	...	...	...	...
		1985/86	...	...	...	7 370	3 953	54
		1990/91	...	...	...	...	...	...
		1992/93	...	...	...	...	...	...
		1993/94	...	...	...	...	...	...
		1994/95	...	...	...	...	...	...
	General	1980/81	...	...	...	7 022	3 679	52
		1985/86	...	...	...	7 111	3 860	54
		1990/91	...	...	...	4 749	2 471	52
		1992/93	...	...	...	6 179	3 289	53
		1993/94	...	...	...	6 431	3 174	49
		1994/95	...	...	...	6 493	3 334	51
	Teacher-training		-	-	-	-	-	-
	Vocational	1985/86	27	7	26	259	93	36
Dominican Republic‡	Total second level	1980/81	...	...	...	356 091	...	...
		1985/86	...	...	...	463 511	...	...
		1993/94	11 605	...	...	232 999	135 087	58
		1994/95	12 054	5 934	49	263 236	151 261	57
	General	1980/81	...	...	...	331 471	...	...
		1985/86	11 754	...	...	438 922	240 898	55
		1993/94	10 301	...	...	211 957	121 738	57
		1994/95	10 757	5 334	50	240 441	138 162	57
	Teacher-training	1980/81	...	...	...	1 722	...	...
		1985/86	...	...	...	3 433	...	...
		1993/94	86	...	...	1 661	947	57
		1994/95	86	60	70	1 292	743	58
	Vocational	1980/81	...	...	...	22 898	...	...
		1985/86	...	...	...	21 156	...	...
		1993/94	1 218	...	...	19 381	12 402	64
		1994/95	1 211	540	45	21 503	12 356	57
El Salvador	Total second level	1980	3 080	844	27	73 030	34 929	48
		1984	...	...	...	...	...	...
		1991	...	...	...	94 268	51 780	55
		1992	...	...	...	105 093	55 572	53
		1993	...	...	...	118 115	61 648	52
	General	1980	1 805	437	24	24 280	10 436	43
		1984	...	...	...	...	...	...
		1991	...	...	...	26 314	13 180	50
		1992	...	...	...	28 032	13 434	48
		1993	...	...	...	29 527	14 227	48
	Teacher-training	1980	65	24	37	3 451	2 560	74
		1991	...	...	...	2 314	1 649	71
		1992	...	...	...	1 961	1 437	73
		1993	...	...	...	1 623	1 204	74
	Vocational	1980	1 210	383	32	45 299	21 933	48
		1991	...	...	...	65 640	36 951	56
		1992	...	...	...	75 100	40 701	54
		1993	...	...	...	86 965	46 217	53
Grenada	Total second level	1980/81	...	...	...	8 626	5 056	59
		1985/86	...	...	...	9 571	5 110	53
		1990/91	...	...	...	9 776	5 215	53
		1991/92	...	...	...	9 896	5 374	54
		1992/93	377	195	52	10 213	5 489	54
	General	1980/81	...	...	...	8 626	5 056	59
		1985/86	...	...	...	9 571	5 110	53
		1990/91	...	...	...	9 776	5 215	53
		1991/92	...	...	...	9 896	5 374	54
		1992/93	377	195	52	10 213	5 489	54
	Teacher-training		-	-	-	-	-	-
	Vocational		-	-	-	-	-	-
Guadeloupe	Total second level	1980/81	...	...	...	49 398	...	...
		1985/86	...	...	...	51 634	27 460	53
		1990/91	3 237	...	...	49 846	26 480	53
		1992/93	3 467	...	...	50 850	25 513	50
		1993/94	...	...	...	50 174	26 002	52
		1994/95	...	...	...	50 899	26 281	52
	General	1985/86	...	...	...	38 510	21 043	55
		1990/91	...	...	...	39 208	21 255	54
		1992/93	...	...	...	38 043	18 932	50
		1993/94	...	...	...	41 139	21 652	53
		1994/95	...	...	...	41 656	21 838	52

Second level: teachers and pupils **3.7**
Second degré: personnel enseignant et élèves
Segundo grado: personal docente y alumnos

Country Pays País	Type of education Type d'enseignement Tipo de enseñanza	Year Année Año	Teaching staff Personnel enseignant Personal docente			Pupils enrolled Élèves inscrits Alumnos matriculados		
			Total	Female Féminin Femenino	% F	Total	Female Féminin Femenino	% F
			(1)	(2)	(3)	(4)	(5)	(6)
Guadeloupe (cont)	Teacher-training		-	-	-	-	-	-
	Vocational	1985/86	...	...	...	13 124	6 417	49
		1990/91	...	...	...	10 638	5 225	49
		1992/93	...	...	...	12 807	6 581	51
		1993/94	...	...	...	9 035	4 350	48
		1994/95	...	...	...	9 243	4 443	48
Guatemala	Total second level	1980	9 613	...	...	171 903	76 918	45
		1985	14 629	...	...	204 049	...	...
		1991	20 717	...	...	294 907	...	...
		1993	20 942	...	...	334 383	156 370	47
	General	1980	...	...	...	119 879	51 299	43
	Teacher-training	1980	...	...	...	22 256	13 880	62
	Vocational	1980	...	...	...	29 768	11 739	39
Haiti	Total second level	1980/81	4 392	...	...	99 894	...	...
		1985/86	...	...	...	143 758	...	...
		1989/90	...	...	...	...	...	...
		1990/91	...	...	...	...	...	...
	General	1980/81	4 034	...	...	96 596	45 867	47
		1985/86	6 978	846	12	139 422	65 367	47
		1989/90	8 814	...	...	176 694	86 486	49
		1990/91	9 470	...	...	184 968	90 534	49
	Teacher-training	1980/81	123	...	...	723	519	72
		1985/86	159	73	46	867	588	68
	Vocational	1980/81	235	...	...	2 575	...	...
		1985/86	...	...	...	3 469	...	...
Honduras	Total second level	1980	4 489	2 152	48	127 293	64 182	50
		1985	...	...	...	184 112	...	...
		1991	8 507	...	...	194 083	106 503	55
		1993	10 203	...	...	203 192	...	...
	General	1980	...	...	...	93 806	46 534	50
		1991	...	...	...	126 582	67 033	53
	Teacher-training	1980	...	...	...	5 156	3 802	74
		1991	...	...	...	8 935	6 544	73
	Vocational	1980	...	...	...	28 331	13 846	49
		1991	...	...	...	58 566	32 926	56
Jamaica‡	Total second level	1980/81	7 525	4 991	66	248 001	131 745	53
		1985/86	8 012	5 317	66	237 713	124 487	52
		1990/91	...	...	...	225 240	115 999	52
		1992/93	10 931	7 333	67	235 071	120 640	51
	General	1980/81	7 110	4 760	67	233 723	122 450	52
		1985/86	7 485	5 041	67	229 023	120 111	52
	Teacher-training		-	-	-	-	-	-
	Vocational	1980/81	415	231	56	14 278	9 295	65
		1985/86	527	276	52	8 690	4 376	50
Martinique‡	Total second level	1980/81	...	...	...	47 745	...	...
		1985/86	...	...	...	47 500	...	...
		1991/92	...	...	...	46 373	24 275	52
		1992/93	...	...	...	43 928	23 657	54
		1993/94	3 451	1 813	53	46 108	23 517	51
		1994/95	...	...	...	46 178	23 258	50
	General	1991/92	...	...	...	32 507	19 528	60
		1992/93	...	...	...	30 912	16 952	55
		1993/94	...	...	...	36 491	19 005	52
		1994/95	...	...	...	36 810	18 991	52
	Teacher-training		-	-	-	-	-	-
	Vocational	1991/92	...	...	...	13 866	4 747	34
		1992/93	...	...	...	13 016	6 705	52
		1993/94	...	...	...	9 617	4 512	47
		1994/95	...	...	...	9 368	4 267	46
Mexico	Total second level	1980/81	268 178	...	...	4 741 850	2 214 442	47
		1985/86	380 774	...	...	6 549 105	3 163 293	48
		1990/91	402 474	...	...	6 704 297	3 329 371	50
		1992/93	412 789	...	...	6 782 886	3 347 884	49
		1993/94	426 157	...	...	6 977 086	3 461 731	50
		1994/95	448 407	...	...	7 264 650	...	...

3.7 Second level: teachers and pupils
Second degré: personnel enseignant et élèves
Segundo grado: personal docente y alumnos

Country / Pays / País	Type of education / Type d'enseignement / Tipo de enseñanza	Year / Année / Año	Teaching staff / Personnel enseignant / Personal docente			Pupils enrolled / Élèves inscrits / Alumnos matriculados		
			Total	Female / Féminin / Femenino	% F	Total	Female / Féminin / Femenino	% F
			(1)	(2)	(3)	(4)	(5)	(6)
Mexico (cont)	General	1980/81	226 532	...	...	4 042 188	1 750 873	43
		1985/86	321 459	...	...	5 717 572	2 645 629	46
		1990/91	344 293	...	...	5 911 816	2 827 425	48
		1992/93	353 072	...	...	5 970 118	2 884 530	48
		1993/94	365 908	...	...	6 179 579	2 988 739	48
		1994/95	386 182	...	...	6 429 571	...	...
	Teacher-training	1980/81	12 988	...	...	207 997	138 669	67
		1985/86	8 491	...	...	64 700	47 117	73
		1990/91	-	-	-	-	-	-
		1992/93	-	-	-	-	-	-
		1993/94	-	-	-	-	-	-
		1994/95	-	-	-	-	-	-
	Vocational	1980/81	28 658	...	...	491 665	324 900	66
		1985/86	50 824	...	...	766 833	470 547	61
		1990/91	58 181	...	...	792 481	501 946	63
		1992/93	59 717	...	...	812 768	463 354	57
		1993/94	60 249	...	...	797 507	472 992	59
		1994/95	62 225	...	...	835 079	...	...
Montserrat	Total second level	1980/81	37	...	...	887	...	...
		1985/86	...	...	...	1 069	545	51
		1991/92	...	...	...	837	414	49
		1992/93	72	...	...	888	...	...
		1993/94	...	...	...	...	...	...
	General	1980/81	32	...	...	828	...	...
		1985/86	...	...	...	1 016	521	51
		1991/92	...	...	...	747	385	52
		1992/93	...	...	...	785	...	...
		1993/94	80	50	63	905	447	49
	Teacher-training		-	-	-	-	-	-
	Vocational	1980/81	5	...	...	59	...	...
		1985/86	...	...	...	53	24	45
		1991/92	...	...	...	90	29	32
		1992/93	...	...	...	103	72	70
Netherlands Antilles	Total second level	1981/82	1 403	...	...	21 249	11 197	53
		1991/92	...	...	...	14 987	...	...
	General	1981/82	669	...	...	10 931	6 808	62
		1991/92	...	...	...	8 740	...	...
	Teacher-training	1981/82	...	...	...	34	34	100
		1991/92	-	-	-	-	-	-
	Vocational	1981/82	...	...	...	10 284	4 355	42
		1991/92	...	...	...	6 247	...	...
Nicaragua	Total second level	1980	4 221	...	...	139 743	74 328	53
		1985	5 204	2 916	56	128 499	86 324	67
		1990	4 865	2 783	57	168 888	97 619	58
		1992	...	...	...	...	...	...
		1993	...	...	...	203 962	107 279	53
		1994	...	...	...	...	...	...
	General	1980	...	...	...	120 522	63 000	52
		1985	3 388	1 961	58	99 984	64 627	65
		1990	3 948	2 292	58	151 959	88 018	58
		1992	4 465	2 522	56	178 342	94 899	53
		1993	6 172	3 380	55	186 722	98 099	53
		1994	5 356	2 975	56	205 716	108 412	53
	Teacher-training	1980	...	...	...	2 560	2 027	79
		1985	296	173	58	4 596	3 855	84
		1990	240	159	66	1 597	1 302	82
		1992	...	...	...	2 433	1 820	75
		1993	175	99	57	2 507	1 928	77
		1994	202	133	66	2 241	1 726	77
	Vocational	1980	...	...	...	16 661	9 301	56
		1985	1 520	782	51	23 919	17 842	75
		1990	677	332	49	15 332	8 299	54
		1993	...	...	...	14 733	7 252	49
Panama	Total second level	1980	8 138	4 319	53	171 273	89 328	52
		1985	9 681	5 155	53	184 536	95 750	52
		1990	9 754	5 284	54	195 903	99 634	51
		1992	10 521	...	...	201 047	...	...
		1993	10 979	...	...	206 509	...	...
		1994	11 241	...	...	209 929	...	...

Second level: teachers and pupils   3.7
Second degré: personnel enseignant et élèves
Segundo grado: personal docente y alumnos

Country Pays País	Type of education Type d'enseignement Tipo de enseñanza	Year Année Año	Teaching staff Personnel enseignant Personal docente			Pupils enrolled Élèves inscrits Alumnos matriculados		
			Total	Female Féminin Femenino	% F	Total	Female Féminin Femenino	% F
			(1)	(2)	(3)	(4)	(5)	(6)
Panama (cont)	General	1980	6 005	3 316	55	130 496	67 037	51
		1985	6 913	3 851	56	134 470	68 782	51
		1990	7 326	4 109	56	144 690	73 416	51
	Teacher-training	1980	48	26	54	984	663	67
		1985	41	18	44	912	599	66
		1990	69	36	52	1 599	1 004	63
	Vocational	1980	2 085	977	47	39 793	21 628	54
		1985	2 727	1 286	47	49 154	26 369	54
		1990	2 359	1 139	48	49 614	25 214	51
Saint Kitts and Nevis‡	Total second level	1980/81	...	...	...	4 214	2 053	49
		1985/86	275	148	54	4 197	*2 046	*49
		1991/92	294	164	56	4 396	2 225	51
		1992/93	312	183	59	4 402	2 242	51
	General	1980/81	...	...	...	4 214	2 053	49
		1985/86	275	148	54	4 197	*2 046	*49
		1991/92	294	164	56	4 396	2 225	51
		1992/93	312	183	59	4 402	2 242	51
	Teacher-training		-	-	-	-	-	-
	Vocational		-	-	-	-	-	-
St. Lucia‡	Total second level	1980/81	...	...	...	4 485	2 461	55
		1985/86	...	...	...	6 833	4 186	61
		1990/91	...	...	...	8 230	*4 864	*59
		1991/92	514	318	62	9 419	5 713	61
		1992/93	558	350	63	10 356	6 476	63
	General	1980/81	229	120	52	4 306	2 400	56
		1985/86	331	193	58	6 239	3 592	58
		1990/91	396	237	60	7 959	*4 604	*58
		1991/92	495	300	61	8 825	5 176	59
		1992/93	524	321	61	9 550	5 710	60
	Teacher-training		-	-	-	-	-	-
	Vocational	1980/81	...	...	...	179	61	34
		1985/86	...	...	...	594	594	100
		1990/91	...	...	...	271	*260	*96
		1991/92	19	18	95	594	537	90
		1992/93	34	29	85	806	766	95
St. Pierre and Miquelon	Total second level	1980/81	62	31	50	748	392	52
		1985/86	74	36	49	821	432	53
		1986/87	71	33	46	800	421	53
	General	1980/81	49	28	57	527	278	53
		1985/86	58	32	55	556	297	53
		1986/87	55	28	51	548	293	53
	Teacher-training		-	-	-	-	-	-
	Vocational	1980/81	13	3	23	221	114	52
		1985/86	16	4	25	265	135	51
		1986/87	16	5	31	252	128	51
St. Vincent and the Grenadines‡	Total second level	1981/82	...	...	...	8 058	4 739	59
		1985/86	...	...	...	6 782	4 015	59
		1990/91	431	226	52	10 719	5 867	55
		1993/94	...	...	...	...	...	...
	General	1981/82	327	171	52	7 771	4 580	59
		1985/86	368	191	52	6 535	3 875	59
		1990/91	382	212	55	10 305	5 584	54
		1993/94	395	202	51	9 870	5 497	56
	Teacher-training	1985/86	...	...	...	119	72	61
		1990/91	12	5	42	118	72	61
	Vocational	1985/86	...	...	...	128	68	53
		1990/91	37	9	24	296	211	71
Trinidad and Tobago‡	Total second level	1980/81	4 377	...	...	89 272	...	...
		1985/86	...	...	...	95 302	...	...
		1990/91	...	...	...	97 493	49 069	50
		1991/92	...	...	...	97 804	48 820	50
		1992/93	...	...	...	100 278	50 287	50
		1993/94	...	...	...	...	...	...

3.7 Second level: teachers and pupils
Second degré: personnel enseignant et élèves
Segundo grado: personal docente y alumnos

Country / Pays / País	Type of education / Type d'enseignement / Tipo de enseñanza	Year / Année / Año	Teaching staff Personnel enseignant Personal docente			Pupils enrolled Élèves inscrits Alumnos matriculados		
			Total	Female Féminin Femenino	% F	Total	Female Féminin Femenino	% F
			(1)	(2)	(3)	(4)	(5)	(6)
Trinidad and Tobago‡ (cont)	General	1980/81	...	...	...	86 833	...	...
		1985/86	...	...	...	94 564	...	...
		1990/91	4 839	2 605	54	96 599	48 810	51
		1991/92	4 844	2 602	54	97 253	48 710	50
		1992/93	4 920	2 712	55	99 590	50 174	50
		1993/94	4 882	2 750	56	100 609	50 923	51
	Teacher-training		-	-	-	-	-	-
	Vocational	1980/81	...	...	...	2 439	917	38
		1985/86	...	...	...	738	255	35
		1990/91	...	...	...	894	259	29
		1991/92	...	...	...	551	110	20
		1992/93	...	...	...	688	113	16
Turks and Caicos Islands	Total second level	1980/81	47	28	60	691	...	...
		1984/85	51	34	67	707	...	...
		1993/94	101	64	63	1 032	519	50
	General	1980/81	47	28	60	691	...	...
		1984/85	51	34	67	707	...	...
		1993/94	71	50	70	943	460	49
	Teacher-training		-	-	-	-	-	-
	Vocational	1980/81	-	-	-	-	-	-
		1984/85	-	-	-	-	-	-
		1993/94	30	14	47	89	59	66
United States‡	Total second level	1980/81	...	...	...	21 585 000	10 631 000	49
		1985/86	...	...	...	20 633 000	10 094 000	49
		1990/91	...	...	...	19 270 000	9 473 000	49
		1992/93	...	...	...	20 516 146	10 000 943	49
		1993/94	1 334 000	720 000	54	20 578 000	9 991 000	49
	General	1980/81	...	...	...	21 585 000	10 631 000	49
		1985/86	...	...	...	20 633 000	10 094 000	49
		1990/91	...	...	...	19 270 000	9 473 000	49
		1992/93	...	...	...	20 516 146	10 000 943	49
		1993/94	1 334 000	720 000	54	20 578 000	9 991 000	49
	Teacher-training		-	-	-	-	-	-
	Vocational		-	-	-	-	-	-
U.S. Virgin Islands‡	Total second level	1980/81	617	...	...	11 326	...	...
		1985/86	...	...	...	13 548	...	...
		1990/91	...	...	...	10 050	5 568	55
		1992/93	...	...	...	12 502	6 191	50
	Teacher-training		-	-	-	-	-	-
	Vocational		-	-	-	-	-	-
America, South								
Argentina	Total second level	1981	...	...	...	1 366 444	725 620	53
		1985	230 093	151 168	66	1 800 049	942 768	52
		1990	...	...	...	2 160 410	...	...
		1991	283 583	...	...	2 262 378	1 159 843	51
		1993	...	...	...	2 026 006	...	...
		1994	233 564	143 824	62	2 238 091	...	...
	General	1981	77 956	58 415	75	528 140	335 653	64
		1985	93 675	69 472	74	715 518	442 107	62
	Teacher-training		-	-	-	-	-	-
	Vocational	1981	...	...	...	838 304	389 967	47
		1985	136 418	81 696	60	1 084 531	500 661	46
Bolivia	Total second level	1980	...	...	...	170 710	73 991	43
		1986	8 523	...	...	209 293	96 690	46
		1990	12 434	6 094	49	219 232	100 748	46
Brazil	Total second level	1980	198 087	105 945	53	2 819 182	1 515 859	54
		1985	206 124	...	...	3 016 175	...	...
		1990	243 246	...	...	3 498 777	...	...
		1992	...	...	...	4 085 631	...	...
		1993	273 539	...	...	4 183 847	...	...
		1994	295 542	...	...	4 510 199	...	...
	General	1985	...	...	...	998 725	...	...
	Teacher-training	1985	...	...	...	536 453	...	...
	Vocational	1985	...	...	...	1 480 997	...	...

Second level: teachers and pupils 3.7
Second degré: personnel enseignant et élèves
Segundo grado: personal docente y alumnos

Country Pays País	Type of education Type d'enseignement Tipo de enseñanza	Year Année Año	Teaching staff Personnel enseignant Personal docente			Pupils enrolled Élèves inscrits Alumnos matriculados		
			Total	Female Féminin Femenino	% F	Total	Female Féminin Femenino	% F
			(1)	(2)	(3)	(4)	(5)	(6)
Chile	Total second level	1980	...	...	...	538 309	284 784	53
		1985	...	...	...	667 797	344 631	52
		1990	...	...	...	719 819	369 855	51
		1991	49 082	26 049	53	699 455	357 440	51
		1993	...	...	...	652 815	334 298	51
		1994	50 187	26 314	52	664 498	338 177	51
	General	1980	...	...	...	369 180	204 802	55
		1985	...	...	...	539 150	280 767	52
		1990	...	...	...	464 423	247 932	53
		1991	...	...	...	436 892	232 116	53
		1993	...	...	...	391 457	210 283	54
		1994	...	...	...	387 272	209 116	54
	Teacher-training		-	-	-	-	-	-
	Vocational	1980	...	...	...	169 129	79 982	47
		1985	...	...	...	128 647	63 864	50
		1990	...	...	...	255 396	121 923	48
		1991	...	...	...	262 563	125 324	48
		1993	...	...	...	261 358	124 015	47
		1994	...	...	...	277 226	129 061	47
Colombia	Total second level	1980	85 135	35 756	42	1 733 192	870 276	50
		1985	95 981	...	...	1 934 032	965 082	50
		1991	119 742	...	...	2 377 947	1 274 580	54
		1992	130 514	...	...	2 686 515	1 442 659	54
		1993	134 161	...	...	2 796 007	1 498 660	54
		1994	140 181	...	...	2 935 830	...	...
	General	1980	61 836	25 290	41	1 313 004	660 502	50
		1985	69 871	...	...	1 468 709	731 399	50
		1991	86 522	...	...	1 781 599	911 400	51
		1992	93 944	...	...	2 011 662	...	...
		1993	97 896	...	...	2 118 205	...	...
	Teacher-training	1980	4 096	2 433	59	67 583	50 958	75
		1985	3 817	...	...	60 721	33 631	55
		1991	4 933	...	...	85 622	61 618	72
		1992	5 455	...	...	93 491	...	...
		1993	5 231	...	...	90 900	...	...
	Vocational	1980	19 203	8 033	42	352 605	158 816	45
		1985	22 293	...	...	404 602	200 052	49
		1991	28 287	...	...	510 726	301 562	59
		1992	31 115	...	...	581 362	...	...
		1993	31 034	...	...	586 902	...	...
Ecuador‡	Total second level	1980/81	34 868	...	...	591 969	...	...
		1985/86	47 506	19 440	41	730 226	367 342	50
		1990/91	...	...	...	...	...	...
		1991/92	...	...	...	...	...	...
		1992/93	...	...	...	814 359	405 655	50
	General	1980/81	27 048	*10 278	*38	516 548	246 141	48
		1985/86	33 557	13 728	41	488 078	230 458	47
		1990/91	60 126	...	...	785 844	...	...
		1991/92	61 396	...	...	811 666	...	...
		1992/93	62 630	27 708	44	534 368	252 876	47
	Teacher-training	1980/81	258	65	25	4 945	3 452	70
		1985/86	...	...	...	7 677	5 007	65
		1992/93	...	...	...	802	427	53
	Vocational	1980/81	7 562	...	...	70 476	...	...
		1985/86	13 949	5 712	41	234 471	131 877	56
		1992/93	...	...	...	279 189	152 352	55
French Guiana	Total second level	1980/81	...	...	...	7 421	...	...
		1990/91	...	...	...	10 722	...	...
		1993/94	...	...	...	13 494	6 829	51
		1994/95	...	...	...	15 034	7 506	50
	General	1993/94	...	...	...	11 303	5 768	51
		1994/95	...	...	...	12 731	6 416	50
	Teacher-training		-	-	-	-	-	-
	Vocational	1993/94	...	...	...	2 191	1 061	48
		1994/95	...	...	...	2 303	1 090	47
Guyana	Total second level	1980/81	...	...	...	...	...	...
		1985/86	2 324	1 097	47	76 546	39 289	51
		1988/89	...	...	...	...	...	...
	General	1980/81	4 236	1 897	45	75 335	38 504	51
		1985/86	2 087	1 051	50	72 679	37 984	52
		1988/89	...	...	...	72 096	*37 700	*52

3.7 Second level: teachers and pupils
Second degré: personnel enseignant et élèves
Segundo grado: personal docente y alumnos

Country Pays País	Type of education Type d'enseignement Tipo de enseñanza	Year Année Año	Teaching staff Personnel enseignant Personal docente			Pupils enrolled Élèves inscrits Alumnos matriculados		
			Total	Female Féminin Femenino	% F	Total	Female Féminin Femenino	% F
			(1)	(2)	(3)	(4)	(5)	(6)
Guyana (cont)	Teacher-training		-	-	-	-	-	-
	Vocational	1985/86	237	46	19	3 867	1 305	34
Paraguay	Total second level	1980	...	...	...	118 828	...	...
		1985	...	...	...	150 736	...	...
		1990	...	...	...	163 734	82 123	50
		1991	12 218	8 201	67	169 167	85 524	51
		1993	20 793	13 711	66	214 272	108 463	51
		1994	...	...	...	240 906	121 356	50
	General	1980	...	...	...	111 905	...	...
		1985	...	...	...	141 461	69 997	49
		1990	...	...	...	153 206	77 382	51
		1991	...	...	...	157 487	80 376	51
		1993	...	...	...	195 677	...	...
		1994	17 668	11 430	65	220 512	112 536	51
	Teacher-training		-	-	-	-	-	-
	Vocational	1980	...	...	...	6 923	...	...
		1985	...	...	...	9 275	...	...
		1990	...	...	...	10 528	4 741	45
		1991	...	...	...	11 680	5 148	44
		1993	...	...	...	18 595	...	...
		1994	...	...	...	20 394	8 820	43
Peru‡	Total second level	1980	...	...	...	1 203 116	547 393	45
		1985	68 541	...	...	1 427 261	667 399	47
		1990	86 247	...	...	1 697 943	...	...
		1992	87 624	...	...	1 703 997	...	...
		1993	85 023	...	...	1 719 854	...	...
		1994	100 698	...	...	1 996 233	...	...
	General	1980	...	...	...	1 151 748	526 780	46
		1985	68 541	...	...	1 427 261	667 399	47
		1990	86 247	...	...	1 697 943	...	...
		1992	87 624	...	...	1 703 997	...	...
		1993	85 023	...	...	1 719 854	...	...
		1994	100 698	...	...	1 996 233	...	...
	Teacher-training		-	-	-	-	-	-
	Vocational	1980	...	...	...	51 368	20 613	40
		1985	-	-	-	-	-	-
		1990	-	-	-	-	-	-
		1992	-	-	-	-	-	-
		1993	-	-	-	-	-	-
		1994	-	-	-	-	-	-
Suriname	Total second level	1980/81	...	...	...	24 027	...	...
		1985/86	4 021	2 091	52	37 630	20 084	53
		1990/91	2 482	1 539	62	33 561	17 793	53
		1991/92	2 496	...	...	35 535	18 946	53
		1992/93	2 487	1 500	60	30 016	15 999	53
		1993/94	...	...	...	...	...	...
	General	1980/81	...	...	...	12 747	...	...
		1985/86	...	...	...	24 996	14 069	56
		1990/91	...	...	...	19 902	11 245	57
		1991/92	...	...	...	19 224	10 842	56
		1992/93	...	...	...	17 709	9 386	53
		1993/94	...	...	...	16 511	9 454	57
	Teacher-training	1980/81	120	...	...	1 529	...	...
		1985/86	...	...	...	2 320	2 095	90
		1990/91	...	...	...	1 954	1 728	88
		1991/92	...	...	...	1 900	1 677	88
		1992/93	...	...	...	1 742	1 543	89
		1993/94	...	...	...	1 654	1 372	83
	Vocational	1980/81	...	...	...	9 751	...	...
		1985/86	...	...	...	10 314	3 920	38
		1990/91	...	...	...	11 705	4 820	41
		1991/92	...	...	...	14 411	6 427	45
		1992/93	...	...	...	10 565	5 070	48
Uruguay‡	Total second level	1980	...	...	...	148 294	78 487	53
		1985	...	...	...	213 774	...	...
		1990	...	...	...	265 947	...	...
		1992	...	...	...	272 622	...	...
		1993	...	...	...	266 840	...	...
		1994	...	...	...	263 180	140 579	53

Second level: teachers and pupils 3.7
Second degré: personnel enseignant et élèves
Segundo grado: personal docente y alumnos

Country Pays País	Type of education Type d'enseignement Tipo de enseñanza	Year Année Año	Teaching staff Personnel enseignant Personal docente			Pupils enrolled Élèves inscrits Alumnos matriculados		
			Total	Female Féminin Femenino	% F	Total	Female Féminin Femenino	% F
			(1)	(2)	(3)	(4)	(5)	(6)
Uruguay‡ (cont)	General	1980	...	...	...	125 438	72 390	58
		1985	...	...	...	188 176	...	...
		1990	...	...	...	223 597	...	...
		1992	...	...	...	227 060	...	...
		1993	...	...	...	221 260	...	...
		1994	...	...	...	220 353	120 447	55
	Teacher-training		-	-	-	-	-	-
	Vocational	1980	...	...	...	22 856	6 097	27
		1985	...	...	...	25 598	11 144	44
		1990	...	...	...	42 350	20 327	48
		1992	...	...	...	45 562	21 726	48
		1993	...	...	...	45 580	...	...
		1994	...	...	...	42 827	20 132	47
Venezuela‡	Total second level	1980/81	...	...	...	222 267	128 340	58
		1985/86	60 112	32 957	55	268 580	151 002	56
		1990/91	30 844	15 860	51	281 419	160 587	57
		1991/92	32 572	16 905	52	289 430	164 685	57
		1992/93	34 183	17 861	52	298 534	171 018	57
		1993/94	33 692	17 903	53	311 209	179 920	58
	General	1980/81	...	...	...	154 626	...	...
		1985/86	...	...	...	213 697	120 860	57
		1990/91	...	...	...	231 659	133 852	58
		1991/92	...	...	...	238 417	137 308	58
		1992/93	...	...	...	245 770	142 198	58
	Teacher-training	1980/81	...	...	...	24 414	...	...
		1985/86	-	-	-	-	-	-
		1990/91	-	-	-	-	-	-
		1991/92	-	-	-	-	-	-
		1992/93	-	-	-	-	-	-
		1993/94	-	-	-	-	-	-
	Vocational	1980/81	...	...	...	43 227	...	...
		1985/86	...	...	...	54 883	30 142	55
		1990/91	...	...	...	49 760	26 735	54
		1991/92	...	...	...	51 013	27 377	54
		1992/93	...	...	...	52 764	28 820	55
Asia								
Afghanistan‡	Total second level	1980	7 532	...	...	136 898	...	...
		1985	...	...	...	...	...	...
		1990	7 356	3 269	44	182 340	92 083	51
		1993	12 448	6 522	52	332 170	85 692	26
		1994	17 548	6 042	34	497 762	101 282	20
		1995	...	...	...	512 851	130 136	25
	General	1980	6 270	1 331	21	124 488	26 143	21
		1985	5 715	1 887	33	105 032	33 248	32
		1990	7 356	3 269	44	182 340	92 083	51
		1993	12 448	6 522	52	332 170	85 692	26
		1994	17 548	6 042	34	497 762	101 282	20
		1995	...	...	...	512 851	130 136	25
	Teacher-training		-	-	-	-	-	-
	Vocational	1980	1 262	...	...	12 410	...	...
		1990	-	-	-	-	-	-
		1993	-	-	-	-	-	-
		1994	-	-	-	-	-	-
		1995	-	-	-	-	-	-
Armenia	Total second level	1993/94	...	...	...	380 113	196 462	52
	General	1993/94	...	...	...	359 084	...	...
	Teacher-training	1993/94	-	-	-	-	-	-
	Vocational	1993/94	...	...	...	21 029	...	...
Azerbaijan	Total second level	1980/81	...	...	...	...	...	...
		1985/86	...	...	...	...	...	...
		1990/91	...	...	...	856 874	418 859	49
		1991/92	...	...	...	869 984	424 661	49
		1992/93	...	...	...	878 598	425 498	48
		1993/94	...	...	...	869 045	417 094	48
	General	1980/81	...	...	...	941 742	...	...
		1985/86	...	...	...	853 074	...	...
		1990/91	...	...	...	816 869	405 488	50
		1991/92	...	...	...	831 338	411 473	49
		1992/93	...	...	...	843 440	412 068	49
		1993/94	...	...	...	838 546	405 155	48

3.7 Second level: teachers and pupils
Second degré: personnel enseignant et élèves
Segundo grado: personal docente y alumnos

Country / Pays / País	Type of education / Type d'enseignement / Tipo de enseñanza	Year / Année / Año	Teaching staff Personnel enseignant Personal docente			Pupils enrolled Élèves inscrits Alumnos matriculados		
			Total	Female Féminin Femenino	% F	Total	Female Féminin Femenino	% F
			(1)	(2)	(3)	(4)	(5)	(6)
Azerbaijan (cont)	Teacher-training	1990/91	...	...	...	576	542	94
		1991/92	...	...	...	678	657	97
		1992/93	...	...	...	786	761	97
		1993/94	...	...	...	721	714	99
	Vocational	1980/81	...	...	...	51 764	16 488	32
		1985/86	...	...	...	62 704	...	...
		1990/91	...	...	...	39 429	12 829	33
		1991/92	...	...	...	37 968	12 531	33
		1992/93	...	...	...	34 372	12 669	37
		1993/94	...	...	...	29 778	11 225	38
Bahrain‡	Total second level	1980/81	1 184	603	51	26 528	12 092	46
		1985/86	2 056	945	46	38 577	18 567	48
		1990/91	2 742	1 370	50	47 005	23 550	50
		1992/93	3 132	1 599	51	51 513	25 804	50
		1993/94	3 166	1 594	50	54 193	27 073	50
		1994/95	3 125	1 580	51	56 057	27 857	50
	General	1980/81	...	...	...	23 718	11 104	47
		1985/86	1 490	815	55	30 707	15 813	51
		1990/91	1 982	1 164	59	40 778	21 934	54
		1992/93	2 309	1 389	60	45 120	24 214	54
		1993/94	2 343	1 413	60	47 417	25 345	53
		1994/95	2 305	1 405	61	48 944	26 089	53
	Teacher-training		-	-	-	-	-	-
	Vocational	1980/81	...	...	...	2 810	988	35
		1985/86	566	130	23	7 870	2 754	35
		1990/91	760	206	27	6 227	1 616	26
		1992/93	823	210	26	6 393	1 590	25
		1993/94	823	181	22	6 776	1 728	26
		1994/95	820	175	21	7 113	1 768	25
Bangladesh	Total second level	1980	111 927	7 489	7	2 659 208	636 584	24
		1985	112 700	9 575	8	3 125 219	875 353	28
		1990	130 949	12 507	10	3 592 995	*1 180 440	*33
	General	1980	110 096	7 314	7	2 632 904	634 372	24
		1985	110 757	9 426	9	3 097 871	868 411	28
		1990	128 389	12 368	10	3 562 194	1 176 122	33
	Teacher-training	1980	772	127	16	6 704	1 782	27
		1985	516	101	20	8 303	5 947	72
		1990	502	91	18	5 010	2 348	47
	Vocational	1980	1 059	48	5	19 600	430	2
		1985	1 427	48	3	19 045	995	5
		1990	2 058	48	2	25 791	*1 970	*8
Bhutan‡	Total second level	1985	...	...	...	6 094	...	...
		1993	...	...	...	...	...	...
		1994	...	...	...	...	...	...
	General	1985	...	...	...	3 780	912	24
		1993	...	...	...	5 321	1 917	36
		1994	...	...	...	7 299	2 805	38
	Teacher-training	1985	...	...	...	95	...	...
		1993	16	...	...	119	46	39
		1994	27	...	...	160	46	29
	Vocational	1985	...	...	...	2 219	...	...
Brunei Darussalam	Total second level	1980	1 413	479	34	17 441	8 716	50
		1985	1 893	...	...	20 462	...	...
		1991	2 172	972	45	25 699	12 937	50
		1992	2 248	1 032	46	26 836	13 710	51
		1993	2 337	1 054	45	28 210	14 381	51
		1994	2 413	1 046	43	28 851	14 605	51
	General	1980	1 214	453	37	16 532	8 349	51
		1985	1 572	...	...	18 889	...	...
		1991	1 865	901	48	24 142	12 306	51
		1992	1 922	952	50	25 115	13 011	52
		1993	1 948	962	49	26 199	13 522	52
		1994	1 975	942	48	26 700	13 691	51
	Teacher-training	1980	81	23	28	450	296	66
		1985	100	...	...	598	...	...
		1991	25	11	44	369	207	56
		1992	26	12	46	358	202	56
		1993	25	12	48	418	225	54
		1994	58	18	31	506	253	50

Second level: teachers and pupils
Second degré: personnel enseignant et élèves
Segundo grado: personal docente y alumnos   **3.7**

Country Pays País	Type of education Type d'enseignement Tipo de enseñanza	Year Année Año	Teaching staff Personnel enseignant Personal docente			Pupils enrolled Élèves inscrits Alumnos matriculados		
			Total	Female Féminin Femenino	% F	Total	Female Féminin Femenino	% F
			(1)	(2)	(3)	(4)	(5)	(6)
Brunei Darussalam (cont)	Vocational	1980	118	3	3	459	71	15
		1985	221	...	...	975	...	...
		1991	282	60	21	1 188	424	36
		1992	300	68	23	1 363	497	36
		1993	364	80	22	1 593	634	40
		1994	380	86	23	1 645	661	40
Cambodia	Total second level	1980/81	...	...	...	...	...	...
		1985/86	...	...	...	314 654	...	...
		1990/91	...	...	...	264 419	...	...
		1993/94	...	...	...	...	...	...
		1994/95	...	...	...	...	...	...
	General	1980/81	699	...	...	17 846	...	...
		1985/86	8 033	...	...	311 795	116 721	37
		1990/91	16 408	4 533	28	248 968	...	...
		1993/94	16 622	...	...	285 779	105 170	37
		1994/95	16 349	4 513	28	297 555	111 798	38
	Teacher-training	1990/91	...	...	...	7 356	...	...
	Vocational	1990/91	...	...	...	8 095	1 395	17
China	Total second level	1980/81	3 171 564	787 700	25	56 778 008	22 341 014	39
		1985/86	2 966 400	835 500	28	50 926 400	20 492 600	40
		1990/91	3 491 200	1 114 900	32	51 054 100	21 557 600	42
		1991/92	3 557 000	1 166 900	33	52 267 900	22 450 900	43
		1992/93	3 624 200	1 222 200	34	53 544 000	23 258 300	43
		1993/94	3 667 800	1 265 900	35	53 837 300	23 748 200	44
	General	1980/81	3 019 700	750 300	25	55 081 000	21 801 000	40
		1985/86	2 651 600	743 900	28	47 059 600	18 931 300	40
		1990/91	3 032 600	955 700	32	45 859 600	19 201 100	42
		1991/92	3 090 000	999 900	32	46 835 000	19 976 400	43
		1992/93	3 141 100	1 045 500	33	47 708 000	20 565 100	43
		1993/94	3 166 800	1 078 100	34	47 391 100	20 716 800	44
	Teacher-training	1980/81	37 664	8 300	22	482 108	125 214	26
		1985/86	46 000	14 200	31	558 200	219 300	39
		1990/91	58 500	20 200	35	677 300	355 000	52
		1991/92	57 200	20 200	35	661 400	351 900	53
		1992/93	57 000	20 700	36	665 600	365 900	55
		1993/94	58 100	21 700	37	722 000	414 000	57
	Vocational	1980/81	114 200	29 100	25	1 214 900	414 800	34
		1985/86	268 800	77 400	29	3 308 600	1 342 000	41
		1990/91	400 100	139 000	35	4 517 200	2 001 500	44
		1991/92	409 800	146 800	36	4 771 500	2 122 600	44
		1992/93	426 100	156 000	37	5 170 400	2 327 300	45
		1993/94	442 900	166 100	38	5 724 200	2 617 400	46
Cyprus‡	Total second level	1980/81	2 953	1 237	42	47 599	23 286	49
		1985/86	3 138	1 367	44	46 159	22 829	49
		1990/91	3 735	1 710	46	44 614	21 971	49
		1992/93	4 217	2 037	48	51 641	25 514	49
		1993/94	4 459	2 169	49	54 687	26 933	49
		1994/95	4 641	2 323	50	57 804	28 390	49
	General	1980/81	2 449	1 140	47	41 794	22 463	54
		1985/86	...	...	...	42 285	22 362	53
		1990/91	3 288	1 630	50	41 584	21 449	52
		1992/93	3 734	1 931	52	48 123	24 879	52
		1993/94	3 935	2 053	52	50 870	26 226	52
		1994/95	4 088	2 184	53	53 738	27 598	51
	Teacher-training		-	-	-	-	-	-
	Vocational	1980/81	504	97	19	5 805	823	14
		1985/86	...	...	...	3 874	467	12
		1990/91	447	80	18	3 030	522	17
		1992/93	483	106	22	3 518	635	18
		1993/94	524	116	22	3 817	707	19
		1994/95	553	139	25	4 066	792	19
Georgia	Total second level	1994/95	...	...	...	...	...	...
	General	1994/95	62 396	37 293	60	417 246	203 695	49
Hong Kong‡	Total second level	1980/81	15 986	7 784	49	468 975	231 238	49
		1985/86	18 773	9 169	49	450 367	222 954	50
		1990/91	...	...	...	...	...	...
		1992/93	...	...	...	...	...	...
		1993/94	...	...	...	...	...	...
		1994/95	...	...	...	...	...	...

3.7 Second level: teachers and pupils
Second degré: personnel enseignant et élèves
Segundo grado: personal docente y alumnos

Country Pays País	Type of education Type d'enseignement Tipo de enseñanza	Year Année Año	Teaching staff Personnel enseignant Personal docente			Pupils enrolled Élèves inscrits Alumnos matriculados		
			Total	Female Féminin Femenino	% F	Total	Female Féminin Femenino	% F
			(1)	(2)	(3)	(4)	(5)	(6)
Hong Kong‡ (cont)	General	1980/81	...	...	...	437 956	221 280	51
		1985/86	...	...	...	411 388	211 197	51
		1990/91	20 159	...	...	431 381	...	...
		1992/93	20 900	...	...	445 785	...	...
		1993/94	21 391	...	...	455 935	...	...
		1994/95	21 444	...	...	458 199	...	...
	Teacher-training		-	-	-	-	-	-
	Vocational	1980/81	...	...	...	31 019	9 958	32
		1985/86	...	...	...	38 979	11 757	30
India‡	Total second level	1980/81	...	...	...	32 748 397	10 391 202	32
		1985/86	...	...	...	44 484 544	14 814 335	33
		1990/91	...	...	...	...	...	...
		1991/92	...	...	...	...	...	...
		1992/93	...	...	...	62 245 635	22 819 986	37
		1993/94	...	...	...	64 115 978	23 887 394	37
	General	1980/81	1 731 978	511 841	30	32 323 173	10 253 252	32
		1985/86	2 126 733	660 079	31	43 807 380	14 614 475	33
		1990/91	2 331 797	768 315	33	54 180 391	19 332 539	36
		1991/92	2 381 408	783 517	33	55 673 664	20 041 128	36
		1992/93	2 435 293	791 747	33	61 418 729	22 714 721	37
		1993/94	2 485 158	836 754	34	63 262 226	23 775 784	38
	Teacher-training	1980/81	977	351	36	15 349	8 300	54
		1985/86	-	-	-	-	-	-
		1990/91	-	-	-	-	-	-
		1991/92	-	-	-	-	-	-
		1992/93	-	-	-	-	-	-
		1993/94	-	-	-	-	-	-
	Vocational	1980/81	...	...	...	409 875	129 650	32
		1985/86	...	...	...	677 164	199 860	30
		1992/93	...	...	...	826 906	105 265	13
		1993/94	...	...	...	853 752	111 610	13
Indonesia	Total second level	1980/81	385 186	...	...	5 721 815	...	...
		1985/86	620 857	...	...	9 479 086	...	...
		1990/91	...	...	...	10 965 430	4 882 717	45
		1991/92	806 384	282 717	35	10 920 580	4 875 804	45
		1992/93	793 558	276 943	35	10 969 305	4 838 238	44
		1993/94	806 396	288 355	36	11 360 349	5 132 921	45
	General	1980/81	...	...	...	4 879 361	...	...
		1985/86	...	...	...	8 311 594	...	...
		1990/91	...	...	...	9 510 766	4 316 625	45
		1991/92	...	...	...	9 506 882	4 320 819	45
		1992/93	...	...	...	9 538 778	4 269 629	45
		1993/94	...	...	...	9 919 480	4 557 307	46
	Teacher-training	1980/81	16 648	...	...	232 024	139 271	60
		1985/86	20 172	...	...	297 651	...	...
		1990/91	...	...	...	40 297	20 154	50
		1991/92	-	-	-	-	-	-
		1992/93	-	-	-	-	-	-
		1993/94	-	-	-	-	-	-
	Vocational	1980/81	...	...	...	610 430	166 872	27
		1985/86	...	...	...	869 841	...	...
		1990/91	...	...	...	1 414 367	545 938	39
		1991/92	...	...	...	1 413 698	554 985	39
		1992/93	...	...	...	1 430 527	568 609	40
		1993/94	...	...	...	1 440 869	575 614	40
Iran, Islamic Republic of	Total second level	1980/81	...	...	...	2 718 461	1 016 145	37
		1985/86	...	...	...	...	...	...
		1990/91	216 273	87 849	41	5 084 832	2 103 856	41
		1992/93	232 758	96 021	41	6 322 988	2 696 570	43
		1993/94	249 812	106 361	43	7 059 037	3 064 706	43
		1994/95	249 307	109 352	44	7 652 829	3 402 131	44
	General	1980/81	...	...	...	2 516 592	984 496	39
		1985/86	195 319	75 689	39	3 204 445	1 297 482	40
		1990/91	197 630	85 054	43	4 822 087	2 047 677	42
		1992/93	211 711	92 524	44	5 995 051	2 619 306	44
		1993/94	227 961	102 648	45	6 683 832	2 969 164	44
		1994/95	228 889	105 882	46	7 284 611	3 310 470	45
	Teacher-training	1980/81	-	-	-	-	-	-
		1990/91	959	226	24	32 684	10 871	33
		1992/93	1 590	514	32	48 256	19 618	41
		1993/94	1 159	334	29	34 721	13 339	38
		1994/95	538	158	29	21 210	7 605	36

Second level: teachers and pupils **3.7**
Second degré: personnel enseignant et élèves
Segundo grado: personal docente y alumnos

Country Pays País	Type of education Type d'enseignement Tipo de enseñanza	Year Année Año	Teaching staff Personnel enseignant Personal docente			Pupils enrolled Élèves inscrits Alumnos matriculados		
			Total	Female Féminin Femenino	% F	Total	Female Féminin Femenino	% F
			(1)	(2)	(3)	(4)	(5)	(6)
Iran, Islamic Rep. of (cont)	Vocational	1980/81	...	...	...	201 869	31 649	16
		1985/86	20 665	2 778	13	195 352	45 942	24
		1990/91	17 684	2 569	15	230 061	45 308	20
		1992/93	19 457	2 983	15	279 681	57 646	21
		1993/94	20 692	3 379	16	340 484	82 203	24
		1994/95	19 880	3 312	17	347 008	84 056	24
Iraq	Total second level	1980/81	33 514	13 400	40	1 033 418	333 771	32
		1985/86	42 998	22 706	53	1 190 833	419 860	35
		1990/91	...	...	...	...	...	...
		1992/93	59 117	32 021	54	1 144 938	433 787	38
	General	1980/81	28 552	11 890	42	954 536	303 154	32
		1985/86	35 143	19 238	55	1 038 627	372 096	36
		1990/91	44 772	27 269	61	1 023 710	398 765	39
		1992/93	48 496	26 551	55	992 617	386 522	39
	Teacher-training	1980/81	814	517	64	21 958	13 939	63
		1985/86	1 110	605	55	26 767	15 764	59
		1992/93	1 303	633	49	22 018	13 571	62
	Vocational	1980/81	4 148	993	24	56 924	16 678	29
		1985/86	6 745	2 863	42	125 439	32 000	26
		1992/93	9 318	4 837	52	130 303	33 694	26
Israel‡	Total second level	1980/81	31 650	18 150	57	199 859	...	...
		1985/86	37 735	...	...	251 466	129 110	51
		1990/91	46 473	29 256	63	309 098	156 653	51
		1991/92	48 677	30 802	63	326 319	165 370	51
		1992/93	50 605	32 650	65	334 290	169 589	51
		1993/94	53 581	34 682	65	338 288	170 029	50
	General	1980/81	...	...	...	117 527	...	...
		1985/86	...	...	...	150 996	84 118	56
		1990/91	...	...	...	194 022	104 377	54
		1991/92	...	...	...	204 581	110 570	54
		1992/93	...	...	...	212 597	114 887	54
		1993/94	...	...	...	215 938	114 667	53
	Teacher-training		-	-	-	-	-	-
	Vocational	1980/81	...	...	...	82 332	38 236	46
		1985/86	...	...	...	100 470	44 992	45
		1990/91	...	...	...	115 076	52 276	45
		1991/92	...	...	...	121 738	54 800	45
		1992/93	...	...	...	121 693	54 702	45
		1993/94	...	...	...	122 350	55 362	45
Japan	Total second level	1980/81	554 078	145 943	26	9 557 563	4 718 610	49
		1985/86	619 105	173 420	28	11 058 133	5 446 781	49
		1990/91	658 569	197 486	30	11 025 720	5 418 667	49
		1991/92	663 215	203 280	31	10 676 866	5 248 048	49
		1992/93	...	...	...	10 255 337	5 054 022	49
		1993/94	695 707	230 677	33	10 202 510	5 013 127	49
	General	1980/81	...	...	...	8 146 845	4 057 997	50
		1985/86	...	...	...	9 635 116	4 786 810	50
		1990/91	...	...	...	9 528 674	4 735 497	50
		1991/92	...	...	...	9 224 769	4 588 120	50
		1993/94	588 460	200 744	34	8 719 312	4 338 597	50
	Teacher-training		-	-	-	-	-	-
	Vocational	1980/81	...	...	...	1 410 718	660 613	47
		1985/86	...	...	...	1 423 017	659 971	46
		1990/91	...	...	...	1 497 046	683 170	46
		1991/92	...	...	...	1 452 097	659 928	45
		1993/94	107 247	29 933	28	1 483 198	674 530	45
Jordan‡	Total second level	1980/81	12 848	5 486	43	266 368	119 022	45
		1985/86	19 174	8 690	45	335 835	159 899	48
		1990/91	6 940	3 257	47	100 953	47 498	47
		1991/92	6 030	2 869	48	109 429	53 188	49
		1992/93	...	...	...	113 910	56 429	50
		1993/94	7 150	3 378	47	123 825	61 710	50
	General	1980/81	11 999	5 248	44	252 367	114 833	46
		1985/86	17 074	7 897	46	305 046	147 809	48
		1990/91	4 876	2 477	51	75 915	38 845	51
		1991/92	3 983	2 067	52	83 930	43 727	52
		1992/93	...	...	...	86 475	46 535	54
		1993/94	4 597	2 425	53	93 773	51 155	55
	Teacher-training		-	-	-	-	-	-

3.7 Second level: teachers and pupils
Second degré: personnel enseignant et élèves
Segundo grado: personal docente y alumnos

Country / Pays / País	Type of education / Type d'enseignement / Tipo de enseñanza	Year / Année / Año	Teaching staff / Personnel enseignant / Personal docente			Pupils enrolled / Élèves inscrits / Alumnos matriculados		
			Total	Female / Féminin / Femenino	% F	Total	Female / Féminin / Femenino	% F
			(1)	(2)	(3)	(4)	(5)	(6)
Jordan‡ (cont)	Vocational	1980/81	849	238	28	14 001	4 189	30
		1985/86	2 100	793	38	30 789	12 090	39
		1990/91	2 064	780	38	25 038	8 653	35
		1991/92	2 047	802	39	25 499	9 461	37
		1992/93	2 107	799	38	27 435	9 894	36
		1993/94	2 553	953	37	30 052	10 555	35
Kazakstan	Total second level	1980/81	...	...	...	1 996 100	...	...
		1985/86	...	...	...	2 173 900	...	...
		1990/91	...	...	...	2 144 400	...	...
		1991/92	...	...	...	2 115 400	...	...
		1992/93	...	...	...	2 064 100	...	...
		1993/94	...	...	...	2 019 700	...	...
	General	1980/81	...	...	...	1 761 000	...	...
		1985/86	123 700	88 400	71	1 910 800	...	...
		1990/91	157 800	116 800	74	1 918 700	...	...
		1991/92	161 500	118 400	73	1 897 000	...	...
		1992/93	174 000	129 700	75	1 861 000	...	...
		1993/94	178 900	133 000	74	1 830 600	944 200	52
	Teacher-training		-	-	-	-	-	-
	Vocational	1980/81	...	...	...	235 100	...	...
		1985/86	...	...	...	263 100	...	...
		1990/91	...	...	...	225 700	...	...
		1991/92	...	...	...	218 400	...	...
		1992/93	...	...	...	203 100	...	...
		1993/94	...	...	...	189 100	...	...
Korea, Democratic People's Rep. of	Total second level	1987/88	...	...	...	...	...	...
	General	1987/88	111 000	67 000	60	2 468 000	1 198 000	49
	Teacher-training	1987/88	-	-	-	-	-	-
Korea, Republic of	Total second level	1980/81	109 546	28 127	26	4 285 889	1 948 972	45
		1985/86	140 942	41 736	30	4 934 975	2 334 562	47
		1990/91	180 724	61 875	34	4 559 557	2 176 401	48
		1993/94	194 809	70 103	36	4 479 463	2 160 591	48
		1994/95	196 839	71 509	36	4 568 829	2 206 746	48
		1995/96	197 494	72 545	37	4 639 728	2 242 264	48
	General	1980/81	82 338	22 744	28	3 404 602	1 561 667	46
		1985/86	109 123	34 547	32	4 038 242	1 890 076	47
		1990/91	145 613	53 379	37	3 735 151	1 738 762	47
		1993/94	152 214	59 413	39	3 619 938	1 702 482	47
		1994/95	155 474	61 058	39	3 717 334	1 757 982	47
		1995/96	155 324	61 629	40	3 727 615	1 761 360	47
	Teacher-training		-	-	-	-	-	-
	Vocational	1980/81	27 208	5 383	20	881 287	387 305	44
		1985/86	31 819	7 189	23	896 733	444 486	50
		1990/91	35 111	8 496	24	824 406	437 639	53
		1993/94	42 595	10 690	25	859 525	458 109	53
		1994/95	41 365	10 451	25	851 495	448 764	53
		1995/96	42 170	10 916	26	912 113	480 904	53
Kuwait	Total second level	1980/81	15 342	7 607	50	181 882	83 227	46
		1985/86	18 795	9 726	52	239 581	112 780	47
		1990/91	...	...	...	...	...	...
		1992/93	16 081	8 517	53	177 675	87 383	49
		1993/94	17 424	9 294	53	187 941	92 507	49
		1994/95	18 287	9 780	53	198 707	97 794	49
	General	1980/81	15 257	7 607	50	181 461	83 227	46
		1985/86	18 650	9 709	52	238 420	112 692	47
		1990/91	13 956	7 332	53	140 324	68 860	49
		1992/93	15 914	8 483	53	176 572	87 167	49
		1993/94	17 245	9 253	54	186 839	92 138	49
		1994/95	18 072	9 726	54	197 326	97 318	49
	Teacher-training		-	-	-	-	-	-
	Vocational	1980/81	85	-	-	421	-	-
		1985/86	145	17	12	1 161	88	8
		1992/93	167	34	20	1 103	216	20
		1993/94	179	41	23	1 102	369	33
		1994/95	215	54	25	1 381	476	34
Kyrgyzstan	Total second level	1980/81	...	...	...	631 400	308 500	49
		1985/86	...	...	...	657 300	320 700	49
		1990/91	...	...	...	651 200	327 400	50
		1992/93	48 700	29 700	61	633 500	319 900	50
		1993/94	46 000	29 300	64	607 700	310 500	51
		1994/95	44 918	30 058	67	606 381	...	...

Second level: teachers and pupils **3.7**
Second degré: personnel enseignant et élèves
Segundo grado: personal docente y alumnos

Country Pays País	Type of education Type d'enseignement Tipo de enseñanza	Year Année Año	Teaching staff Personnel enseignant Personal docente			Pupils enrolled Élèves inscrits Alumnos matriculados		
			Total	Female Féminin Femenino	% F	Total	Female Féminin Femenino	% F
			(1)	(2)	(3)	(4)	(5)	(6)
Kyrgyzstan (cont)	General	1980/81	29 200	16 800	58	580 200	282 900	49
		1985/86	34 000	21 300	63	592 000	288 100	49
		1990/91	42 900	29 400	69	600 700	302 200	50
		1992/93	43 600	28 000	64	586 200	296 300	51
		1993/94	41 500	27 800	67	565 600	289 500	51
		1994/95	40 718	28 458	70	565 681	289 151	51
	Teacher-training		-	-	-	-	-	-
	Vocational	1980/81	...	...	...	51 200	25 600	50
		1985/86	...	...	...	65 300	32 600	50
		1990/91	...	...	...	50 500	25 200	50
		1992/93	5 100	1 700	33	47 300	23 600	50
		1993/94	4 500	1 500	33	42 100	21 000	50
		1994/95	4 200	1 600	38	40 700	...	...
Lao People's Democratic Republic	Total second level	1980/81	4 703	...	...	90 435	34 913	39
		1985/86	10 146	3 510	35	113 630	46 490	41
		1989/90	11 720	4 548	39	137 898	55 027	40
		1991/92	10 198	2 877	28	125 702	48 964	39
		1992/93	13 020	4 934	38	140 777	53 592	38
		1993/94	12 713	4 831	38	155 366	60 023	39
	General	1980/81	3 764	967	26	78 925	30 306	38
		1985/86	8 032	3 034	38	97 197	41 033	42
		1989/90	10 048	4 002	40	125 636	50 009	40
		1991/92	8 936	2 454	27	117 504	45 749	39
		1992/93	10 956	4 322	39	126 976	48 717	38
		1993/94	11 066	4 331	39	143 673	55 942	39
	Teacher-training	1980/81	650	223	34	9 508	4 048	43
		1985/86	1 246	303	24	9 634	3 796	39
		1989/90	1 105	429	39	7 699	3 512	46
		1991/92	718	297	41	4 495	1 973	44
		1992/93	842	293	35	5 398	2 273	42
		1993/94	611	228	37	4 065	1 720	42
	Vocational	1980/81	289	...	...	2 002	559	28
		1985/86	868	173	20	6 799	1 661	24
		1989/90	567	117	21	4 563	1 506	33
		1991/92	544	126	23	3 703	1 242	34
		1992/93	1 222	319	26	8 403	2 602	31
		1993/94	1 036	272	26	7 628	2 361	31
Lebanon	Total second level	1980/81	...	...	...	287 310		...
		1986/87	...	...	...	...	...	...
		1991/92	...	...	...	...	...	...
		1993/94	...	...	...	...	...	...
		1994/95	...	...	...	...	...	...
	General	1980/81	21 344	...	...	254 444	...	...
		1986/87	...	...	...	279 849	...	...
		1991/92	...	...	...	248 097	131 352	53
		1993/94	...	...	...	261 341	137 547	53
		1994/95	...	...	...	277 646	146 780	53
	Teacher-training	1980/81	392	123	31	1 663	1 316	79
	Vocational	1980/81	...	...	...	31 203	...	...
		1986/87	4 400	...	...	31 045	*12 480	*40
		1991/92	4 240	310	7	37 403	14 400	39
		1993/94	3 866	301	8	39 933	15 834	40
		1994/95	...	...	...	45 776	21 441	47
Macau	Total second level	1989/90	...	...	...	16 687	8 760	52
		1991/92	...	...	...	18 978	9 884	52
		1992/93	...	...	...	20 383	10 721	53
	General	1989/90	...	...	...	15 990	8 725	55
		1991/92	...	...	...	18 224	9 828	54
		1992/93	...	...	...	19 526	10 635	54
	Vocational	1989/90	...	...	...	697	35	5
		1991/92	...	...	...	754	56	7
		1992/93	...	...	...	857	86	10
Malaysia	Total second level	1980	47 625	21 436	45	1 083 818	516 114	48
		1985	58 630	27 728	47	1 294 990	635 995	49
		1989/90	74 400	38 130	51	1 456 497	740 060	51
		1991/92	84 744	45 351	54	1 566 790	794 246	51
		1992/93	...	...	...	...	...	...
		1993/94	...	...	...	...	...	...

3.7 Second level: teachers and pupils
Second degré: personnel enseignant et élèves
Segundo grado: personal docente y alumnos

Country / Pays / País	Type of education / Type d'enseignement / Tipo de enseñanza	Year / Année / Año	Teaching staff Personnel enseignant Personal docente			Pupils enrolled Élèves inscrits Alumnos matriculados		
			Total	Female Féminin Femenino	% F	Total	Female Féminin Femenino	% F
			(1)	(2)	(3)	(4)	(5)	(6)
Malaysia (cont)	General	1980	46 163	21 117	46	1 065 787	510 817	48
		1985	56 931	27 320	48	1 274 270	629 983	49
		1989/90	71 439	37 187	52	1 391 037	707 921	51
		1991/92	81 250	44 159	54	1 476 711	755 093	51
		1992/93	...	...	...	1 531 893	788 588	51
		1993/94	84 062	...	...	1 592 099		...
	Teacher-training		-	-	-	-	-	-
	Vocational	1980	1 462	319	22	18 031	5 297	29
		1985	1 699	408	24	20 720	6 012	29
		1989/90	2 961	943	32	65 460	32 139	49
		1991/92	3 494	1 192	34	90 079	39 153	43
Maldives	Total second level	1980	...	...	...	998	...	...
		1992	...	...	...	...	...	...
		1993	...	...	...	...	...	...
	General	1980	...	...	...	875	...	...
		1992	...	...	...	15 933	7 822	49
		1993	...	...	...	18 678	9 268	50
	Teacher-training	1980	-	-	-	-	-	-
		1993	...		...	298	190	64
	Vocational	1980	...	...	...	123	...	...
		1992	...	...	...	154	5	3
Mongolia	Total second level	1980/81	...	...	...	245 600	...	...
		1985/86	...	...	...	...	...	...
		1990/91	...	...	...	...	...	...
		1991/92	...	...	...	...	...	...
		1994/95	12 938	8 585	66	229 769	131 532	57
	General	1980/81	...	...	...	226 900	117 000	52
		1985/86	12 027	...	...	262 600	...	...
		1990/91	14 712	...	...	274 700	...	...
		1991/92	14 251	...	...	257 100	...	...
		1994/95	12 353	8 255	67	222 214	127 868	58
	Teacher-training	1994/95	2	2	100	75	70	93
	Vocational	1985/86	1 842	...	...	23 236	...	...
		1990/91	1 817	...	...	26 431	...	...
		1991/92	1 142	...	...	17 961	...	...
		1994/95	583	328	56	7 480	3 594	48
Myanmar	Total second level	1980/81	31 248	...	...	1 066 300	...	...
		1985/86	53 501	...	...	1 283 586	...	...
		1990/91	...	...	...	...	...	...
		1992/93	...	...	...	...	...	...
		1993/94	...	...	...	...	...	...
		1994/95	...	...	...	...	...	...
	General	1980/81	30 048	...	...	1 046 100	...	...
		1985/86	51 827	34 348	66	1 262 186	589 649	47
		1990/91	65 188	45 166	69	1 271 115	623 992	49
		1992/93	69 983	...	...	1 428 604	...	...
		1993/94	69 441	...	...	1 519 215	...	...
		1994/95	...	...	...	1 779 503	...	...
	Teacher-training	1980/81	394	...	...	5 700	...	...
		1985/86	450	...	...	4 200	...	...
	Vocational	1980/81	806	...	...	14 500	...	...
		1985/86	1 224	...	...	17 200	...	...
		1994/95	599	...	...	6 040	...	...
Nepal‡	Total second level	1980	16 376	1 498	9	512 434	102 502	20
		1985	18 362	...	...	496 921	113 162	23
		1990	22 820	...	...	708 663	205 288	29
		1991	24 632	2 423	10	773 808	232 742	30
		1992	25 357	2 969	12	855 137	272 237	32
		1993	25 881	...	...	910 114		...
Oman	Total second level	1980/81		...	...	16 776	4 058	24
		1985/86	3 845	...	...	48 096	15 556	32
		1990/91	6 533	...	...	102 021	44 805	44
		1992/93	8 537	...	...	140 761	65 437	46
		1993/94	9 449	...	...	162 959	76 470	47
		1994/95	...	...	...	...	...	...
	General	1980/81	1 733	461	27	15 280	3 828	25
		1985/86	3 416	1 117	33	44 931	15 227	34
		1990/91	6 059	2 595	43	99 170	44 587	45
		1992/93	8 112	3 704	46	137 947	65 045	47
		1993/94	9 099	4 231	47	160 654	76 077	47
		1994/95	10 165	4 834	48	178 226	85 017	48

Second level: teachers and pupils 3.7
Second degré: personnel enseignant et élèves
Segundo grado: personal docente y alumnos

Country Pays País	Type of education Type d'enseignement Tipo de enseñanza	Year Année Año	Teaching staff Personnel enseignant Personal docente			Pupils enrolled Élèves inscrits Alumnos matriculados		
			Total	Female Féminin Femenino	% F	Total	Female Féminin Femenino	% F
			(1)	(2)	(3)	(4)	(5)	(6)
Oman (cont)	Teacher-training	1980/81	65	28	43	483	230	48
		1985/86	26	9	35	161	63	39
		1990/91	-	-	-	-	-	-
		1992/93	-	-	-	-	-	-
		1993/94	-	-	-	-	-	-
		1994/95	-	-	-	-	-	-
	Vocational	1980/81	...	...	...	1 013	-	-
		1985/86	403	...	...	3 004	266	9
		1990/91	474	...	...	2 851	218	8
		1992/93	425	...	...	2 814	392	14
		1993/94	350	...	...	2 305	393	17
Pakistan	Total second level	1980/81	123 817	36 815	30	2 165 832	558 029	26
		1985/86	...	...	...	2 923 188	790 805	27
		1990/91	...	...	...	4 345 464	1 350 117	31
		1991/92	...	...	...	5 022 416	1 613 275	32
		1992/93	...	...	...	...	...	...
		1993/94	...	...	...	...	...	...
	General	1980/81	120 646	36 104	30	2 125 418	551 305	26
		1985/86	157 600	49 300	31	2 871 520	779 490	27
		1990/91	...	...	...	4 254 998	1 325 998	31
		1991/92	...	...	...	*4 933 000	*1 588 000	*32
	Teacher-training	1980/81	1 177	316	27	6 922	916	13
		1985/86	...	...	...	10 476	2 116	20
		1990/91	3 309	1 439	43	36 295	13 927	38
		1991/92	2 654	1 408	53	33 149	13 305	40
	Vocational	1980/81	1 994	395	20	33 492	5 808	17
		1985/86	...	...	...	41 192	9 199	22
		1990/91	4 093	1 127	28	54 171	10 192	19
		1991/92	4 047	1 269	31	56 267	11 970	21
		1992/93	6 772	2 790	41	*91 000	*29 000	*32
		1993/94	6 850	2 860	42	*92 000	*30 000	*33
Philippines	Total second level	1980/81	85 779	...	...	2 928 525	1 559 313	53
		1985/86	99 468	...	...	3 214 159	1 608 549	50
		1990/91	121 887	...	...	4 033 597	...	...
		1992/93	...	...	...	4 421 649	...	...
		1993/94	134 898	...	...	4 590 037	...	...
		1994/95	131 831	...	...	4 762 877	...	...
	General	1980/81	85 779	...	...	2 928 525	1 559 313	53
		1985/86	99 468	...	...	3 214 159	1 608 549	50
		1990/91	121 887	...	...	4 033 597	...	...
		1992/93	...	...	...	4 421 649	...	...
		1993/94	134 898	...	...	4 590 037	...	...
		1994/95	131 831	...	...	4 762 877	...	...
	Teacher-training		-	-	-	-	-	-
	Vocational		-	-	-	-	-	-
Qatar	Total second level	1980/81	1 624	817	50	15 901	7 680	48
		1985/86	2 539	1 344	53	22 574	11 310	50
		1990/91	3 547	1 993	56	30 031	15 063	50
		1992/93	5 016	2 973	59	35 013	17 364	50
		1993/94	3 823	2 261	59	36 292	17 828	49
		1994/95	3 858	2 258	59	37 635	18 424	49
	General	1980/81	1 538	817	53	15 461	7 680	50
		1985/86	2 434	1 344	55	21 874	11 310	52
		1990/91	3 420	1 993	58	29 154	15 063	52
		1992/93	4 888	2 973	61	34 231	17 364	51
		1993/94	3 695	2 261	61	35 518	17 828	50
		1994/95	3 738	2 258	60	36 964	18 424	50
	Teacher-training		-	-	-	-	-	-
	Vocational	1980/81	86	-	-	440	-	-
		1985/86	105	-	-	700	-	-
		1990/91	127	-	-	877	-	-
		1992/93	128	-	-	782	-	-
		1993/94	128	-	-	774	-	-
		1994/95	120	-	-	671	-	-
Saudi Arabia‡	Total second level	1980/81	26 634	8 980	34	348 996	132 368	38
		1985/86	42 892	17 280	40	603 127	229 633	38
		1990/91	71 149	29 123	41	892 585	392 136	44
		1991/92	73 230	33 263	45	965 305	426 961	44
		1992/93	92 975	37 553	40	1 073 361	472 972	44
		1993/94	108 820	45 781	42	1 198 607	531 647	44

3.7 Second level: teachers and pupils
Second degré: personnel enseignant et élèves
Segundo grado: personal docente y alumnos

Country Pays País	Type of education Type d'enseignement Tipo de enseñanza	Year Année Año	Teaching staff Personnel enseignant Personal docente			Pupils enrolled Élèves inscrits Alumnos matriculados		
			Total	Female Féminin Femenino	% F	Total	Female Féminin Femenino	% F
			(1)	(2)	(3)	(4)	(5)	(6)
Saudi Arabia‡ (cont)	General	1980/81	24 254	8 058	33	328 328	122 307	37
		1985/86	40 552	16 839	42	582 017	224 785	39
		1990/91	67 956	28 168	41	859 642	379 843	44
		1991/92	69 543	31 929	46	930 186	413 134	44
		1992/93	89 171	36 260	41	1 033 521	455 456	44
		1993/94	102 798	43 837	43	1 151 945	509 683	44
	Teacher-training	1980/81	1 619	922	57	15 562	10 061	65
		1985/86	995	441	44	10 433	4 848	46
		1990/91	639	634	99	8 128	8 106	100
		1991/92	699	699	100	9 945	9 945	100
		1992/93	911	911	100	13 884	13 884	100
		1993/94	1 216	1 216	100	18 589	18 589	100
	Vocational	1980/81	761	-	-	5 106		-
		1985/86	1 345	-	-	10 677	-	-
		1990/91	2 554	321	13	24 815	4 187	17
		1991/92	2 988	635	21	25 174	3 882	15
		1992/93	2 893	382	13	25 956	3 632	14
		1993/94	4 806	728	15	28 073	3 375	12
Singapore‡	Total second level	1980	9 298	4 863	52	180 817	90 306	50
		1985	...	...	...	...	...	...
		1990	...	...	...	...	...	...
		1991	...	...	...	...	...	...
	General	1980	8 275	4 613	56	171 426	88 182	51
		1985	8 562	4 994	58	190 328	96 503	51
		1990	9 197	...	...	191 459	...	...
		1991	9 200	...	...	185 693	...	...
	Teacher-training		-	-	-	-	-	-
	Vocational	1980	1 023	250	24	9 391	2 124	23
Sri Lanka‡	Total second level	1980	...	...	...	1 267 323	...	...
		1985	...	...	...	1 462 794	757 738	52
		1990	108 944	...	...	2 081 842	1 064 399	51
		1992	108 489	63 687	59	2 185 277	1 119 945	51
		1993	106 141	67 864	64	2 246 642	1 149 602	51
		1994	105 916	66 939	63	2 315 541	1 190 755	51
	General	1980	...	...	...	1 258 002	641 045	51
		1985	...	...	...	1 462 794	757 738	52
		1990	108 944	...	...	2 081 842	1 064 399	51
		1992	108 489	63 687	59	2 185 277	1 119 945	51
		1993	106 141	67 864	64	2 246 642	1 149 602	51
		1994	105 916	66 939	63	2 315 541	1 190 755	51
	Teacher-training	1980	689	...	...	9 321	...	...
		1985	-	-	-	-	-	-
		1990	-	-	-	-	-	-
		1992	-	-	-	-	-	-
		1993	-	-	-	-	-	-
		1994	-	-	-	-	-	-
	Vocational		-	-	-	-	-	-
Syrian Arab Republic	Total second level	1980/81	...	...	25	604 327	220 939	37
		1985/86	53 250	13 504	25	870 383	346 467	40
		1990/91	54 115	22 383	41	914 250	379 261	41
		1992/93	58 659	24 580	42	916 950	399 763	44
		1993/94	61 510	25 422	41	923 030	404 597	44
		1994/95	62 080	26 583	43	928 882	412 868	44
	General	1980/81	29 573	6 536	22	577 990	213 345	37
		1985/86	45 912	12 326	27	814 917	332 455	41
		1990/91	44 875	20 151	45	847 783	352 975	42
		1992/93	47 889	21 418	45	845 631	369 642	44
		1993/94	49 951	21 683	43	846 550	370 997	44
		1994/95	50 779	22 720	45	841 964	373 481	44
	Teacher-training	1980/81	...	...	...	147	88	60
		1985/86	-	-	-	-	-	-
		1990/91	-	-	-	-	-	-
		1992/93	-	-	-	-	-	-
		1993/94	-	-	-	-	-	-
		1994/95	-	-	-	-	-	-
	Vocational	1980/81	3 280	...	16	26 190	7 506	29
		1985/86	7 338	1 178	16	55 466	14 012	25
		1990/91	9 240	2 232	24	66 467	26 286	40
		1992/93	10 770	3 162	29	71 319	30 121	42
		1993/94	11 559	3 739	32	76 480	33 600	44
		1994/95	11 301	3 863	34	86 918	39 387	45
Tajikistan	Total second level	1992/93	...	...	...	...	...	...
		1993/94	...	...	...	...	...	...

Second level: teachers and pupils　**3.7**
Second degré: personnel enseignant et élèves
Segundo grado: personal docente y alumnos

Country Pays País	Type of education Type d'enseignement Tipo de enseñanza	Year Année Año	Teaching staff Personnel enseignant Personal docente			Pupils enrolled Élèves inscrits Alumnos matriculados		
			Total	Female Féminin Femenino	% F	Total	Female Féminin Femenino	% F
			(1)	(2)	(3)	(4)	(5)	(6)
Tajikistan (cont)	General	1992/93	64 000	22 000	34	736 700	354 900	48
		1993/94	62 700	21 900	35	652 700	308 500	47
Thailand‡	Total second level	1980/81	...	...	...	1 919 967	...	...
		1985/86	...	...	...		...	...
		1990/91	133 882	...	...	2 230 403	1 076 896	48
		1992/93	141 632	...	...	2 717 672	1 323 630	49
		1993/94	151 008	...	...	3 174 062	...	...
		1994/95	...	...	...	3 432 431	...	...
	General	1980/81	70 201	39 818	57	1 617 465	740 077	46
		1985/86	102 763	...	...	1 870 360	...	...
		1990/91	106 264	...	...	1 864 465	917 289	49
		1992/93	112 073	...	...	2 269 498	1 123 538	50
		1993/94	...	...	...	2 684 397	...	...
		1994/95	...	...	...	2 886 640	...	...
	Teacher-training	1980/81	...	...	...	5 388	2 746	51
		1990/91	-	-	-	-	-	-
		1992/93	-	-	-	-	-	-
		1993/94	-	-	-	-	-	-
		1994/95	-	-	-	-	-	-
	Vocational	1980/81	...	...	...	297 114	...	...
		1985/86	*19 278	...	...	373 013	...	...
		1990/91	27 618	...	...	365 938	159 607	44
		1992/93	29 559	...	...	448 174	200 092	45
		1993/94	...	...	...	489 665	...	...
		1994/95	...	...	...	545 791	...	...
Turkey	Total second level	1980/81	112 178	...	...	2 217 909	...	...
		1985/86	138 640	49 601	36	2 927 692	1 030 948	35
		1990/91	159 401	61 696	39	3 808 142	1 426 071	37
		1991/92	170 611	66 399	39	3 987 423	1 514 908	38
		1992/93	178 802	70 156	39	4 299 810	1 653 221	38
		1993/94	188 545	74 635	40	4 522 963	1 755 686	39
	General	1980/81	77 197	27 775	36	1 681 792	589 994	35
		1985/86	94 325	33 992	36	2 300 052	853 588	37
		1990/91	109 136	42 545	39	2 897 655	1 115 578	38
		1991/92	114 496	44 897	39	2 997 900	1 167 498	39
		1992/93	119 291	47 129	40	3 216 418	1 261 940	39
		1993/94	126 627	50 640	40	3 380 772	1 332 867	39
	Teacher-training	1980/81	1 012	...	...	15 785	...	...
		1985/86	1 022	306	30	11 357	3 964	35
		1990/91	924	258	28	10 282	4 059	39
		1991/92	1 116	341	31	12 607	4 937	39
		1992/93	1 239	366	30	17 217	6 911	40
		1993/94	-	-	-	-	-	...
	Vocational	1980/81	33 969	...	...	520 332	...	...
		1985/86	43 293	15 303	35	616 283	173 306	28
		1990/91	49 341	18 893	38	900 205	306 434	34
		1991/92	54 999	21 161	38	976 916	342 473	35
		1992/93	58 272	22 661	39	1 066 175	384 370	36
		1993/94	61 918	23 995	39	1 142 191	422 819	37
United Arab Emirates‡	Total second level	1980/81	...	...	...	32 362	14 451	45
		1985/86	4 237	2 077	49	62 082	29 880	48
		1990/91	8 565	4 695	55	107 881	54 342	50
		1992/93	10 537	5 876	56	129 683	65 756	51
		1993/94	11 637	6 464	56	145 143	73 403	51
		1994/95	12 602	6 978	55	159 840	80 380	50
	General	1980/81	2 829	1 344	48	31 940	14 451	45
		1985/86	...	...	...	61 478	29 880	49
		1990/91	...	...	...	107 115	54 342	51
		1992/93	...	...	...	128 643	65 756	51
		1993/94	...	...	...	144 000	73 403	51
		1994/95	12 281	6 978	57	157 584	80 380	51
	Teacher-training		-	-	-	-	-	-
	Vocational	1980/81	...	...	...	422	-	-
		1985/86	...	...	...	604	-	-
		1990/91	...	...	...	766	-	-
		1992/93	...	...	...	1 040	-	-
		1993/94	...	...	...	1 143	-	-
		1994/95	321	-	-	2 256	-	-
Uzbekistan	Total second level	1980/81	192 100	...	...	2 879 300	...	...
		1985/86	226 300	...	...	3 115 000	...	...
		1990/91	302 400	...	...	3 194 600	...	...
		1992/93	324 300	...	...	3 194 000	...	...
		1993/94	337 200	...	...	3 218 800	...	...
		1994/95	340 200	...	...	3 318 900	...	...

3.7 Second level: teachers and pupils
Second degré: personnel enseignant et élèves
Segundo grado: personal docente y alumnos

Country Pays País	Type of education Type d'enseignement Tipo de enseñanza	Year Année Año	Teaching staff Personnel enseignant Personal docente			Pupils enrolled Élèves inscrits Alumnos matriculados		
			Total	Female Féminin Femenino	% F	Total	Female Féminin Femenino	% F
			(1)	(2)	(3)	(4)	(5)	(6)
Uzbekistan (cont)	General	1980/81	186 200	90 200	48	2 656 200	1 211 500	46
		1985/86	218 900	106 200	49	2 824 400	1 331 900	47
		1990/91	293 900	141 200	48	2 965 800	1 456 300	49
		1992/93	316 300	152 900	48	2 979 800	1 443 700	48
		1993/94	328 900	158 900	48	2 992 800	1 454 400	49
		1994/95	332 300	162 400	49	3 104 400	1 492 300	48
	Teacher-training		-	-	-	-	-	-
	Vocational	1980/81	5 900	...	...	223 100	...	...
		1985/86	7 400	...	...	290 600	...	...
		1990/91	8 500	...	...	228 800	...	...
		1992/93	8 000	...	...	214 200	...	...
		1993/94	8 300	...	...	226 000	...	...
		1994/95	7 900	...	...	214 500	...	...
Viet Nam	Total second level	1980/81	...	...	...	...	...	...
		1985/86	...	...	...	...	...	...
		1990/91	...	...	...	...	...	...
		1992/93	...	...	...	...	...	...
		1993/94	...	...	...	...	...	...
		1994/95	...	...	...	...	...	...
	General	1980/81	148 973	86 182	58	3 846 737	1 808 028	47
		1985/86	177 344	112 192	63	4 022 858	1 902 929	47
		1990/91	179 493	...	...	3 235 992	...	...
		1992/93	160 166	...	...	3 390 724	...	...
		1993/94	167 538	...	...	3 825 864	...	...
		1994/95	179 300	...	...	4 539 900	...	...
	Teacher-training	1980/81	...	...	...	20 397	4 601	23
	Vocational	1985/86	17 814	...	...	220 339	...	...
		1990/91	15 814	...	...	188 989	...	...
		1992/93	15 092	...	...	144 101	...	...
		1993/94	12 197	...	...	127 530	...	...
		1994/95	15 796	...	...	177 900	...	...
Yemen	Total second level	1993/94	...	...	...	212 129	37 791	18
Former Democratic Yemen	Total second level	1980/81	1 649	329	20	31 490	9 183	29
		1985/86	...	...	...	36 282	10 864	30
		1990/91	...	...	...	...	...	...
	General	1980/81	1 199	276	23	26 160	8 557	33
		1985/86	...	...	...	29 954	10 068	34
	Teacher-training	1980/81	81	8	10	1 229	266	22
		1985/86	...	...	...	1 548	267	17
		1990/91	126	27	21	2 752	596	22
	Vocational	1980/81	369	45	12	4 101	360	9
		1985/86	...	...	...	4 780	529	11
		1990/91	532	110	21	6 351	1 115	18
Former Yemen Arab Republic	Total second level	1980/81	41 155	...	...	41 155	*5 402	*13
		1985/86	7 197	...	...	146 133	15 850	11
		1990/91	13 353	1 359	10	420 697	63 297	15
	General	1980/81	...	...	...	38 293	*4 637	*12
		1985/86	6 461	404	6	133 622	12 881	10
		1990/91	12 106	1 250	10	394 578	59 312	15
	Teacher-training	1980/81	...	...	...	1 548	673	43
		1985/86	457	...	...	10 314	2 807	27
		1990/91	783	89	11	21 051	3 550	17
	Vocational	1980/81	...	...	...	1 314	92	7
		1985/86	279	-	-	2 197	162	7
		1990/91	464	20	4	5 068	435	9
Palestine	Total second level	1994/95	...	...	...	213 609	102 523	48
	General	1994/95	...	...	...	212 141	102 288	48
	Teacher-training	1994/95	-	-	-	-	-	-
	Vocational	1994/95	124	...	...	1 468	235	16
Gaza Strip	Total second level	1986/87	2 169	...	...	59 241	...	...
		1989/90	...	...	...	68 033	31 315	46
		1991/92	...	...	...	73 124	...	...
		1993/94	...	...	...	75 494	...	...

Second level: teachers and pupils **3.7**
Second degré: personnel enseignant et élèves
Segundo grado: personal docente y alumnos

Country Pays País	Type of education Type d'enseignement Tipo de enseñanza	Year Année Año	Teaching staff Personnel enseignant Personal docente			Pupils enrolled Élèves inscrits Alumnos matriculados		
			Total	Female Féminin Femenino	% F	Total	Female Féminin Femenino	% F
			(1)	(2)	(3)	(4)	(5)	(6)
Gaza Strip (cont)	General	1986/87	2 067	...	...	58 147	...	...
		1989/90	...	...	...	67 845	31 218	46
		1991/92	2 584	...	...	72 943	...	...
		1993/94	...	...	...	75 339	36 161	48
	Teacher-training		-	-	-	-	-	-
	Vocational	1986/87	102	...	...	1 094	...	...
		1989/90	20	4	20	188	97	52
		1991/92	...	...	...	181	76	42
		1993/94	...	...	...	155	...	...
West Bank	Total second level	1987/88	6 060	2 337	39	120 825	52 773	44
		1990/91	...	...	...	110 205	49 200	45
		1991/92	...	...	...	119 910	52 568	44
		1993/94	...	...	...	125 305	57 395	46
	General	1987/88	5 892	2 325	39	118 671	52 436	44
		1990/91	...	...	...	108 610	49 033	45
		1991/92	...	...	...	118 867	52 482	44
		1993/94	...	...	...	124 006	57 255	46
	Teacher-training		-	-	-	-	-	-
	Vocational	1987/88	168	12	7	2 154	337	16
		1990/91	170	10	6	1 595	167	10
		1991/92	...	...	...	1 043	86	8
		1993/94	...	...	...	1 299	140	11
Europe								
Albania	Total second level	1980/81	5 392	1 903	35	163 866	73 288	45
		1985/86	7 072	2 816	40	177 679	80 174	45
		1990/91	9 708	...	...	205 774	92 061	45
		1993/94	7 834	3 892	50	103 291	52 042	50
		1994/95	6 365	3 264	51	93 830	46 176	49
	General	1980/81	1 008	468	46	30 780	18 070	59
		1985/86	1 470	845	57	42 133	24 049	57
		1990/91	3 318	1 231	37	67 589	37 415	55
		1993/94	4 149	2 417	58	73 259	40 896	56
		1994/95	4 965	2 564	52	73 216	39 813	54
	Teacher-training	1980/81	21	19	90	604	532	88
		1985/86	102	56	55	2 417	1 621	67
		1990/91	...	...	...	2 250	1 595	71
		1993/94	...	...	...	945	722	76
		1994/95	-	-	-	-	-	-
	Vocational	1980/81	4 363	1 416	32	132 482	54 686	41
		1985/86	5 500	1 915	35	133 129	54 504	41
		1990/91	...	...	...	135 935	53 051	39
		1993/94	...	...	...	29 087	10 424	36
		1994/95	1 400	700	50	20 614	6 363	31
Austria	Total second level	1980/81	68 492	33 594	49	937 484	433 494	46
		1985/86	74 014	38 883	53	847 188	394 872	47
		1990/91	76 295	41 451	54	746 272	349 612	47
		1991/92	78 069	42 711	55	756 385	354 667	47
		1992/93	80 980	45 182	56	768 176	361 570	47
		1993/94	82 696	46 594	56	778 006	367 347	47
	General	1980/81	47 841	25 861	54	583 382	284 271	49
		1985/86	51 431	29 158	57	495 755	239 496	48
		1990/91	52 511	30 777	59	427 286	207 322	49
		1991/92	53 583	31 688	59	441 996	215 231	49
		1992/93	56 313	33 995	60	459 011	224 013	49
		1993/94	57 740	35 237	61	469 915	230 108	49
	Teacher-training	1980/81	708	574	81	5 339	5 289	99
		1985/86	849	680	80	5 363	5 241	98
		1990/91	1 081	858	79	10 227	7 121	70
		1991/92	1 138	904	79	10 785	7 318	68
		1992/93	1 180	943	80	9 913	7 238	73
		1993/94	1 231	978	79	10 682	7 868	74
	Vocational	1980/81	19 943	7 159	36	348 763	143 934	41
		1985/86	21 734	9 045	42	346 070	150 135	43
		1990/91	22 703	9 816	43	308 759	135 169	44
		1991/92	23 348	10 119	43	303 604	132 118	44
		1992/93	23 487	10 244	44	299 252	130 319	44
		1993/94	23 725	10 379	44	297 409	129 371	43

3.7 Second level: teachers and pupils
Second degré: personnel enseignant et élèves
Segundo grado: personal docente y alumnos

Country / Pays / País	Type of education / Type d'enseignement / Tipo de enseñanza	Year / Année / Año	Teaching staff / Personnel enseignant / Personal docente			Pupils enrolled / Élèves inscrits / Alumnos matriculados		
			Total	Female / Féminin / Femenino	% F	Total	Female / Féminin / Femenino	% F
			(1)	(2)	(3)	(4)	(5)	(6)
Belarus‡	Total second level	1980/81	...	...	...	759 700	...	...
		1985/86	...	...	...	716 700	...	...
		1990/91	...	...	...	968 200	...	...
		1992/93	...	...	...	970 300	...	...
		1993/94	...	...	...	993 900	...	...
		1994/95	...	...	...	1 024 600	...	...
	General	1980/81	...	...	...	645 200	...	...
		1985/86	...	...	...	586 700	...	...
		1990/91	...	...	...	843 700	...	...
		1992/93	...	...	...	851 100	433 400	51
		1993/94	...	...	...	867 500	441 700	51
		1994/95	...	...	...	902 100	454 200	50
	Teacher-training	1980/81	...	...	...	3 700	...	...
		1985/86	...	...	...	7 200	...	...
		1990/91	...	...	...	9 600	...	...
		1992/93	...	...	...	7 400	...	...
		1993/94	...	...	...	6 800	...	...
		1994/95	...	...	...	6 600	...	...
	Vocational	1980/81	...	...	...	110 800	...	...
		1985/86	...	...	...	122 800	...	...
		1990/91	...	...	...	114 900	...	...
		1992/93	...	...	...	111 800	...	...
		1993/94	...	...	...	119 600	...	...
		1994/95	...	...	...	115 900	...	...
Belgium	Total second level	1980/81	...	...	...	835 524	415 108	50
		1985/86	...	...	...	824 997	405 651	49
		1990/91	106 372	55 873	53	769 438	377 568	49
		1991/92	110 599	58 751	53	765 672	375 520	49
	General	1985/86	...	...	...	450 662	228 164	51
	Teacher-training		-	-	-	-	-	-
	Vocational	1985/86	...	...	...	374 335	177 487	47
Bulgaria‡	Total second level	1980/81	25 666	13 656	53	314 753	151 529	48
		1985/86	26 851	15 397	57	374 565	183 214	49
		1990/91	27 340	16 697	61	391 550	194 979	50
		1992/93	30 005	18 976	63	374 514	186 999	50
		1993/94	30 642	19 840	65	363 138	181 592	50
		1994/95	31 305	20 770	66	371 102	186 732	50
	General	1980/81	7 159	4 604	64	91 863	62 673	68
		1985/86	9 392	6 318	67	163 417	104 400	64
		1990/91	9 873	7 154	72	152 683	101 432	66
		1992/93	11 329	8 477	75	152 801	103 648	68
		1993/94	11 806	8 861	75	151 903	102 046	67
		1994/95	12 420	9 570	77	158 701	106 984	67
	Teacher-training		-	-	-	-	-	-
	Vocational	1980/81	18 507	9 052	49	222 890	88 856	40
		1985/86	17 459	9 079	52	211 148	78 814	37
		1990/91	17 467	9 543	55	238 867	93 547	39
		1992/93	18 676	10 499	56	221 713	83 351	38
		1993/94	18 836	10 979	58	211 235	79 546	38
		1994/95	18 885	11 200	59	212 401	79 748	38
Croatia	Total second level	1990/91	11 958	...	...	186 090	95 012	51
		1992/93	12 278	7 382	60	190 926	98 053	51
		1993/94	14 965	9 022	60	207 013	104 634	51
		1994/95	15 338	9 226	60	197 027	99 988	51
	General	1992/93	...	...	...	43 205	28 124	65
		1993/94	3 636	2 509	69	48 083	31 418	65
		1994/95	3 770	2 558	68	49 013	31 625	65
	Teacher-training		-	-	-	-	-	-
	Vocational	1992/93	...	...	...	147 721	69 929	47
		1993/94	11 329	6 513	57	158 930	73 216	46
		1994/95	11 568	6 668	58	148 014	68 363	46
Former Czechoslovakia	Total second level	1980/81	60 820	22 455	37	780 811	377 086	48
		1985/86	74 021	25 693	35	744 059	379 768	51
		1990/91	86 143	38 840	45	864 215	437 269	51
	General	1980/81	32 241	14 674	46	420 108	235 340	56
		1985/86	31 943	15 852	50	390 986	223 355	57
		1990/91	37 909	20 169	53	471 511	267 954	57

Second level: teachers and pupils 3.7
Second degré: personnel enseignant et élèves
Segundo grado: personal docente y alumnos

Country / Pays / País	Type of education / Type d'enseignement / Tipo de enseñanza	Year / Année / Año	Teaching staff Personnel enseignant Personal docente			Pupils enrolled Élèves inscrits Alumnos matriculados		
			Total	Female Féminin Femenino	% F	Total	Female Féminin Femenino	% F
			(1)	(2)	(3)	(4)	(5)	(6)
Former Czechoslovakia (cont)								
	Teacher-training	1980/81	986	606	61	14 457	14 293	99
		1985/86	752	499	66	8 821	8 694	99
		1990/91	821	554	67	9 399	9 120	97
	Vocational	1980/81	27 593	7 175	26	346 246	127 453	37
		1985/86	41 326	9 342	23	344 252	147 719	43
		1990/91	47 413	18 117	38	383 305	160 195	42
Czech Republic	Total second level	1992/93	103 103	...	...	1 181 026	591 221	50
		1993/94	105 000	61 972	59	1 119 738	558 272	50
		1994/95	111 999	71 257	64	1 146 838	572 872	50
	General	1992/93	...	...	...	931 171	489 977	53
		1993/94	75 010	49 718	66	874 238	457 621	52
		1994/95	80 977	54 201	67	899 634	468 624	52
	Teacher-training	1992/93	517	337	65	4 898	4 648	95
		1993/94	593	408	69	4 701	4 484	95
		1994/95	492	347	71	5 172	4 725	91
	Vocational	1992/93	...	...	...	244 957	96 596	39
		1993/94	29 397	11 846	40	240 799	96 167	40
		1994/95	30 530	16 709	55	242 032	99 523	41
Denmark	Total second level	1980/81	...	...	...	498 944	242 206	49
		1985/86	...	...	...	487 526	237 437	49
		1990/91	...	...	...	464 555	228 598	49
		1991/92	...	...	...	455 639	224 690	49
		1992/93	...	...	...	455 677	225 610	50
		1993/94	...	...	...	443 841	220 585	50
	General	1980/81	...	...	...	372 948	190 742	51
		1985/86	38 821	...	...	336 754	172 832	51
		1990/91	...	...	...	316 748	163 022	51
		1991/92	...	...	...	310 049	159 526	51
		1992/93	...	...	...	301 690	155 353	51
		1993/94	...	...	...	297 496	153 911	52
	Teacher-training		-	-	-	-	-	-
	Vocational	1980/81	...	...	...	125 996	51 464	41
		1985/86	...	...	...	150 772	64 605	43
		1990/91	...	...	...	147 807	65 576	44
		1991/92	...	...	...	145 590	65 164	45
		1992/93	...	...	...	153 987	70 257	46
		1993/94	...	...	...	146 345	66 674	46
Estonia	Total second level	1985/86	...	...	...	124 532	...	...
		1990/91	...	...	...	132 646	...	...
		1992/93	11 868	9 319	79	121 708	01 025	50
		1993/94	11 896	9 732	82	120 983	63 335	52
		1994/95	14 183	11 194	79	125 052	64 856	52
	General	1985/86	...	...	...	82 596	44 340	54
		1990/91	...	...	...	96 197	50 731	53
		1992/93	10 169	8 440	83	92 185	47 895	52
		1993/94	10 324	8 595	83	92 869	49 267	53
		1994/95	11 307	9 351	83	97 246	51 468	53
	Teacher-training	1985/86	...	...	...	1 784	1 745	98
		1990/91	...	...	...	1 563	...	...
		1992/93	...	...	...	945	914	97
		1993/94	...	...	...	700	697	100
		1994/95	43	29	67	538	530	99
	Vocational	1985/86	...	...	...	40 152	...	...
		1990/91	...	...	...	34 886	...	...
		1992/93	...	...	...	28 668	12 216	43
		1993/94	...	...	...	27 414	13 371	49
		1994/95	2 833	1 814	64	27 268	12 858	47
Finland	Total second level	1980/81	...	...	...	449 322	232 244	52
		1985/86	...	...	...	424 076	224 125	53
		1990/91	...	...	...	426 864	227 534	53
		1991/92	...	...	...	446 207	239 554	54
		1992/93	...	...	...	463 121	247 798	54
		1993/94	...	...	...	459 108	243 719	53
	General	1980/81	19 822	...	...	341 054	181 292	53
		1985/86	...	...	...	300 748	160 420	53
		1990/91	...	...	...	305 979	161 089	53
		1991/92	...	...	...	315 866	167 572	53
		1992/93	...	...	...	323 762	172 126	53
		1993/94	...	...	...	322 555	170 589	53

3.7 Second level: teachers and pupils
Second degré: personnel enseignant et élèves
Segundo grado: personal docente y alumnos

Country Pays País	Type of education Type d'enseignement Tipo de enseñanza	Year Année Año	Teaching staff Personnel enseignant Personal docente			Pupils enrolled Élèves inscrits Alumnos matriculados		
			Total	Female Féminin Femenino	% F	Total	Female Féminin Femenino	% F
			(1)	(2)	(3)	(4)	(5)	(6)
Finland (cont)	Teacher-training	1980/81	...	...	...	872	574	66
		1985/86	...	...	...	954	631	66
		1990/91	-	-	-	-	-	-
		1991/92	-	-	-	-	-	-
		1992/93	-	-	-	-	-	-
		1993/94	-	-	-	-	-	-
	Vocational	1980/81	13 948	5 834	42	107 396	50 378	47
		1985/86	15 700	...	...	122 374	63 074	52
		1990/91	...	...	...	120 885	66 445	55
		1991/92	...	...	...	130 341	71 982	55
		1992/93	...	...	...	139 359	75 672	54
		1993/94	...	...	...	136 553	73 130	54
France‡	Total second level	1980/81	256 369	...	...	5 013 666	2 677 574	53
		1985/86	...	...	...	5 371 593	2 730 395	51
		1990/91	441 452	253 119	57	5 521 862	2 770 286	50
		1991/92	449 511	258 602	58	5 614 894	2 810 871	50
		1992/93	457 644	264 103	58	5 573 582	2 779 489	50
		1993/94	454 000	262 400	58	5 737 358	2 843 564	50
	General	1980/81	...	...	...	3 911 054	1 929 406	49
		1985/86	...	...	...	4 043 246	2 116 554	52
		1990/91	...	...	...	4 275 891	2 196 794	51
		1991/92	...	...	...	4 289 886	2 210 156	52
		1992/93	...	...	...	4 355 952	2 241 029	51
		1993/94	...	...	...	4 486 063	2 274 567	51
	Teacher-training		-	-	-	-	-	-
	Vocational	1980/81	...	...	...	1 102 612	748 168	68
		1985/86	...	...	...	1 328 347	613 841	46
		1990/91	...	...	...	1 245 971	573 492	46
		1991/92	...	...	...	1 325 008	600 715	45
		1992/93	...	...	...	1 217 630	538 460	44
		1993/94	...	...	...	1 251 295	568 997	45
Germany	Total second level	1990/91	...	...	...	7 398 011	...	...
		1991/92	...	...	...	7 500 078	3 607 097	48
		1992/93	527 009	239 738	45	7 662 797	3 682 085	48
		1993/94	521 310	235 412	45	7 796 256	3 757 360	48
	General	1990/91	...	...	...	5 101 924	...	...
		1991/92	...	...	...	5 228 015	2 604 525	50
		1992/93	414 358	201 477	49	5 386 212	2 688 732	50
		1993/94	408 663	196 422	48	5 532 012	2 765 480	50
	Teacher-training		-	-	-	-	-	-
	Vocational	1990/91	...	...	...	2 296 087	...	...
		1991/92	...	...	...	2 272 063	1 002 572	44
		1992/93	112 651	38 261	34	2 276 585	993 353	44
		1993/94	112 647	38 990	35	2 264 244	991 880	44
Former German Democratic Rep.	Total second level	1980/81	164 382	75 616	46	1 895 579	911 282	48
		1985/86	167 310	86 127	51	1 519 152	727 611	48
	General	1980/81	108 652	59 611	55	1 413 213	702 816	50
		1985/86	112 076	67 772	60	1 140 391	565 408	50
	Teacher-training		-	-	-	-	-	-
	Vocational	1980/81	55 730	16 005	29	482 366	208 466	43
		1985/86	55 234	18 355	33	378 761	162 203	43
Federal Republic of Germany‡	Total second level	1980/81	...	...	...	6 561 297	3 266 392	50
		1985/86	...	...	...	7 101 250	3 400 188	48
	General	1980/81	...	...	...	5 950 897	2 938 495	49
		1985/86	*359 219	*161 629	*45	4 573 005	2 258 687	49
	Teacher-training		-	-	-	-	-	-
	Vocational	1980/81	60 621	21 341	35	610 400	327 897	54
		1985/86	...	...	...	2 528 245	1 141 501	45
Gibraltar	Total second level	1980/81	...	...	...	1 811	899	50
		1984/85	144	52	36	1 806	885	49
	General	1980/81	123	52	42	1 770	899	51
		1984/85	125	51	41	1 749	881	50
	Teacher-training		-	-	-	-	-	-
	Vocational	1980/81	...	...	...	41	-	-
		1984/85	19	1	5	57	4	7

Second level: teachers and pupils 3.7
Second degré: personnel enseignant et élèves
Segundo grado: personal docente y alumnos

Country Pays País	Type of education Type d'enseignement Tipo de enseñanza	Year Année Año	Teaching staff Personnel enseignant Personal docente			Pupils enrolled Élèves inscrits Alumnos matriculados		
			Total	Female Féminin Femenino	% F	Total	Female Féminin Femenino	% F
			(1)	(2)	(3)	(4)	(5)	(6)
Greece	Total second level	1980/81	39 571	19 429	49	740 058	337 816	46
		1985/86	50 388	26 475	53	813 534	387 134	48
		1990/91	60 303	32 057	53	851 353	408 580	48
		1991/92	62 798	33 405	53	870 235	418 384	48
		1992/93	71 677	38 504	54	843 403	410 840	49
		1993/94	75 270	40 495	54	851 294	403 086	47
	General	1980/81	31 737	17 547	55	639 633	317 863	50
		1985/86	42 250	23 733	56	704 119	355 389	50
		1990/91	49 802	28 342	57	716 404	364 437	51
		1991/92	50 732	29 029	57	720 511	366 113	51
		1992/93	56 787	32 185	57	709 081	360 889	51
		1993/94	59 137	33 395	56	713 659	355 827	50
	Teacher-training		-	-	-	-	-	-
	Vocational	1980/81	7 834	1 882	24	100 425	19 953	20
		1985/86	8 138	2 742	34	109 415	31 745	29
		1990/91	10 501	3 715	35	134 949	44 143	33
		1991/92	12 066	4 376	36	149 724	52 271	35
		1992/93	14 890	6 319	42	134 322	49 951	37
		1993/94	16 133	7 100	44	137 635	47 259	34
Hungary	Total second level	1980/81	...	...	...	357 334	165 679	46
		1985/86	...	...	...	422 323	205 114	49
		1990/91	...	...	...	514 076	251 505	49
		1991/92	...	...	...	531 051	259 450	49
		1993/94	...	...	...	529 445	263 211	50
		1994/95	...	...	...	523 068	261 038	50
	General	1980/81	6 639	4 027	61	89 400	58 286	65
		1985/86	7 923	5 051	64	105 794	68 832	65
		1990/91	10 246	6 747	66	123 427	81 991	66
		1991/92	10 732	7 040	66	130 378	86 001	66
		1993/94	11 959	8 053	67	138 198	88 712	64
		1994/95	...	...	...	140 352	88 819	63
	Teacher-training	1980/81	...	...	...	5 897	5 894	100
		1985/86	...	...	...	5 081	5 079	100
		1990/91	...	...	...	4 510	4 510	100
		1991/92	...	...	...	3 865	3 862	100
		1993/94	...	...	...	2 257	2 257	100
		1994/95	...	...	...	1 306	1 276	98
	Vocational	1980/81	...	...	...	262 037	101 499	39
		1985/86	...	...	...	311 448	131 203	42
		1990/91	...	...	...	386 139	165 004	43
		1991/92	...	...	...	396 808	169 587	43
		1993/94	...	...	...	388 990	172 242	44
		1994/95	...	...	...	381 410	170 943	45
Iceland	Total second level	1980/81	...	...	...	26 643	12 447	47
		1985/86	...	...	...	27 559	12 962	47
		1990/91	...	...	...	29 465	14 132	48
		1991/92	...	...	...	29 985	14 455	48
		1992/93	...	...	...	30 233	14 689	49
		1993/94	...	...	...	30 914	15 155	49
	General	1980/81	...	...	...	19 091	...	...
		1985/86	...	...	...	20 097	10 180	51
		1990/91	...	...	...	23 143	11 968	52
		1991/92	...	...	...	24 022	12 448	52
		1992/93	...	...	...	24 368	12 708	52
		1993/94	...	...	...	24 863	12 956	52
	Teacher-training	1980/81	...	...	...	168	...	...
		1985/86	...	...	...	297	249	84
		1990/91	...	...	...	373	333	89
		1991/92	...	...	...	462	407	88
		1992/93	...	...	...	481	423	88
		1993/94	...	...	...	516	466	90
	Vocational	1980/81	...	...	...	7 384	...	...
		1985/86	...	...	...	7 165	2 533	35
		1990/91	...	...	...	5 949	1 831	31
		1991/92	...	...	...	5 501	1 600	29
		1992/93	...	...	...	5 384	1 558	29
		1993/94	...	...	...	5 535	1 733	31
Ireland‡	Total second level	1980/81	19 878	...	...	300 601	155 304	52
		1985/86	20 611	...	...	338 256	173 158	51
		1990/91	20 830	...	...	345 941	176 335	51
		1991/92	21 371	...	...	352 408	179 272	51
		1992/93	22 268	...	...	362 230	183 847	51
		1993/94	...	...	...	...	...	...

3.7 Second level: teachers and pupils
Second degré: personnel enseignant et élèves
Segundo grado: personal docente y alumnos

Country / Pays / País	Type of education / Type d'enseignement / Tipo de enseñanza	Year / Année / Año	Teaching staff Personnel enseignant Personal docente			Pupils enrolled Élèves inscrits Alumnos matriculados		
			Total	Female Féminin Femenino	% F	Total	Female Féminin Femenino	% F
			(1)	(2)	(3)	(4)	(5)	(6)
Ireland‡ (cont)	General	1980/81	...	...	...	286 619	145 295	51
		1985/86	...	...	...	315 584	158 583	50
		1990/91	...	...	...	321 477	160 682	50
		1991/92	...	...	...	327 817	164 024	50
		1992/93	...	...	...	336 681	168 241	50
		1993/94	...	...	...	346 742	173 354	50
	Teacher-training		-	-	-	-	-	-
	Vocational	1980/81	...	...	...	13 982	10 009	72
		1985/86	...	...	...	22 672	14 575	64
		1990/91	...	...	...	24 464	15 653	64
		1991/92	...	...	...	24 591	15 248	62
		1992/93	...	...	...	25 549	15 606	61
Italy	Total second level	1980/81	519 128	302 040	58	5 307 989	2 550 177	48
		1985/86	562 196	341 719	61	5 361 579	2 607 247	49
		1990/91	589 655	367 419	62	5 117 897	2 498 371	49
		1991/92	590 692	370 008	63	5 010 467	2 447 449	49
		1992/93	579 690	362 634	63	4 892 194	2 388 788	49
		1993/94	584 642	366 690	63	4 715 635	2 309 247	49
	General	1980/81	325 718	209 981	64	3 484 339	1 680 440	48
		1985/86	347 638	233 956	67	3 381 434	1 649 137	49
		1990/91	336 215	234 965	70	2 994 957	1 477 109	49
		1991/92	333 137	234 013	70	2 900 114	1 434 986	49
		1992/93	324 506	227 890	70	2 805 158	1 391 426	50
		1993/94	327 239	230 776	71	2 741 999	1 361 304	50
	Teacher-training	1980/81	22 308	15 447	69	237 471	223 310	94
		1985/86	21 484	15 414	72	197 349	185 144	94
		1990/91	21 618	15 804	73	184 802	171 988	93
		1991/92	22 281	16 435	74	183 711	170 944	93
		1992/93	22 073	16 282	74	181 040	168 451	93
		1993/94	22 264	16 423	74	183 714	170 938	93
	Vocational	1980/81	171 102	76 612	45	1 586 179	646 427	41
		1985/86	193 074	92 349	48	1 782 796	772 966	43
		1990/91	231 822	116 650	50	1 938 138	849 274	44
		1991/92	235 274	119 560	51	1 926 642	841 519	44
		1992/93	233 111	118 462	51	1 905 996	828 911	43
		1993/94	235 139	119 491	51	1 789 922	777 005	43
Latvia‡	Total second level	1980/81	...	...	...	280 945	...	...
		1985/86	...	...	...	289 226	...	...
		1990/91	...	...	...	264 475	129 795	49
		1992/93	...	...	...	246 877	122 854	50
		1993/94	...	...	...	245 130	124 897	51
		1994/95	...	...	...	243 673	124 241	51
	General	1980/81	25 638	...	...	205 038	...	...
		1985/86	26 542	...	...	210 127	...	...
		1990/91	31 583	...	...	197 066	98 533	50
		1992/93	32 964	...	...	191 565	97 421	51
		1993/94	23 710	19 005	80	195 686	102 023	52
		1994/95	23 288	...	...	198 470	103 723	52
	Teacher-training	1980/81	163	...	...	1 452	...	...
		1985/86	195	...	...	1 741	...	...
		1990/91	352	...	...	3 067	2 952	96
		1992/93	323	...	...	2 108	2 033	96
		1993/94	...	...	...	788	781	99
		1994/95	...	...	...	137	136	99
	Vocational	1980/81	7 097	...	...	74 455	...	...
		1985/86	7 362	...	...	77 358	...	...
		1990/91	6 333	...	...	64 342	28 310	44
		1992/93	6 045	...	...	53 204	23 400	44
		1993/94	...	...	...	48 656	22 093	45
		1994/95	5 141	...	...	45 066	20 382	45
Lithuania	Total second level	1980/81	...	...	...	...	...	...
		1985/86	...	...	...	466 166	...	...
		1990/91	...	...	...	388 903	...	...
		1992/93	...	...	...	350 791	173 585	49
		1993/94	...	...	...	342 524	...	...
		1994/95	...	...	...	351 517	177 399	50
	General	1980/81	20 240	17 168	85	415 974	...	...
		1985/86	22 808	17 792	78	370 989	...	...
		1990/91	26 529	21 242	80	315 854	...	...
		1992/93	28 719	23 394	81	295 715	152 556	52
		1993/94	28 751	23 574	82	290 308	...	...
		1994/95	30 495	24 979	82	301 714	156 442	52
	Teacher-training		-	-	-	-	-	-

Second level: teachers and pupils 3.7
Second degré: personnel enseignant et élèves
Segundo grado: personal docente y alumnos

Country Pays País	Type of education Type d'enseignement Tipo de enseñanza	Year Année Año	Teaching staff Personnel enseignant Personal docente			Pupils enrolled Élèves inscrits Alumnos matriculados		
			Total	Female Féminin Femenino	% F	Total	Female Féminin Femenino	% F
			(1)	(2)	(3)	(4)	(5)	(6)
Lithuania (cont)	Vocational	1985/86	...	...	...	95 177	...	...
		1990/91	...	...	...	73 049	...	...
		1992/93	...	...	...	55 076	21 029	38
		1993/94	...	...	...	52 216	21 330	41
		1994/95	...	...	...	49 803	20 957	42
Luxembourg	Total second level	1980/81	1 944	...	...	27 487	...	...
		1985/86	1 908	...	...	25 656	12 438	48
		1990/91	...	...	...	...	...	...
		1991/92	...	...	...	...	...	...
		1992/93	...	...	...	...	...	...
	General	1980/81	...	...	...	9 037	4 910	54
		1985/86	...	...	...	7 951	4 355	55
		1990/91	...	...	...	7 594		
		1991/92	...	...	...	8 465	4 531	54
		1992/93	...	...	...	8 712	4 710	54
	Teacher-training	1980/81	...	...	...	53	50	94
		1985/86	...	...	...	86	67	78
	Vocational	1980/81	...	...	...	18 397	...	...
		1985/86	...	...	...	17 619	8 016	45
Malta	Total second level	1980/81	2 141	783	37	25 501	11 458	45
		1985/86	2 315	779	34	27 779	13 294	48
		1990/91	2 688	956	36	32 544	15 196	47
		1991/92	...	...	...	34 358	15 956	46
		1992/93	...	...	...	34 619	16 072	46
		1993/94	3 268	1 403	43	34 955	16 027	46
	General	1980/81	1 691	695	41	21 377	10 562	49
		1985/86	1 724	659	38	21 421	11 959	56
		1990/91	1 978	805	41	25 891	13 746	53
		1991/92	...	...	...	27 797	14 736	53
		1992/93	...	...	...	28 419	15 089	53
		1993/94	2 617	1 290	49	29 082	15 148	52
	Teacher-training		-	-	-	-	-	-
	Vocational	1980/81	450	88	20	4 124	896	22
		1985/86	591	120	20	6 358	1 335	21
		1990/91	710	151	21	6 653	1 450	22
		1991/92	707	141	20	6 561	1 220	19
		1992/93	690	121	18	6 200	983	16
		1993/94	651	113	17	5 873	879	15
Moldova	Total second level	1980/81	...	...	...	...	...	...
		1985/86	31 857	21 664	68	...	...	...
		1990/91	36 299	25 116	69	459 701	237 626	52
		1992/93	37 888	26 531	70	441 955	229 857	52
		1993/94	38 568	26 928	70	444 422	229 890	52
		1994/95	...	...	...	...	...	...
	General	1980/81	...	...	...	415 228	211 766	51
		1985/86	...	...	...	427 727	218 141	51
		1990/91	...	...	...	419 153	213 768	51
		1992/93	...	...	...	399 586	203 789	51
		1993/94	...	...	...	405 969	207 044	51
		1994/95	...	...	...	407 338	206 612	51
	Teacher-training	1990/91	...	...	...	2 072	1 927	93
		1992/93	...	...	...	2 549	2 371	93
		1993/94	...	...	...	2 576	2 396	93
		1994/95	...	...	...	2 354	2 166	92
	Vocational	1990/91	...	...	...	38 476	21 931	57
		1992/93	...	...	...	39 820	23 697	60
		1993/94	...	...	...	35 877	20 450	57
Monaco‡	Total second level	1980/81	...	...	...	2 065	...	...
		1990/91	...	...	...	2 785	1 378	49
		1991/92	...	...	...	2 858	1 391	49
		1993/94	...	...	...	2 835	1 381	49
		1994/95	...	...	...	2 861	1 413	49
	General	1980/81	...	...	...	1 314	...	...
		1990/91	180	103	57	2 415	1 242	51
		1991/92	181	104	57	2 383	1 220	51
		1993/94	188	121	64	2 385	1 199	50
		1994/95	195	141	72	2 358	1 202	51
	Teacher-training		-	-	-	-	-	-

3.7 Second level: teachers and pupils
Second degré: personnel enseignant et élèves
Segundo grado: personal docente y alumnos

Country Pays País	Type of education Type d'enseignement Tipo de enseñanza	Year Année Año	Teaching staff Personnel enseignant Personal docente			Pupils enrolled Élèves inscrits Alumnos matriculados		
			Total	Female Féminin Femenino	% F	Total	Female Féminin Femenino	% F
			(1)	(2)	(3)	(4)	(5)	(6)
Monaco‡ (cont)	Vocational	1980/81	...	...	...	751	383	51
		1990/91	145	63	43	370	136	37
		1991/92	73	25	34	475	171	36
		1993/94	61	38	62	450	182	40
		1994/95	84	45	54	503	211	42
Netherlands‡	Total second level	1980/81	...	...	...	1 391 485	663 695	48
		1985/86	...	...	...	1 620 011	774 422	48
		1990/91	89 370	25 900	29	1 401 739	657 882	47
		1991/92	87 200	25 800	30	1 377 768	649 622	47
		1992/93	86 000	25 800	30	1 369 507	653 200	48
		1993/94	88 229	27 010	31	1 352 464	629 841	47
	General	1980/81	54 369	13 997	26	823 730	428 252	52
		1985/86	53 361	14 377	27	803 782	425 118	53
		1990/91	...	...	...	683 662	356 407	52
		1991/92	...	...	...	673 592	351 418	52
		1992/93	...	...	...	668 094	349 283	52
		1993/94	53 781	16 351	30	668 426	349 415	52
	Teacher-training	1980/81	1 124	583	52	7 190	7 119	99
		1985/86	234	95	41	2 138	2 097	98
		1990/91	-	-	-	-	-	-
		1991/92	-	-	-	-	-	-
		1992/93	-	-	-	-	-	-
		1993/94	-	-	-	-	-	-
	Vocational	1980/81	...	...	...	560 565	228 324	41
		1985/86	...	...	...	814 091	347 207	43
		1990/91	...	...	...	718 077	301 475	42
		1991/92	...	...	...	704 176	298 204	42
		1992/93	...	...	...	701 413	303 917	43
		1993/94	34 448	10 659	31	684 038	280 426	41
Norway	Total second level	1980/81	...	...	...	360 776	180 226	50
		1985/86	...	...	...	387 990	194 162	50
		1990/91	...	...	...	370 779	184 225	50
		1991/92	...	...	...	367 395	180 904	49
		1992/93	...	...	...	380 916	183 861	48
		1993/94	...	...	...	380 315	182 366	48
	General	1980/81	...	...	...	279 266	141 888	51
		1985/86	...	...	...	280 357	142 314	51
		1990/91	...	...	...	250 664	128 290	51
		1991/92	...	...	...	248 003	126 983	51
		1992/93	...	...	...	246 615	126 694	51
		1993/94	...	...	...	248 240	126 995	51
	Teacher-training	1980/81	...	...	...	345	288	83
		1985/86	...	...	...	630	577	92
		1990/91	...	...	...	1 154	1 081	94
		1991/92	...	...	...	1 336	1 255	94
		1992/93	...	...	...	1 888	1 799	95
		1993/94	...	...	...	2 192	2 046	93
	Vocational	1980/81	...	...	...	81 165	38 050	47
		1985/86	...	...	...	107 003	51 271	48
		1990/91	...	...	...	118 961	54 854	46
		1991/92	...	...	...	118 056	52 666	45
		1992/93	...	...	...	132 413	55 368	42
		1993/94	...	...	...	129 883	53 325	41
Poland	Total second level	1980/81	93 346	...	...	1 673 869	840 888	50
		1985/86	95 552	...	...	1 567 641	793 568	51
		1990/91	103 814	...	...	1 887 667	945 044	50
		1992/93	105 214	...	...	2 030 842	1 017 918	50
		1993/94	108 902	...	...	2 109 161	1 059 743	50
		1994/95	118 056	...	...	2 442 967	1 199 273	49
	General	1980/81	21 287	...	...	345 214	244 242	71
		1985/86	21 309	...	...	337 563	245 843	73
		1990/91	24 307	...	...	444 597	323 132	73
		1992/93	27 532	...	...	555 379	400 792	72
		1993/94	29 510	...	...	601 864	427 038	71
		1994/95	33 148	...	...	713 897	484 827	68
	Teacher-training	1980/81	1 402	...	...	18 703	16 277	87
		1985/86	1 643	...	...	22 723	20 730	91
		1990/91	2 267	...	...	25 886	23 367	90
		1992/93	281	...	...	2 931	1 403	48
		1993/94	167	...	...	1 832	885	48
		1994/95	69	...	...	921	272	30

Second level: teachers and pupils **3.7**
Second degré: personnel enseignant et élèves
Segundo grado: personal docente y alumnos

Country Pays País	Type of education Type d'enseignement Tipo de enseñanza	Year Année Año	Teaching staff Personnel enseignant Personal docente			Pupils enrolled Élèves inscrits Alumnos matriculados		
			Total	Female Féminin Femenino	% F	Total	Female Féminin Femenino	% F
			(1)	(2)	(3)	(4)	(5)	(6)
Poland (cont)	Vocational	1980/81	70 657	...	...	1 309 952	580 369	44
		1985/86	72 600	...	...	1 207 355	526 995	44
		1990/91	77 240	...	...	1 417 184	598 545	42
		1992/93	77 401	...	...	1 472 532	615 723	42
		1993/94	79 225	...	...	1 505 465	631 820	42
		1994/95	84 839	...	...	1 728 149	714 174	41
Portugal	Total second level	1980/81	32 028	18 963	59	398 320	190 612	48
		1985/86	...	...	...	580 248	...	...
		1990/91	64 513	42 513	66	670 035	354 490	53
		1991/92	...	...	...	759 639	...	...
		1993/94	69 095	...	...	778 465	...	...
	General	1980/81	32 028	18 963	59	398 320	190 612	48
		1985/86	39 685	25 014	63	572 697	302 815	53
		1990/91	...	...	...	637 761	342 712	54
		1991/92	...	...	...	728 283	...	...
		1993/94	...	...	...	749 838	...	...
	Teacher-training		-	-	-	-	-	-
	Vocational	1980/81	-	-	-	-	-	-
		1985/86	...	...	...	7 551	...	...
		1990/91	...	...	...	32 274	11 778	36
		1991/92	...	...	...	31 356	...	...
		1993/94	...	...	...	28 627	...	...
Romania‡	Total second level	1980/81	48 082	20 829	43	871 257	412 381	47
		1986/87	48 648	23 577	48	1 477 349	692 799	47
		1990/91	157 474	96 150	61	2 837 948	1 379 805	49
		1992/93	165 311	101 341	61	2 451 624	1 194 698	49
		1993/94	167 316	102 927	62	2 336 322	1 154 187	49
		1994/95	168 982	104 547	62	2 252 053	1 114 438	49
	General	1980/81	8 254	4 353	53	80 879	52 330	65
		1986/87	7 202	3 883	54	103 379	73 158	71
		1990/91	114 314	74 704	65	1 621 501	821 089	51
		1992/93	119 460	77 125	65	1 659 362	860 764	52
		1993/94	118 427	77 402	65	1 559 075	817 637	52
		1994/95	118 675	77 010	65	1 468 039	774 916	53
	Teacher-training	1980/81	1 134	689	61	6 317	6 019	95
		1986/87	733	447	61	4 679	4 450	95
		1990/91	1 208	764	63	10 716	10 169	95
		1992/93	1 796	1 150	64	16 598	15 736	95
		1993/94	2 035	1 285	63	18 909	17 919	95
		1994/95	2 270	1 465	65	19 967	18 873	95
	Vocational	1980/81	38 694	15 787	41	784 061	354 032	45
		1986/87	40 713	19 247	47	1 369 291	615 191	45
		1990/91	41 952	20 682	49	1 205 731	548 547	45
		1992/93	44 055	23 066	52	775 664	318 198	41
		1993/94	46 854	24 240	52	758 338	318 631	42
		1994/95	48 037	26 072	54	764 047	320 649	42
Russian Federation	Total second level	1980/81	...	...	...	12 991 000	...	...
		1985/86	...	...	...	13 341 000	...	...
		1990/91	...	...	...	13 956 000	...	...
		1991/92	...	...	...	13 890 000	...	...
		1992/93	...	...	...	13 724 000	...	...
		1993/94	...	...	...	13 732 000	...	...
	General	1980/81	738 000	558 000	76	11 351 000	5 735 000	51
		1985/86	775 000	596 000	77	11 675 000	5 836 000	50
		1990/91	944 000	731 000	77	12 363 000	6 300 000	51
		1991/92	983 000	764 000	78	12 313 000	6 317 000	51
		1992/93	1 026 000	806 000	79	12 306 000	6 331 000	51
		1993/94	1 070 000	844 000	79	12 424 000	6 399 000	52
	Teacher-training	1980/81	...	...	...	241 000	220 000	91
		1985/86	...	...	...	288 000	268 000	93
		1990/91	...	...	...	341 000	318 000	93
		1991/92	...	...	...	342 000	318 000	93
		1992/93	...	...	...	322 000	298 000	93
		1993/94	...	...	...	301 000	277 000	92
	Vocational	1980/81	...	...	...	1 399 000	...	...
		1985/86	...	...	...	1 378 000	...	...
		1990/91	...	...	...	1 252 000	...	...
		1991/92	...	...	...	1 235 000	...	...
		1992/93	...	...	...	1 096 000	...	...
		1993/94	...	...	...	1 007 000	...	...

3.7 Second level: teachers and pupils
Second degré: personnel enseignant et élèves
Segundo grado: personal docente y alumnos

Country Pays País	Type of education Type d'enseignement Tipo de enseñanza	Year Année Año	Teaching staff Personnel enseignant Personal docente			Pupils enrolled Élèves inscrits Alumnos matriculados		
			Total	Female Féminin Femenino	% F	Total	Female Féminin Femenino	% F
			(1)	(2)	(3)	(4)	(5)	(6)
San Marino	Total second level	1980/81	112	69	62	1 219	593	49
		1985/86	...	...	...	1 248	597	48
		1990/91	...	...	...	1 182	616	52
		1991/92	...	...	...	1 158	571	49
		1992/93	...	...	...	1 159	561	48
		1993/94	...	...	...	1 157	550	48
	General	1980/81	112	69	62	1 219	593	49
		1985/86	...	...	...	1 248	597	48
		1990/91	...	...	...	1 045	580	56
		1991/92	...	...	...	1 021	535	52
		1992/93	...	...	...	1 001	511	51
		1993/94	...	...	...	994	495	50
	Teacher-training		-	-	-	-	-	-
	Vocational	1980/81	-	-	-	-	-	-
		1985/86	-	-	-	-	-	-
		1990/91	...	...	...	137	36	26
		1991/92	...	...	...	137	36	26
		1992/93	...	...	...	158	50	32
		1993/94	...	...	...	163	55	34
Slovakia	Total second level	1992/93	48 340	32 061	66	657 010	327 920	50
		1993/94	42 679	29 917	70	658 228	328 239	50
		1994/95	43 339	30 740	71	663 647	332 820	50
	General	1992/93	29 386	21 582	73	416 982	212 618	51
		1993/94	28 256	21 100	75	412 575	210 376	51
		1994/95	28 493	21 421	75	409 594	208 479	51
	Teacher-training	1992/93	308	237	77	2 730	2 651	97
		1993/94	244	184	75	2 787	2 666	96
		1994/95	227	171	75	2 832	2 669	94
	Vocational	1992/93	18 646	10 242	55	237 298	112 651	47
		1993/94	14 179	8 633	61	242 866	115 197	47
		1994/95	14 619	9 148	63	251 221	121 672	48
Slovenia	Total second level	1992/93	13 749	9 384	68	211 426	104 544	49
		1993/94	13 605	9 331	69	211 739	104 415	49
		1994/95	13 919	9 600	69	214 042	105 637	49
	General	1992/93	8 717	6 506	75	137 414	71 412	52
		1993/94	8 306	6 312	76	137 578	71 364	52
		1994/95	8 291	6 323	76	137 580	71 223	52
	Teacher-training	1992/93	148	146	99	1 895	1 671	88
		1993/94	147	112	76	824	808	98
		1994/95	149	113	76	802	778	97
	Vocational	1992/93	4 884	2 732	56	72 117	31 461	44
		1993/94	5 152	2 907	56	73 337	32 243	44
		1994/95	5 479	3 164	58	75 660	33 636	44
Spain	Total second level	1980/81	190 251	76 767	40	3 976 747	1 979 208	50
		1985/86	217 364	97 672	45	4 555 541	2 304 983	51
		1990/91	285 557	145 444	51	4 755 322	2 396 541	50
		1991/92	294 438	148 597	50	4 773 349	2 419 992	51
		1992/93	292 864	147 423	50	4 744 204	2 415 482	51
		1993/94	297 697	149 713	50	4 734 401	2 423 305	51
	General	1980/81	149 555	64 106	43	3 088 026	1 569 844	51
		1985/86	160 723	77 838	48	3 349 211	1 687 735	50
		1990/91	210 167	112 897	54	3 653 552	1 854 703	51
		1991/92	212 640	113 359	53	3 618 326	1 828 102	51
		1992/93	...	...	...	3 583 992	1 811 736	51
		1993/94	...	...	...	3 564 992	1 814 851	51
	Teacher-training		-	-	-	-	-	-
	Vocational	1980/81	40 696	12 661	31	888 721	409 364	46
		1985/86	56 641	19 834	35	1 206 330	617 248	51
		1990/91	75 390	32 547	43	1 101 770	541 838	49
		1991/92	81 798	35 238	43	1 155 023	591 890	51
		1992/93	...	...	...	1 160 212	603 746	52
		1993/94	...	...	...	1 169 409	608 454	52
Sweden	Total second level	1980/81	...	...	...	606 833	311 945	51
		1985/86	...	...	...	624 835	...	...
		1990/91	...	...	...	588 474	293 856	50
		1991/92	* ...	...	...	585 527	292 138	50
		1992/93	65 410	33 468	51	602 703	296 338	49
		1993/94	64 244	32 900	51	607 219	297 879	49

Second level: teachers and pupils 3.7
Second degré: personnel enseignant et élèves
Segundo grado: personal docente y alumnos

Country Pays País	Type of education Type d'enseignement Tipo de enseñanza	Year Année Año	Teaching staff Personnel enseignant Personal docente			Pupils enrolled Élèves inscrits Alumnos matriculados		
			Total	Female Féminin Femenino	% F	Total	Female Féminin Femenino	% F
			(1)	(2)	(3)	(4)	(5)	(6)
Sweden (cont)	General	1980/81	...	...	...	443 355	226 649	51
		1990/91	...	...	...	377 191	196 586	52
		1991/92	...	...	...	373 132	195 474	52
		1992/93	...	...	...	381 295	199 386	52
		1993/94	...	...	...	397 991	204 248	51
	Teacher-training	1980/81	...	...	...	73	43	59
		1985/86	-	-	-	-	-	-
		1990/91	-	-	-	-	-	-
		1991/92	-	-	-	-	-	-
		1992/93	-	-	-	-	-	-
		1993/94	-	-	-	-	-	-
	Vocational	1980/81	...	...	...	163 405	85 253	52
		1990/91	...	...	...	211 283	97 270	46
		1991/92	...	...	...	212 395	96 664	46
		1992/93	...	...	...	221 408	96 952	44
		1993/94	...	...	...	209 228	93 631	45
Switzerland	Total second level	1980/81	...	...	...	661 315	306 240	46
		1985/86	...	...	...	634 750	295 115	46
		1990/91	...	...	...	567 396	267 784	47
		1991/92	...	...	...	562 465	266 225	47
		1992/93	...	...	...	561 470	266 447	47
		1993/94	...	...	...	558 920	266 101	48
	General	1980/81	...	...	...	427 193	211 198	49
		1985/86	...	...	...	382 442	189 861	50
		1990/91	...	...	...	337 958	168 580	50
		1991/92	...	...	...	343 735	171 980	50
		1992/93	...	...	...	351 991	176 659	50
		1993/94	...	...	...	358 761	180 450	50
	Teacher-training	1980/81	...	...	...	9 882	7 717	78
		1985/86	...	...	...	9 221	7 465	81
		1990/91	...	...	...	8 119	6 413	79
		1991/92	...	...	...	8 803	6 979	79
		1992/93	...	...	...	9 162	7 216	79
		1993/94	...	...	...	9 375	7 465	80
	Vocational	1980/81	...	...	...	224 240	87 325	39
		1985/86	...	...	...	243 087	97 789	40
		1990/91	...	...	...	221 319	92 791	42
		1991/92	...	...	...	209 927	87 266	42
		1992/93	...	...	...	200 317	82 572	41
		1993/94	...	...	...	190 784	78 186	41
The Former Yugoslav Rep. of Macedonia	Total second level	1980/81	4 277	...	...	82 465	...	...
		1985/86	4 193	...	...	77 023	...	...
		1990/91	4 227	...	...	70 696	...	...
		1992/93	4 345	2 212	51	73 381	36 003	49
		1993/94	4 520	2 318	51	74 583	36 644	49
		1994/95	4 682	2 401	51	77 804	37 857	49
	General	1992/93	...	...	...	20 727	12 760	62
		1993/94	...	...	...	21 649	13 261	61
		1994/95	...	...	...	23 181	13 915	60
	Teacher-training	1992/93	-	-	-	-	-	-
		1993/94	...	...	...	386	136	35
		1994/95	...	...	...	424	134	32
	Vocational	1992/93	...	...	...	52 654	23 243	44
		1993/94	...	...	...	52 548	23 247	44
		1994/95	...	...	...	54 199	23 808	44
Ukraine‡	Total second level	1980/81	...	...	...	3 406 400	...	...
		1985/86	...	...	...	3 401 100	...	...
		1990/91	...	...	...	3 407 500	...	...
		1991/92	...	...	...	3 354 400	...	...
		1992/93	...	...	...	4 701 000	...	...
		1993/94	...	...	...	4 731 200	...	...
	General	1980/81	...	...	...	2 904 000	...	...
		1985/86	316 600	...	...	2 824 400	...	...
		1990/91	353 500	...	...	2 863 900	...	...
		1991/92	359 800	...	...	2 803 600	...	...
		1992/93	371 300	...	...	4 156 700	2 120 900	51
		1993/94	377 000	...	...	4 202 200	2 139 400	51
	Teacher-training	1980/81	...	...	...	22 500	...	...
		1985/86	...	...	...	19 400	...	...
		1990/91	...	...	...	20 700	...	...
		1991/92	...	...	...	22 100	...	...
		1992/93	...	...	...	22 600	...	...
		1993/94	...	...	...	21 300	...	...

Second level: teachers and pupils
Second degré: personnel enseignant et élèves
Segundo grado: personal docente y alumnos

Country / Pays / País	Type of education / Type d'enseignement / Tipo de enseñanza	Year / Année / Año	Teaching staff Personnel enseignant Personal docente			Pupils enrolled Élèves inscrits Alumnos matriculados		
			Total	Female Féminin Femenino	% F	Total	Female Féminin Femenino	% F
			(1)	(2)	(3)	(4)	(5)	(6)
Ukraine‡ (cont)	Vocational	1980/81	...	...	...	479 900	...	...
		1985/86	...	...	...	557 300	...	...
		1990/91	...	...	...	522 900	...	...
		1991/92	...	...	...	528 700	...	...
		1992/93	...	...	...	521 700	...	...
		1993/94	...	...	...	507 700	...	...
United Kingdom	Total second level	1980/81	...	...	...	5 341 849	2 644 645	50
		1985/86	...	...	...	4 877 000	2 424 000	50
		1990/91	...	...	...	4 335 600	2 153 800	50
		1991/92	...	...	...	4 433 500	2 205 900	50
		1992/93	...	...	...	4 537 000	2 253 100	50
		1993/94	...	...	...	...	...	...
	General	1980/81	332 585	162 490	49	5 087 036	2 498 999	49
		1985/86	321 000	160 000	50	4 474 000	2 193 000	49
		1990/91	286 900	153 200	53	3 855 200	1 892 900	49
		1991/92	288 600	155 300	54	3 883 500	1 912 800	49
		1992/93	288 000	156 700	54	3 951 000	1 947 200	49
		1993/94	299 583	168 113	56	4 020 212	1 965 703	49
	Teacher-training		-	-	-	-	-	-
	Vocational	1980/81	...	...	...	254 813	145 646	57
		1985/86	...	...	...	403 000	231 000	57
		1990/91	...	...	...	480 400	260 900	54
		1991/92	...	...	...	550 000	293 100	53
		1992/93	...	...	...	586 000	305 900	52
Former Yugoslavia‡	Total second level	1980/81	131 348	64 735	49	2 426 164	1 140 238	47
		1985/86	132 912	67 237	51	2 352 985	1 114 980	47
		1990/91	141 480	74 550	53	2 344 331	1 128 037	48
	General	1980/81	...	...	...	1 835 636	873 550	48
		1985/86	...	...	...	1 745 439	835 092	48
		1990/91	...	...	...	1 548 408	767 175	50
	Teacher-training	1980/81	...	...	...	2 633	2 195	83
		1985/86	...	...	...	20 390	17 097	84
		1990/91	...	...	...	15 852	13 717	87
	Vocational	1980/81	...	...	...	587 895	264 493	45
		1985/86	...	...	...	587 156	262 791	45
		1990/91	...	...	...	780 071	347 145	45
Federal Republic of Yugoslavia	Total second level	1990/91	...	...	...	788 170	386 756	49
		1991/92	55 165	30 165	55	816 143	398 081	49
		1992/93	55 745	30 679	55	831 506	405 211	49
		1993/94	...	...	...	812 473	398 869	49
	General	1991/92	...	...	...	540 426	272 912	50
		1992/93	...	...	...	551 905	279 324	51
		1993/94	...	...	...	543 128	276 103	51
	Teacher-training	1991/92	...	...	...	3 568	3 269	92
		1992/93	...	...	...	1 783	1 619	91
		1993/94	...	...	...	1 338	787	59
	Vocational	1991/92	...	...	...	272 149	121 900	45
		1992/93	...	...	...	277 818	124 268	45
		1993/94	...	...	...	268 007	121 979	46
Oceania								
American Samoa	Total second level	1980/81	...	...	...	3 000	...	...
		1985/86	203	73	36	3 342	1 559	47
		1989/90	222	87	39	3 437	1 650	48
		1991/92	266	103	39	3 643	1 680	46
	General	1989/90	207	83	40	3 298	1 639	50
		1991/92	245	99	40	3 483	1 673	48
	Teacher-training		-	-	-	-	-	-
	Vocational	1989/90	15	4	27	139	11	8
		1991/92	21	4	19	160	7	4
Australia‡	Total second level	1980	85 340	38 604	45	1 100 468	545 897	50
		1985	105 955	50 960	48	1 278 272	632 578	49
		1990	103 298	51 743	50	1 278 163	635 691	50
		1992	104 110	52 710	51	1 294 596	639 470	49
		1993	103 385	52 881	51	1 282 309	634 060	49
		1994	101 477	52 101	51	1 273 640	631 453	50

Second level: teachers and pupils 3.7
Second degré: personnel enseignant et élèves
Segundo grado: personal docente y alumnos

Country Pays País	Type of education Type d'enseignement Tipo de enseñanza	Year Année Año	Teaching staff Personnel enseignant Personal docente			Pupils enrolled Élèves inscrits Alumnos matriculados		
			Total	Female Féminin Femenino	% F	Total	Female Féminin Femenino	% F
			(1)	(2)	(3)	(4)	(5)	(6)
Australia‡ (cont)	General	1980	85 340	38 604	45	1 100 468	545 897	50
		1985	105 955	50 960	48	1 278 272	632 578	49
		1990	103 298	51 743	50	1 278 163	635 691	50
		1992	104 110	52 710	51	1 294 596	639 470	49
		1993	103 385	52 881	51	1 282 309	634 060	49
		1994	101 477	52 101	51	1 273 640	631 453	50
	Teacher-training		-	-	-	-	-	-
	Vocational		-	-	-	-	-	-
Cook Islands	Total second level	1985	...	...	...	...	...	...
		1988	...	...	...	...	...	...
	General	1985	...	...	...	2 559	...	...
		1988	...	...	...	2 165	...	...
	Teacher-training	1988	...	...	...	22	20	91
Fiji	Total second level	1980	2 564	1 043	41	49 963	25 380	51
		1985	2 954	1 256	43	45 093	22 421	50
		1989	...	...	...	...	...	...
		1991	...	...	...	61 614	29 278	48
		1992	3 631	1 654	46	66 890	32 673	49
	General	1980	2 254	962	43	47 119	23 747	50
		1985	2 669	1 185	44	41 505	20 689	50
		1989	2 605	...	...	47 686	...	...
		1991	...	...	...	55 622	27 469	49
		1992	3 045	1 438	47	60 237	30 950	51
	Teacher-training	1980	75	20	27	514	247	48
		1985	-	-	-	-	-	-
		1989	-	-	-	-	-	-
		1991	-	-	-	-	-	-
		1992	-	-	-	-	-	-
	Vocational	1980	235	61	26	2 330	1 386	59
		1985	285	71	25	3 588	1 732	48
		1991	...	...	...	5 992	1 809	30
		1992	586	216	37	6 653	1 723	26
French Polynesia	Total second level	1981/82	...	540	...	...	...	...
		1986/87	1 240	540	44	17 878	9 822	55
		1990/91	1 497	670	45	20 311	10 766	53
		1992/93	1 592	730	46	22 366	12 241	55
	General	1986/87	855	419	49	13 765	7 819	57
		1990/91	1 174	577	49	16 806	9 444	56
		1992/93	1 276	631	49	18 636	10 492	56
	Teacher-training		-	-	-	-	-	-
	Vocational	1986/87	385	121	31	4 113	2 003	49
		1990/91	323	93	29	3 505	1 322	38
		1992/93	316	99	31	3 730	1 749	47
Guam‡	Total second level	1980/81	553	...	...	14 935	...	...
		1985/86	589	...	...	14 557	...	...
		1988/89	678	...	...	16 017	...	...
Kiribati	Total second level	1980	154	60	39	2 440	1 112	46
		1985	160	60	38	2 196	1 099	50
		1990	247	79	32	3 003	1 463	49
		1991	...	...	...	...	...	...
		1992	237	95	40	3 357	1 732	52
		1993	...	...	...	...	...	...
	General	1980	70	30	43	957	490	51
		1985	88	44	50	1 437	734	51
		1990	172	69	40	2 713	1 399	52
		1991	182	78	43	2 795	1 497	54
		1992	194	83	43	3 069	1 601	52
		1993	179	79	44	3 152	1 688	54
	Teacher-training	1980	13	4	31	107	56	52
		1985	12	4	33	97	68	70
		1990	16	4	25	39	24	62
		1991	15	4	27	51	31	61
		1992	12	3	25	54	33	61
		1993	9	3	33	63	38	60
	Vocational	1980	71	26	37	1 376	566	41
		1985	60	12	20	662	297	45
		1990	59	6	10	251	40	16
		1992	31	9	29	234	98	42

3.7 Second level: teachers and pupils
Second degré: personnel enseignant et élèves
Segundo grado: personal docente y alumnos

Country Pays País	Type of education Type d'enseignement Tipo de enseñanza	Year Année Año	Teaching staff Personnel enseignant Personal docente			Pupils enrolled Élèves inscrits Alumnos matriculados		
			Total	Female Féminin Femenino	% F	Total	Female Féminin Femenino	% F
			(1)	(2)	(3)	(4)	(5)	(6)
Nauru	Total second level	1985	40	18	45	482	242	50
	General	1985	36	18	50	465	234	50
	Teacher-training	1985	-	-	-	-	-	-
	Vocational	1985	4	-	-	17	8	47
New Caledonia	Total second level	1980	839	...	...	11 945	6 449	54
		1985	1 265	...	...	18 351	9 530	52
		1990	1 544	...	...	20 673	10 673	52
		1991	1 669	...	...	21 908	11 307	52
	General	1980	545	...	...	9 139	4 988	55
		1985	...	...	...	12 922	7 017	54
		1990	...	...	...	14 011	7 688	55
		1991	...	...	...	14 889	8 149	55
	Teacher-training		-	-	-	-	-	-
	Vocational	1980	294	94	32	2 806	1 461	52
		1985	...	...	...	5 429	2 513	46
		1990	...	...	...	6 662	2 985	45
		1991	...	...	...	7 019	3 158	45
New Zealand‡	Total second level	1980	...	...	...	352 427	174 175	49
		1985	...	...	...	354 080	176 311	50
		1990	...	...	...	340 915	168 503	49
		1992	...	...	...	350 112	171 673	49
		1993	...	...	...	376 947	185 120	49
		1994	28 358	16 023	57	404 563	200 427	50
	General	1980	13 278	*5 485	*41	349 356	171 668	49
		1985	18 663	8 502	46	351 618	174 299	50
		1990	...	...	...	332 014	164 123	49
		1992	22 195	11 938	54	331 962	163 439	49
		1993	...	...	...	328 361	161 764	49
		1994	24 569	14 172	58	340 905	170 246	50
	Teacher-training		-	-	-	-	-	-
	Vocational	1980	...	...	...	3 071	2 507	82
		1985	...	...	...	2 462	2 012	82
		1990	...	...	...	8 901	4 380	49
		1992	...	...	...	18 150	8 234	45
		1993	...	...	...	48 586	23 356	48
		1994	3 789	1 851	49	63 658	30 181	47
Niue‡	Total second level	1980	25	...	...	397	...	...
		1985	31	...	...	321	...	...
		1988	27	13	48	194	87	45
		1991	27	...	...	302	159	53
	General	1980	25	...	...	397	...	...
		1985	31	...	...	321	...	...
		1988	27	13	48	194	87	45
		1991	27	...	...	302	159	53
	Teacher-training		-	-	-	-	-	-
	Vocational		-	-	-	-	-	-
Papua New Guinea‡	Total second level	1981	2 289	738	32	49 334	...	...
		1987	2 922	978	33	63 391	*21 874	*35
		1990	...	...	...	65 643	24 935	38
		1993	...	...	...	77 665	30 392	39
		1994	...	...	...	83 252	32 804	39
		1995	...	...	...	78 759	30 858	39
	General	1981	1 625	513	32	39 701	13 065	33
		1987	2 200	765	35	53 752	19 564	36
		1990	...	...	...	55 797	21 458	38
		1993	...	...	...	65 406	26 181	40
		1994	...	...	...	70 392	28 580	41
		1995	...	...	...	68 818	27 693	40
	Teacher-training	1981	165	68	41	1 649	619	38
		1987	154	52	34	1 640	687	42
		1990	...	...	...	2 232	850	38
		1993	142	31	22	1 793	845	47
		1994	143	30	21	1 799	827	46
		1995	155	33	21	1 960	915	47

Second level: teachers and pupils 3.7
Second degré: personnel enseignant et élèves
Segundo grado: personal docente y alumnos

Country Pays País	Type of education Type d'enseignement Tipo de enseñanza	Year Année Año	Teaching staff Personnel enseignant Personal docente			Pupils enrolled Élèves inscrits Alumnos matriculados		
			Total	Female Féminin Femenino	% F	Total	Female Féminin Femenino	% F
			(1)	(2)	(3)	(4)	(5)	(6)
Papua New Guinea‡ (cont)	Vocational	1981	499	157	31	7 984	...	...
		1987	568	161	28	7 999	*1 623	*20
		1990	...	...	...	7 614	2 627	35
		1993	555	190	34	10 466	3 366	32
		1994	618	194	31	11 061	3 397	31
		1995	...	...	...	7 981	2 250	28
Samoa‡	Total second level	1980	...	...	...	19 785	9 691	49
		1986	...	...	...	20 604	...	...
	General	1980	475	213	45	19 299	9 459	49
		1986	513	238	46	20 168	10 108	50
	Teacher-training	1980	15	7	47	222	124	56
		1986	34	15	44	280	...	...
	Vocational	1980	35	16	46	264	108	41
		1986	19	5	26	156	...	...
Solomon Islands	Total second level	1980	257	67	26	4 030	...	...
		1985	...	...	...	...	...	...
		1990	...	...	...	5 636	2 068	37
		1992	...	...	...	6 666	2 442	37
		1993	...	...	...	7 351	2 658	36
		1994	...	...	...	7 811	2 940	38
	General	1980	196	61	31	3 547	1 063	30
		1985	270	...	...	5 240	...	...
		1990	...	...	...	5 636	2 068	37
		1992	...	...	...	6 666	2 442	37
		1993	...	...	...	7 351	2 658	36
		1994	...	...	...	7 811	2 940	38
	Teacher-training	1980	24	3	13	116	...	...
		1985	28	...	...	125	...	...
		1990	-	-	-	-	-	-
		1992	-	-	-	-	-	-
		1993	-	-	-	-	-	-
	Vocational	1980	37	3	8	367	18	5
		1990	-	-	-	-	-	-
		1992	-	-	-	-	-	-
		1993	-	-	-	-	-	-
Tokelau	Total second level	1983	...	...	...	488	245	60
		1991	...	...	...	...	...	...
	General	1983	...	...	...	108	56	52
		1991	...	...	...	113	53	47
	Teacher-training		-	-	-	-	-	-
	Vocational	1983	...	...	...	380	189	50
Tonga	Total second level	1981	...	...	...	16 566	7 812	47
		1985	840	381	45	15 232	7 694	51
		1990	832	411	49	14 749	7 076	48
		1991	876	395	45	14 825	7 258	49
		1992	...	...	...	...	...	...
		1993	...	...	...	16 570	7 908	48
	General	1981	686	337	49	15 760	7 447	47
		1985	770	347	45	14 641	7 321	50
		1990	767	375	49	13 877	6 681	48
		1991	...	...	...	13 839	6 814	49
		1992	...	...	...	13 318	6 352	48
		1993	847	265	31	15 573	7 450	48
	Teacher-training	1981	14	8	57	182	113	62
		1985	12	9	75	126	87	69
		1990	20	13	65	210	104	50
		1991	...	...	...	223	110	49
		1992	...	...	...	226	118	52
		1993	18	11	61	210	128	61
	Vocational	1981	...	...	...	624	252	40
		1985	58	25	43	465	286	62
		1990	45	23	51	662	291	44
		1991	...	...	...	763	334	44
		1993	...	...	...	787	330	42
Tuvalu	Total second level	1980	...	...	...	248	...	...
		1987	...	...	...	...	...	...
		1990	31	10	32	345	178	52
	General	1987	...	...	...	293	168	57
		1990	21	10	48	314	178	57

3.7 Second level: teachers and pupils
Second degré: personnel enseignant et élèves
Segundo grado: personal docente y alumnos

Country Pays País	Type of education Type d'enseignement Tipo de enseñanza	Year Année Año	Teaching staff Personnel enseignant Personal docente			Pupils enrolled Élèves inscrits Alumnos matriculados		
			Total	Female Féminin Femenino	% F	Total	Female Féminin Femenino	% F
			(1)	(2)	(3)	(4)	(5)	(6)
Tuvalu (cont)								
	Teacher-training		-	-	-	-	-	-
	Vocational	1990	10	-	-	31	-	-
Vanuatu, Republic of	Total second level	1980	185	...	...	2 426	1 018	42
		1990	...	...	...	...	...	...
		1991	...	...	...	4 184	1 797	43
		1992	...	...	...	...	...	...
	General	1980	...	...	...	1 970	866	44
		1991	208	65	31	3 799	1 642	43
		1992	220	79	36	4 269	1 894	44
	Teacher-training	1980	...	...	...	106	59	56
		1990	...	...	...	94	36	38
		1991	...	...	...	124	57	46
	Vocational	1980	45	...	...	350	93	27
		1990	...	...	...	199	76	38
		1991	...	...	...	261	98	38
		1992	...	...	...	444	140	32

This table gives the number of teaching staff and pupils in each of the three types of education at the second level, i.e. general, teacher-training, and technical and vocational. Unless otherwise stated, data cover public and private schools.

In most cases, data include part-time teachers whose proportion is particularly substantial in technical and vocational education. Personnel without teaching functions (e.g. librarians, guidance personnel, certain principals, etc.) are excluded.

Second level, General: This term refers to education in *second level schools* that provide general or specialized education based upon at least four years' previous instruction at the first level, and which do not aim at preparing the pupils directly for a given trade or occupation. Such schools may be called high schools, middle schools, lyceums, gymnasiums, etc., and offer programmes of which completion is a minimum condition for admission to third level education. In many countries, because of the desire to broaden the curricula there has been the development of schools providing both academic and vocational education. These *composite* schools are also classified as *second level general*.

Second level, Teacher-training: This term refers to education in second level schools with the purpose of training students for the teaching profession.

Second level, Technical and vocational: This term is used here to cover education provided in those *second level schools* which aim at preparing the pupils directly for a trade or occupation other than teaching. Such schools have many different names and vary greatly as to type and duration of training. Part-time courses and short courses abound and are excluded inasmuch as they refer to adult education. The abbreviation *vocational education* has been used in the table headings.

For international comparisons, this table should be consulted in conjunction with Tables 3.1, 3.1a and 3.1b. Please note that for all countries where education at the second level consists of two stages the data refer to both stages.

Ce tableau indique le nombre du personnel enseignant et des élèves inscrits dans chacun des trois types d'enseignement du second degré: général, normal et technique et professionnel. Sauf indication contraire, les données se réfèrent aux écoles publiques et privées.

Dans la plupart des cas, les chiffres comprennent les enseignants à temps partiel qui sont particulièrement nombreux dans l'enseignement technique et professionnel. Le personnel qui n'exerce pas de fonctions d'enseignement est exclu (par exemple les bibliothécaires, les orienteurs, certains chefs d'établissements, etc.).

Second degré, enseignement général: Cette formule désigne l'enseignement, général ou spécialisé, dispensé dans les *écoles du second degré* à des enfants ayant déjà fait au moins quatre années d'études dans le premier degré, et qui ne vise pas à préparer directement les élèves à une profession ou à un emploi. Les écoles de ce type s'appellent collèges, lycées, gymnases, etc., et elles dispensent un enseignement qu'il faut obligatoirement avoir terminé pour pouvoir être admis dans l'enseignement du troisième degré. Dans de nombreux pays, où l'on souhaite dispenser des formations plus diversifiées aux élèves on assiste au développement d'écoles qui offrent une formation tant générale que technique. Ces écoles *composites* sont également classées dans la catégorie *second degré, enseignement général*.

Second degré, enseignement normal: Cette formule désigne l'enseignement dispensé dans les écoles du second degré dont le but est de préparer à la profession d'enseignant.

Enseignement technique et professionnel: Cette formule désigne ici l'enseignement dispensé dans des *écoles du second degré* qui visent à préparer directement les élèves a un emploi ou une profession autre que l'enseignement. Ces écoles peuvent porter divers noms et la formation qu'elles dispensent varie largement quant à sa nature et à sa durée. Ce type d'enseignement comporte fréquemment des cours à mi-temps ou des cours de brève durée, qui ont été exclus dans la mesure où ils se réfèrent à l'éducation des adultes. La formule abrégée *enseignement technique* est utilisée dans les en-têtes des tableaux.

Pour effectuer des comparaisons internationales, ce tableau doit être consulté conjointement avec les tableaux 3.1, 3.1a et 3.1b. Il convient de noter que, pour tous les pays où l'enseignement du second degré se compose de deux cycles, les chiffres se réfèrent à l'ensemble des deux cycles.

Este cuadro indica el número de personal docente y de alumnos matriculados en cada uno de los tres tipos de enseñanza de segundo grado (general, normal, y técnica y profesional). Si no se indica lo contrario, los datos se refieren a las escuelas públicas y privadas.

En la mayoría de los casos, las cifras engloban a los profesores de jornada parcial, cuyo número es particularmente importante en la enseñanza técnica y profesional. En la medida de lo posible, ha quedado excluído el personal que no ejerce funciones docentes (por ejemplo, bibliotecarios, el personal de orientación, ciertos directores de establecimientos de enseñanza, etc.).

Segundo grado, enseñanza general: Esta categoría incluye las *escuelas de segundo grado* (es decir, las que dan una enseñanza general o especializada que implica cuatro años como mínimo de estudios previos en el primer grado) cuya finalidad no consiste en preparar directamente a los alumnos para un oficio o una profesión determinada. Esas escuelas, que pueden llamarse escuelas secundarias, escuelas medias, liceos, gimnasios, etc., tienen un plan de estudios que conduce a la obtención de un diploma que es condición indispensable para el ingreso en la enseñanza superior. Bastantes países, para ofrecer otros tipos de formación a los alumnos, han creado escuelas donde se da una instrucción a la vez

Second level: teachers and pupils 3.7
Second degré: personnel enseignant et élèves
Segundo grado: personal docente y alumnos

general y técnica. Esas escuelas de carácter mixto estan agrupadas bajo la rúbrica *enseñanza general de segundo grado*.

Segundo grado, enseñanza normal (formación de personal docente): Esta expresión se refiere a la enseñanza en escuelas secundarias destinadas a preparar para la profesión docente.

Segundo grado, enseñanza técnica y profesional: Esta expresión se utiliza aqui para designar las *escuelas de segundo grado* que tienen como finalidad preparar directamente a los alumnos para un oficio o una profesión determinada que no sea la docente. El nombre

y el tipo de esas escuelas varían considerablemente. Son frecuentes los ciclos de estudios de horario parcial y los de breve duración, que han sido excluídos en la medida en que se refieren a la educación de adultos. Por razones prácticas, se ha utilizado el término *enseñanza técnica* en los títulos de los cuadros.

Para efectuar comparaciones internacionales, este cuadro debe consultarse conjuntamente con los cuadros 3.1, 3.1a y 3.1b. Nótese que, para todos los países donde la enseñanza de segundo grado comprende dos ciclos, los datos se refieren al total de los dos ciclos.

AFRICA:
Algeria:
E--> See Table 3.1B.
FR-> Voir le tableau 3.1B.
ESP> Véase el cuadro 3.1B.

Benin:
E--> For 1990/1991 and 1991/1992, data refer to public education only.
FR-> En 1990/1991 et 1991/1992, les données se réfèrent à l'enseignement public seulement.
ESP> Para 1990/1991 y 1991/1992, los datos se refieren a la enseñanza pública solamente.

Cape Verde:
E--> See Table 3.1B.
FR-> Voir le tableau 3.1B
ESP> Véase el cuadro 3.1B.

Côte d'Ivoire:
E--> *General education:* Data on teachers refer to public education only. *Vocational education:* Data refer to schools attached to the Ministry of Education only.
FR-> *Enseignement général:* Les données relatives au personnel enseignant se réfèrent à l'enseignement public seulement. *Enseignement technique:* Les données se réfèrent aux écoles rattachées au Ministère de l'Education seulement.
ESP> *Enseñanza general:* Los datos relativos al personal docente se refieren a la enseñanza pública solamente. *Enseñanza técnica:* Los datos se refieren a las escuelas dependientes del Ministerio de Educación solamente.

Djibouti:
E--> *General education:* From 1985/86, data on teachers refer to public education only. *Vocational education:* For 1985/86 data on teachers refer to public education only.
FR-> *Enseignement général:* A partir de 1985/86, les données relatives au personnel enseignant se réfèrent à l'enseignement public seulement. *Enseignement technique:* Pour 1985/86 les données relatives au personnel enseignant se réfèrent à l'enseignement public seulement.
ESP> *Enseñanza general:* A partir de 1985/86, los datos relativos al personal docente se refieren a la enseñanza pública solamente. *Enseñanza técnica:* Para 1985/86, los datos sobre el personal docente se refieren a la enseñanza pública solamente.

Egypt:
E--> See Table 3.1B. *General education:* All data on teachers and those on pupils for 1992/93 and 1994/95 do not include Al Azhar. *Teacher training:* All data on teachers and those on pupils from 1990/91 do not include Al Azhar.
FR-> Voir le tableau 3.1B. *Enseignement général:* Toutes Les données relatives au personnel enseignant et celles relatives aux élèves pour 1992/93 et 1994/95 ne comprennent pas Al Azhar. *Enseignement normal:* Toutes les données sur les enseignants et celles sur les élèves à partir de 1990/91 n'incluent pas Al Azhar.
ESP> Véase el cuadro 3.1B. *Enseñanza general:* Todos los datos relativos al personal docente y aquellos sobre los alumnos para 1992/93 y 1994/95 no incluyen Al Azhar. *Enseñanza normal:* Todos los datos sobre el personal docente y aquellos sobre los alumnos desde 1990/91 no incluyen Al Azhar.

Equatorial Guinea:
E--> In 1992/93 data refer to public education only.
FR-> En 1992/93 les données se réfèrent à l'enseignement public seulement.
ESP> Para 1992/93 los datos se refieren a la enseñanza pública solamente.

Gabon:
E--> *General education:* In 1991/92 data on teachers refer to public education only.
FR-> *Enseignement général:* En 1991/92, les données relatives au personnel enseignant se réfèrent à l'enseignement public seulement.
ESP> *Enseñanza general:* Para 1991/92, los datos relativos al personal docente se refieren a la enseñanza pública solamente.

Ghana:
E--> *General and vocational education:* Except for 1980/81 and 1991/92 data refer to public education only.

FR-> *Enseignement général et technique:* A l'exception de 1980/81 et de 1991/92 les données se réfèrent à l'enseignement public seulement.
ESP> *Enseñanza general y técnica:* Excepto para 1980/81 y 1991/92 los datos se refieren a la enseñanza pública solamente.

Guinea:
E--> See Table 3.1B.
FR-> Voir le tableau 3.1B.
ESP> Véase el cuadro 3.1B.

Kenya:
E--> See Table 3.1B. *Teacher training:* For 1980 data on teachers include teacher training at the third level of education.
FR-> Voir le tableau 3.1B. *Enseignement normal:* Pour 1980 les données relatives au personnel enseignant comprennent l'enseignement normal du troisième degré.
ESP> Véase el cuadro 3.1B. *Enseñanza normal:* Para 1980 los datos relativos al personal docente incluyen la enseñanza normal de tercer grado.

Lesotho:
E--> *Teacher training:* Data on teachers include teacher training at the third level of education.
FR-> *Enseignement normal:* Les données relatives au personnel enseignant comprennent l'enseignement normal du troisième degré.
ESP> *Enseñanza normal:* Los datos relativos al personal docente incluyen la enseñanza normal de tercer grado.

Libyan Arab Jamahiriya:
E--> See Table 3.1B.
FR-> Voir le tableau 3.1B.
ESP> Véase el cuadro 3.1B.

Madagascar:
E--> *General education:* Data for 1979/80 and 1984/85 refer to public education only. *Vocational education:* Data for 1991/92 and 1992/93 refer to public education only.
FR-> *Enseignement général:* Les données pour 1979/80 et 1984/85 se réfèrent à l'enseignement public seulement. *Enseignement technique:* Les données pour 1991/92 et 1992/93 se réfèrent à l'enseignement public seulement.
ESP> *Enseñanza general:* Los datos para 1979/80 y 1984/85 se refieren a la enseñanza pública solamente. *Enseñanza técnica:* Los datos para 1991/92 y 1992/93 se refieren a la enseñanza pública solamente.

Mauritania:
E--> *Vocational education:* From 1990/91 data do not include health-related programmes.
FR-> *Enseignement technique:* A partir de 1990/91 les données n'incluent pas les programmes relatifs à la santé.
ESP> *Enseñanza técnica:* A partir de 1990/91 los datos excluyen los programas relativos a la salud.

Morocco:
E--> See Table 3.1B. *Vocational education:* All data do not include professional schools, except for 1985/86 where they exclude public professional schools only.
FR-> Voir le tableau 3.1B. *Enseignement technique:* Toutes les données ne comprennent pas les écoles professionnelles, à l'exception de 1985/86 ou elles excluent seulement les écoles publiques professionnelles.
ESP> Véase el cuadro 3.1B. *Enseñanza técnica:* Todos los datos no incluyen las escuelas profesionales, excepto para 1985/86 donde ellos excluyen solamente las escuelas públicas profesionales.

Mozambique:
E--> See Table 3.1B.
FR-> Voir le tableau 3.1B.
ESP> Véase el cuadro 3.1B.

Nigeria:
E--> See Table 3.1B. From 1990, the school year corresponds to the calendar year.
FR-> Voir le tableau 3.1B. A partir de 1990, l'année scolaire correspond à l'année du calendrier.
ESP> Véase el cuadro 3.1B. A partir de 1990, el año escolar corresponde al año calendario.

Rwanda:
E--> From 1990/91 data on teaching staff do not include *integrated rural and craft education.*

3.7 Second level: teachers and pupils
Second degré: personnel enseignant et élèves
Segundo grado: personal docente y alumnos

FR-> A partir de 1990/91 les données sur les enseignants n'incluent pas l'enseignement *rural et artisanal intégré*.

ESP> A partir de 1990/91 los datos sobre el personal docente no incluyen la *enseñanza rural y artesanal integrada*.

Senegal:
E--> *General education:* Data on teachers refer to public education only, and for 1990/91 and 1991/92 include teaching staff of vocational education.

FR-> *Enseignement général:* Les données sur le personnel enseignant se réfèrent à l'enseignement public seulement, et en 1990/91 et 1991/92 incluent les professeurs de l'enseignement technique.

ESP> *Enseñanza general:* Los datos sobre el personal docente se refieren a la enseñanza pública solamente, y en 1990/91 y 1991/92 incluyen los profesores de la enseñanza técnica.

Seychelles:
E--> See Table 3.1B.
FR-> Voir le tableau 3.1B.
ESP> Véase el cuadro 3.1B.

South Africa:
E--> Data for 1986 and 1993 do not include the former Independent States (Transkei, Bophuthatswana, Venda and Ciskei).

FR-> Les données pour 1986 et 1993 n'incluent pas les anciens Etats indépendants (Transkei, Bophuthatswana, Venda et Ciskei).

ESP> Los datos para 1986 y 1993 no incluyen los antiguos Estados independientes (Transkei, Bophuthatswana, Venda y Ciskei).

Uganda:
E--> *General education:* Data refer to government-maintained and aided schools only.

FR-> *Enseignement général:* Les données se rapportent aux écoles publiques et subventionnées seulement.

ESP> *Enseñanza general:* Los datos se refieren a las escuelas públicas y subvencionadas solamente.

United Republic of Tanzania:
E--> Data refer to Tanzania Mainland only.
FR-> Les données se réfèrent à la Tanzanie continentale seulement.
ESP> Los datos se refieren a Tanzania continental solamente.

Zambia:
E--> *General education:* Data refer to government-maintained and aided schools only.

FR-> *Enseignement général:* Les données se rapportent aux écoles publiques et subventionnées seulement.

ESP> *Enseñanza general:* Los datos se refieren a las escuelas públicas y subvencionadas solamente.

AMERICA, NORTH:
Bahamas:
E--> For 1980/81 and 1985/86, data on teaching staff do not include senior departments of all-age schools (included in first level).

FR-> Pour 1980/81 et 1985/86, les données sur le personnel enseignant n'incluent pas les classes supérieures des *all-age schools* (comprises dans le premier degré).

ESP> Para 1980/81 y 1985/86, los datos sobre el personal docente no incluyen las clases superiores de *all-age schools* (incluídas en el primer grado).

Barbados:
E--> For 1980/81, data on teachers refer to public education only.

FR-> Pour 1980/81, les données relatives au personnel enseignant se réfèrent à l'enseignement public seulement.

ESP> Para 1980/81, los datos relativos al personal docente se refieren a la enseñanza pública solamente.

Dominica:
E--> *General education:* Data on teachers are included with education at the first level.

FR-> *Enseignement général:* Les données relatives au personnel enseignant sont incluses dans l'enseignement du premier degré.

ESP> *Enseñanza general:* Los datos sobre el personal docente están incluídos en la enseñanza de primer grado.

Dominican Republic:
E--> See Table 3.1B.
FR-> Voir le tableau 3.1B.
ESP> Véase el cuadro 3.1B.

Jamaica:
E--> For 1990/91 data refer to public education only. *General education:* All data on teachers refer to public education only. *Vocational education:* Except for data on pupils for 1980/81, all figures refer to public education only.

FR-> Pour 1990/91 les données se réfèrent à l'enseignement public seulement. *Enseignement général:* Les données relatives au personnel enseignant se réfèrent à l'enseignement public seulement. *Enseignement technique:* A l'exception des données

sur les élèves en 1980/81, les chiffres se réfèrent à l'enseignement public seulement.

ESP> Para 1990/91 los datos se refieren a la enseñanza pública solamente. *Enseñanza general:* Los datos relativos al personal docente se refieren a la enseñanza pública solamente. *Enseñanza técnica:* Con excepción de los datos sobre los alumnos en 1980/81, las cifras se refieren a la enseñanza pública solamente.

Martinique:
E--> Data on teachers refer to public education only.
FR-> Les données relatives au personnel enseignant se réfèrent à l'enseignement public seulement.
ESP> Los datos relativos al personal docente se refieren a la enseñanza pública solamente.

St. Kitts and Nevis:
E--> *General education:* For 1992/93 data on teachers refer to public education only.

FR-> *Enseignement général:* En 1992/93 les données relatives au personnel enseignant se réfèrent à l'enseignement public seulement.

ESP> *Enseñanza general:* Para 1992/93 los datos relativos al personal docente se refieren a la enseñanza pública solamente.

St. Lucia:
E--> *General education:* Data on teaching staff for 1990/91 refer to public education only.

FR-> *Enseignement général:* Les données sur le personnel enseignant pour 1990/91 se réfèrent à l'enseignement public seulement.

ESP> *Enseñanza general:* Los datos sobre el personal docente para 1990/91, se refieren a la enseñanza pública solamente.

St. Vincent and the Grenadines:
E--> *General education:* Data for 1985/86 do not include secondary classes attached to primary schools.

FR-> *Enseignement général:* Les données pour 1985/86 n'incluent pas les classes secondaires rattachées aux écoles primaires.

ESP> *Enseñanza general:* Los datos para 1985/86 no incluyen las clases secundarias adscritas a las escuelas primarias.

Trinidad and Tobago:
E--> *General education:* Data include courses in vocational and technical education.

FR-> *Enseignement général:* Les données incluent des cours d'enseignement professionnel et technique.

ESP> *Enseñanza general:* Los datos incluyen cursos de enseñanza profesional y técnica.

United States:
E--> Revised data series, corresponding to grades 7 to 12.
FR-> Les données ont été révisées et se réfèrent aux classes allant de la septième à la douzième année d'études.
ESP> Los datos han sido revisados y se refieren a las clases comprendidas entre el septimo y el doceaba año de estudio.

U.S. Virgin Islands:
E--> Revised data. Data on teaching staff and data for 1990/91 refer to public education only.

FR-> Données révisées. Les données relatives au personnel enseignant et celles pour 1990/91 se réfèrent à l'enseignement public seulement.

ESP> Datos revisados. Los datos relativos al personal docente y los datos para 1990/91 se refieren a la enseñanza pública solamente.

AMERICA, SOUTH:
Ecuador:
E--> *General education:* For 1990/91 and 1991/92 data include vocational education. *General and vocational education:* Due to a change in classification, from 1985/86 data are not comparable with those of previous years.

FR-> *Enseignement général:* Pour 1990/91 et 1991/92 les données incluent l'enseignement technique. *Enseignement général et technique:* Suite à un changement de classification, à partir de 1985/86 les données ne sont pas comparables à celles des années antérieures.

ESP> *Enseñanza general:* Para 1990/91 y 1991/92 los datos incluyen la enseñanza técnica. *Enseñanza general y técnica:* Debido a un cambio de clasificación, a partir de 1985/86 los datos no son comparables con los de los años anteriores.

Peru:
E--> *General education:* For 1994, data include adult education.

FR-> *Enseignement général:* En 1994, les données incluent l'enseignement des adultes.

ESP> *Enseñanza general:* En 1994, los datos incluyen la enseñanza de adultos.

Uruguay:
E--> *General education:* For 1980 data do not include courses of U.T.U. (Universidad del Trabajo del Uruguay).

FR-> *Enseignement général:* Pour 1980 les données ne comprennent pas les cours de la U.T.U. (Universidad del Trabajo del Uruguay).

Second level: teachers and pupils **3.7**
Second degré: personnel enseignant et élèves
Segundo grado: personal docente y alumnos

ESP> *Enseñanza general:* Para 1980 los datos no incluyen los cursos de la U.T.U. (Universidad del Trabajo del Uruguay).
Venezuela:
E--> For 1985/86, data on teaching staff refer to grades 7 to 11. All other data refer to grades 10 and 11.
FR-> Pour 1985/86, les données sur le personnel enseignant se réfèrent aux années d'études 7 à 11. Toutes les autres données se réfèrent aux années d'études 10 et 11.
ESP> Para 1985/86, los datos sobre el personal docente se refieren a los años de estudios 7 a 11. Todos los otros datos se refieren a los años de estudios 10 y 11.
ASIA:
Afghanistan:
E--> See table 3.1B.
FR-> Voir le tableau 3.1B.
ESP> Véase el cuadro 3.1B.
Bahrain:
E--> *General education:* Data on teachers refer to public education only and for 1985/86 exclude a part of intermediate education.
FR-> *Enseignement général:* Les données relatives au personnel enseignant se réfèrent à l'enseignement public seulement et pour 1985/86 excluent une partie de l'enseignement intermédiaire.
ESP> *Enseñanza general:* Los datos relativos al personal docente se refieren a la enseñanza pública solamente y para 1985/86 excluyen una parte de la enseñanza intermedia.
Bhutan:
E--> See Table 3.1B.
FR-> Voir le tableau 3.1B.
ESP> Véase el cuadro 3.1B.
Cyprus:
E--> Not including Turkish schools. *General and vocational education:* From 1985/86, data on commercial schools are included with general education.
FR-> Non compris les écoles turques. *Enseignement général et technique:* A partir de 1985/86, les données relatives aux écoles commerciales sont comprises avec l'enseignement général.
ESP> Excluídas las escuelas turcas. *Enseñanza general y técnica:* A partir de 1985/86, los datos relativos a las escuelas comerciales están incluídos en la enseñanza general.
Hong Kong:
E--> Since 1990/91, data on teachers do not include teachers in international and English Foundation schools (9,755 pupils in 1994/95).
FR-> A partir de 1990/91, les données sur les enseignants n'incluent pas les enseignants des écoles internationales et de la *English Foundation* (9 755 élèves in 1994/95).
ESP> A partir de 1990/91, los datos relativos al personal docente no incluyen los docentes de las escuelas internacionales y de la *English Foundation* (9 755 alumnos en 1994/95).
India:
E--> *General education:* Data on teachers include primary classes attached to secondary schools.
FR-> *Enseignement général:* Les données relatives au personnel enseignant comprennent les classes primaires rattachées aux écoles secondaires.
ESP> *Enseñanza general:* Los datos relativos al personal docente incluyen las clases primarias adscritas a las escuelas secundarias.
Israel:
E--> Data on teaching staff include intermediate classes attached to primary schools.
FR-> Les données relatives au personnel enseignant incluent les classes intermédiaires rattachées aux écoles primaires.
ESP> Los datos relativos al personal docente incluyen las clases intermedias adscritas a las escuelas primarias.
Jordan:
E--> See Table 3.1B.
FR-> Voir le tableau 3.1B.
ESP> Véase el cuadro 3.1B.
Nepal:
E--> See Table 3.1B.
FR-> Voir le tableau 3.1B.
ESP> Véase el cuadro 3.1B.
Saudi Arabia:
E--> *Teacher training:* For 1985/86, data on teachers refer to full-time only.
FR-> *Enseignement normal:* Pour 1985/86, les données sur le personnel enseignant se réfèrent au personnel à plein temps seulement.
ESP> *Enseñanza normal:* Para 1985/86, los datos sobre el personal docente se refieren al personal de jornada completa solamente.
Singapore:
E--> See Table 3.1B.
FR-> Voir le tableau 3.1B.

ESP> Véase el cuadro 3.1B.
Sri Lanka:
E--> See Table 3.1B.
FR-> Voir le tableau 3.1B.
ESP> Véase el cuadro 3.1B.
Thailand:
E--> *General education:* For 1980/81 data on teachers refer to public education only.
FR-> *Enseignement général:* Pour 1980/81, les données relatives au personnel enseignant se réfèrent à l'enseignement public seulement.
ESP> *Enseñanza general:* Para 1980/81 los datos relativos al personal docente se refieren a la enseñanza pública solamente.
United Arab Emirates:
E--> For 1980/81 and 1985/86, data on teachers refer to public education only.
FR-> En 1980/81 et 1985/86, les données relatives au personnel enseignant se réfèrent à l'enseignement public seulement.
ESP> Para 1980/81 y 1985/86, los datos relativos al personal docente se refieren a la enseñanza pública solamente.
EUROPE:
Belarus:
E--> See Table 3.1B. *General education:* Data on teachers are included with education at the first level.
FR-> Voir le tableau 3.1B. *Enseignement général:* Les données relatives au personnel enseignant sont incluses dans l'enseignement du premier degré.
ESP> Véase el cuadro 3.1B. *Enseñanza general:* Los datos relativos al personal docente quedan incluídos en la enseñanza de primer grado.
Bulgaria:
E--> See Table 3.1B.
FR-> Voir le tableau 3.1B.
ESP> Véase el cuadro 3.1B.
France:
E--> In 1980/81 data on teaching staff refer to public education only.
FR-> Pour 1980/81 les données relatives au personnel enseignant se réfèrent à l'enseignement public seulement.
ESP> Para 1980/81 los datos relativos al personal docente se refieren a la enseñanza pública solamente.
Germany:
Federal Republic of Germany:
E--> For 1980/81, data do not include technical education consisting of both on the job training and school education.
FR-> Pour 1980/81, les données n'incluent pas l'enseignement technique dispensé à la fois dans les institutions scolaires et auprès des entreprises.
ESP> Para 1980/81, los datos no incluyen la enseñanza técnica que se imparte a la vez en las instituciones escolares y en las empresas.
Ireland:
E--> The number of teachers is expressed in full-time equivalent.
FR-> Le nombre de professeurs est compté en équivalent plein temps.
ESP> El número de profesores se presenta en equivalentes de jornada completa.
Latvia:
E--> *General education:* The number of teachers includes those at the primary level.
FR-> *Enseignement général:* Le personnel enseignant inclut celui du premier degré.
ESP> *Enseñanza general:* El personal docente incluye el del primer grado.
Monaco:
E--> Data for 1980/81 refer to public education only. *General education:* Data on teaching staff refer to public education only.
FR-> Les données pour 1980/81 se réfèrent à l'enseignement public seulement. *Enseignement général:* Les données relatives au personnel enseignant se réfèrent à l'enseignement public seulement.
ESP> Los datos para 1980/81 se refieren a la enseñanza pública solamente. *Enseñanza general:* Los datos relativos al personal docente se refieren a la enseñanza pública solamente.
Netherlands:
E--> *Vocational education:* In 1980/81 data do not include apprenticeships and health care training.
FR-> *Enseignement technique:* En 1980/81 les données ne comprennent pas l'apprentissage et les programmes relatifs à la santé.
ESP> *Enseñanza técnica:* Para 1980/81 los datos no incluyen el aprentizaje y los programas relativos a la salud.
Romania:
E--> See Table 3.1B.
FR-> Voir le tableau 3.1B.

3.7 Second level: teachers and pupils
Second degré: personnel enseignant et élèves
Segundo grado: personal docente y alumnos

ESP> Véase el cuadro 3.1B.

Ukraine:

E--> See Table 3.1B. *General education:* All data on teachers refer to grades 5-11, whereas enrolment data refer to these grades only since 1992/93.

FR-> Voir le tableau 3.1B. *Enseignement général:* Toutes les données relatives au personnel enseignant se réfèrent aux années d'études 5 à 11 alors que les élèves ne se réfèrent à ces années d'études qu'à partir de 1992/93.

ESP> Véase el cuadro 3.1B. *Enseñanza general:* Todos Los datos relativos al personal docente se refieren a los años de estudio 5 a 11 aunque los alumnos solo se refieren a estos años de estudios a partir de 1992/93.

Former Yugoslavia:

E--> For 1980/81, data on pupils in vocational education include a part of enrolment in teacher training.

FR-> Pour 1980/81, les données sur les élèves de l'enseignement technique incluent une partie des effectifs de l'enseignement normal.

ESP> Para 1980/81, los datos sobre los alumnos de la enseñanza técnica incluyen una parte de la matrícula de la enseñanza normal.

OCEANIA:

Australia:

E--> From 1990, data on teaching staff are expressed in full-time equivalent.

FR-> A partir de 1990, les données relatives au personnel enseignant sont exprimées en équivalents plein temps.

ESP> A partir de 1990, los datos relativos al personal docente se presentan en equivalentes de jornada completa.

Guam:

E--> Data on teaching staff refer to public education only.

FR-> Les données sur le personnel enseignant se réfèrent à l'enseignement public seulement.

ESP> Los datos sobre el personal docente se refieren a la enseñanza pública solamente.

New Zealand:

E--> *General education:* For 1980, data on teachers do not include forms I and II. *Vocational education:* From 1993, data include part-time students.

FR-> *Enseignement général:* Pour 1980, les données relatives au personnel enseignant n'incluent pas les *forms* I et II. *Enseignement technique:* A partir de 1993, les données incluent les étudiants à temps partiel.

ESP> *Enseñanza general:* Para 1980, los datos sobre el personal docente no incluyen las *forms* I y II. *Enseñanza técnica:* A partir de 1993, los datos incluyen los estudiantes de jornada parcial.

Niue:

E--> See Table 3.1B.

FR-> Voir le tableau 3.1B.

ESP> Véase el cuadro 3.1B.

Papua New Guinea:

E--> Data do not include colleges of distance education.

FR-> Les données n'incluent pas les établissements d'enseignement à distance.

ESP> Los datos no incluyen los establecimientos de enseñanza a distancia.

Samoa:

E--> *General education:* Data on teaching staff do not include intermediate education (Forms I and II).

FR-> *Enseignement général:* Les données relatives au personnel enseignant n'incluent pas l'enseignement intermédiaire (*forms* I et II).

ESP> *Enseñanza general:* Los datos sobre el personal docente no incluyen la enseñanza intermedia (*forms* I y II).

Second level (general): enrolment by grade
Second degré (général): effectifs par année d'études
Segundo grado (general): matrícula escolar por año de estudios

3.8

3.8 Education at the second level (general): distribution of enrolment by grade

Enseignement du second degré (général): répartition des effectifs par année d'études

Enseñanza de segundo grado (general): distribución de la matrícula escolar por año de estudios

Please refer to the explanatory text at the end of the table

Prière de se référer au texte explicatif à la fin du tableau

Referirse al texto explicativo al final del cuadro

\# For countries shown with this symbol data refer to all second level education.

\# Pour les pays présentés avec ce symbole les données se réfèrent à l'ensemble de l'enseignement du second degré.

\# Para los países presentados con este símbolo, los datos se refieren al total de la enseñanza de segundo grado.

Country Pays País	Year Année Año	Sex Sexe Sexo	Grades / Années d'études / Años de estudios									
			I	II	III	IV	V	VI	VII	VIII	IX	X
Africa												
Algeria	1988/89	MF	25	22	25	12	8	9				
		F	24	21	23	14	9	10				
	1990/91	MF	25	22	23	10	9	11				
		F	24	21	21	11	10	13				
	1993/94	MF	25	22	23	12	7	11				
		F	24	21	22	12	9	12				
	1994/95	MF	25	22	23	12	7	10				
		F	23	21	22	12	9	12				
Angola	1985/86	MF	50	28	13	7	2	——>				
	1990/91	MF	47	28	13	9	4	——>				
Benin	1985/86	MF	22	21	20	19	7	6	6			
		F	24	22	22	18	5	4	5			
	1989/90	MF	22	23	19	17	6	6	7			
		F	25	25	20	16	5	4	5			
Botswana	1985	MF	33	32	21	7	6					
		F	33	34	22	5	5					
	1990	MF	39	30	12	11	8					
		F	42	30	11	10	7					
	1993	MF	37	36	10	9	8					
		F	37	37	9	9	8					
	1994	MF	36	36	10	10	9					
Burkina Faso	1985/86	MF	28	21	15	15	7	6	8			
		F	30	23	15	15	6	4	6			
	1990/91	MF	28	21	20	17	5	4	5			
		F	31	22	20	17	4	3	4			
	1992/93	MF	29	22	18	18	6	4	4			
		F	32	22	18	18	4	2	3			
	1993/94	MF	29	21	18	18	6	4	4			
		F	32	22	18	18	4	3	3			
Burundi	1985/86	MF	28	22	17	12	8	7	6			
		F	29	23	18	12	7	6	4			
	1990/91	MF	25	23	20	17	7	5	4			
		F	25	24	21	18	5	4	3			

Second level (general): enrolment by grade
Second degré (général): effectifs par année d'études
Segundo grado (general): matrícula escolar por año de estudios

Country Pays País	Year Année Año	Sex Sexe Sexo	Grades / Années d'études / Años de estudios									
			I	II	III	IV	V	VI	VII	VIII	IX	X
Burundi (cont)	1991/92	MF	25	22	20	17	7	5	4			
		F	27	22	21	17	6	4	3			
	1992/93	MF	27	22	19	16	7	5	5			
		F	29	22	20	16	5	4	4			
Cameroon	1985/86	MF	23	20	18	18	8	7	5			
		F	26	22	19	18	6	5	3			
	1990/91	MF	21	18	18	18	9	9	7			
		F	23	19	19	19	8	7	5			
Cape Verde	1985/86	MF	43	21	19	17	——>					
		F	46	21	19	14	——>					
	1989/90	MF	43	28	17	5	7					
		F	44	28	18	4	6					
	1993/94	MF	33	27	22	7	7	4				
		F	33	27	22	7	7	4				
Central African Republic	1985/86	MF	26	19	16	16	7	7	7			
		F	32	21	16	14	6	5	4			
	1989/90	MF	30	20	16	13	8	5	8			
		F	35	21	15	13	6	4	6			
Chad	1987/88	MF	25	18	16	17	9	7	8			
		F	32	20	18	18	5	4	4			
	1990/91	MF	29	20	15	15	8	5	7			
		F	*33	*22	*16	*16	*6	*3	*4			
	1991/92	MF	29	20	17	15	7	5	7			
	1993/94	MF	23	22	16	17	7	6	9			
		F	27	23	16	16	7	5	7			
Comoros	1985/86	MF	23	22	18	18	10	6	4			
		F	25	23	18	18	9	4	3			
	1991/92	MF	19	20	14	17	13	8	9			
		F	21	20	15	17	13	7	8			
	1992/93	MF	19	17	16	15	13	10	10			
		F	21	17	17	16	12	8	8			
	1993/94	MF	25	17	15	14	8	9	11			
		F	26	17	15	15	8	9	10			
Congo	1986/87	MF	29	21	17	20	5	3	6			
		F	32	23	17	19	4	2	3			
	1990/91	MF	29	19	16	21	7	4	4			
		F	32	20	17	21	4	2	3			
	1991/92	MF	28	20	15	19	9	5	5			
		F	31	21	16	20	6	3	3			
	1993/94	MF	27	18	15	19	10	5	6			
		F	31	20	17	20	6	3	3			
Côte d'Ivoire	1985/86	MF	24	21	20	18	6	7	3			
		F	28	23	20	18	5	5	2			
	1990/91	MF	21	20	18	17	8	7	8			
		F	25	22	19	17	7	5	6			
	1991/92	MF	22	19	18	17	8	7	10			
		F	24	21	18	16	7	6	8			
	1993/94	MF	23	18	17	17	8	6	10			
		F	25	19	18	17	8	5	9			
Djibouti	1985/86	MF	25	25	19	19	6	4	4			
		F	29	26	19	16	4	3	4			
	1990/91	MF	26	25	19	16	5	5	5			
		F	27	25	18	17	4	4	4			
	1992/93	MF	27	23	19	17	5	5	4			
		F	27	23	19	19	4	4	3			
	1993/94	MF	26	23	20	17	5	4	5			
		F	26	23	19	18	5	5	5			
Egypt	1987/88	MF	29	24	26	6	6	8				
		F	31	25	26	6	6	7				

Second level (general): enrolment by grade 3.8
Second degré (général): effectifs par année d'études
Segundo grado (general): matrícula escolar por año de estudios

Country Pays País	Year Année Año	Sex Sexe Sexo	I	II	III	IV	V	VI	VII	VIII	IX	X
			Grades / Années d'études / Años de estudios									
Egypt (cont)	1990/91	MF	33	34	18	5	5	6				
		F	33	35	18	5	5	5				
	1993/94	MF	29	24	25	6	7	8				
		F	30	25	25	6	7	8				
Equatorial Guinea	1993/94	MF	36	23	17	13	3	4	3			
		F	46	24	15	11	2	1	1			
Eritrea	1988/89	MF	22	27	18	13	12	8				
	1990/91	MF	20	26	16	15	13	10				
	1993/94	MF	27	23	22	13	9	6				
		F	29	24	24	11	8	4				
	1994/95	MF	27	22	21	15	10	5				
		F	29	23	22	14	8	4				
Ethiopia	1985/86	MF	32	24	18	11	9	6				
		F	31	25	20	11	9	6				
	1990/91	MF	23	24	18	14	12	8				
		F	23	26	20	14	11	7				
	1992/93	MF	26	23	17	12	12	10				
		F	26	24	18	12	11	8				
	1993/94	MF	25	25	19	12	11	8				
		F	24	26	20	12	10	7				
Gabon‡	1985/86	MF	31	21	17	12	8	6	6			
		F	34	22	16	12	7	5	4			
	1991/92	MF	26	19	17	15	9	8	7			
		F	26	20	15	18	8	7	5			
Gambia #	1985/86	MF	25	24	24	21	5	1	——>			
		F	26	25	24	19	5	2	——>			
	1990/91	MF	26	27	24	17	4	2				
		F	28	30	24	15	3	1				
	1991/92	MF	25	24	23	21	4	1				
		F	27	26	24	20	3	1				
	1992/93	MF	28	24	22	20	5	1				
		F	29	25	22	19	4	1				
Ghana	1986/87	MF	28	26	23	19	3	1	1			
	1991/92	MF	34	30	26	5	4	1	1			
		F	36	30	25	4	3	1	0			
Guinea	1985/86	MF	20	18	17	18	10	16	1			
		F	21	19	18	19	10	13	0			
	1990/91	MF	25	20	18	17	7	10	4			
		F	24	22	20	20	5	8	1			
	1992/93	MF	23	21	16	18	9	9	4			
		F	23	22	15	19	10	8	3			
	1993/94	MF	25	19	18	17	8	9	4			
		F	26	20	18	18	7	8	3			
Guinea-Bissau	1986/87	MF	47	25	16	6	6					
		F	54	25	15	3	4					
	1988/89	MF	45	25	18	4	8					
		F	48	23	23	3	4					
Kenya	1985	MF	34	31	27	4	4					
		F	36	32	26	4	3					
	1991	MF	28	26	24	22						
		F	28	26	24	21						
	1992	MF	28	26	24	22						
		F	28	26	24	21						
	1993	MF	*28	*25	*24	*22						
		F	*29	*26	*23	*21						
Lesotho	1985	MF	36	27	19	10	7					
		F	36	28	19	10	7					
	1990	MF	36	26	19	11	8					
		F	37	27	19	11	7					

3.8 Second level (general): enrolment by grade
Second degré (général): effectifs par année d'études
Segundo grado (general): matrícula escolar por año de estudios

Country / Pays / País	Year / Année / Año	Sex / Sexe / Sexo	\multicolumn{10}{c}{Grades / Années d'études / Años de estudios}
			I	II	III	IV	V	VI	VII	VIII	IX	X
Lesotho (cont)	1993	MF	36	27	19	10	8					
		F	37	27	19	10	7					
	1994	MF	37	27	19	11	7					
		F	37	27	19	10	7					
Libyan Arab Jamahiriya	1985/86	MF	41	31	27							
		F	50	30	20							
	1992/93	MF	41	30	29							
		F	42	31	27							
Madagascar	1987/88	MF	24	18	15	19	7	8	9			
		F	26	17	16	20	7	6	8			
	1990/91	MF	25	19	16	19	7	6	7			
		F	25	20	16	20	7	6	7			
	1993/94	MF	23	20	17	19	7	5	8			
		F	23	20	17	19	7	5	8			
Malawi	1985/86	MF	29	28	21	22						
		F	30	30	19	21						
	1989/90	MF	25	26	24	25						
		F	26	28	23	24						
	1993/94	MF	25	25	25	25						
		F	25	26	25	25						
	1994/95	MF	25	25	25	25						
		F	25	26	25	25						
Mali	1985/86	MF	34	23	30	5	5	3				
	1990/91	MF	35	23	27	5	7	3				
		F	38	24	27	4	5	2				
	1993/94	MF	31	24	24	10	6	6				
		F	32	26	25	8	5	5				
Mauritania	1985/86	MF	23	21	18	15	13	11				
		F	26	22	18	15	10	8				
	1990/91	MF	22	19	17	15	12	16				
		F	*22	*20	*16	*14	*12	*16				
	1992/93	MF	25	19	16	14	12	15				
		F	25	18	16	15	11	14				
	1993/94	MF	22	20	15	14	12	17				
		F	23	22	14	14	11	16				
Mauritius	1985	MF	18	17	17	20	19	4	5			
		F	19	17	17	20	18	4	4			
	1990	MF	18	20	19	19	15	5	5			
		F	18	20	19	19	14	5	5			
	1992	MF	20	18	16	19	16	5	5			
		F	20	18	16	19	17	5	5			
	1993	MF	20	18	17	17	16	5	6			
		F	21	18	17	17	16	5	6			
Morocco	1985/86	MF	21	18	16	18	10	8	10			
		F	22	18	16	18	9	7	10			
	1990/91	MF	22	20	29	12	9	8				
		F	21	20	30	11	9	8				
	1993/94	MF	24	20	26	11	10	9				
		F	23	20	26	11	10	9				
	1994/95	MF	24	21	26	11	9	9				
		F	23	20	27	12	9	9				
Mozambique	1985	MF	48	35	8	5	3	1	1			
		F	50	34	8	4	3	1	1			
	1990	MF	51	30	6	5	6	1	1			
		F	53	29	6	5	5	1	1			
	1994	MF	47	31	9	6	5	1	1			
		F	47	31	10	6	4	1	1			
	1995	MF	46	31	10	6	5	1	1			
		F	46	31	10	6	4	1	1			

Second level (general): enrolment by grade   **3.8**
Second degré (général): effectifs par année d'études
Segundo grado (general): matrícula escolar por año de estudios

Country Pays País	Year Année Año	Sex Sexe Sexo	Grades / Années d'études / Años de estudios									
			I	II	III	IV	V	VI	VII	VIII	IX	X
Namibia	1986	MF	38	24	22	8	6					
	1990	MF	35	29	23	7	5	0				
		F	36	30	24	6	4	0				
	1993	MF	31	24	25	13	7	0				
		F	31	24	26	13	7	0				
	1994	MF	29	23	24	11	12	0				
		F	29	24	25	10	12	0				
Niger	1985/86	MF	25	21	21	21	4	4	4			
		F	29	24	22	17	3	2	3			
	1990/91	MF	32	20	20	16	5	3	4			
		F	36	21	19	16	3	2	3			
	1992/93	MF	27	21	20	18	5	4	6			
		F	27	22	22	19	4	3	3			
	1993/94	MF	38	19	17	15	4	4	4			
Nigeria #	1987	MF	21	20	20	20	18					
		F	21	21	21	20	17					
	1990	MF	25	21	18	15	12	9				
		F	25	21	17	16	12	9				
	1991	MF	24	21	17	15	13	10				
		F	25	21	17	15	13	10				
	1992	MF	25	21	17	14	12	11				
		F	25	21	16	14	12	11				
Reunion	1986/87	MF	25	24	15	15	7	7	7			
		F	23	22	16	16	8	7	7			
	1993/94	MF	21	20	18	16	9	8	9			
		F	19	18	18	17	10	8	10			
	1994/95	MF	20	19	18	18	9	8	9			
		F	18	18	17	18	11	8	10			
Rwanda	1985/86	MF	24	20	22	20	13	1				
		F	28	20	25	18	9	-				
	1990/91	MF	26	21	17	15	12	9				
		F	28	23	17	14	11	7				
	1991/92	MF	41	17	13	11	10	7				
		F	46	16	13	10	9	6				
St. Helena	1985/86	MF	19	23	26	26	4	2				
		F	18	21	24	29	5	3				
Sao Tome and Principe	1986/87	MF	47	25	11	8	6	2	1			
		F	50	26	10	8	4	1	0			
	1989/90	MF	30	31	17	9	10	2	2			
		F	30	33	17	9	8	1	2			
Senegal	1985/86	MF	23	21	18	16	9	8	4			
		F	24	21	19	17	9	7	3			
	1989/90	MF	20	26	16	15	*10	*8	*6			
		F	21	26	17	15	*9	*7	*5			
	1991/92	MF	20	19	19	18	10	7	7			
		F	20	20	19	18	10	7	7			
Seychelles	1985	MF	51	49								
		F	54	46								
	1991	MF	21	19	19	19	21					
		F	21	20	19	20	20					
	1993	MF	21	22	20	18	18					
		F	21	22	20	19	19					
	1994	MF	21	20	21	19	19					
		F	21	20	21	19	19					
Sierra Leone	1986/87	MF	29	23	20	17	10	1	1			
		F	32	23	20	15	9	0	0			
	1990/91	MF	29	23	20	17	10	1	1			
		F	31	24	19	16	9	1	0			

3.8 Second level (general): enrolment by grade
Second degré (général): effectifs par année d'études
Segundo grado (general): matrícula escolar por año de estudios

Country / Pays / País	Year / Année / Año	Sex / Sexe / Sexo	I	II	III	IV	V	VI	VII	VIII	IX	X
Somalia	1985/86	MF	24	19	23	33						
		F	23	19	22	35						
South Africa	1990	MF	27	23	19	16	14					
		F	27	23	19	17	14					
	1991	MF	27	23	19	16	15					
		F	26	23	19	16	15					
	1994	MF	26	23	19	17	15					
Sudan	1985/86	MF	24	23	22	10	10	11				
		F	24	23	22	10	9	10				
	1990/91	MF	24	21	20	10	9	16				
		F	23	20	20	10	9	17				
	1991/92	MF	24	21	20	12	11	11				
		F	24	21	20	13	11	11				
Swaziland	1985	MF	32	28	20	12	8					
		F	34	28	19	11	8					
	1990	MF	31	27	18	15	9					
		F	32	27	17	15	8					
	1993	MF	29	26	18	17	10					
		F	30	27	18	16	9					
	1994	MF	29	25	18	17	10					
		F	30	26	18	17	9					
Togo	1985/86	MF	30	19	20	18	4	4	4			
		F	35	21	20	16	2	2	3			
	1990/91	MF	23	23	22	16	6	7	4			
		F	28	25	21	15	4	4	2			
	1991/92	MF	24	19	21	17	7	7	5			
		F	30	22	21	16	4	5	2			
	1993/94	MF	28	21	19	17	6	5	4			
		F	32	22	19	17	4	3	2			
Tunisia	1985/86	MF	22	19	17	13	11	8	8			
		F	23	20	18	13	11	8	8			
	1990/91	MF	22	20	18	11	9	9	11			
		F	21	20	19	11	9	8	11			
	1993/94	MF	22	19	17	14	12	8	10			
		F	21	19	17	14	12	7	10			
	1994/95	MF	22	18	16	14	12	9	10			
		F	22	18	16	14	12	8	10			
Uganda‡	1986	MF	29	27	21	16	4	4				
		F	30	28	21	15	4	3				
	1990	MF	26	25	22	18	4	5				
		F	28	26	22	17	3	3				
	1992	MF	25	24	22	18	5	5				
		F	28	24	22	17	5	3				
United Republic of Tanzania	1985	MF	25	25	23	21	3	3				
		F	27	25	24	21	2	2				
	1990	MF	28	25	21	19	3	3				
		F	30	27	21	19	2	2				
	1992	MF	27	26	21	19	4	3				
		F	29	28	20	18	2	2				
	1993	MF	25	26	22	19	4	3				
		F	26	28	22	19	3	2				
Zaire	1987/88	MF	43	27	11	8	6	5				
		F	50	29	10	6	3	3				
	1991/92	MF	29	19	20	13	10	9				
		F	37	21	19	11	7	5				
	1992/93	MF	29	19	20	13	10	9				
		F	37	21	19	11	7	5				
	1993/94	MF	40	27	12	9	7	5				
		F	46	28	11	6	5	3				

Second level (general): enrolment by grade
Second degré (général): effectifs par année d'études
Segundo grado (general): matrícula escolar por año de estudios

3.8

Country / Pays / País	Year / Année / Año	Sex / Sexe / Sexo	Grades / Années d'études / Años de estudios									
			I	II	III	IV	V	VI	VII	VIII	IX	X
Zambia‡	1985	MF	37	30	12	11	10					
		F	38	32	11	10	9					
	1988	MF	35	33	11	11	10					
		F	34	35	11	11	9					
	1994	MF	31	34	11	12	11					
		F	34	36	10	11	10					
Zimbabwe	1985	MF	31	28	20	19	1	1				
		F	33	28	20	18	1	0				
	1990	MF	29	27	24	18	1	1				
		F	31	28	24	15	1	1				
	1992	MF	28	25	24	21	1	1				
		F	29	26	23	20	1	1				
	1993	MF	27	25	24	21	1	1				
		F	29	26	24	19	1	1				
America, North												
Antigua and Barbuda	1991/92	MF	27	22	27	14	10					
		F	26	20	27	15	12					
Bahamas	1985/86	MF	19	18	18	18	15	12				
		F	18	17	18	18	16	13				
	1990/91	MF	18	18	18	17	16	13				
	1992/93	MF	18	18	17	17	17	13				
	1993/94	MF	19	18	18	16	16	13				
Barbados	1988/89	MF	19	19	20	19	19	6				
		F	18	18	19	19	20	7				
	1989/90	MF	19	19	19	19	18	5				
		F	19	18	19	19	19	7				
Belize‡	1985/86	MF	31	25	24	20						
		F	30	26	24	19						
	1990/91	MF	34	28	22	15						
		F	33	29	23	16						
	1992/93	MF	33	28	22	17						
		F	32	28	22	18						
	1994/95	MF	34	26	22	18						
		F	34	26	23	18						
British Virgin Islands	1991/92	MF	23	21	22	17	16					
		F	23	20	22	15	19					
	1993/94	MF	26	21	23	17	14					
		F	22	20	26	17	15					
Canada	1985/86	MF	17	17	18	17	16	15				
		F	16	16	18	17	17	15				
	1990/91	MF	17	17	17	17	16	16				
		F	17	17	17	17	16	16				
	1992/93	MF	17	16	17	17	16	17				
		F	17	16	17	17	16	17				
	1993/94	MF	17	16	17	17	16	18				
		F	16	16	17	17	16	18				
Costa Rica	1985	MF	30	23	19	15	12	0				
		F	29	23	20	16	13	0				
	1990	MF	37	23	18	13	9	0				
		F	35	23	18	14	9	0				
	1993	MF	36	23	18	14	9	0				
		F	35	23	18	14	10	0				
	1994	MF	36	23	18	14	9	0				
		F	35	23	18	14	10	0				
Cuba	1985/86	MF	27	27	24	9	7	6				
		F	26	26	24	10	8	6				
	1990/91	MF	21	22	23	13	11	10				
		F	19	20	22	15	12	12				

Second level (general): enrolment by grade
Second degré (général): effectifs par année d'études
Segundo grado (general): matrícula escolar por año de estudios

Country / Pays / País	Year / Année / Año	Sex / Sexe / Sexo	Grades / Années d'études / Años de estudios									
			I	II	III	IV	V	VI	VII	VIII	IX	X
Cuba (cont)												
	1993/94	MF	27	25	24	7	7	9				
		F	25	23	23	9	9	11				
	1994/95	MF	32	25	23	8	5	6				
		F	30	24	22	10	7	8				
Dominica	1985/86	MF	28	24	30	9	8	1				
		F	25	24	29	12	9	1				
	1990/91	MF	28	24	22	14	11	1				
		F	26	22	22	15	13	2				
	1993/94	MF	26	25	24	15	10					
		F	23	24	24	17	11					
	1994/95	MF	26	25	24	15	11					
		F	23	24	24	17	12					
Dominican Republic‡	1985/86	MF	24	19	18	15	13	10				
		F	24	19	18	15	13	11				
	1993/94	MF	31	26	23	19						
		F	31	26	23	19						
	1994/95	MF	33	25	20	22						
		F	33	25	20	22						
El Salvador	1989	MF	38	32	30							
		F	38	31	31							
	1991	MF	40	33	28							
		F	39	32	28							
	1992	MF	39	34	27							
		F	39	33	28							
	1993	MF	38	33	28							
		F	37	34	30							
Grenada	1992/93	MF	28	28	16	14	13					
		F	26	26	18	15	15					
Guadeloupe	1985/86	MF	26	24	17	15	6	6	6			
		F	23	23	17	17	7	6	7			
	1990/91	MF	19	20	*16	*17	9	9	9			
		F	17	18	*16	*17	10	11	10			
	1993/94	MF	20	19	17	16	9	9	11			
		F	18	18	17	16	9	10	12			
	1994/95	MF	19	20	18	17	9	8	10			
		F	17	18	17	17	10	9	12			
Haiti	1985/86	MF	26	20	17	14	11	10	3			
		F	27	20	17	14	11	10	2			
	1990/91	MF	26	20	17	14	11	10	3			
		F	27	21	17	14	10	8	2			
Honduras #	1986	MF	26	18	15	18	13	9				
	1991	MF	27	20	17	15	12	8	1			
	1993	MF	27	20	17	15	12	7	3			
		F	27	20	17	15	12	7	3			
Jamaica‡	1989/90	MF	23	23	22	16	15	1	0			
		F	22	23	22	16	15	1	1			
	1990/91	MF	22	23	23	16	14	1	0			
		F	22	23	23	16	14	1	1			
	1991/92	MF	23	23	22	17	15	1	1			
		F	22	23	22	17	15	1	1			
Martinique	1989/90	MF	22	23	22	20	8	4	2			
		F	20	22	21	21	8	5	3			
	1993/94	MF	19	19	18	17	9	9	9			
		F	17	17	17	18	10	10	11			
	1994/95	MF	19	19	18	17	10	9	9			
		F	17	18	17	17	11	10	10			
Mexico	1985/86	MF	28	24	21	12	9	5				
		F	29	25	22	11	8	5				
	1990/91	MF	26	24	21	13	9	7				
		F	26	24	22	12	9	7				

Second level (general): enrolment by grade
Second degré (général): effectifs par année d'études
Segundo grado (general): matrícula escolar por año de estudios
3.8

Country Pays País	Year Année Año	Sex Sexe Sexo	I	II	III	IV	V	VI	VII	VIII	IX	X
Mexico (cont)	1992/93	MF	27	23	21	13	9	7				
		F	26	23	21	12	9	7				
	1993/94	MF	27	23	20	13	9	7				
		F	26	24	21	12	10	7				
Nicaragua	1985	MF	37	23	19	13	9					
		F	35	23	19	13	9					
	1990	MF	36	23	17	13	10					
		F	35	23	18	13	11					
	1993	MF	36	22	18	14	11					
		F	35	22	18	14	11					
	1994	MF	35	24	17	13	10					
		F	34	24	17	14	11					
Panama #	1985	MF	24	21	18	15	13	10				
		F	22	21	18	15	13	10				
	1990	MF	22	21	18	15	13	11				
		F	21	20	18	15	14	12				
Saint Kitts and Nevis #	1985/86	MF	22	23	23	16	12	4				
		F	22	24	21	17	13	3				
	1988/89	MF	22	22	27	15	10	4				
		F	21	22	26	15	13	4				
	1991/92	MF	20	20	24	20	12	4				
		F	19	20	23	20	14	4				
St. Lucia	1985/86	MF	25	21	27	15	12					
		F	26	20	28	15	11					
	1990/91	MF	23	22	22	18	15					
		F	23	23	20	19	14					
	1991/92	MF	24	20	21	19	16					
		F	24	20	21	19	15					
	1992/93	MF	23	22	21	19	16					
		F	22	22	21	19	15					
St. Pierre and Miquelon	1985/86	MF	27	24	13	16	8	6	5			
		F	26	23	13	16	11	7	5			
Trinidad and Tobago	1986/87	MF	21	20	19	17	18	5				
		F	20	20	19	17	18	5				
	1990/91	MF	22	21	20	17	16	5				
		F	22	21	19	16	16	5				
	1991/92	MF	20	20	19	18	18	5				
		F	20	20	19	18	19	6				
	1992/93	MF	20	19	19	17	19	5				
		F	20	19	19	17	19	6				
United States	1985/86	MF	16	16	19	18	16	15				
		F	16	16	18	17	16	16				
	1990/91	MF	18	17	18	17	15	14				
		F	17	18	18	17	15	15				
	1993/94	MF	18	18	19	17	15	14				
		F	18	18	18	17	15	14				
U.S. Virgin Islands‡	1985/86	MF	22	19	20	17	13	9				
	1990/91	MF	24	18	17	16	13	13				
		F	21	17	16	18	13	15				
	1992/93	MF	23	17	19	16	13	12				
		F	25	18	18	15	13	11				
America, South												
Argentina #	1991	MF	29	23	19	14	12	2				
		F	28	24	19	15	13	1				
Bolivia #	1986	MF	34	27	22	17						
		F	34	26	23	17						
	1990	MF	34	27	22	18						
		F	33	27	22	18						

3.8 Second level (general): enrolment by grade
Second degré (général): effectifs par année d'études
Segundo grado (general): matrícula escolar por año de estudios

Country Pays País	Year Année Año	Sex Sexe Sexo	Grades / Années d'études / Años de estudios									
			I	II	III	IV	V	VI	VII	VIII	IX	X
Brazil #	1987	MF	44	31	22	2						
	1990	MF	44	30	23	3						
	1993	MF	46	30	21	2						
	1994	MF	45	31	22	2						
Chile‡	1985	MF	35	29	21	16						
		F	33	29	21	17						
	1991	MF	29	25	23	19	4					
		F	28	25	24	19	4					
	1992	MF	29	25	23	19	4					
		F	28	24	24	20	4					
	1994	MF	31	27	22	21						
		F	30	27	22	21						
Colombia #	1985	MF	25	20	17	15	13	11				
		F	25	20	17	15	13	11				
	1991	MF	30	20	16	13	12	10				
		F	30	20	16	13	12	10				
	1992	MF	27	20	17	14	12	10				
	1993	MF	28	21	17	13	12	10				
Ecuador #	1986/87	MF	24	19	17	16	13	11				
		F	22	19	17	16	14	11				
	1987/88	MF	23	19	17	17	13	11				
		F	22	19	17	17	14	12				
	1992/93	MF	22	19	17	17	14	12				
		F	21	18	17	17	14	12				
French Guiana	1993/94	MF	27	22	18	15	7	6	6			
		F	26	21	19	15	7	6	7			
	1994/95	MF	27	22	18	16	7	5	5			
		F	27	21	18	16	7	5	6			
Guyana	1986/87	MF	27	24	22	19	8	0				
		F	26	23	22	19	9	0				
Paraguay #	1985	MF	24	21	18	15	12	10				
		F	23	20	18	15	13	11				
	1990	MF	27	21	17	15	11	10				
		F	25	20	17	15	12	10				
	1993	MF	29	22	17	14	11	8				
		F	28	21	17	14	11	9				
	1994	MF	31	23	18	12	9	7				
		F	30	23	18	12	9	8				
Peru	1985	MF	29	22	18	16	14					
		F	30	22	18	16	14					
	1988	MF	28	22	19	17	14					
	1993	MF	28	22	19	16	14					
Uruguay	1987	MF	22	21	17	14	15	10				
	1990	MF	22	20	19	15	14	10				
	1991	MF	22	20	18	15	15	9				
	1994	MF	22	19	18	15	15	10				
		F	20	19	18	16	16	12				
Venezuela #	1985/86	MF	57	41	2							
		F	57	41	2							
	1990/91	MF	56	43	1							
		F	56	44	0							
	1991/92	MF	57	42	1							
		F	57	43	0							
	1992/93	MF	56	43	1							
		F	56	43	0							

Second level (general): enrolment by grade **3.8**
Second degré (général): effectifs par année d'études
Segundo grado (general): matrícula escolar por año de estudios

Country / Pays / País	Year / Année / Año	Sex / Sexe / Sexo	Grades / Années d'études / Años de estudios									
			I	II	III	IV	V	VI	VII	VIII	IX	X
Asia												
Afghanistan	1985	MF	36	26	21	17						
		F	39	26	20	16						
	1989	MF	37	29	*19	*15						
	1993	MF	23	22	21	13	11	11				
		F	23	22	21	13	11	11				
	1995	MF	22	21	20	13	23	--->				
Armenia #	1993/94	MF	19	17	16	15	13	11	10			
		F	19	17	15	15	13	11	11			
Azerbaijan	1992/93	MF	17	17	15	15	15	10	10			
		F	17	16	15	15	15	10	11			
	1993/94	MF	18	17	17	15	15	9	9			
		F	18	17	17	16	15	9	9			
Bahrain‡	1985/86	MF	28	24	22	9	9	8				
		F	25	22	20	12	11	10				
	1990/91	MF	24	22	19	12	11	10	1	1		
		F	23	20	18	14	12	11	1	1		
	1994/95	MF	20	18	17	16	14	13	1	0		
		F	19	18	18	16	15	13	1	0		
Bangladesh	1986	MF	27	21	19	13	11	5	4			
		F	28	21	18	14	12	5	3			
	1990	MF	22	20	18	13	11	9	7			
		F	25	22	18	12	10	7	7			
Bhutan	1985	MF	30	29	23	10	8					
		F	34	27	24	8	8					
	1988	MF	37	33	16	14						
		F	42	36	13	9						
	1993	MF	42	31	16	11						
		F	46	32	13	9						
	1994	MF	46	26	19	10						
		F	49	28	16	7						
Brunei Darussalam	1991	MF	24	27	17	13	14	3	2			
		F	21	27	18	13	15	3	2			
	1993	MF	22	19	22	16	15	3	2			
		F	21	18	22	17	17	3	3			
	1994	MF	22	20	19	17	18	2	2			
		F	21	20	18	17	19	3	3			
Cambodia	1985/86	MF	38	33	25	2	2	1				
	1988/89	MF	30	29	31	5	4	2				
	1993/94	MF	32	26	21	9	7	6				
		F	37	28	20	8	5	3				
	1994/95	MF	29	28	26	8	7	2				
		F	29	31	26	5	6	2				
China	1985/86	MF	31	29	25	6	6	5				
		F	31	29	25	5	6	5				
	1990/91	MF	31	28	25	6	5	5				
		F	31	28	26	5	5	5				
	1992/93	MF	31	29	25	5	5	5				
		F	32	29	26	5	4	4				
	1993/94	MF	32	29	25	5	4	5				
		F	32	29	26	4	4	4				
Cyprus‡#	1985/86	MF	14	18	18	17	18	14	1			
		F	14	17	18	17	19	15	1			
	1990/91	MF	21	20	19	15	13	11	1			
		F	21	19	18	16	13	12	1			
	1993/94	MF	21	20	19	14	13	12	1			
		F	19	19	18	16	14	13	1			

Second level (general): enrolment by grade
Second degré (général): effectifs par année d'études
Segundo grado (general): matrícula escolar por año de estudios

Country / Pays / País	Year / Année / Año	Sex / Sexe / Sexo	Grades / Années d'études / Años de estudios									
			I	II	III	IV	V	VI	VII	VIII	IX	X
Cyprus‡# (cont)	1994/95	MF	21	19	19	15	13	12	2			
		F	20	18	18	16	14	13	1			
Georgia	1994/95	MF	17	17	17	16	15	9	8			
		F	17	17	17	16	15	9	9			
Hong Kong‡	1986/87	MF	21	20	18	16	17	5	3			
		F	21	20	18	17	18	4	3			
	1990/91	MF	21	20	18	17	17	4	3			
	1993/94	MF	20	19	18	16	16	6	5			
	1994/95	MF	20	19	18	16	16	6	5			
India	1985/86	MF	24	20	18	15	12	6	5			
		F	26	22	18	14	11	6	4			
	1988/89	MF	25	21	19	15	12	5	4			
		F	26	22	18	14	11	4	3			
	1992/93	MF	24	21	18	14	12	6	5			
		F	25	22	19	13	11	5	4			
	1993/94	MF	24	21	19	13	12	6	6			
		F	25	22	19	13	11	6	5			
Indonesia‡	1985/86	MF	28	24	21	10	9	9				
	1990/91	MF	24	22	22	11	10	11				
		F	25	22	22	11	10	10				
	1992/93	MF	25	23	21	10	11	10				
		F	26	22	21	10	11	10				
	1993/94	MF	27	23	21	10	10	10				
		F	27	23	21	10	10	10				
Iran, Islamic Republic of‡	1985/86	MF	30	21	17	11	8	6	6			
		F	28	21	17	11	9	7	7			
	1990/91	MF	28	21	19	12	8	7	6			
		F	27	20	18	12	9	7	6			
	1993/94	MF	25	21	17	14	9	8	6			
		F	25	21	18	14	9	8	6			
	1994/95	MF	23	21	18	14	10	8	7			
		F	23	21	18	14	10	8	6			
Iraq	1985/86	MF	29	26	21	8	7	9				
		F	30	26	19	10	7	8				
	1988/89	MF	30	26	22	7	7	9				
		F	30	25	21	8	7	10				
	1992/93	MF	31	26	23	6	6	7				
		F	31	25	22	8	8	7				
Israel	1985/86	MF	40	22	20	18						
		F	38	23	20	19						
	1990/91	MF	37	23	21	19						
		F	35	23	21	20						
	1992/93	MF	35	23	22	20						
		F	33	24	23	21						
	1993/94	MF	35	23	22	21						
		F	33	23	22	22						
Japan	1985/86	MF	21	21	20	13	13	12	0			
	1990/91	MF	18	19	20	15	15	14	0			
	1991/92	MF	18	19	19	14	15	15	0			
	1993/94	MF	18	19	19	15	15	15	0			
Jordan	1985/86	MF	27	23	19	12	10	10				
		F	26	23	18	13	11	10				
	1990/91	MF	50	50								
		F	52	48								
	1992/93	MF	51	49								
		F	52	48								

Second level (general): enrolment by grade 3.8
Second degré (général): effectifs par année d'études
Segundo grado (general): matrícula escolar por año de estudios

Country / Pays / País	Year / Année / Año	Sex / Sexe / Sexo	Grades / Années d'études / Años de estudios									
			I	II	III	IV	V	VI	VII	VIII	IX	X
Jordan (cont)	1993/94	MF	51	49								
		F	53	47								
Kazakstan	1993/94	MF	18	17	16	15	15	10	9	0		
		F	17	17	16	15	15	11	10	-		
Korea, Democratic People's Rep. of	1987/88	MF	14	14	15	18	19	20				
		F	14	14	15	18	19	21				
Korea, Rep. of	1985/86	MF	23	24	22	11	10	10				
		F	24	24	23	10	10	9				
	1990/91	MF	20	20	21	13	13	13				
		F	21	20	22	12	12	12				
	1994/95	MF	23	22	22	11	11	11				
		F	23	23	23	10	10	10				
	1995/96	MF	22	23	22	12	11	11				
		F	22	23	23	11	10	10				
Kuwait	1991/92	MF	17	15	14	14	14	10	9	7		
		F	16	15	14	13	14	11	10	8		
	1993/94	MF	17	16	14	12	16	10	8	7		
		F	17	16	14	12	15	11	9	7		
	1994/95	MF	18	15	14	12	15	10	8	7		
		F	17	15	14	12	14	11	8	8		
Kyrgyzstan	1994/95	MF	19	17	17	15	14	9	9	0	0	
		F	18	17	16	15	14	10	10	0	0	
Lao People's Democratic Rep.	1985/86	MF	32	24	20	10	8	6				
		F	32	24	21	10	7	5				
	1991/92	MF	30	24	21	11	8	7				
		F	31	25	21	10	7	7				
	1992/93	MF	30	23	21	11	8	7				
		F	31	24	21	10	8	6				
	1993/94	MF	31	23	20	11	8	7				
		F	32	23	19	11	8	7				
Macau	1989/90	MF	26	22	19	15	12	6				
		F	25	21	20	15	12	6				
	1991/92	MF	24	20	18	15	13	10				
		F	22	20	19	16	14	10				
	1992/93	MF	25	20	16	15	13	10				
		F	24	19	17	16	14	10				
Malaysia	1985	MF	30	21	21	12	12	2	2			
		F	30	21	21	12	12	2	2			
	1989/90	MF	29	21	20	13	12	2	2			
		F	28	20	20	13	13	3	2			
	1990/91	MF	29	22	20	13	12	2	2			
		F	28	21	20	13	13	3	2			
	1991/92	MF	30	21	21	14	12	2	2			
		F	28	20	20	14	13	2	2			
Maldives	1992	MF	37	27	18	10	5	*1	*1			
		F	38	26	19	11	5	*1	*1			
	1993	MF	36	29	16	11	6	*1	*1			
		F	36	29	15	11	6	*1	*1			
Mongolia	1986/87	MF	18	18	17	17	16	7	7			
	1994/95	MF	17	10	15	27	15	9	7			
		F	15	10	14	27	15	11	9			
Myanmar	1994/95	MF	32	19	15	13	11	11				
Nepal #	1988	MF	27	23	19	16	15					
		F	28	23	19	16	15					
	1991	MF	27	22	20	17	14					
		F	29	22	19	16	14					
	1992	MF	29	22	19	17	14					
		F	30	23	18	16	13					

Second level (general): enrolment by grade
Second degré (général): effectifs par année d'études
Segundo grado (general): matrícula escolar por año de estudios

Country / Pays / País	Year / Année / Año	Sex / Sexe / Sexo	I	II	III	IV	V	VI	VII	VIII	IX	X
Oman	1985/86	MF	33	23	18	10	9	7				
		F	33	24	18	11	8	6				
	1990/91	MF	34	24	16	12	8	6				
		F	33	24	15	13	9	7				
	1993/94	MF	30	21	17	15	10	8				
		F	27	21	18	15	11	8				
	1994/95	MF	27	21	18	15	11	8				
		F	24	21	18	15	12	9				
Pakistan	1985/86	MF	27	22	18	13	10	6	5			
		F	27	21	18	13	10	6	5			
	1989/90	MF	26	22	20	13	10	5	4			
		F	26	22	18	13	10	7	4			
Philippines	1985/86	MF	29	26	24	21						
		F	29	27	23	21						
	1989/90	MF	30	27	23	20						
		F	30	27	23	20						
	1992/93	MF	31	25	22	21						
	1993/94	MF	30	26	23	20						
Qatar‡	1985/86	MF	24	20	18	14	12	12				
		F	22	19	18	16	13	12				
	1990/91	MF	25	19	18	15	11	11				
		F	22	19	18	16	12	12				
	1993/94	MF	22	19	17	17	14	12				
		F	19	19	17	17	15	13				
	1994/95	MF	21	19	17	16	13	13				
		F	19	18	18	17	14	14				
Saudi Arabia	1989/90	MF	27	22	18	15	9	9				
		F	26	22	18	15	10	10				
	1990/91	MF	27	22	18	15	10	9				
		F	26	22	18	15	10	10				
	1991/92	MF	26	22	18	15	11	9				
		F	25	22	18	14	11	9				
	1992/93	MF	28	22	17	15	9	9				
		F	27	22	18	14	10	9				
Singapore	1985	MF	22	20	20	22	9	6	1			
		F	22	19	20	22	10	6	2			
	1989	MF	19	18	20	21	13	8	1			
		F	19	18	19	20	14	9	1			
Sri Lanka	1985	MF	19	18	17	14	22	5	5			
		F	19	17	17	14	22	5	5			
	1990	MF	18	16	14	13	11	18	4	6		
		F	17	16	14	13	12	19	4	6		
	1993	MF	18	17	15	13	12	16	4	5		
		F	17	16	15	13	12	16	5	6		
	1994	MF	17	16	15	14	12	17	4	5		
		F	16	16	15	14	12	17	5	5		
Syrian Arab Rep.	1985/86	MF	29	21	22	8	9	10				
		F	28	22	22	9	9	10				
	1990/91	MF	30	23	24	6	5	11				
		F	29	23	24	6	6	11				
	1992/93	MF	31	24	25	5	6	8				
		F	30	24	25	6	7	8				
	1993/94	MF	31	24	25	5	5	9				
		F	29	24	26	6	6	9				
Thailand	1985/86	MF	24	25	21	11	10	9				
	1990/91	MF	28	26	22	9	8	7				
		F	28	25	22	10	8	8				
Turkey	1985/86	MF	32	23	18	13	8	7	0			
		F	28	22	18	14	9	8	0			

Second level (general): enrolment by grade
Second degré (général): effectifs par année d'études
Segundo grado (general): matrícula escolar por año de estudios

3.8

Country / Pays / País	Year / Année / Año	Sex / Sexe / Sexo	Grades / Années d'études / Años de estudios									
			I	II	III	IV	V	VI	VII	VIII	IX	X
Turkey (cont)	1990/91	MF	31	22	19	13	7	7	0			
		F	29	22	19	14	8	8	0			
	1991/92	MF	29	23	19	13	9	7	0			
		F	28	22	18	14	10	8	0			
	1992/93	MF	27	23	19	11	11	8	0			
		F	26	22	19	12	12	9	0			
United Arab Emirates	1985/86	MF	26	22	18	14	11	9				
		F	25	22	18	14	11	9				
	1990/91	MF	26	21	17	16	11	8				
		F	25	21	17	17	11	9				
	1993/94	MF	25	21	18	15	11	9				
		F	24	21	18	16	12	9				
	1994/95	MF	25	21	18	16	11	9				
		F	23	20	18	16	12	10				
Viet Nam	1985/86	MF	29	23	20	7	8	7	6			
		F	29	24	20	7	8	7	6			
Yemen‡												
Former Democratic Yemen	1985/86	MF	33	26	22	19						
		F	31	24	23	22						
	1989/90	MF	36	24	20	20						
		F	32	24	22	22						
Former Yemen Arab Republic‡	1985/86	MF	36	24	20	9	7	5				
		F	34	23	21	9	8	6				
	1987/88	MF	35	25	18	10	7	5				
		F	39	26	16	9	6	5				
Palestine	1994/95	MF	24	21	18	15	11	10				
		F	25	22	19	15	11	9				
Gaza Strip	1989/90	MF	22	22	17	16	14	8				
		F	24	22	18	15	13	7				
	1993/94	MF	24	20	19	14	11	12				
		F	24	20	19	14	11	12				
West Bank	1987/88	MF	25	21	18	14	11	10				
		F	26	22	18	14	11	9				
	1990/91	MF	24	21	19	14	12	10				
		F	26	21	19	14	11	9				
	1991/92	MF	24	22	17	14	11	10				
		F	26	22	18	15	11	9				
	1993/94	MF	24	22	19	15	11	10				
		F	25	22	19	14	11	9				
Europe												
Albania	1985/86	MF	34	26	21	17	2					
		F	33	26	22	18	2					
	1990/91	MF	32	24	23	19	3					
		F	31	25	23	20	2					
	1993/94	MF	34	25	24	15	1					
		F	30	26	26	17	1					
Austria	1985/86	MF	19	19	20	20	10	4	4	4	0	
		F	19	19	20	21	8	4	4	4	0	
	1990/91	MF	21	20	20	19	9	4	4	3	0	
		F	21	20	20	20	8	4	4	4	0	
	1992/93	MF	21	21	20	19	8	4	3	3	0	
		F	21	21	20	19	7	4	4	4	0	
	1993/94	MF	21	21	21	19	8	4	3	3	0	
		F	21	21	20	19	7	4	4	3	0	
Belarus	1985/86	MF	25	25	24	13	13	0				
	1990/91	MF	15	17	17	17	16	9	9	0		

Second level (general): enrolment by grade
Second degré (général): effectifs par année d'études
Segundo grado (general): matrícula escolar por año de estudios

Country / Pays / País	Year / Année / Año	Sex / Sexe / Sexo	I	II	III	IV	V	VI	VII	VIII	IX	X
Belarus (cont)	1993/94	MF	18	17	17	15	16	8	8			
		F	18	16	17	14	16	10	9			
	1994/95	MF	18	18	17	17	14	9	8			
		F	17	17	16	16	14	10	9			
Belgium #	1985/86	MF	18	18	18	17	15	12	2			
		F	17	18	18	17	15	13	2			
	1990/91	MF	17	17	18	17	16	13	3			
		F	17	17	17	16	16	14	3			
	1991/92	MF	17	17	18	17	16	13	2			
		F	17	17	17	16	16	14	2			
Bulgaria	1985/86	MF	38	32	29	1						
		F	38	32	29	1						
	1990/91	MF	39	32	28	2						
		F	39	32	27	1						
	1992/93	MF	46	27	25	2						
		F	46	27	26	2						
	1994/95	MF	45	27	25	3						
		F	45	26	26	3						
Croatia	1992/93	MF	30	28	25	17						
		F	30	29	26	16						
	1993/94	MF	27	26	25	22						
		F	27	26	25	23						
	1994/95	MF	27	25	25	23						
		F	26	25	25	24						
Former Czechoslovakia	1985/86	MF	26	24	24	26						
		F	26	24	24	26						
	1990/91	MF	27	26	25	23						
		F	26	26	25	23						
	1991/92	MF	25	26	25	24						
		F	24	26	25	25						
Czech Republic	1993/94	MF	15	15	16	17	13	9	8	8		
		F	14	14	15	16	14	10	9	9		
	1994/95	MF	15	15	15	16	13	9	8	8		
		F	14	14	14	15	15	10	9	9		
Denmark	1985/86	MF	22	22	21	19	8	8				
		F	21	21	20	20	9	9				
	1990/91	MF	20	21	22	20	9	8				
		F	19	20	21	20	11	10				
	1991/92	MF	20	20	21	21	9	9				
		F	19	19	20	21	11	10				
Estonia	1992/93	MF	21	22	22	14	12	9				
		F	20	21	21	16	14	10				
	1993/94	MF	22	21	21	14	13	9				
		F	20	19	20	16	14	10				
	1994/95	MF	21	21	20	14	12	11				
		F	19	20	18	16	14	13				
Finland	1985/86	MF	20	21	23	12	13	11				
		F	18	19	21	14	14	13				
	1990/91	MF	22	22	23	13	11	9				
		F	21	21	21	15	12	11				
	1992/93	MF	20	21	22	14	12	10				
		F	19	19	21	16	14	11				
	1993/94	MF	22	22	23	13	11	9				
		F	21	21	22	14	12	10				
France	1985/86	MF	22	23	17	16	9	6	6			
		F	21	22	17	17	10	7	7			
	1990/91	MF	19	19	17	17	11	9	8			
		F	18	18	17	17	12	9	9			
	1992/93	MF	20	19	17	17	10	8	8			
		F	19	18	17	17	12	8	9			

Second level (general): enrolment by grade
Second degré (général): effectifs par année d'études
Segundo grado (general): matrícula escolar por año de estudios

3.8

Country / Pays / País	Year / Année / Año	Sex / Sexe / Sexo	Grades / Années d'études / Años de estudios									
			I	II	III	IV	V	VI	VII	VIII	IX	X
France (cont)	1993/94	MF	19	19	18	17	11	8	8			
		F	18	18	17	17	12	8	9			
Germany	1992/93	MF	16	16	16	15	15	11	4	4	3	
		F	16	16	16	15	15	11	5	4	3	
	1993/94	MF	16	16	16	15	15	11	4	4	3	
		F	15	15	16	15	14	12	5	4	3	
Former German Democratic Rep.	1985/86	MF	15	15	15	19	18	18				
		F	15	15	15	19	19	18				
	1989/90	MF	20	19	17	16	14	14				
		F	20	19	17	16	14	14				
Federal Republic of Germany	1985/86	MF	13	13	14	16	17	13	5	5	5	
		F	12	13	14	16	17	13	5	5	5	
	1990/91	MF	16	15	15	15	15	11	4	4	4	
		F	15	15	15	15	15	11	5	4	5	
	1991/92	MF	16	15	15	15	15	11	4	4	4	
		F	16	15	15	15	15	11	5	4	4	
Greece	1985/86	MF	24	21	18	15	12	11	0			
		F	22	19	17	16	14	12	0			
	1990/91	MF	23	21	18	15	12	11	0			
		F	21	19	18	16	14	12	0			
	1991/92	MF	23	20	18	15	12	12	0			
		F	21	19	18	16	13	13	0			
Hungary	1985/86	MF	26	26	24	24						
		F	27	26	24	24						
	1990/91	MF	29	27	23	20						
		F	30	27	23	20						
	1993/94	MF	27	25	24	23						
		F	27	25	24	24						
	1994/95	MF	27	25	24	23						
		F	27	25	25	23						
Ireland	1985/86	MF	22	22	21	19	16					
		F	21	21	21	20	17					
	1990/91	MF	21	20	20	19	19					
		F	21	20	19	20	20					
	1992/93	MF	21	21	20	19	19					
		F	21	21	20	20	20					
	1993/94	MF	20	20	20	21	19					
		F	20	20	20	21	19					
Italy	1985/86	MF	29	27	25	5	4	4	3	3		
		F	27	27	25	5	4	4	4	3		
	1990/91	MF	25	25	25	6	5	5	5	4		
		F	24	24	25	6	6	6	5	5		
	1992/93	MF	25	24	25	6	5	5	5	5		
		F	24	23	24	7	6	6	6	5		
	1993/94	MF	25	24	24	6	6	5	5	5		
		F	23	23	23	7	6	6	6	6		
Latvia	1992/93	MF	18	18	17	16	16	7	5	3		
		F	17	17	16	16	16	8	7	4		
	1993/94	MF	19	17	17	15	15	7	6	5		
		F	18	16	16	15	14	9	7	6		
	1994/95	MF	18	18	17	16	14	7	6	5		
		F	17	17	16	15	14	9	7	6		
Lithuania	1992/93	MF	15	17	15	15	15	8	7	7		
		F	14	16	14	15	15	9	8	8		
	1993/94	MF	16	16	17	15	15	8	7	6		
	1994/95	MF	16	16	15	16	14	9	7	7		
		F	15	15	14	15	14	10	9	8		
Luxembourg	1985/86	MF	15	16	17	15	13	11	13			
		F	15	16	17	15	13	11	13			

Second level (general): enrolment by grade
Second degré (général): effectifs par année d'études
Segundo grado (general): matrícula escolar por año de estudios

Country Pays País	Year Année Año	Sex Sexe Sexo	Grades / Années d'études / Años de estudios									
			I	II	III	IV	V	VI	VII	VIII	IX	X
Luxembourg (cont)	1987/88	MF	20	16	12	13	14	13	12			
		F	20	16	12	13	15	12	12			
Malta	1985/86	MF	23	23	19	13	12	7	3			
		F	21	22	21	13	13	6	3			
	1990/91	MF	22	22	16	16	12	8	4			
		F	20	21	17	17	13	8	4			
	1992/93	MF	21	20	17	15	13	9	4			
		F	19	19	18	16	14	9	4			
	1993/94	MF	21	20	17	16	13	8	4			
		F	19	18	18	17	15	9	4			
Moldova	1991/92	MF	18	17	17	17	17	7	6			
		F	18	16	17	17	17	9	7			
	1994/95	MF	16	19	18	18	16	7	6	0		
		F	16	19	18	17	16	8	6	0		
Monaco	1991/92	MF	19	17	15	14	11	12	12			
		F	17	17	14	15	12	13	12			
	1993/94	MF	16	17	15	16	13	13	11			
		F	15	18	15	16	12	12	12			
	1994/95	MF	16	16	16	16	13	12	11			
		F	15	16	17	16	13	12	12			
Netherlands	1985/86	MF	19	21	20	23	12	5				
		F	19	21	21	23	12	4				
	1990/91	MF	21	20	19	22	12	5				
		F	21	20	20	22	12	5				
	1991/92	MF	21	21	19	21	12	5				
		F	21	21	20	22	12	5				
	1992/93	MF	22	21	19	21	12	5				
		F	22	21	20	21	12	5				
Norway	1985/86	MF	23	23	23	13	9	9				
		F	22	23	22	14	10	9				
	1990/91	MF	21	21	23	14	10	11				
		F	20	21	22	16	11	11				
	1992/93	MF	21	21	21	15	10	12				
		F	20	20	20	16	11	13				
	1993/94	MF	21	21	21	15	11	12				
		F	20	20	20	16	11	12				
Poland	1985/86	MF	29	26	23	22						
		F	29	49	——>	22						
	1990/91	MF	30	26	23	21						
		F	30	49	——>	21						
	1993/94	MF	29	26	25	21						
		F	28	50	——>	21						
	1994/95	MF	30	26	23	22						
		F	29	49	——>	22						
Portugal	1985/86	MF	24	20	15	41	——>	——>				
		F	22	20	15	42	——>	——>				
	1990/91	MF	24	21	17	13	12	12				
		F	23	21	17	14	13	13				
	1991/92	MF	23	20	18	14	12	14				
Romania‡	1991/92	MF	22	21	21	21	5	4	3	3	0	
		F	20	20	20	20	6	5	4	3	0	
	1992/93	MF	14	14	14	13	12	15	10	7	2	
		F	13	14	14	14	13	14	10	8	1	
Russian Federation	1993/94	MF	19	18	17	16	15	8	7			
		F	18	17	16	16	15	9	9			
San Marino	1985/86	MF	26	25	26	10	6	3	2	2		
		F	26	26	28	6	6	3	3	2		
	1990/91	MF	24	26	25	5	5	5	5	4		
		F	22	24	25	6	7	5	5	5		

Second level (general): enrolment by grade 3.8
Second degré (général): effectifs par année d'études
Segundo grado (general): matrícula escolar por año de estudios

Country Pays País	Year Année Año	Sex Sexe Sexo	Grades / Années d'études / Años de estudios									
			I	II	III	IV	V	VI	VII	VIII	IX	X
San Marino (cont)	1992/93	MF	23	24	26	8	5	5	5	4		
		F	20	22	25	10	5	5	8	5		
	1993/94	MF	24	23	24	7	7	5	5	5		
		F	22	20	23	9	9	5	6	7		
Slovakia	1992/93	MF	21	21	21	22	4	4	4	3		
		F	20	20	21	21	5	5	4	4		
	1993/94	MF	21	21	21	21	4	4	4	4		
		F	20	20	20	21	5	5	5	4		
	1994/95	MF	22	21	21	20	4	4	4	4		
		F	21	20	20	20	5	5	5	5		
Slovenia	1992/93	MF	21	21	21	19	5	5	5	3		
		F	19	20	19	19	6	6	6	4		
	1993/94	MF	20	21	21	20	5	5	5	4		
		F	18	20	20	19	6	6	7	5		
	1994/95	MF	20	20	21	20	5	5	4	4		
		F	18	19	20	19	6	6	6	6		
Spain	1985/86	MF	23	21	19	11	10	8	8			
		F	22	20	19	12	10	9	8			
	1990/91	MF	19	19	18	13	12	10	9			
		F	18	18	18	14	12	11	10			
	1991/92	MF	19	18	18	13	12	10	10			
		F	17	17	18	14	13	11	10			
	1992/93	MF	18	18	18	14	12	11	10			
		F	17	17	17	14	13	11	11			
Sweden	1986/87	MF	28	28	28	6	6	4				
	1990/91	MF	26	27	28	8	7	5				
		F	24	25	26	10	9	6				
	1992/93	MF	26	25	26	10	8	6				
		F	24	23	24	11	10	7				
	1993/94	MF	25	25	24	12	9	6				
		F	24	24	23	12	11	8				
Switzerland	1985/86	MF	5	9	22	23	22	8	5	4	3	
		F	5	9	22	22	22	9	5	4	2	
	1990/91	MF	6	10	22	21	21	8	5	4	3	
		F	6	9	21	21	21	9	5	5	3	
	1992/93	MF	6	10	22	21	20	9	5	5	3	
		F	6	9	21	20	20	10	6	5	3	
	1993/94	MF	6	10	22	21	20	9	5	5	3	
		F	5	10	21	21	20	10	6	5	3	
The Former Yugoslav Rep. of Macedonia	1992/93	MF	30	27	23	20						
		F	28	27	24	21						
	1993/94	MF	28	26	24	21						
		F	27	26	25	22						
	1994/95	MF	29	25	24	22						
		F	28	25	24	23						
Ukraine	1985/86	MF	25	26	25	13	12	0				
	1990/91	MF	25	25	25	13	13	0				
	1992/93	MF	17	17	16	17	16	8	8			
		F	17	16	16	16	16	10	9			
	1993/94	MF	18	17	17	16	16	8	8			
		F	18	16	16	16	16	10	9			
Former Yugoslavia	1985/86	MF	21	20	20	19	8	7	5	——>		
		F	21	20	20	19	8	7	6	——>		
Federal Republic of Yugoslavia #	1990/91	MF	15	15	15	14	13	12	11	6		
		F	15	14	14	14	12	12	11	7		
Oceania												
American Samoa #	1985/86	MF	28	26	25	21						
		F	28	27	24	21						

3.8   Second level (general): enrolment by grade
       Second degré (général): effectifs par année d'études
       Segundo grado (general): matrícula escolar por año de estudios

Country Pays País	Year Année Año	Sex Sexe Sexo	Grades / Années d'études / Años de estudios									
			I	II	III	IV	V	VI	VII	VIII	IX	X
American Samoa # (cont)	1989/90	MF	29	27	23	21						
		F	28	26	24	22						
	1991/92	MF	28	28	24	21						
		F	27	27	25	21						
Australia	1985	MF	14	22	22	20	14	9				
		F	13	22	22	20	14	10				
	1990	MF	12	19	19	19	16	13				
		F	12	19	19	19	17	14				
	1993	MF	12	19	19	19	17	15				
		F	12	19	19	18	17	15				
	1994	MF	12	20	19	19	16	14				
		F	12	19	19	18	16	15				
Cook Islands	1988	MF	21	19	17	17	13	10	3			
Fiji	1985	MF	10	10	25	25	18	11	1			
		F	11	10	25	25	19	10	1			
	1991	MF	10	9	24	22	17	16	3			
		F	10	9	24	22	18	15	2			
	1992	MF	9	9	24	21	17	16	4			
		F	9	9	24	21	18	16	4			
French Polynesia	1986/87	MF	29	26	16	15	7	3	3			
		F	28	26	17	15	7	3	4			
	1990/91	MF	24	23	15	15	9	7	7			
	1992/93	MF	24	22	16	16	8	7	7			
		F	22	21	15	16	8	8	9			
Kiribati	1985	MF	29	26	23	13	6	3				
		F	27	28	25	13	6	3				
	1990	MF	21	27	22	17	10	2	1			
		F	21	28	21	18	10	2	1			
	1992	MF	21	24	23	17	11	3	1			
		F	21	25	21	18	12	2	1			
	1993	MF	20	25	22	16	12	3	1			
		F	19	26	22	16	13	3	1			
Nauru	1985	MF	29	26	25	16	4					
		F	24	24	29	17	7					
New Caledonia	1985	MF	30	28	16	14	6	3	3			
		F	29	26	17	15	7	4	3			
	1990	MF	27	24	16	16	8	4	4			
		F	26	24	16	16	9	5	4			
	1991	MF	28	25	16	15	8	5	4			
		F	26	24	16	16	9	5	4			
New Zealand	1985	MF	17	17	18	18	18	9	3			
		F	17	17	18	18	18	10	3			
	1990	MF	16	16	16	16	18	13	7			
		F	16	15	16	16	18	13	7			
	1993	MF	16	16	15	15	16	13	8			
		F	16	16	15	16	16	13	9			
	1994	MF	15	15	15	15	18	14	8			
		F	15	15	15	15	18	14	9			
Niue	1986	MF	18	25	19	28	10					
		F	18	25	20	27	10					
	1988	MF	31	22	33	14						
		F	30	24	33	13						
	1991	MF	18	16	17	19	23	7				
		F	19	19	14	18	23	6				
Papua New Guinea	1987	MF	30	27	21	19	2	2				
		F	30	27	21	19	1	1				
	1990	MF	30	26	22	19	2	2				
		F	30	27	22	18	2	1				

Second level (general): enrolment by grade   3.8
Second degré (général): effectifs par année d'études
Segundo grado (general): matrícula escolar por año de estudios

Country / Pays / País	Year / Année / Año	Sex / Sexe / Sexo	I	II	III	IV	V	VI	VII	VIII	IX	X
Papua New Guinea (cont)	1994	MF	28	27	23	18	2	2				
		F	28	28	23	18	2	1				
	1995	MF	28	25	22	20	3	2				
		F	27	25	24	20	3	2				
Samoa	1986	MF	22	22	17	16	14	6	2			
		F	22	21	18	17	15	5	1			
Solomon Islands #	1990	MF	30	27	26	8	8	1				
		F	32	27	27	7	6	1				
	1993	MF	28	26	24	12	9	2				
		F	28	27	26	10	7	1				
	1994	MF	27	26	24	11	11	2				
		F	28	26	24	11	9	1				
Tonga	1985	MF	16	19	19	17	18	9	2			
		F	15	18	18	19	20	8	2			
	1990	MF	24	19	18	16	16	7	-			
		F	24	20	19	15	16	6	-			
	1993	MF	20	16	16	18	23	8	0			
		F	20	16	15	18	23	8	0			
Tuvalu	1987	MF	16	17	20	19	14	14				
		F	18	14	22	18	13	14				
	1990	MF	16	18	18	16	18	15				
		F	18	19	19	13	18	14				
Vanuatu, Republic of	1989	MF	22	25	25	20	4	3	1			
		F	22	28	23	19	4	2	1			
	1991	MF	27	22	21	20	5	4	0			
		F	28	22	21	21	4	3	0			
	1992	MF	27	26	20	18	4	4	1			
		F	30	25	20	18	4	3	1			

This table presents for total (MF) and female (F) enrolment at the second level general education a percentage distribution by grade. In general, these percentages are given for the school years beginning in 1985, 1990 and the two latest years for which data are available.

Ce tableau présente la répartition en pourcentage par année d'études des effectifs totaux (MF) et des effectifs féminins (F) de l'enseignement général du second degré. En général, ces pourcentages sont présentés pour les années scolaires commençant en 1985, 1990 et des deux dernières années pour lesquelles les données sont disponibles.

Este cuadro presenta la distribución porcentual por año de estudios del total de la matrícula escolar (MF) y de la matrícula femenina (F) de la enseñanza general de segundo grado. En general, los porcentajes se refieren a los años escolares empezaron en 1985, 1990 y los dos últimos años para los que se dispone de datos.

AFRICA:
Gabon:
E--> For 1991/92, data refer to all second level education.
FR-> Pour 1991/92, les données se réfèrent à l'ensemble de l'enseignement du second degré.
ESP> Para 1991/92, los datos se refieren al total de la enseñanza de segundo grado.
Uganda:
E--> Data refer to government-maintained and aided schools only.
FR-> Les données se réfèrent aux écoles publiques et subventionnées seulement.
ESP> Los datos se refieren a las escuelas públicas y subvencionadas solamente.
Zambia:
E--> For 1994, data refer to government-maintained and aided schools only.
FR-> Pour 1994, les données se réfèrent aux écoles publiques et subventionnées seulement.
ESP> Para 1994, los datos se refieren a las escuelas públicas y subvencionadas solamente.

AMERICA, NORTH:
Belize:
E--> For 1992/93 and 1994/95, data refer to all second level education.
FR-> Pour 1992/93 et 1994/95, les données se réfèrent à l'ensemble de l'enseignement du second degré.
ESP> Para 1992/93 y 1994/95, los datos se refieren al total de la enseñanza de segundo grado.
Dominican Republic:
E--> For 1985/86, data refer to public education only.
FR-> Pour 1985/86, les données se réfèrent à l'enseignement public seulement.
ESP> Para 1985/86, los datos se refieren a la enseñanza pública solamente.
Jamaica:
E--> For 1989/90 and 1990/91, data refer to all second level education.
FR-> Pour 1989/90 et 1990/91, les données se réfèrent à l'ensemble de l'enseignement du second degré.
ESP> Para 1989/90 y 1990/91, los datos se refieren al total de la enseñanza de segundo grado.

3.8 Second level (general): enrolment by grade
Second degré (général): effectifs par année d'études
Segundo grado (general): matrícula escolar por año de estudios

U.S. Virgin Island:
    E—> Revised data. For 1990/91, data refer to public education only.
    FR–> Données révisées. Pour 1990/91, les données se réfèrent à l'enseignement public seulement.
    ESP> Datos revisados. Para 1990/91, los datos se refieren a la enseñanza pública solamente.
AMERICA, SOUTH:
Chile:
    E—> For 1991 and 1992, data refer to all second level education.
    FR–> Pour 1991 et 1992, les données se réfèrent à l'ensemble de l'enseignement du second degré.
    ESP> Para 1991 y 1992, los datos se refieren al total de la enseñanza de segundo grado.
ASIA:
Bahrain:
    E—> For 1985/86, data refer to public education only.
    FR–> Pour 1985/86, les données se réfèrent à l'enseignement public seulement.
    ESP> Para 1985/86, los datos se refieren a la enseñanza pública solamente.
Cyprus:
    E—> Not including Turkish schools.
    FR–> Non compris les écoles turques.
    ESP> Excluídas las escuelas turcas.
Hong Kong:
    E—> For 1986/87, data refer to all second level education.
    FR–> Pour 1986/87, les données se réfèrent à l'ensemble de l'enseignement du second degré.
    ESP> Para 1986/87, los datos se refieren al total de la enseñanza de segundo grado.

Indonesia:
    E—> Data do not include religious schools.
    FR–> Les données ne comprennent pas les écoles religieuses.
    ESP> Los datos no comprenden las escuelas religiosas.
Iran, Islamic Republic of:
    E—> For 1993/94 and 1994/95, data refer to all second level education.
    FR–> Pour 1993/94 et 1994/95, les données se réfèrent à l'ensemble de l'enseignement du second degré.
    ESP> Para 1993/94 y 1994/95, los datos se refieren al total de la enseñanza de segundo grado.
Qatar:
    E—> Data refer to public education only.
    FR–> Les données se réfèrent à l'enseignement public seulement.
    ESP> Los datos se refieren a la enseñanza pública solamente.
Yemen:
Former Yemen Arab Republic:
    E—> Data refer to public education only.
    FR–> Les données se réfèrent à l'enseignement public seulement.
    ESP> Los datos se refieren a la enseñanza pública solamente.
EUROPE:
Romania:
    E—> For 1992/93, data refer to all second level education.
    FR–> Pour 1992/93, les données se réfèrent à l'ensemble de l'enseignement du second degré.
    ESP> Para 1992/93, los datos se refieren al total de la enseñanza de segundo grado.

Third level: number of students per 100,000 inhabitants   3.9
Troisième degré: nombre d'étudiants par 100 000 habitants
Tercer grado: número de estudiantes por 100 000 habitantes

3.9 Education at the third level: number of students per 100,000 inhabitants

Enseignement du troisième degré: nombre d'étudiants par 100 000 habitants

Enseñanza de tercer grado: número de estudiantes por 100 000 habitantes

The years indicated refer to the beginning of the academic year for each country.

\# For countries with this symbol see the annex at the end of the table.

Les années indiquées se réfèrent au début de l'année académique en vigueur dans chaque pays.

\# Pour les pays dont le nom est accompagné de ce symbole voir l'annexe en fin de tableau.

Los años indicados se refieren al inicio del año académico en cada país.

\# Para los países cuyo nombre figura con este símbolo, véase el anexo al final del cuadro.

Country Pays País	Sex Sexe Sexo	Number of students per 100,000 inhabitants Nombre d'étudiants par 100 000 habitants Número de estudiantes por 100 000 habitantes					
		1980	1985	1990	1992	1993	1994
Africa							
Algeria	MF	530	798	1 147	1 160	...	...
	M	789	1 081	...	1 469	...	...
	F	275	508	...	844	...	...
Angola #	MF	39	63	71	...	...	...
	M	67	...	120	...	...	...
	F	12	...	23	...	...	...
Benin	MF	139	227	235	202	208	209
	M	...	388	413	342	348	...
	F	...	71	60	66	71	...
Botswana	MF	119	180	299	332	362	471
	M	163	205	327	326	347	...
	F	79	157	273	338	376	...
Burkina Faso	MF	24	52	60	93	90	...
	M	37	81	94	144	138	...
	F	10	24	28	42	43	...
Burundi	MF	45	59	65	73	...	...
	M	71	92	98	110	...	...
	F	22	28	34	38	...	...
Cameroon	MF	135	191	288	...	...	...
Central African Republic #	MF	74	102	150	...	...	...
	M	142	189	252	...	...	...
	F	12	21	55	...	...	...
Chad #	MF	...	43	70	70	70	...
	M	...	80	...	131	131	...
	F	...	7	...	11	11	...
Comoros #	MF	...	...	47	...	...	...
	M	...	...	80	...	...	...
	F	...	...	14	...	...	...
Congo	MF	435	555	478	582	...	...
	M	759	962	806	...	...	...
	F	126	169	165	...	...	...
Côte d'Ivoire #	MF	240	218	204	...	...	...
	M	386	345	319	...	...	...
	F	86	86	85	...	...	...

3.9   Third level: number of students per 100,000 inhabitants
      Troisième degré: nombre d'étudiants par 100 000 habitants
      Tercer grado: número de estudiantes por 100 000 habitantes

Country / Pays / País	Sex / Sexe / Sexo	Number of students per 100,000 inhabitants / Nombre d'étudiants par 100 000 habitants / Número de estudiantes por 100 000 habitantes					
		1980	1985	1990	1992	1993	1994
Djibouti #	MF	...	...	10	11	...	...
	M	...	...	14	10	...	...
	F	...	...	6	12	...	...
Egypt	MF	1 636	1 725	1 598	1 560	1 542	...
	M	2 205	2 283	2 097	2 047	2 023	...
	F	1 048	1 149	1 083	1 056	1 043	...
Equatorial Guinea #	MF	...	...	164	...	...	...
	M	...	...	292	...	...	...
	F	...	...	41	...	...	...
Eritrea	MF		...	...	...	...	91
	M		...	...	...	...	159
	F		...	...	...	...	24
Ethiopia #	MF	40	66	72	68	...	...
	M	70	108	117	109	...	...
	F	11	24	26	26	...	...
Gabon #	MF	216	402	373	...	...	...
	M	342	584	525	...	...	...
	F	94	225	225	...	...	...
Gambia	MF	...	...	...	...	...	147
	M	...	...	...	...	...	191
	F	...	...	...	...	...	105
Ghana	MF	144	132	126	...	...	...
	M	231	210	200	...	...	...
	F	59	56	54	...	...	...
Guinea	MF	410	176	93	...	...	...
	M	663	302	174	...	...	...
	F	157	51	12	...	...	...
Kenya	MF	78	109	142	...	...	...
	M	126	161	204	...	...	...
	F	30	57	79	...	...	...
Lesotho #	MF	152	155	154	196	206	...
	M	113	121	160	183	187	...
	F	188	188	148	209	224	...
Libyan Arab Jamahiriya #	MF	663	792	1 548	...	...	...
	M	936	...	1 605	...	...	...
	F	356	...	1 486	...	...	...
Madagascar	MF	250	360	285	318	...	...
	M	...	449	317	359	...	...
	F	...	273	253	278	...	...
Malawi #	MF	56	54	63	70	69	...
	M	80	79	92	98	97	...
	F	34	30	34	42	43	...
Mali	MF	71	86	73	...	...	...
	M	127	152	128	...	...	...
	F	18	22	19	...	...	...
Mauritania #	MF	...	256	285	356	393	...
	M	...	...	491	613	657	...
	F	...	...	83	104	135	...
Mauritius	MF	107	114	330	389	431	...
	M	151	146	419	...	...	...
	F	65	83	241	...	...	...
Morocco	MF	580	830	1 011	1 044	1 040	1 019
	M	886	1 123	1 276	1 286	1 261	1 204
	F	273	537	745	800	820	834
Mozambique	MF	8	11	...	31	35	...
	M	12	17	...	47	52	...
	F	5	5	...	16	18	...
Namibia #	MF	...	...	300	...	665	756
	M	...	...	217	...	516	595
	F	...	...	382	...	813	916
Niger #	MF	26	49	60	56	...	...
	M	42	81	104	...	...	...
	F	10	17	18	...	...	...
Nigeria #	MF	208	321	360	...	...	...
	M	...	477	551	...	...	...
	F	...	168	172	...	...	...

Third level: number of students per 100,000 inhabitants 3.9
Troisième degré: nombre d'étudiants par 100 000 habitants
Tercer grado: número de estudiantes por 100 000 habitantes

Country Pays País	Sex Sexe Sexo	Number of students per 100,000 inhabitants Nombre d'étudiants par 100 000 habitants Número de estudiantes por 100 000 habitantes					
		1980	1985	1990	1992	1993	1994
Rwanda #	MF	24	33	50	...	...	...
	M	44	57	82	...	...	...
	F	5	9	19	...	...	...
Senegal #	MF	246	209	287	298	...	...
	M	402	330	433	...	...	...
	F	90	89	140	...	...	...
Sierra Leone #	MF	67	159	129	...	...	...
	M	...	272	218	...	...	...
	F	...	50	45	...	...	...
Somalia #	MF	45	194		...	...	...
	M	...	315	...	...	...	...
	F	...	76	...	...	...	...
South Africa	MF	...	...	1 184	1 264	1 394	1 524
	M	...	...	1 324	1 361	1 509	1 593
	F	...	...	1 047	1 168	1 281	1 455
Sudan	MF	154	174	266	...	...	...
	M	224	219	285	...	...	...
	F	84	128	247	...	...	...
Swaziland #	MF	335	383	430	419	544	...
	M	412	478	516	466	678	...
	F	260	298	352	377	422	...
Togo #	MF	182	173	229	224	235	274
	M	314	302	402	397	416	479
	F	53	47	60	55	57	73
Tunisia	MF	499	573	848	1 044	1 121	1 176
	M	692	728	1 017	1 215	1 282	1 324
	F	300	413	676	869	957	1 024
Uganda	MF	45	67	98	112	121	...
	M	70	104	142	161	171	...
	F	20	31	55	63	72	...
United Republic of Tanzania #	MF	22	22	21	...	...	...
	M	36	39	...	...	...	...
	F	8	6	...	...	...	...
Zaire #	MF	105	129	176	...	...	...
	M	...	...	...	...	...	...
	F	...	...	...	...	...	...
Zambia #	MF	127	169	183	...	...	...
	M	205	288	268	...	...	...
	F	52	55	102	...	...	...
Zimbabwe #	MF	117	420	573	588	...	...
	M	...	615	847	860	...	...
	F	...	228	304	320	...	...
America, North							
Bahamas	MF	1 948	1 934	...	...	...	...
Barbados #	MF	1 620	2 075	2 670	2 415	...	2 493
	M	1 579	2 215	2 497	...	...	2 070
	F	1 656	1 948	2 829	...	...	2 887
Canada	MF	5 770	6 320	6 897	7 096	6 980	...
	M	5 775	5 803	6 376	6 664	6 668	...
	F	5 765	6 830	7 410	7 522	7 287	...
Costa Rica	MF	2 433	2 414	2 461	2 767	...	...
Cuba	MF	1 563	2 328	2 288	1 840	1 620	1 285
	M	1 595	2 125	1 938	1 548	1 392	...
	F	1 530	2 535	2 640	2 134	1 851	...
Dominican Republic	MF	...	1 941	...	...	...	...
El Salvador	MF	1 178	1 488	1 512	...	1 598	...
	M	1 343	1 695	1 738	...	1 639	...
	F	1 018	1 285	1 296	...	1 559	...
Guatemala	MF	736	741	...	...	...	...
Haiti	MF	87	107	...	...	...	...
	M	124	162	...	...	...	...
	F	52	54	...	...	...	...
Honduras	MF	724	875	907	852	865	916
	M	897	1 084	1 079	958	997	1 068
	F	548	663	732	745	731	762

Third level: number of students per 100,000 inhabitants
Troisième degré: nombre d'étudiants par 100 000 habitants
Tercer grado: número de estudiantes por 100 000 habitantes

Country Pays País	Sex Sexe Sexo	Number of students per 100,000 inhabitants Nombre d'étudiants par 100 000 habitants Número de estudiantes por 100 000 habitantes					
		1980	1985	1990	1992	1993	1994
Jamaica #	MF	656	475	677	668	...	...
	M	...	539	765	766	...	...
	F	...	411	590	571	...	...
Mexico	MF	1 387	1 599	1 551	1 477	1 509	...
	M	1 859	2 033	1 798	1 622	1 630	...
	F	912	1 165	1 304	1 333	1 388	...
Nicaragua	MF	1 258	898	836	903	...	...
	M	...	801	841	942	...	...
	F	...	991	832	867	...	...
Panama	MF	2 071	2 552	2 220	2 563	2 736	2 721
	M	1 836	2 131	...	...	...	...
	F	2 313	2 985	...	...	...	...
Trinidad and Tobago	MF	522	567	586	646	673	...
	M	601	700	666	768	805	...
	F	444	436	508	527	543	...
United States	MF	5 311	5 136	5 486	5 677	5 546	...
	M	5 298	5 005	5 120	5 241	5 107	...
	F	5 324	5 260	5 834	6 092	5 965	...
America, South							
Argentina #	MF	1 748	2 790	3 268	3 206	...	3 076
	M	1 757	2 689	...	...	...	2 822
	F	1 740	2 889	...	...	...	3 321
Bolivia #	MF	1 557	2 110	2 154	2 214	...	...
	M	...	...	...	...	...	...
	F	...	...	...	...	...	...
Brazil #	MF	1 162	1 053	1 078	1 079	1 080	1 081
	M	1 187	...	1 080	938	871	806
	F	1 137	...	1 076	1 220	1 288	1 354
Chile	MF	1 306	1 635	1 941	2 336	2 369	...
	M	1 503	1 876	...	...	...	...
	F	1 114	1 400	...	...	...	...
Colombia #	MF	1 024	1 328	1 554	...	...	1 703
	M	1 142	1 376	1 530	...	...	1 693
	F	908	1 280	1 578	...	...	1 713
Ecuador #	MF	3 389	3 164	2 012	...	...	...
	M	4 221	...	...	...	...	...
	F	2 547	...	...	...	...	...
Guyana #	MF	325	295	588	...	1 012	...
	M	369	310	678	...	1 073	...
	F	281	279	499	...	951	...
Paraguay	MF	858	869	762	...	907	...
	M	...	...	815	...	867	...
	F	...	...	707	...	949	...
Peru	MF	1 769	2 318	3 158	3 264	...	3 240
	M	2 273	...	...	...	...	...
	F	1 256	...	...	...	...	...
Suriname #	MF	620	730	1 079	...	...	...
	M	688	684	1 029	...	...	...
	F	554	775	1 127	...	...	...
Uruguay	MF	1 339	...	2 314	2 179	...	...
	M	1 258	...	...	...	...	...
	F	1 416	...	...	...	...	...
Venezuela #	MF	2 035	2 585	2 820	2 757	...	...
	M	...	3 013	...	...	...	...
	F	...	2 149	...	...	...	...
Asia							
Afghanistan #	MF	142	156	162	...	...	...
	M	235	260	217	...	...	...
	F	44	45	102	...	...	...
Armenia #	MF	3 577	3 178	3 410	3 711	...	...
	M	...	...	...	...	...	...
	F	...	...	...	...	...	...
Azerbaijan	MF	3 021	2 735	2 303	1 969	1 753	1 618
	M	...	...	...	2 441	2 049	1 774
	F	...	...	...	1 519	1 470	1 468
Bahrain	MF	550	1 011	1 402	1 493	1 436	...
	M	555	693	1 071	1 113	1 050	...
	F	542	1 467	1 859	2 011	1 959	...

Third level: number of students per 100,000 inhabitants
Troisième degré: nombre d'étudiants par 100 000 habitants
Tercer grado: número de estudiantes por 100 000 habitantes

3.9

Country / Pays / País	Sex / Sexe / Sexo	Number of students per 100,000 inhabitants / Nombre d'étudiants par 100 000 habitants / Número de estudiantes por 100 000 habitantes					
		1980	1985	1990	1992	1993	1994
Bangladesh	MF	272	468	405	...	...	...
	M	455	733	661	...	...	...
	F	78	185	133	...	...	...
Bhutan #	MF	26	18	...	...	...	...
	M	41	28	...	...	...	...
	F	11	7	...	...	...	...
Brunei Darussalam #	MF	74	258	...	516	...	...
	M	69	243	...	425	...	...
	F	80	275	...	617	...	...
Cambodia	MF	172	151	131	...	126	117
	M	...	...	...	...	218	205
	F	...	...	...	...	41	36
China	MF	166	327	329	359	377	...
	M	229	453	453	497	520	...
	F	99	193	197	213	224	...
Cyprus‡	MF	379	575	1 116	1 011	1 069	...
	M	446	600	1 086	1 029	997	...
	F	312	551	1 146	994	1 141	...
Georgia	MF	2 757	2 715	2 710	...	...	3 083
	M	...	...	...	...	...	2 834
	F	...	...	...	...	...	3 309
Hong Kong #	MF	1 198	1 426	1 484	1 540	1 677	...
	M	1 603	1 804	1 730	1 749	1 876	...
	F	758	1 020	1 226	1 320	1 468	...
India	MF	515	582	582	...	...	...
	M	732	789	753	...	...	...
	F	281	360	399	...	...	...
Indonesia #	MF	367	597	955	951	...	...
	M	508	813	...	1 155	...	...
	F	227	384	...	749	...	...
Iran, Islamic Republic of	MF	...	377	852	1 079	1 148	1 184
	M	...	531	1 165	1 477	1 571	1 595
	F	...	219	529	669	711	759
Iraq #	MF	820	1 108	1 240	...	...	...
	M	1 101	1 383	1 510	...	...	...
	F	530	822	959	...	...	...
Israel	MF	2 503	2 742	2 855	3 078	2 979	...
	M	2 437	2 915	2 926	3 157	...	...
	F	2 570	2 570	2 784	3 000	...	...
Japan #	MF	2 065	1 943	2 340	...	...	...
	M	2 820	2 574	2 836	...	...	...
	F	1 333	1 333	1 861	...	...	...
Jordan #	MF	1 648	1 995	2 230	2 225	...	...
	M	1 712	2 100	2 072	2 203	...	...
	F	1 577	1 881	2 404	2 248	...	...
Kazakstan #	MF	3 524	3 492	3 224	3 098	2 915	2 835
	M	...	...	...	...	2 707	2 614
	F	...	...	...	...	3 111	3 045
Korea, Republic of	MF	1 698	3 568	3 946	4 253	4 756	4 930
	M	2 531	4 974	5 366	5 624	6 101	6 314
	F	848	2 137	2 507	2 866	3 398	3 532
Kuwait #	MF	991	1 377	1 370	1 589	...	2 144
	M	739	1 118	1 068	1 299	...	1 843
	F	1 330	1 716	1 757	1 942	...	2 464
Kyrgyzstan #	MF	2 897	2 734	2 359	2 179	1 837	...
	M	...	...	...	...	1 805	...
	F	...	...	...	...	1 867	...
Lao People's Democratic Republic #	MF	44	150	116	128	134	...
	M	60	192	160	185	199	...
	F	28	107	74	72	71	...
Lebanon #	MF	2 962	2 980	3 275	...	...	...
	M	3 854	...	3 513	...	...	...
	F	2 101	...	3 051	...	...	...
Malaysia	MF	419	595	679	854	884	...
	M	512	656	716	...	...	...
	F	325	533	640	...	...	...

3.9 Third level: number of students per 100,000 inhabitants
Troisième degré: nombre d'étudiants par 100 000 habitants
Tercer grado: número de estudiantes por 100 000 habitantes

Country / Pays / País	Sex / Sexe / Sexo	Number of students per 100,000 inhabitants / Nombre d'étudiants par 100 000 habitants / Número de estudiantes por 100 000 habitantes					
		1980	1985	1990	1992	1993	1994
Mongolia #	MF	2 234	1 991	1 424	...	...	1 377
	M	1 656	1 588	...	...	...	835
	F	2 816	2 399	...	...	...	1 927
Myanmar #	MF	483	478	459	559	528	...
	M	...	443	411	476		...
	F	...	512	506	641	...	...
Nepal	MF	259	412	487	512	490	...
	M	408	...	736	...	...	...
	F	101	...	229	...	...	...
Oman #	MF	2	71	341	400	...	...
	M	...	84	362	389	...	...
	F	...	57	317	413	...	...
Pakistan #	MF	189	261	294	...	...	...
	M	264	370	367	...	...	...
	F	107	143	215	...	...	...
Philippines	MF	2 641	2 565	2 813	2 696	2 716	...
	M	2 455	...	2 355	2 257	2 209	...
	F	2 828	...	3 276	3 140	3 230	...
Qatar	MF	990	1 494	1 336	1 408	1 389	1 443
	M	594	847	602	598	609	621
	F	1 682	2 816	2 871	3 072	2 970	3 084
Saudi Arabia	MF	646	898	959	1 145	1 175	...
	M	863	972	955	1 092	1 145	...
	F	392	803	965	1 215	1 212	...
Singapore	MF	963	1 560	2 058	2 380	2 642	2 729
	M	1 150	1 925	2 386	2 695	2 972	3 029
	F	768	1 182	1 721	2 056	2 303	2 422
Sri Lanka #	MF	288	368	488	504	...	552
	M	320	435	591	607	...	653
	F	255	300	384	402	...	451
Syrian Arab Republic	MF	1 611	1 734	1 795	1 700	...	...
	M	2 231	2 225	2 178	1 976	...	...
	F	964	1 230	1 403	1 419	...	...
Tajikistan #	MF	2 450	2 091	2 084	2 298	...	...
Thailand #	MF	1 481	2 009	1 738	2 029	...	2 166
	M	...	...	...	1 921	...	...
	F	...	...	...	2 138	...	...
Turkey	MF	554	934	1 337	1 567	1 918	1 932
	M	808	1 228	1 729	2 002	2 346	2 329
	F	292	622	924	1 111	1 469	1 516
Turkmenistan	MF	2 437	2 351	2 078	...	...	...
United Arab Emirates	MF	282	564	610	601	...	...
	M	210	356	278	281	...	...
	F	442	967	1 228	1 185	...	...
Uzbekistan #	MF	3 237	3 132	2 951	3 054	...	...
Viet Nam	MF	214	255	293	...	316	...
	M	336	...	...	...	...	...
	F	98	...	...	...	...	...
Yemen #	MF	...	...	447	...	...	...
	M	...	...	754	...	...	...
	F	...	...	151	...	...	...
Europe							
Albania	MF	824	1 080	973	981	891	...
	M	834	1 080	978	969	813	...
	F	812	1 080	967	994	972	...
Austria	MF	1 812	2 292	2 670	2 836	2 893	...
	M	2 223	2 641	3 012	3 129	3 152	...
	F	1 444	1 978	2 353	2 560	2 647	...
Belarus	MF	3 530	3 439	3 148	3 060	2 941	...
	M	...	...	3 258	3 162	3 039	...
	F	...	...	3 052	2 969	2 855	...
Belgium	MF	2 111	2 511	2 776	...	...	...
	M	2 451	2 793	2 939	...	...	...
	F	1 787	2 242	2 621	...	...	...
Bulgaria	MF	1 144	1 270	2 096	2 191	2 324	2 529
	M	1 006	1 163	2 067	1 907	1 949	2 036
	F	1 281	1 376	2 125	2 466	2 687	3 005

Third level: number of students per 100,000 inhabitants
Troisième degré: nombre d'étudiants par 100 000 habitants
Tercer grado: número de estudiantes por 100 000 habitantes

3.9

Country / Pays / País	Sex / Sexe / Sexo	Number of students per 100,000 inhabitants / Nombre d'étudiants par 100 000 habitants / Número de estudiantes por 100 000 habitantes					
		1980	1985	1990	1992	1993	1994
Croatia	MF	1 484	1 249	1 601	1 720	1 826	1 826
	M	...	...	...	1 846	1 976	1 922
	F	...	...	...	1 603	1 685	1 736
Czech Republic	MF	1 165	1 060	1 147	1 132	1 484	1 604
	M	...	...	...	1 298	1 605	1 745
	F	...	...	...	974	1 370	1 470
Denmark	MF	2 074	2 275	2 782	3 045	3 284	...
	M	2 148	2 340	2 708	2 940	3 250	...
	F	2 001	2 211	2 853	3 147	3 318	...
Estonia	MF	1 810	1 607	1 743	1 659	1 595	1 654
	M	1 806	1 438	1 886	1 793	1 656	1 699
	F	1 813	1 753	1 618	1 539	1 542	1 613
Finland	MF	2 577	2 611	3 323	3 739	3 902	...
	M	2 761	2 760	3 275	3 615	3 768	...
	F	2 404	2 470	3 368	3 856	4 028	...
France #	MF	2 125	2 318	2 995	3 409	3 623	...
	M	2 245	2 361	2 884	3 202	3 372	...
	F	2 011	2 276	3 101	3 605	3 860	...
Germany	MF	...	...	2 581	2 269	2 319	...
	M	...	...	...	2 821	2 854	...
	F	...	...	...	1 748	1 813	...
Greece	MF	1 256	1 831	1 907	2 893	3 026	...
	M	1 498	1 902	1 930	2 972	3 274	...
	F	1 023	1 763	1 884	2 817	2 785	...
Hungary	MF	945	939	988	1 145	1 312	...
	M	980	904	1 022	1 178	1 295	...
	F	912	972	956	1 113	1 327	...
Iceland	MF	1 592	1 957	2 051	2 179	2 300	...
	M	1 263	1 732	1 739	1 842	1 986	...
	F	1 927	2 184	2 365	2 518	2 615	...
Ireland	MF	1 610	1 979	2 578	3 087	3 338	...
	M	1 901	2 238	2 793	3 208	3 458	...
	F	1 316	1 718	2 363	2 967	3 219	...
Italy	MF	1 981	2 088	2 547	2 829	2 944	...
	M	2 336	2 318	2 750	2 878	2 973	...
	F	1 644	1 870	2 355	2 782	2 917	...
Latvia	MF	1 863	1 680	1 722	1 559	1 452	1 473
	M	1 739	1 468	1 667	1 571	1 367	1 408
	F	1 968	1 862	1 770	1 549	1 525	1 529
Lithuania	MF	2 884	2 691	2 493	2 049	1 898	1 912
	M	2 538	2 084	2 390	1 882	1 673	1 687
	F	3 192	3 231	2 585	2 198	2 101	2 115
Luxembourg	MF	205	207	...	...	...	...
	M	271	279	...	...	...	...
	F	142	139	...	...	...	...
Malta	MF	292	428	882	1 300	1 433	...
	M	454	586	1 002	1 365	1 486	...
	F	139	275	765	1 236	1 382	...
Moldova	MF	2 747	2 700	2 403	...	2 291	2 282
	M	...	...	...	...	...	2 221
	F	...	...	...	...	...	2 338
Netherlands	MF	2 546	2 794	3 203	3 339	3 352	...
	M	3 091	3 333	3 606	3 646	3 644	...
	F	2 008	2 266	2 809	3 038	3 067	...
Norway	MF	1 936	2 279	3 360	3 890	4 111	...
	M	2 039	2 212	3 194	3 656	3 841	...
	F	1 836	2 345	3 523	4 120	4 375	...
Poland	MF	1 656	1 221	1 429	1 611	1 952	...
	M	1 504	1 109	1 290	1 440	1 734	...
	F	1 800	1 327	1 562	1 774	2 159	...
Portugal	MF	944	1 046	1 882	2 514	2 808	...
	M	1 008	1 004	1 728	2 626	...	...
	F	883	1 085	2 026	2 409	...	...
Romania #	MF	868	703	710	1 019	1 086	...
	M	1 010	786	...	1 102	1 177	...
	F	730	623	...	939	998	...

3.9 Third level: number of students per 100,000 inhabitants
Troisième degré: nombre d'étudiants par 100 000 habitants
Tercer grado: número de estudiantes por 100 000 habitantes

Country Pays País	Sex Sexe Sexo	Number of students per 100,000 inhabitants Nombre d'étudiants par 100 000 habitants Número de estudiantes por 100 000 habitantes					
		1980	1985	1990	1992	1993	1994
Russian Federation	MF	4 107	3 806	3 444	3 169	3 104	3 025
	M	3 898	3 533	3 313	3 013	3 004	2 848
	F	4 286	4 043	3 560	3 307	3 193	3 182
Slovakia	MF	...	...	...	1 247	1 369	1 542
	M	...	...	...	1 324	1 438	1 610
	F	...	...	...	1 173	1 303	1 477
Slovenia #	MF	...	...	1 995	2 033	2 077	2 227
	M	...	...	1 944	1 916	1 910	2 010
	F	...	...	2 042	2 143	2 234	2 430
Spain	MF	1 859	2 431	3 112	3 474	3 719	...
	M	2 132	2 521	3 103	3 417	3 710	...
	F	1 595	2 343	3 120	3 530	3 728	...
Sweden #	MF	2 423	2 115	2 250	2 622	2 697	...
	M	2 669	2 048	2 106	2 458	2 479	...
	F	2 182	2 180	2 391	2 783	2 910	...
Switzerland	MF	1 347	1 685	2 012	2 095	2 107	...
	M	1 931	2 346	2 665	2 714	2 694	...
	F	794	1 056	1 376	1 490	1 531	...
The Former Yugoslav Rep. of Macedonia	MF	2 579	1 979	1 296	1 260	1 290	1 357
	M	...	...	1 244	1 208	1 209	1 240
	F	...	...	1 349	1 313	1 373	1 476
Ukraine #	MF	3 370	3 264	3 173	3 152	...	...
	M	...	...	3 357	3 382	...	...
	F	...	...	3 014	2 954	...	...
United Kingdom	MF	1 468	1 824	2 192	2 646	2 788	...
	M	1 911	2 040	2 324	2 732	2 822	...
	F	1 049	1 618	2 065	2 565	2 755	...
Federal Republic of Yugoslavia #	MF	...	...	1 296	1 370	...	1 338
	M	...	...	1 243	1 291	...	1 235
	F	...	...	1 348	1 448	...	1 438
Oceania							
Australia	MF	2 222	2 366	2 872	3 219	3 267	3 135
	M	2 434	2 485	2 721	3 003	3 047	2 904
	F	2 011	2 247	3 024	3 435	3 488	3 365
Fiji #	MF	275	331	1 076	...	...	...
	M	329	406	...	...	...	...
	F	219	254	...	...	...	...
French Polynesia #	MF	18	...	114	...	...	...
	M	25	...	115	...	...	...
	F	10	...	113	...	...	...
Guam #	MF	3 018	5 771	...	...	...	...
	M	2 606	5 105	...	...	...	...
	F	3 467	6 517	...	...	...	...
New Caledonia	MF	306	492	...	...	...	...
	M	364	535	...	...	...	...
	F	244	446	...	...	...	...
New Zealand	MF	2 462	2 950	3 318	4 251	4 675	4 798
	M	2 941	3 232	3 239	3 983	4 336	4 342
	F	1 988	2 673	3 395	4 512	5 005	5 241
Papua New Guinea	MF	163	147	...	...	...	...
	M	243	217	...	...	...	...
	F	76	71	...	...	...	...
Samoa #	MF	404	...	...	...	...	...
	M	729	...	...	...	...	...
	F	58	...	...	...	...	...

Third level: number of students per 100,000 inhabitants 3.9
Troisième degré: nombre d'étudiants par 100 000 habitants
Tercer grado: número de estudiantes por 100 000 habitantes

Annex: Countries shown with the symbol #.
Annexe: Pays dont le nom est accompagné du symbole #.
Anexo: Países en los que aparece el símbolo #.

Country Pays País	Data for Les données pour Los datos para 1980 Refer to Se refèrent à Se refieren a	Data for Les données pour Los datos para 1985 Refer to Se refèrent à Se refieren a	Data for Les données pour Los datos para 1990 Refer to Se refèrent à Se refieren a	Data for Les données pour Los datos para 1992 Refer to Se refèrent à Se refieren a
Africa				
Angola	1981		1989	
Central African Republic			1991	
Chad		1986	1988	
Comoros			1989	
Côte d'Ivoire			1988	
Djibouti			1991	
Equatorial Guinea	1981			
Ethiopia	1981			1991
Gabon	1979	1986	1991	
Lesotho	1981			
Libyan Arab Jamahiriya			1991	
Malawi			1989	
Mauritania			1991	
Namibia			1991	
Niger		1986	1989	1991
Nigeria			1989	
Rwanda			1080	
Senegal			1991	
Sierra Leone			1989	
Somalia	1979	1986		
Swaziland		1986		
Togo			1989	
United Republic of Tanzania	1981		1989	
Zaire			1988	
Zambia	1981		1989	
Zimbabwe		1986	1989	
America, North				
Barbados		1984	1991	
Jamaica				1991
America, South				
Argentina			1991	
Bolivia				1991
Brazil		1986		
Colombia			1991	
Ecuador		1984		
Guyana			1989	
Suriname	1979			
Venezuela				1991

3.9 Third level: number of students per 100,000 inhabitants
Troisième degré: nombre d'étudiants par 100 000 habitants
Tercer grado: número de estudiantes por 100 000 habitantes

Country Pays País	Data for Les données pour Los datos para 1980 Refer to Se refèrent à Se refieren a	Data for Les données pour Los datos para 1985 Refer to Se refèrent à Se refieren a	Data for Les données pour Los datos para 1990 Refer to Se refèrent à Se refieren a	Data for Les données pour Los datos para 1992 Refer to Se refèrent à Se refieren a
Asia				
Afghanistan	1979	1986		
Armenia				1991
Bhutan		1984		
Brunei Darussalam		1986		
Hong Kong		1984	1991	
Indonesia	1981	1984	1991	
Iraq			1988	
Japan			1991	
Jordan			1989	
Kazakstan				1991
Kuwait			1991	
Kyrgyzstan				1991
Lao People's Democratic Rep.			1989	
Lebanon			1991	
Mongolia	1981	1986		
Myanmar			1991	
Oman				1991
Pakistan	1979		1991	
Sri Lanka				1991
Tajikistan				1991
Thailand			1989	
Uzbekistan				1991
Yemen			1991	
Europe				
France	1981			
Romania			1989	
Slovenia			1991	
Sweden	1979			
Ukraine				1991
Federal Republic of Yugoslavia			1991	
Oceania				
Fiji	1981		1991	
French Polynesia			1991	
Guam		1986		
Samoa	1981			

This table shows the number of students enrolled at the third level of education per 100,000 inhabitants. The ratios have been calculated using the enrolment data shown in table 3.10 and the population figures provided by the Population Division of the United Nations. When data in Table 3.10 are incomplete, estimates have been used in order to maintain the comparability of the ratios presented for different years.

Ce tableau présente le nombre d'étudiants inscrits dans l'enseignement du troisième degré par 100 000 habitants. Les taux ont été calculés en utilisant les effectifs indiqués dans le tableau et les chiffres de population fournis par la Division de la Population des Nations Unies. Lorsque les données du tableau 3.10 sont incomplètes, des estimations ont été utilisées afin de maintenir la comparabilité des taux présentés pour les différentes années.

Este cuadro presenta el número de estudiantes inscritos en la enseñanza de tercer grado por 100 000 habitantes. Las tasas se calcularon utilizando la matrícula escolar que figura en el cuadro 3.10 y las cifras de población que nos fueron comunicadas por la División de la Población de las Naciones Unidas. Cuando los datos presentados en el cuadro 3.10 eran incompletos, se prepararon estimaciones que mantuvieran la comparabilidad de las tasas presentadas para los diferentes años.

ASIA:
Cyprus:
　E--> Not including Turkish enrolment and population.

FR-> Non compris les effectifs et la population turques.
ESP> Excluídos la matricula y la población turcas.

Third level: teachers and students 3.10
Troisième degré: professeurs et étudiants
Tercer grado: profesores y estudiantes

3.10 Education at the third level: teachers and students by type of institution

Enseignement du troisième degré: personnel enseignant et étudiants par type d'établissement

Enseñanza de tercer grado: personal docente y estudiantes por tipo de establecimiento

All institutions	= Total des établissements	= Todos los establecimientos
Universities and equiv. insts.	= Universités et étab. équiv.	= Universidades y estab. equiv.
Distance-learning insts.	= Enseignement à distance	= Enseñanza a distancia
Other third level insts.	= Autres étab. du troisième degré	= Otros estab. de tercer grado

Please refer to the explanatory text at the end of the table / Prière de se référer au texte explicatif à la fin du tableau / Referirse al texto explicativo al final del cuadro

Country Pays País	Type of institution Type d'établissement Tipo de establecimiento	Year Année Año	Teaching staff Personnel enseignant Personal docente			Students enrolled Étudiants inscrits Estudiantes matriculados		
			Total	Female Féminin Femenino	% F	Total	Female Féminin Femenino	% F
			(1)	(2)	(3)	(4)	(5)	(6)
Africa								
Algeria‡	All institutions	1980/81	8 962	...	...	79 351	21 014	26
		1985/86	11 464	...	...	132 057	41 558	...
		1990/91	20 040	...	...	285 930	...	...
		1991/92	20 336	...	...	298 117	...	...
		1992/93	19 291	...	...	303 111	...	...
	Universities and equiv. insts.	1980/81	8 962	...	...	79 351	21 014	26
		1985/86	11 464	...	...	132 057	41 558	...
		1990/91	15 171	...	...	212 413	...	...
		1991/92	14 496	...	...	236 185	93 471	40
		1992/93	15 450	3 405	22	257 379	106 928	42
	Distance-learning insts.	1990/91	...	...	...	30 504	...	...
		1991/92	1 742	...	...	26 881	...	...
		1992/93	1 698	...	...	23 883	...	...
	Other third level insts.	1990/91	4 869	...	...	43 013	...	...
		1991/92	4 098	...	...	35 051	...	...
		1992/93	2 143	...	...	21 849	...	...
Angola	All institutions	1980/81	225	...	...	2 333	...	...
		1985/86	666	...	...	5 034	...	...
		1989/90	736	...	...	6 281	1 033	16
		1990/91	986	...	...	6 534	...	...
		1991/92	787	...	...	6 331	...	...

3.10 Third level: teachers and students
Troisième degré: professeurs et étudiants
Tercer grado: profesores y estudiantes

Country Pays País	Type of institution Type d'établissement Tipo de establecimiento	Year Année Año	Teaching staff Personnel enseignant Personal docente			Students enrolled Étudiants inscrits Estudiantes matriculados		
			Total	Female Féminin Femenino	% F	Total	Female Féminin Femenino	% F
			(1)	(2)	(3)	(4)	(5)	(6)
Angola (cont)	Universities and equiv. insts.	1980/81	225	...	...	2 333	...	...
		1985/86	666	...	...	5 034	...	...
		1989/90	736	...	...	6 281	1 033	16
		1990/91	986	...	...	6 534	...	...
		1991/92	787	...	...	6 331	...	...
Benin	All institutions	1980	...	...	...	4 822	...	...
		1985	...	...	...	9 063	1 427	16
		1990	956	...	...	10 873	1 416	13
		1991	1 379	199	14	10 611	1 656	16
		1992	1 424	251	18	9 964	1 634	16
		1993	957	...	...	10 586	1 835	17
		1994	...	...	...	10 986	...	...
Botswana‡	All institutions	1980/81	140	...	...	1 078	372	35
		1985/86	190	...	...	1 938	875	45
		1990/91	...	...	...	...	...	...
		1992/93	...	...	...	...	...	...
		1993/94	...	...	...	...	...	...
		1994/95	...	...	...	...	...	...
	Universities and equiv. insts.	1980/81	140	...	...	1 078	372	35
		1985/86	178	...	...	1 773	801	45
		1990/91	300	...	...	3 365	1 481	44
		1992/93	376	...	...	3 976	1 946	49
		1993/94	...	...	...	4 466	2 228	50
		1994/95	...	...	...	5 062	...	...
	Other third level insts.	1985/86	12	-	-	165	74	45
Burkina Faso	All institutions	1980/81	...	...	...	1 644	354	22
		1985/86	...	...	...	4 085	946	23
		1990/91	387	...	...	5 425	1 254	23
		1991/92	...	...	...	7 387	1 666	23
		1992/93	547	12	2	8 813	2 013	23
		1993/94	571	...	...	8 815	2 131	24
	Universities and equiv. insts.	1980/81	140	...	...	1 520	285	19
		1985/86	...	...	...	3 856	844	22
		1990/91	381	...	...	5 086	1 108	22
		1991/92	...	...	...	6 912	1 429	21
		1992/93	525	10	2	8 276	1 777	21
	Other third level insts.	1980/81	...	...	...	124	69	56
		1985/86	...	...	...	229	102	45
		1990/91	6	...	...	336	146	43
		1991/92	...	...	...	475	237	50
		1992/93	22	2	9	537	236	44
Burundi	All institutions	1980/81	...	...	...	1 879	464	25
		1985/86	467	31	7	2 783	676	24
		1990/91	436	36	8	3 592	957	27
		1991/92	539	60	11	3 830	1 013	26
		1992/93	556	61	11	4 256	1 127	26
	Universities and equiv. insts.	1980/81	...	...	...	1 793	438	24
		1985/86	315	26	8	2 111	504	24
		1990/91	436	36	8	3 592	957	27
		1991/92	539	60	11	3 830	1 013	26
		1992/93	556	61	11	4 256	1 127	26
	Other third level insts.	1980/81	...	...	...	86	26	30
		1985/86	152	5	3	672	172	26
		1990/91	-	-	-	-	-	-
		1991/92	-	-	-	-	-	-
		1992/93	-	-	-	-	-	-
Cameroon‡	All institutions	1980/81	...	...	...	11 686	...	...
		1985/86	...	...	...	...	...	...
		1990/91	1 086	...	...	33 177	...	...
	Universities and equiv. insts.	1980/81	...	...	...	10 631	...	...
		1985/86	871	...	...	17 071	...	...
		1990/91	761	...	...	31 360	...	...
	Other third level insts.	1980/81	...	...	...	1 055	...	...
		1990/91	325	...	...	1 817	...	...
Central African Republic‡	All institutions	1980/81	444	68	15	1 719	143	8
		1985/86	489	38	8	2 651	287	11
		1989/90	...	...	...	3 482	568	16
		1991/92	...	...	...	...	...	...

Third level: teachers and students **3.10**
Troisième degré: professeurs et étudiants
Tercer grado: profesores y estudiantes

Country Pays País	Type of institution Type d'établissement Tipo de establecimiento	Year Année Año	Teaching staff Personnel enseignant Personal docente				Students enrolled Étudiants inscrits Estudiantes matriculados		
			Total	Female Féminin Femenino	% F		Total	Female Féminin Femenino	% F
			(1)	(2)	(3)		(4)	(5)	(6)
Central African Republic‡ (cont)	Universities and equiv. insts.	1980/81 1985/86 1989/90 1991/92	379 139	63 15	17 11		1 394 2 374 2 818 3 783	119 272 302 557	9 11 11 15
	Other third level insts.	1980/81 1985/86 1989/90	65	5	8		325 277 664	24 15 266	7 5 40
Chad‡	All institutions	1984/85 1988/89 1992/93 1993/94	141	11	8		1 643 2 983	142	9 ... ...
	Universities and equiv. insts.	1984/85 1988/89 1992/93 1993/94	104 ... 187 ...	5	5		1 470 2 923 2 842 2 941	139 ... 298 308	9 ... 10 10
	Other third level insts.	1984/85 1988/89	37 ...	6 ...	16 ...		173 60	3 ...	2 ...
Comoros	All institutions	1989/90 1991/92 1992/93	32	10	31		248 223 229	36 63 ...	15 28 ...
	Other third level insts.	1989/90 1991/92 1992/93	32	10	31		248 223 229	36 63 ...	15 28 ...
Congo‡	All institutions	1980/81 1985/86 1990/91 1991/92 1992/93	292 ... 1 112 1 159 656	27 ... 95 91 52	9 ... 9 8 8		7 255 10 684 10 671 12 045 13 806	1 079 1 665 1 885 2 241 ...	15 16 18 19 ...
	Universities and equiv. insts.	1980/81 1985/86 1990/91 1991/92 1992/93	292 ... 1 112 1 159 656	27 ... 95 91 52	9 ... 9 8 8		7 255 10 684 10 671 12 045 13 806	1 079 1 665 1 885 2 241 ...	15 16 18 19 ...
Côte d'Ivoire	All institutions	1980/81 1984/85 1986/87 1988/89	... ...	... ...	... ...		19 633 19 660 23 642 ...	... ... 4 285 ...	... ... 18 ...
	Universities and equiv. insts.	1980/81 1984/85 1986/87 1988/89	625	... ...	... ...		12 742 11 300 15 849 15 501	2 376 2 333 2 959 2 901	19 21 19 19
	Other third level insts.	1980/81 1984/85 1986/87	... ...	... ...	... ...		6 891 8 360 7 793	... ... 1 326	 17
Djibouti	All institutions	1991/92 1992/93	... ...	... ...	... ...		53 61	16 34	30 56
	Other third level insts.	1991/92 1992/93	... ...	... ...	... ...		53 61	16 34	30 56
Egypt‡	All institutions	1980/81 1985/86 1990/91 1991/92 1992/93 1993/94	... 31 903	... ...	... ...		715 701 854 584 708 417	225 562 254 528 244 700	32 30 35 ... ...
	Universities and equiv. insts.	1980/81 1985/86 1990/91 1991/92 1992/93 1993/94	... 29 889 34 553 36 609 37 608 38 828	... 8 042 10 006 10 627 10 999 11 596	... 27 29 29 29 30		663 418 753 190 600 680 518 645 562 658 620 145	210 072 225 873 210 159 191 263 210 154 240 099	32 30 35 37 37 39
	Other third level insts.	1980/81 1985/86 1990/91	... 2 014 ...	... ...	... ...		52 283 101 394 107 737	15 490 28 655 34 541	30 28 32
Equatorial Guinea	All institutions	1990/91	58	7	12		578	73	13
	Universities and equiv. insts.	1990/91	9	1	11		71	3	4
	Distance-learning insts.	1990/91	49	6	12		507	70	14

3.10 Third level: teachers and students
Troisième degré: professeurs et étudiants
Tercer grado: profesores y estudiantes

Country / Pays / País	Type of institution / Type d'établissement / Tipo de establecimiento	Year / Année / Año	Teaching staff Personnel enseignant Personal docente			Students enrolled Étudiants inscrits Estudiantes matriculados		
			Total	Female Féminin Femenino	% F	Total	Female Féminin Femenino	% F
			(1)	(2)	(3)	(4)	(5)	(6)
Eritrea	All institutions	1994/95	...	...	...	3 137	424	14
	Universities and equiv. insts.	1994/95	136	11	8	3 081	422	14
	Other third level insts.	1994/95	...	...	...	56	2	4
Ethiopia‡	All institutions	1980/81	1 051	...	...	14 368	...	...
		1985/86	1 314	116	9	27 338	4 881	18
		1990/91	1 690	127	8	34 076	6 092	18
		1991/92	1 697	87	5	26 218	4 977	19
	Universities and equiv. insts.	1980/81	787	...	...	9 291	...	...
		1985/86	1 034	...	...	21 601	3 055	14
		1990/91	1 439	109	8	29 066	4 485	15
		1991/92	1 440	70	5	20 948	3 387	16
	Other third level insts.	1980/81	264	...	...	5 077	...	...
		1985/86	280	...	...	5 737	1 826	32
		1990/91	251	18	7	5 010	1 607	32
		1991/92	257	17	7	5 270	1 590	30
Gabon	All institutions	1986/87	...	...	...	4 089	1 168	29
		1991/92	...	...	...	...	...	...
	Universities and equiv. insts.	1986/87	364	...	...	2 741	853	31
		1991/92	299	...	...	3 000	852	28
	Other third level insts.	1986/87	...	...	...	1 348	315	23
Gambia	All institutions	1994/95	155	36	23	1 591	573	36
	Other third level insts.	1994/95	155	36	23	1 591	573	36
Ghana	All institutions	1980/81	...	...	...	...	...	...
		1985/86	...	...	...	...	...	...
		1990/91	...	...	...	...	...	...
	Universities and equiv. insts.	1980/81	987	...	...	7 951	1 588	20
		1985/86	1 097	...	...	8 324	1 417	17
		1990/91	...	...	...	9 609	2 158	22
Guinea	All institutions	1980/81	1 289	40	3	18 270	3 497	19
		1985/86	1 107	40	4	8 801	1 267	14
		1990/91	...	...	...	5 366	350	7
	Universities and equiv. insts.	1980/81	577	31	5	5 319	726	14
		1985/86	1 004	40	4	8 393	1 195	14
	Other third level insts.	1980/81	712	9	1	12 951	2 771	21
		1985/86	103	-	-	408	72	18
Kenya	All institutions	1980/81	...	...	...	12 986	...	...
		1985/86	...	...	...	21 756	5 710	26
		1989/90	...	...	...	31 287	...	...
		1990/91	...	...	...	...	...	...
	Universities and equiv. insts.	1980/81	...	...	...	9 155	2 302	25
		1985/86	...	...	...	9 148	2 635	29
		1989/90	...	...	...	22 840	7 034	31
		1990/91	4 392	...	...	35 421	9 769	28
	Other third level insts.	1980/81	...	...	...	3 831	...	...
		1985/86	829	156	19	12 608	3 075	24
		1989/90	...	...	...	8 447	...	...
Lesotho	All institutions	1980/81	192	...	...	1 889	...	...
		1985/86	...	...	...	2 428	1 507	62
		1990/91	431	...	...	2 758	1 353	49
		1991/92	479	...	...	2 982	1 448	49
		1992/93	490	...	...	3 704	2 013	54
		1993/94	492	...	...	4 001	2 223	56
	Universities and equiv. insts.	1980/81	137	...	...	995	...	...
		1985/86	225	...	...	1 504	779	52
		1990/91	273	...	...	1 753	998	57
		1991/92	307	...	...	1 878	1 098	58
		1992/93	316	...	...	2 094	1 252	60
		1993/94	321	...	...	2 347	1 417	60
	Other third level insts.	1980/81	55	...	...	894	761	85
		1985/86	...	...	...	924	728	79
		1990/91	158	14	9	1 035	355	34
		1991/92	172	18	10	1 104	350	32
		1992/93	174	19	11	1 610	761	47
		1993/94	171	11	6	1 654	806	49

Third level: teachers and students 3.10
Troisième degré: professeurs et étudiants
Tercer grado: profesores y estudiantes

Country / Pays / País	Type of institution / Type d'établissement / Tipo de establecimiento	Year / Année / Año	Teaching staff Personnel enseignant Personal docente			Students enrolled Étudiants inscrits Estudiantes matriculados		
			Total	Female Féminin Femenino	% F	Total	Female Féminin Femenino	% F
			(1)	(2)	(3)	(4)	(5)	(6)
Libyan Arab Jamahiriya	All institutions	1980/81	...	...	...	20 166	5 096	25
		1985/86	...	...	...	30 000	...	...
		1989/90	...	...	...	50 471	...	...
		1991/92	...	...	...	72 899	33 336	46
	Universities and equiv. insts.	1980/81	...	...	...	20 166	5 096	25
		1985/86	...	...	...	30 000	...	...
		1989/90	...	...	...	50 471	...	...
		1991/92	...	...	...	72 899	33 336	46
Madagascar	All institutions	1980/81	451	...	...	22 632	...	...
		1985/86	773	...	...	38 310	14 703	38
		1990/91	939	251	27	35 824	16 079	45
		1992/93	855	...	...	42 681	...	...
	Universities and equiv. insts.	1980/81	451	...	...	22 632	...	...
		1985/86	773	...	...	38 310	14 703	38
		1990/91	939	251	27	35 824	16 079	45
		1992/93	819	243	30	33 375	14 909	45
	Distance-learning insts.	1992/93	36	...	...	9 306	...	...
Malawi	All institutions	1980/81	281	...	...	3 476	1 078	31
		1985/86	402	...	...	3 928	1 129	29
		1990/91	...	...	...	6 356	...	...
		1992/93	...	...	...	7 065	2 172	31
		1993/94	...	...	...	7 308	2 289	31
		1994/95	...	...	...	...	...	...
	Universities and equiv. insts.	1980/81	173	34	20	1 722	427	25
		1985/86	278	...	...	1 974	359	18
		1990/91	...	...	...	3 117	...	...
		1992/93	...	...	...	3 521	775	22
		1993/94	309	74	24	3 684	860	23
	Other third level insts.	1980/81	108	...	...	1 754	651	37
		1985/86	124	...	...	1 954	770	39
		1990/91	...	...	...	3 239	1 124	35
		1992/93	...	...	...	3 544	1 397	39
		1993/94	...	...	...	3 624	1 429	39
		1994/95	...	...	...	3 890	1 516	39
Mali	All institutions	1981/82	475	...	...	4 498	495	11
		1985/86	...	...	...	6 768	874	13
		1990/91	701	...	...	6 703	905	14
	Universities and equiv. insts.	1981/82	475	...	...	4 498	495	11
		1985/86	...	...	...	6 768	874	13
		1990/91	701	...	...	6 703	905	14
Mauritania	All institutions	1985/86	...	...	...	4 526	...	...
		1991/92	250	...	...	5 850	867	15
		1992/93	266	...	...	7 501	1 112	15
		1993/94	...	...	...	8 495	1 471	17
	Universities and equiv. insts.	1991/92	195	...	...	5 723	866	15
		1992/93	248	...	...	7 401	1 106	15
		1993/94	...	...	...	7 647	1 195	16
	Other third level insts.	1991/92	55	...	...	127	1	1
		1992/93	18	...	...	100	6	6
		1993/94	...	...	...	820	276	34
Mauritius	All institutions	1980/81	210	32	15	1 038	317	31
		1985/86	236	27	11	1 161	421	36
		1990/91	414	81	20	3 485	1 273	37
		1991/92	526	124	24	4 032	1 690	42
		1992/93	...	...	...	...	...	...
		1993/94	...	...	...	...	...	...
	Universities and equiv. insts.	1980/81	125	8	6	470	88	19
		1985/86	130	8	6	507	114	22
		1990/91	274	42	15	1 658	530	32
		1991/92	306	51	17	1 799	607	34
		1992/93	...	...	...	1 858	...	...
		1993/94	...	...	...	2 161	...	...
	Other third level insts.	1980/81	85	24	28	568	229	40
		1985/86	106	19	18	654	307	47
		1990/91	140	39	28	1 827	743	41
		1991/92	220	73	33	2 233	1 083	49

3.10 Third level: teachers and students
Troisième degré: professeurs et étudiants
Tercer grado: profesores y estudiantes

Country Pays País	Type of institution Type d'établissement Tipo de establecimiento	Year Année Año	Teaching staff Personnel enseignant Personal docente			Students enrolled Étudiants inscrits Estudiantes matriculados		
			Total	Female Féminin Femenino	% F	Total	Female Féminin Femenino	% F
			(1)	(2)	(3)	(4)	(5)	(6)
Morocco‡	All institutions	1980/81	...	...	...	112 405	...	...
		1985/86	...	...	...	181 087	58 549	32
		1990/91	...	...	...	221 217	80 004	36
		1992/93	...	...	...	...	...	...
		1993/94	...	...	...	...	...	...
		1994/95	10 458	...	...	250 919	102 720	41
	Universities and equiv. insts.	1980/81	2 757	486	18	86 731	21 663	25
		1985/86	5 310	889	17	150 795	49 545	33
		1990/91	...	...	...	206 725	76 763	37
		1992/93	7 327	1 560	21	230 081	89 593	39
		1993/94	7 777	1 678	22	234 946	94 260	40
		1994/95	8 562	1 901	22	242 053	100 278	41
	Other third level insts.	1980/81	...	...	...	25 674	...	...
		1985/86	...	...	...	30 292	9 004	30
		1990/91	...	...	...	14 492	3 241	22
		1994/95	1 896	...	...	8 866	2 442	28
Mozambique	All institutions	1980/81	300	...	...	1 000	...	...
		1985/86	331	70	21	1 442	332	23
		1992/93	720	182	25	4 600	1 211	26
		1993/94	877	173	20	5 250	1 357	26
	Universities and equiv. insts.	1980/81	300	...	...	1 000	...	...
		1985/86	331	70	21	1 442	332	23
		1992/93	720	182	25	4 600	1 211	26
		1993/94	877	173	20	5 250	1 357	26
Namibia	All institutions	1991	331	165	50	4 157	2 664	64
		1993	...	...	...	9 714	5 969	61
		1994	...	...	...	11 344	6 904	61
	Universities and equiv. insts.	1991	141	71	50	1 496	978	65
	Distance-learning insts.	1991	8	5	63	574	321	56
	Other third level insts.	1991	182	89	49	2 087	1 365	65
Niger	All institutions	1980/81	224	29	13	1 435	285	20
		1984/85	314	33	11	2 863	526	18
		1989/90	...	...	...	4 506	675	15
		1991/92	232	26	11	4 513	...	...
	Universities and equiv. insts.	1980/81	224	29	13	1 435	285	20
		1984/85	314	33	11	2 863	526	18
		1989/90	...	...	...	4 506	675	15
		1991/92	232	26	11	4 513	...	...
Nigeria‡	All institutions	1980/81	10 742	...	...	150 072	...	...
		1985/86	...	...	...	266 679	70 724	27
		1989/90	19 601	...	...	335 824	81 315	24
	Universities and equiv. insts.	1980/81	5 475	589	11	70 395	...	...
		1985/86	11 016	1 359	12	135 783	32 540	24
		1989/90	11 936	1 157	10	180 871	48 855	27
	Other third level insts.	1980/81	5 267	...	...	79 677	...	...
		1985/86	...	...	...	130 896	37 984	29
		1989/90	7 665	...	...	154 953	32 460	21
Rwanda	All institutions	1980/81	240	21	9	1 243	122	10
		1985/86	331	20	6	1 987	269	14
		1989/90	646	33	5	3 389	639	19
	Universities and equiv. insts.	1980/81	126	11	9	920	101	11
		1985/86	284	19	7	1 669	252	15
		1989/90	469	26	6	2 489	534	21
	Other third level insts.	1980/81	114	10	9	323	21	7
		1985/86	47	1	2	318	17	5
		1989/90	177	7	4	900	105	12
Senegal	All institutions	1980/81	1 084	...	...	13 626	2 507	18
		1985/86	710	...	...	13 354	...	...
		1990/91	...	...	...	18 689	...	...
		1991/92	949	124	13	21 562	5 262	24
		1992/93	965	...	...	23 001	...	...
	Universities and equiv. insts.	1980/81	652	...	...	12 673	2 412	19
		1985/86	710	88	12	12 711	2 640	21
	Other third level insts.	1980/81	433	...	...	953	95	10
		1985/86	...	...	...	643	...	...

Third level: teachers and students 3.10
Troisième degré: professeurs et étudiants
Tercer grado: profesores y estudiantes

Country / Pays / País	Type of institution / Type d'établissement / Tipo de establecimiento	Year / Année / Año	Teaching staff Personnel enseignant Personal docente			Students enrolled Étudiants inscrits Estudiantes matriculados		
			Total	Female Féminin Femenino	% F	Total	Female Féminin Femenino	% F
			(1)	(2)	(3)	(4)	(5)	(6)
Sierra Leone	All institutions	1980/81	270	...	...	2 166	...	...
		1985/86		...	...	5 690	...	...
		1989/90	734	...	...	5 060	...	...
		1990/91	600	...	...	4 742	...	...
	Universities and equiv. insts.	1980/81	270	...	...	2 166	...	...
		1985/86	...	...	...	2 386	447	19
		1989/90	286	...	...	2 649	457	17
		1990/91	257	...	...	2 571	...	...
	Other third level insts.	1985/86	...	...	...	3 304	...	...
		1989/90	348	78	22	2 412	...	...
		1990/91	343	74	22	2 171	...	...
Somalia	All institutions	1986/87	817	...	...	15 672	3 093	20
	Universities and equiv. insts.	1986/87	817	...	...	15 672	3 093	20
South Africa‡	All institutions	1989	16 303	5 513	34	421 152	193 706	46
		1990	16 697	5 756	34	439 007	195 043	44
		1992	16 861	...	...	490 112	227 712	46
		1993	21 225	7 560	36	552 948	255 572	46
		1994	27 099	10 132	37	617 897	296 844	48
	Universities and equiv. insts.	1989	9 584	2 696	28	286 359	131 269	46
		1990	9 765	2 850	29	285 986	133 582	47
		1992	9 971	...	...	318 965	155 016	49
		1993	12 671	4 095	32	329 926	163 433	50
		1994	13 326	4 750	36	353 958	180 563	51
	Other third level insts.	1989	6 719	2 817	42	134 793	62 437	46
		1990	6 932	2 906	42	153 021	61 461	40
		1992	6 890	...	...	171 147	72 696	42
		1993	8 584	3 465	40	223 022	92 139	41
		1994	13 723	5 382	39	263 939	116 281	44
Sudan	All institutions	1980/81	1 276	98	8	28 788	7 791	27
		1985/86	2 165	213	10	37 367	13 742	37
		1989/90	2 522	398	16	60 134	24 164	40
		1990/91	...	...	...	...	...	...
	Universities and equiv. insts.	1980/81	1 027	41	4	25 699	7 026	27
		1985/86	1 635	133	8	33 934	13 090	39
		1989/90	1 933	226	12	54 558	22 493	41
		1990/91	2 043	265	13	59 824	28 615	48
	Other third level insts.	1980/81	249	57	23	3 089	765	25
		1985/86	530	80	15	3 433	652	19
		1989/90	589	172	29	5 576	1 671	30
Swaziland‡	All institutions	1980/81	183	64	35	1 875	741	40
		1985/86	...	...	...	2 732	...	...
		1990/91	447	168	38	3 198	1 371	43
		1991/92	452	183	40	3 224	1 510	47
		1992/93	...	...	...	3 023	1 280	42
		1993/94	515	...	...	4 183	1 866	45
	Universities and equiv. insts.	1980/81	108	37	34	1 009	370	37
		1985/86	115	...	...	1 287	...	...
		1990/91	231	61	26	1 677	732	44
		1991/92	240	71	30	1 689	740	44
		1992/93	247	71	29	1 739	777	45
		1993/94	278	73	26	2 466	1 184	48
	Other third level insts.	1980/81	75	27	36	866	371	43
		1985/86	...	...	...	1 445	...	...
		1990/91	216	107	50	1 521	639	42
		1991/92	212	112	53	1 535	770	50
		1992/93	...	...	...	1 284	503	39
		1993/94	237	...	...	1 717	682	40
Togo	All institutions	1980/81	297	37	12	4 750	703	15
		1985/86	...	...	...	...	...	...
		1989/90	...	...	...	7 826	1 032	13
		1992/93	...	...	...	8 438	1 037	12
		1993/94	...	...	...	9 120	1 119	12
		1994/95	...	...	...	10 994	1 480	13
	Universities and equiv. insts.	1980/81	272	35	13	4 345	664	15
		1985/86	269	33	12	5 055	678	13
		1989/90	...	...	...	7 732	1 030	13
	Other third level insts.	1980/81	25	2	8	405	39	10
		1989/90	...	...	...	94	2	2

3.10 Third level: teachers and students
Troisième degré: professeurs et étudiants
Tercer grado: profesores y estudiantes

Country Pays País	Type of institution Type d'établissement Tipo de establecimiento	Year Année Año	Teaching staff Personnel enseignant Personal docente			Students enrolled Étudiants inscrits Estudiantes matriculados		
			Total	Female Féminin Femenino	% F	Total	Female Féminin Femenino	% F
			(1)	(2)	(3)	(4)	(5)	(6)
Tunisia‡	All institutions	1980/81	4 031	357	9	31 827	9 437	30
		1985/86	5 194	...	...	41 594	14 824	36
		1990/91	4 550	984	22	68 535	26 989	39
		1992/93	5 360	1 284	24	87 780	36 121	41
		1993/94	5 655	1 386	25	96 101	40 570	42
		1994/95	5 944	1 519	26	102 682	44 230	43
	Universities and equiv. insts.	1980/81	4 031	357	9	31 827	9 437	30
		1985/86	5 194	...	...	41 594	14 824	36
		1990/91	4 550	984	22	68 535	26 989	39
		1992/93	5 360	1 284	24	87 780	36 121	41
		1993/94	5 655	1 386	25	96 101	40 570	42
		1994/95	5 944	1 519	26	102 682	44 230	43
Uganda	All institutions	1980/81				5 856	1 323	23
		1985/86				10 103	2 349	23
		1990/91	1 555	...	...	17 578	4 949	28
		1991/92	2 024	266	13	21 281	5 856	28
		1992/93	2 327	344	15	21 489	6 132	29
		1993/94	1 959	276	14	24 122	7 202	30
	Universities and equiv. insts.	1980/81	...	...	...	4 035	795	20
		1985/86	*500	...	...	5 390	1 227	23
		1990/91	725	...	...	7 618	1 919	25
		1991/92	1 163	180	15	8 552	2 183	26
		1992/93	1 351	244	18	9 017	2 516	28
		1993/94	1 080	186	17	9 959	3 033	30
	Other third level insts.	1980/81	...	...	...	1 821	528	29
		1985/86	...	...	...	4 713	1 122	24
		1990/91	830	...	...	9 960	3 030	30
		1991/92	861	86	10	12 729	3 673	29
		1992/93	976	100	10	12 472	3 616	29
		1993/94	879	90	10	14 163	4 169	29
United Rep. of Tanzania‡	All institutions	1985/86	1 239	...	...	4 863	710	15
		1986/87	1 366	...	...	4 987	689	14
		1989/90	1 206	...	...	5 254	...	...
	Universities and equiv. insts.	1985/86	1 025	...	...	3 414	547	16
		1986/87	1 136	...	...	3 437	533	16
		1989/90	939	...	...	3 327	...	...
	Other third level insts.	1985/86	214	...	...	1 449	163	11
		1986/87	230	16	7	1 550	156	10
		1989/90	267	...	...	1 927	...	...
Zaire‡	All institutions	1980/81	...	...	...	28 493	...	...
		1985/86	3 272	...	...	40 878	...	...
		1988/89	3 873	...	...	61 422	...	...
	Universities and equiv. insts.	1980/81	...	...	...	9 927	...	...
		1985/86	1 387	...	...	16 239	...	...
		1988/89	1 636	...	...	27 166	...	...
	Other third level insts.	1980/81	...	...	...	18 566	...	...
		1985/86	1 885	...	...	24 639	...	...
		1988/89	2 237	...	...	34 256	...	...
Zambia	All institutions	1980	...	...	...	...	...	...
		1985	...	...	...	...	...	...
		1989	...	...	...	14 465	4 063	28
		1990	...	...	...	15 343	...	...
	Universities and equiv. insts.	1980	...	...	...	3 425	...	...
		1985	613	78	13	4 680	810	17
		1989	...	...	...	6 247	1 072	17
		1990	...	...	...	7 361	...	...
	Other third level insts.	1989	...	...	...	8 218	2 991	36
		1990	...	...	...	7 982	...	...
Zimbabwe‡	All institutions	1980	...	...	...	8 339	...	...
		1985	...	...	...	30 843	...	...
		1990	2 308	...	...	49 361	...	...
		1991	2 585	...	...	43 950	11 722	27
		1992	3 076	...	...	61 553	16 878	27
	Universities and equiv. insts.	1980	...	...	...	1 873	...	...
		1985	...	...	...	4 742	...	...
		1990	558	...	...	9 300	...	...
		1991	585	153	26	9 784	2 262	23
		1992	976	153	16	9 048	2 340	26

Third level: teachers and students 3.10
Troisième degré: professeurs et étudiants
Tercer grado: profesores y estudiantes

Country Pays País	Type of institution Type d'établissement Tipo de establecimiento	Year Année Año	Teaching staff Personnel enseignant Personal docente			Students enrolled Étudiants inscrits Estudiantes matriculados		
			Total	Female Féminin Femenino	% F	Total	Female Féminin Femenino	% F
			(1)	(2)	(3)	(4)	(5)	(6)
Zimbabwe‡ (cont)	Other third level insts.	1980	262	...	...	6 466	1 528	24
		1985	372	80	22	26 101	...	...
		1990	1 750	...	...	40 061	...	...
		1991	2 000	...	...	34 166	9 460	28
		1992	2 100	...	...	52 505	14 538	28
America, North								
Bahamas	All institutions	1980/81	127	...	...	4 093	...	...
		1985/86	...	...	...	4 531	...	...
		1987/88	249	119	48	5 305	3 625	68
Barbados	All institutions	1980/81	317	90	28	4 033	2 170	54
		1984/85	544	...	...	5 227	2 565	49
		1990/91	...	...	...	6 651	...	...
		1991/92	...	...	...	6 888	3 797	55
		1992/93	...	...	...	6 252	...	...
		1994/95	...	...	...	...	...	...
	Universities and equiv. insts.	1980/81	140	32	23	1 606	778	48
		1984/85	242	...	...	1 767	967	55
		1990/91	...	...	...	2 408	...	...
		1991/92	...	...	...	2 580	1 523	59
		1992/93	...	...	...	2 572	...	...
		1994/95	...	...	...	2 862	1 790	63
	Other third level insts.	1980/81	177	58	33	2 427	1 392	57
		1984/85	302	...	...	3 460	1 598	46
		1990/91	...	...	...	4 243	...	...
		1991/92	83	40	48	4 308	2 274	53
		1992/93	...	...	...	3 680	...	...
Canada‡	All institutions	1980/81	53 434	12 565	24	1 172 750	587 720	50
		1985/86	57 443	13 655	24	1 639 410	736 680	45
		1990/91	61 682	16 085	26	1 916 801	1 038 194	54
		1991/92	67 122	18 679	28	1 942 814	1 053 723	54
		1992/93	67 074	20 078	30	2 021 550	1 080 754	53
		1993/94	68 053	20 602	30	2 011 485	1 059 353	53
	Universities and equiv. insts.	1980/81	33 015	5 105	15	627 617	312 169	50
		1985/86	35 245	6 019	17	752 276	392 437	52
		1990/91	37 500	7 000	19	841 330	465 426	55
		1991/92	36 800	7 560	21	867 352	480 958	55
		1992/93	37 222	7 938	21	890 011	493 987	56
		1993/94	37 616	8 090	22	874 604	484 957	55
	Other third level insts.	1980/81	20 419	7 460	37	545 133	275 551	51
		1985/86	22 198	7 636	34	887 134	344 243	39
		1990/91	24 182	9 085	38	1 075 471	572 768	53
		1991/92	30 322	11 119	37	1 070 108	572 765	54
		1992/93	29 852	12 140	41	1 131 539	586 787	52
		1993/94	30 437	12 512	41	1 136 881	574 396	51
Costa Rica‡	All institutions	1980	...	...	...	55 593	...	...
		1985	...	...	...	63 771	...	...
		1990	...	...	...	74 681	...	...
		1991	...	...	...	80 442	...	...
		1992	...	...	...	88 324	...	...
	Universities and equiv. insts.	1980	4 382	...	...	47 340	...	...
		1985	...	...	...	50 047	...	...
		1990	...	...	...	57 541	...	...
		1991	...	...	...	61 364	...	...
		1992	...	...	...	65 268	...	...
	Distance-learning insts.	1980	...	...	...	3 472	...	...
		1985	397	146	37	8 346	4 807	58
		1990	219	...	...	9 591	...	...
		1991	235	...	...	10 170	...	...
		1992	...	...	...	10 666	...	...
	Other third level insts.	1980	...	...	...	4 781	...	...
		1985	...	...	...	5 378	...	...
		1990	...	...	...	7 549	...	...
		1991	...	...	...	8 908	...	...
		1992	...	...	...	12 390	...	...
Cuba	All institutions	1980/81	10 680	...	...	151 733	73 413	48
		1985/86	19 552	8 328	43	235 224	127 054	54
		1990/91	24 668	10 968	44	242 434	139 171	57
		1992/93	25 264	11 901	47	198 474	114 584	58
		1993/94	24 900	...	...	176 228	100 199	57
		1994/95	23 300	...	...	140 800	...	...

3.10 Third level: teachers and students
Troisième degré: professeurs et étudiants
Tercer grado: profesores y estudiantes

Country Pays País	Type of institution Type d'établissement Tipo de establecimiento	Year Année Año	Teaching staff Personnel enseignant Personal docente			Students enrolled Étudiants inscrits Estudiantes matriculados		
			Total	Female Féminin Femenino	% F	Total	Female Féminin Femenino	% F
			(1)	(2)	(3)	(4)	(5)	(6)
Cuba (cont)	Universities and equiv. insts.	1980/81	10 680	...	...	151 733	73 413	48
		1985/86	19 552	8 328	43	235 224	127 054	54
		1990/91	24 668	10 968	44	242 434	137 171	57
		1992/93	25 264	11 901	47	198 474	114 584	58
		1993/94	24 900	...	...	176 228	100 199	57
		1994/95	23 300	...	...	140 800	...	...
Dominica‡	All institutions	1980/81	17	12	71	63	14	22
		1984/85	*17	*11	*65	60	40	67
		1990/91	34	11	32	430	177	41
		1991/92	40	13	33	658	364	55
		1992/93	34	11	32	484	207	43
	Other third level insts.	1980/81	17	12	71	63	14	22
		1984/85	*17	*11	*65	60	40	67
		1990/91	34	11	32	430	177	41
		1991/92	40	13	33	658	364	55
		1992/93	34	11	32	484	207	43
Dominican Republic	All institutions	1985/86	6 539	...	...	123 748	...	...
El Salvador‡	All institutions	1980	893	208	23	16 838	5 202	31
		1985	4 197	1 054	25	70 499	30 832	44
		1990	4 216	1 097	26	78 211	25 878	33
		1993	...	...	...	...	...	...
	Universities and equiv. insts.	1980	445	72	16	12 740	3 999	31
		1985	3 109	754	24	57 131	24 019	42
		1990	3 452	895	26	66 092	20 158	31
		1993	4 643	3 346	72	77 359	39 545	51
	Distance-learning insts.	1985	295	50	17	3 863	1 739	45
		1990	174	60	34	6 317	2 714	43
	Other third level insts.	1980	448	136	30	4 098	1 203	29
		1985	793	250	32	9 505	5 074	53
		1990	590	142	24	5 802	3 006	52
		1993	409	329	80	2 789	1 059	38
Guatemala‡	All institutions	1980	4 024	...	...	50 890	...	...
		1985	...	...	...	48 283	...	...
		1986	...	...	...	51 860	...	...
	Universities and equiv. insts.	1980	4 024	...	...	50 890	...	...
		1985	...	...	...	48 283	...	...
		1986	...	...	...	51 860	...	...
Haiti	All institutions	1980/81	690	75	11	4 671	1 410	30
		1985/86	654	243	37	6 288	1 625	26
	Universities and equiv. insts.	1980/81	523	66	13	3 441	1 209	35
		1985/86	479	81	17	4 471	1 276	29
	Other third level insts.	1980/81	167	9	5	1 230	201	16
		1985/86	175	162	93	1 817	349	19
Honduras	All institutions	1980	1 653	...	...	25 825	9 736	38
		1985	2 662	917	34	36 620	...	...
		1990	3 430	...	...	44 233	...	...
		1992	3 000	948	32	44 148	19 159	43
		1993	...	...	...	46 144	19 351	42
		1994	4 078	1 165	29	50 323	20 764	41
	Universities and equiv. insts.	1980	1 439	...	...	24 021	9 025	38
		1985	2 274	762	34	30 623	12 721	42
		1990	*3 258	...	...	39 324	16 870	43
		1992	2 927	962	33	40 456	16 950	42
	Distance-learning insts.	1990	*48	...	...	3 906	...	...
		1991	54	15	28	3 631	1 434	39
		1992	65	26	40	3 600	2 209	61
	Other third level insts.	1980	214	...	...	1 804	711	39
		1985	388	155	40	5 997	...	...
		1990	124	...	...	1 003	...	...
		1992	8	-	-	92	-	-
Jamaica	All institutions	1980/81	...	...	...	13 999	...	...
		1985/86	...	...	...	10 969	...	...
		1990/91	...	...	...	16 018	...	...
		1991/92	395	...	...	15 891	...	...

Third level: teachers and students **3.10**
Troisième degré: professeurs et étudiants
Tercer grado: profesores y estudiantes

Country / Pays / País	Type of institution / Type d'établissement / Tipo de establecimiento	Year / Année / Año	Teaching staff Personnel enseignant Personal docente			Students enrolled Étudiants inscrits Estudiantes matriculados		
			Total	Female Féminin Femenino	% F	Total	Female Féminin Femenino	% F
			(1)	(2)	(3)	(4)	(5)	(6)
Jamaica (cont)	Universities and equiv. insts.	1980/81	397	...	...	4 548	...	...
		1985/86	295	87	29	5 126	2 914	57
		1990/91	418	...	...	6 083	3 785	62
		1991/92	395	...	...	6 284	3 958	63
	Distance-learning insts.	1990/91	...	...	...	802	...	...
		1991/92	...	...	...	452	...	...
	Other third level insts.	1980/81	...	...	...	9 451	...	...
		1985/86	...	...	...	5 843	...	...
		1990/91	654	...	...	9 133	...	...
		1991/92	...	...	...	9 155	...	...
Mexico	All institutions	1980/81	77 653	...	...	929 865	305 052	33
		1985/86	108 002	...	...	1 207 779	...	...
		1990/91	134 424	...	...	1 310 835	...	...
		1991/92	...	...	...	...	...	...
		1992/93	...	...	...	...	...	...
		1993/94	...	...	...	...	...	46
	Universities and equiv. insts.	1980/81	72 742	...	...	817 558	248 062	30
		1985/86	...	...	...	1 199 120	454 366	38
		1990/91	...	...	...	1 252 027	536 070	43
		1991/92	136 692	...	...	1 280 006	574 000	45
		1992/93	138 811	...	...	1 302 590	588 571	45
		1993/94	145 789	...	...	1 358 271	625 736	46
	Distance-learning insts.	1985/86	...	...	...	8 659	...	...
		1990/91	...	...	...	58 808	...	...
	Other third level insts.	1980/81	4 911	...	...	112 307	56 990	51
Nicaragua‡	All institutions	1980	...	...	...	35 268	...	...
		1985	2 536	...	...	29 001	16 355	56
		1990	2 289	...	...	30 733	15 963	52
		1991	2 130	635	30	31 499	15 509	49
		1992	2 274	566	25	35 730	17 795	50
	Universities and equiv. insts.	1980	...	...	...	32 958	...	...
		1985	2 151	...	...	24 430	14 009	57
		1990	2 180	...	...	29 780	15 615	52
		1991	2 058	631	31	30 483	15 103	50
		1992	2 222	553	25	35 102	17 477	50
	Distance-learning insts.	1990	109	...	...	821	226	28
		1991	52	4	8	874	278	32
		1992	./.	./.	./.	./.	./.	./.
	Other third level insts.	1980	...	...	...	2 310	...	...
		1985	385	...	...	4 571	2 346	51
		1990	...	...	...	132	122	92
		1991	20	-	-	142	128	90
		1992	52	...	...	628	318	51
Panama	All institutions	1980	2 673	...	...	40 369	22 168	55
		1985	3 986	...	...	55 303	31 856	58
		1990	3 328	...	...	53 235	...	...
		1992	3 771	...	...	63 848	...	...
		1993	4 108	...	...	69 451	...	...
		1994	4 291	...	...	70 327	...	...
	Universities and equiv. insts.	1980	2 673	...	...	40 369	22 168	55
		1985	3 986	...	...	55 303	31 856	58
		1990	3 270	...	...	52 673	...	...
		1992	3 724	...	...	63 303	...	...
		1993	4 033	...	...	68 724	...	...
		1994	4 215	...	...	69 519	...	...
	Other third level insts.	1990	58	...	...	562	...	...
		1992	47	...	...	545	...	...
		1993	75	...	...	727	...	...
		1994	76	...	...	808	...	...
Saint Kitts and Nevis	All institutions	1985/86	27	9	33	212	90	42
		1991/92	38	16	42	325	121	37
		1992/93	51	31	61	394	215	55
	Other third level insts.	1985/86	27	9	33	212	90	42
		1991/92	38	16	42	325	121	37
		1992/93	51	31	61	394	215	55
St. Lucia	All institutions	1980/81	...	...	...	301	157	52
		1984/85	76	28	37	346	158	46
		1987/88	62	21	34	389	212	54
		1992/93	...	...	...	870	529	61

3.10 Third level: teachers and students
Troisième degré: professeurs et étudiants
Tercer grado: profesores y estudiantes

Country / Pays / País	Type of institution / Type d'établissement / Tipo de establecimiento	Year / Année / Año	Teaching staff Personnel enseignant Personal docente			Students enrolled Étudiants inscrits Estudiantes matriculados		
			Total	Female Féminin Femenino	% F	Total	Female Féminin Femenino	% F
			(1)	(2)	(3)	(4)	(5)	(6)
St. Lucia (cont)	Other third level insts.	1980/81	...	...	...	301	157	52
		1984/85	76	28	37	346	158	46
		1987/88	62	21	34	389	212	54
		1992/93	...	...	...	870	529	61
St. Vincent and the Grenadines‡	All institutions	1985/86	35	13	37	736	509	69
		1986/87	34	11	32	795	505	64
		1989/90	96	51	53	677	458	68
	Distance-learning insts.	1989/90	16	7	44	86	63	73
	Other third level insts.	1985/86	35	13	37	736	509	69
		1986/87	34	11	32	795	505	64
		1989/90	80	44	55	591	395	67
Trinidad and Tobago‡	All institutions	1980/81	...	...	...	5 649	2 401	43
		1985/86	...	...	...	6 582	2 540	39
		1990/91	...	...	...	7 249	3 164	44
		1991/92	...	...	...	7 513	3 035	40
		1992/93	...	...	...	8 170	3 360	41
		1993/94	...	...	...	...	...	...
	Universities and equiv. insts.	1980/81	...	...	...	2 923	1 111	38
		1985/86	...	...	...	3 663	1 660	45
		1990/91	289	...	...	4 090	1 987	49
		1991/92	292	43	15	4 529	2 187	48
		1992/93	288	39	14	4 947	2 402	49
		1993/94	...	...	...	5 191	2 580	50
	Other third level insts.	1980/81	...	...	...	2 726	1 290	47
		1985/86	...	...	...	2 919	880	30
		1990/91	...	...	...	3 159	1 177	37
		1991/92	...	...	...	2 984	848	28
		1992/93	...	...	...	3 223	958	30
United States‡	All institutions	1980/81	395 992	104 663	26	12 096 895	6 222 521	51
		1985/86	694 000	...	...	12 247 055	6 428 605	52
		1990/91	833 844	293 415	35	13 710 150	7 471 643	54
		1991/92	826 000	...	...	14 360 965	...	...
		1992/93	835 000	...	...	14 422 975	...	...
		1993/94	842 000	...	...	14 473 106	...	...
	Universities and equiv. insts.	1980/81	305 982	71 980	24	7 572 657	3 745 958	49
		1985/86	494 000	...	...	7 715 978	3 899 762	51
		1990/91	589 799	182 640	31	8 529 132	4 498 360	53
	Other third level insts.	1980/81	90 010	32 683	36	4 524 238	2 476 563	55
		1985/86	200 000	...	...	4 531 077	2 528 843	56
		1990/91	244 045	110 775	45	5 181 018	2 973 283	57
U.S. Virgin Is.	All institutions	1980/81	...	...	...	2 148	1 533	71
		1985/86	221	95	43	2 602	1 876	72
		1990/91	226	92	41	2 466	1 843	75
		1992/93	266	128	48	2 924	2 166	74
	Universities and equiv. insts.	1980/81	...	...	...	2 148	1 533	71
		1985/86	221	95	43	2 602	1 876	72
		1990/91	226	92	41	2 466	1 843	75
		1992/93	266	128	48	2 924	2 166	74
America, South								
Argentina	All institutions	1980	46 267	20 039	43	491 473	247 656	50
		1985	70 699	32 694	46	846 145	444 636	53
		1991	89 609	...	...	1 077 212	...	...
		1992	102 201	...	...	...	...	...
		1994	...	...	...	1 051 542	...	...
	Universities and equiv. insts.	1980	30 602	9 273	30	397 828	169 412	43
		1985	44 038	14 222	32	664 200	302 509	46
		1991	49 200	...	...	816 888	...	...
		1992	...	...	...	700 099	...	...
		1994	...	...	...	740 545	383 737	52
	Other third level insts.	1980	15 665	10 766	69	93 645	78 244	84
		1985	26 661	18 472	69	181 945	142 127	78
		1991	40 409	...	...	260 324	...	...
		1994	43 103	...	...	310 997	...	...
Bolivia	All institutions	1980	...	...	...	...	...	...
		1985	...	...	...	...	...	...
		1990	...	...	...	...	...	...
		1991	...	...	...	...	...	...

Third level: teachers and students 3.10
Troisième degré: professeurs et étudiants
Tercer grado: profesores y estudiantes

Country Pays País	Type of institution Type d'établissement Tipo de establecimiento	Year Année Año	Teaching staff Personnel enseignant Personal docente			Students enrolled Étudiants inscrits Estudiantes matriculados		
			Total	Female Féminin Femenino	% F	Total	Female Féminin Femenino	% F
			(1)	(2)	(3)	(4)	(5)	(6)
Bolivia (cont)	Universities and equiv. insts.	1980	...	...	...	60 900	...	...
		1985	3 286	...	...	88 175	...	...
		1990	4 234	...	...	102 001	...	...
		1991	4 261	...	...	109 503	...	...
Brazil‡	All institutions	1980	109 788	33 238	30	1 409 243	680 445	48
		1986	117 211	...	...	1 451 191	...	...
		1990	131 641	53 503	41	1 540 080	806 547	52
		1992	134 403	50 144	37	1 535 788	822 961	54
		1993	137 156	52 672	38	1 594 668	865 803	54
		1994	141 482	53 509	38	1 661 034	907 677	55
	Universities and equiv. insts.	1980	109 788	33 238	30	1 409 243	680 445	48
		1986	117 211	...	...	1 451 191	...	...
		1990	131 641	53 503	41	1 540 080	806 547	52
		1992	134 403	50 144	37	1 535 788	822 961	54
		1993	137 156	52 672	38	1 594 668	865 803	54
		1994	141 482	53 509	38	1 661 034	907 677	55
Chile‡	All institutions	1980	...	...	...	145 497	62 804	43
		1985	...	...	...	197 437	85 600	43
		1990	...	...	...	255 358	...	...
		1992	...	...	...	317 728	...	...
		1993	...	...	...	327 435	...	...
		1995	...	...	...	342 788	156 614	46
	Universities and equiv. insts.	1980	...	...	...	120 168	48 462	40
		1990	...	...	...	189 371	...	...
		1992	17 182	...	...	234 633	...	...
		1993	18 084	...	...	250 291	...	...
		1995	...	...	...	271 899	123 390	45
	Other third level insts.	1980	804	264	33	25 329	14 342	57
		1990	...	...	...	65 987	31 382	48
		1992	...	...	...	83 095	...	...
		1993	...	...	...	77 144	...	...
		1995	...	...	...	70 889	33 224	47
Colombia‡	All institutions	1980	31 136	6 184	20	271 630	121 115	45
		1985	43 227	10 494	24	391 490	189 937	49
		1989	51 725	13 066	25	474 787	245 340	52
		1991	54 164	14 074	26	510 649	261 237	51
		1994	58 208	15 552	27	588 322	298 385	51
	Universities and equiv. insts.	1980	26 930	5 181	19	234 705	100 587	43
		1985	35 890	8 304	23	317 987	143 575	45
		1989	42 704	10 241	24	403 523	203 297	50
		1991	44 820	11 282	25	430 399	215 374	50
	Distance-learning insts.	1980	./.	./.	./.	./.	./.	./.
		1986	880	266	30	24 049	16 896	70
		1989	544	185	34	6 933	4 370	63
		1991	661	201	30	8 488	5 326	63
	Other third level insts.	1980	4 206	1 003	24	36 925	20 528	56
		1985	6 448	1 924	30	49 454	29 466	60
		1989	8 477	2 640	31	64 331	37 673	59
		1991	8 683	2 591	30	71 762	40 537	56
Ecuador	All institutions	1980/81	...	...	...	269 775	...	...
		1984/85	...	...	...	280 594	...	...
		1989/90	...	...	...	...	...	...
		1990/91	12 856	...	...	206 541	...	...
	Universities and equiv. insts.	1980/81	11 326	...	...	264 136	97 350	37
		1984/85	11 495	...	...	277 799	...	...
		1989/90	12 520	...	...	186 456	...	...
	Distance-learning insts.	1989/90	150	...	...	11 158	...	...
	Other third level insts.	1980/81	...	65	...	5 639	...	...
		1984/85	...	...	...	2 795	...	...
Guyana	All institutions	1980/81	442	118	27	2 465	1 078	44
		1985/86	527	119	23	2 328	1 113	48
		1989/90	450	...	...	4 665	2 001	43
		1993/94	492	...	...	8 257	3 922	47
	Universities and equiv. insts.	1980/81	322	68	21	1 681	535	32
		1985/86	390	65	17	1 598	640	40
		1989/90	309	...	...	2 192	1 081	49
		1993/94	301	...	...	3 607	1 951	54
	Distance-learning insts.	1993/94	33	...	...	891	531	60

3.10 Third level: teachers and students
Troisième degré: professeurs et étudiants
Tercer grado: profesores y estudiantes

Country / Pays / País	Type of institution / Type d'établissement / Tipo de establecimiento	Year / Année / Año	Teaching staff Personnel enseignant Personal docente			Students enrolled Étudiants inscrits Estudiantes matriculados		
			Total	Female Féminin Femenino	% F	Total	Female Féminin Femenino	% F
			(1)	(2)	(3)	(4)	(5)	(6)
Guyana (cont)	Other third level insts.	1980/81	120	50	42	784	543	69
		1985/86	137	54	39	730	473	65
		1989/90	141	46	33	2 473	920	37
		1993/94	184	77	42	3 759	1 440	38
Paraguay‡	All institutions	1980	...	...	...	26 915	...	...
		1985	...	...	...	32 090	...	...
		1990	...	...	...	32 884	...	...
		1993	...	...	...	42 654	19 295	45
	Universities and equiv. insts.	1980	1 893	...	...	25 333	...	...
		1985	...	...	...	29 154	...	...
		1990	...	...	...	29 447	13 618	46
		1993	...	...	...	36 645	14 691	40
	Other third level insts.	1980	...	...	...	1 582	...	...
		1985	...	...	...	2 936	...	...
		1990	...	...	...	3 437	...	...
		1993	...	...	...	6 009	4 604	77
Peru	All institutions	1980	15 816	...	...	306 353	107 980	35
		1985	26 118	...	...	452 462	...	...
		1990	39 830	...	...	681 801	...	...
		1991	...	...	...	728 666	...	...
		1992	45 241	...	...	732 688	...	...
		1994	46 807	...	...	755 929	...	...
	Universities and equiv. insts.	1980	14 384	2 343	16	246 510	83 791	34
		1985	20 123	...	...	354 888	...	...
		1990	27 405	...	...	442 932	...	...
		1991	28 719	...	...	475 709	...	...
		1992	30 098	...	...	463 499	...	...
		1994	29 313	...	...	465 320	...	...
	Other third level insts.	1980	1 432	...	...	59 843	24 189	40
		1985	5 995	...	...	97 574	...	...
		1990	12 425	...	...	238 869	...	...
		1991	...	...	...	252 957	...	...
		1992	15 143	...	...	269 189	...	...
		1994	17 494	...	...	290 609	...	...
Suriname	All institutions	1980/81	...	...	...	2 378	...	...
		1985/86	...	...	...	2 751	1 475	54
		1990/91	495	...	...	4 319	2 276	53
	Universities and equiv. insts.	1980/81	...	...	...	1 217	...	...
		1985/86	187	...	...	1 070	462	43
		1990/91	254	...	...	2 373	1 051	44
	Other third level insts.	1980/81	...	...	...	1 161	...	...
		1985/86	...	...	...	1 681	1 013	60
		1990/91	241	...	...	1 946	1 225	63
Uruguay	All institutions	1980	...	...	...	...	...	...
		1990	...	...	...	71 612	...	...
		1991	...	...	...	73 660	...	...
		1992	...	...	...	68 227	...	...
	Universities and equiv. insts.	1980	3 847	1 141	30	36 298	19 236	53
		1990	6 808	...	...	62 433	...	...
		1991	6 899	...	...	62 587	...	...
		1992	6 442	...	...	56 760	...	...
	Other third level insts.	1990	...	...	...	9 179	...	...
		1991	...	...	...	11 073	...	...
		1992	...	...	...	11 467	...	...
Venezuela	All institutions	1980/81	28 052	...	...	307 133	...	...
		1985/86	30 844	...	...	443 064	182 455	41
		1990/91	46 137	...	...	550 030	...	...
		1991/92	43 833	...	...	550 783	...	...
	Universities and equiv. insts.	1980/81	23 984	...	...	271 583	...	...
		1985/86	23 951	...	...	347 618	...	...
	Distance-learning insts.	1985/86	433	...	...	20 689	...	...
	Other third level insts.	1980/81	4 068	...	...	35 550	...	...
		1985/86	6 460	...	...	74 757	...	...

Third level: teachers and students 3.10
Troisième degré: professeurs et étudiants
Tercer grado: profesores y estudiantes

Country / Pays / País	Type of institution / Type d'établissement / Tipo de establecimiento	Year / Année / Año	Teaching staff Personnel enseignant Personal docente			Students enrolled Étudiants inscrits Estudiantes matriculados		
			Total	Female Féminin Femenino	% F	Total	Female Féminin Femenino	% F
			(1)	(2)	(3)	(4)	(5)	(6)
Asia								
Afghanistan	All institutions	1986	...	...	...	22 306	3 124	14
		1990	1 342	323	24	24 333	7 469	31
	Universities and equiv. insts.	1990	444	97	22	9 367	3 970	42
	Other third level insts.	1990	898	226	25	14 966	3 499	23
Armenia	All institutions	1980/81	...	...	...	109 900	...	...
		1985/86	...	...	...	102 700	...	...
		1990/91	5 370	...	...	114 300	...	...
		1991/92	5 473	...	...	125 900	...	...
Azerbaijan‡	All institutions	1980/81	14 599	...	...	186 000	...	...
		1985/86	17 155	...	...	182 100	...	...
		1990/91	17 166	...	...	163 900	...	...
		1992/93	18 080	...	...	143 688	56 633	39
		1993/94	18 184	...	...	129 469	55 460	43
		1994/95	...	...	...	120 870	56 005	46
	Universities and equiv. insts.	1980/81	...	...	...	107 000	...	...
		1985/86	...	...	...	76 000	...	...
		1990/91	...	...	...	77 100	...	...
		1992/93	...	...	...	100 985	38 655	38
		1993/94	...	...	...	95 572	39 917	42
		1994/95	...	...	...	90 475	39 256	43
	Distance-learning insts.	1980/81	...	...	...	./.	./.	./.
		1985/86	...	...	...	29 900	...	...
		1990/91	...	...	...	28 000	...	...
		1992/93	...	...	...	./.	./.	./.
		1993/94	...	...	...	./.	./.	./.
		1994/95	...	...	...	./.	./.	./.
	Other third level insts.	1980/81	...	...	...	79 000	...	...
		1985/86	...	...	...	76 200	...	...
		1990/91	...	...	...	58 800	...	...
		1992/93	...	...	...	42 703	17 978	42
		1993/94	...	...	...	33 877	15 543	46
		1994/95	...	...	...	30 395	16 749	55
Bahrain	All institutions	1980/81	159	21	13	1 908	786	41
		1985/86	434	159	37	4 180	2 490	60
		1990/91	557	163	29	6 868	3 824	56
		1991/92	605	169	28	7 147	4 157	58
		1992/93	582	165	28	7 763	4 424	57
		1993/94	655	189	29	7 676	4 444	58
	Universities and equiv. insts.	1980/81	70	18	26	317	260	82
		1985/86	294	128	44	2 011	1 512	75
		1990/91	464	95	20	6 194	3 371	54
		1991/92	504	94	19	6 412	3 614	56
		1992/93	487	93	19	6 996	3 850	55
		1993/94	558	119	21	7 011	4 022	57
	Other third level insts.	1980/81	89	3	3	1 591	526	33
		1985/86	140	31	22	2 169	978	45
		1990/91	93	68	73	674	463	69
		1991/92	101	75	74	735	543	74
		1992/93	95	72	76	767	574	75
		1993/94	97	70	72	665	422	63
Bangladesh	All institutions	1980	12 428	1 305	11	240 181	33 348	14
		1985	...	...	...	461 073	...	...
		1990	...	...	...	...	...	...
	Universities and equiv. insts.	1980	2 421	191	8	36 530	6 552	18
		1985	2 705	238	9	41 780	7 294	17
		1990	2 959	357	12	51 775	10 519	20
	Distance-learning insts.	1980	-	-	-	-	-	-
		1985	...	...	...	3 211	...	...
	Other third level insts.	1980	10 007	1 114	11	203 651	26 796	13
		1985	13 482	2 703	20	416 082	80 461	19
		1990	19 488	2 504	13	382 534	58 347	15
Bhutan	All institutions	1980	37	10	27	322	70	22
		1984	...	...	...	...	...	...
	Universities and equiv. insts.	1980	15	3	20	180	14	8
		1984	19	...	...	220	45	20

3.10 Third level: teachers and students
Troisième degré: professeurs et étudiants
Tercer grado: profesores y estudiantes

Country Pays País	Type of institution Type d'établissement Tipo de establecimiento	Year Année Año	Teaching staff Personnel enseignant Personal docente			Students enrolled Étudiants inscrits Estudiantes matriculados		
			Total	Female Féminin Femenino	% F	Total	Female Féminin Femenino	% F
			(1)	(2)	(3)	(4)	(5)	(6)
Bhutan (cont)	Other third level insts.	1980	22	7	32	142	56	39
Brunei Darussalam	All institutions	1980/81	57	18	32	143	72	50
		1986/87	151	24	16	601	302	50
		1992/93	238	40	17	1 388	789	57
	Universities and equiv. insts.	1980/81	-	-	-	-	-	-
		1986/87	98	17	17	446	236	53
		1992/93	199	38	19	1 181	677	57
	Other third level insts.	1980/81	57	18	32	143	72	50
		1986/87	53	7	13	155	66	43
		1992/93	39	2	5	207	112	54
Cambodia	All institutions	1980/81	...	...	...	601	...	...
		1985/86	...	...	...	2 213	...	...
		1990/91	...	...	...	6 659	...	...
		1993/94	784	215	27	12 218	2 081	17
		1994/95	784	195	25	11 652	1 841	16
	Universities and equiv. insts.	1993/94	784	215	27	12 218	2 081	17
		1994/95	784	195	25	11 652	1 841	16
China	All institutions	1980/81	...	...	...	...	...	...
		1985/86	...	...	...	...	...	...
		1990/91	...	...	...	...	...	...
		1991/92	...	...	...	...	...	...
		1992/93	...	...	...	...	...	...
		1993/94	522 086	157 640	30	4 505 215	1 300 218	29
	Universities and equiv. insts.	1980/81	246 862	62 469	25	1 161 440	270 255	23
		1985/86	344 262	91 879	27	1 778 608	524 995	30
		1990/91	394 567	114 826	29	2 146 853	713 370	33
		1991/92	390 771	115 778	30	2 124 121	701 365	33
		1992/93	387 585	115 778	...	2 270 772	757 815	33
		1993/94	408 528	120 416	29	2 642 288	879 689	33
	Distance-learning insts.	1993/94	30 647	8 775	29	1 031 363	192 070	19
	Other third level insts.	1993/94	82 911	28 449	34	831 564	228 459	27
Cyprus‡	All institutions	1980/81	227	57	25	1 940	806	42
		1985/86	343	108	31	3 134	1 507	48
		1990/91	688	283	41	6 554	3 377	52
		1992/93	700	256	37	6 263	3 088	49
		1993/94	725	276	38	6 732	3 604	54
		1994/95	815	314	39	7 765	4 373	56
	Universities and equiv. insts.	1980/81	-	-	-	-	-	-
		1985/86	-	-	-	-	-	-
		1990/91	-	-	-	-	-	-
		1992/93	64	14	22	486	428	88
		1993/94	127	33	26	974	842	86
		1994/95	155	42	27	1 510	1 253	83
	Other third level insts.	1980/81	227	57	25	1 940	806	42
		1985/86	343	108	31	3 134	1 507	48
		1990/91	688	283	41	6 554	3 377	52
		1992/93	636	242	38	5 777	2 660	46
		1993/94	598	243	41	5 758	2 762	48
		1994/95	660	272	41	6 255	3 120	50
Georgia	All institutions	1980/81	...	...	...	139 200	...	...
		1985/86	...	...	...	142 600	...	...
		1990/91	...	...	...	146 800	...	...
		1994/95	24 430	...	...	168 011	94 367	56
	Universities and equiv. insts.	1994/95	19 084	...	...	135 773	75 496	56
	Distance-learning insts.	1994/95	-	-	-	-	-	-
	Other third level insts.	1994/95	5 346	...	...	32 238	18 871	59
Hong Kong‡	All institutions	1980/81	...	...	...	...	...	...
		1984/85	...	...	...	...	...	...
		1991/92	5 978	1 481	25	85 214	34 367	40
		1992/93	6 027	1 489	25	88 950	37 246	42
		1993/94	6 504	1 656	25	97 392	41 665	43

Third level: teachers and students **3.10**
Troisième degré: professeurs et étudiants
Tercer grado: profesores y estudiantes

Country Pays País	Type of institution Type d'établissement Tipo de establecimiento	Year Année Año	Teaching staff Personnel enseignant Personal docente			Students enrolled Étudiants inscrits Estudiantes matriculados		
			Total	Female Féminin Femenino	% F	Total	Female Féminin Femenino	% F
			(1)	(2)	(3)	(4)	(5)	(6)
Hong Kong‡ (cont)	Universities and equiv. insts.	1980/81	1 073	208	19	11 689	4 021	34
		1984/85	1 569	287	18	14 436	5 101	35
		1991/92	4 821	1 056	22	63 177	23 992	38
		1992/93	4 873	1 126	23	68 238	27 433	40
		1993/94	4 931	1 152	23	69 907	29 657	42
	Distance-learning insts.	1991/92	590	200	34	14 434	5 235	36
		1992/93	612	156	25	13 902	5 138	37
		1993/94	656	193	29	16 182	6 547	40
	Other third level insts.	1980/81	1 987	...	...	26 464	5 722	22
		1984/85	4 359	1 151	26	62 408	21 441	34
		1991/92	567	225	40	7 603	5 140	68
		1992/93	542	207	38	6 810	4 675	69
		1993/94	917	311	34	11 303	5 421	48
India	All institutions	1980/81	...	...	...	3 545 318	933 405	26
		1985/86	302 843	63 517	21	4 470 844	1 336 216	30
		1990/91	...	...	...	4 950 974	1 637 610	33
	Universities and equiv. insts.	1990/91	263 125	49 888	19	4 425 247	1 436 887	32
	Distance-learning insts.	1990/91	...	...	...	525 727	200 723	38
Indonesia	All institutions	1984/85	75 589	13 634	18	980 162	316 273	32
		1989/90	...	...	...	1 515 689	...	...
		1991/92	134 949	...	...	1 773 459	...	...
		1992/93	134 672	10 887	8	1 795 453	708 643	39
	Universities and equiv. insts.	1984/85	...	...	...	852 104	271 406	32
	Distance-learning insts.	1991/92	...	...	...	111 579	...	...
		1992/93	790	287	36	177 641	79 587	45
	Other third level insts.	1984/85	...	...	...	128 058	44 867	35
Iran, Islamic Republic of‡	All institutions	1985/86	14 878	2 281	15	184 442	52 780	29
		1990/91	23 376	...	...	312 076	85 325	27
		1992/93	30 262	5 539	18	374 734	105 667	28
		1993/94	32 934	5 800	18	436 564	124 350	28
		1994/95	36 366	6 490	18	478 455	145 353	30
	Universities and equiv. insts.	1985/86	10 229	1 311	13	121 459	37 010	30
		1990/91	19 320	3 988	21	244 227	71 185	29
		1992/93	25 167	4 992	20	282 148	81 282	29
		1993/94	25 947	5 280	20	306 667	88 455	29
		1994/95	27 981	5 755	21	327 129	99 544	30
	Distance-learning insts.	1985/86	350	24	7	4 508	1 175	26
		1990/91	958	62	6	28 342	9 386	33
		1992/93	2 089	193	9	60 992	21 045	35
		1993/94	2 560	51	2	86 963	29 886	34
		1994/95	3 177	207	7	104 631	38 881	37
	Other third level insts.	1985/86	4 299	946	22	58 475	14 595	25
		1990/91	3 098	...	...	39 507	4 754	12
		1992/93	3 006	354	12	31 594	3 340	11
		1993/94	4 427	469	11	42 934	6 009	14
		1994/95	5 208	528	10	46 695	6 928	15
Iraq	All institutions	1980/81	6 703	1 107	17	106 709	33 869	32
		1985/86	8 818	2 089	24	169 665	61 749	36
		1988/89	11 072	2 767	25	209 818	79 704	38
	Universities and equiv. insts.	1980/81	4 627	738	16	81 782	26 496	32
	Other third level insts.	1980/81	2 076	369	18	24 927	7 373	30
Israel‡	All institutions	1980/81	...	...	...	97 097	49 861	51
		1985/86	...	...	...	116 062	54 490	47
		1990/91	...	...	...	...	...	...
		1991/92	...	...	...	...	...	...
		1992/93	...	...	...	...	...	...
		1993/94	...	...	...	...	...	...
	Universities and equiv. insts.	1980/81	10 237	*3 275	*32	55 840	26 133	47
		1985/86	...	...	...	62 514	30 891	49
		1990/91	...	...	...	71 190	36 333	51
		1991/92	...	...	...	78 640	...	...
		1992/93	...	...	...	84 990	45 574	54
		1993/94	...	...	...	91 480	...	...
	Distance-learning insts.	1980/81	...	...	...	11 906	6 453	54
		1985/86	...	...	...	11 914	6 393	54

3.10 Third level: teachers and students
Troisième degré: professeurs et étudiants
Tercer grado: profesores y estudiantes

Country Pays País	Type of institution Type d'établissement Tipo de establecimiento	Year Année Año	Teaching staff Personnel enseignant Personal docente			Students enrolled Étudiants inscrits Estudiantes matriculados		
			Total	Female Féminin Femenino	% F	Total	Female Féminin Femenino	% F
			(1)	(2)	(3)	(4)	(5)	(6)
Israel‡ (cont)	Other third level insts.	1980/81	...	...	...	29 351	*17 275	*59
		1985/86	...	...	...	41 634	17 206	41
		1990/91	...	...	...	47 934	21 646	45
		1992/93	...	...	...	58 190	27 239	47
Japan	All institutions	1980/81	213 537	29 389	14	2 412 117	791 264	33
		1985/86	243 507	34 868	14	2 347 463	818 978	35
		1989/90	271 109	42 181	16	2 683 035	1 033 937	39
		1991/92	286 166	46 286	16	2 899 143	1 173 841	40
	Universities and equiv. insts.	1980/81	168 739	16 002	9	1 937 124	447 256	23
		1985/86	191 533	19 166	10	1 932 785	470 914	24
		1989/90	210 791	23 554	11	2 156 528	586 530	27
		1991/92	221 311	26 102	12	2 311 618	675 766	29
	Distance-learning insts.	1980/81	-	-	-	-	-	-
		1985/86	443	59	13	8 157	3 904	48
		1989/90	791	122	15	17 719	8 686	49
		1991/92	958	152	16	23 481	11 668	50
	Other third level insts.	1980/81	44 798	13 387	30	474 993	344 008	72
		1985/86	51 531	15 643	30	406 521	344 160	85
		1989/90	59 527	18 505	31	508 788	438 721	86
		1991/92	63 897	20 032	31	564 044	486 407	86
Jordan‡	All institutions	1980/81	...	...	...	36 549	16 682	46
		1985/86	2 307	468	20	53 753	24 162	45
		1990/91	...	...	...	80 442	38 890	48
		1991/92	3 753	689	18	84 226	40 773	48
		1992/93	4 014	737	18	88 506	43 394	49
		1993/94	4 280	783	18	85 936	41 283	48
	Universities and equiv. insts.	1980/81	...	...	...	17 103	7 068	41
		1985/86	1 295	168	13	26 711	10 403	39
		1990/91	1 931	242	13	39 668	16 581	42
		1991/92	2 123	254	12	46 068	19 763	43
		1992/93	2 457	302	12	56 530	23 653	42
		1993/94	2 832	354	13	60 644	25 747	42
	Other third level insts.	1980/81	...	...	...	19 446	9 614	49
		1985/86	1 012	300	30	27 042	13 759	51
		1990/91	...	...	...	40 774	22 309	55
		1991/92	1 630	435	27	38 158	21 011	55
		1992/93	1 557	435	28	31 976	19 741	62
		1993/94	1 448	429	30	25 292	15 536	61
Kazakstan	All institutions	1980/81	...	...	...	525 400	...	...
		1985/86	...	...	...	551 000	...	...
		1990/91	...	...	...	537 441	...	...
		1991/92	...	...	...	...	...	...
		1993/94	...	...	...	494 152	271 033	55
		1994/95	...	...	...	482 690	266 241	55
	Universities and equiv. insts.	1980/81	...	...	...	260 000	...	...
		1985/86	19 500	...	...	273 400	...	...
		1990/91	22 000	...	...	289 791	...	...
		1991/92	23 200	...	...	290 840	...	...
		1993/94	27 189	...	...	272 091	140 344	52
		1994/95	27 189	...	...	266 724	*141 129	*53
	Other third level insts.	1980/81	...	...	...	265 400	...	...
		1985/86	...	...	...	277 600	...	...
		1990/91	...	...	...	247 700	...	...
		1993/94	...	...	...	222 061	130 689	59
		1994/95	...	...	...	214 280	125 112	58
Korea, Democr. People's Rep.	All institutions	1987/88	27 000	5 000	19	390 000	131 000	34
	Universities and equiv. insts.	1987/88	23 000	4 000	17	325 000	93 000	29
	Other third level insts.	1987/88	4 000	1 000	25	65 000	38 000	58
Korea, Rep. of‡	All institutions	1980/81	...	...	...	647 505	...	...
		1985/86	34 300	...	...	1 455 759	432 385	30
		1990/91	72 954	16 236	22	1 691 429	534 053	32
		1993/94	87 495	21 024	24	2 099 021	745 862	36
		1994/95	96 640	24 028	25	2 196 895	783 172	36
		1995/96	106 407	27 759	26	2 342 786	848 033	36

Third level: teachers and students **3.10**
Troisième degré: professeurs et étudiants
Tercer grado: profesores y estudiantes

Country / Pays / País	Type of institution / Type d'établissement / Tipo de establecimiento	Year / Année / Año	Teaching staff / Personnel enseignant / Personal docente			Students enrolled / Étudiants inscrits / Estudiantes matriculados		
			Total	Female Féminin Femenino	% F	Total	Female Féminin Femenino	% F
			(1)	(2)	(3)	(4)	(5)	(6)
Korea, Rep. of‡ (cont)	Universities and equiv. insts.	1980/81	14 969	2 289	15	436 918	96 420	22
		1985/86	27 082	4 387	16	1 018 236	275 787	27
		1990/91	57 179	11 918	21	1 143 037	325 979	29
		1993/94	66 427	15 209	23	1 213 596	373 938	31
		1994/95	72 012	16 893	23	1 260 711	394 444	31
		1995/96	77 697	19 196	25	1 320 113	424 780	32
	Distance-learning insts.	1980/81	...	...	...	32 053	...	...
		1985/86	405	...	...	177 934	65 169	37
		1990/91	991	66	7	200 620	80 542	40
		1993/94	2 666	294	11	473 626	200 630	42
		1994/95	3 692	509	14	412 367	196 156	48
		1995/96	4 396	652	15	435 647	202 452	46
	Other third level insts.	1980/81	6 204	981	16	178 534	51 656	29
		1985/86	6 813	1 580	23	259 589	91 429	35
		1990/91	14 784	4 252	29	347 772	127 532	37
		1993/94	18 402	5 521	30	411 799	171 294	42
		1994/95	20 936	6 626	32	523 817	192 572	37
		1995/96	24 314	7 911	33	587 026	220 801	38
Kuwait‡	All institutions	1980/81	1 151	270	23	13 630	7 807	57
		1985/86	...	...	...	23 678	12 754	54
		1991/92	1 771	383	22	20 787	13 577	65
		1992/93	...	...	...	22 113	14 358	65
		1993/94	1 887	363	19	...	...	...
		1994/95	...	...	...	...	...	...
	Universities and equiv. insts.	1980/81	608	61	10	9 388	5 466	58
		1985/86	858	...	...	16 359	9 004	55
		1991/92	677	152	22	10 031	6 614	66
		1992/93	...	...	...	10 091	6 990	69
		1993/94	794	116	15	...	...	...
		1994/95	835	...	...	14 027	9 399	67
	Other third level insts.	1980/81	543	209	38	4 242	2 341	55
		1985/86	...	...	...	7 319	3 750	51
		1991/92	1 094	231	2	10 756	6 963	65
		1992/93	1 129	239	21	12 022	7 368	61
		1993/94	1 093	247	23	12 889	...	...
Kyrgyzstan	All institutions	1980/81	...	...	...	55 400	...	...
		1985/86	...	...	...	58 200	...	...
		1990/91	5 186	...	...	59 466	...	...
		1991/92	5 142	...	...	58 649	...	...
		1993/94	4 918	...	...	55 229	28 652	52
Lao People's Democr. Rep.‡	All institutions	1980/81	140	25	18	1 408	441	31
		1985/86	534	132	25	5 382	1 918	36
		1989/90	698	130	19	4 730	1 531	32
		1992/93	...	...	...	5 016	1 355	27
		1993/94	998	276	28	6 179	1 669	27
	Universities and equiv. insts.	1980/81	140	25	18	1 408	441	31
		1985/86	446	119	27	3 915	1 682	43
		1989/90	476	120	25	3 425	1 448	42
		1993/94	463	155	33	3 287	1 159	36
	Other third level insts.	1980/81	-	-	-	-	-	-
		1985/86	88	13	15	1 467	236	16
		1989/90	222	10	5	1 305	83	6
		1993/94	535	121	23	2 892	510	18
Lebanon	All institutions	1980/81	...	...	...	79 073	28 531	36
		1985/86	...	...	...	79 500	...	...
		1991/92	5 400	1 318	24	85 495	40 923	48
	Universities and equiv. insts.	1980/81	...	...	...	79 073	28 531	36
		1985/86	...	...	...	79 500	...	...
		1991/92	5 400	1 318	24	85 495	40 923	48
Macau	All institutions	1990/91	505	174	34	7 425	3 062	41
		1991/92	594	193	32	7 420	3 201	43
		1992/93	...	...	...	...	...	...
	Universities and equiv. insts.	1990/91	383	114	30	6 857	2 534	37
		1991/92	492	143	29	6 871	2 694	39
		1992/93	...	...	...	6 803	2 699	40
	Other third level insts.	1990/91	122	60	49	568	528	93
		1991/92	102	50	49	549	507	92

3.10 Third level: teachers and students
Troisième degré: professeurs et étudiants
Tercer grado: profesores y estudiantes

Country Pays País	Type of institution Type d'établissement Tipo de establecimiento	Year Année Año	Teaching staff Personnel enseignant Personal docente			Students enrolled Étudiants inscrits Estudiantes matriculados		
			Total	Female Féminin Femenino	% F	Total	Female Féminin Femenino	% F
			(1)	(2)	(3)	(4)	(5)	(6)
Malaysia‡	All institutions	1980/81	5 541	1 415	26	57 650	22 199	39
		1985/86	8 213	1 801	22	93 249	41 468	44
		1990/91	10 169	...	...	121 412	54 370	45
		1991/92	11 239	...	...	137 826	...	...
		1992/93	13 590	...	...	160 566	...	...
		1993/94	11 490	...	...	170 145	...	...
	Universities and equiv. insts.	1980/81	3 299	766	23	26 287	9 105	35
		1985/86	4 718	1 149	24	43 295	17 066	39
		1990/91	5 260	...	...	57 059	26 286	46
		1991/92	5 503	...	...	63 397	...	...
		1992/93	6 242	...	...	77 829	...	...
		1993/94	5 432	...	...	82 971	...	...
	Other third level insts.	1980/81	2 242	649	29	31 363	13 094	42
		1985/86	3 495	652	19	49 954	24 402	49
		1990/91	4 909	...	...	64 353	28 084	44
		1991/92	5 736	...	...	74 429	...	...
		1992/93	7 348	...	...	82 737	...	...
		1993/94	6 058	...	...	87 174	...	...
Mongolia	All institutions	1985/86	2 747	...	...	40 099	...	...
		1990/91	2 689	...	...	31 006	...	...
		1991/92	2 601	...	...	28 209	...	...
		1994/95	3 905	...	...	32 535	22 590	69
	Universities and equiv. insts.	1985/86	1 510	...	...	18 487	...	...
		1990/91	1 429	...	...	13 397	...	...
		1991/92	1 341	...	...	13 223	...	...
		1994/95	...	...	...	16 037	9 944	62
	Other third level insts.	1985/86	1 237	...	...	21 612	...	...
		1990/91	1 260	...	...	17 609	...	...
		1991/92	1 260	...	...	14 986	...	...
		1994/95	...	...	...	16 498	12 646	77
Myanmar	All institutions	1980/81	4 509	...	...	163 197	...	...
		1985/86	4 758	...	...	179 366	...	...
		1991/92	5 497	...	...	196 052	108 663	55
		1992/93	5 442	...	...	244 208	140 432	58
		1993/94	5 989	...	...	235 256	...	...
	Universities and equiv. insts.	1980/81	...	...	...	24 215	...	...
		1985/86	...	...	...	63 262	33 771	53
		1991/92	...	...	...	91 926	53 616	58
		1992/93	...	...	...	89 768	54 236	60
		1993/94	...	...	...	79 391	...	...
	Distance-learning insts.	1980/81	...	...	...	85 395	...	...
		1985/86	...	...	...	88 898	...	...
		1991/92	...	...	...	88 225	47 460	54
		1992/93	...	...	...	133 320	76 116	57
		1993/94	...	...	...	133 418	...	...
	Other third level insts.	1980/81	...	...	...	53 587	...	...
		1985/86	...	...	...	27 206	...	...
		1991/92	...	...	...	15 901	7 587	48
		1992/93	...	...	...	20 782	10 080	49
		1993/94	...	...	...	22 447	...	...
Nepal‡	All institutions	1980/81	2 918	480	16	34 094	7 358	22
		1985/86	...	...	...	54 452	...	...
		1990/91	...	...	...	93 753	21 654	23
		1991/92	4 925	...	...	110 239	26 221	24
		1992/93	...	...	...	103 840	...	...
		1993/94	...	...	...	102 018	...	...
	Universities and equiv. insts.	1980/81	2 918	480	16	34 094	7 358	22
		1985/86	...	...	...	54 452	...	...
		1990/91	...	...	...	93 753	21 654	23
		1991/92	4 925	...	...	110 239	26 221	24
		1992/93	...	...	...	103 840	...	...
		1993/94	...	...	...	102 018	...	...
Oman	All institutions	1980/81	8	...	...	18	-	-
		1985/86	154	...	...	990	378	38
		1990/91	732	...	...	5 962	2 627	44
		1991/92	...	...	...	7 322	3 577	49
	Universities and equiv. insts.	1980/81	-	-	-	-	-	-
		1985/86	-	-	-	-	-	-
		1990/91	433	...	...	3 021	1 412	47
		1991/92	...	...	...	3 615	1 917	53

Third level: teachers and students **3.10**
Troisième degré: professeurs et étudiants
Tercer grado: profesores y estudiantes

Country Pays País	Type of institution Type d'établissement Tipo de establecimiento	Year Année Año	Teaching staff Personnel enseignant Personal docente			Students enrolled Étudiants inscrits Estudiantes matriculados		
			Total	Female Féminin Femenino	% F	Total	Female Féminin Femenino	% F
			(1)	(2)	(3)	(4)	(5)	(6)
Oman (cont)	Other third level insts.	1980/81	8	...	...	18	-	-
		1985/86	154	...	...	990	378	38
		1990/91	299	...	...	2 941	1 215	41
		1991/92	...	...	...	3 707	1 660	45
Pakistan‡	All institutions	1985/86	7 805	1 303	17	267 742	69 868	26
		1989/90	...	...	...	336 689	109 690	33
	Universities and equiv. insts.	1985/86	7 744	1 279	17	233 989	61 774	26
		1989/90	...	...	...	275 341	84 986	31
	Distance-learning insts.	1985/86	61	24	39	33 753	8 094	24
		1989/90	85	29	34	61 348	24 704	40
Philippines	All institutions	1980/81	43 770	23 381	53	1 276 016	681 140	53
		1985/86	57 000	...	...	1 402 000	...	...
		1990/91	...	...	...	1 709 486	...	...
		1991/92	...	...	...	1 656 815	975 250	59
		1992/93	...	...	...	...	...	...
		1993/94	...	...	...	...	...	...
	Universities and equiv. insts.	1980/81	...	...	...	1 143 702	613 197	54
		1985/86	50 821	...	...	1 167 000	...	...
		1990/91	...	...	...	1 549 639	880 847	57
		1991/92	...	...	...	1 525 868	...	...
		1992/93	...	...	...	1 532 152	863 153	56
		1993/94	...	...	...	1 583 820	884 088	56
	Other third level insts.	1980/81	...	...	...	132 314	67 943	51
		1985/86	6 179	...	...	235 000	...	...
		1990/91	...	...	...	159 847	...	...
		1991/92	...	...	...	130 947	...	...
Qatar	All institutions	1980/81	283	87	31	2 269	1 403	62
		1985/86	...	...	...	5 344	3 309	62
		1990/91	...	...	...	6 485	4 507	69
		1992/93	605	193	32	7 283	5 204	71
		1993/94	637	207	32	7 351	5 195	71
		1994/95	637	202	32	7 794	5 558	71
	Universities and equiv. insts.	1980/81	283	87	31	2 269	1 403	62
		1985/86	...	...	...	5 344	3 309	62
		1990/91	...	...	...	6 485	4 507	69
		1992/93	605	193	32	7 283	5 204	71
		1993/94	637	207	32	7 351	5 195	71
		1994/95	637	202	32	7 794	5 558	71
Saudi Arabia	All institutions	1980/81	7 448	1 419	19	62 074	17 311	28
		1985/86	10 923	2 652	24	113 529	44 697	39
		1990/91	13 260	3 331	25	153 967	66 417	43
		1991/92	11 682	3 049	26	163 688	64 732	40
		1992/93	14 803	3 938	27	192 625	88 484	46
		1993/94	14 394	2 824	20	201 090	90 602	45
	Universities and equiv. insts.	1980/81	6 598	1 306	20	56 552	16 472	29
		1985/86	9 297	2 239	24	104 046	40 754	39
		1991/92	10 564	2 522	24	151 649	57 128	38
		1992/93	12 669	3 231	26	174 788	78 037	45
		1993/94	12 484	2 190	18	182 121	80 155	44
	Other third level insts.	1980/81	850	113	13	5 822	839	14
		1985/86	1 626	493	30	9 483	3 943	42
		1991/92	1 118	527	47	12 039	7 604	63
		1992/93	2 134	707	33	17 837	10 447	59
		1993/94	1 910	634	33	18 969	10 447	55
Singapore	All institutions	1980/81	2 270	422	19	23 256	9 087	39
		1985/86	...	...	...	39 913	14 838	37
		1990/91	...	...	...	55 672	22 980	41
		1992/93	...	...	...	65 771	28 068	43
		1993/94	...	...	...	73 772	31 754	43
		1994/95	6 225	1 781	29	76 985	33 729	44
	Universities and equiv. insts.	1980/81	1 433	244	17	9 078	4 011	44
	Other third level insts.	1980/81	837	178	21	14 178	5 076	36
Sri Lanka‡	All institutions	1980	...	...	...	...	...	...
		1985	3 359	...	...	59 377	23 974	40
		1990	...	...	...	...	...	...
		1991	2 358	...	...	55 190	17 483	32
		1994	...	...	...	59 790	26 318	44

3.10 Third level: teachers and students
Troisième degré: professeurs et étudiants
Tercer grado: profesores y estudiantes

Country / Pays / País	Type of institution / Type d'établissement / Tipo de establecimiento	Year / Année / Año	Teaching staff Personnel enseignant Personal docente			Students enrolled Étudiants inscrits Estudiantes matriculados		
			Total	Female Féminin Femenino	% F	Total	Female Féminin Femenino	% F
			(1)	(2)	(3)	(4)	(5)	(6)
Sri Lanka‡ (cont)	Universities and equiv. insts.	1980	1 827	...	...	18 111	7 214	40
		1985	2 189	...	...	24 222	10 378	43
		1990	2 013	600	30	38 424	15 256	40
		1991	2 093	625	30	36 659	13 199	36
		1994	...	...	...	39 607	17 738	45
	Distance-learning insts.	1985	74	...	...	9 851	3 671	37
		1990	103	39	38	15 459	5 551	36
		1991	110	41	37	17 309	3 594	21
		1994	110	41	37	17 872	7 147	40
	Other third level insts.	1980	2 991	...	...	24 583	11 300	46
		1985	1 092	...	...	25 304	9 925	39
		1991	155	...	...	1 222	690	56
		1994	...	...	...	2 311	1 433	62
Syrian Arab Republic‡	All institutions	1980/81	...	...	...	140 180	41 074	29
		1985/86	...	...	...	179 473	62 731	35
		1990/91	...	...	...	221 628	85 734	39
		1991/92	...	...	...	183 079	67 674	37
		1992/93	...	...	...	194 371	74 148	38
	Universities and equiv. insts.	1980/81	...	...	...	110 832	29 565	27
		1985/86	4 504	756	17	135 191	42 968	32
		1990/91	...	...	...	169 913	62 657	37
		1991/92	4 327	797	18	166 710	61 450	37
		1992/93	5 997	1 196	20	178 526	67 993	38
	Other third level insts.	1980/81	...	...	...	29 348	11 509	39
		1985/86	...	...	...	44 282	19 763	45
		1990/91	...	...	...	51 715	23 077	45
		1991/92	...	...	...	16 369	6 224	38
		1992/93	...	...	...	15 845	6 155	39
Tajikistan	All institutions	1980/81	...	...	...	96 900	...	...
		1985/86	...	...	...	95 300	...	...
		1990/91	5 265	...	...	110 200	...	...
		1991/92	5 434	...	...	125 100	...	...
Thailand	All institutions	1980/81	...	...	...	...	...	...
		1985/86	30 905	...	...	1 026 952	...	...
		1989/90	52 317	...	...	952 012	...	...
		1992/93	49 466	21 471	43	1 156 174	607 822	53
		1994/95	...	...	...	...	...	...
	Universities and equiv. insts.	1980/81	10 350	...	...	100 401	...	...
		1985/86	14 666	...	...	150 355	...	...
		1989/90	18 083	...	...	197 539	...	...
		1992/93	18 336	9 391	51	266 107	139 940	53
		1994/95	22 015	...	...	325 893	...	...
	Distance-learning insts.	1985/86	921	...	...	569 869	...	...
		1989/90	1 025	...	...	459 059	...	...
		1992/93	1 055	603	57	472 158	234 249	50
		1994/95	1 106	...	...	490 363	...	...
	Other third level insts.	1980/81	9 244	...	...	178 860	...	...
		1985/86	15 318	...	...	306 728	...	...
		1989/90	33 209	...	...	295 414	...	...
		1992/93	30 075	11 477	38	417 909	233 633	56
Turkey‡	All institutions	1980/81	21 577	5 312	25	246 183	...	...
		1985/86	22 968	6 950	30	469 992	152 047	32
		1990/91	34 469	10 929	32	749 921	252 487	34
		1992/93	38 468	12 519	33	915 765	316 690	35
		1993/94	42 439	13 750	32	1 143 083	427 290	37
		1994/95	44 086	14 456	33	1 174 299	449 771	38
	Universities and equiv. insts.	1980/81	16 162	3 734	23	165 647	42 839	26
		1985/86	20 353	5 867	29	300 836	101 601	34
		1990/91	32 915	10 579	32	416 752	150 624	36
		1992/93	36 387	11 999	33	478 090	178 673	37
		1993/94	40 005	13 124	33	570 672	214 106	38
		1994/95	41 258	13 676	33	737 542	305 096	41
	Distance-learning insts.	1980/81	./.	./.	./.	9 742	...	...
		1985/86	77	21	27	99 063	26 515	27
		1990/91	./.	./.	./.	260 962	80 076	31
		1992/93	./.	./.	./.	347 145	109 384	32
		1993/94	./.	./.	./.	465 766	177 398	38
		1994/95	./.	./.	./.	308 835	99 919	32

Third level: teachers and students 3.10
Troisième degré: professeurs et étudiants
Tercer grado: profesores y estudiantes

Country / Pays / País	Type of institution / Type d'établissement / Tipo de establecimiento	Year / Année / Año	Teaching staff Personnel enseignant Personal docente			Students enrolled Étudiants inscrits Estudiantes matriculados		
			Total	Female Féminin Femenino	% F	Total	Female Féminin Femenino	% F
			(1)	(2)	(3)	(4)	(5)	(6)
Turkey‡ (cont)	Other third level insts.	1980/81	5 415	1 578	29	70 794	18 718	26
		1985/86	2 538	1 062	42	70 093	23 931	34
		1990/91	1 554	350	23	72 207	21 787	30
		1992/93	2 081	520	25	90 530	28 633	32
		1993/94	2 434	626	26	106 645	35 786	34
		1994/95	2 828	780	28	127 922	44 756	35
Turkmenistan	All institutions	1980/81	...	...	...	69 800	...	...
		1985/86	...	...	...	75 800	...	...
		1990/91	...	...	...	76 000	...	...
United Arab Emirates	All institutions	1980/81	257	20	8	2 861	1 389	49
		1985/86	445	47	11	7 772	4 531	58
		1990/91	841	115	14	10 196	7 182	70
		1991/92	1 082	155	14	10 405	7 831	75
		1992/93	...	...	...	10 641	7 429	70
	Universities and equiv. insts.	1980/81	207	10	5	2 646	1 209	46
		1985/86	295	15	5	7 248	4 057	56
		1990/91	494	28	6	8 496	6 063	71
		1991/92	728	64	9	8 668	6 721	78
	Other third level insts.	1980/81	50	10	20	215	180	84
		1985/86	150	32	21	524	484	92
		1990/91	347	87	25	1 700	1 119	66
		1991/92	354	91	26	1 737	1 110	64
Uzbekistan	All institutions	1980/81	...	...	...	515 800	...	...
		1985/86	...	...	...	567 200	...	...
		1990/91	23 062	...	...	602 700	...	...
		1991/92	24 787	...	...	638 200	...	...
Viet Nam	All institutions	1980/81	17 242	3 857	22	114 701	27 090	24
		1985/86	...	...	...	...	...	...
		1990/91	...	...	...	...	...	...
		1993/94	...	...	...	...	...	...
	Universities and equiv. insts.	1980/81	17 242	3 857	22	114 701	27 090	24
		1985/86	18 614	...	...	121 159	...	...
		1990/91	20 871	...	...	121 570	...	...
		1993/94	21 184	...	...	122 893	...	...
	Other third level insts.	1980/81	-	-	-	-	-	-
Yemen	All institutions	1991/92	1 800	210	12	53 082	9 079	17
	Universities and equiv. insts.	1991/92	1 800	210	12	53 082	9 079	17
Former Democr. Yemen	All institutions	1986/87	634	96	15	4 541	1 794	40
	Universities and equiv. insts.	1986/87	634	96	15	4 541	1 794	40
Former Yemen Arab Rep.	All institutions	1986/87	451	...	...	15 055	...	...
	Universities and equiv. insts.	1986/87	451	...	...	15 055	...	...
Palestine Gaza Strip	All institutions	1986/87	258	...	...	5 313	...	...
		1989/90	296	21	7	6 548	2 038	31
		1991/92	217	...	...	4 701	2 052	44
		1994/95	602	29	5	12 483	4 583	37
	Universities and equiv. insts.	1986/87	203	...	...	4 483	1 606	36
		1989/90	146	6	4	4 623	1 655	36
		1991/92	104	18	17	2 280	902	40
		1994/95	336	12	4	9 857	3 431	35
	Other third level insts.	1986/87	55	...	...	830	...	...
		1989/90	150	15	10	1 925	383	20
		1991/92	113	...	...	2 421	1 150	48
		1994/95	266	17	6	2 626	1 152	44
West Bank	All institutions	1986/87	2 271	...	...	19 872	8 696	44
		1989/90	...	...	...	14 434	...	...
		1991/92	1 552	243	16	20 682	9 547	46
		1994/95	1 513	236	16	21 339	11 577	54
	Universities and equiv. insts.	1986/87	917	...	...	10 414	4 197	40
		1989/90	664	...	...	10 260	3 856	38
		1991/92	941	150	16	12 242	4 955	40
		1994/95	882	156	18	14 776	8 136	55

3.10 Third level: teachers and students
Troisième degré: professeurs et étudiants
Tercer grado: profesores y estudiantes

Country / Pays / País	Type of institution / Type d'établissement / Tipo de establecimiento	Year / Année / Año	Teaching staff / Personnel enseignant / Personal docente			Students enrolled / Étudiants inscrits / Estudiantes matriculados		
			Total	Female / Féminin / Femenino	% F	Total	Female / Féminin / Femenino	% F
			(1)	(2)	(3)	(4)	(5)	(6)
West Bank (cont)	Distance-learning insts.	1986/87	-	-	-	-	-	-
		1989/90	...	...	...	271	-	...
		1991/92	17	2	12	2 546	833	33
		1994/95	159	7	4	3 865	1 825	47
	Other third level insts.	1986/87	1 354	...	...	9 458	4 499	48
		1989/90	324	...	...	3 903	1 680	43
		1991/92	594	91	15	5 894	3 743	64
		1994/95	472	73	15	2 698	1 616	60
Europe								
Albania‡	All institutions	1980/81	1 103	222	20	14 568	7 221	50
		1985/86	1 468	347	24	21 995	9 995	45
		1990/91	1 806	513	28	22 059	11 384	52
		1991/92	1 805	489	27	28 001	14 536	52
		1992/93	1 680	497	30	22 835	11 836	52
		1993/94	1 774	480	27	30 185	16 069	53
	Universities and equiv. insts.	1980/81	1 103	222	20	14 568	7 221	50
		1985/86	1 468	347	24	21 995	9 995	45
		1990/91	1 806	513	28	22 059	11 384	52
		1991/92	1 623	438	27	25 569	14 053	55
		1992/93	1 523	449	29	21 666	11 447	53
		1993/94	1 596	440	28	19 086	10 430	55
	Distance-learning insts.	1993/94	...	...	...	9 433	5 116	54
	Other third level insts.	1980/81	-	-	-	-	-	-
		1985/86	-	-	-	-	-	-
		1990/91	-	-	-	-	-	-
		1991/92	182	51	28	1 432	483	34
		1992/93	157	48	31	1 169	389	33
		1993/94	178	40	22	1 666	523	31
Austria‡	All institutions	1980/81	14 086	2 067	15	136 774	57 491	42
		1985/86	12 135	2 455	20	173 215	78 593	45
		1990/91	14 568	3 498	24	205 767	94 004	46
		1991/92	15 201	3 824	25	216 529	99 917	46
		1992/93	16 188	4 277	26	221 389	103 030	47
		1993/94	24 732	6 109	25	227 444	107 013	47
	Universities and equiv. insts.	1980/81	12 572	1 599	13	127 423	50 200	39
		1985/86	10 252	1 854	18	160 904	69 509	43
		1990/91	12 698	2 812	22	191 793	84 306	44
		1991/92	13 315	3 096	23	201 615	89 422	44
		1992/93	14 218	3 481	24	205 769	91 847	45
		1993/94	22 609	5 239	23	210 639	94 988	45
	Other third level insts.	1980/81	1 514	468	31	9 351	7 291	78
		1985/86	1 883	601	32	12 311	9 084	74
		1990/91	1 870	686	37	13 974	9 698	69
		1991/92	1 886	728	39	14 914	10 495	70
		1992/93	1 970	796	40	15 620	11 183	72
		1993/94	2 123	870	41	16 805	12 025	72
Belarus‡	All institutions	1980/81	...	...	...	339 800	...	...
		1985/86	...	...	...	342 400	...	...
		1990/91	40 400	...	...	321 500	99 600	...
		1991/92	39 800	...	...	313 500	98 400	...
		1992/93	39 300	...	...	312 400	95 800	...
		1993/94	39 200	...	...	299 640	91 800	...
Belgium‡	All institutions	1980/81	...	...	...	196 153	86 947	44
		1985/86	...	...	...	247 499	113 120	46
		1990/91	28 058	9 119	33	276 248	133 339	48
	Universities and equiv. insts.	1980/81	...	...	...	95 246	35 107	37
		1985/86	...	...	...	103 598	42 593	41
		1990/91	11 050	2 343	21	111 845	49 951	45
	Other third level insts.	1980/81	...	...	...	100 907	51 840	51
		1985/86	...	...	...	143 901	70 527	49
		1990/91	17 008	6 776	40	164 403	83 388	51
Bulgaria	All institutions	1980/81	14 412	5 592	39	101 359	56 946	56
		1985/86	15 252	5 592	37	113 795	62 035	55
		1990/91	23 663	9 353	40	188 479	96 807	51
		1992/93	21 976	8 459	38	195 447	111 759	57
		1993/94	21 148	8 049	38	206 179	121 250	59
		1994/95	24 274	9 913	41	223 030	134 958	61

Third level: teachers and students **3.10**
Troisième degré: professeurs et étudiants
Tercer grado: profesores y estudiantes

Country Pays País	Type of institution Type d'établissement Tipo de establecimiento	Year Année Año	Teaching staff Personnel enseignant Personal docente			Students enrolled Étudiants inscrits Estudiantes matriculados		
			Total	Female Féminin Femenino	% F	Total	Female Féminin Femenino	% F
			(1)	(2)	(3)	(4)	(5)	(6)
Bulgaria (cont)	Universities and equiv. insts.	1980/81	12 622	4 638	37	87 335	46 491	53
		1985/86	14 409	5 157	36	104 259	54 950	53
		1990/91	20 716	7 781	38	156 536	75 689	48
		1992/93	18 895	6 950	37	165 186	90 715	55
		1993/94	18 158	6 561	36	178 388	101 031	57
		1994/95	21 227	8 360	39	197 869	116 263	59
	Other third level insts.	1980/81	1 790	954	53	14 024	10 455	75
		1985/86	843	435	52	9 536	7 085	74
		1990/91	2 947	1 572	53	31 943	21 118	66
		1992/93	3 081	1 509	49	30 261	21 044	70
		1993/94	2 990	1 488	50	27 791	20 219	73
		1994/95	3 047	1 553	51	25 161	18 695	74
Croatia‡	All institutions	1980/81	...	...	...	64 966	...	...
		1985/86	...	...	...	55 886	...	...
		1990/91	6 633	...	...	72 342	...	...
		1992/93	6 550	2 264	35	77 689	37 358	48
		1993/94	6 429	2 148	33	82 361	39 239	48
		1994/95	6 169	2 022	33	82 251	40 362	49
	Universities and equiv. insts.	1980/81	...	...	...	64 966	...	...
		1985/86	...	...	...	55 886	...	...
		1990/91	6 633	...	...	72 342	...	...
		1992/93	6 550	2 264	35	77 689	37 358	48
		1993/94	6 429	2 148	33	82 361	39 239	48
		1994/95	6 169	2 022	33	82 251	40 362	49
Former Czechoslovakia	All institutions	1980/81	22 478	5 816	26	197 041	81 975	42
		1985/86	23 944	6 591	28	169 344	72 066	43
		1990/91	22 974	6 793	30	190 409	83 885	44
	Universities and equiv. insts.	1980/81	22 478	5 816	26	197 041	81 975	42
		1985/86	23 944	6 591	28	169 344	72 066	43
		1990/91	22 974	6 793	30	190 409	83 885	44
Czech Republic	All institutions	1980/81	...	...	...	119 850	...	...
		1985/86	...	...	...	109 273	...	...
		1990/91	...	...	...	118 194	...	...
		1992/93	14 798	4 321	29	116 560	51 502	44
		1993/94	...	...	...	152 804	72 356	47
		1994/95	...	...	...	165 106	77 577	47
	Universities and equiv. insts.	1992/93	7 979	2 679	34	60 431	33 558	56
		1993/94	15 711	4 825	31	129 391	57 015	44
		1994/95	...	...	...	136 566	59 369	43
	Other third level insts.	1992/93	6 819	1 642	24	56 129	17 944	32
		1993/94	...	...	...	23 413	15 341	66
		1994/95	...	...	...	28 540	18 208	64
Denmark	All institutions	1980/81	...	...	...	106 241	51 923	49
		1985/86	...	...	...	116 319	57 380	49
		1990/91	...	...	...	142 968	74 385	52
		1991/92	...	...	...	150 159	78 891	53
		1992/93	...	...	...	157 006	82 224	52
		1993/94	9 000	2 700	30	169 619	86 784	51
	Universities and equiv. insts.	1980/81	...	...	...	85 388	36 318	43
		1985/86	...	...	...	91 450	40 402	44
		1990/91	...	...	...	120 125	61 019	51
		1991/92	...	...	...	124 942	64 051	51
		1992/93	...	...	...	133 128	68 618	52
	Other third level insts.	1980/81	...	...	...	20 853	15 605	75
		1985/86	...	...	...	24 869	16 978	68
		1990/91	...	...	...	22 843	13 366	59
		1991/92	...	...	...	25 217	14 840	59
		1992/93	...	...	...	23 878	13 606	57
Estonia‡	All institutions	1980/81	...	...	...	25 500	14 000	55
		1985/86	...	...	...	23 500	14 000	60
		1990/91	...	...	...	25 900	13 000	50
		1992/93	...	...	...	24 464	12 264	50
		1993/94	...	...	...	24 768	12 676	51
		1994/95	...	...	...	25 483	13 162	52
	Universities and equiv. insts.	1992/93	...	...	...	22 875	11 522	50
		1993/94	...	...	...	21 261	11 051	52
	Other third level insts.	1992/93	...	...	...	1 589	742	47
		1993/94	...	...	...	3 507	1 625	46

3.10 Third level: teachers and students
Troisième degré: professeurs et étudiants
Tercer grado: profesores y estudiantes

Country / Pays / País	Type of institution / Type d'établissement / Tipo de establecimiento	Year / Année / Año	Teaching staff / Personnel enseignant / Personal docente			Students enrolled / Étudiants inscrits / Estudiantes matriculados		
			Total	Female / Féminin / Femenino	% F	Total	Female / Féminin / Femenino	% F
			(1)	(2)	(3)	(4)	(5)	(6)
Finland	All institutions	1980/81	...	...	...	123 165	59 356	48
		1985/86	...	...	...	127 976	62 467	49
		1990/91	...	...	...	165 714	86 468	52
		1991/92	...	...	...	173 702	91 574	53
		1992/93	...	...	...	188 162	99 791	53
		1993/94	...	...	...	197 367	104 713	53
	Universities and equiv. insts.	1980/81	6 194	...	...	84 176	41 746	50
		1985/86	7 169	...	...	92 230	46 704	51
		1990/91	7 798	...	...	112 921	58 401	52
		1991/92	7 802	...	...	115 358	59 692	52
		1992/93	7 917	...	...	121 736	63 210	52
		1993/94	7 905	...	...	124 370	64 627	52
	Other third level insts.	1980/81	...	...	...	38 989	17 610	45
		1985/86	...	...	...	35 746	15 763	44
		1990/91	...	...	...	52 793	28 067	53
		1991/92	...	...	...	58 344	31 882	55
		1992/93	...	...	...	66 426	36 581	55
		1993/94	...	...	...	72 997	40 086	55
France‡	All institutions	1980/81	...	...	...	1 076 717	...	...
		1985/86	...	...	...	1 278 581	643 429	50
		1990/91	...	...	...	1 698 938	902 557	53
		1991/92	...	...	...	1 840 307	989 443	54
		1992/93	...	...	...	1 951 994	1 058 884	54
		1993/94	...	...	...	2 083 232	1 138 302	55
	Universities and equiv. insts.	1980/81	...	...	...	869 788	...	...
		1985/86	45 211	11 620	26	978 519	510 275	52
		1990/91	48 248	...	...	1 191 823	645 442	54
		1991/92	50 331	13 992	28	1 246 989	679 928	55
		1992/93	52 663	...	...	1 296 459	710 525	55
		1993/94	56 339	...	...	1 395 103	772 135	55
	Other third level insts.	1980/81	...	...	...	206 929	80 104	39
		1985/86	...	...	...	300 062	133 154	44
		1990/91	...	...	...	507 115	257 115	51
		1991/92	...	...	...	593 318	309 515	52
		1992/93	...	...	...	655 535	348 359	53
		1993/94	...	...	...	688 129	366 167	53
Germany‡	All institutions	1990/91	...	...	...	2 048 627	...	...
		1991/92	...	...	...	2 033 702	841 850	41
		1992/93	...	...	...	1 823 100	724 000	40
		1993/94	...	...	...	1 875 099	753 671	40
Former German Democr. Rep.	All institutions	1980/81	38 699	10 498	27	400 799	232 336	58
		1985/86	42 336	...	...	432 672	235 755	54
	Universities and equiv. insts.	1980/81	28 848	6 509	23	137 554	65 297	47
		1985/86	30 082	7 940	26	148 650	70 105	47
	Other third level insts.	1980/81	9 851	3 989	40	263 245	167 039	63
		1985/86	12 254	...	...	284 022	165 650	58
Federal Rep. of Germany‡	All institutions	1980/81	171 708	...	...	1 223 221	503 448	41
		1985/86	...	...	...	1 550 211	646 631	42
	Universities and equiv. insts.	1980/81	127 383	...	...	1 031 590	378 556	37
		1985/86	...	...	...	1 336 395	505 722	38
	Other third level insts.	1980/81	44 325	13 847	31	191 631	124 892	65
		1985/86	...	...	...	213 816	140 909	66
Greece	All institutions	1990/91	...	...	...	283 415	...	...
		1991/92	14 817	4 725	32	271 718	132 770	49
		1992/93	...	...	...	299 023	147 765	49
		1993/94	18 168	6 433	35	314 002	146 693	47
	Universities and equiv. insts.	1990/91	...	...	...	201 505	...	...
		1991/92	9 124	2 554	28	191 070	96 316	50
		1992/93	6 924	2 444	35	85 718	36 335	42
	Other third level insts.	1990/91	...	...	...	81 910	...	...
		1991/92	5 693	2 171	38	80 648	36 454	45
Holy See‡	All institutions	1980/81	1 349	90	7	9 104	3 538	39
		1985/86	1 498	111	7	9 775	3 219	33
		1990/91	1 502	117	8	10 938	3 502	32
		1991/92	1 584	131	8	11 681	3 594	31
		1992/93	1 588	131	8	12 253	3 886	32

Third level: teachers and students 3.10
Troisième degré: professeurs et étudiants
Tercer grado: profesores y estudiantes

Country Pays País	Type of institution Type d'établissement Tipo de establecimiento	Year Année Año	Teaching staff Personnel enseignant Personal docente			Students enrolled Étudiants inscrits Estudiantes matriculados		
			Total	Female Féminin Femenino	% F	Total	Female Féminin Femenino	% F
			(1)	(2)	(3)	(4)	(5)	(6)
Holy See‡ (cont)	Universities and equiv. insts.	1980/81	1 349	90	7	9 104	3 538	39
		1985/86	1 498	111	7	9 775	3 219	33
		1990/91	1 502	117	8	10 938	3 502	32
		1991/92	1 584	131	8	11 681	3 594	31
		1992/93	1 588	131	8	12 253	3 886	32
Hungary	All institutions	1980/81	13 890	4 046	29	101 166	50 314	50
		1985/86	14 850	4 496	30	99 344	53 188	54
		1990/91	17 302	5 592	32	102 387	51 507	50
		1991/92	17 477	5 604	32	107 079	53 791	50
		1992/93	17 743	5 824	33	117 460	59 457	51
		1993/94	18 687	6 191	33	133 956	70 560	53
	Universities and equiv. insts.	1980/81	10 616	2 872	27	61 767	29 099	47
		1985/86	11 460	3 200	28	61 163	30 172	49
		1990/91	12 949	3 830	30	67 384	32 767	49
		1991/92	13 036	3 830	29	71 452	34 771	49
		1992/93	13 349	4 117	31	76 096	37 549	49
		1993/94	14 044	4 463	32	84 632	44 006	52
	Other third level insts.	1980/81	3 274	1 174	36	39 399	21 215	54
		1985/86	3 390	1 296	38	38 181	23 016	60
		1990/91	4 353	1 762	40	35 003	18 740	54
		1991/92	4 441	1 774	40	35 627	19 020	53
		1992/93	4 394	1 707	39	41 364	21 908	53
		1993/94	4 643	1 728	37	49 324	26 554	54
Iceland	All institutions	1980/81	...	...	...	3 633	2 179	60
		1985/86	...	...	...	4 724	2 621	55
		1990/91	...	...	...	5 225	3 001	57
		1991/92	...	...	...	6 161	3 608	59
		1992/93	...	...	...	5 672	3 266	58
		1993/94	...	...	...	6 050	3 426	57
Ireland	All institutions	1980/81	...	...	...	54 746	22 248	41
		1985/86	6 002	...	...	70 301	30 385	43
		1990/91	5 598	...	...	90 296	41 440	46
		1991/92	5 929	...	...	101 108	47 568	47
		1992/93	6 267	...	...	108 394	52 182	48
		1993/94	...	...	...	117 641	56 816	48
	Universities and equiv. insts.	1980/81	...	...	...	33 173	15 819	48
		1985/86	3 332	...	...	39 120	18 912	48
		1990/91	2 695	...	...	47 955	24 409	51
		1991/92	2 837	...	...	52 288	26 941	52
		1992/93	2 980	...	...	56 190	29 340	52
	Other third level insts.	1980/81	2 688	...	...	21 573	6 429	30
		1985/86	2 670	...	...	31 181	11 473	37
		1990/91	2 903	...	...	42 341	17 031	40
		1991/92	3 092	...	...	48 820	20 627	42
		1992/93	3 287	...	...	52 204	22 842	44
Italy	All institutions	1980/81	...	...	...	1 117 742	476 028	43
		1985/86	51 539	...	...	1 185 304	545 902	46
		1990/91	55 766	...	...	1 452 286	690 490	48
		1991/92	57 283	...	...	1 533 202	759 251	50
		1992/93	58 359	...	...	1 615 150	816 632	51
		1993/94	59 770	...	...	1 681 949	856 396	51
	Universities and equiv. insts.	1980/81	42 531	...	...	1 110 547	471 919	42
		1985/86	50 996	...	...	1 176 726	540 431	46
		1990/91	54 991	...	...	1 442 413	683 855	47
		1991/92	56 522	...	...	1 522 824	752 515	49
		1992/93	57 690	...	...	1 604 216	809 171	50
		1993/94	59 001	...	...	1 668 906	847 520	51
	Other third level insts.	1980/81	...	...	...	7 195	4 109	57
		1985/86	543	...	...	8 578	5 471	64
		1990/91	775	...	...	9 873	6 635	67
		1991/92	761	...	...	10 378	7 006	68
		1992/93	669	...	...	10 934	7 461	68
		1993/94	769	191	25	13 043	8 876	68
Latvia‡	All institutions	1980/81	4 834	...	...	47 200	26 921	57
		1985/86	...	...	...	43 900	26 187	60
		1990/91	4 430	...	...	46 000	25 274	55
		1992/93	4 478	...	...	41 138	21 886	53
		1993/94	4 712	...	...	37 907	21 365	56
		1994/95	4 229	1 993	47	38 046	21 225	56

3.10 Third level: teachers and students
Troisième degré: professeurs et étudiants
Tercer grado: profesores y estudiantes

Country Pays País	Type of institution Type d'établissement Tipo de establecimiento	Year Année Año	Teaching staff Personnel enseignant Personal docente			Students enrolled Étudiants inscrits Estudiantes matriculados		
			Total	Female Féminin Femenino	% F	Total	Female Féminin Femenino	% F
			(1)	(2)	(3)	(4)	(5)	(6)
Latvia‡ (cont)	Universities and equiv. insts.	1980/81	...	...	...	33 900	...	...
		1985/86	...	...	...	30 100	...	...
		1990/91	...	...	...	32 400	...	...
		1992/93	...	...	...	30 938	...	...
		1993/94	...	...	...	29 507	...	...
	Distance-learning insts.	1980/81	...	...	...	13 300	...	...
		1985/86	...	...	...	13 800	...	...
		1990/91	...	...	...	13 600	...	...
		1992/93	...	...	...	10 200	...	...
		1993/94	...	...	...	8 400	...	...
Lithuania‡	All institutions	1980/81	11 984	...	...	70 995	38 726	55
		1985/86	10 324	...	...	93 235	59 973	64
		1990/91	11 443	...	...	88 668	...	...
		1992/93	10 914	...	...	72 148	41 339	57
		1993/94	11 366	5 305	47	70 460	41 043	58
		1994/95	11 799	5 476	46	70 863	41 258	58
	Universities and equiv. insts.	1985/86	...	...	...	65 274	40 592	62
		1990/91	...	...	...	67 312	...	...
		1992/93	...	...	...	55 138	29 260	53
		1993/94	8 162	3 136	38	52 840	29 169	55
		1994/95	8 446	3 204	38	51 482	28 139	55
	Other third level insts.	1985/86	...	...	...	27 961	19 381	69
		1990/91	...	...	...	21 356	...	...
		1992/93	...	...	...	17 010	12 070	71
		1993/94	3 204	2 169	68	17 620	11 874	67
		1994/95	3 353	2 272	68	19 381	13 119	68
Luxembourg‡	All institutions	1980/81	250	...	...	748	264	35
		1985/86	366	41	11	759	261	34
	Other third level insts.	1980/81	250	...	...	748	264	35
		1985/86	366	41	11	759	261	34
Malta	All institutions	1980/81	129	7	5	947	231	24
		1985/86	156	9	6	1 474	482	33
		1990/91	252	27	11	3 123	1 371	44
		1991/92	320	46	14	3 602	1 685	47
		1992/93	330	46	14	4 662	2 243	48
		1993/94	381	50	13	5 177	2 525	49
	Universities and equiv. insts.	1980/81	129	7	5	947	231	24
		1985/86	156	9	6	1 474	482	33
		1990/91	252	27	11	3 123	1 371	44
		1991/92	320	46	14	3 602	1 685	47
		1992/93	330	46	14	4 662	2 243	48
		1993/94	381	50	13	5 177	2 525	49
Moldova	All institutions	1980/81	...	...	...	110 200	...	...
		1985/86	...	...	...	113 800	...	...
		1990/91	...	...	...	104 800	...	...
		1993/94	...	...	...	...	...	...
		1994/95	9 418	3 552	38	100 833	54 003	54
	Universities and equiv. insts.	1980/81	...	...	...	51 300	...	...
		1985/86	...	...	...	53 200	...	...
		1990/91	...	...	...	54 700	...	...
		1993/94	...	...	...	47 506	...	...
		1994/95	4 895	1 870	38	56 969	30 931	54
	Other third level insts.	1980/81	...	...	...	58 900	...	...
		1985/86	...	...	...	60 600	...	...
		1990/91	...	...	...	50 100	...	...
		1994/95	4 523	1 682	37	43 864	23 072	53
Netherlands	All institutions	1980/81	...	...	...	360 033	143 083	40
		1985/86	...	...	...	404 866	165 993	41
		1990/91	...	...	...	478 869	212 425	44
		1991/92	41 217	10 654	26	493 563	224 205	45
		1992/93	40 288	10 446	26	506 580	233 027	46
		1993/94	48 629	11 690	24	512 403	236 866	46
	Universities and equiv. insts.	1980/81	...	...	...	149 524	46 227	31
		1985/86	...	...	...	168 858	62 051	37
		1990/91	...	...	...	190 448	78 994	41
		1991/92	21 310	4 575	21	198 442	85 096	43
		1992/93	20 355	4 251	21	205 595	89 919	44
		1993/94	28 225	5 362	19	187 958	84 649	45

Third level: teachers and students
Troisième degré: professeurs et étudiants
Tercer grado: profesores y estudiantes 3.10

Country / Pays / País	Type of institution / Type d'établissement / Tipo de establecimiento	Year / Année / Año	Teaching staff Personnel enseignant Personal docente			Students enrolled Étudiants inscrits Estudiantes matriculados		
			Total	Female Féminin Femenino	% F	Total	Female Féminin Femenino	% F
			(1)	(2)	(3)	(4)	(5)	(6)
Netherlands (cont)	Distance-learning insts.	1980/81	-	-	-	-	-	-
		1985/86	...	...	...	14 546	5 172	36
		1990/91				36 075	13 881	38
		1991/92	869	359	41	35 256	13 570	38
		1992/93	914	384	42	35 536	13 504	38
		1993/94	444	103	23	54 900	21 000	38
	Other third level insts.	1980/81	...	...	...	210 509	96 856	46
		1985/86	15 082	4 188	28	221 462	98 770	45
		1990/91	...	...		252 346	119 550	47
		1991/92	19 038	5 720	30	259 865	125 539	48
		1992/93	19 019	5 811	31	265 449	129 604	49
		1993/94	19 960	6 225	31	269 545	131 217	49
Norway	All institutions	1980/81	7 763	1 490	19	79 117	37 831	48
		1985/86	8 898	2 278	26	94 658	49 233	52
		1990/91	9 504	3 702	39	142 521	75 542	53
		1991/92	...	...	...	154 180	82 211	53
		1992/93	...	...	...	166 499	89 114	54
		1993/94	8 085	2 290	28	176 722	95 030	54
	Universities and equiv. insts.	1980/81	3 903	511	13	40 620	16 642	41
		1985/86	4 265	716	17	41 658	19 533	47
		1990/91	4 516	951	21	63 307	32 853	52
		1991/92	...	...	...	68 249	35 575	52
		1992/93	...	...	...	73 778	38 662	52
		1993/94	4 491	970	22	77 951	40 807	52
	Other third level insts.	1980/81	3 860	979	25	38 497	21 189	55
		1985/86	4 630	1 562	34	*53 000	*29 700	*56
		1990/91	4 988	2 751	55	79 214	42 689	54
		1991/92	...	...	...	85 931	46 636	54
		1992/93	...	...	...	92 721	50 452	54
		1993/94	3 594	1 320	37	98 771	54 223	55
Poland	All institutions	1980/81	...	...	...	589 134	328 416	56
		1985/86	...	...	...	454 190	252 937	56
		1990/91	...	...	...	544 893	305 279	56
		1991/92	...	...	...	549 308	310 534	57
		1992/93	...	...	...	616 400	347 959	56
		1993/94	...	...	...	747 638	424 107	57
	Universities and equiv. insts.	1980/81	57 083	19 726	35	453 652	226 658	50
		1985/86	57 280	20 113	35	359 245	181 310	50
		1990/91	61 463	...	...	436 608	222 073	51
		1991/92	60 528	...	...	448 448	231 444	52
		1992/93	60 783	22 865	38	520 550	273 624	53
		1993/94	65 558	24 237	37	635 777	341 525	54
	Other third level insts.	1980/81	...	...	...	135 482	101 758	75
		1985/86	...	...	...	94 945	71 627	75
		1990/91	...	...	...	108 285	83 206	77
		1991/92	...	...	...	100 860	79 090	78
		1992/93	...	...	...	95 850	74 335	78
		1993/94	...	...	...	110 861	82 582	74
Portugal‡	All institutions	1980/81	10 695	3 364	31	92 152	44 549	48
		1985/86	12 476	4 585	37	103 585	55 599	54
		1990/91	14 432	...	...	185 762	103 475	56
		1991/92	...	...	...	190 856	115 443	60
		1992/93	...	...	...	247 523	...	...
		1993/94	...	...	...	276 263		
	Universities and equiv. insts.	1980/81	6 906	2 038	30	67 652	32 269	48
		1985/86	7 614	2 431	32	70 244	36 732	52
		1990/91	11 239	...	...	128 468	71 772	56
		1991/92	...	...	...	150 510	91 679	61
		1992/93	22 078	...	...	245 599	121 789	50
		1993/94	22 442	...	...	273 118	...	...
	Distance-learning insts.	1980/81	-	-	-	-	-	-
		1985/86	-	-	-	-	-	-
		1990/91	63	...	...	330	276	84
		1991/92	...	...	...	./.	./.	./.
		1992/93	...	...	...	1 924	...	...
		1993/94	...	...	...	3 145	...	...
	Other third level insts.	1980/81	3 789	1 326	35	24 500	12 280	50
		1985/86	4 862	2 154	44	33 341	18 867	57
		1990/91	3 130	...	...	56 964	31 427	55
		1991/92	...	...	...	40 346	23 764	59
		1992/93	...	...	...	-	-	-
		1993/94	...	...	...	-	-	-

3.10 Third level: teachers and students
Troisième degré: professeurs et étudiants
Tercer grado: profesores y estudiantes

Country Pays País	Type of institution Type d'établissement Tipo de establecimiento	Year Année Año	Teaching staff Personnel enseignant Personal docente			Students enrolled Étudiants inscrits Estudiantes matriculados		
			Total	Female Féminin Femenino	% F	Total	Female Féminin Femenino	% F
			(1)	(2)	(3)	(4)	(5)	(6)
Romania	All institutions	1980/81	14 592	4 364	30	192 769	82 113	43
		1985/86	12 961	3 750	29	159 798	71 658	45
		1989/90	11 696	...	...	164 507	...	...
		1992/93	18 123	5 359	30	235 669	110 035	47
		1993/94	19 130	5 894	31	250 087	116 511	47
	Universities and equiv. insts.	1980/81	14 592	4 364	30	192 769	82 113	43
		1985/86	12 961	3 750	29	159 798	71 658	45
		1989/90	11 696	...	...	164 507	...	...
		1992/93	18 123	5 359	30	235 669	110 035	47
		1993/94	19 130	5 894	31	250 087	116 511	47
Russian Federation‡	All institutions	1980/81	...	...	...	5 700 000	3 200 000	56
		1985/86	...	...	...	5 400 000	3 100 000	57
		1990/91	...	...	...	5 100 000	2 800 000	55
		1992/93	...	...	...	4 692 000	2 600 000	55
		1993/94	363 508	...	...	4 587 045	2 505 048	55
		1994/95	382 897	...	...	4 458 363	2 489 458	56
	Universities and equiv. insts.	1992/93	247 000	...	...	...	...	...
		1993/94	247 218	...	...	2 593 218	1 333 927	51
		1994/95	270 400	...	...	2 587 510	1 362 222	53
	Distance-learning insts.	1992/93	./.	...	...	...	...	...
		1993/94	./.	...	...	./.	./.	...
		1994/95	./.	...	...	./.	./.	...
	Other third level insts.	1993/94	116 290	...	...	1 993 827	1 171 121	59
		1994/95	112 497	...	...	1 870 853	1 127 236	60
Slovakia	All institutions	1992/93	...	...	...	66 002	31 782	48
		1993/94	...	...	...	72 726	35 450	49
		1994/95	...	...	...	82 223	40 344	49
	Universities and equiv. insts.	1992/93	9 351	3 100	33	65 759	31 629	48
		1993/94	8 392	2 873	34	71 916	34 979	49
		1994/95	8 760	2 967	34	80 360	39 060	49
	Other third level insts.	1992/93	...	...	...	243	153	63
		1993/94	...	...	...	810	471	58
		1994/95	...	...	...	1 863	1 284	69
Slovenia‡	All institutions	1991/92	2 609	609	23	38 388	20 257	53
		1992/93	2 783	703	25	39 264	21 338	54
		1993/94	3 172	819	26	40 239	22 318	55
		1994/95	3 229	843	26	43 249	24 346	56
	Universities and equiv. insts.	1991/92	2 609	609	23	38 388	20 257	53
		1992/93	2 783	703	25	39 264	21 338	54
		1993/94	3 172	819	26	40 239	22 318	55
		1994/95	3 229	843	26	43 249	24 346	56
Spain	All institutions	1980/81	42 831	8 997	21	697 789	304 838	44
		1985/86	47 504	12 552	26	935 126	459 105	49
		1990/91	65 736	19 318	29	1 222 089	623 868	51
		1991/92	70 410	21 630	31	1 301 748	667 143	51
		1992/93	73 412	22 144	30	1 370 689	708 791	52
		1993/94	80 642	25 716	32	1 469 468	749 509	51
	Universities and equiv. insts.	1980/81	42 260	8 775	21	690 801	300 204	43
		1985/86	46 740	12 258	26	882 798	437 604	50
		1990/91	64 820	18 958	29	1 129 815	582 416	52
		1991/92	69 431	21 301	31	1 206 681	624 592	52
		1992/93	72 325	21 782	30	1 263 507	662 004	52
	Distance-learning insts.	1980/81	./.	./.	./.	./.	./.	./.
		1985/86	510	185	36	48 891	19 438	40
		1990/91	821	332	40	87 032	38 802	45
		1991/92	776	306	39	86 120	38 175	44
		1992/93	854	341	40	92 821	39 742	43
	Other third level insts.	1980/81	571	222	39	6 988	4 634	66
		1985/86	254	109	43	3 437	2 063	60
		1990/91	95	28	29	5 242	2 650	51
		1991/92	203	23	11	8 947	4 376	49
		1992/93	233	21	9	14 361	7 045	49
Sweden	All institutions	1980/81	...	...	...	171 356	...	...
		1985/86	...	...	...	176 589	92 141	52
		1990/91	...	...	...	192 611	103 552	54
		1991/92	...	...	...	207 265	111 888	54
		1992/93	...	...	...	226 830	121 713	54
		1993/94	...	...	...	234 466	127 873	55

Third level: teachers and students 3.10
Troisième degré: professeurs et étudiants
Tercer grado: profesores y estudiantes

Country / Pays / País	Type of institution / Type d'établissement / Tipo de establecimiento	Year / Année / Año	Teaching staff Personnel enseignant Personal docente			Students enrolled Étudiants inscrits Estudiantes matriculados		
			Total	Female Féminin Femenino	% F	Total	Female Féminin Femenino	% F
			(1)	(2)	(3)	(4)	(5)	(6)
Switzerland	All institutions	1980/81	...	...	...	85 127	25 766	30
		1985/86	...	...	...	110 111	35 373	32
		1990/91	...	...	...	137 486	47 647	35
		1991/92	...	...	...	143 067	50 293	35
		1992/93	...	...	...	146 266	52 575	36
		1993/94	...	...	...	148 664	54 571	37
	Universities and equiv. insts.	1980/81	5 942	457	8	61 374	19 915	32
		1985/86	6 236	...	...	74 806	26 774	36
		1990/91	7 331	835	11	85 924	33 371	39
		1991/92	7 344	851	12	89 031	35 201	40
		1992/93	7 515	928	12	90 741	36 377	40
		1993/94	7 502	966	13	91 037	37 012	41
	Other third level insts.	1980/81	...	...	...	23 753	5 851	25
		1985/86	...	...	...	35 305	8 599	24
		1990/91	...	...	...	51 562	14 276	28
		1991/92	...	...	...	54 036	15 092	28
		1992/93	...	...	...	55 525	16 198	29
		1993/94	...	...	...	57 627	17 559	30
The Former Yugoslav Rep. of Macedonia‡	All institutions	1980/81	...	...	...	46 281	...	...
		1985/86	...	...	...	38 065	...	...
		1990/91	2 117	...	...	26 515	13 678	52
		1992/93	2 273	811	36	26 405	13 649	52
		1993/94	2 320	850	37	27 340	14 434	53
		1994/95	2 407	909	38	29 057	15 692	54
	Universities and equiv. insts.	1992/93	...	...	...	23 764	12 023	51
		1993/94	2 204	832	38	24 257	12 689	52
		1994/95	...	...	...	25 610	13 591	53
	Other third level insts.	1992/93	...	...	...	2 641	1 626	62
		1993/94	116	18	16	3 083	1 745	57
		1994/95	...	...	...	3 447	2 101	61
Ukraine‡	All institutions	1980/81	...	...	...	880 400	...	...
		1985/86	...	...	...	853 100	...	...
		1990/91	72 300	...	...	894 700	443 200	50
		1991/92	75 900	...	...	890 192	441 000	50
United Kingdom	All institutions	1980/81	...	...	...	827 146	302 972	37
		1985/86	79 621	12 062	15	1 032 491	469 948	46
		1990/91	86 200	18 000	21	1 258 188	607 040	48
		1991/92	89 500	17 900	20	1 385 072	675 345	49
		1992/93	92 067	19 275	21	1 528 389	757 937	50
		1993/94	97 274	20 823	21	1 614 652	816 113	51
	Universities and equiv. insts.	1980/81	34 297	6 107	18	339 925	126 438	37
		1985/86	31 412	3 666	12	352 419	141 215	40
		1990/91	36 500	7 100	19	428 858	188 062	44
		1991/92	37 200	5 900	16	468 095	208 074	44
		1992/93	37 969	6 339	17	511 123	232 347	45
	Distance-learning insts.	1980/81	5 633	1 421	25	67 740	30 001	44
		1985/86	5 723	1 538	27	78 723	36 464	46
		1990/91	6 900	2 200	32	94 953	45 627	48
		1991/92	7 400	2 500	34	99 255	48 047	48
		1992/93	7 724	2 677	35	104 772	51 667	49
	Other third level insts.	1980/81	...	...	...	419 481	146 533	35
		1985/86	42 484	6 858	16	601 349	292 269	49
		1990/91	42 800	8 700	20	734 377	373 351	51
		1991/92	44 900	9 500	21	817 722	419 224	51
		1992/93	46 374	10 259	22	912 494	473 923	52
Former Yugoslavia‡	All institutions	1980/81	24 449	5 785	24	411 995	186 991	45
		1985/86	25 862	6 784	26	350 334	160 494	46
		1990/91	27 042	8 060	30	327 092	165 273	51
	Universities and equiv. insts.	1980/81	19 981	4 799	24	310 650	142 517	46
		1985/86	22 204	5 943	27	287 907	132 421	46
		1990/91	24 150	7 363	30	285 094	143 166	50
	Other third level insts.	1980/81	4 468	986	22	101 345	44 474	44
		1985/86	3 658	841	23	62 427	28 073	45
		1990/91	2 892	697	24	41 998	22 107	53
Federal Rep. of Yugoslavia‡	All institutions	1991/92	11 647	3 538	30	133 331	69 807	52
		1992/93	11 605	3 643	31	143 268	76 177	53
		1994/95	11 831	3 884	33	143 951	77 851	54

3.10 Third level: teachers and students
Troisième degré: professeurs et étudiants
Tercer grado: profesores y estudiantes

Country Pays País	Type of institution Type d'établissement Tipo de establecimiento	Year Année Año	Teaching staff Personnel enseignant Personal docente			Students enrolled Étudiants inscrits Estudiantes matriculados		
			Total	Female Féminin Femenino	% F	Total	Female Féminin Femenino	% F
			(1)	(2)	(3)	(4)	(5)	(6)
Federal Rep. of Yugoslavia‡ (cont)	Universities and equiv. insts.	1991/92	9 617	3 017	31	106 361	55 670	52
		1992/93	9 695	3 156	33	116 413	62 485	54
		1994/95	10 125	3 365	33	118 566	65 280	55
	Distance-learning insts.	1991/92	-	-	-	-	-	-
		1992/93	-	-	-	-	-	-
		1994/95	-	-	-	-	-	-
	Other third level insts.	1991/92	2 030	521	26	26 970	14 137	52
		1992/93	1 910	487	25	26 855	13 692	51
		1994/95	1 706	519	30	25 385	12 571	50
Oceania								
American Samoa	All institutions	1980/81	...	...	...	976	551	56
		1985/86	...	...	...	758	392	52
		1986/87	...	...	...	900	476	53
	Other third level insts.	1980/81	...	...	...	976	551	56
		1985/86	...	...	...	758	392	52
		1986/87	...	...	...	900	476	53
Australia‡	All institutions	1980	22 134	...	...	323 716	146 676	45
		1985	22 659	5 114	23	370 048	176 178	48
		1990	27 824	9 203	33	485 075	255 655	53
		1992	27 442	8 626	31	559 365	298 812	53
		1993	...	...	...	964 159	466 760	48
		1994	...	...	...	932 969	460 307	49
	Universities and equiv. insts.	1980	22 134	...	...	323 716	146 676	45
		1985	22 659	5 114	23	370 048	176 178	48
		1990	27 824	9 203	33	485 075	255 655	53
		1992	27 442	8 626	31	559 365	298 812	53
		1993	27 780	8 876	32	575 617	307 631	53
		1994	26 555	8 548	32	559 682	300 870	54
	Other third level insts.	1980	-	-	-	-	-	-
		1985	-	-	-	-	-	-
		1990	-	-	-	-	-	-
		1992	-	-	-	-	-	-
		1993	...	...	...	388 542	159 129	41
		1994	...	...	...	373 287	159 437	43
Fiji	All institutions	1980	...	...	...	1 666	...	...
		1985	249	44	18	2 313	875	38
		1989	326	...	...	3 509	...	...
		1991	277	92	33	7 908	...	...
	Universities and equiv. insts.	1980	...	...	...	1 391	...	...
		1985	148	25	17	1 932	710	37
		1989	265	...	...	2 711	...	...
		1991	213	53	25	3 621	...	...
	Distance-learning insts.	1991	4	1	25	3 426	...	...
	Other third level insts.	1980	...	...	...	275	102	37
		1985	101	19	19	381	165	43
		1989	61	35	57	798	...	...
		1991	60	38	63	861	619	72
French Polynesia	All institutions	1980/81	14	1	7	27	7	26
		1991/92	...	...	...	301	150	50
	Other third level insts.	1980/81	14	1	7	27	7	26
		1991/92	...	...	...	301	150	50
Guam	All institutions	1980/81	...	...	...	3 217	1 768	55
		1986/87	257	106	41	7 052	3 754	53
		1988/89	...	...	...	...		...
	Universities and equiv. insts.	1980/81	...	...	...	3 217	1 768	55
		1986/87	174	67	39	5 235	2 982	57
		1988/89	202	69	34	4 257	2 529	59
	Other third level insts.	1986/87	83	39	47	1 817	772	42
New Caledonia	All institutions	1980	97	47	48	438	169	39
		1985	63	...	...	761	336	44
	Other third level insts.	1980	97	47	48	438	169	39
		1985	63	...	...	761	336	44

Third level: teachers and students 3.10
Troisième degré: professeurs et étudiants
Tercer grado: profesores y estudiantes

Country / Pays / País	Type of institution / Type d'établissement / Tipo de establecimiento	Year / Année / Año	Teaching staff Personnel enseignant Personal docente			Students enrolled Étudiants inscrits Estudiantes matriculados		
			Total	Female Féminin Femenino	% F	Total	Female Féminin Femenino	% F
			(1)	(2)	(3)	(4)	(5)	(6)
New Zealand‡	All institutions	1980	7 694	1 377	18	76 643	31 101	41
		1985	8 300	2 014	24	95 793	43 797	46
		1990	11 302	3 794	34	111 504	57 804	52
		1992	12 096	4 870	40	146 215	78 639	54
		1993	12 427	5 214	42	162 932	88 356	54
		1994	...	...	...	169 421	93 725	55
	Universities and equiv. insts.	1980	4 780	647	14	43 933	18 379	42
		1985	5 226	1 062	20	47 799	22 135	46
		1990	6 651	1 840	28	65 606	32 589	50
		1992	4 521	1 172	26	93 113	48 639	52
		1993	4 740	1 277	27	105 555	55 611	53
	Distance-learning insts.	1980	./.	./.	./.	./.	./.	./.
		1985	./.	./.	./.	11 324	7 017	62
		1990	./.	./.	./.	13 312	7 924	60
		1992	./.	./.	./.	./.	./.	./.
		1993	./.	./.	./.	./.	./.	./.
	Other third level insts.	1980	2 914	730	25	32 710	12 722	39
		1985	3 074	952	31	36 670	14 645	40
		1990	4 651	1 954	42	32 586	17 291	53
		1992	7 575	3 698	49	53 102	30 000	56
		1993	7 687	3 937	51	57 377	32 745	57
Papua New Guinea	All institutions	1980	*638	...	...	*5 040	*1 112	*22
		1985	5 068	...	...	5 068	1 174	23
		1995	...	...	...	13 663	4 353	32
	Universities and equiv. insts.	1980	473	...	...	2 872	305	11
		1985	...	...	...	3 181	515	16
		1995	517	...	...	4 669	1 156	25
	Distance-learning insts.	1995	...	...	...	4 210	1 149	27
	Other third level insts.	1980	*165	...	...	*2 168	*807	*37
		1985	...	...	...	1 887	659	35
		1995	442	...	...	4 784	2 048	43
Tonga	All institutions	1980	...	...	...	...	...	...
		1985	...	...	...	705	397	56
	Universities and equiv. insts.	1985	17	3	18	85	19	22
	Other third level insts.	1980	36	14	39	371	180	49
		1985	...	...	...	620	378	61

The data in this table refer to teaching staff and students enrolled in all institutions, both public and private, at the third level of education. For most countries and territories data are shown separately by type of institution: (a) universities and equivalent degree-granting institutions; (b) distance-learning university institutions; (c) other third level educational institutions - these include all other education at the third level in non-university institutions (teacher training colleges, technical colleges, etc.).

Collection of separate information on distance-learning university institutions was initiated by UNESCO in the academic year 1985/86. The programmes included here are only those which lead to recognized third level degrees. Consequently those which cannot be assimilated to programmes of the regular system are excluded.

It should be noted, however, that the criteria applied for determining the three types of institutions may not be exactly the same in each of the countries and territories covered. Moreover, following reforms in the educational system, some non-university institutions in a given country may be attached to universities or recognized as equivalent institutions from one year to the next. The breakdown by type of institution must therefore be used with caution.

As far as possible, the figures include both full-time and part-time teachers and students. Figures referring to teaching staff include, in principle, auxiliary teachers (assistants, demonstrators, etc.) but exclude staff with no teaching duties (administrators, laboratory technicians, etc.).

Ces données se rapportent au personnel enseignant et aux étudiants inscrits dans tous les établissements, publics et privés, d'enseignement du troisième degré. Pour la plupart des pays et territoires, les données sont présentées séparément par type d'établissement: (a) universités et établissements conférant des grades équivalents; (b) établissements universitaires d'enseignement à distance; (c) autres établissements du troisième degré: ceux-ci incluent l'ensemble des autres formes d'enseignement du troisième degré dispensées dans des établissements non-universitaires (écoles normales supérieures, écoles techniques supérieures, etc.).

A partir de l'année académique 1985/86, l'UNESCO a commencé à recueillir séparément les informations sur les établissements universitaires d'enseignement à distance. Les programmes ici inclus sont uniquement ceux qui conduisent à des diplômes universitaires reconnus. Par conséquent, les programmes universitaires d'enseignement à distance qui ne peuvent pas être assimilés aux programmes du système ordinaire sont exclus.

Il faut cependant souligner que le critère appliqué pour déterminer les trois types d'établissements peut ne pas être exactement le même dans chacun des pays et territoires concernés. De plus, il se peut

3.10 Third level: teachers and students
Troisième degré: professeurs et étudiants
Tercer grado: profesores y estudiantes

que dans un même pays, à la suite des réformes du système d'enseignement, plusieurs établissements non universitaires soient, d'une année à l'autre, rattachés aux universités ou considérés comme des établissements équivalents. C'est pourquoi cette répartition par type d'établissement doit être utilisée avec précaution.

Dans la mesure du possible, ces statistiques couvrent aussi bien les professeurs et étudiants à plein temps que ceux à temps partiel. Les chiffres relatifs au personnel enseignant incluent en principe le personnel auxiliaire (assistants, chefs de travaux, etc.) mais non le personnel qui n'exerce pas de fonctions d'enseignement (administrateurs, techniciens de laboratoire, etc.).

Estos datos se refieren al personal docente y a los estudiantes inscritos en todos los establecimientos, públicos y privados, de la enseñanza de tercer grado. Para la mayoría de los países y territorios, los datos se presentan por separado, por tipo de establecimiento: (a) universidades e instituciones que conceden títulos equivalentes; (b) instituciones universitarias de enseñanza a distancia; (c) todas las otras modalidades de enseñanza de tercer grado, dispensada en instituciones no universitarias (escuelas normales superiores, escuelas técnicas superiores, etc.)

La colecta por separado de estadísticas sobre los establecimientos universitarios de enseñanza a distancia fue iniciada por la UNESCO en el año académico 1985/86. Se incluyen aquí únicamente los programas que conducen a títulos universitarios reconocidos. Por consiguiente, aquellos programas universitarios de enseñanza a distancia que no pueden ser asimilados a los programas del sistema ordinario están excluidos.

Procede señalar, sin embargo, que los criterios aplicados para determinar los tres tipos de establecimientos pueden no ser exactamente los mismos en cada uno de los países y territorios. Además, es posible que, en un mismo país, debido a una reforma del sistema de enseñanza, ciertos establecimientos no universitarios queden, de un año para el otro, adscritos a las universidades o considerados como establecimientos docentes equivalentes. Por todo ello, convendría utilizar con precaución esta distribución por tipo de establecimientos de enseñanza.

En la medida de lo posible, estas estadísticas abarcan a la vez a los profesores y estudiantes de jornada completa y de jornada parcial. Las cifras relativas al personal docente comprenden, en principio, el personal auxiliar (adjuntos, encargados de prácticas, etc.) pero no el personal que no ejerce funciones docentes (administradores, técnicos de laboratorio, etc.).

AFRICA:
Algeria:
E--> For 1980/81 and 1985/86, data on students refer only to institutions under the authority of the Ministry of Education. Those relating to female students in 1985/86 exclude post-graduates.

FR-> Pour 1980/81 et 1985/86, les données sur les étudiants se rapportent aux institutions sous la tutelle du Ministère de l'Education seulement. Celles relatives aux étudiantes en 1985/86 excluent le niveau universitaire supérieur.

ESP> Para 1980/81 y 1985/86, los datos relativos a los estudiantes se refieren solamente a las instituciones bajo la tutela del Ministerio de Educación. Los datos relativos a las estudiantes en 1985/86 excluyen el nivel post-universitario.

Botswana:
E--> For 1980/81, data on female students refer to full-time only.

FR-> Pour 1980/81, les données relatives aux étudiantes se rapportent à l'enseignement à plein temps seulement.

ESP> Para 1980/81, los datos relativos a las estudiantes se refieren a la enseñanza de jornada completa solamente.

Cameroon:
E--> For 1980/81, data exclude the *Ecole Nationale d'Administration et de Magistrature.*

FR-> Pour 1980/81, les données excluent l'Ecole Nationale d'Administration et de Magistrature.

ESP> Para 1980/81, los datos excluyen la *Ecole Nationale d'Administration et de Magistrature.*

Central African Republic:
E--> For 1991/92, data on teaching staff in universities and equivalent degree-granting institutions refer to full-time only.

FR-> Pour 1991/92, les données relatives au personnel enseignant dans les universités et les établissements conférant des grades équivalents se réfèrent au plein temps seulement.

ESP> Para 1991/92, los datos relativos al personal docente de las universidades e instituciones que otorgan títulos equivalentes se refieren a la jornada completa solamente.

Chad:
E--> For 1988/89, data do not include the University of Law which had 751 students in 1986/87, of which 44 were female.

FR-> Pour 1988/89 les donnnées ne comprennent pas l'Université des Sciences juridiques qui comptait en 1986/87, 751 étudiants dont 44 de sexe féminin.

ESP> Para 1988/89, los datos excluyen la Universidad de Derecho 751 estudiantes (F44) en 1986/87).

Congo:
E--> For 1992/93, data on teaching staff refer to full-time only.

FR-> Pour 1992/93, les données relatives au personnel enseignant se réfèrent à l'enseignement à plein temps seulement.

ESP> Para 1992/93, los datos relativos al personal docente se refieren a la enseñanza de jornada completa solamente.

Egypt:
E--> Data for female students in 1985/86 and all data from 1990/91 do not include private institutions. All data on teachers, and data on students from 1991/92 exclude Al Azhar university.

FR-> Les données relatives aux étudiantes en 1985/86, et toutes les données à partir de 1990/91 ne comprennent pas les institutions privées. Toutes les données relatives au personnel enseignant et à partir de 1991/92 celles relatives aux étudiants excluent l'université Al Azhar.

ESP> Los datos relativos a las estudiantes en 1985/86, y todos los datos a partir de 1990/91 no incluyen las instituciones privadas.

Todos los datos relativos al personal docente, y a partir de 1991/92, los relativos a los estudiantes no incluyen la universidad de Al Azhar.

Ethiopia:
E--> Data for 1991/92 do not include Asmara University and Kotebe college.

FR-> Les données pour 1991/92 ne comprennent pas l'Université d'Asmara et le collège Kotebe.

ESP> Los datos de 1991/92 no incluyen la Universidad de Asmara y el colegio Kotebe.

Morocco:
E--> For 1980/81 and 1985/86, data on female teachers refer to universities only. For 1990/91 and 1994/95, data on technical education provided in other third level institutions are incomplete.

FR-> Pour 1980/81 et 1985/86, les données sur le personnel enseignant feminin se réfèrent aux universités seulement. En 1990/91 et 1994/95, les données relatives à l'enseignement technique dispensé dans les autres établissements du troisième degré sont incomplètes.

ESP> Para 1980/81 y 1985/86, los datos relativos al personal docente femenino se refieren a las universidades solamente. En 1990/91 y 1994/95, los datos sobre la enseñanza técnica impartida en los otros establecimientos de tercer grado son incompletos.

Nigeria:
E--> For 1989/90 data on students in other third level institutions refer to teacher training only.

FR-> Pour 1989/90, les données relatives aux étudiants dans les autres établissements du troisième degré se réfèrent à l'enseignement normal seulement.

ESP> Para 1989/90, los datos relativos a los estudiantes de los otros establecimientos de tercer grado se refieren a la enseñanza normal solamente.

South Africa:
E--> From 1989 to 1993 data exclude the former Independant States (Transkei, Bophuthatswana, Venda and Ciskei). From 1990 data include distance learning institutions.

FR-> De 1989 à 1993 les données excluent les anciens Etats indépendants (Transkei, Bophuthatswana, Venda et Ciskei). A partir de 1990, les données incluent les établissements d'enseignement à distance.

ESP> De 1989 a 1993, los datos excluyen los antiguos Estados independientes (Transkei, Bophuthatswana, Venda y Ciskei). A partir de 1990, los datos incluyen los establecimientos de enseñanza a distancia.

Swaziland:
E--> From 1980/81, data on students include nationals studying abroad. For 1992/93 and 1993/94, data on other third level institutions do not include students of medical science and health-related.

FR-> Pour 1980/81, les données relatives aux étudiants incluent les étudiants à l'étranger. Pour 1992/93 et 1993/94, les données sur les autres établissements du troisième degré n'incluent pas les étudiants des sciences médicales de la santé et de l'hygiène.

ESP> Para 1980/81, los datos relativos a los estudiantes incluyen los estudiantes en el extranjero. Para 1992/93 y 1993/94, los datos relativos a los otros establecimientos de tercer grado no incluyen los estudiantes de las ciencias medicas, de sanidad e higiene.

Tunisia:
E--> Since 1990/91, data on teaching staff refer to full-time only.

Third level: teachers and students **3.10**
Troisième degré: professeurs et étudiants
Tercer grado: profesores y estudiantes

FR-> A partir de 1990/91, les données se réfèrent au personnel enseignant à plein temps seulement.

ESP> A partir de 1990/91, los datos se refieren al personal docente de jornada completa solamente.

United Republic of Tanzania:

E--> Data on students in 1985/86 and 1986/87 refer to full-time only and exclude post-graduate level.

FR-> Les données relatives aux étudiants en 1985/86 et 1986/87 se réfèrent au plein temps seulement et excluent le niveau universitaire supérieur.

ESP> Los datos relativos a los estudiantes en 1985/86 y 1986/87 se refieren a la jornada completa solamente y excluyen el nivel post-universitario.

Zaire:

E--> For 1980/81 and 1985/86, data on other third level institutions include evening courses.

FR-> Pour 1980/81 et 1985/86, les données des autres établissements du troisième degré incluent les cours du soir.

ESP> Para 1980/81 y 1985/86, los datos de los otros establecimientos de tercer grado incluyen los cursos nocturnos.

Zimbabwe:

E--> Female students in 1980 and all data in 1985 for other third level institutions refer to teacher training only.

FR-> Les étudiantes en 1980 et les données pour 1985 relatives aux autres établissements du troisième degré se réfèrent à l'enseignement normal seulement.

ESP> Las estudiantes en 1980 y los datos de 1985 relativos a los otros establecimientos de tercer grado sólo se refieren a la enseñanza normal.

AMERICA, NORTH:

Canada:

E--> Data on teaching staff refer to full-time only. Those relating to enrolment in 1980/81 and female enrolment in 1985/86 do not include trade and vocational programmes.

FR-> Les données relatives au personnel enseignant se réfèrent au plein temps seulement. Celles concernant les étudiants en 1980/81 et les étudiants en 1985/86 ne comprennent pas les programmes d'enseignement technique et commercial.

ESP> Los datos relativos al personal docente se refieren a la jornada completa solamente. Los datos relativos a los estudiantes en 1980/81 y a las estudiantes en 1985/86 no incluyen los programas de enseñanza técnica y comercial.

Costa Rica:

E--> Data refer only to institutions recognized by the National Council for Higher Education.

FR-> Les données se réfèrent seulement aux institutions reconnues par le Conseil National pour l'Education supérieure.

ESP> Los datos se refieren solamente a las instituciones reconocidas por el Consejo Nacional para la Educación Superior.

Dominica:

E--> From 1990/91, data do not include teacher training.

FR-> A partir de 1990/91, les données n'incluent pas l'enseignement normal.

ESP> A partir de 1990/91, los datos no incluyen la enseñanza normal.

El Salvador:

E--> For 1980, data exclude *la Universidad Nacional de El Salvador*.

FR-> Pour 1980, les données excluent *la Universidad Nacional de El Salvador*.

ESP> Para 1980, los datos excluyen *la Universidad Nacional de El Salvador*.

Guatemala:

E--> Except for students in 1980, data refer to the University of San Carlos only.

FR-> A l'exception des étudiants en 1980, les données se réfèrent à l'Université de San Carlos seulement.

ESP> Con excepción de los estudiantes en 1980, los datos se refieren a la Universidad de San Carlos solamente.

Nicaragua:

E--> For 1992, data on distance learning institutions are included with universities.

FR-> Pour 1992, les données relatives à l'enseignement à distance sont comprises avec celles des universités.

ESP> Para 1992, los datos relativos a la enseñanza a distancia están incluídos en los de las universidades.

St. Vincent and the Grenadines:

E--> Data for 1985/86 and 1986/87 on teaching staff refer to full-time only.

FR-> Les données pour 1985/86 et 1986/87 relatives au personnel enseignant se réfèrent au plein temps seulement.

ESP> Los datos de 1985/86 y 1986/87 relativos al personal docente se refieren a la jornada completa solamente.

Trinidad and Tobago:

E--> For 1980/81 and 1991/92, data on female students in universities refer to nationals only. For 1991/92 and 1992/93, data do not include teacher training.

FR-> Pour 1980/81 et 1991/92, les données relatives aux étudiantes des universités se réfèrent aux étudiantes nationales seulement. Pour 1991/92 et 1992/93, les données n'incluent pas l'enseignement normal.

ESP> Para 1980/81 y 1991/92, los datos relativos a las estudiantes en las universidades se refieren a la matrícula nacional solamente. Para 1991/92 y 1992/93, los datos no incluyen la enseñanza normal.

United States:

E--> For 1980/81, data on teaching staff refer to full-time only.

FR-> Pour 1980/81, les données relatives au personnel enseignant se réfèrent au plein temps seulement.

ESP> Para 1980/81, los datos relativos al personal docente se refieren a la jornada completa solamente.

AMERICA, SOUTH:

Brazil:

E--> All data on students since 1990 as well as female students in 1980 exclude the post-graduate level.

FR-> Toutes les données relatives aux étudiants depuis 1990, ainsi qu'aux étudiantes en 1980 excluent le niveau universitaire supérieur.

ESP> Todos los datos relativos a los estudiantes desde 1990 y a las estudiantes en 1980 excluyen el nivel post-universitario.

Chile:

E--> For 1992 and 1993, data on teaching staff refer to public universities only.

FR-> Pour 1992 et 1993, les données se réfèrent au personnel enseignant des universités publiques seulement.

ESP> Para 1992 y 1993, los datos se refieren al personal docente de las universidades públicas solamente.

Colombia:

E--> In 1980, data on universities include distance learning institutions.

FR-> En 1980, les données relatives aux universités incluent l'enseignement à distance.

ESP> Para 1980, los datos relativos a las universidades incluyen la enseñanza a distancia.

Paraguay:

E--> In 1993, data on female students do not include 10 private universities.

FR-> In 1993, les données relatives aux étudiantes ne comprennent pas 10 universités privés.

ESP> En 1993, los datos relativos a las estudiantes no incluyen 10 universidades privadas.

ASIA:

Azerbaijan:

E--> Apart from 1985/86 and 1990/91, data on distance-learning institutions are included with universities.

FR-> A l'exception de 1985/86 et 1990/91, les données relatives à l'enseignement à distance sont comprises avec celles des universités.

ESP> Con excepción de 1985/86 y 1990/91, los datos relativos a la enseñanza a distancia están incluídos en los de las universidades.

Cyprus:

E--> Not including Turkish institutions. In 1980/81 and 1985/86, data on teaching staff refer to full-time only.

FR-> Non compris les institutions turques. En 1980/81 et 1985/86, les données relatives au personnel enseignant se réfèrent au plein temps seulement.

ESP> No incluyen los instituciones turcos. En 1980/81 y 1985/86, los datos relativos al personal docente se refieren a la jornada completa solamente.

Hong Kong:

E--> Data on ùother third level institutions in 1980/81 refer to Hong Kong Polytechnic only.

FR-> Les données relatives aux ùautres établissements du troisième degré en 1980/81 se réfèrent à *Hong Kong Polytechnic* seulement.

ESP> Los datos relativos a los ùotros establecimientos de tercer grado en 1980/81 se refieren al *Hong Kong Polytechnic* solamente.

Iran, Islamic Republic of:

E--> Data on universities refer to public universities only.

FR-> Les données sur les universités se réfèrent aux universités publiques seulement.

ESP> Los datos sobre las universidades se refieren a las universidades públicas solamente.

Israel:

E--> Data on other third level institutions in 1980/81 exclude the Jewish studies institutes.

FR-> Les données relatives aux autres établissements du troisième degré en 1980/81 excluent les *Jewish studies institutes*.

ESP> Los datos relativos a los otros establecimientos de tercer grado en 1980/81 excluyen los *Jewish studies institutes*.

Jordan:

E--> Data for 1985/86 on teaching staff refer to full-time only.

3.10 Third level: teachers and students
Troisième degré: professeurs et étudiants
Tercer grado: profesores y estudiantes

FR–> Les données pour 1985/86 relatives au personnel enseignant se réfèrent au plein temps seulement.

ESP> Los datos de 1985/86 relativos al personal docente se refieren a la jornada completa solamente.

Korea, Republic of:

E––> For 1980/81 and 1985/86, data on teaching staff refer to full-time only.

FR–> Pour 1980/81 et 1985/86, les données relatives au personnel enseignant se réfèrent au plein temps seulement.

ESP> Para 1980/81 y 1985/86, los datos relativos al personal docente se refieren a la jornada completa solamente.

Kuwait:

E––> Data in 1991/92, 1992/93, and 1993/94 relating to other third level institutions do not include teacher training.

FR–> Les données pour 1991/92, 1992/93, et 1993/94 relatives aux autres établissements du troisième degré ne comprennent pas l'enseignement normal.

ESP> Los datos para 1991/92, 1992/93 y 1993/94 relativos a los otros establecimientos de tercer grado no incluyen la enseñanza normal.

Lao, People's Democratic Republic:

E––> Data in 1992/93 relating to other third level institutions do not include teacher training.

FR–> Les données en 1992/93 relatives aux autres établissements du troisième degré ne comprennent pas l'enseignement normal.

ESP> Los datos para 1992/93 relativos a los otros establecimientos de tercer grado no incluyen la enseñanza normal.

Malaysia:

E––> In 1990/91, data on female students in other third level institutions do not include a part of vocational education.

FR–> En 1990/91, les données relatives aux étudiantes dans les autres établissements du troisième degré ne comprennent pas une partie de l'enseignement technique.

ESP> En 1990/91, los datos relativos a las estudiantes en los otros establecimientos de tercer grado no incluyen una parte de la enseñanza técnica.

Nepal:

E––> For 1980/81 and 1985/86, data refer to public universities only.

FR–> Pour 1980/81 y 1985/86, les données se réfèrent aux universités publiques seulement.

ESP> Para 1980/81 y 1985/86, los datos se refieren a las universidades públicas solamente.

Pakistan:

E––> Not including data on teaching staff in arts and sciences colleges.

FR–> Non compris les données relatives au personnel enseignant des *arts and sciences colleges*.

ESP> Excluídos los datos relativos al personal docente de los *arts and sciences colleges*.

Sri Lanka:

E––> Data for universities in 1980 and for teaching staff in other third level institutions in 1985 refer to full-time only. Data for 1991 and 1994 do not include part of vocational education.

FR–> Les données relatives aux universités en 1980 et au personnel enseignant dans les autres établissements du troisième degré en 1985 se réfèrent au plein temps seulement. Les données pour 1991 et 1994 ne comprennent pas une partie de l'enseignement technique.

ESP> Los datos relativos a las universidades en 1980 y al personal docente en los otros establecimientos de tercer grado en 1985 se refieren a la jornada completa solamente. Los datos para 1991 y 1994 no incluyen una parte de la enseñanza técnica.

Syrian Arab Republic:

E––> In 1991/92 and 1992/93, data do not include a part of vocational education in other third level institutions.

FR–> En 1991/92 et 1992/93, les données ne comprennent pas une partie de l'enseignement technique dans les autres établissements du troisième degré.

ESP> En 1991/92 y 1992/93, los datos no incluyen una parte de la enseñanza técnica en los otros establecimientos de tercer grado.

Turkey:

E––> Except for 1985/86, data on teaching staff in universities and equivalent degree-granting institutions include distance learning institutions.

FR–> A l'exception de 1985/86, les données relatives au personnel enseignant dans les universités et les établissements conférant des grades équivalents comprennent l'enseignement à distance.

ESP> Con excepción de 1985/86, los datos relativos al personal docente en las universidades e instituciones que otorgan títulos equivalentes incluyen la enseñanza a distancia.

EUROPE:

Albania:

E––> Apart from students in 1993/94, data do not include distance learning institutions.

FR–> A l'exception des étudiants en 1993/94, les données ne comprennent pas l'enseignement à distance.

ESP> Con excepción de los estudiantes en 1993/94, los datos excluyen la enseñanza a distancia.

Austria:

E––> From 1985/86, data on teaching staff in universities refer to full-time only.

FR–> A partir de 1985/86, les données relatives au personnel enseignant dans les universités se réfèrent au plein temps seulement.

ESP> A partir de 1985/86, los datos relativos al personal docente en las universidades se refieren a la jornada completa solamente.

Belarus:

E––> Not including female students enrolled in third level programmes in secondary specialized schools.

FR–> Non compris les étudiantes inscrites aux programmes du troisième cycle dans les écoles secondaires specializées.

ESP> No incluyen las estudiantes matriculadas en los programas de tercer ciclo en las escuelas secundarias especializadas.

Belgium:

E––> For 1980/81, data on students in other third level institutions refer to full-time only.

FR–> Pour 1980/81, les données relatives aux étudiants dans les autres établissements du troisième degré se réfèrent au plein temps seulement.

ESP> Para 1980/81, los datos relativos a los estudiantes en los otros establecimientos de tercer grado se refieren a la jornada completa solamente.

Croatia:

E––> Not including post-graduate students as registration is not required.

FR–> Non compris les étudiants de niveau universitaire supérieur pour lequel l'inscription n'est pas exigée.

ESP> No incluyen los estudiantes del nivel post-universitario porque la inscripción no es exigida.

Estonia:

E––> Not including students enrolled in third level programmes in secondary specialized schools.

FR–> Non compris les étudiants inscrits aux programmes du troisième cycle dans les écoles secondaires specialisées.

ESP> No incluyen los estudiantes matriculados en los programas de tercer ciclo en las escuelas secundarias especializadas.

France:

E––> Data on teaching staff in 1985/86 refer to public universities only.

FR–> Les données relatives au personnel enseignant en 1985/86 se réfèrent aux universités publiques seulement.

ESP> Los datos relativos al personal docente en 1985/86 se refieren a las universidades públicas solamente.

Germany:

E––> Not including post-graduate students as registration is not required.

FR–> Non compris les étudiants de niveau universitaire supérieur pour lequel l'inscription n'est pas exigée.

ESP> No incluyen los estudiantes del nivel post-universitario porque la inscripción no es exigida.

Federal Republic of Germany:

E––> Not including post graduate students as registration is not required.

FR–> Non compris les étudiants de niveau universitaire supérieur pour lequel l'inscription n'est pas exigée.

ESP> No incluyen los estudiantes del nivel post-universitario porque la inscripción no es exigida.

Holy See:

E––> Data refer to teaching staff and students enrolled in higher institutions under the authority of the Holy See.

FR–> Les données se réfèrent aux enseignants et étudiants dans les institutions du troisième degré sous l'autorité du Saint-Siège.

ESP> Los datos se refieren al personal docente y a los estudiantes en los institutos de tercer grado bajo la autoridad de la Santa Sede.

Latvia:

E––> Not including students enrolled in third level programmes in secondary specialized schools.

FR–> Non compris les étudiants inscrits aux programmes du troisième cycle dans les écoles secondaires specialisées.

ESP> No incluyen los estudiantes matriculados en los programas de tercer ciclo en las escuelas secundarias especializadas.

Lithuania:

E––> Data for students in 1980/81 refer to universities and equivalent degree granting institutions only and in 1985/86, 1990/91 and 1992/93 they exclude post-graduates.

Third level: teachers and students **3.10**
Troisième degré: professeurs et étudiants
Tercer grado: profesores y estudiantes

FR–> Les données relatives aux étudiants en 1980/81 se réfèrent aux universités et aux établissements conférant des grades équivalents seulement, et en 1985/86, 1990/91 et 1992/93, elles ne comprennent pas le niveau universitaire supérieur.

ESP> Los datos relativos a los estudiantes en 1980/81 se refieren a los universidades e instituciones que otorgan títulos equivalentes solamente y en 1985/86, 1990/91 y 1992/93 ellos no incluyen el nivel post-universitario.

Luxembourg:

E––> Data refer to students enrolled in institutions located in Luxembourg. At university level, the majority of students pursue their studies in the following countries: Austria, Belgium, France, Germany and Switzerland.

FR–> Les données se réfèrent seulement aux étudiants inscrits dans les institutions du Luxembourg. La plus grande partie des étudiants luxembourgeois poursuivent leurs études universitaires dans les pays suivants: Allemagne, Autriche, Belgique, France et Suisse.

ESP> Los datos se refieren solamente a los estudiantes matriculados en las instituciones en Luxemburgo. La mayoría de los estudiantes de Luxemburgo cursan sus estudios universitarios en los países siguientes: Alemania, Austria, Bélgica, Francia y Suiza.

Portugal:

E––> In 1985/86, excluding the University of Porto. Data on teaching staff in 1990/91 refer only to institutions attached to the Ministry of Education.

FR–> En 1985/86, non compris l'Université de Porto. Les données relatives aux personnel enseignant en 1990/91 se réfèrent seulement aux institutions attachées au Ministère de l'Education.

ESP> En 1985/86, excluída la Universidad de Porto. Los datos relativos al personal docente en 1990/91 se refieren a los instituciones dependientes del Ministerio de la Educacion.

Russian Federation:

E––> Data on students in 1993/94 and 1994/95 and all data on teaching staff include distance learning institutions with universities and equivalent degree-granting institutions.

FR–> Les données relatives aux étudiants en 1993/94 et 1994/95 ainsi que toutes les données relatives au personnel enseignant incluent l'enseignement à distance avec les universités et les établissements conférant des grades équivalents.

ESP> Los datos relativos a los estudiantes en 1993/94 y 1994/95 asi como todos los datos relativos al personal docente incluyen la enseñanza a distancia en las universidades e instituciones que otorgan títulos equivalentes.

Slovenia:

E––> Not including post-graduate students as registration is not required.

FR–> Non compris les étudiants de niveau universitaire supérieur pour lequel l'inscription n'est pas exigée.

ESP> No incluyen los estudiantes del nivel post-universitario porque la inscripción no es exigida.

The Former Yugoslav Republic of Macedonia:

E––> Not including post graduate students as registration is not required.

FR–> Non compris les étudiants de niveau universitaire supérieur pour lequel l'inscription n'est pas exigée.

ESP> No incluyen los estudiantes del nivel post-universitario porque la inscripción no es exigida.

Ukraine:

E––> Not including students enrolled in third level programmes in secondary specialized schools. Data on female students do not include the post-graduate level.

FR–> Non compris les étudiants inscrits aux programmes du troisième cycle dans les écoles secondaires specialisées. Les données relatives aux étudiantes ne comprennent pas le niveau universitaire supérieur.

ESP> No incluyen los estudiantes matriculados en los programas de tercer ciclo en las escuelas secundarias especializadas. Los datos relativos a las estudiantes no incluyen el nivel post-universitario.

Former Yugoslavia:

E––> Not including post-graduate students as registration is not required.

FR–> Non compris les étudiants de niveau universitaire supérieur pour lequel l'inscription n'est pas exigée.

ESP> No incluyen los estudiantes del nivel post-universitario porque la inscripción no es exigida.

Federal Republic of Yugoslavia:

E––> Not including post graduate students as registration is not required.

FR–> Non compris les étudiants de niveau universitaire supérieur pour lequel l'inscription n'est pas exigée.

ESP> No incluyen los estudiantes del nivel post-universitario porque la inscripción no es exigida.

OCEANIA:

Australia:

E––> Until 1990, data on teaching staff are expressed in full-time equivalent. For 1993 and 1994, data include Vocational Education and Training Institutes (VETS).

FR–> Jusqu'à 1990, les données relatives au personnel enseignant sont exprimées en équivalents plein temps. Pour 1993 et 1994, les données incluent l'Education Technique et les Instituts de Formation Professionnelle *VETS*.

ESP> Hasta 1990, los datos relativos al personal docente se presentan en equivalentes de jornada completa. Para 1993 y 1994, los datos incluyen la Educación Technica y los Institutos de Formación Profesional *VETS*.

New Zealand:

E––> Data on universities and equivalent degree granting institutions for students in 1980, 1992 and 1993 and for teaching staff in all years include distance learning institutions.

FR–> Les données relatives aux universités et aux établissements conférant des grades équivalents pour les étudiants en 1980, 1992 et 1993 et pour le personnel enseignant pour toutes les années incluent l'enseignement à distance.

ESP> Los datos relativos a las universidades e instituciones que otorgan títulos equivalentes, para los estudiantes en 1980, 1992 y 1993 y para el personal docente en todos los años incluyen la enseñanza a distancia.

3.11 Third level: students by level and field of study
Troisième degré: étudiants par niveau et domaine d'études
Tercer grado: estudiantes por nivel y sector de estudios

3.11 Education at the third level: students by ISCED level and field of study

Enseignement du troisième degré: étudiants par niveau et domaine d'études de la CITE

Enseñanza de tercer grado: estudiantes por nivel y sector de estudios de la CINE

Education science and teacher training	= Sciences de l'éducation et formation d'enseignants	= Ciencias de la educación y formación de personal docente
Humanities, religion and theology	= Lettres, religion et théologie	= Humanidades, religión y teología
Fine and applied arts	= Beaux-arts et arts appliqués	= Bellas artes y artes aplicadas
Law	= Droit	= Derecho
Social and behavioural science	= Sciences sociales et sciences du comportement	= Ciencias sociales y del comportamiento
Commercial and business administration	= Formation au commerce et à l'administration des entreprises	= Enseñanza comercial y de administración de empresas
Mass communication and documentation	= Information et documentation	= Documentación y comunicación social
Home economics (domestic science)	= Enseignement ménager	= Economía doméstica (enseñanza del hogar)
Service trades	= Formation pour le secteur tertiaire	= Formación para el sector de los servicios
Natural science	= Sciences exactes et naturelles	= Ciencias naturales
Mathematics and computer science	= Mathématiques et informatique	= Matemáticas e informática
Medical science and health-related	= Sciences médicales, santé et hygiène	= Ciencias médicas, sanidad e higiene
Engineering	= Sciences de l'ingénieur	= Ingeniería y tecnología
Architecture & town planning	= Architecture et urbanisme	= Arquitectura y urbanismo
Trade, craft & industrial programmes	= Métiers de la production industrielle	= Artes y oficios industriales
Transport and communications	= Transport et télécommunications	= Transportes y comunicaciones
Agriculture, forestry and fishery	= Agriculture, sylviculture et halieutique	= Enseñanza agronómica, dasonómica y pesquera
Other and not specified	= Autres programmes et non spécifiés	= Otros programas y sin especificar

Level 5 — Programmes leading to an award not equivalent to a first university degree	Niveau 5 — Programmes conduisant à un diplôme n'équivalant pas à un premier grade universitaire	Nivel 5 — Programas que conducen a un diploma que no equivale a un primer grado universitario
Level 6 — Programmes leading to a first university degree or equivalent qualification	Niveau 6 — Programmes conduisant à un premier grade universitaire ou à un diplôme équivalent	Nivel 6 — Programas que conducen a un primer grado universitario o a un diploma equivalente
Level 7 — Programmes leading to a post-graduate university degree or equivalent qualification	Niveau 7 — Programmes conduisant à un grade universitaire supérieur ou à un diplôme équivalent	Nivel 7 — Programas que conducen a un grado universitario superior o a un diploma equivalente

Please refer to the explanatory text at the end of the table

Prière de se référer au texte explicatif à la fin du tableau

Referirse al texto explicativo al final del cuadro

Unless otherwise specified, data for the field of study in which they symbol ./. appears are included in the figure above.

Sauf précision contraire, les données du domaine d'études où figure le symbole ./. sont comprises avec le chiffre du domaine présenté au-dessus.

Salvo indicación contraria, los datos relativos al sector de estudios donde figura el símbolo ./. están incluídos en la cifra del sector precedente.

1985 refers to the beginning of the academic year for each country.

1985 se réfère au début de l'année académique en vigueur dans chaque pays.

1985 se refiere al inicio del año académico en cada país.

Data shown as 1985 for countries with this symbol actually refer to 1984 or 1986.

Les données pour les pays présentés avec ce symbole se réfèrent à 1984 ou 1986 au lieu de 1985.

Los datos de los países presentados con este símbolo se refieren a 1984 ó 1986 en lugar de 1985.

Third level: students by level and field of study **3.11**
Troisième degré: étudiants par niveau et domaine d'études
Tercer grado: estudiantes por nivel y sector de estudios

Country Field of study Pays Domaines d'études País Sectores de estudios	Year Année Año	Students by ISCED level of programme Étudiants par niveau de programmes de la CITE Estudiantes por nivel de programas de la CINE								Students all levels, 1985 Étudiants tous niveaux, 1985 Estudiantes todos los niveles 1985	
		Level 5 Niveau 5 Nivel 5		Level 6 Niveau 6 Nivel 6		Level 7 Niveau 7 Nivel 7		All levels Tous niveaux Todos los niveles			
		MF	F	MF	F	MF	F	MF	F	MF	F
		(1)	(2)	(3)	(4)	(5)	(6)	(7)	(8)	(9)	(10)
Africa											
Algeria‡ Total	1992/93	40 685	13 742	202 766	88 507	13 982	...	257 379	...	132 057	41 558
Education science		-	-	5 061	2 428	-	-	5 061	...	5 701	1 311
Humanities & religion		39	12	29 566	17 958	1 485	...	31 090	...	11 843	5 802
Fine & applied arts		-	-	197	71	245	...	442	...	59	10
Law		-	-	17 097	7 484	1 402	...	18 499	...	11 813	3 045
Social & behav. sc.		217	89	24 109	11 494	2 261	...	26 587	...	12 411	3 219
Business administr.		6 712	2 937	3 189	866	23	...	9 924	...	1 215	440
Communic. & doc.		347	232	2 752	1 561	110	...	3 209	...	1 177	497
Home economics		-	-	-	-	-	-	-	-	-	-
Service trades		-	-	-	-	-	-	-	-	-	-
Natural science		3 013	1 740	23 081	13 151	1 911	...	28 005	...	4 787	1 619
Maths. & computer sc.		5 405	2 407	10 636	3 740	840	...	16 881	...	4 298	1 213
Health-related prg.		228	74	21 682	10 982	3 007	...	24 917	...	29 238	10 804
Engineering		20 627	4 800	47 401	11 586	1 574	...	69 602	...	6 135	719
Archit. & town plng.		1 442	438	5 139	1 811	185	...	6 766	...	3 684	892
Trade, craft & indust.		339	169	533	137	80	...	952	...	184	58
Transport & communic.		258	40	213	23	29	...	500	...	740	33
Agriculture		1 679	594	9 986	4 177	711	...	12 376	...	3 782	980
Other & not specified		325	210	2 124	1 038	119	...	2 568	...	34 990	10 916
Angola Total	1991/92	...	...	...	...	...	...	6 331	...	...	...
Education science		...	...	...	...	...	...	1 846	...	...	...
Humanities & religion		...	...	...	...	...	...	-	-	...	...
Fine & applied arts		...	...	...	...	...	...	-	-	...	...
Law		...	...	...	...	...	...	875	...	...	...
Social & behav. sc.		...	...	...	...	...	...	-	-	...	...
Business administr.		...	...	...	...	...	...	935	...	...	...
Communic. & doc.		...	...	...	...	...	...	-	-	...	...
Home economics		...	...	...	...	...	...	-	-	...	...
Service trades		...	...	...	...	...	...	-	-	...	...
Natural science		...	...	...	...	...	...	671	...	...	...
Maths. & computer sc.		...	...	...	...	...	...	-	-	...	...
Health-related prg.		...	...	...	...	...	...	754	...	...	...
Engineering		...	...	...	...	...	...	861	...	...	...
Archit. & town plng.		...	...	...	...	...	...	-	-	...	...
Trade, craft & indust.		...	...	...	...	...	...	-	-	...	...
Transport & communic.		...	...	...	...	...	...	-	-	...	...
Agriculture		...	...	...	...	...	...	389	...	...	...
Other & not specified		...	...	...	...	...	...	-	-	...	...
Benin‡# Total	1994	...	...	...	...	...	...	10 986	...	8 870	1 397
Education science		...	...	...	...	...	...	2 846	...	430	51
Humanities & religion		...	...	...	...	...	...	./.	...	2 074	413
Fine & applied arts		...	...	...	...	...	...	-	-	-	-
Law		...	...	...	...	...	...	4 176	...	2 417	441
Social & behav. sc.		...	...	...	...	...	...	858	...	1 467	186
Business administr.		...	...	...	...	...	...	./.	...	176	9
Communic. & doc.		...	...	...	...	...	...	-	-	./.	./.
Home economics		...	...	...	...	...	...	-	-	78	44
Service trades		...	...	...	...	...	...	-	-	-	-
Natural science		...	...	...	...	...	...	1 978	...	884	135
Maths. & computer sc.		...	...	...	...	...	...	30	...	459	28
Health-related prg.		...	...	...	...	...	...	446	...	373	56
Engineering		...	...	...	...	...	...	./.	...	-	-
Archit. & town plng.		...	...	...	...	...	...	-	-	-	-
Trade, craft & indust.		...	...	...	...	...	...	471	...	290	21
Transport & communic.		...	...	...	...	...	...	-	-	-	-
Agriculture		...	...	...	...	...	...	119	...	222	13
Other & not specified		...	...	...	...	...	...	62	...	-	-

3.11 Third level: students by level and field of study
Troisième degré: étudiants par niveau et domaine d'études
Tercer grado: estudiantes por nivel y sector de estudios

Country Field of study Pays Domaines d'études País Sectores de estudios	Year Année Año	Students by ISCED level of programme Étudiants par niveau de programmes de la CITE Estudiantes por nivel de programas de la CINE								Students all levels, 1985 Étudiants tous niveaux, 1985 Estudiantes todos los niveles 1985	
		Level 5 Niveau 5 Nivel 5		Level 6 Niveau 6 Nivel 6		Level 7 Niveau 7 Nivel 7		All levels Tous niveaux Todos los niveles			
		MF	F	MF	F	MF	F	MF	F	MF	F
		(1)	(2)	(3)	(4)	(5)	(6)	(7)	(8)	(9)	(10)
Botswana‡											
Total	1993/94	962	634	3 286	1 484	218	110	4 466	2 228	1 434	...
Education science		84	44	367	219	135	92	586	355	464	...
Humanities & religion		-	-	1 259	675	21	1	1 280	676	308	...
Fine & applied arts		-	-	-	-	-	-	-	-	-	-
Law		27	3	142	54	-	-	169	57	-	-
Social & behav. sc.		-	-	-	-	-	-	-	-	468	...
Business administr.		656	477	350	173	46	11	1 052	661	./.	...
Communic. & doc.		66	37	28	23	8	5	102	65	-	-
Home economics		-	-	-	-	-	-	-	-	-	-
Service trades		-	-	-	-	-	-	-	-	-	-
Natural science		-	-	954	249	5	-	959	249	194	...
Maths. & computer sc.		39	20	71	13	-	-	110	33	./.	...
Health-related prg.		-	-	-	-	-	-	-	-	-	-
Engineering		-	-	-	-	-	-	-	-	-	-
Archit. & town plng.		-	-	-	-	-	-	-	-	-	-
Trade, craft & indust.		-	-	-	-	-	-	-	-	-	-
Transport & communic.		-	-	-	-	-	-	-	-	-	-
Agriculture		-	-	-	-	-	-	-	-	-	-
Other & not specified		90	53	115	78	3	1	208	132	-	-
Burkina Faso‡											
Total	1993/94	...	...	...	...	...	...	8 815	2 131	4 085	946
Education science		...	...	...	...	...	...	623	97	-	-
Humanities & religion		...	...	...	...	...	...	2 956	897	712	174
Fine & applied arts		...	...	...	...	...	...	-	-	-	-
Law		...	...	...	...	...	...	838	236	545	178
Social & behav. sc.		...	...	...	...	...	...	./.	./.	748	244
Business administr.		...	...	...	...	...	...	2 024	579	681	180
Communic. & doc.		...	...	...	...	...	...	-	-	66	22
Home economics		...	...	...	...	...	...	-	-	-	-
Service trades		...	...	...	...	...	...	-	-	-	-
Natural science		...	...	...	...	...	...	1 392	132	551	69
Maths. & computer sc.		...	...	...	...	...	...	96	7	279	4
Health-related prg.		...	...	...	...	...	...	803	172	285	55
Engineering		...	...	...	...	...	...	-	-	-	-
Archit. & town plng.		...	...	...	...	...	...	-	-	-	-
Trade, craft & indust.		...	...	...	...	...	...	-	-	-	-
Transport & communic.		...	...	...	...	...	...	-	-	-	-
Agriculture		...	...	...	...	...	...	83	11	218	20
Other & not specified		...	...	...	...	...	...	-	-	-	-
Burundi‡											
Total	1991/92	-	-	3 830	1 013	./.	./.	3 830	1 013	2 783	676
Education science		-	-	431	124	./.	./.	431	124	342	87
Humanities & religion		-	-	559	166	./.	./.	559	166	622	166
Fine & applied arts		-	-	-	-	-	-	-	-	-	-
Law		-	-	292	91	./.	./.	292	91	229	76
Social & behav. sc.		-	-	-	-	-	-	-	-	229	68
Business administr.		-	-	924	329	./.	./.	924	329	255	123
Communic. & doc.		-	-	-	-	-	-	-	-	28	16
Home economics		-	-	-	-	-	-	-	-	-	-
Service trades		-	-	-	-	-	-	-	-	-	-
Natural science		-	-	651	156	./.	./.	651	156	207	25
Maths. & computer sc.		-	-	51	9	./.	./.	51	9	-	-
Health-related prg.		-	-	298	80	./.	./.	298	80	262	62
Engineering		-	-	56	2	./.	./.	56	2	125	1
Archit. & town plng.		-	-	135	3	./.	./.	135	3	69	12
Trade, craft & indust.		-	-	-	-	-	-	-	-	-	-
Transport & communic.		-	-	-	-	-	-	-	-	-	-
Agriculture		-	-	331	49	./.	./.	331	49	252	34
Other & not specified		-	-	102	4	./.	./.	102	4	163	6

Third level: students by level and field of study **3.11**
Troisième degré: étudiants par niveau et domaine d'études
Tercer grado: estudiantes por nivel y sector de estudios

Country Field of study Pays Domaines d'études País Sectores de estudios	Year Année Año	Students by ISCED level of programme Étudiants par niveau de programmes de la CITE Estudiantes por nivel de programas de la CINE								Students all levels, 1985 Étudiants tous niveaux, 1985	
		Level 5 Niveau 5 Nivel 5		Level 6 Niveau 6 Nivel 6		Level 7 Niveau 7 Nivel 7		All levels Tous niveaux Todos los niveles		Estudiantes todos los niveles 1985	
		MF	F	MF	F	MF	F	MF	F	MF	F
		(1)	(2)	(3)	(4)	(5)	(6)	(7)	(8)	(9)	(10)
Cameroon‡ 　Total	1990/91	...	...	...	...	...	...	33 177	...	...	...
Education science		...	...	...	...	...	...	2 590	...	...	...
Humanities & religion		...	...	...	...	...	...	./.	...	...	...
Fine & applied arts		...	...	...	...	...	...	-	-	...	...
Law		...	...	...	...	...	...	13 713	...	...	...
Social & behav. sc.		...	...	...	...	...	...	6 452	2 578	...	...
Business administr.		...	...	...	...	...	...	181	...	...	...
Communic. & doc.		...	...	...	...	...	...	62	18	...	...
Home economics		...	...	...	...	...	...	-	-	...	...
Service trades		...	...	...	...	...	...	216		...	...
Natural science		...	...	...	...	...	...	7 560	1 267	...	...
Maths. & computer sc.		...	...	...	...	...	...	./.	./.	...	...
Health-related prg.		...	...	...	...	...	...	602	79	...	...
Engineering		...	...	...	...	...	...	830	7	...	...
Archit. & town plng.		...	...	...	...	...	...	./.	./.	...	...
Trade, craft & indust.		...	...	...	...	...	...	365	11	...	...
Transport & communic.		...	...	...	...	...	...	-	-	...	...
Agriculture		...	...	...	...	...	...	549	57	...	...
Other & not specified		...	...	...	...	...	...	57	7	...	...
Central African 　Republic‡ 　Total	1991/92	...	...	...	...	...	...	3 783	557	2 651	287
Education science		...	...	...	...	...	...	111	5	223	11
Humanities & religion		...	...	...	...	...	...	253	28	717	39
Fine & applied arts		...	...	...	...	...	...	-	-	-	-
Law		...	...	...	...	...	...	1 135	105	925	87
Social & behav. sc.		...	...	...	...	...	...	760	67	./.	./.
Business administr.		...	...	...	...	...	...	128	24	97	24
Communic. & doc.		...	...	...	...	...	...	-	-	-	-
Home economics		...	...	...	...	...	...	-	-	-	-
Service trades		...	...	...	...	...	...	-	-	-	-
Natural science		...	...	...	...	...	...	165	12	86	9
Maths. & computer sc.		...	...	...	...	...	...	18	-	-	-
Health-related prg.		...	...	...	...	...	...	965	299	459	113
Engineering		...	...	...	...	...	...	149	5	71	4
Archit. & town plng.		...	...	...	...	...	...	-	-	-	-
Trade, craft & indust.		...	...	...	...	...	...	-	-	-	-
Transport & communic.		...	...	...	...	...	...	-	-	-	-
Agriculture		...	...	...	...	...	...	-	-	73	-
Other & not specified		...	...	...	...	...	...	99	12	-	-
Chad‡ 　Total	1992/93	-	-	2 109	...	733	...	2 842	...	...	...
Education science		-	-	1 116	...	365	...	1 481	...	...	...
Humanities & religion		-	-	-	-	-	-	-	-	...	...
Fine & applied arts		-	-	-	-	-	-	-	-	...	...
Law		-	-	594	...	259	...	853	...	...	...
Social & behav. sc.		-	-	-	-	-	-	-	-	...	...
Business administr.		-	-	-	-	-	-	-	-	...	...
Communic. & doc.		-	-	-	-	-	-	-	-	...	...
Home economics		-	-	-	-	-	-	-	-	...	...
Service trades		-	-	-	-	-	-	-	-	...	...
Natural science		-	-	291	...	109	...	400	...	...	...
Maths. & computer sc.		-	-	./.	...	./.	...	./.	...	...	...
Health-related prg.		-	-	76	...	-	-	76	...	...	...
Engineering		-	-	-	-	-	-	-	-	...	...
Archit. & town plng.		-	-	-	-	-	-	-	-	...	...
Trade, craft & indust.		-	-	-	-	-	-	-	-	...	...
Transport & communic.		-	-	-	-	-	-	-	-	...	...
Agriculture		-	-	-	-	-	-	-	-	...	...
Other & not specified		-	-	32	...	-	-	32	...	...	...

3.11 Third level: students by level and field of study
Troisième degré: étudiants par niveau et domaine d'études
Tercer grado: estudiantes por nivel y sector de estudios

Country Field of study Pays Domaines d'études País Sectores de estudios	Year Année Año	Students by ISCED level of programme Étudiants par niveau de programmes de la CITE Estudiantes por nivel de programas de la CINE								Students all levels, 1985 Étudiants tous niveaux, 1985 Estudiantes todos los niveles 1985	
		Level 5 Niveau 5 Nivel 5		Level 6 Niveau 6 Nivel 6		Level 7 Niveau 7 Nivel 7		All levels Tous niveaux Todos los niveles			
		MF	F	MF	F	MF	F	MF	F	MF	F
		(1)	(2)	(3)	(4)	(5)	(6)	(7)	(8)	(9)	(10)
Comoros											
Total	1989/90	248	36	-	-	-	-	248	36	...	...
Education science		-	-	-	-	-	-	-	-	...	...
Humanities & religion		135	20	-	-	-	-	135	20	...	...
Fine & applied arts		-	-	-	-	-	-	-	-	...	...
Law		-	-	-	-	-	-	-	-	...	...
Social & behav. sc.		-	-	-	-	-	-	-	-	...	...
Business administr.		40	9	-	-	-	-	40	9	...	...
Communic. & doc.		-	-	-	-	-	-	-	-	...	...
Home economics		-	-	-	-	-	-	-	-	...	...
Service trades		-	-	-	-	-	-	-	-	...	...
Natural science		73	7	-	-	-	-	73	7	...	...
Maths. & computer sc.		-	-	-	-	-	-	-	-	...	...
Health-related prg.		-	-	-	-	-	-	-	-	...	...
Engineering		-	-	-	-	-	-	-	-	...	...
Archit. & town plng.		-	-	-	-	-	-	-	-	...	...
Trade, craft & indust.		-	-	-	-	-	-	-	-	...	...
Transport & communic.		-	-	-	-	-	-	-	-	...	...
Agriculture		-	-	-	-	-	-	-	-	...	...
Other & not specified		-	-	-	-	-	-	-	-	...	...
Congo											
Total	1992/93	1 773	...	9 363	...	2 670	...	13 806	...	10 684	1 665
Education science		687	...	210	...	-	-	897	...	1 119	195
Humanities & religion		-	-	500	...	169	...	669	...	2 026	306
Fine & applied arts		-	-	-	-	-	-	-	-	-	-
Law		6	...	684	...	365	...	1 055	...	5 730	981
Social & behav. sc.		10	...	3 986	...	1 532	...	5 528	...	./.	./.
Business administr.		251	...	28	...	-	-	279	...	./.	./.
Communic. & doc.		-	-	296	...	203	...	499	...	-	-
Home economics		-	-	-	-	-	-	-	-	-	-
Service trades		-	-	-	-	-	-	-	-	-	-
Natural science		-	-	979	...	117	...	1 096	...	643	41
Maths. & computer sc.		-	-	2	...	46	...	48	...	./.	./.
Health-related prg.		-	-	61	...	238	...	299	...	472	96
Engineering		-	-	-	-	-	-	-	-	-	-
Archit. & town plng.		-	-	-	-	-	-	-	-	-	-
Trade, craft & indust.		-	-	-	-	-	-	-	-	-	-
Transport & communic.		-	-	-	-	-	-	-	-	-	-
Agriculture		166	...	153	...	-	-	319	...	376	36
Other & not specified		653	...	2 464	...	-	-	3 117	...	318	-
Djibouti											
Total	1991/92	53	16	-	-	-	-	53	16	...	...
Education science		21	8	-	-	-	-	21	8	...	...
Humanities & religion		-	-	-	-	-	-	-	-	...	...
Fine & applied arts		-	-	-	-	-	-	-	-	...	...
Law		-	-	-	-	-	-	-	-	...	...
Social & behav. sc.		-	-	-	-	-	-	-	-	...	...
Business administr.		-	-	-	-	-	-	-	-	...	...
Communic. & doc.		-	-	-	-	-	-	-	-	...	...
Home economics		-	-	-	-	-	-	-	-	...	...
Service trades		32	8	-	-	-	-	32	8	...	...
Natural science		-	-	-	-	-	-	-	-	...	...
Maths. & computer sc.		-	-	-	-	-	-	-	-	...	...
Health-related prg.		-	-	-	-	-	-	-	-	...	...
Engineering		-	-	-	-	-	-	-	-	...	...
Archit. & town plng.		-	-	-	-	-	-	-	-	...	...
Trade, craft & indust.		-	-	-	-	-	-	-	-	...	...
Transport & communic.		-	-	-	-	-	-	-	-	...	...
Agriculture		-	-	-	-	-	-	-	-	...	...
Other & not specified		-	-	-	-	-	-	-	-	...	...

Third level: students by level and field of study **3.11**
Troisième degré: étudiants par niveau et domaine d'études
Tercer grado: estudiantes por nivel y sector de estudios

Country Field of study Pays Domaines d'études País Sectores de estudios	Year Année Año	Students by ISCED level of programme Étudiants par niveau de programmes de la CITE Estudiantes por nivel de programas de la CINE								Students all levels, 1985 Étudiants tous niveaux, 1985 Estudiantes todos los niveles 1985	
		Level 5 Niveau 5 Nivel 5		Level 6 Niveau 6 Nivel 6		Level 7 Niveau 7 Nivel 7		All levels Tous niveaux Todos los niveles				
		MF	F	MF	F	MF	F	MF	F	MF	F
		(1)	(2)	(3)	(4)	(5)	(6)	(7)	(8)	(9)	(10)
Egypt‡ Total	1992/93	-	-	464 814	179 859	97 844	30 295	562 658	210 154	601 843	201 460
Education science		-	-	80 244	41 722	19 854	8 762	100 098	50 484	80 591	37 783
Humanities & religion		-	-	72 994	35 377	8 372	3 438	81 366	38 815	83 996	39 250
Fine & applied arts		-	-	7 368	4 038	1 066	431	8 434	4 469	7 313	3 215
Law		-	-	60 810	17 089	9 787	996	70 597	18 085	87 464	17 891
Social & behav. sc.		-	-	6 501	2 906	1 554	436	8 055	3 342	5 397	2 326
Business administr.		-	-	109 552	35 494	12 133	3 158	121 685	38 652	146 910	44 150
Communic. & doc.		-	-	1 039	760	277	134	1 316	894	1 727	926
Home economics		-	-	2 891	2 200	208	135	3 099	2 335	2 273	1 709
Service trades		-	-	2 065	999	588	311	2 653	1 310	1 099	724
Natural science		-	-	15 482	7 190	7 930	2 761	23 412	9 951	26 770	8 838
Maths. & computer sc.		-	-	3 924	698	353	105	4 277	803	1 095	294
Health-related prg.		-	-	36 074	17 555	17 199	5 396	53 273	22 951	53 465	21 093
Engineering		-	-	35 512	5 470	8 104	1 086	43 616	6 556	53 726	6 866
Archit. & town plng.		-	-	./.	./.	./.	./.	./.	./.	./.	./.
Trade, craft & indust.		-	-	./.	./.	./.	./.	./.	./.	./.	./.
Transport & communic.		-	-	./.	./.	./.	./.	./.	./.	./.	./.
Agriculture		-	-	21 367	5 692	8 960	2 715	30 327	8 407	42 386	13 696
Other & not specified		-	-	8 991	2 669	1 459	431	10 450	3 100	7 631	2 699
Equatorial Guinea Total	1990/91	188	21	390	52	-	-	578	73	...	...
Education science		27	11	44	25	-	-	71	36	...	...
Humanities & religion		6	1	4	-	-	-	10	1	...	...
Fine & applied arts		-	-	-	-	-	-	-	-	...	...
Law		22	2	91	9	-	-	113	11	...	...
Social & behav. sc.		6	1	14	2	-	-	20	3	...	...
Business administr.		1	1	43	1	-	-	44	2	...	...
Communic. & doc.		-	-	-	-	-	-	-	-	...	...
Home economics		-	-	-	-	-	-	-	-	...	...
Service trades		-	-	-	-	-	-	-	-	...	...
Natural science		1	-	3	-	-	-	4	-	...	...
Maths. & computer sc.		2	-	-	-	-	-	2	-	...	...
Health-related prg.		-	-	-	-	-	-	-	-	...	...
Engineering		9	-	9	-	-	-	18	-	...	...
Archit. & town plng.		-	-	-	-	-	-	-	-	...	...
Trade, craft & indust.		-	-	-	-	-	-	-	-	...	...
Transport & communic.		-	-	-	-	-	-	-	-	...	...
Agriculture		-	-	-	-	-	-	-	-	...	...
Other & not specified		114	5	182	15	-	-	296	20	...	...
Eritrea Total	1994/95	303	65	2 834	359	-	-	3 137	424	...	...
Education science		56	2	-	-	-	-	56	2	...	...
Humanities & religion		-	-	112	19	-	-	112	19	...	...
Fine & applied arts		-	-	-	-	-	-	-	-	...	...
Law		31	3	93	7	-	-	124	10	...	...
Social & behav. sc.		-	-	240	23	-	-	240	23	...	...
Business administr.		216	60	608	85	-	-	824	145	...	...
Communic. & doc.		-	-	-	-	-	-	-	-	...	...
Home economics		-	-	-	-	-	-	-	-	...	...
Service trades		-	-	-	-	-	-	-	-	...	...
Natural science		-	-	396	51	-	-	396	51	...	...
Maths. & computer sc.		-	-	240	18	-	-	240	18	...	...
Health-related prg.		-	-	-	-	-	-	-	-	...	...
Engineering		-	-	-	-	-	-	-	-	...	...
Archit. & town plng.		-	-	-	-	-	-	-	-	...	...
Trade, craft & indust.		-	-	-	-	-	-	-	-	...	...
Transport & communic.		-	-	-	-	-	-	-	-	...	...
Agriculture		-	-	323	25	-	-	323	25	...	...
Other & not specified		-	-	822	131	-	-	822	131	...	...

3.11 Third level: students by level and field of study
Troisième degré: étudiants par niveau et domaine d'études
Tercer grado: estudiantes por nivel y sector de estudios

Country Field of study / Pays Domaines d'études / País Sectores de estudios	Year Année Año	Students by ISCED level of programme Étudiants par niveau de programmes de la CITE Estudiantes por nivel de programas de la CINE								Students all levels, 1985 Étudiants tous niveaux, 1985 Estudiantes todos los niveles 1985	
		Level 5 Niveau 5 Nivel 5		Level 6 Niveau 6 Nivel 6		Level 7 Niveau 7 Nivel 7		All levels Tous niveaux Todos los niveles			
		MF	F	MF	F	MF	F	MF	F	MF	F
		(1)	(2)	(3)	(4)	(5)	(6)	(7)	(8)	(9)	(10)
Ethiopia‡											
Total	1991/92	12 454	3 077	13 065	1 848	699	52	26 218	4 977	27 338	4 881
Education science		1 430	268	786	157	60	1	2 276	426	3 478	664
Humanities & religion		286	130	704	195	90	7	1 080	332	1 436	271
Fine & applied arts		-	-	34	5	-	-	34	5	54	5
Law		260	39	224	23	-	-	484	62	637	54
Social & behav. sc.		-	-	2 591	571	60	3	2 651	574	3 162	452
Business administr.		4 278	1 574	1 892	401	-	-	6 170	1 975	7 061	2 431
Communic. & doc.		260	119	176	52	19	4	455	175	124	22
Home economics		21	6	-	-	-	-	21	6	72	27
Service trades		-	-	-	-	-	-	-	-	-	-
Natural science		233	99	1 700	110	82	2	2 015	211	2 878	217
Maths. & computer sc.		441	147	468	42	32	1	941	190	1 273	161
Health-related prg.		688	173	929	58	247	34	1 864	265	1 384	198
Engineering		1 760	170	2 070	101	13	-	3 843	271	1 728	57
Archit. & town plng.		211	23	104	11	-	-	315	34	119	11
Trade, craft & indust.		578	53	-	-	-	-	578	53	506	27
Transport & communic.		-	-	-	-	-	-	-	-	-	-
Agriculture		2 008	276	1 387	122	96	-	3 491	398	3 426	284
Other & not specified		-	-	-	-	-	-	-	-	-	-
Gabon‡#											
Total	1988/89	1 342	428	2 665	799	./.	./.	4 007	1 227	4 089	1 168
Education science		46	11	254	56	./.	./.	300	67	293	54
Humanities & religion		-	-	347	114	./.	./.	347	114	389	114
Fine & applied arts		-	-	-	-	-	-	-	-	-	-
Law		-	-	478	154	./.	./.	478	154	461	140
Social & behav. sc.		-	-	737	237	./.	./.	737	237	900	280
Business administr.		369	194	249	69	./.	./.	618	263	585	231
Communic. & doc.		81	35	91	26	./.	./.	172	61	234	80
Home economics		-	-	-	-	-	-	-	-	44	-
Service trades		-	-	-	-	-	-	-	-	44	-
Natural science		141	17	-	-	./.	-	141	17	91	90
Maths. & computer sc.		187	34	46	-	./.	-	233	34	278	50
Health-related prg.		143	102	322	132	./.	./.	465	234	366	164
Engineering		171	13	76	4	./.	./.	247	17	188	17
Archit. & town plng.		-	-	38	5	./.	./.	38	5	50	6
Trade, craft & indust.		85	1	-	-	-	-	85	1	75	3
Transport & communic.		27	8	-	-	-	-	27	8	39	11
Agriculture		92	13	-	-	-	-	92	13	70	7
Other & not specified		-	-	27	2	-	-	27	2	26	1
Ghana‡											
Total	1990/91	958	272	8 002	1 791	649	95	9 609	2 158	4 540	...
Education science		20	8	410	84	64	12	494	104	213	...
Humanities & religion		237	72	2 339	724	183	21	2 759	817	446	...
Fine & applied arts		120	61	346	106	47	6	513	173	232	...
Law		-	-	39	19	1	-	40	19	-	-
Social & behav. sc.		114	36	804	217	31	4	949	257	311	...
Business administr.		71	17	639	145	58	10	768	172	694	...
Communic. & doc.		-	-	-	-	38	16	38	16	-	-
Home economics		20	20	27	18	4	4	51	42	-	-
Service trades		-	-	-	-	-	-	-	-	-	-
Natural science		135	47	955	145	89	12	1 179	204	808	...
Maths. & computer sc.		-	-	206	22	21	4	227	26	272	...
Health-related prg.		12	1	824	188	35	1	871	190	336	...
Engineering		63	-	635	19	14	1	712	20	733	...
Archit. & town plng.		-	-	282	38	46	4	328	42	251	...
Trade, craft & indust.		-	-	-	-	-	-	-	-	-	-
Transport & communic.		-	-	-	-	-	-	-	-	-	-
Agriculture		166	10	479	51	18	-	663	61	244	...
Other & not specified		-	-	17	15	-	-	17	15	-	-

Third level: students by level and field of study **3.11**
Troisième degré: étudiants par niveau et domaine d'études
Tercer grado: estudiantes por nivel y sector de estudios

Country / Field of study / Pays / Domaines d'études / País / Sectores de estudios	Year / Année / Año	Students by ISCED level of programme / Étudiants par niveau de programmes de la CITE / Estudiantes por nivel de programas de la CINE								Students all levels, 1985 / Étudiants tous niveaux, 1985 / Estudiantes todos los niveles 1985	
		Level 5 / Niveau 5 / Nivel 5		Level 6 / Niveau 6 / Nivel 6		Level 7 / Niveau 7 / Nivel 7		All levels / Tous niveaux / Todos los niveles			
		MF	F	MF	F	MF	F	MF	F	MF	F
		(1)	(2)	(3)	(4)	(5)	(6)	(7)	(8)	(9)	(10)
Guinea‡											
Total	1990/91	...	...	...	...	...	...	5 366	350	8 801	1 267
Education science		...	...	...	...	...	...	1 772	130	1 855	217
Humanities & religion		...	...	...	...	...	...	./.	./.	./.	./.
Fine & applied arts		...	...	...	...	...	...	-	-	-	-
Law		...	...	...	...	...	...	579	29	./.	./.
Social & behav. sc.		...	...	...	...	...	...	./.	./.	./.	./.
Business administr.		...	...	...	...	...	...	-	-	210	65
Communic. & doc.		...	...	...	...	...	...	-	-	-	-
Home economics		...	...	...	...	...	...	-	-	-	-
Service trades		...	...	...	...	...	...	-	-	-	-
Natural science		...	...	...	...	...	...	1 539	90	3 016	488
Maths. & computer sc.		...	...	...	...	...	...	./.	./.	./.	./.
Health-related prg.		...	...	...	...	...	...	551	70	458	67
Engineering		...	...	...	...	...	...	824	31	548	21
Archit. & town plng.		...	...	...	...	...	...	./.	./.	176	7
Trade, craft & indust.		...	...	...	...	...	...	./.	./.	240	46
Transport & communic.		...	...	...	...	...	...	./.	./.	120	15
Agriculture		...	...	...	...	...	...	101	-	2 178	341
Other & not specified		...	...	...	...	...	...	-	-		
Guinea-Bissau											
Total	1988/89	404	24	-	-	-	-	404	24	-	-
Education science		171	5	-	-	-	-	171	5	-	-
Humanities & religion		-	-	-	-	-	-	-	-	-	-
Fine & applied arts		-	-	-	-	-	-	-	-	-	-
Law		-	-	-	-	-	-	-	-	-	-
Social & behav. sc.		-	-	-	-	-	-	-	-	-	-
Business administr.		-	-	-	-	-	-	-	-	-	-
Communic. & doc.		-	-	-	-	-	-	-	-	-	-
Home economics		-	-	-	-	-	-	-	-	-	-
Service trades		-	-	-	-	-	-	-	-	-	-
Natural science		-	-	-	-	-	-	-	-	-	-
Maths. & computer sc.		-	-	-	-	-	-	-	-	-	-
Health-related prg.		-	-	-	-	-	-	-	-	-	-
Engineering		-	-	-	-	-	-	-	-	-	-
Archit. & town plng.		-	-	-	-	-	-	-	-	-	-
Trade, craft & indust.		233	19	-	-	-	-	233	19	-	-
Transport & communic.		-	-	-	-	-	-	-	-	-	-
Agriculture		-	-	-	-	-	-	-	-	-	-
Other & not specified		-	-	-	-	-	-	-	-	-	-
Kenya‡											
Total	1990/91	...	...	...	...	...	...	35 421	9 769	21 756	5 710
Education science		...	...	...	...	...	...	12 666	4 950	5 595	2 069
Humanities & religion		...	...	...	...	...	...	7 179	1 784	./.	./.
Fine & applied arts		...	...	...	...	...	...	38	9	19	10
Law		...	...	...	...	...	...	649	204	390	154
Social & behav. sc.		...	...	...	...	...	...	2 241	476	1 453	414
Business administr.		...	...	...	...	...	...	2 421	429	1 770	678
Communic. & doc.		...	...	...	...	...	...	-	-	118	56
Home economics		...	...	...	...	...	...	806	514	185	165
Service trades		...	...	...	...	...	...	-	-	-	-
Natural science		...	...	...	...	...	...	3 598	452	1 306	181
Maths. & computer sc.		...	...	...	...	...	...	-	-	131	36
Health-related prg.		...	...	...	...	...	...	1 458	405	1 132	280
Engineering		...	...	...	...	...	...	1 046	49	3 325	55
Archit. & town plng.		...	...	...	...	...	...	629	121	392	69
Trade, craft & indust.		...	...	...	...	...	...	437	28	4 765	1 310
Transport & communic.		...	...	...	...	...	...	-	-	-	-
Agriculture		...	...	...	...	...	...	2 253	348	1 175	233
Other & not specified		...	...	...	...	...	...	-	-	-	-

3.11 Third level: students by level and field of study
Troisième degré: étudiants par niveau et domaine d'études
Tercer grado: estudiantes por nivel y sector de estudios

Country / Field of study — Pays / Domaines d'études — País / Sectores de estudios	Year Année Año	Students by ISCED level of programme — Étudiants par niveau de programmes de la CITE — Estudiantes por nivel de programas de la CINE								Students all levels, 1985 — Étudiants tous niveaux, 1985 — Estudiantes todos los niveles 1985	
		Level 5 / Niveau 5 / Nivel 5		Level 6 / Niveau 6 / Nivel 6		Level 7 / Niveau 7 / Nivel 7		All levels / Tous niveaux / Todos los niveles			
		MF	F	MF	F	MF	F	MF	F	MF	F
		(1)	(2)	(3)	(4)	(5)	(6)	(7)	(8)	(9)	(10)
Lesotho # Total	1993/94	2 332	1 322	1 592	860	77	41	4 001	2 223	2 339	1 479
Education science		906	745	477	320	26	16	1 409	1 081	1 594	1 149
Humanities & religion		35	22	83	57	4	2	122	81	94	54
Fine & applied arts		./.	./.	./.	./.	./.	./.	./.	./.	-	-
Law		-	-	156	68	39	19	195	87	668	65
Social & behav. sc.		-	-	128	74	4	3	132	77	34	19
Business administr.		538	434	268	150	-	-	806	584	229	119
Communic. & doc.		-	-					-	-	-	-
Home economics		30	28	-	-	-	-	30	28	-	-
Service trades		331	16	-	-	-	-	331	16	-	-
Natural science		-	-	371	125	4	1	375	126	198	59
Maths. & computer sc.		48	16	26	18	-	-	74	34	9	5
Health-related prg.		-	-	-	-	-	-	-	-	13	9
Engineering		133	22	-	-	-	-	133	22	-	-
Archit. & town plng.		31	9	-	-	-	-	31	9	-	-
Trade, craft & indust.		252	15	-	-	-	-	252	15	-	-
Transport & communic.		-	-	-	-	-	-	-	-	-	-
Agriculture		19	15	83	48	-	-	102	63	-	-
Other & not specified		9	-	-	-	-	-	9	-	-	-
Madagascar‡ Total	1992/93	26 363	7 830	15 291	6 679	1 027	400	42 681	14 909	38 310	14 703
Education science		-	-	791	287	-	-	791	287	1 100	346
Humanities & religion		4 252	2 836	1 833	1 205	33	18	6 118	4 059	5 856	3 329
Fine & applied arts		-	-	-	-	-	-	-	-	-	-
Law		5 608	1 575	911	392	671	279	7 190	2 246	4 896	2 095
Social & behav. sc.		2 357	981	1 254	472	16	7	3 627	1 460	4 808	1 674
Business administr.		8 026	616	1 942	807	1	1	9 969	1 424	3 652	1 248
Communic. & doc.		-	-	-	-	-	-	-	-	-	-
Home economics		-	-	-	-	-	-	-	-	-	-
Service trades		-	-	-	-	-	-	-	-	-	-
Natural science		4 458	1 524	1 915	772	240	86	6 613	2 382	7 820	2 886
Maths. & computer sc.		956	218	384	69	54	5	1 394	292	1 627	295
Health-related prg.		-	-	5 338	2 441	-	-	5 338	2 441	5 912	2 576
Engineering		706	80	449	63	-	-	1 155	143	2 349	175
Archit. & town plng.		-	-	-	-	-	-	-	-	-	-
Trade, craft & indust.		-	-	-	-	-	-	-	-	-	-
Transport & communic.		-	-	-	-	-	-	-	-	57	1
Agriculture		-	-	474	171	12	4	486	175	233	78
Other & not specified		-	-	-	-	-	-	-	-	-	-
Malawi Total	1993/94	4 775	1 755	2 493	527	40	7	7 308	2 289	3 928	1 129
Education science		3 624	1 429	456	102	-	-	4 080	1 531	2 396	874
Humanities & religion		-	-	136	55	-	-	136	55	66	9
Fine & applied arts		-	-	./.	./.	-	-	./.	./.	./.	./.
Law		-	-	72	19	-	-	72	19	45	3
Social & behav. sc.		-	-	535	116	23	5	558	121	130	24
Business administr.		-	-	636	96	-	-	636	96	275	42
Communic. & doc.		-	-	-	-	-	-	-	-	-	-
Home economics		-	-	-	-	-	-	-	-	-	-
Service trades		158	22	18	-	-	-	176	22	-	-
Natural science		-	-	320	67	-	-	320	67	195	25
Maths. & computer sc.		-	-	./.	./.	-	-	./.	./.	./.	./.
Health-related prg.		262	207	53	42	-	-	315	249	145	83
Engineering		388	25	126	2	-	-	514	27	221	-
Archit. & town plng.		./.	./.	./.	./.	-	-	./.	./.	./.	-
Trade, craft & indust.		-	-	-	-	-	-	-	-	-	-
Transport & communic.		-	-	-	-	-	-	-	-	-	-
Agriculture		343	72	141	28	17	2	501	102	385	64
Other & not specified		-	-	-	-	-	-	-	-	70	5

Third level: students by level and field of study 3.11
Troisième degré: étudiants par niveau et domaine d'études
Tercer grado: estudiantes por nivel y sector de estudios

Country Field of study Pays Domaines d'études País Sectores de estudios	Year Année Año	Students by ISCED level of programme Étudiants par niveau de programmes de la CITE Estudiantes por nivel de programas de la CINE								Students all levels, 1985 Étudiants tous niveaux, 1985 Estudiantes todos los niveles 1985	
		Level 5 Niveau 5 Nivel 5		Level 6 Niveau 6 Nivel 6		Level 7 Niveau 7 Nivel 7		All levels Tous niveaux Todos los niveles			
		MF	F	MF	F	MF	F	MF	F	MF	F
		(1)	(2)	(3)	(4)	(5)	(6)	(7)	(8)	(9)	(10)
Mali‡ Total	1990/91	1 733	325	4 970	580	./.	./.	6 703	905	6 768	874
Education science		-	-	737	95	./.	./.	737	95	1 843	168
Humanities & religion		-	-	1 009	157	./.	./.	1 009	157	./.	./.
Fine & applied arts		-	-	./.	./.	./.	./.	./.	./.	-	-
Law		-	-	482	54	./.	./.	482	54	./.	./.
Social & behav. sc.		-	-	./.	./.	./.	./.	./.	./.	-	-
Business administr.		498	141	338	24	./.	./.	836	165	2 417	404
Communic. & doc.		-	-	-	-	-	-	-	-	-	-
Home economics		-	-	-	-	-		-	-	-	-
Service trades		-	-	-	-	-	-	-	-	-	-
Natural science		-	-	107	3	./.	./.	107	3	-	-
Maths. & computer sc.		-	-	61	3	./.	./.	61	3	-	-
Health-related prg.		-	-	771	166	./.	./.	771	166	456	104
Engineering		-	-	571	11	./.	./.	571	11	700	24
Archit. & town plng.		-	-	-	-	-	-	-	-	-	-
Trade, craft & indust.		-	-	-	-	-	-	-	-	-	-
Transport & communic.		74	24	172	26	./.	./.	246	50	233	62
Agriculture		1 161	160	722	41	./.	./.	1 883	201	1 119	112
Other & not specified		-	-	-	-	-		-	-	-	-
Mauritania Total	1993/94	820	276	7 675	1 195	-	-	8 495	1 471	...	...
Education science		820	276	112	7	-	-	932	283	...	...
Humanities & religion		-	-	2 184	383	-	-	2 184	383	...	...
Fine & applied arts		-	-	-	-	-	-	-	-	...	...
Law		-	-	2 213	238	-	-	2 213	238	...	...
Social & behav. sc.		-	-	2 464	459	-	-	2 464	459	...	...
Business administr.		-	-	28	10	-	-	28	10	...	...
Communic. & doc.		-	-	-	-	-	-	-	-	...	...
Home economics		-	-	-	-	-	-	-	-	...	...
Service trades		-	-	-	-	-	-	-	-	...	...
Natural science		-	-	550	90	-	-	550	90	...	...
Maths. & computer sc.		-	-	53	7	-	-	53	7	...	...
Health-related prg.		-	-	-	-	-	-	-	-	...	...
Engineering		-	-	41	-	-	-	41	-	...	...
Archit. & town plng.		-	-	-	-	-	-	-	-	...	...
Trade, craft & indust.		-	-	30	1	-	-	30	1	...	...
Transport & communic.		-	-	-	-	-	-	-	-	...	...
Agriculture		-	-	-	-	-	-	-	-	...	...
Other & not specified		-	-	-	-	-	-	-	-	...	...
Mauritius Total	1991/92	2 967	1 304	869	331	196	55	4 032	1 690	1 161	421
Education science		1 340	682	107	48	148	46	1 595	776	654	307
Humanities & religion		43	41	85	76	-	-	128	117	-	-
Fine & applied arts		680	340	-	-	-	-	680	340	-	-
Law		-	-	51	29	-	-	51	29	-	-
Social & behav. sc.		59	14	60	26	-	-	119	40	30	6
Business administr.		368	111	135	62	22	-	525	173	183	47
Communic. & doc.		33	12	-	-	-	-	33	12	15	12
Home economics		-	-	-	-	-	-	-	-	-	-
Service trades		38	19	-	-	-	-	38	19	-	-
Natural science		-	-	86	38	-	-	86	38	-	-
Maths. & computer sc.		61	23	69	17	-	-	130	40	29	8
Health-related prg.		187	38	-	-	16	5	203	43	47	16
Engineering		56	1	208	9	5	1	269	11	124	3
Archit. & town plng.		-	-	-	-	-	-	-	-	-	-
Trade, craft & indust.		49	13	-	-	-	-	49	13	19	-
Transport & communic.		-	-	-	-	-	-	-	-	-	-
Agriculture		53	10	68	26	5	3	126	39	60	22
Other & not specified		-	-	-	-	-	-	-	-	-	-

3.11 Third level: students by level and field of study
Troisième degré: étudiants par niveau et domaine d'études
Tercer grado: estudiantes por nivel y sector de estudios

Country / Field of study / Pays / Domaines d'études / País / Sectores de estudios	Year / Année / Año	Students by ISCED level of programme / Étudiants par niveau de programmes de la CITE / Estudiantes por nivel de programas de la CINE								Students all levels, 1985 / Étudiants tous niveaux, 1985 / Estudiantes todos los niveles 1985	
		Level 5 / Niveau 5 / Nivel 5		Level 6 / Niveau 6 / Nivel 6		Level 7 / Niveau 7 / Nivel 7		All levels / Tous niveaux / Todos los niveles			
		MF	F	MF	F	MF	F	MF	F	MF	F
		(1)	(2)	(3)	(4)	(5)	(6)	(7)	(8)	(9)	(10)
Morocco‡											
Total	1994/95	10 552	3 101	223 692	94 594	16 675	5 025	250 919	102 720	143 023	47 952
Education science		-	-	73	40	172	35	245	75	255	91
Humanities & religion		160	26	71 354	37 657	4 587	1 318	76 101	39 001	65 426	27 569
Fine & applied arts		-	-	-	-	-	-	-	-	-	-
Law		378	-	50 144	22 374	4 822	1 508	55 344	23 882	20 987	4 854
Social & behav. sc.		109	66	32 296	12 802	2 946	1 012	35 351	13 880	12 053	3 222
Business administr.		1 018	394	219	98	-	-	1 237	492	./.	./.
Communic. & doc.		630	369	-	-	-	-	630	369	./.	./.
Home economics		-	-	-	-	-	-	-	-	-	-
Service trades		460	197	-	-	-	-	460	197	-	-
Natural science		-	-	61 169	17 787	3 939	1 090	65 108	18 877	36 939	10 075
Maths. & computer sc.		-	-	./.	./.	./.	./.	./.	./.	./.	./.
Health-related prg.		-	-	7 447	3 672	-	-	7 447	3 672	6 761	2 075
Engineering		740	40	990	164	209	62	1 939	266	602	66
Archit. & town plng.		400	158	-	-	-	-	400	158	-	-
Trade, craft & indust.		1 686	659	-	-	-	-	1 686	659	-	-
Transport & communic.		536	9	-	-	-	-	536	9	-	-
Agriculture		2 659	577	-	-	-	-	2 659	577	-	-
Other & not specified		1 776	606	-	-	-	-	1 776	606	-	-
Mozambique											
Total	1993/94	-	-	5 250	1 357	-	-	5 250	1 357	1 442	332
Education science		-	-	676	206	-	-	676	206	91	30
Humanities & religion		-	-	298	114	-	-	298	114	11	4
Fine & applied arts		-	-	-	-	-	-	-	-	-	-
Law		-	-	513	123	-	-	513	123	-	-
Social & behav. sc.		-	-	855	224	-	-	855	224	247	56
Business administr.		-	-	./.	./.	-	-	./.	./.	-	-
Communic. & doc.		-	-	-	-	-	-	-	-	-	-
Home economics		-	-	-	-	-	-	-	-	-	-
Service trades		-	-	-	-	-	-	-	-	-	-
Natural science		-	-	837	230	-	-	837	230	69	21
Maths. & computer sc.		-	-	162	40	-	-	162	40	-	-
Health-related prg.		-	-	389	208	-	-	389	208	162	82
Engineering		-	-	946	65	-	-	946	65	541	42
Archit. & town plng.		-	-	150	31	-	-	150	31	-	-
Trade, craft & indust.		-	-	-	-	-	-	-	-	-	-
Transport & communic.		-	-	-	-	-	-	-	-	-	-
Agriculture		-	-	394	110	-	-	394	110	321	97
Other & not specified		-	-	30	6	-	-	30	6	-	-
Namibia											
Total	1991	2 266	1 424	1 694	1 109	197	131	4 157	2 664	...	...
Education science		1 650	1 144	711	447	55	20	2 416	1 611	...	...
Humanities & religion		-	-	171	68	39	20	210	88	...	...
Fine & applied arts		-	-	./.	./.	./.	./.	./.	./.	...	...
Law		-	-	-	-	-	-	-	-	...	...
Social & behav. sc.		-	-	56	49	10	8	66	57	...	...
Business administr.		477	248	187	72	-	-	664	320	...	...
Communic. & doc.		-	-	-	-	-	-	-	-	...	...
Home economics		-	-	-	-	-	-	-	-	...	...
Service trades		-	-	-	-	-	-	-	-	...	...
Natural science		-	-	83	28	-	-	83	28	...	...
Maths. & computer sc.		-	-	./.	./.	-	-	./.	./.	...	...
Health-related prg.		-	-	486	445	93	83	579	528	...	...
Engineering		-	-	-	-	-	-	-	-	...	...
Archit. & town plng.		-	-	-	-	-	-	-	-	...	...
Trade, craft & indust.		-	-	-	-	-	-	-	-	...	...
Transport & communic.		-	-	-	-	-	-	-	-	...	...
Agriculture		48	14	-	-	-	-	48	14	...	...
Other & not specified		91	18	-	-	-	-	91	18	...	...

Third level: students by level and field of study **3.11**
Troisième degré: étudiants par niveau et domaine d'études
Tercer grado: estudiantes por nivel y sector de estudios

Country Field of study Pays Domaines d'études País Sectores de estudios	Year Année Año	Students by ISCED level of programme Étudiants par niveau de programmes de la CITE Estudiantes por nivel de programas de la CINE								Students all levels, 1985 Étudiants tous niveaux, 1985 Estudiantes todos los niveles 1985	
		Level 5 Niveau 5 Nivel 5		Level 6 Niveau 6 Nivel 6		Level 7 Niveau 7 Nivel 7		All levels Tous niveaux Todos los niveles			
		MF	F	MF	F	MF	F	MF	F	MF	F
		(1)	(2)	(3)	(4)	(5)	(6)	(7)	(8)	(9)	(10)
Niger #											
Total	1989/90	739	111	3 767	564	-	-	4 506	675	3 317	590
Education science		-	-	384	106	-	-	384	106	292	51
Humanities & religion		-	-	709	101	-	-	709	101	943	246
Fine & applied arts		-	-	-	-	-	-	-	-	-	-
Law		-	-	851	27	-	-	851	27	386	65
Social & behav. sc.		-	-	636	132	-	-	636	132	714	119
Business administr.		-	-	115	23	-	-	115	23	-	-
Communic. & doc.		-	-	98	32	-	-	98	32	-	-
Home economics		-	-	-	-	-	-	-	-	-	-
Service trades		-	-	-	-	-	-	-	-	-	-
Natural science		412	17	280	18	-	-	692	35	245	19
Maths. & computer sc.		-	-	-	-	-	-	-	-	238	8
Health-related prg.		-	-	432	111	-	-	432	111	311	71
Engineering		-	-	98	4	-	-	98	4	-	-
Archit. & town plng.		-	-	-	-	-	-	-	-	-	-
Trade, craft & indust.		-	-	-	-	-	-	-	-	-	-
Transport & communic.		-	-	-	-	-	-	-	-	-	-
Agriculture		-	-	164	10	-	-	164	10	188	11
Other & not specified		327	94	-	-	-	-	327	94	-	-
Nigeria‡											
Total	1989/90	...	...	...	...	...	...	180 871	...	...	...
Education science		...	...	...	...	...	...	27 529	...	...	...
Humanities & religion		...	...	...	...	...	...	23 377	...	...	...
Fine & applied arts		...	...	...	...	...	...	./.	...	...	...
Law		...	...	...	...	...	...	9 761	...	...	...
Social & behav. sc.		...	...	...	...	...	...	21 841	...	...	...
Business administr.		...	...	...	...	...	...	12 683	...	...	...
Communic. & doc.		...	...	...	...	...	...	-	-	...	...
Home economics		...	...	...	...	...	...	-	-	...	...
Service trades		...	...	...	...	...	...	-		...	...
Natural science		...	...	...	...	...	...	29 526	...	...	...
Maths. & computer sc.		...	...	...	...	...	...	./.	...	...	...
Health-related prg.		...	...	...	...	...	...	13 276	...	...	...
Engineering		...	...	...	...	...	...	15 085	...	...	...
Archit. & town plng.		...	...	...	...	...	...	6 091	...	...	...
Trade, craft & indust.		...	...	...	...	...	...	-	-	...	...
Transport & communic.		...	...	...	...	...	...	-	-	...	...
Agriculture		...	...	...	...	...	...	14 391	...	...	...
Other & not specified		...	...	...	...	...	...	7 311	...	...	...
Rwanda											
Total	1989/90	2 905	557	484	82	-	-	3 389	639	1 987	269
Education science		187	61	85	21	-	-	272	82	194	52
Humanities & religion		508	55	108	18	-	-	616	73	482	39
Fine & applied arts		-	-	-	-	-	-	-	-	-	-
Law		138	43	63	16	-	-	201	59	143	24
Social & behav. sc.		336	115	38	8	-	-	374	123	172	44
Business administr.		466	119	41	4	-	-	507	123	214	47
Communic. & doc.		-	-	-	-	-	-	-	-	-	-
Home economics		132	60	-	-	-	-	132	60	29	10
Service trades		-	-	-	-	-	-	-	-	-	-
Natural science		227	34	58	4	-	-	285	38	194	12
Maths. & computer sc.		151	15	5	-	-	-	156	15	170	5
Health-related prg.		119	31	53	9	-	-	172	40	164	25
Engineering		132	5	-	-	-	-	132	5	95	-
Archit. & town plng.		-	-	-	-	-	-	-	-	-	-
Trade, craft & indust.		-	-	-	-	-	-	-	-	5	5
Transport & communic.		-	-	-	-	-	-	-	-	-	-
Agriculture		109	7	33	2	-	-	142	9	120	2
Other & not specified		400	12	-	-	-	-	400	12	5	4

3.11 Third level: students by level and field of study
Troisième degré: étudiants par niveau et domaine d'études
Tercer grado: estudiantes por nivel y sector de estudios

Country Field of study Pays Domaines d'études País Sectores de estudios	Year Année Año	Students by ISCED level of programme Étudiants par niveau de programmes de la CITE Estudiantes por nivel de programas de la CINE								Students all levels, 1985 Étudiants tous niveaux, 1985 Estudiantes todos los niveles 1985	
		Level 5 Niveau 5 Nivel 5		Level 6 Niveau 6 Nivel 6		Level 7 Niveau 7 Nivel 7		All levels Tous niveaux Todos los niveles			
		MF	F	MF	F	MF	F	MF	F	MF	F
		(1)	(2)	(3)	(4)	(5)	(6)	(7)	(8)	(9)	(10)
Senegal‡ Total	1991/92	-	-	20 763	5 110	799	152	21 562	5 262	12 711	2 640
Education science		-	-	567	114	-	-	567	114	429	47
Humanities & religion		-	-	7 223	2 134	245	29	7 468	2 163	2 672	591
Fine & applied arts		-	-	-	-	-	-	-	-	-	-
Law		-	-	5 976	1 374	117	14	6 093	1 388	3 770	661
Social & behav. sc.		-	-	202	58	-	-	202	58	./.	./.
Business administr.		-	-	234	65	-	-	234	65	./.	./.
Communic. & doc.		-	-	206	71	-	-	206	71	294	75
Home economics		-	-	-	-	-	-	-	-	-	-
Service trades		-	-	-	-	-	-	-	-	171	48
Natural science		-	-	3 517	292	290	61	3 807	353	2 348	266
Maths. & computer sc.		-	-	177	22	-	-	177	22	./.	./.
Health-related prg.		-	-	2 310	874	147	48	2 457	922	2 486	861
Engineering		-	-	351	106	-	-	351	106	207	29
Archit. & town plng.		-	-	-	-	-	-	-	-	-	-
Trade, craft & indust.		-	-	-	-	-	-	-	-	-	-
Transport & communic.		-	-	-	-	-	-	-	-	-	-
Agriculture		-	-	-	-	-	-	-	-	258	16
Other & not specified		-	-	-	-	-	-	-	-	76	46
Sierra Leone Total	1989/90	...	...	...	...	...	...	5 060	...	5 690	...
Education science		...	...	...	...	...	...	2 946	...	3 837	...
Humanities & religion		...	...	...	...	...	...	793	187	818	189
Fine & applied arts		...	...	...	...	...	...	-	-	-	-
Law		...	...	...	...	...	...	77	13	32	5
Social & behav. sc.		...	...	...	...	...	...	429	58	325	61
Business administr.		...	...	...	...	...	...	./.	./.	./.	./.
Communic. & doc.		...	...	...	...	...	...	-	-	-	-
Home economics		...	...	...	...	...	...	-	-	-	-
Service trades		...	...	...	...	...	...	-	-	-	-
Natural science		...	...	...	...	...	...	173	27	155	38
Maths. & computer sc.		...	...	...	...	...	...	./.	./.	./.	./.
Health-related prg.		...	...	...	...	...	...	76	19	-	-
Engineering		...	...	...	...	...	...	238	16	179	12
Archit. & town plng.		...	...	...	...	...	...	-	-	-	-
Trade, craft & indust.		...	...	...	...	...	...	-	-	-	-
Transport & communic.		...	...	...	...	...	...	-	-	-	-
Agriculture		...	...	...	...	...	...	328	70	344	71
Other & not specified		...	...	...	...	...	...	-	-	-	-
South Africa‡ Total	1994	218 892	105 165	213 372	109 952	35 822	15 483	468 086	230 600	...	...
Education science		74 441	47 453	13 827	9 471	8 752	4 870	97 020	61 794	...	...
Humanities & religion		13 257	7 407	34 737	22 177	3 283	1 499	51 277	31 083	...	...
Fine & applied arts		3 851	2 228	2 830	1 958	313	220	6 994	4 406	...	...
Law		13 111	3 726	22 437	8 678	3 009	1 189	38 557	13 593	...	...
Social & behav. sc.		9 636	4 938	48 868	28 221	4 593	2 390	63 097	35 549	...	...
Business administr.		53 164	21 017	33 388	14 269	7 866	2 353	94 418	37 639	...	...
Communic. & doc.		2 954	2 162	3 288	2 435	515	390	6 757	4 987	...	...
Home economics		2 962	2 427	690	663	62	54	3 714	3 144	...	...
Service trades		-	-	-	-	-	-	-	-	...	...
Natural science		6 384	3 164	13 491	6 080	1 818	713	21 693	9 957	...	...
Maths. & computer sc.		15 092	5 852	14 489	4 542	917	259	30 498	10 653	...	...
Health-related prg.		3 282	2 069	13 206	8 342	2 468	1 196	18 956	11 607	...	...
Engineering		13 379	598	5 457	485	1 122	74	19 958	1 157	...	...
Archit. & town plng.		2 007	390	1 901	538	340	82	4 248	1 010	...	...
Trade, craft & indust.		2 366	639	9	-	1	-	2 376	639	...	...
Transport & communic.		-	-	-	-	-	-	-	-	...	...
Agriculture		2 335	625	1 313	292	506	79	4 154	996	...	...
Other & not specified		671	470	3 441	1 801	257	115	4 369	2 386	...	...

Third level: students by level and field of study **3.11**
Troisième degré: étudiants par niveau et domaine d'études
Tercer grado: estudiantes por nivel y sector de estudios

Country / Field of study / Pays / Domaines d'études / País / Sectores de estudios	Year / Année / Año	Students by ISCED level of programme / Étudiants par niveau de programmes de la CITE / Estudiantes por nivel de programas de la CINE								Students all levels, 1985 / Étudiants tous niveaux, 1985 / Estudiantes todos los niveles 1985	
		Level 5 / Niveau 5 / Nivel 5		Level 6 / Niveau 6 / Nivel 6		Level 7 / Niveau 7 / Nivel 7		All levels / Tous niveaux / Todos los niveles			
		MF	F	MF	F	MF	F	MF	F	MF	F
		(1)	(2)	(3)	(4)	(5)	(6)	(7)	(8)	(9)	(10)
Sudan‡ Total	1990/91	...	...	...	...	...	...	59 824	28 615	33 432	13 480
Education science		...	...	...	...	...	...	3 477	1 181	1 365	471
Humanities & religion		...	...	...	...	...	...	10 138	4 645	9 295	3 946
Fine & applied arts		...	...	...	...	...	...	479	134	257	37
Law		...	...	...	...	...	...	10 424	4 502	5 866	2 144
Social & behav. sc.		...	...	...	...	...	...	3 132	985	7 031	4 065
Business administr.		...	...	...	...	...	...	2 353	1 036	./.	./.
Communic. & doc.		...	...	...	...	...	...	836	200	-	-
Home economics		...	...	...	...	...	...	70	7	706	705
Service trades		...	...	...	...	...	...	-	-	-	-
Natural science		...	...	...	...	...	...	2 171	944	1 184	389
Maths. & computer sc.		...	...	...	...	...	...	868	260	87	19
Health-related prg.		...	...	...	...	...	...	3 219	1 353	2 011	723
Engineering		...	...	...	...	...	...	3 620	502	2 448	212
Archit. & town plng.		...	...	...	...	...	...	168	48	132	25
Trade, craft & indust.		...	...	...	...	...	...	103	69	-	-
Transport & communic.		...	...	...	...	...	...	-	-	-	-
Agriculture		...	...	...	...	...	...	2 930	965	3 050	744
Other & not specified		...	...	...	...	...	...	15 836	11 784	-	-
Swaziland‡ Total	1993/94	2 619	1 090	1 394	687	170	89	4 183	1 866	2 555	...
Education science		1 169	604	210	88	123	71	1 502	763	629	...
Humanities & religion		9	9	323	212	-	-	332	221	173	...
Fine & applied arts		-	-	-	-	-	-	-	-	-	-
Law		37	7	-	-	47	18	84	25	148	...
Social & behav. sc.		-	-	449	226	-	-	449	226	161	...
Business administr.		418	200	69	28	-	-	487	228	244	...
Communic. & doc.		-	-	-	-	-	-	-	-	-	-
Home economics		86	86	41	41	-	-	127	127	53	...
Service trades		10	1	-	-	-	-	10	1	-	-
Natural science		16	3	302	92	-	-	318	95	260	...
Maths. & computer sc.		./.	./.	./.	./.	-	-	./.	./.	./.	...
Health-related prg.		-	-	-	-	-	-	-	-	-	-
Engineering		301	11	-	-	-	-	301	11	-	-
Archit. & town plng.		-	-	-	-	-	-	-	-	-	-
Trade, craft & indust.		194	14	-	-	-	-	194	14	690	...
Transport & communic.		-	-	-	-	-	-	-	-	-	-
Agriculture		168	41	-	-	-	-	168	41	197	...
Other & not specified		211	114	-	-	-	-	211	114	-	-
Togo‡ Total	1993/94	...	...	...	...	...	...	9 120	1 119	5 055	678
Education science		...	...	...	...	...	...	42	10	86	4
Humanities & religion		...	...	...	...	...	...	3 258	481	1 169	203
Fine & applied arts		...	...	...	...	...	...	./.	./.	./.	./.
Law		...	...	...	...	...	...	1 785	253	878	163
Social & behav. sc.		...	...	...	...	...	...	2 021	168	-	-
Business administr.		...	...	...	...	...	...	./.	./.	1 012	100
Communic. & doc.		...	...	...	...	...	...	-	-	-	-
Home economics		...	...	...	...	...	...	-	-	-	-
Service trades		...	...	...	...	...	...	-	-	-	-
Natural science		...	...	...	...	...	...	718	35	742	34
Maths. & computer sc.		...	...	...	...	...	...	./.	./.	./.	./.
Health-related prg.		...	...	...	...	...	...	647	100	508	84
Engineering		...	...	...	...	...	...	215	3	73	-
Archit. & town plng.		...	...	...	...	...	...	90	12	92	1
Trade, craft & indust.		...	...	...	...	...	...	-	-	-	-
Transport & communic.		...	...	...	...	...	...	-	-	-	-
Agriculture		...	...	...	...	...	...	282	9	379	8
Other & not specified		...	...	...	...	...	...	62	48	116	81

3.11 Third level: students by level and field of study
Troisième degré: étudiants par niveau et domaine d'études
Tercer grado: estudiantes por nivel y sector de estudios

Country / Field of study / Pays / Domaines d'études / País / Sectores de estudios	Year / Année / Año	Students by ISCED level of programme / Étudiants par niveau de programmes de la CITE / Estudiantes por nivel de programas de la CINE								Students all levels, 1985 / Étudiants tous niveaux, 1985 / Estudiantes todos los niveles 1985	
		Level 5 / Niveau 5 / Nivel 5		Level 6 / Niveau 6 / Nivel 6		Level 7 / Niveau 7 / Nivel 7		All levels / Tous niveaux / Todos los niveles			
		MF	F	MF	F	MF	F	MF	F	MF	F
		(1)	(2)	(3)	(4)	(5)	(6)	(7)	(8)	(9)	(10)
Tunisia Total	1994/95	7 500	3 772	80 426	34 735	14 756	5 723	102 682	44 230	41 594	14 824
Education science		3 426	1 629	-	-	-	-	3 426	1 629	2 611	806
Humanities & religion		-	-	26 578	15 188	2 616	747	29 194	15 935	10 419	4 536
Fine & applied arts		-	-	552	388	13	10	565	398	374	182
Law		-	-	12 525	5 284	786	258	13 311	5 542	3 295	1 255
Social & behav. sc.		-	-	11 866	4 551	267	243	12 133	4 794	2 562	875
Business administr.		-	-	7 254	2 994	943	175	8 197	3 169	3 744	1 345
Communic. & doc.		-	-	1 139	795	-	-	1 139	795	502	280
Home economics		-	-	-	-	-	-	-	-	180	71
Service trades		-	-	-	-	-	-	-	-	327	66
Natural science		-	-	9 603	3 439	328	148	9 931	3 587	3 792	1 220
Maths. & computer sc.		-	-	2 370	520	558	121	2 928	641	1 775	382
Health-related prg.		1 979	1 439	-	-	7 351	3 535	9 330	4 974	5 812	3 036
Engineering		102	58	4 014	524	852	162	4 968	744	3 750	359
Archit. & town plng.		-	-	-	-	793	261	793	261	377	70
Trade, craft & indust.		-	-	-	-	-	-	-	-	86	15
Transport & communic.		81	34	251	90	39	7	371	131	672	71
Agriculture		841	282	754	242	210	56	1 805	580	1 316	255
Other & not specified		1 071	330	3 520	720	-	-	4 591	1 050	-	-
Uganda Total	1993/94	14 786	4 389	8 399	2 568	937	245	24 122	7 202	10 103	2 349
Education science		6 621	1 739	1 665	654	335	87	8 621	2 480	3 225	774
Humanities & religion		-	-	1 197	355	95	16	1 292	371	525	170
Fine & applied arts		80	33	120	35	-	-	200	68	135	44
Law		-	-	348	126	10	2	358	128	204	64
Social & behav. sc.		-	-	1 136	411	81	26	1 217	437	1 019	281
Business administr.		6 398	2 238	658	183	94	30	7 150	2 451	1 479	608
Communic. & doc.		8	3	185	103	3	1	196	107	70	27
Home economics		-	-	-	-	-	-	-	-	-	-
Service trades		494	286	-	-	-	-	494	286	-	-
Natural science		-	-	863	192	77	18	940	210	760	118
Maths. & computer sc.		-	-	204	44	64	13	268	57	174	15
Health-related prg.		-	-	749	208	89	28	838	236	467	118
Engineering		1 124	78	344	27	6	1	1 474	106	256	5
Archit. & town plng.		-	-	40	6	-	-	40	6	-	-
Trade, craft & indust.		61	12	-	-	-	-	61	12	1 151	26
Transport & communic.		-	-	-	-	-	-	-	-	-	-
Agriculture		-	-	733	133	83	23	816	156	537	91
Other & not specified		-	-	157	91	-	-	157	91	101	8
Zambia‡ Total	1989	8 769	2 999	5 491	1 032	205	32	14 465	4 063	4 680	810
Education science		5 001	2 049	1 290	293	47	3	6 338	2 345	1 246	239
Humanities & religion		-	-	1 161	325	65	14	1 226	339	909	262
Fine & applied arts		144	62	-	-	-	-	144	62	-	-
Law		-	-	145	33	16	4	161	37	153	41
Social & behav. sc.		-	-	./.	./.	./.	./.	./.	./.	./.	./.
Business administr.		1 007	656	786	145	-	-	1 793	801	356	75
Communic. & doc.		-	-	-	-	-	-	-	-	-	-
Home economics		-	-	-	-	-	-	-	-	-	-
Service trades		-	-	-	-	-	-	-	-	-	-
Natural science		-	-	757	103	37	4	794	107	690	63
Maths. & computer sc.		-	-	./.	./.	./.	./.	./.	./.	./.	./.
Health-related prg.		244	44	349	99	23	5	616	148	302	94
Engineering		963	15	551	4	10	-	1 524	19	544	-
Archit. & town plng.		-	-	-	-	-	-	-	-	-	-
Trade, craft & indust.		1 060	59	-	-	-	-	1 060	59	-	-
Transport & communic.		-	-	-	-	-	-	-	-	-	-
Agriculture		-	-	228	15	7	2	235	17	291	14
Other & not specified		350	114	224	15	-	-	574	129	189	22

Third level: students by level and field of study 3.11
Troisième degré: étudiants par niveau et domaine d'études
Tercer grado: estudiantes por nivel y sector de estudios

Country / Field of study / Pays / Domaines d'études / País / Sectores de estudios	Year / Année / Año	Level 5 / Niveau 5 / Nivel 5 MF	F	Level 6 / Niveau 6 / Nivel 6 MF	F	Level 7 / Niveau 7 / Nivel 7 MF	F	All levels / Tous niveaux / Todos los niveles MF	F	Students all levels, 1985 MF	F
		(1)	(2)	(3)	(4)	(5)	(6)	(7)	(8)	(9)	(10)
Zimbabwe‡ Total	1992	29 006	10 954	8 903	...	./.	./.	37 909	...	...	...
Education science		16 365	7 447	919	...	./.	...	17 284	...	...	...
Humanities & religion		-	-	1 381	...	./.	...	1 381	...	...	...
Fine & applied arts		199	39	-	-	-	-	199	39	...	...
Law		-	-	374	...	./.	...	374	...	...	...
Social & behav. sc.		-	-	1 682	...	./.	...	1 682	...	...	...
Business administr.		5 369	2 327	1 216	340	./.	./.	6 585	2 667	...	...
Communic. & doc.		270	89	-	-	-	-	270	89	...	...
Home economics		248	245	-	-	-	-	248	245	...	...
Service trades		195	81	-	-	-	-	195	81	...	...
Natural science		660	257	1 139	...	./.	...	1 799	...	...	...
Maths. & computer sc.		399	158	-	-	-	-	399	158	...	...
Health-related prg.		-	-	904	...	./.	...	904	...	...	...
Engineering		3 808	134	910	200	./.	./.	4 718	334	...	...
Archit. & town plng.		-	-	-	-	-	-	-	-	...	...
Trade, craft & indust.		1 451	167	-	-	-	-	1 451	167	...	...
Transport & communic.		-	-	-	-	-	-	-	-	...	...
Agriculture		42	10	378	60	./.	./.	420	70	...	...
Other & not specified		-	-	-	-	-	-	-	-	...	...
America, North											
Barbados‡# Total	1994/95	-	-	2 583	1 652	279	138	2 862	1 790	5 227	2 565
Education science		-	-	19	10	27	16	46	26	373	234
Humanities & religion		-	-	595	465	49	31	644	496	706	472
Fine & applied arts		-	-	-	-	-	-	-	-	66	43
Law		-	-	328	228	30	16	358	244	297	165
Social & behav. sc.		-	-	1 105	708	91	41	1 196	749	1 344	898
Business administr.		-	-	-	-	-	-	-	-	./.	./.
Communic. & doc.		-	-	-	-	-	-	-	-	-	-
Home economics		-	-	-	-	-	-	-	-	47	47
Service trades		-	-	-	-	-	-	-	-	265	174
Natural science		-	-	489	219	62	26	551	245	773	312
Maths. & computer sc.		-	-	-	-	2	-	2	-	./.	./.
Health-related prg.		-	-	47	22	18	8	65	30	142	89
Engineering		-	-	-	-	-	-	-	-	117	4
Archit. & town plng.		-	-	-	-	-	-	-	-	-	-
Trade, craft & indust.		-	-	-	-	-	-	-	-	1 003	78
Transport & communic.		-	-	-	-	-	-	-	-	40	12
Agriculture		-	-	-	-	-	-	-	-	54	37
Other & not specified		-	-	-	-	-	-	-	-		
Canada‡ Total	1993/94	992 345	491 949	902 454	513 287	116 686	54 117	2 011 485	1 059 353	1 127 011	590 110
Education science		12 584	11 437	63 074	46 894	16 865	11 701	92 523	70 032	71 856	52 096
Humanities & religion		32 578	17 833	64 098	40 466	12 680	6 526	109 356	64 825	51 768	31 634
Fine & applied arts		24 692	14 334	25 375	16 394	2 119	1 260	52 186	31 988	38 208	23 355
Law		-	-	13 223	6 964	1 167	593	14 390	7 557	12 294	5 683
Social & behav. sc.		35 850	22 486	102 168	63 054	12 259	6 320	150 277	91 860	108 346	62 948
Business administr.		110 386	73 071	100 247	51 273	16 492	6 214	227 125	130 558	167 072	85 503
Communic. & doc.		8 088	4 483	9 032	5 738	1 881	1 270	19 001	11 491	13 756	7 969
Home economics		-	-	5 431	4 778	569	464	6 000	5 242	5 282	4 914
Service trades		10 679	4 256	-	-	-	-	10 679	4 256	3 041	1 501
Natural science		-	-	38 502	19 117	8 676	2 760	47 178	21 877	37 149	14 407
Maths. & computer sc.		21 563	6 959	27 485	8 010	3 776	884	52 824	15 853	47 091	14 776
Health-related prg.		48 203	39 511	39 230	29 230	15 577	7 721	103 010	76 462	79 421	57 839
Engineering		42 558	4 200	49 134	8 763	11 839	1 893	103 531	14 856	88 457	8 537
Archit. & town plng.		8 610	1 821	3 157	1 222	599	223	12 366	3 266	8 984	2 028
Trade, craft & indust.		103 256	6 505	-	-	-	-	103 256	6 505	-	-
Transport & communic.		4 759	319	-	-	-	-	4 759	319	1 186	120
Agriculture		19 792	5 258	5 181	2 940	1 967	732	26 940	8 930	17 523	5 890
Other & not specified		508 747	279 476	357 117	208 444	10 220	5 556	876 084	493 476	375 577	210 910

3.11 Third level: students by level and field of study
Troisième degré: étudiants par niveau et domaine d'études
Tercer grado: estudiantes por nivel y sector de estudios

Country / Field of study Pays / Domaines d'études País / Sectores de estudios	Year Année Año	Students by ISCED level of programme Étudiants par niveau de programmes de la CITE Estudiantes por nivel de programas de la CINE								Students all levels, 1985 Étudiants tous niveaux, 1985 Estudiantes todos los niveles 1985	
		Level 5 Niveau 5 Nivel 5		Level 6 Niveau 6 Nivel 6		Level 7 Niveau 7 Nivel 7		All levels Tous niveaux Todos los niveles				
		MF	F	MF	F	MF	F	MF	F	MF	F
		(1)	(2)	(3)	(4)	(5)	(6)	(7)	(8)	(9)	(10)
Costa Rica‡											
Total	1992	12 390	...	75 934	...	./.	...	88 324	...	58 393	...
Education science		-		10 192		./.		10 192		6 209	...
Humanities & religion		-	-	2 446	...	./.	...	2 446	...	11 421	...
Fine & applied arts		36	...	1 446	...	./.	...	1 482	...	1 323	...
Law		-	-	4 543	...	./.	...	4 543	...	3 884	...
Social & behav. sc.		-		5 102	...	./.	...	5 102	...	6 162	...
Business administr.		8 783	...	14 349	...	./.	...	23 132	...	6 815	...
Communic. & doc.		-		1 178	...	./.	...	1 178	...	1 314	...
Home economics		-	-	-	-	-	-	-	-	-	-
Service trades		650	...	-	-	-	-	650	...	264	...
Natural science		-	-	706		./.		706	...	1 604	...
Maths. & computer sc.		1 952	...	3 421	...	./.	...	5 373	...	2 354	...
Health-related prg.		142	...	3 266	...	./.	...	3 408	...	3 130	...
Engineering		184	...	6 097	...	./.	...	6 281	...	4 962	...
Archit. & town plng.		-	-	1 852	...	./.	...	1 852	...	947	...
Trade, craft & indust.		392	...	-	-	-	-	392	...	-	-
Transport & communic.		-	-	-	-	-	-	-	-	-	-
Agriculture		123	...	1 422	...	./.	...	1 545	...	2 058	...
Other & not specified		128	...	19 914	...	./.	...	20 042	...	5 946	...
Cuba											
Total	1992/93	-	-	198 474	114 584	-	-	198 474	114 584	235 224	127 054
Education science		-	-	77 688	54 989	-	-	77 688	54 989	107 399	67 572
Humanities & religion		-	-	1 814	1 244	-	-	1 814	1 244	1 966	1 383
Fine & applied arts		-	-	1 457	783	-	-	1 457	783	952	400
Law		-	-	2 149	1 499	-	-	2 149	1 499	1 803	1 171
Social & behav. sc.		-	-	5 551	3 406	-	-	5 551	3 406	24 012	14 120
Business administr.		-	-	4 525	3 022	-	-	4 525	3 022	5 376	3 517
Communic. & doc.		-	-	737	455	-	-	737	455	678	228
Home economics		-	-	-	-	-	-	-	-	-	-
Service trades		-	-	-	-	-	-	-	-	-	-
Natural science		-	-	2 332	1 396	-	-	2 332	1 396	2 090	1 078
Maths. & computer sc.		-	-	2 176	889	-	-	2 176	889	1 474	756
Health-related prg.		-	-	40 478	27 330	-	-	40 478	27 330	28 101	16 424
Engineering		-	-	22 564	7 455	-	-	22 564	7 455	25 398	8 115
Archit. & town plng.		-	-	6 411	2 611	-	-	6 411	2 611	7 104	3 213
Trade, craft & indust.		-	-	201	138	-	-	201	138	-	-
Transport & communic.		-	-	1 817	313	-	-	1 817	313	3 130	408
Agriculture		-	-	10 646	4 646	-	-	10 646	4 646	15 718	6 426
Other & not specified		-	-	17 928	4 408	-	-	17 928	4 408	10 023	2 243
Dominica											
Total	1992/93	484	227	-	-	-	-	484	227	...	...
Education science		-	-	-	-	-	-	-	-	...	...
Humanities & religion		52	40	-	-	-	-	52	40	...	...
Fine & applied arts		-	-	-	-	-	-	-	-	...	...
Law		-	-	-	-	-	-	-	-	...	...
Social & behav. sc.		112	70	-	-	-	-	112	70	...	...
Business administr.		38	38	-	-	-	-	38	38	...	...
Communic. & doc.		./.	./.	-	-	-	-	./.	./.	...	...
Home economics		-	-	-	-	-	-	-	-	...	...
Service trades		-	-	-	-	-	-	-	-	...	...
Natural science		106	56	-	-	-	-	106	56	...	...
Maths. & computer sc.		./.	./.	-	-	-	-	./.	./.	...	...
Health-related prg.		-	-	-	-	-	-	-	-	...	...
Engineering		-	-	-	-	-	-	-	-	...	...
Archit. & town plng.		-	-	-	-	-	-	-	-	...	...
Trade, craft & indust.		176	23	-	-	-	-	176	23	...	...
Transport & communic.		-	-	-	-	-	-	-	-	...	...
Agriculture		-	-	-	-	-	-	-	-	...	...
Other & not specified		-	-	-	-	-	-	-	-	...	...

Third level: students by level and field of study 3.11
Troisième degré: étudiants par niveau et domaine d'études
Tercer grado: estudiantes por nivel y sector de estudios

Country / Field of study Pays / Domaines d'études País / Sectores de estudios	Year Année Año	Students by ISCED level of programme Étudiants par niveau de programmes de la CITE Estudiantes por nivel de programas de la CINE								Students all levels, 1985 Étudiants tous niveaux, 1985 Estudiantes todos los niveles 1985	
		Level 5 Niveau 5 Nivel 5		Level 6 Niveau 6 Nivel 6		Level 7 Niveau 7 Nivel 7		All levels Tous niveaux Todos los niveles			
		MF	F	MF	F	MF	F	MF	F	MF	F
		(1)	(2)	(3)	(4)	(5)	(6)	(7)	(8)	(9)	(10)
Dominican Republic Total	1985/86	...	...	...	...	...	...	123 748	...	123 748	...
Education science		...	...	...	...	...	...	17 139	...	17 139	...
Humanities & religion		...	...	...	...	...	...	979	...	979	...
Fine & applied arts		...	...	...	...	...	...	868	...	868	...
Law		...	...	...	...	...	...	8 833	...	8 833	...
Social & behav. sc.		...	...	...	...	...	...	5 412	...	5 412	...
Business administr.		...	...	...	...	...	...	30 892	...	30 892	...
Communic. & doc.		...	...	...	...	...	...	1 945	...	1 945	...
Home economics		...	...	...	...	...	...	-	-	-	-
Service trades		...	...	...	...	...	...				
Natural science		...	...	...	...	...	...	4 791	...	4 791	...
Maths. & computer sc.		...	...	...	...	...	...	6 315	...	6 315	...
Health-related prg.		...	...	...	...	...	...	16 461	...	16 461	...
Engineering		...	...	...	...	...	...	13 095	...	13 095	...
Archit. & town plng.		...	...	...	...	...	...	4 141	...	4 141	...
Trade, craft & indust.		...	...	...	...	...	...	644	...	644	...
Transport & communic.		...	...	...	...	...	...	35	...	35	...
Agriculture		...	...	...	...	...	...	5 018	...	5 018	...
Other & not specified		...	...	...	...	...	...	7 180	...	7 180	...
El Salvador‡ Total	1993	16 361	9 984	63 787	30 620	./.	./.	80 148	40 604	70 499	20 058
Education science		10 068	6 558	1 922	1 405	./.	./.	11 990	7 963	12 009	5 799
Humanities & religion		-	-	1 776	964	./.	./.	1 776	964	1 654	299
Fine & applied arts		-	-	145	57	./.	./.	145	57	197	132
Law		-	-	7 325	3 487	./.	./.	7 325	3 487	4 735	647
Social & behav. sc.		-	-	2 318	1 657	./.	./.	2 318	1 657	5 883	1 706
Business administr.		787	476	16 680	8 090	./.	./.	17 467	8 566	16 715	5 730
Communic. & doc.		276	239	3 737	2 473	./.	./.	4 013	2 712	951	331
Home economics		-	-	719	302	./.	./.	719	302	-	-
Service trades		14	11	-	-	-	-	14	11	69	50
Natural science		-	-	238	137	./.	./.	238	137	1 887	141
Maths. & computer sc.		892	434	1 241	632	./.	./.	2 133	1 066	295	-
Health-related prg.		2 033	1 654	11 779	7 313	./.	./.	13 812	8 967	7 118	1 617
Engineering		413	203	12 298	2 849	./.	./.	12 711	3 052	10 851	1 042
Archit. & town plng.		135	21	1 806	844	./.	./.	1 941	865	2 723	1 129
Trade, craft & indust.		1 312	253	260	173	./.	./.	1 572	426	319	73
Transport & communic.		-	-	-	-	-	-	-	-	-	-
Agriculture		294	12	1 543	237	./.	./.	1 837	249	3 045	150
Other & not specified		137	123	-	-	-	-	137	123	2 048	1 212
Honduras Total	1994	562	318	49 481	20 340	280	106	50 323	20 764	36 620	...
Education science		-	-	6 838	4 663	-	-	6 838	4 663	6 234	...
Humanities & religion		46	-	719	346	-	-	765	346	244	...
Fine & applied arts		38	32	11	5	-	-	49	37	23	...
Law		-	-	6 719	2 863	-	-	6 719	2 863	3 546	...
Social & behav. sc.		-	-	1 651	890	63	25	1 714	915	3 145	...
Business administr.		300	152	11 802	*4 743	56	17	12 158	4 912	6 239	...
Communic. & doc.		94	74	1 085	529	-	-	1 179	603	449	...
Home economics		-	-	-	-	-	-	-	-	-	-
Service trades		33	29	118	*70	-	-	151	99		
Natural science		-	-	187	91	-	-	187	91	335	...
Maths. & computer sc.		14	7	2 651	170	-	-	2 665	177	196	...
Health-related prg.		-	-	6 193	3 588	130	52	6 323	3 640	5 691	...
Engineering		-	-	8 205	1 623	31	12	8 236	1 635	8 533	...
Archit. & town plng.		-	-	645	258	-	-	645	258	444	...
Trade, craft & indust.		37	24	-	-	-	-	37	24	-	...
Transport & communic.		-	-	-	-	-	-	-	-	-	-
Agriculture		-	-	1 917	423	-	-	1 917	423	1 256	...
Other & not specified		-	-	*740	*78	-	-	740	78	285	...

3.11 Third level: students by level and field of study
Troisième degré: étudiants par niveau et domaine d'études
Tercer grado: estudiantes por nivel y sector de estudios

Country Field of study Pays Domaines d'études País Sectores de estudios	Year Année Año	Students by ISCED level of programme Étudiants par niveau de programmes de la CITE Estudiantes por nivel de programas de la CINE								Students all levels, 1985 Étudiants tous niveaux, 1985 Estudiantes todos los niveles 1985	
		Level 5 Niveau 5 Nivel 5		Level 6 Niveau 6 Nivel 6		Level 7 Niveau 7 Nivel 7		All levels Tous niveaux Todos los niveles			
		MF	F	MF	F	MF	F	MF	F	MF	F
		(1)	(2)	(3)	(4)	(5)	(6)	(7)	(8)	(9)	(10)
Jamaica‡											
Total	1991/92	9 553	...	5 402	...	936	575	15 891	...	5 126	2 914
Education science		3 718	...	313	...	179	148	4 210	...	358	276
Humanities & religion		13	...	1 354	...	131	101	1 498	...	1 217	882
Fine & applied arts		219	...	-	-	-	-	219	...	-	-
Law		-	-	43	...	-	-	43	...	41	26
Social & behav. sc.		19	...	1 767	...	365	189	2 151	...	1 480	848
Business administr.		2 480	...	-	-	-	-	2 480	...	./.	./.
Communic. & doc.		./.	...	./.	...	./.	./.	./.	...	126	79
Home economics		25	...	-	-	-	-	25	...	-	-
Service trades		364	...	16	...	-	-	380	...	-	-
Natural science		-	-	1 260	...	134	74	1 394	...	1 260	537
Maths. & computer sc.		376	...	53	...	-	-	429	...	./.	./.
Health-related prg.		475	...	504	...	127	63	1 106	...	644	266
Engineering		957	...	47	...	-	-	1 004	...	-	-
Archit. & town plng.		429	...	45	...	-	-	474	...	-	-
Trade, craft & indust.		-	-	-	-	-	-	-	-	-	-
Transport & communic.		-	-	-	-	-	-	-	-	-	-
Agriculture		245	...	-	-	-	-	245	...	-	-
Other & not specified		233	...	-	-	-	-	233	...	-	-
Mexico‡											
Total	1993/94	-	-	1 303 361	605 200	54 910	20 536	1 358 271	625 736	1 199 120	454 366
Education science		-	-	140 729	92 685	6 263	3 307	146 992	95 992	156 168	91 099
Humanities & religion		-	-	14 715	8 491	1 821	928	16 536	9 419	22 298	11 510
Fine & applied arts		-	-	24 079	13 571	240	119	24 319	13 690	1 236	645
Law		-	-	132 769	59 464	2 593	933	135 362	60 397	112 295	38 146
Social & behav. sc.		-	-	69 648	43 763	6 458	2 804	76 106	46 567	81 278	48 486
Business administr.		-	-	320 581	171 339	11 769	4 115	332 350	175 454	218 150	96 783
Communic. & doc.		-	-	36 365	24 065	247	114	36 612	24 179	23 472	14 906
Home economics		-	-	2 656	2 217	56	38	2 712	2 255	-	-
Service trades		-	-	27 985	20 579	26	14	28 011	20 593	-	-
Natural science		-	-	39 201	21 988	3 256	1 184	42 457	23 172	26 836	10 325
Maths. & computer sc.		-	-	95 432	39 599	2 143	580	97 575	40 179	34 342	11 862
Health-related prg.		-	-	94 056	53 613	12 960	4 842	107 016	58 455	148 709	70 978
Engineering		-	-	217 868	30 347	3 999	710	221 867	31 057	209 357	24 267
Archit. & town plng.		-	-	46 732	13 748	1 069	301	47 801	14 049	55 106	14 658
Trade, craft & indust.		-	-	-	-	-	-	-	-	-	-
Transport & communic.		-	-	1 611	158	69	9	1 680	167	-	-
Agriculture		-	-	36 935	9 098	1 738	474	38 673	9 572	97 639	12 762
Other & not specified		-	-	1 999	475	203	64	2 202	539	12 234	7 939
Nicaragua											
Total	1991	1 124	646	30 042	14 766	333	97	31 499	15 509	29 001	16 355
Education science		-	-	4 028	2 396	31	19	4 059	2 415	5 856	4 150
Humanities & religion		-	-	258	194	-	-	258	194	112	105
Fine & applied arts		-	-	154	106	-	-	154	106	142	105
Law		-	-	2 632	1 242	-	-	2 632	1 242	446	235
Social & behav. sc.		-	-	753	560	-	-	753	560	2 760	1 650
Business administr.		350	200	5 517	2 695	-	-	5 867	2 895	3 528	2 068
Communic. & doc.		-	-	435	306	-	-	435	306	360	294
Home economics		-	-	153	137	-	-	153	137	244	239
Service trades		-	-	-	-	-	-	-	-	-	-
Natural science		-	-	905	688	-	-	905	688	712	486
Maths. & computer sc.		64	37	2 241	1 196	-	-	2 305	1 233	395	255
Health-related prg.		243	225	3 905	2 457	288	75	4 436	2 757	4 339	2 728
Engineering		55	39	5 723	1 495	-	-	5 778	1 534	4 013	1 290
Archit. & town plng.		-	-	495	285	-	-	495	285	404	246
Trade, craft & indust.		-	-	-	-	-	-	-	-	69	57
Transport & communic.		-	-	-	-	-	-	-	-	46	4
Agriculture		412	145	2 843	1 009	14	3	3 269	1 157	4 477	2 039
Other & not specified		-	-	-	-	-	-	-	-	1 098	404

Third level: students by level and field of study 3.11
Troisième degré: étudiants par niveau et domaine d'études
Tercer grado: estudiantes por nivel y sector de estudios

Country Field of study Pays Domaines d'études País Sectores de estudios	Year Année Año	Students by ISCED level of programme Étudiants par niveau de programmes de la CITE Estudiantes por nivel de programas de la CINE								Students all levels, 1985 Étudiants tous niveaux, 1985 Estudiantes todos los niveles 1985	
		Level 5 Niveau 5 Nivel 5		Level 6 Niveau 6 Nivel 6		Level 7 Niveau 7 Nivel 7		All levels Tous niveaux Todos los niveles			
		MF	F	MF	F	MF	F	MF	F	MF	F
		(1)	(2)	(3)	(4)	(5)	(6)	(7)	(8)	(9)	(10)
Panama‡ Total	1994	...	...	...	...	...	...	70 327	...	55 303	31 856
Education science		...	...	...	...	...	...	2 490	...	3 567	2 756
Humanities & religion		...	...	...	...	...	...	5 457	...	2 082	1 531
Fine & applied arts		...	...	...	...	...	...	493	...	498	286
Law		...	...	...	...	...	...	3 015	...	2 439	1 043
Social & behav. sc.		...	...	...	...	...	...	986	...	3 987	2 152
Business administr.		...	...	...	...	...	...	11 694	...	17 620	11 692
Communic. & doc.		...	...	...	...	...	...	2 599	...	2 854	1 977
Home economics		...	...	...	...	...	...	-	-	217	217
Service trades		...	...	...	...	...	...			7	4
Natural science		...	...	...	...	...	...	3 479	...	1 737	865
Maths. & computer sc.		...	...	...	...	...	...	2 666	...	794	394
Health-related prg.		...	...	...	...	...	...	2 544	...	3 855	3 057
Engineering		...	...	...	...	...	...	4 218	...	10 195	2 675
Archit. & town plng.		...	...	...	...	...	...	2 928	...	787	235
Trade, craft & indust.		...	...	...	...	...	...	./.	...	585	279
Transport & communic.		...	...	...	...	...	...	./.	...	-	-
Agriculture		...	...	...	...	...	...	751	...	245	51
Other & not specified		...	...	...	...	...	...	27 007	...	3 834	2 642
St. Kitts and Nevis Total	1992/93	394	215	-	-	-	-	394	215	212	90
Education science		58	48	-	-	-	-	58	48	52	41
Humanities & religion		20	10	-	-	-	-	20	10	-	-
Fine & applied arts		-	-	-	-	-	-	-	-	-	-
Law		-	-	-	-	-	-	-	-	-	-
Social & behav. sc.		-	-	-	-	-	-	-	-	-	-
Business administr.		35	15	-	-	-	-	35	15	-	-
Communic. & doc.		-	-	-	-	-	-	-	-	-	-
Home economics		-	-	-	-	-	-	-	-	-	-
Service trades		12	11	-	-	-	-	12	11	-	-
Natural science		18	15	-	-	-	-	18	15	-	-
Maths. & computer sc.		67	31	-	-	-	-	67	31	-	-
Health-related prg.		45	45	-	-	-	-	45	45	-	-
Engineering		-	-	-	-	-	-	-	-	-	-
Archit. & town plng.		10	2	-	-	-	-	10	2	-	-
Trade, craft & indust.		129	38	-	-	-	-	129	38	160	49
Transport & communic.		-	-	-	-	-	-	-	-	-	-
Agriculture		-	-	-	-	-	-	-	-	-	-
Other & not specified		-	-	-	-	-	-	-	-	-	-

**St. Vincent and the
  Grenadines**
  Total
	1989/90	677	458	-	-	-	-	677	458	736	509

Education science		112	83	-	-	-	-	112	83	119	72
Humanities & religion		180	97	-	-	-	-	180	97	-	-
Fine & applied arts		-	-	-	-	-	-	-	-	-	-
Law		2	-	-	-	-	-	2	-	-	-
Social & behav. sc.		71	52	-	-	-	-	71	52	-	-
Business administr.		-	-	-	-	-	-	-	-	444	407
Communic. & doc.		-	-	-	-	-	-	-	-	-	-
Home economics		-	-	-	-	-	-	-	-	-	-
Service trades		-	-	-	-	-	-	-	-	-	-
Natural science		-	-	-	-	-	-	-	-	-	-
Maths. & computer sc.		-	-	-	-	-	-	-	-	-	-
Health-related prg.		120	116	-	-	-	-	120	116	-	-
Engineering		-	-	-	-	-	-	-	-	144	6
Archit. & town plng.		-	-	-	-	-	-	-	-	-	-
Trade, craft & indust.		179	99	-	-	-	-	179	99	-	-
Transport & communic.		-	-	-	-	-	-	-	-	-	-
Agriculture		-	-	-	-	-	-	-	-	29	24
Other & not specified		13	11	-	-	-	-	13	11	-	-

3.11 Third level: students by level and field of study
Troisième degré: étudiants par niveau et domaine d'études
Tercer grado: estudiantes por nivel y sector de estudios

Country Field of study / Pays Domaines d'études / País Sectores de estudios	Year Année Año	Students by ISCED level of programme / Étudiants par niveau de programmes de la CITE / Estudiantes por nivel de programas de la CINE								Students all levels, 1985 / Étudiants tous niveaux, 1985 / Estudiantes todos los niveles 1985	
		Level 5 Niveau 5 Nivel 5		Level 6 Niveau 6 Nivel 6		Level 7 Niveau 7 Nivel 7		All levels Tous niveaux Todos los niveles			
		MF	F	MF	F	MF	F	MF	F	MF	F
		(1)	(2)	(3)	(4)	(5)	(6)	(7)	(8)	(9)	(10)
Trinidad and Tobago‡ Total	1993/94	424	271	3 867	1 920	900	389	5 191	2 580	6 083	2 469
Education science		137	91	45	34	82	55	264	180	547	399
Humanities & religion		46	23	670	502	60	41	776	566	652	460
Fine & applied arts		./.	./.	./.	./.	./.	./.	./.	./.	./.	./.
Law		-	-	41	31	-	-	41	31	34	16
Social & behav. sc.		232	157	790	483	245	109	1 267	749	707	419
Business administr.		./.	./.	./.	./.	./.	./.	./.	./.	638	345
Communic. & doc.		./.	./.	./.	./.	./.	./.	./.	./.	-	-
Home economics		-	-	-	-	-	-	-	-	19	19
Service trades		-	-	-	-	-	-	-	-	-	-
Natural science		-	-	660	347	93	48	753	395	697	327
Maths. & computer sc.		-	-	./.	./.	./.	./.	./.	./.	109	42
Health-related prg.		-	-	580	261	37	16	617	277	-	-
Engineering		-	-	807	147	243	60	1 050	207	529	74
Archit. & town plng.		-	-	-	-	-	-	-	-	349	20
Trade, craft & indust.		-	-	./.	./.	./.	./.	./.	./.	1 324	188
Transport & communic.		-	-	./.	./.	./.	./.	./.	./.	64	1
Agriculture		9	-	274	115	140	60	423	175	414	159
Other & not specified		-	-	-	-	-		-		-	
United States Total	1990/91	5 181 018	...	6 681 892	...	1 847 240	...	13 710 150	...	...	...
Education science		189 677	...	469 430	...	302 758	...	961 865	...	...	...
Humanities & religion		580 312	...	590 463	...	136 909	...	1 307 684	...	...	...
Fine & applied arts		126 720	...	298 272	...	47 148	...	472 140	...	...	...
Law		122 960	...	45 091	...	137 130	...	305 181	...	...	...
Social & behav. sc.		84 573	...	525 291	...	121 361	...	731 225	...	...	...
Business administr.		937 592	...	1 220 755	...	263 108	...	2 421 455	...	...	...
Communic. & doc.		78 651	...	161 092	...	36 430	...	276 173	...	...	...
Home economics		116 508	...	187 253	...	22 701	...	326 462	...	...	...
Service trades		39 675	...	23 356	...	6 963	...	69 994	...	...	...
Natural science		107 436	...	299 623	...	89 356	...	496 415	...	...	...
Maths. & computer sc.		199 462	...	254 958	...	70 647	...	525 067	...	...	...
Health-related prg.		630 990	...	546 182	...	230 729	...	1 407 901	...	...	...
Engineering		238 554	...	472 932	...	89 640	...	801 126	...	...	...
Archit. & town plng.		39 606	...	72 295	...	8 926	...	120 827	...	...	...
Trade, craft & indust.		214 520	...	-	-	-	-	214 520	...	...	...
Transport & communic.		17 721	...	55 544	...	37 864	...	111 129	...	...	...
Agriculture		24 993	...	50 880	...	12 460	...	88 333	...	...	...
Other & not specified		1 431 068	...	1 408 475	...	233 110	...	3 072 653	...	...	...
U.S. Virgin Isl.‡ Total	1992/93	-	-	2 713	1 991	211	175	2 924	2 166	706	...
Education science		-	-	291	247	149	117	440	364	86	...
Humanities & religion		-	-	59	48	-	-	59	48	53	...
Fine & applied arts		-	-	-	-	-	-	-	-	-	-
Law		-	-	-	-	-	-	-	-	-	
Social & behav. sc.		-	-	155	129	-	-	155	129	68	...
Business administr.		-	-	932	742	62	58	994	800	257	...
Communic. & doc.		-	-	27	26	-	-	27	26	-	-
Home economics		-	-	-	-	-	-	-	-	-	
Service trades		-	-	-	-	-	-	-	-	-	
Natural science		-	-	152	83	-	-	152	83	81	...
Maths. & computer sc.		-	-	89	60	-	-	89	60	20	...
Health-related prg.		-	-	130	125	-	-	130	125	98	...
Engineering		-	-	-	-	-	-	-	-	15	...
Archit. & town plng.		-	-	-	-	-	-	-	-	-	
Trade, craft & indust.		-	-	-	-	-	-	-	-	-	
Transport & communic.		-	-	-	-	-	-	-	-	-	
Agriculture		-	-	-	-	-	-	-	-	2	...
Other & not specified		-	-	878	531	-	-	878	531	26	...

Third level: students by level and field of study 3.11
Troisième degré: étudiants par niveau et domaine d'études
Tercer grado: estudiantes por nivel y sector de estudios

Country Field of study Pays Domaines d'études País Sectores de estudios	Year Année Año	Students by ISCED level of programme Étudiants par niveau de programmes de la CITE Estudiantes por nivel de programas de la CINE								Students all levels, 1985 Étudiants tous niveaux, 1985 Estudiantes todos los niveles 1985	
		Level 5 Niveau 5 Nivel 5		Level 6 Niveau 6 Nivel 6		Level 7 Niveau 7 Nivel 7		All levels Tous niveaux Todos los niveles			
		MF	F	MF	F	MF	F	MF	F	MF	F
		(1)	(2)	(3)	(4)	(5)	(6)	(7)	(8)	(9)	(10)
America, South											
Argentina‡ Total	1994	...	...	...	...	...	...	740 545	383 737	...	...
Education science		...	...	...	...	...	...	12 214	9 759	...	...
Humanities & religion		...	...	...	...	...	...	61 307	47 652	...	...
Fine & applied arts		...	...	...	...	...	...	22 974	14 538	...	...
Law		...	...	...	...	...	...	119 740	66 088	...	...
Social & behav. sc.		...	...	...	...	...	...	43 930	29 489	...	...
Business administr.		...	...	...	...	...	...	148 737	69 223	...	...
Communic. & doc.		...	...	...	...	...	...	./.	./.	...	...
Home economics		...	...	...	...	...	...	-	-	...	...
Service trades		...	...	...	...	...	...			...	...
Natural science		...	...	...	...	...	...	69 727	39 288	...	...
Maths. & computer sc.		...	...	...	...	...	...	./.	./.	...	...
Health-related prg.		...	...	...	...	...	...	101 444	62 403	...	...
Engineering		...	...	...	...	...	...	96 205	18 149	...	...
Archit. & town plng.		...	...	...	...	...	...	28 560	11 982	...	...
Trade, craft & indust.		...	...	...	...	...	...	-	-	...	...
Transport & communic.		...	...	...	...	...	...	-	-	...	...
Agriculture		...	...	...	...	...	...	25 444	8 802	...	...
Other & not specified		...	...	...	...	...	...	10 263	6 364	...	...
Bolivia‡ Total	1991	...	...	...	...	...	...	109 503	...	88 175	...
Education science		...	...	...	...	...	...	761	...	736	...
Humanities & religion		...	...	...	...	...	...	2 197	...	2 255	...
Fine & applied arts		...	...	...	...	...	...	211	...	200	...
Law		...	...	...	...	...	...	13 594	...	10 013	...
Social & behav. sc.		...	...	...	...	...	...	7 058	...	9 574	...
Business administr.		...	...	...	...	...	...	19 027	...	15 997	...
Communic. & doc.		...	...	...	...	...	...	3 017	...	1 236	...
Home economics		...	...	...	...	...	...	349	...	468	...
Service trades		...	...	...	...	...	...	1 461	...	726	...
Natural science		...	...	...	...	...	...	2 930	...	1 671	...
Maths. & computer sc.		...	...	...	...	...	...	5 435	...	1 509	...
Health-related prg.		...	...	...	...	...	...	21 695	...	16 098	...
Engineering		...	...	...	...	...	...	17 087	...	17 681	...
Archit. & town plng.		...	...	...	...	...	...	3 186	...	2 795	...
Trade, craft & indust.		...	...	...	...	...	...	3 307	...	2 918	...
Transport & communic.		...	...	...	...	...	...	-	-	-	-
Agriculture		...	...	...	...	...	...	2 776	...	1 344	...
Other & not specified		...	...	...	...	...	...	5 412	...	2 954	...
Brazil‡ Total	1994	-	-	1 661 034	907 677	...	...	1 661 034	907 677	1 451 191	...
Education science		-	-	192 368	156 190	...	...	192 368	156 190	224 503	...
Humanities & religion		-	-	138 525	101 587	...	...	138 525	101 587	141 333	...
Fine & applied arts		-	-	10 158	6 584	...	...	10 158	6 584	10 684	...
Law		-	-	190 712	90 125	...	...	190 712	90 125	143 276	...
Social & behav. sc.		-	-	157 534	93 895	...	...	157 534	93 895	148 756	...
Business administr.		-	-	306 501	138 281	...	...	306 501	138 281	233 754	...
Communic. & doc.		-	-	55 089	35 286	...	...	55 089	35 286	41 502	...
Home economics		-	-	11 071	10 393	...	...	11 071	10 393	10 525	...
Service trades		-	-	9 235	6 250	...	...	9 235	6 250	4 681	...
Natural science		-	-	46 322	24 084	...	...	46 322	24 084	44 948	...
Maths. & computer sc.		-	-	92 701	37 413	...	...	92 701	37 413	42 460	...
Health-related prg.		-	-	154 797	102 304	...	...	154 797	102 304	127 925	...
Engineering		-	-	149 660	28 733	...	...	149 660	28 733	146 256	...
Archit. & town plng.		-	-	24 932	15 780	...	...	24 932	15 780	20 540	...
Trade, craft & indust.		-	-	19 269	6 252	...	...	19 269	6 252	8 161	...
Transport & communic.		-	-	286	60	...	...	286	60	180	...
Agriculture		-	-	39 780	14 310	...	...	39 780	14 310	37 501	...
Other & not specified		-	-	62 094	40 150	...	...	62 094	40 150	64 206	...

3.11   Third level: students by level and field of study
Troisième degré: étudiants par niveau et domaine d'études
Tercer grado: estudiantes por nivel y sector de estudios

Country Field of study / Pays Domaines d'études / País Sectores de estudios	Year Année Año	Level 5 Niveau 5 Nivel 5 MF	F	Level 6 Niveau 6 Nivel 6 MF	F	Level 7 Niveau 7 Nivel 7 MF	F	All levels Tous niveaux Todos los niveles MF	F	Students all levels, 1985 Étudiants tous niveaux, 1985 Estudiantes todos los niveles 1985 MF	F
		(1)	(2)	(3)	(4)	(5)	(6)	(7)	(8)	(9)	(10)
Chile‡#											
Total	1995	90 479	40 162	244 975	113 235	7 334	3 217	342 788	156 614	188 665	80 652
Education science		878	855	24 208	19 055	1 410	916	26 496	20 826	19 278	15 222
Humanities & religion		604	469	18 560	12 916	1 367	782	20 531	14 167	13 961	8 725
Fine & applied arts		./.	./.	./.	./.	./.	./.	./.	./.	7 614	4 335
Law		1 142	759	15 904	6 449	179	44	17 225	7 252	4 314	1 235
Social & behav. sc.		2 416	1 183	45 333	23 602	760	285	48 509	25 070	5 087	2 714
Business administr.		40 420	24 203	26 793	11 403	760	154	67 973	35 760	36 430	14 701
Communic. & doc.		./.	./.	./.	./.	./.	./.	./.	./.	652	428
Home economics		-	-	-	-	-	-	-	-	528	440
Service trades		-	-	-	-	-	-	-	-	298	213
Natural science		1 067	588	6 692	3 098	818	323	8 577	4 009	9 535	4 623
Maths. & computer sc.		./.	./.	./.	./.	./.	./.	./.	./.	8 051	3 017
Health-related prg.		2 400	1 870	15 140	9 737	811	372	18 351	11 979	15 485	8 729
Engineering		29 196	5 902	55 680	10 308	607	82	85 483	16 292	54 412	11 211
Archit. & town plng.		4 334	1 790	17 243	9 377	275	147	21 852	11 314	2 554	741
Trade, craft & indust.		./.	./.	-	-	-	-	./.	./.	1 575	441
Transport & communic.		-		-		-		-		-	
Agriculture		8 022	2 543	19 422	7 290	347	112	27 791	9 945	3 888	1 288
Other & not specified		-	-	-	-	-	-	-	-	5 003	2 589
Colombia‡											
Total	1994	...	...	...	...	...	...	588 322	298 386	391 490	189 937
Education science		...	...	...	...	...	...	88 387	59 915	74 783	50 866
Humanities & religion		...	...	...	...	...	...	4 294	1 898	2 677	1 334
Fine & applied arts		...	...	...	...	...	...	18 406	10 647	8 765	5 324
Law		...	...	...	...	...	...	65 826	38 101	48 405	27 373
Social & behav. sc.		...	...	...	...	...	...	./.	./.	./.	./.
Business administr.		...	...	...	...	...	...	179 066	95 530	104 334	51 967
Communic. & doc.		...	...	...	...	...	...	-	-	./.	./.
Home economics		...	...	...	...	...	...	-	-	./.	./.
Service trades		...	...	...	...	...	...	-	-	./.	./.
Natural science		...	...	...	...	...	...	10 881	5 052	6 477	2 439
Maths. & computer sc.		...	...	...	...	...	...	./.	./.	./.	./.
Health-related prg.		...	...	...	...	...	...	51 492	34 713	39 904	22 589
Engineering		...	...	...	...	...	...	153 840	47 168	95 280	25 212
Archit. & town plng.		...	...	...	...	...	...	./.	./.	./.	./.
Trade, craft & indust.		...	...	...	...	...	...	-	-	./.	./.
Transport & communic.		...	...	...	...	...	...	-	-	./.	./.
Agriculture		...	...	...	...	...	...	16 130	5 362	10 865	2 833
Other & not specified		...	...	...	...	...	...	-	-	-	-
Ecuador #											
Total	1990/91	...	...	...	...	...	...	206 541	...	280 594	...
Education science		...	...	...	...	...	...	51 211	...	53 520	...
Humanities & religion		...	...	...	...	...	...	1 235	...	14 264	...
Fine & applied arts		...	...	...	...	...	...	796	...	2 634	...
Law		...	...	...	...	...	...	16 903	...	13 803	...
Social & behav. sc.		...	...	...	...	...	...	23 800	...	21 116	...
Business administr.		...	...	...	...	...	...	35 623	...	41 993	...
Communic. & doc.		...	...	...	...	...	...	6 779	...	1 882	...
Home economics		...	...	...	...	...	...	548	...	389	...
Service trades		...	...	...	...	...	...	95	...	314	...
Natural science		...	...	...	...	...	...	7 170	...	8 797	...
Maths. & computer sc.		...	...	...	...	...	...	294	...	5 255	...
Health-related prg.		...	...	...	...	...	...	23 715	...	28 824	...
Engineering		...	...	...	...	...	...	25 214	...	54 876	...
Archit. & town plng.		...	...	...	...	...	...	5 117	...	10 672	...
Trade, craft & indust.		...	...	...	...	...	...	702	...	900	...
Transport & communic.		...	...	...	...	...	...	-	-	-	-
Agriculture		...	...	...	...	...	...	5 666	...	4 043	...
Other & not specified		...	...	...	...	...	...	1 673	...	17 312	...

Third level: students by level and field of study 3.11
Troisième degré: étudiants par niveau et domaine d'études
Tercer grado: estudiantes por nivel y sector de estudios

Country Field of study Pays Domaines d'études País Sectores de estudios	Year Année Año	Students by ISCED level of programme Étudiants par niveau de programmes de la CITE Estudiantes por nivel de programas de la CINE								Students all levels, 1985 Étudiants tous niveaux, 1985	
		Level 5 Niveau 5 Nivel 5		Level 6 Niveau 6 Nivel 6		Level 7 Niveau 7 Nivel 7		All levels Tous niveaux Todos los niveles		Estudiantes todos los niveles 1985	
		MF	F	MF	F	MF	F	MF	F	MF	F
		(1)	(2)	(3)	(4)	(5)	(6)	(7)	(8)	(9)	(10)
Guyana											
Total	1989/90	3 205	1 225	1 382	738	78	38	4 665	2 001	2 328	1 113
Education science		576	478	143	91	47	26	766	595	769	546
Humanities & religion		-	-	190	136	6	2	196	138	125	76
Fine & applied arts		-	-	-	-	-	-	-	-	-	-
Law		-	-	25	11	-	-	25	11	25	13
Social & behav. sc.		54	39	332	202	18	7	404	248	195	92
Business administr.		404	280	349	178	-	-	753	458	242	107
Communic. & doc.		39	24	41	24	-	-	80	48	21	7
Home economics		-	-	-	-	-	-	-	-	-	-
Service trades		-	-	-	-	-	-	-	-	1	-
Natural science		21	11	112	44	7	3	140	58	137	45
Maths. & computer sc.		-	-	12	2	-	-	12	2	30	8
Health-related prg.		190	102	51	16	-	-	241	118	98	41
Engineering		426	32	63	6	-	-	489	38	224	17
Archit. & town plng.		21	6	-	-	-	-	21	6	13	-
Trade, craft & indust.		1 383	205	-	-	-	-	1 383	205	-	-
Transport & communic.		-	-	-	-	-	-	-	-	-	-
Agriculture		8	3	64	28	-	-	72	31	280	77
Other & not specified		83	45	-	-	-	-	83	45	168	84
Paraguay‡											
Total	1993	6 148	4 718	30 486	14 542	45	35	36 679	19 295	32 090	...
Education science		6 148	4 718	697	571	-	-	6 845	5 289	3 324	...
Humanities & religion		-	-	688	285	-	-	688	285	4 439	...
Fine & applied arts		-	-	-	-	-	-	-	-	-	-
Law		-	-	4 938	2 404	45	35	4 983	2 439	4 230	...
Social & behav. sc.		-	-	916	487	-	-	916	487	732	...
Business administr.		-	-	8 259	3 736	-	-	8 259	3 736	7 223	...
Communic. & doc.		-	-	274	186	-	-	274	186	306	...
Home economics		-	-	-	-	-	-	-	-	-	-
Service trades		-	-	65	48	-	-	65	48	-	-
Natural science		-	-	1 113	893	-	-	1 113	893	520	...
Maths. & computer sc.		-	-	2 639	1 215	-	-	2 639	1 215	1 115	...
Health-related prg.		-	-	2 127	1 352	-	-	2 127	1 352	2 991	...
Engineering		-	-	1 793	309	-	-	1 793	309	4 228	...
Archit. & town plng.		-	-	1 389	692	-	-	1 389	692	1 578	...
Trade, craft & indust.		-	-	318	29	-	-	318	29	81	...
Transport & communic.		-	-	-	-	-	-	-	-	-	-
Agriculture		-	-	1 825	650	-	-	1 825	650	1 323	...
Other & not specified		-	-	3 445	1 685	-	-	3 445	1 685	-	...
Peru‡											
Total	1991	...	...	...	...	...	...	475 709	...	452 462	...
Education science		...	...	...	...	...	...	54 240	...	57 514	...
Humanities & religion		...	...	...	...	...	...	6 942	...	7 462	...
Fine & applied arts		...	...	...	...	...	...	665	...	6 323	...
Law		...	...	...	...	...	...	43 715	...	26 715	...
Social & behav. sc.		...	...	...	...	...	...	55 417	...	47 444	...
Business administr.		...	...	...	...	...	...	90 085	...	71 641	...
Communic. & doc.		...	...	...	...	...	...	7 277	...	7 363	...
Home economics		...	...	...	...	...	...	1 283	...	990	...
Service trades		...	...	...	...	...	...	2 663	...	-	-
Natural science		...	...	...	...	...	...	15 506	...	11 430	...
Maths. & computer sc.		...	...	...	...	...	...	10 273	...	6 973	...
Health-related prg.		...	...	...	...	...	...	54 418	...	34 646	...
Engineering		...	...	...	...	...	...	82 433	...	66 708	...
Archit. & town plng.		...	...	...	...	...	...	7 325	...	5 621	...
Trade, craft & indust.		...	...	...	...	...	...	-	-	65 457	...
Transport & communic.		...	...	...	...	...	...	-	-	-	-
Agriculture		...	...	...	...	...	...	21 784	...	20 412	...
Other & not specified		...	...	...	...	...	...	21 683	...	15 763	...

3.11 Third level: students by level and field of study
Troisième degré: étudiants par niveau et domaine d'études
Tercer grado: estudiantes por nivel y sector de estudios

Country / Field of study — Pays / Domaines d'études — País / Sectores de estudios	Year Année Año	Students by ISCED level of programme — Étudiants par niveau de programmes de la CITE — Estudiantes por nivel de programas de la CINE								Students all levels, 1985 — Étudiants tous niveaux, 1985 — Estudiantes todos los niveles 1985	
		Level 5 Niveau 5 Nivel 5		Level 6 Niveau 6 Nivel 6		Level 7 Niveau 7 Nivel 7		All levels Tous niveaux Todos los niveles			
		MF	F	MF	F	MF	F	MF	F	MF	F
		(1)	(2)	(3)	(4)	(5)	(6)	(7)	(8)	(9)	(10)
Suriname Total	1990/91	2 348	...	1 971	...	-	-	4 319	...	2 751	1 475
Education science		1 946	...	-	-	-	-	1 946	...	1 583	963
Humanities & religion		-	-	-	-	-	-	-	-	-	-
Fine & applied arts		-	-	42	...	-	-	42	...	21	7
Law		26	...	514	...	-	-	540	...	64	42
Social & behav. sc.		26	...	725	...	-	-	751	...	74	49
Business administr.		-	-	73	...	-	-	73	...	120	62
Communic. & doc.		-	-	38	...	-	-	38	-	18	8
Home economics		-	-	-	-	-	-	-	-	54	25
Service trades		-	-	-	-	-	-	-	-	-	-
Natural science		-	-	-	-	-	-	-	-	27	1
Maths. & computer sc.		-	-	-	-	-	-	-	-	-	-
Health-related prg.		-	-	356	...	-	-	356	...	110	47
Engineering		44	...	223	...	-	-	267	...	-	-
Archit. & town plng.		-	-	-	-	-	-	-	-	23	1
Trade, craft & indust.		-	-	-	-	-	-	-	-	-	-
Transport & communic.		-	-	-	-	-	-	-	-	-	-
Agriculture		-	-	-	-	-	-	-	-	19	9
Other & not specified		306	...	-	-	-	-	306	...	638	261
Uruguay‡ Total	1990	8 019	...	63 593	...	./.	...	71 612	...	...	...
Education science		7 321	...	-	-	-	-	7 321	...	...	...
Humanities & religion		-	-	3 730	...	./.	...	3 730	...	...	...
Fine & applied arts		-	-	2 370	...	./.	...	2 370	...	...	...
Law		-	-	14 380	...	./.	...	14 380	...	...	...
Social & behav. sc.		-	-	3 482	...	./.	...	3 482	...	...	...
Business administr.		-	-	9 604	...	./.	...	9 604	...	...	...
Communic. & doc.		-	-	1 195	...	./.	...	1 195	...	...	...
Home economics		-	-	136	...	./.	...	136	...	...	...
Service trades		-	-	-	-	-	-	-	-	...	...
Natural science		-	-	994	...	./.	...	994	...	...	...
Maths. & computer sc.		-	-	./.	...	./.	...	./.	...		
Health-related prg.		-	-	12 020	...	./.	...	12 020	...	...	...
Engineering		-	-	8 159	...	./.	...	8 159	...	...	...
Archit. & town plng.		-	-	3 404	...	./.	...	3 404	...	...	...
Trade, craft & indust.		-	-	52	...	./.	...	52	...	...	...
Transport & communic.		-	-	-	-	-	-	-	-	...	...
Agriculture		-	-	3 451	...	./.	...	3 451	...	...	...
Other & not specified		698	...	616	...	./.	...	1 314	...	...	...
Venezuela Total	1988/89	101 578	...	398 717	...	...	...	500 295	...	443 064	...
Education science		3 805	...	101 524	...	...	...	105 329	...	82 550	...
Humanities & religion		88	...	5 509	...	...	...	5 597	...	4 830	...
Fine & applied arts		86	...	1 146	...	...	...	1 232	...	651	...
Law		-	-	35 205	...	...	...	35 205	...	37 456	...
Social & behav. sc.		1 399	...	30 001	...	...	...	31 400	...	44 213	...
Business administr.		48 478	...	57 242	...	...	...	105 720	...	76 815	...
Communic. & doc.		230	...	5 649	...	...	...	5 879	...	6 539	...
Home economics		-	-	312	...	...	...	312	...	-	-
Service trades		1 961	...	159	...	...	...	2 120	...	393	...
Natural science		674	...	5 317	...	...	...	5 991	...	7 300	...
Maths. & computer sc.		14 702	...	3 829	...	...	...	18 531	...	8 623	...
Health-related prg.		2 175	...	45 506	...	...	...	47 681	...	46 465	...
Engineering		11 159	...	62 188	...	...	...	73 347	...	78 271	...
Archit. & town plng.		-	-	6 279	...	...	...	6 279	...	6 424	...
Trade, craft & indust.		6 397	...	-	-	-	-	6 397	...		
Transport & communic.		-	-	-	-	-	-	-	-	220	...
Agriculture		8 457	...	10 754	...	...	...	19 211	...	11 539	...
Other & not specified		1 967	...	28 097	...	...	...	30 064	...	30 775	...

Third level: students by level and field of study 3.11
Troisième degré: étudiants par niveau et domaine d'études
Tercer grado: estudiantes por nivel y sector de estudios

Country / Field of study / Pays / Domaines d'études / País / Sectores de estudios	Year / Année / Año	Students by ISCED level of programme / Étudiants par niveau de programmes de la CITE / Estudiantes por nivel de programas de la CINE								Students all levels, 1985 / Étudiants tous niveaux, 1985 / Estudiantes todos los niveles 1985	
		Level 5 / Niveau 5 / Nivel 5		Level 6 / Niveau 6 / Nivel 6		Level 7 / Niveau 7 / Nivel 7		All levels / Tous niveaux / Todos los niveles			
		MF	F	MF	F	MF	F	MF	F	MF	F
		(1)	(2)	(3)	(4)	(5)	(6)	(7)	(8)	(9)	(10)
Asia											
Afghanistan‡ Total	1990	14 966	3 499	9 367	3 970	./.	./.	24 333	7 469	...	...
Education science		6 245	3 357	478	260	./.	./.	6 723	3 617	...	...
Humanities & religion		8 721	142	1 482	801	./.	./.	10 203	943	...	...
Fine & applied arts		-	-	400	53	./.	./.	400	53	...	...
Law		-	-	1 092	464	./.	./.	1 092	464	...	...
Social & behav. sc.		-	-	660	323	./.	./.	660	323	...	...
Business administr.		-	-	906	327	./.	./.	906	327	...	...
Communic. & doc.		-	-	643	300	./.	./.	643	300	...	...
Home economics		-	-	-	-	-	-	-	-	...	...
Service trades		-	-	-	-	-	-	-	-	...	...
Natural science		-	-	1 237	666	./.	./.	1 237	666	...	...
Maths. & computer sc.		-	-	./.	./.	./.	./.	./.	./.	...	...
Health-related prg.		-	-	655	286	./.	./.	655	286	...	...
Engineering		-	-	504	183	./.	./.	504	183	...	...
Archit. & town plng.		-	-	./.	./.	./.	./.	./.	./.	...	...
Trade, craft & indust.		-	-	-	-	-	-	-	-	...	...
Transport & communic.		-	-	-	-	-	-	-	-	...	...
Agriculture		-	-	1 256	307	./.	./.	1 256	307	...	...
Other & not specified		-	-	54	-	./.	-	54	-	...	...
Azerbaijan‡ Total	1994/95	30 305	16 740	90 475	...	./.	...	120 870	...	...	...
Education science		3 880	3 504	34 672	...	./.	...	38 552	...	...	...
Humanities & religion		./.	./.	./.	...	./.	...	./.	...	...	...
Fine & applied arts		3 531	2 502	2 595	...	./.	...	6 126	...	...	...
Law		2 999	1 366	11 163	...	./.	...	14 162	...	...	...
Social & behav. sc.		./.	./.	./.	...	./.	...	./.	...	...	...
Business administr.		./.	./.	./.	...	./.	...	./.	...	...	...
Communic. & doc.		835	390	./.	...	./.	...	835	...	...	...
Home economics		-	-	-	-	-	-	-	...	...	...
Service trades		-	-	-	-	-	-	-	...	...	...
Natural science		-	-	./.	...	./.	...	./.	...	...	...
Maths. & computer sc.		./.	./.	./.	...	./.	...	./.	...	...	...
Health-related prg.		4 911	4 531	7 946	...	./.	...	12 857	...	...	...
Engineering		6 531	2 992	21 108	...	./.	...	27 639	...	...	...
Archit. & town plng.		600	119	4 872	...	./.	...	5 472	...	...	...
Trade, craft & indust.		./.	./.	./.	...	./.	...	./.	...	...	...
Transport & communic.		2 118	182	258	...	./.	...	2 376	...	...	...
Agriculture		4 725	1 068	5 954	...	./.	...	10 679	...	...	...
Other & not specified		265	95	1 907	...	./.	...	2 172	...	...	...
Bahrain Total	1993/94	...	...	...	...	...	...	7 676	4 444	4 180	2 490
Education science		...	...	...	...	...	...	1 960	1 331	1 254	967
Humanities & religion		...	...	...	...	...	...	./.	./.	./.	./.
Fine & applied arts		...	...	...	...	...	...	-	-	-	-
Law		...	...	...	...	...	...	-	-	-	-
Social & behav. sc.		...	...	...	...	...	...	-	-	-	-
Business administr.		...	...	...	...	...	...	1 721	1 217	1 074	638
Communic. & doc.		...	...	...	...	...	...	-	-	-	-
Home economics		...	...	...	...	...	...	-	-	-	-
Service trades		...	...	...	...	...	...	-	-	-	-
Natural science		...	...	...	...	...	...	1 199	789	336	252
Maths. & computer sc.		...	...	...	...	...	...	./.	./.	./.	./.
Health-related prg.		...	...	...	...	...	...	981	625	757	545
Engineering		...	...	...	...	...	...	1 815	482	759	88
Archit. & town plng.		...	...	...	...	...	...	./.	./.	./.	./.
Trade, craft & indust.		...	...	...	...	...	...	./.	./.	./.	./.
Transport & communic.		...	...	...	...	...	...	-	-	-	-
Agriculture		...	...	...	...	...	...	-	-	-	-
Other & not specified		...	...	...	...	...	...	-	-	-	-

3.11   Third level: students by level and field of study
Troisième degré: étudiants par niveau et domaine d'études
Tercer grado: estudiantes por nivel y sector de estudios

Country / Field of study / Pays / Domaines d'études / País / Sectores de estudios	Year / Année / Año	Students by ISCED level of programme / Étudiants par niveau de programmes de la CITE / Estudiantes por nivel de programas de la CINE								Students all levels, 1985 / Étudiants tous niveaux, 1985 / Estudiantes todos los niveles 1985	
		Level 5 / Niveau 5 / Nivel 5		Level 6 / Niveau 6 / Nivel 6		Level 7 / Niveau 7 / Nivel 7		All levels / Tous niveaux / Todos los niveles			
		MF	F	MF	F	MF	F	MF	F	MF	F
		(1)	(2)	(3)	(4)	(5)	(6)	(7)	(8)	(9)	(10)
Bangladesh‡											
Total	1989	-	-	340 275	55 004	30 625	3 750	370 900	58 754	461 073	87 755
Education science		-	-	3 844	1 343	-	-	3 844	1 343	7 789	1 755
Humanities & religion		-	-	95 671	16 053	15 165	2 023	110 836	18 076	155 094	33 647
Fine & applied arts		-	-	108	1	-	-	108	1	-	-
Law		-	-	18 787	985	235	68	19 022	1 053	-	-
Social & behav. sc.		-	-	81 963	14 563	5 304	509	87 267	15 072	115 308	21 061
Business administr.		-	-	44 245	5 354	3 467	243	47 712	5 597	59 522	9 653
Communic. & doc.		-	-	-	-	-	-	-	-	-	-
Home economics		-	-	861	861	282	282	1 143	1 143	./.	./.
Service trades		-	-	-	-	-	-	-	-	-	-
Natural science		-	-	71 829	12 198	3 674	218	75 503	12 416	94 323	16 673
Maths. & computer sc.		-	-	6 930	1 129	593	246	7 523	1 375	9 157	1 955
Health-related prg.		-	-	7 393	2 031	248	56	7 641	2 087	9 051	2 434
Engineering		-	-	4 883	163	947	68	5 830	231	4 671	154
Archit. & town plng.		-	-	164	48	132	21	296	69	345	31
Trade, craft & indust.		-	-	-	-	-	-	-	-	433	19
Transport & communic.		-	-	-	-	-	-	-	-	-	-
Agriculture		-	-	3 597	275	578	16	4 175	291	4 849	265
Other & not specified		-	-	-	-	-	-	-	-	531	108
Brunei Darussalam #											
Total	1992/93	513	328	841	448	34	13	1 388	789	607	386
Education science		306	216	577	291	22	7	905	514	591	379
Humanities & religion		-	-	-	-	-	-	-	-	-	-
Fine & applied arts		-	-	-	-	-	-	-	-	-	-
Law		-	-	-	-	-	-	-	-	-	-
Social & behav. sc.		-	-	32	13	-	-	32	13	-	-
Business administr.		67	40	-	-	-	-	67	40	-	-
Communic. & doc.		-	-	-	-	-	-	-	-	-	-
Home economics		-	-	-	-	-	-	-	-	-	-
Service trades		-	-	-	-	-	-	-	-	-	-
Natural science		-	-	-	-	-	-	-	-	-	-
Maths. & computer sc.		56	38	32	15	-	-	88	53	-	-
Health-related prg.		-	-	-	-	-	-	-	-	-	-
Engineering		80	32	10	-	-	-	90	32	-	-
Archit. & town plng.		-	-	-	-	-	-	-	-	-	-
Trade, craft & indust.		-	-	-	-	-	-	-	-	-	-
Transport & communic.		-	-	-	-	-	-	-	-	-	-
Agriculture		-	-	-	-	-	-	-	-	16	7
Other & not specified		4	2	190	129	12	6	206	137	-	-
China‡											
Total	1993/94	2 799 852	...	1 598 592	...	106 771	...	4 505 215	...	1 778 608	...
Education science		685 437	...	340 166	...	1 625	...	1 027 228	...	425 931	...
Humanities & religion		200 770	...	76 801	...	8 555	...	286 126	...	133 918	...
Fine & applied arts		40 223	...	13 169	...	356	...	53 748	...	12 968	...
Law		111 897	...	37 906	...	4 543	...	154 346	...	38 825	...
Social & behav. sc.		807 332	...	161 983	...	7 581	...	976 896	...	151 617	...
Business administr.		./.	...	./.	...	./.	...	./.	...	./.	...
Communic. & doc.		-	-	-	-	-	-	-	-	-	-
Home economics		-	-	-	-	-	-	-	-	-	-
Service trades		-	-	-	-	-	-	-	-	-	-
Natural science		21 412	...	57 133	...	16 947	...	95 492	...	81 883	...
Maths. & computer sc.		104 182	...	63 722	...	6 958	...	174 862	...	59 022	...
Health-related prg.		152 029	...	157 668	...	10 818	...	320 515	...	166 008	...
Engineering		557 198	...	560 818	...	38 719	...	1 156 735	...	466 276	...
Archit. & town plng.		6 355	...	12 083	...	898	...	19 336	...	90 563	...
Trade, craft & indust.		-	-	-	-	-	-	-	-	-	-
Transport & communic.		31 375	...	27 872	...	5 780	...	65 027	...	27 601	...
Agriculture		68 014	...	77 565	...	3 737	...	149 316	...	110 028	...
Other & not specified		13 628	...	11 706	...	254	...	25 588	...	13 968	...

Third level: students by level and field of study 3.11
Troisième degré: étudiants par niveau et domaine d'études
Tercer grado: estudiantes por nivel y sector de estudios

Country Field of study Pays Domaines d'études País Sectores de estudios	Year Année Año	Students by ISCED level of programme Étudiants par niveau de programmes de la CITE Estudiantes por nivel de programas de la CINE								Students all levels, 1985 Étudiants tous niveaux, 1985 Estudiantes todos los niveles 1985	
		Level 5 Niveau 5 Nivel 5		Level 6 Niveau 6 Nivel 6		Level 7 Niveau 7 Nivel 7		All levels Tous niveaux Todos los niveles			
		MF	F	MF	F	MF	F	MF	F	MF	F
		(1)	(2)	(3)	(4)	(5)	(6)	(7)	(8)	(9)	(10)
Cyprus‡ Total	1994/95	6 024	3 055	1 510	1 253	231	65	7 765	4 373	3 134	1 507
Education science		383	381	612	543	6	2	1 001	926	415	323
Humanities & religion		-	-	241	206	-	-	241	206	-	-
Fine & applied arts		160	111	-	-	12	9	172	120	-	-
Law		38	20	-	-	-	-	38	20	-	-
Social & behav. sc.		26	15	189	157	-	-	215	172	-	-
Business administr.		2 509	1 262	253	200	205	51	2 967	1 513	1 097	604
Communic. & doc.		196	137	-	-	-	-	196	137	-	-
Home economics		23	22	-	-	-	-	23	22	-	-
Service trades		753	446	-	-	-	-	753	446	226	109
Natural science		-	-	39	25	-	-	39	25	-	-
Maths. & computer sc.		553	170	176	122	-	-	729	292	228	88
Health-related prg.		524	380	-	-	-	-	524	380	209	155
Engineering		531	76	-	-	-	-	531	76	531	107
Archit. & town plng.		18	13	-	-	-	-	18	13	-	-
Trade, craft & indust.		264	22	-	-	-	-	264	22	154	8
Transport & communic.		-	-	-	-	-	-	-	-	7	3
Agriculture		46	-	-	-	1	-	47	-	36	-
Other & not specified		-	-	-	-	7	3	7	3	231	110
Georgia Total	1994/95	32 238	18 871	134 339	74 626	1 434	870	168 011	94 367	...	...
Education science		2 813	2 509	10 221	9 178	71	39	13 105	11 726	...	...
Humanities & religion		-	-	14 228	11 044	310	225	14 538	11 269	...	...
Fine & applied arts		3 159	2 763	5 598	4 626	67	45	8 824	7 434	...	...
Law		838	437	6 985	3 271	43	17	7 866	3 725	...	...
Social & behav. sc.		6 383	4 415	12 424	4 876	265	155	19 072	9 446	...	...
Business administr.		1 160	448	3 907	1 718	-	-	5 067	2 166	...	...
Communic. & doc.		-	-	-	-	-	-	-	-	...	...
Home economics		-	-	-	-	-	-	-	-	...	...
Service trades		-	-	-	-	-	-	-	-	...	...
Natural science		-	-	10 881	9 253	184	149	11 065	9 402	...	...
Maths. & computer sc.		-	-	1 702	1 063	128	43	1 830	1 106	...	...
Health-related prg.		4 868	4 396	11 553	6 716	147	91	16 568	11 203	...	...
Engineering		7 610	2 999	34 408	15 455	159	66	42 177	18 520	...	...
Archit. & town plng.		1 773	93	7 137	2 254	14	13	8 924	2 360	...	...
Trade, craft & indust.		193	-	2 080	550	-	-	2 273	550	...	...
Transport & communic.		1 314	320	3 543	1 339	-	-	4 857	1 659	...	...
Agriculture		2 127	491	9 672	3 283	46	27	11 845	3 801	...	...
Other & not specified		-	-	-	-	-	-	-	-	...	...
Hong Kong Total	1993/94	29 106	12 398	56 626	25 526	11 660	3 741	97 392	41 665	...	...
Education science		3 574	2 707	744	463	2 102	1 050	6 420	4 220	...	...
Humanities & religion		995	743	5 776	4 553	966	476	7 737	5 772	...	...
Fine & applied arts		./.	./.	./.	./.	./.	./.	./.	./.	...	...
Law		159	87	617	331	722	250	1 498	668	...	...
Social & behav. sc.		59	59	3 949	2 684	1 058	530	5 066	3 273	...	...
Business administr.		5 709	3 661	8 768	5 049	1 987	651	16 464	9 361	...	...
Communic. & doc.		-	-	640	482	18	12	658	494	...	...
Home economics		-	-	-	-	-	-	-	-	...	...
Service trades		666	420	320	237	5	-	991	657	...	...
Natural science		2 804	815	8 787	2 726	1 793	327	13 384	3 868	...	...
Maths. & computer sc.		./.	./.	./.	./.	./.	./.	./.	./.	...	...
Health-related prg.		620	431	3 037	1 317	486	191	4 143	1 939	...	...
Engineering		7 690	333	6 776	591	2 084	97	16 550	1 021	...	...
Archit. & town plng.		1 474	117	693	195	364	116	2 531	428	...	...
Trade, craft & indust.		1 688	960	594	331	43	18	2 325	1 309	...	...
Transport & communic.		164	53	-	-	-	-	164	53	...	...
Agriculture		-	-	-	-	-	-	-	-	...	...
Other & not specified		3 504	2 012	15 925	6 567	32	23	19 461	8 602	...	...

3.11   Third level: students by level and field of study
Troisième degré: étudiants par niveau et domaine d'études
Tercer grado: estudiantes por nivel y sector de estudios

Country / Field of study / Pays / Domaines d'études / País / Sectores de estudios	Year / Année / Año	Students by ISCED level of programme / Étudiants par niveau de programmes de la CITE / Estudiantes por nivel de programas de la CINE								Students all levels, 1985 / Étudiants tous niveaux, 1985 / Estudiantes todos los niveles 1985	
		Level 5 / Niveau 5 / Nivel 5		Level 6 / Niveau 6 / Nivel 6		Level 7 / Niveau 7 / Nivel 7		All levels / Tous niveaux / Todos los niveles			
		MF	F	MF	F	MF	F	MF	F	MF	F
		(1)	(2)	(3)	(4)	(5)	(6)	(7)	(8)	(9)	(10)
India‡											
Total	1990/91	57 521	14 699	3 898 663	1 262 937	469 063	159 251	4 425 247	1 436 887	4 470 844	1 336 216
Education science		2 560	1 111	89 722	48 501	7 331	3 581	99 613	53 193	186 584	87 654
Humanities & religion		20 926	4 941	1 540 226	681 452	228 328	97 967	1 789 480	784 360	1 651 795	652 288
Fine & applied arts		./.	./.	./.	./.	./.	./.	./.	./.	39 621	27 075
Law		2 368	253	227 291	22 566	4 879	635	234 538	23 454	200 780	20 176
Social & behav. sc.		./.	./.	./.	./.	./.	./.	./.	./.	./.	./.
Business administr.		5 834	625	890 307	191 084	73 741	10 026	969 882	201 735	827 865	180 362
Communic. & doc.		./.	./.	./.	./.	./.	./.	./.	./.	3 959	1 334
Home economics		./.	./.	./.	./.	./.	./.	./.	./.	-	-
Service trades		./.	./.	./.	./.	./.	./.	./.	./.	-	-
Natural science		3 231	1 996	761 207	250 174	104 681	37 247	869 119	289 417	739 087	239 519
Maths. & computer sc.		./.	./.	./.	./.	./.	./.	./.	./.	./.	./.
Health-related prg.		7 825	2 130	126 043	42 634	16 590	3 834	150 458	48 598	166 819	54 653
Engineering		6 466	570	199 433	15 776	10 938	784	216 837	17 130	494 711	43 234
Archit. & town plng.		./.	./.	./.	./.	./.	./.	./.	./.	./.	./.
Trade, craft & indust.		./.	./.	./.	./.	./.	./.	./.	./.	./.	./.
Transport & communic.		./.	./.	./.	./.	./.	./.	./.	./.	./.	./.
Agriculture		1 002	67	43 773	3 214	13 196	1 003	57 971	4 284	56 018	4 459
Other & not specified		7 309	3 006	20 661	7 536	9 379	4 174	37 349	14 716	103 605	25 462
Indonesia‡											
Total	1992/93	1 096 672	...	698 781	...	./.	...	1 795 453	...	...	...
Education science		195 986	...	125 652	...	./.	...	321 638	...	...	...
Humanities & religion		20 894	...	32 417	...	./.	...	53 311	...	...	...
Fine & applied arts		1 610	...	5 222	...	./.	...	6 832	...	...	...
Law		118 276	...	28 696	...	./.	...	146 972	...	...	...
Social & behav. sc.		177 178	...	144 600	...	./.	...	321 778	...	...	...
Business administr.		318 305	...	166 099	...	./.	...	484 404	...	...	...
Communic. & doc.		10 882	...	3 745	...	./.	...	14 627	...	...	...
Home economics		-	-	-	-	-	-	-	...	...	...
Service trades		1 733	...	15 344	...	./.	...	17 077	...	...	...
Natural science		6 446	...	15 948	...	./.	...	22 394	...	...	...
Maths. & computer sc.		3 920	...	9 197	...	./.	...	13 117	...	...	...
Health-related prg.		13 185	...	23 723	...	./.	...	36 908	...	...	...
Engineering		149 735	...	55 351	...	./.	...	205 086	...	...	...
Archit. & town plng.		22 027	...	6 237	...	./.	...	28 264	...	...	...
Trade, craft & indust.		304	...	2 225	...	./.	...	2 529	...	...	...
Transport & communic.		1 691	...	5 336	...	./.	...	7 027	...	...	...
Agriculture		54 500	...	58 989	...	./.	...	113 489	...	...	...
Other & not specified		-	-	-	-		-	-	-	...	...
Iran, Islamic Republic of‡											
Total	1994/95	64 431	16 323	383 394	122 796	30 630	6 234	478 455	145 353	184 442	52 780
Education science		4 326	534	58 170	22 018	709	173	63 205	22 725	52 552	15 217
Humanities & religion		356	186	45 978	20 701	3 059	541	49 393	21 428	11 373	4 945
Fine & applied arts		1 346	879	3 493	1 636	425	133	5 264	2 648	2 058	963
Law		84	-	5 799	911	660	29	6 543	940	3 430	559
Social & behav. sc.		345	120	34 728	10 703	2 301	423	37 374	11 246	14 054	5 577
Business administr.		3 209	233	43 535	9 246	1 065	62	47 809	9 541	5 748	1 793
Communic. & doc.		608	102	2 206	737	370	57	3 184	896	860	387
Home economics		23	23	31	20	-	-	54	43	604	450
Service trades		-	-	-	-	-	-	-	-	19	9
Natural science		317	98	27 926	11 962	2 432	480	30 675	12 540	11 283	4 450
Maths. & computer sc.		2 572	743	18 327	6 250	860	142	21 759	7 135	5 709	1 649
Health-related prg.		21 276	11 696	69 414	31 329	7 277	3 403	97 967	46 428	31 262	13 863
Engineering		24 032	1 001	59 415	5 718	5 289	197	88 736	6 916	36 967	1 861
Archit. & town plng.		806	177	200	36	2 340	421	3 346	634	2 019	521
Trade, craft & indust.		-	-	-	-	-	-	-	-	551	160
Transport & communic.		-	-	-	-	-	-	-	-	50	1
Agriculture		4 622	531	14 156	1 529	3 506	173	22 284	2 233	5 751	373
Other & not specified		509	-	16	-	337	-	862	-	152	2

Third level: students by level and field of study 3.11
Troisième degré: étudiants par niveau et domaine d'études
Tercer grado: estudiantes por nivel y sector de estudios

Country / Field of study / Pays Domaines d'études / País Sectores de estudios	Year Année Año	Students by ISCED level of programme / Étudiants par niveau de programmes de la CITE / Estudiantes por nivel de programas de la CINE								Students all levels, 1985 / Étudiants tous niveaux, 1985 / Estudiantes todos los niveles 1985	
		Level 5 Niveau 5 Nivel 5		Level 6 Niveau 6 Nivel 6		Level 7 Niveau 7 Nivel 7		All levels Tous niveaux Todos los niveles			
		MF	F	MF	F	MF	F	MF	F	MF	F
		(1)	(2)	(3)	(4)	(5)	(6)	(7)	(8)	(9)	(10)
Israel‡											
Total	1992/93	58 190	27 239	58 633	31 669	26 357	13 905	143 180	72 813	104 148	48 097
Education science		34 358	17 820	16 806	12 433	7 255	5 210	58 419	35 463	41 018	24 101
Humanities & religion		./.	./.	./.	./.	./.	./.	./.	./.	./.	./.
Fine & applied arts		./.	./.	./.	./.	./.	./.	./.	./.	./.	./.
Law		-	-	2 861	1 332	265	97	3 126	1 429	2 513	1 001
Social & behav. sc.		8 623	3 351	16 624	9 285	8 078	4 201	33 325	16 837	19 267	8 525
Business administr.		./.	./.	./.	./.	./.	./.	./.	./.	./.	./.
Communic. & doc.		./.	./.	./.	./.	./.	./.	./.	./.	./.	./.
Home economics		./.	./.	./.	./.	./.	./.	./.	./.	./.	./.
Service trades		./.	./.	./.	./.	./.	./.	./.	./.	./.	./.
Natural science		-	-	4 192	2 280	3 780	1 895	7 972	4 175	5 489	2 785
Maths. & computer sc.		-	-	4 952	1 771	1 192	358	6 144	2 129	4 435	1 597
Health-related prg.		2 175	1 825	3 796	2 710	2 486	1 282	8 457	5 817	6 723	4 189
Engineering		11 815	3 401	8 731	1 582	2 661	572	23 207	5 555	21 946	4 476
Archit. & town plng.		./.	./.	./.	./.	./.	./.	-	-	./.	./.
Trade, craft & indust.		-	-	-	-	-	-	-	-	-	-
Transport & communic.		-	-	-	-	-	-	-	-	-	-
Agriculture		-	-	671	276	640	290	1 311	566	1 207	452
Other & not specified		1 219	842	-	-	-	-	1 219	842	1 550	971
Japan‡											
Total	1991/92	564 044	486 407	2 236 449	670 607	98 650	16 827	2 899 143	1 173 841	2 347 463	818 978
Education science		82 476	81 144	139 897	83 126	6 232	2 481	228 605	166 751	219 808	154 858
Humanities & religion		130 376	127 987	345 119	226 685	10 007	4 190	485 502	358 862	363 132	245 163
Fine & applied arts		25 362	22 717	49 793	32 930	1 683	869	76 838	56 516	66 165	47 359
Law		90 891	64 631	869 129	147 307	10 054	2 613	970 074	214 551	756 954	100 248
Social & behav. sc.		./.	./.	./.	./.	./.	./.	./.	./.	./.	./.
Business administr.		./.	./.	./.	./.	./.	./.	./.	./.	./.	./.
Communic. & doc.		./.	./.	./.	./.	./.	./.	./.	./.	./.	./.
Home economics		121 441	121 072	42 355	41 803	513	483	164 309	163 358	133 455	133 019
Service trades		-	-	-	-	-	-	-	-	-	-
Natural science		-	-	50 075	9 326	8 955	1 059	59 030	10 385	49 743	7 682
Maths. & computer sc.		226	217	19 298	3 852	1 367	149	20 891	4 218	17 282	3 935
Health-related prg.		28 631	25 419	116 447	45 937	15 007	2 335	160 085	73 691	149 605	58 597
Engineering		44 872	8 875	406 947	19 029	36 880	1 450	488 699	29 354	409 610	13 485
Archit. & town plng.		./.	./.	./.	./.	./.	./.	./.	./.	./.	./.
Trade, craft & indust.		./.	./.	./.	./.	./.	./.	./.	./.	./.	./.
Transport & communic.		472	21	1 341	59	119	9	1 932	89	2 666	62
Agriculture		3 406	1 375	63 225	15 093	6 161	819	72 852	18 087	63 808	10 452
Other & not specified		35 831	32 949	132 823	44 660	1 672	370	170 326	77 979	117 901	44 180
Jordan											
Total	1993/94	25 292	15 536	55 830	24 504	4 814	1 243	85 936	41 283	53 753	24 162
Education science		2 777	2 540	2 842	1 735	1 035	242	6 654	4 517	11 203	8 699
Humanities & religion		3 600	3 007	9 649	6 335	1 165	351	14 414	9 693	6 994	3 722
Fine & applied arts		1 884	1 164	906	517	-	-	2 790	1 681	-	-
Law		13	7	3 356	910	71	17	3 440	934	500	158
Social & behav. sc.		497	447	4 823	2 424	738	244	6 058	3 115	496	272
Business administr.		5 520	3 004	9 478	2 832	319	84	15 317	5 920	12 572	4 227
Communic. & doc.		335	268	445	228	-	-	780	496	-	-
Home economics		189	189	43	12	-	-	232	201	89	89
Service trades		141	-	59	7	-	-	200	7	171	2
Natural science		182	163	4 095	2 101	324	95	4 601	2 359	6 230	2 387
Maths. & computer sc.		2 943	1 684	4 048	1 504	116	31	7 107	3 219	./.	./.
Health-related prg.		3 857	2 330	6 014	2 947	230	51	10 101	5 328	5 420	2 898
Engineering		2 300	196	6 620	1 305	509	44	9 429	1 545	7 026	1 049
Archit. & town plng.		246	100	666	432	43	11	955	543	./.	./.
Trade, craft & indust.		-	-	-	-	-	-	-	-	-	-
Transport & communic.		-	-	-	-	-	-	-	-	103	9
Agriculture		230	33	1 761	810	196	57	2 187	900	1 103	426
Other & not specified		578	404	1 025	405	68	16	1 671	825	1 846	224

3.11 Third level: students by level and field of study
Troisième degré: étudiants par niveau et domaine d'études
Tercer grado: estudiantes por nivel y sector de estudios

Country Field of study Pays Domaines d'études País Sectores de estudios	Year Année Año	Students by ISCED level of programme Étudiants par niveau de programmes de la CITE Estudiantes por nivel de programas de la CINE								Students all levels, 1985 Étudiants tous niveaux, 1985 Estudiantes todos los niveles 1985	
		Level 5 Niveau 5 Nivel 5		Level 6 Niveau 6 Nivel 6		Level 7 Niveau 7 Nivel 7		All levels Tous niveaux Todos los niveles			
		MF	F	MF	F	MF	F	MF	F	MF	F
		(1)	(2)	(3)	(4)	(5)	(6)	(7)	(8)	(9)	(10)
Kazakstan											
Total	1994/95	214 280	125 112	266 724	140 229	1 686	...	482 690	...	...	...
Education science		38 625	29 398	40 043	24 848	665	...	79 333	...	...	...
Humanities & religion		-	-	42 984	31 378	-	-	42 984	...	...	...
Fine & applied arts		11 071	8 271	4 855	4 427	-	-	15 926	...	...	...
Law		4 500	785	11 502	3 003	10	...	16 012	...	...	...
Social & behav. sc.		-	-	4 209	1 160	92	...	4 301	...	...	...
Business administr.		7 428	6 685	37 715	16 189	-	...	45 143	...	...	...
Communic. & doc.		-	-	1 559	442	-	-	1 559	...	...	...
Home economics		-	-	-	-	-	-	-	-	...	...
Service trades		5 230	3 661	-	-	-	-	5 230	...	...	...
Natural science		-	-	9 096	5 730	-	-	9 096	...	...	...
Maths. & computer sc.		-	-	6 476	2 502	-	-	6 476	...	...	...
Health-related prg.		25 418	22 625	20 553	12 949	228	...	46 199	...	...	...
Engineering		37 029	15 393	37 249	11 158	417	...	74 695	...	...	...
Archit. & town plng.		10 569	3 544	779	381	35	...	11 383	...	...	...
Trade, craft & indust.		-	-	7 356	5 012	-	-	7 356	...	...	...
Transport & communic.		16 409	6 207	8 270	786	-	-	24 679	...	...	...
Agriculture		47 473	22 019	19 319	5 912	224	...	67 016	...	...	...
Other & not specified		10 528	6 524	14 759	14 352	15	...	25 302	...	...	...
Korea, Republic of											
Total	1995/96	587 026	220 801	1 403 560	504 674	112 728	31 675	2 103 314	757 150	1 277 825	367 216
Education science		17 383	17 009	102 909	74 596	19 657	9 701	139 949	101 306	141 627	86 284
Humanities & religion		32 076	15 159	214 729	121 829	11 002	4 387	257 807	141 375	169 208	69 180
Fine & applied arts		59 571	35 003	62 491	39 885	4 569	3 367	126 631	78 255	66 974	43 486
Law		1 334	318	57 619	10 499	2 123	222	61 076	11 039	30 247	2 184
Social & behav. sc.		8 810	6 033	91 384	31 494	5 412	1 514	105 606	39 041	65 385	12 908
Business administr.		92 081	42 499	217 766	53 904	17 905	1 790	327 752	98 193	197 604	24 077
Communic. & doc.		932	666	13 136	6 557	1 317	539	15 385	7 762	12 503	6 934
Home economics		26 133	19 919	42 202	38 702	1 414	1 358	69 749	59 979	30 376	28 497
Service trades		15 765	7 047	6 790	2 486	446	132	23 001	9 665	12 445	5 247
Natural science		-	-	75 181	24 106	6 041	1 691	81 222	25 797	62 170	18 542
Maths. & computer sc.		92 013	21 563	76 142	27 438	2 992	847	171 147	49 848	36 647	8 826
Health-related prg.		56 142	35 828	53 655	24 796	10 307	2 799	120 104	63 423	77 657	36 925
Engineering		125 463	9 510	290 832	20 350	21 242	986	437 537	30 846	204 319	5 122
Archit. & town plng.		25 907	2 698	8 833	1 413	566	84	35 306	4 195	72 557	2 648
Trade, craft & indust.		1 581	417	-	-	-	-	1 581	417	13 637	3 154
Transport & communic.		10 417	489	-	-	-	-	10 417	489	10 776	1 058
Agriculture		13 321	3 376	65 831	18 828	4 227	880	83 379	23 084	52 620	5 384
Other & not specified		8 097	3 267	24 060	7 791	3 508	1 378	35 665	12 436	21 073	6 760
Kuwait											
Total	1988/89	11 636	5 767	14 106	8 819	338	164	26 080	14 750	23 678	12 754
Education science		240	185	2 417	2 040	-	-	2 657	2 225	4 311	3 147
Humanities & religion		443	238	2 038	1 379	10	5	2 491	1 622	3 091	1 792
Fine & applied arts		381	303	-	-	-	-	381	303	-	-
Law		137	-	988	417	-	-	1 125	417	968	318
Social & behav. sc.		1 003	36	1 988	1 266	-	-	2 991	1 302	2 660	1 432
Business administr.		2 445	1 533	1 446	823	-	-	3 891	2 356	4 224	2 465
Communic. & doc.		-	-	-	-	-	-	-	-	-	-
Home economics		235	235	-	-	-	-	235	235	-	-
Service trades		49	-	-	-	-	-	49	-	-	-
Natural science		315	247	1 625	952	54	35	1 994	1 234	2 830	1 618
Maths. & computer sc.		878	499	994	704	54	38	1 926	1 241	27	21
Health-related prg.		1 061	758	1 022	660	44	39	2 127	1 457	1 561	1 096
Engineering		2 074	350	1 588	578	176	47	3 838	975	1 309	478
Archit. & town plng.		40	-	-	-	-	-	40	-	-	-
Trade, craft & indust.		183	-	-	-	-	-	183	-	1 645	-
Transport & communic.		486	165	-	-	-	-	486	165	-	-
Agriculture		-	-	-	-	-	-	-	-	-	-
Other & not specified		1 666	1 218	-	-	-	-	1 666	1 218	1 052	387

Third level: students by level and field of study 3.11
Troisième degré: étudiants par niveau et domaine d'études
Tercer grado: estudiantes por nivel y sector de estudios

Country / Field of study / Pays / Domaines d'études / País / Sectores de estudios	Year / Année / Año	Students by ISCED level of programme / Étudiants par niveau de programmes de la CITE / Estudiantes por nivel de programas de la CINE								Students all levels, 1985 / Étudiants tous niveaux, 1985 / Estudiantes todos los niveles 1985	
		Level 5 / Niveau 5 / Nivel 5		Level 6 / Niveau 6 / Nivel 6		Level 7 / Niveau 7 / Nivel 7		All levels / Tous niveaux / Todos los niveles			
		MF	F	MF	F	MF	F	MF	F	MF	F
		(1)	(2)	(3)	(4)	(5)	(6)	(7)	(8)	(9)	(10)
Kyrgyzstan Total	1993/94	...	...	...	...	...	...	55 229	28 652	...	...
Education science		...	...	...	...	...	...	17 604	13 138	...	...
Humanities & religion		...	...	...	...	...	...	2 255	1 214	...	...
Fine & applied arts		...	...	...	...	...	...	136	27	...	...
Law		...	...	...	...	...	...	226	105	...	...
Social & behav. sc.		...	...	...	...	...	...	-	-	...	...
Business administr.		...	...	...	...	...	...	1 101	314	...	...
Communic. & doc.		...	...	...	...	...	...	-	-	...	...
Home economics		...	...	...	...	...	...	759	298	...	...
Service trades		...	...	...	...	...	...	304	220	...	...
Natural science		...	...	...	...	...	...	4 090	2 670	...	...
Maths. & computer sc.		...	...	...	...	...	...	1 872	1 359	...	...
Health-related prg.		...	...	...	...	...	...	4 690	3 156	...	...
Engineering		...	...	...	...	...	...	1 560	593	...	...
Archit. & town plng.		...	...	...	...	...	...	2 888	655	...	...
Trade, craft & indust.		...	...	...	...	...	...	-	-	...	...
Transport & communic.		...	...	...	...	...	...	1 262	49	...	...
Agriculture		...	...	...	...	...	...	3 651	503	...	...
Other & not specified		...	...	...	...	...	...	12 831	4 351	...	...
Lao People's Democr. Republic‡ Total	1992/93	1 650	99	3 366	1 256	-	-	5 016	1 355	5 382	1 918
Education science		-	-	1 169	444	-	-	1 169	444	2 722	1 130
Humanities & religion		-	-	551	219	-	-	551	219	./.	./.
Fine & applied arts		-	-	-	-	-	-	-	-	-	-
Law		73	6	-	-	-	-	73	6	-	-
Social & behav. sc.		-	-	320	138	-	-	320	130	./.	./.
Business administr.		-	-	-	-	-	-	-	-	-	-
Communic. & doc.		-	-	-	-	-	-	-	-	-	-
Home economics		-	-	-	-	-	-	-	-	-	-
Service trades		-	-	-	-	-	-	-	-	-	-
Natural science		-	-	81	33	-	-	81	33	-	-
Maths. & computer sc.		-	-	217	62	-	-	217	62	./.	./.
Health-related prg.		-	-	634	316	-	-	634	316	981	521
Engineering		204	15	394	52	-	-	598	67	212	31
Archit. & town plng.		344	25	-	-	-	-	344	25	575	102
Trade, craft & indust.		-	-	-	-	-	-	-	-	-	-
Transport & communic.		510	27	-	-	-	-	510	27	703	111
Agriculture		519	26	-	-	-	-	519	26	-	-
Other & not specified		-	-	-	-	-	-	-	-	189	23
Malaysia‡ Total	1990/91	62 704	26 495	53 727	25 711	4 981	2 164	121 412	54 370	93 249	41 468
Education science		23 006	12 914	4 847	2 800	2 142	1 236	29 995	16 950	24 121	15 256
Humanities & religion		-	-	9 486	5 295	738	255	10 224	5 550	1 597	733
Fine & applied arts		386	185	800	365	-	-	1 186	550	700	295
Law		-	-	2 210	1 131	97	24	2 307	1 155	956	478
Social & behav. sc.		227	149	5 904	2 913	301	97	6 432	3 159	9 797	4 482
Business administr.		15 961	8 225	8 639	4 736	127	26	24 727	12 987	14 310	6 807
Communic. & doc.		18	4	1 752	1 090	66	37	1 836	1 131	410	166
Home economics		-	-	-	-	-	-	-	-	174	88
Service trades		652	320	-	-	-	-	652	320	3 042	2 293
Natural science		750	454	7 575	3 405	451	184	8 776	4 043	6 300	2 583
Maths. & computer sc.		3 072	1 609	1 372	678	113	35	4 557	2 322	2 238	1 000
Health-related prg.		16	16	2 680	1 465	448	151	3 144	1 632	2 920	1 373
Engineering		6 662	933	5 792	861	239	32	12 693	1 826	11 767	1 646
Archit. & town plng.		1 699	539	661	207	52	11	2 412	757	3 484	706
Trade, craft & indust.		640	258	-	-	-	-	640	258	912	265
Transport & communic.		-	-	-	-	-	-	-	-	618	138
Agriculture		2 465	739	1 607	644	207	76	4 279	1 459	2 242	454
Other & not specified		7 150	150	402	121	-	-	7 552	271	7 661	2 705

3.11 Third level: students by level and field of study
Troisième degré: étudiants par niveau et domaine d'études
Tercer grado: estudiantes por nivel y sector de estudios

Country Field of study Pays Domaines d'études País Sectores de estudios	Year Année Año	Students by ISCED level of programme Étudiants par niveau de programmes de la CITE Estudiantes por nivel de programas de la CINE								Students all levels, 1985 Étudiants tous niveaux, 1985 Estudiantes todos los niveles 1985	
		Level 5 / Niveau 5 / Nivel 5		Level 6 / Niveau 6 / Nivel 6		Level 7 / Niveau 7 / Nivel 7		All levels / Tous niveaux / Todos los niveles				
		MF	F	MF	F	MF	F	MF	F	MF	F
		(1)	(2)	(3)	(4)	(5)	(6)	(7)	(8)	(9)	(10)
Mongolia #											
Total	1994/95	5 849	4 507	26 265	17 896	421	187	32 535	22 590	39 072	23 409
Education science		671	585	6 065	5 086	3	3	6 739	5 674	5 723	4 202
Humanities & religion		62	53	5 176	3 970	-	-	5 238	4 023	764	561
Fine & applied arts		1 246	720	516	283	14	12	1 776	1 015	1 579	878
Law		-	-	544	309	8	3	552	312	491	262
Social & behav. sc.		11	7	1 780	1 152	89	34	1 880	1 193	2 292	1 533
Business administr.		106	95	2 377	1 539	1	-	2 484	1 634	-	-
Communic. & doc.		69	59	215	164	-	-	284	223	30	13
Home economics		-	-	-	-	-	-	-	-	-	-
Service trades		15	14	-	-	-	-	15	14	1 954	1 492
Natural science		76	58	1 011	614	108	44	1 195	716	583	415
Maths. & computer sc.		-	-	533	267	10	1	543	268	519	300
Health-related prg.		2 121	2 046	2 410	1 912	61	37	4 592	3 995	5 899	5 190
Engineering		544	219	3 951	1 805	112	46	4 607	2 070	9 589	4 123
Archit. & town plng.		-	-	72	37	-	-	72	37	62	9
Trade, craft & indust.		302	287	-	-	-	-	302	287	-	-
Transport & communic.		360	193	-	-	-	-	360	193	3 152	1 333
Agriculture		240	158	985	610	14	6	1 239	774	5 788	2 744
Other & not specified		26	13	630	148	1	1	657	162	647	354
Nepal‡											
Total	1993/94	54 273	...	36 470	...	11 275	...	102 018	...	54 452	...
Education science		4 786	...	6 636	...	730	...	12 152	...	3 630	...
Humanities & religion		22 146	...	10 953	...	5 144	...	38 243	...	21 310	...
Fine & applied arts		./.	...	./.	...	./.	...	./.	...	./.	
Law		3 427	...	2 690	...	-	-	6 117	...	4 907	...
Social & behav. sc.		./.	...	./.	...	./.	...	./.	...	./.	...
Business administr.		12 840	...	10 440	...	3 774	...	27 054	...	12 067	...
Communic. & doc.		-	-	-	-	-	-	-	-	-	-
Home economics		-	-	-	-	-	-	-	-	-	-
Service trades		-	-	-	-	-	-	-	-	-	-
Natural science		8 036	...	4 513	...	1 560	...	14 109	...	7 308	...
Maths. & computer sc.		./.	...	./.	...	./.	...	./.	...	./.	...
Health-related prg.		782	...	249	...	67	...	1 098	...	1 385	...
Engineering		1 663	...	366	...	-	-	2 029	...	2 180	...
Archit. & town plng.		-	-	-	-	-	-	-	-	-	-
Trade, craft & indust.		-	-	-	-	-	-	-	-	-	-
Transport & communic.		-	-	-	-	-	-	-	-	-	-
Agriculture		593	...	623	...	-	-	1 216	...	1 665	...
Other & not specified		-	-	-	-	-	-	-	-	-	-
Oman											
Total	1991/92	3 707	1 660	3 524	1 860	91	57	7 322	3 577	...	...
Education science		2 823	1 213	1 418	1 030	81	52	4 322	2 295	...	...
Humanities & religion		-	-	191	99	10	5	201	104	...	...
Fine & applied arts		-	-	28	18	-	-	28	18	...	...
Law		-	-	-	-	-	-	-	-	...	...
Social & behav. sc.		-	-	90	44	-	-	90	44	...	...
Business administr.		114	33	-	-	-	-	114	33	...	...
Communic. & doc.		-	-	128	54	-	-	128	54	...	...
Home economics		-	-	-	-	-	-	-	-	...	...
Service trades		-	-	-	-	-	-	-	-	...	...
Natural science		-	-	320	201	-	-	320	201	...	...
Maths. & computer sc.		-	-	61	36	-	-	61	36	...	...
Health-related prg.		340	250	471	228	-	-	811	478	...	...
Engineering		-	-	484	43	-	-	484	43	...	...
Archit. & town plng.		-	-	-	-	-	-	-	-	...	...
Trade, craft & indust.		430	164	-	-	-	-	430	164	...	...
Transport & communic.		-	-	-	-	-	-	-	-	...	...
Agriculture		-	-	230	25	-	-	230	25	...	...
Other & not specified		-	-	103	82	-	-	103	82	...	...

Third level: students by level and field of study 3.11
Troisième degré: étudiants par niveau et domaine d'études
Tercer grado: estudiantes por nivel y sector de estudios

Country / Field of study Pays / Domaines d'études País / Sectores de estudios	Year Année Año	Level 5 Niveau 5 Nivel 5 MF	F	Level 6 Niveau 6 Nivel 6 MF	F	Level 7 Niveau 7 Nivel 7 MF	F	All levels Tous niveaux Todos los niveles MF	F	Students all levels, 1985 Étudiants tous niveaux, 1985 Estudiantes todos los niveles 1985 MF	F
		(1)	(2)	(3)	(4)	(5)	(6)	(7)	(8)	(9)	(10)
Philippines‡#											
Total	1993/94	168 315	137 774	1 378 626	721 678	36 879	24 636	1 583 820	884 088	1 115 832	...
Education science		656	421	169 250	37 898	18 285	13 720	188 191	52 039	158 374	...
Humanities & religion		-	-	5 277	385	845	119	6 122	504	164 950	...
Fine & applied arts		584	81	5 468	2 871	433	7	6 485	2 959	./.	...
Law		-	-	14 235	5 636	18	11	14 253	5 647	22 042	...
Social & behav. sc.		-	-	16 238	11 340	346	240	16 584	11 580	-	-
Business administr.		92 605	82 302	314 829	205 479	8 431	4 688	415 865	292 469	359 476	-
Communic. & doc.		36	25	7 126	5 729	32	31	7 194	5 785	-	-
Home economics		404	374	3 505	3 038	-	-	3 909	3 412	-	-
Service trades		652	604	6 301	4 971	-	-	6 953	5 575	-	-
Natural science		192	114	16 831	10 552	421	182	17 444	10 848	./.	...
Maths. & computer sc.		1	-	5 578	3 022	30	22	5 609	3 044	./.	...
Health-related prg.		52 907	45 088	214 828	156 480	1 725	1 404	269 460	202 972	136 827	...
Engineering		3 710	463	197 653	35 369	338	105	201 701	35 937	240 154	-
Archit. & town plng.		-	-	16 311	3 211	-	-	16 311	3 211	-	-
Trade, craft & indust.		-	-	-	-	-	-	-	-	-	-
Transport & communic.		-	-	-	-	-	-	-	-	-	-
Agriculture		15 912	8 093	41 635	20 478	204	96	57 751	28 667	34 009	...
Other & not specified		656	209	343 561	215 219	5 771	4 011	349 988	219 439	-	-
Qatar‡											
Total	1994/95	435	268	7 064	5 055	295	235	7 794	5 558	5 344	3 309
Education science		5	1	1 867	1 695	260	214	2 132	1 910	3 881	2 631
Humanities & religion		-	-	1 547	1 255	20	7	1 567	1 262	850	425
Total		-	-	./.	./.	./.	./.	./.	./.	-	-
Law		-	-	./.	./.	./.	./.	./.	./.	-	-
Social & behav. sc.		-	-	./.	./.	./.	./.	./.	./.	-	-
Business administr.		-	-	650	231	-	-	650	231	103	41
Communic. & doc.		-	-	-	-	-	-	-	-	-	-
Home economics		-	-	-	-	-	-	-	-	./.	./.
Service trades		-	-	-	-	-	-	-	-	-	-
Natural science		-	-	778	487	-	-	778	487	354	212
Maths. & computer sc.		-	-	./.	./.	-	-	./.	./.	./.	./.
Health-related prg.		-	-	-	-	-	-	-	-	-	-
Engineering		-	-	318	-	-	-	318	-	156	-
Archit. & town plng.		-	-	-	-	-	-	-	-	-	-
Trade, craft & indust.		-	-	-	-	-	-	-	-	-	-
Transport & communic.		-	-	-	-	-	-	-	-	-	-
Agriculture		-	-	-	-	-	-	-	-	-	-
Other & not specified		430	267	1 904	1 387	15	14	2 349	1 668	-	-
Saudi Arabia											
Total	1993/94	21 260	10 738	173 862	78 477	5 968	1 387	201 090	90 602	113 529	44 697
Education science		10 706	10 497	59 600	33 208	914	322	71 220	44 027	29 059	15 275
Humanities & religion		511	238	56 986	26 656	2 448	530	59 945	27 424	42 380	17 698
Fine & applied arts		-	-	429	246	35	19	464	265	-	-
Law		-	-	-	-	-	-	-	-	-	-
Social & behav. sc.		-	-	1 436	913	-	-	1 436	913	14 471	4 247
Business administr.		111	-	10 939	2 445	608	160	11 658	2 605	310	-
Communic. & doc.		-	-	3 389	1 050	-	-	3 389	1 050	-	-
Home economics		-	-	2 549	2 549	-	-	2 549	2 549	-	-
Service trades		-	-	-	-	-	-	-	-	-	-
Natural science		-	-	12 878	6 116	420	195	13 298	6 311	11 345	4 230
Maths. & computer sc.		26	3	2 630	1 006	115	-	2 771	1 009	./.	./.
Health-related prg.		166	-	6 371	2 252	235	109	6 772	2 361	5 989	2 497
Engineering		653	-	6 992	-	562	-	8 207	-	7 152	124
Archit. & town plng.		-	-	1 015	30	272	-	1 287	30	./.	./.
Trade, craft & indust.		6 346	-	302	-	-	-	6 648	-	266	-
Transport & communic.		765	-	-	-	-	-	765	-	-	-
Agriculture		-	-	2 150	272	223	21	2 373	293	2 557	626
Other & not specified		1 976	-	6 196	1 734	136	31	8 308	1 765	-	-

3.11 Third level: students by level and field of study
Troisième degré: étudiants par niveau et domaine d'études
Tercer grado: estudiantes por nivel y sector de estudios

Country Field of study Pays Domaines d'études País Sectores de estudios	Year Année Año	Students by ISCED level of programme Étudiants par niveau de programmes de la CITE Estudiantes por nivel de programas de la CINE								Students all levels, 1985 Étudiants tous niveaux, 1985 Estudiantes todos los niveles 1985	
		Level 5 Niveau 5 Nivel 5		Level 6 Niveau 6 Nivel 6		Level 7 Niveau 7 Nivel 7		All levels Tous niveaux Todos los niveles			
		MF	F	MF	F	MF	F	MF	F	MF	F
		(1)	(2)	(3)	(4)	(5)	(6)	(7)	(8)	(9)	(10)
Sri Lanka‡											
Total	1994	14 054	5 173	36 998	17 099	8 738	4 046	59 790	26 318	59 377	23 974
Education science		594	593	6	1	4 972	2 944	5 572	3 538	6 082	4 161
Humanities & religion		3 353	1 904	-	-	312	50	3 665	1 954	-	-
Fine & applied arts		-	-	1 313	1 061	-	-	1 313	1 061	711	592
Law		-	-	2 438	905	61	19	2 499	924	1 072	416
Social & behav. sc.		1 115	299	9 652	5 602	1 131	405	11 898	6 306	8 002	3 829
Business administr.		4 571	1 374	5 450	2 430	535	77	10 556	3 881	12 038	6 705
Communic. & doc.		339	75	-	-	-	-	339	75	-	-
Home economics		212	185	-	-	-	-	212	185	110	110
Service trades		276	110	-	-	-	-	276	110	-	-
Natural science		50	33	7 907	3 509	241	81	8 198	3 623	5 521	2 350
Maths. & computer sc.		115	42	-	-	33	7	148	49	./.	./.
Health-related prg.		-	-	5 366	2 483	804	310	6 170	2 793	3 227	1 477
Engineering		667	122	3 031	406	167	17	3 865	545	11 751	2 329
Archit. & town plng.		-	-	224	83	117	43	341	126	155	60
Trade, craft & indust.		-	-	-	-	-	-	-	-	1 777	76
Transport & communic.		-	-	-	-	-	-	-	-	-	-
Agriculture		222	107	1 323	571	319	90	1 864	768	1 344	675
Other & not specified		2 540	329	288	48	46	3	2 874	380	7 587	1 194
Syrian Arab Rep.‡											
Total	1992/93	15 845	6 155	173 486	66 027	5 040	1 966	194 371	74 148	179 473	62 731
Education science		-	-	2 705	1 578	1 911	961	4 616	2 539	25 038	16 600
Humanities & religion		-	-	40 390	24 697	393	189	40 783	24 886	30 003	15 990
Fine & applied arts		-	-	583	226	14	4	597	230	747	208
Law		-	-	35 093	8 789	78	14	35 171	8 803	20 338	3 106
Social & behav. sc.		-	-	10 266	4 799	171	68	10 437	4 867	2 572	506
Business administr.		5 685	2 661	14 675	4 534	225	49	20 585	7 244	15 395	4 697
Communic. & doc.		-	-	2 048	950	-	-	2 048	950	33	12
Home economics		-	-	-	-	-	-	-	-	-	-
Service trades		-	-	-	-	-	-	-	-	218	53
Natural science		-	-	14 863	6 219	333	141	15 196	6 360	11 538	4 543
Maths. & computer sc.		786	160	548	250	-	-	1 334	410	6 498	2 220
Health-related prg.		2 959	1 543	17 897	5 619	1 152	333	22 008	7 495	17 319	5 851
Engineering		2 716	1 079	8 367	2 547	266	66	11 349	3 692	38 675	6 670
Archit. & town plng.		-	-	1 880	784	58	16	1 938	800	2 721	896
Trade, craft & indust.		1 991	181	17 642	3 546	229	53	19 862	3 780	858	60
Transport & communic.		-	-	-	-	-	-	-	-	-	-
Agriculture		1 525	504	5 154	1 437	202	70	6 881	2 011	7 520	1 319
Other & not specified		183	27	1 375	52	8	2	1 566	81	-	-
Thailand‡											
Total	1994/95	4 616	...	766 317	...	45 323	...	816 256	...	...	...
Education science		-	-	41 361	...	10 481	...	51 842	...	...	...
Humanities & religion		-	-	27 470	...	1 046	...	28 516	...	...	...
Fine & applied arts		42	...	8 834	...	122	...	8 998	...	...	...
Law		-	-	105 993	...	1 243	...	107 236	...	...	...
Social & behav. sc.		216	...	434 023	...	15 763	...	450 002	...	...	...
Business administr.		./.	...	./.	...	./.	...	./.	...	...	...
Communic. & doc.		./.	...	./.	...	./.	...	./.	...	...	...
Home economics		./.	...	./.	...	./.	...	./.	...	...	...
Service trades		-	-	-	-	-	-	-	-	-	-
Natural science		159	...	35 395	...	3 491	...	39 045	...	...	...
Maths. & computer sc.		./.	...	./.	...	./.	...	./.	...	...	...
Health-related prg.		577	...	43 852	...	2 541	...	46 970	...	...	...
Engineering		3 495	...	45 606	...	2 848	...	51 949	...	...	...
Archit. & town plng.		-	-	3 193	...	375	...	3 568	...	...	...
Trade, craft & indust.		-	-	-	-	-	-	-	-	...	...
Transport & communic.		-	-	-	-	-	-	-	-	...	...
Agriculture		127	...	19 694	...	1 683	...	21 504	...	...	...
Other & not specified		-	-	896	...	5 730	...	6 626	...	...	...

Third level: students by level and field of study 3.11
Troisième degré: étudiants par niveau et domaine d'études
Tercer grado: estudiantes por nivel y sector de estudios

Country / Field of study / Pays Domaines d'études / País Sectores de estudios	Year / Année / Año	Level 5 Niveau 5 Nivel 5 MF (1)	F (2)	Level 6 Niveau 6 Nivel 6 MF (3)	F (4)	Level 7 Niveau 7 Nivel 7 MF (5)	F (6)	All levels Tous niveaux Todos los niveles MF (7)	F (8)	Students all levels, 1985 Étudiants tous niveaux, 1985 Estudiantes todos los niveles 1985 MF (9)	F (10)
Turkey Total	1994/95	296 402	132 228	810 918	293 684	66 979	23 859	1 174 299	449 771	469 992	152 047
Education science		64	63	103 612	44 138	4 723	2 014	108 399	46 215	59 780	25 858
Humanities & religion		651	218	41 261	19 405	6 290	1 911	48 202	21 534	26 276	10 075
Fine & applied arts		2 620	1 435	9 499	5 278	1 265	607	13 384	7 320	5 191	2 558
Law		1 519	679	18 121	5 698	1 009	339	20 649	6 716	17 811	5 822
Social & behav. sc.		73 630	22 055	241 153	84 879	11 823	3 964	326 606	110 898	124 644	37 155
Business administr.		46 032	22 062	160 276	50 525	1 956	693	208 264	73 280	50 242	15 617
Communic. & doc.		11 180	7 558	10 094	5 529	952	454	22 226	13 541	4 970	2 368
Home economics		17 541	13 915	870	813	38	35	18 449	14 763	604	597
Service trades		19 381	7 443	6 009	1 967	-	-	25 390	9 410	3 899	970
Natural science		305	149	35 541	16 111	3 481	1 515	39 327	17 775	16 241	7 312
Maths. & computer sc.		4 509	795	19 498	7 209	1 269	345	25 276	8 349	8 848	3 605
Health-related prg.		60 130	46 954	47 824	22 490	15 242	6 080	123 196	75 524	44 043	17 308
Engineering		50 863	5 488	71 822	14 407	11 723	2 655	134 408	22 550	81 176	13 941
Archit. & town plng.		358	269	9 342	4 611	2 255	1 227	11 955	6 107	8 001	4 093
Trade, craft & indust.		3 280	1 792	1 365	775	-	-	4 645	2 567	1 219	515
Transport & communic.		14	1	-	-	183	27	197	28	86	10
Agriculture		4 325	1 352	26 403	9 587	4 770	1 993	35 498	12 932	16 961	4 243
Other & not specified		-	-	8 228	262	-	-	8 228	262	-	-
United Arab Emirates‡ Total	1992/93	...	...	9 732	7 318	...	...	...	...	7 772	4 531
Education science		...	...	2 126	1 953	...	...	...	...	1 203	1 027
Humanities & religion		...	...	-	-	...	...	...	...	1 359	1 055
Fine & applied arts		...	...	-	-	...	...	...	...	-	-
Law		...	...	143	39	...	...	...	...	305	95
Social & behav. sc.		...	...	822	572	...	...	...	...	1 431	940
Business administr.		...	...	948	557	...	...	...	...	996	550
Communic. & doc.		...	...	-	-	...	...	...	...	322	139
Home economics		...	...	-	-	...	...	...	...	-	-
Service trades		...	...	-	-	...	...	...	...	-	-
Natural science		...	...	-	-	...	...	...	...	630	456
Maths. & computer sc.		...	...	-	-	...	...	...	...	95	72
Health-related prg.		...	...	213	144	...	...	...	...	-	-
Engineering		...	...	458	192	...	...	...	...	186	65
Archit. & town plng.		...	...	./.	./.	...	...	...	...	73	39
Trade, craft & indust.		...	...	-	-	...	...	...	...	-	-
Transport & communic.		...	...	-	-	...	...	...	...	-	-
Agriculture		...	...	184	107	...	...	...	...	36	-
Other & not specified		...	...	4 838	3 754	...	...	...	...	1 136	93
Yemen Total	1991/92	...	...	...	...	...	...	53 082	9 079	...	...
Education science		...	...	...	...	...	...	22 971	4 255	...	...
Humanities & religion		...	...	...	...	...	...	5 349	1 730	...	...
Fine & applied arts		-	-	-	-	-	-	-	-	...	...
Law		...	...	...	...	...	...	8 642	300	...	...
Social & behav. sc.		...	...	...	...	...	...	1 005	339	...	...
Business administr.		...	...	...	...	...	...	8 366	900	...	...
Communic. & doc.		...	...	...	...	...	...	65	10	...	...
Home economics		-	-	-	-	-	-	-	-	...	...
Service trades		-	-	-	-	-	-	-	-	...	...
Natural science		...	...	...	...	...	...	1 176	281	...	...
Maths. & computer sc.		...	...	...	...	...	...	72	19	...	...
Health-related prg.		...	...	...	...	...	...	2 451	948	...	...
Engineering		...	...	...	...	...	...	1 872	197	...	...
Archit. & town plng.		...	...	...	...	...	...	156	39	...	...
Trade, craft & indust.		-	-	-	-	-	-	-	-	...	...
Transport & communic.		-	-	-	-	-	-	-	-	...	...
Agriculture		...	...	...	...	...	...	957	61	...	...
Other & not specified		-	-	-	-	-	-	-	-	...	...

3.11 Third level: students by level and field of study
Troisième degré: étudiants par niveau et domaine d'études
Tercer grado: estudiantes por nivel y sector de estudios

Country / Field of study / Pays / Domaines d'études / País / Sectores de estudios	Year / Année / Año	Students by ISCED level of programme / Étudiants par niveau de programmes de la CITE / Estudiantes por nivel de programas de la CINE								Students all levels, 1985 / Étudiants tous niveaux, 1985 / Estudiantes todos los niveles 1985	
		Level 5 / Niveau 5 / Nivel 5		Level 6 / Niveau 6 / Nivel 6		Level 7 / Niveau 7 / Nivel 7		All levels / Tous niveaux / Todos los niveles			
		MF	F	MF	F	MF	F	MF	F	MF	F
		(1)	(2)	(3)	(4)	(5)	(6)	(7)	(8)	(9)	(10)
Palestine											
Gaza Strip											
Total	1994/95	2 616	1 152	9 835	3 425	22	6	12 473	4 583	...	...
Education science		-	-	3 475	1 498	5	1	3 480	1 499	...	...
Humanities & religion		850	609	2 717	761	11	4	3 578	1 374	...	...
Fine & applied arts		-	-	-	-	-	-	-	-	...	...
Law		-	-	-	-	-	-	-	-	...	...
Social & behav. sc.		-	-	270	123	-	-	270	123	...	...
Business administr.		239	99	1 185	303	-	-	1 424	402	...	...
Communic. & doc.		-	-	158	58	-	-	158	58	...	...
Home economics		-	-	-	-	-	-	-	-	...	...
Service trades		-	-	-	-	-	-	-	-	...	...
Natural science		241	180	1 186	458	-	-	1 427	638	...	...
Maths. & computer sc.		440	210	-	-	6	1	446	211	...	...
Health-related prg.		155	53	481	193	-	-	636	246	...	...
Engineering		28	-	249	31	-	-	277	31	...	...
Archit. & town plng.		55	1	-	-	-	-	55	1	...	...
Trade, craft & indust.		-	-	-	-	-	-	-	-	...	...
Transport & communic.		-	-	-	-	-	-	-	-	...	...
Agriculture		-	-	114	-	-	-	114	-	...	...
Other & not specified		608	-	-	-	-	-	608	-	...	...
West Bank											
Total	1994/95	2 698	1 616	18 543	9 927	98	34	21 339	11 577	...	...
Education science		320	308	1 531	997	98	34	1 949	1 339	...	...
Humanities & religion		446	378	5 774	3 593	-	-	6 220	3 971	...	...
Fine & applied arts		35	24	180	85	-	-	215	109	...	...
Law		-	-	-	-	-	-	-	-	...	...
Social & behav. sc.		149	137	1 965	1 112	-	-	2 114	1 249	...	...
Business administr.		714	345	2 856	1 088	-	-	3 570	1 433	...	...
Communic. & doc.		8	2	-	-	-	-	8	2	...	...
Home economics		33	33	-	-	-	-	33	33	...	...
Service trades		-	-	104	53	-	-	104	53	...	...
Natural science		20	13	2 127	1 083	-	-	2 147	1 096	...	...
Maths. & computer sc.		359	183	1 605	622	-	-	1 964	805	...	...
Health-related prg.		291	158	889	694	-	-	1 180	852	...	...
Engineering		248	4	808	225	-	-	1 056	229	...	...
Archit. & town plng.		20	20	395	301	-	-	415	321	...	...
Trade, craft & indust.		-	-	-	-	-	-	-	-	...	...
Transport & communic.		-	-	-	-	-	-	-	-	...	...
Agriculture		-	-	309	74	-	-	309	74	...	...
Other & not specified		55	11	-	-	-	-	55	11	...	...

Third level: students by level and field of study **3.11**
Troisième degré: étudiants par niveau et domaine d'études
Tercer grado: estudiantes por nivel y sector de estudios

Country / Field of study Pays / Domaines d'études País / Sectores de estudios	Year Année Año	Students by ISCED level of programme / Étudiants par niveau de programmes de la CITE / Estudiantes por nivel de programas de la CINE						All levels Tous niveaux Todos los niveles		Students all levels, 1985 Étudiants tous niveaux, 1985 Estudiantes todos los niveles 1985	
		Level 5 / Niveau 5 / Nivel 5		Level 6 / Niveau 6 / Nivel 6		Level 7 / Niveau 7 / Nivel 7					
		MF	F	MF	F	MF	F	MF	F	MF	F
		(1)	(2)	(3)	(4)	(5)	(6)	(7)	(8)	(9)	(10)
Europe											
Albania‡ Total	1993/94	...	...	...	...	...	...	30 185	16 069	21 995	9 995
Education science		...	...	...	...	...	...	8 992	5 930	3 380	1 814
Humanities & religion		...	...	...	...	...	...	4 105	2 728	1 126	656
Fine & applied arts		...	...	...	...	...	...	600	216	544	178
Law		...	...	...	...	...	...	2 497	892	405	173
Social & behav. sc.		...	...	...	...	...	...	1 328	804	3 006	2 025
Business administr.		...	...	...	...	...	...	1 226	762	-	-
Communic. & doc.		...	...	...	...	...	...	70	32	-	-
Home economics		...	...	...	...	...	...	1 182	479	-	-
Service trades		...	...	...	...	...	...	129	49	-	-
Natural science		...	...	...	...	...	...	1 003	560	1 104	646
Maths. & computer sc.		...	...	...	...	...	...	143	65	./.	./.
Health-related prg.		...	...	...	...	...	...	1 993	1 044	1 084	524
Engineering		...	...	...	...	...	...	2 660	696	4 890	1 433
Archit. & town plng.		...	...	...	...	...	...	129	49	-	-
Trade, craft & indust.		...	...	...	...	...	...	111	91	-	-
Transport & communic.		...	...	...	...	...	...	-	-	-	-
Agriculture		...	...	...	...	...	...	3 067	1 398	5 945	2 429
Other & not specified		...	...	...	...	...	...	950	274	511	117
Austria‡ Total	1993/94	18 820	12 694	233 318	102 833	19 330	6 888	271 468	122 415	191 581	85 044
Education science		8 939	7 211	7 888	5 413	837	514	17 664	13 138	12 284	8 695
Humanities & religion		140	129	28 162	17 802	2 972	1 644	31 274	19 575	29 204	18 158
Fine & applied arts		189	131	12 100	7 195	449	292	12 738	7 618	10 340	5 745
Law		-	-	23 703	10 051	2 640	895	26 343	10 946	16 944	5 891
Social & behav. sc.		1 262	923	25 924	14 251	1 416	698	28 602	15 872	17 128	9 023
Business administr.		1 020	570	42 426	17 375	3 079	1 024	46 525	18 969	30 079	11 339
Communic. & doc.		-	-	4 299	2 431	152	87	4 451	2 518	2 851	1 478
Home economics		37	31	908	742	26	19	971	792	178	168
Service trades		918	644	-	-	-	-	918	644	771	600
Natural science		-	-	14 105	5 608	1 673	536	15 778	6 144	10 686	4 066
Maths. & computer sc.		1 355	296	14 786	3 215	1 023	193	17 164	3 704	6 935	1 777
Health-related prg.		2 178	1 870	18 258	9 945	155	89	20 591	11 904	23 608	12 289
Engineering		2 376	720	23 885	1 909	2 010	164	28 271	2 793	15 137	1 001
Archit. & town plng.		-	-	8 864	3 265	337	99	9 201	3 364	4 609	1 307
Trade, craft & indust.		189	169	-	-	-	./.	189	169	-	-
Transport & communic.		-	-	-	-						
Agriculture				7 239	3 337	721	249	7 960	3 586	6 177	1 973
Other & not specified		217	-	771	294	1 840	385	2 828	679	4 650	1 534
Belarus‡ Total	1993/94	...	...	175 400	90 700	2 616	...	178 016	...	181 900	...
Education science		...	...	38 400	30 600	231	...	38 631	...	59 000	...
Humanities & religion		...	...	32 900	20 300	207	...	33 107	...	./.	...
Fine & applied arts		...	...	./.	./.	./.	...	./.	...	1 400	...
Law		...	...	./.	./.	./.	...	./.	...	19 500	...
Social & behav. sc.		...	...	13 900	9 800	391	...	14 291	...	./.	...
Business administr.		...	...	./.	./.	./.	...	./.	...	./.	...
Communic. & doc.		...	...	./.	./.	./.	...	./.	...	./.	...
Home economics		...	...	./.	./.	./.	...	./.	...	./.	...
Service trades		...	...	...	...	...	...	...	...	...	...
Natural science		...	...	./.	./.	518	...	518	...	./.	...
Maths. & computer sc.		...	...	./.	./.	./.	...	./.	...	./.	...
Health-related prg.		...	...	14 800	8 500	346	...	15 146	...	12 900	...
Engineering		...	...	52 100	16 200	777	...	52 877	...	65 200	...
Archit. & town plng.		...	...	./.	./.	./.	...	./.	...	./.	...
Trade, craft & indust.		...	...	./.	./.	./.	...	./.	...	./.	...
Transport & communic.		...	...	17 600	5 200	146	...	17 746	...	23 900	...
Agriculture		...	...	./.				./.		./.	...
Other & not specified		...	...	5 700	100	-	-	5 700	...	./.	...

3.11 Third level: students by level and field of study
Troisième degré: étudiants par niveau et domaine d'études
Tercer grado: estudiantes por nivel y sector de estudios

Country / Field of study / Pays / Domaines d'études / País / Sectores de estudios	Year / Année / Año	Students by ISCED level of programme / Étudiants par niveau de programmes de la CITE / Estudiantes por nivel de programas de la CINE								Students all levels, 1985 / Étudiants tous niveaux, 1985 / Estudiantes todos los niveles 1985	
		Level 5 / Niveau 5 / Nivel 5		Level 6 / Niveau 6 / Nivel 6		Level 7 / Niveau 7 / Nivel 7		All levels / Tous niveaux / Todos los niveles			
		MF	F	MF	F	MF	F	MF	F	MF	F
		(1)	(2)	(3)	(4)	(5)	(6)	(7)	(8)	(9)	(10)
Belgium											
Total	1990/91	123 970	69 292	136 664	59 107	15 614	4 940	276 248	133 339	247 499	113 120
Education science		25 926	18 885	1 992	1 283	307	121	28 225	20 289	30 451	20 066
Humanities & religion		144	78	10 998	7 030	953	375	12 095	7 483	14 740	8 549
Fine & applied arts		4 801	2 548	2 132	1 397	146	70	7 079	4 015	4 527	1 941
Law		-	-	13 688	7 039	1 043	436	14 731	7 475	13 724	6 024
Social & behav. sc.		58 061	31 556	42 399	19 544	3 744	1 159	104 204	52 259	20 060	10 109
Business administr.		./.	./.	./.	./.	./.	./.	./.	./.	55 455	26 870
Communic. & doc.		-	-	2 419	1 405	371	226	2 790	1 631	386	230
Home economics		369	324	73	61	-	-	442	385	-	-
Service trades		-	-	-	-	-	-	-	-	-	-
Natural science		-	-	4 537	2 167	2 349	729	6 886	2 896	20 358	7 361
Maths. & computer sc.				3 123	851	896	168	4 019	1 019	./.	./.
Health-related prg.		16 566	12 822	16 460	9 264	3 160	1 063	36 186	23 149	42 903	25 647
Engineering		191	6	30 655	5 553	1 794	265	32 640	5 824	35 846	4 283
Archit. & town plng.		56	14	3 813	1 487	97	39	3 966	1 540	./.	./.
Trade, craft & indust.		15 410	2 455	143	8	-	-	15 553	2 463	./.	./.
Transport & communic.		-	-	-	-	-	-	-	-	183	61
Agriculture		1 744	404	1 890	833	156	56	3 790	1 293	5 037	1 308
Other & not specified		702	200	2 342	1 185	598	233	3 642	1 618	3 829	671
Bulgaria											
Total	1994/95	25 161	18 695	196 046	115 542	1 823	721	223 030	134 958	113 795	62 035
Education science		4 891	3 918	27 261	21 762	83	58	32 235	25 738	15 476	12 883
Humanities & religion		776	634	14 523	11 814	217	136	15 516	12 584	10 998	7 424
Fine & applied arts		-	-	3 761	1 965	63	28	3 824	1 993	2 671	1 377
Law		-	-	12 772	7 698	33	13	12 805	7 711	2 211	1 010
Social & behav. sc.		-	-	7 352	4 874	348	108	7 700	4 982	1 010	701
Business administr.		3 309	2 521	53 377	33 320	-	-	56 686	35 841	14 895	7 908
Communic. & doc.		91	86	1 529	990	1	1	1 621	1 077	444	249
Home economics		-	-	-	-	-	-	-	-	-	-
Service trades		1 845	1 389	1 690	1 319	-	-	3 535	2 708	925	658
Natural science		-	-	4 949	3 102	266	121	5 215	3 223	6 045	2 997
Maths. & computer sc.		-	-	3 284	1 798	79	39	3 363	1 837	2 615	1 426
Health-related prg.		7 228	6 700	10 759	5 440	151	48	18 138	12 188	12 624	5 757
Engineering		5 058	2 976	41 290	17 494	464	140	46 812	20 610	36 001	16 019
Archit. & town plng.		-	-	840	362	4	1	844	363	576	272
Trade, craft & indust.		-	-	-	-	-	-	-	-	-	-
Transport & communic.		819	339	1 560	671	28	1	2 407	1 011	1 475	702
Agriculture		-	-	5 740	2 691	86	27	5 826	2 718	5 829	2 652
Other & not specified		1 144	132	5 359	242	-	-	6 503	374	-	-
Croatia‡											
Total	1994/95	18 284	6 498	63 967	33 864	...	...	82 251	40 362	...	...
Education science		715	695	7 084	5 502	...	...	7 799	6 197	...	...
Humanities & religion		325	196	5 245	3 657	...	...	5 570	3 853	...	...
Fine & applied arts		206	173	1 043	608	...	...	1 249	781	...	...
Law		1 402	913	6 271	4 070	...	...	7 673	4 983	...	...
Social & behav. sc.		-	-	1 888	1 207	...	...	1 888	1 207	...	...
Business administr.		1 797	1 120	11 097	6 728	...	...	12 894	7 848	...	...
Communic. & doc.		-	-	636	421	...	...	636	421	...	...
Home economics		-	-	299	260	...	...	299	260	...	...
Service trades		983	624	-	-	...	...	983	624	...	...
Natural science		-	-	1 146	696	...	...	1 146	696	...	...
Maths. & computer sc.		-	-	838	292	...	...	838	292	...	...
Health-related prg.		866	668	4 973	3 294	...	...	5 839	3 962	...	...
Engineering		5 903	696	16 306	3 615	...	...	22 209	4 311	...	...
Archit. & town plng.		90	50	1 073	735	...	...	1 163	785	...	...
Trade, craft & indust.		1 006	569	-	-	...	...	1 006	569	...	...
Transport & communic.		2 406	359	-	-	...	...	2 406	359	...	...
Agriculture		602	194	4 135	1 884	...	...	4 737	2 078	...	...
Other & not specified		1 983	241	1 933	895	...	...	3 916	1 136	...	...

Third level: students by level and field of study **3.11**
Troisième degré: étudiants par niveau et domaine d'études
Tercer grado: estudiantes por nivel y sector de estudios

Country / Field of study / Pays / Domaines d'études / País / Sectores de estudios	Year / Année / Año	Students by ISCED level of programme — Étudiants par niveau de programmes de la CITE — Estudiantes por nivel de programas de la CINE								Students all levels, 1985 — Étudiants tous niveaux, 1985 — Estudiantes todos los niveles 1985	
		Level 5 / Niveau 5 / Nivel 5		Level 6 / Niveau 6 / Nivel 6		Level 7 / Niveau 7 / Nivel 7		All levels / Tous niveaux / Todos los niveles			
		MF	F	MF	F	MF	F	MF	F	MF	F
		(1)	(2)	(3)	(4)	(5)	(6)	(7)	(8)	(9)	(10)
Czech Republic Total	1994/95	28 540	18 208	129 453	57 459	7 113	1 910	165 106	77 577	...	...
Education science		1 322	1 139	24 143	16 646	186	89	25 651	17 874	...	...
Humanities & religion		367	90	8 454	5 116	453	218	9 274	5 424	...	...
Fine & applied arts		1 105	706	2 906	1 504	88	34	4 099	2 244	...	...
Law		2 595	2 062	6 518	2 940	536	237	9 649	5 239	...	...
Social & behav. sc.		186	108	3 002	1 485	301	118	3 489	1 711	...	...
Business administr.		12 763	7 672	19 707	9 308	558	159	33 028	17 139	...	...
Communic. & doc.		303	247	546	334	10	8	859	589	...	...
Home economics		-	-	-	-	-	-	-	-	...	...
Service trades		-	-	-	-	-	-	-	-	...	...
Natural science		-	-	2 296	1 164	872	312	3 168	1 476	...	...
Maths. & computer sc.		-	-	2 813	377	575	84	3 388	461	...	...
Health-related prg.		4 787	4 124	11 054	6 650	301	117	16 142	10 891	...	...
Engineering		3 354	1 189	35 827	7 023	2 250	273	41 431	8 485	...	...
Archit. & town plng.		11	3	1 377	554	55	22	1 443	579	...	...
Trade, craft & indust.		-	-	-	-	-	-	-	-	...	...
Transport & communic.		332	111	1 155	196	5	-	1 492	307	...	...
Agriculture		694	298	8 099	3 259	488	143	9 281	3 700	...	...
Other & not specified		721	459	1 556	903	435	96	2 712	1 458	...	...
Denmark‡ Total	1992/93	23 878	13 606	133 128	68 618	./.	./.	157 006	82 224	116 319	57 380
Education science		6 715	5 638	11 494	8 054	./.	./.	18 209	13 692	17 973	12 734
Humanities & religion		1 966	1 732	24 407	16 751	./.	./.	26 373	18 483	16 384	10 986
Fine & applied arts		937	600	3 288	1 941	./.	./.	4 225	2 541	4 067	2 369
Law		-	-	5 505	2 937	./.	./.	5 505	2 937	4 587	2 172
Social & behav. sc.		402	180	14 260	6 637	./.	./.	14 662	6 817	11 010	4 723
Business administr.		5 814	2 589	17 060	6 070	./.	./.	22 874	8 659	9 543	2 600
Communic. & doc.		36	29	2 234	1 269	./.	./.	2 270	1 298	1 549	841
Home economics		-	-	-	-	-	-	-	-	-	-
Service trades		128	122	-	-	-	-	128	122	182	181
Natural science		-	-	5 738	2 418	./.	./.	5 738	2 418	3 866	1 176
Maths. & computer sc.		-	-	6 700	1 812	./.	./.	6 700	1 812	4 102	939
Health-related prg.		1 243	1 093	15 846	12 994	./.	./.	17 089	14 087	17 520	13 725
Engineering		2 866	722	17 748	3 748	./.	./.	20 614	4 470	15 110	1 831
Archit. & town plng.		14	7	1 995	936	./.	./.	2 009	943	1 956	782
Trade, craft & indust.		2 405	336	-	-	-	-	2 405	336	1 125	102
Transport & communic.		256	26	-	-	-	-	256	26	1 311	16
Agriculture		191	30	3 135	1 734	./.	./.	3 326	1 764	2 893	1 094
Other & not specified		905	502	3 718	1 317	./.	./.	4 623	1 819	3 141	1 109
Estonia‡ Total	1994/95	5 793	3 073	17 376	9 068	2 314	1 021	25 483	13 162	...	...
Education science		1 111	1 001	1 927	1 560	156	126	3 194	2 687	...	...
Humanities & religion		417	204	1 594	1 216	240	153	2 251	1 573	...	...
Fine & applied arts		199	145	986	636	116	71	1 301	852	...	...
Law		616	311	613	305	43	14	1 272	630	...	...
Social & behav. sc.		1 646	898	1 322	743	400	178	3 368	1 819	...	...
Business administr.		199	93	2 177	1 261	170	58	2 546	1 412	...	...
Communic. & doc.		118	111	220	144	46	35	384	290	...	...
Home economics		-	-	23	23	-	-	23	23	...	...
Service trades		-	-	242	205	-	-	242	205	...	...
Natural science		84	33	688	295	298	108	1 070	436	...	...
Maths. & computer sc.		-	-	423	197	59	30	482	227	...	...
Health-related prg.		-	-	1 246	923	125	76	1 371	999	...	...
Engineering		470	47	4 150	791	377	44	4 997	882	...	...
Archit. & town plng.		71	33	93	36	21	4	185	73	...	...
Trade, craft & indust.		-	-	-	-	-	-	-	-	...	...
Transport & communic.		232	19	106	-	1	-	339	19	...	...
Agriculture		74	16	1 141	512	166	75	1 381	603	...	...
Other & not specified		556	162	425	221	96	49	1 077	432	...	...

3.11 Third level: students by level and field of study
Troisième degré: étudiants par niveau et domaine d'études
Tercer grado: estudiantes por nivel y sector de estudios

Country / Field of study / Pays / Domaines d'études / País / Sectores de estudios	Year / Année / Año	Students by ISCED level of programme / Étudiants par niveau de programmes de la CITE / Estudiantes por nivel de programas de la CINE								Students all levels, 1985 / Étudiants tous niveaux, 1985 / Estudiantes todos los niveles 1985	
		Level 5 / Niveau 5 / Nivel 5		Level 6 / Niveau 6 / Nivel 6		Level 7 / Niveau 7 / Nivel 7		All levels / Tous niveaux / Todos los niveles			
		MF	F	MF	F	MF	F	MF	F	MF	F
		(1)	(2)	(3)	(4)	(5)	(6)	(7)	(8)	(9)	(10)
Finland Total	1993/94	46 008	30 497	135 157	67 183	16 202	7 033	197 367	104 713	127 976	62 467
Education science		1 339	875	17 722	13 793	793	476	19 854	15 144	12 060	8 844
Humanities & religion		73	62	19 703	14 617	2 114	1 249	21 890	15 928	18 051	13 059
Fine & applied arts		2 237	1 366	2 411	1 317	159	96	4 807	2 779	2 439	1 468
Law		-	-	3 722	1 878	336	120	4 058	1 998	4 019	1 641
Social & behav. sc.		-	-	9 970	6 369	1 609	796	11 579	7 165	9 472	5 649
Business administr.		950	868	18 400	9 514	1 463	520	20 813	10 902	12 217	5 948
Communic. & doc.		-	-	-	-	-	-	-	-	277	145
Home economics		1 336	1 273	141	116	18	18	1 495	1 407	532	521
Service trades		2 060	1 602	-	-	-	-	2 060	1 602	264	154
Natural science		-	-	8 178	4 180	1 728	805	9 906	4 985	8 389	3 988
Maths. & computer sc.		1 892	446	9 483	1 840	1 057	162	12 432	2 448	7 753	2 137
Health-related prg.		25 310	22 614	7 865	5 968	3 333	1 973	36 508	30 555	16 338	13 307
Engineering		9 227	947	31 075	4 478	2 943	544	43 245	5 969	30 109	3 173
Archit. & town plng.		-	-	1 503	649	180	68	1 683	717	1 477	582
Trade, craft & indust.		-	-	-	-	-	-	-	-		
Transport & communic.		-	-	-	-	-	-	-	-	86	5
Agriculture		1 566	444	4 011	1 900	394	174	5 971	2 518	4 141	1 636
Other & not specified		18	-	973	564	75	32	1 066	596	352	210
France‡ Total	1993/94	461 734	244 409	1 415 784	800 223	205 714	93 670	2 083 232	1 138 302	...	...
Education science		-	-	80 078	59 418	-	-	80 078	59 418	...	...
Humanities & religion		-	-	444 968	323 842	44 306	24 954	489 274	348 796	...	...
Fine & applied arts		./.	./.	30 209	17 876	-	-	30 209	17 876	...	...
Law		13 177	7 399	155 025	95 025	23 493	12 028	191 695	114 452	...	...
Social & behav. sc.		./.	./.	./.	./.	./.	./.	./.	./.	...	...
Business administr.		35 564	15 975	158 301	82 092	18 523	7 708	212 388	105 775	...	...
Communic. & doc.		./.	./.	./.	./.	./.	./.	./.	./.	...	...
Home economics		./.	./.	./.	./.	./.	./.	./.	./.	...	...
Service trades		202 884	129 225	-	-	-	-	202 884	129 225	...	...
Natural science		./.	./.	256 065	94 769	48 028	16 056	304 093	110 825	...	...
Maths. & computer sc.		./.	./.	./.	./.	./.	./.	./.	./.	...	...
Health-related prg.		82 348	68 741	83 260	47 974	70 684	32 657	236 292	149 372	...	...
Engineering		-	-	50 845	10 770	-	-	50 845	10 770	...	...
Archit. & town plng.				18 304	7 555	-	-	18 304	7 555	...	...
Trade, craft & indust.		108 536	17 312	-	-	-	-	108 536	17 312	...	...
Transport & communic.		./.	./.	./.	./.	./.	./.	./.	./.	...	...
Agriculture		19 225	5 757	./.	./.	./.	./.	19 225	5 757	...	...
Other & not specified		-	-	138 729	60 902	680	267	139 409	61 169	...	...
Germany‡ Total	1993/94	...	...	...	...	...	...	1 875 099	753 671	...	...
Education science		...	...	...	...	...	...	406 416	256 987	...	...
Humanities & religion		...	...	...	...	...	...	./.	./.	...	...
Fine & applied arts		...	...	...	...	...	...	78 119	46 700	...	...
Law		...	...	...	...	...	...	543 547	220 304	...	...
Social & behav. sc.		...	...	...	...	...	...	./.	./.	...	...
Business administr.		...	...	...	...	...	...	./.	./.	...	...
Communic. & doc.		...	...	...	...	...	...	./.	./.	...	...
Home economics		...	...	...	...	...	...	./.	./.	...	...
Service trades		...	...	...	...	...	...	./.	./.	...	...
Natural science		...	...	...	...	...	...	310 435	106 184	...	...
Maths. & computer sc.		...	...	...	...	...	...	./.	./.	...	...
MEDICA AN		...	...	...	...	...	...	106 184	47 826	...	...
Engineering		...	...	...	...	...	...	389 182	56 176	...	...
Archit. & town plng.		...	...	...	...	...	...	./.	./.	...	...
Trade, craft & indust.		...	...	...	...	...	...	./.	./.	...	...
Transport & communic.		...	...	...	...	...	...	./.	./.	...	...
Agriculture		...	...	...	...	...	...	38 665	18 759	...	...
Other & not specified		...	...	...	...	...	...	2 551	735	...	...

Third level: students by level and field of study 3.11
Troisième degré: étudiants par niveau et domaine d'études
Tercer grado: estudiantes por nivel y sector de estudios

Country Field of study Pays Domaines d'études País Sectores de estudios	Year Année Año	Students by ISCED level of programme Étudiants par niveau de programmes de la CITE Estudiantes por nivel de programas de la CINE								Students all levels, 1985 Étudiants tous niveaux, 1985 Estudiantes todos los niveles 1985	
		Level 5 Niveau 5 Nivel 5		Level 6 Niveau 6 Nivel 6		Level 7 Niveau 7 Nivel 7		All levels Tous niveaux Todos los niveles			
		MF	F	MF	F	MF	F	MF	F	MF	F
		(1)	(2)	(3)	(4)	(5)	(6)	(7)	(8)	(9)	(10)
Former German Democr. Rep. Total	1988/89	121 057	47 029	161 577	112 320	156 296	70 299	438 930	229 648	432 672	235 755
Education science		-	-	25 046	21 325	32 037	22 375	57 083	43 700	55 132	42 770
Humanities & religion		-	-	1 806	893	7 910	3 424	9 716	4 317	8 791	4 427
Fine & applied arts		264	69	1 009	665	3 572	1 545	4 845	2 279	4 577	2 194
Law		-	-	-	-	4 779	1 280	4 779	1 280	4 346	1 548
Social & behav. sc.		-	-	11 148	9 864	11 427	5 719	22 575	15 583	23 176	16 167
Business administr.		586	505	23 972	19 763	13 577	8 488	38 135	28 756	38 576	29 353
Communic. & doc.		-	-	1 630	1 395	1 045	526	2 675	1 921	2 731	2 038
Home economics		-	-	-	-	-	-	-	-	-	-
Service trades		3 827	2 720	-	-	-	-	3 827	2 720	3 389	2 493
Natural science		-	-	-	-	7 337	2 895	7 337	2 895	7 156	3 086
Maths. & computer sc.		670	442	1 264	656	4 774	1 711	6 708	2 809	4 769	2 317
Health-related prg.		-	-	43 930	41 932	14 602	8 002	58 532	49 934	61 633	53 398
Engineering		-	-	42 143	11 395	44 855	10 000	86 998	21 395	85 824	23 394
Archit. & town plng.		-	-	-	-	1 315	608	1 315	608	1 289	568
Trade, craft & indust.		49 324	9 909	-	-	-	-	49 324	9 909	47 871	10 131
Transport & communic.		3 923	1 215	-	-	-	-	3 923	1 215	4 016	1 225
Agriculture		5 782	2 588	9 629	4 432	9 066	3 726	24 477	10 746	23 722	11 542
Other & not specified		56 681	29 581	-	-	-	-	56 681	29 581	55 674	29 104
Federal Republic of Germany‡ Total	1991/92	228 028	124 618	1 639 463	636 041	...	...	1 867 491	760 659	1 550 211	646 631
Education science		1 201	784	78 454	56 473	...	...	79 655	57 257	93 971	69 043
Humanities & religion		1 407	1 268	230 357	141 862	...	...	231 764	143 130	200 220	121 170
Fine & applied arts		1 657	849	50 699	27 265	...	...	52 356	28 114	48 734	25 336
Law		-	-	90 717	38 495	...	...	90 717	38 495	86 499	33 787
Social & behav. sc.		-	-	387 444	156 400	...	...	387 444	156 400	287 334	112 638
Business administr.		10 800	4 351	39 069	17 101	...	...	49 869	21 452	31 823	12 943
Communic. & doc.		-	-	10 513	5 927	...	...	10 513	5 927	7 674	4 050
Home economics		3 810	3 781	8 368	7 069	...	...	12 178	10 850	15 787	14 731
Service trades		312	160	-	-	...	...	312	160	419	319
Natural science		-	-	139 730	44 163	...	...	139 730	44 163	117 095	36 132
Maths. & computer sc.		3 470	1 205	96 174	22 277	...	...	99 644	23 482	61 455	14 491
Health-related prg.		89 291	73 917	107 680	49 828	...	...	196 971	123 745	219 745	143 410
Engineering		60 001	3 618	294 348	25 023	...	...	354 349	28 641	258 588	16 850
Archit. & town plng.		-	-	49 595	19 709	...	...	49 595	19 709	44 625	16 834
Trade, craft & indust.		7 719	1 077	-	-	...	...	7 719	1 077	5 826	513
Transport & communic.		264	3	-	-	...	...	264	3	-	-
Agriculture		8 969	782	35 143	14 886	...	...	44 112	15 668	45 251	13 074
Other & not specified		39 127	32 823	21 172	9 563	...	...	60 299	42 386	25 165	11 310
Greece‡ Total	1992/93	83 696	39 608	213 595	107 533	...	...	297 291	147 141	181 901	88 963
Education science		666	193	50 417	36 872	...	...	51 083	37 065	13 844	10 391
Humanities & religion		365	-	7 341	3 305	...	...	7 706	3 305	29 580	19 438
Fine & applied arts		3 466	2 166	1 657	1 077	...	...	5 123	3 243	1 793	1 040
Law		-	-	21 627	13 343	...	...	21 627	13 343	13 564	7 478
Social & behav. sc.		-	-	2 959	2 010	...	...	2 959	2 010	12 096	5 966
Business administr.		8 455	5 145	47 704	22 265	...	...	56 159	27 410	21 810	10 909
Communic. & doc.		-	-	744	566	...	...	744	566	688	494
Home economics		53	49	-	-	...	...	53	49	466	195
Service trades		20 907	11 851	239	134	...	...	21 146	11 985	3 403	1 873
Natural science		-	-	15 069	5 630	...	...	15 069	5 630	8 461	3 483
Maths. & computer sc.		1 402	262	12 051	4 115	...	...	13 453	4 377	7 963	2 853
Health-related prg.		15 841	12 156	16 501	7 298	...	...	32 342	19 454	24 549	14 450
Engineering		23 085	4 308	23 266	4 772	...	...	46 351	9 080	29 991	5 270
Archit. & town plng.		-	-	2 248	1 237	...	...	2 248	1 237	1 472	748
Trade, craft & indust.		-	-	172	73	...	...	172	73	796	397
Transport & communic.		1 737	31	284	151	...	...	2 021	182	1 038	31
Agriculture		4 905	2 051	5 990	1 875	...	...	10 895	3 926	10 387	3 947
Other & not specified		2 814	1 396	5 326	2 810	...	...	8 140	4 206	-	-

3.11 Third level: students by level and field of study
Troisième degré: étudiants par niveau et domaine d'études
Tercer grado: estudiantes por nivel y sector de estudios

Country / Field of study Pays / Domaines d'études País / Sectores de estudios	Year Année Año	Students by ISCED level of programme Étudiants par niveau de programmes de la CITE Estudiantes por nivel de programas de la CINE								Students all levels, 1985 Étudiants tous niveaux, 1985 Estudiantes todos los niveles 1985	
		Level 5 Niveau 5 Nivel 5		Level 6 Niveau 6 Nivel 6		Level 7 Niveau 7 Nivel 7		All levels Tous niveaux Todos los niveles			
		MF	F	MF	F	MF	F	MF	F	MF	F
		(1)	(2)	(3)	(4)	(5)	(6)	(7)	(8)	(9)	(10)
Holy See‡ Total	1992/93	2 717	1 773	3 723	1 045	5 813	1 068	12 253	3 886	9 775	3 219
Education science		181	96	73	69	710	438	964	603	466	147
Humanities & religion		2 388	1 592	3 484	949	3 962	420	9 834	2 961	8 375	2 931
Fine & applied arts		25	12	-	-	98	27	123	39	69	26
Law		20	9	46	4	796	111	862	124	553	37
Social & behav. sc.		-	-	17	3	119	23	136	26	152	47
Business administr.		-	-	-	-	-	-	-	-	-	-
Communic. & doc.		-	-	-	-	-	-	-	-	-	-
Home economics		-	-	-	-	-	-	-	-	-	-
Service trades		-	-	-	-	-	-	-	-	-	-
Natural science		-	-	-	-	-	-	-	-	-	-
Maths. & computer sc.		-	-	-	-	-	-	-	-	-	-
Health-related prg.		-	-	-	-	-	-	-	-	-	-
Engineering		-	-	-	-	-	-	-	-	-	-
Archit. & town plng.		-	-	-	-	-	-	-	-	-	-
Trade, craft & indust.		-	-	-	-	-	-	-	-	-	-
Transport & communic.		-	-	-	-	-	-	-	-	-	-
Agriculture		-	-	-	-	-	-	-	-	-	-
Other & not specified		103	64	103	20	128	49	334	133	160	31
Hungary‡ Total	1993/94	58 508	32 629	75 448	37 931	./.	./.	133 956	70 560	99 344	53 188
Education science		17 814	15 349	31 613	20 170	./.	./.	49 427	35 519	38 619	28 804
Humanities & religion		2 516	1 169	3 238	2 418	./.	./.	5 754	3 587	2 512	1 492
Fine & applied arts		-	-	1 340	666	./.	./.	1 340	666	1 286	579
Law		1 732	1 006	5 025	2 597	./.	./.	6 757	3 603	5 836	3 138
Social & behav. sc.		95	31	6 194	3 196	./.	./.	6 289	3 227	2 994	1 397
Business administr.		7 814	4 817	-	-	-	-	7 814	4 817	6 949	4 654
Communic. & doc.		-	-	-	-	-	-	-	-	-	-
Home economics		-	-	-	-	-	-	-	-	-	-
Service trades		1 596	1 086	-	-	-	-	1 596	1 086	825	476
Natural science		-	-	1 766	625	./.	./.	1 766	625	1 148	382
Maths. & computer sc.		971	286	617	128	./.	./.	1 588	414	1 068	368
Health-related prg.		2 533	2 267	8 711	4 264	./.	./.	11 244	6 531	9 912	6 466
Engineering		2 638	428	7 976	1 090	./.	./.	10 614	1 518	9 259	1 104
Archit. & town plng.		2 509	717	2 535	682	./.	./.	5 044	1 399	4 494	1 089
Trade, craft & indust.		7 007	1 560	379	212	./.	./.	7 386	1 772	6 319	1 052
Transport & communic.		3 324	1 013	752	36	./.	./.	4 076	1 049	1 395	314
Agriculture		3 148	1 512	4 973	1 846	./.	./.	8 121	3 358	6 045	1 740
Other & not specified		4 811	1 388	329	1	./.	./.	5 140	1 389	683	133
Iceland Total	1991/92	...	...	...	...	...	...	6 161	3 608	4 724	2 621
Education science		...	...	...	...	...	...	971	755	508	428
Humanities & religion		...	...	...	...	...	...	1 273	833	880	549
Fine & applied arts		...	...	...	...	...	...	-	-	10	2
Law		...	...	...	...	...	...	385	196	352	161
Social & behav. sc.		...	...	...	...	...	...	559	364	271	179
Business administr.		...	...	...	...	...	...	766	312	684	284
Communic. & doc.		...	...	...	...	...	...	89	70	73	66
Home economics		...	...	...	...	...	...	36	17	43	27
Service trades		...	...	...	...	...	...	-	-	-	-
Natural science		...	...	...	...	...	...	299	136	264	103
Maths. & computer sc.		...	...	...	...	...	...	225	49	253	60
Health-related prg.		...	...	...	...	...	...	1 095	812	987	715
Engineering		...	...	...	...	...	...	427	58	384	38
Archit. & town plng.		...	...	...	...	...	...	-	-	-	-
Trade, craft & indust.		...	...	...	...	...	...	-	-	-	-
Transport & communic.		...	...	...	...	...	...	-	-	-	-
Agriculture		...	...	...	...	...	...	36	6	9	3
Other & not specified		...	...	...	...	...	...	-	-	6	6

Third level: students by level and field of study 3.11
Troisième degré: étudiants par niveau et domaine d'études
Tercer grado: estudiantes por nivel y sector de estudios

Country Field of study Pays Domaines d'études País Sectores de estudios	Year Année Año	Students by ISCED level of programme Étudiants par niveau de programmes de la CITE Estudiantes por nivel de programas de la CINE								Students all levels, 1985 Étudiants tous niveaux, 1985 Estudiantes todos los niveles 1985	
		Level 5 Niveau 5 Nivel 5		Level 6 Niveau 6 Nivel 6		Level 7 Niveau 7 Nivel 7		All levels Tous niveaux Todos los niveles			
		MF	F	MF	F	MF	F	MF	F	MF	F
		(1)	(2)	(3)	(4)	(5)	(6)	(7)	(8)	(9)	(10)
Ireland Total	1992/93	...	...	...	...	...	...	108 394	52 182	70 301	30 385
Education science		...	...	...	...	...	...	3 654	2 697	4 630	3 308
Humanities & religion		...	...	...	...	...	...	17 700	11 248	11 443	6 722
Fine & applied arts		...	...	...	...	...	...	3 007	1 945	2 028	1 357
Law		...	...	...	...	...	...	1 904	992	984	446
Social & behav. sc.		...	...	...	...	...	...	3 615	2 574	1 637	934
Business administr.		...	...	...	...	...	...	21 666	11 146	11 050	5 066
Communic. & doc.		...	...	...	...	...	...	392	247	324	196
Home economics		...	...	...	...	...	...	-	-	-	-
Service trades		...	...	...	...	...	...	1 812	1 273	-	-
Natural science		...	...	...	...	...	...	14 191	7 200	10 517	5 012
Maths. & computer sc.		...	...	...	...	...	...	2 554	758	./.	./.
Health-related prg.		...	...	...	...	...	...	4 859	2 746	3 893	1 818
Engineering		...	...	...	...	...	...	13 885	1 463	9 586	908
Archit. & town plng.		...	...	...	...	...	...	1 573	407	971	233
Trade, craft & indust.		...	...	...	...	...	...	172	58	-	-
Transport & communic.		...	...	...	...	...	...	-	-	-	-
Agriculture		...	...	...	...	...	...	1 674	671	1 351	295
Other & not specified		...	...	...	...	...	...	15 736	6 757	11 887	4 090
Italy Total	1993/94	13 043	8 876	1 628 715	828 362	40 191	19 158	1 681 949	856 396	1 185 304	545 902
Education science		-	-	33 868	27 033	999	905	34 867	27 938	38 171	33 541
Humanities & religion		-	-	239 996	192 640	2 555	2 135	242 551	194 775	160 454	127 890
Fine & applied arts		13 043	8 876	6 337	3 696	-	-	19 380	12 572	14 367	8 804
Law		-	-	287 219	156 826	1 420	744	288 639	157 570	175 244	81 628
Social & behav. sc.		-	-	384 461	189 794	2 256	1 038	386 717	190 832	221 489	93 458
Business administr.		-	-	51 525	23 307	-	-	51 525	23 307	17 524	5 035
Communic. & doc.		-	-	6 676	4 573	52	38	6 728	4 611	86	36
Home economics		-	-	-	-	-	-	-	-	-	-
Service trades		-	-	-	-	-	-	-	-	-	-
Natural science		-	-	92 636	46 414	1 125	721	93 761	47 135	78 783	41 619
Maths. & computer sc.		-	-	64 020	29 824	79	35	64 099	29 859	39 322	17 684
Health-related prg.		-	-	133 970	71 403	29 346	12 604	163 316	84 007	215 466	85 295
Engineering		-	-	200 155	24 922	594	279	200 749	25 201	99 938	5 956
Archit. & town plng.		-	-	88 198	39 989	519	308	88 717	40 297	66 998	25 063
Trade, craft & indust.		-	-	-	-	-	-	-	-	-	-
Transport & communic.		-	-	-	-	-	-	-	-	-	-
Agriculture		-	-	33 360	12 457	1 031	238	34 391	12 695	37 396	9 647
Other & not specified		-	-	6 294	5 484	215	113	6 509	5 597	20 066	10 246
Latvia‡ Total	1994/95	...	...	37 623	21 024	423	201	38 046	21 225		
Education science		...	...	8 525	6 872	79	68	8 604	6 940	...	...
Humanities & religion		...	...	3 053	2 530	36	17	3 089	2 547	...	...
Fine & applied arts		...	...	1 045	664	4	1	1 049	665	...	...
Law		...	...	1 691	968	9	7	1 700	975	...	...
Social & behav. sc.		...	...	1 505	1 056	55	35	1 560	1 091	...	...
Business administr.		...	...	5 934	3 251	-	-	5 934	3 251	...	...
Communic. & doc.		...	...	381	323	-	-	381	323	...	...
Home economics		...	...	322	210	-	-	322	210	...	...
Service trades		...	...	76	52	-	-	76	52	...	...
Natural science		...	...	948	518	94	38	1 042	556	...	...
Maths. & computer sc.		...	...	1 464	410	18	7	1 482	417	...	...
Health-related prg.		...	...	2 063	1 418	2	1	2 065	1 419	...	...
Engineering		...	...	5 636	1 044	93	12	5 729	1 056	...	...
Archit. & town plng.		...	...	247	97	-	-	247	97	...	...
Trade, craft & indust.		...	...	-	-	-	-	-	-	...	...
Transport & communic.		...	...	1 408	112	-	-	1 408	112	...	...
Agriculture		...	...	2 852	1 388	33	15	2 885	1 403	...	...
Other & not specified		...	...	473	111	-	-	473	111	...	...

3.11   Third level: students by level and field of study
Troisième degré: étudiants par niveau et domaine d'études
Tercer grado: estudiantes por nivel y sector de estudios

Country Field of study Pays Domaines d'études País Sectores de estudios	Year Année Año	Students by ISCED level of programme Étudiants par niveau de programmes de la CITE Estudiantes por nivel de programas de la CINE								Students all levels, 1985 Étudiants tous niveaux, 1985	
		Level 5 Niveau 5 Nivel 5		Level 6 Niveau 6 Nivel 6		Level 7 Niveau 7 Nivel 7		All levels Tous niveaux Todos los niveles		Estudiantes todos los niveles 1985	
		MF	F	MF	F	MF	F	MF	F	MF	F
		(1)	(2)	(3)	(4)	(5)	(6)	(7)	(8)	(9)	(10)
Malta											
Total	1993/94	1 256	632	3 585	1 688	336	205	5 177	2 525	1 474	482
Education science		146	70	776	477	40	91	962	638	318	186
Humanities & religion		263	124	767	403	174	62	1 204	589	7	2
Fine & applied arts		3	2	-	-	-	-	3	2	-	-
Law		-	-	378	197	-	-	378	197	102	33
Social & behav. sc.		95	70	10	8	-	-	105	78	-	-
Business administr.		174	31	668	286	33	9	875	326	350	98
Communic. & doc.		-	-	-	-	-	-	-	-	-	-
Home economics		-	-	-	-	-	-	-	-	-	-
Service trades		-	-	-	-	-	-	-	-	-	-
Natural science		-	-	190	68	40	20	230	88	-	-
Maths. & computer sc.		-	-	./.	./.	./.	./.	./.	./.	-	-
Health-related prg.		487	318	440	219	35	21	962	558	379	146
Engineering		-	-	298	16	5	1	303	17	203	11
Archit. & town plng.		-	-	58	14	4	-	62	14	115	6
Trade, craft & indust.		-	-	-	-	-	-	-	-	-	-
Transport & communic.		-	-	-	-	-	-	-	-	-	-
Agriculture		22	2	-	-	-	-	22	2	-	-
Other & not specified		66	15	-	-	5	1	71	16	-	-
Moldova‡											
Total	1994/95	43 864	23 072	56 249	30 590	720	...	100 833	53 662	...	...
Education science		5 714	5 314	18 001	13 782	16	...	23 731	19 096	...	...
Humanities & religion		-	-	133	48	102	...	235	48	...	...
Fine & applied arts		1 810	869	1 727	914	14	...	3 551	1 783	...	...
Law		1 164	17	1 475	74	19	...	2 658	91	...	...
Social & behav. sc.		3 915	2 623	5 291	3 217	82	...	9 288	5 840	...	...
Business administr.		-	-	-	-	-	-	-	-	...	...
Communic. & doc.		-	-	-	-	-	-	-	-	...	...
Home economics		-	-	-	-	-	-	-	-	...	...
Service trades		-	-	-	-	-	-	-	-	...	...
Natural science		-	-	-	-	154	...	154	-	...	...
Maths. & computer sc.		-	-	-	-	81	...	81	-	...	...
Health-related prg.		5 990	5 271	5 011	3 284	111	...	11 112	8 555	...	...
Engineering		13 246	5 828	14 647	5 969	94	...	27 987	11 797	...	...
Archit. & town plng.		3 491	768	-	-	2	...	3 493	768	...	...
Trade, craft & indust.		-	-	-	-	-	-	-	-	...	...
Transport & communic.		2 431	524	-	-	-	-	2 431	524	...	...
Agriculture		4 916	1 573	5 664	1 807	45	...	10 625	3 380	...	...
Other & not specified		1 187	285	4 300	1 495	-	-	5 487	1 780	...	...
Netherlands‡											
Total	1993/94	./.	./.	269 545	131 217	187 958	84 649	457 503	215 866	390 320	160 821
Education science		./.	./.	57 919	37 725	545	299	58 464	38 024	71 021	36 099
Humanities & religion		./.	./.	974	760	24 647	15 903	25 621	16 663	30 638	17 178
Fine & applied arts		./.	./.	13 868	7 589	3 858	2 832	17 726	10 421	20 126	10 791
Law		./.	./.	604	167	28 439	14 062	29 043	14 229	28 054	11 415
Social & behav. sc.		./.	./.	50 522	29 501	53 637	25 962	104 159	55 463	61 604	28 377
Business administr.		./.	./.	52 344	19 076	18 663	5 794	71 007	24 870	26 378	7 007
Communic. & doc.		./.	./.	7 723	4 786	404	349	8 127	5 135	3 550	2 231
Home economics		./.	./.	442	241	559	512	1 001	753	2 331	1 727
Service trades		./.	./.	5 280	3 363	-	-	5 280	3 363	1 615	848
Natural science		./.	./.	4 806	1 723	9 711	2 946	14 517	4 669	11 115	2 566
Maths. & computer sc.		./.	./.	4 689	309	4 203	599	8 892	908	2 649	382
Health-related prg.		./.	./.	25 512	20 076	18 199	10 535	43 711	30 611	40 133	23 548
Engineering		./.	./.	3 460	3 539	20 889	3 380	55 490	6 919	22 475	1 896
Archit. & town plng.		./.	./.	./.	./.	./.	./.	./.	./.	./.	./.
Trade, craft & indust.		./.	./.	./.	./.	./.	./.	./.	./.	38 092	4 392
Transport & communic.		./.	./.	1 552	88	-	-	1 552	88	3 668	129
Agriculture		./.	./.	8 709	2 274	4 155	1 463	12 864	3 737	14 707	4 167
Other & not specified		./.	./.	-	-	49	13	49	13	12 164	8 068

Third level: students by level and field of study 3.11
Troisième degré: étudiants par niveau et domaine d'études
Tercer grado: estudiantes por nivel y sector de estudios

Country Field of study / Pays Domaines d'études / País Sectores de estudios	Year Année Año	Students by ISCED level of programme / Étudiants par niveau de programmes de la CITE / Estudiantes por nivel de programas de la CINE								Students all levels, 1985 / Étudiants tous niveaux, 1985 / Estudiantes todos los niveles 1985	
		Level 5 Niveau 5 Nivel 5		Level 6 Niveau 6 Nivel 6		Level 7 Niveau 7 Nivel 7		All levels Tous niveaux Todos los niveles			
		MF	F	MF	F	MF	F	MF	F	MF	F
		(1)	(2)	(3)	(4)	(5)	(6)	(7)	(8)	(9)	(10)
Norway Total	1993/94	55 478	29 339	77 329	45 469	43 915	20 222	176 722	95 030	94 658	49 233
Education science		1 500	1 023	23 679	16 987	1 137	718	26 316	18 728	13 011	9 442
Humanities & religion		10 931	7 112	3 658	2 408	5 272	3 015	19 861	12 535	7 386	4 461
Fine & applied arts		277	176	1 078	675	300	181	1 655	1 032	1 046	622
Law		-	-	-	-	8 266	4 326	8 266	4 326	4 878	2 323
Social & behav. sc.		5 786	3 565	3 527	1 983	7 317	4 281	16 630	9 829	7 349	4 065
Business administr.		17 296	7 986	9 465	3 611	525	123	27 286	11 720	18 911	9 143
Communic. & doc.		457	252	1 929	1 103	15	6	2 401	1 361	564	400
Home economics		-	-	69	65	-	-	69	65	49	44
Service trades		963	725	-	-	-	-	963	725	59	28
Natural science		3 345	1 407	1 783	725	4 769	1 855	9 897	3 987	6 275	1 999
Maths. & computer sc.		666	251	536	102	-	-	1 202	353	1 554	375
Health-related prg.		495	416	13 766	11 832	3 525	2 010	17 786	14 258	10 653	8 242
Engineering		270	52	10 490	1 685	7 674	1 698	18 434	3 435	12 072	2 595
Archit. & town plng.		-	-	-	-	713	368	713	368	691	304
Trade, craft & indust.		60	1	134	73	-	-	194	74	208	120
Transport & communic.		1 152	101	-	-	-	-	1 152	101	898	224
Agriculture		252	95	580	126	1 459	778	2 291	999	1 221	488
Other & not specified		12 028	6 177	6 635	4 094	2 943	863	21 606	11 134	7 833	4 358
Poland Total	1993/94	110 861	82 582	561 955	298 948	74 822	42 577	747 638	424 107	454 190	252 937
Education science		14 197	11 902	75 480	62 971	14 117	10 313	103 794	85 186	88 606	70 925
Humanities & religion		-	-	68 211	50 231	13 190	8 383	81 401	58 614	38 656	24 994
Fine & applied arts		326	208	9 161	5 360	592	283	10 079	5 851	8 127	4 151
Law		-	-	37 747	19 726	2 190	1 167	39 937	20 893	13 788	6 420
Social & behav. sc.		-	-	55 180	32 344	4 575	2 550	59 755	34 894	12 284	6 990
Business administr.		51 201	38 913	62 009	34 418	6 221	2 943	119 431	76 274	67 378	41 896
Communic. & doc.		-	-	4 023	3 289	715	293	4 738	3 582	2 812	2 164
Home economics		-	-	6 025	4 118	755	442	6 780	4 560	428	363
Service trades		9 234	7 202	-	-	-	-	9 234	7 202	-	-
Natural science		-	-	17 960	11 562	1 087	408	19 047	11 970	14 558	9 767
Maths. & computer sc.		-	-	11 563	6 679	1 256	535	12 819	7 214	5 631	3 674
Health-related prg.		20 338	17 166	34 950	21 671	21 175	12 939	76 463	51 776	61 411	45 462
Engineering		-	-	115 949	21 123	3 963	543	119 912	21 666	71 466	12 024
Archit. & town plng.		-	-	5 683	2 768	280	152	5 963	2 920	3 863	1 860
Trade, craft & indust.		14 447	6 676	-	-	-	-	14 447	6 676	13 040	2 789
Transport & communic.		179	92	4 127	246	1 812	273	6 118	611	3 746	162
Agriculture		584	193	38 114	16 317	1 765	596	40 463	17 106	35 759	14 787
Other & not specified		355	230	15 773	6 125	1 129	757	17 257	7 112	12 637	4 509
Portugal‡ Total	1993/94	-	-	267 218	...	9 045	...	276 263	...	103 585	55 599
Education science		-	-	34 045	...	1 320	...	35 365	...	11 996	10 331
Humanities & religion		-	-	16 818	...	1 571	...	18 389	...	13 284	9 865
Fine & applied arts		-	-	5 309	...	77	...	5 386	...	1 760	1 005
Law		-	-	20 790	...	101	...	20 891	...	12 765	5 587
Social & behav. sc.		-	-	27 662	...	1 963	...	29 625	...	10 062	5 914
Business administr.		-	-	52 639	...	726	...	53 365	...	9 754	4 280
Communic. & doc.		-	-	9 076	...	304	...	9 380	...	1 235	889
Home economics		-	-	283	...	-	-	283	...	-	-
Service trades		-	-	-	-	-	-	-	-	-	-
Natural science		-	-	8 235	...	422	...	8 657	...	3 172	1 990
Maths. & computer sc.		-	-	11 151	...	324	...	11 475	...	3 231	1 777
Health-related prg.		-	-	15 361	...	675	...	16 036	...	8 635	5 845
Engineering		-	-	44 495	...	781	...	45 276	...	17 896	4 312
Archit. & town plng.		-	-	5 389	...	83	...	5 472	...	1 728	639
Trade, craft & indust.		-	-	-	-	-	-	-	-	273	153
Transport & communic.		-	-	-	-	-	-	-	-	-	-
Agriculture		-	-	10 535	...	471	...	11 006	...	3 883	1 738
Other & not specified		-	-	5 430	...	227	...	5 657	...	3 911	1 274

3.11 Third level: students by level and field of study
Troisième degré: étudiants par niveau et domaine d'études
Tercer grado: estudiantes por nivel y sector de estudios

Country / Field of study / Pays / Domaines d'études / País / Sectores de estudios	Year / Année / Año	Students by ISCED level of programme — Étudiants par niveau de programmes de la CITE — Estudiantes por nivel de programas de la CINE								Students all levels, 1985 / Étudiants tous niveaux, 1985 / Estudiantes todos los niveles 1985	
		Level 5 / Niveau 5 / Nivel 5		Level 6 / Niveau 6 / Nivel 6		Level 7 / Niveau 7 / Nivel 7		All levels / Tous niveaux / Todos los niveles			
		MF	F	MF	F	MF	F	MF	F	MF	F
		(1)	(2)	(3)	(4)	(5)	(6)	(7)	(8)	(9)	(10)
Romania‡											
Total	1993/94	...	...	...	...	...	...	250 087	116 511	159 798	...
Education science		...	...	...	...	...	...	4 444	1 430	6 271	...
Humanities & religion		...	...	...	...	...	...	20 840	12 953	./.	...
Fine & applied arts		...	...	...	...	...	...	4 186	2 004	899	...
Law		...	...	...	...	...	...	14 854	4 538	2 380	...
Social & behav. sc.		...	...	...	...	...	...	5 465	4 007	16 485	...
Business administr.		...	...	...	...	...	...	35 741	22 989	./.	...
Communic. & doc.		...	...	...	...	...	...	2 214	1 889	./.	...
Home economics		...	...	...	...	...	...	-		./.	...
Service trades		...	...	...	...	...	...	3 422	2 288	./.	...
Natural science		...	...	...	...	...	...	12 768	9 212	8 146	...
Maths. & computer sc.		...	...	...	...	...	...	10 088	5 833	./.	...
Health-related prg.		...	...	...	...	...	...	25 738	15 879	18 833	...
Engineering		...	...	...	...	...	...	88 480	24 870	81 992	...
Archit. & town plng.		...	...	...	...	...	...	1 676	720	14 332	...
Trade, craft & indust.		...	...	...	...	...	...	4 083	3 143	./.	...
Transport & communic.		...	...	...	...	...	...	1 458	169	3 455	...
Agriculture		...	...	...	...	...	...	9 681	4 479	7 005	...
Other & not specified		...	...	...	...	...	...	4 949	108	-	-
Russian Federation											
Total	1994/95	1 870 853	1 127 236	2 533 969	1 336 676	53 541	...	4 458 363	2 463 912	...	...
Education science		259 260	236 193	190 150	160 085	3 271	...	452 681	396 278	...	...
Humanities & religion		-	-	231 008	184 935	3 872	...	234 880	184 935	...	...
Fine & applied arts		51 983	36 660	35 547	22 222	1 201	...	88 731	58 882	...	...
Law		32 600	21 611	87 677	41 736	1 418	...	121 695	63 347	...	...
Social & behav. sc.		251 760	224 458	248 325	167 634	8 245	...	508 330	392 092	...	...
Business administr.		142 328	104 641	181 629	128 452	-	...	323 957	233 093	...	...
Communic. & doc.		13 311	10 438	24 683	18 002	-	...	37 994	28 440	...	...
Home economics		-	-	25	25	-	...	25	25	...	...
Service trades		1 756	1 558	-	-	-	...	1 756	1 558	...	...
Natural science		7 520	4 577	140 207	74 762	5 528	...	153 255	79 339	...	...
Maths. & computer sc.		11 183	7 207	137 454	77 510	5 399	...	154 036	84 717	...	...
Health-related prg.		203 442	181 529	166 903	114 601	6 954	...	377 299	296 130	...	...
Engineering		609 533	129 349	787 263	211 813	15 168	...	1 411 964	341 162	...	...
Archit. & town plng.		2 693	1 894	8 980	5 556	248	...	11 921	7 450	...	...
Trade, craft & indust.		77 587	65 008	-	-	-	...	77 587	65 008	...	...
Transport & communic.		48 176	17 330	-	-	-	...	48 176	17 330	...	...
Agriculture		120 685	55 980	182 736	89 769	2 231	...	305 652	145 749	...	...
Other & not specified		37 036	28 803	111 382	39 574	6	...	148 424	68 377	...	...
Slovakia											
Total	1994/95	1 863	1 284	77 321	37 928	3 039	1 132	82 223	40 344	...	...
Education science		-	-	13 562	10 089	137	71	13 699	10 160	...	...
Humanities & religion		-	-	5 181	3 060	215	101	5 396	3 161	...	...
Fine & applied arts		374	190	1 328	657	21	12	1 723	859	...	...
Law		-	-	3 539	1 809	199	98	3 738	1 907	...	...
Social & behav. sc.		133	98	561	366	47	36	741	500	...	...
Business administr.		203	117	11 159	6 372	128	51	11 490	6 540	...	...
Communic. & doc.		-	-	459	270	16	8	475	278	...	...
Home economics		-	-	-	-	-	-	-	-	...	...
Service trades		312	234	-	-	-	-	312	234	...	...
Natural science		-	-	2 005	1 101	475	186	2 480	1 287	...	...
Maths. & computer sc.		-	-	717	129	129	42	846	171	...	...
Health-related prg.		652	605	5 897	3 663	319	156	6 868	4 424	...	...
Engineering		189	40	25 428	7 256	1 044	252	26 661	7 548	...	...
Archit. & town plng.		-	-	914	345	46	29	960	374	...	...
Trade, craft & indust.		-	-	-	-	-	-	-		...	
Transport & communic.		-	-	-	-	-	-			...	
Agriculture		-	-	6 171	2 700	263	90	6 434	2 790	...	...
Other & not specified		-	-	400	111	-	-	400	111	...	...

Third level: students by level and field of study 3.11
Troisième degré: étudiants par niveau et domaine d'études
Tercer grado: estudiantes por nivel y sector de estudios

Country / Field of study — Pays / Domaines d'études — País / Sectores de estudios	Year Année Año	Students by ISCED level of programme / Étudiants par niveau de programmes de la CITE / Estudiantes por nivel de programas de la CINE								Students all levels, 1985 / Étudiants tous niveaux, 1985 / Estudiantes todos los niveles 1985	
		Level 5 Niveau 5 Nivel 5		Level 6 Niveau 6 Nivel 6		Level 7 Niveau 7 Nivel 7		All levels Tous niveaux Todos los niveles			
		MF	F	MF	F	MF	F	MF	F	MF	F
		(1)	(2)	(3)	(4)	(5)	(6)	(7)	(8)	(9)	(10)
Slovenia‡ Total	1994/95	13 832	7 289	29 417	17 057	...	...	43 249	24 346	...	...
Education science		645	614	5 064	3 945	...	...	5 709	4 559	...	...
Humanities & religion		-	-	2 598	1 928	...	...	2 598	1 928	...	...
Fine & applied arts		6	4	695	417	...	...	701	421	...	...
Law		-	-	2 141	1 397	...	...	2 141	1 397	...	...
Social & behav. sc.		-	-	1 915	1 306	...	...	1 915	1 306	...	...
Business administr.		7 288	4 605	4 914	2 844	...	...	12 202	7 449	...	...
Communic. & doc.		-	-	861	700	...	...	861	700	...	...
Home economics		./.	./.	./.	./.	...	...	./.	./.	...	...
Service trades		./.	./.	./.	./.	...	...	./.	./.	...	...
Natural science		2	1	1 029	557	...	...	1 031	558	...	...
Maths. & computer sc.		20	9	198	75	...	...	218	84	...	...
Health-related prg.		989	890	1 817	1 236	...	...	2 806	2 126	...	...
Engineering		3 136	676	5 333	997	...	...	8 469	1 673	...	...
Archit. & town plng.		-	-	732	377	...	...	732	377	...	...
Trade, craft & indust.		-	-	-	-	...	...	-	-	...	...
Transport & communic.		660	208	256	68	...	...	916	276	...	...
Agriculture		609	183	1 288	722	...	...	1 897	905	...	...
Other & not specified		477	99	576	488	...	...	1 053	587	...	...
Spain Total	1993/94	17 858	8 676	1 397 326	715 419	54 284	25 414	1 469 468	749 509	935 126	459 105
Education science		1 459	1 325	96 398	67 552	2 904	1 562	100 761	70 439	111 327	80 188
Humanities & religion		-	-	108 097	68 130	9 388	5 287	117 485	73 417	117 218	76 298
Fine & applied arts		770	431	17 277	10 137	899	499	18 946	11 067	11 553	6 215
Law		-	-	263 849	147 874	4 952	2 234	268 801	150 108	138 184	64 191
Social & behav. sc.		-	-	80 201	54 330	2 462	1 419	82 663	55 749	112 662	53 059
Business administr.		6 264	3 878	258 677	125 866	3 984	1 654	268 925	131 398	44 520	19 433
Communic. & doc.		338	250	31 250	20 479	1 154	570	32 742	21 299	17 978	9 763
Home economics		-	-	-	-	-	-	-	-	-	-
Service trades		1 632	858	19 596	15 223	-	-	21 228	16 081	11 223	7 965
Natural science		-	-	83 090	39 531	6 315	2 738	89 405	42 269	62 570	28 464
Maths. & computer sc.		-	-	74 229	23 018	1 547	412	75 776	23 430	29 287	10 993
Health-related prg.		204	170	98 378	68 034	13 133	6 730	111 715	74 934	103 624	60 838
Engineering		-	-	188 466	40 106	3 194	635	191 660	40 741	93 412	9 959
Archit. & town plng.		58	18	42 122	14 502	1 415	425	43 595	14 945	26 407	5 574
Trade, craft & indust.		5 111	748	-	-	-	-	5 111	748	-	-
Transport & communic.		518	36	-	-	-	-	518	36	-	-
Agriculture		273	84	12 463	6 872	703	306	13 439	7 262	13 389	5 066
Other & not specified		1 231	878	23 233	13 765	2 234	943	26 698	15 586	41 772	21 099
Sweden‡ Total	1993/94	./.	./.	219 163	122 364	15 303	5 509	234 466	127 873	176 589	92 141
Education science		./.	./.	36 938	28 674	531	342	37 469	29 016	23 176	17 619
Humanities & religion		./.	./.	29 017	19 154	2 052	911	31 069	20 065	20 217	12 989
Fine & applied arts		./.	./.	3 749	2 109	257	113	4 006	2 222	5 831	3 457
Law		./.	./.	10 789	5 673	189	79	10 978	5 752	7 945	3 790
Social & behav. sc.		./.	./.	22 435	14 470	1 443	563	23 878	15 033	14 785	9 223
Business administr.		./.	./.	22 444	10 874	735	213	23 179	11 087	22 127	10 375
Communic. & doc.		./.	./.	2 770	1 864	55	31	2 825	1 895	1 915	1 300
Home economics		./.	./.	282	268	4	4	286	272	415	393
Service trades		-	-	-	-	-	-	-	-	198	152
Natural science		./.	./.	8 290	4 040	2 292	716	10 582	4 756	8 277	3 054
Maths. & computer sc.		./.	./.	11 983	3 478	909	151	12 892	3 629	9 223	2 457
Health-related prg.		./.	./.	28 446	22 308	3 603	1 521	32 049	23 829	27 033	19 812
Engineering		./.	./.	35 821	6 720	2 459	569	38 280	7 289	27 612	4 565
Archit. & town plng.		./.	./.	1 151	567	75	32	1 226	599	1 433	650
Trade, craft & indust.		./.	./.	906	96	-	-	906	96	1 577	140
Transport & communic.		./.	./.	691	80	96	21	787	101	530	42
Agriculture		./.	./.	2 531	1 313	603	243	3 134	1 556	2 173	670
Other & not specified		./.	./.	920	676	-	-	920	676	2 122	1 453

3.11 Third level: students by level and field of study
Troisième degré: étudiants par niveau et domaine d'études
Tercer grado: estudiantes por nivel y sector de estudios

Country / Field of study / Pays / Domaines d'études / País / Sectores de estudios	Year / Année / Año	Students by ISCED level of programme / Étudiants par niveau de programmes de la CITE / Estudiantes por nivel de programas de la CINE								Students all levels, 1985 / Étudiants tous niveaux, 1985 / Estudiantes todos los niveles 1985	
		Level 5 / Niveau 5 / Nivel 5		Level 6 / Niveau 6 / Nivel 6		Level 7 / Niveau 7 / Nivel 7		All levels / Tous niveaux / Todos los niveles			
		MF	F	MF	F	MF	F	MF	F	MF	F
		(1)	(2)	(3)	(4)	(5)	(6)	(7)	(8)	(9)	(10)
Switzerland Total	1993/94	60 806	19 211	72 614	30 458	15 244	4 902	148 664	54 571	110 111	35 373
Education science		4 702	3 265	2 235	1 627	217	136	7 154	5 028	5 461	3 308
Humanities & religion		1 867	1 190	12 974	7 364	2 223	1 069	17 064	9 623	15 790	8 410
Fine & applied arts		2 794	1 793	1 296	872	187	101	4 277	2 766	3 251	2 176
Law		84	8	9 799	4 351	1 331	403	11 214	4 762	9 180	3 022
Social & behav. sc.		4 528	2 623	8 672	5 110	1 441	710	14 641	8 443	18 670	6 971
Business administr.		18 684	5 374	11 012	2 641	2 034	425	31 730	8 440	10 041	2 080
Communic. & doc.		57	32	76	36	1	-	134	68	59	30
Home economics		3 192	1 881	-	-	-	-	3 192	1 881	1 502	682
Service trades		-	-	-	-	-	-	-	-	-	-
Natural science		649	184	6 757	2 154	3 990	1 062	11 396	3 400	9 236	2 190
Maths. & computer sc.		2	-	2 465	341	483	83	2 950	424	2 579	365
Health-related prg.		2 449	1 957	7 932	3 967	1 749	634	12 130	6 558	10 248	4 151
Engineering		15 944	540	5 140	370	1 133	141	22 217	1 051	16 693	578
Archit. & town plng.		1 536	233	2 751	952	180	65	4 467	1 250	2 140	633
Trade, craft & indust.		3 766	115	-	-	-	-	3 766	115	2 788	26
Transport & communic.		115	4	-	-	-	-	115	4	25	-
Agriculture		437	12	1 383	648	275	73	2 095	733	2 448	751
Other & not specified		-	-	122	25	-	-	122	25	-	-
The Former Yugoslav Rep. of Macedonia Total	1994/95	3 447	2 101	25 610	13 591	...	...	29 057	15 692	...	...
Education science		1 310	1 136	569	452	...	...	1 879	1 588	...	...
Humanities & religion		-	-	2 502	1 931	...	...	2 502	1 931	...	...
Fine & applied arts		-	-	609	340	...	...	609	340	...	...
Law		-	-	2 009	1 193	...	...	2 009	1 193	...	...
Social & behav. sc.		-	-	4 902	3 134	...	...	4 902	3 134	...	...
Business administr.		-	-	-	-	...	...	-	-	...	...
Communic. & doc.		-	-	647	204	...	...	647	204	...	...
Home economics		-	-	-	-	...	...	-	-	...	...
Service trades		112	49	707	411	...	...	819	460	...	...
Natural science		-	-	1 256	879	...	...	1 256	879	...	...
Maths. & computer sc.		-	-	822	527	...	...	822	527	...	...
Health-related prg.		537	463	2 826	1 895	...	...	3 363	2 358	...	...
Engineering		1 129	298	5 806	1 498	...	...	6 935	1 796	...	...
Archit. & town plng.		-	-	526	300	...	...	526	300	...	...
Trade, craft & indust.		-	-	-	-	...	...	-	-	...	...
Transport & communic.		-	-	159	37	...	...	159	37	...	...
Agriculture		359	155	1 718	674	...	...	2 077	829	...	...
Other & not specified		-	-	552	116	...	...	552	116	...	...
Ukraine‡ Total	1991/92	-	-	876 200	441 000	13 992	...	890 192	...	853 100	...
Education science		-	-	165 900	121 400	592	...	166 492	...	232 200	...
Humanities & religion		-	-	117 000	74 800	4 685	...	121 685	...	./.	...
Fine & applied arts		-	-	6 700	3 700	153	...	6 853	...	6 300	...
Law		-	-	7 600	2 700	232	...	7 832	...	75 600	...
Social & behav. sc.		-	-	./.	./.	./.	...	./.	...	./.	...
Business administr.		-	-	56 200	39 900	2 011	...	58 211	...	./.	...
Communic. & doc.		-	-	./.	./.	./.	...	./.	...	./.	...
Home economics		-	-	./.	./.	./.	...	./.	...	./.	...
Service trades		-	-	./.	./.	./.	...	./.	...	./.	...
Natural science		-	-	./.	./.	./.	...	./.	...	./.	...
Maths. & computer sc.		-	-	./.	./.	./.	...	./.	...	./.	...
Health-related prg.		-	-	61 900	34 000	825	...	62 725	...	58 400	...
Engineering		-	-	369 400	133 500	4 686	...	374 086	...	392 200	...
Archit. & town plng.		-	-	./.	./.	./.	...	./.	...	./.	...
Trade, craft & indust.		-	-	./.	./.	./.	...	./.	...	./.	...
Transport & communic.		-	-	./.	./.	./.	...	./.	...	./.	...
Agriculture		-	-	91 500	31 000	792	...	92 292	...	88 400	...
Other & not specified		-	-	-	-	16	...	16	...	-	...

Third level: students by level and field of study 3.11
Troisième degré: étudiants par niveau et domaine d'études
Tercer grado: estudiantes por nivel y sector de estudios

Country / Field of study / Pays / Domaines d'études / País / Sectores de estudios	Year / Année / Año	Students by ISCED level of programme / Étudiants par niveau de programmes de la CITE / Estudiantes por nivel de programas de la CINE								Students all levels, 1985 / Étudiants tous niveaux, 1985 / Estudiantes todos los niveles 1985	
		Level 5 / Niveau 5 / Nivel 5		Level 6 / Niveau 6 / Nivel 6		Level 7 / Niveau 7 / Nivel 7		All levels / Tous niveaux / Todos los niveles			
		MF	F	MF	F	MF	F	MF	F	MF	F
		(1)	(2)	(3)	(4)	(5)	(6)	(7)	(8)	(9)	(10)
United Kingdom‡ Total	1992/93	452 709	240 614	855 804	422 433	219 876	94 890	1 528 389	757 937	1 032 491	469 948
Education science		17 530	12 627	56 928	45 137	44 123	28 528	118 581	86 292	83 715	54 471
Humanities & religion		25 926	14 604	118 536	73 254	19 439	9 746	163 901	97 604	83 251	50 007
Fine & applied arts		./.	./.	./.	./.	./.	./.	./.	./.	46 339	26 584
Law		./.	./.	./.	./.	./.	./.	./.	./.	247 695	106 949
Social & behav. sc.		23 977	16 152	94 158	49 513	24 632	12 093	142 767	77 758	./.	./.
Business administr.		129 875	68 561	82 021	39 248	40 472	13 592	252 368	121 401	./.	./.
Communic. & doc.		2 106	1 180	7 509	4 875	2 920	1 803	12 535	7 858	35 363	14 719
Home economics		./.	./.	./.	./.	./.	./.	./.	./.	./.	./.
Service trades		./.	./.	./.	./.	./.	./.	./.	./.	./.	./.
Natural science		8 887	4 074	75 770	33 924	21 326	7 465	105 983	45 463	134 697	44 901
Maths. & computer sc.		21 527	5 670	44 176	11 093	10 727	2 595	76 430	19 358	./.	./.
Health-related prg.		109 912	93 931	55 096	35 560	15 099	8 469	180 107	137 960	151 637	117 946
Engineering		83 409	7 854	108 601	16 457	27 068	4 981	219 078	29 292	159 041	12 261
Archit. & town plng.		./.	./.	./.	./.	./.	./.	./.	./.	./.	./.
Trade, craft & indust.		./.	./.	./.	./.	./.	./.	./.	./.	./.	./.
Transport & communic.		./.	./.	./.	./.	./.	./.	./.	./.	./.	./.
Agriculture		4 660	1 672	7 676	3 770	2 470	933	14 806	6 375	8 856	3 213
Other & not specified		24 900	14 289	205 333	109 602	11 600	4 685	241 833	128 576	81 897	38 897
Former Yugoslavia‡ Total	1990/91	41 891	22 097	285 201	143 176	...	...	327 092	165 273	350 334	160 494
Education science		12 260	9 199	12 606	8 003	...	...	24 866	17 202	30 563	18 262
Humanities & religion		-	-	28 298	20 795	...	...	28 298	20 795	26 712	17 983
Fine & applied arts		-	-	4 634	2 687	...	...	4 634	2 687	4 412	2 336
Law		809	541	22 754	14 113	...	...	23 563	14 654	33 768	17 582
Social & behav. sc.		5 038	3 350	43 090	28 013	...	...	48 128	31 363	56 018	30 199
Business administr.		464	229	3 269	1 517	...	...	3 733	1 746	5 595	2 222
Communic. & doc.		-	-	-	-	...	...	-	-	262	212
Home economics											
Service trades		547	306	2 494	1 445	...	...	3 041	1 751	4 033	1 873
Natural science		-	-	20 037	12 810	...	...	20 037	12 810	18 507	10 632
Maths. & computer sc.		-	-	./.	./.	...	...	./.	./.	./.	./.
Health-related prg.		2 559	2 062	25 804	15 475	...	...	28 363	17 537	30 375	18 916
Engineering		13 438	3 579	86 664	24 922	...	...	100 102	28 501	91 354	22 357
Archit. & town plng.		-	-	4 168	2 346	...	...	4 168	2 346	4 874	2 518
Trade, craft & indust.		1 216	882	564	245	...	...	1 780	1 127	2 192	1 174
Transport & communic.		1 302	370	6 992	1 585	...	...	8 294	1 955	8 419	1 921
Agriculture		2 075	922	23 720	9 210	...	...	25 795	10 132	29 545	11 323
Other & not specified		2 183	657	107	10	...	...	2 290	667	3 705	984
Federal Republic of Yugoslavia‡ Total	1994/95	25 385	12 571	118 566	65 280	...	...	143 951	77 851	...	...
Education science		2 306	2 100	5 412	3 262	...	...	7 718	5 362	...	...
Humanities & religion		-	-	15 990	12 946	...	...	15 990	12 946	...	...
Fine & applied arts		361	265	2 713	1 646	...	...	3 074	1 911	...	...
Law		-	-	12 099	7 727	...	...	12 099	7 727	...	...
Social & behav. sc.		4 553	2 972	15 320	10 355	...	...	19 873	13 327	...	...
Business administr.		501	193	1 431	595	...	...	1 932	788	...	...
Communic. & doc.		-	-	-	-	...	...	-	-	...	...
Home economics											
Service trades		797	520	145	64	...	...	942	584	...	...
Natural science		-	-	10 369	7 178	...	...	10 369	7 178	...	...
Maths. & computer sc.		-	-	./.	./.	...	...	./.	./.	...	...
Health-related prg.		1 986	1 617	11 682	7 697	...	...	13 668	9 314	...	...
Engineering		10 689	3 231	29 237	7 828	...	...	39 926	11 059	...	...
Archit. & town plng.		-	-	1 509	904	...	...	1 509	904	...	...
Trade, craft & indust.		817	674	-	-	...	...	817	674	...	...
Transport & communic.		1 338	510	2 616	770	...	...	3 954	1 280	...	...
Agriculture		689	318	9 655	4 128	...	...	10 344	4 446	...	...
Other & not specified		1 348	171	388	180	...	...	1 736	351	...	...

3.11 Third level: students by level and field of study
Troisième degré: étudiants par niveau et domaine d'études
Tercer grado: estudiantes por nivel y sector de estudios

Country / Field of study / Pays / Domaines d'études / País / Sectores de estudios	Year / Année / Año	Students by ISCED level of programme / Étudiants par niveau de programmes de la CITE / Estudiantes por nivel de programas de la CINE								Students all levels, 1985 / Étudiants tous niveaux, 1985 / Estudiantes todos los niveles 1985	
		Level 5 / Niveau 5 / Nivel 5		Level 6 / Niveau 6 / Nivel 6		Level 7 / Niveau 7 / Nivel 7		All levels / Tous niveaux / Todos los niveles			
		MF	F	MF	F	MF	F	MF	F	MF	F
		(1)	(2)	(3)	(4)	(5)	(6)	(7)	(8)	(9)	(10)
Oceania											
Australia‡ Total	1993	425 525	177 813	430 204	234 825	113 643	56 131	969 372	468 769	370 048	176 178
Education science		16 319	10 892	43 702	32 954	27 125	18 373	87 146	62 219	92 910	60 119
Humanities & religion		1 250	777	65 801	44 716	9 491	5 598	76 542	51 091	./.	./.
Fine & applied arts		1 437	710	12 629	8 538	2 182	1 293	16 248	10 541		
Law		676	280	15 091	7 510	3 741	1 542	19 508	9 332	9 945	4 217
Social & behav. sc.		3 931	1 720	16 174	8 984	5 949	3 251	26 054	13 955	./.	./.
Business administr.		30 499	20 935	86 615	40 161	21 367	7 119	138 481	68 215	68 411	21 974
Communic. & doc.		143 913	75 464	6 970	4 922	2 212	1 583	153 095	81 969	-	-
Home economics		-	-	489	432	2	2	491	434	-	-
Service trades		123	66	1 034	608	187	93	1 344	767	-	-
Natural science		27 085	10 248	43 158	20 367	8 838	3 266	79 081	33 881	52 547	19 089
Maths. & computer sc.		1 273	336	18 484	5 142	5 837	1 477	25 594	6 955	./.	./.
Health-related prg.		24 043	17 439	54 940	41 561	12 157	8 367	91 140	67 367	23 431	13 876
Engineering		80 737	5 449	36 623	4 812	7 233	819	124 593	11 080	28 285	1 466
Archit. & town plng.		28 605	3 045	9 234	3 024	2 312	672	40 151	6 741	7 988	1 845
Trade, craft & indust.		296	182	2 328	1 361	43	22	2 667	1 565	-	-
Transport & communic.		33 652	18 458	-	-	-	-	33 652	18 458	-	-
Agriculture		21 975	6 744	8 171	3 474	2 422	817	32 568	11 035	8 068	2 729
Other & not specified		9 711	5 068	8 761	6 259	2 545	1 837	21 017	13 164	3 301	1 607
Fiji Total	1989	2 096	...	1 367	...	46	...	3 509	...	2 313	875
Education science		456	230	103	...	18	...	577	...	514	242
Humanities & religion		-	-	-	-	-	-	-	-	9	6
Fine & applied arts		-	-	-	-	-	-	-	-	-	-
Law		-	-	-	-	-	-	-	-		
Social & behav. sc.		180	...	776	...	21	...	977	...	1 043	398
Business administr.		162	...	19	...	-	-	181	...		
Communic. & doc.		140	...	-	-	-	-	140	...	-	-
Home economics		10	...	-	-	-	-	10	...	-	-
Service trades		-	-	-	-	-	-	-	-	-	-
Natural science		272	...	322	...	7	...	601	...	489	144
Maths. & computer sc.		123	...	-	-	-	-	123	...	6	1
Health-related prg.		473	355	136	49	-	-	609	404	252	84
Engineering		-	-	-	-	-	-	-	-	-	-
Archit. & town plng.		-	-	-	-	-	-	-	-	-	-
Trade, craft & indust.		-	...	-	-	-	-	-	...	-	-
Transport & communic.		-	-	-	-	-	-	-	-	-	-
Agriculture		170	...	-	-	-	-	170	...	-	-
Other & not specified		110	...	11	-	-	...	121	...	-	-
Guam‡ Total	1988/89	-	-	3 769	...	488	...	4 257	...	...	...
Education science		-	-	964	...	367	...	1 331	...	...	...
Humanities & religion		-	-	38	...	1	...	39	...	...	...
Fine & applied arts		-	-	60	...	1	...	61	...	...	...
Law		-	-	-	-	-	-	-	-	...	...
Social & behav. sc.		-	-	348	...	-	-	348	...	...	...
Business administr.		-	-	1 674	...	85	...	1 759	...	...	...
Communic. & doc.		-	-	94	...	-	-	94	...	...	...
Home economics		-	-	-	-	-	-	-	-	...	...
Service trades		-	-	-	-	-	-	-	-	...	...
Natural science		-	-	141	...	22	...	163	...	...	...
Maths. & computer sc.		-	-	79	...	-	-	79	...	...	...
Health-related prg.		-	-	304	...	-	-	304	...	...	...
Engineering		-	-	-	-	-	-	-	-	...	...
Archit. & town plng.		-	-	-	-	-	-	-	-	...	...
Trade, craft & indust.		-	-	-	-	-	-	-	-	...	...
Transport & communic.		-	-	-	-	-	-	-	-	...	...
Agriculture		-	-	34	...	-	-	34	...	...	...
Other & not specified		-	-	33	...	12	...	45	...	...	...

Third level: students by level and field of study 3.11
Troisième degré: étudiants par niveau et domaine d'études
Tercer grado: estudiantes por nivel y sector de estudios

Country Field of study / Pays Domaines d'études / País Sectores de estudios	Year Année Año	Students by ISCED level of programme / Étudiants par niveau de programmes de la CITE / Estudiantes por nivel de programas de la CINE								Students all levels, 1985 / Étudiants tous niveaux, 1985 / Estudiantes todos los niveles 1985	
		Level 5 Niveau 5 Nivel 5		Level 6 Niveau 6 Nivel 6		Level 7 Niveau 7 Nivel 7		All levels Tous niveaux Todos los niveles			
		MF	F	MF	F	MF	F	MF	F	MF	F
		(1)	(2)	(3)	(4)	(5)	(6)	(7)	(8)	(9)	(10)
New Zealand‡ Total	1994	50 378	27 686	100 194	56 639	18 849	9 400	169 421	93 725	98 405	44 920
Education science		8 806	6 935	11 053	9 199	1 442	1 079	21 301	17 213	6 027	4 525
Humanities & religion		1 277	816	24 971	16 342	3 108	1 959	29 356	19 117	18 226	12 406
Fine & applied arts		1 602	937	2 474	1 369	136	76	4 212	2 382	917	555
Law		628	519	5 202	2 824	809	420	6 639	3 763	5 123	2 522
Social & behav. sc.		1 527	1 121	3 110	2 255	1 418	1 012	6 055	4 388	2 530	1 587
Business administr.		16 795	8 502	22 432	10 621	4 587	1 766	43 814	20 889	25 788	10 023
Communic. & doc.		291	256	386	280	74	48	751	584	449	246
Home economics		-	-	-	-	-	-	-	-	354	323
Service trades		997	628	34	23	-	-	1 031	651	173	100
Natural science		1 394	738	11 148	4 572	2 219	922	14 761	6 232	9 433	3 620
Maths. & computer sc.		500	154	363	77	230	49	1 093	280	352	99
Health-related prg.		4 868	4 273	5 649	3 820	1 047	729	11 564	8 822	6 805	5 024
Engineering		4 469	309	4 065	684	482	65	9 016	1 058	9 272	621
Archit. & town plng.		1 241	329	1 629	593	91	36	2 961	958	3 640	960
Trade, craft & indust.		1 949	453	15	1	87	49	2 051	503	3 559	337
Transport & communic.		329	22	233	26	-	-	562	48	353	17
Agriculture		1 282	502	1 757	654	669	201	3 708	1 357	4 459	1 344
Other & not specified		2 423	1 192	5 673	3 299	2 450	989	10 546	5 480	945	611
Papua New Guinea‡ Total	1995	4 784	1 859	4 648	1 151	21	5	9 453	3 015	5 068	1 174
Education science		1 714	828	506	192	-	-	2 220	1 020	650	177
Humanities & religion		./.	./.	./.	./.	-	-	./.	./.	431	86
Fine & applied arts		-	-	355	98	-	-	355	98	55	4
Law		-	-	236	72	-	-	236	72	246	36
Social & behav. sc.		./.	./.	54	22	-	-	54	22	153	17
Business administr.		-	-	786	275	-	-	786	275	613	93
Communic. & doc.		-	-	46	14	-	-	46	14	90	54
Home economics		-	-	-	-	-	-	-	-	-	-
Service trades		47	19	-	-	-	-	47	19	-	-
Natural science		-	-	212	43	21	5	233	48	348	47
Maths. & computer sc.		-	-	83	27	-	-	83	27	-	-
Health-related prg.		./.	./.	64	12	-	-	64	12	989	575
Engineering		-	-	599	38	-	-	599	38	472	15
Archit. & town plng.		-	-	28	4	-	-	28	4	83	3
Trade, craft & indust.		1 023	371	-	-	-	-	1 023	371	-	-
Transport & communic.		-	-	-	-	-	-	-	-	43	4
Agriculture		294	41	119	21	-	-	413	62	689	36
Other & not specified		1 706	600	1 560	333	-	-	3 266	933	206	27

This table, which gives more detail to the data shown in Table 3.10, presents enrolment at the third level of education classified by both ISCED level and field of study for the latest year available, as well as by field of study for 1985. The definitions used are based on the International Standard Classification of Education (ISCED). The three level categories identified in this table by their ISCED codes 5, 6, and 7 are defined as follows:

Level 5: Programmes leading to an award not equivalent to a first university degree. Programmes of this type are usually practical in orientation in that they are designed to prepare students for particular vocational fields in which they can qualify.

Level 6: Programmes leading to a first university degree or equivalent qualification, such as a Bachelors's degree.

Level 7: Programmes leading to a post-graduate university degree or equivalent qualification. These programmes are for persons already holding a first university degree or equivalent qualification and are intended to reflect specialization within a given subject area.

Field of Study should be taken to mean the student's main area of specialization. The subjects falling within each of the major fields according to ISCED are shown in the introductory text to Chapter 3.

Ce tableau, donnant des statistiques complémentaires au tableau 3.10, présente la répartition des étudiants inscrits dans l'enseignement du troisième degré par niveau de la CITE et domaine d'études pour la dernière année disponible, et par domaine d'études en 1985. Les définitions utilisées sont celles de la Classification Internationale Type de l'Education (CITE).

Les trois niveaux, désignés dans ce tableau par leurs codes 5, 6 et 7 de la CITE, sont définis comme suit:

Niveau 5: Programmes conduisant à un diplôme n'équivalant pas à un premier grade universitaire. Ces programmes ont généralement un caractère pratique en

ce sens qu'ils ont pour objectif la formation professionnelle des étudiants dans des domaines précis où ils pourront se qualifier.

Niveau 6: Programmes conduisant à un premier grade universitaire ou à un diplôme équivalent tel que la licence.

Niveau 7: Programmes conduisant à un grade universitaire supérieur ou à un diplôme équivalent. Ces programmes s'adressent aux personnes déjà titulaires d'un premier grade universitaire ou d'un diplôme équivalent. Il s'agit de programmes d'études post-universitaires qui prévoient habituellement une

3.11 Third level: students by level and field of study
Troisième degré: étudiants par niveau et domaine d'études
Tercer grado: estudiantes por nivel y sector de estudios

spécialisation à l'intérieur même de la discipline choisie.
Par *domaine d'études* il faut entendre le domaine principal de spécialisation de l'étudiant. Les sujets compris dans chacune des

disciplines principales en accord avec la CITE sont précisés dans le texte d'introduction du chapitre 3.

Este cuadro, que completa las estadísticas del cuadro 3.10, presenta a los estudiantes inscritos en la enseñanza de tercer grado por nivel de la CINE y por sector de estudios para el último año disponible, y por sector de estudios en 1985. Las definiciones utilizadas se basan en la Clasificación Internacional Normalizada de la Educación (CINE).
Los tres niveles designados en este cuadro según la codificación 5, 6 y 7 de la CINE se definen como sigue:
Nivel 5: Programas que conducen a un diploma que no equivale a un primer grado universitario. Los programas de este tipo suelen ser de orientación práctica, y están destinados a preparar a los estudiantes para determinadas ramas profesionales en las que podrán calificarse.

Nivel 6: Programas que conducen a un primer grado universitario o a un diploma equivalente, tales como el *Bachelor's degree*, o la *licence*.
Nivel 7: Programas que conducen a un grado universitario superior o a un diploma equivalente. Estos programas se destinan en general a las personas titulares de un primer grado universitario o calificación equivalente. Se trata de programas de enseñanza de nivel superior que entrañan en general una especialización en el mismo sector que el que correspondió al primer título.
Por *sector de estudios* se comprende el campo principal de especialización del estudiante. Las materias que figuran en cada una de las ramas principales según la CINE se muestran en el texto de introducción del capítulo 3.

AFRICA:
Algeria:
E--> Data refer to universities and equivalent degree-granting institutions under the Ministry of Education. Female students for 1985/86 exclude post-graduates.
FR-> Les données se réfèrent aux universités et établissements conférant des grades équivalents sous l'autorité du Ministère de l'Education. Les données sur les étudiantes en 1985/86 excluent le niveau universitaire supérieur.
ESP> Los datos sólo se refieren a las universidades y establecimientos que otorgan títulos equivalentes bajo la autoridad del Ministerio de Educación. Los datos relativos a las estudiantes en 1985/86 excluyen el nivel post-universitario.
Benin:
E--> In 1994, natural science includes engineering. In 1985 law includes mass communication and documentation.
FR-> En 1994, les sciences exactes et naturelles incluent les sciences de l'ingénieur. En 1985, le droit inclut l'information et la documentation.
ESP> En 1994, las ciencias naturales incluyen la ingeniería y tecnología. En 1985, el derecho incluye la documentación y comunicación social.
Botswana:
E--> Data for 1985/86 refer to full-time students only and for 1993/94 to universities only.
FR-> Les données pour 1985/86 se réfèrent aux étudiants à temps complet seulement, et pour 1993/94 aux universités seulement.
ESP> Los datos de 1985/86 se refieren a los estudiantes de jornada completa solamente, y para 1993/94 a las universidades solamente.
Burkina Faso:
E--> Humanities, religion and theology include social and behavioural science.
FR-> Les lettres, la religion et la théologie incluent les sciences sociales et sciences du comportement.
ESP> Las humanidades, la religión y la teología incluyen las ciencias sociales y del comportamiento.
Burundi:
E--> Level 6 includes level 7.
FR-> Le niveau 6 inclut le niveau 7.
ESP> El nivel 6 incluye el nivel 7.
Cameroon:
E--> Law includes economics; social and behavioural science include humanities, religion and theology.
FR-> Le droit inclut les sciences économiques; les sciences sociales et du comportement incluent les lettres, la religion et la théologie.
ESP> El derecho incluye las ciencias económicas; las ciencias sociales y del comportamiento incluyen las humanidades, la religión y la teología.
Central African Republic:
E--> For 1991/92, data refer to universities only.
FR-> Pour 1991/92, les données se réfèrent aux universités seulement.
ESP> Para 1991/92, los datos se refieren a las universidades solamente.
Chad:
FR-> Data refer to universities only.
FR-> Les données se réfèrent aux universités seulement.
ESP> Los datos se refieren a las universidades solamente.
Egypt:
E--> Data refer to universities and equivalent degree-granting institutions only but exclude Al Azhar University.

FR-> Les données se réfèrent aux universités et établissements conférant des grades équivalents seulement, mais ne comprennent pas l'Université d' Al Azhar.
ESP> Los datos se refieren a las universidades y establecimientos que otorgan títulos equivalentes solamente pero no comprenden la Universidad Al Azhar.
Ethiopia:
E--> Data for 1991/92 do not include Asmara University and Kotebe college.
FR-> Les données pour 1991/92 ne comprennent pas l'Université d'Asmara et le *Kotebe college*.
ESP> Los datos de 1991/92 excluyen la Universidad de Asmara y el *Kotebe college*.
Gabon:
E--> Level 6 includes level 7.
FR-> Le niveau 6 inclut le niveau 7.
ESP> El nivel 6 incluye el nivel 7.
Ghana:
E--> Data refer to universities only but for 1985/86, they do not include University of Ghana.
FR-> Les données se réfèrent aux universités seulement, mais pour 1985/86, elles n'incluent pas l'Université du Ghana.
ESP> Los datos se refieren a las universidades solamente, pero en 1985/86, ellos no incluyen la Universidad de Ghana.
Guinea:
E--> In 1985/86, education science and teacher training include humanities, religion and theology and social and behavioural science; commercial and business administration includes law.
FR-> En 1985/86, les sciences de l'éducation et la formation d'enseignants incluent les lettres, la religion et la théologie et les sciences sociales et sciences du comportement; la formation au commerce et à l'administration des entreprises inclut le droit.
ESP> En 1985/86, las ciencias de la educación y la formación del personal docente incluyen las humanidades, la religión y la teología y las ciencias sociales y del comportamiento; la enseñanza comercial y de administración de empresas incluye el derecho.
Kenya:
E--> In 1985/86, social and behavioural science include humanities, religion and theology. Data for 1990/91 refer to universities and equivalent degree-granting institutions only.
FR-> En 1985/86, les sciences sociales et sciences du comportement incluent les lettres, la religion et la théologie Les données pour 1990/91 se réfèrent aux universités et établissements conférant des grades équivalents seulement.
ESP> En 1985/86, las ciencias sociales y del comportamiento incluyen las humanidades, la religión y la teología. Los datos de 1990/91 sólo se refieren a las universidades y a los establecimientos que otorgan títulos equivalentes.
Madagascar:
E--> For 1992/93, female students do not include distance learning institutions.
FR-> Pour 1992/93, les données relatives aux étudiants ne comprennent pas l'enseignement à distance.
ESP> Para 1992/93, los datos relativos a las estudiantes no incluyen la enseñanza a distancia.
Mali:
E--> Level 6 includes level 7. In 1985/86, commercial and business administration includes law. In 1990/91, humanities, religion and theology include fine and applied arts and social and behavioural science.
FR-> Le niveau 6 inclut le niveau 7. En 1985/86, la formation au commerce et à l'administration des entreprises inclut le droit. En 1990/91, les lettres, la religion et la théologie incluent les beaux-arts et les arts appliqués, et les sciences sociales et sciences du comportement.

Third level: students by level and field of study **3.11**
Troisième degré: étudiants par niveau et domaine d'études
Tercer grado: estudiantes por nivel y sector de estudios

ESP> El nivel 6 incluye el nivel 7. En 1985/86 la enseñanza comercial y de administración de empresas incluye el derecho. En 1990/91, las humanidades, la religión y la teología incluyen las bellas artes y artes aplicadas, y las ciencias sociales y del comportamiento.

Morocco:

E--> Data for 1985/86 refer to universities only. For 1985/86 and 1994/95, humanities include some students enrolled in social and behavioural science. For 1994/95, data exclude some technical training in other third level institutions.

FR-> Les données pour 1985/86 se réfèrent aux universités seulement. Pour 1985/86 et 1994/95, les lettres incluent un certain nombre d' étudiants inscrits dans les sciences sociales et sciences du comportement. Pour 1994/95 les données n'incluent pas une partie de l'enseignement technique dispensé dans les autres établissements du troisième degré.

ESP> Los datos de 1985/86 se refieren a las universidades solamente. Para 1985/86 y 1994/95, las humanidades incluyen algunos estudiantes inscritos en las ciencias sociales y del comportamiento. Para 1994/95, los datos no incluyen una parte de la enseñanza técnica de los otros establecimientos de tercer grado.

Nigeria:

E--> Data refer to universities only.

FR-> Les données se réfèrent aux universités seulement.

ESP> Los datos se refieren a las universidades solamente.

Senegal:

E--> For 1985/86, data refer to universities only.

FR-> Pour 1985/86, les données se réfèrent aux universités seulement.

ESP> Para 1985/86, los datos se refieren a las universidades solamente.

South Africa:

E--> Data on students are expressed in full-time equivalent.

FR-> Les données relatives aux étudiants sont exprimées en équivalents plein temps.

ESP> Los datos relativos a los estudiantes se presentan en equivalentes de jornada completa.

Sudan:

E--> For 1985/86, data do not include post-graduate students and for 1990/91, they refer to universities and equivalent degree-granting institutions only.

FR-> Pour 1985/86, les données ne comprennent pas les étudiants du niveau universitaire supérieur et pour 1990/91, elles se réfèrent aux universités et établissements conférant des grades équivalents seulement.

ESP> Para 1985/86, los datos excluyen los estudiantes del nivel post-universitario y para 1990/91, ellos se refieren a las universidades y establecimientos que otorgan títulos equivalentes solamente.

Swaziland:

E--> For 1993/94, data do not include medical science and health related students.

FR-> Pour 1993/94, les données n'incluent pas les étudiants des sciences de la santé et de l'hygiène.

ESP> Para 1993/94, los datos no incluyen los estudiantes de las ciencias de sanidad e higiene.

Togo:

E--> For 1985/86, data refer to universities and equivalent degree-granting institutions only.

FR-> Pour 1985/86, les données se réfèrent aux universités et établissements conférant des grades équivalents seulement.

ESP> Para 1985/86, los datos sólo se refieren a las universidades y establecimientos que otorgan títulos equivalentes solamente.

Zambia:

E--> Humanities, religion and theology include social and behavioural science. Data for 1985 refer to universities and equivalent degree-granting institutions only.

FR-> Les lettres, la religion et la théologie comprennent les sciences sociales et sciences du comportement. Les données pour 1985 se réfèrent aux universités et établissements conférant des grades équivalents.

ESP> Las humanidades, religión y teología incluyen las ciencias sociales y del comportamiento. Los datos de 1985 se refieren a las universidades y a los establecimientos que otorgan títulos equivalentes solamente.

Zimbabwe:

E--> Data exclude some part-time students in vocational training centres. Level 6 includes level 7.

FR-> Les données excluent un certain nombre d'étudiants à temps partiel dans les centres de formation technique. Le niveau 6 inclut le niveau 7.

ESP> Los datos excluyen algunos estudiantes de jornada parcial en los centros de formación técnica. El nivel 6 incluye el nivel 7.

AMERICA, NORTH:

Barbados:

E--> For 1994/95 data refer to university only.

FR-> Pour 1994/95 les données se réfèrent à l'université seulement.

ESP> Para 1994/95 los datos se refieren a la universidad solamente.

Canada:

E--> In 1985/86, not including some part-time students in other third level institutions. For the same year female data do not include trade and vocational programmes.

FR-> En 1985/86, non compris un certain nombre d' étudiants à temps partiel dans les autres établissements du troisième degré. Pour la même année les données concernant les étudiantes n'incluent pas les programmes d'enseignement techniques et commerciaux.

ESP> En 1985/86, excluídos algunos estudiantes de jornada parcial en los otros establecimientos de tercer grado. Para el mismo año, los datos relativos a las estudiantes no incluyen los programas de enseñanza técnica y comercial.

Costa Rica:

E--> For 1985, data do not include other third level institutions. In 1992, level 6 includes level 7.

FR-> Pour 1985, les données ne comprennent pas les autres établissements du troisième degré. En 1992, le niveau 6 inclut le niveau 7.

ESP> Para 1985, los datos excluyen los otros establecimientos de tercer grado. En 1992, el nivel 6 incluye el nivel 7.

El Salvador:

E--> Data for 1985 on female students exclude the National University and for 1993, do not include distance learning institutions.

FR-> Les données pour 1985 relatives aux étudiantes excluent l'Université Nationale et pour 1993, elles excluent l'enseignement à distance.

ESP> Los datos de 1985 relativos a las estudiantes excluyen la Universidad Nacional y para 1993, ellos excluyen la enseñanza a distancia.

Jamaica:

E--> For 1985/86, data refer to the University of West Indies only. In 1991/92 social and behavioural science include mass communication and documentation.

FR-> Pour 1985/86, les données se réfèrent à l'Université de West Indies seulement. En 1991/92, les sciences sociales et sciences du comportement incluent l'information et la documentation.

ESP> Para 1985/86, los datos se refieren a la Universidad de West Indies solamente. En 1991/92, las ciencias sociales y del comportamiento incluyen la documentación y comunicación social.

Mexico:

E--> Data refer to universities and equivalent degree-granting institutions only.

FR-> Les données se réfèrent aux universités et établissements conférant des grades équivalents seulement.

ESP> Los datos sólo se refieren a las universidades y a los establecimientos que otorgan títulos equivalentes.

Panama:

E--> For 1994, engineering includes trade, craft and industrial programmes and transport and communications.

FR-> Pour 1994, les sciences de l'ingénieur incluent les métiers de la production industrielle et les transports et télécommunications.

ESP> Para 1994, la ingeniería y tecnología incluyen las artes y oficios industriales y los transportes y comunicaciones.

Trinidad and Tobago:

E--> For 1985/86 data refer to national students. For 1993/94, data refer to universities only; and engineering includes trade, craft and industrial programmes and transport and communications.

FR-> Les données de 1985/86 se réfèrent aux étudiants nationaux. Pour 1993/94, les données se réfèrent aux universités seulement; et les sciences de l'ingénieur incluent les métiers de la production industrielle et les transports et télécommunications.

ESP> Los datos de 1985/86 se refieren a los estudiantes nacionales. Para 1993/94, los datos se refieren a las universidades solamente; y la ingeniería y tecnología incluyen las artes y oficios industriales y los transportes y comunicaciones.

U.S. Virgin Islands:

E--> Data for 1985/86 refer to full-time students only.

FR-> Les données pour 1985/86 se réfèrent aux étudiants à plein temps seulement.

ESP> Los datos de 1985/86 se refieren a los estudiantes de jornada completa solamente.

AMERICA, SOUTH:

Argentina:

E--> Data refer to universities and equivalent degree-granting institutions only.

FR-> Les données se réfèrent aux universités et établissements conférant des grades équivalents seulement.

ESP> Los datos sólo se refieren a las universidades y establecimientos que otorgan títulos equivalentes.

Bolivia:

E--> Data refer to universities and equivalent degree-granting institutions only.

FR-> Les données se réfèrent aux universités et établissements conférant des grades équivalents seulement.

ESP> Los datos sólo se refieren a las universidades y establecimientos que otorgan títulos equivalentes.

3.11 Third level: students by level and field of study
Troisième degré: étudiants par niveau et domaine d'études
Tercer grado: estudiantes por nivel y sector de estudios

Brazil:
E--> Data do not include post-graduate students.
FR-> les données ne conprennent pas les étudiants du niveau universitaire supérieur.
ESP> Los datos excluyen los estudiantes del nivel post-universitario.

Chile:
E--> For 1995, humanities include some students enrolled in social and behavioural sciences. Architecture and town planning include fine and applied arts. Social and behavioural sciences include mass communication and documentation. Engineering includes trade, craft and industrial programmes.
FR-> Pour 1995, les lettres incluent un certain nombre d'étudiants inscrits dans les sciences sociales et du comportement. L'Architecture et l'urbanisme incluent les beaux-arts et arts appliqués. Les sciences sociales et sciences du comportement incluent l'information et la documentation. Les sciences de l'ingénieur incluent les métiers de la production industrielle.
ESP> Para 1995, las humanidades incluyen algunos estudiantes inscritos en las ciencias sociales y del comportamiento. La arquitectura y urbanismo incluyen las bellas artes y artes aplicadas. Las ciencias sociales y del comportamiento incluyen la documentación y comunicación social. La enginiería y tecnología incluyen artes y oficios industriales.

Colombia:
E--> In 1985, fine arts include home economics.
FR-> En 1985, les beaux-arts incluent l'enseignement ménager.
ESP> En 1985, las bellas artes incluyen la economía doméstica.

Paraguay:
E--> In 1993, data do not include 10 private universities.
FR-> En 1993, les données ne comprennent pas 10 universités privées.
ESP> En 1993, los datos no incluyen 10 universidades privadas.

Peru:
E--> Data for 1991 refer to universities only.
FR-> Les données pour 1991 se réfèrent aux universités seulement.
ESP> Los datos de 1991 se refieren a las universidades solamente.

Uruguay:
E--> Level 6 includes 7.
FR-> Le niveau 6 inclut le niveau 7.
ESP> El nivel 6 incluye el nivel 7.

ASIA:
Afghanistan:
E--> Level 6 includes 7.
FR-> Le niveau 6 inclut le niveau 7.
ESP> El nivel 6 incluye el nivel 7.

Azerbaijan:
E--> Level 6 includes level 7. Engineering includes trade, craft and industrial programmes.
FR-> Le niveau 6 inclut le niveau 7. Les sciences de l'ingénieur comprennent les métiers de la production industrielle.
ESP> El nivel 6 incluye el nivel 7. La ingeniería y tecnología incluyen los artes y oficios industriales

Bangladesh:
E--> In 1985, natural science includes home economics and data on female students do not include distance learning institutions.
FR-> En 1985, les sciences exactes et naturelles incluent l'enseignement ménager et les données relatives aux étudiantes ne comprennent pas l'enseignement à distance.
ESP> En 1985, las ciencias naturales incluyen la economía doméstica y los datos relativos a las estudiantes no incluyen la enseñanza a distancia.

China:
E--> For 1985/86, data refer to universities and equivalent degree-granting institutions only.
FR-> Pour 1985/86, les données se réfèrent aux universités et établissements conférant des grades équivalents seulement.
ESP> Para 1985/86, los datos se refieren a las universidades y establecimientos que otorgan títulos equivalentes solamente.

Cyprus:
E--> Not including Turkish institutions.
FR-> Non compris les institutions turques.
ESP> Excluídas las instituciones turcas.

India:
E--> Humanities, religion and theology include social and behavioural science and in 1990/91 they also include fine and applied arts. For 1990/91, data refer to universities and equivalent degree-granting institutions only.
FR-> Les lettres, la religion et la théologie incluent les sciences sociales et sciences du comportement et en 1990/91 elles incluent également les beaux arts et les arts appliqués. En 1990/91, les données se réfèrent aux universités et établissements conférant des grades équivalents seulement.
ESP> Las humanidades, religión y teología incluyen las ciencias sociales y del comportamiento y en 1990/91 ellas incluyen tambíen

las bellas artes y artes aplicadas. En 1990/91 los datos sólo se refieren a las universidades y establecimientos que otorgan títulos equivalentes.

Indonesia:
E--> Level 6 includes level 7.
FR-> Le niveau 6 inclut le niveau 7.
ESP> El nivel 6 incluye el nivel 7.

Iran, Islamic Republic of:
E--> Data refer to public institutions only. In 1994/95, medical science at level 6 includes part of level 7.
FR-> Les données se réfèrent aux établissements publics seulement. En 1994/95, les sciences médicales au niveau 6 incluent une partie du niveau 7.
ESP> Los datos se refieren a los establecimientos públicos solamente. En 1994/95, las ciencias médicas del nivel 6 incluyen una parte del nivel 7.

Israel:
E--> Data do not include distance learning institutions.
FR-> Les données ne comprennent pas l'enseignement à distance.
ESP> Los datos no incluyen la enseñanza a distancia.

Japan:
E--> Humanities, religion and theology include mass communication and documentation.
FR-> Les lettres, la religion et la théologie comprennent l'information et la documentation.
ESP> Las humanidades, religión y teología comprenden la documentación y comunicación social.

Korea, Republic of:
E--> Data do not include some distance learning institutions.
FR-> Les données excluent quelques institutions d'enseignement à distance.
ESP> Los datos no incluyen algunas instituciones de la enseñanza a distancia.

Lao People's Democratic Republic:
E--> For 1985/86, education science and teacher training includes humanities, religion and theology, social and behavioural science, mathematics and computer science.
FR-> Pour 1985/86, les sciences de l'éducation et la formation d'enseignants incluent les lettres, la religion et la théologie, les sciences sociales et sciences du comportement et les mathématiques et l'informatique.
ESP> Para 1985/86, las ciencias de la educación y formación de personal docente incluyen las humanidades, religión y teología, las ciencias sociales y del comportamiento y las matemáticas e informática.

Malaysia:
E--> In 1990/91, data on female students do not include a part of vocational education.
FR-> Pour 1990/91, les données relatives aux étudiantes ne comprennent pas une partie de l'enseignement technique.
ESP> En 1990/91, los datos relativos a las estudiantes no incluyen una parte de la enseñanza técnica.

Nepal:
E--> Humanities, religion and theology include social and behavioural science. Data for 1985/86 refer to public universities only.
FR-> Les lettres, la religion et la théologie comprennent les sciences sociales et sciences du comportement. Les données de 1985/86 se réfèrent aux universités publiques seulement.
ESP> Las humanidades, religión y teología comprenden las ciencias sociales y del comportamiento. Los datos de 1985/86 se refieren a las universidades públicas solamente.

Philippines:
E--> Data refer to universities only; in 1985/86 humanities include natural science, mathematics and computer science.
FR-> Les données se réfèrent aux universités seulement; en 1985/86 les lettres incluent les sciences exactes et naturelles, les mathématiques et l'informatique.
ESP> Los datos se refieren a las universidades solamente; en 1985/86 las humanidades incluyen las ciencias naturales, y las matemáticas e informática.

Qatar:
E--> In 1985/86, education science and teacher training include home economics.
FR-> En 1985/86, les sciences de l'éducation et la formation d'enseignants incluent l'enseignement ménager.
ESP> En 1985/86, las ciencias de la educación y formación de personal docente incluyen la economía doméstica.

Sri Lanka:
E--> In 1994, not including part of vocational education.
FR-> En 1994, non compris une partie de l'enseignement technique.
ESP> En 1994, no se incluye una parte de la enseñanza técnica.

Syrian Arab Republic:
E--> In 1992/93, not including part of vocational education.
FR-> En 1992/93, non compris une partie de l'enseignement technique.

Third level: students by level and field of study **3.11**
Troisième degré: étudiants par niveau et domaine d'études
Tercer grado: estudiantes por nivel y sector de estudios

ESP> En 1992/93, no se incluye una parte de la enseñanza técnica.

Thailand:
E--> Data do not include other third level institutions.
FR-> Les données ne comprennent pas les autres établissements du troisième degré.
ESP> Los datos no incluyen los otros establecimientos de tercer grado.

United Arab Emirates:
E--> Data for 1992/93 do not include teacher training.
FR-> Les données pour 1992/93 ne comprennent pas la formation d'enseignants.
ESP> Los datos de 1992/93 excluyen la formación del personal docente.

EUROPE:

Albania:
E--> In 1985/86, not including distance learning institutions.
FR-> En 1985/86, non compris l'enseignement à distance.
ESP> En 1985/86, excluída la enseñanza a distancia.

Austria:
E--> Data include multiple counting of students enrolled in more than one field of study.
FR-> Les données incluent les étudiants inscrits dans plusieurs domaines d'études.
ESP> Los datos incluyen los estudiantes inscritos en varios sectores de estudios.

Belarus:
E--> The figures have been provided by the authorities of Belarus, according to their own system of classification. Not including students enrolled in third level programmes in secondary specialized schools.
FR-> Ces chiffres sont fournis par les autorités de Belarus, selon leur propre système de classification. Non compris les étudiants inscrits aux programmes du troisième cycle dans les écoles secondaires spécialisées.
ESP> Estas cifras han sido facilitadas por las autoridades de Belarús, con arreglo a su propio sistema de clasificación. No incluyen los estudiantes matriculados en los programas de tercer ciclo en las escuelas secundarias especializadas.

Croatia:
E--> Not including post-graduate students as registration is not required.
FR-> Non compris les étudiants du niveau universitaire supérieur pour lequel l'inscription n'est pas exigée.
ESP> No incluyen los estudiantes del nivel post-universitario por que la inscripción no esta exigida.

Denmark:
E--> Level 6 includes level 7.
FR-> Le niveau 6 inclut le niveau 7.
ESP> El nivel 6 incluye el nivel 7.

Estonia:
E--> Not including students enrolled in third level programmes in secondary specialized schools.
FR-> Non compris les étudiants inscrits aux programmes du troisième cycle dans les écoles secondaires spécialisées.
ESP> No incluyen los estudiantes matriculados en los programas de tercer ciclo en las escuelas secundarias especializadas.

France:
E--> At level 5: service trades include fine and applied arts, social and behavioural science, mass communication and documentation, home economics, computer science, transport and communications; trade craft and industrial programmes include natural science and mathematics. At levels 6 and 7: commercial and business administration include social and behavioural science, mass communication and documentation, home economics, computer science, transport and communications; natural science includes mathematics, agriculture, forestry and fishing.
FR-> Au niveau 5: la formation pour le secteur tertiaire inclut les beaux-arts et arts appliqués, les sciences sociales et sciences du comportement, l'information et documentation, l'enseignement ménager, l'informatique, les transports et télécommunications; les métiers de la production industrielle incluent les sciences exactes et naturelles et les mathémathiques. Aux niveaux 6 et 7: la formation au commerce et à l'administration des entreprises inclut les sciences sociales et sciences du comportement, l'information et documentation, l'enseignement ménager, l'informatique, les transports et télécommunications; les sciences exactes et naturelles incluent les mathématiques, l'agriculture, sylviculture et halieutique.
ESP> En el nivel 5: La formación para el sector de los servicios comprende bellas artes y artes aplicadas, ciencias sociales y del comportamiento, documentación y comunicación social, economía doméstica, informática, transportes y comunicaciones; los artes y oficios industriales comprenden las ciencias naturales y las matemáticas. A los niveles 6 y 7: la enseñanza comercial y de administración de empresas comprenden las ciencias sociales y del comportamiento, la documentación y comunicación social, la economía doméstica, la informática, transportes y comunicaciones;

las ciencias naturales comprenden las matemáticas, la enseñanza agronómica, dasonómica y pesquera.

Germany:
E--> Not including post-graduate students as registration is not required.
FR-> Non compris les étudiants de niveau universitaire supérieur pour lequel l'inscription n'est pas exigée.
ESP> No incluyen los estudiantes del nivel post-universitario por que la inscripción no esta exigida.

Federal Republic of Germany:
E--> Not including post-graduate students as registration is not required.
FR-> Non compris les étudiants de niveau universitaire supérieur pour lequel l'inscription n'est pas exigée.
ESP> No incluyen los estudiantes del nivel post-universitario por que la inscripción no esta exigida.

Greece:
E--> In 1992/93, data do not include post graduate students.
FR-> En 1992/93, les données ne comprennent pas les étudiants du niveau universitaire supérieur.
ESP> En 1992/93, los datos no incluyen los datos del nivel post-universitario.

Holy See:
E--> Data refer to students enrolled in higher institutions under the authority of the Holy See.
FR-> Les données se réfèrent aux étudiants dans les institutions du troisième degré sous l'autorité du Saint-Siège.
ESP> Los datos se refieren a los estudiantes en instituciones de tercer grado bajo la autoridad de la Santa Sede.

Hungary:
E--> Level 6 includes level 7.
FR-> Le niveau 6 inclut le niveau 7.
ESP> El nivel 6 incluye el nivel 7.

Latvia:
E--> Not including students enrolled in third level programmes in secondary specialized schools.
FR-> Non compris les étudiants inscrits aux programmes du troisième cycle dans les écoles secondaires spécialisées.
ESP> No incluyen los estudiantes matriculados en los programas de tercer ciclo en las escuelas secundarias especializadas.

Moldova:
E--> Data on female students do not include post graduates.
FR-> Les données relatives aux étudiantes ne comprennent pas le niveau universitaire supérieur.
ESP> Los datos relativos a las estudiantes no incluyen el nivel post-universitario.

Netherlands:
E--> Not including distance learning institutions. In 1993/94 level 6 includes level 5.
FR-> Non compris l'enseignement à distance. En 1993/94 le niveau 6 inclut le niveau 5.
ESP> Excluída la enseñanza a distancia. En 1993/94 el nivel 6 incluye el nivel 5.

Portugal:
E--> In 1985/86, not including the University of Porto.
FR-> En 1985/86, non compris l'Université de Porto.
ESP> En 1985/86, excluída la Universidad de Porto.

Romania:
E--> In 1985/86, engineering includes trade, craft and industrial programmes.
FR-> En 1985/86, les sciences de l'ingénieur comprennent les métiers de la production industrielle.
ESP> En 1985/86, la ingeniería y tecnología incluye las artes y oficios industriales.

Russian Federation:
E--> Data on female students do not include post-graduates.
FR-> Les données relatives aux étudiantes ne comprennent pas le niveau universitaire supérieur.
ESP> Los datos relativos a las estudiantes no incluyen el nivel post-universitario.

Slovenia:
E--> Not including post-graduate students as registration is not required.
FR-> Non compris les étudiants du niveau universitaire supérieur pour lequel l'inscription n'est pas exigée.
ESP> No incluyen los estudiantes del nivel post-universitario por que la inscripción no esta exigida.

Sweden:
E--> Level 6 includes level 5.
FR-> Le niveau 6 inclut le niveau 5.
ESP> El nivel 6 incluye el nivel 5.

The Former Yugoslav Republic of Macedonia:
E--> Not including post-graduate students as registration is not required.
FR-> Non compris les étudiants du niveau universitaire supérieur pour lequel l'inscription n'est pas exigée .
ESP> No incluyen los estudiantes del nivel post-universitario por que la inscripción no esta exigida.

3.11 **Third level: students by level and field of study**
Troisième degré: étudiants par niveau et domaine d'études
Tercer grado: estudiantes por nivel y sector de estudios

Ukraine:

E––> The figures have been provided by the authorities of Ukraine, according to their own system of classification. Not including students enrolled in third level programmes in secondary specialized schools.

FR–> Ces chiffres sont fournis par les autorités d'Ukraine, selon leur propre système de classification. Non compris les étudiants inscrits aux programmes du troisième cycle dans les écoles secondaires spécialisées.

ESP> Estas cifras han sido facilitadas por las autoridades de Ucrania con arreglo a su propio sistema de clasificación. No incluyen los estudiantes matriculados en los programas de tercer ciclo en las escuelas secundarias especializadas.

United Kingdom:

E––> In 1985/86, mass communication includes home economics, service trades, architecture and town planning, transport and communications; engineering include trade craft and industrial programmes.

FR–> En 1985/86, l'information inclut l'enseignement ménager, la formation pour le secteur tertiaire, l'architecture et l'urbanisme, les transports et télécommunications; les sciences de l'ingénieur incluent les métiers de la production industrielle.

ESP> En 1985/86, la comunicación social incluye la economía doméstica, la formación para el sector de los servicios, la arquitectura y urbanismo y los transportes y comunicaciones; la ingeniería y tecnología incluye las artes y oficios industriales.

Former Yugoslavia:

E––> Not including post-graduate students as registration is not required.

FR–> Non compris les étudiants du niveau universitaire supérieur pour lequel l'inscription n'est pas exigée.

ESP> No incluyen los estudiantes del nivel post-universitario por que la inscripción no esta exigida.

Federal Republic of Yugoslavia:

E––> Not including post-graduate students as registration is not required.

FR–> Non compris les étudiants du niveau universitaire supérieur pour lequel l'inscription n'est pas exigée.

ESP> No incluyen los estudiantes del nivel post-universitario por que la inscripción no esta exigida.

OCEANIA:
Australia:

E––> In 1985, humanities, religion and theology include fine and applied arts and social and behavioural science. Data for 1993 include Vocational Education and Training Institutes (VETS) and include multiple counting of students enrolled in more than one field of study.

FR–> En 1985, les lettres, la religion et la théologie incluent les beaux arts et les arts appliqués, et les sciences sociales et du comportement. Les données pour 1993 incluent l'Education Technique et les Instituts de Formation Professionnelle (VETS) et incluent les étudiants inscrits dans plusieurs domaines d'études.

ESP> Las humanidades, religión y teología incluyen las bellas artes y artes aplicadas y las ciencias sociales y del comportamiento. Los datos de 1993 incluyen la Educación Técnica y los Institutos de Formación Profesional (VETS) y incluyen los estudiantes inscritos en varios sectores de estudios.

Guam:

E––> University only.

FR–> Université seulement.

ESP> Universidad solamente.

New Zealand:

E––> In 1985, data include multiple counting of students enrolled in more than one field of study.

FR–> En 1985, les données incluent les étudiants inscrits dans plusieurs domaines d'études.

ESP> En 1985, los datos incluyen los estudiantes inscritos en varios sectores de estudios.

Papua New Guinea:

E––> In 1995, other and not specified include humanities, religion and theology, some students of social and behavioural science, and students from medical science and health-related.

FR–> En 1995, les autres programmes incluent les lettres, la religion et la théologie, un certain nombre d'étudiants des sciences sociales et sciences du comportement, et des étudiants des sciences médicales, santé et hygiène.

ESP> En 1995, los otros programas incluyen las humanidades, religión y teología, algunos estudiantes de las ciencias sociales y del comportamiento, y estudiantes de las ciencias médicas, sanidad e higiene.

Third level: graduates by level and field of study 3.12
Troisième degré: diplomés par niveau et domaine d'études
Tercer grado: diplomados por nivel y sector de estudios

3.12 Education at the third level: graduates by ISCED level and field of study

Enseignement du troisième degré: diplomés par niveau et domaine d'études de la CITE

Enseñanza de tercer grado: diplomados por nivel y sector de estudios de la CINE

Education science and teacher training	= Sciences de l'éducation et formation d'enseignants	= Ciencias de la educación y formación de personal docente
Humanities, religion and theology	= Lettres, religion et théologie	= Humanidades, religión y teología
Fine and applied arts	= Beaux-arts et arts appliqués	= Bellas artes y artes aplicadas
Law	= Droit	= Derecho
Social and behavioural science	= Sciences sociales et sciences du comportement	= Ciencias sociales y del comportamiento
Commercial and business administration	= Formation au commerce et à l'administration des entreprises	= Enseñanza comercial y de administración de empresas
Mass communication and documentation	= Information et documentation	= Documentación y comunicación social
Home economics (domestic science	= Enseignement ménager	= Economía doméstica (enseñanza del hogar)
Service trades	= Formation pour le secteur tertiaire	= Formación para el sector de los servicios
Natural science	= Sciences exactes et naturelles	= Ciencias naturales
Mathematics and computer science	= Mathématiques et informatique	= Matemáticas e informática
Medical science and health-related	= Sciences médicales, santé et hygiène	= Ciencias médicas, sanidad higiene
Engineering	= Sciences de l'ingénieur	= Ingeniería y tecnología
Architecture & town planning	= Architecture et urbanisme	= Arquitectura y urbanismo
Trade, craft & industrial programmes	= Métiers de la production industrielle	= Artes y oficios industriales
Transport and communications	= Transports et télécommunications	= Transportes y comunicaciones
Agriculture, forestry and fishery	= Agriculture, sylviculture et halieutique	= Enseñanza agronómica, dasonómica y pesquera
Other and not specified	= Autres programmes et non spécifiés	= Otros programas y sin especificar

Level 5	Programmes leading to an award not equivalent to a first university degree	Niveau 5	Programmes conduisant à un diplôme n'équivalant pas à un premier grade universitaire	Nivel 5	Programas que conducen a un diploma que no equivale a un primer grado universitario
Level 6	Programmes leading to a first university degree or equivalent qualification	Niveau 6	Programmes conduisant à un premier grade universitaire ou à un diplôme équivalent	Nivel 6	Programas que conducen a un primer grado universitario o a un diploma equivalente
Level 7	Programmes leading to a post-graduate university degree or equivalent qualification	Niveau 7	Programmes conduisant à un grade universitaire supérieur ou à un diplôme équivalent	Nivel 7	Programas que conducen a un grado universitario superior o a un diploma equivalente

Please refer to the explanatory text at the end of the table

Prière de se référer au texte explicatif à la fin du tableau

Referirse al texto explicativo al final del cuadro

Unless otherwise specified, data for the field of study in which the symbol ./. appears are included in the figure above.

Sauf précision contraire, les données du domaine d'études où figure le symbole domaine présenté au-dessus.

Salvo indicación contraria, los datos relativos al sector de estudio donde figura el símbolo ./. están incluídos en la cifra del sector precedente

3.12 Third level: graduates by level and field of study
Troisième degré: diplomés par niveau et domaine d'études
Tercer grado: diplomados por nivel y sector de estudios

Country Field of study Pays Domaine d'études País Sectores de estudios	Year Année Año	Graduates by ISCED level of programme Diplômés par niveau de programmes de la CITE Diplomados por nivel de programas de la CINE							
		All levels Tous niveaux Todos los niveles		Level 5 Niveau 5 Nivel 5		Level 6 Niveau 6 Nivel 6		Level 7 Niveau 7 Nivel 7	
		MF	F	MF	F	MF	F	MF	F
		(1)	(2)	(3)	(4)	(5)	(6)	(7)	(8)
Africa									
Algeria‡									
Total	1981	...	...	-	-	7 428	...	...	...
	1986	...	...	684	-	13 413	...	...	...
	1991	25 281	9 209	2 752	914	22 529	8 295	./.	./.
Total	1993	29 374	12 419	5 589	2 136	23 785	10 283	./.	./.
Education science		2 403	1 073	-	-	2 403	1 073	./.	./.
Humanities & religion		4 046	2 272	-	-	4 046	2 272	./.	./.
Fine & applied arts		15	-	-	-	15	-	./.	./.
Law		2 037	822	-	-	2 037	822	./.	./.
Social & behav. sc.		3 094	1 250	-	-	3 094	1 250	...	./.
Business administr.		1 436	592	982	470	454	122	./.	./.
Communic. & doc.		615	349	105	67	510	282	./.	./.
Home economics		-	-	-	-	-	-	./.	./.
Service trades		-	-	-	-	-	-	./.	./.
Natural science		1 791	1 174	387	292	1 404	882	./.	./.
Maths. & computer sc.		1 572	805	796	412	776	393	./.	./.
Health-related prg.		2 995	1 481	25	11	2 970	1 470	./.	./.
Engineering		6 555	1 604	2 578	651	3 977	953	./.	./.
Archit. & town plng.		883	300	332	103	551	197	./.	./.
Trade, craft & indust.		128	25	60	17	68	8	./.	./.
Transport & communic.		76	11	45	9	31	2	./.	./.
Agriculture		1 558	597	229	75	1 329	522	./.	./.
Other & not specified		170	64	50	29	120	35	./.	./.
Angola									
Total	1991	536	...	...	...	...	...	...	...
Total	1992	383	...	...	...	...	...	...	...
Education science		50	...	...	...	...	...	...	...
Humanities & religion		-	-	...	...	...	...	...	...
Fine & applied arts		-	-	...	...	...	...	...	...
Law		15	...	...	...	...	...	...	...
Social & behav. sc.		-	-	...	...	...	...	...	...
Business administr.		101	...	...	...	...	...	...	...
Communic. & doc.		-	-	...	...	...	...	...	...
Home economics		-	-	...	...	...	...	...	...
Service trades		-	-	...	...	...	...	...	...
Natural science		38	...	...	...	...	...	...	...
Maths. & computer sc.		-	-	...	...	...	...	...	...
Health-related prg.		66	...	...	...	...	...	...	...
Engineering		79	...	...	...	...	...	...	...
Archit. & town plng.		-	-	...	...	...	...	...	...
Trade, craft & indust.		-	-	...	...	...	...	...	...
Transport & communic.		-	-	...	...	...	...	...	...
Agriculture		34	...	...	...	...	...	...	...
Other & not specified		-	-	...	...	...	...	...	...
Benin‡									
Total	1979	834	...	27	...	598	...	209	...
Total	1986	933	...	297	...	636	...	./.	...
Education science		237	...	27	...	210	...	./.	...
Humanities & religion		68	...	-	-	68	...	./.	...
Fine & applied arts		-	-	-	-	-	-	-	-
Law		130	...	-	-	130	...	./.	...
Social & behav. sc.		-	-	-	-	-	...	-	-
Business administr.		95	...	46	...	49	...	./.	...
Communic. & doc.		-	-	-	-	-	-	-	-
Home economics		-	-	-	-	-	-	-	-
Service trades		138	...	77	...	61	...	./.	...
Natural science		32	...	-	-	32	...	./.	...
Maths. & computer sc.		./.	...	-	-	./.	...	./.	...
Health-related prg.		114	...	60	...	54	...	./.	...
Engineering		-	-	-	-	-	-	-	-
Archit. & town plng.		-	-	-	-	-	-	-	-
Trade, craft & indust.		87	...	87	...	-	-	-	-
Transport & communic.		-	-	-	-	-	-	-	-
Agriculture		32	...	-	-	32	...	./.	...
Other & not specified		-	-	-	-	-	-	-	-

Third level: graduates by level and field of study 3.12
Troisième degré: diplomés par niveau et domaine d'études
Tercer grado: diplomados por nivel y sector de estudios

Country Field of study Pays Domaine d'études País Sectores de estudios	Year Année Año	Graduates by ISCED level of programme Diplômés par niveau de programmes de la CITE Diplomados por nivel de programas de la CINE							
		All levels Tous niveaux Todos los niveles		Level 5 Niveau 5 Nivel 5		Level 6 Niveau 6 Nivel 6		Level 7 Niveau 7 Nivel 7	
		MF	F	MF	F	MF	F	MF	F
		(1)	(2)	(3)	(4)	(5)	(6)	(7)	(8)
Botswana									
Total	1982	190	75	45	13	145	62	-	-
	1985	458	...	228	...	182	...	48	...
Total	1991	772	...	318	...	371	...	83	...
Education science		151	...	87	...	62	...	2	...
Humanities & religion		218	...	35	...	102	...	81	...
Fine & applied arts		-	-	-	-	-	-	-	-
Law		57	...	28	...	29	...	-	-
Social & behav. sc.		136	...	34	...	102	...	-	-
Business administr.		188	...	134	...	54	...	-	-
Communic. & doc.		-	-	-	-	-	-	-	-
Home economics		-	-	-	-	-	-	-	-
Service trades		-	-	-	-	-	-	-	-
Natural science		22	...	-	-	22	...	-	-
Maths. & computer sc.		-	-	-	-	-	-	-	-
Health-related prg.		-	-	-	-	-	-	-	-
Engineering		-	-	-	-	-	-	-	-
Archit. & town plng.		-	-	-	-	-	-	-	-
Trade, craft & indust.		-	-	-	-	-	-	-	-
Transport & communic.		-	-	-	-	-	-	-	-
Agriculture		-	-	-	-	-	-	-	-
Other & not specified		-	-	-	-	-	-	-	-
Burkina Faso‡									
Total	1981	564		...	...	...	...	...	...
	1987	1 818	...	850	...	968	...	-	-
Total	1992	3 613	...	...	...	...	...	...	...
Education science		170	...	...	...	...	...	...	...
Humanities & religion		1 467	...	...	...	...	...	...	...
Fine & applied arts		-	-	...	...	...	...	...	...
Law		257	...	...	...	...	...	...	...
Social & behav. sc.		./.	...	...	...	...	...	...	...
Business administr.		857	...	...	...	...	...	...	...
Communic. & doc.		-	-	...	...	...	...	...	...
Home economics		-	-	...	...	...	...	...	...
Service trades		-	-	...	...	...	...	...	...
Natural science		402	...	...	...	...	...	...	...
Maths. & computer sc.		49	...	...	...	...	...	...	...
Health-related prg.		306	...	...	...	...	...	...	...
Engineering		-	-	...	...	...	...	...	...
Archit. & town plng.		-	-	...	...	...	...	...	...
Trade, craft & indust.		-	-	...	...	...	...	...	...
Transport & communic.		-	-	...	...	...	...	...	...
Agriculture		105	...	...	...	...	...	...	...
Other & not specified		-	-	...	...	...	...	...	...
Burundi‡									
Total	1981	300	...	...	...	...	...	./.	...
	1987	671	...	355	...	316	...	./.	...
	1991	1 453	375	...	...	...	...	...	...
Total	1992	1 192	292	-	-	1 192	292	./.	./.
Education science		146	45	-	-	146	45	./.	./.
Humanities & religion		206	58	-	-	206	58	./.	./.
Fine & applied arts		-	-	-	-	-	-	-	-
Law		104	32	-	-	104	32	./.	./.
Social & behav. sc.		./.	./.	-	-	./.	./.	./.	./.
Business administr.		257	73	-	-	257	73	./.	./.
Communic. & doc.		./.	./.	-	-	./.	./.	./.	./.
Home economics		-	-	-	-	-	-	-	-
Service trades		-	-	-	-	-	-	-	-
Natural science		132	24	-	-	132	24	./.	./.
Maths. & computer sc.		30	4	-	-	30	4	./.	./.
Health-related prg.		96	26	-	-	96	26	./.	./.
Engineering		28	1	-	-	28	1	./.	./.
Archit. & town plng.		37	1	-	-	37	1	-	-
Trade, craft & indust.		-	-	-	-	-	-	-	-
Transport & communic.		-	-	-	-	-	-	-	-
Agriculture		129	25	-	-	129	25	./.	./.
Other & not specified		27	3	-	-	27	3	./.	./.

3.12 Third level: graduates by level and field of study
Troisième degré: diplomés par niveau et domaine d'études
Tercer grado: diplomados por nivel y sector de estudios

Country Field of study Pays Domaine d'études País Sectores de estudios	Year Année Año	Graduates by ISCED level of programme Diplômés par niveau de programmes de la CITE Diplomados por nivel de programas de la CINE							
		All levels Tous niveaux Todos los niveles		Level 5 Niveau 5 Nivel 5		Level 6 Niveau 6 Nivel 6		Level 7 Niveau 7 Nivel 7	
		MF	F	MF	F	MF	F	MF	F
		(1)	(2)	(3)	(4)	(5)	(6)	(7)	(8)
Central African Republic									
Total	1982	255	9	30	2	194	7	31	-
	1986	573	66	...	...	...	...	...	...
Total	1989	650	...	342	...	308	...	-	-
Education science		45	...	33	-	12	...	-	-
Humanities & religion		255	...	112	9	143	2	-	-
Fine & applied arts		-	-	-	-	-	7	-	-
Law		128	...	45	...	83	...	-	-
Social & behav. sc.		56	...	32	...	24	...	-	-
Business administr.		17	4	-	-	17	4	-	-
Communic. & doc.		-	-	-	-	-	-	-	-
Home economics		-	-	-	-	-	-	-	-
Service trades		-	-	-	-	-	-	-	-
Natural science		15	1	15	1	-	-	-	-
Maths. & computer sc.		-	-	-	-	-	-	-	-
Health-related prg.		61	35	61	35	-	-	-	-
Engineering		11	1	-	-	11	1	-	-
Archit. & town plng.		-	-	-	-	-	-	-	-
Trade, craft & indust.		-	-	-	-	-	-	-	-
Transport & communic.		-	-	-	-	-	-	-	-
Agriculture		18	1	-	-	18	1	-	-
Other & not specified		44	-	44	-	-	-	-	-
Chad‡									
Total	1985	335	25	335	25	-	-	-	-
Total	1993	537	...	-	-	464	...	73	...
Education science		323	...	-	-	295	...	28	...
Humanities & religion		-	-	-	-	-	-	-	-
Fine & applied arts		-	-	-	-	-	-	-	-
Law		145	...	-	-	111	...	34	...
Social & behav. sc.		-	-	-	-	-	-	-	-
Business administr.		-	-	-	-	-	-	-	-
Communic. & doc.		-	-	-	-	-	-	-	-
Home economics		-	-	-	-	-	-	-	-
Service trades		-	-	-	-	-	-	-	-
Natural science		69	...	-	-	58	...	11	...
Maths. & computer sc.		./.	...	-	-	./.	...	./.	...
Health-related prg.		-	-	-	-	-	-	-	-
Engineering		-	-	-	-	-	-	-	-
Archit. & town plng.		-	-	-	-	-	-	-	-
Trade, craft & indust.		-	-	-	-	-	-	-	-
Transport & communic.		-	-	-	-	-	-	-	-
Agriculture		-	-	-	-	-	-	-	-
Other & not specified		-	-	-	-	-	-	-	-
Congo									
Total	1981	1 291	...	451	...	642	...	198	...
Total	1988	1 095	...	555	...	494	...	46	...
Education science		403	...	403	...	-	-	-	-
Humanities & religion		174	...	71	...	103	...	-	-
Fine & applied arts		-	-	-	-	-	-	-	-
Law		91	...	-	-	91	...	-	-
Social & behav. sc.		69	...	-	-	69	...	-	-
Business administr.		113	...	81	...	32	...	-	-
Communic. & doc.		27	...	-	-	27	...	-	-
Home economics		-	-	-	-	-	-	-	-
Service trades		-	-	-	-	-	-	-	-
Natural science		55	...	-	-	55	...	-	-
Maths. & computer sc.		16	...	-	-	16	...	-	-
Health-related prg.		72	...	-	-	26	...	46	...
Engineering		75	...	-	-	75	...	-	-
Archit. & town plng.		-	-	-	-	-	-	-	-
Trade, craft & indust.		-	-	-	-	-	-	-	-
Transport & communic.		-	-	-	-	-	-	-	-
Agriculture		-	-	-	-	-	-	-	-
Other & not specified		-	-	-	-	-	-	-	-

Third level: graduates by level and field of study 3.12
Troisième degré: diplômés par niveau et domaine d'études
Tercer grado: diplomados por nivel y sector de estudios

Country Field of study Pays Domaine d'études País Sectores de estudios	Year Année Año	Graduates by ISCED level of programme Diplômés par niveau de programmes de la CITE Diplomados por nivel de programas de la CINE							
		All levels Tous niveaux Todos los niveles		Level 5 Niveau 5 Nivel 5		Level 6 Niveau 6 Nivel 6		Level 7 Niveau 7 Nivel 7	
		MF	F	MF	F	MF	F	MF	F
		(1)	(2)	(3)	(4)	(5)	(6)	(7)	(8)
Egypt‡									
Total	1981	80 443	25 892	-	-	74 143	24 356	6 300	1 536
	1986	116 854	41 937	-	-	105 073	38 801	11 781	3 136
	1990	115 191	42 384	-	-	94 300	35 436	20 891	6 948
Total	1993	110 737	42 812	-	-	92 488	36 209	18 249	6 603
Education science		21 150	10 788	-	-	16 064	7 995	5 086	2 793
Humanities & religion		17 309	8 432	-	-	16 484	8 100	825	332
Fine & applied arts		1 422	752	-	-	1 294	704	128	48
Law		13 710	2 967	-	-	12 923	2 863	787	104
Social & behav. sc.		1 609	795	-	-	1 396	730	213	65
Business administr.		22 472	7 746	-	-	20 659	7 351	1 813	395
Communic. & doc.		330	223	-	-	295	210	35	13
Home economics		492	413	-	-	455	384	37	29
Service trades		385	254	-	-	318	221	67	33
Natural science		3 852	1 436	-	-	2 812	1 054	1 040	382
Maths. & computer sc.		1 276	297	-	-	676	142	600	155
Health-related prg.		10 346	4 499	-	-	5 651	2 893	4 695	1 606
Engineering		7 258	1 101	-	-	6 195	933	1 063	168
Archit. & town plng.		./.	./.	-	-	./.	./.	./.	./.
Trade, craft & indust.		./.	./.	-	-	./.	./.	./.	./.
Transport & communic.		./.	./.	-	-	./.	./.	./.	./.
Agriculture		6 778	2 327	-	-	5 237	1 906	1 541	421
Other & not specified		2 348	782	-	-	2 029	723	319	59
Eritrea									
Total	1995	245	53	113	36	132	17		
Education science		-	-	-	-	-	-	-	-
Humanities & religion		-	-	-	-	-	-	-	-
Fine & applied arts		-	-	-	-	-	-	-	-
Law		30	3	30	3	-	-		
Social & behav. sc.		24	3	-	-	24	3		
Business administr.		138	45	83	33	55	12		
Communic. & doc.		-	-	-	-	-	-	-	-
Home economics		-	-	-	-	-	-	-	-
Service trades		-	-	-	-	-	-	-	-
Natural science		27	1	-	-	27	1	-	-
Maths. & computer sc.		6	-	-	-	6	-	-	-
Health-related prg.		-	-	-	-	-	-	-	-
Engineering		-	-	-	-	-	-	-	-
Archit. & town plng.		-	-	-	-	-	-	-	-
Trade, craft & indust.		-	-	-	-	-	-	-	-
Transport & communic.		-	-	-	-	-	-	-	-
Agriculture		20	1	-	-	20	1	-	-
Other & not specified		-	-	-	-	-	-		
Ethiopia‡									
Total	1981	2 762	...	1 986	...	743	...	33	...
	1986	5 615	...	3 548	...	2 017	...	50	...
	1991	6 747	967	4 479	787	2 132	171	136	9
Total	1992	5 194	987	3 269	812	1 791	164	134	11
Education science		1 237	239	1 103	230	117	9	17	-
Humanities & religion		146	32	18	12	114	20	14	-
Fine & applied arts		12	2	-	-	12	2	-	-
Law		95	20	52	14	43	6	-	-
Social & behav. sc.		232	37	-	-	225	36	7	1
Business administr.		1 193	423	880	374	313	49	-	-
Communic. & doc.		59	23	47	19	-	-	12	4
Home economics		14	4	14	4	-	-	-	-
Service trades		-	-	-	-	-	-	-	-
Natural science		267	17	20	8	230	8	17	1
Maths. & computer sc.		167	26	33	13	120	12	14	1
Health-related prg.		355	48	219	39	103	5	33	4
Engineering		449	23	201	15	243	8	5	-
Archit. & town plng.		71	15	56	15	15	-	-	-
Trade, craft & indust.		90	3	90	3	-	-	-	-
Transport & communic.		-	-	-	-	-	-	-	-
Agriculture		807	75	536	66	256	9	15	-
Other & not specified		-	-	-	-	-	-		

3.12 Third level: graduates by level and field of study
Troisième degré: diplomés par niveau et domaine d'études
Tercer grado: diplomados por nivel y sector de estudios

Country Field of study Pays Domaine d'études País Sectores de estudios	Year Année Año	Graduates by ISCED level of programme Diplômés par niveau de programmes de la CITE Diplomados por nivel de programas de la CINE							
		All levels Tous niveaux Todos los niveles		Level 5 Niveau 5 Nivel 5		Level 6 Niveau 6 Nivel 6		Level 7 Niveau 7 Nivel 7	
		MF	F	MF	F	MF	F	MF	F
		(1)	(2)	(3)	(4)	(5)	(6)	(7)	(8)
Gabon‡									
Total	1980	330	...	51	...	221	...	58	...
	1986	712	...	246	...	365	...	101	...
Total	1989	730	...	380	...	350	...	./.	...
Education science		78	...	31	...	47	...	./.	...
Humanities & religion		116	...	52	...	64	...	./.	...
Fine & applied arts		-	-	-	-	-	-	-	-
Law		61	...	41	...	20	...	./.	...
Social & behav. sc.		116	...	22	...	94	...	./.	...
Business administr.		133	...	82	...	51	...	./.	...
Communic. & doc.		8	...	5	...	3	...	./.	...
Home economics		-	-	-	-	-	-	-	-
Service trades		-	-	-	-	-	-	-	-
Natural science		21	...	21	...	-	-	-	-
Maths. & computer sc.		47	...	47	...	-	-	-	-
Health-related prg.		47	...	17	...	30	...	./.	...
Engineering		18	...	-	...	18	...	./.	...
Archit. & town plng.		6	...	-	-	6	...	./.	...
Trade, craft & indust.		4	...	4	...	-	-	-	-
Transport & communic.		51	...	51	...	-	-	-	-
Agriculture		15	...	7	...	8	...	./.	...
Other & not specified		9	...	-	-	9	...	./.	...
Ghana‡									
Total	1980	2 821	393	796	124	1 617	210	408	59
	1985	2 277	...	392	...	1 684	...	201	...
Total	1991	2 739	589	551	154	1 728	358	460	77
Education science		82	26	35	19	42	7	5	-
Humanities & religion		857	199	187	53	527	123	143	23
Fine & applied arts		177	44	50	17	76	21	51	6
Law		40	19	1	-	39	19	-	-
Social & behav. sc.		269	70	53	17	195	49	21	4
Business administr.		247	49	45	8	170	36	32	5
Communic. & doc.		52	21	-	-	-	-	52	21
Home economics		25	19	13	13	12	6	-	-
Service trades		-	-	-	-	-	-	-	-
Natural science		309	47	19	2	239	36	51	9
Maths. & computer sc.		102	24	36	17	45	3	21	4
Health-related prg.		195	43	-	-	175	42	20	1
Engineering		133	11	26	-	61	7	46	4
Archit. & town plng.		-	-	-	-	-	-	-	-
Trade, craft & indust.		-	-	-	-	-	-	-	-
Transport & communic.		-	-	-	-	-	-	-	-
Agriculture		251	17	86	8	147	9	18	-
Other & not specified		-	-	-	-	-	-	-	-
Guinea									
Total	1986	1 806	291	...	...	...	...	...	...
Total	1988	891	157	...	...	...	...	...	...
Education science		86	27	...	...	...	...	...	...
Humanities & religion		126	18	...	...	...	...	...	...
Fine & applied arts		-	-	...	...	...	...	...	...
Law		-	-	...	...	...	...	...	...
Social & behav. sc.		124	17	...	...	...	...	...	...
Business administr.		./.	./.	...	...	...	...	...	...
Communic. & doc.		-	-	...	...	...	...	...	...
Home economics		-	-	...	...	...	...	...	...
Service trades		-	-	...	...	...	...	...	...
Natural science		327	76	...	...	...	...	...	...
Maths. & computer sc.		52	2	...	...	...	...	...	...
Health-related prg.		58	7	...	...	...	...	...	...
Engineering		111	9	...	...	...	...	...	...
Archit. & town plng.		./.	./.	...	...	...	...	...	...
Trade, craft & indust.		./.	./.	...	...	...	...	...	...
Transport & communic.		-	-	...	...	...	...	...	...
Agriculture		7	1	...	...	...	...	...	...
Other & not specified		-	-	...	...	...	...	...	...

Third level: graduates by level and field of study 3.12
Troisième degré: diplômés par niveau et domaine d'études
Tercer grado: diplomados por nivel y sector de estudios

Country Field of study Pays Domaine d'études País Sectores de estudios	Year Année Año	Graduates by ISCED level of programme Diplômés par niveau de programmes de la CITE Diplomados por nivel de programas de la CINE							
		All levels Tous niveaux Todos los niveles		Level 5 Niveau 5 Nivel 5		Level 6 Niveau 6 Nivel 6		Level 7 Niveau 7 Nivel 7	
		MF	F	MF	F	MF	F	MF	F
		(1)	(2)	(3)	(4)	(5)	(6)	(7)	(8)
Kenya‡									
Total	1987	2 859	...	37	...	2 338	...	484	...
Total	1991	10 701	2 902	...	...	...	...	...	...
Education science		3 661	1 451	...	...	...	...	...	...
Humanities & religion		1 993	422	...	...	...	...	...	...
Fine & applied arts		5	2	...	...	...	...	...	...
Law		135	66	...	...	...	...	...	...
Social & behav. sc.		647	159	...	...	...	...	...	...
Business administr.		751	143	...	...	...	...	...	...
Communic. & doc.		-	-	...	...	...	...	...	...
Home economics		269	171	...	...	...	...	...	...
Service trades		-	-	...	...	...	...	...	...
Natural science		1 099	151	...	...	...	...	...	...
Maths. & computer sc.		-	-	...	...	...	...	...	...
Health-related prg.		619	135	...	...	...	...	...	...
Engineering		349	19	...	...	...	...	...	...
Archit. & town plng.		310	41	...	...	...	...	...	...
Trade, craft & indust.		112	15	...	...	...	...	...	...
Transport & communic.		-	-	...	...	...	...	...	...
Agriculture		751	127	...	...	...	...	...	...
Other & not specified		-	-	...	...	...	...	...	...
Lesotho									
Total	1983	617	...	348	...	266	...	3	...
	1987	884	...	659	...	202	...	23	...
	1991	1 069	...	846	...	206	...	17	...
Total	1993	1 013	...	702	...	280	...	31	...
Education science		369	...	236	...	114	...	19	...
Humanities & religion		7	...	6	...	1	...	-	-
Fine & applied arts		./.	...	./.	...	./.	...	-	-
Law		36	...	-	-	24	...	12	...
Social & behav. sc.		66	...	-	-	66	...	-	-
Business administr.		242	...	214	...	28	...	-	-
Communic. & doc.		-	-	-	-	-	-	-	-
Home economics		-	-	-	-	-	-	-	-
Service trades		123	...	123	...	-	-	-	-
Natural science		39	...	-	-	39	...	-	-
Maths. & computer sc.		7	...	7	...	-	-	-	-
Health-related prg.		-	-	-	-	-	-	-	-
Enginooring		-	-	-	-	-	-	-	-
Archit. & town plng.		24	...	24	...	-	-	-	-
Trade, craft & indust.		75	...	75	...	-	-	-	-
Transport & communic.		-	-	-	-	-	-	-	-
Agriculture		25	...	17	...	8	...	-	-
Other & not specified		-	-	-	-	-	-	-	-
Madagascar									
Total	1986	3 884	...	...	...	...	...	...	...
	1990	4 332	...	1 841	...	2 252	987	239	78
Total	1992	5 619	2 358	2 225	977	3 092	1 269	302	112
Education science		145	53	-	-	145	53	-	-
Humanities & religion		814	515	386	253	415	259	13	3
Fine & applied arts		-	-	-	-	-	-	-	-
Law		610	267	327	153	121	47	162	67
Social & behav. sc.		545	216	279	118	265	98	1	-
Business administr.		1 319	575	633	283	686	292	-	-
Communic. & doc.		-	-	-	-	-	-	-	-
Home economics		-	-	-	-	-	-	-	-
Service trades		-	-	-	-	-	-	-	-
Natural science		1 027	383	375	140	566	207	86	36
Maths. & computer sc.		201	31	85	13	107	17	9	1
Health-related prg.		620	275	-	-	620	275	-	-
Engineering		307	34	140	17	146	14	21	3
Archit. & town plng.		-	-	-	-	-	-	-	-
Trade, craft & indust.		-	-	-	-	-	-	-	-
Transport & communic.		-	-	-	-	-	-	-	-
Agriculture		31	9	-	-	21	7	10	2
Other & not specified		-	-	-	-	-	-	-	-

3.12 Third level: graduates by level and field of study
Troisième degré: diplômés par niveau et domaine d'études
Tercer grado: diplomados por nivel y sector de estudios

Country / Field of study / Pays / Domaine d'études / País / Sectores de estudios	Year / Année / Año	Graduates by ISCED level of programme / Diplômés par niveau de programmes de la CITE / Diplomados por nivel de programas de la CINE							
		All levels / Tous niveaux / Todos los niveles		Level 5 / Niveau 5 / Nivel 5		Level 6 / Niveau 6 / Nivel 6		Level 7 / Niveau 7 / Nivel 7	
		MF	F	MF	F	MF	F	MF	F
		(1)	(2)	(3)	(4)	(5)	(6)	(7)	(8)
Malawi‡									
Total	1981	1 303	332	...	...	...	...	...	
	1986	1 559	...	1 294	...	249	...	16	...
	1990	2 352	...	2 018	...	334	...	./.	...
Total	1994	3 815	1 352	3 083	1 212	715	131	17	9
Education science		2 776	1 111	2 680	1 092	96	19	-	-
Humanities & religion		14	2	-	-	14	2	-	-
Fine & applied arts		./.	./.	-	-	./.	./.	-	-
Law		18	3	-	-	18	3	-	-
Social & behav. sc.		157	29	-	-	143	21	14	8
Business administr.		197	34	13	1	184	33	-	-
Communic. & doc.		-	-	-	-	-	-	-	-
Home economics		-	-	-	-	-	-	-	-
Service trades		42	6	32	6	10	-	-	-
Natural science		75	18	-	-	72	17	3	1
Maths. & computer sc.		./.	./.	-	-	./.	./.	./.	./.
Health-related prg.		147	113	109	92	38	21	-	-
Engineering		189	9	127	7	62	2	-	-
Archit. & town plng.		./.	./.	./.	./.	./.	./.	-	-
Trade, craft & indust.		-	-	-	-	-	-	-	-
Transport & communic.		-	-	-	-	-	-	-	-
Agriculture		200	27	122	14	78	13	-	-
Other & not specified		-	-	-	-	-	-	-	-
Mauritania									
Total	1994	1 353	...	620	166	733	...	-	-
Education science		704	171	620	166	84	5	-	-
Humanities & religion		170	...	-	-	170	...	-	-
Fine & applied arts		-		-	-	-		-	-
Law		157	-	-	-	157	-	-	-
Social & behav. sc.		196	-	-	-	196	-	-	-
Business administr.		10	1	-	-	10	1	-	-
Communic. & doc.		-	-	-	-	-	-	-	-
Home economics		-	-	-	-	-	-	-	-
Service trades		-	-	-	-	-	-	-	-
Natural science		15	6	-	-	15	6	-	-
Maths. & computer sc.		./.	./.	-	-	./.	./.	-	-
Health-related prg.		-	-	-	-	-	-	-	-
Engineering		66	13	-	-	66	13	-	-
Archit. & town plng.		-	-	-	-	-	-	-	-
Trade, craft & indust.		35	-	-	-	35	-	-	-
Transport & communic.		-	-	-	-	-	-	-	-
Agriculture		-	-	-	-	-	-	-	-
Other & not specified		-	-	-	-	-	-	-	-
Mauritius									
Total	1981	237	72	209	68	26	4	2	-
	1985	307	107	294	106	-	-	13	1
	1991	598	190	513	162	81	28	4	-
Total	1992	1 729	691	1 367	525	345	157	17	9
Education science		815	307	613	214	200	93	2	-
Humanities & religion		77	45	77	45	-	-	-	-
Fine & applied arts		311	156	289	140	8	7	14	9
Law		22	13	-	-	22	13	-	-
Social & behav. sc.		54	19	25	5	29	14	-	-
Business administr.		175	79	144	62	31	17	-	-
Communic. & doc.		13	5	13	5	-	-	-	-
Home economics		-	-	-	-	-	-	-	-
Service trades		-	-	-	-	-	-	-	-
Natural science		14	7	-	-	14	7	-	-
Maths. & computer sc.		58	19	58	19	-	-	-	-
Health-related prg.		44	12	44	12	-	-	-	-
Engineering		68	3	34	-	33	3	1	-
Archit. & town plng.		-	-	-	-	-	-	-	-
Trade, craft & indust.		24	5	24	5	-	-	-	-
Transport & communic.		-	-	-	-	-	-	-	-
Agriculture		54	21	46	18	8	3	-	-
Other & not specified		-	-	-	-	-	-	-	-

Third level: graduates by level and field of study 3.12
Troisième degré: diplômés par niveau et domaine d'études
Tercer grado: diplomados por nivel y sector de estudios

Country Field of study Pays Domaine d'études País Sectores de estudios	Year Année Año	Graduates by ISCED level of programme Diplômés par niveau de programmes de la CITE Diplomados por nivel de programas de la CINE							
		All levels Tous niveaux Todos los niveles		Level 5 Niveau 5 Nivel 5		Level 6 Niveau 6 Nivel 6		Level 7 Niveau 7 Nivel 7	
		MF	F	MF	F	MF	F	MF	F
		(1)	(2)	(3)	(4)	(5)	(6)	(7)	(8)
Morocco‡									
Total	1981	6 096	...	...	...	...	...	...	...
	1986	9 429	3 078	40	28	9 389	3 050	-	-
	1991	23 543	7 914	807	228	21 686	7 548	1 050	138
Total	1995	26 859	...	3 191	...	23 007	9 084	661	138
Education science		60	...	-	-	50	34	10	3
Humanities & religion		8 946	...	77	...	8 689	4 170	180	37
Fine & applied arts		-	-	-	-	-	-	-	-
Law		4 172	...	129	...	3 994	1 506	49	9
Social & behav. sc.		2 743	...	49	...	2 647	1 015	47	6
Business administr.		318	...	318	...	-	-	-	-
Communic. & doc.		154	...	154	...	-	-	-	-
Home economics		-	-	-	-	-	-	-	-
Service trades		260	...	260	-	-	-	-	-
Natural science		6 947	...	-	-	6 584	2 011	363	81
Maths. & computer sc.		./.	...	-	-	./.	./.	./.	./.
Health-related prg.		762	...	-	-	762	302	-	-
Engineering		533	...	240	...	281	46	12	2
Archit. & town plng.		73	...	73	...	-	-	-	-
Trade, craft & indust.		679	...	679	...	-	-	-	-
Transport & communic.		-	-	-	-	-	-	-	-
Agriculture		613	...	613	...	-	-	-	-
Other & not specified		599	...	599	-	-	-	-	-
Mozambique									
Total	1981	115	41	-	-	115	41	-	-
	1985	165	...	-	-	165	...	-	-
Total	1994	249	81	39	11	210	70	-	-
Education science		19	4	7	-	12	4	-	-
Humanities & religion		24	15	5	2	19	13	-	-
Fine & applied arts		-	-	-	-	-	-	-	-
Law		4	-	-	-	4	-	-	-
Social & behav. sc.		23	10	8	4	15	6	-	-
Business administr.		8	3	-	-	8	3	-	-
Communic. & doc.		-	-	-	-	-	-	-	-
Home economics		-	-	-	-	-	-	-	-
Service trades		-	-	-	-	-	-	-	-
Natural science		44	13	19	5	25	8	-	-
Maths. & computer sc.		./.	./.	-	-	./.	./.	-	-
Health-related prg.		34	22	-	-	34	22	-	-
Engineering		39	2	-	-	39	2	-	-
Archit. & town plng.		22	4	-	-	22	4	-	-
Trade, craft & indust.		-	-	-	-	-	-	-	-
Transport & communic.		-	-	-	-	-	-	-	-
Agriculture		11	-	-	-	11	-	-	-
Other & not specified		21	8	-	-	21	8	-	-
Namibia									
Total	1991	1 063	...	719	...	236	176	108	69
Education science		709	...	569	...	85	68	55	27
Humanities & religion		41	14	-	-	30	10	11	4
Fine & applied arts		./.	./.	-	-	./.	./.	./.	./.
Law		-	-	-	-	-	-	-	-
Social & behav. sc.		14	12	-	-	5	5	9	7
Business administr.		129	29	114	26	15	3	-	-
Communic. & doc.		-	-	-	-	-	-	-	-
Home economics		-	-	-	-	-	-	-	-
Service trades		-	-	-	-	-	-	-	-
Natural science		9	5	-	-	9	5	-	-
Maths. & computer sc.		-	-	-	-	-	-	-	-
Health-related prg.		125	116	-	-	92	85	33	31
Engineering		-	-	-	-	-	-	-	-
Archit. & town plng.		-	-	-	-	-	-	-	-
Trade, craft & indust.		-	-	-	-	-	-	-	-
Transport & communic.		-	-	-	-	-	-	-	-
Agriculture		8	2	8	2	-	-	-	-
Other & not specified		28	3	28	3	-	-	-	-

3.12 Third level: graduates by level and field of study
Troisième degré: diplomés par niveau et domaine d'études
Tercer grado: diplomados por nivel y sector de estudios

Country Field of study Pays Domaine d'études País Sectores de estudios	Year Année Año	Graduates by ISCED level of programme Diplômés par niveau de programmes de la CITE Diplomados por nivel de programas de la CINE							
		All levels Tous niveaux Todos los niveles		Level 5 Niveau 5 Nivel 5		Level 6 Niveau 6 Nivel 6		Level 7 Niveau 7 Nivel 7	
		MF	F	MF	F	MF	F	MF	F
		(1)	(2)	(3)	(4)	(5)	(6)	(7)	(8)
Nigeria‡									
Total	1982	17 215	...	-	-	15 951	...	1 264	...
Total	1990	31 322	...	...	...	...	...	...	...
Education science		7 229	...	...	...	...	...	...	...
Humanities & religion		3 803	...	...	...	...	...	...	...
Fine & applied arts		./.	...	...	...	...	...	...	...
Law		1 999	...	...	...	...	...	...	...
Social & behav. sc.		4 271	...	...	...	...	...	...	...
Business administr.		1 988	...	...	...	...	...	...	...
Communic. & doc.		-	-	...	...	...	...	...	...
Home economics		-	-	...	...	...	...	...	...
Service trades		-	-	...	...	...	...	...	...
Natural science		3 311	...	...	...	...	...	...	...
Maths. & computer sc.		./.	...	...	...	...	...	...	...
Health-related prg.		1 703	...	...	...	...	...	...	...
Engineering		1 939	...	...	...	...	...	...	...
Archit. & town plng.		768	...	...	...	...	...	...	...
Trade, craft & indust.		-	-	...	...	...	...	...	...
Transport & communic.		-	-	...	...	...	...	...	...
Agriculture		1 518	...	...	...	...	...	...	...
Other & not specified		2 793	...	...	...	...	...	...	...
Rwanda‡									
Total	1982	324	28	189	18	135	10	-	-
	1986	451	65	240	47	211	18	-	-
Total	1990	724	137	568	106	156	31	-	-
Education science		61	17	32	10	29	7	-	-
Humanities & religion		166	14	125	8	41	6	-	-
Fine & applied arts		-	-	-	-	-	-	-	-
Law		63	15	31	6	32	9	-	-
Social & behav. sc.		73	23	60	21	13	2	-	-
Business administr.		98	27	87	26	11	1	-	-
Communic. & doc.		-	-	-	-	-	-	-	-
Home economics		46	14	46	14	-	-	-	-
Service trades		-	-	-	-	-	-	-	-
Natural science		74	13	62	8	12	5	-	-
Maths. & computer sc.		44	6	44	6	-	-	-	-
Health-related prg.		39	6	27	5	12	1	-	-
Engineering		25	-	25	-	-	-	-	-
Archit. & town plng.		-	-	-	-	-	-	-	-
Trade, craft & indust.		-	-	-	-	-	-	-	-
Transport & communic.		-	-	-	-	-	-	-	-
Agriculture		35	2	29	2	6	-	-	-
Other & not specified		-	-	-	-	-	-	-	-
Senegal‡									
Total	1986	4 054	...	...	...	...	...	...	...
Total	1989	4 917	...	3 464	...	1 453	...	-	-
Education science		271	...	271	...	-	-	-	-
Humanities & religion		1 698	...	1 227	...	471	...	-	-
Fine & applied arts		-	-	-	-	-	-	-	-
Law		1 389	...	935	...	454	...	-	-
Social & behav. sc.		-	-	-	-	-	-	-	-
Business administr.		-	-	-	-	-	-	-	-
Communic. & doc.		101	...	66	...	35	...	-	-
Home economics		-	-	-	-	-	-	-	-
Service trades		263	...	220	...	43	...	-	-
Natural science		906	...	684	...	222	...	-	-
Maths. & computer sc.		./.	...	./.	...	./.	...	-	-
Health-related prg.		181	...	-	-	181	...	-	-
Engineering		-	-	-	-	-	-	-	-
Archit. & town plng.		-	-	-	-	-	-	-	-
Trade, craft & indust.		-	-	-	-	-	-	-	-
Transport & communic.		-	-	-	-	-	-	-	-
Agriculture		47	...	-	-	47	...	-	-
Other & not specified		61	...	61	...	-	-	-	-

Third level: graduates by level and field of study **3.12**
Troisième degré: diplômés par niveau et domaine d'études
Tercer grado: diplomados por nivel y sector de estudios

Country Field of study / Pays Domaine d'études / País Sectores de estudios	Year Année Año	Graduates by ISCED level of programme Diplômés par niveau de programmes de la CITE Diplomados por nivel de programas de la CINE							
		All levels Tous niveaux Todos los niveles		Level 5 Niveau 5 Nivel 5		Level 6 Niveau 6 Nivel 6		Level 7 Niveau 7 Nivel 7	
		MF	F	MF	F	MF	F	MF	F
		(1)	(2)	(3)	(4)	(5)	(6)	(7)	(8)
South Africa Total	1990	60 976	30 024	...	...	...	...	...	...
Total	1994	147 391	79 358	92 287	50 655	32 597	17 562	22 507	11 141
Education science		63 542	38 221	52 727	33 010	3 617	1 792	7 198	3 419
Humanities & religion		8 963	5 568	3 226	1 731	3 975	2 784	1 762	1 053
Fine & applied arts		1 908	1 243	1 247	744	496	375	165	124
Law		4 391	1 939	293	172	2 435	1 099	1 663	668
Social & behav. sc.		11 115	6 530	1 763	891	6 494	3 809	2 858	1 830
Business administr.		25 206	11 708	14 796	6 880	5 948	2 777	4 462	2 051
Communic. & doc.		4 026	2 241	3 156	1 453	519	417	351	371
Home economics		1 093	902	884	709	178	164	31	29
Service trades		-	-					-	-
Natural science		4 421	2 054	1 567	770	1 556	723	1 298	561
Maths. & computer sc.		6 046	2 724	4 394	2 138	1 065	386	587	200
Health-related prg.		5 729	3 814	1 722	1 178	3 074	2 034	933	602
Engineering		6 502	494	4 488	334	1 489	126	525	34
Archit. & town plng.		1 417	316	728	130	495	138	194	48
Trade, craft & indust.		437	223	437	223	-	-	-	-
Transport & communic.		-	-	-	-	-	-	-	-
Agriculture		1 105	218	506	95	316	68	283	55
Other & not specified		1 490	1 163	353	197	940	870	197	96
Sudan‡ Total	1982	4 667	...	919	...	3 748	...	./.	./.
	1986	6 413	2 291	1 043	271	5 370	2 020	./.	./.
Total	1991	7 588	3 208	...	...	...	...	...	...
Education science		387	150	...	...	...	...	...	...
Humanities & religion		1 310	468	...	...	...	...	...	...
Fine & applied arts		84	24	...	...	...	...	...	...
Law		875	356	...	...	...	...	...	...
Social & behav. sc.		821	263	...	...	...	...	...	...
Business administr.		1 273	666	...	...	...	...	...	...
Communic. & doc.		-	-	-	-	-	-	-	-
Home economics		15	1	...	...	...	...	...	...
Service trades		-	-	-	-	-	-	-	-
Natural science		210	91	...	...	...	...	...	...
Maths. & computer sc.		38	7	...	...	...	...	...	...
Health-related prg.		872	303	...	...	...	...	...	...
Engineering		176	15	...	...	...	...	...	...
Archit. & town plng.		13	4	...	...	...	...	...	...
Trade, craft & indust.		-	-	-	-	-	-	-	-
Transport & communic.		-	-	-	-	-	-	-	-
Agriculture		695	199	...	...	...	...	...	...
Other & not specified		819	661	...	...	...	...	...	...
Swaziland‡ Total	1981	801	349	...	...	...	...	...	...
	1991	874	447	610	305	251	139	13	3
Total	1995	988	361	594	174	339	163	55	24
Education science		188	97	106	59	49	20	33	18
Humanities & religion		54	39	5	5	49	34	-	-
Fine & applied arts		-	-	-	-	-	-	-	-
Law		74	20	12	1	40	13	22	6
Social & behav. sc.		51	32	-	-	51	32	-	-
Business administr.		226	104	157	76	69	28	-	-
Communic. & doc.		-	-	-	-	-	-	-	-
Home economics		30	30	13	13	17	17	-	-
Service trades		5	-	5	-	-	-	-	-
Natural science		57	18	-	-	57	18	-	-
Maths. & computer sc.		./.	./.	-	-	./.	./.	-	-
Health-related prg.		-	-	-	-	-	-	-	-
Engineering		214	2	214	2	-	-	-	-
Archit. & town plng.		-	-	-	-	-	-	-	-
Trade, craft & indust.		17	-	17	-	-	-	-	-
Transport & communic.		-	-	-	-	-	-	-	-
Agriculture		57	17	50	16	7	1	-	-
Other & not specified		15	2	15	2	-	-	-	-

3.12 Third level: graduates by level and field of study
Troisième degré: diplômés par niveau et domaine d'études
Tercer grado: diplomados por nivel y sector de estudios

Country / Field of study / Pays / Domaine d'études / País / Sectores de estudios	Year / Année / Año	Graduates by ISCED level of programme / Diplômés par niveau de programmes de la CITE / Diplomados por nivel de programas de la CINE							
		All levels / Tous niveaux / Todos los niveles		Level 5 / Niveau 5 / Nivel 5		Level 6 / Niveau 6 / Nivel 6		Level 7 / Niveau 7 / Nivel 7	
		MF	F	MF	F	MF	F	MF	F
		(1)	(2)	(3)	(4)	(5)	(6)	(7)	(8)
Togo									
Total	1980	576	102	-	-	576	102	-	-
Total	1989	1 227	...	695	...	532	...	-	-
Education science		10	...	10	...	-	...	-	-
Humanities & religion		333	...	173	...	160	...	-	-
Fine & applied arts		./.	...	./.	...	./.	...	-	-
Law		156	...	69	...	87	...	-	-
Social & behav. sc.		389	...	209	...	180	...	-	-
Business administr.		45	...	45	...	-	...	-	-
Communic. & doc.		-	-	-	-	-	-	-	-
Home economics		-	-	-	-	-	-	-	-
Service trades		-	-	-	-	-	-	-	-
Natural science		66	...	44	...	22	...	-	-
Maths. & computer sc.		23	...	9	...	14	...	-	-
Health-related prg.		81	...	59	...	22	...	-	-
Engineering		46	...	29	...	17	...	-	-
Archit. & town plng.		-	-	-	-	-	-	-	-
Trade, craft & indust.		-	-	-	-	-	-	-	-
Transport & communic.		-	-	-	-	-	-	-	-
Agriculture		30	...	-	-	30	...	-	-
Other & not specified		48	...	48	...	-	-	-	-
Tunisia									
Total	1981	4 774	1 173	...	...	...	...	...	...
	1986	5 045	1 718	1 629	673	3 111	983	305	62
	1991	6 915	2 745	2 267	1 096	3 602	1 269	1 046	380
Total	1995	11 654	4 984	3 388	1 632	7 169	2 954	1 097	398
Education science		1 231	639	1 231	639	-	-	-	-
Humanities & religion		2 112	983	-	-	2 112	983	-	-
Fine & applied arts		71	52	-	-	71	52	-	-
Law		1 036	463	-	-	1 036	463	-	-
Social & behav. sc.		424	162	-	-	424	162	-	-
Business administr.		2 182	911	890	359	1 292	552	-	-
Communic. & doc.		221	138	92	65	129	73	-	-
Home economics		-	-	-	-	-	-	-	-
Service trades		-	-	-	-	-	-	-	-
Natural science		958	340	-	-	958	340	-	-
Maths. & computer sc.		130	25	-	-	89	20	41	5
Health-related prg.		1 283	690	435	330	-	-	848	360
Engineering		1 227	269	483	86	593	169	151	14
Archit. & town plng.		36	15	-	-	-	-	36	15
Trade, craft & indust.		-	-	-	-	-	-	-	-
Transport & communic.		155	62	64	26	70	32	21	-
Agriculture		177	47	-	-	177	47	-	4
Other & not specified		411	188	193	127	218	61	-	-
Uganda									
Total	1981	1 447	...	...	...	...	...	...	...
	1986	2 428	524	1 127	267	1 290	256	11	1
	1991	4 239	1 124	2 215	697	1 717	358	307	69
Total	1994	7 075	1 658	4 394	924	2 228	621	453	113
Education science		3 632	818	2 796	576	545	177	291	65
Humanities & religion		400	117	-	-	389	114	11	3
Fine & applied arts		72	21	39	12	31	8	2	1
Law		58	25	-	-	58	25	-	-
Social & behav. sc.		360	103	-	-	322	88	38	15
Business administr.		1 132	283	1 018	254	114	29	-	-
Communic. & doc.		52	30	-	-	52	30	-	-
Home economics		-	-	-	-	-	-	-	-
Service trades		152	57	152	57	-	-	-	-
Natural science		280	53	-	-	257	47	23	6
Maths. & computer sc.		99	24	-	-	63	15	36	9
Health-related prg.		134	42	-	-	110	34	24	8
Engineering		409	24	332	20	77	4	-	-
Archit. & town plng.		-	-	-	-	-	-	-	-
Trade, craft & indust.		57	5	57	5	-	-	-	-
Transport & communic.		-	-	-	-	-	-	-	-
Agriculture		189	35	-	-	161	29	28	6
Other & not specified		49	21	-	-	49	21	-	-

Third level: graduates by level and field of study **3.12**
Troisième degré: diplômés par niveau et domaine d'études
Tercer grado: diplomados por nivel y sector de estudios

Country Field of study / Pays Domaine d'études / País Sectores de estudios	Year Année Año	Graduates by ISCED level of programme Diplômés par niveau de programmes de la CITE Diplomados por nivel de programas de la CINE							
		All levels Tous niveaux Todos los niveles		Level 5 Niveau 5 Nivel 5		Level 6 Niveau 6 Nivel 6		Level 7 Niveau 7 Nivel 7	
		MF	F	MF	F	MF	F	MF	F
		(1)	(2)	(3)	(4)	(5)	(6)	(7)	(8)
Zambia									
Total	1981	2 088	...	1 294	...	742	...	52	...
	1984	2 186	...	1 475	...	696	...	15	...
Total	1989	4 374	...	3 595	...	748	142	31	4
Education science		2 467	...	2 294	...	171	...	2	-
Humanities & religion		2	-	-	-	-	-	2	-
Fine & applied arts		179	...	75	...	96	...	8	-
Law		60	...	2	...	45	...	13	3
Social & behav. sc.		-	-	-	-	-	-	-	-
Business administr.		558	...	431	...	121	...	6	1
Communic. & doc.		-	-	-	-	-	-	-	-
Home economics		-	-	-	-	-	-	-	-
Service trades		-	-	-	-	-	-	-	-
Natural science		62	...	-	-	62	...	-	-
Maths. & computer sc.		./.	...	60	...	./.	...	-	-
Health-related prg.		167	...	60	...	107	...	-	-
Engineering		204	...	111	...	93	...	-	-
Archit. & town plng.		-	-	-	-	-	-	-	-
Trade, craft & indust.		462	...	462	...	-	-	-	-
Transport & communic.		-	-	-	-	-	-	-	-
Agriculture		53	...	-	-	53	...	-	-
Other & not specified		160	...	160	...	-	-	-	-
Zimbabwe‡									
Total	1981	454	129	93	40	315	77	46	12
	1986	3 134	...	2 097	...	864	...	173	...
Total	1990	14 087	...	12 027	...	1 880	...	180	...
Education science		6 899	...	6 735	...	164	...	-	-
Humanities & religion		331	...	-	-	331	...	-	-
Fine & applied arts		18	...	18	...	-	-	-	-
Law		143	...	-	-	143	...	-	-
Social & behav. sc.		405	...	-	-	405	...	-	-
Business administr.		2 324	...	2 019	...	305	...	-	-
Communic. & doc.		65	...	65	...	-	-	-	-
Home economics		-	-	-	-	-	-	-	-
Service trades		64	...	64	...	-	-	-	-
Natural science		278	...	57	...	221	...	-	-
Maths. & computer sc.		100	...	100	...	-	-	-	-
Health-related prg.		110	...	-	-	110	...	-	-
Engineering		1 257	...	1 162	...	95	...	-	-
Archit. & town plng.		-	-	-	-	-	-	-	-
Trade, craft & indust.		1 807	...	1 807	...	-	-	-	-
Transport & communic.		-	-	-	-	-	-	-	-
Agriculture		106	...	-	-	106	...	-	-
Other & not specified		180	...	-	-	-	-	180	...
America, North									
Canada‡									
Total	1981	159 149	81 740	45 776	26 975	97 582	49 118	15 791	5 647
	1986	198 481	105 266	59 768	32 842	118 905	64 051	19 808	8 373
	1991	210 066	118 329	57 739	34 115	130 164	74 007	22 163	10 207
Total	1994	671 322	333 853	497 717	235 480	147 001	85 764	26 604	12 609
Education science		30 482	22 950	3 852	3 488	22 359	16 457	4 271	3 005
Humanities & religion		35 130	21 023	15 331	8 673	17 131	10 950	2 668	1 400
Fine & applied arts		10 691	6 625	5 565	3 185	4 615	3 138	511	302
Law		4 271	2 216	-	-	3 882	2 001	389	215
Social & behav. sc.		37 944	23 018	9 035	5 865	26 067	15 741	2 842	1 412
Business administr.		59 051	35 894	30 330	21 975	23 649	12 083	5 072	1 836
Communic. & doc.		5 443	3 308	2 111	1 119	2 612	1 682	720	507
Home economics		1 302	1 156	-	-	1 159	1 049	143	107
Service trades		6 367	2 529	6 367	2 529	-	-	-	-
Natural science		9 768	4 375	-	-	7 820	3 763	1 948	612
Maths. & computer sc.		10 172	3 226	3 990	1 363	5 341	1 657	841	206
Health-related prg.		29 743	22 700	17 911	14 280	9 481	6 998	2 351	1 422
Engineering		19 531	2 476	8 464	830	8 482	1 286	2 585	360
Archit. & town plng.		2 393	598	1 665	336	615	225	113	37
Trade, craft & indust.		71 351	4 138	71 351	4 138	-	-	-	-
Transport & communic.		2 980	184	2 980	184	-	-	-	-
Agriculture		9 485	2 521	7 912	1 775	1 099	557	474	189
Other & not specified		325 218	174 916	310 853	165 740	12 689	8 177	1 676	999

3.12 Third level: graduates by level and field of study
Troisième degré: diplomés par niveau et domaine d'études
Tercer grado: diplomados por nivel y sector de estudios

Country Field of study Pays Domaine d'études País Sectores de estudios	Year Année Año	Graduates by ISCED level of programme Diplômés par niveau de programmes de la CITE Diplomados por nivel de programas de la CINE							
		All levels Tous niveaux Todos los niveles		Level 5 Niveau 5 Nivel 5		Level 6 Niveau 6 Nivel 6		Level 7 Niveau 7 Nivel 7	
		MF	F	MF	F	MF	F	MF	F
		(1)	(2)	(3)	(4)	(5)	(6)	(7)	(8)
Costa Rica‡									
Total	1981	4 288	...	628	...	3 509	...	151	...
	1985	4 908	...	711	...	4 012	...	185	...
	1989	6 799	...	2 366	...	4 165	...	268	...
Total	1992	9 813	...	3 266	...	6 210	...	337	...
Education science		1 816	...	894	...	921	...	1	...
Humanities & religion		249	...	5	...	234	...	10	...
Fine & applied arts		147	...	31	...	116	...	-	-
Law		623	...	1	...	578	...	44	...
Social & behav. sc.		550	...	34	...	501	...	15	...
Business administr.		3 124	...	1 618	...	1 375	...	131	...
Communic. & doc.		190	...	19	...	171	...	-	-
Home economics		-	-	-	-	-	-	-	-
Service trades		56	...	56	...	-	-	-	-
Natural science		79	...	9	...	59	...	11	...
Maths. & computer sc.		309	...	159	...	150	...	-	-
Health-related prg.		1 551	...	66	...	1 367	...	118	...
Engineering		600	...	132	...	468	...	-	-
Archit. & town plng.		71	...	9	...	62	...	-	-
Trade, craft & indust.		-	-	-	-	-	-	-	-
Transport & communic.		-	-	-	-	-	-	-	-
Agriculture		242	...	34	...	201	...	7	...
Other & not specified		206	...	199	...	7	...	-	-
Cuba									
Total	1981	25 898	...	-	-	25 898	...	-	-
	1986	23 579	12 263	-	-	23 579	12 263	-	-
	1990	35 144	19 719	-	-	35 144	19 719	-	-
Total	1992	37 591	21 292	-	-	37 591	21 292	-	-
Education science		18 817	12 415	-	-	18 817	12 415	-	-
Humanities & religion		205	135	-	-	205	135	-	-
Fine & applied arts		242	152	-	-	242	152	-	-
Law		550	369	-	-	550	369	-	-
Social & behav. sc.		2 401	1 131	-	-	2 401	1 131	-	-
Business administr.		1 191	780	-	-	1 191	780	-	-
Communic. & doc.		134	97	-	-	134	97	-	-
Home economics		-	-	-	-	-	-	-	-
Service trades		-	-	-	-	-	-	-	-
Natural science		398	245	-	-	398	245	-	-
Maths. & computer sc.		298	162	-	-	298	162	-	-
Health-related prg.		5 468	3 217	-	-	5 468	3 217	-	-
Engineering		3 589	1 106	-	-	3 589	1 106	-	-
Archit. & town plng.		805	332	-	-	805	332	-	-
Trade, craft & indust.		27	16	-	-	27	16	-	-
Transport & communic.		183	50	-	-	183	50	-	-
Agriculture		1 623	626	-	-	1 623	626	-	-
Other & not specified		1 660	459	-	-	1 660	459	-	-
Dominica									
Total	1981	3	1	3	1	-	-	-	-
	1992	205	...	205	...	-	-	-	-
Total	1993	197	75	197	75	-	-	-	-
Education science		-	-	-	-	-	-	-	-
Humanities & religion		24	17	24	17	-	-	-	-
Fine & applied arts		-	-	-	-	-	-	-	-
Law		-	-	-	-	-	-	-	-
Social & behav. sc.		28	19	28	19	-	-	-	-
Business administr.		13	13	13	13	-	-	-	-
Communic. & doc.		./.	./.	./.	./.	-	-	-	-
Home economics		-	-	-	-	-	-	-	-
Service trades		-	-	-	-	-	-	-	-
Natural science		51	26	51	26	-	-	-	-
Maths. & computer sc.		./.	./.	./.	./.	-	-	-	-
Health-related prg.		-	-	-	-	-	-	-	-
Engineering		-	-	-	-	-	-	-	-
Archit. & town plng.		-	-	-	-	-	-	-	-
Trade, craft & indust.		81	-	81	-	-	-	-	-
Transport & communic.		-	-	-	-	-	-	-	-
Agriculture		-	-	-	-	-	-	-	-
Other & not specified		-	-	-	-	-	-	-	-

Third level: graduates by level and field of study 3.12
Troisième degré: diplômés par niveau et domaine d'études
Tercer grado: diplomados por nivel y sector de estudios

Country Field of study Pays Domaine d'études País Sectores de estudios	Year Année Año	Graduates by ISCED level of programme Diplômés par niveau de programmes de la CITE Diplomados por nivel de programas de la CINE							
		All levels Tous niveaux Todos los niveles		Level 5 Niveau 5 Nivel 5		Level 6 Niveau 6 Nivel 6		Level 7 Niveau 7 Nivel 7	
		MF	F	MF	F	MF	F	MF	F
		(1)	(2)	(3)	(4)	(5)	(6)	(7)	(8)
El Salvador‡									
Total	1985	3 825	1 940	2 004	1 222	1 821	718	./.	./.
	1990	4 619	2 499	1 106	684	3 490	1 812	23	3
Total	1993	7 306	...	2 100	...	5 206	...	./.	./.
Education science		3 652	...	1 408	...	2 244	...	./.	./.
Humanities & religion		164	...	-	-	164	...	./.	./.
Fine & applied arts		-	-	-	-	-	-		
Law		354	...	-	-	354	...	./.	./.
Social & behav. sc.		424	...	-	-	424	...	./.	./.
Business administr.		879	...	145	...	734	...	./.	./.
Communic. & doc.		100	...	17	...	83	...	...	./.
Home economics		75	...	-	-	75	...	./.	./.
Service trades		19	...	19	...	-	-	-	-
Natural science		21	...	-	-	21	...	./.	./.
Maths. & computer sc.		42	...	7	...	35	...	./.	./.
Health-related prg.		728	...	186	...	542	...	./.	./.
Engineering		629	...	180	...	449	...	./.	./.
Archit. & town plng.		64	...	7	...	57	...	./.	./.
Trade, craft & indust.		61	...	61	...	-	-	-	-
Transport & communic.		-	-	-	-	-	-	-	-
Agriculture		47	...	45	...	2	...	./.	./.
Other & not specified		47	...	25	...	22	...	./.	./.
Honduras									
Total	1980	918	288	-	-	918	288	-	-
	1985	1 430	...	...		1 183	...	...	...
	1989	1 736	...	553	227				
Total	1992	1 649	834	33	26	1 561	789	55	19
Education science		78	62	-	-	76	61	2	1
Humanities & religion		18	1	-	-	18	1	-	-
Fine & applied arts		5	5	5	5	-	-	-	-
Law		102	43	-	-	102	43	-	-
Social & behav. sc.		128	85	-	-	113	77	15	8
Business administr.		329	186	17	15	308	168	4	3
Communic. & doc.		17	10	-	-	17	10	-	-
Home economics		-	-	-	-	-	-	-	-
Service trades		-	-	-	-	-	-	-	-
Natural science		10	5	-	-	10	5	-	-
Maths. & computer sc.		54	8	1	-	53	8	-	-
Health-related prg.		622	369	-	-	588	362	34	7
Engineering		254	44	-	-	254	44	-	-
Archit. & town plng.		5	3	-	-	5	3	-	-
Trade, craft & indust.		-	-	-	-	-	-	-	-
Transport & communic.		-	-	-	-	-	-	-	-
Agriculture		17	7	-	-	17	7	-	-
Other & not specified		10	6	10	6	-	-	-	-
Jamaica									
Total	1981	4 266	...	3 320	...	879	...	67	...
	1987	3 537	...	1 505	...	1 823	...	209	...
Total	1992	1 575	...	355	...	1 104	759	116	...
Education science		192	...	74	...	109	96	9	...
Humanities & religion		338	...	1	...	324	254	13	...
Fine & applied arts		-	-	-	-	-	-	-	-
Law		-	-	-	-	-	-	-	-
Social & behav. sc.		448	...	5	...	416	268	27	...
Business administr.		204	...	204	...	-	-	-	
Communic. & doc.		24	...	24	...	-	-	-	-
Home economics		-	-	-	-	-	-	-	-
Service trades		-	-	-	-	-	-	-	-
Natural science		218	...	-		195	100	23	...
Maths. & computer sc.		./.	...	-		./.	./.	./.	
Health-related prg.		151	...	47	...	60	41	44	...
Engineering		-	-	-	-	-	-	-	-
Archit. & town plng.		-	-	-	-	-	-	-	-
Trade, craft & indust.		-	-	-	-	-	-	-	-
Transport & communic.		-	-	-	-	-	-	-	-
Agriculture		-	-	-	-	-	-	-	-
Other & not specified		-	-	-	-	-	-	-	-

3.12 Third level: graduates by level and field of study
Troisième degré: diplômés par niveau et domaine d'études
Tercer grado: diplomados por nivel y sector de estudios

Country Field of study Pays Domaine d'études País Sectores de estudios	Year Année Año	Graduates by ISCED level of programme Diplômés par niveau de programmes de la CITE Diplomados por nivel de programas de la CINE							
		All levels Tous niveaux Todos los niveles		Level 5 Niveau 5 Nivel 5		Level 6 Niveau 6 Nivel 6		Level 7 Niveau 7 Nivel 7	
		MF	F	MF	F	MF	F	MF	F
		(1)	(2)	(3)	(4)	(5)	(6)	(7)	(8)
Mexico‡									
Total	1981	69 572	...	-	-	69 572	...	-	-
	1986	113 050	...	-	-	106 923	...	6 127	...
	1991	157 353	...	-	-	146 085	...	11 268	...
Total	1994	152 316	...	-	-	140 256	...	12 060	...
Education science		4 830	...	-	-	3 213	...	1 617	...
Humanities & religion		1 849	...	-	-	1 533	...	316	...
Fine & applied arts		2 683	...	-	-	2 601	...	82	...
Law		15 758	...	-	-	15 101	...	657	...
Social & behav. sc.		10 544	...	-	-	9 124	...	1 420	...
Business administr.		43 699	...	-	-	41 129	...	2 570	...
Communic. & doc.		5 434	...	-	-	5 413	...	21	...
Home economics		889	...	-	-	819	...	70	...
Service trades		1 963	...	-	-	1 959	...	4	...
Natural science		9 131	...	-	-	8 463	...	668	...
Maths. & computer sc.		9 966	...	-	-	9 524	...	442	...
Health-related prg.		14 639	...	-	-	11 580	...	3 059	...
Engineering		20 212	...	-	-	19 504	...	708	...
Archit. & town plng.		4 209	...	-	-	4 058	...	151	...
Trade, craft & indust.		-	-	-	-	-	-	-	-
Transport & communic.		420	...	-	-	358	...	62	...
Agriculture		5 838	...	-	-	5 641	...	197	...
Other & not specified		252	...	-	-	236	...	16	...
Nicaragua									
Total	1980	4 173	...	1 026	...	3 113	...	34	...
	1985	1 636	810	635	226	1 001	584	-	-
	1990	1 766	1 029	543	273	1 223	756	-	-
Total	1991	2 291	1 397	497	318	1 768	1 071	26	8
Education science		251	194	-	-	251	194	-	-
Humanities & religion		9	5	-	-	9	5	-	-
Fine & applied arts		23	18	-	-	23	18	-	-
Law		126	52	-	-	126	52	-	-
Social & behav. sc.		51	43	-	-	51	43	-	-
Business administr.		635	431	228	164	407	267	-	-
Communic. & doc.		51	39	-	-	51	39	-	-
Home economics		8	8	-	-	8	8	-	-
Service trades		-	-	-	-	-	-	-	-
Natural science		48	39	-	-	48	39	-	-
Maths. & computer sc.		101	69	62	46	39	23	-	-
Health-related prg.		506	288	72	26	408	254	26	8
Engineering		136	54	24	19	112	35	-	-
Archit. & town plng.		27	12	-	-	27	12	-	-
Trade, craft & indust.		-	-	-	-	-	-	-	-
Transport & communic.		-	-	-	-	-	-	-	-
Agriculture		319	145	111	63	208	82	-	-
Other & not specified		-	-	-	-	-	-	-	-
Panama‡									
Total	1980	2 505	1 394	672	399	1 833	995	-	-
	1985	3 280	1 979	1 117	772	2 160	1 206	3	1
	1989	3 174	...	...	...	...	...	...	...
Total	1990	3 351	...	...	...	...	...	...	...
Education science		589	...	...	...	...	...	...	...
Humanities & religion		377	...	...	...	...	...	...	...
Fine & applied arts		-	-	...	...	...	...	...	...
Law		106	...	...	...	...	...	...	...
Social & behav. sc.		24	...	...	...	...	...	...	...
Business administr.		885	...	...	...	...	...	...	...
Communic. & doc.		59	...	...	...	...	...	...	...
Home economics		-	-	...	...	...	...	...	...
Service trades		-	-	...	...	...	...	...	...
Natural science		285	...	...	...	...	...	...	...
Maths. & computer sc.		126	...	...	...	...	...	...	...
Health-related prg.		474	...	...	...	...	...	...	...
Engineering		293	...	...	...	...	...	...	...
Archit. & town plng.		104	...	...	...	...	...	...	...
Trade, craft & indust.		./.	...	...	...	...	...	...	...
Transport & communic.		./.	...	...	...	...	...	...	...
Agriculture		29	...	...	...	...	...	...	...
Other & not specified		-	-	...	...	...	...	...	...

Third level: graduates by level and field of study 3.12
Troisième degré: diplômés par niveau et domaine d'études
Tercer grado: diplomados por nivel y sector de estudios

Country Field of study Pays Domaine d'études País Sectores de estudios	Year Année Año	Graduates by ISCED level of programme Diplômés par niveau de programmes de la CITE Diplomados por nivel de programas de la CINE							
		All levels Tous niveaux Todos los niveles		Level 5 Niveau 5 Nivel 5		Level 6 Niveau 6 Nivel 6		Level 7 Niveau 7 Nivel 7	
		MF	F	MF	F	MF	F	MF	F
		(1)	(2)	(3)	(4)	(5)	(6)	(7)	(8)
St. Kitts and Nevis									
Total	1986	135	62	135	62	-	-	-	-
Total	1993	183	96	183	96	-	-	-	-
Education science		29	21	29	21	-	-	-	-
Humanities & religion		10	6	10	6	-	-	-	-
Fine & applied arts		-	-	-	-	-	-	-	-
Law		-	-	-	-	-	-	-	-
Social & behav. sc.		-	-	-	-	-	-	-	-
Business administr.		18	7	18	7	-	-	-	-
Communic. & doc.		-	-	-	-	-	-	-	-
Home economics		-	-	-	-	-	-	-	-
Service trades		12	11	12	11	-	-	-	-
Natural science		8	6	8	6	-	-	-	-
Maths. & computer sc.		28	18	28	18	-	-	-	-
Health-related prg.		10	10	10	10	-	-	-	-
Engineering		-	-	-	-	-	-	-	-
Archit. & town plng.		10	2	10	2	-	-	-	-
Trade, craft & indust.		58	15	58	15	-	-	-	-
Transport & communic.		-	-	-	-	-	-	-	-
Agriculture		-	-	-	-	-	-	-	-
Other & not specified		-	-	-	-	-	-	-	-
Trinidad and Tobago‡									
Total	1982	394	195	-	-	394	195	-	-
	1987	806	286	-	-	...	...	...	...
	1990	1 110	565	117	63	779	388	214	114
Total	1993	998	...	238	...	663	343	97	...
Education science		134	...	127	...	-	-	7	...
Humanities & religion		139	...	-	-	131	113	8	...
Fine & applied arts		12	...	12	...	-	-	-	-
Law		-	-	-	-	-	-	-	-
Social & behav. sc.		228	...	51	...	172	110	5	...
Business administr.		78	...	48	...	-	-	30	...
Communic. & doc.		./.	...	./.	...	-	-	./.	...
Home economics		-	-	-	-	-	-	-	-
Service trades		-	-	-	-	-	-	-	-
Natural science		125	...	-	-	121	63	4	...
Maths. & computer sc.		2	...	-	-	-	-	2	
Health-related prg.		35	...	-	-	31	10	4	...
Engineering		164	...	-	-	144	21	20	...
Archit. & town plng.		-	"	-	-	-	-	-	-
Trade, craft & indust.		-	-	-	-	-	-	-	-
Transport & communic.		-	-	-	-	-	-	-	-
Agriculture		81	...	-	-	64	26	17	...
Other & not specified		-	-	-	-	-	-	-	-
United States									
Total	1981	1 752 995	870 601	416 377	227 739	935 468	464 906	401 150	177 956
	1986	1 830 284	928 911	456 550	253 250	979 477	496 949	394 257	178 712
	1991	2 024 668	1 096 905	481 720	283 086	1 094 538	590 493	448 410	223 326
Total	1993	2 294 970	1 265 611	724 317	420 233	1 159 931	629 390	410 722	215 988
Education science		221 618	170 053	10 779	7 511	107 781	84 548	103 058	77 994
Humanities & religion		304 479	181 699	163 358	97 395	117 190	71 404	23 931	12 900
Fine & applied arts		74 965	45 358	16 882	10 462	47 761	29 151	10 322	5 745
Law		15 680	11 893	11 341	9 767	2 056	1 389	2 283	737
Social & behav. sc.		247 090	136 267	5 938	3 729	207 912	114 438	33 240	18 100
Business administr.		489 731	256 706	141 928	103 096	256 842	121 269	90 961	32 341
Communic. & doc.		65 146	38 242	4 930	2 180	54 706	32 678	5 510	3 384
Home economics		35 564	30 615	17 640	14 848	15 100	13 462	2 824	2 305
Service trades		11 138	6 466	11 138	6 466	-	-	-	-
Natural science		87 456	38 493	3 923	1 874	64 583	29 916	18 950	6 703
Maths. & computer sc.		71 643	26 970	16 407	8 424	39 012	13 782	16 224	4 764
Health-related prg.		243 022	200 043	148 448	122 796	67 089	55 742	27 485	21 505
Engineering		162 357	21 244	49 737	5 197	78 051	11 215	34 569	4 832
Archit. & town plng.		13 553	5 005	430	303	9 167	3 227	3 956	1 475
Trade, craft & indust.		59 762	5 740	59 372	5 633	388	107	2	-
Transport & communic.		12 597	1 489	8 172	1 028	3 930	422	495	39
Agriculture		33 833	12 064	11 917	4 584	16 778	5 698	5 138	1 782
Other & not specified		145 336	77 264	41 977	14 940	71 585	40 942	31 774	21 382

3.12 Third level: graduates by level and field of study
Troisième degré: diplomés par niveau et domaine d'études
Tercer grado: diplomados por nivel y sector de estudios

Country / Field of study Pays / Domaine d'études País / Sectores de estudios	Year Année Año	Graduates by ISCED level of programme Diplômés par niveau de programmes de la CITE Diplomados por nivel de programas de la CINE							
		All levels Tous niveaux Todos los niveles		Level 5 Niveau 5 Nivel 5		Level 6 Niveau 6 Nivel 6		Level 7 Niveau 7 Nivel 7	
		MF	F	MF	F	MF	F	MF	F
		(1)	(2)	(3)	(4)	(5)	(6)	(7)	(8)
U.S. Virgin Isl.									
Total	1982	221	...	51	...	139	...	31	...
	1986	247	171	79	59	136	95	32	17
	1991	263	215	61	56	153	119	49	40
Total	1993	278	211	-	-	239	183	39	28
Education science		56	49	-	-	32	30	24	19
Humanities & religion		12	11	-	-	12	11	-	-
Fine & applied arts		-	-	-	-	-	-	-	-
Law		-	-	-	-	-	-	-	-
Social & behav. sc.		8	5	-	-	8	5	-	-
Business administr.		158	117	-	-	143	108	15	9
Communic. & doc.		-	-	-	-	-	-	-	-
Home economics		-	-	-	-	-	-	-	-
Service trades		-	-	-	-	-	-	-	-
Natural science		12	4	-	-	12	4	-	-
Maths. & computer sc.		8	4	-	-	8	4	-	-
Health-related prg.		16	16	-	-	16	16	-	-
Engineering		-	-	-	-	-	-	-	-
Archit. & town plng.		-	-	-	-	-	-	-	-
Trade, craft & indust.		-	-	-	-	-	-	-	-
Transport & communic.		-	-	-	-	-	-	-	-
Agriculture		8	5	-	-	8	5	-	-
Other & not specified		-	-	-	-	-	-	-	-
America, South									
Argentina‡									
Total	1979	36 621	16 262	...	...	...	...	...	...
Total	1991	40 599	...	...	...	...	...	...	...
Education science		1 456	...	...	...	...	...	...	...
Humanities & religion		4 064	...	...	...	...	...	...	...
Fine & applied arts		498	...	...	...	...	...	...	...
Law		7 565	...	...	...	...	...	...	...
Social & behav. sc.		1 918	...	...	...	...	...	...	...
Business administr.		5 483	...	...	...	...	...	...	...
Communic. & doc.		./.	...	...	...	...	...	...	...
Home economics		-	-	-	-	-	-	-	-
Service trades		-	-	-	-	-	-	-	-
Natural science		4 933	...	...	...	...	...	...	...
Maths. & computer sc.		./.	...	...	...	...	...	...	...
Health-related prg.		7 487	...	...	...	...	...	...	...
Engineering		3 569	...	...	...	...	...	...	...
Archit. & town plng.		2 096	...	...	...	...	...	...	...
Trade, craft & indust.		-	-	-	-	-	-	-	-
Transport & communic.		-	-	-	-	-	-	-	-
Agriculture		1 530	...	...	...	...	...	...	...
Other & not specified		-	...	...	...	...	...	...	...
Bolivia‡									
Total	1985	4 422	...	...	...	...	...	...	...
	1990	4 610	...	...	...	...	...	...	...
Total	1991	4 348	...	...	...	...	...	...	...
Education science		56	...	...	...	...	...	...	...
Humanities & religion		121	...	...	...	...	...	...	...
Fine & applied arts		-	-	-	-	-	-	-	-
Law		496	...	...	...	...	...	...	...
Social & behav. sc.		396	...	...	...	...	...	...	...
Business administr.		882	...	...	...	...	...	...	...
Communic. & doc.		138	...	...	...	...	...	...	...
Home economics		16	...	...	...	...	...	...	...
Service trades		30	...	...	...	...	...	...	...
Natural science		97	...	...	...	...	...	...	...
Maths. & computer sc.		54	...	...	...	...	...	...	...
Health-related prg.		894	...	...	...	...	...	...	...
Engineering		682	...	...	...	...	...	...	...
Archit. & town plng.		69	...	...	...	...	...	...	...
Trade, craft & indust.		251	...	...	...	...	...	...	...
Transport & communic.		-	-	-	-	-	-	-	-
Agriculture		126	...	...	...	...	...	...	...
Other & not specified		40	...	...	...	...	...	...	...

Third level: graduates by level and field of study 3.12
Troisième degré: diplômés par niveau et domaine d'études
Tercer grado: diplomados por nivel y sector de estudios

Country Field of study Pays Domaine d'études País Sectores de estudios	Year Année Año	Graduates by ISCED level of programme Diplômés par niveau de programmes de la CITE Diplomados por nivel de programas de la CINE							
		All levels Tous niveaux Todos los niveles		Level 5 Niveau 5 Nivel 5		Level 6 Niveau 6 Nivel 6		Level 7 Niveau 7 Nivel 7	
		MF	F	MF	F	MF	F	MF	F
		(1)	(2)	(3)	(4)	(5)	(6)	(7)	(8)
Brazil‡									
Total	1980	237 654	...	-	-	226 423	...	11 231	...
	1986	228 074	...	-	-	228 074	...	...	...
	1990	230 271	137 518	-	-	230 271	137 518	...	...
Total	1993	240 269	144 342	-	-	240 269	144 342	...	...
Education science		43 204	36 179	-	-	43 204	36 179	...	...
Humanities & religion		22 519	17 395	-	-	22 519	17 395	...	...
Fine & applied arts		1 097	706	-	-	1 097	706	...	...
Law		26 535	12 354	-	-	26 535	12 354	...	...
Social & behav. sc.		21 268	14 430	-	-	21 268	14 430	...	...
Business administr.		43 209	20 437	-	-	43 209	20 437	...	...
Communic. & doc.		7 381	4 954	-	-	7 381	4 954	...	...
Home economics		1 638	1 520	-	-	1 638	1 520	...	...
Service trades		1 191	917	-	-	1 191	917	...	...
Natural science		4 810	2 953	-	-	4 810	2 953	...	...
Maths. & computer sc.		9 859	4 206	-	-	9 859	4 206	...	...
Health-related prg.		24 271	15 887	-	-	24 271	15 887	...	...
Engineering		14 846	2 744	-	-	14 846	2 744	...	...
Archit. & town plng.		2 714	1 662	-	-	2 714	1 662	...	...
Trade, craft & indust.		2 377	681	-	-	2 377	681	...	...
Transport & communic.		86	16	-	-	86	16	...	...
Agriculture		5 159	1 573	-	-	5 159	1 573	...	...
Other & not specified		8 105	5 728	-	-	8 105	5 728	...	...
Chile†									
Total	1980	13 925	7 216	-	-	13 925	7 216	-	-
	1984	20 256	9 945	1 462	350	18 581	9 505	213	90
	1991	14 900	...	903	...	12 081	...	1 916	...
Total	1993	15 414	...	1 006	...	11 644	...	2 764	...
Education science		3 506	...	-	-	2 188	...	1 318	...
Humanities & religion		415	...	-	-	362	...	53	...
Fine & applied arts		294	...	-	-	292	...	2	...
Law		430	...	-	-	312	...	118	...
Social & behav. sc.		524	...	-	-	481	...	43	...
Business administr.		2 049	...	86	...	1 518	...	445	...
Communic. & doc.		227	...	30	...	189	...	8	...
Home economics		-	-	-	-	-	-	-	-
Service trades		12	...	12	...	-	-	-	-
Natural science		518	...	1	...	418	...	99	...
Maths. & computer sc.		312	...	66	...	210	...	36	...
Health-related prg.		2 166	...	15	...	1 806	...	345	...
Engineering		3 749	...	437	...	3 138	...	174	...
Archit. & town plng		215	...	29	...	175	...	11	...
Trade, craft & indust.		123	...	123	...	-	-	-	-
Transport & communic.		-	-	-	-	-	-	-	-
Agriculture		787	...	207	...	555	...	25	...
Other & not specified		87	...	-	-	-	-	87	...
Colombia									
Total	1980	26 658	...	...	...	...	...	...	...
	1985	48 736	25 083	12 408	7 901	33 689	16 076	2 639	1 106
	1989	68 443	36 150	16 155	9 730	47 723	24 488	4 565	1 932
Total	1994	82 271	45 390	...	...	...	...	...	...
Education science		17 576	12 624	...	...	...	...	...	...
Humanities & religion		567	288	...	...	...	...	...	...
Fine & applied arts		2 849	1 842	...	...	...	...	...	...
Law		9 774	5 982	...	...	...	...	...	...
Social & behav. sc.		./.	./.	...	...	...	...	...	...
Business administr.		22 487	12 191	...	...	...	...	...	...
Communic. & doc.		-	-	-	-	-	-	-	-
Home economics		-	-	-	-	-	-	-	-
Service trades		-	-	-	-	-	-	-	-
Natural science		1 384	656	...	...	...	...	...	...
Maths. & computer sc.		./.	./.	...	...	...	...	...	...
Health-related prg.		7 380	4 694	...	...	...	...	...	...
Engineering		17 870	6 334	...	...	...	...	...	...
Archit. & town plng.		./.	./.	-	-	-	-	-	-
Trade, craft & indust.		-	-	-	-	-	-	-	-
Transport & communic.		-	-	-	-	-	-	-	-
Agriculture		2 384	779	...	...	...	...	...	...
Other & not specified		-	-	-	-	-	-	-	-

3.12 Third level: graduates by level and field of study
Troisième degré: diplômés par niveau et domaine d'études
Tercer grado: diplomados por nivel y sector de estudios

Country Field of study Pays Domaine d'études País Sectores de estudios	Year Année Año	Graduates by ISCED level of programme Diplômés par niveau de programmes de la CITE Diplomados por nivel de programas de la CINE							
		All levels Tous niveaux Todos los niveles		Level 5 Niveau 5 Nivel 5		Level 6 Niveau 6 Nivel 6		Level 7 Niveau 7 Nivel 7	
		MF	F	MF	F	MF	F	MF	F
		(1)	(2)	(3)	(4)	(5)	(6)	(7)	(8)
Ecuador‡									
Total	1982	15 441	6 262	...	...	...	...	...	...
Total	1991	11 722	...	...	...	...	...	...	...
Education science		2 417	...	...	...	...	...	...	...
Humanities & religion		66	...	...	...	...	...	...	...
Fine & applied arts		32	...	...	...	...	...	...	...
Law		737	...	...	...	...	...	...	...
Social & behav. sc.		1 155	...	...	...	...	...	...	...
Business administr.		2 122	...	...	...	...	...	...	...
Communic. & doc.		129	...	...	...	...	...	...	...
Home economics		35	...	...	...	...	...	...	...
Service trades		3	...	...	...	...	...	...	...
Natural science		294	...	...	...	...	...	...	...
Maths. & computer sc.		-	-	...	...	...	...	...	...
Health-related prg.		2 926	...	...	...	...	...	...	...
Engineering		954	...	...	...	...	...	...	...
Archit. & town plng.		209	...	...	...	...	...	...	...
Trade, craft & indust.		./.	...	...	...	...	...	...	...
Transport & communic.		-	...	...	...	...	...	...	...
Agriculture		444	...	...	...	...	...	...	...
Other & not specified		199	...	...	...	...	...	...	...
Guyana									
Total	1980	1 018	449	782	386	236	63	-	-
	1986	711	328	508	245	196	83	7	-
Total	1990	1 073	485	...	...	...	...	...	...
Education science		275	226	...	...	...	...	...	...
Humanities & religion		36	29	...	...	...	...	...	...
Fine & applied arts		-	-	...	...	...	...	...	...
Law		-	-	...	...	...	...	...	...
Social & behav. sc.		59	35	...	...	...	...	...	...
Business administr.		137	83	...	...	...	...	...	...
Communic. & doc.		10	8	...	...	...	...	...	...
Home economics		-	-	...	...	...	...	...	...
Service trades		-	-	...	...	...	...	...	...
Natural science		26	13	...	...	...	...	...	...
Maths. & computer sc.		./.	./.	...	...	...	...	...	...
Health-related prg.		39	21	...	...	...	...	...	...
Engineering		140	16	...	...	...	...	...	...
Archit. & town plng.		9	1	...	...	...	...	...	...
Trade, craft & indust.		320	47	...	...	...	...	...	...
Transport & communic.		-	-	...	...	...	...	...	...
Agriculture		22	6	...	...	...	...	...	...
Other & not specified		-	-	...	...	...	...	...	...
Paraguay									
Total	1985	2 243	...	...	...	...	...	...	...
	1988	2 431	...	...	...	...	...	...	...
Total	1992	3 669	2 250	1 194	969	2 475	1 281	-	-
Education science		1 214	985	1 194	969	20	16	-	-
Humanities & religion		129	89	-	-	129	89	-	-
Fine & applied arts		-	-	-	-	-	-	-	-
Law		432	210	-	-	432	210	-	-
Social & behav. sc.		174	91	-	-	174	91	-	-
Business administr.		623	319	-	-	623	319	-	-
Communic. & doc.		50	30	-	-	50	30	-	-
Home economics		-	-	-	-	-	-	-	-
Service trades		-	-	-	-	-	-	-	-
Natural science		63	49	-	-	63	49	-	-
Maths. & computer sc.		170	102	-	-	170	102	-	-
Health-related prg.		329	233	-	-	329	233	-	-
Engineering		156	45	-	-	156	45	-	-
Archit. & town plng.		58	13	-	-	58	13	-	-
Trade, craft & indust.		26	5	-	-	26	5	-	-
Transport & communic.		-	-	-	-	-	-	-	-
Agriculture		218	64	-	-	218	64	-	-
Other & not specified		27	15	-	-	27	15	-	-

Third level: graduates by level and field of study 3.12
Troisième degré: diplômés par niveau et domaine d'études
Tercer grado: diplomados por nivel y sector de estudios

Country / Field of study / Pays / Domaine d'études / País / Sectores de estudios	Year / Année / Año	Graduates by ISCED level of programme / Diplômés par niveau de programmes de la CITE / Diplomados por nivel de programas de la CINE							
		All levels / Tous niveaux / Todos los niveles		Level 5 / Niveau 5 / Nivel 5		Level 6 / Niveau 6 / Nivel 6		Level 7 / Niveau 7 / Nivel 7	
		MF	F	MF	F	MF	F	MF	F
		(1)	(2)	(3)	(4)	(5)	(6)	(7)	(8)
Peru‡									
Total	1980	18 530	...	...	...	...	...	...	...
	1990	39 008	...	...	...	...	...	...	...
Total	1991	27 428	...	...	...	...	...	...	...
Education science		3 555	...	...	...	...	...	...	...
Humanities & religion		233	...	...	...	...	...	...	...
Fine & applied arts		11	...	...	...	...	...	...	...
Law		1 955	...	...	...	...	...	...	...
Social & behav. sc.		3 690	...	...	...	...	...	...	...
Business administr.		5 730	...	...	...	...	...	...	...
Communic. & doc.		480	...	...	...	...	...	...	...
Home economics		41	...	...	...	...	...	...	...
Service trades		-	-	-	-	-	-	-	-
Natural science		611	...	...	...	...	...	...	...
Maths. & computer sc.		236	...	...	...	...	...	...	...
Health-related prg.		3 096	...	...	...	...	...	...	...
Engineering		4 128	...	...	...	...	...	...	...
Archit. & town plng.		379	...	...	...	...	...	...	...
Trade, craft & indust.		-	-	-	-	-	-	-	-
Transport & communic.		-	-	-	-	-	-	-	-
Agriculture		1 634	...	...	...	...	...	...	...
Other & not specified		1 649	...	...	...	...	...	...	...
Surinam									
Total	1991	155	...	126	...	29	...	-	-
Education science		138	...	123	...	15	...	-	-
Humanities & religion		-	-	-	-	-	-	-	-
Fine & applied arts		1	...	-	-	1	...	-	-
Law		10	...	1	...	9	...	-	-
Social & behav. sc.		-	-	-	-	-	-	-	-
Business administr.		2	...	1	...	1	...	-	-
Communic. & doc.		-	-	-	-	-	-	-	-
Home economics		-	-	-	-	-	-	-	-
Service trades		-	-	-	-	-	-	-	-
Natural science		-	-	-	-	-	-	-	-
Maths. & computer sc.		-	-	-	-	-	-	-	-
Health-related prg.		2	...	-	-	2	...	-	-
Engineering		2	...	1	...	1	...	-	-
Archit. & town plng.		-	-	-	-	-	-	-	-
Trade, craft & indust.		-	-	-	-	-	-	-	-
Transport & communic.		-	-	-	-	-	-	-	-
Agriculture		-	-	-	-	-	-	-	-
Other & not specified		-	-	-	-	-	-	-	-
Uruguay‡									
Total	1980	2 295	1 134	486	396	1 797	729	12	9
	1985	2 632	1 515	789	632	1 843	883	-	-
	1990	4 125	...	2 159	...	1 966	...	-	-
Total	1991	5 609	...	2 300	...	3 309	...	-	-
Education science		1 189	...	1 168	...	21	...	-	-
Humanities & religion		47	...	-	-	47	...	-	-
Fine & applied arts		1	...	-	-	1	...	-	-
Law		820	...	-	-	820	...	-	-
Social & behav. sc.		531	...	-	-	531	...	-	-
Business administr.		544	...	166	...	378	...	-	-
Communic. & doc.		6	...	-	-	6	...	-	-
Home economics		-	-	-	-	-	-	-	-
Service trades		-	-	-	-	-	-	-	-
Natural science		73	...	-	-	73	...	-	-
Maths. & computer sc.		195	...	178	...	17	...	-	-
Health-related prg.		1 277	...	553	...	724	...	-	-
Engineering		197	...	-	-	197	...	-	-
Archit. & town plng.		185	...	-	-	185	...	-	-
Trade, craft & indust.		29	...	29	...	-	-	-	-
Transport & communic.		-	-	-	-	-	-	-	-
Agriculture		302	...	-	-	302	...	-	-
Other & not specified		213	...	206	...	7	...	-	-

3.12 Third level: graduates by level and field of study
Troisième degré: diplômés par niveau et domaine d'études
Tercer grado: diplomados por nivel y sector de estudios

Country Field of study Pays Domaine d'études País Sectores de estudios	Year Année Año	Graduates by ISCED level of programme							
		All levels Tous niveaux Todos los niveles		Level 5 Niveau 5 Nivel 5		Level 6 Niveau 6 Nivel 6		Level 7 Niveau 7 Nivel 7	
		MF	F	MF	F	MF	F	MF	F
		(1)	(2)	(3)	(4)	(5)	(6)	(7)	(8)
Venezuela									
Total	1981	15 819	...	3 098	...	12 721	...	-	
	1986	29 406	...	7 490	...	21 916	...	-	-
Total	1989	32 787	...	10 914	...	21 873	...	...	...
Education science		5 399	...	1 002	...	4 397	...	...	...
Humanities & religion		292	...	31	...	261	...	...	...
Fine & applied arts		32	...	-	-	32	...	...	...
Law		2 239	...	-	-	2 239	...	...	...
Social & behav. sc.		3 904	...	1 613	...	2 291	...	...	...
Business administr.		6 123	...	3 369	...	2 754	...	...	...
Communic. & doc.		740	...	377	...	363	...	...	...
Home economics		83	...	-	-	83	...	...	...
Service trades		124	...	124	...	-	-	...	...
Natural science		429	...	81	...	348	...	...	...
Maths. & computer sc.		1 093	...	945	...	148	...	...	...
Health-related prg.		3 787	...	217	...	3 570	...	...	...
Engineering		5 166	...	1 051	...	4 115	...	...	...
Archit. & town plng.		824	...	-	-	824	...	...	...
Trade, craft & indust.		886	...	886	...	-	-	...	...
Transport & communic.		43	...	43	...	-	-	...	...
Agriculture		1 521	...	1 073	...	448	...	...	...
Other & not specified		102	...	102	...	-	-	...	...
Asia									
Afghanistan									
Total	1982	2 989	...	1 253	...	1 736	...	-	-
	1986	2 457	1 296	...	...	...	...	...	...
Total	1990	2 429	1 197	...	...	...	...	...	...
Education science		739	525	...	...	...	...	...	...
Humanities & religion		755	154	...	...	...	...	...	...
Fine & applied arts		23	9	...	...	...	...	...	...
Law		157	87	...	...	...	...	...	...
Social & behav. sc.		87	56	...	...	...	...	...	...
Business administr.		148	53	...	...	...	...	...	...
Communic. & doc.		75	47	...	...	...	...	...	...
Home economics		-	-	...	...	...	...	...	...
Service trades		-	-	...	...	...	...	...	...
Natural science		163	141	...	...	...	...	...	...
Maths. & computer sc.		./.	./.	...	...	...	...	...	...
Health-related prg.		110	52	...	...	...	...	...	...
Engineering		47	32	...	...	...	...	...	...
Archit. & town plng.		./.	./.	...	...	...	...	...	...
Trade, craft & indust.		-	-	...	...	...	...	...	...
Transport & communic.		-	-	...	...	...	...	...	...
Agriculture		125	41	...	...	...	...	...	...
Other & not specified		-	-	...	...	...	...	...	...
Azerbaijan‡									
Total	1995	27 902	...	11 471	...	16 431	...	./.	...
Education science		6 819	...	1 537	...	5 282	...	./.	...
Humanities & religion		./.	...	./.	...	./.	...	./.	...
Fine & applied arts		1 381	...	785	...	596	...	./.	...
Law		3 078	...	1 620	...	1 458	...	./.	...
Social & behav. sc.		./.	...	./.	...	./.	...	./.	...
Business administr.		./.	...	./.	...	./.	...	./.	...
Communic. & doc.		311	...	311	...	./.	...	./.	...
Home economics		-	-	-	-	-	-	-	-
Service trades		-	-	-	-	-	-	-	-
Natural science		./.	...	-	-	./.	...	./.	...
Maths. & computer sc.		./.	...	./.	...	./.	...	./.	...
Health-related prg.		2 701	...	1 274	...	1 427	...	./.	...
Engineering		7 885	...	3 529	...	4 356	...	./.	...
Archit. & town plng.		1 715	...	436	...	1 279	...	./.	...
Trade, craft & indust.		./.	...	./.	...	./.	...	./.	...
Transport & communic.		568	...	568	...	-		./.	...
Agriculture		2 869	...	1 367	...	1 502	...	./.	...
Other & not specified		575	...	44	...	531	...	./.	...

Third level: graduates by level and field of study 3.12
Troisième degré: diplômés par niveau et domaine d'études
Tercer grado: diplomados por nivel y sector de estudios

Country Field of study Pays Domaine d'études País Sectores de estudios	Year Année Año	Graduates by ISCED level of programme Diplômés par niveau de programmes de la CITE Diplomados por nivel de programas de la CINE							
		All levels Tous niveaux Todos los niveles		Level 5 Niveau 5 Nivel 5		Level 6 Niveau 6 Nivel 6		Level 7 Niveau 7 Nivel 7	
		MF	F	MF	F	MF	F	MF	F
		(1)	(2)	(3)	(4)	(5)	(6)	(7)	(8)
Bahrain									
Total	1985	608	356	...	...	...	...	...	...
	1991	865	411	283	130	518	243	64	38
Total	1994	1 382	826	...	...	...	...	...	...
Education science		317	245	...	...	...	...	...	...
Humanities & religion		113	55	...	...	...	...	...	...
Fine & applied arts		-	-	...	...	...	...	...	...
Law		-	-	...	...	...	...	...	...
Social & behav. sc.		-	-	...	...	...	...	...	...
Business administr.		372	216	...	...	...	...	...	...
Communic. & doc.		-	-	...	...	...	...	...	...
Home economics		-	-	...	...	...	...	...	...
Service trades		-	-	...	...	...	...	...	...
Natural science		108	57	...	...	...	...	...	...
Maths. & computer sc.		./.	./.	...	...	...	...	...	...
Health-related prg.		233	178	...	...	...	...	...	...
Engineering		239	75	...	...	...	...	...	...
Archit. & town plng.		./.	./.	...	...	...	...	...	...
Trade, craft & indust.		./.	./.	...	...	...	...	...	...
Transport & communic.		-	-	...	...	...	...	...	...
Agriculture		-	-	...	...	...	...	...	...
Other & not specified		-	-	...	...	...	...	...	...
Bangladesh									
Total	1980	27 100	...	213	...	21 316	...	5 571	...
	1983	42 337	...	465	...	36 704	...	5 168	...
Total	1987	69 278	...	180	...	60 952	...	8 146	...
Education science		4 949	...	9	...	4 913	...	27	...
Humanities & religion		35 047	...	168	...	32 202	...	2 677	...
Fine & applied arts		253	...	-	-	253	...	-	-
Law		2 289	...	-	-	2 104	...	185	...
Social & behav. sc.		3 556	...	-	-	1 786	...	1 770	...
Business administr.		10 849	...	-	-	8 882	...	1 967	...
Communic. & doc.		75	...	-	-	75	...	-	-
Home economics		92	...	-	-	92	...	-	-
Service trades		-	...	-	-	-	-	-	-
Natural science		8 468	...	-	-	7 587	...	881	...
Maths. & computer sc.		676	...	-	-	399	...	277	...
Health-related prg.		1 226	...	-	-	1 055	...	171	...
Engineering		785	...	-	-	742	...	43	...
Archit. & town plng.		37	...	-	-	29	...	8	...
Trade, craft & indust.		57	...	3	-	54	...	-	-
Transport & communic.		-	...	-	-	-	-	-	-
Agriculture		813	...	-	-	673	...	140	...
Other & not specified		106	...	-	-	106	...	-	-
China‡									
Total	1981	147 111	...	-	...	146 635	...	476	...
	1986	330 313	...	114 499	...	201 885	...	13 929	...
	1991	645 510	...	305 749	...	307 865	...	31 896	...
Total	1994	1 040 135	...	664 853	...	347 068	...	28 214	...
Education science		294 178	...	208 722	...	85 003	...	453	...
Humanities & religion		67 680	...	49 555	...	15 760	...	2 365	...
Fine & applied arts		10 889	...	8 351	...	2 447	...	91	...
Law		31 198	...	22 776	...	7 208	...	1 214	...
Social & behav. sc.		199 105	...	165 514	...	31 656	...	1 935	...
Business administr.		./.	...	./.	...	./.	...	./.	...
Communic. & doc.		-	-	-	-	-	-	-	-
Home economics		-	-	-	-	-	-	-	-
Service trades		-	-	-	-	-	-	-	-
Natural science		21 462	...	5 612	...	11 087	...	4 763	...
Maths. & computer sc.		26 619	...	12 141	...	12 520	...	1 958	...
Health-related prg.		66 550	...	30 696	...	33 048	...	2 806	...
Engineering		262 647	...	131 867	...	120 831	...	9 949	...
Archit. & town plng.		3 986	...	1 405	...	2 388	...	193	...
Trade, craft & indust.		-	-	-	-	-	-	-	-
Transport & communic.		13 274	...	6 218	...	5 594	...	1 462	...
Agriculture		36 389	...	18 457	...	16 994	...	938	...
Other & not specified		6 158	...	3 539	...	2 532	...	87	...

3.12 Third level: graduates by level and field of study
Troisième degré: diplômés par niveau et domaine d'études
Tercer grado: diplomados por nivel y sector de estudios

Country Field of study Pays Domaine d'études País Sectores de estudios	Year Année Año	Graduates by ISCED level of programme Diplômés par niveau de programmes de la CITE Diplomados por nivel de programas de la CINE							
		All levels Tous niveaux Todos los niveles		Level 5 Niveau 5 Nivel 5		Level 6 Niveau 6 Nivel 6		Level 7 Niveau 7 Nivel 7	
		MF	F	MF	F	MF	F	MF	F
		(1)	(2)	(3)	(4)	(5)	(6)	(7)	(8)
Cyprus‡									
Total	1981	696	274	696	274	-	-	-	-
	1986	1 289	753	1 289	753	-	-	-	-
	1991	1 783	937	1 783	937	-	-	-	-
Total	1994	1 714	936	1 636	908	-	-	78	28
Education science		109	109	109	109	-	-	-	-
Humanities & religion		-	-	-	-	-	-	-	-
Fine & applied arts		54	42	54	42	-	-	-	-
Law		15	6	15	6	-	-	-	-
Social & behav. sc.		5	1	5	1	-	-	-	-
Business administr.		701	400	628	375	-	-	73	25
Communic. & doc.		41	29	41	29	-	-	-	-
Home economics		5	3	5	3	-	-	-	-
Service trades		246	160	246	160	-	-	-	-
Natural science		-	-	-	-	-	-	-	-
Maths. & computer sc.		146	60	146	60	-	-	-	-
Health-related prg.		104	87	104	87	-	-	-	-
Engineering		257	31	257	31	-	-	-	-
Archit. & town plng.		10	5	10	5	-	-	-	-
Trade, craft & indust.		-	-	-	-	-	-	-	-
Transport & communic.		-	-	-	-	-	-	-	-
Agriculture		17	-	16	-	-	-	1	-
Other & not specified		4	3	-	-	-	-	4	3
Georgia									
Total	1995	23 130	...	6 848	...	15 904	...	378	...
Education science		1 738	...	850	...	875	...	13	...
Humanities & religion		1 892	...	867	...	952	...	73	...
Fine & applied arts		1 051	...	568	...	465	...	18	...
Law		1 491	...	221	...	1 265	...	5	...
Social & behav. sc.		1 893	...	875	...	943	...	75	...
Business administr.		1 151	...	290	...	861		-	-
Communic. & doc.		-	-	-	-	-	-	-	-
Home economics		-	-	-	-	-	-	-	-
Service trades		-	-	-	-	-	-	-	-
Natural science		1 122	...	-	-	1 056		66	...
Maths. & computer sc.		698	...	-	-	675		23	...
Health-related prg.		1 822	...	596	...	1 172	...	54	...
Engineering		4 818	...	1 231	...	3 555	...	32	...
Archit. & town plng.		1 470	...	443	...	1 027	...	-	-
Trade, craft & indust.		464	...	48	...	416	...	-	-
Transport & communic.		1 036	...	328	...	708	...	-	-
Agriculture		2 484	...	531	...	1 934	...	19	...
Other & not specified		-	-	-	-	-		-	
Hong Kong									
Total	1981	5 975	1 934	2 413	702	2 576	867	986	365
	1985	20 004	7 302	15 322	557	93 405	1 245	1 277	478
	1992	19 047	7 673	9 527	375	77 138	3 024	2 382	892
Total	1994	23 515	9 989	8 576	3 564	11 362	5 153	3 577	1 272
Education science		2 111	1 325	1 063	788	121	78	927	459
Humanities & religion		2 178	1 645	333	266	1 611	1 253	234	126
Fine & applied arts		./.	./.	./.	./.	./.	./.	./.	./.
Law		739	335	63	36	194	108	482	191
Social & behav. sc.		1 616	1 075	143	115	1 233	823	240	137
Business administr.		5 305	2 883	2 013	1 250	2 662	1 434	630	199
Communic. & doc.		242	192	87	71	149	117	6	4
Home economics		-	-	-	-	-	-	-	-
Service trades		183	122	139	90	44	32	-	-
Natural science		3 629	914	813	238	2 370	601	446	75
Maths. & computer sc.		./.	./.	./.	./.	./.	./.	./.	./.
Health-related prg.		1 030	550	357	243	600	282	73	25
Engineering		4 861	290	2 626	113	1 822	168	413	9
Archit. & town plng.		472	99	233	23	132	40	107	36
Trade, craft & indust.		821	421	625	316	195	104	1	1
Transport & communic.		81	15	81	15	-	-	-	-
Agriculture		-	-	-	-	-	-	-	-
Other & not specified		247	123	-	-	229	113	18	10

Third level: graduates by level and field of study   3.12
Troisième degré: diplomés par niveau et domaine d'études
Tercer grado: diplomados por nivel y sector de estudios

Country Field of study Pays Domaine d'études País Sectores de estudios	Year Année Año	Graduates by ISCED level of programme Diplômés par niveau de programmes de la CITE Diplomados por nivel de programas de la CINE							
		All levels Tous niveaux Todos los niveles		Level 5 Niveau 5 Nivel 5		Level 6 Niveau 6 Nivel 6		Level 7 Niveau 7 Nivel 7	
		MF	F	MF	F	MF	F	MF	F
		(1)	(2)	(3)	(4)	(5)	(6)	(7)	(8)
India‡									
Total	1987	860 725	260 322	...	...	...	...	...	...
Total	1991	1 213 387	...	...	...	...	...	...	...
Education science		104 907	...	...	...	...	...	...	...
Humanities & religion		585 362	...	...	...	...	...	...	...
Fine & applied arts		1 352	...	...	...	...	...	...	...
Law		36 021	...	...	...	...	...	...	...
Social & behav. sc.		./.	...	...	...	...	...	...	...
Business administr.		234 405	...	...	...	...	...	...	...
Communic. & doc.		27	...	...	...	...	...	...	...
Home economics		7 067	...	...	...	...	...	...	...
Service trades		-	-	-	-	-	-	-	-
Natural science		164 414	...	...	...	...	...	...	...
Maths. & computer sc.		./.	...	...	...	...	...	...	...
Health-related prg.		21 992	...	...	...	...	...	...	...
Engineering		33 509	...	...	...	...	...	...	...
Archit. & town plng.		./.	...	...	...	...	...	...	...
Trade, craft & indust.		./.	...	...	...	...	...	...	...
Transport & communic.		./.	...	...	...	...	...	...	...
Agriculture		13 406	...	...	...	...	...	...	...
Other & not specified		10 925	...	...	...	...	...	...	...
Indonesia‡									
Total	1982	64 668	20 674	14 441	6 603	33 914	9 871	16 313	4 200
	1985	73 627	24 907	16 178	7 553	31 224	9 067	20 225	8 287
	1992	149 401	23 939	42 560	...	106 841	...	...	...
Total	1993	177 725	71 201	99 070	39 073	78 655	32 128	...	...
Education science		44 084	21 289	26 692	13 228	17 392	8 061	...	...
Humanities & religion		4 237	2 353	1 964	1 060	2 273	1 293	...	...
Fine & applied arts		868	519	377	220	491	299	...	...
Law		14 699	5 597	9 950	3 625	4 749	1 972	...	...
Social & behav. sc.		29 230	12 117	15 271	6 484	13 959	5 633	...	...
Business administr.		39 641	17 507	25 896	10 280	13 745	7 227	...	...
Communic. & doc.		1 538	543	862	354	676	189	...	...
Home economics		-	-	-	-	-	-	-	-
Service trades		1 109	523	263	134	846	389	...	...
Natural science		1 790	619	223	122	1 567	497	...	...
Maths. & computer sc.		1 275	575	217	93	1 058	482	...	...
Health-related prg.		3 360	1 942	826	489	2 534	1 453	...	...
Engineering		20 860	2 458	11 047	1 284	9 813	1 174	...	...
Archit. & town plng.		1 861	433	1 266	269	595	164	...	...
Trade, craft & indust.		270	70	31	4	239	66	...	...
Transport & communic.		323	60	4	2	310	58	...	...
Agriculture		12 580	4 596	4 181	1 425	8 399	3 171	-	-
Other & not specified		-	-						
Iran, Islamic Republic of‡									
Total	1983	5 793	2 280	1 789	621	3 003	1 354	1 001	305
	1986	28 868	9 325	7 586	2 547	19 346	6 241	1 936	537
	1991	42 857	11 704	13 287	2 041	24 376	8 210	5 194	1 453
Total	1994	63 866	19 553	15 648	3 890	43 604	14 540	4 614	1 123
Education science		8 272	2 918	592	99	7 263	2 709	417	110
Humanities & religion		4 881	2 032	31	4	4 478	1 953	372	75
Fine & applied arts		793	377	164	135	611	239	18	3
Law		1 262	199	24	-	1 204	197	34	2
Social & behav. sc.		3 237	975	239	48	2 688	863	310	64
Business administr.		3 131	543	686	74	2 343	461	102	8
Communic. & doc.		261	118	88	39	135	67	38	12
Home economics		-	-	-	-	-	-	-	-
Service trades		-	-	-	-	-	-	-	-
Natural science		2 924	1 039	57	28	2 569	949	298	62
Maths. & computer sc.		2 170	720	428	145	1 615	555	127	20
Health-related prg.		20 509	9 904	6 370	3 090	12 568	6 098	1 571	716
Engineering		13 090	602	6 058	210	6 331	377	701	15
Archit. & town plng.		229	35	69	4	8	1	152	30
Trade, craft & indust.		-	-	-	-	-	-	-	-
Transport & communic.		-	-	-	-	-	-	-	-
Agriculture		3 000	91	735	14	1 791	71	474	6
Other & not specified		107	-	107					

3.12 Third level: graduates by level and field of study
Troisième degré: diplomés par niveau et domaine d'études
Tercer grado: diplomados por nivel y sector de estudios

Country / Field of study / Pays / Domaine d'études / País / Sectores de estudios	Year / Année / Año	Graduates by ISCED level of programme / Diplômés par niveau de programmes de la CITE / Diplomados por nivel de programas de la CINE							
		All levels Tous niveaux Todos los niveles		Level 5 Niveau 5 Nivel 5		Level 6 Niveau 6 Nivel 6		Level 7 Niveau 7 Nivel 7	
		MF	F	MF	F	MF	F	MF	F
		(1)	(2)	(3)	(4)	(5)	(6)	(7)	(8)
Israel‡									
Total	1980	8 978	4 023	-	-	6 451	2 853	2 527	1 170
	1986	12 050	5 883	-	-	8 919	4 377	3 131	1 506
	1990	13 915	7 033	-	-	10 192	5 269	3 723	1 764
Total	1993	15 573	8 240	-	-	11 144	5 961	4 429	2 279
Education science		3 915	2 862	-	-	2 605	1 925	1 310	937
Humanities & religion		./.	./.	-	-	./.	./.	./.	./.
Fine & applied arts		./.	./.	-	-	./.	./.	./.	./.
Law		506	214	-	-	483	201	23	13
Social & behav. sc.		4 946	2 597	-	-	3 801	2 014	1 145	583
Business administr.		./.	./.	-	-	./.	./.	./.	./.
Communic. & doc.		./.	./.	-	-	./.	./.	./.	./.
Home economics		./.	./.	-	-	./.	./.	./.	./.
Service trades		-	-	-	-	-	-	-	-
Natural science		1 665	926	-	-	939	573	726	353
Maths. & computer sc.		685	241	-	-	517	194	168	47
Health-related prg.		1 510	918	-	-	1 043	696	467	222
Engineering		2 038	340	-	-	1 542	253	496	87
Archit. & town plng.		./.	./.	-	-	./.	./.	./.	./.
Trade, craft & indust.		-	-	-	-	-	-	-	-
Transport & communic.		-	-	-	-	-	-	-	-
Agriculture		308	142	-	-	214	105	94	37
Other & not specified		-	-	-	-	-	-	-	-
Japan‡									
Total	1981	582 761	252 587	177 420	154 419	388 136	96 347	17 205	1 821
	1986	585 665	258 830	183 451	161 295	378 667	94 800	23 547	2 735
Total	1992	697 292	333 406	232 518	206 178	431 758	122 407	33 016	4 821
Education science		65 358	53 344	35 802	35 599	27 490	16 989	2 066	756
Humanities & religion		125 348	102 363	57 440	56 727	65 093	44 475	2 815	1 161
Fine & applied arts		21 614	17 106	10 141	9 347	10 827	7 442	646	317
Law		198 528	44 575	26 182	21 728	169 431	22 193	2 915	654
Social & behav. sc.		./.	./.	./.	./.	./.	./.	./.	./.
Business administr.		./.	./.	./.	./.	./.	./.	./.	./.
Communic. & doc.		./.	./.	./.	./.	./.	./.	./.	./.
Home economics		65 123	64 870	56 051	55 921	8 885	8 769	187	180
Service trades		-	-	-	-	-	-	-	-
Natural science		13 590	2 267	-	-	10 452	1 917	3 138	350
Maths. & computer sc.		4 370	1 045	156	137	3 765	857	449	51
Health-related prg.		34 944	17 831	8 929	7 988	22 044	9 291	3 971	552
Engineering		120 321	6 655	18 601	3 274	87 397	2 914	14 323	467
Archit. & town plng.		./.	./.	./.	./.	./.	./.	./.	./.
Trade, craft & indust.		./.	./.	./.	./.	./.	./.	./.	./.
Transport & communic.		696	28	289	3	363	23	44	2
Agriculture		17 038	3 319	1 453	561	13 572	2 535	2 013	223
Other & not specified		30 362	20 003	17 474	14 893	12 439	5 002	449	108
Jordan									
Total	1981	7 326	...	4 935	...	2 108	846	283	40
	1986	15 186	7 674	9 818	5 413	4 923	2 147	445	114
	1991	17 058	9 243	10 976	6 463	5 270	2 578	812	202
Total	1994	20 653	11 402	11 150	7 069	8 452	4 093	1 051	240
Education science		2 416	1 916	1 750	1 589	379	262	287	65
Humanities & religion		4 390	3 171	2 268	1 817	1 940	1 305	182	49
Fine & applied arts		911	504	731	403	180	101	-	-
Law		517	156	6	4	482	149	29	3
Social & behav. sc.		1 213	726	394	332	661	342	158	52
Business administr.		3 396	1 493	1 967	1 026	1 363	453	66	14
Communic. & doc.		277	159	182	111	95	48	-	-
Home economics		49	49	49	49	-	-	-	-
Service trades		18	-	18	-	-	-	-	-
Natural science		910	514	100	76	739	417	71	21
Maths. & computer sc.		1 399	693	912	483	462	206	25	4
Health-related prg.		2 201	1 230	1 491	861	680	360	30	9
Engineering		1 745	261	803	74	822	181	120	6
Archit. & town plng.		226	118	126	55	94	62	6	1
Trade, craft & indust.		-	-	-	-	-	-	-	-
Transport & communic.		-	-	-	-	-	-	-	-
Agriculture		444	165	39	4	356	151	49	10
Other & not specified		541	247	314	185	199	56	28	6

Third level: graduates by level and field of study 3.12
Troisième degré: diplômés par niveau et domaine d'études
Tercer grado: diplomados por nivel y sector de estudios

Country Field of study Pays Domaine d'études País Sectores de estudios	Year Année Año	Graduates by ISCED level of programme Diplômés par niveau de programmes de la CITE Diplomados por nivel de programas de la CINE							
		All levels Tous niveaux Todos los niveles		Level 5 Niveau 5 Nivel 5		Level 6 Niveau 6 Nivel 6		Level 7 Niveau 7 Nivel 7	
		MF	F	MF	F	MF	F	MF	F
		(1)	(2)	(3)	(4)	(5)	(6)	(7)	(8)
Kazakstan									
Total	1995	106 008	...	60 148	...	45 536	...	324	...
Education science		20 591	...	10 992	...	9 456	...	143	...
Humanities & religion		8 350	...	-	-	8 350	...	-	-
Fine & applied arts		1 114	...	320	...	794	...	-	-
Law		2 684	...	1 144	...	1 540	...	-	-
Social & behav. sc.		978	...	-	-	952	...	26	-
Business administr.		9 608	...	4 749	...	4 859	...		
Communic. & doc.		213	...	-	-	213	...	-	-
Home economics		-	-	-	-	-	-	-	-
Service trades		2 310	...	2 310	...	-	-	-	-
Natural science		2 230	...	-	-	2 230	...	-	-
Maths. & computer sc.		1 149	...	-	-	1 149	...	-	-
Health-related prg.		14 612	...	10 942	...	3 670	...	-	-
Engineering		15 310	...	9 652	...	5 521	...	137	...
Archit. & town plng.		2 732	...	2 617	...	97	...	18	...
Trade, craft & indust.		1 083	...	-	-	1 083	...	-	-
Transport & communic.		4 735	...	3 044	...	1 691	...	-	-
Agriculture		15 339	...	11 939	...	3 400	...	-	-
Other & not specified		2 970	...	2 439	...	531	...	-	-
Korea, Republic of									
Total	1981	109 764	32 919	54 477	16 104	49 735	15 812	5 552	1 003
	1986	210 548	79 260	73 927	33 260	118 584	42 771	18 037	3 229
	1991	293 684	116 688	90 313	47 309	181 107	64 344	22 264	5 035
Total	1995	345 206	155 440	132 229	71 996	183 372	75 634	29 605	7 810
Education science		29 291	21 367	7 134	7 029	17 164	12 205	4 993	2 133
Humanities & religion		38 074	22 444	6 723	4 243	28 484	17 130	2 867	1 071
Fine & applied arts		24 495	19 122	12 508	10 107	10 717	8 100	1 270	915
Law		6 279	1 041	313	116	5 547	889	419	36
Social & behav. sc.		31 422	7 828	2 853	2 395	27 169	5 056	1 400	377
Business administr.		37 065	19 027	21 296	13 569	11 572	5 165	4 197	293
Communic. & doc.		3 137	2 097	621	564	2 215	1 412	301	121
Home economics		15 066	14 046	8 832	8 073	5 757	5 504	477	469
Service trades		4 567	2 501	3 480	2 132	929	317	158	52
Natural science		13 115	5 843	-	-	11 443	5 339	1 672	504
Maths. & computer sc.		27 969	11 007	18 324	6 679	8 784	4 062	861	266
Health-related prg.		25 127	15 055	15 043	11 178	6 770	3 060	3 314	817
Engineering		60 643	4 667	21 952	2 269	33 279	2 199	5 412	199
Archit. & town plng.		6 071	808	4 707	540	1 055	230	309	38
Trade, craft & indust.		392	152	392	152	-	-	-	-
Transport & communic.		1 272	209	1 272	209	-	-	-	-
Agriculture		14 991	5 342	4 617	1 692	9 209	3 444	1 165	206
Other & not specified		6 230	2 884	2 162	1 049	3 278	1 522	790	313
Kuwait									
Total	1981	2 593	1 621	1 087	693	1 506	928	-	-
	1987	4 736	2 937	2 052	1 329	2 684	1 608	-	-
Total	1992	3 341	1 792	1 319	453	1 968	1 314	54	25
Education science		467	407	-	-	467	407	-	-
Humanities & religion		399	225	-	-	399	225	-	-
Fine & applied arts		7	6	-	-	7	6	-	-
Law		371	214	36	-	335	214	-	-
Social & behav. sc.		19	18	19	18	-	-	-	-
Business administr.		570	342	322	187	248	155	-	-
Communic. & doc.		-	-	-	-	-	-	-	-
Home economics		32	32	-	-	32	32	-	-
Service trades		-	-	-	-	-	-	-	-
Natural science		303	196	-	-	289	184	14	12
Maths. & computer sc.		130	68	108	52	22	16	-	-
Health-related prg.		257	115	149	70	106	43	2	2
Engineering		397	96	297	53	62	32	38	11
Archit. & town plng.		67	-	67	-	-	-	-	-
Trade, craft & indust.		-	-	-	-	-	-	-	-
Transport & communic.		171	73	171	73	-	-	-	-
Agriculture		13	-	13	-	1	-	-	-
Other & not specified		138	-	137	-	1	-	-	-

3.12 Third level: graduates by level and field of study
Troisième degré: diplômés par niveau et domaine d'études
Tercer grado: diplomados por nivel y sector de estudios

Country Field of study / Pays Domaine d'études / País Sectores de estudios	Year Année Año	Graduates by ISCED level of programme Diplômés par niveau de programmes de la CITE Diplomados por nivel de programas de la CINE							
		All levels Tous niveaux Todos los niveles		Level 5 Niveau 5 Nivel 5		Level 6 Niveau 6 Nivel 6		Level 7 Niveau 7 Nivel 7	
		MF	F	MF	F	MF	F	MF	F
		(1)	(2)	(3)	(4)	(5)	(6)	(7)	(8)
Lao People's Democratic Republic									
Total	1982	360	101	131	27	229	74	-	-
	1986	1 231	629	252	68	979	561	-	-
	1993	1 163	396	241	14	922	382	-	-
Total	1994	1 645	538	826	199	819	339	-	-
Education science		461	185	176	71	285	114	-	-
Humanities & religion		116	38	-	-	116	38	-	-
Fine & applied arts		-	-	-	-	-	-	-	-
Law		-	-	-	-	-	-	-	-
Social & behav. sc.		206	93	116	49	90	44	-	-
Business administr.		-	-	-	-	-	-	-	-
Communic. & doc.		-	-	-	-	-	-	-	-
Home economics		-	-	-	-	-	-	-	-
Service trades		-	-	-	-	-	-	-	-
Natural science		73	36	53	24	20	12	-	-
Maths. & computer sc.		133	40	74	20	59	20	-	-
Health-related prg.		188	100	-	-	188	100	-	-
Engineering		61	11	-	-	61	11	-	-
Archit. & town plng.		71	9	71	9	-	-	-	-
Trade, craft & indust.		-	-	-	-	-	-	-	-
Transport & communic.		163	14	163	14	-	-	-	-
Agriculture		120	4	120	4	-	-	-	-
Other & not specified		53	8	53	8	-	-	-	-
Macau									
Total	1990	1 021	292	...	...	...	...	...	...
Education science		38	29	...	...	...	...	...	...
Humanities & religion		108	53	...	...	...	...	...	...
Fine & applied arts		-	-	...	...	...	...	...	...
Law		146	26	...	...	...	...	...	...
Social & behav. sc.		81	28	...	...	...	...	...	...
Business administr.		492	107	...	...	...	...	...	...
Communic. & doc.		-	-	...	...	...	...	...	...
Home economics		-	-	...	...	...	...	...	...
Service trades		3	2	...	...	...	...	...	...
Natural science		94	30	...	...	...	...	...	...
Maths. & computer sc.		57	15	...	...	...	...	...	...
Health-related prg.		-	-	...	...	...	...	...	...
Engineering		-	-	...	...	...	...	...	...
Archit. & town plng.		-	-	...	...	...	...	...	...
Trade, craft & indust.		-	-	...	...	...	...	...	...
Transport & communic.		-	-	...	...	...	...	...	...
Agriculture		-	-	...	...	...	...	...	...
Other & not specified		2	2	...	...	...	...	...	...
Malaysia‡									
Total	1981	16 712	6 777	12 485	5 211	4 078	1 508	149	58
	1986	24 853	11 823	17 988	8 863	6 806	2 950	59	10
Total	1991	20 886	9 680	8 575	3 481	10 511	5 218	1 800	981
Education science		2 312	1 461	-	-	1 161	720	1 151	741
Humanities & religion		1 777	1 044	-	-	1 572	947	205	97
Fine & applied arts		228	106	97	43	131	63	-	-
Law		467	235	-	-	423	224	44	11
Social & behav. sc.		2 319	1 216	48	37	2 198	1 151	73	28
Business administr.		5 791	2 998	4 212	2 190	1 511	792	68	16
Communic. & doc.		307	175	13	-	283	169	11	6
Home economics		-	-	-	-	-	-	-	-
Service trades		245	116	245	116	-	-	-	-
Natural science		1 394	667	210	136	1 148	515	36	16
Maths. & computer sc.		1 098	502	668	334	372	153	58	15
Health-related prg.		546	289	-	-	480	269	66	20
Engineering		2 752	409	1 836	283	877	113	39	13
Archit. & town plng.		538	142	375	102	157	39	6	1
Trade, craft & indust.		95	40	95	40	-	-	-	-
Transport & communic.		-	-	-	-	-	-	-	-
Agriculture		813	230	616	161	165	56	32	13
Other & not specified		204	50	160	39	33	7	11	4

Third level: graduates by level and field of study **3.12**
Troisième degré: diplómés par niveau et domaine d'études
Tercer grado: diplomados por nivel y sector de estudios

Country / Field of study — Pays / Domaine d'études — País / Sectores de estudios	Year Année Año	Graduates by ISCED level of programme — Diplômés par niveau de programmes de la CITE — Diplomados por nivel de programas de la CINE							
		All levels Tous niveaux Todos los niveles		Level 5 Niveau 5 Nivel 5		Level 6 Niveau 6 Nivel 6		Level 7 Niveau 7 Nivel 7	
		MF	F	MF	F	MF	F	MF	F
		(1)	(2)	(3)	(4)	(5)	(6)	(7)	(8)
Mongolia									
Total	1982	8 000	...	...	...	...	...	..	..
	1987	9 978	6 533	6 121	4 323	3 857	2 210	..	..
Total	1995	5 820	4 175	2 050	1 588	3 689	2 544	81	43
Education science		1 446	1 239	207	189	1 239	1 050	-	-
Humanities & religion		551	432	20	16	517	406	14	10
Fine & applied arts		244	95	167	60	77	35	-	-
Law		65	31	-	-	65	31	-	-
Social & behav. sc.		37	24	-	-	37	24	-	-
Business administr.		379	253	107	75	269	177	3	1
Communic. & doc.		99	77	66	57	33	20	-	-
Home economics		-	-	-	-	-	-	-	-
Service trades		13	13	13	13	-	-	-	-
Natural science		182	108	9	6	167	97	6	5
Maths. & computer sc.		70	33	-	-	65	33	5	-
Health-related prg.		1 270	1 114	775	747	472	351	23	16
Engineering		748	317	248	99	470	207	30	11
Archit. & town plng.		10	2	-	-	10	2	-	-
Trade, craft & indust.		200	194	200	194	-	-	-	-
Transport & communic.		110	47	110	47	-	-	-	-
Agriculture		265	166	112	76	153	90	-	-
Other & not specified		131	30	16	9	115	21	-	-
Oman‡									
Total	1988	2 404	872	2 404	872	-	-	-	-
Total	1992	1 879	883	1 265	577	558	268	56	38
Education science		1 582	793	1 265	577	261	178	56	38
Humanities & religion		37	16	-	-	37	16	-	-
Fine & applied arts		-	-	-	-	-	-	-	-
Law									
Social & behav. sc.		21	9	-	-	21	9	-	-
Business administr.		-	-	-	-	-	-	-	-
Communic. & doc.		51	17	-	-	51	17	-	-
Home economics		-	-	-	-	-	-	-	-
Service trades									
Natural science		53	29	-	-	53	29	-	-
Maths. & computer sc.		7	2	-	-	7	2	-	-
Health-related prg.		-	-	-	-	-	-	-	-
Engineering		69	1	-	-	69	1	-	-
Archit. & town plng.		-	-	-	-	-	-	-	-
Trade, craft & indust.		-	-	-	-	-	-	-	-
Transport & communic.		-	-	-	-	-	-	-	-
Agriculture		59	16	-	-	59	16	-	-
Other & not specified		-	-	-	-	-	-	-	-
Philippines‡									
Total	1981	208 767	120 052	...	...	...	...	...	...
	1985	254 899	142 289	...	...	...	...	...	...
	1991	277 322	161 803	...	...	...	...	...	...
Total	1994	342 015	...	...	...	...	...	...	...
Qatar‡									
Total	1981	357	224	-	-	301	196	56	28
	1986	840	451	./.	./.	738	400	102	51
	1992	1 055	762	./.	./.	1 001	725	54	37
Total	1994	1 041	774	115	71	921	698	5	5
Education science		465	400	58	43	402	352	5	5
Humanities & religion		271	216	15	7	256	209	-	-
Fine & applied arts		./.	./.	./.	./.	./.	./.	-	-
Law		./.	./.	-	-	./.	./.	-	-
Social & behav. sc.		./.	./.	-	-	./.	./.	-	-
Business administr.		73	32	-	-	73	32	-	-
Communic. & doc.		-	-	-	-	-	-	-	-
Home economics		-	-	-	-	-	-	-	-
Service trades		-	-	-	-	-	-	-	-
Natural science		143	105	-	-	143	105	-	-
Maths. & computer sc.		./.	./.	-	-	./.	./.	-	-
Health-related prg.		-	-	-	-	-	-	-	-
Engineering		47	-	-	-	47	-	-	-
Archit. & town plng.		-	-	-	-	-	-	-	-
Trade, craft & indust.		-	-	-	-	-	-	-	-
Transport & communic.		-	-	-	-	-	-	-	-
Agriculture		-	-	-	-	-	-	-	-
Other & not specified		42	21	42	21	-	-	-	-

3.12 Third level: graduates by level and field of study
Troisième degré: diplômés par niveau et domaine d'études
Tercer grado: diplomados por nivel y sector de estudios

Country Field of study Pays Domaine d'études País Sectores de estudios	Year Année Año	Graduates by ISCED level of programme Diplômés par niveau de programmes de la CITE Diplomados por nivel de programas de la CINE							
		All levels Tous niveaux Todos los niveles		Level 5 Niveau 5 Nivel 5		Level 6 Niveau 6 Nivel 6		Level 7 Niveau 7 Nivel 7	
		MF	F	MF	F	MF	F	MF	F
		(1)	(2)	(3)	(4)	(5)	(6)	(7)	(8)
Saudi Arabia‡									
Total	1981	8 188	1 840	1 917	310	6 271	1 530	./.	./.
	1986	18 988	8 845	3 548	1 349	14 735	7 311	705	185
	1990	22 782	10 458	6 926	2 885	15 273	7 431	583	142
Total	1994	27 684	11 715	5 341	3 415	21 373	7 945	970	355
Education science		13 306	8 291	3 411	3 411	9 659	4 724	236	156
Humanities & religion		6 753	2 122	55	4	6 154	1 932	544	186
Fine & applied arts		62	29	-	-	62	29	-	-
Law		-	-	-	-	-	-	-	-
Social & behav. sc.		173	16	-	-	165	12	8	4
Business administr.		1 992	257	17	-	1 944	255	31	2
Communic. & doc.		243	105	-	-	243	105	-	-
Home economics		30	30	-	-	30	30	-	-
Service trades		-	-	-	-	-	-	-	-
Natural science		1 130	490	-	-	1 093	488	37	2
Maths. & computer sc.		412	113	-	-	398	113	14	-
Health-related prg.		598	205	87	-	489	200	22	5
Engineering		833	-	104	-	667	-	62	-
Archit. & town plng.		74	-	-	-	67	-	7	-
Trade, craft & indust.		1 703	-	1 645	-	58	-	-	-
Transport & communic.		-	-	-	-	-	-	-	-
Agriculture		292	57	-	-	283	57	9	-
Other & not specified		83	-	22	-	61	-	-	-
Sri Lanka‡									
Total	1979	3 645	1 458	311	120	3 293	1 327	41	11
	1986	14 663	...	10 331	...	4 138	...	194	...
Total	1989	6 452	...	1 325	...	4 725	2 161	402	82
Education science		317	...	314	...	-	-	3	2
Humanities & religion		1 212	...	920	...	163	35	129	7
Fine & applied arts		1 487	892	-	-	1 487	892	-	-
Law		103	50	-	-	103	50	-	-
Social & behav. sc.		318	181	-	-	297	174	21	7
Business administr.		936	395	-	-	844	382	92	13
Communic. & doc.		8	4	-	-	8	4	-	-
Home economics		-	-	-	-	-	-	-	-
Service trades		-	-	-	-	-	-	-	-
Natural science		806	332	-	-	766	316	40	16
Maths. & computer sc.		22	11	-	-	22	11	-	-
Health-related prg.		452	174	-	-	375	147	77	27
Engineering		454	81	-	-	454	81	-	-
Archit. & town plng.		39	13	-	-	39	13	-	-
Trade, craft & indust.		91	...	91	...	-	-	-	-
Transport & communic.		-	-	-	-	-	-	-	-
Agriculture		207	66	-	-	167	56	40	10
Other & not specified		-	-	-	-	-	-	-	-
Syrian Arab Republic‡									
Total	1981	16 625	3 852	...	...	10 262	...	...	...
	1986	29 650	12 993	18 084	9 070	10 262	3 329	1 304	594
	1991	...	...	13 957	7 103	14 813	5 165	...	...
Total	1993	18 686	7 660	3 487	1 700	13 760	5 224	1 439	736
Education science		777	482	-	-	207	131	570	351
Humanities & religion		2 622	1 754	-	-	2 334	1 580	288	174
Fine & applied arts		148	55	-	-	148	55	-	-
Law		1 801	312	-	-	1 780	309	21	3
Social & behav. sc.		522	218	-	-	492	202	30	16
Business administr.		2 215	1 022	843	527	1 281	469	91	26
Communic. & doc.		106	45	-	-	106	45	-	-
Home economics		-	-	-	-	-	-	-	-
Service trades		-	-	-	-	-	-	-	-
Natural science		1 377	679	-	-	1 304	639	73	40
Maths. & computer sc.		23	7	-	-	23	7	-	-
Health-related prg.		3 573	1 508	1 064	559	2 340	886	169	63
Engineering		1 899	727	841	414	1 002	294	56	19
Archit. & town plng.		306	122	-	-	280	110	26	12
Trade, craft & indust.		2 148	396	302	30	1 804	357	42	9
Transport & communic.		-	-	-	-	-	-	-	-
Agriculture		963	319	376	162	527	137	60	20
Other & not specified		206	14	61	8	132	3	13	3

Third level: graduates by level and field of study **3.12**
Troisième degré: diplômés par niveau et domaine d'études
Tercer grado: diplomados por nivel y sector de estudios

Country Field of study Pays Domaine d'études País Sectores de estudios	Year Année Año	Graduates by ISCED level of programme Diplômés par niveau de programmes de la CITE Diplomados por nivel de programas de la CINE							
		All levels Tous niveaux Todos los niveles		Level 5 Niveau 5 Nivel 5		Level 6 Niveau 6 Nivel 6		Level 7 Niveau 7 Nivel 7	
		MF	F	MF	F	MF	F	MF	F
		(1)	(2)	(3)	(4)	(5)	(6)	(7)	(8)
Thailand									
Total	1993	209 162	117 273	87 388	47 349	116 301	67 843	5 473	2 081
Education science		31 565	19 154	2 341	941	27 621	17 394	1 603	819
Humanities & religion		4 884	3 743	-	-	4 718	3 642	166	101
Fine & applied arts		31 111	21 221	13 762	9 056	17 303	12 137	46	28
Law		5 582	983	-	-	5 494	969	88	14
Social & behav. sc.		7 341	3 082	-	-	6 812	2 888	529	194
Business administr.		60 639	45 812	35 539	29 059	23 840	16 471	1 260	282
Communic. & doc.		2 115	1 183	-	-	1 945	1 157	170	26
Home economics		2 774	2 687	2 259	2 185	513	500	2	2
Service trades		82	52	-	-	80	50	2	2
Natural science		11 834	5 301	4 155	1 819	7 554	3 408	125	74
Maths. & computer sc.		295	52	-	-	13	9	282	43
Health-related prg.		12 233	9 887	2 259	2 259	9 514	7 341	460	287
Engineering		30 854	1 510	23 718	941	6 794	523	342	46
Archit. & town plng.		306	102	-	-	258	90	48	12
Trade, craft & indust.		499	84	-	-	478	70	21	14
Transport & communic.		160	160	160	160	-	-	-	-
Agriculture		6 437	2 067	3 195	929	3 042	1 056	200	82
Other & not specified		451	193	-	-	322	138	129	55
Turkey									
Total	1986	61 098	21 271	14 551	5 165	43 297	14 983	3 250	1 123
	1991	91 317	31 979	16 640	5 251	67 215	24 143	7 462	2 585
Total	1994	124 861	51 256	36 486	18 623	80 392	29 541	7 983	3 092
Education science		15 818	6 838	27	27	15 181	6 540	610	271
Humanities & religion		5 746	2 498	169	31	4 876	2 232	701	235
Fine & applied arts		1 845	1 107	509	325	1 183	702	153	80
Law		2 590	823	233	110	2 256	674	101	39
Social & behav. sc.		19 413	6 520	1 681	552	16 576	5 470	1 156	498
Business administr.		13 573	5 956	6 389	3 486	6 844	2 347	340	123
Communic. & doc.		1 468	677	46	18	1 325	613	97	46
Home economics		999	901	836	744	160	154	3	3
Service trades		1 755	568	1 102	408	653	160	-	-
Natural science		4 577	2 215	19	12	4 114	2 012	444	191
Maths. & computer sc.		2 979	1 199	667	190	2 133	950	179	59
Health-related prg.		22 469	15 093	13 134	10 998	7 221	3 264	2 114	831
Engineering		21 849	3 708	10 016	1 130	10 561	2 224	1 272	354
Archit. & town plng.		1 631	871	89	66	1 349	682	193	123
Trade, craft & indust.		845	473	668	364	177	109	-	-
Transport & communic.		24	2	9	-	-	-	15	2
Agriculture		5 350	1 807	892	162	3 853	1 408	605	237
Other & not specified		1 930	-	-	-	1 930	-	-	-
United Arab Emirates‡									
Total	1981	783	427	...	...	...	...	...	...
	1986	2 337	1 114	500	450	1 837	664	...	...
	1991	1 428	1 016	277	225	1 122	762	29	29
Total	1992	1 371	922	64	32	1 288	881	19	9
Education science		496	424	-	-	480	418	16	6
Humanities & religion		100	59	-	-	100	59	-	-
Fine & applied arts		18	18	-	-	18	18	-	-
Law		34	6	-	-	34	6	-	-
Social & behav. sc.		158	112	-	-	155	109	3	3
Business administr.		307	170	42	32	265	138	-	-
Communic. & doc.		35	11	-	-	35	11	-	-
Home economics		-	-	-	-	-	-	-	-
Service trades		-	-	-	-	-	-	-	-
Natural science		90	70	-	-	90	70	-	-
Maths. & computer sc.		43	34	-	-	43	34	-	-
Health-related prg.		-	-	-	-	-	-	-	-
Engineering		57	8	22	-	35	8	-	-
Archit. & town plng.		10	1	-	-	10	1	-	-
Trade, craft & indust.		-	-	-	-	-	-	-	-
Transport & communic.		-	-	-	-	-	-	-	-
Agriculture		23	9	-	-	23	9	-	-
Other & not specified		-	-	-	-	-	-	-	-

3.12 Third level: graduates by level and field of study
Troisième degré: diplômés par niveau et domaine d'études
Tercer grado: diplomados por nivel y sector de estudios

Country Field of study Pays Domaine d'études País Sectores de estudios	Year Année Año	Graduates by ISCED level of programme Diplômés par niveau de programmes de la CITE Diplomados por nivel de programas de la CINE							
		All levels Tous niveaux Todos los niveles		Level 5 Niveau 5 Nivel 5		Level 6 Niveau 6 Nivel 6		Level 7 Niveau 7 Nivel 7	
		MF	F	MF	F	MF	F	MF	F
		(1)	(2)	(3)	(4)	(5)	(6)	(7)	(8)
Yemen									
Total	1992	9 080	...	3 267	...	4 698	1 194	1 115	...
Education science		5 413	1 233	2 532	347	2 418	800	463	86
Humanities & religion		380	123	-	-	240	103	140	20
Fine & applied arts		-	-	-	-	-	-	-	-
Law		558	...	-	-	488	36	70	...
Social & behav. sc.		110	35	-	-	110	35	-	-
Business administr.		1 697	...	562	...	870	132	265	15
Communic. & doc.		26	7	26	7	-	-	-	-
Home economics		-	-	-	-	-	-	-	-
Service trades		-	-	-	-	-	-	-	-
Natural science		140	43	-	-	110	40	30	3
Maths. & computer sc.		28	10	-	-	28	10	-	-
Health-related prg.		279	...	147	...	70	6	62	...
Engineering		193	...	-	-	140	20	53	...
Archit. & town plng.		38	11	-	-	38	11	-	-
Trade, craft & indust.		-	-	-	-	-	-	-	-
Transport & communic.		-	-	-	-	-	-	-	-
Agriculture		218	...	-	-	186	1	32	...
Other & not specified		-	-	-	-	-	-	-	-
Palestine									
Gaza Strip									
Total	1986	353	...	106	...	247	...	-	-
	1990	1 245	...	1 104	-	141	-	-	-
Total	1994	747	125	483	37	264	88	-	-
Education science		150	47	-	-	150	47	-	-
Humanities & religion		85	34	19	5	66	29	-	-
Fine & applied arts		-	-	-	-	-	-	-	-
Law		-	-	-	-	-	-	-	-
Social & behav. sc.		8	4	-	-	8	4	-	-
Business administr.		63	22	43	19	20	3	-	-
Communic. & doc.		-	-	-	-	-	-	-	-
Home economics		-	-	-	-	-	-	-	-
Service trades		-	-	-	-	-	-	-	-
Natural science		20	5	-	-	20	5	-	-
Maths. & computer sc.		26	3	26	3	-	-	-	-
Health-related prg.		62	10	62	10	-	-	-	-
Engineering		4	-	4	-	-	-	-	-
Archit. & town plng.		8	-	8	-	-	-	-	-
Trade, craft & indust.		-	-	-	-	-	-	-	-
Transport & communic.		-	-	-	-	-	-	-	-
Agriculture		-	-	-	-	-	-	-	-
Other & not specified		321	-	321	-	-	-	-	-
West Bank									
Total	1986	1 886	...	523	...	1 363	...	-	-
	1991	3 652	1 506	901	505	2 751	1 001	-	-
Total	1994	2 621	1 300	1 101	560	1 516	739	4	1
Education science		406	265	129	119	273	145	4	1
Humanities & religion		678	357	200	111	478	246	-	-
Fine & applied arts		16	9	14	9	2	-	-	-
Law		-	-	-	-	-	-	-	-
Social & behav. sc.		182	88	50	17	132	71	-	-
Business administr.		465	173	296	106	169	67	-	-
Communic. & doc.		-	-	-	-	-	-	-	-
Home economics		18	18	18	18	-	-	-	-
Service trades		18	8	-	-	18	8	-	-
Natural science		165	74	13	13	152	61	-	-
Maths. & computer sc.		195	93	147	77	48	16	-	-
Health-related prg.		323	194	136	78	187	116	-	-
Engineering		117	4	80	-	37	4	-	-
Archit. & town plng.		15	8	5	5	10	3	-	-
Trade, craft & indust.		-	-	-	-	-	-	-	-
Transport & communic.		-	-	-	-	-	-	-	-
Agriculture		10	2	-	-	10	2	-	-
Other & not specified		13	7	13	7	-	-	-	-

Third level: graduates by level and field of study 3.12
Troisième degré: diplomés par niveau et domaine d'études
Tercer grado: diplomados por nivel y sector de estudios

Country Field of study / Pays Domaine d'études / País Sectores de estudios	Year Année Año	Graduates by ISCED level of programme Diplômés par niveau de programmes de la CITE Diplomados por nivel de programas de la CINE							
		All levels Tous niveaux Todos los niveles		Level 5 Niveau 5 Nivel 5		Level 6 Niveau 6 Nivel 6		Level 7 Niveau 7 Nivel 7	
		MF	F	MF	F	MF	F	MF	F
		(1)	(2)	(3)	(4)	(5)	(6)	(7)	(8)
Europe									
Albania‡									
Total	1983	3 800	1 950	-	-	3 800	1 950	-	-
	1986	3 623	1 626	-	-	3 623	1 626	-	-
	1990	3 353	1 890	-	-	3 353	1 890	-	-
Total	1994	3 963	2 106	-	-	3 963	2 106	-	-
Education science		1 004	683	-	-	1 004	683	-	-
Humanities & religion		363	257	-	-	363	257	-	-
Fine & applied arts		124	42	-	-	124	42	-	-
Law		75	38	-	-	75	38	-	-
Social & behav. sc.		165	128	-	-	165	128	-	-
Business administr.		113	74	-	-	113	74	-	-
Communic. & doc.		-	-	-	-	-	-	-	-
Home economics		57	24	-	-	57	24	-	-
Service trades		50	37	-	-	50	37	-	-
Natural science		121	42	-	-	121	42	-	-
Maths. & computer sc.		19	10	-	-	19	10	-	-
Health-related prg.		445	204	-	-	445	204	-	-
Engineering		535	164	-	-	535	164	-	-
Archit. & town plng.		15	8	-	-	15	8	-	-
Trade, craft & indust.		25	17	-	-	25	17	-	-
Transport & communic.		-	-	-	-	-	-	-	-
Agriculture		756	354	-	-	756	354	-	-
Other & not specified		96	24	-	-	96	24	-	-
Austria‡									
Total	1981	8 921	3 010	28	6	7 634	2 637	1 259	367
	1986	14 467	7 200	4 783	3 495	9 001	3 540	683	165
	1991	16 707	8 039	5 042	3 166	10 457	4 553	1 208	320
Total	1994	18 687	9 446	5 376	3 789	11 730	5 200	1 581	457
Education science		3 462	2 733	2 922	2 368	487	340	53	25
Humanities & religion		1 707	1 045	16	14	1 497	951	194	80
Fine & applied arts		821	468	46	35	746	415	29	18
Law		1 470	562	-	-	1 237	495	233	67
Social & behav. sc.		1 371	839	377	267	899	529	95	43
Business administr.		2 390	987	257	155	1 979	807	154	25
Communic. & doc.		247	163	-	-	234	157	13	6
Home economics		29	28	10	9	15	15	4	4
Service trades		318	226	318	226	-	-	-	-
Natural science		894	295	-	-	644	236	250	59
Maths. & computer sc.		759	163	43	17	633	140	83	6
Health-related prg.		1 789	1 104	437	372	1 327	720	25	12
Engineering		2 169	355	762	241	1 146	77	261	37
Archit. & town plng.		360	106	-	-	347	105	13	1
Trade, craft & indust.		54	49	54	49	-	-	-	-
Transport & communic.		-	-	-	-	-	-	-	-
Agriculture		709	285	87	36	478	190	144	59
Other & not specified		138	38	47	-	61	23	30	15
Belarus‡									
Total	1981	31 300	...	...	...	...	...	...	...
	1991	29 348	...	...	...	28 600	...	748	...
Total	1994	36 476	...	...	...	35 800	...	676	...
Education science		7 246	...	...	...	7 200	...	46	...
Humanities & religion		6 373	...	...	...	6 200	...	173	...
Fine & applied arts		300	...	...	...	300	...	./.	...
Law		./.	...	...	...	./.	...	./.	...
Social & behav. sc.		3 508	...	...	...	3 400	...	108	...
Business administr.		./.	...	...	...	./.	...	./.	...
Communic. & doc.		./.	...	...	...	./.	...	./.	...
Home economics		./.	...	...	...	./.	...	./.	...
Service trades		./.	...	...	...	./.	...	./.	...
Natural science		./.	...	...	...	./.	...	./.	...
Maths. & computer sc.		./.	...	...	...	./.	...	./.	...
Health-related prg.		2 782	...	...	...	2 700	...	82	...
Engineering		11 533	...	...	...	11 300	...	233	...
Archit. & town plng.		./.	...	...	...	./.	...	./.	...
Trade, craft & indust.		./.	...	...	...	./.	...	./.	...
Transport & communic.		./.	...	...	...	./.	...	./.	...
Agriculture		3 634	...	...	...	3 600	...	34	...
Other & not specified		1 100	...	...	...	1 100	...	-	...

3.12 Third level: graduates by level and field of study
Troisième degré: diplômés par niveau et domaine d'études
Tercer grado: diplomados por nivel y sector de estudios

Country Field of study Pays Domaine d'études País Sectores de estudios	Year Année Año	Graduates by ISCED level of programme Diplômés par niveau de programmes de la CITE Diplomados por nivel de programas de la CINE							
		All levels Tous niveaux Todos los niveles		Level 5 Niveau 5 Nivel 5		Level 6 Niveau 6 Nivel 6		Level 7 Niveau 7 Nivel 7	
		MF	F	MF	F	MF	F	MF	F
		(1)	(2)	(3)	(4)	(5)	(6)	(7)	(8)
Belgium‡									
Total	1981	16 922	6 802	...	...	...	...	...	...
	1986	48 626	22 797	24 915	13 566	23 711	9 231	./.	./.
Total	1990	55 897	28 850	30 646	18 199	20 992	9 210	4 259	1 441
Education science		7 479	5 233	5 314	3 928	2 056	1 272	109	33
Humanities & religion		1 997	1 204	18	12	1 686	1 066	293	126
Fine & applied arts		1 085	619	790	418	256	181	39	20
Law		2 043	931	-	-	1 678	779	365	152
Social & behav. sc.		490	325	490	325	-	-	-	-
Business administr.		21 605	11 673	14 769	8 718	5 409	2 500	1 427	455
Communic. & doc.		626	392	24	19	496	291	106	82
Home economics		245	234	214	206	31	28	-	-
Service trades		12	8	12	8	-	-	-	-
Natural science		1 227	531	-	-	797	404	430	127
Maths. & computer sc.		904	244	220	40	495	156	189	48
Health-related prg.		7 470	5 247	4 647	3 779	2 243	1 240	580	228
Engineering		5 097	825	43	5	4 671	788	383	32
Archit. & town plng.		455	163	12	2	396	136	47	25
Trade, craft & indust.		3 630	624	3 615	624	15	-	-	-
Transport & communic.		-	-	-	-	-	-	-	-
Agriculture		869	244	478	115	245	94	146	35
Other & not specified		663	353	-	-	518	275	145	78
Bulgaria									
Total	1981	25 756	15 837	7 377	5 845	18 164	9 899	215	93
	1986	20 374	11 488	3 455	2 607	16 312	8 658	607	223
	1992	31 361	18 098	8 033	5 893	22 825	12 080	503	125
Total	1995	30 403	18 218	8 196	6 217	21 951	11 912	256	89
Education science		5 909	4 784	1 826	1 443	4 083	3 341	-	-
Humanities & religion		1 437	1 134	187	171	1 225	947	25	16
Fine & applied arts		483	202	-	-	481	200	2	2
Law		382	196	-	-	378	196	4	-
Social & behav. sc.		512	305	-	-	478	292	34	13
Business administr.		4 180	2 531	614	483	3 566	2 048	-	-
Communic. & doc.		180	98	25	25	155	73	-	-
Home economics		-	-	-	-	-	-	-	-
Service trades		392	308	307	254	85	54	-	-
Natural science		528	316	-	-	462	290	66	26
Maths. & computer sc.		504	256	-	-	493	254	11	2
Health-related prg.		4 885	3 804	3 094	2 829	1 768	965	23	10
Engineering		7 484	3 532	1 585	917	5 823	2 598	76	17
Archit. & town plng.		86	35	-	-	85	35	1	-
Trade, craft & indust.		-	-	-	-	-	-	-	-
Transport & communic.		689	241	216	77	468	164	5	-
Agriculture		1 057	457	-	-	1 048	454	9	3
Other & not specified		1 695	19	342	18	1 353	1	-	-
Croatia‡									
Total	1981	14 844	...	...	...	...	...	...	...
	1986	13 105	...	...	...	...	...	...	...
	1990	11 518	...	...	...	...	...	...	...
Total	1995	9 304	5 157	2 853	1 553	5 638	3 227	813	377
Education science		1 150	986	509	486	621	484	20	16
Humanities & religion		396	245	1	1	350	211	45	33
Fine & applied arts		143	96	22	20	111	70	10	6
Law		568	375	125	98	421	270	22	7
Social & behav. sc.		252	150	-	-	152	107	100	43
Business administr.		1 486	1 065	322	208	1 147	845	17	12
Communic. & doc.		50	39	-	-	50	39	-	-
Home economics		24	22	-	-	24	22	-	-
Service trades		166	110	166	110	-	-	-	-
Natural science		251	139	-	-	105	69	146	70
Maths. & computer sc.		138	44	1	1	116	36	21	7
Health-related prg.		1 188	814	324	277	643	420	221	117
Engineering		1 973	500	587	108	1 261	355	125	37
Archit. & town plng.		137	94	25	13	109	80	3	1
Trade, craft & indust.		163	109	163	109	-	-	-	-
Transport & communic.		261	57	261	57	-	-	-	-
Agriculture		536	203	87	35	377	141	72	27
Other & not specified		422	109	260	30	151	78	11	1

Third level: graduates by level and field of study **3.12**
Troisième degré: diplômés par niveau et domaine d'études
Tercer grado: diplomados por nivel y sector de estudios

Country Field of study Pays Domaine d'études País Sectores de estudios	Year Année Año	Graduates by ISCED level of programme Diplômés par niveau de programmes de la CITE Diplomados por nivel de programas de la CINE							
		All levels Tous niveaux Todos los niveles		Level 5 Niveau 5 Nivel 5		Level 6 Niveau 6 Nivel 6		Level 7 Niveau 7 Nivel 7	
		MF	F	MF	F	MF	F	MF	F
		(1)	(2)	(3)	(4)	(5)	(6)	(7)	(8)
Czech Republic‡									
Total	1992	18 160	8 551	...	...	...	...	...	...
Total	1995	19 684	9 535	...	...	19 566	9 512	118	23
Education science		4 002	2 837	...	...	4 001	2 837	1	-
Humanities & religion		515	258	...	...	506	256	9	2
Fine & applied arts		433	183	...	...	432	182	1	1
Law		705	386	...	...	698	386	7	-
Social & behav. sc.		363	242	...	...	354	241	9	1
Business administr.		3 442	2 070	...	...	3 441	2 070	1	-
Communic. & doc.		196	120	...	...	196	120	-	-
Home economics		-	-	...	...	-	-	-	-
Service trades		-	-	...	...	-	-	-	-
Natural science		369	196	...	...	344	188	25	8
Maths. & computer sc.		537	129	...	...	519	126	18	3
Health-related prg.		1 772	1 117	...	...	1 769	1 114	3	3
Engineering		5 574	1 315	...	...	5 532	1 310	42	5
Archit. & town plng.		164	75	...	...	164	75	-	-
Trade, craft & indust.		-	-	...	...	-	-	-	-
Transport & communic.		28	6	...	...	28	6	-	-
Agriculture		1 448	515	...	...	1 447	515	1	-
Other & not specified		136	86	...	...	135	86	1	-
Denmark‡									
Total	1981	18 343	9 968	7 580	5 319	10 763	4 649	./.	./.
	1986	18 891	10 253	8 682	5 650	10 209	4 603	./.	./.
	1991	22 525	11 881	7 807	4 186	14 718	7 695	./.	./.
Total	1992	22 840	12 265	7 270	4 039	15 570	8 226	./.	./.
Education science		4 171	3 278	2 656	2 231	1 515	1 047	./.	./.
Humanities & religion		1 655	1 372	225	210	1 430	1 162	./.	./.
Fine & applied arts		394	246	201	134	193	112	./.	./.
Law		312	188	-	-	312	188	./.	./.
Social & behav. sc.		924	436	105	51	819	385	./.	./.
Business administr.		3 628	1 382	726	424	2 902	958	./.	./.
Communic. & doc.		349	215	20	14	329	201	./.	./.
Home economics		-	-	-	-	-	-	-	-
Service trades		60	60	60	60	-	-	-	-
Natural science		267	101	-	-	267	101	./.	./.
Maths. & computer sc.		276	73	-	-	276	73	./.	./.
Health-related prg.		3 656	3 218	442	406	3 214	2 812	./.	./.
Engineering		3 786	823	917	252	2 869	571	./.	./.
Archit. & town plng.		258	122	33	13	225	109	./.	./.
Trade, craft & indust.		1 044	108	1 044	108	-	-	-	-
Transport & communic.		59	1	59	1	-	-	-	-
Agriculture		611	226	229	31	382	195	./.	./.
Other & not specified		1 390	416	553	104	837	312	./.	./.
Estonia‡									
Total	1993	2 988	1 804	116	114	2 872	1 690	./.	./.
Total	1995	3 254	1 892	310	278	2 772	1 537	172	77
Education science		548	474	196	190	329	269	23	15
Humanities & religion		169	118	3	-	147	107	19	11
Fine & applied arts		220	131	53	34	164	94	3	3
Law		143	64	-	-	142	64	1	-
Social & behav. sc.		96	58	-	-	69	47	27	11
Business administr.		526	365	-	-	518	361	8	4
Communic. & doc.		104	93	48	47	53	43	3	3
Home economics		-	-	-	-	-	-	-	-
Service trades		51	40	-	-	51	40	-	-
Natural science		130	58	-	-	92	49	38	9
Maths. & computer sc.		48	27	-	-	33	22	15	5
Health-related prg.		291	211	-	-	284	205	7	6
Engineering		587	103	-	-	576	101	11	2
Archit. & town plng.		21	6	-	-	21	6	-	-
Trade, craft & indust.		-	-	-	-	-	-	-	-
Transport & communic.		20	-	-	-	20	-	-	-
Agriculture		207	96	-	-	199	90	8	6
Other & not specified		93	48	10	7	74	39	9	2

3.12   Third level: graduates by level and field of study
Troisième degré: diplômés par niveau et domaine d'études
Tercer grado: diplomados por nivel y sector de estudios

Country Field of study Pays Domaine d'études País Sectores de estudios	Year Année Año	Graduates by ISCED level of programme Diplômés par niveau de programmes de la CITE Diplomados por nivel de programas de la CINE							
		All levels Tous niveaux Todos los niveles		Level 5 Niveau 5 Nivel 5		Level 6 Niveau 6 Nivel 6		Level 7 Niveau 7 Nivel 7	
		MF	F	MF	F	MF	F	MF	F
		(1)	(2)	(3)	(4)	(5)	(6)	(7)	(8)
Finland									
Total	1981	26 321	13 519	15 635	8 021	10 076	5 364	610	134
	1986	22 420	11 566	12 667	6 640	9 036	4 726	717	200
	1991	26 235	14 949	12 139	8 129	12 386	6 153	1 710	667
Total	1993	30 830	18 259	14 826	10 578	14 122	6 919	1 882	762
Education science		3 982	3 132	337	234	3 586	2 865	59	33
Humanities & religion		1 142	784	18	14	945	698	179	72
Fine & applied arts		665	462	473	348	180	106	12	8
Law		464	214	-	-	434	208	30	6
Social & behav. sc.		954	584	-	-	807	515	147	69
Business administr.		1 934	1 148	335	315	1 515	809	84	24
Communic. & doc.		-	-	-	-	-	-	-	-
Home economics		464	450	456	442	8	8	-	-
Service trades		613	495	613	495	-	-	-	-
Natural science		871	421	-	-	626	321	245	100
Maths. & computer sc.		1 924	446	786	295	1 052	141	86	10
Health-related prg.		10 058	8 768	8 501	7 845	807	548	750	375
Engineering		6 224	865	2 455	348	3 544	477	225	40
Archit. & town plng.		113	45	-	-	104	43	9	2
Trade, craft & indust.		-	-	-	-	-	-	-	-
Transport & communic.		-	-	-	-	-	-	-	-
Agriculture		1 357	437	834	242	469	174	54	21
Other & not specified		65	8	18	-	45	6	2	2
France									
Total	1981	266 037	...	47 904	...	164 888	78 596	53 245	18 789
	1986	312 096	153 379	126 774	67 199	133 319	65 170	52 003	21 010
	1991	462 310	...	204 644	119 812	194 928	...	62 738	...
Total	1992	484 662	...	214 437	123 553	201 167	...	69 058	...
Germany									
Total	1993	309 367	137 720	...	...	...	...	...	...
Education science		5 314	3 898	...	...	...	...	...	...
Humanities & religion		18 419	12 411	...	...	...	...	...	...
Fine & applied arts		6 947	3 967	...	...	...	...	...	...
Law		10 083	4 089	...	...	...	...	...	...
Social & behav. sc.		40 303	17 815	...	...	...	...	...	...
Business administr.		14 257	6 496	...	...	...	...	...	...
Communic. & doc.		1 277	819	...	...	...	...	...	...
Home economics		2 735	2 551	...	...	...	...	...	...
Service trades		2 564	1 325	...	...	...	...	...	...
Natural science		17 028	4 942	...	...	...	...	...	...
Maths. & computer sc.		11 762	3 868	...	...	...	...	...	...
Health-related prg.		59 390	39 988	...	...	...	...	...	...
Engineering		68 112	6 784	...	...	...	...	...	...
Archit. & town plng.		5 364	2 124	...	...	...	...	...	...
Trade, craft & indust.		5 367	375	...	...	...	...	...	...
Transport & communic.		314	3	...	...	...	...	...	...
Agriculture		12 380	3 600	...	...	...	...	...	...
Other & not specified		27 751	22 665	...	...	...	...	...	...
Former German Democratic Rep.									
Total	1981	110 398	63 966	38 814	18 888	43 542	32 138	28 042	12 940
	1986	125 426	67 993	48 689	20 178	45 100	33 809	31 637	14 006
Total	1988	128 588	67 533	50 776	19 831	43 020	31 309	34 792	16 393
Education science		14 128	11 104	-	-	6 960	5 931	7 168	5 173
Humanities & religion		2 384	1 295	-	-	281	138	2 103	1 157
Fine & applied arts		962	463	80	21	205	153	677	289
Law		897	282	-	-	-	-	897	282
Social & behav. sc.		5 759	3 531	-	-	3 119	2 214	2 640	1 317
Business administr.		8 422	6 224	145	128	5 111	4 158	3 166	1 938
Communic. & doc.		617	452	-	-	419	359	198	93
Home economics		-	-	-	-	-	-	-	-
Service trades		1 447	1 014	1 447	1 014	-	-	-	-
Natural science		1 825	688	-	-	-	-	1 825	688
Maths. & computer sc.		1 131	521	223	152	240	137	668	232
Health-related prg.		18 512	15 962	-	-	14 341	13 736	4 171	2 226
Engineering		18 862	5 263	-	-	9 733	3 151	9 129	2 112
Archit. & town plng.		278	110	-	-	-	-	278	110
Trade, craft & indust.		18 132	3 495	18 132	3 495	-	-	-	-
Transport & communic.		1 631	466	1 631	466	-	-	-	-
Agriculture		6 319	2 997	1 836	889	2 611	1 332	1 872	776
Other & not specified		27 282	13 666	27 282	13 666	-	-	-	-

Third level: graduates by level and field of study 3.12
Troisième degré: diplômés par niveau et domaine d'études
Tercer grado: diplomados por nivel y sector de estudios

Country / Field of study / Pays / Domaine d'études / País / Sectores de estudios	Year / Année / Año	Graduates by ISCED level of programme / Diplômés par niveau de programmes de la CITE / Diplomados por nivel de programas de la CINE							
		All levels Tous niveaux Todos los niveles		Level 5 Niveau 5 Nivel 5		Level 6 Niveau 6 Nivel 6		Level 7 Niveau 7 Nivel 7	
		MF	F	MF	F	MF	F	MF	F
		(1)	(2)	(3)	(4)	(5)	(6)	(7)	(8)
Federal Republic of Germany									
Total	1981	190 706	86 103	70 163	45 046	108 260	38 566	12 283	2 491
	1985	230 237	107 084	83 317	53 068	131 969	50 418	14 951	3 598
Total	1991	256 703	109 613	84 762	45 808	152 919	58 432	19 022	5 373
Education science		14 142	9 839	303	228	13 451	9 403	388	208
Humanities & religion		10 552	6 223	594	545	8 539	5 158	1 419	520
Fine & applied arts		5 357	2 944	535	296	4 739	2 628	83	20
Law		9 481	3 878	-	-	8 532	3 703	949	175
Social & behav. sc.		35 906	15 222	-	-	34 531	14 937	1 375	285
Business administr.		12 665	5 483	3 284	1 203	9 376	4 279	5	1
Communic. & doc.		1 112	716	-	-	1 083	705	29	11
Home economics		3 377	3 253	2 507	2 502	793	702	77	49
Service trades		328	137	328	137	-	-	-	-
Natural science		15 644	4 414	-	-	11 221	3 390	4 423	1 024
Maths. & computer sc.		7 389	1 529	966	322	6 005	1 151	418	56
Health-related prg.		52 282	35 582	32 176	27 071	12 914	5 947	7 192	2 564
Engineering		51 257	3 514	18 743	1 125	30 910	2 321	1 604	68
Archit. & town plng.		5 159	2 083	-	-	5 101	2 074	58	9
Trade, craft & indust.		5 139	508	5 139	508	-	-	-	-
Transport & communic.		192	6	192	6	-	-	-	-
Agriculture		12 290	2 579	6 617	525	4 713	1 680	960	374
Other & not specified		14 431	11 703	13 378	11 340	1 011	354	42	9
Greece									
Total	1981	24 649	10 306	9 178	3 950	14 914	6 240	557	116
	1986	27 309	15 070	11 258	7 236	15 369	7 606	682	228
	1991	28 504	15 056	8 782	4 779	18 432	9 832	1 290	445
Total	1993	26 581	15 058	7 170	3 915	18 556	10 838	855	305
Education science		6 910	5 489	-	-	6 823	5 439	87	50
Humanities & religion		838	443	-	-	803	433	35	10
Fine & applied arts		264	179	168	114	96	65	-	-
Law		1 334	830	-	-	1 227	771	107	59
Social & behav. sc.		223	152	-	-	221	150	2	2
Business administr.		3 357	1 708	848	449	2 491	1 252	18	7
Communic. & doc.		-	-	-	-	-	-	-	-
Home economics		112	107	112	107	-	-	-	-
Service trades		1 723	978	1 723	978	-	-	-	-
Natural science		1 552	644	-	-	1 351	584	201	60
Maths. & computer sc.		779	315	60	13	710	300	9	2
Health-related prg.		4 332	2 598	2 082	1 637	1 950	868	300	93
Engineering		3 394	788	1 539	342	1 785	433	70	13
Archit. & town plng.		218	123	-	-	217	123	1	-
Trade, craft & indust.		-	-	-	-	-	-	-	-
Transport & communic.		-	-	-	-	-	-	-	-
Agriculture		1 022	409	500	210	509	194	13	5
Other & not specified		523	295	138	65	373	226	12	4
Holy See‡									
Total	1981	2 203	518	276	200	656	67	1 271	251
	1986	2 848	978	1 540	799	977	163	331	16
	1991	2 618	500	603	241	924	157	1 091	102
Total	1993	2 994	596	647	213	932	183	1 415	200
Education science		285	144	40	21	21	18	224	105
Humanities & religion		2 338	399	572	176	845	158	921	65
Fine & applied arts		23	10	4	2	-	-	19	8
Law		264	9	11	1	43	3	210	5
Social & behav. sc.		25	8	-	-	5	2	20	6
Business administr.		-	-	-	-	-	-	-	-
Communic. & doc.		-	-	-	-	-	-	-	-
Home economics		-	-	-	-	-	-	-	-
Service trades		-	-	-	-	-	-	-	-
Natural science		-	-	-	-	-	-	-	-
Maths. & computer sc.		-	-	-	-	-	-	-	-
Health-related prg.		-	-	-	-	-	-	-	-
Engineering		-	-	-	-	-	-	-	-
Archit. & town plng.		-	-	-	-	-	-	-	-
Trade, craft & indust.		-	-	-	-	-	-	-	-
Transport & communic.		-	-	-	-	-	-	-	-
Agriculture		-	-	-	-	-	-	-	-
Other & not specified		59	26	20	13	18	2	21	11

3.12 Third level: graduates by level and field of study
Troisième degré: diplomés par niveau et domaine d'études
Tercer grado: diplomados por nivel y sector de estudios

Country / Field of study Pays / Domaine d'études País / Sectores de estudios	Year Année Año	Graduates by ISCED level of programme Diplômés par niveau de programmes de la CITE Diplomados por nivel de programas de la CINE							
		All levels Tous niveaux Todos los niveles		Level 5 Niveau 5 Nivel 5		Level 6 Niveau 6 Nivel 6		Level 7 Niveau 7 Nivel 7	
		MF	F	MF	F	MF	F	MF	F
		(1)	(2)	(3)	(4)	(5)	(6)	(7)	(8)
Hungary‡									
Total	1981	26 863	14 850	12 976	7 681	4 280	3 151	9 607	4 018
	1986	25 137	14 393	12 694	7 863	4 249	3 075	8 194	3 455
	1991	24 103	13 292	11 635	6 578	12 468	6 714	./.	./.
Total	1994	23 615	12 965	10 674	6 149	12 941	6 816	./.	./.
Education science		9 918	7 348	3 720	3 255	6 198	4 093	./.	./.
Humanities & religion		888	522	113	32	775	490	./.	./.
Fine & applied arts		287	137	6	-	281	137	./.	./.
Law		1 225	645	352	217	873	428	./.	./.
Social & behav. sc.		160	78	31	9	129	69	./.	./.
Business administr.		2 360	1 474	1 938	1 263	422	211	./.	./.
Communic. & doc.		-	-	-	-	-	-	-	-
Home economics		-	-	-	-	-	-	-	-
Service trades		172	110	172	110	-	-	-	-
Natural science		243	106	-	-	243	106	./.	./.
Maths. & computer sc.		279	74	190	56	89	18	./.	./.
Health-related prg.		1 845	1 147	464	441	1 381	706	./.	./.
Engineering		1 791	274	466	79	1 325	195	./.	./.
Archit. & town plng.		749	173	425	113	324	60	./.	./.
Trade, craft & indust.		1 473	293	1 399	252	74	41	./.	./.
Transport & communic.		177	46	136	41	41	5	./.	./.
Agriculture		1 070	347	429	165	641	182	./.	./.
Other & not specified		978	191	833	116	145	75	./.	./.
Ireland‡									
Total	1981	8 674	3 952	820	543	5 115	2 075	2 739	1 334
	1987	15 785	4 730	5 031	254	9 541	4 090	1 213	386
	1991	22 725	10 613	8 843	3 880	11 925	5 936	1 957	797
Total	1992	25 643	12 157	9 737	4 269	13 449	6 861	2 457	1 027
Education science		1 485	1 077	64	58	1 371	991	50	28
Humanities & religion		3 795	2 282	101	24	3 283	2 026	411	232
Fine & applied arts		870	554	576	364	224	148	70	42
Law		411	208	-	-	267	139	144	69
Social & behav. sc.		1 145	758	235	206	614	410	296	142
Business administr.		6 391	3 506	3 596	2 228	2 285	1 111	510	167
Communic. & doc.		211	148	45	30	139	96	27	22
Home economics		-	-	-	-	-	-	-	-
Service trades		62	58	62	58	-	-	-	-
Natural science		3 115	1 642	1 311	725	1 442	745	362	172
Maths. & computer sc.		1 657	567	702	260	846	286	109	21
Health-related prg.		948	496	52	50	774	390	122	56
Engineering		4 487	416	2 700	179	1 553	211	234	26
Archit. & town plng.		220	60	120	17	79	31	21	12
Trade, craft & indust.		-	-	-	-	-	-	-	-
Transport & communic.		-	-	-	-	-	-	-	-
Agriculture		448	156	58	24	289	94	101	38
Other & not specified		398	229	115	46	283	183	-	-
Italy									
Total	1982	87 731	37 910	5 355	3 005	70 512	31 088	11 864	3 817
	1986	91 643	40 994	4 304	2 567	72 970	33 387	14 369	5 040
	1992	106 043	...	1 765	1 229	90 669	45 530	13 609	...
Total	1994	116 305	59 666	2 116	1 464	98 961	51 748	15 228	6 454
Education science		3 177	2 774	-	-	2 908	2 544	269	230
Humanities & religion		15 536	12 998	-	-	14 651	12 272	885	726
Fine & applied arts		2 448	1 648	2 116	1 464	332	184	-	-
Law		14 224	7 370	-	-	13 961	7 239	263	131
Social & behav. sc.		21 151	10 380	-	-	20 344	10 091	807	289
Business administr.		3 005	1 210	-	-	3 005	1 210	-	-
Communic. & doc.		87	47	-	-	52	28	35	19
Home economics		-	-	-	-	-	-	-	-
Service trades		-	-	-	-	-	-	-	-
Natural science		7 446	3 907	-	-	7 253	3 797	193	110
Maths. & computer sc.		3 631	1 844	-	-	3 607	1 830	24	14
Health-related prg.		27 353	12 574	-	-	15 398	7 870	11 955	4 704
Engineering		10 315	1 827	-	-	10 258	1 810	57	17
Archit. & town plng.		4 738	2 132	-	-	4 680	2 101	58	31
Trade, craft & indust.		-	-	-	-	-	-	-	-
Transport & communic.		-	-	-	-	-	-	-	-
Agriculture		3 154	940	-	-	2 491	769	663	171
Other & not specified		40	15	-	-	21	3	19	12

Third level: graduates by level and field of study **3.12**
Troisième degré: diplômés par niveau et domaine d'études
Tercer grado: diplomados por nivel y sector de estudios

Country / Field of study — Pays / Domaine d'études — País / Sectores de estudios	Year Année Año	Graduates by ISCED level of programme — Diplômés par niveau de programmes de la CITE — Diplomados por nivel de programas de la CINE							
		All levels Tous niveaux Todos los niveles		Level 5 Niveau 5 Nivel 5		Level 6 Niveau 6 Nivel 6		Level 7 Niveau 7 Nivel 7	
		MF	F	MF	F	MF	F	MF	F
		(1)	(2)	(3)	(4)	(5)	(6)	(7)	(8)
Latvia‡									
Total	1981	6 903	...	...	...	...	...	...	...
	1986	6 971	...	...	...	...	...	...	...
	1991	5 668	...	...	...	...	...	...	...
Total	1995	6 909	...	...	...	6 865	...	44	...
Education science		1 528	...	...	...	1 522	...	6	...
Humanities & religion		451	...	...	...	445	...	6	...
Fine & applied arts		200	...	...	...	200	...	-	-
Law		196	...	...	...	195	...	1	...
Social & behav. sc.		162	...	...	...	159	...	3	...
Business administr.		1 245	...	...	...	1 245	...	-	
Communic. & doc.		68	...	...	...	68	...	-	-
Home economics		43	...	...	...	43	...	-	-
Service trades		5	...	...	...	5	...	-	-
Natural science		226	...	...	...	216	...	10	...
Maths. & computer sc.		262	...	...	...	255	...	7	...
Health-related prg.		423	...	...	...	423	...	-	...
Engineering		1 236	...	...	...	1 225	...	11	...
Archit. & town plng.		41	...	...	...	41	...	-	
Trade, craft & indust.		-	-	-	-	-	-	-	-
Transport & communic.		271	...	...	...	271	...	-	
Agriculture		450	...	...	...	450	...	-	
Other & not specified		102	...	...	...	102	...	-	
Malta									
Total	1981	204	49	76	12	109	32	19	5
	1986	216	49	-	-	212	49	4	-
	1991	405	177	29	10	376	167	-	-
Total	1994	942	437	231	111	676	313	35	13
Education science		163	110	*61	*50	92	59	*10	*1
Humanities & religion		173	87	21	9	142	75	10	3
Fine & applied arts		-	-	-	-	-	-	-	-
Law		27	17	-	-	27	17	-	-
Social & behav. sc.		-	-	-	-	-	-	-	-
Business administr.		238	105	10	1	221	102	7	2
Communic. & doc.		44	6	44	6	-	-	-	-
Home economics		-	-	-	-	-	-	-	-
Service trades		-	-	-	-	-	-	-	-
Natural science		44	14	-	-	41	12	3	2
Maths. & computer sc.		./.	./.	-	-	./.	./.	-	-
Health-related prg.		154	86	65	38	84	43	5	5
Engineering		69	5	-	*	69	5	-	-
Archit. & town plng.		-	-	-	-	-	-	-	-
Trade, craft & indust.		-	-	-	-	-	-	-	-
Transport & communic.		-	-	-	-	-	-	-	-
Agriculture		1	-	1	-	-	-	-	-
Other & not specified		29	7	29	7	-	-	-	-
Moldova									
Total	1994	20 527	...	11 375	...	9 044	...	108	...
Total	1995	20 756	...	11 771	...	8 866	...	119	...
Education science		4 808	...	1 482	...	3 325	...	1	...
Humanities & religion		13	...	-	...	-	-	13	...
Fine & applied arts		934	...	599	...	335	...	-	...
Law		185	...	182	...	-	...	3	...
Social & behav. sc.		1 640	...	849	...	783	...	8	...
Business administr.		-	-	-	-	-	-	-	
Communic. & doc.		-	-	-	-	-	-	-	-
Home economics		-	-	-	-	-	-	-	-
Service trades		-	-	-	-	-	-	-	-
Natural science		26	...	-	-	-	-	26	...
Maths. & computer sc.		16	...	-	...	-	-	16	...
Health-related prg.		2 971	...	1 986	...	958	...	27	...
Engineering		6 302	...	3 803	...	2 485	...	14	...
Archit. & town plng.		996	...	996	...	-	...	-	
Trade, craft & indust.		-	*	-	-	-	-	-	
Transport & communic.		542	...	542	...	-	...	-	
Agriculture		2 072	...	1 332	...	729	...	11	...
Other & not specified		251	...	-	...	251	...	-	

3.12 Third level: graduates by level and field of study
Troisième degré: diplômés par niveau et domaine d'études
Tercer grado: diplomados por nivel y sector de estudios

Country / Field of study / Pays / Domaine d'études / País / Sectores de estudios	Year / Année / Año	Graduates by ISCED level of programme / Diplômés par niveau de programmes de la CITE / Diplomados por nivel de programas de la CINE							
		All levels / Tous niveaux / Todos los niveles		Level 5 / Niveau 5 / Nivel 5		Level 6 / Niveau 6 / Nivel 6		Level 7 / Niveau 7 / Nivel 7	
		MF	F	MF	F	MF	F	MF	F
		(1)	(2)	(3)	(4)	(5)	(6)	(7)	(8)
Netherlands‡									
Total	1981	50 326	23 111	35 157	18 786	15 169	4 325	./.	./.
	1986	58 731	26 148	41 190	20 364	17 541	5 784	./.	./.
	1991	68 937	29 787	./.	./.	66 390	29 288	2 547	499
Total	1994	69 168	33 235	./.	./.	45 478	22 564	23 690	10 671
Education science		9 485	6 140	./.	./.	9 485	6 140	-	-
Humanities & religion		3 347	2 240	./.	./.	197	167	3 150	2 073
Fine & applied arts		2 515	1 459	./.	./.	2 091	1 148	424	311
Law		3 569	1 799	./.	./.	81	32	3 488	1 767
Social & behav. sc.		14 263	7 653	./.	./.	7 588	4 485	6 675	3 168
Business administr.		8 617	3 186	./.	./.	6 576	2 542	2 041	644
Communic. & doc.		984	657	./.	./.	938	619	46	38
Home economics		166	149	./.	./.	-	-	166	149
Service trades		874	596	./.	./.	874	596	-	-
Natural science		2 339	798	./.	./.	964	373	1 375	425
Maths. & computer sc.		1 343	119	./.	./.	732	51	611	68
Health-related prg.		7 908	5 687	./.	./.	5 562	4 272	2 346	1 415
Engineering		9 503	1 422	./.	./.	6 917	1 041	2 586	381
Archit. & town plng.		./.	./.	./.	./.	./.	./.	./.	./.
Trade, craft & indust.		./.	./.	./.	./.	./.	./.	./.	./.
Transport & communic.		429	74	./.	./.	429	74	-	-
Agriculture		2 203	510	./.	./.	1 421	278	782	232
Other & not specified		1 623	746	./.	./.	1 623	746	-	-
Norway									
Total	1986	38 340	21 143	23 676	13 582	10 102	6 094	4 562	1 467
	1991	53 575	29 118	27 555	14 156	20 919	13 104	5 101	1 858
Total	1993	60 686	33 919	29 415	15 812	25 218	15 742	6 053	2 365
Education science		13 027	9 130	1 518	1 052	11 252	7 940	257	138
Humanities & religion		9 589	6 231	8 257	5 396	885	608	447	227
Fine & applied arts		951	550	414	224	392	232	145	94
Law		1 511	783	943	528	-	-	568	255
Social & behav. sc.		7 690	4 598	6 330	3 832	763	419	597	347
Business administr.		11 079	5 066	7 643	3 566	3 274	1 451	162	49
Communic. & doc.		791	449	450	249	312	186	29	14
Home economics		-	-	-	-	-	-	-	-
Service trades		516	427	516	427	-	-	-	-
Natural science		1 184	532	66	34	630	272	488	226
Maths. & computer sc.		473	128	167	65	149	25	157	38
Health-related prg.		4 385	3 591	135	115	3 618	3 160	632	316
Engineering		3 625	742	31	4	2 120	383	1 474	355
Archit. & town plng.		117	70	-	-	-	-	117	70
Trade, craft & indust.		39	17	9	-	30	17	-	-
Transport & communic.		875	33	875	33	-	-	-	-
Agriculture		596	214	191	61	91	15	314	138
Other & not specified		4 238	1 358	1 870	226	1 702	1 034	666	98
Poland									
Total	1981	117 373	69 181	39 816	29 938	13 806	5 079	63 751	34 164
	1986	110 895	66 778	37 329	29 106	55 602	30 120	17 964	7 552
	1991	108 101	67 829	39 547	31 517	50 058	27 043	18 496	9 269
Total	1994	134 367	83 097	41 092	32 642	60 224	31 157	33 051	19 298
Education science		23 348	19 046	9 218	7 508	10 263	8 305	3 867	3 233
Humanities & religion		9 208	6 479	-	-	7 389	5 278	1 819	1 201
Fine & applied arts		1 575	890	198	134	1 223	667	154	89
Law		3 916	2 141	-	-	2 584	1 377	1 332	764
Social & behav. sc.		5 924	3 424	-	-	4 940	2 972	984	452
Business administr.		20 256	13 278	13 934	11 373	4 283	894	2 039	1 011
Communic. & doc.		685	577	-	-	525	449	160	128
Home economics		779	520	-	-	573	391	206	129
Service trades		2 712	2 230	2 712	2 230	-	-	-	-
Natural science		2 168	1 415	-	-	1 986	1 339	182	76
Maths. & computer sc.		1 662	1 101	-	-	1 525	1 030	137	71
Health-related prg.		33 376	23 840	9 771	8 786	6 783	4 269	16 822	10 785
Engineering		11 518	1 806	-	-	9 680	1 381	1 838	425
Archit. & town plng.		611	289	-	-	481	234	130	55
Trade, craft & indust.		4 681	2 352	4 681	2 352	-	-	-	-
Transport & communic.		2 725	389	49	15	767	14	1 909	360
Agriculture		5 665	2 143	343	126	4 275	1 645	1 047	372
Other & not specified		3 558	1 177	186	118	2 947	912	425	147

Third level: graduates by level and field of study 3.12
Troisième degré: diplômés par niveau et domaine d'études
Tercer grado: diplomados por nivel y sector de estudios

Country Field of study Pays Domaine d'études País Sectores de estudios	Year Année Año	Graduates by ISCED level of programme Diplômés par niveau de programmes de la CITE Diplomados por nivel de programas de la CINE							
		All levels Tous niveaux Todos los niveles		Level 5 Niveau 5 Nivel 5		Level 6 Niveau 6 Nivel 6		Level 7 Niveau 7 Nivel 7	
		MF	F	MF	F	MF	F	MF	F
		(1)	(2)	(3)	(4)	(5)	(6)	(7)	(8)
Portugal									
Total	1980	14 834	8 035	1 778	1 491	12 807	6 540	249	4
	1985	13 510	7 801	2 860	2 404	10 614	5 382	36	15
	1990	12 053	...	-	-	12 053	...	...	...
Total	1993	23 896	...	-	-	22 882	...	1 014	...
Education science		5 277	...	-	-	5 185	...	92	...
Humanities & religion		2 287	...	-	-	2 173	...	114	...
Fine & applied arts		811	...	-	-	810	...	1	...
Law		1 094	...	-	-	1 090	...	4	...
Social & behav. sc.		1 905	...	-	-	1 797	...	108	...
Business administr.		3 565	...	-	-	3 305	...	260	...
Communic. & doc.		790	...	-	-	787	...	3	...
Home economics		31	...	-	-	31	...	-	-
Service trades		-	-	-	-	-	-	-	-
Natural science		461	...	-	-	423	...	38	...
Maths. & computer sc.		465	...	-	-	402	...	63	...
Health-related prg.		2 726	...	-	-	2 616	...	110	...
Engineering		2 565	...	-	-	2 414	...	151	...
Archit. & town plng.		342	...	-	-	342	...	-	...
Trade, craft & indust.		-	-	-	-	-	-	-	-
Transport & communic.		-	-	-	-	-	-	-	-
Agriculture		959	...	-	-	889	...	70	...
Other & not specified		618	...	-	-	618	...	-	...
Romania									
Total	1981	38 615	...	...	...	...	...	...	...
	1986	30 643	...	...	...	...	...	...	...
	1989	27 703	...	...	...	...	...	...	...
Total	1994	34 240	17 064	...	...	...	...	...	...
Education science		751	284	...	...	...	...	...	...
Humanities & religion		2 368	1 241	...	...	...	...	...	...
Fine & applied arts		427	223	...	...	...	...	...	...
Law		1 013	524	...	...	...	...	...	...
Social & behav. sc.		287	192	...	...	...	...	...	...
Business administr.		3 518	2 554	...	...	...	...	...	...
Communic. & doc.		330	281	...	...	...	...	...	...
Home economics		-	-	...	...	...	...	...	...
Service trades		373	242	...	...	...	...	...	...
Natural science		1 669	1 238	...	...	...	...	...	...
Maths. & computer sc.		821	484	...	...	...	...	...	...
Health-related prg.		3 260	2 012	...	...	...	...	...	...
Engineering		16 114	6 045	...	...	...	...	...	...
Archit. & town plng.		259	135	...	...	...	...	...	...
Trade, craft & indust.		934	771	...	...	...	...	...	...
Transport & communic.		369	59	...	...	...	...	...	...
Agriculture		1 495	779	...	...	...	...	...	...
Other & not specified		252	-	...	...	...	...	...	...
Russian Federation‡									
Total	1992	1 030 000	...	623 000	...	407 000	...	./.	...
Total	1995	950 488	560 224	531 669	345 578	406 527	214 646	12 292	...
Education science		113 042	99 896	75 976	69 216	36 442	30 680	624	...
Humanities & religion		35 980	28 093	-	-	35 091	28 093	889	...
Fine & applied arts		16 617	11 071	10 640	7 503	5 709	3 568	268	...
Law		15 537	8 450	6 197	4 108	9 122	4 342	218	...
Social & behav. sc.		107 573	86 397	68 741	61 286	37 199	25 111	1 633	...
Business administr.		72 651	52 823	51 594	37 932	21 057	14 891	-	-
Communic. & doc.		9 651	7 292	4 632	3 632	5 019	3 660	-	-
Home economics		-	-	-	-	-	-	-	-
Service trades		861	763	861	763	-	-	-	-
Natural science		28 622	14 666	1 737	1 057	25 523	13 609	1 362	...
Maths. & computer sc.		28 066	15 364	2 912	1 876	23 920	13 488	1 234	...
Health-related prg.		125 657	104 387	93 842	83 734	30 080	20 653	1 735	...
Engineering		279 330	65 972	143 811	30 518	131 777	35 454	3 742	...
Archit. & town plng.		1 706	1 066	553	388	1 097	678	56	...
Trade, craft & indust.		25 087	21 019	25 087	21 019	-	-	-	...
Transport & communic.		11 528	4 146	11 528	4 146	-	-	-	...
Agriculture		51 463	24 353	24 401	11 318	26 536	13 035	526	...
Other & not specified		27 117	14 466	9 157	7 082	17 955	7 384	5	...

3.12 Third level: graduates by level and field of study
Troisième degré: diplomés par niveau et domaine d'études
Tercer grado: diplomados por nivel y sector de estudios

Country / Field of study / Pays / Domaine d'études / País / Sectores de estudios	Year / Année / Año	All levels Tous niveaux Todos los niveles		Level 5 Niveau 5 Nivel 5		Level 6 Niveau 6 Nivel 6		Level 7 Niveau 7 Nivel 7	
		MF	F	MF	F	MF	F	MF	F
		(1)	(2)	(3)	(4)	(5)	(6)	(7)	(8)
Slovakia‡									
Total	1993	10 667	5 183	-	-	10 667	5 183	./.	./.
Total	1995	9 361	4 800	212	116	9 149	4 684	./.	./.
Education science		2 154	1 647	-	-	2 154	1 647	./.	./.
Humanities & religion		614	377	-	-	614	377	./.	./.
Fine & applied arts		375	204	175	100	200	104	./.	./.
Law		313	156	-	-	313	156	./.	./.
Social & behav. sc.		112	60	-	-	112	60	./.	./.
Business administr.		665	436	-	-	665	436	...	...
Communic. & doc.		123	74	-	-	123	74	./.	./.
Home economics		-	-	-	-	-	-	./.	./.
Service trades		-	-	-	-	-	-	-	-
Natural science		309	196	-	-	309	196	./.	./.
Maths. & computer sc.		87	32	-	-	87	32	./.	./.
Health-related prg.		773	471	37	16	736	455	./.	./.
Engineering		3 059	820			3 059	820	./.	./.
Archit. & town plng.		84	33	-	-	84	33	./.	./.
Trade, craft & indust.		-	-	-	-	-	-	-	-
Transport & communic.		-	-	-	-	-	-	-	-
Agriculture		618	274	-	-	618	274	./.	./.
Other & not specified		75	20	-	-	75	20	./.	./.
Slovenia									
Total	1992	6 060	3 450	3 046	1 932	2 410	1 292	604	226
Total	1995	6 549	3 779	2 668	1 584	3 144	1 881	737	314
Education science		762	605	145	138	591	452	26	15
Humanities & religion		228	167	-	-	173	142	55	25
Fine & applied arts		115	65	22	15	84	48	9	2
Law		326	211	94	66	220	142	12	3
Social & behav. sc.		185	129	8	8	124	97	53	24
Business administr.		1 797	1 307	1 150	870	567	402	80	35
Communic. & doc.		41	33	-	-	40	32	1	1
Home economics		-	-	-	-	-	-	-	-
Service trades		-	-	-	-	-	-	-	-
Natural science		214	119	3	-	134	79	77	40
Maths. & computer sc.		55	29	13	8	38	19	4	2
Health-related prg.		602	417	190	159	202	151	210	107
Engineering		1 537	357	670	163	720	166	147	28
Archit. & town plng.		78	44	-	-	72	40	6	4
Trade, craft & indust.		-	-	-	-	-	-	-	-
Transport & communic.		79	12	79	12	-	-	-	-
Agriculture		247	140	53	26	151	91	43	23
Other & not specified		283	144	241	119	28	20	14	5
Spain									
Total	1981	78 065	37 197	881	594	75 248	36 118	1 936	485
	1986	99 984	54 138	822	716	96 294	52 441	2 868	981
	1991	131 546	74 396	3 089	1 451	123 789	71 282	4 668	1 663
Total	1993	150 155	82 753	7 139	3 428	137 823	77 302	5 193	2 023
Education science		15 044	11 328	362	336	14 408	10 877	274	115
Humanities & religion		13 953	8 889	-	-	13 153	8 517	800	372
Fine & applied arts		2 647	1 451	93	56	2 473	1 369	81	26
Law		25 668	14 662	-	-	25 485	14 602	183	60
Social & behav. sc.		5 908	4 121	-	-	5 714	4 026	194	95
Business administr.		23 996	11 855	2 237	1 412	21 571	10 384	188	59
Communic. & doc.		4 508	2 714	245	176	4 195	2 512	68	26
Home economics		-	-	-	-	-	-	-	-
Service trades		5 152	3 830	870	411	4 282	3 419	-	-
Natural science		8 193	3 781	-	-	7 084	3 326	1 109	455
Maths. & computer sc.		5 336	1 780	-	-	5 248	1 751	88	29
Health-related prg.		16 721	11 171	45	40	15 069	10 512	1 607	619
Engineering		11 116	1 860	-	-	10 817	1 801	299	59
Archit. & town plng.		2 414	661	-	-	2 373	651	41	10
Trade, craft & indust.		1 414	147	1 414	147	-	-	-	-
Transport & communic.		206	15	206	15	-	-	-	-
Agriculture		1 637	777	61	24	1 472	701	104	52
Other & not specified		6 242	3 711	1 606	811	4 479	2 854	157	46

The table heading: Graduates by ISCED level of programme / Diplômés par niveau de programmes de la CITE / Diplomados por nivel de programas de la CINE

Third level: graduates by level and field of study **3.12**
Troisième degré: diplômés par niveau et domaine d'études
Tercer grado: diplomados por nivel y sector de estudios

Country / Field of study Pays / Domaine d'études País / Sectores de estudios	Year Année Año	Graduates by ISCED level of programme Diplômés par niveau de programmes de la CITE Diplomados por nivel de programas de la CINE							
		All levels Tous niveaux Todos los niveles		Level 5 Niveau 5 Nivel 5		Level 6 Niveau 6 Nivel 6		Level 7 Niveau 7 Nivel 7	
		MF	F	MF	F	MF	F	MF	F
		(1)	(2)	(3)	(4)	(5)	(6)	(7)	(8)
Sweden‡									
Total	1980	40 734	21 994	24 434	14 283	15 405	7 498	895	213
	1991	36 470	20 058	19 910	11 297	15 227	8 450	1 610	437
Total	1994	34 689	21 298	13 524	9 748	15 770	8 753	5 395	2 797
Education science		8 462	6 997	4 177	3 691	3 241	2 542	1 044	764
Humanities & religion		1 018	614	16	14	741	480	261	120
Fine & applied arts		620	350	106	54	457	260	57	36
Law		896	495	16	10	813	448	67	37
Social & behav. sc.		1 633	1 166	24	16	1 312	997	297	153
Business administr.		4 425	2 299	537	314	3 220	1 655	668	330
Communic. & doc.		409	311	7	5	287	239	115	67
Home economics		67	65	-	-	61	60	6	5
Service trades		51	45	49	43	2	2	-	-
Natural science		1 098	499	7	4	609	325	482	170
Maths. & computer sc.		1 380	303	283	72	837	192	260	39
Health-related prg.		8 582	6 938	5 935	5 186	1 306	820	1 341	932
Engineering		4 603	890	1 396	223	2 504	558	703	109
Archit. & town plng.		148	70	-	-	133	61	15	9
Trade, craft & indust.		542	45	531	38	11	7	-	-
Transport & communic.		155	10	117	5	28	4	10	1
Agriculture		538	159	263	31	206	103	69	25
Other & not specified		62	42	60	42	2	-	-	-
Switzerland‡									
Total	1980	8 620	2 263	469	230	5 948	1 586	2 203	447
	1986	10 103	3 197	962	515	6 203	2 023	2 938	659
	1991	12 211	4 118	938	565	8 685	2 864	2 588	689
Total	1993	12 916	4 651	793	503	9 165	3 272	2 958	876
Education science		435	269	192	142	220	115	23	12
Humanities & religion		2 007	1 120	429	297	1 284	691	294	132
Fine & applied arts		81	51	-	-	67	47	14	4
Law		1 717	637	-	-	1 520	587	197	50
Social & behav. sc.		1 114	575	-	-	924	495	190	80
Business administr.		1 957	482	26	8	1 655	404	276	70
Communic. & doc.		24	16	24	16	-	-	-	-
Home economics		-	-	-	-	-	-	-	-
Service trades		-	-	-	-	-	-	-	-
Natural science		1 799	468	122	40	961	258	716	170
Maths. & computer sc.		376	49	-	-	310	45	66	4
Health-related prg.		1 819	754	-	-	977	460	842	294
Engineering		987	41	-	-	777	26	210	15
Archit. & town plng.		282	73	-	-	277	71	5	2
Trade, craft & indust.		-	-	-	-	-	-	-	-
Transport & communic.		-	-	-	-	-	-	-	-
Agriculture		318	116	-	-	193	73	125	43
Other & not specified		-	-	-	-	-	-	-	-
The former Yugoslav Rep. of Macedonia									
Total	1992	3 526	1 842	890	443	2 464	1 340	172	59
Total	1995	2 780	1 538	534	339	2 179	1 174	67	25
Education science		294	262	248	227	43	33	3	2
Humanities & religion		205	151	6	3	186	140	13	8
Fine & applied arts		96	37	-	-	96	37	-	-
Law		259	159	-	-	259	159	-	-
Social & behav. sc.		465	293	57	30	400	259	8	4
Business administr.		-	-	-	-	-	-	-	-
Communic. & doc.		3	3	-	-	3	3	-	-
Home economics		-	-	-	-	-	-	-	-
Service trades		18	11	16	9	2	2	-	-
Natural science		126	85	-	-	107	77	19	8
Maths. & computer sc.		31	23	-	-	31	23	-	-
Health-related prg.		291	176	27	26	264	150	-	-
Engineering		667	220	144	30	499	187	24	3
Archit. & town plng.		49	27	-	-	49	27	-	-
Trade, craft & indust.		-	-	-	-	-	-	-	-
Transport & communic.		-	-	-	-	-	-	-	-
Agriculture		246	89	36	14	210	75	-	-
Other & not specified		30	2	-	-	30	2	-	-

3.12 Third level: graduates by level and field of study
Troisième degré: diplômés par niveau et domaine d'études
Tercer grado: diplomados por nivel y sector de estudios

Country / Field of study / Pays / Domaine d'études / País / Sectores de estudios	Year / Année / Año	Graduates by ISCED level of programme / Diplômés par niveau de programmes de la CITE / Diplomados por nivel de programas de la CINE							
		All levels / Tous niveaux / Todos los niveles		Level 5 / Niveau 5 / Nivel 5		Level 6 / Niveau 6 / Nivel 6		Level 7 / Niveau 7 / Nivel 7	
		MF	F	MF	F	MF	F	MF	F
		(1)	(2)	(3)	(4)	(5)	(6)	(7)	(8)
Ukraine‡									
Total	1981	148 100	...	...	...	...	...	...	...
	1986	147 800	...	...	...	...	...	...	...
Total	1991	140 218	...	...	...	137 000	...	3 218	...
Education science		28 121	...	...	...	28 000	...	121	...
Humanities & religion		19 711	...	...	...	18 700	...	1 011	...
Fine & applied arts		1 238	...	...	...	1 200	...	38	...
Law		1 537	...	...	...	1 500	...	37	...
Social & behav. sc.		./.	...	...	...	./.	...	./.	...
Business administr.		12 899	...	...	...	12 500	...	399	...
Communic. & doc.		./.	...	...	...	./.	...	./.	...
Home economics		./.	...	...	...	./.	...	./.	...
Service trades		./.	...	...	...	./.	...	./.	...
Natural science		./.	...	...	...	./.	...	./.	...
Maths. & computer sc.		./.	...	...	...	./.	...	./.	...
Health-related prg.		9 199	...	...	...	9 000	...	199	...
Engineering		52 314	...	...	...	51 100	...	1 214	...
Archit. & town plng.		./.	...	...	...	./.	...	./.	...
Trade, craft & indust.		./.	...	...	...	./.	...	./.	...
Transport & communic.		./.	...	...	...	./.	...	./.	...
Agriculture		15 199	...	...	...	15 000	...	199	...
Other & not specified		-	-	-	-	-	-	-	-
United Kingdom									
Total	1981	140 735	...	22 826	...	91 904	...	26 005	...
	1986	297 784	133 930	117 245	59 531	139 468	59 564	41 071	14 835
	1991	371 818	183 168	145 267	79 325	161 542	75 932	65 009	27 911
Total	1994	462 981	237 310	184 777	102 116	203 595	100 701	74 609	34 493
Education science		27 408	19 091	1 806	1 155	7 000	5 660	18 602	12 276
Humanities & religion		58 874	35 264	13 085	7 058	37 425	23 520	8 364	4 686
Fine & applied arts		./.	./.	./.	./.	./.	./.	./.	./.
Law		15 792	8 733	3 944	2 594	8 658	4 647	3 190	1 492
Social & behav. sc.		33 160	18 337	8 282	5 446	18 179	9 758	6 699	3 133
Business administr.		94 912	44 752	58 304	28 020	26 937	13 470	9 671	3 262
Communic. & doc.		4 532	2 754	1 140	618	2 172	1 405	1 220	731
Home economics		./.	./.	./.	./.	./.	./.	./.	./.
Service trades		./.	./.	./.	./.	./.	./.	./.	./.
Natural science		32 784	14 318	3 982	1 672	21 850	10 181	6 952	2 465
Maths. & computer sc.		25 854	7 677	9 919	3 228	12 257	3 447	3 678	1 002
Health-related prg.		59 746	48 902	43 682	38 943	11 235	7 198	4 829	2 761
Engineering		64 273	12 881	28 631	7 260	27 189	4 209	8 453	1 412
Archit. & town plng.		./.	./.	./.	./.	./.	./.	./.	./.
Trade, craft & indust.		./.	./.	./.	./.	./.	./.	./.	./.
Transport & communic.		./.	./.	./.	./.	./.	./.	./.	./.
Agriculture		5 571	2 258	2 549	915	1 852	925	1 170	418
Other & not specified		40 075	22 343	9 453	5 207	28 841	16 281	1 781	855
Former Yugoslavia									
Total	1981	60 456	25 962	25 415	11 099	31 954	14 132	3 087	731
	1986	52 804	26 083	21 555	11 204	28 227	13 987	3 022	892
Total	1991	47 750	24 338	16 559	9 116	27 584	13 955	3 607	1 267
Education science		5 318	3 813	4 129	3 312	1 126	486	63	15
Humanities & religion		3 751	2 680	116	81	3 313	2 444	322	155
Fine & applied arts		855	506	45	30	745	443	65	33
Law		3 695	1 991	665	379	2 904	1 585	126	27
Social & behav. sc.		8 175	4 691	3 568	2 177	4 258	2 409	349	105
Business administr.		875	375	337	141	470	219	68	15
Communic. & doc.		21	8	-	-	-	-	21	8
Home economics		-	-	-	-	-	-	-	-
Service trades		395	210	273	145	122	65	-	-
Natural science		1 992	1 143	89	57	1 507	901	396	185
Maths. & computer sc.		./.	./.	./.	./.	./.	./.	./.	./.
Health-related prg.		5 697	3 695	1 303	1 055	3 589	2 251	805	389
Engineering		10 456	2 816	3 670	985	5 959	1 674	827	157
Archit. & town plng.		683	395	15	12	623	366	45	17
Trade, craft & indust.		212	113	201	108	11	5	-	-
Transport & communic.		1 417	291	1 027	211	378	80	12	-
Agriculture		3 555	1 392	601	233	2 523	1 025	431	134
Other & not specified		653	219	520	190	56	2	77	27

Third level: graduates by level and field of study **3.12**
Troisième degré: diplômés par niveau et domaine d'études
Tercer grado: diplomados por nivel y sector de estudios

Country Field of study Pays Domaine d'études País Sectores de estudios	Year Année Año	Graduates by ISCED level of programme Diplômés par niveau de programmes de la CITE Diplomados por nivel de programas de la CINE							
		All levels Tous niveaux Todos los niveles		Level 5 Niveau 5 Nivel 5		Level 6 Niveau 6 Nivel 6		Level 7 Niveau 7 Nivel 7	
		MF	F	MF	F	MF	F	MF	F
		(1)	(2)	(3)	(4)	(5)	(6)	(7)	(8)
Federal Republic of **Yugoslavia**									
Total	1992	20 605	10 569	7 411	4 210	11 561	5 690	1 633	669
Total	1995	17 453	9 750	5 886	3 777	10 179	5 391	1 388	582
Education science		2 757	2 089	2 060	1 791	664	279	33	19
Humanities & religion		1 193	928	-	-	1 084	872	109	56
Fine & applied arts		436	272	67	46	316	197	53	29
Law		1 134	641	106	56	983	569	45	16
Social & behav. sc.		2 124	1 387	1 031	695	994	669	99	23
Business administr.		272	118	168	81	83	35	21	2
Communic. & doc.		-	-	-	-	-	-	-	-
Home economics		-	-	-	-	-	-	-	-
Service trades		172	98	172	98	-	-	-	-
Natural science		814	527	-	-	682	455	132	72
Maths. & computer sc.		./.	./.	./.	-	./.	./.	./.	./.
Health-related prg.		2 117	1 325	234	175	1 493	931	390	219
Engineering		4 268	1 471	1 351	535	2 601	852	316	84
Archit. & town plng.		160	89	-	-	140	79	20	10
Trade, craft & indust.		143	95	143	95	-	-	-	-
Transport & communic.		360	139	241	102	107	35	12	2
Agriculture		1 307	530	140	71	1 032	418	135	41
Other & not specified		196	41	173	32	-	-	23	9
Oceania									
Australia									
Total	1981	66 069	...	19 192	...	37 357	...	9 520	...
	1985	73 563	36 958	24 887	14 515	44 349	21 197	4 327	1 246
	1990	94 399	52 775	14 186	10 072	58 182	31 153	22 031	11 550
Total	1993	132 860	76 080	7 933	4 675	90 146	52 988	34 781	18 417
Education science		25 316	18 648	2 461	1 908	11 462	8 923	11 393	7 817
Humanities & religion		15 099	10 159	203	180	12 711	8 672	2 185	1 307
Fine & applied arts		3 814	2 525	353	173	2 813	1 949	648	403
Law		4 846	2 293	264	96	2 980	1 478	1 602	719
Social & behav. sc.		5 679	3 100	49	30	4 051	2 215	1 579	855
Business administr.		24 541	10 822	652	235	17 592	8 457	6 297	2 130
Communic. & doc.		2 535	1 886	39	35	1 646	1 210	850	641
Home economics		51	48	-	-	51	48	-	-
Service trades		322	189	24	14	237	142	61	33
Natural science		11 083	5 021	241	81	9 176	4 347	1 666	593
Maths. & computer sc.		5 015	1 458	244	64	3 271	1 012	1 500	382
Health-related prg.		18 719	14 746	1 675	1 290	13 640	10 979	3 404	2 477
Engineering		6 909	834	449	27	4 857	625	1 603	182
Archit. & town plng.		2 415	787	60	14	1 695	590	660	183
Trade, craft & indust.		627	386	119	71	504	313	4	2
Transport & communic.		-	-	-	-	-	-	-	-
Agriculture		3 248	1 235	902	311	1 655	706	691	218
Other & not specified		2 641	1 943	198	146	1 805	1 322	638	475
Fiji									
Total	1981	356	108	203	70	153	38	-	-
	1985	519	225	...	...	...	...	-	-
Total	1988	557	...	205	...	352	...	-	-
Education science		109	...	80	...	29	...	-	-
Humanities & religion		22	...	19	...	3	...	-	-
Fine & applied arts		2	...	-	...	2	...	-	-
Law		18	...	-	...	18	...	-	-
Social & behav. sc.		192	...	-	...	192	...	-	-
Business administr.		43	...	43	...	-	...	-	-
Communic. & doc.		-	-	-	-	-	-	-	-
Home economics		-	-	-	-	-	-	-	-
Service trades		-	-	-	-	-	-	-	-
Natural science		56	...	-	...	56	...	-	-
Maths. & computer sc.		23	...	23	...	-	...	-	-
Health-related prg.		45	...	15	...	30	...	-	-
Engineering		-	-	-	...	-	-	-	-
Archit. & town plng.		-	-	-	...	-	-	-	-
Trade, craft & indust.		-	-	-	...	-	-	-	-
Transport & communic.		-	-	-	...	-	-	-	-
Agriculture		47	...	25	...	22	...	-	-
Other & not specified		-	-	-	...	-	-	-	-

3.12 Third level: graduates by level and field of study
Troisième degré: diplômés par niveau et domaine d'études
Tercer grado: diplomados por nivel y sector de estudios

Country Field of study Pays Domaine d'études País Sectores de estudios	Year Année Año	Graduates by ISCED level of programme Diplômés par niveau de programmes de la CITE Diplomados por nivel de programas de la CINE							
		All levels Tous niveaux Todos los niveles		Level 5 Niveau 5 Nivel 5		Level 6 Niveau 6 Nivel 6		Level 7 Niveau 7 Nivel 7	
		MF	F	MF	F	MF	F	MF	F
		(1)	(2)	(3)	(4)	(5)	(6)	(7)	(8)
New Zealand‡									
Total	1980	11 496	5 188	3 567	2 275	6 304	2 379	1 625	534
	1985	11 274	5 043	2 303	1 329	6 322	2 733	2 649	981
	1990	13 269	6 247	789	402	9 102	4 396	3 378	1 449
Total	1992	17 648	8 733	3 522	1 567	10 120	5 207	4 006	1 959
Education science		1 189	937	373	313	516	421	300	203
Humanities & religion		4 383	2 829	99	76	3 339	2 187	945	566
Fine & applied arts		208	125	-	-	162	96	46	29
Law		1 073	547	373	196	488	251	212	100
Social & behav. sc.		798	543	87	61	390	265	321	217
Business administr.		4 329	1 611	2 183	762	1 794	708	352	141
Communic. & doc.		98	71	1	-	-	-	97	71
Home economics		-	-	-	-	-	-	-	-
Service trades		12	9	12	9	-	-	-	-
Natural science		2 614	1 036	-	-	1 775	737	839	299
Maths. & computer sc.		89	16	-	-	43	7	46	9
Health-related prg.		854	420	59	38	522	239	273	143
Engineering		602	64	1	-	464	47	137	17
Archit. & town plng.		276	94	-	-	249	84	27	10
Trade, craft & indust.		3	1	-	-	-	-	3	1
Transport & communic.		5	1	-	-	5	1	-	-
Agriculture		732	229	201	38	282	111	249	80
Other & not specified		383	200	133	74	91	53	159	73

This table shows the number of students who have successfully completed their studies. The graduates are classified according to the ISCED level of degree or diploma obtained and their field of study for the latest year available, while for 1981, 1986 and 1991, they are distributed by ISCED level only.

The year shown refers to the calendar year in which the qualification is obtained. For example, 1994 refer to degrees awarded at the end of the academic year 1993/1994. More information on this point is given in the introductory text to Chapter 3.

The three level categories, identified in this table by their ISCED codes 5, 6 and 7 are defined as follows:

Level 5: Diplomas and certificates not equivalent to a first university degree awarded after higher studies which last generally less than three years.

Level 6: First university degrees or equivalent qualifications represent higher studies of three to five years duration which lead to qualifications such as a Bachelor's degree.

Level 7: Post-graduate university degrees or equivalent qualifications, which persons who already possess a first university degree (or equivalent qualification) can obtain by continuing their studies; for example, the Master's degree or the various types of Doctorates.

The classification according to level is intended to establish a distinction between the different degrees and diplomas and to facilitate international comparability on third-level qualifications. It should be noted however that the classification by ISCED level category in no way implies an equivalence of the degrees and diplomas either within a country or between countries.

With regard to the subjects included in the various fields of study, see the definitions in the introductory text to Chapter 3.

Ce tableau présente le nombre d'étudiants qui ont terminé leurs études avec succès. Pour la dernière année disponible, les diplômés sont répartis selon le niveau de la CITE du grade ou diplôme obtenu et par domaine d'études tandis qu'en 1981, en 1986 et en 1991, ils sont repartis par niveau de la CITE seulement.

L'année indiquée est l'année de calendrier durant laquelle le diplôme a été obtenu par exemple, 1994 indique que le diplôme a été obtenu à la fin de l'année universitaire 1993/94.

Les trois niveaux indiqués ici par leurs codes 5, 6 et 7 de la CITE sont définis comme suit:

Niveau 5: Les diplômes et certificats non équivalant à un premier grade universitaire sont ceux décernés à la fin d'études supérieures de durée, en général, de moins de trois ans.

Niveau 6: Les premiers grades universitaires ou diplômes équivalents sont ceux qui sanctionnent des études supérieures de durée de trois à cinq ans qui mènent aux qualifications telles que la licence.

Niveau 7: Les grades universitaires supérieurs ou diplômes équivalents, que peuvent obtenir, en poursuivant leurs études, les personnes déjà titulaires d'un premier grade universitaire (ou d'un diplôme équivalent). Par exemple la maîtrise ou les divers types de doctorats.

Le classement selon le niveau a été effectué afin d'établir une distinction entre les différents grades et diplômes et dans l'espoir de faciliter la comparabilité internationale des statistiques sur les diplômes de l'enseignement du troisième degré. Il faut néanmoins souligner que le classement par niveau CITE n'implique en aucune manière une équivalence des grades et diplômes, que ce soit à l'intérieur du pays considéré ou par rapport à d'autres pays.

En ce qui concerne les sujets inclus dans les divers domaines d'études, voir les définitions présentées dans le texte d'introduction du chapitre 3.

Este cuadro presenta el número de estudiantes que terminaron sus estudios con éxito. Para el último año disponible se distribuye a los diplomados por nivel de la CINE del título o diploma obtenido y por sector de estudio, mientras que para 1981, 1986 y 1991 se presentan por nivel de la CINE solamente.

El año indicado se refiere al año calendario en el cual se obtuvo el título. Por ejemplo, 1994 se refiere a los diplomas concedidos al final del año universitario 1993/1994. Para obtener más detalles, refiérase a la introducción general del capítulo 3.

Los tres niveles que se designan en este cuadro según su codificación 5, 6 y 7 de la CINE se definen como sigue:

Nivel 5. Diplomas y certificados no equivalentes a un primer título universitario, concedidos al final de estudios

Third level: graduates by level and field of study 3.12
Troisième degré: diplomés par niveau et domaine d'études
Tercer grado: diplomados por nivel y sector de estudios

superiores de una duración en general de menos de tres años.

Nivel 6. Primeros títulos universitarios o diplomas equivalentes, que sancionan unos estudios superiores de duración en general de 3 a 5 años, y que conducen a calificaciones como la *Bachelor's degree* o la *licence*.

Nivel 7. Títulos universitarios superiores o diplomas equivalentes, que pueden obtener, continuando los estudios, quienes tienen ya un primer título universitario (o un diploma equivalente). Por ejemplo, la *Master's degree* o los diversos tipos de doctorado.

La clasificación según el nivel se ha efectuado con vistas a establecer una distinción entre los diferentes títulos y diplomas y con la esperanza de facilitar la comparabilidad internacional de las estadísticas relativas a los diplomados de la enseñanza de tercer grado. Sin embargo, cabe recalcar que la clasificación por nivel no implica necesariamente una equivalencia de los títulos o diplomas, ya sea en el propio país o con respecto a otros países.

En lo que se refiere a las materias incluídas en las diversas disciplinas, véase la nota de definiciones en el texto de introducción del capítulo 3.

AFRICA:

Algeria:

E--> Data refer to universities and equivalent degree-granting institutions under the Ministry of Education. In 1991 and 1993, level 6 includes level 7.

FR-> Les données se réfèrent aux universités et établissements conférant des grades équivalents qui sont sous la tutelle du Ministère de l'Education. En 1991 et 1993, le niveau 6 inclut le niveau 7.

ESP> Los datos se refieren a las universidades y establecimientos que otorgan títulos equivalentes bajo la tutela del Ministerío de Educaciòn. En 1991 y 1993, el nivel 6 incluye el nivel 7.

Benin:

E--> In 1986, level 6 includes level 7.

FR-> En 1986, le niveau 6 inclut le niveau 7.

ESP> En 1986, el nivel 6 incluye el nivel 7.

Burkina Faso:

E--> In 1981 and 1987, data refer to universities and equivalent degree-granting institutions only. In 1992, humanities, religion and theology include social and behavioural sciences.

FR-> En 1981 et 1987, les données se réfèrent aux universités et établissements conférant des grades équivalents seulement. En 1992, les lettres, la religion et la théologie incluent les sciences sociales et sciences du comportement.

ESP> En 1981 y 1987, los datos sólo se refieren a las universidades y establecimientos que otorgan títulos equivalentes. En 1992, las humanidades, la religión y la teología incluyen las ciencias sociales y del comportamiento.

Burundi:

E--> Level 6 includes level 7.

FR-> Le niveau 6 inclut le niveau 7.

ESP> El nivel 6 incluye el nivel 7.

Chad:

E--> For 1993, data refer to universities only.

FR-> Pour 1993, les données se réfèrent aux universités seulement.

ESP> Para 1993, los datos se refieren a las universidades solamente.

Egypt:

E--> Data refer to universities and equivalent degree-granting institutions only but exclude Al Azhar University.

FR-> Les données se réfèrent aux universités et établissements conférant des grades équivalents seulement, non compris l'Université d'Al Azhar.

ESP> Los datos sólo se refieren a las universidades y establecimientos que otorgan títulos equivalentes excluída la Universidad Al Azhar.

Ethiopia:

E--> Data for 1992 do not include Kotebe college and Asmara University.

FR-> Les données pour 1992 ne comprennent pas *Kotebe college* et l'Université d'Asmara.

ESP> Los datos de 1992 no incluyen *Kotebe college* y la Universidad de Asmara.

Gabon:

E--> Data refer to universities and degree-granting institutions only.

FR-> Les données se réfèrent aux universités et établissements conférant des grades équivalents seulement.

ESP> Los datos se refieren a las universidades y a los establecimientos que otorgan títulos equivalentes solamente.

Ghana:

E--> Data refer to universities only.

FR-> Les données se réfèrent aux universités seulement.

ESP> Los datos se refieren a las universidades solamente.

Kenya:

E--> Data refer to universities and degree-granting institutions only.

FR-> Les données se réfèrent aux universités et établissements conférant des grades équivalents seulement.

ESP> Los datos se refieren a las universidades y a los establecimientos que otorgan títulos equivalentes solamente.

Malawi:

E--> In 1990, level 6 includes level 7.

FR-> En 1990, le niveau 6 inclut le niveau 7.

ESP> En 1990, el nivel 6 incluye el nivel 7.

Morocco:

E--> Until 1991, data refer to universities and equivalent degree-granting institutions only. In 1995, a part of social sciences is included with humanities, religion and theology; data exclude some technical training in other third level institutions.

FR-> Jusqu'en 1991, les données se réfèrent aux universités et établissements conférant des grades équivalents seulement. En 1995, une partie des sciences sociales est comprise dans les lettres, la religion et la théologie; les données n'incluent pas une partie de l'enseignement technique dispensé dans les autres établissements du troisième degré.

ESP> Hasta 1991, los datos sólo se refieren a las universidades y establecimientos que otorgan títulos equivalentes. En 1995, una parte de la ciencias sociales está incluída en humanidades, religión y teología; los datos no incluyen una parte de la enseñanza técnica de los otros establecimientos de tercer grado.

Nigeria:

E--> Data refer to universities only.

FR-> Les données se réfèrent aux universités seulement.

ESP> Los datos se refieren a las universidades solamente.

Rwanda:

E-> For 1982, data refer to universities only.

FR-> Pour 1982, les données se réfèrent aux universités seulement.

ESP> Para 1982, los datos se refieren a las universidades solamente.

Senegal:

E--> For 1986, data refer to universities only.

FR-> Pour 1986, les données se réfèrent aux universités seulement.

ESP> Para 1986, los datos se refieren a las universidades solamente.

Sudan:

E--> Level 6 includes level 7. For 1991, data refer to universities and equivalent degree-granting institutions only.

FR-> Le niveau 6 inclut le niveau 7. Pour 1991, les données se réfèrent aux universités et établissements conférant des grades équivalents seulement.

ESP> El nivel 6 incluye el nivel 7. Para 1991, los datos se refieren a las universidades y establecimientos que otorgan títulos equivalentes solamente.

Swaziland:

E--> For 1991, data refer to the University of Swaziland only. For 1995, not including medical sciences and health related graduates.

FR-> Pour 1991, les données se réfèrent à l'Université de Swaziland seulement. En 1995, non compris les diplômés des sciences médicales, santé, hygiène.

ESP> Para 1991, los datos se refieren a la Universidad de Swaziland solamente. Para 1995, no incluídos los diplomados de las ciencias médicas, sanidad e higiene.

Zimbabwe:

E--> For 1986, data refer to universities and equivalent degree-granting institutions and teacher training colleges and for 1981, to universities only.

FR-> Pour 1986, les données se réfèrent aux universités et établissements conférant des grades équivalents ainsi qu'aux écoles normales et pour 1981, aux universités seulement.

ESP> Para 1986, los datos se refieren a las universidades y establecimientos que otorgan títulos equivalentes y a las escuelas normales y para 1981, a las universidades solamente.

AMERICA, NORTH:

Canada:

E--> Data for 1981, 1986 and 1991 do not include trade and vocational programmes.

FR-> Les données pour 1981, 1986 et 1991 ne comprennent pas les programmes d'enseignement techniques et commerciaux.

ESP> Los datos de 1981, 1986 y 1991 no incluyen los programas de enseñanza técnica y comercial.

Costa Rica:

E--> Data for 1981 and 1986 do not include other third level institutions.

FR-> Les données pour 1981 et 1986 n'incluent pas les autres établissements du troisième degré.

ESP> En 1990, el nivel 6 incluye el nivel 7.

3.12 Third level: graduates by level and field of study
Troisième degré: diplomés par niveau et domaine d'études
Tercer grado: diplomados por nivel y sector de estudios

ESP> Los datos de 1981 y 1986 no incluyen los otros establecimientos de tercer grado.

El Salvador:

E--> For 1985 and 1990, data do not include *la Universidad Nacional de El Salvador*. Except for 1990, level 6 includes level 7.

FR-> Pour 1985 et 1990, les données ne comprennent pas *la Universidad Nacional de El Salvador*. Sauf pour 1990, le niveau 6 inclut le niveau 7.

ESP> Para 1985 y 1990, los datos no incluyen la Universidad Nacional de El Salvador. Con excepción de 1990, el nivel 6 incluye el nivel 7.

Mexico:

E--> For 1981 and 1986, data refer to universities and equivalent degree-granting institutions only.

FR-> Pour 1981 et 1986, les données se réfèrent aux universités et établissements conférant des grades équivalents seulement.

ESP> Para 1981 y 1986, los datos se refieren a las universidades y establecimientos que otorgan títulos equivalentes solamente.

Panama:

E--> For 1990, engineering includes trade, craft and industrial programmes and transport and communication.

FR-> Pour 1990, les sciences de l'ingénieur incluent les métiers de la production industrielle, les transports et télécommunications.

ESP> Para 1990, la ingeniería y tecnología incluyen las artes y oficios industriales, los transportes y comunicaciones.

Trinidad and Tobago:

E--> Data refer to the University of West Indies only. Social and behavioural sciences include mass communication and documentation.

FR-> Les données se réfèrent à l'Université de *West Indies* seulement. Les sciences sociales et sciences du comportement incluent l'information et la documentation.

ESP> Los datos se refieren a la Universidad de *West Indies* solamente. Las ciencias sociales y del comportamiento incluyen la documentación y comunicación social.

AMERICA, SOUTH:

Argentina:

E--> Data refer to universities and equivalent degree-granting institutions only. Social and behaviourial science include mass communication and documentation.

FR-> Les données se réfèrent aux universités et établissements conférant des grades équivalents seulement. Les sciences sociales et sciences du comportement incluent l'information et la documentation.

ESP> Los datos se refieren a las universidades solamente y establecimientos que otorgan títulos equivalentes. Las ciencias sociales y del comportamiento incluyen la documentación y la comunicación social.

Bolivia:

E--> Data refer to universities and equivalent degree-granting institutions only. For 1991, data do not include teacher-training at other third level institutions.

FR-> Les données se réfèrent aux universités et établissements conférant des grades équivalents seulement, et en 1991, ne comprennent pas l'enseignement normal dispensé dans les autres établissements du troisième degré.

ESP> Los datos se refieren a las universidades y establecimientos que otorgan grados equivalentes solamente y, en 1991, excluyen la enseñanza normal en los otros establecimientos de tercer grado.

Brazil:

E--> Except for 1980, data do not include post-graduates.

FR-> Sauf pour 1980, les données ne comprennent pas les diplômés du niveau universitaire supérieur.

ESP> Con excepción de 1980, los datos excluyen los diplomados del nivel universitario superior.

Chile:

E--> Data for 1991 and 1993 refer to public universities only.

FR-> Les données pour 1991 et 1993 se réfèrent aux universités publiques seulement.

ESP> Los datos de 1991 y 1993 se refieren a las universidades públicas solamente.

Ecuador:

E--> Engineering includes trade, craft and industrial programmes.

FR-> Les sciences de l'ingénieur incluent les métiers de la production industrielle.

ESP> La ingeniería y tecnología incluyen las artes y oficios industriales.

Peru:

E--> Except for 1990, data refer to universities only.

FR-> Sauf pour 1990, les données se réfèrent aux universités seulement.

ESP> Con excepción de 1990, los datos sólo se refieren a las universidades.

Uruguay:

E--> For 1980 and 1985, data refer to universities and equivalent degree-granting institutions only.

FR-> Pour 1980 et 1985, les données se réfèrent aux universités et établissements conférant des grades équivalents seulement.

ESP> Para 1980 y 1985, los datos sólo se refieren a las universidades y establecimientos que otorgan títulos equivalentes.

ASIA:

Azerbaijan:

E--> Engineering includes trade, craft and industrial programmes.

FR-> Les sciences de l'ingénieur incluent les métiers de la production industrielle.

ESP> Ingeniería y tecnología incluyen las artes y oficios industriales.

China:

E--> For 1986 and 1991, data refer to universities only.

FR-> Pour 1986 et 1991, les données se réfèrent aux universités seulement.

ESP> Para 1986 y 1991, los datos se refieren a las universidades solamente.

Cyprus:

E--> Not including Turkish institutions.

FR-> Non compris les institutions turques.

ESP> Excluídas las instituciones turcas.

India:

E--> Humanities, religion and theology include social and behavioural sciences.

FR-> Les lettres, la religion et la théologie incluent les sciences sociales et sciences du comportement.

ESP> Las humanidades, religión y teología incluyen las ciencias sociales y del comportamiento.

Indonesia:

E--> For 1992 and 1993, data do not include post-graduates.

FR-> Pour 1992 et 1993, les données n'incluent pas les diplômés du niveau universitaire supérieur.

ESP> Para 1992 y 1993, los datos no incluyen los diplomados del nivel universitario superior.

Iran, Islamic Republic of:

E--> Data for 1986, 1991 and 1994 refer to public institutions only and for 1986, exclude teacher training. For 1994, medical science at level 6 includes some graduates at level 7.

FR-> Les données pour 1986, 1991 et 1994 se réfèrent aux institutions publiques seulement et pour 1986, ne comprennent pas l'enseignement normal. Pour 1994, les sciences médicales au niveau 6 incluent une partie des diplômés du niveau 7.

ESP> Los datos para 1986, 1991 y 1994 se refieren a las instituciones públicas solamente y para 1986 excluyen la enseñanza normal. Para 1994, las ciencias médicas del nivel 6 incluyen una parte de los diplomados del nivel 7.

Israel:

E--> Data refer to universities and equivalent degree-granting institutions only.

FR-> Les données se réfèrent aux universités et établissements conférant des grades équivalents seulement.

ESP> Los datos se refieren a las universidades y establecimientos que otorgan títulos equivalentes solamente.

Japan:

E--> Humanities, religion and theology include mass communication and documentation.

FR-> Les lettres, la religion et la théologie comprennent l'information et la documentation.

ESP> Las humanidades, religión y teología comprenden la documentación y comunicación social.

Malaysia:

E--> For 1991, data do not include polytechnics and teacher training.

FR-> Pour 1991, les données ne comprennent pas les *polytechnics* et l'enseignement normal.

ESP> Para 1991, los datos no incluyen los *polytechnics* y la enseñanza normal.

Oman:

E--> Data for 1992 refer to the University of Qaboos and teacher training colleges. For 1988, they concern only other third level institutions.

FR-> Les données pour 1992 se réfèrent à l'Université du Qaboos et à l'enseignement normal. Pour 1988, les données se réfèrent aux autres établissements du troisième degré seulement.

ESP> Los datos de 1992 se refieren a la Universidad de Qaboos y formación de personal docente. Para 1988, los datos se refieren a los otros establecimientos de tercer grado solamente.

Philippines:

E--> Data refer to universities and equivalent degree-granting institutions only.

FR-> Les données se réfèrent aux universités et établissements conférant des grades équivalents seulement.

ESP> Los datos se refieren a las universidades y establecimientos que otorgan títulos equivalentes solamente.

Third level: graduates by level and field of study 3.12
Troisième degré: diplômés par niveau et domaine d'études
Tercer grado: diplomados por nivel y sector de estudios

Qatar:
E--> In 1986 and 1992, level 6 includes level 5.
FR-> En 1986 et 1992, le niveau 6 inclut le niveau 5.
ESP> En 1986 y 1992, el nivel 6 incluye el nivel 5.

Saudi Arabia:
E--> In 1981, level 6 includes level 7. In 1994, not including graduates in telecommunications.
FR-> En 1981, le niveau 6 inclut le niveau 7. En 1994, non compris les diplômés en télécommunications.
ESP> En 1981, el nivel 6 incluye el nivel 7. En 1994, excluídos los diplomados de telecomunicaciones.

Sri Lanka:
E--> Data for 1990 refer to universities and equivalent degree-granting institutions only.
FR-> Les données pour 1990 se réfèrent aux universités et établissements conférant des grades équivalents seulement.
ESP> Los datos de 1990 sólo se refieren a las universidades y establecimientos que ortogan títulos equivalentes.

Syrian Arab Republic:
E--> For 1981 and 1993, data do not include teacher training and for 1993, they also exclude technical education.
FR-> Pour 1981 et 1993, les données ne comprennent pas l'enseignement normal et pour 1993 elles excluent aussi l'enseignement technique.
ESP> Para 1981 y 1993, los datos excluyen la enseñanza normal y para 1993 excluída también la enseñanza técnica.

United Arab Emirates:
E--> For 1992, data do not include teacher training at non university institutions.
FR-> Pour 1992, les données ne comprennent pas l'enseignement normal dans les établissements non universitaires.
ESP> Para 1992, los datos excluyen la enseñanza normal en los establecimientos no universitarios.

EUROPE:
Albania:
E--> Data for 1983, 1986 and 1990 do not include distance learning institutions.
FR-> Les données pour 1983, 1986 et 1990 ne comprennent pas l'enseignement à distance.
ESP> Los datos de 1983, 1986 y 1990 excluyen la enseñanza a distancia.

Austria:
E--> Data for 1981 refer to universities and equivalent degree-granting institutions only.
FR-> Les données pour 1981 se réfèrent aux universités et établissements conférant des grades équivalents seulement.
ESP> Los datos de 1981 se refieren a las universidades y establecimientos que otorgan títulos equivalentes solamente.

Belarus:
E--> Not including graduates of specialized secondary schools. The figures have been provided by the authorities of Belarus according to their own system of classification.
FR-> Non compris les diplômés des écoles secondaires spécialisées. Ces chiffres sont fournis par les autorités de Bélarus selon son propre système de classification.
ESP> No incluídos los graduados de las escuelas secundarias espezializadas. Estas cifras han sido facilitadas por las autoridades de Belarús con arreglo a su propio sistema de clasificación.

Belgium:
E--> Data for 1981 refer to universities and equivalent degree-granting institutions only. In 1986, level 6 includes level 7.
FR-> Les données pour 1981 se réfèrent aux universités et établissements conférant des grades équivalents seulement. En 1986, le niveau 6 inclut le niveau 7.
ESP> Los datos de 1981 se refieren a las universidades y establecimientos que otorgan títulos equivalentes solamente. En 1986, el nivel 6 incluye el nivel 7.

Croatia:
E--> Data for 1981, 1986 and 1990 do not include post-graduates.
FR-> Les données pour 1981, 1986 et 1990 ne comprennent pas les diplômés du niveau universitaire supérieur.
ESP> Los datos de 1981, 1986 y 1990 excluyen los diplomados del nivel universitario superior.

Czech Republic:
E--> Data refer to universities and degree-granting institutions only.
FR-> Les données se réfèrent aux universités et établissements conférant des grades équivalents seulement.
ESP> Los datos se refieren a las universidades y a los establecimientos que otorgan títulos equivalentes solamente.

Denmark:
E--> Level 6 includes level 7.
FR-> Le niveau 6 inclut le niveau 7.

ESP> El nivel 6 incluye el nivel 7.
Estonia:
E--> In 1993, level 6 includes level 7.
FR-> En 1993, le niveau 6 inclut le niveau 7.
ESP> En 1993, el nivel 6 incluye el nivel 7.

Holy See:
E--> Data refer to students graduating from higher institutions under the authority of the Holy See.
FR-> Les données se réfèrent aux diplômés des institutions du troisième degré sous l'autorité du Saint-Siège.
ESP> Los datos se refieren a los diplomados de los instituciones de tercer grado bajo la autoridad de la Santa Sede.

Hungary:
E--> In 1991 and 1994, level 6 includes level 7.
FR-> En 1991 et 1994, le niveau 6 inclut le niveau 7.
ESP> En 1991 et 1994, el nivel 6 incluye el nivel 7.

Ireland:
E--> Data for 1981 refer to universities and equivalent degree-granting institutions only.
FR-> Les données pour 1981 se réfèrent aux universités et établissements conférant des grades équivalents seulement.
ESP> Los datos de 1981 se refieren a las universidades y establecimientos que otorgan títulos equivalentes solamente.

Latvia:
E--> Data refer to universities and degree-granting institutions only.
FR-> Les données se réfèrent aux universités et établissements conférant des grades équivalents seulement.
ESP> Los datos se refieren a las universidades y a los establecimientos que otorgan títulos equivalentes solamente.

Netherlands:
E--> In 1981 and 1986, level 6 includes level 7. In 1991 and 1994, level 6 includes level 5.
FR-> En 1981 et 1986, le niveau 6 inclut le niveau 7. En 1991 et 1994, le niveau 6 inclut le niveau 5.
ESP> En 1981 y 1986, el nivel 6 incluye el nivel 7. En 1991 y 1994, el nivel 6 incluye el nivel 5.

Russian Federation:
E--> For 1992, level 6 includes level 7. For 1995, data for female students do not include post-graduates.
FR-> Pour 1992, le niveau 6 inclut le niveau 7. Pour 1995, les données pour les étudiantes ne comprennent pas les diplômées du niveau universitaire supérieur.
ESP> Para 1992, el nivel 6 incluye el nivel 7. Para 1995, los datos para las estudiantes excluyen las diplomadas del nivel universitario superior.

Slovakia:
E--> Level 6 includes level 7.
FR-> Le niveau 6 inclut le niveau 7.
ESP> El nivel 6 incluye el nivel 7.

Sweden:
E--> For 1991, the totals are net figures excluding double counting and thus do not agree with the sums by level.
FR-> Pour 1991, les totaux sont des nombres nets excluant les doubles comptes et ne sont pas la somme de la répartition par niveau.
ESP> Para 1991, los totales son cifras netas que excluyen a los graduados inscritos en varios niveles de estudios y que no son, por lo tanto, la suma de los niveles.

Switzerland:
E--> Data for 1980 and 1986 refer to universities only.
FR-> Les données pour 1980 et 1986 se réfèrent aux universités seulement.
ESP> Los datos de 1980 y 1986 se refieren a las universidades solamente.

Ukraine:
E--> The figures have been provided by the authorities of Ukraine according to their own system of classification. Data refer to universities and degree-granting institutions only.
FR-> Ces chiffres sont fournis par les autorités de l'Ukraine selon son propre système de classification. Les données se réfèrent aux universités et établissements conférant des grades équivalents seulement.
ESP> Estas cifras han sido facilitadas por las autoridades de Ucrania con arreglo a su propio sistema de clasificación. Los datos se refieren a las universidades y a los establecimientos que otorgan títulos equivalentes solamente.

OCEANIA:
New Zealand:
E--> Data refer to universities only.
FR-> Les données se réfèrent aux universités seulement.
ESP> Los datos se refieren a las universidades solamente.

3.13 Third level: foreign students
Troisième degré: étudiants étrangers
Tercer grado: estudiantes extranjeros

3.13 Education at the third level: number of foreign students enrolled

Enseignement du troisième degré: nombre d'étudiants étrangers inscrits

Enseñanza de tercer grado: número de estudiantes extranjeros matriculados

The years indicated refer to the beginning of the academic year for each country.

Les années indiquées se réfèrent au début de l'année académique en vigueur dans chaque pays.

Los años indicados se refieren al inicio del año académico en cada país.

\# For countries with this symbol, see the annex at the end of the table.

\# Pour les pays dont le nom est accompagné de ce symbole voir l'Annexe en fin de tableau.

\# Para los países cuyo nombre figura con este símbolo, véase el anexo al final del cuadro.

Host country Pays d'accueil País huesped	Foreign students enrolled (MF) Étudiants étrangers inscrits (MF) Estudiantes extranjeros matriculados (MF)					
	1980	1985	1990	1992	1993	1994
Africa						
Algeria #	1 810	2 479	2 614	2 550	...	...
Benin #	128	216	295	...	707	738
Botswana #	204	102	312	...	344	...
Burkina Faso #	85	233	...	325	414	...
Burundi	471	374	449	379	...	...
Cameroon	173	...	172	...	...	...
Central African Republic #	...	295	151	...	...	...
Chad	...	...	...	50	...	...
Congo #	544	...	222	...	...	...
Egypt‡	21 751	12 235	7 273	5 752	6 818	...
Ethiopia‡#	46	62	78	65	...	...
Ghana‡#	...	54	99	...	...	...
Guinea #	13	24	50	...	...	...
Lesotho‡#	200	231	173	177	183	...
Madagascar‡#	40	...	367	335	...	...
Malawi	5	...	...	...	26	...
Mauritania	...	...	...	...	503	...
Mauritius‡	5	18	22	...	...	...
Morocco‡	1 641	2 064	4 318	3 157	3 339	3 617
Mozambique	183	149	...	128	135	...
Namibia #	...	...	405	...	...	...
Rwanda‡#	87	193	320	...	...	...
Senegal‡#	3 065	2 378	1 903	...	...	...
South Africa	...	...	...	...	...	*12 625
Sudan #	1 679	361	775	...	...	...
Swaziland‡#	225	...	128	102	168	...
Togo‡#	1 114	675	674	...	210	...
Tunisia	781	1 349	2 434	2 663	2 615	2 679
America, North						
Canada‡	28 443	29 496	35 187	37 478	35 451	...
Cuba	2 026	3 161	5 654	4 811	...	...
El Salvador‡	...	...	133	...	241	...
Honduras	493	709	794	...	708	521
Jamaica‡	46	94	107	82	...	...
Nicaragua	...	214	127	63	...	...
Trinidad and Tobago		37		48	47	...
United States	311 882	343 780	407 530	438 618	449 749	...
U.S. Virgin Islands	...	130	...	136	...	...
America, South						
Argentina‡	...	...	...	...	...	12 678
Chile‡#	534	501	590	...	...	...
Guyana‡#	11	20	13	...	40	...

Third level: foreign students 3.13
Troisième degré: étudiants étrangers
Tercer grado: estudiantes extranjeros

Host country Pays d'accueil País huesped	Foreign students enrolled (MF) Étudiants étrangers inscrits (MF) Estudiantes extranjeros matriculados (MF)					
	1980	1985	1990	1992	1993	1994
Asia						
Afghanistan #	37	...	161	...	...	...
Azerbaijan	...	...	...	...	...	1 455
Bahrain‡	102	104	528	139	525	...
Bangladesh #	240	185	240	...	...	...
China	1 381	3 250	8 495	13 993	22 755	...
Cyprus	331	544	1 184	1 301	1 277	1 434
Hong Kong #	142	208	...	722	1 030	...
Iran, Islamic Republic of	...	135	290	363	412	372
Japan‡#	6 543	12 442	45 066	...	...	...
Jordan‡#	722	2 231	2 498	5 545	8 064	...
Kazakstan	...	...	...	...	1 562	2 215
Korea, Republic of	1 015	978	2 237	1 447	1 908	1 879
Kuwait‡#	2 892	5 985	2 592	...	...	...
Lao People's Democratic Rep.	2	...	...	59	...	...
Mongolia	...	...	...	...	...	239
Pakistan‡#	2 229	1 109	936	...	...	...
Philippines #	7 901	4 460	5 238	4 908	4 139	...
Qatar	1 099	...	...	1 102	1 190	1 311
Saudi Arabia	14 298	17 607	12 408	8 961	6 419	...
Sri Lanka #	44	51	...	...	...	55
Syrian Arab Republic‡#	6 267	12 909	13 173	13 438	...	...
Turkey #	6 655	7 021	7 661	7 850	13 354	15 000
United Arab Emirates	660	1 021	685	...	...	...
Europe						
Albania	...	...	...	...	494	...
Austria†#	12 885	15 388	18 434	21 980	23 911	...
Belarus	...	...	...	2 941	2 656	...
Belgium‡	12 875	24 761	27 378	...	...	...
Bulgaria‡	3 988	7 254	8 768	7 826	7 873	8 058
Croatia	...	...	...	4 329	1 592	1 349
Czech Republic	...	...	3 122	2 505	3 614	2 836
Denmark	3 035	3 167	6 728	7 637	...	...
Finland‡	610	979	1 617	2 182	2 348	...
France‡	110 763	131 979	136 015	138 477	139 562	...
Germany	...	...	107 005	...	...	...
Former German Democratic Rep.	7 106	9 231	...	...	...	...
Federal Republic of Germany	61 841	79 354	...	...	...	...
Greece	7 673	...	1 474	...	...	...
Holy See‡	9 104	9 775	10 938	12 253	...	...
Hungary‡	2 742	2 485	3 310	6 248	6 324	...
Ireland‡	2 845	2 606	3 282	4 160	...	...
Italy‡	29 447	26 268	21 788	20 811	22 618	...
Latvia	...	...	...	2 637	1 572	948
Lithuania‡	...	...	...	...	290	265
Malta	36	25	61	...	72	...
Moldova	...	...	...	...	474	1 068
Netherlands‡	4 128	5 705	8 876	11 389	...	...
Norway #	1 114	...	6 907	8 065	11 290	...
Poland	2 912	2 986	4 259	4 931	4 968	...
Portugal	1 318	2 047	3 773	...	...	...
Romania	15 888	10 774	...	13 200	11 868	...
Russian Federation	...	...	...	...	82 744	73 172
Slovakia	...	...	...	1 466	2 414	2 142
Slovenia #	...	...	990	749	657	548
Spain	10 997	...	10 268	12 578	...	...
Sweden #	...	10 401	10 650	...	...	...
Switzerland	14 716	17 396	22 621	24 844	25 304	...
The Former Yugoslav Republic of Macedonia	...	...	...	1 184	493	...
Ukraine	...	...	...	...	...	22 618
United Kingdom‡	56 003	53 694	80 183	95 944	...	...
Former Yugoslavia	4 426	7 384	5 967	...	...	...
Federal Republic of Yugoslavia	...	...	...	2 642	...	1 149
Oceania						
Australia‡	8 777	16 075	28 993	39 490	42 415	...
Fiji #	...	16	905	...	...	...
New Zealand‡	2 464	2 618	3 229	3 999	4 489	...

3.13 Third level: foreign students
Troisième degré: étudiants étrangers
Tercer grado: estudiantes extranjeros

Annex: Countries shown with the symbol #.
Annexe: Pays dont le nom est accompagné du symbole #.
Anexo: Países en los que aparece el símbolo #.

Country Pays País	Data for Les données pour Los datos para 1980 refer to se réfèrent à se refieren a	Data for Les données pour Los datos para 1985 refer to se réfèrent à se refieren a	Data for Les données pour Los datos para 1990 refer to se réfèrent à se refieren a
Africa			
Algeria			1991
Benin	1981		1991
Botswana		1984	
Bukina Faso		1984	
Central African Republic	1981		1991
Congo			1991
Ethiopia	1981		
Ghana	1979	1984	
Guinea	1981		1988
Lesotho		1984	1991
Madagascar	1979		
Namibia			1991
Rwanda			1989
Senegal			1989
Sudan		1986	
Swaziland	1981		
Togo		1984	1989
America, South			
Chile		1984	
Guyana			1989
Asia			
Afghanistan	1979		
Bangladesh			1989
Hong Kong		1984	
Japan			1991
Jordan		1984	
Kuwait			1991
Pakistan	1979		1991
Philippines		1984	1991
Sri Lanka	1979		
Syrian Arab Republic			1991
Turkey	1979		
Europe			
Austria	1981		
Norway	1979		
Slovenia		1991	
Sweden		1984	1988
Oceania			
Fiji		1984	1991

Third level: foreign students **3.13**
Troisième degré: étudiants étrangers
Tercer grado: estudiantes extranjeros

According to the UNESCO definition, a foreign student is *a person enrolled at an institution of higher education in a country or territory in which he is not a permanent resident.* However, most of the countries have established their statistics on the basis of nationality.

The differences resulting from the application of these two criteria can, in certain cases, be quite appreciable; for example, as concerns those immigrants who have not taken the nationality of the host country but who are permanent residents.

Selon la définition de l'UNESCO, un étudiant étranger est *une personne inscrite dans un établissement d'enseignement supérieur d'un pays ou d'un territoire où elle n'a pas son domicile permanent.* Il faut signaler cependant que la plupart des pays ont établi leurs statistiques d'après le concept de nationalité. Les différences

résultant de l'application de ce concept peuvent être importantes dans certains cas où les statistiques tiennent compte, par exemple, des immigrants qui, n'ayant pas acquis la nationalité du pays hôte, y résident cependant de façon permanente.

De acuerdo con la definición de la UNESCO, un estudiante extranjero es *una persona matriculada en un establecimiento de enseñanza superior de un país o territorio en el que no tiene su domicilio fijo.* Sin embargo, se debe señalar que la mayoría de los países han establecido sus estadísticas ateniéndose al concepto de

nacionalidad. Las diferencias motivadas por la aplicación de este concepto pueden ser importantes en ciertos casos donde las estadísticas toman en consideración, por ejemplo, a los inmigrantes, que no habiendo adquirido la nacionalidad del país huésped, residen sin embargo en el mismo de manera permanente.

AFRICA:
Egypt:
　　E--> Data exclude Al Azhar University and from 1985 refer to universities only.
　　FR-> Les données n'incluent pas l'Université d'Al Azhar et depuis 1985 se réfèrent aux universités seulement.
　　ESP> Los datos excluyen la Universidad de Al Azhar y desde 1985 se refieren a las universidades solamente.
Ethiopia:
　　E--> Data for 1992 refer to 1991.
　　FR-> Les données pour 1992 se réfèrent à 1991.
　　ESP> Los datos para 1992 se refieren a 1991.
Ghana:
　　E--> Data for 1984 and 1990 refer to universities only.
　　FR-> Les données pour 1984 et 1990 se réfèrent aux universités seulement.
　　ESP> Los datos de 1984 y 1990 se refieren a las universidades solamente.
Lesotho:
　　E--> Data refer to the National University of Lesotho only.
　　FR-> Les données se réfèrent à l'Université nationale du Lesotho seulement.
　　ESP> Los datos se refieren a la Universidad Nacional de Lesotho solamente.
Madagascar:
　　E--> Data for 1992 refer to University only.
　　FR-> Les données pour 1992 se réfèrent aux universités seulement.
　　ESP> Los datos para 1992 se refieren a las universidades solamente.
Mauritius:
　　E--> Data for 1980 refer to the University of Mauritius only.
　　FR-> Les données pour 1980 se réfèrent à l'Université de Maurice seulement.
　　ESP> Los datos de 1980 se refieren a la Universidad de Mauricio solamente.
Morocco:
　　E--> Except for 1990, data refer to universities only.
　　FR-> A l'exception de 1990, les données se réfèrent aux universités seulement.
　　ESP> Con excepción de 1990, los datos se refieren a las universidades solamente.
Rwanda:
　　E--> Data for 1980 refer to the National University of Rwanda only.
　　FR-> Les données pour 1980 se réfèrent à l'Université nationale du Rwanda seulement.
　　ESP> Los datos de 1980 se refieren a la Universidad Nacional de Rwanda solamente.
Senegal:
　　E--> Data for 1985 refer to the University of Dakar only.
　　FR-> Les données pour 1985 se réfèrent à l'Université de Dakar seulement.
　　ESP> Los datos de 1985 se refieren a la Universidad de Dakar solamente.
Swaziland:
　　E--> Data refer to universities only.
　　FR-> Les données se réfèrent aux universités seulement.
　　ESP> Los datos se refieren a las universidades solamente.
Togo:
　　E--> Data refer to the University of Benin only.
　　FR-> Les données se réfèrent à l'Université du Bénin seulement.

ESP> Los datos se refieren a la Universidad de Benin solamente.
AMERICA, NORTH:
Canada:
　　E--> Data refer to universities only.
　　FR-> Les données se réfèrent aux universités seulement.
　　ESP> Los datos se refieren a las universidades solamente.
El Salvador:
　　E--> Data refer to universities only.
　　FR-> Les données se réfèrent aux universités seulement.
　　ESP> Los datos se refieren a las universidades solamente.
Jamaica:
　　E--> Data for 1992 refer to 1991.
　　FR-> Les données pour 1992 se réfèrent à 1991.
　　ESP> Los datos para 1992 se refieren a 1991.
AMERICA, SOUTH:
Argentina:
　　E--> Data refer to public universities only.
　　FR-> Les données se réfèrent aux universités publiques seulement.
　　ESP> Los datos se refieren a las universidades públicas solamente.
Chile:
　　E--> Data refer to public universities only.
　　FR-> Les données se réfèrent aux universités publiques seulement.
　　ESP> Los datos se refieren a las universidades públicas solamente.
Guyana:
　　E--> Data for 1980 refer to the University of Guyana only.
　　FR-> Les données pour 1980 se réfèrent à l'Université du Guyana seulement.
　　ESP> Los datos de 1980 se refieren a la Universidad de Guyana solamente.
ASIA:
Bahrain:
　　E--> Data for 1985 refer to universities only.
　　FR-> Les données pour 1985 se réfèrent aux universités seulement.
　　ESP> Los datos de 1985 se refieren a las universidades solamente.
Japan:
　　E--> Data refer to universities and junior colleges only.
　　FR-> Les données se réfèrent aux universités et *junior colleges* seulement.
　　ESP> Los datos se refieren a las universidades y *junior colleges* solamente.
Jordan:
　　E--> Data for 1980 refer to universities only.
　　FR-> Les données pour 1980 se réfèrent aux universités seulement.
　　ESP> Los datos de 1980 se refieren a las universidades solamente.
Kuwait:
　　E--> Data for 1991 refer to the University of Kuwait only.
　　FR-> Les données pour 1991 se réfèrent à l'Université du Koweit seulement.
　　ESP> Los datos de 1991 se refieren a la Universidad de Kuwait solamente.
Pakistan:
　　E--> Data for 1985 refer to universities only.
　　FR-> Les données pour 1985 se réfèrent aux universités seulement.

3.13 Third level: foreign students
Troisième degré: étudiants étrangers
Tercer grado: estudiantes extranjeros

ESP> Los datos de 1985 se refieren a las universidades solamente.

Syrian Arab Republic:
E--> Data for 1980 refer to the University of Damascus only.
FR-> Les données pour 1980 se réfèrent à l'Université de Damas seulement.
ESP> Los datos de 1980 se refieren a la Universidad de Damasco solamente.

EUROPE:
Austria:
E--> Data refer to universities and equivalent degree-granting institutions only.
FR-> Les données se réfèrent aux universités et établissements conférant des grades équivalents seulement.
ESP> Los datos se refieren a las universidades y establecimientos que otorgan grados equivalentes solamente.

Belgium:
E--> Data for 1980 refer to universities and equivalent degree-granting institutions only.
FR-> Les données pour 1980 se réfèrent aux universités et établissements conférant des grades équivalents seulement.
ESP> Los datos de 1980 se refieren a las universidades y establecimientos que otorgan grados equivalentes solamente.

Bulgaria:
E--> Data for 1980 refer to universities only.
FR-> Les données pour 1980 se réfèrent aux universités seulement.
ESP> Los datos de 1980 se refieren a las universidades solamente.

Finland:
E--> Data refer to universities and equivalent degree-granting institutions only.
FR-> Les données se réfèrent aux universités et établissements conférant des grades équivalents seulement.
ESP> Los datos se refieren a las universidades y establecimientos que otorgan grados equivalentes solamente.

France:
E--> Data refer to universities, and from 1990 to public universities only.
FR-> Les données se réfèrent aux universités et, à partir de 1990, aux universités publiques seulement.
ESP> Los datos se refieren a las universidades, y a partir de 1990, a las universidades públicas solamente.

Holy See:
E--> Data refer to foreign students enrolled in higher education institutions under the authority of the Holy See.
FR-> Les données se réfèrent aux étudiants étrangers inscrits dans des institutions du troisième degré sous l'autorité du Saint-Siège.
ESP> Los datos se refieren a los estudiantes extranjeros inscritos en instituciones de tercer grado bajo la autoridad de la Santa Sede.

Hungary:
E--> From 1992, data refer to full-time students only.
FR-> A partir de 1992, les données se réfèrent aux étudiants à plein temps seulement.

ESP> A partir de 1992, los datos se refieren a los estudiantes de jornada completa solamente.

Ireland:
E--> Data for 1992 refer to full-time students only.
FR-> Les données pour 1992 se réfèrent aux étudiants à plein temps seulement.
ESP> Los datos de 1992 se refieren a los estudiantes de jornada completa solamente.

Italy:
E--> From 1990, data refer to foreign students enrolled at ISCED level 6.
FR-> A partir de 1990, les données se réfèrent aux étudiants étrangers inscrits au niveau 6 de la CITE.
ESP> A partir de 1990, los datos se refieren a los estudiantes inscritos en el nivel 6 de la CINE.

Lithuania:
E--> Data refer to universities only.
FR-> Les données se réfèrent aux universités seulement.
ESP> Los datos se refieren a las Universidades solamente.

Netherlands:
E--> Until 1985, data refer to full-time students only.
FR-> Jusqu'à 1985, les données se réfèrent aux étudiants à plein temps seulement.
ESP> Hasta 1985, los datos se refieren a los estudiantes de jornada completa solamente.

United Kingdom:
E--> Data refer to foreign students enrolled at universities (for full-time study or research), technical colleges (advanced courses) and colleges of education.
FR-> Les données se réfèrent aux étudiants étrangers inscrits dans les universités (pour études ou recherches à plein temps), *technical colleges (advanced courses)* et *colleges of education*.
ESP> Los datos se refieren a los estudiantes extranjeros matriculados en las universidades (para realizar estudios o investigaciones en régimen de jornada completa), en los *technical colleges (advanced courses)* y en los *colleges of education*.

OCEANIA:
Australia:
E--> Data do not include Technical and Further Education Institutions (TAFE).
FR-> Les données ne comprennent pas les *Technical and Further Education Institutions* (TAFE).
ESP> Los datos no incluyen *Technical and Further Education Institutions* (TAFE).

New Zealand:
E--> Data for 1980 and 1985 do not include foreign part-time students enrolled at polytechnics and and technical correspondence institute.
FR-> Les données pour 1980 et 1985 ne comprennent pas les étudiants étrangers à temps partiel inscrits dans les écoles polytechniques et l'institut technique par correspondance.
ESP> Los datos de 1980 y 1985 no incluyen a los estudiantes extranjeros de jornada parcial inscritos en las escuelas politécnicas y el instituto técnico de enseñanza por correspondancia.

Third level: foreign students by country of origin **3.14**
Troisième degré: étudiants étrangers par pays d'origine
Tercer grado: estudiantes extranjeros por país de origen

3.14 Education at the third level: foreign students
by country of origin, in 50 selected countries

Enseignement du troisième degré: étudiants étrangers
apr pays d'origine, dans 50 pays choisis

Enseñanza de tercer grado: estudiantes extranjeros
por país de origen, en 50 países seleccionados

3.14 **Third level: foreign students by country of origin**
Troisième degré: étudiants étrangers par pays d'origine
Tercer grado: estudiantes extranjeros por país de origen

Host country‡ / Pays d'accueil‡ / País huésped‡	Year / Année / Año	Total		Country of origin / Pays d'origine / País de origen					
				Africa	Algeria	Angola	Benin	Botswana	Burkina Faso
United States	1993/94	449 749		20 569	245	81	54	336	41
France‡	1993/94	139 562		73 688	19 542	123	1 213	3	635
Germany‡	1991/92	116 474		7 916	268	22	55	3	43
United Kingdom‡	1992/93	95 594		8 505	101	63	5	577	2
Russian Federation	1994/95	73 172		3 762	120	241	110	3	70
Japan‡	1991/92	45 066		335	8	-	-	-	-
Australia‡	1993	42 415		828	-	-	-	-	-
Canada‡	1993/94	35 451		5 842	259	4	88	97	68
Belgium	1990/91	27 378		9 318	431	15	65	1	70
Switzerland	1993/94	25 304		1 366	239	9	43	-	7
Austria‡	1993/94	23 911		993	23	-	-	-	4
China	1993/94	22 755		277	7	-	9	1	-
Italy‡	1993/94	22 618		2 721	-	-	-	-	-
Ukraine	1994/95	18 302		3 853	86	212	57	1	68
Turkey	1994/95	15 000		650	7	-	-	-	-
Syrian Arab Republic	1992/93	13 438		1 955	64	-	-	-	3
Argentina‡	1994/95	12 678		-	-	-	-	-	-
South Africa	1994	12 625		7 701	-	5	-	143	-
Spain	1992/93	12 578		1 732	35	17	18	-	-
Holy See‡	1992/93	12 253		1 022	-	16	14	-	16
Romania	1993/94	11 868		816	3	1	-	-	-
Netherlands	1992/93	11 389		1 142	10	-	2	1	-
Norway	1993/94	11 290		1 129	17	-	1	1	1
Jordan	1993/94	8 064		341	8	-	-	-	-
Bulgaria	1994/95	8 058		659	19	63	10	-	-
Denmark	1992/93	7 637		140	11	-	-	5	-
Egypt‡	1993/94	6 818		2 189	16	-	-	-	-
Saudi Arabia	1993/94	6 419		776	17	-	9	-	5
Hungary‡	1993/94	6 324		350	1	27	4	-	-
Poland	1993/94	4 968		776	24	53	8	-	2
Philippines	1992/93	4 908		222	-	-	-	-	-
Cuba	1992/93	4 811		3 040	-	611	51	1	7
New Zealand	1993/94	4 489		70	-	-	-	4	-
Ireland‡	1992	4 160		163	1	-	-	11	-
Morocco‡	1994/95	3 617		2 648	178	19	23	-	77
Portugal	1989/90	3 608		2 224	1	809	-	-	-
Czech Republic	1994/95	2 836		445	3	66	15	-	3
Tunisia	1994/95	2 679		1 595	201	-	-	-	-
Belarus	1993/94	2 656		719	10	82	9	1	17
Kuwait‡	1991/92	2 592		236	2	-	1	-	-
Algeria	1992/93	2 550		1 408	.	2	11	-	44
Finland‡	1993/94	2 348		302	12	-	1	-	-
Slovakia	1994/95	2 142		292	1	50	5	-	-
Korea, Republic of	1994/95	1 879		22	-	-	2	-	-
Kazakstan	1993/94	1 562		255	1	10	-	-	11
Azerbaijan	1994/95	1 455		110	4	31	-	-	-
Cyprus	1994/95	1 434		51	-	-	-	-	-
Croatia	1994/95	1 349		14	-	1	-	-	-
Qatar	1994/95	1 311		216	-	-	-	-	-
Federal Republic of Yugoslavia	1994/95	1 149		18	1	1	-	-	-
Total (50 countries)		1 352 693		175 401	21 976	2 634	1 883	1 189	1 194

Third level: foreign students by country of origin 3.14
Troisième degré: étudiants étrangers par pays d'origine
Tercer grado: estudiantes extranjeros por país de origen

Host country‡ / Pays d'accueil‡ / País huésped‡	Year / Année / Año	Country of origin / Pays d'origine / País de origen							
		Burundi	Cameroon	Cape Verde	Central African Republic	Chad	Comoros	Congo	Cote d'Ivoire
United States	1993/94	73	832	87	26	27	7	35	372
France‡	1993/94	99	4 676	74	441	189	468	2 679	2 569
Germany‡	1991/92	33	737	15	11	39	3	30	72
United Kingdom‡	1992/93	7	177	2	-	4	7	2	15
Russian Federation	1994/95	47	65	34	-	77	14	167	20
Japan‡	1991/92	-	1	-	-	-	-	1	12
Australia‡	1993	-	-	-	-	-	-	-	-
Canada‡	1993/94	101	308	2	25	20	11	58	284
Belgium	1990/91	163	775	14	8	10	1	34	117
Switzerland	1993/94	29	49	4	2	4	1	12	13
Austria‡	1993/94	1	7	15	1	-	-	4	8
China	1993/94	8	12	-	-	4	-	12	4
Italy‡	1993/94	-	-	-	-	-	-	-	70
Ukraine	1994/95	31	66	34	1	42	10	229	9
Turkey	1994/95	-	2	-	-	1	1	-	-
Syrian Arab Republic	1992/93	-	-	-	-	3	-	-	-
Argentina‡	1994/95	-	-	-	-	-	-	-	-
South Africa	1994	-	-	-	-	-	-	-	-
Spain	1992/93	1	18	3	4	1	-	2	9
Holy See‡	1992/93	23	38	4	6	2	-	9	18
Romania	1993/94	-	13	-	1	-	-	87	-
Netherlands	1992/93	-	5	12	1	-	-	1	3
Norway	1993/94	1	7	3	-	-	-	-	-
Jordan	1993/94	-	-	-	-	-	-	-	-
Bulgaria	1994/95	2	3	-	-	-	-	36	1
Denmark	1992/93	-	1	-	-	-	1	1	-
Egypt‡	1993/94	-	-	-	-	10	-	-	4
Saudi Arabia	1993/94	2	-	-	-	6	7	-	10
Hungary‡	1993/94	-	1	-	-	-	-	3	-
Poland	1993/94	2	1	2	2	1	-	4	2
Philippines	1992/93	-	-	-	-	-	-	-	-
Cuba	1992/93	-	-	41	-	-	-	172	-
New Zealand	1993/94	-	-	-	-	-	-	-	-
Ireland‡	1992	1	2	-	-	-	-	-	-
Morocco‡	1994/95	-	48	4	11	29	63	23	64
Portugal	1989/90	-	-	406	1	-	-	1	-
Czech Republic	1994/95	4	-	3	-	-	-	23	-
Tunisia	1994/95	-	-	-	-	-	-	-	-
Belarus	1993/94	3	13	2	-	11	1	49	-
Kuwait‡	1991/92	-	-	-	-	1	-	-	-
Algeria	1992/93	12	1	-	-	110	9	23	11
Finland‡	1993/94	1	-	-	-	-	-	-	2
Slovakia	1994/95	3	-	-	-	1	-	9	1
Korea, Republic of	1994/95	-	-	-	-	-	-	-	-
Kazakstan	1993/94	1	1	-	-	-	-	5	-
Azerbaijan	1994/95	-	-	-	-	-	-	4	-
Cyprus	1994/95	2	-	-	-	-	-	-	-
Croatia	1994/95	-	-	-	-	-	-	-	-
Qatar	1994/95	-	-	-	-	-	-	-	-
Federal Republic of Yugoslavia	1994/95	-	-	-	-	-	-	-	-
Total (50 countries)		650	7 859	761	541	592	604	3 715	3 690

3.14 Third level: foreign students by country of origin
Troisième degré: étudiants étrangers par pays d'origine
Tercer grado: estudiantes extranjeros por país de origen

Host country‡ Pays d'accueil‡ País huésped‡	Year Année Año	Country of origin / Pays d'origine / País de origen							
		Egypt	Ethiopia	Gabon	Gambia	Ghana	Guinea	Guinea-Bissau	Kenya
United States	1993/94	1 537	1 510	77	320	1 113	63	16	2 399
France‡	1993/94	488	99	1 225	21	48	358	25	41
Germany‡	1991/92	1 052	499	33	6	411	49	5	100
United Kingdom‡	1992/93	251	270	5	117	45	3	1	1 274
Russian Federation	1994/95	41	286	8	5	176	66	92	23
Japan‡	1991/92	85	6	-	-	60	5	-	27
Australia‡	1993	28	-	-	-	-	-	-	102
Canada‡	1993/94	188	88	213	22	301	115	5	423
Belgium	1990/91	44	46	31	2	34	38	3	27
Switzerland	1993/94	76	12	-	2	14	12	1	9
Austria‡	1993/94	322	41	-	1	29	2	3	15
China	1993/94	16	8	6	1	6	10	-	5
Italy‡	1993/94	88	253	-	-	-	-	-	-
Ukraine	1994/95	190	231	13	3	179	69	49	20
Turkey	1994/95	103	9	-	3	71	1	1	59
Syrian Arab Republic	1992/93	80	-	-	1	-	10	-	-
Argentina‡	1994/95	-	-	-	-	-	-	-	-
South Africa	1994	-	-	-	-	-	-	-	-
Spain	1992/93	25	3	10	1	7	12	1	9
Holy See‡	1992/93	19	45	3	-	29	1	6	40
Romania	1993/94	172	5	1	-	10	9	-	6
Netherlands	1992/93	44	60	-	2	20	2	2	1
Norway	1993/94	12	175	-	50	310	2	-	51
Jordan	1993/94	37	6	-	-	10	-	-	-
Bulgaria	1994/95	10	49	-	-	22	19	-	10
Denmark	1992/93	3	27	-	2	9	1	-	4
Egypt‡	1993/94	.	3	-	-	-	3	-	6
Saudi Arabia	1993/94	154	37	-	14	32	29	-	13
Hungary‡	1993/94	44	34	-	-	5	6	-	3
Poland	1993/94	4	44	-	1	19	26	1	47
Philippines	1992/93	3	34	-	-	8	-	-	29
Cuba	1992/93	-	401	-	-	319	74	18	1
New Zealand	1993/94	-	2	-	-	3	-	-	13
Ireland‡	1992	2	-	-	-	7	-	-	5
Morocco‡	1994/95	16	1	41	2	-	97	1	6
Portugal	1989/90	-	-	-	-	-	-	297	-
Czech Republic	1994/95	31	96	-	-	6	19	5	6
Tunisia	1994/95	-	-	-	-	-	-	-	-
Belarus	1993/94	22	69	2	-	24	8	6	5
Kuwait‡	1991/92	148	7	-	-	-	-	-	-
Algeria	1992/93	8	1	2	-	-	42	-	-
Finland‡	1993/94	19	38	-	1	56	1	-	12
Slovakia	1994/95	58	36	-	-	5	13	-	1
Korea, Republic of	1994/95	-	-	2	-	-	-	-	1
Kazakstan	1993/94	91	20	1	-	16	3	2	-
Azerbaijan	1994/95	-	21	-	-	-	-	-	-
Cyprus	1994/95	10	-	-	-	2	-	-	6
Croatia	1994/95	1	1	-	-	-	-	-	-
Qatar	1994/95	84	7	-	-	-	-	-	-
Federal Republic of Yugoslavia	1994/95	1	-	-	-	1	-	-	-
Total (50 countries)		5 607	4 580	1 673	577	3 407	1 168	540	4 799

Third level: foreign students by country of origin 3.14
Troisième degré: étudiants étrangers par pays d'origine
Tercer grado: estudiantes extranjeros por país de origen

Host country‡ Pays d'accueil‡ País huésped‡	Year Année Año	Country of origin / Pays d'origine / País de origen							
		Lesotho	Liberia	Libyan Arab Jamahiriya	Madagascar	Malawi	Mali	Mauritania	Mauritius
United States	1993/94	76	383	69	90	265	149	36	164
France‡	1993/94	3	10	-	2 712	4	468	604	935
Germany‡	1991/92	2	12	41	91	4	103	37	14
United Kingdom‡	1992/93	147	5	610	9	245	11	5	444
Russian Federation	1994/95	-	6	3	187	3	230	131	18
Japan‡	1991/92	-	3	2	4	-	-	-	1
Australia‡	1993	-	-	-	-	39	-	21	-
Canada‡	1993/94	36	4	127	35	50	85	30	102
Belgium	1990/91	-	2	11	72	1	59	4	20
Switzerland	1993/94	-	-	5	74	1	1	6	7
Austria‡	1993/94	-	1	16	2	2	7	2	-
China	1993/94	-	-	7	7	-	13	5	13
Italy‡	1993/94	-	-	168	-	-	-	-	-
Ukraine	1994/95	1	7	16	144	-	148	67	8
Turkey	1994/95	-	-	6	3	11	-	4	-
Syrian Arab Republic	1992/93	-	-	32	-	-	9	309	-
Argentina‡	1994/95	-	-	-	-	-	-	-	-
South Africa	1994	268	-	-	-	124	-	-	-
Spain	1992/93	-	3	10	-	1	37	1	5
Holy See‡	1992/93	4	2	-	23	8	2	-	1
Romania	1993/94	-	4	3	2	-	1	6	-
Netherlands	1992/93	1	1	1	-	-	-	-	1
Norway	1993/94	-	8	4	13	-	-	1	6
Jordan	1993/94	-	-	42	-	-	-	24	-
Bulgaria	1994/95	-	-	-	4	-	5	-	1
Denmark	1992/93	1	-	-	-	-	1	-	-
Egypt‡	1993/94	-	-	322	-	3	4	63	2
Saudi Arabia	1993/94	-	4	11	-	-	25	28	-
Hungary‡	1993/94	-	-	30	2	-	7	-	3
Poland	1993/94	-	4	52	3	-	22	6	1
Philippines	1992/93	-	-	-	-	-	-	-	-
Cuba	1992/93	23	1	-	28	3	24	1	-
New Zealand	1993/94	-	-	-	-	-	-	-	1
Ireland‡	1992	6	-	47	-	4	-	-	10
Morocco‡	1994/95	-	6	128	-	-	104	306	-
Portugal	1989/90	-	-	-	-	1	1	1	1
Czech Republic	1994/95	-	-	19	11	-	8	1	-
Tunisia	1994/95	-	-	-	-	-	-	376	-
Belarus	1993/94	1	2	7	27	-	66	2	3
Kuwait‡	1991/92	-	1	7	-	-	2	4	1
Algeria	1992/93	-	-	3	15	-	86	138	-
Finland‡	1993/94	-	-	7	-	-	1	-	1
Slovakia	1994/95	-	9	-	8	-	3	2	-
Korea, Republic of	1994/95	-	12	-	-	-	-	-	-
Kazakstan	1993/94	-	-	-	5	-	10	-	-
Azerbaijan	1994/95	-	-	-	25	-	-	-	-
Cyprus	1994/95	-	-	8	-	-	-	-	-
Croatia	1994/95	-	-	1	-	-	-	-	-
Qatar	1994/95	-	-	-	-	-	-	18	-
Federal Republic of Yugoslavia‡	1994/95	-	-	1	-	-	1	-	-
Total (50 countries)		569	490	1 816	3 596	769	1 693	2 239	1 763

3.14 Third level: foreign students by country of origin
Troisième degré: étudiants étrangers par pays d'origine
Tercer grado: estudiantes extranjeros por país de origen

Host countryø / Pays d'accueilø / País huéspedø	Year / Année / Año	Country of origin / Pays d'origine / País de origen							
		Morocco	Mozambique	Niger	Nigeria	Rwanda	Sao Tome and Principe	Senegal	Seychelles
United States	1993/94	946	74	60	2 285	100	8	373	21
France‡	1993/94	20 277	58	320	195	128	35	3 307	18
Germany‡	1991/92	1 456	20	8	264	87	1	96	1
United Kingdom‡	1992/93	37	116	7	875	8	4	17	102
Russian Federation	1994/95	271	79	45	230	64	21	50	1
Japan‡	1991/92	5	-	-	14	-	-	3	-
Australia‡	1993	-	-	-	-	-	-	-	-
Canada‡	1993/94	613	2	65	223	94	2	308	7
Belgium	1990/91	3 409	-	42	85	323	-	91	-
Switzerland	1993/94	283	1	8	11	64	-	45	1
Austria‡	1993/94	35	-	4	168	41	-	10	1
China	1993/94	10	12	6	8	3	-	5	2
Italy‡	1993/94	203	-	-	205	-	-	-	-
Ukraine	1994/95	682	96	31	307	33	26	36	-
Turkey	1994/95	3	6	2	7	1	1	2	-
Syrian Arab Republic	1992/93	53	-	-	6	-	-	4	-
Argentina‡	1994/95	-	-	-	-	-	-	-	-
South Africa	1994	-	76	-	-	-	-	-	-
Spain	1992/93	1 177	13	2	17	-	3	5	-
Holy See‡	1992/93	2	13	4	223	36	1	11	-
Romania	1993/94	212	2	-	8	2	-	1	-
Netherlands	1992/93	825	2	-	17	1	-	1	1
Norway	1993/94	93	1	-	71	-	-	4	-
Jordan	1993/94	30	-	-	5	-	-	10	-
Bulgaria	1994/95	58	6	-	79	2	1	1	1
Denmark	1992/93	14	2	-	4	-	-	-	-
Egypt‡	1993/94	12	-	-	11	-	-	3	-
Saudi Arabia	1993/94	9	-	-	54	1	-	24	-
Hungary‡	1993/94	6	6	29	-	-	-	-	-
Poland	1993/94	82	20	2	53	12	7	19	-
Philippines	1992/93	-	-	-	52	4	-	-	-
Cuba	1992/93	-	146	20	19	16	37	1	8
New Zealand	1993/94	-	-	-	3	-	-	-	-
Ireland‡	1992	2	-	-	7	-	-	-	-
Morocco‡	1994/95	.	-	78	18	-	-	173	-
Portugal	1989/90	2	512	-	-	-	118	1	-
Czech Republic	1994/95	9	6	3	10	-	2	6	3
Tunisia	1994/95	1 018	-	-	-	-	-	-	-
Belarus	1993/94	75	15	6	71	10	1	7	-
Kuwait‡	1991/92	5	-	-	3	-	-	6	-
Algeria	1992/93	523	2	47	-	11	-	34	-
Finland‡	1993/94	16	-	1	60	1	-	2	-
Slovakia	1994/95	10	8	-	3	-	-	11	2
Korea, Republic of	1994/95	-	-	-	3	-	-	-	-
Kazakstan	1993/94	50	6	6	-	-	-	-	-
Azerbaijan	1994/95	-	-	-	-	-	-	-	-
Cyprus	1994/95	-	-	-	2	-	-	-	4
Croatia	1994/95	1	1	-	-	-	-	-	-
Qatar	1994/95	10	-	-	-	-	-	-	-
Federal Republic of Yugoslavia	1994/95	1	-	-	1	-	-	-	-
Total (50 countries)		32 525	1 301	796	5 677	1 042	268	4 667	173

Third level: foreign students by country of origin 3.14
Troisième degré: étudiants étrangers par pays d'origine
Tercer grado: estudiantes extranjeros por país de origen

Host country‡ Pays d'accueil‡ País huésped‡	Year Année Año	Country of origin / Pays d'origine / País de origen							
		Sierra Leone	Somalia	South Africa	Sudan	Swaziland	Togo	Tunisia	Uganda
United States	1993/94	318	136	1 853	485	180	122	328	560
France‡	1993/94	19	10	55	100	-	1 118	6 020	21
Germany‡	1991/92	78	76	117	186	5	110	753	102
United Kingdom‡	1992/93	100	13	577	220	81	4	23	292
Russian Federation	1994/95	89	39	2	240	-	37	97	53
Japan‡	1991/92	-	-	-	13	-	-	32	-
Australia‡	1993	-	-	103	-	-	-	-	38
Canada‡	1993/94	21	60	94	33	33	72	410	65
Belgium	1990/91	3	13	18	14	1	32	345	14
Switzerland	1993/94	2	3	12	4	-	24	117	4
Austria‡	1993/94	-	2	6	53	-	14	66	25
China	1993/94	7	7	3	11	-	5	6	8
Italy‡	1993/94	-	263	68	-	-	-	143	-
Ukraine	1994/95	48	19	1	218	-	50	101	43
Turkey	1994/95	4	21	-	147	-	3	70	2
Syrian Arab Republic	1992/93	7	42	-	580	-	-	605	-
Argentina‡	1994/95	-	-	-	-	-	-	-	-
South Africa	1994	-	-	-	-	360	-	-	-
Spain	1992/93	1	1	-	12	1	2	10	-
Holy See‡	1992/93	4	-	8	9	7	14	-	56
Romania	1993/94	-	11	1	210	-	1	21	-
Netherlands	1992/93	3	21	55	7	-	3	12	-
Norway	1993/94	27	101	24	14	2	3	16	27
Jordan	1993/94	1	10	-	82	-	-	7	1
Bulgaria	1994/95	5	6	1	80	-	2	29	-
Denmark	1992/93	2	10	7	4	-	1	8	3
Egypt‡	1993/94	7	85	2	1 538	-	-	7	1
Saudi Arabia	1993/94	8	64	1	102	-	8	33	9
Hungary‡	1993/94	2	5	-	108	-	-	6	-
Poland	1993/94	8	1	2	67	-	-	29	10
Philippines	1992/93	-	22	-	63	-	-	-	-
Cuba	1992/93	10	-	12	38	-	-	-	22
New Zealand	1993/94	-	-	12	-	-	-	-	2
Ireland‡	1992	2	1	21	9	1	-	-	1
Morocco‡	1994/95	5	5	-	140	-	-	923	-
Portugal	1989/90	-	-	52	-	-	-	-	-
Czech Republic	1994/95	-	-	-	36	-	-	9	-
Tunisia	1994/95	-	-	-	-	-	-	.	-
Belarus	1993/94	9	3	-	19	-	10	7	15
Kuwait‡	1991/92	1	10	-	33	-	-	2	2
Algeria	1992/93	1	1	-	12	-	-	257	-
Finland‡	1993/94	1	15	3	11	-	-	1	2
Slovakia	1994/95	1	3	-	20	-	-	3	-
Korea, Republic of	1994/95	-	-	-	-	-	-	-	1
Kazakstan	1993/94	1	3	-	5	-	-	1	2
Azerbaijan	1994/95	-	-	-	10	-	-	10	-
Cyprus	1994/95	-	5	-	-	-	-	-	-
Croatia	1994/95	-	-	-	7	-	-	1	-
Qatar	1994/95	-	51	-	34	-	-	7	-
Federal Republic of Yugoslavia	1994/95	-	1	-	6	-	-	-	-
Total (50 countries)		795	1 139	3 110	4 980	671	1 635	10 515	1 381

3.14 Third level: foreign students by country of origin
Troisième degré: étudiants étrangers par pays d'origine
Tercer grado: estudiantes extranjeros por país de origen

Host country‡ / Pays d'accueil‡ / País huésped‡	Year / Année / Año	Country of origin / Pays d'origine / País de origen							
		United Republic of Tanzania	Zaire	Zambia	Zimbabwe	Africa-other and not specified		America, North	Antigua and Barbuda
United States	1993/94	667	371	356	640	203		47 826	226
France‡	1993/94	11	1 393	5	11	835		5 772	-
Germany‡	1991/92	81	241	28	29	387		5 505	-
United Kingdom‡	1992/93	484	14	584	451	92		7 915	13
Russian Federation	1994/95	104	24	17	16	40		287	-
Japan‡	1991/92	21	18	13	1	-		1 491	-
Australia‡	1993	67	-	66	-	364		1 101	-
Canada‡	1993/94	126	205	54	180	26		4 580	41
Belgium	1990/91	31	2 769	11	2	17		527	-
Switzerland	1993/94	1	151	-	2	1		752	-
Austria‡	1993/94	12	43	2	3	2		614	-
China	1993/94	12	4	6	-	8		2 573	-
Italy‡	1993/94	-	89	-	-	1 171		849	-
Ukraine	1994/95	101	26	12	11	21		132	-
Turkey	1994/95	91	3	3	2	-		30	-
Syrian Arab Republic	1992/93	-	-	-	-	147		9	-
Argentina‡	1994/95	-	-	-	-	-		-	-
South Africa	1994	-	-	78	2 855	3 792		349	-
Spain	1992/93	2	18	2	3	230		1 354	-
Holy See‡	1992/93	82	195	12	6	10		1 064	-
Romania	1993/94	3	12	5	1	2		96	-
Netherlands	1992/93	2	16	4	-	2		411	-
Norway	1993/94	39	7	9	7	21		906	-
Jordan	1993/94	-	3	-	-	65		19	-
Bulgaria	1994/95	-	1	21	21	92		60	-
Denmark	1992/93	6	1	5	4	1		289	-
Egypt‡	1993/94	2	2	-	-	83		-	-
Saudi Arabia	1993/94	1	4	-	-	55		18	-
Hungary‡	1993/94	12	-	3	3	-		209	-
Poland	1993/94	53	35	24	21	-		139	-
Philippines	1992/93	7	-	-	-	-		266	-
Cuba	1992/93	-	-	40	746	149		558	3
New Zealand	1993/94	8	-	7	13	2		162	-
Ireland‡	1992	13	-	7	1	2		803	-
Morocco‡	1994/95	-	40	-	-	19		-	-
Portugal	1989/90	1	16	-	3	-		138	-
Czech Republic	1994/95	15	4	12	8	3		57	-
Tunisia	1994/95	-	-	-	-	-		-	-
Belarus	1993/94	14	2	4	5	4		37	-
Kuwait‡	1991/92	-	-	-	-	-		5	-
Algeria	1992/93	-	1	-	-	1		-	-
Finland‡	1993/94	14	1	2	3	17		150	-
Slovakia	1994/95	12	4	4	6	-		31	-
Korea, Republic of	1994/95	-	1	-	-	-		433	-
Kazakstan	1993/94	2	-	1	1	-		11	-
Azerbaijan	1994/95	-	-	-	-	5		-	-
Cyprus	1994/95	2	-	3	3	4		14	-
Croatia	1994/95	-	-	-	-	-		16	-
Qatar	1994/95	-	-	-	-	5		1	-
Federal Republic of Yugoslavia	1994/95	-	-	3	-	-		7	-
Total (50 countries)		2 099	5 714	1 403	5 058	7 878		87 566	283

Third level: foreign students by country of origin 3.14
Troisième degré: étudiants étrangers par pays d'origine
Tercer grado: estudiantes extranjeros por país de origen

Host country‡ Pays d'accueil‡ País huésped‡	Year Année Año	Country of origin / Pays d'origine / País de origen							
		Bahamas	Barbados	Belize	Bermuda	Canada	Costa Rica	Cuba	Dominican Republic
United States	1993/94	1 808	461	307	633	22 655	885	87	1 045
France‡	1993/94	16	2	-	-	1 091	49	21	54
Germany‡	1991/92	1	5	1	-	425	78	13	17
United Kingdom‡	1992/93	77	159	20	97	1 287	30	13	7
Russian Federation	1994/95	-	-	-	-	2	19	27	12
Japan‡	1991/92	-	-	1	-	105	6	3	9
Australia‡	1993	-	-	-	-	176	-	-	-
Canada‡	1993/94	184	138	14	267	.	32	20	25
Belgium	1990/91	-	1	-	-	74	26	3	1
Switzerland	1993/94	-	1	1	-	157	9	8	1
Austria‡	1993/94	-	1	-	-	59	5	5	3
China	1993/94	-	1	1	-	301	3	29	-
Italy‡	1993/94	-	-	-	-	278	16	-	12
Ukraine	1994/95	-	-	-	-	-	7	1	4
Turkey	1994/95	-	-	-	-	11	1	-	-
Syrian Arab Republic	1992/93	-	-	-	-	1	-	4	-
Argentina‡	1994/95	-	-	-	-	-	-	-	-
South Africa	1994	-	-	-	-	-	-	-	-
Spain	1992/93	-	4	-	-	67	30	98	43
Holy See‡	1992/93	-	-	-	-	105	21	-	15
Romania	1993/94	1	-	-	-	19	4	3	1
Netherlands	1992/93	-	-	-	-	73	-	3	4
Norway	1993/94	-	2	-	-	113	4	2	-
Jordan	1993/94	-	-	-	-	6	-	-	-
Bulgaria	1994/95	-	-	-	-	1	2	-	-
Denmark	1992/93	-	-	-	-	48	-	1	-
Egypt‡	1993/94	-	-	-	-	-	-	-	-
Saudi Arabia	1993/94	1	-	-	-	2	-	-	-
Hungary‡	1993/94	2	-	-	-	28	-	2	-
Poland	1993/94	-	-	-	-	38	7	8	1
Philippines	1992/93	-	-	-	-	13	-	-	-
Cuba	1992/93	1	-	27	.	.	.	.	14
New Zealand	1993/94	-	1	-	-	40	-	-	-
Ireland‡	1992	-	1	-	-	88	1	-	-
Morocco‡	1994/95	-	-	-	-	-	-	-	-
Portugal	1989/90	-	-	-	-	83	-	-	-
Czech Republic	1994/95	-	-	-	-	8	2	2	1
Tunisia	1994/95	-	-	-	-	-	-	-	-
Belarus	1993/94	-	-	-	-	-	3	1	-
Kuwait‡	1991/92	-	-	-	-	4	-	-	-
Algeria	1992/93	-	-	-	-	-	-	-	-
Finland‡	1993/94	-	-	-	-	28	1	3	-
Slovakia	1994/95	-	-	-	-	4	3	-	1
Korea, Republic of	1994/95	-	-	-	-	33	-	-	-
Kazakstan	1993/94	-	-	-	-	-	-	-	-
Azerbaijan	1994/95	-	-	-	-	-	-	-	-
Cyprus	1994/95	-	-	-	-	-	-	-	3
Croatia	1994/95	-	-	-	-	2	-	11	-
Qatar	1994/95	-	-	-	-	-	-	-	-
Federal Republic of Yugoslavia	1994/95	-	-	-	-	3	-	-	-
Total (50 countries)		2 091	777	372	997	27 428	1 244	368	1 273

3.14 Third level: foreign students by country of origin
Troisième degré: étudiants étrangers par pays d'origine
Tercer grado: estudiantes extranjeros por país de origen

Host country‡ / Pays d'accueil‡ / País huésped‡	Year / Année / Año	Country of origin / Pays d'origine / País de origen							
		El Salvador	Grenada	Guatemala	Haiti	Honduras	Jamaica	Mexico	Netherlands Antilles
United States	1993/94	872	151	708	768	962	2 998	8 021	407
France‡	1993/94	34	5	35	331	19	18	617	-
Germany‡	1991/92	64	-	29	35	18	14	258	-
United Kingdom‡	1992/93	6	13	9	3	9	88	419	18
Russian Federation	1994/95	1	-	2	15	9	21	36	-
Japan‡	1991/92	1	-	7	-	3	1	86	-
Australia‡	1993	3	-	-	-	-	-	9	-
Canada‡	1993/94	6	26	17	96	11	149	257	4
Belgium	1990/91	7	-	3	48	3	4	47	-
Switzerland	1993/94	5	-	4	26	11	5	62	-
Austria‡	1993/94	4	-	34	-	3	3	56	-
China	1993/94	-	-	-	-	-	3	13	-
Italy‡	1993/94	-	-	-	-	-	-	-	-
Ukraine	1994/95	-	-	-	-	-	12	16	-
Turkey	1994/95	-	-	-	-	-	-	-	-
Syrian Arab Republic	1992/93	-	-	-	-	-	-	-	-
Argentina‡	1994/95	-	-	-	-	-	-	-	-
South Africa	1994	-	-	-	-	-	-	-	-
Spain	1992/93	27	-	14	14	24	1	448	-
Holy See‡	1992/93	22	1	15	25	4	1	383	-
Romania	1993/94	-	-	-	-	-	-	-	-
Netherlands	1992/93	5	-	2	-	2	2	13	-
Norway	1993/94	4	-	3	-	5	2	15	1
Jordan	1993/94	-	-	-	-	-	-	-	-
Bulgaria	1994/95	-	-	-	-	-	-	2	-
Denmark	1992/93	-	-	-	-	1	1	12	-
Egypt‡	1993/94	-	-	-	-	-	-	-	-
Saudi Arabia	1993/94	-	-	-	-	-	-	-	-
Hungary‡	1993/94	-	-	-	-	1	3	3	-
Poland	1993/94	-	-	-	-	-	-	8	-
Philippines	1992/93	-	-	-	-	-	-	-	-
Cuba	1992/93	3	5	7	35	6	33	16	-
New Zealand	1993/94	-	2	-	-	-	2	15	-
Ireland‡	1992	-	-	-	-	-	-	5	-
Morocco‡	1994/95	-	-	-	-	-	-	-	-
Portugal	1989/90	-	-	-	1	-	-	-	1
Czech Republic	1994/95	-	1	-	-	1	-	2	-
Tunisia	1994/95	-	-	-	-	-	-	-	-
Belarus	1993/94	-	-	-	-	-	-	4	-
Kuwait‡	1991/92	-	-	-	-	-	-	-	-
Algeria	1992/93	-	-	-	-	-	-	-	-
Finland‡	1993/94	-	-	-	-	-	2	6	-
Slovakia	1994/95	4	-	-	-	-	1	-	5
Korea, Republic of	1994/95	-	-	-	-	-	-	1	-
Kazakstan	1993/94	-	-	-	-	-	-	-	-
Azerbaijan	1994/95	-	-	-	-	-	-	-	-
Cyprus	1994/95	-	-	-	-	-	-	-	-
Croatia	1994/95	-	-	-	-	-	-	-	-
Qatar	1994/95	-	-	-	-	-	-	-	-
Federal Republic of Yugoslavia	1994/95	-	-	-	-	-	-	-	-
Total (50 countries)		1 068	204	889	1 397	1 092	3 364	10 830	436

Third level: foreign students by country of origin 3.14
Troisième degré: étudiants étrangers par pays d'origine
Tercer grado: estudiantes extranjeros por país de origen

Host country‡ / Pays d'accueil‡ / País huésped‡	Year / Année / Año	Country of origin / Pays d'origine / País de origen							
		Nicaragua	Panama	St. Lucia	St. Vincent and the Granadines	Trinidad and Tobago	United States	America, North-other and not specified	
United States	1993/94	564	1 545	114	77	1 855	.	677	
France‡	1993/94	28	24	9	7	7	3 392	13	
Germany‡	1991/92	34	16	1	1	10	4 229	256	
United Kingdom‡	1992/93	5	62	36	16	202	5 161	165	
Russian Federation	1994/95	88	48	-	1	-	3	3	
Japan‡	1991/92	3	7	-	1	1	1 257	-	
Australia‡	1993	-	-	-	-	-	903	10	
Canada‡	1993/94	15	19	80	12	400	2 687	80	
Belgium	1990/91	17	3	-	-	2	284	4	
Switzerland	1993/94	3	4	1	-	1	453	-	
Austria‡	1993/94	2	1	-	-	1	436	1	
China	1993/94	6	-	-	-	-	2 213	3	
Italy‡	1993/94	11	14	-	-	-	518	-	
Ukraine	1994/95	67	25	-	-	-	-	-	
Turkey	1994/95	-	-	-	-	1	17	-	
Syrian Arab Republic	1992/93	-	-	-	-	-	4	-	
Argentina‡	1994/95	-	-	-	-	-	-	-	
South Africa	1994	-	-	-	-	-	-	349	
Spain	1992/93	43	97	1	1	-	438	4	
Holy See‡	1992/93	12	7	-	-	1	448	4	
Romania	1993/94	2	-	-	-	-	66	-	
Netherlands	1992/93	1	5	-	-	1	288	12	
Norway	1993/94	2	2	-	-	5	740	6	
Jordan	1993/94	-	-	-	-	-	13	-	
Bulgaria	1994/95	35	1	-	-	-	17	2	
Denmark	1992/93	-	-	-	-	1	225	-	
Egypt‡	1993/94	-	-	-	-	-	-	-	
Saudi Arabia	1993/94	-	-	-	-	-	15	-	
Hungary‡	1993/94	4	-	-	-	-	166	-	
Poland	1993/94	9	8	-	-	-	60	-	
Philippines	1992/93	-	-	-	-	-	253	-	
Cuba	1992/93	275	39	45	9	8	-	32	
New Zealand	1993/94	-	-	-	1	1	100	-	
Ireland‡	1992	-	-	-	-	16	690	2	
Morocco‡	1994/95	-	-	-	-	-	-	-	
Portugal	1989/90	-	-	-	-	-	53	-	
Czech Republic	1994/95	20	7	-	-	-	13	-	
Tunisia	1994/95	-	-	-	-	-	-	-	
Belarus	1993/94	24	4	-	-	-	1	-	
Kuwait‡	1991/92	-	-	-	-	-	1	-	
Algeria	1992/93	-	-	-	-	-	-	-	
Finland‡	1993/94	3	-	-	-	-	107	-	
Slovakia	1994/95	10	1	-	-	-	2	-	
Korea, Republic of	1994/95	-	-	-	-	-	399	-	
Kazakstan	1993/94	4	1	-	-	-	6	-	
Azerbaijan	1994/95	-	-	-	-	-	-	-	
Cyprus	1994/95	-	-	-	-	-	11	-	
Croatia	1994/95	-	-	-	-	-	3	-	
Qatar	1994/95	-	-	-	-	-	1	-	
Federal Republic of Yugoslavia	1994/95	-	1	-	-	-	3	-	
Total (50 countries)		1 287	1 941	287	126	2 513	25 676	1 623	

3.14 Third level: foreign students by country of origin
Troisième degré: étudiants étrangers par pays d'origine
Tercer grado: estudiantes extranjeros por país de origen

Host country‡ Pays d'accueil‡ País huesped‡	Year Année Año	Country of origin / Pays d'origine / País de origen							
		America South	Argentina	Bolivia	Brazil	Chile	Colombia	Ecuador	Guyana
United States	1993/94	20 708	2 036	816	4 977	940	3 077	1 356	415
France‡	1993/94	4 161	437	87	1 543	389	796	106	6
Germany‡	1991/92	3 385	357	242	983	513	426	94	5
United Kingdom‡	1992/93	1 429	61	17	874	55	97	31	51
Russian Federation	1994/95	522	7	100	18	11	121	62	11
Japan‡	1991/92	567	69	16	345	15	20	4	-
Australia‡	1993	76	14	-	24	15	11	-	-
Canada‡	1993/94	933	103	6	315	46	117	20	74
Belgium	1990/91	698	28	40	150	139	120	49	-
Switzerland	1993/94	842	77	70	149	72	127	28	2
Austria‡	1993/94	322	34	9	108	21	52	10	-
China	1993/94	69	10	7	15	1	9	6	-
Italy‡	1993/94	1 041	188	25	142	64	56	30	-
Ukraine	1994/95	407	2	101	2	2	61	45	-
Turkey	1994/95	2	1	-	-	1	-	-	-
Syrian Arab Republic	1992/93	34	3	-	-	-	-	-	-
Argentina‡	1994/95	9 505	.	1 393	349	1 635	-	-	-
South Africa	1994	146	-	-	-	-	-	-	-
Spain	1992/93	3 454	667	61	368	316	390	93	2
Holy See‡	1992/93	1 144	196	26	432	91	217	30	-
Romania	1993/94	32	-	5	2	-	3	12	-
Netherlands	1992/93	1 488	16	3	33	53	26	3	-
Norway	1993/94	306	21	12	28	157	33	3	1
Jordan	1993/94	9	-	-	8	-	1	-	-
Bulgaria	1994/95	25	-	1	2	3	6	4	-
Denmark	1992/93	78	8	-	28	25	4	4	3
Egypt‡	1993/94	-	-	-	-	-	-	-	-
Saudi Arabia	1993/94	4	-	-	-	4	-	-	-
Hungary‡	1993/94	15	2	1	-	-	4	2	-
Poland	1993/94	135	10	6	17	3	33	12	5
Philippines	1992/93	-	-	-	-	-	-	-	-
Cuba	1992/93	507	6	92	13	48	43	206	1
New Zealand	1993/94	32	1	1	15	4	3	2	-
Ireland‡	1992	7	-	-	1	-	2	1	2
Morocco‡	1994/95	-	-	-	-	-	-	-	-
Portugal	1989/90	873	9	-	527	-	1	-	-
Czech Republic	1994/95	41	-	3	2	1	11	4	1
Tunisia	1994/95	-	-	-	-	-	-	-	-
Belarus	1993/94	69	-	25	-	-	11	12	-
Kuwait‡	1991/92	-	-	-	-	-	-	-	-
Algeria	1992/93	-	-	-	-	-	-	-	-
Finland‡	1993/94	42	5	1	4	13	2	-	2
Slovakia	1994/95	17	-	-	2	1	5	2	-
Korea, Republic of	1994/95	111	43	5	18	8	3	1	1
Kazakstan	1993/94	5	-	5	-	-	-	-	-
Azerbaijan	1994/95	15	-	5	-	-	5	-	-
Cyprus	1994/95	-	-	-	-	-	-	-	-
Croatia	1994/95	-	-	-	-	-	-	-	-
Qatar	1994/95	-	-	-	-	-	-	-	-
Federal Republic of Yugoslavia	1994/95	6	-	1	-	2	-	-	-
Total (50 countries)		53 262	4 411	3 182	11 494	4 648	5 893	2 232	582

Third level: foreign students by country of origin 3.14
Troisième degré: étudiants étrangers par pays d'origine
Tercer grado: estudiantes extranjeros por país de origen

Host country‡ Pays d'accueil‡ País huésped‡	Year Année Año	Country of origin / Pays d'origine / País de origen							
		Paraguay	Peru	Suriname	Uruguay	Venezuela	America South-other and not specified		
United States	1993/94	290	2 587	151	272	3 742	49		
France‡	1993/94	27	365	3	85	317	-		
Germany‡	1991/92	48	536	2	61	118	-		
United Kingdom‡	1992/93	11	60	3	16	99	54		
Russian Federation	1994/95	1	175	-	2	14	-		
Japan‡	1991/92	20	52	-	4	22	-		
Australia‡	1993	-	3	-	9	-	-		
Canada‡	1993/94	6	75	3	22	145	1		
Belgium	1990/91	6	113	39	5	7	2		
Switzerland	1993/94	1	277	-	22	17	-		
Austria‡	1993/94	1	63	-	5	19	-		
China	1993/94	4	8	1	-	8	-		
Italy‡	1993/94	7	101	-	-	336	92		
Ukraine	1994/95	-	175	-	1	18	-		
Turkey	1994/95	-	-	-	-	-	-		
Syrian Arab Republic	1992/93	-	-	-	-	31	-		
Argentina‡	1994/95	1 379	3 275	-	1 474	-	-		
South Africa	1994	-	-	-	-	-	146		
Spain	1992/93	17	639	-	160	741	-		
Holy See‡	1992/93	12	74	-	19	45	2		
Romania	1993/94	1	5	-	-	4	-		
Netherlands	1992/93	1	18	1 311	8	16	-		
Norway	1993/94	1	36	-	10	3	1		
Jordan	1993/94	-	-	-	-	-	-		
Bulgaria	1994/95	1	7	-	-	1	-		
Denmark	1992/93	-	3	-	2	1	-		
Egypt‡	1993/94	-	-	-	-	-	-		
Saudi Arabia	1993/94	-	-	-	-	-	-		
Hungary‡	1993/94	-	4	-	1	1	-		
Poland	1993/94	1	30	-	-	18	-		
Philippines	1992/93	-	-	-	-	-	-		
Cuba	1992/93	1	56	-	8	32	1		
New Zealand	1993/94	-	1	-	4	-	1		
Ireland‡	1992	-	-	-	1	-	-		
Morocco‡	1994/95	-	-	-	-	-	-		
Portugal	1989/90	-	-	-	-	336	-		
Czech Republic	1994/95	-	16	-	2	1	-		
Tunisia	1994/95	-	-	-	-	-	-		
Belarus	1993/94	-	21	-	-	-	-		
Kuwait‡	1991/92	-	-	-	-	-	-		
Algeria	1992/93	-	-	-	-	-	-		
Finland‡	1993/94	-	8	-	-	7	-		
Slovakia	1994/95	-	7	-	-	-	-		
Korea, Republic of	1994/95	31	-	1	-	-	-		
Kazakstan	1993/94	-	-	-	-	-	-		
Azerbaijan	1994/95	-	5	-	-	-	-		
Cyprus	1994/95	-	-	-	-	-	-		
Croatia	1994/95	-	-	-	-	-	-		
Qatar	1994/95	-	-	-	-	-	-		
Federal Republic of Yugoslavia	1994/95	3	-	-	-	-	-		
Total (50 countries)		1 870	8 795	1 514	2 193	6 099	349		

3.14 Third level: foreign students by country of origin
Troisième degré: étudiants étrangers par pays d'origine
Tercer grado: estudiantes extranjeros por país de origen

Host country‡ / Pays d'accueil‡ / País huésped‡	Year / Année / Año	Country of origin / Pays d'origine / País de origen							
		Asia	Afghanistan	Armenia	Azerbaijan	Bahrain	Bangladesh	Bhutan	Brunei Darus-salam
United States	1993/94	294 091	103	42	36	330	3 236	16	26
France‡	1993/94	19 612	129	6	-	4	32	2	1
Germany‡	1991/92	50 132	569	-	-	2	103	1	-
United Kingdom‡	1992/93	36 133	9	6	-	221	416	22	692
Russian Federation	1994/95	39 190	880	2 211	2 590	7	143	-	-
Japan‡	1991/92	41 559	9	-	-	1	423	4	4
Australia‡	1993	31 409	-	-	-	-	87	-	167
Canada‡	1993/94	17 029	3	1	1	16	143	11	25
Belgium	1990/91	2 759	1	-	-	-	99	-	-
Switzerland	1993/94	1 818	21	9	-	-	2	2	-
Austria‡	1993/94	4 817	14	4	1	-	72	-	-
China	1993/94	16 790	2	2	5	-	-	-	-
Italy‡	1993/94	3 689	-	-	-	-	-	-	-
Ukraine	1994/95	8 011	307	174	174	9	-	-	-
Turkey	1994/95	11 248	313	1	1 662	1	48	-	-
Syrian Arab Republic	1992/93	11 404	14	-	-	9	-	-	-
Argentina‡	1994/95	-	-	-	-	-	-	-	-
South Africa	1994	658	-	-	-	-	-	-	-
Spain	1992/93	994	12	-	-	1	-	-	1
Holy See‡	1992/93	1 485	-	1	-	-	15	-	-
Romania	1993/94	2 828	-	-	-	26	5	-	-
Netherlands	1992/93	2 913	15	-	-	-	4	-	1
Norway	1993/94	3 574	13	-	-	-	69	-	-
Jordan	1993/94	7 599	-	-	-	23	1	-	-
Bulgaria	1994/95	1 665	158	3	-	2	28	-	-
Denmark	1992/93	1 507	10	-	-	1	1	-	-
Egypt‡	1993/94	4 553	20	-	1	245	6	-	-
Saudi Arabia	1993/94	3 053	177	-	-	114	61	-	-
Hungary‡	1993/94	1 454	24	-	-	2	8	-	-
Poland	1993/94	1 403	54	9	17	-	20	-	-
Philippines	1992/93	4 289	-	-	-	-	53	5	2
Cuba	1992/93	690	-	-	-	2	-	-	-
New Zealand	1993/94	1 902	-	-	-	-	6	-	3
Ireland‡	1992	1 045	-	-	-	24	2	-	11
Morocco‡	1994/95	437	3	-	-	1	6	-	-
Portugal	1989/90	17	-	-	-	-	-	-	-
Czech Republic	1994/95	704	37	8	1	11	12	-	-
Tunisia	1994/95	102	-	-	-	-	-	-	-
Belarus	1993/94	1 672	147	-	-	-	22	-	-
Kuwait‡	1991/92	2 008	5	-	-	96	5	-	-
Algeria	1992/93	1 103	-	-	-	-	-	-	-
Finland‡	1993/94	731	1	-	1	-	114	-	-
Slovakia	1994/95	494	46	-	-	20	5	-	-
Korea, Republic of	1994/95	1 247	-	-	-	-	1	-	5
Kazakstan	1993/94	1 279	67	-	-	-	-	-	-
Azerbaijan	1994/95	1 269	21	-	-	-	8	-	-
Cyprus	1994/95	729	-	-	-	-	169	-	-
Croatia	1994/95	37	-	-	-	-	1	-	1
Qatar	1994/95	1 091	3	-	-	109	-	-	-
Federal Republic of Yugoslavia	1994/95	195	-	-	-	-	-	-	-
Total (50 countries)		644 418	3 187	2 477	4 489	1 277	5 426	63	939

Third level: foreign students by country of origin 3.14
Troisième degré: étudiants étrangers par pays d'origine
Tercer grado: estudiantes extranjeros por país de origen

Host country‡ / Pays d'accueil‡ / País huésped‡	Year / Année / Año	Country of origin / Pays d'origine / País de origen							Iran, Islamic Republic of
		Cambodia	China	Cyprus	Georgia	Hong Kong	India	Indonesia	
United States	1993/94	74	81 962	1 798	77	13 752	34 796	11 744	3 621
France‡	1993/94	803	1 508	19	3	46	199	247	2 621
Germany‡	1991/92	24	6 237	413	-	9	629	2 178	10 723
United Kingdom‡	1992/93	1	1 448	1 888	2	6 579	1 100	491	657
Russian Federation	1994/95	306	146	40	4 940	-	573	3	10
Japan‡	1991/92	-	25 697	2		455	126	1 032	93
Australia‡	1993	9	2 657	16	-	6 778	488	2 716	571
Canada‡	1993/94	3	3 241	28	-	5 735	1 051	502	1 053
Belgium	1990/91	7	601	3	-	-	93	104	324
Switzerland	1993/94	11	473	10	2	4	70	16	272
Austria‡	1993/94	34	600	88	13	-	89	45	1 393
China	1993/94	-		2	3	-	47	179	36
Italy‡	1993/94	-	54	89	-	-	66	-	1 145
Ukraine	1994/95	96	214	28	240	-	1 127	-	252
Turkey	1994/95	-	18	3 761	19	-	16	4	616
Syrian Arab Republic	1992/93	-	2	2	-	-	2	15	82
Argentina‡	1994/95	-	-	-	-	-	-	-	-
South Africa	1994	-	-	-	-	-	-	-	-
Spain	1992/93	-	28	1	-	3	28	4	130
Holy See‡	1992/93	-	14	3	2	5	646	84	3
Romania	1993/94	2	6	13	-	-	23	5	548
Netherlands	1992/93	-	139	3	-	1	41	601	424
Norway	1993/94	-	265	5	-	23	236	8	975
Jordan	1993/94	-	12	-	-	-	5	20	10
Bulgaria	1994/95	13	-	61	1	-	23	2	57
Denmark	1992/93	-	87	1	-	-	10	3	955
Egypt‡	1993/94	1	-	-	-	-	6	8	4
Saudi Arabia	1993/94	1	12	2	-	-	158	71	2
Hungary‡	1993/94	20	11	106	-	-	50	1	243
Poland	1993/94	48	4	15	13	-	43	1	33
Philippines	1992/93	-	516	-	-	-	74	472	146
Cuba	1992/93	-	-	-	-	-	12	-	1
New Zealand	1993/94	-	125	-	-	229	40	153	18
Ireland‡	1992	-	61	1	-	8	29	3	26
Morocco‡	1994/95	-	-	-	-	-	1	7	3
Portugal	1989/90	-	2	-	-	-	9	-	5
Czech Republic	1994/95	18	-	11	5	-	12	1	34
Tunisia	1994/95	-	-	-	-	-	-	-	-
Belarus	1993/94	40	141	3	-	-	91	-	131
Kuwait‡	1991/92	-	-	-	-	-	9	2	23
Algeria	1992/93	-	1	-	-	-	1	4	2
Finland‡	1993/94	-	379	1	1	1	26	1	66
Slovakia	1994/95	8	-	17	1	-	4	-	65
Korea, Republic of	1994/95	-	174	-	-	6	5	4	7
Kazakstan	1993/94	35	85	-	-	-	132	-	5
Azerbaijan	1994/95	5	-	-	180	-	30	-	80
Cyprus	1994/95	-	19	-	18	-	121	-	23
Croatia	1994/95	-	1	2	-	-	-	-	2
Qatar	1994/95	-	-	-	-	-	3	-	45
Federal Republic of Yugoslavia	1994/95	-	1	1	-	-	1	-	123
Total (50 countries)		1 559	126 941	8 433	5 520	33 634	42 341	20 730	27 658

3.14 Third level: foreign students by country of origin
Troisième degré: étudiants étrangers par pays d'origine
Tercer grado: estudiantes extranjeros por país de origen

Host country‡ Pays d'accueil‡ País huésped‡	Year Année Año	Country of origin / Pays d'origine / País de origen							
		Iraq	Israel	Japan	Jordan	Kazakstan	Korea, Democratic People's Republic of	Korea, Republic of	Kuwait
United States	1993/94	330	2 913	43 770	2 826	40	72	31 076	2 556
France‡	1993/94	145	223	1 157	196	-	14	1 642	92
Germany‡	1991/92	376	1 106	1 236	1 049	-	40	4 486	18
United Kingdom‡	1992/93	107	952	2 042	325	1	27	573	392
Russian Federation	1994/95	37	122	5	406	14 327	8	5	31
Japan‡	1991/92	8	20	.	10	-	-	9 843	-
Australia‡	1993	4	21	675	-	-	54	704	-
Canada‡	1993/94	19	118	774	94	-	46	252	49
Belgium	1990/91	36	55	33	18	-	6	27	2
Switzerland	1993/94	21	54	89	9	2	4	39	1
Austria‡	1993/94	104	43	251	73	-	6	351	1
China	1993/94	3	27	8 526	14	11	95	6 433	2
Italy‡	1993/94	102	929	46	456	-	-	25	-
Ukraine	1994/95	28	430	12	941	201	15	-	8
Turkey	1994/95	74	128	7	342	1 037	3	18	13
Syrian Arab Republic	1992/93	265	-	-	2 888	-	1	-	63
Argentina‡	1994/95	-	-	-	-	-	-	-	-
South Africa	1994	-	-	-	-	-	-	-	-
Spain	1992/93	15	52	40	121	-	2	82	10
Holy See‡	1992/93	11	10	38	13	-	5	159	-
Romania	1993/94	24	1 265	3	319	4	-	3	4
Netherlands	1992/93	21	98	41	13	-	4	54	-
Norway	1993/94	43	32	46	4	-	433	5	-
Jordan	1993/94	399	-	-	.	-	-	5	10
Bulgaria	1994/95	22	180	-	75	-	1	3	4
Denmark	1992/93	68	21	18	7	-	-	5	-
Egypt‡	1993/94	35	-	1	366	65	-	4	528
Saudi Arabia	1993/94	13	-	-	225	-	-	1	70
Hungary‡	1993/94	17	207	12	120	3	-	37	-
Poland	1993/94	47	28	8	96	93	-	13	9
Philippines	1992/93	17	-	56	201	-	1 170	-	-
Cuba	1992/93	1	4	-	3	-	-	25	-
New Zealand	1993/94	-	1	109	-	-	18	5	-
Ireland‡	1992	10	1	29	3	-	-	1	88
Morocco‡	1994/95	18	-	-	126	2	-	9	17
Portugal	1989/90	-	-	-	-	-	-	-	-
Czech Republic	1994/95	13	43	-	32	1	-	2	3
Tunisia	1994/95	-	-	-	-	-	-	-	-
Belarus	1993/94	14	25	-	97	-	8	-	-
Kuwait‡	1991/92	198	-	-	910	-	-	-	-
Algeria	1992/93	34	-	-	9	-	4	-	3
Finland‡	1993/94	4	10	39	7	-	3	-	-
Slovakia	1994/95	-	26	3	50	1	-	1	1
Korea, Republic of	1994/95	-	-	392	-	1	-	.	-
Kazakstan	1993/94	1	52	2	89	.	24	9	-
Azerbaijan	1994/95	-	5	-	50	-	-	-	-
Cyprus	1994/95	7	-	-	28	-	-	-	-
Croatia	1994/95	-	-	-	7	-	-	1	-
Qatar	1994/95	5	-	-	183	-	-	-	20
Federal Republic of Yugoslavia	1994/95	1	-	-	16	-	-	-	1
Total (50 countries)		2 697	9 201	59 460	12 817	15 789	2 063	55 898	3 996

Third level: foreign students by country of origin 3.14
Troisième degré: étudiants étrangers par pays d'origine
Tercer grado: estudiantes extranjeros por país de origen

Host country‡ / Pays d'accueil‡ / País huésped‡	Year / Année / Año	Country of origin / Pays d'origine / País de origen							
		Kyrgyzstan	Lao People's Democratic Republic	Lebanon	Malaysia	Mongolia	Myanmar	Nepal	Oman
United States	1993/94	22	63	2 165	13 718	22	398	1 166	532
France‡	1993/94	-	455	3 838	122	4	-	12	7
Germany‡	1991/92	-	16	322	58	18	26	22	7
United Kingdom‡	1992/93	-	4	74	8 529	3	23	94	481
Russian Federation	1994/95	2 466	162	477	-	465	1	83	-
Japan‡	1991/92	-	10	3	1 742	19	145	64	-
Australia‡	1993	-	64	11	7 849	-	38	-	-
Canada‡	1993/94	-	8	169	1 407	-	10	43	5
Belgium	1990/91	-	2	353	83	-	3	6	3
Switzerland	1993/94	-	5	76	8	2	4	3	1
Austria‡	1993/94	-	1	52	7	3	-	17	-
China	1993/94	7	32	5	257	82	5	53	5
Italy‡	1993/94	-	-	480	-	-	-	-	-
Ukraine	1994/95	26	60	742	-	140	-	187	-
Turkey	1994/95	468	4	113	14	70	30	5	1
Syrian Arab Republic	1992/93	-	-	1 004	1	-	-	-	5
Argentina‡	1994/95	-	-	-	-	-	-	-	-
South Africa	1994	-	-	-	-	-	-	-	-
Spain	1992/93	-	3	130	2	-	-	2	-
Holy See‡	1992/93	-	-	104	10	-	9	-	-
Romania	1993/94	-	-	72	-	9	-	1	2
Netherlands	1992/93	-	-	13	2	-	-	2	-
Norway	1993/94	-	-	33	10	1	2	7	-
Jordan	1993/94	-	-	76	562	-	-	-	284
Bulgaria	1994/95	-	-	15	-	41	-	2	-
Denmark	1992/93	-	-	23	3	-	-	1	-
Egypt‡	1993/94	2	-	62	-	-	-	-	256
Saudi Arabia	1993/94	-	-	23	34	-	-	6	47
Hungary‡	1993/94	-	15	10	-	50	-	8	-
Poland	1993/94	5	15	43	-	17	-	5	-
Philippines	1992/93	-	-	7	57	-	14	200	-
Cuba	1992/93	-	1	19	-	-	-	-	6
New Zealand	1993/94	-	-	-	763	1	-	9	-
Ireland‡	1992	-	-	3	420	-	-	2	29
Morocco‡	1994/95	-	-	32	24	-	-	-	18
Portugal	1989/90	-	-	-	-	-	-	-	-
Czech Republic	1994/95	-	5	27	1	61	-	6	1
Tunisia	1994/95	-	-	-	-	-	-	-	-
Belarus	1993/94	-	16	291	-	8	-	111	-
Kuwait‡	1991/92	-	-	76	10	-	-	-	17
Algeria	1992/93	-	-	47	7	-	-	-	-
Finland‡	1993/94	1	-	3	1	-	-	6	-
Slovakia	1994/95	-	11	12	-	28	-	-	-
Korea, Republic of	1994/95	-	-	-	96	11	-	7	1
Kazakstan	1993/94	-	4	6	-	414	-	6	-
Azerbaijan	1994/95	-	-	-	-	-	-	-	-
Cyprus	1994/95	-	-	45	-	-	-	-	-
Croatia	1994/95	-	-	4	-	-	-	-	-
Qatar	1994/95	-	-	13	-	-	-	-	119
Federal Republic of Yugoslavia	1994/95	-	-	6	-	-	-	-	-
Total (50 countries)		2 997	956	11 079	35 797	1 469	708	2 136	1 827

3.14 Third level: foreign students by country of origin
Troisième degré: étudiants étrangers par pays d'origine
Tercer grado: estudiantes extranjeros por país de origen

Host country‡ / Pays d'accueil‡ / País huésped‡	Year / Année / Año	Pakistan	Palestine	Philippines	Qatar	Saudi Arabia	Singapore	Sri Lanka	Syrian Arab Republic
United States	1993/94	7 299	-	3 528	432	3 721	4 823	2 201	761
France‡	1993/94	61	-	30	12	105	23	40	2 282
Germany‡	1991/92	206	-	125	6	43	28	143	525
United Kingdom‡	1992/93	1 106	-	94	90	563	3 359	675	102
Russian Federation	1994/95	42	158	11	-	-	-	115	838
Japan‡	1991/92	68	-	477	-	21	103	145	20
Australia‡	1993	185	-	357	-	-	5 374	527	6
Canada‡	1993/94	159	4	124	2	241	973	284	17
Belgium	1990/91	30	-	51	-	2	2	19	71
Switzerland	1993/94	15	1	13	-	6	1	16	36
Austria‡	1993/94	22	-	18	-	24	3	14	110
China	1993/94	63	15	96	-	2	304	26	22
Italy‡	1993/94	-	-	-	-	26	-	-	84
Ukraine	1994/95	177	136	15	-	-	-	172	872
Turkey	1994/95	102	145	-	-	22	-	1	193
Syrian Arab Republic	1992/93	10	5 817	14	81	102		-	.
Argentina‡	1994/95	-	-	-	-	-	-	-	-
South Africa	1994	-	-	-	-	-	-	-	-
Spain	1992/93	4	-	73	2	10	1	1	120
Holy See‡	1992/93	9	-	217	-	-	5	27	40
Romania	1993/94	50	3	-	-	-	-	1	144
Netherlands	1992/93	11	-	9	1	1	7	14	22
Norway	1993/94	256	-	73	-	-	4	423	12
Jordan	1993/94	9	4 876	11	24	67	-	-	251
Bulgaria	1994/95	1	76	-	3	2	-	3	303
Denmark	1992/93	22	-	2	-	1	1	34	2
Egypt‡	1993/94	18	1 538	4	185	203	4	-	237
Saudi Arabia	1993/94	146	391	67	65	.	2	1	211
Hungary‡	1993/94	35	51	-	-	1	-	7	107
Poland	1993/94	-	122	-	8	-	-	14	267
Philippines	1992/93	888	86	.	-	14	4	29	6
Cuba	1992/93	-	59	1	-	229	-	47	94
New Zealand	1993/94	7	-	34	-	-	180	33	-
Ireland‡	1992	30	16	4	36	6	127	4	5
Morocco‡	1994/95	1	73	-	5	9	-	-	43
Portugal	1989/90	1	-	-	-	-	-	-	-
Czech Republic	1994/95	9	-	1	-	3	1	10	67
Tunisia	1994/95	-	102	-	-	-	-	-	-
Belarus	1993/94	80	9	2	-	-	-	65	236
Kuwait‡	1991/92	10	227	7	7	175	1	-	70
Algeria	1992/93	1	930	-	-	5	-	-	-
Finland‡	1993/94	9	-	3	-	1	-	7	7
Slovakia	1994/95	7	1	-	1	23	-	-	44
Korea, Republic of	1994/95	2	-	8	-	-	1	1	-
Kazakstan	1993/94	30	3	5	-	-	-	-	134
Azerbaijan	1994/95	20	-	-	-	-	-	-	50
Cyprus	1994/95	226	16	-	-	2	-	9	31
Croatia	1994/95	2	3	-	-	-	1	-	12
Qatar	1994/95	9	236	3	.	73	-	-	40
Federal Republic of Yugoslavia	1994/95	2	26	-	-	-	-	-	16
Total (50 countries)		11 440	15 120	5 477	960	5 703	15 332	5 108	8 510

Third level: foreign students by country of origin 3.14
Troisième degré: étudiants étrangers par pays d'origine
Tercer grado: estudiantes extranjeros por país de origen

Host country‡ / Pays d'accueil‡ / País huésped‡	Year / Année / Año	Country of origin / Pays d'origine / País de origen							
		Tajikistan	Thailand	Turkey	Turkmeni-stan	United Arab Emirates	Uzbekistan	Viet Nam	Yemen
United States	1993/94	14	9 537	5 474	2	1 670	41	507	427
France‡	1993/94	-	190	1 657	-	9	2	1 054	45
Germany‡	1991/92	-	230	16 872	-	16	-	1 154	45
United Kingdom‡	1992/93	-	601	842	-	266	-	42	87
Russian Federation	1994/95	1 281	-	9	961	-	4 500	395	434
Japan‡	1991/92	-	898	29	-	-	-	61	4
Australia‡	1993	-	870	16	-	9	-	138	-
Canada‡	1993/94	-	180	109	-	7	1	52	3
Belgium	1990/91	-	53	612	-	-	-	50	1
Switzerland	1993/94	1	14	409	1	2	-	92	1
Austria‡	1993/94	1	29	1 298	-	-	-	24	12
China	1993/94	1	202	30	-	-	28	67	27
Italy‡	1993/94	-	-	-	-	-	-	52	-
Ukraine	1994/95	72	-	39	251	-	179	269	418
Turkey	1994/95	5	-	.	1 428	4	538	-	24
Syrian Arab Republic	1992/93	-	7	113	-	6	-	-	901
Argentina‡	1994/95	-	-	-	-	-	-	-	-
South Africa	1994	-	-	-	-	-	-	-	-
Spain	1992/93	-	3	4	-	6	-	4	3
Holy See‡	1992/93	-	32	10	-	-	-	12	-
Romania	1993/94	-	2	29	-	19	-	6	240
Netherlands	1992/93	-	7	1 274	-	-	-	90	-
Norway	1993/94	-	25	113	-	-	-	448	1
Jordan	1993/94	-	35	32	-	58	-	-	829
Bulgaria	1994/95	-	-	231	-	-	-	70	232
Denmark	1992/93	-	6	162	-	-	-	63	-
Egypt‡	1993/94	-	2	-	-	174	2	-	576
Saudi Arabia	1993/94	-	38	71	10	35	-	-	898
Hungary‡	1993/94	-	-	59	-	6	2	91	152
Poland	1993/94	3	-	3	-	2	6	111	231
Philippines	1992/93	-	220	-	-	-	-	46	7
Cuba	1992/93	-	-	-	-	-	-	27	147
New Zealand	1993/94	-	115	1	-	1	-	2	-
Ireland‡	1992	-	5	2	-	50	-	4	1
Morocco‡	1994/95	-	2	1	-	11	1	-	24
Portugal	1989/90	-	-	-	-	-	-	-	-
Czech Republic	1994/95	1	-	1	-	42	-	88	135
Tunisia	1994/95	-	-	-	-	-	-	-	-
Belarus	1993/94	-	-	8	-	-	-	41	86
Kuwait‡	1991/92	-	1	4	-	25	-	-	125
Algeria	1992/93	-	8	1	-	-	-	1	45
Finland‡	1993/94	-	3	27	-	1	-	4	1
Slovakia	1994/95	2	-	-	-	8	-	43	66
Korea, Republic of	1994/95	-	1	4	-	-	1	8	-
Kazakstan	1993/94	-	2	127	-	-	-	1	46
Azerbaijan	1994/95	-	-	700	-	-	-	10	110
Cyprus	1994/95	-	-	3	-	4	-	-	8
Croatia	1994/95	-	-	-	-	-	-	-	-
Qatar	1994/95	-	-	1	-	29	-	-	90
Federal Republic of Yugoslavia	1994/95	-	-	1	-	-	-	-	-
Total (50 countries)		1 381	13 318	30 378	2 653	2 460	5 301	5 126	6 482

3.14 Third level: foreign students by country of origin
Troisième degré: étudiants étrangers par pays d'origine
Tercer grado: estudiantes extranjeros por país de origen

Host country‡ / Pays d'accueil‡ / País huésped‡	Year / Année / Año	Country of origin / Pays d'origine / País de origen						
		Asia-other not specified	Europe	Albania	Austria	Belarus	Belgium	Bosnia and Herzegovina
United States	1993/94	372	59 607	90	832	41	882	79
France‡	1993/94	575	35 775	156	333	9	1 574	1
Germany‡	1991/92	1 071	47 175	20	5 971	-	790	-
United Kingdom‡	1992/93	1 147	40 386	11	247	1	1 152	8
Russian Federation	1994/95	2	29 411	2	-	5 982	-	-
Japan‡	1991/92	23	806	4	17	-	28	-
Australia‡	1993	1 018	1 353	1	12	-	6	-
Canada‡	1993/94	66	6 175	5	42	-	100	-
Belgium	1990/91	9	13 486	5	27	-	.	-
Switzerland	1993/94	-	18 345	53	788	-	224	24
Austria‡	1993/94	-	16 820	52	.	3	57	243
China	1993/94	74	2 334	5	9	11	45	-
Italy‡	1993/94	135	14 154	391	87	-	231	-
Ukraine	1994/95	-	5 898	-	-	250	-	-
Turkey	1994/95	-	2 991	68	9	-	-	494
Syrian Arab Republic	1992/93	-	34	-	-	-	1	-
Argentina‡	1994/95	-	552	-	-	-	-	-
South Africa	1994	658	3 607	-	-	-	-	-
Spain	1992/93	96	4 973	10	119	-	202	-
Holy See‡	1992/93	1	6 980	13	60	5	48	9
Romania	1993/94	-	8 085	128	20	1	2	-
Netherlands	1992/93	-	5 313	7	85	-	774	-
Norway	1993/94	9	4 016	8	48	-	23	8
Jordan	1993/94	-	87	-	1	-	-	-
Bulgaria	1994/95	53	5 649	54	2	-	2	-
Denmark	1992/93	-	2 899	1	22	-	12	-
Egypt‡	1993/94	-	76	-	1	-	-	-
Saudi Arabia	1993/94	101	92	23	-	-	-	9
Hungary‡	1993/94	-	4 291	1	9	-	1	-
Poland	1993/94	-	2 508	1	10	326	3	2
Philippines	1992/93	-	120	-	-	-	-	-
Cuba	1992/93	12	9	-	-	-	-	-
New Zealand	1993/94	49	184	-	1	-	-	-
Ireland‡	1992	4	2 115	4	18	-	39	-
Morocco‡	1994/95	-	42	-	-	-	-	8
Portugal	1989/90	-	345	-	-	-	7	-
Czech Republic	1994/95	1	1 570	2	3	9	2	21
Tunisia	1994/95	-	-	-	-	-	-	-
Belarus	1993/94	-	159	-	-	.	-	-
Kuwait‡	1991/92	5	6	-	-	-	-	-
Algeria	1992/93	-	30	-	-	-	-	12
Finland‡	1993/94	3	1 063	-	13	1	7	1
Slovakia	1994/95	-	1 308	6	-	-	-	4
Korea, Republic of	1994/95	511	43	-	1	-	1	-
Kazakstan	1993/94	-	7	-	-	-	-	-
Azerbaijan	1994/95	-	61	-	-	-	-	-
Cyprus	1994/95	-	595	3	-	-	-	-
Croatia	1994/95	-	903	6	4	-	-	530
Qatar	1994/95	110	3	-	2	-	-	-
Federal Republic of Yugoslavia	1994/95	-	915	9	1	-	-	-
Total (50 countries)		6 105	353 356	1 139	8 794	6 639	6 213	1 453

Third level: foreign students by country of origin 3.14
Troisième degré: étudiants étrangers par pays d'origine
Tercer grado: estudiantes extranjeros por país de origen

Host country‡ / Pays d'accueil‡ / País huésped‡	Year / Année / Año	Country of origin / Pays d'origine / País de origen							
		Bulgaria	Croatia	Former Czecho-slovakia	Czech Republic	Denmark	Estonia	Finland	France
United States	1993/94	1 195	273	671	-	984	106	922	5 976
France‡	1993/94	570	53	20	-	447	15	252	.
Germany‡	1991/92	292	-	-	702	433	-	771	4 158
United Kingdom‡	1992/93	89	12	-	135	731	12	356	6 338
Russian Federation	1994/95	134	-	30	-	1	1 599	28	2
Japan‡	1991/92	25	-	-	17	16	-	11	116
Australia‡	1993	4	-	12	-	18	-	95	73
Canada‡	1993/94	66	4	-	76	51	2	64	2 199
Belgium	1990/91	22	-	-	9	35	-	16	2 734
Switzerland	1993/94	74	62	90	-	70	8	70	2 681
Austria‡	1993/94	546	385	55	-	42	3	99	274
China	1993/94	20	3	8	-	31	1	24	457
Italy‡	1993/94	102	-	-	-	36	-	78	654
Ukraine	1994/95	53	6	14	-	-	20	1	3
Turkey	1994/95	389	-	3	-	-	-	4	10
Syrian Arab Republic	1992/93	2	-	-	-	-	-	-	3
Argentina‡	1994/95	-	-	-	-	-	-	-	-
South Africa	1994	-	-	-	-	-	-	-	-
Spain	1992/93	25	-	-	13	28	-	10	1 145
Holy See‡	1992/93	17	38	-	144	3	-	1	177
Romania	1993/94	141	1	-	-	-	-	-	16
Netherlands	1992/93	23	-	-	32	79	-	73	236
Norway	1993/94	35	1	1	38	766	6	167	123
Jordan	1993/94	5	-	-	-	-	-	-	5
Bulgaria	1994/95	.	-	4	-	-	-	2	1
Denmark	1992/93	11	-	-	19	.	-	52	78
Egypt‡	1993/94	1	-	-	-	-	-	-	1
Saudi Arabia	1993/94	2	-	-	-	-	-	-	1
Hungary‡	1993/94	63	-	82	-	3	2	17	12
Poland	1993/94	138	11	244	-	5	5	8	28
Philippines	1992/93	-	-	-	-	-	-	-	-
Cuba	1992/93	1	-	-	-	-	-	-	-
New Zealand	1993/94	-	-	-	-	2	-	1	9
Ireland‡	1992	1	-	-	5	32	-	5	163
Morocco‡	1994/95	1	-	-	-	-	-	-	18
Portugal	1989/90	-	-	-	-	-	-	1	177
Czech Republic	1994/95	59	23	.	-	1	6	2	2
Tunisia	1994/95	-	-	-	-	-	-	-	-
Belarus	1993/94	9	2	4	-	-	-	1	3
Kuwait‡	1991/92	2	-	-	-	-	-	-	-
Algeria	1992/93	3	-	-	-	-	-	-	7
Finland‡	1993/94	28	2	1	-	28	156	.	26
Slovakia	1994/95	15	6	745	-	-	1	-	1
Korea, Republic of	1994/95	1	-	-	-	-	-	2	4
Kazakstan	1993/94	1	2	-	-	-	-	-	-
Azerbaijan	1994/95	-	-	-	-	-	-	-	-
Cyprus	1994/95	42	-	3	-	-	4	4	-
Croatia	1994/95	2	.	2	-	-	-	-	-
Qatar	1994/95	-	-	-	-	-	-	-	-
Federal Republic of Yugoslavia	1994/95	1	-	-	-	1	-	-	-
Total (50 countries)		4 210	884	1 989	1 190	3 843	1 946	3 137	27 911

3.14 Third level: foreign students by country of origin
Troisième degré: étudiants étrangers par pays d'origine
Tercer grado: estudiantes extranjeros por país de origen

Host country‡ / Pays d'accueil‡ / País huésped‡	Year / Année / Año	Germany	Greece	Hungary	Iceland	Ireland	Italy	Latvia	Liechten-stein
United States	1993/94	8 508	4 144	867	627	931	2 569	114	9
France‡	1993/94	5 949	2 931	364	81	593	3 174	8	6
Germany‡	1991/92	.	7 090	700	245	366	4 293	-	11
United Kingdom‡	1992/93	7 079	5 943	200	146	6 767	2 122	3	2
Russian Federation	1994/95	96	29	61	1	-	-	867	-
Japan‡	1991/92	161	18	20	3	5	50	-	-
Australia‡	1993	160	25	9	-	23	33	-	-
Canada‡	1993/94	594	181	48	44	91	109	2	-
Belgium	1990/91	513	898	23	2	28	3 649	-	-
Switzerland	1993/94	5 704	383	105	5	36	3 969	6	357
Austria‡	1993/94	5 053	393	518	9	27	5 360	8	63
China	1993/94	460	2	14	1	24	153	-	-
Italy‡	1993/94	1 487	6 550	76	8	24	.	-	-
Ukraine	1994/95	14	43	4	-	-	-	29	-
Turkey	1994/95	48	1 056	5	7	-	20	-	-
Syrian Arab Republic	1992/93	3	13	-	-	-	1	-	-
Argentina‡	1994/95	-	-	-	-	-	-	-	-
South Africa	1994	-	-	-	-	-	-	-	-
Spain	1992/93	1 073	44	17	2	54	450	-	-
Holy See‡	1992/93	237	28	44	1	127	4 459	6	1
Romania	1993/94	350	3 646	31	-	-	17	2	-
Netherlands	1992/93	1 756	134	50	16	27	344	-	-
Norway	1993/94	442	30	28	200	17	51	5	-
Jordan	1993/94	2	6	-	-	-	-	-	-
Bulgaria	1994/95	19	4 295	14	-	1	-	-	-
Denmark	1992/93	573	17	18	412	21	42	-	1
Egypt‡	1993/94	-	7	-	-	-	1	-	-
Saudi Arabia	1993/94	-	1	-	-	-	-	-	-
Hungary‡	1993/94	568	848	.	-	-	7	1	-
Poland	1993/94	164	48	58	-	1	7	47	-
Philippines	1992/93	3	-	-	-	-	-	-	-
Cuba	1992/93	-	-	-	-	-	-	-	-
New Zealand	1993/94	56	4	1	1	5	1	-	-
Ireland‡	1992	329	21	2	1	.	41	-	-
Morocco‡	1994/95	-	-	-	-	-	2	-	-
Portugal	1989/90	55	-	-	-	-	12	-	-
Czech Republic	1994/95	42	430	33	-	2	2	4	-
Tunisia	1994/95	-	-	-	-	-	-	-	-
Belarus	1993/94	7	12	-	-	-	-	-	-
Kuwait‡	1991/92	2	-	1	-	-	-	-	-
Algeria	1992/93	-	-	1	-	-	-	-	-
Finland‡	1993/94	140	15	45	15	6	29	5	-
Slovakia	1994/95	21	124	41	-	-	-	3	-
Korea, Republic of	1994/95	10	-	-	-	-	1	-	-
Kazakstan	1993/94	1	1	2	-	-	-	-	-
Azerbaijan	1994/95	-	-	-	-	-	-	-	-
Cyprus	1994/95	-	180	-	-	-	-	-	-
Croatia	1994/95	12	9	11	-	-	90	-	-
Qatar	1994/95	-	-	-	-	-	-	-	-
Federal Republic of Yugoslavia	1994/95	13	824	4	-	-	-	-	-
Total (50 countries)		41 704	40 423	3 415	1 827	9 176	31 058	1 110	450

Third level: foreign students by country of origin 3.14
Troisième degré: étudiants étrangers par pays d'origine
Tercer grado: estudiantes extranjeros por país de origen

Host country‡ / Pays d'accueil‡ / País huésped‡	Year / Année / Año	Country of origin / **Pays d'origine** / País de origen							
		Lithuania	Luxembourg	Malta	Moldova	Monaco	Nether-lands	Norway	Poland
United States	1993/94	108	55	63	16	21	1 887	2 473	1 424
France‡	1993/94	26	1 066	4	6	164	842	354	1 221
Germany‡	1991/92	-	1 139	10	-	1	2 377	1 023	2 570
United Kingdom‡	1992/93	13	202	100	1	9	1 371	1 864	290
Russian Federation	1994/95	899	-	1	2 029	-	-	-	130
Japan‡	1991/92	-	2	3	-	-	20	5	33
Australia‡	1993	-	-	5	-	-	42	12	24
Canada‡	1993/94	2	3	9	5	1	134	89	75
Belgium	1990/91	-	1 307	1	-	-	1 946	16	97
Switzerland	1993/94	5	232	-	-	-	288	164	215
Austria‡	1993/94	22	287	4	3	-	88	87	475
China	1993/94	3	1	-	2	-	101	15	23
Italy‡	1993/94	-	30	34	-	11	110	38	199
Ukraine	1994/95	23	-	-	1 347	-	-	-	43
Turkey	1994/95	-	2	-	139	-	2	1	3
Syrian Arab Republic	1992/93	-	-	-	-	-	-	-	-
Argentina‡	1994/95	-	-	-	-	-	-	-	-
South Africa	1994	-	-	-	-	-	-	-	-
Spain	1992/93	-	7	15	-	1	159	31	42
Holy See‡	1992/93	25	3	43	1	1	16	-	413
Romania	1993/94	-	1	1	3 127	-	1	3	10
Netherlands	1992/93	-	18	1	-	-	.	136	91
Norway	1993/94	1	1	-	-	-	136	.	241
Jordan	1993/94	-	-	-	-	-	-	-	-
Bulgaria	1994/95	-	-	1	306	-	-	2	40
Denmark	1992/93	3	1	-	-	-	78	654	106
Egypt‡	1993/94	-	-	-	-	-	-	-	-
Saudi Arabia	1993/94	-	-	-	-	-	-	-	-
Hungary‡	1993/94	5	-	-	4	-	11	24	104
Poland	1993/94	366	1	-	6	-	6	14	.
Philippines	1992/93	-	-	-	-	-	-	-	-
Cuba	1992/93	-	-	-	-	-	-	-	-
New Zealand	1993/94	-	-	1	-	-	12	2	1
Ireland‡	1992	-	8	1	-	-	29	9	9
Morocco‡	1994/95	-	-	-	-	-	-	-	-
Portugal	1989/90	-	-	-	-	-	3	-	1
Czech Republic	1994/95	15	-	-	-	-	1	5	98
Tunisia	1994/95	-	-	-	-	-	-	-	-
Belarus	1993/94	-	-	-	-	-	-	5	107
Kuwait‡	1991/92	-	-	-	-	-	-	-	-
Algeria	1992/93	-	-	-	-	-	-	-	1
Finland‡	1993/94	6	-	-	-	-	16	32	47
Slovakia	1994/95	-	-	-	-	-	1	1	56
Korea, Republic of	1994/95	-	-	-	-	-	1	-	-
Kazakstan	1993/94	-	-	-	-	-	-	-	-
Azerbaijan	1994/95	-	-	-	4	-	-	-	-
Cyprus	1994/95	-	-	-	-	-	-	-	4
Croatia	1994/95	-	1	-	-	-	1	-	1
Qatar	1994/95	-	-	-	-	-	-	-	-
Federal Republic of Yugoslavia	1994/95	-	-	-	-	-	1	-	2
Total (50 countries)		1 522	4 367	297	6 996	209	9 680	7 059	8 196

3.14 Third level: foreign students by country of origin
Troisième degré: étudiants étrangers par pays d'origine
Tercer grado: estudiantes extranjeros por país de origen

Host country‡ / Pays d'accueil‡ / País huésped‡	Year / Année / Año	Country of origin / Pays d'origine / País de origen							
		Portugal	Romania	Russian Federation	San Marino	Slovakia	Slovenia	Spain	Sweden
United States	1993/94	720	875	1 582	-	79	90	5 246	3 226
France‡	1993/94	3 525	1 500	784	2	1	10	3 252	759
Germany‡	1991/92	955	425	-	3	-	-	3 071	592
United Kingdom‡	1992/93	741	79	48	2	-	10	2 763	519
Russian Federation	1994/95	9	30		-	-	-	16	2
Japan‡	1991/92	21	6	.	-	-	-	35	17
Australia‡	1993	30	6	65	-	-	-	13	73
Canada‡	1993/94	101	94	179	-	-	13	107	144
Belgium	1990/91	321	36	-	-	-	-	1 339	24
Switzerland	1993/94	272	152	150	-	49	18	1 259	176
Austria‡	1993/94	35	236	218	-	77	277	163	161
China	1993/94	16	13	214	-	2	1	98	85
Italy‡	1993/94	28	169	78	462	81		161	113
Ukraine	1994/95	6	26	3 956	-	-	-	9	3
Turkey	1994/95	-	29	408	-	-	-	3	6
Syrian Arab Republic	1992/93	-	-	-	-	-	-	-	-
Argentina‡	1994/95	-	-	-	-	-	-	552	-
South Africa	1994	-	-	-	-	-	-	-	-
Spain	1992/93	295	29	-	-	-	-	.	68
Holy See‡	1992/93	71	99	6	-	-	28	481	10
Romania	1993/94	-	.	22	-	2	254	1	26
Netherlands	1992/93	92	35	-	-	-	-	346	99
Norway	1993/94	30	35	19	-	1		55	850
Jordan	1993/94	-	1	3	-	-	-	-	3
Bulgaria	1994/95	2	120	64	-	1	-	-	
Denmark	1992/93	11	51	2	-	-	1	26	265
Egypt‡	1993/94	-	-	51	-	-	-	-	
Saudi Arabia	1993/94	-	-	40	-	-	-	-	-
Hungary‡	1993/94	3	1 121	167	-	174	16	2	80
Poland	1993/94	2	29	218	-	41	1	6	57
Philippines	1992/93	4	-	-	-	-	-	-	
Cuba	1992/93	-	-	-	-	-	-	8	-
New Zealand	1993/94	3	-	-	-	-	-	-	10
Ireland‡	1992	9	2	-	-	-	-	119	18
Morocco‡	1994/95	-	4	-	-	-	-	8	-
Portugal	1989/90	.	-	-	-	-	-	47	3
Czech Republic	1994/95	4	8	57	-	567	7	3	9
Tunisia	1994/95	-	-	-	-	-	-	-	
Belarus	1993/94	-	2	-	-	3	-	-	1
Kuwait‡	1991/92	-	-	-	-	-	-	-	
Algeria	1992/93	-	1	-	-	-	-	4	
Finland‡	1993/94	5	15	114	-	-	-	15	214
Slovakia	1994/95	1	81	8	-	.	13	1	-
Korea, Republic of	1994/95	1	2	6	-	-	2	7	1
Kazakstan	1993/94	-	-	-	-	-	-	-	
Azerbaijan	1994/95	-	-	56	-	-	-	-	
Cyprus	1994/95	-	12	191	-	2	-	-	6
Croatia	1994/95	-	4	2	-	1	85	-	1
Qatar	1994/95	-	-	-	-	-	-	-	
Federal Republic of Yugoslavia	1994/95	-	45	4	-	2	-	-	4
Total (50 countries)		7 313	5 372	8 712	469	1 083	826	19 216	7 625

Third level: foreign students by country of origin 3.14
Troisième degré: étudiants étrangers par pays d'origine
Tercer grado: estudiantes extranjeros por país de origen

Host country‡ / Pays d'accueil‡ / País huésped‡	Year / Année / Año	Country of origin / Pays d'origine / País de origen							
		Switzerland	The Former Yugoslav Republic of Macedonia	United Kingdom	Ukraine	Former Yugoslavia	Federal Republic of Yugoslavia	Europe-other and not specified	
United States	1993/94	1 575	-	7 828	313	1 739	-	467	
France‡	1993/94	610	7	4 194	45	537	-	330	
Germany‡	1991/92	1 480	-	2 376	-	-	4 881	430	
United Kingdom‡	1992/93	553	-	.	15	-	134	318	
Russian Federation	1994/95	-	-	-	17 411	51	-	1	
Japan‡	1991/92	23	-	136	-	-	14		
Australia‡	1993	34	-	526	-	19	-	33	
Canada‡	1993/94	118	61	1 334	23	-	-	5	
Belgium	1990/91	81	-	281	-	-	76	-	
Switzerland	1993/94	.	-	333	11	309	-	3	
Austria‡	1993/94	216	-	188	33	811	-	249	
China	1993/94	62	-	402	14	14	-	-	
Italy‡	1993/94	1 484	-	400	-	949	-	83	
Ukraine	1994/95	-	-	.	.	48	-	-	
Turkey	1994/95	2	103	142	38	-	-	-	
Syrian Arab Republic	1992/93	-	-	4	-	6	-	1	
Argentina‡	1994/95	-	-	-	-	-	-	-	
South Africa	1994	-	-	-	-	-	-	3 607	
Spain	1992/93	448	-	507	-	14	-	165	
Holy See‡	1992/93	50	-	175	52	80	6	2	
Romania	1993/94	4	4	1	273	-	-	-	
Netherlands	1992/93	93	-	612	-	-	150	4	
Norway	1993/94	58	-	489	3	81	-	19	
Jordan	1993/94	1	-	10	-	50	-	-	
Bulgaria	1994/95	3	160	-	279	77	-	200	
Denmark	1992/93	37	-	314	1	-	70	-	
Egypt‡	1993/94	1	6	4	-	2	-	1	
Saudi Arabia	1993/94	-	-	5	-	11	-	-	
Hungary‡	1993/94	15	-	29	275	640	-	7	
Poland	1993/94	8	3	6	605	33	-	-	
Philippines	1992/93	-	-	113	:	-	-	-	
Cuba	1992/93	-	-	-	-	-	-	-	
New Zealand	1993/94	3	-	71	-	-	-	-	
Ireland‡	1992	15	-	1 214	-	-	6	15	
Morocco‡	1994/95	-	-	1	-	-	-	-	
Portugal	1989/90	-	-	39	-	-	:	-	
Czech Republic	1994/95	1	55	45	52	-	-	-	
Tunisia	1994/95	-	-	-	-	-	-	-	
Belarus	1993/94	1	-	1	-	1	-	-	
Kuwait‡	1991/92	-	-	1	-	-	-	-	
Algeria	1992/93	-	-	-	1	-	-	-	
Finland‡	1993/94	12	-	55	7	7	-	-	
Slovakia	1994/95	1	3	1	32	142	-	-	
Korea, Republic of	1994/95	-	-	-	1	:	-	2	
Kazakstan	1993/94	-	-	-	-	-	-	-	
Azerbaijan	1994/95	-	-	-	1	-	-	-	
Cyprus	1994/95	-	8	37	14	85	-	-	
Croatia	1994/95	-	61	-	23	57	-	-	
Qatar	1994/95	-	-	1	-	-	-	-	
Federal Republic of Yugoslavia	1994/95	4	-	-	-	.	-	-	
Total (50 countries)		6 993	471	21 875	19 522	5 763	5 337	5 942	

3.14 Third level: foreign students by country of origin
Troisième degré: étudiants étrangers par pays d'origine
Tercer grado: estudiantes extranjeros por país de origen

Host country‡ Pays d'accueil‡ País huésped‡	Year Année Año	Country of origin / Pays d'origine / País de origen							
		Oceania	Australia	Fiji	New Zealand	Pacific Islands	Papua New Guinea	Samoa	Tonga
United States	1993/94	3 857	2 249	75	724	-	25	49	39
France‡	1993/94	175	108	11	25	26	1	1	2
Germany‡	1991/92	175	136	1	28	-	1	-	1
United Kingdom‡	1992/93	886	590	44	208	-	24	4	4
Russian Federation	1994/95	-	-	-	-	-	-	-	-
Japan‡	1991/92	259	154	8	50	28	12	4	3
Australia‡	1993	6 246	.	661	4 457	-	435	-	154
Canada‡	1993/94	359	225	14	106	1	4	-	1
Belgium	1990/91	11	10	-	-	-	1	-	-
Switzerland	1993/94	36	27	-	6	1	1	-	1
Austria‡	1993/94	43	39	-	3	-	1	-	-
China	1993/94	574	535	2	33	-	1	1	-
Italy‡	1993/94	127	120	-	7	-	-	-	-
Ukraine	1994/95	1	1	-	-	-	-	-	-
Turkey	1994/95	27	19	-	-	-	-	-	-
Syrian Arab Republic	1992/93	-	-	-	-	-	-	-	-
Argentina‡	1994/95	-	-	-	-	-	-	-	-
South Africa	1994	164	-	-	-	-	-	-	-
Spain	1992/93	48	45	1	1	-	1	-	-
Holy See‡	1992/93	56	35	4	9	1	1	5	-
Romania	1993/94	11	11	-	-	-	-	-	-
Netherlands	1992/93	63	54	-	7	-	1	1	-
Norway	1993/94	37	29	-	8	-	-	-	-
Jordan	1993/94	-	-	-	-	-	-	-	-
Bulgaria	1994/95	-	-	-	-	-	-	-	-
Denmark	1992/93	19	13	-	6	-	-	-	-
Egypt‡	1993/94	-	-	-	-	-	-	-	-
Saudi Arabia	1993/94	-	-	-	-	-	-	-	-
Hungary‡	1993/94	5	5	-	-	-	-	-	-
Poland	1993/94	7	7	-	-	-	-	-	-
Philippines	1992/93	11	9	2	-	-	-	-	-
Cuba	1992/93	-	-	-	-	-	-	-	-
New Zealand	1993/94	1 996	634	728	.	208	69	139	218
Ireland‡	1992	25	22	-	-	-	2	-	-
Morocco‡	1994/95	-	-	-	-	-	-	-	-
Portugal	1989/90	11	8	-	-	-	-	-	-
Czech Republic	1994/95	2	2	-	-	-	-	-	-
Tunisia	1994/95	-	-	-	-	-	-	-	-
Belarus	1993/94	-	-	-	-	-	-	-	-
Kuwait‡	1991/92	-	-	-	-	-	-	-	-
Algeria	1992/93	-	-	-	-	-	-	-	-
Finland‡	1993/94	11	10	-	1	-	-	-	-
Slovakia	1994/95	-	-	-	-	-	-	-	-
Korea, Republic of	1994/95	22	22	-	-	-	-	-	-
Kazakstan	1993/94	-	-	-	-	-	-	-	-
Azerbaijan	1994/95	-	-	-	-	-	-	-	-
Cyprus	1994/95	-	-	-	-	-	-	-	-
Croatia	1994/95	2	2	-	-	-	-	-	-
Qatar	1994/95	-	-	-	-	-	-	-	-
Federal Republic of Yugoslavia	1994/95	5	4	-	-	-	-	-	-
Total (50 countries)		15 271	5 125	1 551	5 679	265	579	204	423

Third level: foreign students by country of origin 3.14
Troisième degré: étudiants étrangers par pays d'origine
Tercer grado: estudiantes extranjeros por país de origen

Host country‡ Pays d'accueil‡ País huésped‡	Year Année Año	Oceania- other not specified	Former U.S.S.R.	Not Specified			
United States	1993/94	696	3 091	-			
France‡	1993/94	1	-	379			
Germany‡	1991/92	8	746	1 440			
United Kingdom‡	1992/93	12	89	251			
Russian Federation	1994/95	-	-	-			
Japan‡	1991/92	-	42	7			
Australia‡	1993	539	-	1 402			
Canada‡	1993/94	8	-	533			
Belgium	1990/91	-	8	571			
Switzerland	1993/94	-	-	2 145			
Austria‡	1993/94	-	-	302			
China	1993/94	2	-	138			
Italy‡	1993/94	-	-	37			
Ukraine	1994/95	-	-	-			
Turkey	1994/95	8	-	52			
Syrian Arab Republic	1992/93	-	2	-			
Argentina‡	1994/95	-	-	2 621			
South Africa	1994	164	-	-			
Spain	1992/93	1	23	-			
Holy See‡	1992/93	1	10	492			
Romania	1993/94	-	-	-			
Netherlands	1992/93	-	49	10			
Norway	1993/94	-	53	1 269			
Jordan	1993/94	-	-	9			
Bulgaria	1994/95	-	-	2 691			
Denmark	1992/93	-	14	-			
Egypt‡	1993/94	-	-	-			
Saudi Arabia	1993/94	-	-	2 476			
Hungary‡	1993/94	-	-	-			
Poland	1993/94	-	-	-			
Philippines	1992/93	-	-	-			
Cuba	1992/93	-	7	-			
New Zealand	1993/94	-	-	143			
Ireland‡	1992	1	-	2			
Morocco‡	1994/95	-	-	490			
Portugal	1989/90	3	-	-			
Czech Republic	1994/95	-	-	17			
Tunisia	1994/95	-	-	982			
Belarus	1993/94	-	-	-			
Kuwait‡	1991/92	-	1	336			
Algeria	1992/93	-	9	-			
Finland‡	1993/94	-	-	49			
Slovakia	1994/95	-	-	-			
Korea, Republic of	1994/95	-	-	1			
Kazakstan	1993/94	-	-	5			
Azerbaijan	1994/95	-	-	-			
Cyprus	1994/95	-	-	45			
Croatia	1994/95	-	-	377			
Qatar	1994/95	-	-	-			
Federal Republic of Yugoslavia	1994/95	1	-	3			
Total (50 countries)		1 445	4 144	19 275			

3.14 Third level: foreign students by country of origin
Troisième degré: étudiants étrangers par pays d'origine
Tercer grado: estudiantes extranjeros por país de origen

This table shows the country or territory of origin of foreign students enrolled in institutions of higher education in the fifty principal host countries, based on the latest year for which such information is available (1993 for most countries). The table also includes as countries of origin the former U.S.S.R., the former Czechoslovakia and the former Yugoslavia since a number of host countries still report foreign students under these classifications. The data presented do not include certain major host countries for which recent data are not available (e.g: Brazil, India, Lebanon, Sweden etc.) The number of foreign students enrolled in these 50 countries represents about 95 per cent of the known world total.

Ce tableau présente, pour les cinquante principaux pays d'accueil, le nombre d'étudiants étrangers inscrits dans des établissements d'enseignement supérieur, avec indication du pays ou territoire d'origine, sur la base de la dernière année pour laquelle ces données étaient disponible (pour la majorité des pays, l'année 1993). Le tableau comprend aussi comme pays d'origine, l'ancienne U.R.S.S., l'ancienne Tchécoslovaquie et l'ancienne Yougoslavie, étant donné que plusieurs pays d'accueil utilisent encore ces désignations pour présenter les données sur les étudiants étrangers. Certains grands pays d'accueil tels que le Brésil, l'Inde, le Liban, ou la Suede ne sont pas présentés dans ce tableau, faute de données récentes disponibles. Le nombre d'étudiants étrangers inscrits dans ces 50 pays représente environ 95% du total mondial connu.

Este cuadro presenta el número de estudiantes extranjeros matriculados en establecimientos de enseñanza superior en los cincuenta principales países huéspedes y sus países o territorios de origen, en base al último año para el que se disponía de datos (en la mayoría de ellos, se trata de 1993). El cuadro también comprende como países de origen, la ex U.R.S.S., la ex Checoslovaquia y la ex Yugoslavia, pues algunos países huéspedes utilizan aún esta clasificación en la presentación sus estadísticas sobre los estudiantes extranjeros. La presentación de los datos no incluye algunos países huéspedes principales para los que no se dispone de datos recientes (Brasil, India, Líbano, Suecia, etc.). El número de estudiantes extranjeros matriculados en esos 50 países equivalen aproximadamente al 95% del total mundial conocido.

General note / Note générale / Nota general:
E--> Due to lack of recent data this table does not include major host countries such as Brazil, India, Lebanon and Sweden. These countries have been presented in previous editions of the Yearbook.
FR-> Faute de données récentes, ce tableau n'inclut pas certains pays hôtes principaux tels que le Brésil, l'Inde, le Liban et la Suède. Ces pays ont été présentés dans les éditions précédentes de l'annuaire.
ESP> Por falta de datos recientes, este cuadro no incluye algunos países huéspedes principales como Brasil, India, Líbano y Suecia. Estos países han sido presentados en ediciones anteriores del anuario.
Argentina:
E--> Data refer to public universities only.
FR-> Les données se réfèrent aux universités publiques seulement.
ESP> Los datos se refieren a las universidades públicas solamente.
Australia:
E--> Data do not include Technical and Further Education Institutions (TAFE).
FR-> Les données ne comprennent pas les *Technical and Further Education Institutions* (TAFE).
ESP> Los datos no incluyen a los *Technical and Further Education Institutions* (TAFE).
Austria:
E--> Data refer to universities and equivalent degree-granting institutions only.
FR-> Les données se réfèrent aux universités et établissements conférant des grades équivalents seulement.
ESP> Los datos se refieren a las universidades y establecimientos que otorgan grados equivalentes solamente.
Canada:
E--> Data refer to universities only.
FR-> Les données se réfèrent aux universités seulement.
ESP> Los datos se refieren a las universidades solamente.
Egypt:
E--> Data refer to universities only but exclude Al Azhar.
FR-> Les données se réfèrent aux universités seulement, mais ne comprennent pas Al Azhar.
ESP> Los datos se refieren a las universidades solamente, pero no incluyen Al Azhar.
Finland:
E--> Data refer to universities and equivalent degree-granting institutions only.
FR-> Les données se réfèrent aux universités et établissements conférant des titres équivalents seulement.
ESP> Los datos se refieren a las universidades y establecimientos que otorgan grados equivalentes solamente.
France:
E--> Data refer to public universities only.
FR-> Les données se réfèrent aux universités publiques seulement.
ESP> Los datos se refieren a las universidades públicas solamente.
Germany:
E--> Data refer to the former territory of the Federal Republic of Germany.
FR-> Les données se réfèrent à l'ancien territoire de la République Fédérale d'Allemagne.
ESP> Los datos se refieren al antiguo territorio de la República Federale de Alemania.
Holy See:
E--> Data refer to foreign students enrolled in higher education institutions under the authority of the Holy See.
FR-> Les données se réfèrent aux étudiants étrangers inscrits dans les institutions d'enseignement du troisième degré sous l'autorité du Saint-Siège.
ESP> Los datos se refieren a los estudiantes extranjeros en los institutos de enseñanza de tercer grado bajo la autoridad de la Santa Sede.
Hungary:
E--> Data refer to full-time students only.
FR-> Les données se réfèrent aux étudiants à plein temps seulement.
ESP> Los datos sólo se refieren a los estudiantes de jornada completa.
Ireland:
E--> Data refer to full-time students only.
FR-> Les données se réfèrent aux étudiants à plein temps seulement.
ESP> Los datos sólo se refieren a los estudiantes de jornada completa.
Italy:
E--> Data refer to foreign students enrolled at ISCED level 6 only.
FR-> Les données se réfèrent aux étudiants étrangers inscrits au niveau 6 de la CITE seulement.
ESP> Los datos sólo se refieren a los estudiantes extranjeros inscritos en el nivel 6 de la CINE.
Japan:
E--> Data refer to universities and junior colleges only.
FR-> Les données se réfèrent aux universités et *junior colleges* seulement.
ESP> Los datos se refieren a las universidades y *junior colleges* solamente.
Kuwait:
E--> Data refer to the University of Kuwait only.
FR-> Les données se réfèrent à l'Université du Koweit seulement.
ESP> Los datos sólo se refieren a la Universidad de Kuwait.
Morocco:
E--> Data refer to universities only.
FR-> Les données se réfèrent aux universités seulement.
ESP> Los datos se refieren a las universidades solamente.
United Kingdom:
E--> Data refer to foreign students enrolled at universities (for full-time study or research), technical colleges (advanced courses) and colleges of education.
FR-> Les données se réfèrent aux étudiants étrangers inscrits dans les universités (pour études ou recherches à plein temps), *technical colleges (advanced courses)* et *colleges of education.*
ESP> Los datos se refieren a los estudiantes extranjeros matriculados en las universidades (para realizar estudios o investigaciones en régimen de jornada completa) en los *technical colleges (advanced courses)* y en los *colleges of education.*

Educational expenditure **4**
Dépenses de l'enseignement
Gastos de la educación

4 Educational expenditure

Dépenses de l'enseignement

Gastos de la educación

This chapter consists of four tables on educational expenditure which is divided into two main categories of expenditure.

Current expenditure covers expenditure on administration, emoluments of teaching and other staff, teaching materials, scholarships and welfare services.

Capital expenditure refers to expenditure on land, buildings, construction, equipment etc. This item also includes loan transactions.

The data presented in this chapter refer solely to *public expenditure on education* i.e. public expenditure on public education plus subsidies for private education. It has not been possible to show private expenditure on education due to lack of data for a great number of countries.

Public expenditure on education includes, unless otherwise indicated, educational expenditure at every level of administration according to the constitution of the country, i.e. central or federal government, state government, provincial or regional authorities and municipal and local authorities.

In general, the statistics do not take into account foreign aid received for education. However, whenever information on the inclusion of foreign aid is available it is indicated in a footnote.

Data are expressed in national currency at current market prices. Exchange rates between national currencies and the United States dollar can be found in Appendix C.

The years stated indicate the calendar year in which the financial year begins. In the majority of countries and territories the financial year begins in January, coinciding with calendar year, but in some seventy countries this is not the case. Appendix B gives information on the dates of commencement of the financial year in each country and territory.

Data presented in this edition of the *Yearbook* which differ from corresponding data for the same year given in earlier editions are the result of revisions made following the receipt of new information.

For countries which participated in the most recent UNESCO/OECD/Eurostat (UOE) survey and which have been able to provide data for years other than those already shown in the 1995 Yearbook, there may be a break in the time series due to conceptual changes, the most important being the inclusion of private spending on education. As a result of this, data in Tables 4.3 and 4.4 refer in theory to public and private expenditure on education, i.e. expenditure for or of (a) public, (b) government-dependent private and (c) private independent institutions. However, it should be noted that for many of the countries concerned, the private component is either incomplete or lacking altogether. Data presented in Tables 4.1 and 4.2 still cover only public expenditure but for certain countries the most recent figures deviate from the previous ones. Therefore, in all the tables countries affected by the above-mentioned changes can be identified by a line separating the latest reference year from preceding ones.

Table 4.1

This table presents total public expenditure on education distributed between current and capital.

Educational expenditure is also expressed as a percentage of the Gross National Product (GNP) and of total public expenditure.

For almost all countries, data on GNP are supplied by the World Bank. These data being revised every year, the percentages of educational expenditure in relation to GNP may sometimes differ from those shown in previous editions of the *Yearbook*.

Table 4.2

Public current expenditure on education in this table is divided into the following categories:

Administration other than personnel: all administrative expenditure with the exception of emoluments of administrative staff.

Emoluments of administrative staff: emoluments at all administrative levels, including inspections, documentation services and educational research.

Emoluments of teaching staff: gross salaries and all other benefits, including contributions to pension funds and social security, paid to teachers and to auxiliary teaching staff.

Emoluments of other personnel: emoluments of maintenance staff, cleaners, drivers, watchmen, etc.

Total personnel emoluments: total of the three previous categories.

Teaching materials: expenditure directly related to instructional activities such as the purchase of textbooks and other scholastic supplies.

Scholarships: scholarships and all other forms of financial aid granted to students for study in the country or abroad.

Welfare services: boarding costs, school meals, transport, medical services, etc.

Other expenditure: expenditure which cannot be classified in one of the above categories and other expenditure attached to the operation and maintenance of buildings and equipment.

Subsidies not distributed: Government subsidies or transfers to public and private institutions which cannot be distributed by purpose, due mainly to the administrative autonomy of the recipient institutions.

As concerns the presentation of this table, two observations must be made: 1) when the symbol ./. is shown without an explanatory note, the corresponding data are included under *other expenditure*; ii) several categories in this table are shown with the symbol ... , due to the fact that the questionnaire reply did not clearly indicate whether the relevant expenditure was nil or was included under other categories.

Table 4.3

This table presents the percentage breakdown of public current expenditure by level of education.

The column *other types* includes special, adult and other types of education which cannot be classified by level.

The column *not distributed* while generally covering unspecified expenditure may sometimes include expenditure on administration for which there is no breakdown by level of education.

4 Educational expenditure
Dépenses de l'enseignement
Gastos de la educación

Table 4.4

This table gives a cross classification of public current expenditure by level of education and by purpose for the latest year available.

The categories used for the breakdown of expenditure by purpose are those described above for Table 4.2.

When the data supplied did not cover all the categories of expenditure used in this table, only the relevant categories have been shown for the countries concerned.

Ce chapitre contient quatre tableaux sur les dépenses de l'enseignement. Ces dépenses sont réparties selon deux grandes catégories:

Dépenses ordinaires: dépenses d'administration, émoluments du personnel enseignant et auxiliaire, matériel pour l'enseignement, bourses d'études et services sociaux.

Dépenses en capital: dépenses relatives aux terrains, bâtiments, constructions, équipements, etc. Cette rubrique comprend également les transactions afférentes aux prêts.

Les données présentées dans ce chapitre se réfèrent uniquement aux *dépenses publiques d'éducation*, c'est-à-dire, aux dépenses publiques pour l'enseignement public plus les subventions à l'enseignement privé. Faute de données pour la plupart des pays, il n'a pas été tenu compte des dépenses privées d'éducation.

Les dépenses publiques d'éducation comprennent, sauf indication contraire, toutes les dépenses effectuées à quelque échelon administratif que ce soit, en fonction de l'organisation politique du pays: gouvernement central ou fédéral, gouvernements d'état, autorités de province ou régionales et autorités municipales et locales.

D'une manière générale, ces statistiques ne tiennent pas compte de l'aide étrangère reçue pour l'éducation. Cependant, une note signale tous les cas pour lesquels les informations disponibles indiquent expressément l'inclusion de l'aide étrangère.

Les données sont exprimées en monnaie nationale aux prix courants du marché. Les taux de change des monnaies nationales en dollars des Etats-Unis sont indiqués dans l'Annexe C.

Les années indiquées sont les années civiles pendant lesquelles commencent les exercices financiers. Dans la plupart des pays et territoires l'exercice financier commence en Janvier et coincide avec l'année civile mais dans quelque soixante dix pays ce n'est pas le cas. L'annexe B fournit des renseignements sur le commencement de l'exercice financier dans chaque pays et territoire.

Lorsque les données présentées dans cette édition de l'*Annuaire* diffèrent des données correspondant à la même année qui figuraient dans les éditions précédentes, on doit considérer qu'il s'agit de chiffres révisés à la suite de nouveaux renseignements reçus.

Pour les pays qui ont participé au programme de la dernière enquête de l'UNESCO/OCDE/Eurostat (UOE) et qui ont été en mesure de fournir des données pour des années autres que celles déjà présentées dans l'annuaire 1995, il peut y avoir une rupture dans les séries temporelles, dû à des changements conceptuels dont le plus important est l'inclusion des dépenses privées pour l'éducation. En conséquence, les données des tableaux 4.3 et 4.4 se réfèrent, en théorie, aux dépenses publiques et privées pour l'éducation, c'est-à-dire aux dépenses des établissements ou à celles liées aux établissements a) publics, b) privés subventionnés et c) privés. Cependant il faut noter que, pour beaucoup de pays concernés, les dépenses privées sont incomplètes ou manquent totalement. En ce qui concerne les données des tableaux 4.1 et 4.2 qui se réfèrent toujours aux dépenses publiques seulement, on peut observer, pour certains pays, un écart entre les chiffres les plus récents et ceux des années précédentes. Donc, dans tous les tableaux, les pays affectés par les changements mentionnés ci-dessus sont identifiables par une ligne qui sépare la dernière année de référence des années antérieures.

Tableau 4.1

Ce tableau présente le total des dépenses publiques d'éducation réparties entre dépenses ordinaires et en capital.

Les dépenses d'éducation sont aussi exprimées en pourcentage du Produit National Brut (PNB) et de l'ensemble des dépenses publiques.

Pour presque tous les pays, les données relatives au PNB sont fournies par la Banque Mondiale. Comme ces données sont révisées tous les ans, les pourcentages des dépenses d'éducation par rapport au PNB peuvent parfois différer des pourcentages parus dans les éditions précédentes de l'*Annuaire*.

Tableau 4.2

Les dépenses publiques ordinaires d'éducation sont réparties dans ce tableau selon les catégories suivantes:

Administration autre que personnel: toutes les dépenses d'administration à l'exclusion des émoluments du personnel administratif.

Emoluments du personnel administratif: émoluments à tous les niveaux administratifs, inspections, services de documentation et recherche éducative inclus.

Emoluments du personnel enseignant: traitements bruts et toutes sortes de primes additionnelles, y compris les contributions aux caisses de retraite et à la sécurité sociale, payés au personnel enseignant et aux enseignants auxiliaires.

Emoluments d'autre personnel: émoluments du personnel d'entretien et du nettoyage, des conducteurs, surveillants, etc.

Total des émoluments du personnel: total des trois catégories précédentes.

Matériel pour l'enseignement: dépenses directement liées à l'enseignement telles que l'achat des manuels et autres fournitures scolaires.

Bourses d'études: bourses et toute autre forme d'aide financière accordée aux élèves pour étudier dans le pays et à l'étranger.

Services sociaux: frais d'internat, repas scolaires, transport scolaire, services médicaux, etc.

Autres dépenses: dépenses ne pouvant pas être classées dans l'une des rubriques ci-dessus mentionnées et autres dépenses liées au fonctionnement et à l'entretien des bâtiments et du matériel.

Subventions non réparties: subventions ou transferts accordés par le Gouvernement aux établissements publics et privés, qui ne peuvent être répartis selon la destination, en raison notamment de l'autonomie administrative des établissements bénéficiaires.

En ce qui concerne la présentation de ce tableau, deux observations doivent être faites: 1) lorsque le symbole ./. est utilisé sans aucune note explicative, les données correspondant à cette rubrique sont comptées avec les *autres dépenses*; ii) plusieurs rubriques de ce tableau sont présentées avec le symbole ... parce que les réponses reçues au questionnaire ne précisent pas si ces rubriques ont été classées avec d'autres rubriques ou si les dépenses correspondantes sont nulles.

Tableau 4.3

Ce tableau présente la répartition en pourcentage des dépenses publiques ordinaires par degré d'enseignement.

La colonne intitulée *autres types* regroupe l'éducation spéciale, l'éducation des adultes et autres types d'enseignement ne pouvant pas être classés par degré.

La colonne intitulée *non réparties*, qui regroupe généralement les diverses dépenses non spécifiées, peut parfois inclure les dépenses d'administration quand celles-ci ne sont pas déjà réparties par degré.

Tableau 4.4

Ce tableau indique, pour la dernière année disponible, la répartition croisée des dépenses publiques ordinaires par degré d'enseignement et selon leur destination.

Les catégories utilisées pour la répartition des dépenses selon leur destination sont celles ci-dessus définies pour le tableau 4.2.

Lorsque les données communiquées ne couvraient pas toutes les catégories de dépenses figurant dans ce tableau, seules les catégories pertinentes ont été présentées, pour les pays concernés.

Este capítulo comprende cuatro cuadros relativos a los gastos destinados a la educación. Estos gastos se distribuyen según las dos categorías principales siguientes:

Gastos ordinarios: gastos de administración, emolumentos del personal docente y auxiliar, material educativo, becas de estudios y servicios sociales.

Gastos de capital: gastos relativos a los terrenos, edificios, construcciones, equipo, etc. Esta rúbrica comprende igualmente las operaciones de préstamos.

Los datos presentados en este capítulo se refieren únicamente a *los gastos públicos destinados a la educación*, es decir, a los gastos públicos para la enseñanza pública más las subvenciones para la enseñanza privada. Careciendo de datos para la mayoría de los países, no se han tenido en cuenta los gastos privados destinados a la educación.

Los gastos públicos destinados a la educación comprenden, salvo indicación contraria, todos los gastos efectuados a cualquier nivel administrativo, en función de la organización política del país: Gobierno Central o Federal, Gobiernos de Estado, autoridades de provincia o de región y autoridades municipales y locales.

En general, estas estadísticas no toman en cuenta la ayuda extranjera recibida para la educación. Sin embargo, en una nota se señalan todos los casos para los que las informaciones disponibles indican expresamente la inclusión de la ayuda extranjera.

Educational expenditure
Dépenses de l'enseignement
Gastos de la educación

4

Los datos se presentan en moneda nacional a precios corrientes del mercado. Los tipos de cambio entre las monedas nacionales y el dólar de los Estados Unidos se indican en el Anexo C.

Los años representan el año civil durante el cual comienza el ejercicio económico. A pesar de que en la mayoría de los países y territorios el ejercicio económico empieza en enero (es decir coincide con el año civil), en unos setenta países se extiende, en forma más o menos pronunciada, sobre el año civil siguiente. En el apéndice B se presentan datos sobre el comienzo del ejercicio económico en cada país y territorio.

Cuando los datos presentados en esta edición del *Anuario* difieren de los datos correspondientes al mismo año que figuraban en las ediciones anteriores, debe considerarse que se trata de cifras revisadas de acuerdo con las nuevas informaciones recibidas.

Los países que participaron en la última encuesta de UNESCO/OCDE/Eurostat (UOE) y que suministraron datos para años diferentes de los que se publicaron en el anuario 1995, pueden presentar cortes en las series temporales debido a cambios conceptuales. El más importante de ellos es la inclusión de los gastos privados de educación. Como consecuencia de estos cambios, los datos de los Cuadros 4.3 y 4.4 se refieren teóricamente a los gastos públicos y privados de educación, a saber, gastos de o destinados a instituciones (a) públicas, (b) privadas subsidiadas por el Gobierno y (c) privadas. Sin embargo, se puede observar que en algunos países el componente privado está incompleto o es inexistente. Los cuadros 4.1 y 4.2 abarcan como siempre los gastos públicos solamente, pero para ciertos países los datos más actuales se alejan de los observados anteriormente. En todos los cuadros se han identificado los países donde han habido cambios por una línea que separa el año de referencia más reciente del año anterior.

Cuadro 4.1

Este cuadro presenta el total de los gastos públicos destinados a la educación, distribuídos entre gastos ordinarios y gastos de capital.

El total de los gastos de la educación también se expresa en porcentaje del Producto Nacional Bruto (PNB) y del total de los gastos públicos.

Para casi todos los países, los datos relativos al PNB son proporcionados por el Banco Mundial. Como estos datos son revisados cada año, los porcentajes de gastos de educación con respecto al PNB pueden ser diferentes de los porcentajes indicados en ediciones anteriores del *Anuario*.

Cuadro 4.2

Los gastos públicos ordinarios destinados a la educación, se distribuyen en este cuadro de acuerdo con las siguientes categorías:

Administración, excluyendo el personal: todos los gastos administrativos, excepto los emolumentos del personal administrativo.

Emolumentos del personal administrativo: emolumentos en todos los niveles administrativos, incluyendo inspecciones, servicios de documentación e investigación educativa.

Emolumentos del personal docente: sueldos brutos y otras primas adicionales, incluyendo las contribuciones al fondo de pensiones y seguro social, relacionados con el personal docente y el personal docente auxiliar.

Emolumentos de otro personal: emolumentos del personal de conservación y de limpieza de los edificios, conductores, conserjes, etc.

Total de emolumentos de personal: total de las tres categorías precedentes.

Material educativo: gastos directamente relacionados con la enseñanza, como la adquisición de libros de texto y otros suministros escolares.

Becas de estudios: becas y toda otra forma de ayuda financiera concedida a los alumnos para estudiar en el país y en el extranjero.

Servicios sociales: gastos de internado, cantinas escolares, transportes escolares, servicios médicos, etc.

Otros gastos: gastos que no pueden ser clasificados en las categorías que preceden y otros gastos relacionados con el funcionamiento y la conservación de los edificios y del material.

Subvenciones sin distribución: aportes, subvenciones o transferencias del Gobierno a los establecimientos públicos y privados, que no pueden ser distribuídas según su destino debido, principalmente, a la autonomía administrativa de los establecimientos concernidos.

En lo que concierne a la presentación de este cuadro, dos observaciones deben ser precisadas: i) cuando el símbolo ./. aparece sin nota explicativa, los datos correspondientes son presentados en *otros gastos*; ii) varias categorías en este cuadro figuran con el símbolo ... que las respuestas al cuestionario no mostraban claramente si estas categorías habían sido incluídas con otras categorías o si los gastos correspondientes eran nulos.

Cuadro 4.3

Este cuadro presenta la distribución en porcentaje de los gastos públicos ordinarios por grado de enseñanza.

La columna titulada *Otros tipos* agrupa la educación especial, la educación de adultos y los otros tipos de enseñanza que no pueden clasificarse por grado.

La columna titulada *Sin distribución* comprende en general los diversos gastos no especificados e incluye a veces los gastos de administración, cuando no han sido distribuidos por grado.

Cuadro 4.4

Este cuadro da la distribución cruzada de los gastos públicos ordinarios por grados de enseñanza y según su destino, para el último año disponible.

Las categorías utilizadas para la distribución de los gastos según su destino, son las definidas más arriba para el cuadro 4.2.

Cuando los datos que nos han sido comunicados no cubren todas las categorías de gastos que figuran en este cuadro, sólo las categorías pertinentes han sido presentadas, para los países correspondientes.

4.1 Public expenditure on education
Dépenses publiques afférentes à l'enseignement
Gastos públicos destinados a la educación

4.1 Public expenditure on education: total and as percentage of GNP and all public expenditure

Dépenses publiques afférentes à l'enseignement: total et pourcentage par rapport au PNB et à l'ensemble des dépenses publiques

Gastos públicos destinados a la educación: total y porcentaje en relación con el PNB y el conjunto de gastos públicos

Country Currency Pays Monnaie País Moneda	Year Année Año	Total educational expenditure Dépenses totales d'éducation Gastos totales de educación			Current educational expenditure Dépenses ordinaires d'éducation Gastos ordinarios de educación				Capital expenditure Dépenses en capital Gastos en capital (000 000)
		Amount Montant Importe (000 000)	As % of gross national product En % du produit national brut En % del producto nacional bruto (%)	As % of total government expenditure En % des dépenses totales du gouvernement En % de los gastos totales del gobierno (%)	Amount Montant Importe (000 000)	As % of the total En % du total En % del total (%)	As % of gross national product En % du produit national brut En % del producto nacional bruto (%)	As % of current government expenditure En % des dépenses ordinaires du gouvernement En % de los gastos ordinarios del gobierno (%)	
		(1)	(2)	(3)	(4)	(5)	(6)	(7)	(8)
Africa									
Algeria‡ Dinar	1980	12 355	7.8	24.3	8 259	66.9	5.2	29.8	4 095
	1985	24 248	8.5	20.7	16 814	69.3	5.9	26.2	7 434
	1990	29 504	5.7	21.1	24 953	84.6	4.8	29.7	4 551
	1992	53 516	5.4	16.3	...	...	...	...	...
	1993	80 841	7.2	19.6	70 134	86.8	6.3	23.1	10 707
	1994	79 889	5.6	17.6	69 689	87.2	4.9	21.6	10 200
Angola‡ Kwansa	1985	9 643	...	10.8	9 419	97.7	...	14.0	224
	1990	12 076	...	10.7	10 856	89.9	...	...	1 220
Benin Franc C.F.A.	1980	...	...	...	12 426	...	4.2	36.8	...
Botswana‡ Pula	1979	37	7.0	16.1	27	75.2	5.3	21.4	9
	1985	111	6.8	15.4	88	79.3	5.4	18.6	23
	1990	437	7.6	17.0	311	71.3	5.4	21.1	126
	1992	611	7.6	15.1	493	80.7	6.2	21.6	118
	1993	758	9.0	17.6	610	80.5	7.3	21.8	148
	1994	872	8.5	...	708	81.2	6.9	...	164
Burkina Faso Franc C.F.A.	1980	7 994	2.6	19.8	7 436	93.0	2.4	21.1	558
	1985	12 901	2.3	21.0	12 292	95.3	2.2	22.4	609
	1989	18 780	2.7	17.5	18 727	99.7	2.7	21.9	53
	1992	23 577	3.1	...	22 002	93.3	2.9	...	1 575
	1994	36 315	3.6	11.1	30 016	82.7	3.0	17.4	6 299
Burundi‡ Franc	1979	2 066	3.0	17.5	1 796	86.9	2.6	...	270
	1985	3 467	2.5	15.5	3 212	92.7	2.4	17.1	254
	1990	6 570	3.4	16.7	6 370	97.0	3.3	19.4	200
	1991	7 403	3.5	17.7	7 208	97.4	3.4	20.2	195
	1992	8 586	3.8	12.2	8 023	93.4	3.6	24.2	563
Cameroon‡ Franc C.F.A.	1980	45 099	3.2	20.3	36 653	81.3	2.6	...	8 446
	1985	109 344	3.0	14.8	90 045	82.4	2.5	20.9	19 299
	1990	107 968	3.4	19.6	97 948	90.7	3.1	26.9	10 020
	1992	88 000	3.0	16.1	...	...	...	...	...
	1993	84 000	3.1	...	...	...	...	...	...
	1994	92 975	3.1	...	...	...	...	...	...

Public expenditure on education **4.1**
Dépenses publiques afférentes à l'enseignement
Gastos públicos destinados a la educación

Country Currency Pays Monnaie País Moneda	Year Année Año	Total educational expenditure Dépenses totales d'éducation Gastos totales de educación			Current educational expenditure Dépenses ordinaires d'éducation Gastos ordinarios de educación				Capital expenditure Dépenses en capital Gastos en capital (000 000)
		Amount Montant Importe (000 000)	As % of gross national product En % du produit national brut En % del producto nacional bruto (%)	As % of total government expenditure En % des dépenses totales du gouvernement En % de los gastos totales del gobierno (%)	Amount Montant Importe (000 000)	As % of the total En % du total En % del total (%)	As % of gross national product En % du produit national brut En % del producto nacional bruto (%)	As % of current government expenditure En % des dépenses ordinaires du gouvernement En % de los gastos ordinarios del gobierno (%)	
		(1)	(2)	(3)	(4)	(5)	(6)	(7)	(8)
Cape Verde Escudo	1985 1991	341 903	3.6 4.4	... 19.9	325 890	95.3 98.6	3.5 4.3	15.2 20.0	16 13
Central African Republic Franc C.F.A.	1979 1986 1990	5 670 9 553 9 862	3.8 2.8 2.8	20.9	5 510 9 313 9 622	97.2 97.5 97.6	3.6 2.8 2.8	... 25.6 ...	160 240 240
Chad Franc C.F.A.	1991 1993 1994	8 284 ... 10 796	2.3 ... 2.2	... ...	8 212 8 768 10 691	99.1 ... 99.0	2.3 2.6 2.1	... ...	72 ... 105
Comoros‡ Franc C.F.A	1985 1990 1992 1993 1994	... ...	... ...	... ...	2 105 2 666 2 829 2 938 3 285	... ...	4.1 4.0 4.0 4.1 3.7	23.1 24.3 22.0 20.5 21.6	... ...
Congo Franc C.F.A	1980 1984 1990 1991	22 942 44 442 37 899 57 092	7.0 5.1 5.7 8.3	23.6 9.8 14.4 ...	21 517 41 033 36 906 56 537	93.8 92.3 97.4 99.0	6.6 4.7 5.6 8.3	24.1 14.7 18.0 19.3	1 424 3 409 993 555
Côte d'Ivoire‡ Franc C.F.A.	1980 1985 1992 1994	147 478	7.2	22.6	123 196 179 447 153 004 168 923	83.5	6.0 6.3 6.7 5.6	36.4	24 282 ... ...
Djibouti‡ Franc	1979 1985 1990 1991	1 368 1 690 2 614 2 872	... 2.7 3.4 3.8	11.5 7.5 10.5 11.1	1 046 1 690 2 614 2 872	76.5 100.0 100.0 100.0	... 2.7 3.4 3.8	9.6 ... 10.5 11.1	322 - - -
Egypt‡ Pound	1981 1985 1990 1991 1992	919 1 878 3 737 4 557 5 839	5.7 6.3 4.9 4.7 5.0	9.4 ... ... 9.7 11.0	722 1 775 3 229 3 941 4 683	78.6 94.5 86.4 86.5 80.2	4.5 5.9 4.2 4.1 4.0	10.1 10.8 ... 11.0 11.0	197 103 508 616 1 156
Equatorial Guinea Franc C.F.A.	1993	734	1.8	5.6	721	98.2	1.7	5.8	14
Eritrea‡ Birr	1994	181	...	...	160	88.4	...	...	21
Ethiopia Birr	1980 1985 1990 1991 1992 1993	279 420 600 608 704 1 107	... ...	10.4 9.5 0.4 13.1 11.9 13.1	222 354 494 528 564 790	79.5 84.3 82.4 86.9 80.1 71.4	... ...	12.7 14.3 11.1 16.7 17.8 ...	57 66 105 80 140 317
Gabon‡ Franc C.F.A	1980 1985 1992	22 204 69 500 41 529	2.7 4.5 3.2	... 9.4 ...	16 055 47 500 34 407	72.3 68.3 82.9	2.0 3.1 2.7	... 21.7 ...	6 149 22 000 7 122
Gambia Dalasi	1980 1985 1990 1991	13 31 95 78	3.3 3.2 3.8 2.7	... ... 11.0 12.9	11 25 73 75	88.1 80.1 77.1 95.8	2.9 2.6 2.9 2.6	... 16.4 11.6 13.2	2 6 22 3
Ghana‡ Cedi	1980 1985 1990	1 319 8 675 61 900	3.1 2.6 3.1	17.1 19.0 24.3	... ... 53 664	... ... 86.7	... ... 2.7	... ... 27.1	... ... 8 236
Guinea Syli	1984 1990 1991 1992 1993	1 491	... ...	15.3	1 486 23 483 35 384 61 123 65 434	99.7	... 1.4 1.7 2.4 2.2	17.2	5 ... ...
Guinea-Bissau Peso	1980 1984	... ...	... ...	... ...	208 539	... ...	4.0 3.2	... 11.2	... ...

4.1 Public expenditure on education
Dépenses publiques afférentes à l'enseignement
Gastos públicos destinados a la educación

Country Currency / Pays Monnaie / País Moneda	Year / Année / Año	Total educational expenditure Dépenses totales d'éducation Gastos totales de educación			Current educational expenditure Dépenses ordinaires d'éducation Gastos ordinarios de educación				Capital expenditure Dépenses en capital Gastos en capital
		Amount / Montant / Importe (000 000)	As % of gross national product / En % du produit national brut / En % del producto nacional bruto (%)	As % of total government expenditure / En % des dépenses totales du gouvernement / En % de los gastos totales del gobierno (%)	Amount / Montant / Importe (000 000)	As % of the total / En % du total / En % del total (%)	As % of gross national product / En % du produit national brut / En % del producto nacional bruto (%)	As % of current government expenditure / En % des dépenses ordinaires du gouvernement / En % de los gastos ordinarios del gobierno (%)	(000 000)
		(1)	(2)	(3)	(4)	(5)	(6)	(7)	(8)
Kenya‡ Shilling	1980	3 526	6.8	18.1	3 247	92.1	6.2	23.6	279
	1985	6 171	6.4	...	5 789	93.8	6.0	...	382
	1990	12 473	6.7	16.1	11 238	90.1	6.1	19.4	1 235
	1991	11 952	5.7	...	10 989	91.9	5.3	...	963
	1992	13 203	5.4	...	12 307	93.2	5.1	...	896
	1993	20 029	6.8	...	18 999	94.9	6.4	...	1 030
Lesotho Maloti	1980	25	5.1	14.8	20	79.9	4.1	19.0	5
	1985	46	4.3	...	...	...	...	...	...
	1990	99	3.7	12.2	81	82.1	3.0	17.4	18
	1991	168	5.6	17.6	145	86.2	4.8	25.3	23
	1992	204	5.9	...	160	78.1	4.6	...	45
	1993	194	4.8	...	192	98.8	4.8	...	2
Liberia Dollar	1980	62	5.7	24.3	53	85.9	4.9	27.0	9
Libyan Arab Jamahiriya Dinar	1980	356	3.4	...	224	63.0	2.1	...	132
	1985	575	7.1	19.8	457	79.6	5.7	38.1	117
Madagascar‡ Franc	1980	36 896	4.4	...	31 548	85.5	3.7	...	5 348
	1985	52 182	2.9	...	49 806	95.4	2.8	...	2 377
	1990	67 038	1.5	...	64 964	96.9	1.5	...	2 074
	1993	116 638	1.9	13.6	104 064	89.2	1.7	...	12 574
Malawi Kwacha	1980	31	3.4	8.4	24	75.6	2.6	...	8
	1985	64	3.5	9.6	46	72.2	2.5	...	18
	1990	165	3.3	10.3	117	71.0	2.4	9.8	48
	1992	...	...	...	227	...	3.5	...	...
Mali‡ Franc C.F.A.	1980	12 903	3.8	30.8	12 752	98.8	3.7	32.1	151
	1985	17 184	3.7	...	17 048	99.2	3.7	...	136
	1993	15 369	2.1	13.2	14 994	97.6	2.0	...	375
Mauritania‡ Ouguiya	1980	...	...	...	1 546	...	5.0	...	...
	1985	...	...	...	3 973	...	8.2	33.2	...
	1990	...	...	...	3 512	...	4.5	...	...
	1992	...	...	...	3 869	...	4.0	...	...
	1993	...	...	...	4 192	...	3.9	...	...
	1994	...	...	...	4 753	...	4.0	...	...
Mauritius Rupee	1980	454	5.3	11.6	408	89.9	4.7	15.5	46
	1985	598	3.8	9.8	555	92.8	3.5	12.4	43
	1990	1 384	3.7	11.8	1 287	93.0	3.4	14.0	97
	1991	...	...	...	1 451	...	3.4	...	...
	1992	...	...	...	1 585	...	3.3	...	...
	1993	...	...	...	1 963	...	3.6	...	...
Morocco‡ Dirham	1980	4 367	6.1	18.5	3 529	80.8	4.9	23.3	838
	1985	7 697	6.3	22.9	6 079	79.0	5.0	28.6	1 618
	1990	11 220	5.5	26.1	10 187	90.8	5.0	33.6	1 033
	1992	13 564	5.8	26.7	11 944	88.1	5.1	32.0	1 620
	1993	14 589	6.2	25.6	12 939	88.7	5.5	30.9	1 650
	1994	14 950	5.4	22.6	13 367	89.4	4.8	28.4	1 583
Mozambique‡ Meticai	1980	2 900	4.4	12.1	2 500	86.2	3.8	17.7	400
	1985	4 400	4.2	10.6	4 100	93.2	3.9	12.3	300
	1990	72 264	6.3	12.0	46 064	63.7	4.0	17.5	26 200
Namibia South African Rand	1981	25	1.5	...	...	...	...	...	...
	1990	480	7.9	...	...	...	...	...	...
	1994	909	8.7	...	...	...	...	...	...
Niger‡ Franc C.F.A.	1980	16 533	3.1	22.9	7 763	47.0	1.5	16.8	8 770
	1989	19 873	2.9	9.0	15 545	78.2	2.3	13.6	4 328
	1991	20 143	3.1	10.8	19 493	96.8	3.0	18.4	650
Nigeria‡ Naira	1981	3 153	6.4	24.7	2 523	80.0	5.1	68.7	630
	1985	814	1.2	8.7	699	85.9	1.0	19.7	115
	1990	2 121	0.9	5.3	...	...	...	...	...
	1991	1 558	0.5	4.1	...	...	...	...	...
	1992	2 405	0.5	6.3	...	...	...	...	...
	1993	7 999	1.3	7.3	...	...	...	...	...

Public expenditure on education 4.1
Dépenses publiques afférentes à l'enseignement
Gastos públicos destinados a la educación

Country Currency Pays Monnaie País Moneda	Year Année Año	Total educational expenditure Dépenses totales d'éducation Gastos totales de educación			Current educational expenditure Dépenses ordinaires d'éducation Gastos ordinarios de educación				Capital expenditure Dépenses en capital Gastos en capital (000 000)
		Amount Montant Importe (000 000)	As % of gross national product En % du produit national brut En % del producto nacional bruto (%)	As % of total government expenditure En % des dépenses totales du gouvernement En % de los gastos totales del gobierno (%)	Amount Montant Importe (000 000)	As % of the total En % du total En % del total (%)	As % of gross national product En % du produit national brut En % del producto nacional bruto (%)	As % of current government expenditure En % des dépenses ordinaires du gouvernement En % de los gastos ordinarios del gobierno (%)	
		(1)	(2)	(3)	(4)	(5)	(6)	(7)	(8)
Reunion‡ French Franc	1980 1985 1990 1991 1992 1993	1 314 2 416 3 375 3 662 4 854 5 208	... ...	... ...	1 264 2 292 3 343 3 570 4 814 5 180	96.1 94.8 99.1 97.5 99.2 99.5	... ...	... ...	51 125 32 92 40 28
Rwanda Franc	1980 1984 1989	2 880 4 997 7 222	2.7 3.1 3.7	21.6 25.1 25.4	2 439 4 887 6 793	84.7 97.8 94.1	2.3 3.1 3.5	21.5 28.1 29.1	442 109 429
Sao Tome and Principe Dobra	1981 1986	91 100	8.0 3.8	... 18.8	... ...	... ...	... ...	... ...	... ...
Senegal Franc C.F.A.	1980 1985 1990 1991 1992 1993	... ...	... ...	... ...	26 818 46 118 60 467 61 686 67 100 67 008	... ...	4.4 4.2 4.1 4.1 4.3 4.4	23.2 23.1 26.8 27.4 32.8 32.6	... ...
Seychelles‡ Rupee	1980 1985 1990 1992 1993 1994	52 125 153 183 148 168	5.8 10.7 8.1 8.5 6.5 7.4	14.4 21.3 14.8 12.9	50 120 153 156	95.7 96.4 100.0 85.6	5.5 10.3 8.1 7.3	14.0 21.9 18.5 12.5	2 4 - 26 ... ...
Sierra Leone Leone	1980 1985 1989	43 112 604	3.8 2.4 1.4	11.8 12.4 ...	41 106 577	95.3 94.9 95.5	3.6 2.3 1.3	14.5 15.5 ...	2 6 27
Somalia‡ Shilling	1980 1985	169 371	1.0 0.5	8.7 4.1	154 274	91.1 73.8	0.9 0.3	... ...	15 97
South Africa‡ Rand	1986 1990 1992 1993	8 108 17 153 23 221 26 336	6.0 6.5 7.0 7.1	... ... 22.1 22.9	6 844 15 265 21 397 23 849	84.4 89.0 92.1 90.6	5.0 5.8 6.5 6.4	... ...	1 264 1 888 1 824 2 487
Sudan‡ Pound	1980 1985	187 ...	4.8 ...	9.1 ...	172 580	92.2 ...	4.4 4.0	12.6 15.0	15 ...
Swaziland‡ Lilangeni	1980 1985 1989 1993 1994	26 52 101 228 285	6.1 5.9 6.0 6.8 ...	... 20.3 22.5 17.5 ...	20 44 88 187 241	76.4 84.3 86.7 82.0 84.5	4.7 5.0 5.2 5.6 ...	23.1 25.9 25.1 21.0 ...	6 8 13 41 44
Togo Franc C.F.A.	1980 1985 1990 1992	13 049 15 880 24 420 27 004	5.6 5.0 5.6 6.1	19.4 19.4 ... 21.6	12 575 15 028 22 720 26 307	96.4 94.6 93.0 97.4	5.4 4.7 5.2 6.0	21.0 19.2 ... 29.0	474 852 1 700 697
Tunisia‡ Dinar	1980 1985 1990 1991 1992 1993	185 389 648 725 789 895	5.4 5.9 6.2 6.3 5.9 6.3	16.4 14.1 13.5 14.3 14.2 ...	162 351 569 639 701 776	87.6 90.2 87.8 88.2 88.9 86.7	4.7 5.3 5.5 5.5 5.3 5.5	23.5 20.8 16.3 17.4 17.6 ...	23 38 79 86 88 119
Uganda‡ Shilling	1980 1984 1990 1991	15 288 20 188 35 026	1.2 3.0 1.5 1.9	11.3 ... 11.5 15.0	14 205 18 527 33 012	88.3 71.1 91.8 94.3	1.1 2.1 1.4 1.8	12.8 ... 15.1 16.5	2 83 1 661 2 014
United Republic of Tanzania Shilling	1980 1985 1990	1 840 4 234 23 426	4.4 3.6 5.0	11.2 14.0 11.4	1 522 3 643 20 599	82.7 86.0 87.9	3.6 3.1 4.4	16.3 15.6 ...	318 591 2 827
Zaire Zaire	1980 1985	1 015 3 291	2.6 1.0	24.2 7.3	998 3 239	98.3 98.4	2.6 1.0	25.3 7.3	17 52

4.1 Public expenditure on education
Dépenses publiques afférentes à l'enseignement
Gastos públicos destinados a la educación

| Country / Currency | Year | Total educational expenditure Dépenses totales d'éducation Gastos totales de educación | | | Current educational expenditure Dépenses ordinaires d'éducation Gastos ordinarios de educación | | | | Capital expenditure |
| Pays / Monnaie | Année | Amount Montant Importe (000 000) | As % of gross national product En % du produit national brut En % del producto nacional bruto (%) | As % of total government expenditure En % des dépenses totales du gouvernement En % de los gastos totales del gobierno (%) | Amount Montant Importe (000 000) | As % of the total En % du total En % del total (%) | As % of gross national product En % du produit national brut En % del producto nacional bruto (%) | As % of current government expenditure En % des dépenses ordinaires du gouvernement En % de los gastos ordinarios del gobierno (%) | Dépenses en capital Gastos en capital (000 000) |
País / Moneda	Año								
		(1)	(2)	(3)	(4)	(5)	(6)	(7)	(8)
Zambia	1980	127	4.5	7.6	120	95.1	4.2	11.1	6
Kwacha	1985	293	4.7	13.4	272	92.9	4.4	14.3	21
	1990	2 737	2.6	*8.7	2 382	87.0	2.3	*8.7	355
Zimbabwe‡	1980	224	6.6	13.7	218	97.4	6.4	14.1	6
Dollar	1986	726	9.1	15.0	721	99.2	9.0	...	6
	1990	1 661	10.5	...	1 648	99.2	10.4	...	13
	1991	1 933	9.4	...	1 913	99.0	9.3	...	20
	1992	2 444	10.1	...	...	...	...	...	...
	1993	2 914	8.3	...	2 893	99.3	8.3	...	21
America, North									
Antigua and Barbuda	1980	9	3.0	...	9	98.9	3.0	...	0.0
E.Caribbean Dollar	1984	12	2.7	...	11	95.8	2.6	...	1
Aruba	1986	47	...	14.1	46	98.9	...	15.4	1
Florins	1990	77	...	18.0	62	81.2	...	19.4	14
	1991	76	...	15.9	60	78.4	...	16.8	16
Bahamas	1980	...	...	...	53	...	4.4	22.1	...
Dollar	1985	86	4.0	18.0	81	94.5	3.8	...	5
	1990	125	4.2	17.8	112	89.2	3.7	...	14
	1991	114	3.9	16.3	103	90.8	3.5	...	11
Barbados	1980	109	6.5	20.5	90	82.8	5.4	...	19
Dollar	1984	139	6.1	...	123	88.2	5.4	...	17
	1990	269	7.9	22.2	218	81.0	6.4	22.1	51
	1991	248	7.6	18.4	212	85.4	6.5	18.7	36
	1992	215	7.0	16.9	192	89.3	6.3	17.5	23
	1993	238	7.5	18.6	230	96.8	7.3	20.0	8
Belize	1986	...	...	...	18	...	4.0	...	...
Dollar	1991	48	5.7	15.5	38	79.9	4.5	21.8	10
Bermuda	1980	26	4.1	...	26	98.0	4.0	...	1
Dollar	1984	33	3.2	18.4	31	95.2	3.0	19.9	2
	1990	53	...	14.5	49	92.5	...	15.7	4
	1991	60	...	...	54	89.2	...	...	6
British Virgin Islands‡	1980	...	...	...	2	...	...	13.3	...
United States Dollar	1985	5	...	16.7	4	90.5	...	...	1
	1990	8	...	12.2	7	89.2	...	...	1
	1991	11	...	15.4	9	80.0	...	...	2
	1992	...	...	...	10	...	...	...	...
	1993	...	...	...	7	...	...	...	...
Canada	1980	20 833	6.9	16.3	19 295	92.6	6.4	...	1 538
Dollar	1985	30 287	6.6	11.9	28 202	93.1	6.1	...	2 085
	1990	43 487	6.8	14.2	40 288	92.6	6.3	...	3 199
	1991	47 764	7.4	...	44 356	92.9	6.9	...	3 408
	1992	49 955	7.6	14.3	46 515	93.1	7.1	...	3 440
Costa Rica‡	1980	3 069	7.8	22.2	2 802	91.3	7.1	26.7	267
Colon	1985	8 181	4.5	22.7	7 787	95.2	4.2	26.2	394
	1990	22 907	4.6	20.8	22 188	96.9	4.5	26.3	719
	1992	38 552	4.4	21.4	36 636	95.0	4.2	25.4	170
	1993	47 656	4.6	20.2	45 717	95.9	4.4	25.8	902
	1994	58 699	4.7	19.2	56 323	96.0	4.5	22.9	1 256
Cuba‡	1980	1 267	7.2	...	1 135	89.5	6.4	...	133
Peso	1985	1 690	6.3	...	1 588	93.9	5.9	...	103
	1990	1 748	6.6	12.3	1 627	93.1	6.1	14.4	121
Dominica	1986	17	5.9	16.7	16	95.9	5.7	18.5	1
E.Caribbean Dollar	1989	22	5.8	10.6	20	91.0	5.2	19.9	2
Dominican Republic‡	1980	139	2.2	16.0	104	...	1.6	...	10
Peso	1985	234	1.8	14.0	204	...	1.6	...	2
	1992	1 502	1.4	8.9	970	...	0.9	...	24
	1993	2 007	1.7	9.9	1 289	...	1.1	...	63
	1994	2 606	1.9	12.2	1 621	...	1.2	...	124

Public expenditure on education **4.1**
Dépenses publiques afférentes à l'enseignement
Gastos públicos destinados a la educación

Country / Currency Pays / Monnaie País / Moneda	Year Année Año	Total educational expenditure Dépenses totales d'éducation Gastos totales de educación			Current educational expenditure Dépenses ordinaires d'éducation Gastos ordinarios de educación				Capital expenditure Dépenses en capital Gastos en capital (000 000)
		Amount Montant Importe (000 000)	As % of gross national product En % du produit national brut En % del producto nacional bruto (%)	As % of total government expenditure En % des dépenses totales du gouvernement En % de los gastos totales del gobierno (%)	Amount Montant Importe (000 000)	As % of the total En % du total En % del total (%)	As % of gross national product En % du produit national brut En % del producto nacional bruto (%)	As % of current government expenditure En % des dépenses ordinaires du gouvernement En % de los gastos ordinarios del gobierno (%)	
		(1)	(2)	(3)	(4)	(5)	(6)	(7)	(8)
El Salvador Colon	1980	340	3.9	17.1	320	94.1	3.7	22.9	20
	1984	336	3.0	12.5	293	87.3	2.6	16.3	43
	1990	722	1.8	...	715	99.0	1.8	...	7
	1991	785	1.7	...	780	99.4	1.7	...	5
	1992	884	1.6	...	883	99.8	1.6	...	2
Grenada E.Caribbean Dollar	1981	...	...	...	14	...	6.0	...	...
	1985	...	...	...	19	...	6.3	...	...
	1990	...	...	...	30	...	5.9	...	...
	1991	...	...	...	32	...	5.8	...	...
	1992	...	...	...	31	...	5.4	...	...
	1993	...	...	...	31	...	5.3	...	...
Guadeloupe‡ French Franc	1980	862	...	...	818	94.9	...	...	44
	1990	1 973	...	...	1 952	98.9	...	...	21
	1991	2 077	...	...	2 022	97.4	...	...	55
	1992	2 663	...	...	2 627	98.6	...	...	36
	1993	2 776	...	...	2 745	98.9	...	...	31
Guatemala‡ Quetzal	1979	131	1.9	16.6	117	89.4	1.7	23.4	14
	1984	163	1.8	12.4	160	97.8	1.7	23.1	4
	1990	468	1.4	11.8	...	...	...	...	...
	1991	606	1.3	13.0	...	...	...	...	...
	1992	774	1.5	...	...	...	...	...	...
	1993	995	1.6	12.8	...	...	...	...	...
Haiti Gourde	1980	107	1.5	14.9	86	80.1	1.2	17.2	21
	1985	118	1.2	16.5	117	99.8	1.2	16.7	1
	1990	216	1.4	20.0	216	99.9	1.4	20.1	-
Honduras Lempira	1980	155	3.2	14.2	141	91.0	2.9	19.5	14
	1985	290	4.2	13.8	286	98.6	4.1	...	4
	1989	416	4.2	15.9	404	97.1	4.1	...	12
	1991	621	4.1	...	606	97.7	4.0	...	14
	1994	988	4.0	16.0	971	98.3	4.0	...	17
Jamaica‡ Dollar	1980	304	7.0	13.1	303	99.6	7.0	19.4	1
	1985	550	5.8	12.1	515	93.7	5.4	15.8	35
	1990	1 472	5.4	12.8	1 276	86.7	4.7	17.3	196
	1992	3 086	4.7	11.8	2 714	87.9	4.1	17.9	372
	1993	5 516	6.2	12.9	5 081	92.1	5.7	15.6	435
	1994	6 206	4.7	...	5 551	89.4	4.2	...	655
Martinique‡ French Franc	1980	931	...	...	887	95.3	...	...	44
	1990	2 013	...	...	1 994	99.1	...	...	19
	1991	2 090	...	...	2 067	98.9	...	...	23
	1992	2 741	...	...	2 716	99.1	...	...	25
	1993	2 842	...	...	2 814	99.0	...	...	28
Mexico‡ Peso	1980	204 326	4.7	...	129 797	...	3.0	...	10 174
	1985	1 767 324	3.9	...	1 229 314	...	2.7	...	99 868
	1990	26 640 958	4.0	...	16 617 522	...	2.5	...	1 045 034
	1992	48 143 389	4.8	...	32 780 581	...	3.2	...	2 217 884
	1993	62 408 008	5.6	...	43 107 371	...	3.9	...	3 134 503
	1994	71 190 760	5.8	...	...	...	...	...	...
Montserrat E.Caribbean Dollar	1990	...	...	...	7	...	...	18.9	...
	1991	...	...	...	8	...	...	19.5	...
	1992	...	...	...	8	...	...	19.3	...
	1993	...	...	...	7	...	...	18.8	...
Netherlands Antilles Guilder	1991	151	...	...	...	...	...	...	...
	1992	171	...	...	...	...	...	...	...
	1993	196	...	...	...	...	...	...	...
Nicaragua‡ Cordoba	1980	0.662	3.4	10.4	0.580	87.5	3.0	...	0.082
	1985	6.409	6.8	10.2	6.196	96.7	6.6	12.2	0.213
	1991	242	4.4	12.7	...	...	...	...	...
	1992	275	4.1	...	...	...	...	...	...
	1993	324	3.9	12.8	...	...	...	...	...
	1994	340	3.8	12.2	327	96.1	3.7	...	13

4.1 Public expenditure on education
Dépenses publiques afférentes à l'enseignement
Gastos públicos destinados a la educación

Country / Currency — Pays / Monnaie — País / Moneda	Year — Année — Año	Total educational expenditure / Dépenses totales d'éducation / Gastos totales de educación			Current educational expenditure / Dépenses ordinaires d'éducation / Gastos ordinarios de educación				Capital expenditure — Dépenses en capital — Gastos en capital (000 000)
		Amount — Montant — Importe (000 000)	As % of gross national product — En % du produit national brut — En % del producto nacional bruto (%)	As % of total government expenditure — En % des dépenses totales du gouvernement — En % de los gastos totales del gobierno (%)	Amount — Montant — Importe (000 000)	As % of the total — En % du total — En % del total (%)	As % of gross national product — En % du produit national brut — En % del producto nacional bruto (%)	As % of current government expenditure — En % des dépenses ordinaires du gouvernement — En % de los gastos ordinarios del gobierno (%)	
		(1)	(2)	(3)	(4)	(5)	(6)	(7)	(8)
Panama Balboa	1980	166	4.8	19.0	156	93.7	4.5	19.8	10
	1985	237	4.8	18.7	231	97.7	4.7	19.9	6
	1990	248	5.2	20.9	241	97.3	5.1	22.2	7
	1991	268	5.1	18.8	262	97.5	5.0	21.1	7
	1992	329	5.6	18.9	307	93.2	5.2	21.9	22
	1994	346	5.2	20.9	334	96.6	5.0	23.4	12
Saint Kitts and Nevis‡ E.Caribbean Dollar	1980	7	5.2	9.4	7	99.5	5.2	13.6	0.0
	1985	12	5.8	18.5	12	99.7	5.7	19.1	0.0
	1990	11	2.7	...	11	100.0	2.7	...	-
	1991	12	2.8	11.6	12	96.4	2.7	11.7	0.0
	1992	15	3.3	13.5	14	95.2	3.1	...	1
	1993	...	...	...	14	...	2.7	...	...
St. Lucia E.Caribbean Dollar	1980	...	...	...	19	...	6.9	...	...
	1986	38	5.5	...	36	94.4	5.2	...	2
	1990	...	...	...	54	...	5.3	...	...
	1991	...	...	...	55	...	5.1	...	...
	1992	...	...	...	63	...	5.2	...	...
St. Pierre and Miquelon‡ French Franc	1980	18	...	...	17	90.7	...	...	2
	1985	41	...	...	37	90.4	...	...	4
	1990	54	...	...	41	75.5	...	...	13
	1991	46	...	...	42	91.1	...	...	4
	1992	57	...	...	54	95.2	...	...	3
	1993	64	...	...	57	88.8	...	...	7
St. Vincent and the Grenadines‡ E.Caribbean Dollar	1986	19	5.8	11.6	18	93.4	5.4	16.8	1
	1990	34	6.7	13.8	26	75.3	5.0	17.2	8
Trinidad and Tobago Dollar	1980	564	4.0	11.5	431	76.4	3.0	17.6	133
	1985	1 042	6.1	...	912	87.5	5.3	...	130
	1990	788	4.0	11.6	727	92.2	3.7	13.5	61
	1992	811	3.8	10.3	772	95.2	3.6	10.7	39
	1993	836	3.6	...	805	96.3	3.5	...	31
	1994	1 170	4.5	...	1 061	90.7	4.1	...	108
United States‡ Dollar	1980	182 849	6.7	...	...	...	...	...	...
	1985	199 372	4.9	15.5	182 875	91.7	4.5	16.3	16 497
	1990	292 944	5.3	12.3	265 074	90.5	4.8	12.3	27 870
	1992	328 396	5.5	...	...	...	...	...	...
U.S. Virgin Islands United States Dollar	1980	58	7.9	...	57	98.7	7.8	...	1
	1984	74	7.5	...	...	...	...	...	...
America, South									
Argentina‡ Peso	1980	1.018	2.7	15.1	0.860	84.5	2.3	18.8	0.158
	1985	740	1.5	...	667	90.1	1.3	...	73
	1990	7 356 595	1.1	...	7 062 974	96.0	1.1	...	293 621
	1992	6 962	3.1	15.7	...	...	...	...	...
	1993	8 310	3.3	12.4	...	...	...	...	...
	1994	10 471	3.8	14.0	...	...	...	...	...
Bolivia‡ Boliviano	1980	0.0051	4.4	...	0.0049	96.0	4.2	...	0.0002
	1985	43	2.1	...	...	...	...	...	...
	1990	363	2.7	...	...	...	...	...	...
	1991	467	2.7	...	...	...	...	...	...
	1994	1 322	5.4	11.2	1 293	97.8	5.3	15.1	28
Brazil‡ Cruzeiro	1980	0.431	3.6	...	...	...	...	...	...
	1985	50	3.8	...	...	...	...	...	...
	1989	56 101	4.6	...	...	...	...	...	...
	1994	5 761	1.6	...	...	...	...	...	...
Chile Peso	1980	47 961	4.6	11.9	45 504	94.9	4.4	13.4	2 457
	1985	101 493	4.4	15.3	...	...	...	...	...
	1990	232 516	2.7	10.4	225 620	97.0	2.6	...	6 896
	1992	407 645	2.8	12.9	392 411	96.3	2.7	15.0	15 234
	1993	477 307	2.7	...	468 452	98.1	2.6	...	8 855
	1994	620 095	2.9	13.4	585 399	94.4	2.8	14.7	34 696

Public expenditure on education 4.1
Dépenses publiques afférentes à l'enseignement
Gastos públicos destinados a la educación

Country Currency / Pays Monnaie / País Moneda	Year Année Año	Total educational expenditure Dépenses totales d'éducation Gastos totales de educación			Current educational expenditure Dépenses ordinaires d'éducation Gastos ordinarios de educación				Capital expenditure Dépenses en capital Gastos en capital (000 000)
		Amount Montant Importe (000 000)	As % of gross national product / En % du produit national brut / En % del producto nacional bruto (%)	As % of total government expenditure / En % des dépenses totales du gouvernement / En % de los gastos totales del gobierno (%)	Amount Montant Importe (000 000)	As % of the total / En % du total / En % del total (%)	As % of gross national product / En % du produit national brut / En % del producto nacional bruto (%)	As % of current government expenditure / En % des dépenses ordinaires du gouvernement / En % de los gastos ordinarios del gobierno (%)	
		(1)	(2)	(3)	(4)	(5)	(6)	(7)	(8)
Colombia‡ Peso	1980	29 240	1.9	14.3	27 286	93.3	1.7	19.9	1 954
	1985	136 570	2.9	...	127 908	93.7	2.7	...	8 662
	1990	526 686	2.8	12.4	...	...	...	...	...
	1992	996 567	3.1	...	...	...	...	...	...
	1993	1 396 031	3.5	12.3	1 231 516	88.2	3.0	19.2	164 515
	1994	1 927 850	3.7	12.9	1 579 822	81.9	3.0	10.6	348 028
Ecuador Sucre	1980	15 580	5.6	33.3	14 649	94.0	5.3	36.0	931
	1985	38 009	3.7	20.6	35 611	93.7	3.5	25.8	2 397
	1989	134 554	2.8	19.1	127 394	94.7	2.7	24.7	7 160
	1991	298 126	2.6	17.5	260 332	87.3	2.3	23.9	37 794
	1992	492 252	2.7	19.2	416 411	84.6	2.3	24.0	75 841
	1993	790 964	3.0	...	720 441	91.1	2.7	...	70 523
French Guiana‡ French Franc	1980	159	...	...	152	96.1	...	...	6
	1990	501	...	...	490	97.8	...	...	11
	1991	537	...	...	518	96.5	...	...	19
	1992	774	...	...	755	97.5	...	...	19
	1993	851	...	...	833	97.9	...	...	18
Guyana Dollar	1979	121	9.7	14.0	89	73.6	7.2	15.2	32
	1985	162	9.8	10.4	135	83.1	8.1	13.0	27
	1990	542	5.0	...	435	80.2	4.0	5.2	107
Paraguay‡ Guarani	1980	8 793	1.5	16.4	...	...	...	...	...
	1985	20 662	1.5	16.7	16 822	81.4	1.2	18.8	3 840
	1990	74 387	1.2	9.1	72 472	97.4	1.1	...	1 915
	1992	249 750	2.6	11.9	223 139	89.3	2.3	...	26 611
	1993	338 107	2.8	16.9	312 757	92.5	2.6	17.1	25 350
	1994	432 812	2.9	...	401 408	92.7	2.7	...	31 404
Peru Inti	1980	176	3.1	15.2	166	94.4	2.9	18.5	10
	1985	5 042	2.9	15.7	4 855	96.3	2.8	17.9	188
Suriname Guilder	1980	105	6.7	22.5	105	100.0	6.7	22.8	-
	1985	158	9.4	...	...	...	...	...	1
	1990	250	8.1	...	249	99.6	8.1	...	1
	1991	266	7.2	...	265	99.6	7.2	...	2
	1992	362	7.2	...	360	99.4	7.1	...	4
	1993	384	3.6	...	380	99.0	3.6	...	
Uruguay Peso	1980	2 035	2.3	10.0	1 927	94.7	2.2	...	108
	1985	12 565	2.8	9.3	12 068	96.0	2.7	9.3	497
	1990	289 354	3.1	15.9	265 660	91.8	2.8	16.7	23 694
	1991	572 456	2.9	16.6	530 330	92.6	2.7	17.0	42 126
	1992	959 087	2.8	15.4	873 317	91.1	2.5	15.5	85 770
	1994	2 049 055	2.5	13.3	1 981 029	96.7	2.5	13.3	68 026
Venezuela Bolivar	1980	13 162	4.4	14.7	12 524	95.1	4.2	24.3	639
	1985	23 068	5.1	20.3	...	...	...	...	...
	1990	69 352	3.1	12.0	...	...	...	...	...
	1992	211 659	5.3	23.5	...	...	...	...	...
	1993	242 827	4.6	22.0	...	...	...	...	...
	1994	434 282	5.1	22.4	419 515	96.6	4.9	31.2	14 767
Asia									
Afghanistan Afghani	1980	3 205	2.0	12.7	2 886	90.0	1.8	14.4	319
	1990	5 667	...	...	5 282	93.2	...	...	385
Armenia Rouble	1990	4	7.4	20.5	...	...	...	...	...
	1993	...	...	...	136	...	3.5	...	...
Azerbaijan Rouble	1990	1 132	7.7	24.2	...	...	...	...	...
	1991	2 066	7.7	24.7	...	...	...	...	...
	1992	16 205	6.5	...	15 704	96.9	6.3	...	501
	1994	917 980	5.5	13.7	...	...	...	...	...
Bahrain‡ Dinar	1980	33	2.9	10.3	28	86.5	2.5	14.7	4
	1985	52	4.0	10.4	49	94.2	3.8	14.6	3
	1990	65	5.0	...	61	94.3	4.7	...	4
	1991	68	5.1	12.8	65	94.6	4.8	14.9	4
	1992	72	5.0	12.3	68	94.2	4.7	14.4	4
	1993	71	4.7	...	69	97.1	4.6	...	2

4.1 Public expenditure on education
Dépenses publiques afférentes à l'enseignement
Gastos públicos destinados a la educación

Country / Currency Pays / Monnaie País / Moneda	Year Année Año	Total educational expenditure / Dépenses totales d'éducation / Gastos totales de educación			Current educational expenditure / Dépenses ordinaires d'éducation / Gastos ordinarios de educación				Capital expenditure Dépenses en capital Gastos en capital
		Amount Montant Importe (000 000)	As % of gross national product En % du produit national brut En % del producto nacional bruto (%)	As % of total government expenditure En % des dépenses totales du gouvernement En % de los gastos totales del gobierno (%)	Amount Montant Importe (000 000)	As % of the total En % du total En % del total (%)	As % of gross national product En % du produit national brut En % del producto nacional bruto (%)	As % of current government expenditure En % des dépenses ordinaires du gouvernement En % de los gastos ordinarios del gobierno (%)	(000 000)
		(1)	(2)	(3)	(4)	(5)	(6)	(7)	(8)
Bangladesh‡ Taka	1980	3 009	1.5	7.8	2 010	66.8	1.0	13.6	999
	1985	7 782	1.9	9.7	6 005	77.2	1.5	15.3	1 777
	1990	14 942	2.0	10.3	11 820	79.1	1.6	14.4	3 122
	1991	18 184	2.2	11.3	13 816	76.0	1.7	15.9	4 368
	1992	20 996	2.3	8.7	16 744	79.7	1.9	10.4	4 252
Bhutan Ngultrum	1992	...	...	...	187	...	2.9	...	...
	1993	...	...	...	192	...	2.7	...	...
Brunei Darussalam‡ Dollar	1980	129	1.2	11.8	115	88.8	1.1	12.5	15
	1984	168	2.1	...	151	89.9	1.9	...	17
	1990	253	3.9	...	229	90.4	3.5	...	24
	1991	235	3.6	...	217	92.5	3.3	...	17
	1992	258	...	...	239	92.7	...	...	19
	1993	287	...	...	273	95.2	...	...	14
China Yuan	1980	11 319	2.5	9.3	10 263	90.7	2.3	...	1 056
	1985	22 489	2.6	12.2	19 770	87.9	2.3	...	2 719
	1990	43 386	2.3	12.8	40 423	93.2	2.2	...	2 963
	1992	53 874	2.0	12.2	48 976	90.9	1.8	13.5	4 898
	1993	64 439	1.9	12.2	59 104	91.7	1.7	...	5 335
	1994	111 769	2.6	...	100 128	89.6	2.3	...	11 641
Cyprus‡ Pound	1980	27	3.5	12.9	25	94.0	3.3	16.2	2
	1985	55	3.7	12.2	53	95.4	3.6	13.4	3
	1990	89	3.5	11.3	84	94.9	3.3	12.3	5
	1992	120	3.9	12.5	112	92.6	3.6	13.1	9
	1993	139	4.3	12.6	127	91.0	3.9	12.9	13
	1994	156	...	14.2	143	91.2	...	14.8	14
Georgia Kupon	1994	6 913 532	1.9	6.9	5 727 212	82.8	1.5	7.5	1 186 320
Hong Kong Dollar	1980	3 446	...	14.6	3 036	88.1	...	25.5	410
	1985	7 532	...	18.4	6 928	92.0	...	...	604
	1990	16 566	...	17.4	...	...	...	...	...
	1991	19 552	...	18.1	16 915	86.5	...	...	2 637
	1992	22 193	...	17.4	20 349	91.7	...	...	1 844
	1993	25 005	...	17.0	...	...	...	...	...
India Rupee	1980	37 924	2.8	10.0	37 462	98.8	2.7	...	463
	1985	87 257	3.4	9.4	85 198	97.6	3.3	13.0	2 059
	1990	207 897	3.9	10.9	205 330	98.8	3.9	13.7	2 567
	1991	232 425	3.8	11.9	228 878	98.5	3.8	13.4	3 547
	1992	260 169	3.8	11.5	257 377	98.9	3.7	13.4	2 792
Indonesia‡ Rupiah	1980	808 087	1.7	...	...	...	...	...	...
	1990	2 089 319	1.1	...	1 441 498	69.0	0.8	...	647 821
	1992	5 479 346	2.2	...	3 585 711	65.4	1.5	...	1 893 635
	1993	3 639 295	1.2	...	2 294 724	63.1	0.7	...	1 344 571
	1994	4 673 672	1.3	...	3 112 751	66.6	0.9	...	1 560 921
Iran, Islamic Republic of Rial	1980	498 268	7.5	15.7	440 298	88.4	6.6	20.1	57 970
	1985	575 519	3.6	17.2	510 081	88.6	3.2	20.6	65 438
	1990	1 493 896	4.1	22.4	1 232 097	82.5	3.4	28.8	261 799
	1992	3 142 954	4.7	28.2	2 582 561	82.2	3.9	31.4	560 393
	1993	4 978 516	5.3	22.8	4 068 840	81.7	4.3	26.4	909 676
	1994	5 838 840	5.9	18.1	4 793 129	82.1	4.9	22.7	1 045 711
Iraq Dinar	1980	418	3.0	...	...	...	...	...	...
	1985	551	4.0	...	...	...	...	...	...
	1991	804	...	...	711	88.5	...	...	93
	1992	902	...	...	896	99.3	...	...	6
Israel Shekel	1980	9	7.9	7.3	8	92.3	7.3	8.9	1
	1985	1 876	6.4	8.6	1 720	91.7	5.9	8.3	156
	1990	6 239	5.8	10.5	5 713	91.6	5.3	10.4	526
	1991	8 157	5.8	10.6	7 420	91.0	5.3	10.9	737
	1992	10 182	6.0	11.1	9 266	91.0	5.5	11.7	916
Japan‡ Yen	1980	13 908 111	5.8	19.6	9 416 591	...	3.9	...	3 920 843
	1985	16 142 654	5.0	17.9	15 280 808	...	4.8	...	5 143 849
	1990	20 258 000	4.7	16.5	...	...	...	...	...
	1991	21 300 000	4.7	16.6	...	...	...	...	...

Public expenditure on education 4.1
Dépenses publiques afférentes à l'enseignement
Gastos públicos destinados a la educación

Country / Currency / Pays Monnaie / País Moneda	Year / Année / Año	Total educational expenditure — Dépenses totales d'éducation — Gastos totales de educación			Current educational expenditure — Dépenses ordinaires d'éducation — Gastos ordinarios de educación				Capital expenditure / Dépenses en capital / Gastos en capital
		Amount / Montant / Importe (000 000)	As % of gross national product / En % du produit national brut / En % del producto nacional bruto (%)	As % of total government expenditure / En % des dépenses totales du gouvernement / En % de los gastos totales del gobierno (%)	Amount / Montant / Importe (000 000)	As % of the total / En % du total / En % del total (%)	As % of gross national product / En % du produit national brut / En % del producto nacional bruto (%)	As % of current government expenditure / En % des dépenses ordinaires du gouvernement / En % de los gastos ordinarios del gobierno (%)	(000 000)
		(1)	(2)	(3)	(4)	(5)	(6)	(7)	(8)
Jordan‡ Dinar	1980	64	...	11.3	51	79.2	...	15.0	13
	1985	105	5.5	13.0	92	87.1	4.8	18.9	14
	1990	101	4.2	8.5	92	91.5	3.8	...	9
	1992	116	3.6	9.1	102	88.3	3.1	10.9	14
	1993	155	4.2	11.6	139	89.5	3.8	13.2	16
	1994	155	3.8	10.5	...	...	...	...	
Kazakstan Tenge	1985	2 174	6.5	18.9	...	...	...	...	...
	1990	3 001	6.5	17.6	...	...	...	...	...
	1991	6 252	7.7	19.1	...	...	...	...	...
	1992	65 247	5.4	25.2	60 549	92.8	5.0	...	4 698
Korea, Republic of Won	1980	1 374 736	3.7	...	1 158 967	84.3	3.1	...	215 769
	1985	3 530 101	4.5	...	2 811 861	79.7	3.5	...	718 240
	1990	6 159 073	3.5	...	5 495 204	89.2	3.1	...	663 869
	1991	8 543 089	4.0	...	6 728 333	78.8	3.1	...	1 814 756
	1992	10 019 080	4.2	14.8	7 996 446	79.8	3.4	15.3	2 022 634
	1993	11 756 385	4.5	16.0	9 344 751	79.5	3.5	17.7	2 411 634
Kuwait Dinar	1980	219	2.4	8.1	204	93.1	2.3	11.2	15
	1986	360	4.9	12.6	344	95.4	4.7	...	16
	1989	432	4.6	14.0	...	...	...	...	...
	1992	450	6.1	11.4	...	...	...	...	...
	1993	466	5.6	11.0	...	...	...	...	...
Kyrgyzstan Som	1980	2	7.2	22.2	...	...	...	...	...
	1985	2	7.9	22.4	2	92.6	7.3	...	0.0
	1990	4	8.5	22.5	3	88.5	7.5	...	1
	1991	6	6.4	22.7	5	96.6	6.2	...	1
	1993	...	...	...	215	...	3.8	21.0	...
	1994	731	6.8	25.6	697	95.4	6.5	25.2	34
Lao People's Democratic Republic Kip	1980	24	...	...	...	...	...	...	...
	1985	463	...	...	...	...	...	...	...
	1992	19 922	2.3	...	15 094	75.8	1.8	...	4 828
Lebanon‡ Pound	1980	511	...	13.2	...	...	...	...	...
	1985	1 639	...	16.8	...	...	...	...	...
	1989	43 711	2.7	...	...	...	...	...	2 480
	1992	206 603	2.1	12.5	204 123	98.8	2.1	...	2 480
	1993	251 874	1.9	...	227 049	90.1	1.7	...	24 825
	1994	316 678	2.0	...	240 091	75.8	1.5	...	96 587
Macau Pataca	1986	125	...	...	...	...	...	...	...
	1990	444	...	10.7	...	...	...	...	...
	1991	602	...	10.4	...	...	...	...	...
	1992	601	...	8.9	...	...	...	...	...
Malaysia‡ Ringgit	1980	3 104	6.0	14.7	2 575	83.0	5.0	18.4	529
	1985	4 754	6.6	16.3	4 062	85.4	5.6	...	692
	1990	6 033	5.4	18.3	4 664	77.3	4.2	19.3	1 369
	1992	7 702	5.5	16.9	6 656	86.4	4.7	19.6	1 046
	1993	8 074	5.2	15.7	7 085	87.8	4.6	17.2	989
	1994	9 363	5.3	15.5	7 821	83.5	4.4	15.9	1 542
Maldives Rufiyaa	1986	24	4.4	*7.2	20	82.4	3.7	...	4
	1990	79	6.3	*10.0	...	...	...	...	...
	1991	176	11.6	*16.0	...	...	...	...	...
	1992	220	12.0	*16.0	...	...	...	...	...
	1993	183	8.1	13.6	132	72.3	5.8	18.0	51
Mongolia Tughrik	1985	716	7.8	...	...	...	...	...	...
	1990	882	8.6	...	...	...	...	...	...
	1991	1 598	8.5	...	...	...	...	...	...
	1994	15 510	5.2	...	15 384	99.2	5.2	...	126
Myanmar‡ Kyat	1980	660	1.7	...	584	88.5	1.5	...	76
	1985	1 084	2.0	...	841	77.6	1.5	...	243
	1989	2 948	2.4	...	2 699	91.6	2.2	...	249
	1994	5 685	...	14.4	4 436	78.0	...	19.0	1 249

Public expenditure on education
Dépenses publiques afférentes à l'enseignement
Gastos públicos destinados a la educación

Country Currency Pays Monnaie País Moneda	Year Année Año	Total educational expenditure Dépenses totales d'éducation Gastos totales de educación			Current educational expenditure Dépenses ordinaires d'éducation Gastos ordinarios de educación				Capital expenditure Dépenses en capital Gastos en capital (000 000)
		Amount Montant Importe (000 000)	As % of gross national product En % du produit national brut En % del producto nacional bruto (%)	As % of total government expenditure En % des dépenses totales du gouvernement En % de los gastos totales del gobierno (%)	Amount Montant Importe (000 000)	As % of the total En % du total En % del total (%)	As % of gross national product En % du produit national brut En % del producto nacional bruto (%)	As % of current government expenditure En % des dépenses ordinaires du gouvernement En % de los gastos ordinarios del gobierno (%)	
		(1)	(2)	(3)	(4)	(5)	(6)	(7)	(8)
Nepal‡ Rupee	1980 1985 1989 1990 1991 1992	430 1 241 2 086 2 079 3 268 4 428	1.8 2.6 2.3 2.0 2.7 2.9	10.5 12.7 10.6 8.5 12.3 13.2	... ...	... ...	... ...	... ...	... ...
Oman‡ Rial	1980 1985 1990 1992 1993 1994	38 123 128 151 170 173	2.1 4.0 3.5 3.9 4.5 4.5	4.1 ... 11.1 16.2 15.2 15.5	31 77 117 135 151 153	81.3 62.7 92.0 89.8 89.1 88.9	1.7 2.5 3.2 3.5 4.0 4.0	4.6 ... 18.8 19.3 19.1 20.0	7 46 10 15 19 19
Pakistan‡ Rupee	1980 1985 1990 1991	4 619 12 645 23 570 27 790	2.0 2.5 2.6 2.7	5.0	3 379 9 390 19 500 24 090	73.1 74.3 82.7 86.7	1.5 1.8 2.2 2.3	5.2	1 240 3 255 4 070 3 700
Philippines‡ Peso	1980 1985 1990 1991 1992 1993	4 191 7 524 31 067 37 033 31 687 36 320	1.7 1.4 2.9 2.9 2.3 2.4	9.1 7.4 10.1 10.5	4 023 7 026 28 713 32 872	96.0 93.4 92.4 88.8	1.7 1.3 2.7 2.6	13.0 10.0 11.1 11.1	168 498 2 354 4 161 ... ...
Qatar Riyal	1980 1985 1990 1992 1993 1994	792 1 012 929 957 976 889	2.6 4.1 3.4 3.4 3.5 ...	7.2	598 767 904 896 891 816	75.5 75.7 97.3 93.6 91.3 91.8	2.0 3.1 3.3 3.2 3.2 ...	7.8	194 246 25 62 85 73
Saudi Arabia Riyal	1980 1985 1990 1992 1993 1994	21 294 23 540 25 460 30 800 31 590 28 817	4.1 6.7 6.0 6.3	8.7 12.0 17.8 17.0	13 526 19 283 24 033 29 428 29 671 27 386	63.5 81.9 94.4 95.5 93.9 95.0	2.6 5.5 5.7 6.0	... ...	7 768 4 257 1 427 1 372 1 919 1 431
Singapore Dollar	1980 1985 1990 1992 1993 1994	686 1 776 2 055 2 598 2 884 3 416	2.8 4.4 3.1 3.2 3.1 3.3	7.3 ... 18.2 21.2 23.0 24.2	587 1 388 1 795 2 043 2 192 2 486	85.6 78.2 87.3 78.6 76.0 72.8	2.4 3.4 2.7 2.5 2.4 2.4	10.3 ... 25.4 24.1 24.0 25.6	99 387 261 555 693 931
Sri Lanka‡ Rupee	1980 1985 1990 1992 1993 1994	1 799 4 183 8 621 13 883 15 515 18 259	2.7 2.6 2.7 3.3 3.1 3.2	7.7 6.9 8.1 8.8 9.0 9.4	1 535 3 530 7 024 10 598 12 604 15 314	85.3 84.4 81.5 76.3 81.2 83.9	2.3 2.2 2.2 2.5 2.6 2.7	13.5 11.4 10.7 10.6 12.2 13.2	264 653 1 597 3 285 2 911 2 945
Syrian Arab Republic Pound	1980 1985 1990 1991 1992 1994	2 347 5 060 10 720 12 025 10 903 17 987	4.6 6.1 4.2 4.2	8.1 11.8 17.3 14.2 11.7 12.5	1 272 2 799 ... ... 9 627 15 621	... ... 88.3 86.8	2.5 3.4	... ...	457 846 ... ... 1 276 2 366
Tajikistan Rouble	1980 1985 1990 1991 1992 1993	396 509 788 1 227 7 207 60 039	8.2 8.6 10.7 9.2 11.2 9.5	29.2 29.5 24.7 24.4 19.2 17.9	366 479 723 1 190 6 976 56 739	92.4 94.1 91.8 97.0 96.8 94.5	7.6 8.1 9.8 8.9 10.8 9.0	... ...	30 30 65 37 231 3 300
Thailand Baht	1980 1985 1990 1992 1993 1994	22 489 39 367 77 420 109 890 128 786 135 358	3.4 3.8 3.6 4.0 4.1 3.8	20.6 18.5 20.0 19.6 20.6 18.9	15 867 33 830 64 702 ... 104 534 108 485	70.6 85.9 83.6 ... 81.2 80.1	2.4 3.3 3.0 ... 3.3 3.0	19.1 19.2 21.0 ... 22.7 21.1	6 622 5 537 12 718 ... 24 252 26 873

Public expenditure on education 4.1
Dépenses publiques afférentes à l'enseignement
Gastos públicos destinados a la educación

Country Currency Pays Monnaie País Moneda	Year Année Año	Total educational expenditure Dépenses totales d'éducation Gastos totales de educación			Current educational expenditure Dépenses ordinaires d'éducation Gastos ordinarios de educación				Capital expenditure Dépenses en capital Gastos en capital
		Amount Montant Importe (000 000)	As % of gross national product En % du produit national brut En % del producto nacional bruto (%)	As % of total government expenditure En % des dépenses totales du gouvernement En % de los gastos totales del gobierno (%)	Amount Montant Importe (000 000)	As % of the total En % du total En % del total (%)	As % of gross national product En % du produit national brut En % del producto nacional bruto (%)	As % of current government expenditure En % des dépenses ordinaires du gouvernement En % de los gastos ordinarios del gobierno (%)	(000 000)
		(1)	(2)	(3)	(4)	(5)	(6)	(7)	(8)
Turkey‡ Lira	1980	117 744	2.8	10.5	98 593	83.7	2.3	...	19 152
	1985	627 104	2.3	...	523 102	83.4	1.9	...	104 002
	1990	8 506 541	2.2	...	7 580 817	89.1	2.0	...	925 724
	1991	14 943 536	2.4	...	13 604 256	91.0	2.2	...	1 339 280
	1992	30 357 203	2.8	...	27 895 167	91.9	2.6	...	2 462 036
	1994	124 763 320	3.3	...	109 162 355	87.5	2.9	...	15 600 965
Turkmenistan Manat	1985	431	7.6	28.0	...	...	...	...	...
	1990	655	8.6	21.0	...	...	...	...	...
	1991	1 159	7.9	19.7	...	...	...	...	...
United Arab Emirates Dirham	1980	1 460	1.3	...	1 153	79.0	1.0	...	307
	1985	1 738	1.7	10.4	1 637	94.2	1.6	10.6	101
	1990	2 280	1.7	14.6	2 174	95.4	1.7	14.3	106
	1992	2 637	2.0	15.2	2 460	93.3	1.8	15.1	177
	1993	2 657	2.0	15.1	2 457	92.5	1.8	14.9	200
	1994	2 927	...	16.3	2 702	92.3	...	15.9	225
Uzbekistan Rouble	1980	1 457	6.4	23.0	1 249	85.7	5.5	...	208
	1985	2 040	7.5	25.1	1 716	84.1	6.3	...	324
	1990	3 070	9.5	20.4	2 450	79.8	7.6	...	620
	1991	5 770	9.4	17.8	4 893	84.8	8.0	...	877
	1992	45 216	10.1	23.3	42 232	93.4	9.4	...	2 984
	1993	486 502	11.0	24.4	475 863	97.8	10.7	...	10 639
Yemen Rial	1993	13 531	...	20.9	12 939	95.6	...	...	592
	1994	16 114	...	20.8	14 577	90.5	...	...	1 537
Former Democratic Yemen	1980	17	...	16.9	...	...	...	...	...
Former Yemen Arab Republic Rial	1981	1 108	...	15.8	...	...	...	...	...
	1985	2 039	...	21.8	1 789	87.7	...	27.4	251
Europe									
Albania Lek	1980	767	...	10.3	...	...	...	...	...
	1990	984	5.8	...	...	...	...	...	...
	1994	5 893	3.0	...	5 353	90.8	2.7	...	540
Austria Schilling	1980	55 016	5.6	8.0	46 955	85.3	4.8	8.4	8 061
	1985	78 639	5.9	7.9	70 847	90.1	5.3	8.6	7 792
	1990	97 301	5.4	7.6	89 868	92.4	5.0	8.8	7 443
	1991	107 329	5.6	7.6	98 054	91.4	5.1	8.6	9 275
	1992	117 519	5.8	7.7	103 693	88.2	5.1	8.6	13 826
	1993	115 780	5.5	...	102 207	88.3	4.8	...	13 573
Belarus‡ Rouble	1980	1 253	5.2	...	1 051	83.9	4.3	...	202
	1985	1 499	4.8	...	1 264	84.3	4.0	...	235
	1990	2 093	5.0	...	1 758	84.0	4.2	...	335
	1992	60 520	6.6	19.3	49 528	81.8	5.4	20.0	10 992
	1993	662 987	5.3	15.9	527 327	79.5	4.2	...	135 660
	1994	1 228 110	6.1	17.3	1 019 890	83.0	5.0	...	208 220
Belgium‡ Franc	1980	208 469	6.1	...	206 227	98.9	6.0	...	2 243
	1985	287 388	6.2	...	272 843	94.9	5.8	...	14 545
	1990	325 282	5.1	...	321 427	98.8	5.1	...	3 855
	1991	342 383	5.1	...	338 707	98.9	5.0	...	3 676
	1992	361 584	5.1	9.0	358 648	99.2	5.1	...	2 936
	1993	409 254	5.6	9.9	403 466	98.6	5.5	...	5 788
Bulgaria Lev	1980	1 145	4.5	...	1 098	95.9	4.3	...	47
	1985	1 784	5.5	...	1 598	89.6	4.9	...	186
	1990	2 357	5.6	...	2 183	92.6	5.2	...	174
	1992	11 729	5.9	...	11 211	95.6	5.6	...	518
	1993	16 307	5.5	...	15 210	93.3	5.1	...	1 097
	1994	23 999	4.5	...	22 620	94.3	4.3	...	1 379
Former Czechoslovakia Koruna	1980	23 181	4.0	...	21 802	94.1	3.8	...	1 379
	1985	28 201	4.2	7.9	26 959	95.6	4.0	8.6	1 242
	1990	37 323	4.6	8.2	35 482	95.1	4.4	8.7	1 841
Czech Republic Koruna	1992	36 915	4.7	...	33 631	91.1	4.3	...	3 284
	1993	53 393	5.9	12.7	49 198	92.1	5.4	...	4 195

Public expenditure on education
Dépenses publiques afférentes à l'enseignement
Gastos públicos destinados a la educación

Country Currency Pays Monnaie País Moneda	Year Année Año	Total educational expenditure Dépenses totales d'éducation Gastos totales de educación			Current educational expenditure Dépenses ordinaires d'éducation Gastos ordinarios de educación				Capital expenditure Dépenses en capital Gastos en capital (000 000)
		Amount Montant Importe (000 000)	As % of gross national product En % du produit national brut En % del producto nacional bruto (%)	As % of total government expenditure En % des dépenses totales du gouvernement En % de los gastos totales del gobierno (%)	Amount Montant Importe (000 000)	As % of the total En % du total En % del total (%)	As % of gross national product En % du produit national brut En % del producto nacional bruto (%)	As % of current government expenditure En % des dépenses ordinaires du gouvernement En % de los gastos ordinarios del gobierno (%)	
		(1)	(2)	(3)	(4)	(5)	(6)	(7)	(8)
Denmark Krone	1980	25 020	6.9	9.5	22 188	88.7	6.1	9.0	2 832
	1985	42 672	7.2	...	...	...	...	...	...
	1989	55 448	7.5	13.0	52 270	94.3	7.1	12.9	3 178
	1991	58 960	7.4	11.8	54 896	93.1	6.9	11.5	4 064
	1993	72 168	8.5	13.0	67 809	94.0	8.0	...	4 359
Estonia Kroon	1992	795	6.2	31.3	729	91.7	5.7	...	66
	1993	1 540	7.1	20.1	1 344	87.3	6.2	20.9	196
	1994	1 988	5.8	23.8	1 748	87.9	5.1	25.7	240
Finland Markka	1980	10 036	5.3	...	9 182	91.5	4.9	12.0	855
	1985	17 682	5.4	11.8	16 356	92.5	5.0	11.9	1 326
	1990	28 770	5.7	11.9	26 757	93.0	5.3	12.1	2 013
	1991	32 412	6.8	11.9	30 670	94.6	6.5	12.2	1 742
	1992	33 086	7.2	11.6	31 791	96.1	7.0	11.9	1 295
	1993	38 197	8.4	12.8	35 933	94.1	7.9	...	2 264
France‡ Franc	1980	142 099	5.0	...	131 441	92.5	4.7	...	10 658
	1985	269 191	5.8	...	254 433	94.5	5.4	...	14 758
	1990	351 867	5.4	...	327 427	93.1	5.1	...	24 440
	1991	388 819	5.8	...	356 336	91.6	5.3	...	32 483
	1992	393 004	5.7	...	362 695	92.3	5.2	...	30 309
	1993	406 772	5.8	10.4	369 289	90.8	5.2	...	37 483
Germany Deutsche Mark	1993	151 033	4.8	9.5	137 345	90.9	4.3	...	13 688
Former German Democratic Rep. DDR Mark	1980	...	...	...	9 836	...	...	...	...
	1985	...	...	...	12 404	...	...	...	...
Federal Republic of Germany‡ Deutsche Mark	1980	70 099	4.7	9.5	60 558	86.4	4.1	...	9 541
	1985	83 691	4.6	9.2	75 566	90.3	4.1	9.4	8 125
	1990	98 412	...	8.6	88 499	89.9	...	8.7	9 913
	1991	107 497	...	11.6	97 255	90.5	...	12.5	10 242
Gibraltar Pound Sterling	1980	5	9.0	...	3	61.0	5.5	...	2
	1984	5	6.0	...	5	100.0	6.0	...	-
Greece Drachma	1979	31 754	2.2	8.4	29 951	94.3	2.0	9.6	1 803
	1985	133 091	2.9	7.5	126 749	95.2	2.8	8.5	6 342
	1990	325 676	3.1	...	306 303	94.1	2.9	...	19 373
	1991	379 864	3.0	...	359 533	94.6	2.8	...	20 331
Hungary Forint	1980	33 099	4.7	5.2	27 516	83.1	3.9	6.4	5 583
	1985	54 061	5.5	6.4	48 125	89.0	4.9	7.4	5 936
	1990	122 120	6.1	7.8	110 382	90.4	5.5	8.6	11 738
	1992	193 772	6.9	7.7	178 954	92.4	6.4	8.6	14 818
	1993	229 000	6.7	7.4	215 195	94.0	6.3	8.3	13 805
	1994	278 322	6.7	6.9	262 917	94.5	6.3	7.9	15 405
Iceland Krona	1980	699	4.4	14.0	...	...	...	...	...
	1985	5 684	4.9	13.8	...	...	...	...	...
	1990	19 747	5.6	...	14 584	73.9	4.2	...	5 163
	1993	21 615	5.4	12.8	19 202	88.8	4.8	...	2 413
Ireland Pound	1980	595	6.3	...	515	86.6	5.4	...	80
	1985	1 058	6.3	8.9	963	91.0	5.8	10.5	95
	1990	1 372	5.7	10.2	1 303	95.0	5.4	12.1	68
	1991	1 479	5.8	9.7	1 416	95.7	5.6	12.2	63
	1992	1 645	6.2	...	1 568	95.3	5.9	...	77
	1993	1 816	6.4	...	1 734	95.5	6.1	...	82
Italy‡ Lira	1979	13 633 022	4.4	11.1	11 791 069	86.5	3.8	10.7	1 841 953
	1985	40 533 126	5.0	8.3	36 859 217	90.9	4.6	10.0	3 673 909
	1990	40 846 282	3.2	...	40 400 136	98.9	3.1	...	446 146
	1991	43 141 268	3.1	...	42 664 531	98.9	3.0	...	476 737
	1992	62 009 503	4.2	...	59 089 471	95.3	4.0	...	2 920 032
	1993	79 310 895	5.2	9.0	73 774 153	93.0	4.8	...	5 536 742
Latvia Lat	1980	1	3.3	15.3	...	...	...	...	...
	1985	2	3.4	12.4	...	...	...	...	...
	1990	2	3.8	10.8	...	...	...	...	...
	1992	46	4.5	22.1	...	...	...	...	...
	1993	89	6.0	16.5	87	97.4	5.8	16.5	2
	1994	125	6.5	16.1	124	98.8	6.4	16.2	1

Public expenditure on education **4.1**
Dépenses publiques afférentes à l'enseignement
Gastos públicos destinados a la educación

Country / Currency — Pays / Monnaie — País / Moneda	Year — Année — Año	Total educational expenditure / Dépenses totales d'éducation / Gastos totales de educación			Current educational expenditure / Dépenses ordinaires d'éducation / Gastos ordinarios de educación				Capital expenditure — Dépenses en capital — Gastos en capital
		Amount / Montant / Importe (000 000)	As % of gross national product / En % du produit national brut / En % del producto nacional bruto (%)	As % of total government expenditure / En % des dépenses totales du gouvernement / En % de los gastos totales del gobierno (%)	Amount / Montant / Importe (000 000)	As % of the total / En % du total / En % del total (%)	As % of gross national product / En % du produit national brut / En % del producto nacional bruto (%)	As % of current government expenditure / En % des dépenses ordinaires du gouvernement / En % de los gastos ordinarios del gobierno (%)	Capital expenditure / Dépenses en capital / Gastos en capital (000 000)
		(1)	(2)	(3)	(4)	(5)	(6)	(7)	(8)
Lithuania Lita	1980	4	5.5	15.4	4	92.0	5.1	...	0.0
	1985	5	5.3	12.9	4	90.3	4.8	...	1
	1990	6	4.8	13.8	6	93.9	4.5	...	0.0
	1992	179	5.5	22.1	171	95.5	5.2	23.5	8
	1993	531	4.4	20.1	499	94.1	4.1	32.2	32
	1994	947	4.5	21.8	886	93.5	4.2	23.9	62
Luxembourg‡ Franc	1980	9 792	5.7	14.9	9 305	95.0	5.4	19.8	486
	1986	12 269	3.8	15.7	10 712	87.3	3.3	15.4	1 557
	1989	16 363	4.1	16.0	13 440	82.1	3.4	...	2 923
	1992	14 027	2.8	...	...	...	...	...	...
	1993	15 677	3.1	...	...	...	...	...	...
	1994	16 586	3.1	...	...	...	...	...	...
Malta Lira	1980	13	3.0	7.8	12	99.3	2.9	9.7	1
	1985	17	3.4	7.7	17	98.2	3.3	9.1	0.0
	1990	32	4.0	8.3	30	94.4	3.8	10.9	2
	1991	35	4.1	8.5	33	94.4	3.9	11.1	2
	1992	42	4.6	10.9	41	97.1	4.5	12.5	1
	1993	50	5.1	11.7	48	94.9	4.9	13.0	3
Moldova Rouble	1980	0.376	...	...	0.315	83.8	...	...	0.61
	1985	0.471	...	...	0.397	84.3	...	...	0.74
	1990	0.706	7.1	17.2	0.557	78.9	5.6	...	0.149
	1992	14	8.6	26.4	12	81.8	7.0	25.4	3
	1993	127	6.0	...	118	93.1	5.6	...	9
	1994	426	5.5	28.9	403	94.7	5.2	25.1	23
Monaco French Franc	1980		...		43	...			
	1989	124	...	5.3	113	91.1	...	7.8	11
	1992	153	...	5.6	140	91.4	...	7.7	13
Netherlands Guilder	1980	26 016	7.6	...	23 947	92.0	7.0	...	2 069
	1985	27 403	6.4	...	25 729	93.9	6.0	...	1 674
	1990	30 697	6.0	...	29 200	95.1	5.7	...	1 497
	1991	31 709	5.9	...	30 312	95.6	5.6	...	1 397
	1993	31 318	5.5	9.2	30 102	96.1	5.2	...	1 216
Norway Krone	1980	19 731	7.2	13.7	16 448	83.4	6.0	14.4	3 283
	1985	31 680	6.5	14.6	27 979	88.3	5.7	15.3	3 701
	1990	51 119	7.9	14.6	44 109	86.3	6.9	14.5	7 010
	1991	54 709	8.2	14.6	47 807	87.4	7.1	15.7	6 902
	1992	59 201	8.7	14.1	51 132	86.4	7.5	15.8	8 069
	1993	65 666	9.2	...	61 627	93.8	8.7	...	4 039
Poland Zloty	1980	...	...	...	79 984	...	3.3	7.0	...
	1985	497 497	4.9	12.2	405 597	81.5	4.0	11.6	91 900
	1990	...	...	...	28 249 871	...	5.3	16.4	...
	1991	41 956 000	5.4	14.6	38 969 000	92.9	5.0	15.0	2 987 000
	1992	62 442 000	5.5	14.0	58 468 000	93.6	5.2	14.2	3 974 000
	1993	83 697 000	5.5	14.0	77 947 000	93.1	5.1	15.5	5 750 000
Portugal‡ Escudo	1980	53 234	3.8	...	45 443	85.4	3.3	...	7 791
	1985	152 886	4.0	...	135 612	88.7	3.6	...	17 274
	1990	412 481	4.3	...	378 252	91.7	4.0	...	34 229
	1991	540 503	4.8	...	508 664	94.1	4.6	...	31 839
	1992	651 768	5.0	...	610 807	93.7	4.7	...	40 961
	1993	739 755	5.4	...	688 511	93.1	5.1	...	51 244
Romania‡ Leu	1980	19 930	3.3	6.7	17 691	88.8	2.9	...	2 239
	1985	17 941	2.2	...	17 345	96.7	2.1	...	596
	1990	24 270	2.8	7.3	23 881	98.4	2.8	9.0	389
	1992	216 465	3.6	14.2	208 881	96.5	3.5	15.5	7 584
	1993	636 952	3.2	9.1	606 683	95.2	3.1	9.6	30 269
	1994	1 490 795	3.1	13.6	...	...	...	...	...
Russian Federation Rouble	1980	12 689	3.5	...	...	...	...	...	...
	1985	14 945	3.2	...	...	...	...	...	...
	1990	22 237	3.5	...	...	...	...	...	...
	1991	49 996	3.9	...	...	...	...	...	...
	1992	679 434	4.0	...	...	...	...	...	...
	1993	6 917 781	4.4	9.6	6 608 548	95.5	4.2	10.0	309 233

4.1 Public expenditure on education
Dépenses publiques afférentes à l'enseignement
Gastos públicos destinados a la educación

Country / Currency / Pays / Monnaie / Moneda	País Año	Total educational expenditure / Dépenses totales d'éducation / Gastos totales de educación			Current educational expenditure / Dépenses ordinaires d'éducation / Gastos ordinarios de educación				Capital expenditure / Dépenses en capital / Gastos en capital
	Year / Année	Amount / Montant / Importe (000 000)	As % of gross national product / En % du produit national brut / En % del producto nacional bruto (%)	As % of total government expenditure / En % des dépenses totales du gouvernement / En % de los gastos totales del gobierno (%)	Amount / Montant / Importe (000 000)	As % of the total / En % du total / En % del total (%)	As % of gross national product / En % du produit national brut / En % del producto nacional bruto (%)	As % of current government expenditure / En % des dépenses ordinaires du gouvernement / En % de los gastos ordinarios del gobierno (%)	Dépenses en capital / Gastos en capital (000 000)
		(1)	(2)	(3)	(4)	(5)	(6)	(7)	(8)
San Marino Lira	1980	7 252	...	7.5	6 263	86.4	...	9.5	989
	1984	11 470	...	10.7	10 474	91.3	...	10.3	996
	1990	22 048	...	...	21 723	98.5	...	...	325
	1992	30 915	...	...	29 221	94.5	...	...	1 694
	1993	34 112	...	...	32 981	96.7	...	...	1 131
	1994	35 990	...	...	35 475	98.6	...	...	515
Slovakia S. Koruna	1992	19 829	6.5	...	17 575	88.6	5.7	...	2 254
	1993	19 400	5.7	...	16 966	87.5	5.0	...	2 434
	1994	19 495	4.9	...	17 152	88.0	4.3	...	2 343
Slovenia Tolar	1991	16 603	4.8	16.1	15 266	91.9	4.4	...	1 337
	1992	55 828	5.6	23.2	52 595	94.2	5.3	24.6	3 233
	1993	83 183	6.2	21.7	76 591	92.1	5.7	...	6 592
	1994	102 496	6.2	12.8	92 722	90.5	5.6	...	9 774
Spain Peseta	1979	342 376	2.6	...	295 443	86.3	2.3	16.7	46 933
	1985	917 076	3.3	...	821 118	89.5	2.9	...	95 958
	1990	2 181 935	4.4	9.4	1 936 203	88.7	3.9	...	245 732
	1991	2 445 957	4.5	...	2 165 629	88.5	4.0	...	280 328
	1992	2 680 764	4.6	9.3	2 423 169	90.4	4.2	...	257 595
	1993	2 841 459	4.7	...	2 588 491	91.1	4.3	...	252 968
Sweden Krona	1980	47 322	9.0	14.1	40 886	86.4	7.7	...	6 437
	1985	65 001	7.7	12.6	57 703	88.8	6.8	...	7 298
	1990	101 363	7.7	13.8	93 083	91.8	7.1	...	8 280
	1991	113 123	8.0	14.0	103 927	91.9	7.4	...	9 196
	1992	116 298	8.4	12.6	105 803	90.9	7.6	...	10 495
Switzerland Franc	1980	8 873	5.0	18.8	7 937	89.5	4.5	20.0	936
	1985	11 696	4.8	18.6	10 638	91.0	4.4	19.9	1 058
	1990	16 215	5.0	18.7	14 395	88.8	4.4	...	1 820
	1991	18 106	5.2	18.8	16 061	88.7	4.7	19.5	2 045
	1993	19 933	5.6	16.1	17 705	88.8	5.0	...	2 228
The Former Yugoslav Rep. of Macedonia Dinar	1992	605	5.4	...	591	97.7	5.2	...	14
	1993	2 939	5.0	21.5	2 863	97.4	4.9	21.3	75
	1994	6 970	5.6	18.3	6 807	97.6	5.5	18.5	164
Ukraine Karbovanets	1980	5 927	5.6	24.5	5 114	86.3	4.8	...	812
	1985	6 721	5.2	21.2	5 708	84.9	4.4	...	1 013
	1990	8 606	5.2	19.7	6 903	80.2	4.2	...	1 704
	1992	327 968	7.8	17.1	280 690	85.6	6.7	...	47 278
	1993	9 006 147	6.1	15.7	7 430 284	82.5	5.1	...	1 575 863
	1994	84 709 688	8.2	...	70 300 981	83.0	6.8	...	14 408 707
United Kingdom Pound Sterling	1980	12 856	5.6	13.9	12 094	94.1	5.2	...	762
	1985	17 501	4.9	...	16 764	95.8	4.7	...	737
	1990	26 677	4.9	...	25 318	94.9	4.7	...	1 359
	1991	29 534	5.2	...	28 045	95.0	5.0	...	1 489
	1992	32 162	5.4	11.2	...	...	...	...	...
Former Yugoslavia Dinar	1980	8	4.7	32.5	7	85.1	4.0	...	1
	1985	42	3.4	...	39	93.2	3.1	...	3
	1990	60 318	6.1	...	55 911	92.7	5.7	...	4 407
Federal Republic of Yugoslavia New Dinar	1992	0.292	...	...	0.274	94.1	...	...	0.018
	1994	842	...	...	750	89.2	...	...	91
Oceania									
American Samoa United States Dollar	1981	11	8.3	16.0	11	98.1	8.1	17.9	0.0
	1986	23	...	...	23	100.0	...	54.4	-
Australia Dollar	1980	7 592	5.5	14.8	6 899	90.9	5.0	16.8	693
	1985	12 925	5.6	12.8	11 848	91.7	5.1	14.2	1 077
	1990	19 364	5.4	14.8	17 889	92.4	4.9	14.8	1 475
	1991	20 417	5.5	14.1	18 983	93.0	5.1	14.6	1 434
	1992	23 304	6.0	14.2	21 252	91.2	5.4	...	2 052
Cook Islands New Zealand Dollar	1981	3	...	13.1	3	98.0	...	...	0.0
	1986	5	...	9.5	4	99.1	...	9.5	1
	1991	8	...	12.4	8	99.9	...	12.7	0.0

Public expenditure on education **4.1**
Dépenses publiques afférentes à l'enseignement
Gastos públicos destinados a la educación

Country Currency Pays Monnaie País Moneda	Year Année Año	Total educational expenditure Dépenses totales d'éducation Gastos totales de educación			Current educational expenditure Dépenses ordinaires d'éducation Gastos ordinarios de educación				Capital expenditure Dépenses en capital Gastos en capital (000 000)
		Amount Montant Importe (000 000)	As % of gross national product En % du produit national brut En % del producto nacional bruto (%)	As % of total government expenditure En % des dépenses totales du gouvernement En % de los gastos totales del gobierno (%)	Amount Montant Importe (000 000)	As % of the total En % du total En % del total (%)	As % of gross national product En % du produit national brut En % del producto nacional bruto (%)	As % of current government expenditure En % des dépenses ordinaires du gouvernement En % de los gastos ordinarios del gobierno (%)	
		(1)	(2)	(3)	(4)	(5)	(6)	(7)	(8)
Fiji‡	1981	61	5.9	11.3	58	94.0	5.5	22.4	4
Dollar	1986	85	6.0	...	83	98.0	5.9	...	2
	1990	94	4.7	...	93	99.1	4.7	...	1
	1991	105	4.8	...	98	93.5	4.5	...	7
	1992	128	5.4	18.6	124	96.9	5.2	...	4
French Polynesia‡	1984	1 030	9.8	...	935	90.7	8.9	...	96
French Franc	1990	1 205	...	...	1 148	95.3	...	...	57
	1991	1 343	...	...	1 248	92.9	...	...	95
	1992	1 785	...	...	1 708	95.7	...	...	77
	1993	1 894	...	...	1 807	95.4	...	...	87
Guam‡	1981	49	8.0	...	48	98.2	7.9	...	1
United States Dollar	1985	60	8.5	...	59	97.7	8.3	...	1
Kiribati	1980	3	...	...	3	100.0	...	17.4	-
Australian Dollar	1985	3	6.7	18.5	3	100.0	6.7	...	-
	1990	4	6.0	18.3	4	100.0	6.0	...	-
	1991	4	6.5	14.8	4	100.0	6.5	...	-
	1992	5	7.4	...	5	100.0	7.4	...	-
New Caledonia‡	1981	628	11.8	...	596	94.9	11.3	...	32
French Franc	1985	1 007	13.5	...	919	91.2	12.3	...	88
	1990	1 137	...	...	1 040	91.5	...	...	97
	1991	1 223	...	...	1 183	96.7	...	...	40
	1992	1 501	...	...	1 458	97.1	...	...	43
	1993	1 652	...	...	1 606	97.2	...	...	46
New Zealand	1980	1 302	5.8	23.1	1 171	89.9	5.2	27.9	131
Dollar	1985	2 028	4.7	18.4	1 849	91.2	4.3	25.5	179
	1990	4 451	6.5	...	4 252	95.5	6.2	...	199
	1991	5 013	7.3	...	4 825	96.2	7.0	...	188
	1992	5 308	7.3	...	5 107	96.2	7.0	...	201
Niue	1980	0.777	...	13.2	0.755	97.2	...	15.9	0.022
New Zealand Dollar	1986	1.394	...	...	1.283	92.0	...	...	0.111
	1991	1.454	...	10.2	1.164	98.0	...	10.8	0.290
Samoa Tala	1990	15	4.2	10.7	14	94.0	3.9	15.8	1
Solomon Islands	1980	5	5.6	11.2	4	76.2	4.3	14.1	1
Solomon Isl. Dollar	1984	10	4.7	12.4	4	40.2	1.9	8.0	6
	1991	24	4.2	7.9	24	100.0	4.2	13.5	-
Tonga	1980	1.558	...	11.6	1.339	89.8	...	13.3	0.159
Pa'anga	1985	4	4.4	16.1	4	100.0	4.4	...	-
	1992	9	4.8	17.3	...	...	...	...	...
Tuvalu Australian Dollar	1990	1	...	16.2	1	100.0	...	16.3	...
Vanuatu, Republic of	1990	831	4.4	...	831	100.0	4.4	19.2	-
Vatu	1991	929	4.8	...	929	100.0	4.8	18.8	-
Former U.S.S.R.									
Former U.S.S.R.‡	1980	33 026	7.3	11.2	28 099	85.1	6.2	...	4 928
Rouble	1985	39 866	7.0	...	33 319	83.6	5.9	...	6 547
	1990	57 608	8.2	...	46 030	79.9	6.5	...	11 578

General note / Note générale / Nota general:

E--> For more information concerning countries which participated in the most recent UNESCO/OECD/Eurostat survey, see special remark on page 1 of this chapter.

FR-> Pour plus d'information concernant les pays qui ont participé au programme de la dernière enquête de l'UNESCO/ OCDE/Eurostat, voir la note spéciale, page 1 de ce chapitre.

ESP> Para más información sobre los países que participaron en la última encuesta de UNESCO/OCDE/Eurostat, remítase a la nota correspondiente que figura en la página 1 de este capítulo.

AFRICA:
Algeria:
E--> From 1990 to 1994, expenditure on third level education is not included.

FR-> De 1990 à 1994, les dépenses relatives à l'enseignement du troisième degré ne sont pas incluses.

ESP> De 1990 a 1994, no se incluyen los gastos relativos a la enseñanza de tercer grado.

Angola:
E--> For 1990, data refer to expenditure of the Ministry of Education only.

FR-> En 1990, les données se réfèrent aux dépenses du Ministère de l'Education seulement.

ESP> En 1990, los datos se refieren a los gastos del Ministerio de Educación solamente.

Botswana:
E--> From 1990 to 1994, data refer to expenditure of the Ministry od Education only.

4.1 Public expenditure on education
Dépenses publiques afférentes à l'enseignement
Gastos públicos destinados a la educación

FR–> De 1990 à 1994, les données se réfèrent aux dépenses du Ministère de l'Education seulement.

ESP> De 1990 a 1994, los datos se refieren a los gastos del Ministerio de Educación solamente.

Burundi:

E––> Except for 1979 and 1992, data refer to expenditure of the Ministry of Education only.

FR–> Sauf pour 1979 et 1992, les données se réfèrent aux dépenses du Ministère de l'Education seulement.

ESP> Salvo para 1979 y 1992, los datos se refieren a los gastos del Ministerio de Educación solamente.

Cameroon:

E––> Except for 1980, data refer to expenditure of the Ministry of Education only. For 1992 to 1994, expenditure on third level is not included.

FR–> Sauf pour 1980, les données se réfèrent aux dépenses du Ministère de l'Education seulement. De 1992 à 1994, les dépenses relatives à l'enseignement du troisième degré ne sont pas incluses.

ESP> Salvo para 1980, los datos se refieren a los gastos del Ministerio de Educación solamente. De 1992 a 1994, no se incluyen los gastos relativos a la enseñanza de tercer grado.

Comoros:

E––> Expenditure of the Ministry of Education only.

FR–> Dépenses du Ministère de l'Education seulement.

ESP> Gastos del Ministerio de Educación solamente.

Côte d'Ivoire:

E––> For 1992, expenditure of the Ministry of Education only. For 1994, expenditure on third level is not included.

FR–> En 1992, dépenses du Ministère de l'Education seulement. En 1994, les dépenses relatives à l'enseignement du troisième degré ne sont pas incluses.

ESP> En 1992, gastos del Ministerio de Educación solamente. En 1994, no se incluyen los gastos relativos a la enseñanza de tercer grado.

Djibouti:

E––> For 1985, data refer to expenditure of the Ministry of Education only.

FR–> En 1985, les données se réfèrent aux dépenses du Ministère de l'Education seulement.

ESP> En 1985, los datos se refieren a los gastos del Ministerio de Educación solamente.

Egypt:

E––> Expenditure relating to Al-Azhar is not included.

FR–> Les dépenses relatives à Al-Azhar ne sont pas incluses.

ESP> No se incluyen los gastos relativos a Al-Azhar.

Eritrea:

E––> Expenditure on third level education is not included.

FR–> Les dépenses relatives à l'enseignement du troisième degré ne sont pas incluses.

ESP> No se incluyen los gastos relativos a la enseñanza de tercer grado.

Gabon:

E––> For 1992, data refer to expenditure of the Ministry of Primary and Secondary Education only.

FR–> En 1992, les données se réfèrent aux dépenses du Ministère des enseignements primaire et secondaire seulement.

ESP> En 1992, los datos se refieren a los gastos del Ministerio de enseñanza primaria y secundaria solamente.

Ghana:

E––> For 1985, data refer to expenditure of the Ministry of Education only.

FR–> En 1985, les données se réfèrent aux dépenses du Ministère de l'Education seulement.

ESP> En 1985, los datos se refieren a los gastos del Ministerio de Educación solamente.

Kenya:

E––> From 1990 to 1993, data refer to expenditure of the Ministry of Education only.

FR> De 1990 à 1993, les données se réfèrent aux dépenses du Ministère de l'Education seulement.

ESP> De 1990 a 1993, los datos se refieren a los gastos del Ministerio de Educación solamente.

Madagascar:

E––> For 1990 and 1993, data refer to expenditure of the Ministry of Primary and Secondary Education only.

FR–> En 1990 et 1993, les données se réfèrent aux dépenses du Ministère des enseignements primaire et secondaire seulement.

ESP> En 1990 y 1993, los datos se refieren a los gastos del Ministerio de enseñanza primaria y secundaria solamente.

Mali:

E––> For 1993, data refer to expenditure of the Ministry of Education only.

FR–> En 1993, les données se réfèrent aux dépenses du Ministère de l'Education seulement.

ESP> En 1993, los datos se refieren a los gastos del Ministerio de Educación solamente.

Mauritania:

E––> From 1990 to 1994, data refer to expenditure of the Ministry of Education only.

FR–> De 1990 à 1994, les données se réfèrent aux dépenses du Ministère de l'Education seulement.

ESP> De 1990 a 1994, los datos se refieren a los gastos del Ministerio de Educación solamente.

Morocco:

E––> Data refer to expenditure of the Ministry of Education only.

FR–> Les données se réfèrent aux dépenses du Ministère de l'Education seulement.

ESP> Los datos se refieren a los gastos del Ministerio de Educación solamente.

Mozambique:

E––> Data include foreign aid received for education.

FR–> Les données comprennent l'aide étrangère reçue pour l'éducation.

ESP> Los datos incluyen la ayuda extranjera recibida para la educación.

Niger:

E––> For 1989 and 1991, data refer to expenditure of the Ministry of Education only and do not include expenditure on third level education.

FR–> En 1989 et 1991, les données se réfèrent aux dépenses du Ministère de l'Education seulement et ne comprennent pas les dépenses relatives à l'enseignement du troisième degré.

ESP> En 1989 y 1991, los datos se refieren a los gastos del Ministerio de Educación solamente y no se incluyen los gastos relativos a la enseñanza de tercer grado.

Nigeria:

E––> Except for 1981, data refer to expenditure of the Federal Government only.

FR–> Sauf pour 1981, les données se réfèrent aux dépenses du gouvernement fédéral seulement.

ESP> Salvo para 1981, los datos se refieren a los gastos del gobierno federal solamente.

Reunion:

E––> For 1992, expenditure on third level education is not included.

FR–> En 1992, les dépenses relatives à l'enseignement du troisième degré ne sont pas incluses.

ESP> En 1992, no se incluyen los gastos relativos a la enseñanza de tercer grado.

Seychelles:

E––> For 1993 and 1994, data refer to the Ministry of Education only.

FR–> En 1993 et 1994, les données se réfèrent aux dépenses du Ministère de l'Education seulement.

ESP> En 1993 y 1994, los datos se refieren a los gastos del Ministerio de Educación solamente.

Somalia:

E––> Expenditure on third level education is not included.

FR–> Les dépenses relatives à l'enseignement du troisième degré ne sont pas incluses.

ESP> No se incluyen los gastos relativos a la enseñanza de tercer grado.

South Africa:

E––> For 1990, data do not include expenditure for the following States: Transkei, Bophuthatswana, Venda and Ciskei (TBVC).

FR–> En 1990, les données ne comprennent pas les dépenses pour les Etats suivants: Transkei, Bophuthatswana, Venda and Ciskei (TBVC).

ESP> En 1990, los datos no incluyen los gastos de los Estados siguientes: Transkei, Bophuthatswana, Venda y Ciskei (TBVC).

Sudan:

E––> For 1985, expenditure on third level education is not included.

FR–> En 1985, les dépenses relatives à l'enseignement du troisième degré ne sont pas incluses.

ESP> En 1985, no se incluyen los gastos relativos a la enseñanza de tercer grado.

Swaziland:

E––> For 1993, data refer to expenditure of the Ministry of Education only.

FR–> En 1993, les données se réfèrent aux dépenses du Ministère de l'Education seulement.

ESP> En 1993, los datos se refieren a los gastos del Ministerio de Educación solamente.

Tunisia:

E––> For 1991 and 1992, data refer to expenditure of the Ministry of Education only.

FR–> En 1991 et 1992, les données se réfèrent aux dépenses du Ministère de l'Education seulement.

ESP> En 1991 y 1992, los datos se refieren a los gastos del Ministerio de Educación solamente.

Uganda:

E––> Data refer to expenditure of the Ministry of Education only.

Public expenditure on education **4.1**
Dépenses publiques afférentes à l'enseignement
Gastos públicos destinados a la educación

FR–> Les données se réfèrent aux dépenses du Ministère de l'Education seulement.

ESP> Los datos se refieren a los gastos del Ministerio de Educación solamente.

Zimbabwe:

E––> From 1990 to 1993, data on current expenditure (column 4) include capital expenditure on universities.

FR–> De 1990 à 1993, les données relatives aux dépenses ordinaires (colonne 4) comprennent les dépenses en capital effectuées par les universités.

ESP> De 1990 a 1993, los datos relativos a los gastos ordinarios (columna 4) incluyen los gastos de capital incurridos por las universidades.

AMERICA, NORTH:

British Virgin Islands:

E––> For 1993, expenditure on third level education is not included.

FR–> En 1993, les dépenses relatives à l'enseignement du troisième degré ne sont pas incluses.

ESP> En 1993, no se incluyen los gastos relativos a la enseñanza de tercer grado.

Costa Rica:

E––> From 1992 to 1994, data on current and capital expenditure (columns 4 to 8) refer to expenditure of the Ministry of Education only.

FR–> De 1992 à 1994, les données ordinaires et en capital (colonnes 4 à 8) se réfèrent aux dépenses du Ministère de l'Education seulement.

ESP> De 1992 a 1994, los datos relativos a los gastos ordinarios y en capital (columnas 4 a 8) se refieren al Ministerio de Educación solamente.

Cuba:

E––> Expenditure on education is calculated as percentage of global social product.

FR–> Les dépenses de l'enseignement sont calculées en pourcentage du produit social global.

ESP> Los gastos relativos a la enseñanza se han calculado como porcentaje del producto social global.

Dominican Republic:

E––> Data on current and capital expenditure (columns 4 to 8) refer to the Ministry of Education only.

FR–> Les données relatives aux dépenses ordinaires et en capital (colonnes 4 à 8) se réfèrent au Ministère de l'Education seulement.

ESP> Los datos relativos a los gastos ordinarios y de capital (columnas 4 a 8) se refieren al Ministerio de Educación solamente.

Guadeloupe:

E––> For 1992, expenditure on third level education is not included.

FR–> En 1992, les dépenses relatives à l'enseignement du troisième degré ne sont pas incluses.

ESP> En 1992, no se incluyen los gastos relativos a la enseñanza de tercer grado.

Guatemala:

E––> From 1990 to 1993, data refer to expenditure of the Ministry of Education only.

FR–> De 1990 à 1993, les données se réfèrent aux dépenses du Ministère de l'Education seulement.

ESP> De 1990 a 1993, los datos se refieren a los gastos del Ministerio de Educación solamente.

Jamaica:

E––> For 1980, 1990, 1993 and 1994, data refer to expenditure of the Ministry of Education only.

FR–> En 1980, 1990, 1993 et 1994, les données se réfèrent aux dépenses du Ministère de l'Education seulement.

ESP> En 1980, 1990, 1993 y 1994, los datos se refieren a los gastos del Ministerio de Educación solamente.

Martinique:

E––> For 1992, expenditure on third level education is not included.

FR–> En 1992, les dépenses relatives à l'enseignement du troisième degré ne sont pas incluses.

ESP> En 1992, no se incluyen los gastos relativos a la enseñanza de tercer grado.

Mexico:

E––> Data on current and capital expenditure (columns 4 to 8) refer to the Ministry of Education only.

FR–> Les données relatives aux dépenses ordinaires et en capital (colonnes 4 à 8) se réfèrent au Ministère de l'Education seulement.

ESP> Los gastos relativos a los gastos ordinarios y de capital (columnas 4 a 8) se refieren al Ministerio de Educación solamente.

Nicaragua:

E––> For 1985, data refer to expenditure of the Ministry of Education only. From 1991 to 1994, data refer to expenditure of the Ministry of Primary and Secondary Education only and are expressed in gold Cordobas.

FR–> En 1985, les données se réfèrent aux dépenses du Ministère de l'Education seulement. De 1991 à 1994, les données se réfèrent aux dépenses du Ministère des enseignements primaire et secondaire seulement et sont exprimées en Cordobas or.

ESP> En 1985, los datos se refieren a los gastos del Ministerio de Educación solamente. De 1991 a 1994, los datos se refieren a los gastos del Ministerio de las enseñanza de primer y segundo grado solamente y están expresados en Córdobas oro.

Saint Kitts and Nevis:

E––> For 1990, 1991 and 1993, expenditure on third level education is not included.

FR–> En 1990, 1991 et 1993, les dépenses relatives à l'enseignement du troisième degré ne sont pas incluses.

ESP> En 1990, 1991 y 1993, no se incluyen los gastos relativos a la enseñanza de tercer grado.

St. Pierre and Miquelon:

E––> From 1990 to 1993, data refer to expenditure of the Ministry of Education only.

FR–> De 1990 à 1993, les données se réfèrent aux dépenses du Ministère de l'Education seulement.

ESP> De 1990 a 1993, los datos se refieren a los gastos del Ministerio de Educación solamente.

St. Vincent and the Grenadines:

E––> For 1990, expenditure on third level education is not included.

FR–> En 1990, les dépenses relatives à l'enseignement du troisième degré ne sont pas incluses.

ESP> En 1990, no se incluyen los gastos relativos a la enseñanza de tercer grado.

United States:

E––> For 1980, data refer to public and private expenditure on education.

FR–> En 1980, les données se réfèrent aux dépenses publiques et privées afférentes à l'enseignement.

ESP> En 1980, los datos se refieren a los gastos públicos y privados destinados a la enseñanza.

AMERICA, SOUTH:

Argentina:

E––> For 1985 and 1990, data refer to expenditure of the Ministry of Education only. From 1980 to 1985, data are expressed in Australes.

FR–> En 1985 et 1990, les données se réfèrent aux dépenses du Ministère de l'Education seulement. De 1980 à 1985, les données sont exprimées en Australes.

ESP> En 1985 y 1990, los datos se refieren a los gastos del Ministerio de Educación solamente. De 1980 a 1985, los datos están expresados en Australes.

Bolivia:

E––> For 1990 and 1991, data refer to expenditure of the Ministry of Education only and expenditure on universities is not included.

FR–> En 1990 et 1991, les données se réfèrent aux dépenses du Ministère de l'Education seulement et les dépenses des universités ne sont pas incluses.

ESP> En 1990 y 1991, los datos se refieren a los gastos del Ministerio de Educación solamente y no se incluyen los gastos relativos a las universidades.

Brazil:

E––> For 1994, data refer to expenditure of the Federal Government only and are expressed in Reais (1 Reais ~ 2,750 thousand Cruzeiros).

FR–> En 1994, les données se réfèrent aux dépenses du gouvernement fédéral seulement et sont exprimées en Reais (1 Reais ~ 2 750 milliers de Cruzeiros).

ESP> En 1994, los datos se refieren a los gastos del gobierno federal solamente y están expresados en Reais (1 Reais ~ 2 750 millones de Cruzeiros).

Colombia:

E––> Data refer to expenditure of the Ministry of Education only.

FR–> Les données se réfèrent aux dépenses du Ministère de l'Education seulement.

ESP> Los datos se refieren a los gastos del Ministerio de Educación solamente.

French Guiana:

E––> For 1992, expenditure on third level education is not included.

FR–> En 1992, les dépenses relatives á l'enseignement du troisième degré ne sont pas incluses.

ESP> En 1992, no se incluyen los gastos relativos a la enseñanza de tercer grado.

Paraguay:

E––> From 1990 to 1994, data refer to expenditure of the Ministry of Education only.

FR–> De 1990 à 1994, les données se rérèrent aux dépenses du Ministère de l'Education seulement.

ESP> De 1990 a 1994, los datos se refieren a los gastos del Ministerio de Educación solamente.

4.1 Public expenditure on education
Dépenses publiques afférentes à l'enseignement
Gastos públicos destinados a la educación

ASIA:
Bahrain:
E--> From 1990 to 1993, expenditure on third level education is not included.
FR-> De 1990 à 1993, les dépenses relatives à l'enseignement du troisième degré ne sont pas incluses.
ESP> De 1990 a 1993, no se incluyen los gastos relativos a la enseñanza de tercer grado.
Bangladesh:
E--> Data refer to expenditure of the Ministry of Education only.
FR-> Les données se réfèrent aux dépenses du Ministère de l'Education seulement.
ESP> Los datos se refieren a los gastos del Ministerio de Educación solamente.
Brunei Darussalam:
E--> From 1991 to 1993, data refer to expenditure of the Ministry of Education only and expenditure on universities is not included.
FR->De 1991 à 1993, les données se réfèrent aux dépenses du Ministère de l'Education seulement et les dépenses relatives aux universites ne sont pas incluses.
ESP> De 1991 a 1993, los datos se refieren a los gastos del Ministerio de Educación solamente y no se incluyen los gastos relativos a las universidades.
Cyprus:
E--> Expenditure of the Office of Greek Education only.
FR-> Dépenses du bureau grec de l'éducation seulement.
ESP> Gastos del servicio griego de educación solamente.
Indonesia:
E--> For 1990, 1993 and 1994, data refer to expenditure of the Ministry of Education only.
FR-> En 1990, 1993 et 1994, les données se réfèrent aux dépenses du Ministère de l'Education seulement.
ESP> En 1990, 1993 y 1994, los datos se refieren a los gastos del Ministerio de educación solamente.
Japan:
E--> For 1980, data on current and capital expenditure (columns 4 to 8) do not include public subsidies to private education. For 1985, these data (columns 4 to 8) refer to total public and private expenditure on education.
FR-> En 1980, les données relatives aux dépenses ordinaires et en capital (colonnes 4 à 8) ne comprennent pas les subventions publiques à l'enseignement privé. En 1985, ces données (colonnes 4 à 8) se réfèrent à la totalité des dépenses publiques et privées afférentes à l'enseignement.
ESP> En 1980, los datos relativos a los gastos ordinarios y de capital (columnas 4 a 8) no incluyen las subvenciones públicas a la enseñanza privada. En 1985, estos datos (columnas 4 a 8) se refieren a la totalidad de gastos públicos y privados destinados a la enseñanza.
Jordan:
E--> From 1990 to 1992 and 1994, expenditure on third level education is not included. For 1993, expenditure on universities is not included.
FR-> De 1990 à 1992 et 1994, les dépenses relatives à l'enseignement du troisième degré ne sont pas incluses. En 1993, les dépenses relatives aux universités ne sont pas incluses.
ESP> De 1990 a 1992 y 1994, no se incluyen los gastos relativos a la enseñanza de tercer grado. En 1993, no se incluyen los gastos relativos a las universidades.
Lebanon:
E--> Data refer to expenditure of the Ministry of Education only.
FR-> Les données se réfèrent aux dépenses du Ministère de l'Education seulement.
ESP> Los datos se refieren a los gastos del Ministerio de Educación solamente.
Malaysia:
E--> From 1990 to 1994, data refer to expenditure of the Ministry of Education only.
FR-> De 1990 a 1994, les données se réfèrent aux dépenses du Ministère de l'Education seulement.
ESP> De 1990 a 1994, los datos se refieren a los gastos del Ministerio de Educación solamente.
Myanmar:
E--> Data refer to expenditure of the Ministry of Education only.
FR-> Les données se réfèrent aux dépenses du Ministère de l'Education seulement.
ESP> Los datos se refieren a los gastos del Ministerio de Educación solamente.
Nepal:
E--> Data refer to 'regular and development' expenditure.
FR-> Les données se réfèrent aux dépenses 'ordinaires et de developpement'.
ESP> Los datos se refieren a los gastos 'ordinarios y de desarrollo'.
Oman:
E--> For 1994, expenditure on universities is not included.

FR-> En 1994, les dépenses relatives aux universités ne sont pas incluses.
ESP> En 1994, no se incluyen los gastos relativos a las universidades.
Pakistan:
E--> For 1990 and 1991, data do not include expenditure on education by 'other ministries' which are not directly related to education.
FR-> En 1990 et 1991, les données ne comprennent pas les dépenses d'éducation effectuées par d'autres ministères' qui ne sont pas en rapport direct avec l'enseignement.
ESP> En 1990 y 1991, los datos no incluyen los gastos de educación incurridos por 'otros ministerios' que no estén relacionados con la educación.
Philippines:
E--> For 1992 and 1993, data refer to expenditure of the Ministry of Education only.
FR-> En 1992 et 1993, les données se réfèrent aux dépenses du Ministère de l'Education seulement.
ESP> En 1992 y 1993, los datos se refieren a los gastos del Ministerio de Educación solamente.
Sri Lanka:
E--> For 1980 and 1985, data refer to expenditure of the Ministry of Education only.
FR-> En 1980 et 1985, les données se réfèrent aux dépenses du Ministère de l'Education seulement.
ESP> En 1980 y 1985, los datos se refieren a los gastos del Ministerio de Educación solamente.
Syrian Arab Republic:
E--> For 1992 and 1994, expenditure on third level education is not included. Data on current and capital expenditure (columns 4 to 8) do not include expenditure on third level education.
FR-> En 1992 et 1994, les dépenses relatives à l'enseignement du troisième degré ne sont pas incluses. Les données relatives aux dépenses ordinaires et en capital (colonnes 4 à 8) ne comprennent pas les dépenses du troisième degré.
ESP> En 1992 y 1994, no se incluyen los gastos relativos a la enseñanza de tercer grado. Los datos relativos a los gastos ordinarios y de capital (columnas 4 a 8) no incluyen los gastos de tercer grado.
Turkey:
E--> From 1990 to 1992, expenditure on third level education is not included.
FR-> De 1990 à 1992, les dépenses relatives à l'enseignement du troisième degré ne sont pas incluses.
ESP> De 1990 a 1992, no se incluyen los gastos relativos a la enseñanza de tercer grado.
EUROPE:
Belarus:
E--> For 1994, data are expressed in B. Rouble.
FR-> En 1994, les données sont exprimées en B. Rouble.
ESP> En 1994, los datos están expresados en B. Rouble.
Belgium:
E--> Except for 1993, data refer to expenditure of the Ministry of Education only.
FR-> Sauf pour 1993, les données se réfèrent aux dépenses du Ministère de l'Education seulement.
ESP> Salvo para 1993, los datos se refieren a los gastos del Ministerio de Educación solamente.
France:
E--> Metropolitan France.
FR-> France métropolitaine.
ESP> Francia metropolitana.
Federal Republic of Germany:
E--> For 1991, data include expenditure for East Berlin.
FR-> En 1991, les données comprennent les dépenses relatives à Berlin Est.
ESP> En 1991, los datos incluyen los gastos relativos a Berlin Este.
Italy:
E--> For 1990 and 1991, data refer to expenditure of the Central government only. From 1990 to 1992, data do not include expenditure on third level education.
FR-> En 1990 et 1991, les données se réfèrent aux dépenses du gouvernement central seulement. De 1990 à 1992, les données ne comprennent pas les dépenses pour l'enseignement du troisième degré.
ESP> De 1990 y 1991, los datos se refieren a los gastos del gobierno central solamente. De 1990 a 1992, los datos no se incluyen los gastos relativos a la enseñanza de tercer grado.
Luxembourg:
E--> From 1992 to 1994, data refer to expenditure of the Ministry of Education only.
FR-> De 1992 à 1994, les données se réfèrent aux dépenses du Ministère de l'Education seulement.
ESP> De 1992 a 1994, los datos se refieren a los gastos del Ministerio de Educación solamente.

Public expenditure on education 4.1
Dépenses publiques afférentes à l'enseignement
Gastos públicos destinados a la educación

Portugal:

E--> For 1990 and 1991, data refer to expenditure of the Ministry of Education only.

FR-> En 1990 et 1991, les données se réfèrent aux dépenses du Ministère de l'Education seulement.

ESP> En 1990 y 1991, los datos se refieren a los gastos del Ministerio de Educación solamente.

Romania:

E--> For 1994 data refer to expenditure of the Central Government only.

FR-> En 1994 les données se réfèrent aux dépenses de l'éducation du gouvernement central seulement.

ESP> En 1994 los datos se refieren a los gastos destinados a la enseñanza del gobierno central solamente.

OCEANIA:

Fiji:

E--> From 1990 to 1992, data refer to expenditure of the Ministry of Education only.

FR-> De 1990 à 1992, les données se réfèrent aux dépenses du Ministère de l'Education seulement.

ESP> De 1990 a 1992, los gastos se refieren a los gastos del Ministerio de Educación solamente.

French Polynesia:

E--> Except for 1984, data refer to expenditure of the Ministry of Education only. For 1992, expenditure on third level education is not included.

FR-> Sauf pour 1984, les données se réfèrent aux dépenses du Ministère de l'Education seulement. En 1992, les dépenses relatives à l'enseignement du troisième degré ne sont pas incluses.

ESP> Salvo para 1984, los datos se refieren a los gastos del Ministerio de Educación solamente. En 1992, no se incluyen los gastos relativos a la enseñanza de tercer grado.

Guam:

E--> For 1985, expenditure on third level education is not included.

FR-> En 1985, les dépenses relatives à l'enseignement du troisième degré ne sont pas incluses.

ESP> En 1985 no se incluyen los gastos relativos a la enseñanza de tercer grado.

New Caledonia:

E--> From 1990 to 1993, data refer to expenditure of the Ministry of Education only. For 1992, expenditure on third level education is not included.

FR-> De 1990 à 1993, les données se réfèrent aux dépenses du Ministère de l'Education seulement. En 1992, les dépenses relatives à l'enseignement du troisième degré ne sont pas incluses.

ESP> De 1990 a 1993, los datos se refieren a los gastos del Ministerio de Educación solamente. En 1992 no se incluyen los gastos relativos a la enseñanza de tercer grado.

FORMER U.S.S.R.:

Former U.S.S.R.:

E--> Expenditure on education is calculated as percentage of net material product.

FR-> Les dépenses d'enseignement sont calculées en pourcentage du produit matériel net.

ESP> Los gastos relativos a la enseñanza se han calculado como porcentaje del producto material neto.

4.2 Public current expenditure by level of education
Dépenses publiques ordinaires par degré d'enseignement
Gastos públicos ordinarios por grado de enseñanza

4.2 Public current expenditure on education: distribution by level of education

Dépenses publiques ordinaires afférentes à l'enseignement: répartition par degré d'enseignement

Gastos públicos ordinarios destinados a la educación: distribución por grado de enseñanza

Country Currency / Pays Monnaie / País Moneda	Year Année Año	Total / Total / Total (000 000)	Pre-primary Pré-primaire Pre-primaria (%)	1st level 1er degré 1er grado (%)	Second level / Second degré / Segundo grado				3rd level 3ème degré 3er grado (%)	Other types Autres types Otros tipos (%)	Not distributed Non ré-parties Sin distri-bución (%)
					Total Total Total (%)	General Général General (%)	Teacher training Normal Normal (%)	Vocational Technique Técnica (%)			
		(1)	(2)	(3)	(4)	(5)	(6)	(7)	(8)	(9)	(10)
Africa											
Algeria‡	1980	8 259	-	28.5	25.2	...	...	...	17.3	19.8	9.3
Dinar	1991	37 934	-	42.8	52.6	...	...	...	-	2.4	2.2
	1992	53 516	-	33.3	62.4	...	...	...	-	2.2	2.2
Angola‡	1985	9 419	<——	86.8	——>	...	...	...	5.0	8.2	-
Kwansa	1990	10 856	<——	96.3	——>	...	...	...	3.7	-	-
Botswana‡	1979	27	-	52.1	29.2	23.3	2.8	3.0	13.2	-	5.6
Pula	1985	88	-	36.3	40.7	29.2	3.0	8.5	17.2	0.9	4.8
	1989	249	0.3	32.5	43.8	34.1	3.7	6.0	20.1	1.1	2.2
	1991	426	-	31.1	48.8	38.8	4.5	5.5	12.2	1.8	6.1
Burkina Faso‡	1980	7 436	-	32.3	19.8	17.4	1.2	1.1	33.7	9.2	5.1
Franc C.F.A.	1985	12 292	-	38.1	20.3	...	...	...	30.7	4.9	6.0
	1989	18 727	-	41.7	25.8	...	...	...	32.1	0.4	-
	1994	30 016	0.0	48.1	46.5	...	...	...	./.	5.4	-
Burundi‡	1979	1 796	-	42.7	31.0	...	...	...	20.6	5.1	0.6
Franc	1985	3 212	-	45.0	32.3	...	...	...	19.8	1.4	1.5
	1990	6 370	-	46.8	29.1	23.2	——>	5.9	22.0	0.9	1.3
	1992	8 023	-	44.5	28.2	23.2	——>	5.0	24.6	-	2.8
Cameroon‡	1981	38 019	<——	76.0	——>	...	...	...	24.0	-	-
Franc C.F.A.	1985	90 045	<——	72.6	——>	...	...	...	27.4	-	-
	1990	97 948	<——	70.5	——>	...	...	...	29.5	-	-
	1991	81 719	<——	86.6	——>	...	...	...	13.4	-	-
Cape Verde	1985	325	-	61.5	15.9	10.9	1.9	3.0	-	3.7	18.9
Escudo	1991	890	-	54.7	17.5	13.9	0.7	2.9	2.7	9.7	15.4
Central African Republic‡	1981	8 441	-	54.9	13.9	...	...	...	16.3	0.2	14.7
Franc C.F.A.	1986	8 340	-	55.2	17.6	13.4	1.3	2.8	18.8	-	8.4
	1990	8 527	<——	52.7	14.6	...	...	...	21.5	-	11.3
Chad	1991	8 212	3.6	43.6	20.9	17.2	1.6	2.0	8.2	0.4	23.4
Franc C.F.A.	1994	10 691	3.2	38.9	21.7	18.0	1.7	2.0	7.6	0.9	27.8
Comoros‡	1990	2 666	-	42.4	28.2	25.2	2.1	0.9	17.3	-	12.1
Franc C.F.A	1993	2 938	-	40.8	32.8	28.4	2.6	1.8	11.9	-	14.4
Congo	1980	21 517	<——	35.8	29.1	21.9	2.3	4.9	24.3	0.1	10.7
Franc C.F.A	1984	41 033	<——	30.0	35.6	...	...	...	34.4	-	-
Côte d'Ivoire‡	1980	123 196	-	46.8	37.2	...	...	...	14.9	-	1.0
Franc C.F.A.	1985	179 447	-	40.2	42.7	...	...	...	17.1	-	-
	1994	168 923	-	60.6	38.8	34.0	-	4.8	-	-	0.6
Djibouti‡	1979	1 046	-	58.4	18.2	...	...	...	19.1	3.6	0.7
Franc	1985	1 690	-	63.7	23.5	...	...	...		-	12.8
	1990	2 614	-	58.0	21.7	...	...	...	11.5	2.6	6.3
	1991	2 872	-	53.4	21.1	...	...	...	13.9	5.9	5.7
Egypt‡	1980	505	<——	<——	69.1	...	...	...	30.9	-	-
Pound	1991	3 941	<——	<——	62.9	...	...	...	37.1	-	-
	1992	4 683	<——	<——	63.5	...	...	...	36.5	-	-

Public current expenditure by level of education 4.2
Dépenses publiques ordinaires par degré d'enseignement
Gastos públicos ordinarios por grado de enseñanza

Country Currency / Pays Monnaie / País Moneda	Year Année Año	Total / Total / Total (000 000)	Pre-primary / Pré-primaire / Pre-primaria (%)	1st level / 1er degré / 1er grado (%)	Second level / Second degré / Segundo grado				3rd level / 3ème degré / 3er grado (%)	Other types / Autres types / Otros tipos (%)	Not distributed / Non ré-parties / Sin distri-bución (%)
					Total / Total / Total (%)	General / Général / General (%)	Teacher training / Normal / Normal (%)	Vocational / Technique / Técnica (%)			
		(1)	(2)	(3)	(4)	(5)	(6)	(7)	(8)	(9)	(10)
Eritrea‡ Birr	1994	160	0.2	43.3	21.4	18.1	1.7	1.6	-	8.4	26.6
Ethiopia Birr	1980	222	-	42.0	29.8	25.9	2.6	1.3	19.0	4.0	5.2
	1986	384	-	51.5	28.3	25.5	1.7	1.1	14.4	2.4	3.5
	1990	494	0.0	53.9	28.1	25.6	1.4	1.0	12.1	1.8	4.0
	1993	790	-	53.6	27.7	25.5	1.4	0.9	10.5	1.7	6.4
Gabon‡ Franc C.F.A.	1992	34 407	-	43.5	56.5	41.3	2.5	12.7	-	-	-
Gambia‡ Dalasi	1980	11	-	49.2	23.5	...	-	...	10.8	1.5	15.1
	1985	25	-	49.0	21.3	10.1	-	11.2	13.8	0.9	15.0
	1990	73	-	41.6	21.2	11.4	-	9.9	17.8	0.6	18.7
	1991	75	-	42.7	21.4	...	-	...	9.1	0.7	26.1
Ghana‡ Cedi	1980	734	-	29.3	38.7	31.5	4.7	2.5	1.8	0.9	29.3
	1984	3 844	-	24.5	29.5	26.4	1.7	1.4	12.5	0.8	32.7
	1990	53 664	-	29.2	34.3	26.3	3.1	4.9	11.0	1.1	24.4
Guinea Syli	1979	1 186	-	24.7	28.9	...	...	...	31.9	0.7	13.8
	1984	1 486	-	30.8	36.9	31.3	-	5.6	23.5	0.3	8.5
	1991	35 384	-	32.8	28.6	19.2	2.5	6.9	14.8	-	23.8
	1993	65 434	-	35.0	29.1	19.4	2.3	7.5	18.4	-	17.4
Guinea-Bissau Peso	1980	208	0.5	75.8	16.2	12.7	1.9	1.5	-	-	7.5
Kenya‡ Shilling	1981	3 319	0.0	64.4	14.9	11.6	2.3	0.9	13.8	1.9	5.0
	1985	5 789	0.1	59.8	...	...	...	...	12.4	1.9	8.2
	1990	11 238	0.1	58.1	17.8	15.8	2.1	...	18.4	0.7	4.9
	1993	18 999	0.1	62.3	19.2	17.7	1.5	...	13.7	0.8	3.8
Lesotho Maloti	1980	20	-	38.6	33.4	25.1	6.0	2.4	21.8	1.9	4.3
	1984	29	-	39.1	32.7	26.4	4.1	2.2	22.3	-	5.9
	1992	160	-	51.0	30.4	25.0	3.0	2.4	15.9	0.9	1.8
	1993	192	-	48.8	30.6	24.7	3.1	2.9	15.8	1.3	3.4
Madagascar‡ Franc	1980	31 548	-	41.4	25.5	15.1	3.3	7.1	27.5	-	5.6
	1985	49 806	-	42.3	26.5	20.1	1.1	5.4	27.2	-	3.9
	1990	64 964	-	49.1	35.6	30.0	0.9	4.8	-	-	15.2
	1993	104 064	-	36.1	45.6	...	...	...	-	-	18.3
Malawi Kwacha	1980	24	-	38.9	15.7	14.4	-	1.4	30.2	-	15.2
	1985	46	-	41.3	15.2	13.7	-	1.5	23.3	4.4	15.8
	1989	106	-	48.1	13.3	11.7	-	1.6	22.0	2.2	14.3
	1992	227	-	55.4	10.7	9.5	-	1.1	19.3	1.3	13.3
Mali‡ Franc C.F.A.	1980	12 752	0.2	38.8	25.1	13.3	4.3	7.5	24.9	-	11.0
	1985	17 048	<——	44.4	21.5	9.4	5.4	6.7	20.1	1.8	12.1
	1993	14 994	<——	47.2	25.5	...	2.7		23.2	0.5	3.6
Mauritania‡ Ouguiya	1980	1 546	-	35.4	50.3	...	...	...	13.5	-	0.8
	1985	3 973	-	25.1	30.3	24.9	3.3	2.2	17.5	-	27.1
	1990	3 512	-	33.3	37.7	32.3	2.6	2.8	24.9	-	4.2
	1994	4 753	-	37.6	36.1	31.4	2.0	2.7	22.4	-	3.9
Mauritius Rupee	1980	408	-	44.1	36.5	34.5	1.3	0.7	7.7	3.5	8.1
	1985	555	0.1	45.1	37.6	36.4	-	1.2	5.6	3.4	8.3
	1990	1 287	0.1	37.5	36.4	35.2	-	1.2	16.6	2.4	7.0
Morocco‡ Dirham	1980	3 529	-	35.4	46.3	...	...	...	18.3	-	-
	1985	6 079	-	35.3	47.6	...	...	...	17.1	-	-
	1990	10 187	-	34.8	48.9	...	...	...	16.2	-	-
	1992	11 944	-	33.0	50.7	...	...	...	16.3	-	-
Mozambique‡ Meticai	1990	46 064	-	49.8	15.7	6.7	2.8	6.2	9.9	4.1	20.5
Niger‡ Franc C.F.A.	1981	16 586	-	36.8	46.2	...	...	...	17.0	0.0	-
	1989	15 545	-	48.5	25.8	...	...	...	-	0.2	25.4
	1991	19 493	-	46.5	30.1	...	...	...	-	0.2	23.1
Nigeria Naira	1981	2 523	-	17.2	39.8	28.4	8.6	2.8	25.0	0.6	17.4
Reunion French Franc	1985	2 292	<——	32.8	57.1	...	...	...	0.0	-	10.1
	1990	3 343	14.4	25.8	53.1	...	...	...	3.0	...	3.8
	1993	5 180	12.8	23.4	57.0	...	...	...	1.7	3.0	2.1
Rwanda‡ Franc	1980	2 439	-	67.1	19.9	...	...	...	9.6	0.0	3.3
	1986	5 737	-	67.6	15.3	...	...	...	11.5	-	5.6
	1989	6 793	-	67.7	14.1	...	...	...	16.2	-	2.0
Sao Tome and Principe‡ Dobra	1986	100	5.6	50.0	27.0	23.4	1.6	2.0	-	17.4	-

Public current expenditure by level of education
Dépenses publiques ordinaires par degré d'enseignement
Gastos públicos ordinarios por grado de enseñanza

Country / Currency / Pays / Monnaie / País / Moneda	Year / Année / Año	Total (000 000)	Pre-primary Pré-primaire Pre-primaria (%)	1st level 1er degré 1er grado (%)	Second level / Second degré / Segundo grado Total / Total (%)	General Général General (%)	Teacher training Normal Normal (%)	Vocational Technique Técnica (%)	3rd level 3ème degré 3er grado (%)	Other types Autres types Otros tipos (%)	Not distributed Non ré- parties Sin distri- bución (%)
		(1)	(2)	(3)	(4)	(5)	(6)	(7)	(8)	(9)	(10)
Senegal Franc C.F.A.	1980	26 818	-	42.8	27.8	22.2	2.9	2.8	25.0	-	4.3
	1985	46 118	1.0	49.1	25.1	19.0	2.5	3.7	19.0	0.4	5.3
	1990	60 467	0.9	43.0	25.7	21.2	1.7	2.7	24.0	0.3	6.1
Seychelles‡ Rupee	1985	120	<——	29.5	54.3	38.3	-	16.0	-	1.1	15.1
	1990	153	<——	28.2	40.7	27.5	1.8	11.4	9.5	1.6	20.1
	1992	156	<——	<——	66.2	...	...	...	10.7	0.8	22.2
Sierra Leone Leone	1985	106	-	40.7	32.3	29.9	0.0	2.3	15.1	...	11.9
	1989	577	-	21.2	31.6	27.0	0.1	4.5	34.8	...	12.5
South Africa‡ Rand	1986	6 844	<——	73.1	——>	...	...	...	24.8	2.0	-
	1990	15 265	<——	75.6	——>	...	...	...	21.5	2.9	-
	1993	23 849	<——	81.4	——>	...	...	...	15.0	3.6	-
Sudan‡ Pound	1980	172	-	48.0	31.0	29.0	0.1	1.9	20.7	0.3	-
	1985	580	-	55.5	31.6	...	...	...	-	<——	12.9
Swaziland Lilangeni	1980	20	-	45.8	34.3	32.0	2.3	-	10.7	1.8	7.4
	1986	57	0.0	37.3	26.6	23.2	2.9	0.6	21.0	0.7	14.4
	1989	88	0.0	32.9	29.0	25.2	2.7	1.0	20.5	1.1	16.5
	1994	241	0.1	33.4	26.5	...	...	...	29.6	1.8	6.2
Togo Franc C.F.A.	1980	12 575	0.7	29.5	31.0	26.8	1.9	2.3	29.8	0.2	8.7
	1986	16 270	-	34.0	29.1	...	...	...	22.8	-	14.2
	1990	22 720	-	30.4	25.8	23.2	-	2.6	10.9	10.7	22.1
	1992	26 307	-	31.8	28.1	25.4	-	2.6	12.4	6.0	21.8
Tunisia Dinar	1980	162	-	41.2	36.6	...	...	...	20.5	-	1.8
	1985	351	-	44.0	37.0	...	...	...	18.2	-	0.9
	1990	569	-	39.8	36.4	...	...	...	18.5	3.7	1.6
	1993	776	-	41.5	35.1	...	...	...	21.2	-	2.2
Uganda‡ Shilling	1981	57	-	16.2	58.0	46.9	6.0	5.1	18.0	-	7.8
	1984	205	-	44.5	33.4	18.9	8.7	5.8	13.2	-	8.9
United Republic of Tanzania Shilling	1981	1 848	-	54.4	21.1	13.8	6.1	1.2	11.1	6.8	6.6
	1985	3 643	-	57.5	20.5	13.0	6.1	1.3	12.7	3.9	5.4
	1989	13 069	-	41.6	32.1	20.0	8.6	3.6	17.1	3.4	5.8
Zaire Zaire	1980	998	-	<——	69.2	...	...	...	30.8	-	-
	1985	3 239	-	<——	71.3	...	...	...	28.7	-	-
Zambia Kwacha	1980	120	0.0	45.3	25.5	18.8	3.1	3.6	18.0	0.2	11.0
	1985	272	-	43.9	26.9	19.0	2.1	5.7	18.3	-	11.0
	1989	1 209	-	31.7	34.5	26.4	3.6	4.6	17.3	-	16.5
Zimbabwe‡ Dollar	1980	218	-	66.5	21.4	21.4	-	-	7.5	-	4.6
	1986	721	-	58.4	28.3	27.3	-	1.0	9.0	0.3	4.0
	1990	1 648	-	54.1	28.6	28.6	-	-	12.3	0.2	4.7
	1993	2 893	0.0	51.5	27.7	27.7	-	-	17.5	0.1	3.2
America, North											
Antigua and Barbuda E. Caribbean Dollar	1980	9	0.2	33.2	24.1	...	...	...	13.8	-	28.8
	1984	11	-	36.6	30.6	...	...	...	12.7	-	20.1
Barbados Dollar	1980	90	<——	32.0	32.0	...	...	...	18.1	1.1	16.8
	1984	123	<——	31.0	32.5	...	...	...	22.3	0.9	13.3
	1990	218	<——	37.5	37.6	31.9	1.3	4.5	19.2	0.2	5.5
Belize Dollar	1986	18	0.7	65.0	31.0	27.3	3.2	0.5	3.4	-	-
Bermuda Dollar	1984	31	4.4	31.1	33.8	33.8	-	-	21.4	9.4	-
	1990	49	4.3	35.7	33.6	33.3	0.3	0.1	20.2	6.2	-
	1991	54	4.4	32.9	26.9	26.6	0.2	0.1	18.5	6.3	11.0
British Virgin Islands‡ United States Dollar	1980	2	-	45.1	42.7	...	...	...	4.3	-	8.0
	1985	4	<——	38.9	35.8	...	...	...	9.7	-	15.6
	1990	7	<——	35.5	35.3	...	...	...	14.8	-	14.4
	1993	7	<——	37.5	45.8	...	...	...	-	-	16.7
Canada‡ Dollar	1980	20 451	<——	<——	65.3	...	...	...	27.4	7.4	-
	1985	30 176	<——	<——	63.6	...	...	...	28.7	7.7	-
	1990	44 319	<——	<——	62.2	...	...	...	28.6	9.2	-
	1992	51 291	<——	<——	60.8	...	...	...	27.9	11.3	-
Costa Rica‡ Colon	1980	2 802	<——	28.0	21.5	14.7	-	6.8	26.1	1.0	23.4
	1985	7 787	<——	35.1	22.3	15.7	-	6.6	41.4	1.2	-
	1991	28 578	3.6	34.5	21.6	14.7	-	7.0	36.1	1.5	2.7
	1994	56 323	<——	38.6	22.9	15.3	-	7.6	31.1	2.8	4.6

Public current expenditure by level of education **4.2**
Dépenses publiques ordinaires par degré d'enseignement
Gastos públicos ordinarios por grado de enseñanza

Country / Currency Pays / Monnaie País / Moneda	Year Année Año	Total Total Total (000 000) (1)	Pre-primary Pré-primaire Pre-primaria (%) (2)	1st level 1er degré 1er grado (%) (3)	Second level — Total (%) (4)	General Général General (%) (5)	Teacher training Normal Normal (%) (6)	Vocational Technique Técnica (%) (7)	3rd level 3ème degré 3er grado (%) (8)	Other types Autres types Otros tipos (%) (9)	Not distributed Non réparties Sin distribución (%) (10)
Cuba Peso	1980 1985 1990	1 135 1 588 1 627	5.1 5.6 7.4	24.4 20.7 18.2	40.8 42.0 39.0	28.6 27.2 23.4	2.2 2.3 1.7	10.0 12.4 13.9	6.9 12.9 14.4	5.9 10.2 20.9	16.9 8.7 -
Dominica E. Caribbean Dollar	1986 1989	16 20	0.1 0.2	62.3 59.3	26.2 27.1	21.7 22.2	- -	4.6 5.0	2.6 2.5	2.6 3.3	6.2 7.6
Dominican Republic‡ Peso	1980 1985 1994	104 204 1 621	- 0.7 <—	36.8 46.6 51.3	22.9 19.7 12.4	17.7 16.1 9.4	1.9 1.1 0.4	3.3 2.5 2.5	23.9 20.8 10.8	10.6 7.7 5.8	5.8 4.5 19.8
El Salvador Colon	1980	320	-	61.9	6.2	5.9	-	0.3	14.2	1.9	15.9
Guadeloupe French Franc	1990 1993	1 952 2 745	13.0 12.4	25.6 25.0	54.4 56.6	... ...	... ...	... ...	3.2 1.1	- 3.6	3.8 1.3
Guatemala‡ Quetzal	1979 1990 1993	109 421 1 081	1.6 1.6 5.0	35.7 29.5 50.4	12.4 12.9 14.9	7.3 9.4 10.7	2.7 1.7 2.1	2.4 1.8 2.0	18.4 21.2 19.5	2.4 5.3 5.8	29.4 29.4 4.5
Haiti Gourde	1980 1985 1990	86 117 216	- - 0.2	59.3 51.0 53.0	20.4 18.1 19.0	8.8 8.6 11.2	2.3 4.0 0.8	9.3 5.5 6.9	9.6 10.8 9.1	4.7 7.7 10.1	6.0 12.4 8.7
Honduras Lempira	1980 1985 1991 1994	141 286 606 971	- <— <— <—	61.9 49.1 49.1 48.5	17.9 16.7 17.2 16.9	... 11.6 10.5 10.9	... 1.3 1.4 1.5	... 3.8 5.3 4.5	19.3 21.3 18.2 19.8	0.9 0.7 0.6 0.7	- 12.3 14.9 14.1
Jamaica‡ Dollar	1980 1985 1990 1994	303 515 1 276 5 551	1.0 2.0 2.7 3.1	33.7 29.9 34.7 24.7	36.9 34.0 33.2 37.4	26.9 30.6 28.8 33.3	5.9 - - -	4.1 3.4 4.5 4.1	19.2 19.4 21.1 25.7	4.3 2.4 2.0 1.7	5.0 12.3 6.3 7.5
Martinique French Franc	1990 1993	1 994 2 814	14.3 13.4	23.9 23.8	55.6 55.1	... ...	... ...	... ...	2.8 1.5	- 4.6	3.4 1.7
Mexico‡ Peso	1980 1985 1990 1993	129 797 1 229 314 16 617 522 43 107 371	1.9 4.1 5.6 6.4	31.7 27.4 26.7 30.8	24.2 26.8 29.6 25.9	... ... 23.0 19.9	... ... —> —>	... ... 6.6 6.0	12.1 17.6 16.5 13.7	<— <— <— <—	30.1 24.2 21.6 23.3
Montserrat E. Caribbean Dollar	1990 1993	7 7	1.9 2.3	23.8 29.1	38.3 38.8	32.2 31.6	- -	6.1 7.2	- -	- -	36.0 29.8
Netherlands Antilles‡ Guilder	1991 1993	151 196	7.9 8.9	35.1 36.2	46.9 44.8	23.9 24.4	1.2 1.0	21.7 19.4	4.6 4.2	5.5 6.0	- -
Nicaragua‡ Cordoba	1980 1985 1989 1994	0.580 6 383 109 327	0.4 2.4 2.5 3.8	44.7 43.3 30.8 60.2	25.1 16.7 7.7 18.1	19.2 11.5 0.2 15.7	1.8 1.7 2.6 2.4	4.2 3.4 5.0 -	10.5 23.2 20.9 -	7.7 5.0 3.4 2.3	11.5 9.5 34.7 15.6
Panama Balboa	1980 1985 1990 1994	156 231 241 334	<— <— <— <—	46.3 38.3 37.0 30.3	22.0 25.2 23.3 20.7	12.3 15.3 14.2 12.5	2.5 0.2 0.2 0.0	7.2 9.6 9.0 8.2	13.4 20.4 21.3 24.8	1.9 2.9 4.6 5.8	16.4 13.3 13.9 18.4
Saint Kitts and Nevis E. Caribbean Dollar	1980 1985 1992	7 12 14	0.4 1.2 3.7	49.6 49.1 31.0	40.6 40.1 45.4	... 40.1 ...	... - ...	... - ...	2.9 2.1 12.2	0.2 0.4 0.1	6.3 7.1 7.6
St. Lucia E. Caribbean Dollar	1980 1986 1990 1992	19 36 54 63	- 0.1 0.3 0.2	45.6 50.8 47.9 47.6	23.7 26.8 23.3 26.1	... ...	... ...	... ...	14.7 4.5 12.8 12.1	0.7 0.8 0.6 1.2	15.3 17.0 15.0 12.8
St. Pierre and Miquelon‡ French Franc	1986 1990 1993	40 41 57	<— 15.6 13.4	35.3 25.9 24.8	56.3 54.5 60.2	... ...	... ...	... ...	- - -	0.6 - -	7.8 4.0 1.6
St. Vincent and the Grenadines‡ E. Caribbean Dollar	1986 1990	18 26	1.2 <—	71.9 64.1	26.6 31.7	20.4 ...	2.4 ...	3.8 ...	0.2 -	0.1 1.8	- 2.4
Trinidad and Tobago‡ Dollar	1980 1985 1990 1994	431 912 727 1 061	- - 0.1 0.2	46.9 47.5 42.4 40.3	34.9 36.8 36.8 33.1	33.1 35.0 33.7 28.6	- - 1.1 1.6	1.8 1.8 2.0 2.9	10.2 8.9 11.9 13.3	- - 0.2 0.1	8.0 6.8 8.7 13.0

4.2

Public current expenditure by level of education
Dépenses publiques ordinaires par degré d'enseignement
Gastos públicos ordinarios por grado de enseñanza

Country / Currency — Pays / Monnaie — País / Moneda	Year — Année — Año	Total — Total (000 000)	Pre-primary — Pré-primaire — Pre-primaria (%)	1st level — 1er degré — 1er grado (%)	Second level / Second degré / Segundo grado — Total — Total — Total (%)	General — Général — General (%)	Teacher training — Normal — Normal (%)	Vocational — Technique — Técnica (%)	3rd level — 3ème degré — 3er grado (%)	Other types — Autres types — Otros tipos (%)	Not distributed — Non réparties — Sin distribución (%)
		(1)	(2)	(3)	(4)	(5)	(6)	(7)	(8)	(9)	(10)
United States‡ Dollar	1980	182 849	<—	36.5	24.9	...	...	...	38.6	-	-
	1985	182 875	<—	44.7	30.3	...	...	...	25.1	-	-
	1990	265 074	<—	38.9	37.0	...	...	...	24.1	-	-
	1992	328 396	3.7	34.7	36.5	...	...	...	25.2	-	-
America, South											
Argentina‡ Peso	1980	0.860	<—	40.1	25.6	18.1	-	7.5	22.7	1.9	9.7
	1986	1 128	<—	5.5	43.3	30.5	-	12.7	30.8	2.4	18.0
	1990	7 062 974	<—	3.4	44.9	32.3	-	12.6	46.7	2.4	2.6
	1994	10 471	<—	72.3	—>	...	...	...	16.5	-	11.3
Bolivia‡ Boliviano	1980	0.0049	<—	58.9	11.4	...	...	...	17.1	2.9	9.7
	1989	268	<—	73.7	13.5	...	...	...	2.9	3.7	6.3
	1994	1 293	2.4	39.5	11.8	10.4	-	1.5	29.5	2.3	14.5
Brazil‡ Cruzeiro	1980	0.431	<—	44.8	7.1	...	...	...	18.9	<—	29.3
	1985	45	<—	45.9	7.7	...	...	...	19.6	<—	26.8
	1989	56 101	<—	48.8	6.9	...	...	...	25.6	1.3	17.5
Chile‡ Peso	1980	45 504	1.9	42.7	18.0	11.2	-	6.8	33.2	0.4	3.8
	1985	101 093	6.0	51.0	19.5	13.7	-	5.8	20.3	-	3.2
	1990	225 620	7.9	52.2	17.3	10.1	-	7.2	20.3	2.4	-
	1994	585 399	8.1	50.3	17.2	8.7	-	8.5	19.7	3.1	1.5
Colombia‡ Peso	1980	27 286	0.2	44.4	27.0	...	...	...	24.1	4.3	0.1
	1985	136 570	<—	39.2	30.8	...	...	...	22.2	3.4	4.3
	1990	526 686	<—	32.1	27.6	...	...	...	20.6	<—	19.7
	1994	1 579 822	<—	38.8	33.1	...	...	...	16.8	<—	11.3
Ecuador Sucre	1980	14 649	<—	20.6	18.5	14.7	0.4	3.5	15.6	2.5	42.7
	1985	35 611	<—	45.5	35.8	24.7	1.2	9.9	17.8	0.9	-
	1991	260 332	<—	31.3	30.8	19.8	1.7	9.3	28.2	1.0	8.8
	1992	416 411	<—	32.1	33.7	22.0	1.7	10.0	22.7	1.8	9.7
French Guiana French Franc	1990	490	14.7	28.8	52.2	...	...	...	1.2	-	3.1
	1993	833	13.6	29.7	51.0	...	...	...	0.2	3.7	1.8
Guyana Dollar	1979	89	8.5	33.1	33.1	27.3	-	5.8	15.2	4.2	6.0
	1985	135	7.6	31.1	23.8	18.9	2.0	2.9	17.8	0.1	19.6
Paraguay‡ Guarani	1985	16 822	-	36.6	29.7	18.7	2.9	8.0	23.8	2.8	7.1
	1990	74 387	-	43.9	22.6	...	...	...	25.8	<—	8.6
	1994	432 812	-	47.9	19.8	...	...	...	17.5	<—	14.7
Peru‡ Inti	1980	166	2.8	45.1	19.9	...	...	...	3.1	3.8	25.2
	1985	4 855	4.0	35.6	20.5	...	...	...	2.7	5.0	32.2
Suriname Guilder	1980	105	-	64.0	8.4	6.1	0.6	1.6	7.4	1.1	19.1
	1986	182	<—	63.7	13.5	...	...	...	7.7	1.3	13.9
	1990	249	<—	60.5	14.5	...	...	...	8.8	0.5	15.6
	1993	380	<—	60.4	14.8	...	...	...	7.6	0.4	16.7
Uruguay‡ Peso	1980	1 927	-	48.4	33.2	20.4	-	12.7	16.1	2.3	-
	1985	12 068	<—	37.7	28.4	17.4	-	11.0	22.4	2.3	9.2
	1990	265 660	<—	0.0	30.3	19.5	-	10.8	22.6	2.0	7.5
	1994	1 981 029	<—	35.6	31.9	20.8	-	11.1	24.9	2.4	5.1
Venezuela‡ Bolivar	1980	11 053	3.6	32.5	—>	...	...	...	39.2	4.6	20.2
	1985	17 558	4.0	25.5	6.2	...	...	...	36.3	3.6	24.4
	1990	57 347	3.3	20.2	4.5	...	...	...	40.7	2.8	28.5
	1994	419 515	3.7	23.9	2.0	...	...	...	34.7	2.8	33.0
Asia											
Afghanistan Afghani	1980	2 886	1.6	41.9	22.3	14.3	3.2	4.8	18.4	4.8	11.0
	1990	5 282	<—	87.6	—>	...	...	...	12.4	...	...
Armenia Rouble	1993	136	19.8	<—	57.7	...	0.3	8.6	22.6	-	-
Azerbaijan Rouble	1992	15 704	13.1	<—	66.1	...	...	5.6	10.4	9.6	0.8
Bahrain‡ Dinar	1986	59	-	25.7	38.4	...	...	...	13.1	22.8	-
	1990	61	-	30.4	45.8	43.3	-	2.6	-	1.2	22.5
	1993	71	-	27.9	45.1	...	...	...	-	1.2	25.8
Bangladesh‡ Taka	1980	2 010	-	45.3	39.2	...	...	...	12.9	0.0	2.5
	1985	6 005	-	46.1	34.7	31.8	—>	2.9	10.4	-	8.8
	1990	11 820	-	45.6	42.2	39.8	—>	2.4	8.7	1.0	2.5
	1992	16 744	-	44.2	43.3	40.3	0.8	2.3	7.9	4.6	-

Public current expenditure by level of education 4.2
Dépenses publiques ordinaires par degré d'enseignement
Gastos públicos ordinarios por grado de enseñanza

Country Currency / Pays Monnaie / País Moneda	Year Année Año	Total Total Total (000 000)	Pre-primary Pré-primaire Pre-primaria (%)	1st level 1er degré 1er grado (%)	Second level / Second degré / Segundo grado — Total Total Total (%)	General Général General (%)	Teacher training Normal Normal (%)	Vocational Technique Técnica (%)	3rd level 3ème degré 3er grado (%)	Other types Autres types Otros tipos (%)	Not distributed Non ré-parties Sin distri-bución (%)
		(1)	(2)	(3)	(4)	(5)	(6)	(7)	(8)	(9)	(10)
Brunei Darussalam‡ Dollar	1980	115	-	31.4	46.0	30.4	8.6	7.1	16.7	3.2	2.6
	1990	229	0.0	24.1	26.1	20.7	-	5.4	9.5	0.2	40.1
	1993	273	0.0	18.9	26.4	18.7	-	7.7	1.1	0.6	53.0
China‡ Yuan	1980	9 418	0.5	27.1	34.3	...	...	...	20.0	18.1	——>
	1985	18 416	0.9	28.6	33.2	28.3	2.9	2.0	21.8	15.5	——>
	1989	31 616	1.2	31.5	34.4	28.7	3.0	2.8	18.6	14.3	——>
	1994	100 128	1.4	35.5	31.5	...	...	...	16.5	15.2	——>
Cyprus‡ Pound	1980	25	2.5	35.4	50.5	41.5	-	9.0	4.1	4.0	3.5
	1985	53	3.7	34.0	50.7	42.0	-	8.7	4.2	4.2	3.2
	1990	84	4.3	34.2	50.3	43.2	-	7.1	3.8	4.2	3.2
	1994	143	4.2	33.2	50.7	44.1	-	6.5	5.9	3.0	3.0
Georgia Rouble	1994	5 727 212	22.0	<——	45.1	...	...	2.8	18.5	11.8	2.7
Hong Kong Dollar	1980	3 036	-	33.7	35.7	33.4	1.3	1.0	24.6	6.1	-
	1984	6 190	0.1	31.4	37.9	33.0	1.2	3.7	25.1	4.6	0.9
	1989	11 705	0.7	29.1	40.7	37.5	-	3.3	28.8	0.4	0.3
	1991	16 915	0.7	26.3	39.3	36.0	-	3.3	30.0	3.2	0.5
India Rupee	1980	37 462	<——	36.9	24.2	...	...	...	13.5	3.0	22.4
	1985	85 198	<——	37.1	25.2	...	...	...	15.5	5.3	16.9
	1990	205 330	<——	38.1	25.5	...	...	...	14.9	5.8	15.7
	1992	257 377	<——	36.5	27.0	...	...	...	14.4	3.2	17.0
Indonesia‡ Rupiah	1994	3 112 751	<——	<——	47.1	...	...	...	17.6	1.4	33.9
Iran, Islamic Republic of Rial	1980	440 298	2.0	41.7	38.1	18.6	13.1	6.4	7.1	3.8	7.4
	1985	510 081	1.1	40.9	37.9	28.4	1.9	7.6	10.7	2.2	7.2
	1990	1 232 097	<——	33.2	39.2	28.1	3.6	7.5	13.6	5.8	8.2
	1994	4 793 129	<——	27.7	36.1	31.8	3.4	0.9	22.0	<——	14.6
Iraq‡ Dinar	1980	418	<——	47.5	17.3	...	...	...	24.1	11.1	-
	1985	551	<——	46.5	19.5	...	...	...	25.0	9.0	-
	1991	711	2.5	53.3	23.6	18.5	——>	5.1	20.6	-	-
Israel‡ Shekel	1980	8	6.6	33.7	29.2	...	...	...	24.8	1.5	4.1
	1985	1 720	7.8	33.3	31.0	15.9	-	15.1	20.4	3.0	4.5
	1990	5 713	8.9	32.6	31.5	16.9	-	14.6	17.3	4.5	5.1
	1992	9 266	8.8	32.2	31.1	16.9	-	14.2	17.6	5.1	5.2
Japan‡ Yen	1980	9 416 591	1.3	38.2	34.6	...	...	...	11.1	6.8	8.0
	1985	15 280 808	3.4	27.8	32.3	...	...	...	21.4	9.0	6.2
Jordan‡ Dinar	1980	51	<——	<——	75.1	...	-	2.4	22.8	1.3	0.7
	1985	92	<——	<——	63.7	...	...	...	32.0	0.2	4.1
	1989	120	<——	<——	64.4	...	0.3	1.2	33.0	0.7	1.9
	1993	139	<——	<——	89.9	...	0.6	1.8	3.2	0.2	6.8
Korea, Republic of Won	1980	1 158 967	-	49.9	33.2	...	...	...	8.7	0.1	8.2
	1985	2 811 861	0.3	46.7	36.7	31.0	-	5.7	10.9	0.6	4.8
	1990	5 495 204	0.1	44.3	34.1	28.6	-	5.5	7.4	1.2	12.8
	1993	9 344 751	1.0	40.9	39.0	33.3	-	5.7	7.6	1.1	10.4
Kuwait‡ Dinar	1980	204	6.3	29.5	41.9	...	...	...	16.5	4.1	1.6
	1986	344	8.2	68.9	——>	...	...	...	16.7	2.9	3.3
	1990	257	10.4	56.7	——>	...	...	...	16.0	3.2	13.9
Kyrgyzstan Som	1985	2	10.9	<——	60.4	...	...	...	8.8	6.4	13.5
	1990	3	8.5	<——	57.9	...	...	...	10.0	7.1	16.6
	1994	697	7.3	<——	68.8	...	...	11.2	10.8	8.5	4.7
Lao People's Democratic Rep. Kip	1992	15 094	2.7	39.5	43.5	25.2	10.9	7.4	3.9	5.3	5.2
Malaysia‡ Ringgit	1980	2 575	-	35.0	34.0	28.0	3.4	2.7	12.4	2.0	16.5
	1985	4 062	-	37.8	37.1	32.1	3.9	1.1	14.6	0.5	10.1
	1990	4 664	-	34.3	34.4	31.8	...	2.6	19.9	0.2	11.1
	1994	7 821	0.3	33.2	37.7	29.8	5.0	2.9	16.8	6.4	5.7
Maldives Rufiyaa	1993	132	...	66.7	31.9	24.5	2.7	4.7	...	1.4	...
Mongolia‡ Tughrik	1985	716	14.1	<——	65.8	...	...	12.7	20.1	-	-
	1990	882	18.8	<——	63.9	...	...	12.2	17.2	-	-
	1994	15 384	23.5	<——	58.6	...	...	5.1	17.8	0.2	-
Myanmar‡ Kyat	1994	4 436	-	47.7	40.3	38.9	-	1.4	11.7	-	0.3

4.2 Public current expenditure by level of education
Dépenses publiques ordinaires par degré d'enseignement
Gastos públicos ordinarios por grado de enseñanza

Country / Currency — Pays / Monnaie — País / Moneda	Year / Année / Año	Total (000 000)	Pre-primary / Pré-primaire / Pre-primaria (%)	1st level / 1er degré / 1er grado (%)	Second level — Second degré — Segundo grado				3rd level / 3ème degré / 3er grado (%)	Other types / Autres types / Otros tipos (%)	Not distributed / Non ré-parties / Sin distri-bución (%)
					Total (%)	General / Général / General (%)	Teacher training / Normal / Normal (%)	Vocational / Technique / Técnica (%)			
		(1)	(2)	(3)	(4)	(5)	(6)	(7)	(8)	(9)	(10)
Nepal‡ Rupee	1980	430	-	58.8	——>	...	...	...	35.0	2.1	4.2
	1985	1 241	-	35.7	19.9	18.4	0.2	1.3	33.4	<——	11.0
	1990	2 079	-	48.2	15.7	14.1	-	1.6	23.3	<——	12.7
	1992	4 428	-	44.5	17.7	14.2	-	3.5	28.1	<——	9.7
Oman Rial	1986	90	-	50.9	32.1	30.8	-	1.4	15.3	1.1	0.5
	1990	117	-	54.1	37.0	36.3	-	0.7	7.4	1.2	0.4
	1993	151	-	47.8	45.3	44.8	-	0.5	5.8	1.0	0.2
Pakistan‡ Rupee	1980	3 379	<——	39.4	31.0	22.6	1.3	7.2	18.8	<——	10.7
	1985	9 390	<——	36.0	33.3	21.4	2.6	9.3	18.2	<——	12.5
	1989	16 217	<——	47.4	19.1	14.2	...	...	18.3	<——	15.2
Philippines Peso	1980	4 023	-	61.4	15.7	...	...	...	22.1	0.1	0.7
	1985	7 026	-	63.9	10.1	...	...	...	22.5	0.0	3.5
Saudi Arabia Riyal	1992	29 428	<——	80.3	——>			3.7	19.7	-	-
Singapore Dollar	1980	587	-	35.8	41.1	36.1	-	5.1	17.1	3.1	3.0
	1986	1 277	<——	30.1	36.9	31.5	-	5.4	28.4	0.5	4.1
	1990	1 795	<——	29.6	36.5	31.8	-	4.7	29.3	0.4	4.1
	1994	2 486	<——	26.8	35.3	30.8	-	4.5	33.0	-	4.8
Sri Lanka‡ Rupee	1980	1 535	<——	<——	91.1	...	...	...	8.9	...	...
	1985	3 530	<——	<——	90.2	...	...	...	9.8	...	...
	1990	6 161	<——	<——	84.3	...	1.4	...	13.4	...	2.4
	1994	15 314	<——	<——	72.1	...	1.2	...	11.3	1.7	14.9
Syrian Arab Rep.‡ Pound	1980	1 890	-	38.8	28.5	25.6	0.4	2.4	32.7	0.1	-
	1985	4 214	-	38.4	25.3	20.2	——>	5.1	33.6	0.2	2.4
	1990	10 720	<——	38.5	28.2	...	...	...	21.3	0.1	11.8
	1994	15 621	<——	65.6	32.0	25.0	<——	6.9	-	-	2.5
Tajikistan Rouble	1980	366	8.7	<——	52.5	...	...	...	9.6	14.5	14.8
	1985	479	9.2	<——	55.7	...	...	...	7.7	13.6	13.8
	1990	723	6.9	<——	57.0	...	...	...	9.1	12.7	14.2
	1993	56 739	12.2	<——	62.1	...	...	...	9.8	13.7	2.3
Thailand Baht	1981	21 465	0.2	55.1	28.3	23.2	-	5.1	13.3	1.8	1.3
	1985	33 830	<——	58.4	21.1	14.7	-	6.4	13.2	2.2	5.1
	1990	64 702	0.2	56.0	21.6	16.2	-	5.4	14.6	2.3	5.3
	1994	108 485	1.8	51.0	21.5	16.1	-	5.4	16.5	2.5	6.6
Turkey‡ Lira	1981	157 268	-	40.0	26.9	17.4	1.5	8.0	25.5	3.7	3.9
	1985	523 102	<——	45.9	22.4	12.2	——>	10.2	23.9	3.3	4.5
	1990	7 580 817	<——	58.1	29.4	12.5	0.5	16.4	-	4.1	8.3
	1994	109 162 355	0.1	46.2	22.5	10.0	0.6	11.9	21.4	6.5	0.1
Uzbekistan Rouble	1993	475 863	16.8	<——	69.9	...	...	14.6	9.7	0.6	3.0
Yemen Former Democratic Yemen‡ Dinar	1980	17	1.6	63.2	——>			...	11.6	-	23.6
Former Yemen Arab Republic Rial	1985	1 789	-	47.7	17.5	15.3	1.7	0.4	3.7	11.1	20.0
Europe											
Albania Lek	1994	5 353	6.7	57.2	20.6	16.9	-	3.7	10.3	1.9	3.3
Austria Schilling	1980	46 955	6.1	17.9	53.2	29.0	1.6	22.6	14.5	4.4	3.8
	1985	70 847	5.9	17.2	46.9	28.2	0.4	18.4	16.6	4.1	9.2
	1990	89 858	6.0	17.7	46.6	26.5	2.7	17.4	19.1	4.3	6.2
	1993	102 207	7.0	18.6	48.7	...	...	...	18.6		7.1
Belarus‡ Rouble	1980	1 051	21.1	35.2	18.0	./.	./.	18.0	13.9	11.8	-
	1985	1 264	22.5	35.7	16.6	./.	./.	16.6	14.0	11.3	-
	1990	1 758	19.5	38.1	16.2	./.	./.	16.2	14.4	11.7	-
	1994	1 019 890	13.8	51.9	16.8	./.	./.	16.8	11.1	4.9	1.5
Belgium‡ Franc	1980	206 227	<——	25.3	47.3	...	...	...	17.3	6.4	3.7
	1985	272 843	<——	24.7	46.4	...	...	...	16.7	7.3	5.0
	1990	321 427	<——	23.3	42.9	...	...	...	16.5	9.3	8.1
	1993	403 466	8.0	19.6	46.3	...	...	...	17.3	.	8.9
Bulgaria Lev	1980	1 098	19.7	45.3	——>	...	...	...	13.6	21.4	-
	1985	1 598	19.2	46.1	——>	...	...	...	12.4	22.4	-
	1990	2 183	20.2	50.5	——>	...	...	...	13.9	15.4	-
	1994	22 620	20.3	55.0	——>	...	...	...	15.5	9.2	-

Public current expenditure by level of education 4.2
Dépenses publiques ordinaires par degré d'enseignement
Gastos públicos ordinarios por grado de enseñanza

| Country Currency / Pays Monnaie / País Moneda | Year Année Año | Total Total Total (000 000) (1) | Pre-primary Pré-primaire Pre-primaria (%) (2) | 1st level 1er degré 1er grado (%) (3) | Second level / Second degré / Segundo grado | | | | 3rd level 3ème degré 3er grado (%) (8) | Other types Autres types Otros tipos (%) (9) | Not dis-tributed Non ré-parties Sin distri-bución (%) (10) |
					Total Total Total (%) (4)	General Général General (%) (5)	Teacher training Normal Normal (%) (6)	Vocational Technique Técnica (%) (7)			
Former Czechoslovakia Koruna	1980	21 802	12.3	40.9	14.2	2.9	<——	11.3	16.1	6.2	10.2
	1985	26 959	11.1	43.8	13.6	3.0	<——	10.6	14.7	6.3	10.5
	1990	35 482	9.4	40.2	18.1	3.2	<——	14.8	15.8	5.4	11.1
Czech Republic Koruna	1992	33 631	9.1	40.9	29.2	...	...	...	13.0	7.3	0.5
	1993	49 198	9.3	38.9	25.8	...	...	...	17.9	7.8	0.3
Denmark‡ Krone	1980	22 188	<——	53.5	18.6	...	...	...	17.6	6.0	4.4
	1986	43 054	<——	46.2	20.3	...	...	...	21.9	8.1	3.4
	1991	54 896	2.4	21.7	43.2	29.1	-	14.1	18.4	14.3	-
	1993	67 809	10.6	19.3	41.9	...	...	...	25.0	.	3.1
Estonia Kroon	1992	729	18.7	<——	55.8	41.7	-	14.1	15.9	9.3	0.3
	1994	1 748	19.2	<——	57.3	47.7	-	9.6	14.0	8.7	0.7
Finland‡ Markka	1980	9 565	-	31.8	40.7	26.6	0.0	14.1	18.9	8.0	0.6
	1985	17 604	-	30.8	41.6	25.3	<——	16.3	18.7	8.4	0.5
	1990	29 300	-	27.9	39.4	22.5	<——	16.9	23.9	8.2	0.6
	1993	35 933	8.6	25.2	35.4	...	...	...	28.7	.	2.1
France‡ Franc	1980	131 441	8.4	22.0	40.3	...	...	...	12.5	11.0	5.8
	1985	254 433	10.0	19.5	40.8	29.4	-	11.4	12.9	11.0	5.8
	1990	327 427	9.8	17.6	40.7	29.2	-	11.4	13.8	12.2	6.0
	1993	369 289	11.1	20.2	50.3	...	...	...	16.7	.	1.6
Germany Deutsche Mark	1993	137 345	<——	<——	73.3			...	21.4	.	5.3
Former German Democratic Rep. DDR Mark	1980	9 836	7.2	<——	54.8	...	-	9.1	20.5	-	17.5
	1985	12 404	12.1	<——	55.6	...	-	9.0	21.8	0.8	9.7
Federal Republic of Germany‡ Deutsche Mark	1980	60 558	3.5	16.0	53.6	...	...	...	15.1	7.3	4.5
	1985	75 566	3.8	14.0	49.2	...	...	...	20.8	7.9	4.4
	1990	88 499	4.6	13.4	47.5	...	...	...	22.4	7.7	4.4
	1991	97 255	5.0	12.9	46.4	...	...	...	23.7	7.6	4.3
Gibraltar Pound Sterling	1980	3	-	47.6	40.8	31.7	6.2	2.9	5.6	0.5	5.6
	1984	5	-	52.9	37.8	35.3	0.5	2.0	6.9	2.4	-
Greece Drachma	1979	29 951	4.8	36.9	36.8	29.4	-	7.3	21.0	0.6	-
	1985	126 749	6.1	31.6	41.3	33.4	-	7.8	20.1	0.9	0.0
	1990	306 303	5.9	28.2	45.1	35.6	-	9.4	19.5	1.4	-
	1991	359 533	5.7	28.1	45.3	35.9	-	9.5	19.6	1.3	-
Hungary‡ Forint	1981	32 655	14.1	38.3	21.6	6.2	-	15.4	19.3	6.5	0.3
	1985	48 125	14.2	36.9	19.9	3.1	-	16.8	16.9	10.8	1.3
	1990	110 382	13.6	41.8	23.9	...	...	...	15.2	3.7	1.8
	1994	262 917	14.3	39.8	23.0	5.8	-	17.1	17.8	5.2	-
Iceland Krona	1990	14 584	<——	59.5	25.6	...	...	...	14.9	-	-
	1993	19 202	4.6	27.4	39.6	...	...	...	24.6	.	3.9
Ireland Pound	1980	515	8.7	26.1	39.2	26.5	-	12.7	17.6	6.1	2.3
	1985	963	10.2	29.1	39.7	37.0	-	2.7	17.7	0.2	3.0
	1990	1 303	8.7	29.0	40.1	37.4	-	2.7	20.4	<——	1.7
	1993	1 734	8.3	27.3	40.5	...	...	...	21.5	.	2.4
Italy‡ Lira	1979	11 791 069	6.0	29.2	41.0	23.9	——>	17.0	9.1	0.0	14.8
	1985	36 859 217	7.0	23.0	35.5	20.7	——>	14.8	10.2	0.0	24.2
	1990	40 400 136	6.4	26.6	63.2	...	...	...	-	0.0	3.8
	1993	73 774 153	8.0	22.6	49.0	...	...	...	13.7	.	6.7
Latvia‡ Lat	1980	1	14.4	<——	56.8	...	...	...	11.2	-	17.6
	1985	1	15.8	<——	56.2	...	...	...	10.3	-	17.8
	1990	2	11.2	<——	56.3	...	...	...	11.6	-	20.9
	1994	125	<——	81.3	——>			14.6	13.3	-	5.4
Lithuania Lita	1992	171	17.8	<——	51.5	...	...	...	9.2	21.0	3.9	5.9
	1994	886	14.1	<——	51.5	...	...	...	8.3	19.0	5.2	10.2
Luxembourg Franc	1980	9 305	<——	49.3	29.1	13.7	-	15.4	1.5	19.1	1.0
	1986	10 712	9.2	34.3	42.7	19.0	-	23.6	3.3	8.8	1.7
	1989	13 440	10.2	34.2	41.9	18.8	-	23.1	3.3	7.7	2.6
Malta Lira	1980	12	<——	31.4	44.3	33.9	-	10.4	9.3	1.5	13.5
	1985	17	3.2	27.8	43.3	31.0	-	12.3	8.2	2.3	15.2
	1990	30	<——	25.1	44.7	31.7	-	13.1	14.6	2.2	13.4
	1992	41	<——	22.5	40.4	28.2	-	12.2	17.9	2.1	17.1
Monaco‡ French Franc	1989	113	3.4	14.8	52.1	...	...	...	-	0.6	29.2
	1992	124	4.8	17.5	61.7	21.3	23.4	17.0	-	2.7	13.3

4.2 Public current expenditure by level of education
Dépenses publiques ordinaires par degré d'enseignement
Gastos públicos ordinarios por grado de enseñanza

Country / Currency — Pays / Monnaie — País / Moneda	Year Année Año	Total (000 000)	Pre-primary Pré-primaire Pre-primaria (%)	1st level 1er degré 1er grado (%)	Second level — Second degré — Segundo grado				3rd level 3ème degré 3er grado (%)	Other types Autres types Otros tipos (%)	Not distributed Non ré-parties Sin distri-bución (%)
					Total Total Total (%)	General Général General (%)	Teacher training Normal Normal (%)	Vocational Technique Técnica (%)			
		(1)	(2)	(3)	(4)	(5)	(6)	(7)	(8)	(9)	(10)
Netherlands‡ Guilder	1980	23 079	5.5	19.2	33.8	19.1	0.3	14.4	27.5	8.7	5.3
	1985	24 796	<—	22.6	35.9	19.2	<—	16.7	26.4	8.7	6.4
	1990	29 005	5.2	16.3	37.7	19.9	-	17.8	32.1	5.6	3.0
	1993	30 102	6.6	22.0	39.3	...	...	...	32.1	.	-
Norway‡ Krone	1980	16 448	-	47.9	24.3	...	...	...	13.6	8.1	6.0
	1985	27 979	-	45.2	28.3	...	...	...	13.5	7.6	5.4
	1990	44 109	-	39.5	24.7	...	...	...	15.2	8.6	12.0
	1993	61 627	<—	<—	65.0	...	...	...	25.9	.	9.1
Poland Zloty	1980	79 984	8.2	28.7	21.0	4.4	-	16.6	23.6	17.8	0.7
	1985	405 597	10.5	33.7	17.9	3.7	-	14.1	18.2	19.7	-
	1990	28 249 871	9.9	32.9	17.5	3.8	-	13.6	22.0	17.8	-
	1993	77 947 000	10.7	39.0	20.5	5.2	-	15.3	16.0	13.9	-
Portugal‡ Escudo	1980	45 443	<—	52.8	25.4	...	...	...	10.5	6.0	5.3
	1985	135 612	1.2	49.8	30.6	...	...	...	12.7	1.6	4.1
	1990	378 252	2.3	42.3	32.5	...	...	...	16.3	3.1	3.5
	1993	688 511	2.5	37.6	35.4	...	...	...	14.2	.	10.3
Romania‡ Leu	1990	23 881	7.1	45.0	22.1	...	...	...	9.6	16.2	-
	1993	636 952	8.4	36.5	23.8	21.2	-	2.7	15.9	15.4	-
San Marino‡ Lira	1980	6 263	<—	96.6	—>	...	...	...	2.7	0.7	-
	1986	13 477	22.3	30.6	33.3	...	...	...	4.2	2.4	7.3
	1990	21 723	19.5	32.2	32.1	...	...	...	6.7	2.4	7.2
	1994	35 475	17.1	31.6	31.7	...	...	...	15.3	2.5	1.9
Slovakia S. Koruna	1992	17 575	10.1	28.5	18.5	...	...	...	15.0	2.7	25.2
	1994	17 152	9.8	29.5	19.0	...	...	...	14.3	2.7	24.7
Slovenia Tolar	1992	52 595	11.5	22.1	44.1	32.9	-	11.2	19.3	2.0	1.0
	1994	92 722	11.4	19.5	45.7	34.1	-	11.5	18.9	3.5	1.1
Spain Peseta	1979	295 443	3.5	58.9	19.3	14.1	-	5.1	14.0	1.7	2.6
	1990	1 936 203	6.0	23.3	45.0	...	...	...	15.4	9.9	0.5
	1993	2 588 491	6.8	22.1	53.2	...	...	...	15.3	.	2.5
Sweden‡ Krona	1980	40 886	0.1	44.6	13.6	...	...	...	9.3	16.1	16.4
	1985	57 703	0.1	47.9	20.1	...	...	...	13.1	11.7	7.1
	1990	93 083	0.1	47.6	19.6	...	...	...	13.2	18.3	1.3
	1992	105 803	0.0	40.7	18.3	...	...	...	15.8	23.7	1.4
Switzerland Franc	1980	7 937	2.8	<—	73.7	...	10.3	13.0	18.6	2.2	2.7
	1985	10 638	3.1	<—	73.6	...	11.2	14.7	18.1	2.9	2.3
	1990	14 395	3.6	<—	71.4	8.2	2.3	14.7	19.7	3.3	1.9
	1993	17 705	3.9	26.9	46.9	...	...	...	20.3	.	2.1
The Former Yugoslav Rep. of Macedonia Dinar	1992	591	-	56.5	23.5	-	-	23.5	17.1	3.0	-
	1994	6 807	-	55.1	23.2	-	-	23.2	21.7	-	-
Ukraine‡ Karbovanets	1980	5 114	24.8	31.5	16.3	./.	./.	16.3	14.0	13.4	-
	1985	5 708	24.9	33.9	15.3	./.	./.	15.3	13.5	12.3	-
	1990	6 903	16.0	38.9	15.0	./.	./.	15.0	15.1	15.0	-
	1994	70 300 981	20.9	41.2	11.3	./.	./.	11.3	9.8	16.8	-
United Kingdom‡ Pound Sterling	1980	12 094	<—	26.6	40.1	...	...	...	22.4	<—	10.8
	1985	16 764	3.0	23.7	45.9	...	...	...	19.8	4.8	2.8
	1990	25 318	3.6	26.1	43.8	...	...	...	19.6	5.1	1.7
	1992	32 162	1.6	30.6	45.4	...	...	...	22.3	.	
Former Yugoslavia Dinar	1980	7	-	73.0	—>	...	-	22.8	18.5	1.8	6.8
	1985	39	-	76.4	—>	...	-	22.6	15.3	1.9	6.4
	1990	55 911	-	75.2	—>	...	-	22.9	17.0	2.2	5.6
Federal Republic of Yugoslavia New Dinar	1992	0.274	-	44.3	25.6	...	...	...	18.8	2.2	9.1
	1994	750	-	42.9	22.8	...	...	...	22.4	3.2	8.7
Oceania											
American Samoa U.S. Dollar	1986	23	5.5	32.3	40.2	34.2	1.3	4.7	15.5	4.2	2.2
Australia Dollar	1980	6 899	1.7	<—	67.0	...	...	...	22.6	2.7	6.0
	1985	11 848	1.6	<—	60.3	...	...	...	30.5	4.4	3.2
	1990	17 889	2.2	<—	57.4	...	...	...	32.0	4.8	3.6
	1992	21 252	1.1	29.7	41.6	...	...	...	26.6	.	1.0
Cook Islands New Zealand Dollar	1981	3	1.8	38.9	27.5	...	...	...	4.5	-	27.3
	1986	4	2.7	35.1	35.8	35.4	...	0.4	6.0	-	20.3
	1991	8	2.1	27.7	33.4	26.6	6.5	0.3	11.9	9.1	15.8

Public current expenditure by level of education 4.2
Dépenses publiques ordinaires par degré d'enseignement
Gastos públicos ordinarios por grado de enseñanza

Country / Currency — Pays / Monnaie — País / Moneda	Year / Année / Año	Total / Total / Total (000 000)	Pre-primary / Pré-primaire / Pre-primaria (%)	1st level / 1er degré / 1er grado (%)	Second level / Second degré / Segundo grado				3rd level / 3ème degré / 3er grado (%)	Other types / Autres types / Otros tipos (%)	Not distributed / Non ré-parties / Sin distri-bución (%)
					Total / Total / Total (%)	General / Général / General (%)	Teacher training / Normal / Normal (%)	Vocational / Technique / Técnica (%)			
		(1)	(2)	(3)	(4)	(5)	(6)	(7)	(8)	(9)	(10)
Fiji Dollar	1981	58	-	53.0	45.1	36.2	1.7	7.2	1.9	-	-
	1989	82	-	50.5	37.0	33.5	0.7	2.8	9.0	1.6	1.9
French Polynesia‡ French Franc	1984	935	-	53.7	40.9	32.8	-	8.0	-	0.1	5.3
	1990	1 148	15.5	29.4	49.0	...	...	...	2.5	-	3.7
	1993	1 807	13.8	27.4	49.0	...	...	...	1.1	3.3	5.4
Guam‡ U.S. Dollar	1985	59	0.8	33.4	61.6	...	...	...	-	4.2	-
Kiribati Australian Dollar	1981	3	-	37.6	44.8	14.3	6.4	24.2	-	-	17.6
	1989	4	-	50.5	28.7	15.8	7.1	5.8	7.9	-	12.9
New Caledonia‡ French Franc	1981	596	-	24.0	75.6	...	...	...	0.4	-	-
	1986	975	-	24.8	74.4	...	...	...	0.8	-	-
	1990	1 040	13.0	29.8	53.0	...	...	...	1.0	-	3.1
	1993	1 606	10.8	21.4	53.0	...	...	...	1.3	2.5	11.1
New Zealand Dollar	1980	1 171	1.4	35.4	29.7	29.7	-	-	28.3	2.6	2.6
	1985	1 849	1.5	36.9	28.5	28.5	-	-	28.3	2.2	2.7
	1990	4 252	3.7	26.9	25.3	25.3	-	-	37.4	3.0	3.8
	1992	5 107	3.9	22.2	20.9	20.9	-	-	36.7	2.4	13.9
Niue‡ New Zealand Dollar	1980	0.755	-	32.2	48.1	...	...	...	-	1.1	18.7
	1986	1.283	-	36.6	44.5	...	...	...	16.8	-	2.0
Samoa Tala	1990	14	-	52.6	25.2	18.6	3.8	2.8	-	-	22.1
Solomon Islands‡ Solomon Isl. Dollar	1979	3	-	44.1	42.2	11.3	9.4	21.5	13.3	0.4	-
	1991	24	0.3	56.3	29.8	...	...	...	13.7	0.1	-
Tonga‡ Pa'anga	1980	1	-	55.0	25.4	19.4	6.1	-	14.7	-	4.9
	1985	4	-	44.7	30.9	18.1	5.4	7.4	17.9	-	6.5
	1992	9	-	38.8	24.2	20.4	3.8	-	7.3	-	29.7
Tuvalu‡ Australian Dollar	1990	0.854	-	35.9	59.0	40.6	-	18.4	-	-	5.0
Vanuatu, Republic of Vatu	1990	831	-	59.8	26.6	...	...	...	3.4	-	10.2
	1991	929	0.1	58.0	29.1	25.7	2.2	1.2	3.2	-	9.6
Former U.S.S.R.											
Former U.S.S.R.‡ Rouble	1980	28 099	23.6	33.9	16.4	./.	./.	16.4	13.8	12.4	-
	1985	33 319	23.7	35.8	14.7	./.	./.	14.7	13.3	12.6	-
	1990	46 030	21.6	41.3	14.4	./.	./.	14.4	12.4	10.2	-

General note / Note générale / Nota general:

E--> For countries which participated in the most recent UNESCO/OECD/Eurostat (see special remark on page 1 of this chapter), expenditures previously given in the column *other types* are distributed among the different levels of education and the symbol for *category not applicable* is used.

FR-> Pour les pays qui ont participé au programme de la dernière enquête de l'UNESCO/OCDE/Eurostat (voir la note spéciale page 1 de ce chapitre), les dépenses présentées antérieurement dans la colonne *autres types* sont distribuées entre les différents niveaux d'enseignement et le symbole pour *catégorie sans objet* à été utilisé dans cette colonne.

ESP> Para los países que participaron en la última encuesta de UNESCO/OCDE/Eurostat (véase la nota correspondiente que figura en la página 1 de este capítulo), los gastos presentados anteriormente en la columna *otros tipos* fueron clasificados en los distintos niveles de educación, utilizándose el símbolo de *categoría sin objeto*.

AFRICA:
Algeria:

E--> For 1991 and 1992, capital expenditure is included and expenditure on third level education is not included.

FR-> En 1991 et 1992, les dépenses en capital sont incluses et les dépenses relatives à l'enseignement du troisième degré ne sont pas incluses.

ESP> En 1991 y 1992, se incluyen los gastos de capital y no se incluyen los gastos relativos a la enseñanza de tercer grado.

Angola:

E--> For 1990, expenditure of the Ministry of Education only.

FR-> For 1990, dépenses du Ministère de l'Education seulement.

ESP> En 1990, gastos del Ministerio de Educación solamente.

Botswana:

E--> For 1989, expenditure of the Ministry of Education only.

FR-> En 1989, dépenses du Ministère de l'Education seulement.

ESP> En 1989, gastos del Ministerio de Educación solamente.

Burkina Faso:

E--> For 1994, expenditure on third level education is included with second level and expenditure on adult education with first level.

FR-> En 1994, les dépenses du troisième degré sont incluses avec l'enseignement du second degré et les dépenses relatives à l'éducation des adultes sont incluses avec l'enseignement du premier degré.

ESP> En 1994, los gastos de tercer grado quedan incluídos en el secundo grado y los gastos relativos a la educación de adultos quedan incluídos en el primer grado.

Burundi:

E--> For 1985 and 1990, expenditure of the Ministry of Education only.

FR-> En 1985 et 1990, dépenses du Ministère de l'Education seulement.

ESP> En 1985 y 1990, gastos del Ministerio de Educación solamente.

Cameroon:

E--> Expenditure of the Ministry of Education only.

FR-> Dépenses du Ministère de l'Education seulement.

ESP> Gastos del Ministerio de Educación solamente.

4.2   Public current expenditure by level of education
Dépenses publiques ordinaires par degré d'enseignement
Gastos públicos ordinarios por grado de enseñanza

Central African Republic:
E--> For 1986 and 1990, expenditure of the Ministry of Education only.
FR-> En 1986 et 1990, dépenses du Ministère de l'Education seulement.
ESP> En 1986 y 1990, gastos del Ministerio de Educación solamente.

Comoros:
E--> Expenditure of the Ministry of Education only.
FR-> Dépenses du Ministère de l'Education seulement.
ESP> Gastos del Ministerio de Educación solamente.

Côte d'Ivoire:
E--> For 1994, expenditure on third level education is not included.
FR-> En 1994, les dépenses relatives à l'enseignement du troisième degré ne sont pas incluses.
ESP> En 1994, no se incluyen los gastos relativos a la enseñanza de tercer grado.

Djibouti:
E--> For 1985, expenditure of the Ministry of Education only. Data in column 8 refer to scholarships for the students at the third level of education.
FR-> En 1985, dépenses du Ministère de l'Education seulement. Les données de la colonne 8 se réfèrent aux bourses octroyées aux étudiants de l'enseignement du troisième degré.
ESP> En 1985, gastos del Ministerio de Educación solamente. Los datos de la columna 8 se refieren a las becas para los estudiantes de la enseñanza de tercer grado.

Egypt:
E--> Expenditure for Al-Azhar is not included.
FR-> Les dépenses relatives à Al-Azhar ne sont pas incluses.
ESP> No se incluyen los gastos relativos a Al-Azhar.

Eritrea:
E--> Expenditure on third level education is not included.
FR-> Les dépenses relatives à l'enseignement du troisième degré ne sont pas incluses.
ESP> No se incluyen los gastos relativos a la enseñanza de tercer grado.

Gabon:
E--> Data refer to expenditure of the Ministry of Primary and Secondary Education only.
FR-> Les données se réfèrent aux dépenses du Ministère des enseignements primaire et secondaire seulement.
ESP> Los datos se refieren a los gastos del Ministerio de la enseñanza de primer y segundo grado solamente.

Gambia:
E--> Expenditure on third level education refers to post-secondary institutions.
FR-> Les dépenses relatives à l'enseignement du troisième degré se réfèrent aux institutions post-secondaires.
ESP> Los gastos relativos a la enseñanza de tercer grado se refieren a los establecimientos post-secundarios.

Ghana:
E--> For 1980, expenditure on universities is not included.
FR-> En 1980, les dépenses des universités ne sont pas incluses.
ESP> En 1980, no se incluyen los gastos de las universidades.

Kenya:
E--> Except for 1985, expenditure of the Ministry of Education only. For 1985, teacher training at the third level is included with second level education.
FR-> Sauf pour 1985, dépenses du Ministère de l'Education seulement. En 1985, l'enseignement normal du troisième degré est inclus avec l'enseignement du second degré.
ESP> Salvo para 1985, gastos del Ministerio de Educación solamente. En 1985, la enseñanza normal del tercer grado queda incluída en el segundo grado de la enseñanza.

Madagascar:
E--> For 1990 and 1993, data refer to expenditure of the Ministry of Primary and Secondary Education only.
FR-> En 1990 et 1993, les données se réfèrent aux dépenses du Ministère des enseignements primaire et secondaire seulement.
ESP> En 1990 y 1993, los datos se refieren a los gastos del Ministerio de la enseñanza de primer y segundo grados solamente.

Mali:
E--> For 1980 and 1985, scholarships and allocations for study abroad for all levels of education are included with third level education. For 1993, expenditure of the Ministry of Education only.
FR-> En 1980 et 1985, les bourses et allocations d'études à l'étranger pour tous les degrés d'enseignement sont incluses avec l'enseignement du troisième degré. En 1993, dépenses du Ministère de l'Education seulement.
ESP> En 1980 y 1985, las becas y los subsidios para los estudios en el extranjero en todos los niveles de enseñanza quedan incluídos en la enseñanza de tercer grado. En 1993, gastos del Ministerio de Educación solamente.

Mauritania:
E--> For 1990 and 1994, expenditure of the Ministry of Education only.
FR-> En 1990 et 1994, dépenses du Ministère de l'Education seulement.
ESP> En 1990 y 1994, gastos del Ministerio de Educación solamente.

Morocco:
E--> Expenditure of the Ministry of Education only.
FR-> Dépenses du Ministère de l'Education seulement.
ESP> Gastos del Ministerio de Educación solamente.

Mozambique:
E--> Data include foreign aid received for education.
FR-> Les données comprennent l'aide étrangère reçue pour l'éducation.
ESP> Los datos incluyen la ayuda extranjera recibida para la educación.

Niger:
E--> For 1989 and 1991, data refer to expenditure of the Ministry of Education only and do not include expenditure on third level education.
FR-> En 1989 et 1991, les données se réfèrent aux dépenses du Ministère de l'Education seulement et ne comprennent pas les dépenses relatives à l'enseignement du troisième degré.
ESP> En 1989 y 1991, los datos se refieren a los gastos del Ministerio de Educación solamente y no se incluyen los gastos relativos a la enseñanza de tercer grado.

Rwanda:
E--> For 1986, data include capital expenditure. From 1986 to 1989, expenditure on 'enseignement rural et artisanal intégré' is included with first level education.
FR-> En 1986, les données incluent les dépenses en capital. De 1986 à 1989, les dépenses relatives à l'enseignement rural et artisanal intégré, sont incluses avec l'enseignement du premier degré.
ESP> En 1986, los datos incluyen los gastos de capital. De 1986 a 1989, los gastos relativos a la 'enseignement rural et artisanal intégré', quedan incluídos en el primer grado.

Sao Tome and Principe:
E--> Data include capital expenditure.
FR-> Les données comprennent les dépenses en capital.
ESP> Los datos incluyen los gastos de capital.

Seychelles:
E--> Data in column 8 refer to scholarships for the students at the third level of education.
FR-> Les données de la colonne 8 se réfèrent aux bourses octroyées aux étudiants de l'enseignement du troisième degré.
ESP> Los datos de la columna 8 se refieren a las becas para los estudiantes de la enseñanza de tercer grado.

South Africa:
E--> Data on pre-primary, first and second level education refer to expenditure on public and private ordinary schools and technical colleges. Data on third level education refer to expenditure on universities, technikons and teacher training. For 1990, data do not include expenditure for the following states: Transkei, Bophuthatswana, Venda and Ciskei (TBVC).
FR-> Les données relatives à l'enseignement préprimaire, primaire et secondaire se réfèrent aux dépenses des écoles publiques et privées et des collèges techniques. Les données relatives à l'enseignement du troisième degré se réfèrent aux dépenses des universités, des *technikons* et des écoles normales. En 1990, les données ne comprennent pas les dépenses pour les Etats suivants : Transkei, Bophuthatswana, Venda et Ciskei (TBVC).
ESP> Los datos relativos a la enseñanza preprimaria, primaria y secundaria se refieren a los gastos de las escuelas públicas y privadas y de las escuelas técnicas. Los datos relativos a la enseñanza de tercer grado se refieren a los gastos de las universidades, *technikons* y de las escuelas normales. En 1990, los datos no incluyen los gastos de los Estados siguientes : Transkei, Bophuthatswana, Venda y Ciskei (TBVC).

Sudan:
E--> For 1985, expenditure on third level education is not included.
FR-> En 1985, les dépenses relatives à l'enseignement du troisième degré ne sont pas incluses.
ESP> En 1985, no se incluyen los gastos relativos a la enseñanza de tercer grado.

Uganda:
E--> Data refer to expenditure of the Ministry of Education only.
FR-> Les données se réfèrent aux dépenses du Ministère de l'Education seulement.
ESP> Los datos se refieren a los gastos del Ministerio de Educación solamente.

Public current expenditure by level of education 4.2
Dépenses publiques ordinaires par degré d'enseignement
Gastos públicos ordinarios por grado de enseñanza

Zimbabwe:
E--> For 1990 and 1993, capital expenditure for education at third level is included.
FR-> En 1990 et 1993, les dépenses en capital du troisième degré sont incluses.
ESP> En 1990 y 1993, se incluyen los gastos de capital relativos a la enseñanza de tercer grado.
AMERICA, NORTH:
British Virgin Islands:
E--> For 1993, expenditure on third level education is not included.
FR-> En 1993, les dépenses relatives à l'enseignement du troisième degré ne sont pas incluses.
ESP> En 1993, no se incluyen los gastos relativos a la enseñanza de tercer grado.
Canada:
E--> Data refer to public and private expenditure on education.
FR-> Les données se réfèrent aux dépenses publiques et privées afférentes à l'enseignement.
ESP> Los datos se refieren a los gastos públicos y privados destinados a la enseñanza.
Costa Rica:
E--> For 1994, expenditure of the Ministry of Education only.
FR-> En 1994, dépenses du Ministère de l'Education seulement.
ESP> En 1994, gastos del Ministerio de Educación solamente.
Dominican Republic:
E--> Expenditure of the Ministry of Education only.
FR-> Dépenses du Ministère de l'Education seulement.
ESP> Gastos del Ministerio de Educación solamente.
Guatemala:
E--> Expenditure of the Ministry of Education only. For 1990 and 1993, figures on current expenditure refer to the allocated budget.
FR-> Dépenses du ministère de l'Education seulement. En 1990 et 1993, les chiffres correspondant aux dépenses courantes se réfèrent au budget alloué.
ESP> Gastos del Ministerio de Educación solamente. En 1990 y 1993, las cifras relativas a los gastos ordinarios se refieren al presupuesto programado.
Jamaica:
E--> Except for 1985, expenditure of the Ministry of Education only.
FR-> Sauf pour 1985, dépenses du Ministère de l'Education seulement.
ESP> Salvo para 1985, gastos del Ministerio de Educación solamente.
Mexico:
E--> Expenditure of the Ministry of Education only.
FR-> Dépenses du Ministère de l'Education seulement.
ESP> Gastos del Ministerio de Educación solamente.
Netherlands Antilles:
E--> Data include capital expenditure.
FR-> Les données comprennent les dépenses en capital.
ESP> Los datos incluyen los gastos de capital.
Nicaragua:
E--> For 1985 and 1989, expenditure of the Ministry of Education only. For 1994, data refer to the Ministry of Primary and Secondary Education only and are expressed in gold Cordobas.
FR-> En 1985 et 1989, dépenses du Ministère de l'Education seulement. En 1994, les données se réfèrent aux dépenses du Ministère des enseignements primaire et secondaire seulement et sont exprimées en Cordobas or.
ESP> En 1985 y 1989, gastos del Ministerio de Educación solamente. En 1994, los datos se refieren a los gastos del Ministerio de las enseñanzas de primer y segundo grados solamente y están expresados en Córdobas oro.
St. Pierre and Miquelon:
E--> For 1990 and 1993, expenditure of the Ministry of Education only.
FR-> En 1990 et 1993, dépenses du Ministère de l'Education seulement.
ESP> En 1990 y 1993, gastos del Ministerio de Educación solamente.
St. Vincent and the Grenadines:
E--> For 1990, expenditure on third level education is not included.
FR-> En 1990, les dépenses relatives à l'enseignement du troisième degré ne sont pas incluses.
ESP> En 1990, no se incluyen los gastos relativos a la enseñanza de tercer grado.
Trinidad and Tobago:
E--> For 1980 and 1985, expenditure on school feeding programme for general second level education is included with first level.

FR-> En 1980 et 1985, les dépenses relatives au programme d'alimentation scolaire dans l'enseignement général du second degré sont incluses avec le premier degré.
ESP> En 1980 y 1985, los gastos relativos al programa de alimentación escolar en la enseñanza general del segundo grado quedan incluídos en el primer grado.
United States:
E--> For 1980, data refer to the total of public and private expenditure on education. For 1980 and 1992 data include capital expenditure.
FR-> En 1980, les données se réfèrent à la totalité des dépenses publiques et privées à l'enseignement. En 1980 et 1992 les données comprennent les dépenses en capital.
ESP> En 1980, los datos se refieren a la totalidad de los gastos públicos y privados relativos a la enseñanza. En 1980 y 1992 incluyen los gastos de capital.
AMERICA, SOUTH:
Argentina:
E--> For 1986 and 1990, expenditure of the Ministry of Education only. For 1994, capital expenditure is included. Prior to 1994, data are expressed in Australes.
FR-> En 1986 et 1990, dépenses du Ministère de l'Education seulement. En 1994, les dépenses en capital sont incluses. Avant 1994, les données sont exprimées en Australes.
ESP> En 1986 y 1990, gastos del Ministerio de Educación solamente. En 1994, se incluyen los gastos de capital. Antes de 1994, los datos están expresados en Australes.
Bolivia:
E--> For 1989, expenditure on universities is not included.
FR-> En 1989, les dépenses des universités ne sont pas incluses.
ESP> En 1989, no se incluyen los gastos de las universidades.
Brazil:
E--> Data include capital expenditure. For 1985, expenditure of the municipalities is not included.
FR-> Les données comprennent les dépenses en capital. En 1985, les dépenses des municipalités ne sont pas incluses.
ESP> Los datos incluyen los gastos de capital. En 1985, no se incluyen los gastos de los municipios.
Chile:
E--> For 1985, capital expenditure on third level education is included.
FR-> En 1985, les dépenses en capital de l'enseignement du troisième degré sont incluses.
ESP> En 1985, se incluyen los gastos de capital relativos a la enseñanza de tercer grado.
Colombia:
E--> Expenditure of the Ministry of Education only. For 1985 and 1990, capital expenditure is included.
FR-> Dépenses du Ministère de l'Education seulement. En 1985 et 1990, les dépenses en capital sont incluses.
ESP> Gastos del Ministerio de Educación solamente. En 1985 y 1990, se incluyen los gastos de capital.
Paraguay:
E--> For 1990 and 1994, data refer to expenditure of the Ministry of Educacion only and include capital expenditure.
FR-> En 1990 et 1994, les données se réfèrent aux dépenses du Ministère de l'Education seulement et comprennent les dépenses en capital.
ESP> En 1990 y 1994, los datos se refieren a los gastos del Ministerio de Educación solamente y incluyen los gastos de capital.
Peru:
E--> Transfers to universities and to other types of institutions as well as some types of pensions and staff benefits are included in column 10.
FR-> Les transferts aux universités et à certains autres établissements ainsi que différents types de pensions et d'indemnités du personnel son inclus dans la colonne 10.
ESP> Las transferencias a las universidades y otros establecimientos así como diferentes tipos de pensiones y indemnizaciones del personal quedan incluídos en la columna 10.
Uruguay:
E--> For 1980, expenditure on special and adult education is included with first level education.
FR-> En 1980, les dépenses relatives à l'éducation spéciale et à l'éducation des adultes sont incluses avec l'enseignement du premier degré.
ESP> En 1980, los gastos relativos a la educación especial y la educación de adultos quedan incluídos en el primer grado.
Venezuela:
E--> For 1980, expenditure of the central government only. For 1985 and 1990, data refer to expenditure of the Ministry of Education only and include capital expenditure.
FR-> En 1980, dépenses du gouvernement central seulement. En 1985 et 1990, les données se réfèrent aux dépenses du Ministère de l'Education seulement et comprennent les dépenses en capital.

4.2 Public current expenditure by level of education
Dépenses publiques ordinaires par degré d'enseignement
Gastos públicos ordinarios por grado de enseñanza

ESP> En 1980, gastos del gobierno central solamente. En 1985 y 1990, los datos se refieren los gastos del Ministerio de Educación solamente y incluyen los gastos de capital.

ASIA:

Bahrain:
E--> For 1986, capital expenditure on third level education is included. For 1990 and 1993, expenditure on third level education is not included. For 1993, capital expenditure is included.
FR-> En 1986, les dépenses en capital de l'enseignement du troisième degré sont incluses. En 1990 et 1993, les dépenses relatives à l'enseignement du troisième degré ne sont pas incluses. En 1993, les dépenses en capital sont incluses.
ESP> En 1986, se incluyen los gastos de capital relativos a la enseñanza de tercer grado. En 1990 y 1993, no se incluyen los gastos relativos a la enseñanza de tercer grado. En 1993, se incluyen los gastos de capital.

Bangladesh:
E--> Data refer to expenditure of the Ministry of Education only.
FR-> Les données se réfèrent aux dépenses du Ministère de l'Education seulement.
ESP> Los datos se refieren a los gastos del Ministerio de Educación solamente.

Brunei Darussalam:
E--> For 1993, data refer to expenditure of the Ministry of Education only and do not include expenditure on universities.
FR-> En 1993, les données se réfèrent aux dépenses du Ministère de l'Education seulement et ne comprennent pas les dépenses des universités.
ESP> En 1993, los datos se refieren a los gastos del Ministerio de Educación solamente y no se incluyen los gastos de las universidades.

China:
E--> Except 1994, expenditure on specialized second level and technical/vocational schools is not included.
FR-> Sauf pour 1994, les dépenses des écoles spécialisées de l'enseignement du second degré et de l'enseignement technique/professionnel ne sont pas incluses.
ESP> Salvo para 1994, los gastos relativos a las escuelas especializadas de enseñanza de segundo grado y de enseñanza técnica/profesional no están incluídos.

Cyprus:
E--> Expenditure of the Office of Greek Education only.
FR-> Dépenses du bureau grec de l'éducation seulement.
ESP> Gastos del servicio griego de educación solamente.

Indonesia:
E--> Data refer to expenditure of the Ministry of Education only. Expenditure on special education is included with second level.
FR-> Les données se réfèrent aux dépenses du Ministère de l'Education seulement. Les dépenses de l'éducation spéciale sont incluses avec le second degré.
ESP> Los datos se refieren a los gastos del Ministerio de Educación solamente. Los gastos relativos a la educación especial quedan incluídos en el segundo grado.

Iraq:
E--> For 1980 and 1985, data include capital expenditure.
FR-> En 1980 et 1985, les données comprennent les dépenses en capital.
ESP> En 1980 y 1985, los datos incluyen los gastos de capital.

Israel:
E--> Expenditure on special education is included with first level.
FR-> Les dépenses de l'éducation spéciale sont incluses avec le premier degré.
ESP> Los gastos relativos a la educación especial quedan incluídos en el primer grado.

Japan:
E--> For 1980, data do not include public subsidies to private education. For 1985, data refer to public and private expenditure on education.
FR-> En 1980, les données ne comprennent pas les subventions publiques à l'enseignement privé. En 1985, les données se réfèrent aux dépenses publiques et privées afférentes à l'enseignement.
ESP> En 1980, los datos no incluyen las subvenciones públicas a la enseñanza privada. En 1985, los datos se refieren a los gastos públicos y privados destinados a la enseñanza.

Jordan:
E--> For 1993, expenditure on universities is not included.
FR-> En 1993, les dépenses des universités ne sont pas incluses.
ESP> En 1993, no se incluyen los gastos de las universidades.

Kuwait:
E--> For 1990, data include capital expenditure.
FR-> En 1990, les données comprennent les dépenses en capital.
ESP> En 1990, los datos incluyen los gastos de capital.

Malaysia:
E--> For 1990 and 1994, expenditure of the Ministry of Education only.
FR-> En 1990 et 1994, dépenses du Ministère de l'Education seulement.
ESP> En 1990 y 1994, gastos del Ministerio de Educación solamente.

Mongolia:
E--> For 1985 and 1990, data include capital expenditure.
FR-> En 1985 et 1990, les données comprennent les dépenses en capital.
ESP> En 1985 y 1990, los datos incluyen los gastos de capital.

Myanmar:
E--> Data refer to expenditure of the Ministry of Education only.
FR-> Les données se réfèrent aux dépenses du Ministère de l'Education seulement.
ESP> Los datos se refieren a los gastos del Ministerio de Educación solamente.

Nepal:
E--> Data refer to 'regular' and 'development' expenditure.
FR-> Les données se réfèrent aux dépenses 'ordinaires' et de 'développement'.
ESP> Los datos se refieren a los gastos 'ordinarios' y de 'desarrollo'.

Pakistan:
E--> For 1989, data do not include expenditure on education by 'other ministries' which are not directly related to education.
FR-> En 1989, les données ne comprennent pas les dépenses d'éducation effectuées par d''autres ministères' qui ne sont pas en rapport direct avec l'enseignement.
ESP> En 1989, los datos no incluyen los gastos de educación incurridos por 'otros ministerios' que no estén relacionados con la educación.

Sri Lanka:
E--> Except 1994, data refer to expenditure of the Ministry of Education only.
FR-> Sauf pour 1994, les données se réfèrent aux dépenses du Ministère de l'Education seulement.
ESP> Salvo para 1994, los datos se refieren a los gastos del Ministerio de Educación solamente,

Syrian Arab Republic:
E--> For 1980 and 1985, capital expenditure for education at the third level is included. For 1990, data include capital expenditure and, for 1994, do not include expenditure on third level.
FR-> En 1980 et 1985, les dépenses en capital de l'enseignement du troisième degré sont incluses. En 1990, les données comprennent les dépenses en capital et, en 1994, ne comprennent pas les dépenses relatives à l'enseignement du troisième degré.
ESP> En 1980 y 1985, se incluyen los gastos de capital relativos a la enseñanza de tercer grado. En 1990, los datos incluyen los gastos de capital y, en 1994, no incluyen los gastos relativos a la enseñanza de tercer grado.

Turkey:
E--> For 1990, expenditure on third level education is not included.
FR-> En 1990, les dépenses relatives à l'enseignement du troisième degré ne sont pas incluses.
ESP> En 1990, no se incluyen los gastos relativos a la enseñanza de tercer grado.

Yemen: Former Democratic Yemen:
E--> Data include capital expenditure.
FR-> Les données comprennent les dépenses en capital.
ESP> Los datos incluyen los gastos de capital.

EUROPE:

Belarus:
E--> See the note for the former U.S.S.R. For 1994 data are expressed in B. Rouble.
FR-> Voir la note pour l'ancienne U.R.S.S. En 1994, les données sont exprimées en B. Rouble.
ESP> Véase la nota de la ex U.R.S.S. En 1994, los datos están expresados en B. Rouble.

Belgium:
E--> Except for 1993, data refer to expenditure of the Ministry of Education only.
FR-> Sauf pour 1993, les données se réfèrent aux dépenses du Ministère de l'Education seulement.
ESP> Salvo para 1993, los datos se refieren a los gastos del Ministerio de Educación solamente.

Denmark:
E--> For 1986, scholarships for second level education are included with third level.
FR-> En 1986, les bourses relatives à l'enseignement du second degré sont incluses avec le troisième degré.
ESP> En 1986, las becas relativas a la enseñanza de segundo grado quedan incluídas en el tercer grado.

Public current expenditure by level of education **4.2**
Dépenses publiques ordinaires par degré d'enseignement
Gastos públicos ordinarios por grado de enseñanza

Finland:
E--> From 1980 to 1990, data refer to public and private expenditure on education.
FR-> De 1980 à 1990, les données se réfèrent aux dépenses publiques et privées afférentes à l'enseignement.
ESP> De 1980 a 1990, los datos se refieren a los gastos públicos y privados destinados a la enseñanza.

France:
E--> France metropolitan.
FR-> France métropolitaine.
ESP> Francia metropolitana.

Federal Republic of Germany:
E--> For 1991, data include expenditure for East Berlin.
FR-> En 1991, les données comprennent les dépenses relatives à Berlin Est.
ESP> En 1991, los datos incluyen los gastos relativos a Berlin Este.

Hungary:
E--> For 1990 and 1994, expenditure on special education is included with first level.
FR-> En 1990 et 1994, les dépenses de l'education spéciale sont incluses avec le premier degré.
ESP> En 1990 y 1994, los gastos relativos a la educación especial quedan incluídos en el primer grado.

Italy:
E--> For 1990, data refer to expenditure of central government and do not include expenditure on third level education.
FR-> En 1990, les données se réfèrent aux dépenses du gouvernement central et ne comprennent pas les dépenses de l'enseignement du troisième degré.
ESP> En 1990, los datos se refieren a los gastos del gobierno central y no incluyen gastos relativos a la enseñanza de tercer grado.

Latvia:
E--> For 1994, data include capital expenditure.
FR-> En 1994, les données comprennent les dépenses en capital.
ESP> En 1994, los datos incluyen los gastos de capital.

Monaco:
E--> For 1992, data do not include public subsidies to private education.
FR-> En 1992, les données ne comprennent pas les subventions publiques à l'enseignement privé.
ESP> En 1992, los datos no incluyen las subvenciones públicas a la enseñanza privada.

Netherlands:
E--> From 1980 to 1990, data refer to public and private expenditure on education.
FR-> De 1980 à1990, les données se réfèrent aux dépenses publiques et privées afférentes à l'enseignement.
ESP> De 1980 a 1990, los datos se refieren a los gastos públicos y privados destinados a la enseñanza.

Norway:
E--> Expenditure on first level (column 3) refers to compulsory education which covers six grades of primary education and the first three grades of secondary education. Expenditure on second level education, therefore, covers only the last three grades (upper secondary school).
FR-> Les dépenses relatives au premier degré (colonne 3) se réfèrent à l'enseignement obligatoire qui comprend six années de l'enseignement primaire et les trois premières années de l'enseignement secondaire. Les dépenses relatives à l'enseignement du second degré ne comprennent donc que les trois dernières années (école secondaire supérieure).
ESP> Los gastos relativos al primer grado (columna 3) se refieren a la enseñanza obligatoria que incluye seis años de la enseñanza primaria y los tres primeros años de la enseñanza secundaria. Los gastos relativos al segundo grado, por consiguiente, incluyen solamente los tres últimos años (escuela secundaria superior).

Portugal:
E--> For 1990, expenditure of the Ministry of Education only.
FR-> En 1990, dépenses du Ministère de l'Education seulement.
ESP> En 1990, gastos del Ministerio de Educación solamente.

Romania:
E--> For 1993, data include capital expenditure.
FR-> En 1993 les données comprennent les dépenses en capital.
ESP> En 1993, los datos incluyen los gastos de capital.

San Marino:
E--> Data in column 8 refer to scholarships for the students at the second and third levels of education.
FR-> Les données de la colonne 8 se réfèrent aux bourses pour les étudiants des enseignements du second et du troisième degré.
ESP> Los datos de la columna 8 se refieren a las becas para los estudiantes de las enseñanzas de segundo y tercer grado.

Sweden:
E--> Expenditure on first level (column 3) refers to compulsory education which covers six grades of primary education and the first three grades of secondary education. Expenditure on second level education, therefore, covers only the last three grades (upper secondary school).
FR-> Les dépenses relatives au premier degré (colonne 3) se réfèrent à l'enseignement obligatoire qui comprend six années de l'enseignement primaire et les trois premières années de l'enseignement secondaire. Les dépenses relatives à l'enseignement du second degré ne comprennent donc que les trois dernières années (école secondaire supérieure).
ESP> Los gastos relativos al primer grado (columna 3) se refieren a la enseñanza obligatoria que incluye seis años de la enseñanza primaria y los tres primeros años de la enseñanza secundaria. Los gastos relativos al segundo grado, por consiguiente, incluyen solamente los tres últimos años (escuela secundaria superior).

Ukraine:
E--> See the note for the former U.S.S.R.
FR-> Voir la note pour l'ancienne U.R.S.S.
ESP> Véase la nota de la ex U.R.S.S.

United Kingdom:
E--> For 1985 and 1990, expenditure on adult education is included with second level education. For 1992, data include capital expenditure.
FR-> En 1985 et 1990, les dépenses relatives à l'éducation des adultes sont incluses avec l'enseignement du second degré. En 1992, les données comprennent les dépenses en capital.
ESP> En 1985 y 1990, los gastos relativos a la educación de adultos quedan incluídos en el segundo grado. En 1992, los datos incluyen los gastos en capital.

OCEANIA:
French Polynesia:
E--> En 1990 and 1993, expenditure of the Ministry of Education only.
FR-> En 1990 et 1993, dépenses du Ministère de l'Education seulement.
ESP> En 1990 y 1993, gastos del Ministerio de Educación solamente.

Guam:
E--> Expenditure on third level education is not included.
FR-> Les dépenses relatives à l'enseignement du troisième degré ne sont pas incluses.
ESP> No se incluyen los gastos relativos a la enseñanza de tercer grado.

New Caledonia:
E--> En 1990 and 1993, expenditure of the Ministry of Education only.
FR-> En 1990 et 1993, dépenses du Ministère de l'Education seulement.
ESP> En 1990 y 1993, gastos del Ministerio de Educación solamente.

Niue:
E--> For 1986, data in column 8 refer to scholarships for the students at the second and third levels of education.
FR-> En 1986, les données de la colonne 8 se réfèrent aux bourses pour les étudiants des enseignements du second et du troisième degré.
ESP> En 1986, los datos de la columna 8 se refieren a las becas para los estudiantes de las enseñanza de segundo y tercer grado.

Solomon Islands:
E--> Data in column 8 refer to scholarships for the students at the third level of education.
FR-> Les données de la colonne 8 se réfèrent aux bourses octroyées aux étudiants de l'enseignement du troisième degré.
ESP> Los datos de la colunma 8 se refieren a la becas para los estudiantes de la enseñanza de tercer grado.

Tonga:
E--> For 1992, data include capital expenditure.
FR-> En 1992, les données comprennent les dépenses en capital.
ESP> En 1992, los datos incluyen los gastos en capital.

Tuvalu:
E--> Data include capital expenditure.
FR-> Les données comprennent les dépenses en capital.
ESP> Los datos incluyen los gastos en capital.

FORMER U.S.S.R.:
Former U.S.S.R.:
E--> Expenditure on pre-primary education includes play centres. General education at the second level is included with first level (column 3). Total second level (column 4) therefore, refers to technical and vocational education only (column 7) which includes teacher-training (column 6). Special education is included partly in column 3 and partly in column 7.

4.2 Public current expenditure by level of education
Dépenses publiques ordinaires par degré d'enseignement
Gastos públicos ordinarios por grado de enseñanza

FR-> Les dépenses de l'enseignement préprimaire comprennent les garderies d'enfants. L'enseignement général du second degré est inclus dans l'enseignement du premier degré (colonne 3). Le total de l'enseignement du second degré (colonne 4) se réfère donc uniquement à l'enseignement technique et professionnel (colonne 7) qui comprend l'enseignement normal (colonne 6). L'enseignement spécial est réparti entre les colonnes 3 et 7.

ESP> Los gastos de la enseñanza preprimaria comprenden las guarderías. La enseñanza general de segundo grado se incluye en la enseñanza de primer grado (columna 3). El total de la enseñanza de segundo grado (columna 4) se refiere pues únicamente a la enseñanza técnica y profesional (columna 7) que comprende la enseñanza normal (columna 6). La educación especial se distribuye entre las columnas 3 y 7.

4.3 Public current expenditure by purpose
Dépenses publiques ordinaires selon leur destination
Gastos públicos ordinarios según su destino

4.3 Public current expenditure on education: distribution by purpose

Dépenses publiques ordinaires afférentes à l'enseignement: répartition selon leur destination

Gastos públicos ordinarios destinados a la educación: distribución según su destino

Country / Currency Pays / Monnaie País / Moneda	Year Année Año	Total Total Total (000 000)	Administration other than personnel Administration autre que personnel Administración excluyendo al personal (%)	Emoluments / Émoluments / Emolumentos			
				Administrative staff Personnel administratif Personal Administrativo (%)	Teaching staff Personnel enseignant Personal docente (%)	Other personnel Autre personnel Otro personal (%)	Total Total Total (%)
		(1)	(2)	(3)	(4)	(5)	(6)
Africa							
Algeria‡	1980	8 259	...	...	63.6	...	...
Dinar	1991	37 934	8.4	13.3	77.0	0.1	90.4
	1992	53 516	7.4	18.1	73.2	0.1	91.3
Angola‡	1985	9 419	...	...	...	...	90.2
Kwansa	1990	10 856	...	...	...	...	86.3
Botswana	1979	27	5.6	——>	57.6	...	...
Pula	1985	88	6.4	——>	52.3	...	...
	1991	426	4.2	3.9	43.3	5.0	52.2
Burkina Faso‡	1980	7 436	./.	...	...	...	61.0
Franc C.F.A.	1985	12 292	-	7.9	52.9	0.2	61.0
	1989	18 727	3.3	5.8	54.0	-	59.8
	1994	30 016	./.	...	...	...	52.7
Burundi‡	1981	2 635	0.6	...	...	...	74.3
Franc	1985	3 212	0.8	1.3	65.0	1.6	68.0
	1990	6 370	1.4	15.6	58.3	1.1	75.0
	1992	8 023	1.7	10.4	56.1	6.9	73.4
Cameroon‡ Franc C.F.A.	1981	38 019	...	...	65.4	...	...
Cape Verde Escudo	1985	325	2.3	12.2	65.6	12.5	90.3
Central African Republic‡	1979	5 510	...	...	69.4	...	...
Franc C.F.A.	1986	8 340	1.1	7.3	66.8	5.2	79.4
	1990	8 527	1.3	4.4	68.1	7.0	79.6
Chad	1991	8 212	2.2	17.1	58.6	0.8	76.4
Franc C.F.A.	1994	10 691	7.4	8.7	64.7	1.5	74.9
Comoros‡	1992	2 829	0.4	4.5	71.3	-	75.8
Franc C.F.A	1993	2 938	5.1	6.0	73.3	-	79.3
Congo‡	1980	21 517	./.	...	70.8	...	...
Franc C.F.A	1991	56 537	1.1	...	...	...	85.2
Côte d'Ivoire‡	1981	150 241	./.	...	...	...	73.0
Franc C.F.A.	1985	179 447	./.	...	...	...	76.3
	1994	168 923	./.	...	...	...	87.0
Djibouti‡	1979	1 046	0.1	...	61.0	...	...
Franc	1985	1 690	./.	...	...	...	74.7
	1990	2 614	./.	...	...	...	70.0
	1991	2 872	./.	...	...	...	76.8
Egypt‡	1981	722	./.	...	...	...	81.0
Pound	1991	3 941	./.	...	...	...	83.3
	1992	4 683	./.	...	...	...	81.8

Public current expenditure by purpose **4.3**
Dépenses publiques ordinaires selon leur destination
Gastos públicos ordinarios según su destino

Teaching materials Matériel pour l'enseignement Material educativo (%)	Scholarships Bourses d'études Becas de estudios (%)	Welfare services / Services sociaux Servicios sociales		Other expenditure Autres dépenses Otros gastos (%)	Subsidies not distributed Subventions non réparties Subvenciones sin distribución (%)	Country Pays País	Year Année Año
		Total Total Total (%)	Of which school meals and board Dont repas scolaires et internat De los cuales comedores escolares e internado (%)				
(7)	(8)	(9)	(10)	(11)	(12)		
						Africa	
0.3	8.9	3.0	...	24.2	-	Algeria‡	1980
0.0	0.6	0.6	0.6	0.0	-	Dinar	1991
0.3	0.4	0.6	0.5	0.0	-		1992
1.0	0.4	2.5	1.9	5.9	-	Angola‡	1985
0.7	1.3	3.2	2.5	8.5	-	Kwansa	1990
16.4	3.8	3.5	...	-	13.2	Botswana	1979
3.5	10.8	./.		19.4	7.6	Pula	1985
4.0	4.7	10.1	10.1	11.6	13.2		1991
0.4	29.9	6.8		1.8	-	Burkina Faso‡	1980
0.1	26.3	3.4	0.8	4.4	4.8	Franc C.F.A.	1985
...	29.0	6.2	-	-	1.7		1989
./.	./.	./.	...	47.3	——>		1994
1.2	9.6	8.6	...	5.6	-	Burundi‡	1981
1.6	8.4	8.8	...	0.8	11.7	Franc	1985
0.8	8.2	9.0	...	2.7	2.4		1990
0.7	9.0	11.1	11.0	2.0	2.1		1992
						Cameroon‡	
...	2.9	...	...	7.8	24.0	Franc C.F.A.	1981
						Cape Verde	
0.2	...	...	...	7.2	-	Escudo	1985
						Central African	
./.	25.9	...	...	4.8	-	Republic‡	1979
2.4	14.7	1.3	...	1.1	-	Franc C.F.A.	1986
1.3	16.7	1.1	0.0	-			1990
1.4	12.7	...	...	2.5	4.7	Chad	1991
1.0	9.4	...	...	2.6	4.8	Franc C.F.A.	1994
./.	11.3	-	-	12.5	——>	Comoros‡	1992
./.	7.4	-	-	8.2	——>	Franc C.F.A	1993
5.5	19.0	1.2	...	3.6	-	Congo‡	1980
...	8.3	5.4	2.6	-	-	Franc C.F.A	1991
./.	7.8	./.	...	15.2	4.0	Côte d'Ivoire‡	1981
./.	7.5	./.	...	12.2	4.0	Franc C.F.A.	1985
...	...	...	...	5.5	7.5		1994
6.3	24.9	5.3	...	2.5	-	Djibouti‡	1979
12.6	-	-	-	4.1	8.7	Franc	1985
7.1	14.5	...	...	2.6	5.7		1990
6.5	16.7	...	...	...	...		1991
0.6	...	...	...	18.4	-	Egypt‡	1981
0.8	...	...	...	15.9	-	Pound	1991
0.8	...	...	...	17.4	-		1992

4.3 Public current expenditure by purpose
Dépenses publiques ordinaires selon leur destination
Gastos públicos ordinarios según su destino

Country Currency / Pays Monnaie / País Moneda	Year / Année / Año	Total / Total / Total (000 000)	Administration other than personnel / Administration autre que personnel / Administración excluyendo al personal (%)	Emoluments / Émoluments / Emolumentos			
				Administrative staff / Personnel administratif / Personal Administrativo (%)	Teaching staff / Personnel enseignant / Personal docente (%)	Other personnel / Autre personnel / Otro personal (%)	Total / Total / Total (%)
		(1)	(2)	(3)	(4)	(5)	(6)
Ethiopia‡	1981	210	8.1	——>	83.4	...	...
Birr	1990	434	6.0	3.0	90.1	...	...
Gabon‡	1980	16 055	...	...	56.7	...	...
Franc C.F.A	1992	34 407	4.6	...	88.6	...	...
Gambia‡	1979	11	3.4	...	...	...	75.6
Dalasi	1985	25	./.	...	58.8	...	71.3
	1990	73	1.4	...	42.6	...	47.5
	1991	75	0.4	0.7	38.5	1.5	40.6
Ghana‡	1984	3 844	4.2	——>	53.6	...	...
Cedi	1990	53 664	./.	...	...	...	62.7
Guinea	1979	1 186	8.3	...	62.8	...	...
Syli	1984	1 486	9.8	...	...	...	82.5
	1992	61 123	6.3	9.0	58.7	-	67.7
	1993	65 434	6.3	11.1	55.6	-	66.7
Guinea-Bissau							
Peso	1980	208	10.8	——>	73.5	...	...
Lesotho	1984	29	3.7	——>	69.9	...	...
Maloti	1988	61	0.8	3.3	74.2	1.0	78.5
Liberia							
Dollar	1980	53	9.0	...	48.9	...	...
Madagascar‡	1981	32 515	5.2	...	78.6	...	...
Franc	1985	49 806	...	...	76.7	...	...
	1993	104 064	9.2	21.5	61.9	-	83.4
Malawi‡	1979	20	12.3	——>	49.1	4.5	...
Kwacha	1985	46	7.4	3.8	45.7	4.6	54.2
	1989	106	6.1	2.9	52.8	-	55.7
Mali	1980	12 752	9.7	——>	51.0	...	...
Franc C.F.A.	1985	17 048	2.4	8.4	63.1	——>	71.6
Mauritania‡	1985	3 973	2.4	18.1	57.8	-	75.9
Ouguiya	1993	4 192	3.1	17.1	52.1	7.4	76.6
Mauritius‡	1980	408	./.	...	31.4	...	54.2
Rupee	1985	555	./.	...	30.2	...	59.7
	1990	1 287	12.7	11.9	53.8	14.5	80.3
Morocco‡	1981	3 992	./.	...	...	...	85.4
Dirham	1985	6 079	./.	...	...	...	86.4
	1990	8 533	./.	...	...	...	91.7
	1991	10 755	./.	...	...	...	88.1
Mozambique‡							
Meticai	1990	46 064	...	...	...	...	74.5
Niger‡	1980	7 763	./.	...	68.2	...	...
Franc C.F.A.	1989	15 545	3.1	18.4	56.6	3.9	78.9
	1991	19 493	4.6	17.3	57.2	3.1	77.6
Reunion	1980	1 264	7.1	——>	71.0	...	...
French Franc	1985	2 292	2.0	...	...	...	91.0
	1991	3 570	0.5	8.3	83.7	-	92.0
	1993	5 180	0.3	8.4	86.2	-	94.7
Rwanda	1980	2 439		...	74.8	...	...
Franc	1989	6 793	4.8	3.0	80.7	0.3	84.0
Sao Tome and Principe‡							
Dobra	1986	100	./.	...	...	...	68.7
Senegal‡	1980	26 818	./.	...	...	...	66.1
Franc C.F.A.	1985	46 118	./.	...	...	...	74.2
	1990	60 467	./.	...	...	...	69.4
	1993	67 008	./.	...	...	...	64.9
Seychelles	1980	50	12.6	...	...	...	64.4
Rupee	1985	120	22.6	——>	41.8	5.8	...
	1990	153	12.4	...	...	...	62.4
	1992	156	16.6	...	...	...	53.9
Somalia‡	1980	154	./.	...	...	...	80.9
Shilling	1986	290	...	...	...	...	65.6

Public current expenditure by purpose **4.3**
Dépenses publiques ordinaires selon leur destination
Gastos públicos ordinarios según su destino

Teaching materials / Matériel pour l'enseignement / Material educativo (%)	Scholarships / Bourses d'études / Becas de estudios (%)	Welfare services / Services sociaux / Servicios sociales		Other expenditure / Autres dépenses / Otros gastos (%)	Subsidies not distributed / Subventions non réparties / Subvenciones sin distribución (%)	Country / Pays / País	Year / Année / Año
		Total / Total / Total (%)	Of which school meals and board / Dont repas scolaires et internat / De los cuales comedores escolares e internado (%)				
(7)	(8)	(9)	(10)	(11)	(12)		
5.8	-	1.7	...	0.9	-	Ethiopia‡	1981
0.9	-	-	...	-	-	Birr	1990
...	27.0	...		16.4	-	Gabon‡	1980
0.5	3.2	3.1	3.1	-	-	Franc C.F.A	1992
5.0	4.0	6.3	...	5.7	-	Gambia‡	1979
4.8	5.8	2.0	...	2.0	14.1	Dalasi	1985
3.8	6.6	3.5	0.7	9.4	27.8		1990
3.9	2.6	2.7	-	25.5	24.3		1991
21.6	-	7.7	...	2.4	10.4	Ghana‡	1984
./.	-	./.	...	26.7	10.6	Cedi	1990
./.	./.	./.	...	28.9	-	Guinea	1979
2.6	0.2	4.5	...	0.4	-	Syli	1984
./.	./.	./.	...	26.0	-		1992
./.	./.	./.	...	26.9	-		1993
						Guinea-Bissau	
./.	./.	./.	...	15.7	-	Peso	1980
2.1	0.2	0.4	...	1.5	22.3	Lesotho	1984
-	18.8	-	-	1.9	-	Maloti	1988
						Liberia	
8.6	8.0	1.4	...	24.1	-	Dollar	1980
1.7	6.5	1.2	...	6.7	-	Madagascar‡	1981
0.3	8.6	0.7	...	9.9	-	Franc	1985
./.	0.5	./.	...	6.9	-		1993
3.2	-	./.	...	3.2	27.7	Malawi‡	1979
2.0	-	1.3	1.3	6.6	28.6	Kwacha	1985
./.	-	./.	...	14.8	23.4		1989
4.2	35.1	-	-	-	-	Mali	1980
1.8	22.9	-	-	0.0	1.3	Franc C.F.A.	1985
3.7	12.9	5.0	...	-	-	Mauritania‡	1985
5.9	<——	14.4	...	-	-	Ouguiya	1993
0.1	-	3.1	...	4.8	37.8	Mauritius‡	1980
-	1.4	1.4	...	1.7	35.7	Rupee	1985
1.6	0.4	0.9	-	2.3	1.9		1990
0.5	11.8	1.0	...	1.4	-	Moroooo‡	1981
./.	./.	./.	...	13.6	-	Dirham	1985
./.	./.	./.	...	8.3	-		1990
./.	7.6	./.	...	4.3	-		1991
						Mozambique‡	
...	...	...	...	...	25.5	Meticai	1990
13.1	9.4	9.4	...	-	-	Niger‡	1980
5.4	2.9	2.8	2.5	7.0	-	Franc C.F.A.	1989
4.7	./.	./.	...	13.1	-		1991
0.2	5.1	2.1	...	14.4	-	Reunion	1980
0.6	4.1	0.0	...	2.3	0.1	French Franc	1985
0.8	4.1	0.4	0.4	2.3	-		1991
0.3	2.6	0.6	0.6	1.5	-		1993
3.6	3.9	5.4	...	0.0	5.7	Rwanda	1980
1.7	5.7	3.6	3.5	0.3	-	Franc	1989
						Sao Tome and Principe‡	
-	-	7.0	...	24.4	...	Dobra	1986
./.	./.	./.	...	33.9	——>	Senegal‡	1980
./.	./.	./.	...	25.8	——>	Franc C.F.A.	1985
./.	./.	./.	...	30.6	——>		1990
./.	./.	./.	...	35.1	——>		1993
9.8	1.4	2.7	...	9.0	-	Seychelles	1980
3.4	4.2	16.6	14.5	5.6	-	Rupee	1985
3.4	9.5	9.8	8.9	2.5	-		1990
4.9	10.5	7.7	2.7	6.4	-		1992
16.6	...	...	...	2.5	-	Somalia‡	1980
18.4	...	...	...	16.0	-	Shilling	1986

4.3 Public current expenditure by purpose
Dépenses publiques ordinaires selon leur destination
Gastos públicos ordinarios según su destino

Country / Currency Pays / Monnaie País / Moneda	Year Année Año	Total Total Total (000 000)	Administration other than personnel Administration autre que personnel Administración excluyendo al personal (%)	Emoluments / Émoluments / Emolumentos			
				Administrative staff Personnel administratif Personal Administrativo (%)	Teaching staff Personnel enseignant Personal docente (%)	Other personnel Autre personnel Otro personal (%)	Total Total Total (%)
		(1)	(2)	(3)	(4)	(5)	(6)
South Africa‡ Rand	1986 1990 1993	6 844 15 265 23 849	... ...	10.2 8.6 ...	69.9 73.3 76.5	3.7 3.4 ...	83.9 85.3 85.4
Swaziland Lilangeni	1981 1986 1989 1994	23 57 88 241	6.0 5.2 1.5 2.6	—> —> 3.8 11.5	... ... 61.6 49.0	... ... 0.0 6.9	86.5 74.2 65.4 67.3
Togo Franc C.F.A.	1980 1990 1992	12 575 22 720 26 307	12.6 3.9 2.3	—> 2.5 2.4	... 54.6 57.6	... 0.2 -	68.3 57.3 60.0
Tunisia‡ Dinar	1980 1985 1990 1993	162 351 464 776	./. ... ./. 7.8	... ... 6.8	... ... 74.8	... ... 3.8	81.3 84.1 92.4 85.3
United Rep. of Tanzania Shilling	1979 1988	1 769 10 566	9.2 9.1	... ...	35.2 ...	... ...	 53.8
Zambia Kwacha	1980 1985	120 272	17.1 1.3	—> ...	52.6 ...	... ...	... 60.8
Zimbabwe‡ Dollar	1980 1986 1991 1992	218 721 1 655 2 040	3.5 ./. 1.2 0.3	... ... 3.2 3.1	75.2 ... 89.7 89.1	... ...	... 83.4 92.9 92.2
America, North							
Bermuda Dollar	1980 1984 1990 1991	26 31 49 54	5.0 7.0	—> —> 3.7 3.5	59.7 68.5 69.8 66.8	... ... - 0.5	... ... 73.4 70.7
British Virgin Islands United States Dollar	1980 1985 1990 1991	2 4 7 9	5.9 ./. ./. ./.	—>	75.0	... ...	75.0 71.8 67.0 61.8
Canada‡ Dollar	1980 1985 1990 1992	20 451 30 176 44 319 51 291	6.9 2.4 3.2 2.5	—> 6.0 6.0 6.1	52.2 51.2 51.9 50.6	... 11.1 13.0 13.0	... 68.3 70.9 69.8
Costa Rica‡ Colon	1980 1986 1991 1994	2 802 10 053 28 578 56 323	./. 2.3 ./. ./.	... —>	50.2 53.5	... ...	... ... 94.5 95.4
Cuba Peso	1980 1985 1990	1 135 1 588 1 627	3.8	—>	38.8	... ...	... 53.1 57.4
Dominica E. Caribbean Dollar	1989	20	...	7.8	59.1	2.8	69.8
Dominican Republic‡ Peso	1980 1985	104 204	6.6 2.6	—> 4.6	62.2 71.7	... —>	 76.2
Guadeloupe French Franc	1980 1991 1993	818 2 022 2 745	8.8 0.5 0.4	—> 9.5 9.4	69.2 83.8 86.3	- - -	... 93.3 95.7
Guatemala‡ Quetzal	1979 1984 1990 1993	117 160 441 1 136	6.2 7.7	—> —>	69.1 70.4	... ...	... ... 42.7 42.2
Haiti Gourde	1980 1985 1990	86 117 216	11.2 4.8 1.9	—> 22.5 ...	66.9 56.2 ...	... 9.7 ...	... 88.5 95.3
Honduras‡ Lempira	1980 1989 1994	141 416 971	6.5 20.2 ./.	—> ... 6.6	71.1 ... 58.2	... ... 0.1	... 78.6 64.9

Public current expenditure by purpose 4.3
Dépenses publiques ordinaires selon leur destination
Gastos públicos ordinarios según su destino

Teaching materials / Matériel pour l'enseignement / Material educativo (%)	Scholarships / Bourses d'études / Becas de estudios (%)	Welfare services / Services sociaux / Servicios sociales		Other expenditure / Autres dépenses / Otros gastos (%)	Subsidies not distributed / Subventions non réparties / Subvenciones sin distribución (%)	Country / Pays / País	Year / Année / Año
		Total / Total / Total (%)	Of which school meals and board / Dont repas scolaires et internat / De los cuales comedores escolares e internado (%)				
(7)	(8)	(9)	(10)	(11)	(12)		
./.	./.	./.	...	16.1	-	South Africa‡	1986
./.	./.	./.	...	14.7	-	Rand	1990
4.4		./.	...	10.2	-		1993
7.5	...	...	...	...	-	Swaziland	1981
...	6.5	2.2	...	2.9	9.0	Lilangeni	1986
...	6.9	8.6	1.9	5.9	11.6		1989
3.1	17.1	8.8	6.0	1.0	-		1994
1.5	15.6	...	...	2.0	-	Togo	1980
./.	10.2	./.	...	10.5	18.1	Franc C.F.A.	1990
0.9	11.7	0.0	...	6.9	18.2		1992
4.9	6.5	2.3	...	5.0	-	Tunisia‡	1980
1.0	5.3	1.1	0.9	6.1	2.4	Dinar	1985
...		1.4	1.0	0.6	1.7	3.4	1990
...	3.4	2.7	1.2	0.8	-		1993
15.9	13.2	7.6	...	19.0	-	United Rep. of Tanzania	1979
13.7	3.2	12.8	...	7.4	-	Shilling	1988
2.6	2.0	5.5	...	9.6	10.7	Zambia	1980
2.7	5.5	6.7	6.7	10.2	12.8	Kwacha	1985
0.5	0.5	4.0	...	11.4	4.8	Zimbabwe‡	1980
5.8	0.9	1.7	...	0.9	7.4	Dollar	1986
3.8	0.1	1.3	1.3	0.5	0.3		1991
2.1	0.0	1.7	1.4	2.5	1.2		1992
						America, North	
16.6	2.7	...	...	16.0	-	Bermuda	1980
5.2	3.5	-	...	15.8	-	Dollar	1984
./.	./.	./.	...	26.6	./.		1990
./.	./.	./.	...	29.3	./.		1991
1.6	4.3	1.2	...	12.1	-	British Virgin Islands	1980
./.	./.	./.	...	18.3	9.9	United States Dollar	1985
./.	./.	./.	...	19.4	13.5		1990
./.	./.	./.	...	21.5	16.7		1991
10.0	3.9	3.8	...	23.3	-	Canada‡	1980
7.0	4.3	4.3	...	12.9	0.9	Dollar	1985
7.2	3.7	4.6	...	10.2	0.3		1990
6.0	5.4	4.5	...	11.6	0.2		1992
0.2	<———	2.0	...	21.6	26.1	Costa Rica‡	1980
-	0.0	4.5	3.4	-	39.7	Colon	1986
./.	./.	./.	...	5.5	./.		1991
./.	./.	./.	...	4.6	./.		1994
6.6	2.5	45.1	...	3.1	-	Cuba	1980
0.8	1.0	21.8	14.0	23.2	-	Peso	1985
1.9	6.9	18.7	12.6	15.2	-		1990
0.9	1.7	-	-	15.8	11.9	Dominica E. Caribbean Dollar	1989
-	2.0	-	-	5.3	23.9	Dominican Republic‡	1980
-	0.5	-	-	-	20.8	Peso	1985
0.2	4.2	1.9	...	15.7	-	Guadeloupe	1980
0.7	3.6	0.4	0.4	1.4	-	French Franc	1991
0.3	2.4	0.3	0.3	0.8	-		1993
0.5	0.6	22.2	...	1.3	-	Guatemala‡	1979
0.3	0.7	0.7	...	5.1	15.1	Quetzal	1984
...	...	...	...	15.1	42.2		1990
...	...	...	...	15.6	42.2		1993
2.2	1.2	0.2	...	18.2	-	Haiti	1980
1.3	1.9	0.1	0.1	2.8	0.6	Gourde	1985
0.0	0.3	0.3	0.3	0.4	1.8		1990
2.6	1.6	0.6	...	0.1	17.5	Honduras‡	1980
0.3	0.8	0.0	-	-	-	Lempira	1989
0.5	0.3	0.1	0.1	7.2	27.0		1994

4.3 Public current expenditure by purpose
Dépenses publiques ordinaires selon leur destination
Gastos públicos ordinarios según su destino

Country / Currency / Pays / Monnaie / País / Moneda	Year / Année / Año	Total (000 000)	Administration other than personnel / Administration autre que personnel / Administración excluyendo al personal (%)	Emoluments / Émoluments / Emolumentos			
				Administrative staff / Personnel administratif / Personal Administrativo (%)	Teaching staff / Personnel enseignant / Personal docente (%)	Other personnel / Autre personnel / Otro personal (%)	Total (%)
		(1)	(2)	(3)	(4)	(5)	(6)
Jamaica‡	1980	303	12.5	——>	65.6	...	...
Dollar	1985	515	17.1	——>	58.8	...	...
	1990	1 276	0.6	4.2	58.3	2.0	64.5
	1994	5 551	1.8	...	57.9	...	68.8
Martinique	1980	887	9.2	——>	78.0	-	...
French Franc	1991	2 067	0.5	10.8	82.8	-	93.6
	1993	2 814	0.4	10.6	85.0	-	95.6
Mexico‡	1990	16 617 522	33.9	...	...	...	64.4
Peso	1992	32 780 581	36.5	...	...	...	63.1
Nicaragua‡	1980	0.580	10.8	——>	69.7	...	...
Cordoba	1985	6.196	2.2	7.8	61.2	-	69.0
	1992	275	19.6	9.4	68.5	0.6	78.5
Panama	1980	156	13.8	——>	65.3	...	...
Balboa	1985	231	9.3	——>	60.7	...	...
	1990	241	8.4	3.6	...	...	63.2
	1994	334	3.6	6.4	...	...	57.7
Saint Kitts and Nevis‡	1984	9	9.0	——>	82.8	...	...
E. Caribbean Dollar	1989	11	0.4	12.0	75.9	4.3	92.2
	1991	12	0.4	12.3	75.5	4.4	92.2
St. Lucia							
E. Caribbean Dollar	1980	19	7.2	——>	66.9	...	...
St. Pierre and Miquelon‡	1980	17	4.7	——>	72.0	...	...
French Franc	1986	40	1.2	4.6	69.8	1.9	76.3
	1991	42	0.5	8.1	85.2	-	93.3
	1993	57	0.5	8.7	85.8	-	94.5
St. Vincent and the Grenadines‡	1986	18	3.4	6.1	86.1	1.3	93.6
E. Caribbean Dollar	1990	26	...	9.6	82.9	0.7	93.1
Trinidad and Tobago	1980	431	7.1	——>	...	...	73.2
Dollar	1985	912	6.1	——>	69.5	...	...
	1990	727	2.7	4.6	69.7	-	74.3
	1994	1 061	./.	...	...	...	66.7
United States							
Dollar	1992	319 375			53.0		75.5
U.S. Virgin Islands							
United States Dollar	1980	57	16.7	——>	45.0	...	...
America, South							
Argentina‡	1980	0.860	./.	...	...	...	86.7
Austral	1990	7 062 974	7.3	18.4	69.6	-	88.0
Bolivia‡	1980	0.0049	6.5	——>	75.7	...	...
Boliviano	1989	268	1.7	...	...	...	98.1
	1994	1 322	1.0	22.5	47.4	-	69.9
Chile							
Peso	1980	45 504	2.5	——>	76.8	...	...
Colombia‡	1980	27 286	...	...	90.7	...	...
Peso	1984	108 896	0.5	...	94.5	...	...
Ecuador‡	1980	14 649	2.2	...	...	...	77.4
Sucre	1985	35 611	./.	6.2	62.9	0.9	70.0
	1989	127 394	./.	...	...	...	81.6
French Guiana	1980	152	10.8	——>	63.6	-	...
French Franc	1991	518	1.0	9.5	85.3	-	94.8
	1993	833	0.7	8.9	87.5	-	96.4
Guyana	1979	89	8.8	——>	66.5	...	...
Dollar	1984	112	10.5	——>	52.6	...	...
Peru‡	1980	166	8.4	——>	59.4	...	...
Inti	1985	4 855	0.7	11.4	55.2	...	66.6
Suriname‡	1980	67	23.3	——>	41.8	...	...
Guilder	1986	182	4.8	8.2	32.5	3.3	44.1
	1990	249	11.8	8.3	33.4	5.2	47.0
	1993	380	12.4	7.8	31.8	4.4	43.9

Public current expenditure by purpose **4.3**
Dépenses publiques ordinaires selon leur destination
Gastos públicos ordinarios según su destino

Teaching materials / Matériel pour l'enseignement / Material educativo (%)	Scholarships / Bourses d'études / Becas de estudios (%)	Welfare services / Services sociaux / Servicios sociales		Other expenditure / Autres dépenses / Otros gastos (%)	Subsidies not distributed / Subventions non réparties / Subvenciones sin distribución (%)	Country / Pays / País	Year / Année / Año
		Total / Total / Total (%)	Of which school meals and board / Dont repas scolaires et internat / De los cuales comedores escolares e internado (%)				
(7)	(8)	(9)	(10)	(11)	(12)		
2.2	0.0	3.9	...	15.7	-	Jamaica‡	1980
2.6	0.0	7.2	...	14.3	-	Dollar	1985
0.5	0.2	2.4	2.4	7.9	23.9		1990
0.7	0.1	3.4	2.5	3.8	21.3		1994
0.2	3.9	2.4	...	6.4	-	Martinique	1980
0.7	3.4	0.6	0.6	1.2	-	French Franc	1991
0.3	2.3	0.7	0.7	0.7	-		1993
...	0.3	...	...	1.4	-	Mexico‡	1990
0.0	0.2	0.1	0.1	0.0	-	Peso	1992
2.2	0.7	3.3	...	5.9	7.4	Nicaragua‡	1980
2.4	0.2	0.7	...	1.8	23.6	Cordoba	1985
0.4	0.4	0.7	...	-	0.4		1992
1.8	3.8	-	-	-	15.3	Panama	1980
0.9	-	-	-	3.6	25.4	Balboa	1985
...	...	...	...	...	28.4		1990
...	...	...	...	...	38.7		1994
2.3	2.0	4.0	...	-	-	Saint Kitts and Nevis‡	1984
1.4	...	4.2	3.4	1.7	0.2	E. Caribbean Dollar	1989
1.4	...	4.1	3.4	1.6	0.2		1991
						St. Lucia	
2.8	0.3	4.0	...	11.4	7.4	E. Caribbean Dollar	1980
5.6	-	-	-	17.6	-	St. Pierre and Miquelon	1980
5.4	9.3	2.6		5.1	-	French Franc	1986
3.6	0.2	-	-	2.4	-		1991
2.9	0.2	-	-	1.9	-		1993
						St. Vincent and the Grenadines‡	1986
1.5	1.3	0.2	0.2	-	-	E. Caribbean Dollar	
2.8	-	0.2	0.2	3.9	-		1990
4.0	3.7	1.0	1.0	1.6	9.5	Trinidad and Tobago	1980
2.7	6.1	5.5	5.5	2.2	7.9	Dollar	1985
./.	./.	./.	...	6.8	16.1		1990
0.1	0.9	6.3	5.9	7.0	19.0		1994
						United States Dollar	1992
						U.S. Virgin Islands	
2.1	0.0	11.3	...	24.8		United States Dollar	1980
						America, South	
7.9	5.0	...	...	0.3	-	Argentina‡	1980
...	0.6	0.1	...	4.0	-	Austral	1990
-	0.2	2.9	...	0.9	13.8	Bolivia‡	1980
-	0.2	0.1	...	-	-	Boliviano	1989
-	0.1	-	-	2.2	26.8		1994
						Chile	
5.1	<——	5.9	...	2.4	7.3	Peso	1980
...	...	...	...	9.3	-	Colombia‡	1980
0.1	./.	0.6	...	4.2	-	Peso	1984
0.8	0.2	./.	...	6.0	13.4	Ecuador‡	1980
...	...	./.	...	12.2	17.8	Sucre	1985
2.0	0.0	./.	...	16.3	——>		1989
1.3	2.7	4.3	...	17.4	-	French Guiana	1980
0.6	1.7	0.2	0.2	1.7	-	French Franc	1991
0.4	1.2	0.2	0.2	1.1	-		1993
6.0	3.2	5.9	...	9.6	...	Guyana	1979
0.8	8.4	0.9	...	14.4	12.5	Dollar	1984
0.9	...	...	...	31.3	——>	Peru‡	1980
0.3	...	0.2	...	32.2	——>	Inti	1985
7.2	5.5	2.8		19.3	-	Suriname‡	1980
2.7	2.2	3.8	0.1	8.9	33.6	Guilder	1986
4.3	2.4	0.2	0.1	3.8	30.4		1990
5.2	2.6	0.3	0.1	7.4	28.2		1993

4.3 Public current expenditure by purpose
Dépenses publiques ordinaires selon leur destination
Gastos públicos ordinarios según su destino

Country / Currency / Pays / Monnaie / País / Moneda	Year / Année / Año	Total (000 000)	Administration other than personnel / Administration autre que personnel / Administración excluyendo al personal (%)	Emoluments / Émoluments / Emolumentos			
				Administrative staff / Personnel administratif / Personal Administrativo (%)	Teaching staff / Personnel enseignant / Personal docente (%)	Other personnel / Autre personnel / Otro personal (%)	Total (%)
		(1)	(2)	(3)	(4)	(5)	(6)
Uruguay	1980	1 927	20.5	——>	56.9	...	...
Peso	1985	12 068	./.		46.3	...	78.3
	1990	265 660	./.	...	...	...	79.3
	1994	1 981 029	./.	...	47.4	...	69.7
Venezuela	1980	12 524	13.7	——>	60.7	...	...
Bolivar	1984	19 629	11.0	——>	60.0	...	...
	1994	419 515	1.0	2.7	21.4	2.9	27.0
Asia							
Afghanistan							
Afghani	1980	2 886	32.8	——>	46.8	...	...
Azerbaijan							
Rouble	1992	15 704	2.5	...	...	...	72.5
Bahrain‡	1980	28	7.7	——>	69.2	...	...
Dinar	1984	46	7.0	——>	80.5	...	...
	1991	65	...	1.2	72.0	9.3	82.5
	1993	69	...	...	...	...	83.8
Bangladesh‡	1980	2 010	./.	...	33.5	...	...
Taka	1986	7 472	./.	...	...	...	54.8
	1991	13 816	1.6	...	...	...	59.0
Bhutan	1992	187	32.8	...	53.6	...	58.1
Ngultrum	1993	192	32.9	...	53.2	...	57.7
Brunei Darussalam‡	1980	115	6.3	——>	43.5	...	...
Dollar	1984	151	./.	...	...	...	62.4
	1990	229	8.6	17.2	33.7	1.4	52.2
	1993	273	18.1	13.7	28.7	2.7	45.1
China‡	1980	9 418	7.7	...	...	...	56.1
Yuan	1985	18 416	7.6	...	...	...	55.3
	1990	35 652	./.	...	...	...	69.7
	1991	38 870	./.	...	...	...	69.7
Cyprus‡	1980	25	8.1	——>	80.0	...	...
Pound	1984	48	7.7	——>	82.4	...	...
	1990	84	...	6.4	82.3	2.7	91.4
	1994	143	...	6.4	80.7	2.8	89.8
Georgia							
Rouble	1994	5 727 212	19.4	...	...	...	52.6
Hong Kong	1980	3 036	15.2	——>	72.9	...	...
Dollar	1984	6 190	10.6	——>	76.5	...	...
India							
Rupee	1985	85 198	...	9.3	63.1	-	72.4
Israel‡	1980	8	4.1	——>	51.1	...	...
Shekel	1984	645	4.3	——>	58.1	...	...
	1990	6 666	1.6	...	...	...	78.3
	1992	10 601	1.7	...	...	...	76.9
Japan‡	1980	9 416 591	7.1	...	49.8	...	...
Yen	1985	15 280 808	...	...	...	...	61.5
	1988	17 278 783	...	...	...	...	60.5
Jordan‡	1980	51	7.3	——>	69.6	...	...
Dinar	1985	92	1.7	9.6	64.0	3.2	76.8
	1990	92	0.8	5.0	...	...	91.1
	1993	134	4.2	——>	...	...	90.3
Korea, Republic of	1981	1 251 286	10.0	——>	69.2	...	...
Won	1985	2 811 861	5.3	7.1	69.4	0.7	77.2
	1990	5 495 204	...	10.2	61.2	-	71.4
	1993	9 344 751	0.1	8.7	59.0	0.0	67.7
Kuwait‡	1980	204	./.	...	46.5	...	78.7
Dinar	1986	344	12.4	12.4	49.1	13.2	74.6
Kyrgyzstan‡	1993	215	./.	...	...	...	40.9
Som	1994	697	./.	...	...	...	51.0
Lao People's Democratic Republic‡							
Kip	1992	15 094	./.	13.0	65.0	0.1	78.0

Public current expenditure by purpose **4.3**
Dépenses publiques ordinaires selon leur destination
Gastos públicos ordinarios según su destino

Teaching materials	Scholarships	Welfare services / Services sociaux Servicios sociales		Other expenditure	Subsidies not distributed	Country	Year
		Total	Of which school meals and board				
Matériel pour l'enseignement	Bourses d'études	Total	Dont repas scolaires et internat	Autres dépenses	Subventions non réparties	Pays	Année
Material educativo (%)	Becas de estudios (%)	Total (%)	De los cuales comedores escolares e internado (%)	Otros gastos (%)	Subvenciones sin distribución (%)	País	Año
(7)	(8)	(9)	(10)	(11)	(12)		
5.1	./.	7.5	...	10.1	-	Uruguay	1980
./.	./.	./.	...	21.7	-	Peso	1985
./.	./.	./.	...	20.7	-		1990
./.	./.	./.	...	30.3	-		1994
1.0	7.4	3.2	...	14.0	-	Venezuela	1980
4.5	4.5	8.0	...	12.0	-	Bolivar	1984
0.2	0.4	14.5	0.2	14.2	42.6		1994
						Asia	
						Afghanistan	
12.7	-	6.1	...	1.5	-	Afghani	1980
						Azerbaijan	
0.2	4.4	5.9	5.9	14.5	-	Rouble	1992
6.5	6.7	2.4	...	7.5	-	Bahrain‡	1980
6.2	3.3	0.2	...	2.8	-	Dinar	1984
2.9	3.4	2.4	...	8.8	-		1991
./.	./.	./.	...	16.2	-		1993
0.1	0.0	16.6	...	9.6	40.2	Bangladesh‡	1980
1.3	0.2	3.3	-	4.6	35.9	Taka	1986
0.1	0.5	...	...	0.3	38.6		1991
6.2	-	1.7	...	1.1	-	Bhutan	1992
6.3	-	1.9	...	1.2	-	Ngultrum	1993
5.1	15.3	20.8	...	9.1	-	Brunei Darussalam‡	1980
2.5	26.5	./.	...	8.7	-	Dollar	1984
./.	./.	./.	./.	39.2	-		1990
./.	./.	./.	./.	36.7	-		1993
4.7	4.4	4.1	...	23.1	——>	China‡	1980
5.8	3.3	3.4	...	24.6	——>	Yuan	1985
./.	./.	./.	...	30.3	——>		1990
./.	./.	./.	...	30.3	——>		1991
2.4	1.0	2.3	...	6.3	-	Cyprus‡	1980
1.0	0.6	2.4	...	6.0	-	Pound	1984
0.9	0.4	2.3	...	4.7	0.3		1990
1.1	0.4	2.7	...	5.3	0.6		1994
						Georgia	
-	2.0	2.2	2.2	0.5	23.4	Rouble	1994
1.3	0.7	0.8	...	9.0	-	Hong Kong	1980
1.9	0.4	1.1	...	9.5	-	Dollar	1984
						India	
1.1	2.3	0.7	0.7	23.6	-	Rupee	1985
5.6	1.5	-	...	-	37.8	Israel‡	1980
5.1	1.0	-	...	-	31.5	Shekel	1984
17.3	2.8	-	-	-	-		1990
17.1	4.2	-	-	-	-		1992
6.5	1.2	5.0	...	30.3	-	Japan‡	1980
./.	./.	./.	...	38.5	-	Yen	1985
./.	./.	./.	...	39.5	-		1988
7.5	5.2	2.4	...	8.1	-	Jordan‡	1980
./.	./.	./.	...	20.1	1.5	Dinar	1985
./.	...	...	...	8.1	-		1990
2.8	...	...	...	2.8	-		1993
1.4	0.0	0.1	...	19.2	-	Korea, Republic of	1981
2.5	0.5	1.0	0.3	12.4	1.1	Won	1985
1.1	0.8	7.1	3.7	13.6	6.1		1990
0.8	0.5	6.7	2.2	13.3	10.9		1993
5.1	4.0	5.5	...	5.9	0.9	Kuwait‡	1980
1.1	1.1	3.8	0.4	3.2	3.7	Dinar	1986
0.4	6.3	7.2	5.5	45.1	-	Kyrgyzstan‡	1993
./.	5.2	7.3	6.4	36.4	-	Som	1994
						Lao People's Democratic Republic‡	
0.4	10.4	0.2	0.0	11.0	0.0	Kip	1992

4.3 Public current expenditure by purpose
Dépenses publiques ordinaires selon leur destination
Gastos públicos ordinarios según su destino

| | | | | Emoluments / Émoluments / Emolumentos | | | |
Country Currency Pays Monnaie País Moneda	Year Année Año	Total Total Total (000 000)	Administration other than personnel Administration autre que personnel Administración excluyendo al personal (%)	Administrative staff Personnel administratif Personal Administrativo (%)	Teaching staff Personnel enseignant Personal docente (%)	Other personnel Autre personnel Otro personal (%)	Total Total Total (%)
		(1)	(2)	(3)	(4)	(5)	(6)
Malaysia‡	1980	2 575	16.4	——>	57.5	...	...
Ringgit	1985	4 062	2.0	3.1	65.0	-	68.2
	1991	5 552	./.	...	...	...	77.5
	1993	7 085	2.1	2.1	60.5	——>	62.6
Mongolia							
Tughrik	1994	15 384	5.3	...	...	...	36.8
Myanmar‡							
Kyat	1994	4 436	./.	...	...	...	56.8
Nepal‡							
Rupee	1980	430	11.7	——>	59.2	...	...
Oman‡	1980	31	16.1	——>	60.3	...	...
Rial	1985	77	4.2	...	...	...	72.2
	1990	117	2.4	...	...	...	83.9
	1994	153	2.4	...	...	...	84.8
Philippines‡	1980	4 023	./.	...	...	...	78.4
Peso	1985	7 026	1.2	...	61.7	...	...
	1990	27 010	./.	...	...	...	96.1
Qatar‡	1980	598	./.	...	...	...	68.7
Riyal	1985	767	./.	...	...	...	70.7
	1990	904	./.	...	...	...	80.9
	1994	816	./.	...	...	...	79.5
Saudi Arabia‡	1980	13 526	./.	...	...	...	65.5
Riyal	1985	19 283	./.	...	...	...	76.5
Singapore							
Dollar	1980	587	1.6	——>	47.5	...	...
Syrian Arab Republic‡	1980	1 272	4.3	——>	...	...	85.9
Pound	1985	2 799	0.3	...	...	...	87.3
	1989	5 748	...	...	...	...	91.1
	1994	15 621	...	...	...	...	91.5
Thailand	1980	15 867	4.5	...	75.0	...	80.3
Baht	1985	33 830	4.2	3.8	75.0	4.8	83.6
	1990	64 702	5.7	13.5	62.0	5.3	80.7
	1994	108 485	6.3	7.0	61.6	5.0	73.7
Turkey‡	1980	98 593	./.	...	...	...	89.7
Lira	1985	523 102	./.	...	...	...	90.7
	1990	7 580 817	0.1	5.8	86.4	-	92.2
	1994	109 162 355	./.	...	...	...	93.7
United Arab Emirates‡	1981	1 158	9.7	...	...	...	51.9
Dirham	1985	1 637	11.6	...	...	...	61.3
	1990	2 174	12.0	...	...	...	69.7
	1994	2 702	./.	...	...	...	87.1
Uzbekistan							
Rouble	1993	475 863	...	...	...	...	58.4
Yemen							
Former Dem. Yemen‡							
Dinar	1980	16	15.2	——>	58.3	...	...
Europe							
Albania							
Lek	1994	5 353	...	...	...	...	75.2
Austria‡	1980	46 955	32.1	——>	53.1	./.	...
Schilling	1985	70 847	14.3	14.5	49.9	./.	64.4
	1990	89 858	14.5	15.0	50.5	./.	65.5
	1993	108 775					69.0
Belgium‡	1980	206 227	3.0	——>	73.0	...	...
Franc	1985	272 843	1.0	——>	79.6	...	...
	1990	321 427	1.8	——>	80.8	...	...
	1993	404 601			76.2		79.4
Bulgaria							
Lev	1994	22 620	...	...	...	...	67.8
Former Czechoslovakia	1980	21 802	0.2	...	...	...	50.0
Koruna	1985	26 959	...	...	...	...	48.1
	1990	35 482	...	...	...	...	50.5

Public current expenditure by purpose **4.3**
Dépenses publiques ordinaires selon leur destination
Gastos públicos ordinarios según su destino

Teaching materials / Matériel pour l'enseignement / Material educativo (%)	Scholarships / Bourses d'études / Becas de estudios (%)	Welfare services / Services sociaux / Servicios sociales		Other expenditure / Autres dépenses / Otros gastos (%)	Subsidies not distributed / Subventions non réparties / Subvenciones sin distribución (%)	Country / Pays / País	Year / Année / Año
		Total / Total / Total (%)	Of which school meals and board / Dont repas scolaires et internat / De los cuales comedores escolares e internado (%)				
(7)	(8)	(9)	(10)	(11)	(12)		
5.8	2.5	2.7	...	3.9	11.3	Malaysia‡	1980
3.0	2.1	0.8	...	8.8	15.0	Ringgit	1985
1.2	1.4	2.6	2.3	1.6	15.7		1991
6.0	1.1	3.1	1.0	7.5	17.7		1993
						Mongolia	
0.1	1.1	7.7	7.6	49.1	-	Tughrik	1994
						Myanmar‡	
...	...	...	...	43.2	...	Kyat	1994
						Nepal‡	
7.1	3.4	-	-	18.6	-	Rupee	1980
6.4	8.6	4.4	...	4.2	-	Oman‡	1980
6.2	8.0	8.8	1.0	0.6	-	Rial	1985
2.5	4.4	6.4	0.7	-	0.4		1990
1.1	...	11.7	1.3	0.0	-		1994
0.3	7.5	2.1	...	11.7	-	Philippines‡	1980
0.9	0.9	1.3	...	13.4	20.6	Peso	1985
0.6	0.0	0.1	0.1	-	3.1		1990
3.7	14.4	9.9	...	3.3	-	Qatar‡	1980
2.5	12.4	5.3	0.4	9.1	-	Riyal	1985
1.6	8.5	2.4	0.4	6.7	-		1990
1.2	5.8	2.1	0.3	11.5	-		1994
./.	./.	./.	...	34.5	-	Saudi Arabia‡	1980
./.	./.	./.	...	23.5	-	Riyal	1985
						Singapore	
0.0	0.3	-	-	7.5	43.1	Dollar	1980
2.0	0.8	2.2	...	4.8	-	Syrian Arab Republic‡	1980
2.9	0.4	1.9	1.9	6.3	0.9	Pound	1985
2.2	0.2	1.3	0.9	3.5	1.7		1989
3.5	0.1	0.7	0.3	3.8	0.5		1994
4.6	4.3	5.3	...	0.9	-	Thailand	1980
4.2	0.4	0.7	0.1	5.0	1.8	Baht	1985
4.0	0.1	0.2	0.1	3.4	5.9		1990
4.5	1.1	3.3	3.3	2.9	8.1		1994
0.5	0.5	2.0	...	7.3	-	Turkey‡	1980
0.5	-	4.6	3.7	4.3	-	Lira	1985
0.3	0.5	1.7	...	5.2	0.0		1990
0.6	1.3	1.5	1.2	3.0	-		1994
11.8	7.8	11.3	...	7.5	-	United Arab Emirates‡	1981
5.7	6.2	1.2	0.5	13.9	-	Dirham	1985
1.2	3.5	0.3	0.0	13.5	-		1990
./.	./.	./.	./.	12.9	-		1994
						Uzbekistan	
0.9	4.7	5.5	5.5	30.5	-	Rouble	1993
						Yemen Former Dem. Yemen‡	
0.2	0.8	5.9	...	19.6	-	Dinar	1980
						Europe	
						Albania	
5.3	3.0	8.4	2.8	4.8	3.3	Lek	1994
./.	2.9	2.7	...	9.3	-	Austria‡	1980
1.3	3.0	1.1	0.1	16.0	-	Schilling	1985
1.1	2.5	1.1	0.2	15.3	-		1990
							1993
0.1	0.8	0.6	...	22.4	-	Belgium‡	1980
0.0	./.	0.7	0.0	17.2	1.4	Franc	1985
...	1.3	0.7	...	15.3	./.		1990
							1993
						Bulgaria	
...	4.8	0.1	0.1	27.3	-	Lev	1994
18.9	2.1	13.4	...	15.5	-	Former Czechoslovakia	1980
20.8	1.4	20.1	18.3	9.5	0.0	Koruna	1985
17.1	1.1	15.1	13.7	16.2	0.0		1990

4.3 Public current expenditure by purpose
Dépenses publiques ordinaires selon leur destination
Gastos públicos ordinarios según su destino

Country / Currency Pays / Monnaie País / Moneda	Year Année Año	Total Total Total (000 000)	Administration other than personnel Administration autre que personnel Administración excluyendo al personal (%)	Emoluments / Émoluments / Emolumentos			
				Administrative staff Personnel administratif Personal Administrativo (%)	Teaching staff Personnel enseignant Personal docente (%)	Other personnel Autre personnel Otro personal (%)	Total Total Total (%)
		(1)	(2)	(3)	(4)	(5)	(6)
Czech Republic	1992	33 631	...	...	...	...	41.1
Koruna	1993	49 198	...	...	...	...	32.2
Denmark	1980	22 188	15.6	—>	49.3	...	...
Krone	1986	43 054	2.1	...	...	...	58.7
	1991	54 896	0.9	...	...	...	57.8
	1993	56 915			52.2		81.1
Estonia	1992	729	15.2	...	...	...	46.0
Kroon	1994	1 748	16.3	...	...	...	50.1
Finland‡	1980	9 565	6.3	—>	50.5	...	...
Markka	1985	17 604	2.3	5.2	47.6	12.0	64.8
	1990	29 300	2.7	5.7	47.7	10.7	64.2
	1993	32 996			52.0		68.6
France‡	1980	131 441	3.5	—>	68.1	...	...
Franc	1985	254 433	0.7	...	...	...	71.7
	1990	327 427	0.7	...	...	...	73.2
	1993	396 287					76.7
Germany							
Deutsche Mark	1993	123 939					82.2
Federal Rep. of Germany	1980	60 558	1.3	—>	71.3	...	...
Deutsche Mark	1985	75 566	0.2	0.9	73.3	—>	74.3
	1990	88 499	0.2	...	...	...	74.3
	1991	97 255	0.3	...	...	...	73.1
Gibraltar	1980	3	5.6	—>	56.4	...	...
Pound Sterling	1984	5	4.7	—>	63.6	...	...
Greece	1981	47 210	...	5.7	84.8	...	90.6
Drachma	1985	126 749	...	7.5	82.9	...	90.4
	1990	306 303	...	6.1	85.2	...	91.3
	1991	359 533	...	6.3	84.4	...	90.7
Hungary‡	1980	27 516	0.3	...	45.2	...	...
Forint	1985	48 125	./.	...	29.1	...	52.1
	1990	110 382	./.	...	...	...	45.2
	1994	262 917	./.	...	...	...	45.7
Iceland	1990	14 584	1.1	6.2	53.5	10.4	70.1
Krona	1993	16 617					72.3
Ireland	1980	515	4.1	—>	67.6	...	...
Pound	1985	963	1.0	1.4	72.9	1.8	76.0
	1990	1 303	./.	...	74.9	...	83.3
	1993	1 792			77.1		87.7
Italy‡	1979	11 791 069	16.9	—>	68.2	...	...
Lira	1985	36 859 217	./.	...	...	...	79.0
	1990	40 400 136	0.3	...	82.4	...	97.6
	1993	73 838 890			63.5		82.2
Lithuania	1992	171	./.	...	...	...	40.8
Lita	1994	886	./.	...	...	...	65.3
Luxembourg‡	1980	6 123	./.	...	...	...	87.8
Franc	1986	10 712	6.4	4.2	73.8	5.4	83.5
	1989	13 440	6.8	4.1	72.9	5.6	82.6
Malta‡	1980	12	./.	...	53.0	...	81.0
Lira	1985	17	7.1	8.5	52.2	16.5	77.2
	1990	30	4.7	7.6	42.4	13.7	63.7
	1992	41	7.2	9.6	38.7	12.7	61.0
Monaco‡	1980	43	3.7	—>	81.3	...	...
French Franc	1992	124	0.2	...	...	...	83.8
Netherlands‡	1980	23 079	3.2	—>	...	...	73.5
Guilder	1985	24 796	2.0	2.1	71.0	—>	73.1
	1990	29 005	2.0	2.2	64.3	—>	66.5
	1993	27 353					77.8
Norway	1980	16 448	2.7	...	...	...	64.3
Krone	1985	27 979	2.8	...	...	...	64.1
	1990	44 109	2.8	...	...	...	61.0
	1993	46 076					77.6

Public current expenditure by purpose 4.3
Dépenses publiques ordinaires selon leur destination
Gastos públicos ordinarios según su destino

Teaching materials	Scholarships	Welfare services / Services sociaux Servicios sociales		Other expenditure	Subsidies not distributed	Country	Year
		Total	Of which school meals and board				
Matériel pour l'enseignement	Bourses d'études	Total	Dont repas scolaires et internat	Autres dépenses	Subventions non réparties	Pays	Année
Material educativo (%)	Becas de estudios (%)	Total (%)	De los cuales comedores escolares e internado (%)	Otros gastos (%)	Subvenciones sin distribución (%)	País	Año
(7)	(8)	(9)	(10)	(11)	(12)		
22.9	0.3	15.2	11.0	10.7	9.9	Czech Republic	1992
28.1	0.3	9.0	8.0	9.5	20.9	Koruna	1993
4.8	2.7	3.9	...	23.7	-	Denmark	1980
25.1	11.5	2.6	-	-	-	Krone	1986
./.	7.7	./.	...	33.6	-		1991
							1993
1.3	6.1	8.7	8.1	22.7	0.1	Estonia	1992
3.2	0.7	5.4	5.2	24.0	0.3	Kroon	1994
5.7	4.1	14.4	...	19.0	-	Finland‡	1980
6.9	4.6	8.5	5.6	12.9	-	Markka	1985
6.9	5.1	7.9	4.9	13.3	-		1990
							1993
0.1	2.1	8.9	...	17.3	-	France‡	1980
2.0	1.9	8.4	5.8	15.2	-	Franc	1985
0.5	2.1	8.6	5.5	15.1	-		1990
							1993
						Germany	
						Deutsche Mark	1993
...	5.3	2.8	...	13.2	6.1	Fed. Rep. of Germany‡	1980
...	1.1	2.7	...	15.6	6.1	Deutsche Mark	1985
...	1.3	2.5	...	14.4	7.2		1990
...	2.4	2.5	...	14.5	7.2		1991
4.2	11.2	0.7	...	21.9	-	Gibraltar	1980
3.3	6.9	0.4	...	21.2	-	Pound Sterling	1984
3.4	0.2	1.1	...	4.7	-	Greece	1981
	0.2	1.2	...	8.2	-	Drachma	1985
...	0.2	1.6	...	6.9	-		1990
...	0.2	1.4	...	7.6	-		1991
./.	3.4	16.3	...	34.8	——>	Hungary‡	1980
./.	2.6	16.2	14.9	29.1	——>	Forint	1985
./.	2.2	11.5	11.3	41.1	——>		1990
./.	./.	8.9	8.9	45.4	——>		1994
1.5	0.6	-	-	26.6	0.1	Iceland	1990
						Krona	1993
0.4	1.5	4.7	...	21.7	-	Ireland	1980
0.4	1.8	4.1	0.8	16.7	-	Pound	1985
0.3	<——	7.4	5.0	9.0	-		1990
							1993
./.	0.6	2.0	...	12.3	-	Italy‡	1979
...	0.2	8.1	...	12.8	——>	Lira	1985
1.2	...	0.0	...	0.5	0.4		1990
							1993
./.	4.2	1.7	1.7	53.4	0.0	Lithuania	1992
1.3	4.2	3.7	3.7	25.5	-	Lita	1994
1.0	1.0	./.	...	10.2	-	Luxembourg‡	1980
1.6	1.5	1.7	0.2	5.3	-	Franc	1986
1.2	1.9	2.0	0.2	5.6	-		1989
0.2	4.7	2.4	...	2.4	9.3	Malta‡	1980
0.1	2.9	2.8	1.1	1.7	8.2	Lira	1985
0.0	1.0	2.5	0.7	13.6	14.6		1990
0.0	0.1	11.6	0.5	9.2	10.9		1992
-	2.6	1.5	...	10.8	-	Monaco‡	1980
2.7	2.9	1.9	...	8.5	-	French Franc	1992
1.1	3.2	1.5	...	17.6	-	Netherlands‡	1980
1.9	4.9	1.5	...	16.6	-	Guilder	1985
1.9	13.5	——>	...	16.1	-		1990
							1993
6.0	5.2	2.4	...	15.0	4.4	Norway	1980
6.3	5.0	2.2	...	14.4	5.1	Krone	1985
8.3	5.7	...	...	16.0	6.2		1990
							1993

Public current expenditure by purpose
Dépenses publiques ordinaires selon leur destination
Gastos públicos ordinarios según su destino

Country Currency Pays Monnaie País Moneda	Year Année Año	Total Total Total (000 000)	Administration other than personnel Administration autre que personnel Administración excluyendo al personal (%)	Emoluments / Émoluments / Emolumentos			
				Administrative staff Personnel administratif Personal Administrativo (%)	Teaching staff Personnel enseignant Personal docente (%)	Other personnel Autre personnel Otro personal (%)	Total Total Total (%)
		(1)	(2)	(3)	(4)	(5)	(6)
Portugal‡ Escudo	1980 1985 1990 1993	45 443 135 612 378 252 688 511	3.7 3.8 5.6	... ... 2.5	... ... 86.1	... ...	82.8 82.7 88.6 83.3
Romania‡ Leu	1990 1993	23 881 606 683	./. ./.	... ...	... ...	... ...	79.3 80.9
San Marino Lira	1980 1984	6 263 10 474	... ...	... ...	84.7 82.5	... ...	... ...
Slovakia S. Koruna	1992 1994	17 575 17 152	... ...	... ...	... ...	... ...	55.3 57.9
Slovenia Tolar	1991 1994	15 266 92 722	16.8 1.2	2.2 1.4	54.9 58.0	9.0 11.2	66.0 70.6
Spain Peseta	1990 1993	1 936 203 2 970 963	10.2	...	...	...	65.6 80.4
Sweden‡ Krona	1980 1985 1990 1992	40 886 57 703 93 083 105 803	./. 3.6 3.2 4.9	... ...	... ...	... ...	49.2 44.9 47.4 38.8
Switzerland Franc	1980 1985 1990 1993	7 937 10 638 14 395 15 689	13.3 ./. ./.	——> 13.2 13.8	61.0 61.8 61.2	... ...	... 75.0 74.9 84.1
The Former Yugoslav Rep. of Macedonia Dinar	1992 1994	591 6 807	... ...	... ...	... ...	... ...	82.7 82.9
United Kingdom Pound Sterling	1980 1985 1990 1992	12 094 16 764 25 318 28 969	./. 2.3 2.3	... 1.8 2.0	52.1 51.6 51.4 52.0	... 15.9 14.6	 69.3 68.1 67.5
Former Yugoslavia Dinar	1980 1985 1990	7 39 55 911	... ...	... ...	... ...	... ...	63.9 62.5 64.1
Federal Republic of Yugoslavia New Dinar	1992 1994	0.274 750	... ...	... ...	... ...	... ...	60.2 41.2
Oceania							
American Samoa United States Dollar	1981 1986	11 23	14.5 0.3	——> 21.0	44.0 33.1	... 9.8	... 63.9
Australia‡ Dollar	1986 1990 1992	12 583 17 889 22 511	./. ./.	... ...	... ...	... ...	81.6 77.0 70.9
Cook Islands New Zealand Dollar	1981 1986 1991	3 4 8	17.5 ... 3.9	——> ... 6.2	... ...	... ...	72.3 78.9 68.1
Fiji‡ Dollar	1981 1989 1992	58 82 124	6.4 2.6 ...	——>	... ...	... ...	86.5 82.2 73.5
French Polynesia‡ French Franc	1984 1990 1993	935 1 148 1 807	7.5 ... 0.6	——> 8.4 8.4	80.2 83.2 85.9	- - -	... 91.6 94.4
Kiribati Australian Dollar	1980 1985 1990 1992	3 3 4 5	9.1 15.6 18.1 ./.	... ...	45.2 58.3	... ...	... ... 60.6 57.7
New Caledonia‡ French Franc	1981 1986 1990 1993	596 975 1 040 1 606	... ... 1.1	... ... 5.0 8.2	85.8 89.4 85.9 79.7	... ... -	... ... 90.9 87.9

Public current expenditure by purpose 4.3
Dépenses publiques ordinaires selon leur destination
Gastos públicos ordinarios según su destino

Teaching materials Matériel pour l'enseignement Material educativo (%)	Scholarships Bourses d'études Becas de estudios (%)	Welfare services / Services sociaux Servicios sociales		Other expenditure Autres dépenses Otros gastos (%)	Subsidies not distributed Subventions non réparties Subvenciones sin distribución (%)	Country Pays País	Year Année Año
		Total Total Total (%)	Of which school meals and board Dont repas scolaires et internat De los cuales comedores escolares e internado (%)				
(7)	(8)	(9)	(10)	(11)	(12)		
0.8	3.9	3.7	...	5.1	-	Portugal‡	1980
0.1	<——	3.6	...	9.9	-	Escudo	1985
...	1.0	2.4	...	...	2.3		1990
							1993
2.7	1.2	8.9	1.8	7.9	-	Romania‡	1990
1.2	3.2	2.5	2.2	11.8	0.4	Leu	1993
2.8	2.7	6.0	...	3.8	-	San Marino	1980
2.2	4.4	6.2	...	4.6	-	Lira	1984
2.9	0.7	11.6	11.6	29.6	-	Slovakia	1992
0.7	0.5	15.2	15.2	25.7	-	S. Koruna	1994
2.6	0.3	11.5	8.3	2.4	0.4	Slovenia	1991
7.5	8.3	7.2	3.9	5.1	0.3	Tolar	1994
...	2.9	1.9	...	7.6	11.9	Spain	1990
						Peseta	1993
2.4	3.8	15.4	...	29.1	——>	Sweden‡	1980
2.7	4.0	7.3	4.3	16.1	21.4	Krona	1985
...	7.0	7.0	4.2	-	35.4		1990
2.8	7.0	4.7	3.3	-	41.8		1992
3.5	2.4	...	...	19.7	——>	Switzerland	1980
3.1	1.8	...	...	13.0	7.1	Franc	1985
3.2	2.2	...	...	12.3	7.4		1990
							1993
...	0.4	3.5	3.5	13.0	0.4	The Former Yugoslav Rep. of Macedonia	1992
0.1	0.9	3.1	3.1	13.1	-	Dinar	1994
3.6	9.1	5.7	...	29.4	-	United Kingdom	1980
3.7	./.	./.	...	24.7	-	Pound Sterling	1985
5.3	7.5	3.0	...	14.0	-		1990
							1992
6.2	1.5	8.4	...	20.1	-	Former Yugoslavia	1980
8.3	1.4	9.0	...	18.8	-	Dinar	1985
12.4	——>	6.9	...	16.6	-		1990
11.8	——>	6.0	...	22.0	-	Federal Republic of Yugoslavia	1992
15.4	0.7	14.1	...	28.7	-	New Dinar	1994
						Oceania	
4.7	6.4	5.3	...	25.1	-	American Samoa	1981
6.4	4.5	16.1	14.3	6.6	2.2	United States Dollar	1986
...	5.3	2.2	...	...	11.0	Australia‡	1986
...	7.2	1.9	...	...	14.0	Dollar	1990
							1992
10.2	-	-	-	-	-	Cook Islands	1981
3.5	0.6	...	...	9.0	8.1	New Zealand Dollar	1986
2.3	0.5	...	...	11.3	14.0		1991
0.2	2.0	0.7	...	2.3	1.9	Fiji‡	1981
3.9	-	2.2	1.0	0.5	8.6	Dollar	1989
...	...	...	...	14.8	11.7		1992
5.2	3.6	./.	...	3.5	-	French Polynesia‡	1984
0.8	./.	3.9	-	3.7	-	French Franc	1990
-	0.1	2.6	-	2.4	-		1993
5.1	5.9	12.4	...	22.4	-	Kiribati	1980
7.1	12.0	7.0	5.9	-	-	Australian Dollar	1985
5.6	6.9	6.1	5.9	2.7	-		1990
./.	./.	./.	...	42.3	-		1992
6.9	3.5	-	-	3.7	-	New Caledonia‡	1981
6.5	4.1	-	-	-	-	French Franc	1986
1.2	0.1	4.7	-	3.1	-		1990
0.8	0.1	6.7	-	3.5	-		1993

4.3 Public current expenditure by purpose
Dépenses publiques ordinaires selon leur destination
Gastos públicos ordinarios según su destino

Country Currency Pays Monnaie País Moneda	Year Année Año	Total Total Total (000 000)	Administration other than personnel Administration autre que personnel Administración excluyendo al personal (%)	Emoluments / Émoluments / Emolumentos			
				Administrative staff Personnel administratif Personal Administrativo (%)	Teaching staff Personnel enseignant Personal docente (%)	Other personnel Autre personnel Otro personal (%)	Total Total Total (%)
		(1)	(2)	(3)	(4)	(5)	(6)
New Zealand	1980	1 171	1.5	...	...	...	69.8
Dollar	1985	1 849	0.0	9.1	53.7	4.3	67.2
	1990	4 252	13.5	1.2	40.4	...	...
	1992	5 107	11.2	0.8	34.4	...	...
Niue	1980	1	20.1	——>	74.2	...	...
New Zealand Dollar	1986	1	2.0	14.8	53.6	4.6	73.0
Samoa							
Tala	1990	14	6.4	11.0	72.3	1.0	84.3
Solomon Islands	1979	3	5.7	——>	62.9	...	...
Solomon Isl. Dollar	1991	24	...	0.4	71.9	-	72.3
Tonga‡	1980	1.339	2.4	...	...	...	76.6
Pa'anga	1985	4	0.5	8.3	57.8	1.5	67.6
	1992	9	./.	...	...	...	70.7
Tuvalu							
Australian Dollar	1990	0.854	2.2	2.8	58.1	-	60.9
Vanuatu, Republic of‡	1990	831	./.	...	...	...	89.8
Vatu	1991	929	./.	...	...	...	90.4

General note / Note générale / Nota general:

E--> For countries which participated in the most recent UNESCO/OECD/Eurostat survey (see special remark on page 1 of this chapter), the previously used purpose breakdown is no longer applicable; therefore only percentages of emoluments are shown while the remaining purpose categories are left blank.

E--> Pour les pays qui ont participé au programme de la dernière enquête UNESCO/OCDE/Eurostat (voir note spéciale, page 1 de ce chapitre), la répartition par destination utilisée antérieurement n'est plus applicable; en conséquence, seuls les pourcentages des émoluments sont présentés et les colonnes des autre catégories restent vides.

ESP> Para los países que participaron en la última enquesta de UNESCO/OCDE/Eurostat (véase la nota correspondiente que figura en la página 1 de este capítulo), la clasificación de los gastos según su destino no se aplica más. Por consiguiente, se han presentado solamente los percentajes de los emolumentos, dejándose en blanco las otras categorías de esta clasificación.

AFRICA:
Algeria:
E--> For 1991 and 1992, capital expenditure is included and expenditure on third level is not included.

FR-> En 1991 et 1992, les dépenses en capital sont incluses et les dépenses relatives à l'enseignement du troisième degré ne sont pas incluses.

ESP> En 1991 y 1992, se incluyen los gastos de capital y no se incluyen los gastos relativos a la enseñanza de tercer grado.

Angola:
E--> For 1990, data refer to expenditure of the Ministry of Education only.

FR-> En 1990, les données se réfèrent aux dépenses du Ministère de l'Education seulement.

ESP> En 1990, los datos se refieren a los gastos del Ministerio de Educación solamente.

Burkina Faso:
E--> For 1980, expenditure on administration other than personnel (column 2) is included with total emolument (column 6).

FR-> En 1980, les dépenses d'administration autre que le personnel (colonne 2) sont incluses avec le total des émoluments (colonne 6).

ESP> En 1980, los gastos de administración excluyendo el personal (columna 2) quedan incluídos en el total de los emolumentos (columna 6).

Burundi:
E--> For 1985 and 1990 data refer to expenditure of the Ministry of Education only.

FR-> En 1985 et 1990, les données se réfèrent aux dépenses du Ministère de l'Education seulement.

ESP> En 1985 y 1990, los datos se refieren a los gastos del Ministerio de Educación solamente.

Cameroon:
E--> Expenditure of the Ministry of Education only.

FR-> Dépenses du Ministère de l'Education seulement.

ESP> Gastos del Ministerio de Educación solamente.

Central African Republic:
E--> For 1986 and 1990, expenditure of the Ministry of Education only.

FR-> En 1986 et 1990, dépenses du Ministère de l'Éducation seulement.

ESP> En 1986 y 1990, gastos del Ministerio de Educación solamente.

Comoros:
E--> Expenditure of the Ministry of Education only.

FR-> Dépenses du Ministère de l'Education seulement.

ESP> Gastos del Ministerio de Educación solamente.

Congo:
E--> For 1980, expenditure on administration other than personnel (column 2) is included with emoluments of teaching staff (column 4).

FR-> En 1980, les dépenses d'administration autre que le personnel (colonne 2) sont incluses avec les émoluments du personnel enseignant (colonne 4).

ESP> En 1980, los gastos de administraciòn excluyendo el personal (columna 2) quedan incluídos en los emolumentos del personal docente (columna 4).

Côte d'Ivoire:
E--> For 1994, expenditure on third level education is not included.

FR-> En 1994, les dépenses relatives à l'enseignement du troisième degré ne sont pas incluses.

ESP> En 1994, no se incluyen los gastos relativos a la enseñanza de tercer grado.

Djibouti:
E--> For 1985 data refer to expenditure of the Ministry of Education only. From 1985 to 1991, expenditure on administration other than personnel (column 2) is included with total emoluments (column 6).

FR-> En 1985, les données se réfèrent aux dépenses du Ministère de l'Education seulement. De 1985 à 1991, les dépenses d'administration autre que le personnel (colonne 2) sont incluses avec le total des émoluments (colonne 6).

ESP> En 1985, los datos se refieren a los gastos del Ministerio de Educación solamente. De 1985 a 1991 los gastos de

Public current expenditure by purpose **4.3**
Dépenses publiques ordinaires selon leur destination
Gastos públicos ordinarios según su destino

Teaching materials / Matériel pour l'enseignement / Material educativo (%)	Scholarships / Bourses d'études / Becas de estudios (%)	Welfare services / Services sociaux / Servicios sociales		Other expenditure / Autres dépenses / Otros gastos (%)	Subsidies not distributed / Subventions non réparties / Subvenciones sin distribución (%)	Country / Pays / País	Year / Année / Año
		Total / Total / Total (%)	Of which school meals and board / Dont repas scolaires et internat / De los cuales comedores escolares e internado (%)				
(7)	(8)	(9)	(10)	(11)	(12)		
5.6	3.7	2.0		4.5	12.9	New Zealand	1980
5.8	4.6	2.7	0.1	4.8	14.8	Dollar	1985
...	7.8	2.2	-	-	34.8		1990
	5.0	1.7	-	-	46.8		1992
2.8	...	2.6	...	0.3	-	Niue	1980
3.1	16.8	-	-	-	5.0	New Zealand Dollar	1986
						Samoa	
0.7	-	1.4	0.7	-	7.3	Tala	1990
8.8	11.1	9.3	...	2.2	-	Solomon Islands	1979
3.9	13.7	10.2	...	-	-	Solomon Isl. Dollar	1991
3.5	8.4	./.	...	9.1	-	Tonga‡	1980
2.4	6.4	1.7	1.7	7.1	14.4	Pa'anga	1985
0.4	4.7	0.3	0.3	16.8	7.0		1992
						Tuvalu	
5.2	-	28.1	20.5	3.6	-	Australian Dollar	1990
./.	./.	./.	...	10.2	-	Vanuatu, Republic of‡	1990
./.	./.	./.	...	9.6	-	Vatu	1991

administración excluyendo el personal (columna 2) quedan incluídos en el total de los emolumentos (columna 6).

Egypt:
E--> Expenditure on administration other than personnel (column 2) is included with total emoluments (column 6). Expenditure for Al-Azhar is not included.
FR-> Les dépenses d'administration autre que le personnel (colonne 2) sont incluses avec le total des émoluments (colonne 6). Les dépenses relatives à Al-Azhar ne sont pas incluses.
ESP> Los gastos de administración excluyendo el personal (columna 2) quedan incluídos en el total de los emolumentos (columna 6). No se incluyen los gastos relativos a Al-Azhar.

Ethiopia:
E--> Expenditure on third level education is not included.
FR-> Les dépenses relatives à l'enseignement du troisième degré ne sont pas incluses.
ESP> No se incluyen los gastos relativos a la enseñanza de tercer grado.

Gabon:
E--> For 1992, data refer to expenditure of the Ministry of Primary and Secondary Education only.
FR-> En 1992, les données se réfèrent aux dépenses du Ministère des enseignements primaire et secondaire seulement.
ESP> En 1992, los datos se refieren a los gastos del Ministerio de la enseñanza de primer et segundo grado solamente.

Gambia:
E--> For 1985, expenditure on administration other than personnel (column 2) is included with total emoluments (column 6).
FR-> En 1985, les dépenses d'administration autre que le personnel (colonne 2) sont incluses avec le total des émoluments (colonne 6).
ESP> En 1993, los gastos de administración excluyendo el personal (columna 2) quedan incluídos en el total de los emolumentos (columna 6).

Ghana:
E--> For 1990, expenditure on administration other than personnel (column 2) is included with total emoluments (column 6).
FR-> En 1990, les dépenses d'administration autre que le personnel (colonne 2) sont incluses avec le total des émoluments (colonne 6).
ESP> En 1990, los gastos de administración excluyendo el personal (columna 2) quedan incluídos en el total de los emolumentos (columna 6).

Madagascar:
E--> For 1993, data refer to expenditure of the Ministry of Primary and Secondary Education only.

FR-> En 1993, les données se réfèrent aux dépenses du Ministère des enseignements primaire et secondaire seulement.
ESP> En 1993, los datos se refieren a los gastos del Ministerio de las enseñanzas de primer et segundo grados solamente.

Malawi:
E--> For 1979, welfare services are included with teaching materials.
FR-> En 1979, les services sociaux sont inclus avec le matériel pour l'enseignement.
ESP> En 1979, los servicios sociales quedan incluídos en el material educativo.

Mauritania:
E--> For 1993, expenditure of the Ministry of Education only.
FR-> En 1993, les dépenses du Ministère de l'Education seulement.
ESP> En 1993, gastos del Ministerio de Educación solamente.

Mauritius:
E--> For 1980 and 1985, expenditure on administration other than personnel (column 2) is included with total emoluments (column 6).
FR-> En 1980 et 1985, les dépenses d'administration autre que le personnel (colonne 2) sont includes avec le total des émoluments (colonne 6).
ESP> En 1980 y 1985, los gastos de administración excluyendo el personal (columna 2) quedan incluídos en el total de los emolumentos (columna 6).

Morocco:
E--> Data refer to expenditure of Ministry of Education only. For 1990, third level is not included. For 1981, expenditure on administration other than personnel (column 2) is included with total emoluments (column 6).
FR-> Les données se réfèrent aux dépenses du Ministère de l'Education seulement. En 1990, les dépenses relatives à l'enseignement du troisième degré ne sont pas incluses. En 1981, les dépenses d'administration autre que le personnel (colonne 2) sont incluses avec le total des émoluments (colonne 6).
ESP> Los datos se refieren a los gastos del Ministerio de Educación solamente. En 1990, no se incluyen los gastos relativos a la enseñanza de tercer grado. En 1981, los datos de administración excluyendo el personal (columna 2) quedan incluídos en el total de los emolumentos (columna 6).

Mozambique:
E--> Data include foreign aid received for education.
FR-> Les données comprennent l'aide étrangère reçue pour l'éducation.
ESP> Los datos incluyen la ayuda extranjera recibida para educación.

Niger:

E--> For 1989 and 1991, data refer to expenditure of the Ministry of Education only and do not include expenditure on third level education. For 1980, expenditure on administration other than personnel (column 2) is included with emoluments of teaching staff (column 4).

FR-> En 1989 et 1991, les données se réfèrent aux dépenses du Ministère de l'Education seulement et ne comprennent pas les dépenses relatives à l'enseignement du troisième degré. En 1980, les dépenses d'administration autre que le personnel enseignant (colonne 2) sont incluses avec les émoluments du personnel enseignant (colonne 4).

ESP> En 1989 y 1991, los datos se refieren a los gastos del Ministerio de Educación solamente y no se incluyen los gastos relativos a la enseñanza de tercer grado. En 1980, los gastos de administración excluyendo el personal (columna 2) quedan incluídos en los emolumentos del personal docente (columna 4).

Sao Tome and Principe:

E--> Data include capital expenditure and expenditure on administration other than personnel (column 2) is included with total emoluments (column 6).

FR-> Les données comprennent les dépenses en capital et les dépenses d'administration autre que le personnel (colonne 2) sont incluses avec le total des émoluments (colonne 6).

ESP> Los gastos incluyen los gastos de capital y los gastos de administración excluyendo el personal (columna 2) quedan incluídos en el total de los emolumentos (columna 6).

Senegal:

E--> Expenditure on administration other than personnel (column 2) is included with total emoluments (column 6).

FR-> Les dépenses d'admnistration autre que le personnel (colonne 2) sont incluses avec le total des émoluments (colonne 6).

ESP> Los gastos de administración excluyendo el personal (columna 2) quedan incluídos en el total de los emolumentos (columna 6).

Somalia:

E--> Expenditure on third level education is not included. For 1980, expenditure on administration other than personnel (column 2) is included with total emoluments (column 6).

FR-> Les dépenses relatives à l'enseignement du troisième degré ne sont pas incluses. En 1980, les dépenses d'administration autre que le personnel (colonne 2) sont incluses avec le total des émoluments (colonne 6).

ESP> No se incluyen los gastos relativos a la enseñanza de tercer grado. En 1980, los gastos de administración excluyendo el personal (columna 2) quedan incluídos en el total de los emolumentos (columna 6).

South Africa:

E--> For 1990, data do not include expenditure for the following states: Transkei, Bophuthatswana, Venda and Ciskei (TBVC).

FR-> En 1990, les données ne comprennent pas les dépenses pour les etats suivants: Transkei, Bophuthatswana, Venda et Ciskei (TBVC).

ESP> En 1990, los datos no incluyen los gastos de los estados siguientes: Transkei, Bophuthatswana, Venda y Ciskei (TBVC).

Tunisia:

E--> For 1990, expenditure on third level education is not included and expenditure on administration other than personnel (column 2) is included with total emoluments column 6).

FR-> En 1990, les dépenses relatives à l'enseignement du troisième degré ne sont pas incluses et les dépenses d'administration autre que le personnel ((colonne 2) sont incluses avec le total des émoluments (colonne 6).

ESP> En 1990, no se incluyen los gastos relativos a la enseñanza de tercer grado y los gastos de administración excluyendo el personal (colomna 2) quedan incluídos en el total de los emolumentos (columna 6).

Zimbabwe:

E--> For 1991 and 1992, expenditure on third level education is not included. For 1992, capital expenditure is included. For 1986, expenditure on administration other than personnel (column 2) is included with total emoluments (column 6).

FR-> En 1991 et 1992, les dépenses relatives à l'enseignement du troisième degré ne sont pas incluses. En 1992 les dépenses en capital sont incluses. En 1986 les dépenses d'administration autre que le personnel (colonne 2) sont incluses avec le total des émoluments (colonne 6).

ESP> En 1991 y 1992, no se incluyen los gastos relativos a la enseñanza de tercer grado. En 1992, se incluyen los gastos de capital. En 1986, los gastos de administración excluyendo el personal (columna 2) quedan incluídos en el total de los emolumentos (columna 6).

AMERICA, NORTH:

Canada:

E--> Data refer to public and private expenditure on education.

FR-> Les données se réfèrent aux dépenses publiques et privées afférentes à l'enseignement.

ESP> Los datos se refieren a los gastos, públicos y privados destinados a la enseñanza.

Costa Rica:

E--> For 1994, expenditure of the Ministry of Education only. For 1991, and 1994, transfers to universities and other types of institutions are included with total emoluments (column 6).

FR-> En 1994, dépenses du Ministère de l'Education seulement. En 1991 et 1994, les transferts de fonds aux universités et à certain autres établissements sont inclus avec le total des émoluments (colonne 6).

ESP> En 1994, gastos del Ministerio de Educación solamente. En 1991 y 1994, las transferencias del gobierno a las universidades y otros establecimientos se incluyen en el total de los emolumentos (columna 6).

Dominican Republic:

E--> Data refer to expenditure of the Ministry of Education only.

FR-> Les données se réfèrent aux dépenses du Ministère de l'Education seulement.

ESP> Los datos se refieren a los gastos del Ministerio de Educacíon solamente.

Guatemala:

E--> For 1990 and 1993, data refer to the allocated budget of the Ministry of Education only and include capital expenditure.

FR-> En 1990 et 1993, les données se réfèrent au budget alloué du Ministère de l'Education seulement et comprennent les dépenses en capital.

ESP> En 1990 y 1993, los datos se refieren al presupuesto programado del Ministerio de Educación solamente y incluyen los gastos de capital.

Honduras:

E--> For 1989, capital expenditure is included.

FR-> En 1989, les dépenses en capital sont incluses.

ESP> En 1989, se incluyen los gastos de capital.

Jamaica:

E--> Except for 1985, data refer to expenditure of the Ministry of Education only.

FR-> Sauf pour 1985, les données se réfèrent aux dépenses du Ministère de l'Education seulement.

ESP> Salvo para 1985, los datos se refieren a los gastos del Ministerio de Educación solamente.

Mexico:

E--> Expenditure of the Ministry of Education only.

FR-> Dépenses du Ministère de l'Education seulement.

ESP> Gastos del Ministerio de Educación solamente.

Nicaragua:

E--> For 1985, data refer to expenditure of the Ministry of Education only. For 1992, data refer to expenditure of the Ministry of Primary and Secondary Education only and are expressed in gold Cordobas.

FR-> En 1985, les données se réfèrent aux dépenses du Ministère de l'Education seulement. En 1992, les données se réfèrent aux dépenses du Ministère des enseignements primaire et secondaire seulement et sont exprimées en Cordobas or.

ESP> En 1985, los datos se refieren a los gastos del Ministerio de Educación solamente. En 1992, los datos se refieren a los gastos del Ministerio de la enseñanza de primer et segundo grado solamente y están expresados en Córdobas oro.

St. Kitts and Nevis:

E--> Expenditure on third level education is not included.

FR-> Les dépenses relatives à l'enseignement du troisième degré ne sont pas incluses.

ESP> No se incluyen los gastos relativos a la enseñanza de tercer grado.

St. Pierre and Miquelon:

E--> For 1991 and 1993, data refer to expenditure of the Ministry of Education only.

FR-> En 1991 et 1993, les données se réfèrent aux dépenses du Ministère de l'Education seulement.

ESP> En 1991 y 1993, los datos se refieren a los gastos del Ministerio de Educación solamente.

St.Vincent and the Grenadines:

E--> For 1990, expenditure on third level education is not included.

FR-> En 1990, les dépenses relatives à l'enseignement du troisième degré ne sont pas incluses.

ESP> En 1990, no se incluyen los gastos relativos a la enseñanza de tercer grado.

AMERICA, SOUTH:

Argentina:

E--> For 1990, data refer to expenditure of the Ministry of Education only. For 1980, expenditure on administration other than personnel (column 2) is included with total emoluments (column 6).

Public current expenditure by purpose **4.3**
Dépenses publiques ordinaires selon leur destination
Gastos públicos ordinarios según su destino

FR–> En 1990, les données se réfèrent aux dépenses du Ministère de l'Education seulement. En 1980, les dépenses d'administration autre que le personnel (colonne 2) sont incluses avec le total des émoluments (colonne 6).

ESP> En 1990, los datos se refieren a los gastos del Ministerio de Educación solamente. En 1980, los gastos de administración excluyendo el personal (columna 2) quedan incluídos en el total de los emolumentos (columna 6).

Bolivia:

E––> For 1989, expenditure on universities is not included. For 1994, capital expenditure is included.

FR–> En 1989, les dépenses des universités ne sont pas incluses. En 1994, les dépenses en capital sont incluses.

ESP> En 1989, no se incluyen los gastos de las universidades. En 1994, se incluyen los gastos de capital.

Colombia:

E––> Expenditure of the Ministry of Education only.

FR–> Dépenses du Ministère de l'Education seulement.

ESP> Gastos del Ministerio de Educación solamente.

Ecuador:

E––> For 1989, expenditure on administration other than personnel (column 2) is included with total emoluments (column 6).

FR–> En 1989, les dépenses d'administration autre que le personnel (colonne 2) sont incluses avec le total des émoluments (colonne 6).

ESP> En 1989, los gastos de administración excluyendo el personal (columna 2) quedan incluídos en el total de los emolumentos (columna 6).

Peru:

E––> Transfers to universities and to other types of institutions as well as some types of pensions and staff benefits are included in column 11.

FR–> Les transferts de fonds aux universités et à certains autres établissements ainsi que différents types de pensions et indemnités du personnel sont inclus dans la colonne 11.

ESP> Las transferencias a las universidades y otros establecimientos así como diferentes tipos de pensiones y indemnizaciones del personal quedan incluídos en la columna 11.

Suriname:

E––> For 1980, data do not include public subsidies to private education.

FR–> En 1980, les données ne comprennent pas les subventions publiques à l'enseignement privé.

ESP> En 1980, los datos no comprenden las subvenciones públicas a la enseñanza privada.

ASIA:

Bahrain:

E––> For 1991 and 1993, expenditure on third level is not included.

FR–> En 1991 et 1993, les dépenses relatives à l'enseignement du troisième degré ne sont pas incluses.

ESP> En 1991 y 1993, no se incluyen los gastos relativos a la enseñanza de tercer grado.

Bangladesh:

E––> Expenditure of the Ministry of Education only.

FR–> Dépenses du Mnistère de l'Education only.

ESP> Gastos del Ministerio de Educación solamente.

Brunei Darussalam:

E––> For 1984, expenditure on administration other than personnel (column 2) is included with total emoluments (column 6). For 1993, data refer to Ministry of Education only and do not include expenditure on universities.

FR–> En 1984, les dépenses d'administration autre que le personnel (colonne 2) sont incluses avec le total des émoluments (colonne 6). En 1993, les données se réfèrent aux dépenses du Ministère de l'Education seulement et ne comprennent pas les universités.

ESP> En 1984, los gastos de administración excluyendo el personal (columna 2) quedan incluídos en el total de los emolumentos (columna 6). En 1993, los datos se refieren a los gastos del Ministerio de Educación solamente y no comprenden las universidades.

China:

E––> Expenditure on specialized second level and technical/vocational schools is not included.

FR–> Les dépenses des écoles spécialisées de l'enseignement du second degré et de l'enseignement technique/professionnel ne sont pas incluses.

ESP> Los gastos relativos a las escuelas especializadas de enseñanza de segundo grado y de enseñanza técnica/profesional no están incluídos.

Cyprus:

E––> Expenditure of the Office of Greek Education only.

FR–> Dépenses du bureau grec de l'éducation seulement.

ESP> Gastos del servicio griego de educación solamente.

Israel:

E––> For 1990 and 1992, data include expenditure from private sources such as donations, fees etc.

FR–> En 1990 et 1992, les données comprennent les dépenses provenant de sources privées, telles que donations, les frais de scolarité etc.

ESP> En 1990 y 1992, los datos incluyen los gastos provenientes de fuentes privadas como donaciones, gastos de inscripción etc.

Japan:

E––> For 1980, data do not include public subsidies to private education. For 1985 and 1988, data refer to public and private expenditure on education.

FR–> En 1980, les données ne comprennent pas les subventions publiques afférentes à l'enseignement privé. En 1985 et 1988, les données se réfèrent aux dépenses publiques et privées afférentes à l'enseignement.

ESP> En 1980, los datos no incluyen las subvenciones públicas a la enseñanza privada. En 1985 y 1988, los datos se refieren a los gastos públicos y privados destinados a la enseñanza.

Jordan:

E––> For 1990 and 1993, expenditure on third level education is not included.

FR–> En 1990 et 1993, les dépenses relatives à l'enseignement du troisième degré ne sont pas incluses.

ESP> En 1990 y 1993, no se incluyen los gastos relativos a la enseñanza de tercer grado.

Kuwait:

E––> For 1980, expenditure on administration other than personnel (column 2) is included with total emoluments (column 6).

FR–> En 1980, les dépenses d'administration autre que le personnel (colonne 2) sont incluses avec le total des émoluments (colonne 6).

ESP> En 1980, los gastos de administración excluyendo el personal (columna 2) quedan incluídos en el total de los emolumentos (columna 6).

Kyrgyzstan:

E––> For 1994, teaching materials are included with welfare services.

FR–> En 1994, les dépenses en matériel pour l'enseignement sont incluses avec les services sociaux.

ESP> En 1994, los gastos de material educativo quedan incluídos en los servicios sociales.

Lao People's Democratic Republic:

E––> Expenditure on administration other than personnel (column 2) is included with total emoluments (column 6).

FR–> Les dépenses d'administration autre que le personnel (colonne 2) sont incluses avec le total des émoluments (colonne 6).

ESP> Los gastos de administración excluyendo el personal (columna 2) quedan incluídos en el total de los emolumentos (columna 6).

Malaysia:

E––> For 1991 and 1993, data refer to expenditure of the Ministry of Education only. For 1991, administration other than personnel(column 2) is included with total emoluments (column 6).

FR–> En 1991 et 1993, les données se réfèrent aux dépenses du Ministère de l'Education seulement. En 1991, l'administration autre que le personnel (colonne 2) est incluse avec le total des émoluments (colonne 6).

ESP> En 1991 y 1993, los datos se refieren a los gastos del Ministerio de Educación solamente. En 1991, la administración otra que la del personal (columna 2) queda incluída en el total de los emolumentos (columna 6).

Myanmar:

E––> Expenditure of the Ministry of Education only.

FR–> Dépenses du Ministère de l'Education seulement.

ESP> Gastos del Ministerio de Educación solamente.

Nepal:

E––> Data refer to *regular* and *development* expenditure.

FR–> Les données se réfèrent aux dépenses *ordinaires* et de *développement*.

ESP> Los datos se refieren a los gastos *ordinarios* y de *desarrollo*.

Oman:

E––> For 1994, expenditure on universities is not included.

FR–> En 1994, les dépenses des universités ne sont pas incluses.

ESP> En 1994, no se incluyen los gastos de las universidades.

Philippines:

E––> Except for 1985, expenditure on administration other than peronnel (column 2) is included with total emoluments (column 6). For 1990, figures on current expenditure refer to the allocated budget while the figures in Table 4.1 refer to actual expenditure.

FR–> Sauf en 1985, les dépenses d'administration autre que le personnel (colonne 2) sont incluses avec le total des émoluments (colonne 6). En 1990, les chiffres correspondant aux dépenses

4.3 Public current expenditure by purpose
Dépenses publiques ordinaires selon leur destination
Gastos públicos ordinarios según su destino

courantes se réfèrent au budget alloué alors que les chiffres présentés dans le tableau 4.1 se réfèrent aux dépenses effectives.

ESP> Salvo para 1985, los gastos de administración excluyendo el personal (columna 2) quedan incluídos en el total de los emolumentos (column 6). En 1990, las cifras relativas a los gastos ordinarios se refieren al presupuesto asignado, mientras que las cifras presentadas en el cuadro 4.1 se refieren a los gastos efectivos.

Qatar:
E--> Expenditure on administration other than personnel (column 2) is included with total emoluments (column 6).
FR-> Les dépenses d'administration autre que le personnel (colonne 2) sont incluses avec le total des émoluments (colonne 6).
ESP> Los gastos de administración excluyendo el personal (columna 2) quedan incluídos en el total de los emolumentos (column 6).

Saudi Arabia:
E--> Expenditure on administration other than personnel (column 2) is included with total emoluments (column 6).
FR-> Les dépenses d'administration autre que le personnel (colonne 2) sont incluses avec le total des émoluments (colonne 6).
ESP> Los gastos de administración excluyendo el personal (columna 2) quedan incluídos en el total de los emolumentos (columna 6).

Syrian Arab Republic:
E--> Expenditure on third level education is not included.
FR-> Les dépenses relatives à l'enseignement du troisième degré ne sont pas incluses.
ESP> No se incluyen los gastos relativos a la enseñanza de tercer grado.

Turkey:
E--> For 1990, expenditure on third level education is not included. For 1980, 1985 and 1994, expenditure on administration other than personnel (column 2) is included with total emoluments (column 6).
FR-> En 1990, les dépenses relatives à l'enseignement du troisième degré ne sont pas incluses. En 1980, 1985 et 1994, les dépenses d'administration autre que le personnel (colonne 2) sont incluses avec le total des émoluments (colonne 6).
ESP> En 1990, no se incluyen los gastos relativos a la enseñanza de tercer grado. En 1980, 1985 y 1994, los gastos de administración excluyendo el personal (columna 2) quedan incluídos en el total de los emolumentos (columna 6).

United Arab Emirates:
E--> For 1994, expenditure on administration other than personnel (column 2) is included with total emoluments (column 6).
FR-> En 1994, les dépenses d'administration autre que le personnel (colonne 2) sont incluses avec le total des émoluments (colonne 6).
ESP> En 1994, los gastos de administración excluyendo el personal (columna 2) quedan incluídos en el total de los emolumentos (columna 6).

Yemen: Former Democratic Yemen:
E--> Expenditure on third level education is not included.
FR-> Les dépenses relatives à l'enseignement du troisième degré ne sont pas incluses.
ESP> No se incluyen los gastos relativos a la enseñanza de tercer grado.

EUROPE:
Austria:
E--> For 1980, data on emoluments of other personnel (column 5) are included with administration other than personnel (column 2); for 1985 and 1990, these data are included with emoluments of administrative staff (column 3).
FR-> En 1980, les données sur les émoluments d'autre personnel (colonne 5) sont incluses avec celles d'administration autre que personnel(colonne 2); en 1985 et 1990, ces données sont incluses avec celles des émoluments du personnel administratif (colonne 3).
ESP> En 1980, los datos sobre los emolumentos de otro personal (columna 5) quedan incluídos con los de la administración excluyendo el personal(columna 2); en 1985 y 1990 estos datos quedan incluídos en los de los emolumentos del personal administrativo (column 3).

Belgium:
E--> From 1980 to 1990, expenditure of the Ministry of Education only.
FR-> De 1980 à 1990, dépenses du Ministère de l'Education seulement.
ESP> De 1980 a 1990, gastos del Ministerio de Educación solamente.

Finland:
E--> From 1980 to 1990, data refer to public and private expenditure on education.
FR-> De 1980 à 1990, les données se réfèrent aux dépenses publiques et privées afférentes à l'enseignement.

ESP> De 1980 a 1990, los datos se refieren a los gastos públicos y privados destinados a la enseñanza.

France:
E--> Metropolitan France.
FR-> France métropolitaine.
ESP> Francia metropolitana.

Federal Republic of Germany:
E--> For 1991, data include expenditure for East Berlin.
FR-> En 1991, les données comprennent les dépenses relatives à Berlin Est.
ESP> En 1991, los datos incluyen los gastos relativos a Berlin Este.

Hungary:
E--> For 1985, expenditure on administration other than personnel (column 2) is included with total emoluments (column 6).
FR-> En 1985, les dépenses d'administration autre que le personnel (colonne 2) sont incluses avec le total des émoluments (colonne 6).
ESP> En 1985, los gastos de administracíon excluyendo el personal (columna 2) quedan incluídos en el total de los emolumentos (columna 6).

Italy:
E--> For 1990, data refer to expenditure of the central government only and expenditure on third level education is not included.
FR-> En 1990, les données se réfèrent aux dépenses du gouvernement central seulement et les dépenses relatives à l'enseignement du troisième degré ne sont pas incluses.
ESP> En 1990, los datos se refieren a los gastos del gobierno central solamente y no se incluyen los gastos relativos a la enseñanza de tercer grado.

Luxembourg:
E--> For 1980, expenditure of the Central Government only.
FR-> En 1980, dépenses du gouvernement central seulement.
ESP> En 1980, gastos del gobierno central solamente.

Malta:
E--> For 1980, expenditure on administration other than personnel (column 2) is included with total emoluments (column 6).
FR-> En 1980, les dépenses d'administration autre que le personnel (colonne 2) sont incluses avec le total des émoluments (colonne 6).
ESP> En 1980, los gastos de administración excluyendo el personal (columna 2) quedan incluídos en el total de los emolumentos (columna 6).

Monaco:
E--> For 1992, data do not include public subsidies to private education.
FR-> En 1992, les données ne comprennent par les subventions publiques à l'enseignement privé.
ESP> En 1992, los datos no comprenden las subvenciones públicas a la enseñanza privada.

Netherlands:
E--> From 1980 to 1990, data refer to public and private expenditure on education.
FR-> De 1980 à 1990, les données se réfèrent aux dépenses publiques et privées afférentes à l'enseignement.
ESP> De 1980 a 1990, los datos se refieren a los gastos públicos y privados destinados a la enseñanza.

Portugal:
E--> For 1990, data refer to the Ministry of Education only.
FR-> En 1990, les données se réfèrent aux dépenses du Ministère de l'Education seulement.
ESP> En 1990, los datos se refieren a los gastos del Ministerio de Educación solamente.

Romania:
E--> Expenditure on administration other than personnel (column 2) is included with total emoluments (column 6).
FR-> Les dépenses d'administration autre que le personnel (colonne 2) sont incluses avec le total des émoluments (colonne 6).
ESP> Los gastos de administración excluyendo el personal (columna 2) quedan incluídos en el total de los emolumentos (columna 6).

Sweden:
E--> For 1980, expenditure on administration other than personnel (column 2) is included with total emoluments (column 6).
FR-> En 1980, les dépenses d'administration autre que le personnel (colonne 2) sont incluses avec le total des émoluments (colonne 6).
ESP> En 1980, los gastos de administración excluyendo el personal (columna 2) quedan incluídos en el total de los emolumentos (columna 6).

OCEANIA:
Australia:
E--> For 1986 and 1990, expenditure on administration other than personnel (column 2) is included with total emoluments (column 6).

Public current expenditure by purpose **4.3**
Dépenses publiques ordinaires selon leur destination
Gastos públicos ordinarios según su destino

FR-> En 1986 et 1990, les dépenses d'administration autre que le personnel (colonne 2) sont incluses avec le total des émoluments (colonne 6).

ESP> En 1986 y 1990, los gastos de administración excluyendo el personal (columna 2) quedan incluídos en el total de los emolumentos (columna 6).

Fiji:

E--> For 1992, data refer to expenditure of the Ministry of Education only.

FR-> En 1992, les données se réfèrent aux dépenses du Ministère de l'Education seulement.

ESP> En 1992, los datos se refieren a los gastos del Ministerio de Educación solamente.

French Polynesia:

E--> For 1990 and 1993, data refer to expenditure of the Ministry of Education only.

FR-> En 1990 et 1993, les données se réfèrent aux dépenses du Ministère de l'Education seulement.

ESP> En 1990 y 1993, los datos se refieren a los gastos del Ministerio de Educación solamente.

New Caledonia:

E--> For 1990 and 1993, data refer to expenditure of the Ministry of Education only.

FR-> En 1990 et 1993, les données se réfèrent aux dépenses du Ministère de l'Education seulement.

ESP> En 1990 y 1993, los datos se refieren a los gastos del Ministerio de Educación solamente.

Tonga:

E--> For 1992, capital expenditure is included and expenditure on administration other than personnel (column 2) is included with total emoluments (column 6).

FR-> En 1992, les dépenses en capital sont incluses et les dépenses d'administration autre que le personnel (colonne 2) sont incluses avec le total des émoluments (colonne 6).

ESP> En 1992, se incluyen los gastos de capital y los gastos de administración excluyendo el personal (columna 2) quedan incluídos en el total de los emolumentos (columna 6).

Vanuatu, Republic of:

E--> Expenditure on administration other than personnel (column 2) is included with total emoluments (column 6).

FR-> Les dépenses d'administration autre que le personnel (colonne 2) sont incluses avec le total des émoluments (colonne 6).

ESP> Los gastos de administración excluyendo el personal (columna 2) quedan incluídos en el total de los emolumentos (columna 6).

4.4 Public current expenditure by level and purpose
Dépenses publiques ordinaires par degré d'enseignement et destination
Gastos públicos ordinarios por grado de enseñanza y destino

4.4 Public current expenditure on education: distribution by level of education and purpose

Dépenses publiques ordinaires afférentes à l'enseignement: répartition par degré d'enseignement et selon leur destination

Gastos públicos ordinarios destinados a la educación: distribución por grado de enseñanza y según su destino

Total administration	= Total des dépenses d'administration / Total de gastos de administración
Admin. expenditure (excl. staff)	= Dépenses admin. (personnel exclu) / Gastos admin. (excl. personal)
Admin. emoluments	= Émoluments personnel admin. / Emolumentos personal admin.
Teachers' emoluments	= Émoluments du personnel enseignant / Emolumentos del personal docente
Other emoluments	= Autres émoluments / Otros emolumentos
Total emoluments	= Total des émoluments / Total de emolumentos
Teaching materials	= Matériel pour l'enseignement / Material educativo
Scholarships	= Bourses d'études / Becas de estudios
Welfare services	= Services sociaux / Servicios sociales
Other expenditure	= Autres dépenses / Otros gastos
Subsidies (not distributed)	= Subventions (non distribuées) / Subvenciones (sin distribución)

# Figures for countries shown with this symbol are in thousands.	# Les chiffres pour les pays accompagnés de ce symbole sont exprimés en milliers.	# Las cifras de los países donde figura este símbolo se expresan en millares.

Country Currency Pays Monnaie País Moneda	Year Année Año	Purpose Destination Destino	Total current expenditure Total des dépenses ordinaires Total de gastos ordinarios (000 000)	Pre- primary Pré- primaire Pre- primaria (000 000)	First level Premier degré Primer grado (000 000)	Second level Second degré Segundo grado (000 000)	Third level Troisième degré Tercer grado (000 000)	Other types and not distributed Autres types et non réparties Otros tipos y sin dis- tribución (000 000)
Africa								
Algeria‡ Dinar	1992	Total current exp. Admin. excl. staff Admin. emoluments Teachers emoluments Other emoluments Teaching materials Scholarships Welfare services Other current exp.	53 516 3 976 9 667 39 147 31 176 213 295 11	- - - - - - - - -	17 798 751 - 16 764 - - 3 280 -	33 373 2 660 8 793 21 754 - 1 165 - -	- - - - - - - - -	2 345 565 874 629 31 175 45 15 11
Angola‡ Kwansa	1990	Total current exp. Total emoluments Teaching materials Scholarships Welfare services Other current exp.	10 856 9 365 80 139 349 923	<—— <—— <—— <—— <—— <——	10 454 9 133 70 105 318 828	——> ——> ——> ——> ——> ——>	402 232 10 34 31 95	- - - - - -
Botswana # Pula	1991	Total current exp. Admin. excl. staff Admin. emoluments Teachers emoluments Other emoluments Teaching materials Scholarships Welfare services Other current exp. Subsidies not distr.	426 387 18 067 16 636 184 494 21 349 17 073 20 048 42 862 49 594 56 264	- - - - - - - - - -	132 500 - 1 810 103 820 695 3 187 - 11 412 11 576 -	207 956 - 6 653 79 120 18 426 13 845 20 048 29 986 35 883 3 995	52 200 - - - - - - - - 52 200	33 731 18 067 8 173 1 554 2 228 41 1 464 2 135 69

Public current expenditure by level and purpose 4.4
Dépenses publiques ordinaires par degré d'enseignement et destination
Gastos públicos ordinarios por grado de enseñanza y destino

Country / Currency — Pays / Monnaie — País / Moneda	Year — Année — Año	Purpose — Destination — Destino	Total current expenditure / Total des dépenses ordinaires / Total de gastos ordinarios (000 000)	Pre-primary / Pré-primaire / Pre-primaria (000 000)	First level / Premier degré / Primer grado (000 000)	Second level / Second degré / Segundo grado (000 000)	Third level / Troisième degré / Tercer grado (000 000)	Other types and not distributed / Autres types et non réparties / Otros tipos y sin distribución (000 000)
Burkina Faso Franc C.F.A.	1989	Total current exp.	18 727	-	7 813	4 832	6 013	69
		Admin. excl. staff	620	-	116	154	350	-
		Admin. emoluments	1 079	-	482	528	-	69
		Teachers emoluments	10 116	-	7 016	2 432	668	-
		Scholarships	5 439	-	-	1 240	4 199	-
		Welfare services	1 154	-	199	342	613	-
		Subsidies not distr.	319	-	-	136	183	-
Burundi Franc	1992	Total current exp.	8 023	-	3 568	2 263	1 970	222
		Admin. excl. staff	140	-	-	7	10	123
		Admin. emoluments	835	-	232	315	195	93
		Teachers emoluments	4 499	-	3 196	883	420	-
		Other emoluments	552	-	127	334	85	6
		Teaching materials	56	-	-	56	-	-
		Scholarships	720	-	-	-	720	-
		Welfare services	888	-	-	660	228	-
		Other current exp.	163	-	13	8	142	-
		Subsidies not distr.	170	-	-	-	170	-
Central African Republic‡ Franc C.F.A.	1990	Total current exp.	8 527	<———	4 491	1 243	1 833	960
		Admin. excl. staff	108	-	-	-	-	108
		Admin. emoluments	376	<———	37	23	-	316
		Teachers emoluments	5 809	<———	4 373	1 089	347	-
		Other emoluments	600	<———	6	5	53	536
		Teaching materials	115	<———	75	40	-	-
		Scholarships	1 422	-	-	81	1 341	-
		Welfare services	97	-	-	5	92	-
Chad Franc C.F.A.	1994	Total current exp.	10 691	338	4 159	2 318	813	3 063
		Admin. excl. staff	788	5	-	9	-	774
		Admin. emoluments	926	-	-	-	-	926
		Teachers emoluments	6 920	309	4 081	2 183	290	57
		Other emoluments	164	24	38	64	6	32
		Teaching materials	102	-	40	20	-	42
		Scholarships	1 000	-	-	42	-	958
		Other current exp.	274	-	-	-	-	274
		Subsidies not distr.	517	-	-	-	517	-
Comoros‡ Franc C.F.A	1993	Total current exp.	2 938	-	1 200	963	351	424
		Admin. excl. staff	149	-	-	-	-	149
		Admin. emoluments	177	-	-	-	-	177
		Teachers emoluments	2 154	-	1 186	856	28	84
		Scholarships	216	-	-	-	216	-
		Other current exp.	242	-	14	107	107	14
Côte d'Ivoire‡ Franc C.F.A.	1994	Total current exp.	168 923	-	102 426	65 488	-	1 009
		Total emoluments	146 959	-	95 335	51 488	-	136
		Other current exp.	9 337	-	3 035	5 429	-	873
		Subsidies not distr.	12 627	-	4 056	8 571	-	-
Djibouti‡ Franc	1991	Total current exp.	2 872	-	1 534	605	400	333
		Total emoluments	2 205	-	1 409	463	-	333
		Teaching materials	187	-	125	62	-	-
		Scholarships	480	-	-	80	400	-
Egypt‡ Pound	1992	Total current exp.	4 683	<———	<———	2 973	1 710	-
		Total emoluments	3 831	<———	<———	2 520	1 311	-
		Teaching materials	39	<———	<———	30	9	-
		Other current exp.	813	<———	<———	423	390	-
Ethiopia‡# Birr	1990	Total current exp.	434 300	100	266 500	138 800	-	28 900
		Admin. excl. staff	26 000	-	2 900	7 000	-	16 100
		Admin. emoluments	12 900	100	-	-	-	12 800
		Teachers emoluments	391 500	-	261 600	129 900	-	-
		Teaching materials	3 900	-	2 000	1 900	-	-
Gabon‡ Franc C.F.A	1992	Total current exp.	34 407	-	14 955	19 452	-	-
		Admin. excl. staff	1 578	-	64	1 514	-	-
		Teachers emoluments	30 500	-	14 833	15 667	-	-
		Teaching materials	178	-	58	120	-	-
		Scholarships	1 100	-	-	1 100	-	-
		Welfare services	1 051	-	-	1 051	-	-

Public current expenditure by level and purpose
Dépenses publiques ordinaires par degré d'enseignement et destination
Gastos públicos ordinarios por grado de enseñanza y destino

Country Currency / Pays Monnaie / País Moneda	Year Année Año	Purpose / Destination / Destino	Total current expenditure / Total des dépenses ordinaires / Total de gastos ordinarios (000 000)	Pre-primary / Pré-primaire / Pre-primaria (000 000)	First level / Premier degré / Primer grado (000 000)	Second level / Second degré / Segundo grado (000 000)	Third level / Troisième degré / Tercer grado (000 000)	Other types and not distributed / Autres types et non réparties / Otros tipos y sin distribución (000 000)
Gambia‡# Dalasi	1991	Total current exp.	75 083	-	32 029	16 096	6 857	20 101
		Admin. excl. staff	319	-	27	18	242	32
		Admin. emoluments	500	-			247	253
		Teachers emoluments	28 878	-	23 375	5 230	181	92
		Other emoluments	1 124	-	865	186	52	21
		Teaching materials	2 952	-	2 450	435	20	47
		Scholarships	1 925	-	-	260	1 665	-
		Welfare services	2 034	-	-	-	-	2 034
		Other current exp.	19 114	-	1 070	177	245	17 622
		Subsidies not distr.	18 237	-	4 242	9 790	4 205	
Ghana‡ Cedi	1990	Total current exp.	53 664	-	15 650	18 408	5 905	13 701
		Total emoluments	33 665	-	15 561	17 414	537	153
		Other current exp.	14 308	-	89	994	83	13 142
		Subsidies not distr.	5 691	-	-	-	5 285	406
Guinea Syli	1993	Total current exp.	65 434	-	22 909	19 067	12 043	11 415
		Admin. excl. staff	4 152	-	-	-	-	4 152
		Admin. emoluments	7 263	-	-	-	-	7 263
		Teachers emoluments	36 407	-	15 702	15 955	4 750	
		Other current exp.	17 612	-	7 207	3 112	7 293	-
Madagascar‡ Franc	1993	Total current exp.	104 064	-	37 568	47 423		19 073
		Admin. excl. staff	9 585	-	-	-		9 585
		Admin. emoluments	22 335	-	3 448	9 399		9 488
		Teachers emoluments	64 402	-	29 244	35 138		
		Scholarships	526	-	-	526		
		Other current exp.	7 216	-	4 876	2 340		-
Malawi # Kwacha	1989	Total current exp.	106 432	-	51 210	14 145	23 448	17 629
		Admin. excl. staff	6 524	-	-	-	-	6 524
		Admin. emoluments	3 065	-	-	-	-	3 065
		Teachers emoluments	56 193	-	45 993	7 010	1 692	1 498
		Other current exp.	15 769	-	4 955	5 394	3 548	1 872
		Subsidies not distr.	24 881	-	262	1 741	18 208	4 670
Mauritania‡ Ouguiya	1993	Total current exp.	4 192	-	1 551	1 645	837	159
		Admin. excl. staff	131	-	2	15	48	66
		Admin. emoluments	716	-	68	493	70	85
		Teachers emoluments	2 182	-	1 241	839	102	
		Other emoluments	312	-	202	64	38	8
		Teaching materials	247	-	38	79	130	-
		Welfare services	604	-	-	155	449	
Mauritius # Rupee	1990	Total current exp.	1 286 900	1 800	482 800	468 300	213 700	120 300
		Admin. excl. staff	163 000	-	9 600	10 700	130 700	12 000
		Admin. emoluments	153 700	-	65 000	23 100	13 200	52 400
		Teachers emoluments	692 800	-	352 700	296 400	36 700	7 000
		Other emoluments	186 900	-	54 100	98 600	28 100	6 100
		Teaching materials	20 700	-	-	20 100	600	
		Scholarships	5 100	-	-	-	-	5 100
		Welfare services	11 000	-	-	5 100	-	5 900
		Other current exp.	29 400	-	1 400	14 300	4 400	9 300
		Subsidies not distr.	24 300	1 800	-	-	-	22 500
Morocco‡ Dirham	1991	Total current exp.	10 755	-	3 540	4 859	1 748	608
		Total emoluments	9 473	-	3 442	4 701	938	392
		Scholarships	817	-	-	93	676	48
		Other current exp.	465	-	98	65	134	168
Mozambique‡ Meticai	1990	Total current exp.	46 064	-	22 943	7 227	4 555	11 339
		Total emoluments	34 299	-	22 321	5 464	2 138	4 376
		Other current exp.	11 765	-	622	1 763	2 417	6 963
Niger‡ Franc C.F.A.	1989	Total current exp.	15 545	-	7 546	4 017	-	3 982
		Admin. excl. staff	480	-	-	-	-	480
		Admin. emoluments	2 854	-	-	-	-	2 854
		Teachers emoluments	8 797	-	7 284	1 513	-	
		Other emoluments	612	-	-	-	-	612
		Teaching materials	832	-	-	832	-	
		Scholarships	447	-	-	447	-	
		Welfare services	437	-	122	315	-	
		Other current exp.	1 086	-	140	910	-	36
Reunion French Franc	1993	Total current exp.	5 180	665	1 213	2 951	88	263
		Admin. excl. staff	16	-	-	-	-	16
		Admin. emoluments	437	88	142	195	4	8
		Teachers emoluments	4 466	561	1 071	2 602	84	148
		Teaching materials	17	-	-	17	-	-
		Scholarships	137	-	-	137	-	-
		Welfare services	29	-	-	-	-	29
		Other current exp.	78	16	-	-	-	62

Public current expenditure by level and purpose 4.4
Dépenses publiques ordinaires par degré d'enseignement et destination
Gastos públicos ordinarios por grado de enseñanza y destino

Country Currency / Pays Monnaie / País Moneda	Year Année Año	Purpose Destination Destino	Total current expenditure / Total des dépenses ordinaires / Total de gastos ordinarios (000 000)	Pre-primary / Pré-primaire / Pre-primaria (000 000)	First level / Premier degré / Primer grado (000 000)	Second level / Second degré / Segundo grado (000 000)	Third level / Troisième degré / Tercer grado (000 000)	Other types and not distributed / Autres types et non réparties / Otros tipos y sin distribución (000 000)
Rwanda‡ Franc	1989	Total current exp.	6 793	-	4 600	956	1 103	134
		Admin. excl. staff	323	-	17	18	257	31
		Admin. emoluments	201	-	9	76	13	103
		Teachers emoluments	5 481	-	4 456	659	366	-
		Other emoluments	21	-	21	-	-	-
		Teaching materials	118	-	91	19	8	-
		Scholarships	389	-	-	-	389	-
		Welfare services	243	-	-	173	70	-
		Other current exp.	17	-	6	11	-	-
Seychelles # Rupee	1992	Total current exp.	156 458	<——	<——	103 565	16 801	36 092
		Admin. excl. staff	26 043	-	-	-	-	26 043
		Total emoluments	84 280	<——	<——	78 488	393	5 399
		Teaching materials	7 627	<——	<——	4 090	-	3 537
		Scholarships	16 376	-	-	-	16 376	-
		Welfare services	12 058	<——	<——	11 863	-	195
		Other current exp.	10 074	<——	<——	9 124	32	918
South Africa‡ Rand	1993	Total current exp.	23 849	<——	19 417	——>	3 578	854
		Total emoluments	20 364	<——	17 243	——>	2 438	683
		Teaching materials	1 046	<——	1 035	——>	4	7
		Other current exp.	2 439	<——	1 139	——>	1 136	164
Swaziland # Lilangeni	1994	Total current exp.	240 643	209	80 453	63 672	71 211	25 098
		Admin. excl. staff	6 192	11	70	215	630	5 266
		Admin. emoluments	27 600	155	8 035	9 138	1 795	8 477
		Teachers emoluments	117 803	-	64 278	45 689	5 481	2 355
		Other emoluments	16 658	-	8 035	6 091	729	1 803
		Teaching materials	7 482	-	23	2 284	4 438	737
		Scholarships	41 150	-	-	-	41 150	-
		Welfare services	21 247	-	12	255	15 996	4 984
		Other current exp.	2 511	43	-	-	992	1 476
Togo Franc C.F.A.	1992	Total current exp.	26 307	-	8 364	7 386	3 256	7 301
		Admin. excl. staff	596	-	83	252	48	213
		Admin. emoluments	625	-	-	61	-	564
		Teachers emoluments	15 151	-	8 198	6 822	131	-
		Teaching materials	249	-	81	168	-	-
		Scholarships	3 077	-	-	-	3 077	-
		Welfare services	7	-	2	5	-	-
		Other current exp.	1 803	-	-	78	-	1 725
		Subsidies not distr.	4 799	-	-	-	-	4 799
Tunisia # Dinar	1993	Total current exp.	776 300	-	322 300	272 770	164 400	16 830
		Admin. excl. staff	60 400	-	6 400	19 170	34 700	130
		Admin. emoluments	52 400	-	16 000	23 400	6 600	6 400
		Teachers emoluments	580 400	-	296 000	222 500	61 900	-
		Other emoluments	29 600	-	-	-	19 300	10 300
		Scholarships	26 600	-	-	-	26 600	-
		Welfare services	20 900	-	3 900	7 700	9 300	-
		Other current exp.	6 000	-	-	-	6 000	-
Zimbabwe‡ Dollar	1992	Total current exp.	2 040	-	1 287	657	-	96
		Admin. excl. staff	7	-	1	1	-	5
		Admin. emoluments	63	-	-	-	-	63
		Teachers emoluments	1 817	-	1 231	583	-	3
		Teaching materials	42	-	15	27	-	-
		Scholarships	1	-	-	-	-	1
		Welfare services	34	-	7	27	-	-
		Other current exp.	52	-	33	19	-	-
		Subsidies not distr.	24	-	-	-	-	24
America, North								
Bermuda # Dollar	1991	Total current exp.	53 735	2 364	17 699	14 452	9 929	9 291
		Admin. emoluments	1 859	189	1 132	365	-	173
		Teachers emoluments	35 869	2 047	15 333	11 294	4 241	2 954
		Other emoluments	253	-	30	223	-	-
		Other current exp.	15 754	128	1 204	2 570	5 688	6 164
British Virgin Islands United States Dollar	1991	Total current exp.	8 869	<——	2 701	2 763	2 240	1 165
		Total emoluments	5 480	<——	2 424	2 165	365	526
		Other current exp.	1 908	<——	238	481	550	639
		Subsidies not distr.	1 481	<——	39	117	1 325	-

4.4 Public current expenditure by level and purpose
Dépenses publiques ordinaires par degré d'enseignement et destination
Gastos públicos ordinarios por grado de enseñanza y destino

Country / Currency / Pays / Monnaie / País / Moneda	Year / Année / Año	Purpose / Destination / Destino	Total current expenditure / Total des dépenses ordinaires / Total de gastos ordinarios (000 000)	Pre-primary / Pré-primaire / Pre-primaria (000 000)	First level / Premier degré / Primer grado (000 000)	Second level / Second degré / Segundo grado (000 000)	Third level / Troisième degré / Tercer grado (000 000)	Other types and not distributed / Autres types et non réparties / Otros tipos y sin distribución (000 000)
Canada‡ Dollar	1992	Total current exp.	51 291	<—	<—	31 192	14 310	5 789
		Admin. excl. staff	1 293	<—	<—	726	373	194
		Admin. emoluments	3 118	<—	<—	1 955	831	332
		Teachers emoluments	25 967	<—	<—	18 497	5 111	2 359
		Other emoluments	6 691	<—	<—	3 258	2 744	689
		Teaching materials	3 095	<—	<—	1 261	1 489	345
		Scholarships	2 747	<—	<—	-	1 450	1 297
		Welfare services	2 323	<—	<—	1 498	657	168
		Other current exp.	5 934	<—	<—	3 997	1 655	282
		Subsidies not distr.	123	-	-	-	-	123
Costa Rica‡ Colon	1994	Total current exp.	56 323	<—	21 734	12 894	17 523	4 172
		Total emoluments	53 754	<—	21 422	11 695	17 523	3 114
		Other current exp.	2 569	<—	312	1 199	-	1 058
Cuba # Peso	1990	Total current exp.	1 627 300	120 900	296 900	634 700	234 700	340 100
		Total emoluments	934 100	69 900	211 000	373 300	126 000	153 900
		Teaching materials	30 400	1 300	7 500	11 000	3 200	7 400
		Scholarships	111 800	200	300	23 900	33 000	54 400
		Welfare services	303 500	35 400	47 000	157 700	31 700	31 700
		Other current exp.	247 500	14 100	31 100	68 800	40 800	92 700
Dominica # E. Caribbean Dollar	1989	Total current exp.	20 104	31	11 924	5 458	511	2 180
		Admin. emoluments	1 574	-	-	-	-	1 574
		Teachers emoluments	11 884	-	9 695	2 026	163	-
		Other emoluments	570	-	246	215	49	60
		Teaching materials	179	-	-	-	179	-
		Scholarships	336	-	-	336	-	-
		Other current exp.	3 177	-	1 763	748	120	546
		Subsidies not distr.	2 384	31	220	2 133	-	-
Guadeloupe French Franc	1993	Total current exp.	2 745	340	687	1 553	30	135
		Admin. excl. staff	11	-	-	-	-	11
		Admin. emoluments	257	47	81	122	2	5
		Teachers emoluments	2 370	293	606	1 349	28	94
		Teaching materials	9	-	-	9	-	-
		Scholarships	67	-	-	67	-	-
		Welfare services	8	-	-	-	-	8
		Other current exp.	23	-	-	6	-	17
Haiti # Gourde	1990	Total current exp.	215 886	343	114 386	40 921	19 587	40 649
		Admin. excl. staff	4 011	-	1 407	311	755	1 538
		Total emoluments	205 670	343	112 229	38 978	17 444	36 676
		Teaching materials	66	-	15	-	-	51
		Scholarships	699	-	-	246	420	33
		Welfare services	604	-	-	125	382	97
		Other current exp.	936	-	34	54	100	748
		Subsidies not distr.	3 900	-	701	1 207	486	1 506
Honduras # Lempira	1994	Total current exp.	971 231	<—	470 721	163 693	192 495	144 322
		Admin. emoluments	64 156	<—	13 711	48 545	-	1 900
		Teachers emoluments	565 507	<—	451 411	110 428	-	3 668
		Other emoluments	805	<—	45	760	-	-
		Teaching materials	4 461	<—	2 381	2 021	-	59
		Scholarships	2 728	-	-	-	-	2 728
		Welfare services	1 160	<—	1 160	-	-	-
		Other current exp.	69 919	<—	2 013	1 939	-	65 967
		Subsidies not distr.	262 495	-	-	-	192 495	70 000
Jamaica‡ Dollar	1994	Total current exp.	5 551	171	1 369	2 076	1 427	508
		Admin. excl. staff	99	-	13	25	-	61
		Total emoluments	3 821	69	1 312	1 931	318	191
		Teaching materials	41	2	10	23	-	6
		Scholarships	8	-	-	-	8	-
		Welfare services	191	-	-	62	8	121
		Other current exp.	211	2	34	35	65	75
		Subsidies not distr.	1 180	98	-	-	1 028	54
Martinique French Franc	1993	Total current exp.	2 814	377	669	1 551	41	176
		Admin. excl. staff	11	-	-	-	-	11
		Admin. emoluments	299	61	93	134	3	8
		Teachers emoluments	2 391	316	576	1 337	38	124
		Teaching materials	9	-	-	9	-	-
		Scholarships	64	-	-	64	-	-
		Welfare services	20	-	-	-	-	20
		Other current exp.	20	-	-	7	-	13

Public current expenditure by level and purpose 4.4
Dépenses publiques ordinaires par degré d'enseignement et destination
Gastos públicos ordinarios por grado de enseñanza y destino

Country / Currency Pays / Monnaie País / Moneda	Year Année Año	Purpose Destination Destino	Total current expenditure Total des dépenses ordinaires Total de gastos ordinarios (000 000)	Pre-primary Pré-primaire Pre-primaria (000 000)	First level Premier degré Primer grado (000 000)	Second level Second degré Segundo grado (000 000)	Third level Troisième degré Tercer grado (000 000)	Other types and not distributed Autres types et non réparties Otros tipos y sin distribución (000 000)
Mexico‡ Peso	1992	Total current exp.	32 780 581	1 994 477	9 372 417	8 719 655	4 834 024	7 860 008
		Admin. excl. staff	11 965 701	112 538	1 132 814	2 552 958	3 443 381	4 724 010
		Total emoluments	20 697 169	1 877 032	8 236 412	6 164 483	1 374 270	3 044 972
		Teaching materials	12 892	4 901	1 290	1 250	918	4 533
		Scholarships	81 053	-	700	-	13 835	66 518
		Welfare services	21 818	6	1 190	194	1 328	19 100
		Other current exp.	1 948	-	11	770	292	875
Nicaragua‡# Cordoba	1992	Total current exp.	270 113	10 430	155 462	49 057	-	55 164
		Admin. excl. staff	49 353	874	12 370	6 306	-	29 803
		Admin. emoluments	25 889	230	6 586	623	-	18 450
		Teachers emoluments	188 063	9 044	135 052	40 112	-	3 855
		Other emoluments	1 568	-	-	-	-	1 568
		Teaching materials	1 139	181	427	126	-	405
		Scholarships	1 198	101	1 027	27	-	43
		Welfare services	1 863	-	-	1 863	-	-
		Subsidies not distr.	1 040	-	-	-	-	1 040
Panama # Balboa	1994	Total current exp.	333 985	<——	101 069	69 170	82 783	80 963
		Admin. excl. staff	12 052	<——	2 279	784	-	8 989
		Total emoluments	192 610	<——	98 677	67 462	-	26 471
		Subsidies not distr.	129 323	<——	113	924	82 783	45 503
Saint Kitts and Nevis‡# E. Caribbean Dollar	1991	Total current exp.	11 591	470	4 480	6 516	-	125
		Admin. excl. staff	51	18	4	25	-	4
		Admin. emoluments	1 421	141	549	697	-	34
		Teachers emoluments	8 751	235	3 242	5 187	-	87
		Other emoluments	512	76	80	356	-	-
		Teaching materials	165	-	65	100	-	-
		Welfare services	480	-	480	-	-	-
		Other current exp.	191	-	60	131	-	-
		Subsidies not distr.	20	-	-	20	-	-
St. Pierre and Miquelon‡# French Franc	1993	Total current exp.	56 940	7 650	14 100	34 280	-	910
		Admin. excl. staff	260	-	-	-	-	260
		Admin. emoluments	4 940	530	990	3 420	-	-
		Teachers emoluments	48 880	7 120	13 110	28 640	-	10
		Teaching materials	1 660	-	-	1 660	-	-
		Scholarships	100	-	-	100	-	-
		Other current exp.	1 100	-	-	460	-	640
St. Vincent and the Grenadines‡# E. Caribbean Dollar	1990	Total current exp.	25 590	<——	16 409	8 115	-	1 066
		Admin. emoluments	2 463	<——	1 682	364	-	417
		Teachers emoluments	21 202	<——	13 746	7 140	-	316
		Other emoluments	169	<——	94	75	-	-
		Teaching materials	710	<——	226	278	-	206
		Welfare services	44	<——	44	-	-	-
		Other current exp.	1 002	<——	617	258	-	127
Trinidad and Tobago Dollar #	1994	Total current exp.	1 061 331	2 000	427 516	351 014	141 326	139 475
		Total emoluments	708 101	-	348 085	316 381	-	43 635
		Teaching materials	575	-	250	325	-	-
		Scholarships	9 635	-	-	9 635	-	-
		Welfare services	66 530	-	63 000	-	-	3 530
		Other current exp.	74 680	-	1 709	11 282	-	61 689
		Subsidies not distr.	201 810	2 000	14 472	13 391	141 326	30 621
United States Dollar	1992	Total current exp.	319 375	11 343	106 279	111 668	90 085	.
		Teachers emoluments	169 117	6 394	59 764	62 793	40 166	.
		Total emoluments	241 257	9 017	84 514	88 799	58 927	.

America, South

Country / Currency	Year	Purpose	Total	Pre-primary	First level	Second level	Third level	Other
Argentina‡ Austral	1990	Total current exp.	7 062 974	<——	240 089	3 170 627	3 299 365	352 893
		Admin. excl. staff	516 620	<——	2 716	111 601	350 274	52 029
		Admin. emoluments	1 299 246	<——	10 672	518 175	702 519	67 880
		Teachers emoluments	4 916 789	<——	215 815	2 364 277	2 215 117	121 580
		Scholarships	40 883	-	-	963	31 454	8 466
		Welfare services	9 148	<——	6 636	-	-	2 512
		Other current exp.	280 288	<——	4 250	175 611	1	100 426
Bolivia‡# Boliviano	1994	Total current exp.	1 322 182	31 064	510 348	152 799	383 631	244 340
		Admin. excl. staff	12 801	-	-	616	-	12 185
		Admin. emoluments	297 981	6 340	76 870	28 857	4 502	181 412
		Teachers emoluments	626 750	24 724	433 478	119 536	25 869	23 143
		Scholarships	718	-	-	-	-	718
		Other current exp.	29 673	-	-	3 790	-	25 883
		Subsidies not distr.	354 259	-	-	-	353 260	999

4.4 Public current expenditure by level and purpose
Dépenses publiques ordinaires par degré d'enseignement et destination
Gastos públicos ordinarios por grado de enseñanza y destino

Country / Currency — Pays / Monnaie — País / Moneda	Year / Année / Año	Purpose / Destination / Destino	Total current expenditure / Total des dépenses ordinaires / Total de gastos ordinarios (000 000)	Pre-primary / Pré-primaire / Pre-primaria (000 000)	First level / Premier degré / Primer grado (000 000)	Second level / Second degré / Segundo grado (000 000)	Third level / Troisième degré / Tercer grado (000 000)	Other types and not distributed / Autres types et non réparties / Otros tipos y sin distribución (000 000)
Ecuador‡ Sucre	1989	Total current exp.	127 394	<——	53 438	40 732	17 308	15 916
		Total emoluments	104 003	<——	50 100	37 996	-	15 907
		Teaching materials	2 573	<——	209	2 355	-	9
		Scholarships	17	<——	17	-	-	-
		Other current exp.	20 801	<——	3 112	381	17 308	-
French Guiana French Franc	1993	Total current exp.	833	113	247	425	2	46
		Admin. excl. staff	6	-	-	-	-	6
		Admin. emoluments	74	15	30	28	-	1
		Teachers emoluments	729	98	217	382	2	30
		Teaching materials	3	-	-	3	-	-
		Scholarships	10	-	-	10	-	-
		Welfare services	2	-	-	-	-	-
		Other current exp.	9	-	-	2	-	7
Suriname # Guilder	1993	Total current exp.	379 959	<——	229 595	56 073	28 989	65 302
		Admin. excl. staff	47 034	<——	20 774	822	213	25 225
		Admin. emoluments	29 558	<——	1 589	3 825	311	23 833
		Teachers emoluments	120 828	<——	83 225	34 500	3 008	95
		Other emoluments	16 592	<——	13 732	2 860	-	-
		Teaching materials	19 834	<——	10 025	6 665	350	2 794
		Scholarships	9 730			-	-	9 730
		Welfare services	1 000	<——	350	-	-	650
		Other current exp.	28 235	<——	20 990	4 655	65	2 525
		Subsidies not distr.	107 148	<——	78 910	2 746	25 042	450
Uruguay Peso	1994	Total current exp.	1 981 029	<——	706 009	632 843	493 618	148 559
		Teachers emoluments	938 512	<——	427 597	381 445	109 119	20 351
		Total emoluments	1 380 720	<——	514 826	467 899	307 211	90 784
		Other current exp.	600 309	<——	191 183	164 944	186 407	57 775
Venezuela Bolivar	1994	Total current exp.	419 515	15 328	100 359	8 263	145 427	150 138
		Admin. excl. staff	4 397	25	139	89	-	4 144
		Admin. emoluments	11 196	508	1 702	357	-	8 629
		Teachers emoluments	89 929	3 491	37 713	4 353	-	44 372
		Other emoluments	12 247	810	7 838	1 767	-	1 832
		Teaching materials	1 033	28	573	140	-	292
		Scholarships	1 580	72	380	194	86	848
		Welfare services	60 845	9 629	47 674	515	-	3 027
		Other current exp.	59 681	733	4 340	848	-	53 760
		Subsidies not distr.	178 607	32	-	-	145 341	33 234
Asia								
Azerbaijan Rouble	1992	Total current exp.	15 704	2 052	<——	10 376	1 636	1 640
		Admin. excl. staff	386	32	<——	230	44	80
		Total emoluments	11 379	1 028	<——	8 437	1 002	912
		Teaching materials	33	-	<——	33	-	-
		Scholarships	698	3	<——	130	436	129
		Welfare services	925	5	<——	887	14	19
		Other current exp.	2 283	984	<——	659	140	500
Bangladesh‡ Taka	1991	Total current exp.	13 816	-	6 654	5 423	1 176	563
		Admin. excl. staff	219	-	39	145	3	32
		Total emoluments	8 151	-	6 578	1 503	3	67
		Teaching materials	14	-	-	14	-	-
		Scholarships	66	-	2	-	-	64
		Other current exp.	38	-	35	3	-	-
		Subsidies not distr.	5 328	-	-	3 758	1 170	400
Brunei Darussalam‡# Dollar	1993	Total current exp.	272 852	55	51 611	71 935	2 936	146 315
		Admin. excl. staff	49 506	-	-	-	-	49 506
		Admin. emoluments	37 325	-	9 190	23 284	174	4 677
		Teachers emoluments	78 428	-	39 564	36 843	2 021	-
		Other emoluments	7 379	-	737	3 593	366	2 683
		Other current exp.	100 214	55	2 120	8 215	375	89 449
Cyprus‡# Pound	1994	Total current exp.	142 541	5 952	47 268	72 230	8 433	8 658
		Admin. emoluments	9 062	37	1 096	3 641	1 072	3 216
		Teachers emoluments	114 995	4 632	39 598	62 124	4 568	4 073
		Other emoluments	3 969	226	1 133	2 041	344	225
		Teaching materials	1 585	85	692	252	525	31
		Scholarships	623	7	7	30	566	13
		Welfare services	3 845	70	1 137	2 495	37	106
		Other current exp.	7 559	344	3 605	1 295	1 321	994
		Subsidies not distr.	903	551	-	352	-	-

Public current expenditure by level and purpose 4.4
Dépenses publiques ordinaires par degré d'enseignement et destination
Gastos públicos ordinarios por grado de enseñanza y destino

Country Currency / Pays Monnaie / País Moneda	Year Année Año	Purpose Destination Destino	Total current expenditure / Total des dépenses ordinaires / Total de gastos ordinarios (000 000)	Pre-primary / Pré-primaire / Pre-primaria (000 000)	First level / Premier degré / Primer grado (000 000)	Second level / Second degré / Segundo grado (000 000)	Third level / Troisième degré / Tercer grado (000 000)	Other types and not distributed / Autres types et non réparties / Otros tipos y sin distribución (000 000)
Georgia Rouble	1994	Total current exp.	5 727 212	1 257 290	<—	2 581 854	1 058 254	829 814
		Admin. excl. staff	1 108 744	-	<—	481 416	418 968	208 360
		Total emoluments	3 013 803	274 932	<—	1 919 480	466 497	352 894
		Scholarships	113 268	-	<—	1 623	111 504	141
		Welfare services	125 162	-	<—	24 772	25	100 365
		Other current exp.	28 773	4 309	<—	7 206	5 268	11 990
		Subsidies not distr.	1 337 462	978 049	<—	147 357	55 992	156 064
Israel‡ Shekel	1992	Total current exp.	10 601	1 013	3 073	2 981	2 521	1 013
		Admin. excl. staff	184	-	-	-	-	184
		Total emoluments	8 152	803	2 549	2 410	1 828	562
		Teaching materials	1 818	205	503	471	463	176
		Scholarships	447	5	21	100	230	91
Jordan‡# Dinar	1993	Total current exp.	134 067	<—	<—	124 389	-	9 678
		Admin. emoluments	5 595	-	-	-	-	5 595
		Teachers emoluments	121 014	<—	<—	117 774	-	3 240
		Teaching materials	3 734	<—	<—	3 734	-	-
		Other current exp.	3 724	<—	<—	2 881		843
Korea, Republic of Won	1993	Total current exp.	9 344 751	92 935	3 821 988	3 644 585	713 282	1 071 961
		Admin. excl. staff	8 851	-	-	228	3 299	5 324
		Admin. emoluments	813 470	26	281 867	189 295	104 597	237 685
		Teachers emoluments	5 509 129	58 011	2 818 559	2 102 145	321 939	208 475
		Other emoluments	1 739	-	-	78	1 497	164
		Teaching materials	77 834	236	53 697	3 815	17 155	2 931
		Scholarships	46 960	-	-	6 271	34 209	6 480
		Welfare services	624 451	5 567	294 080	213 892	53 603	57 309
		Other current exp.	1 244 557	24 792	373 048	267 178	105 646	473 893
		Subsidies not distr.	1 017 760	4 303	737	861 683	71 337	79 700
Kyrgyzstan‡# Som	1994	Total current exp.	696 927	50 628	<—	479 217	75 503	91 579
		Total emoluments	355 760	19 493	<—	270 497	29 314	36 456
		Scholarships	36 350	-	<—	6 009	19 897	10 444
		Welfare services	50 971	1 287	<—	45 831	1 024	2 829
		Other current exp.	253 846	29 848	<—	156 880	25 268	41 850
Lao People's Democratic Rep.‡ Kip	1992	Total current exp.	15 094	401	5 964	6 565	588	1 576
		Total emoluments	11 780	364	5 657	4 636	200	923
		Teaching materials	60	-	-	22	38	-
		Scholarships	1 572	-	-	990	181	401
		Welfare services	23	-	-	2	21	-
		Other current exp.	1 655	37	307	915	144	252
		Subsidies not distr.	4	-	-	-	4	-
Malaysia‡ Ringgit	1993	Total current exp.	7 085	14	2 430	2 741	1 226	674
		Admin. excl. staff	147	-	-	3	-	144
		Total emoluments	4 434	9	2 127	2 146	-	152
		Teaching materials	424	-	184	240	-	-
		Scholarships	80	-	-	-	-	80
		Welfare services	221	1	-	125	-	95
		Other current exp.	528	4	119	227	-	178
		Subsidies not distr.	1 251	-	-	-	1 226	25
Mongolia Tughrik	1994	Total current exp.	15 384	3 608	<—	9 008	2 744	24
		Admin. excl. staff	808	297	<—	451	57	3
		Total emoluments	5 664	1 009	<—	3 770	877	8
		Teaching materials	11	-	<—	3	8	-
		Scholarships	164	-	<—	4	160	-
		Welfare services	1 187	781	<—	355	51	-
		Other current exp.	7 550	1 521	<—	4 425	1 591	13
Myanmar‡ Kyat	1994	Total current exp.	4 436	-	2 117	1 786	519	14
		Total emoluments	2 521	-	1 995	247	273	6
		Other current exp.	1 915	-	122	1 539	246	8
Oman‡# Rial	1994	Total current exp.	153 449	-	71 732	75 661	4 642	1 414
		Admin. excl. staff	3 681	-	1 631	1 744	283	23
		Total emoluments	130 118	-	61 098	64 370	3 346	1 304
		Teaching materials	1 726	-	808	871	39	8
		Welfare services	17 922	-	8 195	8 676	974	77
		Other current exp.	2	-	-	-	-	2

Public current expenditure by level and purpose
Dépenses publiques ordinaires par degré d'enseignement et destination
Gastos públicos ordinarios por grado de enseñanza y destino

Country / Currency Pays / Monnaie País / Moneda	Year Année Año	Purpose Destination Destino	Total current expenditure Total des dépenses ordinaires Total de gastos ordinarios (000 000)	Pre-primary Pré-primaire Pre-primaria (000 000)	First level Premier degré Primer grado (000 000)	Second level Second degré Segundo grado (000 000)	Third level Troisième degré Tercer grado (000 000)	Other types and not distributed Autres types et non réparties Otros tipos y sin distribución (000 000)
Syrian Arab Rep.‡ Pound	1994	Total current exp.	15 621	<—	10 245	4 993	-	383
		Total emoluments	14 289	<—	9 775	4 326	-	188
		Teaching materials	544	<—	118	379	-	47
		Scholarships	15	<—	4	7	-	4
		Welfare services	111	<—	46	30	-	35
		Other current exp.	589	<—	296	251	-	42
		Subsidies not distr.	73	<—	6	-	-	67
Thailand Baht	1994	Total current exp.	108 485	1 944	55 322	23 359	17 946	9 914
		Admin. excl. staff	6 839	17	1 708	2 125	1 686	1 303
		Admin. emoluments	7 601	-	2 137	466	2 976	2 022
		Teachers emoluments	66 830	-	44 266	16 930	5 400	234
		Other emoluments	5 471	-	1 956	1 477	1 536	502
		Teaching materials	4 897	227	2 286	1 127	955	302
		Scholarships	1 203	-	283	730	145	45
		Welfare services	3 625	1 700	1 904	-	15	6
		Other current exp.	3 186	-	655	462	1 443	626
		Subsidies not distr.	8 833	-	127	42	3 790	4 874
Turkey‡ Lira	1994	Total current exp.	109 162 355	112 540	50 436 597	24 609 241	23 340 555	10 663 422
		Total emoluments	102 256 662	91 540	49 283 622	22 386 572	22 177 662	8 317 266
		Teaching materials	699 410	400	34 800	50 250	532 890	81 070
		Scholarships	1 379 120	-	-	216 000	388 620	774 500
		Welfare services	1 583 110	-	503 725	753 839	-	325 546
		Other current exp.	3 244 053	20 600	614 450	1 202 580	241 383	1 165 040
Uzbekistan Rouble	1993	Total current exp.	475 863	80 055	<—	332 780	46 290	16 738
		Total emoluments	277 730	25 165	<—	223 652	20 190	8 723
		Teaching materials	4 376	-	<—	943	-	3 433
		Scholarships	22 570	-	<—	9 839	12 697	34
		Welfare services	26 043	-	<—	26 040	3	-
		Other current exp.	145 144	54 890	<—	72 306	13 400	4 548
Europe								
Albania Lek	1994	Total current exp.	5 353	360	3 060	1 105	550	278
		Total emoluments	4 028	320	2 510	865	300	33
		Teaching materials	285	20	150	60	25	30
		Scholarships	160	-	-	-	160	-
		Welfare services	447	10	220	160	30	27
		Other current exp.	255	10	180	20	35	10
		Subsidies not distr.	178	-	-	-	-	178
Austria Schilling	1993	Total current exp.	108 775	9 189	19 105	51 426	21 475	.
		Total emoluments	75 019	5 762	15 827	40 929	11 063	.
Belgium Franc	1993	Total current exp.	404 601	33 030	80 994	187 096	68 680	.
		Teachers emoluments	308 186	25 185	64 819	154 689	46 718	.
		Total emoluments	321 327	25 697	66 619	158 974	47 354	.
Bulgaria Lev	1994	Total current exp.	22 620	4 599	12 436	—>	3 507	2 078
		Total emoluments	15 341	2 948	9 408	—>	2 119	866
		Scholarships	1 085	-	507	—>	556	22
		Welfare services	23	23	-	-	-	-
		Other current exp.	6 171	1 628	2 521	—>	832	1 190
Former Czechoslovakia Koruna	1990	Total current exp.	35 482	3 326	14 281	6 408	5 601	5 866
		Total emoluments	17 922	2 135	7 036	4 060	2 441	2 250
		Teaching materials	6 050	538	2 228	972	1 062	1 250
		Scholarships	402	-	-	9	238	155
		Welfare services	5 354	-	2 655	411	642	1 646
		Other current exp.	5 741	653	2 359	954	1 210	565
		Subsidies not distr.	13	-	3	2	8	-
Czech Republic Koruna	1993	Total current exp.	49 198	4 571	19 133	12 710	8 784	4 000
		Total emoluments	15 846	2 254	7 037	2 707	2 503	1 345
		Teaching materials	13 846	1 893	4 982	4 593	1 254	1 124
		Scholarships	145	-	-	3	142	-
		Welfare services	4 449	-	3 666	453	330	-
		Other current exp.	4 650	329	1 136	594	1 868	723
		Subsidies not distr.	10 262	95	2 312	4 360	2 687	808
Denmark Krone	1993	Total current exp.	56 915	8 334	12 765	24 480	9 972	.
		Total emoluments	46 166	6 825	10 455	19 817	7 978	.

Public current expenditure by level and purpose **4.4**
Dépenses publiques ordinaires par degré d'enseignement et destination
Gastos públicos ordinarios por grado de enseñanza y destino

Country / Currency Pays / Monnaie País / Moneda	Year Année Año	Purpose Destination Destino	Total current expenditure Total des dépenses ordinaires Total de gastos ordinarios (000 000)	Pre-primary Pré-primaire Pre-primaria (000 000)	First level Premier degré Primer grado (000 000)	Second level Second degré Segundo grado (000 000)	Third level Troisième degré Tercer grado (000 000)	Other types and not distributed Autres types et non réparties Otros tipos y sin distribución (000 000)
Estonia # Kroon	1994	Total current exp.	1 747 773	336 245	<—	1 002 056	245 294	164 178
		Admin. excl. staff	284 153	54 895	<—	167 233	36 245	25 780
		Total emoluments	876 386	168 804	<—	509 659	117 791	80 132
		Teaching materials	55 599	2 147	<—	33 637	15 447	4 368
		Scholarships	12 352	-	<—	5 074	7 263	15
		Welfare services	95 077	28 821	<—	55 253	6 478	4 525
		Other current exp.	419 093	81 578	<—	230 509	62 070	44 936
		Subsidies not distr.	5 113	-	<—	691	-	4 422
Finland Markka	1993	Total current exp.	32 996	3 089	9 072	12 075	8 004	.
		Teachers emoluments	17 158	1 550	5 729	6 985	2 894	.
		Total emoluments	22 620	2 087	6 922	8 428	4 774	.
France‡ Franc	1993	Total current exp.	396 287	43 504	78 887	200 582	67 402	.
		Total emoluments	303 790	35 029	62 536	157 080	46 294	.
Germany Deutsche Mark	1993	Total current exp.	123 939	7 864	19 313	62 593	28 557	.
		Total emoluments	101 914	6 474	16 762	54 663	20 914	.
Federal Republic of Germany‡ Deutsche Mark	1991	Total current exp.	97 255	4 867	12 530	45 162	23 070	11 626
		Admin. excl. staff	299	-	-	-	-	299
		Total emoluments	71 071	2 288	10 928	36 433	15 835	5 587
		Scholarships	2 364	-	-	659	1 705	
		Welfare services	2 459	-	-	99	304	2 056
		Other current exp.	14 070	491	1 517	5 166	5 024	1 872
		Subsidies not distr.	6 992	2 088	85	2 805	202	1 812
Greece Drachma	1991	Total current exp.	359 533	20 391	100 942	163 001	70 470	4 729
		Admin. emoluments	22 765	280	2 386	7 868	11 492	739
		Teachers emoluments	303 506	19 356	95 321	148 650	36 630	3 549
		Scholarships	691	-	-	77	609	5
		Welfare services	5 107	1	22	1 104	3 827	153
		Other current exp.	27 464	754	3 213	5 302	17 912	283
Hungary Forint	1994	Total current exp.	262 917	37 638	104 715	60 345	46 670	13 549
		Total emoluments	120 187	18 076	50 633	27 908	17 963	5 607
		Welfare services	23 485		14 712	6 961	1 812	
		Other current exp.	119 245	19 562	39 370	25 476	26 895	7 942
Iceland Krona	1993	Total current exp.	16 617	875	5 254	6 896	2 851	.
		Total emoluments	12 011	626	3 758	5 063	2 265	.
Ireland Pound	1993	Total current exp.	1 792	144	476	715	418	.
		Teachers emoluments	1 381	131	433	577	230	.
		Total emoluments	1 572	135	446	610	359	.
Italy‡ Lira	1992	Total current exp.	59 089 471	5 280 471	15 311 231	27 764 365	-	10 733 404
		Admin. excl. staff	254 891	-	-	-	-	254 891
		Admin. emoluments	10 320 503	-	2 212 245	3 123 425	-	4 984 833
		Teachers emoluments	38 407 337	2 966 708	11 613 236	23 531 670	-	295 723
		Teaching materials	491 366	29 263	59 970	402 133	-	-
		Welfare services	23 258					23 258
		Other current exp.	9 564 743	2 284 500	1 425 780	706 023	-	5 148 440
		Subsidies not distr.	27 373	-	-	1 114	-	26 259
Lithuania # Lita	1994	Total current exp.	885 512	125 021	<—	455 793	123 680	181 018
		Total emoluments	577 809	75 571	<—	318 944	78 728	104 566
		Teaching materials	11 839	32	<—	2 018	522	9 267
		Scholarships	37 315		<—	12 367	18 193	6 755
		Welfare services	32 938	18 256	<—	3 762	31	10 889
		Other current exp.	225 611	31 162	<—	118 702	26 206	49 541
Luxembourg Franc	1989	Total current exp.	13 440	1 371	4 596	5 630	447	1 396
		Admin. excl. staff	918	127	389	289	16	97
		Admin. emoluments	549	6	30	375	31	107
		Teachers emoluments	9 802	1 077	3 629	4 349	131	616
		Other emoluments	748	90	276	216	27	139
		Teaching materials	156	-	18	49	16	73
		Scholarships	250	-	-	22	176	52
		Welfare services	270	4	13	161	2	90
		Other current exp.	747	67	241	169	48	222

4.4   Public current expenditure by level and purpose
Dépenses publiques ordinaires par degré d'enseignement et destination
Gastos públicos ordinarios por grado de enseñanza y destino

Country Currency / Pays Monnaie / País Moneda	Year Année Año	Purpose Destination Destino	Total current expenditure / Total des dépenses ordinaires / Total de gastos ordinarios (000 000)	Pre-primary / Pré-primaire / Pre-primaria (000 000)	First level / Premier degré / Primer grado (000 000)	Second level / Second degré / Segundo grado (000 000)	Third level / Troisième degré / Tercer grado (000 000)	Other types and not distributed / Autres types et non réparties / Otros tipos y sin distribución (000 000)
Malta # Lira	1992	Total current exp.	41 211	<——	9 287	16 631	7 373	7 920
		Admin. excl. staff	2 946	-	-	-	-	2 946
		Admin. emoluments	3 968	<——	-	-	-	3 968
		Teachers emoluments	15 947	<——	6 560	8 847	-	540
		Other emoluments	5 225	<——	2 193	2 876	-	156
		Teaching materials	20	<——	1	5	-	14
		Scholarships	39	-	-	-	-	39
		Welfare services	4 799	<——	339	1 330	2 873	257
		Other current exp.	3 767	<——	194	3 573	-	-
		Subsidies not distr.	4 500	-	-	-	4 500	-
Monaco‡# French Franc	1992	Total current exp.	123 516	5 967	21 636	76 152	-	19 761
		Admin. excl. staff	211	32	68	69	-	42
		Total emoluments	103 506	5 815	21 202	73 307	-	3 182
		Teaching materials	3 396	120	366	2 776	-	134
		Scholarships	3 600	-	-	-	-	3 600
		Welfare services	2 313	-	-	-	-	2 313
		Other current exp.	10 490	-	-	-	-	10 490
Netherlands Guilder	1993	Total current exp.	27 353	1 965	6 526	11 038	7 824	.
		Total emoluments	21 273	1 508	5 050	9 093	5 622	.
		Other current exp.	6 080	457	1 476	1 945	2 202	.
Norway Krone	1993	Total current exp.	46 076	<——	<——	34 316	9 222	.
		Total emoluments	35 762	<——	<——	28 414	5 698	.
Portugal Escudo	1993	Total current exp.	688 511	16 949	258 766	244 032	98 068	.
		Total emoluments	573 293	16 330	244 289	219 910	75 161	.
Slovakia S. Koruna	1994	Total current exp.	17 152	1 684	5 053	3 257	2 457	4 701
		Total emoluments	9 934	1 225	3 821	2 077	1 423	1 388
		Teaching materials	119	-	-	-	-	119
		Scholarships	91	-	-	-	-	91
		Welfare services	2 606	-	-	-	291	2 315
		Other current exp.	4 402	459	1 232	1 180	743	788
Slovenia Tolar	1994	Total current exp.	92 722	10 555	18 075	42 332	17 528	4 232
		Admin. excl. staff	1 096	-	254	385	85	372
		Admin. emoluments	1 309	16	-	290	358	645
		Teachers emoluments	53 781	7 151	12 616	25 032	6 998	1 984
		Other emoluments	10 358	1 948	2 226	4 150	1 589	445
		Teaching materials	6 908	309	685	2 915	2 482	487
		Scholarships	7 703	-	-	-	3 901	3 802	-
		Welfare services	6 637	-	1 353	3 666	1 493	125
		Other current exp.	4 695	1 131	941	1 795	654	174
		Subsidies not distr.	235	-	-	168	67	-
Spain Peseta	1993	Total current exp.	2 970 963	262 065	644 919	1 521 493	4 775 523	.
		Total emoluments	2 389 141	192 766	527 073	1 228 759	388 358	.
Sweden‡ Krona	1992	Total current exp.	105 803	40	43 032	19 390	16 710	26 631
		Admin. excl. staff	5 226	-	3 165	1 479	104	478
		Teachers emoluments	40 991	-	22 062	7 646	5 711	5 572
		Teaching materials	2 962	-	1 523	1 327	-	112
		Scholarships	7 432	-	-	2 843	2 853	1 736
		Welfare services	4 943	-	3 550	1 352	-	41
		Subsidies not distr.	44 249	40	12 732	4 743	8 042	18 692
Switzerland Franc	1993	Total current exp.	15 689	671	4 543	6 916	3 251	.
		Total emoluments	13 202	616	3 860	5 930	2 562	.
The Former Yugoslav Rep. of Macedonia # Dinar	1994	Total current exp.	6 806 588	-	3 748 957	1 582 363	1 475 268	-
		Total emoluments	5 641 287	-	3 342 310	1 301 549	997 428	-
		Teaching materials	4 400	-	-	2 000	2 400	-
		Scholarships	60 000	-	-	30 000	30 000	-
		Welfare services	208 986	-	33 986	25 000	15 000	-
		Other current exp.	891 915	-	372 661	223 814	295 440	-
United Kingdom Pound Sterling	1992	Total current exp.	28 969	501	9 440	13 597	5 431	.
		Teachers emoluments	15 073	248	5 490	7 854	1 481	.
		Total emoluments	19 548	360	6 909	9 845	2 434	.
Former Yugoslavia‡ Dinar	1990	Total current exp.	55 911	-	42 067	——>	9 511	4 333
		Total emoluments	35 827	-	28 776	——>	5 747	1 304
		Teaching materials	6 936	-	4 456	——>	1 195	1 285
		Welfare services	3 869	-	2 259	——>	1 012	598
		Other current exp.	9 279	-	6 576	——>	1 557	1 146

Public current expenditure by level and purpose 4.4
Dépenses publiques ordinaires par degré d'enseignement et destination
Gastos públicos ordinarios por grado de enseñanza y destino

Country Currency Pays Monnaie País Moneda	Year Année Año	Purpose Destination Destino	Total current expenditure Total des dépenses ordinaires Total de gastos ordinarios (000 000)	Pre- primary Pré- primaire Pre- primaria (000 000)	First level Premier degré Primer grado (000 000)	Second level Second degré Segundo grado (000 000)	Third level Troisième degré Tercer grado (000 000)	Other types and not distributed Autres types et non réparties Otros tipos y sin dis- tribución (000 000)
Federal Republic of Yugoslavia # New Dinar	1994	Total current exp. Total emoluments Teaching materials Scholarships Welfare services Other current exp.	750 404 308 835 115 361 4 912 105 695 215 601	- - - - - -	321 833 159 757 43 233 - 35 886 82 957	170 934 77 277 21 181 - 23 276 49 200	168 076 61 648 18 994 - 27 878 59 556	89 561 10 153 31 953 4 912 18 655 23 888
Oceania								
Australia Dollar	1992	Total current exp. Total emoluments	22 511 15 969	- -	6 791 5 277	9 070 6 920	6 650 3 772	. .
Cook Islands # New Zealand Dollar	1991	Total current exp. Admin. excl. staff Total emoluments Teaching materials Scholarships Other current exp. Subsidies not distr.	8 225 321 5 598 188 40 928 1 150	170 - 170 - - - -	2 281 - 2 163 82 - 34 2	2 745 - 2 522 103 40 76 4	979 - - - - - 979	2 050 321 743 3 - 818 165
Fiji # Dollar	1989	Total current exp. Admin. excl. staff Total emoluments Teaching materials Welfare services Other current exp. Subsidies not distr.	81 740 2 099 67 211 3 198 1 796 398 7 038	- - - - - - -	41 302 1 872 39 358 59 1 12 -	30 275 173 25 880 2 967 927 268 -	7 333 7 240 9 39 - 7 038	2 830 47 1 733 163 769 118 -
French Polynesia‡ French Franc	1993	Total current exp. Admin. excl. staff Admin. emoluments Teachers emoluments Scholarships Welfare services Other current exp.	1 807 11 152 1 553 1 47 43	250 - 25 225 - - -	496 - 43 453 - - -	885 - 80 801 1 - 3	19 - 1 18 - - -	157 11 3 56 - 47 40
Kiribati # Australian Dollar	1989	Total current exp. Admin. excl. staff Total emoluments Teaching materials Scholarships Welfare services Other current exp.	3 511 520 2 208 198 278 201 106	- - - - - - -	1 772 133 1 524 105 - - 10	1 009 150 503 84 - 201 71	278 - - - 278 - -	452 237 181 9 - - 25
New Caledonia‡ French Franc	1993	Total current exp. Admin. excl. staff Admin. emoluments Teachers emoluments Teaching materials Scholarships Welfare services Other current exp.	1 606 17 131 1 280 13 1 107 57	173 - 18 155 - - - -	343 - 32 311 - - - -	851 - 78 754 13 1 - 5	21 - 1 20 - - - -	218 17 2 40 - - 107 52
New Zealand Dollar	1992	Total current exp. Admin. excl. staff Admin. emoluments Teachers emoluments Scholarships Welfare services Subsidies not distr.	5 107 574 40 1 758 255 88 2 392	200 97 4 95 - - 4	1 135 250 12 824 - 44 5	1 066 224 12 761 19 44 6	1 874 1 - - 236 - 1 637	832 2 12 78 - - 740
Solomon Islands # Solomon Isl. Dollar	1991	Total current exp. Total emoluments Teaching materials Scholarships Welfare services	23 965 17 326 930 3 272 2 437	60 - 60 - -	13 482 12 612 870 - -	7 136 4 699 - - 2 437	3 272 - - 3 272 -	15 15 - - -
Tonga‡# Pa'anga	1992	Total current exp. Total emoluments Teaching materials Scholarships Welfare services Other current exp. Subsidies not distr.	8 833 6 246 37 415 29 1 488 618	- - - - - - -	3 428 3 393 4 - - 31 -	2 138 1 790 16 - 16 44 272	641 219 17 - 13 46 346	2 626 844 - 415 - 1 367 -
Tuvalu # Australian Dollar	1990	Total current exp. Admin. excl. staff Admin. emoluments Teachers emoluments Teaching materials Welfare services Other current exp.	854 19 24 496 44 240 31	- - - - - - -	307 - - 277 30 - -	504 - - 219 14 240 31	- - - - - - -	43 19 24 - - - -

4.4 Public current expenditure by level and purpose
Dépenses publiques ordinaires par degré d'enseignement et destination
Gastos públicos ordinarios por grado de enseñanza y destino

General note / Note générale / Nota general:

E--> For further details concerning the categories included in *other expenditure*, see Table 4.2. For countries which participated in the most recent UNESCO/OECD/Eurostat survey, please refer to the special remark on page 1 of this chapter and the general notes in Tables 4.2 and 4.3.

FR-> Pour plus de détails sur les catégories inclus dans la rubrique *autre dépenses* se référer au tableau 4.2. Pour les pays qui ont participé au programme de la dernière enquête de l'UNESCO/OCDE/Eurostat, veuillez vous référez à la note spéciale, page 1 de ce chapitre ainsi qu'aux notes générales des tableaux 4.2 et 4.3

ESP> Para obtener más detalles sobre las categorías comprendidas en la rubrica *otros gastos* véase el cuadro 4.2. Para los países que participaron en la última encuesta de UNESCO/OCDE/Eurostat, refiérase a la nota correspondiente que figura en la página 1 de este capítulo y a las notas generales de los cuadros 4.2 y 4.3.

AFRICA:

Algeria:
E--> Capital expenditure is included and expenditure on education at the third level is not included.
FR-> Les dépenses en capital sont incluses et les dépenses de l'enseignement du troisième degré ne sont pas incluses.
ESP> Se incluyen los gastos de capital y no se incluyen los gastos relativos a la enseñanza de tercer grado.

Angola:
E--> Expenditure of the Ministry of Education only.
FR-> Dépenses du Ministère de l'Education seulement.
ESP> Gastos del Ministerio de Educación solamente.

Central African Republic:
E--> Expenditure of the Ministry of Education only.
FR-> Dépenses du Ministère de l'Education seulement.
ESP> Gastos del Ministerio de Educación solamente.

Comoros:
E--> Expenditure of the Ministry of Education only.
FR-> Dépenses du Ministère de l'education seulement.
ESP> Gastos del Ministerio de Educación solamente.

Côte d'Ivoire:
E--> Expenditure on education at the third level is not included.
FR-> Les dépenses de l'enseignement du troisième degré ne sont pas incluses.
ESP> No se incluyen los gastos relativos a la enseñanza de tercer grado.

Djibouti:
E--> Expenditure on administration other than personnel is included with total emoluments.
FR-> Les dépenses d'administration autre que le personnel sont incluses avec le total des émoluments.
ESP> Los gastos de administración excluyendo el personal quedan incluídos en el total de los emolumentos.

Egypt:
E--> Expenditure for Al-Azhar is not included. Expenditure on administration other than personnel is included with total emoluments.
FR-> Les dépenses relatives à Al-Azhar ne sont pas incluses. Les dépenses d'administration autre que le personnel sont incluses avec le total des émoluments.
ESP> No se incluyen los gastos relativos a Al-Azhar. Los gastos de administración excluyendo el personal quedan incluídos en el total de los emolumentos.

Ethiopia:
E--> Expenditure on education at the third level is not included.
FR-> Les dépenses de l'enseignement du troisième degrè ne sont pas incluses.
ESP> No se incluyen los gastos relativos a la enseñanza de tercer grado.

Gabon:
E--> Data refer to expenditure of the Ministry of Primary and Secondary Education only.
FR-> Les données se réfèrent aux dépenses du Ministère des enseignements primaire et secondaire seulement.
ESP> Los datos se refieren a los gastos del Ministerio de la enseñanza de primer y secundo grado solamente.

Gambia:
E--> Expenditure on third level education refers to post-secondary institutions.
FR-> Les dépenses relatives à l'enseignement du troisième degrè se réfèrent aux institutions post-secondaires.
ESP> Los gastos relativos a la enseñanza de tercer grado se refieren a los establecimientos post-secundarios.

Ghana:
E--> Expenditure on administration other than personnel is included with total emoluments.
FR-> Les dépenses d'administration autre que le personnel sont incluses avec le total des émoluments.

ESP> Los gastos de administración excluyendo el personal quedan incluídos en el total de los emolumentos.

Madagascar:
E--> Data refer to expenditure of the Ministry of Primary and Secondary Education only.
FR-> Les données se réfèrent aux dépenses du Ministère des enseignements primaire et secondaire seulement.
ESP> Los datos se refieren a los gastos del Ministerio de las enseñanzas de primer y secundo grado solamente.

Mauritania:
E--> Expenditure of the Ministry of Education only. Scholarships are included with welfare services.
FR-> Dépenses du Ministère de l'Education seulement. Les bourses d'études sont incluses avec les services sociaux.
ESP> Gastos del Ministerio de Educación solamente. Las becas de estudio quedan incluídas en los servicios sociales.

Morocco:
E--> Expenditure of the Ministry of Education only.
FR-> Dépenses du Ministère de l'Education seulement.
ESP> Gastos del Ministerio de Educación solamente.

Mozambique:
E--> Data include foreign aid received for education.
FR-> Les données comprennent l'aide étrangère rec+ue pour l'éducation.
ESP> Los datos incluyen la ayuda extranjera recibida para educación.

Niger:
E--> Data refer to expenditure of the Ministry of Education only and do not include expenditure on third level education.
FR-> Les données se réfèrent aux dépenses du Ministère de l'Education seulement et ne comprennent pas les dépenses relatives à l'enseignement du troisième degrè.
ESP> Los datos se refieren a los gastos del Ministerio de Educación solamente y no se incluyen los gastos relativos a la enseñanza de tercer grado.

Rwanda:
E--> Expenditure on *enseignement rural et artisanal intégré* is included with first level education.
FR-> Les dépenses relatives à l'enseignement rural et artisanal intégré sont incluses avec l'enseignement du premier degré.
ESP> Los gastos relativos a la *enseignement rural et artisanal intégré* quedan incluídos en el primer grado.

South Africa:
E--> Data on pre-primary, first and second level education refer to expenditure on public and private ordinary schools and technical colleges. Data on third level education refer to expenditure on universities, technikons and teacher training.
FR-> Les données relatives à l'enseignement préprimaire, primaire et secondaire se réfèrent aux dépenses des écoles publiques et privées et des collèges techniques. Les données relatives à l'enseignement du troisième degré se réfèrent aux dépenses des universités, des *technikons* et des écoles normales.
ESP> Los datos relativos a la enseñanza preprimaria, primaria y secundaria se refieren a los gastos de las escuelas públicas y privadas y de las escuelas técnicas. Los datos relativos a la enseñanza de tercer grado se refieren a los gastos de las universidades, *technikons* y de las escuelas normales.

Zimbabwe:
E--> Data include capital expenditure and do not include expenditure on third level education.
FR-> Les données comprennent les dépenses en capital et les dépenses relatives à l'enseignement du troisième degré ne sont pas incluses.
ESP> Los datos incluyen los gastos de capital y no incluyen los gastos relativos a la enseñanza de tercer grado.

AMERICA, NORTH:

Canada:
E--> Data refer to public and private expenditure on education.
FR-> Les données se réfèrent aux dépenses publiques et privées afférentes à l'enseignement.
ESP> Los datos se refieren a los gastos públicos y privados destinados a la enseñanza.

Costa Rica:
E--> Expenditure of the Ministry of Education only. Transfers to universities and other types of institutions are included with total emoluments.
FR-> Dépenses du Ministère de l'Education seulement. Les transferts de fonds aux universitées et à certain autres établissements sont inclus avec le total des émoluments.
ESP> Gastos del Ministerio de Educación solamente. Las transferencias del gobierno a las universidades y otros establecimientos se incluyen en el total de los emolumentos.

Jamaica:
E--> Expenditure of the Ministry of Education only.

Public current expenditure by level and purpose **4.4**
Dépenses publiques ordinaires par degré d'enseignement et destination
Gastos públicos ordinarios por grado de enseñanza y destino

FR–> Dépenses du Ministère de l'Education seulement.
ESP> Gastos del Ministerio de Educación solamente.

Mexico:
E––> Expenditure of the Ministry of Education only.
FR–> Dépenses du Ministère de l'Education seulement.
ESP> Gastos del Ministerio de Educación solamente.

Nicaragua:
E––> Data refer to the Ministry of Primary and Secondary Education only and are expressed in gold Cordobas.
FR–> Les dépenses se réfèrent aux dépenses du Ministère des enseignements primaire et secondaire seulement et sont exprimées en Cordobas or.
ESP> Los datos se refieren a los gastos del Ministerio de la enseñanza de primer y segundo grados solamente y están expresados en Córdobas oro.

St. Kitts and Nevis:
E––> Expenditure on education at the third level is not included.
FR–> Les dépenses de l'enseignement du troisième degré ne sont pas incluses.
ESP> No se incluyen los gastos relativos a la enseñanza de tercer grado.

St. Pierre and Miquelon:
E––> Expenditure of the Ministry of Education only.
FR–> Dépenses du Ministère de l'Education seulement.
ESP> Gastos del Ministerio de Educación solamente.

St. Vincent and the Grenadines:
E––> Expenditure on education at the third level is not included.
FR–> Les dépenses de l'enseignement du troisième degré ne sont pas incluses.
ESP> No se incluyen los gastos relativos a la enseñanza de tercer grado.

AMERICA, SOUTH:
Argentina:
E––> Expenditure of the Ministry of Education only.
FR–> Dépenses du Ministère de l'Education seulement.
ESP> Gastos del Ministerio de Educación solamente.

Bolivia:
E––> Capital expenditure is included.
FR–> Les dépenses en capital sont incluses.
ESP> Se incluyen los gastos de capital.

Ecuador:
E––> Expenditure on administration other than personnel is included with total emoluments.
FR–> Les dépenses d'administration autre que le personnel sont incluses avec le total des émoluments.
ESP> Los gastos de administración excluyendo el personal quedan incluídos en el total de los emolumentos.

ASIA:
Bangladesh:
E––> Expenditure of the Ministry of Education only.
FR–> Dépenses du Ministère de l'Education seulement.
ESP> Gastos del Ministerio de Educación solamente.

Brunei Darussalam:
E––> Data refer to expenditure of the Ministry of Education only and do not include expenditure on universities.
FR–> Les données se réfèrent aux dépenses du Ministère de l'Education seulement et ne comprennent pas les dépenses des universités.
ESP> Los datos se refieren a los gastos del Ministerio de Educación solamente y no se incluyen los gastos de las universidades.

Cyprus:
E––> Expenditure of the Office of Greek Education only.
FR–> Dépenses du bureau grec de l'Education seulement.
ESP> Gastos del servicio griego de Educación solamente.

Israel:
E––> Data include expenditure from private sources such as donations, fees, etc.
FR–> Les données comprennent les dépenses provenant de sources privées, telles que les donations, les frais de scolarité, etc.
ESP> Los datos incluyen los gastos provenientes de fuentes privadas como donaciones, gastos de inscripción, etc.

Jordan:
E––> Expenditure on education at third level is not included.
FR–> Les dépenses de l'enseignement du troisième degré ne sont pas incluses.
ESP> No se incluyen los gastos relativos a la enseñanza de tercer grado.

Kyrgyzstan:
E––> Expenditure on teaching materials is included with welfare services.
FR–> Les dépenses en matériel pour l'éducation sont incluses avec les services sociaux.
ESP> Los gastos de material educativo quedan incluídos en los servicio sociales.

Lao People's Democratic Republic:
E––> Expenditure on administration other than personnel is included with total emoluments.
FR–> Les dépenses d'administration autre que le personnel sont incluses avec le total des émoluments.
ESP> Los gastos de administración excluyendo el personal quedan incluídos en el total de los emolumentos.

Malaysia:
E––> Expenditure of the Ministry of Education only.
FR–> Dépenses du Ministère de l'Education seulement.
ESP> Gastos del Ministerio de Educación solamente.

Myanmar:
E––> Expenditure of the Ministry of Education only.
FR–> Dépenses du Ministère de l'Education seulement.
ESP> Gastos del Ministerio de Educación solamente.

Oman:
E––> Expenditure on universities is not included.
FR–> Les dépenses des universités ne sont pas incluses.
ESP> No se incluyen los gastos de las universidades.

Syrian Arab Republic:
E––> Expenditure on education at the third level is not included.
FR–> Les dépenses de l'enseignement du troisième degré ne sont pas incluses.
ESP> No se incluyen los gastos relativos a la enseñanza de tercer grado.

Turkey:
E––> Expenditure on administration other than personnel is included with total emoluments.
FR–> Les dépenses d'administration autre que le personnel sont incluses avec le total des émoluments.
ESP> Los gastos de administración excluyendo el personal quedan incluídos en el total de los emolumentos.

EUROPE:
France:
E––> Data refer to Metropolitan France.
FR–> Les données se réfèrent à la France métropolitaine.
ESP> Los datos se refieren a la Francia metropolitana.

Germany: Federal Republic of Germany:
E––> Data include expenditure for East Berlin.
FR–> Les données comprennent les dépenses relatives à Berlin Est.
ESP> Los datos incluyen los gastos relativos a Berlin Este.

Italy:
E––> Expenditure on third level education is not included.
FR–> Les dépenses de l'enseignement du troisième degré ne sont pas incluses.
ESP> No se incluyen los gastos relativos a la enseñanza de tercer grado.

Monaco:
E––> Data do not include public subsidies to private education.
FR–> Les données ne comprennent pas les subventions publiques à l'enseignement privé.
ESP> Los datos no incluyen las subvenciones públicas a la enseñanza privada.

Sweden:
E––> Expenditure on first level (column 3) refers to compulsory education which covers six grades of primary education and the first three grades of secondary education. Expenditure on second level education, therefore, covers only the last three grades (upper secondary school).
FR–> Les dépenses relatives au premier degré (colonne 3) se réfèrent à l'enseignement obligatoire qui comprend six années de l'enseignement primaire et les trois premières années de l'enseignement secondaire. Les dépenses relatives à l'enseignement du second degré ne comprennent donc que les trois dernières années (école secondaire supérieure).
ESP> Los gastos relativos al primer grado (columna 3) se refieren a la enseñanza obligatoria que incluye seis años de la enseñanza primaria y los tres primeros años de la enseñanza secundaria. Los gastos relativos al segundo grado, por consiguiente, incluyen solamente los tres últimos años (escuela secundaria superior).

Former Yugoslavia:
E––> Scholarships are included with teaching materials.
FR–> Les bourses d'études sont incluses avec le matériel pour l'enseignement.
ESP> Las becas de estudio quedan incluídas en el material educativo.

OCEANIA:
French Polynesia:
E––> Expenditure of the Ministry of Education only.
FR–> Dépenses du Ministère de l'Education seulement.
ESP> Gastos del Ministerio de Educación solamente.

New Caledonia:
E––> Data refer to expenditure of the Ministry of Education only.
FR–> Les données se réfèrent aux dépenses du Ministère de l'Education seulement.

4.4 Public current expenditure by level and purpose
Dépenses publiques ordinaires par degré d'enseignement et destination
Gastos públicos ordinarios por grado de enseñanza y destino

ESP> Los datos se refieren a los gastos del Ministerio de Educación solamente.
Tonga:
E——> Data include capital expenditure and expenditure on administration other than personnel is included with total emoluments.

FR—> Les données comprennent les dépenses en capital et les dépenses d'administration autre que le personnel sont incluses avec le total des émoluments.
ESP> Los datos incluyen los gastos de capital y los gastos de administración excluyendo el personal quedan incluídos en el total de los emolumentos.

Science and technology
Science et technologie
Ciencia y tecnología   5

5 Science and technology

Science et technologie

Ciencia y tecnología

This chapter presents selected results of the data collection effort by UNESCO in the field of science and technology. Most of the data were obtained from replies to statistical questionnaires on manpower and expenditure for research and experimental development (R&D), sent to the Member States of UNESCO supplemented by data collected from official reports and publications.

The definitions and concepts used in the R&D questionnaire are based on the *Recommendation concerning the International Standardization of Statistics on Science and Technology* and can be found in the corresponding *Manual* (doc. UNESCO ST-84/WS/12).

Abridged versions of the definitions set out in the above-mentioned Recommendation are given below.

Type of personnel

The following three categories of scientific and technical personnel are defined according to the work they are engaged in and their qualifications:

(1) *Scientists and engineers*, comprising persons working in those capacities, i.e. as persons with scientific or technological training (usually completion of third level education) in any field of science as defined below, who are engaged in professional work on R&D activities, administrators and other high-level personnel who direct the execution of R&D activities.

(2) *Technicians* comprising persons engaged in that capacity in R&D activities who have received vocational or technical training in any branch of knowledge or technology of a specified standard (usually at least three years after the first stage of second-level education).

(3) *Auxiliary personnel*, comprising persons whose work is *directly* associated with the performance of R&D activities, i.e. clerical, secretarial and administrative personnel, skilled, semi-skilled and unskilled workers in the various trades and all other auxiliary personnel. *Excludes* security, janitorial and maintenance personnel engaged in general house-keeping activities.

It should be noted that in general all personnel are considered for inclusion in the appropriate categories regardless of citizenship status or country of origin.

Full- and part-time R&D personnel and full-time equivalent

Data concerning personnel are normally calculated in FTE, especially in the case of scientists and engineers.

Full-time equivalent (FTE). This is a measurement unit representing one person working full-time for a given period; this unit is used to convert figures relating to the number of part-time workers into the equivalent number of full-time workers.

Research and experimental development (R&D)

In general R&D is defined as any creative systematic activity undertaken in order to increase the stock of knowledge, including knowledge of man, culture and society, and the use of this knowledge to devise new applications. It includes fundamental research (i.e. experimental or theoretical work undertaken with no immediate practical purpose in mind), applied research in such fields as agriculture, medicine, industrial chemistry, etc., (i.e. research directed primarily towards a special practical aim or objective), and experimental development work leading to new devices, products or processes.

Sectors of performance

The sectors of performance identify those areas of the economy in which R&D work is performed. The term *sector of performance* distinguishes the execution or the performance of R&D activities from their financing.

Three major sectors of performance can be distinguished: the productive sector, the higher education sector and the general service sector, the productive sector being measured on two *levels* - R&D activities *integrated* and those *not integrated* with production. The productive sector thus covers domestic and foreign industrial and trading establishments which produce and distribute goods and services for sale; the higher education sector relates to establishments of education at the third level and also includes those research institutes, experimental stations, etc. serving them, whilst the general service sector includes various public or government establishments serving the community as a whole.

R&D expenditure

The measurement of R&D expenditure is calculated on the basis of intramural current expenditure, including overheads, and intramural capital expenditure. The sum of the intramural expenditures incurred by the national institutions provides the total domestic expenditure which is the information presented at the international level.

Total domestic expenditure on R&D activities refers to all expenditure made for this purpose in the course of a reference year in institutions and installations established in the national territory, as well as installations physically situated abroad.

The total *expenditure for R&D* as defined above comprises *current expenditure*, including overheads, and *capital expenditure*. Current intramural expenditure is further separated into labour costs and other current costs.

Source of funds

The following sources of finance for domestic expenditure on R&D activities permit the identification of the financial supporters of such activities:

Government funds: include funds provided by the central (federal), State or local authorities.

Productive enterprise funds and special funds: funds allocated to R&D activities by institutions classified in the productive sector and all sums received from the 'Technical and Economic Progress Fund' and other similar funds.

Foreign funds: funds received from abroad for national R&D activities.

Other funds: funds that cannot be classified under any of the preceding headings.

Table Notes

The tables in this chapter are set out in three sections. The first section (A) comprises a table (*5.1*) which presents selected indicators for R&D scientists and engineers and expenditure.

The following two sections comprise 5 tables presenting basic data obtained from the UNESCO statistical surveys and from official reports and publications.

The second section (B) consists of 2 tables relating to human resources.

5 Science and technology
Science et technologie
Ciencia y tecnología

Table 5.2 provides data for the scientists, engineers and technicians engaged in research and experimental development activities, with some data for women when available. In this table, unless otherwise indicated, the data are shown in full-time equivalent.

Table 5.3 covers all personnel engaged in R&D and shows their distribution according to the three sectors of performance (Productive, Higher education and General service), providing both the absolute numbers (in full-time equivalent unless otherwise indicated) and the percentage distribution. Because of the different structure of the Productive sector in countries with different socio-economic systems, to facilitate comparisons two 'integration levels' are also shown within this sector. This provides an indication of the degree of linkage between R&D and production in the different socio-economic systems. The different types of personnel performing in these sectors are also shown.

The third section (C) comprises 3 tables and provides a general picture of the cost of R&D activities. The data are given in national currencies.

The absolute figures for R&D expenditure should not be compared country by country. Such comparisons would require the conversion of national currencies into a common currency by means of the official exchange rates, since special R&D exchange rates do not exist. Official exchange rates do not always reflect the real costs of R&D activities and comparisons based on such rates can result in misleading conclusions. However, they do have some limited value in indicating at least a gross order of magnitude of expenditure on R&D. For the rates of exchange between national currencies and the United States dollar, the reader is referred to Appendix C.

In *Table 5.4* total expenditure for R&D is subdivided by type of expenditure - capital and current, further subdivided into labour and other current costs - and the current as percentage of total expenditure is provided.

The structure of the financing of R&D can be seen in *Table 5.5* which gives the distribution of total expenditure (or alternatively current expenditure) by four main categories of sources of funds. Again, the data are presented in national currencies and in percentages where the information is considered sufficiently complete to enable the reader to compare amongst countries the efforts of different financial supporters of R&D activities.

Table 5.6 shows the distribution of total and current expenditure by the three sectors of performance. As in Table 5.3, the Productive sector is further broken down into two *integration levels*. The expenditures are presented in absolute numbers and to facilitate country-wise comparisons, where sufficiently complete data are available, the percentage distribution among the sectors is also given.

Research workers interested in obtaining further details or clarification pertaining to particular countries as regards national definitions, coverage or limitations of the data presented in the tables may address their enquiries to the Division of Statistics.

Le lecteur trouvera consignés dans ce chapitre quelques résultats sélectionnés des efforts que l'UNESCO a déployés pour rassembler des données statistiques concernant la science et la technologie. Les données proviennent pour la plupart des réponses aux questionnaires statistiques sur le personnel et les dépenses de recherche et de développement expérimental (R-D) que l'UNESCO a adressés aux Etats membres. Elles ont été complétées par des renseignements recueillis auparavant à l'aide des rapports officiels et publications.

Les définitions et concepts proposés pour être utilisés dans le questionnaire de R-D sont basés sur la *Recommandation concernant la normalisation internationale des statistiques relatives à la science et à la technologie* et figurent dans le *Manuel* correspondant (doc. UNESCO ST-84/WS/12).

On trouvera ci-dessous des versions abrégées des définitions proposées dans la Recommandation sus-mentionnée.

Catégories du personnel

Les trois catégories de personnel scientifique et technique suivantes sont définies d'après leurs fonctions et qualifications:

(1) *Scientifiques et ingénieurs* comprenant les personnes qui travaillent en tant que tels, c'est-à-dire comme personnel de conception dans les activités de R-D et qui ont reçu une formation scientifique ou technique (d'ordinaire des études complètes du troisième degré) dans n'importe quel domaine de la science, cité ci-dessous, les administrateurs et autre personnel de haut niveau qui dirigent l'exécution des activités de R-D.

(2) *Techniciens* comprenant les personnes qui travaillent en tant que tels dans des activités de R-D et qui ont reçu une formation professionnelle ou technique dans n'importe quelle branche du savoir ou de la technologie d'un niveau spécifié (d'ordinaire au moins trois années d'études après achèvement du premier cycle de l'enseignement du second degré).

(3) *Personnel auxiliaire* comprenant les personnes dont les fonctions sont *directement* associées à l'exécution des activités de R-D à savoir le personnel de bureau, de secrétariat et d'administration, les ouvriers qualifiés, semi-qualifiés et non qualifiés dans les divers métiers et tout autre personnel auxiliaire. Il *ne comprend pas* le personnel de sécurité, de gardiennage et d'entretien général.

Il est à noter que d'une manière générale, dans les catégories appropriées, tout le personnel doit être pris en considération, quels que soient la nationalité et le pays d'origine.

Personnel de R-D travaillant à plein temps et à temps partiel et équivalent plein temps

En principe, les données concernant les personnel sont calculées en EPT, surtout dans le cas des scientifiques et ingénieurs.

Equivalent plein temps (EPT). Unité d'évaluation qui correspond à une personne travaillant à plein temps pendant une période donnée. On se sert de cette unité pour convertir en nombre de personnes à plein temps le nombre de celles qui travaillent à temps partiel.

Recherche et développement expérimental (R-D)

En général, la recherche scientifique et le développement expérimental (R-D) englobent tous les travaux systématiques et créateurs entrepris afin d'accroître le stock de connaissances, y compris celles qui concernent l'homme, la culture et la société, et l'utilisation de ce stock de connaissances pour imaginer de nouvelles applications. Elle comprend la recherche fondamentale (c'est-à-dire, travaux expérimentaux ou théoriques entrepris principalement sans qu'une application ou utilisation particulière ou spécifique soit recherchée), la recherche appliquée dans des domaines tels que l'agriculture, la médecine, la chimie industrielle, etc. (c'est-à-dire, recherche originale visant principalement un but ou objectif pratique spécifique), et le développement expérimental conduisant à la mise au point de nouveaux produits, dispositifs ou procédés.

Secteurs d'exécution

Les secteurs d'exécution sont les secteurs de l'économie dans lesquels s'exercent les activités de R-D. La notion de *secteur d'exécution* permet de distinguer entre l'exécution des activités de R-D et leur financement.

On peut distinguer trois grands secteurs d'exécution: le secteur de la production, le secteur de l'enseignement supérieur et le secteur de service général, le secteur de la production se subdivisant en deux *niveaux* d'intégration - les activités de R-D *intégrées* à la production et les activités *non-intégrées* à la production. Le secteur de la production comprend donc les entreprises industrielles et commerciales nationales et étrangères qui produisent et distribuent des biens et des services contre rémunération, le secteur de l'enseignement supérieur comprend tous les établissements d'enseignement du troisième degré ainsi que les instituts de recherche, stations d'essais, etc. qui desservent ces établissements, et le secteur de service général comprend tous les organismes, ministères et établissements des administrations publiques - administrations centrales ou administrations des Etats - qui desservent l'ensemble de la communauté.

Dépenses de R-D

Le coût des activités de R-D est calculé sur la base des dépenses courantes intra-muros y compris les frais généraux, et les dépenses en capital intra-muros. La somme des dépenses intra-muros effectuées par les institutions nationales conduit à un agrégat total des dépenses intérieures, qui est l'information présentée à l'échelon international.

Le total des dépenses intérieures pour des activités de R-D peut être défini donc comme l'ensemble des dépenses effectuées à ce titre, au cours d'une année de référence, dans les institutions et installations situées sur le territoire national, y compris dans les installations qui sont géographiquement situées à l'étranger.

Les *dépenses totales pour les activités de R-D*, telles qu'elles sont définies ci-dessus, comprennent toutes les dépenses courantes, y compris les frais généraux et les dépenses en capital. Les dépenses courantes intra-muros sont subdivisées en dépenses totales de personnel et autres dépenses courantes.

Sources de financement

Afin de pouvoir identifier l'origine du financement des activités de R-D, les catégories de sources de financement pour les dépenses de R-D se définissent comme suit:

Fonds publics: comprend les fonds fournis par le gouvernement central ou par les autorités locales.

Fonds provenant des entreprises de production et fonds spéciaux: comprend les fonds affectés aux activités de R-D par les institutions classées dans le secteur de la production comme des établissements ou des entreprises de production et tous les fonds provenant des *Fonds de développement technique et économique* et d'autres fonds analogues.

Fonds étrangers: comprend les fonds reçus de l'étranger pour les activités de R-D nationales.

Fonds divers: comprend les fonds qui ne peuvent être classés dans l'une des rubriques précédentes.

Notes sur les tableaux

Les tableaux de ce chapitre sont classés en trois sections. La première section (A) comprend un tableau (*5.1*) qui fournit des indicateurs selectionnés pour les scientifiques et ingénieurs engagés dans la R-D ainsi que pour les dépenses.

Science and technology
Science et technologie
Ciencia y tecnología

5

Les deux sections suivantes comprennent 5 tableaux qui présentent les données de base recueillies au moyen des enquêtes statistiques de l'UNESCO et des rapports officiels et publications.

La deuxième section (B) comprend 2 tableaux concernant les ressources humaines.

Le *tableau 5.2* présente les données relatives aux scientifiques, ingénieurs et techniciens qui sont employés à des travaux de recherche et de développement expérimental, avec le nombre correspondant de femmes lorsque cette information est connue. Dans ce tableau, sauf indication contraire, les données sont exprimées en *équivalent plein temps*.

Le *tableau 5.3* concerne tout le personnel employé à des travaux de R-D et montre leur répartition entre les trois secteurs d'exécution (secteurs de la production, de l'enseignement supérieur et de service général). Il donne à la fois les chiffres absolus (exprimés en équivalent plein temps, sauf indication contraire) et la distribution en pourcentage du personnel. Compte tenu des différentes structures du secteur de la production dans des pays aux systèmes socio-économiques différents et pour en faciliter la comparaison, les données de ce secteur sont classées suivant deux *niveaux d'intégration* qui indiquent le degré du lien existant entre la R-D et la production dans les différents systèmes socio-économiques. Les différentes catégories de personnel employé dans ces secteurs sont aussi présentées.

La troisième section (C) comprend 3 tableaux et donne un profil du coût des activités de R-D. Les données sont présentées en monnaie nationale.

Il faut éviter de comparer, d'un pays à l'autre, les chiffres absolus qui concernent les dépenses de R-D. On ne pourrait procéder à de telles comparaisons qu'en convertissant en une même monnaie les sommes libellées en monnaie nationale et, comme il n'existe pas de taux de change qui soit spécialement applicable aux activités de R-D, il faudrait nécessairement se fonder, pour cela, sur les taux de change officiels. Or ces taux ne reflètent pas toujours le coût réel des activités de R-D et les comparaisons risquent alors d'être trompeuses. De telles comparaisons ne sont cependant pas totalement dénuées d'intérêt, car elles donnent au moins une idée de l'ordre de grandeur des dépenses de R-D. Le lecteur trouvera dans l'Annexe C les taux de change applicables à la conversion des monnaies nationales en dollars des Etats-Unis.

Dans le *tableau 5.4*, les dépenses totales de R-D sont subdivisées par type de dépenses (en capital et courantes - ces dernières à leur tour subdivisées en dépenses de personnel et autres dépenses courantes) et les dépenses courantes en pourcentage du total sont aussi présentées.

Quant à la structure du financement de la R-D, elle est présentée dans le *tableau 5.5* où les dépenses totales (ou à défaut les dépenses courantes) sont distribuées d'après les quatre grandes catégories de sources de financement. Les données sont toujours présentées en monnaie nationale et en pourcentage, lorsque des informations complètes sont disponibles, pour permettre au lecteur de comparer les efforts réalisés dans les différents pays par ceux qui assurent le financement des activités de R-D.

Le *tableau 5.6* présente la distribution des dépenses totales et courantes selon les trois secteurs d'exécution. Comme dans le tableau 5.3, les données pour le secteur de la production sont réparties selon les deux niveaux d'intégration. Les dépenses sont présentées en chiffres absolus et, pour faciliter les comparaisons entre les pays, lorsque des données complètes sont disponibles, leur distribution en pourcentage selon les secteurs est indiquée.

Les chercheurs qui souhaiteraient obtenir d'autres détails ou des éclaircissements sur un pays particulier en ce qui concerne les définitions nationales, la portée ou les limitations des données présentées dans les tableaux, peuvent adresser leur demande à la Division des Statistiques.

El presente capítulo contiene una selección de los resultados alcanzados por la UNESCO gracias al esfuerzo hecho para reunir datos estadísticos relativos a la ciencia y la tecnología. Los datos proceden, en su mayor parte, de las respuestas al cuestionario estadístico sobre el personal y gastos de investigación y desarrollo experimental (I y D), que la UNESCO envió a los Estados Miembros, habiendo sido completados con informaciones procedentes de informes oficiales y publicaciones.

Las definiciones propuestas para su empleo en el cuestionario de I y D, están basadas en la *Recomendación sobre la normalización internacional de las estadísticas relativas a la ciencia y la tecnología* y que pueden encontrarse en el *Manual* correspondiente (doc. UNESCO ST-84/WS/12).

A continuación encontrarán las versiones resumidas de las definiciones propuestas en la Recomendación arriba mencionada.

Categoría de personal

Las tres categorías siguientes de personal científico y técnico se definen según su función y calificaciones.

(1) *Científicos e ingenieros*, que son las personas que trabajan como tales, es decir, como personal de concepción en las actividades de I y D y que han recibido formación científica o técnica (normalmente enseñanza de tercer grado completa) en no importa qué campo de la ciencia, que se indica más abajo, los administradores y demás personal de categoría superior que dirigen la ejecución de las actividades de I y D.

(2) *Técnicos*, que son las personas que trabajan como tales en actividades de I y D y que han recibido formación profesional técnica en cualquiera de las ramas del saber o de la tecnología, (normalmente con un mínimo de tres años de estudios después de haber terminado el primer ciclo de la enseñanza de segundo grado).

(3) *Personal auxiliar*, que son las personas cuyas funciones están directamente asociadas a la ejecución de las actividades de I y D, a saber, el personal administrativo, de secretaría y de oficina, los obreros especializados, semiespecializados y no especializados en los diversos oficios y los demás tipos de personal auxiliar. *Exclúyase* el personal de seguridad, de guardia y mantenimiento dedicado en general a la conservación de los edificios.

Hay que tener en cuenta que de una manera general, y en las categorías apropiadas, debe tomarse en consideración todo el personal, independientemente de su nacionalidad o país de origen.

Personal de I y D que trabaja a jornada completa, a jornada parcial y en equivalente de jornada completa

En principio, los datos relativos al personal se calculan en EJC sobre todo en el caso de los científicos e ingenieros.

Equivalente de jornada completa (EJC). Unidad de evaluación que corresponde a una persona que trabaja en régimen de plena dedicación durante un período dado. Se emplea esta unidad para convertir las cifras relativas al número de personas que trabajan en régimen de jornada parcial en un número equivalente de personas que trabajan a jornada completa.

Investigación y desarrollo experimental (I y D)

Por I y D se entiende, en general, cualquier trabajo sistemático y creador realizado con el fin de aumentar el caudal de conocimientos, inclusive el conocimiento del hombre, la cultura y la sociedad, y de utilizar estos conocimientos para descubrir nuevas aplicaciones. Comprende la investigación fundamental (es decir, trabajo experimental o teórico efectuado principalmente sin prever ninguna aplicación determinada o específica), la investigación aplicada en ramas tales como la agricultura, la medicina, la química industrial, etc., (es decir, investigación original encaminada principalmente hacia una finalidad u objetivo práctico determinado), y el desarrollo experimental que conduce a la creación de nuevos dispositivos o procedimientos.

Sectores de ejecución

Los sectores de ejecución son aquellos sectores de la economía en los que se realizan actividades de I y D. El término *Sector de Ejecución* distingue la realización o ejecución de actividades de I y D y de su financiamiento.

Se pueden distinguir tres grandes sectores de ejecución: el sector productivo, el sector de enseñanza superior y el sector de servicio general, el sector productivo se reparten según dos *niveles* de integración - actividades de I y D *integradas* a la producción y las actividades *no integradas* a la producción. El sector productivo engloba las empresas industriales y comerciales nacionales y extranjeras, situadas en el país, que producen y distribuyen bienes y servicios a cambio de una remuneración. El sector de enseñanza superior comprende todos los centros de enseñanza de tercer grado así como los institutos de investigación, estaciones de ensayo, etc. que prestan servicios a esos centros. El sector de servicio general comprende todos los organismos, ministerios y establecimientos de la administración pública - administración central o administración de los Estados de una federación que prestan servicios a toda la comunidad.

Gastos de I y D

El cálculo de los gastos relativos a las actividades de I y D se efectuará sobre la base de los gastos ordinarios intramuros, incluídos los gastos generales y los gastos de capital intramuros. La suma de los gastos intramuros de todas las instituciones nacionales constituye un total final que recibe el nombre de *gastos interiores totales* que se utilizan cuando se presenta información a escala internacional.

El total de los gastos interiores para actividades de I y D pueden definirse como todos los gastos efectuados a este respecto durante el año de referencia, en las instituciones e instalaciones situadas en el territorio nacional, comprendidos los relativos a las instalaciones situadas geográficamente en el extranjero.

Los *gastos totales para I y D* tal como se definen en el párrafo anterior, comprenden los gastos corrientes intramuros, incluídos los gastos generales, y los gastos de capital intramuros. Los gastos corrientes intramuros se distribuirán en gastos totales de personal y gastos corrientes varios.

5 Science and technology
Science et technologie
Ciencia y tecnología

Origen de los fondos

Con el fin de poder identificar el origen de financiamiento de las actividades de I y D, las categorías de fuentes de financiamiento para los gastos interiores de I y D se definen como sigue:

Fondos públicos: comprende los fondos proporcionados por las autoridades centrales (federales), estatales o locales.

Fondos procedentes de empresas de producción y fondos especiales: comprende los fondos asignados a actividades de I y D por las instituciones clasificadas en el sector productivo como establecimientos o empresas de producción y todos los fondos procedentes de los *Fondos de Desarrollo Técnico y Económico* y otros fondos análogos.

Fondos extranjeros: comprende los fondos recibidos del extranjero para la realización de actividades nacionales de I y D.

Fondos varios: comprende los fondos que no queda clasificar en ninguna de las categorías anteriores.

Notas sobre los cuadros

Los cuadros en este capítulo se han clasificados en tres secciones. La primera sección (A) consiste de un cuadro (*5.1*) que presenta de indicadores seleccionados para los científicos e ingenieros empleados en I y D también que los gastos.

Las dos secciones siguientes comprenden 5 cuadros y muestran datos básicos obtenidos por las encuestas estadísticas de la UNESCO et de informes officiales y publicaciones.

La segunda sección (B) comprende 2 cuadros que se refieren a los recursos humanos. El potencial humano científico y técnico se presenta en el *cuadro 5.2*.

El *cuadro 5.2* indica los datos que se refieren a los científicos e ingenieros empleados en trabajos de investigación y de desarrollo experimental con algunos datos sobre mujeres empleadas, cuando éstos son proporcionados. En este cuadro, salvo cuando se indica lo contrario, los datos figuran en equivalente de jornada completa.

El *cuadro 5.3* se refiere a todo el personal empleado en trabajos de I y D repartido entre los tres sectores de ejecución (sectores productivo, de enseñanza superior y de servicio general). Da a la vez las cifras absolutas (indicadas en equivalente de jornada completa salvo cuando se indica lo contrario) y la repartición en porcentaje del personal. Teniendo en cuenta las diversas estructuras del sector productivo en países con sistemas socioeconómicos diferentes y con vistas a facilitar su comparación, los datos de este sector se han clasificado siguiendo dos *niveles de integración*, que indican el grado de relación existente entre la I y D y la producción en los diferentes sistemas socioeconómicos. Se presentan

igualmente las diferentes categorías de personal empleado en esos sectores.

La tercera sección (C) comprende 3 cuadros y da una idea del costo de las actividades de I y D. Los datos se presentan en moneda nacional.

Debe evitarse comparar, de un país a otro, las cifras absolutas referentes a los gastos de I y D. Sólo se podrían efectuar comparaciones semejantes convirtiendo en una misma moneda las sumas que figuran en moneda nacional, y como no existe un tipo de cambio especialmente aplicable a las actividades de I y D, sería necesario basarse para ello en los tipos de cambio oficiales. Como sea que tales tipos no siempre reflejan el costo real de las actividades de I y D, se corre el riesgo de que dichas comparaciones sean erróneas. Sin embargo, no carecen totalmente de interés ya que como mínimo dan una idea del orden de magnitud de los gastos de I y D. En el Anexo C pueden verse los tipos de cambio aplicables a la conversión de las monedas nacionales en dólares de los Estados Unidos.

En el *cuadro 5.4*, los gastos totales de I y D se desglosan por tipo de gastos (de capital y corrientes - estos últimos subdivido a su vez en gastos de personal y gastos corrientes varios), estableciéndose una relación en porcentaje entre los gastos corrientes y los gastos totales.

En cuanto a la estructura del financiamiento de la I y D, se indica en el *cuadro 5.5*, donde los gastos totales (o en su defecto los gastos corrientes) se desglosan según las cuatro grandes categorías de fuentes de financiamiento. Los datos se presentan como siempre en moneda nacional y en porcentaje cuando se dispone de datos completos, para que el lector pueda comparar los esfuerzos realizados en los diferentes países por parte de quienes aseguran el financiamiento de las actividades de I y D.

El *cuadro 5.6* presenta la repartición de los gastos totales y corrientes para los tres sectores de ejecución. Como en el cuadro 5.3 los datos para el sector productivo se reparten según dos niveles de integración. Los gastos se presentan en cifras absolutas y, para facilitar las comparaciones entre los países cuando se dispone de datos completos, se indica su repartición entre los sectores en porcentaje.

Los investigadores que deseen obtener otros detalles o aclaraciones sobre un país en particular en lo que se refiere a las definiciones nacionales, el alcance o las limitaciones de los datos presentados en los cuadros, pueden dirigir su petición a la División de Estadística.

5.1 Selected science and technology indicators

Indicateurs sélectionnés du développement scientifique et technologique

Indicadores seleccionados del desarrollo científico y tecnologico

For more information on the national R&D data used in the calculations of the indicators below, please refer to the corresponding footnotes of tables 5.2 and 5.4.

Pour plus de renseignements sur les données de R-D nationales utilisées pour le calcul des indicateurs cidessous, veuillez vous référer aux notes correspondantes des tableaux 5.2 et 5.4.

Para mayor información sobre los datos nacionales de I y D utilizados en el cálculo de los indicadores presentados más abajo, consúltense las notas correspondientes de los cuadros 5.2 y 5.4

Country / Pays / País	Year / Année / Año	Personnel engaged in R&D / Personnel employé à des travaux de R-D / Personal dedicado a actividades de I y D			Year / Année / Año	Expenditure for R&D / Dépenses consacrées à R-D / Gastos dedicados a la I y D		
		Scientists and engineers per million population / Scientifiques et ingénieurs par million d'habitants / Científicos e ingenieros por millón de habitantes	Technicians per million population / Techniciens par million d'habitants / Técnicos por millón de habitantes	Number of technicians per scientist or engineer / Nombre de techniciens par scientifique ou ingénieur / Número de técnicos por científico o ingeniero		As percentage of gross national product (GNP) / En pourcentage du produit national brut (PNB) / En porcentaje del producto nacional bruto (PNB)	Per capita (in national currency) / Par habitant (en monnaie nationale) / Por persona (en moneda nacional)	Annual average per R&D scientist or engineer (in national currency) / Moyenne annuelle par scientifique ou ingénieur de R-D (en monnaie nationale) / Promedio anual por científico o ingeniero de I y D (en moneda nacional)
		(1)	(2)	(3)		(4)	(5)	(6)
Africa								
Benin	1989	177	54	0.3	1989	0.7	745	4 216 240
Burundi	1989	32	31	1.0	1989	0.3	100	3 154 041
Central African Republic	1990	55	31	0.6	1984	0.2	268	3 473 423
Congo	1984	461	788	1.7	1984	0.0	14	29 617
Egypt	1991	458	340	0.7	1991	*1.0	*17	*36 164
Gabon	1987	189	17	0.1	1986	0.0	373	1 801
Guinea	1984	264	126	0.5	1984	...	...	...
Libyan Arab Jamahiriya	1980	361	493	1.4	1980	0.2	8	20 795
Madagascar	1989	22	79	3.6	1988	0.5	1 222	63 032 961
Mauritius	1992	361	158	0.4	1992	0.4	164	455 013
Nigeria	1987	15	69	4.5	1987	0.1	1	64 477
Rwanda	1985	12	*11	*0.9	1985	0.5	152	12 937 465
Senegal	1981	342	467	1.4	1981	...	...	...
Seychelles	1983	281	94	0.3	1983	1.3	201	714 111
South Africa	1991	319	132	0.4	1991	1.0	73	230 217
Tunisia	1992	*388	*71	*0.2	1992	0.3	5 353	*13 803 681
America, North								
Canada	1991	2 322	978	0.4	1994	1.6	400	...
Costa Rica	1992	539	...	...	1986	0.3	225	
Cuba	1992	1 369	878	0.6	1992	*0.9	23	16 786
El Salvador	1992	19	299	0.1	1992	0.0	201	10 623 127
Guatemala	1988	99	107	1.1	1988	0.2	4	37 132

Country / Pays / País	Year / Année / Año	Personnel engaged in R&D / Personnel employé à des travaux de R-D / Personal dedicado a actividades de I y D			Year / Année / Año	Expenditure for R&D / Dépenses consacrées à R-D / Gastos dedicados a la I y D		
		Scientists and engineers per million population / Scientifiques et ingénieurs par million d'habitants / Científicos e ingenieros por millón de habitantes	Technicians per million population / Techniciens par million d'habitants / Técnicos por millón de habitantes	Number of technicians per scientist or engineer / Nombre de techniciens par scientifique ou ingénieur / Número de técnicos por científico o ingeniero		As percentage of gross national product (GNP) / En pourcentage du produit national brut (PNB) / En porcentaje del producto nacional bruto (PNB)	Per capita (in national currency) / Par habitant (en monnaie nationale) / Por persona (en moneda nacional)	Annual average per R&D scientist or engineer (in national currency) / Moyenne annuelle par scientifique ou ingénieur de R-D (en monnaie nationale) / Promedio anual por científico o ingeniero de I y D (en moneda nacional)
		(1)	(2)	(3)		(4)	(5)	(6)
Jamaica	1986	8	6	0.8	1986	0.0	2	223 111
Mexico	1993	95	27	0.3	1993	0.3	40	...
Nicaragua	1987	214	89	0.4	1987	...	292	1 364 097
St. Lucia	1984	434	705	1.6	1992	0.0	3	...
Trinidad and Tobago	1984	240	222	0.9	1984	0.8	125	520 935
United States	1993	*3 732	...	...	1995	...	*650	*177 625
America, South								
Argentina	1988	*350	*197	*0.6	1992	*0.3	*20	...
Bolivia	1991	250	154	0.6	1991	1.7	42	168 292
Brazil	1995	165	58	0.3	1994	0.4	9	...
Chile	1988	364	231	0.6	1994	*0.8	*10 365	...
Colombia	1982	39	37	0.9	1982	0.1	99	2 543 188
Ecuador	1990	169	215	1.3	1990	0.1	823	4 874 711
Guyana	1982	115	230	2.0	1982	0.2	4	31 461
Peru	1981	273	...	...	1984	0.2	8 331	...
Venezuela	1992	*208	*32	*0.2	1992	0.5	960	*4 608 314
Asia								
Brunei Darussalam	1984	91	527	5.8	1984	0.1	49	544 000
China	1993	537	187	0.5	1993	0.6	16	46 834
Cyprus	1992	205	230	1.1	1992	0.2	8	37 946
India	1990	*151	114	*0.8	1990	0.8	49	*326 973
Indonesia	1988	181	...	...	1988	0.2	1 467	8 092 983
Iran, Islamic Republic of	1985	65	38	0.6	1985	0.1	450	6 891 269
Israel	1984	4 826	1 032	0.2	1992	2.2	727	...
Japan	1992	5 677	869	0.2	1991	3.0	111 137	19 987 872
Jordan	1986	106	7	0.1	1986	0.3	1	13 366
Korea, Republic of	1994	2 636	317	0.1	1994	2.8	117 159	67 220 220
Kuwait	1984	924	343	0.4	1984	0.9	44	47 097
Lebanon	1980	67	2	0.0	1980	...	8	122 222
Malaysia	1992	87	88	1.0	1992	0.4	29	337 231
Nepal	1980	22	5	0.2	1980	...	...	...
Pakistan	1990	54	76	1.4	1987	0.9	51	...
Philippines	1984	90	35	0.4	1984	0.1	11	127 000
Qatar	1986	593	158	0.3	1986	0.0	17	29 039
Singapore	1994	2 512	1 524	0.6	1994	1.1	415	165 114
Sri Lanka	1985	173	43	0.2	1984	0.2	16	98 052
Thailand	1991	173	51	0.3	1991	0.2	70	402 800
Turkey	1991	209	23	0.1	1991	0.8	58 158	278 711 667
Uzbekistan	1992	*1 760	*313	*0.2	1992	...	...	...
Viet Nam	1985	334	...	...	1985	0.4	8	24 900
Europe								
Austria	1993	1 604	801	0.5	1993	1.5	3 841	2 393 931
Belarus	1992	3 300	515	0.2	1992	0.9	841	255 036
Belgium	1991	*1 814	*2 200	*1.2	1991	*1.7	*11 229	*6 189 727
Bulgaria	1992	4 240	1 205	0.3	1992	1.7	348	82 057
Croatia	1992	1 977	845	0.4	1992	...	4 844	2 450 150
Czech Republic	1994	1 285	949	0.7	1994	1.3	1 261	981 701
Denmark	1993	2 647	2 656	1.0	1993	1.9	3 039	1 147 883
Estonia	1994	3 296	550	0.2	1994	0.6	141	42 685
Finland	1993	3 675	2 360	0.6	1993	2.3	2 111	574 408
France	1993	2 537	2 926	1.2	1993	2.5	3 021	1 190 700

Country Pays País	Year Année Año	Personnel engaged in R&D Personnel employé à des travaux de R-D Personal dedicado a actividades de I y D			Year Année Año	Expenditure for R&D Dépenses consacrées à R-D Gastos dedicados a la I y D		
		Scientists and engineers per million population Scientifiques et ingénieurs par million d'habitants Científicos e ingenieros por millón de habitantes	Technicians per million population Techniciens par million d'habitants Técnicos por millón de habitantes	Number of technicians per scientist or engineer Nombre de techniciens par scientifique ou ingénieur Número de técnicos por científico o ingeniero		As percentage of gross national product (GNP) En pourcentage du produit national brut (PNB) En porcentaje del producto nacional bruto (PNB)	Per capita (in national currency) Par habitant (en monnaie nationale) Por persona (en moneda nacional)	Annual average per R&D scientist or engineer (in national currency) Moyenne annuelle par scientifique ou ingénieur de R-D (en monnaie nationale) Promedio anual por científico o ingeniero de I y D (en moneda nacional)
		(1)	(2)	(3)		(4)	(5)	(6)
Germany	1991	3 016	1 607	0.5	1991	2.6	933	309 452
Greece	1993	774	314	0.4	1993	0.5	9 681	12 510 585
Hungary	1993	1 157	588	0.5	1993	1.0	3 397	2 935 014
Iceland	1989	3 067	1 603	0.5	1989	1.1	12 393	4 040 103
Ireland	1993	1 871	510	0.3	1993	1.4	114	60 710
Italy	1993	1 303	796	0.6	1993	1.3	341 675	262 230 526
Latvia	1994	1 165	3	0.2	1994	...	...	...
Lithuania	1992	1 278	...	...	1992	...	...	...
Malta	1988	.	.	0.1	1988	0.0	0	294
Netherlands	1991	2 656	1 774	0.7	1991	1.9	689	259 525
Norway	1993	3 434	1 705	0.5	1993	1.9	3 318	966 104
Poland	1992	1 083	1 380	1.3	1992	0.9	249 773	230 624 131
Portugal	1990	599	381	0.6	1990	0.6	5 273	8 807 075
Romania	1994	1 382	613	0.4	1994	0.7	14 719	10 652 279
Russian Federation	1993	4 358	905	0.2	1993	*0.8	*8 876	*2 036 838
Slovakia	1994	1 922	796	0.4	1994	1.1	839	436 473
Slovenia	1992	2 998	2 390	0.8	1992	1.5	7 794	2 599 849
Spain	1993	1 098	342	0.3	1993	0.9	14 008	12 853 135
Sweden	1993	3 714	3 173	0.9	1993	3.5	5 565	1 498 451
Switzerland	1992	...	...	...	1992	2.6	1 302	...
The Former Yugoslav Rep. of Macedonia	1991	1 258	334	0.3	1991	...	...	...
Ukraine	1989	6 761	...	...	1989	...	...	...
United Kingdom	1993	2 417	1 019	0.4	1993	2.2	239	98 779
Federal Rep. of Yugoslavia	1992	1 476	400	0.4	1992	...	0	30
Oceania								
Australia	1990	2 477	943	0.4	1990	1.4	301	121 605
Fiji	1986	.	.	2.5	1986	0.3	5	105 556
French Polynesia	1983	.	.	0.9	1983	0.2	1 968	19 101 176
Guam	1991	.	.	0.5	1991	...	16	96 304
Kiribati	1980	.	.	0.5	1980	...	...	...
New Caledonia	1985	.	.	0.9	1985	0.6	5 167	10 400 260
New Zealand	1993	1 778	822	0.5	1993	1.1	237	133 140
Tonga	1981	.	.	0.4	1980	0.9	5	42 600

5.2 Scientific and technical personnel in R&D
Personnel scientifique et technique dans la R-D
Personal científico y técnico en I y D

5.2 Number of scientists, engineers and technicians engaged in research and experimental development

Nombre de scientifiques, d'ingénieurs et de techniciens employés à des travaux de recherche et de développement expérimental

Número de científicos, ingenieros y técnicos empleados en trabajos de investigación y de desarrollo experimental

Please refer to introduction for definitions of categories included in this table.	Pour les définitions des catégories présentées dans ce tableau, se référer à l'introduction.

En la introducción se dan las definiciones de las categorías que figuran en este cuadro.

SET = Scientists, engineers and technicians

SET = Scientifiques, ingénieurs et techniciens

SET = Científicos, ingenieros y técnicos

Data are expressed in full-time equivalent (FTE) except for certain countries where the symbole # indicates the number of full-time plus part-time R&D personnel.

Les données en équivalent plein temps (EPT) sauf pour certains pays ou le symbole # indique le nombre de personnel de R-D à plein temps et à temps partiel.

Los datos se expresan en equivalente de jornada completa 9EJC) salvo para ciertos países donde el símbolo # indica el número de personal de I y D de jornada completa y de jornada parcial.

Country Pays País	Year Année Año	Total (FTE) Total (EPT) Total (EJC)	Scientists and engineers Scientifiques et ingénieurs Científicos e ingenieros		Technicians Techniciens Técnicos	
		SET	Total	F	Total	F
		(1)	(2)	(3)	(4)	(5)
Africa						
Benin‡	1989	1 036	794	100	242	64
Burundi‡#	1989	338	170	17	168	...
Central African Republic #	1990	254	162	16	92	5
Congo‡#	1984	2 335	862	...	1 473	...
Egypt‡	1991	46 022	26 415	...	19 607	...
Gabon‡#	1987	217	199	...	18	...
Guinea	1984	1 893	1 282	...	611	...
Libyan Arab Jamahiriya	1980	2 600	1 100	...	1 500	...
Madagascar‡#	1989	1 225	269	84	956	...
Mauritius‡	1992	559	389	...	170	...
Nigeria‡	1987	7 380	1 338	...	6 042	...
Rwanda	1985	*138	71	...	*67	...
Senegal	1981	4 610	1 948	...	2 662	...
Seychelles	1983	24	18	...	6	...
South Africa	1991	17 108	12 102	...	5 006	...
Tunisia‡	1992	*3 860	*3 260	...	*600	...
America, North						
British Virgin Islands	1984	-	-	-	-	-
Canada‡	1991	92 870	65 350	...	27 520	...
Costa Rica #	1992	...	1 722	...	...	...
Cuba‡	1992	24 235	14 770	6 383	9 465	5 251
El Salvador‡	1992	1 714	102	...	1 612	...
Guatemala‡	1988	1 783	858	...	925	...
Jamaica‡	1986	33	18	10	15	3
Mexico‡	1993	11 072	8 595	...	2 477	...
Nicaragua #	1987	1 027	725	...	302	...
St. Lucia	1984	139	53	...	86	...

Scientific and technical personnel in R&D 5.2
Personnel scientifique et technique dans la R-D
Personal científico y técnico en I y D

Country / Pays / País	Year / Année / Año	Total (FTE) / Total (EPT) / Total (EJC) SET	Scientists and engineers / Scientifiques et ingénieurs / Científicos e ingenieros Total	F	Technicians / Techniciens / Técnicos Total	F
		(1)	(2)	(3)	(4)	(5)
Trinidad and Tobago	1984	529	275	58	254	44
Turks and Caicos Islands	1984	-	-	-	-	-
United States‡	1993	...	*962 700	...	...	...
America, South						
Argentina	1988	*17 329	*11 088	4 798	*6 241	...
Bolivia‡	1991	2 720	1 681	700	1 039	500
Brazil‡	1995	36 081	26 754	...	9 327	...
Chile‡#	1988	7 570	4 630	...	2 940	...
Colombia‡	1982	2 107	1 083	...	1 024	...
Ecuador	1990	3 936	1 732	...	2 204	...
Guyana‡	1982	267	89	...	178	...
Paraguay #	1981	807		...	...	...
Peru‡	1981	...	4 858	...	...	...
Uruguay #	1987	...	2 093	720	...	...
Venezuela	1992	*4 908	*4 258	*1 490	*650	*205
Asia						
Brunei Darussalam‡#	1984	136	20	...	116	...
China‡	1993	442 500	418 500	...	224 000	...
Cyprus	1992	312	147	...	165	...
India‡	1990	*224 773	*128 036	7 710	96 737	6 138
Indonesia #	1988	...	32 038	...	...	...
Iran, Islamic Republic of	1985	5 048	3 194	...	1 854	...
Israel‡	1984	24 400	20 100	10 400	4 300	1 400
Japan‡	1992	813 360	705 346	...	108 014	...
Jordan‡	1986	447	418	54	29	6
Korea, Republic of‡	1994	131 587	117 486	9 502	14 141	...
Kuwait‡#	1984	2 072	1 511	334	561	113
Lebanon‡	1980	186	180	...	6	...
Malaysia	1992	3 288	1 633	501	1 655	507
Maldives	1986	-	-	-	-	-
Nepal‡	1980	409	334	...	75	...
Pakistan‡	1990	15 940	6 626	464	9 314	...
Philippines #	1984	6 685	4 830	2 319	1 855	...
Qatar‡#	1986	290	229	58	61	2
Singapore‡	1994	11 384	7 086	...	4 298	...
Sri Lanka	1985	3 483	2 790	667	693	188
Tajikistan‡	1992	...	3 974	1 144	...	...
Thailand #	1991	12 650	9 752	...	2 898	...
Turkey‡	1991	13 277	11 948	...	1 329	...
Uzbekistan	1992	*44 312	*37 625	*17 005	*6 687	...
Viet Nam‡	1985	...	20 000	...	...	...
Europe						
Austria	1993	19 217	12 820	...	6 397	...
Belarus	1992	38 939	33 685	5 463	5 254	...
Belgium‡	1991	*40 063	*18 105	...	*21 958	...
Bulgaria	1992	48 577	37 825	17 362	10 752	6 555
Croatia	1992	12 746	8 928	3 339	3 818	2 332
Czech Republic‡	1994	23 096	13 225	...	9 771	...
Denmark‡	1993	27 390	13 673	...	13 717	...
Estonia #	1994	5 927	5 079	2 098	848	588
Finland‡	1993	30 527	18 588	...	11 939	...
France‡	1993	314 170	145 898	...	168 272	...
Germany	1991	369 119	240 803	...	128 316	...
Greece	1993	11 287	8 030	...	3 257	...
Hungary‡	1993	17 821	11 818	...	6 003	...
Iceland‡	1989	1 177	773	...	404	...
Ireland	1993	8 389	6 592	...	1 797	...
Italy	1993	119 933	74 434	...	45 499	...
Latvia	1994	3 954	3 010	...	944	...
Lithuania	1992	...	4 750	1 518	...	...
Malta‡	1988	39	34	...	5	...
Netherlands‡	1991	66 710	40 000	...	26 710	...

5.2 Scientific and technical personnel in R&D
Personnel scientifique et technique dans la R-D
Personal científico y técnico en I y D

Country Pays País	Year Année Año	Total (FTE) Total (EPT) Total (EJC) SET	Scientists and engineers Scientifiques et ingénieurs Científicos e ingenieros Total	 F	Technicians Techniciens Técnicos Total	 F
		(1)	(2)	(3)	(4)	(5)
Norway‡	1993	22 091	14 763	...	7 328	...
Poland‡	1992	94 250	41 440	...	52 810	...
Portugal	1990	9 663	5 908	...	3 755	...
Romania	1994	44 944	31 672	14 048	13 272	7 991
Russian Federation #	1993	778 800	644 900	377 300	133 900	42 400
San Marino	1986	-	-	-	-	-
Slovakia‡	1994	14 493	10 249	...	4 244	...
Slovenia	1992	10 404	5 789	1 745	4 615	2 197
Spain‡	1993	56 863	43 367	11 899	13 496	3 093
Sweden‡	1993	59 876	32 288	...	27 588	...
The Former Yugoslav Rep. of Macedonia‡	1991	3 296	2 605	1 008	691	386
Ukraine‡	1989	...	348 600	...	...	...
United Kingdom	1993	199 000	140 000	...	59 000	...
Federal Rep. of Yugoslavia‡	1992	15 429	11 246	...	4 183	1 858
Oceania						
Australia	1990	57 759	41 837	...	15 922	...
Fiji‡#	1986	126	36	4	90	10
French Polynesia‡	1983	33	17	...	16	...
Guam‡	1991	34	23	5	11	5
Kiribati	1980	3	2	-	1	-
New Caledonia‡	1985	148	77	7	71	...
New Zealand	1993	9 064	6 198	...	2 866	...
Tonga‡#	1981	15	11	-	4	1

AFRICA:

Benin:

E--> Not including data for the productive sector (non-integrated R&D).

FR-> Non compris les données relatives au secteur de la production (activités de R-D non intégrées).

ESP> Excluídos los datos relativos al sector productivo (actividades de I y D no integradas).

Burundi:

E--> Not including data for the productive sector. 51 of the scientists and engineers in column 2 are foreigners.

FR-> Non compris les données relatives au secteur de la production. 51 scientifiques et ingénieurs de la colonne 2 sont ressortissants étrangers.

ESP> Excluídos los datos relativos al sector productivo. 51 científicos e ingenieros de la columna 2 son extranjeros.

Congo:

E--> 206 of the scientists and engineers in column 2 are foreigners. Not including military and defence R&D.

FR-> 206 scientifiques et ingénieurs de la colonne 2 sont ressortissants étrangers. Non compris les activités de R-D de caractère militaire ou relevant de la défense nationale.

ESP> 206 científicos e ingenieros de la columna 2 son extranjeros. Excluídas las actividades militares y de defensa de I y D.

Egypt:

E--> Not including military and defence R&D.

FR-> Non compris les activités de R-D de caractère militaire ou relevant de la défense nationale.

ESP> Excluídas las actividades militares y de defensa de I y D.

Gabon:

E--> Data for scientists and engineers in column 2 do not include the productive sector, whilst technicians in column 4 relate only to those in the general service sector.

FR-> Les données relatives aux scientifiques et ingénieurs de la colonne 2 ne comprennent pas le secteur de la production et celles relatives aux techniciens de la colonne 4 ne se réfèrent qu'au secteur de service général.

ESP> Para los científicos e ingenieros de la columna 2 los datos no incluyen el sector productivo y para los técnicos de la columna 4 sólo se refieren al sector de servicio general.

Madagascar:

E--> Not including data for the higher education sector.

FR-> Non compris les données relatives au secteur de l'enseignement supérieur.

ESP> Excluídos los datos relativos al sector de enseñanza superior.

Mauritius:

E--> Not including data for the productive sector.

FR-> Non compris les données relatives au secteur de la production.

ESP> Excluídos los datos relativos al sector productivo.

Nigeria:

E--> Data relate only to 23 out of 26 national research institutes under the Federal Ministry of Science and Technology.

FR-> Les données ne concernent que 23 des 26 instituts de recherche nationaux sous tutelle du Ministère fédéral de la Science et de la Technologie.

ESP> Los datos sólo se refieren a 23 de los 26 centros nacionales de investigación bajo tutela del Ministerio Federal de Ciencia y Tecnología.

Tunisia:

E--> Not including data for the productive sector.

FR-> Non compris les données relative au secteur de la production.

ESP> Excluídos los datos relativos al sector productivo.

AMERICA, NORTH:

Canada:

E--> Not including social sciences and humanities in the productive sector (integrated R&D).

FR-> Non compris les sciences sociales et humaines dans le secteur de la production (activités de R-D intégrées).

ESP> Excluídas las ciencias sociales y humanas del sector productivo (actividades de I y D integradas).

Cuba:

E--> Not including military and defence R&D.

FR-> Non compris les activités de R-D de caractère militaire ou relevant de la défense nationale.

ESP> Excluídas las actividades militares y de defensa de I y D.

El Salvador:

E--> Data refer to scientists and engineers and technicians engaged in public enterprises. Not including data for the higher education sector.

FR-> Les données se réfèrent aux scientifiques et ingénieurs et techniciens employés dans les entreprises publiques. Non

Scientific and technical personnel in R&D **5.2**
Personnel scientifique et technique dans la R-D
Personal científico y técnico en I y D

compris les données relatives au secteur de l'enseignement supérieur.

ESP> Los datos se refieren a los científicos e ingenieros y técnicos empleados en las empresas públicas. Excluídos los datos relativos al sector de enseñanza superior.

Guatemala:

E--> Data relate to the productive sector (integrated R&D) and the higher education sector only. 88 of the scientists and engineers in column 2 are foreigners.

FR-> Les données ne concernent que le secteur de la production (activités de R-D intégrées) et le secteur de l'enseignement supérieur. 88 scientifiques et ingénieurs de la colonne 2 sont ressortissants étrangers.

ESP> Los datos conciernen el sector productivo (actividades de I y D integradas) y el sector de enseñanza superior solamente. 88 científicos e ingenieros de la columna 2 son extranjeros.

Jamaica:

E--> Data relate to the Scientific Research Council only.

FR-> Les données se réfèrent au *Scientific Research Council* seulement.

ESP> Los datos se refieren al *Scientific Research Council* solamente.

Mexico:

E--> Data relate to the productive sector (integrated R&D) and the higher education sector only.

FR-> Les données ne concernent que le secteur de la production (activités de R-D intégrées) et le secteur de l'enseignement supérieur.

ESP> Los datos conciernen el sector productivo (actividades de I y D integradas) y el sector de enseñanza superior solamente.

United States:

E--> Not including military personnel engaged in R&D.

FR-> Non compris le personnel militaire employé à des travaux de R-D.

ESP> Excluído el personal militar empleado en trabajos de I y D.

AMERICA, SOUTH:

Bolivia:

E--> Data refer to full-time scientists and engineers and technicians.

FR-> Les données se réfèrent aux scientifiques et ingénieurs et techniciens à plein temps.

ESP> Los datos se refieren a los científicos e ingenieros y técnicos de jornada completa.

Brazil:

E--> Data for scientists and engineers refer to researchers listed in the Directory of Research Groups in Brazil by the *Conselho Nacional de Desenvolvimento Científico e Tecnológico (CNPq)*.

FR-> Les données relatives aux scientifiques et ingénieurs se réfèrent aux chercheurs figurant dans le Répertoire des Groupes des Chercheurs élaboré par le *Conselho Nacional de Desenvolvimento Científico e Tecnológico (CNPq)*.

ESP> Los datos relativos a los científicos e ingenieros se refieren a los investigadores que figuran en el Directorio de los Grupos de Investigadores preparado por el *Conselho Nacional de Desenvolvimento Científico e Tecnológico (CNPq)*.

Chile:

E--> Not including military and defence R&D.

FR-> Non compris les activités de R-D de caractère militaire ou relevant de la défense nationale.

ESP> Excluídas las actividades militares y de defensa de I y D.

Colombia:

E--> Not including data for the productive sector (non-integrated R&D).

FR-> Non compris les données relatives au secteur de la production (activités de R-D non intégrées).

ESP> Excluídos los datos relativos al sector productivo (actividades de I y D no integradas).

Guyana:

E--> Not including military and defence R&D. Data for the general service sector and for medical sciences in the higher education sector are also excluded.

FR-> Non compris les activités de R-D de caractère militaire ou relevant de la défense nationale. Les données relatives au secteur de service général et les sciences médicales du secteur de l'enseignement supérieur sont aussi exclues.

ESP> Excluídas las actividades militares y de defensa de I y D. Se excluyen también los datos relativos al sector de servicio general y las ciencias médicas del sector de enseñanza superior.

Peru:

E--> Data for scientists and engineers refer only to full-time.

FR-> Pour les scientifiques et ingénieurs, les données se réfèrent seulement aux effectifs à plein temps.

ESP> Para los científicos e ingenieros los datos se refieren solamente a los efectivos de jornada completa.

ASIA:

Brunei Darussalam:

E--> Data relate to 2 research institutes only.

FR-> Les données ne concernent que 2 instituts de recherche.

ESP> Los datos se refieren a 2 centros de investigación solamente.

China:

E--> Data in columns 1 and 4 include auxiliary personnel.

FR-> Les chiffres des colonnes 1 et 4 comprennent le personnel auxiliaire.

ESP> Las cifras de las columnas 1 y 4 incluyen el personal auxiliar.

India:

E--> Data for scientists and engineers include 22,100 (estimate for 1982) personnel in the higher education sector. Data for women scientists and engineers and for technicians in the higher education sector are not included.

FR-> Les données relatives aux scientifiques et ingénieurs comprennent 22 100 personnes (estimation pour 1982) dans le secteur de l'enseignement supérieur. Les données pour les femmes scientifiques et ingénieurs et pour les techniciens dans l'enseignement supérieur ne sont pas comprises.

ESP> Los datos para los científicos e ingenieros incluyen 22 100 personas (estimación para 1982) en el sector de enseñanza superior. Se excluyen los datos relativos a las mujeres científicos e ingenieros e a los técnicos del sector de enseñanza superior.

Israel:

E--> In column 3, the number relating to female scientists and engineers is counted in full-time plus part-time.

FR-> Dans la colonne 3, les scientifiques et ingénieurs de sexe féminin sont comptés en plein temps et temps partiel.

ESP> En la columna 3, la cifra que se refiere a los científicos e ingenieros de sexo feminino se cuenta en jornada completa y jornada parcial.

Japan:

E--> Data refer to full-time scientists and engineers and technicians. Not including social sciences and humanities in the productive sector (integrated R&D).

FR-> Les données se réfèrent aux scientifiques et ingénieurs et techniciens à plein temps. Non compris les sciences sociales et humaines dans le secteur de la production (activités de R-D intégrées).

ESP> Los datos se refieren a los científicos e ingenieros y técnicos de jornada completa. Excluídas las ciencias sociales y humanas en el sector productivo (actividades de I y D integradas).

Jordan:

E--> Not including military and defence R&D.

FR-> Non compris les activités de R-D de caractère militaire ou relevant de la défense nationale.

ESP> Excluídas las actividades militares y de defensa de I y D.

Korea, Republic of:

E--> Excluding military and defence R&D and social sciences and humanities.

FR-> Non compris les activités de R-D de caractère militaire ou relevant de la défense nationale ni les sciences sociales et humaines.

ESP> Excluídas las actividades militares y de defensa de I y D y las ciencias sociales y humanas.

Kuwait:

E--> Data refer to scientific and technological activities (STA). 1,027 (F: 179) of the scientists and engineers in columns 2 and 3, and 113 (F: 67) of the technicians in columns 4 and 5 are foreigners.

FR-> Les données se réfèrent aux activités scientifiques et techniques (AST). 1,027 (F: 179) scientifiques et ingénieurs des colonnes 2 et 3, et 113 (F. 67) techniciens des colonnes 4 et 5 sont ressortissants étrangers.

ESP> Los datos se refieren a las actividades científicas y tecnológicas (ACT). 1,027 (F: 179) científicos e ingenieros de las columnas 2 y 3, y 113 (F: 67) técnicos de las columnas 4 y 5 son extranjeros.

Lebanon:

E--> Data refer to the Faculty of Science at the University of Lebanon only.

FR-> Les données ne se réfèrent qu'à la Faculté des Sciences de l'Université du Liban.

ESP> Los datos se refieren a la Facultad de Ciencias de la Universidad del Líbano solamente.

Nepal:

E--> Data refer to scientific and technological activities (STA) and do not include social sciences and humanities. Data relate to full-time scientists and engineers and technicians.

FR-> Les données se réfèrent aux activités scientifiques et techniques (AST) et ne comprennent pas les sciences sociales et humaines. Les données se réfèrent aux scientifiques et ingénieurs et techniciens à plein temps.

ESP> Los datos se refieren a las actividades científicas y tecnológicas (ACT) y no incluyen las ciencias sociales y humanas.

5.2 Scientific and technical personnel in R&D
Personnel scientifique et technique dans la R-D
Personal científico y técnico en I y D

Los datos se refieren a los científicos e ingenieros y técnicos de jornada completa.

Pakistan:

E--> Data relate to R&D activities concentrated mainly in government-financed research establishments only. Not including military and defence R&D.

FR-> Les données se réfèrent aux activités de R-D se trouvant pour la plupart dans les établissements de recherche financés par le gouvernement. Non compris les activités de R-D de caractère militaire ou relevant de la défense nationale.

ESP> Los datos se refieren a las actividades de I y D concentradas principalmente en los establecimientos de investigación subvencionados por el gobierno. Excluídas las actividades militares y de defensa de I y D.

Qatar:

E--> 138 of the scientists and engineers in column 2 and 54 of the technicians in column 4 are foreigners. Not including social sciences and humanities in the higher education sector.

FR-> 138 scientifiques et ingénieurs de la colonne 2 et 54 techniciens de la colonne 4 sont ressortissants étrangers. Compte non tenu des sciences sociales et humaines dans le secteur de l'enseignement supérieur.

ESP> 138 científicos e ingenieros de la columna 2 y 54 técnicos de la columna 4 son extranjeros. Excluídas las ciencias sociales y humanas del sector de enseñanza superior.

Singapore:

E--> Data in columns 1 and 4 include non-degree researchers (1,574) and auxiliary personnel.

FR-> Les chiffres des colonnes 1 et 4 comprennent les chercheurs non diplômés (1 574) et le personnel auxiliaire.

ESP> Las cifras de las columnas 1 y 4 incluyen los investigadores no diplomados (1 574) y el personal auxiliar.

Tajikistan:

E--> Data refer to full-time scientists and engineers.

FR-> Les données se réfèrent aux scientifiques et ingénieurs à plein temps.

ESP> Los datos se refieren a los científicos e ingenieros de jornada completa.

Turkey:

E--> Not including social sciences and humanities in the general service sector. Data relating to technicians in columns 1 and 4 do not include the higher education sector.

FR-> Compte non tenu des sciences sociales et humaines dans le secteur de service général. Les données relatives aux techniciens des colonnes 1 et 4 ne comprennent pas le secteur de l'enseignement supérieur.

ESP> Excluídas las ciencias sociales y humanas del sector de servicio general. Para los técnicos de las columnas 1 y 4, los datos no incluyen el sector de enseñanza superior.

Viet Nam:

E--> Not including data for the general service sector.

FR-> Non compris les données pour le secteur de service général.

ESP> Excluídos los datos relativos al sector de servicio general.

EUROPE:

Belgium:

E--> Data in columns 1 and 4 include auxiliary personnel.

FR-> Les chiffres des colonnes 1 et 4 comprennent le personnel auxiliaire.

ESP> Las cifras de las columnas 1 y 4 incluyen el personal auxiliar.

Czech Republic:

E--> Not including military and defence R&D.

FR-> Non compris les activités de R-D de caractère militaire ou relevant de la défense nationale.

ESP> Excluídas las actividades militares y de defensa de I y D.

Denmark:

E--> Data in columns 1 and 4 include auxiliary personnel.

FR-> Les chiffres des colonnes 1 et 4 comprennent le personnel auxiliaire.

ESP> Las cifras de las columnas 1 y 4 incluyen el personal auxiliar.

Finland:

E--> Data in columns 1 and 4 include auxiliary personnel.

FR-> Les chiffres des colonnes 1 et 4 comprennent le personnel auxiliaire.

ESP> Las cifras de las columnas 1 y 4 incluyen el personal auxiliar.

France:

E--> Data in columns 1 and 4 include auxiliary personnel.

FR-> Les chiffres des colonnes 1 et 4 comprennent le personnel auxiliaire.

ESP> Las cifras de las columnas 1 y 4 incluyen el personal auxiliar.

Hungary:

E--> Not including scientists and engineers engaged in the administration of R&D; data in columns 1 and 4 include skilled workers. Of military R&D, only that part carried out in civil establishments is included.

FR-> Non compris les scientifiques et ingénieurs employés dans les services administratifs de R-D; les chiffres des colonnes 1 et 4 comprennent les ouvriers qualifiés. Pour la R-D de caractère militaire, seule la partie effectuée dans les établissements civils a été considérée.

ESP> No incluyen los científicos e ingenieros empleados en los servicios administrativos de I y D; las cifras de las columnas 1 y 4 comprenden los obreros calificados. Para las actividades de I y D de carácter militar, sólo se ha considerado la parte correspondiente a los establecimientos civiles.

Iceland:

E--> Data in columns 1 and 4 include auxiliary personnel.

FR-> Les chiffres des colonnes 1 et 4 incluent le personnel auxiliaire.

ESP> Las cifras de las columnas 1 y 4 incluyen el personal auxiliar.

Malta:

E--> Data relate to the higher education sector only.

FR-> Les données ne concernent que le secteur de l'enseignement supérieur.

ESP> Los datos se refieren exclusivamente al sector de enseñanza superior.

Netherlands:

E--> Data in columns 1 and 4 include auxiliary personnel.

FR-> Les chiffres des colonnes 1 et 4 comprennent le personnel auxiliaire.

ESP> Las cifras de las columnas 1 y 4 incluyen el personal auxiliar.

Norway:

E--> Data in columns 1 and 4 include auxiliary personnel.

FR-> Les chiffres des colonnes 1 et 4 comprennent le personnel auxiliaire.

ESP> Las cifras de las columnas 1 y 4 incluyen el personal auxiliar.

Poland:

E--> Not including military and defence R&D.

FR-> Non compris les activités de R-D de caractère militaire ou relevant de la défense nationale.

ESP> Excluídas las actividades militares y de defensa de I y D.

Slovakia:

E--> Not including military and defence R&D.

FR-> Non compris les activités de R-D de caractère militaire ou relevant de la défense nationale.

ESP> Excluídas las actividades militares y de defensa de I y D.

Spain:

E--> Data relating to technicians in columns 1 and 4 do not include the higher education sector.

FR-> Les données relatives aux techniciens des colonnes 1 et 4 ne comprennent pas le secteur de l'enseignement supérieur.

ESP> Para los técnicos de las columnas 1 y 4, los datos no incluyen el sector de enseñanza superior.

Sweden:

E--> Data in columns 1 and 4 include auxiliary personnel.

FR-> Les chiffres des colonnes 1 et 4 comprennent le personnel auxiliaire.

ESP> Las cifras de las columnas 1 y 4 incluyen el personal auxiliar.

The Former Yugoslav Republic of Macedonia:

E--> Data for the higher education sector refer to full-time plus part-time scientists and engineers and technicians.

FR-> Les données pour le secteur de l'enseignement supérieur se réfèrent aux scientifiques et ingénieurs, et téchniciens à plein temps et à temps partiel.

ESP> Los datos relativos al sector de enseñanza superior se refieren a los científicos e técnicos de jornada completa et de jornada parcial.

Ukraine:

E--> Data in column 2 refer to scientific workers, i.e. all persons with a higher scientific degree or scientific title, regardless of the nature of their work, persons undertaking research work in scientific establishments and scientific teaching staff in institutions of higher education; they also include persons undertaking scientific work in industrial enterprises.

FR-> Les données de la colonne 2 se réfèrent aux travailleurs scientifiques, c.-à-d., à toutes les personnes ayant un diplôme scientifique supérieur ou un titre scientifique, sans considération de la nature de leur travail, aux personnes qui effectuent un travail de recherche dans des institutions scientifiques et au personnel scientifique enseignant dans des établissements d'enseignement supérieur; sont incluses aussi les personnes qui effectuent des travaux scientifiques dans les entreprises industrielles.

Scientific and technical personnel in R&D **5.2**
Personnel scientifique et technique dans la R-D
Personal científico y técnico en I y D

ESP> Los datos de la columna 2 se refieren a los trabajadores científicos, es decir, a todas las personas que poseen un diploma científico superior o un título científico, sin tener en cuenta la naturaleza de su trabajo, a las personas que efectuan un trabajo de investigación en las instituciones científicas y al personal científico que ejerce funciones docentes en los establecimientos de enseñanza superior; también se incluyen las personas que efectuan trabajos científicos en las empresas industriales.

Federal Republic of Yugoslavia:
E--> Not including military and defence R&D.
FR-> Non compris les activités de R-D de caractère militaire ou relevant de la défense nationale.
ESP> Excluídas las actividades militares y de defensa de I y D.

OCEANIA:

Fiji:
E--> Data relate to one research institute only.
FR-> Les données ne concernent qu'un institut de recherche .
ESP> Los datos se refieren a un centro de investigación solamente.

French Polynesia:
E--> Data relate to full-time personnel in one research institute only.
FR-> Les données concernent les effectifs à plein temps dans un seul institut de recherche.

ESP> Los datos se refieren a los efectivos de jornada completa en un centro de investigación solamente.

Guam:
E--> Data relate to the higher education sector only.
FR-> Les données ne concernent que le secteur de l'enseignement supérieur.
ESP> Los datos se refieren exclusivamente al sector de enseñanza superior.

New Caledonia:
E--> Data refer only to 6 out of 11 research institutes.
FR-> Les données ne se rapportent qu'à 6 instituts de recherche sur 11.
ESP> Los datos sólo se refieren a 6 de los 11 centros de investigación.

Tonga:
E--> Data relate to one research institute only, where 8 of the scientists and engineers are foreigners.
FR-> Les données ne concernent qu'un institut de recherche, où 8 des scientifiques et ingénieurs sont ressortissants étrangers.
ESP> Los datos se refieren a un centro de investigación solamente, donde 8 de los científicos e ingenieros son extranjeros.

5.3 R&D personnel by sector of performance
Personnel de R-D par secteur d'exécution
Personal de I y D por sector de ejecución

5.3 Total personnel engaged in research and experimental development by sector of performance and by category of personnel

Total du personnel employé à des travaux de recherche et de développement expérimental, par secteur d'exécution et par catégorie de personnel

Personal empleado en trabajos de investigación y de desarrollo experimental, por sector de ejecución y por categoría de personal

Please refer to introduction for definitions of categories included in this table.

Pour les définitions des catégories présentées dans ce tableau, se référer à l'introduction.

En la introducción se dan las definiciones de las categorías que figuran en este cuadro.

Data are expressed in full-time equivalent (FTE) except for certain countries where the symbol # indicates the number of full-time plus part-time R&D personnel.

Les données sont exprimées en équivalent plein temps (EPT) sauf pour certains pays où le symbole # indique le nombre de personnel de R-D à plein temps et à temps partiel.

Los datos se expresan en equivalente de jornada completa (EJC) salvo para ciertos países donde el símbolo # indica el número de personal de I y D de jornada completa y de jornada parcial.

Country Pays País	Year Année Año	Category of personnel Catégorie de personnel Categoría de personal	Sector of performance/Secteur d'exécution/Sector de ejecución				
			All sectors (FTE) Tous les secteurs (EPT) Todos los sectores (EJC)	Productive sector / Secteur de la production / Sector productivo		Higher education Enseigne-ment supérieur Enseñanza superior	General service Service général Servicio general
				Integrated R&D Activités de R-D intégrées Actividades de I y D integradas	Non-inte-grated R&D Activités de R-D non intégrées Actividades de I y D no integradas		
			(1)	(2)	(3)	(4)	(5)
Africa							
Benin	1989	Total in R&D	...	947	...	1 209	531
		Scientists and engineers	...	150	...	497	147
		Technicians	...	64	...	89	89
		Auxiliary personnel	...	733	...	623	295
Burundi #	1989	Total in R&D	...	...	...	73	741
		Scientists and engineers	...	...	...	56	114
		Technicians	...	...	...	6	162
		Auxiliary personnel	...	...	...	11	465
Central African Republic #	1990	Total in R&D	...	...	...	63	...
		Scientists and engineers	...	...	...	51	...
		Technicians	...	...	...	11	...
		Auxiliary personnel	...	...	...	1	...
Congo‡#	1984	Scientists and engineers	862	205	163	473	21
		Technicians	1 473	585	828	52	8
Egypt‡	1991	Total in R&D	102 296	12 968	8 113	61 124	20 091
		% by sector	100	12.7	7.9	59.8	19.6
		Scientists and engineers	26 415	3 805	772	14 065	7 773
		Technicians	19 607	3 400	1 694	10 347	4 166
		Auxiliary personnel	56 274	5 763	5 647	36 712	8 152
Gabon #	1987	Total in R&D	...	...	...	...	90
		Scientists and engineers	...	...	...	157	42
		Technicians	...	...	...	...	18
		Auxiliary personnel	...	...	...	...	30

R&D personnel by sector of performance **5.3**
Personnel de R-D par secteur d'exécution
Personal de I y D por sector de ejecución

Country / Pays / País	Year / Année / Año	Category of personnel / Catégorie de personnel / Categoría de personal	All sectors (FTE) Tous les secteurs (EPT) Todos los sectores (EJC)	Sector of performance/Secteur d'exécution/Sector de ejecución		Higher education Enseignement supérieur Enseñanza superior	General service Service général Servicio general
				Productive sector / Secteur de la production / Sector productivo			
				Integrated R&D Activités de R-D intégrées Actividades de I y D integradas	Non-integrated R&D Activités de R-D non intégrées Actividades de I y D no integradas		
			(1)	(2)	(3)	(4)	(5)
Guinea	1984	Total in R&D	2 357	562	627	780	388
		% by sector	100	23.8	26.6	33.1	16.5
		Scientists and engineers	1 282	210	235	634	203
		Technicians	611	182	255	75	99
		Auxiliary personnel	464	170	137	71	86
Libyan Arab Jamahiriya	1980	Scientists and engineers	1 100	200	——>	800	100
Madagascar #	1989	Total in R&D	...	1 638	106	...	93
		Scientists and engineers	...	206	33	...	30
		Technicians	...	873	52	...	31
		Auxiliary personnel	...	559	21	...	32
Mauritius	1992	Total in R&D	...	...	...	349	813
		Scientists and engineers	...	...	...	163	226
		Technicians	...	...	...	43	127
		Auxiliary personnel	...	...	...	143	460
Nigeria‡	1987	Total in R&D	...	...	...	...	12 880
		Scientists and engineers	...	...	...	...	1 338
		Technicians	...	...	...	...	6 042
		Auxiliary personnel	...	...	...	...	5 500
Rwanda	1985	Total in R&D	*183	*23	——>	52	108
		% by sector	100	*12.6	——>	28.4	59.0
		Scientists and engineers	74	4	3	33	34
		Technicians	72	6	5	12	49
		Auxiliary personnel	45	*13	——>	7	25
Senegal	1981	Scientists and engineers	1 948	285	——>	826	837
		Technicians	2 662	913	——>	156	1 593
Seychelles‡	1983	Total in R&D	33	-	7	-	26
		% by sector	100	-	21.2	-	78.8
		Scientists and engineers	18	-	2	-	16
		Technicians	6	-	5	-	10
		Auxiliary personnel	9	-	./.	-	./.
South Africa	1991	Total in R&D	22 224	8 480	./.	6 533	7 211
		% by sector					
		Scientists and engineers	12 102	3 395	./.	5 984	2 723
		Technicians	5 006	2 785	./.	289	1 932
		Auxiliary personnel	5 116	2 300	./.	260	2 556
Tunisia	1992	Total in R&D	...	...	...	*5 446	1 755
		Scientists and engineers	...	...	...	*2 718	542
		Technicians	...	...	...	*399	201
		Auxiliary personnel	...	...	...	*2 329	1 012
America, North							
Canada‡	1991	Total in R&D	114 500	53 730	./.	41 860	18 910
		% by sector	100	46.9	./.	36.6	16.5
		Scientists and engineers	65 350	30 290	./.	27 570	7 490
		Technicians	27 520	15 870	./.	6 400	5 250
		Auxiliary personnel	21 630	7 570	./.	7 890	6 170
Costa Rica	1992	Scientists and engineers	1 722	74	——>	1 197	451
Cuba‡	1992	Total in R&D	35 996	1 790	16 111	5 347	12 748
		% by sector	100	5.0	44.8	14.9	35.4
		Scientists and engineers	14 770	790	4 697	4 219	5 064
		Technicians	9 465	479	4 783	372	3 831
		Auxiliary personnel	11 761	521	6 631	756	3 853
El Salvador‡	1992	Total in R&D	...	1 059	./.	...	655
Guatemala	1988	Scientists and engineers	...	557	...	301	...
Jamaica‡	1986	Total in R&D	...	...	...	...	104
		Scientists and engineers	...	...	...	...	18
		Technicians	...	...	...	...	15
		Auxiliary personnel	...	...	...	...	71

5.3   R&D personnel by sector of performance
Personnel de R-D par secteur d'exécution
Personal de I y D por sector de ejecución

Country / Pays / País	Year / Année / Año	Category of personnel / Catégorie de personnel / Categoría de personal	All sectors (FTE) / Tous les secteurs (EPT) / Todos los sectores (EJC)	Productive sector / Secteur de la production / Sector productivo — Integrated R&D / Activités de R-D intégrées / Actividades de I y D integradas	Productive sector — Non-integrated R&D / Activités de R-D non intégrées / Actividades de I y D no integradas	Higher education / Enseignement supérieur / Enseñanza superior	General service / Service général / Servicio general
			(1)	(2)	(3)	(4)	(5)
Mexico	1993	Total in R&D	...	1 932	——>	10 988	...
		Scientists and Engineers	...	867	——>	7 728	...
		Technicians	...	732	——>	1 745	...
		Auxiliary personnel	...	333	——>	1 515	...
Nicaragua #	1985	Total in R&D	1 803	1 429	——>	315	59
		% by sector	100	79.3	——>	17.5	3.3
		Scientists and engineers	650	469	——>	138	43
		Technicians	212	143	——>	64	5
		Auxiliary personnel	941	817	——>	113	11
Trinidad and Tobago	1984	Total in R&D	806	217	179	307	103
		% by sector	100	26.9	22.2	38.1	12.8
		Scientists and engineers	275	61	51	149	14
		Technicians	254	41	79	114	20
		Auxiliary personnel	277	115	49	44	69
United States‡	1993	Scientists and engineers	*962 700	*764 500	——>	*128 000	*60 000
America, South							
Argentina	1988	Total in R&D	22 855	612	5 916	8 836	7 491
		% by sector	100	2.7	25.9	38.7	32.8
		Scientists and engineers	11 088	196	2 098	5 602	3 192
		Technicians	6 241	*273	1 500	2 037	2 431
		Auxiliary personnel	5 526	143	2 318	1 197	1 868
Chile‡#	1988	Total in R&D	8 740	700	1 000	6 550	490
		% by sector	100	8.0	11.4	74.9	5.6
		Scientists and engineers	4 630	250	550	3 500	330
		Technicians	2 940	370	250	2 200	120
		Auxiliary personnel	1 170	80	200	850	40
Colombia	1982	Total in R&D	...	91	...	1 474	2 144
		Scientists and engineers	...	33	...	687	363
		Technicians	...	34	...	388	602
		Auxiliary personnel	...	24	...	399	1 179
Guyana‡	1982	Total in R&D	...	469	——>	154	...
		Scientists and engineers	...	67	——>	22	...
		Technicians	...	134	——>	44	...
		Auxiliary personnel	...	268	——>	88	...
Peru‡	1981	Scientists and engineers	7 464	896	——>	3 600	2 968
		Technicians	5 064	373	——>	1 153	3 538
Venezuela‡#	1983	Total in R&D	10 687	903	337	5 913	3 534
		% by sector	100	8.5	3.2	55.3	33.1
		Scientists and engineers	4 568	347	117	2 921	1 183
		Technicians	2 692	97	126	1 297	1 172
		Auxiliary personnel	3 427	459	94	1 695	1 179
Asia							
China‡	1993	Total in R&D	642 500	175 700	55 700	141 100	270 000
		% by sector	100	27.3	8.7	22.0	42.0
		Scientists and engineers	418 500	64 500	28 100	131 400	194 500
		Technicians	224 000	111 200	27 600	9 700	75 500
		Auxiliary personnel	./.	./.	./.	./.	./.
Cyprus	1992	Total in R&D	366	50	-	2	314
		% by sector	100	13.7	-	0.5	85.8
		Scientists and engineers	147	27	-	1	119
		Technicians	165	16	-	1	148
		Auxiliary personnel	54	7	-	-	47
India‡	1990	Total in R&D	...	61 377	——>		239 500
		Scientists and engineers	*128 036	31 366	——>	*22 100	74 570
		Technicians	...	20 354	——>	...	76 383
		Auxiliary personnel	...	9 657	——>	...	88 547
Israel #	1992	Total in R&D	...	11 615	...	...	...
		Scientists and engineers	...	7 056	...	...	...
		Technicians	...	3 530	...	...	...
		Auxiliary personnel	...	1 029	...	...	...

R&D personnel by sector of performance   5.3
Personnel de R-D par secteur d'exécution
Personal de I y D por sector de ejecución

Country / Pays / País	Year / Année / Año	Category of personnel / Catégorie de personnel / Categoría de personal	Sector of performance/Secteur d'exécution/Sector de ejecución				
			All sectors (FTE) Tous les secteurs (EPT) Todos los sectores (EJC)	Productive sector Secteur de la production Sector productivo		Higher education Enseigne-ment supérieur Enseñanza superior	General service Service général Servicio general
				Integrated R&D Activités de R-D intégrées Actividades de I y D integradas	Non-inte-grated R&D Activités de R-D non intégrées Actividades de I y D no integradas		
			(1)	(2)	(3)	(4)	(5)
Japan‡	1992	Total in R&D	910 051	563 018	./.	264 055	82 978
		% by sector	100	61.9	./.	29.0	9.1
		Scientists and engineers	705 346	428 659	./.	224 766	51 921
		Technicians	108 014	85 129	./.	12 363	10 522
		Auxiliary personnel	96 691	49 230	./.	26 926	20 535
Jordan‡	1986	Scientists and engineers	418	23	-	255	140
		Technicians	29	4	-	15	10
Korea, Republic of‡	1994	Total in R&D	190 298	89 284	——>	74 877	26 137
		% by sector	100	46.9	——>	39.3	13.8
		Scientists and engineers	117 446	59 281	——>	42 700	15 465
		Technicians	14 141	8 140	——>	1 760	4 241
		Auxiliary personnel	58 711	21 863	——>	30 417	6 431
Kuwait‡#	1984	Total in R&D	2 539	298	148	448	1 645
		% by sector	100	11.7	5.8	17.6	64.8
		Scientists and engineers	1 511	194	102	414	801
		Technicians	561	72	8	25	456
		Auxiliary personnel	467	32	38	9	388
Lebanon‡	1980	Total in R&D	...	...	...	206	...
		Scientists and engineers	...	...	...	180	...
		Technicians	...	...	...	6	...
		Auxiliary personnel	...	...	...	20	...
Malaysia‡	1992	Total in R&D	4 563	1 078	./.	1 155	2 330
		% by sector	100	23.6	./.	25.3	51.1
		Scientists and engineers	1 633	394	./.	519	720
		Technicians	1 655	405	./.	505	745
		Auxiliary personnel	1 275	279	./.	131	865
Pakistan‡	1990	Total in R&D	29 040	-	23 460	5 580	./.
		% by sector	100	-	80.8	19.2	./.
		Scientists and engineers	6 626	-	5 460	1 166	./.
		Technicians	9 314	-	7 613	1 701	./.
		Auxiliary personnel	13 100	-	10 387	2 713	./.
Philippines #	1984	Total in R&D	10 185	1 148	487	1 618	6 932
		% by sector	100	11.3	4.8	15.9	68.1
		Scientists and engineers	4 830	645	210	945	3 030
		Technicians	1 855	166	49	207	1 433
		Auxiliary personnel	3 500	337	228	466	2 469
Qatar‡#	1986	Scientists and engineers	229	-	44	185	-
		Technicians	61	-	7	54	-
Singapore‡	1994	Total in R&D	11 384	6 445	<——	<——	4 939
		% by sector	100	56.6	<——	<——	43.4
		Scientists and engineers	7 086	3 561	<——	<——	3 525
		Technicians	4 298	2 884	<——	<——	1 414
		Auxiliary personnel	./.	./.	./.	./.	./.
Sri Lanka	1985	Scientists and engineers	2 790	204	——>	1 242	1 344
		Technicians	693	43	——>	188	462
Thailand	1987	Total in R&D	10 621	6 179	-	4 115	327
		% by sector	100	58.2	-	38.7	3.1
		Scientists and engineers	5 539	2 863	-	2 518	158
		Technicians	2 785	2 095	-	614	76
		Auxiliary personnel	2 297	1 221	-	983	93
Turkey‡	1991	Total in R&D	...	2 509	——>	...	3 692
		Scientists and engineers	11 948	1 280	——>	8 768	1 900
		Technicians	...	805	——>	...	524
		Auxiliary personnel	...	424	——>	...	1 268
Uzbekistan	1991	Total in R&D	76 722	1 461	53 793	18 969	2 499
		% by sector	100	1.9	70.1	24.7	3.3
		Scientists and engineers	47 166	953	27 495	17 615	1 103
		Technicians	10 091	113	9 134	292	552
		Auxiliary personnel	19 465	395	17 164	1 062	844
Viet Nam	1985	Scientists and engineers	...	13 800	——>	6 200	...

R&D personnel by sector of performance
Personnel de R-D par secteur d'exécution
Personal de I y D por sector de ejecución

Country / Pays / País	Year / Année / Año	Category of personnel / Catégorie de personnel / Categoría de personal	Sector of performance/Secteur d'exécution/Sector de ejecución				
			All sectors (FTE) / Tous les secteurs (EPT) / Todos los sectores (EJC)	Productive sector / Secteur de la production / Sector productivo		Higher education / Enseignement supérieur / Enseñanza superior	General service / Service général / Servicio general
				Integrated R&D / Activités de R-D intégrées / Actividades de I y D integradas	Non-integrated R&D / Activités de R-D non intégrées / Actividades de I y D no integradas		
			(1)	(2)	(3)	(4)	(5)
Europe							
Austria	1993	Total in R&D	24 458	13 759	1 355	7 136	2 208
		% by sector	100	56.3	5.5	29.2	9.0
		Scientists and engineers	12 820	6 506	489	4 856	969
		Technicians	6 397	4 612	307	1 099	379
		Auxiliary personnel	5 241	2 641	559	1 181	860
Belarus	1992	Scientists and engineers	33 685	23 524	——>	2 399	7 762
Belgium‡	1991	Total in R&D	*40 063	*22 313	*339	*14 800	*2 611
		% by sector	100	*55.7	*0.8	*36.9	*6.5
		Scientists and engineers	*18 105	*8 749	*166	*8 405	*785
		Technicians	*21 958	*13 564	*173	*6 395	*1 826
		Auxiliary personnel	./.	./.	./.	./.	./.
Bulgaria	1992	Total in R&D	57 655	16 370	——>	21 926	19 359
		% by sector	100	28.4	——>	38.0	33.6
		Scientists and engineers	37 825	9 346	——>	15 919	12 560
		Technicians	10 752	4 044	——>	3 039	3 669
		Auxiliary personnel	9 078	2 980	——>	2 968	3 130
Croatia	1992	Total in R&D	17 233	2 239	2 037	8 223	4 734
		% by sector	100	13.0	11.8	47.7	27.5
		Scientists and engineers	8 928	985	680	5 080	2 183
		Technicians	3 818	867	590	850	1 511
		Auxiliary personnel	4 487	387	767	2 293	1 040
Czech Republic	1994	Total in R&D	37 779	23 114	./.	3 397	11 268
		% by sector	100	61.2	./.	9.0	29.8
		Scientists and engineers	13 325	6 628	./.	1 731	4 966
		Technicians	9 771	6 983	./.	187	2 601
		Auxiliary personnel	14 683	9 503	./.	1 479	3 701
Denmark‡	1993	Total in R&D	27 390	15 973	./.	6 216	5 202
		% by sector	100	58.3	./.	22.7	19.0
		Scientists and engineers	13 673	5 884	./.	4 627	3 161
		Technicians	13 717	10 083	./.	1 589	2 041
		Auxiliary personnel	./.	./.	./.	./.	./.
Estonia #	1994	Total in R&D	9 100	-	-	5 169	3 931
		% by sector	100	-	-	56.8	43.2
		Scientists and engineers	5 079	-	-	3 023	2 056
		Technicians	848	-	-	206	642
		Auxiliary personnel	3 173	-	-	1 940	1 233
Finland‡	1993	Total in R&D	30 527	15 180	——>	8 422	6 925
		% by sector	100	49.7	——>	27.6	22.7
		Scientists and engineers	18 588	8 481	——>	6 173	3 935
		Technicians	11 939	6 699	——>	2 248	2 991
		Auxiliary personnel	./.	./.	./.	./.	./.
France‡	1993	Total in R&D	314 170	164 384	./.	74 856	74 930
		% by sector	100	52.3	./.	23.8	23.9
		Scientists and engineers	145 898	66 455	./.	49 862	29 581
		Technicians	168 272	97 929	./.	24 994	45 349
		Auxiliary personnel	./.	./.	./.	./.	./.
Germany	1991	Total in R&D	515 258	321 756	——>	103 864	89 636
		% by sector	100	62.4	——>	20.2	17.4
		Scientists and engineers	240 803	141 084	——>	62 171	37 548
		Technicians	128 316	86 490	——>	17 789	24 037
		Auxiliary personnel	146 139	94 182	——>	23 904	28 053
Greece	1993	Total in R&D	14 549	2 880	-	6 767	4 902
		% by sector	100	19.9	-	46.5	33.6
		Scientists and engineers	8 030	1 319	-	4 773	1 938
		Technicians	3 257	923	-	1 350	984
		Auxiliary personnel	3 262	638	-	644	1 980

R&D personnel by sector of performance 5.3
Personnel de R-D par secteur d'exécution
Personal de I y D por sector de ejecución

			All sectors (FTE) Tous les secteurs (EPT) Todos los sectores (EJC)	Sector of performance/Secteur d'exécution/Sector de ejecución			
				Productive sector Secteur de la production Sector productivo		Higher education Enseigne-ment supérieur Enseñanza superior	General service Service général Servicio general
Country Pays País	Year Année Año	Category of personnel Catégorie de personnel Categoría de personal		Integrated R&D Activités de R-D intégrées Actividades de I y D integradas	Non-inte-grated R&D Activités de R-D non intégrées Actividades de I y D no integradas		
			(1)	(2)	(3)	(4)	(5)
Hungary‡	1993	Total in R&D	22 609	5 669	2 348	7 776	6 816
		% by sector	100	25.1	10.4	34.4	30.1
		Scientists and engineers	11 818	2 637	866	4 546	3 769
		Technicians	6 003	2 395	421	1 660	1 527
		Auxiliary personnel	4 788	637	1 061	1 570	1 520
Iceland‡	1989	Total in R&D	1 177	221	——>	317	639
		% by sector	100	18.8	——>	26.9	54.3
		Scientists and engineers	773	134	——>	241	398
		Technicians	404	87	——>	76	241
		Auxiliary personnel	./.	./.	./.	./.	./.
Ireland‡	1993	Total in R&D	9 534	4 499	./.	3 589	1 446
		% by sector	100	47.2	./.	37.6	15.2
		Scientists and engineers	6 592	2 576	./.	3 290	726
		Technicians	1 797	1 119	./.	204	474
		Auxiliary personnel	1 145	804	./.	95	246
Italy‡	1993	Total in R&D	142 171	61 993	./.	47 014	33 164
		% by sector	100	43.6	./.	33.1	23.3
		Scientists and engineers	74 434	27 932	./.	33 204	13 298
		Technicians	45 499	22 272	./.	9 234	13 993
		Auxiliary personnel	22 238	11 789	./.	4 576	5 873
Latvia	1994	Total in R&D	5 239	833	——>	2 025	2 381
		% by sector	100	15.9	——>	38.7	45.4
		Scientists and engineers	3 010	377	——>	1 289	1 344
		Technicians	944	76	——>	482	386
		Auxiliary personnel	1 285	380	——>	254	651
Malta	1988	Total in R&D	...	...	...	46	...
		Scientists and engineers	...	...	...	34	...
		Technicians	...	...	...	5	...
		Auxiliary personnel	...	...	...	7	...
Netherlands‡	1991	Total in R&D	66 710	29 590	380	20 090	16 650
		% by sector	100	44.4	0.6	30.1	25.0
		Scientists and engineers	40 000	17 710	210	10 390	11 690
		Technicians	20 440	7 470	70	9 700	3 200
		Auxiliary personnel	6 270	4 410	100	./.	1 760
Norway‡	1993	Total in R&D	22 091	7 732	2 957	6 658	4 744
		% by sector	100	35.0	13.4	30.1	21.5
		Scientists and engineers	14 763	5 233	1 908	4 737	2 885
		Technicians	7 328	2 499	1 049	1 921	1 859
		Auxiliary personnel	./.	./.	./.	./.	./.
Poland‡	1992	Scientists and engineers	41 440	11 550	7 560	15 210	7 120
		Technicians	52 810	29 020	16 360	5 830	1 600
Portugal	1990	Total in R&D	12 043	1 997	976	4 840	4 230
		% by sector	100	16.6	8.1	40.2	35.1
		Scientists and engineers	5 909	437	622	3 755	1 095
		Technicians	3 754	1 125	182	612	1 835
		Auxiliary personnel	2 379	435	171	473	1 300
Romania	1994	Total in R&D	59 102	...	...	...	...
		Scientists and engineers	31 672	...	...	...	...
		Technicians	13 272	...	...	...	...
		Auxiliary personnel	14 158	...	...	...	...
Russian Federation #	1993	Total in R&D	1 315 000	87 400	999 500	53 200	174 900
		% by sector	100	6.6	76.0	4.0	13.3
		Scientists and engineers	644 900	43 800	458 300	40 000	102 800
		Technicians	133 900	14 900	104 400	2 500	12 100
		Auxiliary personnel	536 200	28 700	436 800	10 700	60 000
Slovakia‡	1994	Total in R&D	17 256	5 695	./.	4 285	7 276
		% by sector	100	33.0	./.	24.8	42.2
		Scientists and engineers	10 249	2 648	./.	3 698	3 903
		Technicians	4 244	1 721	./.	510	2 013
		Auxiliary personnel	2 763	1 326	./.	7.7	1 360

5.3   R&D personnel by sector of performance
      Personnel de R-D par secteur d'exécution
      Personal de I y D por sector de ejecución

				Sector of performance/Secteur d'exécution/Sector de ejecución			
			All sectors (FTE)	Productive sector Secteur de la production Sector productivo		Higher education	General service
Country	Year	Category of personnel	Tous les secteurs (EPT)	Integrated R&D Activités de R-D intégrées	Non-inte-grated R&D Activités de R-D non intégrées	Enseigne-ment supérieur	Service général
Pays	Année	Catégorie de personnel					
País	Año	Categoría de personal	Todos los sectores (EJC)	Actividades de I y D integradas	Actividades de I y D no integradas	Enseñanza superior	Servicio general
			(1)	(2)	(3)	(4)	(5)
Slovenia	1992	Total in R&D	12 653	3 314	934	4 363	4 042
		% by sector	100	26.2	7.4	34.5	31.9
		Scientists and engineers	5 789	1 206	333	1 924	2 326
		Technicians	4 615	1 747	397	1 515	956
		Auxiliary personnel	2 249	361	204	924	760
Spain‡	1993	Total in R&D	74 998	27 781	——>	29 103	18 114
		% by sector	100	37.0	——>	38.8	24.2
		Scientists and engineers	43 367	11 256	——>	24 006	8 105
		Technicians	13 496	9 287	——>	./.	4 209
		Auxiliary personnel	18 135	7 238	——>	5 097	5 800
Sweden‡	1993	Total in R&D	59 876	35 588	——>	17 765	6 523
		% by sector	100	59.4	——>	29.7	10.9
		Scientists and engineers	32 288	16 219	——>	11 738	4 331
		Technicians	27 588	19 369	——>	6 027	2 192
		Auxiliary personnel	./.	./.	./.	./.	./.
Switzerland‡	1992	Total in R&D	48 310	33 900	./.	12 650	1 760
		% by sector	100	70.2	./.	26.2	3.6
The Former Yugoslav Rep. of Macedonia‡	1991	Total in R&D	4 500	656	228	2 501	1 115
		% by sector	100	14.6	5.0	55.6	24.8
		Scientists and engineers	2 605	347	91	1 574	593
		Technicians	691	214	53	272	152
		Auxiliary personnel	1 204	95	84	655	370
United Kingdom‡	1993	Total in R&D	279 000	164 000	./.	66 000	49 000
		% by sector	100	58.8	./.	23.7	17.6
		Scientists and engineers	140 000	87 000	./.	32 000	21 000
		Technicians	59 000	40 000	./.	10 000	9 000
		Auxiliary personnel	80 000	37 000	./.	24 000	19 000
Federal Republic of Yugoslavia‡	1992	Total in R&D	25 656	4 753	6 709	10 701	3 493
		% by sector	100	18.5	26.2	41.7	13.6
		Scientists and engineers	11 246	1 807	2 961	4 191	2 287
		Technicians	4 183	1 618	1 583	621	361
		Auxiliary personnel	10 227	1 328	2 165	5 889	845
Oceania							
Australia‡	1990	Total in R&D	67 796	19 985	./.	27 081	20 730
		% by sector	100	29.5	./.	39.9	30.6
		Scientists and engineers	41 837	11 675	./.	20 666	9 496
		Technicians	15 922	5 540	./.	4 166	6 216
		Auxiliary personnel	10 038	2 770	./.	2 249	5 019
Fiji‡#	1986	Total in R&D	...	156	-	...	...
		Scientists and engineers	...	36	-	...	...
		Technicians	...	90	-	...	...
		Auxiliary personnel	...	30	-	...	...
French Polynesia‡	1983	Total in R&D	97	-	-	-	97
		% by sector	100	-	-	-	100.0
		Scientists and engineers	17	-	-	-	17
		Technicians	16	-	-	-	16
		Auxiliary personnel	64	-	-	-	64
Guam	1991	Total in R&D	...	...	...	55	...
		Scientists and engineers	...	...	...	23	...
		Technicians	...	...	...	11	...
		Auxiliary personnel	...	...	...	21	...
Kiribati	1980	Total in R&D	3	-	3	-	-
		% by sector	100	-	100.0	-	-
		Scientists and engineers	2	-	2	-	-
		Technicians	1	-	1	-	-
		Auxiliary personnel	-	-	-	-	-
New Caledonia‡	1985	Total in R&D	334	-	81	-	253
		% by sector	100	-	24.3	-	75.7
		Scientists and engineers	77	-	10	-	67
		Technicians	71	-	32	-	39
		Auxiliary personnel	186	-	39	-	147

R&D personnel by sector of performance 5.3
Personnel de R-D par secteur d'exécution
Personal de I y D por sector de ejecución

Country Pays País	Year Année Año	Category of personnel Catégorie de personnel Categoría de personal	Sector of performance/Secteur d'exécution/Sector de ejecución				
			All sectors (FTE) Tous les secteurs (EPT) Todos los sectores (EJC)	Productive sector Secteur de la production Sector productivo		Higher education Enseigne-ment supérieur Enseñanza superior	General service Service général Servicio general
				Integrated R&D Activités de R-D intégrées Actividades de I y D integradas	Non-inte-grated R&D Activités de R-D non intégrées Actividades de I y D no integradas		
			(1)	(2)	(3)	(4)	(5)
New Zealand	1993	Total in R&D	10 488	2 078	701	3 735	3 974
		% by sector	100	19.8	6.7	35.6	37.9
		Scientists and engineers	6 198	1 261	246	3 025	1 666
		Technicians	2 866	579	316	497	1 474
		Auxiliary personnel	1 424	238	139	213	834
Tonga‡#	1981	Total in R&D	15	-	-	-	15
		% by sector	100	-	-	-	100.0
		Scientists and engineers	11	-	-	-	11
		Technicians	4	-	-	-	4

AFRICA:
Congo:
E--> Not including military and defence R&D.
FR-> Non compris les activités de R-D de caractère militaire ou relevant de la défense nationale.
ESP> Excluídas las actividades militares y de defensa de I y D.
Egypt:
E--> Not including military and defence R&D.
FR-> Non compris les activités de R-D de caractère militaire ou relevant de la défense nationale.
ESP> Excluídas las actividades militares y de defensa de I y D.
Nigeria:
E--> Data relate only to 23 out of 26 national research institutes under the Federal Ministry of Science and Technology.
FR-> Les données ne se rapportent qu'à 23 des 26 instituts de recherche nationaux sous tutelle du Ministère fédéral de la Science et de la Technologie.
ESP> Los datos sólo se refieren a 23 de los 26 centros de investigación bajo tutela del Ministerio federal de Ciencia y Tecnología.
Seychelles:
E--> Auxiliary personnel and technicians in columns 3 and 5 are counted together. Not including military and defence R&D.
FR-> Le personnel auxiliaire et les techniciens des colonnes 3 et 5 sont comptés ensemble. Non compris les activités de R-D de caractère militaire ou relevant de la défense nationale.
ESP> El personal auxiliar y los técnicos de las columnas 3 y 5 son considerados conjuntamente. Excluídas las actividades militares y de defensa de I y D.
AMERICA, NORTH:
Canada:
E--> Not including social sciences and humanities in the productive sector (integrated R&D). Data for the productive sector (non-integrated R&D) are included with the general service sector. Those for the higher education sector also include private non-profit organizations.
FR-> Non compris les sciences sociales et humaines dans le secteur de la production (activités de R-D intégrées). Les données relatives au secteur de la production (activités de R-D non intégrées) sont comprises avec celles du secteur de service général. Celles concernant le secteur de l'enseignement supérieur comprennent aussi les organisations privées a but non lucratif.
ESP> Excluídas las ciencias sociales y humanas del sector productivo (actividades de I y D integradas). Los datos correspondientes al sector productivo (actividades de I y D no integradas) están incluídos en el sector de servicio general. Los relativos al sector de enseñanza superior también incluyen las organizaciones privadas de caracter no lucrativo.
Cuba:
E--> Not including military and defence R&D.
FR-> Non compris les activités de R-D de caractère militaire ou relevant de la défense nationale.
ESP> Excluídas las actividades militares y de defensa de I y D.
El Salvador:
E--> Data relate to scientists and engineers and technicians engaged in public enterprises. Those for the productive sector (non-integrated R&D) are included with the general service sector.

FR-> Les données se réfèrent aux scientifiques et ingénieurs et techniciens employés dans les entreprises publiques. Celles relatives au secteur de la production (activités de R-D non intégrées) sont comprises avec celles de service gènéral.
ESP> Los datos se refieren a los científicos ingenieros y técnicos empleados en las empresas públicas. Los correspondientes al sector productivo (actividades de I y D no integradas) están incluidos en el sector de servicio general.
Jamaica:
E--> Data relate to the Scientific Research Council only.
FR-> Les données se réfèrent au *Scientific Research Council* seulement.
ESP> Los datos se refieren al *Scientific Research Council* solamente.
United States:
E--> Not including military personnel engaged in R&D.
FR-> Non compris le personnel militaire employé à des travaux de R-D.
ESP> Excluído el personal militar empleado en trabajos de I y D.
AMERICA, SOUTH:
Chile:
E--> Not including military and defence R&D.
FR-> Non compris les activités de R-D de caractère militaire ou relevant de la défense nationale.
ESP> Excluídas las actividades militares y de defensa de I y D.
Guyana:
E--> Excluding military and defence R&D and medical sciences in the higher education sector.
FR-> Non compris les activités de R-D de caractère militaire ou relevant de la défense nationale ni les sciences médicales du secteur de l'enseignement supérieur.
ESP> Excluídas las actividades militares y de defensa de I y D y las ciencias médicas del sector de enseñanza superior.
Peru:
E--> Data refer to full-time scientists and engineers and technicians engaged in scientific and technological activities (STA).
FR-> Les données se réfèrent aux scientifiques et ingénieurs et techniciens à plein temps employés dans les activités scientifiques et techniques (AST).
ESP> Los datos se refieren a los científicos e ingenieros y técnicos de jornada completa empleados en las actividades científicas y tecnológicas (ACT).
Venezuela:
E--> Not including military and defence R&D.
FR-> Non compris les activités de R-D de caractère militaire ou relevant de la défense nationale.
ESP> Excluídas las actividades militares y de defensa de I y D.
ASIA:
China:
E--> Auxiliary personnel and technicians are counted together.
FR-> Le personnel auxiliaire et les techniciens sont comptés ensemble.
ESP> El personal auxiliar y los técnicos son considerados conjuntamente.

5.3 R&D personnel by sector of performance
Personnel de R-D par secteur d'exécution
Personal de I y D por sector de ejecución

India:
E--> The estimated figure for the higher education sector refers to 1982.
FR-> Le chiffre estimé pour le secteur de l'enseignement supérieur se rapporte à 1982.
ESP> La cifra estimada para el sector de enseñanza superior se refiere a 1982.

Japan:
E--> Data refer to full-time personnel. Not including social sciences and humanities in the productive sector (integrated R&D). Data for the productive sector (non-integrated R&D) are included with the general service sector.
FR-> Les données se réfèrent aux effectifs à plein temps. Compte non tenu des sciences sociales et humaines dans le secteur de la production (activités de R-D intégrées). Les données relatives au secteur de la production (activités de R-D non intégrées) sont comprises avec celles du secteur de service général.
ESP> Los datos se refieren a los efectivos de jornada completa. Excluídas las ciencias sociales y humanas del sector productivo (actividades de I y D integradas). Los datos correspondientes al sector productivo (actividades de I y D no integradas) están incluídos en el sector de servicio general.

Jordan:
E--> Not including military and defence R&D.
FR-> Non compris les activités de R-D de caractère militaire ou relevant de la défense nationale.
ESP> Excluídas las actividades militares y de defensa de I y D.

Korea, Republic of:
E--> Excluding military and defence R&D and social sciences and humanities.
FR-> Non compris les activités de R-D de caractère militaire ou relevant de la défense nationale ni les sciences sociales et humaines.
ESP> Excluídas las actividades militares y de defensa de I y D y las ciencias sociales y humanas.

Kuwait:
E--> Data refer to scientific and technological activities (STA).
FR-> Les données se réfèrent aux activités scientifiques et techniques (AST).
ESP> Los datos se refieren a las actividades científicas y tecnológicas (ACT).

Lebanon:
E--> Data refer to the Faculty of Science at the University of Lebanon only.
FR-> Les données ne se réfèrent qu'à la Faculté des Sciences de l'Université du Liban.
ESP> Los datos se refieren a la Facultad de Ciencias de la Universidad del Líbano solamente.

Malaysia:
E--> Data for the productive sector (non-integrated R&D) are included with the general service sector.
FR-> Les données relatives au secteur de la production (activités de R-D non intégrées) sont comprises avec celles du secteur de service général.
ESP> Los datos correspondientes al sector productivo (actividades de I y D no integradas) están incluídos en el sector de servicio general.

Pakistan:
E--> Not including military and defence R&D. Data relate to R&D activities concentrated mainly in government-financed research establishments only. For the productive sector (non-integrated R&D), data also include the general service sector.
FR-> Non compris les activités de R-D de caractère militaire ou relevant de la défense nationale. Les données se réfèrent aux activités de R-D se trouvant pour la plupart dans les établissements de recherche financés par le gouvernement. Pour le secteur de la production (activités de R-D non intégrées), les données comprennent aussi le secteur de service général.
ESP> Excluídas las actividades militares y de defensa de I y D. Los datos se refieren a las actividades de I y D concentradas principalmente en los establecimientos de investigación subvencionados por el gobierno. Para el sector productivo (actividades de I y D no integradas), los datos también incluyen el sector de servicio general.

Qatar:
E--> Not including social sciences and humanities in the higher education sector.
FR-> Non compris les sciences sociales et humaines dans le secteur de l'enseignement supérieur.
ESP> Excluídas las ciencias sociales y humanas del sector de enseñanza superior.

Singapore:
E--> Data relating to technicians include non-degree researchers and auxiliary personnel.
FR-> Les données relatives aux techniciens comprennent les chercheurs non diplômés et le personnel auxiliaire.

ESP> Los datos relativos a los técnicos incluyen los investigadores no diplomados et el personal auxiliar.

Turkey:
E--> Not including social sciences and humanities in the general service sector.
FR-> Compte non tenu des sciences sociales et humaines dans le secteur de service général.
ESP> Excluídas las ciencias sociales y humanas del sector de servicio general.

EUROPE:

Belgium:
E--> Auxiliary personnel and technicians are counted together.
FR-> Le personnel auxiliaire et les techniciens sont comptés ensemble.
ESP> El personal auxiliar y los técnicos son considerados conjuntamente.

Czech Republic:
E--> Not including military and defence R&D.
FR-> Non compris les activités de R-D de caractère militaire ou relevant de la défense nationale.
ESP> Excluídas las actividades militares y de defensa de I y D.

Denmark:
E--> Auxiliary personnel and technicians are counted together.
FR-> Le personnel auxiliaire et les techniciens sont comptés ensemble.
ESP> El personal auxiliar y los técnicos son considerados conjuntamente.

Finland:
E--> Auxiliary personnel and technicians are counted together.
FR-> Le personnel auxiliaire et les techniciens sont comptés ensemble.
ESP> El personal auxiliar y los técnicos son considerados conjuntamente.

France:
E--> Auxiliary personnel and technicians are counted together. Data for the productive sector (non-integrated R&D) are included with the general service sector.
FR-> Le personnel auxiliaire et les techniciens sont comptés ensemble. Les données relatives au secteur de la production (activités de R-D non intégrées) sont comprises avec celles du secteur de service général.
ESP> El personal auxiliar y los técnicos son considerados conjuntamente. Los datos correspondientes al sector productivo (actividades de I y D no integradas) están incluídos en el sector de servicio general.

Hungary:
E--> Of military R&D, only that part carried out in civil establishments is included. Not including personnel engaged in the administration of R&D. Skilled workers are counted with technicians rather than with auxiliary personnel. The latter also includes security, maintenance and repair personnel.
FR-> Pour la R-D de caractère militaire, seule la partie effectuée dans les établissements civils a été considérée. Compte non tenu du personnel employé dans les services administratifs de R-D. Les ouvriers qualifiés sont comptés avec les techniciens plutôt qu'avec le personnel auxiliaire. Celui-ci comprend aussi le personnel de sécurité et d'entretien.
ESP> Para la I y D de carácter militar, sólo se ha considerado la parte correspondiente a los establecimientos civiles. Excluído el personal empleado en los servicios administrativos de I y D. Los trabajadores calificados están más bien incluídos con los técnicos que con el personal auxiliar. Este comprende también el personal de seguridad y de mantenimiento.

Iceland:
E--> Auxiliary personnel and technicians are counted together.
FR-> Le personnel auxiliaire et les techniciens sont comptés ensemble.
ESP> El personal auxiliar y los técnicos son considerados conjuntamente.

Ireland:
E--> Data for the productive sector (non-integrated R&D) are included with the general service sector.
FR-> Les données relatives au secteur de la production (activités de R-D non intégrées) sont comprises avec celles du secteur de service général.
ESP> Los datos correspondientes al sector productivo (actividades de I y D no integradas) están incluídos en el sector de servicio general.

Italy:
E--> Data for the productive sector (non-integrated R&D) are included with the general service sector.
FR-> Les données relatives au secteur de la production (activités de R-D non intégrées) sont comprises avec celles du secteur de service général.
ESP> Los datos correspondientes al sector productivo (actividades de I y D no integradas) están incluídos en el sector de servicio general.

R&D personnel by sector of performance **5.3**
Personnel de R-D par secteur d'exécution
Personal de I y D por sector de ejecución

Netherlands:
E--> Data relating to technicians in columns 1 and 4 include also auxiliary personnel in the higher education sector.
FR-> Les données des colonnes 1 et 4 relatives aux techniciens comprennent aussi le personnel auxiliaire du secteur de l'enseignement supérieur.
ESP> Los datos relativos a los técnicos de las columnas 1 y 4 incluyen también el personal auxiliar del sector de enseñanza superior.

Norway:
E--> Auxiliary personnel and technicians are counted together.
FR-> Le personnel auxiliaire et les techniciens sont comptés ensemble.
ESP> El personal auxiliar y los técnicos son considerados conjuntamente.

Poland:
E--> Not including military and defence R&D.
FR-> Non compris les activités de R-D de caractère militaire ou relevant de la défense nationale.
ESP> Excluídas las actividades militares y de defensa de I y D.

Slovakia:
E--> Not including military and defence R&D. Data for the productive sector (non-integrated R&D) are included with the general service sector.
FR-> Non compris les activités de R&D de caractère militaire ou relevant de la défense nationale. Les données relatives au secteur de la production (activités de R-D non intégrées) sont comprises avec celles du secteur de service général.
ESP> Excluídas las actividades militares y de defensa de I y D. Los datos correspondientes al sector productivo (actividades de I y D no integradas) están incluídos en el sector de servicio general.

Spain:
E--> Data relating to auxiliary personnel in columns 1 and 4 include also technicians in the higher education sector.
FR-> Les données des colonnes 1 et 4 relatives au personnel auxiliaire comprennent aussi les techniciens du secteur de l'enseignement supérieur.
ESP> Los datos relativos al personal auxiliar de las columnas 1 y 4 incluyen también los técnicos del sector de enseñanza superior.

Sweden:
E--> Auxiliary personnel and technicians are counted together.
FR-> Le personnel auxiliaire et les techniciens sont comptés ensemble.
ESP> El personal auxiliar y los técnicos son considerados conjuntamente.

Switzerland:
E--> Data are not comparable with those for previous years due to discontinuity in series. Data for the productive sector (non-integrated R&D) are included with the general service sector.
FR-> Les données ne sont pas comparables avec celles des années précédentes en raison de discontinuité dans la série. Les données relatives au secteur de la production (activités de R-D non intégrées) sont comprises avec celles du secteur de service général.
ESP> Los datos no son comparables con los de años anteriores debido a la discontinuidad de la serie. Los datos correspondientes al sector productivo (actividades de I y D no integradas) están incluídos en el sector de servicio general.

The Former Yugoslav Republic of Macedonia:
E--> Data for the higher education sector refer to full-time plus part-time R&D personnel.
FR-> Les données relatives au secteur de l'enseignement supérieur se réfèrent au personnel de R-D à plein temps et à temps partiel.
ESP> Los datos relativos al sector de enseñanza superior se refieren al personal de I y D de jornada completa y parcial.

United Kingdom:
E--> Data for the productive sector (non-integrated R&D) are included with the general service sector.
FR-> Les données relatives au secteur de la production (activités de R-D non intégrées) sont comprises avec celles du secteur de service général.
ESP> Los datos correspondientes al sector productivo (actividades de I y D no integradas) están incluídos en el sector de servicio general.

Federal Republic of Yugoslavia:
E--> Not including military and defence R&D.
FR-> Non compris les activités de R-D de caractère militaire ou relevant de la défense nationale.
ESP> Excluídas las actividades militares y de defensa de I y D.

OCEANIA:
Australia:
E--> Data for the productive sector (non-integrated R&D) are included with the general service sector.
FR-> Les données relatives au secteur de la production (activités de R-D non intégrées) sont comprises avec celles du secteur de service général.
ESP> Los datos correspondientes al sector productivo (actividades de I y D no integradas) están incluídos en el sector de servicio general.

Fiji:
E--> Data relate to one research institute.
FR-> Les données ne concernent qu'un institut de recherche.
ESP> Los datos se refieren a un centro de investigación.

French Polynesia:
E--> Data relate to full-time personnel in one research institute only.
FR-> Les données concernent les effectifs à plein temps dans un seul institut de recherche.
ESP> Los datos se refieren a los efectivos de jornada completa en un centro de investigación solamente.

New Caledonia:
E--> Data refer only to 6 out of 11 research institutes.
FR-> Les données ne se rapportent qu'à 6 instituts de recherche sur 11.
ESP> Los datos sólo se refieren a 6 de los 11 centros de investigacíon.

Tonga:
E--> Data refer to one research institute only. Not including auxiliary personnel.
FR-> Les données ne concernent qu'un seul institut de recherche. Non compris le personnel auxiliaire.
ESP> Los datos se refieren a un centro de investigación solamente. No incluye el personal auxiliar.

5.4 R&D expenditure by type
Dépenses de R-D par type
Gastos de I y D por tipo

5.4 Total expenditure for research and experimental development by type of expenditure

Dépenses totales consacrées à la recherche et au développement expérimental, par type de dépenses

Gastos totales dedicados a la investigación y al desarrollo experimental, por tipo de gastos

Please refer to introduction for definitions of categories included in this table.

Pour les définitions des catégories présentées dans ce tableau, se référer à l'introduction.

En la introducción se dan las definiciones de las categorías que figuran en este cuadro.

Country / Pays / País	Reference year / Année de référence / Año de referencia	Currency / Monnaie / Moneda	Total / Total / Total (000)	Type of expenditure / Type de dépenses / Tipo de gastos				Current as % of total / Courantes en % du total / Corrientes en % del total
				Capital / En capital / De capital (000)	Current / Courantes / Corrientes			
					Total / Total / Total (000)	Labour costs / Dépenses de personnel / Gastos de personal (000)	Other current costs / Autres dépenses courantes / Otros gastos corrientes (000)	
			(1)	(2)	(3)	(4)	(5)	(6)
Benin‡	1989	Franc C.F.A.	...	...	3 347 695	2 347 364	1 000 331	...
Burundi‡	1989	Franc	536 187	...	...	...	...	...
Central African Republic‡	1984	Franc C.F.A.	680 791	...	...	...	...	...
Congo‡	1984	Franc C.F.A.	25 530	14 263	11 267	...	...	44.1
Egypt‡	1991	Pound	*955 273	*281 463	*673 810	*513 086	*160 724	*70.5
Gabon‡	1986	Franc C.F.A.	380 000	130 000	250 000	...	...	65.8
Libyan Arab Jamahiriya	1980	Dinar	22 875	...	...	...	...	...
Madagascar	1988	Franc	14 371 515	13 378 000	993 515	...	...	6.9
Mauritius‡	1992	Rupee	177 000	48 000	129 000	...	...	72.9
Nigeria‡	1987	Naira	86 270	16 655	69 615	...	...	80.7
Rwanda	1985	Franc	918 560	819 280	99 280	...	...	10.8
Seychelles‡	1983	Rupee	12 854	6 771	6 083	...	...	47.3
South Africa	1991	Rand	2 786 086	240 764	2 545 322	1 409 107	1 136 215	91.4
Tunisia‡	1992	Dinar	45 000 000	11 000 000	34 000 000	24 000 000	10 000 000	75.6
America, North								
Canada	1994	Dollar	*11 649 000	...	...	...	...	...
Costa Rica	1986	Colon	612 000	...	...	...	...	...
Cuba‡	1992	Peso	247 925	91 216	156 709	82 057	74 652	63.2
El Salvador‡	1992	Colon	1 083 559	131 377	382 603	...	...	74.4
Guatemala‡	1988	Quetzal	31 859	...	...	...	...	...
Jamaica‡	1986	Dollar	4 016	130	3 886	...	...	96.8
Mexico‡	1993	Peso	3 566 158	830 260	2 735 898	1 047 883	1 688 015	76.7
Nicaragua‡	1987	Cordoba	...	...	988 970	...	...	...
Panama‡	1986	Balboa	173	-	173	...	...	100.0
St. Lucia	1992	E.C. Dollar	...	...	*449	...	...	...

R&D expenditure by type 5.4
Dépenses de R-D par type
Gastos de I y D por tipo

Country / Pays / País	Reference year / Année de référence / Año de referencia	Currency / Monnaie / Moneda	Total / Total / Total (000) (1)	Type of expenditure / Type de dépenses / Tipo de gastos				Current as % of total / Courantes en % du total / Corrientes en % del total (6)
				Capital / En capital / De capital (000) (2)	Current / Courantes / Corrientes			
					Total / Total / Total (000) (3)	Labour costs / Dépenses de personnel / Gastos de personal (000) (4)	Other current costs / Autres dépenses courantes / Otros gastos corrientes (000) (5)	
Trinidad and Tobago	1984	Dollar	143 257	33 336	109 921	...	...	76.7
Turks and Caicos Islands	1984	U.S. Dollar	-	-	-	-	-	-
United States‡	1995	Dollar	171 000 000	...	...	...	...	...
America, South								
Argentina	1992	Austral	*664 700	*142 300	*522 400	*277 900	*244 500	*78.6
Bolivia	1991	Boliviano	282 899 000	200 536 000	82 363 000	...	...	29.1
Brazil‡	1994	Reais	1 491 165	...	...	...	...	...
Chile‡	1992	Peso	*102 196 000	...	...	...	...	...
Colombia‡	1982	Peso	2 754 273	...	...	...	...	...
Ecuador	1990	Sucre	8 443 000	...	...	...	...	...
Guyana‡	1982	Dollar	2 800	...	...	...	...	...
Peru‡	1984	Inti	159 024 000	...	...	...	...	...
Venezuela‡	1992	Bolivar	19 622 200	...	...	...	...	...
Asia								
Brunei Darussalam‡	1984	Dollar	10 880	2 660	8 220	3 840	4 380	75.6
China	1993	Yuan	19 600 000	...	...	...	...	...
Cyprus	1992	Pound	5 578	772	4 806	3 830	976	86.2
India	1990	Rupee	41 864 300	8 475 300	33 389 000	...	...	79.8
Indonesia‡	1988	Rupiah	259 283 000	64 645 000	194 638 000	...	...	75.1
Iran, Islamic Republic of‡	1985	Rial	22 010 713	9 464 315	12 546 398	...	...	57.0
Israel‡	1992	Shekel	3 663 100	200 600	3 462 500	2 272 000	1 190 500	94.5
Japan‡	1991	Yen	13 771 524	2 149 488	11 622 036	5 956 397	5 665 639	84.4
Jordan‡	1986	Dinar	5 587	1 287	4 300	2 348	1 952	77.0
Korea, Republic‡	1994	Won	7 894 746	2 332 835	5 561 911	...	...	70.5
Kuwait‡	1984	Dinar	71 163	8 147	63 016	57 127	5 889	88.6
Lebanon‡	1980	Pound	22 000	...	...	...	...	...
Malaysia	1992	Ringgit	550 699	212 520	338 179	196 931	141 248	61.4
Maldives	1986	Rufiyaa	-	-	-	-	-	...
Pakistan‡	1987	Rupee	5 582 081	1 926 257	3 655 824	...	...	65.5
Philippines	1984	Peso	613 410	98 610	514 800	245 970	268 830	83.9
Qatar	1986	Riyal	6 650	-	6 650	...	...	100.0
Singapore	1994	Dollar	1 170 000	...	...	...	...	...
Sri Lanka	1984	Rupee	256 799	82 464	174 335	95 762	78 573	67.9
Thailand	1991	Baht	3 928 100	828 600	3 099 500	...	...	78.9
Turkey‡	1991	Lira	3 330 047	1 293 048	2 036 999	1 102 518	934 481	61.2
Viet Nam‡	1985	Dong	498 000	...	...	...	...	...
Europe								
Austria	1993	Schilling	30 692 586	4 524 986	26 167 600	15 835 849	10 331 751	85.3
Belarus	1992	Rouble	8 590 900	2 258 700	6 332 200	...	...	73.7
Belgium	1991	Franc	*112 065 000	...	...	...	...	...
Bulgaria	1992	Lev	3 103 800	256 100	2 847 700	1 288 300	1 559 400	91.7
Croatia	1992	Croatian Dinar	...	...	21 874 940	8 506 200	13 368 740	...
Czech Republic‡	1994	Koruna	12 983 000	1 768 000	11 215 000	3 578 000	7 637 000	86.4
Denmark‡	1993	Krone	15 695 000	1 760 000	13 935 000	8 615 000	5 320 000	88.8
Estonia‡	1994	Kroon	216 798	14 767	201 693	113 095	88 598	93.2
Finland	1993	Markka	10 677 100	943 100	9 734 000	6 150 000	3 584 000	91.2
France	1993	Franc	173 721 000	14 701 000	159 020 000	...	...	91.5
Germany‡	1991	D. Mark	74 517 000	7 704 000	66 152 000	42 455 000	23 697 000	89.6
Greece	1993	Drachma	100 460 000	...	...	...	...	...
Hungary‡	1993	Forint	34 686 000	3 593 000	31 093 000	8 568 000	15 878 000	89.6
Iceland	1989	Krona	3 123 000	...	...	...	...	...
Ireland	1993	Pound	400 201	...	...	...	...	...
Italy‡	1993	Lira	19 518 867	2 059 375	17 459 492	9 798 538	7 660 954	89.4
Latvia‡	1992	Lat	2 380	...	...	...	...	...
Malta‡	1988	Lira	10	1	9	...	...	90.0
Netherlands‡	1991	Guilder	10 381 000	1 059 000	9 322 000	5 666 000	3 656 000	89.8
Norway	1993	Krone	14 262 600	1 637 800	12 624 900	7 258 400	5 366 500	88.5

5.4 R&D expenditure by type
Dépenses de R-D par type
Gastos de I y D por tipo

Country / Pays / País	Reference year / Année de référence / Año de referencia	Currency / Monnaie / Moneda	Total / Total / Total (000)	Type of expenditure / Type de dépenses / Tipo de gastos				Current as % of total / Courantes en % du total / Corrientes en % del total
				Capital / En capital / De capital (000)	Current / Courantes / Corrientes			
					Total / Total / Total (000)	Labour costs / Dépenses de personnel / Gastos de personal (000)	Other current costs / Autres dépenses courantes / Otros gastos corrientes (000)	
			(1)	(2)	(3)	(4)	(5)	(6)
Poland‡	1992	Zloty	9 557 064	743 185	8 813 879	...	...	92.2
Portugal	1990	Escudo	52 032 200	10 483 400	41 548 800	31 370 600	10 178 200	79.9
Romania	1994	Leu	...	...	337 379 000	195 845 000	141 534 000	...
Russian Federation‡	1993	Rouble	*1 313 557	*102 579	*1 210 978	...	...	*92.2
San Marino	1986	Lira	-	-	-	-	-	-
Slovakia‡	1994	Koruna	4 473 412	385 684	4 087 728	...	...	91.4
Slovenia	1992	Tolar	15 050 524	1 365 784	13 684 740	7 990 830	5 693 910	90.9
Spain	1993	Peseta	557 401 895	103 605 003	453 796 892	326 858 351	126 938 541	81.4
Sweden	1993	Krona	48 382 000	3 162 000	45 220 000	21 977 000	23 243 000	93.5
Switzerland	1992	Franc	9 090 000	...	...	...	...	...
United Kingdom	1993	Pound Stg.	13 829 000	...	...	...	...	...
Federal Rep. of Yugoslavia‡	1992	Dinar	335	196	139	48	91	41.5
Oceania								
Australia	1990	Dollar	5 087 600	698 800	4 388 800	2 809 600	1 579 200	86.3
Fiji‡	1986	Dollar	3 800	800	3 000	...	...	78.9
French Polynesia	1983	Franc C.F.P.	324 720	16 280	308 440	253 750	54 690	95.0
Guam‡	1991	U.S. Dollar	2 215	...	...	...	...	...
New Caledonia‡	1985	Franc C.F.P.	800 820	93 273	707 547	489 929	217 618	88.4
New Zealand	1993	Dollar	825 200	96 500	728 700	421 500	307 200	88.3
Tonga‡	1980	Pa'anga	426	147	279	237	42	65.5

AFRICA:
Benin:
E--> Not including data for the productive sector (non-integrated R&D).
FR-> Non compris les données relatives au secteur de la production (activités de R-D non intégrées).
ESP> Excluídos los datos relativos al sector productivo (actividades de I y D no integradas).
Burundi:
E--> Not including data for the productive sector and labour costs at the Ministry of Public Health.
FR-> Non compris les données relatives au secteur de la production ni les dépenses de personnel au Ministère de la Santé Publique.
ESP> Excluídos los datos relativos al sector productivo y los gastos de personal en el Ministerio de la Sanidad Pública.
Central African Republic:
E--> Not including data for the general service sector.
FR-> Non compris les données pour le secteur de service général.
ESP> Excluídos los datos relativos al sector de servicio general.
Congo:
E--> Not including military and defence R&D.
FR-> Non compris les activités de R-D de caractère militaire ou relevant de la défense nationale.
ESP> Excluídas las actividades militares y de defensa de I y D.
Egypt:
E--> Data refer to estimated budget for R&D.
FR-> Les données se réfèrent au budget estimé pour la R-D.
ESP> Los datos se refieren al presupuesto estimado para I y D.
Gabon:
E--> Not including data for the productive sector.
FR-> Non compris les données pour le secteur de la production.
ESP> Excluídos los datos relativos al sector productivo.
Mauritius:
E--> Not including data for the productive sector.
FR-> Non compris les données pour le secteur de la production.
ESP> Excluídos los datos relativos al sector productivo.

Nigeria:
E--> Data relate only to 23 out of 26 national research institutes under the Federal Ministry of Science and Technology.
FR-> Les données ne concernent que 23 des 26 instituts de recherche nationaux sous tutelle du Ministère fédéral de la Science et de la Technologie.
ESP> Los datos sólo se refieren a 23 de los 26 centros de investigación nacionales bajo tutela del Ministerio Federal de Ciencia y Tecnología.
Seychelles:
E--> Not including military and defence R&D.
FR-> Non compris les activités de R-D de caractère militaire ou relevant de la défense nationale.
ESP> Excluídas las actividades militares y de defensa de I y D.
Tunisia:
E--> Not including data for the productive sector.
FR-> Non compris les données pour le secteur de la production.
ESP> Excluídos los datos relativos al sector productivo.
AMERICA NORTH:
Cuba:
E--> Data relate to government funds only and do not include military and defence R&D.
FR-> Les données ne concernent que les fonds publics et ne comprennent pas les activités de R-D de caractère militaire ou relevant de la défense nationale.
ESP> Los datos se refieren a los fondos públicos solamente y excluyen las actividades militares y de defensa de I y D.
El Salvador:
E--> Data refer to the R&D activities performed in public enterprises. Data in column 1 include 569,579 thousand colons for which a distribution by sector of performance and by type of expenditure is not known; this figure has been excluded from the percentage calculation in column 6.
FR-> Les données se réfèrent aux activités de R-D exercées dans les entreprises publiques. Les données de la colonne 1 comprennent 569 579 milliers de colones dont la répartition par secteur d'exécution et par type de dépenses n'est pas disponible; ce chiffre n'a pas été pris en compte pour calculer le pourcentage de la colonne 6.
ESP> Los datos se refieren a las actividades de I y D que se ejecutan en las empresas públicas. Los datos de la columna 1

R&D expenditure by type **5.4**
Dépenses de R-D par type
Gastos de I y D por tipo

incluyen 569 579 miles de colones cuya repartición por sector de ejecución y por tipo de gastos no está disonible; esta cifra no se ha considerado en el cálculo del porcentaje de la columna 6.

Guatemala:
E--> Data refer to the productive sector (integrated R&D) and the higher education sector only.
FR-> Les données ne concernent que le secteur de la production (activités de R-D intégrées) et le secteur de l'enseignement supérieur.
ESP> Los datos se refieren al sector productivo (actividades de I y D integradas) y al sector de enseñanza superior solamente.

Jamaica:
E--> Data relate to the Scientific Research Council only.
FR-> Les données se réfèrent au *Scientific Research Council* seulement.
ESP> Los datos se refieren al *Scientific Research Council* solamente.

Mexico:
E--> Figures in millions.
FR-> Chiffres en millions.
ESP> Cifras en millones.

Nicaragua:
E--> Not including military and defence R&D.
FR-> Non compris les activités de R-D de caractère militaire ou relevant de la défense nationale.
ESP> Excluídas las actividades militares y de defensa de I y D.

Panama:
E--> Data refer to the central government only.
FR-> Les données ne concernent que le gouvernement central.
ESP> Los datos sólo se refieren al gobierno central.

United States:
E--> Total expenditure does not include capital expenditure except that of the federal government institutions. Data relating to the general service sector cover only the federal government and the private non-profit organizations. R&D expenditure in the productive sector (integrated R&D) includes also depreciation costs. Humanities in the higher education sector is excluded.
FR-> Le total des dépenses ne comprend pas les dépenses en capital, à l'exception de celles des institutions du gouvernement fédéral. Les données relatives au secteur de service général couvrent seulement le gouvernement fédéral et les organisations privées à but non lucratif. Les dépenses de R-D du secteur de la production (activités de R-D intégrées) comprennent aussi les coûts d'amortissement. Les sciences humaines ne sont pas comprises dans le secteur de l'enseignement supérieur.
ESP> El total de los gastos no incluye los gastos de capital, salvo los de instituciones del Gobierno Federal. Los datos del sector de servicio general comprenden solamente el Gobierno Federal y las organizaciones privadas de carácter no lucrativo. Los gastos de I y D del sector productivo (actividades de I y D integradas) incluyen también los gastos de depreciación. No se incluyen las ciencias humanas en la enseñanza superior.

AMERICA, SOUTH:
Brazil:
E--> Data relate to government and productive enterprise funds only.
FR-> Les données ne concernent que les fonds publics et les fonds des enterprises de production.
ESP> Los datos sólo se refieren a los fondos públicos y los de las empresas de producción.

Chile:
E--> Not including military and defence R&D.
FR-> Non compris les activités de R-D de caractère militaire ou relevant de la défense nationale.
ESP> Excluídas las actividades militares y de defensa de I y D.

Colombia:
E--> Not including data for the productive sector (non-integrated R&D).
FR-> Non compris les données pour le secteur de la production (activités de R-D non intégrées).
ESP> Excluídos los datos relativos al sector productivo (actividades de I y D no integradas).

Guyana:
E--> Not including military and defence R&D. Data for the general service sector and for medical sciences in the higher education sector are also excluded.
FR-> Non compris les activités de R-D de caractère militaire ou relevant de la défense nationale. Les données relatives au secteur de service général et les sciences médicales du secteur de l'enseignement supérieur sont aussi exclues.
ESP> Excluídas las actividades militares y de defensa de I y D. Se excluyen también los datos relativos al sector de servicio general y las ciencias médicas del sector de enseñanza superior.

Peru:
E--> Data refer to the budget allotment for science and technology.

FR-> Les données se réfèrent aux crédits budgétaires relatifs à la science et à la technologie.
ESP> Los datos se refieren a las consignaciones presupuestarias relativas a la ciencia y la tecnología.

Venezuela:
E--> Data relate to government expenditure on scientific and technological activities (STA) and do not include military and defence R&D.
FR-> Les données concernent les dépenses du gouvernement relatives aux activités scientifiques et techniques (AST) et ne comprennent pas les activités de R-D de caractère militaire ou relevant de la défense nationale.
ESP> Los datos se refieren a los gastos del gobierno relativos a las actividades científicas y tecnológicas y excluyen las actividades militares y de defensa de I y D.

ASIA:
Brunei Darussalam:
E--> Data relate to 2 research institutes only.
FR-> Les données se réfèrent à 2 instituts de recherche seulement.
ESP> Los datos se refieren a 2 centros de investigación solamente.

Indonesia:
E--> Data relate to the general service sector only.
FR-> Les données ne concernent que le secteur de service général.
ESP> Los datos se refieren al sector de servicio general solamente.

Iran, Islamic Republic of:
E--> Data refer to government expenditure only.
FR-> Les données ne concernent que les dépenses du gouvernement.
ESP> Los datos se refieren a los gastos del gobierno solamente.

Israel:
E--> Data refer to the civilian sector only.
FR-> Les données ne concernent que le secteur civil.
ESP> Los datos se refieren solamente al sector civil.

Japan:
E--> Figures in millions. Not including data for social sciences and humanities in the productive sector (integrated R&D).
FR-> Chiffres en millions. Non compris les données pour les sciences sociales et humaines dans le secteur de la production (activités de R-D intégrées).
ESP> Cifras en millones. Excluídos los datos relativos a las ciencias sociales y humanas del sector productivo (actividades de I y D integradas).

Jordan:
E--> Not including military and defence R&D.
FR-> Non compris les activités de R-D de caractère militaire ou relevant de la défense nationale.
ESP> Excluídas las actividades militares y de defensa de I y D.

Korea, Republic of:
E--> Figures in millions. Excluding military and defence R&D and social sciences and humanities.
FR-> Chiffres en millions. Non compris les activités de R-D de caractère militaire ou relevant de la défense nationale ni les sciences sociales et humaines.
ESP> Cifras en millones. Excluídas las actividades militares y de defensa de I y D y las ciencias sociales y humanas.

Kuwait:
E--> Data refer to scientific and technological activities (STA).
FR-> Les données se réfèrent aux activités scientifiques et techniques (AST).
ESP> Los datos se refieren a las actividades científicas y tecnológicas (ACT).

Lebanon:
E--> Data refer to the Faculty of Science at the University of Lebanon only.
FR-> Les données ne se réfèrent qu'à la Faculté des Sciences de l'Université du Liban.
ESP> Los datos se refieren a la Facultad de Ciencias de la Universidad del Líbano solamente.

Pakistan:
E--> Data relate to R&D activities concentrated mainly in government-financed research establishments only. Not including military and defense R&D.
FR-> Les données se réfèrent aux activités de R-D se trouvant pour la plupart dans les établissements de recherche financés par le gouvernement. Non compris les activités de R-D de caractère militaire ou relevant de la défense nationale.
ESP> Los datos se refieren a las actividades de I y D concentradas principalmente en los establecimientos de investigación subvencionados por el gobierno. Excluídas las actividades militares y de defensa de I y D.

5.4 R&D expenditure by type
Dépenses de R-D par type
Gastos de I y D por tipo

Turkey:
E--> Figures in millions.
FR-> Chiffres en millions.
ESP> Cifras en millones.
Viet Nam:
E--> Data refer to government expenditure only.
FR-> Les données ne concernent que les dépenses du gouvernement.
ESP> Los datos se refieren a los gastos del gobierno solamente.
EUROPE:
Czech Republic:
E--> Not including military and defence R&D. Data include depreciation costs.
FR-> Non compris les activités de R-D de caractère militaire ou relevant de la défense nationale. Les données comprennent les coûts d'amortissement.
ESP> Excluídas las actividades militares y de defensa de I y D. Los datos incluyen los gastos de depreciación.
Denmark:
E--> Data for current expenditure do not include those relating to the productive sector (non-integrated R&D).
FR-> Les données relatives aux dépenses courantes ne comprennent pas celles du secteur de la production (activités de R-D non integrées).
ESP> Los datos relativos a los gastos corrientes no incluyen los del sector productivo (actividades de I y D no integradas).
Estonia:
E--> Data in column 1 include 338,000 kroons for which a distribution by type of expenditure is not available; this figure has been excluded from the percentage calculation in column 6.
FR-> Les données de la colonne 1 comprennent 338 000 kroons dont la répartition par type de dépenses n'est pas disponible; ce chiffre n'a pas été pris en compte pour calculer le pourcentage de la colonne 6.
ESP> Los datos de la columna 1 incluyen 338 000 kroones cuya repartición por tipo de gastos no está disponible; esta cifra no se ha considerado en el cálculo del porcentaje de la columna 6.
Germany:
E--> Data in column 1 include 661 million Deutsche marks for which a distribution by type of expenditure is not available; this figure has been excluded from the percentage calculation in column 6. Not including data for social sciences and humanities in the productive sector.
FR-> Les données de la colonne 1 comprennent 661 millions de deutsche marks dont la répartition par type de dépenses n'est pas disponible; ce chiffre n'a pas été pris en compte pour calculer le pourcentage de la colonne 6. Non compris les sciences sociales et humaines dans le secteur de la production.
ESP> Los datos de la columna 1 incluyen 661 millones de marcos cuya repartición por tipo de gastos no está disponible; esta cifra no se ha considerado en el cálculo del porcentaje de la columna 6. No se incluyen las ciencias sociales y humanas del sector productivo.
Hungary:
E--> Of military R&D, only that part carried out in civil establishments is included. The total in column 3 includes 6,647 million forints for which a breakdown by type of current expenditure is not known.
FR-> Pour la R-D de caractère militaire, seule la partie effectuée dans les établissements civils a été considérée. Le total de la colonne 3 comprend 6 647 millions de forints dont la répartition par type de dépenses courantes n'est pas disponible.
ESP> Para las actividades de I y D de carácter militar, sólo se ha considerado la parte correspondiente a los establecimientos civiles. El total de la columna 3 incluye 6 647 millones de forints, cuya repartición por tipo de gastos corrientes no está disponible.
Italy:
E--> Figures in millions.

FR-> Chiffres en millions.
ESP> Cifras en millones.
Latvia:
E--> Data relate to government funds only.
FR-> Les données ne concernent que les fonds publics.
ESP> Los datos se refieren a los fondos públicos solamente.
Malta:
E--> Data relate to the higher education sector only.
FR-> Les données ne concernent que le secteur de l'enseignement supérieur.
ESP> Los datos se refieren al sector de enseñanza superior solamente.
Netherlands:
E--> Not including data for social sciences and humanities in the productive sector (integrated R&D).
FR-> Non compris les données pour les sciences sociales et humaines du secteur de la production (activités de R-D intégrées).
ESP> Excluídos los datos relativos a las ciencias sociales y humanas del sector productivo (actividades de I y D integradas).
Poland:
E--> Figures in millions. Not including military and defence R&D.
FR-> Chiffres en millions. Non compris les activités de R-D de caractère militaire ou relevant de la défense nationale.
ESP> Cifras en millones. Excluídas las actividades militares y de defensa de I y D.
Russian Federation:
E--> Figures in millions.
FR-> Chiffres en millions.
ESP> Cifras en millones.
Slovakia:
E--> Not including military and defence R&D.
FR-> Non compris les activités de R-D de caractère militaire ou relevant de la défense nationale.
ESP> Excluídas las actividades militares y de defensa de I y D.
Federal Republic of Yugoslavia:
E--> Not including military and defence R&D.
FR-> Non including les activités de R-D de caractère militaire ou relevant de la défense nationale.
ESP> Excluídas las actividades militares y de defensa de I y D.
OCEANIA:
Fiji:
E--> Data relate to one research institute only.
FR-> Les données ne concernent qu'un institut de recherche.
ESP> Los datos se refieren a un centro de investigación solamente.
French Polynesia:
E--> Data relate to one research institute only.
FR-> Les données ne concernent qu'un institut de recherche.
ESP> Los datos se refieren a un centro de investigación solamente.
Guam:
E--> Data relate to the higher education sector only.
FR-> Les données ne concernent que le secteur de l'enseignement supérieur.
ESP> Los datos se refieren exclusivamente al sector de enseñanza superior.
New Caledonia:
E--> Data refer only to 6 out of 11 research institutes.
FR-> Les données ne se rapportent qu'à 6 instituts de recherche sur 11.
ESP> Los datos sólo se refieren a 6 de los 11 centros de investigación.
Tonga:
E--> Data relate to one research institute only.
FR-> Les données ne concernent qu'un centre de recherche.
ESP> Los datos se refieren a un centro de investigación solamente.

R&D expenditure by source of funds 5.5
Dépenses de R-D selon la source de financement
Gastos de I y D según la fuente de financiación

5.5 Total expenditure for the performance of research and experimental development by source of funds

Dépenses totales consacrées à la recherche et au développement expérimental, selon la source de financement

Gastos totales dedicados a la investigación y al desarrollo experimental, según la fuente de financiación

Please refer to introduction for definitions of categories included in this table.

Pour les définitions des catégories présentées dans ce tableau, se référer à l'introduction.

En la introducción se dan las definiciones de las categorías que figuran en este cuadro.

Country Pays País	Reference year Année de référence Año de referencia	Currency Monnaie Moneda	All sources of funds Toutes les sources de financement Todas las fuentes de financia-ción (000)	Source of funds / Source de financement / Fuente de financiación			
				Government funds Fonds publics Fondos públicos (000)	Productive enterprise funds and special funds Fonds des entreprises de production et fonds spéciaux Fondos de empresas de producción y fondos especiales (000)	Foreign funds Fonds étrangers Fondos extranjeros (000)	Other funds Fonds divers Otros Fondos (000)
			(1)	(2)	(3)	(4)	(5)
Africa							
Burundi†	1989	Franc	536 187 % 100	211 064 39.4	- -	325 123 60.6	- -
Central African Republic‡	1984	Franc C.F.A.	680 791 % 100	406 684 59.7	144 515 21.2	75 592 11.1	54 000 7.9
Congo‡	1984	Franc C.F.A.	25 530 % 100	17 575 68.8	6 500 25.5	1 455 5.7	- -
Mauritius‡	1989	Rupee	54 300 % 100	19 000 35.0	1 300 2.4	- -	34 000 62.6
Nigeria‡	1987	Naira	...	86 270	...	...	...
Rwanda‡	1984	Franc	235 540 % 100	189 040 80.3	- -	46 500 19.7	- -
Seychelles‡	1983	Rupee	12 854 % 100	6 274 48.8	- -	6 580 51.2	- -
South Africa	1991	Rand	2 786 087 % 100	903 288 32.4	1 303 967 46.8	- -	578 832 20.8
America, North							
Canada	1994	Dollar	*11 649 000 % 100	*3 796 000 *32.6	*5 299 000 *44.9	*1 258 000 *10.8	*1 366 000 *11.7

R&D expenditure by source of funds
Dépenses de R-D selon la source de financement
Gastos de I y D según la fuente de financiación

Country / Pays / País	Reference year / Année de référence / Año de referencia	Currency / Monnaie / Moneda	All sources of funds / Toutes les sources de financement / Todas las fuentes de financiación (000)	Source of funds / Source de financement / Fuente de financiación			
				Government funds / Fonds publics / Fondos públicos (000)	Productive enterprise funds and special funds / Fonds des entreprises de production et fonds spéciaux / Fondos de empresas de producción y fondos especiales (000)	Foreign funds / Fonds étrangers / Fondos extranjeros (000)	Other funds / Fonds divers / Otros Fondos (000)
			(1)	(2)	(3)	(4)	(5)
Costa Rica	1986	Colon	612 000 % 100	562 000 91.8	./. ./.	50 000 8.2	- -
Cuba‡	1992	Peso	247 925 % 100	247 925 100.0	- -	- -	- -
El Salvador	1992	Colon	1 083 559 % 100	513 980 47.4	- -	569 579 52.6	- -
Guatemala‡	1988	Quetzal	31 859 % 100	11 692 36.7	170 0.5	5 430 17.0	14 567 45.7
Mexico‡	1993	Peso	3 566 158 % 100	2 935 669 82.3	332 553 9.3	26 153 0.7	271 783 7.6
Nicaragua‡	1987	Cordoba	*988 970 % 100	*799 470 *80.8	-	*189 500 *19.2	-
Panama	1986	Balboa	173 % 100	173 100.0	-	-	-
Trinidad and Tobago	1984	Dollar	143 257 % 100	131 005 91.4	6 276 4.4	4 090 2.9	1 886 1.3
United States‡	1995	Dollar	*171 000 000 % 100	*60 700 000 *45.9	*101 650 000 *50.2	- -	*8 650 000 *3.9
America, South							
Argentina	1992	Austral	*664 700 % 100	*565 000 *85.0	*53 200 *8.0	*13 300 *2.0	*33 200 *5.0
Brazil	1994	Reais	...	1 220 988	270 177	...	...
Chile‡	1988	Peso	23 161 300 % 100	16 308 900 70.4	4 218 200 18.2	757 500 3.3	1 876 700 8.1
Peru‡	1984	Inti	159 024 000 % 100	76 289 000 48.0	43 255 000 27.2	33 367 000 21.0	6 113 000 3.8
Venezuela	1992	Bolivar	19 622 200 % 100	19 622 200 100.0	-	-	-
Asia							
Cyprus	1992	Pound	5 578 % 100	4 170 74.8	773 13.9	105 1.9	530 9.5
India	1990	Rupee	41 864 300 % 100	36 602 100 87.4	5 262 200 12.6	./. ./.	./. ./.
Israel‡	1992	Shekel	3 663 100 % 100	1 360 600 37.1	1 361 400 37.2	280 000 7.6	661 100 18.1
Japan‡	1991	Yen	13 771 524 % 100	2 504 463 18.2	11 255 016 81.7	12 044 0.1	-
Korea, Republic of‡	1994	Won	7 894 746 % 100	1 257 133 15.9	6 634 542 84.0	3 071 0.1	-
Kuwait‡	1984	Dinar	71 163 % 100	24 437 34.3	45 736 64.3	-	990 1.4
Malaysia	1992	Ringgit	550 699 % 100	292 299 53.1	236 554 43.0	10 032 1.8	11 814 2.1
Pakistan‡	1987	Rupee	5 582 081 % 100	5 582 081 100.0	-	-	-
Philippines‡	1984	Peso	612 750 % 100	373 290 60.9	144 860 23.6	79 740 13.0	14 860 2.4

R&D expenditure by source of funds 5.5
Dépenses de R-D selon la source de financement
Gastos de I y D según la fuente de financiación

Country Pays País	Reference year Année de référence Año de referencia	Currency Monnaie Moneda	All sources of funds Toutes les sources de financement Todas las fuentes de financia- ción (000)	Source of funds Source de financement Fuente de financiación			
				Government funds Fonds publics Fondos públicos (000)	Productive enterprise funds and special funds Fonds des entreprises de production et fonds spéciaux Fondos de empresas de producción y fondos especiales (000)	Foreign funds Fonds étrangers Fondos extranjeros (000)	Other funds Fonds divers Otros Fondos (000)
			(1)	(2)	(3)	(4)	(5)
Qatar	1986	Riyal	6 650 % 100	6 650 100.0	-	-	-
Sri Lanka	1984	Rupee	256 799 % 100	214 960 83.7	——> ——>	41 839 16.3	- -
Thailand	1987	Baht	2 664 380 % 100	1 825 780 68.5	259 450 9.7	387 550 14.5	191 600 7.2
Turkey‡	1991	Lira	3 330 047 % 100	2 332 807 70.1	949 311 28.5	5 385 0.2	42 544 1.3
Europe							
Austria	1993	Schilling	30 692 586 % 100	14 208 356 46.3	15 527 103 50.6	821 389 2.7	135 738 0.4
Belarus	1992	Rouble	8 590 900 % 100	3 545 500 41.3	4 825 100 56.2	-	220 300 2.5
Belgium	1991	Franc	*112 065 000 % 100	*35 029 100 *31.3	*72 665 000 *64.8	*3 311 200 *3.0	*1 059 700 *0.9
Bulgaria	1992	Lev	3 103 800 % 100	876 800 38.5	2 227 000 61.5	-	-
Czech Republic‡	1994	Koruna	12 983 000 % 100	3 627 000 27.9	9 356 000 72.1	——> ——>	——> ——>
Denmark	1993	Krone	15 695 000 % 100	5 941 000 37.8	7 809 000 49.8	1 162 000 7.4	783 000 5.0
Estonia	1994	Kroon	216 798 % 100	165 320 76.2	20 825 9.6	15 103 7.0	15 550 7.2
Finland	1993	Markka	10 667 100 % 100	4 252 800 39.8	6 044 900 56.6	192 500 1.8	187 000 1.8
France	1993	Franc	173 721 000 % 100	76 959 900 44.3	80 273 000 46.2	14 147 000 8.1	2 341 100 1.4
Germany‡	1991	D. Mark	74 517 000 % 100	26 686 000 35.8	46 007 000 61.7	1 443 000 1.9	380 000 0.5
Greece	1993	Drachma	100 460 000 % 100	46 013 000 45.8	20 297 000 20.2	30 453 000 30.3	3 697 000 3.7
Hungary‡	1993	Forint	34 686 000 % 100	14 034 000 40.5	18 406 000 53.1	855 000 2.5	1 391 000 4.0
Iceland	1989	Krona	3 123 000 % 100	2 186 100 70.0	718 290 23.0	93 690 3.0	124 920 4.0
Ireland	1993	Pound	400 201 % 100	111 196 27.8	253 893 63.4	31 378 7.8	3 734 1.0
Italy‡	1993	Lira	19 518 867 % 100	9 337 450 47.8	9 398 935 48.2	782 482 4.0	-
Malta‡	1988	Lira	10 % 100	10 100.0	-	-	-
Netherlands‡	1991	Guilder	10 381 000 % 100	4 651 000 44.8	5 325 000 51.3	207 000 2.0	198 000 1.9
Norway	1993	Krone	14 262 600 % 100	6 996 600 49.0	6 313 000 44.3	771 800 5.4	181 200 1.3
Portugal	1990	Escudo	52 032 200 % 100	30 250 700 58.1	14 067 100 27.0	2 413 500 4.6	5 300 900 10.2
Romania‡	1994	Leu	337 379 000 % 100	228 768 000 67.8	67 198 000 19.9	1 439 000 0.4	39 974 000 11.8

5.5 R&D expenditure by source of funds
Dépenses de R-D selon la source de financement
Gastos de I y D según la fuente de financiación

Country Pays País	Reference year Année de référence Año de referencia	Currency Monnaie Moneda	All sources of funds Toutes les sources de financement Todas las fuentes de financia- ción (000)	Source of funds Source de financement Fuente de financiación			
				Government funds Fonds publics Fondos públicos (000)	Productive enterprise funds and special funds Fonds des entreprises de production et fonds spéciaux Fondos de empresas de producción y fondos especiales (000)	Foreign funds Fonds étrangers Fondos extranjeros (000)	Other funds Fonds divers Otros Fondos (000)
			(1)	(2)	(3)	(4)	(5)
Slovakia‡	1994	Koruna	4 473 412 % 100	1 727 740 38.6	2 679 760 59.9	58 594 1.3	7 318 0.2
Slovenia	1992	Tolar	15 050 524 % 100	5 401 468 35.9	7 685 248 51.1	704 796 4.7	1 259 012 8.3
Spain	1993	Peseta	557 401 895 % 100	287 538 300 51.6	228 695 994 41.0	35 693 807 6.4	5 473 794 1.0
Sweden	1993	Krona	48 382 000 % 100	16 098 000 33.3	29 796 000 61.6	1 119 000 2.3	1 368 000 2.8
Switzerland	1992	Franc	9 090 000 % 100	2 580 000 28.4	6 130 000 67.4	170 000 1.9	210 000 2.3
United Kingdom	1993	Pound Sterling	13 829 000 % 100	4 522 000 32.7	7 172 000 51.9	1 617 000 11.7	518 000 3.7
Oceania							
Australia	1990	Dollar	5 087 600 % 100	2 815 300 55.3	2 012 400 39.6	65 700 1.3	194 200 3.8
Fiji‡	1986	Dollar	3 800 % 100	2 800 73.7	- -	1 000 26.3	- -
French Polynesia‡	1983	Franc C.F.P.	324 720 % 100	269 950 83.1	3 820 1.2	- -	50 950 15.7
Guam‡	1991	U. S. Dollar	2 215 % 100	1 943 87.7	- -	- -	272 12.3
New Caledonia‡	1983	Franc C.F.P.	83 000 % 100	61 500 74.1	21 500 25.9	- -	- -
New Zealand	1993	Dollar	825 200 % 100	451 200 54.7	280 100 33.9	20 100 2.4	73 800 8.9
Tonga‡	1980	Pa'anga	426 % 100	106 24.9	- -	320 75.1	- -

AFRICA:
Burundi:
    E--> Not including data for the productive sector nor labour costs at the Ministry of Public Health.
    FR-> Non compris les données relatives au secteur de la production ni les dépenses de personnel au Ministère de la Santé Publique.
    ESP> Excluídos los datos relativos al sector productivo y los gastos de personal en el Ministerio de la Sanidad Pública.
Central African Republic:
    E--> Not including data for the general service sector.
    FR-> Non compris les données pour le secteur de service général.
    ESP> Excluídos los datos relativos al sector de servicio general.
Congo:
    E--> Not including military and defence R&D.
    FR-> Non compris les activités de R-D de caractère militaire ou relevant de la défense nationale.
    ESP> Excluídas las actividades militares y de defensa de I y D.
Mauritius:
    E--> Data refer to current expenditure only.
    FR-> Les données se réfèrent aux dépenses courantes seulement.
    ESP> Los datos se refieren a los gastos corrientes solamente.

Nigeria:
    E--> Data relate only to 23 out of 26 national research institutes under the Federal Ministry of Science and Technology.
    FR-> Les données ne concernent que 23 des 26 instituts de recherche nationaux sous tutelle du Ministère fédéral de la Science et de la Technologie.
    ESP> Los datos sólo se refieren a 23 de los 26 centros de investigación nacionales bajo tutela del Ministerio Federal de Ciencia y Tecnología.
Rwanda:
    E--> Not including data for the productive sector.
    FR-> Compte non tenu des données pour le secteur de la production.
    ESP> Excluídos los datos relativos al sector productivo.
Seychelles:
    E--> Not including military and defence R&D.
    FR-> Non compris les activités de R-D de caractère militaire ou relevant de la défense nationale.
    ESP> Excluídas las actividades militares y de defensa de I y D.
AMERICA, NORTH:
Cuba:
    E--> Not including military and defence R&D.
    FR-> Non compris les activités de R-D de caractère militaire ou relevant de la défense nationale.
    ESP> Excluídas las actividades militares y de defensa de I y D.

R&D expenditure by source of funds **5.5**
Dépenses de R-D selon la source de financement
Gastos de I y D según la fuente de financiación

Guatemala:

E--> Data refer to the productive sector (integrated R&D) and the higher education sector only.

FR-> Les données ne concernent que le secteur de la production (activités de R-D intégrées) et le secteur de l'enseignement supérieur.

ESP> Los datos se refieren al sector productivo (actividades de I y D integradas) y al sector de enseñanza superior solamente.

Mexico:

E--> Figures in millions.

FR-> Chiffres en millions.

ESP> Cifras en millones.

Nicaragua:

E--> Data refer to current expenditure only. Not including military and defence R&D.

FR-> Les données se réfèrent aux dépenses courantes seulement. Non compris les activités de R-D de caractère militaire ou relevant de la défense nationale.

ESP> Los datos se refieren a los gastos corrientes solamente. Excluídas las actividades militares y de defensa de I y D.

United States:

E--> Except for the federal government institutions, data do not include capital expenditure. Data relating to the general service sector cover only the federal government and the private non-profit organizations. R&D expenditure in the productive sector (integrated R&D) includes also depreciation costs. Humanities in the higher education sector is excluded.

FR-> Sauf pour les institutions du gouvernement fédéral, les données n'incluent pas les dépenses en capital. Les données relatives au secteur de service général couvrent seulement le gouvernement fédéral et les organisations privées à but non lucratif. Les dépenses de R-D du secteur de la production (activités de R-D intégrées) comprennent aussi les coûts d'amortissement. Les sciences humaines ne sont pas comprises dans le secteur de l'enseignement supérieur.

ESP> Salvo las instituciones del Gobierno Federal, los datos no incluyen los gastos de capital. Los datos del sector de servicio general comprenden solamente el Gobierno Federal y las organizaciones privadas de carácter no lucrativo. Los gastos de I y D del sector productivo (actividades de I y D integradas) incluyen también los gastos de depreciación. No se incluyen las ciencias humanas en la enseñanza superior.

AMERICA, SOUTH:

Chile:

E--> Not including military and defence R&D.

FR-> Non compris les activités de R-D de caractère militaire ou relevant de la défense nationale.

ESP> Excluídas las actividades militares y de defensa de I y d.

Peru:

E--> Data refer to the budget allotment for science and technology.

FR-> Les données se réfèrent aux crédits budgétaires relatifs à la science et à la technologie.

ESP> Los datos se refieren a las consignaciones presupuestarias relativas a la ciencia y la tecnología.

ASIA:

Israel:

E--> Data refer to the civilian sector only.

FR-> Les données ne concernent que le secteur civil.

ESP> Los datos se refieren solamente al sector civil.

Japan:

E--> Figures in millions. Not including data for social sciences and humanities in the productive sector (integrated R&D).

FR-> Chiffres en millions. Non compris les données pour les sciences sociales et humaines dans le secteur de la production (activités de R-D intégrées).

ESP> Cifras en millones. Excluídos los datos relativos a las ciencias sociales y humanas del sector productivo (actividades de I y D integradas).

Korea, Republic of:

E--> Figures in millions. Excluding military and defence R&D and social sciences and humanities.

FR-> Chiffres en millions. Non compris les activités de R-D de caractère militaire ou relevant de la défense nationale ni les sciences sociales et humaines.

ESP> Cifras en millones. Excluídas las actividades militares y de defensa de I y D y las ciencias sociales y humanas.

Kuwait:

E--> Data refer to scientific and technological activities (STA).

FR-> Les données se réfèrent aux activités scientifiques et techniques (AST).

ESP> Los datos se refieren a las actividades científicas y tecnologícas (ACT).

Pakistan:

E--> Data relate to R&D activities concentrated mainly in government-financed research establishments only. Not including military and defence R&D.

FR-> Les données se réfèrent aux activités de R-D se trouvant pour la plupart dans les établissements de recherche financés par le gouvernement. Compte non tenu des activités de R-D de caractère militaire ou relevant de la défense nationale.

ESP> Los datos se refieren a las actividades de I y D concentradas principalmente en los establecimientos de investigación subvencionados por el gobierno. Excluídas las actividades militares y de defensa de I y D.

Philippines:

E--> Not including 670 thousand pesos for which a distribution by source of funds is not available.

FR-> Non compris 670 mille pesos dont la ventilation par source de financement n'est pas disponible.

ESP> Excluídos 670 miles de pesos cuya repartición por fuente de financiación no está disponible.

Turkey:

E--> Figures in millions.

FR-> Chiffres en millions.

ESP> Cifras en millones.

EUROPE:

Czech Republic:

E--> Not including military and defence R&D. Data include depreciation costs.

FR-> Non compris les activités de R-D de caractère militaire ou relevant de la défense nationale. Les données comprennent les coûts d'amortissement.

ESP> Excluídas las actividades militares y de defensa de I y D. Los datos incluyen los gastos de depreciación.

Germany:

E--> Not including data for social sciences and humanities in the productive sector.

FR-> Non compris les données relatives aux sciences sociales et humaines dans le secteur de la production.

ESP> No se incluyen los datos relativos a las ciencias sociales y humanas del sector productivo.

Hungary:

E--> Of military R&D, only that part carried out in civil establishments is included.

FR-> Pour la R-D de caractère militaire, seule la partie effectuée dans les établissements civils a été considérée.

ESP> Para las actividades de I y D de carácter militar, sólo se ha considerado la parte correspondiente a los establecimientos civiles.

Italy:

E--> Figures in millions.

FR-> Chiffres en millions.

ESP> Cifras en millones.

Malta:

E--> Data relate to the higher education sector only.

FR-> Les données ne concernent que le secteur de l'enseignement supérieur.

ESP> Los datos se refieren exclusivamente al sector de enseñanza superior.

Netherlands:

E--> Not including data for social sciences and humanities in the productive sector (integrated R&D).

FR-> Non compris les données pour les sciences sociales et humaines du secteur de la production (activités de R-D intégrées).

ESP> Excluídos los datos relativos a las ciencias sociales y humanas del sector productivo (actividades de I y D integradas).

Romania:

E--> Data refer to current expenditure only.

FR-> Les données se réfèrent aux dépenses courantes seulement.

ESP> Los datos se refieren a los gastos corrientes solamente.

Slovakia:

E--> Not including military and defence R&D.

FR-> Non compris les activités de R-D de caractère militaire ou relevant de la défense nationale.

ESP> Excluídas las actividades militares y de defensa de I y d.

OCEANIA:

Fiji:

E--> Data relate to one research institute only.

FR-> Les données ne concernent qu'un institut de recherche.

ESP> Los datos se refieren a un centro de investigación solamente.

French Polynesia:

E--> Data relate to one research institute only.

FR-> Les données ne concernent qu'un institut de recherche.

ESP> Los datos se refieren a un centro de investigación solamente.

Guam:

E--> Data relate to the higher education sector only.

FR-> Les données ne concernent que le secteur de l'enseignement supérieur.

ESP> Los datos se refieren al sector de enseñanza superior solamente.

5.5 R&D expenditure by source of funds
Dépenses de R-D selon la source de financement
Gastos de I y D según la fuente de financiación

New Caledonia:
 E--> Data relate to 2 research institutes only.
 FR-> Les données ne concernent que 2 instituts de recherche.
 ESP> Los datos se refieren a 2 centros de investigación solamente.

Tonga:
 E--> Data relate to one research institute only.
 FR-> Les données ne concernent qu'un institut de recherche.
 ESP> Los datos se refieren a un centro de investigación solamente.

R&D expenditure by sector of performance 5.6
Dépenses de R-D par secteur d'exécution
Gastos de I y D por sector de ejecución

5.6 Total and current expenditure for research and experimental development by sector of performance

Dépenses totales et courantes consacrées à la recherche et au développement expérimental, par secteur d'exécution

Gastos totales y corrientes dedicados a la investigación y al desarrollo experimental, por sector de ejecución

Please refer to introduction for definitions of categories included in this table.

Pour les définitions des catégories presentées dans ce tableau, se référer à l'introduction.

En la introducción se dan las definiciones de las categorías que figuran en este cuadro.

Current expenditure = Dépenses courantes = Gastos corrientes

Country / Pays / País	Reference year / Année de référence / Año de referencia	Currency / Monnaie / Moneda	Type of expenditure / Type de dépenses / Tipo de gastos	Sector of performance/Secteur d'exécution/Sector de ejecución				
				All sectors / Tous les secteurs / Todos los sectores (000)	Productive sector / Secteur de la production / Sector productivo		Higher education / Enseignement supérieur / Enseñanza superior (000)	General service / Service général / Servicio general (000)
					Integrated R&D / Activitiés de R-D intégrées / Actividades de I y D integradas (000)	Non integrated R&D / Activitiés de R-D non intégrées / Actividades de I y D no integradas (000)		
				(1)	(2)	(3)	(4)	(5)
Africa								
Burundi‡	1989	Franc	Total	...	...	...	32 226	503 961
Central African Republic	1984	Franc C.F.A.	Total	...	616 312	-	64 479	...
Congo‡	1984	Franc C.F.A	Total	25 530	20 394	4 106	622	408
			%	100	79.9	16.1	2.4	1.6
			Current	11 267	6 831	3 925	372	139
			%	100	60.6	34.8	3.3	1.2
Mauritius	1992	Rupee	Total	...	...	...	18 000	159 000
			Current	...	...	...	11 000	118 000
Nigeria‡	1987	Naira	Total	...	...	...	...	86 270
			Current	...	...	...	...	69 615
Rwanda	1985	Franc	Total	918 560	99 280	...	...	...
			%	100	10.8	...	...	...
Seychelles‡	1983	Rupee	Total	12 854	-	730	-	12 124
			%	100	-	5.7	-	94.3
			Current	6 083	-	400	-	5 683
			%	100	-	6.6	-	93.4
South Africa	1991	Rand	Total	2 786 086	1 297 622	./.	690 439	798 025
			%	100	46.6	./.	24.8	28.6
			Current	2 545 322	1 126 485	./.	660 377	758 460
			%	100	44.3	./.	25.9	29.8
Tunisia	1992	Dinar	Total	...	...	...	20 000 000	25 000 000
			Current	...	...	...	16 000 000	18 000 000

R&D expenditure by sector of performance
Dépenses de R-D par secteur d'exécution
Gastos de I y D por sector de ejecución

Country / Pays / País	Reference year / Année de référence / Año de referencia	Currency / Monnaie / Moneda	Type of expenditure / Type de dépenses / Tipo de gastos	Sector of performance/Secteur d'exécution/Sector de ejecución				
				All sectors / Tous les secteurs / Todos los sectores (000)	Productive sector / Secteur de la production / Sector productivo		Higher education / Enseignement supérieur / Enseñanza superior (000)	General service / Service général / Servicio general (000)
					Integrated R&D / Activitiés de R-D intégrées / Actividades de I y D integradas (000)	Non integrated R&D / Activitiés de R-D non intégrées / Actividades de I y D no integradas (000)		
				(1)	(2)	(3)	(4)	(5)
America, North								
Canada‡	1994	Dollar	Total	*11 649 000	*6 473 000	./.	2 876 000	2 030 000
			%	100	*57.9	./.	24.7	*17.4
Costa Rica	1986	Colon	Total	612 000	./.	./.	282 000	330 000
			%	100	./.	./.	46.1	53.9
Cuba‡	1992	Peso	Total	247 925	9 827	107 667	40 656	89 775
			%	100	4.0	43.4	16.4	36.2
			Current	156 709	2 478	73 646	19 610	60 975
			%	100	1.6	47.0	12.5	38.9
El Salvador‡	1992	Colon	Total	513 980	114 426	./.	105 862	293 692
			%	100	22.3	./.	20.6	57.1
			Current	382 603	113 810	./.	85 147	183 646
			%	100	29.7	./.	22.3	48.0
Guatemala	1988	Quetzal	Total	...	25 592	...	6 267	...
Jamaica‡	1986	Dollar	Total	...	...	...	...	4 016
			Current	...	...	...	...	3 886
Mexico‡	1993	Peso	Total	3 566 158	286 188	./.	1 485 696	1 794 274
			%	100	8.0	./.	41.7	50.3
			Current	2 735 898	229 520	./.	1 188 829	1 317 549
			%	100	8.4	./.	43.4	48.2
Nicaragua‡	1987	Cordoba	Current	988 970	...	...	141 345	...
			%	100	...	...	14.3	...
Trinidad and Tobago	1984	Dollar	Total	143 257	19 503	17 394	92 444	13 916
			%	100	13.6	12.1	64.5	9.7
United States‡	1995	Dollar	Total	*171 000 000	*121400000	——>	*26 900 000	*22 700 000
			%	100	*71.0	——>	*15.7	*13.3
America, South								
Argentina	1992	Austral	Total	*664 700	*53 200	*186 100	*199 400	*226 000
			%	100	*8.0	*28.0	*30.0	*34.0
			Current	*522 400	*31 900	*119 600	*174 100	*196 800
			%	100	*6.1	*22.9	*33.3	*37.7
Brazil‡	1994	Reais	Total	1 491 165	270 177	——>	483 815	737 173
			%	100	18.1	——>	32.4	49.4
Chile	1992	Peso	Total	*102 196 000	...	...	36 597 000	...
			%	100	...	...	*35.8	...
Colombia	1982	Peso	Total	...	42 579	...	422 272	2 289 422
Guyana‡	1982	Dollar	Total	...	900	——>	1 900	...
Venezuela‡	1992	Bolivar	Total	19 662 200	6 887 000	3 770 000	1 838 400	7 126 800
			%	100	35.0	19.2	9.4	36.2
Asia								
Brunei Darussalam‡	1984	Dollar	Total	10 880	9 440	-	-	1 440
			%	100	86.8	-	-	13.2
			Current	8 220	7 130	-	-	1 090
			%	100	86.7	-	-	13.3
China	1993	Yuan	Total	19 600 000	4 450 000	1 890 000	347 000	9 790 000
			%	100	22.7	9.6	17.7	49.9
Cyprus	1992	Pound	Total	5 578	785	-	10	4 783
			%	100	14.1	-	0.2	85.7
			Current	4 806	553	-	5	4 248
			%	100	11.5	-	0.1	88.4
India	1990	Rupee	Total	41 864 300	9 702 900	——>	510 100	31 651 300
			%	100	23.2	——>	1.2	75.6
			Current	33 389 000	6 695 000	——>	423 400	26 270 600
			%	100	20.1	——>	1.3	78.7

R&D expenditure by sector of performance 5.6
Dépenses de R-D par secteur d'exécution
Gastos de I y D por sector de ejecución

Country / Pays / País	Reference year / Année de référence / Año de referencia	Currency / Monnaie / Moneda	Type of expenditure / Type de dépenses / Tipo de gastos	All sectors / Tous les secteurs / Todos los sectores (000)	Productive sector / Secteur de la production / Sector productivo		Higher education / Enseignement supérieur / Enseñanza superior (000)	General service / Service général / Servicio general (000)
					Integrated R&D / Activitiés de R-D intégrées / Actividades de I y D integradas (000)	Non integrated R&D / Activitiés de R-D non intégrées / Actividades de I y D no integradas (000)		
				(1)	(2)	(3)	(4)	(5)
Indonesia‡	1988	Rupiah	Total	...	...	...	...	259 283 000
			Current					194 638 000
Iran, Islamic Republic of‡	1984	Rial	Total	21 527 000	17 534 000	——>	3 298 000	695 000
			%	100	81.5	——>	15.3	3.2
			Current	11 584 000	8 325 000	——>	2 564 000	695 000
			%	100	71.9	——>	22.1	6.0
Israel‡	1992	Shekel	Total	3 663 100	1 731 100	./.	1 218 500	713 500
			%	100	47.3	./.	33.3	19.5
			Current	3 462 500	1 629 900	./.	1 143 200	689 400
			%	100	47.1	./.	33.0	19.9
Japan‡	1991	Yen	Total	13 771 524	9 743 048	./.	2 407 927	1 620 549
			%	100	70.7	./.	17.5	11.8
			Current	11 622 036	8 217 495	./.	2 113 477	1 291 063
			%	100	70.7	./.	18.2	11.1
Jordan‡	1986	Dinar	Total	5 587	315	-	3 831	1 441
			%	100	5.6	-	68.6	25.8
Korea, Republic of‡	1994	Won	Total	7 894 746	5 420 040	325 240	608 851	1 540 615
			%	100	68.7	4.1	7.7	19.5
			Current	5 561 911	3 688 849	249 515	452 919	1 170 618
			%	100	66.3	4.5	8.1	21.0
Kuwait‡	1984	Dinar	Total	71 163	43 324	1 543	1 480	24 816
			%	100	60.9	2.2	2.1	34.9
			Current	63 016	44 148	——>	751	18 117
			%	100	70.1	——>	1.2	28.8
Lebanon‡	1980	Pound	Total	...	...	...	22 000	...
Malaysia‡	1992	Ringgit	Total	550 699	246 335	./.	50 685	253 679
			%	100	44.7	./.	9.2	46.1
			Current	338 179	125 409	./.	31 142	181 628
			%	100	37.1	./.	9.2	53.7
Pakistan†	1987	Rupee	Total	5 582 081	-	4 476 632	1 105 449	./.
			%	100	-	80.2	19.8	./.
			Current	3 655 824	-	2 828 365	827 459	./.
			%	100	-	77.4	22.6	./.
Philippines‡	1984	Peso	Total	613 410	118 890	77 250	38 070	379 200
			%	100	19.4	12.6	6.2	61.8
			Current	514 800	93 520	./.	36 330	384 950
			%	100	18.2	./.	7.1	74.8
Qatar	1986	Riyal	Total	6 650	-	3 300	3 350	-
			%	100	-	49.6	50.4	-
			Current	6 650	-	3 300	3 350	-
			%	100	-	49.6	50.4	-
Singapore‡	1994	Dollar	Total	1 170 000	733 590	./.	179 010	257 400
			%	100	62.7	./.	15.3	22.0
Sri Lanka	1984	Rupee	Total	256 799	24 318	——>	16 138	216 343
			%	100	9.5	——>	6.3	84.2
			Current	174 335	15 980	——>	14 515	143 840
			%	100	9.2	——>	8.3	82.5
Thailand	1991	Baht	Total	3 928 100	...	...	793 640	...
			%	100	...	...	20.2	...
Turkey‡	1991	Lira	Total	3 330 047	702 255	——>	2 366 100	261 692
			%	100	21.1	——>	71.1	7.9
			Current	2 036 999	404 199	——>	1 422 026	210 774
			%	100	19.8	——>	69.8	10.3
Viet Nam‡	1985	Dong	Total	498 000	231 000	——>	31 000	*236 000
			%	100	46.4	——>	6.2	*47.4

5.6 R&D expenditure by sector of performance
Dépenses de R-D par secteur d'exécution
Gastos de I y D por sector de ejecución

Country / Pays / País	Reference year / Année de référence / Año de referencia	Currency / Monnaie / Moneda	Type of expenditure / Type de dépenses / Tipo de gastos	Sector of performance/Secteur d'exécution/Sector de ejecución				
				All sectors / Tous les secteurs / Todos los sectores (000)	Productive sector / Secteur de la production / Sector productivo		Higher education / Enseignement supérieur / Enseñanza superior (000)	General service / Service général / Servicio general (000)
					Integrated R&D / Activitiés de R-D intégrées / Actividades de I y D integradas (000)	Non integrated R&D / Activitiés de R-D non intégrées / Actividades de I y D no integradas (000)		
				(1)	(2)	(3)	(4)	(5)
Europe								
Austria	1993	Schilling	Total	30 692 586	15 756 370	1 477 567	10 663 909	2 794 740
			%	100	51.4	4.8	34.7	9.1
			Current	26 167 600	14 419 103	1 325 609	8 065 403	2 357 485
			%	100	55.1	5.1	30.8	9.0
Belarus	1992	Rouble	Current	6 332 200	4 765 100	——>	440 600	1 126 500
			%	100	75.2	——>	7.0	17.8
Belgium	1991	Franc	Total	*112 065 000	*74 515 000	./.	*29 372 100	*8 177 400
			%	100	*66.5	./.	*26.2	*7.3
Bulgaria	1992	Lev	Total	3 103 800	1 576 800	——>	251 800	1 275 200
			%	100	50.8	——>	8.1	41.1
			Current	2 847 700	1 403 900	——>	243 100	1 200 700
			%	100	49.3	——>	8.5	42.2
Croatia	1992	Croatian Dinar	Current	21 874 940	8 090 995	3 626 831	5 321 980	4 835 134
			%	100	37.0	16.6	24.3	22.1
Czech Republic‡	1994	Koruna	Total	12 983 000	8 699 000	./.	580 000	3 704 000
			%	100	67.0	./.	4.5	28.5
Denmark‡	1993	Krone	Total	15 695 000	7 966 000	1 185 000	3 587 000	2 957 000
			%	100	50.8	7.6	22.8	18.8
			Current	...	7 989 000	...	3 229 000	2 716 000
Estonia	1994	Kroon	Total	216 798	-	-	59 242	157 566
			%	100	-	-	27.3	72.7
Finland	1993	Markka	Total	10 677 100	6 234 100	——>	2 185 200	2 257 800
			%	100	58.4	——>	20.5	21.1
			Current	9 734 000	5 697 100	——>	2 059 100	1 977 800
			%	100	58.5	——>	21.2	20.3
France‡	1993	Franc	Current	159 020 100	99 687 500	./.	25 095 000	34 237 600
			%	100	62.7	./.	15.8	21.5
Germany‡	1991	D. Mark	Total	74 517 000	51 675 000	——>	12 169 000	10 673 000
			%	100	69.3	——>	16.3	14.3
			Current	66 152 000	46 585 000	——>	10 640 000	8 927 000
			%	100	70.4	——>	16.1	13.5
Greece	1993	Drachma	Total	100 460 000	26 924 000	-	40 841 000	32 695 000
			%	100	28.8	-	39.5	31.7
Hungary‡	1993	Forint	Total	28 039 000	8 796 000	2 477 000	7 843 000	8 923 000
			%	100	31.4	8.8	28.0	31.8
			Current	24 466 000	7 681 000	2 055 000	6 776 000	7 934 000
			%	100	31.4	8.4	27.7	32.5
Iceland	1989	Krona	Total	3 123 000	593 370	——>	780 750	1 748 880
			%	100	19.0	——>	25.0	56.0
Ireland‡	1988	Pound	Total	400 201	271 239	./.	84 162	44 800
			%	100	67.8	./.	21.0	11.2
Italy‡	1993	Lira	Total	19 518 867	11 051 861	./.	4 397 616	4 069 390
			%	100	56.7	./.	22.5	20.8
			Current	17 459 492	10 133 660	./.	3 896 276	3 429 556
			%	100	58.1	./.	22.3	19.6
Malta	1988	Lira	Total	...	...	...	10	...
			Current	...	...	...	9	...
Netherlands‡	1991	Guilder	Total	10 381 000	5 460 000	60 000	2 569 000	2 292 000
			%	100	52.6	0.6	24.7	22.1
			Current	9 322 000	4 941 000	55 000	2 334 000	1 992 000
			%	100	53.0	0.6	25.0	21.4

R&D expenditure by sector of performance   **5.6**
Dépenses de R-D par secteur d'exécution
Gastos de I y D por sector de ejecución

Country / Pays / País	Reference year / Année de référence / Año de referencia	Currency / Monnaie / Moneda	Type of expenditure / Type de dépenses / Tipo de gastos	Sector of performance/Secteur d'exécution/Sector de ejecución				
					Productive sector / Secteur de la production / Sector productivo		Higher education / Enseignement supérieur / Enseñanza superior	General service / Service général / Servicio general
				All sectors / Tous les secteurs / Todos los sectores (000)	Integrated R&D / Activitiés de R-D intégrées / Actividades de I y D integradas (000)	Non inte-grated R&D / Activitiés de R-D non intégrées / Actividades de I y D no integradas (000)	(000)	(000)
				(1)	(2)	(3)	(4)	(5)
Norway	1993	Krone	Total	14 262 600	5 827 000	1 805 000	3 893 700	2 736 900
			%	100	40.9	12.7	27.3	19.2
			Current	12 624 900	5 067 600	1 665 700	3 422 500	2 469 100
			%	100	40.1	13.2	27.1	19.6
Poland‡	1992	Zloty	Current	8 813 879	787 740	3 960 655	1 998 925	2 066 559
			%	100	8.9	44.9	22.7	23.4
Portugal	1990	Escudo	Total	52 032 200	13 585 600	6 458 400	18 748 000	13 240 200
			%	100	26.1	12.4	36.0	25.4
			Current	41 548 800	9 906 000	3 718 300	16 863 100	11 061 400
			%	100	23.8	8.9	40.6	26.6
Romania	1992	Leu	Current	39 527 000	29 643 000	——>	1 294 000	8 590 000
			%	100	75.0	——>	3.3	21.7
Russian Federation‡	1993	Rouble	Total	*1 254 879	*89 929	*936 996	*68 263	*159 691
			%	100	*7.2	*74.7	*5.4	*12.7
Slovakia‡	1994	Koruna	Total	4 473 412	2 358 676	./.	219 199	1 895 537
			%	100	52.7	./.	4.9	42.4
			Current	4 087 728	2 219 531	./.	195 079	1 673 118
			%	100	54.3	./.	4.8	40.9
Slovenia	1992	Tolar	Total	15 050 524	5 253 082	1 003 099	3 268 071	5 526 272
			%	100	34.9	6.7	21.7	36.7
			Current	13 684 740	4 804 716	864 004	2 963 752	5 052 268
			%	100	35.1	6.3	21.7	36.9
Spain	1993	Peseta	Total	557 401 895	266 174 510	——>	174 341 668	116 885 717
			%	100	47.8	——>	31.3	20.9
			Current	453 796 892	233 210 072	——>	131 971 346	88 615 474
			%	100	51.4	——>	29.1	19.5
Sweden	1993	Krona	Current	45 220 000	30 700 000	——>	10 400 000	4 120 000
			%	100	67.9	——>	23.0	9.1
Switzerland‡	1992	Franc	Total	9 090 000	6 370 000	./.	2 270 000	450 000
			%	100	70.1	./.	25.0	4.9
United Kingdom‡	1993	Pound Stg.	Total	13 829 000	9 069 000	./.	2 312 000	2 448 000
			%	100	65.6	./.	16.7	17.7
			Current	...	8 042 000	...	...	...
Federal Republic of Yugoslavia‡	1992	Dinar	Total	335	38	23	260	14
			%	100	11.3	6.9	77.6	4.2
			Current	139	16	22	91	10
			%	100	11.5	15.8	65.5	7.2
Oceania								
Australia‡	1990	Dollar	Total	5 087 600	2 017 400	./.	1 350 800	1 719 400
			%	100	39.7	./.	26.6	33.8
			Current	4 388 800	1 772 700	./.	1 129 400	1 486 700
			%	100	40.4	./.	25.7	33.9
Fiji‡	1986	Dollar	Total	...	3 800	-	...	...
			Current	...	3 000	-	...	...
French Polynesia‡	1983	Franc C.F.P.	Total	324 720	-	-	-	324 720
			%	100	-	-	-	100.0
			Current	308 440	-	-	-	308 440
			%	100	-	-	-	100.0
Guam	1991	U.S. Dollar	Total	...	...	...	2 215	...
New Caledonia‡	1985	Franc C.F.P.	Total	800 820	-	472 400	-	328 420
			%	100	-	59.0	-	41.0
			Current	707 547	-	398 500	-	309 047
			%	100	-	56.3	-	43.7

5.6 R&D expenditure by sector of performance
Dépenses de R-D par secteur d'exécution
Gastos de I y D por sector de ejecución

				Sector of performance/Secteur d'exécution/Sector de ejecución				
					Productive sector Secteur de la production Sector productivo			
Country	Reference year	Currency	Type of expenditure	All sectors	Integrated R&D	Non inte-grated R&D	Higher education	General service
Pays	Année de référence	Monnaie	Type de dépenses	Tous les secteurs	Activitiés de R-D intégrées	Activitiés de R-D non intégrées	Enseigne-ment supérieur	Service général
País	Año de referencia	Moneda	Tipo de gastos	Todos los sectores (000)	Actividades de I y D integradas (000)	Actividades de I y D no integradas (000)	Enseñanza superior (000)	Servicio general (000)
				(1)	(2)	(3)	(4)	(5)
New Zealand	1993	Dollar	Total %	825 200 100	189 800 23.0	58 800 7.1	233 500 28.3	343 100 41.6
Tonga‡	1980	Pa'anga	Total % Current %	426 100 279 100	- -	- -	- -	426 100.0 279 100.0

AFRICA:
Burundi:
E--> Not including labour costs at the Ministry of Public Health in the general service sector.
FR-> Non compris les dépenses de personnel au Ministère de la Santé Publique dans le secteur de service général.
ESP> Excluídos los gastos de personal al Ministerio de la Sanidad Pública en el sector de servicio general.
Congo:
E--> Not including military and defence R&D.
FR-> Non compris les activités de R-D de caractère militaire ou relevant de la défense nationale.
ESP> Excluídas las actividades militares y de defensa de I y D.
Nigeria:
E--> Data relate only to 23 out of 26 national research institutes under the Federal Ministry of Science and Technology.
FR-> Les données ne concernent que 23 des 26 instituts de recherche nationaux sous tutelle du Ministère fédéral de la Science et de la Technologie.
ESP> Los datos sólo se refieren a 23 de los 26 centros de investigación nacionales bajo tutela del Ministerio Federal de Ciencia y Tecnología.
Seychelles:
E--> Not including data for military and defence R&D.
FR-> Non compris les activités de R-D de caractère militaire ou relevant de la défense nationale.
ESP> Excluídas las actividades militares y de defensa de I y D.
AMERICA, NORTH:
Canada:
E--> Data for the productive sector (non-integrated R&D) are included with the general service sector.
FR-> Les données relatives au secteur de la production (activités de R-D non intégrées) sont comprises avec celles du secteur de service général.
ESP> Los datos relativos al sector productivo (actividades de I y D no integradas) se incluyen en el sector de servicio general.
Cuba:
E--> Data refer to government funds only. Not including military and defence R&D.
FR-> Les données ne concernent que les fonds publics. Non compris les activités de R-D de caractère militaire ou relevant de la défense nationale.
ESP> Los datos se refieren a los fondos públicos solamente. Excluídas las actividades militares y de defensa de I y D.
El Salvador:
E--> Data relate to R&D activities performed in public enterprises. Not including 569,579 thousand colons for which a distribution by sector of performance and by type of expenditure is not known.
FR-> Les données se réfèrent aux activités de R-D exercées dans les entreprises publiques. Non compris 569 579 milliers de colones dont la répartition par secteur d'éxécution et par type de dépenses n'est pas disponible.
ESP> Los datos se refieren a las actividades de I y D que se ejecutan en las empresas públicas. Excluídos 569 579 miles de colones cuya repartición por sector de ejecución y por tipo de gastos se desconoce.
Jamaica:
E--> Data relate to the Scientific Research Council only.

FR-> Les données se réfèrent au *Scientific Research Council* seulement.
ESP> Los datos se refieren al *Scientific Research Council* solamente.
Mexico:
E--> Not including private non profit organizations. Data for the productive sector (non-integrated R&D) are included with the general service sector.
FR-> Non compris les organisations privées à but non lucratif. Les données relatives au secteur de la production (activités de R-D non intégrées) sont comprises avec celles du secteur de service général.
ESP> Excluídas las organizaciones privadas de carácter no lucrativo. Los datos relativos al sector productivo (actividades de I y D no integradas) se incluyen en el sector de servicio general.
Nicaragua:
E--> Not including military and defence R&D.
FR-> Non compris les activités de R-D de caractère militaire ou relevant de la défense nationale.
ESP> Excluídas las actividades militares y de defensa de I y D.
United States:
E--> Except for the federal government institutions, data do not include capital expenditure. Data for the general service sector cover only the federal government and the private non-profit organizations. R&D expenditure in the productive sector (integrated R&D) includes also depreciation costs. Humanities in the higher education sector is excluded.
FR-> Sauf pour les institutions du gouvernement fédéral, les données n'incluent pas les dépenses en capital. Les données relatives au secteur de service général couvrent seulement le gouvernement fédéral et les organisations privées à but non lucratif. Les dépenses de R-D du secteur de la production (activités de R-D intégrées) comprennent aussi les coûts d'amortissement. Les sciences humaines ne sont pas comprises dans le secteur de l'enseignement supérieur.
ESP> Salvo las instituciones del Gobierno Federal, los datos no incluyen los gastos de capital. Los datos del sector de servicio general comprenden solamente el Gobierno Federal y las organizaciones privadas de carácter no lucrativo. Los gastos de I y D del sector productivo (actividades de I y D integradas) incluyen también los gastos de depreciación. No se incluyen las ciencias humanas en la enseñanza superior.
AMERICA, SOUTH:
Brazil:
E--> Data relate to government and productive enterprise funds only.
FR-> Les données ne concernent que les fonds publics et les fonds des enterprises de production.
ESP> Los datos sólo se refieren a los fondos públicos y los de las empresas de producción.
Guyana:
E--> Not including military and defence R&D. Data for the general service sector and for medical sciences in the higher education sector are also excluded.
FR-> Non compris les activités de R-D de caractère militaire ou relevant de la défense nationale. Les données relatives au secteur de service général et les sciences médicales du secteur de l'enseignement supérieur sont aussi exclues.

R&D expenditure by sector of performance **5.6**
Dépenses de R-D par secteur d'exécution
Gastos de I y D por sector de ejecución

ESP> Excluídas las actividades militares y de defensa de I y D. Se excluyen también los datos relativos al sector de servicio general y las ciencias médicas del sector de enseñanza superior.

Venezuela:
E--> Data refer to government funds only.
FR-> Les données ne concernent que les fonds publics.
ESP> Los datos se refieren a los fondos públicos solamente.

ASIA:
Brunei Darussalam:
E--> Data relate to 2 research institutes only.
FR-> Les données se réfèrent à 2 instituts de recherche seulement.
ESP> Los datos se refieren a 2 centros de investigación solamente.

Indonesia:
E--> Data refer to government expenditure only.
FR-> Les données ne concernent que les dépenses du gouvernement.
ESP> Los datos se refieren a los gastos del gobierno solamente.

Iran, Islamic Republic of:
E--> Data relate to the budget allotment.
FR-> Les données se réfèrent aux crédits budgétaires.
ESP> Los datos se refieren a las consignaciones presupuestarias.

Israel:
E--> Data refer to the civilian sector only. Data for the productive sector (non-integrated R&D) are included with the general service sector.
FR-> Les données ne concernent que le secteur civil. Les données relatives au secteur de la production (activités de R-D non intégrées) sont comprises avec celles du secteur de service général.
ESP> Los datos se refieren solamente al sector civil. Los datos relativos al sector productivo (actividades de I y D no integradas) se incluyen en el sector de servicio general.

Japan:
E--> Figures in millions. Not including data for social sciences and humanities in the productive sector (integrated R&D). Data for the productive sector (non-integrated R-D) are included with the general service sector.
FR-> Chiffres en millions. Non compris les données pour les sciences sociales et humaines dans le secteur de la production (activités de R-D intégrées). Les données relatives au secteur de la production (activités de R-D non intégrées) sont comprises avec celles du secteur de service général.
ESP> Cifras en millones. Excluídos los datos relativos a las ciencias sociales y humanas del sector productivo (actividades de I y D integradas). Los datos relativos al sector productivo (actividades de I y D no integradas) se incluyen en el sector de servicio general.

Jordan:
E--> Not including military and defence R&D.
FR-> Non compris les activités de R-D de caractère militaire ou relevant de la défense nationale.
ESP> Excluídas las actividades militares y de defensa de I y D.

Korea, Republic of:
E--> Figures in millions. Not including military and defence R&D nor social sciences and humanities.
FR-> Chiffres en millions. Non compris les activités de R-D de caractère militaire ou relevant de la défense nationale ni les sciences sociales et humaines.
ESP> Cifras en millones. Excluídas las actividades militares y de defensa de I y D y las ciencias sociales y humanas.

Kuwait:
E--> Data refer to scientific and technological activities (STA).
FR-> Les données se réfèrent aux activités scientifiques et techniques (AST).
ESP> Los datos se refieren a las actividades científicas y tecnológicas (ACT).

Lebanon:
E--> Data refer to the Faculty of Science at the University of Lebanon only.
FR-> Les données ne se réfèrent qu'à la Faculté des Sciences de l'Université du Liban.
ESP> Los datos se refieren a la Facultad de Ciencias de la Universidad del Líbano solamente.

Malaysia:
E--> Data for the productive sector (non-integrated R&D) are included with the general service sector.
FR-> Les données relatives au secteur de la production (activités de R-D non intégrées) sont comprises avec celles du secteur de service général.
ESP> Los datos relativos al sector productivo (actividades de I y D no integradas) se incluyen en el sector de servicio general.

Pakistan:
E--> Data refer to R&D activities concentrated mainly in government-financed research establishments only; those relating to the general service sector are included with the production sector (non-integrated). Not including military and defence R&D.
FR-> Les données se réfèrent aux activités de R-D se trouvant pour la plupart dans les établissements de recherche financés par le gouvernement; celles relatives au secteur de service général sont comprises avec le secteur de la production (activités de R-D non intégrées). Compte non tenu des activités de R-D de caractère militaire ou relevant de la défense nationale.
ESP> Los datos se refieren a las actividades de I y D concentradas principalmente en los establecimientos de investigación subvencionados por el gobierno; los del sector de servicio general se incluyen en el sector productivo (actividades de I y D no integradas). Excluídas las actividades militares y de defensa de I y D.

Philippines:
E--> Data referring to current expenditure in the productive sector (non-integrated) R&D are included with the general service sector.
FR-> Les données concernant les dépenses courantes dans le secteur de la production (activités de R-D non intégrées) sont comprises avec celles du secteur de service général.
ESP> Los datos relativos a los gastos corrientes en el sector productivo (actividades de I y D no integradas) se incluyen en el sector de servicio general.

Singapore:
E--> Data for the productive sector (non-integrated R&D) are included with the general service sector.
FR-> Les données relatives au secteur de la production (activités de R-D non intégrées) sont comprises avec celles du secteur de service général.
ESP> Los datos relativos al sector productivo (actividades de I y D no integradas) se incluyen en el sector de servicio general.

Turkey:
E--> Figures in millions.
FR-> Chiffres en millions.
ESP> Cifras en millones.

Viet Nam:
E--> Data refer to government expenditure only.
FR-> Les données ne concernent que les dépenses du gouvernement.
ESP> Los datos se refieren a los gastos del gobierno solamente.

EUROPE:
Czech Republic:
E--> Not including military and defence R&D. Data include depreciation costs.
FR-> Non compris les activités de R-D de caractère militaire ou relevant de la défense nationale. Les données comprennent les coûts d'amortissement.
ESP> Excluídas las actividades militares y de defensa de I y D. Los datos incluyen los gastos de depreciación.

France:
E--> Data for the productive sector (non-integrated R&D) are included with the general service sector.
FR-> Les données relatives au secteur de la production (activités de R-D non intégrées) sont comprises avec celles du secteur de service général.
ESP> Los datos relativos al sector productivo (actividades de I y D no integradas) se incluyen en el sector de servicio general.

Germany:
E--> Data relating to current expenditure do not include the relevant part of 661 million Deutsche marks (343 in the productive sector and 318 in the higher education sector) for which a distribution between capital and current expenditure is unknown. Not including data for social sciences and humanities in the productive sector.
FR-> Les données relatives aux dépenses courantes ne comprennent pas la partie de la somme de 661 millions de deutsche marks (343 dans le secteur de la production et 318 dans le secteur de l'enseignement supérieur) dont la répartition entre les dépenses en capital et les dépenses courantes n'a pas été précisée. Non compris les données pour les sciences sociales et humaines dans le secteur de la production.
ESP> Los datos relativos a los gastos corrientes excluyen la parte correspondiente de la suma de 661 millones de marcos (343 en el sector productivo y 318 en el sector de enseñanza superior) cuya repartición entre gastos corrientes y gastos de capital no se ha precisado. Excluídos los datos relativos a las ciencias sociales y humanas del sector productivo.

Hungary:
E--> Not including 6,647 million forints (all current expenditure) for which a breakdown by sector of performance is not available. Of military R&D, only that part carried out in civil establishments is included.

5.6

R&D expenditure by sector of performance
Dépenses de R-D par secteur d'exécution
Gastos de I y D por sector de ejecución

FR–> Compte non tenu de 6 647 millions de forints (dépenses courantes) dont la répartition par secteur d'exécution n'est pas disponible. Pour de R-D de caractère militaire, seule la partie effectuée dans les établissements civils a été considérée.

ESP> Excluídos 6 647 millones de forints (gastos corrientes) cuya repartición por sector de ejecución se desconoce. Para las actividades de I y D de carácter militar, sólo se ha considerado la parte correspondiente a los establecimientos civiles.

Ireland:

E––> Data for to the productive sector (non-integrated R&D) are included with the general service sector.

FR–> Les données relatives au secteur de la production (activités de R-D non intégrées) sont comprises avec celles du secteur de service général.

ESP> Los datos relativos al sector productivo (actividades de I y D no integradas) se incluyen en el sector de servicio general.

Italy:

E––> Figures in millions. Data for the productive sector (non-integrated R&D) are included with the general service sector.

FR–> Chiffres en millions. Les données relatives au secteur de la production (activités de R-D non intégrées) sont comprises avec celles du secteur de service général.

ESP> Cifras en millones. Los datos relativos al sector productivo (actividades de I y D no integradas) se incluyen en el sector de servicio general.

Netherlands:

E––> Not including data for social sciences and humanities in the productive sector (integrated R&D).

FR–> Non compris les données pour les sciences sociales et humaines du secteur de la production (activités de R-D intégrées).

ESP> Excluídos los datos relativos a las ciencias sociales y humanas del sector productivo (actividades de I y D integradas).

Poland:

E––> Figures in millions. Not including military and defence R&D.

FR–> Chiffres en millions. Non compris les activités de R-D de caractère militaire ou relevant de la défense nationale.

ESP> Cifras en millones. Excluídas las actividades militares y de defensa de I y D.

Russian Federation:

E––> Figures in millions. Not including 58,678 million roubles for which a breakdown by sector of performance is not available.

FR–> Chiffres en millions. Compte non tenu de 58 678 millions de roubles dont la répartition par secteur d'exécution n'est pas disponible.

ESP> Cifras en millones. Excluídos 58 678 millones de rublos cuya repartición por sector de ejecución se desconoce.

Slovakia:

E––> Not including military and defence R&D. Data for the productive sector (non-integrated R&D) are included with the general service sector.

FR–> Non compris les activités de R-D de caractère militaire ou relevant de la défense nationale. Les données relatives au secteur de la production (activités de R-D non intégrées) sont comprises avec celles du secteur de service général.

ESP> Excluídas las actividades militares y de defensa de I y D. Los datos correspondientes al sector productivo (actividades de I y D no integradas) están incluídos en el sector de servicio general.

Switzerland:

E––> Data for the productive sector (non-integrated R&D) are included with the general service sector. The latter also includes private non-profit organizations.

FR–> Les données relatives au secteur de la production (activités de R-D non intégrées) sont comprises avec celles du secteur de service général. Ce dernier comprend aussi les organisations privées à but non lucratif.

ESP> Los datos relativos al sector productivo (actividades de I y D no integradas) se incluyen en el sector de servicio general. También incluyen las organizaciones privadas de carácter no lucrativo.

United Kingdom:

E––> Data for the productive sector (non-integrated R&D) are included with the general service sector.

FR–> Les données relatives au secteur de la production (données de R-D non intégrées) sont comprises avec celles du secteur de service général.

ESP> Los datos relativos al sector productivo actividades de I y D non integradas) se incluyen en el sector de servicio general.

Federal Republic of Yugoslavia:

E––> Not including military and defence R&D.

FR–> Non compris les activités de R-D de caractère militaire ou relevant de la défense nationale.

ESP> Excluídas las actividades militares y de defensa de I y D.

OCEANIA:

Australia:

E––> Data for the productive sector (non-integrated R&D) are included with the general service sector.

FR–> Les données relatives au secteur de la production (activités de R-D non intégrées) sont comprises avec celles du secteur de service général.

ESP> Los datos relativos al sector productivo (actividades de I y D no integradas) se incluyen en el sector de servicio general.

Fiji:

E––> Data refer to one research institute only.

FR–> Les données ne concernent qu'un institut de recherche.

ESP> Los datos se refieren a un centro de investigación solamente.

French Polynesia:

E––> Data refer to one research institute only.

FR–> Les données ne concernent qu'un institut de recherche.

ESP> Los datos se refieren a un centro de investigación solamente.

New Caledonia:

E––> Data refer only to 6 out of 11 research institutes.

FR–> Les données ne se rapportent qu'à 6 instituts de recherche sur 11.

ESP> Los datos sólo se refieren a 6 de los 11 centros de investigación.

Tonga:

E––> Data refer to one research institute only.

FR–> Les données ne concernent qu'un institut de recherche.

ESP> Los datos se refieren a un centro de investigación solamente.

Summary tables for culture and communication 6
Tableaux récapitulatifs pour la culture et la communication
Cuadros recapitulativos para la cultura y la comunicación

6 Summary tables for culture and communication subjects by continents, major areas and groups of countries

Tableaux récapitulatifs pour la culture et la communication, par continents, grandes régions et groupes de pays

Cuadros recapitulativos para la cultura y la comunicación, por continentes, grandes regiones y grupos de países

This chapter provides a number of summary tables on selected subjects in the field of culture and communication. The statistics contained in these tables are shown by continents, major areas and groups of countries, the composition of which is given in page xii of this *Yearbook*. The subjects dealt with are the following: daily newspapers, cultural paper, and radio and television receivers.

It should be pointed out that due to difficulties in assessing the reliability of the statistics available and to the lack of information for many countries the world and regional figures given in this chapter represent only a rough approximation of the existing situation. Also, the presentation of regional estimation on book production and the film industry have been discontinued because of the inadequacy of the data.

Table 6.1
This table gives world and regional estimates for daily newspapers in 1980 and 1994. The statistics relate to the number of newspapers, their circulation and the circulation per 1,000 inhabitants.

Tables 6.2 and 6.3
On the basis of the statistics made available to UNESCO by the Food and Agriculture Organization of the United Nations (FAO), world and regional estimates have been calculated for the production and consumption of *cultural paper* (newsprint and other printing and writing paper) for the years 1970, 1980, 1990 and 1994.

Table 6.4
Table 6.4 gives regional figures for the total number of radio receivers and the number per 1,000 inhabitants in 1970, 1980, 1990 and 1994.

Table 6.5
Table 6.5 gives the total number of television receivers and the number per 1,000 inhabitants in 1970, 1980, 1990 and 1994.

Ce chapitre présente une série de tableaux récapitulatifs sur des sujets sélectionnés relatifs au domaine de la culture et de la communication. Les statistiques qui figurent dans ces tableaux sont présentées par continents, grandes régions et groupes de pays, dont la composition est indiquée en page xii de cet *Annuaire*. Les sujets considérés sont les suivants: journaux quotidiens, papier culturel, et récepteurs de radio et de télévision.

Il faut préciser que les difficultés qui existent pour déterminer la fiabilité des statistiques disponibles et les lacunes qui se manifestent dans les informations communiquées par plusieurs pays font que les données mondiales et régionales qui figurent dans ce chapitre ne représentent qu'une estimation approximative de la situation réelle. Aussi la présentation des estimations régionales de l'édition de livres et de la production de films a été arrêtée parce que les données étaient insuffisantes.

Tableau 6.1
Ce tableau présente des estimations mondiales et régionales sur les journaux quotidiens en 1980 et 1994. Les statistiques se réfèrent au nombre de journaux, à leur diffusion et à la diffusion pour 1 000 habitants.

Tableaux 6.2 et 6.3
Sur la base des statistiques disponibles, procurées à l'UNESCO par l'Organisation des Nations Unies pour l'Alimentation et l'Agriculture (FAO), des estimations mondiales et régionales ont été effectuées sur la production et la consommation de *papier culturel* (papier journal et papier d'impression et d'écriture) pour les années 1970, 1980 et 1994.

Tableau 6.4
Ce tableau présente, par régions, le nombre total de récepteurs de radio ainsi que leur nombre pour 1 000 habitants pour 1970, 1980, 1990 et 1994.

Tableau 6.5
Le tableau 6.9 présente le nombre total de récepteurs de télévision ainsi que leur nombre pour 1 000 habitants pour 1970, 1980, 1990 et 1994.

6 Summary tables for culture and communication
Tableaux récapitulatifs pour la culture et la communication
Cuadros recapitulativos para la cultura y la comunicación

Este capítulo presenta una serie de cuadros recapitulativos sobre temas seleccionados relativos al área de la cultura y de la comunicación. Los datos que figuran en estos cuadros se representan en estos cuadros se presentan por continentes, grandes regiones y grupos de países y su composición se indica en la página xii de este *Anuario*. Los temas considerados son los siguientes: papel cultural/ y receptores de radio y de televisión.

Es necesario precisar que, debido a las dificultades que existen para determinar la fiabilidad de las estadísticas disponibles y a la falta de la información para muchos países, las cifras correspondientes al mundo y regionales que figuran en este capítulo son sólo una aproximación de la situación real. No se presentan más las estimaciónes regionales sobre producción de libros e industria cinematográfica debido a falta de fiabilidad de los datos.

Cuadro 6.1

Este cuadro presenta estimaciones para el mundo y regionales sobre periódicos diarios en 1980 y 1994. Los datos se refieren al número de periódicos, su circulación y circulación por 1 000 habitantes.

Cuadros 6.2 y 6.3

En base a las estadísticas disponibles, proporcionadas a la UNESCO por la Organización de las Naciones Unidas para la Alimentatión y la Agricultura (FAO), se han efectuado estimaciones a nivel mundial y regional de la producción y el consumo de *papel cultural* (papel de periódico y papel de imprenta y de escribir) para los años 1970, 1980, 1990 y 1994.

Cuadro 6.4

El cuadro 6.4 presenta cifras regionales sobre el número total de receptores de radio y el número por 1 000 habitantes para 1970, 1980, 1990 y 1994.

Cuadro 6.5

El cuadro 6.9 presenta el número total de receptores de televisión y el número por 1 000 habitantes para 1970, 1980, 1990 y 1994.

Number and circulation of daily newspapers **6.1**
Nombre et tirage des journaux quotidiens
Número y tirada de los periódicos diarios

6.1 Number and circulation of daily newspapers

Nombre et tirage des journaux quotidiens

Número y tirada de los periódicos diarios

Continents, major areas and groups of countries Continents, grandes régions et groupes de pays Continentes, grandes regiones y grupos de países	Number of dailies Nombre de quotidiens Número de diarios		Estimated circulation Tirage (estimation) Tirada (estimación)			
			Total (millions) (millones)		per 1,000 inhabitants pour 1 000 habitants por 1 000 habitantes	
	1980	1994	1980	1994	1980	1994
World total	8 206	8 896	393	539	88	96
Africa	169	204	7	12	16	17
America	3 112	2 854	97	103	159	135
Asia	2 440	3 536	149	215	56	63
Europe	2 380	2 188	134	202	193	278
Oceania	105	114	6	6	257	214
Developing countries	3 712	4 808	122	194	37	44
Sub-Saharan Africa	134	157	5	6	12	10
Arab States	113	136	5	11	27	44
Latin America and the Caribbean	1 244	1 199	30	38	83	80
Eastern Asia and Oceania	344	404	60	99	42	56
Southern Asia	1 432	2 790	17	35	18	27
Least developed countries	158	179	2	4	5	7
Developed countries	4 494	4 088	271	345	242	286

6.2 Newsprint production and consumption
Production et consommation de papier journal
Producción y consumo de papel de periódico

6.2 Newsprint production and consumption

Production et consommation de papier journal

Producción y consumo de papel de periódico

MT = Millions of metric tons

MT = Millions de tonnes métriques

MT = Millones de toneladas métricas

Continents, major areas and groups of countries / Continents, grandes régions et groupes de pays / Continentes, grandes regiones y grupos de países	Newsprint / Papier journal / Papel de periódico					
	Production Production Producción (MT)	Consumption / Consommation / Consumo				
		Total (MT)	Per inhabitant (kg) Par habitant (kg) Por habitante (kg)			
	1994	1994	1970	1980	1990	1994
World total	33.8	33.4	5.8	5.8	6.2	5.9
Africa	0.4	0.5	0.8	0.7	0.8	0.8
America	16.5	14.3	21.0	21.0	20.7	18.8
Asia	5.4	7.8	1.4	1.7	2.1	2.3
Europe	10.7	9.9	10.3	10.5	13.8	13.7
Oceania	0.8	0.8	28.4	28.3	28.7	28.2
Developing countries	3.7	6.6	0.9	1.0	1.2	1.5
Sub-Saharan Africa	0.4	0.4	0.9	0.6	0.7	0.7
Arab States	-	0.2	0.5	0.9	0.8	0.9
Latin America and the Caribbean	0.8	1.7	3.6	3.5	3.4	3.6
Eastern Asia and Oceania	2.0	3.3	0.7	0.9	1.2	1.9
Southern Asia	0.4	0.6	0.3	0.4	0.5	0.5
Least developed countries	0.05	0.06	0.2	0.1	0.1	0.1
Developed countries	30.1	26.8	18.3	19.9	23.4	22.2

Production and consumption of other cultural paper **6.3**
Production et consommation des autres papiers culturels
Producción y consumo de otros papeles culturales

6.3 Production and consumption of other printing and writing paper

Production et consommation des autres papiers d'impression et d'écriture

Producción y consumo de otros papeles de imprenta y de escribir

| MT = Millions of metric tons | MT = Millions de tonnes métriques | | MT = Millones de toneladas métricas | | | |

Continents, major areas and groups of countries Continents, grandes régions et groupes de pays Continentes, grandes regiones y grupos de países	Other printing and writing paper Autres papiers d'impression et d'écriture Otros papeles de imprenta y de escribir					
	Production Production Producción (MT)	Consumption / Consommation / Consumo				
		Total (MT)	Per inhabitant (kg) Par habitant (kg) Por habitante (kg)			
	1994	1994	1970	1980	1990	1994
World total	81.3	79.3	7.1	9.2	13.2	14.1
Africa	0.6	1.1	1.0	1.2	1.5	1.5
America	30.4	30.6	22.2	28.5	36.6	40.1
Asia	22.0	23.5	1.9	2.8	5.8	6.9
Europe	28.4	23.2	15.9	21.5	31.8	31.9
Oceania	0.4	1.0	14.6	19.3	35.8	34.8
Developing countries	15.3	18.0	1.2	1.9	3.1	4.1
Sub-Saharan Africa	0.4	0.6	0.9	1.0	1.2	1.1
Arab States	0.2	0.7	1.3	2.2	2.5	2.9
Latin America and the Caribbean	3.1	3.2	3.5	5.7	5.3	6.9
Eastern Asia and Oceania	10.7	11.6	0.9	1.8	4.4	6.5
Southern Asia	1.3	1.6	0.8	0.7	1.2	1.2
Least developed countries	0.07	0.2	0.2	0.2	0.2	0.3
Developed countries	66.0	61.3	22.4	30.8	47.7	50.8

6.4 Radio receivers
Récepteurs de radio
Receptores de radio

6.4 Number of radio receivers and receivers per 1,000 inhabitants

Nombre de récepteurs de radiodiffusion sonore et de récepteurs pour 1 000 habitants

Número de receptores de radiodifusión sonora y de receptores por 1 000 habitantes

Continents, major areas and groups of countries Continents, grandes régions et groupes de pays Continentes, grandes regiones y grupos de países	Number of radio broadcasting receivers Nombre de récepteurs de radiodiffusion sonore Número de receptores de radiodifusión sonora							
	Total (millions/millones)				per 1,000 inhabitants pour 1 000 habitants por 1 000 habitantes			
	1970	1980	1990	1994	1970	1980	1990	1994
World total	771	1 307	1 877	2 008	209	294	355	357
Africa	19	49	108	122	51	104	171	173
America	350	566	711	756	687	926	991	991
Asia	78	254	568	621	37	96	178	183
Europe	314	418	464	481	481	604	643	662
Oceania	10	20	26	28	526	871	996	1007
Developing countries	123	323	724	790	46	97	177	179
Sub-Saharan Africa	10	36	77	88	35	92	151	152
Arab States	14	28	55	62	110	166	247	251
Latin America and the Caribbean	45	93	153	168	160	261	348	354
Eastern Asia and Oceania	29	117	328	349	25	82	196	197
Southern Asia	18	42	102	114	24	45	85	88
Least developed countries	7	20	48	55	23	51	95	98
Developed countries	648	984	1 153	1 218	629	881	969	1009

Television receivers 6.5
Récepteurs de télévision
Receptores de televisión

6.5 Number of television receivers and receivers per 1,000 inhabitants

Nombre de récepteurs de télévision et de récepteurs
pour 1 000 habitants

Número de receptores de televisión y de receptores
por 1 000 habitantes

Continents, major areas and groups of countries / Continents, grandes régions et groupes de pays / Continentes, grandes regiones y grupos de países	Number of television receivers / Nombre de récepteurs de télévision / Número de receptores de televisión							
	Total (millions/millones)				per 1,000 inhabitants / pour 1 000 habitants / por 1 000 habitantes			
	1970	1980	1990	1994	1970	1980	1990	1994
World total	298	561	915	1 096	81	128	176	195
Africa	1.6	8.2	23	29	4.5	17	37	40
America	108	202	292	314	212	331	406	412
Asia	41	102	317	443	19	39	101	130
Europe	144	243	274	299	219	350	380	412
Oceania	3.6	6.8	9.9	11	190	300	381	386
Developing countries	26	86	343	457	9.8	27	83	104
Sub-Saharan Africa	0.4	4.4	13	16	1.4	12	25	28
Arab States	2.7	9.3	22	26	21	55	98	104
Latin America and the Caribbean	16	35	71	81	57	99	163	171
Eastern Asia and Oceania	2.9	24	187	275	2.4	17	111	156
Southern Asia	0.7	6.1	34	46	0.9	6.4	28	35
Least developed countries	0.2	1.3	4.4	5.7	0.6	3.4	8.8	10
Developed countries	272	475	575	639	264	425	483	526

7 Printed matter

Imprimés

Impresos

This chapter is divided into four sections. The first section (Tables 7.1 and 7.2) gives statistics on libraries. The second section (Tables 7.3 to 7.8) contains statistics on book production. The third section is concerned with statistics on newspapers and periodicals (Tables 7.9 to 7.11), while the last section presents data on the production, importation, exportation and consumption of newsprint and other printing and writing paper (Table 7.12).

Section 1

This first section contains two tables. Table 1 shows national statistics on different categories of libraries, their collections, additions and registered users. The other table provides more detailed statistics on acquisitions, loans, expenditure, personnel, etc. of libraries of institutions of higher education. For the relevant information on national and public libraries the reader should refer to the 1995 edition of this *Yearbook*.

From 1950 UNESCO collected library statistics every alternate year. This periodicity was changed to three years following the Recommendation concerning the International Standardization of Library Statistics, adopted by the General Conference of UNESCO at its sixteenth session in 1970. The first three surveys conducted after the adoption of the 1970 Recommendation requested data for 1971, 1974 and 1977 respectively. In order to facilitate the collection of data and improve the response rate from Member States, it was decided as from 1980 to survey not more than two categories of library at any one time. The questionnaire on libraries was therefore divided into three parts dealing respectively with (1) national and public libraries, (2) libraries of institutions of higher education and school libraries and (3) special libraries, each part being sent out in turn. Thus, the 1985, 1988, 1991 and 1994 surveys dealt with national and public libraries while those carried out in early 1983, 1986, 1989, 1992 and 1995 concentrated on libraries of institutions of higher education and school libraries. Statistics on special libraries were obtained from the 1984 and 1987 surveys but for various reasons, these surveys had to be suspended.

The majority of the definitions that follow are taken from the above-mentioned Recommendation. There are, nevertheless, a few such as those concerning audio-visual and other library materials or registered users which are either not covered by the Recommendation or have undergone modifications in order to better respond to certain developments in librarianship.

1. *Library*: irrespective of its title, any organized collection of printed books and periodicals or any other graphic or audio-visual materials, and the services of a staff to provide and facilitate the use of such materials as are required to meet the informational, research, educational or recreational needs of its users.

Libraries thus defined are counted in numbers of administrative units and service points, as follows: (a) *administrative unit*, any independent library, or group of libraries, under a single director or a single administration; (b) *service point*, any library which provides in separate quarters a service for users, whether it is an independent library or part of a larger administrative unit.

Libraries are classified as follows:

2. *National libraries*: libraries which, irrespective of their title, are responsible for acquiring and conserving copies of all significant publications produced in the country and functioning as a *deposit* library, either by law or other arrangement, and normally compiling a national bibliography.

3. *Libraries of institutions of higher education*: libraries primarily serving students and teachers in universities and other institutions of education at the third level.

4. *Other major non-specialized libraries*: non-specialized libraries of a learned character which are neither libraries of institutions of higher education nor national libraries, though they may fulfil the functions of a national library for a specified geographical area.

5. *School libraries*: those attached to all types of schools below the third level of education and serving primarily the pupils and teachers of such schools, even though they may also be open to the general public.

6. *Special libraries*: those maintained by an association, government service, parliament, research institution (excluding university institutes), learned society, professional association, museum, business firm, industrial enterprise, chamber of commerce, etc. or other organized group, the greater part of their collections covering a specific field or subject, e.g. natural sciences, social sciences, agriculture, chemistry, medicine, economics, engineering, law, history.

7. *Public (or popular) libraries*: those which serve the population of a community or region free of charge or for a nominal fee; they may serve the general public or special categories of users such as children, members of the armed forces, hospital patients, prisoners, workers and employees.

With respect to library holdings, acquisitions, loans, expenditure, personnel, etc., the following definitions and classifications are given:

8. *Collection*: all library materials provided by the library for its users.

Statistics relating to library collections cover the following *documents available to users* including an allowance for material on loan: (a) books and bound periodicals; (b) manuscripts; (c) microforms; (d) audio-visual documents and (e) other library materials.

9. *Annual additions*: all materials added to collections during the year whether by purchase, donation, exchange or any other method. Statistics relating to additions cover the same items as those on collections.

10. *Volume*: any printed or manuscript work contained in one binding or portfolio.

11. *Audio-visual materials*: non-book, non-microform library materials which require the use of special equipment to be seen and/or heard. This includes materials such as records, tapes, cassettes, motion pictures, slides, transparencies, video recordings, etc.

12. *Other library materials*: all materials other than books, bound periodicals, manuscripts, microforms and audio-visual materials. This includes materials such as maps, charts, art prints, photographs, dioramas, etc.

13. *Registered user*: a person registered with a library in order to use materials of its collection on or off the premises.

14. *Current expenditure*: expenditure incurred in the running of the library, i.e., expenditure on staff, acquisitions, etc.

15. *Trained librarians*: all persons employed in libraries who have received a general training in librarianship or information science.

The training may be by formal methods or by means of an extended period of work under supervision in a library.

16. *Population served*: (a) by *public libraries*: the total number of inhabitants in the districts served by public libraries proper, i.e. those libraries receiving financial support, in whole or in large part, from the public authorities (municipal or regional libraries); (b) by *school libraries*: the total number of pupils and teachers in primary and secondary schools provided with school library services; (c) by *libraries of institutions of higher education*: the total number of students, faculty and staff eligible to use the services of libraries in universities and other institutions of education at the third level.

Table 7.1

Table 7.1 presents selected statistics on collections, annual additions and registered users for the different categories of libraries.

Table 7.2

Table 7.2 refers to libraries of institutions of higher education. This table includes only those countries whose statistics give more information than that shown in Table 7.1

Section 2

Up to 1985, national book *production* statistics were compiled in accordance with the definitions and classifications set forth in the Recommendation concerning the International Standardization of Statistics relating to Book Production and Periodicals adopted in 1964 by the General Conference of UNESCO. From 1986 onwards, the international collection and reporting of statistics on books (as well as on newspapers and periodicals) has been guided by a revised version of the 1964 Recommendation which was adopted by the General Conference of UNESCO at its twenty-third session in November 1985.

According to the 1985 Recommendation, book production statistics should cover printed non-periodic publications which are published in a particular country, made available to the public and which, in general, should be included in the national bibliographies of the various countries, *with the exception* of the following categories:

a) *Publications issued for advertising purposes*, provided that the literary or scientific text is subsidiary and that the publications are distributed free of charge (trade catalogues, prospectuses and other types of commercial, industrial and tourist advertising; publications drawing attention to the products or services supplied by the publisher even though they may be describing activities or technical progress in some branch of industry or commerce);

b) *Publications belonging to the following categories, when they are considered to be of a transitory character*: timetables, price-lists, telephone directories, etc.; programmes of entertainment, exhibitions, fairs, etc.; regulations and reports of business firms, company directives, circulars, etc.; calendars, etc.;

c) *Publications belonging to the following categories in which the text is not the most important part*: musical works (scores or music books), provided that the music is more important than the words; maps and charts, with the exception of atlases.

The following types of publication, *inter alia, should be included* in book production statistics:

1. *Government publications*, i.e. publications issued by public administrations or their subsidiary bodies, except for those which are confidential or designed for internal distribution only.
2. *School textbooks*, i.e. books prescribed for pupils receiving education at the first and second levels.
3. *University theses*.
4. *Offprints*, i.e. reprints of a part of a book or a periodical already published, provided that they have a title and a separate pagination and that they constitute a distinct work.
5. *Publications which form part of a series*, but which constitute separate bibliographical units.
6. *Illustrated works*: (i) collections of prints, reproductions of works of art, drawings, etc. when such collections form complete paginated volumes and when the illustrations are accompanied by an explanatory text, however short, referring to these works or to the artists themselves; (ii) albums, illustrated books and pamphlets written in the form of continuous narratives, with pictures illustrating certain episodes; (iii) albums and picture books for children; (iv) comic books.

When compiling these statistics, the following definitions should be used:

a) A publication is considered to be *non-periodic* if it is published at one time, or at intervals, by volumes, the number of which is generally determined in advance;

b) The term *printed* includes reproduction by any method of mechanical impression, whatever it may be;

c) A publication is considered to be *published in a particular country* if the publisher has his registered office in the country where the statistics are compiled, the place of printing or place of circulation being irrelevant here. When a publication is issued by one or more publishers who have registered offices in two or more countries, it is considered as having been published in the country or countries where it is issued;

d) A publication is considered as being *made available to the public* when it is obtainable either by purchase or by distribution free of charge. Publications intended for a restricted public, such as certain government publications, those of learned societies, political or professional organizations, etc., are also considered as being available to the public at large;

e) A *book* is a non-periodic printed publication of at least 49 pages, exclusive of the cover pages, published in the country and made available to the public;

f) A *pamphlet* is a non-periodic printed publication of at least 5 but not more than 48 pages, exclusive of the cover pages, published in a particular country and made available to the public;

g) A *first edition* is the first publication of an original or translated manuscript;

h) A *re-edition* is a publication distinguished from previous editions by changes made in the contents (revised edition) or layout (new edition) and which requires a new ISBN;

i) A *reprint* is unchanged in contents and layout, apart from correction of typographical errors in previous editions and does not require a new ISBN. A reprint by any publisher other than the original publisher is regarded as a re-edition;

j) A *translation* is a publication which reproduces a work in a language other than the original language;

k) A *title* is a term used to designate a printed publication which forms a separate whole, whether issued in one or several volumes.

This section comprises seven tables which cover production as a whole.

Tables 7.3 to 7.8 present data collected each year by means of questionnaires sent to approximately 200 countries and territories. Unless otherwise indicated these data cover books and pamphlets of original works or translations. However, certain categories of publications which, according to the Recommendation, *should be included* in book production statistics (e.g. government publications, school textbooks, university theses, offprints, illustrated works) or *excluded* from such statistics (e.g. publications issued for advertising purposes, publications of a transitory nature, publications in which the text is not the most important part) are classified differently, for statistical purposes, in different countries. In the absence of complete and precise information, it has not been possible to indicate certain differences of this kind between the various national statistics and the Recommendation.

Only those countries able to present statistics in accordance with the classification by subject set forth in the 1985 Recommendation are included in Tables 7.5 and 7.8. The classification given below, which is based upon the Universal Decimal Classification (UDC) is taken from this Recommendation (the corresponding UDC headings are shown in parentheses):

1. Generalities (0)
2. Philosophy, Psychology (1)
3. Religion, Theology (2)
4. Sociology, Statistics (30-31)
5. Politics, Economics (32-33)
6. Law, Public Administration, Social Relief and Welfare, Insurance (34,351-354,36)
7. Military Art and Science (335-359)
8. Education, Teaching, Training, Leisure (37)
9. Trade, Communication, Transport, Tourism (38)
10. Ethnography, Cultural Anthropology (customs, folklore, mores, tradition) (39)
11. Philology, Languages, Linguistics (4)
12. Mathematics (51)
13. Natural Science (52-59)
14. Medical Sciences, Public Health (61)
15. Engineering, Technology, Industries, Trades and Crafts (62, 66-69)
16. Agriculture, Forestry, Stockbreeding, Hunting and Fisheries (63)
17. Domestic Science (64)
18. Management, Administration and Organization (65)
19. Physical Planning, Town and Country Planning, Architecture (70-72)
20. Plastic and Graphic Arts, Photography (73-77)
21. Music, Performing Arts, Theatre, Film and Cinema (78, 791-792)
22. Games and Sport (793-799)
23. Literature (8)
(a) History of Literature and Literary Criticism
(b) Literary Texts
24. Geography (91)
25. History, Biography (92-99)

Whenever a total does not correspond to the sum of its component items, the difference either represents the number of works not distributed among the ten main branches of the Universal Decimal Classification or the twenty-five subject groups or is explained by the rounding-off of figures. Tables 7.3 and 7.6 show for each country a total figure and the number of books only, the difference being the number of pamphlets.

Table 7.3
This table presents data for the years 1991 to 1994 on the number of titles of *first editions* and *re-editions* of original works (or translations) by the ten main UDC classes. It contains only those countries for which UNESCO can produce statistics relating to at least one of the three years under review.

Table 7.4
The figures given in Table 7.4 refer to the number of titles of both *first editions* and *re-editions* by subject groups. For countries where the total number of editions is identical to that of first editions, it should be presumed that either there were no re-editions or that their number is unknown. Similarly, where the total number of titles and the total number of books do not differ, it may be assumed that either no pamphlets were published or that their number is unknown.

Table 7.5
This table presents data for the years 1991 to 1994 on the number of copies of *first editions, re-editions* and *reprints* of original works (or translations) by UDC classes.

Table 7.6
The figures given in Table 7.6 refer to the number of copies of *first editions, re-editions* and *reprints* by subject groups. The comments on Table 7.4 concerning total editions and first editions also apply to this table.

Table 7.7
The figures in this table refer to both *first editions* and *re-editions* of school textbooks which are defined in the Recommendation as books prescribed for pupils receiving education at the first and second levels.

Table 7.8
The figures in Table 7.8 refer to both *first editions* and *re-editions* of children's books.

Section 3
The statistics in Tables 7.9 to 7.11 cover daily newspapers, non-dailies and periodicals.

In general, national statistics on newspapers and periodicals should be drawn up in accordance with the definitions and classifications set out in the 1985 Revised Recommendation concerning the International Standardization of Statistics on the Production and Distribution of Books, Newspapers and Periodicals. Data given in Tables 7.9 and 7.10 are published regularly in this *Yearbook*, while those on periodicals by type are presented every other year. According to the 1985 Recommendation, national statistics on the press should cover printed periodic publications which are published in a particular country and made available to the public, with the exception of publications issued for advertising purposes, those of a transitory character, and those in which the text is not the most important part. However, the following types of publications, *inter alia, should be included* in statistics on newspapers and periodicals: government periodicals, academic and scientific journals, periodicals of professional, trade union, political or sports organizations, etc., publications appearing annually or less frequently, parish magazines, school magazines and school newspapers, *house organs*, and entertainment, radio and television programmes, if the literary text in them is substantial.

When compiling these statistics, the following definitions should be used:
1. A publication is considered to be *periodic* if it constitutes one issue in a continuous series under the same title, published at regular or irregular intervals over an indefinite period, individual issues in the series being numbered consecutively or each issue being dated.
2. Periodic publications are subdivided into two categories: newspapers and periodicals.
a) *Newspapers* are periodic publications intended for the general public and mainly designed to be a primary source of written information on current events connected with public affairs, international questions, politics, etc. A newspaper thus defined, issued at least four times a week, is considered to be a daily newspaper; those appearing three times a week or less frequently are considered as non-daily newspapers;
b) *Periodicals* are those periodic publications which either are concerned with subjects of very general interest or else mainly carry studies and factual information on specialized subjects such as legislation, finance, trade, medicine, fashion, sports, etc. This definition covers specialized journals, reviews, magazines and other periodicals with the exception of publications listed under a) to c) in the second paragraph of Section 2 of this chapter.
3. *Circulation* figures show the average daily circulation, or the average circulation per issue in the case of non-daily publications. These figures should include the number of copies (a) sold directly, (b) sold by subscription and (c) mainly distributed free of charge both inside the country and abroad.
When interpreting data in the following tables, it should be borne in mind that in some cases, methods of enumeration, definitions and classifications applied by certain countries do not entirely conform to the standards recommended by UNESCO. For example, circulation data should refer to the number of copies distributed as defined above. It appears, however, that some countries have reported the number of copies printed, which is usually higher than the distribution figure.

Table 7.9
This table presents data on the number, total circulation and circulation per 1,000 inhabitants of daily newspapers for the years, 1980, 1985, 1990 and 1994.

Table 7.10
This table gives data for the latest year available in the period 1989-1994 on the number, total circulation and circulation per 1,000 inhabitants of non-daily newspapers and periodicals.

Table 7.11
This table gives data on periodicals by type for the latest year available in the period 1989-1994. The reader's attention is drawn to the fact that the addition of the two subtotals shown in this table should be identical to the total shown for periodicals in Table 7.10. However this is not always the case, probably because data originate form different sources or because it is not yet possible for certain countries to apply the international standards. It has nevertheless been considered preferable to publish data for as many countries as possible rather than restrict the number to those fpr which statistics are complete and consistent. For this reason the information provided in this table should be interpreted and used with caution, not forgetting that in many cases the figures represent at the most a very rough aprroximation of the existing situation.

Section 4
The data given in Table 7.12 relate to the production, importation, exportation and consumption of *cultural paper*, i.e. newsprint as well as printing paper (other than newsprint) and writing paper for the years 1970, 1975, 1980, 1985, 1990 and 1994. As in preceding years, these data have been supplied by the *Food and Agriculture Organization of the United Nations* (FAO). Readers needing additional information should refer to the *Yearbook of Forest Products* published by the FAO.

The term *newsprint* (item 641.1 of the Standard International Trade Classification, Revision 2) designates the bleached, unsized or slack-sized printing paper, without coating, of the type usually used for newspapers. Newsprint weighs from 45 to 60 grammes per square metre, at least 70 per cent of the weight of fibrous material usually being derived from mechanical pulp.

The expression *other printing and writing paper* (item 641.2 of the Standard International Trade Classification, Revision 2) covers paper other than newsprint in rolls or sheets, suitable for use in printing and writing. It does not cover articles manufactured from printing and writing paper, such as stationery, exercise books, registers, etc.

For countries where no separate information for the two above-mentioned categories of paper is available, the totals are shown under the category *newsprint*.

Ce chapitre est divisé en quatre sections. La première section (tableaux 7.1 et 7.2) présente les statistiques relatives aux bibliothèques. La section 2 (tableaux 7.3 à 7.8) se réfère aux statistiques sur l'édition de livres. La section 3 concerne les statistiques relatives aux journaux et périodiques (tableaux 7.9 à 7.11); la dernière section, présente des données sur la production, l'importation, l'exportation et la consommation de papier journal et autre papier d'impression et d'écriture (tableau 7.12).

Section 1
Cette première section comprend deux tableaux. Le tableau 1 présente les statistiques nationales sur les différents types de bibliothèques, leurs collections, leurs acquisitions et les usagers inscrits. L'autre tableau contient des statistiques plus détaillées sur les acquisitions, les prêts, les dépenses, le personnel, etc. des bibliothèques d'établissements d'enseignement supérieur. Pour les données relatives aux bibliothèques nationales et bibliothèques publiques, le lecteur doit se référer à l'édition 1995 de l'*Annuaire Statistique*.

Depuis 1950, l'UNESCO rassemblait des statistiques sur les bibliothèques tous les deux ans. Conformément à la Recommandation concernant la normalisation internationale des statistiques relatives aux bibliothèques, adoptée par la Conférence générale de l'UNESCO à sa seizième session, en 1970, la périodicité a été portée à trois ans. Dans les trois premières enquêtes qui ont été effectuées après l'adoption de la Recommandation de 1970, les données demandées concernaient respectivement les années 1971, 1974 et 1977. Il a été décidé en 1980 de n'enquêter que sur deux catégories de bibliothèques à la fois, afin de faciliter la collecte des données et d'améliorer le taux de réponse des Etats membres. Le questionnaire sur les bibliothèques a été par conséquent divisé en trois parties séparées, comme suit: (1) bibliothèques nationales et publiques, (2) bibliothèques d'établissements d'enseignement supérieur et bibliothèques scolaires et (3) bibliothèques spécialisées, chacune d'entre elles étant envoyée à tour de rôle. Les enquêtes de 1985, 1988, 1991 et 1994 concernaient les bibliothèques nationales et publiques, tandis que celles réalisées au début de

1983, 1986, 1989, 1992 et 1995 ont été axées sur les bibliothèques d'établissements d'enseignement supérieur et les bibliothèques scolaires. Les statistiques relatives aux bibliothèques spécialisées ont été recueillies dans les enquêtes de 1984 et 1987, mais pour diverses raisons, ces enquêtes ont été différées.

Les définitions suivantes sont en grande majorité tirées de la Recommandation sus-mentionnée. Néanmoins, il y en a quelques unes comme celles concernant les matériels audiovisuels et les autres matériels de bibliothèque ou les usagers inscrits qui, soit ne sont pas couvertes par la Recommandation ou, soit ont subi des modifications dans le but d'améliorer certains développements dans le domaine bibliothécaire.

1. *Bibliothèque*: est considérée comme bibliothèque, quelle que soit sa dénomination, toute collection organisée de livres et de périodiques imprimés ou de tous autres documents, notamment graphiques et audiovisuels, ainsi que les services du personnel chargé de faciliter l'utilisation de ces documents par les usagers à des fins d'information, de recherche, d'éducation ou de récréation.

Les bibliothèques ainsi définies sont comptées en nombre d'unités administratives et de points de desserte. Est considérée comme: (a) *unité administrative*, toute bibliothèque indépendante ou tout groupe de bibliothèques ayant un directeur ou une administration unique; (b) *point de desserte*, toute bibliothèque desservant les usagers dans un local séparé, qu'elle soit indépendante ou fasse partie d'un groupe de bibliothèques constituant une unité administrative.

Les bibliothèques sont classées comme suit:

2. *Bibliothèques nationales*: bibliothèques, quelle que soit leur appellation, qui sont responsables de l'acquisition et de la conservation d'exemplaires de toutes les publications éditées dans le pays et fonctionnant comme bibliothèques de *dépôt*, soit en vertu d'une loi, soit en vertu d'un accord particulier et qui, normalement établissent une bibliographie nationale.

3. *Bibliothèques d'établissements d'enseignement supérieur*: bibliothèques qui sont, en premier lieu, au service des étudiants et du personnel enseignant des universités et autres établissements d'enseignement du troisième degré.

4. *Autres bibliothèques importantes non spécialisées*: bibliothèques non spécialisées, de caractère savant, qui ne sont ni des bibliothèques d'établissements d'enseignement supérieur ni des bibliothèques nationales, même si certaines remplissent les fonctions d'une bibliothèque nationale pour une aire géographique déterminée.

5. *Bibliothèques scolaires*: bibliothèques qui dépendent d'établissements d'enseignement de n'importe quel type au-dessous du niveau de l'enseignement du troisième degré et qui doivent avant tout être au service des élèves et des professeurs de ces établissements même si elles sont, par ailleurs, ouvertes au public.

6. *Bibliothèques spécialisées*: bibliothèques qui relèvent d'une association, d'un service gouvernemental, d'un parlement, d'une institution de recherche (à l'exclusion des instituts d'université), d'une société savante, d'une association professionnelle, d'un musée, d'une entreprise commerciale ou industrielle, d'une chambre de commerce, etc., ou d'un autre organisme, la plus grande partie de leurs collections couvrant une discipline ou un domaine particulier, par exemple: sciences naturelles, sciences sociales, agriculture, chimie, médecine, sciences économiques, sciences de l'ingénieur, droit, histoire.

7. *Bibliothèques publiques (ou populaires)*: bibliothèques servant, gratuitement ou contre une cotisation de principe, une collectivité et, notamment, une collectivité locale ou régionale, et s'adressant soit à l'ensemble du public, soit à certaines catégories d'usagers, telles que les enfants, les membres des forces armées, les malades des hôpitaux, les prisonniers, les ouvriers et les employés.

En ce qui concerne les collections, acquisitions, prêts, dépenses, personnel etc., les définitions et classifications sont les suivantes:

8. *Collection d'une bibliothèque*: l'ensemble des documents mis à la disposition des usagers.

Les statistiques concernant les collections des bibliothèques doivent porter sur les documents suivants mis à la disposition des usagers, y compris les documents prêtés au-dehors: (a) livres et périodiques reliés; (b) manuscrits; (c) microcopies; (d) matériels audiovisuels et (e) autres matériels de bibliothèque.

9. *Acquisitions annuelles*: ensemble des documents qui sont venus enrichir les collections au cours de l'année, par voie d'achat, de don, d'échange ou de toute autre manière.

Les statistiques sur les acquisitions couvrent les mêmes documents que ceux indiqués dans la rubrique collection.

10. *Volume*: documents imprimés ou manuscrits contenus dans une reliure ou un carton.

11. *Matériels audiovisuels*: matériels de bibliothèque autres que les livres et les microcopies qui ont besoin d'un équipement spécial pour être vus et/ou entendus. Ceci comprend des matériels tels que disques, bandes, cassettes, films, diapositives, transparences, enregistrements vidéo, etc.

12. *Autres matériels de bibliothèque*: tous les matériels de bibliothèque autres que les livres, périodiques reliés, manuscrits, microcopies et matériels audiovisuels. Ceci comprend des matériels tels que cartes, graphiques, reproductions artistiques, photographies, dioramas, etc.

13. *Usager inscrit*: toute personne inscrite à une bibliothèque pour utiliser les matériels de la collection à l'intérieur ou à l'extérieur des locaux.

14. *Dépenses ordinaires*: toutes dépenses qui résultent du fonctionnement de la bibliothèque, c'est-à-dire dépenses relatives au personnel, aux acquisitions, etc.

15. *Bibliothécaire professionnel*: toute personne employée dans une bibliothèque ayant reçu une formation générale en bibliothéconomie ou en science de l'information. Cette formation peut consister en un enseignement théorique ou en un stage prolongé sous contrôle dans une bibliothèque.

16. *Population desservie*: (a) *par les bibliothèques publiques*: nombre total d'habitants des localités desservies par les bibliothèques publiques proprement dites, c'est-à-dire les bibliothèques financées en totalité ou en majeure partie par les pouvoirs publics (bibliothèques municipales ou régionales); (b) *par les bibliothèques scolaires*: nombre total d'élèves et de professeurs des écoles du premier et du second degré (écoles primaires et secondaires) desservis par les bibliothèques scolaires; (c) *par les bibliothèques des établissements d'enseignement supérieur*: nombre total d'étudiants et du personnel autorisés à utiliser les services des bibliothèques universitaires et des bibliothèques d'autres établissements d'enseignement supérieur.

Tableau 7.1

Le tableau 7.1 présente des statistiques sélectionnées sur les collections, les acquisitions annuelles et les usagers inscrits pour les différentes catégories de bibliothèques.

Tableau 7.2

Le tableau 7.2 se réfère aux bibliothèques des établissements d'enseignement supérieur. Ce tableau comprend les pays dont les informations statistiques sont plus détaillées que ceux qui figurent dans le tableau 7.1.

Section 2

Jusqu'en 1985 les statistiques nationales de l'édition de livres ont été établies conformément aux définitions et aux classifications figurant dans la Recommandation concernant la normalisation internationale des statistiques de l'édition de livres et de périodiques adoptée en 1964 par la Conférence Générale de l'UNESCO. A partir de 1986, la collecte internationale de la présentation de statistiques des livres (et également des journaux et périodiques) a été guidée par une version révisée de la Recommandation de 1964 qui a été adoptée par la Conférence générale de l'UNESCO à sa vingt-troisième session en novembre 1985.

Selon les termes de la Recommandation de 1985, les statistiques de l'*édition* de livres devraient porter sur les publications non périodiques imprimées qui sont éditées dans le pays, offertes au public et devraient, en général, figurer dans les bibliographies nationales des différents pays, à l'*exception* des catégories suivantes:

a) *Publications éditées à des fins publicitaires*, à condition que le texte littéraire ou scientifique ne prédomine pas et que ces publications soient distribuées gratuitement (catalogues, prospectus et autres publications de propagande commerciale, industrielle et touristique; publications attirant l'attention sur les produits ou les services fournis par l'éditeur, même si elles traitent de l'activité ou de l'évolution technique d'une branche de l'industrie ou du commerce);

b) *Publications appartenant aux catégories suivantes, lorsqu'elles sont considérées comme ayant un caractère éphémère*: horaires, tarifs, annuaires téléphoniques, etc.; programmes de spectacles, d'expositions, de foires, etc.; statuts et bilans des sociétés, directives des entreprises, circulaires, etc.; calendriers, etc.;

c) *Publications appartenant aux catégories suivantes, dont le contenu prédominant n'est pas le texte*: les oeuvres musicales (partitions, cahiers de musique), à condition que la notation musicale soit plus importante que le texte; la production cartographique, excepté les atlas.

Les catégories suivantes de publications, notamment, *devraient être comptées* dans les statistiques de l'édition de livres:

1. *Publications officielles*, c'est-à-dire imprimés publiés par les administrations publiques ou les organismes qui en dépendent, à l'exception de ceux qui sont confidentiels ou réservés à la distribution intérieure;

2. *Livres de classe* (manuels scolaires), c'est-à-dire ouvrages prescrits aux élèves de l'enseignement du premier degré et du second degré;

3. *Thèses universitaires*;

4. *Tirages à part*, c'est-à-dire réimpressions d'une partie d'un livre ou d'une publication périodique déjà parus, à condition qu'ils aient un titre et une pagination distincts et qu'ils constituent un ouvrage distinct;

5. *Publications faisant partie d'une série*, mais dont chacune constitue une unité bibliographique;

6. *Ouvrages illustrés*: (i) recueils de gravures, de reproductions d'oeuvres d'art, de dessins, etc., pour autant que ces collections constituent des ouvrages complets et paginés et que les illustrations soient accompagnées d'un texte explicatif, même sommaire, se rapportant à ces oeuvres ou à leurs auteurs; (ii)

albums, livres et brochures illustrés, rédigés sous la forme d'une narration continue et ornés d'images illustrant certains épisodes; (iii) albums et livres d'images pour les enfants; (iv) albums de bandes dessinées.

Pour l'établissement de ces statistiques, les définitions ci-après devraient être utilisées:

a) Une publication est considérée comme *non périodique* si elle est publiée en une seule fois, ou à intervalles, par volumes dont le nombre est généralement déterminé d'avance;

b) Le terme *imprimé* recouvre tous les divers procédés d'impression, quels qu'ils soient;

c) Est considérée comme *éditée dans le pays* toute publication dont l'éditeur a son siège social dans le pays établissant les statistiques, sans qu'il soit tenu compte ni du lieu d'impression ni du lieu de distribution. Lorsqu'une publication est faite par un ou des éditeurs ayant leur siège social dans deux ou plusieurs pays, elle est considérée comme étant éditée dans celui ou ceux de ces pays où elle est distribuée;

d) Une publication est considérée comme *offerte au public* lorsqu'il peut se la procurer soit en la payant, soit gratuitement. Sont également considérées comme offertes au grand public les publications destinées à un public restreint, telles que certaines publications officielles, les publications de sociétés savantes, d'organisations politiques ou professionnelles, etc.;

e) Un *livre* est une publication non périodique imprimée comptant au moins 49 pages (pages de couverture non comprises), éditée dans le pays et offerte au public;

f) Une *brochure* est une publication non périodique imprimée comptant au moins 5, mais pas plus de 48 pages (pages de couverture non comprises), éditée dans le pays et offerte au public;

g) Une *première édition* est la première publication d'un manuscrit original ou traduit;

h) Une *réédition* est une édition qui se distingue des éditions antérieures par des modifications apportées au contenu (édition révisée) ou à la présentation (édition nouvelle) et qui nécessite l'attribution d'un nouveau numéro ISBN;

i) Une *réimpression* ne comporte pas, par rapport à l'édition antérieure, de modifications de contenu ou de présentation autres que des corrections typographiques et ne nécessite pas l'attribution d'un nouveau numéro ISBN. Une réimpression faite par un éditeur autre que l'éditeur précédent est considérée comme une réédition;

j) Une *traduction* est une publication qui reproduit un ouvrage dans une langue autre que la langue originale;

k) Un *titre* est un terme utilisé pour désigner une publication imprimée constituant un tout distinct, qu'elle soit en un ou en plusieurs volumes.

La présente section comprend sept tableaux, qui se rapportent à la totalité de l'édition.

Les données présentées dans les tableaux 7.3 à 7.8 sont rassemblées chaque année au moyen de questionnaires adressés approximativement à 200 pays et territoires. Sauf indication contraire, elles englobent les livres et les brochures d'ouvrages originaux ou de traductions. Toutefois, certaines catégories de publications qui, selon la Recommandation, *devraient être* soit comprises dans les statistiques de l'édition de livres - par exemple les publications officielles, les livres de classe (manuels scolaires), les thèses universitaires, les tirages à part, les ouvrages illustrés - soit *exclues* de ces statistiques (telles les publications éditées à des fins publicitaires, les publications de caractère éphémère et celles dont le contenu prédominant n'est pas le texte) sont traitées différemment, suivant les pays, lorsqu'il s'agit d'établir les statistiques. Faute de renseignements complets et précis, il n'a pas été possible d'indiquer dans quelle mesure les différentes statistiques nationales s'écartent, à cet égard, des normes formulées dans la Recommandation.

Seuls les pays qui ont été en mesure de présenter des statistiques établies selon la classification par catégories de sujets préconisée dans la Recommandation de 1985 figurent dans les tableaux 7.5 et 7.8. La classification ci-après, fondée sur la Classification Décimale Universelle (CDU) est extraite de cette Recommandation (entre parenthèses : indices correspondants de la CDU):

1. Généralités (0)
2. Philosophie, psychologie (1)
3. Religion, théologie (2)
4. Sociologie, statistique (30-31)
5. Sciences politiques, sciences économiques (32-33)
6. Droit, administration publique, prévoyance et aide sociale, assurances (34, 351-354, 36)
7. Art et science militaire (355-359)
8. Education, enseignement, formation, loisirs (37)
9. Commerce, communication, transports, tourisme (38)
10. Ethnographie, anthropologie culturelle (coutumes, folklore, moeurs, tradition) (39)
11. Philologie, langues, linguistique (4)
12. Mathématiques (51)
13. Sciences naturelles (52-59)
14. Sciences médicales, santé publique (61)

15. Art de l'ingénieur, technologie, industries, métiers (62, 66-69)
16. Agriculture, sylviculture, élevage, chasse et pêche (63)
17. Science ménagère (64)
18. Gestion, administration et organisation (65)
19. Aménagement du territoire, urbanisme, architecture (70-72)
20. Arts graphiques et plastiques, photographie (73-77)
21. Musique, arts du spectacle, théâtre, film et cinéma (78, 791-792)
22. Jeux et sports (793-799)
23. Littérature (8)
(a) Histoire et critique littéraires
(b) Textes littéraires
24. Géographie (91)
25. Histoire, biographie (92-99)

Quand un total ne correspond pas à la somme des éléments qui la composent, la différence qui en résulte, soit représente le nombre d'ouvrages non répartis entre les dix catégories de la Classification Décimale Universelle ou entre les 25 groupes de sujets, soit s'explique par le fait que les chiffres sont arrondis. Les tableaux 7.3 et 7.6 indiquent, pour chaque pays, un chiffre total et le nombre de livres, la différence entre ces deux chiffres représentant le nombre de brochures.

Tableau 7.3
Ce tableau présente les données pour les années 1991 à 1994 et ne se réfère qu'aux pays pour lesquels l'UNESCO dispose de statistiques concernant au moins l'une des trois années considérées. Sauf indication contraire, les données de ce tableau comprennent le nombre de titres des *premières éditions* et des *rééditions* d'ouvrages originaux ou de traductions selon les dix catégories principales de la CDU.

Tableau 7.4
Les chiffres du tableau 7.4 se rapportent au nombre de titres des *premières éditions* et des *rééditions* par groupes de sujets. Pour les pays où le nombre total des éditions et le nombre des premières éditions sont identiques, on doit considérer qu'il n'y a pas de rééditions ou que leur nombre est inconnu. De même lorsque le nombre de titres est égal au nombre de livres, on peut supposer qu'aucune brochure n'a été publiée ou que leur nombre est inconnu.

Tableau 7.5
Ce tableau présente pour les années 1991 à 1994 les données sur le nombre d'exemplaires des *premières éditions*, *rééditions* et *réimpressions* d'ouvrages originaux (ou de traductions) classés d'après la C.D.U.

Tableau 7.6
Les chiffres du tableau 7.6 se rapportent au nombre d'exemplaires des *premières éditions*, des *rééditions* et aux *réimpressions* par groupes de sujets. Les observations du tableau 7.4 concernant le total d'éditions et les premières éditions s'appliquent également à ce tableau.

Tableau 7.7
Les chiffres de ce tableau se réfèrent aux *premières éditions* et aux *rééditions* de manuels scolaires qui, dans la Recommandation, sont définis comme ouvrages prescrits aux élèves de l'enseignement du premier degré et du second degré.

Tableau 7.8
Les données du tableau 7.8 se réfèrent aux *premières éditions* et aux *rééditions* de livres pour enfants.

Section 3
Les tableaux 7.9 à 7.11 contiennent des données relatives aux journaux quotidiens, non quotidiens, ainsi qu'aux périodiques.

D'une manière générale, les statistiques nationales des journaux et des autres périodiques devraient être établies conformément aux définitions et aux classifications figurant dans la Recommandation révisée de 1985 concernant la normalisation internationale des statistiques relatives à la production et à la distribution de livres, de journaux et de périodiques. Les données présentées dans les tableaux 7.9 et 7.10 sont publiées régulièrement dans cet annuaire tandis que celles relatives aux périodiques classés par type, sont présentées une fois tous les deux ans. Selon les termes de la Recommandation de 1985, les statistiques nationales sur la presse devraient porter sur les publications périodiques imprimées qui sont édités dans le pays et offertes au public, à l'exception des publications éditées à des fins publicitaires, celles à caractère éphémère et celles dont le contenu prédominant n'est pas le texte. Cependant les catégories de publications ci-après, notamment, *devraient être comptées* dans les statistiques des journaux et périodiques: périodiques officiels, périodiques académiques et scientifiques, périodiques des organisations professionnelles, syndicales, politiques, sportives, etc., publications annuelles ou à périodicité plus espacée, bulletins paroissiaux, bulletins des écoles, journaux d'entreprise, et programmes de spectacles, de radio et de télévision, à condition que le texte littéraire en soit d'une certaine importance.

Pour l'établissement de ces statistiques, les définitions ci-après devraient être utilisées:

1. Une publication est considérée comme *périodique* si elle est publiée en série continue sous un même titre, à intervalles

réguliers ou irréguliers pendant une période indéterminée, les différents numéros de la série étant numérotés consécutivement ou chaque numéro étant daté.

2. Les publications périodiques sont subdivisées en deux catégories: journaux et périodiques.

a) Les *journaux* sont des publications périodiques destinées au grand public, qui ont essentiellement pour objet de constituer une source originale d'information écrite sur les événements d'actualité intéressant les affaires publiques, les questions internationales, la politique, etc. Un journal répondant à cette définition qui paraît au moins quatre fois par semaine est considéré comme un quotidien, un journal paraissant trois fois par semaine ou moins fréquemment est classé dans la catégorie des journaux non quotidiens;

b) Les *périodiques* sont des publications périodiques qui traitent des sujets d'intérêt très général ou qui sont spécialement consacrés à des études et informations documentaires sur des questions particulières: législation, finances, commerce, médecine, mode, sports, etc. Cette définition englobe des journaux spécialisés, les revues, les magazines et les autres périodiques à l'exception des publications inscrites de a) à c) dans le deuxième paragraphe de la section 2 de ce chapitre.

3. Les chiffres concernant la *diffusion* représentent la diffusion quotidienne moyenne, ou la diffusion moyenne par numéro dans le cas des publications non quotidiennes. Ces chiffres devraient comprendre le nombre d'exemplaires (a) vendus directement, (b) vendus par abonnement, (c) distribués en général gratuitement dans le pays et à l'étranger.

En interprétant les données des tableaux ci-après, il ne faut pas perdre de vue que dans certains cas les méthodes de recensement, les définitions et les classifications utilisées par certains pays ne s'ajustent pas entièrement aux normes préconisées par l'UNESCO. Ainsi, par exemple, les tirages mentionnés devraient se référer au nombre d'exemplaires distribués ainsi qu'il est défini ci-dessus. Cependant, il apparaît que quelques pays ont reporté le nombre d'exemplaires imprimés qui est généralement plus important que les chiffres concernant la distribution.

Tableau 7.9
On trouvera dans le tableau 7.9 des données sur le nombre, la diffusion totale et la diffusion pour 1 000 habitants des journaux quotidiens en 1980, 1985, 1990 et 1992.

Tableau 7.10
Ce tableau indique, pour la dernière année disponible de 1989 à 1994, le nombre, la diffusion totale et la diffusion pour 1 000 habitants des journaux non quotidiens et des périodiques.

Tableau 7.11
Ce tableau présente, pour la dernière année disponible de 1989 à 1994 des données relatives aux périodiques classés par type. Il faut souligner à l'attention des lecteurs que la somme des deux totaux partiels qui figurent dans ce tableau devrait correspondre au total indiqué sous la rubrique périodiques du tableau 7.10. Cependant, on constatera que ce n'est pas toujours le cas, probablement parce que les données proviennent de sources différentes ou qu'il n'a pas encore été possible à certains pays d'appliquer les normes internationales. Néanmoins, il a été jugé préférable d'inclure dans ce tableau le plus grand nombre de pays possible, plutôt que de limiter leur nombre aux seuls pays pour lesquels nous possédons des statistiques complètes et conséquentes. Pour cette raison, il est évident que les données publiées doivent être utilisées et interprétées avec circonspection, sans oublier que les chiffres ne représentent souvent tout au plus qu'une approximation très grossière de la situation réelle.

Section 4
Les données qui figurent dans le tableau 7.12 se rapportent à la production, à l'importation, à l'exportation et à la consommation de *papier culturel*, c'est-à-dire, de papier journal, de papier d'impression (autre que le papier journal) et de papier d'écriture pour les années 1970, 1975, 1980, 1985, 1990 et 1994. Comme pour les années précédentes, ces données nous ont été fournies par l'*Organisation des Nations Unies pour l'Alimentation et l'Agriculture* (FAO). Les lecteurs qui souhaiteraient obtenir des renseignements complémentaires doivent se référer à l'*Annuaire des Produits Forestiers* publié par la FAO.

Le terme *papier journal* (sous-groupe 641.1 de la Classification Type pour le Commerce International, Révision 2) désigne le papier d'impression blanchi, non collé ou peu encollé, non couché, du type utilisé d'ordinaire pour les journaux. Le papier journal a un poids de 45 à 60 grammes au mètre carré et contient en général au moins 70 pour cent en poids de matière fibreuse tirée de la pâte mécanique.

L'expression *autres papiers d'impression et papier d'écriture* (sous-groupe 641.2 de la Classification Type pour le Commerce International, Révision 2) désigne les différents types de papiers (en feuilles ou en rouleaux) autres que le papier journal qui sont destinés à l'impression ainsi qu'à l'écriture. N'entrent pas dans cette catégorie les produits manufacturés tels que fournitures de bureau, cahiers, registres, etc.

Pour les pays sur lesquels on ne dispose pas de données séparées pour les deux catégories de papier définies ci-dessus, les chiffres globaux sont présentés sous la rubrique *papier journal*.

Este capítulo se divide en cuatro secciones. La primera sección (cuadros 7.1 y 7.2) se refiere a las estadísticas sobre bibliotecas. La segunda sección (cuadros 7.3 a 7.8) contiene datos sobre la edición de libros. La sección 3 concierne las estadísticas relativas a los periódicos diarios y otras publicaciones periódicas (cuadros 7.9 a 7.11) ; la última sección presenta datos sobre la producción, la importación, la exportación y el consumo de papel de periódico y otro papel de imprenta y de escribir (cuadro 7.12).

Sección 1
Esta primera sección contiene dos cuadros. El primer cuadro presenta datos nacionales relativos a las diferentes categorías de bibliotecas, sus fondos, adquisiciones y usuarios inscritos. El otro presenta datos más detallados sobre las adquisiciones, préstamos, gastos, personal, etc. de bibliotecas de enseñanza superior. Para más información sobre las bibliotecas nacionales y públicas, el lector deberá referirse a la edición 1995 del *Anuario estadístico*.

Desde 1950, la UNESCO reúne cada dos años datos estadísticos sobre bibliotecas. De acuerdo con la Recomendación sobre la normalización internacional de las estadísticas relativas a las bibliotecas, aprobada por la Conferencia General de la UNESCO en su décimosexta reunión en 1970, la recolección de datos fue ficida a tres años. En las tres primeras encuestas efectuadas a raíz de la adopción de la Recommendación de 1970, se solicitaron datos para 1971, 1974 y 1977, respectivamente. Se decidió que a partir de 1980, sólo se efecturian encuestas sobre dos categorias de bibliotecas a la vez. Para facilitar la recolección de datos y de mejorar la tasa de respuestas de los Estados Miembros. Por consiguiente, se dividió el cuestionario sobre las bibliotecas en tres partes separadas, a saber: (1) bibliotecas nacionales y públicas, (2) bibliotecas de instituciones de enseñanza superior y bibliotecas escolares y (3) bibliotecas especializadas, enviándose cada uno de ellos a la vez. Las encuestas de 1985, 1988, 1991 y 1994 se referían a las bibliotecas nacionales y públicas; las encuestas llevadas a cabo en los primeros meses de 1983, 1986, 1989, 1992 y 1995 estaban orientadas a las bibliotecas de instituciones de enseñanza superior y a las bibliotecas escolares. Las estadísticas sobre las bibliotecas especializadas fueron obtenidas a partir de las encuestas de 1984 y 1987. No obstante esto, se debid suspender por razones diversas las encuestas sobre las bibliotecas especializadas.

Las definiciones a continuación fueron extraídas en su gran mayoría de la Recomendación arriba mencionada. Sin embargo, hay algunas como aquéllas que conciernen los materiales audiovisuales y otros materiales de bibliotecas o los usuarios inscritos que no figuran en la Recomendación o que han sido modificadas a fin de adaptarse desarrollo de la biblioteconomía.

1. *Biblioteca*: Se entenderá por biblioteca, sea cual fuere su denominación, toda colección organizada de libros y publicaciones periódicas impresas o de cualesquiera otros documentos, en especial gráficos y audiovisuales, así como los servicios del personal que facilite a los usuarios la utilización de estos documentos, con fines informativos, de investigación, de educación o recreativos.

Esas bibliotecas son consignadas según el número de unidades administrativas y de puntos de servicio. Se entenderá por: a) *unidad administrativa*, toda biblioteca independiente, o todo grupo de bibliotecas que tengan una misma dirección o una administración única; b) *punto de servicio*, toda biblioteca que preste servicios a los usuarios en un local aparte, tanto si es independiente, como si forma parte de un grupo de bibliotecas que constituyan una unidad administrativa.

Las bibliotecas se clasifican como sigue:

2. *Bibliotecas nacionales*: bibliotecas que, cualquiera que sea su denominación, son responsables de la adquisición y conservación de ejemplares de todas las publicaciones impresas en el país y que funcionan como bibliotecas de *depósito*, en virtud de una disposición sobre el depósito legal o de otras disposiciones y que normalmente elaboran una bibliografía nacional.

3. *Bibliotecas de instituciones de enseñanza superior*: bibliotecas dedicadas primordialmente al servicio de los estudiantes y del personal docente de las universidades y demás instituciones de enseñanza superior.

4. *Otras bibliotecas importantes no especializadas*: bibliotecas no especializadas, de carácter científico o erudito, que no son ni universitarias ni nacionales, aunque puedan ejercer funciones de biblioteca nacional en un área geográfica determinada.

5. *Bibliotecas escolares*: bibliotecas que dependen de instituciones de enseñanza de cualquier categoría inferior a la enseñanza superior y que, ante todo, están al servicio de los alumnos y profesores de esos establecimientos, aunque estén abiertas al público.

6. *Bibliotecas especializadas*: bibliotecas que dependen de una asociación, servicio oficial, parlamento, centro de investigación (excluídos los centros universitarios), sociedad erudita, asociación profesional, museo, empresa comercial o industrial, cámara de comercio, etc., o de cualquier otro organismo y cuyos fondos cubren en su mayor parte a una disciplina o una rama particular, por ejemplo: ciencias naturales, ciencias sociales, agricultura, química, medicina, ciencias económicas, ingeniería, derecho, historia.

7. *Bibliotecas públicas (o populares)*: bibliotecas que están, gratuitamente o por una módica suma, al servicio de una comunidad, especialmente de una comunidad local o regional, para atender al público en general o a cierta categoría de usuarios como niños, militares, enfermos de los hospitales y empleados.

En lo que se refiere a los fondos, adquisiciones, préstamos, gastos, personal, etc., las definiciones y clasificaciones son las siguientes:

8. *Fondos de una biblioteca*: conjunto de documentos puestos a disposición de los usuarios.

Los datos referentes a los fondos de las bibliotecas deben comprender los documentos siguientes puestos a disposición de los usuarios, incluídos los préstamos: a) libros y publicaciones periódicas encuadernadas; b) manuscritos; c) microcopias; d) materiales audiovisuales y e) otros materiales de biblioteca.

9. *Adquisiciones anuales*: conjunto de documentos que han ido enriqueciendo el fondo durante el año, por compra, donación, intercambio o de cualquier otro modo.

Las estadísticas referentes a las adquisiciones toman en cuenta los mismo documentos que están indicados en la rúbrica fondos.

10. *Volumen*: documentos impresos o manuscritos contenidos en una encuadernación o carpeta.

11. *Materiales audiovisuales*: materiales de biblioteca además de libros y microcopias que precisan de un equipo especial para ser vistos y/o oídos. Comprende materiales tales como discos, cintas, cassettes, películas, diapositivas, proyecciones de transparencia, grabaciones, video, etc.

12. *Otros materiales de biblioteca*: materiales de biblioteca además de libros, publicaciones periódicas encuadernadas, manuscritos, microcopias y material audiovisual. Comprende materiales tales como mapas, gráficos, reproducciones artísticas, fotografías, dioramas, etc.

13. *Usuario inscrito*: toda persona inscrita en una biblioteca con el fin de utilizar materiales dentro o fuera de ella.

14. *Gastos ordinarios*: todos los gastos que ocasione el funcionamiento de la biblioteca, es decir gastos relativos al personal, a las adquisiciones, etc.

15. *Bibliotecario profesional*: toda persona empleada en una biblioteca que ha adquirido una formación general en biblioteconomía o en ciencia de la información. Esta formación puede haberla adquirido mediante una enseñanza teórica o trabajando durante un tiempo prolongado, bajo control, en una biblioteca.

16. *Población servida*: a) *Por las bibliotecas públicas*: el número total de habitantes de las localidades servidas por las bibliotecas públicas propiamente dichas, es decir, las bibliotecas financiadas totalmente o en su mayor parte, por los poderes públicos (bibliotecas municipales o regionales); b) *por las bibliotecas escolares*: el número total de alumnos y personal docente de las escuelas de primero y segundo grado (escuelas primarias y secundarias) provistas de servicios de bibliotecas escolares; c) *por las bibliotecas de instituciones de enseñanza superior*: el número total de estudiantes y personal autorizado para utilizar los servicios de las bibliotecas universitarias y de las bibliotecas de las demás instituciones de enseñanza superior.

Cuadro 7.1

Este cuadro presenta estadísticas seleccionadas sobre los fondos, las adquisiciones anuales y los usuarios inscritos para las diferentes categorías de bibliotecas.

Cuadro 7.2

El cuadro 7.2 se refiere a las bibliotecas de instituciones de enseñanza superior. Este cuadro sólo incluye aquellos países cuya información estadística es más completa la información presentada en el cuadro 7.1.

Sección 2

Hasta 1985, las estadísticas nacionales de edición de libros fueron calculadas de acuerdo con las definiciones y clasificaciones que figuran en la Recomendación sobre la Normalización Internacional de las Estadísticas Relativas a la Edición de Libros y Publicaciones Periódicas aprobada en 1964 por la Conferencia General de la UNESCO. A partir de 1986, la recolección y presentación de estadísticas de libros (así como periódicos diarios y otros periódicos), fué guiada por una versión revisada de la Recomendación de 1964 que fué adoptada por la Conferencia General de la UNESCO en su vigésima tercera reunión, en Noviembre de 1985.

De acuerdo con la Recomendación de 1985, las estadísticas de *edición* de libros deberían referirse a las publicaciones no periódicas impresas, editadas en el país, puestas a la disposición del público y, en general, publicaciones que deberían incluirse en las bibliografías nacionales de los diferentes países, *con excepción* de las siguientes categorías:

a) *Publicaciones editadas con fines publicitarios*, siempre que no predomine en ellas el texto literario o científico, y que su distribución sea gratuita (catálogos, prospectos y otras publicaciones de propaganda comercial, industrial y turística; publicaciones en las que se señalen a la atención de los lectores los productos o servicios suministrados por su editor, aun cuando se refieran a la actividad o la evolución técnica de alguna rama de la industría o del comercio);

b) *Publicaciones pertenecientes a las siguientes categorías, siempre que sean consideradas de carácter efímero*: horarios, tarifas, guías telefónicas, etc.; programas de espectáculos, exposiciones, ferias, etc.; estatutos y balances de sociedades, instrucciones formuladas por empresas, circulares, etc; calendarios, etc.;

c) *Publicaciones pertenecientes a las siguientes categorías y cuya parte más importante no es el texto*: las obras musicales (partituras, cuadernos de música) siempre que la música sea más importante que el texto; la producción cartográfica, excepto los atlas.

En las estadísticas relativas a la edición de libros, *no deberían omitirse* las siguientes categorías de publicaciones:

1. *Publicaciones oficiales*: es decir, las obras editadas por las administraciones públicas o los organismos que de ellas dependen, excepto las que tengan carácter confidencial o sean distribuidas únicamente en el servicio interesado;

2. *Libros de texto*: es decir, obras prescritas a los alumnos que reciben enseñanza de primero o de segundo grado;

3. *Tesis universitarias*;

4. *Separatas*: es decir, las reimpresiones de partes de un libro o de una publicación periódica ya editados, siempre que tengan título y paginación propios y que constituyan una obra independiente;

5. *Publicaciones que forman parte de una serie* pero que constituyen una unidad bibliográfica diferente;

6. *Obras ilustradas*: (i) colecciones de grabados, reproducciones de obras de arte, dibujos, etc., siempre que tales colecciones constituyan obras completas y paginadas, y que los grabados vayan acompañados de un texto explicativo, por breve que sea, referente a esas obras o a sus autores; (ii) álbumes, libros y folletos ilustrados cuyo texto se presente como narración continua acompañada de imágenes para ilustrar determinados episodios: (iii) álbumes y libros de imágenes para niños; (iv) historietas ilustradas.

Al compilar las estadísticas deberían utilizarse las siguientes definiciones:

a) Se entiende por publicación *no periódica* la obra editada, de una sola vez o a intervalos, en varios volúmenes y cuyo número se determina generalmente con antelación;

b) El término *impreso* comprende los diversos procedimientos de impresión que se puedan utilizar;

c) Se considera como *editada en el país* cualquier publicación cuyo editor tenga su domicilio social en el país en que se compilan las estadísticas; no se toman en consideración el lugar de impresión ni el de distribución. Las publicaciones hechas por uno o varios editores con domicilio social en dos o más países se considerarán como editadas en el país o países donde se distribuyan;

d) Se considerarán como *puestas a disposición del público* las publicaciones que éste pueda obtener pagando o gratuitamente. Se considerarán también como puestas a disposición del público en general las publicaciones destinadas a un público restringido, por ejemplo, ciertas publicaciones oficiales de sociedades eruditas, de organizaciones políticas o profesionales, etc.;

e) Se entiende por *libro* una publicación impresa no periódica que consta como mínimo de 49 páginas sin contar las de cubierta, editada en el país y puesta a disposición del público;

f) Se entiende por *folleto* una publicación impresa no periódica que consta de 5 a 48 páginas sin las de cubierta, impresa, editada en el país y puesta a disposición del público;

g) Se entiende por *primera edición* la primera publicación de un manuscrito original o traducido;

h) Se entiende por *reedición* una edición que se distingue de las ediciones anteriores por algunas modificaciones introducidas en el contenido (edición revisada) o en la presentación (nueva edición) y requiera un nuevo ISBN;

i) Una *reimpresión* no contiene otras modificaciones de contenido o de presentación sino las correcciones tipográficas realizadas en el texto de ediciones anteriores y no requiere un nuevo ISBN; toda reimpresión hecha por un editor distinto del editor anterior se considera como una reedición;

j) Se entiende por *traducción* la publicación en que se reproduce una obra en un idioma distinto del original;

k) Un *título* es un término utilizado para designar una publicación impresa que constituye un todo único, tanto si consta de uno como de varios volúmenes.

Esta sección comprende siete cuadros, que se refieren a la edición de libros en su totalidad.

En los cuadros 7.3 a 7.8 figuran datos compilados cada año mediante los cuestionarios que se envían aproximadamente a 200 países y territorios. Salvo indicación contraria, cabe suponer que esos datos abarcan a la vez libros y folletos de obras originales o de traducciones. Ahora bien, ciertas categorías de publicaciones que, según la Recomendación, *deberían quedar comprendidas* en las estadísticas de edición de libros (por ejemplo, las publicaciones oficiales, los libros de texto, las tesis universitarias, las separatas, las obras ilustradas) *o excluidas* de esas estadísticas (por ejemplo, las publicaciones editadas con fines publicitarios, las de carácter efímero y aquellas otras cuyo contenido predominante no es un texto escrito) reciben un trato distinto según los países, cuando se trata de preparar las estadísticas. Al no disponerse de datos completos y precisos, no ha sido posible indicar en qué medida las diferentes estadísticas nacionales se apartan a este respecto de las normas formuladas en la Recomendación.

Sólo los países que han podido proporcionarnos estadísticas establecidas de acuerdo con la clasificación por categorías de materias, preconizada en la Recomendación de 1985, figuran en los cuadros 7.5 y 7.8. La siguiente clasificación, basada en la Clasificación Decimal Universal (CDU), está tomada de esta Recomendación (se indican entre paréntesis los índices correspondientes de la CDU) :

1. Generalidades (0)
2. Filosofía, psicología (1)
3. Religión, teología (2)
4. Sociología, estadística (30-31)
5. Ciencias políticas, ciencias económicas (32-33)
6. Derecho, administración pública, previsión y asistencia social, seguros (34, 351-354, 36)
7. Arte y ciencia militar (355-359)
8. Educación, enseñanza, formación, distracciones (37)
9. Comercio, comunicaciones, transportes, turismo (38)
10. Etnografía, antropología cultural (costumbres, folklore, hábitos, tradición) (39)
11. Filología, idiomas, lingüística (4)
12. Matemáticas (51)
13. Ciencias naturales (52-59)
14. Ciencias médicas, sanidad (61)
15. Ingeniería, tecnología, industrias, oficios (62, 66-69)
16. Agricultura, silvicultura, ganadería, caza y pesca (63)
17. Ciéncia doméstica (64)
18. Gestión, administración y organización (65)
19. Acondicionamiento del territorio, urbanismo, arquitectura (70-72)
20. Artes plásticas y gráficas, fotografía (73-77)
21. Música, artes del espectáculo, teatro, películas y cine (78, 791-792)
22. Juegos y deportes (793-799)
23. Literatura (8)
(a) Historia y crítica literarias
(b) Textos literarios
24. Geografía (91)
25. Historia, biografía (92-99)

Cuando el total no corresponde a la suma de sus componentes, la diferencia será sea el número de obras no desglosadas entre las diez materias principales de la Clasificación Decimal Universal o los veinticinco grupos de categorías de temas, sea números redondos.

Cuadro 7.3 y 7.6 indican, para cada país, el total de las publicaciones y el número de libros; la diferencia entre estas cifras representa el número de folletos.

Cuadro 7.3
Este cuadro presenta para los años 1991 a 1994. Sólo incluye los países con respecto a los cuales la UNESCO dispone de estadísticas relativas por lo menos a uno de esos tres años, los datos de este cuadro comprenden datos relativos al número de títulos de las *primeras ediciones* y de las *reediciones* de obras originales y de traducciones clasificadas según las diez materias principales de la CDU.

Cuadro 7.4
Las cifras del cuadro 7.4 se refieren al número de títulos de las *primeras ediciones* y a las *reediciones* por categorías de temas. Para los países en los que el número total de ediciones y el número de primeras ediciones son idénticos, se deberá considerar que no hubieron reediciones o que el número de reediciones no es conocido. De la misma forma, cuando el número total de títulos es igual al número total de libros, se supondrá que ningún folleto fue publicado, o que su número no es conocido.

Cuadro 7.5
Este cuadro presenta para los años 1991 a 1994, datos sobre el número de ejemplares de las *primeras ediciones*, *reediciones* y *reimpresiones* de obras originales (o de traducciones) clasificados por materias (C.D.U.).

Cuadro 7.6
Las cifras del cuadro 7.6 se refieren al número de ejemplares de las *primeras ediciones*, las *reediciones* y a las *reimpresiones* por categorías de temas. Las observaciones del cuadro 7.5 sobre el total de ediciones y de primeras ediciones también deben ser tomadas en cuenta para este cuadro.

Cuadro 7.7
Las cifras de este cuadro se refieren a las *primeras ediciones* y a las *reediciones* de los libros de texto escolares que, en la

Recomendación, se definen como obras prescritas a los alumnos que reciben enseñanza de primero o de segundo grado.

Cuadro 7.8
Los datos del cuadro 7.8 se refieren a las *primeras ediciones* y a las *reediciones* de libros para niños.

Sección 3
Los cuadros 7.9 a 7.11 contienen datos relativos a los periódicos diarios, no diarios y revistas.

En general, las estadísticas nacionales de los diarios y publicaciones periódicas deberían establecerse de conformidad con las definiciones y las clasificaciones que figuran en la Recomendación revisada en 1985 sobre la normalización internacional de las estadísticas relativas a la producción y distribución de libros, diarios y otras publicaciones periódicas. Los datos presentados en los cuadros 7.9 y 7.10 son publicados regularmente en este *Annuario estadístico*, mientras que para los datos relativos a las publicaciones periódicas clasificadas por tipo son publicados cada año. De acuerdo con la Recomendación de 1985, las estadísticas nacionales relativas a la prensa deberían referirse a las publicaciones periódicas impresas en el país y ofrecidas al público, exceptuando las publicaciones editadas con fines publicitarios, de carácter efímero y de aquéllas cuyo contenido predominante no es el texto. En cambio, las categorías de publicaciones, en particular las siguientes, *deberían incluirse* en las estadísticas de periódicos y revistas: publicaciones periódicas oficiales, publicaciones periódicas académicas y científicas, publicaciones periódicas de entidades profesionales, sindicales, políticas, deportivas, etc., publicaciones anuales o de menor frecuencia de aparición, boletines parroquiales, boletines escolares, periódicos de empresa y programas de espectáculos, de radio y televisión, si predomina el texto literario.

Para calcular esas estadísticas, deberían utilizarse las definiciones siguientes:
1. Se entiende por publicación *periódica* la editada en serie continua con el mismo título, a intervalos regulares o irregulares durante un período indeterminado de forma que los números de la serie lleven una numeración consecutiva o cada número esté fechado.
2. Las publicaciones periódicas se subdividen en dos categorías: periódicos corrientes y y otro periódicos.
a) *Periódicos corrientes*: son las publicaciones periódicas destinadas al gran público y que tengan esencialmente por objeto constituir una fuente de información escrita sobre los acontecimientos de actualidad relacionados con asuntos públicos, cuestiones internacionales, política, etc. Un periódico que responda a esa definición y que se publique al menos cuatro veces por semana se considerará como un diario; un periódico que aparezca tres veces por semana o con menor frecuencia, se clasificará en la categoría de los periódicos no diarios;
b) *Otros periódicos*: son los que tratan de temas muy amplios o los dedicados especialmente a estudios e informaciones documentales sobre determinadas cuestiones: legislación, hacienda, comercio, medicina, modas, deportes, etc. Esta definición abarca los periódicos especializados, las revistas, las revistas ilustradas y las demás publicaciones periódicas, a la excepción de las publicaciones a) a c) citadas en el segundo párrafo de la sección 2 de este capítulo.
3. Las cifras concernientes a la *difusión* expresan el promedio de difusión cotidiana o, en el caso de las publicaciones no diarias, el promedio por número. En todo caso, las cifras correspondientes deberían comprender el número de (a) ejemplares vendidos directamente, (b) por suscripción, y (c) principalmente distribuidos en forma gratuita tanto en el país como en el extranjero.

Al interpretar los datos de los cuadros que figuran a continuación, no hay que perder de vista que en ciertos casos los métodos de compilación, y las definiciones y clasificaciones que aplican algunos países no se ajustan enteramente a las normas preconizadas por la UNESCO. Por ejemplo, las tiradas que se mencionan deberían referirse al número de ejemplares distribuidos como definido anteriormente. Sin embargo, parece que algunos países han indicado el número de ejemplares impresos que es generalmente más importante que las cifras relativas a la distribución.

Cuadro 7.9
En el cuadro 7.9 figuran datos sobre el número, la circulación total y la circulación por 1 000 habitantes de los diarios de información general en 1980, 1985, 1990 y 1992.

Cuadro 7.10
Este cuadro indica el número, la circulación total y la circulación por 1 000 habitantes de los periódicos no diarios y otras publicaciones periódicas, durante el último año del período 1989-1994 para el cual se poseen cifras.

Cuadro 7.11
Est cuadro presenta los datos sobre otras publicaciones periódicas por categorías, durante el último ãno del período 1989-1994 para el cual se dispone de datos. Hay que señalar a la atención de los lectores que la suma de los dos totales parciales que figuran en ses cuadro debe correspnder al total indicado bajo el epígrafe otras

publicaciones periódicas del cuadro 7.10. Se observará que no es ese siempre el caso, probablemente porque las fuentes nacionales utilizadas son diferentes o porque en algunos países no ha sido todavía posible aplicar las normas internacionales. No obstante, se ha estimado preferible incluir en ese cuadro el mayor número posible de países en lugar de limitario únicamente a los países cuyas estadísticas son completas y seguras. Por esta razón, los datos publicados deberán utilizarse e interpretarse con circunspección, sin olvidar que, con frequencia, las cifras no constituyen a lo sumo más que una aproximación muy relativa de la situación real.

Sección 4

Los datos que figuran en el cuadro 7.12 se refieren a la producción, a la importación, a la exportación y al consumo de *papel cultural*, es decir, de papel de periódico, de papel de imprenta (distinto al papel de periódico) y de papel de escribir para los años 1970, 1975, 1980, 1985, 1990 y 1994. Como para los años anteriores, estos datos nos han sido procurados por la *Organización de las Naciones Unidas para la Alimentación y la Agricultura* (FAO). Los lectores deseosos de obtener información complementaria deben referirse al *Anuario de Productos Forestales* publicado por la FAO.

El término *papel de periódico* (subgrupo 641.1 de la Clasificación Tipo para el Comercio Internacional, Revisión 2) se refiere al papel de imprenta blanqueado, no encolado o poco encolado, no cuché, del tipo utilizado corrientemente para los periódicos. El papel de periódico tiene un peso de 45 a 60 gramos por metro cuadrado y contiene, en general, al menos un 70 por ciento en peso de materia fibrosa extraída de la pasta mecánica.

La expresión *otros papeles de imprenta y papel de escribir* (subgrupo 641.2 de la Clasificación Tipo para el Comercio Internacional, Revision 2) designa las diferentes clases de papel en hojas o en rollo que no sean el papel periódico y que se destinan a la impresión y escritura. No se incluyen en esa categoría los productos manufacturados tales como material de oficina, cuadernos, libros de registro, etc.

Para los países sobre los cuales no se dispone de datos separados relativos a las dos categorías de papel arriba definidas, las cifras globales se presentan bajo la rúbrica *papel de periódico*.

7.1 Libraries by category
Bibliothèques par catégorie
Bibliotecas por categoría

7.1 Libraries by category: number, collections, additions, registered users

Bibliothèques par catégorie: nombre, collections, acquisitions, usagers inscrits

Bibliotecas por categoría: número, fondos, adquisiciones, usuarios inscritos

Categories of library:	Catégories de bibliothèques:	Categorías de bibliotecas:
a. National	a. Nationales	a. Nacionales
b. Non-specialized	b. Non-spécialisées	b. No especializadas
c. Public	c. Publiques	c. Públicas
d. Higher education	d. Enseignement supérieur	d. Enseñanza superior

Country / Pays / País	Year / Année / Año	Category of library / Catégorie de bibliothèques / Categoría de bibliotecas	Adminis-trative units / Unités admini-stratives / Unidades admini-strativas	Service points / Points de service / Puntos de servicio	Collections		Annual additions (volumes) / Acquisitions annuelles (volumes) / Adquisicones anuales (volúmenes)	Registered users / Usagers inscrits / Usuarios inscritos
					Number of volumes (000) / Nombre de volumes (000) / Número de volúmenes (000)	Metres of shelving / Mètres de rayonnage / Metros de estantes		
			(1)	(2)	(3)	(4)	(5)	(6)
Africa								
Benin	1989	a. National	1	...	6	177	1 102	158
	1989	b. Non-specialized	4	4	40	1 100	...	...
	1989	c. Public	12	12	28	777	2 008	689
Burundi	1989	b. Non-specialized	174	...	174	...	...	500
	1989	c. Public	60	60	...	...	...	20 000
Cameroon	1989	a. National	1	7	40	1 000	25 000	5 000
	1989	b. Non-specialized	1	14	50	...	3 500	3 000
Congo	1989	a. National	1	1	9	125	2 000	995
	1989	c. Public	1	4	15	360	1 200	22 365
Egypt	1991	a. National	1	52	2 195	...	...	...
	1991	b. Non-specialized	105	105	832	...	...	...
	1989	d. Higher education	272	272	35 790	...	...	65 900
Equatorial Guinea	1993	b. Non-specialized	1	1	5	...	...	...
	1992	c. Public	3	3	...	...	...	...
Ethiopia	1994	a. National	1	9	100	...	...	420
Gabon	1992	a. National	1	1	...	...	454	2 382
Gambia	1992	a. National	1	5	2	220	300	1 350
	1992	c. Public	2	6	94	...	4 900	...
Ghana	1989	c. Public	13	47	1 576	...	32 200	56 211
Kenya	1989	a. National	1	22	603	...	10 260	178 978
Lesotho	1989	c. Public	1	3	24	672	...	607
Malawi	1992	c. Public	1	7	237	3 000	18 223	36 976
Mauritius	1992	a. National	1	1	38	467	2 603	...
Nigeria‡	1992	a. National	1	12	865	...	16 384	34 373
	1992	c. Public	12	76	611	...	24 895	14 927

Libraries by category 7.1
Bibliothèques par catégorie
Bibliotecas por categoría

Country Pays País	Year Année Año	Category of library Catégorie de bibliothèques Categoría de bibliotecas	Adminis-trative units Unités admini-stratives Unidades admini-strativas	Service points Points de service Puntos de servicio	Collections		Annual additions (volumes) Acquisitions annuelles (volumes) Adquisicones anuales (volúmenes)	Registered users Usagers inscrits Usuarios inscritos
					Number of volumes (000) Nombre de volumes (000) Número de volúmenes (000)	Metres of shelving Mètres de rayonnage Metros de estantes		
			(1)	(2)	(3)	(4)	(5)	(6)
Reunion	1990	d. Higher education	1	1	52	2 429	4 375	2 961
Senegal	1994	d. Higher education	7	...	380	13 894	7 432	12 906
Seychelles‡	1989	c. Public	1	4	42	...	1 285	16 664
	1990	d. Higher education	1	5	26	510	2 270	*1 610
South Africa	1989	a. National	2	5	1 455	...	...	...
	1989	c. Public	671	1 029	15 683	...	...	...
	1989	d. Higher education	84	166	8 120	...	...	...
Swaziland	1989	a. National	1	...	3	32	20	...
Togo	1993	a. National	1	...	16	...	600	500
	1989	c. Public	1	26	63	600	2 000	7 706
Tunisia	1992	c. Public	250	...	2 493	...	255 980	...
Uganda	1992	c. Public	1	17	82	...	4 184	53 476
	1993	d. Higher education	5	10	1 096	56 300	9 223	34 700
Zambia	1992	a. National	1	1	16		98	120
Zimbabwe	1993	a. National	1	1	96	...	785	46 605
	1989	c. Public	76	83	1 038	...	3 195	151 563
	1990	d. Higher education	25	31	764	...	7 609	30 707
America, North								
Barbados‡	1992	a. National	1	...	38	...	1 011	...
	1992	c. Public	1	9	175	...	5 069	56 094
	1993	d. Higher education	1	1	29	365	616	195
Belize‡	1992	a. National	1	...	*150	...	...	25 096
	1992	c. Public	1	26	*130	47 079	...	*14 999
	1990	d. Higher education	1	1	6	...	...	312
Bermuda	1989	c. Public	1	4	148	...	4 934	26 361
	1989	d. Higher education	1	1	25	...	800	443
British Virgin Islands‡	1989	c. Public	1	6	48	...	2 102	8 815
Canada‡	1991	a. National	1	...	...	...	207 297	*7 500
	1990	c. Public	1 027	3 301	60 955	...	4 800 203	...
Cayman Islands	1991	c. Public	2	6	16	...	2 520	5 513
	1990	d. Higher education	1	1	1.5	...	50	50
Costa Rica	1990	d. Higher education	4	4	633	...	25 145	...
Cuba‡	1992	a. National	1	1	2 431	...	55 900	13 299
	1992	c. Public	353	4 627	5 326	...	337 500	207 411
	1993	d. Higher education	86	86	2 525	...	2 340	270 540
Dominica	1992	c. Public	1	3	29	400	2 727	9 470
El Salvador	1989	a. National	1	3	10	334	12 309	...
	1989	c. Public	44	83	55	...	8 145	21 490
Greenland	1990	a. National	1	...	...	...	...	...
	1990	c. Public	17	...	245	...	...	...
	1990	d. Higher education	1	...	...	...	...	...
Grenada	1992	c. Public	4	8	64	...	1 540	1 245
Guadeloupe‡	1990	d. Higher education	1	3	90	4 195	6 453	3 649
Jamaica	1989	c. Public	1	202	1 169	...	45 271	689 593
Mexico	1989	a. National	1	...	1 500	...	17 169	110 313
	1993	c. Public	4 894	4 894	19 875	...	...	72 559 000
	1993	d. Higher education	1 139	1 139	12 776	...	1 008 570	1 010 090
Nicaragua	1990	d. Higher education	13	18	187	...	8 544	27 633
St. Vincent and the Grenadines	1989	c. Public	1	16	100	...	5 000	...
	1990	d. Higher education	2	2	12	...	550	1 100
Trinidad and Tobago	1993	d. Higher education	1	10	305	...	6 864	5 290

7.1   Libraries by category
Bibliothèques par catégorie
Bibliotecas por categoría

Country Pays País	Year Année Año	Category of library Catégorie de bibliothèques Categoría de bibliotecas	Adminis- trative units Unités admini- stratives Unidades admini- strativas	Service points Points de service Puntos de servicio	Collections		Annual additions (volumes) Acquisitions annuelles (volumes) Adquisicones anuales (volúmenes)	Registered users Usagers inscrits Usuarios inscritos
					Number of volumes (000) Nombre de volumes (000) Número de volúmenes (000)	Metres of shelving Mètres de rayonnage Metros de estantes		
			(1)	(2)	(3)	(4)	(5)	(6)
Turks and Caicos Islands‡	1992	c. Public	1	2	7	171	1 116	...
America, South								
Argentina	1989	a. National	3	11	1 950	...	115 419	...
Brazil	1993	a. National	1	2	5 280	38 548	67 175	465 506
	1994	c. Public	2 739	...	...	...	...	...
Chile	1993	a. National	1	3	3 554	...	2 590	...
	1992	c. Public	289	289	1 121	...	...	2 221 889
	1989	d. Higher education	178	...	5 669	...	...	...
Colombia	1993	a. National	1	1	463	17 534	12 636	3 676
	1993	c. Public	1 378	...	...	...	...	...
Paraguay	1990	a. National	1	...	...	...	...	...
	1990	c. Public	28	...	...	...	...	...
	1990	d. Higher education	26	...	...	...	...	...
Peru	1992	a. National	1	...	3 890	...	163 165	8 696
	1992	c. Public	609	...	...	...	...	...
Venezuela	1993	a. National	1	...	5 115	...	...	99 274
	1993	c. Public	23	672	3 459	...	...	12 699 641
	1989	d. Higher education	78	168	...	...	...	...
Asia								
Armenia	1992	a. National	2	...	4 094	...	24 727	33 940
	1992	c. Public	42	1 306	14 685	...	151 487	1 066 928
Azerbaijan	1992	a. National	1	13	2 360	...	14 508	25 028
	1992	b. Non-specialized	1	14	1 725	...	13 124	16 160
	1992	c. Public	4 650	...	40 087	...	1 364 820	3 021 880
Bahrain‡	1989	c. Public	1	10	218	...	...	...
	1990	d. Higher education	1	1	35	790	1 267	1 800
Bangladesh	1989	a. National	1	1	15	328	...	...
	1989	c. Public	57	61	521	...	26 600	...
Brunei Darussalam	1992	c. Public	1	5	285	...	23 426	41 001
	1990	d. Higher education	2	3	150	...	10 854	1 504
China‡	1989	a. National	1	...	13 768	290 000	476 796	166 861
	1993	c. Public	2 579	...	314 100	7 970 000	7 900 000	7 130 000
	1993	d. Higher education	1 075	*5 000	406 471	...	10 170 199	4 271 724
Cyprus	1992	a. National	1	2	54	...	2 070	6 500
	1992	c. Public	20	...	318	...	20 800	43 050
Georgia	1992	a. National	1	...	7 524	90 351	37 498	462 285
	1992	c. Public	4 048	...	32 319	...	1 119 616	*2 500 000
Hong Kong‡	1992	c. Public	2	55	4 189	...	348 158	2 646 832
	1990	d. Higher education	17	33	3 370	...	225 078	123 125
Indonesia	1989	d. Higher education	45	137	1 735	...	...	534 798
Iran, Islamic Republic of	1992	a. National	1	5	392	10 364	17 616	2 902
	1990	c. Public	488	...	...	...	...	...
	1994	d. Higher education	113	168	2 323	...	...	280 877
Iraq	1989	a. National	1	3				
Japan‡	1990	a. National	1	3	5 528	...	...	452 000
	1990	c. Public	1 475	1 950	161 694	...	15 205 000	16 038 000
	1990	d. Higher education	507	704	181 839	...	...	1 370 000
Jordan	1992	a. National	1	1	...	2 890	1 640	...
	1990	d. Higher education	33	44	1 227	...	36 182	51 369
Kazakstan	1993	a. National	1	...	5 209	...	94 000	46 000
	1993	c. Public	8 770	...	104 362	...	5 026 000	6 501 000
Korea, Republic of	1994	a. National	1	2	2 343	...	...	2 164 149
	1989	b. Non-specialized	1	1	686	...	48 709	108 049
	1994	c. Public	277	277	8 442	...	...	30 525 908
	1994	d. Higher education	340	...	35 758	...	...	61 559 059

Libraries by category 7.1
Bibliothèques par catégorie
Bibliotecas por categoría

Country / Pays / País	Year / Année / Año	Category of library / Catégorie de bibliothèques / Categoría de bibliotecas	Adminis-trative units / Unités admini-stratives / Unidades admini-strativas	Service points / Points de service / Puntos de servicio	Collections		Annual additions (volumes) / Acquisitions annuelles (volumes) / Adquisicones anuales (volúmenes)	Registered users / Usagers inscrits / Usuarios inscritos
					Number of volumes (000) / Nombre de volumes (000) / Número de volúmenes (000)	Metres of shelving / Mètres de rayonnage / Metros de estantes		
			(1)	(2)	(3)	(4)	(5)	(6)
Kuwait	1992	b. Non-specialized	3	11	135	...	18 000	12 500
	1992	c. Public	1	18	272	4 530	43 440	...
Kyrgyzstan	1992	a. National	1	-	3 076	...	...	33 417
	1992	b. Non-specialized	1 249	2 015	14 609	...	265 800	1 274 201
	1992	c. Public	57	3 264	...	...	...	...
Lebanon	1993	d. Higher education	72	-	*2 075	...	...	...
Malaysia‡	1992	a. National	1	90	858	...	81 033	134 956
	1992	c. Public	13	350	8 144	...	1 005 750	1 443 564
	1990	d. Higher education	48	73	3 412	...	383 873	...
Mongolia‡	1990	d. Higher education	9	...	1 581	...	1 100	20 100
Myanmar	1993	a. National	1	...	4.2	...	...	14 081
Oman‡	1992	a. National	1	2	3.6	155	8	168
	1993	d. Higher education	1	4	78	1 945	*8 852	*6 000
Pakistan	1992	a. National	1	1	78	621	3 486	...
	1992	c. Public	4	10	543	6 468	7 339	62 325
	1993	d. Higher education	31	113	3 955	135 367	29 163	49 268
Philippines	1993	a. National	1	4	902	...	71 932	189 798
	1989	c. Public	1	517	5 756	...	...	1 595 194
Qatar	1992	a. National	1	1	185	...	4 898	6 292
	1992	c. Public	6	6	169	...	5 088	4 565
	1993	d. Higher education	2	7	329	...	5 000	6 000
Saudi Arabia	1993	d. Higher education	21	65	4 844	113 849	98 664	483 611
Singapore‡	1992	a. National	1	8	2 891	...	164 520	875 056
	1990	d. Higher education	5	12	2 354	14 865	137 181	77 934
Sri Lanka	1993	a. National	1	1	157	...	...	96
	1989	c. Public	15	154	481	3 030	10 500	98 006
	1990	d. Higher education	11	36	829	...	26 321	30 727
Syrian Arab Republic‡	1992	a. National	1	...	150	...	15 000	...
	1992	b. Non-specialized	1	...	8	...	20	400
	1993	d. Higher education	1	...	10	250	25	...
Thailand	1992	a. National	1	25	1 528	6 200	138 129	1 456 000
	1992	c. Public	589	589	...	...	...	...
Turkey	1992	a. National	1	1	1 079	45 402	20 505	10 100
	1992	c. Public	...	910	9 042	...	545 994	...
	1993	d. Higher education	212	212	5 700	...	...	...
United Arab Emirates	1990	d. Higher education	3	22	248	11 177	34 009	12 519
Uzbekistan	1993	d. Higher education	58	304	2 358	158 738	940 828	263 446
Viet Nam	1993	c. Public	4	566	12 737	...	...	...
Europe								
Austria‡	1992	a. National	1	1	3 069	...	40 748	360 656
	1992	b. Non-specialized	7	9	1 562	...	37 335	84 351
	1992	c. Public	2 129	2 129	9 202	...	...	960 125
	1993	d. Higher education	21	...	16 953	...	459 477	4 094 407
Belarus	1992	a. National	1	2	6 868	...	109 900	37 000
	1992	b. Non-specialized	7	16	4 511	...	115 900	226 500
	1992	c. Public	5 743	11 329	77 142	...	...	4 296 800
	1993	d. Higher education	38	...	20 428	...	636 429	192 683
Belgium‡	1990	a. National	1	1	*4 278	*57 591	...	*104 544
	1990	b. Non-specialized	*5	*6	*1 402	*24 139	...	*55 262
	1990	c. Public	38	1 151	29 678	*823 936	...	*1 743 269
	1990	d. Higher education	16	140	*5 988	*147 413	65 853	87 400
Bulgaria	1993	a. National	1	...	*2 266	...	...	*24 000
	1992	b. Non-specialized	27	...	10 655	...	301 859	232 546
	1992	c. Public	4 879	...	57 092	...	1 414 734	1 342 761
	1993	d. Higher education	81	...	7 520	...	154 190	149 946

7.1 Libraries by category
Bibliothèques par catégorie
Bibliotecas por categoría

Country / Pays / País	Year / Année / Año	Category of library / Catégorie de bibliothèques / Categoría de bibliotecas	Administrative units / Unités administratives / Unidades administrativas (1)	Service points / Points de service / Puntos de servicio (2)	Collections		Annual additions (volumes) / Acquisitions annuelles (volumes) / Adquisicones anuales (volúmenes) (5)	Registered users / Usagers inscrits / Usuarios inscritos (6)
					Number of volumes (000) / Nombre de volumes (000) / Número de volúmenes (000) (3)	Metres of shelving / Mètres de rayonnage / Metros de estantes (4)		
Croatia	1992	a. National	1	...	2 333	61 725	19 785	223 239
	1992	b. Non-specialized	5	...	2 457	44 456	23 703	96 366
	1992	c. Public	250	...	4 631	104 082	232 784	6 122 295
	1992	d. Higher education	128	136	3 433	75 073	80 464	101 500
Czech Republic‡	1993	a. National	11		16 184	...	...	279 500
	1993	c. Public	6 227	7 848	37 749	...	...	1 142 000
	1993	d. Higher education	58	1 149	8 551	...	208 862	183 834
Denmark‡	1992	a. National	1	4	4 388	103 745	72 414	...
	1992	b. Non-specialized	5	13	*5 252	131 314	136 702	...
	1992	c. Public	251	904	32 479	...	2 059	...
	1993	d. Higher education	20	52	12 584	290 172	275 499	116 932
Estonia‡	1992	a. National	2	2	2 688	...	72 364	1 690
	1992	b. Non-specialized	1	1	2 790	...	21 200	18 316
	1994	c. Public	605	...	10 148	...	...	344 900
	1993	d. Higher education	13	27	4 815	95 004	130 579	67 863
Faeroe Islands	1993	a. National	1	...	123	...	...	...
	1992	c. Public	15	...	192	...	...	...
Finland	1993	a. National	1	1	2 952	...	...	...
	1993	b. Non-specialized	31	427	130 363	362 370	339 271	...
	1993	c. Public	444	1 339	36 300	...	1 800 000	2 404 631
	1993	d. Higher education	30	...	12 279	...	...	...
France‡	1992	a. National	1	...	12 000	...	...	...
	1991	b. Non-specialized	1	1	400	15 500	19 500	3 713 644
	1992	c. Public	1 325	...	...	...	...	...
	1991	d. Higher education	73	232	...	...	538 000	858 000
Germany‡	1992	a. National	8	9	29 438	...	757 382	150 181
	1992	b. Non-specialized	38	45	17 062	...	439 860	222 102
	1992	c. Public	14 019	14 019	128 922	...	...	8 938 841
	1993	d. Higher education	271	...	126 117	...	3 818 000	1 802 862
Gibraltar	1989	c. Public	1	1	28	1 150	12 000	5 494
Greece	1990	a. National	2	2	2 633	36 500	13 043	...
	1989	b. Non-specialized	758	758	7 492	194 430	216 221	1 221 072
	1990	c. Public	680	680	7 400	151 526	227 873	...
	1990	d. Higher education	*39	*70	6 482	*167 639	...	*128 391
Holy See‡	1990	d. Higher education	15	28	3 216	139 168	42 395	46 745
Hungary	1992	a. National	1	...	2 660	...	...	25 460
	1992	b. Non-specialized	1	...	1 296	...	...	6 856
	1993	c. Public	3 032	5 264	49 102	...	...	1 609 000
	1993	d. Higher education	29	...	12 803	...	...	132 751
Iceland	1992	a. National	1	1	431	...	7 271	10 332
	1993	c. Public	137	...	1 945	...	...	93 263
	1991	d. Higher education	6	6	382	11 472	13 767	...
Ireland	1990	a. National	1	2	750	14 530	10 000	28 300
	1990	b. Non-specialized	2	4	383	*5 993	344	10 323
	1991	c. Public	...	364	11 046	...	...	808 042
	1990	d. Higher education	*15	33	5 018	177 832	113 000	*51 049
Italy‡	1992	a. National	2	2	10 960	175 346	98 478	605 417
	1992	b. Non-specialized	34	34	7 835	433 448	77 565	752 952
	1992	c. Public	42	...	27 518	...	...	257 622
	1993	d. Higher education	10	11	6 190	158 140	33 578	841 644
Latvia‡	1993	a. National	1	...	4 335	...	518 100	24 800
	1994	c. Public	1 046	...	21 800	...	...	...
	1993	d. Higher education	15	...	7 100	...	221 122	53 814
Liechtenstein	1992	a. National	1	1	160	...	4 500	15 750
	1992	c. Public	3	3	26	...	1 145	1 800
	1990	d. Higher education	1	1	*30	*783	...	*262
Lithuania	1993	c. Public	1 623	...	...	...	...	...
	1993	d. Higher education	27	...	12 053	...	...	...
Luxembourg‡	1990	a. National	1	1	675	26 400	...	24 650
	1990	c. Public	2	5	*613	*17 015	...	*43 505
	1990	d. Higher education	1	1	269	*7 134	...	*5 321
Malta	1992	a. National	1	2	373	6 928	1 534	...
	1992	c. Public	1	61	331	4 350	15 995	120 000

Libraries by category 7.1
Bibliothèques par catégorie
Bibliotecas por categoría

Country / Pays / País	Year / Année / Año	Category of library / Catégorie de bibliothèques / Categoría de bibliotecas	Administrative units Unités administratives Unidades administrativas	Service points Points de service Puntos de servicio	Collections		Annual additions (volumes) Acquisitions annuelles (volumes) Adquisicones anuales (volúmenes)	Registered users Usagers inscrits Usuarios inscritos
					Number of volumes (000) Nombre de volumes (000) Número de volúmenes (000)	Metres of shelving Mètres de rayonnage Metros de estantes		
			(1)	(2)	(3)	(4)	(5)	(6)
Moldova	1993	a. National	1	1	2 950	...	25 100	16 800
	1993	b. Non-specialized	28	28	605	...	24 100	34 600
	1993	c. Public	1 598	3 143	18 874	...	1 086 800	1 235 400
	1993	d. Higher education	15	...	5 844	...	134 444	...
Monaco‡	1992	a. National	1	2	285	6 350	5 700	10 000
Netherlands‡	1990	a. National	1	4	2 482	*54 000	...	96 770
	1990	b. Non-specialized	*3	*5	*876	*51 100	...	*80 518
	1992	c. Public	603	1 192	41 781	...	...	4 512 000
	1993	d. Higher education	369	...	25 266	721 000	...	...
Norway	1992	a. National	2	3	2 186	66 377	97 802	...
	1992	b. Non-specialized	20	...	938	...	11 042	...
	1992	c. Public	439	1 214	19 893	...	973 399	...
	1993	d. Higher education	95	209	9 412	267 841	336 708	236 166
Poland	1991	a. National	1	...	2 209	...	45 291	6 293
	1991	b. Non-specialized	261	...	10 629	...	174 839	99 023
	1993	c. Public	9 605	...	135 928	...	4 890 512	6 670 991
	1993	d. Higher education	126	1 027	43 182	...	1 071 918	988 681
Portugal‡	1993	a. National	1	1	*2 530	...	28 983	64 484
	1993	b. Non-specialized	8	...	*2 150	...	12 004	43 433
	1993	c. Public	161	...	*3 910	...	294 024	633 077
	1993	d. Higher education	242	343	6 279	...	200 559	349 111
Romania	1993	a. National	6	...	20 040	...	...	115 000
	1993	c. Public	2 917	...	46 406	...	...	2 007 000
	1993	d. Higher education	64	348	20 919	309 300	493 736	614 000
Russian Federation	1993	a. National	2	2	68 271	...	1 002 599	1 362 820
	1993	b. Non-specialized	7	7	10 266	...	151 091	153 077
	1993	c. Public	51 111	...	884 754	...	52 569 950	62 449 000
	1993	d. Higher education	519	...	324 696	...	12 478 481	3 730 272
Slovakia‡	1992	a. National	1	1	3 580	...	32 420	4 806
	1992	c. Public	2 682	3 012	19 757	...	588 012	715 002
	1993	d. Higher education	33	546	4 738	...	104 183	108 334
Slovenia	1992	a. National	1	1	1 749	22 300	44 096	9 251
	1992	c. Public	60	833	5 283	...	233 770	365 888
	1992	d. Higher education	68	69	2 863	79 567	80 866	211 210
Spain‡	1990	a. National	1	2	3 500	*71 148	-	55 909
	1992	b. Non-specialized	59	...	...	...	...	...
	1992	c. Public	3 993	4 609	29 718	...	2 045 263	4 384 521
	1992	d. Higher education	648	1 131	18 618	783 100	959 271	1 647 868
Sweden	1992	a. National	1	4	*3 168	79 208	*42 880	...
	1990	b. Non-specialized	26	72	*18 035	*452 390	...	*94 335
	1993	c. Public	286	1 734	45 147	...	1 863 000	...
	1991	d. Higher education	25	...	*18 500	460 619	...	...
Switzerland‡	1992	a. National	1	1	2 653	...	51 825	7 534
	1992	b. Non-specialized	34	34	7 697	...	250 674	382 693
	1990	c. Public	*46	*2 555	27 674	*768 290	...	*351 444
	1993	d. Higher education	9	...	14 427	362 308	277 832	200 711
The Former Yugoslav Rep. of Macedonia	1992	a. National	1	1	2 169	61 655	10 656	152 800
	1992	b. Non-specialized	1	1	142	2 582	872	2 428
	1992	c. Public	62	122	2 729	30 289	68 454	987 483
	1992	d. Higher education	26	43	1 135	26 323	7 833	496 906
Ukraine	1992	c. Public	25 300	...	400 883	...	*21 246 800	21 691 500
United Kingdom‡	1990	a. National	*3	23	27 500	790 000	542 606	82 945
	1990	b. Non-specialized	*26	*23	*8 026	*214 295	...	*316 460
	1993	c. Public	167	5 185	133 134	...	12 753 643	*33 505 000
	1990	d. Higher education	215	*860	89 832	1 804 000	1 910 000	1 331 000
Federal Republic of Yugoslavia‡	1992	a. National	3	3	5 607	180 272	83 829	176 101
	1992	b. Non-specialized	10	10	1 171	10 324	15 770	352
	1992	c. Public	407	924	15 337	...	267 436	7 892 223
	1992	d. Higher education	166	310	7 052	108 242	116 108	1 744 537

7.1   Libraries by category
Bibliothèques par catégorie
Bibliotecas por categoría

Country Pays País	Year Année Año	Category of library Catégorie de bibliothèques Categoría de bibliotecas	Adminis- trative units Unités admini- stratives Unidades admini- strativas	Service points Points de service Puntos de servicio	Collections		Annual additions (volumes) Acquisitions annuelles (volumes) Adquisicones anuales (volúmenes)	Registered users Usagers inscrits Usuarios inscritos
					Number of volumes (000) Nombre de volumes (000) Número de volúmenes (000)	Metres of shelving Mètres de rayonnage Metros de estantes		
			(1)	(2)	(3)	(4)	(5)	(6)
Oceania								
Australia‡	1991 1994	a. National d. Higher education	1 43	... 231	4 625 33 000	... ...	... *1 500 000	... *550 000
Fiji	1989	d. Higher education	7	7	65	1 905	2 250	800
Nauru	1990	d. Higher education	1	1	1	...	...	80
New Caledonia‡	1990	d. Higher education	1	2	8.6	269	3 879	665
New Zealand	1990	d. Higher education	7	33	5 910	...	181 848	...
Niue‡	1989 1990	c. Public d. Higher education	1 1	1 1	7 3	117 70	480 *40	713 30
Papua New Guinea	1989 1989	a. National c. Public	1 19	4 ...	60 151	4 000 ...	2 408 6 000	3 600 46 095
Vanuatu, Republic of‡	1989	a. National	1	1	50	700	1 000	200

AFRICA:

Nigeria:

E--> Data on public libraries refer only to libraries financed by public authorities.

FR-> Les données relatives aux bibliothèques publiques se réfèrent seulement aux bibliothèques financées par les pouvoirs publics.

ESP> Los datos relativos a las bibliotecas públicas se refiere sólo a las bibliotecas financiadas por los poderes públicos.

Seychelles:

E--> The figure in column 5 on public libraries refer to the number of titles only.

FR-> Le chiffre de la colonne 5 relatifs aux bibliothèques publiques se réfèrent au nombre de titres seulement.

ESP> La cifra de la columna 5 relativas a las bibliotecas públicas se refieren al número de titulos solamente.

AMERICA, NORTH:

Barbados:

E--> Data on libraries of higher education refer only to the library of Erdiston Teacher Training College.

FR-> Les données relatives aux bibliothèques d'établissements d'enseignement supérieur se réfèrent seulement à la bibliothèques de *Erdiston Teacher Training College*.

ESP> Los datos para las bibliotecas de instituciones de enseñanza superior se refieren solamente a la biblioteca del *Erdiston Teacher Training College*.

Belize:

E--> The public library also serves as the national library.

FR-> La bibliothèque publique remplit également la fonction de bibliothèque nationale.

ESP> La biblioteca pública desempeña al mismo tiempo la función de biblioteca nacional.

British Virgin Islands:

E--> The public library also serves as the national library.

FR-> La bibliothèque publique remplit également la fonction de bibliothèque nationale.

ESP> La biblioteca pública desempeña al mismo tiempo la función de biblioteca nacional.

Canada:

E--> Data for public libraries refer only to libraries financed by public authorities.

FR-> Les données relatives aux bibliothèques publiques se réfèrent seulement aux bibliothèques financées par les pouvoirs publics.

ESP> Los datos relativos a las bibliotecas públicas se refieren sólo a las bibliotecas financiadas por los poderes públicos.

Cuba:

E--> Data on libraries of institutions of higher education refer only to main or central university libraries.

FR-> Les données pour les bibliothèques d'établissements d'enseignement supérieur se réfèrent seulement aux bibliothèques universitaires principales ou centrales.

ESP> Los datos relativos a las bibliotecas de instituciones de enseñanza superior se refieren solamente a las bibliotecas universitarias principales o centrales.

Guadeloupe:

E--> Data on libraries of institutions of higher education refer to the only one universitary library for Antilles and French Guiana. Data are also counted with those for France.

FR-> Les données relatives aux bibliothèques d'établissements d'enseignement supérieur se rèfèrent à la seule bibliothèque universitaire des Antilles et de la Guyane française. Les données sont également comptées avec celle de la France.

ESP> Los datos relativos a las bibliotecas de instituciones de enseñanza superior se refieren solamente a la biblioteca universitaria para las Antillas y la Guyana Francesa. Los datos se cuentan igualmente con los de Francia.

Trinidad and Tobago:

E--> Data on libraries of institutions of higher education refer only to the main or central library of the University of the West Indies in St Augustine.

FR-> Les données relatives aux bibliothèques d'établissements d'enseignement supérieur se réfèrent seulement à la bibliothèque principale ou centrale de l'Université de *West Indies* à St. Augustine.

ESP> Los datos relativos a las bibliotecas de instituciones de enseñanza superior se refieren solamente a la biblioteca principal o central de la Universidad de *West Indies*„ a St Augustine.

Turks and Caicos Islands:

E--> The public library also serves as the national library.

FR-> La bibliothèque publique remplit également la fonction de bibliothèque nationale.

ESP> La biblioteca pública desempeña al mismo tiempo la función de biblioteca nacional.

ASIA:

Bahrain:

E--> Data on libraries of institutions of higher education refer only to the library of the University *Ahmed Al-Farsi*.

FR-> Les données relatives aux bibliothèques d'établissements d'enseignement supérieur se réfèrent seulement à la bibliothèque de l'université de *Ahmed Al-Farsi*.

Libraries by category 7.1
Bibliothèques par catégorie
Bibliotecas por categoría

ESP> Los datos relativos a las bibliotecas de instituciones de enseñanza superior se refieren solamente a la biblioteca de la universidad *Ahmed Al-Farsi*.

China:

E--> The figure in column 5 on libraries of institutions of higher education refers to the number of titles only.

FR-> Le chiffre de la colonne 5 relatif aux bibliothèques d'établissements d'enseignement supérieur se réfère au nombre de titres seulement.

ESP> La cifra de la columna 5 relativa a las bibliotecas de instituciones de enseñanza superior se refiere al nùmero de titulos solamente.

Hong Kong:

E--> The public libraries also serve as national libraries.

FR-> Les bibliothèques publiques servent également de bibliothèques nationales.

ESP> Las bibliotecas públicas desempeñan al mismo tiempo al función de las bibliotecas nacionales.

Japan:

E--> The figure in column 3 on national library refers to books only and in column 6 to the number of readers. Data on libraries of institutions of higher education refer to university libraries only.

FR-> Le chiffre de la colonne 3 de la bibliothèque nationale se réfère aux livres seulement et celui de la colonne 6 au nombre de lecteurs. Les données relatives aux bibliothèques d'établissements d'enseignement supérieur se réfèrent aux bibliothèques universitaires seulement.

ESP> La cifra de la columna 3 a la biblioteca nacional se refiere a los libros solamente y la cifra de la columna 6 al número de lectores. Los datos relativos a las bibliotecas de instituciones de enseñanza superior se refieren a las bibliotecas universitarias solamente.

Malaysia:

E--> Data on public libraries refer only to libraries financed by public authorities.

FR-> Les données relatives aux bibliothèques publiques se réfèrent seulement aux bibliothèques financées par les pouvoirs publics.

ESP> Los datos relativos a las bibliotecas públicas se refieren solamente a las bibliotecas financiadas por los poderes públicos.

Mongolia:

E--> Data on libraries of institutions of higher education refer to main or central university libraries only.

FR-> Les données relatives aux bibliothèques d'enseignement supérieur se réfèrent aux bibliothèques universitaires principales ou centrales seulement.

ESP> Los datos relativos a las bibliotecas de instituciones de enseñanza superior se refieren a las bibliotecas universitarias principales o centrales solamente.

Oman:

E--> Data on libraries of institutions of higher education refer to main or central university libraries only.

FR-> Les données relatives aux bibliothèques d'établissements d'enseignement supérieur se réfèrent aux bibliothèques universitaires principales ou centrales seulement.

ESP> Los datos relativos a las bibliotecas de instituciones de enseñanza superior se refieren a las bibliotecas universitarias principales o centrales solamente.

Singapore:

E--> The national library also serves as a public library and the figure in column 4 on libraries of institutions of higher education refers to 4 libraries only.

FR-> La bibliothèque nationale sert également de bibliothèque publique et le chiffre de la colonne 4 relatif aux bibliothèques d'enseignement superieur se réfère à 4 bibliothèques seulement.

ESP> La biblioteca nacional desempeña al mismo tiempo al función de biblioteca pública y la cifra de la columna 4 relativa a las bibliotecas de instituciones de enseñanza superior se refiere a 4 bibliotecas solamente.

Syrian Arab Republic:

E--> Data on libraries of institutions of higher education refer to the University of Damascus only.

FR-> Les données relatives aux bibliothèques d'établissements d'enseignement supérieur se réfèrent à l'Université de Damas seulement.

ESP> Los datos para las bibliotecas de instituciones de enseñanza superior se refieren a la Universidad de Damasco solamente.

EUROPE:

Austria:

E--> Data on libraries of institutions of higher education refer to 19 main or central university libraries, to an unknown number of libraries of institutes or departments and to 2 libraries of institutions of higher education which are not part of a university.

FR-> Les données relatives aux bibliothèques d'enseignement supérieur se réfèrent à 19 bibliothèques universitaires principales ou centrales, à un nombre inconnu de bibliothèques d'instituts ou

de départements et à 2 bibliothèques d'instituts d'établissements d'enseignement supérieur ne faisant pas partie d'une université.

ESP> Los datos relativos a las bibliotecas de las instituciones de enseñanza superior se refieren a 19 bibliotecas principales o centrales, a un nùmero desconocido de bibliotecas de institutos o departamentos y a 2 bibliotecas de institutos de instituciones de enseñanza superior que no forman parte de una universidad.

Belgium:

E--> The figure in column 6 on national library refers to the number of readers only.

FR-> Le chiffre de la colonne 6 relatif a la bibliothéque nationale se réfère au nombre de lecteurs seulement.

ESP> La cifra de la columna 6 relativa a la biblioteca nacional se refiere al número de lectores solamente.

Czech Republic:

E--> Data on libraries of institutions of higher education refer only to main or central university libraries.

FR-> Les données relatives aux bibliothèques d'établissements d'enseignement supérieur se réfèrent seulement aux bibliothèques universitaires principales ou centrales.

ESP> Los datos relativos a las bibliotecas de las institucíones de enseñanza superior se refieren solamente a las bibliotecas universitarias principales o centrales.

Denmark:

E--> Data on libraries of institutions of higher education do not include 132 libraries which are not administered by the main library.

FR-> Les données relatives aux bibliothèques d'établissements d'enseignement supérieur ne tiennent pas compte des 132 bibliothèques qui ne sont pas administrées par la bibliothèque principale.

ESP> Los datos relativos a las bibliotecas de las instituciones de enseñanza superior no toman en consideracion 132 bibliotecas que no están administradas por la biblioteca principal.

Estonia:

E--> Data on libraries of institutions of higher education do not include libraries which are not administered by the main library.

FR-> Les données relatives aux bibliothèques d'enseignement supérieur ne tiennent pas compte des bibliothèques qui ne sont pas administrées par la bibliothèque principale.

ESP> Los datos relativos a las bibliotecas de las instituciones de enseñanza superior no toman en consideracíon las bibliotecas que no están administradas por la biblioteca principal.

France:

E--> All data refer to Metropolitan France and overseas departments. Data on non-specialized libraries refer only to the *Bibliothèque publique d'Information (BPI) de Beaubourg* and the figures in column 6 refer to the number of visitors.

FR-> Toutes les données se réfèrent à la France métropolitaine et aux départements d'Outre-Mer. Les données relatives aux bibliothèques non-spécialisées se réfèrent seulement à la Bibliothèque Publique d'Information (BPI) de Beaubourg et les chiffres de la colonne 6 se réfèrent au nombre de visiteurs.

ESP> Todos los datos se refieren a la Francia metropolitana y a los departamentos de Ultramar. Los datos relativos a las bibliotecas no especializadas se refieren unicamente a la *Bibliothèque Publique d'Information (BPI) do Beaubourg* y las cifras de la columna 6 se refiere al número de visitores.

Germany:

E--> Data on national libraries include central specialized libraries. Data on libraries of institutions of higher education refer to 235 out of 271 libraries.

FR-> Les données relatives aux bibliothèques nationales incluent les bibliothèques centrales spécialisées. Les données relatives aux bibliothèques d'établissements d'enseignement supérieur se réfèrent à 235 bibliothèques pour un nombre total de 271.

ESP> Los datos relativos a las bibliotecas nacionales incluyen las bibliotecas centrales especializados. Los datos relativos a las bibliotecas de las instituciones de enseñanza superior se refieren a 235 bibliotecas para el número total de 271.

Holy See:

E--> Data on libraries of institutions of higher education refer only to main or central university libraries.

FR-> Les données relatives aux bibliothèques d'établissements d'enseignement supérieur se réfèrent seulement aux bibliothèques universitaires principales ou centrales.

ESP> Los datos relativos a las bibliotecas de las instituciones de enseñanza superior se refieren solamente a las bibliotecas universitarias principales o centrales.

Italy:

E--> Data relating to public libraries refer only to libraries dependent of the Ministry of Culture and Environment and the figure in column 3 includes the number of volumes of books and booklets. Data on libraries of institutions of higher education refer only to main or central university libraries.

7.1 Libraries by category
Bibliothèques par catégorie
Bibliotecas por categoría

FR–> Les données relatives aux bibliothèques publiques se réfèrent seulement aux bibliothèques dépendantes du Ministère de la Culture et de l'Environnement et le chiffre de la colonne 3 inclut le nombre de volumes de livres et de livrets. Les données relatives aux bibliothèques d'établissements d'enseignement supérieur se réfèrent seulement aux bibliothèques universitaires principales ou centrales.

ESP> Los datos que conciernen las bibliotecas públicas se refieren solamente a las bibliotecas dependientes del Ministerio de la Cultura y del Medio Ambiente y la cifra de la columna 3 incluye al nùmero de volumenes de libros y de folletos. Los datos relativos a las bibliotecas de las institucíones de enseñanza superior se refieren solamente a las bibliotecas universitarías principales o centrales.

Latvia:
E––> Data on libraries of institutions of higher education refer to 15 out of 18 libraries.

FR–> Les données relatives aux bibliothèques d'établissements d'enseignement supérieur se réfèrent à 15 bibliothèques pour un nombre total de 18.

ESP> Los datos relativos a las bibliotecas de las institucíones de enseñanza superior se refieren a 15 bibliotecas para el nùmero total de 18.

Luxembourg:
E––> The figure in column 6 on national library refers to the number of readers only.

FR–> Le chiffre de la colonne 6 relatif à la bibliothèque nationale se réfère au nombre de lecteurs seulement.

ESP> La cifra de la columna 6 relativa a la biblioteca nacional se refiere al nùmero de lectores solamente.

Monaco:
E––> The national library also serves as the public library.

FR–> La bibliothèque nationale remplit également la fonction de la bibliothèque publique.

ESP> La biblioteca nacional desempeña al mismo tiempo la función de la biblioteca pública.

Netherlands:
E––> The figure in column 6 on national library refers to the number of readers only.

FR–> Le chiffre de la colonne 6 relatif à la bibliothèque nationale se réfère au nombre de lecteurs seulement.

ESP> La cifra de la columna 6 relativa a la biblioteca nacional se refiere al número de lectores solamente.

Norway:
E––> Data on libraries of institutions of higher education do not include libraries which are not administered by the main lilbrary.

FR–> Les données relatives aux bibliothèques d'établissements d'enseignement supérieur n'incluent pas les bibliothèques qui ne sont pas administrées par la bibliothèque principale.

ESP> Los datos relativos a las bibliotecas de institucíones de enseñanza superior no incluyen las bibliotecas que no están administradas por la biblioteca principal.

Portugal:
E––> Data on libraries of institutions of higher education refer only to main or central university libraries.

FR–> Les données pour les bibliothèques d'établissements d'enseignement supérieur se réfèrent seulement aux bibliothèques universitaires principales ou centrales.

ESP> Los datos relativos a las bibliotecas de institucíones de enseñanza superior se refieren solamente a las bibliotecas universitarias principales o centrales.

Slovakia:
E––> Data on libraries of institutions of higher education refer only to main or central university libraries.

FR–> Les données pour les bibliothèques d'établissements d'enseignement supérieur se réfèrent seulement aux bibliothèques universitaires principales ou centrales.

ESP> Los datos relativos a las bibliotecas de institucíones de enseñanza superior se refieren solamente a las bibliotecas universitarias principales o centrales.

Spain:
E––> The figures in column 6 on public libraries and libraries of institutions of higher education refer to registered borrowers and that on national libraries refer to the number of readers only.

FR–> Les chiffres de la colonne 6 relatifs aux bibliothèques publiques ainsi qu'aux bibliothèques d'établissements d'enseignement supérieur se réfèrent aux emprunteurs inscrits et ceux relatifs aux bibliothèques nationales se réfèrent au nombre de lecteurs seulement.

ESP> La cifras de la columna 6 relativas a las bibliotecas públicas y las bibliotecas de instituciones de enseñanza superior se refieren a los prestatarios inscritos y la cifra relativa a las bibliotecas nacionales se refiere al número de lectores solamente.

Switzerland:
E––> Data on libraries of institutions of higher education refer only to main or central university libraries .

FR–> Les données pour les bibliothèques d'établissements d'enseignement supérieur se réfèrent seulement aux bibliothèques universitaires principales ou centrales.

ESP> Los datos relativos a las bibliotecas de instituciones de enseñanza superior se refieren solamente a las bibliotecas universitarias principales o centrales.

United Kingdom:
E––> The figures in column 6 on national libraries do not include data for *The National Library of Scotland.*

FR–> Les chiffres de la colonne 6 relatifs aux bibliothèques nationales ne comprennent pas les données de la bibliothèque nationale d'Ecosse.

ESP> Las cifras de la columna 6 relativos a las bibliotecas nacionales no incluye datos de la biblioteca nacional de la Escosia.

Fed. Rep. of Yugoslavia:
E––> Data on public libraries refer only to independent libraries and those incorporated in enterprises and the figure in column 6 refers to the number of readers only.

FR–> Les données relatives aux bibliothèques publiques se réfèrent seulement aux bibliothèques indépendantes ainsi qu'a celles faisant partie des entreprises et le chiffre de la colonne 6 se réfère au nombre de lecteurs seulement.

ESP> Los datos relativos a las bibliotecas públicas se refiere solamente a las bibliotecas independantes y a las bibliotecas que forman porte de las empresas y la cifra de la columna 6 se refiere al número de lectores solamente.

OCEANIA:
Australia:
E––> The figure in column 3 on national library includes manuscripts and microforms.

FR–> Le chiffre de la colonne 3 relatif à la bibliothèque nationale inclut les manuscrits et les microcopies.

ESP> La cifra de la columna 3 relativa a la biblioteca nacionale incluye los manuscritos y las microcopias.

New Caledonia:
E––> Data refer to the only one university library for Pacific (French Polynesia and New Caledonia).

FR–> Les données se réfèrent à la seule bibliothèque universitaire du Pacifique (Polynesie française et Nouvelle Calédonie).

ESP> Los datos se refieren solamente a la biblioteca universitaria para el Pacifico (Polynesia Francesa y Nueva Caledonia).

Niue:
E––> The public library also serves as the national library.

FR–> La bibliothèque publique remplit également la fonction de bibliothèque nationale.

ESP> La biblioteca pública desenpeña al mismo tiempo la función de biblioteca nacional

Vanuatu, Republic of:
E––> The national library also serves as a public library.

FR–> La bibliothèque nationale sert également de bibliothèque publique.

ESP> La biblioteca nacional desempeña al mismo tiempo la función de biblioteca pública.

7.2 Libraries of institutions of higher education
Bibliothèques d'établissements d'enseignement supérieur
Bibliotecas de instituciones de enseñanza superior

7.2 Libraries of institutions of higher education: collections, registered users, works loaned out, current expenditure, employees

Bibliothèques d'établissements d'enseignement supérieur: collections, usagers inscrits, documents prêtés au-dehors, dépenses ordinaires, personnel

Bibliotecas de instituciones de enseñanza superior: fondos, usarios inscritos, documentos prestados al exterior, gastos ordinarios, personal

Country / Pays / País	Year / Année / Año	Administrative units / Unités administratives / Unidades administrativas	Service points / Points de service / Puntos de servicio	Collections / Collections / Fondos				
				Books/Livres/Libros		Microforms / Microcopies / Microcopias	Audio-visual documents / Matériels audio-visuels / Materiales audio-visuales	Other library materials / Autres matériels de bibliothèque / Otros materiales de biblioteca
				Number of volumes (000) / Nombre de volumes (000) / Número de volumenes (000)	Metres of shelving / Mètres de rayonnage / Metros de estantes			
		(1)	(2)	(3)	(4)	(5)	(6)	(7)
Africa								
Egypt	1989	272	272	35 790	...	9 700	6 700	57 800
Reunion‡	1990	1	1	52	2 429	1 260	...	...
Senegal‡	1994	7	...	380	13 894	2 474	1 653	145
Seychelles	1990	1	5	26	510	...	*40	...
Uganda	1993	5	10	1 096	56 300	734	...	...
Zimbabwe‡	1990	25	31	764	...	286	402	...
America, North								
Barbados‡	1993	1	1	29	365	-	453	484
Belize	1990	1	1	6	...	...	20	...
Bermuda	1989	1	1	25	...	1	760	-
Cayman Islands‡	1990	1	1	2	...	-	-	100
Costa Rica‡	1990	4	4	633	...	...	...	...
Cuba‡	1993	86	86	2 525	...	...	...	...
Guadeloupe‡	1990	1	3	90	4 195	54 000	...	...
Mexico‡	1993	1 139	1 139	12 776	...	369 889	599 571	1 857 414
Nicaragua	1990	13	18	187	...	1 146	1 392	1 111
St. Vincent and the Grenadines	1990	2	2	12	...	...	...	...
Trinidad and Tobago‡	1993	1	10	305	...	9 302	21 403	3 610
America, South								
Chile	1989	178	...	5 669	...	317 353	104 623	608 112
Asia								
Bahrain‡	1990	1	1	35	790	...	500	...
Brunei Darussalam	1990	2	3	150	...	530	2 449	1 293
China‡	1993	1 075	*5 000	406 471	...	19 653 547	1 138 072	...
Hong Kong	1990	17	33	3 370	...	...	255 048	...
Indonesia‡	1989	45	137	1 735	...	...	3 936	...

Libraries of institutions of higher education 7.2
Bibliothèques d'établissements d'enseignement supérieur
Bibliotecas de instituciones de enseñanza superior

Annual additions		Registered users	Loans to users	Inter-library loans	Current expenditure		Library employees		
Acquisitions annuelles					Dépenses ordinaires		Personnel des bibliothèques		
Adquisiciones anuales					Gastos ordinarios		Personal de las bibliotecas		
Volumes	Other materials	Usagers inscrits	Prêts aux usagers	Prêts entre biblio-thèques	Total (000)	Staff (%)	Total	Holding a diploma	Trained on the job
Volumes	Autres matériels				Total (000)	Personnel (%)	Total	Diplomé	Formé sur le tas
Volumenes	Otros materiales	Usarios inscritos	Prestamos a los usarios	Prestamos entre bibliotecas	Total (000)	Personal (%)	Total	Diplomado	Formado en ejercicio
(8)	(9)	(10)	(11)	(12)	(13)	(14)	(15)	(16)	(17)
...	...	65 900	...	...	...	...	2 413	...	...
4 375	2 961	2 961	27 000	12	1 158	...	14	4	...
7 432	...	12 906	117 664	502	75 981	...	85	35	7
2 270	...	*1 610	12 882	...	322	66	10	2	7
9 223	...	34 700	904 400	...	484 000	28	171	25	35
7 609	...	30 707	1 202 660	2 296	...	...	224	121	...
616	181	195	1 982	...	105 224	91	5	1	2
...	...	312	...	...	73	94	5	2	...
800	60	443	4 562	30	128	66	4	1	...
50	5	50	200	...	7	...	1	...	...
25 145	301	...	...	1 585	...	...	...	...	...
2 340	...	270 540	395 118	...	...	...	740	220	...
6 453	...	3 649	115 000	173	7 849	46	23	11	...
1 008 570	231 870	1 010 090	69 997 153	252 181	...	...	7 247	1 515	5 732
8 544	-	27 633	168 051	43 075	...	...	97	10	33
550	...	1 100	...	...	28	...	4	1	3
6 864	3 912	5 290	283 622	265	...	...	94	21	...
...	...	...	10 590 012	...	...	...	1 124	298	64
1 267	...	1 800	9 074	...	...	...	9	3	...
10 854	337	1 504	64 600	...	...	...	55	18	33
10 170 199	598 673	4 271 724	...	...	316 408	...	44 417	30 894	...
225 078	...	123 125	...	...	186 440	50	648	114	15
...	...	534 798	...	...	922 215	...	2 078	789	...

Libraries of institutions of higher education
Bibliothèques d'établissements d'enseignement supérieur
Bibliotecas de instituciones de enseñanza superior

Country / Pays / País	Year / Année / Año	Administrative units / Unités administratives / Unidades administrativas	Service points / Points de service / Puntos de servicio	Collections / Collections / Fondos				
				Books/Livres/Libros		Microforms / Microcopies / Microcopias	Audio-visual documents / Matériels audio-visuels / Materiales audio-visuales	Other library materials / Autres matériels de bibliothèque / Otros materiales de biblioteca
				Number of volumes (000) / Nombre de volumes (000) / Número de volumenes (000)	Metres of shelving / Mètres de rayonnage / Metros de estantes			
		(1)	(2)	(3)	(4)	(5)	(6)	(7)
Iran, Islamic Republic of	1994	113	168	2 323	...	...	...	...
Japan‡	1990	507	704	181 839	...	...	...	...
Jordan	1990	33	44	1 227	...	34 105	11 390	2 736
Korea, Republic of	1994	340	...	35 758	...	...	...	...
Lebanon	1993	72	...	*2 075	...	...	...	...
Malaysia	1990	48	73	3 412	...	1 794 904	32 320	4 786
Mongolia‡	1990	9	...	1 581	...	...	...	-
Oman‡	1993	1	4	78	1 945	176 000	...	-
Pakistan	1993	31	113	3 955	135 367	23 500	6 260	103 502
Qatar	1993	2	7	329	...	23 520	666	2 125
Saudi Arabia	1993	21	65	4 844	113 849	741 274	9 333	138 344
Singapore‡	1990	5	12	2 354	14 865	255 809	75 967	3 987
Sri Lanka	1990	11	36	829	...	5 212	1 706	5 841
Syrian Arab Republic‡	1993	1	...	10	250	...	...	...
Turkey‡	1993	212	212	5 700	...	...	73 828	216 435
United Arab Emirates‡	1990	3	22	248	11 177	...	8 560	105
Uzbekistan‡	1993	58	304	2 358	158 738	14 344	1 620	952 121
Europe								
Austria‡	1993	21	...	16 953	...	...	...	...
Belarus‡	1993	38	...	20 428	...	...	...	...
Belgium‡	1990	16	140	*5 988	*147 413	*566 649	*178 386	*179 101
Bulgaria	1993	81	...	7 520	...	11 555	32 815	312 086
Croatia‡	1992	128	136	3 433	75 073	111	35 644	77 327
Czech Republic‡	1993	58	1 149	8 551	...	...	...	...
Denmark‡	1993	20	52	12 584	290 172	7 370 601	780 069	11 738 252
Estonia‡	1993	13	27	4 815	95 004	674 356	9 537	532 014
Finland	1993	30	...	12 279	...	...	...	...
France‡	1991	73	232	...	...	...	...	...
Germany‡	1993	235	...	126 117	...	25 978 612	952 621	17 509 522
Greece‡	1990	*39	*70	6 482	*167 639	*509 297	*160 331	*802 928
Holy See‡	1990	15	28	3 216	139 168	3 691	236	125 816
Hungary‡	1993	29	...	12 803	...	...	...	...
Iceland	1991	6	6	382	11 472	...	630	...
Ireland‡	1990	*15	33	5 018	177 832	*202 498	*63 748	*319 247
Italy‡	1993	10	11	6 190	158 140	69 497	40 994	51 081
Latvia‡	1993	15	...	7 100	...	-	-	-
Liechtenstein‡	1990	1	1	*30	*783	2 252	539	3 148
Luxembourg‡	1990	1	1	269	*7 134	*21 109	*6 645	33 279
Moldova‡	1993	15	...	5 844	...	...	...	...
Netherlands	1993	369	...	25 266	721 000	1 754 000	...	...
Norway‡	1993	95	209	9 412	267 841	464 807	76 826	...
Poland	1993	126	1 027	43 182	...	1 652 721	402 111	11 384 158
Portugal‡	1993	242	343	6 279	...	75 970	85 970	315 157
Romania	1993	64	348	20 919	309 300	143 029	229 169	780 312
Russian Federation‡	1993	519	...	324 696	...	...	...	...
Slovakia‡	1993	33	546	4 738	...	...	...	...
Slovenia	1992	68	69	2 863	79 567	47 819	15 004	345 205
Spain‡	1992	648	1 131	18 618	783 100	737 569	500 858	236 873
Sweden	1991	25	...	*18 500	460 619	342 573	...	...
Switzerland‡	1993	9	...	14 427	362 308	2 274 718	775 721	98 374
The Former Yugoslav Rep. of Macedonia	1992	26	43	1 135	26 323	-	17 927	1 470
United Kingdom‡	1990	215	*860	89 832	1 804 000	*3 182 376	1 636 000	5 064 469
Federal Republic of Yugoslavia‡	1992	166	310	7 052	108 242	1 771	70 661	42 995
Oceania								
Australia‡	1994	43	231	33 000	...	5 000 000	555 000	2 005 000
Fiji	1989	7	7	65	1 905	...	...	...
Nauru	1990	1	1	1	...	...	130	...
New Caledonia‡	1990	1	2	8.6	269	4 800	...	515
New Zealand	1990	7	33	5 910	...	730 818	25 791	569 325
Niue	1990	1	1	3	70	...	...	...

Libraries of institutions of higher education **7.2**
Bibliothèques d'établissements d'enseignement supérieur
Bibliotecas de instituciones de enseñanza superior

| Annual additions / Acquisitions annuelles / Adquisiciones anuales | | Registered users / Usagers inscrits / Usarios inscritos | Loans to users / Prêts aux usagers / Prestamos a los usarios | Inter-library loans / Prêts entre bibliothèques / Prestamos entre bibliotecas | Current expenditure / Dépenses ordinaires / Gastos ordinarios | | Library employees / Personnel des bibliothèques / Personal de las bibliotecas | | |
Volumes / Volumes / Volumenes	Other materials / Autres matériels / Otros materiales				Total (000) / Total (000) / Total (000)	Staff (%) / Personnel (%) / Personal (%)	Total / Total / Total	Holding a diploma / Diplomé / Diplomado	Trained on the job / Formé sur le tas / Formado en ejercicio
(8)	(9)	(10)	(11)	(12)	(13)	(14)	(15)	(16)	(17)
...	...	280 877	...	...	...	...	630	...	...
...	...	1 370 000	16 928 000	...	...	...	11 708	...	...
36 182	6 566	51 369	913 913	...	1 998	33	351	73	183
...	...	61 559 059	45 495 895	...	101 475 898	...	3 525	...	...
...	...	...	...	...	238	...	449	57	...
383 873	115 350	...	2 189 318	-	...	...	1 754	329	...
1 100	...	20 100	...	...	...	...	100	...	...
*8 852	*5 654	*6 000	61 009	19	...	...	68	35	...
29 163	...	49 268	363 735	...	13 010	...	569	88	41
5 000	5 000	6 000	...	...	...	...	132	14	61
98 664	67 803	483 611	...	9 825	17 865	32	512	161	117
137 181	5 953	77 934	2 130 254	2 104	...	...	398	98	8
26 321	11	30 727	461 881	421	110 425	42.3	415	28	55
25	...	...	*5 000	...	8	...	2	1	1
...	...	...	...	...	254 733 000	...	1 310	263	749
34 009	1 345	12 519	...	-	7 159	...	129	19	35
940 828	8 636	263 446	14 344 031	935	3 392	26	1 602	1 060	383
459 477	...	4 094 407	2 106 042	...	308 421	...	942	...	...
636 429	...	192 683	...	11 367	...	...	1 311	784	...
65 853	...	87 400	704 766	...	*30 660	*60	*6 599	*220	...
154 190	5 908	149 946	3 324 945	...	64 257	45	498	410	88
80 464	37 209	101 500	1 102 827	1 542	179 469	...	281	234	...
208 862	...	183 834	2 714 305	42 733	47 988	...	562	...	...
275 499	136 251	116 932	2 698 232	460 042	474 740	58	1 147	332	182
130 579	11 666	67 863	3 240 020	1 250	7 395	53	505	227	...
...	...	...	3 553 000	...	...	...	...	...	...
538 000	...	858 000	...	...	...	...	3 208	...	...
3 818 000	2 842 516	1 802 862	52 450 901	...	1 117 336	69	8 941	...	...
...	...	*128 391	*1 766 360	...	33 191	60	831	*243	...
42 395	116	46 745	...	...	...	...	80	40	40
...	...	132 751	1 242 412	54 444	389 755	...	908	...	...
13 767	...	...	75 229	...	...	...	44	28	16
113 000	...	*51 049	1 164 000	...	13 433	62	441	125	...
33 578	8 540	841 644	825 914	10 234	7 325 288	...	836	100	138
221 122	...	63 814	3 437 977	...	223	...	392	...	...
...	...	*262	*9 352	...	*151	60	3	1	...
...	...	*5 321	*73 210	...	*1 376	60	5	1	...
134 444	...	...	...	1 798	...	...	201	114	...
...	...	...	4 782 000	...	...	...	2 058	...	...
336 708	132 027	236 166	1 550 210	217 263	288 492	49	852	426	426
1 071 918	318 017	988 681	7 273 253	100 956	...	...	5 842	2 118	...
200 559	28 141	349 111	790 151	3 036	1 643 597	48	960	151	323
493 736	47 595	614 000	8 948 000	...	...	...	1 059	488	...
12 478 481	...	3 730 272	272 377 965	116 748	...	...	22 118	15 366	...
104 183	...	108 334	2 084 920	17 727	61 830	53	504	455	95
80 866	14 370	211 210	1 565 921	64 287	724 847	39	313	193	53
959 271	225 648	1 647 868	7 894 738	229 703	13 629 351	58	3 567	1 163	1 085
...	...	...	2 067 025	...	399 803	62	1 198	608	*590
277 832	133 190	200 711	1 598 973	142 827	113 546	65	709	196	...
7 833	494	496 906	146	1 061	37 244	...	58	51	7
1 910 000	48 000	1 331 000	34 897 000	...	279 301	55	7 858	2 946	...
116 108	1 842	1 744 537	3 297 120	...	20 181	...	443	261	182
1 500 000	...	550 000	21 000 000	390 000	361 000	53	4 785	1 578	...
2 250	...	800	104 000	...	380	95	14	1	13
...	...	80	...	...	...	...	1	-	1
3 879	5 315	665	6 500	...	1 235	40	2	1	...
181 848	65 832	...	2 578 439	53 059	36 239	39	592	119	133
*40	...	30	*200	9	...	...	...	...	...

7.2 Libraries of institutions of higher education
Bibliothèques d'établissements d'enseignement supérieur
Bibliotecas de instituciones de enseñanza superior

AFRICA:
Reunion:
E--> The figure in column 12 refers only to loans at national level and the figure in column 13 refers to expenditure on acquisitions.
FR-> Le chiffre de la colonne 12 se réfère seulement aux prêts nationaux et celui de la colonne 13 aux dépenses pour les acquisitions.
ESP> La cifra de la columna 12 se refiere solamente a los préstamos nacionales y la cifra de la columna 13 a los gastos relativos a las adquisiciónes.
Senegal:
E--> The figure in column 12 refers only to loans at international level and the figure in column 13 does not include expenditure on employees.
FR-> Le chiffre de la colonne 12 se réfère seulement aux prêts internationaux et le chiffre de la colonne 13 n'inclut pas les dépenses pour le personnel.
ESP> La cifra de la columna 12 se refiere solamente a los préstamos internacionales y la cifra de la columna 13 no incluyen los gastos de personal.
Zimbabwe:
E--> The figure in column 12 refers to loans at international level only.
FR-> Le chiffre de la colonne 12 se réfère aux prêts internationaux seulement.
ESP> La cifra de la columna 12 se refiere a los prestamos internacionales solamente.
AMERICA, NORTH:
Barbados:
E--> Data refer to Erdiston Teacher Training College only.
FR-> Les données se réfèrent à la bibliothèque de *Erdiston Teacher Training College* seulement.
ESP> Los datos se refieren a la biblioteca del *Erdiston Teacher Training College* solamente.
Cayman Islands:
E--> The figure in column 13 refers to expenditure on acquisitions only.
FR-> Le chiffre de la colonne 13 se réfère aux dépenses pour les acquisitions seulement.
ESP> La cifra de la columna 13 se refiere a los gastos relativos a las adquisiciones solamente.
Costa Rica:
E--> The figure in column 12 refers to loans at national level only.
FR-> Le chiffre de la colonne 12 se réfère aux prêts nationaux seulement.
ESP> La cifra de la columna 12 se refiere a los prestamos nacionales solamente.
Cuba:
E--> Data refer only to the main or central university libraries and the figure in column 8 refers to number of titles.
FR-> Les données se réfèrent seulement aux bibliothèques universitaires principales ou centrales et le chiffre de la colonne 8 se réfère au nombre de titres.
ESP> Los datos se refieren solamente a las bibliotecas universitarias principales o centrales y la cifra de la columna 8 se refiere al número de títulos.
Guadeloupe:
E--> Data are also counted with those for France and refer to the only university library for Antilles and French Guiana. The figure in column 12 refers to loans at national level only.
FR-> Les données sont également comptées avec celles de la France et se réfèrent à la seule bibliothèque universitaire des Antilles et de la Guyane française. Le chiffre de la colonne 12 se réfère aux prêts nationaux seulement.
ESP> Los datos se cuentan igualmente con los de Francia y se refieren solamente a la biblioteca universitaria para las Antilles y la Guyona Francesca. La cifra de la columna 12 se refiere a los prestamos nacionales solamente.
Mexico:
E--> The figure in column 12 refers to loans at national level only.
FR-> Le chiffre de la colonne 12 se réfère aux prêts nationaux seulement.
ESP> La cifra de la columna 12 se refiere a los prestamos nacionales solamente.
Trinidad and Tobago:
E--> Data refer to the main or central library of the University of the West Indies in St. Augustine.
FR-> Les données se réfèrent à la bibliothèque principale ou centrale de l'Université de *West Indies* à St. Augustine seulement.
ESP> Lo datos se refieren a la biblioteca principal o central de la Universidad de *West Indies* a St. Augustine solamente.

ASIA:
Bahrain:
E--> Data refer only to the library of the University *Ahmed Al-Farsià* (College of Health Sciences).
FR-> Les données se réfèrent seulement à la bibliothèque de l'université de *Ahmed Al-Farsià* (College of Health Sciences).
ESP> Los datos se refieren solamente a la biblioteca de la universidad *Ahmed Al-Farsià* (College of Health Sciences).
China:
E--> The figure in column 8 refers to the number of titles and the figure in column 13 does not include expenditure on employees.
FR-> Le chiffre de la colonne 8 se réfère au nombre de titres et le chiffre de la colonne 13 n'inclut pas les dépenses pour le personnel.
ESP> La cifra de la columna 8 se refiere al número de títulos y la cifra de la columna 13 no incluye los gastos de personal.
Indonesia:
E--> The figure in column 13 does not include expenditure on employees.
FR-> Le chiffre de la colonne 13 n'inclut pas les dépenses pour le personnel.
ESP> La cifra de la columna 13 no incluye los gastos de personal.
Japan:
E--> Data refer to University libraries only.
FR-> Les données se réfèrent aux bibliothèques universitaires seulement.
ESP> Los datos se refieren a los bibliotecas universitarias solamente.
Mongolia:
E--> Data refer only to the main or central university libraries.
FR-> Les données se réfèrent seulement aux bibliothèques universitaires principales ou centrales.
ESP> Los datos se refieren solamente a los bibliotecas universitarias principales o centrales.
Oman:
E--> Data refer only to the main or central university libraries.
FR-> Les données se réfèrent seulement aux bibliothèques universitaires principales ou centrales.
ESP> Los datos se refieren solamente a los bibliotecas universitarias principales o centrales.
Singapore:
E--> Data in columns 4,6, 7 and 12 refer to 4 libraries and those in column 9 to 3 libraries. The figure in column 7 refers to computer files of 4 libraries and that in column 17 refers to libraries which are not part of university.
FR-> Les données des colonnes 4,6, 7 et 12 se réfèrent à 4 bibliothèques, celles de la colonne 9 à 3 bibliothèques. Le chiffre de la colonne 7 se réfère au nombre de fiches d'ordinateurs classés pour 4 bibliothèques et celui de la colonne 17 se réfère aux bibliothèques d'établissements d'enseignement supérieur ne faisant pas partie d'une université.
ESP> Los datos de la columnas 4,6, 7 y 12 se refieren a 4 bibliotecas y la cifra de la columna 9 se refiere a 3 bibliotecas .La cifra de la columna 7 se refiere a el número de archivar de la computador para 4 bibliotecas y la cifra de la columna 17 se refiere a las bibliotecas de instituciones de enseñanza superior que no forman parte de una universidad.
Syrian Arab Republic:
E--> Data refer to the University of Damascus only. The figure in column 13 does not include expenditure on acquisitions.
FR-> Les données se rapportent à l'université de Damas seulement. Le chiffre de la colonne 13 n'inclut pas les dépenses pour les acquisitions.
ESP> Las datos se refieren a la universidad de Damasco solamente. La cifra de la columna 13 no incluye los gastos destinados a las adquisiciones.
Turkey:
E--> The figure in column 13 refers to expenditure on acquisitions only.
FR-> Le chiffre de la colonne 13 se réfère aux dépenses pour les acquisitions seulement.
ESP> La cifra de la columna 13 se refiere a los gastos destinados a las adquisiciones solamente.
United Arab Emirates:
E--> The figure in column 13 refers only to expenditure on acquisitions.
FR-> Le chiffre de la colonne 13 se réfère seulement aux dépenses pour les acquisitions.
ESP> La cifra de la columna 13 se refiere a los gastos destinados a las adquisiciones solamente.
Uzbekistan:
E--> The figure in column 12 refers to loans at national level only.

Libraries of institutions of higher education 7.2
Bibliothèques d'établissements d'enseignement supérieur
Bibliotecas de instituciones de enseñanza superior

FR-> Le chiffre de la colonne 12 se réfère aux prêts nationaux seulement.

ESP> La cifra de la columna 12 se refiere a los prestamos nacionales solamente.

EUROPE:
Austria:
E--> Data refer to 19 main or central university libraries, to an unknown number of libraries of institutes or departments and to 2 libraries of institutions of higher education which are not part of a university. The figure in column 13 refers to expenditure on acquisitions only.

FR-> Les données se réfèrent à 19 bibliothèques universitaires principales ou centrales, à un nombre inconnu de bibliothèques d'instituts ou de départements et à 2 bibliothèques d'instituts d'établissements d'enseignement supérieur ne faisant pas partie d'une université. Le chiffre de la colonne 13 se réfère aux dépenses pour les acquisitions seulement.

ESP> Los datos se refieren a 19 bibliotecas principales o centrales, a un número desconocido de bibliotecas de institutos o departamentos y a 2 bibliotecas de institutos de instituciones de enseñanza superior que no forman parte de una universidad. La cifra de la columna 13 se refiere a los gastos destinados a las adquisiciones solamente.

Belarus:
E--> The figure in column 12 refers to loans at national level only.

FR-> Le chiffre de la colonne 12 se réfère aux prêts nationaux seulement.

ESP> La cifra de la columna 12 se refiere a los prestamos nacionales solamente.

Belgium:
E--> The figure in column 13 is shown in thousands of Ecu'S (European Currency Unit) expressed at 1990 constant prices.

FR-> Le chiffre de la colonne 13 est montré en milliers d'Ecus (monnaie européenne commune) et s'exprime en valeur constante de 1990.

ESP> La cifra de la columna 13 se expressa en millares de Ecu's (moneda común europea) en valores constantes en 1990.

Croatia:
E--> The figure in column 12 refers to loans at national level only.

FR-> Le chiffre de la colonne 12 se réfère aux prêts nationaux seulement.

ESP> La cifra de la columna 12 se refiere a los prestamos nacionales solamente.

Czech Republic:
E--> Data refer to main or central university libraries only. The figure in column 12 refers only to loans at national level, those in column 13 refer to expenditure on acquisitions.

FR-> Les données se réfèrent aux bibliothèques principales on centrales seulement. Le chiffre de la colonne 12 se rapporte seulement aux prêts nationaux et celui de la colonne 13 se réfère aux dépenses pour les acquisitions.

ESP> Los datos se refieren a las bibliotecas universitarias principales o centrales solamente. La cifra de la columna 12 se refiere solamente a los préstamos nacionales y esa de la columna 13 se refiere a los gastos para las acquisiciones.

Denmark:
E--> Data do not include 132 libraries which are not administered by the main library

FR-> Les données ne tiennent pas compte des 132 bibliothèques qui ne sont pas administrées par la bibliothèque principale.

ESP> Los datos no toman en consideración las 132 bibliotecas que no están administradas por la biblioteca principal.

Estonia:
E--> Data do not include libraries which are not administered by the main library.

FR-> Les données excluent les bibliothéques qui ne sont pas administrées par la bibliothèque principale.

ESP> Los datos no incluyen las bibliotecas que no están administrados por la biblioteca principal.

France:
E--> Data refer to Metropolitan France and overseas departments.

FR-> Les données se réfèrent à la France métropolitaine et aux départements d'Outre-mer.

ESP> Los datos se refieren a Francia metropolitana y a los departamentos de Ultramar.

Germany:
E--> Data refer to 235 libraries for a total number of 271 libraries. The figure in column 13 refers to expenditure on employees and acquisitions.

FR-> Les données se réfèrent à 235 bibliothèques pour un nombre total de 271 bibliothèques. Le chiffre de la colonne 13 se réfère aux dépenses pour le personnel et les acquisitions.

ESP> Los datos se refieren a 235 bibliotecas para el número total de 271 bibliotecas. La cifra de la columna 13 se refieren a los gastos para al personal y adquisiciones.

Greece:
E--> The figure in column 13 is shown in thousands of Ecu's (European Currency Unit) expressed at 1990 constant prices.

FR-> Le chiffre de la colonne 13 est montré en milliers d'Ecus (monnaie européenne commune) et s'exprime en valeur constante de 1990.

ESP> La cifra de la columna 13 se expressa en millares de Ecu's (moneda común europea) en valores constantes en 1990.

Holy See:
E--> Data refer only to main or central university libraries.

FR-> Les données se réfèrent seulement aux bibliothèques universitaires principales ou centrales.

ESP> Los datos se refieren solamente a los bibliotecas universitarias principales o centrales.

Hungary:
E--> Data refer only to main or central university libraries. The figure in column 13 refers to the expenditure on acquisitions only.

FR-> Les données se réfèrent seulement aux bibliothèques universitaires principales ou centrales. Le chiffre de la colonne 13 se réfère aux dépenses pour les acquisitions seulement.

ESP> Los datos se refieren solamente a los bibliotecas universitarias principales o centrales. La cifra de la columna 13 se refiere a los gastos relativos a las adquisiciones solamente.

Ireland:
E--> The figure in column 13 is shown in thousands of Ecu's (European Currency Unit) expressed at 1990 constant prices.

FR-> Le chiffre de la colonne 13 est montré en milliers d'Ecus (monnaie européenne commune) et s'exprime en valeur constante de 1990.

ESP> La cifra de la columna 13 se expressed en millares de Ecu's (moneda común europea) en valores constantes en 1990.

Italy:
E--> Data refer to main or central University libraries only. The figure in column 13 does not include expenditure for employees.

FR-> Les données se réfèrent aux bibliothèques universitaires principales ou centrales seulement. Le chiffre de la colonne 13 n'inclut pas les dépenses pour le personnel.

ESP> Los datos se refieren a las bibliotecas universitarias principales o centrales solamente. La cifra de la columna 13 no incluye los gastos de personal.

Latvia:
E--> Data refer to 15 libraries for a total number of 18 libraries.

FR-> Les données se réfèrent à 15 bibliothèques pour un nombre total de 18 bibliothèques.

ESP> Los datos se refieren a 15 bibliotecas para el número total de 18 bibliotecas.

Liechtenstein:
E--> The figure in column 13 is shown in thousands of Ecu's (European Currency Unit) expressed at 1990 constant prices.

FR-> Le chiffre de la colonne 13 est montré en milliers d'Ecus (monnaie européenne commune) et s'exprime en valeur constante de 1990.

ESP> La cifra de la columna 13 se expressa en millares de Ecu's (moneda común europea) en valores constantes en 1990.

Luxembourg:
E--> The figure in column 13 is shown in thousands of Ecu's (European Currency Unit) expressed at 1990 constant prices.

FR-> Le chiffre de la colonne 13 est montré en milliers d'Ecus (monnaie européenne commune) et s'exprime en valeur constante de 1990.

ESP> La cifra de la columna 13 se expressa en millares de Ecu's (moneda común europea) en valores constantes en 1990.

Moldova:
E--> The figure in column 12 refers to loans at national level only.

FR-> Le chiffre de la colonne 12 se réfère aux prêts nationaux seulement.

ESP> La cifra de la columna 12 se refiere a los prestamos nacionales solamente.

Norway:
E--> Data do not include libraries which are not administered by the main library.

FR-> Les données n'incluent pas les bibliothèques qui ne sont pas administrées par la bibliothèque principale.

ESP> Los datos no incluyen los bibliotecas que no están administradas por la biblioteca principal.

Portugal:
E--> Data refer to main or central University libraries only.

FR-> Les données se réfèrent aux bibliothèques universitaires ou centrales seulement.

ESP> Los datos se refieren a los bibliotecas universitarias principales o centrales.

7.2 Libraries of institutions of higher education
Bibliothèques d'établissements d'enseignement supérieur
Bibliotecas de instituciones de enseñanza superior

Russian Federation:

E--> The figure in column 12 refers to loans at national level only.

FR-> Le chiffre de la colonne 12 se rèfère aux prêts nationaux seulement.

ESP> La cifra de la columna 12 se refiere a los prestamos nacionales solamente.

Slovakia:

E--> Data refer to main or central university libraries only. The figure in column 12 refers to loans at national level and that in column 13 refers to expenditure on employees and acquisitions.

FR-> Les données se réfèrent aux bibliothèques universitaires principales ou centrales. Le chiffre de la colonne 12 se réfère aux prêts nationaux et celui de la colonne 13 se rèfère aux dèpenses pour le personnel et les acquisitions.

ESP> Los datos se refieren a los bibliotecas universitarias principales o centrales. La cifra de la columna 12 se refiere a los prestamos nacionales y esa de la columna 13 se refiere a los gastos relativos a las adquisiciones y personal.

Spain:

E--> The figure in column 10 refers to registered borrowers.

FR-> Le chiffre de la colonne 10 se réfère aux emprunteurs inscrits.

ESP> La cifra de la columna 10 se refiere a los prestatorios.

Switzerland:

E--> Data refer to main or central university libraries only.

FR-> Les données se réfèrent aux bibliothèques universitaires principales ou centrales seulement.

ESP> Los datos se refieren a las bibliotecas universitarias principales o centrales solamente.

United Kingdom:

E--> The figure in column 13 is shown in thousands of Ecu's (European Currency Unit) expressed at 1990 constant prices.

FR-> Le chiffre de la colonne 13 est montré en milliers d'Ecus (monnaie européenne commune) et s'exprime en valeur constante de 1990.

ESP> La cifra de la columna 13 se expressa en millares de Ecu's (moneda común europea) en valores constantes en 1990.

Federal Republic of Yugoslavia:

E--> The figure in column 13 refers to expenditure on acquisitions only.

FR-> Le chiffre de la colonne 13 se réfère aux dépenses pour les acquisitions seulement.

ESP> La cifra de la columna 13 se refiere a los gastos relativos a las adquisiciones solamente.

OCEANIA:
Australia:

E--> The figure in column 12 refers to loans at national level only.

FR-> Le chiffre de la colonne 12 se réfère aux prêts nationaux seulement.

ESP> La cifra de la columna 12 se refiere a los prestamos nacionales solamente.

New Caledonia:

E--> Data refer to the only one university library for Pacific (New caledonia and French Polynesia).

FR-> Les données se réfèrent à la seule bibliothèque universitaire du Pacifique (Nouvelle- Caledonie et Polynésie Française).

ESP> Los datos se refieren solamente a la biblioteca universataria para el Pacifico (Nueva Caledonia y Polinesia Francesa).

Number of titles by UDC classes **7.3**
Nombre de titres classés d'après la CDU
Número de títulos clasificados por materias (CDU)

7.3 Book production: number of titles by UDC classes

Edition de livres: nombre de titres classés d'après la CDU

Edición de libros: número de títulos clasificados por materias según la CDU

Country / Pays / País	Year / Année / Año	Total / Total / Total	Gener-alities / Généra-lités / Genera-lidades	Philos-ophy / Philo-sophie / Filo-sofía	Religion / Religion / Religión	Social sciences / Sciences sociales / Ciencias sociales	Phil-ology / Philo-logie / Filo-logía	Pure sciences / Sciences pures / Ciencias puras	Applied sciences / Sciences appl. / Ciencias aplicadas	Arts / Arts / Artes	Litera-ture / Litté-rature / Litera-tura	Geog./ history / Géogr./ histoire / Geogr./ histopria
		(1)	(2)	(3)	(4)	(5)	(6)	(7)	(8)	(9)	(10)	(11)
Africa												
Algeria	1992	506	18	10	42	153	28	71	77	19	54	34
	1994	323	22	21	9	97	4	42	14	10	72	32
Benin‡	1992	647	10	4	-	534	7	12	77	-	-	3
	1994	84	5	-	1	22	6	6	37	1	5	1
Egypt‡	1993	3 108	289	58	329	220	238	190	280	118	378	176
Eritrea	1993	106	-	-	-	37	33	29	7	-	-	-
Gambia	1994	21	-	-	4	5	4	6	1	-	-	1
Ghana	1992	28	-	1	6	7	3	-	5	2	4	-
Madagascar‡	1992	85	-	2	33	25	-	1	13	1	7	3
	1993	143	1	3	25	47	12	8	23	-	14	10
	1994	114	-	6	37	29	6	6	11	-	11	8
Malawi	1992	189	12	-	15	75	7	19	31	6	15	9
	1003	206	12	-	29	56	8	13	53	4	20	11
	1994	243	10	-	41	92	11	11	40	10	24	4
Mauritius	1992	80	1	1	3	21	13	5	5	1	20	10
	1993	96	1	1	2	24	30	7	5	-	23	3
	1994	84	9	1	1	35	3	1	6	1	15	12
Morocco‡	1994	354	21	4	40	128	./.	2	24	8	76	51
Nigeria	1992	1 562	55	14	142	733	104	71	196	30	148	69
Reunion	1992	69	1	-	-	20	-	4	5	12	14	13
South Africa	1992	4 738	176	41	661	1 203	225	312	808	210	870	232
	1993	4 751	123	35	584	1 080	332	345	938	173	966	175
	1994	4 574	116	40	491	1 034	315	363	911	189	907	208
Tunisia‡	1992	1 165	130	100	35	194	-	68	108	20	310	200
	1993	539	10	12	13	69	2	3	18	5	116	31
Uganda‡	1992	162	4	2	-	77	-	-	78	-	-	1
	1993	314	-	-	4	10	43	35	14	-	4	11
Zaire‡	1992	64	-	1	30	27	-	-	5	-	-	1
Zimbabwe	1992	232	6	-	15	107	15	3	48	7	24	7
America, North												
Belize‡	1993	70	-	-	-	4	-	1	-	-	6	3
Canada‡	1993	22 208	528	340	409	6 188	425	940	2 409	794	3 196	1 101
Costa Rica‡	1994	963	21	11	38	474	15	45	113	34	162	50

7.3 Number of titles by UDC classes
Nombre de titres classés d'après la CDU
Número de títulos clasificados por materias (CDU)

Country / Pays / País	Year / Année / Año	Total / Total / Total	Gener-alities / Généra-lités / Genera-lidades	Philos-ophy / Philo-sophie / Filo-sofía	Religion / Religion / Religión	Social sciences / Sciences sociales / Ciencias sociales	Phil-ology / Philo-logie / Filo-logía	Pure sciences / Sciences pures / Ciencias puras	Applied sciences / Sciences appl. / Ciencias aplicadas	Arts / Arts / Artes	Litera-ture / Litté-rature / Litera-tura	Geog./history / Géogr./histoire / Geogr./histopria
		(1)	(2)	(3)	(4)	(5)	(6)	(7)	(8)	(9)	(10)	(11)
Cuba	1992	957	46	16	5	241	18	48	161	54	344	24
	1993	568	25	14	2	134	-	34	112	25	214	8
	1994	932	77	7	5	85	22	14	414	44	254	10
Honduras	1993	22	-	-	1	6	1	-	-	-	11	3
Trinidad and Tobago‡	1993	26	-	-	-	26	-	-	-	-	-	-
United States‡	1992	49 276	2 153	1 806	2 540	10 147	617	2 729	8 144	2 851	8 816	4 329
	1993	49 757	1 870	1 764	2 633	10 379	699	2 678	8 222	3 063	8 592	4 388
	1994	51 863	2 208	1 741	2 730	11 072	700	3 021	8 384	3 146	8 836	4 704
America, South												
Argentina‡	1992	5 628	144	338	407	1 571	53	108	572	358	1 712	365
	1994	9 065	279	996	607	2 594	86	28	920	404	2 778	373
Brazil‡	1992	27 557	1 749	1 388	3 175	5 022	376	352	683	391	3 037	721
	1993	20 141	1 480	1 225	3 005	4 430	919	1 451	2 355	491	3 713	1 072
	1994	21 574	2 013	2 281	2 823	5 629	941	773	2 341	1 051	2 358	1 364
Chile	1992	1 820	13	59	127	587	34	58	183	43	548	168
Ecuador‡	1994	11	-	-	-	-	1	-	-	1	9	-
Guyana‡	1994	33	-	-	-	5	9	10	9	-	-	-
Paraguay	1993	152	11	2	4	71	6	4	14	2	28	10
Peru	1992	1 657	52	39	45	540	47	86	316	130	222	180
	1993	2 106	68	87	60	743	51	99	354	150	303	191
	1994	1 993	65	81	59	697	39	88	321	111	328	204
Venezuela‡	1992	3 879	86	130	121	935	79	275	843	386	680	344
	1993	3 934	129	147	86	1 038	57	203	960	324	749	241
	1994	3 660	147	141	138	1 003	86	160	794	301	625	265
Asia												
Armenia‡	1994	224	-	4	3	19	17	15	14	10	84	28
Azerbaijan	1992	599	9	15	9	131	25	36	63	13	241	57
	1994	375	12	11	20	157	17	1	20	4	128	5
Brunei Darussalam‡	1992	45	4	3	7	24	2	2	1	1	-	1
China‡	1993	92 972	3 098	1 222	./.	48 796	2 724	3 248	15 311	5 560	9 488	3 525
	1994	100 951	3 013	1 156	./.	55 380	3 175	3 673	15 783	5 350	9 735	3 686
Cyprus	1992	900	37	11	69	210	41	19	197	79	191	46
	1993	942	24	7	68	223	32	26	250	61	209	42
	1994	1 040	25	4	62	241	25	16	244	95	285	43
Georgia‡	1994	314	-	11	12	41	30	16	33	9	137	25
India	1992	15 778	231	418	907	3 254	200	463	4 747	366	3 887	1 305
	1993	12 768	219	399	769	3 399	196	543	1 441	356	4 309	1 040
	1994	11 460	307	412	848	2 188	233	584	1 183	297	4 350	1 058
Indonesia‡	1992	6 303	191	148	892	1 192	294	186	788	64	231	246
Iran, Islamic Republic of‡	1992	6 822	346	372	1 009	585	629	451	967	402	1 620	441
	1994	10 753	341	404	1 932	998	910	617	1 319	439	1 849	603
Israel‡	1992	4 608	58	104	543	489	282	289	231	81	1 488	370
Japan‡	1992	35 496	539	1 539	638	8 529	917	1 142	6 276	5 532	8 525	1 859
Jordan‡	1992	790	-	3	64	299	1	109	5	29	251	17
	1993	500	15	11	77	115	14	13	37	10	136	72
Kazakstan‡	1992	1 226	-	21	16	293	85	117	313	23	304	54
	1994	1 148	-	24	17	342	69	49	158	51	222	65
Korea, Rep. of	1992	27 889	3 044	659	2 063	2 635	1 741	1 491	2 880	5 954	6 270	1 152
	1993	30 861	633	803	2 068	4 925	2 217	1 767	3 589	6 281	7 230	1 348
	1994	34 204	579	640	1 844	6 584	2 371	2 025	3 856	6 315	8 885	1 105
Kuwait‡	1992	196	17	5	17	18	-	102	6	15	13	3
Kyrgyzstan	1994	328	31	2	3	193	16	3	29	5	46	-

Number of titles by UDC classes **7.3**
Nombre de titres classés d'après la CDU
Número de títulos clasificados por materias (CDU)

Country / Pays / País	Year / Année / Año	Total / Total / Total	Gener-alities / Généra-lités / Genera-lidades	Philos-ophy / Philo-sophie / Filo-sofía	Religion / Religion / Religión	Social sciences / Sciences sociales / Ciencias sociales	Phil-ology / Philo-logie / Filo-logía	Pure sciences / Sciences pures / Ciencias puras	Applied sciences / Sciences appl. / Ciencias aplicadas	Arts / Arts / Artes	Litera-ture / Litté-rature / Litera-tura	Geog./ history / Géogr./ histoire / Geogr./ histopria
		(1)	(2)	(3)	(4)	(5)	(6)	(7)	(8)	(9)	(10)	(11)
Lao People's Dem. Rep.‡	1992	64	-	-	1	7	11	-	6	-	36	3
Malaysia	1993	3 799	56	29	288	480	709	309	323	141	1 292	172
	1994	4 050	53	25	488	716	883	413	291	122	827	232
Mongolia‡	1992	285	26	12	5	36	6	17	20	9	135	19
Myanmar‡	1992	3 785	11	78	720	18	./.	66	26	1 274	1 584	8
	1993	3 660	-	73	713	26	./.	82	22	1 171	1 551	22
Oman‡	1992	24	1	-	3	-	9	-	1	-	-	10
Pakistan‡	1992	70	10	-	-	14	-	14	4	-	6	4
	1993	247	2	9	20	16	46	74	25	-	37	18
	1994	124	51	2	1	8	18	12	17	-	12	3
Philippines‡	1992	1 016	78	4	6	735	13	13	88	11	58	10
	1994	1 233	36	13	51	323	70	45	159	187	47	45
Qatar	1992	372	23	14	31	186	19	36	24	11	17	11
	1993	368	11	6	42	141	19	63	43	8	17	18
	1994	371	23	6	26	149	15	60	41	4	11	36
Sri Lanka	1992	4 225	263	46	312	2 209	179	71	400	75	531	139
	1993	3 204	298	41	279	1 446	132	59	231	84	509	125
	1994	2 929	218	32	251	1 601	88	58	211	49	297	124
Syrian Arab Republic‡	1992	598	144	24	62	79	13	1	89	25	112	49
Tajikistan‡	1994	231	-	3	1	24	7	16	47	8	60	22
Thailand	1992	7 626	413	189	302	2 341	234	591	2 235	443	457	421
Turkey‡	1992	6 549	159	204	526	1 591	176	140	811	236	1 371	463
	1993	5 978	74	129	385	1 459	117	144	712	230	1 238	454
	1994	4 473	332	143	309	1 329	82	63	544	147	1 237	287
Turkmenistan	1992	565	47	5	6	147	21	72	74	18	136	39
United Arab Emirates‡	1992	302	10	3	46	20	85	99	9	3	-	27
	1993	293	-	3	68	2	83	99	9	2	-	27
Uzbekistan‡	1992	1 267	4	150	./.	72	86	./.	188	./.	407	./.
	1993	1 340	./.	118	./.	54	71	./.	136	./.	605	./.
Viet Nam‡	1992	4 707	./.	./.	./.	683	./.	./.	603	./.	1 024	./.
	1993	5 581	./.	./.	./.	647	./.	./.	646	./.	1 502	./.
Europe												
Andorra‡	1992	56	3	-	1	15	1	3	4	7	10	12
	1994	57	-	-	-	24	-	3	4	5	15	6
Austria‡	1992	4 986	156	193	164	1 552	124	449	501	528	919	400
	1993	5 628	171	175	167	1 813	167	585	613	585	908	444
	1994	7 987	229	246	284	2 758	229	847	703	922	1 181	588
Belarus	1992	2 364	112	41	27	665	123	140	674	80	418	84
	1993	2 926	151	45	144	711	168	142	690	110	667	98
	1994	3 346	161	68	184	790	169	187	792	77	813	105
Bulgaria	1992	4 773	127	151	146	814	1	264	729	145	2 191	205
	1993	5 771	194	236	211	1 016	157	275	821	154	2 448	259
	1994	5 925	252	270	165	1 176	130	236	798	156	2 445	297
Croatia‡	1993	2 094	39	50	166	453	59	88	412	65	448	75
	1994	2 671	44	94	220	679	68	102	463	158	608	58
Czech Republic	1992	6 743	330	178	244	1 045	353	684	1 107	423	1 981	398
	1993	8 203	299	252	267	1 849	358	636	1 111	382	2 465	584
	1994	9 309	302	283	331	1 458	305	806	1 164	511	3 498	651
Denmark	1992	11 761	271	510	316	2 225	361	932	2 723	773	2 505	1 145
	1993	11 492	339	485	269	2 188	339	891	2 794	714	2 367	1 106
	1994	11 973	403	503	332	2 377	293	964	2 859	767	2 366	1 109
Estonia	1992	1 557	63	42	73	320	-	161	314	87	437	60
	1993	1 965	87	50	58	412	-	174	290	140	631	123
	1994	2 291	125	52	75	517	-	194	393	140	667	128
Finland	1992	11 033	291	181	456	2 603	403	1 080	2 774	761	1 816	668
	1993	11 785	319	245	319	2 862	346	1 108	3 196	794	1 738	858
	1994	12 539	320	230	341	3 066	405	1 209	3 167	828	1 861	1 112

Number of titles by UDC classes
Nombre de titres classés d'après la CDU
Número de títulos clasificados por materias (CDU)

Country / Pays / País	Year / Année / Año	Total / Total / Total	Generalities / Généralités / Generalidades	Philosophy / Philosophie / Filosofía	Religion / Religion / Religión	Social sciences / Sciences sociales / Ciencias sociales	Philology / Philologie / Filología	Pure sciences / Sciences pures / Ciencias puras	Applied sciences / Sciences appl. / Ciencias aplicadas	Arts / Arts / Artes	Literature / Littérature / Literatura	Geog./ history / Géogr./ histoire / Geogr./ histopria
		(1)	(2)	(3)	(4)	(5)	(6)	(7)	(8)	(9)	(10)	(11)
France	1992	45 379	755	1 642	1 402	13 062	1 040	2 038	5 094	3 525	11 659	5 162
	1993	41 234	731	1 890	1 322	7 893	1 010	1 971	5 578	3 308	12 401	5 130
	1994	45 311	1 029	2 053	1 407	8 306	1 029	2 140	6 226	3 538	13 524	6 059
Germany‡	1992	67 277	5 914	3 132	3 595	15 104	./.	2 141	9 441	5 734	13 426	8 790
	1993	67 206	6 126	3 403	3 620	14 816	-	2 326	9 688	5 743	12 501	8 983
	1994	70 643	6 255	3 594	3 815	16 259	-	2 532	10 062	5 797	13 015	9 314
Holy See‡	1992	205	5	37	117	31	7	-	-	-	-	8
Hungary	1992	8 536	249	237	312	1 432	439	557	1 711	551	2 452	596
	1993	9 170	264	286	368	1 418	454	565	1 669	601	2 876	669
	1994	10 108	261	342	421	1 499	459	636	1 764	737	3 193	796
Iceland	1992	1 649	34	19	52	273	150	144	192	130	491	164
	1993	1 327	38	34	42	207	96	103	172	77	429	129
	1994	1 429	36	22	37	276	123	110	166	124	382	153
Italy	1992	29 351	880	1 678	1 752	6 223	612	1 042	3 613	3 620	7 143	2 788
	1993	30 110	1 107	1 623	1 767	6 134	720	1 111	3 590	3 459	7 678	2 921
	1994	32 673	800	1 751	2 013	6 039	824	1 140	3 687	3 429	8 978	4 012
Latvia‡	1992	1 509	67	50	74	169	72	64	283	66	361	77
	1993	1 614	62	30	57	206	70	61	197	69	428	118
	1994	1 677	49	59	77	222	53	36	144	50	529	66
Lithuania	1992	2 361	179	71	66	416	130	189	559	127	500	124
	1993	2 224	168	57	73	434	155	177	437	76	516	131
	1994	2 885	197	68	110	520	155	185	571	138	787	154
Luxembourg	1992	586	44	9	10	240	2	9	61	108	48	55
	1993	640	19	-	11	292	5	7	85	118	46	57
	1994	681	64	13	15	246	2	19	49	118	67	88
Malta	1992	395	9	7	76	155	17	6	17	22	34	52
	1993	417	8	11	80	163	18	4	16	29	41	47
Moldova	1992	802	24	13	12	174	27	57	204	20	225	46
	1993	354	-	3	5	48	27	48	71	17	84	51
	1994	797	11	18	24	364	23	35	171	19	100	32
Netherlands‡	1992	15 997	71	628	833	1 701	233	358	2 502	874	3 251	1 393
	1993	34 067	70	710	788	1 883	334	215	2 310	2 826	2 950	1 364
Norway‡	1992	4 881	196	139	193	1 096	107	270	658	378	1 432	412
	1993	4 943	166	145	168	983	136	189	566	326	1 860	404
	1994	6 846	156	186	458	1 223	228	280	760	490	2 683	382
Poland	1992	10 727	211	333	514	1 801	423	1 000	2 147	631	2 691	976
	1993	9 788	157	354	684	1 493	414	796	1 753	495	2 668	974
	1994	10 874	212	342	566	1 785	428	939	2 190	479	2 982	951
Portugal‡	1992	6 462	92	764	./.	./.	./.	./.	373	154	1 974	./.
	1993	6 089	286	./.	./.	830	./.	./.	410	159	2 021	./.
	1994	6 667	./.	./.	./.	789	./.	401	./.	192	1 934	./.
Romania	1992	3 662	71	83	133	254	201	382	758	118	1 442	220
	1993	6 130	109	167	255	490	350	694	1 307	191	2 237	330
	1994	4 074	85	119	148	431	183	425	870	85	1 534	194
Russian Federation	1992	28 716	3 354	480	585	4 550	722	2 727	7 681	690	6 975	952
	1993	29 017	1 430	756	778	4 630	817	2 751	8 661	624	7 581	989
	1994	30 390	2 860	896	957	5 965	995	2 644	6 849	704	7 176	1 344
Slovakia	1992	3 308	75	94	197	577	147	325	850	168	734	141
	1993	3 285	73	93	212	671	165	264	713	126	817	151
	1994	3 481	63	143	164	656	139	271	774	146	938	187
Slovenia	1992	2 136	94	60	83	517	86	234	327	235	354	146
	1994	2 906	57	117	106	536	125	263	481	393	631	197
Spain	1992	41 816	1 342	1 447	1 760	7 638	1 631	2 512	5 873	3 116	12 098	4 399
	1993	40 758	1 550	1 509	1 919	8 334	1 401	2 101	5 571	3 344	11 220	3 809
	1994	44 261	1 680	1 562	1 908	8 482	1 362	2 483	5 925	3 453	13 619	3 787
Sweden	1992	12 813	305	346	404	2 451	405	912	2 696	842	3 222	1 230
	1993	12 895	336	271	502	2 394	471	902	2 894	826	3 176	1 123
	1994	13 822	317	401	577	2 722	428	919	3 038	923	3 226	1 271
Switzerland‡	1992	14 663	282	508	846	3 188	230	1 344	3 285	1 406	1 839	876
	1993	14 870	241	647	867	3 358	239	1 475	3 238	1 457	1 782	729
	1994	15 378	262	709	814	3 654	220	1 610	3 414	1 363	1 616	694
The Former Yugoslav Rep. of Macedonia	1994	672	11	10	5	363	12	18	45	23	151	34

Number of titles by UDC classes 7.3
Nombre de titres classés d'après la CDU
Número de títulos clasificados por materias (CDU)

Country / Pays / País	Year / Année / Año	Total / Total / Total	Gener-alities / Généra-lités / Genera-lidades	Philos-ophy / Philo-sophie / Filo-sofía	Religion / Religion / Religión	Social sciences / Sciences sociales / Ciencias sociales	Phil-ology / Philo-logie / Filo-logía	Pure sciences / Sciences pures / Ciencias puras	Applied sciences / Sciences appl. / Ciencias aplicadas	Arts / Arts / Artes	Litera-ture / Litté-rature / Litera-tura	Geog./ history / Géogr./ histoire / Geogr./ histopria
		(1)	(2)	(3)	(4)	(5)	(6)	(7)	(8)	(9)	(10)	(11)
Ukraine	1992	4 410	7	70	94	837	144	513	1 439	69	1 050	187
	1993	5 002	7	114	115	930	181	798	1 358	89	1 112	298
United Kingdom	1992	86 573	2 385	2 888	3 252	17 286	2 434	9 490	14 695	6 294	17 601	10 248
	1994	95 015	2 445	3 063	4 278	19 791	3 858	10 764	10 969	9 927	19 139	10 781
Federal Rep. of Yugoslavia	1992	2 618	43	42	71	775	3	110	400	308	784	82
	1994	2 799	117	62	48	908	4	76	409	165	846	164
Oceania												
Australia	1994	10 835	218	151	246	4 453	157	511	1 730	700	1 812	857
Fiji‡	1994	401	-	-	-	22	21	40	39	2	-	21

AFRICA:
Benin:
E--> Data are all first editions and, for 1992, do not include pamphlets.
FR-> Tous les ouvrages recensés sont des premières éditions et, en 1992, ne comprennent pas les brochures.
ESP> Todas las obras consideradas son primeras ediciones y, en 1992, no incluyen los folletos.
Egypt:
E--> School textbooks (809) and children's books (23) are included in the total but not in the class breakdown.
FR-> Les manuels scolaires (809) et les livres pour enfants (23) sont compris dans le total mais ne sont pas répartis par catégories.
ESP> Los libros de texto (809) y los libros para niños (23) quedan incluídos en el total pero no están repartidos por categorías.
Madagascar:
E--> For 1992, all first editions.
FR-> En 1992, tous les ouvrages recensés sont des premières éditions.
ESP> En 1992, todas las obras consideradas son primeras ediciones.
Morocco:
E--> Works on philology are distributed, without specification, among other classes.
FR-> Les ouvrages relatifs à la philologie sont distribués, sans spécification, entre les autres catégories.
ESP> Las obras relativas a la filología se desglosan, sin especificación, entre las otras categorías.
Tunisia:
E--> Data do not include pamphlets. For 1993, data refer only to first editions; school textbooks (61), children's books (129) and government publications (62) as well as 8 books without specification are included in the total but not in the class breakdown.
FR-> Les données ne tiennent pas compte des brochures. En 1993, les données se réfèrent seulement aux premières éditions; les manuels scolaires (61), les livres pour enfants (129) et les publications officielles (62) ainsi que 8 livres sans spécification sont inclus dans le total mais ne sont pas répartis par catégories.
ESP> Los datos no incluyen los folletos. En 1993, los datos se refieren solamente a las primeras ediciones; los libros de texto (61), los libros para niños (129) y las publicaciones oficiales (62) así como 8 libros sin especificación quedan incluídos en el total pero no están repartidos por categorías.
Uganda:
E--> Data do not include pamphlets and government publications but include school textbooks (94) and children's books (99) for which a class breakdown is not available.
FR-> Les données ne comprennent pas les brochures et les publications officielles mais comprennent les manuels scolaires (94) et les livres pour enfants (99) pour lesquels une répartition par catégories n'est pas disponible.
ESP> Los datos no incluyen los folletos y las publicaciones oficiales pero incluyen los libros de texto (94) y los libros para niños (99) para los cuales la repartición por categorías no está disponible.
Zaire:
E--> All first editions.
FR-> Tous les ouvrages recensés sont des premières éditions.

ESP> Todas las obras consideradas son primeras ediciones.
AMERICA, NORTH:
Belize:
E--> Data are all first editions and include 20 school textbooks, 6 children's books and 30 government publications for which a class breakdown is not available.
FR-> Les données sont toutes des premières éditions et comprennent 20 manuels scolaires, 6 livres pour enfants et 30 publications officielles pour lesquelles une répartition par catégories n'est pas disponible.
ESP> Los datos son todas primeras ediciones y incluyen 20 libros de texto, 6 libros para niños y 30 publicaciones oficiales para los cuales la repartición por categorías no está disponible.
Canada:
E--> Data include 5,878 titles (first editions only) for which a class breakdown is not available.
FR-> Les données comprennent 5 878 titres (premières éditions seulement) pour lesquels une répartition par catégories n'est pas disponible.
ESP> Los datos incluyen 5 878 títulos (primeras ediciones solamente) para los cuales la repartición por categorías no está disponible.
Costa Rica:
E--> Data do not include pamphlets.
FR-> Les données ne tiennent pas compte des brochures.
ESP> Los datos no incluyen los folletos.
Trinidad and Tobago:
E--> Data refer only to first editions of one school textbook and 25 children's books.
FR-> Les données se réfèrent seulement aux premières éditions d'un manuel scolaire et de 25 livres pour enfants.
ESP> Los datos se refieren solamente a las primeras ediciones de uno libro de texto y de 25 libros para niños.
United States:
E--> Data do not include pamphlets, school textbooks, government publications and university theses but include juvenile titles (1992: 5,144; 1993: 5,469; 1994:5,321) for which a class breakdown is not available.
FR-> Les données ne comprennent pas les brochures, les manuels scolaires, les publications officielles et les thèses universitaires mais tiennent compte des livres pour enfants (1992: 5 144; 1993: 5 469; 1994:5 321) pour lesquels une répartition par catégories n'est pas disponible.
ESP> Los datos no incluyen los folletos, los libros de texto, las publicaciones oficiales y las tesis universitarias pero incluyen los libros para niños (1992: 5 144; 1993: 5 469; 1994:5 321) para los cuales la repartición por categorías no está disponible.
AMERICA, SOUTH:
Argentina:
E--> For 1994, data do not include pamphlets.
FR-> En 1994, les données ne tiennent pas compte des brochures.
ESP> En 1994, los datos no incluyen los folletos.
Brazil:
E--> Data exclude pamphlets but include reprints. For 1992, school textbooks (2,754) and children's books (7,909) are included in the total but not in the class breakdown.

Number of titles by UDC classes
Nombre de titres classés d'après la CDU
Número de títulos clasificados por materias (CDU)

FR-> Les données excluent les brochures mais incluent les réimpressions. En 1992, les manuels scolaires (2 754) et les livres pour enfants (7 909) sont inclus dans le total mais ne sont pas répartis par catégories.

ESP> Los datos excluyen los folletos pero incluyen las reimpresiones. En 1992, los libros de texto (2 754) y los libros para niños (7 909) quedan incluídos en el total pero no están repartidos por categorías.

Ecuador:
E--> Data refer only to first editions
FR-> Les données ne se réfèrent qu'aux premières éditions.
ESP> Los datos se refieren solamente a las primeras ediciones.

Guyana:
E--> Data refer only to first editions of 32 school textbooks and one children's book.
FR-> Les données se réfèrent seulement aux premières éditions de 32 manuels scolaires et d'un livre pour enfants.
ESP> Los datos se refieren solamente a las primeras ediciones de 32 libros de texto y de uno libro para niños.

Venezuela:
E--> Data refer only to first editions.
FR-> Les données ne se réfèrent qu'aux premières éditions.
ESP> Los datos se refieren solamente a las primeras ediciones.

ASIA:
Armenia:
E--> All first editions. School textbooks (21) and children's books (9) are included in the total but not in the class breakdown.
FR-> Tous les ouvrages recensés sont des premières éditions. Les manuels scolaires (21) et les livres pour enfants (9) sont compris dans le total mais ne sont pas répartis par catégories.
ESP> Todas las obras consideradas son primeras ediciones. Los libros de texto (21) y los libros para niños (9) quedan incluídos en el total pero no están repartidos por categorías.

Brunei Darussalam:
E--> Data do not include pamphlets and refer only to first editions.
FR-> Les données ne comprennent pas les brochures et ne se réfèrent qu'aux premières éditions.
ESP> Los datos no incluyen los folletos y se refieren solamente a las primeras ediciones.

China:
E--> Works of UDC class 3 (religion) are distributed among other classes without specification.
FR-> Les ouvrages de la catégorie 3 de la CDU (religion) sont distribués, sans spécification, entre les autres catégories.
ESP> Las obras de la categoría 3 de la CDU (religión) se desglosan, sin especificación, entre las otras categorías.

Georgia:
E--> All first editions
Fr-> Tous les ouvrages recensés sont des premières éditions.
ESP> Todas las obras consideradas son primeras ediciones.

Indonesia:
E--> Data refer only to first editions. School textbooks (715), children's books (134) and government publications (272) are included in the total but not in the class breakdown.
FR-> Les données ne se réfèrent qu'aux premières éditions. Les manuels scolaires (715), les livres pour enfants (134) et les publications officielles (272) sont inclus dans le total mais ne sont pas répartis par catégories.
ESP> Los datos se refieren solamente a las primeras ediciones. Los libros de texto (715), los libros para niños (134) y las publicaciones oficiales (272) quedan incluídos en el total pero no están repartidos por categorías.

Iran, Islamic Republic of:
E--> For 1992, data do not include pamphlets. For 1994, children's books (1,201) are included in the total but not in the class breakdown.
FR-> En 1992, les données ne comprennent pas les brochures. En 1994, les livres pour enfants (1 201) sont inclus dans le total mais ne sont pas répartis par catégories.
ESP> En 1992, los datos no incluyen los folletos. En 1994, los libros para niños (1 201) quedan incluídos en el total pero no están repartidos por categorías.

Israel:
E--> Data include government publications (657) and also 16 titles for which a class breakdown is not available.
ESP> Les données comprennent les publications officielles (657) et aussi 16 titres pour lesquels une répartition n'est pas disponible.
ESP> Los datos incluyen las publicaciones oficiales (657) and also 16 títulos para los cuales la repartición por categorías no está disponible.

Japan:
E--> Data do not include pamphlets and refer only to first editions.

FR-> Les données ne comprennent pas les brochures et ne se réfèrent qu'aux premières éditions.
ESP> Los datos no incluyen los folletos y se refieren solamente a las primeras ediciones.

Jordan:
E--> Data do not include pamphlets and are first editions only. For 1992, data include 13 titles for which a class breakdown is not available.
FR-> Les données ne tiennent pas compte des brochures et ne sont que des premières éditions. En 1992, les données comprennent 13 titres pour lesquels une répartition par catégories n'est pas disponible.
ESP> Los datos no incluyen los folletos y son primeras ediciones solamente. En 1992, los datos incluyen 13 títulos para los cuales la repartición no está disponible.

Kazakstan:
E--> For 1994, data are first editions only and include 151 titles for which a class breakdown is not available.
FR-> En 1994, les données ne se réfèrent qu'aux premières éditions et comprennent 151 titres pour lesquels une répartition par catégories n'est pas disponible.
ESP> En 1994, los datos se refieren solamente a las primeras ediciones y incluyen 151 títulos para los cuales la repartición por categorías no está disponible.

Kuwait:
E--> Data refer to government publications only.
FR-> Les données ne se réfèrent qu'aux publications officielles.
ESP> Los datos se refieren qu'aux publicaciones oficiales.

Lao People's Democratic Republic:
E--> All first editions.
FR-> Tous les ouvrages recensés sont des premières éditions.
ESP> Todas las obras consideradas son primeras ediciones.

Mongolia:
E--> All first editions.
FR-> Tous les ouvrages recensés sont des premières éditions.
ESP> Todas las obras consideradas son primeras ediciones.

Myanmar:
E--> Data on philology are included with those on literature.
FR-> Les données relatives à la philologie sont comprises avec celles de la littérature.
ESP> Los datos relativos a la filología quedan incluídos con los de la literatura.

Oman:
E--> Data do not include pamphlets.
FR-> Les données ne tiennent pas compte des brochures.
ESP> Los datos no incluyen los folletos.

Pakistan:
E--> For 1992, all first editions; school textbooks (10), children's books (7) and government publications (1) are included in the total but not in the class breakdown. For 1993, data include 59 titles for which a class breakdown is not available.
FR-> En 1992, tous les ouvrages recensés sont des premières éditions; les manuels scolaires (10), les livres pour enfants (7) et les publications officielles (1) sont inclus dans le total mais ne sont pas répartis par catégories. En 1993, les données comprennent 59 titres pour lesquels une répartition par catégories n'est pas disponible.
ESP> En 1992, todas las obras consideradas son primeras ediciones; los libros de texto (10), los libros para niños (7) y las publicaciones oficiales (1) quedan incluídos en el total pero no están repartidos por categorías. En 1993, los datos incluyen 59 títulos para los cuales la repartición por categorías no está disponible.

Philippines:
E--> For 1994, data do not include pamphlets.
FR-> En 1994, les données ne tiennent pas compte des brochures.
ESP> En 1994, los datos no incluyen los folletos.

Syrian Arab Republic:
E--> Data do not include pamphlets.
FR-> Les données ne tiennent pas compte des brochures.
ESP> Los datos no incluyen los folletos.

Tajikistan:
E--> School textbooks (21), children's books (11) and government publications (11) are included in the total but not in the class breakdown.
FR-> Les manuels scolaires (21), les livres pour enfants (11) et les publications officielles (11) sont compris dans le total mais ne sont pas répartis par catégories.
ESP> Los libros de texto (21), los libros para niños (11) y las publicaciones oficiales (11) quedan incluídos en el total pero no están repartidos por categorías.

Turkey:
E--> School textbooks (1992: 503; 1993: 603) and children's books (1992: 369; 1993: 433), are included in the total but not in the class breakdown.

Number of titles by UDC classes 7.3
Nombre de titres classés d'après la CDU
Número de títulos clasificados por materias (CDU)

FR–> Les manuels scolaires (1992: 503; 1993: 603) et les livres pour enfants (1992: 369; 1993: 433), sont inclus dans le total mais ne sont pas répartis par catégories.

ESP> Los libros de texto (1992: 503; 1993: 603) y los libros para niños (1992: 369; 1993: 433), quedan incluídos en el total pero no están repartidos por categorías.

United Arab Emirates:

E––> For 1993, data refer only to school textbooks.

FR–> En 1993, les données se réfèrent seulement aux manuels scolaires.

ESP> En 1993, los datos se refieren solamente a los libros de texto.

Uzbekistan:

E––> School textbooks (1992: 196; 1993: 194), children's books (1992: 61; 1993: 42) and government publications (1992: 103; 1993: 120) are included in the total but not in the class breakdown. Works not broken down are distributed among other classes without specification.

FR–> Les manuels scolaires (1992: 196; 1993: 194), les livres pour enfants (1992: 61; 1993: 42), et les publications officielles (1992: 103; 1993: 120) sont inclus dans le total mais ne sont pas répartis par catégories. Les ouvrages non répartis sont ventilés entre les autres catégories sans spécification.

ESP> Los libros de texto (1992: 196; 1993: 194), los libros para niños (1992: 61; 1993: 42), y las publicaciones oficiales (1992: 103; 1993: 120) quedan incluídos en el total pero no están repartidos por categorías. Las obras no repartidas quedan distribuidas entre las otras categorías sin especificación.

Viet Nam:

E––> Works of UDC classes indicated by the symbol ./. are distributed, without specification, among other classes for which a figure is shown. School textbooks (1992: 792; 1993: 1,370) and children's books (1992: 869; 1993: 683) as well as titles without specification (192: 736; 1993: 733) are included in the total but not in the class breakdown.

FR–> Les ouvrages des catégories de la CDU représentés par le symbole ./. sont distribués, sans spécification, entre les autres catégories pour lesquelles un chiffre est donné. Les manuels scolaires (1992: 792; 1993: 1 370) et les livres pour enfants (1992: 869; 1993: 683) ainsi que des titres sans spécification (1992: 736; 1993: 733) sont compris dans le total mais ne sont pas répartis par catégories.

ESP> Las obras de las categorías de la CDU indicadas por el simbolo ./. han sido distribuidas, sin especificación, entre las otras categorías para las cuales se ha presentado una cifra. Los libros de texto (1992: 792; 1993: 1 370) y los libros para niños (1992: 869; 1993: 683) así como títulos sin especificación (1992: 736; 1993: 733) quedan incluídos en el total pero no están repartidos por categorías.

EUROPE:

Andorra:

E––> Data do not include pamphlets.

FR–> Les données ne comprennent pas les brochures.

ESP> Los datos no incluyen los folletos.

Austria:

E––> Data do not include school textbooks.

FR–> Les données ne comprennent pas les manuels scolaires.

ESP> Los datos no incluyen los libros de texto.

Croatia:

E––> Data include titles (1993: 239; 1994: 177) for which a class breakdown is not available.

FR–> Les données comprennent des titres (1993: 239; 1994: 177) pour lesquels une répartition par catégories n'est pas disponible.

ESP> Los datos incluyen títulos (1993: 239; 1994: 177) para los cuales la repartición por categorías no está disponible.

Germany:

E––> For 1992, data on philology are included with those on literature.

FR–> En 1992, les données relatives à la philologie sont comprises avec celles de la littérature.

ESP> En 1992, los datos relativos a la filología quedan incluídos con los de la literatura.

Holy See:

E––> Data do not include pamphlets.

FR–> Les données ne tiennent pas compte des brochures.

ESP> Los datos no incluyen los folletos.

Latvia:

E––> School textbooks (1992: 118; 1993: 161; 1994: 202), children's books (1992: 107; 1993: 154; 1994: 188) and government publications (1992: 1; 1993: 1; 1994; 2) are included in the total but not in the class breakdown.

FR–> Les manuels scolaires (1992: 118; 1993: 161; 1994: 202), les livres pour enfants (1992: 107; 1993: 154; 1994: 188) et les publications officielles (1992: 1; 1993: 1; 1994: 2) sont inclus dans le total mais ne sont pas répartis par catégories.

ESP> Los libros de texto (1992: 118; 1993: 161; 1994: 202), los libros para niños (1992: 107; 1993: 154; 1994: 188) y las publicaciones oficiales (1992: 1; 1993: 1; 1994: 2) quedan incluídos en el total pero no están repartidos por categorías.

Netherlands:

E––> Data do not include pamphlets. School textbooks (1992: 2,196; 1993: 11,002) and children's books (1992: 1,954; 1993: 9,615) are included in the total but not in the class breakdown.

FR–> Les données n'incluent pas les brochures. Les manuels scolaires (1992: 2 196; 1993: 11 002) et les livres pour enfants (1992: 1 954; 1993: 9 615) sont compris dans le total mais ne sont pas répartis par catégories.

ESP> Los datos no incluyen los folletos. Los libros de texto (1992: 2 196; 1993: 11 002) y los libros para niños (1992: 1 954; 1993: 9 615) quedan incluídos en el total pero no están repartidos por categorías.

Norway:

E––> Data do not include school textbooks and government publications.

FR–> Les données n'incluent pas les manuels scolaires et les publications officielles.

ESP> Los datos excluyen los libros de texto y las publicaciones oficiales.

Portugal:

E––> Works of UDC classes indicated by the symbol ./. are distributed, without specification, among other classes for which a figure is shown. Data exclude pamphlets but include reprints. School textbooks (1992: 1,606; 1993: 1,391 1994: 1,381), children's books (1992: 1,042; 1993: 992 1994: 1,025) and comic books (1992: 96) as well as titles without specification (1992: 361; 1994: 945) are included in the total but not in the class breakdown.

FR–> Les ouvrages des catégories de la CDU représentés par le symbole ./. sont distribués, sans spécification, entre les autres catégories pour lesquelles un chiffre est donné. Les données excluent les brochures mais incluent les réimpressions. Les manuels scolaires (1992: 1 606; 1993: 1 391; 1994: 1 381), les livres pour enfants (1992: 1 042; 1993: 992; 1994:1 025) et les bandes dessinées (1992: 96) ainsi que des titres sans spécification (1992: 361; 1994: 945) sont compris dans le total mais ne sont pas répartis par catégories.

ESP> Las obras de las categorías de la CDU indicadas por el símbolo ./. han sido distribuidas sin especificación, entre las categorías para las cuales se ha presentado una cifra. Los datos excluyen los folletos pero incluyen las reimpressiones. Los libros de texto (1992: 1 606; 1993: 1 391; 1994: 1 381), los libros para niños (1992: 1 042; 1993: 992; 1994: 1 025) y las historietas illustradas (1992: 96) así como títulos sin especificación (1992: 361; 1994: 945) quedan incluídos en el total pero no están repartidos por categorías.

Switzerland:

E––> School textbooks (1992: 344; 1993: 247; 1994: 381) and children's books (1992: 515; 1993: 590; 1994: 641) are included in the total but not in the class breakdown.

FR–> Les manuels scolaires (1992: 344; 1993: 247; 1994: 381) et les livres pour enfants (1992: 515; 1993: 590; 1994: 641) sont compris dans le total mais ne sont pas répartis par catégories.

ESP> Los libros de texto (1992: 344; 1993: 247; 1994: 381) y los libros para niños (1992: 515; 1993: 590; 1994: 641) quedan comprendidos en el total pero no están repartidos por categorías.

OCEANIA:

Fiji:

E––> Data refer only to books published by the Ministry of Education and the Government printing department. School textbooks (223) and government publications (33) are included in the total but not in the class breakdown.

FR–> Les données se réfèrent seulement aux livres publiés par le Ministère de l'Education et le *Government printing department*. Les manuels scolaires (223) et les publications officielles (33) sont compris dans le total mais ne sont pas répartis par catégories.

ESP> Los datos se refieren solamente a los libros publicados por el Ministerio de Educación y el *Government printing department*. Los libros de texto (223) y las publicaciones oficiales (33) quedan incluídos en el total pero no están repartidos por categorías.

7.4 Number of titles by subject group
Nombre de titres par groupes de sujets
Número de títulos por categorías de temas

7.4 Book production: number of titles by subject group

Edition de livres: nombre de titres par groupes de sujets

Edición de libros: número de títulos por categorías de temas

All editions: First editions and re-editions Toutes éditions: Premières éditions et rééditions Todas ediciones: Primeras ediciones y reediciones		First editions only Premières éditions seulement Primeras ediciones solamente	
Total (books and pamphlets) Total (livres et brochures) Total (libros y folletos)	of which: books dont: livres del cual: libros	Total (books and pamphlets) Total (livres et brochures) Total (libros y folletos)	of which: books dont: livres del cual: libros

For the subject breakdown, based upon the Universal Decimal Classification (UDC), see section 2 of the introductory text to this chapter.

Pour la ventilation par sujet, fondée sur la classification décimale (CDU), voir la section 2 du texte d'introduction à ce chapitre.

Para la repartición por tema, basada en la clasificación decimal universal (CDU), véase la sección 2 del texto de introducción a este capítulo.

Africa

Subject group Groupe de sujets Categoría de temas	Algeria (1994)				Benin‡ (1994)			
	All editions		First editions		All editions		First editions	
	Total	of which: books	Total	of which: books	Total	of which: books	Total	of which: books
Total	323	322	284	283	84	83	84	83
1. Generalities	22	22	17	17	5	5	5	5
2. Philosophy, psychology	21	21	21	21	-	-	-	-
3. Religion, theology	9	9	9	9	1	1	1	1
4. Sociology, statistics	9	9	9	9	4	4	4	4
5. Political science	37	37	10	10	14	14	14	14
6. Law, public administration	30	30	30	30	1	1	1	1
7. Military art	-	-	-	-	-	-	-	-
8. Education, leisure	13	13	13	13	2	1	2	1
9. Trade, transport	7	7	5	5	1	1	1	1
10. Ethnography, folklore	1	1	1	1	-	-	-	-
11. Linguistics, philology	4	3	4	3	6	6	6	6
12. Mathematics	31	31	28	28	6	6	6	6
13. Natural sciences	11	11	11	11	./.	./.	./.	./.
14. Medical sciences	-	-	-	-	32	32	32	32
15. Engineering, crafts	8	8	6	6	-	-	-	-
16. Agriculture	5	5	5	5	5	5	5	5
17. Domestic science	1	1	1	1	./.	./.	./.	./.
18. Management, administration	-	-	-	-	-	-	-	-
19. Planning, architecture	3	3	3	3	-	-	-	-
20. Plastic arts	2	2	2	2	./.	./.	./.	./.
21. Performing arts	-	-	-	-	1	1	1	1
22. Games, sports	5	5	5	5	./.	./.	./.	./.
23. Literature								
(A) History and criticism	17	17	17	17	./.	./.	./.	./.
(B) Literary texts	55	55	55	55	5	5	5	5
24. Geography, travel	2	2	2	2	./.	./.	./.	./.
25. History, biography	30	30	30	30	1	1	1	1

Number of titles by subject group 7.4
Nombre de titres par groupes de sujets
Número de títulos por categorías de temas

Subject group / Groupe de sujets / Categoría de temas	Egypt‡ (1993) All editions Total	of which: books	First editions Total	of which: books	Eritrea‡ (1993) All editions Total	of which: books	First editions Total	of which: books
Total	3 108	2 754	1 323	1 183	106	83	25	19
1. Generalities	289	210	151	120	-	-	-	-
2. Philosophy, psychology	58	57	32	31	-	-	-	-
3. Religion, theology	329	294	152	142	-	-	-	-
4. Sociology, statistics	220	195	129	113	11	-	1	-
5. Political science	./.	./.	./.	./.	9	5	6	5
6. Law, public administration	./.	./.	./.	./.	13	10	13	10
7. Military art	./.	./.	./.	./.	-	-	-	-
8. Education, leisure	./.	./.	./.	./.	2	2	-	-
9. Trade, transport	./.	./.	./.	./.	-	-	-	-
10. Ethnography, folklore	./.	./.	./.	./.	2	1	2	1
11. Linguistics, philology	238	214	58	51	33	33	-	-
12. Mathematics	190	165	45	41	11	11	-	-
13. Natural sciences	./.	./.	./.	./.	18	18	-	-
14. Medical sciences	280	247	116	106	-	-	-	-
15. Engineering, crafts	./.	./.	./.	./.	7	3	3	3
16. Agriculture	./.	./.	./.	./.	-	-	-	-
17. Domestic science	./.	./.	./.	./.	-	-	-	-
18. Management, administration	./.	./.	./.	./.	-	-	-	-
19. Planning, architecture	118	108	51	45	-	-	-	-
20. Plastic arts	./.	./.	./.	./.	-	-	-	-
21. Performing arts	./.	./.	./.	./.	-	-	-	-
22. Games, sports	./.	./.	./.	./.	-	-	-	-
23. Literature								
(A) History and criticism	378	359	229	222	-	-	-	-
(B) Literary texts	./.	./.	./.	./.	-	-	-	-
24. Geography, travel	176	167	112	109	-	-	-	-
25. History, biography	./.	./.	./.	./.	-	-	-	-

Subject group / Groupe de sujets / Categoría de temas	Gambia (1994) All editions Total	of which: books	First editions Total	of which: books	Ghana (1992) All editions Total	of which: books	First editions Total	of which: books
Total	21	16	1	-	28	13	27	12
1. Generalities	-	-	-	-	-	-	-	-
2. Philosophy, psychology	-	-	-	-	1	-	1	-
3. Religion, theology	4	1	-	-	6	2	5	1
4. Sociology, statistics	1	1	-	-	1	-	1	-
5. Political science	-	-	-	-	1	-	1	-
6. Law, public administration	2	-	1	-	2	-	2	-
7. Military art	-	-	-	-	-	-	-	-
8. Education, leisure	1	1	-	-	3	3	3	3
9. Trade, transport	1	1	-	-	-	-	-	-
10. Ethnography, folklore	-	-	-	-	-	-	-	-
11. Linguistics, philology	4	4	-	-	3	3	3	3
12. Mathematics	3	3	-	-	-	-	-	-
13. atural sciences	3	3	-	-	-	-	-	-
14. Medical sciences	-	-	-	-	1	1	1	1
15. Engineering, crafts	-	-	-	-	4	1	4	1
16. Agriculture	-	-	-	-	-	-	-	-
17. Domestic science	-	-	-	-	-	-	-	-
18. Management, administration	1	1	-	-	-	-	-	-
19. Planning, architecture	-	-	-	-	-	-	-	-
20. Plastic arts	-	-	-	-	-	-	-	-
21. Performing arts	-	-	-	-	2	-	2	-
22. Games, sports	-	-	-	-	-	-	-	-
23. Literature								
(A) History and criticism	-	-	-	-	-	-	-	-
(B) Literary texts	-	-	-	-	4	3	4	3
24. Geography, travel	-	-	-	-	-	-	-	-
25. History, biography	1	1	-	-	-	-	-	-

7.4 Number of titles by subject group
Nombre de titres par groupes de sujets
Número de títulos por categorías de temas

Subject group / Groupe de sujets / Categoría de temas	Madagascar (1994) All editions		First editions		Malawi (1994) All editions		First editions	
	Total	of which: books	Total	of which: books	Total	of which: books	Total	of which: books
Total	114	72	110	69	243	137	158	90
1. Generalities	-	-	-	-	10	9	8	7
2. Philosophy, psychology	6	3	6	3	-	-	-	-
3. Religion, theology	37	23	33	20	41	26	25	16
4. Sociology, statistics	1	1	1	1	6	3	2	1
5. Political science	7	5	7	5	50	23	24	10
6. Law, public administration	7	2	7	2	20	9	11	7
7. Military art	-	-	-	-	1	-	1	-
8. Education, leisure	9	8	9	8	8	5	7	5
9. Trade, transport	-	-	-	-	6	4	4	2
10. Ethnography, folklore	5	3	5	3	1	1	-	-
11. Linguistics, philology	6	3	6	3	11	8	5	2
12. Mathematics	-	-	-	-	3	3	1	1
13. Natural sciences	6	4	6	4	8	4	5	4
14. Medical sciences	5	2	5	2	4	3	2	1
15. Engineering, crafts	-	-	-	-	8	2	8	2
16. Agriculture	6	4	6	4	24	10	18	8
17. Domestic science	-	-	-	-	3	2	3	2
18. Management, administration	-	-	-	-	1	1	1	1
19. Planning, architecture	-	-	-	-	-	-	-	-
20. Plastic arts	-	-	-	-	4	1	4	1
21. Performing arts	-	-	-	-	6	5	5	5
22. Games, sports	-	-	-	-	-	-	-	-
23. Literature								
(A) History and criticism	1	1	1	1	1	1	1	1
(B) Literary texts	10	7	10	7	23	14	20	12
24. Geography, travel	1	1	1	1	2	2	2	2
25. History, biography	7	5	7	5	2	1	1	-

Subject group / Groupe de sujets / Categoría de temas	Mauritius (1994) All editions		First editions		Morocco‡ (1994) All editions		First editions	
	Total	of which: books	Total	of which: books	Total	of which: books	Total	of which: books
Total	84	63	71	50	354		333	
1. Generalities	9	5	9	5	21		20	
2. Philosophy, psychology	1	-	1	-	4		4	
3. Religion, theology	1	1	1	1	40		37	
4. Sociology, statistics	1	1	1	1	15		14	
5. Political science	2	2	2	2	42		41	
6. Law, public administration	10	6	10	6	28		23	
7. Military art	-	-	-	-	8		8	
8. Education, leisure	15	14	5	4	23		21	
9. Trade, transport	-	-	-	-	8		7	
10. Ethnography, folklore	7	6	7	6	4		4	
11. Linguistics, philology	3	1	3	1	./.		./.	
12. Mathematics	-	-	-	-	./.		./.	
13. Natural sciences	1	-	1	-	2		2	
14. Medical sciences	-	-	-	-	1		1	
15. Engineering, crafts	-	-	-	-	3		3	
16. Agriculture	2	1	2	1	5		5	
17. Domestic science	1	1	1	1	5		5	
18. Management, administration	3	3	3	3	10		8	
19. Planning, architecture	-	-	-	-	1		1	
20. Plastic arts	-	-	-	-	1		1	
21. Performing arts	1	1	1	1	1		1	
22. Games, sports	-	-	-	-	5		5	
23. Literature								
(A) History and criticism	1	1	1	1	./.		./.	
(B) Literary texts	14	11	13	10	76		72	
24. Geography, travel	2	1	1	-	7		7	
25. History, biography	10	8	9	7	44		43	

Number of titles by subject group 7.4
Nombre de titres par groupes de sujets
Número de títulos por categorías de temas

Subject group / Groupe de sujets / Categoría de temas	Nigeria (1992) All editions Total	of which: books	First editions Total	of which: books	Reunion (1992) All editions Total	of which: books	First editions Total	of which: books
Total	1 562	1 022	1 536	1 002	69	50	65	49
1. Generalities	55	21	55	21	1	1	1	1
2. Philosophy, psychology	14	8	14	8	-	-	-	-
3. Religion, theology	142	82	142	82	-	-	-	-
4. Sociology, statistics	67	45	66	44	8	5	6	5
5. Political science	216	142	214	140	5	5	5	5
6. Law, public administration	206	131	205	130	-	-	-	-
7. Military art	1	-	1	-	-	-	-	-
8. Education, leisure	216	126	213	126	1	1	1	1
9. Trade, transport	24	13	23	13	3	2	3	2
10. Ethnography, folklore	3	3	3	3	3	3	3	3
11. Linguistics, philology	104	83	95	76	-	-	-	-
12. Mathematics	23	19	23	19	-	-	-	-
13. Natural sciences	48	40	46	38	4	1	4	1
14. Medical sciences	62	35	62	35	1	-	-	-
15. Engineering, crafts	24	14	24	14	-	-	-	-
16. Agriculture	64	30	64	30	1	1	1	1
17. Domestic science	4	4	4	4	-	-	-	-
18. Management, administration	42	29	42	29	3	3	3	3
19. Planning, architecture	6	6	6	6	1	1	1	1
20. Plastic arts	8	4	8	4	10	5	10	5
21. Performing arts	12	10	12	10	-	-	-	-
22. Games, sports	4	2	4	2	1	1	1	1
23. Literature								
(A) History and criticism	10	8	10	8	2	2	1	1
(B) Literary texts	138	108	134	104	12	12	12	12
24. Geography, travel	11	11	11	11	4	2	4	2
25. History, biography	58	48	55	45	9	5	9	5

Subject group / Groupe de sujets / Categoría de temas	South Africa‡ (1994) All editions Total	of which: books	First editions Total	of which: books	Tunisia‡ (1993) All editions Total	of which: books	First editions Total	of which: books
Total	4 574	2 873	4 149	2 549	539		539	
1. Generalities	116	74	103	62	10		10	
2. Philosophy, psychology	40	34	36	31	12		12	
3. Religion, theology	491	317	454	293	13		13	
4. Sociology, statistics	114	88	108	83	8		8	
5. Political science	87	54	85	52	11		11	
6. Law, public administration	298	223	273	201	30		30	
7. Military art	6	4	6	4	-		-	
8. ducation, leisure	176	110	160	95	6		6	
9. Trade, transport	262	166	248	153	7		7	
10. Ethnography, folklore	91	18	80	17	7		7	
11. Linguistics, philology	315	148	276	111	2		2	
12. Mathematics	119	97	102	80	-		-	
13. Natural sciences	244	141	204	114	3		3	
14. Medical sciences	115	91	101	78	5		5	
15. Engineering, crafts	466	128	423	118	2		2	
16. Agriculture	63	54	58	49	3		3	
17. Domestic science	134	100	122	91	-		-	
18. Management, administration	133	119	99	85	8		8	
19. Planning, architecture	9	7	9	7	1		1	
20. Plastic arts	86	65	82	65	1		1	
21. Performing arts	45	28	42	26	3		3	
22. Games, sports	49	41	33	26	-		-	
23. Literature								
(A) History and criticism	907	606	863	570	33		33	
(B) Literary texts	./.	./.	./.	./.	83		83	
24. Geography, travel	103	72	82	55	1		1	
25. History, biography	105	88	100	83	30		30	

7.4 Number of titles by subject group
Nombre de titres par groupes de sujets
Número de títulos por categorías de temas

Subject group / Groupe de sujets / Categoría de temas	Uganda‡ (1993) All editions Total	of which: books	First editions Total	of which: books	Zaire‡ (1992) All editions Total	of which: books	First editions Total	of which: books
Total	314	314	63	63	64	64	64	64
1. Generalities	-	-	-	-	-	-	-	-
2. Philosophy, psychology	-	-	-	-	1	1	1	1
3. Religion, theology	4	4	-	-	30	30	30	30
4. Sociology, statistics	-	-	-	-	4	4	4	4
5. Political science	9	9	6	6	8	8	8	8
6. Law, public administration	1	1	-	-	2	2	2	2
7. Military art	-	-	-	-	-	-	-	-
8. Education, leisure	-	-	-	-	10	10	10	10
9. Trade, transport	-	-	-	-	2	2	2	2
10. Ethnography, folklore	-	-	-	-	1	1	1	1
11. Linguistics, philology	43	43	7	7	-	-	-	-
12. Mathematics	20	20	1	1	-	-	-	-
13. Natural sciences	15	15	1	1	-	-	-	-
14. Medical sciences	5	5	-	-	3	3	3	3
15. Engineering, crafts	-	-	-	-	2	2	2	2
16. Agriculture	9	9	-	-	-	-	-	-
17. Domestic science	-	-	-	-	-	-	-	-
18. Management, administration	-	-	-	-	-	-	-	-
19. Planning, architecture	-	-	-	-	-	-	-	-
20. Plastic arts	-	-	-	-	-	-	-	-
21. Performing arts	-	-	-	-	-	-	-	-
22. Games, sports	-	-	-	-	-	-	-	-
23. Literature								
(A) History and criticism	-	-	-	-	-	-	-	-
(B) Literary texts	4	4	3	3	-	-	-	-
24. Geography, travel	5	5	2	2	1	1	1	1
25. History, biography	6	6	4	4	-	-	-	-

America, North

Subject group / Groupe de sujets / Categoría de temas	Zimbabwe (1992) All editions Total	of which: books	First editions Total	of which: books	Belize‡ (1993) All editions Total	of which: books	First editions Total	of which: books
Total	232	151	229	148	70	70	70	70
1. Generalities	6	6	4	4	-	-	-	-
2. Philosophy, psychology	-	-	-	-	-	-	-	-
3. Religion, theology	15	12	15	12	-	-	-	-
4. Sociology, statistics	8	7	8	7	1	1	1	1
5. Political science	32	17	32	17	1	1	1	1
6. Law, public administration	52	26	52	26	-	-	-	-
7. Military art	-	-	-	-	-	-	-	-
8. Education, leisure	9	4	9	4	-	-	-	-
9. Trade, transport	5	3	5	3	1	1	1	1
10. Ethnography, folklore	1	-	1	-	1	1	1	1
11. Linguistics, philology	15	12	15	12	-	-	-	-
12. Mathematics	-	-	-	-	-	-	-	-
13. Natural sciences	3	2	3	2	1	1	1	1
14. Medical sciences	7	3	7	3	-	-	-	-
15. Engineering, crafts	10	8	10	8	-	-	-	-
16. Agriculture	19	11	19	11	-	-	-	-
17. Domestic science	2	2	2	2	-	-	-	-
18. Management, administration	10	5	10	5	-	-	-	-
19. Planning, architecture	-	-	-	-	-	-	-	-
20. Plastic arts	6	4	6	4	-	-	-	-
21. Performing arts	1	1	1	1	-	-	-	-
22. Games, sports	-	-	-	-	-	-	-	-
23. Literature								
(A) History and criticism	2	2	2	2	6	6	6	6
(B) Literary texts	22	21	21	20	-	-	-	-
24. Geography, travel	3	2	3	2	-	-	-	-
25. History, biography	4	3	4	3	3	3	3	3

Number of titles by subject group **7.4**
Nombre de titres par groupes de sujets
Número de títulos por categorías de temas

Subject group / Groupe de sujets / Categoría de temas	Canada‡ (1993) All editions Total	of which: books	First editions Total	of which: books	Costa Rica (1994) All editions Total	of which: books	First editions Total	of which: books
Total	22 208		20 375		963	963		
1. Generalities	528		463		21	21		
2. Philosophy, psychology	340		295		11	11		
3. Religion, theology	409		379		38	38		
4. Sociology, statistics	541		505		33	33		
5. Political science	1 819		1 738		121	121		
6. Law, public administration	2 768		2 519		143	143		
7. Military art	38		36		2	2		
8. Education, leisure	593		547		157	157		
9. Trade, transport	323		286		15	15		
10. Ethnography, folklore	106		105		3	3		
11. Linguistics, philology	425		391		15	15		
12. Mathematics	302		260		8	8		
13. Natural sciences	638		597		37	37		
14. Medical sciences	574		500		21	21		
15. Engineering, crafts	699		539		2	2		
16. Agriculture	316		291		55	55		
17. Domestic science	238		196		23	23		
18. Management, administration	582		460		12	12		
19. Planning, architecture	185		175		1	1		
20. Plastic arts	302		291		14	14		
21. Performing arts	122		101		17	17		
22. Games, sports	185		165		2	2		
23. Literature								
(A) History and criticism	3 196		2 687		9	9		
(B) Literary texts	./.		./.		153	153		
24. Geography, travel	157		126		8	8		
25. History, biography	944		845		42	42		

Subject group / Groupe de sujets / Categoría de temas	Cuba (1994) All editions Total	of which: books	First editions Total	of which: books	Honduras (1993) All editions Total	of which: books	First editions Total	of which: books
Total	932	390	830	301	22	22	15	15
1. Generalities	77	55	67	45	-	-	-	-
2. Philosophy, psychology	7	7	6	6	-	-	-	-
3. Religion, theology	5	3	5	3	1	1	1	1
4. Sociology, statistics	13	8	12	7	1	1	1	1
5. Political science	9	8	4	3	2	2	1	1
6. Law, public administration	2	2	-	-	1	1	-	-
7. Military art	1	1	1	1	-	-	-	-
8. Education, leisure	28	21	14	7	-	-	-	-
9. Trade, transport	21	2	20	1	2	2	2	2
10. Ethnography, folklore	11	9	10	8	2	2	2	2
11. Linguistics, philology	22	16	8	4	1	1	1	1
12. Mathematics	6	6	1	1	-	-	-	-
13. Natural sciences	8	7	7	6	-	-	-	-
14. Medical sciences	372	18	368	14	-	-	-	-
15. Engineering, crafts	26	23	10	7	-	-	-	-
16. Agriculture	6	6	3	3	-	-	-	-
17. Domestic science	2	1	2	1	-	-	-	-
18. Management, administration	8	3	6	1	-	-	-	-
19. Planning, architecture	2	2	-	-	-	-	-	-
20. Plastic arts	8	5	8	5	-	-	-	-
21. Performing arts	19	14	16	12	-	-	-	-
22. Games, sports	15	5	14	4	-	-	-	-
23. Literature								
(A) History and criticism	72	49	68	49	2	2	2	2
(B) Literary texts	182	113	172	108	9	9	4	4
24. Geography, travel	4	3	2	2	-	-	-	-
25. History, biography	6	3	6	3	3	3	3	3

7.4 Number of titles by subject group
Nombre de titres par groupes de sujets
Número de títulos por categorías de temas

Subject group / Groupe de sujets / Categoría de temas	Trinidad and Tobago‡ (1993)				United States‡ (1994)			
	All editions		First editions		All editions		First editions	
	Total	of which: books	Total	of which: books	Total	of which: books	Total	of which: books
Total	26	26	26	26	51 863	51 863	42 454	42 454
1. Generalities	-	-	-	-	2 208	2 208	1 855	1 855
2. Philosophy, psychology	-	-	-	-	1 741	1 741	1 485	1 485
3. Religion, theology	-	-	-	-	2 730	2 730	2 396	2 396
4. Sociology, statistics	-	-	-	-	8 038	8 038	6 976	6 976
5. Political science	-	-	-	-	./.	./.	./.	./.
6. Law, public administration	-	-	-	-	1 168	1 168	784	784
7. Military art	-	-	-	-	./.	./.	./.	./.
8. Education, leisure	1	1	1	1	1 310	1 310	1 130	1 130
9. Trade, transport	25	25	25	25	556	556	408	408
10. Ethnography, folklore	-	-	-	-	./.	./.	./.	./.
11. Linguistics, philology	-	-	-	-	700	700	567	567
12. Mathematics	-	-	-	-	3 021	3 021	2 500	2 500
13. Natural sciences	-	-	-	-	./.	./.	./.	./.
14. Medical sciences	-	-	-	-	3 147	3 147	2 359	2 359
15. Engineering, crafts	-	-	-	-	2 085	2 085	1 668	1 668
16. Agriculture	-	-	-	-	532	532	429	429
17. Domestic science	-	-	-	-	1 004	1 004	817	817
18. Management, administration	-	-	-	-	1 616	1 616	1 254	1 254
19. Planning, architecture	-	-	-	-	./.	./.	./.	./.
20. Plastic arts	-	-	-	-	1 621	1 621	1 417	1 417
21. Performing arts	-	-	-	-	364	364	277	277
22. Games, sports	-	-	-	-	1 161	1 161	892	892
23. Literature								
(A) History and criticism	-	-	-	-	8 836	8 836	6 311	6 311
(B) Literary texts	-	-	-	-	./.	./.	./.	./.
24. Geography, travel	-	-	-	-	./.	./.	./.	./.
25. History, biography	-	-	-	-	4 704	4 704	4 069	4 069

America, South

Subject group / Groupe de sujets / Categoría de temas	Argentina (1994)				Brazil‡ (1994)			
	All editions		First editions		All editions		First editions	
	Total	of which: books	Total	of which: books	Total	of which: books	Total	of which: books
Total	9 065	9 065			21 574	21 574	7 884	7 884
1. Generalities	279	279			2 013	2 013	1 055	1 055
2. Philosophy, psychology	996	996			2 281	2 281	1 060	1 060
3. Religion, theology	607	607			2 823	2 823	1 019	1 019
4. Sociology, statistics	189	189			276	276	38	38
5. Political science	343	343			782	782	353	353
6. Law, public administration	711	711			2 642	2 642	459	459
7. Military art	9	9			-	-	-	-
8. Education, leisure	1 225	1 225			1 408	1 408	367	367
9. Trade, transport	72	72			430	430	208	208
10. Ethnography, folklore	45	45			91	91	30	30
11. Linguistics, philology	86	86			941	941	176	176
12. Mathematics	28	28			773	773	100	100
13. Natural sciences	-	-			./.	./.	./.	./.
14. Medical sciences	413	413			2 341	2 341	1 113	1 113
15. Engineering, crafts	60	60			./.	./.	./.	./.
16. Agriculture	83	83			./.	./.	./.	./.
17. Domestic science	112	112			./.	./.	./.	./.
18. Management, administration	252	252			./.	./.	./.	./.
19. Planning, architecture	28	28			1 051	1 051	446	446
20. Plastic arts	100	100			./.	./.	./.	./.
21. Performing arts	213	213			./.	./.	./.	./.
22. Games, sports	63	63			./.	./.	./.	./.
23. Literature								
(A) History and criticism	43	43			2 358	2 358	1 100	1 100
(B) Literary texts	2 735	2 735			./.	./.	./.	./.
24. Geography, travel	41	41			1 364	1 364	360	360
25. History, biography	332	332			./.	./.	./.	./.

Number of titles by subject group **7.4**
Nombre de titres par groupes de sujets
Número de títulos por categorías de temas

Subject group Groupe de sujets Categoría de temas	Chile (1992)				Ecuador (1994)			
	All editions		First editions		All editions		First editions	
	Total	of which: books	Total	of which: books	Total	of which: books	Total	of which: books
Total	1 820	1 493	422	372	11	11	11	11
1. Generalities	13	12	3	3	-	-	-	-
2. Philosophy, psychology	59	56	13	13	-	-	-	-
3. Religion, theology	127	98	26	19	-	-	-	-
4. Sociology, statistics	57	40	10	10	-	-	-	-
5. Political science	132	84	38	38	-	-	-	-
6. Law, public administration	153	137	35	31	-	-	-	-
7. Military art	-	-	-	-	-	-	-	-
8. Education, leisure	216	172	20	19	-	-	-	-
9. Trade, transport	11	9	-	-	-	-	-	-
10. Ethnography, folklore	18	17	2	2	-	-	-	-
11. Linguistics, philology	34	30	5	5	1	1	1	1
12. Mathematics	12	12	3	3	-	-	-	-
13. Natural sciences	46	42	14	13	-	-	-	-
14. Medical sciences	57	50	14	12	-	-	-	-
15. Engineering, crafts	35	14	20	5	-	-	-	-
16. Agriculture	33	23	3	3	-	-	-	-
17. Domestic science	29	17	8	7	-	-	-	-
18. Management, administration	29	27	-	-	-	-	-	-
19. Planning, architecture	6	4	7	7	-	-	-	-
20. Plastic arts	15	9	5	5	-	-	-	-
21. Performing arts	15	9	-	-	1	1	1	1
22. Games, sports	7	4	-	-	-	-	-	-
23. Literature								
(A) History and criticism	7	7	6	6	-	-	-	-
(B) Literary texts	541	465	150	133	9	9	9	9
24. Geography, travel	29	26	5	5	-	-	-	-
25. History, biography	139	129	35	33	-	-	-	-

Subject group Groupe de sujets Categoría de temas	Guyana‡ (1994)				Paraguay (1993)			
	All editions		First editions		All editions		First editions	
	Total	of which: books	Total	of which: books	Total	of which: books	Total	of which: books
Total	33	33	33	33	152	129		
1. Generalities	-	-	-	-	11	8		
2. Philosophy, psychology	-	-	-	-	2	1		
3. Religion, theology	-	-	-	-	4	2		
4. Sociology, statistics	5	5	5	5	5	4		
5. Political science	./.	./.	./.	./.	25	21		
6. Law, public administration	./.	./.	./.	./.	27	24		
7. Military art	./.	./.	./.	./.	1	1		
8. Education, leisure	./.	./.	./.	./.	4	3		
9. Trade, transport	./.	./.	./.	./.	1	1		
10. Ethnography, folklore	./.	./.	./.	./.	8	6		
11. Linguistics, philology	9	9	9	9	6	5		
12. Mathematics	5	5	5	5	-	-		
13. Natural sciences	5	5	5	5	4	4		
14. Medical sciences	-	-	-	-	1	1		
15. Engineering, crafts	3	3	3	3	-	-		
16. Agriculture	3	3	3	3	9	4		
17. Domestic science	3	3	3	3	-	-		
18. Management, administration	-	-	-	-	4	4		
19. Planning, architecture	-	-	-	-	1	1		
20. Plastic arts	-	-	-	-	-	-		
21. Performing arts	-	-	-	-	1	1		
22. Games, sports	-	-	-	-	-	-		
23. Literature								
(A) History and criticism	-	-	-	-	28	28		
(B) Literary texts	-	-	-	-	-	-		
24. Geography, travel	-	-	-	-	2	2		
25. History, biography	-	-	-	-	8	8		

7.4   Number of titles by subject group
Nombre de titres par groupes de sujets
Número de títulos por categorías de temas

Subject group Groupe de sujets Categoría de temas	Peru (1994)				Venezuela (1994)			
	All editions		First editions		All editions		First editions	
	Total	of which: books	Total	of which: books	Total	of which: books	Total	of which: books
Total	1 993	1 310	1 763	1 181	3 660	2 580	3 660	2 580
1. Generalities	65	48	51	38	147	118	147	118
2. Philosophy, psychology	81	60	68	54	141	115	141	115
3. Religion, theology	59	43	48	39	138	105	138	105
4. Sociology, statistics	167	115	134	99	231	160	231	160
5. Political science	138	106	113	87	239	181	239	181
6. Law, public administration	145	115	111	92	126	106	126	106
7. Military art	24	15	16	10	19	6	19	6
8. Education, leisure	146	98	143	96	293	230	293	230
9. Trade, transport	54	31	49	29	54	37	54	37
10. Ethnography, folklore	23	13	18	10	41	29	41	29
11. Linguistics, philology	39	23	32	20	86	56	86	56
12. Mathematics	37	21	33	19	32	23	32	23
13. Natural sciences	51	27	44	25	128	88	128	88
14. Medical sciences	115	72	109	68	144	93	144	93
15. Engineering, crafts	40	23	36	21	370	227	370	227
16. Agriculture	66	38	61	36	53	41	53	41
17. Domestic science	45	25	42	23	40	22	40	22
18. Management, administration	55	34	49	31	187	153	187	153
19. Planning, architecture	31	16	29	16	18	13	18	13
20. Plastic arts	31	18	27	16	149	91	149	91
21. Performing arts	26	15	23	13	87	54	87	54
22. Games, sports	23	13	21	12	47	22	47	22
23. Literature								
(A) History and criticism	144	98	136	95	34	14	34	14
(B) Literary texts	184	102	178	99	591	398	591	398
24. Geography, travel	59	38	56	36	21	20	21	20
25. History, biography	145	103	136	97	244	178	244	178

Asia

Subject group Groupe de sujets Categoría de temas	Armenia‡ (1994)				Azerbaijan (1994)			
	All editions		First editions		All editions		First editions	
	Total	of which: books	Total	of which: books	Total	of which: books	Total	of which: books
Total	224	197	224	197	375	329	361	315
1. Generalities	-	-	-	-	12	8	12	8
2. Philosophy, psychology	4	3	4	3	11	11	11	11
3. Religion, theology	3	2	3	2	20	15	20	15
4. Sociology, statistics	-	-	-	-	-	-	-	-
5. Political science	10	7	10	7	21	18	21	18
6. Law, public administration	4	4	4	4	5	4	5	4
7. Military art	3	3	3	3	2	2	2	2
8. Education, leisure	1	-	1	-	81	58	70	47
9. Trade, transport	-	-	-	-	3	2	3	2
10. Ethnography, folklore	1	1	1	1	45	42	44	41
11. Linguistics, philology	17	17	17	17	17	15	17	15
12. Mathematics	-	-	-	-	-	-	-	-
13. Natural sciences	15	13	15	13	1	1	1	1
14. Medical sciences	11	11	11	11	15	12	15	12
15. Engineering, crafts	-	-	-	-	3	3	3	3
16. Agriculture	-	-	-	-	2	2	2	2
17. Domestic science	3	3	3	3	-	-	-	-
18. Management, administration	-	-	-	-	-	-	-	-
19. Planning, architecture	-	-	-	-	-	-	-	-
20. Plastic arts	2	2	2	2	-	-	-	-
21. Performing arts	5	4	5	4	4	4	4	4
22. Games, sports	3	2	3	2	-	-	-	-
23. Literature								
(A) History and criticism	-	-	-	-	10	9	10	9
(B) Literary texts	84	76	84	76	118	118	116	116
24. Geography, travel	-	-	-	-	5	5	5	5
25. History, biography	28	25	28	25	-	-	-	-

Number of titles by subject group 7.4
Nombre de titres par groupes de sujets
Número de títulos por categorías de temas

Subject group / Groupe de sujets / Categoría de temas	Brunei Darussalam (1992) All editions Total	of which: books	First editions Total	of which: books	China‡ (1994) All editions Total	of which: books	First editions Total	of which: books
Total	45	45	45	45	100 951			
1. Generalities	4	4	4	4	3 013			
2. Philosophy, psychology	3	3	3	3	1 156			
3. Religion, theology	7	7	7	7	./.			
4. Sociology, statistics	-	-	-	-	987			
5. Political science	3	3	3	3	10 835			
6. Law, public administration	-	-	-	-	./.			
7. Military art	-	-	-	-	510			
8. Education, leisure	17	17	17	17	42 376			
9. Trade, transport	-	-	-	-	672			
10. Ethnography, folklore	4	4	4	4	./.			
11. Linguistics, philology	2	2	2	2	3 175			
12. Mathematics	2	2	2	2	3 673			
13. Natural sciences	-	-	-	-	./.			
14. Medical sciences	-	-	-	-	3 844			
15. Engineering, crafts	-	-	-	-	9 887			
16. Agriculture	-	-	-	-	2 052			
17. Domestic science	1	1	1	1	./.			
18. Management, administration	-	-	-	-	./.			
19. Planning, architecture	-	-	-	-	5 350			
20. Plastic arts	-	-	-	-	./.			
21. Performing arts	1	1	1	1	./.			
22. Games, sports	-	-	-	-	./.			
23. Literature								
(A) History and criticism	-	-	-	-	9 735			
(B) Literary texts	-	-	-	-	./.			
24. Geography, travel	-	-	-	-	3 686			
25. History, biography	1	1	1	1	./.			

Subject group / Groupe de sujets / Categoría de temas	Cyprus (1994) All editions Total	of which: books	First editions Total	of which: books	Georgia (1994) All editions Total	of which: books	First editions Total	of which: books
Total	1 040	557	784	489	314	261	314	261
1. Generalities	25	21	23	20	-	-	-	-
2. Philosophy, psychology	4	3	4	3	11	11	11	11
3. Religion, theology	62	33	48	28	12	8	12	8
4. Sociology, statistics	32	10	30	10	-	-	-	-
5. Political science	30	13	17	10	12	10	12	10
6. Law, public administration	16	5	10	4	5	3	5	3
7. Military art	39	1	13	1	-	-	-	-
8. Education, leisure	67	20	49	13	6	3	6	3
9. Trade, transport	45	7	33	6	3	3	3	3
10. Ethnography, folklore	12	9	11	8	15	9	15	9
11. Linguistics, philology	25	17	19	14	30	25	30	25
12. Mathematics	10	7	5	2	4	4	4	4
13. Natural sciences	6	6	3	3	12	9	12	9
14. Medical sciences	52	8	26	8	21	17	21	17
15. Engineering, crafts	36	9	33	8	6	2	6	2
16. Agriculture	115	42	30	13	6	4	6	4
17. Domestic science	14	2	12	2	-	-	-	-
18. Management, administration	27	4	14	4	-	-	-	-
19. Planning, architecture	17	5	14	5	1	1	1	1
20. Plastic arts	15	7	14	6	-	-	-	-
21. Performing arts	50	7	50	7	4	3	4	3
22. Games, sports	13	3	8	2	4	4	4	4
23. Literature								
(A) History and criticism	18	18	18	18	-	-	-	-
(B) Literary texts	267	267	263	263	137	121	137	121
24. Geography, travel	28	18	22	16	2	2	2	2
25. History, biography	15	15	15	15	23	22	23	22

7.4 Number of titles by subject group
Nombre de titres par groupes de sujets
Número de títulos por categorías de temas

Subject group / Groupe de sujets / Categoría de temas	India (1994) All editions Total	of which: books	India (1994) First editions Total	of which: books	Indonesia‡ (1992) All editions Total	of which: books	Indonesia‡ (1992) First editions Total	of which: books
Total	11 460	11 163	10 689	10 392	6 303	6 128	6 303	6 128
1. Generalities	307	305	299	297	191	100	191	100
2. Philosophy, psychology	412	412	379	379	148	148	148	148
3. Religion, theology	848	843	763	758	892	880	892	880
4. Sociology, statistics	438	438	420	420	148	144	148	144
5. Political science	850	811	837	798	417	412	417	412
6. Law, public administration	523	316	517	310	358	358	358	358
7. Military art	26	26	26	26	-	-	-	-
8. Education, leisure	173	172	153	152	181	176	181	176
9. Trade, transport	87	85	87	85	39	36	39	36
10. Ethnography, folklore	91	91	87	87	49	48	49	48
11. Linguistics, philology	233	232	213	212	294	284	294	284
12. Mathematics	170	170	163	163	64	64	64	64
13. Natural sciences	414	414	396	396	122	120	122	120
14. Medical sciences	390	387	360	357	210	210	210	210
15. Engineering, crafts	388	379	358	349	217	216	217	216
16. Agriculture	154	153	150	149	211	190	211	190
17. Domestic science	88	86	82	80	41	34	41	34
18. Management, administration	163	163	160	160	109	108	109	108
19. Planning, architecture	63	63	54	54	19	16	19	16
20. Plastic arts	41	41	41	41	7	6	7	6
21. Performing arts	149	147	134	132	19	18	19	18
22. Games, sports	44	42	41	39	19	16	19	16
23. Literature								
(A) History and criticism	1 084	1 080	988	984	143	141	143	141
(B) Literary texts	3 266	3 254	3 023	3 011	88	88	88	88
24. Geography, travel	181	181	177	177	90	88	90	88
25. History, biography	877	872	781	776	156	156	156	156

Subject group / Groupe de sujets / Categoría de temas	Iran, Islamic Republic of‡ (1994) All editions Total	of which: books	Iran, Islamic Republic of‡ (1994) First editions Total	of which: books	Israel‡ (1992) All editions Total	of which: books	Israel‡ (1992) First editions Total	of which: books
Total	10 753	10 613	5 563	5 491	4 608		1 689	
1. Generalities	341	341	203	203	58		22	
2. Philosophy, psychology	404	404	168	168	104		53	
3. Religion, theology	1 932	1 932	902	902	543		182	
4. Sociology, statistics	998	998	557	557	146		76	
5. Political science	./.	./.	./.	./.	159		88	
6. Law, public administration	./.	./.	./.	./.	62		43	
7. Military art	./.	./.	./.	./.	8		6	
8. Education, leisure	./.	./.	./.	./.	87		36	
9. Trade, transport	./.	./.	./.	./.	27		14	
10. Ethnography, folklore	./.	./.	./.	./.	./.		./.	
11. Linguistics, philology	910	910	416	416	282		92	
12. Mathematics	617	617	313	313	171		53	
13. Natural sciences	./.	./.	./.	./.	118		48	
14. Medical sciences	1 319	1 319	843	843	22		8	
15. Engineering, crafts	./.	./.	./.	./.	89		44	
16. Agriculture	./.	./.	./.	./.	24		2	
17. Domestic science	./.	./.	./.	./.	96		31	
18. Management, administration	./.	./.	./.	./.	./.		./.	
19. Planning, architecture	439	439	244	244	./.		./.	
20. Plastic arts	./.	./.	./.	./.	34		11	
21. Performing arts	./.	./.	./.	./.	19		8	
22. Games, sports	./.	./.	./.	./.	28		12	
23. Literature								
(A) History and criticism	1 849	1 849	1 095	1 095	1 488		683	
(B) Literary texts	./.	./.	./.	./.	./.		./.	
24. Geography, travel	603	603	373	373	63		22	
25. History, biography	./.	./.	./.	./.	307		151	

Number of titles by subject group 7.4
Nombre de titres par groupes de sujets
Número de títulos por categorías de temas

Subject group / Groupe de sujets / Categoría de temas	Japan‡ (1992) All editions		First editions		Jordan (1993) All editions		First editions	
	Total	of which: books	Total	of which: books	Total	of which: books	Total	of which: books
Total	35 496	35 496	35 496	35 496	500	500	500	500
1. Generalities	539	539	539	539	15	15	15	15
2. Philosophy, psychology	1 539	1 539	1 539	1 539	11	11	11	11
3. Religion, theology	638	638	638	638	77	77	77	77
4. Sociology, statistics	1 943	1 943	1 943	1 943	5	5	5	5
5. Political science	2 229	2 229	2 229	2 229	15	15	15	15
6. Law, public administration	904	904	904	904	20	20	20	20
7. Military art	./.	./.	./.	./.	5	5	5	5
8. Education, leisure	1 571	1 571	1 571	1 571	55	55	55	55
9. Trade, transport	1 589	1 589	1 589	1 589	10	10	10	10
10. Ethnography, folklore	293	293	293	293	5	5	5	5
11. Linguistics, philology	917	917	917	917	14	14	14	14
12. Mathematics	167	167	167	167	5	5	5	5
13. Natural sciences	975	975	975	975	8	8	8	8
14. Medical sciences	1 445	1 445	1 445	1 445	5	5	5	5
15. Engineering, crafts	2 482	2 482	2 482	2 482	12	12	12	12
16. Agriculture	316	316	316	316	7	7	7	7
17. Domestic science	-	-	-	-	3	3	3	3
18. Management, administration	2 033	2 033	2 033	2 033	10	10	10	10
19. Planning, architecture	579	579	579	579	2	2	2	2
20. Plastic arts	2 390	2 390	2 390	2 390	2	2	2	2
21. Performing arts	1 055	1 055	1 055	1 055	1	1	1	1
22. Games, sports	1 508	1 508	1 508	1 508	5	5	5	5
23. Literature								
(A) History and criticism	1 980	1 980	1 980	1 980	16	16	16	16
(B) Literary texts	6 545	6 545	6 545	6 545	120	120	120	120
24. Geography, travel	225	225	225	225	22	22	22	22
25. History, biography	1 634	1 634	1 634	1 634	50	50	50	50

Subject group / Groupe de sujets / Categoría de temas	Kazakhstan‡ (1994) All editions		First editions		Korea, Republic of (1994) All editions		First editions	
	Total	of which: books	Total	of which: books	Total	of which: books	Total	of which: books
Total	1 148		1 148		34 204	31 977	31 580	29 361
1. Generalities	-		-		579	464	539	431
2. Philosophy, psychology	24		24		640	613	602	575
3. Religion, theology	17		17		1 844	1 739	1 786	1 681
4. Sociology, statistics	3		3		670	668	640	638
5. Political science	83		83		996	996	826	826
6. Law, public administration	35		35		911	910	819	818
7. Military art	2		2		17	16	17	16
8. Education, leisure	182		182		2 416	2 109	1 726	1 419
9. Trade, transport	37		37		1 513	1 508	1 513	1 508
10. Ethnography, folklore	-		-		61	60	60	59
11. Linguistics, philology	69		69		2 371	2 093	2 196	1 918
12. Mathematics	38		38		1 214	651	1 166	603
13. Natural sciences	11		11		811	732	772	693
14. Medical sciences	73		73		659	650	637	628
15. Engineering, crafts	51		51		2 434	2 410	2 324	2 300
16. Agriculture	-		-		63	62	58	57
17. Domestic science	34		34		371	360	361	350
18. Management, administration	-		-		329	319	304	294
19. Planning, architecture	19		19		258	245	251	238
20. Plastic arts	-		-		558	504	548	494
21. Performing arts	14		14		375	350	369	344
22. Games, sports	18		18		5 124	5 123	5 107	5 106
23. Literature								
(A) History and criticism	60		60		208	208	201	201
(B) Literary texts	162		162		8 677	8 132	7 742	7 198
24. Geography, travel	14		14		167	131	160	124
25. History, biography	51		51		938	924	856	842

7.4 Number of titles by subject group
Nombre de titres par groupes de sujets
Número de títulos por categorías de temas

Subject group / Groupe de sujets / Categoría de temas	Kuwait‡ (1992) All editions Total	of which: books	First editions Total	of which: books	Kyrgyzstan (1994) All editions Total	of which: books	First editions Total	of which: books
Total	196	187	42	42	328	222	319	215
1. Generalities	17	15	3	3	31	31	31	31
2. Philosophy, psychology	5	5	5	5	2	2	2	2
3. Religion, theology	17	17	5	5	3	3	3	3
4. Sociology, statistics	5	5	1	1	-	-	-	-
5. Political science	1	1	1	1	34	9	34	9
6. Law, public administration	8	5	2	2	17	9	17	9
7. Military art	-	-	-	-	-	-	-	-
8. Education, leisure	2	1	1	1	124	70	115	63
9. Trade, transport	2	2	2	2	2	1	2	1
10. Ethnography, folklore	-	-	-	-	16	15	16	15
11. Linguistics, philology	-	-	-	-	16	15	16	15
12. Mathematics	-	-	-	-	3	3	3	3
13. Natural sciences	102	102	2	2	-	-	-	-
14. Medical sciences	3	3	3	3	10	8	10	8
15. Engineering, crafts	1	1	-	-	2	2	2	2
16. Agriculture	-	-	-	-	14	13	14	13
17. Domestic science	-	-	-	-	3	2	3	2
18. Management, administration	2	-	-	-	-	-	-	-
19. Planning, architecture	-	-	-	-	-	-	-	-
20. Plastic arts	-	-	-	-	-	-	-	-
21. Performing arts	13	13	13	13	3	3	3	3
22. Games, sports	2	1	-	-	2	1	2	1
23. Literature								
(A) History and criticism	2	2	2	2	-	-	-	-
(B) Literary texts	11	11	-	-	46	35	46	35
24. Geography, travel	-	-	-	-	-	-	-	-
25. History, biography	3	3	2	2	-	-	-	-

Subject group / Groupe de sujets / Categoría de temas	Lao People's Democratic Republic (1992) All editions Total	of which: books	First editions Total	of which: books	Malaysia (1994) All editions Total	of which: books	First editions Total	of which: books
Total	64	64	64	64	4 050	3 944	4 042	3 936
1. Generalities	-	-	-	-	53	41	53	41
2. Philosophy, psychology	-	-	-	-	25	25	24	24
3. Religion, theology	1	1	1	1	488	487	488	487
4. Sociology, statistics	-	-	-	-	110	88	110	88
5. Political science	4	4	4	4	177	155	176	154
6. Law, public administration	2	2	2	2	207	191	206	190
7. Military art	-	-	-	-	5	5	5	5
8. Education, leisure	-	-	-	-	141	136	141	136
9. Trade, transport	1	1	1	1	23	20	23	20
10. Ethnography, folklore	-	-	-	-	53	53	53	53
11. Linguistics, philology	11	11	11	11	883	883	881	881
12. Mathematics	-	-	-	-	285	285	284	284
13. Natural sciences	-	-	-	-	128	125	128	125
14. Medical sciences	3	3	3	3	59	57	58	56
15. Engineering, crafts	-	-	-	-	59	59	59	59
16. Agriculture	3	3	3	3	86	77	86	77
17. Domestic science	-	-	-	-	25	25	25	25
18. Management, administration	-	-	-	-	62	61	61	60
19. Planning, architecture	-	-	-	-	7	7	7	7
20. Plastic arts	-	-	-	-	35	35	35	35
21. Performing arts	-	-	-	-	32	32	32	32
22. Games, sports	-	-	-	-	48	46	48	46
23. Literature								
(A) History and criticism	-	-	-	-	20	20	20	20
(B) Literary texts	36	36	36	36	807	807	807	807
24. Geography, travel	-	-	-	-	60	59	60	59
25. History, biography	3	3	3	3	172	165	172	165

Number of titles by subject group 7.4
Nombre de titres par groupes de sujets
Número de títulos por categorías de temas

Subject group / Groupe de sujets / Categoría de temas	Mongolia (1992)				Myanmar‡ (1993)			
	All editions		First editions		All editions		First editions	
	Total	of which: books	Total	of which: books	Total	of which: books	Total	of which: books
Total	285	121	285	121	3 660			
1. Generalities	26	6	26	6	-			
2. Philosophy, psychology	12	4	12	4	73			
3. Religion, theology	5	-	5	-	713			
4. Sociology, statistics	-	-	-	-	26			
5. Political science	4	2	4	2	./.			
6. Law, public administration	7	4	7	4	./.			
7. Military art	1	1	1	1	./.			
8. Education, leisure	9	3	9	3	./.			
9. Trade, transport	10	2	10	2	./.			
10. Ethnography, folklore	5	2	5	2	./.			
11. Linguistics, philology	6	4	6	4	./.			
12. Mathematics	6	6	6	6	82			
13. Natural sciences	11	2	11	2	./.			
14. Medical sciences	6	5	6	5	22			
15. Engineering, crafts	3	2	3	2	./.			
16. Agriculture	4	3	4	3	./.			
17. Domestic science	4	4	4	4	./.			
18. Management, administration	3	3	3	3	./.			
19. Planning, architecture	2	1	2	1	1 171			
20. Plastic arts	1	1	1	1	./.			
21. Performing arts	3	2	3	2	./.			
22. Games, sports	3	2	3	2	./.			
23. Literature								
(A) History and criticism	3	3	3	3	1 551			
(B) Literary texts	132	52	132	52	./.			
24. Geography, travel	5	3	5	3	22			
25. History, biography	14	4	14	4	./.			

Subject group / Groupe de sujets / Categoría de temas	Oman (1992)				Pakistan (1994)			
	All editions		First editions		All editions		First editions	
	Total	of which: books	Total	of which: books	Total	of which: books	Total	of which: books
Total	24	24			124	124	90	90
1. Generalities	1	1			51	51	51	51
2. Philosophy, psychology	-	-			2	2	1	1
3. Religion, theology	3	3			1	1	1	1
4. Sociology, statistics	-	-			2	2	2	2
5. Political science	-	-			-	-	-	-
6. Law, public administration	-	-			-	-	-	-
7. Military art	-	-			-	-	-	-
8. Education, leisure	-	-			6	6	-	-
9. Trade, transport	-	-			-	-	-	-
10. Ethnography, folklore	-	-			-	-	-	-
11. Linguistics, philology	9	9			18	18	1	1
12. Mathematics	-	-			-	-	-	-
13. Natural sciences	-	-			12	12	10	10
14. Medical sciences	-	-			4	4	-	-
15. Engineering, crafts	-	-			12	12	8	8
16. Agriculture	1	1			1	1	1	1
17. Domestic science	-	-			-	-	-	-
18. Management, administration	-	-			-	-	-	-
19. Planning, architecture	-	-			-	-	-	-
20. Plastic arts	-	-			-	-	-	-
21. Performing arts	-	-			-	-	-	-
22. Games, sports	-	-			-	-	-	-
23. Literature								
(A) History and criticism	-	-			-	-	-	-
(B) Literary texts	-	-			12	12	12	12
24. Geography, travel	-	-			-	-	-	-
25. History, biography	10	10			3	3	3	3

7.4 Number of titles by subject group
Nombre de titres par groupes de sujets
Número de títulos por categorías de temas

Subject group / Groupe de sujets / Categoría de temas	Philippines (1994) All editions Total	of which: books	First editions Total	of which: books	Qatar (1994) All editions Total	of which: books	First editions Total	of which: books
Total	1 233	1 233			371	371	232	232
1. Generalities	36	36			23	23	20	20
2. Philosophy, psychology	13	13			6	6	6	6
3. Religion, theology	51	51			26	26	25	25
4. Sociology, statistics	39	39			12	12	12	12
5. Political science	58	58			9	9	9	9
6. Law, public administration	60	60			5	5	5	5
7. Military art	1	1			-	-	-	-
8. Education, leisure	117	117			118	118	23	23
9. Trade, transport	28	28			4	4	3	3
10. Ethnography, folklore	20	20			1	1	1	1
11. Linguistics, philology	70	70			15	15	6	6
12. Mathematics	22	22			15	15	8	8
13. Natural sciences	23	23			45	45	36	36
14. Medical sciences	65	65			5	5	5	5
15. Engineering, crafts	17	17			9	9	8	8
16. Agriculture	44	44			1	1	1	1
17. Domestic science	12	12			13	13	12	12
18. Management, administration	21	21			13	13	11	11
19. Planning, architecture	14	14			2	2	2	2
20. Plastic arts	1	1			-	-	-	-
21. Performing arts	160	160			-	-	-	-
22. ames, sports	12	12			2	2	2	2
23. Literature (A) History and criticism	13	13			4	4	4	4
(B) Literary texts	34	34			7	7	7	7
24. Geography, travel	11	11			13	13	7	7
25. History, biography	34	34			23	23	19	19

Subject group / Groupe de sujets / Categoría de temas	Sri Lanka (1994) All editions Total	of which: books	First editions Total	of which: books	Syrian Arab Republic (1992) All editions Total	of which: books	First editions Total	of which: books
Total	2 929	1 089	2 645	893	598	598		
1. Generalities	218	97	209	90	144	144		
2. Philosophy, psychology	32	28	22	18	24	24		
3. Religion, theology	251	113	204	80	62	62		
4. Sociology, statistics	64	47	54	39	20	20		
5. Political science	87	48	83	45	23	23		
6. Law, public administration	1 247	127	1 197	124	11	11		
7. Military art	2	-	2	-	-	-		
8. Education, leisure	119	73	115	69	7	7		
9. Trade, transport	69	27	66	24	5	5		
10. Ethnography, folklore	13	11	9	7	13	13		
11. Linguistics, philology	88	58	62	38	13	13		
12. Mathematics	42	36	31	25	1	1		
13. Natural sciences	16	9	15	8	-	-		
14. Medical sciences	82	56	64	40	54	54		
15. Engineering, crafts	57	15	55	14	21	21		
16. Agriculture	53	18	51	17	9	9		
17. Domestic science	5	4	5	4	4	4		
18. Management, administration	14	7	12	5	1	1		
19. Planning, architecture	27	27	23	23	8	8		
20. Plastic arts	-	-	-	-	8	8		
21. Performing arts	18	6	17	5	6	6		
22. Games, sports	4	-	4	-	3	3		
23. Literature (A) History and criticism	162	83	147	74	73	73		
(B) Literary texts	135	111	98	75	39	39		
24. Geography, travel	6	2	3	2	20	20		
25. History, biography	118	86	97	67	29	29		

Number of titles by subject group 7.4
Nombre de titres par groupes de sujets
Número de títulos por categorías de temas

Subject group Groupe de sujets Categoría de temas	Tajikistan‡ (1994)				Thailand (1992)			
	All editions		First editions		All editions		First editions	
	Total	of which: books	Total	of which: books	Total	of which: books	Total	of which: books
Total	231	194	216	179	7 626	7 565	7 378	7 318
1. Generalities	-	-	-	-	413	409	404	400
2. Philosophy, psychology	3	2	3	2	189	187	187	185
3. Religion, theology	1	1	1	1	302	295	271	265
4. Sociology, statistics	-	-	-	-	262	260	255	253
5. Political science	5	5	5	5	396	393	383	380
6. Law, public administration	11	10	11	10	351	349	342	340
7. Military art	2	2	2	2	129	128	126	125
8. Education, leisure	6	6	6	6	752	750	682	680
9. Trade, transport	-	-	-	-	215	215	210	210
10. Ethnography, folklore	-	-	-	-	236	234	232	230
11. Linguistics, philology	7	7	7	7	234	233	231	230
12. Mathematics	-	-	-	-	156	155	151	150
13. Natural sciences	16	12	16	12	435	430	425	420
14. Medical sciences	15	13	15	13	617	610	608	601
15. Engineering, crafts	11	9	11	9	299	296	293	290
16. Agriculture	21	5	18	2	692	690	683	681
17. Domestic science	-	-	-	-	243	241	237	235
18. Management, administration	-	-	-	-	384	383	376	375
19. Planning, architecture	-	-	-	-	166	165	161	160
20. Plastic arts	-	-	-	-	86	85	81	80
21. Performing arts	8	6	8	6	109	105	104	100
22. Games, sports	-	-	-	-	82	81	81	80
23. Literature								
(A) History and criticism	13	13	13	13	236	235	231	230
(B) Literary texts	47	44	46	43	221	220	216	215
24. Geography, travel	-	-	-	-	182	180	177	175
25. History, biography	22	18	22	18	239	236	231	228

Subject group Groupe de sujets Categoría de temas	Turkey (1994)				Turkmenistan (1992)			
	All editions		First editions		All editions		First editions	
	Total	of which: books	Total	of which: books	Total	of which: books	Total	of which: books
Total	4 473	4 157	3 924	3 608	565	386	552	374
1. Generalities	332				47	12	47	12
2. Philosophy, psychology	143				5	5	5	5
3. Religion, theology	309				6	4	6	4
4. Sociology, statistics	211				3	3	3	3
5. Political science	470				72	37	72	37
6. Law, public administration	95				18	13	18	13
7. Military art	49				1	1	1	1
8. Education, leisure	444				43	41	30	29
9. Trade, transport	12				5	4	5	4
10. Ethnography, folklore	48				5	4	5	4
11. Linguistics, philology	82				21	17	21	17
12. Mathematics	49				18	15	18	15
13. Natural sciences	14				54	38	54	38
14. Medical sciences	360				19	11	19	11
15. Engineering, crafts	70				29	16	29	16
16. Agriculture	61				24	19	24	19
17. Domestic science	26				2	1	2	1
18. Management, administration	27				-	-	-	-
19. Planning, architecture	48				-	-	-	-
20. Plastic arts	40				-	-	-	-
21. Performing arts	57				14	9	14	9
22. Games, sports	2				4	1	4	1
23. Literature								
(A) History and criticism	1 145				15	14	15	14
(B) Literary texts	92				121	89	121	89
24. Geography, travel	70				11	7	11	7
25. History, biography	217				28	25	28	25

7.4   Number of titles by subject group
Nombre de titres par groupes de sujets
Número de títulos por categorías de temas

Subject group Groupe de sujets Categoría de temas	United Arab Emirates‡ (1993)				Uzbekistan‡ (1993)			
	All editions		First editions		All editions		First editions	
	Total	of which: books	Total	of which: books	Total	of which: books	Total	of which: books
Total	293	293			1 340			
1. Generalities	-	-			./.			
2. Philosophy, psychology	3	3			118			
3. Religion, theology	68	68			./.			
4. Sociology, statistics	1	1			./.			
5. Political science	1	1			./.			
6. Law, public administration	-	-			./.			
7. Military art	-	-			./.			
8. Education, leisure	-	-			54			
9. Trade, transport	-	-			./.			
10. Ethnography, folklore	-	-			./.			
11. Linguistics, philology	83	83			71			
12. Mathematics	40	40			./.			
13. Natural sciences	59	59			./.			
14. Medical sciences	-	-			45			
15. Engineering, crafts	1	1			66			
16. Agriculture	-	-			25			
17. Domestic science	8	8			./.			
18. Management, administration	-	-			./.			
19. Planning, architecture	-	-			./.			
20. Plastic arts	-	-			./.			
21. Performing arts	2	2			./.			
22. Games, sports	-	-			./.			
23. Literature								
(A) History and criticism	-	-			605			
(B) Literary texts	-	-			./.			
24. Geography, travel	21	21			./.			
25. History, biography	6	6			./.			

Europe

Subject group Groupe de sujets Categoría de temas	Viet Nam‡ (1993)				Andorra (1994)			
	All editions		First editions		All editions		First editions	
	Total	of which: books	Total	of which: books	Total	of which: books	Total	of which: books
Total	5 581				57	57		
1. Generalities	./.				-	-		
2. Philosophy, psychology	./.				-	-		
3. Religion, theology	./.				-	-		
4. Sociology, statistics	647				2	2		
5. Political science	./.				5	5		
6. Law, public administration	./.				8	8		
7. Military art	./.				-	-		
8. Education, leisure	./.				5	5		
9. Trade, transport	./.				1	1		
10. Ethnography, folklore	./.				3	3		
11. Linguistics, philology	./.				-	-		
12. Mathematics	./.				-	-		
13. Natural sciences	./.				3	3		
14. Medical sciences	646				-	-		
15. Engineering, crafts	./.				1	1		
16. Agriculture	./.				2	2		
17. Domestic science	./.				-	-		
18. Management, administration	./.				1	1		
19. Planning, architecture	./.				1	1		
20. Plastic arts	./.				3	3		
21. Performing arts	./.				-	-		
22. Games, sports	./.				1	1		
23. Literature								
(A) History and criticism	1 502				-	-		
(B) Literary texts	./.				15	15		
24. Geography, travel	./.				5	5		
25. History, biography	./.				1	1		

Number of titles by subject group 7.4
Nombre de titres par groupes de sujets
Número de títulos por categorías de temas

Subject group / Groupe de sujets / Categoría de temas	Austria‡ (1994)				Belarus (1994)			
	All editions		First editions		All editions		First editions	
	Total	of which: books	Total	of which: books	Total	of which: books	Total	of which: books
Total	7 987				3 346	2 330	3 189	2 211
1. Generalities	229				161	98	160	97
2. Philosophy, psychology	246				68	52	68	52
3. Religion, theology	284				184	131	183	130
4. Sociology, statistics	1 075				18	11	17	10
5. Political science	184				221	122	221	122
6. Law, public administration	444				95	69	92	66
7. Military art	./.				22	13	22	13
8. Education, leisure	655				423	279	319	212
9. Trade, transport	117				1	-	1	-
10. Ethnography, folklore	283				10	10	9	9
11. Linguistics, philology	229				169	121	162	114
12. Mathematics	339				59	36	59	36
13. Natural sciences	508				128	84	128	84
14. Medical sciences	207				208	113	197	102
15. Engineering, crafts	292				309	193	301	186
16. Agriculture	204				173	68	171	66
17. Domestic science	./.				45	34	39	28
18. Management, administration	./.				57	41	56	40
19. Planning, architecture	./.				11	8	11	8
20. Plastic arts	523				15	8	15	8
21. Performing arts	263				18	10	18	10
22. Games, sports	136				33	17	33	17
23. Literature								
(A) History and criticism	./.				32	24	32	24
(B) Literary texts	1 181				781	700	774	693
24. Geography, travel	./.				4	4	4	4
25. History, biography	588				101	84	97	80

Subject group / Groupe de sujets / Categoría de temas	Bulgaria (1994)				Croatia‡ (1994)			
	All editions		First editions		All editions		First editions	
	Total	of which: books	Total	of which: books	Total	of which: books	Total	of which: books
Total	5 925	5 027	5 452	4 580	2 671	1 941	2 153	1 669
1. Generalities	252	150	241	144	44	30	41	28
2. Philosophy, psychology	270	260	238	228	94	83	78	69
3. Religion, theology	165	144	151	130	220	175	181	141
4. Sociology, statistics	59	56	59	56	14	12	12	10
5. Political science	390	347	375	333	106	84	94	77
6. Law, public administration	240	188	211	159	85	55	67	45
7. Military art	33	27	32	26	60	37	56	34
8. Education, leisure	412	355	361	309	346	268	200	155
9. Trade, transport	3	3	2	2	57	44	56	43
10. Ethnography, folklore	39	37	34	32	11	8	11	8
11. Linguistics, philology	130	127	105	102	68	61	38	34
12. Mathematics	82	78	71	67	22	13	16	8
13. Natural sciences	154	146	118	110	80	67	74	64
14. Medical sciences	248	231	225	208	210	157	208	155
15. Engineering, crafts	302	285	261	245	117	79	114	77
16. Agriculture	86	73	83	70	47	40	46	39
17. Domestic science	90	81	86	77	9	8	7	6
18. Management, administration	72	66	58	52	80	60	73	56
19. Planning, architecture	10	10	10	10	32	25	31	24
20. Plastic arts	37	32	36	31	92	30	91	29
21. Performing arts	40	38	35	34	13	11	13	11
22. Games, sports	69	66	69	66	21	17	20	16
23. Literature								
(A) History and criticism	115	114	101	100	608	529	573	496
(B) Literary texts	2 330	1 836	2 212	1 729	./.	./.	./.	./.
24. Geography, travel	15	13	12	11	7	5	7	5
25. History, biography	282	264	266	249	51	43	46	39

7.4 Number of titles by subject group
Nombre de titres par groupes de sujets
Número de títulos por categorías de temas

Subject group / Groupe de sujets / Categoría de temas	Czech Republic (1994) All editions Total	of which: books	First editions Total	of which: books	Denmark‡ (1994) All editions Total	of which: books	First editions Total	of which: books
Total	9 309	7 957	8 392	7 105	11 973	8 023	10 156	6 583
1. Generalities	302	197	291	186	403	313	362	280
2. Philosophy, psychology	283	262	254	234	503	359	419	279
3. Religion, theology	331	248	302	227	332	237	296	206
4. Sociology, statistics	255	223	249	217	245	171	228	155
5. Political science	249	194	236	183	799	458	702	383
6. Law, public administration	369	309	327	268	725	466	470	305
7. Military art	51	45	50	45	82	57	69	47
8. Education, leisure	350	236	311	208	437	295	405	268
9. Trade, transport	151	84	136	71	./.	./.	./.	./.
10. Ethnography, folklore	33	20	32	19	89	50	76	39
11. Linguistics, philology	305	279	246	220	293	202	253	173
12. Mathematics	436	354	378	298	227	120	209	109
13. Natural sciences	370	313	308	254	737	449	684	408
14. Medical sciences	289	259	271	242	763	497	656	428
15. Engineering, crafts	373	312	309	248	1 208	804	1 069	691
16. Agriculture	148	100	138	90	343	196	307	166
17. Domestic science	163	103	141	88	162	111	123	86
18. Management, administration	191	176	178	165	383	285	311	224
19. Planning, architecture	27	20	24	17	117	63	113	60
20. Plastic arts	145	105	130	90	300	168	280	155
21. Performing arts	201	165	181	145	134	90	123	82
22. Games, sports	138	113	130	106	216	127	184	102
23. Literature								
(A) History and criticism	90	82	81	73	70	63	63	56
(B) Literary texts	3 408	3 198	3 099	2 907	2 296	1 621	1 804	1 196
24. Geography, travel	79	52	67	45	360	245	295	190
25. History, biography	572	508	523	459	749	576	655	495

Subject group / Groupe de sujets / Categoría de temas	Estonia (1994) All editions Total	of which: books	First editions Total	of which: books	Finland (1994) All editions Total	of which: books	First editions Total	of which: books
Total	2 291	1 547	2 026	1 326	12 539	9 478	11 705	8 737
1. Generalities	125	74	124	73	320	233	295	211
2. Philosophy, psychology	52	45	47	41	230	219	207	196
3. Religion, theology	75	47	72	44	341	273	314	253
4. Sociology, statistics	34	18	34	18	236	197	216	183
5. Political science	135	70	134	69	996	695	959	664
6. Law, public administration	125	84	122	81	956	710	908	675
7. Military art	5	2	5	2	111	92	104	88
8. Education, leisure	120	66	118	65	660	485	650	476
9. Trade, transport	79	29	79	29	-	-	-	-
10. Ethnography, folklore	19	15	17	13	107	97	103	93
11. Linguistics, philology	-	-	-	-	405	363	349	309
12. Mathematics	62	41	43	24	221	130	202	113
13. Natural sciences	132	89	119	80	988	688	949	655
14. Medical sciences	91	56	85	52	588	464	549	433
15. Engineering, crafts	140	79	134	76	1 306	906	1 258	863
16. Agriculture	121	62	112	58	399	279	387	268
17. Domestic science	28	19	27	18	145	127	125	108
18. Management, administration	13	6	12	5	729	515	678	467
19. Planning, architecture	27	14	27	14	199	129	197	127
20. Plastic arts	57	31	57	31	357	222	325	202
21. Performing arts	20	12	20	12	109	95	104	90
22. Games, sports	36	23	34	22	163	119	156	113
23. Literature								
(A) History and criticism	193	143	133	102	57	50	54	47
(B) Literary texts	474	407	367	304	1 804	1 414	1 556	1 176
24. Geography, travel	36	28	31	25	109	98	100	90
25. History, biography	92	87	73	68	1 003	878	960	837

Number of titles by subject group 7.4
Nombre de titres par groupes de sujets
Número de títulos por categorías de temas

Subject group / Groupe de sujets / Categoría de temas	France‡ (1994) All editions Total	of which: books	France‡ First editions Total	of which: books	Germany (1994) All editions Total	of which: books	Germany First editions Total	of which: books
Total	45 311				70 643		52 767	
1. Generalities	1 029				6 255		4 359	
2. Philosophy, psychology	2 053				3 594		2 381	
3. Religion, theology	1 407				3 815		2 850	
4. Sociology, statistics	573				1 115		897	
5. Political science	1 952				4 641		3 725	
6. Law, public administration	4 134				4 109		2 995	
7. Military art	50				350		288	
8. Education, leisure	975				5 457		4 068	
9. Trade, transport	268				400		321	
10. Ethnography, folklore	354				187		138	
11. Linguistics, philology	1 029				-		-	
12. Mathematics	772				533		409	
13. Natural sciences	1 368				1 999		1 672	
14. Medical sciences	1 635				3 788		2 879	
15. Engineering, crafts	1 923				2 843		2 022	
16. Agriculture	613				1 013		738	
17. Domestic science	585				757		494	
18. Management, administration	1 470				1 661		1 445	
19. Planning, architecture	1 123				1 179		891	
20. Plastic arts	1 309				2 706		2 172	
21. Performing arts	433				1 051		877	
22. Games, sports	673				861		601	
23. Literature								
(A) History and criticism	853				2 923		2 370	
(B) Literary texts	12 671				10 092		6 680	
24. Geography, travel	1 194				6 082		4 812	
25. History, biography	4 865				3 232		2 683	

Subject group / Groupe de sujets / Categoría de temas	Holy See (1992) All editions Total	of which: books	Holy See First editions Total	of which: books	Hungary (1994) All editions Total	of which: books	Hungary First editions Total	of which: books
Total	205	205	135	135	10 108	9 383	8 144	7 492
1. Generalities	5	5	5	5	261	252	200	191
2. Philosophy, psychology	37	37	21	21	342	337	267	263
3. Religion, theology	117	117	82	82	421	363	373	316
4. Sociology, statistics	10	10	5	5	156	147	146	137
5. Political science	-	-	-	-	327	304	315	292
6. Law, public administration	11	11	3	3	378	369	358	350
7. Military art	-	-	-	-	31	31	31	31
8. Education, leisure	9	9	6	6	437	407	399	369
9. Trade, transport	-	-	-	-	59	59	51	51
10. Ethnography, folklore	1	1	1	1	111	97	96	85
11. Linguistics, philology	7	7	4	4	459	426	266	245
12. Mathematics	-	-	-	-	194	192	107	107
13. Natural sciences	-	-	-	-	442	403	284	249
14. Medical sciences	-	-	-	-	304	288	256	240
15. Engineering, crafts	-	-	-	-	780	756	357	337
16. Agriculture	-	-	-	-	201	190	157	146
17. Domestic science	-	-	-	-	166	165	114	113
18. Management, administration	-	-	-	-	313	293	259	240
19. Planning, architecture	-	-	-	-	172	114	138	98
20. Plastic arts	-	-	-	-	300	200	267	176
21. Performing arts	-	-	-	-	147	142	115	111
22. Games, sports	-	-	-	-	118	116	101	100
23. Literature								
(A) History and criticism	-	-	-	-	385	361	320	301
(B) Literary texts	-	-	-	-	2 808	2 632	2 493	2 321
24. Geography, travel	-	-	-	-	279	245	234	203
25. History, biography	8	8	8	8	517	494	440	420

7.4   Number of titles by subject group
       Nombre de titres par groupes de sujets
       Número de títulos por categorías de temas

Subject group	Iceland‡ (1994)				Italy (1994)			
Groupe de sujets	All editions		First editions		All editions		First editions	
Categoría de temas	Total	of which: books	Total	of which: books	Total	of which: books	Total	of which: books
Total	1 429	965	1 089	746	32 673	29 936	29 177	26 547
1. Generalities	36	26	26	19	800	723	694	624
2. Philosophy, psychology	22	16	19	14	1 751	1 719	1 553	1 521
3. Religion, theology	37	27	31	22	2 013	1 750	1 855	1 600
4. Sociology, statistics	71	51	23	18	896	844	831	779
5. Political science	90	53	80	46	1 175	1 134	1 011	972
6. Law, public administration	61	36	54	31	2 057	2 026	1 518	1 493
7. Military art	-	-	-	-	112	104	110	102
8. Education, leisure	33	17	24	12	1 106	968	921	789
9. Trade, transport	15	13	12	11	202	185	177	160
10. Ethnography, folklore	6	3	4	1	491	474	454	437
11. Linguistics, philology	123	66	52	38	824	784	637	605
12. Mathematics	56	31	18	5	369	287	313	232
13. Natural sciences	54	32	38	25	771	640	672	542
14. Medical sciences	29	18	19	15	1 334	1 168	1 213	1 048
15. Engineering, crafts	54	24	45	19	1 399	1 165	1 259	1 025
16. Agriculture	41	19	40	18	280	268	263	252
17. Domestic science	24	17	16	9	402	395	322	315
18. Management, administration	18	15	15	13	272	249	158	145
19. Planning, architecture	89	44	82	40	625	593	561	529
20. Plastic arts	./.	./.	./.	./.	1 428	1 269	1 305	1 148
21. Performing arts	./.	./.	./.	./.	665	583	617	540
22. Games, sports	35	25	33	23	711	550	641	503
23. Literature								
(A) History and criticism	8	7	6	6	695	678	657	640
(B) Literary texts	374	310	321	264	8 283	7 549	7 769	7 050
24. Geography, travel	25	13	21	12	941	871	818	755
25. History, biography	128	102	110	85	3 071	2 960	2 848	2 741

Subject group	Latvia‡ (1994)				Lithuania (1994)			
Groupe de sujets	All editions		First editions		All editions		First editions	
Categoría de temas	Total	of which: books	Total	of which: books	Total	of which: books	Total	of which: books
Total	1 677	1 371	1 249	974	2 885	2 214	2 688	2 036
1. Generalities	49	42	46	40	197	129	193	125
2. Philosophy, psychology	59	53	47	43	68	53	66	51
3. Religion, theology	77	59	66	48	110	89	107	86
4. Sociology, statistics	32	24	31	23	19	14	19	14
5. Political science	59	48	55	44	173	123	161	115
6. Law, public administration	42	34	35	27	165	123	163	122
7. Military art	-	-	-	-	7	6	7	6
8. Education, leisure	55	38	53	36	132	79	130	78
9. Trade, transport	21	18	21	18	-	-	-	-
10. Ethnography, folklore	13	7	10	6	24	17	23	17
11. Linguistics, philology	53	48	38	34	155	130	113	94
12. Mathematics	-	-	-	-	57	36	46	28
13. Natural sciences	36	22	35	21	128	100	117	91
14. Medical sciences	32	27	31	26	146	83	142	80
15. Engineering, crafts	21	19	20	18	216	144	216	144
16. Agriculture	47	23	46	22	105	74	104	73
17. Domestic science	19	15	17	13	27	21	26	20
18. Management, administration	25	18	24	17	77	61	77	61
19. Planning, architecture	3	3	3	3	34	27	32	25
20. Plastic arts	17	8	16	8	16	7	16	7
21. Performing arts	17	14	15	12	43	27	42	26
22. Games, sports	13	7	13	7	45	28	45	28
23. Literature								
(A) History and criticism	25	18	22	16	25	21	23	19
(B) Literary texts	504	500	263	259	762	695	670	603
24. Geography, travel	14	7	14	7	19	14	17	12
25. History, biography	52	45	42	37	135	113	133	111

Number of titles by subject group 7.4
Nombre de titres par groupes de sujets
Número de títulos por categorías de temas

Subject group / Groupe de sujets / Categoría de temas	Luxembourg (1994) All editions		First editions		Malta (1993) All editions		First editions	
	Total	of which: books	Total	of which: books	Total	of which: books	Total	of which: books
Total	681	408	645	377	417	320	413	316
1. Generalities	64	38	60	34	8	6	8	6
2. Philosophy, psychology	13	8	9	5	11	6	11	6
3. Religion, theology	15	6	14	6	80	50	80	50
4. Sociology, statistics	17	8	16	7	10	8	10	8
5. Political science	96	37	95	37	22	16	22	16
6. Law, public administration	39	27	35	23	94	80	94	80
7. Military art	1	1	1	1	5	5	5	5
8. Education, leisure	69	37	67	35	14	12	14	12
9. Trade, transport	23	16	21	13	12	7	12	7
10. Ethnography, folklore	1	-	1	-	6	5	6	5
11. Linguistics, philology	2	2	2	2	18	13	16	11
12. Mathematics	12	11	12	11	1	1	1	1
13. Natural sciences	7	6	7	6	3	3	3	3
14. Medical sciences	20	4	20	4	2	1	2	1
15. Engineering, crafts	18	8	18	8	7	6	7	6
16. Agriculture	8	3	7	2	1	1	1	1
17. Domestic science	3	3	3	3	4	4	4	4
18. Management, administration	-	-	-	-	2	1	2	1
19. Planning, architecture	10	6	9	5	7	5	7	5
20. Plastic arts	33	19	33	19	5	5	5	5
21. Performing arts	37	21	35	21	6	5	6	5
22. Games, sports	38	24	38	24	11	8	11	8
23. Literature								
(A) History and criticism	21	20	21	20	-	-	-	-
(B) Literary texts	46	37	42	33	41	30	39	28
24. Geography, travel	3	2	3	2	26	22	26	22
25. History, biography	85	64	76	56	21	20	21	20

Subject group / Groupe de sujets / Categoría de temas	Moldova (1994) All editions		First editions		Netherlands‡ (1993) All editions		First editions	
	Total	of which: books	Total	of which: books	Total	of which: books	Total	of which: books
Total	797	458	786	450	34 067	34 067	8 858	8 858
1. Generalities	11	5	11	5	70	70	56	56
2. Philosophy, psychology	18	15	18	15	710	710	533	533
3. Religion, theology	24	23	24	23	788	788	585	585
4. Sociology, statistics	4	4	4	4	296	296	257	257
5. Political science	98	24	98	24	392	392	358	358
6. Law, public administration	26	18	26	18	842	842	628	628
7. Military art	1	1	1	1	17	17	17	17
8. Education, leisure	224	137	217	133	270	270	221	221
9. Trade, transport	10	5	10	5	32	32	28	28
10. Ethnography, folklore	1	1	1	1	34	34	30	30
11. Linguistics, philology	23	18	23	18	334	334	268	268
12. Mathematics	10	4	10	4	93	93	86	86
13. Natural sciences	25	12	25	12	122	122	117	117
14. Medical sciences	36	27	36	27	561	561	431	431
15. Engineering, crafts	66	22	66	22	887	887	788	788
16. Agriculture	62	11	62	11	178	178	130	130
17. Domestic science	4	4	4	4	277	277	213	213
18. Management, administration	3	1	3	1	407	407	303	303
19. Planning, architecture	3	2	3	2	408	408	359	359
20. Plastic arts	4	4	4	4	1 941	1 941	-	-
21. Performing arts	6	6	6	6	38	38	34	34
22. Games, sports	6	4	5	3	439	439	318	318
23. Literature								
(A) History and criticism	7	6	7	6	178	178	157	157
(B) Literary texts	93	75	90	72	2 772	2 772	1 912	1 912
24. Geography, travel	5	3	5	3	400	400	304	304
25. History, biography	27	26	27	26	964	964	725	725

7.4 Number of titles by subject group
Nombre de titres par groupes de sujets
Número de títulos por categorías de temas

Subject group / Groupe de sujets / Categoría de temas	Norway‡ (1994) All editions Total	of which: books	First editions Total	of which: books	Poland (1994) All editions Total	of which: books	First editions Total	of which: books
Total	6 846	6 031	5 951	5 209	10 874	9 640	8 899	7 772
1. Generalities	156	125	137	112	212	148	194	130
2. Philosophy, psychology	186	167	157	139	342	325	293	277
3. Religion, theology	458	384	410	343	566	502	477	420
4. Sociology, statistics	168	155	150	137	125	119	109	103
5. Political science	242	220	218	196	619	503	577	462
6. Law, public administration	510	464	399	358	558	499	483	429
7. Military art	./.	./.	./.	./.	46	45	42	41
8. Education, leisure	194	187	162	158	395	351	364	320
9. Trade, transport	43	35	42	34	-	-	-	-
10. Ethnography, folklore	66	55	61	50	42	42	40	40
11. Linguistics, philology	228	202	157	140	428	411	292	279
12. Mathematics	66	57	45	36	257	228	172	144
13. Natural sciences	214	177	191	157	682	601	513	435
14. Medical sciences	267	252	223	209	548	495	471	423
15. Engineering, crafts	142	131	88	79	934	876	717	664
16. Agriculture	94	84	85	75	304	222	265	189
17. Domestic science	112	94	85	71	101	92	88	80
18. Management, administration	145	144	95	94	303	282	259	240
19. Planning, architecture	59	44	58	43	134	120	125	111
20. Plastic arts	170	119	151	107	141	128	121	108
21. Performing arts	261	222	224	187	126	115	110	100
22. Games, sports	./.	./.	./.	./.	78	72	67	61
23. Literature								
(A) History and criticism	103	97	58	54	311	284	264	240
(B) Literary texts	2 580	2 274	2 413	2 124	2 671	2 301	2 010	1 696
24. Geography, travel	61	60	55	54	195	175	151	136
25. History, biography	321	282	287	252	756	704	695	644

Subject group / Groupe de sujets / Categoría de temas	Portugal‡ (1994) All editions Total	of which: books	First editions Total	of which: books	Romania‡ (1994) All editions Total	of which: books	First editions Total	of which: books
Total	6 667		4 189		4 074	3 741	4 007	
1. Generalities	./.		./.		85	84	82	
2. Philosophy, psychology	./.		./.		119	116	117	
3. Religion, theology	./.		./.		148	136	134	
4. Sociology, statistics	789		506		22	21	22	
5. Political science	./.		./.		148	126	145	
6. Law, public administration	./.		./.		100	98	92	
7. Military art	./.		./.		-	-	-	
8. Education, leisure	./.		./.		144	94	141	
9. Trade, transport	./.		./.		-	-	-	
10. Ethnography, folklore	./.		./.		17	16	17	
11. Linguistics, philology	./.		./.		183	179	178	
12. Mathematics	401		316		204	183	203	
13. Natural sciences	./.		./.		221	207	220	
14. Medical sciences	./.		./.		175	147	174	
15. Engineering, crafts	./.		./.		483	403	481	
16. Agriculture	./.		./.		99	92	97	
17. Domestic science	./.		./.		18	18	17	
18. Management, administration	./.		./.		95	85	95	
19. Planning, architecture	192		90		12	9	12	
20. Plastic arts	./.		./.		19	16	19	
21. Performing arts	./.		./.		34	32	33	
22. Games, sports	./.		./.		20	20	20	
23. Literature								
(A) History and criticism	1 934		1 499		1 534	1 471	1 520	
(B) Literary texts	./.		./.		./.	./.	./.	
24. Geography, travel	./.		./.		158	154	36	
25. History, biography	./.		./.		36	34	152	

Number of titles by subject group 7.4
Nombre de titres par groupes de sujets
Número de títulos por categorías de temas

Subject group / Groupe de sujets / Categoría de temas	Russian Federation‡ (1994)				Slovakia (1994)			
	All editions		First editions		All editions		First editions	
	Total	of which: books	Total	of which: books	Total	of which: books	Total	of which: books
Total	30 390	23 537	29 471	22 741	3 481	3 266	1 619	1 534
1. Generalities	2 860	1 244	2 762	1 207	63	59	33	32
2. Philosophy, psychology	896	791	878	775	143	142	68	67
3. Religion, theology	957	808	932	786	164	151	77	69
4. Sociology, statistics	345	294	345	294	32	30	16	16
5. Political science	1 738	1 383	1 699	1 345	210	201	93	89
6. Law, public administration	949	747	933	733	80	79	43	43
7. Military art	74	67	73	66	6	4	5	4
8. Education, leisure	2 340	1 935	2 057	1 672	309	281	141	137
9. Trade, transport	347	244	336	234	9	9	1	1
10. Ethnography, folklore	172	146	172	146	10	10	3	3
11. Linguistics, philology	995	761	942	708	139	134	72	69
12. Mathematics	548	368	539	361	57	57	22	22
13. Natural sciences	2 096	1 486	2 068	1 460	214	208	101	96
14. Medical sciences	1 488	1 206	1 415	1 139	164	161	47	47
15. Engineering, crafts	4 111	2 936	3 987	2 823	283	281	136	134
16. Agriculture	675	499	645	473	139	133	78	73
17. Domestic science	277	254	265	242	43	41	20	18
18. Management, administration	298	192	276	171	145	139	96	92
19. Planning, architecture	499	413	489	403	34	28	8	6
20. Plastic arts	./.	./.	./.	./.	35	32	12	11
21. Performing arts	./.	./.	./.	./.	34	30	20	18
22. Games, sports	205	146	200	142	43	42	18	18
23. Literature								
(A) History and criticism	384	347	381	344	71	52	39	28
(B) Literary texts	6 792	6 048	6 748	6 010	867	799	408	385
24. Geography, travel	179	153	176	150	79	74	25	24
25. History, biography	1 165	1 069	1 153	1 057	108	89	37	32

Subject group / Groupe de sujets / Categoría de temas	Slovenia (1994)				Spain‡ (1994)			
	All editions		First editions		All editions		First editions	
	Total	of which: books	Total	of which: books	Total	of which: books	Total	of which: books
Total	2 906	2 207	2 417	1 777	44 261	39 300	38 102	33 420
1. Generalities	57	41	47	32	1 680	1 494	1 523	1 345
2. Philosophy, psychology	117	113	101	98	1 562	1 502	1 295	1 246
3. Religion, theology	106	87	90	71	1 908	1 732	1 552	1 398
4. Sociology, statistics	57	53	52	49	1 021	925	985	890
5. Political science	124	100	99	76	1 136	1 029	1 046	939
6. Law, public administration	93	90	78	75	2 432	2 216	2 083	1 871
7. Military art	6	5	6	5	133	124	131	122
8. Education, leisure	208	165	157	124	2 549	2 339	2 330	2 130
9. Trade, transport	13	9	10	7	425	389	407	372
10. Ethnography, folklore	35	30	32	27	786	675	712	602
11. Linguistics, philology	125	103	91	69	1 362	1 331	1 164	1 133
12. Mathematics	171	153	113	99	646	618	589	564
13. Natural sciences	92	74	51	37	1 837	1 656	1 708	1 538
14. Medical sciences	156	121	123	92	1 975	1 810	1 813	1 655
15. Engineering, crafts	128	92	103	71	1 627	1 500	1 473	1 349
16. Agriculture	71	50	62	41	724	610	661	562
17. Domestic science	39	27	27	19	450	422	404	378
18. Management, administration	87	80	72	67	1 149	1 102	1 008	962
19. Planning, architecture	47	34	45	32	423	369	409	355
20. Plastic arts	256	68	248	62	1 934	1 351	1 865	1 291
21. Performing arts	48	18	43	15	636	598	593	557
22. Games, sports	42	35	38	31	460	434	425	399
23. Literature								
(A) History and criticism	44	42	29	28	-	-	-	-
(B) Literary texts	587	457	533	417	13 619	11 566	10 642	8 738
24. Geography, travel	147	120	120	95	1 416	1 272	1 220	1 092
25. History, biography	50	40	47	38	2 371	2 236	2 064	1 932

7.4   Number of titles by subject group
Nombre de titres par groupes de sujets
Número de títulos por categorías de temas

Subject group / Groupe de sujets / Categoría de temas	Sweden (1994) All editions Total	of which: books	First editions Total	of which: books	Switzerland‡ (1994) All editions Total	of which: books	First editions Total	of which: books
Total	13 822	10 760	11 711	8 948	15 378		15 114	
1. Generalities	317	248	277	217	262		259	
2. Philosophy, psychology	401	350	321	273	709		669	
3. Religion, theology	577	431	498	371	814		783	
4. Sociology, statistics	154	123	134	105	723		722	
5. Political science	678	510	573	423	1 187		1 170	
6. Law, public administration	1 170	851	982	706	767		747	
7. Military art	67	54	62	50	50		50	
8. Education, leisure	402	298	361	268	456		446	
9. Trade, transport	176	127	146	101	263		262	
10. Ethnography, folklore	75	63	70	58	208		206	
11. Linguistics, philology	428	373	357	306	220		210	
12. Mathematics	109	93	93	77	182		181	
13. Natural sciences	810	554	755	505	1 428		1 420	
14. Medical sciences	1 241	930	1 129	841	1 772		1 756	
15. Engineering, crafts	917	722	827	642	1 004		1 001	
16. Agriculture	258	185	213	145	228		222	
17. Domestic science	179	149	148	121	113		110	
18. Management, administration	443	383	372	314	297		292	
19. Planning, architecture	222	137	179	123	229		228	
20. Plastic arts	302	231	281	212	692		691	
21. Performing arts	161	123	150	114	263		261	
22. Games, sports	238	164	213	144	179		173	
23. Literature								
(A) History and criticism	198	182	176	161	440		422	
(B) Literary texts	3 028	2 398	2 288	1 741	1 176		1 164	
24. Geography, travel	568	483	480	402	276		276	
25. History, biography	703	598	626	528	418		415	

Subject group / Groupe de sujets / Categoría de temas	The Former Yugoslav Rep. of Macedonia (1994) All editions Total	of which: books	First editions Total	of which: books	Ukraine‡ (1993) All editions Total	of which: books	First editions Total	of which: books
Total	672	589	380	338	5 002	4 145	4 804	3 957
1. Generalities	11	11	11	11	7	5	7	5
2. Philosophy, psychology	10	10	9	9	114	105	112	103
3. Religion, theology	5	2	5	2	115	85	114	84
4. Sociology, statistics	3	3	3	3	12	8	12	8
5. Political science	8	8	8	8	236	176	235	175
6. Law, public administration	2	2	1	1	107	83	103	79
7. Military art	3	3	3	3	1	1	1	1
8. Education, leisure	346	303	104	87	434	335	346	250
9. Trade, transport	-	-	-	-	127	98	120	91
10. Ethnography, folklore	1	1	1	1	13	11	11	9
11. Linguistics, philology	12	12	11	11	181	159	174	152
12. Mathematics	4	4	2	2	218	214	217	213
13. Natural sciences	14	14	14	14	580	535	576	531
14. Medical sciences	7	7	5	5	229	179	225	175
15. Engineering, crafts	25	25	20	20	818	660	814	656
16. Agriculture	9	9	9	9	228	184	212	168
17. Domestic science	2	2	2	2	76	64	63	51
18. Management, administration	2	2	2	2	7	6	7	6
19. Planning, architecture	-	-	-	-	58	35	57	34
20. Plastic arts	6	6	4	4	./.	./.	./.	./.
21. Performing arts	16	6	7	5	./.	./.	./.	./.
22. Games, sports	1	1	1	1	31	26	30	25
23. Literature								
(A) History and criticism	5	5	5	5	68	63	66	61
(B) Literary texts	146	120	119	100	1 044	851	1 011	825
24. Geography, travel	2	2	2	2	64	56	64	56
25. History, biography	32	31	32	31	234	206	227	199

Number of titles by subject group **7.4**
Nombre de titres par groupes de sujets
Número de títulos por categorías de temas

Subject group / Groupe de sujets / Categoría de temas	United Kingdom (1994)				Federal Republic of Yugoslavia (1994)			
	All editions		First editions		All editions		First editions	
	Total	of which: books	Total	of which: books	Total	of which: books	Total	of which: books
Total	95 015	88 032	73 317	67 391	2 799	2 475	1 814	1 544
1. Generalities	2 445	2 364	1 859	1 791	117	88	104	82
2. Philosophy, psychology	3 063	2 973	2 388	2 314	62	56	39	34
3. Religion, theology	4 278	3 933	3 550	3 248	48	38	30	21
4. Sociology, statistics	3 610	3 523	3 029	2 961	24	19	13	13
5. Political science	6 227	5 884	5 054	4 754	192	175	148	141
6. Law, public administration	5 302	4 830	4 199	3 773	242	190	206	157
7. Military art	442	402	342	304	-	-	-	-
8. Education, leisure	2 330	2 041	1 958	1 691	444	422	48	33
9. Trade, transport	1 413	1 280	1 087	985	5	5	4	4
10. Ethnography, folklore	467	431	326	298	1	-	-	-
11. Linguistics, philology	3 858	3 693	3 188	3 041	4	2	2	2
12. Mathematics	5 059	4 738	4 311	4 052	35	34	21	20
13. Natural sciences	5 705	5 484	4 382	4 198	41	38	32	31
14. Medical sciences	3 912	3 744	3 088	2 948	109	95	73	62
15. Engineering, crafts	1 238	1 141	965	883	126	100	90	65
16. Agriculture	1 678	1 606	1 257	1 195	50	40	46	36
17. Domestic science	3 325	3 215	2 453	2 354	12	12	8	8
18. Management, administration	816	739	677	609	112	100	83	73
19. Planning, architecture	3 378	3 036	2 830	2 509	19	14	19	14
20. Plastic arts	1 634	1 505	1 353	1 234	14	10	14	10
21. Performing arts	2 017	1 814	1 551	1 408	122	99	89	66
22. Games, sports	2 898	2 171	2 504	1 798	10	6	8	4
23. Literature								
(A) History and criticism	2 308	2 246	1 968	1 911	15	15	12	12
(B) Literary texts	16 831	15 419	11 010	9 960	831	766	616	560
24. Geography, travel	2 610	2 317	1 490	1 287	94	86	69	61
25. History, biography	8 171	7 503	6 498	5 885	70	65	40	35

Oceania

Subject group / Groupe de sujets / Categoría de temas	Australia‡ (1994)				Fiji‡ (1994)			
	All editions		First editions		All editions		First editions	
	Total	of which: books	Total	of which: books	Total	of which: books	Total	of which: books
Total	10 835		10 027		401	178	229	25
1. Generalities	218		187		-	-	-	-
2. Philosophy, psychology	151		143		-	-	-	-
3. Religion, theology	246		221		-	-	-	-
4. Sociology, statistics	430		408		1	1	1	1
5. Political science	1 314		1 239		14	14	14	14
6. Law, public administration	1 950		1 812		5	1	5	1
7. Military art	19		18		-	-	-	-
8. Education, leisure	430		416		2	2	2	2
9. Trade, transport	254		241		-	-	-	-
10. Ethnography, folklore	56		52		-	-	-	-
11. Linguistics, philology	157		140		21	2	19	-
12. Mathematics	125		118		11	-	10	-
13. Natural sciences	386		348		29	5	24	-
14. Medical sciences	391		343		6	3	6	3
15. Engineering, crafts	425		409		17	-	17	-
16. Agriculture	396		371		8	-	8	-
17. Domestic science	247		215		8	-	8	-
18. Management, administration	271		209		-	-	-	-
19. Planning, architecture	153		147		-	-	-	-
20. Plastic arts	254		251		-	-	-	-
21. Performing arts	98		87		1	1	-	-
22. Games, sports	195		170		1	1	-	-
23. Literature								
(A) History and criticism	1 812		1 730		-	-	-	-
(B) Literary texts	./.		./.		-	-	-	-
24. Geography, travel	213		158		18	8	11	1
25. History, biography	644		594		3	1	2	-

7.4 Number of titles by subject group
Nombre de titres par groupes de sujets
Número de títulos por categorías de temas

AFRICA:
Benin:

E--> Works not broken down are distributed among other classes without specification.

FR-> Les ouvrages non répartis sont ventilés entre les autres catégories sans spécification.

ESP> Las obras no repartidas quedan distribuidas entre las categorías sin especificación.

Egypt:

E--> Works of groups 5 to 10 are included in group 4; 13 in group 12; 15 to 18 in group 14; 20 to 22 in group 19; 23b in group 23a; 25 in group 24. School textbooks (809 of which 237 first editions) and children's books (23 of which 11 first editions) are included in the total but not identified in the 25 groups.

FR-> Les ouvrages des groupes 5 à 10 sont inclus dans le groupe 4; 13 dans le groupe 12; 15 à 18 dans le groupe 14; 20 à 22 dans le groupe 19; 23b dans le groupe 23a; 25 dans le groupe 24. Les manuels scolaires (809 dont 237 premières éditions) et les livres pour enfants (23 dont 11 premières éditions) sont compris dans le total mais ne sont pas répartis entre les 25 groupes.

ESP> Las obras de los grupos 5 a 10 quedan incluídas en el grupo 4; 13 en el grupo 12; 15 a 18 en el grupo 14; 20 a 22 en el grupo 19; 23b en el grupo 23a; 25 en el grupo 24. Los libros de texto (809 cuyas 237 primeras ediciones) y los libros para niños (23 cuyas 11 primeras ediciones) quedan incluídos en el total pero no se desglosan entre los 25 grupos.

Eritrea:

E--> The total number of books refers only to school textbooks (64) and government publications (19). The number of books of first editions refers only to government publications.

FR-> Le nombre total des livres se réfère seulement aux manuels scolaires (64) et aux publications officielles (19). Le nombre des livres des premières éditions se réfèrent seulement aux publications officielles.

ESP> El número total de los libros se refiere solamente a los libros de texto (64) y a las publicaciones oficiales (19). El número de los libros de las primeras ediciones se refiere solamente a las publicaciones oficiales.

Morocco:

E--> Works of groups 11, 12 and 23a are distributed, without specification, among the other subjects.

FR-> Les ouvrages des groupes 11, 12 et 23a sont répartis, sans spécification, entre les autres sujets.

ESP> Las obras de los grupos 11, 12 y 23a se deglosan, sin especificación, entre los otros temas.

South Africa:

E--> Works of group 23b are included in group 23a.

FR-> Les ouvrages du groupe 23b sont inclus dans le groupe 23a.

ESP> Las obras del grupo 23b quedan incluídas en el grupo 23a.

Tunisia:

E--> School textbooks (61), children's books (129) and government publications (62) as well as 8 books without specification are included in the total but not identified in the 25 groups.

FR-> Les manuels scolaires (61), les livres pour enfants (129) et les publications officielles (62) ainsi que 8 livres sans spécification sont compris dans le total mais ne sont pas répartis entre les 25 groupes.

ESP> Los libros de texto (61), los libros para niños (129) y las publicaciones oficiales (62) así como 8 libros sin especificación quedan incluídos en el total pero no se desglosan entre los 25 grupos.

Uganda:

E--> Data do not include government publications but include school textbooks (94 of which 19 first editions) and children's books (99 of which 20 first editions) for which a subject breakdown is not available.

FR-> Les données ne comprennent pas les publications officielles mais comprennent les manuels scolaires (94 dont 19 premières éditions) et les livres pour enfants (99 dont 20 premières éditions) pour lesquels une répartition par sujets n'est pas disponible.

ESP> Los datos no incluyen las publicaciones oficiales pero incluyen los libros de texto (94 cuyas 19 primeras ediciones) y los libros para niños (99 cuyas 20 primeras ediciones) para los cuales la repartición por temas no está disponible.

AMERICA, NORTH:
Belize:

E--> Data include first editions of 20 school textbooks, 6 children's books and 30 government publications for which a subject breakdown is not available.

FR-> Les données comprennent les premières éditions de 20 manuels scolaires, de 6 livres pour enfants et de 30 publications officielles pour lesquelles une répartition par sujets n'est pas disponible.y

ESP> Los datos incluyen las primeras ediciones de 20 libros de texto, de 6 libros para niños, y de 30 publicaciones oficiales para las cuales la repartición por temas no está disponible.

Canada:

E--> Works of group 23b are included in group 23a. Data include 5,878 first editions for which a subject breakdown is not available.

FR-> Les ouvrages du groupe 23b sont compris dans le groupe 23a. Les données comprennent 5 878 premières éditions pour lesquelles une répartition par sujets n'est pas disponible.

ESP> Las obras del grupo 23b quedan incluídas en el grupo 23a. Los datos incluyen 5 878 primeras ediciones para las cuales la repartición por temas no está disponible.

Trinidad and Tobago:

E--> Data refer only to first editions of one school textbook and 25 children's books.

FR-> Les données se réfèrent seulement aux premières éditions d'un manuel scolaire et de 25 livres pour enfants.

ESP> Los datos se refieren solamente a las primeras ediciones de uno libro de texto y de 25 libros para niños.

United States:

E--> Works of group 5 are included in group 4, 13 in group 12 and 23b in group 23a while those of groups 7, 10, 19 and 24 are distributed among other subjects without specification. Data dot not include pamphlets, school textbooks, government publications and university theses but include juvenile titles (5,321 of which 4,860 first editions) for which a subject breakdown is not available.

FR-> Les ouvrages du groupe 5 sont compris dans le groupe 4, 13 dans le groupe 12 et 23b dans le groupe 23a tandis que ceux des groupes 7, 10, 19 et 24 sont répartis, sans spécification, entre les autres sujets. Les données ne comprennent pas les brochures, les manuels scolaires, les publications officielles et les thèses universitaires mais tiennent compte des livres pour enfants (5 321 dont 4 860 premières éditions) pour lesquels une répartition par sujets n'est pas disponible.

ESP> Las obras del grupo 5 quedan incluídas en el grupo 4, 13 en el grupo 12 y 23b en el grupo 23a mientras que las de los grupos 7, 10, 19 y 24 se desglosan, sin especificación, entre los otros temas. Los datos no incluyen los folletos, los libros de texto, las publicaciones oficiales y las tesis universitarias pero incluyen los libros para niños (5 321 cuyas 4 860 primeras ediciones) para los cuales la repartición por temas no está disponible.

AMERICA, SOUTH:
Brazil:

E--> Data include reprints. Works of group 13 are included in group 12; 15 to 18 in group 14; 20 to 22 in group 19; 23b in group 23a; 25 in group 24.

FR-> Les données comprennent les réimpressions. Les ouvrages du groupe 13 sont inclus dans le groupe 12; 15 à 18 dans le groupe 14; 20 à 22 dans le groupe 19; 23b dans le groupe 23a; 25 dans le groupe 24.

ESP> Los datos incluyen las reimpresiones. Las obras del grupo 13 quedan incluídas en el grupo 12; 15 a 18 en el grupo 14; 20 a 22 en el grupo 19; 23b en el grupo 23a; 25 en el grupo 24.

Guyana:

E--> Data refer only to first editions of 32 school textbooks and one children's book. Works of groups 5 to 10 are included in group 4.

FR-> Les données se réfèrent seulement aux premières éditions de 32 manuels scolaires et d'un livre pour enfants. Les ouvrages des groupes 5 à 10 sont inclus dans le groupe 4.

ESP> Los datos se refieren solamente a las primeras ediciones de 32 libros de texto y de uno libro para niños. Las obras de los grupos 5 a 10 quedan incluídas en el grupo 4.

ASIA:
Armenia:

E--> School textbooks (21) and children's books (9) are included in the total but not identified in the 25 groups.

FR-> Les manuels scolaires (21) et les livres pour enfants (9) sont compris dans le total mais ne sont pas répartis entre les 25 groupes.

ESP> Los libros de texto (21) y los libros para niños (9) quedan incluídos en el total pero no están repartidos entre los 25 grupos.

China:

E--> Works of group 6 are included in group 5, 10 and 22 in group 8, 13 in group 12; 20 and 21 in group 19; 23b in group 23a and 25 in group 24 while those of groups 3, 17 and 18 are distributed among other subjects, without specification.

FR-> Les ouvrages du groupe 6 sont inclus dans le groupe 5, 10 et 22 dans le groupe 8; 13 dans le groupe 12; 20 et 21 dans le groupe 19; 23b dans le groupe 23a et 25 dans le groupe 24 tandis que ceux des groupes 3, 17 et 18 sont répartis, sans spécification, entre les autres sujets.

ESP> Las obras del grupo 6 quedan incluídas en el grupo 5, 10 y 22 en el grupo 8, 13 en el grupo 12; 22 y 21 en el grupo 19; 23b en el grupo 23a y 25 en el grupo 24 mientras que las de

Number of titles by subject group **7.4**
Nombre de titres par groupes de sujets
Número de títulos por categorías de temas

los grupos 3, 17 y 18 se desglosan, sin especificación, entre los otros temas.

Indonesia:

E--> School textbooks (715), children's books (134) and government publications (272) are included in the total but not identified in the 25 groups.

FR-> Les manuels scolaires (715), les livres pour enfants (134) et les publications officielles (272) sont inclus dans le total mais ne sont pas répartis entre les 25 groupes.

ESP> Los libros de texto (715), los libros para niños (134) y las publicaciones oficiales (272) quedan incluídos en el total pero no se desglosan entre los 25 grupos.

Iran, Islamic Republic of:

E--> Works of groups 5 to 10 are included in group 4; 13 in group 12; 15 to 18 in group 14; 20 to 22 in group 19; 23b in group 23a; 25 in group 24. Children's books (1,201) are included in the total but not in the 25 groups.

FR-> Les ouvrages des groupes 5 à 10 sont inclus dans le groupe 4; 13 dans le groupe 12; 15 à 18 dans le groupe 14; 20 à 22 dans le groupe 19; 23b dans le groupe 23a; 25 dans le groupe 24. Les livres pour enfants (1 201) sont inclus dans le total mais ne sont pas répartis entre les 25 groupes.

ESP> Las obras de los grupos 5 a 10 quedan incluídas en el grupo 4; 13 en el grupo 12; 15 a 18 en el grupo 14; 20 a 22 en el grupo 19; 23b en el grupo 23a; 25 en el grupo 24. Los libros para niños (1 201) quedan incluídos en el total pero no están repartidos entre los 25 grupos.

Israel:

E--> Works of group 10 are included in group 4; 18 in group 17; 19 in group 15; 23b in group 23a. Data include government publications (657) and also titles (16 of which 4 first editions) for which a subject breakdown is not available.

FR-> Les ouvrages du groupe 10 sont inclus dans le groupe 4; 18 dans le groupe 17; 19 dans le groupe 15; 23b dans le groupe 23a. Les données comprennent les publications officielles et aussi des titres (16 dont 4 premières éditions) pour lesquels une répartition par sujets n'est pas disponible.

ESP> Las obras del grupo 10 quedan incluídas en el grupo 4; 18 en el grupo 17; 19 en el grupo 15; 23b en el grupo 23a. Los datos incluyen las publicaciones oficiales así como títulos (16 cuyas 4 primeras ediciones) para los cuales la repartición por temas no está disponible.

Japan:

E--> Works on *statistics* (group 4) are included with *economics* (group 5) and those on *military art* (group 7) with *politics* (group 5).

FR-> Les ouvrages relatifs aux *statistiques* (groupe 4) sont compris avec les *sciences économiques* (groupe 5) et ceux relatifs à *art et science militaire* (groupe 7) avec les *sciences politiques* (groupe 5).

ESP> Las obras relativas a la *estadistica* (grupo 4) quedan incluídas con las *ciencias economicas* (grupo 5) y las de las relativas a *arte y ciencia militar* (grupo 7) con las *ciencias politicas* (grupo 5).

Kazakstan:

E--> Data include titles (151) for which a subject breakdown is not available.

FR-> Les données comprennent les titres (151) pour lesquels une répartition par sujets n'est pas disponible.

ESP> Los datos incluyen títulos (151) para los cuales la repartición por temas no está disponible.

Kuwait:

E--> Data refer to government publications only.

FR-> Les données se réfèrent aux publications officielles seulement.

ESP> Los datos se refieren a las publicaciones oficiales solamente.

Myanmar:

E--> Works of groups 5 to 10 are included in group 4; 13 in group 12; 15 to 18 in group 14; 20 to 22 in group 19; 11 and 23b in group 23a; 25 in group 24.

FR-> Les ouvrages des groupes 5 à 10 sont inclus dans le groupe 4; 13 dans le groupe 12; 15 à 18 dans le groupe 14; 20 à 22 dans le groupe 19; 11 et 23b dans le groupe 23a; 25 dans le groupe 24.

ESP> Las obras de los grupos 5 a 10 quedan incluídas en el grupo 4; 13 en el grupo 12; 15 a 18 en el grupo 14; 20 a 22 en el grupo 19; 11 y 23b en el grupo 23a; 25 en el grupo 24.

Tajikistan:

E--> School textbooks (21 of which 11 first editions), children's books (11 first editions) and government publications (11 first editions) are included in the total but not in the class breakdown.

FR-> Les manuels scolaires (21 dont 11 premières éditions), les livres pour enfants (11 premières éditions) et les publications officielles (11 premières éditions) sont compris dans le total mais ne sont pas répartis par catégories.

ESP> Los libros de texto (21 cuyas 11 primeras ediciones), los libros para niños (11 primeras ediciones) y las publicaciones oficiales (11 primeras ediciones) quedan incluídos en el total pero no están repartidos por categorías.

United Arab Emirates:

E--> Data refer only to school textbooks.

FR-> Les données se réfèrent seulement aux manuels scolaires.

ESP> Los datos se refieren solamente a los libros de texto.

Uzbekistan:

E--> School textbooks (194), children's books (42) and government publications (120) are included in the total but not identified in the 25 groups. Works not broken down are distributed among other subjects without specification.

FR-> Les manuels scolaires (194), les livres pour enfants (42) et les publications officielles (120) sont compris dans le total mais ne sont pas répartis entre les 25 groupes. Les ouvrages non répartis sont ventilés entre les autres sujets sans spécification.

ESP> Los libros de texto (194), los libros para niños (42) y las publicaciones oficiales (120) quedan incluídos en el total pero no se desglosan entre los 25 grupos. Las obras no repartidas quedan distribuidas entre los otros temas sin especificación.

Viet Nam:

E--> Works of groups 5 to 10 are included in group 4; 15 to 18 in group 14; 23b in group 23a while those of other groups are distributed without specification among other subjects . School textbooks (1,370) and children's books (683) as well as 733 titles without specification are included in the total but not in the 25 groups.

FR-> Les ouvrages des groupes 5 à 10 sont inclus dans le groupe 4; 15 à 18 dans le groupe 14; 23b dans le groupe 23a, tandis que ceux des autres groupes sont répartis, sans spécification, entre les autres sujets. Les manuels scolaires (1 370) et les livres pour enfants (683) ainsi que 733 titres sans spécification sont compris dans le total mais ne sont pas répartis entre les 25 groupes.

ESP> Las obras de los grupos 5 a 10 quedan incluídas en el grupo 4; 15 a 18 en el grupo 14; 23b en el grupo 23a, mientras que las de los otros grupos se desglosan, sin especificación entre los otros temas. Los libros de texto (1 370) y los libros para niños (683) así como 733 títulos sin especificación quedan incluídos en el total pero no están repartidos entre los 25 grupos.

EUROPE:

Austria:

E--> Data do not include school textbooks. Works of group 7 are included in group 5; 10 in group 24; 11 in group 23a; 17 in group 16; 18 in groups 4 and 5; 19 in groups 15 and 20.

FR-> Les données ne comprennent pas les manuels scolaires. Les ouvrages du groupe 7 sont inclus dans le groupe 5; 10 dans le groups 24; 11 dans le groupe 23a; 17 dans le groupe 16; 18 dans les groupes 4 et 5; 19 dans les groupes 15 et 20.

ESP> Los datos no incluyen los libros de texto. Las obras del grupo 7 quedan incluídas en el grupo 5; 10 en el grupo 24; 11 en el grupo 23a; 17 en el grupo 16; 18 en los grupos 4 y 5; 19 en los grupos 15 y 20.

Croatia:

E--> Works of group 23b are included in group 23a. The total number of all editions include 177 titles for which a subject breakdown is not available.

FR-> Les ouvrages du groupe 23b sont compris dans le groupe 23a. Le nombre total de toutes les éditions comprennent 177 titres pour lesquels une répartition par sujet n'est pas disponible.

ESP> Las obras del grupo 23b quedan incluídas en el grupo 23a. El número total de todas las edicíones incluyen 177 títulos para los cuales la repartición por temas no está disponible.

Denmark:

E--> Works of group 9 are included in group 18.

FR-> Les ouvrages du groupe 9 sont inclus dans le groupe 18.

ESP> Las obras del grupo 9 quedan incluídas en el grupo 18.

France:

E--> Works of group 12 include also 159 titles on science in general.

FR-> Les ouvrages du groupe 12 comprennent aussi 159 titres relatifs aux sciences en général.

ESP> Los obras del grupo 12 incluyen también 159 títulos relativos a las ciencias en general.

Iceland:

E--> Works of groups 20 and 21 are included in group 19.

FR-> Les ouvrages des groupes 20 et 21 sont inclus dans le groupe 19.

ESP> Las obras de los grupos 20 y 21 quedan incluídas en el grupo 19.

Latvia:

E--> School textbooks (202 of which 146 first editions), children's books (188 of which 138 first editions) and government publications (two first editions) are included in the total but not identified in the 25 groups.

7.4 Number of titles by subject group
Nombre de titres par groupes de sujets
Número de títulos por categorías de temas

FR-> Les manuels scolaires (202 dont 146 premières éditions), les livres pour enfants (188 dont 138 premières éditions) et les publications officielles (deux premières éditions) sont inclus dans le total mais ne sont pas répartis entre les 25 groupes.

ESP> Los libros de texto (202 cuyas 146 primeras ediciones), los libros para niños (188 cuyas 138 primeras ediciones) y las publicaciones oficiales (dos primeras ediciones) quedan incluídas en el total pero no se deglosan entre los 25 grupos.

Netherlands:

E--> School textbooks (11,002) and children's books (9,615) are included in the total of *all editions* but not in the class breakdown.

FR-> Les manuels scolaires (11 002) et les livres pour enfants (9 615) sont compris dans le total de *toutes les éditions* mais ne sont pas répartis par catégories.

ESP> Los libros de texto (11 002) y los libros para niños (9 615) quedan incluídos en el total de *todas las ediciones* pero no están repartidos por categorías.

Norway:

E--> Data do not include school textbooks and government publications. Works of group 7 are included in group 6; 22 in group 21.

FR-> Les données ne comprennent pas les manuels scolaires et les publications officielles. Les ouvrages du groupe 7 sont compris dans le groupe 6; 22 dans le groupe 21.

ESP> Los datos excluyen los libros de texto y las publicaciones oficiales. Las obras del grupo 7 quedan incluídas en el grupo 6; 22 en el grupo 21.

Portugal:

E--> Data include reprints. Works of groups 5 to 10 are included in group 4; 15 to 18 in group 14; 20 to 22 in group 19; 23b in group 23a while those of other groups are distributed among other subjects without specification. School textbooks (1,381 of which 599 first editions) and children's books (1,025 of which 630 first editions) as well as 945 titles of which 549 first editions without specification are included in the total but not identified in the 25 groups.

FR-> Les données comprennent les réimpressions. Les ouvrages des groupes 5 à 10 sont inclus dans le groupe 4; 15 à 18 dans le groupe 14; 20 à 22 dans le groupe 19; 23b dans le groupe 23a tandis que ceux des autres groupes sont répartis, sans spécification, entre les autres sujets. Les manuels scolaires (1 381 dont 599 premières éditions) et les livres pour enfants (1 025 dont 630 premières éditions) ainsi que 945 titres dont 549 premières éditions sans spécification sont compris dans le total mais ne sont pas répartis entre les 25 groupes.

ESP> Los datos incluyen las reimpresiones. Las obras de los grupos 5 a 10 quedan incluídos en el grupo 4; 15 a 18 en el grupo 14; 20 a 22 en el grupo 19; 23b en el grupo 23a mientras que las de los otros grupos se desglosan, sin especificación, entre los otros temas. Los libros de texto (1 381 cuyas 599 primeras ediciones), y los libros para niños (1 025 cuyas 630 primeras ediciones) así como 945 títulos cuyas 549 primeras ediciones quedan incluídos en el total pero no se desglosan entre los 25 grupos.

Romania:

E--> Works of group 23b are included in group 23a.

FR-> Les ouvrages du groupe 23b sont inclus dans le groupe 23a.

ESP> Las obras del grupo 23b quedan incluídas en el grupo 23a.

Russian Federation:

E--> Works of groups 20 and 21 are included in group 19.

FR-> Les ouvrages des groupes 20 et 21 sont inclus dans le groupe 19.

ESP> Las obras de los grupos 20 y 21 quedan incluídas en el grupo 19.

Spain:

E--> Works of group 23b are included in group 23a.

FR-> Les ouvrages du groupe 23b sont inclus dans le groupe 23a.

ESP> Las obras del grupo 23b quedan incluídas en el grupo 23a.

Switzerland:

E--> School textbooks (381 of which 350 first editions) and children's books (641 of which 628 first editions) are included in the total but not identified in the 25 groups.

FR-> Les manuels scolaires (381 dont 350 premières éditions) et les livres pour enfants (641 dont 628 premières éditions) sont compris dans le total mais ne sont pas répartis entre les 25 groupes.

ESP> Los libros de texto (381 cuyas 350 primeras ediciones) y los libros para niños (641 cuyas 628 primeras ediciones) quedan comprendidos en el total pero no se desglosan entre los 25 grupos.

Ukraine:

E--> Works of groups 20 and 21 are included in group 19.

FR-> Les ouvrages des groupes 20 et 21 sont inclus dans le groupe 19.

ESP> Las obras de los grupos 20 y 21 quedan incluídas en el grupo 19.

OCEANIA:

Australia:

E--> Works of group 23b are included in group 23a.

FR-> les ouvrages du groupe 23b sont inclus dans le groupe 23a.

ESP> Las obras del grupo 23b quedan incluídas en el grupo 23a.

Fiji:

E--> Data refer only to books published by the Ministry of Education and the Government printing department. School textbooks (223 of which 102 first editions) and government publications (33) are included in the total but not in the 25 groups.

FR-> Les données se réfèrent seulement aux livres publiés par le ministère de l'éducation et le *Government printing department*. Les manuels scolaires (223 dont 102 premières éditions) et les publications officielles (33) sont compris dans le total mais ne sont pas répartis entre les 25 groupes.

ESP> Los datos se refieren solamente a los libros publicados por el Ministerio de Educación y el *Government printing department*. Los libros de texto (223 cuyas 102 primeras ediciones) y las publicaciones oficiales (33) quedan incluídos en el total pero no están repartidos entre los 25 grupos.

Number of copies by UDC classes 7.5
Nombre d'exemplaires classés d'après la CDU
Número de ejemplares clasificados por materias (CDU)

7.5 Book production: number of copies by UDC classes

Edition de livres: nombre d'exemplaires classés d'après la CDU

Edición de libros: número de ejemplares clasificados por materias (CDU)

Data are presented in thousands　　　　　Les données sont présentées en milliers　　　　　Los datos se presentan en millares

Country / Pays / País	Year / Année / Año	Total / Total / Total	Gener-alities / Généra-lités / Genera-lidades	Philos-ophy / Philo-sophie / Filo-sofía	Religion / Religion / Religión	Social sciences / Sciences sociales / Ciencias sociales	Phil-ology / Philo-logie / Filo-logía	Pure sciences / Sciences pures / Ciencias puras	Applied sciences / Sciences appl. / Ciencias aplicadas	Arts / Arts / Artes	Litera-ture / Litté-rature / Litera-tura	Geog./ history / Géogr./ histoire / Geogr./ historia
		(1)	(2)	(3)	(4)	(5)	(6)	(7)	(8)	(9)	(10)	(11)
Africa												
Benin‡	1992	874	18	7	-	692	12	24	109	-	-	12
	1994	42	2	-	1	11	3	3	18	0	3	1
Egypt‡	1993	108 042	4 185	586	11 196	4 605	9 417	11 538	8 571	3 073	2 643	2 384
Eritrea	1993	420	-	-	-	85	229	93	13	-	-	-
Gambia	1994	20	-	-	3	2	4	6	0	-	-	5
Madagascar‡	1992	*402	-	4	*35	*340	-	3	*8	1	*8	3
	1993	537	5	9	80	169	26	23	89	-	128	8
	1994	287	-	18	85	97	12	1	51	-	12	11
Mauritius	1992	99	1	1	2	15	28	20	6	0	11	15
	1993	135	1	1	2	31	45	9	7	-	34	5
	1994	100	7	1	4	43	7	2	10	2	12	12
Morocco‡	1994	1 380	234	11	133	470	./.	1	71	3	163	294
South Africa	1992	42 935	115	87	6 861	3 728	9 794	3 694	7 022	595	8 266	2 773
	1993	36 813	52	75	6 104	2 480	9 151	3 666	4 308	462	8 170	2 345
	1994	37 561	109	72	6 110	2 072	9 477	5 107	3 519	578	7 221	3 296
Tunisia‡	1992	94	15	4	3	14	-	16	17	2	20	3
Uganda‡	1993	2 229	-	-	8	19	269	287	90	-	6	90
Zaire‡	1992	535	-	6	240	232	-	-	50	-	-	7
America, North												
Cuba	1992	7 162	276	47	10	2 743	610	846	749	287	1 264	330
	1993	2 087	125	12	3	895	-	22	225	58	586	161
	1994	4 610	269	5	8	1 984	594	668	158	202	556	166
Honduras	1993	80	-	-	2	15	1	-	-	-	58	4
Trinidad and Tobago‡	1993	30	-	-	-	30	-	-	-	-	.	.
America, South												
Argentina‡	1992	49 293	384	1 587	3 379	7 173	418	356	1 963	2 559	10 272	21 202
	1994	48 882	804	3 832	4 008	10 363	937	70	3 866	3 926	17 591	3 485
Brazil‡	1992	189 933	13 102	3 320	14 402	12 152	1 119	4 496	1 571	979	11 910	2 569
	1993	131 251	5 051	2 775	14 935	14 145	32 007	30 337	14 542	2 863	9 573	5 023
	1994	104 397	10 030	5 490	9 953	19 673	21 277	15 828	6 389	2 166	5 602	7 989
Ecuador‡	1994	40	-	-	-	-	2	-	-	2	36	-
Guyana‡	1994	508	-	-	-	26	192	212	78	.	-	-
Venezuela‡	1994	8 180	175	332	557	2 435	314	274	1 906	497	986	704

7.5 Number of copies by UDC classes
Nombre d'exemplaires classés d'après la CDU
Número de ejemplares clasificados por materias (CDU)

Country / Pays / País	Year / Année / Año	Total / Total / Total	Gener-alities / Généra-lités / Genera-lidades	Philos-ophy / Philo-sophie / Filo-sofía	Religion / Religion / Religión	Social sciences / Sciences sociales / Ciencias sociales	Phil-ology / Philo-logie / Filo-logía	Pure sciences / Sciences pures / Ciencias puras	Applied sciences / Sciences appl. / Ciencias aplicadas	Arts / Arts / Artes	Litera-ture / Litté-rature / Litera-tura	Geog./history / Géogr./histoire / Geogr./historia
		(1)	(2)	(3)	(4)	(5)	(6)	(7)	(8)	(9)	(10)	(11)
Asia												
Armenia‡	1994	1 739	-	9	5	92	105	31	48	12	402	65
Azerbaijan	1992	8 954	25	185	99	2 911	587	144	617	52	3 356	978
	1994	5 557	39	134	306	3 744	99	6	183	68	967	11
China‡	1993	5 855 140	31 390	10 810	./.	5 178 470	65 070	47 490	232 440	108 370	115 940	65 160
	1994	5 945 320	31 020	9 880	./.	5 298 300	76 570	47 010	225 860	78 090	122 470	56 120
Cyprus	1992	1 359	33	5	80	468	145	31	303	80	149	65
	1993	1 354	26	5	80	500	85	40	345	71	145	57
	1994	1 530	22	5	70	560	91	46	407	133	153	43
Georgia‡	1994	1 131	-	37	76	237	117	30	76	12	476	70
Iran, Islamic Republic of‡	1992	26 275	1 256	1 302	4 028	2 227	2 427	1 574	3 180	1 858	6 326	2 097
Israel‡	1992	9 368	152	118	1 273	1 183	1 084	1 180	397	470	2 648	830
Japan‡	1992	316 725	4 811	13 698	4 224	36 201	5 762	5 005	20 436	56 347	157 353	12 888
Kazakstan‡	1992	30 512	-	181	419	9 792	1 590	241	2 714	58	14 616	901
	1994	18 999	-	168	320	11 075	455	45	438	169	3 051	612
Korea, Rep. of	1992	136 392	50 225	4 755	4 538	8 332	13 505	17 465	7 274	9 709	16 009	4 580
	1993	151 344	9 151	3 617	5 578	43 250	20 270	15 954	7 943	12 875	27 385	5 321
	1994	160 305	5 072	2 636	5 774	43 733	25 419	24 258	7 939	15 351	26 427	3 696
Kyrgyzstan	1994	1 875	119	12	180	874	87	6	50	3	544	-
Lao People's Democr. Rep.‡	1992	136	-	-	1	13	31	-	10	-	73	8
Malaysia	1993	13 960	76	75	1 538	1 533	3 657	1 761	692	485	3 197	946
	1994	17 424	81	114	1 976	2 667	5 365	1 987	788	518	2 097	1 831
Mongolia‡	1992	959	104	48	15	115	12	82	65	21	405	92
Oman‡	1992	25	1	-	3	-	9	-	1	-	-	11
Pakistan‡	1992	317	8	-	-	5	-	14	5	-	6	1
	1994	714	114	2	1	166	387	12	17	-	12	3
Sri Lanka	1992	26 777	734	176	1 428	15 348	2 296	1 289	1 555	199	1 445	2 307
	1993	16 931	376	108	1 256	5 970	3 449	1 726	1 167	129	1 313	1 437
	1994	15 337	428	109	1 030	5 379	3 045	1 095	1 120	87	1 304	1 740
Tajikistan‡	1994	2 561	-	25	30	128	24	66	367	18	516	61
Turkmenistan	1992	6 604	159	24	180	2 390	69	93	224	74	3 209	182
United Arab Emirates‡	1992	5 558	30	39	460	53	2 306	1 902	160	10	-	598
	1993	5 117	-	28	631	21	1 902	1 819	145	4	-	567
Uzbekistan‡	1992	47 657	910	5 355	./.	887	588	./.	3 582	./.	16 490	./.
	1993	44 033	./.	2 054	./.	414	923	./.	2 207	./.	17 451	...
Viet Nam‡	1992	71 500	./.	./.	./.	1 912	./.	./.	980	./.	2 160	./.
	1993	83 000	./.	./.	./.	1 475	./.	./.	1 308	./.	4 014	...
Europe												
Belarus	1992	71 940	1 055	964	4 409	15 004	1 665	311	8 010	417	39 599	506
	1993	98 351	3 269	539	13 946	17 392	1 813	294	11 082	1 086	47 782	1 148
	1994	80 606	3 438	584	11 511	18 446	1 439	284	8 860	301	34 849	894
Bulgaria	1992	53 677	1 328	1 416	1 606	10 687	10	1 287	3 813	803	30 499	2 228
	1993	55 356	2 292	1 714	1 395	12 613	1 118	1 740	4 322	748	27 359	2 055
	1994	42 746	2 690	1 389	692	10 312	1 008	1 252	3 578	584	20 091	1 150
Estonia	1992	15 960	402	728	769	1 592	-	589	2 274	375	8 811	420
	1993	12 313	186	240	430	937	-	643	1 030	668	7 433	746
	1994	8 592	256	226	260	1 274	-	798	772	530	3 999	477
Holy See‡	1992	153	3	29	85	22	5	-	-	-	-	9
Hungary	1992	88 097	4 046	2 667	2 040	2 920	6 579	9 098	8 213	3 661	43 440	5 433
	1993	77 157	3 189	1 624	2 291	3 112	5 047	6 214	6 768	3 062	41 328	4 522
	1994	75 645	2 731	1 701	2 033	3 163	4 075	7 124	7 071	3 708	39 307	4 732
Italy	1992	223 655	11 425	7 645	14 725	40 797	7 943	11 005	18 479	20 205	72 992	18 439
	1993	251 066	16 788	10 278	12 118	37 189	8 837	11 328	20 261	17 673	98 794	17 800
	1994	289 100	19 264	9 737	15 995	37 891	9 272	12 942	19 224	18 658	118 270	27 847

Number of copies by UDC classes 7.5
Nombre d'exemplaires classés d'après la CDU
Número de ejemplares clasificados por materias (CDU)

Country / Pays / País	Year / Année / Año	Total / Total / Total (1)	Generalities / Généralités / Generalidades (2)	Philosophy / Philosophie / Filosofía (3)	Religion / Religion / Religión (4)	Social sciences / Sciences sociales / Ciencias sociales (5)	Philology / Philologie / Filología (6)	Pure sciences / Sciences pures / Ciencias puras (7)	Applied sciences / Sciences appl. / Ciencias aplicadas (8)	Arts / Arts / Artes (9)	Literature / Littérature / Literatura (10)	Geog./history / Géogr./histoire / Geogr./historia (11)
Latvia‡	1992	21 980	576	938	1 358	810	375	60	2 870	930	8 314	576
	1993	14 410	397	316	744	965	601	58	1 386	339	4 757	522
	1994	10 835	298	365	395	575	324	64	749	179	3 388	190
Lithuania	1992	30 954	3 015	1 041	1 812	2 385	2 660	1 498	3 328	1 353	12 504	1 358
	1993	19 242	1 546	517	1 171	1 129	2 354	1 502	1 636	317	8 169	901
	1994	19 627	1 780	256	1 085	1 094	2 207	1 489	2 401	452	7 886	977
Moldova	1992	363	1	0	3	244	5	0	11	1	95	3
	1993	5 619	-	7	168	320	531	459	278	145	3 118	593
	1994	5 850	5	337	271	1 896	281	130	407	199	2 174	150
Poland	1992	125 820	3 487	3 621	4 427	6 409	13 606	15 716	12 841	5 725	46 983	13 005
	1993	102 533	1 299	2 075	5 197	4 686	9 740	10 547	10 667	4 455	44 474	9 393
	1994	98 612	3 809	1 920	3 190	4 569	7 926	11 312	11 178	5 030	40 631	9 047
Portugal‡	1992	24 324	582	1 507	./.	./.	./.	./.	429	374	2 776	./.
	1993	21 234	1 664	./.	./.	1 815	./.	./.	630	233	2 981	./.
	1994	26 942	./.	./.	./.	2 285	./.	869	./.	369	3 407	./.
Romania	1992	66 598	589	1 436	1 830	3 942	6 255	8 026	2 715	1 615	36 017	4 173
	1993	75 907	949	1 767	2 513	4 327	8 276	8 574	4 600	2 183	37 558	5 160
	1994	50 230	605	922	1 448	3 844	4 532	6 466	2 912	872	25 222	3 407
Russian Federation	1992	1 312 964	54 293	15 430	33 917	269 561	24 734	10 116	135 927	15 364	734 212	19 410
	1993	949 861	29 447	15 632	34 372	192 883	12 123	6 074	91 870	7 171	546 658	13 631
	1994	594 323	38 626	12 446	27 946	154 489	10 986	3 870	62 534	5 491	267 464	10 471
Slovakia	1992	13 258	624	250	1 206	2 326	924	879	1 703	2 956	1 704	686
	1993	8 355	161	215	525	2 060	637	1 008	2 026	496	865	362
	1994	6 139	64	189	445	1 969	290	555	1 264	126	734	503
Spain	1992	194 785	4 846	4 335	9 698	24 787	11 428	9 798	19 002	11 372	79 848	19 671
	1993	183 229	5 301	5 078	11 759	26 611	10 620	9 035	20 508	10 199	69 374	14 744
	1994	180 181	6 273	4 566	9 232	23 315	8 832	10 941	20 341	10 210	69 626	16 845
The Former Yugoslav Rep. of Macedonia	1994	2 918	10	6	40	2 515	9	15	21	87	183	32
Ukraine	1992	128 471	233	645	3 556	29 807	2 501	1 533	16 111	1 087	70 918	2 080
	1993	87 567	110	578	1 353	24 896	2 308	2 065	13 391	576	40 331	1 959
Federal Rep. of Yugoslavia	1992	11 351	61	78	200	7 077	3	121	868	798	2 031	114
	1994	11 905	712	107	92	8 392	3	69	610	203	1 402	315
Oceania												
Fiji‡	1994	2 256	-	-	-	88	325	290	94	2	-	148

AFRICA:
Benin:
E--> Data are all first editions and, for 1992, do not include pamphlets.
FR-> Tous les ouvrages recensés sont des premières éditions et, en 1992, ne comprennent pas les brochures.
ESP> Todas las obras consideradas son primeras ediciones y, en 1992, no incluyen los folletos.
Egypt:
E--> School textbooks (49.3 million) and children's books (583,000) are included in the total but not in the class breakdown.
FR-> Les manuels scolaires (49,3 millions) et les livres pour enfants (583 000) sont compris dans le total mais ne sont pas répartis par catégories.
ESP> Los libros de texto (49,3 millones) y los libros para niños (583 000) quedan incluídos pero no se desglosan por categorías.
Madagascar:
E--> For 1992, all first editions.
FR-> En 1992, tous les ouvrages recensés sont des premières éditions.
ESP> En 1992, todas las obras consideradas son primeras ediciones.
Morocco:
E--> Works on philology are distributed, without specification, among other classes.
FR-> Les ouvrages relatifs à la philologie sont distribués, sans spécification, entre les autres catégories.
ESP> Las obras relativas a la filología se desglosan, sin especificación, entre las otras categorías.
Tunisia:
E--> Data do not include pamphlets.
FR-> Les données ne tiennent pas compte des brochures.
ESP> Los datos no incluyen les folletos.
Uganda:
E--> Data do not include pamphlets and government publications but include school textbooks (720,000) and children's books (740,000) for which a class breakdown is not available.
FR-> Les données ne comprennent pas les brochures et les publications officielles mais comprennent les manuels scolaires (720 000) et les livres pour enfants (740 000) pour lesquels une répartition par catégories n'est pas disponible.
ESP> Los datos no incluyen los folletos y las publicaciones oficiales pero incluyen los libros de texto (720 000) y los libros para niños (740 000) para los cuales la repartición por categorías no está disponible.
Zaire:
E--> All first editions.
FR-> Tous les ouvrages recensés sont des premières éditions.
ESP> Todas las obras consideradas son primeras ediciones.
AMERICA, NORTH:
Trinidad and Tobago:
E--> Data refer only to first editions of school textbooks (10,000) and children's books (20,000).

7.5 Number of copies by UDC classes
Nombre d'exemplaires classés d'après la CDU
Número de ejemplares clasificados por materias (CDU)

FR–> Les données se réfèrent seulement aux premières éditions des manuels scolaires (10 000) et des livres pour enfants (20 000).

ESP> Los datos se refieren solamente a las primeras ediciones de los libros de texto (10 000) y de los libros para niños (20 000).

AMERICA, SOUTH:

Argentina:

E––> For 1994, data do not include pamphlets.

FR–> En 1994, les données ne tiennent pas compte des brochures.

ESP> En 1994, los datos no incluyen los folletos.

Brazil:

E––> Data exclude pamphlets but include reprints. For 1992, school textbooks (73.9 million) and children's books (50.5 million) are included in the total but not in the class breakdown.

FR–> Les données excluent les brochures mais incluent les réimpressions. En 1992, les manuels scolaires (73,9 millions) et les livres pour enfants (50,5 millions) sont compris dans le total mais ne sont pas répartis par catégories.

ESP> Los datos excluyen los folletos pero incluyen las reimpresiones. En 1992, los libros de texto (73,9 millones) y los libros para niños (50,5 millones) quedan incluídos en el total pero no están repartidos por categorías.

Ecuador:

E––> Data refer only to first editions.

FR–> Les données ne se réfèrent qu'aux premières éditions.

ESP> Los datos se refieren solamente a las primeras ediciones.

Guyana:

E––> Data refer only to first editions of school textbooks (468,000) and children's books (40,000).

FR–> Les données se réfèrent seulement aux premières éditions des manuels scolaires (468 000) et des livres pour enfants (40 000).

ESP> Los datos se refieren solamente a las primeras ediciones de los libros de texto (468 000) y de los libros para niños (40 000).

Venezuela:

E––> Data refer only to first editions.

FR–> Les données ne se réfèrent qu'aux premières éditions.

ESP> Los datos se refieren solamente a las primeras ediciones.

ASIA:

Armenia:

E––> All first editions. School textbooks (902,000) and children's books (68,000) are included in the total but not in the class breakdown.

FR–> Tous les ouvrages recensés sont des premières éditions. Les manuels scolaires (902 000) et les livres pour enfants (68 000) sont compris dans le total mais ne sont pas répartis par catégories.

ESP> Todas las obras consideradas son primeras ediciones. Los libros de texto (902 000) y los libros para niños (68 000) quedan incluídos en el total pero no están repartidos por categorías.

China:

E––> Works of UDC class 3 (religion) are distributed, without specification, among other classes.

FR–> Les ouvrages de la catégorie 3 de la CDU (religion) sont distribués, sans spécification, entre les les autres catégories.

ESP> Las obras de la categoría 3 de la CDU (religión) se desglosan, sin especificación, entre las otras categorías.

Georgia:

E––> All first editions.

FR–> Tous les ouvrages recensés sont des premières éditions.

ESP> Todas las obras consideradas son primeras ediciones.

Iran, Islamic Republic of:

E––> Data do not include pamphlets.

FR–> Les données ne tiennent pas compte des brochures.

ESP> Los datos no incluyen los folletos.

Israel:

E––> Data include copies of books (33,000) for which a class breakdown is not available.

FR–> Les données comprennent des exemplaires de livres (33 000) pour lesquels une répartition par catégories n'est pas disponible.

ESP> Los datos incluyen ejemplares de libros (33 000) para los cuales la repartición por categorías no está disponible.

Japan:

E––> Data do not include pamphlets and refer only to first editions.

FR–> Les données ne comprennent pas les brochures et ne se réfèrent qu'aux premières éditions.

ESP> Los datos no incluyen los folletos y se refieren a las primeras ediciones solamente.

Kazakstan:

E––> For 1994, data are first editions only and include 2.7 million copies for which a class breakdown is not available.

FR–> En 1994, les données ne se réfèrent qu'aux premières éditions et comprennent 2,7 millions d'exemplaires pour lesquels une répartition par catégories n'est pas disponible.

ESP> En 1994, los datos se refieren solamente a las primeras ediciones y incluyen 2,7 millones de ejemplares para los cuales la repartición por categorías no está disponible.

Lao People's Democratic Republic:

E––> All first editions.

FR–> Tous les ouvrages recensés sont des premières éditions.

ESP> Todas las obras consideradas son primeras ediciones.

Mongolia:

E––> All first editions.

FR–> Tous les ouvrages recensés sont des premières éditions.

ESP> Todas las obras consideradas son primeras ediciones.

Oman:

E––> Data do not include pamphlets.

FR–> Les données ne tiennent pas compte des brochures.

ESP> Los datos no incluyen los folletos.

Pakistan:

E––> For 1992, all first editions; school textbooks (252,000), children's books (25,000) and government publications (1,000) are included in the total but not in the class breakdown.

FR–> En 1992, tous les ouvrages recensés sont des premières éditions; les manuels scolaires (252 000), les livres pour enfants (25 000) et les publications officielles (1 000) sont inclus dans le total mais ne sont pas répartis par catégories.

ESP> En 1992, todas las obras consideradas son primeras ediciones; los libros de texto (252 000), los libros para niños (25 000) y las publicaciones oficiales (1 000) quedan incluídos en el total pero no están repartidos por categorías.

Tajikistan:

E––> School textbooks (1.21 million), children's books (97,000) and government publications (19,000) are included in the total but not in the class breakdown.

FR–> Les manuels scolaires (1,21 million), les livres pour enfants (97 000) et les publications officielles (19 000) sont compris dans le total mais ne sont pas répartis par catégories.

ESP> Los libros de texto (1,21 millón), los libros para niños (97 000) y las publicaciones oficiales (19 000) quedan incluídos en el total pero no están repartidos por categorías.

United Arab Emirates:

E––> For 1993, data refer only to school textbooks.

FR–> En 1993, les données se réfèrent seulement aux manuels scolaires.

ESP> En 1993, los datos se refieren solamente a los libros de texto.

Uzbekistan:

E––> School textbooks (1992: 18.1 million; 1993: 20.1 million), children's books (1992: 1.6 million; 1993: 806,000) and government publications (1992: 163,000; 1993: 109,000) are included in the total but not in the class breakdown. Works not broken down are distributed among other classes without specification.

FR–> Les manuels scolaires (1992: 18,1 millions; 1993: 20,1 millions), les livres pour enfants (1992: 1,6 million; 1993: 806 000) et les publications officielles (1992: 163 000; 1993: 109 000) sont compris dans le total mais ne sont pas répartis par catégories. Les ouvrages non répartis sont ventilés entre les autres catégories sans spécification.

ESP> Los libros de texto (1992: 18,1 millones; 1993: 20,1 millones), los libros para niños (1992: 1,6 millón; 1993: 806 000) y las publicaciones oficiales (1992: 163 000; 1993: 109 000) quedan incluídos en el total pero no se desglosan por categorías. Las obras no repartidas quedan distribuidas entre las otras categorías, sin especificación.

Viet Nam:

E––> Works of UDC classes indicated by the symbol ./. are distributed, without specification, among other classes for which a figure is shown. School textbooks (1992: 62 million; 1993: 66 million) and children's books (1992: 2.8 million; 1993: 8.6 million) as well as copies of titles without specification (1992: 1.7 million: 1993: 1.6 million) are included in the total but not in the class breakdown.

FR–> Les ouvrages des catégories de la CDU représentés par le symbole ./. sont distribués sans spécification, entre les autres catégories pour lesquelles un chiffre est donné. Les manuels scolaires (1992: 62 millions; 1993: 66 millions) et les livres pour enfants (1992: 2,8 millions; 1993: 8,6 millions) ainsi que des exemplaires de titres sans spécification (1992: 1,7 million; 1993: 1,6 million) sont compris dans le total mais ne sont pas répartis par catégories.

ESP> Las obras de categorías de la CDU indicadas por el símbolo ./. han sido distribuidas, sin especificación, entre las otras categorías para las cuales se ha presentado una cifra. Los libros de texto (1992: 62 millones; 1993: 66 millones) y los libros para niños (1992: 2,8 millones; 1993: 8,6 millones) así como ejemplares

Number of copies by UDC classes **7.5**
Nombre d'exemplaires classés d'après la CDU
Número de ejemplares clasificados por materias (CDU)

de títulos sin especificación (1992: 1,7 millón; 1993: 1,6 millón) quedan incluídos en el total pero no están repartidos por categorías.

EUROPE:

Holy See:

E--> Data do not include pamphlets.

FR-> Les données ne tiennent pas compte des brochures.

ESP> Los datos no incluyen los folletos.

Latvia:

E--> School textbooks (1992: 2.0 million; 1993: 2.2 million; 1994: 2.3 million), children's books (1992: 3.1 million; 1993: 2.1 million; 1994: 2.0 million) and government publications (1992: 10,000; 1994: 4,000) are included in the total but not in the class breakdown.

FR-> Les manuels scolaires (1992: 2,0 millions; 1993: 2,2 millions; 1994: 2,3 millions), les livres pour enfants (1992: 3,1 millions; 1993: 2,1 millions; 1994: 2,0 millions) et les publications officielles (1992: 10 000; 1994: 4 000) sont compris dans le total mais ne sont pas répartis par catégories.

ESP> Los libros de texto (1992: 2,0 millones; 1993: 2,2 millones; 1994: 2,3 millones), los libros para niños (1992: 3,1 millones; 1993: 2,1 millones; 1994: 2,0 millones) y las publicaciones oficiales (1992: 10 000; 1994: 4 000) quedan incluídos en el total pero no se desglosan por categorías.

Portugal:

E--> Works of UDC classes indicated by the symbol ./. are distributed, without specification, among other classes for which a figure is shown. School textbooks (1992: 10.9 million; 1993: 10.6 million; 1994: 10.3 million), children's books (1992: 2.7 million; 1993: 3.3 million; 1994: 4.0 million) and comic books (1992: 0.3 million) as well as copies without specification (1992: 4.8 million; 1994: 5.7 million) are included in the total but not in the class breakdown.

FR-> Les ouvrages des catégories de la CDU représentés par le symbole ./. sont distribués, sans spécification, entre les autres catégories pour lesquelles un chiffre est donné.Les manuels scolaires (1992: 10,9 millions; 1993: 10,6 millions; 1994: 10,3 millions), les livres pour enfants (1992: 2,7 millions; 1993: 3,3 millions; 1994: 4,0 millions) et les bandes dessinées (1992: 0,3 million) ainsi que des exemplaires sans spécification (1992: 4,8 millions; 1994: 5,7 millions) sont inclus dans le total mais ne sont pas répartis par catégories.

ESP> Las obras de categorías de la CDU indicadas por el símbolo ./. han sido distribuidas, sin especificación, entre las otras categorías para las cuales se ha presentado una cifra. Los libros de texto (1992: 10,9 millones; 1993: 10,6 millones; 1994: 10,3 millones), los libros para niños (1992: 2,7 millones; 1993: 3,3 millones; 1994: 4,0 millones) y las historietas ilustradas (1992: 0.3 millón) así como ejemplares sin especificación (1992: 4,8 millones; 1994: 5,7 millones) quedan incluídos en el total pero no se desglosan por categorías.

OCEANIA:

Fiji:

E--> Data refer only to books published by the Ministry of Education and the Government printing department. School textbooks (1.3 million) and government publications (58,000) are included in the total but not in the class breakdown.

FR-> Les données se réfèrent seulement aux livres publiés par le ministère de l'éducation et le *Government printing department*. Les manuels scolaires (1,3 million) et les publications officielles (58 000) sont compris dans le total mais ne sont pas répartis par catégories.

ESP> Los datos se refieren solamente a los libros publicados por el Ministerio de Educación y el *Government printing department*. Los libros de texto (1,3 millón) y las publicaciones oficiales (58 000) quedan incluídos en el total pero no están repartidos por categorías.

7.6 Number of copies by subject group
Nombre d'exemplaires par groupes de sujets
Número de ejemplares por categorías de temas

7.6 Book production: number of copies by subject group

Edition de livres: nombre d'exemplaires par groupes de sujets

Edición de libros: número de ejemplares por categorías de temas

All editions: First editions and re-editions Toutes éditions: Premières éditions et rééditions Todas ediciones: Primeras ediciones y reediciones		First editions only Premières éditions seulement Primeras ediciones solamente	
Total (books and pamphlets) Total (livres et brochures) Total (libros y folletos)	of which: books dont: livres del cual: libros	Total (books and pamphlets) Total (livres et brochures) Total (libros y folletos)	of which: books dont: livres del cual: libros

For the subject breakdown, based upon the Universal Decimal Classification (UDC), see section 2 of the introductory text to this chapter.

Pour la ventilation par sujet, fondée sur la classification décimale universelle (CDU), voir la section 2 du texte d'introduction à ce chapitre.

Para la repartición por tema, basada en la clasificación decimal universal (CDU), véase la sección 2 del texto de introducción a este capítulo.

Data are presented in thousands

Les données sont présentées en milliers

Los datos se presentan en millares

Africa

Subject group Groupe de sujets Categoría de temas	Benin‡ (1994)				Egypt‡ (1993)			
	All editions		First editions		All editions		First editions	
	Total	of which: books	Total	of which: books	Total	of which: books	Total	of which: books
Total	42	41	42	41	108 042	89 721	31 795	21 591
1. Generalities	2	2	2	2	4 185	2 000	2 685	930
2. Philosophy, psychology	-	-	-	-	586	585	395	394
3. Religion, theology	1	1	1	1	11 196	9 477	3 359	2 629
4. Sociology, statistics	2	2	2	2	4 605	4 057	1 565	1 089
5. Political science	7	7	7	7	./.	./.	./.	./.
6. Law, public administration	1	1	1	1	./.	./.	./.	./.
7. Military art	-	-	-	-	./.	./.	./.	./.
8. Education, leisure	1	0	1	0	./.	./.	./.	./.
9. Trade, transport	0	0	0	0	./.	./.	./.	./.
10. Ethnography, folklore	-	-	-	-	./.	./.	./.	./.
11. Linguistics, philology	3	3	3	3	9 417	7 777	1 964	1 202
12. Mathematics	3	3	3	3	11 538	10 649	2 352	2 043
13. Natural sciences	./.	./.	./.	./.	./.	./.	./.	./.
14. Medical sciences	16	16	16	16	8 571	7 013	2 181	1 203
15. Engineering, crafts	-	-	-	-	./.	./.	./.	./.
16. Agriculture	2	2	2	2	./.	./.	./.	./.
17. Domestic science	./.	./.	./.	./.	./.	./.	./.	./.
18. Management, administration	-	-	-	-	./.	./.	./.	./.
19. Planning, architecture	-	-	-	-	3 073	2 081	1 010	926
20. Plastic arts	./.	./.	./.	./.	./.	./.	./.	./.
21. Performing arts	0	0	0	0	./.	./.	./.	./.
22. Games, sports	./.	./.	./.	./.	./.	./.	./.	./.
23. Literature								
(A) History and criticism	./.	./.	./.	./.	2 643	2 534	1 300	1 251
(B) Literary texts	3	3	3	3	./.	./.	./.	./.
24. Geography, travel	./.	./.	./.	./.	2 384	2 301	686	628
25. History, biography	1	1	1	1	./.	./.	./.	./.

Number of copies by subject group **7.6**
Nombre d'exemplaires par groupes de sujets
Número de ejemplares por categorías de temas

Subject group / Groupe de sujets / Categoría de temas	Etritrea‡ (1993)				Gambia (1994)			
	All editions		First editions		All editions		First editions	
	Total	of which: books	Total	of which: books	Total	of which: books	Total	of which: books
Total	420	360	51	36	20	11	0	-
1. Generalities	-	-	-	-	-	-	-	-
2. Philosophy, psychology	-	-	-	-	4	1	-	-
3. Religion, theology	-	-	-	-	0	0	-	-
4. Sociology, statistics	30	-	3	-	-	-	-	-
5. Political science	22	15	15	14	-	-	-	-
6. Law, public administration	26	20	26	20	0	-	0	-
7. Military art	-	-	-	-	-	-	-	-
8. Education, leisure	1	1	-	-	1	1	-	-
9. Trade, transport	-	-	-	-	1	1	-	-
10. Ethnography, folklore	6	1	6	1	-	-	-	-
11. Linguistics, philology	229	229	-	-	3	3	-	-
12. Mathematics	34	34	-	-	3	-	-	-
13. Natural sciences	59	59	-	-	3	-	-	-
14. Medical sciences	-	-	-	-	-	-	-	-
15. Engineering, crafts	13	1	1	1	-	-	-	-
16. Agriculture	-	-	-	-	-	-	-	-
17. Domestic science	-	-	-	-	-	-	-	-
18. Management, administration	-	-	-	-	0	0	-	-
19. Planning, architecture	-	-	-	-	-	-	-	-
20. Plastic arts	-	-	-	-	-	-	-	-
21. Performing arts	-	-	-	-	-	-	-	-
22. Games, sports	-	-	-	-	-	-	-	-
23. Literature								
(A) History and criticism	-	-	-	-	-	-	-	-
(B) Literary texts	-	-	-	-	-	-	-	-
24. Geography, travel	-	-	-	-	-	-	-	-
25. History, biography	-	-	-	-	5	5	-	-

Subject group / Groupe de sujets / Categoría de temas	Madagascar (1994)				Mauritius (1994)			
	All editions		First editions		All editions		First editions	
	Total	of which: books	Total	of which: books	Total	of which: books	Total	of which: books
Total	287	181	271	165	100	81	86	67
1. Generalities	-	-	-	-	7	5	7	5
2. Philosophy, psychology	18	11	18	11	1	-	1	-
3. Religion, theology	85	60	69	44	4	4	4	4
4. Sociology, statistics	0	0	0	0	4	4	4	4
5. Political science	6	6	6	6	6	6	6	6
6. Law, public administration	25	3	25	3	10	7	10	7
7. Military art	-	-	-	-	-	-	-	-
8. Education, leisure	61	57	61	57	14	14	5	5
9. Trade, transport	-	-	-	-	-	-	-	-
10. Ethnography, folklore	5	2	5	2	9	8	9	8
11. Linguistics, philology	12	4	12	4	7	3	7	3
12. Mathematics	-	-	-	-	-	-	-	-
13. Natural sciences	1	1	1	1	2	-	2	-
14. Medical sciences	45	15	45	15	-	-	-	-
15. Engineering, crafts	-	-	-	-	-	-	-	-
16. Agriculture	6	4	6	4	5	3	5	3
17. Domestic science	-	-	-	-	2	2	2	2
18. Management, administration	-	-	-	-	3	3	3	3
19. Planning, architecture	-	-	-	-	-	-	-	-
20. Plastic arts	-	-	-	-	-	-	-	-
21. Performing arts	-	-	-	-	2	2	2	2
22. Games, sports	-	-	-	-	-	-	-	-
23. Literature								
(A) History and criticism	2	2	2	2	2	2	2	2
(B) Literary texts	10	7	10	7	10	8	9	7
24. Geography, travel	3	3	3	3	3	2	1	-
25. History, biography	8	6	8	6	9	8	7	6

7.6 Number of copies by subject group
Nombre d'exemplaires par groupes de sujets
Número de ejemplares por categorías de temas

Subject group / Groupe de sujets / Categoría de temas	Morocco‡ (1994)				South Africa‡ (1994)			
	All editions		First editions		All editions		First editions	
	Total	of which: books	Total	of which: books	Total	of which: books	Total	of which: books
Total	1 380		1 307		37 561	30 757	28 480	22 392
1. Generalities	234		223		109	102	93	87
2. Philosophy, psychology	11		11		72	67	66	61
3. Religion, theology	133		123		6 110	3 324	4 495	1 934
4. Sociology, statistics	38		36		265	235	204	181
5. Political science	255		249		184	73	182	71
6. Law, public administration	44		36		177	133	151	107
7. Military art	13		13		2	2	2	2
8. Education, leisure	96		87		678	562	576	463
9. Trade, transport	16		14		362	310	251	202
10. Ethnography, folklore	8		8		404	289	298	192
11. Linguistics, philology	./.		./.		9 477	8 574	7 381	6 585
12. Mathematics	./.		./.		3 062	2 996	2 507	2 441
13. Natural sciences	1		1		2 045	1 767	1 465	1 204
14. Medical sciences	1		1		587	527	499	441
15. Engineering, crafts	0		0		321	232	233	148
16. Agriculture	5		5		596	571	465	440
17. Domestic science	15		15		811	725	716	630
18. Management, administration	50		40		1 204	1 200	639	635
19. Planning, architecture	0		0		17	17	17	17
20. Plastic arts	0		0		215	185	211	185
21. Performing arts	1		1		242	202	231	197
22. Games, sports	2		2		104	83	79	64
23. Literature								
(A) History and criticism	./.		./.		7 221	6 100	5 426	4 422
(B) Literary texts	163		155		./.	./.	./.	./.
24. Geography, travel	7		7		2 529	1 726	1 686	1 088
25. History, biography	287		280		767	755	607	595

Subject group / Groupe de sujets / Categoría de temas	Uganda‡ (1993)				Zaire (1992)			
	All editions		First editions		All editions		First editions	
	Total	of which: books	Total	of which: books	Total	of which: books	Total	of which: books
Total	2 229	2 229			535	535	535	535
1. Generalities	-	-			-	-	-	-
2. Philosophy, psychology	-	-			6	6	6	6
3. Religion, theology	8	8			240	240	240	240
4. Sociology, statistics	-	-			27	27	27	27
5. Political science	18	18			59	59	59	59
6. Law, public administration	1	1			20	20	20	20
7. Military art	-	-			-	-	-	-
8. Education, leisure	-	-			82	82	82	82
9. Trade, transport	-	-			14	14	14	14
10. Ethnography, folklore	-	-			30	30	30	30
11. Linguistics, philology	269	269			-	-	-	-
12. Mathematics	137	137			-	-	-	-
13. Natural sciences	150	150			-	-	-	-
14. Medical sciences	45	45			28	28	28	28
15. Engineering, crafts	-	-			22	22	22	22
16. Agriculture	45	45			-	-	-	-
17. Domestic science	-	-			-	-	-	-
18. Management, administration	-	-			-	-	-	-
19. Planning, architecture	-	-			-	-	-	-
20. Plastic arts	-	-			-	-	-	-
21. Performing arts	-	-			-	-	-	-
22. Games, sports	-	-			-	-	-	-
23. Literature								
(A) History and criticism	-	-			-	-	-	-
(B) Literary texts	6	6			-	-	-	-
24. Geography, travel	55	55			7	7	7	7
25. History, biography	35	35			-	-	-	-

Number of copies by subject group **7.6**
Nombre d'exemplaires par groupes de sujets
Número de ejemplares por categorías de temas

America, North

Subject group / Groupe de sujets / Categoría de temas	Cuba (1994) All editions Total	of which: books	First editions Total	of which: books	Honduras (1993) All editions Total	of which: books	First editions Total	of which: books
Total	4 610	3 691	1 187	616	80	80	35	35
1. Generalities	269	108	239	77	-	-	-	-
2. Philosophy, psychology	5	5	5	5	-	-	-	-
3. Religion, theology	8	6	8	6	2	2	2	2
4. Sociology, statistics	4	4	2	2	2	2	2	2
5. Political science	39	37	11	9	4	4	2	2
6. Law, public administration	3	3	-	-	5	5	-	-
7. Military art	1	1	1	1	-	-	-	-
8. Education, leisure	1 914	1 893	37	16	-	-	-	-
9. Trade, transport	13	8	6	1	-	-	-	-
10. Ethnography, folklore	10	9	10	9	4	4	4	4
11. Linguistics, philology	594	410	6	4	1	1	1	1
12. Mathematics	658	658	1	1	-	-	-	-
13. Natural sciences	10	9	9	8	-	-	-	-
14. Medical sciences	123	38	113	28	-	-	-	-
15. Engineering, crafts	28	28	9	9	-	-	-	-
16. Agriculture	5	5	4	4	-	-	-	-
17. Domestic science					-	-	-	-
18. Management, administration	2	2	2	2	-	-	-	-
19. Planning, architecture	1	1	-	-	-	-	-	-
20. Plastic arts	25	4	25	4	-	-	-	-
21. Performing arts	31	22	15	12	-	-	-	-
22. Games, sports	145	29	143	27	-	-	-	-
23. Literature								
(A) History and criticism	70	41	65	41	4	4	4	4
(B) Literary texts	486	364	463	346	54	54	16	16
24. Geography, travel	156	5	3	3	-	-	-	-
25. History, biography	10	1	10	1	4	4	4	4

America, South

Subject group / Groupe de sujets / Categoría de temas	Trinidad and Tobago‡ (1993) All editions Total	of which: books	First editions Total	of which: books	Argentina (1994) All editions Total	of which: books	First editions Total	of which: books
Total	30	30	30	30	48 882	48 882		
1. Generalities	-	-	-	-	804	804		
2. Philosophy, psychology	-	-	-	-	3 832	3 832		
3. Religion, theology	-	-	-	-	4 008	4 008		
4. Sociology, statistics	-	-	-	-	412	412		
5. Political science	-	-	-	-	677	677		
6. Law, public administration	-	-	-	-	1 545	1 545		
7. Military art	-	-	-	-	33	33		
8. Education, leisure	10	10	10	10	7 255	7 255		
9. Trade, transport	20	20	20	20	319	319		
10. Ethnography, folklore	-	-	-	-	122	122		
11. Linguistics, philology	-	-	-	-	937	937		
12. Mathematics	-	-	-	-	70	70		
13. Natural sciences	-	-	-	-	-			
14. Medical sciences	-	-	-	-	2 515	2 515		
15. Engineering, crafts	-	-	-	-	125	125		
16. Agriculture	-	-	-	-	97	97		
17. Domestic science	-	-	-	-	805	805		
18. Management, administration	-	-	-	-	324	324		
19. Planning, architecture	-	-	-	-	37	37		
20. Plastic arts	-	-	-	-	554	554		
21. Performing arts	-	-	-	-	2 090	2 090		
22. Games, sports	-	-	-	-	1 245	1 245		
23. Literature								
(A) History and criticism	-	-	-	-	48	48		
(B) Literary texts	-	-	-	-	17 543	17 543		
24. Geography, travel	-	-	-	-	488	488		
25. History, biography	-	-	-	-	2 997	2 997		

7.6 Number of copies by subject group
Nombre d'exemplaires par groupes de sujets
Número de ejemplares por categorías de temas

Subject group Groupe de sujets Categoría de temas	Brazil‡ (1994)				Ecuador (1994)			
	All editions		First editions		All editions		First editions	
	Total	of which: books	Total	of which: books	Total	of which: books	Total	of which: books
Total	104 397	104 397	31 897	31 897	40	40	40	40
1. Generalities	10 030	10 030	4 146	4 146	-	-	-	-
2. Philosophy, psychology	5 490	5 490	1 981	1 981	-	-	-	-
3. Religion, theology	9 953	9 953	2 905	2 905	-	-	-	-
4. Sociology, statistics	355	355	102	102	-	-	-	-
5. Political science	1 447	1 447	726	726	-	-	-	-
6. Law, public administration	4 667	4 667	926	926	-	-	-	-
7. Military art	-	-	-	-	-	-	-	-
8. Education, leisure	8 976	8 976	4 488	4 488	-	-	-	-
9. Trade, transport	4 078	4 078	1 858	1 858	-	-	-	-
10. Ethnography, folklore	150	150	51	51	-	-	-	-
11. Linguistics, philology	21 277	21 277	1 398	1 398	2	2	2	2
12. Mathematics	15 828	15 828	2 624	2 624	-	-	-	-
13. Natural sciences	./.	./.	./.	./.	-	-	-	-
14. Medical sciences	6 389	6 389	3 614	3 614	-	-	-	-
15. Engineering, crafts	./.	./.	./.	./.	-	-	-	-
16. Agriculture	./.	./.	./.	./.	-	-	-	-
17. Domestic science	./.	./.	./.	./.	-	-	-	-
18. Management, administration	./.	./.	./.	./.	-	-	-	-
19. Planning, architecture	2 166	2 166	1 419	1 419	-	-	-	-
20. Plastic arts	./.	./.	./.	./.	-	-	-	-
21. Performing arts	./.	./.	./.	./.	2	2	2	2
22. Games, sports	./.	./.	./.	./.	-	-	-	-
23. Literature								
(A) History and criticism	5 602	5 602	2 649	2 649	-	-	-	-
(B) Literary texts	./.	./.	./.	./.	36	36	36	36
24. Geography, travel	7 989	7 989	3 010	3 010	-	-	-	-
25. History, biography	./.	./.	./.	./.	-	-	-	-

Subject group Groupe de sujets Categoría de temas	Guyana‡ (1994)				Venezuela (1994)			
	All editions		First editions		All editions		First editions	
	Total	of which: books	Total	of which: books	Total	of which: books	Total	of which: books
Total	508	508	508	508	8 180	5 271	8 180	5 271
1. Generalities	-	-	-	-	175	141	175	141
2. Philosophy, psychology	-	-	-	-	332	296	332	296
3. Religion, theology	-	-	-	-	557	481	557	481
4. Sociology, statistics	26	26	26	26	280	185	280	185
5. Political science	./.	./.	./.	./.	249	205	249	205
6. Law, public administration	./.	./.	./.	./.	283	217	283	217
7. Military art	./.	./.	./.	./.	41	10	41	10
8. Education, leisure	./.	./.	./.	./.	1 451	1 190	1 451	1 190
9. Trade, transport	./.	./.	./.	./.	35	29	35	29
10. Ethnography, folklore	./.	./.	./.	./.	96	75	96	75
11. Linguistics, philology	192	192	192	192	314	304	314	304
12. Mathematics	146	146	146	146	116	112	116	112
13. Natural sciences	66	66	66	66	158	140	158	140
14. Medical sciences	-	-	-	-	1 510	306	1 510	306
15. Engineering, crafts	26	26	26	26	131	36	131	36
16. Agriculture	26	26	26	26	68	42	68	42
17. Domestic science	26	26	26	26	113	40	113	40
18. Management, administration	-	-	-	-	84	77	84	77
19. Planning, architecture	-	-	-	-	91	62	91	62
20. Plastic arts	-	-	-	-	215	128	215	128
21. Performing arts	-	-	-	-	121	87	121	87
22. Games, sports	-	-	-	-	70	42	70	42
23. Literature								
(A) History and criticism	-	-	-	-	0	0	0	0
(B) Literary texts	-	-	-	-	986	596	986	596
24. Geography, travel	-	-	-	-	40	24	40	24
25. History, biography	-	-	-	-	664	446	664	446

Number of copies by subject group 7.6
Nombre d'exemplaires par groupes de sujets
Número de ejemplares por categorías de temas

Asia

Subject group / Groupe de sujets / Categoría de temas	Armenia‡ (1994)				Azerbaijan (1994)			
	All editions		First editions		All editions		First editions	
	Total	of which: books	Total	of which: books	Total	of which: books	Total	of which: books
Total	1 739	1 656	1 739	1 656	5 557	5 133	4 860	4 436
1. Generalities	-	-	-	-	39	32	39	32
2. Philosophy, psychology	9	4	9	4	134	134	134	134
3. Religion, theology	5	5	5	5	306	261	306	261
4. Sociology, statistics	-	-	-	-	-	-	-	-
5. Political science	27	27	27	27	82	67	82	67
6. Law, public administration	9	9	9	9	12	12	12	12
7. Military art	49	49	49	49	4	4	4	4
8. Education, leisure	2	-	2	-	3 128	2 879	2 484	2 235
9. Trade, transport	-	-	-	-	120	70	120	70
10. Ethnography, folklore	5	5	5	5	398	367	388	357
11. Linguistics, philology	105	105	105	105	99	97	99	97
12. Mathematics	-	-	-	-	-	-	-	-
13. Natural sciences	31	29	31	29	6	6	6	6
14. Medical sciences	18	18	18	18	171	146	171	146
15. Engineering, crafts	-	-	-	-	3	3	3	3
16. Agriculture	-	-	-	-	9	9	9	9
17. Domestic science	30	30	30	30	-	-	-	-
18. Management, administration	-	-	-	-	-	-	-	-
19. Planning, architecture	-	-	-	-	-	-	-	-
20. Plastic arts	5	5	5	5	-	-	-	-
21. Performing arts	3	3	3	3	68	68	68	68
22. Games, sports	4	2	4	2	-	-	-	-
23. Literature								
(A) History and criticism	-	-	-	-	47	47	47	47
(B) Literary texts	402	373	402	373	920	920	877	877
24. Geography, travel	-	-	-	-	11	11	11	11
25. History, biography	65	65	65	65	-	-	-	-

Subject group / Groupe de sujets / Categoría de temas	China‡ (1994)				Cyprus (1994)			
	All editions		First editions		All editions		First editions	
	Total	of which: books	Total	of which: books	Total	of which: books	Total	of which: books
Total	5 945 320				1 530	584	1 067	452
1. Generalities	31 020				22	15	20	14
2. Philosophy, psychology	9 880				5	3	5	3
3. Religion, theology	./.				70	37	58	34
4. Sociology, statistics	6 720				32	4	29	4
5. Political science	153 400				27	6	14	4
6. Law, public administration	./.				12	2	7	2
7. Military art	3 650				111	1	36	1
8. Education, leisure	5 124 930				223	85	163	58
9. Trade, transport	9 600				143	27	113	23
10. Ethnography, folklore	./.				12	6	11	5
11. Linguistics, philology	76 570				91	64	75	58
12. Mathematics	47 010				30	21	15	6
13. Natural sciences	./.				16	16	8	8
14. Medical sciences	36 880				66	5	30	5
15. Engineering, crafts	172 700				90	16	84	15
16. Agriculture	16 280				188	85	54	25
17. Domestic science	./.				22	1	20	1
18. Management, administration	./.				41	5	21	5
19. Planning, architecture	78 090				20	2	15	2
20. Plastic arts	./.				16	4	16	4
21. Performing arts	./.				78	3	78	3
22. Games, sports	./.				19	1	12	1
23. Literature								
(A) History and criticism	122 470				8	8	8	8
(B) Literary texts	./.				145	145	143	143
24. Geography, travel	56 120				36	15	25	13
25. History, biography	./.				7	7	7	7

7.6 Number of copies by subject group
Nombre d'exemplaires par groupes de sujets
Número de ejemplares por categorías de temas

Subject group / Groupe de sujets / Categoría de temas	Georgia (1994) All editions		First editions		Israel‡ (1992) All editions		First editions	
	Total	of which: books	Total	of which: books	Total	of which: books	Total	of which: books
Total	1 131	1 056	1 131	1 056	9 368		3 943	
1. Generalities	-	-	-	-	152		54	
2. Philosophy, psychology	37	37	37	37	118		62	
3. Religion, theology	76	57	76	57	1 273		391	
4. Sociology, statistics	-	-	-	-	325		129	
5. Political science	34	28	34	28	211		96	
6. Law, public administration	163	161	163	161	48		38	
7. Military art	-	-	-	-	17		17	
8. Education, leisure	18	17	18	17	115		46	
9. Trade, transport	13	13	13	13	467		431	
10. Ethnography, folklore	9	5	9	5	./.		./.	
11. Linguistics, philology	117	112	117	112	1 084		302	
12. Mathematics	2	2	2	2	474		117	
13. Natural sciences	28	27	28	27	706		134	
14. Medical sciences	50	48	50	48	35		11	
15. Engineering, crafts	9	8	9	8	80		44	
16. Agriculture	17	7	17	7	29		1	
17. Domestic science	-	-	-	-	253		68	
18. Management, administration	-	-	-	-	./.		./.	
19. Planning, architecture	2	2	2	2	./.		./.	
20. Plastic arts	-	-	-	-	381		345	
21. Performing arts	3	1	3	1	17		5	
22. Games, sports	7	7	7	7	72		20	
23. Literature								
(A) History and criticism	-	-	-	-	2 648		1 314	
(B) Literary texts	476	454	476	454	./.		./.	
24. Geography, travel	2	2	2	2	260		70	
25. History, biography	68	68	68	68	570		237	

Subject group / Groupe de sujets / Categoría de temas	Japan‡ (1992) All editions		First editions		Kazakstan‡ (1994) All editions		First editions	
	Total	of which: books	Total	of which: books	Total	of which: books	Total	of which: books
Total	316 725	316 725	316 725	316 725	18 999		18 999	
1. Generalities	4 811	4 811	4 811	4 811	-		-	
2. Philosophy, psychology	13 698	13 698	13 698	13 698	168		168	
3. Religion, theology	4 224	4 224	4 224	4 224	320		320	
4. Sociology, statistics	10 260	10 260	10 260	10 260	1		1	
5. Political science	8 103	8 103	8 103	8 103	410		410	
6. Law, public administration	2 264	2 264	2 264	2 264	307		307	
7. Military art	./.	./.	./.	./.	9		9	
8. Education, leisure	3 372	3 372	3 372	3 372	10 280		10 280	
9. Trade, transport	10 900	10 900	10 900	10 900	68		68	
10. Ethnography, folklore	1 302	1 302	1 302	1 302	-		-	
11. Linguistics, philology	5 762	5 762	5 762	5 762	455		455	
12. Mathematics	483	483	483	483	33		33	
13. Natural sciences	4 522	4 522	4 522	4 522	12		12	
14. Medical sciences	2 839	2 839	2 839	2 839	307		307	
15. Engineering, crafts	7 451	7 451	7 451	7 451	82		82	
16. Agriculture	1 471	1 471	1 471	1 471	-		-	
17. Domestic science	-	-	-	-	49		49	
18. Management, administration	8 675	8 675	8 675	8 675	-		-	
19. Planning, architecture	1 173	1 173	1 173	1 173	15		15	
20. Plastic arts	27 408	27 408	27 408	27 408	-		-	
21. Performing arts	8 691	8 691	8 691	88691	130		130	
22. Games, sports	19 075	19 075	19 075	19 075	24		24	
23. Literature								
(A) History and criticism	17 092	17 092	17 092	17 092	638		638	
(B) Literary texts	140 261	140 261	140 261	140 261	2 413		2 413	
24. Geography, travel	1 040	1 040	1 040	1 040	29		29	
25. History, biography	11 848	11 848	11 848	11 848	583		583	

Number of copies by subject group 7.6
Nombre d'exemplaires par groupes de sujets
Número de ejemplares por categorías de temas

Subject group Groupe de sujets Categoría de temas	Korea, Republic of (1994)				Kyrgyzstan (1994)			
	All editions		First editions		All editions		First editions	
	Total	of which: books	Total	of which: books	Total	of which: books	Total	of which: books
Total	160 305	144 642	129 946	119 310	1 875	1 613	1 412	1 301
1. Generalities	5 072	4 845	4 906	4 693	119	119	119	119
2. Philosophy, psychology	2 636	1 438	2 510	1 312	12	12	12	12
3. Religion, theology	5 774	5 067	4 758	4 051	180	180	180	180
4. Sociology, statistics	2 807	2 792	2 437	2 422	-	-	-	-
5. Political science	3 404	3 404	2 223	2 223	50	41	50	41
6. Law, public administration	2 427	2 427	0	0	71	59	71	59
7. Military art	2 420	2 300	2 419	2 299	-	-	-	-
8. Education, leisure	32 312	28 612	24 685	22 985	669	489	206	177
9. Trade, transport	229	229	202	202	3	3	3	3
10. Ethnography, folklore	134	131	131	128	81	71	81	71
11. Linguistics, philology	25 419	23 018	22 726	20 325	87	87	87	87
12. Mathematics	18 171	15 882	14 015	12 726	6	6	6	6
13. Natural sciences	6 087	5 463	5 097	4 473	-	-	-	-
14. Medical sciences	979	944	941	906	40	39	40	39
15. Engineering, crafts	4 948	4 900	3 159	3 111	0	0	0	0
16. Agriculture	84	81	71	68	6	5	6	5
17. Domestic science	1 311	1 211	1 213	1 113	4	3	4	3
18. Management, administration	617	607	590	580	-	-	-	-
19. Planning, architecture	314	263	305	254	-	-	-	-
20. Plastic arts	1 618	1 436	1 571	1 390	-	-	-	-
21. Performing arts	2 111	2 075	1 823	1 787	1	1	1	1
22. Games, sports	11 308	11 308	11 288	11 288	2	1	2	1
23. Literature								
(A) History and criticism	462	462	450	450	-	-	-	-
(B) Literary texts	25 965	22 202	19 431	17 668	544	497	544	497
24. Geography, travel	956	820	917	781	-	-	-	-
25. History, biography	2 740	2 725	2 078	2 075	-	-	-	-

Subject group Groupe de sujets Categoría de temas	Lao People's Democratic Republic (1992)				Malaysia (1994)			
	All editions		First editions		All editions		First editions	
	Total	of which: books	Total	of which: books	Total	of which: books	Total	of which: books
Total	136	136	136	136	17 424	16 778	17 395	16 749
1. Generalities	-	-	-	-	81	51	81	51
2. Philosophy, psychology	-	-	-	-	114	114	104	104
3. Religion, theology	1	1	1	1	1 976	1 974	1 976	1 974
4. Sociology, statistics	-	-	-	-	462	228	462	228
5. Political science	9	9	9	9	885	742	884	741
6. Law, public administration	3	3	3	3	414	327	412	325
7. Military art	-	-	-	-	14	14	14	14
8. Education, leisure	-	-	-	-	691	680	691	680
9. Trade, transport	1	1	1	1	103	73	103	73
10. Ethnography, folklore	-	-	-	-	98	98	98	98
11. Linguistics, philology	31	31	31	31	5 365	5 365	5 354	5 354
12. Mathematics	-	-	-	-	1 422	1 422	1 422	1 422
13. Natural sciences	-	-	-	-	565	559	563	557
14. Medical sciences	4	4	4	4	159	119	158	118
15. Engineering, crafts	-	-	-	-	146	146	146	146
16. Agriculture	6	6	6	6	175	163	175	163
17. Domestic science	-	-	-	-	114	114	114	114
18. Management, administration	-	-	-	-	194	184	192	182
19. Planning, architecture	-	-	-	-	32	32	32	32
20. Plastic arts	-	-	-	-	95	95	95	95
21. Performing arts	-	-	-	-	213	213	213	213
22. Games, sports	-	-	-	-	178	177	178	177
23. Literature								
(A) History and criticism	-	-	-	-	97	97	97	97
(B) Literary texts	73	73	73	73	2 000	2 000	2 000	2 000
24. Geography, travel	-	-	-	-	962	962	962	962
25. History, biography	8	8	8	8	869	829	869	829

7.6 Number of copies by subject group
Nombre d'exemplaires par groupes de sujets
Número de ejemplares por categorías de temas

Subject group / Groupe de sujets / Categoría de temas	Mongolia (1992)				Oman (1992)			
	All editions		First editions		All editions		First editions	
	Total	of which: books	Total	of which: books	Total	of which: books	Total	of which: books
Total	959	438	959	438	25	25		
1. Generalities	104	30	104	30	1	1		
2. Philosophy, psychology	48	16	48	16	-	-		
3. Religion, theology	15	-	15	-	3	3		
4. Sociology, statistics	-	-	-	-	-	-		
5. Political science	12	6	12	6	-	-		
6. Law, public administration	21	12	21	12	-	-		
7. Military art	2	2	2	2	-	-		
8. Education, leisure	45	15	45	15	-	-		
9. Trade, transport	20	4	20	4	-	-		
10. Ethnography, folklore	15	6	15	6	-	-		
11. Linguistics, philology	12	8	12	8	9	9		
12. Mathematics	60	60	60	60	-	-		
13. Natural sciences	22	4	22	4	-	-		
14. Medical sciences	18	15	18	15	-	-		
15. Engineering, crafts	9	6	9	6	-	-		
16. Agriculture	20	15	20	15	1	1		
17. Domestic science	12	12	12	12	-	-		
18. Management, administration	6	6	6	6	-	-		
19. Planning, architecture	4	2	4	2	-	-		
20. Plastic arts	2	2	2	2	-	-		
21. Performing arts	6	4	6	4	-	-		
22. Games, sports	9	6	9	6	-	-		
23. Literature								
(A) History and criticism	9	9	9	9	-	-		
(B) Literary texts	396	156	396	156	-	-		
24. Geography, travel	50	30	50	30	-	-		
25. History, biography	42	12	42	12	11	11		

Subject group / Groupe de sujets / Categoría de temas	Pakistan (1994)				Sri Lanka (1994)			
	All editions		First editions		All editions		First editions	
	Total	of which: books	Total	of which: books	Total	of which: books	Total	of which: books
Total	714	714	152	152	15 337	10 328	6 698	2 897
1. Generalities	114	114	114	114	428	242	416	234
2. Philosophy, psychology	2	2	1	1	109	100	61	52
3. Religion, theology	1	1	1	1	1 030	663	322	15
4. Sociology, statistics	1	1	1	1	1 187	872	141	74
5. Political science	-	-	-	-	147	99	117	74
6. Law, public administration	-	-	-	-	3 673	1 063	3 632	1 060
7. Military art	-	-	-	-	10	-	10	-
8. Education, leisure	165	165	-	-	188	147	182	141
9. Trade, transport	-	-	-	-	151	47	144	40
10. Ethnography, folklore	-	-	-	-	23	19	15	11
11. Linguistics, philology	387	387	1	1	3 045	2 656	575	516
12. Mathematics	-	-	-	-	1 056	1 034	65	43
13. Natural sciences	12	12	10	10	39	16	36	13
14. Medical sciences	4	4	-	-	933	903	125	97
15. Engineering, crafts	12	12	8	8	54	19	50	17
16. Agriculture	1	1	1	1	109	26	104	26
17. Domestic science	-	-	-	-	6	5	6	5
18. Management, administration	-	-	-	-	18	11	13	6
19. Planning, architecture	-	-	-	-	63	63	55	55
20. Plastic arts	-	-	-	-	-	-	-	-
21. Performing arts	-	-	-	-	22	7	20	5
22. Games, sports	-	-	-	-	2	-	2	-
23. Literature								
(A) History and criticism	-	-	-	-	1 043	933	241	144
(B) Literary texts	12	12	12	12	261	208	178	126
24. Geography, travel	-	-	-	-	528	31	33	31
25. History, biography	3	3	3	3	1 212	1 164	155	112

Number of copies by subject group 7.6
Nombre d'exemplaires par groupes de sujets
Número de ejemplares por categorías de temas

Subject group / Groupe de sujets / Categoría de temas	Tajikistan‡ (1994)				Turkmenistan (1992)			
	All editions		First editions		All editions		First editions	
	Total	of which: books	Total	of which: books	Total	of which: books	Total	of which: books
Total	2 561	2 374	2 075	1 888	6 604	4 435	5 524	3 440
1. Generalities	-	-	-	-	159	104	159	104
2. Philosophy, psychology	25	5	25	5	24	24	24	24
3. Religion, theology	30	30	30	30	180	100	180	100
4. Sociology, statistics	-	-	-	-	4	4	4	4
5. Political science	28	28	28	28	296	133	296	133
6. Law, public administration	19	18	19	18	134	20	134	20
7. Military art	12	12	12	12	7	7	7	7
8. Education, leisure	69	69	69	69	1 906	1 811	826	816
9. Trade, transport	-	-	-	-	1	1	1	1
10. Ethnography, folklore	-	-	-	-	42	32	42	32
11. Linguistics, philology	24	24	24	24	69	63	69	63
12. Mathematics	-	-	-	-	37	36	37	36
13. Natural sciences	66	56	66	56	56	36	56	36
14. Medical sciences	212	132	212	132	25	13	25	13
15. Engineering, crafts	147	130	147	130	10	7	10	7
16. Agriculture	8	6	7	5	114	112	114	112
17. Domestic science	-	-	-	-	75	50	75	50
18. Management, administration	-	-	-	-	-	-	-	-
19. Planning, architecture	-	-	-	-	-	-	-	-
20. Plastic arts	-	-	-	-	-	-	-	-
21. Performing arts	18	15	18	15	40	22	40	22
22. Games, sports	-	-	-	-	34	3	34	3
23. Literature								
(A) History and criticism	59	59	59	59	82	81	82	81
(B) Literary texts	457	432	432	407	3 127	1 621	3 127	1 621
24. Geography, travel	-	-	-	-	7	5	7	5
25. History, biography	61	47	61	47	175	150	175	150

Subject group / Groupe de sujets / Categoría de temas	United Arab Emirates‡ (1993)				Uzbekistan‡ (1993)			
	All editions		First editions		All editions		First editions	
	Total	of which: books	Total	of which: books	Total	of which: books	Total	of which: books
Total	5 117	5 117			44 033			
1. Generalities	-	-			./.			
2. Philosophy, psychology	28	28			2 054			
3. Religion, theology	631	631			./.			
4. Sociology, statistics	10	10			./.			
5. Political science	11	11			./.			
6. Law, public administration	-	-			./.			
7. Military art	-	-			./.			
8. Education, leisure	-	-			414			
9. Trade, transport	-	-			./.			
10. Ethnography, folklore	-	-			./.			
11. Linguistics, philology	1 902	1 902			923			
12. Mathematics	771	771			./.			
13. Natural sciences	1 048	1 048			./.			
14. Medical sciences	-	-			653			
15. Engineering, crafts	22	22			1 286			
16. Agriculture	-	-			268			
17. Domestic science	123	123			./.			
18. Management, administration	-	-			./.			
19. Planning, architecture	-	-			./.			
20. Plastic arts	-	-			./.			
21. Performing arts	4	4			./.			
22. Games, sports	-	-			./.			
23. Literature								
(A) History and criticism	-	-			17 451			
(B) Literary texts	-	-			./.			
24. Geography, travel	406	406			./.			
25. History, biography	161	161			./.			

7.6 Number of copies by subject group
Nombre d'exemplaires par groupes de sujets
Número de ejemplares por categorías de temas

Europe

Subject group / Groupe de sujets / Categoría de temas	Viet Nam‡ (1993) All editions		First editions		Belarus (1994) All editions		First editions	
	Total	of which: books	Total	of which: books	Total	of which: books	Total	of which: books
Total	83 000				80 606	63 688	67 837	55 338
1. Generalities	./.				3 438	2 357	3 428	2 347
2. Philosophy, psychology	./.				584	337	584	337
3. Religion, theology	./.				11 511	6 877	11 473	6 839
4. Sociology, statistics	1 475				13	12	11	10
5. Political science	./.				482	408	482	408
6. Law, public administration	./.				846	370	825	349
7. Military art	./.				357	194	357	194
8. Education, leisure	./.				16 581	10 917	6 715	5 469
9. Trade, transport	./.				1	-	1	-
10. Ethnography, folklore	./.				166	166	146	146
11. Linguistics, philology	./.				1 439	1 424	1 014	999
12. Mathematics	./.				88	84	88	84
13. Natural sciences	./.				196	187	196	187
14. Medical sciences	1 308				2 570	2 249	1 818	1 497
15. Engineering, crafts	./.				1 821	1 714	1 290	1 184
16. Agriculture	./.				1 077	992	927	842
17. Domestic science	./.				2 825	2 310	2 265	1 750
18. Management, administration	./.				567	530	557	520
19. Planning, architecture	./.				50	49	50	49
20. Plastic arts	./.				30	26	30	26
21. Performing arts	./.				57	54	57	54
22. Games, sports	./.				164	161	164	161
23. Literature								
(A) History and criticism	4 014				111	102	111	102
(B) Literary texts	./.				34 738	31 343	34 428	31 033
24. Geography, travel	./.				1	1	1	1
25. History, biography	./.				893	824	819	750

Subject group / Groupe de sujets / Categoría de temas	Bulgaria (1994) All editions		First editions		Estonia (1994) All editions		First editions	
	Total	of which: books	Total	of which: books	Total	of which: books	Total	of which: books
Total	42 746	34 277	37 364	29 545	8 592	6 454	6 964	5 163
1. Generalities	2 690	1 118	2 578	1 085	256	188	255	187
2. Philosophy, psychology	1 389	1 362	1 286	1 259	226	216	209	200
3. Religion, theology	692	548	604	460	260	155	250	145
4. Sociology, statistics	114	113	114	113	26	12	26	12
5. Political science	1 009	847	961	802	225	146	225	146
6. Law, public administration	1 181	1 002	1 014	835	259	111	251	103
7. Military art	71	50	69	48	5	4	5	4
8. Education, leisure	7 803	5 417	5 459	3 442	176	106	172	104
9. Trade, transport	3	3	0	0	532	389	532	389
10. Ethnography, folklore	131	126	106	101	51	39	44	32
11. Linguistics, philology	1 008	994	730	716	-	-	-	-
12. Mathematics	449	443	233	227	372	299	152	100
13. Natural sciences	803	763	453	413	426	265	311	192
14. Medical sciences	1 219	1 082	1 138	1 001	208	144	201	139
15. Engineering, crafts	870	817	778	726	205	140	190	126
16. Agriculture	378	329	266	217	147	82	142	80
17. Domestic science	903	875	872	844	183	153	178	148
18. Management, administration	208	194	159	145	29	14	23	8
19. Planning, architecture	8	8	8	8	73	33	73	33
20. Plastic arts	94	67	89	62	318	101	318	101
21. Performing arts	116	115	81	80	53	16	53	16
22. Games, sports	366	347	366	347	86	63	86	63
23. Literature								
(A) History and criticism	575	572	453	450	1 363	1 045	741	612
(B) Literary texts	19 516	16 068	18 569	15 294	2 636	2 311	2 128	1 860
24. Geography, travel	148	101	49	22	216	168	175	146
25. History, biography	1 002	916	929	848	261	254	224	217

Number of copies by subject group **7.6**
Nombre d'exemplaires par groupes de sujets
Número de ejemplares por categorías de temas

Subject group / Groupe de sujets / Categoría de temas	Holy See (1992) All editions Total	of which: books	First editions Total	of which: books	Hungary (1994) All editions Total	of which: books	First editions Total	of which: books
Total	153	153	107	107	75 645	70 291	56 005	51 345
1. Generalities	3	3	3	3	2 731	2 719	1 936	1 924
2. Philosophy, psychology	29	29	20	20	1 701	1 695	1 343	1 338
3. Religion, theology	85	85	56	56	2 033	1 805	1 615	1 387
4. Sociology, statistics	4	4	3	3	177	170	125	117
5. Political science	-	-	-	-	658	621	598	561
6. Law, public administration	8	8	5	5	940	822	874	757
7. Military art	-	-	-	-	116	116	116	116
8. Education, leisure	9	9	6	6	905	865	764	723
9. Trade, transport	-	-	-	-	93	93	72	72
10. Ethnography, folklore	1	1	1	1	274	239	164	152
11. Linguistics, philology	5	5	4	4	4 075	3 749	1 632	1 444
12. Mathematics	-	-	-	-	2 820	2 800	753	753
13. Natural sciences	-	-	-	-	4 304	3 982	1 855	1 599
14. Medical sciences	-	-	-	-	1 151	1 112	955	917
15. Engineering, crafts	-	-	-	-	2 923	2 902	1 249	1 240
16. Agriculture	-	-	-	-	584	567	433	416
17. Domestic science	-	-	-	-	1 279	1 278	849	848
18. Management, administration	-	-	-	-	1 134	1 024	773	664
19. Planning, architecture	-	-	-	-	862	565	514	377
20. Plastic arts	-	-	-	-	996	841	856	727
21. Performing arts	-	-	-	-	1 247	1 232	626	617
22. Games, sports	-	-	-	-	603	592	473	467
23. Literature								
(A) History and criticism	-	-	-	-	2 424	2 329	1 262	1 192
(B) Literary texts	-	-	-	-	36 883	33 696	34 161	31 009
24. Geography, travel	-	-	-	-	2 028	1 811	725	669
25. History, biography	9	9	9	9	2 704	2 666	1 282	1 259

Subject group / Groupe de sujets / Categoría de temas	Italy (1994) All editions Total	of which: books	First editions Total	of which: books	Latvia‡ (1994) All editions Total	of which: books	First editions Total	of which: books
Total	289 100	266 104	185 852	168 499	10 835	8 878	7 636	5 927
1. Generalities	19 264	17 582	10 274	8 791	290	287	288	281
2. Philosophy, psychology	9 737	8 987	6 204	6 118	365	325	299	266
3. Religion, theology	15 995	11 747	9 761	6 391	395	337	368	310
4. Sociology, statistics	2 229	2 153	1 789	1 713	32	13	31	12
5. Political science	4 782	4 661	3 442	3 322	143	101	132	90
6. Law, public administration	7 808	7 714	4 152	4 085	124	94	110	80
7. Military art	499	490	472	463	-	-	-	-
8. Education, leisure	18 914	16 959	8 469	7 448	132	103	128	99
9. Trade, transport	2 151	795	1 968	612	99	98	99	98
10. Ethnography, folklore	1 508	1 490	1 137	1 120	45	37	40	34
11. Linguistics, philology	9 272	9 048	3 248	3 078	324	286	230	196
12. Mathematics	5 047	4 990	1 557	1 513	-	-	-	-
13. Natural sciences	7 895	6 211	4 834	3 253	64	43	63	42
14. Medical sciences	5 235	4 657	3 810	3 254	98	91	88	81
15. Engineering, crafts	4 817	4569	2443	2202	34	33	29	28
16. Agriculture	1 302	1245	931	902	217	192	217	192
17. Domestic science	5 645	5628	2874	2857	348	335	332	319
18. Management, administration	2 225	2147	566	515	52	40	50	38
19. Planning, architecture	1 954	1915	1558	1519	14	14	14	14
20. Plastic arts	7 163	6162	3979	3573	41	13	38	13
21. Performing arts	3 323	3141	2247	2094	54	51	46	43
22. Games, sports	6 218	4739	3693	2784	70	50	70	50
23. Literature								
(A) History and criticism	4 185	4 159	2 199	2 173	37	34	32	30
(B) Literary texts	114 085	109 167	88 055	83 934	3 351	3 320	1 648	1 617
24. Geography, travel	11 262	10 421	4 174	4 001	42	14	42	14
25. History, biography	16 585	15 327	12 016	10 784	148	117	118	91

Number of copies by subject group
Nombre d'exemplaires par groupes de sujets
Número de ejemplares por categorías de temas

Subject group / Groupe de sujets / Categoría de temas	Lithuania (1994) All editions Total	of which: books	First editions Total	of which: books	Moldova (1994) All editions Total	of which: books	First editions Total	of which: books
Total	19 627	15 986	16 661	13 538	5 850	5 171	5 646	4 968
1. Generalities	1 780	1 303	1 740	1 263	5	4	5	4
2. Philosophy, psychology	256	220	249	213	337	337	337	337
3. Religion, theology	1 085	702	1 048	665	271	266	271	266
4. Sociology, statistics	32	28	32	28	7	7	7	7
5. Political science	419	296	406	287	145	135	145	135
6. Law, public administration	241	190	228	187	113	111	113	111
7. Military art	13	12	13	12	0	0	0	0
8. Education, leisure	259	183	253	178	1 566	1 480	1 473	1 388
9. Trade, transport	-	-	-	-	60	59	60	59
10. Ethnography, folklore	130	92	126	92	5	5	5	5
11. Linguistics, philology	2 207	1 691	1 143	937	281	231	281	231
12. Mathematics	659	377	321	156	104	102	104	102
13. Natural sciences	830	715	521	472	26	25	26	25
14. Medical sciences	915	636	783	510	187	186	187	186
15. Engineering, crafts	183	148	183	148	49	44	49	44
16. Agriculture	343	295	342	294	19	4	19	4
17. Domestic science	308	239	296	227	152	152	152	152
18. Management, administration	652	380	652	380	0	0	0	0
19. Planning, architecture	77	60	66	49	6	6	6	6
20. Plastic arts	38	17	38	17	4	4	4	4
21. Performing arts	260	175	247	162	17	17	17	17
22. Games, sports	77	49	77	49	172	162	72	62
23. Literature								
(A) History and criticism	198	196	146	144	46	46	46	46
(B) Literary texts	7 688	7 132	6 819	6 263	2 128	1 638	2 117	1 627
24. Geography, travel	161	104	141	84	0	0	0	0
25. History, biography	816	746	791	721	150	150	150	150

Subject group / Groupe de sujets / Categoría de temas	Poland (1994) All editions Total	of which: books	First editions Total	of which: books	Portugal‡ (1994) All editions Total	of which: books	First editions Total	of which: books
Total	98 612	90 555	64 826	57 916	26 942		12 949	
1. Generalities	3 809	1 362	3 282	835	./.		./.	
2. Philosophy, psychology	1 920	1 856	1 599	1 539	./.		./.	
3. Religion, theology	3 190	2 831	2 290	1 992	./.		./.	
4. Sociology, statistics	264	262	219	217	2 285		988	
5. Political science	1 069	956	923	815	./.		./.	
6. Law, public administration	1 742	1 639	1 318	1 227	./.		./.	
7. Military art	341	340	132	131	./.		./.	
8. Education, leisure	937	821	835	719	./.		./.	
9. Trade, transport	-	-	-	-	./.		./.	
10. Ethnography, folklore	216	216	198	198	./.		./.	
11. Linguistics, philology	7 926	7 771	2 615	2 480	./.		./.	
12. Mathematics	4 685	4 602	1 123	1 045	869		646	
13. Natural sciences	6 627	6 392	2 561	2 347	./.		./.	
14. Medical sciences	3 123	2 802	2 361	2 071	./.		./.	
15. Engineering, crafts	2 204	1 997	1 279	1 076	./.		./.	
16. Agriculture	1 279	930	1 118	779	./.		./.	
17. Domestic science	3 704	3 644	3 279	3 229	./.		./.	
18. Management, administration	868	848	675	660	./.		./.	
19. Planning, architecture	471	444	423	396	369		341	
20. Plastic arts	1 456	1 441	413	398	./.		./.	
21. Performing arts	2 781	2 751	597	567	./.		./.	
22. Games, sports	322	292	283	253	./.		./.	
23. Literature								
(A) History and criticism	2 610	2 464	931	810	3 407		2 662	
(B) Literary texts	38 021	35 552	32 429	30 393	./.		./.	
24. Geography, travel	4 565	4 012	1 394	1 341	./.		./.	
25. History, biography	4 482	4 330	2 549	2 398	./.		./.	

Number of copies by subject group **7.6**
Nombre d'exemplaires par groupes de sujets
Número de ejemplares por categorías de temas

Subject group / Groupe de sujets / Categoría de temas	Romania‡ (1994)				Russian Federation‡ (1994)			
	All editions		First editions		All editions		First editions	
	Total	of which: books	Total	of which: books	Total	of which: books	Total	of which: books
Total	50 230	48 000	49 519		594 323	529 826	518 238	456 926
1. Generalities	605	570	554		38 626	28 660	35 717	26 117
2. Philosophy, psychology	922	911	905		12 446	11 141	12 170	10 866
3. Religion, theology	1 448	1 361	1 270		27 946	20 714	25 686	18 655
4. Sociology, statistics	74	74	74		1 463	1 393	1 463	1 393
5. Political science	588	578	583		9 973	9 060	9 714	8 802
6. Law, public administration	650	649	583		9 062	7 717	8 867	7 524
7. Military art	-	-	-		712	710	707	705
8. Education, leisure	2 379	1 175	2 368		128 428	116 796	70 039	60 122
9. Trade, transport	-	-	-		4 117	3 900	4 033	3 818
10. Ethnography, folklore	153	151	153		734	691	734	691
11. Linguistics, philology	4 532	4 511	4 472		10 986	10 458	9 626	9 098
12. Mathematics	3 933	3 915	3 933		878	806	824	753
13. Natural sciences	2 533	2 532	2 523		2 992	2 784	2 703	2 549
14. Medical sciences	653	638	651		21 966	20 716	17 778	16 843
15. Engineering, crafts	1 338	1 316	1 337		15 100	13 823	12 706	11 631
16. Agriculture	283	282	276		7 142	5 591	6 630	5 090
17. Domestic science	158	158	149		13 929	13 386	13 442	12 899
18. Management, administration	480	479	480		4 397	3 459	3 961	3 033
19. Planning, architecture	67	67	67		3 258	3 091	3 023	2 856
20. Plastic arts	67	56	66		./.	./.	./.	./.
21. Performing arts	597	594	589		./.	./.	./.	./.
22. Games, sports	141	141	141		2 233	1 966	2 122	1 856
23. Literature								
(A) History and criticism	25 222	24 444	24 997		1 675	1 559	1 624	1 508
(B) Literary texts	./.	./.	./.		265 789	241 225	264 512	240 251
24. Geography, travel	1 289	1 281	1 289		1 098	967	1 077	946
25. History, biography	2 118	2 117	2 059		9 373	9 213	9 080	8 920

Subject group / Groupe de sujets / Categoría de temas	Slovakia (1994)				Spain (1994)			
	All editions		First editions		All editions		First editions	
	Total	of which: books	Total	of which: books	Total	of which: books	Total	of which: books
Total	6 139	5 729	3 364	3 212	180 181	162 009	137 956	121 162
1. Generalities	64	55	42	38	6 273	5 822	4 705	4 286
2. Philosophy, psychology	189	188	114	113	4 566	4 412	3 289	3 208
3. Religion, theology	445	389	148	148	9 232	8 385	5 591	4 845
4. Sociology, statistics	58	57	22	22	1 747	1 597	1 622	1 477
5. Political science	307	306	186	185	3 029	2 752	2 448	2 172
6. Law, public administration	289	289	183	183	5 384	4 871	4 083	3 584
7. Military art	19	19	19	19	494	472	472	450
8. Education, leisure	1 292	1 195	392	388	9 516	8 610	7 918	7 049
9. Trade, transport	2	2	1	1	881	745	753	618
10. Ethnography, folklore	2	2	0	0	2 264	2 041	1 959	1 737
11. Linguistics, philology	290	287	209	206	8 832	8 755	5 340	5 268
12. Mathematics	181	181	131	131	3 688	3 659	2 154	2 128
13. Natural sciences	374	368	226	225	7 253	6 336	5 409	4 523
14. Medical sciences	277	276	203	203	6 240	5 547	4 973	4 346
15. Engineering, crafts	405	405	249	249	3 266	3 052	2 640	2 444
16. Agriculture	298	297	211	210	2 174	1 571	1 840	1 318
17. Domestic science	2	2	2	2	3 865	3 554	3 458	3 154
18. Management, administration	282	279	180	177	4 796	4 752	3 819	3 784
19. Planning, architecture	16	16	6	6	917	676	855	615
20. Plastic arts	4	4	0	0	5 247	4 417	4 521	3 741
21. Performing arts	49	39	32	32	2 392	2 259	2 056	1 960
22. Games, sports	57	56	24	24	1 654	1 539	1 483	1 402
23. Literature								
(A) History and criticism	88	54	34	15	-	-	-	-
(B) Literary texts	646	536	450	341	69 626	61 243	52 878	45 187
24. Geography, travel	284	273	235	235	8 001	6 712	6 704	5 478
25. History, biography	219	154	65	59	8 844	8 230	6 986	6 388

7.6 Number of copies by subject group
Nombre d'exemplaires par groupes de sujets
Número de ejemplares por categorías de temas

Subject group / Groupe de sujets / Categoría de temas	The Former Yugoslav Republic of Macedonia (1994)				Ukraine‡ (1993)			
	All editions		First editions		All editions		First editions	
	Total	of which: books	Total	of which: books	Total	of which: books	Total	of which: books
Total	2 918	2 434	888	634	87 567	74 151	71 899	59 318
1. Generalities	10	10	10	10	110	100	110	100
2. Philosophy, psychology	6	6	6	6	578	517	528	467
3. Religion, theology	40	2	40	2	1 353	1 072	1 353	1 072
4. Sociology, statistics	2	2	2	2	29	27	29	27
5. Political science	8	8	8	8	811	740	800	729
6. Law, public administration	11	11	1	1	888	759	829	700
7. Military art	1	1	1	1	50	50	50	50
8. Education, leisure	2 487	2 120	593	402	22 091	19 703	17 081	15 188
9. Trade, transport	-	-	-	-	790	710	760	680
10. Ethnography, folklore	6	6	6	6	237	236	112	111
11. Linguistics, philology	9	9	8	8	2 08	2 239	2 040	1 971
12. Mathematics	4	4	2	2	529	418	525	414
13. Natural sciences	11	11	11	11	1 536	975	1 514	953
14. Medical sciences	4	4	2	2	4 700	4 308	4 525	4 133
15. Engineering, crafts	11	11	9	9	2 172	2 095	2 101	2 024
16. Agriculture	4	4	4	4	2 692	2 240	2 316	1 864
17. Domestic science	1	1	1	1	3 815	3 311	3 138	2 634
18. Management, administration	1	1	1	1	12	11	12	11
19. Planning, architecture	-	-	-	-	213	187	163	137
20. Plastic arts	32	32	22	22	./.	./.	./.	./.
21. Performing arts	54	9	9	4	./.	./.	./.	./.
22. Games, sports	1	1	1	1	363	357	353	347
23. Literature								
(A) History and criticism	4	4	4	4	676	642	660	626
(B) Literary texts	179	145	115	95	39 655	31 675	31 136	23 496
24. Geography, travel	1	1	1	1	180	171	180	171
25. History, biography	31	31	31	31	1 779	1 608	1 584	1 413

Oceania

Subject group / Groupe de sujets / Categoría de temas	Federal Republic of Yugoslavia (1994)				Fiji‡ (1994)			
	All editions		First editions		All editions		First editions	
	Total	of which: books	Total	of which: books	Total	of which: books	Total	of which: books
Total	11 905	11 021	3 236	2 634	2 256	550	1 739	90
1. Generalities	712	585	657	545	-	-	-	-
2. Philosophy, psychology	107	103	70	70	-	-	-	-
3. Religion, theology	92	79	49	48	-	-	-	-
4. Sociology, statistics	19	15	11	11	0	0	0	0
5. Political science	241	207	206	178	79	79	79	79
6. Law, public administration	458	249	408	202	4	0	4	0
7. Military art	-	-	-	-	-	-	-	-
8. Education, leisure	7 661	7 510	140	126	5	5	5	5
9. Trade, transport	7	7	5	5	-	-	-	-
10. Ethnography, folklore	6	-	-	-	-	-	-	-
11. Linguistics, philology	3	2	2	2	325	23	302	-
12. Mathematics	28	28	12	12	153	-	150	-
13. Natural sciences	41	39	35	33	137	10	127	0
14. Medical sciences	139	109	86	68	47	2	47	2
15. Engineering, crafts	205	128	124	55	0	-	0	-
16. Agriculture	42	36	36	30	24	-	24	-
17. Domestic science	51	51	45	45	23	-	23	-
18. Management, administration	173	158	139	126	-	-	-	-
19. Planning, architecture	8	6	8	6	-	-	-	-
20. Plastic arts	9	5	6	3	-	-	-	-
21. Performing arts	169	101	79	68	1	1	-	-
22. Games, sports	17	4	16	3	1	1	-	-
23. Literature								
(A) History and criticism	17	17	14	14	-	-	-	-
(B) Literary texts	1 385	1 331	840	797	-	-	-	-
24. Geography, travel	229	168	192	134	143	15	128	0
25. History, biography	86	83	56	53	5	3	2	-

Number of copies by subject group **7.6**
Nombre d'exemplaires par groupes de sujets
Número de ejemplares por categorías de temas

AFRICA:
Benin:
E--> Works not broken down are distributed among other classes without specification.

FR-> Les ouvrages non répartis sont ventilés entre les autres catégories sans spécification.

ESP> Las obras no repartidas quedan distribuidas entre las categorías sin especificación.

Egypt:
E--> Works of groups 5 to 10 are included in group 4; 13 in group 12; 15 to 18 in group 14; 20 to 22 in group 19; 23b in group 23a; 25 in group 24. School textbooks (49.3 million of which 14.1 million of first editions) and children's books (583,000 of which 175,000 first editions) are included in the total but not identified in the 25 groups.

FR-> Les ouvrages des groupes 5 à 10 sont inclus dans le groupe 4; 13 dans le groupe 12; 15 à 18 dans le groupe 14; 20 à 22 dans le groupe 19; 23b dans le groupe 23a; 25 dans le groupe 24. Les manuels scolaires (49,3 millions dont 14.1 millions de premières éditions) et les livres pour enfants (583 000 dont 175 000 premières éditions) sont compris dans le total mais ne sont pas répartis entre les 25 groupes.

ESP> Las obras de los grupos 5 a 10 quedan incluídas en el grupo 4; 13 en el grupo 12; 15 a 18 en el grupo 14; 20 a 22 en el grupo 19; 23b en el grupo 23a; 25 en el grupo 24. Los libros de texto (49,3 millones 14,1 millones de primeras ediciones) y los libros para niños (583 000 cuyas 175 000 primeras ediciones) quedan incluídos en el total pero no se desglosan entre los 25 grupos.

Eritrea:
E--> The total number of copies of books refers only to school textbooks (323,000) and government publications (37,000). The number of copies of books of first editions refers only to government publications.

FR-> Le nombre total des exemplaires de livres se réfère aux manuels scolaires (323 000) et aux publications officielles (37 000). Le nombre des exemplaires de livres des premières éditions se réfère seulement aux publications officielles.

ESP> El número total de los ejemplares de libros se refiere solamente a los libros de texto (323 000) y a las publicaciones oficiales (37 000). El número de los ejemplares de libros de las primeras ediciones se refiere solamente a las publicaciones oficiales.

Morocco:
E--> Works of groups 11, 12 and 23a are distributed among other subjects, without specification.

FR-> Les ouvrages des groupes 11, 12 et 23a sont répartis entre les autres sujets, sans spécification.

ESP> Las obras de los grupos 11, 12 y 23a se desglosan entre los otros temas, sin especificación.

South Africa:
E--> Works of group 23b are included in group 23a.

FR-> Les ouvrages du groupe 23b sont inclus dans le groupe 23a.

ESP> Las obras del grupo 23b quedan incluídas en el grupo 23a.

Uganda:
E--> Data do not include government publications but include school textbooks (720,000) and children's books (740,000) for which a subject breakdown is not available.

FR-> Les données ne comprennent pas les publications officielles mais comprennent les manuels scolaires (720 000) et les livres pour enfants (740 000) pour lesquels une répartition par sujets n'est pas disponible.

ESP> Los datos no incluyen las publicaciones oficiales pero incluyen los libros de texto (720 000) y los libros para niños (740 000) para los cuales la repartición por temas no está disponible.

AMERICA, NORTH:
Trinidad and Tobago:
E--> Data refer only to first editions of school textbooks (10,000) and children's books (20,000).

FR-> Les données se réfèrent seulement aux premières éditions des manuels scolaires (10 000) et des livres pour enfants (20 000).

ESP> Los datos se refieren solamente a las primeras ediciones de los libros de texto (10 000) y de los libros para niños (20 000).

AMERICA, SOUTH:
Brazil:
E--> Works of group 13 are included in group 12; 15 to 18 in group 14; 20 to 22 in group 19; 23b in group 23a; 25 in group 24.

FR-> Les ouvrages du groupe 13 sont inclus dans le groupe 12; 15 à 18 dans le groupe 14; 20 à 22 dans le groupe 19; 23b dans le groupe 23a; 25 dans le groupe 24.

ESP> Las obras del grupo 13 quedan incluídas en el grupo 12; 15 a 18 en el grupo 14; 20 a 22 en el grupo 19; 23b en el grupo 23a; 25 en el grupo 24.

Guyana:
E--> Data refer only to first editions of school textbooks (468,000) and children's books (40,000). Works of groups 5 to 10 are included in group 4.

FR-> Les données se réfèrent seulement aux premières éditions des manuels scolaires (468 000) et des livres pour enfants (40 000). Les ouvrages des groupes 5 à 10 sont inclus dans le groupe 4.

ESP> Los datos se refieren solamente a las primeras ediciones de los libros de texto (468 000) y de los libros para niños (40 000). Las obras de los grupos 5 a 10 quedan incluídas en el grupo 4.

ASIA:
Armenia:
E--> School textbooks (902,000) and children's books (68,000) are included in the total but not in the 25 groups.

FR-> Les manuels scolaires (902 000) et les livres pour enfants (68 000) sont compris dans le total mais ne sont pas répartis entre les 25 groupes.

ESP> Los libros de texto (902 000) y los libros para niños (68 000) quedan incluídos en el total pero no están repartidos entre los 25 grupos.

China:
E--> Works of group 6 are included in group 5; 10 and 22 in group 8; 13 in group 12; 20 and 21 in group 19; 23b in group 23a and 25 in group 24 while those of groups 3, 17 and 18 are distributed among the other subjects without specification.

FR-> Les ouvrages du groupe 6 sont inclus dans le groupe 5; 10 et 22 dans le groupe 8; 13 dans le groupe 12, 20 et 21 dans le groupe 19; 23b dans le groupe 23a et 25 dans le groupe 24 tandis que ceux des groupes 3, 17 et 18, sont répartis entre les autres sujets sans spécification.

ESP> Las obras del grupo 6 quedan incluídas en el grupo 5; 10 y 22 en el grupo 8; 13 en el grupo 12; 20 y 21 en el grupo 19; 23b en el grupo 23a y 25 en el grupo 24 mientras que las de los grupos 3, 17 y 18, se deglosan entre los otros temas sin especificación.

Israel:
E--> Works of group 10 are included in group 4; 18 in group 17; 19 in group 15; 23b in group 23a. Data include copies of books (33,000 of which 11,000 first editions) for which a subject breakdown is not available.

FR-> Les ouvrages du groupe 10 sont inclus dans le groupe 4; 18 dans le groupe 17; 19 dans le groupe 15; 23b dans le groupe 23a. Les données comprennent des exemplaires de livres (33 000 dont 11 000 premières éditions) pour lesquels une répartition par sujets n'est pas disponible.

ESP> Las obras del grupo 10 quedan incluídas en el grupo 4; 18 en el grupo 17; 19 en el grupo 15; 23b en el grupo 23a. Los datos incluyen ejemplares de libros (33 000 cuyas 11 000 primeras ediciones) para los cuales la repartición por temas no está disponible.

Japan:
E--> Works on *statistics* (group 4) are included with *economics* (group 5) and those on *military art* (group 7) with *politics* (group 5).

FR-> Les ouvrages relatifs aux *statistiques* (groupe 4) sont compris avec les *sciences économiques* (groupe 5) et ceux relatifs à *art et science militaire* (groupe 7) avec les *sciences politiques* (groupe 5).

ESP> Las obras relativas a la *estadística* (grupo 4) quedan incluídas con las *ciencias económicas* (grupo 5) y las relativas a *arte y ciencia militar* (grupo 7) con las *ciencias políticas* (grupo 5).

Kazakstan:
E--> Data include copies of books (2.7 million) for which a subject breakdown is not available.

FR-> Les données comprennent des exemplaires de livres (2,7 millions) pour lesquels une répartition par sujets n'est pas disponible.

ESP> Los datos incluyen ejemplares de libros (2,7 millones) para los cuales la repartición por temas no está disponible.

Tajikistan:
E--> School textbooks (1.21 million of which 750,000 first editions), children's books (97,000 first editions) and government publications (19,000 first editions) are included in the total but not in the class breakdown.

FR-> Les manuels scolaires (1,21 million dont 750 000 premières éditions), les livres pour enfants (97 000) premières éditions) et les publications officielles (19 000 premières éditions) sont compris dans le total mais ne sont pas répartis par catégories.

ESP> Los libros de texto (1,21 millon cuyas 750 000 primeras ediciones), los libros para niños (97 000 primeras ediciones) y las publicaciones oficiales (19 000 primeras ediciones) quedan incluídos en el total pero no están repartidos por categorías.

United Arab Emirates:
E--> Data refer to school textbooks only.

FR-> Les données se réfèrent aux manuels scolaires seulement.

7.6 Number of copies by subject group
Nombre d'exemplaires par groupes de sujets
Número de ejemplares por categorías de temas

ESP> Los datos se refieren a los libros de texto solamente.
Uzbekistan:

E--> School textbooks (20.1 million), children's books (806,000) and governement publications (109,000) are included in the total but not identified in the 25 groups. Works not broken down are distributed among other subjects without specification.

FR-> Les manuels scolaires (20,1 millions), les livres pour enfants (806 000) et les publications officielles (109 000) sont compris dans le total mais ne sont pas répartis entre les 25 groupes. Les ouvrages non répartis sont ventilés entre les autres sujets sans spécification.

ESP> Los libros de texto (20,1 millones), los libros para niños (806 000) y las publicaciones oficiales (109 000) quedan incluídos en el total pero no se desglosan entre los 25 grupos. Las obras no repartidas quedan distribuidas entre los otros temas sin especificación.
Viet-Nam:

E--> Works of groups 5 to 10 are included in group 4; 15 to 18 in group 14; 23b in group 23a while those of other groups are distributed among subjects without specification. School textbooks (66 million) and children's books (8.6 million) as well as copies of titles without specification (1.6 million) are included in the total but not in the 25 groups.

FR-> Les ouvrages des groupes 5 à 10 sont inclus dans le groupe 4; 15 à 18 dans le groupe 14; 23b dans le groupe 23a tandis que ceux des autres groupes sont répartis, sans spécification, entre les autres sujets. Les manuels scolaires (66 millions) et les livres pour enfants (8,6 millions) ainsi que des exemplaires de titres sans spécification (1,6 million) sont compris dans le total mais ne sont pas répartis entre les 25 groupes.

ESP> Las obras de los grupos 5 a 10 quedan incluídas en el grupo 4; 15 a 18 en el grupo 14; 23b en el grupo 23a mientras que las de los grupos se deglosan, sin especificación, entre los otros temas. Los libros de texto (66 millones) y los libros para niños (8,6 millones) así como ejemplares de títulos sin especificación (1,6 millon) quedan incluídos en el total pero no están repartidos entre los 25 grupos.
EUROPE:
Latvia:

E--> School textbooks (2.3 million of which 1.6 million first editions), children's books (2.0 million of which 1.5 million first editions) and government publications (4,000 first editions) are included in the total but not identified in the 25 groups.

FR-> Les manuels scolaires (2,3 millions dont 1.6 million de premières éditions), les livres pour enfants (2.0 millions dont 1,5 million de premières éditions) et les publications officielles (4 000 premières éditions) sont compris dans le total mais ne sont pas répartis entre les 25 groupes.

ESP) Los libros de texto (2,3 millones cuyas 1.6 millón de primeras ediciones), los libros para niños (2.0 millones cuyas 1.5 millón de primeras ediciones) y las publicaciones oficiales (4 000 primeras ediciones) quedan incluídos en el total pero no están repartidos entre los 25 grupos.
Portugal:

E--> Works of groups 5 to 10 are included in group 4; 13 to 18 in group 12; 20 to 22 in group 19; 23a in group 23b; 25 in group 24 while those of other groups are distributed among other subjects without specification. School textbooks (10.3 million of which 3.7 million first edition), children's books (4.0 million of which 2.8 million

first editions) as well as 5.7 million copies of which 1.8 million first editions without specification are included in the total but not identified in the 25 groups.

FR-> Les ouvrages des groupes 5 à 10 sont compris dans le groupe 4; 13 à 18 dans le groupe 12; 20 à 22 dans le dans le groupe 19; 23a dans le groupe 23b; 25 dans le groupe 24 tandis que ceux des autres groupes sont répartis, sans spécification, entre les autres sujets. Les manuels scolaires (10,3 millions dont 3,7 millions de premières éditions), les livres pour enfants (4,0 millions dont 2,8 millions de premières éditions) ainsi que 5,7 millions d'exemplaires dont 1,8 million de premières éditions sans spécification sont compris dans le total mais ne sont pas répartis entre les 25 groupes.

ESP> Las obras de los grupos 5 a 10 quedan incluídas en el grupo 4; 13 a 18 en el grupo 12; 20 a 22 en el grupo 19; 23a en el grupo 23b; 25 en el grupo 24 mientras que las de los otros grupos se desglosan, sin especificación, entre los otros temas. Los libros de texto (10,3 millones cuyas 3,7 millones de primeras ediciones), los libros para niños (4,0 millones cuyas 2,8 millones de primeras ediciones) así como 5,7 millones de ejemplares cuyas 1,8 millón de primeras ediciones sin especificación quedan incluídos en el total pero no se desglosan entre los 25 grupos.
Romania:

E--> Works of group 23b are included in group 23a.

FR-> Les ouvrages du groupe 23b sont inclus dans le groupe 23a.

ESP> Las obras del grupo 23b quedan incluídas en el grupo 23a.
Russian Federation:

E--> Works of groups 20 and 21 are included in group 19.

FR-> Les ouvrages des groupes 20 et 21 sont inclus dans le groupe 19.

ESP> Las obras de los grupos 20 y 21 quedan incluídas en el grupo 19.
Ukraine:

E--> Works of groups 20 and 21 are included in group 19.

FR-> Les ouvrages des groupes 20 et 21 sont inclus dans le groupe 19.

ESP> Las obras de los grupos 20 y 21 quedan incluídas en el grupo 19.
OCEANIA:
Fiji:

E--> Data refer only to books published by the Ministry of Education and the Government printing department. School textbooks (1.3 million of which 848,000 first editions) and government publications (58,000) are included in the total but not in the 25 groups.

FR-> Les données se réfèrent seulement aux livres publiés par le ministère de l'éducation et le *Government printing department*. Les manuels scolaires (1,3 million dont 848 000 premières éditions) et les publications officielles (58 000) sont compris dans le total mais ne sont pas répartis entre les 25 groupes.

ESP> Los datos se refieren solamente a los libros publicados por el Ministerio de Educacion y el *Government printing department*. Los libros de texto (1,3 millón cuyas 848 000 primeras ediciones) y las publicaciones oficiales (58 000) quedan incluídos en el total pero no están repartidos entre los 25 grupos.

School textbooks: number of titles and copies 7.7
Manuels scolaires: nombre de titres et d'exemplaires
Libros de texto: número de títulos y de ejemplares

7.7 Production of school textbooks: number of titles and copies

Edition de manuels scolaires: nombre de titres et d'exemplaires

Edición de libros de texto: número de títulos y de ejemplares

Data for countries shown with this symbol are all first editions.

Toutes les données relatives aux pays accompagnés de ce symbole sont des premières éditions.

Todos los datos relativos a los países donde figura este símbolo son primeras ediciones.

Country / Pays / País	Year / Année / Año	Number of titles / Nombre de titres / Número de títulos			Number of copies / Nombre d'exemplaires / Número de ejemplares		
		Books / Livres / Libros	Pamphlets / Brochures / Folletos	Total	Books / Livres / Libros (000)	Pamphlets / Brochures / Folletos (000)	Total (000)
Africa							
Algeria	1992	15	...	15	...	...	...
Benin #	1992	6	...	6	9		9
Egypt	1993	735	74	809	41 149	8 112	49 261
Eritrea	1993	64	-	64	323	-	323
Gambia	1994	2	-	2	6	-	6
Madagascar #	1994	14	3	17	56	4	60
Malawi	1994	8	12	20	...	...	...
Mauritius	1994	14	1	15	16	1	17
Morocco	1994	...	...	23	...	...	96
Nigeria	1992	340	67	407	...	...	...
Reunion #	1992	1	-	1	...	...	...
South Africa	1994	215	57	272	16 087	210	16 297
Tunisia #	1993	...	...	61	...	...	...
Uganda	1993	94	...	94	720	...	720
Zaire #	1992	14	-	14	112	-	112
Zimbabwe #	1992	6	2	8	...	...	...
America, North							
Belize #	1993	20	-	20	...	-	...
Canada	1993	...	...	1 240	...	...	...
Cuba	1994	102	48	150	549	76	625
Trinidad and Tobago #	1993	1	-	1	10	-	10
America, South							
Argentina	1992	736	-	736	4 720	-	4 720
Brazil	1994	5 454	...	5 454	82 222	...	82 222
Chile	1992	148	21	169	...	...	...
Guyana #	1994	32	-	32	468	-	468
Paraguay	1993	25	-	25	...	-	...
Peru #	1994	34	5	39	...	...	...
Asia							
Armenia #	1994	21	-	21	902	-	902
Azerbaijan	1994	41	1	42	2 807	150	2 957
Cyprus	1994	52	47	99	272	142	414
Georgia #	1994	2	-	2	5	-	5
India	1994	191	-	191	...	-	...
Indonesia #	1992	715	-	715	...	-	...
Israel	1992	...	...	1 092	...	...	3 731
Japan #	1992	2 512	...	2 512	12 190	...	12 190
Korea, Republic of	1994	3 568	902	4 470	72 488	6 864	79 352
Kyrgyzstan	1994	11	2	13	379	151	530
Lao People's Democratic Republic	1992	-	-	-	-	-	-
Malaysia	1994	1 023	-	1 023	7 799	-	7 799
Mongolia #	1992	37	-	37	370	-	370
Pakistan #	1992	10	-	10	252	-	252
Philippines	1994	207	...	207	...	...	...

7.7 School textbooks: number of titles and copies
Manuels scolaires: nombre de titres et d'exemplaires
Libros de texto: número de títulos y de ejemplares

Country / Pays / País	Year / Année / Año	Number of titles / Nombre de titres / Número de titulos			Number of copies / Nombre d'exemplaires / Número de ejemplares		
		Books Livres Libros	Pamphlets Brochures Folletos	Total	Books Livres Libros (000)	Pamphlets Brochures Folletos (000)	Total (000)
Qatar	1994	228	-	228	...	-	...
Sri Lanka	1994	9	5	14	7 695	1 280	8 975
Tajikistan	1994	21	-	21	1 210	-	1 210
Thailand	1992	640	-	640	...	-	...
Turkey	1994	...	...	355	...	...	...
Turkmenistan	1992	27	1	28	1 678	85	1 763
United Arab Emirates	1993	293	-	293	5 117	-	5 117
Uzbekistan	1993	...	...	194	...	...	20 069
Viet Nam	1993	...	...	1 370	...	...	66 049
Europe							
Andorra	1992	5	-	5	...	-	...
Belarus	1994	123	49	172	9 329	5 632	14 961
Bulgaria	1994	1 052	72	1 124	9 057	2 224	11 281
Croatia	1994	208	66	274	...	...	...
Czech Republic	1994	337	74	411	...	...	...
Denmark	1994	...	...	844	...	...	...
Estonia	1994	167	59	226	1 655	500	2 155
Finland	1994	461	33	494	...	...	...
France	1994	...	...	891	...	...	...
Germany	1994	...	...	3 551	...	...	...
Hungary	1994	1 588	62	1 650	18 189	707	18 896
Iceland	1994	156	120	276	...	...	...
Italy	1994	1 967	198	2 165	44 671	1 768	46 439
Latvia	1994	168	34	202	1 819	495	2 314
Liechtenstein	1994	...	...	...	...	...	...
Lithuania	1994	136	42	178	3 142	1 208	4 350
Luxembourg #	1994	7	4	11	...	...	...
Malta #	1993	14	9	23	...	...	...
Moldova	1994	43	-	43	866	-	866
Netherlands	1993	11 002	...	11 002	...	...	...
Poland	1994	535	39	574	26 823	878	27 701
Portugal	1994	...	...	1 381	...	...	10 348
Romania	1994	361	1	362	14 885	10	14 895
Russian Federation	1994	...	...	1 031	...	...	108 373
Slovakia	1994	170	38	208	2 258	10	2 268
Slovenia	1994	437	44	481	...	...	...
Spain	1994	2 285	61	2 346	22 286	265	22 551
Sweden	1994	488	75	563	...	...	...
Switzerland	1994	...	...	381	...	...	...
The Former Yugoslav Rep. of Macedonia	1994	358	44	402	2 148	371	2 519
Ukraine	1993	156	11	167	17 667	1 236	18 903
United Kingdom	1994	2 157	999	3 156	...	...	...
Federal Republic of Yugoslavia	1994	577	32	609	7 777	160	7 937
Oceania							
Fiji	1994	124	99	223	407	844	1 251

Children's books: number of titles and copies **7.8**
Livres pour enfants: nombre de titres et d'exemplaires
Libros para niños: número de títulos y de ejemplares

7.8 Production of children's books: number of titles and copies

Edition de livres pour enfants: nombre de titres et d'exemplaires

Edición de libros para niños: número de títulos y de ejemplares

Data for countries shown with this symbol are all first editions.

Toutes les données relatives aux pays accompagnés de ce symbole sont des premières éditions.

Todos los datos relativos a los países donde figura este símbolo son primeras ediciones.

Country / Pays / País	Year / Année / Año	Number of titles / Nombre de titres / Número de títulos			Number of copies / Nombre d'exemplaires / Número de ejemplares		
		Books Livres Libros	Pamphlets Brochures Folletos	Total	Books Livres Libros (000)	Pamphlets Brochures Folletos (000)	Total (000)
Africa							
Algeria	1992	17	...	17	...	...	...
Egypt	1993	3	20	23	98	485	583
Eritrea	1993	-	-	-	-	-	-
Madagascar #	1994	-	1	1	-	3	3
Malawi #	1994	-	4	4	-	...	...
Mauritius	1994	-	-	-	-	-	-
Morocco #	1994	...	...	9	...	...	19
Nigeria #	1992	7	30	37	...	...	...
Reunion #	1992	2	2	4	...	...	...
South Africa	1994	93	433	526	2 844	1 269	4 113
Tunisia #	1993	...	...	129	...	...	...
Uganda	1993	99	...	99	740	...	740
Zaire #	1992	1	-	1	8	-	8
Zimbabwe #	1992	1	4	5	...	...	...
America, North							
Belize #	1993	6	-	6	...	-	...
Canada	1993	...	...	971	...	...	...
Cuba	1994	30	39	69	2 396	483	2 879
Honduras	1993	3	-	3	9	-	9
Trinidad and Tobago #	1993	25	-	25	20	-	20
United States	1994	5 321	...	5 321	...		...
America, South							
Argentina	1992	807	-	807	4 847	-	4 847
Brazil	1994	10 354	...	10 354	44 998	...	44 998
Chile	1992	107	41	148	...	...	...
Ecuador #	1994	9	-	9	36	-	36
Guyana #	1994	1	-	1	40	-	40
Paraguay	1993	3	-	3	...	-	...
Peru	1994	20	9	29	...	...	...
Asia							
Armenia #	1994	3	6	9	25	43	68
Azerbaijan	1994	20	-	20	319	-	319
China	1994	...	...	3 064	...	...	131 730
Cyprus	1994	20	-	20	18	-	18
Georgia	1994	3	1	4	14	1	15
India	1994	400	-	400	...	-	...
Indonesia #	1992	1 084	-	1 084	...	-	...
Iran, Islamic Republic of	1994	1 201	...	1 201	...	...	...
Japan #	1992	2 889	...	2 889	18 780	...	18 780
Jordan #	1993	28	...	28	...	...	...

7.8 Children's books: number of titles and copies
Livres pour enfants: nombre de titres et d'exemplaires
Libros para niños: número de títulos y de ejemplares

Country Pays País	Year Année Año	Number of titles Nombre de titres Número de títulos			Number of copies Nombre d'exemplaires Número de ejemplares		
		Books Livres Libros	Pamphlets Brochures Folletos	Total	Books Livres Libros (000)	Pamphlets Brochures Folletos (000)	Total (000)
Kazakstan	1992	...	...	104	...	...	7 002
Korea, Republic of	1994	4 169	1 179	5 348	18 573	4 009	22 582
Kyrgyzstan #	1994	1	3	4	2	39	41
Lao People's Democratic Rep. #	1992	13	-	13	34	-	34
Malaysia #	1994	1 843	1	1 844	7 047	1	7 048
Mongolia #	1992	20	5	25	80	20	100
Pakistan #	1992	7	-	7	25	-	25
Philippines #	1994	15	...	15	...	...	...
Qatar	1994	1	-	1	...	-	...
Sri Lanka	1994	9	76	85	16	158	174
Syrian Arab Republic	1992	34	...	34	...	...	...
Tajikistan #	1994	10	1	11	83	14	97
Thailand	1992	439	-	439	...	-	...
Turkey	1994	...	...	269	...	...	...
Turkmenistan #	1992	33	14	47	819	988	1 807
Uzbekistan	1993	...	...	42	...	...	806
Viet Nam	1993	...	...	683	...	...	8 596
Europe							
Andorra	1992	1	-	1	...	-	...
Austria	1994	...	...	463	...	...	...
Belarus	1994	166	66	232	7 194	3 559	10 753
Bulgaria	1994	130	299	429	1 532	4 497	6 029
Czech Republic	1994	155	79	234	...	...	...
Denmark	1994	...	...	1 147	...	...	...
Estonia	1994	72	54	126	327	500	827
Finland	1994	364	429	793	...	...	...
France	1994	...	...	2 768	...	...	...
Germany	1994	...	...	4 777	...	...	...
Hungary	1994	559	140	699	5 727	3 163	8 890
Iceland	1994	49	62	111	...	...	...
Italy	1994	1 037	708	1 745	11 958	6 402	18 360
Latvia	1994	104	84	188	1 027	963	1 990
Lithuania	1994	109	66	175	1 524	898	2 422
Luxembourg	1994	4	2	6	...	...	...
Malta #	1993	7	5	12	...	...	...
Moldova	1994	37	12	49	1 153	460	1 613
Netherlands	1993	9 615	...	9 615	...	...	...
Norway	1994	440	...	440	...	...	...
Poland	1994	363	129	492	4 023	1 956	5 979
Portugal	1994	...	...	1 025	...	...	3 969
Russian Federation	1994	...	...	1 742	...	...	80 713
Slovakia	1994	833	6	839	10	O	10
Slovenia	1994	154	206	360	...	...	...
Spain	1994	2 059	1 667	3 726	10 539	8 507	19 046
Sweden	1994	574	611	1 185	...	...	...
Switzerland	1994	...	...	641	...	...	...
The Former Yugoslav Rep. of Macedonia	1994	23	9	32	55	17	72
Ukraine	1993	410	165	575	8 629	8 744	17 373
United Kingdom	1994	5 708	1 787	7 495	...	...	...
Federal Republic of Yugoslavia	1994	66	5	71	251	9	260
Oceania							
Fiji	1994	-	-	-	-	-	-

7.9 Daily newspapers: number and circulation (total and per 1,000 inhabitants)

Journaux quotidiens: nombre et diffusion
(total et pour 1 000 habitants)

Periódicos diarios: número y circulación
(total y por 1 000 habitantes)

Country / Pays / País	Daily newspapers / Journaux quotidiens / Periódicos diarios											
	Number / Nombre / Número				Circulation / Diffusion / Difusión							
					Total (in thousands) / Total (en milliers) / Total (en millares)				Per 1,000 inhabitants / Pour 1 000 habitants / Por 1 000 habitantes			
	1980	1985	1990	1994	1980	1985	1990	1994	1980	1985	1990	1995
	(1)	(2)	(3)	(4)	(5)	(6)	(7)	(8)	(9)	(10)	(11)	(12)
Africa												
Algeria	4	5	10	6	448	570	1 274	1 250	24	26	51	46
Angola	4	4	4	4	143	103	*115	*117	20	13	*13	*11
Benin	1	1	1	1	1	1	12	12	0.3	0.3	3	2
Botswana	1	1	1	1	19	18	18	35	21	17	14	24
Burkina Faso	1	2	1	1	2	4	3	3	0.2	0.4	0.3	0.3
Burundi	1	1	1	1	1	2	20	20	0.2	0.4	4	3
Cameroon	2	1	2	1	65	35	*80	*50	8	4	*7	*4
Central African Republic	-	-	1	1	-	-	*2	*2	-	-	*1	*1
Chad	1	1	1	1	1	1	2	2	0.2	0.2	0.4	0.4
Congo	1	1	5	6	3	8	*17	*19	2	4	*8	*8
Côte d'Ivoire	2	1	1	1	81	90	90	90	10	9	8	7
Egypt	12	12	14	17	1 701	2 383	*2 400	3 949	39	48	*43	64
Equatorial Guinea	2	2	2	1	*2	*2	*2	1	*7	*5	*6	3
Ethiopia	3	3	6	4	40	41	*100	*81	1	1	*2	*2
Gabon	1	1	1	1	15	20	*20	*20	19	20	*17	*16
Gambia	-	6	2	2	-	4	*2	*2	-	6	*2	*2
Ghana	5	5	2	4	*500	*510	200	*310	*47	*40	13	*18
Guinea-Bissau	1	1	1	1	6	6	6	6	8	7	6	6
Kenya	3	4	5	5	216	283	*330	*358	13	14	*14	*13
Lesotho	3	4	4	2	44	47	20	14	33	30	11	7
Liberia	3	5	8	8	11	*28	*35	*35	6	*13	*14	*14
Libyan Arab Jamahiriya	3	3	3	4	*55	*65	*70	*70	*18	*17	*15	*13
Madagascar	6	7	5	7	55	67	50	60	6	6	4	4
Malawi	*2	1	1	1	*20	15	25	25	*3	2	3	2
Mali	2	2	2	2	*4	*10	*10	*40	*1	*1	*1	*4
Mauritania	-	-	1	1	-	-	*1	*1	-	-	*0.5	*0.5
Mauritius	10	7	7	6	80	*70	80	75	83	*69	76	68
Morocco	11	14	13	13	*270	320	*320	*344	*14	*15	*13	*13
Mozambique	2	2	2	2	54	81	81	81	4	6	6	5
Namibia	4	3	6	4	27	21	220	153	26	17	163	102
Niger	1	1	1	4	3	4	5	11	1	1	1	1
Nigeria	16	19	31	27	*1 100	*1 400	*1 700	*1 950	*15	*17	*18	*18
Reunion	3	2	3	3	56	49	*55	55	111	89	*91	85
Rwanda	1	1	1	1	0.3	0.3	0.5	0.5	0.1	0.1	0.1	0.1
Senegal	1	3	1	3	35	53	50	48	6	8	7	6
Seychelles	1	1	1	1	3	3	3	3	48	49	46	44
Sierra Leone	1	1	1	1	10	10	10	10	3	3	3	2
Somalia	2	2	1	1	*5	*7	9	9	*1	*1	1	1
South Africa	*24	24	22	17	*1 400	1 440	1 340	1 346	*48	44	36	33
Sudan	6	5	5	5	105	*250	*610	*620	6	*12	*25	*23

7.9 Daily newspapers
Journaux quotidiens
Periódicos diarios

Country / Pays / País	Number / Nombre / Número				Circulation / Diffusion / Difusión — Total (in thousands)				Per 1,000 inhabitants			
	1980	1985	1990	1994	1980	1985	1990	1994	1980	1985	1990	1995
	(1)	(2)	(3)	(4)	(5)	(6)	(7)	(8)	(9)	(10)	(11)	(12)
Swaziland	1	2	3	3	9	10	*11	*12	15	15	*15	*14
Togo	3	2	1	1	*16	*11	10	10	*6	*4	3	2
Tunisia	5	6	6	7	272	*280	*345	*403	43	*39	*43	*46
Uganda	1	1	2	2	25	25	30	*35	2	2	2	2
United Republic of Tanzania	3	2	3	3	208	101	*200	*220	11	5	*8	*8
Zaire	5	4	5	9	*60	*50	*75	*112	*2	*2	*2	*3
Zambia	2	2	2	2	110	95	99	70	19	14	12	8
Zimbabwe	2	3	2	2	133	203	206	195	19	24	21	18
America, North												
Antigua and Barbuda	1	1	1	-	6	6	6	-	98	97	94	-
Aruba	...	...	12	14	...	...	53	52	...	...	796	757
Bahamas	3	3	3	3	33	39	35	35	157	167	137	129
Barbados	2	2	2	2	39	40	30	41	156	158	117	159
Belize	1	1	-	-	3	3	-	-	21	18	-	-
Bermuda	1	1	1	1	14	18	*18	16	257	321	*295	254
Canada	123	117	108	107	5 425	5 566	*5 800	*5 500	221	215	*209	*189
Cayman Islands	-	-	1	1	-	-	6	8	-	-	212	250
Costa Rica	4	6	5	5	251	*280	*306	333	110	*106	*101	99
Cuba	17	17	19	17	1 050	1 207	1 824	1 315	108	119	172	120
Dominican Republic	7	7	12	11	220	216	*230	264	39	34	*32	34
El Salvador	7	4	5	6	291	243	270	284	64	51	52	50
Grenada	1	-	-	-	*4	-	-	-	*45	-	-	-
Guadeloupe	1	2	1	1	*32	*33	*34	35	*98	*93	*87	83
Guatemala	9	9	5	5	*200	*250	190	240	*29	*31	21	23
Haiti	4	5	4	4	*36	*50	45	45	*7	*9	7	6
Honduras	6	7	5	5	212	293	199	*240	59	70	41	*44
Jamaica	3	4	3	3	109	*140	*160	*160	51	*61	*68	*66
Martinique	1	1	1	1	28	32	32	32	86	94	88	84
Mexico	317	332	*285	309	8 322	9 964	*11 237	10 420	124	132	*133	113
Netherlands Antilles	8	6	6	6	*52	*54	*54	53	*299	*297	*284	269
Nicaragua	3	3	6	4	136	*160	*180	130	49	*50	*49	30
Panama	5	7	8	7	*110	245	*234	160	*56	113	*98	62
Puerto Rico	4	5	3	3	512	599	618	670	160	178	175	184
Trinidad and Tobago	4	4	4	*4	*155	173	175	175	*143	149	142	135
United States	1 745	1 676	1 611	1 548	62 200	62 800	62 328	59 305	273	263	249	228
U.S. Virgin Islands	3	3	2	2	17	21	19	26	170	214	188	245
America, South												
Argentina	220	218	159	187	*4 000	*3 940	*4 000	*4 705	*142	*130	*123	*138
Bolivia	14	14	17	11	226	*290	*400	*500	42	*49	*61	*69
Brazil	343	322	356	317	5 482	6 534	*8 100	*7 200	45	48	*55	*45
Chile	34	*38	*45	32	...	...	*1 923	1 411	...	...	*146	100
Colombia	36	*46	45	46	*1 400	*1 800	*2 000	*2 200	*53	*61	*62	*64
Ecuador	18	26	25	24	558	*800	*820	808	70	*88	*80	72
French Guiana	1	1	1	1	1	1	1	2	15	11	9	11
Guyana	1	2	2	2	58	78	*80	80	76	99	*101	97
Paraguay	5	6	5	5	*160	*170	*165	203	*51	*46	*38	42
Peru	66	70	66	48	*1 400	*1 600	*1 700	*2 000	*81	*82	*79	*86
Suriname	4	5	2	3	*45	*55	40	*43	*127	*146	100	*103
Uruguay	24	25	30	32	*700	*680	*720	*750	*240	*226	*233	*237
Venezuela	66	55	54	89	2 937	*2 700	*2 800	*4 600	195	*158	*144	*215
Asia												
Afghanistan	13	13	14	15	*90	*110	*180	216	*6	*8	*12	11
Armenia	.	.	.	7	.	.	.	*80	.	.	.	*23
Azerbaijan	.	.	.	3	.	.	.	*210	.	.	.	*28
Bahrain	3	2	2	3	*14	19	29	*70	*40	45	59	*128
Bangladesh	44	60	52	51	274	591	*700	*710	3	6	*6	*6
Brunei Darussalam	-	-	1	1	-	-	10	20	-	-	39	71
China	50	70	44	38	34 375	*39 000	*48 000	27 790	34	*36	*42	23
Cyprus	12	10	11	15	*80	83	78	81	*127	125	110	110
Hong Kong	41	46	38	43	*3 600	*4 100	*4 250	*4 200	*714	*751	*745	*719
India	...	...	...	...	14 531	19 804	*0...	...	21	26	*0...	...
Indonesia	84	97	64	56	2 281	3 010	5 144	*3 800	15	18	28	*20
Iran, Islamic Republic of	*45	15	21	12	*970	*1 250	*1 500	*1 200	*25	*26	*25	*18
Iraq	5	6	6	4	*340	*600	*650	532	*26	*39	*36	27
Israel	36	21	30	34	*1 000	*1 100	*1 200	1 534	*258	*260	*258	281
Japan	151	124	125	121	66 258	68 296	72 524	71 924	567	565	587	576

Country Pays País	Daily newspapers / Journaux quotidiens / Periódicos diarios											
	Number Nombre Número				Circulation / Diffusion / Difusión							
					Total (in thousands) Total (en milliers) Total (en millares)				Per 1,000 inhabitants Pour 1 000 habitants Por 1 000 habitantes			
	1980	1985	1990	1994	1980	1985	1990	1994	1980	1985	1990	1995
	(1)	(2)	(3)	(4)	(5)	(6)	(7)	(8)	(9)	(10)	(11)	(12)
Jordan	4	4	4	4	66	155	225	250	23	40	53	48
Korea, Democratic People's Rep. of	11	11	11	11	*4 000	*4 500	*5 000	*5 000	*219	*226	*230	*213
Korea, Republic of	30	35	39	62	8 000	*10 000	*12 000	*18 000	210	*245	*280	*404
Kuwait	8	8	9	9	305	380	*450	655	222	221	*210	401
Kyrgyzstan	.	.	.	3	.	.	.	53	.	.	.	11
Lao People's Democratic Rep.	3	3	3	3	*14	*13	*14	*14	*4	*4	*3	*3
Lebanon	14	13	*14	16	*290	*300	*320	*500	*109	*112	*125	*172
Macau	6	9	8	9	*70	*250	*240	*250	*289	*880	*702	*628
Malaysia	40	32	45	44	*810	*1 500	*2 500	*2 800	*59	*96	*140	*142
Maldives	2	2	*2	2	1	2	*3	3	6	8	*12	12
Mongolia	2	2	1	1	177	177	162	207	106	93	74	88
Myanmar	7	7	2	5	*350	511	*700	1 032	*10	14	*17	23
Nepal	28	28	28	28	*120	*130	*150	*162	*8	*8	*8	*8
Oman	-	3	4	4	-	51	62	63	-	37	35	30
Pakistan	106	118	398	273	*1 032	1 149	1 826	2 840	*12	11	15	21
Philippines	22	15	47	42	2 000	2 170	*3 400	4 286	41	40	*56	65
Qatar	3	4	5	4	*30	60	*80	80	*131	168	*165	148
Saudi Arabia	11	13	12	19	*350	*450	*600	*950	*36	*36	*37	*54
Singapore	12	10	8	8	690	*706	763	1 027	286	*276	282	364
Sri Lanka	21	17	18	9	450	390	*550	*450	30	24	*32	*25
Syrian Arab Republic	7	7	10	8	*114	*163	*260	261	*13	*16	*21	18
Tajikistan	.	.	.	2	.	.	.	*80	.	.	.	*13
Thailand	27	32	34	35	2 680	4 350	*4 500	2 766	57	85	*81	48
Turkey	...	...	*68	57	*2 500	*3 020	*3 499	2 679	*56	*60	*62	44
United Arab Emirates	9	13	8	8	152	290	250	300	149	210	150	161
Uzbekistan	.	.	.	4	.	.	.	160	.	.	.	7
Viet Nam	4	4	5	4	*520	*540	*560	*570	*10	*9	*8	*8
Yemen	*6	*4	*5	3	*98	*125	*135	230	*12	*13	*12	17
Europe												
Albania	2	2	2	3	145	135	135	185	54	46	41	54
Andorra	-	-	-	3	-	-	-	*4	-	-	-	*63
Austria	30	33	25	23	2 651	2 729	2 706	3 736	351	361	351	472
Belarus	27	28	28	10	2 343	2 446	2 937	*1 899	243	246	288	*187
Belgium	26	24	33	32	2 289	2 171	*3 000	3 231	232	220	*301	321
Bosnia and Herzegovina‡	...	...	...	2	...	...	...	518	...	...	...	131
Bulgaria	14	17	24	17	2 244	2 626	4 065	1 843	253	293	452	209
Croatia	...	8	9	6	...	...	*2 400	*2 600	...	...	*531	*575
Czech Republic	...	...	...	23	...	...	...	2 259	...	...	...	219
Denmark	48	47	47	51	1 874	1 855	1 810	1 886	366	363	352	365
Estonia	.	.	.	4	.	.	.	373	.	.	.	242
Finland	58	65	66	56	2 414	2 661	2 780	2 405	505	543	558	473
France	90	92	79	118	10 332	10 670	11 792	13 685	192	193	208	237
Germany‡	*368	*358	414	411	*29 388	*30 428	24 174	25 757	*375	*392	305	317
Gibraltar	1	1	2	2	2	3	*4	6	83	107	*143	214
Greece	128	140	130	168	*1 160	*1 210	1 250	1 622	*120	*122	122	156
Holy See	1	1	1	1	70	70	70	70	.	.	.	.
Hungary	27	28	34	27	2 648	2 717	2 460	2 321	247	257	237	228
Iceland	6	6	6	5	125	113	*130	*137	548	467	*510	*515
Ireland	7	7	7	8	779	685	591	600	229	193	169	170
Italy	82	72	76	74	4 775	5 511	*6 000	5 985	85	97	*105	105
Latvia	.	.	.	22	.	.	.	589	.	.	.	228
Liechtenstein	2	2	*2	2	14	14	*18	18	540	504	*621	581
Lithuania	.	.	.	16	.	.	.	506	.	.	.	136
Luxembourg	5	4	5	5	135	140	143	154	371	381	375	384
Malta	5	4	3	3	*60	*56	*54	64	*185	*163	*153	176
Moldova	.	.	.	4	.	.	.	106	.	.	.	24
Monaco	2	2	1	1	10	*10	8	*8	381	*357	267	*250
Netherlands	84	88	45	46	4 612	4 496	*4 500	5 138	326	310	*301	334
Norway	85	82	85	83	1 892	2 120	2 588	2 623	463	510	610	607
Poland	43	45	67	66	8 407	7 714	4 889	5 404	236	207	128	141
Portugal	28	25	24	23	*480	413	446	404	*49	42	45	41
Romania	35	36	65	69	*4 024	*3 601	*6 300	*6 800	*181	*158	*271	*297
Russian Federation				17				39 301				267
San Marino	3	.	.	-	1	.	.	-	48	.	.	-
Slovakia‡	...	...	18	21	.	.	1 410	1 363	.	.	267	256
Slovenia	3	3	4	6	198	216	303	360	108	115	158	185
Spain	111	102	*125	148	3 487	3 078	3 450	*4 100	93	80	88	*104
Sweden	114	115	107	94	4 386	4 389	4 499	4 219	528	526	526	483
Switzerland	89	97	94	80	2 483	3 213	3 063	2 920	393	492	448	409

Country / Pays / País	Daily newspapers / Journaux quotidiens / Periódicos diarios											
	Number Nombre Número				Circulation / Diffusion / Difusión							
					Total (in thousands) Total (en milliers) Total (en millares)				Per 1,000 inhabitants Pour 1 000 habitants Por 1 000 habitantes			
	1980	1985	1990	1994	1980	1985	1990	1994	1980	1985	1990	1995
	(1)	(2)	(3)	(4)	(5)	(6)	(7)	(8)	(9)	(10)	(11)	(12)
The former Yugoslav Rep. of Macedonia	...	...	2	3	...	...	*55	44	...	...	*27	21
Ukraine‡	...	...	127	90	...	...	13 026	6 083	...	...	252	118
United Kingdom	113	104	*103	103	23 472	22 495	*22 350	20 372	417	397	*389	351
Federal Republic of Yugoslavia‡	12	12	11	9	537	425	973	966	56	43	94	90
Oceania												
American Samoa	2	3	-	-	10	*9	-	-	319	*226	-	-
Australia	62	62	62	69	*4 700	*4 300	*4 200	*4 600	*323	*275	*249	*258
Cook Islands	1	1	1	1	2	2	2	2	111	118	111	105
Fiji	3	3	1	1	64	68	27	35	102	97	37	45
French Polynesia	2	3	2	4	*13	23	21	*24	*86	132	107	*112
Guam	1	1	1	1	18	18	22	25	169	151	161	170
New Caledonia	1	1	1	3	15	19	19	*23	105	123	113	*129
New Zealand	32	33	35	31	1 059	1 075	*1 100	*1 050	340	331	*327	*297
Papua New Guinea	1	2	2	2	27	45	49	65	9	13	13	15
Tonga	-	-	1	1	-	-	7	7	-	-	73	73

General note / Note générale / Nota general:

E--> For 1994, it is known or believed that no daily newspapers were published in the following 37 countries and territories: Africa: Cape Verde, Comoros, Djibouti, Eritrea, Guinea, St Helena, Sao Tome and Principe, Western Sahara, America, North: Anguilla, Antigua and Barbuda, Aruba, Belize, British Virgin Islands, Dominica, Greenland, Grenada, Montserrat, St Kitts and Nevis, St Lucia, St Pierre and Miquelon, St Vincent and the Grenadines, Turks and Caicos Islands, America, South: Falkland Islands (Malvinas), Asia: Bhutan, Cambodia, East Timor. Europe: Faeroe Islands, San Marino, Oceania: American Samoa, Kiribati, Nauru, Niue, Norfolk Island, Pacific Islands, Samoa, Solomon Islands, Tokelau, Tuvalu, Vanuatu.

FR-> Pour 1994, les renseignements disponibles indiquent ou permettent de penser qu'il n'est paru aucun journal quotidien dans les 37 pays ou territoires dont la liste suit: Afrique: Cap-Vert, Comores, Djibouti, Erythree, Guinée, Sahara occidental, Sainte-Hélène, Sao Tomé et Principe. Amérique du Nord: Anguilla, Antigua et Barbuda, Aruba, Belize, Dominique, Grenade, Groënland, Iles Turques et Caïques, Iles Vierges britanniques, Montserrat, Saint Kitts et Nevis, St Lucie, Saint-Pierre et Miquelon, Saint Vincent-et-Grenadines, Amérique du Sud: Iles Falkland (Malvinas). Asie: Bhoutan, Cambodge, Timor Oriental. Europe: Iles Féroé, San Marino, Océanie: Ile Norfolk, Iles du Pacifique, Iles Salomon, Kiribati, Nauru, Nioué, Samoa, Samoa américaines, Tokelaou, Tuvalu, Vanuatu.

ESP> Para 1994, la información disponible indica o permite pensar que no se ha publicado ningún periódico diario en los 37 países y territorios siguientes: Africa: Cabo Verde, Comoras, Eritrea, Guinea, Sáhara Occidental, Santa Elena, Santo Tomé y Príncipe, Djibuti, América del Norte: Anguilla, Antigua y Barbuda, Aruba, Belice, Dominica, Granada, Groenlandia, Islas Turcas y Caicos, Islas Virgenes Británicas, Montserrat, Saint Kitts y Nevis, Santa Lucia, San Pedro y Miquelón, San Vicente y las Granadinas. América del Sur: Islas Falkland (Malvinas). Asia: Bhután, Camboja, Timor Oriental. Europa: Islas Feroé, San Marino, Oceanía: Isla Norfolk, Islas del Pacifico, Islas Salomón, Kiribati, Nauru, Niue, Samoa, Samoa Americanas, Tokelau, Tuvalu, Vanuatu.

EUROPE:

Bosnia and Herzegovina:

E--> Data for 1994 refer to 1992 and only to the territory that is under the control of the Government of the Republic of Bosnia and Herzegovina.

FR-> Les données pour 1994 se réfèrent à 1992 et seulement au territoire qui est sous le contrôle du gouvernement de la République de Bosnie-Herzégovine.

ESP> Los datos para 1994 se refieren a 1992 y solamente al territorio bajo control del gobierno de la República de Bosnia y Herzegovina.

Germany:

E--> Data for 1990 refer to 1991.

FR-> Les données pour 1990 se réfèrent à 1991.

ESP> Los datos para 1990 se refieren a 1991.

Slovakia:

E--> Data for 1990 refer to 1991.

FR-> Les données pour 1990 se réfèrent à 1991.

ESP> Los datos se para 1990 se refieren a 1991.

Ukraine:

E--> Data for 1994 refer to 1992.

FR-> Les données pour 1994 se réfèrent à 1992.

ESP> Los datos para 1994 se refieren a 1992.

Fed. Rep. of Yugoslavia:

E--> Data for 1990 refer to 1991.

FR-> Les données pour 1990 se réfèrent à 1991.

ESP> Los datos para 1990 se refieren a 1991.

Non-daily newspapers and periodicals 7.10
Journaux non quotidiens et périodiques
Periódicos no diarios y revistas

7.10 Non-daily newspapers and periodicals: number and circulation (total and per 1,000 inhabitants)

Journaux non quotidiens et périodiques: nombre et diffusion (total et pour 1 000 habitants)

Periódicos no diarios y revistas:
número y circulación (total y por 1 000 habitantes)

Country / Pays / País	Year / Année / Año	Non-daily newspapers / Journaux non quotidiens / Periódicos no diarios					Periodicals / Périodiques / Revistas		
		Number / Nombre / Número			Circulation Diffusion Difusión			Circulation Diffusion Difusión	
		Total Total Total	1 - 3 times a week 1 à 3 fois par semaine 1 a 3 veces por semana	Issued less frequently Paraissant moins fréquemment Publicados con menor frecuencia	Total (000) Total (000) Total (000)	Per 1,000 inhabitants Pour 1000 habitants Por 1 000 habitantes	Number Nombre Número	Total (000) Total (000) Total (000)	Per 1,000 inhabitants Pour 1 000 habitants Por 1 000 habitantes
		(1)	(2)	(3)	(4)	(5)	(6)	(7)	(8)
Africa									
Algeria	1990	37	24	13	1 409	57	48	803	32
Botswana	1992	4	4	-	61	45	14	177	130
Burkina Faso	1990	10	2	8	14	2	37	24	3
Congo‡	1990	3	1	2	139	62	3	34	15
Djibouti‡	1989	...	...	...	...	...	7	6	14
Egypt	1991	35	17	18	1 502	26	266	1 815	31
Gambia	1990	6	3	3	*7	*8	10	885	958
Ghana	1990	87	83	4	1 111	74	121	774	52
Guinea	1990	*1	1	-	*1	*.2	*3	*5	*1
Madagascar	1994	31	9	22	*90	*6	55	*108	*8
Malawi	1992	4	3	1	133	13	...	...	...
Mauritius‡	1994	28	18	10	...	...	62	...	...
Namibia	1990	18	11	7	71	53	...	...	...
Rwanda	1992	15	2	13	*155	*22	15	101	14
Senegal	1994	87	29	58	...	...	...	...	...
South Africa	1991	10	10	-	1 527	40	11	2 149	57
Uganda	1990	...	...	...	...	...	26	158	10
Zaire	1990	77	76	1	...	...	...	...	...
Zimbabwe	1990	...	...	...	...	...	28	680	69
America, North									
Antigua and Barbuda	1992	4	...	...	...	...	...	...	...
Barbados	1990	4	4	-	*95	*370	...	...	...
Belize	1990	7	7	-	37	196	...	...	...
Bermuda	1990	3	2	1	35	566	...	...	...
British Virgin Islands	1990	2	2	-	4	250	...	...	...
Canada‡	1992	1 627	...	...	22 043	804	1 400	37 108	1 303
Costa Rica	1991	12	5	7	106	34	...	...	...
Cuba‡	1990	4	4	-	36	3	160	2 797	264
Dominica	1992	1	1	-	5	63	...	...	...
Grenada	1992	2	2	-	*5	*55	...	...	...
Mexico	1994	45	38	7	1 274	14	158	13 097	143
Montserrat	1990	2	2	-	2	200	...	...	...
Saint Kitts and Nevis	1993	2	2	-	6	143	10	44	*1 048
St. Lucia	1992	3	3	-	18	131	...	...	...
St. Pierre and Miquelon	1992	1	1	-	2	317	...	...	...
Trinidad and Tobago	1990	5	5	-	125	101	...	...	...
Turks and Caicos Islands	1992	1	1	-	10	769	...	...	...
United States	1994	9 728	9 728	...	...	...	...	...	...

7.10 Non-daily newspapers and periodicals
Journaux non quotidiens et périodiques
Periódicos no diarios y revistas

Country / Pays / País	Year / Année / Año	Non-daily newspapers Journaux non quotidiens Periódicos no diarios					Periodicals Périodiques Revistas		
		Number / Nombre / Número			Circulation Diffusion Difusión		Number Nombre Número	Circulation Diffusion Difusión	
		Total	1 - 3 times a week / 1 à 3 fois par semaine / 1 a 3 veces por semana	Issued less frequently Paraissant moins fréquemment Publicados con menor frecuencia	Total (000)	Per 1,000 inhabitants / Pour 1000 habitants / Por 1 000 habitantes		Total (000)	Per 1,000 inhabitants / Pour 1 000 habitants / Por 1 000 habitantes
		(1)	(2)	(3)	(4)	(5)	(6)	(7)	(8)
America, South									
Argentina	1992	*7	*6	*1	*350	*11	...	...	...
Chile	1992	48	33	15	102	7	417	*3 450	*254
Ecuador	1992	...	...	...	...	...	199	...	...
Suriname	1992	1	1	-	*5	*12	...	...	...
Asia									
Afghanistan	1992	13	9	4	...	...	...	...	...
Armenia	1992	57	48	9	*200	*58	40	5 064	1 472
Azerbaijan	1992	273	185	88	3 476	476	49	801	110
Bahrain	1993	5	5	-	17	31	26	73	137
Bhutan	1992	1	...	...	11	7	...	...	...
Brunei Darussalam	1992	2	...	...	57	212	15	132	489
China‡	1992	875	...	...	134 409	114	6 486	205 060	173
Cyprus	1992	30	8	22	133	185	37	167	232
Hong Kong‡	1992	17	-	17	...	...	598	...	...
Indonesia	1992	92	92	-	3 501	19	117	3 985	21
Iran, Islamic Republic of	1990	50	41	9	*470	*8	318	6 166	105
Japan	1992	*16	*10	*6	*9 100	*73	2 926	...	...
Jordan	1990	6	5	1	122	29	31	43	10
Kuwait	1989	21	21	-	...	...	...	...	...
Kyrgyzstan	1994	137	98	39	720	154	...	...	...
Macau	1992	*3	*2	*1	...	...	16	...	...
Malaysia	1992	8	8	-	1 530	81	25	996	53
Mongolia	1990	55	31	24	1 133	520	45	6 361	2 920
Oman	1992	5	5	-	...	...	15	...	...
Pakistan‡	1991	719	...	...	1 957	16	...	...	...
Philippines	1990	306	247	59	*610	*10	1 570	*9 468	*156
Qatar	1994	1	*1	-	7	13	12	157	291
Saudi Arabia	1994	3	3	-	...	...	471	...	...
Singapore	1994	7	6	1	1 035	367	...	...	...
Sri Lanka	1994	80	43	37	...	...	...	...	...
Tajikistan	1994	96	75	21	...	...	22	50	8
Thailand	1992	395	260	135	...	...	1 522	...	...
Turkey	1994	1 100	480	*620	...	...	3 554	...	...
United Arab Emirates	1990	...	...	...	...	...	80	922	614
Uzbekistan	1994	313	74	239	*2 000	*90	70	2 032	91
Europe									
Albania	1989	42	...	...	65	20	143	3 477	1 074
Andorra	1992	4	...	...	*8	*138	...	...	...
Austria	1993	141	...	...	...	...	2 481	...	...
Belarus	1992	338	212	126	4 749	465	155	3 765	369
Belgium	1992	3	3	-	*40	*4	13 706	...	...
Bosnia and Herzegovina	1992	22	7	15	2 508	636	...	...	...
Bulgaria‡	1993	874	322	552	8 280	933	745	3 097	347
Croatia	1990	563	124	439	*2 781	*616	352	6 357	1 407
Czech Republic	1993	168	168	...	64	6	1 168	81 387	7 905
Denmark	1992	11	11	-	1 490	289	205	7 838	1 520
Estonia	1994	196	...	...	...	...	470	...	...
Faeroe Islands	1992	7	...	...	6	128	...	...	...
Finland‡	1994	171	171	-	1 095	215	5 711	...	...
France	1991	227	218	9	3 068	54	2 672	120 018	2 106
Germany	1992	35	35	-	5 322	66	9 010	395 036	4 916
Gibraltar	1992	*5	5	-	*6	*221	...	...	...
Holy See	1992	...	...	...	...	...	48	102	...
Hungary	1991	279	54	225	4 603	446	1 203	14 927	1 447
Iceland	1994	77	16	61	...	...	938	...	...
Italy	1994	231	197	34	1 428	25	9 951	80 469	1 408
Latvia	1994	235	121	114	...	...	213	1 660	643
Liechtenstein	1991	3	-	3	3	97	...	...	...
Lithuania	1994	429	136	293	3 200	863	269	...	...
Luxembourg	1990	...	...	...	...	...	508	...	...
Malta	1992	8	7	1	...	...	359	...	...

Non-daily newspapers and periodicals 7.10
Journaux non quotidiens et périodiques
Periódicos no diarios y revistas

Country / Pays / País	Year / Année / Año	Non-daily newspapers Journaux non quotidiens Periódicos no diarios					Periodicals Périodiques Revistas		
		Number / Nombre / Número			Circulation Diffusion Difusión			Circulation Diffusion Difusión	
		Total	1 - 3 times a week 1 à 3 fois par semaine 1 a 3 veces por semana	Issued less frequently Paraissant moins fréquemment Publicados con menor frecuencia	Total (000)	Per 1,000 inhabitants Pour 1000 habitants Por 1 000 habitantes	Number Nombre Número	Total (000)	Per 1,000 inhabitants Pour 1000 habitants Por 1 000 habitantes
		(1)	(2)	(3)	(4)	(5)	(6)	(7)	(8)
Moldova	1994	157	103	54	1 195	270	76	196	44
Monaco	1992	...	...	...	...	...	3	38	1 226
Netherlands	1990	...	...	...	...	...	367	19 283	1 290
Norway	1994	69	69	-	366	85	8 017	...	...
Poland	1994	48	48	-	1 880	49	3 999	77 735	2 027
Portugal	1994	*175	175	-	*3 729	*379	984	10 208	1 038
Romania‡	1993	24	24	-	*812	*35	987	...	...
Russian Federation	1992	4 498	3 500	998	86 677	585	2 592	918 218	6 201
San Marino	1994	8	-	8	13	520	17	11	440
Slovakia	1992	262	91	171	2 091	395	424	8 725	1 648
Slovenia	1994	163	34	129	...	...	784		
Sweden‡	1994	71	71	-	459	53	4 272		
Switzerland‡	1994	138	138	-	1 281	180	60	4 561	640
The Former Yugoslav Rep. of Macedonia	1991	*112	...	...	...	...	*74	*347	*168
Ukraine	1992	1 605	1 238	367	18 194	352	321	3 491	68
Federal Republic of Yugoslavia	1994	514	81	433	...	...	395	...	...
Oceania									
American Samoa	1992	2	2	-	4	86	...	...	...
Niue	1992	1	1	-	2	950	8	5.4	3
Norfolk Island	1992	1	1	-	1	...	...	...	...
Tuvalu	1992	1	1	-	0.3	33	...	...	...
Vanuatu, Rep. of	1992	1	1	-	2	11	...	...	...

AFRICA:
Congo:
 E––> Data on periodicals refer only to periodicals for the general public.
 FR–> Les données relatives aux périodiques se réfèrent seulement aux périodiques destinés au grand public.
 ESP> Los datos relativos a las revistas se refieren solamente a las revistas para el público en general.
Djibouti:
 E––> Data on periodicals refer only to periodicals for the general public.
 FR–> Les données relatives aux périodiques se réfèrent seulement aux périodiques destinés au grand public.
 ESP> Los datos relativos a las revistas se refieren solamente a las revistas para el público en general.
Mauritius:
 E––> Data on periodicals refer to 1992.
 FR–> Les données relatives aux périodiques se réfèrent à 1992.
 ESP> Los datos relativos a las revistas se refieren a 1992.
AMERICA NORTH:
Canada:
 E––> Data on non-dailies refer to 1989.
 FR–> Les données pour les non-quotidiens se réfèrent à 1989.
 ESP> Datos relativos a los periódicos no diarios se refieren a 1989.
Cuba:
 E––> Data on non-dailies refer to 1989.
 FR–> Les données pour les non-quotidiens se réfèrent à 1989.
 ESP> Datos relativos a los periodicos no diarios se refieren a 1989.
ASIA:
China:
 E––> Data on non-dailies include daily newspapers.
 FR–> Les données relatives aux non-quotidiens comprennent les quotidiens.
 ESP> Los datos relativos a los periodicos no diarios incluyen los diarios.

Hong Kong:
 E––> Data on periodicals refer only to periodicals for the general public.
 FR–> Les données relatives aux périodiques se réfèrent seulement aux périodiques destinés au grand public.
 ESP> Los datos relativos a las revistas se refieren solamente a las revistas para el público en general.
Pakistan:
 E––> Data on non-dailies include periodicals.
 FR–> Les données relatives aux non-quotidiens comprennent les périodiques.
 ESP> Los datos relativos a los periódicos no diarios incluyen las revistas.
EUROPE:
Bulgaria:
 E––> Data on non-daily newspapers include regional editions and data on periodicals refer to 1992.
 FR–> Les données relatives aux journaux non-quotidiens comprennent les éditions régionales et les données relatives aux périodiques se réfèrent à 1992.
 ESP> Los datos relativos a los periódicos no diarios incluyen las ediciones regionales y los datos relativos a las revistas se refieren a 1992.
Finland:
 E––> Data on periodicals refer to 1990
 FR–> Les données relatives aux periodiques se réfèrent à 1990.
 ESP> Los datos relativos a las revistas se refieren a 1990.
Romania:
 E––> Data on non-dailies refer to 1989.
 FR–> Les données pour les non-quotidiens se rèfèrent à 1989.
 ESP> Los datos relativos a los periodicos no diarios se refieren a 1989.
Sweden:
 E––> Data on periodicals refer to 1993 and to periodicals for the general public only.
 FR–> Les données relatives aux périodiques se réfèrent à 1993 et aux périodiques destinés au grand public seulement.
 ESP> Los datos relativos a las revistas se refieren a 1993 y a las revistas para el público en general solamente.

7.10 Non-daily newspapers and periodicals
Journaux non quotidiens et périodiques
Periódicos no diarios y revistas

Switzerland:

E--> Data on non-dailies refer only to newspapers purchased and do not include satellites publications. Figures on periodicals refer to periodicals for the general public only.

FR-> Les données relatives aux non-quotidiens se réfèrent seulement aux journaux payants et n'incluent pas les éditions satellites. Les chiffres pour les périodiques se réfèrent aux périodiques destinés au grand public seulement.

ESP> Los datos relativos a los periódicos no diarios se refieren solamente a los periódicos vendidos y no incluyen las ediciónes satelites. Las cifras sobre las revistas se refieren a las revistas para el público en general solamente.

Former Yugoslav Rep. of Macedonia:

E--> Data on periodicals refer only to periodicals for the general public.

FR-> Les données relatives aux périodiques se réfèrent seulement aux périodiques destinés au grand public.

ESP> Los datos relativos a las revistas se refieren solamente a las revistas para el público en general.

Periodicals: number and circulation by type 7.11
Périodiques: nombre et diffusion par type
Revistas: número y circulación por tipos

7.11 Periodicals by type: number and circulation

Périodiques classés par type: nombre et diffusion

Revistas clasificadas por tipos: número y circulación

A. Total - periodicals for the general public	A. Total - périodiques destinés au grand public	A. Total - revistas para el público en general
1. Illustrated magazines providing news and reporting	1. Magazines illustrés d'information et de reportage	1. Revistas ilustradas que contienen noticias y reportajes
2. Politics, philosophy religion, culture	2. Politiques, philosophie, religion, culture	2. Política, filosofía, religión, cultura
3. Women's, mens's and family magazines	3. Magazines féminins, masculins et de presse familiale	3. Revistas femeninas, masculinas y para el hogar
4. Radio, television and cinema magazines	4. Magazines de radiotélévision et de cinéma	4. Revistas de radio, televisión y cine
5. Tourism, travel, leisure and sports	5. Tourisme, voyages, loisirs, sports	5. Turismo, viajes, ocio y deportes
6. Popular history and geography	6. Vulgarisation historique et géographique	6. Indole histórica y geográfica popular
7. Popular science and technology	7. Vulgarisation scientifique et technique	7. Vulgarización científica y técnica
8. Publications for young persons and children, comics	8. Publications pour la jeunesse et l'enfance, bandes dessinées	8. Publicaciones para jovenes y niños, historietas
9. Other periodicals for the general public	9. Autres périodiques destinés au grand public	9. Otras revistas para el público en general
B. Total - periodicals for specific readership	B. Total - périodiques s'adressant à un public spécifique	B. Total - revistas dirigidas a un público determinado
1. Professional journals	1. Revues professionnelles	1. Revistas profesionales
2. Trade union, political party, association journals	2. Organes de syndicats, de partis politiques, d'associations	2. Revistas sindicales, de partidos políticos, asociaciones
3. Mutual benefit societies	3. Revues mutualistes	3. Boletines de sociedades de ayuda mutua
4. Business house organs	4. Revues d'entreprise	4. Boletines de empresa
5. Parish magazines	5. Bulletins paroissiaux	5. Boletines parroquiales
6. Other periodicals for specific readership	6. Autres périodiques destinés à un public restreint	6. Otras revistas dirigidas a un público determinado

Number = Number of titles

Circulation = Total average circulation (or copies printed)

Nombre = Nombre de titres

Diffusion = Diffusion moyenne totale (ou tirage)

Número = Número de títulos

Circulación = Promedio de la circulación total (o tirada)

7.11 Periodicals: number and circulation by type
Périodiques: nombre et diffusion par type
Revistas: número y circulación por tipos

Africa

Types of publications / Types de périodiques / Tipos de revistas	Algeria 1990		Burkina Faso 1990		Congo 1990	
	Number Nombre Número	Circulation Diffusion Circulación (000)	Number Nombre Número	Circulation Diffusion Circulación (000)	Number Nombre Número	Circulation Diffusion Circulación (000)
Total A+B	48	802.7	37	...	...	...
A. Total - periodicals for the general public	34	414.7	15	19.9	3	33.6
1. Illustrated magazines	4	2.0	3	8.1	2	25.0
2. Politics, philosophy, religion, culture	6	15.0	1	...	1	8.6
3. Women's, men's and family magazines	3	25.0	1	3.0	-	-
4. Radio, television and cinema magazines	3	10.0	1	3.0	-	-
5. Tourism, travel, leisure and sports	5	90.0	-	-	-	-
6. Popular history and geography	-	-	1	2.0	-	-
7. Popular science and technology	9	215.0	6	1.8	-	-
8. Publications for young persons and children	3	51.0	2	2.0	-	-
9. Other periodicals for the general public	1	6.7	-	-	-	-
B. Total - periodicals for specific readership	14	388.0	22	...	...	...
1. Professional journals	2	52.0	2	1.4	...	...
2. Trade union, political party journals	9	294.5	3	...	...	...
3. Mutual benefit societies	-	-	2	...	...	...
4. Business house organs	-	-	-	-	...	...
5. Parish magazines	-	-	10	2.0	...	...
6. Other periodicals for specific readership	3	41.5	5	1.1	...	...

Types of publications / Types de périodiques / Tipos de revistas	Djibouti 1989		Egypt 1991		Ghana 1990	
	Number Nombre Número	Circulation Diffusion Circulación (000)	Number Nombre Número	Circulation Diffusion Circulación (000)	Number Nombre Número	Circulation Diffusion Circulación (000)
Total A+B	...	...	266	1 815.0	121	774.0
A. Total - periodicals for the general public	7	6.9	159	991.0	63	507.0
1. Illustrated magazines	-	-	25	376.0	10	70.0
2. Politics, philosophy, religion, culture	2	2.5	41	292.0	37	265.0
3. Women's, men's and family magazines	-	-	-	-	3	25.0
4. Radio, television and cinema magazines	-	-	-	-	1	5.0
5. Tourism, travel, leisure and sports	-	-	-	-	6	50.0
6. Popular history and geography	-	-	-	-	-	-
7. Popular science and technology	1	0.8	93	323.0	-	-
8. Publications for young persons and children	-	-	-	-	6	92.0
9. Other periodicals for the general public	4	3.6	-	-	-	-
B. Total - periodicals for specific readership	...	...	107	824.0	58	267.0
1. Professional journals	...	...	71	285.0	12	60.0
2. Trade union, political party journals	...	...	-	-	13	120.0
3. Mutual benefit societies	...	...	-	-	5	7.0
4. Business house organs	...	...	-	-	28	80.0
5. Parish magazines	...	...	-	-	-	-
6. Other periodicals for specific readership	...	...	36	539.0	-	-

Periodicals: number and circulation by type 7.11
Périodiques: nombre et diffusion par type
Revistas: número y circulación por tipos

Types of publications Types de périodiques Tipos de revistas	Guinea 1990		Madagascar 1994		Mauritius 1992	
	Number Nombre Número	Circulation Diffusion Circulación (000)	Number Nombre Número	Circulation Diffusion Circulación (000)	Number Nombre Número	Circulation Diffusion Circulación (000)
Total A + B	*5	*10.0	55	*108.5	62	...
A. Total - periodicals for the general public	*4	*6.0	38	*84.5	...	...
1. Illustrated magazines	*4	*6.0	5	*11.0	...	...
2. Politics, philosophy, religion, culture	-	-	14	*10.0	...	...
3. Women's, men's and family magazines	-	-	-	-	...	...
4. Radio, television and cinema magazines	-	-	-	-	...	...
5. Tourism, travel, leisure and sports	-	-	1	0.5	...	...
6. Popular history and geography	-	-	-	-	...	...
7. Popular science and technology	-	-	9	56.0	...	...
8. Publications for young persons and children	-	-	2	1.0	...	...
9. Other periodicals for the general public			7	6.0		
B. Total - periodicals for specific readership	*1	*4.0	17	*24.0	...	...
1. Professional journals	*1	*4.0	10	*8.0	...	...
2. Trade union, political party journals	-	-	3	*1.0	...	...
3. Mutual benefit societies	-	-	-	-	...	...
4. Business house organs	-	-	-	-	...	...
5. Parish magazines	-	-	4	15.0	...	...
6. Other periodicals for specific readership	-	-	-	-	...	...

Types of publications Types de périodiques Tipos de revistas	Rwanda 1992		Uganda 1990		Zimbabwe 1990	
	Number Nombre Número	Circulation Diffusion Circulación (000)	Number Nombre Número	Circulation Diffusion Circulación (000)	Number Nombre Número	Circulation Diffusion Circulación (000)
Total A + B	14	101.2	26	158.0	28	680.0
A. Total - periodicals for the general public	9	92.7	11	50.0	22	580.0
1. Illustrated magazines	4	4.6	2	10.0	6	180.0
2. Politics, philosophy, religion, culture	1	0.3	3	15.0	2	60.0
3. Women's, men's and family magazines	-	-	1	5.0	4	120.0
4. Radio, television and cinema magazines	-	-	-	-	1	60.0
5. Tourism, travel, leisure and sports	1	2.0	3	12.0	2	40.0
6. Popular history and geography	-	-	-	-	2	120.0
7. Popular science and technology	2	5.8	-	-	2	50.0
8. Publications for young persons and children	1	80.0	1	5.0	3	50.0
9. Other periodicals for the general public	-	-	1	3.0	-	-
B. Total - periodicals for specific readership	5	8.5	15	108.0	6	100.0
1. Professional journals	2	3.5	10	60.0	1	10.0
2. Trade union, political party journals	-	-	1	3.0	2	40.0
3. Mutual benefit societies	-	-	1	20.0	1	10.0
4. Business house organs	1	1.0	2	15.0	2	40.0
5. Parish magazines	1	1.0	1	10.0	-	-
6. Other periodicals for specific readership	1	3.0	-	-	-	-

7.11   Periodicals: number and circulation by type
Périodiques: nombre et diffusion par type
Revistas: número y circulación por tipos

America, North

Types of publications Types de périodiques Tipos de revistas	Canada 1992		Cuba 1990		Saint Kitts and Nevis 1993	
	Number Nombre Número	Circulation Diffusion Circulación (000)	Number Nombre Número	Circulation Diffusion Circulación (000)	Number Nombre Número	Circulation Diffusion Circulación (000)
Total A + B	1 400	37 108.0	160	2 796.8	9	42.7
A. Total - periodicals for the general public	551	26 118.0	94	2 521.8	7	40.4
1. Illustrated magazines	...	...	14	559.4	1	2.0
2. Politics, philosophy, religion, culture	...	...	35	352.4	-	-
3. Women's, men's and family magazines	...	...	9	520.2	-	-
4. Radio, television and cinema magazines	...	...	2	14.0	-	-
5. Tourism, travel, leisure and sports	...	...	3	643.1	1	35.0
6. Popular history and geography	...	...	5	1.9	1	0.8
7. Popular science and technology	...	...	6	16.8	-	-
8. Publications for young persons and children	...	...	9	308.0	-	-
9. Other periodicals for the general public	...	...	11	106.0	4	2.6
B. Total - periodicals for specific readership	849	10 990.0	66	275.0	2	2.3
1. Professional journals	222	640.0	44	89.5	-	-
2. Trade union, political party journals	-	-	22	185.5	-	-
3. Mutual benefit societies	-	-	-	-	-	-
4. Business house organs	378	5 673.0	-	-	2	2.3
5. Parish magazines	188	3 597.0	-	-	-	-
6. Other periodicals for specific readership	61	1 080.0	-	-	-	-

America, South   Asia

Types of publications Types de périodiques Tipos de revistas	Ecuador 1992		Armenia 1992		Azerbaijan 1992	
	Number Nombre Número	Circulation Diffusion Circulación (000)	Number Nombre Número	Circulation Diffusion Circulación (000)	Number Nombre Número	Circulation Diffusion Circulación (000)
Total A + B	199	...	40	5 064.2	49	801.5
A. Total - periodicals for the general public	166	...	19	4 637.5	21	632.5
1. Illustrated magazines	125	...	1	174.6	-	-
2. Politics, philosophy, religion, culture	10	...	10	105.4	2	76.0
3. Women's, men's and family magazines	1	...	1	1 210.0	-	-
4. Radio, television and cinema magazines	10	...	2	1 493.0	-	-
5. Tourism, travel, leisure and sports	6	...	-	-	1	0.5
6. Popular history and geography	4	...	1	1.1	1	2.0
7. Popular science and technology	6	...	1	150.0	-	-
8. Publications for young persons and children	4	...	3	1 503.4	2	117.0
9. Other periodicals for the general public	-	-	-	-	15	437.0
B. Total - periodicals for specific readership	33	...	21	426.7	28	169.0
1. Professional journals	20	...	14	331.6	20	136.0
2. Trade union, political party journals	4	...	6	90.1	4	15.0
3. Mutual benefit societies	1	...	1	5.0	-	-
4. Business house organs	6	...	-	-	-	-
5. Parish magazines	1	...	-	-	-	-
6. Other periodicals for specific readership	1	...	-	-	4	18.0

Periodicals: number and circulation by type 7.11
Périodiques: nombre et diffusion par type
Revistas: número y circulación por tipos

Types of publications Types de périodiques Tipos de revistas	Bahrain 1992		Cyprus 1991		Hong Kong 1992	
	Number Nombre Número	Circulation Diffusion Circulación (000)	Number Nombre Número	Circulation Diffusion Circulación (000)	Number Nombre Número	Circulation Diffusion Circulación (000)
Total A + B	33	93.1	37	166.5	...	...
A. Total - periodicals for the general public	16	59.8	37	166.5	598	...
1. Illustrated magazines	3	12.5	6	50.0	200	...
2. Politics, philosophy, religion, culture	3	9.0	5	7.0	66	...
3. Women's, men's and family magazines	2	18.5	5	20.0	13	...
4. Radio, television and cinema magazines	1	3.0	3	30.0	118	...
5. Tourism, travel, leisure and sports	2	4.0	6	15.0	108	...
6. Popular history and geography	2	6.0	4	7.5	3	...
7. Popular science and technology	-	-	4	12.0	32	...
8. Publications for young persons and children	-	-	4	25.0	25	...
9. Other periodicals for the general public	3	6.8	-	-	33	...
B. Total - periodicals for specific readership	17	33.3	-	-	...	...
1. Professional journals	2	2.0	-	-	...	...
2. Trade union, political party journals	1	3.7	-	-	...	...
3. Mutual benefit societies	1	2.0	-	-	...	...
4. Business house organs	5	7.6	-	-	...	...
5. Parish magazines	-	-	-	-	...	...
6. Other periodicals for specific readership	8	18.0	-	-	...	...

Types of publications Types de périodiques Tipos de revistas	Indonesia 1992		Iran, Islamic Republic of 1990		Jordan 1990	
	Number Nombre Número	Circulation Diffusion Circulación (000)	Number Nombre Número	Circulation Diffusion Circulación (000)	Number Nombre Número	Circulation Diffusion Circulación (000)
Total A + B	888	...	318	6 167.0	31	43.0
A. Total - periodicals for the general public	117	3 985.0	258	5 943.9	28	40.0
1. Illustrated magazines	29	758.2	22	243.8	6	8.0
2. Politics, philosophy, religion, culture	20	470.9	119	1 699.9	5	5.0
3. Women's, men's and family magazines	19	1 199.3	4	169.0	-	-
4. Radio, television and cinema magazines	3	199.5	6	76.8	1	1.0
5. Tourism, travel, leisure and sports	4	51.0	14	547.0	3	5.0
6. Popular history and geography	2	71.5	5	17.5	1	2.0
7. Popular science and technology	12	210.6	61	685.4	8	12.0
8. Publications for young persons and children	18	774.6	27	2 504.5	3	6.0
9. Other periodicals for the general public	10	249.4	-	-	1	1.0
B. Total - periodicals for specific readership	771	...	60	223.1	3	3.0
1. Professional journals	...	...	51	184.6	1	1.0
2. Trade union, political party journals	...	...	8	33.5	-	-
3. Mutual benefit societies	...	...	-	-	-	-
4. Business house organs	...	...	1	5.0	-	-
5. Parish magazines	...	...	-	-	2	2.0
6. Other periodicals for specific readership	...	...	-	-	-	-

7.11 Periodicals: number and circulation by type
Périodiques: nombre et diffusion par type
Revistas: número y circulación por tipos

Types of publications / Types de périodiques / Tipos de revistas	Malaysia 1992 Number Nombre Número	Malaysia 1992 Circulation Diffusion Circulación (000)	Mongolia 1989 Number Nombre Número	Mongolia 1989 Circulation Diffusion Circulación (000)	Philippines 1990 Number Nombre Número	Philippines 1990 Circulation Diffusion Circulación (000)
Total A + B	25	995.9	41	6 949.0	1 570	9 468.0
A. Total - periodicals for the general public	24	975.5	34	6 061.3	120	9 445.0
1. Illustrated magazines	-	-	1	1 711.9	31	*1 767.0
2. Politics, philosophy, religion, culture	-	-	8	1 094.6		
3. Women's, men's and family magazines	6	385.7	1	371.0	8	758.0
4. Radio, television and cinema magazines	4	253.6	-	-	2	160.0
5. Tourism, travel, leisure and sports	2	66.9	-	-	-	-
6. Popular history and geography	-	-	4	445.8	-	-
7. Popular science and technology	-	-	6	828.6		
8. Publications for young persons and children	7	212.9	7	945.7	79	6 760.0
9. Other periodicals for the general public	5	56.4	7	663.7		
B. Total - periodicals for specific readership	1	20.4	7	887.7	1 450	23.0
1. Professional journals	-	-	7	887.7	-	-
2. Trade union, political party journals	-	-	-	-	-	-
3. Mutual benefit societies	-	-	-	-	-	-
4. Business house organs	-	-	-	-	-	-
5. Parish magazines	-	-	-	-	-	-
6. Other periodicals for specific readership	1	20.4	-	-	1 450	23.0

Types of publications / Types de périodiques / Tipos de revistas	Qatar 1994 Number Nombre Número	Qatar 1994 Circulation Diffusion Circulación (000)	Saudi Arabia 1994 Number Nombre Número	Saudi Arabia 1994 Circulation Diffusion Circulación (000)	Tajikistan 1994 Number Nombre Número	Tajikistan 1994 Circulation Diffusion Circulación (000)
Total A + B	12	157.0	471	...	22	50.3
A. Total - periodicals for the general public	11	154.5	194		14	42.3
1. Illustrated magazines	3	64.0	15		-	-
2. Politics, philosophy, religion, culture	-	-	64	...	4	11.4
3. Women's, men's and family magazines	1	28.0	13	...	-	-
4. Radio, television and cinema magazines	-	-	5	...	-	-
5. Tourism, travel, leisure and sports	4	11.5	19	...	-	-
6. Popular history and geography	-	-	17	...	-	-
7. Popular science and technology	1	3.0	18		3	8.5
8. Publications for young persons and children	1	28.0	13		7	22.4
9. Other periodicals for the general public	1	20.0	30		-	-
B. Total - periodicals for specific readership	1	2.5	277	...	8	8.0
1. Professional journals	1	2.5	82	...	7	7.6
2. Trade union, political party journals	-	-	3	...	1	0.4
3. Mutual benefit societies	-	-	14	...		
4. Business house organs	-	-	98	...	-	-
5. Parish magazines	-	-	-	-	-	-
6. Other periodicals for specific readership	-	-	80		-	-

Periodicals: number and circulation by type **7.11**
Périodiques: nombre et diffusion par type
Revistas: número y circulación por tipos

Types of publications Types de périodiques Tipos de revistas	Thailand 1992		Turkey 1990		United Arab Emirates 1990	
	Number Nombre Número	Circulation Diffusion Circulación (000)	Number Nombre Número	Circulation Diffusion Circulación (000)	Number Nombre Número	Circulation Diffusion Circulación (000)
Total A + B	1 484	...	1 325	1 325.0	80	922.0
A. Total - periodicals for the general public	950	...	854	854.0	63	862.0
1. Illustrated magazines	100	...	...	...	5	100.0
2. Politics, philosophy, religion, culture	72	...	...	...	25	200.0
3. Women's, men's and family magazines	144	...	...	...	8	200.0
4. Radio, television and cinema magazines	42	...	...	...	1	2.0
5. Tourism, travel, leisure and sports	96	...	...	...	10	100.0
6. Popular history and geography	25	...	...	...	4	50.0
7. Popular science and technology	163	...	...	...	2	10.0
8. Publications for young persons and children	56	...	...	...	8	200.0
9. Other periodicals for the general public	252	...	...	...	-	-
B. Total - periodicals for specific readership	534	...	471	471.0	17	60.0
1. Professional journals	263	...	...	...	4	10.0
2. Trade union, political party journals	15	...	...	...	-	-
3. Mutual benefit societies	110	...	...	...	13	50.0
4. Business house organs	22	...	...	...	-	-
5. Parish magazines	50	...	...	...	-	-
6. Other periodicals for specific readership	74	...	...	...	-	-

Europe

Types of publications Types de périodiques Tipos de revistas	Uzbekistan 1994		Belarus 1992		Belgium 1992	
	Number Nombre Número	Circulation Diffusion Circulación (000)	Number Nombre Número	Circulation Diffusion Circulación (000)	Number Nombre Número	Circulation Diffusion Circulación (000)
Total A + B	70	2 032.0	155	3 765.0	13 706	...
A. Total - periodicals for the general public	34	1 805.1	60	3 313.0	10 786	...
1. Illustrated magazines	1	14.9	1	10.0	1 711	...
2. Politics, philosophy, religion, culture	15	237.5	17	192.0	1 521	...
3. Women's, men's and family magazines	3	215.3	7	1 916.0	2 360	...
4. Radio, television and cinema magazines	5	864.3	4	117.0	433	...
5. Tourism, travel, leisure and sports	-	-	4	54.0	1 269	...
6. Popular history and geography	-	-	1	3.0	422	...
7. Popular science and technology	5	159.0	1	118.0	1 277	...
8. Publications for young persons and children	5	314.1	8	463.0	367	...
9. Other periodicals for the general public	-	-	17	440.0	1 426	...
B. Total - periodicals for specific readership	36	226.9	95	452.0	2 920	...
1. Professional journals	32	219.6	26	36.0	730	...
2. Trade union, political party journals	1	0.3	1	9.0	581	...
3. Mutual benefit societies	-	-	3	57.0	351	...
4. Business house organs	-	-	3	57.0	305	...
5. Parish magazines	-	-	-	-	11	...
6. Other periodicals for specific readership	3	7.0	62	293.0	942	...

7.11 Periodicals: number and circulation by type
Périodiques: nombre et diffusion par type
Revistas: número y circulación por tipos

Types of publications / Types de périodiques / Tipos de revistas	Bulgaria 1992		Czech Republic 1992		Denmark 1992	
	Number Nombre Número	Circulation Diffusion Circulación (000)	Number Nombre Número	Circulation Diffusion Circulación (000)	Number Nombre Número	Circulation Diffusion Circulación (000)
Total A + B	681	3 042.0	1 907	...	205	7 838.0
A. Total - periodicals for the general public	307	2 269.0	977	...	38	3 089.0
1. Illustrated magazines	34	401.0	63	...	2	516.0
2. Politics, philosophy, religion, culture	67	235.0	250	...	-	-
3. Women's, men's and family magazines	12	151.0	68	...	8	1 283.0
4. Radio, television and cinema magazines	2	22.0	40	...	-	-
5. Tourism, travel, leisure and sports	47	606.0	133	...	-	-
6. Popular history and geography	14	53.0	78	...	-	-
7. Popular science and technology	5	11.0	53	...	-	-
8. Publications for young persons and children	28	399.0	71	...	2	154.0
9. Other periodicals for the general public	98	391.0	221	...	26	1 136.0
B. Total - periodicals for specific readership	374	773.0	930	...	167	4 749.0
1. Professional journals	268	373.0	560	...	...	...
2. Trade union, political party journals	13	20.0	55	...	...	...
3. Mutual benefit societies	-	-	48	...	...	...
4. Business house organs	2	2.0	97	...	...	...
5. Parish magazines	4	2.0	4	...	...	...
6. Other periodicals for specific readership	87	376.0	166	...	...	...

Types of publications / Types de périodiques / Tipos de revistas	Estonia 1994		France‡ 1991		Germany 1992	
	Number Nombre Número	Circulation Diffusion Circulación (000)	Number Nombre Número	Circulation Diffusion Circulación (000)	Number Nombre Número	Circulation Diffusion Circulación (000)
Total A + B	470	16 619.9	2 686	123 067.0	9 010	395 036.0
A. Total - periodicals for the general public	191	13 296.3	1 417	110 820.0	5 689	319 593.0
1. Illustrated magazines	-	-	13	3 627.0	288	66 057.0
2. Politics, philosophy, religion, culture	33	420.6	98	3 972.0	913	18 664.0
3. Women's, men's and family magazines	110	9 802.9	98	17 986.0	104	28 719.0
4. Radio, television and cinema magazines	-	-	51	12 940.0	./.	./.
5. Tourism, travel, leisure and sports	14	446.4	453	15 774.0	699	39 581.0
6. Popular history and geography	1	60.2	-	-	./.	./.
7. Popular science and technology	5	209.0	15	1 686.0	1 848	70 552.0
8. Publications for young persons and children	28	2 357.2	94	5 638.0	74	5 409.0
9. Other periodicals for the general public	-	-	595	49 197.0	1 763	90 611.0
B. Total - periodicals for specific readership	279	3 323.5	1 269	12 247.0	3 321	75 443.0
1. Professional journals	51	462.5	1 269	12 247.0	1 747	13 842.0
2. Trade union, political party journals	7	102.5	-	-	./.	./.
3. Mutual benefit societies	46	265.5	-	-	./.	./.
4. Business house organs	53	632.8	-	-	127	54 988.0
5. Parish magazines	72	477.6	-	-	-	-
6. Other periodicals for specific readership	50	1 382.6	-	-	1 447	6 613.0

Periodicals: number and circulation by type 7.11
Périodiques: nombre et diffusion par type
Revistas: número y circulación por tipos

Types of publications Types de périodiques Tipos de revistas	Holy See 1990		Hungary 1991		Italy 1994	
	Number Nombre Número	Circulation Diffusion Circulación (000)	Number Nombre Número	Circulation Diffusion Circulación (000)	Number Nombre Número	Circulation Diffusion Circulación (000)
Total A + B	47	56.7	1 203	14 927.4	10 256	3 906.2
A. Total - periodicals for the general public	12	7.4	465	12 744.2	5 671	3 660.5
1. Illustrated magazines	-	-	2	15.4	1 738	2 323.3
2. Politics, philosophy, religion, culture	9	5.1	151	1 579.1	1 053	234.1
3. Women's, men's and family magazines	-	-	10	406.5	149	179.1
4. Radio, television and cinema magazines	-	-	10	1 998.5	222	173.9
5. Tourism, travel, leisure and sports	-	-	110	4 004.8	378	461.1
6. Popular history and geography	2	1.3	5	46.9	304	13.4
7. Popular science and technology	-	-	10	857.7	297	30.0
8. Publications for young persons and children	-	-	97	1 364.0	162	81.3
9. Other periodicals for the general public	1	1.0	70	2 471.3	1 368	164.3
B. Total - periodicals for specific readership	35	49.3	738	2 183.2	4 585	245.7
1. Professional journals	34	46.5	368	986.4	923	59.0
2. Trade union, political party journals	-	-	34	151.2	2 380	128.1
3. Mutual benefit societies	-	-	-		566	49.4
4. Business house organs	-	-	309	734.9	-	-
5. Parish magazines	-	-	26	262.7	716	9.2
6. Other periodicals for specific readership	1	2.8	1	48.0	-	-

Types of publications Types de périodiques Tipos de revistas	Latvia 1994		Lithuania 1994		Luxembourg 1990	
	Number Nombre Número	Circulation Diffusion Circulación (000)	Number Nombre Número	Circulation Diffusion Circulación (000)	Number Nombre Número	Circulation Diffusion Circulación (000)
Total A + B	213	1 660.0	269	...	508	...
A. Total - periodicals for the general public	100	1 265.0	175	...	142	...
1. Illustrated magazines	3	49.0	5	...	14	...
2. Politics, philosophy, religion, culture	21	81.0	53	...	37	...
3. Women's, men's and family magazines	17	488.0	29	...	7	...
4. Radio, television and cinema magazines	1	7.0	1	...	3	...
5. Tourism, travel, leisure and sports	9	92.0	16	...	7	...
6. Popular history and geography	-	-	12	...	10	...
7. Popular science and technology	4	39.0	37	...	17	...
8. Publications for young persons and children	19	126.0	20	...	12	...
9. Other periodicals for the general public	26	383.0	2	...	35	...
B. Total - periodicals for specific readership	113	395.0	94	...	366	...
1. Professional journals	14	14.0	42	...	31	...
2. Trade union, political party journals	3	7.0	13	...	224	...
3. Mutual benefit societies	12	33.0	-	-	-	-
4. Business house organs	24	267.0	16	...	15	...
5. Parish magazines	8	7.0	-	-	11	...
6. Other periodicals for specific readership	52	67.0	23	...	85	...

7.11   Periodicals: number and circulation by type
Périodiques: nombre et diffusion par type
Revistas: número y circulación por tipos

Types of publications Types de périodiques Tipos de revistas	Malta 1992		Moldova 1994		Monaco 1992	
	Number Nombre Número	Circulation Diffusion Circulación (000)	Number Nombre Número	Circulation Diffusion Circulación (000)	Number Nombre Número	Circulation Diffusion Circulación (000)
Total A + B	359	...	76	196.0	3	3.8
A. Total - periodicals for the general public	249	...	31	106.0	3	3.8
1. Illustrated magazines	1	...	2	2.0	3	3.8
2. Politics, philosophy, religion, culture	128	...	10	31.0	-	-
3. Women's, men's and family magazines	12	...	1	16.0	-	-
4. Radio, television and cinema magazines	4	...	4	10.0	-	-
5. Tourism, travel, leisure and sports	36	...	-	-	-	-
6. Popular history and geography	3	...	2	5.0	-	-
7. Popular science and technology	8	...	-	-	-	-
8. Publications for young persons and children	7	...	6	35.0	-	-
9. Other periodicals for the general public	50	...	6	7.0	-	-
B. Total - periodicals for specific readership	110	...	45	90.0	-	-
1. Professional journals	15	...	10	29.0	-	-
2. Trade union, political party journals	19	...	1	2.0	-	-
3. Mutual benefit societies	5	...	-	-	-	-
4. Business house organs	9	...	-	-	-	-
5. Parish magazines	40	...	-	-	-	-
6. Other periodicals for specific readership	22	...	34	59.0	-	-

Types of publications Types de périodiques Tipos de revistas	Netherlands 1990		Norway 1994		Poland 1994	
	Number Nombre Número	Circulation Diffusion Circulación (000)	Number Nombre Número	Circulation Diffusion Circulación (000)	Number Nombre Número	Circulation Diffusion Circulación (000)
Total A + B	367	19 283.0	11 191	...	3 999	77 735.0
A. Total - periodicals for the general public	74	15 463.0	8 759	...	1 623	70 707.0
1. Illustrated magazines	8	900.0	...	...	272	6 309.0
2. Politics, philosophy, religion, culture	4	211.0	...	...	237	4 602.0
3. Women's, men's and family magazines	26	4 747.0	...	...	175	17 172.0
4. Radio, television and cinema magazines	9	4 842.0	...	...	62	6 534.0
5. Tourism, travel, leisure and sports	14	3 325.0	...	...	314	18 206.0
6. Popular history and geography	2	473.0	...	...	26	127.0
7. Popular science and technology	2	25.0	...	...	82	3 190.0
8. Publications for young persons and children	9	940.0	...	...	145	9 192.0
9. Other periodicals for the general public	-	-	...	...	310	5 375.0
B. Total - periodicals for specific readership	293	3 820.0	2 432	...	2 376	7 028.0
1. Professional journals	293	3 820.0	...	...	1 633	3 597.0
2. Trade union, political party journals	-	-	...	...	127	809.0
3. Mutual benefit societies	-	-	...	...	120	408.0
4. Business house organs	-	-	...	...	145	968.0
5. Parish magazines	-	-	...	...	113	437.0
6. Other periodicals for specific readership	-	-	...	...	238	809.0

Periodicals: number and circulation by type 7.11
Périodiques: nombre et diffusion par type
Revistas: número y circulación por tipos

Types of publications Types de périodiques Tipos de revistas	Portugal 1994		San Marino 1992		Slovakia 1992	
	Number Nombre Número	Circulation Diffusion Circulación (000)	Number Nombre Número	Circulation Diffusion Circulación (000)	Number Nombre Número	Circulation Diffusion Circulación (000)
Total A + B	984	...	18	...	424	11 239.0
A. Total - periodicals for the general public	712	...	6	...	243	6 221.0
1. Illustrated magazines	375	...	-	-	24	1 193.0
2. Politics, philosophy, religion, culture	160	...	2	...	48	1 001.0
3. Women's, men's and family magazines	16	...	-	-	28	900.0
4. Radio, television and cinema magazines	-	-	-	-	8	303.0
5. Tourism, travel, leisure and sports	1	...	2	...	22	408.0
6. Popular history and geography	15	...	-	-	4	98.0
7. Popular science and technology	122	...	-	-	6	153.0
8. Publications for young persons and children	17	...	-	-	27	620.0
9. Other periodicals for the general public	6	...	2	...	76	1 545.0
B. Total - periodicals for specific readership	272	...	12	...	181	5 018.0
1. Professional journals	100	...	4	...	92	2 550.0
2. Trade union, political party journals	19	...	7	...	13	384.0
3. Mutual benefit societies	-	-	-	-	10	303.0
4. Business house organs	84	...	-	-	16	367.0
5. Parish magazines	-	-	-	-	3	92.0
6. Other periodicals for specific readership	69	...	1	...	47	1 322.0

Types of publications Types de périodiques Tipos de revistas	Switzerland 1994		The Former Yugoslav Rep. of Macedonia 1989		Federal Republic of Yugoslavia 1994	
	Number Nombre Número	Circulation Diffusion Circulación (000)	Number Nombre Número	Circulation Diffusion Circulación (000)	Number Nombre Número	Circulation Diffusion Circulación (000)
Total A + B	...	...	...	...	395	3 190.0
A. Total - periodicals for the general public	60	4 561.3	70	266.0	184	2 362.0
1. Illustrated magazines	5	443.1	-	-	-	-
2. Politics, philosophy, religion, culture	-	-	13	56.0	21	41.0
3. Women's, men's and family magazines	23	2 490.6	-	-	1	20.0
4. Radio, television and cinema magazines	5	760.2	1	1.0	-	-
5. Tourism, travel, leisure and sports	-	-	-	-	1	114.0
6. Popular history and geography	-	-	4	5.0	-	-
7. Popular science and technology	-	-	50	201.0	153	2 165.0
8. Publications for young persons and children	17	440.8	-	-	1	10.0
9. Other periodicals for the general public	10	426.6	2	3.0	7	12.0
B. Total - periodicals for specific readership	...	...	...	...	211	828.0
1. Professional journals	...	...	...	...	170	602.0
2. Trade union, political party journals	...	...	...	...	4	7.0
3. Mutual benefit societies	...	...	...	...	-	-
4. Business house organs	...	...	...	...	-	-
5. Parish magazines	...	...	...	...	9	67.0
6. Other periodicals for specific readership	...	...	...	...	28	152.0

7.11   Periodicals: number and circulation by type
Périodiques: nombre et diffusion par type
Revistas: número y circulación por tipos

Oceania

Types of publications Types de périodiques Tipos de revistas	Niue 1991	
	Number Nombre Número	Circulation Diffusion Circulación (000)
Total A + B	4	2.4
A. Total - periodicals for the general public	3	1.9
1. Illustrated magazines	-	-
2. Politics, philosophy, religion, culture	-	-
3. Women's, men's and family magazines	-	-
4. Radio, television and cinema magazines	-	-
5. Tourism, travel, leisure and sports	-	-
6. Popular history and geography	-	-
7. Popular science and technology	-	-
8. Publications for young persons and children	-	-
9. Other periodicals for the general public	3	1.9
B. Total - periodicals for specific readership	1	0.5
1. Professional journals	-	-
2. Trade union, political party journals	-	-
3. Mutual benefit societies	-	-
4. Business house organs	-	-
5. Parish magazines	-	-
6. Other periodicals for specific readership	1	0.5

EUROPE:
France:
   E--> For periodicals, 373 titles and 36,530 copies of the free press are included in the total of group A.

FR-> Pour les périodiques, 373 titres et 36 530 copies de la presse gratuite sont inclus dans le total du groupe A.
   ESP> Para las revistas, 373 títulos y 36 530 ejemplares de la presa gratuita se incluídas en el total del grupo A.

Newsprint, printing and writing paper **7.12**
Papier journal, papier d'impression et papier d'écriture
Papel de periódico, papel de imprenta y papel de escribir

7.12 Newsprint and other printing and writing paper: production, imports, exports and consumption (total and per 1,000 inhabitants)

Papier journal et autre papier d'impression et d'écriture: production, importations, exportations et consommation (total et pour 1 000 habitants)

Papel de periódico y otro papel de imprenta y de escribir: producción, importaciones, exportaciones y consumo (total y por 1 000 habitantes)

| Production, imports, exports and consumption are expressed in metric tons; consumption per 1,000 inhabitants is expressed in kilograms. | Production, importations, exportations et consommation sont exprimées en tonnes métriques; la consommation pour 1 000 habitants est exprimée en kilogrammes. | Producción, importaciones, exportaciones y consumo se expresan en toneladas métricas; consumo por 1 000 habitantes se expresa en kilogramos. |

Country / Year — Pays / Année — País / Año	Newsprint / Papier journal / Papel de periódico					Other printing and writing paper / Autre papier d'impression et d'écriture / Otro papel de imprenta y de escribir				
	Production / Production / Producción	Imports / Importations / Importaciones	Exports / Exportations / Exportaciones	Consumption / Consommation / Consumo	Consumption per 1,000 inh. / Consommation pour 1 000 hab. / Consumo por 1 000 hab.	Production / Production / Producción	Imports / Importations / Importaciones	Exports / Exportations / Exportaciones	Consumption / Consommation / Consumo	Consumption per 1,000 inh. / Consommation pour 1 000 hab. / Consumo por 1 000 hab.
Africa										
Algeria										
1970		6 200		6 200	451	23 000	19 000		42 000	3 055
1975		8 900		8 900	556	18 000	7 200		25 200	1 573
1980		12 000		12 000	640	26 000	3 200		29 200	1 558
1985		15 600		15 600	713	30 000	26 500		56 500	2 581
1990		30 000		30 000	1 203	39 000	26 000		65 000	2 607
1994		17 864		17 864	654	36 000	26 593	21	62 572	2 290
Angola										
1970		100	200			1 500	2 000		3 500	626
1975		1 100		1 100	180	3 000			3 000	491
1980		1 500		1 500	214	3 000			3 000	429
1985		500		500	63					
1990		100		100	11					
1993		401		401	39		2 100		2 100	204
1994		401		401	38		1 327	4	1 323	124
Benin										
1970										
1975		100		100	33		500		500	165
1980		100		100	29		100		100	29
1985		100		100	25		500		500	125
1990							721		721	156
1993		30		30	6		848		848	167
1994		30		30	6		648		648	124
Burkina Faso										
1970										
1975										
1980										
1985										
1990										
1993							680		680	70
1994							680		680	68

7.12 Newsprint, printing and writing paper
Papier journal, papier d'impression et papier d'écriture
Papel de periódico, papel de imprenta y papel de escribir

Country Year / Pays Année / País Año	Newsprint Papier journal Papel de periódico					Other printing and writing paper Autre papier d'impression et d'écriture Otro papel de imprenta y de escribir				
	Production / Production / Producción	Imports / Importa-tions / Importa-ciones	Exports / Exporta-tions / Exporta-ciones	Consumption / Consom-mation / Consumo	Consump-tion per 1,000 inh. / Consomma-tion pour 1 000 hab. / Consumo por 1 000 hab.	Production / Production / Producción	Imports / Importa-tions / Importa-ciones	Exports / Exporta-tions / Exporta-ciones	Consumption / Consom-mation / Consumo	Consump-tion per 1,000 inh. / Consomma-tion pour 1 000 hab. / Consumo por 1 000 hab.
Burundi										
1970										
1975										
1980										
1985							400		400	84
1990							700		700	127
1993							249	160	89	15
1994							400		400	64
Cameroon										
1970		100		100	15		1 300		1 300	197
1975							2 000		2 000	266
1980		500		500	58		4 000		4 000	462
1985		2 100		2 100	211		4 600		4 600	461
1990		4 000		4 000	347		3 200		3 200	278
1993		2 727		2 727	218		7 255		7 255	579
1994		426		426	33		6 380		6 380	496
Cape Verde										
1970										
1975										
1980										
1985										
1990										
1993		31		31	84		165		165	446
1994		31		31	81		11		11	29
Central African Republic										
1970							200		200	108
1975										
1980										
1985										
1990										
1993							212		212	67
1994							212		212	66
Chad										
1970										
1975							100		100	25
1980							200		200	45
1985							100		100	20
1990							200		200	36
1993							163		163	27
1994							250		250	40
Comoros										
1970										
1975										
1980										
1985										
1990										
1993		12		12	20		215		215	354
1994		12		12	19		412		412	654
Congo										
1970							200		200	158
1975							200		200	138
1980							100		100	60
1985							500		500	260
1990							300		300	134
1993		224		224	92		380	94	286	117
1994		45		45	18		192	94	98	39
Côte d'Ivoire										
1970		900		900	163					
1975		800		800	118		4 200		4 200	622
1980		800		800	98		4 200		4 200	513
1985		1 400		1 400	141		8 400		8 400	846
1990		3 200		3 200	267					
1993		1 424		1 424	107		9 278	15	9 263	696
1994		1 800		1 800	131		9 278	15	9 263	672

Newsprint, printing and writing paper **7.12**
Papier journal, papier d'impression et papier d'écriture
Papel de periódico, papel de imprenta y papel de escribir

Country / Year / Pays / Année / País / Año	Newsprint — Papier journal — Papel de periódico					Other printing and writing paper — Autre papier d'impression et d'écriture — Otro papel de imprenta y de escribir				
	Production / Producción	Imports / Importations / Importaciones	Exports / Exportations / Exportaciones	Consumption / Consommation / Consumo	Consumption per 1,000 inh. / Consommation pour 1 000 hab. / Consumo por 1 000 hab.	Production / Producción	Imports / Importations / Importaciones	Exports / Exportations / Exportaciones	Consumption / Consommation / Consumo	Consumption per 1,000 inh. / Consommation pour 1 000 hab. / Consumo por 1 000 hab.
Djibouti										
1970										
1975										
1980										
1985										
1990										
1993							55	23	32	57
1994		8		8	14		67	23	44	78
Egypt										
1970		32 900		32 900	932	40 000	5 000		45 000	1 275
1975		40 200		40 200	1 035	24 000	34 000		58 000	1 493
1980		67 000		67 000	1 531	66 000	53 600		119 600	2 734
1985		35 300		35 300	710	52 000	129 000		181 000	3 638
1990		58 200		58 200	1 034	73 000	110 900		183 900	3 266
1993		75 300		75 300	1 248	85 000	170 000	3 263	251 737	4 173
1994		69 800		69 800	1 132	70 000	167 300	1 300	236 000	3 829
Equatorial Guinea										
1970										
1975										
1980										
1985										
1990										
1993							16		16	42
1994							16		16	41
Ethiopia										
1970		900		900	31		900		900	31
1975		400		400	12	3 500	2 800		6 300	196
1980		2 000		2 000	55	3 500	200		3 700	102
1985		2 200		2 200	53	8 000	5 700		13 700	333
1990		2 300		2 300	49	7 000	1 300		8 300	175
1993										
1994										
Gabon										
1970							100		100	198
1975							12 600		12 600	19 780
1980							1 300		1 300	1 613
1985							2 700		2 700	2 741
1990							1 500		1 500	1 309
1993							1 339		1 339	1 073
1994							897		897	699
Gambia										
1970										
1975										
1980										
1985										
1990										
1993		26		26	25		185		185	178
1994		27		27	25		238	15	223	206
Ghana										
1970		3 600		3 600	418		7 600		7 600	882
1975		7 300		7 300	743		6 700		6 700	682
1980		1 500		1 500	140		3 300		3 300	307
1985		4 000		4 000	312		5 500		5 500	428
1990		6 000		6 000	399		7 300		7 300	486
1993		2 040		2 040	124		6 077	1	6 076	369
1994		1 144		1 144	68		5 889	30	5 859	346
Guinea										
1970										
1975										
1980										
1985										
1990										
1993							294		294	47
1994		3		3			252		252	39
Guinea-Bissau										
1970										
1975		100		100	159					
1980		100		100	126					
1985		200		200	229					
1990										
1993		5		5	5		125		125	122
1994		5		5	5		107		107	102

7.12 Newsprint, printing and writing paper
Papier journal, papier d'impression et papier d'écriture
Papel de periódico, papel de imprenta y papel de escribir

Country Year / Pays Année / País Año	Newsprint — Papier journal — Papel de periódico					Other printing and writing paper — Autre papier d'impression et d'écriture — Otro papel de imprenta y de escribir				
	Production / Producción	Imports / Importations / Importaciones	Exports / Exportations / Exportaciones	Consumption / Consommation / Consumo	Consumption per 1,000 inh. / Consommation pour 1 000 hab. / Consumo por 1 000 hab.	Production / Producción	Imports / Importations / Importaciones	Exports / Exportations / Exportaciones	Consumption / Consommation / Consumo	Consumption per 1,000 inh. / Consommation pour 1 000 hab. / Consumo por 1 000 hab.
Kenya										
1970		5 000		5 000	435	8 000	6 900	100	6 800	591
1975		3 900		3 900	284	8 000	3 000	400	10 600	771
1980		7 900		7 900	475	19 000	1 900	8 300	12 600	758
1985	7 000	2 600		9 600	483	30 000	100	300	29 800	1 499
1990	6 000	965		6 965	295	28 000	5 600	155	33 445	1 416
1993	16 000	298		16 298	618	32 000	9 545	105	41 440	1 570
1994	16 000	1 006		17 006	622	32 000	8 166	105	40 061	1 465
Liberia										
1970		100		100	72		200		200	144
1975							450		450	280
1980							300		300	160
1985		200		200	91		100		100	45
1990		29		29	11		2 638		2 638	1 024
1993							165		165	58
1994							165		165	56
Libyan Arab Jamahiriya										
1970		800		800	403		1 400		1 400	705
1975		100		100	41		8 700		8 700	3 557
1980		800		800	263		3 500		3 500	1 150
1985		2 000		2 000	528		7 400		7 400	1 955
1990		865		865	190		5 982		5 982	1 316
1993							11 300		11 300	2 239
1994		181		181	35		4 669		4 669	894
Madagascar										
1970	300			300	44	3 900		1 300	2 600	378
1975	817			817	105	8 200		800	7 400	950
1980	3 500			3 500	386		600		600	66
1985	800			800	75	6 600	2 300		8 900	837
1990	350			350	28	3 000	516		3 516	280
1993	320	10		330	24	4 100	1 088	29	5 159	372
1994	320			320	22	3 700	1 200		4 900	343
Malawi										
1970		200		200	44		2 500		2 500	553
1975		500		500	95		2 200		2 200	420
1980		600		600	97		9 700		9 700	1 569
1985		600		600	83		100		100	14
1990							1 548		1 548	165
1993		42		42	4		312		312	30
1994		42	61				429		429	40
Mali										
1970		200		200	36					
1975		100		100	16		200		200	32
1980							200		200	29
1985							300		300	38
1990							300		300	33
1993		7		7	1		652	160	492	49
1994		32		32	3		977	88	889	85
Mauritania										
1970										
1975										
1980										
1985										
1990										
1993		4		4	2		942		942	436
1994		4		4	2		942		942	425
Mauritius										
1970		600		600	726		800		800	969
1975		600		600	673		1 000		1 000	1 121
1980		500		500	518		1 600		1 600	1 656
1985		1 400		1 400	1 378		1 700		1 700	1 673
1990		2 800		2 800	2 649		5 200		5 200	4 920
1993		3 400		3 400	3 116		7 500	3	7 497	6 872
1994		4 200		4 200	3 804		8 300	100	8 200	7 428

Newsprint, printing and writing paper **7.12**
Papier journal, papier d'impression et papier d'écriture
Papel de periódico, papel de imprenta y papel de escribir

Country Year Pays Année País Año	Newsprint Papier journal Papel de periódico					Other printing and writing paper Autre papier d'impression et d'écriture Otro papel de imprenta y de escribir				
	Production Production Producción	Imports Importa- tions Importa- ciones	Exports Exporta- tions Exporta- ciones	Consumption Consom- mation Consumo	Consump- tion per 1,000 inh. Consomma- tion pour 1 000 hab. Consumo por 1 000 hab.	Production Production Producción	Imports Importa- tions Importa- ciones	Exports Exporta- tions Exporta- ciones	Consumption Consom- mation Consumo	Consump- tion per 1,000 inh. Consomma- tion pour 1 000 hab. Consumo por 1 000 hab.
Morocco										
1970		3 100		3 100	202	10 000	2 000		12 000	784
1975		2 800		2 800	162	16 500	1 300		17 800	1 029
1980		5 400		5 400	279	25 000	3 200		28 200	1 455
1985		4 800		4 800	220	24 000	4 000		28 000	1 283
1990		12 100		12 100	497	29 000	25 800		54 800	2 252
1993		23 387	19	23 368	901	25 000	21 652	208	46 444	1 790
1994		19 863	605	19 258	727	29 000	28 930	530	57 400	2 167
Mozambique										
1970		200		200	21					
1975		1 700		1 700	162					
1980		1 500		1 500	124		4 000		4 000	331
1985		100		100	7		100		100	7
1990		1 100		1 100	78		1 000		1 000	70
1993		261		261	17		1 542		1 542	102
1994		118		118	8		616		616	40
Niger										
1970										
1975		150		150	31		100		100	21
1980		100		100	18		100		100	18
1985		100		100	15		1 100		1 100	166
1990		100		100	13		600		600	78
1993		32		32	4		199		199	23
1994		122		122	14		464	3	461	52
Nigeria										
1970		17 100		17 100	311	2 000	25 200		27 200	494
1975		23 700		23 700	378	2 000	29 000		31 000	494
1980		29 000		29 000	403	3 500	41 900		45 400	630
1985		14 800		14 800	178	4 500	50 000		54 500	656
1990	30 000	2 768		32 768	341	5 000	70 989		75 989	790
1993	12 000	7 355		19 355	184		50 053	19	50 034	475
1994	12 000	6 011		18 011	166		44 769	19	44 750	413
Reunion										
1970		400		400	868		300		300	651
1975		500		500	1 035					
1980		1 000		1 000	1 976					
1985		3 100		3 100	5 636		1 600		1 600	2 909
1990		3 900		3 900	6 457		3 900		3 900	6 457
1993		5 730	12	5 718	9 019		6 201	153	6 048	9 539
1994		5 186	24	5 162	8 016		5 574	12	5 562	8 637
Rwanda										
1970										
1975										
1980										
1985							400		400	66
1990							1 200		1 200	172
1993							244	10	234	31
1994		19		19	2		208	8	200	26
St. Helena										
1970										
1975										
1980										
1985										
1990										
1993							6		6	1 000
1994		15		15	2 500		48		48	8 000
Sao Tome and Principe										
1970										
1975										
1980										
1985										
1990										
1993		1		1	8		69		69	543
1994		1		1	8		5		5	38

7.12 Newsprint, printing and writing paper
Papier journal, papier d'impression et papier d'écriture
Papel de periódico, papel de imprenta y papel de escribir

Country Year / Pays Année / País Año	Newsprint / Papier journal / Papel de periódico					Other printing and writing paper / Autre papier d'impression et d'écriture / Otro papel de imprenta y de escribir				
	Production / Production / Producción	Imports / Importations / Importaciones	Exports / Exportations / Exportaciones	Consumption / Consommation / Consumo	Consumption per 1,000 inh. / Consommation pour 1 000 hab. / Consumo por 1 000 hab.	Production / Production / Producción	Imports / Importations / Importaciones	Exports / Exportations / Exportaciones	Consumption / Consommation / Consumo	Consumption per 1,000 inh. / Consommation pour 1 000 hab. / Consumo por 1 000 hab.
Senegal										
1970		500		500	120		3 300		3 300	794
1975		1 800		1 800	375		1 200		1 200	250
1980		900		900	163		1 800		1 800	325
1985		1 000		1 000	157		7 000		7 000	1 098
1990		500		500	68		4 500		4 500	614
1993		361		361	46		4 658		4 658	589
1994		500		500	62		4 658		4 658	575
Seychelles										
1970										
1975										
1980										
1985										
1990										
1993							33		33	458
1994		192		192	2 667		63		63	875
Sierra Leone										
1970		200		200	75		200		200	75
1975		100		100	34					
1980		200		200	62					
1985		200		200	56		200		200	56
1990							300		300	75
1993		325		325	76		537	94	443	103
1994		70		70	16		732	5	727	165
Somalia										
1970		500		500	104		100		100	21
1975		300		300	55		100		100	18
1980		200		200	30		1 300		1 300	194
1985		100		100	13		100		100	13
1990							152		152	18
1993							27		27	3
1994							144		144	16
South Africa										
1970	160 000	52 500		212 500	9 462	70 000	130 500	3 600	196 900	8 767
1975	210 000	300	14 500	195 800	7 628	77 000	74 000	6 800	144 200	5 618
1980	224 000		70 000	154 000	5 279	177 000	92 600	14 400	255 200	8 749
1985	325 000	100	205 000	120 100	3 635	256 000	84 000	56 000	284 000	8 595
1990	355 000	51	75 562	279 489	7 540	395 000	69 234	21 596	442 638	11 942
1993	140 000	1 400	77 450	63 950	1 612	400 000	106 037	46 496	459 541	11 587
1994	367 000	5 503	41 796	330 707	8 155	380 000	122 727	24 428	478 299	11 794
Sudan										
1970		2 700		2 700	195		3 700		3 700	267
1975		3 400		3 400	212		5 000		5 000	312
1980		1 500		1 500	80		7 200		7 200	385
1985		8 500		8 500	396		6 900		6 900	321
1990		900		900	37		3 200		3 200	130
1993		676	16	660	25		3 139		3 139	118
1994		957	16	941	34		5 147		5 147	188
Togo										
1970										
1975										
1980										
1985							1 800		1 800	594
1990							1 200		1 200	340
1993		54		54	14		644		644	166
1994		33	25	8	2		657		657	164
Tunisia										
1970										
1975		2 900		2 900	517	15 000		3 800	11 200	1 996
1980		5 500		5 500	862	18 000	11 100	100	29 000	4 543
1985		9 900		9 900	1 363	26 000	4 700		30 700	4 227
1990		11 100		11 100	1 374	29 000	7 423		36 423	4 508
1993		5 790		5 790	676	36 000	12 069	18	48 051	5 607
1994		15 825	181	15 644	1 791	36 000	14 778	2 334	48 444	5 547
Uganda										
1970		1 000		1 000	102		2 600		2 600	265
1975		500		500	45		400		400	36
1980		200		200	15		500		500	38
1985		200		200	13		400		400	26
1990		1		1			1 276		1 276	71
1993		61		61	3		2 242		2 242	112
1994		61		61	3		2 465		2 465	120

Newsprint, printing and writing paper **7.12**
Papier journal, papier d'impression et papier d'écriture
Papel de periódico, papel de imprenta y papel de escribir

Country Year Pays Année País Año	Newsprint Papier journal Papel de periódico					Other printing and writing paper Autre papier d'impression et d'écriture Otro papel de imprenta y de escribir				
	Production Production Producción	Imports Importa- tions Importa- ciones	Exports Exporta- tions Exporta- ciones	Consumption Consom- mation Consumo	Consump- tion per 1,000 inh. Consomma- tion pour 1 000 hab. Consumo por 1 000 hab.	Production Production Producción	Imports Importa- tions Importa- ciones	Exports Exporta- tions Exporta- ciones	Consumption Consom- mation Consumo	Consump- tion per 1,000 inh. Consomma- tion pour 1 000 hab. Consumo por 1 000 hab.
United Rep. of Tanzania										
1970		1 500		1 500	110		5 100		5 100	372
1975		4 500		4 500	283		5 000		5 000	314
1980		3 500		3 500	188		7 000		7 000	377
1985		2 500		2 500	115		4 200		4 200	193
1990	8 000	212		8 212	321	6 000	1 163		7 163	280
1993	8 000	4 200		12 200	435	6 000	1 700	11	7 689	274
1994	8 000	400		8 400	291	6 000	2 600	11	8 589	298
Zaire										
1970		500		500	25		2 400		2 400	118
1975		1 000		1 000	43		2 000		2 000	86
1980		1 000		1 000	37		2 700		2 700	100
1985		1 000		1 000	32		4 900		4 900	155
1990		800		800	21		2 000		2 000	53
1993		152		152	4		5 176		5 176	126
1994		150		150	4		9 859		9 859	232
Zambia										
1970		2 100		2 100	501		5 300		5 300	1 265
1975		4 300		4 300	888		4 400		4 400	909
1980		3 000		3 000	523		6 300		6 300	1 098
1985		3 000		3 000	437	1 000	800		1 800	262
1990		4 000		4 000	491	900	3 000		3 900	479
1993		1 700		1 700	190	2 000	1 700	6	3 694	413
1994		1 700		1 700	185	1 000	369	6	1 363	148
Zimbabwe										
1970	10 000			10 000	1 901					
1975	12 000			12 000	1 953					
1980	16 000			16 000	2 245		8 500		8 500	1 193
1985	18 000	400		18 400	2 192		4 900		4 900	584
1990	21 000	1 610		22 610	2 283		7 600		7 600	767
1993	15 000	16	25	14 991	1 396		3 535		3 535	329
1994	17 000	16	25	16 991	1 544		6 535		6 535	594
America, North										
Anguilla										
1970										
1975										
1980										
1985										
1990										
1993		2		2	250		419		419	52 375
1994										
Antigua and Barbuda										
1970										
1975										
1980										
1985										
1990										
1993		34	28	6	92		167		167	2 569
1994		13	28				376	149	227	3 439
Aruba										
1970										
1975										
1980										
1985										
1990										
1993		233		233	3 377		447		447	6 478
1994		573		573	8 304		251		251	3 638
Bahamas										
1970		1 000		1 000	5 882		500		500	2 941
1975		600		600	3 158		200		200	1 053
1980		900		900	4 286		100		100	476
1985		400		400	1 709		100		100	427
1990		1 400		1 400	5 469		300		300	1 172
1993		489		489	1 825		1 412	100	1 312	4 896
1994		503		503	1 849		1 863	165	1 698	6 243

7.12   Newsprint, printing and writing paper
Papier journal, papier d'impression et papier d'écriture
Papel de periódico, papel de imprenta y papel de escribir

Country / Year / Pays / Année / País / Año	Newsprint — Papier journal — Papel de periódico					Other printing and writing paper — Autre papier d'impression et d'écriture — Otro papel de imprenta y de escribir				
	Production / Producción	Imports / Importations / Importaciones	Exports / Exportations / Exportaciones	Consumption / Consommation / Consumo	Consumption per 1,000 inh. / Consommation pour 1 000 hab. / Consumo por 1 000 hab.	Production / Producción	Imports / Importations / Importaciones	Exports / Exportations / Exportaciones	Consumption / Consommation / Consumo	Consumption per 1,000 inh. / Consommation pour 1 000 hab. / Consumo por 1 000 hab.
Barbados										
1970		900		900	3 766		500		500	2 092
1975		500		500	2 033		800		800	3 252
1980		1 500		1 500	6 024		2 800		2 800	11 245
1985		1 400		1 400	5 534		3 100		3 100	12 253
1990		1 700		1 700	6 615		800		800	3 113
1993		2 245		2 245	8 635		3 264	1	3 263	12 550
1994		3 844		3 844	14 728		3 151	1	3 150	12 069
Belize										
1970		200		200	1 626		100		100	813
1975		200		200	1 493		100		100	746
1980		200		200	1 370		300		300	2 055
1985		200		200	1 205		200		200	1 205
1990		200		200	1 058		300		300	1 587
1993		80		80	392		253	99	154	755
1994		211		211	1 005		290	99	191	910
Bermuda										
1970										
1975										
1980										
1985										
1990										
1993		1 624		1 624	26 194		1 187		1 187	19 145
1994		1 392		1 392	22 095		987		987	15 667
British Virgin Islands										
1970										
1975										
1980										
1985										
1990										
1993							117	1	116	6 444
1994							117	1	116	6 105
Canada										
1970	7 996 000		7 339 300	656 700	30 796	821 000	35 000	300 100	555 900	26 069
1975	7 010 000		6 348 800	661 200	28 489	679 000	146 700	275 600	550 100	23 702
1980	8 625 000		7 706 800	918 200	37 334	1 511 000	126 800	652 700	985 100	40 054
1985	8 991 000		8 274 700	716 300	27 612	2 141 000	242 300	731 200	1 652 100	63 684
1990	9 069 000		8 722 300	346 700	12 475	3 599 000	443 700	1 864 800	2 177 900	78 367
1993	9 165 000	14 576	9 029 000	150 576	5 225	4 194 000	506 166	2 117 000	2 583 166	89 640
1994	9 321 000	10 000	9 387 000			4 472 000	560 000	2 380 000	2 652 000	91 006
Cayman Islands										
1970										
1975										
1980										
1985										
1990										
1993		191		191	6 586		101	585		
1994		292		292	9 733		271	155	116	3 867
Costa Rica										
1970		11 100		11 100	6 412		4 000		4 000	2 311
1975		11 200		11 200	5 691		2 800		2 800	1 423
1980		12 000		12 000	5 252		7 600		7 600	3 326
1985		11 000		11 000	4 164		6 100		6 100	2 309
1990		15 000		15 000	4 942		11 000		11 000	3 624
1993		18 801	24	18 777	5 742		25 420	2	25 418	7 773
1994		18 073	21	18 052	5 393		19 692	148	19 544	5 839
Cuba										
1970		22 800		22 800	2 676	20 000	6 500		26 500	3 110
1975		26 700		26 700	2 869	30 000	22 000		52 000	5 588
1980		32 000		32 000	3 296	31 300	15 400		46 700	4 809
1985		43 200		43 200	4 276	59 000	17 000		76 000	7 523
1990		38 600		38 600	3 642	39 000	13 200		52 200	4 925
1993						14 000	707		14 707	1 352
1994		79		79	7	14 000	1 315	43	15 272	1 393

Newsprint, printing and writing paper 7.12
Papier journal, papier d'impression et papier d'écriture
Papel de periódico, papel de imprenta y papel de escribir

Country / Year — Pays / Année — País / Año	Newsprint — Papier journal — Papel de periódico					Other printing and writing paper — Autre papier d'impression et d'écriture — Otro papel de imprenta y de escribir				
	Production — Producción	Imports — Importations — Importaciones	Exports — Exportations — Exportaciones	Consumption — Consommation — Consumo	Consumption per 1,000 inh. — Consommation pour 1 000 hab. — Consumo por 1 000 hab.	Production — Producción	Imports — Importations — Importaciones	Exports — Exportations — Exportaciones	Consumption — Consommation — Consumo	Consumption per 1,000 inh. — Consommation pour 1 000 hab. — Consumo por 1 000 hab.
Dominica										
1970										
1975										
1980										
1985							204		204	2 873
1990										
1993		651		651	9 169		524		524	7 380
1994		651		651	9 169		200		200	2 817
Dominican Rep.										
1970		4 200		4 200	950		3 600		3 600	814
1975		6 600		6 600	1 307		5 900		5 900	1 169
1980		12 400		12 400	2 177		25 900		25 900	4 546
1985		7 800		7 800	1 223		23 400		23 400	3 670
1990		15 000		15 000	2 110		31 081		31 081	4 371
1993		18 403		18 403	2 440		19 936	67	19 869	2 634
1994		14 254		14 254	1 855		23 543	67	23 476	3 055
El Salvador										
1970		13 000		13 000	3 623		2 100		2 100	585
1975		10 300	100	10 200	2 497		4 100	400	3 700	906
1980		15 000		15 000	3 315			500		
1985		12 700		12 700	2 680		2 000	500	1 500	317
1990		12 000		12 000	2 320		15 000		15 000	2 900
1993		25 078	9	25 069	4 544		16 249		16 249	2 945
1994		22 800	9	22 791	4 040		14 300		14 300	2 535
Greenland										
1970										
1975										
1980										
1985										
1990										
1993		154		154	2 702		517		517	9 070
1994		100		100	1 724		110		110	1 897
Grenada										
1970										
1975										
1980										
1985										
1990										
1993		2		2	22		80		80	870
1994		2		2	22		69		69	750
Guadeloupe										
1970										
1075										
1980										
1985							900		900	2 535
1990							1 300		1 300	3 325
1993		85		85	206		4 849		4 849	11 741
1994		23		23	55		1 952	105	1 847	4 387
Guatemala										
1970		8 300		8 300	1 582	6 700	1 100	4 100	3 700	705
1975	600	7 500		8 100	1 345	9 000	1 600	4 400	6 200	1 029
1980		17 000		17 000	2 458	14 700	5 600	13 500	6 800	983
1985	100	7 100		7 200	904	9 000	17 800	1 800	25 000	3 140
1990		13 000		13 000	1 414	10 000	2 000	1 000	11 000	1 196
1993		38 000	9	37 991	3 788	10 000	25 538	16	35 522	3 542
1994		21 200	100	21 100	2 044	10 000	18 600	150	28 450	2 756
Haiti										
1970		700		700	155		300		300	66
1975		800		800	163		300		300	61
1980		300		300	56		600		600	112
1985		913		913	156		2 530		2 530	431
1990		468		468	72		2 005		2 005	309
1993							3 199		3 199	464
1994		21		21	3		2 570		2 570	365
Honduras										
1970		2 700		2 700	1 042		2 500		2 500	965
1975		2 100		2 100	696		2 500	200	2 300	762
1980		6 500		6 500	1 821		5 400		5 400	1 513
1985		6 400		6 400	1 529		3 100		3 100	741
1990		4 800		4 800	984					
1993		7 819		7 819	1 466		12 793	2	12 791	2 398
1994		8 700		8 700	1 584		7 600		7 600	1 384

7.12 Newsprint, printing and writing paper
Papier journal, papier d'impression et papier d'écriture
Papel de periódico, papel de imprenta y papel de escribir

Country Year Pays Année País Año	Newsprint Papier journal Papel de periódico					Other printing and writing paper Autre papier d'impression et d'écriture Otro papel de imprenta y de escribir				
	Production Production Producción	Imports Importa- tions Importa- ciones	Exports Exporta- tions Exporta- ciones	Consumption Consom- mation Consumo	Consump- tion per 1,000 inh. Consomma- tion pour 1 000 hab. Consumo por 1 000 hab.	Production Production Producción	Imports Importa- tions Importa- ciones	Exports Exporta- tions Exporta- ciones	Consumption Consom- mation Consumo	Consump- tion per 1,000 inh. Consomma- tion pour 1 000 hab. Consumo por 1 000 hab.
Jamaica										
1970		8 600		8 600	4 601		4 100		4 100	2 194
1975		8 700		8 700	4 322		6 300		6 300	3 130
1980		3 500		3 500	1 641		6 900		6 900	3 235
1985		4 500		4 500	1 947		3 800		3 800	1 644
1990		8 000		8 000	3 381		5 700		5 700	2 409
1993		9 300		9 300	3 857		9 000		9 000	3 733
1994		7 500		7 500	3 088		9 300		9 300	3 829
Martinique										
1970										
1975										
1980		800		800	2 454					
1985		1 200		1 200	3 519					
1990		3 600		3 600	10 000					
1993		5 453	1	5 452	14 656		1 351	10	1 341	3 605
1994		4 300	1	4 299	11 464		2 154	11	2 143	5 715
Mexico										
1970	40 000	118 800		158 800	3 147	122 000	236 800		358 800	7 111
1975	29 000	185 600		214 600	3 645	256 000	64 000		320 000	5 436
1980	116 000	110 000		226 000	3 370	526 000	65 300		591 300	8 818
1985	260 000	37 500		297 500	3 939	456 000	63 600		519 600	6 880
1990	398 000	56 600		454 600	5 379	528 000	40 100		568 100	6 722
1993	216 000	163 300	333	378 967	4 209	462 000	215 000	24 900	652 100	7 243
1994	214 000	228 300	333	441 967	4 811	402 000	225 300	24 900	602 400	6 558
Montserrat										
1970										
1975										
1980										
1985										
1990										
1993							4		4	364
1994							3		3	273
Netherlands **Antilles**										
1970		600		600	3 774		600		600	3 774
1975		500		500	3 012		600		600	3 614
1980		600		600	3 448		1 100		1 100	6 322
1985		2 100		2 100	11 538		800		800	4 396
1990		1 200		1 200	6 316		1 400		1 400	7 368
1993		2 539		2 539	13 021		2 175		2 175	11 154
1994		1 964		1 964	9 970		1 701	795	906	4 599
Nicaragua										
1970		3 700		3 700	1 794		2 500		2 500	1 212
1975		4 000		4 000	1 649		1 800		1 800	742
1980		3 000		3 000	1 071		1 900		1 900	678
1985		5 000		5 000	1 548		2 900		2 900	898
1990		6 400		6 400	1 741		1 200		1 200	326
1993		3 300		3 300	802		2 015		2 015	490
1994		4 000		4 000	936		2 615	4	2 611	611
Panama										
1970		5 900		5 900	3 918		5 900		5 900	3 918
1975		3 400		3 400	1 973		3 200		3 200	1 857
1980		2 600		2 600	1 333	3 000	1 800		4 800	2 462
1985		6 300		6 300	2 907		9 000		9 000	4 153
1990		9 700		9 700	4 045		10 100		10 100	4 212
1993		11 500	1 735	9 765	3 848		13 100	89	13 011	5 126
1994		11 900	3 800	8 100	3 133		10 500		10 500	4 062
St. Lucia										
1970										
1975										
1980										
1985										
1990										
1993		45		45	326		293		293	2 123
1994		35		35	250		1 026		1 026	7 329

Newsprint, printing and writing paper 7.12
Papier journal, papier d'impression et papier d'écriture
Papel de periódico, papel de imprenta y papel de escribir

Country / Year / Pays / Année / País / Año	Newsprint — Papier journal — Papel de periódico					Other printing and writing paper — Autre papier d'impression et d'écriture — Otro papel de imprenta y de escribir				
	Production / Producción	Imports / Importations / Importaciones	Exports / Exportations / Exportaciones	Consumption / Consommation / Consumo	Consumption per 1,000 inh. / Consommation pour 1 000 hab. / Consumo por 1 000 hab.	Production / Producción	Imports / Importations / Importaciones	Exports / Exportations / Exportaciones	Consumption / Consommation / Consumo	Consumption per 1,000 inh. / Consommation pour 1 000 hab. / Consumo por 1 000 hab.
St. Pierre and Miquelon										
1970										
1975										
1980										
1985										
1990										
1993						10			10	1 667
1994						13			13	2 167
St. Vincent and the Grenadines										
1970										
1975										
1980										
1985						3 700			3 700	36 275
1990						196			196	1 832
1993		36		36	327	108			108	982
1994		36		36	324	51			51	459
Trinidad and Tobago										
1970		5 600		5 600	5 767		2 800		2 800	2 884
1975		6 300		6 300	6 225		1 900		1 900	1 877
1980		5 100		5 100	4 713		4 300		4 300	3 974
1985		11 900		11 900	10 250		8 400		8 400	7 235
1990		3 700		3 700	2 991		16 100		16 100	13 015
1993		4 451	2	4 449	3 478		7 478	66	7 412	5 795
1994		4 400	2	4 398	3 404		9 200	50	9 150	7 082
Turks and Caicos Islands										
1970										
1975										
1980										
1985										
1990										
1993										
1994						4			4	286
United States										
1970	3 143 000	6 019 300	130 300	9 032 000	44 048	9 684 000	259 200	164 900	9 778 300	47 687
1975	3 348 000	5 305 000	149 800	8 503 200	39 372	9 708 000	331 400	360 400	9 679 000	44 816
1980	4 238 000	6 593 600	158 600	10 673 000	46 861	13 829 000	848 200	278 900	14 398 300	63 218
1985	4 923 000	7 685 700	285 200	12 323 500	51 678	16 408 000	2 072 800	171 700	18 369 100	77 030
1990	6 001 000	7 529 300	526 600	13 003 700	52 031	20 092 000	2 032 200	355 000	21 769 200	87 103
1993	6 419 000	7 062 000	925 297	12 555 703	48 680	21 511 000	2 891 000	1 017 000	23 385 000	90 666
1994	6 339 000	7 150 000	862 000	12 627 000	48 448	22 891 000	3 172 000	1 357 000	24 706 000	94 793
America, South										
Argentina										
1970	3 200	274 300	100	277 400	11 577	122 700	4 200	4 200	122 700	5 121
1975		148 800		148 800	5 712	94 000	6 200	1 500	98 700	3 789
1980	97 000	174 000	200	270 800	9 632	152 000	38 000	11 000	179 000	6 367
1985	201 000	12 500	10 200	203 300	6 704	157 000	10 000	2 300	164 700	5 431
1990	208 000	15 000	55 000	168 000	5 162	170 000	16 000	30 000	156 000	4 793
1993	141 000	154 082	265	294 817	8 728	204 000	135 529	8 581	330 948	9 797
1994	142 000	95 654	61	237 593	6 951	203 000	162 361	2 911	362 450	10 604
Bolivia										
1970		4 700		4 700	1 116		3 900		3 900	926
1975		4 700		4 700	988		3 900		3 900	820
1980		6 000		6 000	1 120		6 000		6 000	1 120
1985		3 000		3 000	509		1 500		1 500	254
1990		7 700		7 700	1 171					
1993		9 200		9 200	1 303		9 126		9 126	1 292
1994		9 500		9 500	1 313		13 600		13 600	1 879
Brazil										
1970	103 000	108 800	200	211 600	2 208	254 000	58 000	900	311 100	3 246
1975	125 000	116 000	300	240 700	2 228	416 000	60 000	6 000	470 000	4 351
1980	105 000	167 100	500	271 600	2 239	870 000	68 000	135 000	803 000	6 621
1985	208 000	95 400	4 400	299 000	2 214	1 146 000	27 000	239 000	934 000	6 916
1990	246 000	123 100	20 200	348 900	2 350	1 321 000	68 400	414 000	975 400	6 569
1993	268 000	190 304	39 220	419 084	2 678	1 670 000	113 058	665 559	1 117 499	7 141
1994	263 000	286 040	19 039	530 001	3 330	1 858 000	157 764	729 744	1 286 020	8 081

7.12 Newsprint, printing and writing paper
Papier journal, papier d'impression et papier d'écriture
Papel de periódico, papel de imprenta y papel de escribir

Country / Year / Pays / Année / País / Año	Newsprint / Papier journal / Papel de periódico					Other printing and writing paper / Autre papier d'impression et d'écriture / Otro papel de imprenta y de escribir				
	Production / Production / Producción	Imports / Importations / Importaciones	Exports / Exportations / Exportaciones	Consumption / Consommation / Consumo	Consumption per 1,000 inh. / Consommation pour 1 000 hab. / Consumo por 1 000 hab.	Production / Production / Producción	Imports / Importations / Importaciones	Exports / Exportations / Exportaciones	Consumption / Consommation / Consumo	Consumption per 1,000 inh. / Consommation pour 1 000 hab. / Consumo por 1 000 hab.
Chile										
1970	124 400		78 300	46 100	4 856		7 900		7 900	832
1975	120 000		78 300	41 700	4 035	41 000	3 000	14 000	30 000	2 903
1980	131 000		63 000	68 000	6 102	48 000	13 000	15 000	46 000	4 128
1985	172 000		116 000	56 000	4 637	63 000	18 600	10 300	71 300	5 904
1990	171 000		115 000	56 000	4 257	60 000	43 000	3 000	100 000	7 602
1993	185 000	7 211	145 985	46 226	3 344	86 000	82 872	5 304	163 568	11 833
1994	186 000	17 000	151 400	51 600	3 674	98 000	75 900	3 400	170 500	12 140
Colombia										
1970		59 200		59 200	2 772	43 800	2 500	3 400	42 900	2 008
1975		44 400		44 400	1 867	44 000	9 200	900	52 300	2 200
1980		71 000		71 000	2 677	71 000	24 300	2 500	92 800	3 499
1985		77 500		77 500	2 629	106 000	4 700	5 300	105 400	3 575
1990		75 900		75 900	2 350	128 000	4 500	3 600	128 900	3 991
1993		79 909	1 538	78 371	2 306	184 000	52 664	10 717	225 947	6 648
1994		94 944	92	94 852	2 746	211 000	57 193	17 665	250 528	7 252
Ecuador										
1970		13 900		13 900	2 328		5 900		5 900	988
1975		10 800		10 800	1 564	3 000	11 000		14 000	2 027
1980		32 600		32 600	4 095	4 200	19 000		23 200	2 914
1985		39 600		39 600	4 352	1 000	28 400		29 400	3 231
1990		24 000		24 000	2 338	8 500	25 000		33 500	3 264
1993		19 100	658	18 442	1 679	2 900	22 167	1 300	23 767	2 164
1994		43 870	658	43 212	3 851	2 900	23 587	1 900	24 587	2 191
Falkland Islands (Malvinas)										
1970										
1975										
1980										
1985										
1990										
1993		128		128	64 000		19	196		
1994		128		128	64 000		25	196		
French Guiana										
1970										
1975										
1980										
1985										
1990										
1993		4		4	30		300		300	2 239
1994		4		4	29		300		300	2 143
Guyana										
1970		1 200		1 200	1 693		1 200		1 200	1 693
1975		1 400		1 400	1 907		1 400		1 400	1 907
1980		1 500		1 500	1 976		800		800	1 054
1985		500		500	633		1 400		1 400	1 772
1990		500		500	628		300		300	377
1993		687		687	842		973	10	963	1 180
1994		487		487	590		820	10	810	982
Paraguay										
1970		4 100		4 100	1 743		500		500	213
1975		3 100		3 100	1 156		1 400		1 400	522
1980		8 000		8 000	2 551	2 000	3 800		5 800	1 849
1985		8 000		8 000	2 166	2 000	3 700		5 700	1 543
1990		10 500		10 500	2 432	2 000	6 900		8 900	2 062
1993		15 440		15 440	3 284		14 947	43	14 904	3 170
1994		15 513		15 513	3 212		16 759	43	16 716	3 461
Peru										
1970		49 400		49 400	3 744	22 000	2 700	2 700	22 000	1 668
1975		51 400	100	51 300	3 384	38 000	4 200		42 200	2 783
1980	30 000	6 500		36 500	2 107	42 400	3 200	400	45 200	2 610
1985		39 000		39 000	1 998	49 000	5 800	900	53 900	2 762
1990		87 600		87 600	4 058	45 000	3 100	900	47 200	2 186
1993		50 565		50 565	2 209	98 000	58 253	1	156 252	6 827
1994		54 500		54 500	2 336	98 000	55 800	1	153 799	6 592

Newsprint, printing and writing paper 7.12
Papier journal, papier d'impression et papier d'écriture
Papel de periódico, papel de imprenta y papel de escribir

Country Year Pays Année País Año	Newsprint Papier journal Papel de periódico					Other printing and writing paper Autre papier d'impression et d'écriture Otro papel de imprenta y de escribir				
	Production Production Producción	Imports Importa- tions Importa- ciones	Exports Exporta- tions Exporta- ciones	Consumption Consom- mation Consumo	Consump- tion per 1,000 inh. Consomma- tion pour 1 000 hab. Consumo por 1 000 hab.	Production Production Producción	Imports Importa- tions Importa- ciones	Exports Exporta- tions Exporta- ciones	Consumption Consom- mation Consumo	Consump- tion per 1,000 inh. Consomma- tion pour 1 000 hab. Consumo por 1 000 hab.
Suriname										
1970		500		500	1 344		2 000		2 000	5 479
1975		400		400	1 096		2 000		2 000	5 634
1980		600		600	1 690		1 000		1 000	2 653
1985		1 000		1 000	2 653		1 000		1 000	2 653
1990		1 000		1 000	2 500		1 200		1 200	3 000
1993		536		536	1 295		1 555	3	1 552	3 749
1994		334		334	797		355	29	326	778
Uruguay										
1970		20 800		20 800	7 407	14 500	100		14 600	5 199
1975		10 600		10 600	3 747	10 800	800	1 000	10 600	3 747
1980		15 200		15 200	5 216	25 400	4 100	8 400	21 100	7 241
1985		8 900		8 900	2 959	15 000	500	7 300	8 200	2 726
1990		17 400		17 400	5 624	16 000	4 900	5 700	15 200	4 913
1993		14 943		14 943	4 745	26 000	10 329	8 275	28 054	8 909
1994		15 096		15 096	4 765	26 000	11 108	8 709	28 399	8 964
Venezuela										
1970		84 300		84 300	7 863	26 200	8 800		35 000	3 265
1975		85 600		85 600	6 722	55 700	5 000		60 700	4 767
1980		141 000		141 000	9 343	84 200	18 400		102 600	6 799
1985		136 000		136 000	7 936	103 000	12 700		115 700	6 751
1990		103 500		103 500	5 307	118 000	3 700		121 700	6 240
1993		112 922	802	112 120	5 361	118 000	32 744	9 898	140 846	6 735
1994		89 219	136	89 083	4 167	153 000	27 639	1 178	179 461	8 395
Asia										
Afghanistan										
1970							400		400	29
1975		1 200		1 200	78		1 300		1 300	85
1980		100		100	6		500		500	31
1985							900		900	62
1990							600		600	40
1993		17		17	1		505		505	29
1994		17		17	1		66	50	16	1
Armenia										
1970		.		.	.		.	.	.	.
1975		.		.	.		.	.	.	.
1980		.		.	.		.	.	.	.
1985		.		.	.		.	.	.	.
1990		.		.	.		.	.	.	.
1993		.		.	.		3	.	3	1
1994		.		.	.		7	.	7	2
Azerbaijan										
1970							.		.	.
1975		.		.	.		.		.	.
1980		.		.	.		.		.	.
1985		.		.	.		.		.	.
1990		.		.	.		.		.	.
1993			19				33	127		
1994			500				100	200		
Bahrain										
1970							400		400	1 818
1975							1 500		1 500	5 515
1980							1 700		1 700	4 899
1985							2 100		2 100	5 072
1990							5 535		5 535	11 296
1993		2 663		2 663	4 978		4 776		4 776	8 927
1994		2 106		2 106	3 836		3 952	62	3 890	7 086
Bangladesh										
1970	36 000			36 000	540	32 000			32 000	480
1975	20 000		5 300	14 700	192	24 000		400	23 600	308
1980	37 000		18 000	19 000	215	27 000		1 000	26 000	295
1985	47 000		18 100	28 900	293	38 000	1 800		39 800	404
1990	46 000			46 000	425	38 000	8 500		46 500	430
1993	46 000	213		46 213	401	45 000	14 502	13	59 489	516
1994	48 000	2		48 002	408	50 000	37 158	1	87 157	740

7.12 Newsprint, printing and writing paper
Papier journal, papier d'impression et papier d'écriture
Papel de periódico, papel de imprenta y papel de escribir

Country Year / Pays Année / País Año	Newsprint / Papier journal / Papel de periódico					Other printing and writing paper / Autre papier d'impression et d'écriture / Otro papel de imprenta y de escribir				
	Production / Production / Producción	Imports / Importations / Importaciones	Exports / Exportations / Exportaciones	Consumption / Consommation / Consumo	Consumption per 1,000 inh. / Consommation pour 1 000 hab. / Consumo por 1 000 hab.	Production / Production / Producción	Imports / Importations / Importaciones	Exports / Exportations / Exportaciones	Consumption / Consommation / Consumo	Consumption per 1,000 inh. / Consommation pour 1 000 hab. / Consumo por 1 000 hab.
Bhutan										
1970										
1975										
1980										
1985										
1990										
1993							100	36	64	40
1994							487	10	477	296
Brunei Darussalam										
1970		100		100	769		200		200	1 538
1975		200		200	1 242		200		200	1 242
1980		200		200	1 036		500		500	2 591
1985		400		400	1 770		1 200		1 200	5 310
1990		500		500	1 946		1 500		1 500	5 837
1993		20	19	1	4		196	8	188	686
1994		2	19				1 760	109	1 651	5 896
Cambodia										
1970	500			500	72	2 400			2 400	346
1975										
1980										
1985										
1990										
1993							532		532	55
1994							532		532	53
China										
1970	386 000	13 600	13 000	386 600	465	778 000	2 100	13 300	766 800	923
1975	340 000	51 300	1 900	389 400	420	1 260 000	3 600	21 300	1 242 300	1 339
1980	373 000	155 500	700	527 800	528	1 769 000	6 700	34 200	1 741 500	1 743
1985	452 000	332 200		784 200	733	3 076 000	78 300	55 300	3 099 000	2 896
1990	475 000	243 100	1 100	717 000	621	4 984 000	167 500	93 300	5 058 200	4 378
1993	631 000	371 528	5 263	997 265	834	6 754 000	531 448	217 219	7 068 229	5 908
1994	727 000	388 824	6 733	1 109 091	917	7 734 000	863 139	283 266	8 313 873	6 878
Cyrus										
1970		1 700		1 700	2 764		4 100		4 100	6 667
1975		1 300		1 300	2 135		1 900		1 900	3 120
1980		2 600		2 600	4 134		3 300		3 300	5 246
1985		3 200		3 200	4 812		4 700		4 700	7 068
1990		3 100		3 100	4 416		5 800		5 800	8 262
1993		5 435		5 435	7 486		15 112	852	14 260	19 642
1994		6 800		6 800	9 264		16 000	100	15 900	21 662
Georgia										
1970		.	.	.	.	.	.	.	.	.
1975		.	.	.	.	.	.	.	.	.
1980		.	.	.	.	.	.	.	.	.
1985		.	.	.	.	.	.	.	.	.
1990		.	.	.	.	.	.	.	.	.
1993		24		.	.		1	2	.	.
1994							105		105	19
Hong Kong										
1970		48 200	3 200	45 000	11 416		53 700	4 300	49 400	12 532
1975		54 700	1 400	53 300	12 125		51 100	4 300	46 800	10 646
1980		90 000	14 200	75 800	15 043		117 400	5 000	112 400	22 306
1985		116 200	2 300	113 900	20 876		95 400	1 600	93 800	17 192
1990		203 400	5 600	197 800	34 671		380 500	41 600	338 900	59 404
1993		214 670	2 005	212 665	36 610		550 626	6 177	544 449	93 725
1994		257 643	3 513	254 130	43 530		684 651	11 049	673 602	115 382
India										
1970	37 300	144 200		181 500	327	444 700	2 800	14 200	433 300	781
1975	52 000	100 800		152 800	246	504 000	2 700	100	506 600	816
1980	40 000	270 000		310 000	450	514 000	12 200	1 500	524 700	762
1985	200 000	188 000		388 000	505	680 000	45 000	200	724 800	944
1990	310 000	85 000		395 000	464	900 000	22 400	7 600	914 800	1 075
1993	320 000	175 673	740	494 933	549	1 085 000	96 259	841	1 180 418	1 309
1994	320 000	159 124	87	479 037	522	1 085 000	65 880	12 994	1 137 886	1 239
Indonesia										
1970	3 000	40 600		43 600	362	6 000	44 000		50 000	416
1975		46 700		46 700	344	45 000	8 000		53 000	391
1980		66 000		66 000	437	121 000	34 700	7 000	148 700	985
1985	63 000	95 400	1 200	157 200	939	201 000	10 500	28 900	182 600	1 091
1990	157 000	13 800	600	170 200	931	504 000	19 100	81 000	442 100	2 418
1993	195 000	8 347	102 626	100 721	525	844 000	50 309	418 254	476 055	2 484
1994	239 000	4 200	67 100	176 100	905	992 000	68 016	395 396	664 620	3 415

Newsprint, printing and writing paper 7.12
Papier journal, papier d'impression et papier d'écriture
Papel de periódico, papel de imprenta y papel de escribir

Country Year / Pays Année / País Año	Newsprint / Papier journal / Papel de periódico					Other printing and writing paper / Autre papier d'impression et d'écriture / Otro papel de imprenta y de escribir				
	Production / Production / Producción	Imports / Importations / Importaciones	Exports / Exportations / Exportaciones	Consumption / Consommation / Consumo	Consumption per 1,000 inh. / Consommation pour 1 000 hab. / Consumo por 1 000 hab.	Production / Production / Producción	Imports / Importations / Importaciones	Exports / Exportations / Exportaciones	Consumption / Consommation / Consumo	Consumption per 1,000 inh. / Consommation pour 1 000 hab. / Consumo por 1 000 hab.
Iran, Islamic Republic of										
1970		10 900		10 900	383	12 000	99 800		111 800	3 933
1975		32 800		32 800	984	36 000	33 800		69 800	2 093
1980		14 000		14 000	357	45 000	32 000		77 000	1 962
1985		18 000		18 000	368	45 000	55 400		100 400	2 052
1990		36 000		36 000	611	72 000	219 000		291 000	4 937
1993		11 880		11 880	185	65 000	66 887	42	131 845	2 055
1994		5 355		5 355	81	85 000	78 645	45	163 600	2 488
Iraq										
1970		3 100		3 100	331		11 100		11 100	1 186
1975		4 900		4 900	445	8 000	5 600		13 600	1 234
1980		14 000		14 000	1 076	9 000	1 500		10 500	807
1985		20 000		20 000	1 306	9 000	27 000		36 000	2 350
1990		34 000		34 000	1 881	16 000	27 000		43 000	2 379
1993						5 000	79		5 079	261
1994						7 000	79		7 079	355
Israel										
1970	9 400	24 600		34 000	11 432	31 800	5 100	1 500	35 400	11 903
1975	7 000	30 700		37 700	10 912	47 000	2 400	1 400	48 000	13 893
1980	4 000	34 100		38 100	9 822	41 000	10 000	2 300	48 700	12 555
1985	1 000	48 700		49 700	11 741	53 000	10 900	300	63 600	15 025
1990	1 000	78 000		79 000	16 953	61 000	32 000	2 000	91 000	19 528
1993		105 421		105 421	20 065	61 000	79 426	1 386	139 040	26 464
1994		114 045	2	114 043	20 895	62 000	86 160	939	147 221	26 973
Japan										
1970	1 917 000	88 000	32 000	1 973 000	18 911	2 410 000	2 000	191 000	2 221 000	21 288
1975	2 160 000	29 500	107 300	2 082 200	18 670	2 772 000	24 500	194 400	2 602 100	23 332
1980	2 674 000	126 900	97 500	2 703 400	23 144	4 137 000	26 300	247 000	3 916 300	33 528
1985	2 592 000	330 400	81 000	2 841 400	23 514	4 746 000	86 000	320 200	4 511 800	37 338
1990	3 479 000	434 900	125 500	3 788 400	30 666	9 250 000	111 400	254 300	9 107 100	73 720
1993	2 917 000	550 053	59 297	3 407 756	27 364	9 543 000	118 000	184 000	9 477 000	76 098
1994	2 972 000	536 300	33 600	3 474 700	27 839	9 805 000	116 800	194 500	9 727 300	77 934
Jordan										
1970		600		600	261		500		500	217
1975		700		700	269		2 000		2 000	769
1980		2 600		2 600	889		7 100		7 100	2 429
1985		8 400		8 400	2 191		7 700		7 700	2 009
1990		5 305		5 305	1 246		19 825		19 825	4 655
1993		8 887		8 887	1 800		53 446	4 110	49 336	9 995
1994		14 022	25	13 997	2 693		24 833	3 460	21 373	4 112
Kazakstan										
1970	.	.	.	.	.	.	.	.	.	.
1975	.	.	.	.	.	.	.	.	.	.
1980	.	.	.	.	.	.	.	.	.	.
1985	.	.	.	.	.	.	.	.	.	.
1990	.	.	.	.	.	.	.	.	.	.
1993		6 064					189		189	11
1994		702					534		534	31
Korea, Democratic People's Rep. of										
1970		1 300		1 300	89		2 100		2 100	144
1975		1 300		1 300	78		2 100		2 100	127
1980		1 300		1 300	71		2 100		2 100	115
1985		3 200		3 200	161		3 500		3 500	176
1990		200		200	9		1 500		1 500	69
1993		1 101		1 101	48		3 835	2 007	1 828	79
1994		2 966	4	2 962	126		6 978	481	6 497	277
Korea, Rep. of										
1970	101 700	6 600		108 300	3 393	22 300	400		22 700	711
1975	155 000		4 400	150 600	4 269	132 000	100	10 900	121 200	3 435
1980	249 000		22 000	227 000	5 954	293 000	400	50 500	242 900	6 371
1985	238 000		7 200	230 800	5 656	483 000	1 400	43 800	440 600	10 797
1990	522 000		40 300	481 700	11 237	919 000	34 900	75 900	878 000	20 481
1993	743 000	149 121	12 237	879 884	19 938	1 116 000	56 346	179 629	992 717	22 495
1994	874 000	135 641	29 059	980 582	22 004	1 350 000	115 987	795 851	670 136	15 038

7.12 Newsprint, printing and writing paper
Papier journal, papier d'impression et papier d'écriture
Papel de periódico, papel de imprenta y papel de escribir

Country Year / Pays Année / País Año	Newsprint / Papier journal / Papel de periódico					Other printing and writing paper / Autre papier d'impression et d'écriture / Otro papel de imprenta y de escribir				
	Production / Production / Producción	Imports / Importations / Importaciones	Exports / Exportations / Exportaciones	Consumption / Consommation / Consumo	Consumption per 1,000 inh. / Consommation pour 1 000 hab. / Consumo por 1 000 hab.	Production / Production / Producción	Imports / Importations / Importaciones	Exports / Exportations / Exportaciones	Consumption / Consommation / Consumo	Consumption per 1,000 inh. / Consommation pour 1 000 hab. / Consumo por 1 000 hab.
Kuwait										
1970							6 700	300	6 400	8 602
1975		4 800		4 800	4 767		12 000	1 200	10 800	10 725
1980		19 000		19 000	13 818		26 500	3 800	22 700	16 509
1985		18 000		18 000	10 465		16 000	1 200	14 800	8 605
1990		2 014		2 014	940		18 623		18 612	8 685
1993		17 593		17 593	9 912		22 715	11	22 715	12 797
1994		20 773		20 773	12 721		27 255		27 255	16 690
Kyrgyzstan										
1970		.		.	.	.	.	.	.	.
1975		.		.	.		.	.	.	.
1980		.		.	.		.	.	.	.
1985		.		.	.		.	.	.	.
1990		.		.	.		.	.	.	.
1993			110				154	3	151	33
1994							23		23	5
Lao People's Democratic Rep.										
1970		300		300	111		400		400	147
1975		200		200	66		500		500	165
1980		200		200	62		500		500	156
1985										
1990										
1993		138		138	30		174		174	38
1994		138		138	29		174		174	37
Lebanon										
1970		5 100		5 100	2 066		23 500		23 500	9 518
1975		6 300		6 300	2 277		25 400		25 400	9 180
1980		7 000		7 000	2 623		33 200		33 200	12 439
1985		4 700		4 700	1 762		20 900		20 900	7 834
1990		3 068		3 068	1 201		23 843		23 843	9 332
1993		4 340		4 340	1 546		43 950	654	43 296	15 424
1994		7 057		7 057	2 421		42 341	129	42 212	14 481
Macau										
1970		3 700		3 700	16 372		2 500		2 500	11 062
1975		2 800		2 800	11 966		1 900		1 900	8 120
1980		6 200		6 200	25 620					
1985							4 900		4 900	17 254
1990		300		300	877		5 400		5 400	15 789
1993		2 961	2	2 959	7 706		3 536	300	3 236	8 427
1994		4 200		4 200	10 553		4 300	500	3 800	9 548
Malaysia										
1970		38 400	200	38 200	3 520		20 500	600	19 900	1 834
1975		34 100	200	33 900	2 766	1 000	31 100	500	31 600	2 578
1980		66 000	100	65 900	4 788	1 000	61 700	100	62 600	4 548
1985		100 000		100 000	6 379	3 000	70 000		73 000	4 657
1990		154 000		154 000	8 607	130 000	157 719	88 604	199 115	11 129
1993		172 673		172 673	8 971	201 000	156 795	20 736	337 059	17 512
1994	2 000	180 400		182 400	9 261	159 000	252 800	53 400	358 400	18 198
Maldives										
1970										
1975										
1980										
1985										
1990		200		200	926		200		200	926
1993							2 300	3	2 297	9 651
1994		114		114	463		116	1	115	467
Mongolia										
1970		2 400		2 400	1 911					
1975		2 600		2 600	1 797		1 700		1 700	1 175
1980		2 300		2 300	1 383		1 900		1 900	1 143
1985		3 800		3 800	1 991		3 100		3 100	1 624
1990		397		397	182		544		544	250
1993		275		275	119		59	5	54	23
1994		114		114	48		342	5	337	143

Newsprint, printing and writing paper 7.12
Papier journal, papier d'impression et papier d'écriture
Papel de periódico, papel de imprenta y papel de escribir

Country Year / Pays Année / País Año	Newsprint Papier journal Papel de periódico					Other printing and writing paper Autre papier d'impression et d'écriture Otro papel de imprenta y de escribir				
	Production Production Producción	Imports Importa-tions Importa-ciones	Exports Exporta-tions Exporta-ciones	Consumption Consom-mation Consumo	Consump-tion per 1,000 inh. Consomma-tion pour 1 000 hab. Consumo por 1 000 hab.	Production Production Producción	Imports Importa-tions Importa-ciones	Exports Exporta-tions Exporta-ciones	Consumption Consom-mation Consumo	Consump-tion per 1,000 inh. Consomma-tion pour 1 000 hab. Consumo por 1 000 hab.
Myanmar										
1970		15 900		15 900	587	400	11 700		12 100	446
1975		6 500		6 500	214	7 000	7 400		14 400	473
1980		4 000		4 000	118	7 000	8 000		15 000	444
1985		5 300		5 300	141	10 000	5 300		15 300	408
1990		3 300		3 300	79	5 000	1 600		6 600	158
1993		1 730		1 730	39	8 000	1 489		9 489	213
1994		400		400	9	8 000	8 200		16 200	356
Nepal										
1970										
1975										
1980										
1985		1 200		1 200	71					
1990										
1993							59	111		
1994							69	121		
Oman										
1970										
1975										
1980		700		700	501		5 900		5 900	4 223
1985		1 200		1 200	685		6 200		6 200	3 541
1990		1 027		1 027	516		7 938	56	7 882	3 957
1993		1 027		1 027	494		12 600	56	12 544	6 039
1994										
Pakistan										
1970		500		500	8	6 300	7 000	400	12 900	196
1975		6 700		6 700	90	17 000	45 000		62 000	830
1980		33 100		33 100	388	28 000	23 200		51 200	600
1985		40 400		40 400	394	34 000	63 500		97 500	951
1990		53 000		53 000	435	55 000	45 200		100 200	822
1993		60 000		60 000	451	52 000	30 000	18	81 982	617
1994		65 000		65 000	476	62 000	38 000	18	99 982	732
Philippines										
1970	30 000	45 500		75 500	2 011	30 000	10 700		40 700	1 084
1975	68 000	800		68 800	1 600	38 000	11 600	100	49 500	1 151
1980	80 000	20 000		100 000	2 070	58 000	12 000	200	69 800	1 445
1985	56 000	2 000		58 000	1 061	31 000	8 200		39 200	717
1990	52 000	200		52 200	859	94 000	11 400		105 400	1 734
1993	110 000	16 800	238	126 562	1 953	103 000	71 000	100	173 900	2 684
1994	110 000	34 800	500	144 300	2 180	103 000	82 100	300	184 800	2 792
Qatar										
1970							600		600	5 405
1975							1 400		1 400	8 187
1980							3 400		3 400	14 847
1985							3 500		3 500	9 777
1990							3 970		3 970	8 186
1993		24		24	45		2 813	4	2 809	5 310
1994		53		53	98		1 932	12	1 920	3 556
Saudi Arabia										
1970		500		500	87		6 700		6 700	1 166
1975		2 300		2 300	317		12 200		12 200	1 683
1980		13 000		13 000	1 354		45 200		45 200	4 706
1985		28 000		28 000	2 214		51 200		51 200	4 048
1990		7 000		7 000	436		77 279		77 279	4 815
1993		29 566		29 566	1 727		106 761	277	106 484	6 220
1994		26 069	150	25 919	1 485		79 347	105	79 242	4 541
Singapore										
1970		24 500	900	23 600	11 373		23 600	3 300	20 300	9 783
1975		30 300	2 100	28 200	12 461		28 900	9 600	19 300	8 529
1980		60 000	4 300	55 700	23 064		71 100	17 900	53 200	22 029
1985		69 500	12 600	56 900	22 244		121 500	24 600	96 900	37 881
1990		106 600	8 900	97 700	36 118		193 300	30 000	163 300	60 370
1993		120 950	205	120 745	43 231		219 127	11 014	208 113	74 512
1994		157 825	9 975	147 850	52 410		317 222	79 828	237 394	84 152
Sri Lanka										
1970		18 300		18 300	1 462	8 900	4 300		13 200	1 055
1975		6 500		6 500	478	9 000	6 200		15 200	1 117
1980		8 000		8 000	540	12 500	15 600		28 100	1 896
1985		17 200		17 200	1 067	14 000	6 000		20 000	1 241
1990		22 700		22 700	1 318	11 700	28 400		40 100	2 328
1993		8 300		8 300	464	15 000	17 706		32 706	1 827
1994		25 548		25 548	1 410	15 000	47 879	48	62 831	3 467

7.12 Newsprint, printing and writing paper
Papier journal, papier d'impression et papier d'écriture
Papel de periódico, papel de imprenta y papel de escribir

Country Year / Pays Année / País Año	Newsprint / Papier journal / Papel de periódico					Other printing and writing paper / Autre papier d'impression et d'écriture / Otro papel de imprenta y de escribir				
	Production / Production / Producción	Imports / Importa-tions / Importa-ciones	Exports / Exporta-tions / Exporta-ciones	Consumption / Consom-mation / Consumo	Consump-tion per 1,000 inh. / Consomma-tion pour 1 000 hab. / Consumo por 1 000 hab.	Production / Production / Producción	Imports / Importa-tions / Importa-ciones	Exports / Exporta-tions / Exporta-ciones	Consumption / Consom-mation / Consumo	Consump-tion per 1,000 inh. / Consomma-tion pour 1 000 hab. / Consumo por 1 000 hab.
Syrian Arab Rep.										
1970		1 500		1 500	240		7 200		7 200	1 151
1975		900		900	121		12 000		12 000	1 613
1980		3 700		3 700	425		30 000		30 000	3 447
1985		5 600		5 600	541		24 500		24 500	2 368
1990		7 064		7 064	572		16 678		16 678	1 351
1993		5 785		5 785	422		21 062	51	21 011	1 534
1994		2 588		2 588	183		33 146	20	33 126	2 338
Tajikistan										
1970	.	.	.	.	.	.	.	.	.	.
1975	.	.	.	.	.	.	.	.	.	.
1980	.	.	.	.	.	.	.	.	.	.
1985	.	.	.	.	.	.	.	.	.	.
1990	.	.	.	.	.	.	.	.	.	.
1993							15	3	12	2
1994							15	3	12	2
Thailand										
1970		36 300		36 300	1 016	32 000	12 500	300	44 200	1 237
1975		63 400		63 400	1 533	51 000	2 100	1 800	51 300	1 240
1980		91 600		91 600	1 961	73 000	8 800	300	81 500	1 745
1985		137 800		137 800	2 695	103 000	21 500		124 500	2 435
1990		194 900		194 900	3 506	190 000	23 200	1 800	211 400	3 803
1993		289 785	618	289 167	5 022	256 000	55 861	2 747	309 114	5 368
1994	39 000	280 000	4 900	314 100	5 398	299 000	58 000	17 700	339 300	5 832
Turkey										
1970	10 700	15 400		26 100	739	42 400	4 300		46 700	1 322
1975	86 000	12 200		98 200	2 453	72 000	2 400		74 400	1 859
1980	86 000	71 400		157 400	3 542	69 000	2 800		71 800	1 616
1985	145 000	17 000		162 000	3 218	91 000	21 300		112 300	2 231
1990	151 000	80 900		231 900	4 134	139 000	65 400		204 400	3 644
1993	94 000	256 340	80	350 260	5 877	111 000	196 865	5 398	302 467	5 075
1994	69 000	124 700	200	193 500	3 184	90 000	104 400	20 400	174 000	2 863
Turkmenistan										
1970	.	.	.	.	.	.	.	.	.	.
1975	.	.	.	.	.	.	.	.	.	.
1980	.	.	.	.	.	.	.	.	.	.
1985	.	.	.	.	.	.	.	.	.	.
1990	.	.	.	.	.	.	.	.	.	.
1993	.	.	.	.	.	.	92	25	67	17
1994							26	25	1	
United Arab Emirates										
1970										
1975										
1980										
1985										
1990										
1993		15 933	349	15 584	8 581		52 909	2 168	50 741	27 941
1994		20 984	160	20 824	11 190		64 224	236	63 988	34 384
Uzbekistan										
1970	.	.	.	.	.	.	.	.	.	.
1975	.	.	.	.	.	.	.	.	.	.
1980	.	.	.	.	.	.	.	.	.	.
1985	.	.	.	.	.	.	.	.	.	.
1990	.	.	.	.	.	.	.	.	.	.
1993							2 786		2 786	127
1994							5 483		5 483	245
Viet Nam										
1970		21 700		21 700	508	19 000	100		19 100	447
1975		2 000		2 000	42	31 000			31 000	645
1980		2 500		2 500	47	23 000			23 000	428
1985	5 000	5 000		10 000	167	38 000			38 000	634
1990	9 000			9 000	135	26 000		9 300	16 700	250
1993	13 000	1 057	1 556	12 501	175	67 000	15 515		82 515	1 157
1994	13 000	2 755	1 556	14 199	195	67 000	24 241	1 519	89 722	1 230
Yemen										
1970							400		400	63
1975		100		100	14		1 800		1 800	257
1980		500		500	61		1 000		1 000	122
1985		300		300	31		300		300	31
1990		300		300	27		300		300	27
1993		900		900	68		13 416		13 416	1 017
1994		900		900	65		6 151	13	6 138	442

Newsprint, printing and writing paper **7.12**
Papier journal, papier d'impression et papier d'écriture
Papel de periódico, papel de imprenta y papel de escribir

Country / Year — Pays / Année — País / Año	Newsprint — Papier journal — Papel de periódico					Other printing and writing paper — Autre papier d'impression et d'écriture — Otro papel de imprenta y de escribir				
	Production / Producción	Imports / Importations / Importaciones	Exports / Exportations / Exportaciones	Consumption / Consommation / Consumo	Consumption per 1,000 inh. / Consommation pour 1 000 hab. / Consumo por 1 000 hab.	Production / Producción	Imports / Importations / Importaciones	Exports / Exportations / Exportaciones	Consumption / Consommation / Consumo	Consumption per 1,000 inh. / Consommation pour 1 000 hab. / Consumo por 1 000 hab.
Europe										
Albania										
1970										
1975										
1980										
1985				8 000	2 432	4 500			4 500	1 368
1990	8 000			8 000	2 466	4 500			5 110	1 508
1993	8 000	378	20	8 358	2 466	4 500	630	20	5 110	1 508
1994	8 000	100		8 100	2 373	4 500	300		4 800	1 406
Andorra										
1970										
1975										
1980										
1985										
1990										
1993		20	80				1 295	37	1 258	20 623
1994		8	80				1 776	28	1 748	27 313
Austria										
1970	170 000	400	67 000	103 400	13 848	394 000	8 100	288 100	114 000	15 267
1975	147 000	4 600	30 800	120 800	15 939	523 000	12 100	409 800	125 300	16 533
1980	176 000	1 500	39 100	138 400	18 334	618 000	56 700	562 100	112 600	14 916
1985	241 000	6 300	133 000	114 300	15 123	850 000	129 400	890 800	88 600	11 723
1990	333 000	38 400	227 000	144 400	18 741	1 377 000	241 000	958 000	660 000	85 659
1993	387 000	73 635	26 064	434 571	55 268	1 574 000	289 468	1 718 020	145 448	18 498
1994	403 000	69 000	6 000	466 000	58 853	1 728 000	339 000	1 965 000	102 000	12 882
Belarus										
1970	.	.	.	.	.	.	.	.	.	.
1975	.	.	.	.	.	.	.	.	.	.
1980	.	.	.	.	.	.	.	.	.	.
1985	.	.	.	.	.	.	.	.	.	.
1990	.	.	.	.	.	.	.	.	.	.
1993		13	66				282	81	201	20
1994							400		400	39
Belgium‡										
1970	95 000	110 300	25 600	179 700	18 610	352 000	208 300	237 400	322 900	33 440
1975	77 000	105 400	20 500	161 900	16 527	330 000	155 500	201 800	283 700	28 961
1980	102 000	126 000	31 000	197 000	19 996	436 000	337 700	288 400	485 300	49 259
1985	109 000	140 100	27 600	221 500	22 471	414 000	357 100	178 300	592 800	60 140
1990	102 000	184 400	46 200	240 200	24 138	733 000	764 600	621 700	875 900	88 021
1993	119 000	146 278	47 555	217 723	21 673	666 000	765 083	633 843	797 240	79 359
1994	122 000	193 074	96 990	218 084	21 635	610 000	1 083 840	848 868	844 972	83 827
Bosnia and Herzegovina										
1970	.	.	.	.	.	.	.	.	.	.
1975	.	.	.	.	.	.	.	.	.	.
1980	.	.	.	.	.	.	.	.	.	.
1985	.	.	.	.	.	.	.	.	.	.
1990	.	.	.	.	.	.	.	.	.	.
1993		5		5	1		509	561		14
1994			15				98		98	28
Bulgaria										
1970		35 400		35 400	4 170	41 000	9 500		50 500	5 948
1975		49 000		49 000	5 618	42 000	18 400		60 400	6 925
1980		46 200		46 200	5 213	36 000	13 400		49 400	5 574
1985		42 300		42 300	4 721	81 000	10 000		91 000	10 156
1990		30 700		30 700	3 415	52 000	6 800		58 800	6 540
1993		4 517	828	3 689	416	8 000	18 220	564	25 656	2 892
1994		7 047	828	6 219	705	8 000	25 941	735	33 206	3 766
Croatia										
1970	.	.	.	.	.	.	.	.	.	.
1975	.	.	.	.	.	.	.	.	.	.
1980	.	.	.	.	.	.	.	.	.	.
1985	.	.	.	.	.	.	.	.	.	.
1990	.	.	.	.	.	.	.	.	.	.
1993		18 342	202	18 140	4 021	2 000	35 166	2 275	34 891	7 735
1994		18 342	202	18 140	4 028	1 600	35 166	2 275	34 491	7 658

7.12 Newsprint, printing and writing paper
Papier journal, papier d'impression et papier d'écriture
Papel de periódico, papel de imprenta y papel de escribir

Country / Year Pays / Année País / Año	Newsprint — Papier journal — Papel de periódico					Other printing and writing paper — Autre papier d'impression et d'écriture — Otro papel de imprenta y de escribir				
	Production Producción	Imports Importations Importaciones	Exports Exportations Exportaciones	Consumption Consommation Consumo	Consumption per 1,000 inh. Consommation pour 1 000 hab. Consumo por 1 000 hab.	Production Producción	Imports Importations Importaciones	Exports Exportations Exportaciones	Consumption Consommation Consumo	Consumption per 1,000 inh. Consommation pour 1 000 hab. Consumo por 1 000 hab.
Czech Republic										
1970	.	.	.	.	.	.	.	.	.	.
1975	.	.	.	.	.	.	.	.	.	.
1980	.	.	.	.	.	.	.	.	.	.
1985	.	.	.	.	.	.	.	.	.	.
1990	.	.	.	.	.	.	.	.	.	.
1993	59 000	31 769	28 000	62 769	6 096	63 000	93 000	55 000	101 000	9 810
1994	85 000	22 100	57 000	50 100	4 866	70 000	127 000	64 000	133 000	12 919
Denmark										
1970		149 200	200	149 000	30 229	71 000	84 600	10 800	144 800	29 377
1975		125 700	400	125 300	24 763	59 000	91 600	14 700	135 900	26 858
1980		153 300	700	152 600	29 787	113 000	135 800	57 600	191 200	37 322
1985		188 800	1 000	187 800	36 723	142 000	149 000	73 000	218 000	42 628
1990		217 100	700	216 400	42 101	124 000	232 100	66 900	289 200	56 265
1993		223 000	565	222 435	43 066	93 000	264 915	57 983	299 932	58 070
1994		238 100	1 300	236 800	45 776	93 000	133 000	76 000	150 000	28 997
Estonia										
1970	.	.	.	.	.	.	.	.	.	.
1975	.	.	.	.	.	.	.	.	.	.
1980	.	.	.	.	.	.	.	.	.	.
1985	.	.	.	.	.	.	.	.	.	.
1990	.	.	.	.	.	.	.	.	.	.
1993		1 634	215	1 419	914	8 700	3 162	35	11 827	7 616
1994		4 500	100	4 400	2 855	8 700	7 400	100	16 000	10 383
Finland										
1970	1 305 000	900	1 187 000	118 900	25 814	981 000	1 600	779 200	203 400	44 160
1975	992 000		776 200	215 800	45 808	1 340 000	3 000	1 176 800	166 200	35 279
1980	1 569 000		1 431 900	137 100	28 682	2 027 000	4 300	1 750 000	281 300	58 849
1985	1 811 000		1 643 400	167 600	34 190	3 166 000	9 000	2 756 800	418 200	85 312
1990	1 430 000		1 202 900	227 100	45 548	4 768 000	30 300	4 172 500	625 800	125 511
1993	1 425 000	19 771	1 251 970	192 801	38 118	5 567 000	28 294	4 903 150	692 144	136 841
1994	1 446 000	17 000	1 253 000	210 000	41 306	6 159 000	31 000	5 554 000	636 000	125 098
France										
1970	430 200	177 000	1 700	605 500	11 926	1 418 000	228 000	158 000	1 488 000	29 307
1975	238 000	165 000	1 000	402 000	7 628	1 311 000	362 000	262 000	1 411 000	26 775
1980	261 000	371 400	3 600	628 800	11 670	2 011 000	596 600	528 200	2 079 400	38 593
1985	264 000	317 800	13 500	568 300	10 301	1 898 000	851 800	621 600	2 128 200	38 575
1990	422 000	497 600	131 500	788 100	13 895	2 773 000	1 342 400	981 300	3 134 100	55 258
1993	802 000	416 623	475 229	743 394	12 927	2 936 000	1 792 000	1 363 000	3 365 000	58 514
1994	844 000	488 000	525 000	807 000	13 975	3 268 000	2 095 000	1 592 000	3 771 000	65 302
Germany										
1970										
1975										
1980										
1985										
1990										
1993	1 302 000	1 314 000	507 000	2 109 000	26 083	4 928 000	2 919 000	2 315 000	5 532 000	68 417
1994	1 499 000	1 293 000	575 000	2 217 000	27 277	5 865 000	3 218 000	2 947 000	6 136 000	75 494
Gibraltar										
1970										
1975										
1980										
1985										
1990										
1993		43		43	1 536		93		93	3 321
1994		38		38	1 357		110	1	109	3 893
Greece										
1970		31 600		31 600	3 594	30 000	5 700		35 700	4 060
1975		48 000	100	47 900	5 295	35 000	34 300	300	69 000	7 627
1980	9 000	40 000	7 900	41 100	4 262	80 000	42 500	28 300	94 200	9 769
1985	12 000	68 800	1 800	79 000	7 952	70 000	46 300	3 200	113 100	11 385
1990	16 000	88 800	4 100	100 700	9 836	75 000	86 500	2 700	158 800	15 511
1993	9 000	59 552	947	67 605	6 515	125 000	138 739	1 676	262 063	25 254
1994	9 000	59 559	328	68 231	6 551	125 000	157 369	763	281 606	27 036
Hungary										
1970		53 600		53 600	5 185	74 200	35 400	1 200	108 400	10 486
1975		56 300		56 300	5 346	101 000	42 700	19 200	124 500	11 821
1980		63 000	2 000	61 000	5 697	115 000	44 000	24 300	134 700	12 579
1985		67 500		67 500	6 381	136 000	31 100	28 700	138 400	13 083
1990		51 600		51 600	4 978	127 000	27 000	36 000	118 000	11 384
1993		25 909	60	25 849	2 532	64 000	112 955	3 233	173 722	17 015
1994		25 000	300	24 700	2 431	80 000	79 000	5 700	153 300	15 087

Newsprint, printing and writing paper 7.12
Papier journal, papier d'impression et papier d'écriture
Papel de periódico, papel de imprenta y papel de escribir

Country / Year / Pays / Année / País / Año	Newsprint — Papier journal — Papel de periódico					Other printing and writing paper — Autre papier d'impression et d'écriture — Otro papel de imprenta y de escribir				
	Production / Producción	Imports / Importations / Importaciones	Exports / Exportations / Exportaciones	Consumption / Consommation / Consumo	Consumption per 1,000 inh. / Consommation pour 1 000 hab. / Consumo por 1 000 hab.	Production / Producción	Imports / Importations / Importaciones	Exports / Exportations / Exportaciones	Consumption / Consommation / Consumo	Consumption per 1,000 inh. / Consommation pour 1 000 hab. / Consumo por 1 000 hab.
Iceland										
1970		3 100		3 100	15 196		1 800		1 800	8 824
1975		3 000		3 000	13 761		1 800		1 800	8 257
1980		4 000		4 000	17 544		3 200		3 200	14 035
1985		5 800		5 800	24 066		2 800		2 800	11 618
1990		4 800		4 800	18 824		4 200		4 200	16 471
1993		5 289		5 289	20 110		8 729	9	8 720	33 156
1994		5 682		5 682	21 361		8 506	149	8 357	31 417
Ireland										
1970	6 000	48 200		54 200	18 348	10 000	5 300	1 000	14 300	4 841
1975	10 000	47 000	300	56 700	17 847	19 000	8 900	2 100	25 800	8 121
1980		60 800	200	60 600	17 818	23 000	22 100	6 700	38 400	11 291
1985		51 400	400	51 000	14 358		42 000	1 100	40 900	11 515
1990		63 000	1 000	62 000	17 699		94 000	5 811	88 189	25 175
1993		77 389	7 600	69 789	19 804		122 000	9 100	112 900	32 037
1994		70 700	1 700	69 000	19 497		130 000	7 200	122 800	34 699
Italy										
1970	311 000	13 800	42 500	282 300	5 245	1 167 000	24 100	133 000	1 058 100	19 659
1975	243 000	11 500	9 600	244 900	4 417	1 054 000	33 900	111 000	976 900	17 621
1980	277 000	63 700	13 000	327 700	5 807	1 799 000	147 900	330 400	1 616 500	28 644
1985	178 000	232 000	28 000	382 000	6 729	1 940 000	331 000	479 000	1 792 000	31 565
1990	233 000	374 000	10 000	597 000	10 469	2 247 000	765 000	528 000	2 484 000	43 561
1993	83 000	468 000	7 471	543 529	9 514	2 381 000	1 000 170	729 862	2 651 308	46 411
1994	154 000	471 000	4 000	621 000	10 865	2 595 000	1 224 000	812 000	3 007 000	52 609
Latvia										
1970	.	.	.	.	.	.	.	.	.	.
1975	.	.	.	.	.	.	.	.	.	.
1980	.	.	.	.	.	.	.	.	.	.
1985	.	.	.	.	.	.	.	.	.	.
1990	.	.	.	.	.	.	.	.	.	.
1993	3 000	15 000		18 000	6 894	1 000	18 000	999	18 001	6 894
1994	2 000	17 000		19 000	7 356	1 000	25 000	1 400	24 600	9 524
Lithuania										
1970		.	.	.	.	.	.	.	.	.
1975		.	.	.	.	.	.	.	.	.
1980		.	.	.	.	.	.	.	.	.
1985		.	.	.	.	.	.	.	.	.
1990	.								.	.
1993		389	2 133			1 900	371	1 710	561	151
1994		5 900	300	5 600	1 511	1 900	2 300	1 200	3 000	809
Malta										
1970		300		300	990		2 900		2 900	9 571
1975		200		200	658		2 400		2 400	7 895
1980		700		700	2 160		2 300		2 300	7 099
1985		1 500		1 500	4 360		4 200		4 200	12 209
1990		2 600		2 600	7 345		6 400		6 400	18 079
1993		2 875		2 875	7 964		16 279	17	16 262	45 047
1994		5 200		5 200	14 286		20 000	17	19 983	54 898
Moldova										
1970	.	.	.	.	.	.	.	.	.	.
1975	.	.	.	.	.	.	.	.	.	.
1980	.	.	.	.	.	.	.	.	.	.
1985	.	.	.	.	.	.	.	.	.	.
1990	.	.	.	.	.	.	.		.	.
1993			4				114		114	26
1994			700				5 000		5 000	1 131
Netherlands										
1970	167 000	247 300	35 600	378 700	29 059	489 000	213 000	151 200	550 800	42 265
1975	125 000	257 400	22 700	359 700	26 346	406 000	249 400	193 900	461 500	33 802
1980	171 000	331 900	45 100	457 800	32 367	571 000	394 300	283 600	681 700	48 197
1985	191 000	270 800	77 600	384 200	26 511	562 000	446 700	379 000	629 700	43 452
1990	300 000	393 900	200 600	493 300	32 992	819 000	934 600	708 100	1 045 500	69 924
1993	326 000	403 481	238 814	490 667	32 101	775 000	1 025 780	772 000	1 028 780	67 307
1994	311 000	432 000	227 000	516 000	33 513	902 000	759 000	743 000	918 000	59 622
Norway										
1970	554 000		475 600	78 400	20 222	317 000	4 900	223 600	98 300	25 355
1975	435 000		380 500	54 500	13 601	292 000	16 400	163 400	145 000	36 187
1980	589 000		522 800	66 200	16 202	337 000	52 800	231 300	158 500	38 791
1985	877 000		761 300	115 700	27 859	304 000	91 200	222 200	173 000	41 657
1990	910 000		822 300	87 700	20 674	339 000	114 400	309 700	143 700	33 876
1993	1 007 000	11 025	821 600	196 425	45 691	495 000	138 423	436 850	196 573	45 725
1994	1 007 000	20 000	770 600	256 400	59 379	606 000	156 400	596 000	166 400	38 536

7.12 Newsprint, printing and writing paper
Papier journal, papier d'impression et papier d'écriture
Papel de periódico, papel de imprenta y papel de escribir

Country Year / Pays Année / País Año	Newsprint — Papier journal — Papel de periódico					Other printing and writing paper — Autre papier d'impression et d'écriture — Otro papel de imprenta y de escribir				
	Production / Production / Producción	Imports / Importations / Importaciones	Exports / Exportations / Exportaciones	Consumption / Consommation / Consumo	Consumption per 1,000 inh. / Consommation pour 1 000 hab. / Consumo por 1 000 hab.	Production / Production / Producción	Imports / Importations / Importaciones	Exports / Exportations / Exportaciones	Consumption / Consommation / Consumo	Consumption per 1,000 inh. / Consommation pour 1 000 hab. / Consumo por 1 000 hab.
Poland										
1970	87 900	15 000	15 000	87 900	2 702	188 100	21 000	100	209 000	6 426
1975	83 000	38 000		121 000	3 557	210 000	56 000	2 000	264 000	7 760
1980	91 000	36 000		127 000	3 570	199 000	28 000	2 000	225 000	6 325
1985	82 000	53 400		135 400	3 639	216 000	17 000		233 000	6 263
1990	25 000	8 000	15 400	17 600	462	243 000	4 300	14 700	232 600	6 102
1993	46 000	41 000	15 000	72 000	1 880	284 000	68 100	31 600	320 500	8 367
1994	68 000	19 500	12 700	74 800	1 951	334 000	85 700	22 700	397 000	10 354
Portugal										
1970	700	43 500	200	44 000	4 865	43 200	1 500	300	44 400	4 909
1975	1 000	28 500	2 100	27 400	3 013	54 000	2 300	14 400	41 900	4 608
1980		41 000		41 000	4 198	87 000	4 300	14 000	77 300	7 915
1985		40 300		40 300	4 069	103 000	16 000	35 400	83 600	8 441
1990		54 000	400	53 600	5 432	167 000	79 500	49 100	197 400	20 004
1993		63 415	921	62 494	6 352	385 000	107 034	146 413	345 621	35 131
1994		62 000	200	61 800	6 287	435 000	121 000	292 000	264 000	26 857
Romania										
1970	53 000	9 500	10 800	51 700	2 553	123 000	4 000	45 100	81 900	4 044
1975	44 000	12 500	12 400	44 100	2 076	121 000	1 200	38 000	84 200	3 963
1980	103 000	12 000	59 000	56 000	2 522	141 000		57 000	84 000	3 784
1985	90 000		30 000	60 000	2 640	139 000		46 000	93 000	4 092
1990	67 000		12 976	54 024	2 328	111 000		46 000	65 000	2 801
1993	57 000	65	1 043	56 022	2 433	52 000	9 789	1 348	60 441	2 625
1994	57 000	3 490	5 791	54 699	2 386	36 000	14 950	13 523	37 427	1 633
Russian Federation										
1970	·	·	·	·	·	·	·	·	·	·
1975	·	·	·	·	·	·	·	·	·	·
1980	·	·	·	·	·	·	·	·	·	·
1985	·	·	·	·	·	·	·	·	·	·
1990	·	·	·	·	·	·	·	·	·	·
1993	845 000	1 628	578 000	268 628	1 818	665 000	15 950	12 111	668 839	4 527
1994	1 038 000	400	677 000	361 400	2 452	429 000	18 900	27 000	420 900	2 856
Slovakia										
1970	·	·	·	·	·	·	·	·	·	·
1975	·	·	·	·	·	·	·	·	·	·
1980	·	·	·	·	·	·	·	·	·	·
1985	·	·	·	·	·	·	·	·	·	·
1990	·	·	·	·	·	·	·	·	·	·
1993	20 000	7 523		27 523	5 179	90 000	15 124	59 338	45 786	8 616
1994	20 000	7 523		27 523	5 161	85 000	15 124	59 338	40 786	7 648
Slovenia										
1970	·	·	·	·	·	·	·	·	·	
1975	·	·	·	·	·	·	·	·	·	
1980	·	·	·	·	·	·	·	·	·	
1985	·	·	·	·	·	·	·	·	·	
1990	·	·	·	·	·	·	·	·	·	
1993	66 000	5 988	17 519	54 469	28 120	45 000	33 599	130 836		
1994	76 000	6 000	19 000	63 000	32 441	44 000	32 000	153 000		
Spain										
1970	115 000	78 800		193 800	5 737	322 800	11 300	15 900	318 200	9 420
1975	103 000	101 800	900	203 900	5 728	521 000	53 000	64 300	509 700	14 319
1980	108 000	57 600	3 200	162 400	4 326	717 000	82 000	42 900	756 100	20 140
1985	134 000	134 600	5 500	263 100	6 838	712 000	110 900	112 700	710 200	18 459
1990	173 000	261 000	24 000	410 000	10 440	832 000	642 800	170 200	1 304 600	33 220
1993	94 000	363 000	16 700	440 300	11 143	812 000	879 000	284 000	1 407 000	35 608
1994	99 000	380 000	14 000	465 000	11 752	874 000	1 010 000	332 000	1 552 000	39 224
Sweden										
1970	1 030 000		686 600	343 400	42 696	537 000	16 100	283 800	269 300	33 483
1975	1 213 000		920 800	292 200	35 665	448 000	18 400	277 500	188 900	23 056
1980	1 534 000		1 238 400	295 600	35 567	998 000	32 700	510 100	520 600	62 640
1985	1 594 000	300	1 352 000	242 300	29 018	1 364 000	64 600	679 400	749 200	89 725
1990	2 273 000	2 900	1 772 100	503 800	58 862	1 655 000	111 300	1 289 800	476 500	55 672
1993	2 325 000	15 766	1 885 000	455 766	52 423	1 884 000	114 485	1 524 390	474 095	54 531
1994	2 415 000	39 000	2 030 000	424 000	48 524	2 060 000	131 000	1 798 000	393 000	44 976
Switzerland										
1970	143 000	24 600	100	167 500	27 073	249 000	77 300	8 900	317 400	51 301
1975	143 000	6 000	8 200	140 800	22 212	180 000	82 400	28 700	233 700	36 867
1980	210 000	24 600	27 600	207 000	32 758	284 000	156 600	76 000	364 600	57 699
1985	232 000	45 000	30 000	247 000	37 791	300 000	205 000	119 000	386 000	59 058
1990	280 000	88 000	58 000	310 000	45 361	370 000	335 000	109 000	596 000	87 211
1993	288 000	105 000	69 400	323 600	45 862	381 000	325 680	188 910	517 770	73 380
1994	288 000	116 000	68 000	336 000	47 118	381 000	397 000	256 000	522 000	73 202

Newsprint, printing and writing paper 7.12
Papier journal, papier d'impression et papier d'écriture
Papel de periódico, papel de imprenta y papel de escribir

Country Year Pays Année País Año	Newsprint Papier journal Papel de periódico					Other printing and writing paper Autre papier d'impression et d'écriture Otro papel de imprenta y de escribir				
	Production Production Producción	Imports Importa- tions Importa- ciones	Exports Exporta- tions Exporta- ciones	Consumption Consom- mation Consumo	Consump- tion per 1,000 inh. Consomma- tion pour 1 000 hab. Consumo por 1 000 hab.	Production Production Producción	Imports Importa- tions Importa- ciones	Exports Exporta- tions Exporta- ciones	Consumption Consom- mation Consumo	Consump- tion per 1,000 inh. Consomma- tion pour 1 000 hab. Consumo por 1 000 hab.
The Former Yugoslav Rep. of Macedonia										
1970										
1975										
1980										
1985										
1990										
1993		2 100		2 100	991		6 100	300	5 800	2 737
1994		3 000		3 000	1 401		11 600	200	11 400	5 322
Ukraine										
1970										
1975										
1980										
1985										
1990										
1993		3	1 288				5 942	1 189	4 753	92
1994		3	1 288				5 942	1 189	4 753	92
United Kingdom										
1970	756 900	789 100	1 800	1 544 200	27 757	1 145 300	274 700	69 000	1 351 000	24 285
1975	319 000	943 000	4 900	1 257 100	22 358	952 000	531 000	58 400	1 424 600	25 337
1980	363 000	1 076 500	58 400	1 381 100	24 518	937 000	814 500	111 800	1 639 700	29 109
1985	382 000	1 242 000	63 000	1 561 000	27 571	965 000	1 342 000	151 000	2 156 000	38 080
1990	696 000	1 307 600	145 000	1 858 600	32 374	1 387 000	2 106 200	476 000	3 017 200	52 554
1993	741 000	1 354 340	163 033	1 932 307	33 359	1 675 000	2 155 120	685 673	3 144 447	54 286
1994	769 000	1 696 000	202 000	2 263 000	38 955	1 819 000	2 653 000	672 000	3 800 000	65 413
Federal Rep. of Yugoslavia										
1970	.	.	.	.	.	.	.	.	.	.
1975	.	.	.	.	.	.	.	.	.	.
1980	.	.	.	.	.	.	.	.	.	.
1985	.	.	.	.	.	.	.	.	.	.
1990	.	.	.	.	.	.	.	.	.	.
1993		690	4 190				2 178	472	1 706	
1994		361	4 190				1 290	472	818	
Oceania										
American Samoa										
1970										
1975										
1980										
1985										
1990										
1993		237		237	4 647		5		5	98
1994		122		122	2 302		14		14	264
Australia										
1970	173 300	275 300	100	448 500	35 780	126 300	123 000	17 100	232 200	18 524
1975	196 000	324 500	200	520 300	37 429	160 000	163 900	12 900	311 000	22 372
1980	221 000	336 800	1 200	556 600	38 204	210 000	181 100	16 200	374 900	25 733
1985	354 000	301 900	4 300	651 600	41 660	227 000	249 900	13 600	463 300	29 621
1990	371 000	288 100	400	658 700	39 004	406 000	451 400	36 000	821 400	48 638
1993	433 000	204 700	5 600	632 100	35 880	304 000	541 000	41 800	803 200	45 592
1994	461 000	206 000	2 700	664 300	37 209	348 000	581 000	46 000	883 000	49 459
Cook Islands										
1970										
1975										
1980										
1985										
1990										
1993		32		32	1 684		42		42	2 211
1994		45		45	2 368		52		52	2 737
Fiji										
1970		800		800	1 538		500		500	962
1975		900		900	1 563		2 600		2 600	4 514
1980		1 700		1 700	2 681		2 400		2 400	3 785
1985		2 000		2 000	2 861		3 000		3 000	4 292
1990		1 400		1 400	1 928		4 900		4 900	6 749
1993		2 475		2 475	3 265		1 257		1 257	1 658
1994		2 700		2 700	3 502		6 400		6 400	8 301

7.12 Newsprint, printing and writing paper
Papier journal, papier d'impression et papier d'écriture
Papel de periódico, papel de imprenta y papel de escribir

Country Year	Newsprint Papier journal Papel de periódico					Other printing and writing paper Autre papier d'impression et d'écriture Otro papel de imprenta y de escribir				
Pays Année País Año	Production Production Producción	Imports Importa-tions Importa-ciones	Exports Exporta-tions Exporta-ciones	Consumption Consom-mation Consumo	Consump-tion per 1,000 inh. Consomma-tion pour 1 000 hab. Consumo por 1 000 hab.	Production Production Producción	Imports Importa-tions Importa-ciones	Exports Exporta-tions Exporta-ciones	Consumption Consom-mation Consumo	Consump-tion per 1,000 inh. Consomma-tion pour 1 000 hab. Consumo por 1 000 hab.
French Polynesia										
1970		400		400	3 604					
1975		300		300	2 308					
1980		100		100	662					
1985										
1990		1 508		1 508	7 655					
1993		1 738		1 738	8 237		999		999	4 735
1994		1 658		1 658	7 712		1 203		1 203	5 595
Guam										
1970										
1975										
1980										
1985										
1990										
1993		552		552	3 833		9		9	63
1994		41		41	279		1		1	7
Kiribati										
1970										
1975										
1980										
1985										
1990										
1993		2		2	26		25		25	329
1994		4		4	51		43		43	551
Nauru										
1970										
1975										
1980										
1985										
1990										
1993							1		1	91
1994							4		4	364
New Caledonia										
1970										
1975		1 100		1 100	8 271					
1980		1 300		1 300	9 091					
1985		300		300	1 935					
1990		1 100		1 100	6 548		1 200		1 200	7 143
1993		933		933	5 331		1 106		1 106	6 320
1994		933		933	5 242		1 106		1 106	6 213
New Zealand										
1970	213 900	500	118 600	95 800	33 972	29 700	16 900	400	46 200	16 383
1975	219 000	2 300	106 400	114 900	37 269	34 000	12 600	300	46 300	15 018
1980	319 000	300	241 200	78 100	25 088	33 000	26 400	1 600	57 800	18 567
1985	298 000	21 100	187 000	132 100	40 684	48 000	58 400	3 500	102 900	31 691
1990	295 000	18 700	224 200	89 500	26 629	38 000	81 300	9 000	110 300	32 818
1993	369 000	624	255 509	114 115	32 745	10 000	108 170	6 065	112 105	32 168
1994	365 000	100	251 600	113 500	32 144	14 000	65 100	2 900	76 200	21 580
Niue										
1970										
1975										
1980										
1985										
1990										
1993										
1994							5		5	2 500
Papua New Guinea										
1970		600		600	248		700		700	289
1975		500		500	183					
1980										
1985										
1990										
1993		2 800		2 800	681		1 061	5	1 056	257
1994		2 940		2 940	699		1 592	5	1 587	377
Samoa										
1970		200		200	1 379		300		300	2 069
1975										
1980										
1985										
1990							100		100	625
1993		55		55	329		117		117	718
1994		140		140	828		61		61	365
							96		96	568

Newsprint, printing and writing paper **7.12**
Papier journal, papier d'impression et papier d'écriture
Papel de periódico, papel de imprenta y papel de escribir

Country Year / Pays Année / País Año	Newsprint / Papier journal / Papel de periódico					Other printing and writing paper / Autre papier d'impression et d'écriture / Otro papel de imprenta y de escribir				
	Production / Production / Producción	Imports / Importations / Importaciones	Exports / Exportations / Exportaciones	Consumption / Consommation / Consumo	Consumption per 1,000 inh. / Consommation pour 1 000 hab. / Consumo por 1 000 hab.	Production / Production / Producción	Imports / Importations / Importaciones	Exports / Exportations / Exportaciones	Consumption / Consommation / Consumo	Consumption per 1,000 inh. / Consommation pour 1 000 hab. / Consumo por 1 000 hab.
Solomon Islands										
1970										
1975										
1980										
1985										
1990										
1993		94		94	266		36		36	102
1994		134		134	366		74		74	202
Tonga										
1970										
1975										
1980										
1985										
1990										
1993		54		54	557		236		236	2 433
1994		72		72	735		126		126	1 286
Tuvalu										
1970										
1975										
1980										
1985										
1990										
1993							2		2	200
1994										
Vanuatu, Rep. of										
1970										
1975										
1980										
1985										
1990										
1993		6		6	37		30		30	186
1994		8		8	48		45		45	273

Belgium:
  E––> Including Luxembourg.

FR–> Y compris le Luxembourg.
ESP> Incluído Luxemburgo.

8 Cultural heritage

Patrimoine culturel

Patrimonio cultural

This chapter refers to cultural heritage as defined in category O of the UNESCO Framework for Cultural Statistics (FCS). Once again, only data on museums and related institutions are shown; for data on archival institutions the reader should refer to the 1990 edition of this *Yearbook*.

UNESCO's first attempt to establish international statistics on museums and related institutions was made in the early 1950s. From 1962 onward, the statistical questionnaire was sent out every two years until 1974, when it was decided that the surveys should be conducted at regular intervals of three years in view of the infrequent changes in this field.

What renders the international collection of museum statistics, and thus their comparability, relatively difficult is the almost complete absence of generally accepted standards and norms. Some countries, for instance, include in their museum statistics historical monuments and archaeological sites but leave out zoological and botanical gardens, aquaria, nature reserves, etc. In other countries it is just the reverse. Furthermore, not all countries take account of museums which are owned by individuals or private organizations.

The lack of internationally accepted definitions and classifications affects in no small measure the quality, quantity and completeness of the statistics collected. Consequently any kind of international comparison should be made with great caution.

In order to achieve at least a minimum degree of comparability the categories and terms used in the surveys since 1977 have been based on definitions established by the *International Council of Museums (ICOM)*.

For the purpose of these surveys the term *museum* is defined as *a non profit-making, permanent institution in the service of society and of its development and open to the public, which acquires, conserves, researches, communicates and exhibits, for purposes of study, education and enjoyment, material evidence of man and his environment.* In addition to museums designated as such, the following entities recognized by ICOM as being of museum nature are also included in the surveys:

    a: Conservation institutes and exhibition galleries permanently maintained by libraries and archive centres;
    b: Natural, archaeological and ethnographical monuments and sites and historical monuments and sites *of a museum nature* for their acquisition, conservation and communication activities;
    c: Institutions displaying live specimens such as botanical and zoological gardens, aquaria, vivaria, etc;
    d: Nature reserves;
    e: Science centres and planetaria.

For statistical purposes, museums and related institutions are counted by number of administrative units rather than by number of collections.

For the classification of museums and related institutions by *predominant subject of exhibits and collections* the following categories have been used:

    a: *Art museums:* museums for the display of works of fine and applied arts. Within this group fall museums of sculpture, picture galleries, museums of photography and cinema, museums of architecture, etc. Also included in

this category are conservation institutes and exhibition galleries permanently maintained by libraries and archive centres;
    b: *Archaeology and history museums:* the aim of history museums is to present the historical evolution of a region, country or province over a limited period or over the centuries. Museums of archaeology are distinguished by the fact that they owe all or part of their collections to excavations. Within this group fall museums of collections of historical objects and relics, memorial museums, museums of archives, military museums, museums of historical figures, museums of archaeology, museums of antiquities, etc;
    c: *Natural history and natural science museums:* museums for the display of subjects related to either one or several disciplines such as biology, geology, botany, zoology, palaeontology and ecology;
    d: *Science and technology museums:* museums in this category relate to one or several exact sciences or technologies such as astronomy, mathematics, physics, chemistry, medical science, construction and building industries, manufactured articles, etc. Also included in this category are planetaria and science centres;
    e: *Ethnography and anthropology museums:* museums displaying materials on culture, social structures, beliefs, customs, traditional arts, etc;
    f: *Specialized museums:* museums which are concerned with research and display of all aspects of a *single theme or subject not covered* in one of the categories (a) to (e);
    g: *Regional museums:* museums which illustrate a more or less extensive region constituting a historical and cultural entity and sometimes also an ethnic, economic or social one, i.e. the collections refer to a specific territory rather than to a specific theme or subject;
    h: *General museums:* museums which have mixed collections and cannot be identified by any one principal field;
    i: *Other museums:* museums and related institutions not included in any of the above categories;
    j: *Historical monuments and archaeological sites:* architectural or sculptural works and topographical areas of special interest from an archaeological, historical, ethnological or anthropological point of view;
    k: *Zoological and botanical gardens, aquaria and nature reserves:* the specific feature of these entities of a museum nature is that they display live specimens.

Figures on *annual attendance* for the different types of museum represent the number of *visitors*.

Data on *receipts* refer to total annual receipts and are given in the national currency.

With regard to *personnel employed* by museums and related institutions a distinction is made between *professional* and *other staff,* whereby:

    Professional staff are defined as employees doing work that requires specialized education, training or

experience. This category includes personnel such as curators, designers, librarians, technicians engaged in restoration work, taxidermists, laboratory technicians, archaeologists, etc;
Other staff (non-professional) include custodial, security and clerical staff, animal attendants, packers, cleaning personnel, etc.
A distinction is also made between *paid personnel* and *volunteers*, the latter performing tasks that otherwise would require the hiring of

paid personnel. Part-time paid staff are expressed in full-time equivalent.
Data on current expenditure refer to total annual expenditure and are shown in national currency.
Table 8.1
The figures given in this table show the number of establishments, annual attendance, receipts, personnel and current expenditure by predominant subject of collection and have been obtained through either the 1992 or 1995 survey.

Ce chapitre se réfère au patrimoine culturel décrit dans la catégorie O du *Cadre de l'UNESCO pour les statistiques culturelles (CSC)*. Une fois de plus, seules les les données relatives aux musées et institutions assimilées seront présentées. En ce qui concerne les données relatives aux institutions d'archives, le lecteur devra se reporter à l'édition de 1990 de cet *Annuaire*.

La première tentative de l'UNESCO pour établir des statistiques internationales relatives aux musées et aux institutions assimilées date du début des années cinquante. A partir de 1962, le questionnaire a été envoyé tous les deux ans jusqu'en 1974; il a été décidé alors que les enquêtes devraient être effectuées à des intervalles réguliers de trois ans, compte tenu des changements peu fréquents qui interviennent dans ce domaine.

Ce qui rend relativement difficile la collecte internationale de données statistiques sur les musées et par conséquent leur comparabilité, est l'absence presque complète de normes et de classifications généralement acceptées. Quelques pays, par exemple, comprennent dans leurs statistiques sur les musées, les monuments historiques et les sites archéologiques mais ne tiennent pas compte des jardins zoologiques et botaniques, des aquariums et réserves naturelles, etc. Pour d'autres pays, c'est juste le contraire qui se produit. De plus, tous les pays ne prennent pas en considération les musées qui appartiennent à des particuliers ou à des organismes privés.

Le manque de définitions et de classifications qui soient acceptées du point de vue international affecte sensiblement la qualité, la quantité et la portée des statistiques recueillies. Par conséquent, toute sorte de comparaison internationale doit être effectuée avec beaucoup de prudence.

Dans le but d'assurer un minimum de comparabilité, les catégories et les termes utilisés dans les enquêtes depuis 1977 ont été choisis sur la base des définitions établies par le *Conseil International des Musées (ICOM)*.

Aux fins de ces enquêtes, par *musée* on entend *une institution permanente sans but lucratif au service de la société et de son développement, ouverte au public, qui acquiert, conserve, étudie, communique et expose, à des fins de recherche et d'éducation et pour l'agrément, des objets portant témoignage sur l'homme et son environnement*. Outre les musées désignés comme tels, les entités ci-après, reconnues par l'ICOM comme ayant la nature de musées, sont également couvertes par les enquêtes:
a: Les instituts de conservation et galeries d'exposition dépendant des bibliothèques et des centres d'archives;
b: Les sites et monuments archéologiques, ethnographiques et naturels, les sites et monuments historiques *ayant un caractère de musée* par leurs activités d'acquisition, de conservation et de communication;
c: Les institutions qui présentent des spécimens vivants, tels que les jardins botaniques et zoologiques, aquariums, vivariums, etc.;
d: Les réserves naturelles;
e: Les centres scientifiques et planétariums.

Les unités statistiques correspondent, pour les musées et institutions assimilées, aux unités administratives et non au nombre de collections.

Pour la classification des musées et institutions assimilées *d'après la nature prédominante des sujets exposés et des collections* les catégories suivantes ont été utilisées:
a: *Musées d'art:* musées consacrés aux beaux-arts et aux arts appliqués. Ce groupe comprend les musées de sculpture, les galeries de peinture, les musées de la photographie et du cinéma, les musées d'architecture, etc. Les instituts de conservation et galeries d'exposition dépendant des bibliothèques et des centres d'archives sont également compris dans cette catégorie.
b: *Musées d'archéologie et d'histoire:* les musées d'histoire ont pour but de présenter l'évolution historique d'une région, d'un pays ou d'une province pour des périodes limitées dans le temps ou au cours des siècles. Les musées d'archéologie se distinguent par le fait que leurs collections proviennent en partie ou en totalité de fouilles. Ce groupe englobe les musées de collections

d'objets historiques ou de vestiges, musées commémoratifs, musées d'archives, musées militaires, musées de personnalités historiques, musées d'archéologie, musées d'antiquités, etc.;
c: *Musées de science et d'histoire naturelles:* musées consacrés aux sujets se rapportant à une ou à plusieurs disciplines telles que la biologie, la géologie, la botanique, la zoologie, la paléontologie et l'écologie;
d: *Musées des sciences et des techniques:* musées consacrés aux sujets se rapportant à une ou plusieurs sciences exactes ou techniques telles que l'astronomie, les mathématiques, la physique, la chimie, les sciences médicales, la construction et les industries du bâtiment, les articles manufacturés, etc. Sont également inclus dans cette catégorie les planétariums et les centres scientifiques.
e: *Musées d'ethnographie et d'anthropologie:* musées qui exposent des matériels se rapportant à la culture, aux structures sociales, aux croyances, aux coutumes, aux arts traditionnels, etc.
f: *Musées spécialisés:* musées concernés par la recherche et l'exposition de tous aspects relatifs à *un thème ou sujet unique* non inclus dans l'une des catégories (a) à (e).
g: *Musées régionaux:* musées dont le thème illustre une région plus ou moins étendue constituant une entité historique et culturelle et parfois même une entité ethnique, économique ou sociale, c'est-à-dire dont les collections se rapportent davantage à un territoire spécifique qu'à un thème ou à un sujet particulier;
h: *Musées généraux:* musées ayant des collections hétérogènes et ne pouvant pas être identifiés par un domaine principal;
i: *Autres musées:* musées et institutions assimilées n'entrant dans aucune des catégories précédentes;
j: *Monuments historiques et sites archéologiques protégés:* travaux architecturaux et sculpturaux et zones topographiques présentant un intérêt spécial des points de vue archéologique, historique, ethnologique ou anthropologique;
k: *Jardins zoologiques et botaniques, aquariums et réserves naturelles:* Leur caractéristique spécifique est qu'ils présentent des spécimens vivants;

Les données statistiques concernant la *fréquentation annuelle* des différents types de musées représentent le nombre de *visiteurs.*

Les données sur les *recettes* se réfèrent au total des recettes annuelles exprimé en monnaie nationale.

En ce qui concerne le *personnel employé* par les musées et autres institutions assimilées une distinction est établie entre le *personnel professionnel* et *l'autre personnel* comme suit:
Le *personnel professionnel* se rapporte aux employés exécutant un travail nécessitant une formation, une instruction ou une expérience spécialisées. Cette catégorie inclut du personnel tel que les administrateurs, réalisateurs, bibliothécaires, restaurateurs, taxidermistes, techniciens de laboratoire, archéologues, etc.
L'*autre personnel* (non professionnel) comprend les gardiens, responsables des services de sécurité, commis, soigneurs d'animaux, emballeurs, personnel de nettoyage, etc.

Une distinction est aussi établie entre les *salariés* et les *volontaires*, ces derniers faisant des travaux qui, autrement, nécessiteraient l'embauche de salariés. Le personnel salarié à temps partiel est indiqué en équivalent plein temps.

Les données sur les *dépenses de fonctionnement* se réfèrent au total annuel de ces dépenses exprimé en monnaie nationale.
Tableau 8.1
Les chiffres présentés dans ce tableau montrent le nombre d'établissements, la fréquentation annuelle, les recettes, les dépenses pour le personnel et les dépenses ordinaires d'après la nature prédominante de leurs collections et proviennent soit de l'enquête de 1992 soit de celle de 1995.

Este capítulo se refiere al patrimonio cultural, tal como se indica en la categoría O del Marco de las Estadísticas Culturales de la UNESCO (MEC). Una vez más se presentan solamente los datos relativos a los museos e instituciones conexas. En lo que concierne las instituciones de archivos el lector deberá referirse a la edición de 1990 del *Anuario Estadístico* de la UNESCO.

La primera tentativa de la UNESCO para establecer estadísticas internacionales relativas a los museos e instituciones conexas se situa a principios de los años cincuenta. A partir de 1962 y hasta 1974 los cuestionarios estadísticos se envían cada dos años, decidiéndose en 1974 que la encuesta se efectuaría a intervalos regulares de tres años, dado que los cambios que se producen en esta materia son poco frecuentes.

Lo que rinde relativamente difícil la recolección internacional de datos estadísticos sobre museos y por consiguiente su comparabilidad, es la ausencia casi completa de normas y de clasificaciones generalmente aceptadas. Algunos países, por ejemplo, comprenden en las estadísticas relativas a los museos los monumentos históricos y lugares arqueológicos pero no tienen en cuenta los jardines zoológicos y botánicos, los acuarios y reservas naturales, etc. En otros países, es lo contrario que se produce. Además, no todos los países toman en consideración los museos que pertenecen a particulares o a organismos privados.

La falta de definiciones y de clasificaciones internacionalmente aceptadas, afecta sensiblemente la calidad, la cantidad y el alcance de las estadísticas reunidas. Por consiguiente, toda clase de comparaciones internacionales deben efectuarse con mucha prudencia.

Con vistas a asegurar un mínimo de comparabilidad, las categorías y los términos utilizados en las encuestas que comenzaron en 1977 han sido redactados sobre la base de las definiciones establecidas por el *Consejo Internacional de Museos (ICOM)*.

Para los fines de esta encuesta, un *museo* significa *una institución permanente, sin fines lucrativos, al servicio de la sociedad y de su desarrollo, abierta al público y que efectua investigaciones sobre los testimonios materiales del hombre y de su medio ambiente, adquiridos, conservados, comunicados y sobre todo expuestos para fines de estudio, de educación y de deleite.* Además de los museos citados, las entidades siguientes, también reconocidas por el ICOM como museos, se tomarán en consideración en esta encuesta:

a: Los institutos de conservación y las galerías de exposición que dependen de las bibliotecas y de los centros de archivo;

b: Los sitios y monumentos arqueológicos, etnográficos y naturales y los lugares y monumentos históricos que por su actividades de adquisición, de conservación y de comunicación tienen *el carácter de un museo;*

c: Las instituciones que exponen especies vivientes, tales como los jardines botánicos y zoológicos, los acuarios, los viveros, etc.;

d: Las reservas naturales;

e: Los planetariums y los centros científicos.

Con referencia a la unidad estadística empleada, los museos y las instituciones conexas son contados según el número de unidades administrativas y no según el número de colecciones.

Para la clasificación de los museos y de las instituciones conexas según la *naturaleza predominante de sus exposiciones y de sus colecciones,* se han utilizado las categorías siguientes:

a: *Museos de arte:* museos para la exposición de obras de bellas artes y de artes aplicadas. Forman parte de este grupo museos tales como las galerías de pintura, los museos de escultura, museos de fotografía y de cinematografía, museos de arquitectura, etc. De esta categoría forman parte también los institutos de conservación y las galerías de exposición que dependen de las bibliotecas y de los centros de archivo;

b: *Museos de arqueología y de historia:* los museos de historia son aquellos cuya finalidad es la de presentar la evolución histórica de una región, país o provincia durante un período determinado o a través de los siglos. Los museos de arqueología se distinguen por el hecho de que sus colecciones provienen en todo o en parte de excavaciones. De este grupo forman parte los museos de

colecciones de objetos históricos y de vestigios, museos conmemorativos, museos de archivos, museos militares, museos de figuras históricas, museos de arqueología, museos de antiguedades, etc.;

c: *Museos de historia y ciencias naturales:* museos para la exposición de temas relacionados con una o varias disciplinas como biología, geología, botánica, zoología, paleontología, ecología;

d: *Museos de ciencia y de tecnología:* los museos de esta categoría se dedican a una o varias ciencias exactas o tecnológicas tales como astronomía, matemáticas, física, química, ciencias médicas, industrias de la construcción, artículos manufacturados, etc.; incluídos igualmente en esta categoría están los planetariums y los centros científicos.

e: *Museos de etnografía y de antropología:* museos que exponen materiales sobre la cultura, las estructuras sociales, las creencias, las costumbres, las artes tradicionales, etc.;

f: *Museos especializados:* museos que se ocupan de la investigación y exposición de todos los aspectos de un solo tema o sujeto que no esté cubierto en ninguna de las categorias a) a e);

g: *Museos regionales:* museos que ilustran una región más o menos extensa que constituye una entidad histórica y cultural y, algunas veces, también étnica, económica o social, es decir, que las colecciones se refieren más a un territorio determinado que a un tema o sujeto particular;

h: *Museos generales:* museos que poseen colecciones mixtas y que no pueden ser identificados por su esfera principal;

i: *Otros museos:* museos e instituciones conexas que no están cubiertos en una de las anteriores categorías.

j: *Monumentos históricos y sitios arqueológicos protegidos:* obras arquitectónicas o esculturales y zonas topográficas que presentan especial interés desde un punto de vista arqueológico, histórico, etnológico o antropológico;

k: *Jardines zoológicos y botánicos, acuarios y reservas naturales:* la característica específica de estas entidades es la de exponer especímenes vivientes;

Los datos sobre la *frecuentación anual* en los diferentes tipos de museos se refieren al número de *visitantes.* ‡Los datos sobre los *ingresos* se refieren al total de los ingresos anuales indicados en moneda nacional.

Con respecto al *personal empleado* en los museos e instituciones conexas, se establece una distinción entre personal *profesional* y *otro* personal, como sigue:

Personal profesional: son los empleados cuyo trabajo requiere una enseñanza, una formación profesional o una experiencia especializadas. Esta categoría incluye los conservadores, dibujantes, bibliotecarios, técnicos de los servicios de restauración, taxidermistas, técnicos de laboratorio, arqueólogos, etc.

Otro personal (no profesional) incluye los guardianes, el servicio de seguridad y los empleados de despacho, los cuidadores de animales, los embaladores, el personal de limpieza, etc.

También se hace una distinción entre los empleados *remunerados* y los *voluntarios,* estos últimos efectuando trabajos que en otro caso requerirían el empleo de personal remunerado. El personal remunerado de jornada parcial será indicado en equivalente a jornada completa.

Los datos sobre los *gastos ordinarios* se refieren al total anual de los gastos ordinarios, que será indicado en moneda nacional.

Cuadro 8.1

Las cifras en este cuadro presentan la cantidad de establecimientos, la frecuentación anual, los ingresos, los gastos de personal y los gastos ordinarios, de acuerdo con la naturaleza predominante de las colecciones cuya descripción proviene, sea de la encuesta de 1992 o de la de 1995.

8.1 Museums and related institutions
Musées et institutions assimilées
Museos e instituciones conexas

8.1 Museums by subject of collection and related institutions by type: number, annual attendance, receipts, personnel and current expenditure

Musées d'après la nature des collections et institutions assimilées par type: nombre, fréquentation annuelle, recettes, personnel et dépenses ordinaires

Museos según la naturaleza de sus colecciones e instituciones conexas según el tipo: número, frecuentación anual, ingresos, personal y gastos ordinarios

Subject of collection or type of institution:
1. Art museums
2. Archaeology and history museums
3. Natural history and natural science museums
4. Science and technology museums
5. Ethnography and anthropology museums
6. Specialized museums
7. Regional museums
8. General museums
9. Other museums

   Historical and archaeological monuments and sites
   Zoos, botanical gardens, etc.

Annual current expenditure and receipts are expressed in national currency

Nature des collections ou type d'institution:
1. Musées d'art
2. Musées d'archéologie et d'histoire
3. Musées de science et d'histoire naturelles
4. Musées des sciences et des techniques
5. Musées d'éthnographie et d'anthropologie
6. Musées spécialisés
7. Musées régionaux
8. Musées généraux
9. Autres musées

   Monuments et sites historiques et archéologiques
   Jardins zoologiques et botaniques, etc.

Les dépenses ordinaires et les recettes annuelles sont exprimées en monnaie nationale

Country / Pays / País	Year / Année / Año	Subject of collection or type of institution / Nature des collections ou type d'institution / Naturaleza de las colecciones o tipo de institución	Total number of museums / Nombre total de musées / Número total de museos	Attendance Fréquentation Frecuentación — Number of museums reporting / Nombre de musées ayant fourni ces données / Número de museos que dieron este dato	Attendance — Number of visitors (000) / Nombre de visiteurs (000) / Número de visitantes (000)	Annual receipts Recettes annuelles Ingresos anuales — Number of museums reporting / Nombre de musées ayant fourni ces données / Número de museos que dieron este dato	Annual receipts — Total (000) / Total (000) / Total (000)
			(1)	(2)	(3)	(4)	(5)
Africa							
Benin‡	1990	Total museums	6	6	8	6	1 884
		Monuments and sites	12	-	...	-	...
		Zoos, botanical gardens, etc.	3	-	...	-	...
Botswana	1993	Total museums	1	1	40	1	40
		8. General museums	1	1	40	1	40
Burkina Faso	1990	Total museums	6	1	300	1	807
		2. Archaeology and history	1	-	...	-	...
		3. Nat. history & nat. science	1	-	...	-	...
		5. Ethnography & anthropology	2	-	...	-	...
		7. Regional museums	2	1	300	1	807
		Monuments and sites	1	-	...	-	...
Burundi	1990	Total museums	2	2	18	2	958
		Monuments and sites	1	1	.3	1	44
Egypt	1993	Total museums	50	50	4 241	50	7 781
		1. Art	35	35	3 600	35	7 693
		3. Nat. history & nat. science	15	15	641	15	88
		Zoos, botanical gardens, etc.	15	15	7 762	15	3 588
Equatorial Guinea‡	1993	Total museums	1	-	...	-	...
		Zoos, botanical gardens, etc.	1	-	...	-	...

Museums and related institutions 8.1
Musées et institutions assimilées
Museos e instituciones conexas

Naturaleza de las colecciones o tipo de institución:
1. Museos de arte
2. Museos de arqueología y de historia
3. Museos de historia y ciencias naturales
4. Museos de ciencia y de tecnología
5. Museos de etnografía y de antropología
6. Museos especializados
7. Museos regionales
8. Museos generales
9. Otros museos

   Monumentos y sitios históricos y arqueológicos
   Jardines zoológicos y botánicos, etc.

Los gastos ordinarios y los ingresos anuales se
presentan en moneda nacional.

Personnel / Personnel / Personal						Annual current expenditure / Dépenses annuelles ordinaires / Gastos ordinarios anuales		
Number of museums reporting / Nombre de musées ayant fourni ces données / Número de museos que dieron este dato	Total staff / Total du personnel / Total de personal	Professional staff / Personnel professionnel / Personal professional		Other staff / Autre personnel / Otro personal		Number of museums reporting / Nombre de musées ayant fourni ces données / Número de museos que dieron este dato	Total (000) / Total (000) / Total (000)	Country / Pays / País
		Paid staff / Salariés / Remunerados	Volunteers / Volontaires / Voluntarios	Paid staff / Salariés / Remunerados	Volunteers / Volontaires / Voluntarios			
(6)	(7)	(8)	(9)	(10)	(11)	(12)	(13)	
								Africa
6	58	58	-	./.	-	6	19 448	Benin‡
-	...	...	...	...	...	-	...	
-	...	...	...	...	...	-	...	
1	114	46	-	68	-	1	115	Botswana
1	114	46	-	68	-	1	115	
1	8	-	-	3	5	1	685	Burkina Faso
-	...	...	...	...	...	-	...	
-	...	...	...	...	...	-	...	
1	8	-	-	3	5	1	685	
-	...	...	...	...	...	-	...	
2	31	3	-	28	-	2	881	Burundi
1	4	1	-	3	-	1	4	
50	1 971	...	...	...	...	-	...	Egypt
35	1 321	...	...	...	...	-	...	
15	650	...	...	...	...	-	...	
15	1 152	...	...	...	...	-	...	
1	5	5	-	-	-	1	1 920	Equatorial Guinea‡
1	20	20	7	-	-	1	5 000	

8.1 Museums and related institutions
Musées et institutions assimilées
Museos e instituciones conexas

Country / Pays / País	Year / Année / Año	Subject of collection or type of institution / Nature des collections ou type d'institution / Naturaleza de las colecciones o tipo de institución	Total number of museums / Nombre total de musées / Número total de museos	Attendance Fréquentation Frecuentación		Annual receipts Recettes annuelles Ingresos anuales	
				Number of museums reporting / Nombre de musées ayant fourni ces données / Número de museos que dieron este dato	Number of visitors (000) / Nombre de visiteurs (000) / Número de visitantes (000)	Number of museums reporting / Nombre de musées ayant fourni ces données / Número de museos que dieron este dato	Total (000)
			(1)	(2)	(3)	(4)	(5)
Eritrea	1993	Total museums	4	4	300	-	...
		2. Archaeology and history	1	-	...	-	...
		3. Nat. history & nat. science	1	-	...	-	...
		5. Ethnography & anthropology	1	-	...	-	...
		9. Other museums	1	-	...	-	...
		Monuments and sites	13	-	...	-	...
		Zoos, botanical gardens, etc.	2	-	...	-	...
Ethiopia	1993	Total museums	1	1	10	1	37
		8. General museums	1	1	10	1	37
Madagascar‡	1990	Total museums	5	5	134	-	...
		2. Archaeology and history	4	4	127	-	...
		5. Ethnography & anthropology	1	1	7	-	...
		Monuments and sites	155	-	...	-	...
Mali	1993	Total museums	3	1	10	-	...
		7. Regional museums	2	-	...	-	...
		8. General museums	1	1	10	-	...
		Zoos, botanical gardens, etc.	1	-	...	-	...
Mauritius	1993	Total museums	5	5	350	-	...
		2. Archaeology and history	1	1	50	-	...
		3. Nat. history & nat. science	1	1	275	-	...
		9. Other museums	3	3	25	-	...
Morocco	1990	Total museums	14	14	222	14	1 940
		1. Art	1	1	1	1	12
		2. Archaeology and history	3	3	12	3	103
		5. Ethnography & anthropology	8	8	189	8	1 653
		6. Specialized museums	2	2	20	2	172
Niger‡	1989	Total museums	3	1	450	1	30 000
		1. Art	1	1	450	1	30 000
		7. Regional museums	2	-	...	-	...
		Monuments and sites	32	-	...	-	...
		Zoos, botanical gardens, etc.	6	-	...	-	...
Nigeria	1990	Total museums	12	12	267	12	19
		2. Archaeology and history	2	2	40	-	...
		5. Ethnography & anthropology	8	8	113	-	...
		6. Specialized museums	1	1	19	-	...
		9. Other museums	1	1	95	-	...
		Monuments and sites	62	-	...	-	...
		Zoos, botanical gardens, etc.	3	-	...	-	...
Seychelles	1990	Total museums	2	2	10	-	...
		8. General museums	1	1	9	-	...
		9. Other museums	1	1	1	-	...
Togo	1993	Total museums	8	-	...	-	...
		Zoos, botanical gardens, etc.	12	2	4	2	6 000

Museums and related institutions 8.1
Musées et institutions assimilées
Museos e instituciones conexas

	Personnel / Personnel / Personal					Annual current expenditure / Dépenses annuelles ordinaires / Gastos ordinarios anuales		
Number of museums reporting		Professional staff / Personnel professionnel / Personal professional		Other staff / Autre personnel / Otro personal		Number of museums reporting	Total (000)	Country
Nombre de musées ayant fourni ces données	Total staff	Paid staff	Volunteers	Paid staff	Volunteers	Nombre de musées ayant fourni ces données	Total (000)	Pays
Número de museos que dieron este dato	Total du personnel / Total de personal	Salariés / Remunerados	Volontaires / Voluntarios	Salariés / Remunerados	Volontaires / Voluntarios	Número de museos que dieron este dato	Total (000)	País
(6)	(7)	(8)	(9)	(10)	(11)	(12)	(13)	
3	17	3	-	14	-	-	...	Eritrea
-	...	...	...	...	...	-	...	
-	...	...	...	...	...	-	...	
-	...	...	...	...	...	-	...	
-	...	...	...	6	...	-	...	
-	...	...	...	...	...		...	
1	35	17	-	18	-	1	35	Ethiopia
1	35	17	-	18	-	1	35	
5	32	32	...	...	...	5	28 502	Madagascar‡
4	30	30	...	...	...	-	...	
1	2	2	...	...	...	-	...	
-	...	...	...	...	...	9	336 999	
1	50	40	-	10	-	-	...	Mali
-	...	...	...	...	...	-	...	
1	50	40	-	10	-	-	...	
-	...	...	...	...	...	-	...	
5	35	7	...	28	-	5	4 600	Mauritius
1	8	2	...	6	...	-	...	
1	17	3	...	14	...	-	...	
3	10	2	...	8	...	-	...	
14	82	...	...	...	...	14	550	Morocco
1	2	...	...	...	...	1	100	
3	25	...	...	...	...	3	52	
8	50	...	...	...	...	8	341	
2	5	...	...	...	...	2	57	
1	87	87	-	-	-	1	30 000	Niger‡
1	87	87	-	-	-	1	30 000	
-	...	...	...	...	...	-	...	
-	...	...	...	...	...	-	...	
-	...	...	...	...	...	-	...	
12	4 000	1 826	-	2 174	-	12	19	Nigeria
-	...	...	...	...	...	-	...	
-	...	...	...	...	...	-	...	
-	...	...	...	...	...	-	...	
-	...	...	...	...	...	-	...	
-	...	...	...	...	...	-	...	
2	13	1	...	12	...	2	937	Seychelles
1	8	1	...	7	...	-	...	
1	5	-	...	5	...	-	...	
2	38	11	-	27	-	-	...	Togo
2	352	352	-	-	-	-	...	

8.1   Museums and related institutions
Musées et institutions assimilées
Museos e instituciones conexas

Country Pays País	Year Année Año	Subject of collection or type of institution Nature des collections ou type d'institution Naturaleza de las colecciones o tipo de institución	Total number of museums Nombre total de musées Número total de museos	Attendance Fréquentation Frecuentación		Annual receipts Recettes annuelles Ingresos anuales	
				Number of museums reporting Nombre de musées ayant fourni ces données Número de museos que dieron este dato	Number of visitors (000) Nombre de visiteurs (000) Número de visitantes (000)	Number of museums reporting Nombre de musées ayant fourni ces données Número de museos que dieron este dato	Total (000) Total (000) Total (000)
			(1)	(2)	(3)	(4)	(5)
United Republic of Tanzania	1993	Total museums	7	4	23	4	87
		2. Archaeology and history	1	1	2	1	9
		3. Nat. history & nat. science	1	1	3	1	11
		5. Ethnography & anthropology	1	1	6	1	23
		7. Regional museums	3	-	...	-	...
		8. General museums	1	1	12	1	44
Zambia	1993	Total museums	10	6	185	-	...
		2. Archaeology and history	1	1	35	-	...
		4. Science and technology	1	1	25	-	...
		5. Ethnography & anthropology	3	2	50	-	...
		6. Specialized museums	3	-	-	-	...
		8. General museums	2	2	75	-	...
		Zoos, botanical gardens, etc.	20	-	...	-	...
Zimbabwe	1990	Total museums	11	11	100	11	1 000
		2. Archaeology and history	2	-	...	-	...
		3. Nat. history & nat. science	1	-	...	-	...
		4. Science and technology	1	-	...	-	...
		5. Ethnography & anthropology	1	-	...	-	...
		9. Other museums	6	-	...	-	...
		Monuments and sites	166	-	...	-	...
		Zoos, botanical gardens, etc.	1	-	...	-	...
America, North							
Bahamas	1993	Total museums	9	2	11 303	2	8 502
		2. Archaeology and history	6	1	7 069	1	5 342
		6. Specialized museums	2	-	...	-	...
		8. General museums	1	1	4 234	1	3 160
		Monuments and sites	3	-	...	-	...
		Zoos, botanical gardens, etc.	2	-	...	-	...
Barbados	1993	Total museums	6	4	62	4	587
		1. Art	2	1	20	1	30
		6. Specialized museums	3	2	8	2	20
		8. General museums	1	1	34	1	537
		Monuments and sites	17	5	281	5	3 217
		Zoos, botanical gardens, etc.	5	4	186	4	1 748
Canada‡	1990	Total museums	1 352	1 327	27 302	1 252	431 319
		1. Art	186	182	5 772	179	128 066
		2. Archaeology and history	149	147	4 392	138	77 269
		3. Nat. history & nat. science	40	40	1 132	37	22 847
		4. Science and technology	63	60	4 226	52	56 246
		6. Specialized museums	66	65	1 606	58	9 181
		7. Regional museums	705	695	3 332	655	31 366
		8. General museums	23	23	3 655	23	77 708
		9. Other museums	120	115	3 187	110	28 636
		Monuments and sites	368	361	16 946	353	118 607
		Zoos, botanical gardens, etc.	196	188	65 512	192	299 698
Costa Rica‡	1994	Total museums	38	19	733	-	...
		1. Art	5	2	69	-	...
		2. Archaeology and history	11	7	436	-	...
		3. Nat. history & nat. science	4	3	57	-	...
		4. Science and technology	2	2	141	-	...
		5. Ethnography & anthropology	1	1	10	-	...
		7. Regional museums	9	4	20	-	...
		9. Other museums	6	-	...	-	...

Museums and related institutions 8.1
Musées et institutions assimilées
Museos e instituciones conexas

		Personnel / Personnel / Personal				Annual current expenditure / Dépenses annuelles ordinaires / Gastos ordinarios anuales		
Number of museums reporting		Professional staff / Personnel professionnel / Personal professional		Other staff / Autre personnel / Otro personal		Number of museums reporting	Total (000)	Country
Nombre de musées ayant fourni ces données	Total staff	Paid staff	Volunteers	Paid staff	Volunteers	Nombre de musées ayant fourni ces données	Total (000)	Pays
Número de museos que dieron este dato	Total du personnel / Total de personal	Salariés / Remunerados	Volontaires / Voluntarios	Salariés / Remunerados	Volontaires / Voluntarios	Número de museos que dieron este dato	Total (000)	País
(6)	(7)	(8)	(9)	(10)	(11)	(12)	(13)	
4	119	119	-	-	-	4	87	United Republic of Tanzania
1	13	13	-	-	-	1	9	
1	15	15	-	-	-	1	11	
1	31	31	-	-	-	-	23	
-	...	...	-	-	-	-	...	
1	60	60	-	-	-	1	44	
4	153	29	-	124	-	4	340	Zambia
-	...	...	-	...	-	-	...	
1	25	2	-	23	-	1	33	
1	40	5	-	35	-	1	74	
-	-	-	-	-	-	-	-	
2	88	22	-	66	-	2	233	
-	...	...	...	...	...	-	...	
11	654	600	4	50	-	5	7 000	Zimbabwe
-	...	...	...	...	...	-	...	
-	...	...	...	...	...	-	...	
-	...	...	...	...	...	-	...	
-	...	...	...	...	...	-	...	
-	...	...	...	...	...	-	...	
-	...	...	...	...	...	-	...	
								America, North
5	22	11	1	10	9	1	7 250	Bahamas
3	6	2	-	4	2	-	...	
1	6	2	1	3	-	-	...	
1	10	7	...	3	7	1	7 250	
-	...	...	...	...	...	-	...	
-	...	...	...	...	...	-	...	
4	87	12	35	30	10	3	829	Barbados
1	6	3	...	3	...	1	134	
2	12	2	-	10	-	1	26	
1	69	7	35	17	10	1	669	
5	65	9	-	56	-	4	308	
4	67	11	10	43	3	3	1 162	
1 239	8 816	7 504	1 312	./.	./.	1 212	412 513	Canada‡
179	2 310	1 937	373	./.	./.	174	126 719	
139	1 308	1 207	101	./.	./.	133	72 604	
38	450	423	27	./.	./.	35	21 220	
53	1 128	1 035	93	./.	./.	49	55 322	
59	329	218	111	./.	./.	57	8 590	
637	1 365	1 014	351	./.	./.	633	29 553	
23	1 357	1 175	182	./.	./.	23	71 209	
111	569	495	74	./.	./.	108	27 296	
347	3 472	3 239	233	./.	./.	345	109 228	
191	5 965	5 855	110	./.	./.	192	248 249	
23	327	94	-	233	-	9	64 650	Costa Rica‡
4	49	13	-	36	-	1	3 200	
7	156	53	-	103	-	6	49 450	
2	10	4	-	6	-	-	...	
2	96	17	-	79	-	-	...	
1	6	3	-	3	-	-	...	
7	10	4	-	6	-	2	12 000	
-	...	...	...	...	...	-	...	

8.1 Museums and related institutions
Musées et institutions assimilées
Museos e instituciones conexas

Country / Pays / País	Year / Année / Año	Subject of collection or type of institution / Nature des collections ou type d'institution / Naturaleza de las colecciones o tipo de institución	Total number of museums / Nombre total de musées / Número total de museos	Attendance Fréquentation Frecuentación		Annual receipts Recettes annuelles Ingresos anuales	
				Number of museums reporting / Nombre de musées ayant fourni ces données / Número de museos que dieron este dato	Number of visitors (000) / Nombre de visiteurs (000) / Número de visitantes (000)	Number of museums reporting / Nombre de musées ayant fourni ces données / Número de museos que dieron este dato	Total (000) / Total (000) / Total (000)
			(1)	(2)	(3)	(4)	(5)
Cuba‡	1990	Total museums	216	216	6 734	-	...
		1. Art	15	15	813	-	...
		2. Archaeology and history	3	3	30	-	...
		3. Nat. history & nat. science	58	58	2 183	-	...
		5. Ethnography & anthropology	1	1	1	-	...
		7. Regional museums	128	128	3 551	-	...
		9. Other museums	11	11	156	-	...
		Zoos, botanical gardens, etc.	10	10	6 969	2	1 981
Mexico‡	1990	Total museums	93	1	9 883	-	...
		2. Archaeology and history	...	1	9 883	-	
Panama	1990	Total museums	11	11	51	9	3 809
		1. Art	1	1	3	1	624
		2. Archaeology and history	1	1	2	-	...
		3. Nat. history & nat. science	1	1	2	1	53
		4. Science and technology	1	1	11	1	936
		6. Specialized museums	1	1	2	1	56
		7. Regional museums	5	5	11	5	2 140
		9. Other museums	1	1	20	-	...
		Monuments and sites	57	-	...	-	...
St. Lucia	1993	Total museums	2	1	53	1	445
		6. Specialized museums	2	1	53	1	445
		Zoos, botanical gardens, etc.	4	2	5	2	118
America, South							
Chile	1993	Total museums	26	25	648	23	133 799
		1. Art	4	4	155	4	33 083
		2. Archaeology and history	7	7	162	5	17 030
		3. Nat. history & nat. science	3	3	162	3	33 724
		5. Ethnography & anthropology	4	4	56	4	13 485
		6. Specialized museums	3	2	54	2	12 656
		7. Regional museums	5	5	59	5	23 821
Guyana	1990	Total museums	2	2	120	-	...
		5. Ethnography & anthropology	1	1	.3	-	...
		8. General museums	1	1	120	-	...
Venezuela	1990	Total museums	165	-	...	-	...
		1. Art	57	-	...	-	...
		2. Archaeology and history	36	-	...	-	...
		3. Nat. history & nat. science	7	-	...	-	...
		4. Science and technology	16	-	...	-	...
		5. Ethnography & anthropology	20	-	...	-	...
		6. Specialized museums	6	-	...	-	...
		7. Regional museums	3	-	...	-	...
		8. General museums	8	-	...	-	...
		9. Other museums	12	-	...	-	...
		Monuments and sites	635	-	...	-	...
Asia							
Armenia	1993	Total museums	74	54	300	54	75 969
		1. Art	22	17	64	17	37 800
		2. Archaeology and history	31	23	136	23	29 450
		5. Ethnography & anthropology	7	5	96	5	1 900
		7. Regional museums	14	9	4	9	6 819
		Monuments and sites	228 000	-	...	-	...
		Zoos, botanical gardens, etc.	6	-	...	-	...

Museums and related institutions 8.1
Musées et institutions assimilées
Museos e instituciones conexas

Number of museums reporting / Nombre de musées ayant fourni ces données / Número de museos que dieron este dato	Total staff / Total du personnel / Total de personal	Professional staff Personnel professionnel Personal professional		Other staff Autre personnel Otro personal		Number of museums reporting / Nombre de musées ayant fourni ces données / Número de museos que dieron este dato	Total (000) / Total (000) / Total (000)	Country / Pays / País
		Paid staff / Salariés / Remunerados	Volunteers / Volontaires / Voluntarios	Paid staff / Salariés / Remunerados	Volunteers / Volontaires / Voluntarios			
(6)	(7)	(8)	(9)	(10)	(11)	(12)	(13)	
216	3 038	683	-	2 355	-	-	...	Cuba‡
15	292	52	-	240	-	-	...	
3	12	7	-	5	-	-	...	
58	879	200	-	679	-	-	...	
1	2	-	-	2	-	-	...	
128	1 755	398	-	1 357	-	-	...	
11	98	26	-	72	-	-	...	
-	...	...	...	...	...	-	...	
1	1 627	242	...	1 253	...	-	...	Mexico‡
1	1 627	242	...	1 253	...	-	...	
11	65	43	22	-	-	-	...	Panama
1	7	7	-	-	-	-	...	
1	8	6	2	-	-	-	...	
1	6	3	3	-	-	-	...	
1	17	5	12	-	-	-	...	
1	3	3	-	-	-	-	...	
5	19	14	5	-	-	-	...	
1	5	5	-	-	-	-	...	
1	35	35	-	-	-	-	...	
1	18	2	-	16	-	1	469	St. Lucia
1	18	2	-	16	-	1	469	
2	17	14	-	3	-	2	124	
								America, South
23	248	84	5	159	-	23	121 052	Chile
4	69	20	5	44	-	4	26 541	
5	34	10	-	24	-	5	15 627	
3	87	38	-	49	-	3	33 122	
4	14	3	-	11	-	4	12 969	
2	8	2	-	6	-	2	10 009	
5	36	11	-	25	-	5	22 784	
2	28	5	-	23	-	2	1 312	Guyana
1	4	2	-	2	-	1	250	
1	24	3	-	21	-	1	1 062	
-	...	...	...	...	...	-	...	Venezuela
-	...	...	...	...	...	-	...	
-	...	...	...	...	...	-	...	
-	...	...	...	...	...	-	...	
-	...	...	...	...	...	-	...	
-	...	...	...	...	...	-	...	
-	...	...	...	...	...	-	...	
-	...	...	...	...	...	-	...	
								Asia
54	1 204	430	-	774	-	54	345 200	Armenia
17	430	155	-	275	-	17	100 200	
23	470	198	-	272	-	23	155 000	
5	214	37	-	177	-	5	52 000	
9	90	40	-	50	-	9	38 000	
-	...	...	...	...	...	-	...	
-	...	...	...	...	...	-	...	

Museums and related institutions
Musées et institutions assimilées
Museos e instituciones conexas

Country / Pays / País	Year / Année / Año	Subject of collection or type of institution / Nature des collections ou type d'institution / Naturaleza de las colecciones o tipo de institución	Total number of museums / Nombre total de musées / Número total de museos	Attendance Fréquentation Frecuentación		Annual receipts Recettes annuelles Ingresos anuales	
				Number of museums reporting / Nombre de musées ayant fourni ces données / Número de museos que dieron este dato	Number of visitors (000) / Nombre de visiteurs (000) / Número de visitantes (000)	Number of museums reporting / Nombre de musées ayant fourni ces données / Número de museos que dieron este dato	Total (000) / Total (000) / Total (000)
			(1)	(2)	(3)	(4)	(5)
Azerbaijan	1993	Total museums	115	115	2 290	115	57 447
		1. Art	27	27	530	27	15 183
		2. Archaeology and history	9	9	541	9	16 359
		6. Specialized museums	7	7	84	7	2 278
		7. Regional museums	48	48	846	48	14 973
		9. Other museums	24	24	289	24	8 654
		Monuments and sites	6 571	-	...	-	...
		Zoos, botanical gardens, etc.	14	-	...	-	...
Bahrain	1993	Total museums	12	2	110	-	...
		1. Art	2	-	...	-	...
		2. Archaeology and history	4	-	...	-	...
		3. Nat. history & nat. science	1	-	...	-	...
		5. Ethnography & anthropology	3	-	...	-	...
		8. General museums	2	2	110	-	-
Brunei Darussalam	1990	Total museums	8	5	142	-	...
		3. Nat. history & nat. science	1	1	.2	-	...
		6. Specialized museums	3	3	3	-	...
		8. General museums	4	1	139	-	...
		Monuments and sites	4	1	.1	-	...
		Zoos, botanical gardens, etc.	9	3	28	-	...
China	1992	Total museums	1 085	...	...	...	...
Cyprus	1993	Total museums	24	19	515	18	224
		2. Archaeology and history	9	7	336	7	157
		3. Nat. history & nat. science	1	1	5	1	3
		5. Ethnography & anthropology	7	6	42	6	13
		6. Specialized museums	4	2	22	1	7
		7. Regional museums	3	3	110	3	44
		Monuments and sites	1 075	21	1 535	16	737
Iraq	1990	Total museums	25	25	311	-	...
		1. Art	25	25	311	-	...
Japan	1990	Total museums	698	698	73 426	-	...
		1. Art	252	252	32 127	-	...
		2. Archaeology and history	258	258	18 583	-	...
		3. Nat. history & nat. science	81	81	12 563	-	...
		8. General museums	96	96	6 578	-	...
		9. Other museums	11	11	3 575	-	...
		Zoos, botanical gardens, etc.	101	101	56 896	-	...
Jordan	1993	Total museums	21	11	429	6	546
		1. Art	1	1	11	-	...
		2. Archaeology and history	13	7	374	4	536
		5. Ethnography & anthropology	5	2	43	2	10
		6. Specialized museums	2	1	1	-	...

Museums and related institutions 8.1
Musées et institutions assimilées
Museos e instituciones conexas

		Personnel Personnel Personal				Annual current expenditure Dépenses annuelles ordinaires Gastos ordinarios anuales		
Number of museums reporting		Professional staff Personnel professionnel Personal professional		Other staff Autre personnel Otro personal		Number of museums reporting	Total (000)	Country
Nombre de musées ayant fourni ces données	Total staff	Paid staff	Volunteers	Paid staff	Volunteers	Nombre de musées ayant fourni ces données	Total (000)	Pays
Número de museos que dieron este dato	Total du personnel	Salariés	Volontaires	Salariés	Volontaires	Número de museos que dieron este dato		
	Total de personal	Remunerados	Voluntarios	Remunerados	Voluntarios		Total (000)	País
(6)	(7)	(8)	(9)	(10)	(11)	(12)	(13)	
115	1 898	535	-	1 363	-	115	55 093	Azerbaijan
27	490	144	-	346	-	27	14 576	
9	482	167	-	315	-	9	16 248	
7	78	29	-	49	-	7	2 122	
48	593	130	-	463	-	48	13 664	
24	255	65	-	190	-	24	8 483	
6 571	50	25	-	25	-	6 571	84 000	
14	494	494	...	...	...	14	9 717	
2	100	100	...	...	...	1	8 84	Bahrain
-	...	...	...	...	...	-	...	
-	...	...	...	...	...	-	...	
2	100	100	-	-	-	1	884	
8	315	15	-	300	-	6	*5 100	Brunei Darussalam
1	3	1	-	2	-	-	...	
3	18	2	-	16	-	2	*100	
4	294	12	-	282	-	4	*5 000	
1	63	1	-	62	-	1	*2 000	
2	141	10	-	131	-	7	*335	
...	...	...	...	...	...	...	...	China
19	128	66	-	62	-	19	969	Cyprus
7	93	54	-	30	-	7	723	
1	1	1	-	-	-	1	7	
6	21	5	-	16	-	6	133	
2	3	1	-	2	-	2	19	
3	10	5	-	5	-	3	87	
17	78	43	-	35	-	101	800	
-	...	...	...	...	...	-	...	Iraq
-	...	...	...	...	...	-	...	
698	7 717	2 297	...	...	...	-	...	Japan
252	2 816	833	...	...	...	-	...	
258	2 209	700	...	...	...	-	...	
81	1 281	352	...	...	...	-	...	
96	1 168	388	...	...	...	-	...	
11	243	24	...	...	...	-	...	
101	3 712	252	...	...	...	-	...	
12	78	41	-	37	-	-	...	Jordan
1	6	3	-	3	-	-	...	
7	56	31	-	25	-	-	...	
2	6	3	-	3	-	-	...	
2	10	4	-	6	-	-	...	

8.1 Museums and related institutions
Musées et institutions assimilées
Museos e instituciones conexas

Country Pays País	Year Année Año	Subject of collection or type of institution Nature des collections ou type d'institution Naturaleza de las colecciones o tipo de institución	Total number of museums Nombre total de musées Número total de museos	Attendance Fréquentation Frecuentación		Annual receipts Recettes annuelles Ingresos anuales	
				Number of museums reporting Nombre de musées ayant fourni ces données Número de museos que dieron este dato	Number of visitors (000) Nombre de visiteurs (000) Número de visitantes (000)	Number of museums reporting Nombre de musées ayant fourni ces données Número de museos que dieron este dato	Total (000) Total (000) Total (000)
			(1)	(2)	(3)	(4)	(5)
Kazakstan	1993	Total museums	180	180	6 536	-	...
		1. Art	32	32	1 200	-	...
		2. Archaeology and history	5	5	500	-	...
		3. Nat. history & nat. science	4	4	73	-	...
		4. Science and technology	2	2	55	-	...
		5. Ethnography & anthropology	6	6	240	-	...
		6. Specialized museums	40	40	1 200	-	...
		7. Regional museums	60	60	3 100	-	...
		8. General museums	25	25	100	-	...
		9. Other museums	6	6	68	-	...
		Monuments and sites	128	15	55	-	...
		Zoos, botanical gardens, etc.	10	6	900	-	...
Kuwait	1995	Total museums	6	6	36	-	...
		2. Archaeology and history	2	2	20	-	...
		5. Ethnography & anthropology	2	2	5	-	...
		6. Specialized museums	1	1	10	-	...
		8. General museums	1	1	1	-	...
		Monuments and sites	80	80	4	-	...
Macau	1993	Total museums	3	1	226	-	...
Malaysia	1993	Total museums	51	1	759	1	6 300
		1. Art	6	-	...	-	...
		2. Archaeology and history	10	-	...	-	...
		3. Nat. history & nat. science	3	-	...	-	...
		4. Science and technology	1	1	759	1	6 300
		5. Ethnography & anthropology	6	-	...	-	...
		6. Specialized museums	6	-	...	-	...
		7. Regional museums	15	-	...	-	...
		8. General museums	4	-	...	-	...
		Monuments and sites	428	-	...	-	...
Oman	1994	Total museums	7	7	57	-	...
		2. Archaeology and history	1	1	16	-	...
		3. Nat. history & nat. science	1	1	20	-	...
		4. Science and technology	1	1	3	-	...
		5. Ethnography & anthropology	1	1	3	-	...
		8. General museums	2	2	11	-	...
		9. Other museums	1	1	4	-	...
		Monuments and sites	32	32	225	-	...
Pakistan	1994	Total museums	12	12	1 305	9	830
		1. Art	5	5	105	3	118
		2. Archaeology and history	6	6	1 196	6	712
		5. Ethnography & anthropology	1	1	4	-	...
		Monuments and sites	300	152	272	2	558
		Zoos, botanical gardens, etc.	22	12	...	-	...
Qatar	1994	Total museums	7	6	78	-	...
		1. Art	1	-	...	-	...
		2. Archaeology and history	1	1	14	-	...
		5. Ethnography & anthropology	2	2	13	-	...
		7. Regional museums	2	2	14	-	...
		8. General museums	1	1	37	-	...
Saudi Arabia	1993	Total museums	12	12	44 147	-	...
		Monuments and sites	10 150	...	71 000	-	...

Museums and related institutions 8.1
Musées et institutions assimilées
Museos e instituciones conexas

	Personnel / Personnel / Personal					Annual current expenditure / Dépenses annuelles ordinaires / Gastos ordinarios anuales		
Number of museums reporting / Nombre de musées ayant fourni ces données / Número de museos que dieron este dato	Total staff / Total du personnel / Total de personal	Professional staff / Personnel professionnel / Personal professional		Other staff / Autre personnel / Otro personal		Number of museums reporting / Nombre de musées ayant fourni ces données / Número de museos que dieron este dato	Total (000) / Total (000) / Total (000)	Country / Pays / País
		Paid staff / Salariés / Remunerados	Volunteers / Volontaires / Voluntarios	Paid staff / Salariés / Remunerados	Volunteers / Volontaires / Voluntarios			
(6)	(7)	(8)	(9)	(10)	(11)	(12)	(13)	
180	2 810	1 310	-	1 500	-	-	...	Kazakstan
32	450	250	-	200	-	-	...	
5	300	130	-	170	-	-	...	
4	65	24	-	41	-	-	...	
2	23	11	-	12	-	-	...	
6	130	65	-	65	-	-	...	
40	470	232	-	238	-	-	...	
60	1 067	470	-	597	-	-	...	
25	240	100	-	140	-	-	...	
6	65	28	-	37	-	-	...	
15	60	13	-	47	-	-	...	
6	425	105	-	320	-	-	...	
6	81	81	-	-	-	-	...	Kuwait
2	15	15	-	-	-	-	...	
2	10	10	-	-	-	-	...	
1	6	6	-	-	-	-	...	
1	50	50	-	-	-	-	...	
4	4	4	-	-	-	-	...	
-	...	...	...	...	...	-	...	Macau
1	206	84	-	122	-	1	17 600	Malaysia
-	...	...	...	...	...	-	...	
-	...	...	...	...	...	-	...	
1	206	84	-	122	-	1	17 600	
-	...	...	...	...	...	-	...	
-	...	...	...	...	...	-	...	
-	...	...	...	...	...	-	...	
-	...	...	...	...	...	-	...	
7	56	37	5	14	-	-	...	Oman
1	2	2	-	-	-	-	...	
1	15	3	5	7	-	-	...	
1	14	14	-	-	-	-	...	
1	7	2	-	5	-	-	...	
2	12	10	-	2	-	-	...	
1	6	6	-	-	-	-	...	
-	85	27	-	58	-	-	...	
12	285	63	-	222	-	11	14 502	Pakistan
5	65	27	-	38	-	5	4 757	
6	207	31	-	176	-	5	8 745	
1	13	5	-	8	-	1	1 000	
122	260	45	20	195	-	2	1 878	
...	9	1	-	8	...	-	...	
-	...	...	...	...	...	-	...	Qatar
-	...	...	...	...	...	-	...	
-	...	...	...	...	...	-	...	
-	...	...	...	...	...	-	...	
-	...	...	...	...	...	-	...	
12	58	...	...	58	...	-	...	Saudi Arabia
-	...	...	...	...	...	-	...	

8.1   **Museums and related institutions**
Musées et institutions assimilées
Museos e instituciones conexas

Country Pays País	Year Année Año	Subject of collection or type of institution Nature des collections ou type d'institution Naturaleza de las colecciones o tipo de institución	Total number of museums Nombre total de musées Número total de museos	Attendance Fréquentation Frecuentación		Annual receipts Recettes annuelles Ingresos anuales	
				Number of museums reporting Nombre de musées ayant fourni ces données Número de museos que dieron este dato	Number of visitors (000) Nombre de visiteurs (000) Número de visitantes (000)	Number of museums reporting Nombre de musées ayant fourni ces données Número de museos que dieron este dato	Total (000) Total (000) Total (000)
			(1)	(2)	(3)	(4)	(5)
Syrian Arab Republic	1990	Total museums	33	12	1 125	33	3 867
		1. Art	2	...	134	-	...
		2. Archaeology and history	13	...	88	-	...
		3. Nat. history & nat. science	1	1	8	-	...
		6. Specialized museums	2	...	1	-	...
		7. Regional museums	13	...	774	-	...
		9. Other museums	2	...	120	-	...
		Monuments and sites	4 096	3 155	792	1 967	1 933
Thailand	1990	Total museums	180	60	1 770	46	81 789
		1. Art	11	1	7	-	...
		2. Archaeology and history	84	44	1 201	42	81 784
		3. Nat. history & nat. science	44	3	4	4	5
		4. Science and technology	8	3	528	-	...
		5. Ethnography & anthropology	11	1	3	-	...
		6. Specialized museums	20	6	8	-	...
		7. Regional museums	1	1	4	-	...
		8. General museums	1	1	15	-	...
		Monuments and sites	203	1	2	-	...
		Zoos, botanical gardens, etc.	34	3	457	-	...
Turkey‡	1993	Total museums	184	157	6 980	157	153 345
		2. Archaeology and history	72	66	3 401	66	84 891
		5. Ethnography & anthropology	54	42	2 987	42	68 307
		8. General museums	58	49	592	49	147
		Monuments and sites	29 522	91	5 502	91	141 895
Uzbekistan	1993	Total museums	64	59	2 949	42	19 738
		1. Art	9	8	1 356	6	1 546
		2. Archaeology and history	26	22	474	14	12 727
		3. Nat. history & nat. science	1	1	62	1	125
		6. Specialized museums	1	1	63	1	202
		7. Regional museums	22	22	949	16	4 153
		9. Other museums	5	5	45	4	985
Europe							
Andorra	1993	Total museums	6	3	28	1	3 425
		1. Art	1	1	1	-	...
		4. Science and technology	2	1	24	1	3 425
		5. Ethnography & anthropology	1	-	...	-	...
		6. Specialized museums	1	...	...	-	...
		9. Other museums	1	1	3	-	...
		Monuments and sites	8	-	...	-	...
Austria	1993	Total museums	712	685	18 277	-	...
		1. Art	48	46	3 442	-	...
		2. Archaeology and history	166	163	5 473	-	...
		3. Nat. history & nat. science	80	78	2 743	-	...
		4. Science and technology	63	58	521	-	...
		5. Ethnography & anthropology	53	51	481	-	...
		6. Specialized museums	100	96	1 644	-	...
		7. Regional museums	158	153	580	-	...
		8. General museums	32	28	1 422	-	...
		9. Other museums	12	12	1 971	-	...
		Monuments and sites	8	8	772	-	...
		Zoos, botanical gardens, etc.	22	21	2 135	-	...

Museums and related institutions   8.1
Musées et institutions assimilées
Museos e instituciones conexas

Number of museums reporting — Nombre de musées ayant fourni ces données — Número de museos que dieron este dato	Total staff — Total du personnel — Total de personal	Professional staff / Personnel professionnel / Personal professional		Other staff / Autre personnel / Otro personal		Number of museums reporting — Nombre de musées ayant fourni ces données — Número de museos que dieron este dato	Total (000) — Total (000) — Total (000)	Country / Pays / País
		Paid staff / Salariés / Remunerados	Volunteers / Volontaires / Voluntarios	Paid staff / Salariés / Remunerados	Volunteers / Volontaires / Voluntarios			
(6)	(7)	(8)	(9)	(10)	(11)	(12)	(13)	
33	272	56	...	216	...	33	2 000	Syrian Arab Republic
2	6	2	...	4	...	-	...	
13	112	25	...	87	...	-	...	
1	5	1	...	4	...	-	...	
2	6	2	...	4	...	-	...	
13	105	24	...	81	...	-	...	
2	38	2	...	36	...	-	...	
13	38	3	...	35	...	4 096	10 000	
58	1 059	431	19	608	1	10	98 227	Thailand
1	13	1	-	12	-	1	15 175	
44	893	321	1	570	1	1	81 748	
4	25	10	4	11	-	2	504	
1	21	5	12	4	-	1	...	
1	5	3	2	-	-	2	400	
6	99	90	-	9	-	2	100	
1	3	1	-	2	-	1	300	
-	...	...	...	...	...	-	...	
1	2	-	-	2	-	-	...	
3	35	8	-	17	10	-	...	
157	3 912	564	-	3 348	-	...	36 712	Turkey‡
66	2 249	317	-	1 932	-	...	36 712	
42	1 469	220	-	1 249	-	-	-	
49	194	27	-	167	-	-	...	
-	...	...	-	...	-	-	...	
64	1 911	...	...	...	...	42	15 928	Uzbekistan
9	268	...	...	...	...	6	1 510	
26	653	...	...	...	...	14	9 072	
1	28	...	...	...	...	1	99	
1	31	...	...	...	...	1	201	
22	784	...	...	...	...	16	4 091	
5	147	...	...	...	...	4	955	
								Europe
5	19	10	-	9	-	1	6 712	Andorra
1	2	1	-	1	-	-	...	
1	5	2	-	3	-	-	...	
1	10	5	-	5	-	-	...	
1	1	1	-	-	-	-	...	
1	1	1	-	-	-	-	6 712	
1	10	-	-	10	-	-	...	
-	...	...	...	...	...	-	...	Austria
-	...	...	...	...	...	-	...	
-	...	...	...	...	...	-	...	
-	...	...	...	...	...	-	...	
-	...	...	...	...	...	-	...	
-	...	...	...	...	...	-	...	
-	...	...	...	...	...	-	...	
-	...	...	...	...	...	-	...	
-	...	...	...	...	...	-	...	

8.1 Museums and related institutions
Musées et institutions assimilées
Museos e instituciones conexas

Country / Pays / País	Year / Année / Año	Subject of collection or type of institution / Nature des collections ou type d'institution / Naturaleza de las colecciones o tipo de institución	Total number of museums / Nombre total de musées / Número total de museos	Attendance / Fréquentation / Frecuentación		Annual receipts / Recettes annuelles / Ingresos anuales	
				Number of museums reporting / Nombre de musées ayant fourni ces données / Número de museos que dieron este dato	Number of visitors (000) / Nombre de visiteurs (000) / Número de visitantes (000)	Number of museums reporting / Nombre de musées ayant fourni ces données / Número de museos que dieron este dato	Total (000) / Total (000) / Total (000)
			(1)	(2)	(3)	(4)	(5)
Belarus	1993	Total museums	139	117	2 682	139	4 343 672
		1. Art	9	7	222	9	586 552
		2. Archaeology and history	59	51	1 011	59	1 258 582
		3. Nat. history & nat. science	3	3	114	3	101 253
		7. Regional museums	65	53	1 320	65	2 027 125
		9. Other museums	3	3	15	3	370 160
		Monuments and sites	14 392	-	...	-	...
		Zoos, botanical gardens, etc.	4	4	17 544	1	22 094
Belgium‡	1993	Total museums	75	75	2 413	63	182 380
		1. Art	15	15	1 360	11	61 415
		2. Archaeology and history	19	19	272	20	29 985
		3. Nat. history & nat. science	3	3	240	3	1 078
		4. Science and technology	10	10	102	8	45 952
		5. Ethnography & anthropology	7	7	84	6	20 456
		6. Specialized museums	5	5	120	120	4
		7. Regional museums	13	13	108	9	12 643
		8. General museums	3	3	127	2	2 312
Bulgaria	1993	Total museums	221	221	3 435	221	197 322
		1. Art	50	50	866	50	35 437
		2. Archaeology and history	117	117	1 862	117	132 444
		3. Nat. history & nat. science	5	5	94	5	3 879
		4. Science and technology	5	5	23	5	3 432
		5. Ethnography & anthropology	7	7	211	7	8 076
		6. Specialized museums	37	37	379	37	14 054
		Monuments and sites	39 399	-	...	...	37 543
		Zoos, botanical gardens, etc.	100	11	1 064	11	34 449
Croatia	1994	Total museums	146	90	580	101	65 613
		1. Art	43	19	102	23	9 891
		2. Archaeology and history	13	9	97	12	18 657
		3. Nat. history & nat. science	5	3	24	3	3 892
		4. Science and technology	7	4	158	4	4 522
		5. Ethnography & anthropology	6	4	13	6	4 031
		6. Specialized museums	9	6	5	4	292
		7. Regional museums	33	23	62	23	6 308
		8. General museums	30	22	119	26	18 020
Czech Republic	1993	Total museums	254	254	9 029	254	1 647
		1. Art	37	37	1 645	37	526
		4. Science and technology	2	2	208	2	55
		8. General museums	3	3	1 005	3	199
		9. Other museums	212	212	6 171	212	867
Denmark	1993	Total museums	288	288	11 197	-	...
		1. Art	55	55	2 671	-	...
		2. Archaeology and history	10	10	1 231	-	...
		3. Nat. history & nat. science	14	14	403	-	...
		6. Specialized museums	75	75	4 189	-	...
		7. Regional museums	128	128	2 544	-	...
		9. Other museums	6	6	159	-	...
		Zoos, botanical gardens, etc.	6	6	2 089	-	...
Estonia	1993	Total museums	88	88	793	88	26 261
		1. Art	12	12	136	12	1 327
		2. Archaeology and history	40	40	268	40	12 819
		3. Nat. history & nat. science	3	3	46	3	413
		5. Ethnography & anthropology	5	5	65	5	1 665
		6. Specialized museums	9	9	114	9	4 820
		7. Regional museums	19	19	164	19	5 217

Museums and related institutions 8.1
Musées et institutions assimilées
Museos e instituciones conexas

| | Personnel / Personnel / Personal | | | | | Annual current expenditure / Dépenses annuelles ordinaires / Gastos ordinarios anuales | | Country |
| Number of museums reporting / Nombre de musées ayant fourni ces données / Número de museos que dieron este dato | Total staff / Total du personnel / Total de personal | Professional staff / Personnel professionnel / Personal professional | | Other staff / Autre personnel / Otro personal | | Number of museums reporting / Nombre de musées ayant fourni ces données / Número de museos que dieron este dato | Total (000) / Total (000) / Total (000) | Pays / País |
		Paid staff / Salariés / Remunerados	Volunteers / Volontaires / Voluntarios	Paid staff / Salariés / Remunerados	Volunteers / Volontaires / Voluntarios			
(6)	(7)	(8)	(9)	(10)	(11)	(12)	(13)	
139	2 210	831	-	1 379	-	139	4 232 838	Belarus
9	244	86	-	158	-	9	578 081	
59	863	292	-	571	-	59	1 221 677	
3	41	13	-	28	-	3	102 092	
65	1 017	417	-	600	-	65	1 977 341	
3	45	23	-	22	-	3	353 647	
-	...	...	-	...	-	-	...	
4	1 019	486	-	533	-	4	1 139 441	
4	956	...	...	...	...	69	441 109	Belgium‡
2	503	...	...	...	...	17	169 046	
-	...	...	...	...	...	20	131 325	
1	266	...	...	...	...	3	2 002	
-	...	...	...	...	...	8	85 645	
-	...	...	...	...	...	6	23 920	
-	...	...	...	...	...	4	7 875	
-	...	...	...	...	...	9	16 234	
1	187	...	...	...	...	2	5 062	
221	2 938	1 611	-	1 327	-	221	182 021	Bulgaria
50	562	271	-	291	-	50	33 829	
117	1 883	1 044	-	839	-	117	119 414	
5	71	43	-	28	-	5	3 597	
5	84	52	-	32	-	5	3 409	
7	104	50	-	54	-	7	7 850	
37	234	151	-	83	-	37	13 922	
...	726	696	-	30	-	...	36 798	
11	266	133	-	133	-	11	31 432	
141	1 245	645	...	600	...	107	62 964	Croatia
42	276	119	...	157	...	30	9 581	
13	223	106	...	117	...	12	18 168	
5	62	43	...	19	...	3	3 871	
7	69	33	...	36	...	4	4 327	
5	75	42	...	33	...	5	3 717	
8	43	20	...	23	...	2	277	
31	145	83	...	62	...	26	6 305	
30	352	199	...	153	...	25	16 718	
254	5 150	5 150	...	...	...	254	1 434	Czech Republic
37	1 215	1 215	...	...	...	37	477	
2	219	219	...	...	...	2	45	
3	905	905	...	...	...	3	179	
212	2 811	2 811	...	...	...	212	733	
-	...	...	...	...	...	-	...	Denmark
-	...	...	...	...	...	-	...	
-	...	...	...	...	...	-	...	
-	...	...	...	...	...	-	...	
-	...	...	...	...	...	-	...	
-	...	...	...	...	...	-	...	
-	...	...	...	...	...	-	...	
88	1 239	423	-	816	-	88	34 697	Estonia
12	242	60	-	182	-	12	9 783	
40	486	167	-	319	-	40	12 705	
3	37	15	-	22	-	3	410	
5	62	18	-	44	-	5	1 752	
9	218	80	-	138	-	9	4 867	
19	194	83	-	111	-	19	5 180	

8.1   Museums and related institutions
Musées et institutions assimilées
Museos e instituciones conexas

Country Pays País	Year Année Año	Subject of collection or type of institution Nature des collections ou type d'institution Naturaleza de las colecciones o tipo de institución	Total number of museums Nombre total de musées Número total de museos	Attendance Fréquentation Frecuentación		Annual receipts Recettes annuelles Ingresos anuales	
				Number of museums reporting Nombre de musées ayant fourni ces données Número de museos que dieron este dato	Number of visitors (000) Nombre de visiteurs (000) Número de visitantes (000)	Number of museums reporting Nombre de musées ayant fourni ces données Número de museos que dieron este dato	Total (000) Total (000) Total (000)
			(1)	(2)	(3)	(4)	(5)
Finland‡	1994	Total museums	249	249	3 677	245	317 089
		1. Art	46	46	1 102	46	102 992
		3. Nat. history & nat. science	17	17	257	16	8 058
		9. Other museums	186	186	2 318	183	206 039
		Monuments and sites	19 100	-	...	-	...
France‡	1992	Total museums	*1 300	35	14 056	35	199 000
		1. Art	...	11	4 324	-	...
		2. Archaeology and history	...	20	4 931	-	...
		4. Science and technology	...	2	63	-	...
		5. Ethnography & anthropology	...	1	65	-	...
		8. General museums	...	1	4 673	-	...
Germany‡	1993	Total museums	4 682	3 768	93 756	-	...
		1. Art	506	414	15 377	-	...
		2. Archaeology and history	250	204	10 170	-	...
		3. Nat. history & nat. science	235	189	6 972	-	...
		4. Science and technology	481	379	13 271	-	...
		6. Specialized museums	652	489	7 602	-	...
		7. Regional museums	2 258	1 826	18 745	-	...
		8. General museums	100	92	9 273	-	...
		9. Other museums	200	175	12 346	-	...
Greece‡	1993	Total museums	268	75	2 359	75	9 510
		1. Art	60	-	...	-	...
		2. Archaeology and history	102	75	2 359	75	9 510
		3. Nat. history & nat. science	19	-	...	-	...
		4. Science and technology	16	-	...	-	...
		5. Ethnography & anthropology	50	-	...	-	...
		6. Specialized museums	16	-	...	-	...
		7. Regional museums	3	-	...	-	...
		8. General museums	2	-	...	-	...
		Monuments and sites	30 129	59	5 618	-	...
		Zoos, botanical gardens, etc.	52	-	...	-	...
Hungary	1993	Total museums	529	...	7 415	-	...
		1. Art	117	...	2 586	-	...
		2. Archaeology and history	73	...	1 467	-	...
		3. Nat. history & nat. science	35	...	550	-	...
		4. Science and technology	89	...	477	-	...
		5. Ethnography & anthropology	59	...	432	-	...
		6. Specialized museums	25	...	374	-	...
		7. Regional museums	109	...	1 432	-	...
		8. General museums	18	...	80	-	...
		9. Other museums	4	...	17	-	...
		Monuments and sites	225	...	1 903	-	...
Iceland	1993	Total museums	56	56	486	-	...
		1. Art	8	8	264	-	...
		2. Archaeology and history	20	20	59	-	...
		3. Nat. history & nat. science	4	4	16	-	...
		6. Specialized museums	1	1	31	-	...
		7. Regional museums	23	23	116	-	...
Italy‡	1992	Total museums	3 442	2 497	39 882	773	87 092
		1. Art	953	720	16 696	298	52 332
		2. Archaeology and history	1 144	797	13 821	258	25 609
		3. Nat. history & nat. science	364	293	2 418	43	1 369
		4. Science and technology	150	101	1 365	21	2 256
		5. Ethnography & anthropology	221	180	1 044	37	595
		6. Specialized museums	301	199	2 853	58	3 219
		7. Regional museums	271	172	1 209	50	818
		8. General museums	38	35	476	8	894
		Zoos, botanical gardens, etc.	112	89	6 875	37	11 929

	Personnel / Personnel / Personal					Annual current expenditure / Dépenses annuelles ordinaires / Gastos ordinarios anuales		
Number of museums reporting	Total staff	Professional staff / Personnel professionnel / Personal professional		Other staff / Autre personnel / Otro personal		Number of museums reporting	Total (000)	Country
Nombre de musées ayant fourni ces données	Total du personnel	Paid staff / Salariés / Remunerados	Volunteers / Volontaires / Voluntarios	Paid staff / Salariés / Remunerados	Volunteers / Volontaires / Voluntarios	Nombre de musées ayant fourni ces données	Total (000)	Pays
Número de museos que dieron este dato	Total de personal					Número de museos que dieron este dato	Total (000)	País
(6)	(7)	(8)	(9)	(10)	(11)	(12)	(13)	
247	1 167	583	-	584	-	247	383 737	Finland‡
46	378	161	-	217	-	46	128 632	
16	91	67		24	-	16	22 881	
185	698	355	-	343	-	185	232 224	
-	...	...	...	...	...	-	...	
35	2 215	...	...	...	...	35	1 300 000	France‡
11	673	...	...	...	...	-	...	
20	600	...	...	...	...	-	...	
2	76	...	...	...	...	-	...	
1	79	...	...	...	...	-	...	
1	787	...	...	...	...	-	...	
-	...	...	...	...	...	-	...	Germany‡
-	...	...	...	...	...	-	...	
-	...	...	...	...	...	-	...	
-	...	...	...	...	...	-	...	
-	...	...	...	...	...	-	...	
-	...	...	...	...	...	-	...	
-	...	...	...	...	...	-	...	
75	1 598	1 273	-	325	-	-	...	Greece‡
-	...	...	...	...	...	-	...	
75	1 598	1 273	-	325	-	-	...	
-	...	...	...	...	...	-	...	
-	...	...	...	...	...	-	...	
-	...	...	...	...	...	-	...	
-	...	...	...	...	...	-	...	
-	...	...	...	...	...	-	...	
-	...	...	...	...	...	-	...	
...	5 912	1 059	...	3 235	...	...	4 491	Hungary
...	1 399	181	...	748	...	...	901	
...	1 147	216	...	650	...	...	889	
...	272	79	...	113	...	...	156	
...	407	59	...	215	...	...	317	
...	394	64	...	224	...	...	236	
...	271	60	...	147	...	...	218	
...	1 951	387	...	1 107	...	...	1 770	
...	61	12	...	28	...	-	4	
...	10	1	...	3	...	-	...	
...	492	28	...	269	...	...	14	
-	...	...	...	...	...	-	...	Iceland
-	...	...	...	...	...	-	...	
-	...	...	...	...	...	-	...	
-	...	...	...	...	...	-	...	
-	...	...	...	...	...	-	...	
2 497	16 031	...	...	...	...	-	...	Italy‡
720	5 535	...	...	...	...	-	...	
797	6 667	...	...	...	...	-	...	
293	1 065	...	...	...	...	-	...	
101	549	...	...	...	...	-	...	
180	681	...	...	...	...	-	...	
199	649	...	...	...	...	-	...	
172	736	...	...	...	...	-	...	
35	149	...	...	...	...	-	...	
89	933	...	...	...	...	-	...	

Museums and related institutions
Musées et institutions assimilées
Museos e instituciones conexas

Country Pays País	Year Année Año	Subject of collection or type of institution Nature des collections ou type d'institution Naturaleza de las colecciones o tipo de institución	Total number of museums Nombre total de musées Número total de museos	Attendance Fréquentation Frecuentación		Annual receipts Recettes annuelles Ingresos anuales	
				Number of museums reporting Nombre de musées ayant fourni ces données Número de museos que dieron este dato	Number of visitors (000) Nombre de visiteurs (000) Número de visitantes (000)	Number of museums reporting Nombre de musées ayant fourni ces données Número de museos que dieron este dato	Total (000) Total (000) Total (000)
			(1)	(2)	(3)	(4)	(5)
Latvia	1993	Total museums	97	97	1 248	97	2 157
		1. Art	8	8	281	8	250
		2. Archaeology and history	51	51	495	51	1 104
		3. Nat. history & nat. science	1	1	86	1	78
		4. Science and technology	4	4	88	4	133
		5. Ethnography & anthropology	2	2	101	2	101
		6. Specialized museums	4	4	55	4	101
		7. Regional museums	9	9	29	9	66
		8. General museums	17	17	112	17	307
		9. Other museums	1	1	1	1	17
		Zoos, botanical gardens, etc.	9	9	133	9	842
Liechtenstein	1990	Total museums	5	4	38	4	717
		1. Art	1	1	21	1	504
		2. Archaeology and history	1	1	13	1	205
		6. Specialized museums	1	-	...	-	...
		7. Regional museums	2	2	4	2	8
Lithuania	1993	Total museums	58	57	1 246	-	...
		1. Art	3	3	533	-	...
		2. Archaeology and history	14	14	313	-	...
		3. Nat. history & nat. science	3	3	118	-	...
		4. Science and technology	4	4	15	-	...
		5. Ethnography & anthropology	1	1	57	-	...
		6. Specialized museums	4	4	3	-	...
		7. Regional museums	29	28	207	-	...
		Monuments and sites	10 784	-	...	-	...
		Zoos, botanical gardens, etc.	2	-	...	-	...
Malta	1993	Total museums	15	15	716	-	...
		1. Art	3	3	61	-	...
		2. Archaeology and history	4	4	288	-	...
		3. Nat. history & nat. science	4	4	337	-	...
		4. Science and technology	1	1	5	-	...
		6. Specialized museums	2	2	23	-	...
		8. General museums	1	1	2	-	...
		Monuments and sites	6	6	552	-	...
Moldova	1993	Total museums	88	62	657	66	630
		1. Art	4	2	81	2	140
		2. Archaeology and history	45	34	387	38	295
		5. Ethnography & anthropology	10	10	109	10	160
		7. Regional museums	29	16	80	16	35
Monaco‡	1990	Total museums	6	4	1 137	3	44 416
		2. Archaeology and history	1	-	...	-	...
		3. Nat. history & nat. science	1	1	974	1	42 721
		5. Ethnography & anthropology	1	1	101	1	603
		6. Specialized museums	1	1	52	1	1 092
		7. Regional museums	2	1	10	-	...
		Zoos, botanical gardens, etc.	2	1	503	1	11 700
Netherlands	1993	Total museums	732	732	22 994	732	570 980
		1. Art	68	68	4 347	68	103 479
		2. Archaeology and history	374	374	7 125	374	184 033
		3. Nat. history & nat. science	71	71	3 443	71	36 074
		4. Science and technology	153	153	4 674	153	90 288
		5. Ethnography & anthropology	17	17	522	17	23 587
		8. General museums	49	49	2 883	49	133 519

Museums and related institutions 8.1
Musées et institutions assimilées
Museos e instituciones conexas

	Personnel / Personnel / Personal					Annual current expenditure / Dépenses annuelles ordinaires / Gastos ordinarios anuales		
Number of museums reporting / Nombre de musées ayant fourni ces données / Número de museos que dieron este dato	Total staff / Total du personnel / Total de personal	Professional staff / Personnel professionnel / Personal professional		Other staff / Autre personnel / Otro personal		Number of museums reporting / Nombre de musées ayant fourni ces données / Número de museos que dieron este dato	Total (000) / Total (000) / Total (000)	Country / Pays / País
		Paid staff / Salariés / Remunerados	Volunteers / Volontaires / Voluntarios	Paid staff / Salariés / Remunerados	Volunteers / Volontaires / Voluntarios			
(6)	(7)	(8)	(9)	(10)	(11)	(12)	(13)	
97	2 054	...	...	...	...	97	2 167	Latvia
8	246	...	...	...	...	8	258	
51	1 017	...	...	...	...	51	1 102	
1	63	...	...	...	...	1	76	
4	117	...	...	...	...	4	133	
2	102	...	...	...	...	2	104	
4	105	...	...	...	...	4	100	
9	94	...	...	...	...	9	64	
17	290	...	...	...	...	17	313	
1	20	...	...	...	...	1	17	
9	648	227	-	421	-	9	961	
5	26	8	-	18	-	5	2 561	Liechtenstein
1	12	3	-	9	-	1	1 747	
1	8	4	-	4	-	1	702	
1	5	-	-	5	-	1	75	
2	1	1	-	-	-	2	37	
57	2 426	676	...	1 750	...	-	...	Lithuania
3	882	203	...	679	...	-	...	
14	512	160	...	352	...	-	...	
13	176	47	...	129	...	-	...	
4	95	27	...	68	...	-	...	
1	109	20	...	89	...	-	...	
4	74	24	...	50	...	-	...	
28	578	195	...	383	...	-	...	
-	...	...	...	...	...	-	...	
-	...	...	...	...	...	-	...	
-	...	...	...	...	...	-	...	Malta
-	...	...	...	...	...	-	...	
-	...	...	...	...	...	-	...	
-	...	...	...	...	...	-	...	
-	...	...	...	...	...	-	...	
-	...	...	...	...	...	-	...	
-	...	...	...	...	...	-	...	
66	724	264	-	460	-	66	590	Moldova
2	102	31	-	71	-	2	120	
38	391	153	-	238	-	38	282	
10	182	55	-	127	-	10	160	
16	49	25	-	24	-	16	28	
4	118	102	...	12	4	3	2 951	Monaco‡
-	...	...	...	...	...	-	...	
1	95	95	-	-	-	1	210	
1	10	5	-	5	-	1	2 670	
1	9	2	-	7	-	1	71	
1	4	-	-	-	4	1	...	
1	44	44	-	-	-	-	...	
732	6 406	4 004	...	678	1 725	732	576 022	Netherlands
68	818	640	...	95	82	68	103 994	
374	2 364	1 225	...	261	880	374	185 719	
71	509	319	...	82	108	71	36 415	
153	12 940	660	...	137	497	153	91 612	
17	210	168	...	14	28	17	23 309	
49	1 211	992	...	89	130	49	134 973	

8.1 Museums and related institutions
Musées et institutions assimilées
Museos e instituciones conexas

Country Pays País	Year Année Año	Subject of collection or type of institution Nature des collections ou type d'institution Naturaleza de las colecciones o tipo de institución	Total number of museums Nombre total de musées Número total de museos	Attendance / Fréquentation / Frecuentación — Number of museums reporting Nombre de musées ayant fourni ces données Número de museos que dieron este dato	Number of visitors (000) Nombre de visiteurs (000) Número de visitantes (000)	Annual receipts / Recettes annuelles / Ingresos anuales — Number of museums reporting Nombre de musées ayant fourni ces données Número de museos que dieron este dato	Total (000) Total (000) Total (000)
			(1)	(2)	(3)	(4)	(5)
Norway	1993	Total museums	475	431	8 219	396	979 953
		1. Art	36	29	1 111	30	207 231
		2. Archaeology and history	344	323	4 753	289	565 916
		3. Nat. history & nat. science	20	16	1 204	14	50 594
		9. Other museums	75	63	1 151	63	156 212
Poland‡	1993	Total museums	567	552	15 629	...	1 011 000
		1. Art	70	66	4 441	-	...
		2. Archaeology and history	112	111	3 215	-	...
		3. Nat. history & nat. science	30	30	1 777	-	...
		4. Science and technology	35	33	573	-	...
		5. Ethnography & anthropology	40	39	794	-	...
		6. Specialized museums	77	73	1 517	-	...
		7. Regional museums	156	153	1 806	-	...
		8. General museums	27	27	862	-	...
		9. Other museums	20	20	644	-	...
		Monuments and sites	500 000	-	...	...	18 900
		Zoos, botanical gardens, etc.	1 426	-	...	...	10 000
Portugal	1993	Total museums	310	276	5 088	169	2 762
		1. Art	80	72	2 340	47	1 715
		2. Archaeology and history	83	78	1 186	44	433
		3. Nat. history & nat. science	13	12	606	8	109
		4. Science and technology	10	10	159	5	55
		5. Ethnography & anthropology	36	30	205	17	147
		6. Specialized museums	23	17	97	9	20
		7. Regional museums	41	36	411	24	241
		8. General museums	24	21	84	15	42
		Monuments and sites	11	10	1 059	7	346
		Zoos, botanical gardens, etc.	7	7	1 055	5	850
Romania	1993	Total museums	404	...	6 518	-	...
		1. Art	81	...	2 095	-	...
		2. Archaeology and history	61	...	684	-	...
		3. Nat. history & nat. science	22	...	775	-	...
		4. Science and technology	11	...	120	-	...
		5. Ethnography & anthropology	53	...	616	-	...
		6. Specialized museums	12	...	318	-	...
		7. Regional museums	3	...	79	-	...
		8. General museums	2	...	183	-	...
		9. Other museums	159	...	1 648	-	...
		Zoos, botanical gardens, etc.	36	...	2 423	-	...
Russian Federation‡	1993	Total museums	1 478	1 375	79 831	1 478	76 291
		1. Art	210	204	16 370	210	25 480
		2. Archaeology and history	511	478	42 481	511	29 381
		3. Nat. history & nat. science	24	21	2 253	24	602
		6. Specialized museums	53	48	1 866	53	2 988
		7. Regional museums	676	621	16 325	676	17 605
		9. Other museums	4	3	536	4	235
		Monuments and sites	55 140	-	...	-	...
San Marino	1993	Total museums	7	-	...	-	...
		1. Art	2	-	...	-	...
		6. Specialized museums	4	-	...	-	...
		9. Other museums	1	-	...	-	...
		Monuments and sites	4	-	...	-	...

Museums and related institutions 8.1
Musées et institutions assimilées
Museos e instituciones conexas

	Personnel / Personnel / Personal					Annual current expenditure / Dépenses annuelles ordinaires / Gastos ordinarios anuales		
Number of museums reporting		Professional staff / Personnel professionnel / Personal professional		Other staff / Autre personnel / Otro personal		Number of museums reporting	Total (000)	Country
Nombre de musées ayant fourni ces données	Total staff	Paid staff	Volunteers	Paid staff	Volunteers	Nombre de musées ayant fourni ces données	Total (000)	Pays
Número de museos que dieron este dato	Total du personnel / Total de personal	Salariés / Remunerados	Volontaires / Voluntarios	Salariés / Remunerados	Volontaires / Voluntarios	Número de museos que dieron este dato	Total (000)	País
(6)	(7)	(8)	(9)	(10)	(11)	(12)	(13)	
228	3 066	2 774	292	-	-	395	998 003	Norway
24	312	310	2	-	-	30	229 846	
158	2 092	1 822	270	-	-	288	568 562	
16	190	187	3	-	-	15	47 748	
30	472	455	17	-	-	62	151 847	
-	...	...	...	...	...	-	...	Poland‡
-	...	...	...	...	...	-	...	
-	...	...	...	...	...	-	...	
-	...	...	...	...	...	-	...	
-	...	...	...	...	...	-	...	
-	...	...	...	...	...	-	...	
-	...	...	...	...	...	-	...	
-	...	...	...	...	...	-	...	
-	...	...	...	...	...	-	...	
233	2 224	945	64	1 179	36	169	4 779	Portugal
60	859	351	20	484	4	47	2 546	
65	597	218	27	345	7	44	925	
11	79	65	-	14	-	8	139	
9	85	39	-	46	-	5	163	
24	182	77	5	92	8	17	281	
15	81	39	4	35	3	9	29	
31	266	115	6	132	13	24	409	
18	75	41	2	31	1	15	287	
9	107	40	-	66	1	7	240	
5	332	227	-	105	-	5	848	
-	...	...	...	...	...	-	...	Romania
-	...	...	...	...	...	-	...	
-	...	...	...	...	...	-	...	
-	...	...	...	...	...	-	...	
-	...	...	...	...	...	-	...	
-	...	...	...	...	...	-	...	
-	...	...	...	...	...	-	...	
-	...	...	...	...	...	-	...	
-	...	...	...	...	...	-	...	
1 478	40 569	12 700	...	27 869	...	1 478	65 823	Russian Federation‡
210	10 703	3 158	...	7 545	...	210	22 273	
511	14 830	4 145	...	10 685	...	511	23 856	
24	877	400	...	477	...	24	560	
53	2 355	757	...	1 598	...	53	2 531	
676	11 712	4 212	...	7 500	...	676	16 397	
4	92	28	-	64	...	4	206	
-	...	...				-		
-	...	...	...	...	...	-	...	San Marino
-	...	...	...	...	...	-	...	
-	...	...	...	...	...	-	...	
-	...	...	...	...	...	-	...	

8.1   Museums and related institutions
Musées et institutions assimilées
Museos e instituciones conexas

Country Pays País	Year Année Año	Subject of collection or type of institution Nature des collections ou type d'institution Naturaleza de las colecciones o tipo de institución	Total number of museums Nombre total de musées Número total de museos	Attendance Fréquentation Frecuentación		Annual receipts Recettes annuelles Ingresos anuales	
				Number of museums reporting Nombre de musées ayant fourni ces données Número de museos que dieron este dato	Number of visitors (000) Nombre de visiteurs (000) Número de visitantes (000)	Number of museums reporting Nombre de musées ayant fourni ces données Número de museos que dieron este dato	Total (000) Total (000) Total (000)
			(1)	(2)	(3)	(4)	(5)
Slovakia	1993	Total museums	70	63	2 825	60	13 300
		2. Archaeology and history	8	7	561	7	6 822
		4. Science and technology	1	1	99	1	107
		6. Specialized museums	19	15	752	13	1 057
		7. Regional museums	40	38	1 196	37	4 556
		8. General museums	2	2	217	2	758
		Monuments and sites	10	-	...	-	...
Slovenia	1994	Total museums	78	77	1 795	65	2 474 302
		1. Art	13	13	287	12	587 420
		2. Archaeology and history	5	5	439	5	377 245
		3. Nat. history & nat. science	1	1	31	1	84 787
		4. Science and technology	2	2	48	2	84 544
		5. Ethnography & anthropology	4	4	25	4	92 694
		6. Specialized museums	12	12	134	7	150 929
		7. Regional museums	14	14	463	14	724 973
		8. General museums	13	13	310	10	344 815
		9. Other museums	14	13	58	10	26 895
		Monuments and sites	1	1	10	1	-
		Zoos, botanical gardens, etc.	5	5	365	3	130 521
Spain	1994	Total museums	758	567	28 474	-	...
		1. Art	221	160	11 916	-	...
		2. Archaeology and history	164	129	4 776	-	...
		3. Nat. history & nat. science	46	33	1 552	-	...
		4. Science and technology	16	11	1 519	-	...
		5. Ethnography & anthropology	67	46	396	-	...
		6. Specialized museums	103	78	2 656	-	...
		7. Regional museums	25	21	438	-	...
		8. General museums	102	80	3 014	-	...
		9. Other museums	14	9	2 207		
Sweden	1993	Total museums	197	197	18 642	197	1 971
		1. Art	27	-	...	-	...
		2. Archaeology and history	8	-	...	-	...
		3. Nat. history & nat. science	6	-	...	-	...
		4. Science and technology	14	-	...	-	...
		5. Ethnography & anthropology	49	-	...	-	...
		6. Specialized museums	32	-	...		...
		7. Regional museums	23	23	3 074	23	451
		8. General museums	15	-	...	-	...
		9. Other museums	23	-	...	-	...
Switzerland	1993	Total museums	776	520	8 792	-	...
		1. Art	126	84	2 086	-	...
		2. Archaeology and history	69	51	1 192	-	...
		3. Nat. history & nat. science	51	37	1 350	-	...
		4. Science and technology	51	36	1 172	-	...
		5. Ethnography & anthropology	15	12	570	-	...
		6. Specialized museums	105	68	805	-	...
		7. Regional museums	352	225	1 054	-	...
		8. General museums	7	7	563	-	...
		Monuments and sites	183	124	1 835		...
		Zoos, botanical gardens, etc.	19	10	2 018	-	...
The former Yugoslav Rep. of Macedonia‡	1994	Total museums	21	20	208	16	47 836
		1. Art	2	2	25	2	9 313
		2. Archaeology and history	2	2	47	2	1 654
		3. Nat. history & nat. science	1	1	10	1	3 921
		8. General museums	16	15	126	11	32 948
		Monuments and sites	7	7	./.	7	38 725
		Zoos, botanical gardens, etc.	8	8	...	8	56 298

Museums and related institutions 8.1
Musées et institutions assimilées
Museos e instituciones conexas

Number of museums reporting / Nombre de musées ayant fourni ces données / Número de museos que dieron este dato	Total staff / Total du personnel / Total de personal	Professional staff — Personnel professionnel — Personal professional		Other staff — Autre personnel — Otro personal		Number of museums reporting / Nombre de musées ayant fourni ces données / Número de museos que dieron este dato	Total (000) / Total (000) / Total (000)	Country / Pays / País
		Paid staff / Salariés / Remunerados	Volunteers / Volontaires / Voluntarios	Paid staff / Salariés / Remunerados	Volunteers / Volontaires / Voluntarios			
(6)	(7)	(8)	(9)	(10)	(11)	(12)	(13)	
63	1 726	803	-	...	-	60	253 889	Slovakia
7	167	60	-	...	...	7	29 880	
1	69	33	-	...	...	1	11 218	
15	339	183	-	...	...	12	48 821	
38	850	399	-	...	...	38	111 522	
2	301	128	-	...	...	2	52 448	
-	...	...	...	...	...	-	...	
78	817	469	70	225	53	63	2 428 410	Slovenia
13	147	82	-	61	4	12	583 053	
5	185	74	54	33	24	5	369 609	
1	29	24	-	5	-	1	78 212	
2	32	16	-	16	-	2	80 220	
4	29	24	-	4	1	4	97 777	
12	49	42	1	3	3	8	147 953	
14	213	135	2	75	1	14	766 502	
13	116	70	3	27	16	10	293 384	
14	17	2	10	1	4	7	11 700	
1	2	1	-	1	-	-	...	
4	47	8	-	39	-	3	121 531	
544	5 554	...	...	...	...	-	...	Spain
152	1 976	...	...	...	...	-	...	
127	1 213	...	...	...	...	-	...	
33	202	...	...	...	...	-	...	
10	64	...	...	...	...	-	...	
41	298	...	...	...	...	-	...	
69	551	...	...	...	...	-	...	
20	110	...	...	...	...	-	...	
81	859	...	...	...	...	-	...	
11	281	...	...	...	...	-	...	
197	4 256	...	...	...	...	197	2 110	Sweden
-	...	...	...	...	...	-	...	
-	...	...	...	...	...	-	...	
-	...	...	...	...	...	-	...	
-	...	...	...	...	...	23	457	
-	...	...	...	...	...	-	...	
-	...	...	...	...	...	-	...	
265	1632	...	...	...	...	-	...	Switzerland
63	325	...	...	...	...	-	...	
29	152	...	...	...	...	-	...	
29	302	...	...	...	...	-	...	
16	166	...	...	...	...	-	...	
10	68	...	...	...	...	-	...	
34	140	...	...	...	...	-	...	
78	186	...	...	...	...	-	...	
6	293	...	...	...	...	-	...	
38	252	...	1 192	...	...	-	...	
14	404	...	25	...	...	-	...	
21	553	374	-	179	-	16	47 268	The Former Yugoslav Rep. of Macedonia‡
2	60	49	-	11	-	2	9 196	
2	18	7	-	11	-	2	1 555	
1	33	20	-	13	-	1	3 907	
16	442	298	-	144	-	11	32 610	
7	280	188	-	92	-	7	38 584	
8	259	...	-	...	-	8	52 519	

8.1 Museums and related institutions
Musées et institutions assimilées
Museos e instituciones conexas

Country Pays País	Year Année Año	Subject of collection or type of institution Nature des collections ou type d'institution Naturaleza de las colecciones o tipo de institución	Total number of museums Nombre total de musées Número total de museos	Attendance Fréquentation Frecuentación		Annual receipts Recettes annuelles Ingresos anuales	
				Number of museums reporting Nombre de musées ayant fourni ces données Número de museos que dieron este dato	Number of visitors (000) Nombre de visiteurs (000) Número de visitantes (000)	Number of museums reporting Nombre de musées ayant fourni ces données Número de museos que dieron este dato	Total (000) Total (000) Total (000)
			(1)	(2)	(3)	(4)	(5)
Ukraine	1993	Total museums	271	271	15 253	271	77 643
		1. Art	49	49	3 940	49	18 038
		2. Archaeology and history	94	94	5 687	94	35 646
		7. Regional museums	100	100	4 542	100	19 363
		9. Other museums	28	28	1 082	28	4 596
		Monuments and sites	145 686	-	...	...	112
Federal Republic of Yugoslavia‡	1994	Total museums	177	159	1 850	83	4 876
		1. Art	40	34	756	-	...
		2. Archaeology and history	40	36	163	-	...
		3. Nat. history & nat. science	5	3	33	-	...
		4. Science and technology	5	5	53	-	...
		5. Ethnography & anthropology	21	19	51	-	...
		8. General museums	66	62	756	-	...
		Zoos, botanical gardens, etc.	1 436	2	2 686	2	2 038
Oceania							
Australia	1991	Total museums	1 893	...	17 960	-	...
		1. Art	236	...	9 710	-	...
Fiji	1994	Total museums	1	1	12	1	348
		5. Ethnography & anthropology	1	1	12	1	348
Niue	1990	Total museums	1	-	...	1	1
		5. Ethnography & anthropology	1	-	...	1	1

Museums and related institutions 8.1
Musées et institutions assimilées
Museos e instituciones conexas

	Personnel Personnel Personal					Annual current expenditure Dépenses annuelles ordinaires Gastos ordinarios anuales		
Number of museums reporting Nombre de musées ayant fourni ces données Número de museos que dieron este dato	Total staff Total du personnel Total de personal	Professional staff Personnel professionnel Personal professional		Other staff Autre personnel Otro personal		Number of museums reporting Nombre de musées ayant fourni ces données Número de museos que dieron este dato	Total (000) Total (000) Total (000)	Country Pays País
		Paid staff Salariés Remunerados	Volunteers Volontaires Voluntarios	Paid staff Salariés Remunerados	Volunteers Volontaires Voluntarios			
(6)	(7)	(8)	(9)	(10)	(11)	(12)	(13)	
271	10 970	5 110	-	6 860	-	271	75 233	Ukraine
49	2 430	779	-	1 651	-	49	17 415	
94	4 328	1 492	-	2 836	-	94	38 305	
100	3 336	1 520	-	1 816	-	100	15 531	
28	876	319	-	557	-	28	3 982	
-	...	...	...	...	...	-	...	
								Federal Republic of Yugoslavia‡
144	1 804	1 157	-	647	-	83	4 742	
34	291	169	-	122	-	-	...	
27	164	104	-	60	-	-	...	
4	48	39	-	9	-	-	...	
4	36	30	-	6	-	-	...	
16	150	99	-	51	-	-	...	
59	1 115	716	-	399	-	-	...	
2	48	24	...	24	...	2	1 656	
								Oceania
779	...	...	...	...	51 861	-	...	Australia
-	...	...	...	...	...	-	...	
1	24	6	-	18	-	1	341	Fiji
1	24	6	-	18	-	1	341	
1	2	1	-	1	-	1	40	Niue
1	2	1	-	1	-	1	40	

8.1   Museums and related institutions
Musées et institutions assimilées
Museos e instituciones conexas

AFRICA:
Benin:

E--> Professional and other staff are counted together.

FR-> Le personnel professionnel et l'autre personnel sont comptés ensemble.

ESP> Se considera a la vez el personal profesional y otro personal.

Equatorial Guinea:

E--> Data for expenditure are expressed in millions.

FR-> Les données relatives aux dépenses sont exprimées en millions.

ESP> Los datos relativos a los gastos se expresan en millones.

Madagascar:

E--> Data refer to national museums only.

FR-> Les données se réfèrent aux musées nationaux seulement.

ESP> Los datos se refieren a los museos nacionales solamente.

Niger:

E--> Data on the art museum include collections on archaeology and history, natural history and natural science, science and technology, ethnography and anthropology.

FR-> Le musée d'art inclut les collections sur l'archéologie et l'histoire, l'histoire et les sciences naturelles, les sciences et les techniques, l'ethnographie et l'anthropologie.

ESP> El museo de arte incluye las colecciones sobre arqueología e historia, historía y ciencias naturales, ciencia y tecnología, etnografía y antropología.

AMERICA, NORTH:
Canada:

E--> Archaeology and history museums include ethnology and anthropology museums. Professional and other staff are counted together.

FR-> Les musées d'archéologie et d'histoire incluent les musées d'ethnographie et d'anthropologie. Le personnel professionnel et l'autre personnel sont comptés ensemble.

ESP> Los museos de arqueología e historia incluyen los museos de etnografía y antropología. Se considera a la vez el personal profesional y otro personal.

Costa Rica:

E--> Data for expenditure are expressed in millions.

FR-> Les données relatives aux dépenses sont exprimées en millions.

ESP> Los datos relativos a los gastos se expresan en millones.

Cuba:

E--> Data on museums include 105 monuments and sites.

FR-> Les données relatives à 105 monuments et sites sont incluses avec celles des musées.

ESP> Los datos relativos a los museos incluyen 105 monumentos y sitios arqueológicos.

Mexico:

E--> Data refer only to the national museum.

FR-> Les données se réfèrent au musée national seulement.

ESP> Los datos se refieren al museo nacional solamente.

ASIA:
Turkey:

E--> Data for receipts and expenditure are expressed in millions.

FR-> Les données relatives aux recettes et dépenses sont exprimées en millions.

ESP> Los datos relativos a los ingresos y gastos se expresan en millones.

EUROPE:
Belgium:

E--> Data refer only to the French community.

FR-> Les données se réfèrent à la communauté française seulement.

ESP> Los datos se refieren solamente a la comunidad francesa.

Finland:

E--> Data on archaeology and history museums, science and technology museums, ethnology and anthropology museums, specialized, regional and general museums are included under other museums.

FR-> Les données relatives aux musées d'archéologie et d'histoire, des sciences et techniques, d'ethnographie et d'anthropologie et aux musées régionaux, généraux et spécialisés sont comptées avec les autres musées.

ESP> Los datos relativos a los museos de arqueología e historia, ciencia y tecnología, etnografía y antropología, museos regionales, generales y especializados, se incluyen en *otros museos.*

France:

E--> Data refer only to national and public museums. Of the estimated 1,300 public museums in France, 35 are national museums controlled by the *Direction des musées de France (DMF).*

FR-> Les données se réfèrent seulement aux musées publics. Sur les 1 300 musées publics estimés en France, 34 sont des musées nationaux contrôlés par la *Direction des musées de France (DMF).*

ESP> Los datos se refieren solamente a los museos nacionales y públicos. De los 1 300 museos estimados en Francia, 34 son museos nacionales controlados por la *Direction des musées de France (DMF).*

Germany:

E--> Specialized museums include ethnology and anthropology museums.

FR-> Les musées spécialisés incluent les musées d'ethnographie et d'anthropologie.

ESP> Los museos especializados incluyen los museos de etnografía y antropología.

Greece:

E--> Data refer only to national and public museums. Data on personnel and expenditure for monuments and sites are included under museums.

FR-> Les données relatives au personnel et aux dépenses pour les monuments et sites sont comprises avec les musées.

ESP> Los datos se refieren solamente a los museos nacionales y públicos. Los datos relativos al personal y a los gastos destinados a los monumentos y sitios arqueológicos se incluyen en museos.

Italy:

E--> Data refer only to government institutions attached to the Ministry of *Beni culturali e ambientali.* Data for receipts are expressed in millions.

FR-> Les données se réfèrent seulement aux institutions gouvernementales dépendant du ministère des *Beni culturali e ambientali.*

ESP> Los datos se refieren solamente a las instituciones gubernamentales dependientes del Ministerio de los *Beni culturali e ambientali.* Los datos se expresan en millones.

Monaco:

E--> Data on expenditure of the anthropology museum do not include expenditure on personnel.

FR-> Les données relatives aux dépenses du musée d'anthropologie ne comprennent pas les dépenses relatives au personnel.

ESP> Los datos relativos a los gastos del museo de antropología no incluyen los gastos de personal.

Poland:

E--> Data on receipts are expressed in millions.

FR-> Les données relatives aux recettes et dépenses sont exprimées en millions.

ESP> Los datos relativos a los ingresos y gastos se expresan en millones.

Russian Federation:

E--> Data on receipts and expenditure are expressed in millions.

FR-> Les données relatives aux recettes et dépenses sont exprimées en millions.

ESP> Los datos relativos a los ingresos y gastos se expresan en millones.

The Former Yugoslav Republic of Macedonia:

E--> Data on attendance in the line total also include attendance at monuments and sites.

FR-> Les données relatives à la fréquentation présentées sur la ligne *Total* incluent aussi la fréquentation de monuments et sites.

ESP> Los datos presentados bajo *Frecuentación* en la linea *Total museos* incluyen también la frecuentación en los monumentos y sitios arqueológicos.

Federal Republic of Yugoslavia:

E--> Data on attendance in the line *Total* include 38,000 visitors for which a distribution by type of museums is not available.

FR-> Les données relatives à la fréquentation présentées sur la ligne *Total* incluent 38 000 visiteurs pour lesquels une répartition par types de musées n'est pas disponible.

ESP> Los datos presentados bajo *Frecuentación* en la linea *Total museos* incluyen 38 000 visitantes para los que no se dispone de repartición port tipos de museos.

9 Broadcasting

Radiodiffusion

Radiodifusión

This chapter presents statistical information on radio and television broadcasting. The figures shown in the five tables of this chapter have been obtained from statistical surveys carried out in 1990, 1992 and 1995. The questionnaire used in these surveys was based on definitions and classifications proposed in the Recommendation concerning the International Standardization of Statistics on Radio and Television adopted by the General Conference in 1976.

The response rate to the surveys on radio and television broadcasting still being somewhat low, Tables 9.3 to 9.5 contain, as in previous editions of the *Yearbook*, only half the number of countries that are shown in the tables on receivers/licences issued, for which the statistics have been supplemented from various sources other than the regular UNESCO questionnaires.

Table 9.1

This table gives information on the number of radio receivers for the years 1970, 1980, 1985, 1990 and 1994. Generally, the data refer to the end of the year indicated and relate to all types of receivers for radio broadcasts to the general public, including those connected to a cable distribution system (wired receivers), individual private receivers such as car radios, portable radio sets and private sets installed in public places as well as communal receivers. Data on receivers are estimates of the number of receivers in use. They vary widely in

reliability from country to country and should be treated with caution.

Table 9.2

This table gives statistics for the years 1970, 1980, 1985, 1990 and 1994 on the number of television receivers and/or licences as well as on receivers and/or licences per 1,000 inhabitants.

As in the case of radio receivers, data relating to television *receivers* represent the estimated total number of receivers in use.

Table 9.3

Table 9.3 shows the latest statistics available on sound broadcasting programmes for the period 1988 to 1994. The total annual broadcasting time has been broken down according to programme functions, e.g., information, education, advertisement, entertainment etc. The table also indicates whether the broadcasting institutions are governmental, public service or commercial.

Table 9.4

This table on television programmes has basically the same structure and content as Table 9.3.

Table 9.5

This table shows the most recent statistics available since 1988 on personnel employed permanently in radio and television broadcasting institutions. In the latest survey carried out in 1995 a distinction was made between male and female personnel.

Ce chapitre donne des renseignements statistiques sur la radio et la télévision. Les chiffres qui apparaissent dans les cinq tableaux de ce chapitre ont été obtenus grâce à des enquêtes statistiques effectuées en 1990, 1992 et 1995. Le questionnaire utilisé pour ces enquêtes a été préparé sur la base des définitions et classifications qui figurent dans la Recommandation concernant la normalisation internationale des statistiques relatives à la radio et à la télévision, adoptée par la Conférence générale en 1976.

Le taux de réponse aux enquêtes sur la radio et la télévision étant toujours bas, les tableaux 9.3 à 9.5 ne présentent, comme dans les éditions précédentes de l'*Annuaire Statistique*, que la moitié des pays qui figurent dans les tableaux sur les récepteurs et les licences délivrées, pour lesquels les statistiques ont été obtenues de différentes sources autres que les questionnaires de l'UNESCO.

Tableau 9.1

Ce tableau présente des renseignements sur le nombre de récepteurs de radio pour les années 1970, 1980, 1985, 1990 et 1994. En général, les données se réfèrent à la fin de l'année indiquée et elles portent sur tous les genres de postes récepteurs destinés à capter les programmes radiodiffusés à l'intention du grand public, y compris les postes récepteurs reliés à un réseau de distribution par câble, ainsi que sur tous les postes individuels privés, comme les récepteurs pour automobiles, les postes portatifs et les postes privés installés dans des lieux publics de même que les récepteurs destinés à l'écoute collective. Les données sur les récepteurs sont des estimations du nombre de récepteurs en service. La fiabilité de ces données varie sensiblement

d'un pays à l'autre et elles doivent donc être considérées avec prudence.

Tableau 9.2

Ce tableau présente des statistiques pour les années 1970, 1980, 1985, 1990 et 1994 sur le nombre de récepteurs de télévision et/ou les licences ainsi que les récepteurs et/ou les licences pour 1 000 habitants.

Comme pour la radio, les données relatives aux récepteurs de télévision représentent une estimation du nombre total des récepteurs en service.

Tableau 9.3

Le tableau 9.3 présente les dernières statistiques disponibles sur les programmes de radiodiffusion sonore pour la période de 1988 à 1994. La durée totale annuelle de diffusion a été répartie selon les fonctions des programmes, c'est-à-dire, information, éducation, publicité, divertissement, etc. De plus, le tableau indique si les organismes de radiodiffusion sont gouvernementaux, de service public ou commerciaux.

Tableau 9.4

Ce tableau se réfère aux programmes de télévision et présente exactement la même structure et le même contenu que le tableau 9.3.

Tableau 9.5

Ce tableau présente les statistiques les plus récentes disponibles depuis 1988 sur le personnel permanent employé dans les organismes de radiodiffusion sonore et visuelle. Dans la dernière enquête réalisée en 1995 une distinction a été faite entre les personnels masculin et féminin.

Este capítulo proporciona información estadística sobre la radio y la televisión. Los datos que figuran en los cinco cuadros de este capítulo han sido obtenidos por medio de encuestas estadísticas efectuadas en 1988, 1990 y 1992. El cuestionario utilizado en estas encuestas esta basado en las definiciones y clasificaciones contenidas en la Recomendación sobre la normalización internacional de las estadísticas relativas a la radio y la televisión, adoptada por la Conferencia General en 1976.

Como la tasa de respuesta a las encuestas sobre la radio y la televisión es todavía baja, los cuadros 9.3 a 9.5 contienen, como en los *Anuarios estadísticos* precedentes, sólo la mitad de los países que figuran en los cuadros sobre los receptores y licencias existentes para los cuales se han obtenido estadísticas de diversas fuentes.

Cuadro 9.1

Este cuadro procura información sobre el número de receptores de radio para 1970, 1980, 1985, 1990 y 1994. En general, los datos se refieren al final del año y a todos los tipos de receptores destinados a captar los programas emitidos para el público en general, incluídos los que están conectados por cable a una red de distribución, los receptores individuales privados, como los de los automóviles, los portátiles y los receptores privados instalados en locales públicos así como los receptores destinados a una escucha colectiva. Los datos sobre los receptores son estimaciones del número de receptores en uso. La fiabilidad de estos datos varía sensiblemente de un país a otro y por eso deben ser considerados con prudencia.

Cuadro 9.2

Este cuadro presenta estadísticas para los años 1970, 1980, 1985, 1990 y 1994 sobre el número de receptores de televisión y/o permisos concedidos y los receptores y/o permisos concedidos por 1 000 habitantes.

Como para la radio, los datos relativos a los receptores de televisión representan una estimación del número total de los receptores en uso.

Cuadro 9.3

El cuadro 9.3 presenta, para el periodo 1988 a 1994, las últimas estadísticas disponibles sobre los programas de radiodifusión. La duración anual total de radiodifusión ha sido repartida según las funciones de los programas, i.e., información, educación, publicidad, programas recreativos, etc. El cuadro indica también si las instituciones de radiodifusión son gubernamentales, de servicio público o comerciales.

Cuadro 9.4

Este cuadro se refiere a los programas de televisión y presenta exactamente la misma estructura y los mismos criterios que el cuadro 9.3.

Cuadro 9.5

El cuadro 9.5 presenta las estadísticas más recientes disponibles desde 1988 sobre el personal permanente empleado en organismos de radiodifusión y teledifusión. Durante la última encuesta realizada en 1995 se estableció la distinción entre personal masculino y femenino.

Radio broadcasting: receivers 9.1
Radiodiffusion sonore: récepteurs
Radiodifusión sonora: receptores

9.1 Radio broadcasting: number of receivers, and receivers per 1,000 inhabitants

Radiodiffusion sonore: nombre de récepteurs, et de récepteurs pour 1 000 habitants

Radiodifusión sonora: número de receptores, y de receptores por 1 000 habitantes

Country Pays País	Number of receivers (thousands) Nombre de postes récepteurs (milliers) Número de receptores (en miles)					Number of receivers per 1,000 inhabitants Nombre de postes récepteurs pour 1 000 habitants Número de receptores por 1 000 habitantes				
	1970	1980	1985	1990	1994	1970	1980	1985	1990	1994
	(1)	(2)	(3)	(4)	(5)	(6)	(7)	(8)	(9)	(10)
Africa										
Algeria	2 500	3 700	4 800	5 810	6 450	182	197	219	233	236
Angola	95	145	217	260	320	17	21	27	28	30
Benin	85	230	300	415	480	32	66	75	90	91
Botswana	20	75	115	150	180	31	83	107	118	125
Burkina Faso	87	125	150	235	280	16	18	19	26	28
Burundi	65	160	250	320	400	18	39	53	58	64
Cameroon	170	760	1 200	1 650	1 900	26	88	120	143	148
Cape Verde	5	41	50	59	67	19	142	161	173	176
Central African Republic	46	120	150	200	235	25	52	58	68	73
Chad	450	750	1 150	1 350	1 520	123	168	229	243	246
Comoros	24	46	56	69	81	87	120	123	127	129
Congo	65	100	138	250	290	51	60	72	112	115
Côte d'Ivoire	75	1 000	1 300	1 700	1 975	14	122	131	142	143
Djibouti	8	21	30	41	46	54	75	77	79	81
Egypt	4 400	6 000	12 000	17 000	18 950	125	137	241	302	307
Equatorial Guinea	70	87	128	147	165	241	401	410	418	424
Eritrea	.	.	.	.	300	.	.	.	.	87
Ethiopia	450	3 000	8 000	9 300	10 550	16	82	194	196	197
Gabon	62	105	132	165	189	123	130	134	144	147
Gambia	48	73	105	148	176	103	114	141	160	163
Ghana	703	1 700	2 500	3 423	3 880	82	158	195	228	229
Guinea	91	135	180	240	280	23	30	36	42	43
Guinea-Bissau	4	25	30	38	42	8	31	34	39	40
Kenya	265	650	1 600	2 000	2 400	23	39	80	85	88

9.1 Radio broadcasting: receivers
Radiodiffusion sonore: récepteurs
Radiodifusión sonora: receptores

Country Pays País	Number of receivers (thousands) Nombre de postes récepteurs (milliers) Número de receptores (en miles)					Number of receivers per 1,000 inhabitants Nombre de postes récepteurs pour 1 000 habitants Número de receptores por 1 000 habitantes				
	1970	1980	1985	1990	1994	1970	1980	1985	1990	1994
	(1)	(2)	(3)	(4)	(5)	(6)	(7)	(8)	(9)	(10)
Lesotho	5	33	44	56	65	5	25	28	31	33
Liberia	195	335	475	580	670	141	179	216	225	228
Libyan Arab Jamahiriya	85	200	800	1 020	1 180	43	66	211	224	226
Madagascar	541	1 600	1 950	2 400	2 740	79	177	183	191	192
Malawi	106	260	1 500	2 000	2 450	23	42	207	214	226
Mali	60	105	250	400	465	11	15	32	43	44
Mauritania	55	150	250	291	327	45	97	142	145	147
Mauritius	110	260	335	385	405	133	269	330	364	367
Morocco	935	3 000	3 850	5 250	5 800	61	155	176	216	219
Mozambique	90	254	450	525	580	10	21	33	37	37
Namibia	...	...	150	180	208	...	...	127	133	139
Niger	60	250	300	460	540	14	45	45	60	61
Nigeria	1 275	7 000	14 500	18 700	21 300	23	97	175	194	196
Reunion	79	100	122	145	158	171	198	222	240	245
Rwanda	30	175	335	450	520	8	34	55	64	67
St. Helena	1	1	2	2	2	140	280	313	383	387
Sao Tome and Principe	6	23	27	32	35	82	245	255	269	270
Senegal	240	360	700	830	945	58	65	110	113	117
Seychelles	7	21	25	32	35	132	333	385	457	490
Sierra Leone	40	450	775	925	1 025	15	139	216	231	233
Somalia	50	112	200	320	375	10	17	25	37	41
South Africa	2 000	8 000	10 000	11 450	12 750	89	274	303	309	314
Sudan	1 200	3 500	5 375	6 280	7 050	87	187	250	255	258
Swaziland	30	81	101	120	136	72	145	156	161	163
Togo	40	530	630	740	850	20	203	208	210	212
Tunisia	388	1 000	1 185	1 550	1 740	76	157	163	192	199
Uganda	200	400	1 250	1 900	2 210	20	30	83	106	107
United Republic of Tanzania	150	290	365	600	740	11	16	17	23	26
Western Sahara	8	22	33	42	50	105	169	179	182	184
Zaire	630	1 500	2 800	3 600	4 150	31	56	88	96	98
Zambia	75	135	500	650	760	18	24	73	80	83
Zimbabwe	145	240	500	832	945	28	34	60	84	86
America, North										
Anguilla	.	.	.	2	3	.	.	.	307	315
Antigua and Barbuda	10	17	21	26	28	174	279	339	406	427
Aruba	...	...	...	...	40	...	...	...	...	581
Bahamas	65	102	120	137	200	382	486	513	535	735
Barbados	89	135	200	225	229	372	542	791	875	877
Belize	48	71	88	109	122	390	486	530	577	581
Bermuda	38	60	68	77	80	717	1 111	1 214	1 254	1 270
British Virgin Islands	5	6	7	8	9	450	458	486	470	474
Canada	15 000	17 734	23 237	28 461	30 640	703	721	896	1 024	1 051
Cayman Islands	3	12	19	25	29	250	706	910	962	967

Radio broadcasting: receivers 9.1
Radiodiffusion sonore: récepteurs
Radiodifusión sonora: receptores

Country / Pays / País	Number of receivers (thousands) / Nombre de postes récepteurs (milliers) / Número de receptores (en miles)					Number of receivers per 1,000 inhabitants / Nombre de postes récepteurs pour 1 000 habitants / Número de receptores por 1 000 habitantes				
	1970	1980	1985	1990	1994	1970	1980	1985	1990	1994
	(1)	(2)	(3)	(4)	(5)	(6)	(7)	(8)	(9)	(10)
Costa Rica	130	190	650	781	870	75	83	246	257	260
Cuba	1 330	2 914	3 282	3 650	3 800	156	300	325	344	347
Dominica	5	31	38	42	43	71	419	528	592	600
Dominican Republic	650	900	1 020	1 210	1 330	147	158	160	170	173
El Salvador	583	1 550	1 900	2 125	2 500	162	343	401	411	443
Greenland	7	15	19	23	24	152	300	358	402	407
Grenada	15	35	45	54	55	160	393	500	588	595
Guadeloupe	30	50	80	89	96	94	153	225	227	228
Guatemala	220	350	450	600	700	42	51	57	65	68
Haiti	76	105	140	290	350	17	20	24	45	50
Honduras	108	500	1 600	1 980	2 240	42	140	382	406	408
Jamaica	500	800	920	1 010	1 060	268	375	398	427	436
Martinique	50	62	67	72	76	153	190	196	200	203
Mexico	5 600	9 000	15 000	21 500	23 500	111	134	199	254	256
Montserrat	5	6	6	6	6	409	458	545	573	582
Netherlands Antilles	115	175	190	202	211	723	1 006	1 044	1 065	1 069
Nicaragua	140	670	802	955	1 120	68	239	248	260	262
Panama	215	300	400	540	586	143	154	185	225	227
Puerto Rico	1 525	2 000	2 300	2 505	2 600	561	624	683	709	713
Saint Kitts and Nevis	...	...	21	27	27	...	...	488	643	666
St. Lucia	58	81	92	100	107	574	704	738	752	764
St. Pierre and Miquelon	2	4	4	4	4	320	583	633	696	702
St. Vincent and the Grenadines	22	42	55	70	74	253	429	539	654	667
Trinidad and Tobago	200	300	500	600	635	206	277	431	485	491
Turks and Caicos Islands	1	4	5	6	7	167	506	510	512	514
United States	290 000	454 500	500 000	529 440	553 000	1 414	1 996	2 097	2 118	2 122
U.S. Virgin Islands	43	82	93	101	105	672	845	939	990	1 005
America, South										
Argentina	9 000	12 000	18 000	21 800	23 000	376	427	594	670	673
Bolivia	402	2 800	3 675	4 380	4 850	95	523	623	666	670
Brazil	11 800	38 000	49 000	57 000	62 500	123	313	363	384	393
Chile	1 400	3 250	4 000	4 500	4 850	147	292	331	342	345
Colombia	2 217	3 300	4 000	5 600	6 150	104	124	136	173	178
Ecuador	1 700	2 425	2 850	3 330	3 670	285	305	313	324	327
Falkland Islands (Malvinas)		1	1	1	1	200	400	500	500	504
French Guiana	7	30	59	75	90	143	441	643	644	645
Guyana	94	310	355	387	405	133	408	449	486	491
Paraguay	150	350	600	730	830	64	112	162	169	172
Peru	1 748	2 750	4 000	5 420	5 950	132	159	205	251	255
Suriname	92	189	230	265	285	247	532	610	663	680
Uruguay	1 000	1 630	1 760	1 865	1 920	356	559	585	603	606
Venezuela	3 800	5 900	7 000	8 600	9 480	354	391	408	441	443

9.1 Radio broadcasting: receivers
Radiodiffusion sonore: récepteurs
Radiodifusión sonora: receptores

Country / Pays / País	Number of receivers (thousands) Nombre de postes récepteurs (milliers) Número de receptores (en miles)					Number of receivers per 1,000 inhabitants Nombre de postes récepteurs pour 1 000 habitants Número de receptores por 1 000 habitantes				
	1970	1980	1985	1990	1994	1970	1980	1985	1990	1994
	(1)	(2)	(3)	(4)	(5)	(6)	(7)	(8)	(9)	(10)
Asia										
Afghanistan	600	1 200	1 450	1 720	2 230	44	75	100	114	118
Bahrain	56	125	210	269	305	255	360	507	549	556
Bangladesh	500	1 500	4 000	4 855	5 500	8	17	41	45	47
Bhutan	3	7	18	24	28	3	6	13	16	17
Brunei Darussalam	15	41	55	68	76	115	212	243	265	271
Cambodia	103	600	800	942	1 080	15	92	106	107	108
China	12 000	55 000	120 000	209 500	222 000	14	55	112	181	184
Cyprus	105	162	190	205	220	171	258	286	292	300
East Timor	3	4	5	6	6	5	7	7	7	8
Georgia	.	.	.	.	3 000	.	.	.	.	550
Hong Kong	694	2 550	3 250	3 800	3 950	176	506	596	666	677
India	11 747	26 000	50 000	67 000	74 000	21	38	65	79	81
Indonesia	2 550	15 000	21 500	26 500	28 800	21	99	128	145	148
Iran, Islamic Republic of	1 800	6 400	10 000	13 428	15 550	63	163	204	228	237
Iraq	1 026	2 100	3 000	3 880	4 335	110	161	196	215	218
Israel	477	950	1 800	2 180	2 610	160	245	425	468	478
Japan	23 250	79 200	95 000	111 000	113 800	223	678	786	899	912
Jordan	370	550	791	1 015	1 265	161	188	206	238	243
Kazakstan	.	.	.	.	6 400	.	.	.	.	376
Korea, Dem. People's Rep.	650	1 500	2 000	2 600	2 950	44	82	101	119	126
Korea, Republic of	4 012	20 000	38 605	43 350	45 300	126	525	946	1 011	1 017
Kuwait	105	390	535	700	726	141	284	311	327	445
Lao People's Democratic Rep.	50	350	430	520	600	18	109	120	124	127
Lebanon	600	2 000	2 050	2 255	2 590	243	749	768	883	889
Macau	21	80	98	120	140	93	331	345	351	352
Malaysia	600	5 650	6 600	7 680	8 500	55	411	421	429	432
Maldives	1	7	19	25	29	11	44	103	116	118
Mongolia	90	160	200	289	322	72	96	105	133	136
Myanmar	400	774	2 500	3 400	3 750	15	23	67	81	82
Nepal	55	300	450	650	745	5	20	27	34	35
Oman	10	300	800	1 010	1 210	14	272	573	577	583
Pakistan	3 000	5 500	8 500	10 650	12 000	46	64	83	87	88
Philippines	1 500	2 100	5 000	8 600	9 500	40	43	91	141	144
Qatar	25	90	150	206	231	225	393	419	425	428
Saudi Arabia	700	2 500	3 545	4 655	5 125	122	260	280	290	294
Singapore	500	900	1 550	1 720	1 820	241	373	606	636	645
Sri Lanka	640	1 454	2 551	3 400	3 650	51	98	158	197	201
Syrian Arab Republic	1 170	1 700	2 200	3 150	3 640	187	195	213	255	257
Thailand	2 775	6 550	8 000	10 300	11 050	78	140	156	185	190
Turkey	3 550	5 000	7 000	9 000	9 850	101	113	139	160	162
United Arab Emirates	20	240	380	515	580	90	236	276	308	312
Uzbekistan	.	.	.	.	1 800	.	.	.	.	81
Viet Nam	2 500	5 000	6 000	6 900	7 600	59	93	100	103	104

Radio broadcasting: receivers 9.1
Radiodiffusion sonore: récepteurs
Radiodifusión sonora: receptores

Country / Pays / País	Number of receivers (thousands) / Nombre de postes récepteurs (milliers) / Número de receptores (en miles)					Number of receivers per 1 000 inhabitants / Nombre de postes récepteurs pour 1 000 habitants / Número de receptores por 1 000 habitantes				
	1970	1980	1985	1990	1994	1970	1980	1985	1990	1994
	(1)	(2)	(3)	(4)	(5)	(6)	(7)	(8)	(9)	(10)
Yemen	.	.	.	310	450	.	.	.	27	32
Europe										
Albania	150	400	493	570	650	70	150	166	173	190
Andorra	4	7	9	11	14	194	200	200	205	211
Austria	3 200	3 830	4 180	4 755	4 900	429	507	553	617	619
Belarus	1 390	2 145	2 450	2 595	2 900	154	223	246	254	285
Belgium	5 400	7 200	7 450	7 660	7 800	559	731	756	770	774
Bosnia and Herzegovina	...	...	...	...	800	...	...	...	...	227
Bulgaria	2 975	3 500	3 750	3 950	4 000	350	395	419	439	454
Croatia	...	1 050	1 075	1 088	1 174	...	240	240	241	261
Czech Republic	...	4	4 400	5 500	6 500	...		427	534	631
Denmark	3 450	4 750	4 875	5 250	5 360	700	927	953	1 021	1 036
Estonia	.	.	.	.	720	.	.	.	.	467
Finland	2 000	4 000	4 830	4 960	5 100	434	837	985	995	1 003
France	25 000	39 900	48 000	50 370	51 450	492	741	870	888	891
Germany	.	.	.	69 650	76 000	.	.	.	878	935
Gibraltar	24	33	34	36	36	889	1 124	1 199	1 289	1 296
Greece	990	3 310	4 000	4 250	4 350	113	343	403	415	418
Hungary	3 600	5 340	6 144	6 275	6 350	348	499	581	605	625
Iceland	125	162	185	200	211	613	711	768	784	793
Ireland	690	1 275	2 050	2 170	2 250	234	375	577	619	636
Italy	30 500	34 000	37 000	45 500	45 850	567	602	652	798	802
Latvia	.	.	.	.	1 710	.	.	.	.	662
Liechtenstein	5	13	18	19	21	238	520	648	655	661
Lithuania	.	.	.	.	1 435	.	.	.	.	387
Luxembourg	157	200	229	240	255	463	549	624	630	636
Malta	120	165	178	186	193	396	509	517	525	530
Moldova	.	.	.	.	3 000	.	.	.	.	679
Monaco	7	26	28	30	33	275	967	1 007	1 012	1 016
Netherlands	7 350	9 200	12 000	13 550	14 000	564	650	828	906	909
Norway	2 455	2 700	3 230	3 370	3 450	633	661	778	794	799
Poland	7 000	10 615	12 250	16 500	16 900	215	298	329	433	441
Portugal	1 400	1 660	2 000	2 240	2 290	155	170	202	227	233
Romania	3 550	3 930	4 100	4 600	4 680	175	177	180	198	204
Russian Federation	.	.	.	49 700	50 000	.	.	.	336	339
San Marino	4	10	12	14	15	222	476	527	587	592
Slovakia	.	.	.	.	3 030	.	.	.	.	568
Slovenia	420	500	650	700	735	251	273	346	365	378
Spain	7 700	9 700	11 300	12 000	12 350	228	258	294	306	312
Sweden	3 750	7 000	7 250	7 500	7 680	466	842	868	876	879
Switzerland	3 700	5 140	5 426	5 682	6 000	598	813	830	831	841
The Former Yugoslav Rep. of Macedonia	...	...	...	367	390	...	...	...	179	182

9.1   Radio broadcasting: receivers
Radiodiffusion sonore: récepteurs
Radiodifusión sonora: receptores

Country Pays País	Number of receivers (thousands) Nombre de postes récepteurs (milliers) Número de receptores (en miles)					Number of receivers per 1,000 inhabitants Nombre de postes récepteurs pour 1 000 habitants Número de receptores por 1 000 habitantes				
	1970	1980	1985	1990	1994	1970	1980	1985	1990	1994
	(1)	(2)	(3)	(4)	(5)	(6)	(7)	(8)	(9)	(10)
Ukraine	18 424	28 941	36 434	41 000	41 800	389	579	716	794	812
United Kingdom	34 706	53 500	57 000	80 000	83 000	624	950	1 007	1 393	1 429
Federal Rep. of Yugoslavia	1 110	1 930	2 020	...	...	128	203	205	...	...
Oceania										
American Samoa	20	31	38	47	53	741	969	974	1 003	1 008
Australia	7 250	16 000	19 500	21 600	23 050	578	1 098	1 247	1 279	1 291
Cook Islands	5	8	10	12	13	238	417	612	678	700
Fiji	150	300	370	430	468	288	473	529	592	607
French Polynesia	50	78	93	108	119	450	517	532	546	553
Guam	75	100	150	185	206	872	935	1 250	1 381	1 401
Kiribati	7	12	13	15	16	140	193	195	203	209
Nauru	2	4	5	6	6	383	557	569	572	577
New Caledonia	25	69	80	94	100	231	479	516	560	562
New Zealand	2 400	2 755	2 950	3 130	3 500	851	885	909	931	991
Niue	1	1	1	1	1	120	317	358	558	563
Papua New Guinea	80	180	230	280	320	33	58	67	73	76
Samoa	19	32	68	74	78	131	201	425	454	462
Solomon Islands	8	20	27	38	45	47	88	100	119	122
Tokelau	.	.	1	1	1	.	.	425	525	605
Tonga	8	20	30	53	55	98	217	330	552	561
Tuvalu	1	2	2	3	3	167	206	238	304	310
Vanuatu, Republic of	10	23	36	43	49	115	197	269	285	294

9.2 Television broadcasting: number of receivers, and receivers per 1,000 inhabitants

Télévision: nombre de récepteurs, et de récepteurs pour 1 000 habitants

Televisión: número de receptores, y de receptores por 1 000 habitantes

R = Estimated number of receivers in use	R = Estimation du nombre de récepteurs en service
L = Number of licences issued or sets declared	L = Nombre de licences délivrées ou de postes déclarés

R = Estimación del número de receptores en funcionamiento

L = Número de permisos existentes o de receptores declarados

Country Pays País	Defi-nition of data Type de données Tipo de datos	Number of receivers in use and/or licenses issued (thousands) Nombre de postes récepteurs en service et/ou de licences délivrées (milliers) Número de receptores en funcionamiento y/o de permisos existentes (en miles)					Number of receivers in use and/or licences issued per 1,000 inhabitants Nombre de postes récepteurs en service et/ou de licences délivrées pour 1 000 habitants Número de receptores en funcionamiento y/o de permisos existentes por 1 000 habitantes				
		1970	1980	1985	1990	1994	1970	1980	1985	1990	1994
		(1)	(2)	(3)	(4)	(5)	(6)	(7)	(8)	(9)	(10)
Africa											
Algeria	R	400	975	1 500	1 840	2 150	29	52	69	74	79
Angola	R	-	30	37	57	70	-	4.3	4.6	6.2	6.6
Benin	R	-	5	15	23	29	-	1.4	3.8	5.0	5.5
Botswana	R	-	-	-	20	24	-	-	-	16	17
Burkina Faso	R	6	20	37	48	55	1.1	2.9	4.7	5.3	5.5
Burundi	R	-	-	0.3	5	9	-	-	0.1	0.6	1.5
Cameroon	R	-	-	-	270	309	-	-	-	23	24
Cape Verde	R	-	-	-	1	1	-	-	-	2.9	3.4
Central African Republic	R	-	1	5	13	16	-	0.3	1.7	4.4	4.9
Chad	R	-	-	-	7	9	-	-	-	1.2	1.4
Comoros	R	-	-	-	0.2	0.2	-	-	-	0.4	0.4
Congo	R	2	4	5	13	18	1.6	2.2	2.8	5.8	7.0
Côte d'Ivoire	R	34	310	500	703	822	6.2	38	50	59	60
Djibouti	R	1	5	12	22	25	6.8	18	31	43	44
Egypt	R	529	1 400	3 860	5 700	6 700	15	32	78	101	109
Equatorial Guinea	R	-	1	2	3	4	-	4.6	7.1	9.4	9.6
Eritrea	R	.	.	.	.	1	.	.	.	.	0.3
Ethiopia	R L	8 7	30 25	70 55	180 57	230 63	0.3 0.2	0.8 0.7	1.7 1.3	3.8 1.2	4.3 1.2
Gabon	R	1	9	22	43	49	2.0	12	22	38	38
Gambia	R	-	-	-	-	3	-	-	-	-	2.8
Ghana	R	16	57	150	246	1 500	1.9	5.3	12	16	89
Guinea	R	-	6	8	40	50	-	1.3	1.7	7.0	7.7
Kenya	R L	16 2	62 9	100 15	225 ...	295 ...	1.4 0.2	3.7 0.5	5.0 0.8	9.5 ...	11 ...
Lesotho	R	-	-	0.5	10	20	-	-	0.3	5.6	10
Liberia	R	7	21	35	47	55	5.1	11	16	18	19

Country Pays País	Defi- nition of data Type de données Tipo de datos	Number of receivers in use and/or licenses issued (thousands) Nombre de postes récepteurs en service et/ou de licences délivrées (milliers) Número de receptores en funcionamiento y/o de permisos existentes (en miles)					Number of receivers in use and/or licences issued per 1,000 inhabitants Nombre de postes récepteurs en service et/ou de licences délivrées pour 1 000 habitants Número de receptores en funcionamiento y/o de permisos existentes por 1 000 habitantes				
		1970	1980	1985	1990	1994	1970	1980	1985	1990	1994
		(1)	(2)	(3)	(4)	(5)	(6)	(7)	(8)	(9)	(10)
Libyan Arab Jamahiriya	R	1	186	235	435	525	0.5	61	62	96	100
Madagascar	R	4	45	100	240	280	0.6	5.0	9.4	19	20
Mali	R	...	-	1	10	14	...	-	0.1	1.1	1.3
Mauritania	R	-	-	1	45	55	-	-	0.3	22	25
Mauritius	R L	25 19	92 83	140 107	233 147	245 ...	30 23	95 86	138 105	220 139	222 ...
Morocco	R L	200 174	890 749	1 370 1 150	1 850 ...	2 100 ...	13 11	46 39	63 53	76 ...	79 ...
Mozambique	R	-	2	7	40	55	-	0.2	0.5	2.8	3.5
Namibia	R	-	5	16	30	34	-	4.9	14	22	23
Niger	R	0.1	5	12	35	44	0.0	0.9	1.8	4.5	4.9
Nigeria	R	75	550	1 000	3 500	4 150	1.4	7.6	12	36	38
Reunion	R L	21 10	81 80	89 87	98 ...	106 ...	46 22	160 158	161 158	162 ...	165 ...
St. Helena	R	-	-	-	-	1	-	-	-	-	167
Sao Tome and Principe	R	-	-	-	-	21	-	-	-	-	162
Senegal	R	1	8	200	265	297	0.2	1.4	31	36	37
Seychelles	R	-	-	2	6	6	-	-	31	86	88
Sierra Leone	R	3	20	30	42	48	1.1	6.2	8.4	11	11
Somalia	R	-	-	1	105	120	-	-	0.1	12	13
South Africa	R	70	2 010	3 000	3 700	4 100	3.1	69	91	100	101
Sudan	R	45	800	1 100	1 800	2 180	3.2	43	51	73	80
Swaziland	R	-	1	8	14	17	-	1.8	12	19	20
Togo	R	-	10	15	22	30	-	3.8	5.0	6.2	7.5
Tunisia	R	72	300	400	625	710	14	47	55	77	81
Uganda	R	8	72	90	180	230	0.8	5.5	6.0	10	11
United Republic of Tanzania	R	4	7	8	40	60	0.3	0.	4.4	1.6	2.1
Western Sahara	R	1	2	4	5	6	13	18	20	20	21
Zaire	R	6	10	13	40	63	0.3	0.4	0.4	1.1	1.5
Zambia	R	17	60	90	210	245	4.1	10	13	26	27
Zimbabwe	R	50	73	178	260	297	9.5	10	21	26	27
America, North											
Antigua and Barbuda	R	5	16	19	23	24	88	262	306	359	370
Aruba	R	.	.	.	.	19	.	.	.	.	277
Bahamas	R	-	31	51	57	61	-	148	218	223	226
Barbados	R	16	52	60	70	73	67	209	237	272	279
Belize	R	-	-	-	31	35	-	-	-	164	167
Bermuda	R	17	30	45	56	58	321	556	804	918	924
British Virgin Islands	R	0.3	2	3	3	4	30	167	201	204	213
Canada	R	7 100	10 617	14 028	17 019	19 973	333	432	541	612	685
Cayman Islands	R	-	2	4	5	6	-	106	190	200	200
Costa Rica	R	100	155	200	420	475	58	68	76	138	142

Country / Pays / País	Defi-nition of data / Type de données / Tipo de datos	Number of receivers in use and/or licenses issued (thousands) / Nombre de postes récepteurs en service et/ou de licences délivrées (milliers) / Número de receptores en funcionamiento y/o de permisos existentes (en miles)					Number of receivers in use and/or licences issued per 1,000 inhabitants / Nombre de postes récepteurs en service et/ou de licences délivrées pour 1 000 habitants / Número de receptores en funcionamiento y/o de permisos existentes por 1 000 habitantes				
		1970	1980	1985	1990	1994	1970	1980	1985	1990	1994
		(1)	(2)	(3)	(4)	(5)	(6)	(7)	(8)	(9)	(10)
Cuba	R	400	1 273	1 940	1 770	1 870	47	131	192	167	171
Dominica	R	-	-	-	5	5	-	-	-	70	75
Dominican Republic	R	100	400	500	600	695	23	70	78	84	90
El Salvador	R	92	300	350	600	2 500	26	66	74	116	443
	L	-	-	-	-	13	-	-	-	-	2.3
Greenland	R	2	3.5	7	11	12	43	70	132	196	203
Grenada	R	-	-	-	30	31	-	-	-	330	337
Guadeloupe	R	8	37	77	102	111	25	113	217	261	262
	L	7	33	70	...	...	22	101	197	...	...
Guatemala	R	72	175	207	475	545	14	25	26	52	53
Haiti	R	11	16	21	30	34	2.4	3.0	3.6	4.6	4.8
Honduras	R	22	65	280	370	428	8.5	18	67	76	78
Jamaica	R	70	170	215	310	345	37	80	93	131	142
Martinique	R	10	38	44	48	51	31	117	129	133	137
	L	10	38	43	...	...	31	117	126	...	...
Mexico	R	1 800	3 820	8 500	12 350	15 000	36	57	113	146	163
Montserrat	R	-	-	-	2	2	-	-	-	148	150
Netherlands Antilles	R	32	43	58	63	66	201	247	319	332	334
Nicaragua	R	55	160	190	240	285	27	57	59	65	67
Panama	R	130	225	350	400	440	86	115	162	167	170
Puerto Rico	R	410	725	850	930	973	151	226	253	263	267
St. Kitts and Nevis	R	3	4	5	9	9	64	91	116	202	213
St. Lucia	R	2	9	17	25	27	15	80	135	188	189
St. Pierre and Miquelon	R	1	3	4	4	4	260	533	600	650	655
St. Vincent and the Grenadines	R	2	5	6	15	16	17	53	59	140	147
Trinidad and Tobago	R	60	210	320	387	410	62	194	276	313	317
United States	R	84 600	155 800	190 000	203 000	213 000	413	684	797	812	817
U.S. Virgin Islands	R	9	50	59	64	66	141	515	596	630	636
America, South											
Argentina	R	3 500	5 140	6 500	7 100	7 500	146	183	214	218	219
Bolivia	R	35	300	420	730	820	8.3	56	71	111	113
Brazil	R	6 100	15 000	25 000	30 800	33 200	64	124	185	207	209
Chile	R	500	1 225	1 750	2 700	2 960	53	110	145	205	211
Colombia	R	810	2 250	2 750	3 600	4 070	38	85	93	111	118
Ecuador	R	150	500	600	880	990	25	63	66	86	88
French Guiana	R	2	13	17	21	25	49	191	184	175	181
	L	2	10	13	...	...	38	154	143	...	...
Guyana	R	-	-	-	28	33	-	-	-	35	39
Paraguay	R	45	68	85	300	400	19	22	23	69	83
Peru	R	395	895	1 500	2 080	2 310	30	52	77	96	99
Suriname	R	28	40	45	55	59	75	113	119	138	141
Uruguay	R	280	368	500	710	735	100	126	166	229	232
Venezuela	R	950	1 710	2 250	3 100	3 500	89	113	131	159	164

Country Pays País	Defi- nition of data Type de données Tipo de datos	Number of receivers in use and/or licenses issued (thousands) Nombre de postes récepteurs en service et/ou de licences délivrées (milliers) Número de receptores en funcionamiento y/o de permisos existentes (en miles)					Number of receivers in use and/or licences issued per 1,000 inhabitants Nombre de postes récepteurs en service et/ou de licences délivrées pour 1 000 habitants Número de receptores en funcionamiento y/o de permisos existentes por 1 000 habitantes				
		1970	1980	1985	1990	1994	1970	1980	1985	1990	1994
		(1)	(2)	(3)	(4)	(5)	(6)	(7)	(8)	(9)	(10)
Asia											
Afghanistan	R	-	45	100	137	185	-	2.8	6.9	9.1	9.8
Armenia	R	.	.	.	.	800	.	.	.	.	225
	L	.	.	.	.	7	.	.	.	.	2.0
Bahrain	R	13	90	170	208	236	59	259	411	424	430
Bangladesh	R	8	80	261	525	685	0.1	0.9	2.6	4.9	5.8
	L	5	45	90	...	...	0.1	0.5	0.9	...	...
Brunei Darussalam	R	5	26	45	60	68	38	135	199	233	241
Cambodia	R	19	35	52	68	80	2.7	5.4	6.9	7.7	8.0
China	R	660	9 020	69 650	150 000	227 880	0.8	9.0	65	130	189
Cyprus	R	54	85	92	215	235	88	135	138	306	320
Georgia	R	.	.	.	.	2 500	.	.	.	.	459
Hong Kong	R	444	1 114	1 275	1 550	1 700	113	221	234	272	291
India	R	28	3 000	10 000	27 000	37 000	0.1	4.4	13	32	40
	L	25	1 548	3 500	...	...	0.0	2.2	4.6	...	...
Indonesia	R	90	3 000	6 438	10 500	12 000	0.7	20	38	57	62
	L	50	2 000	6 384	...	...	0.4	13	38	...	...
Iran, Islamic Republic of	R	533	2 000	2 600	3 620	4 076	19	51	53	61	62
Iraq	R	350	650	900	1 300	1 500	37	50	59	72	75
Israel	R	534	900	1 100	1 245	1 500	180	232	260	267	275
	L	356	480	520	...	...	120	124	123	...	...
Japan	R	35 000	62 976	70 000	75 500	85 000	335	539	579	611	681
	L	22 883	29 140	31 509	33 543	...	219	249	261	272	...
Jordan	R	46	172	240	315	395	20	59	63	74	76
Kazakstan	R	.	.	.	.	4 250	.	.	.	.	250
Korea, Democratic People's Rep. of	R	-	130	200	330	1 000	-	7.1	10	15	43
Korea, Republic of	R	600	6 300	7 721	9 000	14 408	19	165	189	210	323
	L	418	6 280	7 200	7 438	...	13	165	176	174	...
Kuwait	R	100	353	450	575	620	134	257	262	268	380
Lao People's Democratic Rep.	R	-	-	-	22	40	-	-	-	5.2	8.4
Lebanon	R	260	750	800	880	1 050	105	281	300	344	360
Macau	R	-	-	-	30	40	-	-	-	88	101
Malaysia	R	130	1 200	1 800	2 640	3 100	12	87	115	148	157
	L	127	1 119	1 567	1 767	...	12	81	100	99	...
Maldives	R	-	1	3	5	6	-	7.0	17	24	25
	L	-	1	3	...	...	-	5.2	16	...	...
Mongolia	R	1	6	45	85	100	0.	83.4	24	39	42
Myanmar	R	-	1	20	101	226	-	0.0	0.5	2.4	5.0
Nepal	R	-	-	20	35	100	-	-	1.2	1.8	4.7
Oman	R	-	35	900	1 130	1 375	-	32	644	645	662
Pakistan	R	99	938	1 304	1 989	2 600	1.5	11	13	16	19
	L	75	655	1 200	1 687	...	1.1	7.7	12	14	...
Philippines	R	400	1 050	1 500	2 700	3 200	11	22	27	44	48
Qatar	R	1	76	120	190	215	4.5	331	335	392	398
Saudi Arabia	R	500	2 100	3 080	3 950	4 455	87	219	243	246	255
Singapore	R	200	750	850	1 020	1 100	96	311	332	377	390
	L	157	397	482	583	646	76	164	188	216	229

Country Pays País	Defi- nition of data Type de données Tipo de datos	Number of receivers in use and/or licenses issued (thousands) Nombre de postes récepteurs en service et/ou de licences délivrées (milliers) Número de receptores en funcionamiento y/o de permisos existentes (en miles)					Number of receivers in use and/or licences issued per 1,000 inhabitants Nombre de postes récepteurs en service et/ou de licences délivrées pour 1 000 habitants Número de receptores en funcionamiento y/o de permisos existentes por 1 000 habitantes				
		1970	1980	1985	1990	1994	1970	1980	1985	1990	1994
		(1)	(2)	(3)	(4)	(5)	(6)	(7)	(8)	(9)	(10)
Sri Lanka	R	-	35	450	600	900	-	2.4	28	35	50
	L	-	31	326	501	...	-	2.1	20	29	...
Syrian Arab Republic	R	116	385	600	740	880	19	44	58	60	62
Thailand	R	250	1 000	4 122	5 900	6 800	7.0	21	81	106	117
Turkey	R	400	3 500	8 000	9 750	11 000	11	79	159	174	181
Turkmenistan	R	.	.	.	.	720	.	.	.	.	180
United Arab Emirates	R	-	89	130	172	200	-	88	94	103	107
Uzbekistan	R	.	.	.	...	4 250	.	.	.	...	190
Viet Nam	R	...	...	2 000	2 600	3 100	...	...	33	39	43
Yemen	R	.	.	.	300	390	.	.	.	27	28
Europe											
Albania	R	2	96	232	280	310	1.0	36	78	85	91
Andorra	R	1	4	6	8	24	81	118	136	154	367
Austria	R	1 900	2 950	3 260	3 650	3 800	254	391	431	474	480
	L	1 420	2 225	2 417	2 500	2 628	190	295	320	324	332
Belarus	R	1 111	2 100	2 500	2 750	2 300	123	218	251	269	226
Belgium	R	2 750	3 815	3 950	4 450	4 565	285	387	401	447	453
	L	2 100	2 934	2 972	3 296	3 473	217	298	302	331	345
Bulgaria	R	1 335	2 150	2 220	2 900	3 200	157	243	248	323	363
	L	1 028	1 652	1 696	1 633	...	121	186	189	182	...
Croatia	R	...	940	976	1 027	1 138	...	215	218	227	253
Czech Republic	R	.	.	.	.	4 920	.	.	.	.	478
	L	.	.	.	.	3 255	.	.	.	.	316
Denmark	R	1 835	2 550	2 675	2 750	2 790	372	498	523	535	539
	L	1 359	1 856	1 975	1 962	2 123	276	362	386	382	410
Estonia	R	.	.	.	.	565	.	.	.	.	367
Finland	R	1 200	1 980	2 300	2 470	2 600	261	414	469	495	511
	L	1 059	1 538	1 784	1 894	1 882	230	322	364	380	370
France	R	12 000	19 000	21 500	22 800	34 100	236	353	390	402	591
	L	10 968	15 978	17 951	19 492	20 093	216	297	325	344	348
Germany	R	.	.	.	44 000	45 500	.	.	.	554	560
	L	.	.	.	24 694	32 314	.	.	.	311	398
Gibraltar	R	5	7	8	10	10	185	240	282	349	351
	L	5	7	8	...	...	167	233	271	...	...
Greece	R	187	1 650	1 896	1 970	2 150	21	171	191	192	206
	L	170	1 500	1 715	...	...	19	156	173	...	...
Hungary	R	2 120	3 320	4 250	4 330	4 360	205	310	402	418	429
	L	1 769	2 766	2 911	2 930	2 738	171	258	275	283	269
Iceland	R	45	65	75	83	93	221	285	311	325	350
	L	41	64	73	77	85	201	281	303	302	320
Ireland	R	447	785	910	1 025	1 070	151	231	256	293	302
	L	438	616	749	895	958	148	181	211	255	271
Italy	R	12 000	22 000	23 600	24 200	25 000	223	390	416	424	437
	L	9 979	13 361	14 521	15 002	15 864	185	237	256	263	278
Latvia	R	.	.	.	.	1 200	.	.	.	.	465
Liechtenstein	R	3	7	9	10	10	119	280	322	332	337
Lithuania	R	.	.	.	.	1 430	.	.	.	.	386
Luxembourg	R	71	90	92	141	150	209	247	251	370	374
Malta	R	130	202	235	262	272	429	623	683	740	747
	L	44	76	117	144	148	145	235	340	407	407

Country Pays País	Defi-nition of data Type de données Tipo de datos	Number of receivers in use and/or licenses issued (thousands) Nombre de postes récepteurs en service et/ou de licences délivrées (milliers) Número de receptores en funcionamiento y/o de permisos existentes (en miles)					Number of receivers in use and/or licences issued per 1,000 inhabitants Nombre de postes récepteurs en service et/ou de licences délivrées pour 1 000 habitants Número de receptores en funcionamiento y/o de permisos existentes por 1 000 habitantes				
		1970	1980	1985	1990	1994	1970	1980	1985	1990	1994
		(1)	(2)	(3)	(4)	(5)	(6)	(7)	(8)	(9)	(10)
Moldova	R	.	.	.	.	1 200	.	.	.	.	271
Monaco	R	15	17	19	22	24	625	630	679	735	741
Netherlands	R	3 086	5 650	6 700	7 200	7 600	237	399	462	482	494
	L	3 086	4 181	4 633	4 879	5 804	237	296	320	326	377
Norway	R	1 025	1 430	1 640	1 790	1 850	264	350	395	422	428
	L	854	1 195	1 369	1 496	1 550	220	292	330	353	359
Poland	R	4 640	8 750	10 400	11 640	11 800	143	246	280	305	308
	L	4 215	7 954	9 468	9 912	9 969	130	224	254	260	260
Portugal	R	505	1 540	1 765	2 950	3 160	56	158	178	299	321
	L	389	1 400	1 605	1 706	...	43	143	162	173	...
Romania	R	1 630	4 085	4 375	4 520	4 600	80	184	193	195	201
	L	1 485	3 714	3 879	3 645	4 054	73	167	171	157	177
Russian Federation	R	.	.	.	53 978	55 500	.	.	.	365	377
	L	.	.	.	...	44 839	.	.	.	...	304
San Marino	R	3	6	7	8	9	139	300	314	350	352
	L	2	6	7	...	...	133	286	305	...	...
Slovakia	R	.	.	.	.	2 530	.	.	.	.	474
	L	.	.	.	.	1 209	.	.	.	.	227
Slovenia	R	...	460	500	550	622	...	251	266	287	320
	L	...	443	468	449	564	...	242	249	234	290
Spain	R	4 115	9 505	10 400	15 500	15 900	122	253	270	395	402
Sweden	R	3 680	3 830	3 875	4 000	4 150	458	461	464	467	475
	L	2 513	3 165	3 257	3 309	3 353	312	381	390	387	384
Switzerland	R	1 500	2 300	2 550	2 725	2 967	242	364	390	399	416
	L	1 281	2 000	2 227	2 435	2 589	207	317	341	356	363
The Former Yugoslav Rep. of Macedonia	R	135	262	310	335	355	86	146	161	164	166
	L	114	254	302	331	...	73	142	157	162	...
Ukraine	R	7 167	12 722	15 190	16 950	17 520	151	255	298	328	340
United Kingdom	R	18 000	22 600	24 500	24 900	25 500	324	401	433	434	439
	L	16 309	18 522	18 716	20 040	21 176	293	329	331	349	365
Federal Republic of Yugoslavia	R	950	1 620	1 710	1 800	1 930	109	170	174	177	179
	L	737	1 596	1 704	1 704	...	85	168	173	168	...
Oceania											
American Samoa	R	2	6	7	10	12	74	173	179	211	221
Australia	R	2 758	5 600	7 000	8 200	8 730	220	384	448	486	489
Cook Islands	R	-	-	-	3	3	-	-	-	167	179
Fiji	R	-	-	-	11	13	-	-	-	15	17
French Polynesia	R	8	18	27	33	37	72	121	155	170	172
Guam	R	40	63	76	88	97	465	589	633	657	660
New Caledonia	R	8	25	40	45	48	74	175	258	268	270
New Zealand	R	790	1 035	1 397	1 500	1 800	280	332	430	446	510
	L	661	862	935	...	-	234	277	288	...	-
Papua New Guinea	R	-	-	-	9	12	-	-	-	2.3	2.9
Samoa	R	-	3	5	6	7	-	16	31	38	39
Solomon Islands	R	-	-	-	-	2	-	-	-	-	6.0
Tonga	R	-	-	-	-	2	-	-	-	-	16
Vanuatu, Rep. of	R	-	-	-	1	2	-	-	-	9.1	13

General note / Note générale / Nota general:

E--> In a few of the countries listed in Table 9.2 for which only the estimated number of receivers in use (R) is shown, a licence system for television receivers may be in force but information on this matter has not been communicated.

FR-> Pour quelques uns des pays figurant dans le tableau 9.2 pour lesquels seule l'estimation du nombre de récepteurs en service (R) est indiquée, il est possible qu'un système de redevances pour les récepteurs de télévision soit en vigueur mais les renseignements à ce sujet n'ont pas été communiqués.

ESP> En algunos de los países que aparecen en el cuadro 9.2 para los cuales la estimación del número de receptores en servicio (R) está indicado, es posible que un sistema de permisos para los receptores de televisión esté en vigor, pero las informaciones al respecto no han sido comunicadas.

9.3 Radio broadcasting: programmes
Radiodiffusion sonore: programmes
Radiodifusión sonora: programas

9.3 Radio broadcasting: programmes by function and by type of institution

Radiodiffusion sonore: programmes d'après leur fonction et le type d'organisme

Radiodifusión sonora: programas clasificados según su función y el tipo de institución

Total annual broadcasting hours	= Total annuel d'heures de diffusion	= Total anual de horas de difusión
of which (in percentage)	= dont (en pourcentage)	= de las cuales (en porcentaje)
Informative programmes	= Programmes d'information	= Programas informativos
News bulletins, etc.	= Bulletins d'information, etc.	= Boletines de noticias, etc.
Other informative programmes	= Autres programmes d'information	= Otros programas informativos
Educational programmes	= Programmes éducatifs	= Programas educativos
Related to a specific curriculum	= Liés à un enseignement particulier	= Relacionados con un programa de estudios específicos
For rural development	= Destinés au développement rural	= Para el desarrollo rural
Other educational programmes	= Autres programmes éducatifs	= Otros programas educativos
Cultural programmes	= Programmes culturels	= Programas culturales
Religious programmes	= Programmes religieux	= Programas religiosos
Advertisements	= Publicité	= Publicidad
Entertainment	= Divertissement	= Programas recreativos
Plays	= Dramatiques	= Dramas
Music	= Musique	= Música
Sports programmes	= Programmes sportifs	= Programas deportivos
Other entertainment programmes	= Autres programmes de divertissement	= Otros programas recreativos
Programmes not classified	= Programmes non classés	= Programas no clasificados

Govt = Governmental	Govt = Gouvernemental	Govt = Gubernamental
Public = Public	Public = Public	Public = Pública
Comm = Commercial	Comm = Commercial	Comm = Comercial

Radio broadcasting: programmes 9.3
Radiodiffusion sonore: programmes
Radiodifusión sonora: programas

Africa

Type of programme by function Programmes d'après leur fonction Programas según su función	Benin (1989) Govt	Botswana (1989) Govt	Burundi (1989) Govt	Chad‡ (1988) Govt	Congo (1989) Govt	Côte d'Ivoire (1994) Govt	Djibouti (1992) Govt
Total annual broadcasting hours	4 655	4 745	10 952	1 518	7 100	3 744	10 868
Informative programmes	39.1	22.6	14.9	14.7	36.7	14.7	10.6
News bulletins, etc.	20.1	9.5	14.2	9.6	36.7	7.5	9.2
Other informative programmes	19.0	13.0	0.6	5.1	-	7.2	1.4
Educational programmes	20.1	42.2	14.0	30.2	6.4	46.2	10.1
Related to a specific curriculum	1.1	37.9	0.7	2.6	3.4	7.7	-
For rural development	11.7	3.1	2.4	19.2	3.0	10.3	3.4
Other educational programmes	7.3	1.1	10.9	8.3	-	28.2	6.7
Cultural programmes	1.1	3.3	2.1	5.4	6.4	5.1	3.4
Religious programmes	1.7	2.7	0.8	8.0	-	20.8	6.7
Advertisements	4.5	-	1.4	0.2	0.3	-	1.8
Entertainment	33.5	25.1	65.6	41.6	28.5	12.2	62.9
Plays	2.8	1.1	1.0	6.0	2.1	2.6	2.2
Music	22.3	11.0	62.8	26.2	20.6	4.5	57.6
Sports programmes	1.7	2.2	1.9	6.9	3.7	-	0.8
Other entertainment programmes	6.7	10.9	-	2.6	2.0	5.1	2.3
Programmes not classified	-	4.1	1.2	-	*21.7	1.0	4.5

Type of programme by function Programmes d'après leur fonction Programas según su función	Egypt (1989) Govt	Ethiopia (1989) Govt	Ghana‡ (1994) Govt	Madagascar (1980)			Malawi (1991) Public
				Total	Govt	Public	
Total annual broadcasting hours	73 236	8 711	34 202	6 628	5 136	1 492	6 935
Informative programmes	8.5	21.7	36.9	16.1	14.7	20.8	15.2
News bulletins, etc.	...	12.2	28.7	15.1	13.7	20.0	8.2
Other informative programmes	...	9.5	8.1	1.0	1.0	0.8	6.9
Educational programmes	1.9	52.9	13.6	25.0	29.4	9.7	17.5
Related to a specific curriculum	...	29.1	2.7	8.3	10.0	2.4	6.4
For rural development	...	16.4	5.4	3.8	4.7	0.8	6.7
Other educational programmes	...	7.5	5.4	12.9	14.7	6.4	4.4
Cultural programmes	18.9	5.2	1.1	25.8	28.4	16.9	9.3
Religious programmes	20.0	-	2.6	3.1	4.1	-	8.0
Advertisements	0.4	0.2	8.8	2.0	1.4	3.8	12.6
Entertainment	41.9	19.9	37.0	28.0	21.9	48.9	34.6
Plays	...	1.1	0.9	4.0	3.0	7.2	2.2
Music	...	17.3	32.6	18.4	14.4	32.2	22.0
Sports programmes	...	0.7	1.5	4.2	3.0	8.0	1.5
Other entertainment programmes	...	0.8	2.0	1.4	1.4	1.4	8.9
Programmes not classified	8.4	-	0.0	-	-	-	2.9

9.3 Radio broadcasting: programmes
      Radiodiffusion sonore: programmes
      Radiodifusión sonora: programas

America, North

Type of programme by function / Programmes d'après leur fonction / Programas según su función	Mozambique (1994) Govt	Niger (1991) Govt	Senegal (1994) Public	Sudan (1991) Govt	United Republic of Tanzania‡ (1990) Govt	Bahamas (1994) Govt	Barbados (1991) Govt
Total annual broadcasting hours	50 295	6 188	12 528	6 357	5 215	8 760	7 300
Informative programmes	17.1	28.0	29.0	21.5	26.2	10.4	20.0
News bulletins, etc.	17.1	...	...	21.5	11.7	10.4	7.9
Other informative programmes	-	...	...	-	14.5	-	12.1
Educational programmes	8.1	27.0	3.9	14.3	8.1	9.5	2.1
Related to a specific curriculum	-	...	...	4.3	8.1	6.5	-
For rural development	-	...	...	7.2	-	3.0	2.1
Other educational programmes	8.1	...	...	2.9	-	-	-
Cultural programmes	16.1	10.0	5.7	10.5	-	-	0.4
Religious programmes	-	-	1.6	9.6	3.2	12.3	3.3
Advertisements	7.6	10.0	4.2	1.9	7.3	-	1.7
Entertainment	48.9	25.0	3.6	29.2	55.2	67.8	68.5
Plays	-	...	...	4.3	1.3	-	-
Music	48.9	...	...	14.4	46.9	67.2	63.0
Sports programmes	-	...	...	3.4	-	0.6	1.4
Other entertainment programmes	-	...	...	7.2	7.0	-	4.1
Programmes not classified	2.3	-	51.9	12.9	-	-	4.1

Type of programme by function / Programmes d'après leur fonction / Programas según su función	Cuba (1994) Govt		El Salvador (1994) Total	Govt	Public	Comm	
Total annual broadcasting hours	293 449		496 800	32 140	124 826	339 834	
Informative programmes	25.0		10.0	2.3	4.4	12.8	
News bulletins, etc.	...		8.0	1.9	4.0	10.0	
Other informative programmes	...		2.0	0.5	0.4	2.7	
Educational programmes	-		10.0	1.2	16.4	8.5	
Related to a specific curriculum	-		5.0	-	-	7.3	
For rural development	-		4.0	-	15.9	-	
Other educational programmes	-		1.0	1.2	0.5	1.2	
Cultural programmes	23.7		8.0	6.2	6.2	8.8	
Religious programmes	-		10.0	1.2	32.0	2.7	
Advertisements	0.7		20.0	-	1.6	28.6	
Entertainment	50.6		41.0	88.0	37.5	37.8	
Plays	6.0		-	-	-	-	
Music	42.4		30.0	9.3	36.1	29.7	
Sports programmes	2.2		10.0	76.5	0.4	7.2	
Other entertainment programmes	-		1.0	2.2	1.0	0.9	
Programmes not classified	-		1.0	0.9	1.9	0.7	

Radio broadcasting: programmes **9.3**
Radiodiffusion sonore: programmes
Radiodifusión sonora: programas

America, South

Type of programme by function / Programmes d'après leur fonction / Programas según su función	Argentina (1989)			Bolivia (1989)			Guyana (1991)
	Total	Govt	Comm	Total	Govt	Comm	Govt
Total annual broadcasting hours	1 109 600	407 340	702 260	40 775	5 140	35 635	21 144
Informative programmes	39.5	41.7	38.2	18.6	0.9	21.1	16.6
News bulletins, etc.	7.9	8.3	7.6	15.4	0.6	17.6	9.5
Other informative programmes	31.6	33.3	30.6	3.1	0.3	3.5	7.1
Educational programmes	5.3	5.6	5.1	4.6	0.4	5.2	10.0
Related to a specific curriculum	2.6	2.8	2.5	0.0	...	0.0	4.0
For rural development	2.6	2.8	2.5	4.5	0.3	5.1	3.3
Other educational programmes	-	-	-	0.0	0.1	0.0	2.7
Cultural programmes	10.5	11.1	10.2	0.2	0.1	0.2	1.4
Religious programmes	2.6	2.8	2.5	1.2	0.1	1.3	4.9
Advertisements	-	-	-	21.9	0.4	25.0	33.3
Entertainment	42.1	38.9	44.0	53.5	98.2	47.0	33.8
Plays	5.3	5.6	5.1	0.0	-	0.0	0.9
Music	21.1	16.7	23.6	53.4	98.1	46.9	28.4
Sports programmes	10.5	11.1	10.2	0.1	0.1	0.1	2.4
Other entertainment programmes	5.3	5.6	5.1	-	-	-	2.1
Programmes not classified	-	-	-	0.0	0.0	0.0	-

Asia

Type of programme by function / Programmes d'après leur fonction / Programas según su función	Armenia (1994)	Bangladesh (1991)	Brunei Darussalam (1989)	Cyprus (1989)	India (1990)	Iran, Islamic Republic of‡ (1994)	Iraq (1994)
	Govt	Govt	Govt	Public	Govt	Public	Govt
Total annual broadcasting hours	14 512	32 875	*9 733	12 845	858 269	77 758	7 650
Informative programmes	12.2	4.0	*35.2	11.7	22.4	33.6	13.7
News bulletins, etc.	5.4	3.6	*11.5	8.8	18.5	14.3	12.5
Other informative programmes	6.8	0.4	*23.7	2.8	3.9	19.3	1.2
Educational programmes	4.2	1.7	-	4.8	6.5	8.2	0.4
Related to a specific curriculum	2.1	0.7	-	1.9	2.5	1.6	-
For rural development	2.1	0.7	-	0.4	4.1	6.6	0.4
Other educational programmes	-	0.2	-	2.4	-	-	-
Cultural programmes	15.8	-	*2.1	8.3	-	30.5	2.6
Religious programmes	0.2	0.9	*13.6	1.0	0.2	16.2	10.5
Advertisements	0.8	13.9	*49.0	2.8	1.9	0.1	-
Entertainment	66.0	68.9	-	69.2	34.8	10.7	72.8
Plays	3.9	1.6	-	1.0	2.2	3.9	72.1
Music	55.0	66.6	-	65.1	32.6	0.1	0.7
Sports programmes	0.9	0.7	-	1.0	-	3.7	-
Other entertainment programmes	6.2	-	-	2.2	-	3.0	-
Programmes not classified	0.8	10.6	-	2.2	38.3	0.8	-

9.3 Radio broadcasting: programmes
Radiodiffusion sonore: programmes
Radiodifusión sonora: programas

Type of programme by function Programmes d'après leur fonction Programas según su función	Korea, Republic of (1994)				Kuwait (1993)	Malaysia (1991)	Oman (1992)
	Total	Govt	Public	Comm	Govt	Govt	Govt
Total annual broadcasting hours	1 100 314	706 523	321 526	72 265	22 710	39 649	12 853
Informative programmes	14.4	16.4	8.3	21.9	10.2	15.0	16.0
News bulletins, etc.	14.0	15.9	8.3	21.9	...	9.0	14.4
Other informative programmes	0.4	0.5	-	-	...	6.0	1.6
Educational programmes	0.7	1.0	-	-	1.4	7.3	8.8
Related to a specific curriculum	...	...	-	-	...	7.3	6.5
For rural development	...	...	-	-	...	-	-
Other educational programmes	...	...	-	-	...	-	2.3
Cultural programmes	35.5	28.3	52.4	30.4	8.5	-	18.5
Religious programmes	2.0	-	-	30.0	20.4	4.6	11.6
Advertisements	-	-	-	-	-	3.3	-
Entertainment	47.5	54.3	39.3	17.7	59.5	69.8	42.5
Plays	...	...	...	...	1.5	1.4	./.
Music	...	...	...	...	-	67.1	./.
Sports programmes	...	...	...	...	-	1.3	2.0
Other entertainment programmes	...	...	...	...	58.0	-	-
Programmes not classified	-	-	-	-	-	-	2.7

Type of programme by function Programmes d'après leur fonction Programas según su función	Pakistan (1991)	Qatar (1994)		Saudi Arabia (1994)	Thailand (1989)		Turkey (1994)
	Govt	Govt		Govt	Govt		Public
Total annual broadcasting hours	98 550	20 138		32 485	*26 304		31 340
Informative programmes	16.5	9.4		17.0	*25.0		3.0
News bulletins, etc.	13.6	6.8		...	...		2.2
Other informative programmes	2.9	2.6		...	...		0.8
Educational programmes	6.6	0.2		35.0	*23.6		4.3
Related to a specific curriculum	-	0.1		...	...		1.1
For rural development	2.6	-		...	...		1.2
Other educational programmes	4.0	0.1		...	...		2.0
Cultural programmes	1.2	7.2		-	-		2.1
Religious programmes	13.0	14.8		20.0	*.1		0.5
Advertisements	10.0	-		-	-		0.9
Entertainment	52.7	65.4		28.0	*45.0		57.8
Plays	1.0	2.9		...	...		1.1
Music	42.9	36.0		...	...		55.2
Sports programmes	2.6	0.0		...	...		0.4
Other entertainment programmes	6.1	26.5		...	...		1.1
Programmes not classified	-	3.0		-	*6.4		31.4

Radio broadcasting: programmes 9.3
Radiodiffusion sonore: programmes
Radiodifusión sonora: programas

Europe

Type of programme by function / Programmes d'après leur fonction / Programas según su función	Albania (1991)				Andorra (1991)	Austria (1994)	
	Total	Public	Comm		Govt	Public	
Total annual broadcasting hours	77 296	24 844	52 452		8 760	68 620	
Informative programmes	14.8	13.0	15.6		20.2	19.9	
News bulletins, etc.	12.6	13.0	12.4		14.2	10.0	
Other informative programmes	2.2	-	3.2		5.9	9.9	
Educational programmes	2.0	-	2.9		-	2.1	
Related to a specific curriculum	-	-	-		-	0.3	
For rural development	-	-	-		-	-	
Other educational programmes	2.0	-	2.9		-	1.7	
Cultural programmes	22.5	29.9	19.1		-	19.3	
Religious programmes	32.6	57.1	20.9		4.9	0.6	
Advertisements	4.0	-	5.9		-	2.3	
Entertainment	23.9	-	35.3		74.9	54.9	
Plays	0.3	-	0.5		...	3.1	
Music	19.1	-	28.1		...	27.0	
Sports programmes	1.6	-	2.4		...	2.4	
Other entertainment programmes	2.9	-	4.3		...	22.4	
Programmes not classified	0.2	-	0.3		-	0.9	

Type of programme by function / Programmes d'après leur fonction / Programas según su función	Belarus (1994)				Belgium‡ (1994)		Bulgaria (1994)
	Total	Govt	Comm		Public		Public
Total annual broadcasting hours	39 418	13 138	26 280		33 323		218 966
Informative programmes	16.6	11.9	19.0		11.7		27.9
News bulletins, etc.	12.2	8.5	14.0		5.0		10.9
Other informative programmes	4.5	3.4	5.0		6.7		17.1
Educational programmes	0.2	0.5	-		0.3		1.3
Related to a specific curriculum	0.0	0.1	-		...		0.7
For rural development	-	-	-		...		0.5
Other educational programmes	0.1	0.4	-		...		0.1
Cultural programmes	4.9	4.8	5.0		3.0		3.9
Religious programmes	0.9	0.6	1.0		0.1		0.2
Advertisements	3.7	1.2	5.0		1.3		5.7
Entertainment	63.3	49.8	70.0		80.2		52.5
Plays	0.4	1.3	-		0.7		0.8
Music	61.4	44.1	70.0		70.4		36.6
Sports programmes	0.1	0.2	-		1.9		2.6
Other entertainment programmes	1.4	4.2	-		7.2		12.4
Programmes not classified	10.4	31.2	-		3.2		8.4

9.3 Radio broadcasting: programmes
Radiodiffusion sonore: programmes
Radiodifusión sonora: programas

Type of programme by function / Programmes d'après leur fonction / Programas según su función	Croatia (1994)			Czech Republic (1994)			Denmark (1989)
	Total	Govt	Public	Total	Public	Comm	Public
Total annual broadcasting hours	346 306	26 719	319 587	378 426	54 640	323 786	16 506
Informative programmes	16.6	21.7	16.2	12.3	31.9	9.0	11.4
News bulletins, etc.	6.8	7.3	6.7	6.7	12.5	5.7	11.4
Other informative programmes	9.8	14.4	9.4	5.7	19.4	3.3	-
Educational programmes	2.6	3.0	2.5	1.6	1.5	1.6	0.7
Related to a specific curriculum	0.7	2.0	0.6	0.3	0.1	0.3	...
For rural development	1.1	0.2	1.2	0.1	0.2	0.1	...
Other educational programmes	0.8	0.8	0.8	1.2	1.3	1.2	...
Cultural programmes	2.6	3.9	2.5	5.2	11.6	4.1	16.6
Religious programmes	1.0	0.3	1.1	0.7	0.9	0.7	1.9
Advertisements	12.0	1.3	12.9	3.0	0.7	3.4	-
Entertainment	65.1	69.9	64.7	49.3	42.1	50.5	56.2
Plays	0.9	1.2	0.8	4.4	1.7	4.9	3.0
Music	52.4	64.2	51.4	40.0	36.0	40.7	45.6
Sports programmes	4.1	1.2	4.4	0.6	0.5	0.6	1.2
Other entertainment programmes	7.8	3.4	8.2	4.3	3.9	4.3	6.3
Programmes not classified	-	-	-	27.8	11.4	30.6	13.3

Type of programme by function / Programmes d'après leur fonction / Programas según su función	Estonia (1994)			Finland (1994)			France (1993)
	Total	Public	Comm	Total	Public	Comm	Govt
Total annual broadcasting hours	104 597	23 615	80 982	329 206	79 206	*250 000	463 506
Informative programmes	18.3	18.9	18.1	12.9	21.9	10.0	18.6
News bulletins, etc.	12.4	12.7	12.3	7.3	14.8	5.0	...
Other informative programmes	5.9	6.2	5.8	5.5	7.1	5.0	...
Educational programmes	2.0	2.3	2.0	0.2	0.8	-	3.4
Related to a specific curriculum	-	-	-	0.1	0.2	-	...
For rural development	-	-	-	-	-	-	...
Other educational programmes	2.0	2.3	2.0	0.1	0.6	-	...
Cultural programmes	9.4	21.9	5.8	0.3	1.4	-	5.5
Religious programmes	1.0	0.3	1.2	0.9	0.6	1.0	-
Advertisements	3.1	1.3	3.6	4.6	-	6.0	-
Entertainment	44.4	39.4	45.8	74.7	48.4	83.0	72.5
Plays	0.4	0.6	0.4	0.2	0.7	-	-
Music	0.4	0.5	0.3	52.6	45.1	55.0	56.0
Sports programmes	1.7	1.9	1.6	1.1	1.2	1.0	-
Other entertainment programmes	41.9	36.3	43.5	20.8	1.4	27.0	16.5
Programmes not classified	21.8	16.0	23.5	6.5	26.9	-	-

Radio broadcasting: programmes   9.3
Radiodiffusion sonore: programmes
Radiodifusión sonora: programas

Type of programme by function Programmes d'après leur fonction Programas según su función	Germany‡ (1992) Public	Greece‡ (1991) Public	Holy See (1994) Total	Hungary (1994) Public	Ireland (1993) Public	Italy (1994) Public	Lithuania (1994) Govt
Total annual broadcasting hours	372 905	73 438	19 963	28 527	21 784	41 549	15 156
Informative programmes	26.1	35.3	78.6	10.5	14.1	26.4	17.2
News bulletins, etc.	14.1	33.3	...	5.2	7.9	20.8	10.0
Other informative programmes	12.0	2.0	...	5.3	6.3	5.6	7.2
Educational programmes	6.5	1.2	-	3.0	0.0	0.1	0.6
Related to a specific curriculum	...	0.2	-	2.2	0.0	-	...
For rural development	...	0.7	-	0.5	-	-	...
Other educational programmes	...	0.3	-	0.3	-	0.1	...
Cultural programmes	./.	1.5	-	4.7	1.5	34.9	49.5
Religious programmes	-	3.6	4.7	0.5	0.5	-	-
Advertisements	1.3	-	-	0.7	-	1.0	-
Entertainment	63.1	52.0	16.8	57.8	65.2	35.2	32.7
Plays	4.8	-	-	3.0	1.7	1.0	...
Music	54.1	33.1	16.8	51.7	55.5	28.4	...
Sports programmes	1.4	4.0	-	1.0	2.3	2.1	...
Other entertainment programmes	2.8	14.9	-	2.1	5.7	3.8	...
Programmes not classified	3.1	6.4	-	22.7	18.6	2.5	-

Type of programme by function Programmes d'après leur fonction Programas según su función	Luxembourg (1994) Total	Luxembourg (1994) Public	Luxembourg (1994) Comm	Malta (1994) Govt	Moldova (1994) Govt	Norway‡ (1994) Public	Poland (1991) Govt
Total annual broadcasting hours	44 370	3 467	40 903	76 114	13 379	22 281	129 320
Informative programmes	14.8	19.1	14.5	12.8	27.2	20.2	43.0
News bulletins, etc.	7.4	14.3	6.8	4.5	10.9	13.6	11.8
Other informative programmes	7.4	4.8	7.6	8.3	16.3	6.6	31.2
Educational programmes	2.8	6.0	2.6	4.9	-	0.8	2.4
Related to a specific curriculum	0.2	-	0.3	...	-	-	0.5
For rural development	0.1	-	0.1	...	-	-	0.2
Other educational programmes	2.5	6.0	2.2	...	-	0.8	1.7
Cultural programmes	4.9	9.0	4.6	1.0	10.3	6.2	12.6
Religious programmes	0.5	-	0.5	1.4	0.1	1.5	0.1
Advertisements	0.9	-	1.0	4.1	0.9	-	6.1
Entertainment	71.5	65.9	72.0	75.8	48.2	64.9	35.7
Plays	0.5	0.1	0.5	-	1.2	0.4	1.0
Music	55.0	44.8	55.9	62.6	37.4	45.5	27.7
Sports programmes	2.9	-	3.2	3.3	0.5	2.6	1.6
Other entertainment programmes	13.0	21.0	12.3	9.9	9.1	16.4	5.4
Programmes not classified	4.6	-	4.9	-	13.3	6.4	0.2

9.3   Radio broadcasting: programmes
Radiodiffusion sonore: programmes
Radiodifusión sonora: programas

Type of programme by function / Programmes d'après leur fonction / Programas según su función	Portugal (1991)			Romania (1994)	Slovakia (1994)	Slovenia (1994)	Sweden (1994)
	Govt	Public	Comm	Public	Comm	Public	Public
Total annual broadcasting hours	33 829	17 520	16 309	58 358	8 760	21 733	125 855
Informative programmes	17.1	18.3	15.9	39.7	6.8	27.5	34.5
News bulletins, etc.	13.8	15.8	11.7	24.7	3.0	13.4	15.8
Other informative programmes	3.3	2.5	4.1	15.0	3.8	14.1	18.7
Educational programmes	1.6	-	3.3	2.8	-	1.8	1.8
Related to a specific curriculum	0.3	-	0.6	-	-	1.5	...
For rural development	0.8	-	1.6	-	-	0.4	...
Other educational programmes	0.5	-	1.1	2.8	-	-	...
Cultural programmes	23.9	44.0	2.3	7.2	1.8	1.2	5.4
Religious programmes	1.9	1.4	2.5	-	-	0.4	0.4
Advertisements	4.9	1.1	9.0	1.3	1.0	2.9	-
Entertainment	38.2	26.3	50.9	47.0	91.1	66.1	55.7
Plays	0.1	0.2	-	1.7	0.7	3.4	-
Music	27.6	16.7	39.4	41.8	87.9	60.3	43.7
Sports programmes	3.5	3.5	3.5	1.2	1.8	1.0	3.3
Other entertainment programmes	6.9	5.9	8.0	2.3	0.7	1.3	8.7
Programmes not classified	12.5	8.9	16.3	2.0	0.7	-	2.2

Type of programme by function / Programmes d'après leur fonction / Programas según su función	Switzerland (1994)		The Former Yugoslav Republic of Macedonia (1994)				Federal Republic of Yugoslavia (1994)
	Public		Total	Public	Comm		Govt
Total annual broadcasting hours	82 880		356 619	118 459	238 160		356 619
Informative programmes	10.9		10.4	16.3	7.5		18.8
News bulletins, etc.	...		7.5	12.6	5.1		...
Other informative programmes	...		2.9	3.8	2.4		...
Educational programmes	0.1		5.9	6.8	5.5		4.4
Related to a specific curriculum	...		4.4	3.8	4.7		...
For rural development	...		0.5	1.2	0.2		...
Other educational programmes	...		0.9	1.8	0.5		...
Cultural programmes	5.0		1.8	2.7	1.4		4.2
Religious programmes	0.6		0.3	0.2	0.4		-
Advertisements	-		10.4	6.6	12.3		10.0
Entertainment	80.9		63.6	49.9	70.4		49.7
Plays	0.7		0.9	1.2	0.7		...
Music	68.1		57.6	41.0	65.9		...
Sports programmes	1.5		1.3	1.7	1.1		...
Other entertainment programmes	10.6		3.8	6.0	2.7		...
Programmes not classified	2.4		7.5	17.4	2.6		12.9

Radio broadcasting: programmes 9.3
Radiodiffusion sonore: programmes
Radiodifusión sonora: programas

Oceania

Type of programme by function Programmes d'après leur fonction Programas según su función	Australia‡ (1991)		Kiribati (1994)
	Public	Comm	Govt
Total annual broadcasting hours	*740 173	*1 270 262	203
Informative programmes	15.3	12.4	-
News bulletins, etc.	3.8	7.9	-
Other informative programmes	11.5	4.5	-
Educational programmes	1.3	./.	88.7
Related to a specific curriculum	1.3	./.	10.8
For rural development	./.	./.	7.4
Other educational programmes	./.	./.	70.4
Cultural programmes	1.6	./.	7.4
Religious programmes	2.5	0.9	-
Advertisements	./.	7.8	-
Entertainment	72.0	74.0	3.9
Plays	./.	./.	-
Music	69.0	71.5	3.9
Sports programmes	2.9	2.5	-
Other entertainment programmes	0.1	-	-
Programmes not classified	7.2	4.9	-

AFRICA:
Chad:
    E--> Data exclude regional programmes.
    FR-> Les données excluent les programmes régionaux.
    ESP> Los datos excluyen los programas regionales.
Ghana:
    E--> Data include 5,014 hours corresponding to public programmes.
    FR-> Les données incluent 5 014 heures correspondant aux programmes publics.
    ESP> Los datos incluyen 5 014 horas de programas públicos.
United Republic of Tanzania:
    E--> Data refer to Radio-Tanzania.
    FR-> Les données se réfèrent à Radio-Tanzania.
    ESP> Los datos se refieren a Radio Tanzania.
ASIA:
Iran, Islamic Republic of:
    E--> Data refer to national programmes only.
    FR-> Les données se réfèrent aux programmes nationaux seulement.
    ESP> Los datos se refieren a los programas nacionales solamente.
EUROPE:
Belgium:
    E--> Data refer to RTBF (Radiodiffusion belge de langue française) and BRTN (Belgische Radio en Televisie).
    FR-> Les données se réfèrent à la RTBF (radiodiffusion belge de langue française) et le BRTN (Belgishe Radio en Televisie).
    ESP> Los datos se refieren a la RTBF (radiodiffusion belge de langue française) y a la BRTN (Belgische Radio en Televisie).
Germany:
    E--> Cultural programmes are included with educational programmes.
    FR-> Les programmes culturels sont comptés avec les programmes éducatifs.

    ESP> Los programmas culturales se incluyen con los programmas educativos.
Greece:
    E--> Data do not include 43,434 hours corresponding to the 5 national programmes.
    FR-> Les données n'incluent pas 43 434 heures correspondant à 5 programmes nationaux.
    ESP> Los datos no incluyen 43 434 horas correspondientes a 5 programas nacionales.
Norway:
    E--> Data refer to the Norwegian Broascasting Corporation (NRK) only.
    FR-> Les données se réfèrent à la Norwegian Broadcasting Corporation (NRK) seulement.
    ESP> Los datos se refieren a la Norwegian Broadcasting Corporation (NRK) solamente.
OCEANIA:
Australia:
    E--> For public radio programmes, advertisements and plays are included under the category *programmes not elsewhere classified*. For commercial radio programmes, educational and cultural programmes and plays are included under the category *programmes not elsewhere classified*.
    FR-> Pour les programmes relatifs à la radio publique, la publicité et les dramatiques sont inclus dans la catégorie des *programmes non classés*. Pour ceux relatifs à la radio commerciale, les programmes éducatifs, culturels et les dramatiques sont inclus dans la catégorie des *programmes non classés*.
    ESP> Los programas de la radio pública, la publicidad y las novelas se incluyen en la categoría de *programas no clasificados*. Los de la radio comercial, los programas educativos y culturales y las novelas se incluyen en la categoría de *programas no clasificados*.

9.4 Television broadcasting: programmes by function and by type of institution

Télévision: programmes d'après leur fonction et le type d'organisme

Televisión: programas clasificados según su función y el tipo de institución

Total annual broadcasting hours	= Total annuel d'heures de diffusion	= Total anual de horas de difusión
of which (in percentage)	= dont (en pourcentage)	= de las cuales (en porcentaje)
Informative programmes	= Programmes d'information	= Programas informativos
News bulletins, etc.	= Bulletins d'information, etc.	= Boletines de noticias, etc.
Other informative programmes	= Autres programmes d'information	= Otros programas informativos
Educational programmes	= Programmes éducatifs	= Programas educativos
Related to a specific curriculum	= Liés à un enseignement particulier	= Relacionados con un programa de estudios específicos
For rural development	= Destinés au développement rural	= Para el desarrollo rural
Other educational programmes	= Autres programmes éducatifs	= Otros programas educativos
Cultural programmes	= Programmes culturels	= Programas culturales
Religious programmes	= Programmes religieux	= Programas religiosos
Advertisements	= Publicité	= Publicidad
Entertainment	= Divertissement	= Programas recreativos
Cinema films	= Films cinématographiques	= Películas cinematográficas
Plays	= Dramatiques	= Dramas
Music programmes	= Musique	= Música
Sports programmes	= Programmes sportifs	= Programas deportivos
Other entertainment programmes	= Autres programmes de divertissement	= Otros programas recreativos
Other not elsewhere classified	= Programmes non classés	= Programas no clasificados

Govt = Governmental
Public = Public
Comm = Commercial

Govt = Gouvernemental
Public = Public
Comm = Commercial

Govt = Gubernamental
Public = Pública
Comm = Comercial

Africa

Type of programme by function / Programmes d'après leur fonction / Programas según su función	Burundi (1989) Govt	Chad (1994) Govt	Congo (1989) Govt	Côte d'Ivoire (1989) Govt	Djibouti (1992) Govt	Egypt (1993) Govt	Ethiopia (1994) Govt
Total annual broadcasting hours	1 990	774	2 523	1 629	2 136	16 748	2 799
Informative programmes	22.6	41.9	32.5	10.1	46.8	12.6	28.8
News bulletins, etc.	18.1	...	...	6.4	38.2	...	15.3
Other informative programmes	4.5	...	...	3.7	8.5	...	13.5
Educational programmes	25.1	3.2	10.5	31.6	6.1	6.7	32.3
Related to a specific curriculum	2.5	...	...	-	-	...	10.6
For rural development	17.6	...	...	1.5	1.9	...	4.0
Other educational programmes	5.0	...	...	20.2	4.3	...	17.7
Cultural programmes	8.0	10.6	19.2	4.9	7.3	44.3	-
Religious programmes	-	2.7	-	4.4	5.9	8.1	-
Advertisements	-	3.9	0.2	0.1	2.1	3.0	5.0
Entertainment	42.7	37.7	37.6	58.7	25.0	25.3	33.9
Cinema films	20.1	26.9	...	32.1	11.7	...	11.5
Plays	2.5	3.1	...	1.5	2.4	...	1.5
Music programmes	12.6	5.8	...	14.7	-	...	5.0
Sport programmes	5.0	1.9	...	10.4	5.8	...	3.3
Other entertainment programmes	2.5	-	...	-	5.1	...	12.6
Programmes not classified	1.5	-	-	-	6.8	-	-

Type of programme by function / Programmes d'après leur fonction / Programas según su función	Ghana (1994) Govt	Madagascar (1989) Govt	Mozambique (1991) Govt	Niger (1991) Govt	Senegal (1994) Public	Sudan (1991) Govt	Togo (1994) Govt
Total annual broadcasting hours	3 627	902	504	1 560	2 480	2 544	2 913
Informative programmes	43.9	35.1	31.0	30.8	29.6	25.0	28.6
News bulletins, etc.	22.5	30.4	25.8	...	25.5	20.0	23.7
Other informative programmes	21.4	4.8	5.2	...	4.1	5.0	4.9
Educational programmes	7.6	16.5	10.3	17.3	7.4	10.0	-
Related to a specific curriculum	-	4.3	-	...	2.6	...	-
For rural development	-	0.7	5.2	...	1.5	...	-
Other educational programmes	7.6	11.5	5.2	...	3.4	...	-
Cultural programmes	0.7	4.8	5.2	16.0	6.3	10.0	4.2
Religious programmes	1.4	0.3	-	-	11.9	20.0	4.5
Advertisements	9.4	0.2	-	1.6	2.5	8.0	0.9
Entertainment	34.5	43.0	53.6	30.8	39.8	25.0	53.6
Cinema films	11.9	17.3	15.5	...	10.5	...	22.3
Plays	6.5	11.5	10.3	...	10.5	...	4.5
Music programmes	9.6	8.6	12.3	...	9.8	...	15.6
Sport programmes	-	5.5	15.5	...	5.9	...	4.0
Other entertainment programmes	6.6	-	-	...	3.1	...	7.1
Programmes not classified	2.5	-	-	3.5	2.4	2.0	8.3

America,
North

Type of programme by function Programmes d'après leur fonction Programas según su función	United Republic of Tanzania‡ (1990) Govt	Zaire (1992) Govt	Zimbabwe (1989) Total	Govt	Public	Comm	Bahamas (1994) Govt
Total annual broadcasting hours	1 243	5 615	5 617	2 093	2 860	664	4 628
Informative programmes	15.5	51.8	37.3	65.8	25.1	-	7.9
News bulletins, etc.	14.7	41.9	13.0	16.8	13.3	-	6.7
Other informative programmes	0.8	9.8	24.3	49.1	11.8	-	1.1
Educational programmes	28.8	1.8	6.5	9.9	5.5	-	5.6
Related to a specific curriculum	10.5	1.3	0.9	1.2	0.9	-	12.4
For rural development	4.7	0.4	5.6	8.7	4.5	-	5.6
Other educational programmes	13.7	-	-	-	-	-	
Cultural programmes	9.7	2.2	-	-	-	-	-
Religious programmes	9.7	4.7	0.9	1.1	0.9	-	2.2
Advertisements	1.0	4.5	3.6	-	-	30.4	1.1
Entertainment	35.1	34.4	43.5	23.2	68.5	-	38.2
Cinema films	10.5	15.9	3.2	-	6.4	-	6.7
Plays	3.2	1.0	0.9	-	1.7	-	-
Music programmes	12.9	9.6	5.7	6.6	6.4	-	0.6
Sport programmes	8.0	3.6	5.2	4.5	7.0	-	3.4
Other entertainment programmes	0.5	4.4	28.5	12.0	47.1	-	27.5
Programmes not classified	0.3	0.6	8.2	-	-	69.6	44.9

Type of programme by function Programmes d'après leur fonction Programas según su función	Barbados (1991) Govt		Canada‡ (1994) Total	Public	Comm		Cuba (1991) Govt
Total annual broadcasting hours	6 237		938 756	508 660	430 096		11 387
Informative programmes	7.7		31.8	32.4	31.0		19.2
News bulletins, etc.	6.8		11.0	11.2	10.8		7.6
Other informative programmes	0.9		20.8	21.2	20.2		11.6
Educational programmes	5.1		10.0	14.5	4.7		0.2
Related to a specific curriculum	0.7		5.2	8.6	1.2		-
For rural development	-		-	-	-		-
Other educational programmes	4.4		4.8	5.9	3.5		0.2
Cultural programmes	1.5		1.0	1.9	0.0		9.8
Religious programmes	1.7		2.5	2.3	2.8		-
Advertisements	2.3		-	-	-		7.4
Entertainment	49.5		53.5	48.4	59.6		63.4
Cinema films	3.5		10.2	8.7	12.0		18.1
Plays	0.4		-	-	-		11.4
Music programmes	0.7		0.9	1.3	0.6		16.9
Sport programmes	3.3		5.8	5.7	5.9		15.7
Other entertainment programmes	41.7		36.6	32.6	41.2		1.3
Programmes not classified	32.0		1.2	0.6	1.8		-

Type of programme by function / Programmes d'après leur fonction / Programas según su función	El Salvador (1994)				Panama (1989)		
	Total	Govt	Public	Comm	Total	Govt	Comm
Total annual broadcasting hours	70 200	7 162	10 484	52 554	17 982	1 701	16 281
Informative programmes	10.0	12.0	3.3	11.1	20.7	77.8	14.8
News bulletins, etc.	8.0	7.8	2.3	9.2	8.7	1.6	9.5
Other informative programmes	2.0	4.2	1.0	1.9	12.0	76.2	5.3
Educational programmes	2.0	16.8	0.5	0.3	-	-	-
Related to a specific curriculum	0.5	4.9	-	-	-	-	-
For rural development	0.5	4.9	-	-	-	-	-
Other educational programmes	1.0	7.0	0.5	0.3	-	-	-
Cultural programmes	15.0	46.1	19.1	10.0	-		-
Religious programmes	10.0	4.2	55.3	1.8	4.2	-	4.6
Advertisements	25.0	-	14.3	30.5	-	-	-
Entertainment	36.0	19.5	4.7	44.5	27.9	22.2	28.5
Cinema films	18.0	5.6	2.3	22.8	19.2	15.9	19.6
Plays	0.5	1.4	-	0.5	-	-	-
Music programmes	10.0	5.6	1.4	12.3	3.9	6.3	3.6
Sport programmes	5.5	2.8	-	7.0	4.8	-	5.3
Other entertainment programmes	2.0	4.2	1.0	1.9	-	-	-
Programmes not classified	2.0	1.4	2.9	1.9	47.1	-	52.1

America, South

Type of programme by function / Programmes d'après leur fonction / Programas según su función	Argentina (1989)				Bolivia (1989)		
	Total	Govt	Comm		Total	Govt	Comm
Total annual broadcasting hours	161 654	67 027	94 627		11 888	2 470	9 418
Informative programmes	33.7	33.7	33.7		16.9	11.3	18.4
News bulletins, etc.	15.3	15.3	15.3		15.4	10.1	16.8
Other informative programmes	18.4	18.4	18.4		1.5	1.2	1.6
Educational programmes	4.9	4.9	4.9		7.5	12.1	6.2
Related to a specific curriculum	3.0	3.0	3.0		4.0	-	5.1
For rural development	1.7	1.7	1.7		-	-	-
Other educational programmes	0.1	0.1	0.1		3.4	12.1	1.1
Cultural programmes	5.3	5.3	5.3		-	-	
Religious programmes	0.9	0.9	0.9		1.2	-	1.5
Advertisements	-	-	-		10.1	8.1	10.6
Entertainment	55.2	55.2	55.2		64.3	68.4	63.2
Cinema films	22.5	22.5	22.5		28.8	20.2	31.0
Plays	5.0	5.0	5.0		4.4	3.6	4.6
Music programmes	5.1	5.1	5.1		16.0	12.1	17.0
Sport programmes	4.5	4.5	4.5		10.1	8.1	10.6
Other entertainment programmes	18.2	18.2	18.2		5.0	24.3	-
Programmes not classified	-	-	-		-	-	-

Type of programme by function Programmes d'après leur fonction Programas según su función	Colombia (1991)			Guyana (1991)			
	Total	Public	Comm	Total	Govt	Public	Comm
Total annual broadcasting hours	10 302	1 931	8 371	18 664	1 664	8 552	8 448
Informative programmes	24.2	20.4	25.1	-	-	-	-
News bulletins, etc.	8.4	-	10.3	-	-	-	-
Other informative programmes	15.8	20.4	14.8	-	-	-	-
Educational programmes	2.0	1.3	2.1	-	-	-	-
Related to a specific curriculum	...	-	...	-	-	-	-
For rural development	...	1.3	...	-	-	-	-
Other educational programmes	...	-	...	-	-	-	-
Cultural programmes	7.1	16.6	5.0	-	-	-	-
Religious programmes	-	-	-	0.5	3.1	0.6	-
Advertisements	-	-	-	2.7	-	-	5.9
Entertainment	65.1	53.2	67.8	96.8	96.9	99.4	94.1
Cinema films	15.8	16.0	15.7	...	...	...	...
Plays	15.6	6.6	17.7	...	...	...	...
Music programmes	3.9	10.7	2.3	...	...	...	...
Sport programmes	2.5	10.8	0.6	...	...	...	...
Other entertainment programmes	27.3	9.2	31.5	...	...	...	...
Programmes not classified	1.6	8.5	-	-	-	-	-

Asia

Type of programme by function Programmes d'après leur fonction Programas según su función	Armenia (1994)	Bangladesh (1991)	Brunei Darussalam (1989)	Cyprus (1989)			Georgia (1994)
	Govt	Govt	Govt	Total	Public	Comm	Govt
Total annual broadcasting hours	4 745	2 795	2 873	2 505	1 184	1 321	6 387
Informative programmes	12.8	22.1	23.1	26.0	46.4	7.7	14.8
News bulletins, etc.	8.9	19.7	11.0	13.3	28.2	-	6.2
Other informative programmes	4.0	2.4	12.1	12.7	18.2	7.7	8.6
Educational programmes	6.6	7.0	5.9	0.7	1.4	-	6.9
Related to a specific curriculum	2.4	4.7	-	...	...	-	3.8
For rural development	0.5	0.4	-	...	...	-	1.6
Other educational programmes	3.6	2.0	5.9	...	...	-	1.6
Cultural programmes	11.2	5.3	...	0.4	0.9	-	7.8
Religious programmes	0.3	6.9	8.1	0.3	0.7	-	0.8
Advertisements	2.6	9.0	1.0	8.7	18.3	-	1.9
Entertainment	62.8	44.4	61.9	60.8	25.8	92.3	66.5
Cinema films	47.7	20.7	14.8	12.9	-	24.5	17.1
Plays	0.5	8.6	21.3	1.4	2.1	0.7	0.8
Music programmes	10.7	6.4	1.1	6.7	4.7	8.4	38.4
Sport programmes	1.7	5.7	7.2	6.1	10.0	2.7	2.3
Other entertainment programmes	2.2	3.0	17.5	33.7	9.0	55.9	8.0
Programmes not classified	3.7	5.2	-	3.1	6.5	-	1.3

Type of programme by function / Programmes d'après leur fonction / Programas según su función	India‡ (1990) Govt	Indonesia‡ (1991) Govt	Iran Islamic Republic of (1994) Public	Korea, Republic of (1994) Total	Govt	Public	Comm
Total annual broadcasting hours	4 338	934	17 671	237 667	133 702	76 404	27 561
Informative programmes	13.5	26.9	30.9	26.5	43.0	2.7	12.8
News bulletins, etc.	11.5	...	13.9	...	...	...	...
Other informative programmes	2.1	...	17.0	...	...	...	...
Educational programmes	39.6	12.0	9.7	1.3	2.4	-	-
Related to a specific curriculum	13.4	...	0.6	...	...	-	-
For rural development	10.5	...	9.0	...	...	-	-
Other educational programmes	15.7	...	-	...	...	-	-
Cultural programmes	8.1	./.	16.2	25.1	7.6	50.2	40.5
Religious programmes	-	-	14.5	-	-	-	-
Advertisements	0.7	-	0.8	-	-	-	-
Entertainment	38.0	38.7	26.7	47.0	47.0	47.1	46.7
Cinema films	10.4	...	3.5	...	...	...	...
Plays	15.3	...	8.2	...	...	...	...
Music programmes	5.4	...	0.7	...	...	...	...
Sport programmes	5.8	...	13.4	...	...	...	...
Other entertainment programmes	1.1	...	0.9	...	...	...	...
Programmes not classified	-	22.4	1.2	-	-	-	-

Type of programme by function / Programmes d'après leur fonction / Programas según su función	Kuwait‡ (1993) Govt	Malaysia (1991) Govt	Oman (1992) Govt	Pakistan (1991) Govt	Qatar (1994) Govt	Saudi Arabia (1994) Govt	Sri Lanka (1991) Govt
Total annual broadcasting hours	9 120	7 085	4 770	20 261	8 488	6 020	2 695
Informative programmes	12.3	30.3	16.3	27.7	9.0	13.5	25.6
News bulletins, etc.	...	...	14.5	12.6	8.5	12.1	14.2
Other informative programmes	...	...	1.8	15.1	0.5	1.4	11.4
Educational programmes	10.2	-	19.7	7.0	0.2	2.0	4.7
Related to a specific curriculum	...	-	8.3	1.1	-	-	0.4
For rural development	...	-	-	0.6	-	-	4.2
Other educational programmes	...	-	11.5	5.3	0.2	2.0	-
Cultural programmes	13.7	-	12.6	3.6	7.8	2.5	0.3
Religious programmes	9.3	8.4	13.5	8.5	9.6	13.7	4.6
Advertisements	1.0	9.1	1.1	4.2	0.8	5.5	10.5
Entertainment	53.7	52.2	35.7	41.5	56.4	18.6	27.7
Cinema films	-	-	27.6	0.7	6.9	0.7	3.2
Plays	27.3	32.4	./.	8.5	25.5	0.5	6.6
Music programmes	-	16.4	./.	4.2	5.8	0.4	3.6
Sport programmes	-	3.4	8.1	13.5	8.5	2.1	4.9
Other entertainment programmes	26.4	-	1.0	14.6	9.6	15.0	9.4
Programmes not classified	-	-	-	7.5	16.2	44.2	26.7

Europe

Type of programme by function / Programmes d'après leur fonction / Programas según su función	Turkey (1994) Public	Yemen (1994) Govt	Austria (1994) Public	Belarus (1994)			Belgium‡ (1994) Public
				Total	Govt	Comm	
Total annual broadcasting hours	32 684	5 929	13 779	26 976	7 266	19 710	5 597
Informative programmes	22.9	27.6	28.4	13.9	11.0	15.0	19.5
News bulletins, etc.	13.0	24.1	26.3	10.2	10.6	10.0	11.4
Other informative programmes	9.9	3.5	2.1	3.8	0.4	5.0	8.1
Educational programmes	18.0	20.0	3.3	0.9	3.3	-	5.1
Related to a specific curriculum	8.8	5.4	3.3	0.9	3.3	-	...
For rural development	0.3	4.3	-	-	-	-	...
Other educational programmes	8.9	10.3	-	-	-	-	...
Cultural programmes	10.3	11.7	7.9	5.0	18.6	-	6.4
Religious programmes	0.6	8.7	0.9	-	-	-	0.8
Advertisements	0.2	4.4	4.0	4.0	1.2	5.0	1.8
Entertainment	45.9	27.5	44.1	76.2	65.9	80.0	53.4
Cinema films	8.7	19.9	30.3	45.8	34.4	50.0	37.9
Plays	11.3	-	-	1.2	4.4	-	-
Music programmes	10.3	3.8	-	23.2	4.7	30.0	3.6
Sport programmes	9.9	3.8	9.0	1.4	5.2	-	11.8
Other entertainment programmes	5.7	-	4.8	4.6	17.3	-	-
Programmes not classified	2.1	-	11.4	-	-	-	13.0

Type of programme by function / Programmes d'après leur fonction / Programas según su función		Bulgaria (1994) Public		Croatia (1994)			
				Total	Govt	Public	Comm
Total annual broadcasting hours		7 178		16 290	10 846	3 728	1 716
Informative programmes		16.3		26.1	25.1	17.9	49.7
News bulletins, etc.		11.6		15.9	14.4	9.8	38.5
Other informative programmes		4.7		10.2	10.7	8.2	11.2
Educational programmes		1.2		4.3	5.0	3.8	1.4
Related to a specific curriculum		1.2		3.2	3.5	3.5	-
For rural development		-		0.5	0.4	0.3	1.4
Other educational programmes		-		0.7	1.0	-	-
Cultural programmes		3.5		4.1	3.8	5.4	2.8
Religious programmes		0.4		1.2	0.9	1.9	1.4
Advertisements		2.2		7.3	1.8	24.4	5.0
Entertainment		48.2		49.2	55.4	36.8	37.0
Cinema films		23.3		11.5	12.6	7.2	13.9
Plays		0.4		10.5	14.9	0.5	4.8
Music programmes		10.6		10.9	8.2	20.7	7.0
Sport programmes		8.2		6.0	7.6	2.9	2.8
Other entertainment programmes		5.8		10.3	12.2	5.5	8.5
Programmes not classified		28.1		7.8	8.0	9.7	2.8

Type of programme by function Programmes d'après leur fonction Programas según su función	Czech Republic (1994)			Denmark (1989)	Estonia‡ (1994)		
	Total	Public	Comm	Public	Total	Public	Comm
Total annual broadcasting hours	27 868	15 336	12 532	2 956	6 457	2 741	3 716
Informative programmes	16.9	27.6	3.9	25.3	15.5	21.5	11.2
News bulletins, etc.	...	21.1	...	13.3	9.6	13.7	6.6
Other informative programmes	...	6.5	...	11.9	5.9	7.8	4.5
Educational programmes	3.2	4.6	1.6	2.4	3.3	4.3	2.5
Related to a specific curriculum	...	1.6	...	2.4	-	-	-
For rural development	...	-	...	-	-	-	-
Other educational programmes	...	3.0	...	-	3.3	4.3	2.5
Cultural programmes	14.8	17.5	11.5	13.2	7.2	7.3	7.1
Religious programmes	0.3	0.6	-	2.1	0.8	1.7	0.1
Advertisements	2.0	0.6	3.6	-	4.5	3.2	5.4
Entertainment	46.7	39.6	55.3	54.1	64.7	56.5	70.7
Cinema films	...	9.6	...	10.9	40.5	23.9	52.7
Plays	...	13.2	...	16.3	./.	./.	./.
Music programmes	...	10.3	...	5.1	1.2	2.0	0.6
Sport programmes	...	4.4	...	7.4	7.3	13.5	2.7
Other entertainment programmes	...	2.1	...	14.4	15.7	17.1	14.6
Programmes not classified	16.1	9.5	24.2	2.9	4.1	5.5	3.0

Type of programme by function Programmes d'après leur fonction Programas según su función	Finland (1994)				France‡ (1994)		
	Total	Public	Comm		Total	Public	Comm
Total annual broadcasting hours	11 512	7 228	4 284		36 773	17 923	18 850
Informative programmes	28.7	30.4	25.8		10.9	13.4	8.5
News bulletins, etc.	7.7	9.1	5.4		6.8	7.5	0.6
Other informative programmes	20.9	21.3	20.4		4.1	5.9	2.4
Educational programmes	4.7	7.1	0.7		0.8	1.6	0.0
Related to a specific curriculum	2.8	4.1	0.7		...	...	...
For rural development	-	-	-		...	...	...
Other educational programmes	1.9	3.0	-		...	...	...
Cultural programmes	5.7	8.6	0.9		20.9	25.5	16.5
Religious programmes	1.1	1.0	1.2		./.	./.	./.
Advertisements	5.6	-	14.9		6.5	5.3	7.7
Entertainment	50.0	48.6	52.5		55.4	47.6	62.8
Cinema films	8.7	8.5	6.6		27.3	21.6	32.8
Plays	12.1	19.2	...		0.2	0.4	0.1
Music programmes	4.2	4.6	3.5		0.7	0.6	0.9
Sport programmes	9.4	9.6	8.9		4.3	6.2	2.5
Other entertainment programmes	15.8	6.6	31.2		22.8	18.8	26.5
Programmes not classified	4.2	4.4	3.9		5.6	6.6	4.6

Type of programme by function / Programmes d'après leur fonction / Programas según su función	Germany‡ (1994)			Greece (1991)	Hungary (1994)	Ireland (1993)	Italy (1994)
	Total	Govt	Public	Public	Public	Govt	Public
Total annual broadcasting hours	10 928	4 904	6 024	11 187	11 559	9 528	31 860
Informative programmes	29.5	21.0	36.4	27.8	34.7	14.2	28.3
News bulletins, etc.	10.6	9.3	11.7	...	12.8	7.7	24.3
Other informative programmes	18.9	11.7	24.7	...	21.9	6.5	4.0
Educational programmes	0.2	-	0.4	4.3	7.2	6.0	5.4
Related to a specific curriculum	-	-	-	...	1.9	1.6	0.3
For rural development	-	-	-	...	-	4.3	-
Other educational programmes	0.2	-	0.4	...	5.3	-	5.1
Cultural programmes	4.2	3.9	4.5	4.0	7.7	4.2	16.2
Religious programmes	1.1	1.0	1.2	1.1	1.1	1.0	-
Advertisements	1.7	1.8	1.6	1.2	2.7	8.8	2.9
Entertainment	63.3	72.2	56.0	56.8	30.2	60.2	43.9
Cinema films	21.7	28.2	16.4	22.4	14.3	41.4	13.2
Plays	22.6	21.1	23.9	16.2	0.5	-	10.6
Music programmes	2.5	0.8	3.9	4.7	2.7	54.4	11.3
Sport programmes	12.4	13.6	11.3	6.4	6.7	7.8	6.1
Other entertainment programmes	4.0	8.5	0.4	7.1	5.9	5.6	2.7
Programmes not classified	-	-	-	4.8	16.5	5.7	3.2

Type of programme by function / Programmes d'après leur fonction / Programas según su función	Lithuania (1994)	Luxembourg (1994)	Malta (1994)	Moldova (1994)	Netherlands‡ (1989)	Norway‡ (1994)	Poland (1991)
	Govt	Comm	Govt	Govt	Public	Public	Govt
Total annual broadcasting hours	3 789	838	3 824	4 746	8 578	3 518	15 944
Informative programmes	24.5	43.4	12.9	13.3	27.7	24.9	33.9
News bulletins, etc.	13.7	43.4	6.9	7.8	4.5	9.6	22.0
Other informative programmes	10.8	-	6.0	5.5	23.2	15.3	11.9
Educational programmes	4.1	3.6	3.4	4.3	6.9	3.8	11.0
Related to a specific curriculum	...	3.6	...	2.3	2.9	1.7	5.7
For rural development	...	-	...	-	-	-	1.0
Other educational programmes	...	-	...	2.0	4.1	2.1	4.3
Cultural programmes	53.8	10.7	4.1	2.5	12.7	8.7	8.9
Religious programmes	-	-	2.7	1.1	2.0	1.5	0.6
Advertisements	-	3.6	4.5	0.8	4.3	-	2.7
Entertainment	17.6	26.3	72.4	66.2	46.2	52.5	35.4
Cinema films	-	-	26.9	33.7	6.0	7.0	19.8
Plays	-	-	8.8	6.7	17.4	7.5	3.5
Music programmes	-	1.8	6.7	20.0	4.8	3.3	5.8
Sport programmes	11.3	7.2	9.9	2.7	5.1	17.9	2.7
Other entertainment programmes	6.3	17.3	20.0	3.0	12.9	16.7	3.6
Programmes not classified	-	12.4	-	11.8	0.2	8.5	7.5

Type of programme by function / Programmes d'après leur fonction / Programas según su función	Portugal‡ (1991) Public	Romania (1994) Public	Slovenia (1994) Public	Spain‡ (1991) Public	Sweden (1992) Public	Switzerland (1994) Public	
Total annual broadcasting hours	21 374	12 083	8 897	7 661	6 668	31 827	
Informative programmes	14.8	17.2	24.4	21.0	7.6	16.9	
News bulletins, etc.	12.3	10.0	9.3	10.4	7.6	9.8	
Other informative programmes	2.5	7.2	15.1	10.6	-	7.2	
Educational programmes	17.4	6.7	1.7	3.6	10.9	1.5	
Related to a specific curriculum	...	-	0.9	-	-	...	
For rural development	...	-	0.7	0.5	-	...	
Other educational programmes	...	6.7	-	3.1	-	...	
Cultural programmes	0.8	12.2	3.7	5.5	27.5	7.2	
Religious programmes	0.7	4.5	0.7	0.7	./.	0.5	
Advertisements	1.5	1.2	3.5	2.0	-	2.2	
Entertainment	61.9	40.1	60.2	63.7	48.3	40.1	
Cinema films	./.	17.8	11.1	10.5	-	7.8	
Plays	./.	1.6	20.1	26.1	1.9	16.4	
Music programmes	./.	12.7	9.8	6.4	12.5	1.8	
Sport programmes	9.1	6.8	11.6	9.0	12.6	9.3	
Other entertainment programmes	-	1.2	7.6	11.6	21.3	4.9	
Programmes not classified	2.9	18.1	5.9	3.5	5.6	31.5	

Type of programme by function / Programmes d'après leur fonction / Programas según su función	The Former Yugoslav Republic of Macedonia (1994) Total	Public	Comm		Federal Republic of Yugoslavia (1994) Total	Govt	Comm
Total annual broadcasting hours	113 986	23 102	90 884		35 071	23 436	11 635
Informative programmes	14.4	24.1	12.0		34.1	34.6	31.7
News bulletins, etc.	10.9	14.6	10.0		19.6	22.6	13.6
Other informative programmes	3.5	9.5	2.0		14.5	12.7	18.1
Educational programmes	3.4	4.8	3.1		4.8	6.9	0.7
Related to a specific curriculum	1.9	4.3	1.3		2.1	3.2	-
For rural development	0.6	0.2	0.7		-	-	-
Other educational programmes	1.0	0.4	1.1		2.7	3.7	0.7
Cultural programmes	2.1	1.0	2.4		2.5	3.0	1.4
Religious programmes	0.7	0.1	0.9		-	-	-
Advertisements	12.3	4.4	14.3		4.0	3.7	4.6
Entertainment	66.1	63.3	66.8		50.7	45.8	60.7
Cinema films	28.6	36.4	26.6		14.8	8.3	28.1
Plays	5.4	1.4	6.4		0.4	0.5	0.2
Music programmes	20.6	16.2	21.7		12.2	12.9	10.8
Sport programmes	3.8	4.1	3.7		5.1	6.3	2.9
Other entertainment programmes	7.8	5.2	8.5		18.2	17.9	18.7
Programmes not classified	0.9	2.3	0.6		3.9	5.3	1.0

Oceania

Type of programme by function Programmes d'après leur fonction Programas según su función	Australia‡ (1991)		
	Total	Public	Comm
Total annual broadcasting hours	268 280	6 280	262 000
Informative programmes	17.6	25.7	17.4
News bulletins, etc.	13.3	21.8	13.1
Other informative programmes	4.3	3.9	4.3
Educational programmes	4.1	22.4	3.6
Related to a specific curriculum	1.9	9.6	1.7
For rural development	-	-	-
Other educational programmes	2.2	12.7	2.0
Cultural programmes	0.1	3.0	-
Religious programmes	1.0	1.3	0.9
Advertisements	./.	-	./.
Entertainment	77.3	47.6	78.0
Cinema films	12.5	3.2	12.7
Plays	-	-	-
Music programmes	2.2	5.0	2.1
Sport programmes	10.2	12.3	10.2
Other entertainment programmes	52.4	27.1	53.0
Programmes not classified	-	-	-

AFRICA:
United Republic of Tanzania:
E--> Data refer to Zanzibar only.
FR-> Les données se réfèrent à Zanzibar seulement.
ESP> Los datos se refieren a Zanzíbar solamente.
AMERICA, NORTH:
Canada:
E--> Advertisements are not identified separately.
FR-> Les programmes de publicité ne sont pas identifiés séparèment.
ESP> Los programas de publicidad no están identificados separadamente.
ASIA:
India:
E--> Data refer to Delhi only.
FR-> Les données se réfèrent à Delhi seulement.
ESP> Los datos se refieren a Delhi solamente.
Indonesia:
E--> Cultural programmes are included with entertainment programmes and religious programmes with educational programmes.
FR-> Les programmes culturels sont comptés avec les programmes de divertissement et les programmes religieux avec les programmes éducatifs.
ESP> Los programas culturales van incluídos con los programas recreativos y los programas religiosos con los programas educativos.
Kuwait:
E--> Figure on cinema films include plays programmes.
FR-> Le chiffre relatif aux films cinématographiques inclut les programmes concernant les dramatiques.
ESP> La clfra relativa a las películas cinematográficas incluye los dramas.
EUROPE:
Belgium:
E--> Data refer to R.T.B.F only.
FR-> Les données se réfèrent à la R.T.B.F seulement.
ESP> Los datos se refieren a la R.T.B.F solamente.
Estonia:
E--> Figure on cinema films include play programmes.
FR-> Le chiffre relatif aux films cinématografica inclut les programm es concernant les dramatiques.
ESP> La chifra relatif a les películas cinematográficas incluye los dramas.
France:
E--> Data concern national programmes only. Religious programmes are included with educational programmes.
FR-> Les données se réfèrent aux programmes nationaux seulement. Les programmes religieux sont comptés avec les programmes éducatifs.

ESP> Los datos se refieren a los programas nacionales solamente. Los programas religiósos han incluídos con los programas educativos.
Germany:
E--> Data refer to *Zweites Deutsches Fernsehen (Z.D.F)* only.
FR-> Les données se réfèrent à la *Zweites Deutsches Fernsehen (Z.D.F)* seulement.
ESP> Los datos se refieren a la *Zweites Deutsches Fernsehen (Z.D.F)* solamente.
Netherlands:
E--> Data concern national programmes only.
FR-> Les données se réfèrent aux programmes nationaux seulement.
ESP> Los datos se refieren a los programas nacionales solamente.
Norway :
E--> Data refer to the Norwegian Broadcasting Corporation (NRK) only.
FR-> Les données se réfèrent à la *Norwegian Broadcasting Corporation (NRK)* seulement.
ESP> Los datos se refieren a la *Norwegian Broadcasting Corporation (NRK)* solamente.
Portugal:
E--> Educational programmes include children's and youth programmes. Entertainment programmes include cinema films and plays ; Cultural programme include music programme.
FR-> Les programmes éducatifs incluent les programmes pour les enfants et la jeunesse. Les programmes de divertissement comprennent les films cinématographiques et les dramatiques. Les programmes culturels incluent les programmes de musique.
ESP> Los programas educativos incluyen los programas para los niños y la juventud. Los programas recreativos incluyen las películas cinematográficas y los dramas. Los programas culturales incluyen los programas de música.
Spain :
E--> Religious programmes are included with cultural programmes.
FR-> Les programmes religieux sont comptés avec les programmes cultur els.
ESP> Los programas religíosos van incluídos con los programas cultur ales.
OCEANIA:
Australia:
E--> The figures for commercial television include advertisements for which the breakdown of data is unknown.
FR-> Les chiffres de la télévision commerciale incluent les programmes de publicité pour lesquels la répartition des données n'est pas connue.
ESP> Las cifras de la televisión comercial incluyen la publicidad, para la cual se desconoce la repartición de los datos.

9.5 Radio and television broadcasting: personnel
Radiodiffusion sonore et télévision: personnel
Radiodifusión sonora y televisión: personal

9.5 Radio and television broadcasting: personnel employed by type of personnel and type of institution

Radiodiffusion sonore et télévison: personnel employé d'après le type de personnel et le type d'organisme

Radiodifusión sonora y televisión: personal que trabaja según el tipo de personal y de institución

Country Year / Pays Année / País Año	Type of institution / Type d'organisme / Tipo de institución	Sex / Sexe / Sexo	Total staff / Personnel total / Personal total	Type of personnel / Type de personnel / Tipo de personal						
				Programme / Des programmes / De programas	Journalistic / Journalistique / Periodístico	Technical production / Technique de production / Técnico de producción	Technical transmission / Technique de diffusion / Técnico de radiodifusión	Other technical / Autre technique / Otro técnico	Administrative / Administratif / Administrativo	Other / Divers / Otros tipos
			(1)	(2)	(3)	(4)	(5)	(6)	(7)	(8)
Africa										
Benin 1989	Radio	Government	MF	107	12.2	16.8	62.6	——>	——>	4.7	3.7
Botswana 1989	Radio	Government	MF	177	18.6	14.1	20.9	5.7	-	12.4	28.2
Burundi 1989	Radio	Government	MF	256	23.4	15.2	10.2	18.4	-	28.9	3.9
	TV	Government	MF	157	31.8	21.7	24.2	9.6	-	12.7	-
Chad 1995	TV	Government	MF	74	20.2	27.0	12.1	13.5	4.0	9.5	13.5
			F	12	41.7	41.7	-	-	-	16.7	-
Congo 1989	Radio	Government	MF	310	9.4	17.1	14.8	47.4	-	3.2	8.1
	TV	Government	MF	588	3.4	8.3	6.6	72.4	4.6	1.2	3.4
Côte d'Ivoire 1994	Radio	Government	MF	84	31.0	6.0	39.3	6.0	6.0	6.0	6.0
			F	11	54.5	9.1	9.1	9.1	-	9.1	9.1
Djibouti 1992	Radio + TV	Government	MF	131	16.8	15.3	18.3	27.5	2.3	3.8	16.0
Ethipopia 1991	Radio	Government	MF	491	5.5	24.4	14.9	5.5	2.9	46.8	-
1994	TV	Government	MF	556	2.9	14.9	20.3	13.8	-	7.2	40.8
			F	202	7.9	10.4	15.3	7.4	-	10.9	48.0
Ghana 1994	Radio + TV	Government	MF	1 549	22.1	6.9	19.8	7.5	12.2	22.6	9.0
			F	255	31.8	10.2	3.5	-	-	43.1	11.4
Madagascar 1989	Radio	Government	MF	164	28.0	10.4	3.7	13.4	4.9	23.8	15.9
	TV	Government	MF	128	10.2	10.9	28.1	5.5	1.6	15.6	28.1
Malawi 1991	Radio	Public	MF	362	16.3	12.4	11.6	9.1	3.6	36.5	10.5
Mauritania 1989	Radio	Government	MF	159	16.4	23.9	19.5	3.1	0.6	13.8	22.6
Mozambique 1994	Radio	Public	MF	170	8.2	6.5	55.9	12.4	8.2	8.8	-

Radio and television broadcasting: personnel 9.5
Radiodiffusion sonore et télévision: personnel
Radiodifusión sonora y televisión: personal

Country Year / Pays Année / País Año		Type of institution / Type d'organisme / Tipo de institución	Sex / Sexe / Sexo	Total staff / Personnel total / Personal total (1)	Type of personnel / Type de personnel / Tipo de personal						
					Programme / Des programmes / De programas (2)	Journal-istic / Journa-listique / Perio-dístico (3)	Technical production / Technique de production / Técnico de producción (4)	Technical trans-mission / Technique de diffusion / Técnico de radio-difusión (5)	Other technical / Autre technique / Otro técnico (6)	Adminis-trative / Adminis-tratif / Adminis-trativo (7)	Other / Divers / Otros tipos (8)
			F	54	...	...	...	...	...	...	-
Niger 1991	Radio	Government	MF	114	14.0	25.4	14.0	13.2	4.4	20.2	8.8
	TV	Government	MF	121	46.3	18.2	21.5	——>	——>	14.1	-
Senegal # 1994	Radio	Public	MF	217	27.2	18.0	24.9	11.1	2.8	8.3	7.8
			F	57	49.1	7.0	19.3	-	-	24.6	-
	TV	Public	MF	145	10.3	20.0	47.6	10.3	4.1	2.8	4.8
			F	27	14.8	33.3	37.0	3.7	-	11.1	-
	Radio + TV	Public	MF	195	-	-	-	-	-	100.0	-
			F	69	-	-	-	-	-	100.0	-
Sudan 1991	Radio	Government	MF	670	55.5	4.5	26.1	10.7	3.3	-	-
	TV	Government	MF	546	39.4	——>	47.1	——>	——>	4.4	9.2
Togo 1994	TV	Government	MF	272	18.4	16.5	36.4	7.4	-	21.3	-
			F	51	29.4	15.7	13.7	-	-	41.2	-
United Republic of Tanzania‡ 1989	Radio	Government	MF	135	13.3	13.3	8.9	17.8	1.5	33.3	11.9
1991	TV	Government	MF	194	29.9	8.2	15.5	10.3	7.7	28.4	
Zaire # 1992	Radio	Government	MF	325	56.3	29.8	11.0	2.8	-	-	-
			F	67	76.1	23.9	-	-	-	-	-
	TV	Government	MF	404	44.1	34.2	6.7	3.0	12.1	-	-
			F	73	61.6	28.8	-	-	9.6	-	-
	Radio + TV	Government	MF	479	-	-	-	-	43.6	56.4	-
			F	67	-	-	-	-	19.4	80.6	-
Zimbabwe 1989	Radio + TV	Public	MF	837	*25.3	9.0	16.5	——>	——>	49.2	-
America, North											
Bahamas 1994	Radio + TV	Government	MF	260	19.2	16.9	13.1	3.5	5.4	3.5	38.5
			F	137	15.3	15.3	4.4	1.5	1.5	2.2	59.9
Barbados 1991	Radio	Government	MF	44	36.4	-	15.9	-	-	25.0	22.7
	TV	Government	MF	157	20.4	13.4	15.9	4.5	-	8.9	36.9
Canada 1994	Radio	Public	MF	642	46.3	——>	11.7	——>	——>	33.0	9.0
		Commercial	MF	9 251	53.9	——>	4.0	——>	——>	15.9	26.2
	TV	Public	MF	1 693	63.9	——>	10.6	——>	——>	19.3	6.3
		Commercial	MF	8 273	65.9	——>	8.1	——>	——>	13.2	12.8
	Radio + TV	Public	MF	12 298	80.0	——>	2.8	——>	——>	13.1	4.1
Cuba‡ 1994	Radio	Government	MF	4 658	40.9	13.4	11.7	——>	——>	12.3	21.7
			F	1 644	...	...	...	...	...	...	...
	TV	Government	MF	3 750	32.6	4.4	22.0	——>	——>	9.4	31.6
			F	1 356	...	...	...	...	...	...	...
El Salvador 1994	Radio	Government	MF	48	10.4	10.4	22.9	16.7	6.3	18.8	14.6
			F	16	12.5	12.5	18.8	12.5	6.3	25.0	12.5
		Public	MF	136	8.8	9.6	33.1	18.4	5.1	14.7	10.3
			F	51	11.8	7.8	29.4	13.7	7.8	19.6	9.8
		Commercial	MF	506	4.0	2.8	29.8	26.3	6.1	21.5	9.5
			F	140	6.4	3.6	39.3	19.3	6.4	17.9	7.1

9.5   Radio and television broadcasting: personnel
Radiodiffusion sonore et télévision: personnel
Radiodifusión sonora y televisión: personal

Country Year / Pays Année / País Año	Type of institution / Type d'organisme / Tipo de institución	Sex / Sexe / Sexo	Total staff / Personnel total / Personal total (1)	Programme / Des programmes / De programas (2)	Journalistic / Journalistique / Periodístico (3)	Technical production / Technique de production / Técnico de producción (4)	Technical transmission / Technique de diffusion / Técnico de radiodifusión (5)	Other technical / Autre technique / Otro técnico (6)	Administrative / Administratif / Administrativo (7)	Other / Divers / Otros tipos (8)
El Salvador (cont) 1994	TV Government	MF	107	11.2	2.8	22.4	14.0	7.5	28.0	14.0
		F	43	9.3	2.3	23.3	11.6	7.0	34.9	11.6
	Public	MF	120	5.0	2.5	25.0	35.0	3.3	21.7	7.5
		F	30	6.7	3.3	20.0	26.7	10.0	23.3	10.0
	Commercial	MF	553	5.4	4.3	32.6	23.5	6.3	18.1	9.8
		F	205	3.9	8.3	39.0	24.4	2.4	9.8	12.2
Mexico 1991	Radio Public	MF	772	22.8	6.5	20.5	14.6	-	28.9	6.7
	Commercial	MF	11 022	28.1	3.4	18.9	4.4	0.2	40.4	4.6
	TV Public	MF	354	8.2	-	11.0	1.7	2.0	39.0	38.1
	Commercial	MF	3 365	17.4	-	13.0	0.8	1.7	39.7	27.3
America, South										
Argentina 1989	Radio Government	MF	2 206	24.9	——>	45.3	——>	——>	20.5	9.3
	Commercial	MF	2 209	35.7	——>	33.9	——>	——>	15.7	14.7
	TV Government	MF	4 013	1.5	2.8	5.5	2.0	8.6	30.2	49.4
	Commercial	MF	1 597	5.0	5.4	5.4	4.4	12.8	24.2	42.9
Bolivia 1989	Radio Government	MF	13	23.1	15.4	7.7	7.7	7.7	30.8	7.7
	Commercial	MF	1 780	-	11.1	0.8	1.6	0.2	29.8	56.4
	TV Government	MF	38	18.4	13.2	5.3	5.3	5.3	39.5	13.2
	Commercial	MF	450	22.2	22.2	8.9	8.9	4.4	22.2	11.1
Chile 1989	Radio Government	MF	700	12.1	11.7	14.3	11.4	2.7	12.9	34.9
	Public	MF	285	9.5	9.5	12.6	8.4	4.2	18.2	37.5
	Commercial	MF	2 978	9.2	10.4	8.0	10.9	4.8	18.1	38.5
Colombia 1989	Radio Government	MF	85	17.6	5.9	28.2	16.5	-	8.2	23.5
	TV Government	MF	1 040	4.9	0.1	19.5	25.7	-	26.1	23.8
Guyana 1991	Radio+TV Government	MF	195	19.5	14.4	1.5	10.3	10.3	8.7	35.4
Asia										
Armenia 1994	Radio Government	MF	1 045	24.3	37.0	7.8	29.7	-	1.1	-
		F	586	23.2	55.6	6.0	14.0	-	1.2	-
	TV Government	MF	1 791	21.4	15.2	21.2	41.2	-	1.0	-
		F	543	28.2	20.1	28.0	22.1	-	1.7	-
Bangaldesh 1991	Radio Government	MF	2 626	8.0	2.5	26.3	——>	——>	63.1	-
	TV Government	MF	1 520	27.8	3.8	16.6	8.5	9.7	18.0	15.6
Brunei Darussalam 1989	Radio+TV Government	MF	994	33.9	6.1	40.2	——>	——>	10.7	9.1
Cyprus 1989	Radio Public	MF	111	49.6	9.9	18.0	-	-	1.8	20.7
	TV Public	MF	346	9.2	2.9	29.5	4.9	4.0	4.0	45.4
Georgia 1994	Radio Government	MF	377	9.3	47.7	29.2	10.1	3.2	0.5	-
		F	196	12.8	66.3	11.2	5.1	4.1	0.5	-
	TV Government	MF	2 505	11.3	35.1	33.8	10.3	-	1.5	8.0
		F	1 114	20.5	29.8	27.6	14.5	-	1.1	6.6

Radio and television broadcasting: personnel 9.5
Radiodiffusion sonore et télévision: personnel
Radiodifusión sonora y televisión: personal

Country Year / Pays Année / País Año	Type of institution / Type d'organisme / Tipo de institución	Sex / Sexe / Sexo	Total staff / Personnel total / Personal total	Type of personnel / Type de personnel / Tipo de personal						
				Programme / Des programmes / De programas	Journal-istic / Journa-listique / Perio-dístico	Technical production / Technique de production / Técnico de producción	Technical trans-mission / Technique de diffusion / Técnico de radio-difusión	Other technical / Autre technique / Otro técnico	Adminis-trative / Adminis-tratif / Adminis-trativo	Other / Divers / Otros tipos
			(1)	(2)	(3)	(4)	(5)	(6)	(7)	(8)
India 1991	Radio — Government	MF	24 185	21.6	——>	6.8	30.9	-	40.8	-
	TV — Government	MF	19 975	24.0	——>	48.9	——>	-	27.1	-
Indonesia 1991	TV — Government	MF	5 659	199	——>	23.5	12.9	13.1	28.0	2.6
Iran, Islamic Republic of 1994	Radio + TV — Public	MF	15 360	28.4	9.2	9.2	8.0	6.1	22.7	16.5
		F	2 602	42.4	16.9	9.6	-	-	31.1	-
Korea, Republic of 1994	Radio — Government	MF	221	19.0	-	-	38.9	-	42.1	-
		F	62	...	...	...	...	...	...	...
	Radio — Commercial	MF	1 199	30.1	14.8	-	16.0	2.3	31.0	5.7
		F	220	...	...	...	...	...	...	...
	TV — Commercial	MF	484	31.6	20.7	-	22.5	-	20.7	4.5
		F	38	...	...	...	...	...	...	...
	Radio + TV — Government	MF	5 709	36.6	11.6	0.3	26.2	0.5	22.9	2.0
		F	602	...	...	...	...	...	...	...
	Public	MF	4 147	26.5	15.4	2.6	19.5	1.7	29.5	4.9
		F	423	...	...	...	...	...	...	...
	Commercial	MF	1 477	44.6	17.6	-	15.2	-	22.7	-
		F	229	...	...	...	...	...	...	...
Kuwait 1989	Radio — Government	MF	685	34.0	16.5	6.6	9.6	15.3	6.3	11.7
	TV — Government	MF	1 808	4.7	——>	37.1	9.7	-	34.3	14.3
Malaysia 1990	Radio + TV — Government	MF	7 218	48.4	3.4	15.9	4.6	0.6	27.2	-
Oman 1990	Radio — Government	MF	215	43.7	9.3	27.4	2.3	-	9.3	7.9
	TV — Government	MF	296	6.4	2.4	47.6	17.2	-	17.2	9.1
Pakistan 1991	Radio — Government	MF	5 729	17.3	4.4	25.9	——>	——>	40.0	12.4
	TV — Government	MF	5 528	15.0	4.1	28.3	——>	——>	44.3	8.3
Qatar 1994	Radio — Government	MF	324	20.7	13.3	8.3	22.2	6.8	18.2	10.5
		F	32	46.9	3.1	6.3	-	-	43.8	-
	TV — Government	MF	501	40.9	8.0	38.7	5.0	1.8	3.0	2.6
		F	19	73.7	5.3	-	-	5.3	15.8	-
Saudi Arabia 1994	Radio — Government	MF	870	40.7	14.0	17.7	6.6	-	9.7	11.4
		F	57	...	...	...	...	...	...	...
	TV — Government	MF	1 177	0.3	1.7	27.1	53.4	17.0	0.3	0.3
Sri Lanka 1991	TV — Government	MF	678	18.4	——>	29.8	——>	——>	33.2	18.6
Turkey 1994	Radio + TV — Public	MF	6 255	46.9	2.6	13.7	-	2.7	25.5	8.5
		F	1 522	57.7	1.9	2.5	-	0.7	33.4	3.8
Europe										
Austria 1991	Radio + TV — Public	MF	3 261	26.6	——>	46.2	——>	——>	22.6	4.6
1994	COM — Public	MF	3 010	29.9	——>	37.3	1.2	7.0	21.2	3.3
Belarus 1994	Radio — Government	MF	517	16.6	7.7	28.6		-	18.6	28.4
		F	317	21.1	6.3	31.5		-	18.9	22.1
	Commercial	MF	62	37.1	12.9	21.0		-	24.2	4.8
		F	24	33.3	20.8	12.5		-	33.3	-

9.5   Radio and television broadcasting: personnel
Radiodiffusion sonore et télévision: personnel
Radiodifusión sonora y televisión: personal

Country Year / Pays Année / País Año	Type of institution / Type d'organisme / Tipo de institución	Sex / Sexe / Sexo	Total staff / Personnel total / Personal total	Programme / Des programmes / De programas	Journalistic / Journalistique / Periodístico	Technical production / Technique de production / Técnico de producción	Technical transmission / Technique de diffusion / Técnico de radiodifusión	Other technical / Autre technique / Otro técnico	Administrative / Administratif / Administrativo	Other / Divers / Otros tipos
			(1)	(2)	(3)	(4)	(5)	(6)	(7)	(8)
Belarus (cont) 1994	TV	Government MF	618	30.3	4.9	28.0	4.2	-	28.3	4.4
		F	378	30.4	3.4	30.4	2.1	-	27.8	5.8
		Commercial MF	162	25.9	14.8	25.9	-	-	28.4	5.0
		F	68	17.6	11.8	20.6	-	-	41.2	8.8
Belgium‡# 1994	Radio	Public MF	726	21.9	22.9	25.6	——>	2.8	20.4	6.5
		F	297	29.0	19.5	3.0	——>	-	41.4	7.1
	TV	Public MF	1 283	27.8	11.2	36.4	——>	10.8	11.8	1.9
		F	403	42.9	10.9	10.2	——>	1.5	31.0	3.5
	Radio + TV	Public MF	3 351	31.4	6.3	25.4	3.3	9.5	19.0	5.1
		F	1 048	43.1	7.1	4.8	——>	5.0	34.1	6.0
Bulgaria 1989	Radio + TV	Government MF	7 172	27.7	25.6	24.2	——>	——>	12.9	9.6
Croatia 1994	Radio	Government MF	450	14.4	58.0	6.2	...	-	15.8	5.6
		Public MF	700	19.1	42.6	20.1	...	-	12.6	5.6
	TV	Government MF	1 447	28.4	14.1	-	18.2	-	19.1	20.2
		Public MF	10	-	50.0	50.0	-	-	-	-
		Commercial MF	56	5.4	44.6	28.6	-	-	19.6	1.8
Denmark 1989	Radio	Public MF	1 378	1.8	44.8	14.2	-	14.9	13.0	11.3
	TV	Public MF	1 961	1.3	31.6	30.5	-	15.6	12.7	8.3
Finland # 1994	Radio	Public MF	1 280	39.6	11.8	29.0	1.9	1.7	7.6	8.4
		F	580	36.4	10.3	34.1	0.2	1.4	11.2	6.4
		Commercial MF	1 040	38.5	26.9	2.9	——>	——>	7.7	24.0
	TV	Public MF	2 041	16.3	9.6	60.7	1.1	5.7	6.3	0.3
		F	780	17.7	9.2	60.0	0.1	0.1	12.2	0.6
		Commercial MF	617	44.7	——>	23.7	——>	5.0	26.6	-
		F	308	...	...	...	...	...	...	-
	Radio + TV	Public MF	1 097	-	-	0.4	31.4	27.0	36.6	4.6
		F	367	-	-	1.1	14.4	11.4	62.1	10.9
Germany‡ 1994	TV	Public MF	5 854	46.9	——>	18.5	8.4	3.8	22.4	...
Greece 1991	Radio + TV	Government MF	3 431	29.5	——>	40.3	——>	——>	29.2	1.0
Holy See 1994	Radio	Government MF	404	52.7	——>	10.1	14.6	10.6	11.9	...
		F	111	88.2	——>	0.9	——>	0.9	10.8	...
Hungary 1994	Radio	Public MF	2 013	19.5	18.0	12.9	3.6	6.4	22.0	17.6
		F	987	18.2	18.0	5.8	1.5	5.3	26.0	25.1
	TV	Public MF	3 644	21.8	9.6	14.3	4.6	2.5	19.9	27.3
		F	1 312	15.8	13.3	6.5	0.3	1.2	40.2	22.6
Ireland 1991	Radio + TV	Government MF	1 927	35.0	2.4	28.2	3.7	5.3	18.4	6.9
Italy # 1994	Radio	Public MF	2 007	18.9	17.5	31.5	1.5	3.4	2.4	24.7
		F	770	29.6	9.0	-	-	1.0	3.9	56.5
	TV	Public MF	5 631	9.8	22.3	57.7	0.7	3.7	1.8	3.9
		F	1 050	43.2	23.7	2.9	-	8.1	8.8	13.3
	Radio + TV	Public MF	4 171	4.4	-	-	20.5	15.2	59.7	0.3
		F	1 660	2.3	-	-	-	1.3	96.4	-

Radio and television broadcasting: personnel 9.5
Radiodiffusion sonore et télévision: personnel
Radiodifusión sonora y televisión: personal

Country Year / Pays Année / País Año	Type of institution / Type d'organisme / Tipo de institución	Sex / Sexe / Sexo	Total staff / Personnel total / Personal total	Type of personnel / Type de personnel / Tipo de personal						
				Programme / Des programmes / De programas	Journal-istic / Journa-listique / Perio-dístico	Technical production / Technique de production / Técnico de producción	Technical trans-mission / Technique de diffusion / Técnico de radio-difusión	Other technical / Autre technique / Otro técnico	Adminis-trative / Adminis-tratif / Adminis-trativo	Other / Divers / Otros tipos
			(1)	(2)	(3)	(4)	(5)	(6)	(7)	(8)
Luxembourg 1995	Radio Public	MF	12	41.7	41.7	-	-	-	16.7	-
		F	5	40.0	40.0	-	-	-	20.0	-
	Commercial	MF	77	28.6	36.4	10.4	3.9	2.6	16.9	1.3
		F	27	25.9	33.3	-	-	-	37.0	3.7
	TV Commercial	MF	50	28.0	26.0	42.0	2.0	-	2.0	-
		F	9	33.3	44.4	11.1	-	-	11.1	-
Malta 1989	Radio Government	MF	97	10.3	12.4	13.4	—>	—>	27.8	36.1
	TV Government	MF	168	16.1	18.5	22.6	—>	—>	31.0	11.9
Moldova 1994	Radio + TV Government	MF	1 811	0.6	22.5	21.5	-	-	2.9	52.5
		F	933	1.0	28.7	19.9	-	-	3.1	47.3
Norway 1994	Radio Public	MF	635	58.7	—>	19.8	—>	—>	21.4	-
		F	251	...	...	...	...	...	...	...
	TV Public	MF	989	44.4	—>	34.4	—>	—>	21.2	-
		F	418	...	...	...	...	...	...	...
	Radio + TV Public	MF	1 336	32.9	—>	25.2	—>	—>	41.9	-
Poland 1991	Radio + TV Government	MF	9 034	25.3	18.7	28.2	-	2.3	16.0	9.5
Potugal 1991	Radio Public	MF	1 947	8.9	12.7	8.3	1.9	4.6	31.2	32.5
	TV Public	MF	2 388	27.7	—>	8.1	32.5	6.4	21.7	3.6
San Marino 1994	Radio + TV Public	MF	41	39.0	—>	34.2	—>	—>	24.4	2.4
		F	22	54.6		-		-	45.5	-
Slovenia 1994	Radio + TV Public	MF	2 408	15.3	14.6	35.1	9.3	-	7.3	18.4
Sweden 1994	Radio Public	MF	2 091	27.2	26.4	13.5	-	6.5	21.4	4.9
		F	828	30.6	27.9	3.7	-	0.8	33.9	3.0
Switzerland‡# 1994	Radio Public	MF	1 549	56.9	—>	11.9	-	3.6	12.7	15.0
	TV Public	MF	2 939	43.4	—>	38.8	-	6.9	10.4	0.5
	Radio + TV Public	MF	196	-	-	-		11.2	88.8	
The Former Yugoslav Rep. of Macedonia # 1994	Radio Public	MF	679	11.8	51.7	17.4	-	7.4	9.6	2.2
	Commercial	MF	107	28.0	17.8	36.4	-	6.5	9.3	1.9
	TV Public	MF	758	19.5	28.0	30.5	-	10.4	6.9	4.7
	Commercial	MF	79	30.4	17.7	31.6	-	3.8	15.2	1.3
	Radio + TV Public	MF	857	5.5	2.8	-	21.5	3.4	23.0	43.9
	Commercial	MF	24	29.2	29.2	-	25.0	8.3	8.3	-
Federal Republic of Yugoslavia 1994	Radio Government	MF	3 750	25.6	37.9	17.5	—>	—>	11.7	7.4
	TV Public	MF	2 842	17.8	22.3	39.5	—>	—>	15.4	5.0
	Commercial	MF	60	31.7	28.3	15.0	—>	—>	8.3	16.7
	Radio + TV Public	MF	1 393	2.7	0.9	4.5	—>	—>	57.8	34.1
	Commercial	MF	131	13.7	26.7	20.6	—>	—>	16.0	22.9

9.5 Radio and television broadcasting: personnel
Radiodiffusion sonore et télévision: personnel
Radiodifusión sonora y televisión: personal

Country Year / Pays Année / País Año	Type of institution / Type d'organisme / Tipo de institución	Sex / Sexe / Sexo	Total staff / Personnel total / Personal total	Type of personnel / Type de personnel / Tipo de personal						
				Programme / Des programmes / De programas	Journal-istic / Journa-listique / Perio-dístico	Technical production / Technique de production / Técnico de producción	Technical trans-mission / Technique de diffusion / Técnico de radio-difusión	Other technical / Autre technique / Otro técnico	Adminis-trative / Adminis-tratif / Adminis-trativo	Other / Divers / Otros tipos
			(1)	(2)	(3)	(4)	(5)	(6)	(7)	(8)
Oceania										
Australia 1991	Radio Public	MF	296	34.8	6.1	8.8	——>	——>	50.3	-
	Commercial	MF	4 029	34.1	9.0	5.0	——>	——>	22.6	29.3
TV	Commercial	MF	5 989	29.8	8.0	24.5	12.8	3.6	12.9	8.4

General note / Note générale / Nota general:

E--> The symbol # indicates that figures shown under Radio and TV combined refer to personnel that cannot be shown separately for these two media.

FR-> Le symbole # indique que les chiffres globaux concernant la radio et la télévision sont présentés lorqu'il est impossible de dissocier le personnel employé par ces deux medias.

ESP> El símbolo # indique que se presentan cifras globales relativas a la radio y la televisión cuando no ha sido posible disociar el personal empleado por ellas.

AFRICA:
United Republic of Tanzania:

E--> Data refer to Zanzibar only.

FR-> Les données se réfèrent à Zanzibar seulement.

ESP> Los datos se refieren a Zanzibar solamente.

AMERICA, NORTH:
Cuba:

E--> Figures on technical staff include data on programme staff.

FR-> Les chiffres relatifs au personnel technique incluent les données concernant le personnel des programmes.

ESP> Las cifras relativos el personal técnico incluyen los datos para el personal de programas.

EUROPE:
Belgium:

E--> Figures do not include data for BRF (*Belgisches Rundfunk- und Fernsehzentrum*).

FR-> Les chiffres n'incluent pas les données pour la BRF (*Belgisches Rundfunk- und Fernsehzentrum*).

ESP> Las cifras no incluyen los datos para la BRF (*Belgisches Rundfunk- und Fernsehzentrum*).

Germany:

E--> Figures refer to *Zweites Deutsches Fernsehen* (Z.D.F) only.

FR-> Les chiffres se réfèrent à la *Zweites Deutsches Fernsehen* (Z.D.F) seulement.

ESP> Las cifras se refieren a la *Zweites Deutsches Fernsehen* (Z.D.F) solamente.

Switzerland:

E--> Transmission is the responsibility of the national post and telegraph service *P.T.T.*.

FR-> La transmission est assurée par le service national des postes et télégraphes (P.T.T.).

ESP> El servicio nacional de correos y telégrafos *P.T.T.* es responsable de la transmisión.

International trade in printed matter
Commerce international en matière d'imprimés
Comercio internacional de impresos

10

10 International trade in printed matter

Commerce international en matière d'imprimés

Comercio internacional de impresos

The two tables in this chapter contain statistics on international trade in printed matter, i.e. books and pamphlets on the one hand, and newspapers and periodicals on the other, both belonging to Category 1 of the UNESCO Framework for Cultural Statistics (FCS). The international collection of this type of data is foreseen in the Revised Recommendation concerning the International Standardization of Statistics on the Production and Distribution of Books, Newspapers and Periodicals, adopted by the UNESCO General Conference at its twenty-third session in Sofia (November, 1985).

Attempts to collect data on the international exchange of printed materials by means of a questionnaire addressed to Member States did not bring the expected results. In view of this, and also in order to avoid a duplication of effort for national agencies supplying statistical information to different organizations of the United Nations family, it was found preferable to publish in this Yearbook data that have been obtained from the Statistical Division of the United Nations, and which correspond to those published in the *U.N. World Trade Annual*.

Table 10.1
The data in this table refer to international trade in books and pamphlets (code 892.11 of the Standard International Trade Classification (SITC), Revision 2) for the years 1980, 1990 and 1994.

Table 10.2
This table gives for the years 1980, 1990 and 1994 statistics on international trade in newspapers and periodicals which correspond to code 892.2 of the SITC, Revision 2.

Les deux tableaux de ce chapître contiennent des statistiques sur le commerce international en matière d'imprimés: livres et brochures d'une part et journaux et périodiques d'autre part, les deux appartenant à la catégorie 1 du Cadre de l'UNESCO pour les statistiques culturelles (CSC). La collecte internationale de ce genre de données est prévue dans la Recommandation révisée concernant la normalisation internationale des statistiques relatives à la production et à la distribution de livres, de journaux et de périodiques, adoptée par la Conférence générale à sa vingt-troisième session à Sofia (novembre, 1985).

Des essais de rassemblement des données sur les échanges internationaux d'imprimés, effectué à l'aide d'un questionnaire adressé aux Etats Membres n'ont pas donné les résultats escomptés. A cause de cela et aussi afin d'éviter un double travail aux institutions nationales qui fournissent des informations statistiques aux différentes organisations de la famille des Nations Unies, on a trouvé préférable de publier dans cet *Annuaire* des données obtenues de la Division de statistique des Nations Unies qui correspondent à celles publiées dans le *U.N. World Trade Annual*.

Tableau 10.1
Les données de ce tableau se réfèrent au commerce international de livres et brochures (code 892.11 de la Classification type pour le commerce international (CTCI), Révision 2) pour les années 1980, 1990 et 1994.

Tableau 10.2
Ce tableau donne, pour les années 1980, 1990 et 1994 des statistiques sur le commerce international de journaux et périodiques qui correspondent au code 892.2 de la CTCI, Révision 2.

Los dos cuadros en este capítulo contienen estadísticas sobre el comercio internacional de impresos, i.e. libros y folletos por un lado, diarios y periódicos por otro; ambos corresponden a la categoría 1 del Marco de las Estadísticas Culturales de la UNESCO (MEC). La recolección internacional de este tipo de datos está prevista en la Recomendación Revisada sobre la normalización internacional de las estadísticas relativas a la producción y distribución de libros diarios y otras publicaciones periódicas, aprobada por la Conferencia General de la UNESCO en su vigésima-tercera reunión, Sofía (noviembre de 1985).

Intentos de recopilación de datos sobre los intercambios internacionales de impresos se llevaron a cabo por medio de un cuestionario, dirigido a los Estados Miembros, que no obtuvo los resultados esperados; como consecuencia de esto y para evitar una duplicación de los esfuerzos hechos por las agencias nacionales para proporcionar información estadística a las diferentes organizaciones de la familia de las Naciones Unidas, se estimó preferible el publicar en este Anuario, datos que han sido obtenidos de la División de Estadística de las Naciones Unidas, y que corresponden a aquellos publicados en el *U.N. World Trade Annual*.

Cuadro 10.1
Los datos en este cuadro se refieren al comercio internacional de libros y folletos (Código 892.11 de la Clasificación Uniforme para el Comercio Internacional (CUCI), Revisión 2) para los años 1980, 1990 y 1994.

Cuadro 10.2
Este cuadro proporciona para los años 1980, 1990 y 1994 estadísticas sobre el comercio internacional sobre diarios y periódicos que corresponden al código 892.2 del CUCI Revisión 2.

10.1 International trade in books and pamphlets
Commerce international de livres et brochures
Comercio internacional de libros y folletos

10.1 Importation and exportation of books and pamphlets: 1980, 1990 and 1994

Importation et exportation de livres et brochures: 1980, 1990 et 1994

Importación y exportación de libros y folletos: 1980, 1990 y 1994

| Amounts shown are in millions of U.S. dollars. | Les montants sont exprimés en millions de dollars des États-Unis. | Los importes se expresan en millones de dólares de los Estados Unidos. |

Country Pays País	1980			1990			1994		
	Exports Exporta- tions Exporta- ciones	Imports Importa- tions Importa- ciones	Balance Balance Balanza	Exports Exporta- tions Exporta- ciones	Imports Importa- tions Importa- ciones	Balance Balance Balanza	Exports Exporta- tions Exporta- ciones	Imports Importa- tions Importa- ciones	Balance Balance Balanza
Africa									
Algeria	0.2	22.5	-22.3	0.1	9.1	-9.0	...	3.2	...
Burkina Faso	0.0	1.1	-1.1	...	...	...	...	...	...
Cameroon	0.7	8.3	-7.6	0.1	94.3	-94.2	...	...	...
Cape Verde	...	0.2	...	...	...	...	...	...	...
Central African Republic	...	0.2	...	...	...	...	...	...	...
Congo	0.0	1.5	-1.5	...	...	...	0.0	1.3	-1.3
Djibouti	...	...	...	0.0	1.7	-1.7	...	...	...
Egypt	...	...	...	7.8	9.9	-2.1	5.9	11.1	-5.2
Gabon	...	2.1	...	...	...	...	0.5	11.0	-10.6
Kenya	1.6	9.0	-7.4	2.0	4.3	-2.3	...	...	...
Liberia	...	1.9	...	...	...	...	...	...	...
Libyan Arab Jamahiriya	...	...	...	0.3	18.5	-18.2	...	...	...
Madagascar	0.0	1.4	-1.4	0.0	2.3	-2.3	0.0	2.2	-2.2
Malawi	0.0	0.0	-0.0	0.0	1.7	-1.6	...	...	...
Mali	...	3.8	...	...	0.4	...	...	...	...
Mauritius	0.0	2.8	-2.7	0.3	5.2	-4.9	0.7	8.9	-8.2
Morocco	0.2	14.6	-14.4	0.9	23.8	-22.9	1.3	23.9	-22.6
Niger	0.0	3.1	-3.1	...	...	...	...	...	...
Reunion	0.1	4.0	-3.9	0.1	15.3	-15.1	0.2	18.4	-18.2
Senegal	0.2	7.4	-7.2	0.0	5.4	-5.3	...	...	...
Seychelles	...	...	...	0.0	0.8	-0.8	...	...	...
Togo	0.0	1.2	-1.2	0.0	2.3	-2.3	...	...	...

International trade in books and pamphlets **10.1**
Commerce international de livres et brochures
Comercio internacional de libros y folletos

Country / Pays / País	1980			1990			1994		
	Exports Exporta-tions Exporta-ciones	Imports Importa-tions Importa-ciones	Balance Balance Balanza	Exports Exporta-tions Exporta-ciones	Imports Importa-tions Importa-ciones	Balance Balance Balanza	Exports Exporta-tions Exporta-ciones	Imports Importa-tions Importa-ciones	Balance Balance Balanza
Tunisia	1.1	5.2	-4.1	1.0	9.1	-8.0	1.2	12.9	-11.7
Zimbabwe	...	...	...	0.9	4.7	-3.8	...	...	...
America, North									
Barbados	0.1	2.2	-2.1	0.4	5.2	-4.9	...	...	...
Belize	...	...	...	...	...	...	0.0	1.6	-1.6
Canada	...	337.1	...	104.1	802.5	-698.4	168.0	920.7	-752.7
Costa Rica	...	...	...	3.5	11.9	-8.4	5.1	20.9	-15.8
El Salvador	...	...	...	0.3	1.7	-1.4	1.1	7.9	-6.8
Greenland	0.0	1.2	-1.2	0.0	1.4	-1.4	0.1	1.9	-1.7
Grenada	...	...	...	...	0.9	...	...	...	...
Guadeloupe	0.2	4.0	-3.8	0.4	14.8	-14.4	0.5	14.9	-14.4
Guatemala	...	...	...	0.4	6.0	-5.7	0.3	9.8	-9.5
Honduras	...	...	...	0.0	2.7	-2.7	0.0	3.5	-3.5
Jamaica	0.2	3.5	-3.3	0.3	11.7	-11.3	...	...	...
Martinique	0.3	5.6	-5.3	0.7	13.9	-13.3	0.2	12.7	-12.5
Mexico	...	...	...	28.4	111.7	-83.4	77.1	325.0	-247.8
Nicaragua	...	...	...	0.0	1.9	-1.9	0.0	5.8	-5.8
Panama	...	...	...	0.2	8.1	-7.9	0.0	11.4	-11.4
St. Lucia	...	...	...	0.0	1.9	-1.9	...	...	...
Trinidad and Tobago	0.2	10.9	-10.7	0.7	7.2	-6.5	1.2	8.7	-7.5
United States	...	...	...	1 491.0	930.8	560.2	1 832.9	1 109.7	723.2
America, South									
Argentina	44.0	70.2	-26.2	21.2	5.8	15.4	36.1	52.1	-16.0
Bolivia	0.0	7.7	-7.7	0.0	4.8	-4.8	0.4	6.0	-5.7
Brazil	...	...	...	5.0	53.5	-48.5	15.4	60.7	-45.3
Chile	...	...	...	10.5	15.6	-5.1	35.3	31.5	3.7
Colombia	24.1	35.8	-11.8	57.9	19.2	38.7	85.3	50.6	34.7
Ecuador	0.8	3.4	-2.6	0.3	9.5	-9.3	0.5	40.4	-39.9
French Guiana	0.0	0.6	-0.5	0.0	3.1	-3.0	0.1	3.0	-2.9
Paraguay	...	...	...	1.2	0.7	0.4	1.4	4.1	-2.7
Peru	1.5	7.7	-6.2	0.7	22.6	-21.9	1.2	16.0	-14.8
Suriname	...	...	...	...	2.0	...	...	...	...
Uruguay	...		...	0.3	0.1	0.2	0.0	0.2	-0.2
Venezuela	...		...	3.5	23.7	-20.2	2.7	32.2	-29.5
Asia									
Bangladesh	0.0	1.0	-1.0	...	...	...	...	...	...
Brunei Darussalam	...	...	...	0.0	4.2	-4.2	...	...	...
China	...	...	...	19.6	30.9	-11.3	56.5	37.5	19.0
Cyprus	0.1	4.9	-4.8	0.8	8.8	-8.0	0.4	12.2	-11.8
Hong Kong	75.7	11.7	64.1	265.4	70.1	195.3	340.8	135.0	205.8
Indonesia	0.0	3.1	-3.0	0.4	19.2	-18.8	0.9	14.3	-13.4

10.1 International trade in books and pamphlets
Commerce international de livres et brochures
Comercio internacional de libros y folletos

Country	1980			1990			1994		
Pays	Exports Exporta-tions Exporta-ciones	Imports Importa-tions Importa-ciones	Balance Balance Balanza	Exports Exporta-tions Exporta-ciones	Imports Importa-tions Importa-ciones	Balance Balance Balanza	Exports Exporta-tions Exporta-ciones	Imports Importa-tions Importa-ciones	Balance Balance Balanza
País									
Israel	...	...	...	19.6	15.5	4.1	19.3	22.0	-2.6
Japan	61.5	100.6	-39.1	218.6	231.7	-13.1	200.4	233.9	-33.5
Jordan	...	...	...	0.3	8.9	-8.7	6.5	7.0	-0.5
Korea, Republic of	3.2	10.4	-7.2	29.2	28.2	1.0	36.3	61.4	-25.0
Kuwait	...	...	...	0.6	5.2	-4.6	1.0	10.9	-9.9
Macau	...	0.7	...	0.1	0.5	-0.4	0.1	1.2	-1.1
Malaysia	2.2	20.8	-18.5	9.7	46.2	-36.5	30.2	74.3	-44.1
Oman	...	...	...	0.3	3.1	-2.8	0.1	2.7	-2.6
Pakistan	...	...	...	1.0	8.0	-7.0	1.3	10.9	-9.6
Philippines	0.1	13.7	-13.7	0.4	14.5	-14.1	0.7	35.1	-34.4
Saudi Arabia	0.4	27.1	-26.8	1.8	26.7	-25.0	...	...	...
Singapore	45.0	31.8	13.2	171.5	87.9	83.6	310.3	135.7	174.5
Sri Lanka	0.0	1.1	-1.1	0.2	3.4	-3.2	0.3	8.3	-8.1
Syrian Arab Republic	0.2	0.9	-0.7	0.4	0.6	-0.2	...	...	...
Thailand	0.1	4.5	-4.4	1.9	17.8	-15.9	8.0	34.7	-26.7
Turkey	...	...	...	2.1	15.8	-13.7	2.6	50.4	-47.7
Europe									
Austria	61.5	129.1	-67.6	87.5	248.8	-161.3	99.4	305.0	-205.5
Belgium‡	166.7	180.5	-13.8	353.4	292.7	60.7	328.4	312.9	15.5
Czech Republic	.	.	.	.	.	.	24.8	43.0	-18.2
Denmark	38.5	43.1	-4.6	128.0	105.0	23.1	118.8	83.0	35.8
Faeroe Islands	...	1.1	...	...	1.6	...	...	0.9	...
Finland	18.9	21.6	-2.7	44.3	54.7	-10.4	42.5	40.5	1.9
Germany	.	.	.	.	.	.	908.9	471.7	437.2
Former German Democratic Republic	403.8	230.6	173.2	855.1	466.9	388.2	...	...	...
Greece	3.7	8.1	-4.4	5.0	31.3	-26.3	7.4	37.7	-30.3
Iceland	0.2	1.9	-1.8	0.2	5.8	-5.6	0.8	5.8	-5.1
Ireland	6.1	32.3	-26.2	32.0	105.4	-73.5	52.4	75.7	-23.4
Italy	171.3	38.5	132.8	387.5	125.3	262.3	452.8	153.7	299.0
Latvia	.	.	.	.	.	.	0.4	1.3	-0.9
Lithuania	.	.	.	.	.	.	0.8	2.0	-1.2
Malta	...	...	...	1.2	4.9	-3.7	...	...	...
Moldova	.	.	.	.	.	.	1.5	3.0	-1.4
Netherlands	166.3	179.2	-12.9	332.4	309.6	22.8	299.9	285.6	14.3
Norway	4.1	37.0	-32.9	22.0	88.5	-66.5	22.2	83.6	-61.4
Poland	...	...	...	...	...	...	9.7	85.2	-75.5
Portugal	13.0	7.5	5.5	26.6	31.7	-5.1	15.7	47.0	-31.3
Romania	...	...	...	2.7	5.3	-2.7	0.5	12.8	-12.4
Slovenia	.	.	.	.	.	.	37.7	7.0	30.7
Spain	358.8	31.5	327.3	293.0	141.3	151.7	461.0	136.9	324.0
Sweden	35.3	68.6	-33.3	73.1	189.5	-116.4	79.2	163.4	-84.2
Switzerland	146.5	187.0	-40.5	145.7	357.5	-211.8	211.1	440.8	-229.7

International trade in books and pamphlets **10.1**
Commerce international de livres et brochures
Comercio internacional de libros y folletos

Country	1980			1990			1994		
Pays	Exports Exporta-tions Exporta-ciones	Imports Importa-tions Importa-ciones	Balance Balance Balanza	Exports Exporta-tions Exporta-ciones	Imports Importa-tions Importa-ciones	Balance Balance Balanza	Exports Exporta-tions Exporta-ciones	Imports Importa-tions Importa-ciones	Balance Balance Balanza
País									
United Kingdom	552.7	288.1	264.6	1 298.6	781.8	516.8	1 449.0	817.2	631.8
Oceania									
Australia	24.2	198.2	-174.0	47.2	388.3	-341.2	67.4	371.1	-303.7
Fiji	0.1	1.0	-0.9	0.0	2.1	-2.0	0.1	3.3	-3.2
French Polynesia	0.0	2.7	-2.7	...	...	...	...	...	...
New Caledonia	0.3	2.8	-2.6	...	...	...	...	...	...
New Zealand	2.7	63.4	-60.8	3.9	87.4	-83.5	9.3	99.2	-89.9
Papua New Guinea	...	...	...	0.0	5.1	-5.1	...	...	...
Samoa	...	0.3	...	...	0.3	...	...	...	...

General note / Note générale / Nota general:

E--> Export values are f.o.b. (free on board) at the frontier of the exporting country. Import values are c.i.f. (cost, insurance, freight) except for Canada and Australia where they are f.o.b. Export data include, where appropriate, re-exports.

FR-> Les valeurs d'exportations sont f.o.b.(franco à bord) à la frontière du pays exportateur. Les valeurs d'importations sont c.i.f. (coût, assurance, frêt) sauf pour le Canada et l'Australie, où elles s'expriment f.o.b. Les exportations comprennent, s'il y a lieu, les re-exportations.

ESP> Los datos sobre las exportaciones son f.o.b. (franco a bordo) a la frontera del país exportador. Los datos sobre las importaciones son c.i.f. (coste, seguro y flete) salvo por Canada y Australia, por los cuales se expresan f.o.b. Las exportaciones incluyen, si necesario, las re-exportaciones.

Belgium:
E--> Including Luxembourg.
FR-> Y compris le Luxembourg.
ESP> Incluído Luxemburgo.

10.2 International trade in newspapers and periodicals
Commerce international de journaux et périodiques
Comercio internacional de publicaciones periódicas

10.2 Exportation and importation of newspapers and periodicals: 1980, 1990 and 1994

Exportation et importation de journaux et périodiques: 1980, 1990 et 1994

Exportación y importación de publicaciones periódicas: 1980, 1990 y 1994

Amounts shown are in millions of U.S. dollars.

Les montants sont exprimés en millions de dollars des États-Unis.

Los importes se expresan en millones de dólares de los Estados Unidos.

Country / Pays / País	1980			1990			1994		
	Exports / Exportations / Exportaciones	Imports / Importations / Importaciones	Balance / Balance / Balanza	Exports / Exportations / Exportaciones	Imports / Importations / Importaciones	Balance / Balance / Balanza	Exports / Exportations / Exportaciones	Imports / Importations / Importaciones	Balance / Balance / Balanza
Africa									
Algeria	...	9.5	...	3.4	7.4	-4.0	0.7	0.1	0.6
Burkina Faso	...	0.5	...	...	...	...	...	...	...
Cameroon	...	3.3	...	0.0	9.7	-9.7	...	...	...
Central African Republic	...	0.1	...	...	...	...	...	...	...
Congo	...	0.2	...	...	...	...	...	0.2	...
Djibouti	...	...	...	...	0.2	...	...	...	...
Egypt	...	...	...	2.1	2.4	-0.3	4.4	3.4	1.0
Gabon	...	0.6	...	...	...	...	...	5.1	...
Kenya	0.0	1.7	-1.7	0.0	0.9	-0.9	...	...	...
Liberia	...	0.5	...	...	...	...	...	...	...
Libyan Arab Jamahiriya	...	...	...	...	3.4	...	...	...	...
Madagascar	0.0	1.6	-1.6	...	0.7	...	...	0.7	...
Malawi	0.0	0.4	-0.4	...	0.4	...	...	...	...
Mali	...	0.4	...	...	0.3	...	...	...	...
Mauritius	...	0.7	...	0.0	1.2	-1.2	0.0	2.8	-2.8
Morocco	...	13.1	...	0.0	3.7	-3.7	0.0	4.1	-4.0
Niger	...	0.5	...	...	...	...	...	...	...
Reunion	0.3	2.0	-1.7	0.2	3.9	-3.7	0.1	9.3	-9.2
Senegal	3.8	1.0	2.8	...	8.4	...	...	...	...
Seychelles	...	0.2	...	...	0.2	...	...	...	...
Togo	0.0	0.1	-0.1	...	0.9	...	...	...	...
Tunisia	0.0	2.6	-2.6	0.6	4.6	-4.0	0.5	5.8	-5.3

International trade in newspapers and periodicals **10.2**
Commerce international de journaux et périodiques
Comercio internacional de publicaciones periódicas

Country	1980			1990			1994		
Pays	Exports / Exportations / Exportaciones	Imports / Importations / Importaciones	Balance / Balance / Balanza	Exports / Exportations / Exportaciones	Imports / Importations / Importaciones	Balance / Balance / Balanza	Exports / Exportations / Exportaciones	Imports / Importations / Importaciones	Balance / Balance / Balanza
País									
Zimbabwe	...	...	...	0.0	0.2	-0.2	...	...	...
America, North									
Barbados	0.2	0.5	-0.2	0.7	1.2	-0.6	...	...	...
Belize	...	...	...	...	...	...	...	0.3	...
Canada	72.6	244.0	-171.4	125.9	572.3	-446.4	136.0	614.3	-478.3
Cayman Islands	...	0.1	...	...	...	...	...	...	...
Costa Rica	...	...	...	0.0	1.3	-1.3	0.2	2.7	-2.5
El Salvador	...	...	...	0.0	0.3	-0.2	0.0	0.6	-0.6
Greenland	...	...	...	0.0	0.0	-0.0	...	...	...
Guadeloupe	0.2	2.2	-2.0	0.0	13.4	-13.4	0.9	15.2	-14.3
Guatemala	...	...	...	0.0	0.7	-0.7	0.0	0.4	-0.4
Honduras	...	...	...	...	0.4	...	...	0.5	-0.5
Jamaica	0.1	...	...	0.2	2.8	-2.6	...	...	...
Martinique	1.1	3.5	-2.4	0.0	0.3	-0.3	0.1	1.6	-1.5
Mexico	...	...	...	7.6	34.3	-26.7	14.8	93.7	-78.9
Nicaragua	...	...	...	...	...	...	0.0	0.5	-0.5
Panama	...	...	...	0.3	4.4	-4.1	...	6.9	...
St. Lucia	...	...	...	...	0.2	...	...	...	...
Trinidad and Tobago	0.1	1.0	-0.9	0.2	1.6	-1.4	0.2	1.0	-0.7
United States	...	...	...	703.3	193.3	510.0	823.4	228.5	594.9
America, South									
Argentina	5.8	9.3	-3.5	3.1	2.7	0.4	17.1	24.2	-7.1
Bolivia	...	0.9	...	...	0.8	...	...	1.0	...
Brazil	...	...	...	7.1	29.1	-22.0	11.8	32.8	-21.0
Chile	...	...	...	9.1	3.0	6.0	34.3	8.4	25.9
Colombia	12.0	5.9	6.1	21.0	5.0	15.9	30.3	9.1	21.2
Ecuador	...	...	...	...	0.8	...	...	4.2	...
French Guiana	...	...	...	...	1.1	...	...	1.1	...
Paraguay	...	...	...	...	0.1	...	0.1	0.5	-0.4
Peru	0.2	5.0	-4.8	0.0	2.4	-2.4	0.1	5.1	-5.0
Suriname	...	...	...	...	0.1	...	...	...	...
Uruguay	...	...	...	...	...	...	1.0	0.0	1.0
Venezuela	...	...	...	1.0	6.2	-5.2	1.0	14.9	-13.9
Asia									
Bangladesh	0.0	0.0	-0.0	...	...	...	...	...	...
Brunei Darussalam	...	...	...	0.0	3.9	-3.9	...	...	...
China	...	...	...	2.3	27.7	-25.4	2.2	8.3	-6.1
Cyprus	0.7	3.2	-2.5	2.9	8.0	-5.1	0.8	10.2	-9.4
Hong Kong	15.4	3.3	12.1	35.9	10.3	25.6	38.9	33.3	5.6
India	0.6	1.9	-1.3	...	...	...	...	...	...
Indonesia	0.0	0.6	-0.6	0.1	2.4	-2.3	0.1	7.4	-7.3

10.2 International trade in newspapers and periodicals
Commerce international de journaux et périodiques
Comercio internacional de publicaciones periódicas

Country / Pays / País	1980			1990			1994		
	Exports Exporta-tions Exporta-ciones	Imports Importa-tions Importa-ciones	Balance Balance Balanza	Exports Exporta-tions Exporta-ciones	Imports Importa-tions Importa-ciones	Balance Balance Balanza	Exports Exporta-tions Exporta-ciones	Imports Importa-tions Importa-ciones	Balance Balance Balanza
Israel	...	...	...	2.8	5.7	-2.9	2.3	6.8	-4.5
Japan	21.7	48.6	-26.9	35.5	112.3	-76.8	49.0	156.6	-107.6
Jordan	...	...	...	0.0	0.5	-0.5	0.0	0.3	-0.3
Korea, Republic of	0.2	3.7	-3.5	1.6	19.4	-17.8	1.8	32.0	-30.2
Kuwait	...	...	...	0.5	3.7	-3.2	0.3	4.4	-4.2
Macau	...	...	...	0.0	0.1	-0.1	0.0	0.0	-0.0
Malaysia	0.8	4.9	-4.1	1.7	13.2	-11.5	1.4	12.8	-11.5
Oman	...	...	...	0.2	2.4	-2.2	0.3	2.1	-1.8
Pakistan	...	...	...	2.3	0.4	1.9	4.0	0.4	3.7
Philippines	0.3	3.6	-3.3	0.5	5.0	-4.5	1.2	8.7	-7.5
Saudi Arabia	0.1	2.1	-2.1	0.1	1.7	-1.6	...	...	...
Singapore	3.2	14.8	-11.6	15.6	21.3	-5.6	33.7	27.8	5.9
Sri Lanka	0.0	0.1	-0.1	0.2	1.8	-1.6	0.7	1.1	-0.4
Syrian Arab Republic	0.0	0.0	-0.0	0.0	0.1	-0.1	...	...	...
Thailand	0.2	0.6	-0.4	3.2	9.4	-6.2	4.8	10.3	-5.5
Turkey	...	...	...	1.6	7.7	-6.0	2.3	11.1	-8.9
Europe									
Austria	18.8	105.4	-86.7	77.0	244.5	-167.5	81.9	250.8	-168.9
Belgium‡	95.3	129.3	-34.0	112.8	341.0	-228.2	107.7	337.5	-229.9
Czech Republic	.	.	.	.	.	.	8.7	18.6	-10.0
Denmark	7.0	7.9	-0.9	31.5	24.7	6.8	48.4	28.3	20.1
Faeroe Islands	...	...	...	...	0.1	...	...	1.5	...
Finland	25.4	6.5	18.9	51.2	23.7	27.5	83.7	19.1	64.6
Germany	.	.	.	.	.	.	921.5	272.2	649.2
Former German Democratic Rep.	376.6	95.4	281.1	879.5	234.8	644.7	...	...	...
Greece	0.9	0.8	0.1	11.7	5.5	6.2	8.1	34.7	-26.5
Iceland	...	1.3	...	0.0	2.6	-2.5	0.1	2.6	-2.5
Ireland	3.6	31.4	-27.8	16.8	60.7	-43.9	13.9	75.6	-61.7
Italy	168.6	32.1	136.4	211.3	50.8	160.5	204.9	107.6	97.3
Latvia	.	.	.	.	.	.	0.3	1.9	-1.6
Lithuania	.	.	.	.	.	.	0.1	1.2	-1.0
Malta	...	...	...	0.1	4.4	-4.3	...	...	...
Moldova	...	...	...	...	...	...	...	...	...
Netherlands	77.0	51.4	25.6	175.3	93.3	82.0	128.8	118.5	10.3
Norway	0.5	15.4	-14.9	1.1	36.9	-35.9	0.7	36.6	-35.9
Poland	...	...	...	...	...	...	4.2	80.6	-76.4
Portugal	2.3	10.4	-8.2	4.5	31.8	-27.3	2.2	59.6	-57.4
Romania	...	...	...	...	...	...	0.9	0.8	0.1
Slovenia	.	.	.	.	.	.	1.6	11.6	-10.0
Spain	20.6	28.4	-7.8	65.5	82.2	-16.7	120.8	110.2	10.7
Sweden	10.7	24.1	-13.5	26.2	68.7	-42.6	13.9	84.9	-71.0
Switzerland	24.9	119.4	-94.5	69.8	276.9	-207.0	78.4	303.4	-225.0

International trade in newspapers and periodicals 10.2
Commerce international de journaux et périodiques
Comercio internacional de publicaciones periódicas

Country Pays País	1980			1990			1994		
	Exports Exporta- tions Exporta- ciones	Imports Importa- tions Importa- ciones	Balance Balance Balanza	Exports Exporta- tions Exporta- ciones	Imports Importa- tions Importa- ciones	Balance Balance Balanza	Exports Exporta- tions Exporta- ciones	Imports Importa- tions Importa- ciones	Balance Balance Balanza
United Kingdom	99.4	55.9	43.4	222.1	214.6	7.5	478.5	158.4	320.1
Oceania									
Australia	10.1	56.3	-46.2	9.1	120.5	-111.3	23.6	162.2	-138.6
Fiji	...	0.1	...	...	...	...	0.0	0.1	-0.1
French Polynesia	...	0.9	...	...	...	...	...	...	...
New Caledonia	...	1.5	...	...	...	...	...	...	...
New Zealand	2.8	20.7	-17.8	0.4	45.8	-45.4	1.2	60.3	-59.2
Papua New Guinea	...	...	...	0.0	0.2	-0.2	...	...	...
Samoa	0.0	0.0	-0.0	...	...	...	...	...	...

General note / Note générale / Nota general:

E--> Export values are f.o.b. (free on board) at the frontier of the exporting country. Import values are c.i.f. (cost, insurance, freight) except for Canada and Australia where they are f.o.b. Export data include, where appropriate, re-exports.

FR-> Les valeurs d'exportations sont f.o.b.(franco à bord) à la frontière du pays exportateur. Les valeurs d'importations sont c.i.f. (coût, assurance, frêt) sauf pour le Canada et l'Australie, où elles s'expriment f.o.b. Les exportations comprennent, s'il y a lieu, les re-exportations.

ESP> Los datos sobre las exportaciones son f.o.b. (franco a bordo) a la frontera del país exportador. Los datos sobre las importaciones son c.i.f. (coste, seguro y flete) salvo por Canada y Australia, por los cuales se expresan f.o.b. Las exportaciones incluyen, si necesario, las re-exportaciones.

EUROPE: Belgium:

E--> Including Luxembourg.
FR-> Y compris le Luxembourg.
ESP> Incluído Luxemburgo.

Appendixes

Annexes

Anexos

Member States and Associate Members
Etats membres et Membres associés
Estados miembros y Miembros asociados

A   Member States and Associate Members of UNESCO

Etats membres et Membres associés de l'UNESCO

Estados miembros y Miembros asociados de la UNESCO

Member State État membre Estado miembro	Date of entry Date d'adhésion Fecha de entrada	Scale of contributions Barème des contributions Escala de contribuciones	Contributions to the budget 1996 Contributions au budget 1996 Contribuciones al presupuesto 1996	
			Portion in French Francs Part en francs français Parte en francos franceses	Portion in U.S. dollars Part en dollars des E.U. Parte en dólares estadounidenses
Afghanistan	4. 5. 1948	0.01	122 325	13 225
Albania	16. 10. 1958	0.01	122 325	13 225
Algeria	15. 10. 1962	0.16	1 957 201	211 602
Andorra	20. 10. 1993	0.01	122 325	13 225
Angola	11. 3. 1977	0.01	122 325	13 225
Antigua and Barbuda	15. 7. 1982	0.01	122 325	13 225
Argentina	15. 9. 1948	0.47	5 749 278	621 580
Armenia	9. 6. 1992	0.08	978 601	105 801
Australia	4. 11. 1946	1.44	17 614 809	1 904 416
Austria	13. 8. 1948	0.84	10 275 305	1 110 909
Azerbaijan	3. 6. 1992	0.16	1 957 201	211 602
Bahamas	23. 4. 1981	0.02	244 650	26 450
Bahrain	18. 1. 1972	0.02	244 650	26 450
Bangladesh	27. 10. 1972	0.01	122 325	13 225
Barbados	24. 10. 1968	0.01	122 325	13 225
Belarus	12. 5. 1954	0.36	4 403 702	476 104
Belgium	29. 11. 1946	0.98	11 987 856	1 296 061
Belize	10. 5. 1982	0.01	122 325	13 225
Benin	18. 10. 1960	0.01	122 325	13 225
Bhutan	13. 4. 1982	0.01	122 325	13 225
Bolivia	13. 11. 1946	0.01	122 325	13 225
Bosnia and Herzegovina	2. 6. 1993	0.02	244 650	26 450
Botswana	16. 1. 1980	0.01	122 325	13 225
Brazil	4. 11. 1946	1.60	19 572 010	2 116 018
Bulgaria	17. 5. 1956	0.10	1 223 251	132 251
Burkina Faso	14. 11. 1960	0.01	122 325	13 225
Burundi	16. 11. 1962	0.01	122 325	13 225
Cambodia	3. 7. 1951	0.01	122 325	13 225
Cameroon	11. 11. 1960	0.01	122 325	13 225
Canada	4. 11. 1946	3.03	37 064 493	4 007 209
Cape Verde	15. 2. 1978	0.01	122 325	13 225
Central African Republic	11. 11. 1960	0.01	122 325	13 225
Chad	19. 12. 1960	0.01	122 325	13 225
Chile	7. 7. 1953	0.08	978 601	105 801
China	4. 11. 1946	0.71	8 685 079	938 983
Colombia	31. 10. 1947	0.11	1 345 576	145 476

Member States and Associate Members
Etats membres et Membres associés
Estados miembros y Miembros asociados

Member State État membre Estado miembro	Date of entry Date d'adhésion Fecha de entrada	Scale of contributions Barème des contributions Escala de contribuciones	Contributions to the budget 1996 Contributions au budget 1996 Contribuciones al presupuesto 1996	
			Portion in French Francs Part en francs français Parte en francos franceses	Portion in U.S. dollars Part en dollars des E.U. Parte en dólares estadounidenses
Comoros	22. 3. 1977	0.01	122 325	13 225
Congo	24. 10. 1960	0.01	122 325	13 225
Cook Islands	25. 10. 1989	0.01	122 325	13 225
Costa Rica	19. 5. 1950	0.01	122 325	13 225
Côte d'Ivoire	27. 10. 1960	0.01	122 325	13 225
Croatia	1. 06. 1992	0.10	1 223 251	132 251
Cuba	29. 08. 1947	0.07	856 276	92 576
Cyprus	6. 02. 1961	0.03	366 975	39 675
Czech Republic	22. 02. 1993	0.31	3 792 077	409 979
Denmark	4. 11. 1946	0.69	8 440 429	912 533
Djibouti	31. 08. 1989	0.01	122 325	13 225
Dominica	9. 01. 1979	0.01	122 325	13 225
Domican Republic	4. 11. 1946	0.01	122 325	13 225
Ecuador	22. 01. 1947	0.02	244 650	26 450
Egypt	4. 11. 1946	0.07	856 276	92 576
El Salvador	28. 04. 1948	0.01	122 325	13 225
Equatorial Guinea	29. 11. 1979	0.01	122 325	13 225
Eritrea	2. 09. 1993	0.01	122 325	13 225
Estonia	14. 10. 1991	0.05	611 625	66 126
Ethiopia	1. 07. 1955	0.01	122 325	13 225
Fiji	14. 07. 1983	0.01	122 325	13 225
Finland	10. 10. 1956	0.60	7 339 504	793 507
France	4. 11. 1946	6.25	76 453 163	8 265 695
Gabon	16. 11. 1960	0.01	122 325	13 225
Gambia	1. 08. 1973	0.01	122 325	13 225
Georgia	7. 10. 1992	0.16	1 957 201	211 602
Germany	11. 07. 1951	8.84	108 135 353	11 690 998
Ghana	11. 04. 1958	0.01	122 325	13 225
Greece	4. 11. 1946	0.36	4 403 702	476 104
Grenada	17. 02. 1975	0.01	122 325	13 225
Guatemala	2. 01. 1950	0.02	244 650	26 450
Guinea	2. 2. 1960	0.01	122 325	13 225
Guinea-Bissau	1. 11. 1974	0.01	122 325	13 225
Guyana	21. 03. 1967	0.01	122 325	13 225
Haïti	18. 11. 1946	0.01	122 325	13 225
Honduras	16. 12. 1947	0.01	122 325	13 225
Hungary	14. 09. 1948	0.15	1 834 876	198 377
Iceland	8. 06. 1964	0.03	366 975	39 675
India	4. 11. 1946	0.31	3 792 077	409 979
Indonesia	27. 05. 1950	0.14	1 712 551	185 152
Iran, Islamic Republic of	6. 09. 1948	0.59	7 217 179	780 282
Iraq	21. 10. 1948	0.14	1 712 551	185 152
Ireland	3. 10. 1961	0.20	2 446 501	264 502
Israel	16. 09. 1949	0.26	3 180 452	343 853
Italy	27. 01. 1948	4.73	57 859 754	6 255 478
Jamaica	7. 11. 1962	0.01	122 325	13 225
Japan	2. 07. 1951	13.79	168 686 258	18 237 429
Jordan	14. 06. 1950	0.01	122 325	13 225

Member States and Associate Members
Etats membres et Membres associés
Estados miembros y Miembros asociados

Member State État membre Estado miembro	Date of entry Date d'adhésion Fecha de entrada	Scale of contributions Barème des contributions Escala de contribuciones	Contributions to the budget 1996 Contributions au budget 1996 Contribuciones al presupuesto 1996	
			Portion in French Francs Part en francs français Parte en francos franceses	Portion in U.S. dollars Part en dollars des E.U. Parte en dólares estadounidenses
Kazakstan	22. 05. 1992	0.26	3 180 452	343 853
Kenya	7. 04. 1964	0.01	122 325	13 225
Kiribati	24. 10. 1989	0.01	122 325	13 225
Korea, Democratic People's Rep	18. 10. 1974	0.04	489 300	52 901
Korea, Republic of	14. 06. 1950	0.79	9 663 680	1 044 784
Kuwait	18. 11. 1960	0.20	2 446 501	264 502
Kyrgyzstan	2. 06. 1992	0.04	489 300	52 901
Lao People's Democratic Rep.	9. 07. 1951	0.01	122 325	13 225
Latvia	14. 10. 1991	0.10	1 223 251	132 251
Lebanon	4. 11. 1946	0.01	122 325	13 225
Lesotho	29. 09. 1967	0.01	122 325	13 225
Liberia	6. 03. 1947	0.01	122 325	13 225
Libyan Arab Jamahiriya	27. 06. 1953	0.21	2 568 826	277 727
Lithuania	7. 10. 1991	0.11	1 345 576	145 476
Luxembourg	27. 10. 1947	0.07	856 276	92 576
Madagascar	10. 11. 1960	0.01	122 325	13 225
Malawi	27. 10. 1964	0.01	122 325	13 225
Malaysia	16. 06. 1958	0.14	1 712 551	185 152
Maldives	18. 07. 1980	0.01	122 325	13 225
Mali	7. 11. 1960	0.01	122 325	13 225
Malta	10. 02. 1965	0.01	122 325	13 225
Marshall Islands	30. 06. 1995	...	...	...
Mauritania	10. 01. 1962	0.01	122 325	13 225
Mauritius	25. 10. 1968	0.01	122 325	13 225
Mexico	4. 11. 1946	0.77	9 419 030	1 018 334
Moldova	27. 05. 1992	0.11	1 345 576	145 476
Monaco	6. 07. 1949	0.01	122 325	13 225
Mongolia	1. 11. 1962	0.01	122 325	13 225
Morocco	7. 11. 1956	0.03	366 975	39 675
Mozambique	11. 10. 1976	0.01	122 325	13 225
Myanmar	27. 06. 1949	0.01	122 325	13 225
Namibia	2. 11. 1978	0.01	122 325	13 225
Nepal	1. 05. 1953	0.01	122 325	13 225
Netherlands	1. 01. 1947	1.56	19 082 710	2 063 117
New Zealand	4. 11. 1946	0.24	2 935 802	317 403
Nicaragua	22. 02. 1952	0.01	122 325	13 225
Niger	10. 11. 1960	0.01	122 325	13 225
Nigeria	14. 11. 1960	0.16	1 957 201	211 602
Niue	26. 10. 1993	0.01	122 325	13 225
Norway	4. 11. 1946	0.54	6 605 553	714 156
Oman	10. 2. 1972	0.04	489 300	52 901
Pakistan	14. 09. 1949	0.06	733 950	79 351
Panama	10. 01. 1950	0.01	122 325	13 225
Papua New Guinea	4. 10. 1976	0.01	122 325	13 225
Paraguay	20. 06. 1955	0.01	122 325	13 225
Peru	21. 11. 1946	0.06	733 950	79 351
Philippines	21. 11. 1946	0.06	733 950	79 351
Poland	6. 11. 1946	0.37	4 526 027	489 329

Member States and Associate Members
Etats membres et Membres associés
Estados miembros y Miembros asociados

Member State État membre Estado miembro	Date of entry Date d'adhésion Fecha de entrada	Scale of contributions Barème des contributions Escala de contribuciones	Contributions to the budget 1996 Contributions au budget 1996 Contribuciones al presupuesto 1996	
			Portion in French Francs Part en francs français Parte en francos franceses	Portion in U.S. dollars Part en dollars des E.U. Parte en dólares estadounidenses
Portugal	12. 03. 1965	0.24	2 935 802	317 403
Qatar	27. 01. 1972	0.04	489 300	52 901
Romania	27. 07. 1956	0.15	1 834 876	198 377
Russian Federation	21. 04. 1954	5.61	68 624 359	7 419 288
Rwanda	7. 11. 1962	0.01	122 325	13 225
Saint Kitts and Nevis	26. 10. 1983	0.01	122 325	13 225
Saint Lucia	6. 03. 1980	0.01	122 325	13 225
St. Vincent and the Grenadines	14. 01. 1983	0.01	122 325	13 225
Samoa	3. 04. 1981	0.01	122 325	13 225
San Marino	12. 11. 1974	0.01	122 325	13 225
Sao Tome and Principe	22. 01. 1980	0.01	122 325	13 225
Saudi Arabia	4. 11. 1946	0.79	9 663 680	1 044 784
Senegal	10. 11. 1960	0.01	122 325	13 225
Seychelles	18. 10. 1976	0.01	122 325	13 225
Sierra Leone	28. 03. 1962	0.01	122 325	13 225
Slovakia	9. 2. 1993	0.10	1 223 251	132 251
Slovenia	27. 05. 1992	0.07	856 276	92 576
Solomon Islands	7. 09. 1993	0.01	122 325	13 225
Somalia	15. 11. 1960	0.01	122 325	13 225
South-Africa	12. 12. 1994	0.34	2 896 780	313 184
Spain	30. 01. 1953	2.21	27 033 838	2 922 750
Sri Lanka	14. 11. 1949	0.01	122 325	13 225
Sudan	26. 11. 1956	0.01	122 325	13 225
Suriname	16. 07. 1976	0.01	122 325	13 225
Swaziland	25. 01. 1978	0.01	122 325	13 225
Sweden	23. 01. 1950	1.21	14 801 332	1 600 239
Switzerland	28. 01. 1949	1.20	14 679 007	1 587 013
Syrian Arab Republic	16. 11. 1946	0.05	611 625	66 126
Tajikistan	6. 04. 1993	0.03	366 975	39 675
Thailand	1. 01. 1949	0.13	1 590 226	171 927
The Former Yugoslav Republic of Macedonia	28. 06. 1993	0.01	122 325	13 225
Togo	17. 11. 1960	0.01	122 325	13 225
Tonga	29. 09. 1980	0.01	122 325	13 225
Trinidad and Tobago	2. 11. 1962	0.04	489 300	52 901
Tunisia	8. 11. 1956	0.03	366 975	39 675
Turkey	4. 11. 1946	0.33	4 036 727	436 429
Turkmenistan	17. 08. 1993	0.04	489 300	52 901
Tuvalu	21. 10. 1991	0.01	122 325	13 225
Uganda	9. 11. 1962	0.01	122 325	13 225
Ukraine	12. 05. 1954	1.46	17 859 459	1 930 866
United Arab Emirates	21. 04. 1972	0.19	2 324 176	251 277
United Republic of Tanzania	6. 03. 1962	0.01	122 325	13 225
Uruguay	8. 11. 1947	0.04	489 300	52 901
Uzbekistan	26. 10. 1993	0.19	2 324 176	251 277
Vanuatu	10. 2. 1994	0.01	122 325	13 225
Venezuela	25. 11. 1946	0.39	4 770 678	515 779
Viet Nam	6. 07. 1951	0.01	122 325	13 225
Yemen	2. 04. 1962	0.01	122 325	13 225

Member States and Associate Members
Etats membres et Membres associés
Estados miembros y Miembros asociados

Member State État membre Estado miembro	Date of entry Date d'adhésion Fecha de entrada	Scale of contributions Barème des contributions Escala de contribuciones	Contributions to the budget 1996 Contributions au budget 1996 Contribuciones al presupuesto 1996	
			Portion in French Francs Part en francs français Parte en francos franceses	Portion in U.S. dollars Part en dollars des E.U. Parte en dólares estadounidenses
Yugoslavia	31. 03. 1950	0.11	1 345 576	145 476
Zaire	25. 11. 1960	0.01	122 325	13 225
Zambia	9. 11. 1964	0.01	122 325	13 225
Zimbabwe	22. 09. 1980	0.01	122 325	13 225
Total		70.00	855 013 150	92 439 309
Associate Members: Membres associés: Miembros asociados:				
Aruba	20. 10. 1987	0.006	73 395	7 935
Bristish Virgin Islands	24. 11. 1983	0.006	73 395	7 935
Netherlands Antilles	26. 10. 1983	0.006	73 395	7 935

School and financial years
Année scolaire et exercice financier
Año escolar y ejercicio económico

B School and financial years

Année scolaire et exercice financier

Año escolar y ejercicio económico

In the following table, the
months are represented by
roman numerals:

January = I
February = II
March = III
April = IV
May = V
June = VI
July = VII
August = VIII
September = IX
October = X
November = XI
December = XII

Dans le tableau suivant, les
mois sont représentés par
des chiffres romains:

Janvier = I
Février = II
Mars = III
Avril = IV
Mai = V
Juin = VI
Juillet = VII
Août = VIII
Septembre = IX
Octobre = X
Novembre = XI
Décembre = XII

En el cuadro siguiente,
los meses están repre-
sentados por cifras romanas:

Enero = I
Febrero = II
Marzo = III
Abríl = IV
Mayo = V
Junio = VI
Julio = VII
Agosto = VIII
Septiembre = IX
Octubre = X
Noviembre = XI
Diciembre = XII

Country / Pays / País	School year / Année scolaire / Año escolar		Start of financial year / Début de l'exercice financier / Comienzo del ejercicio económico
	Start / Début / Comienzo	End / Fin / Fin	
Africa			
Algeria	IX	VI	I
Angola	IX	VII	I
Benin	X	VII	I
Botswana	I	XII	IV
Burkina Faso	X	VII	I
Burundi	IX	VI	I
Cameroon (1)	IX	VI	VII
(2)	X	VI	
Cape Verde	X	VI	I
Central African Republic	X	VI	I
Chad	IX	VI	I
Comoros	X	VI	I
Congo	X	VI	I
Cote d'Ivoire	IX	VI	I
Djibouti	IX	VI	I
Egypt	IX	V	VII
Equatorial Guinea	IX	VI	I
Ethiopia	IX	VI	VII
Gabon	X	VI	II
Gambia	IX	VII	VII
Ghana	IX	VII	I
Guinea	X	VI	I
Guinea-Bissau	X	VII	I
Kenya	I	XI	VII
Lesotho	I	XII	IV
Liberia	III	XII	VII
Libyan Arab Jamahiriya	X	VI	I
Madagascar	X	VII	I
Malawi	X	VII	IV
Mali	X	VI	I
Mauritania	IX	VI	I
Mauritius	I	XI	VII
Morocco	IX	VI	I
Mozambique	II	XI	I
Namibia	I	XII	IV
Niger	X	VI	I
Nigeria	X	VIII	IV
Reunion	IX	VIII	I
Rwanda	IX	VI	I
St. Helena	IX	VIII	I
Sao Tome and Principe	X	VII	I
Senegal	X	VI	I
Seychelles	I	XII	I
Sierra Leone	IX	VII	VII
Somalia	XI	VI	I
South Africa	I	XII	IV
Sudan	VII	III	VII
Swaziland	I	XII	IV
Togo	IX	VI	I
Tunisia	IX	VI	I
Uganda	I	XII	VII
United Rep. of Tanzania	I	XII	VII
Western Sahara	IX	VIII	...
Zaire	IX	VII	I
Zambia	I	XII	I
Zimbabwe	I	XII	VII
America, North			
Anguilla	IX	VII	...
Antigua and Barbuda	IX	VII	I
Bahamas	IX	VI	I
Barbados	IX	VII	IV
Belize	IX	VI	IV

School and financial years
Année scolaire et exercice financier
Año escolar y ejercicio económico

Country / Pays / País	School year / Année scolaire / Año escolar — Start / Début / Comienzo	End / Fin / Fin	Start of financial year / Début de l'exercice financier / Comienzo del ejercicio económico
British Virgin Islands	IX	VII	I
Canada	IX	VI	IV
Cayman Islands	IX	VII	I
Costa Rica	III	XI	I
Cuba	IX	VI	I
Dominica	IX	VI	I
Dominican Republic (1)	IX	VI	I
(2)	I	IX	
El Salvador	II	XI	I
Grenada	IX	VII	I
Guadeloupe	IX	VI	I
Guatemala	I	X	I
Haiti	X	XI	X
Honduras	III	XI	I
Jamaica	IX	VII	IV
Martinique	IX	VI	I
Mexico	IX	VI	I
Montserrat	IX	VII	...
Netherlands Antilles	VIII	VII	I
Nicaragua	III	XI	I
Panama	IV	XII	I
Puerto Rico	IX	VI	VII
St. Kitts and Nevis	IX	VII	I
St. Lucia	IX	VII	IV
St. Pierre and Miquelon	IX	VI	I
St. Vincent and the Grenadines	IX	VII	I
Trinidad and Tobago	IX	VII	I
Turks and Caicos Islands	IX	VII	III
United States	IX	VI	VII
U.S. Virgin Islands	IX	VI	VII
America, South			
Argentina (1)	III	XI	I
(2)	IX	V	
Bolivia	II	X	I
Brazil	III	XII	I
Chile	III	XII	I
Colombia (1)	II	XI	I
(2)	IX	VI	
Ecuador (1)	X	VII	I
(2)	V	I	
Falkland Isl. (Malvinas)	II	XII	VII
French Guiana	IX	VI	I
Guyana	IX	VII	I
Paraguay	III	XI	I
Peru	IV	XII	I
Suriname	X	VIII	I
Uruguay	III	XII	I
Venezuela	X	VII	I
Asia			
Afghanistan (1)	III	XII	III
(2)	IX	VI	
Armenia	...	...	I
Azerbaijan	IX	V	I
Bahrain	X	VI	I
Bangladesh	I	XII	VII
Bhutan	III	XII	IV
Brunei Darussalam	I	XII	I
Cambodia	X	VI	...
China	IX	VII	I
Cyprus	IX	VI	I
East Timor	X	VII	...
Hong Kong	IX	VII	IV
India (1)	IV	III	IV
(2)	I	XII	
Indonesia	VII	VI	IV
Iran, Islamic Rep. of	IX	VI	III

Country / Pays / País	School year / Année scolaire / Año escolar — Start / Début / Comienzo	End / Fin / Fin	Start of financial year / Début de l'exercice financier / Comienzo del ejercicio económico
Iraq	X	VI	I
Israel	IX	VI	IV
Japan	IV	III	IV
Jordan	IX	VI	I
Kazakstan	IX	VI	I
Korea, Dem. People's Rep.	IX	VIII	...
Korea, Republic of	III	II	I
Kuwait	IX	V	VII
Kyrgyzstan	IX	V	I
Lao People's Dem. Rep.	IX	VI	I
Lebanon	X	VI	I
Macau	IX	VI	...
Malaysia	XII	X	I
Maldives	II	XII	I
Mongolia	IX	VI	I
Myanmar	IV	III	IV
Nepal (1)	III	XII	VII
(2)	XII	XI	
Oman	IX	VI	I
Pakistan	IV	III	VII
Philippines	VI	III	I
Qatar	IX	VI	IV
Saudi Arabia	X	VI	IV
Singapore	I	XII	IV
Sri Lanka	I	XII	I
Syrian Arab Republic	IX	V	I
Tajikistan	IX	V	I
Thailand	V	IV	X
Turkey	IX	VI	I
United Arab Emirates	IX	VI	I
Uzbekistan	...	...	I
Viet Nam	IX	V	I
Yemen	...	...	I
Former Dem. Yemen	X	VI	I
Former Yemen Arab Rep.	IX	VI	I
Palestine	IX	V	...
Europe			
Albania	IX	VI	I
Andorra	IX	VI	I
Austria	IX	VI	I
Belarus	IX	VI	I
Belgium	IX	VI	I
Bulgaria	IX	VI	I
Croatia	IX	VIII	...
Former Czechoslovakia	IX	VI	I
Czech Republic	IX	VI	I
Denmark	VIII	VI	I
Estonia	IX	V	I
Finland	VIII	VI	I
France	IX	VII	I
Germany	VIII	VII	I
Former German Dem. Rep.	IX	VII	I
Federal Rep. of Germany	VIII	VII	I
Gibraltar	IX	VII	IV
Greece	IX	VI	I
Hungary	IX	VI	I
Iceland	IX	V	I
Ireland	IX	VI	I
Italy	IX	VI	I
Latvia	IX	V	I
Liechtenstein	IV	III	I
Lithuania	IX	VI	I
Luxembourg	IX	VII	I
Malta	IX	VII	I
Moldova	IX	VI	I
Monaco	IX	VI	I
Netherlands	VIII	VII	I
Norway	VIII	VI	I

School and financial years
Année scolaire et exercice financier
Año escolar y ejercicio económico

Country / Pays / País	School year / Année scolaire / Año escolar		Start of financial year / Début de l'exercice financier / Comienzo del ejercicio económico
	Start / Début / Comienzo	End / Fin / Fin	
Poland	IX	VIII	I
Portugal	IX	VI	I
Romania	IX	VI	I
Russian Federation	IX	VI	I
San Marino	IX	VI	I
Slovakia	IX	VI	I
Slovenia	IX	VIII	I
Spain	X	VI	I
Sweden	VIII	VI	VII
Switzerland	VIII	VII	I
The Former Yugoslav Rep. of Macedonia	IX	VI	I
Ukraine	IX	V	I
United Kingdom	IX	VII	IV
Former Yugoslavia	IX	VI	I
Fed. Rep. of Yugoslavia	IX	VI	I
Oceania			
American Samoa	IX	VI	X
Australia	I	XII	VII
Cook Islands	II	XII	IV
Fiji	I	XII	I
French Polynesia	IX	VI	I

Country / Pays / País	School year / Année scolaire / Año escolar		Start of financial year / Début de l'exercice financier / Comienzo del ejercicio económico
	Start / Début / Comienzo	End / Fin / Fin	
Guam	IX	VI	X
Kiribati	II	XII	I
Nauru	I	XI	VII
New Caledonia	III	XII	I
New Zealand	II	XII	VII
Niue	II	XII	VII
Pacific Islands	IX	VI	X
Papua New Guinea	I	XII	I
Samoa	I	XII	I
Solomon Islands	I	XI	I
Tokelau	I	XII	III
Tonga	II	XII	VII
Tuvalu	I	XII	I
Vanuatu, Republic of	II	XII	I
Former U.S.S.R.			
Former U.S.S.R.	.	.	I

General Note

For certain countries, 2 lines are given as concerns the
start and the end of the school year. The following table
indicates the areas to which these lines refer.

Note générale

Pour certains pays les données relatives au début et à la fin de
l'année scolaire sont présentées en deux lignes. Le tableau
suivant montre les régions auxquelles se réfèrent ces lignes.

Nota general

Para ciertos países los datos relativos al comienzo y al fin
del año escolar se presentan en dos líneas. El cuadro siguiente
muestra las regiones a las que se refieren dichas líneas.

Country / Pays / País	Line / Ligne / Línea	Region / Région / Región
Cameroon	1 2	Western / occidental Eastern / oriental
Dominican Republic	2	Coffee-growing region / Région des plantations de café/ zona cafetalera
Argentina	2	Cold regions / Régions froides / Regiones frías
Colombia	2	Valle, Cauca and Narino Departments / Départements de Valle, Cauca et Narino / Departamentos de Valle, Cauca y Narino
Ecuador	1 2	Sierra Coastal region / Région côtière / Región costera
Afghanistan	2	Warm regions / Régions chaudes / Regiones calidas
India	2	Bihar - Meghalaya - Tripura
Nepal	1 2	Cold regions / Régions froides / Regiones frías Warm regions / Régions chaudes / Regiones calidas

Exchange rates
Cours des changes
Tipos de cambio

C Exchange rates

Cours des changes

Tipos de cambio

The following table lists rates of exchange for the figures on expenditure expressed in national currencies which appear in Tables 2.11, 4.1 to 4.4 and 5.4 to 5.6. The exchange rates are expressed in terms of the number of units of national currency corresponding to one United States Dollar.

The reader's attention is drawn to the fact that most countries and territories whose monetary unit is that of another country have been omitted from the table of exchange rates; the relevant information can however easily be found by referring to the data for the country with which the currency is identified.

For most countries, the data were provided by the International Monetary Fund, and refer to average annual exchange rates. For additional information concerning the methodology used to calculate these rates the reader may wish to consult the monthly bulletin *International Financial Statistics* published by the International Monetary Fund. For the remaining countries (indicated by a note) the exchange rates have been extracted from the *Monthly Bulletin of Statistics* of the United Nations.

Le tableau ci-après présente les cours des changes applicables aux données relatives aux dépenses qui sont exprimées en monnaie nationale dans les tableaux 2.11, 4.1 à 4.4 et 5.4 à 5.6. Les cours des changes sont exprimés en nombre d'unités de monnaie nationale pour un dollar des États-Unis.

Le lecteur est prié de noter que les pays ou territoires dont l'unité monétaire est la même que celle d'un autre pays ont été supprimés du tableau des cours des changes. On peut cependant trouver facilement l'information pertinente en se référant aux données du pays dont la monnaie est originaire.

Pour la plupart des pays, les données nous ont été fournies par le Fonds Monétaire International et se réfèrent au cours moyen de l'année. Pour plus de renseignements sur la méthodologie appliquée pour le calcul de ces cours, le lecteur peut consulter le bulletin mensuel *International Financial Statistics* du Fonds Monétaire International. Pour les autres pays (signalés par une note), les cours des changes ont été tirés du *Bulletin Mensuel de Statistiques* des Nations Unies.

En el cuadro que figura a continuación, se indican los tipos de cambio que deben aplicarse a los datos relativos a los gastos expresados en moneda nacional en los cuadros 2.11, 4.1 a 4.4 y 5.4 a 5.6. Las tasas de cambio están expresadas en el número de unidades de moneda nacional por Dólar de los Estados Unidos.

Nos permitimos indicar al lector que los países o territorios cuya unidad monetaria es la misma que la de otro país, han sido suprimidos del cuadro; la información correspondiente puede ser obtenida referiéndose a los datos del país de orígen.

Para la mayor parte de los países, los datos nos han sido proporcionados por el Fondo Monetario Internacional y se refieren al curso medio del año. Para mayor información sobre la metodología aplicada para el cálculo de los tipos de cambio, el lector puede consultar el boletín mensual *International Financial Statistics* del Fondo Monetario Internacional. Para los demás países (indicados por una nota), los tipos de cambio han sido obtenidos del *Monthly Bulletin of Statistics* (Boletín Mensual de Estadísticas) de las Naciones Unidas.

Exchange rates
Cours des changes
Tipos de cambio

# #

# Data for countries shown with this symbol are non-commercial rates and have been taken from the *Monthly Bulletin of Statistics* published by the United Nations.	# Les données concernant les pays signalés par ce symbole sont les taux non-commerciaux et ont été extraites du *Bulletin mensuel de statistiques* publié par les Nations Unies.

Country Pays País	National currency Monnaie nationale Moneda nacional	National currency per United States dollar Valeur du dollar des États-Unis en monnaie nationale Valor del dolar de los Estados Unidos en moneda nacional				
		1980	1982	1983	1984	1985
Africa						
Algeria	Dinar	3.838	4.592	4.789	4.983	5.028
Angola	Kwansa	30.000	30.000	30.000	30.000	30.000
Benin	Franc C.F.A.	211.280	328.610	381.070	436.960	449.260
Botswana	Pula	0.777	1.030	1.097	1.298	1.903
Burkina Faso	Franc C.F.A.	211.280	328.610	381.070	436.960	449.260
Burundi	Franc	90.000	90.000	92.948	119.709	120.691
Cameroon	Franc C.F.A.	211.280	328.610	381.070	436.960	449.260
Cape Verde	Escudo	40.175	58.293	71.686	84.878	91.632
Central African Republic	Franc C.F.A.	211.280	328.610	381.070	436.960	449.260
Chad	Franc C.F.A.	211.280	328.610	381.070	436.960	449.260
Comoros	Franc C.F.A	211.280	328.607	381.067	436.958	449.264
Congo	Franc C.F.A	211.280	328.610	381.070	436.960	449.260
Côte d'Ivoire	Franc C.F.A.	211.280	328.610	381.070	436.960	449.260
Djibouti	Franc	177.721	177.721	177.721	177.721	177.721
Egypt	Pound	0.700	0.700	0.700	0.700	0.700
Equatorial Guinea	Franc C.F.A	211.280	328.610	381.070	436.960	449.260
Ethiopia	Birr	2.070	2.070	2.070	2.070	2.070
Gabon	Franc C.F.A	211.280	328.610	381.070	436.960	449.260
Gambia	Dalasi	1.721	2.290	2.639	3.584	3.894
Ghana	Cedi	2.750	2.750	8.830	35.986	54.365
Guinea	Syli	18.969	22.366	23.095	24.090	24.333
Guinea-Bissau	Peso	33.810	39.870	42.100	104.560	159.270
Kenya	Shilling	7.420	10.922	13.312	14.414	16.432
Lesotho	Maloti	0.779	1.086	1.114	1.475	2.229
Liberia	Dollar	1.000	1.000	1.000	1.000	1.000
Libyan Arab Jamahiriya	Dinar	0.296	0.296	0.296	0.296	0.296
Madagascar	Franc	211.280	349.740	430.450	576.640	662.480
Malawi	Kwacha	0.812	1.056	1.175	1.413	1.719
Mali	Franc C.F.A.	211.280	328.610	381.070	436.960	449.260
Mauritania	Ouguiya	45.914	51.769	54.812	63.803	77.085
Mauritius	Rupee	7.684	10.873	11.706	13.800	15.443
Morocco	Dirham	3.937	6.023	7.111	8.811	10.063
Mozambique	Meticai	32.400	37.800	40.200	42.400	43.200
Namibia	South African Rand	0.779	1.086	1.114	1.475	2.229
Niger	Franc C.F.A.	211.280	328.610	381.070	436.960	449.260
Nigeria	Naira	0.547	0.674	0.724	0.767	0.894
Reunion	French Franc	4.226	6.572	7.621	8.739	8.985
Rwanda	Franc	92.840	92.840	94.343	100.172	101.262
St. Helena	Pound Sterling	0.430	0.572	0.660	0.752	0.779
Sao Tome and Principe	Dobra	34.771	40.999	42.335	44.159	44.604
Senegal	Franc C.F.A.	211.280	328.610	381.070	436.960	449.260
Seychelles	Rupee	6.392	6.553	6.768	7.059	7.134
Sierra Leone	Leone	1.050	1.239	1.885	2.510	5.094
Somalia	Shilling	6.295	10.750	15.788	20.019	39.487
South Africa	Rand	0.779	1.086	1.114	1.475	2.229

Exchange rates
Cours des changes
Tipos de cambio

\# Los datos para los países indicados por este símbolo
corresponden a los tipos de cambio no-comerciables y
han sidos extraidos del *Monthly Bulletin of
Statistics* (Boletín mensual de estadísticas)
publicado por las Naciones Unidas.

National currency per United States dollar / Valeur du dollar des États-Unis en monnaie nationale / Valor del dolar de los Estados Unidos en moneda nacional								
1986	1987	1988	1989	1990	1991	1992	1993	1994
4.702	4.850	5.915	7.609	8.958	18.473	21.836	23.345	35.059
30.000	30.000	30.000	30.000	30.000	55.000	251.000	2 660.000	59 515.000
346.310	300.540	297.850	319.010	272.260	282.110	264.690	283.160	555.200
1.879	1.679	1.829	2.015	1.861	2.022	2.110	2.423	2.685
346.310	300.540	297.850	319.010	272.260	282.110	264.690	283.160	555.200
114.171	123.564	140.395	158.667	171.255	181.513	208.303	242.780	252.663
346.310	300.540	297.850	319.010	272.260	282.110	264.690	283.160	555.200
80.145	72.466	72.068	77.978	70.031	71.408	68.018	80.427	81.891
346.310	300.540	297.850	319.010	272.260	282.110	264.690	283.160	555.200
346.310	300.540	297.850	319.010	272.260	282.110	264.690	283.160	555.200
346.307	300.537	297.849	319.009	272.265	282.108	264.692	283.163	416.403
346.310	300.540	297.850	319.010	272.260	282.110	264.690	283.160	555.200
346.310	300.540	297.850	319.010	272.260	282.110	264.690	283.160	555.200
177.721	177.721	177.721	177.721	177.721	177.721	177.721	177.721	177.721
0.700	0.700	0.700	0.867	1.550	3.138	3.322	3.353	3.385
346.310	300.540	297.850	319.010	272.260	282.110	264.690	283.160	555.200
2.070	2.070	2.070	2.070	2.070	2.070	2.803	5.000	5.465
346.310	300.540	297.850	319.010	272.260	282.110	264.690	283.160	555.200
6.938	7.074	6.709	7.585	7.883	8.803	8.888	9.129	9.576
89.204	153.733	202.346	270.000	326.332	367.831	437.087	649.061	956.711
333.453	428.403	474.396	591.646	660.167	753.858	902.001	955.490	976.636
203.630	559.010	1 109.710	1 810.150	2 185.460	3 658.610	6 933.910	10 081.900	12 892.140
16.226	16.455	17.747	20.573	22.915	27.508	32.217	58.001	56.051
2.285	2.036	2.273	2.623	2.587	2.761	2.852	3.268	3.551
1.000	1.000	1.000	1.000	1.000	1.000	1.000	1.000	1.000
0.296	0.273	0.286	0.300	0.283	0.281	0.285	0.305	0.321
676.340	1 069.210	1 407.110	1 603.440	1 494.150	1 835.360	1 863.970	1 913.780	3 067.340
1.861	2.209	2.561	2.760	2.729	2.803	3.603	4.403	8.736
346.310	300.540	297.850	319.010	272.260	282.110	264.690	283.160	555.200
74.375	73.878	75.261	83.051	80.609	81.946	87.027	120.806	123.575
13.466	12.878	13.438	15.250	14.864	15.652	15.563	17.648	17.960
9.104	8.359	8.209	8.488	8.242	8.707	8.538	9.299	9.203
40.400	290.700	524.600	744.900	929.100	1 434.500	2 516.500	3 874.200	6 038.600
2.285	2.036	2.273	2.623	2.587	2.761	2.852	3.268	3.551
346.310	300.540	297.850	319.010	272.260	282.110	264.690	283.160	555.200
1.755	4.016	4.537	7.365	8.038	9.910	17.298	22.065	21.996
6.926	6.011	5.957	6.380	5.445	5.642	5.294	5.663	5.552
87.640	79.673	76.445	79.977	82.597	125.140	133.350	168.197	
0.682	0.612	0.562	0.611	0.563	0.569	0.569	0.666	0.653
38.589	54.211	86.343	124.672	143.331	201.816	321.337	429.854	732.628
346.310	300.540	297.850	319.010	272.260	282.110	264.690	283.160	555.200
6.177	5.600	5.384	5.646	5.337	5.289	5.122	5.182	5.056
16.092	34.043	32.514	59.813	151.446	295.344	499.442	567.459	586.740
72.000	105.177	170.453	490.675	...	...	...	...	...
2.285	2.036	2.273	2.623	2.587	2.761	2.852	3.268	3.551

Exchange rates
Cours des changes
Tipos de cambio

Country Pays País	National currency Monnaie nationale Moneda nacional	National currency per United States dollar Valeur du dollar des États-Unis en monnaie nationale Valor del dolar de los Estados Unidos en moneda nacional				
		1980	1982	1983	1984	1985
Sudan	Pound	0.500	0.952	1.300	1.300	2.304
Swaziland	Lilangeni	0.779	1.086	1.114	1.475	2.223
Togo	Franc C.F.A.	211.280	328.610	381.070	436.960	449.260
Tunisia	Dinar	0.405	0.591	0.679	0.777	0.835
Uganda	Shilling	0.070	0.940	1.540	3.600	6.720
United Republic of Tanzania	Shilling	8.197	9.283	11.143	15.292	17.472
Zaire‡	Zaire‡	2.800	5.750	12.889	36.129	49.873
Zambia	Kwacha	0.789	0.929	1.259	1.813	3.140
Zimbabwe	Dollar	0.643	0.759	1.013	1.258	1.614
America, North						
Antigua and Barbuda	E.Caribbean Dollar	2.700	2.700	2.700	2.700	2.700
Aruba	Florins	...	...	...	...	...
Bahamas	Dollar	1.000	1.000	1.000	1.000	1.000
Barbados	Dollar	2.011	2.011	2.011	2.011	2.011
Belize	Dollar	2.000	2.000	2.000	2.000	2.000
Bermuda	Dollar	1.000	1.000	1.000	1.000	1.000
British Virgin Islands	United States Dollar	1.000	1.000	1.000	1.000	1.000
Canada	Dollar	1.169	1.234	1.232	1.295	1.365
Costa Rica	Colon	8.570	37.407	41.094	44.533	50.453
Cuba £	Peso	0.710	0.850	0.870	0.900	0.910
Dominica	E.Caribbean Dollar	2.700	2.700	2.700	2.700	2.700
Dominican Republic	Peso	1.000	1.000	1.000	1.000	3.113
El Salvador	Colon	2.500	2.500	2.500	2.500	2.500
Grenada	E.Caribbean Dollar	2.700	2.700	2.700	2.700	2.700
Guadeloupe	French Franc	4.226	6.572	7.621	8.739	8.985
Guatemala	Quetzal	1.000	1.000	1.000	1.000	1.000
Haiti	Gourde	5.000	5.000	5.000	5.000	5.000
Honduras	Lempira	2.000	2.000	2.000	2.000	2.000
Jamaica	Dollar	1.781	1.781	1.932	3.943	5.559
Martinique	French Franc	4.226	6.572	7.621	8.739	8.985
Mexico	Peso	22.950	56.400	120.090	167.830	256.870
Montserrat	E.Caribbean Dollar	2.700	2.700	2.700	2.700	2.700
Netherlands Antilles	Guilder	1.800	1.800	1.800	1.800	1.800
Nicaragua‡	Cordoba	0.003	0.003	0.003	0.003	0.0078
Panama	Balboa	1.000	1.000	1.000	1.000	1.000
Saint Kitts and Nevis	E.Caribbean Dollar	2.700	2.700	2.700	2.700	2.700
St. Lucia	E.Caribbean Dollar	2.700	2.700	2.700	2.700	2.700
St. Pierre and Miquelon	French Franc	4.226	6.572	7.621	8.739	8.985
St. Vincent and the Grenadines	E.Caribbean Dollar	2.700	2.700	2.700	2.700	2.700
Trinidad and Tobago	Dollar	2.400	2.400	2.400	2.400	2.450
United States	Dollar	1.000	1.000	1.000	1.000	1.000
U.S. Virgin Islands	United States Dollar	1.000	1.000	1.000	1.000	1.000
America, South						
Argentina‡	Peso	0.018	0.259	1.053	6.760	60.180
Bolivia‡	Boliviano	24.520	64.070	231.630	3 135.910	0.440
Brazil‡	Cruzeiro	52.710	179.510	577.040	1 848.020	0.006
Chile	Peso	39.000	50.909	78.842	98.656	161.081
Colombia	Peso	47.280	64.085	78.854	100.817	142.312
Ecuador	Sucre	25.000	30.030	44.120	62.540	69.560
French Guiana	French Franc	4.226	6.572	7.621	8.739	8.985
Guyana	Dollar	2.550	3.000	3.000	3.832	4.252
Paraguay	Guarani	126.000	126.000	126.000	201.000	306.670
Peru‡	Inti	0.289	0.698	1.629	3.467	10.974
Suriname	Guilder	1.785	1.785	0.179	1.785	1.785
Uruguay	Peso	9.100	13.910	34.540	56.120	101.430
Venezuela	Bolivar	4.293	4.293	4.298	7.018	7.500
Asia						
Afghanistan	Afghani	44.129	50.600	50.600	50.600	50.600
Bahrain	Dinar	0.377	0.376	0.376	0.376	0.376
Bangladesh	Taka	15.454	22.118	24.615	25.354	27.995
Bhutan	Ngultrum	7.863	9.455	10.099	11.363	12.369
Brunei Darussalam	Dollar	2.150	2.149	2.129	2.141	2.226
Cambodia	Riel	...	...	...	...	...
China	Yuan	1.498	1.893	1.976	2.320	2.937
Cyprus	Pound	0.353	0.475	0.527	0.588	0.613
Hong Kong	Dollar	4.976	6.070	7.265	7.818	7.791
India	Rupee	7.863	9.455	10.099	11.363	12.369
Indonesia	Rupiah	626.990	661.420	909.260	1 025.940	1 110.580
Iran, Islamic Republic of	Rial	70.615	83.603	86.358	90.030	91.052
Iraq	Dinar	0.295	0.299	0.311	0.311	0.311
Israel	Shekel	0.005	0.024	0.056	0.293	1.179
Japan	Yen	226.740	249.080	237.510	237.520	238.540

Exchange rates
Cours des changes
Tipos de cambio

	National currency per United States dollar Valeur du dollar des États-Unis en monnaie nationale Valor del dolar de los Estados Unidos en moneda nacional							
1986	1987	1988	1989	1990	1991	1992	1993	1994
2.500	3.000	4.500	4.500	4.500	6.956	97.432	159.314	289.609
2.285	2.036	2.273	2.623	2.587	2.761	2.852	3.268	3.551
346.310	300.540	297.850	319.010	272.260	282.110	264.690	283.160	555.200
0.794	0.829	0.858	0.949	0.878	0.925	0.884	1.004	1.012
14.000	42.840	106.140	223.090	428.850	734.010	1 133.830	1 195.020	979.450
32.698	64.260	99.292	143.377	195.056	219.157	297.708	405.274	509.631
59.625	112.403	187.070	381.445	718.580	15 587.000	645 420.000	2.514	1 194.119
7.788	9.519	8.266	13.814	30.289	64.640	172.214	452.763	669.371
1.667	1.662	1.806	2.119	2.452	3.621	5.098	6.483	8.151
2.700	2.700	2.700	2.700	2.700	2.700	2.700	2.700	2.700
1.790	1.790	1.790	1.790	1.790	1.790	1.790	1.790	1.790
1.000	1.000	1.000	1.000	1.000	1.000	1.000	1.000	1.000
2.011	2.011	2.011	2.011	2.011	2.011	2.011	2.011	2.011
2.000	2.000	2.000	2.000	2.000	2.000	2.000	2.000	2.000
1.000	1.000	1.000	1.000	1.000	1.000	1.000	1.000	1.000
1.000	1.000	1.000	1.000	1.000	1.000	1.000	1.000	1.000
1.390	1.326	1.231	1.184	1.167	1.146	1.209	1.290	1.366
55.986	62.776	75.805	81.504	91.579	122.432	134.506	142.172	157.067
0.793	0.773	0.776	0.791	0.700	0.700	0.700	0.700	...
2.700	2.700	2.700	2.700	2.700	2.700	2.700	2.700	2.700
2.904	3.845	6.113	6.340	8.525	12.692	12.774	12.676	13.160
4.852	5.000	5.000	5.000	6.848	8.017	8.361	8.703	8.729
2.700	2.700	2.700	2.700	2.700	2.700	2.700	2.700	2.700
6.926	6.011	5.957	6.380	5.445	5.642	5.294	5.663	5.552
1.875	2.500	2.620	2.816	4.486	5.029	5.171	5.635	5.751
5.000	5.000	5.000	5.000	5.000	6.034	9.802	12.823	15.040
2.000	2.000	2.000	2.000	4.112	5.317	5.498	6.472	8.409
5.478	5.487	5.489	5.745	7.184	12.116	22.960	24.949	33.086
6.926	6.011	5.957	6.380	5.445	5.642	5.294	5.663	5.552
611.770	1 378.180	2 273.110	2 461.470	2 812.600	3 018.430	3 095.000	3 116.000	3 375.000
2.700	2.700	2.700	2.700	2.700	2.700	2.700	2.700	2.700
1.800	1.800	1.800	1.793	1.790	1.790	1.790	1.790	1.790
0.0195	0.0205	53.95	0.0031	0.141	4.271	5.000	5.620	6.723
1.000	1.000	1.000	1.000	1.000	1.000	1.000	1.000	1.000
2.700	2.700	2.700	2.700	2.700	2.700	2.700	2.700	2.700
2.700	2.700	2.700	2.700	2.700	2.700	2.700	2.700	2.700
6.926	6.011	5.957	6.380	5.445	5.642	5.294	5.663	5.552
2.700	2.700	2.700	2.700	2.700	2.700	2.700	2.700	2.700
3.600	3.600	3.844	4.250	4.250	4.250	4.250	5.351	5.925
1.000	1.000	1.000	1.000	1.000	1.000	1.000	1.000	1.000
1.000	1.000	1.000	1.000	1.000	1.000	1.000	1.000	1.000
94.300	214.430	875.300	0.042	0.488	0.954	0.991	0.999	0.999
1.922	2.055	2.350	2.692	3.173	3.581	3.900	4.265	4.621
0.014	0.039	0.263	2.834	68.300	406.609	4 512.600	88 449.000	0.639
193.010	219.540	245.048	267.155	305.062	349.373	362.588	404.349	420.077
194.261	242.608	299.174	382.568	502.259	633.045	759.282	863.065	844.836
122.780	170.460	301.610	526.350	767.750	1 046.250	1 533.960	1 919.110	2 196.730
6.926	6.011	5.957	6.380	5.445	5.642	5.294	5.663	5.552
4.272	9.756	10.000	27.159	39.533	111.811	125.003	126.730	138.290
339.170	550.000	550.000	1 056.220	1 229.810	1 325.180	1 500.260	1 744.350	1 911.550
13.948	16.836	128.830	2666.190	0.188	0.773	1.246	1.988	2.195
1.785	1.785	1.785	1.785	1.785	1.785	1.785	1.785	134.117
151.990	226.670	359.440	605.510	1 171.050	2 018.820	3 027.000	3 948.000	5 053.000
8.083	14.500	14.500	34.682	46.901	56.816	68.376	90.826	148.503
50.600	50.600	50.600	50.600	50.600	50.600	50.600	50.600	50.600
0.376	0.376	0.376	0.376	0.376	0.376	0.376	0.376	0.376
30.407	30.950	31.733	32.270	34.569	36.596	38.951	39.567	40.212
12.611	12.962	13.917	16.226	17.505	22.742	25.918	30.493	31.374
2.220	2.107	2.014	1.951	1.813	1.730	...	...	...
...	...	...	...	...	...	1 266.600	2 689.000	2 545.300
3.453	3.722	3.722	3.765	4.783	5.323	5.515	5.762	8.619
0.518	0.481	0.467	0.495	0.458	0.464	0.450	0.497	0.492
7.803	7.798	7.806	7.800	7.790	7.771	7.741	7.736	7.728
12.611	12.962	13.917	16.226	17.504	22.742	25.918	30.493	31.374
1 282.560	1 643.850	1 685.700	1 770.060	1 842.810	1 950.320	2 029.920	2 087.100	2 160.750
78.760	71.460	68.683	72.015	68.096	67.505	65.552	1 267.772	1 748.751
0.311	0.311	0.311	0.311	0.311	0.311	0.311	0.311	0.311
1.488	1.595	1.599	1.916	2.016	2.279	2.459	2.830	3.011
168.520	144.640	128.150	137.960	144.790	134.710	126.650	111.200	102.210

Exchange rates
Cours des changes
Tipos de cambio

Country Pays País	National currency Monnaie nationale Moneda nacional	National currency per United States dollar Valeur du dollar des États-Unis en monnaie nationale Valor del dolar de los Estados Unidos en moneda nacional				
		1980	1982	1983	1984	1985
Jordan	Dinar	0.298	0.352	0.363	0.384	0.395
Kazakstan	Tenge					
Korea, Republic of	Won	607.430	731.080	775.750	805.980	870.020
Kuwait	Dinar	0.270	0.288	0.291	0.296	0.301
Kyrgyzstan #	Som					
Lao People's						
Democratic Republic	Kip	10.000	35.000	35.000	35.000	55.000
Lebanon	Pound	3.440	4.740	4.530	6.510	16.420
Macau	Pataca	5.095	6.226	7.464	8.045	7.941
Malaysia	Ringgit	2.177	2.335	2.321	2.344	2.483
Maldives	Rufiyaa	7.550	7.174	7.050	7.050	7.098
Mongolia‡	Tughrik	2.850	3.270	3.390	3.790	3.710
Myanmar	Kyat	6.598	7.790	8.035	8.386	8.475
Nepal	Rupee	12.000	13.244	14.545	16.459	18.246
Oman	Rial	0.345	0.345	0.345	0.345	0.345
Pakistan	Rupee	9.900	11.848	13.117	14.046	15.928
Philippines	Peso	7.511	8.540	11.113	16.699	18.607
Qatar	Riyal	3.657	3.640	3.640	3.640	3.640
Saudi Arabia	Riyal	3.327	3.428	3.455	3.524	3.622
Singapore	Dollar	2.141	2.140	2.113	2.133	2.200
Sri Lanka	Rupee	16.534	20.812	23.529	25.438	27.163
Syrian Arab Republic	Pound	3.925	3.925	3.925	3.925	3.925
Thailand	Baht	20.476	23.000	23.000	23.639	27.159
Turkey	Lira	76.040	162.550	225.460	366.680	521.980
Turkmenistan #	Manat					
United Arab Emirates	Dirham	3.707	3.671	3.671	3.671	3.671
Viet Nam	Dong	0.210	0.940	1.000	1.030	8.300
Yemen	Rial					
Former Democratic Yemen	Dinar	0.345	0.345	0.345	0.345	0.345
Former Yemen Arab Republic	Rial	4.563	4.563	4.579	5.353	7.363
Europe						
Albania #	Lek	7.000	7.000	7.000	7.000	7.000
Austria	Schilling	12.938	17.059	17.963	20.009	20.690
Belarus #	Rouble					
Belgium	Franc	29.242	45.691	51.132	57.784	59.378
Bulgaria‡	Lev	0.850	0.850	0.980	0.980	1.030
Croatia #	Kuna					
Former Czechoslovakia	Koruna	14.270	13.710	14.160	16.610	17.140
Czech Republic	Koruna					
Denmark	Krone	5.636	8.332	9.145	10.357	10.596
Estonia	Kroon					
Finland	Markka	3.730	4.820	5.570	6.010	6.198
France	Franc	4.226	6.572	7.621	8.739	8.985
Germany	Deutsche Mark					
Former German Democratic Rep. #	DDR Mark	1.950	2.500	2.700	3.050	2.600
Federal Republic of Germany	Deutsche Mark	1.818	2.427	2.553	2.846	2.944
Gibraltar	Pound Sterling	0.430	0.572	0.660	0.752	0.779
Greece	Drachma	42.617	66.803	88.064	112.717	138.119
Hungary	Forint	32.532	36.631	42.671	48.042	50.119
Iceland	Krona	4.798	12.352	24.843	31.694	41.508
Ireland	Pound	0.487	0.705	0.805	0.923	0.946
Italy	Lira	856.450	1 352.510	1 518.850	1 756.960	1 909.440
Latvia	Lat					
Liechtenstein	Swiss Franc	1.676	2.030	2.099	2.350	2.457
Lithuania	Lita					
Luxembourg	Franc	29.242	45.691	51.132	57.784	59.378
Malta	Lira	0.345	0.412	0.432	0.461	0.469
Monaco	French Franc	4.226	6.572	7.621	8.739	8.985
Netherlands	Guilder	1.988	2.670	2.854	3.209	3.321
Norway	Krone	4.939	6.454	7.296	8.161	8.597
Poland	Zloty	44.200	84.800	91.600	113.200	147.100
Portugal	Escudo	50.062	79.473	110.780	146.390	170.395
Romania	Leu	18.000	15.000	17.179	21.280	17.141
Russian Federation #	Rouble					
San Marino	Lira	856.450	1 352.510	1 518.850	1 756.960	1 909.440
Slovakia	S. Koruna					
Slovenia	Tolar					
Spain	Peseta	71.702	109.859	143.430	160.761	170.044
Sweden	Krona	4.230	6.283	7.667	8.272	8.604
Switzerland	Franc	1.676	2.030	2.099	2.350	2.457
Ukraine #	Karbovanets					
United Kingdom	Pound Sterling	0.430	0.572	0.660	0.752	0.779
Former Yugoslavia‡	Dinar	2.464	5.028	9.284	0.015	0.027
Federal Rep. of Yugoslavia #	New Dinar					

Exchange rates
Cours des changes
Tipos de cambio

National currency per United States dollar / Valeur du dollar des États-Unis en monnaie nationale / Valor del dolar de los Estados Unidos en moneda nacional								
1986	1987	1988	1989	1990	1991	1992	1993	1994
0.350	0.338	0.374	0.575	0.664	0.681	0.680	0.693	0.699
						...	...	36.180
881.450	822.570	731.470	671.460	707.760	733.350	780.650	802.670	803.450
0.291	0.279	0.279	0.294	0.288	0.284	0.293	0.302	0.297
					...	...	9.400	...
95.000	187.500	400.375	591.500	707.750	702.083	716.083	716.250	717.667
38.370	224.600	409.230	496.690	695.090	928.230	1 712.790	1 741.360	1 680.070
8.357	8.050	8.050	8.050	8.050	8.050	8.050	8.050	8.050
2.581	2.520	2.619	2.709	2.705	2.751	2.547	2.574	2.624
7.151	9.223	8.785	9.041	9.552	10.253	10.569	10.957	11.586
3.180	2.890	2.950	2.990	4.670	9.520	42.560	295.422	412.720
7.330	6.653	6.395	6.705	6.339	6.284	6.105	6.157	5.975
21.230	21.819	23.289	27.189	29.369	37.255	42.718	48.607	49.398
0.382	0.385	0.385	0.385	0.385	0.385	0.385	0.385	0.385
16.648	17.398	18.003	20.542	21.707	23.801	25.083	28.107	30.567
20.386	20.568	21.095	21.737	24.311	27.479	25.513	27.120	26.417
3.640	3.640	3.640	3.640	3.640	3.640	3.640	3.640	3.640
3.703	3.745	3.745	3.745	3.745	3.745	3.745	3.745	3.745
2.177	2.106	2.012	1.950	1.813	1.728	1.629	1.616	1.527
28.017	29.445	31.807	36.047	40.063	41.372	43.830	48.322	49.415
3.925	3.925	11.225	11.225	11.225	11.225	11.225	11.225	11.225
26.299	25.723	25.294	25.702	25.585	25.517	25.400	25.320	25.150
674.510	857.210	1 422.350	2 121.680	2 608.640	4 171.820	6 872.420	10 984.630	29 608.680
							2.000	...
3.671	3.671	3.671	3.671	3.671	3.671	3.671	3.671	3.671
22.740	78.290	606.520	4 463.950	6 482.800	10 037.030	11 202.190	10 640.960	10 962.130
				...	12.010	12.010	12.010	12.010
0.345	0.345	0.345	0.345	...				
9.639	10.342	9.772	9.760	...				
7.000	7.000	6.000	6.400	15.000	25.000	97.000	95.000	...
15.267	12.643	12.348	13.231	11.370	11.676	10.989	11.632	11.422
					...	...	5 710.000	
44.672	37.334	36.768	39.404	33.418	34.148	32.150	34.597	33.457
0.940	0.870	0.830	0.840	2.190	17.790	23.340	27.590	54.130
								5.700
14.990	13.690	14.360	15.050	17.950	29.480	29.150	29.150	28.790
8.091	6.840	6.732	7.310	6.189	6.397	6.036	6.484	6.361
						13.223	13.223	12.991
5.070	4.396	4.183	4.291	3.824	4.044	4.479	5.712	5.224
6.926	6.011	5.957	6.380	5.445	5.642	5.294	5.663	5.552
					1.660	1.562	1.653	1.623
2.000	1.650	1.870	1.790	1.500	1.616			
2.171	1.797	1.756	1.880	...				
0.682	0.612	0.562	0.611	0.563	0.567	0.570	0.667	0.653
139.981	135.430	141.861	162.417	158.514	182.266	190.624	229.250	242.603
45.832	46.971	50.413	59.066	63.206	74.735	78.988	91.933	105.160
41.104	38.677	43.014	57.042	58.284	58.996	57.546	67.603	69.944
0.743	0.673	0.656	0.706	0.605	0.621	0.588	0.677	0.669
1 490.810	1 296.070	1 301.630	1 372.090	1 198.100	1 240.610	1 232.410	1 573.670	1 612.440
					...	0.737	0.675	0.560
1.799	1.491	1.463	1.636	1.389	1.434	1.406	1.478	1.368
					...	1.770	4.340	3.980
44.672	37.334	36.768	39.404	33.418	34.148	32.150	34.597	33.457
0.393	0.345	0.331	0.348	0.318	0.323	0.319	0.382	0.378
6.926	6.011	5.957	6.380	5.445	5.642	5.294	5.663	5.552
2.450	2.026	1.977	2.121	1.821	1.870	1.758	1.857	1.820
7.395	6.737	6.517	6.905	6.260	6.483	6.215	7.094	7.058
175.300	265.100	430.500	1 439.200	9 500.000	10 576.100	13 626.400	18 115.000	22 722.800
149.587	140.882	143.954	157.458	142.555	144.482	134.998	160.800	165.993
16.153	14.557	14.277	14.922	22.432	76.387	307.953	760.051	1 655.086
					1.670	...	1 200.000	...
1 490.810	1 296.070	1 301.630	1 372.090	1 198.100	1 240.610	1 232.410	1 573.670	1 612.440
						30.770	30.770	32.040
						97.000	124.000	117.000
140.048	123.478	116.487	118.378	101.934	103.912	102.379	127.260	133.958
7.124	6.340	6.127	6.447	5.919	6.046	5.824	7.783	7.716
1.799	1.491	1.463	1.636	1.389	1.434	1.406	1.478	1.368
					...	637.7	25 000.000	...
0.682	0.612	0.562	0.611	0.563	0.567	0.570	0.667	0.653
0.038	0.074	0.252	2.876	11.318	19.638			
						97.000	124.000	122.700

Exchange rates
Cours des changes
Tipos de cambio

Country Pays País	National currency Monnaie nationale Moneda nacional	National currency per United States dollar Valeur du dollar des États-Unis en monnaie nationale Valor del dolar de los Estados Unidos en moneda nacional				
		1980	1982	1983	1984	1985
Oceania						
Australia	Dollar	0.878	0.986	1.110	1.140	1.432
Fiji	Dollar	0.818	0.932	1.017	1.083	1.154
French Polynesia	French Franc	76.829	119.493	138.569	158.893	163.368
New Caledonia	French Franc	76.829	119.493	138.569	158.893	163.368
New Zealand	Dollar	1.027	1.333	1.497	1.764	2.023
Papua New Guinea	Kina	0.671	0.738	0.836	0.899	1.000
Samoa	Tala	0.919	1.207	1.549	1.862	2.245
Solomon Islands	Solomon Isl. Dollar	0.830	0.971	1.149	1.274	1.481
Tonga	Pa'anga	0.878	0.986	1.110	1.140	1.432
Vanuatu, Republic of	Vatu	68.292	96.208	99.368	99.233	106.032
Former U.S.S.R.						
Former U.S.S.R. #	Rouble	0.660	0.730	0.766	0.850	0.770

Exchange rates
Cours des changes
Tipos de cambio

National currency per United States dollar Valeur du dollar des États-Unis en monnaie nationale Valor del dolar de los Estados Unidos en moneda nacional								
1986	1987	1988	1989	1990	1991	1992	1993	1994
1.496	1.428	1.280	1.265	1.281	1.284	1.362	1.471	1.368
1.133	1.244	1.430	1.483	1.481	1.476	1.503	1.542	1.464
125.929	109.285	108.308	116.002	99.005	102.584	96.255	94.653	...
125.929	109.285	108.308	116.002	99.005	102.584	96.255	94.653	...
1.913	1.695	1.526	1.672	1.676	1.734	1.862	1.851	1.687
0.971	0.908	0.867	0.859	0.955	0.952	0.965	0.978	1.011
2.236	2.122	2.080	2.270	2.315	2.398	2.466	2.570	2.528
1.742	2.003	2.083	2.293	2.529	2.715	2.928	3.188	3.291
1.496	1.428	1.275	1.261	1.280	1.296	1.347	1.384	1.320
106.076	109.849	104.426	116.042	117.061	111.675	113.392	121.581	116.405
0.684	0.602	0.612	0.633	1.600	.	.	.	.

AFRICA:

Zaire:

E--> For 1993 and 1994, exchange rates are expressed in New Zaires (1 New Zaire = 3 million Old Zaires).

FR-> En 1993 et 1994, les cours des changes sont exprimés en Nouveaux Zaires (1 Nouveau Zaire = 3 million Anciens Zaires).

ESP> En 1993 y 1994, los tipos de cambio están expresados en Nuevos Zaire (1 Nuevo Zaire = 3 millón Zaires Antiguos).

AMERICA, NORTH:

Nicaragua:

E--> Prior to 1989, exchange rates are expressed in Cordobas oro per million U.S.dollars.

FR-> Avant 1989, les cours des changes sont exprimés en Cordobas oro par million de dollars des États-Unis.

ESP> Antes de 1989, los tipos de cambio están expresados en Córdobas oro por millón de dólares de los Estados Unidos.

AMERICA, SOUTH:

Argentina:

E--> Prior to 1988. exchange rates are expressed in Pesos per million U.S. Dollars.

FR-> Avant 1988, les cours des changes sont exprimés en Pesos par million de dollars des États-Unis.

ESP> Antes de 1988, los tipos de cambio están expresados en Pesos por millón de dólares de los Estados Unidos.

Bolivia:

E--> Prior to 1985. exchange rates are expressed in Bolivianos per million U.S. Dollars.

FR-> Avant 1985, les cours des changes sont exprimés en Bolivianos par million de dollars des États-Unis.

ESP> Antes de 1985, los tipos de cambio están expresados en Bolivianos por millón de dólares de los Estados Unidos.

Brazil:

E--> Prior to 1985, exchange rates are expressed in Cruzeiros per million U.S.Dollars. For 1994, exchange rates are expressed in Reais (1 Reais = 2,750 thousand Cruzeiros).

FR-> Avant 1985, les cours des changes sont exprimés en Cruzeiros par million de dollars des États-Unis. En 1994, les cours des changes sont exprimés en Reais (1 Reais = 2 750 milliers de Cruzeiros).

ESP> Antes de 1985, los tipos de cambio están expresados en Cruzeiros por millón de dólares de los Estados Unidos. En 1994, los tipos de cambio están expresados en Reais (1 Reais = 2 750 millares de Cruzeiros).

Peru:

E--> From 1990 to 1994, exchanged rates are expressed in New Soles (1 New Sol = 1 million Intis).

FR-> De 1990 à 1994, les cours des changes sont exprimés en Nouveaux Soles (1 Nouveau Sol = 1 million d'Intis).

ESP> De 1990 a 1994, los tipos de cambio están expresados en Nuevos Soles (1 Nuevo Sol = 1 millón de Intis).

ASIA:

Mongolia:

E--> Prior to 1985, data refer to non-commercial rates applied to tourism and to remittances from outside the rouble area, and have been taken from the Monthly Bulletin of Statistics published by the United Nations.

FR-> Avant 1985, les données se réfèrent aux taux non-commerciaux appliqués aux tourisme et envois de fonds provenant des pays extérieurs à la zone rouble, et ont été extraites du Bulletin Mensuel de Statistiques publié par les Nations Unies.

ESP> Antes de 1985, los datos se refieren a los tipos de cambio no comerciables utilizados para el turismo y envíos de fondos que provienen de los países externos a la zona de rublos, y han sido extraídos del Boletin Mensual de Estadísticas publicado por Naciones Unidas.

EUROPE:

Bulgaria:

E--> Prior to 1985, data refer to non-commercial rates applied to tourism and to remittances from outside the rouble area, and have been taken from the Monthly Bulletin of Statistics published by the United Nations.

FR-> Avant 1985, les données se réfèrent aux taux non-commerciaux appliqués aux tourisme et envois de fonds provenant des pays extérieurs à la zone rouble, et ont été extraites du Bulletin Mensuel de Statistiques publié par les Nations Unies.

ESP> Antes de 1985, los datos se refieren a los tipos de cambio no comerciables utilizados para el turismo y envios de fondos que provienen de los países externos a la zona de rublos, y han sido extraídos del Boletin Mensual de Estadísticas publicado por Naciones Unidas.

Former Yugoslavia:

E--> Data refer to the New Dinar (1 New Dinar = 10,000 Old Dinars).

FR-> Les données se rapportent au Nouveau Dinar (1 Nouveau Dinar = 10 000 Anciens Dinars).

ESP> Los datos se refieren al Nuevo Dinar (1 Nuevo Dinar = 10 000 Dinares Antiguos).

Selected list of UNESCO statistical publications
Liste sélective d'ouvrages statistiques publiés par l'UNESCO
Lista selectiva de obras estadísticas publicadas por la UNESCO

D Selected list of UNESCO statistical publications

Liste sélective d'ouvrages statistiques publiés par l'UNESCO

Lista selectiva de obras estadísticas publicadas por la UNESCO

This appendix presents three lists of selected statistical publications, according to the language in which they were published: English, French and Spanish. Details regarding different language versions are shown in brackets at the end of each entry, referring the reader to one or both of the other two lists, as well as giving information on works existing in Arabic or Russian. All publications, except for the Statistical Yearbook and Statistical Reports and Studies, can be obtained free of charge from the Division of Statistics, which should also be contacted for information on publications prior to 1992 and not shown in this list.

. . . .

Cette annexe présente trois listes sélectives de publications statistiques, selon la langue dans laquelle elles ont été publiées (anglais, français et espagnol). Le détail des différentes versions linguistiques est indiqué entre parenthèses après chaque titre; le lecteur pourra ainsi se reporter aux deux autres listes et également savoir si l'ouvrage a été publié en arabe ou en russe. Toutes les publications, à l'exception de l'Annuaire statistique et des Rapports et études statistiques, peuvent être obtenues gratuitement en s'adressant à la Division des statistiques de l'UNESCO. Pour tous renseignements concernant les publications antérieures à 1992, qui ne figurent pas sur cette liste, le lecteur est prié de s'adresser également à la Division des statistiques.

. . . .

Este apéndice presenta tres listas con una selección de publicaciones estadísticas, según el idioma en que fueron publicadas, a saber, inglés, francés y español. Las indicaciones sobre las diferentes versiones existentes figuran entre paréntesis al final del título de la publicación. Esas indicaciones remiten el lector a una de las dos otras listas o ambas y dan información sobre las publicaciones en árabe o ruso. Todas las publicaciones, salvo el Anuario estadístico, pueden obtenerse gratuitamente escribiendo a la División de Estadística de la UNESCO. Asimismo se ruega dirigirse a esta División por obtener mayor información sobre las publicaciones anteriores a 1992 que no figuran en esta lista.

Selected list of UNESCO statistical publications
Liste sélective d'ouvrages statistiques publiés par l'UNESCO
Lista selectiva de obras estadísticas publicadas por la UNESCO

Identification	Title	Published in
ISBN 92-3-003032-5	UNESCO Statistical Yearbook, published annually since 1963 (Trilingual: English/French/Spanish, explanatory texts also in Arabic and Russian)	annually
	Statistical reports and studies	
No. 32	International Flows of Selected Cultural Goods 1970-1987 (English only)	1992
No. 34	Towards a Standardized Definition of Educational Expenditure (also published in French)	1994
No. 35	Compendium of Statistics on Illiteracy - 1995 edition (also published in French and Spanish)	1995
	Current surveys and research in statistics (CSR)	
CSR-S-24	Human and Financial Resources for Research and Experimental Development in the Higher Education Sector (also published in French and Spanish)	1990
CSR-S-25	Estimated World Resources for Research and Experimental Development 1980 and 1985 (also published in French and Spanish)	1991
CSR-E-61	China: Educational Financing in the 1980s (English only)	1991
CSR-E-62	Literacy Assessment and its Implications for Statistical Measurement (also published in French and Spanish)	1992
CSR-E-63	Trends and Projections of Enrolment by Level of Education, by age and by sex, 1960-2025 (as assessed in 1993) (also published in French)	1993
CSR-E-64	Use of Sample Survey Techniques in Educational Statistics (also published in French)	1993
	Statistical Issues	
STE/8	The Impact of Primary Education on Literacy (also published in French and Spanish)	1992
STE/9	Primary education—Age in Grade 1 (also published in French and Spanish)	1992
STE/10	Special Survey on Primary Education—Urban and Rural Schools (also published in French and Spanish)	1992
STE/11	Foreign Students in Higher Education - Comparative Statistical Data for 1980 and 1990 (English only)	1993
STE/12	Secondary General Education : Repetition (also published in French and Spanish)	1993
STE/13	Demographic Pressure on Primary Education (1993 update) (also published in French and Spanish)	1993
STE/14	Adult Illiteracy in China (also published in French and Spanish)	1994
STE/16	Statistics on Adult Illiteracy: Preliminary Results of the 1994 Estimations and Projections (English only)	1994
STE/17	Technical and Vocational Education at the Second Level: Female Participation in the Different Fields of Study, 1980 and 1992. (also published in French and Spanish)	1995

Selected list of UNESCO statistical publications
Liste sélective d'ouvrages statistiques publiés par l'UNESCO
Lista selectiva de obras estadísticas publicadas por la UNESCO

Identification	Title	Published in
STE/18	Methodology used in the 1994 Estimation and Projection of Adult Illiteracy (also published in French)	1995
STC/1	World Press Trends, 1965-1988 (also published in French and Spanish)	1992
STC/2	Number of Speakers of the World's Principal Languages in 1989 (also published in French and Spanish)	1992

International recommendations

	Recommendation concerning the International Standardization of Library Statistics, adopted by the General Conference at its sixteenth session, Paris, 13 November 1970 (Multilingual: English/Spanish/French/Russian)	1970
	Recommendation concerning the International Standardization of Statistics on Radio and Television, adopted by the General Conference at its nineteenth session, Nairobi, 22 November 1976. (Multilingual: English/Spanish/French/Russian/Arabic)	1976
	Revised Recommendation concerning the International Standardization of Educational Statistics, adopted by the General Conference at its twentieth session, Paris, 27 November 1978 (Multilingual: English/Spanish/French/Russian/Arabic)	1978
	Recommendation concerning the International Standardization of Statistics on Science and Technology, adopted by the General Conference at its twentieth session, Paris, 27 November 1978 (Multilingual: English/Spanish/French/Russian/Arabic)	1978
	Recommendation concerning the International Standardization of Statistics on the Public Financing of Cultural Activities, adopted by the General Conference at its twenty-first session, Belgrade, 27 October 1980 (Multilingual: English/Spanish/French/Russian Arabic/Chinese)	1980
	Revised Recommendation Concerning the International Standardization of Statistics on the Production and Distribution of Books, Newspapers and Periodicals, adopted by the General Conference at its twenty-third session, Sofia, 1 November 1985 (Multilingual: English/Spanish/French/Russian Arabic/Chinese)	1985

Miscellaneous reports and documents

ED/BIE/confinted 43/ref. 1	Statistical Document on Education and Culture International Conference on Education 43rd Session September 1992 (also published in French)	1992
ED-91/MINEDAF/ ref. 1	Development of Education in Africa: a Statistical Review (also published in French)	1991
ED-93/MINEDAP/ ref. 2	Development of Education in Asia and the Pacific: a Statistical Review (English only)	1993
ED-94/MINEDARAB/ ref.2	Development of Education in the Arab States: a Statistical Review and Projections (English only)	1994
Working paper. No. 10	Proposals for a set of Cultural Indicators. joint ECE/UNESCO work session on Cultural Statistics (Paris, 26-28 April 1993) (English only)	1993
ISBN 9966- 831-30-4	Female Participation in Education in Sub-Saharan Africa (also published in French)	1995

Selected list of UNESCO statistical publications
Liste sélective d'ouvrages statistiques publiés par l'UNESCO
Lista selectiva de obras estadísticas publicadas por la UNESCO

Identification	Titre	Publie en
ISBN 92-3-003032-5	Annuaire statistique de l'UNESCO publié chaque année depuis 1963 (trilingue: anglais/français/espagnol, textes explicatifs également en arabe et en russe)	annuellement
	Rapports et études statistiques	
No. 33	Les dépenses d'enseignement dans le monde: évolution passée et perspective à moyen terme (publié en français seulement)	1992
No. 34	Eléments pour une définition harmonisée des dépenses d'éducation (publié également en anglais)	1994
No. 35	Compendium des statistiques relatives à l'analphabétisme, édition de 1995 (publié également en anglais et en espagnol)	1995
	Enquêtes et recherches statistiques	
	Travaux en cours (CSR)	
CSR-S-24	Ressources humaines et financicères consacrées à la recherche et au développement expérimental dans le secteur de l'enseignement supérieur (publié également en anglais et en espagnol)	1990
CSR-S-25	Estimation des ressources mondiales consacrées à la recherche et au développement expérimental, 1980 et 1985 (publié également en anglais et en espagnol)	1991
CSR-E-62	L'évaluation de l'alphabétisation et les problèmes de mesure statistique (publié également en anglais et en espagnol)	1992
CSR-E-63	Tendances et projections des effectifs scolaires par degré d'enseignement, par âge et par sexe, 1960-2025 (évaluées en 1993) (pubié également en anglais)	1993
CSR-E-64	Application des techniques de sondage aux statistiques de l'éducation (publié également en anglais)	1994
	Notes statistiques	
STE/8	L'impact de l'enseignement primaire sur l'alphabétisation (publié également en anglais et espagnol)	1992
STE/9	Enseignement primaire - âge en première année d'études (publié également en anglais et en espagnol)	1992
STE/10	Enquête spéciale sur l'enseignement primaire: écoles urbaines et écoles rurales (publié également en anglais et en espagnol)	1992
STE/12	Enseignement général du second degré: redoublement (publié également en anglais et en espagnol)	1993
STE/13	La pression démographique sur l'enseignement primaire (actualisation de 1993) (publié également en anglais et en espagnol)	1993
STE/14	L'analphabétisme des adultes en Chine (publié également en anglais et en espagnol)	1994
STE/17	Enseignement technique et professionnel du second degré: la participation féminine dans les différents domaines d'études, 1980 et 1992 (publié également en anglais et en espagnol)	1995

Selected list of UNESCO statistical publications
Liste sélective d'ouvrages statistiques publiés par l'UNESCO
Lista selectiva de obras estadísticas publicadas por la UNESCO

Identification	Titre	Publie en
STE/18	Analphabétisme ches les adultes: méthodes utilisées dans les estimations et les projections de 1994 (publié également en anglais)	1995
	- -	
STC/1	Tendances de la presse dans le monde 1965-1988 (publié également en anglais et en espagnol)	1992
STC/2	Nombre de locuteurs des principales langues parlées dans le monde en 1989 (publié également en anglais et en espagnol)	1992
	Recommandations internationales.	
	Recommandation concernant la normalisation internationale des statistiques relatives aux bibliothèques, adoptée par la Conférence générale à sa seizième session, Paris, 13 novembre 1970 (plurilingue: anglais/espagnol/français/russe)	1970
	Recommandation concernant la normalisation internationale des statistiques relatives à la radio et à la télévision, adoptée par la Conférence générale à sa dix-neuvième session, Nairobi, 22 novembre 1976 (plurilingue: anglais/espagnol/français/russe/arabe)	1976
	Recommandation révisée concernant la normalisation internationale des statistiques de l'éducation, adoptée par la Conférence générale à sa vingtième session, Paris, 27 novembre 1978 (plurilingue: anglais/espagnol/français/russe/arabe)	1978
	Recommandation concernant la normalisation internationale des statistiques relatives à la science et à la technologie, adoptée par la Conférence générale à sa vingtième session, Paris, 27 novembre 1978 (plurilingue: anglais/espagnol/français/russe/arabe)	1978
	Recommandation concernant la normalisation internationale des statistiques relatives au financement public des activités culturelles, adoptée par la Conférence générale à sa vingt et unième session, Belgrade, 27 octobre 1980 (plurilingue: anglais/espagnol/français/russe arabe/chinois)	1980
	Recommandation révisée concernant la normalisation internationale des statistiques relatives à la production et à la distribution de livres, de journaux et de périodiques, adoptée par la Conférence générale à sa vingt-troisième session, Sofia, 1er novembre 1985. (plurilingue: anglais/arabe/espagnol/français/russe/chinois)	1985
	Rapports et documents divers	
ED/BIE/confinted 43/ref.1	Document statistique sur l'éducation et la culture Conférence internationale sur l'éducation 43ème session, septembre 1992 (publié également en anglais)	1992
ED-91/MINEDAF/ ref. 1	Développement de l'éducation en Afrique: étude statistique (publié également en anglais)	1991
ISBN 9966-831-36-3	La participation des femmes à l'éducation en Afrique subsaharienne (publié également en anglais)	1995

Selected list of UNESCO statistical publications
Liste sélective d'ouvrages statistiques publiés par l'UNESCO
Lista selectiva de obras estadísticas publicadas por la UNESCO

Identificacion	Titulo	Publicado en
ISBN 92-3-003032-5	Anuario estadístico de la UNESCO publicado anualmente desde 1963 (trilingüe: inglés/español/francés, textos explicativos igualmente en árabe y ruso)	anual
	Informes y estudios estadísticos	
No. 35	Compendio de estadísticas relativas al analfabetismo, edición de 1995 (publicado igualmente en inglés y en francés)	1995
	Encuestas e investigaciones estadísticas:	
	trabajos en curso (CSR):	
CSR-S-24	Recursos humanos y financieros para la investigación y el desarrollo experimental en el sector de enseñanza superior (publicado igualmente en inglés y en francés)	1988
CSR-S-25	Estimación de los recursos mundiales dedicados a la investigación y al desarrollo experimental 1980-1985 (publicado igualmente en inglés y en francés)	1991
- - - - - - - -	- - - - - - - - - - - - - - - -	- - - - -
CSR-E-62	La evaluación de la alfabetización y sus repercusiones en las mediciones estadísticas (publicado igualmente en inglés y en francés)	1992
	Notas estadísticas	
STE/8	Las repercusiones de la enseñanza primaria en la alfabetización (publicado igualmente en inglés y en francés)	1991
STE/9	La enseñanza primaria—Edad de la matrícula de primer año de estudio (publicado igualmente en inglés y en francés)	1992
STE/10	Encuesta especial sobre la enseñanza primaria Escuelas urbanas y rurales (publicado igualmente en inglés y en francés)	1992
STE/12	La repetición de curso en la enseñanza secundaria general (publicado igualmente en inglés y en francés)	1993
STE/13	La presión demografica en la educación primaria (actualización de 1993) (publicado igualmente en inglés y en francés)	1993
STE/14	El analfabetismo de adultos en china (publicado igualmente en inglés y en francés)	1994
STE/17	Enseñanza técnica y profesional de nivel secundario: participación femenina en los diferentes sectores de estudios en 1980 y 1992 (publicado igualmente en inglés y en francés)	1995
- - - - - - - -	- - - - - - - - - - - - - - - -	- - - - -
STC/1	Las tendencias de la prensa en el mundo entre 1965 y 1988 (publicado igualmente en inglés y en francés)	1992
STC/2	Número de personas que hablaban los principales idiomas del mundo en 1989 (publicado igualmente en inglés y en francés)	1992
	Recomandaciónes internacionales	
	Recomendación sobre la normalización internacional de las estadísticas relativas a las bibliotecas, aprobada por la Conferencia General en su decimosexta reunión, París, 13 de noviembre de 1970 (plurilingüe: inglés/español/francés/ruso)	1970

Selected list of UNESCO statistical publications
Liste sélective d'ouvrages statistiques publiés par l'UNESCO
Lista selectiva de obras estadísticas publicadas por la UNESCO

Identificacion	Titulo	Publicado en
	Recomendación sobre la normalización internacional de las estadísticas relativas a la radio y la televisión, aprobada por la Conferencia General en su decimo-novena reunión, Nairobi, 22 de noviembre de 1976 (plurilingüe: inglés/español/francés/ruso/árabe)	1976
	Recomendación revisada sobre la normalización internacional de las estadísticas relativas a la educación, aprobada por la Conferencia General en su vigésima reunión, París, 27 de noviembre de 1978 (plurilingüe: inglés/español/francés/ruso/árabe)	1978
	Recomendación sobre la normalización internacional de las estadísticas relativas a la ciencia y la tecnología aprobada por la Conferencia General en su vigésima reunión, París, 27 de noviembre de 1978 (plurilingüe: inglés/español/francés/ruso/árabe)	1978
	Recomendación sobre la normalización internacional de las estadísticas relativas al financiamiento público de las actividades culturales, aprobada por la Conferencia General en su 21a. reunión, Belgrado, 27 de octubre de 1980 (plurilingüe: inglés/español/francés/ruso/árabe/chino)	1980
	Recomendación revisada sobre la normalización internacional de las estadísticas relativas a la producción y distribución de libros, diarios y otras publicaciones periódicas, aprobada por la Conferencia General en su 23a reunión, Sofía, 1° de noviembre de 1985 (plurilingüe: inglés/español/francés/ruso/árabe/chino)	1985

E   Tables omitted

Tableaux supprimés

Cuadros suprimidos

Table Title	Last published as table no. and in the edition specified below
Summary tables for all levels of education, continents, major areas and groups of countries	
Number of countries by characteristics of their education systems	1991, table 2.1
Distribution of countries according to the pupil-teacher ratio at the first level of education	1991, table 2.7
Estimated enrolment ratios by age-group	1994, table 2.9
Science and technology	
Scientific and technical manpower: estimates for 1980, and 1985	1993, table 5.1
Scientists and engineers engaged in R&D and expenditure for R&D: estimates for 1980, 1985 and 1990	1994, table 5.1
Scientific and technical manpower	1995, table 5.2
Number of scientists and engineers engaged in research and experimental development, by their field of study	1995, table 5.4
Number of scientists and engineers engaged in research and experimental development, performed in the productive sector, by branch of economic activity	1994, table 5.6
Number of scientists and engineers engaged in research and experimental development performed in the higher education and the general service sectors, by field of science and technology	1994, table 5.7
Current expenditure for research and experimental development by type of R&D activity	1994, table 5.10
Total expenditure for the performance of research and experimental development in the productive sectors, by branch of economic activity	1994, table 5.12
Total expenditure for the performance for research and experimental development in the higher education and the general service sectors, by field of science and technology	1994, table 5.13
Expenditure for national research and experimental development activities by major socio-economic aim	1994, table 5.14
Personnel engaged in research and experimental development: selected data for recent years	1992, table 5.16
Expenditure for research and experimental development: selected data for recent years	1992, table 5.17

Table Title	Last published as table no. and in the edition specified below
Summary tables for culture and communication subjects by continents, major areas and groups of countries	
Number of book titles published	1995, table 6.1
Production of long films	1995, table 6.5
Number and seating capacity of fixed cinemas	1995, table 6.6
Annual cinema attendance	1995, table 6.7
Number of radio broadcasting transmitters	1990, table 6.8
Number of television transmitters	1990, table 6.10
Libraries	
National libraries: collections, registered users, works loaned out, current expenditure, employees	1995, table 7.2
Public libraries: collections, registered users, works loaned out, current expenditure, employees	1995, table 7.3
School librairies: collections, registered users, works loaned out, current expenditure, employees	1993, table 7.3
Book production	
Book production: number of titles by language of publication	1995, table 7.6
Translations by country of publication and by UDC classes	1993, table 7.11
Translations by original language and by UDC classes	1993, table 7.12
Translations by country of publication and by selected languages from which translated	1993, table 7.13
Translations by original language and by selected language into which translated	1993, table 7.14
Authors most frequently translated	1993, table 7.15
Film and Cinema	
Long films: number of films produced	1995, table 8.1
Long films: number of long films imported, by country of origin	1995, table 8.2
Cinemas: number, seating capacity, annual attendance and box office receipts	1995, table 8.3

Table Title	Last published as table no. and in the edition specified below
Broadcasting	
Radio and television broadcasting: annual revenue by source and by type of institution..	1993, table 9.6
Radio and television broadcasting; annual current expenditure by purpose and by type of institution...	1993, table 9.7
Cultural heritage	
Archival institutions: holdings, accessions, reference service, personnel and current expenditure..	1990, table 8.2

Titre du tableau	Publié avec le no. du tableau et dans l'édition indiqué ci-dessous
Tableaux récapitulatifs pour tous les degrés d'enseignement, par continents, grandes régions et groupes de pays	
Nombre de pays selon les caractéristiques de leurs systèmes d'enseignement	1991, tableau 2.1
Répartition des pays selon le nombre d'élèves par maître pour le premier degré d'enseignement	1991, tableau 2.7
Estimation des taux d'inscription par groupe d'âge	1994, tableau 2.9
Science et technologie	
Potentiel humain scientifique et technique: estimations pour 1980 et 1985	1993, tableau 5.1
Scientifiques et ingénieurs employés à des travaux de R-D et dépenses consacrées; R-D:estimations pour 1980, 1985 et 1990	1994, tableau 5.1
Potentiel humain scientifique et technique	1995, tableau 5.2
Nombre de scientifique et d'ingénieurs employés à des travaux de recherche et de développement expérimental, par leur domaine d'études	1995, tableau 5.4
Nombre de scientifiques et d'ingénieurs employés; des travaux de recherche et de développement expérimental effectués dans le secteur de la production, par branche d'activité économique.	1994, tableau 5.6
Nombre de scientifiques et d'ingénieurs employés à des travaux de recherche et de développement expérimental effectués dans les secteurs de l'enseignement supérieur et de service général, par domaine de la science et de la technologie	1994, tableau 5.7
Dépenses courantes consacrées à la recherche et au développement expérimental, par type d'activité de R-D	1994, tableau 5.10
Dépenses totales pour l'exécution de travaux de recherche et de développement expérimental dans le secteur de la production, par branche d'activité économique	1994, tableau 5.12
Dépenses totales pour l'exécution de travaux de recherche et de développement expérimental dans les secteurs de l'enseignement supérieur et de service général, par domaine de la science et de la technologie	1994, tableau 5.13
Dépenses afférentes aux activités nationales de recherche et de développement expérimental par finalités socio-économiques principales	1994, tableau 5.14
Personnel employé à des travaux de recherche et de développement expérimental: données sélectionnées pour des années récentes	1992, tableau 5.16
Dépenses consacrées à la recherche et au développement expérimental: données sélectionnées pour des années récentes	1992, tableau 5.17

Titre du tableau	Publié avec le no. du tableau et dans l'édition indiqué ci-dessous
Tableaux récapitulatifs pour la culture et la communication, par continents, grandes régions et groupes de pays	
Nombre de titres de livres publiés	1995, tableau 6.1
Production de films de long métrage	1995, tableau 6.5
Nombre de cinémas fixes et de sièges	1995, tableau 6.6
Fréquentation annuelle de cinémas	1995, tableau 6.7
Nombre d'émetteurs de radiodiffusion sonore	1990, tableau 6.8
Nombre d'émetteurs de télévision	1990, tableau 6.10
Bibliothèques	
Bibliothèques nationales: collections, usagers inscrits, documents prêtés au-dehors, dépenses ordinaires, personnel	1995, tableau 7.2
Bibliothèques publiques: collections, usagers inscrits, documents prêtés au-dehors, dépenses ordinaires, personnel	1995, tableau 7.3
Bibliothèques scolaires: collections, usagers inscrits, documents prêtés au-dehors, dépenses ordinaires, personnel	1993, tableau 7.3
Edition de livres	
Édition de livres: nombre de titre classés d'après la langue de publication	1995, tableau 7.6
Traductions classées par pays de publication et d'après les groupes de sujets de la CDU	1993, tableau 7.11
Traductions classées d'après la langue originale et les groupes de sujets de la CDU	1993, tableau 7.12
Traductions classées par pays de publication et d'après les langues sélectionnées à partir desquelles elles sont traduites	1993, tableau 7.13
Traductions classées, pour des langues sélectionnées, d'après la langue originale et la langue dans laquelle elles sont traduites	1993, tableau 7.14
Auteurs les plus traduits	1993, tableau 7.15
Films et cinémas	
Films de long métrage: nombre de films produits	1995, tableau 8.1
Films de long métrage: nombre de films importés, par pays d'origine	1995, tableau 8.2
Cinémas: nombre d'établissements, nombre de sièges, fréquentation annuelle et recettes guichet	1995, tableau 8.3

Titre du tableau	Publié avec le no. du tableau et dans l'édition indiqué ci-dessous
Radiodiffusion	
Radiodiffusion sonore et télévision: ressources financières annuelles d'après l'origine des ressources et le type d'organisme..	1993, tableau 9.6
Radiodiffusion sonore et télévision: dépenses courantes annuelles d'après leur destination et le type d'organisme	1993, tableau 9.7
Patrimoine culturel	
Institutions d'archives: fonds et collections, entrées, services de renseignements, personnel et dépenses courantes	1990, tableau 8.2

Título del cuadro	Publicado con el número de cuadro y en la edición indicada más abajo
Cuadros recapitulativos para todos los grados de enseñanza, por continentes, grandes regiones y grupos de países	
Número de países según las características de sus sistemas de enseñanza.................................	1991, cuadro 2.1
Distribución de los países según el número de alumnos por maestro para el primer grado de enseñanza..	1991, cuadro 2.7
Estimación de las tasas de escolarización por grupo de edad	1994, cuadro 2.9
Ciencia y tecnología	
Recursos humanos científicos e técnicos potenciales: estimaciones para 1980 y 1985.....................	1993, cuadro 5.1
Científicos e ingenieros empleados en trabajos de I y D y gastos dedicados a la I y D: estimaciones para 1980, 1985 y 1990	1994, cuadro 5.1
Recursos humanos científicos y técnicos	1995, cuadro 5.2
Número de científicos e ingenieros empleados en trabajos de investigación y de desarrollo experimental, según el sector de estudios....................................	1995, cuadro 5.4
Número de científicos e ingenieros empleados en trabajos de investigación y de desarrollo experimental efectuados en el sector productivo, por rama de actividad económica	1994, cuadro 5.6
Número de científicos e ingenieros empleados en trabajos de investigación y de desarrollo experimental efectuado en los sectores de enseñanza superior y de servicio general, por campo de la ciencia y de la tecnología	1994, cuadro 5.7
Gastos corrientes dedicados a la investigación y al desarrollo experimental por tipo de actividad de I y D	1994, cuadro 5.10
Gastos totales para la ejecución de trabajos de investigación y de desarrollo experimental en el sector productivo, por rama de actividad económica	1994, cuadro 5.12
Gastos totales para la ejecución de trabajos de investigación y de desarrollo experimental en los sectores de enseñanza superior y de servicio general, por campo de la ciencia y de la tecnología	1994, cuadro 5.13
Gastos destinados a las actividades nacionales de investigación y de desarrollo experimental, por finalidades socio-económicas principales	1994, cuadro 5.14
Personal empleado en actividades de investigación y de desarrollo experimental: datos seleccionados sobre los últimos años..	1992, cuadro 5.16
Gastos dedicados a la investigación y al desarrollo experimental: datos seleccionados sobre los últimos años..	1992, cuadro 5.17
Cuadros recapitulativos para la cultura y la comunicación, por continentes, grandes regiones y grupos de países	
Número de títulos de libros publicados..	1995, cuadro 6.1
Producción de películas de largo metraje..	1995, cuadro 6.5
Número de cines fijos y de asientos	1995, cuadro 6.6
Frecuentación anual de cines..	1995, cuadro 6.7

Título del cuadro	Publicado con el número de cuadro y en la edición indicada más abajo
Número de transmisores de radiodifusión sonora	1990, cuadro 6.8
Número de transmisores de televisión	1990, cuadro 6.10

Bibliotecas

Bibliotecas nacionales: fondos, usuarios inscritos, documentos prestados al exterior, gastos ordinarios, personal	1995, cuadro 7.2
Bibliotecas públicas: fondos, usuarios inscritos, documentos prestados al exterior, gastos ordinarios, personal	1995, cuadro 7.3
Bibliotecas escolares: fondos, usuarios inscritos, documentos prestados al exterior, gastos ordinarios, personal	1993, cuadro 7.3

Edición de libros

Edición de libros: número de títulos clasificados según la lengua en que se publican	1995, cuadro 7.6
Traducciones clasificadas según el país de publicación y según los grupos de materias de la CDU	1993, cuadro 7.11
Traducciones clasificadas según la lengua original y los grupos de materias de la CDU	1993, cuadro 7.12
Traducciones clasificadas por país de publicación y según las lenguas seleccionadas a partir de las cuales fueron traducidas	1993, cuadro 7.13
Traduccciones clasificadas, por idiomas seleccionados, según la lenga original y la lengua en que han sido traducidas	1993, cuadro 7.14
Autores más traducidos	1993, cuadro 7.15

Películas y cines

Películas de largo metraje: número de películas producidas	1995, cuadro 8.1
Películas de largo metraje: número de películas importadas, por país de origen	1995, cuadro 8.2
Cines: número de establecimientos, número de asientos, frecuentación anual y recaudación de taquilla	1995, cuadro 8.3

Radiodifusión

Radiodifusión sonora y televisión: fuentes de ingreso anuales, según el origen de los fondos y el tipo de institución	1993, cuadro 9.6
Radiodifusión sonora y televisión: gastos ordinarios anuales, según su destino y el tipo de institución	1993, cuadro 9.7

Patrimonio cultural

Instituciones de archivos: fondos y colecciones, ingresos, servicio de informaciones, personal y gastos corrientes	1990, cuadro 8.2

Introductory texts in Russian
Textes d'introduction en russe
Textos de introducción en ruso

F Introductory texts in Russian

Textes d'introduction en russe

Textos de introducción en ruso

Introductory texts in Russian
Textes d'introduction en russe
Textos de introducción en ruso

Предисловие

Настоящее издание *Статистического ежегодника* ЮНЕСКО было подготовлено Отделом статистики в сотрудничестве с национальными комиссиями по делам ЮНЕСКО, национальными статистическими службами и другими национальными учреждениями.

В соответствии со статьей VIII Устава ЮНЕСКО каждому государству-члену предлагается периодически представлять Организации доклады о своих законах, положениях и статистических данных, относящихся к жизни и деятельности в области образования, науки и культуры. Сбор данных осуществляется, главным образом, из официальных ответов от около 200 стран и территорий на вопросники и специальных обследований ЮНЕСКО, а также из официальных докладов и публикаций, дополняемых информацией, доступной Секретариату из национальных и международных источников, в частности из Статистического отдела и Отдела народонаселения ООН. Там, где имеющиеся данные не соответствуют принятым рекомендациям или другим концепциям и определениям, применяемым ЮНЕСКО, соблюдается национальная статистическая практика и по возможности даются примечания.

Около 200 стран и территорий отвечают в пределах своих возможностей непосредственно на вопросники ЮНЕСКО, и данные, которые они любезно предоставили, включены в этот *Ежегодник*. Совершенствование таблиц и представленная дополнительная информация отражены в предисловиях к каждой тематической главе.

Пояснительные тексты к таблицам, представленные на английском, французском и испанском языках, были включены в тексты предисловий в начале каждой главы, кроме главы 3, где эти тексты можно найти в конце каждой отдельной таблицы. В качестве подспорья для читателей *Ежегодника*, владеющих арабским и русским языками, тексты предисловий к каждой главе, были переведены на оба эти языка. Их можно найти в Дополнениях F и G *Ежегодника*.

Внимание читателя обращается на то, что некоторые таблицы, которые были помещены в предыдущих изданиях *Ежегодника*, не включены в настоящее издание. Перечень этих таблиц приведен в Дополнении Е с указанием последнего издания, в котором можно найти данные таблицы.

Все вопросы и замечания, а также предложения по дальнейшему улучшению последующих изданий *Ежегодника* будут с благодарностью приняты Отделом статистики ЮНЕСКО по адресу: Division of Statistics, UNESCO, 75352 Paris 07 SP, France.

Introductory texts in Russian
Textes d'introduction en russe
Textos de introducción en ruso

Пояснения

Данные, представленные в этой публикации, относятся, как правило, к территориальным единицам в пределах их нынешних границ «де факто». Полный список стран и территорий приводится сразу после настоящих Пояснений. Изменения, происшедшие в некоторых странах за последние годы, находят отражение в названиях стран, фигурирующих в этом списке и используемых в таблицах *Ежегодника*.

Необходимо отметить следующее:

- Данные, представленные по *Иордании*, за исключением Таблицы 1.1, относятся только к Восточному берегу реки Иордан.

- Статистика, касающаяся Палестины, ограничена только *Сектором Газа* и *Западным берегом реки Иордан* и приводится после стран Азии в каждой из соответствующих таблиц.

- Данные, которые относятся к *Германии* до 1990 г., представлены отдельно по *Федеративной Республике Германия* и по бывшей *Германской Демократической Республике*.

- Это следует отметить также в отношении Йемена, где данные до 1990 г. приводятся отдельно по *Демократическому Йемену* и бывшей *Йеменской Арабской Республике*.

- В 1991 г. *Союз Советских Социалистических Республик* официально распался на пятнадцать отдельных стран (Азербайджан, Армения, Беларусь, Грузия, Казахстан, Кыргызстан, Латвия, Литва, Республика Молдова, Российская Федерация, Таджикистан, Туркменистан, Узбекистан, Украина, Эстония). По мере возможности, данные приводятся по каждой отдельной стране.

- Данные по бывшей *Югославии* и бывшей *Чехословакии* относятся, как правило, к периоду, предшествующему происшедшим в этих странах изменениям. При наличии соответствующей статистики приводятся данные по отдельным республикам.

- Данные, представленные по *Ватикану*, относятся к государству - городу Ватикану.

- До 1991 г. данные по Эфиопии включают Эритрею; однако данные по последней имеются за период, предшествующий 1991 г., они приводятся отдельно от Эфиопии.

В этом издании *Ежегодника* могут быть представлены пересмотренные данные, отличающиеся таким образом от соответствующих данных за тот же год в предыдущих изданиях.

Итоговые данные и промежуточные итоги, показанные в таблицах, не всегда точно соответствуют сумме составляющих их компонентов вследствие округления цифр.

Пояснения, касающиеся отдельных цифр, отмечены условным обозначением «C» у названия соответствующих континентов, регионов, стран или территорий. Тексты этих пояснений приводятся в конце каждой таблицы: каждое примечание включает название континента, региона, страны или территории (на английском языке) с последующим необходимым пояснением, для которого перед английским текстом приводится обозначение E→, французским текстом – FR→ и испанским текстом – ESP→. Для ряда таблиц дается также общее примечание, которое предшествует примечаниям по отдельным странам.

В *Ежегоднике* используются следующие условные обозначения:

–	Незначительная величина
0 или 0.0	Величина меньше половины используемой единицы измерения
...	Данные отсутствуют
.	Категория не применима
★	Предварительные или оценочные данные
./.	Данные, указанные в другом месте и включенные в иную категорию
→	Цифра, расположенная непосредственно слева от стрелки, включает данные, касающиеся тех столбцов, где приводится это условное обозначение
←	Цифра, расположенная непосредственно справа от стрелки, включает данные, касающиеся тех столбцов, где приводится это условное обозначение

Разрыв в последовательности временного ряда обозначен вертикальной или горизонтальной линией.

Introductory texts in Russian
Textes d'introduction en russe
Textos de introducción en ruso

1 Вводные таблицы

Первая глава *Ежегодника* состоит из трех таблиц: одной - по населению, одной - по неграмотности и одной - по достигнутому уровню образования населения. Они представляют основные справочные данные для всех других таблиц, которые касаются вопросов образования, науки, культуры и средств массовой информации.

Численность и плотность населения страны непосредственно влияют на развитие ее учреждений и материальных возможностей в области образования.

Данные по неграмотности и достигнутому уровню образования дают образовательный профиль взрослого населения, который может служить дополнением к статистике численности учащихся школ и университетов.

Таблица 1.1

Таблица 1.1 содержит данные об общей численности населения, площади и плотности населения для некоторых групп стран и отдельных стран. Цифры, представленные в этой таблице, соответствуют среднему варианту пересмотра 1994 года оценок и прогнозов численности населения, подготовленного Отделом народонаселения Организации Объединенных Наций.

Данные о площади включают площади внутренних водоемов. Данные о плотности населения (количество жителей на один квадратный километр) не приводятся по территориям площадью менее 1 000 квадратных километров. Читателям, интересующимся более подробной информацией о территории, населении и возрастной структуре, рекомендуется обратиться к различным изданиям *Демографического ежегодника* и *Статистического ежегодника* Организации Объединенных Наций.

Таблица 1.2

В Таблице 1.2 представлены данные, касающиеся неграмотного взрослого населения и процента неграмотных на основе последних переписей или обследований, которые проводились после 1979 г. Эти данные предоставлены Статистическим отделом Организации Объединенных Наций или получены из национальных публикаций. В таблице приводятся также последние оценки численности неграмотного взрослого населения за 1995 г., сделанные Статистическим отделом ЮНЕСКО в 1994 г. Читатели, которых интересует сравнительная статистика за предыдущие годы, а также оценочные временные ряды по отдельным развивающимся странам, могут обратиться к публикации ЮНЕСКО «Компендиум статистики неграмотности» - издание 1995 г.

Таблица 1.3

В Таблице 1.3 показано процентное распределение взрослого населения в зависимости от наивысшего уровня образования. Данные получены из национальных переписей или выборочных обследований, предоставлены Статистическим отделом Организации Объединенных Наций или взяты из национальных публикаций.

Читателям, интересующимся данными за более ранние годы, рекомендуется обратиться к публикации Статистика достигнутого уровня образования и неграмотности. 1970-1980 гг. CSR-E-44 (ЮНЕСКО 1983 г.).

Шесть уровней достигнутого образования концептуально основаны на ряде категорий Международной стандартной классификации образования (МСКО) и могут быть определены следующим образом:

Без школьного образования. Этот термин применяется к лицам, которые имеют школьное образование менее 1 года.

Неполное образование первой ступени. Эта категория включает всех лиц, которые закончили по крайней мере один год обучения первой ступени, но не завершили последний год обучения этой ступени. Продолжительность образования на первой ступени может различаться в разных странах: соответствующая информация приводится в Таблице 3.1.

Полное образование первой ступени. В эту группу включены лица, завершившие последний год обучения первой ступени (категория «1» МСКО), но не начали обучение на второй ступени.

S-1. Первый этап образования второй ступени. В эту группу входят лица, достигнутый уровень образования которых ограничен нижним этапом образования второй ступени согласно Таблице 3.1 и соответствует категории «2» МСКО.

S-2. Второй этап образования второй ступени. Эта группа соответствует категории «3» МСКО и охватывает лиц, перешедших с нижнего на более высокий этап образования второй ступени, но не продолживших обучение на третьей ступени.

Послесреднее образование. К этой группе можно отнести тех, кто обучался на третьей ступени (категории «5», «6» или «7» МСКО), независимо от завершения полного курса обучения.

В возрастной группе 15-24 года доля лиц с тем или иным уровнем образования третьей ступени зачастую меньше доли таких лиц в возрастной группе 25-34 года, поскольку значительную часть в возрастной группе 15-24 года составляет молодежь, не достигшая возраста поступления в учебные заведения третьей ступени. По этой причине для целей данной таблицы взят общий возрастной диапазон взрослого населения 25+ (а не 15+) лет.

Introductory texts in Russian
Textes d'introduction en russe
Textos de introducción en ruso

Образование

В следующих трех главах *Ежегодника* приводится большая часть собранной и обобщенной ЮНЕСКО базовой статистической информации в отношении населения, неграмотности взрослых, а также государственных и частных учебных заведений всех уровней. В тридцати таблицах приводятся общемировые статистические данные по таким аспектам, как число школ; численность учителей и учащихся с разбивкой по ступени и типу образования; численность студентов и выпускников высших учебных заведений с разбивкой по специализации и уровню программ; число иностранных студентов в высших учебных заведениях с разбивкой по посылающим и принимающим странам; государственные расходы на образование с разбивкой по целям и ступеням образования. Данные по возможности относятся к учебным годам, начинающимся в 1980 г., 1985 г. и 1990 г., а также к трем последним годам.

Для целей этих таблиц по возможности применялись определения и классификации, установленные пересмотренной Рекомендацией о международной стандартизации статистики в области образования, принятой Генеральной конференцией ЮНЕСКО на ее двадцатой сессии (Париж, 1978 г.), а также Международной стандартной классификацией образования (МСКО). В соответствии с этими документами образование классифицируется по ступеням следующим образом:

Образование, предшествующее первой ступени (ступень 0 МСКО), которое обеспечивает воспитание детей, еще не достигших того возраста, когда они могут поступить в школу первой ступени (например в яслях, детских садах).

Образование первой ступени (ступень 1 МСКО), главной функцией которого является обеспечение базовых элементов образования (например в начальной школе).

Образование второй ступени (ступени 2 и 3 МСКО), обеспечиваемое в средних школах, педагогических училищах на этом уровне, школах профессионального или технического характера. Эта ступень образования основана на предшествующем по крайней мере 4-летнем обучении первой ступени и обеспечивает общую и/или специализированную подготовку.

Образование третьей ступени (ступени 5, 6 и 7 МСКО), которое обеспечивается в университетах, педагогических колледжах, высших профессиональных школах и для доступа к которому требуется как минимум успешное завершение образования второй ступени или свидетельство о приобретении эквивалентного уровня знаний.

Специальное образование, охватывающее все типы образования, предоставляемого детям с физическими и умственными недостатками, дефектами зрения, слуха или речи, ущербных в плане социального общения или испытывающих трудности в чтении или письме.

Следующие определения воспроизводятся из Рекомендации:

Ученик (учащийся) - лицо, зачисленное в школу для систематического обучения на какой-либо ступени образования.

Преподаватель - лицо, непосредственно обучающее группу учеников (учащихся). Руководители учебных заведений, инспекторы или другой персонал рассматриваются в качестве преподавателей только тогда, когда они регулярно выполняют преподавательские функции.

Школа (учебное заведение) - группа учеников (учащихся) одного или более лет обучения, организованная для получения образования данного типа и на данной ступени под руководством одного или нескольких преподавателей при непосредственном контроле со стороны руководителя учебного заведения.

(a) *Государственная школа* - школа, находящаяся в ведении государственных органов (национальных, федеральных, штата или провинции или местных), независимо от того, кто ее финансирует.

(b) *Частная школа* - школа, которая не находится в ведении какого-либо государственного органа, независимо от того, финансируется она такими органами или нет. Частные школы можно определить соответственно как получающие помощь и не получающие помощь, в зависимости от того, получают ли они финансовую поддержку от государственных органов или нет.

Данные о численности учащихся, приводимые в этих таблицах, относятся, как правило, к началу учебного или академического года. В этой связи следует отметить, что данные о численности могут существенно варьироваться в зависимости от даты учета (т.е. в начале, середине, конце учебного года, среднегодовая оценка и т.д.).

Указанные годы означают учебный или академический год. В Дополнении B приводится информация о датах начала и окончания учебного и финансового года в каждой стране и территории.

Introductory texts in Russian
Textes d'introduction en russe
Textos de introducción en ruso

2 Сводные таблицы для всех уровней образования по континентам, крупным регионам и группам стран

В этой главе, включающей 11 таблиц, приводятся сводные данные о численности населения, а также статистические данные по всем ступеням образования. Вместе эти таблицы дают общую картину количественных изменений после 1980 г., а также нынешней ситуации в том, что касается неграмотности взрослых, образования и расходов на образование во всем мире и в каждом крупном регионе и группе стран.

Таблица 2.1

В Таблице 2.1 представлены оценки и прогнозы в отношении общей численности населения, а также численности лиц младше 25 лет для всего мира, по континентам, крупным регионам и группам стран за 1970 г., 1980 г., 1990 г., 1995 г., 2000 г. и 2010 г. Отдельные оценки приводятся по возрастным группам 0-4, 5-9, 10-14, 15-19 и 20-24 лет, охватывающим возрастные категории, имеющие наибольшее отношение к образованию. Цифры, представленные в этой таблице, соответствуют среднему варианту пересмотра 1994 года оценок и прогнозов численности населения, подготовленного Отделом народонаселения Организации Объединенных Наций.

Таблица 2.2

В этой таблице представлены данные за 1980 г., 1985 г., 1990 г. и 1995 г., касающиеся оценок численности неграмотного взрослого населения и процента неграмотных по континентам, крупным регионам и группам стран, подготовленных Статистическим отделом ЮНЕСКО в 1994 г.

Таблица 2.3

Эта таблица составлена, главным образом, на основе данных о численности учащихся и преподавательского состава по каждой отдельной стране и территории, приведенных в Таблице 3.3.

Таблицы 2.4-2.8

Эти таблицы представляют региональные тенденции в отношении численности учащихся и преподавательского состава по ступеням образования. Определения каждой ступени образования даны в вводной части к разделу «Образование». Данные в этих таблицах основаны, главным образом, на статистике численности учащихся и преподавательского состава, приводимой по каждой отдельной стране или территории в таблицах 3.4, 3.7 и 3.10 *Ежегодника*. Однако в случае изменений в национальных системах образования данные были стандартизированы для отражения последней структуры образования по каждой стране. Следует отметить, что разбивка и процентное распределение по ступеням образования зависят от продолжительности обучения на каждой ступени, которая в свою очередь зависит от критериев, применяемых в национальных определениях соответствующих ступеней (см. Таблицу 3.1). Поскольку эти критерии, особенно в отношении начального и среднего образования, варьируются по странам, следует осторожно подходить к сравнениям между регионами.

Таблица 2.9

Эта таблица показывает распределение численности учащихся и преподавательского состава на второй ступени в зависимости от типа образования. Эти данные основаны, главным образом, на показателях численности учащихся и преподавательского состава по каждой отдельной стране и территории, которые приводятся в Таблице 3.7. Следует проявлять осторожность при сравнениях между регионами и при толковании изменений, наблюдавшихся в пределах того или иного региона в течение рассматриваемого периода, в силу различий в учебных программах и классификаций, используемых странами и территориями для определения роли и функции педагогического образования, а также технического и профессионального образования второй ступени.

Таблица 2.10

В этой таблице приводятся скорректированные брутто-коэффициенты охвата с разбивкой по ступеням образования и по признаку пола. Данные основаны на оценках численности учащихся, представленных в Таблице 2.4 и в среднем варианте пересмотра 1994 года оценок и прогнозов в отношении населения, подготовленном Отделом народонаселения Организации Объединенных Наций. Брутто-коэффициент охвата для данной ступени образования получают делением общей численности учащихся данной ступени образования вне зависимости от возраста на численность населения той возрастной группы, которая в соответствии с национальными законами подлежит зачислению в учебные заведения этой ступени. Термин «скорректированный» означает, что группы населения, использованные для получения этих коэффициентов для того или иного конкретного региона, взяты с учетом структуры образования каждой страны в регионе. Однако для третьей ступени образования для всех стран использована стандартная продолжительность обучения в 5 лет по завершении общего образования второй ступени. Все коэффициенты выражены в процентах и могут превышать 100 в силу позднего зачисления, второгодничества и т.д.

Таблица 2.11

Цель данной таблицы состоит в том, чтобы показать общие тенденции государственных расходов на образование, выраженных в долларах США в текущих рыночных ценах.

Для большинства стран статистические данные по валовому национальному продукту (ВНП) и обменные курсы получены соответственно от Мирового банка и Международного валютного фонда.

Данные, приведенные в этой таблице, следует рассматривать в качестве общих приблизительных показателей государственных средств, выделяемых на образование. Сравнительный анализ данных, выраженных в долларах США, следует воспринимать с большой долей осторожности в силу того, что официальные обменные курсы, использованные для пересчета, дают нереалистичную стоимость в долларах США для ряда стран. Кроме того, эта стоимость выражена в текущих ценах и поэтому подвержена инфляции.

Introductory texts in Russian
Textes d'introduction en russe
Textos de introducción en ruso

3 Образование

В этой главе представлены статистические данные по образованию, предшествующему первой ступени, а также данные по образованию первой, второй и третьей ступеней. Приводятся также данные о системах образования и коэффициентах охвата разных ступеней. Данные о численности учащихся и преподавателей даются по всем ступеням образования; данные о числе учебных заведений приводятся в отношении образования, предшествующего первой ступени, и образования первой ступени; данные о численности учащихся и выпускников учебных заведений, дающих образование третьей ступени, приводятся с различной разбивкой.

Таблицы в этой главе можно подразделить на три группы.

Первая группа, которая включает таблицы 3.1 и 3.2, содержит сведения по странам относительно вступительных возрастов и продолжительности обязательного обучения на первой и второй ступенях общего образования, а также о коэффициентах охвата по ступеням образования.

Вторая группа состоит из шести таблиц 3.3-3.8, касающихся образования, предшествующего первой ступени, а также образования первой и второй ступеней. При использовании этих таблиц следует также учитывать сведения о продолжительности обучения и т.п., которые содержатся в таблицах 3.1, 3.1a и 3.1b. В целом, во всех этих таблицах приводятся данные за учебные годы, начинающиеся в 1980 г., 1985 г. и 1990 г., а также за четыре последних года, по которым имеются данные.

Третья группа включает шесть таблиц 3.9-3.14 по развитию образования третьей ступени.

В соответствии с принятым ЮНЕСКО определением для поступления на третью ступень образования в качестве минимального условия требуется успешное завершение образования на второй ступени или свидетельство о приобретении эквивалентных знаний или опыта. Такое образование можно получить в учебных заведениях различного типа, таких, как университеты, педагогические институты, технические институты и т.д.

Таблица 3.1

Эта таблица содержит суммарные данные по отдельным элементам систем образования. Приводимая здесь информация облегчает правильное толкование цифр, содержащихся в других таблицах по образованию.

Первые два столбца содержат данные о положениях, касающихся обязательного образования. В первом столбце указываются нижние и верхние возрастные пределы. Так, 6-14 лет, например, означает, что на детей распространяется действие закона об обязательном образовании с возраста 6 и до 14 лет, если не предусмотрены исключения. Во втором столбце указано число лет обязательного посещения школы. Например, соответствующие положения могут предусматривать, что продолжительность обязательного обучения составляет 6 лет в возрасте с 6 до 14. Это означает, что действие этих положений в отношении ребенка прекращается по достижении им возраста 14 лет, или по завершении шестилетнего обучения (хотя ему может быть только 12 или 13 лет).

Однако во многих странах и территориях, где неотложной проблемой является обеспечение достаточного числа школ для всех детей, существование законов об обязательном образовании может представлять чисто академический интерес, поскольку почти все такие правовые положения освобождают ребенка от посещения школы, если пригодного учебного заведения нет на разумном расстоянии от его дома.

В третьем столбце указан возраст, в котором дети принимаются для обучения, предшествующего первой ступени. В большинстве стран такое обучение обеспечивается все еще на ограниченной основе, зачастую только в городах, но даже там во многих случаях лишь незначительная доля детей возрастных категорий, указанных в данной таблице, реально получает дошкольное образование.

Диаграммы для всех стран и территорий, которые соответствуют этим трем столбцам, дают наглядное представление о продолжительности обучения и вступительном возрасте для общего образования первой и второй ступеней согласно действующей в настоящее время системе образования.

Данные о педагогическом образовании и профессионально-техническом обучении не представлены. Условное обозначение «p» показывает продолжительность образования первой ступени, «S1» - первый этап общего образования второй ступени и «S2» - продолжительность второго этапа общего образования второй ступени. Следует отметить, что для некоторых стран и территорий не проводится различия между двумя этапами общего образования второй ступени. В этих случаях продолжительность образования данной ступени показана условным обозначением «S». Для ряда стран вступительный возраст и продолжительность образования для этих двух ступеней варьируют в зависимости от района или типа школы. На диаграмме показана наиболее характерная система.

В Таблице 3.1a представлены другие существующие варианты, а в Таблице 3.1b показаны изменения системы образования, которые произошли с 1980 г. К этой таблице следует обращаться при использовании данных о числе учащихся, приводимых в таблицах 3.3-3.8.

Таблица 3.2

В этой таблице представлены коэффициенты охвата по странам и территориям, население которых превышает 150 000 человек. Для стран с населением менее 150 000 человек демографических данных по отдельным возрастным группам не имеется. Демографическая статистика основывается на оценках и прогнозах Отдела народонаселения Организации Объединенных Наций, разработанных в 1994 г., а данные о численности учащихся, использованные для расчета брутто-коэффициентов охвата, приводятся в таблицах 3.3, 3.4, 3.7 и 3.10 настоящего *Ежегодника*. В тех случаях, когда имеются также данные о числе учащихся по возрастным группам для первой и второй ступеней образования, рассчитывался нетто-коэффициент охвата.

Все коэффициенты выражены в процентах. Брутто-коэффициент охвата учащихся получают делением общего числа учащихся всех возрастных групп на численность населения официальной возрастной группы, соответствующей конкретной ступени образования. Нетто-коэффициент охвата рассчитывался с учетом только той части контингента учащихся, которая соответствует возрастной группе рассматриваемой ступени образования.

Брутто-коэффициент охвата в системе дошкольного воспитания представляет собой общую численность детей,

Introductory texts in Russian
Textes d'introduction en russe
Textos de introducción en ruso

охваченных образованием, предшествующим первой ступени, независимо от возраста, в процентном выражении от возрастной группы населения, соответствующей национальным нормам для этой ступени образования. Поскольку нормы для этой ступени являются чрезвычайно гибкими, при проведении сравнений между странами следует проявлять осторожность.

Коэффициенты для первой и второй ступеней образования рассчитаны с учетом различий национальных систем образования и продолжительности обучения первой и второй ступеней общего образования. Для третьей ступени коэффициенты выражены в виде процентной доли, которая приходится на население пятилетней возрастной группы, следующей за официальным возрастом завершения среднего образования.

Возрастные группы, используемые для расчета коэффициентов охвата первой и второй ступеней, которые приводятся в данной таблице, определены в соответствии со следующими правилами:

1. Для стран с единой школьной системой каждой ступени возрастная группа определяется в соответствии с обычным возрастом начала обучения и нормальной продолжительностью общего школьного образования первой и второй ступеней, как указано в Таблице 3.1.

2. В отношении стран с несколькими системами образования различной продолжительности использована система, которой охвачено большинство учащихся.

3. Применялись сроки обучения, которые действовали в указанном году.

Возрастная группа для сводного коэффициента первой и второй ступеней определена путем учета общей численности лиц, входящих в эти две возрастные группы, определенные для первой и второй ступеней.

Коэффициенты охвата для второй ступени рассчитаны на основе общей численности учащихся, включая общее образование, педагогическое и профессионально-техническое образование. Более подробная информация о численности учащихся приводится в Таблице 3.7. Следует отметить, что брутто-коэффициенты охвата для дошкольного воспитания и для первой и второй ступеней включают учащихся всех возможных возрастов, в то время как соответствующее население ограничено официальными школьными возрастами, определенными в соответствии с вышеупомянутыми правилами. Поэтому для стран, где всеобщим образованием первой ступени охвачено почти все население школьного возраста, брутто-коэффициент охвата будет превышать 100, если фактическое возрастное распределение учащихся выходит за рамки официального школьного возраста.

Кроме того, в некоторых странах, где образованием первой ступени охвачено 100 процентов населения, неттокоэффициент охвата может быть меньше 100, если некоторые дети начального школьного возраста еще посещают дошкольные учреждения.

Таблица 3.3

Эти данные касаются образования, предшествующего первой ступени, например в яслях, детских садах, а также в дошкольных классах при школах. Детские комнаты, группы присмотра за детьми, игровые детские группы и т.п. были исключены. Если иного не оговорено, данные относятся как

к государственным, так и к частным заведениям. Данные о воспитателях относятся, как правило, к персоналу как на полной ставке, так и на неполной ставке. Показана также процентная доля учащихся частных учебных заведений (получающих и не получающих финансовую помощь) от общего числа детей, охваченных образованием, предшествующим первой ступени. В некоторых случаях данные этой таблицы следует рассматривать в качестве приблизительных показателей масштаба дошкольного образования - поскольку полных сведений не имеется. Дополнительная информация приводится в Таблице 3.1.

Таблица 3.4

Как правило, в этой таблице приводятся данные по частным и государственным заведениям первой ступени образования, включая начальные классы средних школ. С учебного года, начинающегося в 1994 г., включается специальное образование. Однако образование взрослых здесь не учитывается. При использовании этой таблицы следует учитывать информацию о продолжительности обучения, которая приводится в таблицах 3.1, 3.1a и 3.1b. Данные о преподавательском составе касаются в основном преподавателей на полных и неполных ставках. Это может сказаться на сопоставимости данных, особенно когда речь идет о соотношении числа учащихся и преподавателей в столбце 8, поскольку доля преподавателей на неполной ставке значительно колеблется по странам. Из этих данных по возможности исключен учебный персонал, который не занимается преподаванием (например некоторые директора школ, библиотекари, наставники и т.д.).

Таблица 3.5

В этой таблице представлено процентное распределение по годам обучения для общей численности учащихся (MF) и численности девочек (F). Как правило, проценты приводятся за учебные годы, начинающиеся в 1985 г., 1990 г. и два последних года, за которые имеются данные.

Таблица 3.6

В этой таблице указано число второгодников на первой ступени обучения и их процентное отношение к общему контингенту учащихся и численности учащихся на каждом году обучения.

В тех случаях, когда отсутствовали данные о численности второгодников в частных учебных заведениях, приводились оценки с целью обеспечения согласованности и последовательности серии данных о второгодниках, а также для облегчения сопоставления этих данных с численностью учащихся по годам обучения, представленной в Таблице 3.5

Как правило, приводятся данные за учебные годы, начинающиеся в 1985 г. и 1990 г., а также за два последних года, по которым они имеются.

Таблица 3.7

В этой таблице представлены данные о числе преподавателей и учащихся для каждого из трех типов образования второй ступени, т.е. общего, педагогического и технического и профессионального. Если не указано иное, данные относятся к государственным и частным школам.

В большинстве случаев данные содержат сведения о преподавателях на неполной ставке, доля которых особенно значительна в техническом и профессиональном образовании. Исключается персонал, не выполняющий учебных

Introductory texts in Russian
Textes d'introduction en russe
Textos de introducción en ruso

функций (например библиотекари, наставники, некоторые директора школ и т.д.).

Общее образование второй ступени: этот термин относится к образованию в школах второй ступени, обеспечивающих общую и специализированную подготовку на основе предшествующего по крайней мере четырехлетнего образования первой ступени и не преследующих цель подготовить учащихся непосредственно к той или иной профессии или роду деятельности. Такие школы могут называться средними или общеобразовательными школами, лицеями, гимназиями и т.д. и предлагать программы, завершение которых является минимальным условием для приема на обучение третьей ступени. В связи с желанием расширить учебную программу во многих странах получили развитие школы, обеспечивающие как общеобразовательную, так и профессиональную подготовку. Такие «комбинированные» школы также относятся к учебным заведениям «общего образования второй ступени».

Педагогическое образование второй ступени: этот термин относится к образованию, которое дают школы второй ступени, обеспечивающие подготовку учащихся для учительской профессии.

Техническое и профессиональное образование второй ступени: этот термин используется здесь для образования, получаемого в «школах второй ступени», целью которых является подготовка учащихся непосредственно по профессии или специальности непедагогического характера. Такие школы имеют много различных названий и значительно отличаются друг от друга по типу и продолжительности подготовки. Существует много курсов, рассчитанных на неполный рабочий день, и краткосрочных курсов, которые исключаются из статистики, поскольку они относятся к образованию взрослых. В заголовках таблиц используется сокращение «профессиональное образование».

Для международных сравнений эту таблицу следует использовать вместе с таблицами 3.1, 3.1а и 3.1b. Следует отметить, что для всех тех стран, где образование второй ступени состоит из двух этапов, данные относятся к обоим этапам.

Таблица 3.8

В этой таблице представлены сведения об общей численности учащихся (MF) и численности девочек (F) на второй ступени общего образования в процентном распределении по годам обучения. Как правило, процентные показатели приводятся за учебные годы, начинающиеся в 1985 г., 1990 г., и за два последних года, по которым имеются данные.

Таблица 3.9

Эта таблица показывает число студентов третьей ступени образования на 100 000 жителей. Относительные показатели рассчитаны на основе данных о численности студентов, представленных в Таблице 3.10, и статистики населения, предоставленной Отделом народонаселения Организации Объединенных Наций. В тех случаях, когда данные в Таблице 3.10 неполны, используются оценочные показатели для сохранения сопоставимости представленных показателей за различные годы.

Таблица 3.10

Данные этой таблицы касаются преподавательского состава и студентов всех учебных заведений как государственных, так и частных, в сфере образования третьей ступени.

Для большинства стран и территорий отдельно приводятся данные по следующим типам учебных заведений: (а) университеты и эквивалентные им учебные заведения, присваивающие ученые степени; (b) заочные учебные заведения университетского типа; (с) другие учебные заведения третьей ступени образования - они охватывают все другие виды образования третьей ступени в учебных заведениях неуниверситетского типа (педагогических колледжах, технических колледжах и т.д.).

Сбор отдельных сведений по заочным учебным заведениям университетского типа был начат в ЮНЕСКО в 1985/86 учебном году.

Сюда включались только те программы, которые позволяют получать признаваемые дипломы об образовании третьей ступени. Соответственно те программы, которые не могут быть приравнены к программам обычной системы образования, не учитываются.

Однако следует отметить, что критерии, применяемые для определения этих трех типов учебных заведений, могут быть не всегда одинаковы для рассматриваемых стран и территорий. Кроме того, вследствие реформ системы образования некоторые учебные заведения неуниверситетского типа в той или иной стране могут в разные годы присоединяться к университетам или признаваться в качестве эквивалентных учебных заведений. Поэтому к разбивке по типу учебных заведений следует подходить осторожно.

По возможности, приводимая статистика включает данные о числе преподавателей и студентов, занятых как полный, так и неполный рабочий день. В цифрах по педагогическому составу отражен в принципе вспомогательный преподавательский персонал (ассистенты, демонстраторы и т.д.), однако исключен персонал, не выполняющий преподавательских функций (администраторы, техники лабораторий и т.д.).

Таблица 3.11

Эта таблица, дополняющая данные Таблицы 3.10, представляет показатели численности студентов третьей ступени образования в соответствии с классификацией МСКО по категориям и областям специализации за последний год, по которому имеются сведения, а также по областям специализации за 1985 г. Используемые определения основаны на Международной стандартной классификации образования (МСКО).

Три категории, выделенные в этой таблице в соответствии с индексами МСКО (5, 6 и 7), могут быть определены следующим образом:

Категория 5: программы, после прохождения которых выдается свидетельство, не эквивалентное первой университетской степени. Программы этого типа обычно имеют «практическую» направленность в том смысле, что они предназначены для подготовки студентов в конкретных профессиональных областях, где они могут получить специальность.

Категория 6: программы, ведущие к получению первой университетской степени или ее эквивалента, например, «степени бакалавра».

Категория 7: программы, ведущие к получению послеуниверситетской ученой степени или ее эквивалента. Для

Introductory texts in Russian
Textes d'introduction en russe
Textos de introducción en ruso

прохождения программ этого типа обычно требуется наличие первой университетской степени или ее эквивалента. Они должны отражать специализацию в конкретной предметной области.

Под областью изучения понимается основная область специализации студента. Предметы, входящие в каждую из основных областей, соответствующих классификации МСКО, указаны во введении к Главе 3.

Таблица 3.12

В этой таблице представлено число студентов, успешно закончивших обучение. За последний год, по которому имеются данные, выпускники классифицируются в соответствии с уровнем (МСКО) полученной степени или диплома, а также по области изучения за 1981 г., 1986 г. и 1991 г. они распределяются только по ступени МСКО.

Указанный год соответствует календарному году, в котором присвоена квалификация. Например, данные, указанные за 1994 г., касаются степеней, присвоенных в конце 1993/94 академического года. Более подробная информация по этому вопросу приводится в предисловии к Главе 3.

Три категории, представленные в этой таблице в соответствии с индексами МСКО (5, 6 и 7), определяются следующим образом:

Категория 5: дипломы и свидетельства, не эквивалентные первой университетской степени. Они соответствуют высшему образованию сокращенной продолжительности, как правило, менее трех лет.

Категория 6: первые университетские степени или их эквиваленты, соответствующие высшему образованию продолжительностью от 3 до 5 лет, ведущему к получению таких квалификаций, как степень «бакалавра».

Категория 7: послеуниверситетские ученые степени или их эквиваленты. Эти степени могут получить посредством продолжения своих занятий лица, уже имеющие первую университетскую степень (или ее эквивалент). Например, степень «магистра», различные типы степени «доктора» и т.д.

Классификация по категориям предназначена устано-

вить различие между разными степенями и дипломами и облегчить международную сопоставимость квалификаций третьей ступени. Следует отметить, что классификация в соответствии с категориями МСКО никоим образом не подразумевает эквивалентности степеней и дипломов ни в рамках какой-либо страны, ни между странами.

Что касается предметов, входящих в различные области изучения, см. определения во введении к Главе 3.

Таблица 3.13

В соответствии с определением ЮНЕСКО, иностранным студентом является лицо, зачисленное в высшее учебное заведение той или иной страны и территории, в которой он не проживает постоянно. Однако большинство стран вели статистику на основе гражданства. Различия, вытекающие из применения этих двух критериев, могут в отдельных странах быть весьма значительными: например, в случае иммигрантов, не принявших гражданство принимающей страны, но постоянно проживающих в ней.

Таблица 3.14

В этой таблице показаны страны или территории происхождения иностранных студентов, зачисленных в высшие учебные заведения в 50 основных принимающих странах; в качестве основы взят последний год, за который имеется такая информация (для большинства стран - 1993 г.).

В таблицу включены также в качестве стран происхождения бывший СССР, бывшая Чехословакия и бывшая Югославия, поскольку ряд принимающих стран все еще проводят статистику иностранных студентов по этим классификациям.

Представленные данные не включают некоторые крупные принимающие страны, по которым не имеются последние данные (например Бразилия, Индия, Ливан, Швеция и т.д.).

Иностранные студенты, зачисленные в учебные заведения этих 50 стран, составляют около 95 процентов известного общемирового показателя.

Introductory texts in Russian
Textes d'introduction en russe
Textos de introducción en ruso

4 Расходы на образование

В этой главе приводятся четыре таблицы по расходам на образование, которые разделены на две основные категории.

Текущие расходы включают расходы на административное управление, заработную плату преподавателей и другого персонала, учебные материалы, стипендии и службы социального обеспечения.

К капитальным расходам относятся расходы на земельные участки, здания, строительство, оборудование и т.д. В эту статью входят также займы.

Данные, представленные в этой главе, относятся только к государственным расходам на образование, т.е. к государственным расходам на государственное образование, а также к субсидиям частным учебным заведениям. Показать частные расходы на образование не представлялось возможным в силу отсутствия данных по большому числу стран.

Государственные расходы на образование включают, если не указано иное, расходы на образование на всех административных уровнях в соответствии с конституционным устройством государств, т.е. на уровне центральных или федеральных правительств, правительств штатов, провинциальных или региональных властей, муниципальных и местных властей.

Как правило, эта статистика не учитывает иностранную помощь, получаемую для целей образования. Однако в тех случаях, когда имеется информация о включении иностранной помощи, это указывается в сноске.

Данные выражены в национальной валюте в текущих рыночных ценах. Обменные курсы между национальными валютами и долларом США приводятся в Приложении С.

Приводимый год соответствует календарному году, в котором начинается финансовый год. Хотя в большинстве стран и территорий финансовый год начинается в январе, т.е. фактически совпадает с календарным годом, приблизительно в 70 странах такого совпадения нет. В Приложении В приводится информация о начале финансового года в каждой стране и территории.

Данные, представленные в этом издании *Ежегодника*, могут отличаться от соответствующих данных за тот же год в предыдущих изданиях в результате пересмотров, связанных с получением дополнительной информации.

По странам, участвовавшим в недавних обследованиях ЮНЕСКО/ОЭЕР/Евростат (ЮОЕ) и предоставивших данные за годы, отличающиеся от тех, которые указаны в *Ежегоднике* 1995 г., могут быть разрывы во временных рядах, вызванные концептуальными изменениями, наиболее важным из которых является включение данных о частном финансировании образования. В результате этого данные в таблицах 4.3 и 4.4 теоретически относятся к государственным и частным расходам на образование, т.е. к расходам на (а) государственные, (b) зависимые от государства частные и (с) независимые частные учреждения, а также расходы самих этих учреждений. Однако следует отметить, что для многих соответствующих стран частный компонент является либо неполным, либо совсем отсутствует. Данные, представленные в таблицах 4.1 и 4.2, охватывают по-прежнему только государственные расходы, однако в случае ряда стран наиболее поздние цифры расходятся с предыдущими. Поэтому во всех таблицах страны, затронутые вышеуказанными изменениями, можно определить по черте, отделяющей последний справочный год от предыдущих.

Таблица 4.1

В этой таблице приводятся общие государственные расходы на образование с разбивкой на текущие и капитальные расходы.

Расходы на образование выражены также в процентах к валовому национальному продукту (ВНП) и к общим государственным расходам.

Почти по всем странам данные о ВНП предоставлены Всемирным банком. Поскольку эти данные ежегодно пересматриваются, процентные доли расходов на образование по отношению к ВНП могут иногда отличаться от тех, которые указаны в предыдущих изданиях *Ежегодника*.

Таблица 4.2

В этой таблице государственные текущие расходы на образование разбиты на следующие категории.

Расходы на управление, исключая персонал: все административные расходы, за исключением заработной платы административного персонала.

Заработная плата административного персонала: заработная плата на всех административных уровнях, включая инспекции, службы документации и педагогические исследования.

Заработная плата педагогического персонала: зарплата до вычетов и все другие дополнительные льготы, включая взносы в пенсионные фонды и фонды социального страхования, выплачиваемые преподавателям и вспомогательному педагогическому персоналу.

Зарплата персонала других категорий: зарплата обслуживающего персонала, уборщиков, шоферов, работников охраны и т.д.

Общая заработная плата персонала: общие выплаты трех предыдущих категорий.

Расходы на учебные материалы: расходы по статьям, непосредственно связанным с учебной деятельностью, таким, как покупка учебников и других школьных принадлежностей.

Стипендии: стипендии и все другие виды финансовой помощи, предоставляемой учащимся для обучения в данной стране или за границей.

Службы социального обеспечения: оплата пансиона, школьное питание, транспорт, медицинское обслуживание и т.д.

Прочие расходы: расходы, которые не могут быть классифицированы по вышеуказанным категориям, и другие расходы, связанные с функционированием и эксплуатацией зданий и оборудования.

Нераспределенные субсидии: правительственные субсидии и переводы государственным и частным учреждениям, которые не могут быть классифицированы по целям, главным образом в силу административной автономии получающих учреждений.

Что касается формы представления материала в данной таблице, следует сделать два замечания: (i) когда дается условное обозначение ./. без пояснения, то соответствующие данные включены в «прочие расходы»; (ii) несколько категорий в этой таблице отмечены условным обозначением ..., поскольку в ответах на вопросник нечетко показано, являются ли соответствующие расходы незначительными или включены в другие категории.

Таблица 4.3

В этой таблице дается процентная разбивка государственных текущих расходов по ступеням образования.

Introductory texts in Russian
Textes d'introduction en russe
Textos de introducción en ruso

В столбце «other types» («другие виды») включены расходы на специальное образование, образование взрослых и другие виды образования, которые не могут быть распределены по ступеням.

В столбце «not distributed» («нераспределенные данные»), как правило охватывающем неклассифицированные расходы, в отдельных случаях могут встречаться расходы на администрацию, в отношении которых нет разбивки по ступеням образования.

Таблица 4.4

В этой таблице приводится перекрестная классификация государственных текущих расходов по ступеням образования и по целям за последний год, по которому имеются данные.

Категории, использованные для разбивки расходов по целям, определяются в примечании к Таблице 4.2 выше.

В тех случаях, когда предоставленные данные не охватывают всех категорий расходов, используемых в этой таблице, для некоторых стран показаны только соответствующие категории.

Introductory texts in Russian
Textes d'introduction en russe
Textos de introducción en ruso

5 Наука и техника

В этой главе приводятся некоторые результаты проводимого ЮНЕСКО сбора данных в области науки и техники. Подавляющая часть данных была получена из ответов на рассылавшиеся государствам - членам ЮНЕСКО ежегодные статистические вопросники по людским ресурсам и расходам в области научных исследований и экспериментальных разработок (НИЭР), дополненных за счет данных, собранных из официальных докладов и публикаций.

Определения и понятия, используемые в вопроснике по научным исследованиям и экспериментальным разработкам, основаны на *Рекомендации о международной стандартизации статистики в области науки и техники* и могут быть найдены в соответствующем *Руководстве* (документ ЮНЕСКО ST-84/WS/12).

Ниже приводятся сокращенные варианты определений, излагаемых в вышеупомянутой Рекомендации.

Категории персонала

Следующие три категории научно-технического персонала определены в соответствии с выполняемой ими работой и квалификацией:

(1) *Научные работники и инженеры* - лица, которые работают в качестве таковых, то есть в качестве лиц, имеющих научно-техническую подготовку (как правило, законченное образование третьей ступени) в любой из определенных ниже областей науки, профессионально занимающихся деятельностью по НИЭР и выполняющих обязанности администраторов и другого персонала высокого уровня, который руководит проведением НИЭР.

(2) *Техники* - лица, занимающиеся в качестве таковых НИЭР и имеющие профессиональную или техническую подготовку определенного уровня в любой отрасли знаний или техники (как правило, не менее трех лет после первого этапа образования второй ступени).

(3) *Вспомогательный персонал* - лица, работа которых непосредственно связана с осуществлением НИЭР, то есть канцелярские служащие, секретари и административный персонал, квалифицированные, полуквалифицированные и неквалифицированные рабочие различных специальностей и любые другие вспомогательные работники. «Исключается» персонал охраны, уборки и обслуживания, занятый общей хозяйственной деятельностью.

Следует отметить, что, как правило, в соответствующие категории включается весь персонал, независимо от гражданства или страны происхождения.

Персонал, занятый НИЭР полный и неполный рабочий день и эквивалент полного рабочего дня.

Данные, касающиеся персонала, как правило, рассчитываются в эквиваленте полного рабочего дня (ЭПРД), особенно в отношении научных работников и инженеров.

Эквивалент полного рабочего дня (ЭПРД). Это единица измерения, которая соответствует одному лицу, занятому полный рабочий день в течение определенного периода времени; эта единица служит для пересчета числа лиц, занятых неполный рабочий день, в число лиц, занятых полный рабочий день.

Научные исследования и экспериментальные разработки (НИЭР)

В целом, НИЭР определяются как любая систематическая творческая деятельность, направленная на увели-чение объема знаний, включая знания о человеке, культуре и обществе, и использование этих знаний для разработки новых прикладных аспектов. К ним относятся фундаментальные исследования (экспериментальная или теоретическая деятельность без какой-либо непосредственной практической цели), прикладные исследования в таких областях, как сельское хозяйство, медицина, промышленная химия и т.д. (т.е. исследования, направленные в первую очередь на достижение какой-либо конкретной практической цели или задачи) и экспериментальные разработки, ведущие к появлению новых устройств, продукций или процессов.

Секторы деятельности

Секторы деятельности определяют те области экономики, в которых осуществляются НИЭР. Термин «сектор деятельности» отличает выполнение или осуществление мероприятий НИЭР от их финансирования.

Выделяются следующие три основных сектора деятельности: сектор производства, сектор высшего образования и сектор общих услуг, причем сектор производства оценивается на двух «уровнях» - деятельность в области НИЭР, «интегрированная» и «неинтегрированная» с производством. Сектор производства, таким образом, включает национальные и иностранные промышленные и коммерческие предприятия, которые производят и распределяют платные товары и услуги; сектор высшего образования включает учреждения образования третьей ступени, а также обслуживающие их научно-исследовательские институты, экспериментальные станции и т.д., в то время как сектор общих услуг включает различные государственные или правительственные учреждения, обслуживающие общество в целом.

Расходы на НИЭР

Расходы на НИЭР рассчитываются на основе внутренних текущих расходов, включая накладные расходы, и внутренних капитальных расходов. Сумма внутренних расходов, производимых национальными учреждениями, дает общий объем расходов страны, который является информацией, предоставляемой на международном уровне.

Общая сумма внутренних расходов на НИЭР представляет собой все расходы, произведенные на эти цели за рассматриваемый год в организациях и учреждениях, созданных на национальной территории, а также в учреждениях, физически находящихся вне ее.

Общая сумма расходов на НИЭР в соответствии с приводимым выше определением включает *текущие расходы*, в том числе накладные расходы, и *капитальные расходы*. Текущие внутренние расходы далее подразделяются на оплату труда и другие текущие расходы.

Источники финансирования

Приведенные ниже источники финансирования внутренних расходов на НИЭР позволяют определить финансовых спонсоров такой деятельности:

Правительственные фонды: средства, предоставляемые центральным (федеральным) правительством, властями штата или местными властями.

Фонды производственных предприятий и специальные фонды: средства, предоставляемые на НИЭР учреждениями, относящимися к сектору производства, и все суммы, полученные из «фондов технического и экономического развития» и других аналогичных фондов.

Introductory texts in Russian
Textes d'introduction en russe
Textos de introducción en ruso

Иностранные фонды: фонды, получаемые из-за границы, на национальные НИЭР.

Прочие фонды: средства, которые нельзя отнести ни к какой из вышеуказанных категорий.

Примечания к таблицам

Таблицы в этой главе представлены в трех разделах. Первый раздел (А) включает **Таблицу 5.1,** в которой приведены отдельные показатели, касающиеся научных работников и инженеров и расходов в области НИЭР.

Следующие два раздела включают 5 таблиц, содержащих базовую информацию, полученную с помощью статистических обследований ЮНЕСКО, а также из официальных докладов и публикаций. Данные, касающиеся Бельгии, Германии, Канады, Турции, Финляндии и Японии, взяты из публикации ОЭСР «Базовая статистика науки и техники» - издание 1995 г.

Второй раздел (В) состоит из 2 таблиц, касающихся людских ресурсов.

Таблица 5.2 содержит данные по научным работникам, инженерам и техникам, участвующим в деятельности в области научных исследований и экспериментальных разработок, с указанием некоторых данных по женщинам, когда такие сведения имеются. В этой таблице, если не указано иное, данные приведены в эквиваленте полного рабочего дня.

Таблица 5.3 охватывает весь персонал, участвующий в НИЭР, и показывает его распределение по трем секторам деятельности (производство, высшее образование и общие услуги) с приведением как абсолютных данных (в эквиваленте полного рабочего дня, если не оговаривается иное), так и процентного распределения. В связи с различиями в структуре сектора производства в странах с различными социально-экономическими системами для облегчения сравнений в рамках этого сектора указывается также два «уровня интеграции». Это позволяет получить представление о степени взаимосвязи между НИЭР и производством в различных социально-экономических системах. Показаны также различные категории персонала, занятого в этих секторах.

Третий раздел (С) включает 3 таблицы и дает общую картину расходов на НИЭР. Данные приводятся в национальной валюте.

Абсолютные показатели расходов на НИЭР не следует сопоставлять по странам. Такие сопоставления потребовали бы перевода национальных валют в какую-либо общую валюту на основе официальных обменных курсов, поскольку специальные обменные курсы для НИЭР не существуют. Официальные обменные курсы не всегда отражают реальные расходы на НИЭР, и сопоставления, основанные на таких курсах, могут привести к неправильным выводам. Тем не менее такие данные представляют определенный интерес, указывая по крайней мере общий порядок расходов на НИЭР. С обменными курсами между национальными валютами и долларом Соединенных Штатов Америки читатель может ознакомиться в Приложении С.

В **Таблице 5.4** общие расходы на НИЭР подразделяются по типам расходов на капитальные и текущие расходы, в которых в свою очередь выделяются расходы на персонал и другие текущие расходы; дается процентное отношение текущих расходов к общей сумме расходов.

Структура финансирования НИЭР приводится в **Таблице 5.5,** где дается распределение общей суммы расходов (или, в качестве варианта, текущих расходов) по четырем основным категориям источников средств. Аналогичным образом, данные приводятся в национальных валютах и в виде процентного соотношения, и эта информация считается достаточно полной, для того чтобы читатель смог сопоставить по странам роль различных источников финансирования НИЭР.

В **Таблице 5.6** дано распределение общих и текущих расходов по трем секторам деятельности. Как и в Таблице 5.3, сектор производства подразделяется на два «уровня интеграции». Расходы представлены в абсолютных цифрах, а для облегчения сопоставления по странам в тех случаях, когда имеются достаточно полные данные, приводится также процентное распределение по секторам.

Научно-исследовательские работники, заинтересованные в получении более подробной информации или разъяснений по какой-либо конкретной стране, в том что касается национальных определений, охвата или ограничений данных, представленных в этих таблицах, могут обращаться со своими запросами в Отдел статистики.

Introductory texts in Russian
Textes d'introduction en russe
Textos de introducción en ruso

6 Сводные таблицы по культуре и коммуникации по континентам, крупным регионам и группам стран

В этой главе приводится ряд сводных таблиц по отдельным темам в области культуры и коммуникации. Статистические данные, содержащиеся в этих таблицах, приводятся по континентам, крупным регионам и группам стран, состав которых указывается на стр. XII этого *Ежегодника*. Здесь рассмотрены следующие темы: ежедневные газеты, типографская и писчая бумага, число радиоприемников и телевизоров.

Следует указать, что в связи с трудностями оценки достоверности имеющихся статистических данных и в связи с отсутствием информации по многим странам, данные по всему миру и регионам, приводимые в этой главе, дают лишь очень приблизительное представление о существующей ситуации.

Кроме того, в силу неадекватности данных прекращено представление региональных оценок выпуска книг и кинопродукции.

Таблица 6.1

В этой таблице приводятся мировые и региональные оценочные данные по ежедневным газетам в 1980 г. и 1994 г.

Статистические данные касаются числа газет, их тиража и тиража на 1 000 жителей.

Таблицы 6.2 и 6.3

Мировые и региональные оценочные данные относительно выпуска и потребления газетной и других видов типографской и писчей бумаги в 1970 г., 1980 г., 1990 г. и 1994 г. были рассчитаны на основе статистических данных, представленных ЮНЕСКО Продовольственной и сельскохозяйственной организацией ООН (ФАО).

Таблица 6.4

В этой таблице приводятся региональные показатели общего числа радиоприемников и их количества в расчете на 1 000 жителей в 1970 г., 1980 г., 1990 г. и 1994 г.

Таблица 6.5

В Таблице 6.5 приводится общее число телевизоров и их количество в расчете на 1 000 жителей в 1970 г., 1980 г., 1990 г. и 1994 г.

Introductory texts in Russian
Textes d'introduction en russe
Textos de introducción en ruso

7 Печатные материалы

Эта глава разбита на четыре раздела. В первом разделе (таблицы 7.1 и 7.2) приводятся статистические данные о библиотеках. Во втором разделе (таблицы 7.3-7.8) помещены статистические сведения о выпуске книг. Третий раздел посвящен статистике газет и периодических изданий (таблицы 7.9-7.11), тогда как последний раздел содержит данные о производстве, импорте, экспорте и потреблении газетной бумаги и другой типографской и писчей бумаги (Таблица 7.12).

Раздел 1

В первом разделе содержатся две таблицы. В Таблице 1 приводятся национальные статистические данные по различным категориям библиотек, их фондам, комплектованию и количеству зарегистрированных пользователей. В другой таблице приводятся более подробные статистические данные о приобретенных фондах, выдаче книг по абонементу, расходах, персонале и т.д. библиотек высших учебных заведений. Для получения соответствующей информации о национальных и публичных библиотеках читателю следует обратиться к изданию 1993 г. *Ежегодника*.

Начиная с 1950 г. ЮНЕСКО раз в два года собирала статистические данные о библиотеках. Эта периодичность была изменена на три года в соответствии с Рекомендацией о международной стандартизации библиотечной статистики, принятой Генеральной конференцией ЮНЕСКО на ее шестнадцатой сессии в 1970 г. В первых трех обследованиях, проведенных после принятия Рекомендации 1970 г., запрашивались данные соответственно за 1971 г., 1974 г. и 1977 г. В целях облегчения сбора данных и увеличения количества ответов от государств-членов было решено с 1980 г. обследовать не более двух категорий библиотек одновременно. В этой связи вопросник по библиотекам был разделен на три части, касающиеся соответственно (1) национальных и публичных библиотек, (2) библиотек высших учебных заведений и школьных библиотек и (3) специальных библиотек, причем каждая из этих частей направляется поочередно. Таким образом, обследования за 1985 г., 1988 г., 1991 г. и 1994 г. касались национальных и публичных библиотек, тогда как обследования, проведенные в 1983 г., в 1986 г., в 1989 г., 1992 г. и 1995 г., сосредоточивались на библиотеках высших учебных заведений и школьных библиотеках. Статистика о специальных библиотеках была получена на основании обследований за 1984 г. и 1987 г., однако по различным причинам проведение этих обследований было приостановлено.

Большинство приводимых ниже определений взято из вышеуказанной Рекомендации. Тем не менее в некоторых случаях, касающихся, например, аудиовизуальных и других библиотечных материалов или зарегистрированных пользователей, они либо не отражены в Рекомендации, либо подверглись изменениям с целью лучшего соответствия некоторым аспектам развития библиотечного дела.

1. *Библиотека*: библиотекой считается, независимо от ее названия, любое организованное собрание печатных книг и периодических изданий или любых других графических или аудиовизуальных материалов, а также обслуживающий персонал, обеспечивающий и облегчающий использование тех материалов, которые необходимы для удовлетворения потребностей пользователей в области информации, научных исследований, образования или досуга.

Подпадающие под это определение библиотеки подсчитываются в качестве административных единиц и пунктов обслуживания следующим образом: (а) *административная единица* - любая независимая библиотека или группа библиотек с одним директором или единой администрацией; (b) *пункт обслуживания* - любая библиотека, обслуживающая читателей в отдельном помещении, независимо от того, является ли она самостоятельной или частью более крупной административной единицы.

Библиотеки классифицируются следующим образом:

2. *Национальные библиотеки*: библиотеки, которые независимо от их названия отвечают за приобретение и хранение экземпляров всех основных публикаций, издаваемых в стране, и выступают в качестве «книгохранилища» на основании закона или других установок и которые обычно составляют национальную библиографию.

3. *Библиотеки высших учебных заведений*: библиотеки, которые, в первую очередь, обслуживают студентов и преподавателей университетов и других учебных заведений третьей ступени.

4. *Другие крупные неспециализированные библиотеки*: неспециализированные библиотеки научного характера, которые не являются ни библиотеками высших учебных заведений, ни национальными библиотеками, даже если они выполняют функции национальной библиотеки для определенного географического района.

5. *Школьные библиотеки*: библиотеки, которые существуют при школах любого типа, дающих образование ниже третьей ступени, и которые должны прежде всего обслуживать учащихся и преподавателей этих школ, даже если они могут быть также открыты для широкой публики.

6. *Специальные библиотеки*: библиотеки, находящиеся в ведении ассоциации, правительственной службы, парламента, научно-исследовательского учреждения (за исключением институтов, принадлежащих университетам), научного общества, профессиональной организации, музея, коммерческого или промышленного предприятия, торговой палаты и т.д. или другой организованной группы, причем наибольшая часть их фондов касается конкретной дисциплины или тематики, например естественных наук, социальных наук, сельского хозяйства, химии, медицины, экономических наук, технических наук, права, истории.

7. *Публичные (или массовые) библиотеки*: библиотеки, обслуживающие бесплатно или за символическую плату жителей населенного пункта или района; они могут обслуживать все население или особые категории читателей, таких, как дети, военнослужащие, больные в больницах, заключенные, рабочие и служащие.

В отношении библиотечных фондов, их пополнения, выдачи книг, расходов, персонала и т.д. приводятся следующие определения и классификации:

8. *Фонды*: все библиотечные материалы, предоставляемые библиотекой читателям.

Статистические данные, касающиеся библиотечных фондов, охватывают следующие *документы для пользователей*, включая материалы, выдаваемые по абонементу:

(а) книги и переплетенные периодические издания;
(b) рукописи;

Introductory texts in Russian
Textes d'introduction en russe
Textos de introducción en ruso

(*c*) микроформы;

(*d*) аудиовизуальные документы;

(*e*) другие библиотечные материалы.

9. *Ежегодное пополнение*: совокупность материалов, которые были дополнительно включены в фонды в течение одного года за счет покупки, даров, обмена или каких-либо других способов.

Статистические данные о пополнениях охватывают те же аспекты, что и статистика фондов.

10. *Том*: любое печатное или рукописное произведение, содержащееся в одном переплете или в папке.

11. *Аудиовизуальные материалы*: библиотечные материалы, не являющиеся книгами или микроформами, для просмотра и/или прослушивания которых требуется использование специального оборудования. Сюда относятся такие материалы, как пластинки, магнитофонные пленки, кассеты, кинофильмы, слайды, диапозитивы, видеозаписи и т.д.

12. *Другие библиотечные материалы*: все материалы, кроме книг, переплетенных периодических изданий, рукописей, микроформ и аудиовизуальных материалов. Сюда относятся такие материалы, как карты, схемы, художественные репродукции, фотографии, диорамы и т.п.

13. *Зарегистрированный пользователь*: лицо, записавшееся в библиотеку с целью пользования материалами из ее фондов в самой библиотеке или вне ее помещений.

14. *Текущие расходы*: расходы на функционирование библиотеки, то есть расходы на персонал, комплектование и т.п.

15. *Квалифицированные библиотекари*: все работающие в библиотеках лица, которые получили общую подготовку в области библиотечного дела или информационных наук. Подготовка может быть получена путем формального образования или посредством продолжительной работы в библиотеке под руководством специалистов.

16. *Обслуживаемое население*: (a) *публичными библиотеками*: общее число жителей районов, обслуживаемых собственно публичными библиотеками, т.е. библиотеками, получающими финансовую помощь полностью или большей частью от государственных властей (муниципальные или районные библиотеки); (b) *школьными библиотеками*: общее число учащихся и преподавателей начальных и средних школ, обслуживаемых школьными библиотеками; (c) *библиотеками высших учебных заведений*: общее число студентов, профессорско-преподавательского состава и сотрудников, имеющих право пользования услугами библиотек в университетах и других учебных заведениях третьей ступени.

Таблица 7.1

В Таблице 7.1 представлены отобранные статистические данные по фондам, ежегодным пополнениям и зарегистрированным пользователям для различных категорий библиотек.

Таблица 7.2

Таблица 7.2 относится к библиотекам высших учебных заведений. В эту таблицу включены только те страны, статистика которых дает больше информации, чем сведения в Таблице 7.1.

Раздел 2

Вплоть до 1985 г. национальная статистика выпуска книг составлялась в соответствии с определениями и классификациями, установленными в Рекомендации о международной стандартизации статистики выпуска книг и периодических изданий, принятой в 1964 г. Генеральной конференцией ЮНЕСКО. Начиная с 1986 г. и далее сбор и предоставление на международном уровне статистических данных о книгах (а также о газетах и периодических изданиях) регламентируется пересмотренным вариантом Рекомендации 1964 г., который был принят Генеральной конференцией ЮНЕСКО на ее двадцать третьей сессии в ноябре 1985 г.

Согласно Рекомендации 1985 г., статистика выпуска книг должна охватывать публикуемые в данной стране печатные непериодические издания, доступные для широкой публики и подлежащие обычно включению в национальные библиографии различных стран, за исключением следующих категорий:

(a) *Публикации, предназначенные для рекламных целей*, при условии, что литературный или научный текст носит вспомогательный характер и что они распространяются бесплатно (торговые каталоги, проспекты и другие виды коммерческой, промышленной и туристической рекламы; публикации, привлекающие внимание к продукции или услугам, предоставляемым издателем, хотя в них может содержаться описание деятельности или технических достижений в некоторых областях промышленности или торговли).

(b) *Публикации, относящиеся к следующим категориям, когда они рассматриваются как имеющие временное значение*: расписания, прейскуранты, телефонные справочники и т.д.; программы спектаклей, выставок, ярмарок и т.д.; уставы и отчеты различных фирм, инструкции, циркуляры и т.д. компаний; календари и т.д.

(c) *Публикации, относящиеся к следующим категориям, в которых текст не является важнейшей составной частью*: музыкальные произведения (партитуры и сборники нот) при условии, что музыка в них занимает более важное место, чем текст; карты и планы, за исключением атласов.

В статистику выпуска книг должны включаться, в частности, следующие виды изданий:

1. *Правительственные издания*, т.е. издания, выпускаемые органами государственной администрации или их вспомогательными учреждениями, за исключением изданий конфиденциального характера или предназначенных только для внутреннего пользования.

2. *Школьные учебники*, т.е. книги, предписанные для учащихся, получающих образование первой и второй ступеней.

3. *Университетские диссертации*.

4. *Оттиски*, т.е. перепечатки части уже вышедшей книги или периодического издания при условии, что они имеют название, самостоятельную нумерацию страниц и представляют собой отдельные произведения.

5. *Публикации, являющиеся частью серии*, но представляющие собой отдельную библиографическую единицу.

6. *Иллюстрированные издания*: (i) сборники эстампов, репродукций художественных произведений, рисунков и т.д., когда такие сборники образуют цельные тома с пронумерованными страницами и иллюстрации в них сопровождаются хотя бы даже самым кратким пояснительным текстом,

Introductory texts in Russian
Textes d'introduction en russe
Textos de introducción en ruso

относящимся к этим произведениям или к их авторам; (ii) альбомы, иллюстрированные книги и брошюры, написанные в форме последовательного изложения с рисунками, иллюстрирующими отдельные эпизоды; (iii) альбомы и иллюстрированные книги для детей; (iv) книги комиксов.

При составлении этой статистики необходимо пользоваться следующими определениями:

(a) *непериодической публикацией* называется издание, выпускаемое одновременно целиком или через определенные промежутки времени отдельными томами, число которых обычно установлено заранее;

(b) термин *печатный* означает воспроизведение любым механическим способом, независимо от его характера;

(c) *опубликованным в данной стране* считается издание, выпущенное издателем, зарегистрированное местопребывание которого находится в стране, где составляется статистика, без учета в данном случае места печатания или распространения издания. Издание, опубликованное одним или несколькими издателями, зарегистрированное местопребывание которых находится в двух или более странах, рассматривается как изданное в стране или странах, где оно вышло в свет;

(d) издание считается *доступным для публики*, если оно может быть приобретено за плату или получено бесплатно. Доступными для публики в целом считаются также издания, предназначенные для ограниченного круга лиц, такие, как некоторые правительственные публикации, издания научных обществ, политических или профессиональных организаций и т.д.;

(e) *книгой* является непериодическое печатное издание объемом не менее 49 страниц, не считая обложки, опубликованное в данной стране и доступное для публики;

(f) *брошюрой* является непериодическое печатное издание объемом не менее 5 и не более 48 страниц, не считая обложки, опубликованное в данной стране и доступное для публики;

(g) *первым изданием* является впервые опубликованная оригинальная или переводная рукопись;

(h) *переиздание* представляет собой публикацию, которая отличается от предыдущих изданий изменениями, внесенными в содержание (пересмотренное издание) или форму (новое издание) и требует нового индекса ISBN;

(i) *перепечатка* - не имеет изменений в содержании и форме, не считая исправления опечаток предыдущего издания и не требует нового индекса ISBN. Перепечатка, осуществленная каким-либо другим издателем, помимо первоначального издателя, считается переизданием;

(j) *перевод* - это публикация, которая воспроизводит произведение на ином языке, нежели язык оригинала;

(к) *название* - термин, применяемый для обозначения печатного издания, образующего единое целое и выпущенного в одном или нескольких томах.

Этот раздел включает семь таблиц, которые охватывают выпуск в целом.

В Таблицах 7.3-7.8 представлены данные, собираемые каждый год посредством вопросников, направляемых примерно в 200 стран и территорий. Если не указано иное, то эти данные охватывают книги и брошюры, содержащие оригинальные работы или переводы. Однако некоторые категории публикаций, которые согласно Рекомендации должны включаться в статистику выпуска книг (например правительственные издания, школьные учебники, университетские диссертации, оттиски, иллюстрированные произведения) или исключаться из такой статистики (например публикации для рекламных целей, издания временного характера, издания, в которых текст не является важнейшей составной частью), в статистических целях по-разному классифицируются в различных странах. В отсутствие полной и точной информации не удалось указать определенные несовпадения такого рода между различными национальными статистическими данными и Рекомендацией.

В Таблицы 7.5 и 7.8 включены только те страны, которые смогли представить статистику в соответствии с классификацией по темам, установленной в Рекомендации 1985 г. Приведенная ниже классификация, которая основывается на Универсальной десятичной классификации (УДК), взята из этой Рекомендации (соответствующие разделы УДК отмечены в скобках).

1. Общее (0);
2. Философия, психология (1);
3. Религия, теология (2);
4. Социология, статистика (30-31);
5. Политика, экономика (32-33);
6. Право, государственная администрация, социальное вспомоществование, обеспечение и страхование (34, 351-354, 36);
7. Военное искусство и наука (335-359);
8. Просвещение, преподавание, подготовка кадров, досуг (37);
9. Торговля, связь, транспорт, туризм (38);
10. Этнография, культурная антропология (обычаи, фольклор, нравы, традиции) (39);
11. Филология, языкознание, лингвистика (4);
12. Математика (51);
13. Естественные науки (52-59);
14. Медицинские науки, общественное здравоохранение (61);
15. Инженерное дело, техника, промышленность, промыслы и ремесла (62, 66-69);
16. Сельское хозяйство, лесоводство, животноводство, охота и рыболовство (63);
17. Домоводство (64);
18. Управление, администрация и организация (65);
19. Материальное планирование, городское и национальное планирование, архитектура (70-72);
20. Пластическое и графическое искусство, фотография (73-77);
21. Музыка, исполнительское искусство, театр, фильмы и кинотеатры (78, 791-792);
22. Игры и спорт (793-799);
23. Литература (8);
    (a) история литературы и литературная критика;
    (b) литературные тексты;
24. География (91);
25. История, биографии (92-99).

В тех случаях, когда общий итог не соответствует сумме составных частей, разница либо представляет собой число произведений, не распределенных по основным десяти

Introductory texts in Russian
Textes d'introduction en russe
Textos de introducción en ruso

разделам Универсальной десятичной классификации или по двадцати пяти тематическим группам, либо объясняется округлением цифр. В таблицах 7.3-7.6 указывается для каждой страны только общая цифра и количество книг, а разница соответствует количеству брошюр.

Таблица 7.3

В этой таблице представлены данные за 1991-1994 гг. о числе названий *первых изданий* и *переизданий* оригинальных произведений (или переводов) по десяти основным разделам УДК. В нее включены только те страны, по которым ЮНЕСКО могла подготовить статистику, относящуюся по крайней мере к одному из трех рассматриваемых годов.

Таблица 7.4

Приведенные в Таблице 7.4 цифры указывают число названий *первых изданий* и *переизданий* по тематическим группам. В отношении тех стран, где общее число изданий соответствует числу первых изданий, следует исходить из того, что там либо отсутствовали переиздания, либо число их неизвестно. Аналогичным образом, в тех случаях, когда общее число названий не отличается от общего количества книг, можно считать, что либо не публиковались брошюры, либо их количество неизвестно.

Таблица 7.5

В этой таблице представлены данные за 1991-1994 гг. о числе экземпляров *первых изданий, переизданий* и *перепечаток* оригинальных произведений (или переводов) по разделам УДК.

Таблица 7.6

Приведенные в Таблице 7.6 цифры означают число экземпляров *первых изданий, переизданий* и *перепечаток* по тематическим группам. Замечания к Таблице 7.4, касающиеся общего числа изданий и первых изданий, относятся также к этой таблице.

Таблица 7.7

Цифры в этой таблице указывают как *первые издания*, так и *переиздания* школьных учебников, которые определяются в Рекомендации как книги, предписанные для учащихся, получающих образование первой и второй ступеней.

Таблица 7.8

Цифры в Таблице 7.8 указывают как *первые издания*, так и *переиздания* детских книг.

Раздел 3

Статистика в Таблицах 7.9 и 7.11 охватывает ежедневные и неежедневные газеты, а также периодические издания.

Как правило, национальная статистика по газетам и другим периодическим изданиям должна составляться в соответствии с определениями и классификацией, установленными в пересмотренной в 1985 г. Рекомендации о международной стандартизации статистики выпуска и распределения книг, газет и периодических изданий. Данные, приводимые в Таблицах 7.9 и 7.11, регулярно публикуются в этом *Ежегоднике*, тогда как данные о периодических изданиях по типам представляются раз в два года. В соответствии с Рекомендацией 1985 г. национальная статистика по прессе должна охватывать опубликованные в данной стране печатные периодические издания, доступные для широкой публики, за исключением публикаций для рекламных целей, публикаций временного характера и

публикаций, в которых текст не является важнейшей составной частью. Однако следующие виды издания, в частности, должны включаться в статистику о газетах и периодических изданиях: правительственные периодические издания, академические и научные журналы, периодические издания профессиональных, профсоюзных, политических, спортивных и других организаций, публикации, выходящие раз в год или реже, приходские бюллетени, школьные газеты и журналы, газеты предприятий, а также программы развлечений, радио и телевидения, если литературный текст в них имеет существенное значение.

При составлении этой статистики необходимо пользоваться следующими определениями:

1. *Периодической* публикацией называется издание, образующее непрерывную серию выпусков под одним и тем же названием, выходящих с регулярными или нерегулярными интервалами в течение неопределенного времени, причем отдельные выпуски серии имеют порядковые номера или каждый выпуск имеет дату.

2. Периодические издания подразделяются на две категории: газеты и периодические публикации.

(a) *Газетами* являются периодические издания, которые предназначены для широкой публики и служат прежде всего первичным источником письменной информации о текущих событиях, связанных с общественными делами, международными проблемами, политикой и т.д. Подпадающие под это определение газеты, выходящие не реже четырех раз в неделю, считаются ежедневными газетами; газеты, выходящие три раза в неделю и реже, не считаются ежедневными газетами.

(b) *Периодическими изданиями* являются периодические публикации, касающиеся вопросов, представляющих весьма широкий интерес, или же содержащие преимущественно исследования и фактическую информацию по таким специализированным темам, как законодательство, финансы, торговля, медицина, мода, спорт и т.д. Под это определение подпадают специализированные журналы, обзорные журналы, иллюстрированные журналы и другие периодические издания за исключением публикаций, перечисленных в подпунктах (a)-(c) во втором пункте раздела 2 данной главы.

3. Данные о *тиражах* показывают средний дневной тираж или средний тираж каждого номера для неежедневных изданий. Эти данные должны включать количество экземпляров, (a) проданных непосредственно, (b) проданных по подписке и (c) распространяемых преимущественно бесплатно как внутри страны, так и за рубежом.

При анализе данных в приведенных таблицах следует иметь в виду, что в некоторых случаях применяемые отдельными странами методы учета, определения и классификации не полностью отвечают стандартам, рекомендованным ЮНЕСКО. Например, данные о тиражах должны относиться к числу распределенных экземпляров, как это указано выше. Однако представляется, что некоторые страны сообщили о количестве отпечатанных экземпляров, которые обычно выше, чем распространяемый тираж.

Таблица 7.9

В этой таблице представляются данные о количестве, общем тираже и тираже на 1 000 жителей ежедневных газет за 1980 г., 1985 г., 1990 г. и 1994 г.

Introductory texts in Russian
Textes d'introduction en russe
Textos de introducción en ruso

Таблица 7.10

Эта таблица представляет данные за последний год в период 1989-1994 гг., по которому имеются сведения о количестве, общем тираже и тираже на 1 000 жителей неежедневных газет и других периодических изданий.

Таблица 7.11

В этой таблице приводятся данные по видам периодических изданий за последний год, по которому имеется статистика в период 1989-1994 гг. Внимание читателя обращается на то, что сумма двух промежуточных итогов в этой таблице должна соответствовать общему количеству периодических изданий в таблице 7.10.

Однако эти цифры не всегда сходятся, возможно в силу того, что данные поступают из различных источников, или из-за того, что некоторые страны все еще не могут применять международные стандарты. Тем не менее было сочтено предпочтительным опубликовать данные по максимальному числу стран, а не ограничиваться теми странами, по которым имеется полная и последовательная статистика. По этой причине следует с осторожностью подходить к интерпретации информации, которая приводится в данной таблице, не забывая о том, что во многих случаях указанные цифры дают весьма приблизительное представление о существующей ситуации.

Раздел 4

Приводимые в Таблице 7.12 данные относятся к производству, импорту, экспорту и потреблению бумаги для печатной продукции, то есть газетной, а также типографской бумаги (помимо газетной) и писчей бумаги за 1970 г., 1975 г., 1980 г., 1985 г., 1990 г. и 1994 г. Как и в предыдущие годы, эти данные представлялись *Продовольственной и сельскохозяйственной организацией Объединенных Наций (ФАО)*. Читатели, нуждающиеся в дополнительной информации, могут почерпнуть ее в публикуемом ФАО сборнике *Yearbook of Forest Products* (Ежегодник лесной продукции).

Термин *газетная бумага* (пункт 641.1, Пересмотр 2, Международной стандартной торговой классификации) означает отбеленную безразмерную или не имеющую точных размеров типографскую бумагу без покрытия, такого типа, который обычно используется для газет. Один квадратный метр газетной бумаги весит от 45 до 60 граммов, и не менее 70 процентов веса волокнистого вещества обычно получается из механически размолотой пульпы.

Определение *другая типографская и писчая бумага* (пункт 641.2, Пересмотр 2, Международной стандартной торговой классификации) означает бумагу, кроме газетной бумаги в рулонах или в листах, пригодную для типографской печати или письма. Оно не охватывает изделий, производимых из типографской или писчей бумаги, таких, как почтовая бумага, тетради для упражнений, регистрационные журналы и т.п.

Для тех стран, по которым отсутствует раздельная информация по двум вышеупомянутым категориям бумаги, в разряде газетной бумаги указана общая цифра.

Introductory texts in Russian
Textes d'introduction en russe
Textos de introducción en ruso

8 Культурное наследие

Эта глава касается культурного наследия, как оно определено в рамках категории ноль в Структуре статистики культуры ЮНЕСКО (ССК). Вновь приводятся только данные, касающиеся музеев и учреждений родственного характера, а данные в отношении архивных учреждений читатель может почерпнуть в издании *Ежегодника* 1990 г.

Первая попытка ЮНЕСКО подготовить международные статистические данные по музеям и родственным учреждениям была предпринята в начале 50-х годов. Начиная с 1962 г. и далее статистический вопросник рассылался каждые два года вплоть до 1974 г., когда было решено, что обследования следует проводить на регулярной основе каждые три года ввиду того, что в этой области изменения происходят нечасто.

Международный сбор статистических данных о музеях и соответственно их сопоставление представляет определенные трудности в связи с почти полным отсутствием общепринятых стандартов и норм. Например, некоторые страны включают в свою статистику о музеях данные об исторических памятниках и археологических объектах, однако не учитывают зоологические и ботанические сады, аквариумы, природные заповедники и т.п. В других странах дело обстоит как раз наоборот. Кроме этого, не все страны учитывают музеи, которые являются собственностью отдельных лиц или частных организаций.

Отсутствие согласовнных в международном плане определений и классификации в немалой степени сказывается на качестве, количестве и полноте собираемых статистических данных. В связи с этим любой вид международного сопоставления данных приходится осуществлять очень осторожно.

Для того чтобы добиться по крайне мере минимальной степени сопоставимости, категории и термины, использовавшиеся в обследованиях с 1977 г., основывались на определениях, принятых *Международным советом музеев (ИКОМ)*.

Для целей этих обследований термин *музей* определяется как *некоммерческое постоянное учреждение, которое стоит на службе общества и развития,* доступно для всех и которое приобретает, сохраняет, изучает, представляет и экспонирует в целях исследования, просвещения и развития досуга материальные предметы человека и окружающей его среды. Помимо определенных таким образом музеев, в обследования включаются следующие объекты, признаваемые ИКОМ как имеющие музейный характер:

(a) хранилища и выставочные галереи, функционирование которых постоянно обеспечивается библиотеками и архивными центрами;

(b) природные, археологические и этнографические памятники и объекты и исторические памятники и объекты, имеющие *музейный характер* в силу того, что они занимаются приобретением, хранением и представлением экпонатов;

(c) учреждения, демонстрирующие живые экспонаты, такие, как ботанические и зоологические сады, аквариумы, виварии и т.д.;

(d) природные заповедники;

(e) научные центры и планетарии.

Для статистических целей музеи и родственные учреждения подсчитываются по количеству административных единиц, а не по числу экспонируемых собраний.

В целях классификации музеев и родственных учреждений по *превалирующей теме выставок и собраний* использовались следующие критерии:

(a) *музеи искусств*: музеи, в которых выставляются произведения изящных и прикладных искусств. В эту группу входят такие музеи, как музеи скульптуры, картинные галереи, музеи фотографий и кино, архитектурные музеи и т.д. В эту категорию также включаются хранилища и выставочные галереи, функционирование которых постоянно обеспечивается библиотеками и архивными центрами;

(b) *археологические и исторические музеи:* цель исторических музеев заключается в том, чтобы показать историческую эволюцию региона, страны или провинции в течение ограниченного периода или на протяжении столетий. Отличительной чертой археологических музеев является то, что все собрание их экспонатов или его часть образованы благодаря археологическим раскопкам. В эту группу входят музеи, имеющие собрания исторических предметов и реликвий, мемориальные музеи, музеи архивов, военные музеи, музеи исторических личностей, археологические музеи, музеи древностей и т.д.

(c) *Музеи естественной истории и естественных наук*: музеи, в которых выставляются экспонаты, касающиеся одной или нескольких дисциплин, таких, как биология, геология, ботаника, зоология, палеонтология и экология;

(d) *Научно-технические музеи*: к этой категории относятся музеи, посвященные одной или нескольким точным наукам или же техническим дисциплинам, таким, как астрономия, математика, физика, химия, медицинская наука, строительно-монтажная промышленность, изделия обрабатывающей промышленности и т.д. В эту категорию также включаются планетарии и научные центры;

(e) *Этнографические и антропологические музеи*: музеи, экспонирующие материалы по культуре, социальным структурам, верованиям, обычаям, традиционным видам искусства и т.д;

(f) *Специализированные музеи*: музеи, которые занимаются исследованиями и демонстрированием всех аспектов одной темы или предмета, которые не входят ни в одну из категорий (a) - (e);

(g) *Региональные музеи:* музеи, которые освещают более или менее обширный регион, представляющий собой единое историческое и культурное пространство, а иногда также - этническое, экономическое или социальное формирование, т.е. его собрания посвящены отдельной территории, а не отдельной теме или предмету;

(h) *Музеи общего характера:* музеи, которые имеют смешанные собрания и не могут быть отнесены ни к одной основной области;

(i) *Другие музеи:* музеи и родственные им учреждения, которые не включены в вышеуказанные категории;

(j) *Исторические памятники и археологические объекты:* архитектурные или скульптурные произведения и топографические районы, представляющие особый интерес с археологической, исторической,

Introductory texts in Russian
Textes d'introduction en russe
Textos de introducción en ruso

этнографической или антропологической точки зрения;
(к) *Зоологические и ботанические сады, аквариумы и природные заповедники:* особая черта этих структур музейного характера заключается в том, что они выставляют живые экспонаты.

Данные о *ежегодном посещении* различных типов музеев представлены в виде количества *посетителей.*

Данные о *кассовой выручке* показывают общую выручку за год и приводятся в национальной валюте.

Что касается *работников музеев* и родственных им учреждений, то они подразделяются на *специалистов* и *другой персонал* следующим образом:

Специалисты это служащие, выполняющие работу, которая требует специального образования, подготовки и опыта. Сюда относятся кураторы, дизайнеры, библиотекари, техники по реставрационным работам, таксидермисты, лаборанты, археологи и т.д.

К другому персоналу (неспециалисты) относятся: смотрители, сторожа и канцелярские работники, лица, ухаживающие за животными, упаковщики, уборщики и т.д.

Также проводится различие между *оплачиваемым персоналом* и *добровольцами*, причем последние выполняют работу, для которой в их отсутствие надо было бы нанимать оплачиваемый персонал. Оплачиваемый персонал, привлекаемый на неполный рабочий день, учитывается в эквиваленте полного рабочего дня.

Данные о текущих расходах касаются общей суммы годовых расходов и приводятся в национальной валюте.

Таблица 8.1

Цифры, приводимые в этой таблице, показывают число учреждений, ежегодную посещаемость, кассовую выручку, численность персонала и текущие расходы в разбивке по превалирующей тематике собрания и были получены на основании обследований за 1992 г. или за 1995 г.

Introductory texts in Russian
Textes d'introduction en russe
Textos de introducción en ruso

9 Радио и телевещание

В этой главе представлена статистическая информация о радио- и телевещании. Представленные в четырех таблицах этой главы цифры получены в результате статистических обследований, проведенных в 1990 г., 1992 г. и 1995 г. Используемый для этих обследований вопросник основывался на определениях и классификациях, предложенных в Рекомендации о международной стандартизации статистики радио и телевидения, принятой Генеральной конференцией в 1976 г.

Поскольку количество ответов на обследования в области радио- и телевещания по-прежнему является довольно ограниченным, таблицы 9.3 - 9.5 включают, как и в предыдущих выпусках *Ежегодника*, лишь половину общего числа стран, указанных в таблицах о радио- и телеприемниках/выданных лицензиях, в отношении которых статистические данные пополнялись из различных источников, помимо ответов на регулярные вопросники ЮНЕСКО.

Таблица 9.1

В этой таблице содержатся сведения о количестве радиоприемников и/или лицензий за 1970 г., 1980 г., 1985 г., 1990 г. и 1994 г. Обычно данные относятся к концу указанного года и касаются всех типов приемников для приема радиопередач, предназначенных для широкой аудитории, включая те из них, которые подключаются к системе кабельного вещания (проводные приемники), отдельные личные приемники, такие, как автомобильные радиоприемники, переносные радиоприемники и индивидуальные приемники, устанавливаемые в общественных местах, а также общественные приемники. Данные о приемниках представляют собой оценочное количество приемников, находящихся в пользовании. Достоверность этих данных весьма различна в разных странах, и они требуют осторожного подхода. Указанное в этой таблице количество лицензий на ридоприемник включает число лицензий на радиоприемники плюс, в соответствующих случаях, количество объединенных радио/телевизионных лицензий.

Таблица 9.2

В этой таблице приводятся статистические данные за 1970 г., 1980 г., 1985 г., 1990 г. и 1994 г. о количестве телевизионных приемников и/или лицензий, а также приемников и/или лицензий на 1 000 жителей.

Как и в отношении радиоприемников, данные, касающиеся телевизионных приемников, представляют собой оценки общего количества находящихся в пользовании приемников.

Таблица 9.3

В Таблице 9.3 представлены последние имеющиеся статистические данные о программах звукового вещания за период с 1988 г. по 1994 г. Общее ежегодное время вещания распределяется в соответствии с такими программными функциями, как, например, информация, образование, реклама, развлекательные передачи и т.д. В таблице также указывается, являются ли учреждения вещания правительственными, общественными или коммерческими.

Таблица 9.4

Эта таблица, содержащая данные о телевизионных программах, имеет в основном ту же структуру и содержание, что и Таблица 9.3.

Introductory texts in Russian
Textes d'introduction en russe
Textos de introducción en ruso

10 Международная торговля печатными материалами

Две таблицы этой главы содержат статистические данные о международной торговле печатными материалами, относящимися к категории 1 Структуры статистики культуры (ССК) ЮНЕСКО, т.е. книгами и брошюрами, с одной стороны, и газетами и периодическими изданиями, с другой. Сбор таких данных на международном уровне предусмотрен пересмотренной Рекомендацией о международной стандартизации статистики выпуска и распространения книг, газет и периодических изданий, принятой Генеральной конференцией ЮНЕСКО на ее двадцать третьей сессии в Софии (ноябрь 1985 г.).

Попытки сбора данных о международном обмене печатными материалами с помощью направляемого государствам-членам вопросника не принесли ожидаемых результатов. В связи с этим, а также с целью избежать дублирования работы для национальных служб, предо-

ставляющих статистическую информацию различным организациям системы ООН, было сочтено предпочтительным опубликовать в настоящем *Ежегоднике* данные, полученные из Статистического отдела Организации Объединенных Наций и соответствующие данным, опубликованным в *Ежегоднике мировой торговли ООН.*

Таблица 10.1

Данные в этой таблице относятся к международной торговле книгами и брошюрами (индекс 892.11 Международной стандартной торговой классификации (МСТК), Пересмотр 2) за 1980 г., 1990 г. и 1994 г.

Таблица 10.2

В этой таблице приводятся статистические данные за 1980 г., 1990 г. и 1994 г. по международной торговле газетами и периодическими изданиями, которые соответствуют индексу 892.2 МСТК, Пересмотр 2.

Introductory texts in Russian
Textes d'introduction en russe
Textos de introducción en ruso

C. Обменные курсы

Следующая таблица показывает обменные курсы для выраженных в национальных валютах данных о расходах или доходах, которые приводятся в таблицах 2.11, 4.1-4.4, 5.4-5.6. Обменные курсы выражены числом единиц национальной валюты, соответствующих одному доллару США.

Внимание читателя обращается на то, что в таблице обменных курсов не приводится большинство стран и территорий, где используются единицы валют других стран; однако соответствующую информацию можно легко найти на основе данных по той стране, чья валюта использовалась.

Для большинства стран данные представлены Международным валютным фондом и относятся к среднегодовым обменным курсам. Для получения дополнительной информации, касающейся методологии, использованной для расчета этих курсов, читатель может обратиться к ежемесячному бюллетеню «International Financial Statistics, издаваемому Международным валютным фондом. Для остальных стран (отмеченных сноской) обменные курсы были взяты из бюллетеня Организации Объединенных Наций «Monthly Bulletin of Statistics».

Introductory texts in Arabic
Textes d'introduction en arabe
Textos de introducción en árabe

G Introductory texts in Arabic

Textes d'introduction en arabe

Textos de introducción en árabe

Introductory texte in Arabic
Textes d'introduction en arabe
Textos de introducción árabe

الملحق C – أسعار تبديل النقد

يتضمن الجدول التالي أسعار تبديل النقد لأرقام الانفاق أو الدخل المعبر عنها بالنقد المحلي والتي تظهر في الجداول 2.11، 4.1 الى 4.4 و5.4 الى 5.6. هذا وتم التعبير عن سعر تبديل النقد بعدد الوحدات من النقد المحلي المقابلة لدولار أمريكي واحد.

ونلفت انتباه القارىء الى أن هذا الجدول لا يتضمن أسعار تبديل النقد لمعظم البلدان أو الأراضي التي نقدها المحلي هو نقد بلدان أخرى. هذا ويمكن الحصول على المعلومات المتعلقة بهذا الموضوع بالعودة الى بيانات البلدان التي أمكن تحديد نقدها.

هذا وتم الحصول على بيانات معظم البلدان من صندوق النقـ الدولي وتعبر عن المتوسط السنوي لأسعار التبديل. وللحصول علـ معلومات اضافية تتعلق بمنهجية حساب هذه الأسعار، يمكن للقارى مراجعة النشرة الشهرية «الاحصاءات المالية الدولية» المنشورة من قبـ صندوق النقد الدولي. أما من أجل بقية البلدان (المشار اليها بحاشيـ فقد تم الحصول على أسعار تبديل النقد من النشرة الاحصائية الشهريـ للأمم المتحدة.

Introductory texte in Arabic
Textes d'introduction en arabe
Textos de introducción árabe

10 – التجارة الدولية للمواد المطبوعة

يتضمن جدولا هذا الفصل احصاءات عن التجارة الدولية في مجال المطبوعات، مثل الكتب والكراسات من ناحية أولى والصحف والدوريات من ناحية ثانية وكلاهما يقع في الفئة الأولى من اطار اليونسكو للاحصاءات الثقافية. ويتوقع جمع هذه البيانات الاحصائية عالميا في اطار التوصيات المعدلة والمتعلقة بالنمط الدولي لاحصاءات انتاج الكتب وتوزيعها، الصحف والدوريات والتي ثم عتمدها المؤتمر العام لليونسكو في اجتماعه الثالث والعشرين في صوفيا (نوفمبر 1985).

ونظرا لأن المحاولة الأولى لجمع بيانات عن التبادل الدولي للمطبوعات باستخدام استمارة وجهت الى الدول الأعضاء، لم تعط نتائجها المتوقعة وتحاشيا لتكرار العبء الواقع على كاهل الأجهزة الوطنية نتيجة تزويد مؤسسات الأمم المتحدة بمختلف المعلومات

الاحصائية، فقد وجدنا من الأفضل أن تتضمن هذا الكتاب السنوي بيانات احصائية تم الحصول عليها من قسم الاحصاء للأمم المتحدة والتي تتطابق مع تلك المنشورة في سنوية التجارة العالمية للأمم المتحدة.

الجدول 10.1 :

تتعلق البيانات الواردة في هذا الجدول بالتجارة الدولية في مجال الكتب والكراسات (الدليل 892.11 من التصنيف الدولي المقنن للتجارة الخارجية، المعدّل 2) للسنوات 1980، 1990 و1994.

الجدول 10.2 :

يقدم هذا الجدول بيانات احصائية عن التجارة الخارجية عن الصحف والدوريات للسنوات 1980، 1990، و1994 (الدليل 892.2 من التصنيف الدولي المقنن للتجارة الخارجية، المعدّل 2).

Introductory texte in Arabic
Textes d'introduction en arabe
Textos de introducción árabe

9 – الاذاعة

يوفر هذا الفصل معلومات احصائية عن الاذاعة والتلفزيون. لقد استندت الأرقام الواردة في جداول هذا الفصل الأربعة على نتائج المسوح الاحصائية التي أجريت في أعوام 1990، 1992 و1995 وقد نظمت الاستبيانات المستعملة في هذه المسوحات على أساس التعاريف والتصنيفات الواردة في التوصية التي اعتمدها المؤتمر العام لليونسكو في عام 1976 والمتعلقة بالتوحيد الدولي لاحصاءات الاذاعة والتلفزيون.

ولقد كان معدل الاجابات على المسوحات الخاصة بالراديو والتلفزيون دائما منخفضا. كما كان الحال في طبعات السنوات الماضية، تتضمن الجداول 9.3 الى 9.5 فقط نصف عدد البلدان المبينة في الجداول الخاصة بعدد أجهزة الاستقبال/ أو التراخيص الممنوحة التي استكملت فيها الاحصاءات من مصادر أخرى متعددة بالاضافة الى استبيانات اليونسكو.

الجدول 9.1 :

يورد هذا الجدول معلومات عن عدد أجهزة الاستقبال اللاسلكي (الراديو) و/أو عن مجموع التراخيص الممنوحة لأعوام 1970، 1980، 1985، 1990 و1994. بصفة عامة تشير البيانات الى نهاية السنة المحددة، وتتناول جميع أنواع أجهزة الاستقبال المخصصة لاستقبال البرامج المذاعة لعامة الجمهور، بما فيها أجهزة الاستقبال الموصولة بشبكة التوزيع بالكابل، أجهزة الاستقبال الفردية كأجهزة الاستقبال في السيارات والأجهزة المتنقلة الفردية وتتضمن كذلك الأجهزة الخاصة الموضوعة في أماكن عامة والأجهزة المخصصة للاستماع الجماعي.

البيانات الخاصة بأجهزة الاستقبال هي تقديرات لعدد أجهزة الاستقبال المستعملة. وتتفاوت اعتمادية هذه البيانات تفاوتا ملموسا

من بلد لاخر وينبغي أن ينظر اليها بحذر. ان عدد تراخيص أجهزة الاستقبال المبين في هذا الجدول يشير الى عدد التراخيص الصوتية فقط (الراديو) والى عدد التراخيص الممنوحة الجامعة بين الصوت (الراديو والتلفزيون فيما لو وجدت.

الجدول 9.2 :

يقدم هذا الجدول احصاءات للأعوام 1970، 1980، 1985، 1990 و1994 عن عدد أجهزة الاستقبال التلفزيوني و/أو الرخص الممنوحة وكذلك أجهزة الاستقبال التلفزيوني و/أو الرخص لكل 1 000 من السكان كما هو الحال بالنسبة الى الراديو تمثل البيانات الخاصة بأجهزة الاستقبال التلفزيوني تقديرا لمجموع عدد أجهزة الاستقبال المستعملة.

الجدول 9.3 :

يورد الجدول 9.3 اخر الاحصاءات المتوفرة عن برامج الاذاعة الصوتية للأعوام 1988-1994 وقد تم توزيع المدة السنوية الاجمالية للارسال حسب وظائف البرامج أي الاعلام، التعليم، الاعلان، الترفيه، الخ. وفضلا عن ذلك يحدد الجدول ما اذا كانت مؤسسات الاذاعة هي حكومية أم اذاعية عامة أم اذاعية تجارية.

الجدول 9.4 :

يشير هذا الجدول الى برامج التلفزيون وله تماما نفس بنية ومحتوى الجدول 9.3.

الجدول 9.5 :

يبين الجدول 9.5 أحدث احصاءات متوفرة منذ عام 1988 عن الموظفين الدائمين العاملين في مؤسسات الراديو والتلفزيون. هذا وقد تم التمييز بين العاملين الذكور والإناث وذلك في آخر مسح نفذ عام 1995.

Introductory texte in Arabic
Textes d'introduction en arabe
Textos de introducción árabe

تمثل البيانات الاحصائية المتعلقة بالارتياد السنوي لأنواع المتاحف المختلفة عدد الزوار.

البيانات المتعلقة بالايرادات تعود الى الايرادات السنوية ومحسوبة بالعملات المحلية.

فيما يتعلق بالموظفين المستخدمين في المتاحف والمؤسسات لمشابهة جرى تفريق بين الموظفين المهنيين وغيرهم من الموظفين على النحو التالي : الموظفون المهنيون هم المستخدمون الذي يقومون بعمل يتطلب اعدادا وخبرة ومعرفة متخصصة. وتتضمن هذه الفئة موظفين كالمديرين والرسامين وأمناء المكتبات والمحنطين ومصلحي التحف الفنية وفنيي المختبرات وعلماء الآثار، الخ. وتتضمن فئة الموظفين الآخرين (الموظفين غير المهنيين) الحراس والكتبة ومستخدمي الأمن والمعتنين بالحيوانات وعمال التغليف ومستخدمي التنظيف، الخ.

وقد أيضا تم التمييز بين العاملين بأجر وبين المتطوعين الذين يمارسون أعمالا تتطلب عادة استخدام موظفين جدد لولا قيامهم بها ودون مقابل. وقد حولت اعداد العاملين بأجر جزئي الى اعداد عاملين بأجر كامل عن طريق معادل للتفرغ.

هذا وتشير أرقام المصروفات الجارية الى مجموع المصروفات السنوية محسوبة بالعملات المحلية.

الجدول 8.1 :

تظهر بيانات هذا الجدول عدد المنشآت، الارتياد السنوي، الدخول، العاملين، والمصروفات الجارية موزعة حسب الموضوع الغالب للمجموعات. وتستند الأرقام الى البيانات المتوفرة من مسح 1992 أو 1995

Introductory texte in Arabic
Textes d'introduction en arabe
Textos de introducción árabe

8 – التراث الثقافي

يقدم هذا الفصل احصاءات خاصة بالتراث الثقافي طبقا للفئة (صفر 1) من اطار اليونسكو للاحصاءات الثقافية. مرة أخرى، وردت فقط البيانات المتعلقة بالمتاحف والمؤسسات المشابهة. أما فيما يتعلق ببيانات مؤسسات المحفوظات، يرجى من القارىء الرجوع الى طبعة 1990 من هذا الكتاب السنوي.

ان محاولة اليونسكو الأولى لوضع احصاءات دولية عن المتاحف والمؤسسات المشابهة ترجع الى أوائل الخمسينات. وقد بدأت اليونسكو منذ عام 1962 بارسال الاستبيانات الاحصائية عن المتاحف كل سنتين. الا انها قررت اعتبارا من عام 1974 اجراء المسح بصورة منتظمة مرة كل ثلاث سنوات لعدم تكرار التغييرات في هذا المجال.

ان ما يجعل جمع البيانات الاحصائية الخاصة بالمتاحف على المستوى الدولي ومقارنتها صعبا نسبيا هو الانعدام شبه الكلي لمعايير وتصنيفات يقبل بها عموما. فبعض البلدان مثلا تضمن احصاءاتها الخاصة بالمتاحف الصروح والأمكنة التاريخية والأثرية ولكنها تصرف النظر عن حدائق الحيوانات والنباتات ومرابي المائيات ومحميات الطبيعة، الخ. هذا ويحدث العكس تماما بالنسبة لدول أخرى وفضلا عن ذلك لا تأخذ كافة البلدان بالاعتبار المتاحف التي يملكها أفراد أو مؤسسات خاصة.

ان انعدام التعاريف والتصنيفات المقبول بها دوليا يؤثر على نحو ظاهر في نوعية وكمية ودلالة البيانات الاحصائية المجمعة. وبالتالي فان اجراء المقارنات الدولية يجب أن يجري بكثير من الحذر.

وبغية الوصول الى حد أدنى من المقارنة فقد وضعت التسميات والفئات المستخدمة في المسوحات الاحصائية التي بدأت عام 1977، استنادا الى التعاريف التي وضعها المجلس الدولي للمتاحف (ايكوم).

ففي اطار تلك المسوحات يقصد بكلمة متحف المؤسسة الدائمة غير الهادفة الى الربح والموضوعة في خدمة المجتمع وتطوره والمفتوحة للجمهور والتي تقوم بالبحث عن الشواهد المادية للانسان ولبيئته فتقتنيها وتحفظها وتتيح الاطلاع عليها، وعلى وجه الخصوص تعرضها من أجل الدراسة والتعلم والاستماع. وقد شملت المسوحات اضافة للمتاحف بعض المؤسسات المشابهة وفق رأي المجلس الدولي للمتاحف هي :

أ) – دوائر حفظ الوثائق وصالات العرض الدائمة التابعة للمكتبات ولدور المحفوظات.

ب) – الأمكنة والصروح الأثرية والاثنوغرافية والطبيعة والأمكنة والصروح التاريخية التي هي من طبيعة المتاحف من نشاطها في اقتناء الشواهد وحفظها واتاحة الاطلاع عليها.

جـ) – المؤسسات التي تعرض نماذج حية كحدائق النباتات والحيوانات ومرابي المائيات والحيوانات البرية، الخ.

د) – محميات الطبيعة.

هـ) – المراكز العلمية والقبب الفلكية الاصطناعية.

لأغراض احصائية، تم عدّ المتاحف والمؤسسات المشابهة اعتمادا على الوحدة الادارية وليس عدد المجموعات المقتناة. أما فيما يتعلق بتصنيف المتاحف والمؤسسات المشابهة وفق الطبيعة الغالبة للمواضيع المعروضة وللمجموعات فقد استخدمت الفئات الرئيسية الاتية :

أ) – مماحف الفنون : متاحف مخصصة للفنون الجميلة وللفنون التطبيقية. وتشمل هذه المجموعة متاحف النحت ومعارض الرسم ومتاحف التصوير الفوتوغرافي والسينما ومتاحف العمارة، الخ.

ب) – متاحف الاثار والتاريخ : تهدف متاحف التاريخ الى ايضاح التطور التاريخي لمنطقة أو بلد أو اقليم خلال فترة محددة من الزمن أو على امتداد العصور. وتتميز متاحف الاثار بكون مجموعاتها تُرد جزئيا أو كليا من الحفريات وتشمل هذه الفئة المتاحف الخاصة بالأشياء التاريخية ومخلفات الماضي، والمتاحف التذكارية ومتاحف المحفوظات والمتاحف العسكرية ومتاحف الشخصيات التاريخية ومتاحف الاثار ومتاحف الأثريات، الخ.

جـ) – متاحف العلوم الطبيعية والتاريخ الطبيعي : متاحف مخصصة لمواضيع تتعلق بواحد أو أكثر من علوم البيولوجيا والنبات والحيوان والمستحاثات والبيئة.

د) – متاحف العلوم والتكنولوجيا : تخصص متاحف هذه الفئة لواحد أو أكثر من العلوم الرياضية أو التقنية كعلم الفلك والرياضيات والفيزياء والكيمياء والعلوم الطبية والانشاءات وصناعة البناء والمواد المصنعة، الخ. وتدخل في هذه الفئة أيضا القبب الفلكية والاصطناعية والمراكز العلمية.

هـ) – متاحف الاثنوغرافيا والانثروبولوجيا : وهي متاحف تعرض مواد تتعلق بالثقافة والبنى الاجتماعية والمعتقدات والعادات والفنون التقليدية، الخ.

و) – المتاحف المتخصصة : متاحف تعنى بتقصي وعرض كافة المظاهر الخاصة ببحث أو بموضوع منفصل غير مشمول في أية من الفئات (أ) الى (هـ).

ز) – المتاحف الاقليمية : وهي متاحف يتركز اهتمامها على منطقة لها بعض الاتساع وتشكل كيانا تاريخيا وثقافيا وحتى في بعض الأحيان اثنيا واقتصاديا واجتماعيا، أي متاحف تتعلق مجموعاتها باقليم معين أكثر مما تتعلق بمادة أو بموضوع خاص.

ح) – المتاحف العامة : متاحف مجموعاتها غير متجانسة ولا يمكن تعريفها بالاستناد الى موضوع رئيسي تهتم به.

ط) – الصروح والأمكنة التاريخية : أعمال عمارة ونحت ومناطق طبوغرافية تشكل موضوع اهتمام خاص من وجهة النظر الأثرية والتاريخية والاثنولوجية والانثروبولوجية.

ى) – حدائق الحيوانات والنباتات ومرابي المائيات ومحميات الطبيعة : تكمن الخاصة النوعية لهذه الكيانات التي هي من طبيعة المتاحف في كونها تعرض نماذج حية.

Introductory texte in Arabic
Textes d'introduction en arabe
Textos de introducción árabe

مكررة. وتنطبق الملاحظات عن عدد مجموع الطبعات والطبعات الأولى الواردة في الجدول 7.4 على هذا الجدول أيضا.

الجدول 7.7 :

يشير هذا الجدول الى الطبعات الأولى والطبعات المعادة للكتب المدرسية التي عرّفت في التوصية ككتب مقررة للتلاميذ الذين يتلقون تعليما على المستوى الأول أو المستوى الثاني.

الجدول 7.8 :

تشير أرقام الجدول 7.8 الى الطبعات الأولى والطبعات المعادة لكتب الأطفال.

القسم الثالث

تغطي الاحصاءات في الجدولين 7.9 و7.11 الصحف اليومية وغير اليومية والدوريات الأخرى.

بصفة عامة يجب اعداد الاحصاءات الخاصة بالصحف والدوريات طبقا للتعاريف والتصنيفات الواردة في التوصية المعدلة لعام 1985 المتعلقة بالتوحيد الدولي للاحصاءات الخاصة بانتاج ونشر الكتب والصحف. ان البيانات الواردة في الجدولين 7.9 و7.10 تنشر بشكل منتظم في هذا الكتاب، أما البيانات المتعلقة بالدوريات حسب النوعية، فهي تنشر مرة كل سنتين. بموجب توصية 1985 يجب أن تغطي الاحصاءات الوطنية الخاصة بالصحافة الدوريات المطبوعة الصادرة في بلد معين والموضوعة في متناول الجمهور باستثناء الدوريات الصادرة لغرض الاعلان والدوريات ذات الصفة العابرة والدوريات التي لا يحتل النص القسم الأكبر منها. هذا ويجب أن تتضمن الاحصاءات الخاصة بالصحف والدوريات بيانات عن: الدوريات الحكومية، اليوميات الأكاديمية والعلمية، دوريات المنظمات المهنية والنقابية والسياسية والرياضية الخ، المنشورات الصادرة كل سنة أو كل أكثر من سنة، نشرات الأبرشيات، النشرات المدرسية، نشرات المؤسسات ونشرات برامج الراديو والتلفزيون شرط أن يكون النص الأدبي ذات أهمية.

لجمع هذه الاحصاءات يتوجب استعمال التعاريف الاتية:

1 – يعتبر المطبوع دوريا ان هو صدر كسلسلة متواصلة تحت عنوان واحد وبفترات منتظمة أو غير منتظمة خلال مدة غير محدودة على أن تكون الأعداد مرقّمة بشكل متتابع أو يكون لكل عدد تاريخه.

2 – تقسم المطبوعات الدورية الى فئتين:

(أ) الصحف والدوريات وهي دوريات مخصصة للجمهور ومصممة كمصدر رئيسي لمعلومات مكتوبة عن الأحداث الجارية المرتبطة بالشؤون العامة وبالمسائل الدولية والسياسية، الخ. وتعتبر صحيفة يومية كل صحيفة تتفق مع هذا التعريف وتصدر على الأقل أربع مرات في الأسبوع. أما الصحف التي تصدر ثلاث مرات أو أقل في الأسبوع فتعتبر صحفا غير يومية.

(ب) الدوريات هي اما تلك التي تتناول مواضيع ذات اهتمام عام أو تلك المخصصة لدراسات ومعلومات وثائقية خاصة كالتشريع والأمور المالية والتجارة والطب والأزياء والرياضة، الخ. ويغطي هذا التعريف باستثناء المطبوعات الواردة ضمن (أ) و(جـ) من المقطع الثاني في القسم الثاني من هذا الفصل، الصحف المتخصصة والمجلات والدوريات الأخرى.

3 – ويجب أن تمثل الأرقام المتعلقة بتداول الصحف والدوريات وسطي التداول اليومي أو وسطي التداول لكل عدد في حال كون المطبوعات غير دورية. يجب أن تتضمن هذه الأرقام (أ) عدد النسخ

المباعة مباشرة (ب) المباعة عن طريق الاشتراك و(جـ) عدد النسخ الموزعة مجانا، داخل أو خارج البلد. لدى تحليل البيانات في الجداول الاتية يجب ألا يغيب عن الذهن أنه في بعض الأحوال لا تنطبق طرائق العدّ والتعريف والتصنيف المتبعة في بعض البلدان، تماما مع المعايير الموصى بها من قبل اليونسكو. مثلا يجب أن تشير بيانات التداول الى عدد النسخ الموزعة كما تم تعريفه انفا. هذا ويظهر أن بعض البلدان تعطي عدد النسخ المطبوعة وهي عادة أعلى من رقم التوزيع.

الجدول 7.9 :

يقدم الجدول 7.9 بيانات عن العدد وعن مجموع التداول وعن التداول لكل ألف من السكان، تتعلق بالصحف اليومية للأعوام 1980، 1985، 1990 و1994.

الجدول 7.10 :

يقدم هذا الجدول البيانات المتوفرة لاخر سنة من 1989 الى 1994 عن العدد والتداول الاجمالي والتداول لكل ألف من السكان لصحف الاعلام العام غير اليومية وللدوريات الأخرى.

الجدول 7.11 :

يقدم هذا الجدول البيانات المتوفرة عن الدوريات حسب النوع وذلك لآخر سنة متوفرة خلال الفترة (1989-1994).

هذا ومن المستحسن تنبيه القارىء الى ضرورة توافق جمع «المجموعين الجزئيين» الواردين في هذا الجدول مع المجموع المتعلق بالدوريات والوارد في الجدول 7.10. ومع ذلك هذا التوافق ليس واردا في بعض الحالات نتيجة اختلاف مصدر البيانات أو عدم استطاعة بعض البلدان استخدام التصنيفات الدولية. وتأتي وجود مثل هذه الحالات في اطار سياسة تقديم بيانات لأوفر عدد من البلدان.

القسم الرابع

تتعلق البيانات الواردة في الجدول 7.12 باستهلاك وانتاج وتصدير واستيراد الورق المستخدم للأغراض الثقافية أي ورق الصحف وورق الطباعة (غير ورق الصحف) وورق الكتابة للأعوام 1970، 1975، 1980، 1985، 1990 و1994 وكما في السنوات السابقة وفرت هذه البيانات منظمة الأغذية والزراعة التابعة للأمم المتحدة (FAO). وعلى القراء الراغبين في الحصول على معلومات اضافية أن يرجعوا الى الكتاب السنوي لمنتجات الغابات الصادر عن تلك المنظمة.

ان التسمية ورق الصحف (البند 641.1 من التصنيف المقنن للتجارة الدولية، المعدل 2) تشير الى ورق الطباعة المقصور، غير المصمغ أو قليل التصميغ، من النوع المستعمل عادة للصحف. يزن ورق الصحف من 45 الى 60 غراما لكل متر مربع ويحتوي بصفة عامة، بنسبة 70 % على الأقل من وزنه، على مواد ليفية مستخرجة من العجينة الورقية المعدة ميكانيكيا.

ان التسمية أوراق الطباعة والكتابة الأخرى (البند 641.2 من التصنيف المقنن للتجارة الدولية، المعدل 2) تشير الى أنواع الورق المختلفة (بشكل لفائف أو صحائف) غير ورق الصحف، المخصصة للطباعة وللكتابة. ولا تدخل في هذه الفئة المنتجات المصنعة كلوازم المكاتب ولا الدفاتر أو السجلات، الخ.

فيما يتعلق بالبلدان التي لم تتوفر بشأنها البيانات المستقلة بالنسبة لفئتي الورق المعرّفتين أعلاه، أدرجت الأرقام الاجمالية تحت عنوان ورق الصحف.

Introductory texte in Arabic
Textes d'introduction en arabe
Textos de introducción árabe

11 – اللغات، اللغويات، فقه اللغة (4)

12 – الرياضيات (51)

13 – العلوم الطبيعية (52-59)

14 – العلوم الطبية، الصحة العامة (61)

15 – العلوم الهندسية، التكنولوجيا، الصناعات، المهن والحرف (62، 66-69)

16 – الزراعة، الغابات، تربية الحيوانات، الصيد، صيد الأسماك (63)

17 – العلوم المنزلية (64)

18 – إدارة الأعمال، الإدارة والتنظيم (65)

19 – التخطيط الإقليمي، تخطيط المدن والأرياف، هندسة العمارة (70-72)

20 – الفنون التشكيلية والتخطيطية، التصوير الفوتوغرافي (73-77)

21 – الموسيقى، الفنون المسرحية، المسرح، الأفلام والسينما (78، 791-792)

22 – الألعاب الرياضية (793-799)

23 – الأدب (8) (أ) تاريخ الأدب والنقد الذهبي (ب) النصوص الأدبية

24 – الجغرافيا (91)

25 – التاريخ، السيرة (92-99)

حينما لا ينطبق أحد المجاميع مع حاصل جمع عناصره، يمثل الفرق عندئذ عدد الأعمال التي لم تصنف في الفئات العشر الرئيسية للتصنيف العشري الجامع أو في فئات المواضيع الخمسة والعشرين أو أنه يكون ناتجا عن تدوير الأرقام.

يورد الجدولان 7.3 و7.6 لكل بلد أرقاما عن الكتب والكراسات معا وكذلك أرقاما عن الكتب فقط. والفرق بين الرقمين يمثل بالطبع عدد الكراسات.

الجدول 7.3 :

يقدم هذا الجدول بيانات من عام 1991 الى عام 1994 عن عدد عناوين الطبعات الأولى والطبعات المعادة لمؤلفات أصلية (أو لترجمات) موزعة حسب فئات التصنيف العشري الجامع. ويتضمن هذا الجدول فقط البلدان التي توفرت بشأنها احصاءات تتعلق بواحدة على الأقل من السنوات الثلاث المشار اليها.

الجدول 7.4 :

تشير البيانات الواردة في الجدول 7.4 الى عدد العناوين حسب مجموعات المواضيع للطبعات الأولى والطبعات المعادة. ويمكن الاعتبار أن البلدان التي يتساوى فيها مجموع العناوين مع عناوين الطبعات الأولى لم تقم بإعادة طبع عناوين (أو أن عدد هذه الأخيرة غير معروف). ويمكن الافتراض أيضا اذا ما كان عدد العناوين المطبوعة مساويا لعدد الكتب المطبوعة أنه لم تطبع نشرات أو أن عدد تلك الأخيرة غير معروف.

الجدول 7.5 :

تشير بيانات هذا الجدول الى عدد نسخ الطبعات الأولى والطبعات المعادة والطبعات المكررة لأعمال أصلية أو لترجمات للأعوام 1991 الى 1994 وذلك حسب فئات التصنيف العشري الجامع.

الجدول 7.6 :

تشير البيانات الواردة في الجدول 7.6 الى توزيع حسب مجموعات المواضيع لعدد نسخ الطبعات الأولى والطبعات المعادة والطبعات

(هـ) الكتاب هو مطبوع غير دوري يحتوي على 49 صفحة على الأقل فيما عدا صفحات الغلاف، وموضوع في متناول الجمهور.

(و) الكراسة هي مطبوع غير دوري يحتوي على 5 صفحات على الأقل و48 صفحة على الأكثر فيما عدا صفحات الغلاف، صادرا في بلد معين وموضوع في متناول الجمهور.

(ز) الطبعة الأولى هي أول نشر لمخطوط أصلي أو مترجم.

(ح) الطبعة المعادة هي مطبوع يختلف عن الطبعات السابقة نتيجة لتغييرات في المحتوى (طبعة منقحة) أو في التصميم (طبعة جديدة) والتي يتطلب اصدارها رقما جديدا في الـ ISBN.

(ط) الطبعة المكررة لا تتضمن أية تغييرات في المحتوى وفي التصميم ما عدا تصحيحا لأخطاء مطبعية وردت في الطبعات السابقة. وتعتبر كل طبعة مكررة يقوم بها ناشر غير الناشر الأصلي كطبعة معادة.

(ي) الترجمة هي مطبوع ينقل عملا الى لغة غير لغته الأصلية.

(ك) العنوان هو صيغة تستعمل للدلالة على مطبوع مستقل سواء كان صادرا بمجلد واحد أو بعدة مجلدات.

يحتوي هذا القسم على سبعة جداول تتعلق بالنشر ككل.

تورد الجداول 7.3 الى 7.8 بيانات تجمع كل سنة بواسطة استبيانات ترسل الى حوالي 200 من البلدان والأراضي الملحقة. ما لم يشر الى عكس ذلك يمكن الافتراض أن هذه البيانات تضم الكتب والكراسات لأعمال أصلية أو مترجمة. بيد أن بعض فئات المطبوعات التي يجب، بموجب نص التوصية، اما أن تُضمَن في احصاءات نشر الكتب (كالمنشورات الحكومية، والكتب المدرسية والرسائل الجامعية والطبعات الخاصة والأعمال المصوَّرة) واما أن تستبعد من تلك الاحصاءات (كالمنشورات التي لا يحتل النص القسم الأكبر منها) قد اختلف تصنيفها باختلاف البلدان. وفي غياب معلومات كاملة ودقيقة لم يكن بالامكان الاشارة الى بعض الاختلافات بين الاحصاءات الوطنية من جهة ونصوص التوصية من جهة أخرى.

لقد ضمنت في الجداول 7.5 و7.8 فقط البلدان التي تمكنت من توفير الاحصاءات التي تتفق مع التصنيف بحسب الموضوع والمحدد في توصية 1985. ان التصنيف الوارد أدناه والذي يقوم على أساس التصنيف العشري الجامع قد استند على التوصية المتعلقة بالتوحيد الدولي للاحصاءات الخاصة بنشر الكتب والدوريات (وقد أشير بين قوسين الى الرموز المقابلة في التصنيف العشري الجامع).

1 – عموميات (صفر)

2 – الفلسفة، علم النفس (1)

3 – الدين، اللاهوت (2)

4 – علم الاجتماع، الاحصاء (31-30)

5 – العلوم السياسية، العلوم الاقتصادية (33-32)

6 – القانون، الادارة العامة، الاسعاف والخدمة الاجتماعية، التأمين (34، 351-354، 36)

7 – العلوم والفنون العسكرية (355-359)

8 – التربية، التعليم، التدريب، الترفيه في أوقات الفراغ (37)

9 – التجارة، المواصلات، النقل، السياحة (28)

10 – الاثنوغرافيا، الانثروبولوجيا الثقافية (العادات، الفولكلور، الأعراف، التقاليد) (39)

Introductory texte in Arabic
Textes d'introduction en arabe
Textos de introducción árabe

10 – المجلد: هو أي عمل مطبوع أو مخطوط محتوى في غلاف لدي أو كرتوني.

11 – المواد السمعية البصرية: بخلاف الكتب ومواد المكتبات ذات أشكال المصغرة التي تتطلب قراءتها أو الاستماع اليها توفر تجهيزات خاصة. تشمل المواد السمعية البصرية مثلا الاسطوانات، الشرائط مغنطيسية، (الكاسيتات)، أفلام السينما، الشرائح المنزلقة، الصور لشفافة، تسجيلات الفيديو.

12 – مواد المكتبات الأخرى: كل مواد المكتبات ما عدا الكتب والدوريات المجلدة والوثائق والأشكال المصغرة والمواد السمعية البصرية. وتشمل أيضا موادا مثل الخرائط، الرسوم البيانية، الصور الفنية والصور الأخرى والديوراما.

13 – المستخدمون المسجلون: أي شخص مسجل لدى مكتبة بقصد استخدام أي من مواد موجوداتها داخل أو خارج بناء المكتبة.

14 – النفقات الجارية: هي النفقات الناتجة عن تسيير المكتبة، مثل الانفاق على الموظفين، المقتنيات... الخ.

15 – أمناء المكاتب المدربون: كل شخص يعمل في المكتبة حاصل على تدريب في أمانة المكتبات أو في حقل المعلومات. ويمكن أن يكون التدريب قد جرى في معاهد متخصصة أو بالمراس خلال العمل في المكتبات لمدة طويلة تحت اشراف أشخاص مدربين.

16 – الجمهور الذي يمكنه الاستفادة من خدمات المكتبات:

(أ) فيما يتعلق بالمكتبات العامة: مجموع عدد السكان في المناطق التي تخدمها المكتبات العامة. أي المكتبات الممولة جزئيا أو كليا من السلطات العامة (المكتبات البلدية أو الجهوية «المناطقية»)؛ (ب) فيما يتعلق بالمكتبات المدرسية: مجموع عدد تلاميذ ومدرسي المدارس الابتدائية والثانوية التي تخدمها تلك المكتبات؛ (ج) فيما يتعلق بمكتبات مؤسسات التعليم العالي: مجموع عدد طلاب ومدرسي مؤسسات التعليم العالي الذين يحق لهم الاستفادة من خدمات مكتبات الجامعات أو مكتبات مؤسسات التعليم العالي في المستوى الثالث.

الجدول 7.1 :

يقدم الجدول 7.1 احصاءات منتقاة عن الموجودات والمقتنيات والرواد المسجلين حسب الفئات المختلفة للمكتبات.

الجدول 7.2

يشير الجدول 7.2 الى مكتبات التعليم العالي. ويتضمن هذا الجدول فقط البلدان التي توفرت بشأنها احصاءات أكثر تفصيلا من التي وردت في الجدول 7.1 .

القسم الثاني

أعدت حتى عام 1985 الاحصاءات الوطنية المتعلقة بنشر الكتب طبقا للتعاريف والتصنيفات الواردة في التوصية المتعلقة بالتوحيد الدولي لاحصاءات نشر الكتب والدوريات التي اعتمدها المؤتمر العام لليونسكو عام 1964. ومنذ عام 1986 جرى جمع احصاءات نشر الكتب (وكذلك احصاءات الصحف اليومية والدوريات) على المستوى الدولي طبقا لتوصية 1964 المعدّلة التي اعتمدها المؤتمر العام لليونسكو في دورته الثالثة والعشرين في نوفمبر 1985.

حسب توصية 1985 يجب أن تغطي الاحصاءات الخاصة بنشر الكتب المطبوعات غير الدورية المطبوعة والصادرة في البلد المعني والمقدمة الى الجمهور والتي من المفروض عموما أن ترد في قوائم

المؤلفات الوطنية لمختلف البلدان، باستثناء الفئات التالية:

(أ) المطبوعات الصادرة لغرض اعلاني بشرط أن لا يحتل النص الأدبي أو العلمي القسم الأكبر منها وأن توزع مجانا (الكتالوجات والكراسات الاعلانية وغيرها من منشورات الاعلان التجاري أو الصناعي أو السياحي، والمنشورات التي تشير الى منتجات الناشر أو الخدمات التي يوفرها حتى لو تناولت النشاط أو التطور التقني لفرع من فروع الصناعة أو التجارة).

(ب) المطبوعات العائدة للفئات التالية، حينما يتعارف على أن لها صفة عابرة: جداول المواعيد، جداول الأسعار، دليل الهاتف الخ، برامج العروض المسرحية وبرامج المعارض والأسواق التجارية الخ، ملاكات وميزانيات الشركات والرسائل الدورية الخ، التقويمات، المفكرات، الخ.

(جـ) المطبوعات العائدة للفئات التالية والتي لا يحتل النص القسم الأكبر منها: الأعمال الموسيقية (التوليفات ودفاتر الموسيقى) بشرط أن تكون النوطة الموسيقية أكبر حجما من النص، انتاج الخرائط باستثناء الأطالس.

ويجب أن تغطي احصاءات نشر الكتب الفئات التالية:

1 – المطبوعات الرسمية أي الأعمال التي تنشرها الادارات العامة أو المؤسسات التابعة لها باستثناء الأعمال ذات الطابع السري أو المخصصة للتوزيع الداخلي،

2 – الكتب المدرسية أي المؤلفات المقررة لتلاميذ التعليم على المستوى الأول والمستوى الثاني،

3 – الرسائل الجامعية،

4 – الطبعات الخاصة أي اعادة طبع جزء من كتاب أو من نشرة دورية سبق وصدر بشرط أن يكون لتلك الطبعات عنوان وترقيم صفحات مختلفان عن الأصل وأن تشكل مؤلفا مختلفا،

5 – المطبوعات التي هي جزء من سلسلة والتي يشكل كل منها وحدة مرجعية.

6 – الأعمال التوضيحية: مجموعات صور ومجموعات نسخ لأعمال فنية أو لرسوم الخ، على أن تشكل هذه المجموعات مجلدات كاملة ذات صفحات مرقمة ولو يرافق فيها نص تفسيري أو مقتضب يتعلق بهذه الأعمال وبأصحابها، الكتب المصورة والكراسات المصورة والمصوغة بشكل قصة متصلة ومزينة برسوم توضح بعض الحلقات، دفاتر صور وكتب رسوم للأطفال وكذلك الكتب الفكاهية.

ولاعداد هذه الاحصاءات يجب استعمال التعاريف التالية:

(أ) يعتبر المطبوع غير دوري اذا صدر مرة واحدة أو بشكل مجلدات تصدر بفترات على وجه العموم محددا بصورة مسبقة.

(ب) تشمل كلمة مطبوعة كافة أساليب الطباعة الميكانيكية أيا كانت،

(جـ) يعتبر المطبوع صادرا في بلد معين اذا كان مقر الناشر في البلد الذي جمعت فيه الاحصاءات بصرف النظر عن مكان الطبع ومكان التوزيع. وعندما يصدر مطبوع عن ناشر واحد أو عدة ناشرين لهم مقرهم في بلدين أو أكثر يعتبر ذلك المطبوع صادرا في البلد أو البلدان حيث نشر.

(د) يعتبر مطبوع موضوعا في متناول الجمهور عندما يمكن الحصول عليه سواء عن طريق الشراء أو عن طريق التوزيع المجاني. ان المطبوعات المخصصة لفئة محصورة من القراء كبعض المطبوعات الحكومية ومطبوعات الجمعيات العلمية والمنظمات السياسية والمهنية تعتبر أيضا موضوعة في متناول الجمهور.

Introductory texte in Arabic
Textes d'introduction en arabe
Textos de introducción árabe

7 – المطبوعات

لقد قسم هذا الفصل الى أربعة أقسام. يبين القسم الأول (الجدولان 7.1 و7.2) الاحصاءات الخاصة بالمكتبات . ويورد القسم الثاني (الجداول 7.3 الى 7.8) الاحصاءات الخاصة بنشر الكتب. ويتعلق القسم الثالث بالاحصاءات الخاصة بالصحف والدوريات (الجداول 7.9 الى 7.11). أما القسم الأخير فيعرض بيانات عن انتاج واستيراد وتصدير واستهلاك ورق الصحف وورق الطباعة والكتابة (الجدول 7.12).

القسم الأول

يتألف هذا القسم من جدولين يعرض الأول الاحصاءات الوطنية عن مختلف أنواع المكتبات ومجموعاتها ومقتنياتها والرواد المسجلين. بينما توفر الجداول الأخرى احصاءات أكثر تفصيلا عن المقتنيات، الاعارة، المصاريف والموظفين (الخ). في المكتبات ومؤسسات التعليم العالي.

أما فيما يتعلق ببيانات المكتبات الوطنية والمكتبات العامة، يرجى من القارىء العودة الى طبعة عام 1995 من هذا الكتاب الاحصائي.

منذ عام 1950 قامت اليونسكو بجمع احصاءات عن المكتبات مرة كل سنتين. وتمشيا مع التوصية المتعلقة بالتوحيد الدولي للاحصاءات الخاصة بالمكتبات، التي اعتمدها المؤتمر العام لليونسكو في دورته السادسة عشرة، عام 1970، أصبح هذا الجمع يجري مرة كل ثلاث سنوات. فالمسوحات الثلاثة التي أجريت منذ ذلك العام طلبت بيانات عن أعوام 1971، 1974، 1977، على التوالي. وبغية تسهيل جمع البيانات ورفع معدلات الاجابة من قبل الدول الأعضاء فقد تقرر منذ عام 1980 عدم شمول أي مسح لأكثر من نوعين من المكتبات في ان واحد. ولذلك قسم الاستبيان الاحصائي لليونسكو الخاص بالمكتبات الى ثلاثة أجزاء يغطي كل جزء على التوالي المواضيع التالية: (١) المكتبات الوطنية والعامة (٢) مكتبات مؤسسات التعليم العالي والمكتبات المدرسية (٣) المكتبات المتخصصة. ويرسل كل جزء بدوره الى الدول لتعبئته. وبينما عالج المسح الذي أجري عام 1985، 1988، 1991 و1994 موضوع المكتبات الوطنية والعامة. تركز مسوحات بداية عام 1983، 1986، 1989، 1992 و1995 على مكتبات مؤسسات التعليم العالي والمكتبات المدرسية بينما وفر مسح كل من عامي 1984 و1987 بيانات عن المكتبات المتخصصة. هذا وقد استبعدت المسوحات لأسباب متعددة.

ان غالبية التعاريف أدناه مأخوذة من التوصيات المذكورة أعلاه ومع ذلك فان البعض المتعلق بالمواد السمعية والبصرية وكذلك المواد الأخرى الخاصة بالمكتبات أو المستعيرون المسجلون فانها اما غير واردة في التوصيات أو خضعت لتعديلات للتناسب مع التطور الحادث في مجال المكتبات:

1 – المكتبة : تعتبر مكتبة، أية كانت تسميتها كل مجموعة منظمة من الكتب والدوريات المطبوعة أو أية وثائق أخرى مكتوبة سمعية – بصرية ومعها موظفون مكلفون بتسهيل استعمالها من قبل الرواد لغرض استقاء المعلومات والبحث والتعليم أو الترفيه عن النفس. ويتم حساب المكتبات وفقا لهذا التعريف على أنها عدد من الوحدات الادارية ومن نقاط الخدمة. (أ) تعتبر وحدة ادارية كل مكتبة مستقلة أو كل مجموعة من المكتبات لها مدير واحد أو ادارة واحدة. (ب) وتعتبر نقطة

خدمة كل مكتبة تلبي طلبات الرواد في مقر منفصل، سواء كانت مستقلة أو كانت جزءا من مجموعة مكتبات تشكل وحدة ادارية.

وتصنف المكتبات كما يلي :

2 – المكتبات الوطنية : وهي المكتبات، أية كانت تسميتها المسؤولة عن اقتناء وحفظ نسخ من كافة المطبوعات الصادرة في البلد نفسه التي تعمل كمكتبات ايداع سواء كان ذلك بموجب قانون أو بموجب اتفاقات خاصة، كما تعد بليوغرافيا وطنية.

3 – مكتبات مؤسسات التعليم العالي : وهي المكتبات التي تقدم خدمات في الدرجة الأولى الى طلاب ومدرسي الجامعات وغيرها من مؤسسات التعليم على المستوى الثالث.

4 – مكتبات أخرى كبيرة غير متخصصة : مكتبات غير متخصصة ذات صفة علمية دون أن تكون مكتبات مؤسسات تعليم عال ولا مكتبات وطنية، حتى ولو كان بعضها يقوم بوظيفة مكتبة وطنية لمنطقة محددة.

5 – المكتبات المدرسية : وهي المكتبات التابعة لمؤسسات تعليم من أي نوع كان دون المستوى الثالث والموضوعة في المرتبة الأولى في خدمة تلاميذ ومعلمي هذه المؤسسات حتى ولو كانت فضلا عن ذلك مفتوحة للجمهور.

6 – المكتبات المتخصصة : وهي المكتبات التابعة لجمعية أو لادارة حكومية أو لبرلمان أو لمؤسسة أبحاث (باستثناء المعاهد الجامعية) أو لجمعية علمية أو لجمعية مهنية أو لمتحف أو لمؤسسة تجارية أو صناعية أو لغرفة تجارة الخ، والتي يتعلق الجزء الأكبر من مجموعاتها بموضوع معين. مثلا العلوم الطبيعية، العلوم الاجتماعية، الزراعة، الكيمياء، الطب، العلوم التجارية، العلوم الهندسية، القانون، التاريخ.

7 – المكتبات العامة (أو الشعبية) : وهي مكتبات تخدم مجانا أو مقابل اشتراك اسمي جماعات محلية أو سكان منطقة وتلبي حاجة اما كافة الجمهور واما بعض فئات الرواد كالأطفال وأعضاء القوات المسلحة ومرضى المستشفيات والمساجين والعمال والموظفين ويجب التفريق بين :

أما التعاريف والتصنيفات المتعلقة بالمجموعات والمقتنيات والاعارة والمصروفات والموظفين، الخ، فهي الاتية :

8 – الموجودات : هي مجمل الوثائق الموضوعة تحت تصرف الرواد. وتغطي الاحصاءات المتعلقة بالموجودات الوثائق التالية الموضوعة تحت تصرف المستفيدين بما في ذلك الوثائق المعارة.

(أ) – الكتب والدوريات المجلدة؛

(ب) – المخطوطات؛

(ج) – الأشكال المصغرة؛

(د) – المواد السمعية البصرية؛

(هـ) – المواد الأخرى الخاصة بالمكتبات.

9 – المقتنيات السنوية: وهي مجموعة الوثائق التي جرى اضافتها الى الموجودات خلال السنة عن طريق الشراء أو الهبة أو المبادلة أو عن أي طريق اخر. وتغطي الاحصاءات عن المقتنيات السنوية نفس البنود المذكورة عن الموجودات.

Introductory texte in Arabi
Textes d'introduction en arab
Textos de introducción árab

6 - جداول اجمالية عن مواضيع الثقافة والاتصال حسب القارات والمناطق الكبرى ومجموعات البلدان

يقدم هذا الفصل عددا من الجداول الاجمالية عن مواضيع منتقاة في مجالات الثقافة والاتصال. وقد وزعت البيانات الاحصائية التي تضمنتها الجداول حسب القارات والمناطق الكبرى ومجموعات البلدان كما تضمنت الصفحة XII من هذا الكتاب السنوي المكونات التركيبية لكل المناطق ومجموعات البلدان. أما المواضيع التي تطرقت اليها الجداول فهي الاتية : الصحف اليومية، الورق المستخدم لأغراض ثقافية، عدد أجهزة ارسال واستقبال الاذاعة والتلفزيون. ومما يجدر الاشارة اليه بأنه نظرا لصعوبة تحديد اعتمادية الاحصاءات المتوفرة ولنقص في المعلومات لبلدان عدة فان الأرقام الواردة في هذا الفصل على المستويين العالمي والاقليمي هي تقديرات تقريبية. كما توقفنا عن تقديم التقديرات على المستوى الاقليمي لنشر الكتب وانتاج الأفلام وذلك لعدم توفر بيانات كافية.

الجدول 6.1 :

يقدم هذا الجدول تقديرات عالمية واقليمية عن الصحف اليومية الصادرة عام 1980 وعام 1994. وتشير الاحصاءات الى عدد الصحف وانتشارها ومعدل الانتشار لكل ألف من السكان.

الجدول 6.2 و6.3 :

يتضمن هذان الجدولان تقديرات على المستويين العالمي والاقليمي لانتاج واستهلاك الورق المستخدم لأغراض ثقافية وتعليمية (ورق الصحف وورق الطباعة وورق الكتابة) وذلك للأعوام 1970، 1980، 1990 و1994. وقد تم حساب هذه التقديرات اعتمادا على احصاءات منظمة الأمم المتحدة للزراعة والتغذية.

الجدول 6.4 :

يقدم الجدول 6.4 بيانات اقليمية عن أجهزة الاستقبال الاذاعية ومعدل عدد الأجهزة لكل ألف من السكان للأعوام 1970، 1980،1990 و1994.

الجدول 6.5 :

يقدم الجدول 6.5 بيانات عن العدد الاجمالي لأجهزة الاستقبال التلفزيوني ومعدل عدد الأجهزة لكل ألف من السكان للأعوام 1970، 1980، 1990 و1994.

Introductory texte in Arabic
Textes d'introduction en arabe
Textos de introducción árabe

المصنفة في قطاع الانتاج وجميع الأموال الواردة من «صناديق الانماء التكنولوجي والاقتصادي» وغيرها من الصناديق الخاصة المماثلة.

الأموال الأجنبية: تشمل هذه الفئة الأموال الواردة من الخارج لأنشطة الـ (ب) و(ت) الوطنية.

أموال متنوعة: ينبغي أن تدرج في هذه الفئة الأموال التي لا يمكن ادراجها في احدى الفئات السابقة.

ملاحظات على الجداول

لقد صنفت الجداول الواردة في هذا الفصل في ثلاثة أقسام. يتضمن القسم الأول (A) الجدول (5.1) الذي يقدم بيانات مختارة عن المعلمين والمهندسين العاملين في الـ (ب) و(ث) وكذلك المصروفات.

يتضمن القسمين التاليين 5 جداول تورد معلومات أساسية مستقاة من مسوحات اليونسكو الاحصائية، التقارير الرسمية والنشرات. أما البيانات المتعلقة ببلجيكا، كندا، فنلندا، ألمانيا، اليابان وتركيا فقد تم الحصول عليها من مطبوع OCDE :

«Basic science and Technology Statistics, 1995 Edition»

أما القسم الثاني (B) فيتضمن 2 جداول تتعلق بالموارد البشرية.

يورد الجدول 5.2 بيانات عن العلميين والمهندسين والتقنيين العاملين بأنشطة البحث العلمي والتنمية التجريبية مع البيانات الخاصة بالنساء حينما توفرت. فان بيانات هذا الجدول، ما لم يشر الى عكس ذلك، أوردت استخدام معادل التفرغ.

الجدول 5.3 يتعلق بجميع العاملين بأنشطة الـ (ب) و(ت) وهو يظهر توزيعهم بين قطاعات التنفيذ الثلاثة (قطاع الانتاج وقطاع التعليم العالي وقطاع الخدمات العامة). وهو يعطي أرقام العاملين المطلقة (محددة بمعادل التفرغ ما لم يشر الى عكس ذلك) وتوزيعهم كنسب مئوية. ونظرا لاختلاف بنى قطاعات الانتاج في البلدان ذات النظم الاجتماعية الاقتصادية المتباينة، وبغية تسهيل المقارنات فقد صنفت بيانات هذا القطاع بحسب مستويي تكامل يشيران الى درجة الارتباط القائم بين الـ (ب) و(ت) والانتاج في النظم الاجتماعية الاقتصادية المختلفة. وقد بيّنت أيضا الفئات المختلفة للعاملين المستخدمين في تلك القطاعات.

يتضمن القسم الثالث (C) 3 جداول رئيسية ويعطي صورة لتكلفة أنشطة الـ (ب) و(ت). وقد حددت البيانات بالعملات الوطنية. ومن الصعب

مقارنة الأرقام المطلقة لمصروفات الـ (ب) و(ت) من بلد الى اخر اذ أن مثل تلك المقارنة توجب تحويل العملات المختلفة الى عملة واحدة وذلك باستعمال أسعار الصرف الرسمية لعدم وجود أسعار صرف خاصة بأنشطة الـ (ب) و(ت). الا أن أسعار الصرف الرسمية لا تعكس في أكثرية الأحوال التكلفة الحقيقية لأنشطة الـ (ب) و(ت) وكل مقارنة تقوم على أساس تلك الأسعار قد تؤدي الى نتائج يشك في دقتها. وبالرغم من هذا التحفظ يمكن لمثل تلك المقارنات توفير صورة تقريبية عن حجم مصروفات الـ (ب) و(ت). وللحصول على أسعار الصرف الرسمية بين العملات المختلفة ودولار الولايات المتحدة الأمريكية يمكن الرجوع الى الملحق C من هذا الكتاب.

في الجدول 5.4 تم تفريع المصروفات الاجمالية لأنشطة الـ (ب) و(ت) بحسب نوع المصروفات (اجمالية، رأسمالية، جارية، وقد فرعت هذه الأخيرة بدورها الى مصروفات العاملين والمصروفات الجارية الأخرى) وأقيمت علاقة بين المصروفات الاجمالية والمصروفات الجارية.

أما بنى تمويل أنشطة الـ (ب) و(ت) فقد وردت في الجدول 5.5 حيث وزعت المصروفات الاجمالية (أو المصروفات الجارية ان لم تتوفر تلك) بحسب الفئات الأربع الكبرى لمصادر التمويل. وقد حددت دائما البيانات بالعملات الوطنية وكنسب مئوية وذلك كلما أتيحت المعلومات الكاملة لكي يتمكن القارىء من مقارنة الجهود المبذولة في مختلف البلدان من جانب أولئك الذين ينهضون بعبء تمويل أنشطة البحث والتنمية التجريبية.

يورد الجدول 5.6 توزيع المصروفات الاجمالية والمصروفات الجارية حسب قطاعات التنفيذ الثلاثة. وكما في الجدول 5.3 وزعت البيانات الخاصة بقطاع الانتاج حسب مستويي التكامل. وقد تم تبيان المصروفات كأرقام مطلقة، وبغية تسهيل المقارنة بين البلدان تم أيضا تبيان توزيعها كنسب مئوية كلما توفرت البيانات لذلك.

ويمكن للباحثين الراغبين في الحصول على تفاصيل أخرى أو ايضاحات بشأن بلد معين فيما يتعلق بالتعاريف الوطنية أو نطاق أو حدود البيانات المندرجة في الجداول أن يتقدموا بطلبهم الى قسم الاحصاء باليونسكو.

Introductory texte in Arabic
Textes d'introduction en arabe
Textos de introducción árabe

5 - العلم والتكنولوجيا

يقدم هذا الفصل بعض النتائج المختارة للجهود التي بذلتها اليونسكو لجمع بيانات تتعلق بالعلم والتكنولوجيا. ولقد استقيت معظم البيانات من الاجابات على الاستبيانات الخاصة بالعاملين في أنشطة البحث والتنمية التجريبية وبمصروفاتها، والتي وجهتها اليونسكو للدول الأعضاء وقد استكملت تلك البيانات بمعلومات استقيت من تقارير رسمية ونشرات.

أما التعاريف والمفاهيم المستعملة في الاستبيان الاحصائي عن (ب) و(ث) فهي مبنية على التوصية بشأن التوحيد الدولي للاحصاءات الخاصة بالعلم والتكنولوجيا ومتضمنة في الدليل التالي (وثيقة اليونسكو ST-84/WS/12.)

وفيما يلي مختصر للتعاريف الواردة في التوصية المذكورة أعلاه:

فئات العاملين

لقد عرّفت فئات العاملين العلميين والتقنيين الثلاث الاتية بحسب نوع عملهم ومؤهلاتهم:

(1) العلميون والمهندسون: وهم يشملون الأشخاص الذين يعملون بهاتين الصفتين، والذين تلقوا اعدادا علميا أو تقنيا في أي من مجالات العلم المذكورة أدناه ويضطلعون بأعمال مهنية في أنشطة البحث والتنمية التجريبية والاداريون وغيرهم من كبار الموظفين الذين يتولون ادارة تنفيذ أنشطة البحث والتنمية التجريبية (ب) و(ت).

(2) التقنيون: وهم يشملون الأشخاص الذين يعملون بهذه الصفة في أنشطة البحث العلمي والتنمية التجريبية والذين تلقوا تدريبا مهنيا أو تقنيا في أي فرع من فروع العلم والتكنولوجيا حسب معيار محدد (عادة ثلاث سنوات على الأقل بعد الانتهاء من المرحلة الأولى من المستوى التعليمي الثاني).

(3) الموظفون المساعدون، وهم يشملون الأشخاص الذين ترتبط وظائفهم ارتباطا مباشرا بتنفيذ أنشطة البحث العلمي والتنمية التجريبية أي موظفي المكاتب والسكرتارية والادارة والعمال المؤهلون وغير المؤهلين في مختلف المهن وغيرهم من الموظفين المساعدين. [لا تتضمن هذه الفئة الأفراد المسؤولين عن الأمن وكذلك المسؤولين عن النظافة والصيانة والأنشطة الحرفية الأخرى] هذا ويجب الاشارة الى أن هذه الفئات تتضمن الأفراد بغض النظر عن الجنسية أو بلد الأصل.

العاملون في البحث العلمي والتنمية التجريبية
المتفرغون وغير المتفرغين ومعادل التفرغ

تحسب عادة البيانات الخاصة بالعاملين بوحدات معادل التفرغ ولاسيما فيما يتعلق بالعلميين والمهندسين.

معادل التفرغ (م ت): يمثل معادل التفرغ وحدة للقياس تناظر شخصا متفرغا للعمل أثناء فترة معينة وتستخدم هذه الوحدة في تحويل عدد الأشخاص غير متفرغين الى عدد من المتفرغين.

البحث العلمي والتنمية التجريبية (ب) و(ت)

بصفة عامة يمكن تعريف البحث العلمي والتنمية التجريبية ((ب) و(ت)) بأنهما الأنشطة المنهجية والابداعية التي تمارس بغية زيادة

رصيد المعارف بما في ذلك المعارف الخاصة بالانسان والثقافة والمجتمع واستخدام رصيد المعارف هذا لابتكار تطبيقات جديدة. ويشمل نطاق البحث العلمي والتنمية التجريبية البحوث الأساسية (أي الأنشطة النظرية والتجريبية التي تجرى بدون هدف تطبيق عملي مباشر) والبحوث التطبيقية في مجالات كالزراعة والطب والكيمياء الصناعية، الخ. (أي الموجهة أساسا نحو هدف عملي محدد)، وأنشطة التنمية التجريبية التي تؤدي الى استحداث أنظمة وطرائق ومنتجات جديدة.

قطاعات التنفيذ

قطاعات التنفيذ هي قطاعات الاقتصاد التي تمارس فيها أنشطة البحث العلمي والتنمية التجريبية الـ (ب) و(ت). ان عبارة قطاع التنفيذ تتيح التمييز بين تنفيذ أنشطة الـ (ب) و(ت) وتمويلها. ويمكن التمييز بين ثلاثة قطاعات كبرى للتنفيذ: قطاع الانتاج، قطاع التعليم العالي وقطاع الخدمات العامة. وتقاس أنشطة الـ (ب) و(ت) في قطاع الانتاج على مستويين: الأنشطة الداخلة في الانتاج والأنشطة الغير الداخلة في الانتاج. ويشمل هذا القطاع المؤسسات الصناعية والتجارية التي تنتج وتوزع السلع والخدمات مقابل أجر. أما قطاع التعليم العالي فيشمل كافة مؤسسات التعليم على المستوى الثالث وكذلك مؤسسات البحوث ومحطات التجارب التي تخدمها بينما يتضمن قطاع الخدمات العامة مختلف المؤسسات العامة والحكومية التي توفر خدمات للمجتمع.

مصروفات الـ (ب) و(ت)

تحسب مصروفات أنشطة الـ (ب) و(ت) على أساس المصروفات الجارية الداخلية بما فيها المصروفات الغير المباشرة من جهة والمصروفات الرأسمالية الداخلية من جهة أخرى. يؤدي مجموع المصروفات الداخلية التي تنفقها كافة المؤسسات الوطنية الى مجموع نهائي للمصروفات الداخلية تتكون منه المعلومات المقدمة على الصعيد الدولي.

مجموع المصروفات الداخلية لأنشطة الـ (ب) و(ت) يمكن تعريفها بأنها جميع المبالغ المنفقة لهذا الغرض أثناء السنة المرجعية في المؤسسات والمنشات الواقعة في الأراضي الوطنية، وكذلك المنشات الواقعة جغرافيا في الخارج.

تشمل المصروفات الاجمالية المنفقة على أنشطة الـ (ب) و(ت) حسبما عرفت أعلاه جميع المصروفات الجارية بما فيها المصروفات الغير مباشرة وكذلك المصروفات الرأسمالية. وتفرع المصروفات الجارية الداخلية بدورها الى تكاليف العاملين والى المصروفات الجارية الأخرى.

مصادر التمويل

تعرف مصادر التمويل لمصروفات الـ (ب) و(ت) من خلال الفئات التالية:

الأموال الحكومية: تشمل هذه الفئة الأموال التي تقدمها الحكومة المركزية (أو حكومات الولايات) والسلطات المحلية.

الأموال الواردة من شركات الانتاج والاعتمادات الخاصة: تشمل هذه الفئة الاعتمادات المخصصة لأنشطة الـ (ب) و(ت) من قبل المؤسسات

Introductory texte in Arabic
Textes d'introduction en arabe
Textos de introducción árabe

الجدول 4.3

يبين الجدول التوزيع المئوي للانفاق العام الجاري على التعليم حسب مستويات التعليم. يضم العمود المدرج تحت عنوان نماذج التعليم الأخرى التربية الخاصة وتعليم الكبار ونماذج أخرى من التعليم لا يمكن تصنيفها حسب المستويات. ان العمود الوارد تحت عنوان المصروفات غير الموزعة والذي يضم بصفة عامة مختلف المصروفات غير المعينة، يمكن أحيانا أن يتضمن مصروفات الادارة حينما لا تكون هذه قد وزعت حسب المستويات.

الجدول 4.4

يعطي هذا الجدول تصنيفا تقاطعيا للانفاق العام الجاري حسب مستوى التعليم والغاية من الانفاق وذلك لاخر سنة تتوفر عنها بيانات. أما الفئات التي تم وفقها تصنيف الانفاق حسب الغاية فهي نفسها المدرجة في حاشية الجدول 4.2.

هذا وعندما لا تغطي البيانات المدرّجة جميع فئات الانفاق الواردة في الجدول، فان الفئات المعنية هي التي تظهر فقط لتعكس انفاق البلدان ذات العلاقة.

Introductory texte in Arabi
Textes d'introduction en arab
Textos de introducción árab

4 – الانفاق على التعليم

يحتوي هذا الفصل على أربعة جداول للنفقات التعليمية. وقد وزعت حسب فئتين كبيرتين :

النفقات الجارية : مصروفات ادارة، أجور المعلمين والمساعدين، ووسائل تعليمية أخرى، منح مدرسية وخدمات اجتماعية.

النفقات الرأسمالية: المصروفات المتعلقة بالأمن والمباني والتشييد والتجهيزات الخ، وتتضمن هذه الفئة أيضا النفقات الخاصة بخدمة الديون.

تشير البيانات المدرجة في هذا الفصل الى الانفاق العام على التعليم فقط، أي الانفاق العام على التعليم الرسمي مضافا اليه الاعانات المالية للتعليم الخاص. ونظرا لعدم توفر البيانات لمعظم البلاد التي لم تؤخذ بالاعتبار مصروفات التعليم الخاص.

يتضمن الانفاق العام على التعليم، ما لم يشر الى عكس ذلك، النفقات على جميع المستويات الادارية، تبعا للتنظيم السياسي للدول: حكومة مركزية أو فدرالية، حكومات الولايات، سلطات مقاطعات أو سلطات اقليمية وسلطات بلدية ومحلية.

وبصفة عامة لا تأخذ الاحصاءات بالاعتبار المساعدات الخارجية للتعليم. بيد أن ثمة اشارة الى جميع الحالات التي تدل المعلومات المتاحة بشأنها بصراحة على تضمنها مثل تلك المساعدات. لقد حددت البيانات بالعملة الوطنية بالأسعار الجارية وأدرجت أسعار صرف العملات الوطنية بالنسبة لدولار الولايات المتحدة الأمريكية في الملحق C. والسنوات المبينة تشير الى السنة التقويمية التي تبتدأ فيها السنة المالية. أن السنة المالية تبتدأ في أغلبية البلدان في شهر كانون الثاني/ يناير أي انها تطابق السنة التقويمية غير ان ليس هو حال حوالي 70 بلدا. ويوفر الملحق B معلومات على تاريخ بدء السنة المالية في كل بلد. ويعود اختلاف بعض البيانات الواردة في هذا الكتاب عن البيانات المقابلة لنفس العام المبينة في الطبعة السابقة الى تعديلات أدخلت بعد وصول معلومات جديدة.

أما فيما يتعلق بالدول المشاركة في أحدث مسح UNESCO/OCDE/ (UOE) EUROSTAT والذي يؤمن بيانات لسنوات غير تلك التي وردت في طبعة 1995. فمن الممكن أن يحصل انقطاع في السلسلة الزمنية ويعود ذلك لتغييرات مفاهيمية من أهمها ادخال المصروفات الخاصة للتعليم. ونتيجة ذلك، تعود نظريا بيانات الجدولين 3.4 الى 4.4 الى المصروفات العامة والخاصة للتعليم، أي المصروفات المتعلقة بالمؤسسات : (أ) العامة، (ب) الخاصة المعانة ماليا من الحكومة و(ث) الخاصة. هذا وتجدر الاشارة الى ان القسم الخاص قد ورد بشكل غير كامل أو لم يرد كليا وذلك لعدة دول معينة. أما فيما يخص بيانات الجدولين 4.1 و4.2 والتي تعود دائما للمصاريف العامة فقط، يمكن ملاحظة فرقا بين الأرقام الحديثة والسابقة وذلك لبعض الدول. اذا وفي جميع الجداول، فإن الدول المتأثرة بالتغييرات المشار اليها أعلاه يمكن تمييزها بخط يفصل بين آخر سنة مرجعية والسنوات السابقة.

الجدول 4.1

يبين هذا الجدول مجموع الانفاق العام على التعليم موزعا بين نفقات جارية ونفقات رأسمالية. ولقد ترجمت نفقات التعليم أيضا الى نسب مئوية من اجمالي الناتج القومي ومن مجمل الانفاق العام. ان البيانات العائدة لاجمالي الناتج القومي قد وفرها البنك الدولي فيما يتعلق بجميع الدول تقريبا. وبما أن هذه البيانات تعدل كل سنة فان النسب المئوية للمصروفات من الناتج القومي قد تختلف أحيانا عن النسب المنشورة في الطبعات السابقة.

الجدول 4.2

لقد وزع الانفاق العام الجاري على التعليم في هذا الجدول حسب الفئات التالية :

الادارة باستثناء الموظفين: جميع النفقات الادارية باستثناء أجور الموظفين الاداريين.

أجور الموظفين الاداريين : أجور الموظفين الاداريين على كافة المستويات الادارية بما فيها التفتيش وخدمات التوثيق والبحوث التربوية.

أجور المعلمين : الرواتب ومختلف المكافآت الاضافية للمعلمين وللموظفين المساعدين الذين يعاونون مباشرة في التعليم بما فيها المدفوعات عنهم لصناديق التقاعد (المعاش) والضمان الاجتماعي.

الأجور الأخرى : أجور موظفي الصيانة والنظافة والسائقين والحراس، الخ.

مجموع الأجور المدفوعة: مجموع الفئات الثلاث السابقة.

الوسائل التعليمية : المصروفات المرتبطة مباشرة بالتعليم كشراء المقررات والكتب وغيرها من اللوازم المدرسية.

المنح الدراسية : المنح ومختلف أشكال المساعدة المالية الأخرى للطلاب، للدراسة في بلدهم أو في الخارج.

الخدمات الاجتماعية: نفقات المدارس الداخلية والوجبات المدرسية والنقل المدرسي والخدمات الطبية، الخ.

نفقات أخرى: المصروفات التي يتعذر تصنيفها في أي من الأبواب المذكورة أعلاه. والمصروفات الأخرى المرتبطة بعمل وبصيانة المباني والأجهزة.

اعانات مالية غير موزعة: الاعانات الحكومية لمؤسسات تعليمية رسمية أو خاصة لم يمكن توزيعها حسب الغرض نظرا للاستقلال الاداري التي تتمتع به المؤسسات المستفيدة.

وفيما يتعلق بهذا الجدول يتوجب ابداء ملاحظتين حينما يستعمل الرمز % في احدى الفئات بدون أي شرح تكون البيانات العائدة لتلك الفئة مصنفة مع فئة «النفقات الأخرى». من جهة أخرى نجد عدة فئات في هذا الجدول وقد رافقها الرمز (...)، ذلك لأن الاجابات الواردة على استبيان اليونسكو لم تحدد ما اذا كانت النفقات العائدة لتلك الفئات قد صنفت مع نفقات فئة أخرى أم انها معدومة.

Introductory texte in Arabic
Textes d'introduction en arabe
Textos de introducción árabe

ان السنة المشار اليها هي السنة التقويمية التي خلالها منحت الشهادة. مثلا عام 1994 يشير الى الشهادة الممنوحة في نهاية السنة الجامعية 1993/94. للحصول على معلومات أكثر تفصيلا (الرجاء مراجعة مقدمة هذا النص).

يمكن تعريف المستويات التي أشير اليها في هذا الجدول بواسطة رموزها (5 و6 و7) في الاسكد كالاتي :

المستوى 5 : الشهادات والدرجات التي لا تعادل الدرجة الجامعية الأولى هي تلك التي تمنح في نهاية دراسة عليا ذات مدة (عموما أقل من ثلاث سنوات).

المستوى 6 : الدرجات الأولى أو الشهادات التي تعادلها هي تلك التي تكلّل دراسات عليا ذات مدة طبيعية (عموما بين 3 و5 سنوات وأحيانا 7 سنوات). وهذه الدرجات أو الشهادات هي الأكثر عددا. فهي تتضمن ليس فقط الدرجات المعروفة كالليسانس ودرجة البكالوريرس، الخ، وبل أيضا الدرجات الأولى ذات الطابع المهني العلوم الهندسية أو القانون الخ.

المستوى 7 : الدرجات الجامعية العليا أو الشهادات التي تعادلها هي تلك التي يمكن أن يحصل عليها أشخاص سبق وحصلوا على درجة جامعية أولى (أو على شهادة تعادلها) ان هم تابعوا دراستهم. مثلا الشهادات المختلفة التي تمنح بعد الدرجة الجامعية الأولى (دبلوم الدراسات العليا) ودرجة الماجستير ومختلف أنواع الدكتوراة الخ.

لقد جرى التصنيف حسب المستويات لكي يتسنى التفريق بين مختلف الدرجات والشهادات وبأمل تسهيل امكانية المقارنة على الصعيد الدولي للاحصاءات المتعلقة بشهادات التعليم على المستوى الثالث. بيد أنه من المستحسن ألا تجرى مقارنات معمقة نظرا لأن التصنيف حسب المستويات لا ينطوي بأية حال على تعادل في

الدرجات والشهادات سواء داخل البلد الواحد أو لدى مقارنة ذلك البلد مع بلد اخر.

فيما يتعلق بالمواضيع المضمنة في مجالات الدراسة المختلفة الرجاء الرجوع الى التعاريف في مقدمة هذا الفصل.

الجدول 3.13

يعرف الطالب الأجنبي حسب اليونسكو بأنه شخص مسجل في مؤسسة تعليم عال لبلد ليس له فيه اقامة دائمة. الا أن معظم البلدان نظمت احصاءاتها على أساس مبدأ الجنسية، ولذلك نجد أن الفوارق الناجمة عن تطبيق هذين المعيارين يمكن أن تكون كبيرة في بعض البلدان التي تراعى فيها الاحصاءات مثلا المهاجرين الذين يقيمون بشكل دائم في البلد المضيف دون أن يكونوا قد حصلوا على جنسيته.

الجدول 3.14

يبين هذا الجدول البيانات المتعلقة بخمسين بلدا مختارا، لعدد الطلاب الأجانب المقيدين في مؤسسات التعليم على المستوى الثالث وذلك حسب بلد أو قطر الأصل.

لقد أختيرت هذه البلدان الخمسون تبعا لعدد الطلاب الأجانب المقيدين (المسجلين) فيها وذلك للسنة الأخيرة التي كان بها توزيع الطلاب حسب بلد الأصل متوفرا (1993 بالنسبة لمعظم البلدان). يتضمن الجدول أيضا بلدان الأصل كالاتحاد السوفياتي سابقا، تشكوسلوفاكيا سابقا ويوغسلافيا سابقا كما انهم أدرجوا بحسب البلدان المضيفة. غير ان عدد كبير من البلدان المضيفة مثل (الهند، لبنان، السويد والبرازيل الخ) لم يردوا في هذا الجدول وذلك لعدم توفر بيانات حديثة.

ويشكل الطلاب الأجانب في الخمسين بلدا المذكورة في الجدول حوالي 95% من مجموع الطلاب الأجانب في العالم.

Introductory texte in Arab
Textes d'introduction en arab
Textos de introducción árab

على ذلك يمكن في البلد الواحد ونتيجة لتعديلات تطرأ على نظام التعليم أن تلحق عدة مؤسسات غير جامعية، بين سنة وأخرى، بالجامعات أو أن تعتبر كمؤسسات معادلة لها. ولذلك فان التوزيع حسب نوع المؤسسات يجب أن يستعمل بحذر.

تغطي احصاءات المستوى الثالث في حدود البيانات المتوفرة الأساتذة والطلاب ذوي الأنصبة الكاملة والأنصبة الجزئية. وتشمل الأرقام العائدة للمدرسين، بصفة مبدئية، موظفي التدريس المعاونين (المدرسين المساعدين والمعيدين الخ)، ولكنها لا تشمل الموظفين الذين لا يمارسون وظيفة تدريسية (موظفي الادارة وفنيي المختبرات الخ).

الجدول 3.11

يبين هذا الجدول المتمم للجدول 3.10 عدد الطلاب المسجلين في المستوى الثالث للتعليم موزعين حسب مستوى الـ (اسكد) ومجال الدراسة والجنس لاخر سنة توفرت فيها المعلومات وحسب مجال الدراسة والجنس لعام 1985. أما التعاريف المستخدمة فتعتمد على التصنيف الدولي المقنن للتعليم (اسكد).

يمكن تعريف المستويات التي أشير اليها في هذا الجدول بواسطة رموزها (5 و6 و7) في الأسكد كالاتي:

المستوى 5 : البرامج التي تؤدي الى شهادة لا تعادل الدرجة الجامعية الأولى. ان لهذه البرامج على وجه العموم طابعا علميا بمعنى أنها تهدف الى التحضير المهني للطلاب في ميادين معينة يمكنهم التأهل فيها كتقنيين مثلا ومعلمين وممرضين ومراقبي انتاج الخ.

المستوى 6 : البرامج التي تؤدي الى الدرجة الجامعية الأولى او الى شهادة تعادلها ويشمل هذا المستوى أيضا البرامج التي تؤدي الى درجة جامعية أولى مثل الليسانس والبكالوريوس الخ. وكذلك البرامج التي تؤدي الى درجة جامعية مهنية أو الى شهادة كشهادة الدكتوراه الممنوحة عند نهاية الدراسات في الطب أو في العلوم الهندسية أو في القانون الخ.

المستوى 7 : البرامج التي تؤدي الى درجة جامعية عليا أو الى شهادة تعادلها. تخصص هذه البرامج بصفة عامة لحملة الدرجة الجامعية الأولى أو شهادة تعادلها. انها برامج دراسة ما بعد جامعية الغرض منها عادة توفير التخصص ضمن مجال معين من الدراسة الجامعية. وتنقسم هذه البرامج الى نوعين: يتضمن أحدهما البرامج التي تلي تلك التي تؤدي الى الدرجة الجامعية الأولى والتي تتضمن بصورة رئيسية دراسات مقررة، والثاني يشمل البرامج التي يكون قوامها أعمال بحث شخصية.

ويقصد بعبارة مجال الدراسة مجال التخصص الرئيسي للطالب. ان المواضيع التي يتضمنها كل من المجالات الكبرى وفقا للاسكد قد تم تحديدها في مقدمة هذا الفصل.

الجدول 3.12

يظهر هذا الجدول عدد الطلاب الذين اتموا دراستهم. وقد وزعوا المتخرجون حسب مستوى الاسكد للدرجة أو الشهادة الممنوحة ومجال الدراسة. أما بالنسبة للأعوام 1981، 1986 و1991 فقد وزعوا حسب مجال الاسكد فقط.

بلدان مدارس متنوعة توفر تهيئة عامة وتعليم تقني في آن معا. وقد صنفت هذه المدارس الخليطة بفئة المستوى الثاني، تعليم عام.

المستوى الثاني، اعداد المعلمين: تشير الصيغة «المستوى الثاني، عداد المعلمين» الى التعليم الذي يعطى في المدارس الثانوية التي هدفها لتهيئة الى مهنة التعليم.

التعليم التقني والمهني: يقصد بهذه الصيغة التعليم الذي يعطى في مدارس ثانوية هدفها تهيئة تلاميذها مباشرة لوظيفة أو لمهنة غير لتعليم. قد تحمل هذه المدارس أسماء مختلفة، والاعداد الذي توفره متباين كثيرا من حيث طبيعته ومدته. وغالبا ما يتضمن نوع التعليم هذا دروسا بنصف وقت أو دروسا ذات مدة قصيرة، وقد استبعدت هذه الدروس كلما أمكن ذلك. وقد استعملت الصيغة المختصرة «التعليم التقني» في عناوين الجداول.

للقيام بمقارنات دولية يراجع هذا الجدول مع الجداول 3.1 و3.1.a، 3.1.b.

من المفيد التنويه أنه في البلدان التي يكون فيها المستوى الثاني من التعليم على مرحلتين فان البيانات تعود الى كلا المرحلتين.

الجدول 3.8

يبين هذا الجدول التوزيع المئوي حسب الصف لمجموع المقيدين (ذكور وإناث) والى المقيدات من الاناث في المستوى الثاني من التعليم العام. بصفة عامة، تعود هذه النسب المئوية للأعوام الدراسية التي تبدأ في 1985/86 و1990/91 وللسنتين الأخيرتين المتوفر عنهما بيانات.

الجدول 3.9

يظهر هذا الجدول على شكل نسب عدد الطلاب المسجلين في التعليم على المستوى الثالث لكل 100 000 من السكان هذا وقد استعملت لحسابها البيانات الخاصة بالمقيدين المدرجة في الجدول 3.10 وأعداد السكان التي وفرها قسم السكان في الأمم المتحدة. وقد أجريت تقديرات لأعداد الطلاب حينما لم تتوفر بيانات عنهم وذلك للوصول الى نسب يمكن مقارنتها من سنة الى أخرى.

الجدول 3.10

تتعلق بيانات هذا الجدول بالمدرسين وبالطلاب المقيدين في كافة مؤسسات التعليم على المستوى الثالث الرسمية منها والخاصة. وفي معظم الحالات أدرجت البيانات بصورة منفصلة حسب نوع المؤسسة:

أ – الجامعات وما عادلها من مؤسسات تؤدي الدراسة فيها الى شهادة جامعية.

ب – المؤسسات الجامعية للتعليم عن بعد.

جـ – مؤسسات تعليمية أخرى على المستوى الثالث. وتشمل هذه مجمل الأنواع الأخرى للتعليم على المستوى الثالث المعطي في مؤسسات غير جامعية (دور معلمين عليا، ومدارس تقنية عليا، الخ).

وقد باشرت اليونسكو بجمع بيانات عن المؤسسات الجامعية للتعليم عن بعد في السنة الجامعية 1985/1986 وقد أوردت تلك البيانات للمرة الأولى في هذه الطبعة من الكتاب الاحصائي. وقد ضمنت فقط المؤسسات الجامعية التي تمنح شهادات في المستوى الثالث من التعليم معترف بها. واستبعدت البرامج التي لا تعادل الدراسة فيها برامج التعليم النظامي.

بيد أنه يجب الاشارة الى أن المعيار المتبع لتحديد الأنواع أعلاه من المؤسسات يمكن أن لا يطبق بحذافيره في كل من البلدان المعنية. وعلاوة

Introductory texte in Arabic
Textes d'introduction en arabe
Textos de introducción árabe

كحد أدنى اذ أن البيانات الكاملة لم تتوفر لجميع الحالات. للحصول على معلومات متممة (الرجاء مراجعة الجدول 3.1).

الجدول 3.4

تتعلق بيانات هذا الجدول بصفة عامة بمؤسسات التعليم على المستوى الأول الرسمية والخاصة بما فيه الصفوف الابتدائية الملحقة بمؤسسات المستوى الثاني، غير انها تشمل التعليم المخصص للمعوقين وتعليم الكبار وذلك اعتبارا من العام الدراسي 1994. لدى مراجعة هذا الجدول يجدر الرجوع الى المعلومات المعطاة عن مدة الدراسة في الجداول 3.1، 3.1.a، و3.1.b.

تعكس بصفة عامة الأرقام العائدة للمعلمين العدد الاجمالي للمعلمين ذوي النصاب الكامل وذوي النصاب الجزئي وبهذا يمكن أن تتأثر صحة مقارنة البيانات وعلى الأخص نسبة تلميذ/ معلم الواردة في العمود 8 حيث تختلف أهمية المعلمين ذوي النصاب الجزئي بصورة كبيرة من بلد لاخر. بصورة عامة، فقد استثنيا الموظفين غير المكلفين بالتعليم (المدراء وأمناء المكتبات ومستشاري التوجيه المهني، الخ).

الجدول 3.5

يقدم هذا الجدول التوزيع المئوي حسب الصف لمجموع المقيدين (ذكور وإناث) والمقيدات الإناث في المستوى الأول للتعليم. وتعود هذه النسب للسنوات المدرسية 1985 و1990 ولاخر سنتين توفرت فيهما البيانات.

الجدول 3.6

يورد هذا الجدول المعيدين في المستوى الأول كما يقدم نسبتهم الى مجموع المسجلين والمسجلين حسب سنة الدراسة.

وبغية توفير سلسلة مترابطة ومنطقية عن المعيدين وتسهيل امكانية المقارنة بين هذه البيانات وتلك المتعلقة بالمسجلين حسب السنة والواردة في الجدول 3.5، تم اجراء تقديرات لعدد المعيدين في المدارس الخاصة في حال عدم توفرها.

بصورة عامة، تعود البيانات الى السنوات المدرسية التي تبدأ في 1985 و1990 ولاخر سنتين توفرت فيهما البيانات.

الجدول 3.7

يبين هذا الجدول عدد المعلمين والتلاميذ في كل من الأنواع الثلاثة للتعليم على المستوى الثاني أي التعليم العام واعداد المعلمين والتعليم التقني والمهني. تتضمن البيانات، ما لم يشر الى عكس ذلك، معلمي وتلاميذ المدارس الرسمية والمدارس الخاصة.

في معظم الأحوال تتضمن الأرقام المعلمين ذوي نصاب التعليم الجزئي وهم عديدون بصورة خاصة في التعليم التقني والمهني.

في كل حدود الامكان استبعد الموظفون الذين لا يقومون بمهمات تعليمية كأمناء المكتبات مثلا والموجهين وبعض مدراء المؤسسات التعليمية، الخ.

المستوى الثاني، التعليم العام : تدل الصيغة «المستوى الثاني، التعليم العام» على التعليم العام والمتخصص، الذي يعطى في مدارس المستوى الثاني لتلاميذ سبق وأتموا أربع سنوات دراسة على الأقل في المستوى الأول، والذي لا يطمح الى اعداد التلاميذ مباشرة لمهنة أو لوظيفة. يمكن تسمية المدارس من هذا النوع ثانويات، متوسطات، جمنازيوم، الخ. وهي تعطي تعليما يجب على التلميذ اتمامه بالضرورة لكي يقبل في التعليم للمستوى الثالث. ولاعداد التلاميذ فقد طورت بعض

عمرية من السكان مطابقة للنظم الوطنية لمستوى هذا التعليم. غير أن نظم هذا المستوى هي في غاية المرونة، لذا يتوجب الحذر عند المقارنة بين بلد واخر. ولحساب نسبة القيد للتعليمين الابتدائي والثانوي فقد استخدم فقط عدد المقيدين الواقعة أعمارهم ضمن حدود الأعمار الرسمية لهذين المستويين. وقد حسبت هذه النسب بعد مراعاة تنوع النظم الوطنية للتعليم ومدة الدراسة على المستويين الأول والثاني. وفيما يتعلق بالتعليم على المستوى الثالث فقد روعيت الفئة العمرية 20-24 سنة. وقد حددت الفئات العمرية المستخدمة لحساب نسب القيد العائدة للتعليمين على المستوى الأول والثاني والمدرجة في الجدول وفقا للمعايير الآتية :

1 – فيما يتعلق بالبلدان التي تتبع نموذجا وحيدا للتعليم على جميع المستويات فقد حددت الفئة العمرية وفقا لعمر القبول العادي وللمدة العادية للدراسة في المستوى الأول والمستوى الثاني المبينة في الجدول 3.1.

2 – فيما يتعلق بالبلدان التي تتبع عدة نماذج للتعليم بمدد مختلفة فقد أختير النظام الذي ينطبق على أكثرية التلاميذ.

3 – ان مدد التعليم التي روعيت هي تلك التي كانت سارية خلال السنة المعنية.

ان الفئة العمرية التي روعيت في حساب النسبة العائدة للمستوى الأول والمستوى الثاني مجتمعين قد حددت بكامل مجال الفئتين العمريتين العائدتين للمستوى الأول والمستوى الثاني معا.

وتتركز نسبة القيد في المستوى الثاني على عدد المقيدين في مجمل النماذج الثلاثة للتعليم على هذا المستوى (التعليم العام، اعداد المعلمين، وغيرهما من التعليم على المستوى الثاني). ويجد القارىء معلومات أكثر تفصيلا عن أعداد المقيدين هذه في الجدول 3.7. وتجدر الاشارة الى أن النسبة الاجمالية للقيد على المستوى الابتدائي والمستوى الأول والمستوى الثاني شملت التلاميذ في جميع أعمار في حين أن فئة السكان تقتصر على أولئك الذين تقابل أعمارهم الفئة العمرية المدرسية الرسمية المحددة فيما ذكر انفا. وبالتالي وفيما يتعلق بالبلدان التي فئة سكانها الكائنة في عمر الدراسة على المستوى الأول مقيدة كليا تقريبا في المدارس قد تصل نسبة القيد الاجمالي فيها الى أكثر من 100 لكون بعض المقيدين ينتمون الى فئة عمرية خارج حدود الأعمار الرسمية.

كما أن بعض البلدان حيث تغطي المرحلة الابتدائية كامل أفراد الفئة العمرية لهذه المرحلة. فان نسبة القيد الاجمالي يمكن أن تكون أقل من 100 لأن عددا من التلاميذ في عمر المدرسة لا يزالون في مرحلة ما قبل الابتدائي.

الجدول 3.3

تتعلق البيانات الواردة في هذا الجدول بالتعليم السابق للمستوى الأول (حدائق الأطفال، مدارس الحضانة، والصفوف المخصصة للأطفال ضمن مدارس ذات مستوى أعلى). وقد استبعدت بقدر الامكان بيوت الحضانة ومراكز لعب الأطفال، الخ. تتعلق البيانات بالمؤسسات الرسمية والمؤسسات الخاصة معا، ما لم يشر الى عكس ذلك. وبصفة عامة، فإن الأرقام العائدة للهيئة التعليمية تشمل المعلمين ذوي النصاب الكامل والمعلمين ذوي النصاب الجزئي. لقد ذكرت النسب المئوية للمقيدين في المؤسسات الخاصة (المعانة وغير المعانة) بالنسبة لمجموع المقيدين في التعليم السابق للمستوى الأول. بيد أنه يجدر اعتبار بيانات هذا الجدول

Introductory texte in Arabic
Textes d'introduction en arabe
Textos de introducción árabe

3 - التعليم

يقدم هذا الفصل احصاءات تتعلق بالتعليم السابق للمستوى الأول والتعليم على المستويات الأول والثاني والثالث فبالاضافة الى بيانات عن النظم الوطنية للتعليم فانه يعرض بيانات عن نسب القيد المدرسية وعن عدد المعلمين والمقيدين بكافة مستويات التعليم وكذلك بيانات عن أعداد المدارس في المستوى السابق للمستوى الأول وفي المستوى الأول، أما الأرقام المتعلقة بالمقيدين في المستوى الثالث للتعليم وبالمتخرجين منه فقد عرضت بحسب أنماط توزيع مختلفة. لقد تم تقسيم الفصل التالي الى ثلاثة أقسام :

يوفر القسم الأول المتضمن الجدولين 3.1 و 3.2 معلومات لكل بلد عن أعمار القبول ومدة التعليم الالزامي على المستوى الأول والمستوى الثاني للتعليم العام وكذلك عن معدلات القيد في هذين المستويين.

يتضمن القسم الثاني ستة جداول، 3.3 الى 3.8، تشير الى التعليم السابق للمستوى الأول والى التعليمين على المستوى الأول والمستوى الثاني. وعند مراجعة جداول هذا الفصل يجب الرجوع الى المعلومات عن مدة الدراسة، الخ، التي تحتويها الجداول 3.1 و 3.1.a و 3.1.b. وبصفة عامة تعود البيانات المدرجة في هذه الجداول للسنوات الدراسية التي تبدأ 1980/81، 1985/86، 1990/91، والسنوات الثلاث الأخيرة التي تتوفر فيها المعلومات.

يتضمن القسم الثالث ستة جداول احصائية، 3.9 الى 3.14، عن تطور التعليم على المستوى الثالث. ان التعليم على المستوى الثالث، حسب التعريف الذي اعتمدته اليونسكو، هو التعليم الذي يستوجب كشرط أدنى للقبول فيه أن يكون طالبه قد تابع بنجاح تعليما كاملا على المستوى الثاني أو أن يتمكن من اثبات حصوله لمعلومات أو معرفة معادلة. ويمكن أن يقدم هذا التعليم في أنواع مختلفة من المؤسسات كالجامعات ودور المعلمين العليا والمدارس التقنية العليا، الخ.

الجدول 3.1

يقدم هذا الجدول بيانات مختصرة منتقاة عن نظم التعليم، والمعلومات المقدمة هنا من شأنها أن تساعد على تفسير صحيح للأرقام المدرجة في الجداول الأخرى المخصصة للتعليم.

يظهر العمودان الأولان البيانات العائدة لأنظمة التعليم الالزامي وقد أدرجت في العمود الأول الحدود الدنيا والعليا للأعمار. وهكذا فان الرقمين 6-14 يعنيان أن القوانين التي تنظم التعليم الالزامي تطبق، الا في الحالات الاستثنائية، على الأطفال من عمر 6 الى 14 سنة. ويبين العمود الثاني عدد السنوات التي يكون فيها الأطفال ملزمين بالذهاب الى المدرسة. فيمكن مثلا أن تنص الأنظمة على أن مدة التعليم الالزامي هي ست سنوات دراسية (بين 6 و14 سنة) وبعبارة أخرى يزول خضوع الطفل للتعليم الالزامي اما عند بلوغه سن الرابعة عشر واما عند اتمامه سنة الدراسة السادسة (حتى ولو لم يبلغ عندئذ الا السنة الثانية عشر أو الثالثة عشر من عمره).

بيد أن المشكلة الأكثر الحاحا في كثير من البلدان والأراضي الملحقة هي مشكلة توفير عدد كاف من المدارس لجميع الأولاد، ذلك أن وجود

قانون للتعليم الالزامي ليس له الا قيمة نظرية لأن معظم هذه الأنظمة تعفي الطفل من المدرسة في حال عدم وجود مدرسة على مسافة معقولة من منزله.

يبين العمود الثالث أعمار قبول الأطفال في التعليم السابق للمستوى الأول، والذي ما زال بالنسبة لمعظم البلدان مقتصرا بصفة عامة على مناطق المدن حيث تستطيع الافادة منه نسبة ضئيلة فقط من الأطفال ذوي العمر المبين.

ان العرض البياني الذي يلي ذلك والذي يجمل الأعمدة الثلاثة يعطي تمثيلا بيانيا لمدة ولعمر القبول في التعليم العام على المستوى الثاني وفقا لنظم التعليم المعتمدة حاليا. ولم يشمل هذا العرض البياني تدريب المعلمين وباقي التعليم على المستوى الثاني. ان الرمز «P» يمثل مدة التعليم على المستوى الأول، ويمثل الرمز «S1» مدة المرحلة الأولى للتعليم العام على المستوى الثاني، أما الرمز «S2» فيمثل مدة المرحلة الثانية للتعليم العام على المستوى الثاني. وتجدر الملاحظة الى أن بعض البلدان لم تفرق ما بين مرحلتي التعليم العام على المستوى الثاني، وبهذه الحال فقد مثلت مدة التعليم على هذا المستوى بالرمز «S». بالاضافة الى ذلك وفيما يتعلق بعدد من البلدان قد يتغير عمر القبول ومدة التعليم على هذين المستويين تبعا للمنطقة أو لنوع المدرسة. لذلك فان النظام الأكثر شيوعا في هذه البلدان هو الذي ظهر في التمثيل البياني. ويبين الجدول 3.1.a الامكانيات الأخرى المتاحة.

وأخيرا يبين الجدول 3.1.b أنه لم يطرأ أي تغييرات على نظام التعليم منذ عام 1980 في عدد من البلدان. ويجب مراجعة هذا الجدول عند الرجوع الى بيانات المقيدين المدرجة في المدارس في الجداول 3.3 الى 3.8.

الجدول 3.2

يورد هذا الجدول نسب القيد في البلدان والأراضي الملحقة التي يزيد عدد سكانها على 150 000 نسمة. أما في البلدان التي يقل عدد سكانها عن هذا الحد فلم تتوفر عنها بيانات سكانية موزعة حسب سنوات الأعمار تسمح بحساب تلك النسب فيها. تعتمد البيانات السكانية على التقديرات والاسقاطات التي أعدها قسم السكان في الأمم المتحدة عام 1994. ان أعداد المقيدين التي استخدمت لحساب معدلات القيد الاجمالية هي تلك التي وردت في الجداول 3.3، 3.4، 3.7، و3.10 من هذا الكتاب. وكلما توفرت أعداد المقيدين موزعة حسب سنوات الأعمار لكل من التعليمين على المستوى الأول والمستوى الثاني حسبت أيضا نسب القيد الصافية. نسب القيد جميعها هي نسب مئوية. ان نسبة القيد الاجمالي هو ناتج قسمة عدد المقيدين في مستوى معين من التعليم، أيا كانت أعمارهم، على عدد السكان الواقعة أعمارهم ضمن حدود الأعمار الرسمية للمستوى. أما نسبة القيد الصافية فقد حسبت باستخدام فقط عدد المقيدين الذي يتناسب أعمارهم للمستوى التعليمي. ان نسبة القيد الاجمالي للتعليم ما قبل الابتدائي هي مجموع القيد لمرحلة التعليم السابق للمستوى الأول، أيا كانت الأعمار، فانها تعتبر كنسبة مئوية لفئة

Introductory texte in Arabic
Textes d'introduction en arabe
Textos de introducción árabe

2 – جداول اجمالية لجميع مستويات التعليم
حسب القارات والمناطق الكبرى ومجموعات البلدان

يقدم هذا الفصل الذي يحتوي على 11 جدول عرضا اجماليا للبيانات الاحصائية عن السكان كذلك البيانات لجميع مستويات التعليم. وتوفر هذه الجداول صورة عامة عن التطور الكمي من عام 1980 وعن الوضع الحالي، للأمية بين الكبار، للتعليم والانفاق على التعليم للعالم ككل ولكل منطقة كبرى ومجموعة بلدان.

الجدول 2.1 :

يعرض الجدول 2.1 التقديرات والاسقاطات لأعوام 1970، 1980، 1990، 1995، 2000 و2010 لمجمل عدد السكان ولعدد السكان الذين هم تحت عمر 25 وذلك للعالم أجمع بحسب القارات والمناطق الكبرى ومجموعات البلدان. ويقدم الجدول أيضا تقديرات منفصلة للفئات العمرية 0-4 و10-14 و15-19 و20-24 سنة وتعتبر الفئات الأكثر أهمية بالنسبة للتعليم. وتقابل الأرقام الواردة في هذا الجدول، متغير الاسقاط الوسط المعدل عام 1994 في التقديرات السكانية والاسقاطات المعدة من قبل قسم السكان في الأمم المتحدة.

الجدول 2.2 :

يقدم هذا الجدول تقديرات بعدد الأميين الكبار لأعوام 1980، 1985، 1990 و1995، كذلك النسبة المئوية للأميين بحسب القارات والمناطق الكبرى ومجموعات البلدان، وقد أعدها قسم الاحصاء باليونسكو عام 1994.

الجدول 2.3 :

تعتمد البيانات في هذا الجدول بصورة رئيسية عدد الطلاب (التلاميذ) الملتحقين في المدارس وعدد المعلمين لكل من البلدان والأراضي الملحقة المبينة في الجدول 3.3 من هذا الكتاب السنوي.

الجدول 2.4 الى 2.8 :

تبين هذه الجداول التطور الكمي للملتحقين بالمدارس ولعدد المعلمين لمختلف مستويات التعليم، تضمن النص التمهيدي المتعلق بالتعليم التعاريف لكل مستويات التعليم. تعتمد البيانات الواردة بشكل رئيسي على أعداد الطلاب/ التلاميذ الملتحقين في المدارس وعدد المعلمين وذلك لكل بلد وأرض ملحقة والواردة في الجداول 3.4، 3.7 و3.10 من هذا الكتاب السنوي. بيد أن، في حال حدوث أي تغير في النظم التربوية الوطنية، فقد تم توحيد البيانات كي تعكس البنى النهائية للتعليم. هذا ويجب الاشارة الى أن التوزيع المطلق والنسبي حسب مستويات التعليم يتأثر بمدة الدراسة في كل مستوى التي تعتمد بدورها على المعايير المستخدمة محليا لتعريف مستويات التعليم المختلفة. (أنظر الجدول 3.1). وبما أن هذه المعايير وخاصة المتعلقة بالتعليمين الابتدائي والثانوي تختلف من بلد الى اخر. فيجب النظر بحذر الى المقارنات بين المناطق.

الجدول 2.9 :

يقدم هذا الجدول توزيع عدد الطلاب والمعلمين للتعليم الثانوي حسب نوع هذا التعليم. تعتمد البيانات المبينة في هذا الجدول على عدد الطلاب (التلاميذ) الملتحقين في المدارس وعدد المعلمين لكل من البلدان والأراضي الملحقة المبينة في الجدول 3.7 من هذا الكتاب السنوي. ويجب النظر بحذر الى المقارنات بين المناطق والى تعليل أسباب التغييرات الملاحظة في كل منطقة خلال الفترة التي تعود اليها البيانات وذلك نظرا للتفاوت في المناهج والتصنيفات المستخدمة لتعريف دور ووظيفة اعداد المعلم والتعليم المهني والتقني في المستوى الثاني.

الجدول 2.10 :

يقدم هذا الجدول نسب قيد مدرسية معدّلة لكل مستوى تعليمي وموزعة حسب الجنس. ان البيانات الواردة في هذا الجدول تعتمد على التقديرات والاسقاطات المبينة في الجدول 2.4، وكذلك على استخدام المتغير الوسط في التقديرات المعدّلة للسكان لعام 1994 التي قام باعدادها قسم السكان في الأمم المتحدة. وتحسب نسبة القيد الاجمالي لمستوى تعليمي بتقسيم مجموع التلاميذ/ الطلاب المقيدين في هذا المستوى أيا كانت أعمارهم على مجموع عدد السكان في الفئة العمرية التي يفترض، حسب النظم الوطنية، أن تلتحق بالدراسة في هذا المستوى. أما عبارة في «المعدّل» فتعني أنه تم اختيار الفئات العمرية المستخدمة لحساب نسبة القيد المدرسي لمنطقة ما بعد الأخذ بعين الاعتبار بنية التعليم لكل بلد من بلدان تلك المنطقة. أما فيما يتعلق بالمستوى الثالث للتعليم فقد اعتمدت في الحساب فترة واحدة لكل البلدان مدتها خمس سنوات بعد نهاية التعليم الثانوي العام. ومما يجب أيضا ملاحظته أن نسب القيد المدرسي مئوية قد تتجاوز في بعض الأحيان 100 نظرا للالتحاق المتأخر وللاعادة، الخ.

الجدول 2.11 :

يهدف هذا الجدول الى اظهار الاتجاهات العامة في الانفاق العام على التعليم بالدولار الأمريكي وبالأسعار الجارية. وقد تم الحصول على بيانات اجمالي الناتج القومي GNP وأسعار الصرف بين العملات الوطنية والدولار الأمريكي من البنك الدولي وصندوق النقد الدولي. ويجب اعتبار البيانات المنشورة في هذا الجدول على أنها مجرد مؤشرات عامة تقريبية عن الموارد العامة المخصصة للتعليم. ويجب أيضا النظر بحذر لأي تحليل مقارن لقيم محسوبة بالدولار الأمريكي اذ أن استخدام أسعار الصرف الرسمية للوصول الى قيم بالدولار قد يؤدي في بعض البلدان الى قيم غير واقعية. بالاضافة الى أن القيم هي بالأسعار الجارية التي تتأثر عادة بالتضخم المالي.

Introductory texte in Arabic
Textes d'introduction en arabe
Textos de introducción árabe

لتعليم

تتضمن الفصول الثلاثة التالية من هذا الكتاب معظم المعلومات الاحصائية الأساسية التي تجمعها اليونسكو عن السكان، أمية الكبار والتعليم الرسمي والخاص على كافة مستويات التعليم. ان أكثر من ثلاثين جدولا يوفر بيانات احصائية للعالم أجمع عن مواضيع مثل : عدد المدارس، عدد المعلمين والتلاميذ موزعين حسب المستوى ونوع التعليم، الطلبة والمتخرجون من التعليم العالي حسب مجالات الدراسة ومستوى البرنامج، الطلاب الأجانب في التعليم العالي حسب بلد الأصل وبلد الدراسة، الانفاق العام على التعليم حسب الغرض ومستوى التعليم. ويقدر الامكان تشير البيانات الى السنوات الدراسية التي تبتدأ في 1980، 1985 و1990 وبالاضافة الى أحدث ثلاث سنوات توفرت بشأنها البيانات.

وقد استخدمت في هذه الجداول التعاريف والتصنيفات المتضمنة في التوصية المعدلة الخاصة بالتوحيد الدولي لاحصاءات التربية التي اعتمدها مؤتمر اليونسكو العام في دورته العشرين (باريس، 1978)، وتلك الواردة في التصنيف الدولي المقنن للتعليم (اسكد) كلما كان ذلك ممكنا. وبناء على ما تقدم يصنف التعليم حسب المستوى كما يلي :

– التعليم السابق للمستوى الأول : (المستوى 0 من اسكد) الذي تقدمه مثلا مدارس الحضانة أو حدائق الأطفال والذي يوفر تعليما للأطفال الذين لم يصلوا الى عمر الالتحاق بالتعليم في المستوى الأول.

– التعليم في المستوى الأول (المستوى 1 من الاسكد) الذي تقدمه مثلا المدارس الأولية أو الابتدائية والذي يهدف بشكل رئيسي الى تقديم العناصر الأولية للمعرفة.

– التعليم في المستوى الثاني (المستويات 2 و3 من الأسكد) ويتبع على الأقل أربع سنوات من التعليم في المستوى الأول ويقدم تعليما عاما وتخصصيا. (في المدارس المتوسطة، الثانويات، مدارس تدريب المعلمين في هذا المستوى، المدارس التقنية أو المهنية).

– التعليم في المستوى الثالث (المستويات 5 و6 و7 من الاسكد) ويتطلب كحد أدنى للالتحاق به اتمام التعليم في المستوى الثاني أو اثبات الحصول على ما يعادله من معرفة (في الجامعات، معاهد تدريب المعلمين، المعاهد المهنية العليا).

– التعليم الموجه لفئات خاصة : ويشمل جميع أنواع التعليم المقدمة الى الأولاد الذين يعانون من معوقات أو عاهات جسدية أو عقلية أو بصرية أو اجتماعية أو سمعية أو كلامية أو يجدون صعوبة في القراءة والكتابة.

ونورد فيما يلي التعاريف المتضمنة في التوصية المعدلة بشأن التوحيد الدولي لاحصاءات التربية :

(أ) التلميذ (الطالب) : هو شخص مقيد و/أو مسجل في برنامج تعليمي.

(ب) المعلم : هو شخص يقوم بتدريس (تعليم) مجموعة من التلاميذ (الطلاب). هذا ولا يعتبر رؤساء المؤسسات التعليمية والموظفون المكلفون بالاشراف معلمين الا اذا كلفوا بمهام تعليمية منتظمة.

(جـ) المدرسة (المؤسسة التعليمية) : هي مجموعة من التلاميذ (الطلاب) من صف أو أكثر منظمة لتلقي تعليما من نوع معين وفي مستوى معين من معلم واحد أو أكثر وباشراف رئيس مباشر.

(1) المدرسة العامة هي مدرسة تديرها سلطة عامة (وطنية أو اتحادية أو اقليمية أو محلية) أيا كان مصدر مواردها المالية.

(2) المدرسة الخاصة : هي مدرسة لا تديرها سلطة عامة، سواء أكانت تتلقى تمويلا أم لا دعما ماليا من السلطات العامة. ويمكن تعريف المدارس الخاصة بأنها معانة أو غير معانة وذلك فيما اذا كانت تحصل أو لا تحصل على دعم مالي من السلطات العامة.

وتعود، بصورة عامة، بيانات قيد التلاميذ (الطلاب) الواردة في هذه الجداول الى بداية السنة الدراسية أو الأكاديمية. ويجدر بهذا الصدد الاشارة الى أن بيانات القيد قد تختلف اختلافا محسوسا تبعا لليوم الذي تمّ فيه العدّ مثلا في بداية السنة، في منتصف السنة أو في نهايتها.

وتشير السنوات المبينة في الجداول الى السنة الدراسية (أو الأكاديمية). ويوفر الملحق B معلومات عن تاريخ بدء ونهاية السنة الدراسية والسنة المالية لكل من البلدان والأراضي المورد عنها بيانات.

Introductory texte in Arabic
Textes d'introduction en arabe
Textos de introducción árabe

1 – جداول مرجعية

يتألف الفصل الأول من الكتاب الاحصائي السنوي من ثلاثة جداول، تتضمن جدولين عن السكان وجدول عن الأمية وجدول عن مستوى التعليم، وتوفر هذه الجداول بيانات يرجع اليها فيما يتعلق بكافة الجداول الأخرى التي تتناول مؤسسات التعليم والعلم والثقافة ووسائل الاتصال الجماهيرية.

يؤثر حجم وكثافة السكان لبلد ما في نمو مؤسسات ووسائل التعليم فيه. وتتمم البيانات الخاصة بالأمية وبالمستوى التعليمي للكبار احصاءات القيد في المدارس والجامعات وغيرها من المؤسسات التعليمية.

الجدول 1.1

يقدم الجدول 1.1 بيانات عن مجموع عدد السكان والمساحة وكثافة السكان وذلك لبعض مجموعات البلدان ولكل بلد. تقابل الأرقام الواردة في هذا الجدول، متغير الاسقاط الوسط المعدّل عام 1994 في التقديرات السكانية والاسقاطات المعدة من قبل قسم السكان في الأمم المتحدة. تتضمن الأرقام المتعلقة بالمساحة المياه الداخلية، ما لم يشر الى عكس ذلك. لم تدرج البيانات عن كثافة السكان (عدد السكان في الكيلومتر المربع الواحد) للمساحات التي تقل عن 1 000 كيلومترا مربعا. يرجى من القراء الراغبين في الحصول على معلومات أكثر تفصيلا عن المساحة وعدد السكان والبنية العمرية الرجوع الى الكتاب الديموغرافي السنوي والكتاب الاحصائي السنوي للأمم المتحدة.

الجدول 1.2

يورد الجدول 1.2 استنادا الى نتائج التعدادات والمسوحات التي أجريت منذ عام 1979 والتي توفرت نتائجها، بيانات عن عدد السكان الكبار الأميين وعن النسبة المئوية للأمية. لقد تم الحصول على هذه الأرقام من مكتب الاحصاء التابع لمنظمة الأمم المتحدة أو استخلصت من المطبوعات الوطنية.

ويورد الجدول أيضا اخر التقديرات عن أمية الكبار لعام 1995 والتي أعدها قسم الاحصاء باليونسكو عام 1994. على القراء الراغبين في الحصول على احصاءات مماثلة للسنوات السابقة و/أو تقديرات زمنية بشأن البلدان النامية يمكنهم الاطلاع على مطبوع اليونسكو :
«Compendiuni of satistics on illiteracy - 1995 Edition».

الجدول 1.3

يظهر الجدول 1.3 التوزيع المئوي للسكان من الكبار حسب أعلى مستوى للتعليم تم تحصيله. وقد استقيت البيانات من التعدادات الوطنية للسكان ومن المسوحات عن طريق العينات الخاصة والمقدمة من قسم

احصاء منظمة الأمم المتحدة أو مستخلصة من النشرات والمطبوعات الوطنية. على القراء الراغبين في الاطلاع على البيانات المتعلقة بسنوات سابقة الرجوع الى مطبوع اليونسكو الصادر عن اليونسكو عام 1983 بعنوان «احصاءات عن المستوى التعليمي والأمية 1970-1980، (CSR-44).

ان مستويات التعليم الستة تقوم على انتقاء لفئات التصنيف الدولي المقنن للتعليم (اسكد) وقد عرفت كما يلي:

(1) بدون أي تعليم مدرسي: ينطبق هذا على الأشخاص الذين لم يكملوا سنة دراسية واحدة.

(2) المستوى الأول غير كامل : تشمل هذه الفئة جميع الأشخاص الذين أكملوا سنة تعليم واحدة على الأقل ولكنهم لم يتموا السنة الأخيرة من هذا المستوى التعليمي. ان مدة التعليم في المستوى الأول يمكن أن تتغير حسب البلد. هذا ويتضمن الجدول 3.1 البيانات المتعلقة بهذا الموضوع.

(3) المستوى الأول كامل : تشمل هذه الفئة الأشخاص الذين أتموا السنة الأخيرة من المستوى الأول للتعليم (مستوى 1 في الاسكد) ولكنهم لم يدخلوا التعليم الثانوي.

(4) (S-1) التحاق بالتعليم على المستوى الثاني. المرحلة الأولى: تتضمن هذه الفئة كل الأشخاص الذين لم تتجاوز دراستهم المرحلة الأولى من التعليم الثانوي حسبما حددت في الجدول 3.1 وتطابق المستوى 2 في الاسكد.

(5) (S-2) التحاق بالتعليم على المستوى الثاني. المرحلة الثانية: ان هذه الفئة تطابق المستوى 3 من اسكد وتضم الأشخاص الذين انتقلوا من المرحلة الأولى الى المرحلة الثانية للتعليم الثانوي ولكنهم لم يتلقوا تعليما فوق الثانوي.

(6) تعليم فوق الثانوي: يدخل في هذه الفئة كل الأشخاص الذين تلقوا تعليما لاحقا للمستوى الثانوي سواء أتموه أم لم يتموه (المستويات 5، 6، و7 في الاسكد).

وفيما يتعلق بمستوى التعليم فوق الثانوي فيلاحظ أن النسبة المئوية لأفراد الفئة العمرية 15-24 المصنفة فيه هي في كثير من الأحيان أدنى من النسبة المئوية المقابلة في الفئة العمرية 25-34 وذلك لأن عددا كبيرا من أفراد الفئة العمرية الأولى لم يصل الى عمر يتيح له التعليم فوق الثانوي. ولهذا السبب أدرج في هذا الجدول مجموع السكان الكبار للفئة العمرية 25 سنة وما فوق ولم تختار فئة الأعمار (15 سنة وما فوق).

Introductory texte in Arabic
Textes d'introduction en arabe
Textos de introducción árabe

بيان توضيحي

تتناول البيانات الواردة في هذا المطبوع بشكل عام البلدان والأراضي الملحقة بحدودها الفعلية.

وقد ألحقت لائحة كاملة بالدول والأراضي. فالتغيرات التي طرأت على تسمية بعض الدول، خلال السنوات الأخيرة قد انعكست في اللائحة والجداول الواردة في هذا الكتاب الاحصائي. غير انه يجب التنبه الى أن :

– البيانات الواردة عن الأردن، باستثناء الجدول 1.1، يتعلق بالضفة الشرقية فقط.

– الاحصاءات المتعلقة بفلسطين تغطي الضفة الغربية وقطاع غزة، وترد هذه البيانات بعد تلك المتعلقة بالدول الاسيوية.

– البيانات المتعلقة بألمانيا ما قبل 1990، قدمت منفصلة تحت اسم (ألمانيا الاتحادية) و(ألمانيا الديمقراطية).

– كذلك الحال بالنسبة لليمن فإن البيانات التي تعود الى ما قبل 1990، وردت تحت اسم اليمن الديمقراطية واليمن العربية.

– في عام 1991 انهار الاتحاد السوفياتي السابق وانقسم الى خمس عشرة دولة (أرمينيا، أذربيجان بيلاروس، استونيا، جورجيا، قازاخستان، قيرغيزستان، لاتفيا، ليتوانيا، جمهورية مولدفا، الاتحاد الروسي، طاجيسكتان، تركمنسان، أوكرانيا، أوزبكستان). كلما أمكن وردة البيانات من الدول المستقلة.

– وبخصوص البيانات المتعلقة بيوغوسلافيا السابقة وتشيكوسلوفاكيا السابقة فان تاريخها يعود الى سنوات ما قبل التغيرات التي حصلت في تلك الدول. عندما تتوفر البيانات المتعلقة بالجمهوريات المنبثقة عن هذه الدول فانها سترد على حدة.

– تشير البيانات الواردة عن الكرسي الرسولي الى دولة الفاتيكان.

– إن البيانات العائدة لاثيوبيا تتضمن أريتريا حتى عام 1991. أما في حال توفر البيانات عن أريتريا ما قبل 1991 فانها قد وردت مستقلة عن اثيوبيا.

– ان البيانات المعدلة الواردة في هذا المطبوع تختلف عن البيانات المقابلة لنفس السنة المذكورة في أعداد سابقة من الكتاب الاحصائي السنوي لليونسكو.

بسبب تدوير الأرقام لا تتطابق في بعض الأحيان تماما المجموعات أو المجموعات الجزئية مع مجموع العناصر التي تشكلها. أشير الى التوضيحات الخاصة ببعض الأرقام بعلامة حاشية رمزها @ وهي تلي مباشرة أسماء القارات والمناطق والبلدان والأراضي الملحقة بها. أما النصوص المقابلة لكل حاشية فقد أوردت في نهاية كل جدول. وتتألف كل حاشية من اسم القارة والمنطقة والبلد أو الأرض (بالانكليزية) يرد بعدها الشرح المطلوب. ويسبق الرمز E ← النص الانكليزي والرمز FR ← النص الفرنسي والرمز ESP ← النص بالاسبانية. وقد تضمنت بعض الجداول أيضا حاشية عامة أوردت بعد نهاية الجدول مباشرة.

جرى استخدام الرموز التالية في هذا المطبوع:

–	رقم مساو لصفر
0 أو00	رقم أقل من نصف الوحدة المستعملة
...	بيانات غير متوفرة
.	فئة لا تنطبق
*	بيانات تمهيدية أو تقديرية
%	بيانات مضمنة في فئة أخرى
←	يتضمن الرقم على يسار السهم مباشرة بيانات الأعمدة المبين فيها ذلك السهم
→	يتضمن الرقم على يمين السهم مباشرة بيانات الأعمدة المبين فيها ذلك السهم

وأشير الى انقطاع تجانس سلسلة زمنية بخط أفقي أو رأسي.

Introductory texte in Arabic
Textes d'introduction en arabe
Textos de introducción árabe

مقدمة

أعد هذا العدد من الكتاب الاحصائي السنوي قسم الاحصاء باليونسكو بالتعاون مع اللجان الوطنية لليونسكو، مصالح الاحصاء ووكالات وطنية أخرى.

بموجب المادة الثامنة من دستور اليونسكو تقوم الدول الأعضاء بتقديم تقارير دورية الى المنظمة عن القوانين والأنظمة والاحصاءات الخاصة بالأنشطة والمؤسسات التعليمية والعلمية والثقافية فيها. وقد جمعت البيانات بشكل رئيسي من الاجابات الرسمية لحوالي 200 بلدا على استبيانات ومسوحات اليونسكو وكذلك من المطبوعات والتقارير الرسمية، واستكملت بالمعلومات المتوفرة من مصادر وطنية ودولية أخرى وبشكل خاص قسم الاحصاء وقسم السكان في الأمم المتحدة. وحينما لم تتطابق البيانات المتوفرة مع التوصيات المعتمدة أو المفاهيم المستعملة من قبل اليونسكو، اعتمدت الممارسات الاحصائية الوطنية مع الاشارة الى ذلك بحاشية كلّما أمكن.

وقد تم عرض النصوص التوضيحية للجداول باللغات الانكليزية والفرنسية والاسبانية وكذلك النصوص التمهيدية في بداية كل فصل باستثناء الفصل الثالث حيث وضعت هذه النصوص في نهاية كل جدول. ولتسهيل استخدام هذا الكتاب من قبل القراء الناطقين باللغة العربية أو الروسية، فقد ترجمت مقدمات الفصول الى هاتين اللغتين، ويمكن ايجادهم في الملحق F، في الملحق G في نهاية الكتاب السنوي.

وننبه القارىء الى أن بعض الجداول التي تم عرضها في الطبعات السابقة من هذا الكتاب، لم ترد في الطبعة الحالية. ويتضمن الملحق E قائمة بهذه الجداول تشير الى الطبعة الأخيرة المتضمنة لهذه الجداول.

هذا ويرجى ارسال أي استفسار أو تعليق أو اقتراح لتحسين الأعداد المقبلة من هذا المطبوع الى قسم الاحصاء باليونسكو، 75352 باريس 07 SP، فرنسا.